CANADIAN
GLOBAL
ALMANAC
2004

CANADIAN
GLOBAL
ALMANAC
2004

John Wiley and Sons Canada
Toronto

Contents

CANADIAN GLOBAL ALMANAC 2004

Managing Editor **NICOLE LANGLOIS**

Contributing Editors **ANDREW BORKOWSKI**
(Arts and Entertainment)

FRANKLIN CARTER
(Politics)

PETER HAMMERSCHMIDT
(News Events)

MICHAEL KELLY
(Sports)

DAVID PHILLIPS
(Climate)

MICHAEL SMITH
(Geography, Science)

DONNA WILLIAMS
(Hall of Fame, Obituaries)

Typesetter **BETH CRANE, HEIDY LAWRANCE ASSOCIATES**

Researchers **SONJA RUTHARD**

ANN McILWRAITH

BOB BALL

Indexer **LIBA BERRY**

Cover Designer **IAN KOO**

Some of the information in this publication is made available through the cooperation of Statistics Canada. Any items credited to Statistics Canada are copyright of Statistics Canada; integral and/or adapted reproductions are published with permission of the Minister of Industry, Science and Technology. Readers wishing further information on any of the subjects credited to Statistics Canada may obtain copies of related publications by contacting Publications Sales, Statistics Canada, Ottawa, Ontario, Canada KIA 0T6, or by calling 1-613-951-7277 or 1-800-267-6677 (toll free in Canada and the United States). Readers may also fax orders by dialing 1-613-951-1584 or fax order line 1-877-287-4369 (toll free in Canada and the United States).

National Library of Canada Cataloguing in Publication Data

The National Library of Canada has catalogued this publication as follows:

The Canadian global almanac.

Annual.
1992–
Imprint varies.
Continues: Canadian world almanac and book of facts, ISSN 0833-532X.
ISSN 1187-4570
ISBN 0-470-83359-9 (2004 edition)

1. Almanacs, Canadian (English). 2. Almanacs.

AY414.C36 1992-   031.02   C92-031173-3

Printed in Canada

CANADA

Canada at-a-Glance

■ LAND

Area	9 976 140 sq. km
Length of coastline	202 080 km (longest in the world)
Length of border with U.S. inc. Alaska	8 890 km
Longitudinal centre of Canada	97°W (close to Winnipeg)
Latitudinal centre of Canada	62°N (close to Yellowknife, Northwest Territories)
Geographic centre of Canada	Arviat, Nunavut (60°06'30"N, 94°03'30"W)
Greatest distance east to west	5 514 km (Cape Spear, Newfoundland, to the Yukon/Alaska border)
Greatest distance north to south	4 634 km (Cape Columbia, Ellesmere Island, to Middle Island, Lake Erie)
Largest island	Baffin Island, Nunavut, 507 451 sq. km
Northernmost point	Cape Columbia, Ellesmere Island, Nunavut, 83°06'N–69°57'W
Southernmost point	Middle Island, Lake Erie, Ontario, 41°41'N–82°40'W
Easternmost point	Cape Spear, Newfoundland, 47°31'N–52°37'W
Westernmost point	Yukon/Alaska boundary, 141°00'W
Northernmost community	Grise Fiord, Ellesmere Island, Nunavut, 76°25'N–82°54'W
Southernmost community	Pelee Island South, Ontario, 41°45'N–82°38'W
Easternmost community	Blackhead, Newfoundland, 47°32'N–52°39'W
Westernmost community	Beaver Creek, Yukon Territory, 62°23'N–140°52'W
Longest river	Mackenzie River, Northwest Territories, 4 241 km
Largest lake (entirely) in Canada	Great Bear Lake, Northwest Territories, 31 328 sq. km
Highest waterfall	Della Falls, Della Lake, B.C., 440 metres (more than one drop)

■ PEOPLE

Population (July 2003 est.)	32 207 113
Population growth rate (2003)	0.94%
Life expectancy at birth (2003 est.)	79.8; men: 76.4; women: 83.4
Age structure of the population	0–19 years: 25.9%; 20–64: 61.1%; 65+: 13%
Official languages	English and French

■ NATION

Confederation	July 1, 1867
Governor General	Her Excellency, the Right Honourable Adrienne Clarkson
Prime Minister	The Right Honourable Jean Chrétien
Motto	*A Mari usque ad Mare* (From Sea to Sea)
National symbols	the Maple Leaf and the Beaver (both official)
National game	lacrosse (summer), hockey (winter)
Anthem	"O Canada" (National), "God Save the Queen" (Royal)
National capital	Ottawa, Ontario
Date of the last general election	November 27, 2000
Largest province	Quebec, 1 542 056 sq. km
Smallest province	Prince Edward Island, 5 660 sq. km

■ ECONOMY

GDP at market prices (June 2003)	$1 090.2 billion
Rate of inflation (July 2003)	2.6%
Rate of unemployment (August 2002)	7.7%

Source: *Canadian Heritage; Natural Resources Canada; Statistics Canada*

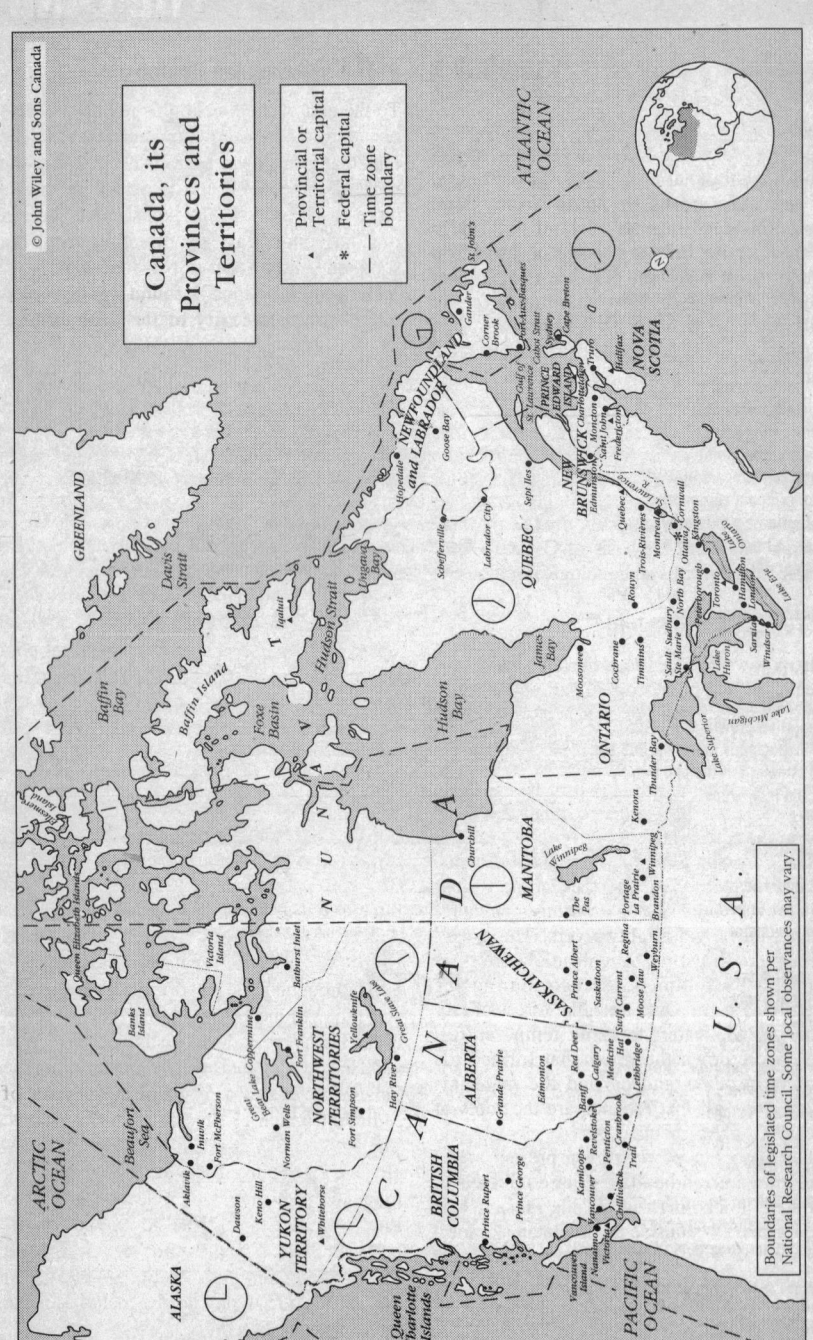

© John Wiley and Sons Canada

Canada, its Provinces and Territories

▲ Provincial or Territorial capital
✷ Federal capital
– – – Time zone boundary

Boundaries of legislated time zones shown per National Research Council. Some local observances may vary.

LANDFORMS

Canada is the largest country in the Western Hemisphere and the second largest in the world, with a total area of 9,970,610 sq. km. It stretches north to south from Cape Columbia on Ellesmere Island to Middle Island in Lake Erie, a distance of 4,634 km. The greatest east-west distance is 5,514 km from Cape Spear, Newfoundland, to the Yukon–Alaska border. Within this vast expanse, Canada contains an extremely wide variety of geographical features: the towering peaks of the Rockies, the flat Prairies, the rugged north and the gently rolling landscape of the east. But within this seemingly wide range of features, five areas with common characteristics are found. These physiographic regions are generally used to describe Canada and form the basis of Canada's geographical landforms and geological regions.

■ The Canadian Shield

Also known as the Precambrian Shield, this area is located in the central part of the continent. Viewed from the air it is a vast, inhospitable land of rocks, lakes and trees. It makes up roughly half of Canada's surface area, sweeping around Hudson Bay like a giant horseshoe, but also is the foundation for the rest of the continent.

The Canadian Shield has not always looked as it does today. Early in the Earth's history this area was the site of towering mountains, deep valleys and mighty rivers. The mountains were thrust up by volcanic activity as long as 3.8 billion years ago, during the Precambrian era. Over time, the forces of erosion—wind, water, freezing temperatures, ice—wore down the rocks that formed the mountain peaks and carried the materials away. Now all that remains are the roots of the once-mighty mountains.

The processes of volcanism present at the time of mountain-building caused minerals to form in the cooling rock of the Precambrian mountains. Deep inside the mountains, minerals such as gold, silver, copper and nickel came together into veins of ore. These ore bodies make the Shield a rich storehouse of mineral wealth.

■ The Appalachian Region

To the east of the Shield, this region was also once the site of massive mountain peaks. The rock that forms these peaks is not as old as the rock of the Shield, and is of a type that is more easily eroded. The Appalachian Region runs in a northeasterly direction from the southern United States to Newfoundland.

The mineral deposits found in the region reflect the complexity of the geology, and include gypsum, barite, salt, copper, zinc, lead, gold and silver. Since the end of the mountain-building period, erosion has worn off the tops of the mountains and filled the valleys with sediments, which gives the area its present-day less rugged appearance.

■ The Interior Plains

West of the Shield, rock which formed at the bottom of ancient lakes and seas gives the Prairies their distinctive flatness.

The Interior Plains occupy the central portion of the continent. Minerals found in the Interior Plains include potash, a substance produced when lakes and shallow seas evaporate, leaving deposits. Potash deposits in Saskatchewan are among the largest in the world. Coal, oil and natural gas were formed from organic materials trapped by the sedimentary layers during Palaeozoic times. An extension of the Interior Plains thrusts up between the Canadian Shield and the Appalachian Region, forming the Great Lakes–St. Lawrence Lowlands landform area. Soils throughout the Interior Plains are fertile, since the sedimentary materials that are found in the Plains break down easily.

Other lowland areas were formed during the Palaeozoic era as a result of the deposit of sediment which created the Interior Plains. The Hudson Bay Lowlands on the southwestern edge of Hudson Bay are relatively thin layers of sedimentary rock on top of the Precambrian Shield. The Arctic Lowlands, between the Shield and the Innuitian Mountains of the high Arctic, are similar in age and characteristics to the material of the Interior Plains.

■ The Western Cordillera

As the Precambrian mountains eroded, the sedimentary layers were deposited over a great distance and formed the Appalachian Region to the east. These deposits also provided the material from which future landforms would be built to the west. These landforms are now known as the Western Cordillera.

When the continent started its westward movement about 200 million years ago, its leading edge was forced against the adjacent oceanic plate and the land moved overtop the ocean. Geologists speculate that the tremendous pressure exerted during this process caused the sedimentary layers of the plate's edge to buckle into a massive dome. Magma, the hot fluid substance below the Earth's crust, flowed into the dome and formed a core which eventually collapsed between 65 and 160 million years ago, breaking the rock layers. This core stretches along the edge of the continental plate and absorbs the pressure of the two plates as they press upon each other.

The Western Cordillera is an area of great complexity; rocks composed of different materials and through different processes are thoroughly mixed. The Coast Ranges which form the leading western edge of the continent are composed of both igneous and metamorphic rock. The interior of the Cordillera is a jumble of plateaus, folded and broken rock layers and recent volcanoes. The sedimentary materials of the Rockies on the eastern edge of the Cordillera were folded and broken during a period of mountain-building in Eocene times, some 40-65 million years ago.

The Cordillera contains minerals associated with all the processes involved in its creation. The igneous rocks of the western part of the Cordillera are a major source of minerals including lead, zinc, silver, copper and gold. The sedimentary deposits of the eastern Cordillera are responsible for the coal and petroleum found there.

■ Innuitian Region

Mountain-building shaped the landforms of the high Arctic during the Devonian period (about 405 million years ago). The most recent activities appear to have occurred about 30 million years ago, which was long after the mountain-building period that thrust up the Rocky Mountains in the Cordillera.

Little detail is known about this region because research is so difficult in the inhospitable climate, but some geologists have suggested mountain-building is the result of the North American plate advancing on the Eurasian plate.

The topography of this region is characterized by low plateau mountains, with ridges as high as 3,000 m. The area is composed mainly of sedimentary rocks but includes some metamorphic and volcanic rocks.

For more information on geological time periods, see the chart in the Science and Nature section.

Highest Point in Each Province and Territory

Province/Territory	Highest Point	Elev. (m)
Newfoundland & Labrador	Mt. Caubvick[1]	1 652
Prince Edward Island	46° 20'—63° 25' (Queen's County)	142
Nova Scotia	46° 42'—60° 36' (Cape Breton Highlands)	532
New Brunswick	Mt. Carleton	817
Quebec	Mont D'Iberville[2]	1 652
Ontario	Ishpatina Ridge	693
Manitoba	Baldy Mtn.	832
Saskatchewan	Cypress Hills	1 468
Alberta	Mt. Columbia	3 747
British Columbia	Fairweather Mtn.	4 663
Yukon Territory	Mt. Logan	5 959
Northwest Territories	61° 52'—127° 42' (unnamed peak, Mackenzie Mtns.)	2 773
Nunavut	Barbeau Peak (Ellesmere Island)	2 616

Source: *Natural Resources Canada*

(1) On the Nfld & Lab./Que. border; also known as Mt. D'Iberville in Quebec; next highest point in Nfld & Lab. is Cirque Mt. at 1,568 m. (2) On the Nfld & Lab./ Que. border; also known as Mt. Caubvick in Nfld & Lab.; next highest point in Que. is Mont Jacques-Cartier at 1,268 m.

Largest Lakes in Canada

Lake	Area[1] (sq. km)	Lake	Area[1] (sq. km)
Superior, Ont.[2]	82 100	Nettilling, NT*	5 542
Huron, Ont.[3]	59 600	Winnipegosis, Man.	5 374
Great Bear, NWT	31 328	Nipigon, Ont.	4 848
Great Slave, NWT	28 568	Manitoba, Man.	4 624
Erie, Ont.[4]	25 700	Dubawnt, NT*	3 833
Winnipeg, Man.	24 387	Lake of the Woods, Ont./Man.[6]	4 472
Ontario, Ont.[5]	18 960	Amadjuak, NT*	3 115
Athabasca, Sask.	7 935	Melville, Nfld/Lab.	3 069
Reindeer, Sask./Man.	6 650	Wollaston, Sask.	2 681
Smallwood Reservoir, Nfld/Lab.	6 527	Lac Mistassini, Que.	2 335

Source: *Natural Resources Canada*   *Nunavut*

(1) Total area, including islands except for the Great Lakes, where area does not include islands larger than 0.052 sq. km. (2) Includes 53,400 sq. km in US. (3) Includes 23,600 sq. km in US. (4) Includes 12,900 sq. km in US. (5) Includes 8,960 sq. km in US. (6) Includes 1,322 sq. km in US.

The Great Lakes

The Great Lakes form the largest body of fresh water in the world and with their connecting waterways are the largest inland water transportation unit. They enable shipping to reach the Atlantic via the St. Lawrence River; the Gulf of Mexico via the Illinois Waterway, from Lake Michigan to the Mississippi River; a third outlet connects with the Hudson River and thence the Atlantic via the New York State Barge Canal System.

	Superior	Michigan	Huron	Erie	Ontario
Length in km	563	494	332	388	311
Breadth in km	257	190	295	92	85
Deepest soundings in metres	405	281	229	64	244
Volume of water in cubic km	12 100	4 920	3 540	484	1 640
Area[1] (sq. km) in US	53 400	57 800	23 600	12 900	8 960
Area[1] (sq. km) in Canada	28 700	0	36 000	12 800	10 000
Total Area[1] (sq. km) US and Canada	**82 100**	**57 800**	**59 600**	**25 700**	**18 960**
National boundary line in km	430	0	446	404	281

Source: *Natural Resources Canada*   (1) Does not include islands larger than 0.052 sq. km.

Longest Rivers in Canada

River	Length (km)	Flows Into	River	Length (km)	Flows Into
Mackenzie	4 241	Arctic Ocean	North Saskatchewan	1 287	Saskatchewan R.
Yukon	3 185	Bering Sea	Ottawa	1 271	St. Lawrence R.
St. Lawrence	3 058	Gulf of St. Lawrence	Athabasca	1 231	Lake Athabasca
Nelson	2 575	Hudson Bay	Liard	1 115	Mackenzie R.
Columbia	2 000	Pacific Ocean	Assiniboine	1 070	Red R.
Saskatchewan	1 939	Lake Winnipeg (via Cedar Lake)	Severn	982	Hudson Bay
			Albany	982	James Bay
Peace	1 923	Lake Athabasca	Back	974	Arctic Ocean
Churchill (Man.)	1 609	Hudson Bay	Thelon	904	Hudson Bay
South Saskatchewan	1 392	Saskatchewan R.	La Grande Rivière	893	James Bay
Fraser	1 370	Pacific Ocean			

Source: *Natural Resources Canada*

Canadian Heritage Rivers System (CHRS)

It's not quite a national holiday, but the second Sunday in June is now Canadian Rivers Day, which was celebrated for the first time **June 8, 2003**. Heritage Minister Sheila Copps proclaimed the special day in mid-2002. Among the groups calling for the special day was the Canadian Heritage Rivers System board, which was established in 1984 as part of a federal-provincial plan to manage Canada's rivers. Individual rivers are administered by the government responsible for the land each flows through. However, the CHRS assists by supporting a management plan with funding and policy initiatives. No management plan is put forward until after public consultation is complete and a consensus has been reached.

The Heritage Rivers System is overseen by a fourteen member board made up of a representative appointed by each of the provincial and territorial governments, plus a federal appointee from the Department of Indian Affairs and Northern Development and another from Canadian Heritage's Parks Canada. This board meets at least once a year to designate funding and program priorities, and to review and approve new guidelines and policies. 30 rivers have been designated for special management and conservation attention; 9 have been nominated for CHRS status (Bay du Nord, Newfoundland; Churchill, Saskatchewan; Clearwater, Alberta section; Cowichan, B.C.; Hayes, Manitoba; Jacques-Cartier, Quebec; Missinaibi, Ontario; Montague-Three Rivers, P.E.I.; Tatshenshini, Yukon. More are under study, including the Coppermine and the Mackenzie.

For information about the CHRS and detailed fact sheets on each river, visit www.chrs.ca.

Designated Rivers	Location	Length
Alsek River	Kluane National Park Reserve, Yukon	90 km section
Arctic Red River	Arctic Red River (Tsiigèhnjik), Northwest Territories	450 km
Athabasca River	Canadian Rocky Mountains National Parks, Alberta and BC	1 538 km
Bloodvein River	Woodland Caribou Provincial Park/Atikaki Wilderness Park, Ontario/Manitoba	306 km section
Bonnet Plume River	Yukon	350 km
Boundary Waters-Voyageur Waterway	Quetico, Middle Falls and Voyageur Provincial Parks, Ontario	250 km section
Clearwater River	Clearwater River Provincial Wilderness Park, Saskatchewan	187 km section in Sask
Detroit River	Ontario	51 km
Fraser River	British Columbia	1 375 km
French River	French River Provincial Park, Ontario	110 km
Grand River	Ontario	627 km
Hillsborough River	Prince Edward Island	45 km
Humber River	Ontario	100 km
Kazan River	Nunavut	850 km
Kicking Horse	Canadian Rocky Mountains National Parks, Alberta and BC	68 km section
Main River	Newfoundland and Labrador	57 km
Margaree-Lake Ainslie River System	Nova Scotia	120 km
Mattawa River	Mattawa River Provincial Park, Ontario	65 km section
North Saskatchewan River	Canadian Rocky Mountains National Parks, Alberta and BC	48.5 headwater section
Rideau Waterway	Ontario	202 km
Seal River	Manitoba	260 km section
Shelburne River	Nova Scotia	53 km
Soper River	Nunavut	248 km
South Nahanni River	Nahanni National Park Reserve, Northwest Territories	540 km
St. Croix	New Brunswick	185 km
St. Marys River	Ontario	125 km
Thames River	Ontario	273 km
Thelon River	Nunavut	545 km section
Upper Restigouche	New Brunswick	55 km section
Yukon River	Yukon	Thirty Mile Section 48 km

Source: *Parks Canada*

VEGETATION

Coniferous forests dominated by spruce, fir and pine cover much of the Canadian landscape, sweeping across the continent in a broad band. Through the rest of the country there is a range of forest conditions. To the north, cold temperatures limit growth and the trees become small and fewer in number. At the tree line, trees grow only in sheltered river valleys. The tree line marks the northern extent of forests and the beginning of tundra conditions (moss, lichens and dwarf vegetation with permanent frozen subsoil).

The massive spruce, fir and pine of the forests along the coast of British Columbia are encouraged by a friendly climate. The moisture-laden winds from the Pacific Ocean keep the land well-supplied with rain. Under these conditions tree growth is rapid: the soils are constantly being replenished with minerals by the rains, and plant decay is also rapid in the damp conditions, thereby releasing more minerals for tree growth. With average monthly temperatures seldom going below freezing, the growing season is long. Coniferous trees thrive under such conditions.

The Interior Plains is one region of Canada that is not covered by forests because there is not enough precipitation, or available moisture, to sustain tree growth. In Alberta, Saskatchewan and Manitoba, forests gradually give way from north to south through a transitional area called the park belt, which contains both trees and grassland, before yielding to grasslands. Within these provinces, there are areas where moisture levels are insufficient to support grasslands and even hardy grasses have difficulty growing. During the 1930s, the lack of rainfall in the Interior Plains led to "dust bowl" conditions because vegetation could not grow enough to anchor the soil.

The forests of southeastern Canada are mixed, containing both coniferous and deciduous trees. Adequate rainfall and warm temperatures allow the less hardy species such as oak, maple, hickory and walnut to flourish in southern Ontario and Quebec and the Maritime provinces.

The Arctic tundra is so very dry and cold that the growing season is extremely limited. The vegetation of the tundra consists of mosses, lichen, dwarf bushes and heather. These plants are able to grow because they have adapted to the difficult conditions through characteristics such as small size and slow growth. Some shrubs and lichen grow so slowly that their development must be measured in centimetres per century.

AGRICULTURE

There are four main types of farms in Canada: livestock farms, grain farms producing such crops as wheat and oats, mixed farms producing both grain and livestock, and special crop farms producing vegetables, fruits, tobacco and other products. Both the type and amount of farming within Canada are affected by climate and location.

■ The Atlantic Region

The Atlantic region is an area of diverse agricultural activity. Newfoundland, because of poorly developed soils and a difficult climate, has a limited agricultural industry supplying only local markets. Encouraged by a moist climate and silty, stone-free soils, farming is the leading industry on Prince Edward Island; potatoes are the main crop. The land also supports mixed grains and dairy farms.

Nova Scotia's main agricultural areas surround the Bay of Fundy and Northumberland Strait where they are protected from Atlantic gales; dairy farming and poultry production are common. Nova Scotia's Annapolis Valley is famous for fruit, mainly apples. In New Brunswick, potatoes and livestock are produced in the Saint John River valley, and there is mixed farming in the northwest of the province.

■ The Central Region

In Canada's central region, the fertile soils and moist climate of southern Ontario and Quebec support a thriving agricultural industry. Although these growing conditions allow a variety of crops, the population concentration in this area encourages specialization in products with high transportation costs. Dairy farms are concentrated around Montreal and in southwestern Ontario, supplying milk, butter and cheese to the major centres such as London, Hamilton, Toronto, Kingston,

Montreal and Quebec City. Vegetable crops are also grown near these centres. Farms specializing in poultry and egg production, sheep and hogs are also common.

The Niagara Peninsula, between lakes Ontario and Erie, is a major fruit-growing centre. The moderating effects of the lakes delay the growth of the fruit trees in the spring until the danger of frost is past. Tender fruit crops—peaches, pears, plums and cherries—as well as grapes thrive in these conditions. Tobacco (and now ginseng) grow well on the glacially created sand plains of southwestern Ontario.

■ The Prairie Provinces

Manitoba, Saskatchewan and Alberta contain 80 percent of Canada's farmland. Here, a combination of flat, easily worked land, fertile soils, long sunny summer days and sufficient precipitation encourages the healthy growth of high-quality grains. This area grows most of Canada's wheat, about 90 percent of its barley and rye, and more than 75 percent of its oats.

Manitoba grows canola and flax in addition to wheat and other grains. Mixed farming in the province emphasizes beef cattle. Dairy farms are common around Winnipeg. Saskatchewan grows about 60 percent of Canada's wheat and large quantities of other grains. Mixed farming, poultry, egg and livestock production contribute to the provincial economy. Alberta, also a major grain producer, has more beef cattle ranches than any other province. They are located mainly in the south of the province and in the foothills of the Rocky Mountains where the steep slopes and dry land is unsuited to growing crops.

■ The Pacific Region

In the Pacific region, only 2 percent of British Columbia is agricultural land. But the pockets of farmland are extremely productive. The lower mainland and the southern tip of Vancouver Island comprise the Georgia Strait agricultural region, an area concentrating on dairy farming and poultry raising to supply the province's population centres. Other crops include raspberries, strawberries, peas, tomatoes and flowers.

The Okanagan Valley contains 90 percent of British Columbia's orchards, producing grapes, apples and tender fruit such as peaches, plums, apricots and cherries. Here, local climatic and physiographic characteristics have resulted in conditions suitable for the orchard industry, although irrigation is often necessary and frost damage is a hazard. Beef cattle and sheep are raised in the interior of the province, where growing conditions are not suitable for crops requiring cultivation, but grazing can be carried out.

■ The North

Canada's North generally has soil and climatic conditions unsuited to agriculture. A small number of farms produce some dairy products, beef cattle and vegetables for the local market.

That Elusive North Pole

*L*ike a giant bar magnet, the Earth has a north pole and a south pole. The north pole is located in the Canadian Arctic Ocean, and the south pole is off the coast of Antarctica. If you were to follow a compass needle north, you would eventually come to the magnetic north pole and in 2004, that would take you to latitude 83.1 degrees north and longitude 110.8 degrees.

But if you made the trip twice, you wouldn't necessarily arrive at the same place—the magnetic pole is slowly drifting across the north, moving approximately northwest at about 40 kilometres a year. But there's more—the position of the pole is an average, and on any given day, it may be displaced by 80 kilometres or more. However, although the pole's motion on any given day is irregular, the average path forms a well-defined oval.

Scientists from the Geological Survey of Canada track the motion of the pole with periodic surveys; the latest ended in 2001. Climate and the remote Arctic location make the job tough: the survey can be carried out only when the sea is frozen, it is warm enough to work, and there is sufficient sunlight to allow safe landing on the ice—basically late April to mid-May. Each observation of the pole requires about one hour on the ice, but its distance from land means scientists can only make about four tests a day.

Source: *Geological Survey of Canada*

CLIMATE

Within Canada, climate is primarily affected by surrounding landforms, proximity to large bodies of water and the degree of latitude.

Landforms Air masses are forced to rise over mountains which lie in their path. As this happens, the air cools and its ability to retain moisture is reduced. Condensation then occurs and precipitation falls in the form of snow or rain. For instance, Prince Rupert on the western side (windward) of the Coastal Mountains receives over 2,500 mm of precipitation annually.

On the leeward side of the mountains (the side away from the wind), the air mass descends, warms and is able to once again retain moisture. Moreover, there may be little moisture left in the air mass. Thus precipitation is light and a rain-shadow effect is created. In a rain-shadow area, such as near Kamloops, B.C., desert-like conditions exist.

Water Parts of Canada near large bodies of water have more moderate climates due to the differing abilities of land and water to gain or lose heat. Whereas water can act like a heat bank, releasing accumulated heat through the fall and early winter and warming the land nearby, the reverse is also true. In the spring and early summer, the water is cooler than the land and can keep the land temperature lower.

Wind direction also determines the degree to which this influence is felt. On the Pacific coast the prevailing westerlies blow off the water onto the land and the influence of the Pacific Ocean is keenly felt. On the Atlantic coast, the westerlies blow off the land onto the water so the effect of the Atlantic Ocean is not

as pronounced. Victoria's lowest monthly average temperature is 4.6°C in January with an annual range of only 11°C between the warmest and coldest months while Halifax's lowest monthly average is –4.8°C in February with an annual range of 22.7°C.

Latitude Latitude is the distance north or south of the equator and is expressed in degrees. Its effects on climate are twofold. Firstly, the further north the location, the more the curvature of the earth results in the sunlight spreading over a greater surface area. This decreases the solar radiation per unit area of ground so that less warmth from the sun is felt. Secondly, solar radiation has to travel a greater distance through the atmosphere at higher latitudes which again reduces the amount of energy reaching the earth.

Other Factors Because the prevailing wind direction is from west to east, the air masses move eastward across the continent picking up moisture from lakes and rivers and releasing it further along. Therefore, generally, precipitation increases with greater distance eastward from the central continent: the average precipitation in Winnipeg is 504 mm, Toronto 781 mm, Montreal 940 mm and Halifax 1,474 mm.

Also, the Labrador Current affects climate on the Atlantic coast. This cold current within the Atlantic Ocean flows south along the coast of Newfoundland and Labrador and reduces the moderating effect of the ocean on the land. It also causes the thick Newfoundland fog when relatively warm air is cooled from below on contact with the cold waters.

Water Institute Wins World Honour

*T*he National Water Research Institute (NWRI) was awarded the prestigious Cannes International Prize for Water and Sciences in mid-June 2003, during the 5th Cannes Water Symposium held in Cannes, France. The prize honoured 30 years of contributions to water science.

The Institute, in Burlington, Ontario, is Canada's pre-eminent freshwater research institute and its scientific investigations are vitally important to the conservation and protection of Canada's water resources. It generates scientific knowledge through ecosystem-based research to support the development of sound government policies and programs, public decision-making, and early identification of environmental problems. NWRI scientists are leading the way in recognizing new threats to the quality and quantity of freshwater and in producing the scientific knowledge needed by policy makers and governments to act swiftly to confront them. Web site: www.nwri.ca.

Source: *Environment Canada*

Average Weather Data for Selected Airports in Canada

Airport	Temperature °C				Precipitation	
	Winter		Summer		Annual Snowfall cm	Total Precipitation mm
	High	Low	High	Low		
Vancouver	6.1	0.5	21.7	13.2	48.2	119.0
Calgary	-2.8	-15.1	22.9	9.4	126.7	412.6
Edmonton	-7.3	-16.0	22.8	12.1	123.5	476.9
Regina	-10.7	-21.6	25.7	11.8	105.9	388.1
Winnipeg	-12.7	-22.8	25.8	13.3	110.6	513.7
Toronto	-2.1	-10.5	26.8	14.8	115.4	792.7
Ottawa	-6.1	-15.3	26.5	15.4	235.7	943.5
Montreal	-5.8	-14.9	26.3	15.5	214.2	966.8
Saint John	-2.7	-13.6	22.4	11.7	256.9	1390.3
Halifax	-0.2	-9.2	22.1	13.5	176.4	1421.4
Charlottetown	-3.3	-12.6	23.2	13.8	311.9	1173.3
St. John's	-0.9	-8.6	20.3	10.5	322.3	1513.7
Iqaluit	-22.5	-30.6	11.6	3.7	235.8	412.0
Yellowknife	-22.7	-30.9	21.1	12.4	151.8	280.7
Whitehorse	-13.3	-22.0	20.5	7.7	145.0	267.4

Airport	Wind			Sunshine	
	Average Speed km/hr	Prevailing Direction	Peak Wind km/hr	Bright Sunshine hours	Possible Sunshine hours
Vancouver	11.8	E	129	1928	4781
Calgary	14.8	N	127	2405	4585
Edmonton	12.1	NW	117	2299	4693
Regina	18.6	SE	153	2338	4679
Winnipeg	16.9	S	129	2372	4646
Toronto	14.7	N	135	2038	4653
Ottawa	12.9	W	135	2061	4631
Montreal	14.3	W	161	2029	4627
Saint John	16.1	SW	146	1950	4515
Halifax	15.1	NW	150	1965	4525
Charlottetown	17.4	SW	177	1859	4610
St. John's	23.3	W	193	1512	4629
Iqaluit	15.4	NW	156	1506	4934
Yellowknife	14.0	E	113	2265	5234
Whitehorse	12.7	S	106	1855	4979

Airport	Annual Number of Days						
	Frost	Wet Weather	Thunder-storms	Freezing Precipitation	Smoke/Haze	Blowing Snow	Fog
Vancouver	46	166	6	1	48	0	23
Calgary	196	114	27	6	14	7	21
Edmonton	179	126	19	7	17	3	10
Regina	200	115	22	13	4	24	27
Winnipeg	194	124	27	12	11	22	16
Toronto	146	146	28	9	83	8	27
Ottawa	159	163	24	17	64	12	34
Montreal	155	165	24	13	51	11	17
Saint John	169	162	11	12	14	10	98
Halifax	142	166	11	13	16	11	100
Charlottetown	166	184	10	18	16	22	44
St. John's	174	216	5	39	11	25	119
Iqaluit	272	155	0	6	0	58	14
Yellowknife	222	119	5	12	9	9	18
Whitehorse	225	122	7	2	2	2	14

Source: Environment Canada

Ocean Currents

Oceans or large bodies of water such as the Great Lakes affect the climate of the land nearby because they act as heat reservoirs and heat exchangers. Water heats up more slowly than land, and it holds that heat for a longer time. Because of this, the climate in the areas closest to water is more moderate than the climate inland: even though the air over the coastal land is warmer in summer and colder in winter than the air over water at the same latitude, it won't be as hot (or as cold) as the air over land that is far away from the coast.

These water bodies also affect rainfall, wind and clouds: when the water is warmer than the air above it, it generates clouds, rain and wind; when the water is colder than the air above, the opposite happens—there is likely to be fog, less rain, and winds are reduced.

As the ocean currents move heat and cold around the world, Canada is affected by the warm Gulf Stream on the Atlantic coast and the weaker but still warm Alaska Current on the Pacific side; both of these flow northward. Cold currents such as the West Greenland Current and the Labrador Current flow south from the Arctic on the east side; the banks of fog off the southeast coast of Newfoundland mark the spot where the Labrador Current meets the Gulf Stream. In general, however, because our weather flows from west to east, it is the currents on the Pacific side that have the greatest effect on Canada's climate.

Inland, the Great Lakes and Hudson Bay are two vast areas of water that affect the climate around them: the Great Lakes act as a huge heat reservoir that moderates the weather in southern Ontario and Quebec, while Hudson Bay is frozen over for six months, and even during the summer months melting ice keeps the surface water temperature close to freezing. Hudson Bay's most common effect is fog in summer and precipitation, cloud and strong winds during the rest of the year.

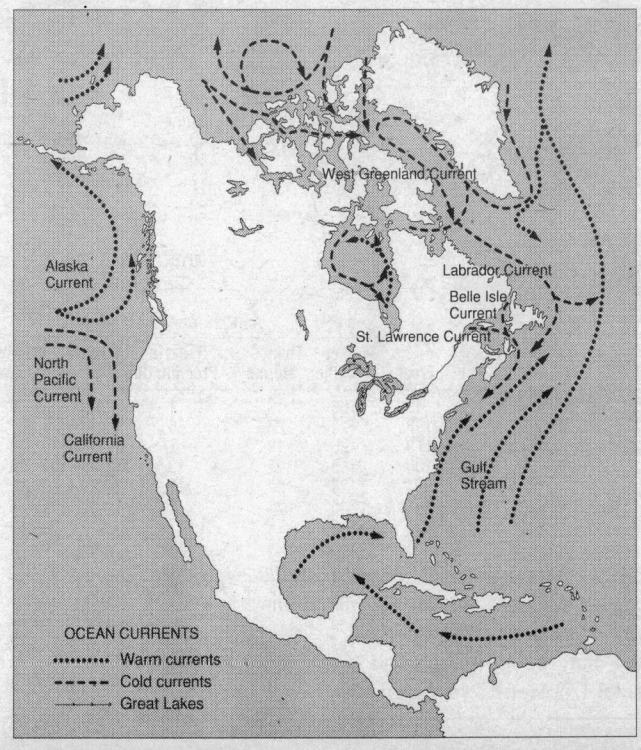

SUMMER AIR MASSES AND CIRCULATION

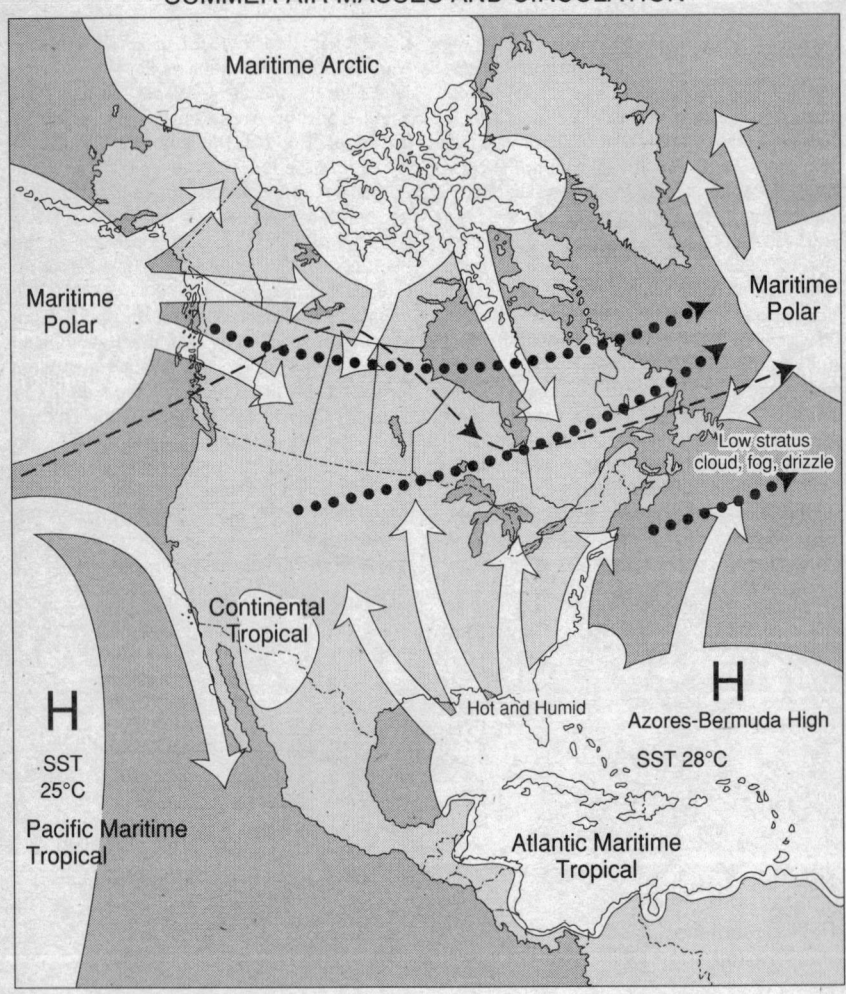

Maritime Arctic

Maritime
Polar

Maritime
Polar

Low stratus
cloud, fog, drizzle

Continental
Tropical

Hot and Humid

H

H

Azores-Bermuda High

SST
25°C

SST 28°C

Pacific Maritime
Tropical

Atlantic Maritime
Tropical

– – – – Polar jet stream
●●●● Primary storm tracks
SST Sea Surface Temperature

Pacific Maritime Tropical: high pressure precludes moist air
Atlantic Maritime Tropical: very hot, humid, unstable
Maritime Arctic: modified by water
Maritime Polar: warmer, more stable than Maritime Arctic air
Continental Tropical: hot, dry, unstable

WINTER AIR MASSES AND CIRCULATION

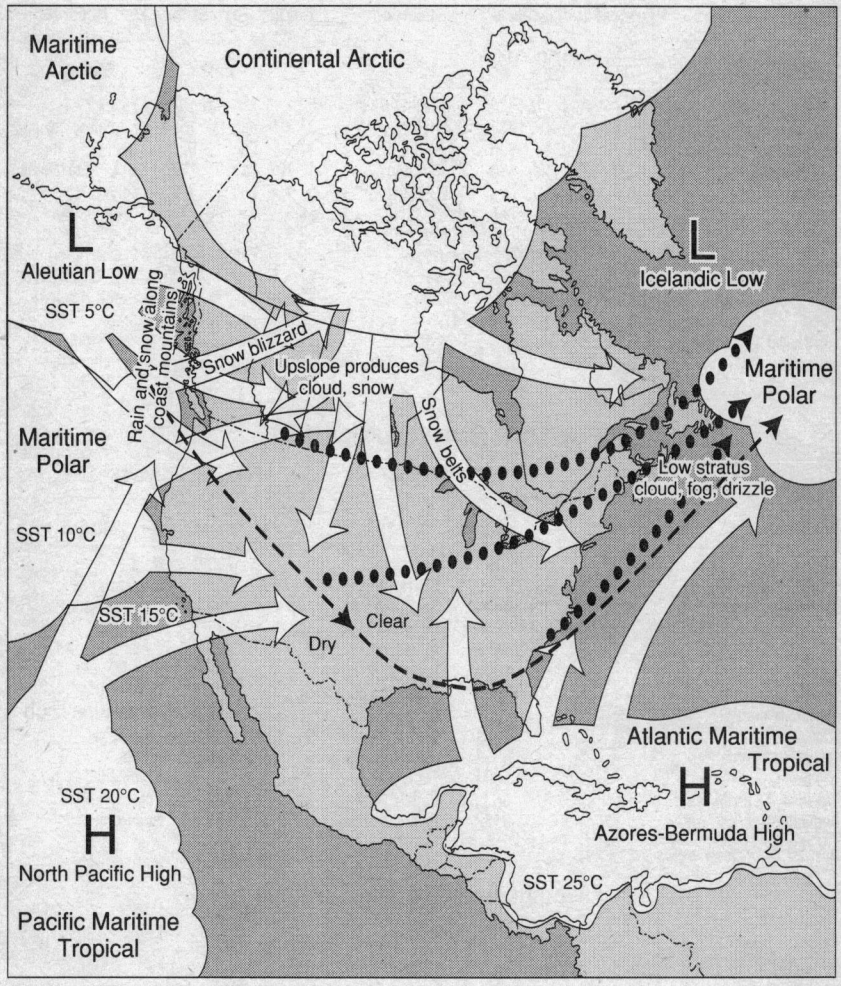

Maritime Arctic

Continental Arctic

Maritime Arctic

L Aleutian Low

SST 5°C

Snow blizzard

Rain and snow along coast mountains

Upslope produces cloud, snow

Snow belts

L Icelandic Low

Maritime Polar

Low stratus cloud, fog, drizzle

Maritime Polar

SST 10°C

SST 15°C

Clear

Dry

Atlantic Maritime Tropical

SST 20°C

H North Pacific High

H Azores-Bermuda High

SST 25°C

Pacific Maritime Tropical

– – – – Polar jet stream

●●●●● Primary storm tracks

SST Sea Surface Temperature

Continental Arctic: very cold, dry, stable
Maritime Arctic: very unstable, clouds, frequent showers or flurries
Maritime Polar: milder, more stable than Arctic air
Pacific Maritime Tropical: stable in lower 1000m
Atlantic Maritime Tropical: warm and humid

Provincial Weather Facts

Province	Warmest Temperature Ever Recorded			Coldest Temperature Ever Recorded		
	°C	Date	Station	°C	Date	Station
Newfoundland & Labrador	41.7	Aug. 11, 1914	Northwest River	-51.1	Feb. 17, 1973	Esker 2
P.E.I.	36.7	Aug. 19, 1935	Charlottetown	-37.2	Jan. 26, 1884	Kilmahumaig
New Brunswick	39.4	Aug. 18, 1935	Nepisiguit Falls	-47.2	Feb. 1, 1955	Sisson Dam
Nova Scotia	38.3	Aug. 19, 1935	Collegeville	-41.1	Jan. 31, 1920	Upper Stewiacke
Quebec	40.0	July 6, 1921	Ville Marie	-54.4	Feb. 5, 1923	Doucet
Ontario	42.2	July 20, 1919	Biscotasing	-58.3	Jan. 23, 1935	Iroquois Falls
Manitoba	44.4	July 11, 1936	St. Albans	-52.8	Jan. 9, 1899	Norway House
Saskatchewan	45.0	July 5, 1937	Midale	-56.7	Feb. 1, 1893	Prince Albert
Alberta	43.3	July 21, 1931	Bassano Dam	-61.1	Jan. 11, 1911	Fort Vermilion
British Columbia	44.4	July 16, 1941	Lillooet	-58.9	Jan. 31, 1947	Smith River
Yukon	36.1	June 14, 1969	Mayo	-63.0	Feb. 3, 1947	Snag
Northwest Territories	39.4	July 18, 1941	Fort Smith	-57.2	Dec. 26, 1917	Fort Smith
Nunavut	33.9	July 22, 1973	Arviat	-57.8	Feb. 13, 1973	Shepherd Bay

Source: *Environment Canada*

Average Annual Precipitation

Province	Greatest		Least	
	mm	Station	mm	Station
Newfoundland & Labrador	1 699.7	Burgeo	739.8	Nain
Prince Edward Island	1 169.4	Charlottetown A	921.0	Montague
New Brunswick	1 444.4	Saint John A	909.6	Upsalquitch Lake
Nova Scotia	1 630.7	Ingonish Beach	973.7	Pugwash
Quebec	1 559.8	Mont Logan	295.9	Cape Hopes Advance
Ontario	1 191.1	West Guilford	569.0	Kenora TCPL
Manitoba	696.1	Peace Gardens	402.3	Churchill A
Saskatchewan	530.1	Brabant Lake	287.9	Nashlyn
Alberta	1 072.0	Waterton Park HQ	270.8	Empress
British Columbia	6 655.0	Henderson Lake	205.6	Ashcroft
Yukon	590.6	Tuchitua	135.9	Komakuk Beach A
Northwest Territories	663.2	Cape Dyer A	137.6	Tuktoyaktuk
Nunavut	355.1	Fort Simpson	61.0	Rea Point

Source: *Environment Canada*

Average Annual Bright Sunshine

Province	Greatest		Least	
	Hrs	Station	Hrs	Station
Newfoundland & Labrador	1 572	Churchill Falls A	1 303	St. Shotts
Prince Edward Island	1 967	Tignish	1 817	East Baltic
New Brunswick	2 010	Chatham A	1 373	Summit Depot
Nova Scotia	1 969	Shearwater A	1 449	Sable Island
Quebec	2 054	Montreal Int'l. A	1 158	Mont Logan
Ontario	2 203	Thunder Bay A	1 635	New Liskeard
Manitoba	2 460	Delta U	1 828	Churchill A
Saskatchewan	2 537	Estevan A	2 073	Cree Lake
Alberta	2 490	Coronation A	1 724	Banff
British Columbia	2 244	Cranbrook A	949	Stewart A
Yukon	1 844	Whitehorse A	1 789	Watson Lake A
Northwest Territories	2 277	Yellowknife A	1 899	Inuvik
Nunavut	2 091	Eureka	1 443	Mould Bay A

Source: *Environment Canada*

Average Annual Snowfall

Province	Greatest		Least	
	cm	Station	cm	Station
Newfoundland & Labrador	322.8	Woody Point	91.6	St. Shotts
Prince Edward Island	330.6	Charlottetown A	173.3	Montague
New Brunswick	448.8	Dawson Settlement	176.2	Southwest Head
Nova Scotia	406.7	Cheticamp	104.1	Baccaro
Quebec	648.4	Mont Logan	161.6	Havre aux Maisons
Ontario	430.0	Searchmount	74.0	Lakeview MOE
Manitoba	332.7	Island Lake	94.9	Lundar
Saskatchewan	348.6	Collins Bay	58.0	Aylesbury
Alberta	642.9	Columbia Icefield	59.9	Empress
British Columbia	1 433.0	Glacier NP Mt. Fidelity	20.4	Carnation Creek
Yukon	365.7	Keno Hill	60.1	Komakuk Beach A
Northwest Territories...............	234.5	Fort McPherson	65.2	Tuktoyaktuk
Nunavut	602.4	Cape Dyer A	28.6	Rea Point

Source: *Environment Canada*

Wind

Province	Highest Average Annual Wind Speed			Highest % of Calms	
	km/hr		Station	%	Station
Newfoundland & Labrador	28.0	(W)	Bonavista	17.1	Wabush Lake A
Prince Edward Island	22.4	(SSW)	Summerside A	4.4	Summerside A
New Brunswick	22.4	(W)	Miscou Island (AUT)	11.8	Fredericton A
Nova Scotia	25.7	(W)	Sable Island	16.9	Greenwood A
Quebec	32.0	(NW)	Grindstone Island	20.4	Gaspé A
Ontario	21.0	(SW)	Bruce Ontario Hydro	30.2	White River
Manitoba	22.7	(WNW)	Churchill A	21.0	Norway House A
Saskatchewan	22.9	(W)	Swift Current A	12.8	La Ronge A
Alberta	21.5	(W)	Pincher Creek	39.7	High Level A
British Columbia	33.7	(NW)	Cape St. James	48.5	Quesnel A
Yukon	14.1	(SSE)	Whitehorse A	57.5	Dawson A
Northwest Territories	19.9	(E)	Nicholson Peninsula	18.9	Fort Simpson
Nunavut	35.3	(NW)	Resolution Island	35.1	Eureka

Source: *Environment Canada*

"Coldest Days" (Wind Chill)

Province	ET/WCF[1]	Location	Date	Temp (°C)	Wind (km/hr)
Newfoundland & Labrador	-71/2814	Wabush Lake	Jan. 20, 1975	-41	40
Prince Edward Island	-57/2450	Charlottetown	Jan. 18, 1982	-32	37
Nova Scotia	-53/2309	Sydney	Jan. 18, 1982	-25	59
New Brunswick	-61/2547	Charlo	Jan. 18, 1982	-31	54
Quebec	-77/3001	Nitchequon	Jan. 20, 1975	-42	56
Ontario	-70/2753	Thunder Bay	Jan. 10, 1982	-36	54
Manitoba	-76/2938	Churchill	Jan. 18, 1975	-41	56
Saskatchewan	-70/2757	Swift Current	Dec. 15, 1964	-34	89
Alberta	-68/2740	Red Deer	Dec. 15, 1964	-35	61
British Columbia	-69/2749	Old Glory Mtn.	Dec. 15, 1964	-36	58
Yukon	-83/3152	Komakuk Beach	Feb. 12, 1975	-50	40
NWT/Nunavut	-92/3357	Pelly Bay	Jan. 13, 1975	-51	56

Source: *Environment Canada*

(1) ET is equivalent wind chill temperature in °C. WCF is wind chill factor in watts/square metre

Weather Highlights July 2002 to June 2003

JULY 2002: Ontario and Quebec started July in a heat wave. By the second week, temperatures in western Canada also climbed into the 30s. In Edmonton, the temperature exceeded 34° on July 11 and 12, breaking daily record highs, and at Princeton, B.C., the thermometer soared just a tenth of a degree short of 40°—likely the highest temperature nationally in 2002. Across Alberta and Saskatchewan, severe heat stress began to take its toll on moisture-starved crops. Then at the end of July, century-old low temperature records were shattered in many parts of the western Prairies when thermometers dipped to freezing.

On July 4, a weak tornado near Ste-Jacques, N.B., uprooted hundreds of trees and damaged several buildings. Winds were estimated at 180 km/h. Trees fell across power lines, cutting hydro to 10,000 people. The main storm system struck Charlotte-town, dumping 74 mm of rain in less than two hours. The deluge flooded streets and basements, and knocked out 60 to 100 power transformers.

On July 6, millions of residents in eastern Canada woke up to the smell of acrid smoke and the sight of hazy skies caused by forest fires south of James Bay in Quebec, the province's worst in a decade. The smoke pall cut visibility to three kilometres in places, and dimmed sunshine for much of north-eastern North America.

A vicious storm swept through central New Brunswick on July 23, inflicting considerable damage at Canadian Forces Base Gagetown.

AUGUST 2002: August got off to a chilly start in western Canada. Temperatures fell below the freezing mark in B.C., Alberta, and Saskatchewan, resulting in frost damage to many already drought-stricken crops. Precipitation varied across much of Canada. The rains that western farmers had begged for in June, and didn't want at harvest time, fell in August at the worst possible time.

Lack of rain created drought concerns in central Canada for the second summer in a row. For Sarnia, London and Kitchener-Waterloo, among others, it was the driest August and driest month ever. Toronto (Pearson airport) had its driest August since 1937. In the Great Lakes region, five of the last six summers have been drier than normal. Across the north, Iqaluit had its third driest August in 57 years, while to the west, Inuvik had its fourth wettest August in 45 years.

In the east, torrid heat along with abundant sunshine and a sluggish circulation meant a record-breaking number of smog episodes in southern Ontario. In the most seriously affected area, between Toronto and Windsor, authorities issued 10 advisories in the summer totaling 27 days—more than last year's record. In Quebec, there were 15 smog days on seven separate occasions. Maritime officials issued smog and health advisories on seven occasions.

SEPTEMBER 2002: Warm, summery weather continued across most of Canada. Ottawa set a record when the temperature on September 9 soared past 35°—the highest temperature ever for so late in the year.

In Toronto, the average June 1 to September 30 temperature was 21.5° a whopping 3.2 degrees warmer than normal and the warmest in 63 years. The number of hot days above 32° was 23 (normal is 5); the number of hot nights above 20° was a record 19 (normal is 5). In Montreal, the June 21 to September 20 period was the driest and warmest ever. Incredibly, total summer rainfall was 25 percent less than the previous summer's, itself a record low.

September saw 8 of the season's 12 tropical storms—an all-time record for a single month in the Atlantic Ocean. Hurricane Gustav was the first hurricane to strike Nova Scotia since 1996, making landfall near Sydney, N.S., on September 12, and snapping utility poles, downing trees and causing minor flooding. Its greatest rainfall (100 mm) occurred near Antigonish, N.S., and highest wind speed (122 km/h) was on Sable Island.

Wine producers in the Okanagan Valley and Ontario's Niagara Peninsula described this year's grape crop as the best ever due to the hot, dry weather in August and September. Across the entire Arctic Ocean, sea ice cover in September was less than in any previous year in the satellite observation period, dating back to 1978.

OCTOBER 2002: British Columbia continued dry in October. In Vancouver, a scant 18.3 mm of rain fell at the International Airport compared to the normal 112.5 mm. In the interior, Vernon experienced its driest ever June-to-October rainfall with only 72 mm— the lowest since record-keeping began in 1900. By the end of October, reservoirs in the Lower Mainland and on Vancouver Island had fallen to about 25 percent of capacity.

Queen Elizabeth II arrived in Iqaluit, Nunavut, on October 2 for the start of her Golden Jubilee tour of Canada. Large crowds came out in sub-freezing temperatures and snow flurries. Two days later, thousands of residents in Victoria greeted the Queen and Prince Philip under clear skies and warm sunshine. But on October 8, in Winnipeg, the temperature hovered close to freezing and strong north-northwesterly winds blew at 35 km/h, gusting to 50. As it turned out, Winnipeg had its coldest October on record and the only October when the average temperature stayed below zero.

NOVEMBER 2002: British Columbia's dry spell eased, following 16 consecutive days of rain. Between November 5 and 21, Vancouver got 147.3 mm of rain, but the month's total of 147.7 mm was still below normal. A parade of storms drenched Halifax in November, making it the wettest on record. Nearly 280 mm of precipitation fell at the International Airport, compared to a norm of 154 mm. At mid-month, a huge storm system stalled southeast of Halifax, dumping a record 120.3 mm of rain on the city.

In mid-month, an early winter snowstorm hammered southern regions of Central Canada with more than 22 cm of snow plus freezing rain, rain and ice pellets. Following a quick melt, authorities issued a flood warning. Between Quebec and Gaspé, the huge storm dumped 30 to 40 cm of snow. Gaspé Airport reported nearly 63 cm of snow in a single day—a record for the area. Then, the intense low stalled just east of Newfoundland's Avalon Peninsula and continued to clobber the east coast for 40 hours or more. More than 30 cm of snow, whipped by

gusts of 100 km/h, created blizzard conditions in St. John's.

DECEMBER 2002: With the exception of Canada's east coast, monthly average temperatures were above normal during December. Nowhere was this more apparent than in the Northwest Territories, where monthly average temperatures exceeded the norm by as much as 10 degrees. By the middle of December, double-digit temperatures were observed in southern Alberta.

With the exception of the Pacific coast, southern regions of Saskatchewan and Manitoba, and Newfoundland, most of Canada had drier than normal conditions in December. A series of intense Pacific storms began pummeling the west coast with strong winds and heavy rain around the middle of December. One storm packed winds in excess of 130 km/h on the outer coast of Vancouver Island, prompting a rare warning for hurricane-force winds in the Strait of Georgia. On Newfoundland's east coast, fierce winds and heavy snow (up to 47 cm) forced officials to cancel flights and close schools. Snow for Christmas was the rule across most of the country, but just barely, with most places in Central Canada getting snow on December 25.

For Canada, 2002 was the tenth consecutive year with above-normal temperatures, but the cool spring broke the unprecedented string of 19 consecutive seasons with warmer-than-normal temperatures, dating back to the summer of 1997.

JANUARY 2003: Except for a few cold days, above-normal temperatures prevailed across most of B.C. and the northern territories in January. Across BC's Lower Mainland, outdoor enthusiasts packed tennis courts and golf courses and enthusiastic gardeners flocked to nurseries.

Some of the El Niño warming spilled across the Prairies during the first week of January. Officials in southern Alberta considered re-opening golf courses. On January 7, Calgary's temperature reached a stunning 17.6°—the hottest January day in the city's history. The unusually high temperatures in the Northwest Territories created havoc for those building ice roads. In Manitoba, 18 of 20 weather stations broke high temperature records. McCreary, Manitoba, logged a high of 14.5°. Maple Creek, Saskatchewan, was the province's hot spot at 18.3°. By the second week of January, though, temperatures in the West plunged well below –20° for the first time this winter.

In the East, there were no El Niño breezes. In the grip of a brutal cold snap, Toronto declared a series of cold weather alerts. Wind chills in the city reached –27°. In Montreal and Ottawa, on only one day during January —New Year's Day—did temperatures rise above the freezing mark. Temperatures surpassed the –30° mark in Bagotville, Quebec, and nearly hit –40° in Timmins, Ontario. Sydney, Nova Scotia, hit a record-low temperature of –23.6° on January 15.

A record snowfall of 45 cm occurred in St. John's on January 24, eclipsing the old record of 22 cm set in 1995. At month's end, the city was buried under 185 cm of new snow, breaking the 1960 record of 162 cm. On January 20. three avalanches near Revelstoke killed seven skiers. At the same time, another winter storm pounded the Maritimes, especially Cape Breton Island, where 25 to 30 cm added to a deepening snow cover. The blizzard closed schools and forced motorists off the roads. On January 27 and 28, another storm swept Cape Breton Island—this time with record rainfall, freezing rain and snow, flooding basements and coating streets in slippery snow and ice.

FEBRUARY 2003: Winter temperatures between December and February inclusive were warmer than normal across the west coast, in the north and across much of the Prairie provinces. It was especially mild in the Yukon where temperatures were more than 6 degrees warmer than normal. For the Pacific coast and the B.C. interior, winter turned out to be the third warmest on record —2 to 3 degrees warmer than normal and the warmest in 12 years. On the other hand, the Great Lakes basin saw the second coldest winter in 18 years. Further, it turned out to be the driest in 56 years—as long as records have been kept.

Between February 2 and 5, New Brunswick was hit with another devastating ice storm that knocked out power to 63,000 customers. On February 15, residents in Badger, Newfoundland, woke up to find icy flood waters from three rivers invading their homes and washing away vehicles. With the freezing temperatures, most of the town was frozen in ice.

A major winter storm blasted southern and eastern Ontario on February 22 and 23. The storm dumped snow over a large region extending from Windsor across Barrie-Huronia into the Ottawa area.

The last week of February saw frigid weather eclipsing records across the Prairies. Drumheller, Alberta, recorded –38°, smashing the 1979 record of –30.5. In Edmonton, the temperature plunged to –36.9, beating the old record of –30.3. February was the coldest in 24 years in Winnipeg—a monthly average of –19.4°, nearly six degrees colder than normal.

MARCH 2003: In early March, wind-whipped snow, heavy drifting, and a flash freeze at near-record low temperatures made surfaces in southern Ontario treacherous for drivers and pedestrians. Environment Canada issued a wind chill warning for the entire eastern half of Canada. In Ottawa, the temperature plunged from a high of 2° to –16° in a matter of two hours. Snow, frigid temperatures and cutting winds prompted officials at the Canada Winter Games in Bathurst, New Brunswick, to postpone some of the outdoor events.

On March 3, the temperature in Toronto dipped to –24.7°—the coldest March day since 1873. In London, the temperature dipped to –25.6°, making it the coldest March day on record. In Montreal, temperatures hovered around –25° and a wind chill made it feel like –40°. Directly on the heels of the cold wave came another major winter storm that raced through southern and eastern Ontario and into Atlantic Canada.

Conditions turned especially cold in the West around March 8. Among the records: Brandon –35.4°; Winnipeg –34.6° and Saskatoon –37.6°C.

For the first time in years, the entire surfaces of Lake Superior, Lake Huron and Lake Erie froze over. In the second week of March, a pair of avalanches closed the Trans-Canada Highway between Revelstoke and Golden, British Columbia, for several days. Two more people died in the Rockies from avalanches and snow slides. The deaths of 25 back-country enthusiasts this winter made this the deadliest season for avalanches in Canada in more than three decades.

APRIL 2003: At the beginning of April, an intense storm moved across Atlantic Canada. Heavy rains of 80 to 120 mm fell over mainland Nova Scotia, southern New Brunswick and western Newfoundland—most of it in 12 hours. The rain storm caused more than $15 million in damage in Nova Scotia.

During the first week of April, back-to-back storms brought between 20 and 40 cm of snow to parts of southern Saskatchewan, pleasing farmers and ranchers but annoying motorists. A day later, the storm struck Winnipeg, dumping 20 cm of snow in gusty winds.

On April 4 and 5, a fierce winter storm struck southern Ontario before moving into Quebec. The freezing rain, snow and ice pellets left roads slick, delayed or cancelled air traffic, and had crews scrambling to recall road-salting trucks and sidewalk plows. Two days later, the area was hit again with another winter storm. Then, by the middle of April, roller-coaster weather brought record warm temperatures across parts of southern Ontario. Toronto made it to 26°—tying the 1942 record set at Pearson airport. Windsor reached 28°.

In Vancouver, April was a dismally dull month with record amounts of cloud and a new low sunshine total of 89.5 hours—a bit more than half April's average of 171 hours. On April 26, a record-breaking snowstorm slammed into southern Alberta, dumping between 30 and 50 cm of heavy, wet snow on the region. As it turned out, the storm may have been the turning point in the drought that has plagued Alberta's agriculture for four years. The storm heaped near-record levels of wet snow on much of the province, including the area that had been, only a few months earlier, going through its driest state since 1869.

MAY 2003: Spring temperatures between March and May were a degree or more above normal across northern Canada, but were generally below normal in the south. Overall, Canada experienced a wetter than normal spring this year—the eleventh wettest out of the 56-year period of record, 8.4 percent above normal. It was −1.1° cooler than normal in Atlantic Canada—the seventh coolest in 56 years. At Rankin, Nunavut, it was the warmest May on record, some 3.9° warmer than normal.

Edmonton had 32.4 cm of snow in May, making it the second snowiest May since 1886. Initially, farmers welcomed the drought-ending snow, but the wet weather delayed seeding and created difficult calving conditions when it continued into the second week of May.

The long weekend in May was cool and wet across the West. In Manitoba, thousands headed out to cottage country only to head home early when sun and warmth turned to rain and cold. Vancouver saw thunder, hail and temperatures 3 to 5 degrees below normal. In southern Ontario, the long weekend in May had glorious weather.

In the final week of May, the temperature at Churchill, Manitoba, reached 29°. In Moosonee, Ontario, the temperature soared above 30°. Cities in southern Ontario had only reached the high twenties.

JUNE 2003: Early in June, high temperature records tumbled in British Columbia. In Victoria, the temperature on June 6 peaked at 33.5°, breaking the all-time high for June. Port Alberni had the Island's high of 34.7°, smashing the old mark of 25.9° for the day. The highest in the province was 35.2° in Squamish and Lillooet. After what for many Eastern residents seemed like the coolest, wettest, and cloudiest spring in several years, Southern Ontario finally got some summer-like weather during the final week with plenty of sunshine and mid-20s temperatures. Just two days into the summer of 2003, Ontario issued its first smog alert of the year. At Moosonee there had been five days above 30°, including 35° on June 22. Toronto hadn't yet had its first +30° reading. On June 23, Ottawa's temperature soared to 33.2°— hot and sticky and breaking the record of 33° for that day set in 1987.

Around June 19, firefighters in northern Alberta welcomed cooler, more humid weather to help them fight forest fires around Fort Mackay. Around June 26 in Ontario, heavy rains and cool temperatures calmed a raging forest fire in the northwestern community of Sioux Lookout. On the last day of June in northwestern Alberta, a severe storm with tornado-like power ripped up trees, moved a large building and destroyed an arena as it cut a swath of destruction through the northwestern Alberta town of Grimshaw.

Seasonal Temperature and Precipitation in Canada

All figures are based on the thirty-year period 1961 to 1990 inclusive.
*Airport station unless * designates city office station.*

Station	January Average Temperature (°C) Mid Afternoon	Early Morning	Total Precipitation (mm)	April Average Temperature (°C) Mid Afternoon	Early Morning	Total Precipitation (mm)
Calgary, Alta.	-2.8	-15.1	11.6	11.3	-2.1	23.9
Charlottetown, P.E.I.	-3.3	-12.6	106.4	6.7	-1.4	87.8
Churchill, Man.	-22.7	-30.7	16.9	-5.0	-14.5	19.0
Dawson, Yk.	-22.5	-30.9	19.2	7.6	-7.5	8.0
Edmonton, Alta	-7.3	-16.0	22.5	11.3	-0.3	26.0
Fredericton, N.B.	-4.0	-15.5	109.6	9.7	-1.1	87.4
Halifax, N.S.	-0.2	-9.2	134.7	8.1	0.2	114.3
Hamilton, Ont.	-2.2	-9.7	65.8	11.2	1.2	78.0
Iqaluit, Nvt	-22.5	-30.6	21.1	-9.9	-19.6	28.2
Kitchener, Ont.	-3.1	-11.0	64.4	11.1	0.4	76.9
London, Ont.	-2.4	-10.1	74.2	11.6	1.0	82.2
Moncton, N.B.	-3.6	-14.3	119.2	8.0	-1.7	99.3
Montreal, Que.	-5.8	-14.9	70.4	10.7	0.7	76.1
Ottawa, Ont.	-6.1	-15.3	70.2	10.8	0.6	72.4
Quebec, Que.	-7.9	-17.6	89.8	7.8	-1.3	81.2
Regina, Sask.	-10.7	-21.6	14.9	10.9	-2.0	23.5
Saint John, N.B.	-2.7	-13.6	139.4	8.3	-1.2	104.2
St. John's, Nfld	-0.9	-8.6	150.0	5.2	-2.0	121.8
Saskatoon, Sask.	-11.8	-22.3	15.2	10.6	-1.9	23.9
Sault Ste. Marie, Ont.	-5.5	-15.5	71.3	8.4	-2.2	68.5
Toronto, Ont.	-2.1	-10.5	52.2	11.5	1.0	68.4
Vancouver, B.C.	6.1	0.5	153.6	13.1	5.3	84.0
Victoria, B.C.	6.9	0.7	136.6	13.4	4.1	44.5
Whitehorse, Yk.	-13.3	-22.0	16.7	6.4	-4.6	7.0
Windsor, Ont.	-0.9	-8.1	57.6	13.4	3.0	85.1
Winnipeg, Man.	-12.7	-22.8	19.7	10.3	-2.4	31.9
Yellowknife, NWT	-22.7	-30.9	14.1	0.4	-11.0	10.8

Oh, Tuponia? Oh, Hochelaga? Oh, Canada!

*A*fter 136 years, we're pretty accustomed to the name "Canada" for our sprawling country, but it wasn't always so. In fact, in the years before Confederation, a fierce debate raged as to what the new country should be called—and the suggestions ranged from A to V. Among the proposals: Albertsland, Albionora, Borealia, Britannia, Cabotia, Colonia, Efisga (a combination of the first letters of England, France, Ireland, Scotland, Germany, and Aboriginal lands), Hochelaga, Norland, Superior, Transatlantia, Tuponia (an acrostic for the United Provinces
of North America), and Victorialand. Politician Thomas D'Arcy McGee, commenting on the host of names in early 1865, said: "I ask any honourable member of this House how he would feel if he woke up some fine morning and found himself instead of a Canadian, a Tuponian or a Hochelagander." As we know, McGee's common-sense position prevailed slightly more than two years later, when the Dominion of Canada was born in Charlottetown on July 1, 1867.

Station	July Average Temperature (°C) Mid Afternoon	July Average Temperature (°C) Early Morning	July Total Precipitation (mm)	October Average Temperature (°C) Mid Afternoon	October Average Temperature (°C) Early Morning	October Total Precipitation (mm)
Calgary, Alta.	22.9	9.4	67.9	12.1	-1.4	13.9
Charlottetown, P.E.I. . . .	23.2	13.8	85.8	11.8	3.8	108.6
Churchill, Man.	17.3	6.8	56.0	1.1	-4.5	46.9
Dawson, Yk.	23.1	8.1	48.4	-0.5	-9.4	31.6
Edmonton, Alta	22.8	12.1	91.7	10.9	0.3	17.9
Fredericton, N.B.	25.6	13.0	87.1	12.8	1.2	97.7
Halifax, N.S.	22.1	13.5	107.4	13.1	5.1	126.6
Hamilton, Ont.	26.3	15.1	86.5	13.8	4.4	72.5
Iqaluit, Nvt	11.6	3.7	59.4	-2.0	-7.7	36.7
Kitchener, Ont.	25.9	13.7	91.8	13.4	2.9	65.6
London, Ont.	26.3	14.6	82.2	14.0	4.0	97.7
Moncton, N.B.	24.5	12.6	103.3	12.4	1.8	103.8
Montreal, Que.	26.3	15.5	90.1	12.5	3.1	77.6
Ottawa, Ont.	26.5	15.4	90.6	12.5	3.0	79.4
Quebec, Que.	25.0	13.4	127.8	10.7	1.7	101.7
Regina, Sask.	25.7	11.8	64.4	11.5	-2.0	21.8
Saint John, N.B.	22.4	11.7	101.5	11.9	2.7	124.8
St. John's, Nfld	20.3	10.5	89.4	10.5	3.3	161.9
Saskatoon, Sask.	24.9	11.4	60.1	10.8	-1.9	16.7
Sault Ste. Marie, Ont. . . .	24.0	11.3	76.8	11.5	2.5	86.7
Toronto, Ont.	26.8	14.8	74.4	13.9	3.9	64.1
Vancouver, B.C.	21.7	13.2	39.6	13.5	6.6	112.6
Victoria, B.C.	21.9	10.8	19.5	14.2	5.3	75.7
Whitehorse, Yk.	20.5	7.7	41.4	4.3	-3.1	23.8
Windsor, Ont.	27.9	17.4	81.8	15.6	6.2	64.9
Winnipeg, Man.	25.8	13.3	70.6	10.8	-0.3	36.0
Yellowknife, NWT	21.1	12.4	35.0	1.0	-4.4	35.0

Source: *Environment Canada*

Icebergs—More Than Meets the Eye

*A*n iceberg is a massive piece of ice that has broken away from a glacier. The shapes of icebergs vary greatly, but to qualify as bergs, they must protrude 5 metres or more above sea-level. Smaller pieces of ice are called "growlers" (less than 1 metre above the water) and "bergy bits" (between 1 and 5 metres). About 90 percent of all icebergs in Canadian waters— between 10,000 and 40,000 every year—come from the glaciers of Western Greenland.

Icebergs float because the density of ice (around 900 kg per cubic metre) is lower than that of seawater (around 1025 kg per cubic metre). That means most of the mass of an iceberg— about seven-eighths—is under water. Large icebergs move mainly because of water motion; an iceberg takes an average of 2 to 3 years to drift from its place of origin on the west coast of Greenland to the Grand Banks of Newfoundland.

Source: *Environment Canada*

Spring and Fall Frost Dates in Canada

Frost occurs whenever temperatures fall to 0°C or lower. All frost dates and values are based on the available data during the period 1951–80. Growing degree-day data are from the period 1961–90. Data reported from airport stations unless * designates city office station.

	1 in 10 Chance Last Spring Frost After Date	1 in 10 Chance First Fall Frost Before Date	Frost-free Period (days)	Growing Degree-Days Above 5°C[1]
Newfoundland & Labrador				
Corner Brook*	June 10	Sept. 8	139	1 432
St. John's*	June 24	Sept. 19	131	1 262
Prince Edward Island				
Charlottetown	May 27	Oct. 6	151	1 636
Nova Scotia				
Halifax	May 28	Sept. 30	155	1 707
New Brunswick				
Fredericton	June 10	Sept. 13	126	1 760
Moncton	June 10	Sept. 14	124	1 649
Saint John	June 10	Sept. 18	139	1 499
Quebec				
Chicoutimi*	June 4	Sept. 18	135	1 575
Gaspé*	June 12	Sept. 11	123	1 336
Montreal	May 19	Sept. 26	157	2 079
Quebec	May 28	Sept. 14	137	1 688
Schefferville	June 27	Aug. 22	77	604
Ontario				
Kitchener*	May 25	Sept. 17	151	1 992
London	May 25	Sept. 23	147	2 121
Moosonee*	July 6	July 30	70	1 078
Ottawa	May 25	Sept. 21	147	2 045
St. Catharines*	May 18	Oct. 5	173	2 451
Sudbury	June 11	Sept. 11	128	1 680
Thunder Bay	June 13	Aug. 29	104	1 427
Timmins	June 23	Aug. 19	91	1 395
Toronto	May 25	Sept. 18	149	2 090
Windsor	May 10	Oct. 3	177	2 544
Manitoba				
Brandon	June 9	Aug. 31	108	1 652
Churchill	July 7	Aug. 20	76	562
Flin Flon	June 10	Sept. 2	115	1 379
Winnipeg	June 10	Sept. 11	121	1 802
Saskatchewan				
Prince Albert	June 21	Aug. 17	95	1 455
Regina	June 14	Aug. 27	109	1 723
Saskatoon	June 10	Sept. 1	117	1 658
Alberta				
Banff*	June 30	Aug. 6	89	1 124
Calgary	June 10	Aug. 27	112	1 435
Edmonton	June 14	Aug. 13	105	1 352
Fort McMurray	June 30	Aug. 2	84	1 352
Lethbridge	May 31	Sept. 2	124	1 779
Medicine Hat	May 27	Sept. 8	129	1 971
Peace River	June 23	Aug. 13	93	1.276
British Columbia				
Fort Nelson	June 7	Aug. 14	106	1 289
Kamloops	May 18	Sept. 19	149	2 259
Penticton	May 23	Sept. 14	148	2 163
Prince George	July 1	Aug. 11	85	1 238
Prince Rupert	May 25	Sept. 28	156	1 181
Vancouver	Apr. 21	Oct. 13	216	2 018
Victoria	Apr. 30	Oct. 17	201	1 864

▶

	1 in 10 Chance Last Spring Frost After Date	1 in 10 Chance First Fall Frost Before Date	Frost-free Period (days)	Growing Degree-Days Above 5°C[1]
▶ **Yukon**				
Dawson*	June 16	Aug. 6	91	1 015
Whitehorse	June 24	Aug. 13	82	871
Northwest Territories				
Yellowknife	June 9	Sept. 3	111	1 039
Nunavut				
Alert*	July 15	July 16	4	30
Iqaluit	July 12	July 26	59	177
Resolute	July 15	July 16	9	29

Source: *Environment Canada*

(1) Growing degree days represent the average total number of heat units (daily mean temp. –5°C) during the growing season

Plant Hardiness Zones in Canada

A plant's hardiness rating is related to its ability to survive in specific climate conditions. Plant hardiness zones were originally based on average minimum winter temperatures in a location, and first developed by the U.S. Department of Agriculture (USDA).

The USDA created 11 zones, each of which have since been split into subzones a and b. Canada's Department of Agriculture took the concept of hardiness further by including other factors besides minimum temperature in designating Canada's plant hardiness zones. They created a weighted equation that took into account such factors as the average minimum temperature of the coldest month; the average length of the frost-free period; average rainfall between June and

November; the average maximum temperature in the hottest month; the amount of snow; and the maximum windspeeds in the last 30 years in any given area.

Canada's zones range from 0a in our coldest regions to 9a in our most temperate locations, and the minimum temperature equivalents are shown below. Canadian gardeners may find themselves in micro-climates that differ from the conditions the zone map indicates; however most should choose perennials based on the zone the garden is in and the hardiness rating of the plant. (A plant can survive in the zone it's rated for or a higher/warmer one.)

To find out what zone you're in, consult a local nursery or visit the map at http://res.agr.ca/CANSIS/SYSTEMS/online_maps.html

Hardiness Zone	Average Minimum Temperature (°C)	Hardiness Zone	Average Minimum Temperature (°C)
0a – 0b	–46 or colder	5a – 5b	–20 to –15
1a – 1b	–46 to –37	6a – 6b	–15 to –12
2a – 2b	–37 to –29	7a – 7b	–12 to –6
3a – 3b	–29 to –23	8a – 8b	–6 to –1
4a – 4b	–23 to –20	9a	–1 to 4 or warmer

Source: *Agriculture Canada*

Farms and Farmers Declining

*T**he number of farms and farmers in Canada is falling, according to Statistics Canada, but the acreage of crops is increasing and so are the numbers of livestock. The 2001 Census of Agriculture reports 346,200 farm operators, 10 percent fewer than the 385,600 reported in 1996. On May 15, 2001, they were operating 246,923 farms, down 10.7 percent from 1996.*

On the other hand, the census found, the farmers reported they were cultivating 89.9 million acres of crops, up 4.2 percent from 1996. As well, livestock numbers increased: cattle were up by 4.4 percent, pigs by 26.4 percent, and sheep by 46 percent.

There are fewer young farmers: Those under 35 represented 11.5 percent of all farmers in 2001, compared with 15.8 percent in 1996 and 19.9 percent in 1991. Both men and women have increased their rate of working off the farm since 1990, and roughly equal proportions of women farm operators (45.6 percent) and men (44.2 percent) worked at non-farm jobs in 2000.

There were 2,230 farms producing organic crops, mostly field crops, such as wheat, alfalfa, canola and barley.

PROVINCES AND TERRITORIES

Latitude, Longitude, Elevation of Canadian Cities

City	Lat. N °	Lat. N '	Long.W °	Long.W '	Elev. (m)	City	Lat. N °	Lat. N '	Long.W °	Long.W '	Elev. (m)
Alert, NT*	82	30	62	22	31	Moose Jaw, Sask.	50	23	105	32	544
Brandon, Man.	49	51	99	57	409	Niagara Falls, Ont.	43	06	79	03	180
Brantford, Ont.	43	08	80	15	215	North Bay, Ont.	46	18	79	27	204
Burlington, Ont.	43	19	79	47	87	Ottawa, Ont.	45	26	75	41	56
Calgary, Alta.	51	02	114	03	1 045	Peterborough, Ont.	44	18	78	19	205
Charlottetown, PEI	46	14	63	07	9	Prince Rupert, BC	54	19	130	19	38
Churchill, Man.	58	45	94	10	29	Quebec, Que.	46	48	71	12	50
Dartmouth, NS	44	39	63	34	7	Regina, Sask.	50	27	104	36	577
Dawson, Yukon	64	03	139	26	369	Saint John, NB	45	16	66	03	8
Edmonton, Alta.	53	32	113	29	666	St. John's, Nfld & Lab.	47	34	52	43	61
Fredericton, NB	45	57	66	38	9	Saskatoon, Sask.	52	07	106	39	484
Guelph, Ont.	43	32	80	14	325	Sault Ste. Marie, Ont.	46	30	84	20	180
Halifax, NS	44	38	63	34	18	Sherbrooke, Que.	45	24	71	53	191
Hamilton, Ont.	43	15	79	52	100	Sudbury, Ont.	46	29	80	59	347
Hull, Que.	45	25	75	42	56	Sydney, NS	46	08	60	11	62
Iqaluit, NT*	63	45	68	31	34	Thunder Bay, Ont.	48	22	89	14	188
Kingston, Ont.	44	13	76	28	80	Toronto, Ont.	43	39	79	23	91
Kitchener, Ont.	43	26	80	29	335	Trois-Rivières, Que.	46	21	72	33	35
LaSalle, Que.	45	25	73	39	34	Vancouver, BC	49	18	123	04	43
Laval, Que.	45	33	73	44	43	Victoria, BC	48	25	123	21	17
Lethbridge, Alta.	49	41	112	49	910	Whitehorse, Yukon	60	43	135	03	703
London, Ont.	42	59	81	14	251	Winnipeg, Man.	49	53	97	08	232
Moncton, NB	46	05	64	46	12	Yellowknife, NWT	62	28	114	22	205
Montreal, Que.	45	30	73	33	27						

Source: *Natural Resources Canada* *Nunavut

Area¹ of Canadian Provinces and Territories

(sq. km)

	Land	Water	Total	% of Total Area of Canada
Newfoundland and Labrador	373 872	31 340	405 212	4.06
Prince Edward Island	5 660	—	5 660	0.06
Nova Scotia	53 338	1 946	55 284	0.55
New Brunswick	71 450	1 458	72 908	0.73
Quebec	1 365 128	176 928	1 542 056	15.44
Ontario	917 741	158 654	1 076 395	10.78
Manitoba	553 556	94 241	647 797	6.49
Saskatchewan	591 670	59 366	651 036	6.52
Alberta	642 317	19 531	661 848	6.63
British Columbia	925 186	19 549	944 735	9.46
Yukon	474 391	8 052	482 443	4.83
Northwest Territories	1 183 085	163 021	1 346 106	13.48
Nunavut	1 936 113	157 077	2 093 190	20.96
Canada	**9 093 507**	**891 163**	**9 984 670**	**100.00**

Source: *Natural Resources Canada*

(1) Calculated from the National Atlas of Canada 1:1000000 scale hydrology base. (—) = zero

Newfoundland & Labrador

□ **CAPITAL:** St. John's, CMA pop. (2001) 172 918. **Date entered Confederation:** Mar. 31, 1949.

□ **POPULATION (2002):** 531 600; **Pop. density:** 1.26 per sq. km. **Pop. growth** (2001–2002); -0.3%. **Pop. urban** (2001): 57%. **Age structure (2001):** 25% under 19; 62.7% 20-64; 12% over 65. **Median age** (2001): 38.4. **Net interprovincial migration** (2000-01): -3 541.

□ **VITAL STATISTICS: Rates** (per 1 000 pop., 2001): birth: 8.8; death: 8.4. **Life expectancy at birth (1999):** 77.7.

□ **GEOGRAPHY: Total area** 405 212 sq. km; **Land area** 373 872 sq. km; **Forested land** 142 000 sq. km; **Length of coastline** 23 232 km. **Climate**: ranges from subarctic in Labrador and northern tip of island to humid continental with cool summers and heavy precipitation. **Topography**: Island of Newfoundland: highlands of the Long Range Mtns. (elev. 900 m) along W coast; barren and rocky central plateau descends to lowlands towards the N east; coast is deeply indented with bays and fjords. Labrador: mountainous in the N; rugged coast and interior plateau.

□ **ECONOMY: Gross Domestic Product** at market prices (2001): $13 000 million; **% change GDP** (2000-01): 1.3%; **Per capita GDP** (2001): $25 345. **Employment distrib.** (2000): goods-producing industries (agriculture, primary ind., mfg, construction) 22%; service-producing industries (transpt., trade, finance, service, pub. admin, unclassified) 78%. **Unemployment rate** (2002): 15.3%. **Principal industries:** mining, manufacturing, fishing, logging and forestry, electricity production, tourism.

□ **EDUCATION: Elem. enrolment** (2001-2): 82 656. **Spending** per full-time equiv. student (1999): $5 841. **Post-sec. degrees** granted (1998): 2 999.

□ **INTERNATIONAL AIRPORTS:** Gander.

□ **NATIONAL PARKS:** Gros Morne, Terra Nova.

□ **PROVINCIAL DATA: Motto:** *Quaerite Prime Regnum Dei:* "Seek Ye First the Kingdom of God." **Flower**: Pitcher plant. **Bird**: Atlantic Puffin (unofficial). **Anthem**: Ode to Newfoundland. **Tartan**: Newfoundland Tartan.

□ **POLITICS: Premier**: Danny Williams (Prog. Cons.). **Leaders, opposition parties:** Jack Harris (NDP), Roger Grimes (Lib.). **Date of last general election**: Oct. 21, 2003. **Lt. Governor:** Hon. Edward M. Roberts.

Prince Edward Island

□ **CAPITAL:** Charlottetown, metro pop. (2001) 32 245. **Date entered Confederation:** July 1, 1873.

□ **POPULATION (2002):** 139 900. **Pop. density:** 23.9 per sq. km. **Pop. growth** (2001–2002): 0.5%. **Pop. urban** (2001): 44.0%. **Age structure** (2001): 27.3% under 19; 59.0% 20-64; 13.7% over 65. **Median age** (2001): 37.7. **Net interprovincial migration** (2000-01): 71.

□ **VITAL STATISTICS: Rates** (per 1 000 pop., 2001): birth: 10.8; death: 9.4. **Life expectancy at birth (1999):** 78.4.

□ **GEOGRAPHY: Total area** 5 660 sq. km; **Land area** 5 660 sq. km; **Forested land** 3 000 sq. km; **Length of coastline** 1 076 km. **Climate**: humid continental with temperatures moderated by maritime location. **Topography**: flat through gently rolling hills; sharply indented coastline; many streams but only small rivers and lakes.

□ **ECONOMY: Gross Domestic Product** at market prices (2001): $3 174 million; **% change GDP** (2000-01): 0.1%; **Per capita GDP** (2001): $23 460. **Employment distrib.** (2000): goods-producing industries (agriculture, primary ind., mfg, construction) 27%; service-producing industries (transpt., trade, finance, service, pub. admin, unclassified) 73%. **Unemployment rate** (2002): 11.2%. **Principal industries:** agriculture, tourism, fishing, manufacturing.

□ **EDUCATION: Elem. enrolment** (2001-2): 24 327. **Spending** per full-time equiv. student (1999): $5 677. **Post-sec. degrees** granted (1998): 407.

□ **INTERNATIONAL AIRPORTS:** none.

□ **NATIONAL PARKS:** Prince Edward Island (north shore).

□ **PROVINCIAL DATA: Motto:** *Parva Sub Ingenti:* "The small under the protection of the great." **Flower:** Lady's slipper. **Bird:** Blue Jay. **Tree:** Red Oak.

□ **POLITICS: Premier:** Pat Binns (Prog. Cons.) **Leaders, opposition parties:** Robert Ghiz (Lib.), Gary Robichaud (NDP). **Date of last general election:** April 17, 2000. **Lt. Governor:** Hon. J. Léonce Bernard.

Nova Scotia

□ **CAPITAL:** Halifax, Reg. CMA. pop. (2001) 359 183. **Date entered Confederation:** July 1, 1867.

□ **POPULATION (2002):** 944 800 **Pop. density:** 16.42 per sq. km. **Pop. growth** (2001–2002): -0%. **Pop. urban** (2001): 55.0%. **Age structure** (2001): 25.0% under 19; 61.1% 20-64; 13.9% over 65. **Median age** (2001): 38.8. **Net interprovincial migration** (2000-01): -824.

□ **VITAL STATISTICS:** Rates (per 1 000 pop., 2001): birth: 9.9; death: 9.0. **Life expectancy at birth** (1999): 78.7.

□ **GEOGRAPHY: Total area** 55 284 sq. km; **Land area** 53 338 sq. km; **Forested land** 41,000 sq. km; **Length of coastline** 6 014 km. **Climate:** humid continental with some moderating effects due to maritime location. **Topography:** Atlantic Uplands are segmented by river valleys; Cape Breton Is. rises from lowland in the S to a high plateau; many rivers, lakes and jagged coastline.

□ **ECONOMY: Gross Domestic Product at market prices (2001):** $23 368 million; **% change GDP** (2000-01): 2.4%; **Per capita GDP (2001):** $25 735. **Employment distrib. (2000):** goods-producing industries (agriculture, primary ind., mfg, construction) 22%; service-producing industries (transpt., trade, finance, service, pub. admin, unclassified) 78%. **Unemployment rate (2002):** 9.8%. **Principal industries:** manufacturing, fishing and trapping, mining, agriculture, pulp and paper.

□ **EDUCATION: Elem. enrolment** (2001-2): 149 111. **Spending** per full-time equiv. student (1999): $5 642. **Post-sec. degrees** granted (1998): 7 811.

□ **INTERNATIONAL AIRPORTS:** Halifax

□ **NATIONAL PARKS:** Cape Breton Highlands, Kejimkujik.

□ **PROVINCIAL DATA: Motto:** _Munit Haec et Altera Vincit:_ "One defends and the other conquers." **Flower:** Mayflower. **Bird:** Osprey. **Tree:** Red Spruce. **Gem:** Agate.

□ **POLITICS: Premier:** Dr. John Hamm (Prog. Cons.). **Leaders, opposition parties:** Danny Graham (Lib.), Darrel Dexter (NDP). **Date of last general election:** Aug. 5, 2003. **Lt. Governor:** Hon. Myra A. Freeman.

New Brunswick

□ **CAPITAL:** Fredericton, metro pop. (2001) 47 560. **Date entered Confederation:** July 1, 1867.

□ **POPULATION (2002):** 756 700. **Pop. density:** 10.0 per sq. km. **Pop. growth** (2001–2002): 0%. **Pop. urban** (2001): 50.0%. **Age structure** (2001): 24.8% under 19; 61.7% 20-64; 13.6% over 65. **Median age** (2001): 38.6. **Net interprovincial migration** (2000-01): -81.

□ **VITAL STATISTICS:** Rates (per 1 000 pop., 2001): birth: 10.2; death: 8.9. **Life expectancy at birth** (1999): 78.4.

□ **GEOGRAPHY: Total area** 72 908 sq. km; **Land area** 71 450 sq. km; **Forested land** 61,000 sq. km; **Length of coastline** 2 298 km. **Climate:** humid continental climate except along the shores where there is a marked maritime effect. **Topography:** northern upland; rolling central plateau; southern lowland plain with many rivers.

□ **ECONOMY: Gross Domestic Product at market prices** (2001): $18 739 million; **% change GDP** (2000-01): 0.7%; **Per capita GDP** (2001): $25 688. **Employment distrib.** (2000): goods-producing industries (agriculture, primary ind., mfg, construction) 25%; service-producing industries (transpt., trade, finance, service, pub. admin, unclassified) 75%. **Unemployment rate** (2002): 10.1%. **Principal industries:** manufacturing, fishing, mining, forestry, pulp and paper, agriculture.

□ **EDUCATION: Elem. enrolment** (2001-2): 116 713. **Spending** per full-time equiv. student (1999): $6 433. **Post-sec. degrees** granted (1998): 4 030.

□ **INTERNATIONAL AIRPORTS:** none.

□ **NATIONAL PARKS:** Fundy, Kouchibouguac.

□ **PROVINCIAL DATA: Motto:** _Spem Reduxit:_ "Hope was restored." **Flower:** Purple Violet. **Bird:** Black- capped Chickadee. **Tree:** Balsam Fir.

□ **POLITICS: Premier:** Bernard Lord (Prog. Cons.). **Leaders, opposition parties:** Shawn Graham (Lib.), Elizabeth Weir (NDP). **Date of last general election:** June 9, 2003. **Lt. Governor:** Hon. Herménégilde Chiasson.

Quebec

☐ **CAPITAL:** Quebec, CMA pop. (2001) 682 757. **Date entered Confederation:** July 1, 1867.

☐ **POPULATION (2002):** 7 455 200. **Pop. density:** 4.69 per sq. km. **Pop. growth (2001–2002):** 0.1%. **Pop. urban (2001):** 80.0%. **Age structure (2001):** 24.2% under 19; 62.5% 20-64; 13.3% over 65. **Median age (2001):** 38.8. **Net interprovincial migration (2000-01):** -11 782.

☐ **VITAL STATISTICS: Rates** (per 1000 pop., 2001): birth: 9.7; death: 7.2. **Life expectancy at birth** (1999): 78.5.

☐ **GEOGRAPHY: Total area** 1 542 056 sq. km; **Land area** 1 356 128 sq. km; **Forested land** 940 000 sq. km; **Length of coastline** 15 208 km. Climate: varies from subarctic to continental. Topography: lowlands along the St. Lawrence R. valley separate the Laurentian Mtns. to the N and the Appalachian Mtns. to the S; Canadian Shield landscape dominates north.

☐ **ECONOMY: Gross Domestic Product at market prices** (2001): $216 988 million; **% change GDP** (2000-01): 0.9%; **Per capita GDP** (2001): $29 985. **Employment distrib.** (2000): goods-producing industries (agriculture, primary ind., mfg, construction) 26%; service-producing industries (transpt., trade, finance, service, pub. admin, unclassified) 74%. **Unemployment rate (2002):** 8.6%. **Principal industries:** manufacturing, electric power, mining, pulp and paper, transportation equipment.

☐ **EDUCATION: Elem. enrolment** (2001-2): 1 022 209. **Spending** per full-time equiv. student (1999): $7 097. **Post-sec. degrees** granted (1998): 51 066.

☐ **INTERNATIONAL AIRPORTS:** Trudeau; Mirabel.

☐ **NATIONAL PARKS:** Forillon, La Mauricie, Mingan Archipelago, Saguenay-St. Lawrence Marine Park.

☐ **PROVINCIAL DATA: Motto:** *Je me souviens:* "I remember." **Flower:** Lys blanc de jardin (White Garden (Madonna) Lily). **Bird:** Harfang des neiges (Snowy Owl).

☐ **POLITICS: Premier:** Jean Charest (Lib.). **Leader, opposition parties:** Bernard Landry (Parti Québécois), Mario Dumont (A.D.). **Date of last general election:** April14, 2003. **Lt. Governor:** Hon. Lise Thibault.

Ontario

☐ **CAPITAL:** Toronto, CMA pop. (2001) 4 682 897. **Date entered Confederation:** July 1, 1867.

☐ **POPULATION (2002):** 12 068 300. **Pop. density:** 10.6 per sq. km. **Pop. growth (2001–2002):** 0.4%. **Pop. urban (2001):** 84.0%. **Age structure (2001):** 26.3% under 19; 60.8% 20-64; 12.9% over 65. **Median age (2001):** 37.2. **Net interprovincial migration (2000-01):** 17 877.

☐ **VITAL STATISTICS: Rates** (per 1 000 pop., 2001): birth: 11.1; death. 7.4; **Life expectancy at birth** (1999): 79.4.

☐ **GEOGRAPHY: Total area** 1 076 395 sq. km; **Land area** 917 741 sq. km; **Forested land** 807 000 sq. km; **Length of coastline** 1 324 km. Climate: ranges from humid continental in south to subarctic in far north; westerly winds bring winter storms; the Great Lakes moderate winter temperatures. **Topography:** Rugged, rocky Canadian Shield plateau is broken by lowlands around Great Lakes, St. Lawrence R. and Hudson Bay.

☐ **ECONOMY: Gross Domestic Product at market prices** (2001): $430 957 million; **% change GDP** (2000–01): 1.0%; **Per capita GDP** (2001): $40 399. **Employment distrib.** (2000): goods-producing industries (agriculture, primary ind., mfg, construction) 27%; service-producing industries (transpt., trade, finance, service, pub. admin, unclassified) 73%. **Unemployment rate** (2002): 7.0%. **Principal industries:** manufacturing, construction, agriculture, forestry, mining.

☐ **EDUCATION: Elem. enrolment** (2001-2): 1 848 807. **Spending** per full-time equiv. student (1999): $7 554. **Post-sec. degrees** granted (1998): 65 899.

☐ **INTERNATIONAL AIRPORTS:** Pearson (Toronto); Ottawa.

☐ **NATIONAL PARKS:** Bruce Peninsula, Fathom Five Marine Park, Georgian Bay Islands, Point Pelee, Pukaskwa, St. Lawrence Islands.

☐ **PROVINCIAL DATA: Motto:** *Ut Incepit Fidelis Sic Permanet:* "Loyal she began, loyal she remains." **Flower:** White trillium. **Bird:** Common Loon. **Tree:** Eastern White Pine. **Gem:** Amethyst.

☐ **POLITICS: Premier:** Dalton McGuinty (Lib.). **Leaders, opposition parties:** Ernie Eves (Prog. Cons.); Howard Hampton (NDP). **Date of last general election:** October 2, 2003. **Lt. Governor:** Hon. James K. Bartleman.

Manitoba

□ **CAPITAL:** Winnipeg, CMA pop. (2001) 671 274. **Date entered Confederation:** July 15, 1870.

□ **POPULATION (2002):** 1 150 038. Pop. density: 1.72 per sq. km. **Pop. growth (2001–2002):** 0.1%. **Pop. urban (2001):** 71.0%. **Age structure (2001):** 28.1% under 19; 58.0% 20-64; 14.0% over 65. **Median age (2001):** 36.8. **Net interprovincial migration (2000-01):** -3 094.

□ **VITAL STATISTICS: Rates** (per 1 000 pop., 2001): birth: 12.4; death: 9.0. **Life expectancy at birth** (1999): 78.0.

□ **GEOGRAPHY: Total area** 647 797 sq. km; **Land area** 553 556 sq. km; **Forested land** 349 000 sq. km; **Length of coastline** 990 km. **Climate:** continental with seasonal extremes. **Topography:** the land rises gradually south and west from Hudson Bay; flat plateau through south central region; countless lakes, streams and bogs.

□ **ECONOMY: Gross Domestic Product** at market prices (2001): $33 305 million; **% change GDP** (2000–01): 1.4%; **Per capita GDP** (2000): $29 748. **Employment distrib.** (2000): goods-producing industries (agriculture, primary ind., mfg, construction) 26%; service-producing industries (transpt., trade, finance, service, pub. admin, unclassified) 74%. **Unemployment rate** (2002): 5.5%. **Principal industries:** manufacturing, agriculture, food industry, mining, construction.

□ **EDUCATION: Elem. enrolment** (2001-2): 207 368. **Spending** per full-time equiv. student (1999): $7 432. **Post-sec. degrees** granted (1998): 5 639.

□ **INTERNATIONAL AIRPORTS:** Winnipeg.

□ **NATIONAL PARKS:** Riding Mountain, Wapusk.

□ **PROVINCIAL DATA: Motto:** Glorious and Free. **Flower:** Prairie Crocus. **Bird:** Great Grey Owl. **Tartan:** Manitoba Tartan.

□ **POLITICS: Premier:** Gary Doer (NDP). **Leaders, opposition parties:** Stuart Murray (Prog. Cons.), Jon Gerrard (Lib.). **Date of last general election:** June 3, 2003. **Lt. Governor:** Hon. Peter M. Liba.

Saskatchewan

□ **CAPITAL:** Regina, CMA pop. (2001) 192 800. **Date entered Confederation:** Sept. 1, 1905.

□ **POPULATION (2002):** 1 011 800. Pop. density: 1.5 per sq. km. **Pop. growth (2001–2002):** -0.2%. **Pop. urban (2001):** 64.0%. **Age structure (2001):** 29.2% under 19; 55.8% 20-64; 15.1% over 65. **Median age (2001):** 36.7. **Net interprovincial migration (2000-01):** -10 453.

□ **VITAL STATISTICS: Rates** (per 1 000 pop., 2001): birth: 12.3; death: 9.1. **Life expectancy at birth** (1999): 78.5.

□ **GEOGRAPHY: Total area** 651 036 sq. km; **Land area** 591 670 sq. km; **Forested land** 178 000 sq. km; **Climate:** continental, with cold winters and hot summers. **Topography:** gently rolling plains through south; higher, hilly plateaus in the SW; north is rugged Canadian Shield.

□ **ECONOMY: Gross Domestic Product** at market prices (2001): $30 836 million; **% change GDP** (2000–01): -1.9%; **Per capita GDP** (2001): $31 500. **Employment distrib.** (2000): goods-producing industries (agriculture, primary ind., mfg, construction) 28%; service-producing industries (transpt., trade, finance, service, pub. admin, unclassified) 72%. **Unemployment rate** (2002): 5.9%. **Principal industries:** agriculture, mining, manufacturing, electric power, construction, chemical prod.

□ **EDUCATION: Elem. enrolment** (2001-2): 192 920. **Spending** per full-time equiv. student (1999): $6 277. **Post-sec. degrees** granted (1998): 5 443.

□ **INTERNATIONAL AIRPORTS:** Saskatoon.

□ **NATIONAL PARKS:** Grasslands, Prince Albert.

□ **PROVINCIAL DATA: Motto:** *Multis E Gentibus Vires:* "from many peoples strength." **Flower:** Western Red Lily. **Bird:** Prairie sharp-tailed grouse. **Tree:** White Birch. **Tartan:** Saskatchewan Tartan.

□ **POLITICS: Premier:** Lorne Calvert (NDP). **Leaders, opposition parties:** Elwin Hermanson (Sask.), David Karwacki (Lib.). **Date of last general election:** Sept. 16, 1999. **Lt. Governor:** Hon. Lynda M. Haverstock.

Alberta

☐ **CAPITAL:** Edmonton, CMA pop. (2001) 937 854. **Date entered Confederation:** Sept. 1, 1905.

☐ **POPULATION (2002):** 3 113 600. **Pop. density:** 4.49 per sq. km. **Pop. growth (2001–2002):** 0.4%. **Pop. urban (2001):** 80.0%. **Age structure (2001):** 28.3% under 19; 61.4% 20-64; 10.4% over 65. **Median age (2001):** 35.0. **Net interprovincial migration (2000-01):** 25 748.

☐ **VITAL STATISTICS: Rates** (per 1 000 pop., 2001): birth: 11.8; death: 5.7. **Life expectancy at birth** (1999): 79.2.

☐ **GEOGRAPHY: Total area** 661 848 sq. km; **Land area** 642 317 sq. km; **Forested land** 349 000 sq. km. **Climate**: great variance in temperatures between regions and seasons; summer highs between 16°C and 32°C; winters as low as -45°C. **Topography**: Rocky Mtns. in SW to rolling prairie throughout southern region; far north is a forested plateau.

☐ **ECONOMY: Gross Domestic Product** at market prices (2001): $123 955 million; **% change GDP** (2000–01): 2.9%; **Per capita GDP** (2001): $41 668. **Employment distrib.** (2000): goods-producing industries (agriculture, primary ind., mfg, construction) 27%; service-producing industries (transpt., trade, finance, service, pub. admin, unclassified) 73%. **Unemployment rate** (2002): 5.3%. **Principal industries:** chemical products, mining, agriculture, food, manufacturing, construction, oil prod. and refinement.

☐ **EDUCATION: Elem. enrolment** (2001-2): 541 596. **Spending** per full-time equiv. student (1999): $6 871. **Post-sec. degrees** granted (1998): 13 003.

☐ **INTERNATIONAL AIRPORTS:** Edmonton; Calgary.

☐ **NATIONAL PARKS:** Banff, Elk Island, Jasper, Waterton Lakes, Wood Buffalo (shared with Northwest Territories).

☐ **PROVINCIAL DATA: Motto:** *Fortis et Liber:* "Strong and free." **Flower:** Wild Rose. **Bird:** Great horned owl. **Tree:** Lodge pole pine. **Tartan:** Alberta Tartan. **Stone:** Petrified wood.

☐ **POLITICS: Premier:** Ralph Klein (Prog. Cons.). **Leaders, opposition parties:** Ken Nicol (Lib.), Raj Pannu (NDP). **Date of last general election:** March 12, 2001. **Lt. Governor:** Hon. Lois E. Hole.

British Columbia

☐ **CAPITAL:** Victoria, CMA pop. (2001) 311 902. **Date entered Confederation:** July 20, 1871.

☐ **POPULATION (2002):** 4 141 300. **Pop. density:** 4.13 per sq. km. **Pop. growth (2001–2002):** 0.2%. **Pop. urban (2001):** 84.0%. **Age structure (2001):** 25.0% under 19; 61.4% 20-64; 13.6% over 65. **Median age (2001):** 38.4. **Net interprovincial migration (2000-01):** -12 689.

☐ **VITAL STATISTICS: Rates** (per 1 000 pop., 2001): birth: 9.8; death: 6.8. **Life expectancy at birth** (1999): 80.0.

☐ **GEOGRAPHY: Total area** 944 735 sq. km; **Land area** 925 186 sq. km; **Forested land** 633 000 sq. km; **Length of coastline** 22 898 km. **Climate**: maritime with mild temperatures and abundant rainfall in the coastal areas; continental climate with temperature extremes in the interior and northeast. **Topography**: mostly mountainous; deep river valleys and gorges, except for the NE area which is an extension of the Great Plains; indented coast with numerous bays and islands.

☐ **ECONOMY: Gross Domestic Product** at market prices (2001): $125 534 million; **% change GDP** (2000-01): 0.9%; **Per capita GDP** (2001): $32 124. Employment distrib. (2000): goods-producing industries (agriculture, primary ind., mfg, construction) 21%; service-producing industries (transpt., trade, finance, service, pub. admin, unclassified) 79%. **Unemployment rate** (2002): 8.7%. **Principal industries:** forestry, wood and paper, mining, tourism, agriculture, fishing, manufacturing.

☐ **EDUCATION: Elem. enrolment** (2001-2): 655 100. **Spending** per full-time equiv. student (1999): $6 985. **Post-sec. degrees** granted (1998): 15 779.

☐ **INTERNATIONAL AIRPORTS:** Vancouver; Victoria.

☐ **NATIONAL PARKS:** Glacier, Kootenay, Mount Revelstoke, Pacific Rim, Gwaii Haanas (South Moresby), Yoho.

☐ **PROVINCIAL DATA: Motto:** *Splendor Sine Occasu:* "Splendor without Diminishment." **Flower:** Dogwood. **Bird:** Stellar's Jay.

☐ **POLITICS: Premier:** Gordon Campbell (Lib). **Leader, opposition parties:** Joy MacPhail (NDP). **Date of last general election:** May 16, 2001. **Lt. Governor:** Hon. Iona Campagnolo.

Yukon Territory

☐ **CAPITAL:** Whitehorse, metro pop. (2001) 19 058. **Date entered Confederation:** June 13, 1898.

☐ **POPULATION (2003):** 29 900. **Pop. density:** 0.05 per sq. km. **Pop. growth (2002–2003):** -0.9%. **Pop. urban (2001):** 58.0%. **Age structure (2001):** 29.0% under 19; 64.9% 20-64; 6.0% over 65. **Median age (2001):** 36.1. **Net interprovincial migration (2000-01):** -846.

☐ **VITAL STATISTICS: Rates** (per 1 000 pop., 2001): birth: 13.3; death: 4.8. **Life expectancy at birth** (1999): 76.9.

☐ **GEOGRAPHY: Total area** 482 443 sq. km; **Land area** 474 391 sq. km; **Forested land** 242 000 sq. km; **Length of coastline** 418 km. **Climate**: great variance in temperatures; warm summers, very cold winters; low precipitation. **Topography**: main feature is the Yukon plateau with 21 peaks exceeding 3 300 m; open tundra in the far north.

☐ **ECONOMY: Gross Domestic Product** at market prices (2001): $1 092 million; **% change GDP** (2000-01): 1.2%; **Per capita GDP** (2001): $38 083. **Unemployment rate** (2000): n.a. **Principal industries:** mining, tourism.

☐ **EDUCATION: Elem. enrolment** (May 31, 2002): 5 432. **Spending** per full-time equiv. student (1999): $12 392.

☐ **INTERNATIONAL AIRPORTS:** Whitehorse.

☐ **NATIONAL PARKS:** Ivvavik, Kluane, Vuntut.

☐ **PROVINCIAL DATA: Flower:** Fireweed. **Bird:** Common Raven.

☐ **POLITICS: Govt. Leader:** Dennis Fentie (Yukon Party), **Leaders, opposition parties:** Pat Duncan (Lib.), Todd Hardy (NDP). **Date of last general election:** Nov. 4, 2002. **Commissioner:** Hon. Jack Cable.

Northwest Territories

☐ **CAPITAL:** Yellowknife, metro pop. (2001) 16 541. **Date entered Confederation:** July 15, 1870.

☐ **POPULATION (2003):** 41 400; **Pop. density:** 0.02 per sq. km.; **Pop. growth (2002–2003):** 0.5%; **Pop. urban (2001):** 58%; **Age structure (2001):** 35.0% under 19; 60.7% 20-64; 4.4% over 65; **Median age (2001):** 30.1; **Net interprovincial migration (2000-01):** -606.

☐ **VITAL STATISTICS: Rates** (per 1 000 pop., 2001): birth: 17.1; death: 3.8. **Life expectancy at birth** (1999): 75.3.

☐ **GEOGRAPHY: Total area** 1 346 106 sq. km; **Land area** 1 183 085 sq. km; **Forested land** 615 000 sq. km; **Length of coastline** 14 734 km. **Climate**: extreme temperatures and low precipitation; arctic and sub-arctic. **Topography**: mostly tundra plains formed on the rocks of the Canadian Shield; the Mackenzie Lowland is a continuation of the Great Plains; the Mackenzie River Valley is forested.

☐ **ECONOMY: Gross Domestic Product** at market prices (2001): $2 725 million; **% change GDP** (2000-01): 20.8%; **Per capita GDP** (2001): $72 939. **Unemployment rate** (2000): n.a. **Principal industries:** construction, mining, utilities, services, tourism.

☐ **EDUCATION: Elem. enrolment** (2001-2): 7 944. **Spending** per full-time equiv. student (1999): $11 261 (incl. Nunavut).

☐ **INTERNATIONAL AIRPORTS:** none.

☐ **NATIONAL PARKS:** Aulavik, Nahanni, Tuktut Nogait, Wood Buffalo (shared with Alberta).

☐ **PROVINCIAL DATA: Flower:** Mountain Avens. **Bird:** Gyrfalcon. **Tree:** Jack pine.

☐ **POLITICS: Premier:** Stephen Kakfwi. **Date of last general election:** Dec. 6, 1999. **Commissioner:** Hon. Glenna F. Hansen.

Provinces on the Web

Newfoundland & Labrador: www.gov.nf.ca
Prince Edward Island: www.gov.pe.ca
Nova Scotia: www.gov.ns.ca
New Brunswick: www.gnb.ca
Quebec: www.gouv.qc.ca
Ontario: www.gov.on.ca
Manitoba: www.gov.mb.ca

Saskatchewan: www.gov.sk.ca
Alberta: www.gov.ab.ca
British Columbia: www.gov.bc.ca
Nunavut: www.gov.nu.ca
Northwest Territories: www.gov.nt.ca
Yukon Territory: www.gov.yk.ca

Nunavut

□ **CAPITAL:** Iqaluit, metro pop. (2001): 5 236. **Date became territory:** April 1, 1999.

□ **POPULATION (2003):** 28 700. **Pop. density:** 0.01 per sq. km. **Pop. growth (2002– 2003): 2.3%. Pop. urban (2001):** 32%. **Age structure (2001):** 46.5% under 19; 51.2% 20-64; 2.2% over 65. **Median age (2001):** 22.1. **Net interprovincial migration (2000-01):** 220.

□ **VITAL STATISTICS: Rates** (per 1 000 pop., 2001): birth: 25.3; death: 5.5. **Life expectancy at birth** (1999): 68.9.

□ **GEOGRAPHY: Total area:** 2 093 190 sq. km; **Land area:** 1 936 113 sq. km. **Length of coastline:** 114 920 km. **Climate:** extreme temperatures and low precipitation; arctic. **Topography:** rocky tun-dra with stunted vegetation located above the tree line; snow-covered most of the year.

□ **ECONOMY: Gross Domestic Product** at market prices (2001): 941 million; **% change GDP** (2000-01): 3.7%; **Per capita GDP** (2001): $35 184. **Unemployment rate** (1996): 15.4. **Principal industries:** mining, tourism, shrimp and scallop fishing, hunting and trapping, arts and crafts production.

□ **EDUCATION (1999–2000 est.):** No. of schools: 42 elem. and sec.; 1 post-sec. **Enrolment:** 7 462 elem. and sec.; 167 post-sec.

□ **INTERNATIONAL AIRPORTS:** Iqaluit.

□ **NATIONAL PARKS:** Auyuittuq, Quttinirpaaq (Ellesmere Island), Sirmilik.

□ **PROVINCIAL DATA:** n.a.

□ **POLITICS: Premier:** Paul Okalik. **Date of last general election:** Feb. 9, 1999. **Commissioner:** Hon. Peter Irniq.

CANADIAN CITIES

A census metropolitan area (CMA) is a very large urban area (known as the urban core) together with adjacent urban and rural areas (known as urban and rural fringes) which have a high degree of social and economic integration with the urban core. A CMA has an urban core population of a least 100 000 based on the previous census. Once an area becomes a CMA, it is retained as a CMA even if the population of its urban core declines below 100 000. All CMAs are subdivided into census tracts. A CMA may be consolidated with adjacent census agglomerations (CAs) if they are socially and economically integrated. This new grouping is known as a consolidated CMA and the component CMA and CA(s) are known as the primary census metropolitan area (PCMA) and primary census agglomeration(s) [PCA(s)]. A CMA may not be consolidated with another CMA.

For the 2001 census, Abbotsford, B.C., and Kingston, Ont., were added to the list of CMAs. Data for all categories will not be available for those two CMAs until the final releases from Statistics Canada in 2003.

Abbotsford, B.C.

Year Incorporated: 1995 Area: 626 sq. km.

□ **DEMOGRAPHICS: CMA Population** (2001): 147 370 Pop. density: 235 per sq. km. **Pop. growth** (1996–2001): 7%. **Immigrant pop.** (1996): n.a. **Age Structure** (2001): Male pop.: under 25: 38%, over 65: 12%; Female pop.: under 25: 35%, over 65: 15%.

□ **OFFICIAL LANGUAGES (1996):** n.a.

□ **FAMILIES (1996):** n.a.

□ **FAMILY INCOME (2000): Median Family Income:** n.a. **Median Income for Husband-Wife Families:** n.a. **Median Income for Lone-parent families:** n.a.

□ **LABOUR FORCE (2001): Labour Force (000s):** n.a. Employed Full-time (000s): n.a. **Employment rate:** n.a. **Unemployed (000s):** n.a. **Unemployment rate:** n.a. **Participation rate:** n.a.

□ **CLIMATE: Avg. day/night temps.:** 5.8°/-0.6° (Jan.); 23.4°/11.5° (July) **Avg. annual sunshine:** 1 866 h **Avg. annual precip.:** 1 573.2 mm **Avg. annual snowfall:** 63.5 cm.

Calgary, Alta

Year Incorporated: 1893. Area: 5 083 sq. km.

□ **DEMOGRAPHICS: CMA Population** (2001): 951 395. Pop. density: 187 per sq. km. **Pop. growth** (1996–2001): 15%. **Immigrant pop.** (1996): 20.8%. **Age Structure** (2001): Male pop.: under 25: 35%, over 65: 8%; Female pop.: under 25: 33%, over 65: 10%.

□ **OFFICIAL LANGUAGES (1996):** 90.7% English; 0.1% French; 7.3% bilingual; 1.9% neither.

□ **FAMILIES (1996): Avg. family size:** 3.2. **Lone-parent families:** 13.2% of families.

□ **FAMILY INCOME (2000): Median Family Income:** $60 700. **Median Income for Husband-**

Wife Families: $66 500. **Median Income for Lone-parent families:** $30 400.

☐ **LABOUR FORCE (2001): Labour Force (000s):** 596.3. Employed Full-time (000s): 477.7. **Employment rate:** 72.1. **Unemployed (000s):** 26.8. **Unemployment rate:** 4.5. **Participation rate:** 75.5.

☐ **CLIMATE:** Avg. day/night temps.: -2.8°/-15.1° (Jan.) 22.9°/9.4° (July) **Avg. annual sunshine:** 2 405 h **Avg. annual precip.:** 412.6 mm **Avg. annual snowfall:** 126.7 cm

Chicoutimi–Jonquière, Que.

Year Incorporated: 1976. Area: 1 754 sq. km.

☐ **DEMOGRAPHICS: CMA Population** (2001): 154 938. Pop. density: 88 per sq. km. **Pop. growth** (1996–2001): -3%. **Immigrant pop.** (1996): 0.7%. **Age Structure** (2001): Male pop.: under 25: 33%, over 65: 11%; Female pop.: under 25: 30%, over 65: 15%.

☐ **OFFICIAL LANGUAGES (1996):** 0.1% English; 82.5% French; 17.4% bilingual.

☐ **FAMILIES (1996):** Avg. family size: 3.1. **Lone-parent families:** 15.0% of families.

☐ **FAMILY INCOME (2000):** Median Family **Income:** $50 900. **Median Income for Husband-Wife Families:** $55 700. **Median Income for Lone-parent families:** $25 200.

☐ **LABOUR FORCE (2001): Labour Force (000s):** 78.9. Employed Full-time (000s): 56.5. **Employment rate:** 52.9. **Unemployed (000s):** 8.8. **Unemployment rate:** 11.2. **Participation rate:** 59.6.

☐ **CLIMATE:** Avg. day/night temps.: -10.3°/–21.7° (Jan.) 24.2°/12.0° (July) **Avg. annual sunshine:** 1 873 h **Avg. annual precip.:** 950.8 mm **Avg. annual snowfall:** 341.6 cm.

Edmonton, Alta

Year Incorporated: 1904. Area: 9 419 sq. km.

☐ **DEMOGRAPHICS: CMA Population** (2001): 937 845. Pop. density: 100 per sq. km. **Pop. growth** (1996–2001): 8%. **Immigrant pop.** (1996): 18.4%. **Age Structure** (2001): Male pop.: under 25: 36%, over 65: 9%; Female pop.: under 25: 34%, over 65: 12%.

☐ **OFFICIAL LANGUAGES (1996):** 90.9% English; 0.1% French; 7.5% bilingual; 1.6% neither.

☐ **FAMILIES (1996):** Avg. family size: 3.2. **Lone-parent families:** 15.0% of families.

☐ **FAMILY INCOME (2000):** Median Family **Income:** $56 300. **Median Income for Husband-Wife Families:** $62 700. **Median Income for**

Lone-parent families: $26 800.

☐ **LABOUR FORCE (2001): Labour Force (000s):** 531.1. Employed Full-time (000s): 408.1. **Employment rate:** 67.1. **Unemployed (000s):** 26.2. **Unemployment rate:** 4.9. **Participation rate:** 70.6.

☐ **CLIMATE:** Avg. day/night temps.: -7.3°/–16° (Jan.) 22.8°/12.1° (July) **Avg. annual sunshine:** 2 299 h **Avg. annual precip.:** 476.9 mm **Avg. annual snowfall:** 123.5 cm.

Halifax, N.S.

Year Incorporated: 1841. Area: 5 496 sq. km.

☐ **DEMOGRAPHICS: CMA Population** (2001): 359 183. Pop. density: 65 per sq. km. **Pop. growth** (1996–2001): 4%. **Immigrant pop.** (1996): 7.1%. **Age Structure** (2001): Male pop.: under 25: 33%, over 65: 9%; Female pop.: under 25: 31%, over 65: 12%.

☐ **OFFICIAL LANGUAGES (1996):** 88.9% English; 0.1% French; 10.7% bilingual; 0.3% neither.

☐ **FAMILIES (1996):** Avg. family size: 3.1. **Lone-parent families:** 15.9% of families.

☐ **FAMILY INCOME (2000):** Median Family **Income:** $53 400. **Median Income for Husband-Wife Families:** $60 200. **Median Income for Lone-parent families:** $23 500.

☐ **LABOUR FORCE (2001): Labour Force (000s):** 197.5. Employed Full-time (000s): 152.5. **Employment rate:** 65.5. **Unemployed (000s):** 13.9. **Unemployment rate:** 7.0. **Participation rate:** 70.5.

☐ **CLIMATE:** Avg. day/night temps.: -0.2°/–9.2° (Jan.) 22.1°/13.5° (July) **Avg. annual sunshine:** 1 965 h **Avg. annual precip.:** 1421.4 mm **Avg. annual snowfall:** 176.4 cm

Hamilton, Ont.

Year Incorporated: 1846. Area: 1 372 sq. km.

☐ **DEMOGRAPHICS: CMA Population** (2001): 662 401. Pop. density: 483 per sq. km. **Pop. growth** (1996–2001): 6%. **Immigrant pop.** (1996): 23.3%. **Age Structure** (2001): Male pop.: under 25: 34%, over 65: 12%; Female pop.: under 25: 31%, over 65: 16%.

☐ **OFFICIAL LANGUAGES (1996):** 91.7% English; 0.1% French; 6.8% bilingual; 1.5% neither.

☐ **FAMILIES (1996):** Avg. family size: 3.1. **Lone-parent families:** 14.3% of families.

☐ **FAMILY INCOME (2000):** Median Family **Income:** $59 700. **Median Income for Husband-Wife Families:** $65 900. **Median Income for Lone-parent families:** $28 000.

☐ **LABOUR FORCE (2001): Labour Force (000s):** 371.1. Employed Full-time (000s): 281.6. **Employment rate:** 63.2. **Unemployed (000s):** 22.8. **Unemployment rate:** 6.1. **Participation rate:** 67.4.

☐ **CLIMATE:** Avg. day/night temps.: -2.2°/–9.7° (Jan.) 26.3°/15.1° (July) **Avg. annual sunshine:** 2 088 h **Avg. annual precip.:** 910.1 mm **Avg. annual snowfall:** 161.8 cm

Kingston, Ont.

Year Incorporated: 1998. Area: 1 907 sq. km.

☐ **DEMOGRAPHICS: CMA Population** (2001): 146 838 Pop. density: 77 per sq. km. **Pop. growth** (1996–2001): 1%. **Immigrant pop.:** n.a. **Age Structure** (2001): Male pop.: under 25: 33%, over 65:.12%; Female pop.: under 25: 31%, over 65: 16%.

☐ **OFFICIAL LANGUAGES:** n.a.

☐ **FAMILIES:** n.a.

☐ **FAMILY INCOME (2000):** Median Family Income: n.a. **Median Income for Husband-Wife Families:** n.a. **Median Income for Lone-parent families:** n.a.

☐ **LABOUR FORCE (2001): Labour Force (000s):** n.a. Employed Full-time (000s): n.a. **Employment rate:** n.a. **Unemployed (000s):** n.a. **Unemployment rate:** n.a. **Participation rate:** n.a.

☐ **CLIMATE:** Avg. day/night temps.: -3.2°/–12.2° (Jan.) 24.8°/15.7° (July) **Avg. annual sunshine:** 1 992 h **Avg. annual precip.:** 968.2 mm **Avg. annual snowfall:** 180.9 cm.

Kitchener, Ont.

Year Incorporated: 1912. Area: 827 sq. km.

☐ **DEMOGRAPHICS: CMA Population** (2001): 414 284. Pop. density: 501 per sq. km. **Pop. growth** (1996–2001): 8%. **Immigrant pop.** (1996): 21.6%. **Age Structure** (2001): Male pop.: under 25: 36%, over 65: 9%; Female pop.: under 25: 33%, over 65: 13%.

☐ **OFFICIAL LANGUAGES (1996):** 91.4% English; 0.1% French; 6.9% bilingual; 1.6% neither.

☐ **FAMILIES (1996):** Avg. family size: 3.2. **Lone-parent families:** 13,7% of families.

☐ **FAMILY INCOME (2000):** Median Family Income: $60 700. **Median Income for Husband-Wife Families:** $66 200. **Median Income for Lone-parent families:** $28 700.

☐ **LABOUR FORCE (2001): Labour Force (000s):** 240.5. Employed Full-time (000s): 186.3. **Employment rate:** 66.0. **Unemployed (000s):**

14.8. **Unemployment rate:** 6.2. **Participation rate:** 70.3.

☐ **CLIMATE:** Avg. day/night temps.: -3.1°/–11° (Jan.) 25.9°/13.7° (July) **Avg. annual sunshine:** 1 920 h **Avg. annual precip.:** 907.9 mm **Avg. annual snowfall:** 159.5 cm.

London, Ont.

Year Incorporated: 1855. Area: 2 333 sq. km.

☐ **DEMOGRAPHICS: CMA Population** (2001): 432 451. Pop. density: 185 per sq. km. **Pop. growth** (1996–2001): 3%. **Immigrant pop.** (1996): 19.1%. **Age Structure** (2001): Male pop.: under 25: 35%, over 65: 11%; Female pop.: under 25: 32%, over 65: 15%.

☐ **OFFICIAL LANGUAGES (1996):** 92.2% English; 6.6% bilingual; 1.1% neither.

☐ **FAMILIES (1996):** Avg. family size: 3.1. **Lone-parent families:** 15.5% of families.

☐ **FAMILY INCOME (2000):** Median Family Income: $56 200. Median Income for Husband-Wife Families: $63 000. **Median Income for Lone-parent families:** $26 300.

☐ **LABOUR FORCE (2001): Labour Force (000s):** 230.7. Employed Full-time (000s): 171.1. **Employment rate:** 63.3. **Unemployed (000s):** 14.7. **Unemployment rate:** 6.4. **Participation rate:** 67.6.

☐ **CLIMATE:** Avg. day/night temps.: -2.4°/–10.1° (Jan.) 26.3°/14.6° (July) **Avg. annual sunshine:** 1 800 h **Avg. annual precip.:** 987.1 mm **Avg. annual snowfall:** 202.4 cm.

Montreal, Que.

Year Incorporated: 1832. Area: 4 047 sq. km.

☐ **DEMOGRAPHICS: CMA Population** (2001): 3 426 350. Pop. density: 847 per sq. km. **Pop. growth** (1996–2001): 3%. **Immigrant pop.** (1996): 17.6%. **Age Structure** (2001): Male pop.: under 25: 33%, over 65: 11%; Female pop.: under 25: 30%, .over 65: 15%.

☐ **OFFICIAL LANGUAGES (1996):** 8.5% English; 39.8% French; 49.7% bilingual; 1.9% neither.

☐ **FAMILIES (1996):** Avg. family size: 3.1. **Lone-parent families:** 17.4% of families.

☐ **FAMILY INCOME (2000):** Median Family Income: $50 000. **Median Income for Husband-Wife Families:** $56 000. **Median Income for Lone-parent families:** $26 600.

☐ **LABOUR FORCE (2001): Labour Force (000s):** 1 857.7. Employed Full-time (000s): 1 426.7. **Employment rate:** 60.4. **Unemployed (000s):**

152.0. **Unemployment rate:** 8.2. **Participation rate:** 65.7.

☐ **CLIMATE: Avg. day/night temps.:** -5.8°/–14.9° (Jan.) 26.3°/15.5° (July) **Avg. annual sunshine:** 2 029 h **Avg. annual precip.:** 966.8 mm **Avg. annual snowfall:** 214.2 cm.

Oshawa, Ont.

Year Incorporated: 1924. Area: 903 sq. km.

☐ **DEMOGRAPHICS: CMA Population** (2001): 296 298. Pop. density: 328 per sq. km. **Pop. growth** (1996–2001): 10%. **Immigrant pop.** (1996) 16.4%. **Age Structure** (2001): Male pop.: under 25: 37%, over 65: 9%; Female pop.: under 25: 34%, over 65: 12%.

☐ **OFFICIAL LANGUAGES (1996):** 92.8% English; 0.1% French; 6.7% bilingual; 0.5% neither.

☐ **FAMILIES (1996): Avg. family size:** 3.2. **Lone-parent families:** 14.1% of families.

☐ **FAMILY INCOME (2000):** Median Family Income: $64 700. **Median Income for Husband-Wife Families:** $71 800. **Median Income for Lone-parent families:** $28 900.

☐ **LABOUR FORCE (2001): Labour Force (000s):** 163.4. Employed Full-time (000s): 127.5. **Employment rate:** 65.2. **Unemployed (000s):** 9.2. **Unemployment rate:** 5.6. **Participation rate:** 69.0.

☐ **CLIMATE: Avg. day/night temps.:** -1.4°/-9.2° (Jan.) 25°/15.5° (July) **Avg. annual sunshine:** 1 893 h **Avg. annual precip.:** 877.9 mm **Avg. annual snowfall:** 118.4 cm.

Ottawa-Hull, Ont./Que.

Year Incorporated: 1854 (Ottawa). Area: 5 318 sq. km.

☐ **DEMOGRAPHICS: CMA Population** (2001): 1 063 664. Pop. density: 200 per sq. km. **Pop. growth** (1996–2001): 6%. **Immigrant pop.** (1996): 16.0%. **Age Structure** (2001): Male pop.: under 25: 34%, over 65: 9%; Female pop.: under 25: 31%, over 65: 12%.

☐ **OFFICIAL LANGUAGES (1996):** 45.8% English; 9.0% French; 44.0% bilingual.

☐ **FAMILIES (1996): Avg. family size:** 3.1. **Lone-parent families:** 15.6% of families.

☐ **FAMILY INCOME (2000):** Median Family Income: $65 500. **Median Income for Husband-Wife Families:** $72 900. **Median Income for Lone-parent families:** $30 500.

☐ **LABOUR FORCE (2001): Labour Force (000s):** 615.0. Employed Full-time (000s): 477.0. **Employment rate:** 65.8. **Unemployed (000s):**

39.0. **Unemployment rate:** 6.3. **Participation rate:** 70.3.

☐ **CLIMATE: CLIMATE: Avg. day/night temps.:** -6.1°/–15.3° (Jan.) 26.5°/15.4° (July) **Avg. annual sunshine:** 2 061 h **Avg. annual precip.:** 943.5 mm **Avg. annual snowfall:** 235.7 cm.

Quebec, Que.

Year Incorporated: 1832. Area: 3 154 sq. km.

☐ **DEMOGRAPHICS: CMA Population** (2001): 682 757. Pop. density: 216 per sq. km. **Pop. growth** (1996–2001): 1%. **Immigrant pop.** (1996): 2.6%. **Age Structure** (2001): Male pop.: under 25: 31%, over 65: 11%; Female pop.: under 25: 28%, over 65: 15%.

☐ **OFFICIAL LANGUAGES (1996):** 0.2% English; 69.6% French; 30.0% bilingual; 0.2% neither.

☐ **FAMILIES (1996): Avg. family size:** 3.0. **Lone-parent families:** 16.1% of families.

☐ **FAMILY INCOME (2000):** Median Family Income: $53 300. **Median Income for Husband-Wife Families:** $58 200. **Median Income for Lone-parent families:** $29 800.

☐ **LABOUR FORCE (2001): Labour Force (000s):** 367.8. Employed Full-time (000s): 270.0. **Employment rate:** 59.7. **Unemployed (000s):** 28.8. **Unemployment rate:** 7.8. **Participation rate:** 64.8.

☐ **CLIMATE: Avg. day/night temps.:** -7.9°/–17.6° (Jan.) 25.0°/13.4° (July) **Avg. annual sunshine:** 1 905 h **Avg. annual precip.:** 1230.3 mm **Avg. annual snowfall:** 315.9 cm.

Regina, Sask.

Year Incorporated: 1903. Area: 3 408 sq. km.

☐ **DEMOGRAPHICS: CMA Population** (2001): 192 800. Pop. density: 57 per sq. km. **Pop. growth** (1996–2001): -1%. **Immigrant pop.** (1996): 7.9%. **Age Structure** (2001): Male pop.: under 25: 37%, over 65: 11%; Female pop.: under 25: 34%, over 65: 14%.

☐ **OFFICIAL LANGUAGES (1996):** 93.9% English; 0.1% French; 5.6% bilingual; 0.4% neither.

☐ **FAMILIES (1996): Avg. family size:** 3.2. **Lone-parent families:** 16.6% of families.

☐ **FAMILY INCOME (2000):** Median Family Income: $56 600. **Median Income for Husband-Wife Families:** $64 700. **Median Income for Lone-parent families:** $25 600.

☐ **LABOUR FORCE (2001): Labour Force (000s):** 111.3. Employed Full-time (000s): 86.6. **Employment rate:** 67.4. **Unemployed (000s):** 6.1. **Unemployment rate:** 5.5. **Participation rate:** 71.3.

☐ **CLIMATE:** Avg. day/night temps.: -10.7°/–21.6° (Jan.) 25.7°/11.8° (July) **Avg. annual sunshine:** 2 338 h **Avg. annual precip.:** 388.1 mm **Avg. annual snowfall:** 105.9 cm.

St. Catharines–Niagara, Ont.

Year Incorporated: 1876. Area: 1 406 sq. km.

☐ **DEMOGRAPHICS: CMA Population** (2001): 377 009. Pop. density: 268 per sq. km. **Pop. growth** (1996–2001): 1%. **Immigrant pop.** (1996): 18.1%. **Age Structure** (2001): Male pop.: under 25: 32%, over 65: 15%; Female pop.: under 25: 29%, over 65: 19%.

☐ **OFFICIAL LANGUAGES (1996):** 90.8% English; 0.2% French; 8.3% bilingual; 0.7% neither.

☐ **FAMILIES (1996):** Avg. family size: 3.0. **Lone-parent families:** 14.8% of families.

☐ **FAMILY INCOME (2000):** Median Family Income: $53 300. **Median Income for Husband-Wife Families:** $59 100. **Median Income for Lone-parent families:** $26 200.

☐ **LABOUR FORCE (2001): Labour Force (000s):** 202.7. Employed Full-time (000s): 150.0. **Employment rate:** 59.0. **Unemployed (000s):** 12.7. **Unemployment rate:** 6.3. **Participation rate:** 63.0.

☐ **CLIMATE:** Avg. day/night temps.: -0.5°/–7.7° (Jan.) 27.1°/16.4° (July) **Avg. annual sunshine:** 2 005 h **Avg. annual precip.:** 873.6 mm **Avg. annual snowfall:** 136.6 cm.

Saint John, N.B.

Year Incorporated: 1785. Area: 3 360 sq. km.

☐ **DEMOGRAPHICS: CMA Population** (2001): 122 678. Pop. density: 37 per sq. km. **Pop. growth** (1996–2001): -3%. **Immigrant pop.** (1996): 3.9%. **Age Structure** (2001): Male pop.: under 25: 34%, over 65: 11%; Female pop.: under 25: 31%, over 65: 15%.

☐ **OFFICIAL LANGUAGES (1996):** 87.5% English; 0.1% French; 12.3% bilingual; 0.1% neither.

☐ **FAMILIES (1996):** Avg. family size: 3.1. **Lone-parent families:** 16.9% of families.

☐ **FAMILY INCOME (2000):** Median Family Income: $47 800. **Median Income for Husband-Wife Families:** $55 200. **Median Income for Lone-parent families:** $20 800.

☐ **LABOUR FORCE (2001): Labour Force (000s):** 64.2. Employed Full-time (000s): 48.6. **Employment rate:** 57.8. **Unemployed (000s):** 6.1. **Unemployment rate:** 9.5. **Participation rate:** 63.8.

☐ **CLIMATE:** Avg. day/night temps.: -2.7°/–13.6° (Jan.) 22.4°/11.7° (July) **Avg. annual sunshine:** 1

950 h Avg. annual precip.: 1 390.3 mm Avg. annual snowfall: 256.9 cm.

St. John's, Nfld and Labrador

Year Incorporated: 1888. Area: 805 sq. km.

☐ **DEMOGRAPHICS: CMA Population** (2001): 176 918. Pop. density: 215 per sq. km. **Pop. growth** (1996–2001): -1%. **Immigrant pop.** (1996): 2.9%. **Age Structure** (2001): Male pop.: under 25: 35%, over 65: 9%; Female pop.: under 25: 32%, over 65: 12%.

☐ **OFFICIAL LANGUAGES (1996):** 94.5% English; 0% French; 5.4% bilingual; 0.1% neither.

☐ **FAMILIES (1996):** Avg. family size: 3.2. **Lone-parent families:** 16.8% of families.

☐ **FAMILY INCOME (2000):** Median Family Income: $48 800. **Median Income for Husband-Wife Families:** $56 300. **Median Income for Lone-parent families:** $21 200.

☐ **LABOUR FORCE (2001): Labour Force (000s):** 94.5. Employed Full-time (000s): 73.4. **Employment rate:** 60.5. **Unemployed (000s):** 8.6. **Unemployment rate:** 9.1. **Participation rate:** 66.6.

☐ **CLIMATE:** Avg. day/night temps.: -0.9°/–1.5° (Jan.) 20.3°/10.5° (July) **Avg. annual sunshine:** 1 512 h **Avg. annual precip.:** 1 513.7 mm **Avg. annual snowfall:** 322.3 cm.

Saskatoon, Sask.

Year Incorporated: 1906. Area: 5 192 sq. km.

☐ **DEMOGRAPHICS: CMA Population** (2001): 225 927. Pop. density: 44 per sq. km. **Pop. growth** (1996–2001): 3%. **Immigrant pop.** (1996): 7.5%. **Age Structure** (2001): Male pop.: under 25: 38%, over 65: 10%; Female pop.: under 25: 36%, over 65: 13%.

☐ **OFFICIAL LANGUAGES (1996):** 92.9% English; 0.0% French; 6.5% bilingual; 0.5% neither.

☐ **FAMILIES (1996):** Avg. family size: 3.2. **Lone-parent families:** 15.9% of families.

☐ **FAMILY INCOME (2000):** Median Family Income: $51 600. **Median Income for Husband-Wife Families:** $58 300. **Median Income for Lone-parent families:** $22 600.

☐ **LABOUR FORCE (2001): Labour Force (000s):** 123.2. Employed Full-time (000s): 91.8. **Employment rate:** 63.7. **Unemployed (000s):** 7.6. **Unemployment rate:** 6.2. **Participation rate:** 67.8.

☐ **CLIMATE:** Avg. day/night temps.: -11.8/–22.3° (Jan) 24.9°/11.4° (July) **Avg. annual sunshine:** 2 328 h **Avg. annual precip.:** 350.0 mm **Avg. annual snowfall:** 97.2 cm.

Sherbrooke, Que.

Year Incorporated: 1875. Area: 1 108 sq. km.

☐ **DEMOGRAPHICS: CMA Population** (2001): 153 811. Pop. density: 139 per sq. km. **Pop. growth** (1996–2001): 2%. **Immigrant pop.** (1996): 4.2%. **Age Structure** (2001): Male pop.: under 25: 34%, over 65: 10%; Female pop.: under 25: 31%, over 65: 16%.

☐ **OFFICIAL LANGUAGES (1996):** 1.9% English; 58.8% French; 39.1% bilingual; 0.3% neither.

☐ **FAMILIES (1996):** Avg. family size: 3.0. **Lone-parent families:** 17.0% of families.

☐ **FAMILY INCOME (2000): Median Family Income:** $47 600. **Median Income for Husband-Wife Families:** $52 900. **Median Income for Lone-parent families:** $26 300.

☐ **LABOUR FORCE (2001): Labour Force (000s):** 80.7 Employed Full-time (000s): 61.4. **Employment rate:** 59.2. **Unemployed (000s):** 6.3. **Unemployment rate:** 7.8. **Participation rate:** 64.2.

☐ **CLIMATE:** Avg. day/night temps.: -5.7°/–18.0° (Jan.) 24.7°/11.4° (July) **Avg. annual sunshine:** 1 850 h **Avg. annual precip.:** 1 144.1 mm **Avg. annual snowfall:** 294.3 cm.

Sudbury, Ont.

Year Incorporated: 1930. Area: 3 536 sq. km.

☐ **DEMOGRAPHICS: CMA Population** (2001): 155 601. Pop. density: 44 per sq. km. **Pop. growth** (1996–2001): -7%. **Immigrant pop.** (1991): 8.1%. **Age Structure** (2001): Male pop.: under 25: 33%, over 65: 12%; Female pop.: under 25: 31%, over 65: 15%.

☐ **OFFICIAL LANGUAGES (1996):** 58.0% English; 1.5% French; 40.1% bilingual; 0.3% neither.

☐ **FAMILIES (1996):** Avg. family size: 3.1. **Lone-parent families:** 15.2% of families.

☐ **FAMILY INCOME (2000): Median Family Income:** $54 400. **Median Income for Husband-Wife Families:** $61 300. **Median Income for Lone-parent families:** $23 100.

☐ **LABOUR FORCE (2001): Labour Force (000s):** 79.4. Employed Full-time (000s): 57.5. **Employment rate:** 56.2. **Unemployed (000s):** 6.9. **Unemployment rate:** 8.7. **Participation rate:** 61.6.

☐ **CLIMATE:** Avg. day/night temps.: -8.4°/–18.6° (Jan.) 24.8°/13.3° (July) **Avg. annual sunshine:** 1 989 h **Avg. annual precip.:** 899.3 mm **Avg. annual snowfall:** 274.4 cm

Thunder Bay, Ont.

Year Incorporated: 1970. Area: 2 548 sq. km.

☐ **DEMOGRAPHICS: CMA Population** (2001): 121 986. Pop. density: 48 per sq. km. **Pop. growth** (1996–2001): -4%. **Immigrant pop.** (1996): 12.2%. **Age Structure** (2001): Male pop.: under 25: 33%, over 65: 13%; Female pop.: under 25: 30%, over 65: 17%.

☐ **OFFICIAL LANGUAGES (1996):** 91.7% English; 0.1% French; 7.4% bilingual; 0.7% neither.

☐ **FAMILIES (1996):** Avg. family size: 3.1. **Lone-parent families:** 16.0% of families.

☐ **FAMILY INCOME (2000): Median Family Income:** $57 100. **Median Income for Husband-Wife Families:** $63 800. **Median Income for Lone-parent families:** $24 500.

☐ **LABOUR FORCE (2001): Labour Force (000s):** 67.5. Employed Full-time (000s): 48.5. **Employment rate:** 61.0. **Unemployed (000s):** 5.4. **Unemployment rate:** 8.0. **Participation rate:** 66.3.

☐ **CLIMATE:** Avg. day/night temps.: -8.6°/–21.1° (Jan.) 24.2°/11.0° (July) **Avg. annual sunshine:** 2 168 h **Avg. annual precip.:** 711.6 mm **Avg. annual snowfall:** 187.6 cm.

Toronto, Ont.

Year Incorporated: 1834. Area: 5 903 sq. km.

☐ **DEMOGRAPHICS: CMA Population** (2001): 4 682 897. Pop. density: 793 per sq. km. **Pop. growth** (1996–2001): 9%. **Immigrant pop.** (1996): 41.6%. **Age Structure** (2001): Male pop.: under 25: 34%, over 65: 10%; Female pop.: under 25: 31%, over 65: 13%.

☐ **OFFICIAL LANGUAGES (1996):** 87.4% English; 0.1% French; 8.0% bilingual; 4.5% neither.

☐ **FAMILIES (1996):** Avg. family size: 3.3. **Lone-parent families:** 15.5% of families.

☐ **FAMILY INCOME (2000): Median Family Income:** $55 000. **Median Income for Husband-Wife Families:** $61 400. **Median Income for Lone-parent families:** $29 400.

☐ **LABOUR FORCE (2001): Labour Force (000s):** 2 745.7. Employed Full-time (000s): 2 177.0. **Employment rate:** 65.1. **Unemployed (000s):** 173.8. **Unemployment rate:** 6.3. **Participation rate:** 69.5.

☐ **CLIMATE:** Avg. day/night temps.: -2.1°/–10.5° (Jan.) 26.8°/14.8° (July) **Avg. annual sunshine:** 2 038 h **Avg. annual precip.:** 792.7 mm **Avg. annual snowfall:** 115.4 cm.

Trois–Rivières, Que.

Year Incorporated: 1857. Area: 880 sq. km.

□ **DEMOGRAPHICS: CMA Population** (2001): 137 507. Pop. density: 156 per sq. km. **Pop. growth** (1996–2001): -2%. **Immigrant pop.** (1996): 1.6%. **Age Structure** (2001): Male pop.: under 25: 31%, over 65: 13%; Female pop.: under 25: 28%, over 65: 18%.

□ **OFFICIAL LANGUAGES (1996):** 0.1% English; 75.4% French; 24.4% bilingual.

□ **FAMILIES (1996): Avg. family size:** 3.0. **Lone-parent families:** 16.1% of families.

□ **FAMILY INCOME (2000): Median Family Income:** $45 900. **Median Income for Husband-Wife Families:** $51 700. **Median Income for Lone-parent families:** $23 800.

□ **LABOUR FORCE (2001): Labour Force (000s):** 72.5. Employed Full-time (000s): 53.5. **Employment rate:** 56.1. **Unemployed (000s):** 7.0. **Unemployment rate:** 9.7. **Participation rate:** 62.1.

□ **CLIMATE: Avg. day/night temps.:** -7.3°/–17.6° (Jan.) 25.5°/14.1° (July) **Avg. annual sunshine:** 1 967 h **Avg. annual precip.:** 1 099.8 mm **Avg. annual snowfall:** 241.3 cm.

Victoria, B.C.

Year Incorporated: 1862. Area: 695 sq. km.

□ **DEMOGRAPHICS: CMA Population** (2001): 311 902. Pop. density: 449 per sq. km. **Pop. growth** (1996–2001): 2%. **Immigrant pop.** (1996): 19.0%. **Age Structure** (2001): Male pop.: under 25: 30%, over 65: 15%; Female pop.: under 25: 27%, over 65: 20%.

□ **OFFICIAL LANGUAGES (1996):** 90.6% English; 0.0% French; 8.6% bilingual; 0.7% neither.

□ **FAMILIES (1996): Avg. family size:** 2.9. **Lone-parent families:** 14.1% of families.

□ **FAMILY INCOME (2000):** Median Family Income: $55 200. Median Income for Husband-Wife Families: $60 800. Median Income for Lone-parent families: $28 100.

□ **LABOUR FORCE (2001): Labour Force (000s):** 158.5. Employed Full-time (000s): 113.3. **Employment rate:** 57.7. **Unemployed (000s):** 9.6. **Unemployment rate:** 6.1. **Participation rate:** 61.4.

□ **CLIMATE: Avg. day/night temps.:** 6.9°/0.7° (Jan.) 21.9°/10.8° (July) **Avg. annual sunshine:** 2 086 h **Avg. annual precip.:** 883.3 mm **Avg. annual snowfall:** 43.8 cm

Vancouver, B.C.

Year Incorporated: 1886. Area: 2 879 sq. km.

□ **DEMOGRAPHICS: CMA Population** (2001): 1 986 965. Pop. density: 690 per sq. km. **Pop. growth** (1996–2001): 8%. **Immigrant pop.** (1996) 34.6%. **Age Structure** (2001): Male pop.: under 25: 32%, over 65: 11%; Female pop.: under 25: 30%, over 65: 14%.

□ **OFFICIAL LANGUAGES (1996):** 87.9% English; 0.1% French; 7.4% bilingual; 4.7% neither.

□ **FAMILIES (1996): Avg. family size:** 3.2. **Lone-parent families:** 13.9% of families.

□ **FAMILY INCOME (2000):** Median Family Income: $50 100. **Median Income for Husband-Wife Families:** $55 200. **Median Income for Lone-parent families:** $26 900.

□ **LABOUR FORCE (2001): Labour Force (000s):** 1 125.1. Employed Full-time (000s): 843.2. **Employment rate:** 61.4. **Unemployed (000s):** 74.0. **Unemployment rate:** 6.6. **Participation rate:** 65.7.

□ **CLIMATE: Avg. day/night temps.:** 6.1°/0.5° (Jan.) 21.7°/13.2° (July) **Avg. annual sunshine:** 1 928 h **Avg. annual precip.:** 1 199.0 mm **Avg. annual snowfall:** 48.2 cm.

Windsor, Ont.

Year Incorporated: 1892. Area: 1 023 sq. km.

□ **DEMOGRAPHICS: CMA Population** (2001): 307 877. Pop. density: 301 per sq. km. **Pop. growth** (1996–2001): 7%. **Immigrant pop.** (1996): 20.4%. **Age Structure** (2001): Male pop.: under 25: 35%, over 65: 11%; Female pop.: under 25: 32%, over 65: 14%.

□ **OFFICIAL LANGUAGES (1996):** 87.8% English; 0.2% French; 10.5% bilingual; 1.5% neither.

□ **FAMILIES (1996): Avg. family size:** 3.2. **Lone-parent families:** 16.0% of families.

□ **FAMILY INCOME (2000):** Median Family Income: $64 200. **Median Income for Husband-Wife Families:** $72 000. **Median Income for Lone-parent families:** $28 200.

□ **LABOUR FORCE (2001): Labour Force (000s):** 165.7. Employed Full-time (000s): 124.7. **Employment rate:** 61.9. **Unemployed (000s):** 11.1. **Unemployment rate:** 6.7. **Participation rate:** 66.3.

□ **CLIMATE: Avg. day/night temps.:** -0.9°/–8.1° (Jan.) 27.9°/17.4° (July) **Avg. annual sunshine:** 2 027 h **Avg. annual precip.:** 918.3 mm **Avg. annual snowfall:** 126.6 cm

Winnipeg, Man.

Year Incorporated: 1873. Area: 4 151 sq. km.

☐ **DEMOGRAPHICS: CMA Population** (2001): 671 274. Pop. density: 162 per sq. km. **Pop. growth** (1996–2001): 0.6%. **Immigrant pop.** (1996): 16.7%. **Age Structure** (2001): Male pop.: under 25: 34%, over 65: 11%; Female pop.: under 25: 31%, over 65: 16%.

☐ **OFFICIAL LANGUAGES (1996):** 87.9% English; 0.1% French; 10.9% bilingual; 1.1% neither.

☐ **FAMILIES (1996): Avg. family size:** 3.1. **Lone-parent families:** 15.8% of families.

☐ **FAMILY INCOME (2000): Median Family Income:** $52 500. **Median Income for Husband-Wife Families:** $58 400. **Median Income for Lone-parent families:** $25 500.

☐ **LABOUR FORCE (2001): Labour Force (000s):** 377.6. Employed Full-time (000s): 290.7. **Employment rate:** 66.7. **Unemployed (000s):** 19.4. **Unemployment rate:** 5.1. **Participation rate:** 70.3.

☐ **CLIMATE:** Avg. day/night temps.: -12.7°/-22.8° (Jan.) 25.8°/13.3° (July) **Avg. annual sunshine:** 2 372 h **Avg. annual precip.:** 513.7 mm **Avg. annual snowfall:** 110.6 cm.

Where Do We Live?

*I**n** the cities—51 percent of us (15.3 million strong) live in four highly urbanized regions: metropolitan Montreal; the Golden Horseshoe in Ontario; the Calgary–Edmonton corridor in Alberta; and the Lower Mainland–south Vancouver Island portion of British Columbia. The other 49 percent of Canada's citizens are scattered across our vast geography—and many of them also live in smaller urban centres.*

While the census of 1871 showed a nation with 19.6 percent of Canadians living in urban areas and 80.4 percent living in rural areas, the 2001 census makes it clear how much times have changed: 79.7 percent of us now live in urban areas and 20.3 percent live in rural areas. As planners at all levels of government begin to work with the new census data, it's clear that the needs of the urban areas, be they social or economic, may necessitate some structural changes to a governing system that was created to serve the rural population of 1871.

The census data also showed that we've continued to move to Ontario and Alberta, as the Atlantic provinces (with the exception of PEI, which held steady), Quebec, Manitoba, Saskatchewan and B.C. experienced a net loss of people through emigration during each of the last five years. The northern territories of Yukon and the Northwest Territories also experienced net losses, while Nunavut has seen very modest net population gains through inter-provincial migration in the last two years.

Growth in some municipalities was explosive: in five years, Cochrane, Alberta, grew by 58.9 percent; Sylvan Lake, Alberta by 44.5 percent and Strathmore, Alberta, by 43.4 percent. Still in Alberta, Calgary grew by 15 percent, Red Deer by 13 percent and Grande Prairie by 18 percent. In contrast, the CMA of Toronto grew only by 9.8 percent; the outlying area of Richmond Hill, Ontario, grew by 29.8 percent. In Toronto's case, however, the relatively modest percentage of growth resulted in absorbing 419,000 newcomers.

In several areas, the population in the core municipality is growing more slowly than in the areas around it, forming a doughnut. The larger the difference in the growth between the two, the more pronounced the "doughnut effect." This phenomenon was particularly prominent in areas such as Saskatoon and Regina.

Globalization may be making urban economies the new focus of attention. The health of urban centres is becoming a hot topic among planners and Canada's cities are ready for a new deal that will give them a better chance to manage their infrastructure (development, transportation and primary services) to build prosperity.

NATIONAL PARKS

Canada's national parks are protected by law to preserve representative natural areas throughout the country. The parks are maintained to enhance public understanding, appreciation and enjoyment of the country's natural heritage, and increasingly, park management efforts are being directed to protect Canada's wide variety of ecosystems for the long term.

In 1988, the National Parks Act was amended to ensure that each park's management plan would maintain the ecological integrity of the area, that is, that the structure and function of the existing ecosystem would not be harmed by human activity. This amendment was made as it became increasingly clear that many ecological features, such as grizzly bear populations, require very large areas and very long time lines if they are to survive, if not thrive. The host of modern environmental stresses also affect protected areas and their inhabitants, and mere protection is not enough; a co-operative parks management structure—including public, corporate, environmental and Aboriginal interest groups—and an ecosystem management approach is the preferred management model to minimize damage.

The goal of the national parks policy is to create at least one national park in each of Canada's 39 natural regions. Thirty-nine national parks and national park reserves currently exist; however, 14 more national parks are needed. Once completed, the parks system will preserve just over 3 percent of the country's land mass. For more information, visit www.parkscanada.ca

Park	Location	Size (sq. km)	Year est.	Description
Aulavik	northern portion of Banks Is., NWT	12 200	(1992)[1]	Thomsen River forms core of a park marked by deep river canyons and desert-like badlands. Area supports high concentration of musk oxen. The Thomsen River is Canada's most northerly navigable river.
Auyuittuq[2]	Cumberland Peninsula, Baffin Is., NT	21 469	1976	Located on the Arctic Circle; this is an isolated and very rugged wilderness area with mountains, fjords, tundra and permafrost. Park protects part of Northern Davis Strait Natural Region and portions of Baffin Island Shelf Marine region. Contains prehistoric and historic resources from ancient Thule settlements.
Banff	Banff, Alta.	6 641	1885	Our first national park is noted for ice-capped peaks, canyons, glaciers, hot springs, and hoodoos (rock pillars, often in fantastic shapes). Wildlife includes bighorn sheep, black and grizzly bears, elk and caribou. Banff is part of UNESCO's Rocky Mountain Parks World Heritage Site.
Bruce Peninsula, including Fathom Five National Marine Park	299 km northwest of Toronto, between Lake Huron and Georgian Bay	154	(1987)[1]	This park was created to protect the Niagara Escarpment and the limestone cliffs on Georgian Bay; contains mixed forests, wetlands and limestone cliffs. Fathom Five National Marine Park includes 19 islands, over 20 shipwrecks, clear water and distinctive underwater geological features.
Cape Breton Highlands	across northern Cape Breton Is., N.S.	948	1936	The scenic Cabot Trail is characterized by a rugged shoreline with plunging cliffs.
Elk Island	45 km east of Edmonton, Alta.	194	1913	A large population of plains and wood bison, elk and moose inhabit the rolling woodlands and lakes. Other wildlife include bear, beaver and coyote.

▶

Park	Location	Size (sq. km)	Year est.	Description
Forillon	northeast tip of Gaspé Peninsula, Que.	244	1970	Protects parts of the Notre-Dame and Mégantic mountains and some of the Gulf of St. Lawrence marine area. Features a rich variety of seabirds and animals, limestone cliffs, Arctic-alpine plants and the highest mountains in eastern Canada.
Fundy	southeastern shore on the Bay of Fundy, N.B.	206	1948	The giant tides of the Bay of Fundy, among the highest in the world, and a bold, irregular coastline.
Georgian Bay Islands	160 km northwest of Toronto, Ont.	25	1929	59 glacier swept islands are home to endangered species, limestone cliffs, caves and archaeological sites. This area was the inspiration for many of the Group of Seven artists.
Glacier	45 km east of Revelstoke, B.C.	1 349	1886	Protects a section of the Columbia Mountains Natural Region that includes habitats for grizzly bear and mountain caribou. Steep angular mountains, deep valleys, icefields, glaciers, waterfalls, avalanche paths and high precipitation characterise the area.
Grasslands	100 km south of Swift Current, Sask.	906	(1975)[1]	Unique natural habitat of short-grass prairie; blacktailed prairie dogs, pronghorn antelope and the prairie falcon are found.
Gros Morne	west coast of Nfld	1 805	(1970)[1]	Park is dominated by a coastal lowland and an alpine plateau that each boast a variety of land mammals, bird species, fish and trees, ferns and flowers. The park has been declared a UNESCO World Heritage Site because of its spectacular geology.
Gwaii Haanas (South Moresby)[2] including Gwaii Haanas, National Marine Conservation Area	southern part of Queen Charlotte Islands, B.C.	1 495	(1987)[1]	Canada's "Galapagos," home to 39 unique plants, an estimated 750,000 seabirds come to nest, and animals such as black bear, pine marten, deer mice, shrews and weasels. Geography features deep fjords, rugged mountains, and one of the finest old-growth temperate rainforest left on Pacific coast.
Ivvavik	northern tip of Yukon	10 168	1984	Migration route for Porcupine caribou herd; major North American waterfowl area; home to grizzly, black and polar bears. Contains unique non-glaciated landscape.
Jasper	340 km west of Edmonton, Alta.	10 878	1907	Contains the largest icefield in the Canadian Rockies—Columbia Icefield—and preserves the headwaters of major rivers, particularly the Athabasca.
Kejimkujik	central southwestern N.S.	404	1974	Gently rolling country with many lakes and rivers. The earliest inhabitants—Maritime Archaic Indians—arrived about 4,500 years ago.
Kluane[2]	southwest corner of Yukon	22 013	1976	Features Mount Logan, Canada's highest peak, Kluane Lake (Yukon's largest), grizzly bears, dall sheep and whitewater rivers.
Kootenay	1 km east of Radium Hot Springs, B.C.	1 406	1920	The park contains Rocky Mountain wilderness and is part of UNESCO's Rocky Mountain Parks World Heritage Site. Hot springs, alpine lakes, canyons, glaciers, home to bighorn sheep, mountain goats.

Park	Location	Size (sq. km)	Year est.	Description
Kouchibouguac	eastern N.B.	239	1979	Swimming, sunbathing on the beaches and dunes; cycling, hiking trails; windsurfing.
La Mauricie	55 km north of Trois-Rivières, Que.	536	1977	Hilly terrain at the edge of the Canadian Shield with transitional forest vegetation from evergreens to deciduous. Beaver, moose and the common loon; an area filled with brooks, lakes and waterfalls.
Mingan Archipelago[2]	N of Anticosti Is. along the St. Lawrence shore, Que.	151	1984	This is a limestone environment that is home to diversified plant species, nesting seabirds and whales, seals and porpoises.
Mount Revelstoke	Revelstoke, B.C.	260	1914	Columbia Mountain ranges. Park is characterised by deep snow accumulation and high annual precipitation. Contains three ecoregions: Interior Alpine Tundra, Interior Sub-alpine Tundra and Interior Cedar Hemlock.
Nahanni[2]	southwestern NWT	4 765	1976	The wild and spectacular South Nahanni river passes through this long, narrow park. The route contains four canyons; the river plunges from twice the height of Niagara Falls at Virginia Falls. Park contains sulphur hotsprings, alpine tundra and vast forests, plus numerous species of birds, mammals and fish.
Pacific Rim[2]	west coast of Vancouver Island, B.C.	500	(1970)[1]	3 sections—Long Beach, Broken Group Islands and West Coast Trail—offer rainforest, beaches and scenic, rugged hiking. Park contains native archaeological sites that indicate settlement for at least 4,300 years.
Point Pelee	southernmost point of Ont.	15	1918	Extensive marshlands and beaches provide refuge for many migratory birds and butterflies. The temperate climate allows over 70 species of tree to survive, as well as a huge variety of reptiles, birds, amphibians, insects and spiders.
Prince Albert	200 km north of Saskatoon, Sask.	3 875	1927	Mixture of forest land and lakes, home to woodland caribou, bison and a pelican colony. Archaeological digs indicate that the area has been inhabited by Aboriginal cultures for at least 6,000 years.
Prince Edward Island	north shore of P.E.I.	22	1937	40 km of fine saltwater beaches, sand dunes, high coastal cliffs, marshes, ponds and woodlands. Green Gables in located in this park.
Pukaskwa	northeastern shore of Lake Superior	1 878	(1971)[1]	Hilly terrain is characterised by ridges and cliffs, and lakes on rocky shores with shallow soil. Park interior features spruce, fir, cedar, aspen and birch. Wildlife includes moose, wolves, black bears and woodland caribou. This park is also the site of rare Arctic plants.
Quttinirpaaq (Ellesmere Island)	northern tip of Canada	37 775	1988	Vast isolated high Arctic wilderness park. Mountains, glaciers, musk-oxen, Peary's caribou. Fragile permafrost environments. Historic sites and artifacts from early Arctic explorers.
Riding Mountain	270 km northwest of Winnipeg, Man.	2 973	1929	Wildlife—wolf, elk, moose, black bear and beaver—abound.

▶

Park	Location	Size (sq. km)	Year est.	Description
Saguenay-St. Lawrence Marine Park	At the confluence of the Saguenay Fjord and St. Lawrence estuary; access through L'Anse-Saint-Jean, on the north shore of the St. Lawrence near Tadoussac		1988	A rich diversity of marine life; whales, seals, plants and birds of all kinds.
Sirmilik[2]	northern Baffin Is., incl Bylot Is. and Borden Penin	22 200	(1992)	Mountains, snowfields, glaciers, tundra. Sparse vegetation: 50 bird species incl. murres, kittiwakes, snow geese. Caribou, wolf, Artic fox, lemming, seals, whales, walrus, polar bear
St. Lawrence Islands	Thousand Islands	8	1904	Park includes over 21 islands and 90 islets between Kingston and Brockville, with 100 acres on the mainland at Mallorytown Landing. The area features Thousand Islands landscape and the St. Lawrence River. The Great Lakes moderate the climate, allowing many animals and plants to exist further north than might otherwise be possible.
Terra Nova	east coast of Nfld on Bonavista Bay	400	1957	Rolling forested hills are remnants of the ancient Appalachian Mountains. Rugged cliffs and sheltered inlets are featured on the coast; the interior has spongy bogs, rolling hills covered with forest and inland ponds.
Tuktut Nogait	east of Inuvik in NWT	16 340	1996	Spectacular river canyons and cliffs dotted by hundreds of archaeological sites. Park protects calving grounds of Bluenose caribou and one of the highest concentrations of birds of prey in North America.
Vuntut	Old Crow Flats, northern Yukon	4 345	(1993)[1]	Yukon's most important waterfowl habitat and home to porcupine caribou, grizzly bear, moose, muskrat and several species of fish. Vertebrate fossils found at over 56 sites within park. The area is only 300 m in elevation and features over 2,000 shallow lakes.
Wapusk	northeast corner of Manitoba	11 475	1996	This region of flat inland expanse of tundra, eskers and permafrost includes one of the world's largest known polar bear denning areas.
Waterton Lakes	southwest corner of Alta.	505	1895	Officially renamed the Waterton-Glacier International Peace Park in 1932; the world's first park established by two governments. Protects transition from prairie grasslands to Rocky Mountains and a rich variety of wildlife.
Wood Buffalo	straddles the Alta.-NWT border	44 802	1922	Canada's largest national park is also a UNESCO World Heritage Site. Home to the largest free-roaming herd of bison; only site of naturally nesting whooping cranes, peregrine falcons and red-sided garter snakes. Geography features sinkholes, underground rivers, caves and sunken valleys.
Yoho	25 km east of Golden, BC	1 313	1886	Contains several of the highest peaks in the Rocky Mountains, icefields, waterfalls and a varied plant and animal life.

Source: *Canadian Heritage, Parks Canada*   (1) Park created by federal/provincial/territorial agreement rather than federal enactment and administered by special legislation. (2) Park reserve, set aside for national park and under jurisdiction of National Parks Act, but lands, fish and wildlife are subject to future settlement of native land claims.

Canadian World Heritage Sites

World Heritage sites are designated around the world by UNESCO to raise local and international awareness of indigenous cultural and natural treasures. "Cultural heritage" consists of monuments, groups of buildings or sites of historical, aesthetic, archaeological, scientific, ethnological or anthropological value. "Natural heritage" refers to outstanding physical, biological and geological features; habitats of threatened plants or animal species and areas of value on scientific or aesthetic grounds or from the point of view of conservation. Thirteen of the organization's World Heritage sites are in Canada. The majority of these sites relate to Canada's natural heritage.

UNESCO has created a World Heritage Educational Resource Kit. Based on an interactive and interdisciplinary approach, the kit invites teachers and students to explore aspects of heritage conservation in the form of a journey through the world's magnificent cultural and natural heritage. More information about the kit can be found at www.whc.unesco.org.

	Province or Territory	Area	Year Designated	Criteria N:Natural C:Cultural
Nahanni National Park	Northwest Territories	4 766 km^2	1978	N
L'Anse aux Meadows Archaeological Site	Newfoundland & Labrador		1978	C
Kluane /Wrangell-St. Elias / Glacier Bay / Tatshenshini—Alsek Park	Canada/US	97 303 km^2 9 850 km^2	1979 Added in 1994	N
Dinosaur Provincial Park	Alberta	7 492 km^2	1979	N
Head-Smashed-In Buffalo Jump Provincial Historic Site	Alberta		1982	C
SGaang Gwaii (Anthony Island)	British Columbia		1981	C
Wood Buffalo National Park	Alberta/Northwest Territories	44 807 km^2	1983	N
CANADIAN ROCKY MOUNTAIN PARKS Banff National Park Jasper National Park Kootenay National Park Yoho National Park Mount Robson Provincial Park Mount Assiniboine Provincial Park Hamber Provincial Park	Alberta/British Columbia	22 990 km^2	1984 and 1990	N
THE HISTORIC DISTRICT OF QUEBEC Fortifications of Quebec National Historic Site Artillery Park National Historic Site	Quebec		1985	C
Gros Morne National Park	Newfoundland & Labrador	1 805 km^2	1987	N
WATERTON—GLACIER INTERNATIONAL PEACE PARK Waterton Lakes National Park (Canada) Glacier National Park (U.S.)	Canada/U.S.	4 600 km^2	1995	N
The Old Town Lunenburg	Nova Scotia		1995	C
Miguasha Park	Quebec	873 km^2	2000	N

Source: *Canadian Heritage, Parks Canada*

THE PEOPLE

POPULATION

Population of Provinces and Territories[1]

(thousands)

	Canada	N&L	PEI	NS	NB	Que	Ont	Man	Sask	Alta	BC	YT	NWT	NVT
1861[2]....	3 230	n.a.	81	331	252	1 112	1 396	*	n.a.	n.a.	52	*	7	n.a.
1871....	3 689	n.a.	94	388	286	1 192	1 621	25	n.a.	n.a.	36	*	48	n.a.
1881....	4 325	n.a.	109	441	321	1 360	1 927	62	n.a.	n.a.	49	*	56	n.a.
1891....	4 833	n.a.	109	450	321	1 489	2 114	153	*	*	98	*	99	n.a.
1901....	5 371	n.a.	103	460	331	1 649	2 183	255	91	73	179	27	20	n.a.
1911....	7 207	n.a.	94	492	352	2 006	2 527	461	492	374	393	9	7	n.a.
1921....	8 788	n.a.	89	524	388	2 361	2 934	610	758	588	525	4	8	n.a.
1931....	10 377	n.a.	88	513	408	2 875	3 432	700	922	732	694	4	9	n.a.
1941....	11 507	n.a.	95	578	457	3 332	3 788	730	896	796	818	5	12	n.a.
1951....	14 009	361	98	643	516	4 056	4 598	777	832	940	1 165	9	16	n.a.
1961....	18 238	458	105	737	598	5 259	6 236	922	925	1 332	1 629	15	23	n.a.
1971....	21 962	531	113	797	643	6 137	7 849	999	932	1 666	2 241	19	36	n.a.
1981....	24 820	575	124	855	706	6 548	8 811	1 036	976	2 294	2 824	24	48	n.a.
1986....	26 101	577	128	889	725	6 708	9 438	1 092	1 029	2 431	3 004	25	55	n.a.
1991....	28 031	580	130	915	746	7 065	10 428	1 110	1 003	2 593	3 373	29	39	22
1996....	29 672	561	136	931	753	7 274	11 101	1 134	1 019	2 781	3 882	32	42	26
2002[3]	31 324	530	139	943	758	7 433	12 029	1 153	1 009	3 111	4 119	29	41	29
2003[3]	31 549	526	139	943	759	7 451	12 178	1 156	1 002	3 155	4 139	28	41	30

Source: © *Census of Canada, Statistics Canada*
(n.a.) Not applicable (*) Included with the Northwest Territories. (1) As of July 1 in non-census years. Includes data from incompletely enumerated population. Totals may not add up due to rounding. (2) Pre-Confederation. (3) Intercensal estimate as of April 1, 2003.

Age Structure of the Population[1]

	Total (000s)	% Under 5 Years	% 5–19 Years	% 20–44 Years	% 45–64 Years	% 65+ Years
1851	2 436	18.51	37.81	31.65	9.40	2.67
1861	3 230	16.81	37.21	32.66	10.15	3.03
1871	3 689	14.67	38.03	32.58	11.14	3.66
1881	4 325	13.85	36.02	33.94	12.14	4.12
1891	4 833	12.64	34.49	35.40	12.91	4.55
1901	5 371	12.03	32.73	36.19	14.00	5.05
1911	7 207	12.35	30.15	38.81	14.06	4.66
1921	8 788	12.05	31.51	36.63	15.02	4.78
1931	10 377	10.36	31.29	36.07	16.74	5.55
1941	11 507	9.14	28.39	37.19	18.61	6.67
1951	14 009	12.29	25.60	36.63	17.74	7.75
1961	18 238	12.37	29.44	33.19	17.37	7.63
1971	21 568	8.42	30.97	33.87	18.66	8.09
1981	24 343	7.32	24.70	39.14	19.13	9.70
1991	27 297	6.99	20.42	41.33	19.66	11.61
1996	29 672	6.62	20.35	39.63	21.32	12.07
2001	30 007	5.65	20.27	36.83	24.29	12.96

Source: © *Census of Canada, Statistics Canada*
(1) As of July 1 each year. Percentages may not add to 100 due to rounding.

Male and Female Population by Age Group
(thousands)

	Total Population	Under 5 Years	5–9 Years	10–14 Years	15–24 Years	25–34 Years	35–44 Years	45–54 Years	55–64 Years	65 Years and Over
1851 MALE	1 250	233	173	152	248	168	116	78	46	35
FEMALE	1 186	218	173	146	252	161	103	67	38	30
1861 MALE	1 660	277	218	203	341	232	156	107	70	54
FEMALE	1 570	266	211	196	337	222	141	92	59	44
1871 MALE	1 869	276	264	243	374	249	175	132	86	74
FEMALE	1 820	265	255	233	385	256	171	120	73	61
1881 MALE	2 189	304	284	262	455	302	217	161	111	94
FEMALE	2 136	295	278	251	464	301	212	153	100	84
1891 MALE	2 460	309	300	282	504	366	263	191	131	115
FEMALE	2 373	302	292	272	499	354	246	180	122	105
1901 MALE	2 752	326	313	297	543	412	331	234	157	139
FEMALE	2 620	320	306	285	530	386	299	214	148	133
1911 MALE	3 822	450	396	356	745	687	475	334	209	171
FEMALE	3 385	440	389	346	653	535	388	286	184	165
1921 MALE	4 530	534	529	462	757	693	630	434	276	215
FEMALE	4 258	525	521	452	761	650	532	366	246	206
1931 MALE	5 375	543	573	543	990	778	707	590	356	295
FEMALE	5 002	531	560	531	962	717	627	485	306	281
1941 MALE	5 901	534	529	556	1 083	920	745	649	494	391
FEMALE	5 606	518	517	545	1 069	891	691	579	421	377
1951 MALE	7 089	879	714	575	1 070	1 066	950	728	557	551
FEMALE	6 921	843	684	556	1 077	1 108	919	679	520	535
1961 MALE	9 219	1 154	1 064	948	1 316	1 258	1 191	959	655	674
FEMALE	9 019	1 102	1 016	908	1 301	1 222	1 199	920	635	717
1971 MALE	10 795	930	1 152	1 181	2 016	1 462	1 286	1 132	854	782
FEMALE	10 773	887	1 102	1 129	1 988	1 428	1 241	1 160	877	963
1981 MALE	12 068	914	912	985	2 356	2 106	1 497	1 256	1 031	1 011
FEMALE	12 275	869	865	936	2 303	2 110	1 471	1 242	1 128	1 350
1991 MALE	13 455	976	978	963	1 944	2 420	2 176	1 487	1 180	1 330
FEMALE	13 842	931	930	915	1 887	2 446	2 196	1 479	1 220	1 840
1996 MALE	14 692	1 007	1 033	1 031	2 059	2 400	2 502	1 891	1 253	1 515
FEMALE	14 980	958	984	978	1 965	2 346	2 499	1 897	1 286	2 067
2001[1] MALE	14 707	868	1 011	1 051	2 034	1 967	2 517	2 185	1 411	1 663
FEMALE	15 300	828	965	1 002	1 975	2 028	2 585	2 235	1 457	2 226

Source: © Census of Canada, Statistics Canada   (1) Unadjusted census count.

Canadian Population Projections[1] by Age Group
(thousands)

	Total Population	Under 5 Years	5–9 Years	10–14 Years	15–24 Years	25–34 Years	35–44 Years	45–54 Years	55–64 Years	65 Yrs and Over
2006										
MALE	15 947.4	841.4	918.4	1 075.8	2 213.4	2 228.3	2 519.7	2 509.1	1 796.5	1 844.8
FEMALE	16 281.2	798.8	872.0	1 020.6	2 109.6	2 167.4	2 482.9	2 517.5	1 855.3	2 457.3
2011										
MALE	16 511.6	855.1	880.0	957.7	2 261.3	2 311.7	2 343.3	2 667.9	2 129.3	2 105.4
FEMALE	16 850.2	811.3	835.9	905.9	2 155.0	2 244.8	2 305.2	2 651.2	2 200.4	2 740.6
2016										
MALE	17 044.8	877.0	893.6	919.8	2 155.4	2 383.3	2 369.6	2 536.7	2 388.1	2 521.0
FEMALE	17 375.0	831.7	848.2	870.3	2 051.3	2 313.1	2 321.5	2 505.9	2 451.9	3 181.1
2021										
MALE	17 531.4	890.6	915.2	933.2	2 003.3	2 430.3	2 449.2	2 374.1	2 545.9	2 989.7
FEMALE	17 850.4	844.3	868.4	882.4	1 904.5	2 356.1	2 394.2	2 337.4	2 582.0	3 681.1
2026										
MALE	17 939.6	880.9	928.6	954.5	1 979.9	2 327.9	2 517.4	2 403.3	2 431.6	3 515.5
FEMALE	18 250.9	834.9	880.8	902.2	1 881.7	2 254.8	2 458.2	2 354.3	2 446.4	4 237.5

Source: © Statistics Canada   (1) Figures represent the medium-growth projection and are based on 2000 population estimates. Due to rounding, the totals may not always add up to the sum of the figures.

Canada's Changing Population

The release of data from the 2001 census gave Canadians a look at how the country is changing. One notable change is visible in the statistics on the age of our citizens.

CANADIANS ARE GETTING OLDER

In 1966, the median age of Canada's population—the age where half the population is older and half is younger—was 25.4 years. In 2001, the median age was 37.6, a gain of 2.3 years from the previous high of 35.3 in the 1996 census. This information has implications for social planners, particularly those who are forecasting the futures of our labour force and our economy, and demands on social services and healthcare systems.

The population age group 45 to 64 increased to 24.3 per cent of the total population; planners forecast that by 2011, nearly one-third of the population will be in that bracket. As increasing numbers of the labour force near age 65, there will be more competition for workers, which could mean higher wages (and higher prices). There may even be a need to change the age for mandatory retirement, particularly in light of the better levels of health and fitness of older Canadians.

While 37.6 was the median age for the country, age distribution varies. As the table below shows, Nova Scotia and Quebec are the "oldest" provinces, with median ages of nearly 39. Nunavut is the youngest, by a wide margin.

Age Distribution, Canada, Provinces and Territories, 2001

| | Median Age | Age Group Distribution | | |
| | | 0–19 | 20–64 | 65+ |
	(years)		(percent)	
Canada	37.6	25.9	61.1	13.0
Newfoundland and Labrador	38.4	25.0	62.7	12.3
Prince Edward Island	37.7	27.3	59.0	13.7
Nova Scotia	38.8	25.0	61.1	13.9
New Brunswick	38.6	24.8	61.7	13.6
Quebec	38.8	24.2	62.5	13.3
Ontario	37.2	26.3	60.8	12.9
Manitoba	36.8	28.1	58.0	14.0
Saskatchewan	36.7	29.2	55.8	15.1
Alberta	35.0	28.3	61.4	10.4
British Columbia	38.4	25.0	61.4	13.6
Yukon Territory	36.1	29.0	64.9	6.0
Northwest Territories	30.1	35.0	60.7	4.4
Nunavut	22.1	46.5	51.2	2.2

Ten Youngest Municipalities with Population More Than 5,000

	Median Age
Mackenzie No. 23, Alberta	22.0
Stanley, Manitoba	25.2
Lloydminster, Saskatchewan	26.8
Hanover, Manitoba	27.8
Slave Lake, Alberta	28.1
Taber, Alberta	28.3
Iqaluit, Nunavut	28.3
Wellesley, Ontario	28.7
Mapleton, Ontario	29.2
Oromocto, New Brunswick	29.3

Ten Oldest Municipalities with Population More Than 5,000

Qualicum Beach, B.C.	58.1
White Rock, B.C.	50.9
Sidney, B.C.	50.7
Cote-Saint-Luc, Quebec	50.5
Parksville, B.C.	49.6
Nanaimo G, B.C.	49.5
Elliot Lake, Ontario	49.4
Columbia-Shuswap C, B.C.	48.8
North Saanich, B.C.	47.8
Oak Bay, B.C.	47.8

Source: *Census,* © Statistics Canada

Canadian Urban and Rural Population

(thousands)

Year	Urban Total	Urban %	Rural Non-Farm	%	+	Farm	%	=	Total	%
1871	722	19.6	n.a.	n.a.		n.a.	n.a.		2 967	80.4
1881	1 110	25.7	n.a.	n.a.		n.a.	n.a.		3 215	74.3
1891	1 537	31.8	n.a.	n.a.		n.a.	n.a.		3 296	68.2
1901	2 014	37.5	n.a.	n.a.		n.a.	n.a.		3 357	62.5
1911	3 273	45.4	n.a.	n.a.		n.a.	n.a.		3 934	54.6
1921	4 352	49.5	n.a.	n.a.		n.a.	n.a.		4 436	50.5
1931	5 469	52.7	1 670	16.1		3 238	31.2		4 908	47.3
1941	6 271	54.5	2 123	18.4		3 113	27.1		5 236	45.5
1951	8 817	62.9	2 423	17.3		2 769	19.8		5 192	37.1
1956	10 715	66.6	2 734	17.0		2 632	16.4		5 366	33.4
1961	12 700	69.6	3 465	19.0		2 073	11.4		5 538	30.4
1966	14 727	73.6	3 374	16.9		1 914	9.6		5 288	26.4
1971	16 410	76.1	3 738	17.3		1 420	6.6		5 158	23.9
1976	17 367	75.5	4 591	20.0		1 035	4.5		5 626	24.5
1981	18 436	75.7	4 867	20.0		1 040	4.3		5 907	24.3
1986	19 352	76.5	5 067	20.0		890	3.5		5 957	23.5
1991	20 907	76.6	5 583	20.5		807	3.0		6 390	23.4
1996	22 415	77.9	5 485	19.1		851	3.0		6 336	22.1
2001	23 908	79.7	n.a.	n.a.		n.a.	n.a.		6 099	20.3

Source: © *Census of Canada, Statistics Canada*   (n.a.) Not available.

Definitions: Urban: persons living in a built-up area having a population of 1 000 or more, and a population density of 400 or more per sq. km; **Rural:** persons living outside "urban areas"; **Rural Farm:** persons living in rural areas who are members of households of farm operators; **Rural Non-Farm:** persons living in rural areas who are not members of households of farm operators.

Urban and Rural Population by Province

Province	1951 Rural	1951 Urban	1991 Rural	1991 Urban	2001[3] Rural	2001[3] Urban
Canada	5 174 555	8 473 458	6 389 724	20 907 135	6 098 883	23 908 211
Nfld and Labrador[1]	n.a.	n.a.	264 023	304 451	216 734	296 196
Prince Edward Island	73 744	24 685	77 952	51 813	74 619	60 675
Nova Scotia	297 753	344 831	418 434	481 508	400 998	507 009
New Brunswick	300 686	215 011	378 686	345 214	361 596	367 902
Quebec	1 358 363	2 697 318	1 544 752	5 351 211	1 420 330	5 817 149
Ontario	1 346 443	3 251 099	1 831 043	8 253 842	1 747 499	9 662 547
Manitoba	336 961	439 580	304 767	787 175	314 262	805 321
Saskatchewan	579 258	252 470	365 531	623 397	349 897	629 036
Alberta	489 826	449 675	514 660	2 030 893	569 647	2 405 160
British Columbia	371 739	793 471	641 922	2 640 139	597 885	3 309 853
Yukon Territory	6 502	2 594	11 462	16 335	11 831	16 843
Northwest Territories	13 280[2]	2 724[2]	36 492[2]	21 157[2]	15 529	21 831
Nunavut[3]	n.a.	n.a.	n.a.	n.a.	18 056	8 689

Source: © *Census of Canada, Statistics Canada*
(1) Newfoundland joined confederation in 1949, and urban/rural split in population was not included in 1951 census data. (2) Includes Nunavut. (3) Unadjusted census count.

Population of Canadian Towns and Cities

(more than 5,000 inhabitants)

Town or city classification is made according to the official designations adopted by provincial or federal authority.

	POPULATION		AREA 2001 (sq. km)
	1996	2001	
■ NEWFOUNDLAND AND LABRADOR			
Bay Roberts	5 472	**5 237**	23.92
Clarenville	5 335	**5 104**	140.73
Conception Bay South	19 265	**19 772**	59.27
Corner Brook*	21 893	**20 103**	148.27
Gander	10 364	**9 651**	104.25
Grand Falls-Windsor	14 160	**13 340**	54.48
Happy Valley-Goose Bay	8 655	**7 969**	305.87
Labrador City	8 455	**7 744**	10.02
Marystown	6 742	**5 908**	61.97
Mount Pearl*	25 531	**24 964**	15.74
Paradise	7 948	**9 598**	29.24
Portugal Cove-St. Philip's	5 773	**5 866**	57.35
St. John's*	101 936	**99 182**	446.04
Stephenville	7 764	**7 109**	35.50
Torbay	5 230	**5 474**	34.88
■ PRINCE EDWARD ISLAND			
Charlottetown*	32 531	**32 245**	44.33
Stratford	5 869	**6 314**	22.48
Summerside*	14 525	**14 654**	28.36
■ NOVA SCOTIA			
Amherst	9 669	**9 470**	12.02
Bridgewater	7 351	**7 621**	13.61
Halifax (Regional. Mun.)	342 851	**359 111**	5 490.90
Kentville	5 551	**5 610**	17.35
New Glasgow	9 812	**9 432**	9.93
Truro	11 938	**11 457**	37.62
Yarmouth	7 568	**7 561**	10.56
■ NEW BRUNSWICK			
Bathurst*	13 815	**12 924**	91.55
Campbellton*	8 404	**7 798**	18.66
Dieppe	12 497	**14 951**	51.16
Edmundston*	17 876	**17 373**	106.90
Fredericton*	46 507	**47 560**	131.23
Grand Falls (Grand-Sault)	6 133	**5 858**	18.06
Miramichi*	19 241	**18 508**	179.83
Moncton*	59 313	**61 046**	141.15
Oromocto	9 194	**8 843**	22.37
Quispamsis	13 579	**13 757**	57.12
Riverview	16 684	**17 010**	33.88
Rothesay	11 470	**11 505**	34.13
Sackville	5 393	**5 361**	74.32

	POPULATION		AREA 2001 (sq. km)
	1996	2001	
Saint John*	72 494	**69 661**	316.31
Woodstock	5 092	**5 198**	13.26
■ QUEBEC			
Acton Vale	7 172	**7 299**	90.74
Alma	26 121	**25 918**	109.28
Amos	13 632	**13 044**	430.27
Amqui	6 800	**6 473**	120.81
Anjou	37 308	**38 015**	13.62
Asbestos	6 793	**6 580**	29.67
Aylmer	34 901	**36 085**	88.96
Baie-Comeau	25 554	**23 079**	338.87
Baie-Saint-Paul	7 366	**7 290**	546.28
Beaconsfield	19 414	**19 310**	11.01
Beauceville	6 371	**6 261**	167.54
Beauharnois	6 435	**6 387**	40.94
Beauport	72 920	**72 813**	74.37
Bécancour	11 489	**11 051**	441.00
Bellefeuille	12 803	**14 066**	49.99
Beloeil	19 294	**19 053**	24.09
Blainville	29 603	**36 029**	55.10
Boisbriand	25 227	**26 729**	27.76
Bois-des-Filion	7 124	**7 712**	4.28
Boucherville	34 989	**36 253**	70.80
Bromptonville	5 583	**5 571**	76.78
Brossard	65 927	**65 026**	45.74
Buckingham	11 678	**11 668**	15.11
Candiac	11 805	**12 675**	17.51
Cap-de-la-Madeleine	33 438	**32 534**	18.25
Cap-Rouge	14 163	**13 700**	6.80
Carignan	5 614	**5 915**	62.42
Chambly	19 716	**20 342**	25.23
Charlemagne	5 739	**5 662**	2.17
Charlesbourg	70 942	**70 310**	66.28
Charny	10 661	**10 507**	8.07
Châteauguay	41 423	**41 003**	35.89
Chibougamau	8 664	**7 922**	699.16
Chicoutimi	63 061	**60 008**	156.11
Coaticook	8 809	**8 988**	218.55
Contrecoeur	5 331	**5 222**	61.19
Côte-Saint-Luc*	29 705	**30 244**	6.94
Cowansville	12 051	**12 032**	46.09
Delson	6 703	**7 024**	7.13
Deux-Montagnes	15 953	**17 080**	6.16
Dolbeau-Mistassini	15 214	**14 879**	295.67 ▶

	POPULATION		AREA 2001		POPULATION		AREA 2001
	1996	2001	(sq. km)		1996	2001	(sq. km)
Dollard-des-Ormeaux ...	47 826	48 206	15.10	Mont-Laurier	8 007	7 365	79.59
Donnacona	5 739	5 479	20.01	Montmagny	11 885	11 654	126.07
Dorval*	17 572	17 706	20.87	Montréal 1 016 376		1 039 534	185.94
Drummondville	44 882	46 599	71.44	Montréal-Nord	81 581	83 600	11.07
Farnham	7 899	7 747	92.04	Montréal-Ouest	5 254	5 172	1.41
Fleurimont	16 262	16 521	35.47	Mont-Royal	18 282	18 682	7.66
Gaspé	16 517	14 932	1 120.63	Mont-Saint-Hilaire	13 064	14 270	44.29
Gatineau	100 684	102 898	146.78	Mont-Tremblant	7 298	8 352	255.23
Granby	43 316	44 121	72.04	Nicolet	7 795	7 928	96.11
Grand-Mère	14 223	13 179	62.95	Otterburn Park	7 320	7 866	5.35
Greenfield Park	17 337	16 978	4.78	Outremont	22 571	22 933	3.83
Hampstead	6 986	6 974	1.79	Pierrefonds	53 151	54 963	24.90
Hull	62 339	66 246	36.49	Pincourt	10 023	10 107	7.54
Iberville	9 635	9 424	5.21	Plessisville	6 810	6 756	4.30
Joliette	17 541	17 837	22.81	Pointe-Claire	28 435	29 286	18.87
Jonquière	56 503	54 842	216.04	Pont-Rouge	6 821	7 146	121.22
Kirkland	18 678	20 434	9.64	Port-Cartier	7 070	6 412	292.86
La Baie	21 057	19 940	262.67	Prévost	7 308	8 280	35.00
La Malbaie	9 274	9 143	459.35	Princeville	5 750	5 703	195.53
La Plaine	14 413	15 673	40.19	Québec 167 264		169 076	92.93
La Prairie	17 128	18 896	43.69	Repentigny	53 824	54 550	24.48
La Sarre	8 345	7 728	148.69	Rimouski	31 773	31 305	76.18
La Tuque	12 102	11 298	579.46	Rivière-du-Loup	17 801	17 772	84.23
Lac-Brome	5 073	5 444	205.13	Roberval	11 640	10 906	152.99
Lachenaie	18 489	21 709	42.07	Rock Forest	16 604	18 667	48.22
Lachine	39 910	40 222	17.83	Rosemère	12 025	13 391	10.77
Lachute	11 556	11 628	108.65	Rouyn-Noranda	30 936	28 270	348.07
Lac-Mégantic	5 864	5 897	21.76	Roxboro	5 785	5 642	2.22
Lac-Saint-Charles	8 540	8 912	34.07	Saint-Antoine	10 806	11 488	9.93
Lafontaine	9 008	9 477	14.36	Saint-Basile-le-Grand ...	11 771	12 385	36.10
L'Ancienne-Lorette	15 895	15 929	7.63	Saint-Bruno-de-Montarville	23 714	23 843	43.28
LaSalle	72 029	73 983	16.75	Saint-Constant	21 933	22 577	57.30
L'Assomption	15 573	15 615	98.91	Sainte-Adèle	8 719	9 215	119.98
Laval 330 393		343 005	247.07	Sainte-Agathe-des-Monts	7 878	7 116	41.01
Le Gardeur	16 853	17 668	37.29	Sainte-Anne-de-Bellevue .	4 700	5 062	10.57
Lévis	40 407	40 926	43.55	Sainte-Anne-des-Monts			
L'Île-Bizard	13 038	13 861	22.77	-Tourelle	7 183	6 835	263.31
L'Île-Perrot	9 178	9 375	5.56	Sainte-Anne-des-Plaines .	12 908	12 908	92.79
Longueuil 127 977		128 016	44.00	Sainte-Catherine	13 724	15 953	10.19
Loretteville	14 168	13 737	6.37	Sainte-Foy	72 330	72 547	83.85
Lorraine	8 876	9 476	6.04	Sainte-Julie	24 030	26 580	49.52
Louiseville	7 911	7 622	62.59	Sainte-Marie	10 966	11 320	107.20
Magog	14 050	14 283	13.94	Sainte-Marthe-du-Cap ...	6 150	6 162	39.89
Marieville	7 636	7 240	62.78	Sainte-Marthe-sur-le-Lac	8 295	8 742	9.31
Mascouche	28 097	29 556	106.63	Saint-Émile	9 889	10 940	8.36
Masson-Angers	7 989	9 799	54.97	Sainte-Thérèse	23 477	24 269	9.58
Matane	12 364	11 635	24.80	Saint-Eustache	39 848	40 378	69.42
Mercier	9 059	9 442	45.95	Saint-Félicien	10 797	10 622	363.57
Mirabel	22 626	27 330	485.41	Saint-Georges	20 057	20 787	25.33
Mont-Joli	6 267	5 886	9.95	Saint-Hubert	77 042	75 912	65.98 ▶

	POPULATION		AREA 2001
	1996	2001	(sq. km)
Saint-Hyacinthe	38 995	**38 739**	37.46
Saint-Jean-Chrysostome	16 161	**17 089**	85.80
Saint-Jean-sur-Richelieu	36 435	**37 386**	47.06
Saint-Jérôme	23 916	**24 583**	16.23
Saint-Lambert	20 971	**21 051**	8.15
Saint-Laurent	74 240	**77 391**	42.88
Saint-Léonard	71 327	**69 604**	13.52
Saint-Lin – Laurentides	12 039	**12 384**	118.68
Saint-Louis-de-France	7 327	**7 246**	60.55
Saint-Luc	18 371	**20 573**	51.51
Saint-Nicéphore	9 251	**9 966**	95.80
Saint-Nicolas	15 594	**16 645**	95.09
Saint-Raymond	8 733	**8 836**	670.58
Saint-Rédempteur	6 358	**6 349**	3.71
Saint-Rémi	5 707	**5 736**	78.79
Saint-Romuald	10 604	**10 825**	17.94
Saint-Timothée	8 495	**8 299**	69.49
Salaberry-de-Valleyfield	26 600	**26 170**	27.45
Sept-Îles	25 224	**23 791**	294.20
Shawinigan	18 943	**17 535**	28.15
Shawinigan-Sud	11 804	**11 544**	48.97
Sherbrooke	76 786	**75 916**	58.15
Sillery	12 003	**11 909**	6.70
Sorel-Tracy	36 021	**34 194**	58.07
Terrebonne	42 214	**43 149**	72.15
Thetford Mines	17 635	**16 628**	36.95
Trois-Rivières	48 419	**46 264**	77.83
Trois-Rivières-Ouest	22 886	**23 287**	29.73
Val-Bélair	20 176	**21 332**	69.88
Val-d'Or	24 479	**22 748**	2 889.53
Vanier	11 174	**11 054**	4.59
Varennes	18 842	**19 653**	92.53
Vaudreuil-Dorion	18 466	**19 920**	72.47
Verdun	59 714	**60 564**	9.82
Victoriaville	38 174	**38 841**	82.65
Westmount	20 420	**19 727**	4.02
Windsor	5 515	**5 321**	14.28

■ ONTARIO

	POPULATION		AREA 2001
	1996	2001	(sq. km)
Ajax	64 430	**73 753**	67.09
Amherstburg	19 273	**20 339**	185.67
Arnprior	7 113	**7 192**	13.03
Aurora	34 857	**40 167**	49.61
Aylmer	7 022	**7 126**	6.05
Barrie*	79 191	**103 710**	76.98
Belleville*	46 195	**45 986**	241.79
Blue Mountains	5 667	**6 116**	286.77
Bluewater	6 874	**6 919**	416.99
Bracebridge	13 223	**13 751**	617.47
Bradford West Gwillimbury	20 213	**22 228**	201.03
Brampton*	268 251	**325 428**	266.53

	POPULATION		AREA 2001
	1996	2001	(sq. km)
Brant*	29 800	**31 669**	845.49
Brantford*	84 764	**86 417**	71.56
Brighton	9 022	**9 449**	222.57
Brockville*	21 752	**21 375**	20.73
Burlington*	136 976	**150 836**	185.71
Caledon	39 893	**50 595**	687.04
Cambridge*	101 429	**110 372**	112.82
Campbellford/Seymour, Percy, Hastings	**12 437**	12 569	511.10
Carleton Place	8 483	**9 083**	8.83
Chatham-Kent*	109 350	**107 341**	2 457.97
Clarence-Rockland*	18 633	**19 612**	296.53
Clarington	60 615	**69 834**	611.06
Cobourg	16 185	**17 172**	22.37
Cochrane	5 955	**5 690**	538.74
Collingwood	15 596	**16 039**	33.46
Cornwall*	47 403	**45 640**	61.83
Dryden*	8 289	**8 198**	65.31
East Gwillimbury	19 770	**20 555**	245.06
Elliot Lake*	13 588	**11 956**	698.12
Erin	10 657	**11 052**	296.98
Espanola	5 796	**5 449**	82.37
Essex	19 437	**20 085**	277.95
Fort Erie	27 183	**28 143**	167.42
Fort Frances	8 790	**8 315**	26.09
Gananoque	5 217	**5 167**	7.29
Georgian Highlands	10 497	**10 381**	589.03
Georgina	34 777	**39 263**	287.72
Goderich	7 553	**7 604**	7.91
Gravenhurst	10 030	**10 899**	517.94
Greater Napanee	14 994	**15 132**	459.71
Greater Sudbury*	165 336	**155 219**	3354.34
Greenstone	6 530	**5 662**	2 780.56
Grimsby	19 585	**21 297**	68.94
Guelph*	95 821	**106 170**	86.66
Haldimand*	42 041	**43 728**	1 252.37
Halton Hills	42 390	**48 184**	276.35
Hamilton*	467 799	**490 268**	1 117.11
Hanover	6 965	**6 869**	9.81
Hawkesbury	10 162	**10 314**	9.45
Hearst	6 049	**5 825**	98.67
Huntsville	15 918	**17 338**	703.29
Huron East	9 937	**9 680**	669.16
Ingersoll	10 502	**10 977**	12.90
Innisfil	24 711	**28 666**	284.18
Iroquois Falls	5 714	**5 217**	599.42
Kapuskasing	10 036	**9 238**	83.98
Kawartha Lakes*	67 926	**69 179**	3 059.22
Kenora*	16 365	**15 838**	211.08
Kingston*	112 605	**114 195**	450.39 ▶

POPULATION		AREA 2001	POPULATION		AREA 2001
1996	2001	(sq. km)	1996	2001	(sq. km)
Kingsville 18 409	**19 619**	246.83	South Huron 10 229	**10 019**	425.35
Kirkland Lake 9 905	**8 616**	262.24	St. Catharines* 130 926	**129 170**	97.11
Kitchener* 178 420	**190 399**	136.86	St. Marys 5 952	**6 293**	12.48
Lakeshore 26 127	**28 746**	530.67	St. Thomas* 31 407	**33 236**	32.24
Lambton Shores* 10 874	**10 571**	331.92	Stratford* 29 007	**29 676**	21.92
LaSalle 20 566	**25 285**	65.25	Tecumseh 23 151	**25 105**	120.31
Leamington 25 389	**27 138**	262.45	Thorold* 17 883	**18 048**	84.82
Lincoln 18 801	**20 612**	162.86	Thunder Bay* 113 662	**109 016**	328.47
London* 325 669	**336 539**	421.77	Tillsonburg 13 211	**14 052**	22.34
Markham 173 383	**208 615**	212.47	Timmins* 47 499	**43 686**	2961.52
Midland 16 347	**16 214**	29.09	Toronto* 2 385 421	**2 481 494**	629.91
Milton 32 104	**31 471**	366.46	Vaughan* 132 549	**182 022**	273.50
Minto 7 854	**8 164**	300.37	Wasaga Beach 8 698	**12 419**	58.45
Mississauga* 544 382	**612 925**	288.42	Waterloo* 77 949	**86 543**	64.09
Mississippi Mills 11 069	**11 647**	509.05	Welland* 48 411	**48 402**	83.47
Mono 6 552	**6 922**	277.77	West Nipissing 13 481	**13 114**	1 909.67
New Tecumseth 22 904	**26 141**	274.18	Whitby 73 794	**87 413**	146.52
Newmarket 57 125	**65 788**	38.07	Whitchurch-Stouffville . . 19 835	**22 008**	206.74
Niagara Falls* 76 917	**78 815**	209.99	Windsor* 197 694	**208 402**	120.63
Niagara-on-the-Lake 13 238	**13 839**	133.67	Woodstock* 32 253	**33 061**	30.44
Norfolk* 60 534	**60 847**	1 606.95	■ **MANITOBA**		
North Bay* 54 332	**52 771**	314.92	Brandon* 39 175	**39 716**	74.53
North Perth 11 808	**12 055**	493.18	Dauphin* 8 266	**8 085**	12.65
Oakville 128 405	**144 738**	138.51	Flin Flon (Part)* 6 572	**6 000**	13.88
Orangeville 21 498	**25 248**	15.57	Morden 5 689	**6 142**	12.86
Orillia* 27 846	**29 121**	28.61	Portage la Prairie* 13 077	**12 976**	24.68
Oshawa* 134 364	**139 051**	145.65	Selkirk* 9 881	**9 752**	24.87
Ottawa* 721 136	**774 072**	2 778.64	Steinbach* 8 478	**9 227**	25.57
Owen Sound* 21 390	**21 431**	23.51	The Pas 5 945	**5 795**	34.74
Parry Sound 6 326	**6 124**	13.33	Thompson* 14 385	**13 256**	17.18
Pelham 14 343	**15 272**	126.42	Winkler 7 241	**7 943**	17.02
Pembroke* 14 177	**13 490**	14.35	Winnipeg* 618 477	**619 544**	465.16
Penetanguishene 7 900	**8 316**	25.36	■ **SASKATCHEWAN**		
Perth 5 902	**6 003**	10.36	Estevan* 10 752	**10 242**	17.53
Petawawa 15 304	**14 398**	164.68	Humboldt* 5 074	**5 161**	11.66
Peterborough* 69 742	**71446**	58.61	Lloydminster (Part)* 7 636	**7 840**	17.34
Pickering* 78 989	**87 139**	231.58	Melfort* 5 759	**5 559**	14.78
Plympton-Wyoming 7 344	**7 359**	318.76	Moose Jaw* 32 973	**32 131**	46.81
Port Colborne* 18 451	**18 450**	123.37	North Battleford* 14 051	**13 692**	33.51
Port Hope and Hope 15 446	**15 605**	278.99	Prince Albert* 34 777	**34 291**	65.76
Prince Edward* 25 046	**24 901**	1 049.99	Regina* 180 404	**178 225**	118.66
Quinte West* 41 676	**41 409**	499.14	Saskatoon* 193 653	**196 811**	148.34
Renfrew 8 125	**7 942**	12.77	Swift Current* 14 890	**14 821**	24.03
Richmond Hill 101 725	**132 030**	100.89	Weyburn* 9 723	**9 534**	15.72
Sarnia* 72 738	**70 876**	164.62	Yorkton* 15 154	**15 107**	24.02
Saugeen Shores 12 084	**11 388**	170.58	■ **ALBERTA**		
Sault Ste. Marie* 80 054	**74 566**	223.45	Airdrie* 15 946	**20 382**	21.48
Sioux Lookout 5 165	**5 336**	378.64	Banff 6 098	**7 135**	4.85 ▶
Smiths Falls 9 131	**9 140**	8.21			
South Bruce Peninsula . . 8 004	**8 090**	531.92			

	POPULATION		AREA 2001 (sq. km)
	1996	2001	
Beaumont	5 838	7 006	10.50
Bonnyville	5 100	5 709	14.09
Brooks	10 093	11 604	17.46
Calgary*	768 082	878 866	701.79
Camrose*	13 728	14 854	25.85
Canmore	8 354	10 792	68.80
Coaldale	5 770	6 008	7.92
Cochrane	7 424	11 798	16.51
Cold Lake*	11 791	11 520	59.30
Crowsnest Pass	6 356	6 262	373.04
Drayton Valley	5 883	5 801	7.96
Drumheller	7 833	7 785	107.93
Edmonton*	616 306	666 104	683.88
Edson	7 399	7 585	29.54
Fort Saskatchewan*	12 408	13 121	45.30
Grande Prairie*	31 353	36 983	60.42
High River	7 359	9 345	11.43
Hinton	9 961	9 405	25.76
Innisfail	6 116	6 928	9.80
Lacombe	8 330	9 384	18.05
Leduc*	14 346	15 032	36.97
Lethbridge*	63 053	67 374	121.83
Lloydminster (Part)*	11 317	13 148	24.19
Medicine Hat*	46 783	51 249	111.99
Morinville	6 226	6 540	11.34
Okotoks	8 528	11 664	17.91
Olds	5 815	6 607	11.05
Peace River	6 536	6 240	24.87
Ponoka	6 152	6 330	10.67
Red Deer*	60 080	67 707	60.90
Rocky Mountain House	5 809	6 208	12.44
Slave Lake	6 553	6 600	14.24
Spruce Grove*	14 271	15 983	26.40
St. Albert*	46 888	53 081	34.61
St. Paul	4 880	5 061	6.85
Stettler	5 228	5 215	9.52
Stony Plain	8 274	9 589	27.07
Strathmore	5 314	7 621	15.59
Sylvan Lake	5 184	7 493	9.48
Taber	7 214	7 671	15.09
Vegreville	5 337	5 376	13.47
Wainwright	5 079	5 117	8.24
Wetaskiwin*	10 959	11 154	15.83
Whitecourt	7 783	8 334	26.14
■ BRITISH COLUMBIA			
Abbotsford*	105 403	115 463	359.18
Burnaby*	179 209	193 954	90.09
Castlegar*	7 030	7 002	18.00
Chilliwack*	60 186	62 927	257.96
Colwood*	13 848	13 745	17.76
Comox	11 069	11 172	14.20
Coquitlam*	101 820	112 890	121.68
Courtenay*	17 404	18 304	17.02
Cranbrook*	18 329	18 476	17.80
Dawson Creek*	11 125	10 754	20.66
Fort St. John*	15 021	16 034	21.54
Kamloops*	76 394	77 281	297.57
Kelowna*	89 442	96 288	211.22
Kimberley*	6 738	6 484	58.31
Ladysmith	6 456	6 587	8.43
Langley*	22 523	23 643	10.22
Merritt*	7 631	7 088	24.90
Nanaimo*	70 130	73 000	89.17
Nelson*	9 585	9 298	7.27
New Westminster*	49 350	54 656	15.40
North Vancouver*	41 475	44 303	11.95
Parksville*	9 472	10 323	14.60
Penticton*	30 987	30 985	42.42
Port Alberni*	18 782	17 743	19.87
Port Coquitlam*	46 682	51 257	28.79
Port Moody*	20 847	23 816	25.62
Prince George*	75 150	72 406	315.99
Prince Rupert*	16 714	14 643	54.90
Qualicum Beach	6 734	6 921	12.45
Quesnel*	10 532	10 044	35.34
Revelstoke*	8 047	7 500	30.72
Richmond*	148 867	164 345	128.69
Sidney	10 701	10 929	5.04
Smithers	5 624	5 414	15.55
Surrey*	304 477	347 825	317.40
Terrace*	12 783	12 109	41.45
Trail*	7 874	7 575	34.78
Vancouver*	514 008	545 671	114.67
Vernon*	32 165	33 494	77.92
Victoria*	73 504	74 125	19.68
View Royal	6 441	7 271	14.48
White Rock*	17 210	18 250	5.28
Williams Lake*	11 235	11 153	33.03
■ YUKON TERRITORY			
Whitehorse*	19 157	19 058	416.44
■ NORTHWEST TERRITORIES			
Yellowknife*	17 275	16 541	105.20
■ NUNAVUT			
Iqaluit	4 220	5 236	52.34

Source: © *Census of Canada, Statistics Canada*

*Indicates a city or *ville* in Quebec; all others are towns.

Population of Census Metropolitan Areas[1] in Canada

Statistics Canada defines a census metropolitan area (CMA) as a very large urban area, together with neighbouring urban and rural areas that have a high degree of economic and social integration with that large urban area. The urban area itself (or urbanized core) must have a population of at least 100,000 based on the previous census. For a more detailed look at these cities, see "Canadian Cities" pages 31–38.

	Population				Land Area (sq. km)
CMA	1976	1986	1996	2001[2]	2001
Abbotsford, B.C.[3]	n.a	n.a.	136 480	147 370	625.94
Calgary, Alta.	469 917	671 453	821 628	951 395	5 083.00
Chicoutimi, Que.	128 643	158 468	160 454	154 938	1 753.67
Edmonton, Alta.	554 228	774 026	862 597	937 845	9 418.62
Halifax, N.S.	267 991	295 922	342 966	359 183	5 495.54
Hamilton, Ont.	529 371	557 029	624 360	662 401	1 371.76
Kingston, Ont.[3]	114 069	122 350	144 528	146 838	1 906.82
Kitchener, Ont.	272 158	311 195	382 940	414 284	826.98
London, Ont.	270 383	342 302	416 546	432 451	2 333.37
Montreal, Que.	2 802 485	2 921 357	3 326 447	3 426 350	4 047.35
Oshawa, Ont.	135 196	203 543	268 773	296 298	903.23
Ottawa-Hull, Ont.-Que.	693 288	819 263	998 718	1 063 664	5 318.36
Quebec, Que.	542 158	603 267	671 889	682 757	3 154.35
Regina, Sask.	151 191	186 521	193 652	192 800	3 407.84
St. Catharines-Niagara, Ont.	301 921	343 258	372 406	377 009	1 406.42
St. John's, Nfld and Lab.	143 390	161 901	174 051	172 918	804.63
Saint John, N.B.	112 974	121 265	125 705	122 678	3 359.61
Saskatoon, Sask.	133 750	200 665	219 056	225 927	5 192.22
Sherbrooke, Que.	104 505	129 960	149 569	153 811	1 108.16
Sudbury, Ont.	157 030	148 877	165 618	155 601	3 536.10
Thunder Bay, Ont.	119 253	122 217	126 643	121 986	2 548.16
Toronto, Ont.	2 803 101	3 431 981	4 263 759	4 682 897	5 902.74
Trois Rivières, Que.	98 583	128 888	139 956	137 507	880.47
Vancouver, B.C.	1 166 348	1 380 729	1 831 665	1 986 965	2 878.52
Victoria, B.C.	218 250	255 225	304 287	311 902	695.34
Windsor, Ont.	247 582	253 988	286 811	307 877	1 022.53
Winnipeg, Man.	578 217	625 304	667 093	671 274	4 151.48

Source: © *Census of Canada, Statistics Canada*

(1) Total land area considered to be part of CMA varied from census to census. (2) Unadjusted census count. (3) Abbotsford, B.C., and Kingston, Ont., were reclassified as Census Metropolitan Areas for the 2001 census. Data for previous years shows Census Agglomeration population, where appropriate.

VITAL STATISTICS

Births in Canada

	Live Births	Birth Rate[1]		Live Births	Birth Rate[1]		Live Births	Birth Rate[1]
1921	264 879	29.3	1977	361 400	15.5	1990	405 417	14.6
1926	240 015	24.7	1978	358 852	15.3	1991	402 528	14.4
1931	247 205	23.2	1979	366 064	15.9	1992	398 642	14.0
1936	227 980	20.3	1980	370 709	15.5	1993	388 394	13.5
1941	263 993	22.4	1981	371 346	15.3	1994	385 112	13.3
1946	343 504	27.2	1982	373 082	15.0	1995	378 011	12.9
1951	381 092	27.2	1983	373 689	15.0	1996	366 200	12.3
1956	450 739	28.0	1984	377 031	15.0	1997	348 598	11.6
1961	475 700	26.1	1985	375 727	14.8	1998	342 418	11.3
1966	387 710	19.4	1986	372 913	14.2	1999	337 249	11.0
1971	362 187	16.8	1987	369 742	13.9	2000	327 882	10.9
1976	359 987	15.7	1988	376 795	14.0	2000–01[2]	329 791	10.7
			1989	392 625	14.4	2001–02[2]	328 417	10.6

Source: © *Statistics Canada*
(1) Per 1 000 population. (2) From July 1 of one year to June 30 of the next year.

Births by Province, 2000–2001[1]

	Births	Birth Rate[2]		Births	Birth Rate[2]
Canada	**328 417**	**10.6**	Manitoba	14 010	12.2
Newfoundland & Labrador	4 745	8.9	Saskatchewan	11 969	11.8
Prince Edward Island	1 430	10.3	Alberta	36 357	11.9
Nova Scotia	8 996	9.5	British Columbia	40 581	9.9
New Brunswick	7 245	9.6	Yukon	356	11.8
Quebec	73 482	9.9	Northwest Territories	659	16
Ontario	127 840	10.7	Nunavut	747	26.6

Source: © *Statistics Canada*   (1) From July 1 to June 30. (2) Rate per 1 000 population.

Age-specific Fertility Rates

(per 1,000 women)

Age-specific fertility rates are calculated by dividing the number of live births in each age group by the total female population (in thousands) in each age group. Trends in the last ten years indicate that while women aged 25-29 are the most likely to give birth (although at a declining rate), births in the younger age groups are generally declining, while the fertility rates among women 30 and over hold steady or show modest increases.

	1986	1991	1996	1997	1999	2002
15-19 years[1]	23.01	25.98	22.34	20.19	18.70	17.0
20-24 years	78.74	77.50	67.28	64.07	60.90	56.7
25-29 years	119.01	120.33	105.82	103.88	100.00	95.8
30-34 years	72.52	83.63	85.51	84.44	85.80	85.5
35-39 years	22.30	28.27	32.22	32.52	33.60	35.3
40-44 years	3.15	3.88	5.06	5.19	5.50	5.7
45-49 years[2]	0.13	0.17	0.20	0.20	0.20	0.2

Source: © *Statistics Canada*
(1) Births to women aged 14 and under are included in the 15–19 age group. (2) Births to women aged 50 and over are included in the 45–49 age group.

Birth by Age of Mother, by Province, 2000

In 1999, despite the birth of 337,249 shown below, Canadian fertility hit a then record low of 1.52 children per woman—since surpassed by a rate of 1.49 in 2000. A comparison with the US revealed the US fertility rate for 1999 was 2.08. Canada's population growth is now only about three-quarters of the growth south of the border. Projections indicate that the growth rate in the US will continue to be higher in the coming years.

Where's the difference? The fertility rate among women aged 30 and over has increased at the same rate on both sides of the border. The fertility difference shows up in the women in their 20s and younger. In Canada, fertility among women aged 20 to 24 has decreased by nearly 40 per cent in the last 20 years; fertility among women aged 25 to 29 has dropped by 25 per cent. An additional factor: American teenage fertility rates continue to be relatively high compared to other industrialized countries. Why the difference? Researchers have suggested everything from the use of more effective birth control methods in Canada to Canadians' relative difficulty in establishing themselves in the work force.

Low fertility means that immigration is the main contributor to population growth. Within 20 years it's likely that deaths will exceed births, and immigration will be the only source of population growth.

Age	Canada	N&L	PEI	NS	NB	Que	Ont	Man	Sask	Alta	BC	YT	NWT	NVT
Under 15 . . .	153	2	1	4	3	19	42	17	25	6	15	0	2	7
15–19	17 350	389	120	581	554	3 183	5 317	1 323	1 338	2 441	1 835	33	82	154
20–24	59 523	1 084	335	1 893	1 795	14 696	18 902	3 185	3 088	7 565	6 527	70	160	223
25–29	101 072	1 580	430	2 906	2 496	24 231	37 360	4 369	3 879	11 414	11 952	92	173	190
30–34	96 353	1 343	376	2 497	1 768	19 894	41 513	3 458	509	10 124	12 514	96	155	106
35–39	45 393	435	152	1 061	660	8 530	20 538	1 502	1 098	4 659	6 564	72	85	37
40–44	7 643	34	27	163	70	1 411	3 505	231	179	773	1 220	7	15	8
45–49	278	2	0	10	1	41	150	4	10	13	44	0	1	2
50+	3	0	0	0	0	0	2	0	0	0	1	0	0	0
Not stated . .	114	0	0	1	0	4	93	1	14	1	0	0	0	0
Total	327 882	4 869	1 441	9 116	7 347	72 009	127 422	14 090	12 140	37 006	40 672	370	673	727

Source: © *Statistics Canada*

The 2001 Census Teacher's Kit

*S*tatistics Canada has developed a teacher's kit of materials related to the census for use in elementary, intermediate and secondary schools across the country. The activities have been classroom tested and meet curriculum requirements. There is a on-line teacher's guide (including 156 lesson plans by grade level and subject) plus activities that can be applied to subjects as varied as English, economics, mathematics, art, social studies, geography, history, family studies, theatre arts, science and phys ed. There are also materials that can be used in an ESL setting in the form of a literacy kit.

All materials can be downloaded from Statistics Canada's web site. They are in PDF format and require Adobe Acrobat Reader to access them at www.statcan.ca/english/kits/2001/tkit.htm (The material is also available in French.)

Expected Years of Life Remaining by Age, 1997

Age	Male Years of Life Remaining	Female Years of Life Remaining	Age	Male Years of Life Remaining	Female Years of Life Remaining
0	75.42	81.15	55	23.91	28.40
1	74.89	80.57	56	23.07	27.52
2	73.92	79.60	57	22.24	26.64
3	72.94	78.62	58	21.42	25.77
4	71.96	77.64	59	20.61	24.91
5	70.98	76.66	60	19.81	24.06
6	69.99	75.67	61	19.03	23.21
7	69.00	74.68	62	18.26	22.37
8	68.01	73.69	63	17.50	21.54
9	67.01	72.69	64	16.76	20.71
10	66.02	71.70	65	16.04	19.90
11	65.03	70.71	66	15.33	19.10
12	64.04	69.72	67	14.64	18.31
13	63.05	68.73	68	13.97	17.54
14	62.07	67.74	69	13.31	16.77
15	61.09	66.76	70	12.67	16.02
16	60.12	65.77	71	12.05	15.27
17	59.16	64.79	72	11.44	14.54
18	58.21	63.82	73	10.85	13.82
19	57.26	62.84	74	10.28	13.12
20	56.31	61.86	75	9.73	12.44
21	55.36	60.88	76	9.19	11.77
22	54.42	59.90	77	8.67	11.12
23	53.47	58.92	78	8.18	10.48
24	52.53	57.94	79	7.70	9.87
25	51.58	56.96	80	7.24	9.28
26	50.63	55.98	81	6.80	8.71
27	49.68	55.00	82	6.39	8.17
28	48.73	54.02	83	5.99	7.64
29	47.78	53.04	84	5.62	7.14
30	46.83	52.06	85	5.26	6.67
31	45.88	51.08	86	4.93	6.22
32	44.94	50.11	87	4.61	5.79
33	43.99	49.13	88	4.31	5.39
34	43.05	48.16	89	4.03	5.01
35	42.11	47.19	90	3.76	4.66
36	41.16	46.22	91	3.50	4.33
37	40.22	45.25	92	3.25	4.03
38	39.29	44.28	93	3.01	3.75
39	38.35	43.32	94	2.81	3.49
40	37.42	42.36	95	2.62	3.24
41	36.49	41.40	96	2.45	3.02
42	35.56	40.44	97	2.29	2.81
43	34.63	39.49	98	2.13	2.62
44	33.71	38.54	99	1.99	2.44
45	32.79	37.60	100	1.86	2.27
46	31.87	36.66	101	1.74	2.12
47	30.96	35.72	102	1.63	1.98
48	30.05	34.79	103	1.52	1.85
49	29.15	33.86	104	1.42	1.74
50	28.26	32.94	105	1.33	1.63
51	27.37	32.02	106	1.25	1.53
52	26.49	31.10	107	1.17	1.43
53	25.62	30.20	108	1.10	1.35
54	24.76	29.30	109	1.03	1.26

Source: © *Census of Canada, Statistics Canada*
(1) Represents the percentage of the population that will die before reaching the next age; in some cases totals do not equal 100 percent due to rounding.

Expected Years of Life Remaining by Sex

	At Birth		At Age 20		At Age 40		At Age 60		At Age 80	
	Male	Female	Male	Female	Male	Female	Male	Female	Male	Female
1921[1]	n.a.	n.a.	49.1	49.2	32.2	33.0	16.6	17.1	6.0	6.1
1931	60.0	62.1	49.1	49.8	32.0	33.0	16.3	17.2	5.6	5.9
1941	63.0	66.3	49.6	51.8	31.9	34.0	16.1	17.6	5.5	6.0
1951	66.3	70.8	50.8	54.4	32.5	35.6	16.5	18.6	5.8	6.4
1956	67.6	72.9	51.2	55.8	32.7	36.7	16.5	19.3	5.9	6.8
1961	68.4	74.2	51.5	56.7	33.0	37.5	16.7	19.9	6.1	6.9
1966	68.8	75.2	51.5	57.4	33.0	38.2	16.8	20.6	6.4	7.3
1971	69.3	76.4	51.7	58.2	33.2	39.0	17.0	21.4	6.4	7.9
1976	70.2	77.5	52.1	59.0	33.6	39.7	17.2	22.0	6.4	8.2
1981	71.9	79.0	53.4	60.1	34.7	40.7	18.0	22.9	6.9	8.8
1986	73.0	79.7	54.3	60.7	35.5	41.2	18.4	23.2	6.9	8.9
1991	74.6	80.9	55.6	61.7	36.8	42.2	19.4	24.0	7.2	9.4
1997	75.4	81.1	56.3	61.9	37.4	42.4	19.8	24.1	7.2	9.3

Source: © *Census Canada, Statistics Canada*   (n.a.) Not available. (1) Excludes Quebec.

Deaths in Canada

	Deaths	Death Rates[1]		Deaths	Death Rates[1]		Deaths	Death Rates[1]
1921[2]	104 531	11.6	**1974**	166 794	7.3	**1988**	190 011	7.1
1926[2]	111 055	11.4	**1975**	167 404	7.2	**1989**	190 965	7.0
1931[3]	108 446	10.2	**1976**	167 009	7.1	**1990**	191 973	6.9
1936[3]	111 111	9.9	**1977**	167 498	7.0	**1991**	195 568	7.0
1941[3]	118 797	10.1	**1978**	168 179	7.0	**1992**	196 535	6.9
1946	118 785	9.4	**1979**	168 183	6.9	**1993**	204 912	7.1
1951	125 823	9.0	**1980**	171 473	7.0	**1994**	207 077	7.1
1956	131 961	8.2	**1981**	171 029	6.9	**1995**	210 733	7.2
1961	140 985	7.7	**1982**	174 413	6.9	**1996**	212 859	7.2
1966	149 863	7.5	**1983**	174 484	6.9	**1997**	215 669	7.2
			1984	175 727	6.8	**1998**	218 091	7.2
1971	157 272	7.3	**1985**	181 323	7.0	**1999**	219 530	7.2
1972	162 413	7.4	**1986**	184 224	7.0	**1999–00**[4]	220 405	7.2
1973	164 039	7.4	**1987**	184 953	7.0	**2000–01**[4]	226 760	7.3

Source: © *Statistics Canada*
(1) Per 1 000 population. (2) Excludes Que., Nfld. & Lab., Yukon and N.W.T. (3) Excludes Nfld. & Lab., Yukon and N.W.T.
(4) From July 1 to June 30.

Deaths by Province, 2001–2002

	Deaths	Death Rate		Deaths	Death Rate
Canada	226 760	7.3	Manitoba	10 190	8.9
Newfoundland & Labrador	4 328	8.1	Saskatchewan	9 294	9.1
Prince Edward Island	1 167	8.4	Alberta	18 068	5.9
Nova Scotia	7 949	8.4	British Columbia	28 371	6.9
New Brunswick	6 307	8.3	Yukon	144	4.8
Quebec	54 068	7.3	Northwest Territories	169	4.1
Ontario	86 569	7.3	Nunavut	136	4.8

Source: © *Statistics Canada*

Leading Causes of Male Death

	1977		1999	
	No. of Deaths	Rate[1]	No. of Deaths	Rate[1]
All Causes	**96 872**	**875.5**	**113 668**	**752.7**
Diseases of the Circulatory System	**45 760**	**413.6**	**39 808**	**263.6**
Ischaemic Heart Disease	31 180	281.8	23 617	156.4
Stroke	7 160	64.7	6 371	42.2
Cancer	**20 378**	**184.2**	**33 026**	**218.7**
Lung	6 142	55.5	10 276	68.0
Prostate	1 833	16.6	3 601	23.8
Respiratory Diseases	**6 828**	**61.7**	**11 517**	**76.3**
Other Chronic Airway Obstructions	2 584	23.4	4 637	30.7
Pneumonia and Influenza	2 764	25.0	4 206	27.9
External Causes of Injury and Poisoning	**11 366**	**102.7**	**9 405**	**62.3**
Suicide	2 459	22.2	3 224	21.3
Motor Vehicle Accidents	3 831	34.6	2 110	14.0
Diseases of the Digestive System	**3 742**	**33.8**	**3 934**	**26.0**
Chronic Liver Disease and Cirrhosis	1 924	17.4	1 391	9.2
Noninfective Enteritis and Colitis	n.a.	n.a.	407	2.7
Endocrine Diseases	**1 616**	**14.6**	**3 829**	**25.4**
Diabetes Mellitus	1 289	11.7	3 065	20.3
Fluid, Electrolyte and Acid-Base Balance	85	0.8	199	1.3
Diseases of the Nervous System	**1 023**	**9.3**	**2 941**	**19.5**
Alzheimer's Disease	n.a.	n.a.	917	6.1
Parkinson's Disease	n.a.	n.a.	742	4.9
Mental Disorders	**763**	**6.9**	**2 472**	**16.4**
Senile and Presenile Dementia	n.a.	n.a.	912	6.0
Psychoses, including Alcoholic	154	1.4	544	3.6
All Other Causes	**5 396**	**48.8**	**6 736**	**44.5**

Source: © *Statistics Canada* (1) Per 100 000 population by gender.

Leading Causes of Female Death

	1977		1999	
	No. of Deaths	Rate[1]	No. of Deaths	Rate[1]
All Causes	**70 626**	**644.3**	**105 861**	**687.5**
Diseases of the Circulatory System	**35 714**	**325.8**	**39 134**	**254.2**
Ischaemic Heart Disease	20 228	184.6	19 002	123.4
Stroke	8 362	76.3	9 038	58.7
Cancer	**16 041**	**146.5**	**28 624**	**185.9**
Lung	1 519	13.9	6 437	41.8
Breast	3 321	30.3	4 762	30.9
Respiratory Diseases	**4 005**	**36.5**	**10 509**	**68.3**
Pneumonia and Influenza	2 392	21.8	4 805	31.2
Other Chronic Airway Obstructions	2 213	20.2	3 328	21.6
External Causes of Injury and Poisoning	**4 635**	**43.4**	**4 591**	**29.8**
Accidental Falls	829	7.6	1 612	10.5
Motor Vehicle Accidents	1 424	13.0	974	6.3
Diseases of the Digestive System	**2 388**	**21.8**	**3 962**	**25.7**
Chronic Liver Disease and Cirrhosis	838	7.7	700	4.5
Noninfective Enteritis and Colitis	n.a.	n.a.	672	4.4
Endocrine Diseases	**2 103**	**19.2**	**4 008**	**26.0**
Diabetes Mellitus	1 721	15.7	3 072	20.0
Fluid, Electrolyte and Acid-Base Balance	98	0.9	323	2.1
Diseases of the Nervous System	**786**	**7.2**	**3 814**	**24.8**
Alzheimer's Disease	n.a.	n.a.	1 941	12.6
Parkinson's Disease	n.a.	n.a.	611	4.0
Mental Disorders	**382**	**3.57**	**4 200**	**27.3**
Senile and Presenile Dementia	n.a.	n.a.	1 985	12.9
Psychoses, including Alcoholic	161	1.47	163	1.1
All Other Causes	**4 572**	**41.71**	**7 019**	**45.5**

Source: © *Statistics Canada* (1) Per 100 000 population by gender.

MIGRATION

How to Become a Canadian Citizen

To become a Canadian citizen, you must be at least 18 years of age, a permanent resident and in Canada legally.

If you are a permanent resident, you must have lived in Canada for at least three of the four years before the date of your application. If you lived in Canada before becoming a permanent resident, that time is counted at half the rate if it was during the four years before your application date.

You must be able to speak and understand spoken English or French, or be able to read and write in simple English or French.

If you are between 18 and 59 years of age, you must learn about Canada before becoming a citizen. When you apply for citizenship, you'll be sent a free publication called *A Look at Canada* on which your citizenship test will be based.

Children under 18 don't need to meet the three-year residency requirement; however, you must already be a Canadian citizen or be applying to become one. Children don't write a citizenship test.

Who Doesn't Qualify

Not everyone can become a Canadian citizen. You cannot become a citizen if :

- you were convicted of an indictable offence in the past three years
- you are under a deportation order
- you were in prison, on parole or on probation in the past four years
- you have been charged with an indictable offence
- you are now charged with an offence under the Citizenship Act
- your Canadian citizenship has been revoked in the past five years
- you are under investigation for war crimes or crimes against humanity

Applying

1. **Get the correct application form.** It should be the "Application for Citizenship." Each child for whom you are applying needs a separate form.

2. **Read the form.** The cost to process your forms isn't refundable, so be sure you are ready to become a citizen and fill the form out carefully. The current fee for citizenship for adults is $200, and the fee for children under 18 is $100.

3. **Complete the application and attach necessary documents.** Photocopies of documents are acceptable, but you may need to bring the original when you take the test. The application form comes with detailed instructions.

4. **Mail the completed application.** Check that you have included all documentation and filled in the application completely.

5. **Prepare for your test.** Read the book *A Look at Canada* that will be sent to you. You may want to take a citizenship class if one is being held near you. A notice detailing the date and time of your citizenship test will be sent to you. The test may be oral or written.

6. **Take the oath.** Once you have met all the requirements, you will receive a notice detailing when and where the citizenship ceremony will take place.

Call Centres and Citizenship Offices

You can get more information on any of the topics discussed here by contacting one of the call centres listed below.

Montreal: (514) 496-1010
Toronto: (416) 973-4444
Vancouver: (604) 666-2171
Toll-free: 1-888-242-2100

Case Processing Centre

P.O. Box 7000
Sydney, NS B1P 6V6

Source: *Citizenship and Immigration Canada*

Canadian Immigration Totals

Year	Total	Year	Total	Year	Total	Year	Total
1855*	25 296	1924	124 164	1950	73 912	1976	149 429
1860*	6 276	1925	84 907	1951	194 391	1977	114 914
1865*	18 958	1926	135 982	1952	164 498	1978	86 313
1870	24 706	1927	158 886	1953	168 868	1979	112 093
1875	27 382	1928	166 783	1954	154 227	1980	143 136
1880	38 505	1929	164 993	1955	109 946	1981	128 639
1885	79 169	1930	104 806	1956	164 857	1982	121 176
1890	75 067	1931	27 530	1957	282 164	1983	89 188
1895	18 790	1932	20 591	1958	124 851	1984	88 273
1900	41 681	1933	14 382	1959	106 928	1985	84 333
1905	141 465	1934	12 476	1960	104 111	1986	99 326
		1935	11 277	1961	71 689	1987	152 001
1910	286 839	1936	11 643	1962	74 586	1988	161 500
1911	331 288	1937	15 101	1963	93 151	1989	191 497
1912	375 756	1938	17 244	1964	112 606	1990	216 398
1913	400 870	1939	16 994	1965	146 758	1991	232 751
1914	150 484	1940	11 324	1966	194 743	1992	254 820
1915	36 665	1941	9 329	1967	222 876	1993	256 739
1916	55 914	1942	7 576	1968	183 974	1994	224 373
1917	72 910	1943	8 504	1969	164 531	1995	212 860
1918	41 845	1944	12 801	1970	147 713	1996	226 044
1919	107 698	1945	22 722	1971	121 900	1997	216 024
1920	138 824	1946	71 719	1972	122 006	1998	174 191
1921	91 728	1947	64 127	1973	184 200	1999	189 922
1922	64 224	1948	125 414	1974	218 465	2000	227 346
1923	133 729	1949	95 217	1975	187 881	2001	250 484
						2002[1]	229 091

Source: *Citizenship and Immigration Canada*   (*) Pre-Confederation. (1) Preliminary figure.

Persons Granted Canadian Citizenship[1]

Year	Number	Year	Number	Year	Number	Year	Number
1920	3 004	1961	56 476	1975	137 507	1989	87 478
1925	13 288	1962	72 082	1976	117 276	1990	104 267
1930	21 221	1963	69 468	1977	123 655	1991	118 630
1935	20 903	1964	64 334	1978	223 214	1992	115 757
1940	18 207	1965	63 844	1979	156 699	1993	150 543
1941	15 594	1966	60 852	1980	118 590	1994	217 320
1942	14 213	1967	59 968	1981	94 457	1995	227 720
1943	12 533	1968	60 055	1982	87 468	1996	166 627
1944	12 827	1969	59 900	1983	90 328	1997	154 624
1945	13 562	1970	57 556	1984	109 504	1998	134 485
1950	10 441	1971	63 669	1985	126 466	1999	189 945
1955	58 711	1972	80 866	1986	103 800	2000	214 568
		1973	104 697	1987	73 638	2001	167 353
1960	62 378	1974	130 278	1988	58 810	2002	141 588

Source: *Citizenship and Immigration Canada*   (1) For fiscal year ending Mar 31 for 1920 to 1951; calendar years 1952 onwards.

Dual Citizenship for Canadians

Canada's Citizenship Act allows a Canadian citizen to acquire a foreign nationality without automatically losing Canadian citizenship. Since 1977, a Canadian citizen acquiring citizenship rights elsewhere may retain Canadian citizenship—unless he or she voluntarily applies to renounce it and that application gets approval from a citizenship judge.

Two or more citizenships and allegiances can be held at the same time for an indefinite period. This means an individual may have the citizen's rights and obligations of each country—when present in that country. When travelling outside both countries, a passport from one of them will be necessary.

Immigration to Canada[1]

	Total Immigrants	United States	Asia[2]	Europe	Caribbean[3]	South America	Africa	Oceania
1956	164 857	9 777	3 537	145 554	1 351	1 551	1 079	1 924
1960	104 111	11 247	4 002	82 922	1 542	1 823	833	1 657
1965	146 758	15 143	11 215	108 285	3 420	2 471	3 196	2 711
1966	194 743	17 514	13 835	148 410	4 357	2 604	3 661	4 057
1967	222 876	19 038	20 740	159 979	9 004	3 090	4 608	6 168
1968	183 974	20 422	21 686	120 702	8 129	2 693	5 204	4 815
1969	161 531	22 785	23 319	88 363	13 908	4 767	3 297	4 411
1970	147 713	24 424	21 170	75 609	13 371	4 943	2 863	4 385
1971	121 900	24 366	22 171	52 031	11 653	5 058	2 841	2 902
1972	122 006	22 618	23 325	51 293	9 218	4 309	8 308	2 143
1973	184 200	25 242	43 193	71 883	20 704	11 057	8 307	2 671
1974	218 465	26 541	50 566	88 694	25 276	12 528	10 450	2 594
1975	187 881	20 155	47 382	72 898	19 483	13 270	9 867	2 174
1976	149 429	17 315	44 328	49 903	16 198	10 628	7 752	1 886
1977	114 914	12 888	31 368	40 748	13 187	7 840	6 372	1 545
1978	86 313	9 945	24 007	30 075	9 240	6 782	4 261	1 233
1979	112 096	9 617	50 540	32 858	7 060	5 898	3 958	1 395
1980	143 117	9 926	71 602	41 168	8 141	5 433	4 330	2 497
1981	128 618	10 559	48 831	46 299	9 625	6 163	4 889	2 253
1982	121 147	9 360	41 686	46 156	10 317	6 871	4 513	2 119
1983	89 157	7 381	36 906	24 312	10 864	4 816	3 659	1 213
1984	88 239	6 922	41 920	20 901	9 706	4 085	3 552	1 151
1985	84 302	6 669	38 597	18 859	11 143	4 356	3 545	1 128
1986	99 219	7 275	41 600	22 709	14 947	6 686	4 770	1 227
1987	152 098	7 967	67 337	37 563	18 100	10 801	8 501	1 827
1988	161 929	6 537	81 136	40 689	15 108	7 255	9 380	1 822
1989	192 001	6 931	93 261	52 105	16 764	8 685	12 199	2 041
1990	213 334	6 057	111 195	51 667	19 459	8 888	13 426	2 642
1991	232 020	20 122[4]	120 736	48 232	12 978	10 632	16 175	3 145[5]
1992	253 345	20 123[4]	139 546	44 933	14 993	10 415	19 669	3 666[5]
1993	255 935	8 025	147 378	46 622	24 315	9 588	16 922	3 085[5]
1994	223 912	6 242	141 600	38 652	13 486	7 919	13 708	2 305[5]
1995	212 463[6]	5 199	128 534	41 127	13 352	7 485	14 560	1 873[5]
1996	226 050[6]	5 896	143 956	40 009	12 958	6 115	14 836	2 058[5]
1997	216 050	5 053	138 018	38 580	8 195	5 682	14 473	2 024
1998	174 162	4 781	101 297	38 482	6 341	4 964	13 672	1 639
1999	189 922[8]	5 528	113 934	38 990	6 758	5 609	15 695	532
2000[7]	227 313[8]	5 814	140 988	42 950	7 149	6 784	19 828	696
2001	250 346[8]	5 894	132 711	43 204	—[10]	20 129	48 278[11]	—[9]
2002	229 091	5 288	118 899	38 841	—[10]	19 417	46 113[11]	—[9]

Source: *Citizenship and Immigration Canada*

(1) By country of last permanent residence. (2) Includes China and Hong Kong. (3) Includes Central America, Greenland and St. Pierre & Miquelon for 1956–76; except for 1991, 1992 when North and Central America were included with U.S. figures (4) Includes North and Central America. (5) Includes Australia and other islands. (6) Includes those whose country of last permanent residence was not stated. (7) Preliminary numbers. (8) Includes those whose last permanent residence was North and Central America and those not stated. (9) Included in Asia. (10) Included in South America. (11) Includes Middle East.

Dual Citizenship for Immigrants

*I*mmigrants to Canada may have several citizenships: if born in a country other than Canada, naturalized in Canada (without the loss of citizenship in the birth country), and naturalized in a third country, an individual may be a citizen of all three. Cases of dual citizenship are most common.

Dual citizenship may carry benefits, but it may bring difficulties—legal proceedings, taxation or financial responsibilities, military service, emigration problems, even imprisonment for failure to comply with citizenship obligations. Canadian officials will not be able to help if a Canadian citizen who is also a citizen elsewhere has difficulties while in their other homeland.

Immigration by Province of Intended Destination

	Totals[1]	N&L	PEI	NS	NB	Que	Ont	Man	Sask	Alta	BC	YT	NWT	NVT
1956	**164 857**	426	112	1 639	852	31 396	90 662	5 796	2 202	9 959	17 812	n.a.	n.a.	n.a.
1960	**104 111**	306	83	1 210	634	23 774	54 491	4 337	2 087	6 949	10 120	n.a.	n.a.	n.a.
1965	**146 758**	604	137	1 612	1 074	30 346	79 702	3 948	2 649	8 049	18 502	n.a.	n.a.	n.a.
1970	**147 713**	630	185	2 007	1 070	23 261	80 732	5 826	1 709	10 405	21 683	n.a.	n.a.	n.a.
1975	**187 881**	1106	235	2 124	2 093	28 042	98 471	7 134	2 837	16 277	29 272	n.a.	n.a.	n.a.
1980	**143 117**	541	190	1 616	1 207	22 538	62 257	7 683	3 603	18 839	24 437	n.a.	n.a.	n.a.
1985	**84 302**	325	113	974	609	14 884	40 730	3 415	1 905	9 001	12 239	n.a.	n.a.	n.a.
1990	**214 230**	546	176	1 563	842	40 842	113 438	6 637	2 361	18 994	28 723	83	75	n.a.
1991	**232 020**	641	150	1 504	685	52 155	119 257	5 659	2 455	17 043	32 263	84	124	n.a.
1992	**253 345**	787	151	2 359	754	48 597	138 453	5 084	2 511	17 696	36 709	133	111	n.a.
1993	**255 935**	807	165	3 021	702	44 964	134 420	4 874	2 403	18 580	45 724	104	171	n.a.
1995	**212 463**	585	167	3 581	639	27 182	115 681	3 603	1 949	14 329	44 541	108	91	n.a.
1996	**226 072**	585	154	3 225	717	29 802	119 072	3 928	1 824	13 896	52 026	87	92	n.a.
1997	**216 048**	431	150	2 873	631	27 905	117 431	3 799	1 759	12 976	47 880	86	101	n.a.
1998	**174 190**	412	136	2 059	750	26 645	92 220	3 015	1 578	11 214	35 998	62	63	n.a.
1999	**189 922**	415	125	1 601	663	29 085	104 010	3 701	1 725	12 059	36 076	79	54	10
2000	**227 313**	410	192	1 591	758	32 424	133 323	4 606	1 888	14 319	37 372	60	82	9
2001	**229 091**	405	110	1419	710	37 627	133 641	4 621	1 665	14 729	34 000	49	61	12

Source: *Citizenship and Immigration Canada*   (1) Includes those whose destination was not stated.

Top Five Provincial Destinations for Immigration

	2000		2001		2002	
	#	%	#	%	#	%
Total Number of Immigrants	**227 313**	**100**	**250 346**	**100**	**229 091**	**100**
Destination:						
Ontario	133 323	58.65	148 425	59.29	133 641	58.34
British Columbia...........	37 372	16.44	38 266	15.29	34 000	14.84
Quebec	32 424	14.27	37 428	14.95	37 627	16.43
Alberta	14 319	6.31	16 371	6.54	14 729	6.43
Manitoba	4 606	2.03	4 574	1.82	4 621	2.01

Source: *Citizenship and Immigration Canada*

Top Ten CMA Destinations for Immigration

	2000		2001		2002	
	#	%	#	%	#	%
Total Number of Immigrants	**227 313**	**100**	**250 346**	**100**	**229 091**	**100**
Destination:						
Toronto	110 059	48.42	125 061	49.96	111 580	48.71
Vancouver	33 292	14.65	34 165	13.65	29 922	13.60
Montreal	28 139	12.38	32 366	12.93	33 004	14.41
Calgary	8 469	3.73	10 169	4.06	9 038	3.95
Ottawa-Hull (ON).........	7 772	3.42	8 448	3.37	7 156	3.12
Edmonton	4 313	1.90	4 580	1.83	4 225	1.84
Winnipeg................	3 700	1.63	3 742	1.49	3 810	1.66
Hamilton	3 167	1.39	2 767	1.11	3 079	1.34
London	1 973	0.87	1 955	0.78	1 710	0.75
Quebec City..............	1 405	0.62	1 829	0.73	1 335	0.58

Source: *Citizenship and Immigration Canada*

FOCUS ON...

The Immigrant Population

The 2001 census has provided important new information on Canada's immigrant population. Immigrants formed a significant, and increasing, proportion of the country's population, reaching 5.4 million in 2001. Immigrants have accounted for the highest recorded share of Canada's population (18.4 percent) since 1931. More than one-third arrived in Canada in the 1991-2001 decade and over 80 percent chose to become Canadian citizens.

Sixty percent of recent immigrants (those who arrived between 1991 and 2001) came from Asia and the Middle East. Not surprisingly, a growing proportion of Canada's newest immigrants (61 percent in 2001, compared to 55 percent in 1991) reported speaking a language other than English or French most often at home, with Chinese spoken in a third of these households. Religious affiliations have also changed: the number of recent immigrants who identified themselves as one of Muslim, Hindu, Sikh or Buddhist has almost doubled.

Immigrants were much more likely to be among the working-age population. Sixty-seven percent were between 25 and 64 years old, compared to only 52 percent of the non-immigrant population. The remaining 33 percent were more likely to be over 65 years but less likely to be under 24. Immigrants were also increasingly well educated. Among working-age immigrants who arrived in the 1990s, 41 percent were university-trained, 13 percent had a college diploma and eight percent had a trade certificate.

Recent immigrants are much more likely than the Canadian-born population to live in a census metropolitan area. Ninety-four percent of immigrants who arrived in the 1990s settled in an urban area compared to 64 percent of the overall population. Taken together, Toronto, Vancouver and Montreal were home to 80 percent of recent immigrant city-dwellers.

■ Employment

Immigrant landings accounted for almost 70 percent of labour force growth between 1991 and 2001, adding about 965,000 people to the work force. Despite comprising only seven percent of the working-age population, recent immigrants aged 25 to 64 constituted an impressive 24 percent of the work force for higher skilled occupations in 2001.

Immigrants accounted for 20 percent of the labour force, an increase of one percent compared to 1996. The employment rates (see note) for immigrants and very recent immigrants (those who arrived in the last five years) were 77.4 percent and 69.4 percent respectively. These percentages represent an improvement over the 1996 figures (72.3 percent and 62.2 percent respectively), but are still below 1991 levels (78.5 percent and 71.7 percent respectively). A significant gap in employment rates, larger for females than males, remained between very recent immigrants and the Canadian-born.

■ Earnings

Male immigrants aged 25 to 54 who arrived in Canada in the 1990s earned $33,900 in 2000, an average of 25 percent less than their Canadian-born counterparts. Similarly, female immigrants aged 25 to 54 earned 24 percent less than their Canadian-born counterparts, their yearly earnings averaging $21,959.

The income of recent arrivals tended to increase the longer they remained in Canada. After ten years, a male immigrant earned an average of 80 percent of his Canadian-born counterpart's salary, compared to only 63 percent after one year in Canada. Despite this improvement, the relative gap between recent immigrants and the Canadian-born widened. Whereas in 1980, a male immigrant who had been in Canada ten years earned an average of $1.04 for every dollar earned by his Canadian-born counterpart, the figure had dropped to $0.90 by 1990 and $0.80 by 2000.

The average real family income for immigrants has increased by 12 percent, from $59,016 in 1995 to $65,825 in 2000, while the increase for non-immigrant families was 11 percent. The distribution of income also changed for the better. In all income groups, there were relatively fewer people with lower incomes in 2000 than in 1995. For example, 46.7 percent of immigrant families earned less than $50,000 in 2000 compared to 51.2 percent in 1995.

■ Children Living in Poverty

Despite these gains, there are a significant number of children in poor immigrant families. Thirty-three percent of children whose parents have been in Canada for less than ten years come from low-income families. This compares to 15.5 percent of children living with Canadian-born parents and 15 percent of children living with immigrant parents who have been in Canada for more than ten years. There were relatively more children from poor immigrant families in 2000 (33 percent) than there were either in 1980 (20 percent) or 1990 (27 percent).

What conclusions can be drawn from these findings? The gap in financial well-being between Canadian-born and immigrant families may be attributed to a number of factors, including the language barrier many immigrants face when they arrive on Canadian soil, and the fact that Canadian educational institutions or business organizations may not recognize the qualifications an immigrant brings from his or her home country. Unfortunately, it is also likely that, in spite of Canada's reputation for tolerance, many immigrants (especially those from visible minorities) experience intolerant attitudes that limit their employment potential and success.

Note: The employment rate as defined here is the product of the proportion of the labour force that is employed and the labour force participation rate.

Immigrant Earnings (10 Years after Arrival in Canada) as a Percentage of Canadian-born Earnings

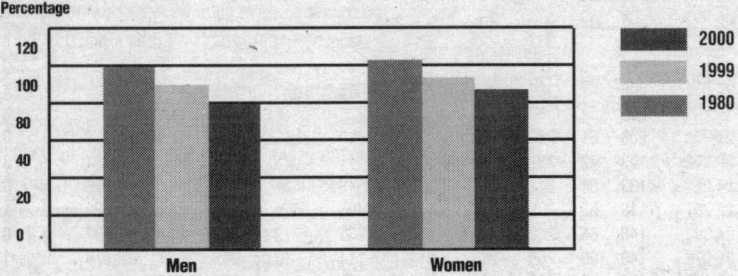

Children Living in Low Income Families, by the Parents' Immigration Status

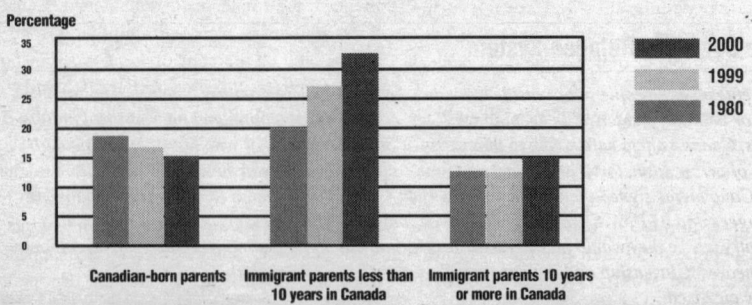

Source: *Citizenship and Immigration Canada*

Refugees to Canada[1]

1962	1 733	1973	2 381	1983	14 062	1993	24 835
1963	2 024	1974	1 656	1984	15 553	1994	19 739
1964	2 279	1975	6 109	1985	17 000	1995	27 753
1965	2 131	1976	5 576	1986	19 485	1996	28 352
1966	2 058	1977	3 670	1987	21 950	1997	24 221
1967	1 499	1978	3 038	1988	27 230	1998	22 787
1968	9 971	1979	27 894	1989	37 361	1999	24 393
1969	3 604	1980	40 638	1990	36 093	2000	30 072
1970	1 361	1981	15 058	1991	35 891	2001	27 899
1971	614	1982	17 000	1992	36 943	2002	25 111
1972	5 204						

Source: *Refugees Branch, Citizenship and Immigration Canada*
(1) Includes persons admitted from abroad as Convention Refugees or members of Designated Classes, as well as persons recognized in Canada as Convention Refugees or members of the special Backlog Clearance Designated Class. Does not include special humanitarian movements of other persons.

Refugees by Province of Destination[1]

	Total[2]	N&L	PEI	NS	NB	Que	Ont	Man	Sask	Alta	BC	YT	NWT
1981	14 997	28	11	119	76	3 257	5 544	822	657	2 751	1 722	6	4
1982	16 991	40	28	161	47	3 200	7 013	1 031	644	3 112	1 706	7	2
1983	14 062	11	17	89	61	2 184	6 100	844	574	2 488	1 692	0	2
1984	15 553	40	20	175	85	2 228	6 900	1 032	773	2 446	1 848	1	5
1985	17 000	55	33	206	165	1 906	8 301	1 131	749	2 529	1 919	1	5
1986	19 485	77	43	253	170	2 530	9 580	1 350	777	2 677	2 018	5	5
1987	21 921	87	45	241	192	3 216	11 026	1 366	791	2 673	2 277	3	4
1988	27 230	93	18	290	208	3 690	14 716	1 653	806	3 265	2 453	7	1
1989	37 361	94	49	329	194	5 137	21 585	1 929	815	4 535	2 679	9	6
1990	36 093	94	50	361	182	5 085	20 644	2 325	776	4 118	2 447	6	5
1991	35 891	265	40	337	211	6 284	21 342	1 579	706	2 738	2 382	4	3
1992	36 943	220	28	176	95	7 111	22 894	1 048	568	2 428	2 374	1	0
1993	24 835	243	41	189	100	5 776	14 433	692	375	1 649	1 325	1	11
1994	19 739	225	64	173	137	4 430	10 485	582	515	1 606	1 520	2	0
1995	27 753	208	61	223	179	6 122	16 413	663	575	1 447	1 854	8	0
1996	28 352	173	72	232	189	8 909	13 937	683	547	1 341	2 264	2	3
1997	24 221	133	63	211	150	7 686	11 646	621	558	1 156	1 996	1	0
1998	22 787	113	58	235	162	6 227	11 496	655	532	1 275	2 033	0	1
1999	24 393	148	66	258	149	7 333	11 961	779	509	1 281	1 892	0	0
2000	30 072	140	109	269	267	8 044	15 114	1 016	649	1 871	2 578	0	1
2001	27 899	157	50	265	230	7 147	14 226	1 161	595	1 875	2 189	0	1

Source: *Refugees Branch, Citizenship and Immigration Canada* (1) Includes Refugees Resettled from Abroad, their Dependants and inland Determination where destination is known. (2) Shows only those whose destination was identified.

The Canadian Refugee System

*R*efugees are people in or outside Canada who fear returning to their country of nationality or habitual residence. In keeping with its humanitarian tradition and international obligations, Canada offers safe haven to thousands of persons every year who have a well-founded fear of persecution, torture, or cruel and unusual treatment or punishment.

Canada has signed the United Nations 1951 Geneva Convention Relating to the Status of Refugees and its 1967 Protocol. This Convention protects refugees from being returned to a country where they would face persecution. To find out about claiming refugee status, contact the nearest Citizenship and Immigration Canada office, or consult their Web site at www.cic.gc.ca.   **Source:** *Citizenship and Immigration Canada*

Where Canadians Move Within Canada

When Canadians move from one province to another, it tends to be related to economic conditions. During 1977–81 the resource boom in Alberta caused an influx from other provinces. Falling oil prices in the early 1980s led to a reversal as Canadians moved east, especially to Ontario.

By the late 1980s, BC was the choice location. For the latter part of the 1990s, up to the present, Ontario and Alberta were on top again. The table shows net interprovincial migration—the number of persons moving into a province minus the number of persons moving out.

	N&L	PEI	NS	NB	Que	Ont	Man	Sask	Alta	BC	YK	NWT	NVT[1]
1977–81	-21 086	-1 451	-8 185	-13 680	-156 817	-60 890	-42 115	-11 729	190 719	131 176	-2 363	-3 579	n.a.
1982–86	-14 117	811	7 442	835	-67 235	165 460	-2 395	-7 057	-82 737	3 226	-2 393	-1 840	n.a.
1987–91	-11 355	-65	-607	-2 063	-45 406	28 876	-39 533	-69 397	-13 198	154 126	871	-2 249	n.a.
1992–95	-18 730	1 826	-5 454	-3 015	-37 711	-32 592	-18 977	-19 418	242	135 036	-129	-1 078	n.a.
1996-97[2]	-8 134	136	-1 648	-1 263	-17 436	1 977	-5 873	-2 794	26 282	9 880	-54	-696	-377
1997-98[2]	-9 490	-416	-2 569	-3 192	-16 958	9 231	-5 276	-1 940	43 089	-10 029	-1 024	-1 316	-110
1998-99[2]	-5 695	193	201	-1 244	-13 065	16 706	-2 113	-4 333	25 191	-14 484	-747	-555	-55
1999-00[2]	-4 263	104	-270	-1 183	-12 146	22 369	-3 456	-7 947	22 674	-14 610	-691	-651	70
2000-01[2]	-4 493	165	-2 077	-1 530	-9 442	18 623	-4 323	-8 410	20 457	-8 286	-572	-160	48
2001-02[2,3]	-2 510	683	-1 266	-871	-8 432	7 266	-5 298	-8 635	26 740	-6 994	-395	-311	23

Source: © *Statistics Canada*   n.a. not applicable   (1) Nunavut became a territory in 1999.   (2) Year ends June 30.   (3) Preliminary data.

Population Growth Components

(thousands)

Population growth is made up of natural increase (births minus deaths) plus net migration (immigration minus emigration). As the birth rate in Canada falls and the death rate continues to rise, the role of immigration becomes an increasingly important factor in population growth. By 2030, natural increase is expected to be close to zero, and immigration will become our sole source of population growth.

	Total Population Growth	Natural Increase		Net Migration	
		Births	Deaths	Immigration	Emigration
1851–1861	793	1 281	670	352	170
1861–1871	459	1 370	760	260	411
1871–1881	636	1 480	790	350	404
1881–1891	508	1 524	870	680	826
1891–1901	538	1 548	880	250	380
1901–1911	1 836	1 925	900	1 550	739
1911–1921	1 581	2 340	1 070	1 400	1 089
1921–1931	1 589	2 415	1 055	1 200	971
1931–1941	1 130	2 294	1 072	149	241
1941–1951	2 141	3 186	1 214	548	379
1951–1956	2 071	2 106	633	783	185
1956–1961	2 157	2 362	687	760	278
1961–1966	1 777	2 249	731	539	280
1966–1971	1 553	1 856	766	890	427
1971–1976	1 626	1 755	824	1 053	358
1976–1981	1 470	1 820	843	771	278
1981–1986	1 386	1 872	885	677	278
1986–1991	1 973	1 933	946	1 199	213
1991–1996	1 848	1 936	1 024	1 137	229
1997–98	261	345	218	194	56
1998–99	261	338	218	173	59
1999–2000	282	337	219	206	63
2000–01	320	326	224	252	67
2001–02	303	327	234	256	71

Source: © *Statistics Canada*   (1) Updated data. Year ends June 30th.   (2) Preliminary data.

SOCIAL TRENDS

Marriages by Province

	1998	1999	2000	2001	Rate (%)
Canada	152 821	152 855	155 399	153 234	4.9
Newfoundland and Labrador	3 150	3 075	3 022	2 967	5.6
Prince Edward Island	882	882	878	876	6.3
Nova Scotia	5 134	5 107	5 074	5 037	5.3
New Brunswick	4 063	4 030	4 003	3 977	5.3
Quebec	22 940	22 815	24 921	21 963	3.0
Ontario	64 533	64 633	65 043	65 677	5.5
Manitoba	6 437	6 426	6 410	6 402	5.6
Saskatchewan	5 740	5 750	5 729	5 679	5.6
Alberta	17 813	18 116	18 374	18 717	6.1
British Columbia	21 749	21 649	21 577	21 575	5.3
Yukon	167	160	156	150	5.0
Northwest Territories	134	132	131	130	3.2
Nunavut	79	80	81	84	3.0

Source: © *Statistics Canada*

Divorces by Province

	1997	1998	1999	2000	2001	Rate (%)
Canada	67 408	69 088	70 910	71 144	71 783	2.3
Newfoundland and Labrador	822	944	892	913	905	1.7
Prince Edward Island	243	279	291	272	272	2.0
Nova Scotia	1 983	1 933	1 954	2 054	2 049	2.2
New Brunswick	1 373	1 473	1 671	1 717	1 714	2.3
Quebec	17 478	16 916	17 144	17 054	17 090	2.3
Ontario	23 629	25 149	26 088	26 148	26 577	2.2
Manitoba	2 625	2 443	2 572	2 430	2 431	2.1
Saskatchewan	2 198	2 246	2 237	2 194	2 181	2.1
Alberta	7 185	7 668	7 931	8 176	8 307	2.7
British Columbia	9 692	9 827	9 935	10 017	10 088	2.5
Yukon	101	117	112	68	68	2.3
Northwest Territories	79	93	52	63	63	1.5
Nunavut			31	38	38	1.4

Source: © *Statistics Canada*

FOCUS ON...

Defining Marriage and Family

A family portrait taken by the census at the outset of the 21st century shows a continuation of many of the changes in families over the last 20 years. The proportion of "traditional" families—mom, dad and the kids—continues to decline, while families with no children at home are on the increase.

As of May 15, 2001, married or common-law couples with children aged 24 and under living at home represented only 44 percent of all families in Canada. In 1991, they accounted for 49 percent of all families, and in 1981 they represented more than one-half (55 percent).

At the same time, couples with no children living at home accounted for 41 percent of all families in 2001, up from 38 percent in 1991 and 34 percent in 1981.

Behind this shift in living arrangements are diverse factors, such as lower fertility rates, couples who are delaying having children or who choose to remain childless. In addition, life expectancy is increasing, with one result being that couples have more of their lives to spend together as "empty-nesters" after their children have grown up and left home.

Some couples with children consist of step families. According to the 2001 General Social Survey, Canada had 503,100 step families in 2001. This represents almost 12 percent of all Canadian couples with children in 2001, compared to 10 percent in 1995.

The 2001 census showed that an increasing proportion of couples choose to live common-law. The proportion of married-couple families was 70 percent in 2001, down from 83 percent in 1981. At the same time, the proportion of common-law families increased from 5.6 percent to 14 percent.

The census counted 5,901,420 married families and 1,158,410 common-law families in 2001. The 1,311,190 lone-parent families represented 16 percent of families in Canada. The trend toward common-law relationship continued to be strongest in Quebec, where 508,520 common-law families represented 30 percent of all couple families in that province.

A recent study based on Statistics Canada's General Social Survey showed that common-law unions have become more and more popular in Quebec, and that trend has started to take hold among younger people in other provinces.

Still, while younger Canadian men and women are more likely to start their conjugal life through a common-law relationship (about 40 percent of men and women aged 30 to 39), most will eventually marry (roughly 75 percent) if trends observed in 2001 continue.

■ Same-sex partnerships in the 2001 census

For the first time, the 2001 census provides data on same-sex partnerships.

Changes in the legal status of same-sex common-law couples was the primary reason for collecting data on same-sex partnerships in the 2001 census. The number of same-sex couples in the census reflects people who identified themselves as living in a same-sex common-law relationship.

The 2001 census did not ask about sexual orientation. Therefore, the data on same-sex partnerships should not be interpreted as an estimation of the number of gays and lesbians in Canada, some of whom may be living alone or with parents or friends.

A total of 34,200 same-sex common-law couples were counted in Canada in 2001, representing 0.5 percent of all couples.

There were 10,360 couples in Quebec and 5,790 couples in British Columbia who identified themselves as same-sex common-law couples, accounting for 0.6 percent of all couples living in each province. Ontario had the largest number of same-sex couples (12,505), representing 0.5 percent of all couples.

Although the actual numbers are small, same sex couples also represented 0.6 percent of all couples (married and common-law) in the Yukon.

Newfoundland and Labrador had the lowest proportion of same-sex couples (0.1 percent of all couples).

There were slightly more male same-sex common-law couples than female. The census counted about 19,000 male same-sex couples, 55 percent of the total.

More female same-sex couples have children living with them. About 15 percent of the 15,200 female same-sex couples are living with children, compared to only 3 percent of male same-sex couples. Less than 10 percent of male and female same-sex couples live with other household members (other than children). The majority of same-sex couples (88 percent of male couples and 77 percent of female couples) had no other people living in their household.

Male couples were more likely to live in census metropolitan areas. Eighty-five percent live in the larger urban areas of Canada, compared with 76 percent of female couples.

The metropolitan areas of Ottawa-Hull (now known as Ottawa-Gatineau) and Vancouver had the highest proportions of same-sex common-law couples (about 0.9 percent of all couples). Close to 4,000 same-sex couples were counted in Vancouver, and 2,170 couples identified themselves as same-sex couples in Ottawa-Hull.

Same-sex common-law couples represented 0.8 percent of all couples in the metropolitan areas of Montreal and Victoria.

Source: © *Census of Canada, Statistics Canada*

Marital Status of the Canadian Population, 2002[1]

	Total Population		Single		Married[2]		Widowed		Divorced	
	Male (000s)	Female (000s)	Male (%)	Female (%)	Male (%)	Female (%)	Male (%)	Female (%)	Male (%)	Female (%)
Total Population 15+12	575.4	13 029.8	33.0	25.6	59.5	57.9	2.3	9.7	5.2	6.8
15-19	1 076.0	1 019.5	99.2	96.8	0.8	3.2	...	...	...	...
20-24	1 094.1	1 050.6	88.0	73.3	13.8	26.4	...	...	0.1	0.3
25-29	1 083.4	1 055.5	58.5	42.4	40.5	65.9	...	0.1	1.0	1.6
30-34	1 147.8	1 126.9	37.7	25.1	59.5	70.9	0.1	0.3	2.7	3.7
35-39	1 309.0	1 286.1	26.0	17.4	68.9	75.7	0.1	0.5	5.0	6.4
40-44	1 345.8	1 341.2	19.3	13.7	73.5	76.3	0.3	1.0	6.9	9.0
45-49	1 226.1	1 232.6	13.9	10.6	76.7	75.8	0.5	1.9	8.9	11.6
50-54	1 064.8	1 073.0	10.1	8.0	79.2	75.1	0.9	3.6	9.8	13.2
55-59	862.9	881.6	7.4	6.4	81.1	73.2	1.6	6.9	9.9	13.5
60-64	654.1	684.9	6.2	5.5	81.8	69.7	2.9	13.1	9.1	11.7
65-69	547.3	591.7	5.8	5.2	80.9	69.0	5.5	22.5	7.8	9.4
70-74	473.3	552.1	5.9	5.4	78.6	52.6	9.1	34.7	6.9	7.2
75-79	345.5	477.1	5.6	5.7	74.8	40.0	15.1	49.2	4.5	5.0
80-84	208.9	346.5	5.1	6.3	68.2	27.5	23.4	62.8	3.3	3.4
85-89	96.2	189.9	4.9	7.5	56.7	14.2	36.1	78.4	2.2	1.9
90+	39.7	111.0	5.7	8.8	37.3	4.4	56.3	86.1	1.7	0.7

Source: © Statistics Canada   (...) Less than 0.1 percent. (1) As of July 1. (2) Includes common-law.

Composition of Canadian Families

(thousands)

	1971		1981		1991		2001	
	No. of Families	%	No. of Families	%	No. of Families	%	No. of Families	%
Total families[1]	5 071	100.0	6 325	100.0	7 356	100.0	8 371	100.0
Without children at home	1 545	30.5	2 013	31.8	2 580	35.1	3 059	36.5
With children at home	3 526	69.5	4 312	68.2	4 776	64.9	5 311	63.4
With one child	1 045	20.6	1 580	25.0	1 945	26.4	2 285	27.2
two children	1 077	21.2	1 648	26.1	1 927	26.2	2 087	24.9
three children[2]	677	13.4	730	11.5	691	9.4	939	11.2
four children	367	7.2	243	3.8	165	2.2	n.a.	n.a.
five children or more	360	7.1	112	1.8	48	0.5	n.a.	n.a.
Lone parent families	471	9.3	653	10.3	955	13.0	1 111	15.6
lone female parent	371	7.3	541	8.6	786	10.7	1 065	12.7
lone male parent	100	2.0	112	1.8	168	2.3	245	2.8

Source: © Census of Canada, Statistics Canada   (n.a.) Not available.

(1) Based on the census family definition: a husband and wife (without children or with children who never married) or a parent with one or more children who never married, living together in the same home. (2) The 2001 census grouped all families of 3 or more children into the "three children" category.

Size of Families in Canada

(thousands)

	1971		1981		1991		2001	
	No. of Families	Avg. Size	No. of Families	Avg. Size	No. of Families	Avg. Size	No. of Families	Avg. Size
Canada	5 071	3.7	6 325	3.3	7 356	3.1	8 371	3
Newfoundland and Labrador	108	4.4	135	3.8	151	3.3	154	2.9
Prince Edward Island	24	4.0	30	3.5	34	3.2	38	3
Nova Scotia	181	3.8	216	3.3	245	3.1	263	2.9
New Brunswick	140	4.0	177	3.4	198	3.1	215	2.9
Quebec	1 357	3.9	1 672	3.3	1 883	3.0	2 020	2.9
Ontario	1 882	3.6	2 279	3.2	2 727	3.1	3 191	3
Manitoba	236	3.6	262	3.2	286	3.1	303	3
Saskatchewan	216	3.7	246	3.3	258	3.2	266	3
Alberta	382	3.7	566	3.3	668	3.1	811	3
British Columbia	534	3.5	728	3.1	888	3.0	1 086	2.9
Yukon	11[1]	4.3[1]	6	3.3	7	3.1	8	3
Northwest Territories	11[1]	4.3[1]	9	4.0	13	3.7	10	3.3
Nunavut	—	—	—	—	—	—	6	3.8

Source: © Census of Canada, Statistics Canada   (1) Includes both the Yukon and Northwest Territories.

Lone-Parent Families by Province, 2001

Province	Lone-Parent Families	Average Family Size	Male Parent	Average Family Size	Female Parent	Average Family Size
Canada	1 369 157	2.5	224 220	2.4	1 144 937	2.6
Newfoundland & Labrador	23 297	2.4	3 260	2.4	20 037	2.4
Prince Edward Island. . . .	6 471	2.6	1 143	2.6	5 328	2.6
Nova Scotia	47 218	2.5	6 893	2.3	40 325	2.6
New Brunswick	33 316	2.4	5 357	2.3	27 959	2.5
Quebec	359 700	2.5	67 403	2.3	292 297	2.5
Ontario	530 652	2.6	77 552	2.4	453 100	2.6
Manitoba	48 068	2.6	7 364	2.5	38 722	2.7
Saskatchewan	41 044	2.7	6 211	2.6	34 833	2.7
Alberta.	111 605	2.6	20 625	2.4	90 980	2.6
British Columbia	169 768	2.6	28 412	2.4	141 356	2.6

Source: © *Statistics Canada*

Lone-Parent Families by Age, 2001

	Total Families	Size of Families		
		2 Members	3 Members	4 or more Members
Headed by Male Parent	**224 220**	**154 934**	**54 623**	**14 663**
Age 15-24.	1 924	1 665	188	71
25-34	20 552	14 613	4 782	1 157
35-44	71 229	43 758	21 583	5 888
45-54	76 627	51 139	20 100	5 388
55-64	25 557	19 528	4 873	1 156
65+.	28 331	24 231	3 097	1 003
Headed by Female Parent	**1 144 937**	**662 512**	**347 330**	**135 095**
Age 15-24.	70 005	51 068	15 959	2 978
25-34	237 167	115 823	82 756	38 588
35-44	374 674	164 575	144 887	65 212
45-54	255 151	155 244	77 379	22 528
55-64	77 506	62 410	12 459	2 637
65+.	130 434	113 392	13 890	3 152

Source: © *Statistics Canada*

Census Families by Size and Structure, 2001

Two-parent Families	Total Families	Families by Size				Average Family Size
		2 members	3 members	4 members	5 members	
Canada	6 988 831	2 875 942	1 468 415	1 776 542	659 058	3.1
Newfoundland & Labrador.	133 551	50 772	36 904	35 380	8 908	3.1
Prince Edward Island	32 120	12 330	7 196	7 685	3 485	3.2
Nova Scotia	212 610	93 696	47 917	50 292	16 463	3.0
New Brunswick	183 979	77 144	46 027	44 206	13 475	3.0
Quebec.	1 660 021	684 583	377 224	419 586	140 352	3.1
Ontario.	2 671 937	1 048 980	556 540	715 873	265 043	3.2
Manitoba	253 874	104 977	50 966	60 613	26 845	3.2
Saskatchewan	224 390	100 325	38 658	49 129	25 681	3.2
Alberta	714 030	297 172	134 928	178 663	76 303	3.2
British Columbia	902 319	405 963	172 055	215 115	82 503	3.1

Source: © *Statistics Canada*

Average Household Expenditure, including Budget Share

(dollars)

	1999		2000		2001	
	Average expenditure ($ current[1])	Share of budget (%)	Average expenditure ($ current[1])	Share of budget (%)	Average expenditure ($ current[1])	Share of budget (%)
Total expenditure	53 470		55 834		57 742	100.0
Personal taxes	11 560	21.6	12 012	21.5	12 218	21.2
Shelter	10 240	19.2	10 498	18.8	10 984	19.0
Transportation	6 880	12.9	7 576	13.6	7 596	13.2
Food.	6 100	11.4	6 217	11.1	6 438	11.1
Recreation	2 960	5.5	3 165	5.7	3 453	6.0
Personal insurance payments and pension contributions	2 840	5.3	3 135	5.6	3 125	5.4
Household operation	2 410	4.5	2 516	4.5	2 619	4.5
Clothing	2 330	4.4	2 351	4.2	2 398	4.2
Household furnishings and equipment	1 480	2.8	1 557	2.8	1 655	2.9
Health care.	1 260	2.4	1 357	2.4	1 420	2.5
Gifts of money and contributions .	1 360	2.5	1 302	2.3	1 259	2.2
Tobacco products and alcoholic beverages	1 180	2.2	1 218	2.2	1 313	2.3
Miscellaneous expenditures	860	1.6	827	1.5	865	1.5
Education.	760	1.4	826	1.5	898	1.6
Personal care	710	1.3	740	1.3	960	1.7
Reading materials and other printed matter	270	0.5	275	0.5	276	0.5
Games of chance expense (net)' . .	270	0.5	261	0.5	267	0.5

Source: © *Statistics Canada*

(1) Not adjusted for inflation.

Kids count when it comes to recreational spending

*O*ver the past two decades, spending on recreation by households with children grew faster than that of others. Two-parent households saw their recreational spending increase by 50 percent and lone-parent households by 57 percent. Couples without children recorded a 36 percent growth in expenditures and one-person households a 17 percent rise.

Purchases of cable television represented the largest single increase in recreational spending for all types of households. The home recreation equipment category also recorded large increases, mainly because this category includes computer equipment and supplies. Sixty-seven percent of two-parent and 44 percent of lone-parent households spent money on computers in 1999, compared with 34 percent of couples only and 19 percent of one-person households. Many parents now feel that owning a computer is no longer a luxury but a necessity to help their children succeed academically.

Source: *Statistics Canada, Canadian Social Trends, 11-008 (Spring 2002)*

Average Household Expenditure by Province

(dollars)

Ontario and Alberta remained the most expensive provinces when it came to maintaining a household in 2001, with householders in Ontario, Alberta, Manitoba and Saskatchewan seeing significant increases in their spending as compared to the previous year. Households in Newfoundland and Labrador once again had the lowest average household spending.

	1998 ($ current[1])	1999 ($ current[1])	2000 ($ current[1])	2001 ($ current[1])
Newfoundland and Labrador	$ 41 080	$ 42 510	$ 43 240	$ 46 646
Prince Edward Island	42 560	45 400	45 080	47 015
Nova Scotia	43 280	45 850	48 620	49 054
New Brunswick	41 350	44 730	47 090	47 623
Quebec	44 090	46 870	48 320	50 170
Ontario.	56 700	58 780	62 740	64 375
Manitoba	46 630	49 410	50 360	51 845
Saskatchewan	45 000	46 900	46 970	48 516
Alberta	56 560	59 210	62 090	65 767
British Columbia	53 920	54 970	55 670	57 352

Source: © *Statistics Canada*

(1) Not adjusted for inflation.

Average Household Expenditure by Metropolitan Area, by Province

(dollars)

Given the statistics above on household spending by province, it is no surprise that households in CMAs in Ontario and Alberta once again captured the top four spots as most expensive cities to live in in 2001.

2000 Rank[1]	2001 Rank		1999 ($ current[2])	2000 ($ current[2])	2001 ($ current[2])
1	3	Toronto, Ont.	$ 65 810	$ 76 619	70 150
2	1	Ottawa, Ont.	61 170	68 800	83 071
3	2	Calgary, Alta	65 010	67 908	73 782
4	4	Edmonton, Alta	58 380	66 402	66 021
5	8	Regina, Sask.	56 200	62 251	56 727
6	5	Vancouver, B.C.	60 600	61 820	64 928
7	7	Halifax, N.S.	52 420	56 997	57 682
8	9	Saskatoon, Sask.	49 540	53 696	56 300
9	14	Saint John, N.B.	47 410	53 476	49 568
10	11	Montreal, Que.	2 020	53 350	54 377
11	10	Winnipeg, Man.	53 060	52 864	55 987
12	13	Victoria, B.C.	52 440	52 602	50 806
13	6	St. John's, Nfld and Lab.	51 940	51 361	60 063
14	15	Charlottetown-Summerside, P.E.I.	43 030	44 234	45 600
15	12	Québec, Que.	48 200	42 260	52 804

Source: © *Statistics Canada*

(1) Yellowknife (#1 in 1999) and Whitehorse (#4 in 1999) not included in 2000 data collection. (2) Not adjusted for inflation.

Body Mass Index of the Canadian Population, % by Age and Sex

Body mass index (BMI) is a measure of weight relative to height. It is a good indicator of possible health concerns that can be obtained without special equipment and can be taken from fairly accessible measures. The table below shows the values for normal, overweight and obesity. Find your height in inches in the left column; find your body weight in pounds along that row. The weight value should fall into one of three categories (underweight is not shown, nor is highly obese). The number at the top of the column where your weight is listed gives a BMI rating.

Why does this matter? Overweight and obesity are linked to the development of a variety of serious health problems, including heart disease, some forms of cancer and diabetes. A BMI in the normal range will give you a better chance of avoiding those (and other) ailments, and give you a much better chance of fighting them successfully if they develop.

How do Canadians rate? The next page shows a comparison of men and women by age, over an 8-year period: our weight is slowly creeping up. (Internationally, the proportion of Canadians who are definitely overweight is higher than that in Australia or Scotland.)

Body Mass Index Table

	Normal						Overweight					Obese									
BMI	19	20	21	22	23	24	25	26	27	28	29	30	31	32	33	34	35	36	37	38	39
Height (inches)												Body Weight (pounds)									
58	91	96	100	105	110	115	119	124	129	134	138	143	148	153	158	162	167	172	177	181	186
59	94	99	104	109	114	119	124	128	133	138	143	148	153	158	163	168	173	178	183	188	193
60	97	102	107	112	118	123	128	133	138	143	148	153	158	163	168	174	179	184	189	194	199
61	100	106	111	116	122	127	132	137	143	148	153	158	164	169	174	180	185	190	195	201	206
62	104	109	115	120	126	131	136	142	147	153	158	164	169	175	180	186	191	196	202	207	213
63	107	113	118	124	130	135	141	146	152	158	163	169	175	180	186	191	197	203	208	214	220
64	110	116	122	128	134	140	145	151	157	163	169	174	180	186	192	197	204	209	215	221	227
65	114	120	126	132	138	144	150	156	162	168	174	180	186	192	198	204	210	216	222	228	234
66	118	124	130	136	142	148	155	161	167	173	179	186	192	198	204	210	216	223	229	235	241
67	121	127	134	140	146	153	159	166	172	178	185	191	198	204	211	217	223	230	236	242	249
68	125	131	138	144	151	158	164	171	177	184	190	197	203	210	216	223	230	236	243	249	256
69	128	135	142	149	155	162	169	176	182	189	196	203	209	216	223	230	236	243	250	257	263
70	132	139	146	153	160	167	174	181	188	195	202	209	216	222	229	236	243	250	257	264	271
71	136	143	150	157	165	172	179	186	193	200	208	215	222	229	236	243	250	257	265	272	279
72	140	147	154	162	169	177	184	191	199	206	213	221	228	235	242	250	258	265	272	279	287
73	144	151	159	166	174	182	189	197	204	212	219	227	235	242	250	257	265	272	280	288	295
74	148	155	163	171	179	186	194	202	210	218	225	233	241	249	256	264	272	280	287	295	303
75	152	160	168	176	184	192	200	208	216	224	232	240	248	256	264	272	279	287	295	303	311
76	156	164	172	180	189	197	205	213	221	230	238	246	254	263	271	279	287	295	304	312	320

Source: *National Heart, Lung and Blood Institute*

Body Mass Index of the Canadian Population, % by Age and Sex[1]

	% Underweight — BMI under 20				% Acceptable weight — BMI 20-24.9			
	1994/95	1996/97	1998/99	2000/01[2]	1994/95	1996/97	1998/99	2000/01[2]
■ 20-64 years								
Total	8.5	8.0	7.2	8.1	42.2	42.2	41.6	42.9
Men	3.6	2.8	3.1	3.9	38.09	37.9	35.5	39.9
Women	13.5	13.4	11.4	12.3	46.6	46.7	47.7	45.9
■ 20-24 years								
Total	16.8	14.9	14.0	17.5	52.1	54.8	56.8	53.8
Men	8.4	5.4	5.7	10.2	54.3	55.8	56.0	56.2
Women	25.0	25.1	22.8	25.2	50.0	53.8	57.7	51.3
■ 25-34 years								
Total	11.0	10.7	9.4	10.3	46.9	45.1	45.3	45.9
Men	4.4	3.6	3.6	4.7	44.2	42.4	40.7	43.3
Women	17.9	18.2	15.4	16.4	49.8	47.9	50.0	48.8
■ 35-44 years								
Total	7.9	7.4	6.4	7.8	43.6	43.5	42.4	43.2
Men	2.9	2.3	1.8	2.9	36.6	36.7	33.4	38.5
Women	13.2	12.6	11.1	12.6	50.8	50.5	51.7	47.9
■ 45-54 years								
Total	5.2	5.0	5.3	4.9	35.5	36.2	35.0	38.8
Men	2.1	1.5	3.0	2.3	20.3	30.0	28.5	34.3
Women	8.7	8.6	7.5	7.4	41.1	42.6	41.3	43.1
■ 55-64 years								
Total	3.9	4.3	3.8	3.7	38.7	34.7	33.4	36.3
Men	2.6	2.2	3.1	2.4	28.4	31.0	27.4	33.6
Women	5.0	6.2	4.4	5.0	38.4	38.1	39.5	39.0

	% With some excess weight — BMI 25-27				% Overweight — BMI higher than 27			
	1994/95	1996/97	1998/99	2000/01[2]	1994/95	1996/97	1998/99	2000/01[2]
■ 20-64 years								
Total	18.7	18.6	19.0	15.6	29.4	28.1	31.2	31.9
Men	24.0	23.9	24.2	19.5	33.8	34.0	36.6	36.1
Women	13.3	13.1	13.6	11.6	24.9	22.2	25.7	27.5
■ 20-24 years								
Total	13.4	13.3	13.9	10.3	16.7	15.0	14.3	17.4
Men	18.8	17.8	19.2	13.5	18.0	20.0	18.3	19.5
Women	8.1	8.5	8.3	6.8	15.5	9.7	10.0	15.3
■ 25-34 years								
Total	16.9	17.9	16.8	14.6	24.2	23.6	27.7	27.7
Men	22.5	23.7	22.4	19.1	28.5	29.0	33.0	32.3
Women	11.1	11.8	11.1	9.7	19.9	17.9	22.3	22.8
■ 35-44 years								
Total	19.1	18.1	19.6	15.6	28.0	27.7	30.9	31.8
Men	26.4	24.6	26.3	20.2	33.6	35.3	38.0	37.7
Women	11.6	11.4	12.7	10.9	22.1	19.9	23.5	25.9
■ 45-54 years								
Total	19.7	20.9	20.5	17.1	38.0	34.5	37.7	37.4
Men	23.1	25.2	24.5	20.9	43.8	41.2	43.4	41.9
Women	16.0	16.0	16.5	13.4	31.9	27.6	32.2	33.1
■ 55-64 years								
Total	23.3	21.0	22.2	18.4	38.1	36.7	39.3	39.8
Men	27.1	25.7	25.9	20.9	40.9	39.4	42.6	42.6
Women	19.9	16.7	18.4	16.0	35.6	34.2	36.0	37.0

Source: © *Statistics Canada*   (1) Excluding pregnant women. (2) Only 2000-01 data includes territories.

Dietary Practices by Age and Sex,[1] 2000–01

	Total Number 2000-01	Consume fruits and vegetables less than 5 times per day		Consume fruits and vegetables 5 to 10 times per day		Consume fruits and vegetables more than 10 times per day		Fruit and vegetable consumption not stated	
		Number	%	**Number**	**%**	Number	%	Number	%
Total, 12 years and over	25 801 719	15 933 145	61.8	**8 630 186**	**33.4**	957 949	3.7	280 440	1.1
MALES	12 705 415	8 536 595	67.2	**3 595 805**	**28.3**	409 237	3.2	163 778	1.3
FEMALES	13 096 304	7 396 550	56.5	**5 034 381**	**38.4**	548 712	4.2	116 662	0.9
12-19 years	3 243 281	1 926 414	59.4	**1 099 754**	**33.9**	174 935	5.4	42 179	1.3
MALES	1 662 580	1 025 623	61.7	**519 292**	**31.2**	93 531	5.6	24 135	1.5
FEMALES	1 580 701	900 791	57.0	**580 462**	**36.7**	81 404	5.1	18 044	1.1
20-24 years	2 130 833	1 368 720	64.2	**635 508**	**29.8**	106 095	5.0	20 510	1.0
MALES	1 081 580	740 027	68.4	**278 533**	**25.8**	49 475	4.6	13 545E	1.3
FEMALES	1 049 253	628 692	59.9	**356 975**	**34.0**	56 620	5.4	6 965E	0.7
25-34 years	4 172 944	2 708 166	64.9	**1 283 725**	**30.8**	145 833	3.5	35 221	0.8
MALES	2 109 632	1 497 030	71.0	**537 297**	**25.5**	55 425	2.6	19 881	0.9
FEMALES	2 063 311	1 211 135	58.7	**746 428**	**36.2**	90 408	4.4	15 340E	0.7
35-44 years	5 319 716	3 489 804	65.6	**1 624 881**	**30.5**	163 684	3.1	41 347	0.8
MALES	2 649 765	1 897 218	71.6	**659 313**	**24.9**	68 657	2.6	24 577	0.9
FEMALES	2 669 951	1 592 586	59.6	**965 568**	**36.2**	95 027	3.6	16 770	0.6
45-54 years	4 449 730	2 804 796	63.0	**1 446 536**	**32.5**	151 367	3.4	47 031	1.1
MALES	2 197 419	1 524 286	69.4	**590 072**	**26.9**	55 642	2.5	27 420	1.2
FEMALES	2 252 312	1 280 510	56.9	**856 464**	**38.0**	95 726	4.3	19 611	0.9
55-64 years	2 837 424	1 672 319	58.9	**1 039 951**	**36.7**	92 599	3.3	32 555	1.1
MALES	1 410 073	925 274	65.6	**420 979**	**29.9**	42 912	3.0	20 907	1.5
FEMALES	1 427 352	747 044	52.3	**618 972**	**43.4**	49 687	3.5	11 648	0.8
65-74 years	2 156 504	1 190 806	55.2	**859 013**	**39.8**	74 753	3.5	31 932	1.5
MALES	1 004 986	605 197	60.2	**350 142**	**34.8**	28 612	2.8	21 035	2.1
FEMALES	1 151 518	585 609	50.9	**508 871**	**44.2**	46 140	4.0	10 897	0.9
75 years and over	1 491 287	772 121	51.8	**640 818**	**43.0**	48 682	3.3	29 666	2.0
MALES	589 380	321 940	54.6	**240 178**	**40.8**	14 983E	2.5E	12 280	2.1
FEMALES	901 906	450 181	49.9	**400 640**	**44.4**	33 699	3.7	17 386	1.9

Source: © *Statistics Canada, Canadian Community Health Survey, 2000/01*

(1) Population aged 12 and over by the average number of times per day that they consume fruits and vegetables.

Canadians with Diabetes[1] by Age Group and Sex, 2000–01

Statistics Canada has been tracking the number of Canadians diagnosed by a health professional as having diabetes since 1994. During that period, an average of 3 percent of Canadians aged 12 or older had developed diabetes. The figure varies with age and gender: in 1998-9, 2 percent of those 35 to 44 had been diagnosed with diabetes, while 12 percent of seniors 75 and over had the disease. Between men and women, 2 percent of men aged 35 to 44 had diabetes, compared to only 1 percent of women, and 16 percent of men over 75 had diabetes, compared to 10 percent of women.

There were no big provincial differences among the population with diabetes. The prevalence of diabetes for all provinces ranged between 3 and 5 percent.

	Total population	With diabetes		Without diabetes	
		Number	%	Number	%
Total, 12 years and over	25 801 719	1 063 698	4.1	24 719 208	95.8
MALES	12 705 415	556 838	4.4	12 138 236	95.5
FEMALES	13 096 304	506 860	3.9	12 580 972	96.1
12-14 years	1 154 646	...	...	1 151 047	99.7
MALES	601 795	...	...	599 897	99.7
FEMALES	552 851	...	...	551 150	99.7
15-19 years	2 088 635	7 858	0.4	2 080 212	99.6
MALES	1 060 785	3 631	0.3	1 057 074	99.7
FEMALES	1 027 850	4 227	0.4	1 023 138	99.5
20-24 years	2 130 833	6 819	0.3	2 122 261	99.6
MALES	1 081 580	3 628	0.3	1 076 546	99.5
FEMALES	1 049 253	3 191	0.3	1 045 715	99.7
25-34 years	4 172 944	42 069	1.0	4 130 776	99.0
MALES	2 109 632	18 367	0.9	2 091 266	99.1
FEMALES	2 063 311	23 702	1.1	2 039 510	98.8
35-44 years	5 319 716	103 807	2.0	5 212 277	98.0
MALES	2 649 765	53 039	2.0	2 594 443	97.9
FEMALES	2 669 951	50 768	1.9	2 617 834	98.0
45-54 years	4 449 730	190 664	4.3	4 257 175	95.7
MALES	2 197 419	100 131	4.6	2 096 418	95.4
FEMALES	2 252 312	90 533	4.0	2 160 757	95.9
55-64 years	2 837 424	246 455	8.7	2 585 162	91.1
MALES	1 410 073	141 650	10.0	1 264 606	89.7
FEMALES	1 427 352	104 805	7.3	1 320 556	92.5
65-74 years	2 156 504	277 333	12.9	1 877 699	87.1
MALES	1 004 986	147 494	14.7	857 056	85.3
FEMALES	1 151 518	129 839	11.3	1 020 643	88.6
75 years and over	1 491 287	185 818	12.5	1 302 598	87.3
MALES	589 380	87 336	14.8	500 930	85.0
FEMALES	901 906	98 483	10.9	801 668	88.9

Source: © *Statistics Canada*

(1) Population aged 12 and over who report that they have been diagnosed by a health professional as having diabetes.

Canadians with Low Incomes,[1] 1998

Statistics Canada defines the "low-income cut off" as spending 20 percent more of income on food, shelter and clothing than the average Canadian (see Average Household Expenditure on pages 71 and 72). In general, families and individuals with low incomes spend more than 55 percent of their income on those three items. While these are not official poverty lines and have no status as such, they do indicate the number of Canadians living in less than affluent circumstances.

Low incomes are not spread evenly across the country: in PEI, 12.7 percent of the popula-tion is below the low-income cut-off; the number is 22.1 percent in Quebec. The rest of the provinces fall in between. Children and seniors are more likely to live in low-income situations; mother-led, lone-parent families are much more likely to fall below the low-income cut-offs than almost any other group. The level of educational attainment (not shown here) also plays a role in determining income. Families headed by people who did not graduate from high school are twice as likely to fall below the low-income cut-offs.

	Canada	N&L	PEI	NS	NB	Que	Ont	Man	Sask	Alta	BC
POPULATION WITH LOW INCOMES (000s)	5 055.9	108.7	17.2	168.3	117.3	1 620.1	1 603.7	218.3	160.0	458.1	584.2
As a % of total population	16.9	20.0	12.7	18.2	15.8	22.1	14.0	20.0	16.3	15.9	15.0
% of Population with Low Income by age											
Under 18	19.2	25.3	n.a.	19.3	18.1	24.0	17.7	23.6	18.8	17.3	14.9
18-64	15.5	18.7	n.a.	18.1	15.0	20.0	12.6	17.4	14.8	15.2	14.3
65 and over	19.7	n.a	n.a.	17.0	15.4	29.9	14.4	25.4	18.3	16.8	18.7
% of Population with Low Income by sex											
Men	15.3	18.7	n.a.	14.5	14.2	20.1	12.7	17.3	13.9	15.1	14.0
Women	18.4	21.3	n.a.	21.8	17.2	24.1	15.3	22.6	18.7	16.7	15.9
% of Population with Low Income											
Aboriginal peoples	28.9	n.a.	n.a.	n.a.	n.a.	36.3	22.1	41.6	27.4	25.7	27.8
Immigrants	18.6	n.a.	n.a.	n.a.	n.a.	44.0	13.3	19.7	n.a.	17.6	16.4
People in a visible minority	24.3	n.a.	n.a.	n.a.	n.a.	56.1	16.7	n.a.	n.a.	27.0	18.1
FAMILIES WITH LOW INCOME											
% of two-parent families with children	10.7	16.2	n.a.	7.6	9.5	13.8	9.3	13.2	10.8	11.3	8.2
% lone-parent families, male head	23.1	n.a.	n.a.	n.a.	n.a.	n.a.	n.a.	36.5	n.a.	n.a.	n.a.
% lone-parent families, female head	52.9	68.6	n.a.	74.3	59.8	56.6	50.5	66.6	40.1	46.5	49.4
% of families with head aged 65 and over	9.7	n.a.	n.a.	n.a.	n.a.	15.6	6.9	14.4	6.3	n.a.	9.5
UNATTACHED INDIVIDUALS WITH LOW INCOME											
Men under 65	33.0	44.9	35.7	34.3	41.2	39.3	30.1	37.6	32.9	32.6	25.8
Women under 65	43.6	66.5	45.9	58.5	44.7	48.6	36.3	53.1	42.6	45.3	41.4
Men over 65	35.1	n.a.	n.a.	n.a.	n.a.	44.3	32.3	39.5	30.1	28.3	36.5
Women over 65	47.9	66.5	38.0	50.4	49.4	63.0	38.4	51.6	41.0	46.2	42.8

Source: © *Statistics Canada*
(1) Statistics Canada defines those with Low Income as those who usually spend more than 55% of their income on food, shelter and clothing. Base year is 1992.

EDUCATION

Canadian Population[1] by Highest Level of Schooling, 2001

(percentage)

	Elementary– Secondary Schooling Only	Post secondary, Non-university Education	University Without a Degree	University With a Degree
Canada	**41.8**	**34.3**	**11.3**	**19.6**
Newfoundland & Labrador	48.7	34.4	10.9	12.4
Prince Edward Island	45.2	34.8	12.3	15.1
Nova Scotia	41.5	35.3	13.3	18.0
New Brunswick	49.1	31.7	11.7	14.4
Quebec	46.9	32.8	6.8	18.6
Ontario	39.9	33.9	12.0	21.4
Manitoba	45.8	31.7	14.0	16.7
Saskatchewan	46.0	32.5	15.2	15.4
Alberta	37.7	38.3	12.5	18.8
British Columbia	36.6	36.7	15.0	20.9
Yukon Territory	29.0	45.7	2.4	26.7
Northwest Territories	38.3	40.6	10.1	17.0
Nunavut	48.5	39.7	4.8	10.0

Source: © *Census of Canada, Statistics Canada*   (1) Over the age of 15; over the age of 20 for 2001 census figures.

Labour Force[1] by Highest Level of Schooling

	2001			2002		
	Population[2] (000s)	% of Pop. by educational attainment	Participation rate[3]	Population[2] (000s)	% of Pop. by educational attainment	Participation rate[3]
Total, all education levels	24 617.8	100	66.0	24 945.1	100	66.9
0–8 years	2413.2	9.8	24.2	2361.4	9.5	25.1
Some high school	4291.0	17.4	51.4	4228.4	17.0	52.3
High school diploma	4798.6	19.5	70.4	4862.6	19.5	71.7
Some post-secondary	2252.0	9.1	68.7	2278.1	9.1	69.3
Post-secondary certificate or diploma	6964.7	28.3	77.0	7150.8	28.7	77.2
University degree	3898.3	15.8	81.2	4063.8	16.3	81.2
Bachelor's degree	2661.8	10.8	81.1	2794.4	11.2	81.4
Above bachelor's degree	1236.5	5.0	81.4	1269.4	5.1	80.7

Source: © *Statistics Canada*   (1) Employed workers and those who are unemployed but actively seeking work. (2) Age 15 years and over. (3) Participation rate is the percent of that population segment that has been able to find work.

Elementary-Secondary Enrolment[1] by Province

(thousands)

	Canada	N&L	PEI	NS	NB	Que	Ont	Man	Sask	Alta	BC	YT	NWT	NVT
1999-2000	4 862.8	88.9	24.4	150.5	120.0	1 027.1	1 862.8	205.4	193.6	530.9	636.2	5.8	9.4	7.7
2000-01	4 867.3	85.7	24.4	149.7	118.3	1 024.4	1 858.9	206.4	193.3	536.1	646.2	6.0	9.6	7.9
2001-02	4 864.9	82.7	24.3	149.1	116.7	1 022.2	1 848.8	207.4	192.9	541.6	655.1	6.0	9.8	7.9

Source: © *Statistics Canada*   (1) Estimates, including public, private, federal and overseas schools.

University Graduates, by Field of Study, by Sex

	1994	1995	1996	1997	1998
Canada	178 074	178 066	178 116	173 937	172 076
MALE	76 470	76 022	75 106	73 041	71 949
FEMALE	101 604	102 044	103 010	100 896	100 127
Social sciences	69 583	68 685	67 862	66 665	67 019
MALE	30 700	29 741	29 029	28 421	27 993
FEMALE	38 883	38 944	38 833	38 244	39 026
Education	30 369	30 643	29 792	27 807	25 956
MALE	9 093	9 400	8 693	8 036	7 565
FEMALE	21 276	21 243	21 099	19 771	18 391
Humanities	23 071	22 511	22 357	21 373	20 816
MALE	8 427	8 428	8 277	8 034	7 589
FEMALE	14 644	14 083	14 080	13 339	13 227
Health professions & occupations	12 183	12 473	12 895	13 073	12 658
MALE	3 475	3 461	3 517	3 460	3 514
FEMALE	8 708	9 012	9 378	9 613	9 144
Engineering & applied sciences	12 597	12 863	13 068	12 768	12 830
MALE	10 285	10 284	10 446	10 125	10 121
FEMALE	2 312	2 579	2 622	2 643	2 709
Agriculture & biological sciences	10 087	10 501	11 400	11 775	12 209
MALE	4 309	4 399	4 756	4 780	4 779
FEMALE	5 778	6 102	6 644	6 995	7 430
Mathematics & physical sciences	9 551	9 879	9 786	9 738	9 992
MALE	6 697	6 941	6 726	6 749	6 876
FEMALE	2 854	2 938	3 060	2 989	3 116
Fine and applied arts	5 308	5 240	5 201	5 206	5 256
MALE	1 773	1 740	1 780	1 706	1 735
FEMALE	3 535	3 500	3 421	3 500	3 521
Arts and sciences	5 325	5 271	5 755	5 532	5 340
MALE	1 711	1 628	1 882	1 730	1 777
FEMALE	3 614	3 643	3 873	3 802	3 563

Source: © *Statistics Canada*   (1) Includes bachelor's and first professional degrees, undergraduate diplomas and certificates, other undergraduate qualifications, master's degrees, doctoral degrees, and graduate diplomas and certificates.

Community College[1] Graduates, by Field of Study, by Sex

	1993-1994	1994-1995	1995-1996	1996-1997	1997-1998
Canada	69 813	72 548	79 544	85 909	91 359
MALE	28 956	30 288	33 836	36 309	38 450
FEMALE	40 857	42 260	45 708	49 600	52 909
Business and commerce	19 227	20 979	22 054	23 327	24 477
MALE	5 921	6 597	7 283	7 726	8 149
FEMALE	13 306	14 382	14 771	15 601	16 328
Engineering and applied sciences	14 685	14 722	16 244	18 279	20 093
MALE	12 158	12 150	13 510	14 976	16 158
FEMALE	2 527	2 572	2 734	3 303	3 935
Social sciences and services	13 526	14 304	15 603	16 779	17 718
MALE	3 741	3 947	4 085	4 119	4 230
FEMALE	9 785	10 357	11 518	12 660	13 488
Health sciences	11 500	11 020	11 628	11 618	11 580
MALE	2 119	2 043	2 276	2 165	1 987
FEMALE	9 381	8 977	9 352	9 453	9 593
Arts	5 796	5 968	6 376	7 192	7 474
MALE	2 421	2 518	2 766	2 965	3 109
FEMALE	3 375	3 450	3 610	4 227	4 365
Natural sciences & primary industries	3 137	3 708	4 227	4 819	5 008
MALE	1 962	2 367	2 572	2 880	2 890
FEMALE	1 175	1 341	1 655	1 939	2 118
Humanities	1 188	1 167	1 176	1 235	1 399
MALE	317	353	386	375	382
FEMALE	871	814	790	860	1 017
Arts and sciences	402	544	1 760	2 531	3 350
MALE	151	242	765	1 053	1 384
FEMALE	251	302	995	1 478	1 966
Not reported	352	136	476	129	260
MALE	166	71	193	50	161
FEMALE	186	65	283	79	99

Source: © *Statistics Canada*

(1) Includes related institutions such as hospital schools, agricultural colleges, arts schools and other specialized colleges.

Expenditures on Education, by Education Level, 1999–2000

($ millions)

	Canada	N&L	PEI	Nova Scotia	New Brunswick	Quebec	Ontario
All expenditures[1]	67 696.7	1 116.4	267.8	1 963.6	1 602.5	15 953.7	25 429.8
LEVEL							
Elementary and secondary	39 309.4	569.3	142.3	1 079.6	885.9	8 530.3	15 773.0
Community college	5 467.9	34.2	21.0	102.7	63.9	2 020.0	1 923.2
University	14 549.0	271.7	57.8	605.8	340.7	3 516.8	5 364.2
Vocational training	8 370.4	241.2	46.7	175.4	312.0	1 886.6	2 369.4
DIRECT SOURCE OF FUNDS							
Federal government[2]	5 567.6	149.1	31.3	172.4	136.9	1 264.5	1 536.5
Provincial governments	39 502.8	807.0	187.7	1 244.1	1 256.4	11 017.9	13 634.1
Municipal governments[3]	10 800.0	0.1	0.0	147.6	0.0	1 023.8	5 825.3
Fees and other sources	11 826.3	160.2	48.8	399.5	209.2	2 647.6	4 433.9

	Manitoba	Saskatchewan	Alberta	British Columbia	Yukon	Northwest Territories	Nunavut
All expenditures[1]	2 694.1	2 419.2	6 918.5	8 702.3	122.0	167.1	175.9
LEVEL							
Elementary & secondary	1 751.2	1 383.4	3 891.4	4 994.4	80.4	85.4	118.2
Community college	104.9	61.2	550.1	521.5	7.6	33.8	20.5
University	540.3	591.7	1 379.8	1 790.9	3.7	4.9	0.8
Vocational training	297.7	382.8	1 097.1	1 395.4	30.4	43.1	36.3
DIRECT SOURCE OF FUNDS							
Federal government[2]	405.4	426.3	573.0	663.7	14.5	15.2	15.9
Provincial governments	1 309.3	1 109.0	3 515.1	5 034.4	100.7	139.2	148.1
Municipal governments[3]	602.1	597.3	1 301.9	1 291.4	0.4	0.9	9.1
Fees and other sources	377.3	286.6	1 528.4	1 712.7	6.5	11.8	2.7

Source: © Statistics Canada

((1) Includes operating, capital, student aid and all departmental expenditures. (2) In addition to the direct funding reported here, the federal government also provides indirect support in respect of post secondary education to provinces and territories under the Federal-Provincial Fiscal Arrangements and Federal Post-secondary Education and Health Contributions Act, 1977 and under the Official Languages in Education Program. (3) Includes local school taxation.

Education Spending: Where the Money Goes

*T*otal school board expenditures and expenditures per student in public elementary-secondary education rose 2.1 percent in 1999 (in current dollars). This was the largest annual increase in school board expenditures and expenditures per student since 1992. (In comparison, the Consumer Price Index (CPI) rose only 1.8 percent in 1999.) School boards spent $32.3 billion in 1999, representing 3.3 percent of the gross domestic product (GDP). This continued a downward trend that started after 1992, when spending by school boards peaked at 4.3 percent of GDP.

From 1994 to 1997, expenditures per full-time equivalent student remained relatively stable at about $6,850 in current dollars. In 1998, they started to rise, reaching over $7,100 in 1999. Expenditures per student increased in 1999 in every jurisdiction except Ontario, British Columbia and the Northwest Territories. For Canada as a whole, average expenditures per student increased about 4 percent in the last five years, compared with an increase of 6 percent in the CPI for the same period. (The expenditures per pupil include all public elementary and secondary education-related expenditures.)

Expenditures by school boards account for about 80 percent of total elementary and secondary education spending. (And teachers' salaries make up over 60 percent of those expenditures.) Other categories of elementary and secondary expenditures include private schools, federal schools, special education schools and departmental expenditures by the ministries of education. About 95 percent of school board revenues come from provincial or territorial governments and local taxation.

School board expenditures include both operating and capital spending. Operating expenditures are salaries, benefits, supplies and services, fees and contractual services, and other operating costs. These expenses can be further broken down by function (instruction, administration, transportation, school facilities and other categories).

Source: The Daily, July 23, 2002 © Statistics Canada

RELIGION

Religious Groups in Canada, 1999

Religious Group	Includes	1999 GSS Population % Distribution
Catholic	Roman Catholic, Ukrainian Catholic, Polish Catholic, Other Catholic	40.9
Protestant	United Church, Presbyterian, Lutheran, Anglican, Baptist, Jehovah's Witnesses, Pentecostal, Mormons, Other Protestant	30.2
Eastern Orthodox	Greek Orthodox, Ukrainian Orthodox, Russian Orthodox, Other Orthodox	1.3
Other Eastern Religions	Islam, Buddhist, Hindu, Sikh, Bahai, Etc.	3.5
Jewish		.8
Other	Atheist, Free Thinker, Humanist, New Age, Scientology, New Thought, Native Indian or Inuit, Etc.	.4
No Religion		16.1
Don't Know/Not Stated		6.8

Source: © *Census of Canada, General Social Survey, Statistics Canada*

FOCUS ON ...

Religious Growth and Decline

■ Canada still predominantly Roman Catholic and Protestant

Seven out of every ten Canadians identify themselves as either Roman Catholic or Protestant, according to new data from the 2001 census.

The census showed a continuation of a long-term downward trend in the population who report Protestant denominations. The number of Roman Catholics increased slightly during the 1990s, but their share of the total population fell marginally.

At the same time, the number of Canadians who reported religions such as Islam, Hinduism, Sikhism and Buddhism has increased substantially.

Much of the shift in the nation's religious make-up during the past several decades is the result of the changing sources of immigrants, which has contributed to a more diverse religious profile. As well, many major Protestant denominations that were dominant in the country 70 years ago, such as Anglican and United Church, are declining in numbers, in part because their members are aging and fewer young people are identifying with these denominations.

In 2001, Roman Catholics were still the largest religious group, drawing the faith of just under 12.8 million people, or 43 percent of the population, down from 45 percent in 1991. The proportion of Protestants, the second largest group, declined from 35 percent of the population to 29 percent, or about 8.7 million people.

Combined, the two groups represented 72 percent of the total population in 2001, compared with 80 percent a decade earlier.

The 2001 census also recorded an increase in those reporting simply that they were "Christian," without specifying a Catholic, Protestant or Christian Orthodox faith. This group more than doubled (+121 percent) during the decade to 780,400, representing 2.6 percent of the population in 2001. This was one of the largest percentage increases among all major religious groups.

In addition, far more Canadians reported in the 2001 census that they had no religion. This group accounted for 16 percent of the population in 2001, compared with 12 percent a decade earlier.

Respondents in the 2001 census were instructed to report a specific denomination or group, even if they were not practising members of their group. Consequently, these data indicate only religious affiliation. Other data sources, principally Statistics Canada's General Social Survey, are available as measures of attendance at religious services.

The census collects information on religious affiliation only, regardless of whether respondents actually practice their religion. Data on the frequency of attendance at religious services have been collected by Statistics Canada's General Social Survey since 1986. The survey samples adults aged 15 and over living in private households in the ten provinces.

According to GSS data, attendance at religious services has fallen dramatically across the country over the past 15 years. Nationally, only one-fifth (20 percent) of individuals aged 15 and over attended religious services on a weekly basis in 2001, compared with 28 percent in 1986. In 2001, four in ten adults (43 percent) reported that they had not attended religious services during the 12 months prior to the survey, compared with only 26 percent in 1986.

GSS data showed that religious attendance is influenced by factors including demographics, immigration patterns and cultural background.

■ Roman Catholics: the largest religious group in Canada

Between 1991 and 2001, the number of Roman Catholics in Canada increased slightly, while the number adhering to Protestant denominations continued a long-term decline. The census enumerated just under 12.8 million Roman Catholics, up 4.8 percent, while the number of Protestants fell 8.2 percent to about 8.7 million.

For more than 100 years in Canada, Protestants outnumbered Catholics. In 1901, Protestant faiths accounted for well over one-half (56 percent) of the total population, compared with 42 percent for Roman Catholics.

This reflected immigration patterns at the time. Prior to 1961, most European immigrants came from the United Kingdom, Italy, Germany and the Netherlands.

However, by 1971, for the first time since Confederation, Catholics outnumbered Protestants as the sources of immigration to Canada began to change. In 1971, Roman Catholics represented 46 percent of the population, and Protestants 44 percent.

The proportion of Protestant faiths in the population has been declining since it peaked at 56 percent in 1921. The proportion of Roman Catholics peaked in 1971.

One reason for the recent growth among Roman Catholics was immigration. Of the 1.8 million immigrants who came to Canada between 1991 and 2001, Roman Catholics accounted for nearly one-quarter (23 percent) of this total, the highest proportion for any major religion among these recent arrivals.

While the proportion of immigrants of Roman Catholic faith entering Canada in the past 40 years has declined, they nevertheless have remained the largest religious denomination within each new wave of immigrants since the 1960s. Roman Catholics represented 39 percent of immigrants who came to Canada before 1961, increasing to 43 percent of those who arrived between 1961 and 1970. Immigrants of Roman Catholic faith represented about one-third of those who came during both the 1970s and 1980s.

■ Protestants still second largest major religion

Protestant denominations still comprised the second largest major religious group in 2001.

Most of the decline in Protestant denominations during the 1990s occurred within the six largest denominations. Only one of these groups recorded growth during the 1990s: Baptist, which increased 10 percent to 729,500.

The two major influences in the declines among the largest Protestant denominations have been immigration and the fact that there are fewer young people reporting these denominations. Many adherents of these faiths are descendants of European immigrants who arrived in Canada prior to 1961.

Since 1961, the proportion of immigrants entering Canada who were Protestant has declined steadily. Protestants represented four out of every 10 immigrants (39 percent) who came to Canada prior to 1961. This ratio declined to one in 10 (11 percent) among those who arrived during the 1990s.

Contributing to the decline of those reporting Protestant denominations was the increase during the decade among those reporting simply "Christian," as well as the increase in those reporting no religion.

■ Growth in Islam, Hinduism, Sikhism and Buddhism

The largest gains in religious affiliations occurred among faiths consistent with changing immigration patterns toward more immigrants from regions outside of Europe, in particular Asia and the Middle East.

Among this group, those who identified themselves as Muslim recorded the biggest increase, more than doubling from 253,300 in 1991 to 579,600 in 2001. These individuals represented 2 percent of the total population in 2001, up from under 1 percent a decade earlier.

The number of people who identified themselves as Hindu increased 89 percent to 297,200. Those who identified themselves as Sikh rose 89 percent to 278,400, while the number of Buddhists increased 84 percent to about 300,300. Each represented around 1 percent of the total population.

Immigration was a key factor in the increases for all these groups. The proportion of immigrants entering Canada with these religions increased with each new wave of arrivals since the 1960s. Of the 1.8 million new immigrants who came during the 1990s, Muslims accounted for 15 percent, Hindus almost 7 percent and Buddhists and Sikhs each about 5 percent.

In terms of age, each of these religions had relatively young populations. The median age of Muslims was 28 years, Sikhs 30, and Hindus 32, all well below the median of 37 for the overall population.

Ontario was home to 73 percent of the Hindu population in 2001, 61 percent of all Muslims, and 38 percent of all Sikhs. Nearly one-half of the Sikh population lived in British Columbia.

■ An increase among Orthodox Christians

Just over 479,600 people identified themselves as members of a Christian Orthodox religion in the 2001 census, a 24 percent increase from 1991. They represented 1.6 percent of the total population, up slightly from 1.4 percent in 1991.

About 215,200 people identified themselves as members of the Greek Orthodox Church, a 7 percent decline from 1991. At the same time, the number of Ukrainian Orthodox adherents declined 5 percent to 32,700. The median age for both groups was older than for the total population, 41 years for Greek Orthodox and 46 years for Ukrainian Orthodox.

The census enumerated just over 20,500 members of the Serbian Orthodox faith, up from just under 10,000 in 1991, and about 15,600 members of the Russian Orthodox, up from 6,600 in 1991. These increases are likely a result of increased immigration to Canada over the past decade from countries of the former Yugoslavian and Soviet republics.

In addition, the number of people reporting their religion as simply "Orthodox" increased during the past decade, contributing to the overall increase in the number of people of Orthodox faith in 2001.

■ Slight increase in Jewish faith

The number of individuals who identified themselves as Jewish increased 3.7 percent during the 1990s to nearly 330,000.

They accounted for 1.1 percent of the population in 2001, virtually unchanged during the decade. Well over one-half of these individuals, about 190,800, lived in Ontario.

According to the census, nearly one-third (31 percent) of people of Jewish faith in 2001 were born outside Canada. However, Jewish people accounted for only 1 percent of the 1.8 million immigrants who came to Canada during the 1990s.

CRIME AND JUSTICE

Selected Criminal Code Incidents by Province, 2000

	Canada	N&L	PEI	NS	NB[3]	Que	Ont
Population	31 081 887	533 761	138 514	942 691	757 077	7 410 504	11 874 436
Homicide							
Number	554	1	2	9	8	140	170
Rate[1]	1.8	0.2	1.4	1.0	1.1	1.9	1.4
Annual % change in rate[2]	0.4	-83.2	-33.5	-40.1	-20.2	-7.1	7.2
Sexual Assault							
Number	24 419	585	108	851	819	3 705	8 790
Rate[1]	79	110	78	90	108	50	74
Annual % change in rate[2]	0.7	3.1	-0.3	13.1	10.7	7.7	-2.1
Assault							
Number	239 163	3 936	857	7 946	5 892	37 602	82 790
Rate[1]	769	737	619	843	778	507	697
Annual % change in rate[2]	1.3	-2.7	2.9	4.8	3.3	0.0	1.9
Robbery							
Number	27 414	67	23	627	184	7 198	8 997
Rate[1]	88	13	17	67	24	97	76
Annual % change in rate[2]	0.4	18.3	52.8	20.4	3.1	-6.2	5.4
Total violent crime							
Number	**309 101**	**4 762**	**1 033**	**9 865**	**7 482**	**53 309**	**107 211**
Rate[1]	**994**	**892**	**746**	**1 046**	**988**	**719**	**903**
Annual % change in rate[2]	**1.3**	**-1.4**	**2.0**	**5.8**	**4.8**	**0.3**	**1.8**
Breaking and Entering							
Number	282 512	3 207	740	6 595	4 773	73 969	85 230
Rate[1]	909	601	534	700	630	998	718
Annual % change in rate[2]	-4.7	-8.4	-9.5	-14.2	-8.6	-7.9	-1.7
Motor Vehicle Theft							
Number	170 213	634	272	2 755	1 765	42 054	50 067
Rate[1]	548	119	196	292	233	567	422
Annual % change in rate[2]	5.1	-1.1	22.7	-4.1	6.8	-1.4	2.2
Other Theft							
Number	687 107	6 887	2 637	18 515	11 875	123 170	224 958
Rate[1]	2 211	1 290	1 904	1 964	1 569	1 662	1 894
Annual % change in rate[2]	-0.6	-5.7	-1.5	-1.3	-2.4	-3.0	1.0
Total property crime							
Number	**1 257 729**	**12 190**	**4 086**	**32 516**	**21 400**	**260 136**	**403 718**
Rate[1]	**4 047**	**2 284**	**2 950**	**3 449**	**2 827**	**3 510**	**3 400**
Annual % change in rate[2]	**-0.6**	**-5.6**	**-2.2**	**-3.6**	**-3.4**	**-3.8**	**0.7**
Offensive weapons							
Number	17 456	190	40	623	391	1 231	7 098
Rate[1]	56	36	29	66	52	17	60
Annual % change in rate[2]	12.8	6.8	20.8	24.4	9.3	6.6	11.2
Mischief							
Number	338 425	5 456	1 602	11 383	7 259	51 775	104 064
Rate[1]	1 089	1 022	1 157	1 208	959	699	876
Annual % change in rate[2]	2.7	4.8	-6.4	-0.6	1.4	-5.6	1.1
Total other criminal code							
Number	**841 191**	**13 127**	**4 262**	**29 609**	**20 168**	**121 477**	**262 000**
Rate[1]	**2 706**	**2 459**	**3 077**	**3 141**	**2 664**	**1 639**	**2 206**
Annual % change in rate[2]	**4.3**	**1.8**	**1.6**	**4.8**	**-0.7**	**-1.1**	**2.8**
TOTAL CRIMINAL CODE[3]							
Number	**2 408 021**	**30 079**	**9 381**	**71 990**	**49 050**	**434 922**	**772 929**
Rate[1]	**7 747**	**5 635**	**6 773**	**7 637**	**6 479**	**5 869**	**6 509**
Annual % change in rate[2]	**1.3**	**-1.8**	**0.0**	**1.0**	**-1.1**	**-2.6**	**1.6** ▶

	Man	Sask	Alta	BC	YK	NWT	NVT
Population	1 150 034	1 015 783	3 064 249	4 095 934	29 885	40 860	28 159
Homicide							
Number . . . . : . . .	34	27	70	85	1	4	3
Rate[1]	3.0	2.7	2.3	2.1	3.3	9.8	
Annual % change in rate[2] . . .	12.9	4.5	16.5	-0.9	-48.8	300.5	-2.6
Sexual Assault							
Number	1 371	1 423	2 676	3 646	76	147	
Rate[1]	119	140	87	89	254	360	
Annual % change in rate[2] . . .	0.7	-6.4	5.2	-2.7	-9.6	-18.7	
Assault							
Number	14 761	14 724	26 484	39 955	960	1 730	1 526
Rate[1]	1 284	1 450	864	975	3 212	4 234	5 419
Annual % change in rate[2] . . .	-1.8	8.7	3.6	-2.6	16.5	5.3	
Robbery							
Number	1 819	1 088	2 726	4 626	27	20	12
Rate[1]	158	107	89	113	90	49	43
Annual % change in rate[2] . . .	-1.8	18.5	5.6	-6.0	112.5	11.2	-2.6
Total violent crime							
Number	**18 626**	**18 307**	**33 672**	**49 851**	**1 121**	**2 011**	**1 851**
Rate[1]	**1 620**	**1 802**	**1 099**	**1 217**	**3 751**	**4 922**	**6 573**
Annual % change in rate[2] .	**-1.5**	**8.0**	**3.8**	**-2.8**	**12.4**	**1.5**	
Breaking and Entering							
Number	13 310	15 103	25 650	51 933	609	705	
Rate[1]	1 157	1 487	837	1 268	2 038	1 725	2 443
Annual % change in rate[2] . . .	-6.7	-3.9	-6.0	-0.8	-19.5	-13.8	
Motor Vehicle Theft							
Number	13 206	7 986	17 467	33 242	239	285	
Rate[1]	1 148	786	570	812	800	698	
Annual % change in rate[2] . . .	11.5	5.2	15.0	12.5	1.1	35.9	
Other Theft							
Number	28 786	30 195	76 024	161 490	1 115	946	
Rate[1]	2 503	2 973	2 481	3 943	3 731	2 315	1 808
Annual % change in rate[2] . . .	3.7	0.1	-1.4	-0.7	-11.9	-21.5	
Total property crime							
Number	**59 070**	**59 548**	**134 995**	**264 246**	**2 157**	**2 118**	**1 549**
Rate[1]	**5 136**	**5 862**	**4 405**	**6 451**	**7 218**	**5 184**	**5 501**
Annual % change in rate[2] .	**3.1**	**-0.3**	**-0.8**	**1.2**	**-11.8**	**-11.5**	
Offensive weapons							
Number	1 183	820	1 867	3 807	57	83	66
Rate[1]	103	81	61	93	191	203	
Annual % change in rate[2] . . .	10.9	17.4	13.2	15.5	-24.2	45.8	
Mischief							
Number	25 939	20 610	43 674	60 343	1 389	3 256	1 675
Rate[1]	2 255	2 029	1 425	1 473	4 648	7 969	5 948
Annual % change in rate[2] . . .	16.2	6.3	5.8	4.6	26.9	4.8	
Total other criminal code							
Number	**53 004**	**58 844**	**108 659**	**154 070**	**4 153**	**8 190**	**3 628**
Rate[1]	**4 609**	**5 793**	**3 546**	**3 762**	**13 897**	**20 044**	**12 884**
Annual % change in rate[2] .	**11.5**	**11.0**	**10.3**	**2.9**	**14.6**	**14.6**	
TOTAL CRIMINAL CODE[3]							
Number	**130 700**	**136 699**	**277 326**	**468 167**	**7 431**	**12 319**	**7 028**
Rate[1]	**11 365**	**13 548**	**9 050**	**11 430**	**24 865**	**30 149**	**24 958**
Annual % change in rate[2] .	**5.6**	**5.4**	**3.9**	**1.3**	**5.1**	**6.9**	

Source: © *Statistics Canada, Uniform Crime Reporting Survey, Canadian Centre for Justice Statistics*
(1) Rates are calculated on the basis of 100 000 population. Population estimates at July 1. (2) In comparison to the previous year. Percent change based on unrounded rates. (3) Without traffic offences.

Rates of Criminal Code Incidents in Canada[1]

	1990	1991	1992	1993	1994	1995
Population[2](000)	27 700.6	28 030.9	28 376.6	28 703.1	29 036.0	29 353.9
Violent crime rate	973	1 059	1 084	1 081	1 046	1 007
Annual % change.	6.8	8.9	2.3	−0.3	−3.2	−3.7
Property crime rate	5 611	6 160	5 902	5 571	5 250	5 283
Annual % change.	6.1	9.8	−4.2	−5.6	−5.8	0.6
Other criminal code rate	2 900	3 122	3 051	2 879	2 817	2 702
Annual % change.	7.8	7.7	−2.3	−5.6	−2.2	−4.1
Total[3] criminal code rate	9 484	10 342	10 036	9 531	9 114	8 993
Annual % change.	6.7	9.0	−3.0	−5.0	−4.4	−1.3

	1996	1997	1998	1999	2000	2001
Population[2](000)	29 671.9	29 987.2	30 246.9	30 491.3	30 750.1	31 081.9
Violent crime rate	1 000	990	979	955	982	994.5
Annual % change.	−0.7	−1.0	−1.1	−2.4	2.8	1.3
Property crime rate	5 264	4 867	4 556	4 266	4 070	4 047
Annual % change.	−0.4	−7.5	−6.4	−6.4	−4.5	−0.6
Other criminal code rate	2 650	2 596	2 602	2 512	2 603	2 706
Annual % change.	−1.9	−2.1	0.3	−3.5	3.7	4.3
Total[3] criminal code rate	8 914	8 453	8 137	7 733	7 655	8 154
Annual % change.	−0.9	−5.2	−3.7	−5.0	−1.0	1.6

Source: *Uniform Crime Reporting Survey, Canadian Centre for Justice Statistics, © Statistics Canada*
(1) Rates are calculated per 100 000 people. (2) Population estimates as of July 1. (3) Does not include traffic violations.

Persons Charged by Gender and Age, 2002

(percentage)

	Age Group[1] by Gender				Total by Age Group[1]	
	Adults		Youth		Adults	Youth
	Male	Female	Male	Female	Adults	Youth
Homicide[2]	89	11	79	21	91	9
Attempted murder.	87	13	92	8	89	11
Assaults	83	17	69	31	85	15
Sexual assaults	98	2	94	6	83	18
Other sexual offences	95	5	94	6	81	19
Abduction	54	46	60	40	96	4
Robbery	91	9	85	15	68	32
Total Violent crime	**84**	**16**	**73**	**27**	**84**	**16**
Break and enter.	93	7	89	11	63	37
Motor vehicle theft	91	9	84	16	60	40
Fraud	70	30	66	34	92	8
Theft over $5,000	76	24	81	19	87	13
Theft $5,000 and under	70	30	63	37	74	26
Total Property crime	**77**	**23**	**75**	**25**	**74**	**26**
Mischief	87	13	86	14	67	33
Arson	85	15	89	11	60	40
Prostitution.	47	53	17	83	99	1
Offensive weapons	93	7	92	8	80	20
Total Criminal Code.	**82**	**18**	**75**	**25**	**80**	**20**
Impaired driving[3]	88	12	85	15	99	1
Cannabis Offences	88	12	88	12	82	18
Cocaine Offences	82	18	77	23	95	5
Other Drugs Offences	83	17	84	16	89	11

Source: *© Statistics Canada, Uniform Crime Report Survey, Canadian Centre for Justice statistics*
(1) Adults are defined as people age 18 and over, Youth between the ages of 12 and 17. (2) Data based on Homicide Survey. (3) Includes impaired operation of a vehicle causing death, causing bodily harm, alcohol rate over 80 mg., failure/refusal to provide a breath/blood sample. Dated based on Incident-based survey.

NATIONAL SYMBOLS

The National Anthem: O Canada

The music of *O Canada* was composed by Calixa Lavallée and the lyrics were written in French by Adolphe-Basile Routhier in Quebec City. Originally called *Chant National*, it was first performed at a banquet in Quebec City on June 24, 1880. The anthem grew in popularity in Quebec but was not heard in English until the early 1900s. There have been several English versions of the work, the most popular of which was written in 1908 by Robert Stanley Weir. In 1967 a Special Joint Committee of the Senate and the House of Commons was formed to recommend official versions of Canada's National and Royal Anthems. With a few minor changes, the official English version of *O Canada* is based on Weir's lyrics. On June 27, 1980, the House of Commons passed Bill C-36 designating both the music and lyrics of *O Canada* as Canada's national anthem. It was proclaimed July 1, 1980.

O Canada

O Canada! Terre de nos aïeux,

Ton front est ceint de fleurons glorieux!

Car ton bras sait porter l'épée,

Il sait porter la croix!

Ton histoire est une épopée

Des plus brillants exploits,

Et ta valeur, de foi trempée,

Protégera nos foyers et nos droits,

Protégera nos foyers et nos droits.

O Canada

O Canada! Our home and native land!

True patriot love in all thy sons command.

With glowing hearts we see thee rise,

The True North strong and free!

From far and wide, O Canada,

We stand on guard for thee.

God keep our land glorious and free!

O Canada, we stand on guard for thee.

O Canada, we stand on guard for thee!

The National Flag

The National Flag was adopted by Parliament December 15, 1964 and proclaimed by Queen Elizabeth II. It was inaugurated on February 15, 1965.

It is a red flag of the proportions two by length and one by width, containing in its centre a white square, the width of the flag, bearing a single, red, stylized maple leaf. The maple leaf has been looked upon as an emblem of Canada since the early 1700s. Red and white were declared Canada's official colours by King George V on November 21, 1921.

The National Flag is to be flown daily at all federal government buildings, airports and military bases and establishments within and outside Canada. When flown with other flags, it should be given a place of honour.

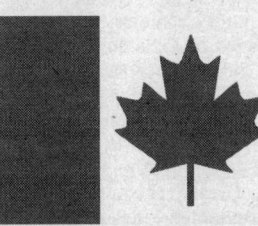

The National Coat of Arms

The creation of coats of arms dates back to the Middle Ages. Centuries ago few could read, nor did they have access to print material, pictures or the other means we now use to identify people. Heraldry was developed as a form of picture-writing, used to create visual emblems that identified individuals or members of a community or nation, particularly in battle.

Over time, such symbols became quite sophisticated; a coat of arms could identify not only the individual but tell if his father was still alive, his birth order, whether or not he was married and the prestige of his branch of the family. In war, the device was painted on a shield; in peace, it would be embroidered on a coat or banner. Because of its significance, heraldry came to be carefully regulated; colleges of arms controlled the grant and use of them.

At the time of Confederation, Canada did not have a coat of arms and used the Royal Arms of the United Kingdom to identify the offices of the Government of Canada. By 1868, however, a Great Seal was required and the government adopted a design that was also used as the Arms of Canada. The design showed the emblems of the original four provinces of the federation—Nova Scotia, New Brunswick, Quebec and Ontario—on a shield. When new provinces joined the federation, their emblems were added to the shield and the design became fragmented and confusing as the provinces multiplied. In 1919, the governor general convened a special committee to study the question of a Canadian coat of arms; a request for a grant of arms was later submitted to the sovereign.

Canada's Coat of Arms was granted by a royal proclamation of King George V on Nov. 21, 1921. Although simplified in 1957 and augmented in 1994, the coat of arms we have now is faithful to that original design.

The most important part of the design is the shield, which shows the emblems of the four founding peoples (English, Scottish, Irish and French) with an added sprig of distinctly Canadian maple leaves. The shield is supported on one side by the lion of England holding the Royal Union flag and the unicorn of Scotland holding a banner of royalist France on the other. A royal helmet and mantle sit above the shield, with a crest showing a royal lion holding a maple leaf on top of the helmet. (The crest is the symbol used on the governor general's standard.) The imperial crown above the crest represents the monarch as Canada's head of state.

Below the shield is Canada's motto, *A Mari usque ad Mare* (From sea to sea) which is based on a verse from Psalm 72 of the Bible: "He shall have dominion from sea to sea and from the river unto the ends of the earth." Around the shield is a ribbon with the motto of the Order of Canada: "Desiderantes Meliorem Patriam" (They desire a better country). The floral emblems of the four founding nations are found at the base of the design: the English rose, the Scottish thistle, the French fleur-de-lis and the shamrock of Ireland.

Canada's coat of arms represents national sovereignty and is used on federal government property such as buildings, official seals, money, passports, proclamations and publications as well as on badges of some members of the armed forces. This national symbol is protected from unauthorized commercial use by the Trade Marks Act.

CANADIAN HISTORY

■ Exploration and First Settlements

The first people who came to North America arrived during the last Ice Age, which began about 80,000 years ago and ended about 12,000 years ago. These Native People were hunters who crosssed from Asia via a land bridge that is now submerged beneath the Bering Sea. Although there is continuing debate among archeologists as to how early humans might have settled in what is now Canada, the earliest accepted occupation site is at the Bluefish Caves in the Yukon; artifacts at least 12,000 to 17,000 years old have been found there. As the glaciers of the Ice Age retreated, human settlements spread across Canada and gradually, these first Canadians developed lifestyles based on the environments in which they lived. They obtained their food by hunting, fishing, gathering, and in the case of Eastern Woodland tribes, by farming. By the time explorers from Europe reached Canada, the Native People had well developed trading patterns, arts and crafts, languages, writing, religious beliefs, laws and government.

There has been much conjecture as to who the first Europeans to come to Canada were. The claim that an Irish monk, St. Brendan, arrived about the year 550 has not been proven. However, the theory that Vikings settled in Newfoundland was confirmed by archeological excavations at L'Anse aux Meadows during the 1960s and 1970s.

A burst of European exploration didn't take place until the Age of Discovery in the 15th and 16th centuries. Explorers found what they called a New World while in search of a route to the Far East. In 1497, Giovanni Caboto (John Cabot), an Italian sailing for England, landed on the Canadian coast, likely in Cape Breton or Newfoundland, and claimed the land for Henry VII of England. Although Cabot probably died on a second expedition in 1498, his voyages helped open up the rich fishing grounds of the Grand Banks.

European navigators and fishermen continued to visit the shores of Canada, but the first serious exploration of the area was undertaken by Jacques Cartier, who discovered the Gulf of St. Lawrence while searching for a passage to Asia, in 1534. The next year he travelled up the St. Lawrence River as far as the native settlements of Stadacona (Quebec) and Hochelaga (Montreal). On this voyage, Cartier picked up the Iroquoian word for village, Kanata (thought to be the origin of "Canada"), and used it to apply to the whole region he had discovered. Cartier's discoveries gave France a claim to Canada and led to the first French settlements.

In 1541–42, Cartier and the Sieur de Roberval established a short-lived settlement at Charlesbourg-Royal just above Quebec. In 1605, the Sieur de Monts and Samuel de Champlain established the colony of Port Royal in what is now Nova Scotia. Champlain went on to establish a settlement at Quebec in 1608, to explore the interior and to draw maps of New France. Champlain also started a fur-trading network (mostly in beaver pelts) with the Algonquins and the Hurons who inhabited the St. Lawrence and Great Lakes regions. This trade relationship became a military alliance as Champlain supported these groups against the Iroquois. This enmity between the French and the Iroquois prevailed throughout most of the history of New France.

Circa 1000   **Leif Ericsson** and other **Vikings** visit Labrador and Newfoundland.

1497   **John Cabot** (Giovanni Caboto) claims Cape Breton Island (or possibly Newfoundland or Labrador) for Henry VII of England (June 24).

1498   **Cabot** makes his second voyage to North America.

1534   **Jacques Cartier** visits the Strait of Belle Isle (Newfoundland), and charts the Gulf of St Lawrence (landing in Gaspé July 14).

1535   **Cartier** sails up the St Lawrence River to **Quebec** and **Montreal**.

1541   Cartier and the Sieur de Roberval found Charlesbourg-Royal, the **first French settlement** in America.

1577   **Martin Frobisher** of England makes the first of his three attempts to find a north-west passage, sailing as far as Hudson Strait.

1600   King Henry IV of France grants a **fur-trading monopoly** in the Gulf of St Lawrence to a group of French merchants.

1605   **Samuel de Champlain** and the Sieur de Monts found Port Royal (Annapolis, NS).

1608   **Champlain** founds Quebec.

1609 Champlain supports the Algonquins against the Iroquois at Lake Champlain.

1610 Étienne Brûlé goes to live among the Huron and eventually becomes the first European to see Lakes Ontario, Huron and Superior. **Henry Hudson** explores Hudson Bay.

1617 Louis Hébert, the **first habitant (farmer)**, arrives in Quebec.

1625 Jesuits arrive in Quebec to begin missionary work among the Indians.

1627 The **Company of One Hundred Associates** is founded (Apr. 29) to establish a French empire in North America.

■ The Growth of New France (1627–1660)

The economic foundation of New France was the fur trade. In fact, the French kings were content to let fur-trading companies run the colony. Although these companies expanded the territory's boundaries, they failed to encourage settlement. One of King Louis XIII's most able advisers, Cardinal Richelieu, tried to remedy this problem by granting a fur-trading monopoly to the Company of One Hundred Associates in 1627, on condition that it bring out several hundred settlers each year. However, war between England and France broke out and Quebec was captured in 1629. Even after peace was restored in 1633, the Company of One Hundred Associates failed to honour its commitment to bring out settlers.

Despite the lack of settlers, the colony was expanding in other ways. As governor, Champlain encouraged the expansion of the fur trade. The Jesuits had arrived in 1625 and were vigorously pursuing their missionary work among the Hurons.

Champlain died in 1635, just two years after the colony was restored to France. No leader possessing his vision or drive emerged to replace him. Next, despite their conviction, the French missionaries made few converts among the native people. Even Sainte-Marie among the Hurons, their central mission-post, was abandoned in 1649 in the face of invasion by the Iroquois, who dispersed the Hurons and disrupted the French fur-trading network. Finally, the security of the centre of the fur trade, Montreal (founded in 1642), and the rest of the colony was threatened by the wars against the Iroquois. When the wars were renewed in 1659–1660, after a brief peace,

there were still only about 3,000 French settlers in the colony. Clearly, the French king would have to act to secure France's foothold in North America.

1629 **David Kirke** captures Quebec for Britain (July 19).

1632 The **Treaty of Saint-Germain-en-Laye** returns Quebec to France.

1634–40 The **Huron nation** is reduced by half from European diseases (smallpox epidemic, 1639).

1637 **Kirke** is named first governor of Newfoundland.

1642 **Montreal** is founded (May 18) by the Sieur **de Maisonneuve**.

1649 The Jesuit Father **Jean de Brébeuf** is martyred by the **Iroquois** at St-Ignace (Mar. 16). The Iroquois disperse the Huron nation (1648–49).

1659 **François de Laval,** later to become Canada's first bishop, arrives in Quebec (June).

1660 **Adam Dollard des Ormeaux** makes his last stand against the Iroquois at Long Sault (May). The small party of French fights so well that the Iroquois decide not to attack Montreal.

■ Royal Government in New France (1663–1700)

In 1663 King Louis XIV made New France a crown colony. Regular troops were sent out and undertook a successful campaign against the Iroquois, which resulted in the signing of a peace treaty in 1667. Several hundred of these regulars stayed on as settlers, thereby adding to the security of the colony. A system of government headed by a governor, an intendant and a bishop was instituted. The governor, who was the king's representative, was charged with defence. The intendant was responsible for industry, trade and administrative affairs. The bishop looked after religious matters, which included education. In theory, this system provided for a clear separation of powers; but, in practice, there were frequent disputes among the three officials. Still, this system survived intact for the remainder of the colony's history, and it provided New France with some remarkably dynamic officials. Two of these arrived in the first years of the Royal Government.

The first intendant of New France, Jean Talon (1665–1672), introduced innovative measures, including awards for early marriage, to boost the population. As well, he tried to build a diversified economy on the St. Lawrence by promoting crafts, farming and local industry. Few subsequent officials in New France shared Talon's concern for settlement or economic diversity. Most were more interested in profits from the fur trade. Count Frontenac, governor for all but seven years between 1672 and 1698, threw his support behind the fur trade, not only raising profits but also encouraging exploration. Under his rule, French adventurers explored the Mississippi River from its upper reaches to the Gulf of Mexico, greatly expanding the fur-trading boundaries of New France. Frontenac gained more fame when he withstood the attack of an English army which besieged Quebec in 1690.

But Frontenac had not only exceeded his powers in promoting territorial expansion, he had also undermined the security of the colony. With its limited population, New France now found itself competing for the fur trade with the more populous English colonies around them. In the north, there was rivalry with the Hudson's Bay Company, founded in 1670. To the south, there was border warfare between French fur traders and their Indian allies, and the English with their Iroquois allies. New France fared well in the limited warfare of the 1680s and 1690s; but in the 18th century there was a series of major wars which resulted in disaster for the colony.

1663 Quebec becomes a **royal province**.

1665 The Carignan-Salières regiment is sent from France to Quebec to deal with the Iroquois. **Jean Talon** becomes Quebec's intendant.

1666 Canada's **first census** counts 3,215 non-native inhabitants in 668 families.

1670 The **Hudson's Bay Company** is formed and granted trade rights over all territory draining into Hudson Bay (May 2).

1672 Count **Frontenac** becomes Governor of Quebec.

1673 **Marquette** and **Jolliet** explore the Mississippi to its junction with the Arkansas.

1674 **Laval** becomes first Bishop of Quebec.

1678–79 **Dulhut** explores the headwaters of the Mississippi.

1682 **La Salle** explores the Mississippi to its mouth.

1686 **De Troyes** and **D'Iberville** capture the English posts of Moose Fort (June 20), Rupert House (July 3) and Fort Albany (July 26) on James Bay.

1689 The Iroquois kill many French settlers at Lachine.

1690 **Sir William Phips captures Port Royal** (May 11). Frontenac repels Phips's attack on Quebec (Oct.).

1697 The **Treaty of Ryswick** restores the status quo in the struggle between England and France. All captured territory is returned.

■ The Collapse of New France (1701–1763)

In the early years of the 18th century, New France stretched from Hudson Bay to the Gulf of Mexico, and from Newfoundland to the Great Lakes. Its population was thinly scattered in the north, south and west but its fur-trading posts in these regions gave legitimacy to its territorial claims. In the Atlantic region, there were several hundred colonists in Newfoundland and another 1,500 in Acadia. The heartland of New France was the settlement of about 20,000 colonists in Montreal, Quebec and in the small communities along the St. Lawrence. The prosperity of the French settlements was to be hurt by long periods of war.

The first of these was the War of the Spanish Succession fought between France and Austria (and their allies) between 1701–1714. Although the British failed to capture their main objective in the North American campaign, the fortress city of Quebec, they made other gains at the bargaining table. In the Treaty of Utrecht, which ended the conflict, France gave up claims to the Hudson Bay territory, all of Acadia except Cape Breton, and Newfoundland.

During a 30-year period of peace, New France enjoyed limited prosperity. The populaton grew, farm yields increased, some industry was established and furs were still exported. But military expenditure necessary to protect the colony was turning it into a financial burden for France. Much of that expenditure went into the huge fortress of

Louisbourg, built on Cape Breton Island to protect the offshore fisheries and guard the St. Lawrence.

Prussia, France, Spain, Naples, Bavaria and Saxony fought Austria and England when the War of Austrian Succession broke out in 1740 and Louisbourg was a natural target. The fortress fell to the British, although it was returned to France at the war's end in 1748. The British established their own military and naval base at Halifax in 1749.

The fragile peace was broken in 1754, when fighting broke out between the English and French colonists in the Ohio Valley. Within two years, Britain and France were officially at war again in what became known as the Seven Years' War. Despite some early victories, the French suffered the loss of Louisbourg in 1758. In the following year, General Wolfe defeated General Montcalm on the Plains of Abraham above the St. Lawrence at Quebec. Although Montreal did not fall until the next year, the loss of Quebec was an irreversible setback. The British army occupied New France, and in 1763 the treaty ending the Seven Years' War confirmed British sovereignty.

New France had fallen because of decisive military defeats at Louisbourg and Quebec, but more significant was the inability of France to supply its colony in the face of British naval supremacy. The British were now masters in North America.

1701 The **War of the Spanish Succession** begins in Europe; the conflict spreads to North America the following year.

1710 Francis Nicholson captures Port Royal for England.

1713 The **Treaty of Utrecht** confirms British possession of Hudson Bay, Newfoundland and Acadia (except Cape Breton Island). France starts building Fort **Louisbourg**.

1739 **La Vérendrye** expedition explores Lake Winnipeg.

1740 The **War of the Austrian Succession** pits Britain against France; the European conflict spreads to North America (**King George's War**) in 1744.

1745 Massachusetts Governor William Shirley takes the French fortress of **Louisbourg**.

1748 Louisbourg is returned to France by the **Treaty of Aix-la-Chapelle**.

1749 Britain founds **Halifax** to counter the French presence at Louisbourg.

1752 Canada's **first newspaper**, the Halifax *Gazette,* appears (Mar. 25).

1753 **George Washington**'s military expedition to the Monogahela is defeated by the French.

1754 Beginning of **French and Indian War** in America. Although war is not officially declared for another two years, this marks the final phase in the struggle between France and Britain in North America.

1755 Britain expels the **Acadians** from Nova Scotia, scattering them throughout her other North American colonies.

1756 Beginning of the **Seven Years' War** in Europe pits Britain against France. The Marquis **de Montcalm** assumes command of French troops in North America.

1758 The British under Generals Amherst and Wolfe take Louisbourg.

1759 **Wolfe takes Quebec**, defeating Montcalm on the Plains of Abraham (Sept. 13). Both generals are killed.

1760 General **James Murray** is appointed military governor of Quebec; he becomes civil governor in **1764**.

■ The First Years of British Rule (1763–1812)

The British had been active on the continent during their search for a northwest passage to the far east; however, their victory over the French encouraged a shift from exploration and fur trading to settlement and the strengthening of British customs in the new territory.

In 1763 a Royal Proclamation was imposed by the British government on the newly acquired territories of New France. The intent of this proclamation was clear. By encouraging the establishment of Protestant schools, by promoting the Church of England, and by stipulating that an assembly be elected, the proclamation aimed at Anglicization. The intent was most visible in the matter of the assembly. Although the French inhabitants were in the majority, under British law no Roman Catholic could hold office. If an assembly were elected, a few hundred British settlers would control about 65,000 Canadiens.

Fortunately for the French in Canada, James Murray, the governor of Quebec from 1760 to 1768, felt that the loyalty of the French colonists could more likely be gained by fair treatment. Murray refused to call elections for the assembly, and allowed French legal practices to continue. Murray's sympathies provoked a storm of protest from the British colonists in Quebec and he was recalled. But his successor, Guy Carleton, also realized that the Royal Proclamation of 1763 would only alienate the recently defeated colonists. Carleton saw that even if Anglicization were carried out, few colonists from the Thirteen Colonies in America or immigrants from Britain would be lured to the rugged colony of Quebec. Consequently, Carleton advised the government in London to replace the proclamation with more liberal legislation.

The result was the Quebec Act of 1774, which dropped the assembly in favour of an appointed council on which Catholics might serve. As well, the French system of civil law and the seigneurial system of land tenure were both guaranteed. Finally, the Quebec Act expanded the borders of the colony to include the rich lands of the Ohio Valley. The British had acted to win the support of the Canadiens. In doing so, however, the British government angered the citizens of the Thirteen Colonies, who resented the special treatment given to their former enemies. These English colonists were especially upset over the loss of the Ohio Valley, a region into which they expected to expand.

The Quebec Act was not the only cause for complaint in the Thirteen Colonies. Protests over British taxation policies and trade restriction led to talk of revolution. That talk led to action, and in 1775 an invading American army took Montreal. Quebec held out against the American siege until relieved by British forces. Although there was some sympathy for the American cause in both Quebec and Nova Scotia, it was not a strong enough sentiment to cause these two colonies to join the revolution.

During and immediately after the American Revolution, some American colonists who wished to retain their British ties fled from the newly created United States into the Maritimes and Quebec. The arrival of about 30,000 of these Loyalists in Nova Scotia resulted in the creation of a new colony, New Brunswick, in 1784. Similarly, the influx of 10,000 Loyalists into Quebec led to division of the colony, and in 1791, the western part of the colony became Upper Canada. The remainder of the old colony was known as Lower Canada.

Despite these changes, fur trading remained an important economic activity in the interior of British North America. In fact, there was keen rivalry for furs between the Hudson's Bay Company and the newly formed (1784) North West Company based in Montreal which led to a flurry of western exploration. Alexander Mackenzie, a partner in the North West Company, explored a river (now known as the Mackenzie) to its mouth on the Beaufort Sea in 1789, and found a route to the Pacific via the Fraser and Bella Coola Rivers in 1793. Two other North West Company employees, Simon Fraser and David Thompson, also carried out voyages of discovery. Fraser followed the river named after him to the Pacific in 1808, and Thompson travelled down the Columbia River to the coast in 1811. These voyages, along with the earlier coastal explorations of James Cook in 1778 and George Vancouver in 1792–1795, helped establish Britain's claim to the northwest part of the continent.

1763 France cedes its North American possessions to Britain by the **Treaty of Paris.** A Royal Proclamation imposes British institutions on Quebec (Oct.). This proclamation also serves as the cornerstone for relations between Canadian aboriginal peoples and the Canadian government, preserving land for their use and giving the government exclusive right to negotiate treaties.

1768 **Guy Carleton** succeeds Murray as governor of Quebec.

1769 Frances Brooke publishes *The History of Emily Montague*, a novel with descriptions of geography, climate and social culture in the New World.

1774 The **Quebec Act** provides for British criminal law but restores French civil law and guarantees religious freedom for Roman Catholic colonists.

1775 Americans under Montgomery capture Montreal (Nov.) and attack Quebec (Dec. 31).

1776 Under Carleton, Quebec withstands American siege until the appearance of a British fleet (May 6).

1778 Captain **James Cook** anchors in Nootka Sound, Vancouver Island (Mar. 29–Apr. 26).

1783 The American Revolutionary War ends; the border between Canada and the US is accepted between the Atlantic Ocean and Lake of the Woods.

1784 **United Empire Loyalists** arrive in Canada. The province of **New Brunswick** is created. The **North West Company** is formed.

1789 **Alexander Mackenzie** journeys to the Beaufort Sea, following what would later be named the Mackenzie River.

1791 **Constitutional Act** divides Quebec into Upper and Lower Canada.

1792 **George Vancouver** begins his explorations of the Pacific coast.

1793 **Alexander Mackenzie** reaches the **Pacific**.

1794 **Jay's Treaty** (Nov. 19) between the US and Britain promises British evacuation of the Ohio Valley forts. The treaty's appointment of officials to settle boundary disputes marks the beginning of international arbitration through its provisions for boundary settlements.

1797 **David Thompson** joins the North West Company as a surveyor and mapmaker.

1806 *Le Canadien*, Quebec nationalist newspaper, is founded.

1808 **Simon Fraser**, a North West Company employee, travels the river named after him to the Pacific.

1811 **David Thompson** charts the Columbia River to the Pacific coast.

■ The War of 1812

Although the British and Americans signed a peace treaty in 1783 to end the American War of Independence, there was still friction between them. One source of conflict was the British fur-trading posts in the Ohio Valley which now belonged to the United States. Although Britain surrendered these posts in 1796 as stipulated by Jay's Treaty (1794), there were still American complaints that the British were arming the local native people. At the same time there was growing American resentment over British interference with shipping. The British, who were at war with France, claimed the right to search American ships for cargoes bound for the enemy. In the process, the British often forced American

sailors on these ships to join the British navy. Resentment grew among Americans until June 1812, when the United States declared war on Britain.

In the first year of the war, the Americans under General William Hull crossed the Detroit River to invade Upper Canada. Hull expected Canadian sympathizers to flock to his cause but he was disappointed. Without fighting a major battle, he retreated to Detroit. British General Isaac Brock and the Shawnees, under Chief Tecumseh, moved against Detroit, and General Hull surrendered. This British and Canadian victory was followed by a victory at Queenston Heights on the Niagara River. Brock was killed in this battle, which nevertheless gave confidence to the defenders of the British colonies.

In 1813, the Americans carried out a successful raid on York (now Toronto), and also gained a foothold in the Niagara district. But by the summer of that year the Americans had been pushed back across the Niagara River by British victories at Stoney Creek and Beaver Dam. Meanwhile, the Americans were building up a large fleet on the Great Lakes, and in September 1813 the Americans won control of Lake Erie at the Battle of Put-in-Bay. This victory prompted the British under General Proctor to abandon Fort Malden on the Detroit River. However, the American General Harrison caught the retreating forces at Moraviantown on the Thames River and defeated Proctor. Tecumseh was killed in this battle. In the east, a two-pronged attack on Montreal was repulsed. The American invaders were defeated on the Chateauguay River and at Crysler's Farm near Cornwall in the fall of 1813.

In 1814, the Americans again invaded the Niagara district but were halted at the Battle of Lundy's Lane. From Halifax, British forces attacked targets in Maine, and occupied most of that state. Another attack from Halifax was launched on the American capital, Washington. The British raiders burned the government buildings there in retaliation for the destruction of York the previous year. Despite these successes, a major British offensive against Plattsburgh on Lake Champlain failed. By now the war was in stalemate and both sides were tired. British and American negotiators signed the Treaty of Ghent in Dec. 1814, to end the war.

In the aftermath of the war, the two sides made an effort to settle outstanding differences. The Rush-Bagot Agreement of 1817 provided for naval disarmament on the Great Lakes. In the following year Britain and the United States agreed to accept the 49th parallel as the international boundary from the Lake of the Woods to the Rocky Mountains. In addition, they agreed to the joint occupation of the Oregon Territory for 10 years.

1812 The US declares war on Britain (June 18), beginning the **War of 1812**. Americans under General William Hull invade Canada from Detroit (July 11). The Red River settlement is begun in Canada's northwest (Aug.–Oct.). Battle of Queenston Heights (Oct. 13): Canadian victory. British **General Isaac Brock** is killed in this battle.

1813 Americans burn York (Apr. 27). Battle of Stoney Creek (June 5): Canadian victory. Battle of Beaver Dams (June 23): Canadian victory; **Laura Secord**, driving a cow, passes American sentries and walks 32 km through dense bush to warn of American attack. Battle of Put-in-Bay, Lake Erie (Sept. 10): American victory. Battle of Moraviantown (Oct. 5): American victory; the Indian Chief **Tecumseh** is killed. Battle of Chateauguay (Oct. 25): Canadian victory. Battle of Crysler's Farm (Nov. 11): Canadian victory.

1814 Battle of Chippewa (July 5): American victory. Battle of Lundy's Lane (July 25): Canadian victory. A British naval force takes Washington (Aug. 24). Battle of Lake Champlain (Sept. 6–11): American victory. The **Treaty of Ghent** ends the War of 1812 (Dec. 24).

■ Rebellion and Reform (1814–1839)

In the years after the War of 1812, there was considerable growth in British North America. The population increased as immigrants from both the United States and Britain arrived to take up land that was free or inexpensive. The economy became more diversified as lumbering, farming and shipbuilding developed in the Canadas and in the Maritimes. Finally, a sense of nationalism began to grow in parts of British North America. This feeling arose partly out of postwar patriotism and partly out of the shared experiences of a demanding colonial life.

As the colonies became more populous, political interest increased. In both the

Canadas and the Maritimes friction between ruling elites and the ordinary colonists developed and was partially fuelled by the form of government in each colony. British governors or lieutenant-governors picked their own officials, including the members of legislative or executive councils. There were elected assemblies in each colony, but their powers were limited. Legislation might pass in the assembly but be turned down by the legislative council. The assemblies, the voice of the people, found themselves frustrated by the power of appointed officials.

By the mid-1830s, economic distress increased the discontent that had been building during the 1820s. In Lower Canada, where cultural prejudice against the Canadiens added to the tension, Louis Joseph Papineau emerged as leader of the radical Patriote Party. When the colonial authorities would not grant the reforms called for by Papineau and his followers, rebellion broke out in November 1837. But loyalist forces quickly defeated the badly organized and poorly led rebels. Papineau and other leaders fled to the United States.

In Upper Canada, the reform movement was able to gain a majority in the assembly in several elections. Still, the reformers could not turn their program into legislation because of Tory control of the Legislative Council. When an anti-reform lieutenant-governor, Sir Francis Bond Head, took over in 1836, some reformers became more radical. Their leader was William Lyon Mackenzie, a newspaper editor and member of the assembly. The Tories won the election of 1836, when Head directly intervened in the campaign. Mackenzie and his followers, spurred on by events in Lower Canada, took up arms in early December 1837. Mackenzie's disorganization, and lack of widespread support among the colonists, doomed the rebellion. After a skirmish north of Toronto the main body of rebels fled. An uprising in the western districts of Upper Canada was equally unsuccessful. Throughout the following year some rebels and American sympathizers mounted raids on Upper Canada from the United States, but these received no popular support.

In the aftermath of the rebellions came political change. The British government sent out Lord Durham to act as Governor General of British North America and investigate the rebellion. The Durham Report of 1839 contained two main recommendations: the first called for the union of Upper and Lower Canada as a first step in the eventual assimilation of the French Canadians; the second recommended the granting of responsible government (in which the executive is responsible to the assembly), a key demand of reformers.

1816 Agents of the North West Company kill Robert Semple, governor of the Hudson's Bay Company's Red River colony, and 21 others at White Oaks (June 19).

1817 The **Rush-Bagot** agreement limits the number of battleships on the Great Lakes.

1818 The **49th parallel** is accepted as **Canada's border** with the US from Lake of the Woods to the Rocky Mountains.

1821 The Hudson's Bay Company and the North West Company are amalgamated as the HBC.

1829 The **Lachine** and **Welland Canals** are completed.

1835 **William Lyon Mackenzie** becomes the first mayor of Toronto.

1836 Opening of Canada's **first railway line,** from St. Johns, Que., to La Prairie, Que.

1837 Unsuccessful **rebellions** in Upper and Lower Canada are led by Mackenzie and Louis-Joseph Papineau.

1839 **Lord Durham's Report** recommends union of Upper and Lower Canada and the establishment of responsible government.

■ The Road to Confederation (1840–1867)

The middle years of the 19th century were both satisfying and disturbing for British North Americans. Immigrants from Europe streamed into the colonies, more land was cleared and towns grew. Local industries were started while lumbering and shipbuilding activities increased. Montreal and Toronto became commercial centres and the ports of the Maritimes were prosperous, fuelled by shipbuilding and trade. Transportation improved as roads, canals and, by the 1850s, railways were built. Some British North Americans looked beyond their borders and began to think of a federation of British colonies that included not only Canada and the Maritimes, but the Red River settlement and the colonies in British Columbia.

Despite the prosperity, there were reasons to consider such an alliance. Until the mid-1840s, the colonies had enjoyed a preferential trading relationship whereby Britain reduced tariffs on colonial products. This advantage was lost in 1846 when Britain adopted free trade. At first, the colonies found some advantage in entering into a limited free trade arrangement with the United States. But the Americans allowed this Reciprocity Treaty of 1854 to lapse in 1866. British North Americans would have to look to themselves as trading partners.

There was also concern in British North America about the United States. That country seemed intent on fulfilling its "Manifest Destiny" to take over North America. The threat was especially clear during and after the American Civil War (1861–65). During the war, the Northern States were angered by British support for the South, and after the war, there was a fear that the large Northern army might march into British territory.

As well, there was a serious political problem in the colony of Canada. The union of Upper and Lower Canada in 1841 had resulted in the creation of a single legislature for the new colony, Canada. By the 1860s, however, this legislature was barely functioning. No single party could gain enough support from both Francophones and Anglophones to gain a majority. There had been 12 different governments in 15 years, and Canadian politicians were desperate for a solution.

Three powerful figures in Canada's legislature, John A. Macdonald, George Brown and George-Étienne Cartier formed a coalition and proposed a larger union of British North America as a way to end the political deadlock. In addition, this proposal would solve the problem of trade and provide security against the American threat. Meanwhile, on the East Coast there was interest in a union too, a union of the Maritimes. A conference had been called for Charlottetown in September 1864 to discuss that topic. When the leaders of the new Canadian coalition heard of this meeting, they asked for an invitation. At Charlottetown the British North American delegates decided on a federation of all the colonies. A second conference at Quebec in October 1864 resulted in a plan for federal union. A federal government would control defence, trade and other matters of national interest. Provincial governments would have power over local matters such as roads and education. The final details were hammered out at another conference in London, England, in 1866.

The British government, which supported this colonial initiative, passed the British North America Act in March 1867. On July 1, 1867, the provinces of Nova Scotia, New Brunswick, Ontario (formerly Canada West) and Quebec (formerly Canada East) became the Dominion of Canada.

1841   The **Act of Union** unites Upper and Lower Canada.

1842   The Ashburton-Webster Treaty settles the Maine–New Brunswick border dispute.

1843   **Fort Victoria** is built to bolster Britain's claim to Vancouver Island.

1846   Great Britain ends a preferential trading policy with the British North American colonies and enters into a **limited free trade agreement** with the United States.

1848   **Responsible government** is achieved in the Canadas and in the Maritimes, thanks to the work of **Robert Baldwin** and **Joseph Howe**.

1849   The boundary of the 49th parallel is extended to the Pacific Ocean. The province of Canada adopts both English and French as official languages. All bills of the United Canada Parliament, now Quebec and Ontario, are given assent in both English and French.

1851   Britain transfers control of the colonial postal system to Canada.

1854   The **Reciprocity Treaty** between Canada and the US is signed (June 6).

1857   **Ottawa** is named **Canada's capital** by Queen Victoria.

1860   Cornerstone of the **Parliament Buildings** is laid (Sept. 1).

1861   The **Grand Trunk Railway** through the length of the Province of Canada is completed.

1864   The **Charlottetown Conference** (Sept. 1–9) takes the first steps toward **Confederation**. The **Quebec Conference** (Oct. 10–27) sets out the basis for union.

1866   The **London Conference** (Dec. 4) passes resolutions which are redrafted to become the **British North America Act**. First raid into Canada by the **Fenians**, a radical Irish-American anti-British group, takes place (June 2). The American government

allows the **Reciprocity Treaty of 1854** to lapse.

1867   **Confederation**. Britain's North American colonies are united by means of the **BNA Act** to become the **Dominion of Canada** (July 1). **Sir John A. Macdonald** is Canada's first prime minister. The BNA Act, now the **Constitution Act, 1867**, confirms the practice of **official bilingualism**, guaranteeing the use of French and English in the debates of the House of Commons and in the Senate, in federal courts and in publications of federal statutes. The provincial legislature, statutes and courts of Quebec are also made bilingual.

■ The Nation Expands (1867–1885)

Soon after the Confederation of Ontario, Quebec, New Brunswick and Nova Scotia in 1867, the new nation of Canada began to acquire more territory. In 1869, guided by the national vision of Prime Minister John A. Macdonald, the federal government bought Rupert's Land from the Hudson's Bay Company. This was a huge territory which included most of modern Manitoba, as well as parts of Saskatchewan, Alberta and the Northwest Territories. The few Ontario immigrants in the Red River Settlement there welcomed this move; but the far more numerous Métis (descendants of French fur traders and native people) were suspicious, especially because they had not been consulted beforehand. When newly appointed Lieutenant-Governor William McDougall tried to enter the settlement before the territory had officially been transferred to Canada, the Métis turned him back. In the absence of a legitimate government, the Métis, under their leader Louis Riel, seized Fort Garry on the Red River and proclaimed a provisional government. The Métis demanded the right to vote, land laws, the official use of both French and English, and the provision of both Roman Catholic and Protestant schools. The Métis list of rights became the terms for negotiating Manitoba's entry into Confederation in 1870.

In the same year, representatives from the colony of British Columbia arrived in Ottawa to discuss union. With the promise from Ottawa to build a transcontinental railway, British Columbia entered Confederation in 1871. Canada now stretched from sea to sea, but the work of nation building was still not complete.

In 1868, Nova Scotia elected an anti-Confederation provincial government and sent a delegation, led by veteran politician Joseph Howe, to London to seek a repeal of the union. But Britain was unsympathetic, and in 1869 Macdonald seized the opportunity to offer Nova Scotia better terms and Howe a cabinet position. With the Nova Scotia situation resolved, Macdonald turned his attention to Prince Edward Island. The Islanders were more attracted to the idea of union after an expensive railway project nearly bankrupted the colony. Macdonald agreed to assume the colony's debts, offered a cash subsidy and promised a steamer service to the mainland. In 1873, Prince Edward Island agreed to the terms and became Canada's seventh province.

In the 1870s and 1880s railways were built to link the provinces of the new nation. The Intercolonial Railway, joining central Canada to the Maritimes, was completed in 1876, but construction of a rail link to British Columbia ran into several delays. First, Macdonald's government was defeated in 1873 over charges of corruption associated with the railway project. The new prime minister, Alexander Mackenzie, refused to fund railway projects because the country was in the midst of a depression. However, after Macdonald's re-election in 1878, railway building began in earnest. In February 1881, the Canadian Pacific Railway Company (CPR) was incorporated, and in November 1885 the last spike was driven at Craigellachie in British Columbia to complete the link to the Pacific.

Even before it was fully completed, the CPR was used to carry troops to quell a rebellion in the spring of 1885. Trouble had started several years earlier when settlers in the North-West Territory (modern Alberta and Saskatchewan) complained to the government about land titles, shipping rates, and their lack of an elected government. Among those who complained were the Métis, some of whom had moved farther west after the Red River troubles of 1870. When the federal government was slow to respond, the Métis, again under Louis Riel, rose up in March 1885 against the territorial council appointed by Ottawa. By late April, 5,000 Canadian soldiers, who had travelled by the new railway, were on the march against Riel and his Métis and native followers. At the Battle of Batoche in May, the forces of General Middleton defeated the rebels. Riel was found guilty of treason by an English-speaking jury and executed.

1868 Confederationist **Thomas D'Arcy McGee** is **assassinated** by a Fenian in Canada's first political assassination.

1869 Canada purchases Rupert's Land from the Hudson's Bay Company for £300,000.

1870 **Louis Riel** leads the Métis in resisting Canadian authority in Canada's northwest. The Métis negotiate with the Canadian government over the right to vote, land laws, the official use of both French and English and the provision of Roman Catholic and Protestant schools. The Manitoba Act creates the province of **Manitoba**.

1871 **British Columbia** joins Confederation upon the promise from Ottawa to build a **transcontinental railway**.

1872 Macdonald's Conservatives win federal re-election.

1873 **Prince Edward Island** joins Confederation. A period of economic depression begins. The North-West Mounted Police are formed. **Alexander Mackenzie** becomes Canada's second prime minister after **Macdonald resigns** over the **Pacific Scandal**.

1874 **Liberals** win federal election.

1875 The **Supreme Court of Canada** is established.

1876 The **Intercolonial Railway** linking central Canada and the Maritimes is completed (July 1). The **Indian Act of 1876** defines special status for aboriginal people living on land reserves and sets out land regulations. Status Indians have no vote in Canadian elections and are exempted from taxation.

1878 Conservatives under Macdonald win federal election.

1879 Macdonald introduces **protective tariffs** as part of his **National Policy**.

1880 **Emily Stowe** receives her medical licence after practising medicine in Toronto since her graduation from a New York medical school in 1867.

1881 The **Canadian Pacific Railway** is incorporated.

1884 **Riel returns** to Canada.

1885 Métis and the NWMP clash at Duck Lake (Mar. 26). The Métis are defeated at Batoche (May 9–12). The **last spike of the transcontinental railway** is driven at Craigellachie in Eagle Pass, BC, by Donald

Smith (Nov. 7). **Louis Riel** is **hanged** in Regina (Nov. 16).

1887 Conservatives win federal election. Liberals choose **Wilfrid Laurier** as leader. The **first provincial premiers' conference** takes place in Quebec City.

1889 The **Dominion Women's Enfranchisement Association** is created to campaign for female voting rights in Canada.

1890 Manitoba Liberals under Thomas Greenway halt public funding of Catholic schools in Manitoba (Mar.).

1891 Conservatives win federal election. **Sir John A. Macdonald dies**. **Sir John Abbott** takes office as prime minister (June 16).

1892 Abbott resigns (Nov. 24). **Sir John Thompson** becomes prime minister (Dec. 5). He establishes the **Canadian Criminal Code**.

1894 Thompson dies (Dec. 12). **Sir Mackenzie Bowell** is asked by the governor general, the Earl of Aberdeen, to form the fourth Conservative government since 1891.

■ The Laurier Era (1896–1911)

Conservative Prime Minister John A. Macdonald died in 1891, soon after winning a federal election. The Conservatives could not find a suitable successor and by 1896 there had been four prime ministers—John Abbott, John Thompson, Mackenzie Bowell and Charles Tupper. During this period, the Conservatives had to deal with a crisis over school legislation introduced in Manitoba. The Manitoba legislature had replaced the dual school system (both Protestant and Catholic schools) which had been guaranteed in the terms of union, with a single Protestant system. Francophone Catholics across Canada were already bitter about Louis Riel's execution. Now the Manitoba schools legislation convinced them that English Protestant Canadians wanted to stamp out French Catholic rights. Extremists on both sides inflamed the issue, and the Conservatives' inability to settle the matter hurt them in the election of 1896. The Liberals, under Wilfrid Laurier, formed a government.

Laurier settled the Manitoba school question by adopting a compromise approach. Religious instruction would be allowed within the single system, and instruction in French could take place where numbers warranted. The issue died down, but Laurier remained sensitive to the tensions between Anglophone Protestants and Francophone Catholics. Many English Canadians were swept up in a great wave of pro-imperial sentiment associated with the Diamond Jubilee of Queen Victoria. In Britain the event was seen as an opportunity to strengthen ties within the British Empire. Laurier acknowledged Canada's support for the Empire, but resisted proposals for a closer relationship with Britain and the other colonies. The prime minister did not wish to yield Canadian autonomy, nor did he wish to lose support in French Canada. The issue of Canada's role in the Empire came to a head in 1899 during the Boer War when the South African Republic (Transvaal) and the Orange Free State fought against Britain. Once again steering a middle course, Laurier agreed to equip and transport Canadian volunteers to South Africa, but sent no official troops. Although this compromise did not satisfy all Canadians, it avoided a bitter dispute. For a time, imperial issues were forgotten, as Canadians enjoyed boom times after the turn of the century.

Laurier summed up the nation's mood when he declared that the "twentieth century is Canada's century." Impressive growth in both industrial and agricultural production provided support for his words. Canada's prospects appealed to immigrants who flocked to the industrial cities and to the farmland of the Prairies. Many of them were attracted by an extensive government advertising campaign and by the lure of free land in the West. As a result of this influx, two new provinces, Alberta and Saskatchewan, were created in 1905. The immigrant tide boosted Canada's population from 5,371,315 in 1901 to 7,206,643 in 1911. The mood of the country was so confident that two new transcontinental railway building projects got under way in the early years of the century.

The international scene, however, was not so bright. In 1903, the British sided with the Americans in the Alaska Boundary Dispute, a disagreement over the international boundary near the Klondike gold fields. Canadians were dismayed, but Britain was less concerned about the Canadian claim than for the need to maintain good relations with the United States. Tension in Europe was increasing and Britain found itself outside of the complicated system of alliances which had developed there. This same concern led both the British government and the Canadian pro-imperialists to pressure

Laurier into providing money to build British warships. Again, Laurier staked out a middle position by introducing a Naval Service Act which created a Canadian navy that could help Britain where the need arose.

Laurier's compromise on naval policy satisfied neither side. Some French Canadians supported the views of Quebec nationalist Henri Bourassa who claimed Laurier had betrayed his people. Anglophone pro-imperialists complained that Laurier's "tin pot navy" was not enough. Canada's naval policy became an issue in the 1911 election, as did the Liberal plan for free trade with the United States. Conservative leader Robert Borden was able to use both to characterize Laurier as not only disloyal to Britain but favouring annexation to the United States. The Conservatives won the election. Borden became prime minister and Laurier stayed on as leader of the Opposition, continuing to advocate conciliatory policies when the interests of French and English Canadians clashed.

1896 The economic depression ends. Bowell resigns, calling his cabinet a "nest of traitors" (Apr. 27). **Sir Charles Tupper** leads an interim government until the Liberals under Laurier win federal election on **Manitoba Schools Question** (June 23). Canada's minister of the interior, **Clifford Sifton**, develops an immigration plan that will bring farmers from Central and Eastern Europe to settle on the Prairies. Gold is discovered in the Klondike (Aug. 16).

1897 Gold Rush begins in the Klondike. **Clara Brett Martin** is the first woman admitted to the bar of Ontario.

1898 Yukon becomes a separate entity from the Northwest Territories. **Kit Coleman**, the first female Canadian war correspondent, covers the Spanish-American War for a Toronto newspaper.

1899 The first **Canadian troops** ever sent overseas are dispatched to the **Boer War** (Oct. 30).

1901 Marconi receives the **first transatlantic radio message** at St. John's, Newfoundland.

1903 Canada loses the **Alaska Boundary Dispute** when British tribunal representative Lord Alverstone sides with the US (Oct. 20). In northern Ontario, Fred LaRose throws hammer at what he thinks are fox's eyes and hits world's richest silver vein.

1904 Liberals win federal election.

1905 The provinces of **Alberta** and **Saskatchewan** are formed.

1907 The **National Council of Women** calls for "equal pay for equal work."

1908 Liberals win federal election.

1909 The Department of External Affairs is formed. John McCurdy's Silver Dart is first heavier-than-air machine to achieve powered flight in Canada at Baddeck, NS. University of Toronto wins **first Grey Cup** football match.

1910 Laurier creates a Canadian navy via the Naval Service Bill.

1911 **Robert Borden** and the Conservatives win federal election, defeating Laurier on the reciprocity issue.

■ Canada and the First World War (1914–1918)

In August 1914, Britain declared war on Germany and Austria–Hungary. The declaration automatically applied to Canada, as part of the British Empire. At first, there was an enthusiastic response, especially among recent British immigrants. When the minister of militia, Sam Hughes, called for 25,000 volunteers, nearly 33,000 appeared. In 1915, when the government asked the Canadian public to buy $50 million in war bonds, they bought $100 million. But enthusiasm for war began to fade as the casualties mounted and the realities of trench warfare became known.

Canadian troops sailed for Europe in October 1914 and, after training in Britain, went into action at Ypres, Belgium, in April 1915. There they gained a reputation for courage, holding their positions in the face of a poison-gas attack, a new weapon at the time. Canadians took part in the costly battles at St. Eloi and Mont Sorrel in 1916. By the Battle of the Somme, in late summer of 1916, Canada had four army divisions in France; in the spring of 1917, all four were deployed in the attack on Vimy Ridge, which resulted in the first real Canadian victory of the war. But by now it was clear that every battle would result in terrible losses. At Passchendaele in October 1917, the Canadians sustained more than 15,000 casualties.

Voluntary recruitment could not keep pace with the high casualty rates. Prime Minister Borden was forced to consider conscription to draft soldiers into the army and took the question to the electorate in 1917, unleashing one of the most bitterly fought campaigns in Canadian history. In Quebec, Henri Bourassa rallied anti-conscription supporters and argued that Canada had done enough. In Ontario, Borden's supporters condemned French-Canadian anti-conscriptionists as traitors. For his part, Borden introduced the Wartime Elections Act to help secure victory. This act removed the right to vote from enemy aliens, even though some were Canadian citizens. It also gave the right to vote to women relatives of soldiers. In the election, Borden won in every province except Quebec where he was soundly rejected. Conscription had created a deep division between Quebec and the rest of Canada and once in practice, it had little impact on the course of the war. When the first 400,000 conscripts were called up, 90 percent of them appealed for exemption, and by the war's end only about 24,000 conscripts had reached the front.

While the conscription crisis raged at home, Canadian soldiers played a major role in the events leading to an Allied victory. They took part in the successful battle at Amiens in August 1918 and helped to roll the Germans back to Mons by November. The Canadians were still fighting at Mons when the armistice was signed Nov. 11, 1918.

Canadians also served with distinction in other theatres of war. By 1918, Canadians made up almost 25 percent of the pilots in Britain's Royal Flying Corps. Other Canadians served in the Royal Navy or on coastal patrol in Canada's own small navy. Some served in forestry corps overseas and others operated the railways behind the British lines. Some, including women, served as ambulance drivers at the front. Many Canadian women also played key roles as nurses overseas and in the munitions factories in Canada.

Canada's war effort won the country a place in the Imperial War Cabinet during the war, and a seat in the League of Nations afterwards. There were other benefits, too. Women's contributions to the war effort helped them win the right to vote in federal elections and in provincial elections in seven of the provinces by 1919. Yet these advances came at a terrible cost. Overseas, 68,300 Canadians had died. At home, bitterness over the conscription issue had created a division between French and English Canadians that would be remembered for decades.

1914   CP ship *Empress of Ireland* sinks in the St Lawrence in 14 minutes after being rammed in fog, with the loss of 1,014 lives (May 29). **Canada is automatically at war** with Germany when Britain declares war (Aug. 4). The first Canadian troops leave for England (Oct. 3). Parliament passes the **War Measures Act**, allowing suspension of civil rights during periods of emergency. European immigration to Canada increases. Over one million settlers come between 1911 and 1913, bringing total immigration to three million since 1891.

1915   Canadians face German gas attack at **Ypres,** Belgium (Apr. 22). John McCrae writes "In Flanders Fields."

1916   **Nellie McClung** succeeds in persuading the Manitoba government to grant women the right to vote and to hold office (Jan.). The Parliament Buildings are destroyed by fire (Feb. 3). Canadian troops fight in the Battle of the **Somme** (July to Nov.); 24,713 Canadians and Newfoundlanders are killed. The unreliable, Canadian-made Ross rifle is withdrawn from war service (Aug.). **Emily Gowan Murphy** is the first woman magistrate appointed within the British Empire.

1917   **Income tax** is introduced as a "temporary wartime measure." Prime Minister Sir Robert Borden sits as a member of the Imperial War Cabinet (Feb. 23), giving Canada a voice in war policy. The Military Service Bill is introduced (June 11), leading to the **Conscription Crisis** between Quebec and English Canada. Unionist government under Borden wins federal election, in which **women vote** for the first time. **Louise McKinney** is elected to the Alberta legislature, the first woman in the British Commonwealth to hold such office. Canadians capture **Vimy Ridge,** France (Apr. 9–12). Canadians take **Passchendaele,** Belgium, (Nov. 7) in one of the war's worst battles; of the 20,000 Canadian troops sent into the two-week battle, 15,654 are killed or wounded. Explosion of a munitions ship in **Halifax harbour** wipes out two square miles (5.2 sq. km) of Halifax, killing almost 2,000 and injuring 9,000 (Dec. 6).

1918 Canadians break through German trenches at Amiens (Aug. 8), "the black day of the German army." The period from this date until the end of the war becomes known as "Canada's Hundred Days." Armistice ends war (Nov. 11).

■ Canada in the 1920s

As the soldiers returned home, many expected to find a Canada ready to reward them for their sacrifices. What they found was a nation in the midst of painful postwar readjustment. Industry had to convert to peacetime production, but interest rates were so high investment capital was scarce. Jobs were hard to find and wages were low, and tariffs on imported goods kept prices high. By 1921, 300,000 men and women—more than 15 percent of the work force—were unemployed. Farmers, especially on the Prairies, also suffered. During the war, the West had become the world's breadbasket: wheat prices had soared and many farmers had borrowed heavily to expand their production. But with the war's end, world markets collapsed; wheat prices fell by almost half within two years.

These conditions, along with resentment over wartime profiteering by big business, created unrest. The One Big Union movement, centred in western Canada, attempted to create a single union to represent all workers. The Winnipeg General Strike of 1919 grew out of the organizers' efforts and the general discontent. Although the Winnipeg workers were striking over such issues as the right to collective bargaining, better wages and improved working conditions, the opponents of the general strike characterized it as a Communist conspiracy by raising the spectre of a revolution similar to the one in Russia two years earlier. The federal government sided with the anti-strike forces. Immigration laws were amended to deport "alien" labour radicals, the strike leaders were arrested and the Royal North West Mounted Police fired into a rioting crowd on June 21, 1919—"Bloody Sunday"— killing one and wounding 30. The six-week strike was over and so was the growth of labour unions. In 1919 alone there were more than 400 strikes, but after the Winnipeg General Strike, the federal government and most governments at the provincial level opposed union activities. Throughout the 1920s there was a decline in union membership.

The reasons for unrest and discontent varied from region to region in the 1920s. The government takeover of five financially troubled railways had led to the creation of the Canadian National Railways in 1919, and railway rates in the Maritimes were raised 40 percent to bring them up to central Canadian levels. Angry over the rail rates and feeling that Ottawa was making decisions on the basis of central Canada's interests, many Maritimers protested by forming the Maritimes Rights movement, aimed at winning transportation concessions and federal subsidies. At the same time it promoted regional rights and pride.

Canadian farmers, resentful over low prices for farm products, high rail rates and high prices for manufactured goods, formed the United Farmers' movement. United Farmers' parties won provincial elections in Ontario in 1919, in Alberta in 1921, and in Manitoba in 1922. At the federal level, the Progressive Party embraced some of the program of the United Farmers' movement. The Progressives called for free trade, nationalization (especially in the case of railways) and more direct democracy (such as the use of a referendum to decide a controversial issue). Although they were a new party, the Progressives were to play an important role in politics in the 1920s.

The election of 1921 marked new directions in Canadian politics. Both major parties had new leaders: Arthur Meighen had replaced Borden as prime minister; William Lyon Mackenzie King had taken over as Liberal leader after Laurier's death. Of even greater significance was that for the first time, Canadians could vote for one of three parties at the federal level: the Liberals, the Conservatives or the Progressives. The Liberals won the 1921 election, but the Progressives finished second and formed the Opposition. Their position in the House of Commons was even more important after the 1925 election in which the Conservatives under Meighen won the most seats, but King remained in power by claiming the support of the Progressives. After 1925 the Progressives declined, and many of their supporters voted Liberal in King's 1926 election victory. But the influence of the Progressive movement was felt as King's government, anxious to keep their support, passed Canada's first Old Age Pension Act in 1927.

In foreign affairs, King made sure that Canada played a cautious role in the League of Nations, because he feared that Canada would be drawn into international disputes. In imperial matters, his insistence on autonomy contributed to a redefinition of the empire at the Imperial Conference of 1926. There it was acknowledged that Canada and the other British dominions were autonomous even in their external affairs. As a result, by 1929, Canada had diplomatic posts in Washington, Paris and Tokyo, and Britain had a high commissioner in Ottawa. The Governor General became a symbolic representative of the Crown rather than a representative of the British government.

At home, there were many signs that good times had finally come to Canada. World markets for Canadian manufactured goods had revived, and wheat prices were soaring to new levels. New mining and lumbering areas were developed. By 1928, more than a billion dollars' worth of products were being extracted from the newly developed primary industries of the Canadian Shield. Immigrants poured into Canada by the hundreds of thousands to provide labour in the growing industrial cities. Cars, radios, telephones, electrical appliances and other consumer goods were being bought, especially by middle-class Canadians, often using credit plans. Credit was also used to buy shares on the stock market, as the country became increasingly optimistic about its future. On both sides of the Canadian-American border, the Roaring Twenties were in full swing and there seemed no end in sight to the good times.

1919 Alcock and Brown take off from St. John's, Nfld, (June 14) on the first successful flight across the Atlantic to Cliften, Ireland. A **general strike paralyzes Winnipeg** (May–June), where an armed charge by the RCMP kills one person and injures 30 (June 21).

1920 Canada joins the **League of Nations** at its inception (Jan. 10). The flow of emigrants from the British Isles and Europe resumes, many going to urban centres. Federal legislation makes **women eligible** to sit in the **House of Commons**. The North West Mounted Police became the Royal Canadian Mounted Police (RCMP).

1921 Liberals under **Mackenzie King** defeat Conservatives under Arthur Meighen in federal election; the Progressive Party comes in second. **Agnes Macphail** becomes the first woman elected to Parliament. The world's fastest fishing schooner, the *Bluenose,* is launched at Lunenburg, NS. (Mar. 26). **Postwar economic depression** puts 300,000 men and women out of work—more than 15 percent of the work force.

1922 Canada declines to rally to Britain's side during the Chanak Crisis. Sir Frederick **Banting**, Dr Charles **Best**, Dr J.J.R. MacLeod and J.B. Collip share Nobel Prize for the **discovery of insulin**.

1923 The Canadian Northern and Canadian Transcontinental are merged to form the **Canadian National Railways**. Canada signs the Halibut Treaty with the US without a corroborating British signature. Mackenzie King leads opposition to a common imperial policy ("one voice for the empire") at an Imperial Conference in London.

1924 The Saskatchewan Wheat Pool begins operations.

1925 Although Conservatives win more seats in federal election, Mackenzie King's Liberals remain in power with the support of the Progressives.

1926 King's Liberals win federal election. An Imperial Conference defines British dominions as autonomous (Balfour Report).

1927 Britain's Privy Council awards Labrador to Newfoundland instead of to Quebec (Mar. 1). The Diamond Jubilee of Confederation (July 1) is marked by Canada's first coast-to-coast radio network broadcast. King's government, with the support of the Progressive Party, passes Canada's first **Old Age Pension Act**.

1928 The Supreme Court of Canada rules that, according to the British North America Act, women are not "persons" who could hold public office. This decision is reversed by British Privy Council in 1929.

■ The Great Depression (1929–1939)

In 1929, Canadians looked with confidence toward the next decade and that confidence made the effects of the Great Depression of the 1930s even more bitter. The Depression was worldwide, but the effects were especially felt in Canada because about a third of the nation's gross national product was based on exports. The first signs of Canadian economic collapse appeared in October 1929 when wheat prices began to fall. In the same month the stock market collapsed, ruining thousands of shareholders, some of whom, on paper at least, had been millionaires. By 1930, the number of unemployed had doubled and the Conservatives, under R.B. Bennett, won the 1930 federal election decisively as voters hoped a change in government would bring a change in fortune. However by 1933, one in five Canadians was unemployed.

Western Canada was hardest hit in "The Dirty Thirties" because of its reliance on wheat. The Prairie provinces also suffered from a drought which led to crop failure during these hard times. The combined results were devastating. In Saskatchewan, provincial income fell by 90 percent and two-thirds of the province's population had to go on welfare. In the 1930s, welfare, or "relief" as it was then known, became a burden for municipal and provincial governments across the country. By 1935, 10 percent of Canadians were on relief.

Bennett's government did not intervene to rebuild the economy. In the 1930s, politicians, economists and business leaders assumed that the Depression, like other downswings in the business cycle, would soon be followed by a recovery. Their experience, and most economic theory at the time, did not encourage them to consider major government spending as a way to stimulate a depressed economy.

One of the few federally financed programs created involved sending single unemployed men to camps where they did manual work in return for their keep and a small allowance. Working in isolated conditions, often at meaningless tasks, did nothing to satisfy the men, and those in the British Columbia camps took action. In 1935, about 1,500 camp inmates decided to present their complaints directly to Bennett in Ottawa. They began the "On to Ottawa" trek by taking over freight trains heading east. By the time they reached Regina, there were about 2,000 protesters and the railway refused to provide further transportation. Representatives of the Trekkers met with Prime Minister Bennett in Ottawa, but the talks were inconclusive. When the delegation returned to Regina, Bennett decided to arrest the protest leaders. On July 1, there was a bloody riot in Regina involving the Trekkers, local police and the RCMP, which left one policeman dead and several dozen rioters, constables and local citizens injured. The Trek was over and the protesters returned home over the next few days; but Bennett's handling of the affair hurt his image. In the election of

1935, the people turned to King again, in the hope that this time he could deal with the Depression.

After 1935, economic conditions began to improve slowly, yet federal politicians did little to speed this recovery. The failure of the Liberals and the Conservatives to deal with the Depression led to the rise of reform parties. A socialist party, the Co-operative Commonwealth Federation (CCF) won seven seats in the 1935 election and elected members to several provincial legislatures. Other new parties appeared at the provincial level. In Alberta, the Social Credit Party promised $25 prosperity certificates to each resident; but the plan fell flat because the province did not have the power to issue currency. In Quebec, Maurice Duplessis established the Union Nationale and promised economic reform. But the Union Nationale, like the other parties, could not end the Depression, the effects of which faded only with the outbreak of World War II in 1939.

1929 The **Great Depression** begins.

1930 **Cairine Wilson** is appointed Canada's first woman senator (Feb. 20). The Canadian Federation of Business and Professional Women's Clubs is organized. Conservatives under **R.B. Bennett** win federal election (Aug. 7).

1931 The **Statute of Westminster** (Dec. 11) grants Canada full legislative authority domestically and in external affairs. The Governor General becomes a representative of the Crown.

1932 Ottawa Agreements provide for preferential trade between Canada and other Commonwealth nations. The **Co-operative Commonwealth Federation (CCF)** is founded at Calgary.

1933 One in five Canadians is unemployed.

1934 The Bank of Canada is formed. The **Dionne quintuplets** are born in Callander, Ont.

1935 Ten percent of Canadians rely on welfare or "relief." The **On to Ottawa** trek by young men from government work camps ends in a riot at Regina (July 1). Liberals under Mackenzie King win federal election. The CCF wins 7 seats. Social Credit claims 17. **William Aberhart** leads Social Credit into office in Alberta. The Canadian Wheat Board is created.

1936 Union Nationale under **Maurice Duplessis** wins its first election in Quebec.

1937 The **Rowell-Sirois Commission** is appointed to investigate the financial relationship between the federal government and the provinces. First regular flight of **Trans Canada Air Lines** (Sept. 1).

1938 Franklin D. Roosevelt becomes first US President in office to visit Canada, meeting Mackenzie King at Kingston.

■ Canada in World War II (1939–1945)

While most Canadians focused attention on the effects of the Depression at home, events in Europe during the 1930s were moving the world closer to another global conflict. After taking over Austria and Czechoslovakia (present-day Czech and Slovak republics), Germany invaded Poland in 1939; Britain and France responded by declaring war. Following Britain's action, King quickly summoned Parliament. On Sept. 10, one week after Britain had entered the conflict, the Canadian Parliament declared war on Germany and its allies.

Parliamentary support for the war declaration was based in part on King's known preference for a limited Canadian role and his assurance that there would be no conscription. Initially, only one Canadian division was sent to Britain. But by 1940, France had fallen and Britain faced invasion. King abandoned the concept of limited participation and decided to dispatch more troops. By late 1942, Canada had five divisions overseas. Canadian soldiers first saw action in December 1941 during the unsuccessful defence of Hong Kong. In August 1942, 5,000 Canadians took part in the disastrous raid on the French port of Dieppe, suffering casualties of 2,200 killed or captured. Despite these setbacks, the Canadian army played a major role in defeating enemy forces in Italy and took part in the Allied landings at Normandy in June 1944. After taking key targets in France, Canadian soldiers moved northward to liberate Holland in 1945.

Canadians contributed to the war effort in other important ways. The Royal Canadian Navy grew from six destroyers and less than 2,000 personnel in 1939 to 471 warships, 99,688 men and 6,500 women by the war's end in 1945. The navy helped win the Battle of the Atlantic against German submarines by providing protection to the convoys of merchant ships carrying essential supplies from North America to Britain. (Despite the protection, German U-boats sank 5,150 merchant ships.) Canadians also fought in the air as members of Britain's Royal Air Force, and, in increasing numbers throughout the war, in the Royal Canadian Air Force (RCAF). By 1945, there were 48 RCAF squadrons overseas. Other members of the RCAF were involved in the British Commonwealth Air Training Plan. Operating from Canadian airfields, this plan trained 131,000 aircrew from around the Commonwealth.

Canada also produced a wide variety of munitions, and provided important food supplies to the Allied war effort. Much of Canada's war production went directly to Britain, so did more than $3 billion in financial assistance.

While the contributions of Canadian men and women to the war effort were significant, the conflict raised disturbing issues at home. In reversing his earlier stand against conscription, Prime Minister King called for a national plebiscite on the issue in 1942. In all provinces except Quebec the electorate voted for conscription; relations between Quebec and the rest of Canada were strained, although not as severely as in World War I.

In a move that would later become controversial, Japanese-Canadians were interned and their property was confiscated in the name of national security after the Japanese attack on Pearl Harbor in 1941. The interned included Japanese-Canadians who had fought for Canada in World War I, and more than 40 years later, the Canadian government would officially apologize to the interned and their families.

By the war's end, more than a million Canadians had served in the armed forces and more than 42,000 had died. Canada's war effort enhanced its international image. At the same time, Canada had developed closer ties with the United States as the country's interests shifted away from Britain and Europe.

1939 **Canada declares war** on Germany (Sept. 10) after remaining neutral for a week following the British declaration. Quebec Premier Maurice Duplessis, who opposed Quebec participation in the war, is defeated by the provincial Liberals on that issue (Oct. 26).

1940 **Unemployment insurance** is introduced. Liberals win federal election (Mar. 26).

The Permanent Joint Board of Defence is formed between Canada and the US. **Thérèse Casgrain** wins women in Quebec the right to vote and to hold provincial office.

1941 Canadians are captured when Hong Kong falls to Japanese (Dec. 25); about 500 of the POWs subsequently die in Japanese camps. Immigration has changed Canadian demographic structure. Canadians of British ancestry now make up 49.7 percent of the population, of French descent 30.3 percent and of other ethnic backgrounds 20 percent.

1942 In the Canadian army's first European war action, many soldiers are captured or killed in the disastrous **Dieppe** raid (Aug. 19). Canadians of Japanese descent are moved inland from the coast of British Columbia as "security risks"; their property is confiscated. A national plebiscite releases Mackenzie King from his pledge of no conscription but reveals deep divisions between Quebec and the rest of Canada.

1943 Canadians participate in the invasion of Sicily (July 10). Canadians win the Battle of Ortona (Dec. 20–28). **Ernest C. Manning** wins first of nine successive elections for the Social Credit in Alberta.

1944 Canadian troops push farther inland than any other Allied unit on D-Day (June 6). Canadian forces fight as a separate army (July 23). Saskatchewan elects Tommy Douglas's CCF, the first socialist government in North America. Maurice Duplessis regains office for the Union Nationale in Quebec.

1945 War in Europe ends (May 8). One million Canadians fought in WW II; 42,042 were killed. Canadians killed while fighting for other Allied forces numbered 4,500. Liberals win federal election (June 11). First **family allowance payments** are **made** (June 20). Canada joins the **United Nations** (June 26). Igor Gouzenko defects from the Soviet embassy in Ottawa (Sept. 5) and reveals the existence in Canada of a Soviet spy network. Canada's first nuclear reactor begins operations at Chalk River, Ontario.

■ **Postwar Canada: 1945–1968**

In the years following World War II, Canadians enjoyed a standard of living that was in stark contrast to the Depression years. The economy had boomed during the war and the gross national product had doubled. The

war had prompted development in new industries which continued to expand in peacetime. Consumer spending had increased dramatically during the war, and continued to rise with the postwar baby boom. This boom, along with large numbers of European immigrants, resulted in a 40 percent population increase between the war's end and 1958. In Canada's quickly growing cities and suburbs, home ownership was made easier by the National Housing Act, designed to make mortgages easier to obtain. This example of government involvement in the economy was characteristic of the times. By 1945, unemployment insurance and family allowance legislation had been passed and other social welfare measures were being discussed.

Prime Minister King retired in 1948, and was followed as Liberal leader by Louis St. Laurent. One of St. Laurent's first achievements was the entry of Newfoundland into Confederation in 1949. In 1951, his government increased old age pensions and, in 1957, introduced a hospital insurance plan. St. Laurent negotiated with the United States to build the St. Lawrence Seaway, an impressive feat of engineering completed in 1959. In 1956, however, the government used closure (a limit on debate) to cut off the parliamentary debate concerning the building of the trans-Canada pipeline for oil and gas. In the election the following year, the Conservatives under John Diefenbaker won a minority victory. In 1958, Diefenbaker called another election to consolidate his position. This time the Conservatives swept the country, winning 208 of 265 seats.

Western agriculture found huge new markets when the government arranged wheat sales to China. In 1960, Diefenbaker's government introduced the Bill of Rights to protect the rights of all Canadians, and granted Native Canadians the right to vote in federal elections.

Despite continuing popular support for the British Commonwealth, the government of Canada signed the North American Air Defence Agreement (NORAD) with the United States to increase security during a time of international tension. But it could not deal with an economic recession that led to a devalued dollar and high unemployment. Also, the prime minister dealt Canada's fledgling aircraft industry a serious blow when he cancelled production of the Canadian-made Avro Arrow fighter jet, and his refusal to allow nuclear warheads on the American missiles based in Canada earned him the emnity of the US government. In the election of 1962, his government was returned to power, but in a minority situation that forced another election in 1963. The 1963 election also resulted in a minority government, but this time, the Liberals, under Lester B. Pearson, were in power.

As prime minister, Pearson, a career diplomat, concentrated on domestic matters. His government relied on the support of the New Democratic Party (formerly the CCF) to hold a majority in the House of Commons, and the partnership produced legislation that broadened social welfare by introducing Medicare, the Canada Pension Plan and the Canada Assistance Plan. Canadian nationalism was heightened with the adoption of the maple leaf flag in 1965, and in the same year another federal election produced a Liberal government one seat short of a clear majority. The opening of the world's fair, Expo in Montreal, in Canada's centennial year, 1967, marked a year of celebration across the country.

During the 1960s, Pearson was sensitive to growing nationalism in Quebec. His government established a Royal Commission on Bilingualism and Biculturalism in 1963, to demonstrate that Quebec's interests could be served by federalism, and he encouraged some of those closely associated with the Quiet Revolution to run for federal office. Quebec had been transformed from traditional to modern attitudes towards education, social reform and industrialization, a movement known as the Quiet Revolution, under Premier Jean Lesage. The Quebec government was implementing the ideas of the Quiet Revolution, and championed provincial rights with its slogan *maîtres chez nous* (masters in our own house). This sentiment took centre stage during Centennial celebrations. Visiting French President Charles de Gaulle ended a Montreal speech with the cry *"Vive le Québec libre!"* ("Long live free Quebec") which set off a storm of diplomatic protest and delighted local nationalists. Despite growing nationalist sentiment, many Quebeckers, including Pierre Trudeau, went to Ottawa. Trudeau was elected to the House of Commons in 1965, and was named minister of justice in 1967. In 1968, following Pearson's retirement, Trudeau became Liberal leader.

1947 Imperial Oil discovers the **Leduc oil field** (Feb. 13).

1948 **Louis St. Laurent** succeeds Mackenzie King as prime minister (Nov. 15).

1949 Under Premier **Joey Smallwood**, **Newfoundland** becomes Canada's tenth province (Mar. 31). Canada joins NATO. Canadian appeals to Britain's Judicial Committee of the Privy Council are abolished: Canada's Supreme Court becomes final court of appeal. Liberals under St Laurent defeat Conservatives under George Drew in federal election (June 3).

1950 The Korean War begins (June 25); Canadian troops participate in the conflict as part of a United Nations force.

1951 The midcentury census reports Canada's population as 14,009,429. **Postwar immigration** to Canada exceeds 100,000 annually during the 1950s, primarily moving from Central and Eastern Europe to hold manufacturing jobs in urban centres. The Massey Royal Commission reports that Canadian cultural life is dominated by American influences. Revisions to the **Indian Act**, beginning in 1951, limit its coverage of aboriginal people. Indian women married to non-Indian men are excluded from the act. This provision was removed in 1985 after much protest of discrimination. **Charlotte Whitton**, the first woman to be mayor of a major Canadian city, is elected in Ottawa.

1952 **Vincent Massey** becomes the first native-born Governor General of Canada. Canada's **first television** stations begin broadcasting in Montreal (Sept. 6) and Toronto (Sept. 8). **W.A.C. Bennett** begins **Social Credit's** administration in British Columbia.

1953 Canada's National Library is established in Ottawa (Jan. 1). The Stratford Festival opens (July 13). The **Korean War** ends (July 27); total Canadian casualties are 314 killed and 1,211 wounded. Liberals under St Laurent defeat Conservatives under Drew in federal election (Aug. 10).

1954 An economic slump interrupts the postwar boom. Canada's **first subway** opens in Toronto (Mar. 30). Roger Bannister and John Landy run the "miracle mile" at the British Empire Games in Vancouver (Aug.), the first to run a mile in less than four minutes. Sixteen-year-old Marilyn Bell becomes the first person to swim Lake Ontario (Sept. 9).

Hurricane Hazel hits Toronto, killing 83 people (Oct. 15). The Geneva Conference on the Far East invites Canada to join India and Poland in **supervising peace in Indochina**. This peacekeeping commitment continues for nearly 20 years to 1973.

1955 The Canadian Labour Congress is formed. The suspension of Montreal Canadiens' hockey star Maurice (Rocket) Richard leads to rioting in Montreal (Mar. 17).

1956 The Liberals use closure to limit the **Pipeline Debate** (May 8–June 6), a manoeuvre that contributes to their electoral defeat the following year.

1957 Conservatives under **John Diefenbaker** win federal election (June 10) and form minority government. Ellen Fairclough becomes the first woman federal cabinet minister. The Canada Council is created to help foster Canadian cultural life. **Lester B. Pearson wins Nobel Prize** (Oct. 12) for his role in resolving the Suez Crisis. Canadian supply and services troops are sent to work with a multinational UN force around the **Gulf of Aqaba**. They stay until 1967 and return there in 1973.

1958 Conservatives under Diefenbaker win 208 seats in federal election (Mar. 31). Coal mine disaster at Springhill, NS, results in death of 74 miners.

1959 The **Avro Arrow** project is terminated, with a loss of almost 14,000 jobs (Feb. 20). The **St. Lawrence Seaway** is **opened** (June 26).

1960 Liberals under **Jean Lesage** win provincial election in Quebec (June 22), inaugurating the **Quiet Revolution**. A **Canadian Bill of Rights** is approved by Parliament. Native people get the right to vote in federal elections. During the 1960s French is recognized as a language of instruction in elementary and secondary schools in New Brunswick, Ontario and Manitoba. It is recognized subsequently in other provincial jurisdictions.

1961 The **New Democratic Party** replaces the CCF.

1962 Conservatives are reduced to minority status in federal election (June 18). Social Credit wins 30 seats and NDP take 19 to control the balance of power in the House of Commons. The Saskatchewan NDP introduces the first Canadian **Medicare** plan (July 1), and is opposed by a doctors' strike. **Trans-Canada Highway** officially opens (Sept. 3). Canadian-made satellite *Alouette* is launched (Sept. 29), making Canada the third nation in space. Canada's last execution, the double hanging of Ronald Turpin and Arthur Lucas, takes place (Dec. 11), at the Don Jail in Toronto.

1963 Liberals under Pearson win federal election (Apr. 8), and form a minority government. The Quebec separatist group **Front de libération du Québec (FLQ)** sets off a series of bombs in Montreal (Apr.–May). A Trans-Canada Airways flight crashes in Quebec, killing all 118 people aboard (Nov. 29). The **Royal Commission on Bilingualism and Biculturalism** begins its work.

1964 Canadians get social insurance cards (Apr.). Canada ends difficult peacekeeping duties in the Congo after four years of service with heavy casualties. Canadian troops join UN forces in Cyprus.

1965 Canada gets a new flag (Feb. 15). The **Autopact** between Canada and the US is signed. Canadian Roman Catholic Churches begin to celebrate mass in English (Mar. 7). Liberals win federal election (Nov. 8) to continue as a minority government. Failure of an Ontario Hydro relay device at Queenston plunges eastern North America into a power blackout (Nov. 9).

1966 The Munsinger Affair becomes Canada's first major parliamentary sex scandal (Mar. 4). The **Canada Pension Plan** is established. The CBC begins colour television broadcasting (Oct. 1).

1967 The Canadian army, navy and air forces are **unified** to become the Canadian **Armed Forces** (Apr. 25). Montreal hosts a world's fair, **Expo 67** (opened Apr. 27). Canada celebrates its **Centennial** (July 1). French President Charles **de Gaulle** delivers his "Vive le Québec Libre" speech in Montreal (July 24). The federal Department of Manpower and Immigration establishes the **"points system"** for immigrants. Patterns shift in the 1960s from European to Third World immigration as humanitarian objectives and family reunification policies increase multicultural immigration.

■ The Trudeau Years (1968–1984)

The Liberals won a majority victory in the election of 1968. Trudeau was a strong federalist, determined to show that Ottawa could promote the rights of French Canada. The Official Languages Act of 1969 recognized both English and French as official languages, and required federal institutions to provide services in both languages. Although the legislation was supported by all parties, it was not universally popular, even in Quebec.

In the October Crisis of 1970, separatist extremists belonging to the FLQ (Front de libération du Québec) kidnapped British trade commissioner James Cross, and killed Quebec Cabinet minister Pierre Laporte. Trudeau used the War Measures Act to apply emergency measures of arrest, detention and martial law. This move was generally accepted but was criticized by advocates of civil rights, especially since the FLQ had little real support and the Act was in effect across the country.

In his early years in power, Trudeau attempted to concentrate decision-making in Ottawa, and his newly created Prime Minister's Office led to western Canadian accusations of an eastern-dominated federal government. At the same time opposition parties charged that Trudeau was undermining both the power of the cabinet and of Parliament. The Liberals were almost defeated in the election of 1972, but retained office through a minority government that saw the New Democrats, under David Lewis, hold the balance of power. During this period the Foreign Investment Review Agency was set up (1973) to protect the Canadian economy against foreign domination; business critics claimed that it discouraged investment.

By 1974, the Liberals had regained a majority; their agenda was dominated by an economy battered by inflation. The government tried a variety of economic measures, including a three-year imposition of wage and price controls under the Anti-Inflation Act of 1975. Although the controls may have had some effect, world conditions, especially the international oil crisis, kept inflation high.

In 1976, the separatist Parti Québécois under René Lévesque defeated the provincial Liberals, led by Robert Bourassa in the Quebec election. This election fuelled public uncertainty over the future of Quebec (and

Canada), while continuing inflation and western alienation also undermined Liberal support. In the 1979 election, the Liberals lost, and Conservative leader Joe Clark took office as head of a minority government. Clark's government was short-lived as it suffered defeat in the House of Commons that same year.

The Liberals won the election of 1980, and Trudeau, lured out of planned retirement by the sudden election, embarked on an eventful term of office. He and members of his government actively campaigned on the victorious NO side in the 1980 Quebec referendum on sovereignty-association. The Liberals brought in the National Energy Program in the same year, again attempting to regulate ownership and control in part of the economy, and again succeeding in alienating foreign and local business interests. Resistance to the NEP, particularly in the West, was deep and persistent.

Then, after a long (18 months) and difficult campaign waged in Parliament, at federal-provincial meetings and in the media, Trudeau succeeded in getting an agreement on patriating the Canadian constitution amongst all provinces except Quebec. Patriation officially took place when Queen Elizabeth II proclaimed the new Constitution Act in Ottawa on April 17, 1982. The Canadian Charter of Rights and Freedoms was also proclaimed, entrenching bilingualism in the federal jurisdiction and providing for minority language education rights across Canada.

By 1984 the country was mired in a recession and in no mood for the international interest Trudeau was pursuing; he retired and John Turner became Liberal leader and prime minister for a brief period. The Liberal government was at the end of its mandate and Parliament was dissolved. After nearly 16 years of Liberal government, the voters were eager for a change.

1968 **Pierre Elliott Trudeau** succeeds Pearson as prime minister (Apr. 6), and leads Liberals to majority in federal election (June 25). A Royal Commission on the Status of Women is appointed. Canadian divorce law is reformed.

1969 Saturday postal deliveries end. Abortion law is liberalized (May). English and French become **official languages** of federal administration (July 9). New Brunswick declares official bilingualism. The Breathalyser comes into use as a test for alcohol-impaired drivers (Dec. 1).

1970 The FLQ kidnaps British trade commissioner James Cross (Oct. 5), precipitating the **October Crisis**. Quebec labour and immigration minister Pierre Laporte is kidnapped (Oct. 10), and found murdered (Oct. 17). The federal government invokes the **War Measures Act** (Oct. 16), leading to the arrest of 465 people.

1971 A policy of **multiculturalism** is adopted by the federal government. Canadian Gerhard Herzberg wins the Nobel Prize in chemistry for his studies of chemical reactions that help produce smog.

1972 Canada defeats the USSR in the first hockey series between the Soviets and Canadian professionals (Aug.–Sept.). Liberals win federal election with 109 seats to the Conservatives' 107, with the NDP holding the balance of power at 31 (Oct. 30).

1973 The separatist Parti Québécois becomes the Official Opposition in Quebec. Canadian troops are sent to the Middle East and serve with the United Nations Emergency Task Force there until 1979.

1974 Liberals under Trudeau win federal election and form majority government (July 8). **Pauline McGibbon** becomes the first female lieutenant-governor (Ontario) in the British Commonwealth.

1975 The **CN Tower**, the world's tallest free-standing structure at 553.339 metres, is completed in Toronto (Apr. 2). Federal government announces (July 18) its intention to screen foreign investment in Canada, via the Foreign Investment Review Agency (FIRA). Television cameras are allowed inside the House of Commons for the first time. Federal government imposes **wage and price controls** in an effort to fight inflation (Oct. 14). **Grace Hartman** is elected president of the Canadian Union of Public Employees.

1976 Canada announces 200-nautical-mile coastal fishing zone (June 4). **Death penalty** is **abolished** in a free vote (130–124) in Parliament (July 14). Montreal hosts **Olympic Games** (July 17–31). Team Canada wins the first **Canada Cup** hockey series

(Sept. 15). The **Parti Québécois** under René Lévesque wins provincial election in Quebec (Nov..15).

1977 Quebec government passes Bill 101, restricting English-language schooling to children whose mother or father had attended English elementary school in Quebec (Aug. 26). Highway signs in most of Canada become metric (Sept. 6).

1978 **Soviet nuclear-powered satellite crashes** in Canadian north (Jan. 24). Sun Life Assurance Co. announces a head office move from Montreal to Toronto because of language laws and political instability in Quebec. **Hilda Watson**, first woman to lead a political party in Canada, wins leadership of Yukon Progressive Conservative party.

1979 Conservatives under **Joe Clark** win federal election (May 22). Canada's first gold bullion coin, the Maple Leaf, goes on sale (Sept. 5). Supreme Court of Canada declares Manitoba and Quebec legislation creating unilingual courts and legislatures unconstitutional (Dec. 13). Federal Conservatives lose non-confidence vote on budget (Dec. 13), forcing the government's resignation. **Antonine Maillet** wins the prestigious French literary prize, the Prix Goncourt, for her novel *Pélagie-la-Charette*.

1980 Canada's ambassador to Iran, Ken Taylor, arranges the successful **escape of six American embassy staff** from Tehran while their colleagues are held hostage (Jan. 28). Liberals win federal election (Feb. 18). Canada boycotts the Olympic Games in Moscow because of the Soviet invasion of Afghanistan. **Jeanne Sauvé** becomes the first female Speaker of the House of Commons (Apr. 14). **Quebec votes "no"** to "sovereignty-association" in a **referendum** (May 22). **"O Canada"** becomes Canada's national anthem (June 27). The Supreme Court awards Rosa Becker half the assets accumulated during a 19-year common-law relationship. **National Energy Program** is created to encourage oil self-sufficiency, increase Canadian ownership in the oil industry and obtain a larger share of Canadian energy revenues.

1981 Quebec bans public signs in English (Sept. 23). The federal government and every province except Quebec reach agreement on a method for patriating Canada's constitution (Nov. 5). The 1981 census indicates significant increases in the percentage of new Canadians from Asia, the Caribbean and Latin America.

1982 Bertha Wilson becomes Canada's first woman to be appointed a justice of the Supreme Court (Mar. 4). The Quebec Court of Appeal rejects the Quebec government's claim of veto power over constitutional change (Apr. 7). Canada gains a new **Constitution** and **Charter of Rights and Freedoms** (Apr. 17). Canada's GNP falls 4.8 percent in the worst recession since the Great Depression of the 1930s.

1983 Canadian pay-TV channels begin operation (Feb. 1). **Jeanne Sauvé** is Canada's first woman to be appointed Governor General (Dec. 23). Canada approves a US plan to test unarmed **cruise missiles** in western Canada beginning in 1984.

■ **Mulroney in Power (1984–1993)**

In the 1984 general election, the Conservatives, under Brian Mulroney, won a decisive victory, taking 211 of 282 seats in the House of Commons, including 58 seats in Quebec, a former Liberal stronghold. In contrast to the previous government, the Conservatives sought to strengthen ties with the United States and took steps to attract more foreign investment to Canada. The recession of the early 80s was over and business and government were both ready to expand.

One of the goals of the Mulroney government was to amend the Constitution Act of 1982 to obtain the support of Quebec. The prime minister and 10 provincial premiers reached an agreement, which became known as the Meech Lake Accord, on such an amendment in 1987; the agreement was to be taken to provincial legislatures and to Parliament for approval by June 23, 1990. Also in 1987, the government negotiated a Canada–US free trade agreement (FTA) which provided for the elimination of all cross-border tariffs over 10 years. But the deal was rejected by both opposition parties and Liberal leader John Turner announced that the Liberal-dominated Senate would not approve free trade unless the Conservatives obtained public support in a general election. Mulroney called an election for November 1988. The campaign that followed was fractious; emotions ran high and there were wide fluctuations in public opinion. Anti-FTA sentiment was split between the opposition parties, and the Conservatives won a second majority government. The FTA was approved in December and took effect Jan. 1, 1989.

As the deadline for ratification of the Meech Lake Accord approached, its confirmation became increasingly uncertain. Provincial governments had changed in the interim and both Manitoba and Newfoundland indicated that they had reservations about the agreement. Despite a last-minute first ministers' conference and a great deal of political pressure, the Manitoba legislature failed to ratify the accord and Newfoundland withdrew its consent; the deal lapsed on June 23, 1990. The following years were marked by numerous federal-provincial conferences, a variety of proposals and pressure from Quebec to include recognition of its distinct society. In August 1992, a new federal-provincial agreement was reached (the Charlottetown Accord) in time to be considered in a referendum Quebec Premier Robert Bourassa had pledged to hold on the future of Quebec. The other provinces also took part in a national referendum on the terms of the accord, which included not only recognition of Quebec as a distinct society, but also provisions to transfer mining, forestry, telecommunications and many other jurisdictions to the provinces. Canadians from all walks of life grappled with the issues raised by the terms of the Charlottetown Accord, and the question dominated national media, (aside from the sports pages, which were distracted by the prospect of a Canadian team, the Toronto Blue Jays, winning the 1992 World Series). The referendum was held on Oct. 26, 1992, and the deal was rejected by 54.8 percent of the voters.

The Conservatives' second term of office was also marked by the introduction of the Goods and Services Tax (GST), a tax designed to replace the manufacturers' tax and spread the tax burden more evenly across the economy. This tax was deeply unpopular and the Liberal-appointed members of the Senate vowed to block its passage in the upper chamber. Mulroney responded by temporarily increasing the number of senators to 112, with new appointees who would support the measure. The tax was the subject of heated debate and much protest across the country as Canadians transferred their frustration over the endless constitutional discussion, the now faltering economy and disappointment over the results of FTA to the government.

The GST took effect on Jan. 1, 1991, and the Conservative government continued to pursue wider trade agreements by joining the US and Mexico in negotiations for a North American Free Trade Agreement that would supersede the FTA. Amid much controversy, the deal was signed in December and the government's popularity continued to plumb the depths of the popularity polls. In February, Mulroney announced his decision to step aside as leader; Kim Campbell became the new leader of the Conservatives and the country's first female prime minister after a June leadership convention. As the Conservative mandate drew to a close, Campbell attempted to present herself as a brand-new prime minister at the head of a brand-new government. In the election in October 1993, Canadian voters made it clear they did not accept this stance: the Liberals under Jean Chrétien won a lopsided victory in an election that changed the political map of the country. The new government took office with a record number of rookie MPs, the Loyal Opposition was made up of members of the separatist Bloc Québécois, with the Reform Party from western Canada nearly matching the BQ's number of seats. The Conservatives elected only two members and the NDP also fared poorly at the hands of the electorate.

1984 **John Turner** succeeds Pierre Trudeau as prime minister (June 30). Conservatives under **Brian Mulroney** win federal election with 211 seats, the largest majority in Canada's history (Sept. 4). The **Pope visits Canada** (Sept. 9–20). **Marc Garneau** becomes the first Canadian in space, aboard US space shuttle *Challenger* (Oct. 5). Council for the Northwest Territories recognizes the use of **aboriginal languages** as well as English and French.

1985 The voyage through the Northwest Passage of US icebreaker *Polar Sea* challenges Canada's **Arctic sovereignty**. Prime Minister Mulroney and US President Reagan declare mutual support for **Star Wars research** and **free trade** between the two nations at "Shamrock Summit" (Mar. 18) in Quebec City. The Quebec provincial Liberals

under Robert Bourassa defeat the Parti Québécois (Dec. 2).

1986 The Canadian dollar hits a then all-time low of 70.20 cents US (Jan. 31). The **Expo 86** world's fair is held in Vancouver (May 2–Oct. 13). Canada joins other Commonwealth nations (Aug. 5) in adopting **economic sanctions against South Africa** because of its apartheid policy. Canada receives a United Nations award (Oct. 6) for providing a haven for world refugees. Canadian John Polanyi shares (with Dudley R. Herschbach and Yuan T. Lee) the Nobel Prize for chemistry.

1987 The Bank of Canada rate drops to a 13-year low of 7.49 percent (Jan. 28); 6-month residential mortgages are as low as 7.5 percent. Prime Minister Brian Mulroney and 10 provincial premiers agree on proposed constitutional amendments in the **Meech Lake Accord** (Apr. 30). Ontario passes the first **pay equity legislation** for the private sector enacted in North America (June). A free vote in Parliament on restoration of **capital punishment** defeats the proposal 148–127 (June). A **free trade** agreement between Canada and the United States is set out (Oct. 3). **Stock prices tumble** (Oct. 19) in Canada and throughout the world. The founding assembly of the **Reform Party of Canada** is held (November).

1988 Canada is left without an **abortion law** (Jan. 28) when the Supreme Court rules that existing legislation is unconstitutional. Canadian sprinter **Ben Johnson** sets a world record and wins a gold medal at the Summer Olympics in Seoul (Sept. 24) but is stripped of both (Sept. 26) after testing positive for steroids. Yukon Territory passes language legislation recognizing the use of aboriginal languages. Brian Mulroney's Progressive Conservatives win a second consecutive majority in the **federal election** (Nov. 21) after a bitter campaign fought over the free trade agreement with the US. Quebec's **French-only sign law** is struck down by the Supreme Court (Dec. 15) but is re-instated by Quebec (Dec. 21) using the "notwithstanding" clause in the Charter of Rights and Freedoms. Free trade legislation passes the House of Commons (Dec. 24) and the Senate (Dec. 30). The "Kamloops Amendment" to the Indian Act grants band councils jurisdiction over all reserve land, including the power to impose taxes.

1989 The Free Trade Agreement takes effect (Jan. 1). The federal government announces a new **goods and services tax** (GST) to take effect in January 1991. Audrey McLaughlin becomes Canada's **first female national party leader** as the NDP chooses a successor to Ed Broadbent (Dec. 2).

1990 Revisions to the Criminal Code provide choice of language in criminal hearings (January). Several Quebec Conservative MPs, led by cabinet minister Lucien Bouchard (May 21), leave the government to form the pro-independence **Bloc Québécois**. The **Meech Lake Accord dies** when both Newfoundland and Manitoba fail to ratify the constitutional agreement by the deadline (June 23). Manitoba MLA **Elijah Harper** refuses the unanimous consent required for debate and a vote on the Meech Lake Accord because the accord does not provide special status for aboriginal peoples as it does for Quebec. Jean Chrétien becomes leader of the federal Liberal party. A land dispute leads to a 78-day armed confrontation between Mohawk warriors and government forces at the Kanesatake reserve near **Oka**, Que. **Canada sends warships** to the Persian Gulf as part of the multinational force being assembled to force Iraq to withdraw from occupied Kuwait. Brian Mulroney's Conservative government stacks the Senate (Sept. 27) with new appointees to ensure passage of the federal **goods and services tax (GST)**, which takes effect Jan. 1.

1991 Canadian military personnel participate with the Allied forces in the assault against Iraq beginning Jan. 16 (the **Gulf War**). Prime Minister Brian Mulroney and US President George Bush sign an **acid rain accord** with the goal of ending acid rain within 10 years. **Rita Johnston** succeeds BC Premier **William Vander Zalm** as premier, the first woman to enter the provincial premier's office in Canada. Mulroney's government announces a **new constitutional reform package** promising aboriginal self-government within 10 years and guaranteeing aboriginal representation in an elected Senate. **Gun control** is passed, imposing tougher controls and banning imported military assault weapons. **Yukon First Nations** sign an umbrella agreement on land claims and self-government; an agreement is reached on creation of Nunavut.

1992 A year-long crisis in the Atlantic **fisheries** results in a two-year shutdown of the cod fishery (July 2), a five-year ban on commercial salmon fishing in Newfoundland (Mar. 6) and international negotiations to protect the fish stocks. **Gwich'in Indians** sign a deal with Ottawa, giving them title to nearly 24,000 sq. km of land in the NWT and Yukon (Apr. 22). The details of the North American Free Trade Agreement (**NAFTA**) are announced Aug. 12. Prime Minister Mulroney signs the deal on Dec. 17. Negotiations on constitutional reform occur throughout the year, and the **Charlottetown Accord**, which wins Quebec's approval, is announced Aug. 19. Proposals include Senate reform, an enlarged House of Commons and self-government for native people. On Oct. 26, a national referendum is held on the accord; the rejectionists claim victory.

1993 The **Sahtu Tribe** of the Great Bear Lake region in the NWT settles a land claim to 41,437 sq. km; the **Cree** in northern Quebec win compensation from Hydro-Quebec for damage done around James Bay. On Jan. 19 Canadian troops begin the planned pull-out from NATO bases. On Feb. 24 Prime Minister Mulroney announces his resignation, to take effect in June. Four members of the **Canadian Airborne Regiment**, in Somalia since January on a peacekeeping mission, are charged in the death of a Somali civilian. NAFTA legislation passes in the House of Commons on May 27. Yukon's 14 First Nations sign the **Umbrella Final Agreement** in Whitehorse on May 29; the settlement includes 41,400 sq. km of land and $280 million. Defence Minister **Kim Campbell** takes over the Conservative government after a second-ballot victory at the leadership convention on June 25. On Oct. 25, the Liberal Party wins a decisive victory in a federal election that sees the emergence of **two new parties**—the Bloc Québécois and the Reform party—and the near demise of the Progressive Conservatives. The cod moratorium of 1992 is extended to include the Gulf of St. Lawrence and is slated to last until the end of the decade.

1994 Most of the country west of the Rockies endures the coldest winter since the 1950s. **Cigarette taxes** are cut federally and provincially in an effort to curb a black market in cigarettes. The Liberals' first budget forecasts cuts in defence spending, UI benefits, tax deductions and foreign aid and freezes transfer payments and public sector salaries. The **Canada Pension Plan** posts a deficit for the first time in 28 years. Members of the **Saskatchewan Wheat Pool** vote to transform the organization, formed in 1924, into a public company. The prime minister and provincial premiers sign an agreement to end trade barriers among the provinces. The Inuit of Quebec sign a self-government deal with the Quebec government. **Canadian troops leave CFB Lahr**, officially ending 27 years of Canadian service for NATO in Europe. The **Algonquins** of Gold Lake, Ont., sign an agreement to begin negotiating an 8.5-million-acre land claim in southern Canada. Canadian sports fans are left hockey-less until the new year by a labour dispute and **NHL lock-out**.

1995 The Canadian Airborne Regiment is disbanded in January after a new scandal compounds damage done by the **Somalia Affair**. Federal fisheries officials seize the Spanish fishing vessel *Estai* in March in a battle over fishing rights on the Grand Banks. A settlement of the dispute in April gives the **North Atlantic Fishing Organization** greater powers; in the same month, Canada loses its triple-A bond rating courtesy of Moody's Investors Service of New York. BC's Fraser River salmon run is shut down in August because fish stocks are too low. In September, Newfoundland voters approve a proposal to shift control of education from the church to the province. In October, **Alexa McDonough** is elected leader of the federal NDP. On Oct. 30, after a bruising campaign that sees federal Opposition Leader Bouchard take over the YES side, the **proposal that Quebec separate from Canada** to form a sovereign state is narrowly defeated in a referendum—49.4 percent Yes, and 50.6 percent against.

1996 The Mint unveils the new $2 coin (Feb. 19). On May 29, Canada and the US sign a **softwood lumber agreement** after 15 years of controversy. On July 9, the **Innu** of Davis Inlet agree to relocate to Sango Bay. On July 20–21, **devastating floods** hit the Saguenay valley in Quebec. On Oct. 2, former Quebec premier **Robert Bourassa** dies. On Oct. 8, Gen. Jean Boyle resigns as head of Canada's armed forces after controversial evidence arises at the **Somalia inquiry**. On Nov. 18, Canada and Chile sign a free trade deal. In December, Canada signs a $4 billion contract with China for two **CANDU** reactors.

1997 The federal government announces an out-of-court settlement with Brian Mulroney in his libel suit over the **Airbus investigation** (Jan. 6). Voters in Alberta give Premier **Ralph Klein** another majority (Mar. 11). On Mar. 6, the federal government's **anti-smoking bill**, which limits tobacco-company funding of arts and sports activities, passes in the House of Commons. Census data taken in 1996 and released on Apr. 15 reveals that Quebec's share of Canada's population has fallen below 25 percent for the first time since 1867. Premier **Gary Filmon** declares an emergency in southern Manitoba as the **Red River** floods across the US border (Apr. 22). An independent auditor confirms that the gold in samples from the **Bre-X claim** in Indonesia are "negligible" (May 4). The **Confederation Bridge** officially opens to traffic between PEI and the mainland (May 31). The federal Liberals win re-election with a reduced majority; the Reform party becomes the Opposition (June 2). Casting ballots in a second referendum on creating secular schools, Newfoundland voters support the change (Sept. 2). A judge rules that the **Red Cross** is negligent in the tainted-blood scandal (Oct. 8). A bus crash in Quebec kills 43 in the worst road accident in Canadian history (Oct. 13). **Saskatchewan Conservatives** vote to mothball their party for at least two provincial elections (Nov. 9). The annual **APEC conference** is held in Vancouver (Nov. 21–25); the RCMP pepper-spray student demonstrators. Canada agrees to the **Kyoto Convention** on greenhouse gas emissions (Dec. 11).

1998 An **ice storm** cripples Quebec and eastern Ontario, leaving one million people without power and food (Jan. 6). Ottawa apologizes to Canada's aboriginals for past mistreatment (Jan. 7). On Feb. 17, **Ontario Hydro** reports a loss of $6.32 billion in 1997—the largest business loss in Canadian history. Canadian athletes at the **Nagano Winter Olympics** win a record 15 medals (Feb. 22). On Mar. 27, federal Conservative leader **Jean Charest** says he will run for leader of Quebec's Liberal party. On the same day, federal and provincial governments announce $1.1 billion in compensation for victims who contracted hepatitis C from tainted blood in 1986–90. Ottawa and Washington agree to save Pacific salmon. The **Nisga'a** people and the BC government sign a historic land claim treaty (July 15). The Supreme Court of Canada rules on **Quebec's proposed secession from Canada:** Canada–Quebec talks must begin after a majority in Quebec votes for independence in a referendum with an unambiguous question (Aug. 20). On Sept. 1, a new blood collection agency replaces the Canadian Red Cross. **Swissair Flight 111** crashes off the coast of Nova Scotia, killing all 229 passengers (Sept. 2). Ten thousand gun owners meet on Parliament Hill to protest firearm registration (Sept. 22). Canada wins a seat on the UN Security Council (Oct. 8). Canada's first diamond mine opens in NWT (Oct. 14). Statistics Canada reports that inflation has sunk to 1960s levels (Oct. 21). The *National Post* publishes its first edition (Oct. 27). Ontario passes the **Energy Competition Act** to end Ontario Hydro's monopoly on power provision in 2001 (Oct. 29). Former prime minister **Joe Clark** is elected leader of the federal Conservative party (Nov. 14). Canada pledges $100 million in hurricane relief to Central America over four years (Nov. 15). The Saskatchewan Court of Appeal rules that **Robert Latimer** must serve at least 10 years in prison for the 1993 killing of his disabled daughter (Nov. 23). **Environment Canada** declares 1998 the warmest year globally in 130–140 years (Nov. 30). On Dec. 1, federal justice minister **Anne McLellan** officially launches Canada's new gun control law. Statistics Canada reports that the national jobless rate fell to 8 percent in November—the lowest level this decade (Dec. 4). Finance Minister Paul Martin prohibits Canadian **bank mergers**, saying they would concentrate economic power in the hands of fewer bankers and reduce competition (Dec. 14).

1999 Toronto's task force on homelessness reports that the fastest-growing groups of **homeless people** are youths under age 18 and families with children (Jan. 14). The next day, snowfall in Toronto surpasses 120 cm for January and breaks an 1871 record for snowfall in one month. Statistics Canada says the number of self-employed and part-time workers steadily grew in the 1990s (Jan. 27). Prime Minister Chrétien gets nine premiers to agree to a **social union accord** after promising more health-care funding for the provinces but fails to secure Quebec's signature (Feb. 4). In his federal budget address, Finance Minister Paul Martin promises an $11.5 billion boost in **health-care transfers** to the provinces over the next five years (Feb. 16). The *Free Press* of Regina and Saskatoon declares bankruptcy

(Feb. 17). In Ottawa, **Kurds** hurl a gasoline bomb at a police line outside the Turkish embassy, setting one officer ablaze (Feb. 17); in Montreal, police and about 100 Kurds clash outside the Israeli consulate (Feb. 22). Ottawa and all provinces except Nova Scotia offer $1.5 billion in relief to 45,000 farm families facing financial hardship caused by falling international grain and hog markets (Feb. 24). Senator **Eric Berntson** becomes the fifteenth Conservative convicted in Saskatchewan's long-running expense-fraud scandal (Feb. 25). The Liberal government moves to bar federal Crown corporations from donating to political parties (Mar. 5). Canadian **CF-18 fighter-bombers** begin taking part in NATO air strikes against **Yugoslavia** (Mar. 24); in Toronto, Serbs throw rocks, paint and Molotov cocktails at the US consulate and police (Mar. 24–25). In Manitoba, an inquiry led by **Alfred Monnin** reports that senior Tories illegally recruited and backed supposedly independent aboriginal candidates in the 1995 provincial election to split popular support for the NDP (Mar. 29). For the first time in Canada, **Mohawks** on Quebec's Kahnawake reserve win the right to collect tax-like levies from non-natives on reserves (Mar. 30). MPs from all federal parties endorse Canadian participation in NATO's air war against **Yugoslavia** (Mar. 31). **Nunavut** becomes Canada's newest territory; **Paul Okalik** becomes its first premier (Apr. 1). Ontario sells **Highway 407** to a Quebec-led consortium for $3.1 billion in the biggest privatization in Canadian history to date (Apr. 13). Statistics Canada reports that the average household is no richer than it was 20 years ago (Apr. 14). **Wayne Gretzky** plays his last professional hockey game (Apr. 18). The Supreme Court of Canada says the courts put too many offenders behind bars, making Canada's incarceration rate one of the highest in the world (Apr. 23). Newfoundland's legislature unanimously votes to change the province's official name to Newfoundland and Labrador (Apr. 29). **David Milgaard**, who spent 22 years in prison for a murder he did not commit, gets a record $10 million in compensation from the Saskatchewan and federal governments (May 17). The Supreme Court of Canada rules that the **Ontario Family Law Act**'s definition of spouse—which applies only to heterosexual couples—is unconstitutional because it discriminates against gays; the court also opens band elections to off-reserve natives for the first time (May 20). Ottawa unanimously passes a law giving victims more voice in the criminal justice system (May 28). Ottawa agrees to liberalize trade with five Andean countries (May 31). The House of Commons passes a Reform party motion that says marriage is a union between man and woman (June 8). Defence Minister **Art Eggleton** announces the departure of another 500 peacekeepers to **Kosovo** (June 11), two days after Western generals and Yugoslavia sign a peace accord. The **Coast Guard** intercepts a cargo ship filled with 123 Chinese **illegal immigrants** off Vancouver Island (July 20). Statistics Canada reports that Canada's crime rate fell for the seventh year in a row and hit a 19-year low (July 21). Canadian goaltender **Steve Vézina** tests positive for banned stimulants at the **Pan American Games**; his roller hockey team is stripped of its gold medals (Aug. 1). In Winnipeg, the Pan American Games close after Canadian athletes win 196 medals, 64 of them gold (Aug. 8). Explosions rock an oil-recycling plant in Calgary (Aug. 9). A second cargo ship dumps 131 Chinese illegal immigrants in the Queen Charlotte Islands (Aug. 11). After 130 years, **Eaton's** files for bankruptcy protection and announces plans to close its stores (Aug. 20). BC Premier **Glen Clark** resigns following the revelation that he was under criminal investigation for awarding a casino license to a friend (Aug. 21). The NDP meets for a national convention in Ottawa; **Alexa McDonough** wins support for a policy of balanced budgets and moderate tax cuts (Aug. 27–29). The Canadian Forces, RCMP and Coast Guard rescue Chinese immigrants aboard a third ship near Vancouver Island (Aug. 31). A BC court sentences **Dave Stupich**, a provincial finance minister in the 1980s, to two years in prison for stealing hundreds of thousands of dollars from an NDP fundraising society in Nanaimo (Sept. 3). Prime Minister Chrétien says Canada will send up to 600 peacekeepers to **East Timor** (Sept. 12). Cape Breton's Phalen coal mine shuts down ahead of schedule; 400 workers lose their jobs (Sept. 13). **Donald Marshall** wins a victory in the Supreme Court of Canada defending historic Mi'kmaq fishing rights (Sept. 17). On Oct. 3, non-natives, angry that aboriginals have been allowed to fish off-season, destroy native lobster traps in **Miramichi Bay** off the coast of northeastern New Brunswick. (The Supreme Court of

Canada judgment on Sept. 17, 1999, ruled that terms of a 1760 Mi'kmaq treaty allowing East Coast natives to earn a moderate livelihood from hunting, fishing and gathering is valid.) On Oct. 10, Fisheries Minister **Herb Dhaliwal** announces future limits on native fishing. On Oct. 13, the **World Trade Organization** rules that the 1965 Canada–US auto pact violates rules that call for freer global trade. On Oct. 29, Ottawa agrees to pay **$3.6 billion in back pay** to thousands of mostly female workers to compensate for wage gaps between men and women. On Nov. 7, a labour dispute shuts down West Coast ports for everything but bulk grain shipments for a week, costing the **Port of Vancouver** alone $90 million a day. On Nov. 23, **Wayne Gretzky** is inducted into the Hockey Hall of Fame. On Nov. 23, Health Canada releases 1,200 pages of industry documents showing Canadian-based Imperial Tobacco Ltd. assessed smokers as young as nine and "fortified" products to increase their addictive qualities. On Dec. 3, the jobless rate is reported at 6.9 percent, the lowest in 18 years. **Air Canada** gains control of **Canadian Airlines** on Dec. 8 and reaches a release agreement with AMR Corp., Canadian's largest shareholder. **Merchant mariners** and the federal government reach a deal (Dec. 15) on compensation for civilian seamen who served aboard cargo ships during the Second World War.

2000 On Jan. 12, **Beverley McLachlin** is sworn in as chief justice of the Supreme Court of Canada—the first woman to hold the office. On Jan. 13, Ottawa announces it will pay $1 billion over the next two years to help farmers through the latest crisis in agricultural prices, but critics say the promised aid isn't enough. On Jan. 27, the Reform party opens the convention destined to create the **Canadian Alliance**. Human Resources Minister **Jane Stewart** spends much of January trying to play down reports that her department had misspent $1 billion on dubious projects. On Jan. 31, Ottawa approves the $8 billion takeover of **Canada Trust** by **Toronto Dominion Bank**. BC Attorney General **Ujjal Dosanjh**'s first ballot win (Feb. 20) at the NDP convention sets the stage for him to become Canada's first Indo-Canadian premier four days later. On Mar. 15, the House of Commons votes overwhelmingly for legislation to clarify the rules if Quebec, or any other province, holds a referendum on secession. On Apr. 11, the federal government's **same-sex bill** passes through the Commons as MPs vote overwhelmingly for the legislation. The bill gives same-sex pairs the same social and tax benefits as heterosexual couples. On Apr. 13, **Nisga'a leaders** smile and fight tears as a land-claim treaty started 113 years ago by their ancestors clears its last parliamentary hurdle. The BC First Nation receives self-government powers and $253 million in cash and economic funding. Ottawa promises $255 million toward the deal that will cost a total of $487 million. In late May, seven deaths in **Walkerton**, Ont., are blamed on the worst *E. coli* outbreak in Canadian history. The contamination by the deadly bacteria is traced to the town's water supply; local officials are accused of failing to alert townspeople to the danger. Alberta's controversial **Bill 11**, authorizing some private health-care services, receives royal assent on May 31; critics of the bill claim that its inclusion of provisions for private health care will make Canada's health-care system open to globalization. On June 4 in Windsor, Ont., **anti-globalization protesters** are blasted with pepper spray and arrested as police riot squads brace for the opening of the annual general assembly of the Organization of American States. On June 15, the Supreme Court upholds the five-year-old **Firearms Act** that requires every gun owner to get a licence and register every firearm by the end of 2000. Baton-wielding riot police dodge bricks, paint bombs and Molotov cocktails on June 15 as more than 1,000 **anti-poverty protesters** attempt to storm the Ontario legislature to protest the policies of the Harris government. Preston Manning places second to **Stockwell Day** on June 24 as the Canadian Alliance votes for its first leader. Manning loses two weeks later in a second ballot. On July 5, federal Agriculture Minister Lyle Vanclief declares that Canada's **agriculture ministers** signed a $5.5-billion deal to take some of the uncertainty out of the farming business. **Matthew Coon Come**, a Cree leader from northern Quebec, unseats Phil Fontaine as national chief of the Assembly of First Nations on July 12. Ninety **Chinese migrants** who arrived in BC by boat in 1999 return to China on July 27 to face jail and fines. On July 31, **CanWest Global Communications Corp.** announces a $3.5-billion takeover of all the major Canadian newspapers held by Conrad Black's **Hollinger Inc.**

On July 31, Ontario's highest court declares the law banning possession of **marijuana** unconstitutional and gives Ottawa one year to amend it. The Ontario Court of Appeal rules that Canada's marijuana law fails to recognize that people who suffer from chronic illnesses can use pot as medicine. On Aug. 3, armed Canadian soldiers drop from helicopters to take charge of the American cargo ship **GTS** *Katie*, loaded with Canadian military equipment, which is refusing to complete its delivery because of a dispute over payment. Victims of Canada's tainted-blood tragedy agree to a $79-million compensation plan on Aug. 30. The people infected by **hepatitis C** and **HIV** were infected before 1986 or after 1990, making them ineligible for the $1.5 billion federal-provincial compensation package announced two years earlier. Premiers strike a **health-care deal** on Sept. 11 with Prime Minister Jean Chrétien that raises federal transfers to $18.3 billion next year. The provinces want federal transfer payments restored to 1994 levels of $18.7 billion, which they say will cost $4.2 billion annually. On Sept. 11, Canadian Alliance leader Stockwell Day and PC leader Joe Clark win seats in **federal by-elections**. On Sept. 13, Groupe Videotron Ltee. agrees to be taken over by **Quebecor Inc.** for $5.4 billion. Finance Minister **Paul Martin** announces Sept. 20 that the surplus for 1999–2000 is $12.3 billion, with a $11.4-billion surplus in the first four months of the latest fiscal year. On Sept. 28, former prime minister **Pierre Trudeau** dies at the age of 80; his body is brought to Ottawa to lie in state on Sept. 30 and his state funeral is held at Montreal's Notre-Dame Basilica on Oct. 3. On Oct. 27, RCMP arrest two men charged in connection with the 15-year-long investigation of the Air India Flight 182 bombing in 1985. **NASDAQ Canada**, the tech-oriented stock exchange, commences trading in Montreal on Nov. 21. On Nov. 27 the Liberals win the general election with a healthy majority of 173 seats; the CA takes 66 to become the Official Opposition. Canadian astronaut **Marc Garneau** lifts off on his third space mission on board the space shuttle *Endeavour* on Nov. 30. His mission is to take and install solar panels on the International Space Station. He returns to Earth on Dec. 11.

2001 Despite a last-minute rush to meet the Jan. 1 deadline, hundreds of thousands of

gun owners fail to register their guns. Two **gay couples**, one male and one female, are married on Jan. 14 in a Toronto church in a campaign to change Canada's ban on same-sex marriages. In a rare settlement, the **Correctional Service of Canada** agrees to pay $215,000 to a sexual-assault victim only hours before her civil suit against the prison system is due to begin. **Lorne Calvert** is elected leader of the NDP in Saskatchewan and the province's premier at a leadership convention in Saskatoon (Jan. 27). Ottawa bans the importation of **Brazilian beef** (Feb. 2) as a precaution against mad cow disease. Claiming there is no danger, Brazil says that the move is just part of a long-running trade battle. **Roger Grimes** becomes premier of Newfoundland and Labrador (Feb. 13). In February, the Supreme Court of Canada rules unanimously against extradition to countries that have **capital punishment**, unless there is assurance that detainees will not be executed if convicted of a crime carrying the death penalty. The ruling comes in the case of two Vancouver men, Glen Sebastian Burns and Atif Ahmad Rafay, wanted in Washington State for several murders. **Bernard Landry** is acclaimed premier of Quebec (Mar. 8). Alberta Premier **Ralph Klein** wins his third term in the Mar. 12 election. Hundreds of tractors and farm vehicles head for Ottawa in a Canada-wide protest to demand more financial support for **farmers**. The federal government had unveiled a $500-million aid package, but farmers—hurt by low commodity prices and poor harvests due to drought-like conditions—say it is not enough (Mar. 14). Canada's **softwood lumber** deal with the US expires on Mar. 31; US companies ask Washington to establish anti-dumping and countervailing duties against Canadian products. Health Minister **Allan Rock** appoints former Saskatchewan premier **Roy Romanow** to investigate Canadian health care and consider the role of private health care. A **VIA train** derails in Stewiacke, NS, injuring 24, after a switch lock is set incorrectly (Apr. 12). A teen is later charged with mischief. Astronaut **Chris Hadfield** becomes the first Canadian to walk in space as he deploys the new Canadarm2 during a mission to space station *Alpha* (Apr. 19). The **Summit of the Americas** is held in Quebec City (Apr. 20-22). More than 30,000 demonstrators march during the meeting of national leaders from North, Central and South America. Several hundred are arrested following battles with police and thousands are tear-gassed. Ontario Chief Justice Patrick LeSage approves a no-fault settlement in a class-action suit arising from the tainted-water tragedy in **Walkerton**, Ont. Under the settlement, all of the town's 5,000 residents plus visitors who got sick receive at least $2,000. American George Gillett buys 80 percent of the **Montreal Canadiens** from Molson Inc. for $275 million (May 7). (The NHL approves the deal in June, which becomes final in July.) On May 15, **eight Alliance MPs** leave their party and form a rebel faction due to leader Stockwell Day's poor performance. Ottawa announces that the last underground coal mine in **Cape Breton** will be shut down by the fall; 500 jobs will disappear along with a 280-year tradition (May 16). Liberal leader **Gordon Campbell** becomes premier of BC after his party defeats the NDP led by **Ujjal Dosanjh** (May 16). BC's NDP is reduced to two seats. Nova Scotia passes legislation giving **gay couples** registered with the Department of Vital Statistics some of the rights formerly reserved for married heterosexual couples. Members of Parliament vote to fast-track a new **pay package** for themselves, which includes a 20 percent raise but ends their tax-free expense allowance (June 5). Calgary-based **Gulf Canada Resources Ltd.** agrees to be taken over by Conoco Inc. of Houston for $9.8 billion. The Ontario government becomes the first provincial government to offer **tax credits** to families with children in private or independent religious schools (June 27). The credit is to be phased in over five years. The total of **Alliance defections** reaches 11 on June 27, putting the rebel group one member shy of official party status. Ontario Premier **Mike Harris** testifies before the Walkerton inquiry that he was never warned of risks to human health posed by funding cuts to the Environment Ministry (June 29). **Nortel Networks** announces the biggest quarterly loss in Canadian corporate history: US$19.4 billion in its second quarter (July 20). MPs from the Canadian Alliance and the Conservative party meet for two days in Halifax; on July 27, the group pledges to work together. Seven children, removed from their Aylmer, Ont., home by **Children's Aid** in a clash over spanking and medical care, are reunited with their Christian parents. On July 30, United Grain Growers and Agricore announce a merger to create **Agricore United**. The new company will control close to 40 percent of western Canadian grain. The **provincial premiers**, in a rare show of solidarity, demand $7 billion from Ottawa for their health-care systems to forestall cuts to service (Aug. 3). The US commerce department levies a 19.3 percent duty on Canadian **softwood lumber** from all provinces outside Atlantic Canada; the duty is made retroactive to mid-May and is projected to cost Canadian producers $4 billion a year (Aug. 10). **Conrad Black** announces the sale of his remaining half interest in the *National Post* to the Asper family's **CanWest Global Communications** (Aug. 24). By Aug. 28, 10 birds in Southern Ontario are found carrying the **West Nile virus**, which can be fatal in humans. On Sept. 11, three of the **Alliance dissidents** return to the party caucus and the remaining eight form a coalition with the Conservatives in the House of Commons. **Hundreds of flights** denied entry into US airspace are grounded in Canada after the terrorist attacks on New York City and Washington; thousands of travellers are put up in Canadian communities, from Gander to Vancouver, in hotels, school gyms and private homes. In the wake of the Sept. 11 attacks, **stricter surveillance** makes it tougher to cross the Canada–U.S. border and delays shipments, forcing thousands of layoffs in the Ontario auto industry. The ban on **air traffic** in Canada is lifted on the afternoon of Sept. 12; however, it takes days for air traffic to return to normal. On Sept. 14, 100,000 gather on Parliament Hill to pay respects to the victims of the terrorist attacks in the US. **Tropical storm Gabrielle** pounds the eastern coast of Newfoundland and Labrador with rain and winds of 111 km an hour (Sept. 19). The damage prompts the provincial government to apply for federal disaster relief. **General Motors** announces the closure of its assembly plant in Broisbriand, Que., for the fall of 2002, eliminating the province's auto industry (Sept. 25). On Sept. 26, Ottawa announces that it will freeze the assets of any group that the US government identifies as having terrorist links. On Oct. 2, Ottawa announces a **$160-million bailout** to help airlines cope with post–Sept. 11 financial losses. On Oct. 8, Defence Minister **Art Eggleton** outlines Canada's military aid to US-led operations in Afghanistan. Assistance includes six ships,

six aircraft and more than 2,000 personnel. An **anti-terrorism bill** in the House of Commons proposes to create new terrorist-related offences. The government considers giving new powers, such as the power to make preventive arrests and to monitor communications going outside Canada, to police and security forces (Oct. 15). A consortium of energy companies signs a deal with the **Mackenzie Valley Aboriginal Pipeline Corp.** and gives aboriginals a one-third stake in a proposed natural gas pipeline (Oct. 15). On Oct. 22, Health Minister **Allan Rock** approves the purchase of a generic version of the drug for treating exposure to **anthrax**; Bayer, holder of the patent for Cipro, threatens a lawsuit. The US Commerce Department places a second duty on Canadian **softwood lumber**, adding a 12.6 percent dumping duty to the existing 19.3 percent countervailing duty (Oct. 31). A Senate committee reviewing the **anti-terrorism bill** recommends placing a five-year limit on any new powers given to police. The committee also recommends that government ministers given new powers under the bill be strictly supervised to guarantee citizens' freedoms (Nov. 1). On Nov. 9, **Canada 3000**, the country's second-largest airline, leaves thousands of travellers stranded when it grounds its fleet and files for bankruptcy. Police and demonstrators clash when the **G-20 group of nations** meets in Ottawa (Nov. 17–18). On Nov. 29, released court documents show that **Samir Ait Mohamed**, an Algerian held in Vancouver and accused of plotting a terrorist attack in 1999 on the Los Angeles airport, had also planned attacks on Jews in Montreal. Alberta introduces regulations allowing some surgery in **private clinics** (Nov. 30). Thousands of Canadians, including Prime Minister Chrétien, take part in a "Canada Loves New York" rally in Manhattan to pay tribute to those who risked and lost their lives on Sept. 11, 2001 (Dec. 1). On Dec. 3, Canada and the US sign a **border security agreement** that includes more information sharing and border patrols by the US National Guard. Newfoundland's name officially changes to Newfoundland and Labrador (Dec. 6). On Dec. 12, the House of Commons releases a report on **reproductive technologies**, setting boundaries for researchers and users. The report calls for a ban on cloning humans and patenting human genes, but allows for experiments on human embryos left over from fertility treatments. **Stockwell Day** resigns as leader of the Canadian Alliance (Dec. 12). On Dec. 12, Ontario Premier Mike Harris announces plans to privatize **Hydro One** and open the province's electricity market to competition. Health Canada announces that **marijuana** grown in Flin Flon, Man., for medical use is available for shipment to eligible users (Dec. 21).

2002 A Montreal man, **Mokhtar Haouri**, is sentenced to 24 years in prison for his role in the plot to bomb the Los Angeles airport on the last day of 1999 (Jan. 16). The dollar hits a record low of US$0.62 (Jan. 17). On Jan 18, the first instalment of the report on **Walkerton** blames the Ontario Conservative government's emphasis on cost-cutting and deregulation for contributing to the May 2000 *E. coli* outbreak that killed seven people and made 2,300 ill. On Jan. 29, Defence Minister Eggleton confirms that **Canadian soldiers** have captured **al-Qaeda and Taliban fighters** and has handed them to US forces during the previous week. Former leader of the Reform party **Preston Manning** retires from politics (Jan. 31). On Feb. 4, 14,000 **Alberta teachers strike**. They are ordered back to work three weeks later. A $3.4-billion deal is signed by leaders of Quebec and the **Cree Nation**, opening Cree territory to future hydroelectric projects (Feb. 7). At the Olympics in Salt Lake City, the near-perfect performance of Canadian figure skaters **Jaime Salé** and **David Pelletier** on Feb. 11 wins them a silver medal. The gold goes to the Russian team, whose performance is flawed. A French judge later admits that she was pressured to favour the Russians. Salé and Pelletier get a new set of gold medals four days later. Federal Solicitor General **Lawrence MacAulay** gives in to provincial demands to create a national sex offender registry (Feb. 13). On Feb. 20, Ontario Premier **Mike Harris** files a $15-million lawsuit over a story in *The Globe and Mail* linking him to the 1995 police shooting of native protester **Dudley George**. An investigation into the **disappearance of 50 women** since 1983 leads police to a pig farm in Port Coquitlam, B.C. On Feb. 22, police charge the farm's owner, Robert William Pickton, with two counts of murder. About 45,000 **Ontario public servants** strike over wages and job security (Mar. 13). On Mar. 14, about 500 Canadian soldiers lead **Operation Harpoon**

against suspected terrorists in Afghanistan. The attack is the Canadian Forces' biggest ground offensive in more than 50 years. On Mar. 17, the **Arctic Winter Games** open in Iqaluit. The event is the largest held to date in Nunavut. **Stephen Harper** is elected leader of the Canadian Alliance (Mar. 20). On Apr. 3, **James Sabzali**, a Canadian living in the US, becomes the first foreign national convicted under the US law barring trade with Cuba. Prime Minister Chrétien begins a tour of six countries in Africa (Apr. 3). The report of an inquiry into **North Battleford's water** is released on Apr. 5, and the Saskatchewan government adopts all its recommendations. In March and April 2001, about 7,000 North Battleford residents became ill from a parasite contaminating the city's water. NDP MP **Svend Robinson** tries to visit **Yasser Arafat** in Ramallah on Apr. 6, but Robinson is removed by Israeli soldiers. Party leader **Alexa McDonough** distances the NDP from his visit and from the perception that the NDP favours either side in the Middle East conflict. **Ernie Eves** is sworn in as premier of Ontario (Apr. 15). In Afghanistan, **four Canadian soldiers die** and eight are wounded when a US F-16 fighter pilot bombs them during a live-fire training exercise at night. (Apr. 17) The pilot says later that he mistook the exercise for hostile fire and acted in self-defence. In Toronto, **Marcia and Tony Dooley** are convicted of murdering their seven-year-old son Randal in one of the worst cases of child abuse in Canadian history (Apr. 19). Two labour unions challenge the Ontario government's decision to sell **Hydro One** in court; on Apr. 19, the court rules that the province lacks the authority to sell. A military panel led by **Maurice Baril**, former chief of the defence staff, begins investigating the **deaths of four Canadian soldiers** killed in Afghanistan (Apr. 22). The federal government unveils a new anti-terrorism bill, the **Public Safety Act**, which replaces the bill tabled in the fall (Apr. 29). On May 1, the **Ontario electricity market** opens to competition. Prices are set by the market, not by a provincial regulator. Moody's Investor Service restores **Canada's Triple-A credit rating** on May 3; it had been downgraded in 1995. A jury finds **Hells Angels** leader Maurice (Mom) Boucher guilty of attempted murder and two counts of first degree murder in the 1997 shooting deaths of two prison guards (May 5). It is Boucher's second trial for the killings. On May 8,

Federal Auditor General **Sheila Fraser** recommends an RCMP investigation into $1.6 million worth of contracts awarded to a Montreal ad agency by **Alfonso Gagliano**, the former minister of public works. Fraser says the department "broke just about every rule in the book" in awarding the contracts, and the agency, Groupaction, may not have done the work. The informal inquiry into the contracts becomes a **criminal investigation** later in the month. On May 14, **1,700 people evacuate their homes** in Notre-Dame-du-Lac, Que., when fire destroys an abattoir and fear spreads that ammonia in the plant might be released. In Quebec City, a **bomb** blasts a hole in a door of the town's only **synagogue** (May 19). Ontario Public Safety Minister **Bob Runciman** announces that provincial police have shut down an **al-Qaeda "sleeper cell"** (May 22). On May 26, Prime Minister **Jean Chrétien** fires Defence Minister **Art Eggleton** for awarding a $36,500 military contract to an ex-girlfriend; Chrétien also takes the public works portfolio away from **Don Boudria**, who faces conflict of interest charges. On June 2, Prime Minister Chrétien dismisses Finance Minister **Paul Martin**. Inco Ltd. and the Newfoundland government sign a $2.9-billion deal to develop **Voisey Bay's** mineral deposit in Labrador in 2006 (June 11). On June 14, the federal government introduces a revised Indian Act: the **First Nations Governance Act**. Candidates for the new Action Démocratique du Québec party defeat their PQ rivals in **three Montreal by-elections** on June 17. On July 3, **B.C. holds a referendum** asking respondents to vote yes or no to eight principles proposed to guide B.C. in aboriginal treaty negotiations. Native groups call for a boycott, and critics say the questions are skewed to ensure agreement. Police reveal on July 10 that they have seized **$100 million worth of drugs** and have arrested 39 people in Halifax—one of the largest drug busts in Canadian history. The Alberta government announces a $324-million **drought relief package** (July 17). The province faces its third consecutive year of drought. Pope John Paul II and 200,000 young people from around the world come to Toronto for **World Youth Day** (July 23–28). Solicitor General **Lawrence MacAulay** bans al-Qaeda and six other extremist groups from Canada (July 23). On July 26, the World Trade Organization initially rules in favour of Canada in the **softwood lumber dispute** between Canada and the US; the WTO denies US claims that Canada unfairly subsidizes producers. Mi'kmaq leaders in Burnt Church, N.B., and the federal government agree to end **the dispute over the lobster fishery** between native and non-native fishers (Aug. 1). Because the summer's drought left prairie farmers without feed for their herds, farmers in Ontario and Quebec launch the **"Hay West"** campaign in July. On Aug. 5, donated hay from Ontario starts arriving in Saskatchewan and Alberta. On Aug. 21, after months of public speculation, Prime Minister **Jean Chrétien** says that he will not run in the next election but will continue to lead Canada until February 2004. A B.C. court finds former premier **Glen Clark** not guilty of charges of breach of trust and accepting a benefit (Aug. 29). Prime Minister Chrétien announces at the World Summit on Sustainable Development that Canada will ratify the **Kyoto Accord** by year's end (Sept. 2). The first Canadian case of **West Nile virus** in a human is confirmed in an Ontario man (Sept. 6). Violence at **Montreal's Concordia University** forces visiting former Israeli prime minister **Benjamin Netanyahu** to cancel a planned speech (Sept. 9). The following day, he receives a standing ovation in Toronto. On Sept. 11, Canadians join in **remembrance ceremonies** for victims of the terrorist attacks in 2001 on the US. Prime Minister Chrétien visits Gander, Nfld, where thousands of air travellers had been stranded in 2001; he also visits New York later in the day. On Sept. 13, the US Air Force charges two pilots in the "friendly fire" incident that killed four Canadian soldiers and wounded eight in Afghanistan in April. Maj. **Harry Schmidt** is charged with involuntary manslaughter and assault; Maj. **William Umbach** is charged with aiding and abetting manslaughter and assault. On Sept. 18, Nova Scotia Premier **John Hamm** announces a $60-million clean-up of Halifax harbour. A **health-care workers strike** in Saskatchewan expands to 27 groups of health professionals—2,500 members of the Health Sciences Association of Saskatchewan—when bargaining breaks off in mid-September. At midnight on Sept. 30, Newfoundland and Labrador's **physicians strike** to gain wage parity with their counterparts in the rest of the Atlantic region. Only emergency room services remain available in the first such strike in the province's history.

Canadian Disasters

Aug. 29, 1583: Canada's first recorded marine disaster took 85 lives when the *Delight* was wrecked on Sable Island.

1710: Ships arriving in Quebec City from the West Indies brought a cargo that included yellow fever. The resulting epidemic killed a number of people, including six nurses; 12 priests and the ship's crew.

Aug. 23, 1711: As many as 950 drowned when ships attached to the British fleet preparing to attack Quebec were grounded and sank on the rocks of Ile-aux-Oeufs.

1746: Typhus broke out on a flotilla of French warships sailing for Port Royal in Acadia. Of the 3,150 soldiers aboard, 1,270 died at sea; another 1,130 died in the Bedford Basin while waiting for an army from Quebec. Typhus then spread to the Mi'kmaq population.

Oct. 5, 1825: A fire destroyed Newcastle and Douglastown, north of the Miramichi River, in New Brunswick. Between 200 and 500 people died.

1832–34: Cholera swept through Lower Canada when diseased Irish and English immigrants arrived in Quebec City. In Montreal, the disease killed at least 947 people between June 10–27, 1832.

Despite attempts by the authorities to quarantine infected immigrants on Grosse Île in the St Lawrence River, between 1833–34, the cholera killed about 3,800 people in Quebec City and 1,900 more in Montreal.

May 17, 1841: On this date, several large boulders from Cap Diamant tumbled down the precipitous cliffs above the Lower Town of Quebec City and demolished eight houses, killing 32 people.

1847: Ireland's potato famine prompted tens of thousands of Irish to sail for North America. Typhus killed about 5,000 immigrants at sea; at Grosse Île, medical inspectors buried at least 5,424 people throughout the year. From Grosse Île, some ships went to Pointe Saint-Charles, Montreal, where another 6,000 Irish immigrants died and were buried. The epidemic also spread to the population of Montreal and Quebec City.

1847–48: Under the command of Sir John Franklin, a British naval officer, 129 men perished of starvation and cold when their ships, HMS *Terror* and HMS *Erebus*, became trapped in pack ice west of King William Island in the Arctic archipelago. Franklin had been searching for the Northwest Passage.

Oct. 27, 1854: In one of the earliest Canadian train disasters, a gravel train running near Baptiste Creek, 24 km west of Chatham, Ont., was hit by an express train on the same line. In the collision, 52 persons were killed and 48 seriously injured.

June 29, 1864: Near St-Hilaire, Que., a passenger train was unable to stop for an open drawbridge at Beloeil on the Richelieu River. The train plunged through the opening onto passing barges, killing 99 and injuring 100 people.

Apr. 1, 1873: Sailing from Liverpool to New York, the steamer *Atlantic* struck Meager's Rock off the coast of Nova Scotia and sank with the loss of 535 people.

May 13, 1873: Sixty men died when a fire and subsequent explosion in a coal mine at Westville, Pictou County, NS, trapped firemen and workers. The mine was eventually sealed to starve the fire of oxygen and it was two years before all the bodies were recovered.

Aug. 25, 1873: The Great Nova Scotia Cyclone swept over Cape Breton Island. The hurricane destroyed 1,200 vessels and 900 buildings, demolished dikes, wharves and bridges and claimed 500 lives.

1885: A smallpox epidemic swept through Montreal killing 3,164 people—2,117 of whom were children. The catastrophe prompted city authorities to vaccinate the population, but some doctors said vaccination merely spread the disease. On Sept. 18, terrified rioters ransacked the home of the chief medical vaccinator, pharmacies, magistrates' homes and city hall.

May 3, 1887: In Nanaimo, BC, an explosion at the Number One mine, which was owned by the Vancouver Coal Mining and Land Company, killed 148 miners.

Jan. 24, 1888: Seventy-seven men lost their lives in a fire in the Number Five mine at Wellington, just outside of Nanaimo, BC.

Feb. 21, 1891: In the first of several major disasters in the coal mines of Springhill, NS, 125 men were killed in an explosion.

May 26, 1896: Fifty-five people were killed when a bridge at Point Ellice in Victoria, BC, collapsed while a streetcar was passing over it. The bridge was too weak to support the weight of a recently built tramline.

Sept. 19, 1899: A massive rockslide from the cliffs above Quebec City's Lower Town demolished most of Champlain St., killing 45 people.

Apr. 29, 1903: Parts of the town of Frank, Alta, were obliterated by a sudden landslide when over 90 million tonnes of limestone came crashing down Turtle Mountain, crossed the 4-km-wide valley floor and rolled up the other side of the valley. Approximately 75 people were killed. The landslide also sealed a mine entrance at the foot of the mountain and trapped 17 miners inside. The men were able to escape by digging a new tunnel to the surface.

Aug. 29, 1907: The Quebec Bridge, 11 km north of Quebec City, was the largest canti-levered bridge in the world at the time. As the bridge was nearing completion, the southern cantilever span collapsed, killing 75 workmen.

Aug. 2, 1908: A fire in BC's Kootenay Valley caused $5 million in damages and killed 70 people.

Mar. 5, 1910: Sixty-two train men and labourers died 2 km west of Rogers Pass, BC, when their engine was hit by an avalanche and hurtled 500 m into Bear Creek. Over 600 volunteers used pickaxes and shovels to dig through 10 m of snow in the search for survivors.

June 30, 1912: The worst tornado in Canadian history swept through Regina, Sask., killing 28 residents, injuring hundreds and causing $75 million damage (est. 1990 dollars).

Nov. 7–13, 1913: Thirty-four ships sank and 270 sailors drowned when a storm swept over Lake Erie and Lake Ontario. Winds reached speeds of 140 km/h. Days later, one ship was found afloat with its dead crew lashed to the mast.

Apr. 1, 1914: Seventy-seven sealers froze to death on the ice during a storm off the southeast coast of Labrador. At the storm's height, from Mar. 31 to Apr. 2, the temperature fell to –23°C and winds reached 64 km/h.

May 29, 1914: The Canadian Pacific liner *Empress of Ireland* collided with a Norwegian coal ship in the St. Lawrence River near Rimouski, Que., and sank in only 14 minutes with the loss of 1,014 lives. This was one of the worst naval disasters in history, with the eighth largest loss of life for a naval accident.

June 19, 1914: The worst coal mine disaster in Canadian history occurred at Hillcrest, Alta, when dust explosions killed 189 men.

July 29, 1916: A forest fire in northern Ontario, thought to have been started by lightning and locomotive sparks, engulfed the towns of Cochrane and Matheson, killing at least 233 persons.

Sept. 11, 1916: The Quebec Bridge was the scene of further tragedy when a new centre span being hoisted into position fell into the river below. Thirteen men were killed, bringing the loss of life during construction of the bridge to 88.

Dec. 6, 1917: Halifax was the scene of Canada's worst single disaster when a French munitions ship filled with explosives collided with a freighter in Halifax harbour. The French ship, the *Mont Blanc*, was split to the waterline; fuel oil spilled over its explosive cargo and started a fire in the hold. The crew abandoned ship without attempting to extinguish the fire.

In the explosion that followed, the *Mont Blanc* was tossed more than 1,000 m into the air. The explosion levelled homes and businesses in a large part of the city and set off explosives stockpiled on shore. The blast, heard as far away as Prince Edward Island, is thought to be the largest-ever accidental explosion, and the largest non-nuclear blast in history. More than 1,600 people were killed, 9,000 injured, and 6,000 left homeless. Property damage was estimated at $35 million.

Oct. 23, 1918: The Canadian Pacific steamship *Princess Sophia* ran onto Vanderbilt Reef while sailing from Alaska to Vancouver. The ship sank two days later on Oct. 25. All 343 aboard were drowned.

Jan. 9, 1927: A small fire that broke out in Montreal's Laurier Palace Theatre was quickly extinguished, but in the panic that ensued 12 people were crushed to death and 64 were asphyxiated, including many children.

Aug. 24–25, 1927: A hurricane struck Newfoundland, killing 56 people at sea. Throughout Atlantic Canada, the storm washed out roads, flooded houses and swamped boats.

Apr. 14, 1928: The 18-gun sloop *Acorn* sank near Halifax with 115 men on board.

Nov. 18, 1929: Newfoundland's Burin Peninsula was struck by a 4.5-m tidal wave. Property damage was extensive and 27 were killed.

June 26, 1930: A store of dynamite blew up when lightning struck the bow of the *John B. King*, a drillship on the St. Lawrence River. The explosion killed 30 people and injured 11 others.

1933–37: Throughout these years, the Prairies received only 60 percent of normal rainfall. The region turned into a dust bowl: Farmers lost thousands of animals to starvation and suffocation, crops withered, and 250,000 people left the Prairies to seek better lives elsewhere.

July 5–17, 1936: During an intense heat wave, 1,180 Canadians died in Manitoba and Ontario. Temperatures exceeding 44°C killed large numbers of infants and seniors; drowning killed about 400 people who went swimming to escape the heat.

Dec. 12, 1942: An arsonist set fire to the Knights of Columbus hostel in St John's. Because the hostel had no emergency lighting, the doors opened inwards and exits were restricted, 99 people died and another 100 were seriously injured.

May–June 1948: BC's worst flood of the century occurred when the Fraser River overflowed. The water destroyed 2,300 homes and forced 16,000 people to flee. Ten people drowned. For three weeks, Vancouver had no rail connection with the rest of Canada.

Sept. 17, 1949: Seven hundred people were aboard the Great Lakes excursion ship *Noronic* when it caught fire and burned at its pier in Toronto harbour. The ship's fire hydrants were dry and no alarm was sent to the city fire department until 15 minutes after the blaze was discovered. In the meantime, the single exit became blocked by fire and 118 lives were lost.

Spring 1950: The Red River flooded, forcing the evacuation of 100,000 people from southern Manitoba and damaging 5,000 homes. The provincial government responded by building the Winnipeg Floodway to forestall future floods.

Oct. 15, 1954: During the worst inland storm in Canadian history, Hurricane Hazel, over 10 cm of rain fell in Toronto in 12 hours. At that time, many houses in Toronto were built on low-lying flood plains. The storm and resulting floods caused 83 deaths and widespread property damage.

Nov. 1, 1956: A second major tragedy struck the coal mines at Springhill, NS, when an accident killed 39 men.

Dec. 9, 1956: A DC-4 North Star flown by Trans-Canada Airways (later Air Canada) crashed into the east face of Mount Slesse, BC, killing all 62 on board.

June 17, 1958: Design errors in Vancouver's Second Narrows Bridge caused one section to collapse. The accident killed 18 men, including the two engineers that an investigation later determined were responsible for the errors.

Oct. 23, 1958: A third mining accident in Springhill, NS, killed 75 when a tunnel collapsed.

June 20, 1959: More than 30 fishermen drowned and 22 salmon boats sank near Esuminac, NB, when a storm suddenly struck the Gulf of St. Lawrence.

Nov. 19, 1963: A Trans-Canada Airways DC-8F crashed after takeoff from Dorval in Montreal, killing 118.

July 5, 1970: At Toronto International Airport, an Air Canada DC-8 lost one starboard engine during a landing attempt. During the pilot's effort to take off and land again, the remaining starboard engine fell off. The aircraft crashed, killing all 109 persons aboard.

May 4, 1971: During a prolonged rainstorm in St-Jean-Vianney, Que., a giant sinkhole appeared in the ground. The hole swallowed 40 houses, several cars and a bus, and 31 people were killed.

Nov. 10, 1975: The 218-m ore carrier *Edmund Fitzgerald*, based in Sault Ste. Marie, broke apart during a storm on Lake Superior and sank in 156 m of water with all 29 members of the crew aboard. Two days later only two rubber rafts and some life preservers from the ship were found.

June 21, 1977: A fire that broke out in the cell block of the city police headquarters of St John, NB, was so hot that the locks on several cell doors were fused. Twenty prisoners were killed and 12 police officers who attempted to rescue the prisoners were injured.

Feb. 11, 1978: A Pacific Western Airlines aircraft crashed at Cranbrook, BC, killing 43 people.

Aug. 4, 1978: The brakes on a chartered bus failed near Eastman, Que. The bus plunged into a lake, and 41 passengers were killed.

Dec. 31, 1979: Forty-four persons were killed during New Year's Eve celebrations at a social club in Chapais, Que., in a fire caused by a man playing with a lighter who set decorations ablaze.

Feb. 15, 1982: The ocean drilling rig *Ocean Ranger* overturned and sank during a storm while operating 265 km east of Newfoundland, killing 84 men. Inadequate safety procedures and equipment were later blamed for the accident.

May 31, 1985: A midafternoon tornado struck Barrie, Ont., killing 12, including four children. Property damage was in the hundreds of millions of dollars.

Dec. 12, 1985: In the worst air crash in Canada, an Arrow Airlines DC-8, after refuelling in Gander en route to Hopkinsville, Ky., crashed seconds after takeoff, killing 256 passengers and crew.

Feb. 8, 1986: A 16-unit VIA Rail passenger train slammed head-on into a 118-unit CN freight train near Hinton, Alta. Twenty-six people were killed and dozens were seriously injured.

July 31, 1987: A tornado touched down in Edmonton, Alta, killing 26 people, injuring 250 others and causing an estimated $250 million damage.

Mar. 10, 1989: An Air Ontario jet crashed immediately after takeoff from Dryden, Ont., killing 24 people.

Feb. 12, 1990: One of the worst tire fires in North America broke out near Hagersville,

Ont., spewing oil and toxic smoke. The dump, which stored 14 million tires for recycling, burned for 16 days; the blaze was extinguished at a cost of $1.5 million.

May 9, 1992: Twenty-six miners died underground in the Westray coal mine near Plymouth, NS, after a methane gas explosion. Fifteen bodies were recovered but the bodies of the remaining victims could not be reached in the debris.

July 16, 1993: Nineteen people died when a truck towing tanks of diesel fuel collided with a van carrying senior citizens near Lac-Bouchette, Que.

July 19–20, 1996: Ten people died in the Lac-St-Jean Saguenay Region when flash floods from overflowing dams and reservoirs wiped out communities along the Saguenay River.

April–May 1997: Manitoba's Red River flooded 2,000 square km of valley land when water rose 12 m above winter levels—the highest for the river in the 20th century. Thousands of volunteers and soldiers fought the flood for days. Damage estimates reached half a billion dollars.

Oct. 13, 1997: Forty-four passengers were killed when the brakes failed on their sightseeing bus; the vehicle missed a turn at the bottom of a steep hill and crashed into a ravine in Les Eboulements, 110 km northeast of Quebec City.

Jan. 4–9, 1998: One of the most destructive ice storms in Canadian history struck Quebec and Eastern Ontario, causing hardship for 4 million people and costing $3 billion. Losses included 130 transmission towers, 120,000 km of power and phone lines, and millions of trees. Power outages lasted up to four weeks.

Sept. 2, 1998: All 229 passengers were killed when a Swissair MD-11 en route from New York to Geneva crashed in the Atlantic near Peggy's Cove, NS. The accident was the second worst in Canadian aviation history.

May 2000: At least seven people died and up to 2,300 people fell ill after drinking tap water infected by *E. coli* bacteria in Walkerton, Ont.

Prime Ministers of Canada

■ Sir John A. Macdonald

Canada's first prime minister, Sir John A. Macdonald, was born in Glasgow, Scotland, Jan. 11, 1815. At age five he came to Canada with his parents who settled at Kingston, Upper Canada.

Called to the bar in 1836, Macdonald practised law in Kingston and then in Toronto. He established a reputation as a corporate lawyer, company director and businessman.

He was elected to the Legislative Assembly of the Province of Canada in 1844 and was re-elected in 1848, 1851, 1854, 1857, 1861 and 1863. In 1864, he joined a coalition with George Brown, leader of the Upper Canadian reformers, dedicated to bringing about Confederation. That same year, Macdonald was a delegate to the Charlottetown and Quebec conferences, and became the principal author of the Confederation resolutions agreed upon in Quebec. He was chairman of the London Conference (1866–67) and played a pivotal role in bringing about Confederation.

Macdonald became Canada's first prime minister when the Conservative party won a majority of seats in Parliament following the first post-Confederation general election in 1867. Though he was re-elected in 1872, Macdonald's second administration was marred by the "Pacific Scandal" in 1873,

when the Liberal Opposition charged that his government had awarded the CPR contract to Sir Hugh Allan in return for political contributions. An investigation into these charges was held, and the government resigned on Nov. 5, 1873.

Macdonald's Liberal-Conservatives were re-elected Sept. 17, 1878, and Macdonald remained prime minister until his death in Ottawa on June 6, 1891.

During his first administration, the Dominion of Canada expanded to include the provinces of British Columbia, Prince Edward Island and the newly created Manitoba.

The building of the transcontinental railway is the most memorable feature of his second administration, but other accomplishments include the establishment of the "National Policy"—a system of tariff protection to aid the development of Canadian industries (1879)—and the increased settlement of the Western provinces that followed the construction of the railway.

■ Alexander Mackenzie

Alexander Mackenzie was born on Jan. 28, 1822 near Dunkeld, Perthshire, Scotland. He left school and became a stonemason at the age of 14.

He emigrated to Canada in 1842 and became a contractor at Lambton, Ontario, and then editor of the *Lambton Shield*. From 1866–74, he was a major in the 27th Lambton Battalion Volunteer Infantry.

In 1861, Mackenzie was elected to the Legislative Assembly of the Province of Canada, where he gave his support to the Confederation plan. When George Brown was defeated in the 1867 election, Mackenzie became *de facto* leader of the Opposition, though it was not until after the 1872 elections that he formally accepted this title.

It was Mackenzie who led the attack on the Macdonald administration over the "Pacific Scandal"; when Macdonald resigned on Nov. 5, 1873, Mackenzie became prime minister.

During his 5-year term of office, Mackenzie introduced changes to election laws that included the secret ballot and universal male suffrage. The Supreme Court of Canada was established under Mackenzie's rule, and Wilfrid Laurier was brought into Mackenzie's cabinet.

Severe economic depression plagued Canada during the Mackenzie years, and in 1878, his Liberal party was routed at the polls.

Mackenzie retained his own seat, however, and was still a member of Parliament when he died Apr. 17, 1892, in Toronto.

■ Sir John Abbott

Sir John Joseph Caldwell Abbott was born Mar. 12, 1821, at St. Andrews, Lower Canada—the first prime minister to be born on Canadian soil.

After taking his law degree from University of McGill College, he was admitted to the bar

in 1847 and practised law in Montreal. From 1855–80 he was dean of the Faculty of Law, McGill University.

Abbott was elected to the Legislative Assembly of the Province of Canada in 1857, re-elected in 1861 and 1863, and sat until Confederation. He was then elected to the House of Commons in 1867, 1872 and 1874. He was last elected in 1882 and appointed to the Senate on May 12, 1887.

When Sir John A. Macdonald died in 1891, Abbott—though a senator—inherited the Conservative leadership. The three other leading Conservatives—Langevin, Tupper and Thompson—were unwilling or unable to assume the post. Abbott held the office of prime minister from June 16, 1891, until his resignation on Nov. 24, 1892. He died in Montreal on Oct. 30, 1893.

■ Sir John Thompson

Sir John Sparrow David Thompson was born in Halifax, NS, on Nov. 10, 1845.

Thompson was called to the Nova Scotia bar in 1865, and was instrumental in founding Dalhousie Law School in 1883, where he eventually became a lecturer.

In May 1882, Thompson became premier of Nova Scotia, but when his government was defeated two months later, he retired from politics and became a judge of the Supreme Court of Nova Scotia.

Prime Minister Macdonald coaxed Thompson back into politics, making him minister of justice in 1885. When Macdonald died in 1891, Thompson declined the leadership, fearing that his conversion to Roman Catholicism in 1870 would hinder his party's fortunes. However, the following year, Thompson changed his mind, and on Dec. 5, 1892, he became prime minister.

Though prime minister for just over 2 years, Thompson was largely responsible for the establishment of the Criminal Code and penetentiary reforms. He very nearly succeeded in bringing Newfoundland into Confederation in 1894, and successfully negotiated fisheries clauses in the Treaty of Washington.

He died while still in office on Dec. 12, 1894.

■ Sir Mackenzie Bowell

Mackenzie Bowell was born at Rickinghall, Suffolk, England, on Dec. 27, 1823, and came to Canada in 1832. In 1834, he became an

apprentice printer at Belleville, Upper Canada, and was later editor and proprietor of the Belleville *Intelligencer*. He served in the militia of the United Province of Canada during the American Civil War and the Fenian raids of 1866.

Bowell was elected to the House of Commons in 1867 for Hastings North, Ont., and was re-elected in 1872, 1874, 1878, 1887 and 1891.

As spokesman for the Orange Association of British America, Bowell was instrumental in having Louis Riel expelled from the Commons in 1874.

On Dec. 5, 1892, Bowell was appointed to the Senate and, after Thompson's death in 1894, was invited by the Governor General to form a government.

Perhaps the thorniest problem facing Prime Minister Bowell was the Manitoba Schools question. In 1890, Manitoba legislation had withdrawn school privileges from the Roman Catholic and primarily French minority in that province. By the time Bowell assumed office, attempts were being made to restore those lost school privileges by federal remedial legislation. Bowell was not equal to the political challenges facing him; he lost control of his cabinet ministers, several of whom eventually called for his resignation. Bowell denounced this cabinet rebellion as a "nest of traitors," but eventually he resigned on Apr. 27, 1896. He died in Belleville, Ont., on Dec. 10, 1917, at age 93.

■ Sir Charles Tupper

Charles Tupper was born at Amherst, NS, July 2, 1821. He took a degree in medicine at Edinburgh University. At the age of 22, he began practising medicine in Amherst and became the first president of the Canadian Medical Association (1867–70).

The 1855 election that brought him to the Legislative Assembly of Nova Scotia was declared void on Feb. 24, 1857. He was subsequently re-elected in a by-election that same year and was elected again in 1859 and 1863.

Tupper was active in the Confederation movement, and was a delegate to the

Charlottetown, Quebec and London Conferences. He was elected to the House of Commons in 1867 and re-elected 1870, 1872, 1874, 1878 and 1882. He resigned in 1884 and served as High Commissioner for Canada in the United Kingdom from May 28 of that year to Jan. 26, 1887. In 1887, he was re-elected to the House of Commons, but resigned the following year and again served as High Commissioner from May 23, 1888, to Jan. 14, 1896.

In 1896, following the rebellion of Bowell's cabinet, Tupper became *de facto* leader of the administration until Bowell formally resigned on Apr. 27, 1896. At that time, the Governor General invited Tupper to form the government. Parliament was dissolved shortly thereafter and in the election that followed on June 23, Tupper's Conservatives were defeated. Tupper stayed on as leader of the Opposition until Feb. 5, 1901, then retired from public life. He died Oct. 30, 1915 at Bexley Heath, Kent, England.

■ Sir Wilfrid Laurier

Wilfrid Laurier was born at St-Lin, Canada East, Nov. 20, 1841. He first attended College de l'Assomption and then took his degree from McGill University.

He was called to the bar of Lower Canada in 1865. He practised law at Montreal and at Arthabaskaville, Que.

First elected to the Legislative Assembly of Quebec in 1871, Laurier resigned in Jan. 1874 and later that year was elected to the House of Commons. He became leader of the Liberal Opposition in June 1887. Then, following the 1896 election that gave his party a 23-seat majority, Laurier became Canada's first French-speaking prime minister on July 11, 1896. The Liberals retained power in 1900 and won a landslide election victory in 1904.

Immigration increased during his time in office as Clifford Sifton, Laurier's minister of the interior from 1896–1905, mounted a powerful campaign to attract immigrants from Britain, the United States and Europe. In 1905, Laurier created the provinces of Alberta and Saskatchewan and established the boundaries of Manitoba. During Laurier's years in power the Canadian West became a major world wheat producer. In 1909, Laurier established the External Affairs Department.

His government's controversial support for the creation of a Canadian navy, and his unpopular attempt to enter into a reciprocal trade agreement with the United States (an agreement that would have reduced or eliminated duties on many imported goods) spelled trouble for Laurier in 1911. His party was defeated in the Sept. 21 election. He remained an Opposition M.P. until his death on Feb. 17, 1919, in Ottawa.

■ Sir Robert Borden

Robert Laird Borden was born at Grand Pré, NS, June 26, 1854. At age 14 he gave up formal schooling to become an assistant master in classical studies. He taught classics and mathematics in New Jersey in 1873, before returning to Nova Scotia to study law. He was admitted to the Nova Scotia bar in 1878 and practised first in Halifax, then in Kentville, NS.

Borden was elected to the House of Commons in 1896 and 1900 and became leader of the Conservative party on Feb. 6, 1901. He served as Leader of the Opposition until 1911, when he led his party to victory in the Sept. 21 election.

Borden was prime minister throughout World War I, and during the war years his government was accused of scandal over British munitions contracts and its staunch support of the Ross Rifle—a weapon known to jam in battle. Borden's government introduced the first federal income tax, nationalized Canadian railways and introduced conscription in 1917.

In the election of Dec. 17, 1917, Borden led a re-organized Union Government made up of Conservatives and pro-conscription Liberals to victory. Borden headed the Canadian dele-

gation at the Paris Peace Conference in 1919, where the autonomy of Canada and other dominions within the British Commonwealth was successfully established. He resigned on July 10, 1920, and died in Ottawa on June 10, 1937.

■ Arthur Meighen

Arthur Meighen was born at Anderson, Ont., June 16, 1874. Following his graduation from university in 1896, Meighen taught high school for a year, then moved to Winnipeg in 1898 to study law. He was called to the Manitoba bar in 1902, and practised at Portage La Prairie.

He was first elected to the House of Commons in 1908, re-elected in 1911, 1913 and 1917, defeated in 1921, and re-elected in 1922 and 1925.

Meighen first achieved national prominence in 1913 when he helped devise a closure rule which permitted the government to end debate on a bill which was to effect a $35-million contribution to the British navy. Prior to closure, the bill had been obstructed by a fierce and protracted Opposition party blockade.

Prime Minister Borden appointed Meighen his solicitor general on Oct. 2, 1915, and Meighen held this post for two years. A strong supporter of conscription, Meighen essentially drafted Canada's 1917 conscription bill, and put it into operation. He was also the chief draughtsman of the Wartime Elections Act.

When Borden resigned on July 10, 1920, Meighen succeeded him as prime minister. In the general election of Dec. 6, 1921, Meighen's party was defeated. Though his Conservatives won the most seats in the election of Oct. 29, 1925, the Liberals were able to stay in power with the support of Progressive and Labour members.

Following the resignation of William Lyon Mackenzie King's government on June 28, 1926, the Governor General invited Meighen to form a new ministry. This government was less than three months old, however, when it was defeated in the House of Commons (by only one vote) and Canadians again went to the polls.

Following a Liberal victory in the election of Sept. 14, 1926, Meighen resigned as Conservative leader in the House of Commons. He was appointed to the Senate on Feb. 3, 1932, during Richard Bennett's ministry and became government leader in the Senate. Then, following King's victory in 1935, he became Senate Opposition leader.

On Nov. 12, 1941, he once again became leader of the Conservative party, but failed in his bid to win a seat in the Commons in a federal by-election on Feb. 2, 1942. Following this defeat, he retired from politics and resumed his law practice in Toronto, where he died Aug. 5, 1960.

■ Mackenzie King

William Lyon Mackenzie King, grandson of William Lyon Mackenzie, was born in Kitchener (then called Berlin), Ont., on Dec. 17, 1874.

He took his B.A. and law degrees from the University of Toronto and also studied at the University of Chicago and Harvard University.

He served as deputy minister of labour from 1900–1908.

He was first elected to the House of Commons in 1908, and succeeded Laurier as leader of the Liberal party in 1919. King became prime minister when the Liberals won the general election of Dec. 6, 1921.

Though Meighen's Conservatives won a majority of seats in the general election of Oct. 29, 1925, King stayed in office with the help of Progressive and Labour members who supported his proposed tariff reductions and old-age pension legislation. King had lost his York North seat in the 1925 election but returned to the House of Commons as the member for Prince Albert, Sask., following a by-election on Feb. 15, 1926. King's government was shaken in 1926 by the revelation that the customs department was tainted with corruption and incompetence. In the furor that followed, King lost the support of many members of Parliament and, although never technically defeated in the House of Commons, decided that he could no longer hold his minority government. He appealed to Governor General Lord Byng to dissolve Parliament, even though the government had not been defeated. Byng refused. King subsequently resigned on June 28, 1926, and the Governor General invited Arthur Meighen to form a government which was subsequently defeated in the House of Commons.

In the general election of Sept. 14, 1926, King's Liberals regained power and held it until 1930. But the disastrous fall in the price of wheat and other Canadian exports in 1929 soured Canadians on their government, and King was defeated by R. B. Bennett's Conservatives in the election of July 28, 1930.

Five years later, King was back in the prime minister's office, following the Liberal victory in the general election of Oct. 14, 1935. In the coming years, King, an ardent supporter of Canada's autonomy within the British Commonwealth, was faced with the issue of Canada's participation in an impending European war. To soothe French-Canadian concerns over Canadian support of Great Britain, King promised there would be no conscription; Canada declared war in September 1939. Later, however, heavy casualties in France and Italy in 1944 prompted King to break his promise and send conscripts overseas.

King's government began introducing postwar recovery legislation even before peace was declared. These measures included reconstruction plans and social security schemes such as mother's allowances.

King resigned as prime minister on Nov. 15, 1948, supporting Louis St Laurent as his successor. In poor health in his final years, King died July 22, 1950, at Kingsmere, his estate in Wright County, Que.

■ Richard Bennett

Richard Bedford Bennett was born at Hopewell, NB, July 3, 1870. Bennett studied law at Dalhousie University. He read and practised law in Chatham, NB, from 1893–97, before moving to Calgary where he entered a legal partnership with Senator James A. Lougheed.

Bennett was first elected to the House of Commons in 1911. He served as minister of justice in Arthur Meighen's 1921 cabinet, and minister of finance and minister of mines in Meighen's 1926 government.

Bennett was chosen to replace Meighen as Conservative leader at the party convention in Winnipeg in 1927. He became prime minister following the Conservative victory in the election of July 28, 1930.

Bennett had the task of governing Canada during the worst years of the Depression. Virtually every measure his government

attempted ended in failure. High unemployment levels continued despite Bennett's efforts to reduce them. Negotiations for a reciprocity treaty with the United States did not succeed. A plan of preferential tariffs agreed to in 1930 at the Imperial Conference did little to ease Canada's economic woes.

Then, in 1935, near the end of his term, Bennett took an unexpected step to the political left. He proclaimed that "the old order is gone" and that it was time for a new economic system. That new system was to include a state-planned economy, new unemployment and health insurance legislation and old-age pension laws.

In the election of Oct. 14, 1935, Bennett's Conservatives suffered a devastating defeat, winning just 39 seats. Bennett remained in Opposition until 1937, when he retired to England. There he was given the title Viscount Bennett of Mickelham, Hopewell and Calgary.

Despite the overwhelming problems of the Great Depression, Bennett's term saw the creation of the Canadian Radio Broadcasting Corporation (the predecessor to the CBC) and the Bank of Canada. As well, it was during Bennett's tenure that the Statute of Westminster gave Canada increased autonomy in 1931.

Bennett died June 27, 1947.

■ Louis St Laurent

Louis Stephen St Laurent was born at Compton, Que., Feb. 1, 1882. Called to the Quebec bar in 1905, he practised law in Quebec City, and became professor of law at Université Laval. He was elected president of the Canadian Bar Association in 1930.

St Laurent became justice minister in Mackenzie King's cabinet on Dec. 10, 1941. On Feb. 9, 1942, he was elected to the House of Commons in a by-election for Quebec East.

Originally planning to hold his cabinet post only during the war, St Laurent was persuaded to stay on. On Dec. 10, 1946, he became secretary of state for external affairs. A firm believer in collective security, St Laurent was one of the architects of the North

Atlantic Treaty Organization (NATO). On Aug. 7, 1948, he accepted his party's nomination to be King's successor, and on Nov. 15 became prime minister.

While in power, St Laurent ended the practice of appealing court cases to the Judicial Committee of the Privy Council in England, and made the Supreme Court of Canada the final Canadian court of appeal. He won the acceptance of a new apportionment of taxes in 1956 and, in negotiation with President Truman, laid the foundation for a US–Canada agreement to develop the St Lawrence Seaway.

In 1958, he retired and returned to Quebec City to practise law. He died July 25, 1973.

■ John Diefenbaker

John George Diefenbaker was born at Neustadt, Ont., Sept. 18, 1895. He received his B.A. from the University of Saskatchewan in 1915 and his M.A. one year later.

After the outbreak of World War I, he joined the Canadian Officers' Training Corps, and served overseas as a lieutenant with the 105th "Saskatoon Fusiliers" Regiment from 1916 to 1917.

Returning to Saskatchewan, he took his law degree from the University of Saskatchewan in 1919 and established a law practice at Wakaw. He later moved to Prince Albert.

After several unsuccessful attempts to gain a seat, first in the federal, then in Saskatchewan's provincial parliament, Diefenbaker was finally elected to the House of Commons in 1940. He was a candidate for leadership of the Progressive Conservative party at the 1942 and 1948 conventions, but did not win the nomination until Dec. 14, 1956.

The PCs won the election of June 10, 1957, by a slim margin, and on June 21, John Diefenbaker officially became prime minister. A year later, he called an election, hoping to turn his Conservative minority government into a clear majority. He was overwhelmingly successful, winning 208 of the 265 seats in the Mar. 31, 1958, election. He fared less well in the 1962 election, when only 116 PCs were elected, and in the general election of 1963, a Liberal victory relegated Diefenbaker to the role of Opposition leader. Diefenbaker remained Conservative leader until Sept. 1967, when he was replaced by Robert Stanfield.

The Diefenbaker years (1957–63) saw the passage of the Canadian Bill of Rights, a "roads-to-resources" program to encourage the development of northern resources, legislation providing support for agriculture, encouragement of technical training and improved health and welfare programs. Regional development was emphasized by significant public works such as construction of the South Saskatchewan Dam, and simultaneous translation was introduced in the House of Commons.

Diefenbaker died Aug. 16, 1979, at his home in Rockliffe Park, Ottawa.

■ Lester Pearson

Lester Bowles Pearson was born at Newtonbrook, Ont., on Apr. 23, 1897. He took his B.A. at the University of Toronto and his M.A. at Oxford University.

After serving overseas in World War I, he became a history professor at the University of Toronto, where he taught from 1924–1928. He joined Canada's foreign service in 1928, became Canada's ambassador to the UN in 1945, was appointed under-secretary of state for external affairs in 1946 and accepted the invitations of King and St Laurent to become minister of external affairs in Sept. 1948.

In 1956, following the Anglo-French-Israeli invasion of Egypt, Pearson's work at the United Nations helped establish a UN Emergency Force which kept peace on the Israeli–Egyptian border for the next decade. His settlement of the Suez crisis brought him the Nobel Peace Prize in 1957—the only time a Canadian has been so honoured.

Pearson was chosen leader of the Liberal party Jan. 15, 1958. In the general election of Apr. 8, 1963, the Liberals won 129 seats in the House of Commons, and Pearson became the leader of a minority government.

In the 1965 election, the Liberals made slight gains, but were still short of a majority. Pearson announced his resignation in Dec. 1967 and, in Apr. 1968, was succeeded by Pierre Trudeau.

Under Pearson, the old age pension was extended and a national health plan created. He secured the adoption of a national flag and established the Royal Commission on Bilingualism and Biculturalism.

Though he retired in 1968, his international reputation prompted the World Bank to commission him to prepare a report on international aid programs.

He died in Ottawa, Dec. 27, 1972.

■ Pierre Trudeau

Pierre Elliott Trudeau was born in Montreal on Oct. 18, 1919. He attended the University of Montreal, Harvard University, Université de Paris and the London School of Economics. He was called to the Quebec bar in 1943. From 1949–51, he was a member of the Privy Council staff in Ottawa. In 1950, he co-founded the magazine *Cité Libre*. From 1952–62, he practised law and was a journalist and broadcaster in Montreal. From 1962–65, he was a law professor at the University of Montreal.

First elected to the House of Commons in 1965, Trudeau was named justice minister in Lester Pearson's cabinet in 1967. The following year, he won the Liberal leadership and became prime minister Apr. 19, 1968. In the general election of the same year, the Liberals won a solid majority.

During his first four years in power, Trudeau faced the FLQ Crisis—the kidnapping of British diplomat James Cross and Quebec cabinet minister Pierre Laporte by the radical separatist organization Front de libération du Québec. (Laporte was later murdered.) In response he invoked the War Measures

Act, a statute giving the state broad powers of arrest and detention.

In the general election of 1972, Trudeau returned to power with a minority government. In 1974, he regained a majority.

In the general election of 1979, the Progressive Conservatives under Joe Clark won a narrow victory and were able to form a minority government. Trudeau announced his intention to retire, but when the Clark government fell later that year, Trudeau led the Liberals in the election and won a majority on Feb. 18, 1980.

Trudeau's final term in office was devoted to constitutional reform which, for the first time, allowed Canada's Parliament to amend the constitution without appeal to the UK government. A constitutionally, entrenched Charter of Rights and Freedoms was also introduced.

Trudeau's introduction of a National Energy Program led to bitter disputes between the federal government and the energy-producing provinces, particularly Alberta. The NEP was aimed at increasing Canadian control of the oil industry, promoting energy self-sufficiency and generating more federal revenues in the energy sector.

During his final year as prime minister Trudeau launched a world peace initiative, visiting more than 40 world leaders to appeal for peace and an end to the nuclear arms race.

In June of 1984, Trudeau resigned. He was succeeded by John Turner and left politics, eventually joining a Montreal law firm.

Trudeau died Sept. 28, 2000 at his home in Montreal.

■ Joe Clark

Charles Joseph "Joe" Clark was born at High River, Alta., on June 5, 1939. He was educated at the University of Alberta.

Clark was first elected to the House of Commons in 1972. In 1976 he became leader of the Progressive Conservative party and, in the general election of 1979, won enough seats to form a minority government. At 39, Clark was Canada's youngest prime minister. But his minority government fell in Dec. 1979 on a vote of non-confidence on its proposed budget. In the Feb. 1980 election that followed, the Liberals returned to power.

At a national general meeting of the Conservative party in Jan. 1983, Clark received the support of only two-thirds of the delegates and called for a national party leadership conven-

tion. In June 1983, Clark lost the leadership to Brian Mulroney on the fourth ballot. He remained an MP and, when Mulroney became prime minister in 1984, Clark joined the cabinet as secretary of state for external affairs.

In 1991, he was appointed as minister responsible for constitutional affairs and given the task of succeeding where the Meech Lake Accord had failed. Late 1991 and the first half of 1992 were marked by weeks of cross-country constitutional negotiations under Clark's

guidance. In August 1992, the Charlottetown Accord—an agreement to amend the Constitution Act of 1982—was agreed upon by all first ministers. The text of the agreement was presented to Canadians and a national referendum was held on Oct. 26, 1992, on the issue of whether or not to approve the deal. The agreement was rejected by the majority of voters across the country.

Clark left federal politics after the 1993 election. In 1998, he re-entered public life when Jean Charest vacated the federal Conservative leadership to run in Quebec's provincial election. On Nov. 14, 1998, Clark was re-elected federal Conservative leader.

■ John Turner

John Napier Turner was born at Richmond, Surrey, England, on June 7, 1929. He attended the University of British Columbia, Oxford University and Université de Paris. He was called to the bar in England in 1953 and the bar in Quebec in 1954. He lectured for a time in the Faculty of Commerce at Sir George Williams University.

First elected to the House of Commons in 1962, Turner entered Lester Pearson's cabinet in 1965. He became minister of consumer and corporate affairs in 1967. In 1968, he was a candidate for the Liberal leadership, finishing third on the final ballot.

In 1968, Turner was appointed minister of justice in Pierre Trudeau's cabinet. In 1972, he became minister of finance, a post he held until his resignation in Sept. 1975. In Feb. 1976, he left politics and joined a Toronto law firm.

Turner remained in private practice until Trudeau's retirement in 1984, when he successfully ran for leader of the Liberal party and became prime minister on June 30, though he did not have a seat in the House of Commons. He dissolved Parliament July 9, and in the ensuing general election the Liberals were overwhelmingly defeated by the Progressive Conservatives.

As leader of the Opposition, Turner used the Liberal majority in the Senate to block passage of the Conservatives' free trade legislation and force an election on the issue in 1988. The Conservatives won the election and were able to form another majority government.

Early in 1989, Turner announced plans to step down as leader; in June 1990, he was succeeded by Jean Chrétien.

■ Brian Mulroney

Martin Brian Mulroney was born at Baie Comeau, Que., Mar. 20, 1939. He attended St. Francis Xavier University and Université Laval. Called to the bar of Quebec in 1965, Mulroney practised law in Montreal. In 1976, he joined the Iron Ore Company of Canada as executive vice-president and was elected company president the following year.

Mulroney made an unsuccessful bid for the Progressive Conservative party leadership in 1976. In 1983 he ran again, defeating the incumbent leader, Joe Clark, on the fourth ballot.

A by-election for the Maritime riding of Central Nova brought Mulroney into Parliament as leader of the Opposition. In the general election of 1984, he led the Conservatives to victory, winning the largest number of seats (211) in Canadian history.

Mulroney's major initiatives between 1984 and 1988 were the Meech Lake Accord—a package of constitutional changes designed to end Quebec's boycott of the 1982 constitutional reform—and the negotiation of a free trade agreement with the United States.

In 1988, with free trade the central election issue, Mulroney won a second majority government. The free trade agreement subse-

quently received final approval and took effect in 1989.

His term from 1988 to 1993 was marked by intense negotiations to bring about a new constitutional agreement to replace the Meech Lake Accord, which was not ratified by all provinces by the June 1990 deadline. Agreement was reached amongst federal and provincial officials in what became known as the Charlottetown Accord, but the proposals were rejected in a national referendum held on Oct. 26, 1992.

The Conservatives under Mulroney continued their free trade initiative and finalized a North American free trade deal (NAFTA) with the US and Mexico.

Mulroney announced his intention to retire in February 1993, and on June 25, 1993, he was replaced by Kim Campbell, newly elected leader of the Conservative party.

■ Kim Campbell

Avril Phaedra (Kim) Campbell was born Mar. 10, 1947, in Port Alberni, BC. She attended the University of British Columbia, earning an honours degree in political science.

After an academic career in BC, she studied law at UBC. In September 1985, she joined BC Premier William Bennett's office as a policy advisor. In May 1986, Campbell ran in the provincial election and won a seat in the legislature, representing Vancouver/Point Grey. She served in the provincial legislature until October 1988 when she resigned her seat to contest the federal riding of Vancouver Centre. An ardent defender of free trade, Campbell joined Prime Minister Mulroney's cabinet with the Indian Affairs and Northern Development portfolio.

In 1990 Campbell became the first woman promoted to the Attorney General and Justice post. In January of 1993 she became Canada's first female defence minister and a candidate in the Conservative leadership contest that year. On June 13, 1993, she was elected leader on the second ballot; on June 25, she was sworn in as Canada's first female prime minister. In the election of Oct. 1993, however, the Conservatives lost all but two

seats in the House of Commons. Campbell's tenure as prime minister ended on Nov. 4; she stepped down as federal Conservative leader on Dec. 14, 1993.

■ Jean Chrétien

Jean Chrétien was born in Shawinigan, Quebec, on Jan. 11, 1934. He studied law at Laval University and was called to the bar of Quebec in 1958.

Chrétien was first elected to the House of Commons in 1963 and after re-election in 1965 served as parliamentary secretary to the prime minister (1965) and the finance minister (1966). He became minister of national revenue in 1968; after the June 1968 election, he became responsible for Indian affairs and northern development. In 1974, he was appointed president of the treasury board; in 1976, he served as minister of industry, trade and commerce. In 1977, he was named

finance minister; in 1980 he became justice minister and attorney general and also served as minister of state for social development. Chrétien played an important role in patriating the Constitution. In 1982, he became minister of energy, mines and resources; in 1984, he became deputy prime minister and secretary of state for external affairs.

In 1984, Chrétien ran second to John Turner in the Liberal leadership race; in the 1984 election, Chrétien kept his seat in the House of Commons. In 1986, when Liberals confirmed Turner's leadership at a party convention, Chrétien resigned his seat to practice law.

In 1990, Turner resigned as Liberal leader after losing a second election to the Conservatives, and Chrétien won the Liberal leadership. He subsequently won a by-election in Beausejour and took his seat in the House of Commons as leader of the Opposition.

Chrétien inherited a party that was disorganized and almost bankrupt. His support for the Charlottetown Accord in 1992 cost him support among Quebec's nationalists. Nonetheless, in the election of Oct. 25, 1993, Chrétien led the Liberals to victory over the ruling Conservatives. He was re-elected in his old riding of Saint-Maurice and was sworn in as Canada's 20th prime minister.

The new government inherited a troubled economy. In 1993, Canada suffered from high unemployment, a large national debt and an alarming annual deficit. Chrétien chose to limit or cut federal programs, including subsidies to the provinces, and to eliminate the national deficit. Chrétien also chose to keep the Goods and Services Tax, despite an election pledge to abolish it.

In his first term, Chrétien also struggled with Quebec's separatists. In 1993, the federal Liberals won only 20 seats in Quebec compared to the 54 seats won by the Bloc Québécois. In the Quebec referendum of Oct. 30, 1995, the federalists sustained the barest margin of victory over the separatists, and Chrétien's role in the federalist campaign was criticized.

In foreign policy, Chrétien stressed international trade. He led a series of well-publicized "Team Canada" missions around the globe and endorsed the North American Free Trade Agreement (NAFTA), which came into force on Jan. 1, 1994. Chrétien also established a cordial relationship with US President Bill Clinton.

In the election of June 2, 1997, Chrétien led his party to another victory, but the number of Liberal seats in the House of Commons fell from 177 to 155. The government continued the economic policies of its first term and, in 1998, the government declared a budget surplus for the first time in 25 years. In 1999, the Chrétien government committed Canadian troops to NATO's war against the Serbs in the Balkans.

In the election of Nov. 27, 2000, Chrétien led the Liberals to a third consecutive victory at the polls. (See pages 113–21 for more information about the Chrétien years.)

Fathers of Confederation

Union of the British North American colonies into the Dominion of Canada was discussed and its terms negotiated at three confederation conferences held at Charlottetown (C), Sept. 1, 1864; Quebec (Q), Oct. 10, 1864; and London (L), Dec. 4, 1866. The names of delegates are followed by the provinces they represented; Canada refers to what are now the provinces of Ontario and Quebec.

Adams G. Archibald, NS	C,Q,L	Hector L. Langevin, Canada	C,Q,L
George Brown, Canada	C,Q	Jonathan McCully, NS	C,Q,L
Alexander Campbell, Canada	C,Q	A.A. Macdonald, PEI	C,Q
Frederick B.T. Carter, Nfld	Q	John A. Macdonald, Canada	C,Q,L
George-Étienne Cartier, Canada	C,Q,L	William McDougall, Canada	C,Q,L
Edward B. Chandler, NB	C,Q	Thomas D'Arcy McGee, Canada	C,Q
Jean-Charles Chapais, Canada	Q	Peter Mitchell, NB	Q,L
James Cockburn, Canada	Q	Oliver Mowat, Canada	Q
George H. Coles, PEI	C,Q	Edward Palmer, PEI	C,Q
Robert B. Dickey, NS	Q	William H. Pope, PEI	C,Q
Charles Fisher, NB	Q,L	John W. Ritchie, NS	L
Alexander T. Galt, Canada	C,Q,L	J. Ambrose Shea, Nfld	Q
John Hamilton Gray, NB	C,Q	William H. Steeves, NB	C,Q
John Hamilton Gray, PEI	C,Q	Sir Étienne-Paschal Taché, Canada	Q
Thomas Heath Haviland, PEI	Q	Samuel Leonard Tilley, NB	C,Q,L
William A. Henry, NS	C,Q,L	Charles Tupper, NS	C,Q,L
William P. Howland, Canada	L	Edward Whelan, PEI	Q
John M. Johnson, NB	C,Q,L	R.D. Wilmot, NB	L

GOVERNMENT OF CANADA

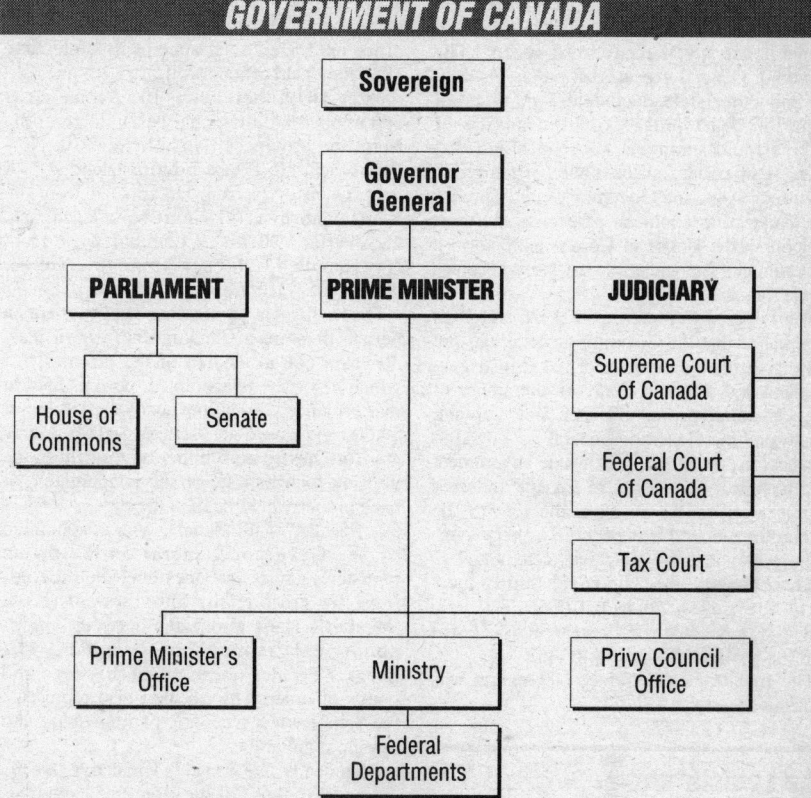

Canada is an independent, self-governing democracy. Its form of government is constitutional monarchy. Government power is divided into three types: legislative, executive and judicial. In Canada the legislative and executive powers are joined, while the judiciary remains separate. The executive proposes legislation, presents budgets and implements laws; the legislature adopts laws and votes on recommendations for taxes or other revenue; the judiciary interprets the laws.

■ The Monarchy

The Queen (crowned Queen Elizabeth II on June 2, 1953) is Canada's official head of state. All government authority is derived from the Queen, and all laws are enacted in her name. The Queen's role is set out in the Constitution Act (formerly the British North America Act, 1867), which also gives the monarch ultimate authority over Canada's armed forces.

In practice, however, the Queen has little or no part to play in Canadian government. She appoints the Governor General, but does so only on the prime minister's recommendation. Once appointed, it is the Governor General who performs the monarch's duties, and these duties have been mainly ceremonial for many years. Only during royal visits does the Queen carry out functions normally performed in her name by the Governor General such as the opening of Parliament.

■ The Governor General

The Governor General is selected by the prime minister and formally appointed by the Queen to act as her representative in Canada. The appointment is usually for five years but has sometimes been extended to seven.

Bills passed in the House of Commons and Senate do not become law until the Governor General has given them royal assent. The Governor General executes all orders-in-council and other state documents, appoints all superior court judges (on the advice of Cabinet) and summons, prorogues and dissolves Parliament (on the advice of the prime minister). Also, the Governor General invites the leader of the political party with the most support in the House of Commons to form a government. The leader of that party becomes prime minister.

The Imperial Conferences of 1926 and 1930 established that the Governor General was not the representative or agent of the British government and should act only on the advice of the Canadian prime minister and Cabinet. Therefore, the Governor General is obliged to respect the principle of responsible government and to follow the wishes of Canada's elected representatives. As a result, the role of the Governor General has become largely symbolic, with duties that are chiefly ceremonial.

Three members of the royal family have held the post: the Marquess of Lorne (1878–83), the Duke of Connaught (1911–16) and the Earl of Athlone (1940–46).

The first Canadian Governor General was Vincent Massey (1952–59).

The Legislature

Canada's legislature or Parliament consists of the Queen, an upper house (known as the Senate) and the House of Commons. Senators are appointed by the Governor General on the advice of the prime minister. The seats in the Senate are distributed on a regional basis. Originally, there were 72 senators, but through the years the Senate has increased as the number of provinces and the population have grown. In 1975 the Senate was increased to 104 members; in 1990 Prime Minister Brian Mulroney employed a never-before-used section of the Constitution Act to increase the number temporarily to 112. The House of Commons is an elected assembly in which each member represents one of 301 electoral districts distributed according to population.

■ The Senate

The Senate is the Upper House of the Canadian Parliament through which all legislation must pass before it becomes law. Its members,

appointed by the Governor General on the recommendation of the prime minister, hold office until age 75. (If appointed before June 1965 they held office for life).

After 1999, there were 105 Senate seats apportioned on a regional basis: 24 from the Maritime provinces (Nova Scotia, 10; New Brunswick, 10; Prince Edward Island, 4); 24 from Quebec; 24 from Ontario; 24 from the Western provinces (Manitoba, 6; Saskatchewan, 6; Alberta, 6; British Columbia, 6); 6 from Newfoundland; 1 each from the Yukon, Northwest Territories and Nunavut.

To be eligible for Senate appointment, a person must be a Canadian citizen, at least 30 years old, a resident of the province for which he or she is appointed, possess land in that province with an unencumbered value of $4,000 and have a net estate of $4,000. A senator for Quebec must either be resident in the division for which he or she is appointed, or have property qualification there.

A Speaker of the Senate, who is appointed by the Governor General on the prime minister's advice, presides over the proceedings. By custom, the appointment to the Speaker's chair alternates between anglophone and francophone members. The Speaker decides questions of privilege and points of order. The Speaker also represents the Senate when receiving parliamentary and foreign dignitaries.

Technically, the Senate's legislative powers are equal to those of the House of Commons with two restrictions: first, on certain constitutional amendments, the Senate may delay resolutions of the House of Commons for up to 180 days but cannot defeat them; second, the Senate cannot initiate money bills.

In practice, however, the Senate's chief role is to provide technical reviews of legislation proposed in the House of Commons rather than initiate political action. These reviews are done by Senate committees, which inspect each bill clause by clause and hear evidence from groups or individuals who may be affected by the proposed legislation.

Three types of Senate committee are worth noting. Standing committees, which are created at the start of a parliamentary session, study ongoing issues such as banking and foreign affairs. Standing committees may sit for up to five years. Special committees, which are created to deal with unusual or temporary issues, usually sit for six months before tabling their final reports in the

Senate. Joint committees, which consist of representatives from the Senate and the House of Commons, work on issues that affect both chambers of Parliament.

Historically, the Senate rarely used its powers to impede legislation originating from the elected House of Commons. From 1984 to 1990, however, the Liberal-dominated Senate attempted several times to stall or block legislation approved by the Conservative majority in the House of Commons. In 1990, when the Senate blocked his government's goods and services tax, Prime Minister Mulroney temporarily increased the size of the Senate and added eight new Conservatives, ensuring that the measure would be made law.

In recent years, there have been repeated calls, especially from the West, for constitutional reform which would include an elected Senate with more representation from the Western provinces and Newfoundland.

■ The House of Commons

The House of Commons is Canada's 301-member elected federal assembly. Its members are chosen in general elections held at least once every five years. By-elections are held if a member dies or resigns between general elections.

All bills governing matters within federal jurisdiction must be passed by a majority of members of Parliament to become law.

Members of Parliament usually belong to a political party and will normally vote with that party on any proposed legislation. Occasionally, members will break with their party on a vote and will leave the party they were affiliated with when elected to sit as independents or to join another political party within the House. Members of Parliament can also be elected as independent candidates who do not belong to a political party.

The prime minister is the leader of the political party able to command the support of a majority of the members of the House of Commons. The prime minister's command of a majority of members in the House also makes the prime minister the leader of the federal government. If no party holds a clear majority of seats, a "minority government" is formed, usually led by the party with the most seats in Parliament, provided it has enough support from the other parties to enable it to pass legislation.

The Opposition consists of parties that win enough votes to elect members to the House but do not have enough seats in the House to form a majority government. These parties sit on benches across from the governing party in the House and debate the government's policies for the life of the legislature—a maximum of five years. The Opposition party with the largest number of seats is given the title of "Her Majesty's Loyal Opposition." The minimum requirement for "official party" status is 12 seats in the House.

When the House of Commons is in session it convenes at two o'clock daily and 11 o'clock on Fridays when the Speaker of the House takes the chair. After the mace is laid on the table in front of the Speaker and the daily prayer is read, business commences. Members of the government sit to the Speaker's right and the Opposition sits on the left. The leaders of other opposition parties sit on the left farther away from the Speaker's chair.

The Speaker of the House, who is elected from and by the members after a general election, presides over the legislature. This official decides all procedural questions and maintains order. The Speaker is impartial at all times, enforcing the House's rules without regard to party loyalty. The Speaker also chairs the Board of Internal Economy, which controls the House of Commons staff and its annual budget. Some Speakers resign their party membership and run as independents in subsequent elections to maintain their impartial standing in the House.

An important feature of Parliament is the daily question period when members question Cabinet ministers about their policies and actions. But most of Parliament's time is spent discussing proposed legislation introduced as "bills." Any member may introduce a bill, although this is usually done by a member of Cabinet. After an initial reading in the House, a bill is forwarded into committee for detailed examination.

The House of Commons features several types of committees. Standing committees, which are the most common, are created at the beginning of a parliamentary session. They investigate ongoing issues and may sit for up to five years. Special committees, which are sometimes called task forces, are created to deal with unusual issues (such as illegal drug use). Special committees usually sit for six months before tabling their final reports in the House. Legislative committees are created solely to examine a bill after its second reading in the House. These committees usually have no more than seven members and cease to exist after reporting to the House.

After a bill is examined by committee and read a third time in the House, members vote on the bill. If a majority of members vote for the bill, it is forwarded to the Senate for consideration.

The leader of the government in the House of Commons—who is a cabinet minister but not the prime minister—shepherds the government's bills through the legislature. The house leader of the government works with the leader of the government in the Senate to coordinate the smooth passage of bills there. The house leader of the government also keeps Opposition members informed about all legislative matters.

Before a vote on a bill occurs, the party whips—who are drawn from their respective caucuses—ensure that their party's members appear in the legislature or at committee meetings to vote. Party whips rely more on persuasion than coercion to ensure member attendance; occasionally whips offer minor rewards (e.g., trips and committee memberships) to party colleagues to ensure that they vote. In 2001, the Liberal government appointed the first woman—Marlene Catterall of Ontario West—to the post of chief government whip in the House of Commons.

When a major piece of legislation introduced by the government is defeated in the House of Commons, the government is obliged to resign. The Governor General may then call on the Leader of the Opposition to form a government but, in most cases, will call a general election so that the electorate can decide which party has the most public support for its policies.

The Executive

■ The Prime Minister

The prime minister is the pre-eminent figure in Canadian politics. The power and authority of the office come from the prime minister's leadership of the party (or group of parties) that has control of the most seats in the House of Commons. The prime minister is an elected member of Parliament as well as national party leader and has a mandate to govern via programs and policies and to speak on behalf of Canada.

The prime minister appoints and dismisses cabinet ministers, senior civil servants and parliamentary secretaries; the prime minister also appoints senators, judges, lieutenant-governors, privy councillors, provincial administrators and Speakers of the Senate. In addition, the prime minister recommends to the monarchy the appointment of the Governor General. The prime minister has the authority to dissolve Parliament and can therefore control the timing of an election. The prime minister also controls the organization of government, including the power to create or shut down Crown corporations; create, modify or merge cabinet portfolios and bureaucratic agencies; and appoint royal commissions.

■ The Cabinet

The Cabinet is a group of government ministers who, chosen and led by the prime minister, determine executive policies and are responsible for them to the House of Commons. Cabinet members are usually given responsibility for heading specific areas of the government such as finance or foreign policy and will introduce legislation pertaining to them in the House of Commons. They will also explain or defend government actions when questioned in the House.

Cabinet ministers are generally chosen from members of the government's party in the House of Commons, although senators are sometimes appointed to provide Cabinet representation from all parts of the country. When senators join the Cabinet they do not usually head a government department because a senator is constitutionally forbidden to introduce tax or "money bill" legislation.

There are five categories of cabinet ministers:

1. department ministers who assume responsibility for running one or more government departments

2. ministers with special parliamentary responsibilities

3. ministers without portfolios who do not have responsibility for running a department and are often appointed to balance regional representation in the Cabinet

4. ministers of state for designated purposes who formulate and develop new policies outside normal departmental responsibilities

5. secretaries of state who may assist departmental ministers, though the departmental minister remains legally responsible for the duties and functions performed by the minister of state

■ The Privy Council Office

The Privy Council Office is directed by the senior member of the public service, the clerk of the Privy Council, who also serves as the secretary to the Cabinet. As part of the executive branch of government, the office staffs the Cabinet secretariat and provides services to ensure the smooth functioning of the Cabinet and Cabinet meetings. The Privy Council Office advises the prime minister on government appointments, relations with Parliament and the monarchy, the roles and responsibilities of ministers and the organization of government. The office assists in the co-ordination of policy, ensuring that new proposals are compatible both with existing policy and the government's objectives. During a transition period between governments, the Privy Council Office assists in the winding down of outgoing administrations and the startup of the newly elected government.

The Privy Council Office's primary responsibilities are to ensure the smooth functioning of the machinery of government and decision-making, provide support to the Cabinet, monitor developments throughout the government, and act as a broker to resolve governmental problems.

■ The Treasury Board

The Treasury Board is a committee of the Privy Council that reviews planned expenditures and programs proposed by government departments and assigns priorities to each. The board is responsible for preparing a long-range and comprehensive fiscal plan that projects government income and expenses for up to four years; it also prepares operational plans for departmental programs. The board's estimates of the costs of existing programs, major statutory payments (such as transfer payments) and public debt charges form the basis of the main estimates, which are tabled by the first of March each year for review by various House committees.

The Treasury Board is also responsible for administrative policy; organization of the public service; and financial, expenditure and personnel management. In 1988, the board was also given responsibility for the policies and programs of the Official Languages Act. The board's secretariat negotiates collective agreements with the federal public service, acting as employer on the government's behalf.

■ Departments

Legislation and government policies are administered through departments, departmental branches and corporations, corporations owned or controlled by the government, special boards and various commissions and advisory bodies. Departments and departmental corporations are accountable to a cabinet minister and ultimately to Parliament; they perform research, administrative, advisory, supervisory or regulatory roles. Crown corporations usually operate in a competitive or commercial environment and some are accountable to Parliament through a minister as well.

The Canadian Judiciary

■ The Supreme Court of Canada

The Supreme Court of Canada is Canada's highest court of law. It was created by federal statute in 1875. Originally, Supreme Court decisions could be appealed to a special tribunal in England, but such appeals were abolished for criminal cases in 1933 and for civil cases in 1949. Since then, the Supreme Court of Canada has been the court of last resort for every case—criminal or civil—commenced in a Canadian court.

The Supreme Court has jurisdiction to hear appeals from the courts of appeal of each province, as well as from the Federal Court of Canada. The Supreme Court is also empowered to consider questions referred to it by the federal Cabinet, and to rule on the legality of bills submitted by the government.

The Constitution Act, 1982, with its new Canadian Charter of Rights and Freedoms, has expanded the role of the courts in general and of the Supreme Court in particular. Though it has always been within the power of Canadian courts to declare laws or other government actions invalid, this power had narrow limits prior to 1982. Legislation could be struck down only if the government introducing it had exceeded its legislative authority as defined in the Constitution Act, 1867 (formerly called the British North America Act, 1867). The federal government was not permitted to legislate on matters within provincial legislative authority, and the provincial governments were not permitted to legislate on matters within federal legislative authority. As long as the legislation satisfied that test, it was valid.

But since the Constitution Act became law in 1982, the courts have had the power to strike down legislation or invalidate other government actions if they infringe or deny any of the fundamental rights and freedoms recognized by the Canadian Charter of Rights and Freedoms. This new power has made Supreme Court judges the watchdogs of Parliament and, ultimately, the guardians of our constitutional rights. As the highest court in the land, the Supreme Court of Canada has the final word on whether laws violate the Constitution.

The Supreme Court consists of nine judges, including the chief justice. Three of the judges must be appointed from Quebec. By convention (although it is not legally required) three have been appointed from Ontario, two from the West and one from Atlantic Canada. All judges are appointed and paid by the federal government, and may hold office until age 75.

■ Federal Court of Canada

This court consists of a trial division and a court of appeal and has jurisdiction over a small range of specialized areas such as admiralty law, income tax, patents and customs. Once called the Exchequer Court, the Federal Court is administered by the federal government.

■ Appellate Courts

When a decision of the provincial superior courts is to be appealed, these courts hear the appeal and decide upon it. An appeal is not a new trial; there are rarely any witnesses called and the judges do not re-hear the whole case. Instead, they examine written transcripts of the trial and listen to legal arguments presented by the parties' lawyers. The appellate courts are provincial institutions and are called either the Court of Appeal, the Supreme Court Appeal Division or Appellate Division; the judges are appointed by the federal government.

■ Superior Court of Original Jurisdiction

This is the highest court at the provincial level, with jurisdiction to hear all civil and criminal cases, unless a statute specifically says otherwise. The name of the superior court differs among provinces. It can be called either the Court of Queen's Bench, the High Court of Justice or the Supreme Court Trial Division. The judges of these courts are appointed and paid by the federal government.

■ District or County Courts

These trial courts hear all but the most serious criminal matters and civil matters up to a certain dollar value. The judges of these courts are also appointed by the federal government.

■ Provincial Courts

This is the lowest rung of the judicial ladder. The jurisdiction of the provincial courts is limited by statute to the less serious criminal matters and civil cases involving relatively small sums of money. These judges are appointed and paid by the province in which they serve.

■ Federal and Provincial Legislative Authority

Because Canada is a federal state, legislative powers are divided between two levels of government: federal and provincial. (Municipal governments only exercise powers delegated to them by the provincial government).

Each level of government has a distinct sphere of authority. With a few exceptions, neither level is permitted to encroach on the legislative authority of the other.

The Constitution Act, 1867 (formerly the BNA Act), lists the classes of subject over which the federal and provincial governments have exclusive authority. The federal government, in addition to a general power to make laws for the "peace, order and good government of Canada," has exclusive power in several areas including criminal law, unemployment insurance, postal service, regulation of trade, external relations, money and banking, transportation, citizenship, Indian affairs and defence. Matters exclusively within provincial legislative authority include property and civil rights, administration of justice, education, health and welfare, municipal institutions and matters of a merely local or private nature.

Many of the subject classes set out in the Constitution Act, 1867, are broadly worded, and considerable debate has arisen over which level of government has authority to pass certain laws. Confusion has also arisen over the proper distribution of powers to regulate matters that could not have been foreseen by the Fathers of Confederation, such as air travel, radio and television broadcasting, etc. These difficulties have led to long political debates and court challenges. The latter arise when a person adversely affected by a particular law claims that the law is invalid because it is *ultra vires*—beyond the powers of the level of government that enacted it. Before the passing of the Constitution Act, 1982, only statutes found to be *ultra vires* could be declared inoperative by the Constitution. Now, there is an additional restraint on the federal Parliament and the provincial legislatures to comply with constitutional provisions, including the Canadian Charter of Rights and Freedoms.

■ The Provincial Governments

Canada's 10 provinces have a system of government which parallels that of the federal government in several ways. A premier, like the prime minister, leads the government by virtue of being leader of the party with the most seats in the provincial legislature and forms a Cabinet from the elected members of the governing party. Members of a provincial legislature, like members of the federal Parliament, represent constituencies and approve legislation within their constitutional jurisdiction. A lieutenant-governor, like the Governor General, gives royal assent to the laws passed by the legislature.

The major difference between the provincial and federal systems is that the provinces have no equivalent body to Canada's Senate.

■ The Territorial Governments

The Yukon, Northwest Territories and Nunavut are governed by elected representatives. Although the administration of each territory is technically in the hands of a commissioner appointed by the federal government, in practice the role of the commissioner has become like a provincial lieutenant-governor's: a commissioner follows the wishes of the elected representatives when exercising their authority.

In the Northwest Territories, the legislature consists of 14 elected members who run for office as independents rather than as members of political parties. This assembly selects the territory's political executives: a premier, who must win more than 50 percent of the vote, and six other cabinet ministers.

In Nunavut, the legislature consists of 19 elected members who also run for office as independents rather than as members of political parties. The territory's executive, which is drawn from this assembly, consists of a premier and six other cabinet ministers.

Yukon has a 18-member legislative assembly, which features political parties. The leader of the party supported by a majority of the assembly's elected representatives is named premier. Executive power is in the hands of an executive council, which functions like a provincial cabinet. Its members are appointed by Yukon's commissioner on the advice of the premier.

In the territories, the elected bodies have jurisdiction over such areas as education, housing, social services and renewable resources.

In 1990, the Northwest Territories established six aboriginal languages (Dogrib, Chipewyan, Gwich'in, Cree, Slavey and Inuktitut) as official languages, in addition to English and French.

■ Mechanics of Government

Formation of Government: General elections for the House of Commons occur at least every five years. But they may take place more often if the prime minister decides to call an early election or if the governing party loses the support of the majority of members of the House.

Following an election, the Governor General calls upon the leader of the party with the greatest House of Commons support to become prime minister. This is almost always the leader of the party with the most seats in the House but, under unusual circumstances, it could be the leader of another party which is able to gain majority support in Parliament.

The prime minister selects the Cabinet, usually from members of his party in the House of Commons. Formally, the prime minister and Cabinet act as advisors to the Governor General. In practice, however, they wield executive power and the Governor General's role is mainly ceremonial.

Passage of Legislation: To become law, proposed legislation (known as bills) must be passed by a majority of members in both the House of Commons and the Senate and then must be given royal assent by the Governor General. Most bills are introduced by members of the government in the House of Commons. Typically, a bill is given three "readings" in the House. The first reading is simply to introduce the bill. The second reading is accompanied by debate on the principle of the bill. The bill is then voted on and, if approved, is sent to a House committee composed of representatives of all parties to be considered clause by clause. The committee prepares a report and submits it to the House of Commons with any proposed amendments. These amendments, plus any others moved by any member of Parliament, are debated and usually voted on. A motion is then brought for the bill to be given third reading. If the vote is favorable, the bill is then introduced in the Senate where it undergoes a similar process. After a bill has been approved by both Houses, the Governor General gives it royal assent in a ceremony that takes place in the Senate chamber.

Defeat of a Government: Between elections, a government can be forced to resign if it is defeated in a vote on a major government bill. When this happens, the government is considered to have lost the support of the majority of Parliament's elected representatives. This typically occurs only when the party in power has formed a minority government—that is, if it holds more seats than any other single party but fewer seats than the combined Opposition parties. This last happened federally in 1979 when a minority Conservative government, elected earlier that year, introduced a budget which was defeated by the combined votes of the Liberal and New Democratic Party members in the House. Parliament was dissolved, an election was called and the Liberals regained power.

■ The Constitution of Canada

Canada's constitution consists of written documents and unwritten conventions. The written constitution is embodied in the Constitution Acts of 1867 and 1982. The 1867 legislation (originally titled the British North America Act) was a British statute that established a federal state with a Parliament modelled on the British system. The Act assembled the colonies of Nova Scotia, New Brunswick and Canada (Ontario and Quebec) into the "Dominion of Canada," created a federal government in Ottawa, and divided the powers of government between Ottawa and the provinces.

The BNA Act gave Ottawa broad jurisdiction over internal matters, including unlimited powers of taxation, while allowing the provinces only a narrow field of local control. In general, the Canadian constitution of the late 19th century was a centralist document.

Under the BNA Act, Britain still had the power to veto Canadian laws or to enact statutes affecting Canada. But the British had no desire to raise revenue in Canada, for example, or to tax Canadians directly. This approach extended to trade and tariffs. Gradually, the practice was established that where money was involved, even in trade treaties, Canada would determine its own policy.

The same was not true of political foreign policy. When Britain declared war on Germany in 1914, Canada, as part of the British Empire, was automatically at war. During this period, British courts also interpreted Canadian statutes, especially those involving the division of power between Ottawa and the provinces. Through this process, the constitution's strong centralist thrust was altered to give more authority to the provinces.

The constitution was also adjusted more directly, through amendments. But because the BNA Act was a British statute, Canada could make formal changes to it only with the consent of the British Parliament. Ottawa tended to seek such amendments only when they did not affect provincial powers or when the provinces agreed with the changes. This process worked at least some of the time: 29 times, in fact, between 1870 and 1975. In 1940, for example, unemployment insurance became a federal responsibility through an amendment to the BNA Act.

In 1931, Britain attempted to tidy up relations with Canada and other self-governing dominions within the Commonwealth by passing the Statute of Westminster. The Statute ceded full powers over foreign affairs and trade to Canada. But because the federal and provincial governments could not agree on a method for amending the BNA Act at home, the British Parliament retained ultimate power over Canada's constitution. Until 1949, British courts continued to review Canadian constitutional cases.

From 1927 until 1982, a succession of federal governments attempted to resolve the problem by getting the provinces to agree to an amending formula. These negotiations failed as the provinces used them as a means to gain concessions from Ottawa.

The catalyst in constitutional discussions during the late 20th century came from Quebec, where provincial governments since 1960 sought to expand the province's jurisdiction. To protect French culture, the Quebec government requested more powers over culture, the economy and social institutions.

Ottawa resisted the move under prime ministers Lester Pearson and Pierre Trudeau. Trudeau argued that without a strong central power a country as sprawling and diverse as Canada would be fatally weakened and might disintegrate.

In lengthy negotiations with the provinces, Trudeau failed to gain agreement on an amending formula, even when he offered increased powers in return. In 1976, the election of the separatist Parti Québécois in Quebec made constitutional compromise even more unlikely and the matter was set aside.

After Quebec's 1980 referendum on sovereignty-association was won by the federalists, constitutional renewal was back on the agenda. However, federal-provincial discussions became mired in disagreement through the summer of 1980. In September, Trudeau announced that the federal government, with the support of only Ontario and New Brunswick, would ask the British Parliament to amend the BNA Act to patriate the constitution and establish a Charter of Rights and Freedoms to protect individual liberties. The Charter would also protect minority rights in education and the mobility rights of Canadian citizens, and change the name of the constitution: the BNA Act became the Constitution Act, 1982.

It took 18 months to get the new amendments approved by the Canadian Parliament, resolve the concerns of eight provincial governments, and get the Act through the British Parliament. But, in April 1982, the Constitution Act was proclaimed—although the consent of the Quebec government was never given.

The Constitution Act, 1982, consolidated all the previous BNA Acts and added an amending formula and a Charter of Rights and Freedoms. The Charter, which provided for basic democratic rights, also contained a "notwithstanding" clause that allowed Parliament or any provincial legislature to over-ride its provisions.

The amending formula provided for two types of constitutional change. The division of powers between the federal and provincial governments could be modified with the consent of the federal Parliament and seven provincial legislatures in provinces totalling more than 50 percent of the Canadian population; matters such as the composition of the Supreme Court or the status of English or French, however, required unanimous consent. The formula also stipulated that no amendment could take longer than three years to be ratified by Ottawa and all 10 provinces.

Visiting Public Galleries in Parliament

When Parliament is in session, visitors may sit in public galleries to watch debates or question period. Visits to the Senate gallery do not require reservations, but visits to the House of Commons do. Individuals who want to watch the House in action should schedule their visit through their MP's office; groups of 10–50 people or more must schedule their visit through their MP's office or through Parliament's reservation office at (613) 996-0896.

Electoral Redistribution

Since 1867, Canada's elected representatives have wrestled with the problem of ensuring that each Canadian citizen receives fair representation in government while also ensuring that each region has a fair say in the nation's business. Representation in both the House of Commons and the Senate has always been based on geography, and Canada's vast and often sparsely populated territory has always made establishing fair representation a challenge.

THE QUEST FOR A FORMULA

The first formula for representation in the House of Commons used the population of Quebec as the benchmark for calculating what is known as the "electoral quotient." First, the population of Quebec was divided by 65 (the number of seats guaranteed by the first Constitution Act). The result was then divided into the populations of each of the other provinces to calculate the number of seats each province would have—giving each voter the same relative representation.

Recognizing the need for a process of future adjustment, Parliament legislated that the number of seats in the House of Commons would be re-examined and redistributed after each 10-year census, beginning in 1871. At the same time, because not all provinces' populations would grow equally, the formula was softened by what was known as the "one-twentieth rule": no province would lose seats unless its percentage of Canada's total population dropped by at least 5 percent between the last two censuses. Despite the rule, people soon realized that the formula was too harsh.

In 1915, a new rule was introduced, stating that no province would have fewer seats in the Commons than it had in the Senate. (Thus PEI was guaranteed four seats.) In 1946, the formula was again amended to calculate the electoral quotient by dividing Canada's total population by the number of seats (255) to ascertain the average population per electoral district. By 1951, emerging population trends (which continue today) threatened to erode the voting power of the smaller provinces too quickly. Nova Scotia, Manitoba and Saskatchewan all faced the loss of seats after the 1951 census. A new rule, known as the "15

percent clause" was adopted. It stated that no province, no matter what its population drop, could lose more than 15 percent of its seats in any one redistribution. The 1961 census showed more population loss in those provinces, as well as in Quebec, and the 15 percent clause again came into effect. The 1971 census added Newfoundland to the number of provinces losing seats as a result of population shifts. Concern over the continuing erosion of the position of some provinces prompted another overhaul of the rules for calculating the allocation of seats when the Representation Act, 1974, was enacted. It was based on the following assumption:

> The objective must be adequate and realistic representation of all Canadians bearing in mind the historical undertakings arising out of Confederation and its responsibilities. The allocation of seats (in the House of Commons) is at the very heart of the Confederation compromise.[1]

The Representation Act made radical changes to the rules for allocating seats:

1) The population of Quebec was again used to calculate the electoral quotient.
2) Quebec was guaranteed 75 seats instead of 65.
3) The number of seats assigned to Quebec was to grow by 4 at each readjustment in order to slow the growth in the average population per electoral district.
4) Categories of provinces were created to assist in balancing representation among large and small provinces. A small province was classed as having a population of less than 1.5 million; an intermediate province, between 1.5 million and 2.5 million; a large province, over 2.5 million.

The new formula was used in 1976 and the House increased to 282 seats. After the 1981

---

(1) The Standing Committee on Privileges and Elections, February 1974.

census, it was clear that the formula of 1974 would send the number of seats in the House soaring—possibly to 369 after 2001. The Representation Act, 1985, simplified the formula. It guides the redistribution triggered by the 2001 census. It provides for the following:

1) Subtract 1 seat for each of the territories (3) from the total number of seats in the House of Commons (282) to reach 279 seats.
2) Divide the total population of the provinces (29,914,315) by 279 seats to reach the national quotient: 107,220 people.
3) Divide a province's population in 2001 by 107,220 to reach the number of seats for the province.
4) Then apply the Special Clauses—the various senatorial and grandfather clauses—to arrive at the final allocation of seats shown in the table below.

Redistribution began on March 12, 2002, as soon as Elections Canada received the census data from the chief statistician. It is clear from the electoral quotient that while the goal is "one elector—one vote," not all votes carry equal weight. The Supreme Court of Canada was asked to address this issue in 1991 and, in its opinion, judged that the formula guaranteed the right of effective representation rather than equality of voting power.

BOUNDARY READJUSTMENT

Changing representation is a two-step process: once seats are allocated, boundaries for constituencies must be adjusted. This job rests with independent provincial commissions set up by Elections Canada. Chaired by a judge appointed by that province's chief justice, each commission includes two appointees named by the speaker of the House of Commons. Deliberations of the commissions are subject to public scrutiny. Maps of proposed changes are published and public hearings are held to ensure public input. The most recent round of hearings ended in 2002, and all 10 provincial commissions filed their reports in the House of Commons by March 28, 2003. Throughout the summer of 2003, the commissions dealt with various objections to their proposed boundary changes from federal MPs. Canada's new electoral boundaries will come into effect no earlier than July 21, 2004.

For more information about Canada's electoral boundaries, visit Elections Canada, the independent body responsible for administering federal elections and referendums, at www.elections.ca

Canada's Current Representation Formula, using 2001 Census Data

Province/ Territory	Minimum Number of Seats[2]	Calculations				Electoral Quotient[3]
		Population 2001	Divided by National Quotient[4] (rounded result)	Adjustments due to Special Clauses	Total Seats	
Newfoundland & Labrador	7	512 930	5	+2	7	73 276
Prince Edward Island	4	135 294	1	+3	4	33 824
Nova Scotia	11	908 007	8	+3	11	82 546
New Brunswick	10	729 498	7	+3	10	72 950
Quebec...............	75	7 237 479	68	+7	75	96 500
Ontario..............	95	11 410 046	106	0	106	107 642
Manitoba	14	1 119 583	10	+4	14	79 970
Saskatchewan	14	978 933	9	+5	14	69 924
Alberta..............	21	2 947 807	28	0	28	106 243
British Columbia	28	3 907 738	36	0	36	108 548
Nunavut	1	n.a.	n.a.	n.a.	1	n.a.
Northwest Territories	1	n.a.	n.a.	n.a.	1	n.a.
Yukon Territory	1	n.a.	n.a.	n.a.	1	n.a.
Total Seats	**282**				**308**	

(2) In accordance with the Constitution Act, 1867 and amendments. (3) Population divided by the actual number of seats.
(4) Population of provinces divided by existing seats allocated to provinces: 29 914 315 / 279 = 107 220

Text of the Canadian Charter of Rights and Freedoms

Whereas Canada is founded upon principles that recognize the supremacy of God and the rule of law:

■ Guarantee of Rights and Freedoms

1 The Canadian Charter of Rights and Freedoms guarantees the rights and freedoms set out in it subject only to such reasonable limits prescribed by law as can be demonstrably justified in a free and democratic society.

■ Fundamental Freedoms

2 Everyone has the following fundamental freedoms: (a) freedom of conscience and religion; (b) freedom of thought, belief, opinion and expression, including freedom of the press and other media of communication; (c) freedom of peaceful assembly; and (d) freedom of association.

■ Democratic Rights

3 Every citizen of Canada has the right to vote in an election of members of the House of Commons or of a legislative assembly and to be qualified for membership therein.

4 (1) No House of Commons and no legislative assembly shall continue for longer than five years from the date fixed for the return of the writs at a general election of its members. (2) In time of real or apprehended war, invasion or insurrection, a House of Commons may be continued by Parliament and a legislative assembly may be continued by the legislature beyond five years if such continuation is not opposed by the votes of more than one-third of the members of the House of Commons or the legislative assembly, as the case may be.

5 There shall be a sitting of Parliament and of each legislature at least once every twelve months.

■ Mobility Rights

6 (1) Every citizen of Canada has the right to enter, remain in and leave Canada. (2) Every citizen of Canada and every person who has the status of a permanent resident of Canada has the right (a) to move to and take up residence in any province; and (b) to pursue the gaining of a livelihood in any province. (3) The rights specified in subsection (2) are subject to (a) any laws or practices of general application in force in a province other than those that discriminate among persons primarily on the basis of province of present or previous residence; and (b) any laws providing for reasonable residency requirements as a qualification for the receipt of publicly provided social services. (4) Subsections (2) and (3) do not preclude any law, program or activity that has as its object the amelioration in a province of conditions of individuals in that province who are socially or economically disadvantaged if the rate of employment in that province is below the rate of employment in Canada.

■ Legal Rights

7 Everyone has the right to life, liberty and security of the person and the right not to be deprived thereof except in accordance with the principles of fundamental justice.

8 Everyone has the right to be secure against unreasonable search or seizure.

9 Everyone has the right not to be arbitrarily detained or imprisoned.

10 Everyone has the right on arrest or detention (a) to be informed promptly of the reasons therefor; (b) to retain and instruct counsel without delay and to be informed of that right; and (c) to have the validity of the detention determined by way of *habeas corpus* and to be released if the detention is not lawful.

11 Any person charged with an offence has the right (a) to be informed without unreasonable delay of the specific offence; (b) to be tried within a reasonable time; (c) not to be compelled to be a witness in proceedings against that person in respect of the offence; (d) to be presumed innocent until proven guilty according to law in a fair and public hearing by an independent

and impartial tribunal; (e) not to be denied reasonable bail without just cause; (f) except in the case of an offence under military law tried before a military tribunal, to the benefit of trial by jury where the maximum punishment for the offence is imprisonment for five years or a more severe punishment; (g) not to be found guilty on account of any act or omission unless, at the time of the act or omission, it constituted an offence under Canadian or international law or was criminal according to the general principles of law recognized by the community of nations; (h) if finally acquitted of the offence, not to be tried for it again and, if finally found guilty and punished for the offence, not to be tried or punished for it again; and (i) if found guilty of the offence and if the punishment for the offence has been varied between the time of commission and the time of sentencing, to the benefit of the lesser punishment.

12 Everyone has the right not to be subjected to any cruel and unusual treatment or punishment.

13 A witness who testifies in any proceedings has the right not to have any incriminating evidence so given used to incriminate that witness in any other proceedings, except in a prosecution for perjury or for the giving of contradictory evidence.

14 A party or witness in any proceedings who does not understand or speak the language in which the proceedings are conducted or who is deaf has the right to the assistance of an interpreter.

■ Equality Rights

15 (1) Every individual is equal before and under the law and has the right to the equal protection and equal benefit of the law without discrimination and, in particular, without discrimination based on race, national or ethnic origin, colour, religion, sex, age or mental or physical disability. (2) Subsection (1) does not preclude any law, program or activity that has as its object the amelioration of conditions of disadvantaged individuals or groups including those that are disadvantaged because of race, national or ethnic origin,

colour, religion, sex, age or mental or physical disability.

■ Official Languages of Canada

16 (1) English and French are the official languages of Canada and have equality of status and equal rights and privileges as to their use in all institutions of the Parliament and government of Canada. (2) English and French are the official languages of New Brunswick and have equality of status and equal rights and privileges as to their use in all institutions of the legislature and government of New Brunswick. (3) Nothing in this Charter limits the authority of Parliament or a legislature to advance the equality of status or use of English and French.

17 (1) Everyone has the right to use English or French in any debates and other proceedings of Parliament. (2) Everyone has the right to use English or French in any debates and other proceedings of the legislature of New Brunswick.

18 (1) The statutes, records and journals of Parliament shall be printed and published in English and French and both language versions are equally authoritative. (2) The statutes, records and journals of the legislature of New Brunswick shall be printed and published in English and French and both language versions are equally authoritative.

19 (1) Either English or French may be used by any person in, or in any pleading in or process issuing from, any court established by Parliament. (2) Either English or French may be used by any person in, or in any pleading in or process issuing from, any court of New Brunswick.

20 (1) Any member of the public in Canada has the right to communicate with, and to receive available services from, any head or central office of an institution of the Parliament or government of Canada in English or French, and has the same right with respect to any other office of any such institution where (a) there is a significant demand for communications with and services from that office in such language; or (b) due to the nature of the office, it is reasonable that communications with and services from that office be available in both English and French. (2) Any member of the public in New Brunswick has the

right to communicate with, and to receive available services from, any office of an institution of the legislature or government of New Brunswick in English or French.

21 Nothing in sections 16 to 20 abrogates or derogates from any right, privilege or obligation with respect to the English and French languages, or either of them, that exists or is continued by virtue of any other provision of the Constitution of Canada.

22 Nothing in sections 16 to 20 abrogates or derogates from any legal or customary right or privilege acquired or enjoyed either before or after the coming into force of this Charter with respect to any language that is not English or French.

■ Minority Language Educational Rights

23 (1) Citizens of Canada (a) whose first language learned and still understood is that of the English or French linguistic minority population of the province in which they reside, or (b) who have received their primary school instruction in Canada in English or French and reside in a province where the language in which they received that instruction is the language of the English or French linguistic minority population of the province, have the right to have their children receive primary and secondary school instruction in that language in that province. (2) Citizens of Canada of whom any child has received or is receiving primary or secondary school instruction in English or French in Canada, have the right to have all their children receive primary and secondary school instruction in the same language. (3) The right of citizens of Canada under subsections (1) and (2) to have their children receive primary and secondary school instruction in the language of the English or French linguistic minority population of a province (a) applies wherever in the province the number of children of citizens who have such a right is sufficient to warrant the provision to them out of public funds of minority language instruction; and (b) includes, where the number of those children so warrants, the right to have them receive that instruction in minority language educational facilities provided out of public funds.

■ Enforcement

24. (1) Anyone whose rights or freedoms, as guaranteed by this Charter, have been infringed or denied may apply to a court of competent jurisdiction to obtain such remedy as the court considers appropriate and just in the circumstances. (2) Where, in proceedings under subsection (1), a court concludes that evidence was obtained in a manner that infringed or denied any rights or freedoms guaranteed by this Charter, the evidence shall be excluded if it is established that, having regard to all the circumstances, the admission of it in the proceedings would bring the administration of justice into disrepute.

■ General

25 The guarantee in this Charter of certain rights and freedoms shall not be construed so as to abrogate or derogate from any aboriginal, treaty or other rights or freedoms that pertain to the aboriginal peoples of Canada including (a) any rights or freedoms that have been recognized by the Royal Proclamation of October 7, 1763; and (b) any rights or freedoms that now exist by way of land claims agreements or may be so acquired.

26 The guarantee in this Charter of certain rights and freedoms shall not be construed as denying the existence of any other rights or freedoms that exist in Canada.

27 This Charter shall be interpreted in a manner consistent with the preservation and enhancement of the multicultural heritage of Canadians.

28 Notwithstanding anything in this Charter, the rights and freedoms referred to in it are guaranteed equally to male and female persons.

29 Nothing in this Charter abrogates or derogates from any rights or privileges guaranteed by or under the Constitution of Canada in respect of denominational, separate or dissentient schools.

30 A reference in this Charter to a province or to the legislative assembly or legislature or a province shall be deemed to include a reference to the Yukon Territory and the Northwest Territories, or to the appropriate legislative authority thereof, as the case may be.

31 Nothing in this Charter extends the legislative powers of any body or authority.

■ Application of Charter

32 (1) This Charter applies (a) to the Parliament and government of Canada in respect of all matters within the authority of Parliament including all matters relating to the Yukon Territory and Northwest Territories; and (b) to the legislature and government of each province in respect of all matters within the authority of the legislature of each province. (2) Notwithstanding subsection (1), section 15 shall not have effect until three years after this section comes into force.

33 (1) Parliament or the legislature of a province may expressly declare in an Act of Parliament or of the legislature, as the case may be, that the Act or a provision thereof shall operate notwithstanding a provision included in section 2 or sections 7 to 15 of this Charter. (2) An Act or a provision of an Act in respect of which a declaration made under this section is in effect shall have such operation as it would have but for the provision of this Charter referred to in the declaration. (3) A declaration made under subsection (1) shall cease to have effect five years after it comes into force or on such earlier date as may be specified in the declaration. (4) Parliament or the legislature of a province may re-enact a declaration made under subsection (1). (5) Subsection (3) applies in respect of a re-enactment made under subsection (4).

■ Citation

34 This Part may be cited as the Canadian Charter of Rights and Freedoms.

Canadian Orders and Decorations

For more information on Canada's orders and decorations, see the Web site of Governor General Adrienne Clarkson at http://www.gg.ca/honours and "Canadian Military Medals and Decorations" at the Web site of Veterans Affairs Canada at http://www.vac-acc.gc.ca/clients.

☐ National Orders

■ The Order of Canada

History   Creation of the Order of Canada was announced by Prime Minister Lester B. Pearson in 1967. It was instituted on the centennial of Canadian Confederation, July 1, 1967.

Basis of Award   To honour Canadians for outstanding achievement and service to their country or humanity. Appointments are announced twice annually, around July 1 and Jan. 1. Investitures occur three times a year, in February, April and October when the awards are given by the Governor General.

Eligibility   Every living Canadian is eligible to become a member. Federal and provincial politicians and judges are ineligible while in office.

Membership   There are three categories of membership. The first is Companion of the Order of Canada (C.C.). No more than 15 companions may be appointed in any one year, and no more than 165 living companions may hold the order at one time.

The second is Officer of the Order of Canada (O.C.). No more than 64 appointments may be made annually.

The third is Member of the Order of Canada (C.M.)., which recognizes service in a locality or a field of activity. No more than 136 appointments may be made annually.

Badge   A stylized snowflake bearing the crown with a ribbon in the same proportions of white and red which appear on the Canadian flag and the Latin motto *Desiderantes Meliorem Patriam*—"They Desire a Better Country." Worn at the neck by companions and officers and on the left breast by members.

■ The Order of Military Merit

History   The Order of Military Merit was instituted on July 1, 1972.

Basis of Award   To recognize exceptional service and conspicuous merit by regular and reserve members of Canada's Armed Forces.

Appointments are made by the Governor General on the recommendation of the chief of defence staff.

Eligibility   Active members of the Canadian Armed Forces, regular and reserve. A formula limits the number of annual appointments per year to one-tenth of one percent of the average number of persons who were members of the Armed Forces during the previous year.

Membership There are three categories of membership. The first is Commander of the Order of Military Merit (C.M.M.). Six percent of annual appointments go to this category of membership.

The second is Officer of the Order of Military Merit (O.M.M.). Thirty percent of annual appointments go to this category of membership.

The third is Member of the Order of Military Merit (M.M.M.). The balance of annual appointments go to this category of membership.

Badge In the form of an enamelled blue cross having expanded arms, with a blue ribbon edged in gold. Bears the words "Merit Merite Canada." Worn at the neck by commanders and on the left breast by officers and members.

☐ Medals for Military Valour

The Military Valour Decorations, consisting of the Victoria Cross (Canadian), the Star of Military Valour and the Medal of Military Valour, enable Canada to recognize members of the Canadian Forces, or members of an allied armed force serving with the Canadian Forces, for deeds of military valour.

■ Victoria Cross (V.C.) (Canadian)

History Approved by Queen Elizabeth II on Feb. 2, 1993. The British Victoria Cross was created by Queen Victoria in 1856 and was awarded to Canadians in all wars until 1945. There have been 94 Canadian recipients of the British V.C. and none of the Canadian version.

Basis of Award In recognition of "the most conspicuous bravery, a daring or pre-eminent act of valour or self-sacrifice or extreme devotion to duty, in the presence of the enemy." The V.C. will be awarded by the Governor General on the advice of the Military Valour Advisory Committee. It is the highest in the order of precedence in Canadian honours.

Eligibility Members of the Canadian Forces or a member of an allied armed force that is serving with or in conjunction with the Canadian Forces on or after Jan. 1, 1993. The V.C. may be awarded posthumously.

Badge The Cross is a bronze straight armed cross, suspended from a crimson ribbon. The face has, in the middle of the cross, a lion guardant standing on the Royal Crown, with the Latin inscription *Pro Valore*—"For Valour." The date of the act for which the decoration is bestowed is engraved in a raised circle on the reverse.

■ The Star of Military Valour (S.M.V.)

History Approved by Queen Elizabeth II on Feb. 2, 1993.

Basis of Award Awarded for distinguished and valiant service in the presence of the enemy.

Eligibility Members of the Canadian Forces or a member of an allied armed force that is serving with or in conjunction with the Canadian Forces on or after Jan. 1, 1993. The S.M.V. may be awarded posthumously.

Badge A gold star with four points with a maple leaf in each of the angles, on the face of which a gold maple leaf is superimposed in the centre of a sanguine field surrounded by a silver wreath of laurel and on the reverse of which the Royal Cypher and Crown and the Latin inscription *Pro Valore*—"For Valour" —appears. The Star shall be worn, suspended from a crimson ribbon with two white stripes, immediately after any order and before the Star of Courage.

■ The Medal of Military Valour (M.M.V.)

History Approved by Queen Elizabeth II on Feb. 2, 1993.

Basis of Award Awarded for an act of valour or devotion to duty in the presence of the enemy.

Eligibility Members of the Canadian Forces or a member of an allied armed force that is serving with or in conjunction with the Canadian Forces on or after Jan. 1, 1993. The M.M.V. may be awarded posthumously.

Badge A circular gold medal, on the face of which there is a maple leaf surrounded by a wreath of laurel and on the reverse of which the Royal Cypher and Crown and the Latin inscription *Pro Valore*—"For Valour"— appears. The medal shall be worn, from a crimson ribbon with three white stripes, immediately after the Meritorious Service Cross and before the Medal of Bravery.

☐ Decorations for Bravery

The Decorations for Bravery, consisting of the Cross of Valour, the Star of Courage and the Medal of Bravery honour those who have risked their lives to save or protect others.

These three Canadian decorations replaced the following non-combatant Commonwealth medals: the George Cross, the George Medal and the Queen's Gallantry Medal, respectively.

■ The Cross of Valour (C.V.)

History Created on May 1, 1972, the Cross of Valour takes precedence before all orders and other decorations except the Victoria Cross.

Basis of Award Awarded for acts of the most conspicuous courage in circumstances of extreme peril.

Eligibility May be awarded to civilians or members of the Canadian Forces. Only 19 have been awarded. May be awarded posthumously.

Badge A gold cross bearing the words "Valour Vaillance."

■ The Star of Courage (S.C.)

History Created on May 1, 1972.

Basis of Award Awarded for acts of conspicuous courage in circumstances of great peril.

Eligibility May be awarded to civilians or members of the Canadian Forces. May be awarded posthumously.

Badge A four-pointed silver star with the word "Courage."

■ The Medal of Bravery (M.B.)

History Created on May 1, 1972.

Basis of Award Awarded for acts of bravery in hazardous circumstances.

Eligibility May be awarded to civilians or members of the Canadian Forces. May be awarded posthumously.

Badge A circular silver medal with the words "Bravery Bravoure."

■ The Meritorious Service Cross (M.S.C.) (military and civilian)

History Military division created in 1984; civilian division created in 1991.

Basis of Award *Military division*: awarded in recognition of a military deed or activity that has been performed in an outstandingly professional manner or according to a rare high standard that brings considerable benefit or great honour to the Canadian Forces. *Civilian division*: awarded in recognition of the performance of a deed or activity performed in an outstandingly professional manner or according to an uncommonly high standard that brings considerable benefit or great honour to Canada.

Eligibility A member of the Canadian and allied forces, persons serving in conjunction with the Canadian Forces or other persons, Canadian or foreign.

Badge A Greek cross of silver, ends splayed and convexed, ensigned with the Royal Crown. On the face appear a maple leaf within a circle and a laurel wreath between the arms. Recipients are entitled to use the letters "M.S.C." after their names.

■ The Meritorious Service Medal (M.S.M.) (military and civilian)

History Created in 1991.

Basis of Award *Military division*: awarded in recognition of a military deed or activity that has been performed in a highly professional manner or is of a very high standard that brings benefit or honour to the Canadian Forces. *Civilian division*: awarded in recognition of the performance of a deed or activity performed in a highly professional manner or of a very high standard that brings benefit or honour to Canada.

Eligibility A member of the Canadian and allied forces, persons serving in conjunction with the Canadian Forces or other persons, Canadian or foreign.

Badge A circular medal of silver ensigned with the Royal Crown. On the face appears the design of the cross. On the reverse appears the Royal Cypher and, within a double circle, the words "Meritorious Service Méritoire." Recipients are entitled to use the letters "M.S.M." after their names.

□ Other Notable Awards

The Governor General also bestows these awards.

■ The Academic Medal

Created in 1873. Awarded for academic excellence. Medals are distributed in March to colleges and universities and in April to high schools.

■ The Governor General's Caring Canadian Award

Created in 1996. Awarded to unpaid volunteers for their extraordinary contributions, performed behind the scenes and for several years, in support of family, community or humanitarian causes.

Governors General of Canada

Name	Date Appointed	Assumed Office	Term
Sir Charles Stanley, Viscount Monck	June 1, 1867	July 1, 1867	1867–69
Sir John Young, Baron Lisgar	Dec. 29, 1868	Feb. 2, 1869	1869–72
Frederick Temple Hamilton Blackwood, Earl of Dufferin	May 22, 1872	June 25, 1872	1872–78
John Douglas Sutherland Campbell, Marquess of Lorne	Oct. 5, 1878	Nov. 20, 1878	1878–83
Henry Charles Keith Petty-Fitzmaurice, Marquess of Lansdowne	Aug. 18, 1883	Oct. 23, 1883	1883–88
Frederick Arthur Stanley, Baron Stanley of Preston	May 1, 1888	June 11, 1888	1888–93
John Campbell Hamilton-Gordon, Earl of Aberdeen	May 22, 1893	Nov. 18, 1893	1893–98
Gilbert John Elliott Murray-Kynynmound, Earl of Minto	July 30, 1898	Nov. 12, 1898	1898–1904
Albert Henry George Grey, Earl Grey	Sept. 26, 1904	Dec. 10, 1904	1904–11
His Royal Highness The Prince Arthur, Field Marshal Duke of Connaught	Mar. 21, 1911	Oct. 13, 1911	1911–16
Victor Christian William Cavendish, Duke of Devonshire	Aug. 19, 1916	Nov. 11, 1916	1916–21
Julian Byng, General Baron Byng of Vimy and of Thorpe	Aug. 2, 1921	Aug. 11, 1921	1921–26
Sir Freeman Freeman-Thomas, Baron Willingdon of Ratton	Aug. 5, 1926	Nov. 2, 1926	1926–31
Vere Brabazon Ponsonby, Earl of Bessborough	Feb. 9, 1931	Apr. 4, 1931	1931–35
John Buchan, Baron Tweedsmuir	Aug. 10, 1935	Nov. 2, 935	1935–40
Alexander George Cambridge, Major General Earl of Athlone	Apr. 3, 1940	June 21, 1940	1940–46
Sir Harold George Alexander, Field Marshal Viscount Alexander of Tunis	Aug. 1, 1945	Apr. 18, 1946	1946–52
The Right Honourable Vincent Massey	Jan. 24, 1952	Feb. 22, 1952	1952–59
General the Right Honourable Georges P. Vanier	Aug. 1, 1959	Sept. 15, 1959	1959–67
The Right Honourable Daniel Roland Michener	Mar. 25, 1967	Apr. 15, 1967	1967–74
The Right Honourable Jules Léger	Oct. 5, 1973	Jan. 14, 1974	1974–79
The Right Honourable Edward Richard Schreyer	Dec. 7, 1978	Jan. 22, 1979	1979–83
The Right Honourable Jeanne Sauvé	Dec. 23, 1983	May 14, 1984	1984–90
The Right Honourable Ramon John Hnatyshyn	Oct. 6, 1989	Jan. 21, 1990	1990–95
The Right Honourable Roméo LeBlanc	Nov. 22, 1994	Feb. 8, 1995	1995–99
The Right Honourable Adrienne Clarkson	Sept. 8, 1999	Oct. 7, 1999	1999–

Prime Ministers of Canada

Prime Minister	Party	Term(s)	Born	P.M. at age	Died
Sir John A. Macdonald	Conservative	July 1, 1867–Nov. 5, 1873 Oct. 9, 1878–June 6, 1891	Jan. 11, 1815	52	June 6, 1891
Alexander Mackenzie	Liberal	Nov. 5, 1873–Oct. 9, 1878	Jan. 28, 1822	51	Apr. 17, 1892
Sir John Abbott	Conservative	June 15, 1891–Nov. 24, 1892	Mar. 12, 1821	70	Oct. 30, 1893
Sir John Thompson	Conservative	Nov. 25, 1892–Dec. 12, 1894	Nov. 10, 1845	48	Dec. 12, 1894
Sir Mackenzie Bowell	Conservative	Dec. 13, 1894–Apr. 27, 1896	Dec. 27, 1823	70	Dec. 10, 1917
Sir Charles Tupper	Conservative	Apr. 27, 1896–July 8, 1896	July 2, 1821	74	Oct. 30, 1915
Sir Wilfrid Laurier	Liberal	July 11, 1896–Oct. 6, 1911	Nov. 20, 1841	54	Feb. 17, 1919
Sir Robert Borden	Conservative/ Unionist	Oct. 10, 1911–Oct. 12, 1917 Oct. 12, 1917–July 10, 1920	June 26, 1854	57	June 10, 1937
Arthur Meighen	Unionist/ Conservative	July 10, 1920–Dec. 29, 1921 June 29, 1926–Sept. 25, 1926	June 16, 1874	46	Aug. 5, 1960
Mackenzie King	Liberal	Dec. 29, 1921–June 28, 1926 Sept. 25, 1926–Aug. 6, 1930 Oct. 23, 1935–Nov. 15, 1948	Dec. 17, 1874	47	July 22, 1950
Richard B. Bennett	Conservative	Aug. 7, 1930–Oct. 23, 1935	July 3, 1870	60	June 27, 1947
Louis St. Laurent	Liberal	Nov. 15, 1948–June 21, 1957	Feb. 1, 1882	66	July 25, 1973
John Diefenbaker	Prog. Cons.	June 21, 1957–Apr. 22, 1963	Sept. 18, 1895	61	Aug. 16, 1979
Lester Pearson	Liberal	Apr. 22, 1963–Apr. 20, 1968	Apr. 23, 1897	65	Dec. 27, 1972
Pierre Trudeau	Liberal	Apr. 20, 1968–June 4, 1979 Mar. 3, 1980–June 30, 1984	Oct. 18, 1919	48	Sept. 28, 2000
Joe Clark	Prog. Cons.	June 4, 1979–Mar. 3, 1980	June 5, 1939	39	
John Turner	Liberal	June 30, 1984–Sept. 17, 1984	June 7, 1929	55	
Brian Mulroney	Prog. Cons.	Sept. 17, 1984–June 25, 1993	Mar. 20, 1939	45	
Kim Campbell	Prog. Cons.	June 25, 1993–Nov. 4, 1993	Mar. 10, 1947	46	
Jean Chrétien	Liberal	Nov. 4, 1993–	Jan. 11, 1934	59	

Canadian Cabinet Ministers and Secretaries of State

(as of October 1, 2003)

Cabinet ministers are the most powerful elected officials in government. They are sworn to the Privy Council and are bound by collective responsibility. They work with their staffs to set policies for their ministries and present (or defend) those policies in the House of Commons. They shepherd their bills through various readings and committees before having their bills voted into law.

Secretaries of state, although sworn to the Privy Council and bound by collective responsibility as well, are not members of the Cabinet. Secretaries of state are assigned to support specific cabinet ministers; they also get smaller staffs and less pay than cabinet ministers. Prime Minister Jean Chrétien introduced the distinction between these "senior" and "junior" officials on Nov. 4, 1993.

■ The Cabinet

The Prime Minister of Canada
The Right Hon. Jean Chrétien
(Saint-Maurice, Quebec)
Telephone: (613) 992-4211
Fax: (613) 941-6900
E-mail: pm@pm.gc.ca

The Deputy Prime Minister of Canada,
Minister of Finance and Minister of Infrastructure
Provides the federal government with an annual budget; provides research and advice on financial issues; regularly monitors the performance of Canada's economy.
The Hon. John Paul Manley
(Ottawa South, Ontario)
Telephone: (613) 992-3269
Fax: (613) 995-1534
E-mail: Manley.J@parl.gc.ca

The Leader of the Government in the Senate
Represents the Cabinet in the Senate.
The Hon. Sharon Carstairs
(Manitoba)
Telephone: (613) 947-7123
Fax: (613) 947-7125
E-mail: carsts@sen.parl.gc.ca

The Minister of Agriculture and Agri-Food
Responsible for production, processing, marketing and protection of crops and livestock, including research and technology; soil conservation; food processing and inspection; and trade policies and support programs.
The Hon. Lyle Vanclief
(Prince Edward–Hastings, Ontario)
Telephone: (613) 992-5321
Fax: (613) 996-8652
E-mail: Vanclief.L@parl.gc.ca

The Minister of Canadian Heritage
Responsible both for Canada's natural heritage (parks) and our historic and cultural heritage, including the arts, sports and multiculturalism.
The Hon. Sheila M. Copps
(Hamilton East, Ontario)
Telephone: (613) 995-2772
Fax: (613) 994-1267
E-mail: Copps.S@parl.gc.ca

The Minister of Citizenship and Immigration
Administers policies and procedures for citizenship and immigration.
The Hon. Denis Coderre
(Bourassa, Quebec)
Telephone: (613) 995-6108
Fax: (613) 995-9755
E-mail: Coderre.D@parl.gc.ca

The Minister of the Environment
Protects and conserves Canada's air and water; monitors climate and pollution.
The Hon. David Anderson
(Victoria, British Columbia)
Telephone: (613) 996-2358
Fax: (613) 952-1458
E-mail: Anderson.D@parl.gc.ca

The Minister of Fisheries and Oceans
Manages Canada's resources in the water, particularly in the ocean, when outside other jurisdictions; oversees public harbours and coastal and inland fisheries.
The Hon. Robert Thibault
(West Nova, Nova Scotia)
Telephone: (613) 995-5711
Fax: (613) 996-9857
E-mail: Thibault.R@parl.gc.ca

▶

The Minister of Foreign Affairs
Creates foreign policy; promotes and protects Canada's interests abroad; manages Canadian embassies and diplomatic staff; ensures Canadian citizens abroad receive fair treatment under foreign laws.
The Hon. Bill Graham
(Toronto Centre–Rosedale, Ontario)
Telephone: (613) 992-5234
Fax: (613) 996-9607
E-mail: Graham.B@parl.gc.ca

The Minister of Health
Provides funding and policies for a national health-care system; sets and enforces health standards.
The Hon. Anne McLellan
(Edmonton West, Alberta)
Telephone: (613) 992-4524
Fax: (613) 943-0044
E-mail: McLellan.A@parl.gc.ca

The Minister of Human Resources Development
Fosters an educated and mobile work force; provides income as necessary for seniors, the unemployed and the disabled.
The Hon. Jane Stewart
(Brant, Ontario)
Telephone: (613) 992-3118
Fax: (613) 992-6382
E-mail: Stewart.J@parl.gc.ca

**The Minister of Indian Affairs
and Northern Development**
Meets the federal government's treaty obligations to Inuit and First Nations people, including the provision of basic services; negotiates and oversees claims settlements.
The Hon. Robert Daniel Nault
(Kenora–Rainy River, Ontario)
Telephone: (613) 996-1161
Fax: (613) 996-1759
E-mail: Nault.R@parl.gc.ca

The Minister of Industry
Drafts major federal bills and programs for consumer and business groups; provides policy advice, business services and industrial information.
The Hon. Allan Rock
(Etobicoke Centre, Ontario)
Telephone: (613) 947-5000
Fax: (613) 947-4276
E-mail: Rock.A@parl.gc.ca

The Minister for International Cooperation
Administers economic and technical aid to the developing world through CIDA.
The Hon. Susan Whelan
(Essex, Ontario)
Telephone: (613) 992-1812
Fax: (613) 995-0033
E-mail: Whelan.S@parl.gc.ca

The Minister for International Trade
Takes part in international trade talks and institutions to promote Canadian business abroad and to resolve trade disputes.
The Hon. Pierre S. Pettigrew
(Papineau–Saint-Denis, Quebec)
Telephone: (613) 995-8872
Fax: (613) 995-9926
E-mail: Pettigrew.P@parl.gc.ca

**The Minister of Justice and
Attorney General of Canada**
Provides legal services to all government departments and agencies; supervises the administration of justice.
The Hon. Martin Cauchon
(Outremont, Quebec)
Telephone: (613) 995-7691
Fax: (613) 995-0114
E-mail: Cauchon.M@parl.gc.ca

The Minister of Labour
Enforces the labour code including health and safety in the workplace; promotes fairness and cooperation between labour and management; provides mediation and conciliation in labour disputes.
The Hon. Claudette Bradshaw
(Moncton–Riverview–Dieppe, New Brunswick)
Telephone: (613) 992-8072
Fax: (613) 992-8083
E-mail: Bradshaw.C@parl.gc.ca

The Minister of National Defence
Administers Canada's Armed Forces, defends citizens at home and meets Canada's military obligations abroad.
The Hon. John McCallum
(Markham, Ontario)
Telephone: (613) 996-3374
Fax: (613) 992-3921
E-mail: McCallum.J@parl.gc.ca

The Minister of National Revenue
Administers the Customs and Excise Acts as well as import and export taxes and permits.
The Hon. Elinor Caplan
(Thornhill, Ontario)
Telephone: (613) 992-0253
Fax: (613) 992-0887
Email: Caplan.E@parl.gc.ca

The Minister of Natural Resources
Proposes and plans national policies for energy, mines and resources (renewable and nonrenewable); researches conservation and development strategies.
The Hon. Harbance Singh (Herb) Dhaliwal
(Vancouver South–Burnaby, British Columbia)
Telephone: (613) 995-7052
Fax: (613) 996-2962
E-mail: Dhaliwal.H@parl.gc.ca

▶

The Minister of Public Works and Government Services, Minister Responsible for the Canadian Wheat Board and Federal Interlocutor for Métis and Non-Status Indians

Buys services for the daily operation of government; provides office space and maintains public buildings; provides telecommunications and information services; prepares public audits and disburses public mónies.
The Hon. Ralph Goodale
(Wascana, Saskatchewan)
Telephone: (819) 997-5421
Fax: (819) 956-8382
E-mail: Goodale.R@parl.gc.ca

The Minister of State and Leader of the Government in the House of Commons

Plans and manages the government's legislative agenda in its pre-parliamentary and parliamentary stages; maintains relations with the Opposition.
The Hon. Donald Boudria
(Glengarry–Prescott–Russell, Ontario)
Telephone: (613) 996-2907
Fax: (613) 996-9123
E-mail: Boudria.D@parl.gc.ca

The Minister of State (Atlantic Canada Opportunities Agency)

Promotes economic growth in Atlantic Canada.
The Hon. Gerry Byrne
(Humber–St Barbe–Baie Verte, Newfoundland and Labrador)
Telephone: (613) 996-5511
Fax: (613) 996-9632
E-mail: Byrne.G@parl.gc.ca

The Minister of Transport

Oversees national policies to ensure competitive, safe and environmentally sustainable transportation.
The Hon. David Michael Collenette
(Don Valley East, Ontario)
Telephone: (613) 995-4988
Fax: (613) 995-1686
E-mail: Collenette.D@parl.gc.ca

The Minister of Veterans Affairs and Secretary of State (Science, Research and Development)

Provides Canadian combat veterans and their families with benefits; preserves the memory veterans' sacrifices and achievements.
The Hon. Rey Pagtakhan
(Winnipeg North–St. Paul, Manitoba)
Telephone: (613) 992-7148
Fax: (613) 996-9125
E-mail: Pagtakhan.R@parl.gc.ca

The President of the Queen's Privy Council for Canada and Minister of Intergovernmental Affairs

Manages federal-provincial relations; provides legal advice on constitutional issues and national unity.
The Hon. Stéphane Dion
(Saint-Laurent–Cartierville, Quebec)
Telephone: (613) 996-5789
Fax: (613) 992-3700
E-mail: Dion.S@parl.gc.ca

The President of the Treasury Board

Functions as the government's chief employer and general manager; responsible for finances, personnel and administration.
The Hon. Lucienne Robillard
(Westmount–Ville Marie, Quebec)
Telephone: (613) 996-7267
Fax: (613) 995-8632
E-mail: Robillard.L@parl.gc.ca

The Solicitor General of Canada

Responsible for prisons, the RCMP, CSIS, parole boards and everything within Parliament's jurisdiction not legally assigned somewhere else.
The Hon. Wayne Easter
(Malpeque, Prince Edward Island)
Telephone: (613) 992-2406
Fax: (613) 995-7408
E-mail: Easter.W@parl.gc.ca

■ Secretaries of State

Secretary of State (Amateur Sport) and Deputy Leader of the Government in the House of Commons

The Hon. Paul DeVillers
(Simcoe North, Ontario)
Telephone: (613) 992-6582
E-mail: DeVillers.P@parl.gc.ca

Secretary of State (Asia-Pacific)

The Hon. Dave Kilgour
(Edmonton Southeast, Alberta)
Telephone: (613) 995-8695
E-mail: Kilgour.D@parl.gc.ca

Secretary of State (Central and Eastern Europe and Middle East)

The Hon. Gar Knutson
(Elgin–Middlesex–London, Ontario)
Telephone: (613) 990-7769
E-mail: Knutson.G@parl.gc.ca

Secretary of State (Children and Youth)

The Hon. Ethel Blondin-Andrew
(Western Arctic, Northwest Territories)
Telephone: (613) 992-4587
E-mail: Blondin-Andrew.E@parl.gc.ca

▶ **Secretary of State (Economic Development Agency of Canada for the Regions of Quebec)**
The Hon. Claude Drouin
(Beauce, Quebec)
Telephone: (613) 992-8053
E-mail: Drouin.C@parl.gc.ca

Secretary of State (Federal Economic Development Initiative for Northern Ontario) (Rural Development)
The Hon. Andrew Mitchell
(Parry Sound–Muskoka, Ontario)
Telephone: (613) 996-3434
E-mail: Mitchell.A@parl.gc.ca

Secretary of State (Francophonie) (Latin America and Africa)
The Hon. Denis Paradis
(Brome–Missisquoi, Quebec)
Telephone: (613) 947-8185
E-mail: Paradis.D@parl.gc.ca

Secretary of State (Indian Affairs and Northern Development) (Western Economic Diversification)
The Hon. Stephen Owen
(Vancouver Quadra, British Columbia)
Telephone: (613) 992-2430
E-mail: Owen.S@parl.gc.ca

Secretary of State (International Financial Institutions)
The Hon. Maurizio Bevilacqua
(Vaughan–King–Aurora, Ontario)
Telephone: (613) 996-4971
E-mail: Bevilacqua.M@parl.gc.ca

Secretary of State (Multiculturalism) (Status of Women)
The Hon. Jean Augustine
(Etobicoke–Lakeshore, Ontario)
Telephone: (613) 995-9364
E-mail: Augustine.J@parl.gc.ca

Secretary of State (Selected Crown Corporations)
The Hon. Steve Mahoney
(Mississauga West, Ontario)
Telephone: (613) 995-7784
E-mail: Mahoney.S@parl.gc.ca

Deputy Prime Ministers of Canada

(as of October 1, 2003)

The title of deputy prime minister is strictly honorary. It is conferred at the prime minister's discretion on a member of the Cabinet. The title has no standing in law and carries no formal duties or tasks. Deputy prime ministers, however, often have other Cabinet portfolios.

Prime Minister Pierre Trudeau named the first deputy prime minister during a press interview after the nomination of his Cabinet on Sept. 16, 1977.

Since then only Prime Minister Joe Clark (1979–80) has not named a deputy prime minister.

In 1984, Prime Minister Brian Mulroney began the practice of appointing the deputy prime minister by "instrument of advice." An instrument of advice is a private letter written by the prime minister to the Crown. Since 1984, all deputy prime ministers have been appointed by this method.

Deputy Prime Minister	Date Appointed	Term Ended	Designated by Prime Minister
Allan J. MacEachen	Sept. 16, 1977	June 3, 1979	Pierre Trudeau
Allan J. MacEachen	Mar. 3, 1980	June 29, 1984	Pierre Trudeau
Jean Chrétien	June 30, 1984	Sept. 16, 1984	John Turner
Erik Nielsen	Sept. 17, 1984	June 29, 1986	Brian Mulroney
Donald Mazankowski	June 30, 1986	June 24, 1993	Brian Mulroney
Jean J. Charest	June 25, 1993	Nov. 3, 1993	Kim Campbell
Sheila M. Copps	Nov. 4, 1993	Apr. 30, 1996	Jean Chrétien
Sheila M. Copps	June 19, 1996	June 10, 1997	Jean Chrétien
Herbert E. Gray	June 11, 1997	Jan. 14, 2002	Jean Chrétien
John Paul Manley	Jan. 15, 2002		Jean Chrétien

Source: *Library of Parliament, Information and Documentation Branch*

Public Accountability in Government

Several federal bodies monitor federal government activity to ensure that responsible actions are taken and the rights of citizens are respected. Independent of Cabinet and political parties, officials in these organizations report government shortcomings to the House of Commons and are often empowered to act on citizens' complaints.

THE AUDITOR GENERAL

The auditor general examines the handling of taxpayers' money. Authorized by the Auditor General Act and the Financial Administration Act, this official ensures that federal institutions keep accurate accounts and collect and spend their budgets as intended. The auditor general, employing a staff of accountants, lawyers, engineers, computer technicians, economists and management experts, looks for efficient spending and exposes fraud and carelessness. Appointed to a 10-year term in May 2001, the current auditor general is Sheila Fraser.

The Office of the Auditor General includes the commissioner of the environment and sustainable development. This commissioner ensures that government is improving the protection of the environment and fostering sustainable development—25 federal departments and agencies must prepare sustainable development strategies. The post was created in 1995 to give the public a way to pressure federal departments on environmental issues through a petition process. The current commissioner is Johanne Gélinas, appointed in August 2000.

Write to the Office of the Auditor General and the Commissioner of the Environment and Sustainable Development, 240 Sparks Street, Ottawa, Ontario KIA OG6 or phone (613) 995-3708. Regional offices exist in Vancouver, Edmonton, Winnipeg, Montreal and Halifax/Dartmouth. Visit http://www.oag-bvg.gc.ca.

PRIVACY COMMISSIONER

Authorized by the Privacy Act, the commissioner monitors the government's collection, use and disclosure of Canadians' personal information. The Act gives Canadians the right to examine any government-held information about them—110 federal organizations can hold personal information. The Act requires that the information be accurate, confidential and used only for its intended purpose. The commissioner investigates complaints about the misuse of government-held information and may act as an ombudsman. Although unable to impose penalties or force compliance, the commissioner may make recommendations to complainants and may take cases before the Federal Court. The commissioner can also launch privacy-related suits against the government in the public interest.

The commissioner usually serves for seven years, but the current official—Robert Marleau—is an interim commissioner. He was appointed in June 2003. Write to the Privacy Commissioner of Canada, 112 Kent Street, Ottawa, Ontario K1A 1H3 or phone 1 (800) 282-1376. Visit http://www.privcom.gc.ca.

INFORMATION COMMISSIONER

Authorized by the Access to Information Act, this commissioner ensures that Canadians obtain non-personal information collected by the government. As an ombudsman, the commissioner investigates complaints when the government denies access to public documents, mediates disputes and makes recommendations. The commissioner may also take cases to the Federal Court.

The commissioner serves for seven years. The current official, John Reid, was appointed in July 1998. Write to the Information Commissioner of Canada, Place de Ville, Tower B, 112 Kent Street, 22nd Floor, Ottawa, Ontario K1A IH3 or phone 1 (800) 267-0441. Visit http://www.infocom.gc.ca.

CANADIAN HUMAN RIGHTS COMMISSIONER

This commissioner is charged with ensuring that the Canadian Human Rights Act is upheld by resolving individual complaints, promoting understanding of human rights, upholding equality principles and assisting in reducing equality barriers in employment and access to services.

The chief commissioner serves for seven years. The current official, Mary Gusella, was appointed in August 2002. Write to the CHRC, 344 Slater Street, 8th Floor, Ottawa, Ontario K1A 1E1 or phone 1 (888) 214-1090. Visit http://www.chrc-ccdp.ca.

Members of Canada's Senate

(as of Oct. 1, 2003)

The Governor General appoints senators under the Great Seal of Canada on the prime minister's advice.

To be eligible for the Senate, a candidate must be a Canadian citizen and at least 30 years old. A candidate must also live in the region the appointment represents—either Ontario, Quebec, the West, the Maritimes or a territory. He or she must own land in that region with an unencumbered value of at least $4,000 and have a net estate worth at least $4,000. A senator from Quebec must either live in or have land in Quebec. A senator must retire at age 75.

Senator	Birthdate	Date Nominated	Appointed by	Province
Willie Adams	June 22, 1934	Apr. 5, 1977	Trudeau	Nun.
Raynell Andreychuk	Aug. 14, 1944	Mar. 11, 1993	Mulroney	Sask.
W. David Angus	July 21, 1937	June 10, 1993	Mulroney	Que.
Norman Atkins	June 27, 1934	July 2, 1986	Mulroney	Ont.
Jacob (Jack) Austin	Mar. 2, 1932	Aug. 19, 1975	Trudeau	BC
Lise Bacon	Aug. 25, 1934	Sept. 18, 1994	Chrétien	Que.
George S. Baker	Sept. 4, 1942	Mar. 26, 2002	Chrétien	Nfld
Tommy Banks	Dec. 17, 1936	Apr. 7, 2000	Chrétien	Alta
Gérald Beaudoin	Apr. 15, 1929	Sept. 26, 1988	Mulroney	Que.
Michel Biron	Mar. 16, 1934	Oct. 4, 2001	Chrétien	Que.
John G. Bryden	Aug. 25, 1937	Nov. 29, 1994	Chrétien	NB
John Buchanan	Apr. 22, 1931	Sept. 12, 1990	Mulroney	NS
Catherine Callbeck	July 25, 1939	Sept. 23, 1997	Chrétien	PEI
Pat Carney	May 26, 1935	Aug. 30, 1990	Mulroney	BC
Sharon Carstairs	Apr. 26, 1942	Sept. 15, 1994	Chrétien	Man.
Thelma Chalifoux	Feb. 8, 1929	Nov. 26, 1997	Chrétien	Alta
Maria Chaput	May 7, 1942	Dec. 12, 2002	Chrétien	Man.
Ione Christensen	Oct. 10, 1933	Sept. 2, 1999	Chrétien	YT
Ethel Cochrane	Sept. 23, 1937	Nov. 17, 1986	Mulroney	Nfld
Gérald J. Comeau	Feb. 1, 1946	Aug. 30, 1990	Mulroney	NS
Joan Cook	Oct. 6, 1934	Mar. 6, 1998	Chrétien	Nfld
Anne C. Cools	Aug. 12, 1943	Jan. 13, 1984	Trudeau	Ont.
Eymard Corbin	Aug. 2, 1934	July 9, 1984	Turner	NB
Jane Marie Cordy	July 2, 1950	June 9, 2000	Chrétien	NS
Joseph A. Day	Jan. 24, 1945	Oct. 4, 2001	Chrétien	NB
Pierre De Bané	Aug. 2, 1938	June 29, 1984	Trudeau	Que.
Consiglio Di Nino	Jan. 24, 1938	Aug. 30, 1990	Mulroney	Ont.
C. William Doody	Feb. 26, 1931	Oct. 3, 1979	Clark	Nfld
Percy Downe	July 8, 1954	June 26, 2003	Chrétien	PEI
John Trevor Eyton	July 12, 1934	Sept. 23, 1990	Mulroney	Ont.
Joyce Fairbairn	Nov. 6, 1939	June 29, 1984	Trudeau	Alta
Marisa Ferretti Barth	Apr. 28, 1931	Sept. 22, 1997	Chrétien	Que.
Isobel Finnerty	July 15, 1930	Sept. 2, 1999	Chrétien	Ont.
D. Ross Fitzpatrick	Feb. 4, 1933	Mar. 6, 1998	Chrétien	BC
John Michael Forrestall	Sept. 23, 1932	Sept. 27, 1990	Mulroney	NS
Joan Fraser	Oct. 12, 1944	Sept. 17, 1998	Chrétien	Que.
George Furey	May 12, 1948	Aug. 11, 1999	Chrétien	Nfld
Jean-Robert Gauthier	Oct. 22, 1929	Nov. 23, 1994	Chrétien	Ont.
Aurélien Gill	Aug. 26, 1933	Sept. 17, 1998	Chrétien	Que.
Jerahmiel S. Grafstein	Jan. 2, 1935	Jan. 13, 1984	Trudeau	Ont.
Alasdair B. Graham	May 21, 1929	Apr. 27, 1972	Trudeau	NS
Leonard J. Gustafson	Nov. 10, 1933	May 26, 1993	Mulroney	Sask.
Daniel Hays	Apr. 24, 1939	June 29, 1984	Trudeau	Alta
Céline Hervieux-Payette	Apr. 22, 1941	Mar. 21, 1995	Chrétien	Que.
Elizabeth Hubley	Sept. 8, 1942	Mar. 8, 2001	Chrétien	PEI
Mobina S.B. Jaffer	Aug. 20, 1949	June 13, 2001	Chrétien	BC

▶

Janis Johnson	Apr. 27, 1946	Sept. 27, 1990	Mulroney	Man.
Serge Joyal	Feb. 1, 1945	Nov. 26, 1997	Chrétien	Que.
James Francis Kelleher	Oct. 2, 1930	Sept. 23, 1990	Mulroney	Ont.
Colin Kenny	Dec. 10, 1943	June 29, 1984	Trudeau	Ont.
Wilbert Joseph Keon	May 17, 1935	Sept. 27, 1990	Mulroney	Ont.[1]
Noel A. Kinsella	Nov. 28, 1939	Sept. 12, 1990	Mulroney	NB
Michael Kirby	Aug. 5, 1941	Jan. 13, 1984	Trudeau	NS
Leo E. Kolber	Jan. 18, 1929	Dec. 23, 1983	Trudeau	Que.
Richard H. Kroft	May 22, 1938	June 11, 1998	Chrétien	Man.
Laurier L. LaPierre	Nov. 21. 1929	June 13, 2001	Chrétien	Ont.
Jean Lapointe	Dec. 6, 1935	June 13, 2001	Chrétien	Que.
Raymond Lavigne	Nov. 16, 1945	Mar. 26, 2002	Chrétien	Que.
Edward M. Lawson	Sept. 24. 1929	Oct. 7, 1970	Trudeau	BC
Marjory LeBreton	July 4, 1940	June 18, 1993	Mulroney	Ont.
Viola Léger	June 29, 1930	June 13, 2001	Chrétien	NB
Rose-Marie Losier-Cool	June 18, 1937	Mar. 21. 1995	Chrétien	NB
John Lynch-Staunton	June 19, 1930	Sept. 23, 1990	Mulroney	Que.
Shirley Maheu	Oct. 7, 1931	Feb. 1, 1996	Chrétien	Que.
Frank Mahovlich	Jan. 10, 1938	June 11, 1998	Chrétien	Ont.
Paul J. Massicotte	Sept. 10, 1951	June 26, 2003	Chrétien	Que.
Michael Arthur Meighen	Mar. 25, 1939	Sept. 27, 1990	Mulroney	Ont.[1]
Pana Merchant	Apr. 2, 1943	Dec. 12, 2002	Chrétien	Sask.
Lorna Milne	Dec. 13, 1934	Sept. 22, 1995	Chrétien	Ont.
Wilfred P. Moore	Jan. 14, 1942	Sept. 26, 1996	Chrétien	NS
Yves Morin	Nov. 28, 1929	Mar. 8, 2001	Chrétien	Que.
Lowell Murray	Sept. 26, 1936	Sept. 13, 1979	Clark	Ont.
Pierre Claude Nolin	Oct. 30, 1950	June 18, 1993	Mulroney	Que.
Donald H. Oliver	Nov. 16, 1938	Sept. 7, 1990	Mulroney	NS
Landon Carter (Lucy) Pearson	Nov. 16, 1930	Sept. 15, 1994	Chrétien	Ont.
Lucie Pépin	Sept. 7, 1936	Apr. 8, 1997	Chrétien	Que.
Gerard A. Phalen	Mar. 28, 1934	Oct. 4, 2001	Chrétien	NS
P. Michael Pitfield	June 18, 1937	Dec. 22, 1982	Trudeau	Ont.
Marie-Paule Poulin	June 21, 1945	Sept. 21, 1995	Chrétien	Ont.
Vivienne Poy	May 15, 1941	Sept. 17, 1998	Chrétien	Ont.
Marcel Prud'homme	Nov. 30, 1934	May 26, 1993	Mulroney	Que.
Pierrette Ringuette	Dec. 31, 1955	Dec. 12, 2002	Chrétien	NB
Jean-Claude Rivest	Jan. 27, 1943	Mar. 11, 1993	Mulroney	Que.
Brenda Mary Robertson	May 23, 1929	Dec. 21, 1984	Mulroney	NB
Fernand Robichaud	Dec. 2, 1939	Sept. 23, 1997	Chrétien	NB
Douglas Roche	June 14,1929	Sept. 17, 1998	Chrétien	Alta.
William Rompkey	May 13, 1936	Sept. 22, 1995	Chrétien	Nfld
Eileen Rossiter	July 14, 1929	Nov. 17, 1986	Mulroney	PEI
Gerry St. Germain	Nov. 6, 1937	June 23, 1993	Mulroney	BC
Nick G. Sibbeston	Nov. 21, 1943	Sept. 2, 1999	Chrétien	NWT
David Paul Smith	May 16, 1941	June 25, 2002	Chrétien	Ont.
Herbert O. Sparrow	Jan. 4, 1930	Feb. 9, 1968	Pearson	Sask.
Mira Spivak	July 12, 1934	Nov. 17, 1986	Mulroney	Man.
Peter A. Stollery	Nov. 29, 1935	July 2, 1981	Trudeau	Ont.
Terrance R. Stratton	Mar. 16, 1938	Mar. 25, 1993	Mulroney	Man.
David Tkachuk	Feb. 18, 1945	June 8, 1993	Mulroney	Sask.
Charlie Watt	June 29, 1944	Jan. 16, 1984	Trudeau	Que.
John (Jack) Wiebe	May 31, 1936	Apr. 7. 2000	Chrétien	Sask.

Source: *Parliamentary Internet (Library of Parliament, Information and Documentation Branch)*
(1) Represents region rather than a province.

Former Soldiers in the Senate

*T*hree sitting senators served in the Canadian military: Joseph A. Day (Liberal) served in the air force (1963–68); William H. Rompkey (Liberal) served in the navy (1955–63); and Gerry St. Germain (Canadian Alliance) also served in the air force.

Members of Parliament

(as of Oct. 1, 2003)

Correspondence to members of Parliament should be addressed individually and may be sent postage free to the following address: (Name of MP), House of Commons, Parliament Buildings, Ottawa, Ontario, K1A 0A6. For general information, call (613) 992-4793.

To contact a government department or minister's office via the Internet, go to http://canada.gc.ca (the Web site for the Government of Canada) and access "About Government."

■ Newfoundland and Labrador

Riding (population 2001)	Member (year of birth)	Party	Occupation	Elected[1]
Bonavista/Trinity/Conception (83 661)	R. John Efford (1944)	Lib.	Businessman	2002*
Burin/St. George's (65 898)	Bill Matthews (1947)	Lib.	Politician	1997
Gander/Grand Falls (70 891)	Rex Barnes (1960)	PC	Paramedic	2002*
Humber/St. Barbe/Baie Verte (67 445)	Gerry Byrne (1966)	Lib.	Civil Servant	1996*
Labrador (27 864)	Lawrence O'Brien (1951)	Lib.	Civil Servant	1996*
St. John's East (101 917)	Norman Doyle (1945)	PC	Politician	1997
St. John's West (95 254)	Loyola Hearn (1943)	PC	Teacher	2000*

■ Prince Edward Island

Riding (population 2001)	Member (year of birth)	Party	Occupation	Elected[1]
Cardigan (30 437)	Lawrence MacAulay (1946)	Lib.	M.P.	1988
Egmont (35 198)	Joe McGuire (1944)	Lib.	M.P.	1988
Hillsborough (35 252)	Shawn Murphy (1951)	Lib.	Lawyer	2000
Malpeque (34 407)	Wayne Easter (1949)	Lib.	Farmer	1993

■ Nova Scotia

Riding (population 2001)	Member (year of birth)	Party	Occupation	Elected[1]
Bras d'Or/Cape Breton (70 879)	Rodger Cuzner (1955)	Lib.	Event Organizer	2000
Cumberland/Colchester (81 912)	Bill Casey (1945)	PC	Financial Advisor	1997
Dartmouth (82 899)	Wendy Lill (1950)	NDP	Social Worker	1997
Halifax (82 518)	Alexa McDonough (1945)	NDP	Social Worker	1997
Halifax West (106 372)	Geoff Regan (1959)	Lib.	Lawyer	2000
Kings/Hants (99 379)	Scott Brison (1967)	PC	Sales Manager	2000
Pictou/Antigonish/Guysborough (76 370)	Peter Mackay (1965)	PC	Crown Attorney	1997
Sackville/Musquodoboit Valley/ Eastern Shore (87 394)	Peter Stoffer (1956)	NDP	Customer Serv.	1997
South Shore (75 545)	Gerald Keddy (1953)	PC	Businessman	1997
Sydney/Victoria (76 575)	Mark Eyking (1960)	Lib.	Farmer	2000
West Nova (68 164)	Robert Thibault (1959)	Lib.	City Admin.	2000

■ New Brunswick

Riding (population 2001)	Member (year of birth)	Party	Occupation	Elected[1]
Acadie/Bathurst (82 929)	Yvon Godin (1955)	NDP	Staff Rep	1997
Beauséjour/Petitcodiac (82 930)	Dominic LeBlanc (1967)	Lib.	Lawyer	2000
Fredericton (75 811)	Andy Scott (1955)	Lib.	Public Servant	1993
Fundy/Royal (72 464)	John Herron (1967)	PC	Manager	1997
Madawaska/Restigouche (69 561)	Jeannot Castonguay (1944)	Lib.	Doctor	2000
Miramichi (57 772)	Charles Hubbard (1940)	Lib.	School Principal	1993
Moncton/Riverview/Dieppe (92 935)	Claudette Bradshaw (1949)	Lib.	Public Servant	1997
New Brunswick Southwest (61 622)	Greg Thompson (1947)	PC	Educator	1997
Saint John (69 821)	Elsie Wayne (1932)	PC	Retired	1993
Tobique/Mactaguac (63 653)	Andy Savoy (1963)	Lib.	Engineer	2000

▶

▶ ■ **Quebec**

Riding (population 2001)	Member (year of birth)	Party	Occupation	Elected[1]
Abitibi/Baie-James/Nunavik (94 381)	Guy St-Julien (1940)	Lib.	Lawyer	1997
Ahuntsic (105 828)	Eleni Bakopanos (1954)	Lib.	Political Admin.	1993
Anjou/Rivière-des-Prairies (97 187)	Yvon Charbonneau (1940)	Lib.	Politician	1997
Argenteuil/Papineau/Mirabel (109 252)	Mario Laframboise (1957)	BQ	Notary	2000
Bas-Richelieu/Nicolet/Bécancour (84 759)	Louis Plamondon (1943)	BQ	Businessman	1984
Beauce (101 739)	Claude Drouin (1956)	Lib.	Civil Servant	1997
Beauharnois/Salaberry (92 882)	Serge Marcil (1944)	Lib.	Businessman	2000
Beauport/Montmorency/Côte-de-Beaupré/Île-d'Orléans (100 576)	Michel Guimond (1953)	BQ	Lawyer	1993
Bellechasse/Etchemins/Montmagny/L'Islet (82 436)	Gilbert Normand (1943)	Lib.	Doctor	1997
Berthier/Montcalm (129 230)	Roger Gaudet (1945)	BQ	Restaurateur	2002*
Bonaventure/Gaspé/Îles-de-la-Madeleine/Pabok (68 934)	Georges Farrah (1957)	Lib.	Administrator	2000
Bourassa (93 595)	Denis Coderre (1963)	Lib.	Editor	1997
Brome/Missisquoi (87 670)	Denis Paradis (1949)	Lib.	Lawyer	1995*
Brossard/La Prairie (100 489)	Jacques Saada (1947)	Lib.	Teacher	1997
Chambly (104 995)	Ghislain Lebel (1946)	Ind.	Notary Public	1993
Champlain (86 686)	Marcel Gagnon (1936)	BQ	Businessman	2000
Charlesbourg/Jacques-Cartier (107 033)	Richard Marceau (1970)	BQ	Lawyer	1997
Charlevoix (74 995)	Gérard Asselin (1950)	BQ	Foreman	1993
Châteauguay (113 635)	Robert Lanctôt (1963)	BQ	Lawyer	2000
Chicoutimi/Le Fjord (82 149)	André Harvey (1941)	Lib.	School Com.	1997
Compton/Stanstead (82 801)	David Price (1945)	Lib.	Mayor	1997
Drummond (88 165)	Pauline Picard (1947)	BQ	Admin. Assistant	1993
Frontenac/Mégantic (68 547)	Gerard Binet (1955)	Lib.	Businessman	2000
Gatineau (124 365)	Mark Assad (1940)	Lib.	Professor	1988
Hochelaga/Maisonneuve (96 902)	Réal Ménard (1962)	BQ	Political Attaché	1993
Hull/Aylmer (101 993)	Marcel Proulx (1946)	Lib.	Administrator	1999*
Joliette (97 932)	Pierre Paquette (1955)	BQ	Professor	2000
Jonquière (67 348)	Jocelyne Girard-Bujold (1943)	BQ	Businesswoman	1997
Kamouraska/Rivière-du-Loup/Témiscouata/Les Basques (86 588)	Paul Crête (1943)	BQ	Personnel Dir.	1993
Lac-Saint-Jean/Saguenay (69 043)	Sébastien Gagnon (1973)	BQ	Exec. Mgr.	2002*
Lac-Saint-Louis (110 372)	Clifford Lincoln (1928)	Lib.	Consultant	1993
LaSalle/Émard (99 767)	Paul Martin (1938)	Lib.	M.P.	1988
Laurentides (133 345)	Monique Guay (1959)	BQ	Businesswoman	1993
Laurier/Sainte-Marie (99 957)	Gilles Duceppe (1947)	BQ	M.P.	1990*
Laval Centre (111 518)	Madeleine Dalphond-Guiral (1938)	BQ	Professor	1993
Laval-Est (110 500)	Carole-Marie Allard (1949)	Lib.	Author	2000
Laval-Ouest (120 987)	Raymonde Folco (1940)	Lib.	Commissioner	1997
Lévis-et-Chutes-de-la-Chaudière (125 848)	Christian Jobin (1952)	Lib.	Mayor	2003*
Longueuil (85 222)	Caroline St-Hilaire (1969)	BQ	Author Agent	1997
Lotbinière/L'Érable (69 314)	Odina Desrochers (1951)	BQ	Civil Servant	1997
Louis-Hébert (98 156)	Hélène Scherrer (1950)	Lib.	Event Organizer	2000
Manicouagan (52 561)	Ghislain Fournier (1938)	BQ	Businessman	1997
Matapédia/Matane (70 417)	Jean-Yves Roy (1949)	BQ	Teacher	2000
Mercier (95 842)	Francine Lalonde (1940)	BQ	Lecturer	1993
Mont-Royal (98 346)	Irwin Cotler (1940)	Lib.	Professor	1999*
Notre-Dame-de-Grâce/Lachine (102 935)	Marlene Jennings (1951)	Lib.	Public Servant	1997
Outremont (98 722)	Martin Cauchon (1962)	Lib.	Lawyer	1993
Papineau/Saint-Denis (108 748)	Pierre Pettigrew (1951)	Lib.	Businessman	1996*
Pierrefonds/Dollard (112 159)	Bernard Patry (1943)	Lib.	Doctor	1993
Pontiac/Gatineau/Labelle (102 277)	Robert Bertrand (1953)	Lib.	Insurance Agent	1993
Portneuf (91 602)	Claude Duplain (1954)	Lib.	Contractor	2000
Québec (102 051)	Christiane Gagnon (1948)	BQ	Real Estate Agent	1993
Québec-Est (109 709)	Jean Guy Carignan (1941)	Ind.	Administrator	2000
Repentigny (127 150)	Benoît Sauvageau (1963)	BQ	Teacher	1997
Richmond/Arthabaska (99 446)	André Bachand (1951)	PC	Educator	1997
Rimouski-Neigette-et-la-Mitis (71 615)	Suzanne Tremblay (1937)	BQ	Professor	1993

▶

▶ Rivière-des-Mille-Îles (117 198) *..... Gilles–A. Perron (1940) .... BQ — Pol. Advisor — 1997
Roberval (70 077) .... Michel Gauthier (1950)................. BQ — Administrator — 1993
Rosemont/Petite-Patrie (103 458) ..... Bernard Bigras (1970) .... BQ — Civil Servant — 1997
Saint-Bruno/Saint-Hubert (99 755) .... Pierrette Venne (1945) .... Ind. — Notary Public — 1988
Saint-Hyacinthe/Bagot (94 084)....... Yvan Loubier (1959)................... BQ — Economist — 1993
Saint-Jean (95 096) .... Claude Bachand (1951) .... BQ — Educator — 1993
Saint-Lambert (85 678) .... Yolande Thibeault (1939) .... Lib. — Director (DRO) — 1997
Saint-Laurent/Cartierville (100 747)... Stéphane Dion (1955)................. Lib. — Professor — 1996*
Saint-Léonard/Saint-Michel (102 302).. Massimo Pacetti (n.a.) .... Lib. — Accountant — 2002*
Saint-Maurice (77 068) .... Jean Chrétien (1934) .... Lib. — Lawyer — 1963
Shefford (94 939) .... Diane St-Jacques (1953) .... Lib. — P.R. — 1997
Sherbrooke (96 630)................... Serge Cardin (1950) .... BQ — Accountant — 1998*
Témiscamingue (80 007)............... Gilbert Barrette (1941) .... Lib. — School Admin. — 2003*
Terrebonne/Blainville (122 665)....... Diane Bourgeois (1949) .... BQ — Teacher — 2000
Trois-Rivières (91 460) .... Yves Rocheleau (1944)............... BQ — Consultant — 1993
Vaudreuil/Soulanges (102 100) .... Nick Discepola (1949) .... Lib. — Mayor — 1993
Verchères/Les-Patriotes (107 658) .... Stéphane Bergeron (1965) .... BQ — Political Attaché — 1993
Verdun/Saint-Henri/Saint-Paul/
  Pointe Saint-Charles (91 795) ...... Liza Frulla (1949) .... Lib. — Communicator — 2002*
Westmount/Ville-Marie (94 061) ...... Lucienne Robillard (1945) .... Lib. — Politician — 1995*

■ Ontario

Riding (population 2001)	Member (year of birth)	Party	Occupation	Elected[1]
Algoma/Manitoulin (73 398)	Brent St. Denis (1950)	Lib.	Parl. Assistant	1993
Ancaster/Dundas/Flamborough/ Aldershot (104 775)	John Bryden (1943)	Lib.	Journalist	1993
Barrie/Simcoe/Bradford (154 942)	Aileen Carroll (1944)	Lib.	Businesswoman	1997
Beaches/East York (112 961)	Maria Minna (1948)	Lib.	Consultant	1993
Bramalea/Gore/Malton/ Springdale (144 714)	Gurbax Singh Malhi (1949)	Lib.	Real Estate Agent	1993
Brampton Centre (119 971)	Sarkis Assadourian (1948)	Lib.	Businessman	1993
Brampton West/Mississauga (189 934)	Colleen Beaumier (1944)	Lib.	Businesswoman	1993
Brant (109 016)	Jane Stewart (1955)	Lib.	Human Resources	1993
Bruce/Grey/Owen Sound (98 532)	Ovid L. Jackson (1939)	Lib.	Teacher	1993
Burlington (101 993)	Paddy Torsney (1962)	Lib.	Consultant	1993
Cambridge (125 952)	Janko Peric (1949)	Lib.	Welder	1993
Chatham/Kent Essex (106 144)	Jerry Pickard (1940)	Lib.	Teacher	1997
Davenport (103 618)	Charles Caccia (1930)	Lib.	Economist	1968
Don Valley East (116 963)	David Collenette (1946)	Lib.	Mgmt. Consultant	1993
Don Valley West (115 539)	John Godfrey (1942)	Lib.	Journalist	1993
Dufferin/Peel/Wellington/Grey (127 673)	Murray Calder (1951)	Lib.	Poultry Producer	1993
Durham (122 101)	Alex Shepherd (1946)	Lib.	C.A.	1993
Eglinton/Lawrence (111 237)	Joseph Volpe (1947)	Lib.	Educator	1988
Elgin/Middlesex/London (103 688)	Gar Knutson (1956)	Lib.	Manager	1993
Erie/Lincoln (98 312)	John Maloney (1945)	Lib.	Lawyer	1993
Essex (121 750)	Susan Whelan (1963)	Lib.	Lawyer	1993
Etobicoke Centre (105 620)	Allan Rock (1947)	Lib.	Lawyer	1993
Etobicoke/Lakeshore (113 914)	Jean Augustine (1937)	Lib.	School Principal	1993
Etobicoke North (118 583)	Roy Cullen (1944)	Lib.	Accountant	1996*
Glengarry/Prescott/Russell (103 922)	Don Boudria (1949)	Lib.	Civil Servant	1984
Guelph/Wellington (122 601)	Brenda Chamberlain (1952)	Lib.	Exec. Director	1993
Haldimand/Norfolk/Brant (101 558)	Bob Speller (1956)	Lib.	M.P.	1988
Haliburton/Victoria/Brock (109 578)	John O'Reilly (1940)	Lib.	Real Estate Broker	1993
Halton (154 033)	Julian Reed (1936)	Lib.	Farmer	1993
Hamilton East (98 163)	Sheila Copps (1952)	Lib.	M.P.	1984
Hamilton Mountain (111 325)	Beth Phinney (1938)	Lib.	M.P.	1988
Hamilton West (102 432)	Stan Keyes (1953)	Lib.	M.P.	1988
Hastings/Frontenac/Lennox & Addington (98 150)	Larry McCormick (1940)	Lib.	Consultant	1993
Huron/Bruce (93 460)	Paul Steckle (1942)	Lib.	Businessman	1993
Kenora/Rainy River (78 758)	Robert D. Nault (1955)	Lib.	M.P.	1988
Kingston & the Islands (112 872)	Peter Milliken (1946)	Lib.	Lawyer	1988 ▶

Riding	Member	Party	Occupation	Year
▶ Kitchener Centre (112 506)	Karen Redman (1953)	Lib.	Councillor	1997
Kitchener/Waterloo (126 142)	Andrew Telegdi (1946)	Lib.	Mun. Politician	1993
Lambton/Kent/Middlesex (98 878)	Rose-Marie Ur (1946)	Lib.	Farmer	1993
Lanark/Carleton (138 398)	Scott Reid (1964)	CA	Author	2000
Leeds/Grenville (96 606)	Joe Jordan (1958)	Lib.	Professor	1997
London/Fanshawe (107 314)	Pat O'Brien (1948)	Lib.	Teacher	1993
London North Centre (107 672)	Joe Fontana (1950)	Lib.	Businessman	1988
London West (110 988)	Sue Barnes (1952)	Lib.	Lawyer	1993
Markham (142 408)	John McCallum (1950)	Lib.	Economist	2000
Mississauga Centre (122 864)	Carolyn Parrish (1946)	Lib.	Public Servant	1993
Mississauga East (108 459)	Albina Guarnieri (1953)	Lib.	M.P.	1988
Mississauga South (101 647)	Paul Szabo (1948)	Lib.	Chartered Acct.	1993
Mississauga West (150 764)	Steve Mahoney (1947)	Lib.	Bus./Politician	1997
Nepean/Carleton (126 638)	David Pratt (1955)	Lib.	Mun. Politician	1997
Niagara Centre (104 146)	Tony Tirabassi (1957)	Lib.	Sales Rep.	2000
Niagara Falls (95 722)	Gary Pillitteri (1936)	Lib.	Farmer	1993
Nickel Belt (79 661)	Raymond Bonin (1942)	Lib.	Professor	1993
Nipissing (74 915)	Bob Wood (1940)	Lib.	M.P.	1988
Northumberland (102 424)	Paul Macklin (1944)	Lib.	Lawyer	2000
Oak Ridges (173 378)	Bryon Wilfert (1952)	Lib.	Teacher	1997
Oakville (104 103)	Bonnie Brown (1941)	Lib.	Social Worker	1993
Oshawa (107 008)	Ivan Grose (1928)	Lib.	Businessman	1993
Ottawa Centre (114 032)	Mac Harb (1953)	Lib.	M.P.	1988
Ottawa/Orleans (108 378)	Eugène Bellemare (1932)	Lib.	M.P.	1988
Ottawa South (118 472)	John Manley (1950)	Lib.	Lawyer	1988
Ottawa/Vanier (106 196)	Mauril Bélanger (1955)	Lib.	M.P.	1995*
Ottawa West/Nepean (112 232)	Marlene Catterall (1939)	Lib.	M.P.	1988
Oxford (99 270)	John Finlay (1929)	Lib.	Retired	1993
Parkdale/High Park (107 968)	Sarmite Bulte (1953)	Lib.	Lawyer	1997
Parry Sound/Muskoka (85 377)	Andy Mitchell (1953)	Lib.	Bank Manager	1993
Perth/Middlesex (97 216)	Gary Schellenberger (1943)	PC	Decorator	2003*
Peterborough (112 111)	Peter Adams (1936)	Lib.	Professor	1993
Pickering/Ajax/Uxbridge (137 518)	Dan McTeague (1962)	Lib.	Media Relations	1993
Prince Edward/Hastings (92 934)	Lyle Vanclief (1943)	Lib.	Agrologist	1988
Renfrew/Nipissing/Pembroke (96 416)	Cheryl Gallant (1960)	CA	Office Manager	2000
Sarnia/Lambton (88 331)	Roger Gallaway (1948)	Lib.	Lawyer	1993
Sault Ste. Marie (74 566)	Carmen Provenzano (1942)	Lib.	Lawyer	1997
Scarborough/Agincourt (114 411)	Jim Karygiannis (1955)	Lib.	Engineer	1988
Scarborough Centre (123 089)	John Cannis (1951)	Lib.	HR Consultant	1993
Scarborough East (115 799)	John McKay (1948)	Lib.	Lawyer	1997
Scarborough/Rouge River (126 382)	Derek Lee (1948)	Lib.	Lawyer	1988
Scarborough Southwest (113 616)	Tom Wappel (1950)	Lib.	M.P.	1988
Simcoe/Grey (123 786)	Paul Bonwick (1964)	Lib.	Businessman	1997
Simcoe North (112 089)	Paul DeVillers (1946)	Lib.	Lawyer	1993
St. Catharines (103 678)	Walt Lastewka (1940)	Lib.	Plant Manager	1993
St. Paul's (108 696)	Carolyn Bennett (1950)	Lib.	Doctor	1997
Stoney Creek (109 970)	Tony Valeri (1957)	Lib.	Insurance	1993
Stormont/Dundas/ Charlottenburgh (94 267)	Bob Kilger (1944)	Lib.	Businessman	1988
Sudbury (79 342)	Diane Marleau (1943)	Lib.	M.P.	1988
Thornhill (116 840)	Elinor Caplan (1944)	Lib.	Provincial Politician	1997
Thunder Bay/Atikokan (76 009)	Stan Dromisky (1931)	Lib.	Retired	1993
Thunder Bay/Superior North (75 237)	Joe Comuzzi (1933)	Lib.	M.P.	1988
Timiskaming/Cochrane (69 901)	Benoît Serré (1951)	Lib.	Businessman	1993
Timmins/James Bay (71 648)	Réginald Bélair (1949)	Lib.	M.P.	1997
Toronto Centre/Rosedale (122 882)	Bill Graham (1939)	Lib.	Lawyer	1993
Toronto/Danforth (103 153)	Dennis Mills (1946)	Lib.	Businessman	1988
Trinity/Spadina (103 368)	Tony Ianno (1957)	Lib.	Businessman	1993
Vaughan/King/Aurora (164 590)	Maurizio Bevilacqua (1960)	Lib.	Consultant	1988
Waterloo/Wellington (119 469)	Lynn Myers (1951)	Lib.	Mayor	1997
Whitby/Ajax (128 164)	Judi Longfield (1947)	Lib.	Exec. Assistant	1997
Willowdale (118 375)	Jim Peterson (1941)	Lib.	Lawyer	1988
Windsor/St. Clair (109 046)	Joe Comartin (1947)	NDP	Director	2000 ▶

▶ Windsor West (117 041) . . . . Brian Masse (1968) . . . . NDP   Professor   2002*
York Centre (107 055) . . . . Arthur C. Eggleton (1943) . . . . Lib.   Consultant   1993
York North (132 038) . . . . Karen Kraft Sloan (1952) . . . . Lib.   Consultant   1993
York South/Weston (114 649) . . . . AlanTonks (1943) . . . . Lib.   Teacher   2000
York West (103 616) . . . . Judy Sgro (1944) . . . . Lib.   Politician   1999*

■ Manitoba

Riding (population 2001)	Member (year of birth)	Party	Occupation	Elected[1]
Brandon/Souris (77 740)	Rick Borotsik (1950)	PC	Mayor	1997
Charleswood St. James/ Assiniboia (74 595)	John Harvard (1938)	Lib.	Broadcaster	1988
Churchill (77 580)	Bev Desjarlais (1955)	NDP	School Trustee	1997
Dauphin/Swan River (74 337)	Inky Mark (1947)	PC	Mayor	1997
Portage/Lisgar (82 486)	Brian Pallister (1954)	CA	Financial Analyst	2000
Provencher (88 155)	Vic Toews (1952)	CA	Lawyer	2000
Saint Boniface (81 239)	Raymond Simard (1958)	Lib.	Business Mgr.	2002*
Selkirk/Interlake (86 072)	Howard Hilstrom (1947)	CA	RCMP Officer	1997
Winnipeg Centre (75 346)	Pat Martin (1955)	NDP	Union Official	1997
Winnipeg North Centre (75 134)	Judy Wasylycia-Leis (1951)	NDP	Provincial Politician	1997
Winnipeg North/St. Paul (81 596)	Rey Pagtakhan (1935)	Lib.	Physician	1988
Winnipeg South (87 989)	Reg Alcock (1948)	Lib.	Politician	1993
Winnipeg South Centre (77 259)	Anita Neville (1942)	Lib.	Economist	2000
Winnipeg/Transcona (80 055)	Bill Blaikie (1951)	NDP	Clergyman	1979

■ Saskatchewan

Riding (population 2001)	Member (year of birth)	Party	Occupation	Elected[1]
Battlefords/Lloydminster (73 386)	Gerry Ritz (1951)	CA	Rancher	1997
Blackstrap (73 725)	Lynne Yelich (1953)	CA	Administrator	2000
Churchill River (64 416)	Rick Laliberte (1958)	Lib.	Education	1997
Cypress Hills/Grasslands (63 412)	David Anderson (1957)	CA	Farmer	2000
Palliser (67 282)	Dick Proctor (1941)	NDP	Journalist	1997
Prince Albert (73 988)	Brian Fitzpatrick (1945)	CA	Lawyer	2000
Regina/Lumsden/Lake Centre (66 374)	Larry Spencer (1941)	CA	Minister	2000
Regina/Qu'Appelle (69 014)	Lorne Nystrom (1947)	NDP	Politician	1968
Saskatoon/Humboldt (74 270)	Jim Pankiw (1966)	Ind.	Chiropractor	1997
Saskatoon/Rosetown/Biggar (71 365)	Carol Skelton (1945)	CA	Rancher	2000
Saskatoon/Wanuskewin (75 955)	Maurice Vellacott (1955)	CA	Minister	1997
Souris/Moose Mountain (66 223)	Roy Bailey (1928)	CA	School Supt.	1997
Wascana (72 508)	Ralph E. Goodale (1949)	Lib.	Business Exec.	1993
Yorkton/Melville (67 015)	Garry Breitkreuz (1945)	CA	Teacher	1993

■ Alberta

Riding (population 2001)	Member (year of birth)	Party	Occupation	Elected[1]
Athabasca (93 191)	David Chatters (1946)	CA	Farmer	1993
Calgary Centre (122 385)	Joe Clark (1939)	PC	Politician	1972
Calgary East (101 882)	Deepak Obhrai (1950)	CA	Entrepreneur	1997
Calgary Northeast (139 649)	Art Hanger (1943)	CA	Police Officer	1993
Calgary/Nose Hill (141 905)	Diane Ablonczy (1949)	CA	Lawyer	1993
Calgary Southeast (121 115)	Jason Kenney (1968)	CA	Exec. Director	1997
Calgary Southwest (115 498)	Stephen Harper (1959)	CA	Economist	1993
Calgary West (131 926)	Rob Anders (1972)	CA	Lobbyist	1997
Crowfoot (99 705)	Kevin Sorenson (1958)	CA	Farmer	2000
Edmonton Centre-East (113 136)	Peter Goldring (1944)	CA	Businessman	1997
Edmonton North (112 475)	Deborah Grey (1952)	CA	Teacher	1989*
Edmonton Southeast (100 774)	David Kilgour (1941)	Lib.	M.P.	1979
Edmonton Southwest (116 867)	James Rajotte (1970)	CA	Researcher	2000
Edmonton/Strathcona (109 177)	Rahim Jaffer (1971)	CA	Entrepreneur	1997
Edmonton West (113 675)	Anne McLellan (1950)	Lib.	Professor	1993
Elk Island (111 632)	Ken Epp (1939)	CA	Instructor	1993
Lakeland (108 870)	Leon E. Benoit (1950)	CA	Civ.servant/Farmer	1993
Lethbridge (105 150)	Rick Casson (1943)	CA	Manager/Printer	1997

▶

▶ Macleod (102 869)................ Grant Hill (1943)................... CA Physician   1993
Medicine Hat (104 915)............ Monte Solberg (1958) .... CA Businessman   1993
Peace River (121 957)............. Charlie Penson (1942) .... CA Farmer   1993
Red Deer (125 651)............... Bob Mills (1941)................... CA Businessman   1993
St Albert (118 053) .... John Williams (1946) .... CA Accountant   1993
Wetaskiwin (111 687)............. Dale Johnston (1941)............... CA Farmer   1993
Wild Rose (134 711)............... Myron Thompson (1936) .... CA Retired   1993
Yellowhead (95 952)............... Bob Merrifield (1953)............... CA Businessman   2000

■ British Columbia

Riding (population 2001)	Member (year of birth)	Party	Occupation	Elected[1]
Burnaby/Douglas (119 998).........	Svend J. Robinson (1952)	NDP	M.P.	1979
Cariboo/Chilcotin (80 469)...........	Philip Mayfield (1937)	CA	Ord. Minister	1993
Delta/South Richmond (124 881)	John Cummins (1942)	CA	Teacher	1993
Dewdney/Alouette (121 477).........	Grant McNally (1962)	CA	Teacher	1997
Esquimalt/Juan de Fuca (110 909).....	Keith Martin (1960)	CA	Physician	1993
Fraser Valley (129 828)	Chuck Strahl (1957)	CA	Logging Cont.	1993
Kamloops/Thompson/				
Highland Valleys (100 452)	Betty Hinton (1950)	CA	Businesswoman	2000
Kelowna (124 335)................	Werner Schmidt (1932)	CA	Businessman	1993
Kootenay/Boundary/Okanagan (91 262)	Jim Gouk (1946)...................	CA	Real Estate Agt.	1993
Kootenay/Columbia (84 308).........	Jim Abbott (1942)	CA	Businessman	1993
Langley/Abbotsford (136 872).......	Randy White (1948)	CA	CMA	1993
Nanaimo/Alberni (112 972)	James D. Lunney (1951)	CA	Chiropractor	2000
Nanaimo/Cowichan (116 754)	Reed Elley (1945)	CA	Minister	1997
New Westminster/				
Coquitlam/Burnaby (123 832)	Paul E. Forseth (1946)	CA	Probation Officer	1993
North Vancouver (128 214).........	Ted White (1949)	CA	Company Pres.	1993
Okanagan/Coquihalla (105 239)......	Stockwell Day (1950)	CA	Politician	2000*
Okanagan/Shuswap (106 166)........	Darrel Stinson (1945)..............	CA	Mining	1993
Port Moody/Coquitlam/				
Port Coquitlam (148 140)	James Moore (1976)	CA	Broadcaster	2000
Prince George/Bulkley Valley (90 005).	Richard M. Harris (1944)	CA	Retired	1993
Prince George/Peace River (94 482) ...	Jay Hill (1952)	CA	Farmer	1993
Richmond (136 893)...............	Joe Peschisolido (1963).............	CA	Lawyer	2000
Saanich/Gulf Islands (110 284)	Gary Lunn (1957)..................	CA	Lawyer	1997
Skeena (77 720)...................	Andy Burton (1942)	CA	Property Manager	2000
South Surrey/White Rock/				
Langley (101 559)	Val Meredith (1949)	CA	Businesswoman	1993
Surrey Central (179 158)	Gurmant Grewal (1957)	CA	Real Estate Agt.	1997
Surrey North (114 620)	Chuck Cadman (1948)	CA	Elec. Eng. Tech.	1997
Vancouver Centre (131 147)	Hedy Fry (1941)	Lib.	Physician	1993
Vancouver East (113 573)	Elizabeth Davies (1953)	NDP	Councillor	1997
Vancouver Island North (109 242) ...	John Duncan (1948)................	CA	Forester	1993
Vancouver Kingsway (119 507)	Sophia Leung (1934)	Lib.	Social Worker	1997
Vancouver Quadra (114 464).........	Stephen Owen (1948)...............	Lib.	Lawyer	2000
Vancouver South/Burnaby (122 765).	Harbance Singh Dhaliwal (1952)	Lib.	Businessman	1993
Victoria (104 561)	David Anderson (1937)..............	Lib.	Env. Consultant	1968
West Vancouver/				
Sunshine Coast (121 650)	John Reynolds (1942)	CA	Businessman	1997

■ Yukon

Riding (population 2001)	Member (year of birth)	Party	Occupation	Elected[1]
Yukon (28 674)	Larry Bagnell (1949)	Lib.	Exec. Director	2000

■ Northwest Territiories

Riding (population 2001)	Member (year of birth)	Party	Occupation	Elected[1]
Western Arctic (37 360)...............	Ethel Blondin-Andrew (1951)...........	Lib.	Politician	1988

■ Nunavut

Riding (population 2001)	Member (year of birth)	Party	Occupation	Elected[1]
Nunavut (26 745).....................	Nancy Karetak-Lindell (1957)	Lib.	Businessperson	1997

(1) General election unless * indicating by-election. (n.a.) not available. PC—Progressive Conservative; Lib.—Liberal; NDP—New Democratic Party; CA—Canadian Alliance; Ind.—Independent.

Standing Committees of the Senate

(as of Oct. 1, 2003)

Standing Committee on	Chair (Party)	Number of Subcommittees	Clerk's Telephone
Aboriginal Peoples	Thelma Chalifoux (Lib.)	—	(613) 990-6160
Agriculture and Forestry	Donald Oliver (PC)	—	(613) 993-9021
Banking, Trade and Commerce	Richard Kroft (Lib.)	—	(613) 993-8129
Energy, the Environment and Natural Resources	Tommy Banks (Lib.)	—	(613) 990-6080
Fisheries and Oceans	Gerald Comeau (PC)	—	(613) 998-0371
Foreign Affairs	Peter Stollery (Lib.)	—	(613) 998-0424
Human Rights	Shirley Maheu (Lib.)	—	(613) 990-6081
Internal Economy, Budgets and Administration	Lise Bacon (Lib.)	—	(613) 992-2493
Legal and Constitutional Affairs	George Furey (Lib.)	—	(613) 943-7865
National Finance	Lowell Murray (PC)	—	(613) 993-4874
National Security and Defence	Colin Kenny (Lib.)	1	(613) 990-6187
Official Languages	Rose-Marie Losier-Cool (Lib.)	—	(613) 998-0371
Rules, Procedures and the Rights of Parliament	Lorna Milne (Lib.)	—	(613) 991-9213
Selection	—	—	(613) 990-5013
Social Affairs, Science and Technology	Michael Kirby (Lib.)	—	(613) 991-0719
Transport and Communications	Joan Fraser (Lib.)	—	(613) 991-3620

Lib.—Liberal; PC—Progressive Conservative.

Standing Committees of the House of Commons

(as of Oct. 1, 2003)

Standing Committee on	Chair (Party)	Number of Subcommittees	Clerk's Telephone
Aboriginal Affairs, Northern Development and Natural Resources	Raymond Bonin (Lib.)	—	(613) 996-1173
Agriculture and Agri-Food	Paul Steckle (Lib.)	1	(613) 947-6732
Canadian Heritage	Clifford Lincoln (Lib.)	—	(613) 947-6729
Citizenship and Immigration	Joe Fontana (Lib.)	—	(613) 995-4026
Environment and Sustainable Development	Charles Caccia (Lib.)	—	(613) 992-5023
Finance	Sue Barnes (Lib.)	1	(613) 992-9753
Fisheries and Oceans	Tom Wappel (Lib.)	1	(613) 996-3105
Foreign Affairs and International Trade	Bernard Patry (Lib.)	3	(613) 996-1540
Government Operations and Estimates	Reg Alcock (Lib.)	3	(613) 995-9469
Health	Bonnie Brown (Lib.)	—	(613) 995-4108
Human Resources Development and the Status of Persons with Disabilities	Judi Longfield (Lib.)	3	(613) 996-1542
Industry, Science and Technology	Walt Lastewka (Lib.)	1	(613) 947-1971
Justice and Human Rights	Andy Scott (Lib.)	2	(613) 996-1553
Liaison	Walt Lastewka (Lib.)	2	(613) 992-3156
National Defence and Veterans Affairs	David Pratt (Lib.)	2	(613) 995-9461
Official Languages	Mauril Bélanger (Lib.)	—	(613) 996-2441
Procedure and House Affairs	Peter Adams (Lib.)	3	(613) 996-0506
Public Accounts	John Williams (CA)	1	(613) 996-1664
Transport	Joe Comuzzi (Lib.)	1	(613) 996-4663

Lib.—Liberal; CA—Canadian Alliance

Government of Canada Primary Internet Site

The Canada Site is the official Web site of the Canadian government. It provides access to information and services about Canada and Canadian governments. The starting point is http://canada.gc.ca/main_e.html, and the information appears in French and English. Across the top of the site, the following web links appear in red:

WHAT'S NEW: This link connects you to an archive of government press releases and reports. The announcements are categorized by date and by government department and agency. You can find current data in Statistics Canada's *The Daily*, the Bank of Canada's *Weekly Financial Statistics* and the Canadian Forest Service's *National Forest Fire Situation Report*.

PUBLICATIONS: This link connects you to Government of Canada Publications. You can find specialized books and CD-ROMs listed by subject, title or government agency. You can check for recent releases and order them online. (Some publications are free!) The "Canadian Library Gateway" allows you to browse through library Web sites and catalogues across Canada.

ABOUT GOVERNMENT: This link leads to sites that describe Canada's federal system of government. You can find an alphabetical list of government departments and agencies, information about the workings of Parliament, lists of Canadian municipalities and so on. This link also provides access to the texts of the throne speech, the federal budget, federal laws (e.g., the Immigration Act) and the auditor general's report.

QUICK TIPS: This link leads to a page that describes how to use web-browsing techniques to search for information on the Canada Site.

PROVINCES AND TERRITORIES: This link connects you to the official sites of Canada's provincial and territorial governments.

On the left of the Canada Site's home page, a vertical bar in black, red and gold provides more web links:

PRIME MINISTER OF CANADA: This link takes you to the official Web site of Prime Minister Jean Chrétien.

GOVERNMENT ANNOUNCEMENTS: This link takes you to a page of information that supplements government ads that have appeared on television or in the newspapers. The site features information about West Nile virus, tourism, climate change and services for children and families.

E-FORMS AND SERVICES: This link connects you to sites with printable government forms for air travel complaints, firearm registration, GST/HST remittance etc. "Shop On-line" links you to sites that allow you to buy videos from the National Film Board or clothing from the RCMP's Musical Ride Boutique.

GOVERNMENT CONTACTS: Do you want to write or speak to a government official? This link connects you to directories of parliamentarians and federal public servants—including Canadian diplomats abroad. You can also find contact information for foreign embassies and consulates in Canada.

The centre of the Canada Site features four "gateway links":

SERVICES FOR CANADIANS: This link connects you to a range of public services and information sites for consumers, job seekers, seniors, aboriginals, youth, rural dwellers, new immigrants and Canadians living abroad.

SERVICES FOR NON-CANADIANS: This links you to "Canada International," a site for tourists, immigrants and foreign investors. Several links connect you to pages that explain Canadian foreign policy and culture to non-Canadians.

SERVICES FOR CANADIAN BUSINESS: This links you to sites on business start-ups, taxation, financing, statistics analysis, mergers, acquisitions and bankruptcy. Other links connect you to sites on employee management, exports and imports, technology, research and development.

ABOUT CANADA: This link connects you to Canadiana: maps, national symbols and landscape photos. Four sublinks lead you to facts about Canada's society, government, land and economy.

The Canada Site: a world of information at the click of a mouse!

If You're Not on the Internet...

*The Government of Canada provides a toll-free telephone inquiry service called 1 (800) O Canada. Operators at **1 (800) 622-6232** will direct callers to a service that will supply the needed information.*

Salaries of Federal Political Figures

(as of October 2003)

The **GOVERNOR GENERAL OF CANADA** receives $106 175 per year.
Each provincial **LIEUTENANT-GOVERNOR** receives $103 800 per year.
Each **SENATOR** receives an annual sessional indemnity of $114 200 plus 64 travel points[1] per year.[2]

The following senators receive salaries on top of their annual sessional indemnities for performing specialized duties:

Leader of the Government in the Senate . . . . $66 816 plus $2 122 car allowance
Leader of the Opposition in the Senate $32 000
Speaker of the Senate . . . . $48 900 plus $3 000 residence allowance and $1 061 car allowance
Speaker pro tempore $20 300
Deputy Leader of the Government $32 000
Deputy Leader of the Opposition $20 300
Government Whip $10 000
Opposition Whip $6 100
Chair of Standing Committee $10 000
Vice-Chair of Standing Committee $5 200

Each **MEMBER OF PARLIAMENT** (MP) in the House of Commons receives an annual sessional indemnity of $139 200 plus 64 travel points[1] per year.[2]

The following MPs receive salaries on top of their annual sessional indemnities for performing specialized duties:

Prime Minister . . . . $139 200 plus $2 122 car allowance
Cabinet Minister . . . . $66 816 plus $2 122 car allowance
Secretary of State $50 112
Speaker of the House . . . . $66 800 plus $1 061 car allowance and $3 000 rent allowance
Deputy Speaker of the House . . . . $34 800 plus $1 500 rent allowance
Leader of the Opposition in the House . . . . $66 800 plus $2 122 car allowance
Leader: Other Party $47 600
Opposition House Leader $34 800
House Leader: Other Party $14 100
Chief Government Whip $25 300
Chief Opposition Whip $25 300
Deputy Government Whip $10 000
Deputy Opposition Whip $10 000
Whip: Other Party $10 000
Parliamentary Secretary $14 100
Deputy Chair, Committee of the Whole House $14 100
Assistant Deputy Chair, Committee of the Whole House $14 100
Chair of Standing or Standing Joint Committee[3] $10 000
Vice-Chair of Standing or Standing Joint Committee[3] $5 200

(1) One travel point is worth a business-class return air trip between Ottawa and a representative's riding. Travel points may be used by representatives, their spouses or dependents. Representatives may also take free trips on VIA Rail Canada for official business. (2) Representatives who travel at least 100 km from their principal residences in Canada on official business may claim as much as $16,000 in expenses for food, lodging etc. (3) Excludes the Liaison Committee and the Standing Joint Committee on the Library of Parliament.

■ **SENATORS' OFFICE BUDGET**

Each senator is entitled to a budget of $127,500 per fiscal year for research and office expenses. The expenses must be incurred while the senator fulfills his or her parliamentary role.

■ **SENATORS' PENSION PLAN**

Senators must contribute 7 percent of their basic salaries (and may contribute up to 7 percent extra) to their pensions. Senators must serve at least six years to be eligible for a monthly pension for life. Senators who retire with fewer than six years' service get their pension contributions returned. Retirement benefits are indexed to the cost of living after age 60. No senator may collect pension benefits before age 55.

The maximum basic pension equals 75 percent of a senator's average best five years after 25 years of service (accrued at 3 percent annually). There is no maximum to extra salary pension, and the amount is accrued at 4 percent annually. After a senator dies, the surviving spouse is entitled to three-fifths of the senator's pension; up to three dependent children are entitled to a further one-tenth each of the deceased senator's pension.

■ MEMBERS' OFFICE BUDGET

Most members of the House of Commons have two offices: one in Ottawa and another in a home riding. These offices serve constituents who have problems when dealing with the federal government. The members' office budgets cover the costs of paying staff salaries, hiring contract labour, and renting, equipping and maintaining their offices. Office budgets also cover travel expenses, both within the riding and within the province.

The amount of money allocated to a member's office budget depends on whether the office is in a rural riding, an urban riding, an urban-rural riding, Nunavut or the Northwest Territories. The amounts allocated range between $227,800 and $244,100 per office. In general, urban offices cost less than rural offices to run. Territorial constituency offices are the most expensive to maintain.

Elector and Geographic Supplements: Members receive supplements for their main office budgets if they represent large constituencies. Offices in ridings that have at least 70,000 voters receive an extra $7,030, while offices in ridings that have at least 150,000 voters receive an extra $42,110. In addition, offices in ridings of at least 8,000 sq. km receive an extra $7,030 while offices in ridings of at least 500,001 sq. km receive an extra $42,280. These annual budgetary supplements cover the costs of hiring additional staff and some travel. Supplements often change after general elections when population sizes or riding boundaries change.

Other Services: To help meet the needs and requests of their constituents, members are also given access to printing, translation, mail and other support services that help them respond to the thousands of letters and requests they receive. (Canadians may write to members of Parliament free of charge from anywhere in Canada.) The services also allow members to keep the public up-to-date on the events in Ottawa through a parliamentary report known as a "householder." Finally, members are provided with desks, computers, photocopiers and other office supplies and equipment required to run an efficient office in Ottawa.

■ MEMBERS' PENSION PLAN

The Members of Parliament Retiring Allowances Act provides MPs with their pensions. Members must contribute 7 percent of their annual sessional allowance of $139,200 when in office. Members who receive extra salaries for being cabinet ministers, whips, parliamentary secretaries, etc., may contribute as much as 7 percent of their salaries as well. To collect, members must serve in the House of Commons for at least six years and be at least 55 years old when they retire, die or lose an election.

Pensions are payable at the rate of 3 percent per year of service (i.e., a minimum of 18 percent: 6 years × 3 percent) to a maximum of 75 percent (25 years of service) of the average of the best consecutive six years of earnings. Members who serve less than six years must withdraw their contributions.

The indexing of pensions begins only when members reach the age of 60, except for extraordinary situations such as disability. Survivors' benefits are payable to spouses and dependent children. If former members in receipt of pensions are re-elected to the House or appointed to the Senate, their pensions are suspended for their time in office. In 1995 the pension plan was amended to allow members to opt out, eliminate "double dipping" (drawing more than one pension after holding several positions), and provide that former members cannot receive pensions until they are at least 55 years old.

Sources: *Rideau Hall; Department of Canadian Heritage; Finance and Human Resources Directorate, House of Commons; Finance Directorate, Senate; Library of Parliament, Information and Documentation Branch.*

Supreme Court Justices of Canada

(as of October 2003)

Name	Date of Birth	Date Appointed	Appointed from
The Rt. Hon. Madam Justice Beverley McLachlin	Sept. 7, 1943	Mar. 30, 1989[1]	Supreme Court of BC
The Hon. Madam Justice Louise Arbour	Feb. 10, 1947	June 10, 1999	Ontario Court of Appeal
The Hon. Mr. Justice Michel Bastarache	June 10, 1947	Oct. 1, 1997	NB Court of Appeal
The Hon. Mr. Justice William Ian Corneil Binnie	Apr. 14, 1939	Jan. 8, 1998	Private law practice
The Hon. Madam Justice Marie Deschamps	Oct. 2, 1952	Aug. 7, 2002	Quebec Court of Appeal
The Hon. Mr. Justice Morris J. Fish	Nov. 16, 1938	July 31, 2003	Quebec Court of Appeal
The Hon. Mr. Justice Frank Iacobucci	June 29, 1937	Jan. 7, 1991	Federal Court of Canada
The Hon. Mr. Justice Louis LeBel	Nov. 30, 1939	Jan. 7, 2000	Quebec Court of Appeal
The Hon. Mr. Justice John Charles Major	Feb. 20, 1931	Nov. 13, 1992	Alberta Court of Appeal

Source: *Supreme Court of Canada*   (1) Appointed Chief Justice Jan. 7, 2000

Chief Justices of the Supreme Court of Canada

Name	Date of Birth	Date Appointed Chief Justice	Term Ended
The Hon. Sir William Buell Richards	May 2, 1815	Sept. 30, 1875	Jan. 10, 1879
The Hon. Sir William Johnston Ritchie.......................	Oct. 28, 1813	Jan. 11, 1879	Sept. 25, 1892
The Rt. Hon. Sir Samuel Henry Strong.....................	Aug. 13, 1825	Dec. 13, 1892	Nov. 18, 1902
The Rt. Hon. Sir Henri-Elzéar Taschereau	Oct. 7, 1836	Nov. 21, 1902	May 2, 1906
The Rt. Hon. Sir Charles Fitzpatrick...........................	Dec. 19, 1853	June 4, 1906	Oct. 21, 1918
The Rt. Hon. Sir Louis Henry Davies..........................	May 6, 1845	Oct. 23, 1918	May 1, 1924
The Rt. Hon. Francis Alexander Anglin.......................	Apr. 2, 1865	Sept. 16, 1924	Feb. 28, 1933
The Rt. Hon. Sir Lyman Poore Duff...........................	Jan. 7, 1865	Mar. 17, 1933	Jan. 7, 1944
The Rt. Hon. Thibaudeau Rinfret................................	June 22, 1879	Jan. 8, 1944	June 22, 1954
The Hon. Patrick Kerwin..	Oct. 25, 1889	July 1, 1954	Feb. 2, 1963
The Rt. Hon. Robert Taschereau	Sept. 10, 1896	Apr. 22, 1963	Sept. 1, 1967
The Rt. Hon. John Robert Cartwright.........................	Mar. 23, 1895	Sept. 1, 1967	Mar. 23, 1970
The Rt. Hon. Joseph Honoré Gérald Fauteux	Oct. 22, 1900	Mar. 23, 1970	Dec. 23, 1973
The Rt. Hon. Bora Laskin	Oct. 5, 1912	Dec. 27, 1973	Mar. 26, 1984
The Rt. Hon. Robert George Brian Dickson.................	May 25, 1916	Apr. 18, 1984	June 30, 1990
The Rt. Hon. Antonio Lamer.......................................	Jul. 8, 1933	July 1, 1990	Jan. 6, 2000
The Rt. Hon. Beverley McLachlin	Sept. 7, 1943	Jan. 7, 2000–	

Source: *Supreme Court of Canada and Canadian Parliamentary Guide*

Contacting the Supreme Court

F or information on the Supreme Court of Canada, turn to page 143. Visit the court's Web site at http://www.scc-csc.gc.ca for more information on judges, history, recent decisions, tours and news. You may also write to the Supreme Court of Canada, 301 Wellington Street, Ottawa, Ontario, K1A 0J1. Phone (613) 995-4330 or e-mail reception@scc-csc.gc.ca

FOCUS ON...

Key Decisions of the Supreme Court of Canada

The Persons Case (1928): The court unanimously decided that women were not "persons" qualified for appointment to the Canadian Senate. In 1929, the British Privy Council overturned the decision on appeal, declaring the exclusion of women from public office "a relic of days more barbarous than ours."

Alberta Press Act Reference (1938): The court struck down an Alberta bill that would have required newspapers, when called upon by government officials, to publish the government's rebuttal of criticism that had appeared in the newspapers. The decision blocked one form of government interference with press freedom.

Saumur v City of Quebec (1953): The court narrowly upheld the province's right to authorize municipal bans on street pamphleteering. (The ban had been challenged by Jehovah's Witnesses who were distributing leaflets.) However, one majority judge declared that a Quebec law guaranteeing religious freedom prevented the authorities from banning the distribution of *religious* pamphlets. Thus the court attempted to protect this form of religious expression.

Switzman v Elbling (1957): The court struck down a Quebec law—the Act Respecting Communistic Propaganda of 1937—which criminalized the publication and distribution of Communist literature. The law, also known as the Padlock Act, empowered the attorney general to close buildings used by Communists for up to a year. The court ruled that the province lacked the constitutional power to pass criminal laws.

Roncarelli v Duplessis (1959): The court ruled that Maurice Duplessis, former premier and attorney general of Quebec, committed a civil wrong when he revoked the liquor licence of Roncarelli, a restaurateur, in 1946. Duplessis had revoked the licence, and had ruined Roncarelli's business, because Roncarelli had aided Jehovah's Witnesses who had been arrested for pamphleteering. The court ordered Duplessis to pay damages.

R. v Drybones (1970): The court used a clause declaring equality before the law in the Bill of Rights to strike down part of the Indian Act that made it an offence for a Native person to be drunk when off a reserve. The court decided that if a federal law cannot be applied without infringing on a citizen's rights, the law must be suspended until Parliament declares that the law still applies—regardless of the Bill of Rights. Then the court ruled that Drybones, an aboriginal man found drunk while away from his reserve, had been punished for his race under a law whose penalty differed for other Canadians.

R. v Kienapple (1975): The court abolished the practice of sentencing defendants twice for offences that amounted to being the same act.

CUPE Local 963 v New Brunswick Liquor Corp. (1979): The court affirmed the growing role of administrative tribunals and established when the courts can interfere with the tribunals' decisions.

Patriation Reference (1981): The court ruled that the federal government could patriate the constitution (then known as the British North America Act) without the consent of the provinces; however, the court also said that the federal government would violate a political tradition if it patriated the constitution without first securing "a substantial degree" of provincial consent.

The Bill 101 Case (1984): The court struck down two sections of Quebec's Bill 101 (The Charter of the French Language) that dealt with anglophone schooling. The sections attempted to make French the language of instruction in elementary schools for anglophones who had moved to Quebec from elsewhere in Canada. The court declared that this was incompatible with minority-language education guarantees in the Canadian Charter of Rights and Freedoms.

Hunter v Southam Inc. (1984): The court struck down two subsections of the Combines Investigation Act because they violated the guarantee in the Canadian Charter of Rights and Freedoms against unreasonable searches and seizures. Hunter, a government official investigating restrictive trade practices, had sent several officers without search warrants to enter Southam's corporate office in Edmonton to examine documents.

R. v Big M Drug Mart (1985): The court struck down the Lord's Day Act, a federal law passed in 1907 that banned business activities on Sundays. The court declared that, by forcing all members of society to observe the Christian Sabbath, the law infringed on the religious freedoms of non-Christian minorities; therefore, the Act was incompatible with the religious freedom guarantees in the Canadian Charter of Rights and Freedoms. Big M Drug Mart had been charged with selling merchandise on Sundays.

Singh et al. v Minister of Employment and Immigration (1985): The court ruled that foreign refugees in Canada may not be deported to countries where their lives or freedom are threatened. The guarantee of personal security in the Canadian Charter of Rights and Freedoms applied to everyone in Canada. The court also ruled that the Immigration Act's method for establishing refugee status failed to meet the Charter's requirements for fundamental justice. People seeking refugee status were entitled to a hearing.

R. v Oakes (1986): The court struck down a section of the Narcotic Control Act that conflicted with the presumption of innocence of accused persons—a presumption guaranteed in the Canadian Charter of Rights and Freedoms. The court also established a two-step test to see whether laws measure up to Charter guarantees. First, the government must prove the existence of a purpose important and urgent enough to justify the suppression of a right; second, the government's legislative methods must be reasonable, fair and proportionate to the goal.

Ford v Quebec (1988): The court struck down two more sections of Quebec's Bill 101. The provisions attempted to impose the exclusive use of French on public and commercial signs in Quebec. The court decided that these provisions violated the freedom of expression guarantees in the Canadian Charter of Rights and Freedoms, although the *predominant* use of French on such signs could be legally justified.

Daigle v Tremblay (1989): The court declared that fetuses have no constitutional rights; constitutional rights begin at the time of live birth. The court also decided that the father of a fetus may not use a court injunction to prevent the mother from exercising her right of choice to have an abortion. Tremblay had tried to stop his partner, Daigle, from aborting their unborn child.

R. v Stinchcombe (1990): The court unanimously affirmed that the Crown must reveal all its evidence against an accused to the defence so the defence can properly defend the accused. This responsibility of the Crown, which had existed in common law, became obligatory rather than merely voluntary. The ruling also required police and prosecutors to disclose all their evidence before the accused chose a mode of trial or entered a plea.

R. v Sparrow (1990): The court affirmed the rights of aboriginal peoples in the Constitution Act and declared that these rights must be interpreted broadly. The authorities had charged Sparrow, an aboriginal man, with breaking a federal fishing law. Sparrow successfully argued that the right to fish was protected by treaty and the constitution. The court also established criteria for interpreting aboriginal rights in the constitution.

Kindler v. Canada (1991): The court ruled that the extradition of a non-Canadian fugitive did not violate the guarantee in the Canadian Charter of Rights and Freedoms to life, liberty and security of person. Extradition also did not violate the Charter's ban on subjecting a person to cruel and unusual punishment. Kindler, an American who had been convicted of murder and kidnapping in Pennsylvania, had escaped from prison and fled to Canada where he was arrested. He faced a possible death sentence if returned to the US.

R. v Généreux (1992): The court found that judges in courts martial were vulnerable to financial and administrative pressures from senior officials in the Canadian Armed Forces. The decision paved the way for parliamentary reforms aimed at strengthening the independence and impartiality of military judges. Généreux, a corporal who had been court martialled for desertion and selling narcotics, had argued that he had not received an impartial trial.

R. v Tran (1994): The court ruled that an accused is entitled to full and contemporaneous translation in his or her native language during a trial. The court then ordered a new trial for Tran, a Vietnamese man who spoke no English or French and who had received inadequate translation service during his trial for sexual assault in Nova Scotia. This case was the first in which the Supreme Court of Canada dealt with an accused's right to an interpreter.

RJR-MacDonald Inc. v Canada (1995): The court declared that Parliament possessed the constitutional authority (in criminal law) to regulate the use of tobacco products. The court also said that Parliament had a valid interest in countering the harmful effects of tobacco on health. However, a 5–4 majority of justices struck down the Tobacco Products Control Act of 1988 because the law's broad ban on tobacco advertising violated the freedom of expression guarantees in the Canadian Charter of Rights and Freedoms.

Cooper v Canada (1996): The court ruled that the Canadian Human Rights Commission lacked the authority and expertise to rule on the constitutional validity of the mandatory age of retirement.

R. v Stillman (1997): The court decided that the common-law power to conduct a search incidental to an arrest excluded the right to seize body substances by force. The police had subjected a suspect, Stillman, to an intrusive body search without consent. The court ruled that such searches must meet three requirements to be legal: the arrest must be legal, the search must be incidental, and the search must be conducted in a reasonable way.

Delgamuukw v British Columbia (1997): The court defined the content and extent of aboriginal title to ancestral lands. The court required aboriginals seeking such title to prove that they occupied the territory before Canada's declaration of sovereignty. The court also decided to consider admitting oral history as evidence.

Godbout v Longueuil (1997): The court unanimously declared that a municipal government may not dictate where its employees live. The City of Longueuil, Quebec, had demanded that its permanent employees live inside the town's limits.

R. v Caslake (1998): The court decided that a police search made for purposes of inventory, conforming to police policy but without a search warrant or permission, is an abusive search. Caslake had been arrested for possessing narcotics; an RCMP search of Caslake's van several hours after the arrest—which led to the seizure of more narcotics—prompted the dispute over "abusive searches" in court.

Quebec Secession Reference (1998): The court ruled unanimously that a unilateral declaration of independence by a province (i.e., Quebec) would be illegal according to the Canadian constitution and international law. However, a constitutional amendment would make secession possible. The court also said that if a clear majority of Quebeckers voted for secession in a referendum, the rest of Canada would be obliged to negotiate the terms of independence. The negotiations would have to respect democracy, federalism, the rule of law and the protection of minorities.

Vriend v Alberta (1998): The court unanimously declared that Alberta's failure to include sexual orientation as an illegal form of discrimination in its Individual Rights Protection Act violated the Canadian Charter of Rights and Freedoms. The court ruled that Vriend, a homosexual, had been wrongfully dismissed from his job at an Edmonton college after he acknowledged his sexual orientation to his employer.

Little Sister's Book and Art Emporium v Canada (2000): The court upheld the authority of customs officials to seize imported books, magazines and videos that may be sexually obscene. The justices also shifted the burden of proving illegal obscenity from importers to customs officials in open court. Little Sister's, a bookstore in Vancouver, had repeatedly complained about the seizure of homosexual erotica by customs agents.

Lieutenant-Governors and Commissioners

(as of October 2003)

On the advice of the prime minister, the Governor General of Canada appoints 10 provincial lieutenant-governors and three territorial commissioners. Lieutenant-governors and commissioners represent the monarch and perform the same duties at the provincial and territorial levels that the Governor General performs at the federal level. They open, prorogue and dissolve legislatures and give royal assent to legislation and orders-in-council.

Lieutenant-governors and commissioners are paid by the federal government and usually serve terms of five years.

Province or Territory	Lieutenant-Governor/ Commissioner	Birthdate	Date Sworn in
Newfoundland and Labrador	Hon. Edward M. Roberts	Sept. 1, 1940	Nov. 1, 2002
Prince Edward Island	Hon. J. Léonce Bernard	May 23, 1943	May 28, 2001
Nova Scotia	Hon. Myra A. Freeman	May 17, 1949	May 17, 2000
New Brunswick	Hon. Herménégilde Chiasson	Apr. 7, 1946	Aug. 26, 2003
Quebec	Hon. Lise Thibault	Apr. 2, 1939	Jan. 30, 1997
Ontario	Hon. James K. Bartleman	Dec. 24, 1939	Mar. 7, 2002
Manitoba	Hon. Peter M. Liba	May 10, 1940	Mar. 2, 1999
Saskatchewan	Hon. Lynda M. Haverstock	Sept. 16, 1948	Feb. 21, 2000
Alberta	Hon. Lois Elsa Hole	1933	Feb. 10, 2000
British Columbia	Hon. Iona Campagnolo	Oct. 18, 1932	Sept. 25, 2001
Nunavut	Hon. Peter Irniq	1947	Apr. 1, 2000
Northwest Territories	Hon. Glenna F. Hansen	Aug. 10, 1956	Mar. 31, 2000
Yukon	Hon. Jack Cable	Aug. 17, 1934	Sept. 30, 2000

Provincial Premiers: An Historical Listing

(as of October 2003)

■ Newfoundland and Labrador

Premier	Term	Party	Elected or sworn in
Joseph R. Smallwood	1949–72	Liberal	Apr. 1, 1949
Frank D. Moores	1972–79	Conservative	Jan. 18, 1972
A. Brian Peckford	1979–89	Conservative	Mar. 26, 1979
Tom Rideout	1989	Conservative	Mar. 22, 1989
Clyde Wells	1989–96	Liberal	May 5, 1989
Brian Tobin	1996–2000	Liberal	Jan. 26, 1996
Beaton Tulk	2000–01	Liberal	Oct. 16, 2000
Roger Grimes	2001–03	Liberal	Feb. 13, 2001
Danny Williams	2003–	Conservative	Oct. 21, 2003

■ Prince Edward Island

Premier	Term	Party	Elected or sworn in
C. Pope	1873	Conservative	Apr., 1873
L. C. Owen	1873–76	Conservative	Sept., 1873
L. H. Davies	1876–79	Liberal (Coalition)	Aug., 1876
W. W. Sullivan	1879–89	Conservative	Apr. 25, 1879
N. McLeod	1889–91	Conservative	Nov., 1889
F. Peters	1891–97	Liberal	Apr. 27, 1891
A. B. Warburton	1897–98	Liberal	Oct., 1897
D. Farquharson	1898–1901	Liberal	Aug., 1898
A. Peters	1901–08	Liberal	Dec. 29, 1901
F. L. Haszard	1908–11	Liberal	Feb. 1, 1908
H. James Palmer	1911	Liberal	May 16, 1911
John A. Mathieson	1911–17	Conservative	Dec. 2, 1911
Aubin Arsenault	1917–19	Conservative	June, 21, 1917
J. H. Bell	1919–23	Liberal	Sept. 9, 1919
James D. Stewart	1923–27	Conservative	Sept. 5, 1923
Albert C. Saunders	1927–30	Liberal	Aug. 12, 1927
Walter M. Lea	1930–31	Liberal	May 20, 1930

▶

▶ James D. Stewart	1931–33	Conservative	Aug. 29, 1931
William J. P. MacMillan	1933–35	Conservative	Oct. 14, 1933
Walter M. Lea	1935–36	Liberal	Aug. 15, 1935
Thane A. Campbell	1936–43	Liberal	Jan. 14, 1936
J. Walter Jones	1943–53	Liberal	May 11, 1943
Alexander W. Matheson	1953–59	Liberal	May 25, 1953
Walter Shaw	1959–66	Prog. Conservative	Sept. 16, 1959
Alexander B. Campbell	1966–78	Liberal	July 28, 1966
William Bennett Campbell	1978–79	Liberal	Sept. 18, 1978
J. Angus MacLean	1979–81	Prog. Conservative	May 3, 1979
James M. Lee	1981–86	Prog. Conservative	Nov. 17, 1981
Joseph A. Ghiz	1986–93	Liberal	May 2, 1986
Catherine Callbeck	1993–96	Liberal	Jan. 25, 1993
Keith Milligan	1996	Liberal	Oct. 10, 1996
Patrick Binns	1996–	Prog. Conservative	Nov. 27, 1996

■ Nova Scotia

Premier	Term	Party	Elected or sworn in
H. Blanchard	1867	Conservative	July 4, 1867
William Annand	1867–75	Liberal	Nov. 7, 1867
P. C. Hill	1875–78	Liberal	May 11, 1875
S. H. Holmes	1878–82	Conservative	Oct. 22, 1878
John S. D. Thompson	1882	Conservative	May 25, 1882
W. T. Pipes	1882–84	Liberal	Aug. 3, 1882
W. S. Fielding	1884–96	Liberal	July 28, 1884
George H. Murray	1896–1923	Liberal	July 20, 1896
E. H. Armstrong	1923–25	Liberal	Jan. 24, 1923
E. N. Rhodes	1925–30	Conservative	July 16, 1925
Col. Gordon S. Harrington	1930–33	Conservative	Aug. 11, 1930
Angus L. Macdonald	1933–40	Liberal	Sept. 5, 1933
A. S. MacMillan	1940–45	Liberal	July 10, 1940
Angus L. Macdonald	1945–54	Liberal	Sept. 8, 1945
Harold Connolly	1954	Liberal	Apr. 13, 1954
Henry D. Hicks	1954–56	Liberal	Sept. 30, 1954
Robert L. Stanfield	1956–67	Prog. Conservative	Nov. 20, 1956
George Smith	1967–70	Prog. Conservative	Sept. 13, 1967
Gerald A. Regan	1970–78	Liberal	Oct. 28, 1970
John Buchanan	1978–90	Prog. Conservative	Oct. 5, 1978
Roger Bacon	1990–91	Prog. Conservative	Sept. 12, 1990
Donald Cameron	1991–93	Prog. Conservative	Feb. 9, 1991
John Savage	1993–97	Liberal	June 11, 1993
Russell MacLellan	1997–99	Liberal	July 18, 1997
John Hamm	1999–	Prog. Conservative	July 27, 1999

■ New Brunswick

Premier	Term	Party	Elected or sworn in
Andrew Wetmore	1867–70	Confederation Party	1867
G.E. King	1870–71	Conservative	1870
George Hatheway	1871–72	Conservative	1871
G.E. King	1872–78	Conservative	1872
James Fraser	1878–82	Conservative	1878
D. L. Hanington	1882–83	Conservative	1882
Andrew Blair	1883–96	Liberal	1883
James Mitchell	1896–97	Liberal	July, 1896
Henry Emmerson	1897–1900	Liberal	Oct. 29, 1897
L. J. Tweedie	1900–07	Liberal	Aug. 31, 1900
William Pugsley	1907	Liberal	Mar. 6, 1907
Clifford Robinson	1907–08	Liberal	May 31, 1907
John Douglas Hazen	1908–11	Conservative	Mar. 24, 1908
James K. Flemming	1911–14	Conservative	Oct. 16, 1911
George J. Clark	1914–17	Conservative	Dec. 17, 1914
James Murray	1917	Conservative	Feb. 1, 1917
Walter E. Foster	1917–23	Liberal	Apr. 4, 1917
Peter Veniot	1923–25	Liberal	Feb. 28, 1923
John B. M. Baxter	1925–31	Conservative	Sept. 14, 1925	▶

▶ Charles D. Richards 1931–33   Conservative   May 19, 1931
Leonard Tilley 1933–35   Conservative   June 1, 1933

	Term	Party	Elected or sworn in
Charles D. Richards	1931–33	Conservative	May 19, 1931
Leonard Tilley	1933–35	Conservative	June 1, 1933
Allison Dysart	1935–40	Liberal	July 16, 1935
John McNair	1940–52	Liberal	Mar. 13, 1940
Hugh J. Flemming	1952–60	Prog. Conservative	Oct. 8, 1952
Louis J. Robichaud	1960–70	Liberal	July 12, 1960
Richard Hatfield	1970–87	Prog. Conservative	Nov. 12, 1970
Frank McKenna	1987–97	Liberal	Oct. 27, 1987
Ray Frenette (interim)	1997–98	Liberal	Oct 14, 1997
Camille Thériault	1998–99	Liberal	May 14, 1998
Bernard Lord	1999–	Prog. Conservative	June 21, 1999

■ Quebec

Premier	Term	Party	Elected or sworn in
Pierre-Joseph-Olivier Chauveau	1867–73	Conservative	July 15, 1867
Gédéon Ouimet	1873–74	Conservative	Feb. 26, 1873
Charles E. Boucher deBoucherville	1874–78	Conservative	Sept. 22, 1874
Henri Joly	1878–79	Liberal	Mar. 8, 1878
J. Adolphe Chapleau	1879–82	Conservative	Oct. 31, 1879
J. Alfred Mousseau	1882–84	Conservative	July 31, 1882
John J. Ross	1884–87	Conservative	Jan. 23, 1884
L. Olivier Taillon	1887	Conservative	Jan. 25, 1887
Honoré Mercier	1887–91	Liberal	Jan. 27, 1887
Charles E. Boucher deBoucherville	1891–92	Conservative	Dec. 21, 1891
L. Olivier Taillon	1892–96	Conservative	Dec. 16, 1892
Edmund J. Flynn	1896–97	Conservative	May 11, 1896
F. Gabriel Marchand	1897–1900	Liberal	May 24, 1897
S. Napoléon Parent	1900–05	Liberal	Oct. 3, 1900
Lomer Gouin	1905–20	Liberal	Mar. 23, 1905
L. Alexandre Taschereau	1920–36	Liberal	July 9, 1920
Adélard Godbout	1936	Liberal	June 11, 1936
Maurice Duplessis	1936–39	Union Nationale	Aug. 26, 1936
Adélard Godbout	1939–44	Liberal	Nov. 8, 1939
Maurice Duplessis	1944–59	Union Nationale	Aug. 30, 1944
Paul Sauvé	1959–60	Union Nationale	Sept. 11, 1959
Antonio Barrette	1960	Union Nationale	Jan. 8, 1960
Jean Lesage	1960–66	Liberal	July 5, 1960
Daniel Johnson	1966–68	Union Nationale	June 16, 1966
Jean-Jacques Bertrand	1968–70	Union Nationale	Oct. 2, 1968
Robert Bourassa	1970–76	Liberal	May 12, 1970
René Lévesque	1976–85	Parti Québécois	Nov. 25, 1976
Pierre-Marc Johnson	1985	Parti Québécois	Oct. 3, 1985
Robert Bourassa	1985–94	Liberal	Dec. 12, 1985
Daniel Johnson	1994–94	Liberal	Jan. 11, 1994
Jacques Parizeau	1994–96	Parti Québécois	Sept. 26, 1994
Lucien Bouchard	1996–2001	Parti Québécois	Jan. 29, 1996
Bernard Landry	2001–03	Parti Québécois	Mar. 8, 2001
Jean Charest	2003–	Liberal	Apr. 29, 2003

■ Ontario

Premier	Term	Party	Elected or sworn in
J.S. Macdonald	1867–71	Coalition	July 16, 1867
Edward Blake	1871–72	Liberal	Dec. 20, 1871
Oliver Mowat	1872–96	Liberal	Oct. 25, 1872
Arthur S. Hardy	1896–99	Liberal	July 25, 1896
George William Ross	1899–1905	Liberal	Oct. 21, 1899
Sir James P. Whitney	1905–14	Conservative	Feb. 8, 1905
Sir William Hearst	1914–19	Conservative	Oct. 2, 1914
Ernest C. Drury	1919–23	United Farmers of Ontario	Nov. 14, 1919
George Howard Ferguson	1923–30	Conservative	July 16, 1923
George Stewart Henry	1930–34	Conservative	Dec. 15, 1930
Mitchell F. Hepburn	1934–42	Liberal	July 10, 1934
Gordon Daniel Conant	1942–43	Liberal	Oct. 21, 1942
Harry C. Nixon	1943	Liberal	May 18, 1943
George Drew	1943–48	Prog. Conservative	Aug. 17, 1943
Thomas L. Kennedy	1948–49	Prog. Conservative	Oct. 19, 1948

▶

▶

Leslie M. Frost	1949–61	Prog. Conservative	May 4, 1949
John P. Robarts	1961–71	Prog. Conservative	Nov. 8, 1961
William G. Davis	1971–85	Prog. Conservative	Mar. 1, 1971
Frank Miller	1985	Prog. Conservative	Feb. 8, 1985
David Peterson	1985–90	Liberal	June 26, 1985
Bob Rae	1990–95	New Democratic	Oct. 1, 1990
Mike Harris	1995–2002	Prog. Conservative	June 28, 1995
Ernie Eves	2002–2003	Prog. Conservative	Apr. 15, 2002
Dalton McGuinty	2003–	Liberal	Oct. 2, 2003

■ Manitoba

Premier	Term	Party	Elected or sworn in
A. Boyd	1870–71	n.a.	Sept. 16, 1870
M. A. Girard	1871–72	Conservative	Dec. 14, 1871
H. H. Clarke	1872–74	n.a.	Mar. 14, 1872
M. A. Girard	1874	Conservative	July 8, 1874
R. A. Davis	1874–78	n.a.	Dec. 3, 1874
John Norquay	1878–87	Conservative	Oct. 16, 1878
D. H. Harrison	1887–88	Conservative	Dec. 26, 1887
T. Greenway	1888–1900	Liberal	Jan. 19, 1888
H. J. Macdonald	1900	Conservative	Jan. 8, 1900
Sir R. P. Roblin	1900–15	Conservative	Oct. 29, 1900
T. C. Norris	1915–22	Liberal	May 12, 1915
John Bracken	1922–43	Coalition[1]	Aug. 8, 1922
S. S. Garson	1943–48	Coalition	Jan. 8, 1943
D. L. Campbell	1948–58	Conservative	Nov. 11, 1948
Duff Roblin	1958–67	Prog. Conservative	June 16, 1958
Walter Weir	1967–69	Prog. Conservative	Nov. 25, 1967
Edward Schreyer	1969–77	New Democratic	July 15, 1969
Sterling Lyon	1977–81	Prog. Conservative	Nov. 24, 1977
Howard Pawley	1981–88	New Democratic	Nov. 30, 1981
Gary Filmon	1988–99	Prog. Conservative	Apr. 26, 1988
Gary Doer	1999–	New Democratic	Oct. 5, 1999

■ Saskatchewan

Premier	Term	Party	Elected or sworn in
Walter Scott	1905–16	Liberal	Sept. 5, 1905
W. M. Martin	1916–22	Liberal	Oct. 20, 1916
C. A. Dunning	1922–26	Liberal	Apr. 5, 1922
J. G. Gardiner	1926–29	Liberal	Feb. 26, 1926
J. T. M. Anderson	1929–34	Conservative	Sept. 9, 1929
J. G. Gardiner	1934–35	Liberal	July 19, 1934
W. J. Patterson	1935–44	Liberal	Nov. 1, 1935
Tommy Douglas	1944–61	C.C.F.[2]	July 10, 1944
W. S. Lloyd	1961–64	C.C.F.—N.D.P.	Nov. 7, 1961
W. Ross Thatcher	1964–71	Liberal	May 22, 1964
Allan E. Blakeney	1971–82	New Democratic	June 30, 1971
Grant Devine	1982–91	Prog. Conservative	May 8, 1982
Roy Romanow	1991–2001	New Democratic	Nov. 1, 1991
Lorne Calvert	2001–	New Democratic	Feb. 8, 2001

■ Alberta

Premier	Term	Party	Elected or sworn in
Alex Rutherford	1905–10	Liberal	Sept. 2, 1905
A. L. Sifton	1910–17	Liberal	May 26, 1910
Charles Stewart	1917–21	Liberal	Oct. 30, 1917
Herbert Greenfield	1921–25	United Farmers of Alberta	Aug. 13, 1921
John E. Brownlee	1925–34	United Farmers of Alberta	Nov. 23, 1925
Richard G. Reid	1934–35	United Farmers of Alberta	July 10, 1934
William Aberhart	1935–43	Social Credit	Sept. 3, 1935
E. C. Manning	1943–68	Social Credit	May 31, 1943
Harry Strom	1968–71	Social Credit	Dec. 12, 1968
Peter Lougheed	1971–85	Prog. Conservative	Sept. 10, 1971
Don Getty	1985–92	Prog. Conservative	Nov. 1, 1985
Ralph P. Klein	1992–	Prog. Conservative	Dec. 14, 1992

▶

▶■ **British Columbia**

Premier	Term	Party	Elected or sworn in
J. F. McCreight	1871–72	n.a.	Nov. 13, 1871
Amor De Cosmos	1872–74	n.a.	Dec. 23, 1872
G. A. Walkem	1874–76	n.a.	Feb. 11, 1874
A. C. Elliott	1876–78	n.a.	Feb. 1, 1876
G. A. Walkem	1878–82	n.a.	June 25, 1878
Robert Beaven	1882–83	n.a.	June 13, 1882
William Smithe	1883–87	n.a.	Jan. 29, 1883
A. E. B. Davie	1887–89	n.a.	May 1, 1887
John Robson	1889–92	n.a.	Aug. 2, 1889
Theodore Davie	1892–95	n.a.	July 2, 1892
J. H. Turner	1895–98	n.a.	Mar. 4, 1895
C. A. Semlin	1898–1900	n.a.	Aug. 15, 1898
Joseph Martin	1900	n.a.	Feb. 28, 1900
James Dunsmuir	1900–02	n.a.	June 15, 1900
E. G. Prior	1902–03	n.a.	Nov. 21, 1902
Richard McBride	1903–15	Conservative	June 1, 1903
William J. Bowser	1915–16	Conservative	Dec. 15, 1915
Harlan C. Brewster	1916–18	Liberal	Nov. 23, 1916
John Oliver	1918–27	Liberal	Mar. 6, 1918
John D. MacLean	1927–28	Liberal	Aug. 20, 1927
Simon F. Tolmie	1928–33	Conservative	Aug. 21, 1928
T. D. Pattullo	1933–41	Liberal	Nov. 15, 1933
John Hart	1941–47	Liberal[3]	Dec. 9, 1941
Byron Johnson	1947–52	Liberal[3]	Dec. 29, 1947
W. A. C. Bennett	1952–72	Social Credit	Aug. 1, 1952
David Barrett	1972–75	New Democratic	Sept. 15, 1972
William R. Bennett	1975–86	Social Credit	Dec. 22, 1975
Bill Vander Zalm	1986–91	Social Credit	Aug. 6, 1986
Rita Johnston	1991–91	Social Credit	Apr. 2, 1991
Michael Harcourt	1991–96	New Democratic	Nov. 5, 1991
Glen Clark	1996–99	New Democratic	Feb. 22, 1996
Dan Miller	1999–2000	New Democratic	Aug. 25, 1999
Ujjal Dosanjh	2000–01	New Democratic	Feb. 24, 2000
Gordon Campbell	2001–	Liberal	June 5, 2001

■ **Nunavut**

Premier	Term	Party	Elected or sworn in
Paul Okalik	1999–	n.a.	Apr. 1, 1999

■ **Northwest Territories**

Premier	Term	Party	Elected or sworn in
George Braden	1980–83	n.a.	July 25, 1980
Richard Nerysoo	1984–85	n.a.	Jan. 12, 1984
Nick Sibbeston	1985–87	n.a.	Nov. 5, 1985
Dennis Patterson	1987–91	n.a.	Nov. 12, 1987
Nellie Cournoyea	1991–95	n.a.	Nov. 13, 1991
Don Morin	1995–98	n.a.	Nov. 20, 1995
James L. Antoine	1998–2000	n.a.	Dec. 10, 1998
Stephen Kakfwi	2000–	n.a.	Jan. 19, 2000

■ **Yukon**

Premier	Term	Party	Elected or sworn in
Chris Pearson	1978–85	Prog. Conservative	
Willard Phelps	1985	Prog. Conservative	Mar. 20, 1985
Tony Penikett	1985–92[4]	New Democratic	May 29, 1985
John Ostashek	1992–96	Yukon Party	Nov. 7, 1992
Piers McDonald	1996–2000	New Democratic	Oct. 19, 1996
Pat Duncan	2000–02	Liberal	May 6, 2000
Dennis Fentie	2002–	Yukon Party	Nov. 30, 2002

Source: *Historical Statistics of Canada; Provincial Archives*

(1) United Farmer/Progressive, 1922–27; Coalition, 1927–37; Liberal—Progressive, 1937–43. (2) Co-operative Commonwealth Federation. (3) Coalition. (4) From 1989–92, Government Leader was designated Premier. (n.a.) not available.

Cabinets of the Provinces and Territories

(as of October 2003)

■ Newfoundland and Labrador:

Danny Williams (P.C.) is premier elect. At press time he had not named a cabinet.

Ministry or Portfolio of Outgoing Government	Minister
Premier	Roger Grimes
Education	Gerry Reid
Environment	Robert Mercer
Finance; Treasury Board	Joan Marie Aylward
Fisheries and Aquaculture; Status of Women	Yvonne Jones
Forest Resources and Agrifoods	Rick Woodford
Government Services and Lands	George Sweeney
Health and Community Services; Strategic Social Plan	Gerald Smith
Human Resources and Employment	Ralph Wiseman
Industry, Trade and Rural Development	Judy Foote
Intergovernmental Affairs; Government House Leader	Tom Lush
Justice and Attorney General	Kelvin Parsons
Labour	Percy Barrett
Labrador and Aboriginal Affairs	Wally Andersen
Mines and Energy	Walter Noel
Municipal and Provincial Affairs	Oliver Langdon
Tourism, Culture and Recreation	Julie Bettney
Works, Services and Transportation	James Walsh
Youth Services and Post-Secondary Education	Anne Thistle

■ New Brunswick

Ministry or Portfolio	Minister
Premier; Regional Development Corp.; Red Tape Reduction; Status of Disabled Persons; Youth	Bernard Lord
Deputy Premier; Supply and Services	Dale Graham
Agriculture, Fisheries and Aquaculture	David Alward
Business New Brunswick	Peter Mesheau
Education	Madeleine Dubé
Energy	Bruce Fitch
Environment and Local Government	Brenda Fowlie
Family and Community Services; Seniors	Tony J. Huntjens
Finance; Liquor; Lotteries; NB Investment Management Corp.	Jeannot Volpé
Health and Wellness	Elvy Robichaud
Human Resources	Rose-May Poirier
Intergovernmental and International Relations; Culture and Sport; Francophonie; Service New Brunswick	Percy Mockler
Justice and Attorney General; Aboriginal Affairs	Bradley Green
Natural Resources	Keith Ashfield
Public Safety	Wayne Steeves
Tourism and Parks	Joan MacAlpine
Training and Employment Development; Status of Women	Margaret-Ann Blaney
Transportation; Acadian Peninsula Fisheries	Paul Robichaud

■ Nova Scotia

Ministry or Portfolio	Minister
Premier; Intergovernmental Affairs	John F. Hamm
Deputy Premier; Transportation and Public Works	Ronald S. Russell
Aboriginal Affairs; Attorney General and Justice; Treasury	Michael G. Baker
Acadian Affairs; Agriculture and Fisheries	Chris A. d'Entremont
African Nova Scotian Affairs; Service Nova Scotia and Municipal Relations	Barry Barnet
Community Services; Disabled Persons	David M. Morse
Economic Development; Emergency Measures; Liquor Control	Ernest L. Fage
Education; Youth	Jamie Muir
Energy	Cecil P. Clarke
Environment and Labour	Kerry Morash
Finance	Peter G. Christie
Health; Senior Citizens	Angus MacIsaac
Health Promotion; Sport and Recreation; Tourism and Culture	Rodney J. MacDonald

►

▶ Human Resources; Public Services; Status of Women .... Carolyn Bolivar-Getson
Natural Resources .... Richard Hurlburt

■ Prince Edward Island

Ministry or Portfolio	Minister
Premier; Intergovernmental Affairs	Patrick G. Binns
Agriculture, Fisheries, Aquaculture and Forestry	Kevin MacAdam
Attorney General; Environment and Energy	James W. Ballem
Community and Cultural Affairs	Elmer MacFadyen
Development and Technology	Michael Currie
Education	Mildred Dover
Health and Social Services	Chester Gillan
Provincial Treasury	P. Mitchell Murphy
Tourism	Philip Brown
Transportation and Public Works	Gail Shea

■ Quebec

Ministry or Portfolio	Minister
Premier	Jean Charest
Deputy Premier; International Relations	Monique Gagnon-Tremblay
Agriculture, Fisheries and Food	Françoise Gauthier
Canadian Intergovernmental Affairs and Native Affairs	Benoît Pelletier
Culture and Communications	Line Beauchamp
Education	Pierre Reid
Employment, Social Solidarity and Family Welfare	Claude Béchard
Environment	Thomas J. Mulcair
Family Welfare	Carole Théberge
Finance	Yves Séguin
Forests, Wildlife and Parks	Pierre Corbeil
Government Administration and Treasury	Monique Jérôme-Forget
Health and Social Services	Philippe Couillard
Health, Social Services and Status of Seniors	Vacant
Justice and Attorney General	Marc Bellemare
Labour	Michel Després
Municipal Affairs, Sports and Recreation	Jean-Marc Fournier
Natural Resources, Wildlife and Parks	Sam Hamad
Public Security	Jacques Chagnon
Reform of Democratic Institutions	Jacques P. Dupuis
Regional and Economic Development	Michel Audet
Regional Development and Tourism	Nathalie Normandeau
Relations with the Citizens and Immigration	Michelle Courchesne
Revenue	Lawrence S. Bergman
Transport	Yvon Marcoux

■ Ontario

Ministry or Portfolio	Minister
Premier; Intergovernmental Affairs	Dalton McGuinty
Agriculture and Food	Steve Peters
Attorney General; Democratic Renewel; Native Affairs	Michael Bryant
Children's Services Citizenship and Immigration	Marie Bountrogianni
Community and Social Services; Women's Issues	Sandra Pupatello
Community Safety and Correctional Services	Monte Kwinter
Consumer and Business Services	Jim Watson
Culture; Francophone Affairs	Madeleine Meilleur
Economic Development and Trade	Joe Cordiano
Education	Gerard Kennedy
Energy; Chair of Cabinet; Government House Leader	Dwight Duncan
Environment	Leona Dombrowsky
Finance	Greg Sorbara
Health and Long-Term Care	George Smitherman
Labour	Chris Bentley
Management Board of Cabinet	Gerry Phillips
Municipal Affairs; Seniors	John Gerretsen
Natural Resources	David Ramsay
Northern Development and Mines	Rick Bartolucci

▶

Public Infastructure Renewal	David Caplan
Tourism and Recreation	Jim Bradley
Training, Colleges and Universities	Mary Anne Chambers
Transportation	Harinder Takhar

■ Manitoba

Ministry or Portfolio	Minister
Premier; Federal-Provincial Relations	Gary Albert Doer
Deputy Premier; Agriculture and Food; Intergovernmental Affairs, Co-operative Development	Rosann Wowchuk
Aboriginal and Northern Affairs	Oscar Lathlin
Advanced Education and Training; Status of Women; Seniors	Diane McGifford
Conservation; Labour and Immigration; Multiculturalism; Workers' Compensation	Steve Ashton
Culture, Heritage and Tourism; Sport	Eric Robinson
Education and Youth	Ron Lemieux
Energy, Science and Technology; Gaming; Hydro	Tim Sale
Family Services and Housing; Persons with Disabilities	Drew Caldwell
Finance; French Language Services; Civil Service; Liquor Control	Gregory F. Selinger
Health	David Walter Chomiak
Industry, Trade and Mines	MaryAnn Mihychuk
Justice and Attorney General; Constitutional Affairs; Government House Leader	Gord Mackintosh
Transportation and Government Services; Emergency Measures	Scott Smith

■ Saskatchewan

Ministry or Portfolio	Minister
Premier	Lorne Calvert
Deputy Premier; Agriculture, Food and Rural Revitalization	Clay Serby
Aboriginal Affairs; Intergovernmental Affairs; Government House Leader	Eldon Lautermilch
Community Resources and Employment; Disability Issues; Gaming	Glenn Hagel
Corrections and Public Safety; Information Technology	Andrew Thomson
Crown Investments Corp.	Maynard Sonntag
Culture, Youth and Recreation; Provincial Secretary	Joanne Crofford
Environment; Northern Affairs	Buckley Belanger
Finance	Jim Melenchuk
Government Relations; Saskatchewan Property Management Corp.	Ron Osika
Health; Seniors	John Nilson
Highways and Transportation	Mark Wartman
Industry and Resources; Justice and Attorney General	Eric Cline
Labour; Status of Women	Deb Higgins
Learning	Judy Junor

■ Alberta

Ministry or Portfolio	Minister
Premier	Ralph Klein
Aboriginal Affairs and Northern Development	Pearl Calahasen
Agriculture, Food and Rural Development	Shirley McClellan
Children's Services	Iris Evans
Community Development	Gene Zwozdesky
Economic Development	Mark Norris
Energy	Murray Smith
Environment	Lorne Taylor
Finance	Patricia Nelson
Gaming	Ron Stevens
Government Services	David Coutts
Health and Wellness	Gary Mar
Human Resources and Employment	Clint Dunford
Infrastructure	Ty Lund
Innovation and Science	Victor Doerksen
International and Intergovernmental Relations	Halvar Jonson
Justice and Attorney General	David Hancock
Learning	Lyle Oberg
Municipal Affairs	Guy Boutilier
Revenue	Greg Melchin
Seniors	Stan Woloshyn

▶ Solicitor General . . . . Heather Forsyth
Sustainable Resource Development . . . . Mike Cardinal
Transportation . . . . Ed Stelmach

■ British Columbia

Ministry or Portfolio*	Minister
Premier	Gordon Campbell
Deputy Premier; Education	Christy Clark
Advanced Education	Shirley Bond
Agriculture, Food and Fisheries	John van Dongen
Attorney General; Treaty Negotiations	Geoff Plant
Children and Family Development	Gordon Hogg
Community, Aboriginal and Women's Services	George Abbott
Competition, Science and Enterprise	Rick Thorpe
Energy and Mines	Richard Neufeld
Finance	Gary Collins
Forests	Michael de Jong
Health Planning	Sindi Hawkins
Health Services	Colin Hansen
Human Resources	Murray Coell
Management Services	Sandy Santori
Provincial Revenue	Bill Barisoff
Public Safety and Solicitor General	Rich Coleman
Skills Development and Labour	Graham Bruce
Sustainable Resource Management	Stan Hagen
Transportation	Judith Reid
Water, Land and Air Protection	Joyce Murray
Min. of State for Community Charter	Ted Nebbeling
Min. of State for Deregulation	Kevin Falcon
Min. of State for Early Childhood Development	Linda Reid
Min. of State for Intergovernmental Relations	Greg Halsey-Brandt
Min. of State for Intermediate, Long Term and Home Care	Katherine Whittred
Min. of State for Mental Health	Gulzar Cheema
Min. of State for Women's Equality	Lynn Stephens

■ Yukon Territory

Ministry or Portfolio	Minister
Premier; Devolution; Finance; Land Claims; Women; Youth	Dennis Fentie
Business, Tourism and Culture; Justice	Elaine Taylor
Community Services; Highways and Public Works; Housing; Liquor	Glenn Hart
Education	John Edzerza
Energy, Mines and Resources	Archie Lang
Environment	Jim Kenyon
Health and Social Services; Yukon Workers' Compensation, Health and Safety	Peter Jenkins

■ Northwest Territories

Ministry or Portfolio	Minister
Premier; Intergovernmental Affairs; Status of Women	Stephen Kakfwi
Deputy Premier; Aboriginal Affairs; Intergovernmental Forum; Resources, Wildlife and Economic Development	Jim Antoine
Education, Culture and Employment	Jake Ootes
Finance; Energy and Hydro; Government House Leader; Transportation	Joseph Handley
Justice; NWT Housing Corp.; Public Utilities; Youth	Roger Allen
Health and Social Services; Persons with Disabilities; Seniors	J.M. Miltenberger
Municipal and Community Affairs; Public Works and Services	Vince Steen

■ Nunavut

Ministry or Portfolio	Minister
Premier; Aboriginal Affairs; Intergovernmental Affairs; Justice	Paul Okalik
Deputy Premier; Finance; Government House Leader; Housing; Workers' Compensation	Kelvin Ng
Culture, Language, Elders and Youth; Community Government and Transportation; Persons with Disabilities; Sport; Status of Women	Peter Kilabuk
Education; Human Resources	Manitok Thompson
Energy; Health and Social Services; Homelessness	Ed Picco
Public Works and Services	Peter Kattuk
Sustainable Development	Olayuk Akesuk

* In B.C. ministers of state are indicated; other officials are ministers.

POLITICS AND ELECTIONS

Registered Federal Political Parties

(as of October 2003)

Federal political parties can only be registered at election time, when they qualify for registration by fielding at least 50 candidates by the nomination deadline in a forthcoming election. In between elections, parties can be founded and organized, and can apply for registration to the chief electoral

Bloc Québécois
Short Name: Bloc Québécois
Party Leader: Gilles Duceppe
National HQ: Ste 307, 3750 Crémazie Blvd E
Montreal, QC H2A 1B6
Tel.: (514) 526-3000
Fax: (514) 526-2868
Website: http://www.blocquebecois.org
Registered: Sept. 11, 1993

Canadian Action Party
Short Name: Canadian Action
Party Leader: Paul T. Hellyer
National HQ: Ste 302, 99 Atlantic Ave
Toronto, ON M6K 3J8
Tel.: (416) 535-4144
Fax: (416) 535-6325
Website: http://www.canadianactionparty.ca
Registered: May 13, 1997

Canadian Reform Conservative Alliance
Short Name: Canadian Alliance
Party Leader: Stephen Harper
National HQ: Ste 300, 717–7th Ave SW
Calgary, AB T2P 0Z3
Tel.: (403) 269-1990
Fax: (403) 266-6748
Website: http://www.canadianalliance.ca
Registered: Oct. 21, 1988

Communist Party of Canada
Short Name: Communist
Party Leader: Miguel Figueroa
National HQ: 290A Danforth Ave
Toronto, ON M4K 1N6
Tel.: (416) 469-2446
Fax: (416) 469-4063
Website: http://www.communist-party.ca
Registered: Nov. 8, 2000

The Green Party of Canada
Short Name: Green Party
Party Leader: Jim Harris
National HQ: PO Box 997, Station B
Ottawa, ON K1P 5R1
Tel.: (613) 235-7687
Fax: (613) 235-5819
Website: http://green.ca
Registered: Aug. 8, 1984

Liberal Party of Canada
Short Name: Liberal
Party Leader: Jean Chrétien
National HQ: Ste 400, 81 Metcalfe St
Ottawa, ON K1P 6M8
Tel.: (613) 237-0740
Fax: (613) 235-7208
Website: http://www.liberal.ca
Registered: Apr. 4, 1972

Marijuana Party
Short Name: Marijuana Party
Party Leader: Marc-Boris St-Maurice
National HQ: 5537 Bourbonnière St
Montreal, QC H1X 2N3
Tel.: (514) 728-4505
Website: http://www.marijuanaparty.com
Registered: Nov. 6, 2000

Marxist-Leninist Party of Canada
Short Name: Marxist-Leninist
Party Leader: Sandra L. Smith
National HQ: 1867 Amherst St
Montreal, QC H2L 3L7
Tel.: 1 (800) 749-9553
Fax: (514) 522-5872
Website: http://www.cpcml.ca
Registered: Sept. 28, 1993

Natural Law Party of Canada
Short Name: Natural Law Party
Party Leader: Allen Faguy
National HQ: Ste 503, 20 Cherrytree Dr
Brampton, ON L6Y 3V1
Tel.: (905) 450-0619
Registered: Sept. 23, 1993

New Democratic Party
Short Name: NDP
Party Leader: Jack Layton
National HQ: Ste 1001, 75 Albert St
Ottawa, ON K1P 5E7
Tel.: (613) 236-3613
Fax: (613) 230-9950
Website: http://www.ndp.ca
Registered: June 7, 1971

Progressive Conservative Party of Canada
Short Name: Progressive Conservative
Party Leader: Peter MacKay
National HQ: Ste 806, 141 Laurier Ave W
Ottawa, ON K1P 5J3
Tel.: (613) 238-6111
Fax: (613) 238-7429
Website: http://www.pcparty.ca
Registered: Feb. 17, 1972

Source: *Elections Canada*

Federal Election Results, 1867–2000

❦ 1867–1904

	1867	1872	1874	1878	1882	1887	1891	1896	1900	1904
Canada										
Conservative	101	103	73	137	139	123	123	89	80	75
Liberal	80	97	133	69	71	92	92	117	133	139
Other	—	—	—	—	—	—	—	7	—	—
Prince Edward Island[1]										
Conservative	—	—	—	5	4	—	2	3	2	3
Liberal	—	—	6	1	2	6	4	2	3	1
Nova Scotia										
Conservative	3	11	4	14	15	14	16	10	5	—
Liberal	16	10	17	7	6	7	5	10	15	18
New Brunswick										
Conservative	7	7	5	5	10	10	13	9	5	6
Liberal	8	9	11	11	6	6	3	5	9	7
Quebec										
Conservative	45	38	32	45	48	33	30	16	7	11
Liberal	20	27	33	20	17	32	35	49	58	54
Other	—	—	—	—	—	—	—	5	—	—
Ontario										
Conservative	46	38	24	59	54	52	48	44	55	48
Liberal	36	50	64	29	37	40	44	43	37	38
Other	—	—	—	—	—	—	—	5	—	—
Manitoba[2]										
Conservative	—	3	2	3	2	4	4	4	4	3
Liberal	—	1	2	1	3	1	1	2	3	7
Other	—	—	—	—	—	—	—	1	—	—
British Columbia[3]										
Conservative		6	6	6	6	6	6	2	2	—
Liberal		—	—	—	—	—	—	4	4	7
Yukon[4]										
Conservative		—	—	—	—	—	—	—	—	1
Northwest Territories[2]										
Conservative	—	—	—	—	—	—	4	4	1	3
Liberal	—	—	—	—	—	—	—	—	2	4	7
Other	—	—	—	—	—	—	—	1	—	—

❦ 1908–1940

	1908	1911	1917[7]	1921	1925	1926	1930	1935	1940
Canada									
Conservative	85	133	153	50	116	91	137	39	39
Liberal	133	86	82	117	101	116	88	171	178
Progressive	—	—	—	64	25	—	2	—	—
CCF	—	—	—	—	—	—	—	7	8
Social Credit	—	—	—	—	—	—	—	17	10
Other	3	2	—	4	3	38	18	11	10
Prince Edward Island									
Conservative	1	2	2	—	2	1	3	—	—
Liberal	3	2	2	4	2	3	1	4	4
Nova Scotia									
Conservative	6	9	12	—	11	12	10	—	1
Liberal	12	9	4	16	3	2	4	12	10
CCF	—	—	—	—	—	—	—	—	1

▶

(1) Entered Confederation July 1, 1873. (2) Entered Confederation July 15, 1870. (3) Entered Confederation July 20, 1871. (4) Entered Confederation June 13, 1898. (5) Entered Confederation Mar. 31, 1949. (6) Entered Confederation Sept. 1, 1905. (7) For the 1917 election, Conservative refers to "Unionists," a coalition of Conservatives and pro-conscription Liberals; Liberals, for the 1917 election, are sometimes called "Laurier Liberals" because of their support for Laurier's anti-conscription stand. (8) The New Democratic Party (NDP) replaced the Co-operative Commonwealth Federation (CCF) in 1961. (9) From 1908–1949 shared one representative. In 1953, the number was increased to two. (10) The Canadian Reform Conservative Alliance (or Canadian Alliance) replaced the Reform party in 2000. (11) Nunavut's first federal election occurred in 2000.

✦ 1908–1940

	1908	1911	1917[7]	1921	1925	1926	1930	1935	1940
New Brunswick									
Conservative	2	5	7	5	10	7	10	1	5
Liberal	11	8	4	5	1	4	1	9	5
Other	—	—	—	1	—	—	—	—	—
Quebec									
Conservative	11	27	3	—	4	4	24	5	—
Liberal	53	37	62	65	60	60	40	55	61
Other	1	1	—	—	1	1	1	5	4
Ontario									
Conservative	48	72	74	37	68	53	59	25	25
Liberal	36	36	8	21	12	23	22	56	55
Progressive	—	—	—	24	2	4	—	—	—
Other	2	1	—	—	—	2	1	1	2
Manitoba									
Conservative	8	8	14	—	7	—	11	1	1
Liberal	2	2	1	2	1	4	1	12	14
CCF	—	—	—	—	—	—	—	2	1
Progressive	—	—	—	12	7	4	—	—	—
Other	—	—	—	1	2	9	5	2	1
Saskatchewan[6]									
Conservative	1	1	16	—	—	—	8	1	2
Liberal	9	9	—	1	15	16	11	16	12
CCF	—	—	—	—	—	—	—	2	5
Progressive	—	—	—	15	6	5	2	—	—
Social Credit	—	—	—	—	—	—	—	2	—
Other	—	—	—	—	—	—	—	—	2
Alberta[6]									
Conservative	3	1	11	—	3	1	4	1	—
Liberal	4	6	1	—	4	3	3	1	7
Progressive	—	—	—	10	9	—	—	—	—
Social Credit	—	—	—	—	—	—	—	15	10
United Farmers of Alta	—	—	—	—	—	11	9	—	—
Other	—	—	—	2	—	1	—	—	—
British Columbia									
Conservative	5	7	13	7	10	12	7	5	4
Liberal	2	—	—	3	3	1	5	6	10
CCF	—	—	—	—	—	—	—	3	1
Progressive	—	—	—	2	1	—	—	—	—
Social Credit	—	—	—	—	—	—	—	—	—
Other	—	—	—	1	—	1	2	2	1
Yukon and Northwest Territories[9]									
Conservative	—	1	—	1	1	1	1	—	1
Liberal	1	—	—	—	—	—	—	—	—
Other	—	—	—	—	—	—	—	1	—

✦ 1945–1968

	1945	1949	1953	1957	1958	1962	1963	1965	1968
Canada									
Conservative	67	41	51	112	208	116	95	97	72
Liberal	125	190	170	105	48	99	129	131	155
NDP (CCF)[8]	28	13	23	25	8	19	17	21	22
Social Credit	13	10	15	19	—	30	24	5	—
Other	12	8	6	4	1	1	—	11	15
Newfoundland[5]									
Conservative	—	2	—	2	2	1	—	—	6
Liberal	—	5	7	5	5	6	7	7	1
NDP (CCF)	—	—	—	—	—	—	—	—	—
Prince Edward Island									
Conservative	1	1	1	4	4	4	2	4	4
Liberal	3	3	3	—	—	—	2	—	—

▶

❖ 1945–1968

	1945	1949	1953	1957	1958	1962	1963	1965	1968
Nova Scotia									
Conservative	3	2	1	10	12	9	7	10	10
Liberal	8	10	10	2	—	2	5	2	1
NDP (CCF)	1	1	1	—	—	1	—	—	—
New Brunswick									
Conservative	3	2	3	5	7	4	4	4	5
Liberal	7	7	7	5	3	6	6	6	5
Other	—	1	—	—	—	—	—	—	—
Quebec									
Conservative	1	2	4	9	50	14	8	8	4
Liberal	54	66	66	63	25	35	47	56	56
NDP (CCF)	—	—	—	—	—	—	—	—	—
Social Credit	—	—	—	—	—	26	20	—	—
Other	10	5	5	3	—	—	—	11	14
Ontario									
Conservative	48	25	33	61	67	35	27	25	17
Liberal	34	56	50	20	14	43	52	51	64
NDP (CCF)	—	—	—	3	3	6	6	9	6
Other	—	2	2	1	1	1	—	—	1
Manitoba									
Conservative	2	1	3	8	14	11	10	10	5
Liberal	10	12	8	1	—	1	2	1	5
NDP (CCF)	5	3	3	5	—	2	2	3	3
Saskatchewan									
Conservative	1	1	1	3	16	16	17	17	5
Liberal	2	14	5	4	—	1	—	—	2
NDP (CCF)	18	5	11	10	1	—	—	—	6
Alberta									
Conservative	2	2	2	3	17	15	14	15	15
Liberal	2	5	4	1	—	—	1	—	4
NDP (CCF)	—	—	—	—	—	—	—	—	—
Social Credit	13	10	11	13	—	2	2	2	—
British Columbia									
Conservative	5	3	3	7	18	6	4	3	—
Liberal	5	11	8	2	—	4	7	7	16
NDP (CCF)	4	3	7	7	4	10	9	9	7
Social Credit	—	—	4	6	—	2	2	3	—
Other	2	1	—	—	—	—	—	—	—
Yukon[9]									
Conservative	1	—	—	—	1	1	1	1	1
Liberal	—	1	2	1	—	—	—	—	—
NDP (CCF)	—	—	—	—	—	—	—	—	—
Northwest Territories[9]									
Conservative	n.a.	n.a.	n.a.	—	—	—	1	—	—
Liberal	n.a.	n.a.	n.a.	1	1	1	—	1	1
NDP (CCF)	n.a.	n.a.	n.a.	—	—	—	—	—	—

❖ 1972–2000

	1972	1974	1979	1980	1984	1988	1993	1997	2000
Canada									
Bloc Québécois	—	—	—	—	—	—	54	44	38
Conservative	107	95	136	103	211	169	2	20	12
Liberal	109	141	114	147	40	83	177	155	172
NDP	31	16	26	32	30	43	9	21	13
Reform/Canadian Alliance[10]	—	—	—	—	—	—	52	60	66
Social Credit	15	11	6	—	—	—	—	—	—
Other	2	1	—	—	1	—	1	1	—
Newfoundland									
Conservative	4	3	2	2	4	2	—	3	2
Liberal	3	4	4	5	3	5	7	4	5
NDP	—	—	1	—	—	—	—	—	—
Prince Edward Island									
Conservative	3	3	4	2	3	—	—	—	—
Liberal	1	1	—	2	1	4	4	4	4
NDP									—

▶ ✦ 1972–2000	1972	1974	1979	1980	1984	1988	1993	1997	2000
Nova Scotia									
Conservative	10	8	8	6	9	5	—	5	4
Liberal	1	2	2	5	2	6	11	—	4
NDP	—	1	1	—	—	—	—	6	—
New Brunswick									
Conservative	5	3	4	3	9	5	1	5	3
Liberal	5	6	6	7	1	5	9	3	6
NDP	—	—	—	—	—	—	—	2	1
Other	—	1	—	—	—	—	—	—	—
Quebec									
Bloc Québécois	—	—	—	—	—	—	54	44	38
Conservative	2	3	2	1	58	63	1	5	1
Liberal	56	60	67	74	17	12	19	26	36
NDP	—	—	—	—	—	—	—	—	—
Social Credit	15	11	6	—	—	—	—	—	—
Other	1	—	—	—	—	—	1	—	—
Ontario									
Conservative	40	25	57	38	67	46	—	1	—
Liberal	36	55	32	52	14	43	98	101	100
NDP	11	8	6	5	13	10	—	—	1
Reform/Canadian Alliance[10]	—	—	—	—	—	—	1	—	2
Other	1	—	—	—	1	—	—	1	—
Manitoba									
Conservative	8	9	7	5	9	7	—	1	1
Liberal	2	2	2	2	1	5	12	6	5
NDP	3	2	5	7	4	2	1	4	4
Reform/Canadian Alliance[10]	—	—	—	—	—	—	1	3	4
Saskatchewan									
Conservative	7	8	10	7	9	4	—	—	—
Liberal	1	3	—	—	—	—	5	1	2
NDP	5	2	4	7	5	10	5	5	2
Reform/Canadian Alliance[10]	—	—	—	—	—	—	4	8	10
Alberta									
Conservative	19	19	21	21	21	25	—	—	1
Liberal	—	—	—	—	—	—	4	2	2
NDP	—	—	—	—	—	1	—	—	—
Reform/Canadian Alliance[10]	—	—	—	—	—	—	22	24	23
British Columbia									
Conservative	8	13	19	16	19	12	—	—	—
Liberal	4	8	1	—	1	1	6	6	5
NDP	11	2	8	12	8	19	2	3	2
Reform/Canadian Alliance[10]	—	—	—	—	—	—	24	25	27
Yukon									
Conservative	1	1	1	1	1	—	—	—	—
Liberal	—	—	—	—	—	—	—	—	1
NDP	—	—	—	—	—	1	1	1	—
Northwest Territories									
Conservative	—	—	1	1	2	—	—	—	—
Liberal	—	—	—	—	—	2	2	2	1
NDP	1	1	1	1	—	—	—	—	—
Nunavut[11]									
Conservative									—
Liberal									1
NDP									—

Minority Party Election Results

*I*n the federal election of 2000, six of the eleven political parties that ran candidates for seats in the House of Commons failed to elect a single person. Of these six parties, the most popular was the Green Party of Canada, which won 104,402 votes. The other parties, ranked in descending order of popularity, were the Marijuana Party (66,258 votes); the Canadian Action Party (27,103 votes); the Natural Law Party of Canada (16,577 votes); the Marxist-Leninist Party of Canada (12,068 votes); and the Communist Party of Canada (8,776 votes).

Source: *Elections Canada*

Federal Election 2000: Total Votes by Province and Party

	Bloc Québécois	Canadian Alliance	Liberal	New Democrat	Progressive Conservative	Other[1]
Newfoundland	—	8 837	103 103	29 993	79 157	8 408
Prince Edward Island	—	3 719	35 021	6 714	28 610	400
Nova Scotia	—	41 752	158 870	104 277	126 557	3 813
New Brunswick	—	60 277	159 803	44 778	116 980	1 174
Quebec	1 377 727	212 874	1 529 642	63 611	192 153	80 891
Ontario	—	1 051 209	2 292 075	368 709	642 438	98 174
Manitoba	—	148 293	158 713	101 741	70 635	8 450
Saskatchewan	—	207 004	89 697	113 626	20 855	2 515
Alberta	—	739 514	263 008	68 363	169 093	16 021
British Columbia	—	797 518	446 624	182 993	117 614	69 972
Yukon	—	3 659	4 293	4 223	991	53
Northwest Territories	—	2 273	5 855	3 430	1 282	—
Nunavut	—	—	5 327	1 410	633	349
Total votes cast	1 377 727	3 276 929	5 252 031	1 093 868	1 566 998	290 220

Source: *Elections Canada. (1) Includes Canadian Action, Communist, Green, Marijuana, Marxist-Leninist, Natural Law, and Independent*

Federal Election 2000: % of Popular Vote by Province and Party

	Bloc Québécois	Canadian Alliance	Liberal	New Democrat	Progressive Conservative	Other[1]
Newfoundland	—	3.9	44.9	13.1	34.5	3.7
Prince Edward Island	—	5.0	47.0	9.0	38.4	0.5
Nova Scotia	—	9.6	36.5	24.0	29.1	0.9
New Brunswick	—	15.7	41.7	11.7	30.5	0.3
Quebec	39.9	6.2	44.2	1.8	5.6	2.3
Ontario	—	23.6	51.5	8.3	14.4	2.2
Manitoba	—	30.4	32.5	20.9	14.5	1.7
Saskatchewan	—	47.7	20.7	26.2	4.8	0.6
Alberta	—	58.9	20.9	5.4	13.5	1.3
British Columbia	—	49.4	27.7	11.3	7.3	4.3
Yukon	—	27.7	32.5	31.9	7.5	0.4
Northwest Territories	—	17.7	45.6	26.7	10.0	—
Nunavut	—	—	69.0	18.3	8.2	4.5
Canada	10.7	25.5	40.8	8.5	12.2	2.3
Total seats	38	66	172	13	12	0

Source: *Elections Canada. (1) Includes Canadian Action, Communist, Green, Marijuana, Marxist-Leninist, Natural Law, and Independent*

Voter Turnout at Canada's Federal Elections, 1867–2000

(percentage of eligible voters casting votes)

Voter turnout[1]	Voter turnout[1]	Voter turnout[1]	Voter turnout[1]	Voter turnout[1]
1867 .... 73%	1900 .... 79%	1930 .... 76%	1958 .... 81%	1979 .... 76%
1872 70	1904 84	1935 75	1962 80	1980 69
1874 75	1908 79	1940 71	1963 80	1984 75
1878 71	1911 72	1945 76	1965 76	1988 76
1882 72	1917 90	1949 75	1968 76	1993 70
1887 70	1921 71	1953 68	1972 77	1997 67
1891 65	1925 69	1957 75	1974 71	2000 61
1896 61	1926 70			

Source: *Elections Canada*

[1]Percentage of actual votes to eligible voters. In many early general elections, several electoral districts were won by acclamation; hence, no eligible voters nor actual votes were recorded. Furthermore, in some of the more remote districts, votes were cast but no voters' lists had been prepared.

Federal Political Party Leaders

■ Progressive Conservative[1] Party

Leader	Term
Sir John A. Macdonald	1854–June 6, 1891
Sir J.J.C. Abbott	June 16, 1891–Dec. 5, 1892
Sir John Thompson	Dec. 5, 1892–Dec. 12, 1894
Sir Mackenzie Bowell	Dec. 21, 1894–Apr. 27, 1896
Sir Charles Tupper	May 1, 1896–Feb. 5, 1901
Sir Robert Borden	Feb. 6, 1901–July 10, 1920
Arthur Meighen	July 10, 1920–Oct. 11, 1926
Hugh Guthrie[2]	Oct. 11, 1926–Oct. 12, 1927
R.B. Bennett	Oct. 12, 1927–July 7, 1938
R.J. Manion	July 7, 1938–May 13, 1940
R.B. Hanson[2]	May 13, 1940–Nov. 12, 1941
Arthur Meighen	Nov. 12, 1941–Dec. 11, 1942
John Bracken	Dec. 11, 1942–Oct. 2, 1948
George A. Drew	Oct. 2, 1948–Dec. 14, 1956
John G. Diefenbaker	Dec. 14, 1956–Sept. 9, 1967
Robert L. Stanfield	Sept. 9, 1967–Feb. 22, 1976
Joe Clark	Feb. 22, 1976–Feb. 8, 1983
Erik Nielsen[2]	Feb. 9, 1983–June 11, 1983
Brian Mulroney	June 11, 1983–June 13, 1993
Kim Campbell	June 13, 1993–Dec. 13, 1993
Jean Charest	Dec. 14, 1993–Apr. 3, 1998
Elsie Wayne[2]	Apr. 6, 1998–Nov. 13, 1998
Joe Clark	Nov. 14, 1998–June 1, 2003
Peter MacKay	June 1, 2003–

■ Liberal Party

Leader	Term
Robert Baldwin	1804–1858
Louis-H. Lafontaine	1807–1864
George Brown	1867–1872
Alexander Mackenzie	Mar. 6, 1873–Apr. 27, 1880
Edward Blake	May 4, 1880–June 2, 1887
Sir Wilfrid Laurier	June 1887–Feb. 17, 1919
Daniel D. McKenzie[2]	Feb. 1919–Aug. 1919
W.L. Mackenzie King	Aug. 7, 1919–Aug. 7, 1948
Louis St. Laurent	Aug. 7, 1948–Jan. 16, 1958
Lester B. Pearson	Jan. 16, 1958–Apr. 2, 1968
Pierre E. Trudeau	Apr. 6, 1968–June 16, 1984
John N. Turner	June 16, 1984–June 23, 1990
Jean Chrétien	June 23, 1990–

■ New Democratic Party[3]

Leader	Term
James S. Woodsworth	Aug. 1932–July 1942
M.J. Coldwell	July 1942–Aug. 1960
Hazen Argue	Aug. 1960–Aug. 1961
Tommy Douglas	Aug. 1961–Apr. 1971
David Lewis	Apr. 24, 1971–July 7, 1975
Ed Broadbent	July 7, 1975–Dec. 2, 1989
Audrey McLaughlin	Dec. 2, 1989–Oct. 1995
Alexa McDonough	Oct. 14, 1995–Jan. 25, 2003
Jack Layton	Jan. 25, 2003–

■ Bloc Québécois

Leader	Term
Lucien Bouchard	June 15, 1991–Jan. 18, 1996
Michel Gauthier	Feb. 17, 1996–Mar. 15, 1997
Gilles Duceppe	Mar. 16, 1997–

■ Canadian Reform Conservative Alliance[4]

Leader	Term
E. Preston Manning	Nov. 1, 1987–July 8, 2000
Stockwell Day	July 8, 2000–Mar. 20, 2002
Stephen Harper	Mar. 20, 2002–

(1) Name changed from Conservative to Progressive Conservative Dec. 1942.
(2) Interim leader appointed to fill a vacancy until a party leadership convention could be held.
(3) Prior to Aug. 1961 party was called the Co-operative Commonwealth Federation (CCF).
(4) Before Jan. 2000, party was called the Reform Party of Canada

Provincial Election Results

■ Newfoundland and Labrador

	1972	1975	1979	1982	1985	1989	1993	1996	1999	2003
Liberal	9	16	19	8	15	31	35	37	32	12
Progressive Conservative	33	30	33	44	36	21	16	9	14	34
New Democratic	—	—	—	—	1	—	1	1	2	2
Other	—	5	—	—	—	—	—	1	—	—
Size of legislature	42	51	52	52	52	52	52	48	48	48

■ Prince Edward Island

	1974	1978	1979	1982	1985	1989	1993	1996	2000	2003
Liberal	26	17	11	14	21	30	31	8	1	4
Progressive Conservative	6	15	21	18	11	2	1	18	26	23
New Democratic	—	—	—	—	—	—	—	1	—	—
Size of legislature	32	32	32	32	32	32	32	27	27	27

■ Nova Scotia

	1970	1974	1978	1981	1984	1988	1993	1998	1999	2003
Liberal	23	31	17	13	6	21	40	19	11	12
New Democratic[1]	2	3	4	1	3	2	3	19	11	15
Progressive Conservative[2]	21	12	31	37	42	28	9	14	30	25
Other	—	—	—	1	1	1	—	—	—	—
Size of legislature	46	46	52	52	52	52	52	52	52	52

■ New Brunswick

	1967	1970	1974	1978	1982	1987	1991	1995	1999	2003
Liberal	32	26	25	28	18	58	46	48	10	26
Progressive Conservative[3]	26	32	33	30	39	—	3	6	44	28
New Democratic	—	—	—	—	1	—	1	1	1	1
Confederation of Regions	—	—	—	—	—	—	8	—	—	—
Size of legislature	58	58	58	58	58	58	58	55	55	55

■ Quebec

	1966	1970	1973	1976	1981	1985	1989	1994	1998	2003
Crédit Social	—	12	2	1	—	—	—	—	—	—
Equality	—	—	—	—	—	—	4	—	—	—
Liberal	50	72	102	26	42	99	92	47	48	76
Parti Québécois[4]	—	7	6	71	80	23	29	77	76	45
Union Nationale	56	17	—	11	—	—	—	—	—	—
Other	2	—	—	1	—	—	—	1	1	4
Size of legislature	108	108	110	110	122	122	125	125	125	125

■ Ontario

	1971	1975	1977	1981	1985	1987	1990	1995	1999	2003
Liberal	20	36	34	34	48	95	36	30	35	72
New Democratic[5]	19	38	33	21	25	19	74	17	9	7
Progressive Conservative[3]	78	51	58	70	52	16	20	82	59	24
Independent	—	—	—	—	—	—	—	1	—	—
Size of legislature	117	125	125	125	125	130	130	130	103	103

■ Manitoba

	1969	1973	1977	1981	1986	1988	1990	1995	1999	2003
Liberal	4	5	1	—	1	20	7	3	1	2
New Democratic[5]	28	31	23	34	30	12	20	23	32	35
Progressive Conservative[6]	22	21	33	23	26	25	30	31	24	20
Other	3	—	—	—	—	—	—	—	—	—
Size of legislature	57	57	57	57	57	57	57	57	57	57

■ Saskatchewan

	1964	1967	1971	1975	1978	1982	1986	1991	1995	1999
Liberal	33	35	15	15	—	—	1	1	11	4
New Democratic[7]	25	24	45	39	44	8	25	55	42	29
Progressive Conservative[8]	1	—	—	7	17	56	38	10	5	—
Saskatchewan Party	—	—	—	—	—	—	—	—	—	25
Size of legislature	59	59	60	61	61	64	64	66	58	58

■ Alberta

	1967	1971	1975	1979	1982	1986	1989	1993	1997	2001
Liberal	3	—	—	—	—	4	8	32[9]	18	7
New Democratic[1]	—	1	1	1	2	16	16	—	22	2
Progressive Conservative[6]	6	49	69	74	75	61	59	51	63	74
Social Credit	55	24	4	4	—	—	—	—	—	—
Other	1	1	1	—	2	2	—	—	—	—
Size of legislature	65	75	75	79	79	83	83	83	83	83

■ British Columbia

	1966	1969	1972	1975	1979	1983	1986	1991	1996	2001
Liberal	6	5	5	1	—	—	—	17	33	77
New Democratic[5]	16	12	38	18	26	21	22	51	39	2
Progressive Conservative[6]	—	—	2	1	—	—	—	—	—	—
Social Credit	33	38	10	35	31	35	47	7	—	—
Other	—	—	—	—	—	1	—	—	3	—
Size of legislature	55	55	55	55	57	57	69	75	75	79

■ Yukon

	1978	1982	1985	1989	1992	1996	2000	2002
Liberal	2	—	2	—	1	3	10	1
New Democratic	1	6	8	9	6	11	6	5
Progressive Conservative	11	10	6	7	—	—	—	—
Yukon Party	—	—	—	—	7	3	1	12
Independent	2	—	—	—	3	—	—	—
Size of legislature	16	16	16	16	17	17	17	18

(1) Known as the Co-operative Commonwealth Federation until 1962. (2) Known as the Conservative Party until 1946. (3) Known as the Conservative Party until 1943. (4) Formed in 1968. (5) Known as the Co-operative Commonwealth Federation until 1961. (6) Known as the Conservative Party until 1944. (7) Known as the Co-operative Commonwealth Federation until 1967. (8) Known as the Conservative Party until 1945. (9) One Alberta Liberal became an independent.

Provincial Party Leaders[1]

(as of October 2003)

■ Newfoundland and Labrador

Progressive Conservative Party		Liberal Party		New Democratic Party	
Tom Rideout	1989–91	Stephen Neary	1984–85	Peter Fenwick	1981–89
Len Simms	1991–95	Leo Barry	1985–87	Cle Newhook	1989–92
Lynn Verge	1995–96	Clyde Wells	1987–96	Jack Harris	1992–
Loyola Sullivan	1996–98	Brian Tobin	1996–2000		
Ed Byrne	1998–2001	Beaton Tulk	2000–01		
Danny Williams	2001–	Roger Grimes	2001–		

■ Prince Edward Island

Progressive Conservative Party		Liberal Party		New Democratic Party	
James M. Lee	1981–87	Catherine Callbeck	1993–96	David Burke	1982–83
Leone Bagnall	1987–88	Keith Milligan	1996–99	Jim Mayne	1983–89
Melbourne Gass	1988–90	Wayne Carew	1999–2000	Larry Duchesne	1991–95
Pat Mella	1990–96	Ron MacKinley	2000–03	Herb Dickieson	1995–2002
Patrick Binns	1996–	Robert Ghiz	2003–	Gary Robichaud	2002–

■ Nova Scotia

Progressive Conservative Party[2]		Liberal Party		New Democratic Party[3]	
George I. Smith	1967–71	J. William Gillis	1985–86	Jeremy Akerman	1968–80
John M. Buchanan	1971–90	Vincent J. MacLean	1986–92	Alexa McDonough	1980–94
Donald Cameron	1991–93	John Savage	1992–97	John Holme	1994–96
Terence R.B. Donahoe	1993–95	Russell MacLellan	1997–2000	Robert Chisholm	1996–2000
Dr. John Hamm	1995–	Wayne Gaudet	2000–02	Helen MacDonald	2000–01
		Danny Graham	2002–	Darrell Dexter	2001–

■ New Brunswick

Progressive Conservative Party		Liberal Party		New Democratic Party	
Richard B. Hatfield	1969–87	Doug Young	1982–83	Elizabeth Weir	1988–
Malcolm MacLeod	1987–89	Frank McKenna	1985–97		
Barbara Baird Filliter	1989–91	Ray Frenette	1997–98		
Dennis Cochrane	1991–95	Camille Theriault	1998–2001		
Bernard Valcourt	1995–97	Bernard Richard	2001–02		
Bernard Lord	1997–	Shawn Graham	2002–		

■ Quebec

Parti Québécois		Parti Libéral		Action démocratique	
René Lévesque	1968–85	Robert Bourassa	1970–77	Mario Dumont	1994–
Pierre-Marc Johnson	1985–88	Claude Ryan	1978–82		
Jacques Parizeau	1988–96	Robert Bourassa	1983–94		
Lucien Bouchard	1996–2001	Daniel Johnson	1994–98		
Bernard Landry	2001–	Jean Charest	1998–		

■ Ontario

Progressive Conservative Party		Liberal Party		New Democratic Party[4]	
Frank Miller	1985	Stuart Smith	1977–81	Stephen H. Lewis	1970–78
Larry Grossman	1985–87	David Peterson	1982–90	Michael Cassidy	1978–82
Andrew Brandt	1987–90	Lyn McLeod	1992–96	Bob Rae	1982–96
Mike Harris	1990–2002	Dalton McGuinty	1996–	Howard Hampton	1996–
Ernie Eves	2002–				

■ Manitoba

Progressive Conservative Party	Liberal Party	New Democratic Party [4]
Sidney Spivak 1971–75	Paul Edwards 1993–96	A. Russell Paulley 1960–69
Sterling Lyon 1975–83	Ginny Hasselfield 1996–98	Edward R. Schreyer 1969–79
Gary Filmon 1983–2000	Neil Gaudry 1998	Howard R. Pawley 1979–88
Bonnie Mitchelson 2000	Jon Gerrard 1998–	Gary Doer 1988–
Stuart Murray 2000–		

■ Saskatchewan

Progressive Conservative Party	Liberal Party	New Democratic Party [4]
Party inactive as of Nov. 9, 1997	Ron Osika 1996	Tommy Douglas 1944–61
	Jim Melenchuk.......... 1996–2001	Woodrow Lloyd 1961–70
Saskatchewan Party	David Karwacki 2001–	Allan Blakeney 1970–78
Ken Karwetz 1997–98		Roy Romanow 1987–2001
Elwin Hermanson 1998–		Lorne Calvert 2001–

■ Alberta

Progressive Conservative Party	Liberal Party	New Democratic Party [4]
Milt Harradance 1962–64	Laurence Decore 1988–94	W. Grant Notley 1968–84
Peter Lougheed 1965–85	Betty Hewes 1994	Ray Martin 1984–94
Donald R. Getty 1985–92	Grant Mitchell 1994–98	Ross Harvey............ 1994–96
Ralph P. Klein 1992–	Nancy MacBeth 1998–2001	Pam Barrett 1996–2000
	Ken Nicol 2001–	Raj Pannu 2000–

■ British Columbia

Reform Party of British Columbia	New Democratic Party	Liberal
Ron Gamble 1993–95	Bob Skelly 1984–87	Jevington Blair Tothill .. 1979–81
Jack Weisgerber 1995–97	Michael Harcourt 1987–96	Shirley McLoughlin 1981–83
Wilf Hanni 1997-98	Glen Clark 1996–99	Arthur Lee 1984–87
Bill Vander Zalm 1998–2001	Dan Miller.............. 1999–2000	Gordon Wilson 1987–93
	Ujjal Dosanjh 2000–01	Gordon Campbell 1993–
	Joy MacPhail........... 2001–	

■ Yukon

Progressive Conservative Party	Liberal Party	New Democratic Party
Willard Phelps.......... 1985–91	Ron Veale 1980–85	Fred Berger 1978–81
Chris Young............ 1991	Roger Coles 1985–92	Tony Penikett 1981–95
	Paul Theriault 1992–95	Piers McDonald 1995–2000
Yukon Party	Ken Taylor 1995–98	Trevor Harding 2000
John Ostashek......... 1991–2000	Pat Duncan 1998–	Eric Fairclough 2001–02
Peter Jenkins........... 2000–02		Todd Hardy 2002–
Dennis Fentie........... 2002–		

(1) Includes 10 provinces and 1 territory (Yukon); excludes the Northwest Territories and Nunavut because they lack party systems.
(2) Known as the Conservative Party until 1946.
(3) Known as the Co-operative Commonwealth Federation until 1962.
(4) Known as the Co-operative Commonwealth Federation until 1961.

DEFENCE

Canadian security policy is based on three elements: defence and collective security, arms control and disarmament, and the peaceful resolution of disputes. The Department of National Defence and the Canadian Forces support this policy by their contributions to strategic deterrence, conventional defence, sovereignty, peacekeeping and arms control.

In addition, the Department of National Defence provides special support to other government depart-

ments for tasks such as search and rescue, fisheries patrols, enforcement of drug prohibitions, disaster relief and aid to civil powers in law enforcement. These tasks are carried out both in emergencies and where they complement military surveillance and control responsibilities.

The Web site of the Department of National Defence and the Canadian Forces is at http://www.forces.gc.ca.

Canadian Regular Armed Forces Strength

Canada has an all-volunteer Armed Forces which, since 1968, has been a single body composed of what had been a separate army, navy and air force.

	Navy	Army	Air Force	Total Armed Forces		Navy	Army	Air Force	Total Armed Forces
1914	379	3 000	—	3 379	1951	11 082	34 986	22 359	68 427
1915	1 255	81 195	—	82 450	1952	13 505	49 278	32 611	95 394
1916	1 557	274 194	—	275 751	1953	15 546	48 458	40 423	104 427
1917	2 220	304 585	—	306 805	1955	19 207	49 409	49 461	118 077
1918	4 792	326 258	—	331 050	1960	20 675	47 185	51 737	119 597
1919	5 495	228 292	—	233 787	1965	19 756	46 264	48 144	114 164
1920	1 048	4 684	—	5 732	1970	—	—	—	93 353
1925	496	3 410	384	4 290	1975	—	—	—	79 817
1930	783	3 510	844	5 137	1980	—	—	—	80 166
1935	860	3 509	794	5 163	1985	—	—	—	83 740
1939	1 585	4 169	2 191	7 945	1990	—	—	—	87 976
1940	6 135	76 678	9 483	92 296	1995	—	—	—	72 079
1941	17 036	194 774	48 743	260 553	1996	—	—	—	61 336
1942	32 067	311 118	111 223	454 408	1997	—	—	—	60 320
1943	56 259	460 387	176 307	692 953	1998	—	—	—	60 942
1944	81 582	495 804	210 089	787 475	1999	—	—	—	58 567
1945	92 529	494 258	174 254	761 041	2000	—	—	—	56 706
1950	9 259	20 652	17 274	47 185	2001	—	—	—	58 479
					2002	—	—	—	60 391
					2003	—	—	—	61 622[1]

Source: *Department of National Defence*   (1) As of July 2003

Senior Canadian Military Personnel

(as of Oct. 1, 2003)

Chief of the Defence Staff...	Gen. Ray R. Henault
Vice-Chief of the Defence Staff.......................................	Lt.-Gen. George Macdonald
Deputy Chief of the Defence Staff.....................................	Vice-Admiral Greg R. Maddison
Chief of the Land Staff..	Lt.-Gen. Rick Hillier
Chief of the Maritime Staff	Vice-Admiral Ron D. Buck
Chief of the Air Staff	Lt.-Gen. Ken Pennie
Canadian Military Representative, North Atlantic Treaty Organization......	Vice-Admiral Bruce MacLean
Deputy Commander-in-Chief, North American Aerospace Defence.........	Lt.-Gen. Eric Findley
Commander, Canadian Defence Liaison Staff (London)	Col. William Neumann
Commander, Canadian Defence Liaison Staff (Washington)..............	Rear Admiral Ian D. Mack

Source: *Department of National Defence*

Canadian Military Ranks

Army/Air Force

General Officers: General, Lieutenant-General, Major-General, Brigadier-General
Senior Officers: Colonel, Lieutenant-Colonel, Major
Junior Officers: Captain, Lieutenant, Second Lieutenant, Officer Cadet
Non-commissioned Members: Chief Warrant Officer, Master Warrant Officer, Warrant Officer, Sergeant, Master Corporal, Corporal, Private

Navy

Flag Officers: Admiral, Vice-Admiral, Rear Admiral, Commodore
Senior Officers: Captain (N), Commander, Lieutenant-Commander
Junior Officers: Lieutenant (N), Sub-Lieutenant, Acting Sub-Lieutenant, Naval Cadet
Non-commissioned Members: Chief Petty Officer 1st class, Chief Petty Officer 2nd class, Petty Officer 1st class, Petty Officer 2nd class, Master Seaman, Leading Seaman, Able Seaman, Ordinary Seaman

Source: *Department of National Defence*

Canadian Forces Units in Canada

National Defence Headquarters in Ottawa oversees a network of military installations across Canada. These installations are classified differently.

Canadian Forces Bases (CFBs) support either land, air or naval units. Canadian Forces Stations (CFSs) are smaller than bases. Stations have fewer resources and personnel; they are organized for operations and lack support capability.

Area Support Units (ASUs) provide food, fuel, maintenance and transportation for nearby operational units. A Canadian Forces Support Unit (CFSU) is similar to an ASU. Forward Operating Locations (FOLs) are unmanned airstrips stocked with aviation fuel for use in emergencies. All FOLs are in the Arctic. The Western Area Training Centre (WATC) is a land force base.

Source: *Department of National Defence*

Air Force Bases:
CFB Bagotville (Que.)
CFB Cold Lake (Alta)
CFB Comox (BC)
CFB Gander (Nfld)
CFB Goose Bay (Nfld)
CFB Greenwood (NS)
CFB Moose Jaw (Sask.)
CFB North Bay (Ont.)
CFB Shearwater (NS)
CFB Trenton (Ont.)
CFB Winnipeg (Man.)

Training Base:
CFB Borden (Ont.)

Land Force Bases:
CFB/ASU Edmonton (Alta)
CFB/ASU Gagetown (NB)
CFB/ASU Kingston (Ont.)
CFB/ASU Montreal (Que.)
CFB/ASU Petawawa (Ont.)
CFB/ASU Shilo (Man.)
CFB/ASU Valcartier (Que.)
CFB Suffield (Alta)
WATC Wainwright (Alta)

Naval Bases:
CFB Esquimalt (BC)
CFB Halifax (NS)

Other Units and Locations:
ASU Calgary (Alta)
ASU Chilliwack (BC)
ASU London (Ont.)
ASU Northern Ontario
ASU Saint-Jean (Que.)
ASU Toronto (Ont.)
CFS St. John's (Nfld)
CFSU Ottawa (Ont.)
FOL Inuvik (NWT)
FOL Iqaluit (Nun.)
FOL Rankin Inlet (Nun.)
FOL Yellowknife (NWT)

Source: *Department of National Defence*

Note: as of October 2003

Operation Athena

Canadian soldiers are keeping order in Afghanistan. Task Force Kabul is working with the NATO-led International Security Assistance Force (ISAF) in the capital city.

The task force consists of:
- soldiers from the 3rd Battalion, Royal Canadian Regiment;
- soldiers from the 2nd Canadian Mechanized Brigade; and
- a National Command Element that liaises with Ottawa.

About 3,600 Canadians will take part in the year-long mission in two six-month rotations of 1,800 troops each. They will provide logistics and air support for the ISAF.

The United Nations authorized the ISAF to provide security for Afghanistan's government and to train the nation's police and military. The ISAF was created on December 6, 2001.

Canadian Participation in UN Peacekeeping and Other Military Missions, 1947–2002

Location	Year	Mission (Canadian participation)
Korea	1947–48	Supervising elections (2)
India, Pakistan	1949–96	Supervising a ceasefire between India and Pakistan (39)
Korea	1950–53	Supervising the Armistice Agreement (6 146)
Korea	1953–2000	Supervising the armistice between North and South (1)
Cambodia, Laos, Vietnam	1954–74	Supervising the withdrawal of French forces (133)
Egypt (Sinai)	1956–67	Supervising the withdrawal of French, British and Israeli forces (1 007)
Lebanon	1958	Preventing infiltration across Lebanese borders (77)
Congo	1960–64	Keeping law and order (421)
West New Guinea (now West Irian)	1962–63	Maintaining peace and security (13)
Yemen	1963–64	Observing the withdrawal of Egyptian troops (36)
Dominican Republic	1965–66	Observing the withdrawal of OAS troops (1)
India, Pakistan	1965–66	Supervising a border ceasefire (112)
Nigeria	1968–70	Observing a ceasefire (2)
Egypt (Sinai)	1973–79	Supervising the redeployment of Israeli and Egyptian forces (1 145)
South Vietnam	1973	Supervising a truce (248)
Southern Lebanon	1978	Confirming the withdrawal of Israeli forces (117)
Afghanistan	1988–90	Confirming the withdrawal of Soviet troops (5)
Iran, Iraq	1988–91	Supervising a ceasefire and the withdrawal of forces (525)
Namibia	1989–90	Aiding the transition to independence (301)
Central America	1989–92	Verifying compliance with the Esquipulas Agreement (174)
Haiti	1990–91	Observing the 1990 elections (11)
Afghanistan, Pakistan	1990–92	Providing military advice (1)
Persian Gulf	1990–91	Securing the liberation of Kuwait
Iraq, Kuwait	1991	Monitoring the demilitarized pre-war boundary at the end of the Persian Gulf War (5)
Iraq, Kuwait	1991–2001	Enforcing UN restrictions on Iraq's trade at sea (236); monitoring the Iraqi-Kuwaiti border (2)
Western Sahara	1991–94	Monitoring a ceasefire; supervising a referendum (34)
Angola	1991–93	Monitoring a ceasefire (15)
Former Yugoslavia and neighbouring states	1991–94	Monitoring a ceasefire (15); reporting on breaches of the Geneva Convention (7)
El Salvador	1991–94	Investigating human rights abuses; monitoring the progress of military reform (55)
El Salvador	1992–95	Investigating human rights abuses; developing a process for military reform and elections (55)
Red Sea	1992	Participating in a naval embargo of Iraq after the Gulf War (250)
Cambodia	1992–93	Monitoring a ceasefire; establishing landmine awareness; monitoring disarmament (240)
Yugoslavia	1992–95	Observing patrols; clearing landmines; building shelters (2 400)
Somalia	1992–93	Providing headquarters staff (12)
Somalia, Kenya	1992–93	Distributing relief supplies (1 250)
Somalia	1993–95	Providing relief and political reconciliation (9)
Haiti	1993–94	Enforcing an embargo (250)
Mozambique	1993–95	Providing security, removing landmines; verifying a ceasefire (4)
Rwanda, Uganda	1993–94	Monitoring the border to enforce a military embargo (3)
Rwanda	1993–96	Providing security for refugees; distributing relief supplies (112)
Yugoslavia	1993–95	Enforcing a no-fly zone (13)
Dominican Republic	1994	Monitoring the DR-Haitian border; providing technical advice to the UN for enforcing a Haitian trade embargo (15)

►

▶ Haiti	1994–96	Providing security and stability for the training of Haiti's military and police and for elections (500)
Guatemala	1996	Verifying a ceasefire agreement (15)
Haiti	1997	Professionalizing the Haitian police (5)
Croatia	1996–2001	Monitoring the demilitarized zone in Prevlaka (1)
Guatemala	1997–98	Monitoring the Comprehensive Agreement on Human Rights (15)
Central African Republic	1998–99	Providing security, police training, advice and technical support (55)
Central Europe	1998–99	Taking part in OSCE military inspections in Macedonia and Slovakia and military evaluations in Estonia and Moldova
Kosovo	1998–2000	Supporting CF-18 fighter jets based in Italy (300)
Kosovo, Macedonia (Former Yugoslav Republic)	1999–2000	Supporting NATO land forces; aiding refugees; rebuilding schools and hospitals
Kosovo	1999–2002	Participating in UN interim administration (1)
Mozambique	1999	Clearing landmines (3)
East Timor	1999–2001	Securing peace and order; supporting a UN mission (650)
Eritrea, Ethiopia	2000–01	Preserving a ceasefire (472)
Eritrea, Ethiopia	2001–03	Monitoring a ceasefire between two countries (6)
Macedonia (Former Yugoslav Republic)	2001	Collecting weapons from armed insurgents (200)

Source: *Department of National Defence*

Canadian Participation in UN Peacekeeping and Other Military Missions

Location	Year	Mission (Canadian participation)
Middle East	1954–	Supervising a 1949 armistice between Israel and Egypt, Lebanon, Jordan and Syria (7)
Cyprus	1964–	Maintaining a ceasefire since 1974 (1)
Israel, Syria	1974–	Supervising a ceasefire at Golan Heights (192)
Egypt (Sinai)	1986–	Supervising the 1979 Camp David Accord (29)
Bosnia-Herzegovina	1995–	Enforcing the Dayton Peace Accords (1 699)
Democratic Republic of Congo	1999–	Investigating ceasefire violations (8)
Sierra Leone	2000–	Monitoring the disarming and demobilizing of combatants (5); reorganizing the government's military (11)
Afghanistan, Arabian Gulf	2001–	Fighting terrorism through maritime and air patrols; providing humanitarian aid; supporting coalition forces (966)
Afghanistan	2003–	Supporting NATO's International Security Assistance Force
Senegal	2003–	Resolving a border dispute between Nigeria and Cameroon (1)
Democratic Republic of Congo	2003–	Supporting a multinational force to restore order at Bunia (50)

Source: *Department of National Defence*

Humanitarian Missions

Aid was brought to		Aid was brought to		Aid was brought to	
1947	Japan	1979	St. Vincent	1996	Haiti
1948	British Columbia	1983	Grenada	1996	Quebec
1960	Congo, Chile	1988–91	Ethiopia	1997	Manitoba
1965	Zambia	1989	Montserrat	1998	Quebec, Ontario,
1967	India	1989–91	Northern Ontario		Nova Scotia, Italy,
1970	Peru	1991	Iraq		Central America
1971	Pakistan	1992	Bahamas, Florida	1999	Turkey
1973	West Africa, Newfoundland	1992–93	Somalia, CIS	2001	Manitoba,
1973–79	Nicaragua	1992–96	Sarajevo		Newfoundland,
1974–89	Manitoba	1993–95	Somalia		Nova Scotia
1974	Saskatchewan	1994, 1996	Rwanda	2002	Afghanistan

Source: *Department of National Defence*

THE ECONOMY

Understanding the Economy: A Glossary of Terms

Appreciation: the increase in the value of a currency relative to other currencies under free market conditions.

Balance of payments: a measure of all yearly business transactions between one country and the rest of the world, i.e., the difference between the value of exports and imports, plus the difference between investment money coming in and leaving.

Balanced budget: when a government's budget is balanced, revenues equal expenditures in a budget year. There is no surplus or deficit, but a national debt may still exist.

Bank of Canada: the sole money-issuing bank in Canada, acting as banker to all other financial institutions and the government. It is responsible for Canada's banking system, sets interest rates and regulates the money supply.

Bank rate: the interest rate at which the Bank of Canada lends money to the chartered banks.

Cartel: a group of companies in a specific industry that band together to restrict output and increase prices to get higher profits. In Canada, cartels are illegal.

Constant dollars: dollars expressed in relation to a specified base year in order to adjust for the effects of inflation (changes in purchasing power). Costs or income expressed in constant dollars compared over a range of time give a truer picture of price changes. Also called "real dollars."

Consumer price index: an indexed measure of the average prices of certain specified household goods to show inflationary trends; compiled monthly by Statistics Canada.

Cost of living: the cost of maintaining a particular standard of living measured in terms of purchased goods and services. The rise in the cost of living is the same as the rate of inflation.

Current dollars: cost of an asset or service expressed at the price in effect when it was acquired, i.e. prices are not adjusted for inflation.

Deficit spending: the practice whereby a government goes into debt to finance some expenditures.

Deflation: a decline in price levels, often caused by a reduction in the supply of money or credit.

Depreciation: the decrease in the value of a currency relative to other currencies under free market conditions. This differs from devaluation.

Depression: a long period of little business activity when prices are low, unemployment is high, and purchasing power decreases sharply.

Devaluation: the official lowering of the value of a nation's currency relative to foreign currencies.

Disposable income: income after taxes available to persons for spending and saving.

Equalization payments: transfers of tax revenues from the Canadian government to provinces with a high proportion of lower-income earners as compensation for their lower per capita tax revenues.

Exchange rate: the price of one country's currency relative to another country's currency.

Fiscal policy: the use of government budget measures (taxation and/or spending) to alleviate economic problems such as low GNP, high unemployment or inflation.

Free trade: the free movement of goods and services, investment money and workers between countries is neither restricted nor encouraged by governments.

Gross domestic product (GDP): the value of all goods and services produced in a country.

Gross national product (GNP): the value of all goods and services produced by citizens of a country both inside and outside the country.

Inflation: a steady rise in the average level of prices in an economy.

Less developed countries (LDCs): also known as Third World countries, these are countries considered economically underdeveloped relative to the western industrialized nations.

Monetary policy: the government's manipulation of interest rates and the money supply to achieve economic growth, employment and price stability.

Money supply: the amount of money in an economy, with money defined as all currency in circulation and in chequing accounts.

National debt: the debt of the central government; in Canada's case, the federal government.

Per capita GNP: also known as per capita income, a nation's gross national product divided by its population.

Prime interest rate: the rate charged by chartered banks on short-term loans to large commercial customers with the best credit ratings.   ▶

▶ **Protectionism:** government policies to protect domestic industries by restricting imports. Policies include customs duties (tariffs) and restrictions on the quantity of imports (quotas).

Real GNP: GNP adjusted for inflation.

Recession: not as severe or long-lasting as a depression but with the same general characteristics: a decline in real GNP for two consecutive quarters, with unemployment and widespread softening in many sectors of the economy.

Stagflation: a high inflation rate combined with a high unemployment rate.

Supply-side economics: a belief that an economy can prosper through policies affecting costs of production—i.e., production incentives to labour and greater financial rewards to investors.

Trade balance: the difference between the value of exports and imports.

Transfer payments: government payments to the provinces where no productive return is provided, such as pensions, EI and welfare.

Wage-price controls: wage, salary and price increases are set by government legislation to curb inflation.

Wage-price spiral: increased wages increase costs to the producers, who in turn increase prices. The increase in prices causes a demand for higher wages, resulting in spiralling inflation.

ECONOMIC INDICATORS

Canadian Gross Domestic Product

(millions of dollars)

Gross domestic product is the unduplicated value of production originating within Canada, regardless of the ownership of the factors of production.

There are three ways to measure the GDP: *Income Based Approach*: adding up all incomes earned in current production; *Expenditure Based Approach*: adding up all sales of current production to final users; or *Value Added Approach*: summing the difference between an industry's total revenue and the costs of materials and services purchased by that company.

In addition, there are two ways to express GDP: at Market Prices or at Factor Cost. At *Market Prices*: GDP is expressed in terms of the prices actually paid by the purchaser of the product or service—including indirect taxes, but excluding subsidies. GDP at *Factor Cost* reflects the costs of the factors of production—expressed in terms of the expenses of the producer rather than the purchase price—again, including subsidies but not indirect taxes.

The costs themselves are then expressed either in Current Dollars—the prices in effect at the time that the data is for, or in Constant Dollars—also known as "real dollars." These are dollar figures adjusted for inflation growth in the economy. Constant Dollars allow us to compare data from different time periods (trends). The table below shows expenditure-based real GDP at market prices.

Expenditure-based GDP at Market Prices[1]

(millions of dollars)

Expenditure-based estimates	1993	1997	2001	2002	2003
Gross Domestic Product (GDP) at market prices ...	772 498	882 734	1 037 714	1 071 389	1 090 242
Personal expenditure on consumer goods and services	452 701	510 695	583 050	603 334	619 590
Government current expenditure on goods and services	178 686	171 756	192 611	198 311	202 780
Government gross fixed capital formation	20 355	20 104	27 033	30 189	31 838
Government investment in inventories	-3	5	13	-40	16
Business gross fixed capital formation	115 277	154 737	187 748	187 901	193 324
Residential structures......................	41 278	43 519	50 492	57 610	60 562
Non-residential structures and equipment	74 150	111 218	137 256	130 291	132 762
Non-residential structures.................	33 436	43 872	48 203	43 211	42 470
Machinery and equipment.................	41 119	67 346	89 053	87 080	90 292
Business investment in inventories............	-1314	8 176	-5406	2327	13 114
Business investment in non-farm inventories	-2640	9 174	-3748	3954	11 554
Business investment in farm inventories.......	1413	-998	-1658	-1627	1 564
Exports of goods and services	244 260	348 604	441 795	440 838	433 394
Deduct: Imports of goods and services........	236 738	331 271	388 078	391 058	404 002
Statistical discrepancy	-2015	-72	-1052	-413	184
Final domestic demand	767 177	857 292	990 442	1 019 735	1 047 532

Source: *Statistics Canada*

(1) Constant (1997) dollars.

Canadian Consumer Price Index by Year

(1992 = 100)

1915	7.3	1962	18.9	1977	40.0	1992	100.0
1920	13.5	1963	19.2	1978	43.6	1993	101.8
1925	10.9	1964	19.6	1979	47.6	1994	102.0
1930	10.9	1965	20.0	1980	52.4	1995	104.2
1935	8.6	1966	20.8	1981	58.9	1996	105.8
1940	9.5	1967	21.5	1982	65.3	1997	107.6
1945	10.8	1968	22.4	1983	69.1	1998	108.6
1950	14.9	1969	23.4	1984	72.1	1999	110.5
1955	16.8	1970	24.2	1985	75.0	2000	113.5
1956	17.1	1971	24.9	1986	78.1	2001	116.4
1957	17.6	1972	26.1	1987	81.5	2002	119.0
1958	18.0	1973	28.1	1988	84.8	2003[1]	122.1
1959	18.2	1974	31.1	1989	89.0		
1960	18.5	1975	34.5	1990	93.3		
1961	18.7	1976	37.1	1991	98.5		

Source: © *Statistics Canada*   (1) As of July 2003.

Canadian Consumer Price Index by Item

(1992 = 100)

This table shows the relative costs, as far back as 1950, of categories of purchases made by Canadian consumers. To compare 2003 costs with those of another year, divide the 2003 index by the index for the year you wish to compare it with; then multiply that by your actual cost in the year for which you are making the comparison.

Example: you spent $65 per week on family food purchases in 1985. To calculate what that would be in today's dollars, divide the 2003 food index (122.6) by the 1985 food index (78.8). Now multiply the result by $65. The answer, $101.13, is what you now must spend to buy the same package of groceries that cost $65 in 1985.

	Food	Shelter	Household Oper. & Furn.	Clothing and Footwear	Trans-portation	Health and Personal Care	Recreation and Education	Tobacco and Alcohol
1950	14.2	n.a	n.a	23.4	14.8	12.0	15.7	11.3
1955	15.5	n.a	n.a	25.3	16.6	14.9	18.9	11.8
1960	16.8	n.a	n.a	26	19.7	18.2	22.3	12.7
1965	18.8	n.a	n.a	28.5	20.7	20.6	23.8	13.4
1970	22.2	n.a	n.a	33.5	24.6	25.5	29.6	16.2
1975	36.4	n.a	n.a	42.5	33.1	34.6	39.3	20.6
1980	58.6	50.2	60.3	60.7	51.4	51.8	53.0	30.4
1985	78.8	74.7	82.3	75.2	79.6	73.0	72.9	52.9
1990	95.8	93.9	95.8	90.6	96.3	91.4	92.5	80.6
1991	100.4	98.2	99.5	99.1	98.0	97.8	98.9	94.4
1992	100.0	100.0	100.0	100.0	100.0	100.0	100.0	100
1993	101.6	101.4	101.0	101.0	103.2	102.7	102.4	101.6
1994	102.1	101.8	101.2	101.8	107.8	103.6	105.4	85.0
1995	104.5	102.9	103.1	101.7	113.4	103.5	109.5	84.9
1996	105.9	103.1	105.3	101.4	117.8	104.1	112.1	86.6
1997	107.6	103.3	106.6	102.7	121.5	105.9	114.9	89.3
1998	109.3	103.7	108.2	103.9	120.5	108.1	117.5	92.6
1999	110.7	105.1	109.0	105.3	124.5	110.2	119.6	94.5
2000	112.2	108.8	110.0	105.5	130.7	112.0	122.5	97.6
2001	117.2	112.8	112.2	106.0	130.8	114.2	124.3	105.1
2002	120.3	113.8	113.8	105.2	134.4	115.5	126.3	123.6
2003	122.6	117.0	114.4	103.0	141.7	116.6	126.9	134.7

Source: © *Statistics Canada*   (n.a.) Not available.

Canadian Inflation Rate by Year

This table shows annual inflation rates, as measured by the percentage change in the Consumer Price Index (CPI) from one year to the next. The CPI, determined monthly by Statistics Canada, is a "weighted" average of the cost of a package of goods and services — such as food, clothing, housing and health care — normally purchased by Canadian households. Weighted average means that some items are given more importance according to the proportion of household income spent on them.

Prices increase for several reasons: rising production costs, limited availability of the commodity, unfavourable exchange rates pushing up import prices, excessive consumer demand and too much currency in the economy.

Year	Rate	Year	Rate	Year	Rate	Year	Rate
1915	1.4	1959	1.7	1975	10.9	1991	5.6
1920	16.4	1960	1.1	1976	7.5	1992	1.5
1925	1.9	1961	1.1	1977	7.8	1993	1.8
1930	-0.9	1962	1.1	1978	9.0	1994	0.2
1935	1.2	1963	1.6	1979	9.2	1995	2.2
1940	3.3	1964	2.1	1980	10.1	1996	1.6
1945	0.9	1965	2.0	1981	12.4	1997	1.6
1950	2.8	1966	4.0	1982	10.9		
1951	10.1	1967	3.4	1983	5.8	1998	0.9
1952	3.0	1968	4.2	1984	4.3	1999	1.7
1953	-1.2	1969	4.5	1985	4.0	2000	2.7
1954	0.6	1970	3.4	1986	4.1	2001	2.6
1955	0.0	1971	2.9	1987	4.4		
1956	1.8	1972	4.8	1988	4.0	2002	1.3
1957	2.9	1973	7.7	1989	5.0	2003[1]	2.6
1958	2.3	1974	10.7	1990	4.8		

Source: © *Statistics Canada*

(1) As of July 2003.

Canadian Unemployment Rates[1]

	1980	1985	1990	1995	1997	1999	2000	2001	2002
Canada	7.5	10.7	8.1	9.4	9.1	7.6	6.8	7.2	7.7
Newfoundland & Labrador	13.1	20.8	16.9	18.1	18.6	16.9	16.7	16.1	16.9
Prince Edward Island	10.5	13.5	14.6	15.0	15.4	14.4	12.0	11.9	12.1
Nova Scotia	9.7	13.6	10.5	12.1	12.1	9.6	9.1	9.7	9.7
New Brunswick	11.1	15.3	12.1	11.2	12.7	10.2	10.0	11.2	10.4
Quebec	10.0	12.2	10.4	11.4	11.4	9.3	8.4	8.7	8.6
Ontario	6.8	8.1	6.2	8.7	8.4	6.3	5.7	6.3	7.1
Manitoba	5.5	8.4	7.3	7.2	6.5	5.6	4.9	5.0	5.2
Saskatchewan	4.2	8.3	7.0	6.6	5.9	6.1	5.2	5.8	5.7
Alberta	3.8	10.0	6.8	7.8	5.8	5.7	5.0	4.6	5.3
British Columbia	6.6	14.5	8.6	8.4	8.4	8.3	7.2	7.7	8.5

Source: © *Statistics Canada*

(1) Percentage of labour force.

1992 = 100

*A*ll indexes measuring changes over time must have a specified time base. The time base is the reference point against which all levels are compared. Without a common time base, the indexes are meaningless. When quoting an index figure, the time base should always be included [e.g., all-items CPI in 1985 was 75.0 (1992 = 100)].

As of January 1998, the time base changed from 1986 to 1992. All constant dollar series were converted to 1992 dollars during the process, including historical tables for CPI.

New Vehicle Sales

	Total, new motor vehicles		Passenger cars		Commercial vehicles[1]	
	Units	Dollars ($ 000)	Units	Dollars ($ 000)	Units	Dollars ($ 000)
1996	1 204 557	31 485 777	660 769	14 510 882	543 788	16 974 894
1997	1 424 380	38 986 224	738 550	16 836 615	685 830	22 149 610
1998	1 428 932	40 255 777	740 809	17 054 244	688 123	23 201 534
1999	1 542 041	45 317 914	806 450	19 017 278	735 591	26 300 638
2000	1 587 561	46 930 514	849 171	20 790 660	738 390	26 139 852
2001	1 597 964	46 886 252	868 633	21 168 628	729 331	25 717 623
2002	1 733 318	52 225 955	934 705	23 191 161	798 618	29 035 793

	Passenger cars made in North America		Passenger cars made overseas		Commercial vehicles[1] made in North America		Commercial vehicles[1] made overseas	
	Units	Dollars ($ 000)	Units	Dollars ($ 000)	Units	Dollars ($ 000)	Units	Dollars ($ 000)
1996	572 581	12 062 092	88 188	2 448 790	517 738	16 115 584	26 050	859 309
1997	629 488	13 809 161	109 062	3 027 455	628 214	20 341 263	57 616	1 808 346
1998	590 667	13 101 703	150 142	3 952 538	627 256	21 165 239	60 867	2 036 296
1999	625 292	14 138 902	181 158	4 878 374	672 444	24 055 653	63 147	2 244 986
2000	640 856	15 089 665	208 315	5 700 993	669 492	23 745 933	68 898	2 393 922
2001	519 810	14 575 745	248 823	6 592 884	647 987	22 958 458	81 344	2 759 162
2002	651 305	15 521 295	283 400	7 659 870	698 870	25 633 136	99 743	3 402 655

Source: *Statistics Canada*   (1) Includes minivans, sport-utility vehicles, light and heavy trucks, vans and buses.

Construction in Canada—Building Permits

(millions of dollars)

	Total	Annual % Change	Residential	Non-Residential Total	Industrial	Commercial	Institutional and Government
1960	2 025	-14.9	944	1 080	184	433	460
1965	3 810	16.6	1 757	2 053	430	783	840
1970	4 700	-4.0	2 312	2 389	498	807	1 084
1975	10 598	14.2	6 129	4 469	876	2 251	1 342
1980	15 452	9.2	7 468	7 984	1 911	4 322	1 751
1985	19 524	25.9	10 883	8 641	1 885	4 640	2 116
1990	32 131	-18.3	17 424	14 706	3 393	7 975	3 338
1991	28 468	-11.4	16 632	11 836	2 120	5 906	3 811
1992	26 995	-5.2	17 161	9 834	1 643	4 918	3 273
1993	25 586	-5.2	16 433	9 154	1 756	4 268	3 130
1994	27 637	8.0	17 590	10 047	2 250	4 993	2 803
1995	24 595	-11.0	13 242	11 353	2 823	5 441	3 089
1996	26 155	6.4	15 718	10 347	2 643	5 567	2 227
1997	30 838	17.9	18 317	12 521	3 455	6 520	2 546
1998	33 341	8.1	17 945	15 395	4 261	8 115	3 019
1999	35 736	7.2	19 957	15 779	3 630	8 463	3 686
2000	36 950	3.4	20 342	16 608	3 976	8 907	3 726
2001	39 555	7.0	21 996	17 560	3 598	8 856	5 105
2002	46 304	17.0	29 424	16 880	3 263	8 212	5 405

Source: © *Statistics Canada*

Industrial Capacity Use Rates

An industry's "capacity use rate" is the ratio of actual production versus estimated potential production. Statistics Canada makes estimates of an industry's potential output from measures of that industry's physical resources and consults companies to produce survey-based industry measures. A company's measure of its level of operation, as a percentage of potential, takes into account changes in the obsoles-cence of facilities, capital-to-labour ratios and other characteristics of production techniques.

Capacity use (or utilization) rate is another measure of the level of economic activity. In September 2002, Statistics Canada reported that, overall, industries were working at 83.2% capacity during the second quarter of the year, up from 81.9% in the first quarter of the year.

Manufacturing

	Total	Machinery	Transportation	Computer and products	Electrical products	Primary Metals
1990	78.2	70.2	74.5	72.1	85.4	85.1
1991	74.2	63.1	72.2	69.6	74.1	81.0
1992	76.4	65.4	71.0	72.8	71.9	83.4
1993	79.9	74.3	77.2	70.5	76.4	90.2
1994	83.5	81.0	81.9	77.3	82.4	93.1
1995	83.9	85.4	86.2	84.9	79.4	88.3
1996	82.8	80.1	84.8	76.2	83.6	88.0
1997	83.6	84.8	86.4	79.3	85.2	89.0
1998	84.3	80.4	86.4	85.0	91.0	93.8
1999	85.8	80.0	89.5	91.2	93.7	91.0
2000	86.2	83.6	89.0	96.8	92.6	90.7
2001	81.9	79.3	86.0	72.1	76.3	88.6
2002	83.5	80.0	88.9	66.8	73.1	91.2

	Wood	Clothing	Paper	Petroleum	Chemicals
1990	74.0	78.1	83.7	87.5	86.6
1991	70.6	76.1	84.5	82.6	80.7
1992	81.6	77.0	88.1	83.6	81.0
1993	90.2	79.7	88.0	86.9	83.9
1994	91.1	80.4	94.3	87.3	84.7
1995	86.7	81.0	92.0	89.5	85.2
1996	86.4	83.0	89.1	92.8	86.3
1997	84.5	85.1	90.4	93.1	80.2
1998	86.5	84.1	86.1	95.5	81.2
1999	83.5	85.6	90.9	94.4	80.9
2000	85.1	84.0	92.1	93.6	80.1
2001	82.0	82.0	88.6	94.9	80.4
2002	93.8	81.9	90.4	96.4	81.1

Non-Manufacturing

	Total non-farm	Construction	Forestry	Mining	Utilities
1990	81.6	91.1	82.2	82.8	80.7
1991	78.3	83.6	78.1	83.6	84.2
1992	78.2	78.8	82.7	83.0	79.7
1993	80.0	76.3	84.8	84.3	81.0
1994	82.4	78.8	81.3	83.7	82.0
1995	81.6	75.8	81.3	81.1	79.7
1996	81.2	78.6	76.0	78.0	82.7
1997	82.5	83.1	81.4	78.1	82.2
1998	83.2	84.4	82.0	77.2	84.3
1999	84.2	86.5	81.8	75.2	83.8
2000	85.4	86.6	82.0	79.2	88.5
2001	82.2	86.4	76.8	76.6	87.5
2002	82.2	84.5	77.2	71.9	88.5

Source: *Statistics Canada*

Annual Bankruptcies in Canada

	Personal	Business	Total		Personal	Business	Total
1970	2 732	2 927	5 659	1992	61 822	14 317	76 139
1975	8 335	2 958	11 293	1993	54 456	12 527	66 983
1980	21 025	6 595	27 620	1994	53 802	11 810	65 612
				1995	65 432	13 258	78 690
1985	19 752	8 663	28 415	1996	79 631	14 229	93 860
1986	21 765	8 502	30 267	1997	85 297	12 200	97 497
1987	24 384	7 659	32 043	1998	75 465	10 791	86 256
1988	25 817	8 031	33 848	1999	72 997	10 026	83 023
1989	29 202	8 664	37 866	2000	75 137	10 055	85 192
1990	42 782	11 642	54 424	2001	79 453	10 405	89 858
1991	62 277	13 496	75 773	2002	78 232	9 472	87 704

Source: *Bankruptcy Branch, Industry Canada*

Commercial Bankruptcies by Industry

	1997	1999	2000	2001	2002
All industries	12 200	10 026	10 055	10 405	9 472
Agriculture and related services	276	287	263	272	228
Fishing and trapping	84	22	18	12	10
Logging and forestry	173	151	143	203	150
Mining, quarrying and oil wells	31	66	66	32	61
Manufacturing	862	750	776	913	804
Construction	1 680	1 445	1 490	1 410	1 361
Transportation and storage	802	715	861	1 074	932
Communications and other utilities	148	116	118	126	135
Wholesale trade	749	479	552	519	480
Retail trade	2 579	1 964	1 821	1 814	1 451
Finance and insurance	92	89	87	120	117
Real estate operators and insurance agents	272	175	190	133	138
Business services	851	725	753	804	758
Government services	17	23	27	39	44
Educational services	42	26	36	62	31
Health and social services	231	128	133	141	123
Accommodation, food and beverage services	1 805	1 396	1 310	1 311	1 033
Other service industries	1 506	1 469	1 411	1 420	1 616

Source: *Statistics Canada*

Consumer Bankruptcies by Province, 2001[1]

	Total Bankruptcies	Total Assets $	Total Liabilities $	Total Deficiency $
Canada	78 232	2 386 961 093	4 421 870 361	2 034 909 268
Newfoundland and Labrador	1 930	55 989 197	82 196 545	26 207 348
Nova Scotia	3 255	99 376 375	139 081 329	39 704 954
Prince Edward Island	165	5 346 130	9 731 869	4 385 739
New Brunswick	1 823	59 409 128	85 188 295	25 779 167
Quebec	21 734	379 707 528	981 268 157	601 560 630
Ontario	27 054	835 267 735	1 695 961 739	860 694 004
Manitoba	2 437	78 413 102	125 948 809	47 535 708
Saskatchewan	2 008	82 949 549	104 196 330	21 246 781
Alberta	8 231	356 134 723	435 341 746	79 207 023
British Columbia	9 531	431 201 161	757 964 634	326 763 474
Northwest Territories	33	1 166 662	2 614 789	1 448 127
Yukon	27	1 833 493	2 015 915	182 422
Nunavut	4	166 311	360 203	193 892

Sources: *Bankruptcy Branch, Industry Canada*   (1) Total consumer bankruptcies reported in the calendar year.

FEDERAL GOVERNMENT SPENDING

Federal Ministry Spending

(millions of dollars)

Department	1987-88	1997-98	2000-01	2001–02
Agriculture and Agri-Food	3 386.6	1 911.7	2 736	2 936
Canada Customs and Revenue Agency	1 328.5	2 441.9	4 561	32 936
Canadian Heritage (Communications)	1 706.5	2 619.6	3 124	3 409
Citizenship and Immigration	—	748.8	1 002	1 048
Consumer and Corporate Affairs	533.7	—[1]	—[1]	—[1]
Energy, Mines & Resources	1 335.8	—[2]	—[2]	—[2]
Environment	784.9	557.9	651	854
Finance	35 973.6	64 439.9	74 342	69 911
Fisheries and Oceans	608.5	1 151.5	1 528	1 512
Foreign Affairs and International Trade (External Affairs)	3 172.8	3 363.8	3 833	4 074
Governor General (and Lieutenant-Governors)	8.1	11.2	16	18
Health	—	1 884.3	2 717	3 210
Human Resources Development	—	24 943.5	27 022	27 873
Indian and Northern Affairs	2 824.1	4 555.9	5 107	5 145
Industry	—	4 523.2	4 077	4 908
Justice	567.9	828.1	1 258	1 373
Labour	222.7	—[3]	—[3]	—[3]
Manpower/Employment and Immigration	4 622.5	—[3]	—[3]	—[3]
National Defence	10 650.4	10 187.3	11 470	12 254
National Health and Welfare	28 973.6	—[4]	—[4]	—[4]
Natural Resources	—	753.3	920	1 186
Parliament	225.2	296.5	345	394
Privy Council	88.2	339.4	469	334
Public Works and Government Services	2 925.1	3 757.0	4 313	4 442
Regional Economic (Industrial) Expansion	1 425.7	—[1]	—[1]	—[1]
Science and Technology	799.2	—[1]	—[1]	—[1]
Secretary of State	3 382.7	—[5]	—[5]	—[5]
Solicitor General	1 905.3	2 738.0	3 135	3 583
Supply & Services	768.8	—[6]	—[6]	—[6]
Transport	4 758.6	2 256.4	940	1 220
Treasury Board	417.8	1 150.6	4 179	1 554
Veterans Affairs	1 611.7	1 934.7	2 109	2 247
Total	**115 110.5**	**141 298.8**	**159 854**	**156 928**

Source: *Public Accounts of Canada*

(1) See Industry.

(2) See Natural Resources.

(3) Responsibilities moved to Human Resources Development.

(4) See Health.

(5) Split between Canadian Heritage and Human Resources Development.

(6) See Public Works.

Statement of Assets and Liabilities

as at March 31, 2002 (millions of dollars)

	2001	2002
Assets		
Cash and Accounts Receivable		
Cash in bank	13 237	12 026
Cash in transit	6 956	7 280
Less outstanding cheques and warrants	(4 599)	(5 839)
Accounts receivable[1]	3 592	3 362
Foreign Exchange Accounts	50 270	52 046
Loans, Investments and Advances		
Enterprise Crown corporations[2]	10 085	9,192
National governments including developing countries and international organizations	7 541	7 342
Provincial and territorial governments and other loans, investments and advances	5 661	10 043
Portfolio investments	1 240	1 240
Less allowance for valuation	(8 485)	(9 071)
Total Assets	**85 498**	**87 621**
Accumulated Deficit	**547 378**	**536 489**
Liabilities		
Current Liabilities and Allowances		
Accounts payable and accrued liabilities	25 028	23 617
Interest and matured debt	9 107	7 817
Allowance for employee benefits	5 558	5 169
Allowance for loan guarantees and for borrowings of Crown corporations ...	3 951	4 076
Interest-Bearing Debt		
Unmatured debt payable in Canadian currency		
Marketable bonds	294 973	293 843
Treasury bills	88 700	94 039
Canada savings bonds	26 099	23 966
Non-marketable bonds and notes	3 473	3 391
Unmatured debt payable in foreign currencies	33 158	27 032
Public sector pensions	129 185	126 921
Due to Canada Pension Plan	6 391	6 770
Other pension and other accounts	7 253	7 469
Total Liabilities	**632 876**	**624 110**

Source: *Public Works and Government Services Canada (Receiver General)*

(1) Net of allowance for doubtful accounts of $1,373 million in 2000; $1,318 million in 2001; $1,178 million in 2002.

(2) Also includes other government business enterprises.

Interest on Public Debt

(millions of dollars)[1]

	Mun.	Prov.	Fed.	Total		Mun.	Prov.	Fed.	Total
1985	3 298	12 549	24 738	40 585	1994	4 219	25 221	40 157	69 597
1986	3 313	13 693	26 216	43 222	1995	4 316	26 957	46 254	77 527
1987	3 340	15 056	27 883	46 279	1996	4 176	26 756	45 352	76 284
1988	3 365	15 730	31 711	50 806	1997	3 949	26 679	43 407	74 035
1989	3 495	17 366	37 424	58 285	1998	3 588	27 978	43 910	75 476
1990	3 722	18 684	41 880	64 286	1999	3 412	27 986	43 632	75 030
1991	3 886	19 587	41 053	64 526	2000	3 204	28 364	45 145	76 713
1992	4 089	21 594	39 558	65 241	2001	3 016	28 286	41 471	72 773
1993	4 295	23 337	39 219	66 851	2002	2 952	27 586	35 734	66 272

Source: *© Statistics Canada*

(1) Expressed in constant dollars, 1992 = 100.

Statement of Revenue and Expenditure

for the Year Ended March 31, 2002 (net, millions of dollars)

	2001	2002
Revenue		
Tax revenue		
Income tax		
Personal	82 305	83 790
Corporation	28 212	24 013
Other income tax revenues	4 312	3 035
Employment insurance premiums	18 731	17 980
Excise tax and duties		
Goods and services tax	24 990	24 910
Energy taxes	4 805	4 758
Customs import duties	2 807	3 017
Other excise taxes and duties	3 514	3 953
Non-tax Revenue		
Return on investments	6 144	5 891
Other non-tax revenue	2 770	1 968
Total Revenue	**178 590**	**173 315**
Expenditure		
Transfer payments		
Old age security benefits, guaranteed income supplements and spouse's allowances	24 256	25 365
Other levels of government	23 724	26 616
Employment insurance benefits	11 444	13 748
Other transfer payments	23 503	19 854
Crown Corporation expenditures	2 903	4 082
Other program expenditures		
National Defence	9 696	10 571
All other departments and agencies	23 822	26 437
Public debt charges	42 094	37 735
Total Expenditure	**161 442**	**164 408**
Surplus	**17 148**	**8 907**

Source: *Public Works and Government Services Canada (Receiver General)*

Annual Federal Government Expenditure

(millions of dollars)[1]

	Total Expenditure	Expenditure on Goods & Services	Transfer Payments[2]	Interest on Public Debt
1975	35 364	9 369	22 290	3 705
1980	60 846	15 335	35 614	9 897
1985	112 318	26 657	60 923	24 738
1990	151 488	34 965	74 643	41 880
1995	172 390	37 777	88 359	46 254
1996	166 086	36 610	84 124	45 352
1997	160 069	35 019	81 643	43 407
1998	163 684	36 268	83 506	43 910
1999	171 865	37 909	90 324	43 632
2000	178 786	42 005	91 636	45 145
2001	183 917	43 077	99 369	41 471
2002	182 552	45 660	101 158	35 734

Source: © *Statistics Canada*

(1) Expressed in constant dollars, 1992 = 100.

(2) Includes payments to persons, businesses, non-residents, and provinces and local administrations.

Federal Transfers to Provinces and Territories

The federal government transfers cash and tax revenues to the provinces and territories every year in order to support the delivery of programs and services in health care, post secondary education, social assistance, social services and early childhood development. The goal is to ensure that, as much as possible, all Canadians receive comparable levels of public services, regardless of where they live.

Most of the transfers are administered through three programs:

- The Canada Health and Social Transfer (CHST) is a combination of cash and tax transfers in a block fund to provide support for health care, post-secondary education, social assistance and social services. In 2001-02, the CHST accounted for $33 billion of federal spending.
- The Equalization Program provides less prosperous provinces with enough revenue to fund reasonably comparable services without unduly increasing taxation. This money is transferred without conditions, for the provincial governments to spend as they feel necessary. In 2001-02, eight provinces received $10.3 billion.
- The Territorial Formula Financing (TFF) was established to ensure that territorial governments can provide comparable services despite the higher costs of doing business in and residing in the North. TFF funding totaled $1.5 billion in 2001-02.
- Several smaller transfer programs, totalling $1.7 billion in 2001-02, also assist the provinces and territories.

In the fiscal year 2001-02, total transfers to the provinces and territories was $46.5 billion, or $1,444 per person, accounting for around 24 per cent of all provincial and territorial revenues.

	2000-01 ($ millions)	2001-02 ($ millions)
NEWFOUNDLAND AND LABRADOR		
- CHST	567	591
- Equalization/ TFF	1 124	1 074
Total[1]	**1 572**	**1 549**
PRINCE EDWARD ISLAND		
- CHST	143	153
- Equalization/TFF	273	260
Total[1]	**389**	**387**
NOVA SCOTIA		
- CHST	981	1 044
- Equalization/TFF	1 408	1 326
Total[1]	**2 258**	**2 244**
NEW BRUNSWICK		
- CHST	784	838
- Equalization/TFF	1 252	1 202
Total[1]	**1 905**	**1 914**
QUEBEC		
- CHST	7 832	8 204
- Equalization/TFF	5 217	4 719
Total[1]	**12 468**	**12 367**
ONTARIO		
- CHST	12 002	13 128
- Equalization/TFF	—	—
Total[1]	**12 002**	**13 128**
MANITOBA		
- CHST	1 189	1 274
- Equalization/TFF	1 277	1 207
Total[1]	**2 351**	**2 369**

	2000-01 ($ millions)	2001-02 ($ millions)
SASKATCHEWAN		
- CHST	1 055	1 126
- Equalization/TFF	276	398
Total[1]	**1 135**	**1 358**
ALBERTA		
- CHST	3 064	3 388
- Equalization/TFF	—	—
Total[1]	**3 064**	**3 388**
BRITISH COLUMBIA		
- CHST	4 181	4 535
- Equalization/TFF	—	132
Total[1]	**4 181**	**4 535**
YUKON TERRITORY		
- CHST	32	33
- Equalization/TFF	340	346
Total[1]	**372**	**379**
NORTHWEST TERRITORIES		
- CHST	52	55
- Equalization/TFF	553	510
Total[1]	**605**	**565**
NUNAVUT		
- CHST	31	31
- Equalization/TFF	578	611
Total[1]	**609**	**642**

Source: *Finance Canada*

(1) Including smaller programs not detailed.

Federal Government Annual Surplus or Deficit

Fiscal Year Ending March 31 (millions of dollars)

	Surplus or Deficit[1]	% of GDP[2]		Surplus or Deficit[1]	% of GDP[2]		Surplus or Deficit[1]	% of GDP[2]
1960	-600	1.7	1974	-1 999	1.3	1988	-28 201	4.6
1961	-529	1.3	1975	-2 009	1.2	1989	-28 951	4.4
1962	-948	2.1	1976	-5 737	2.9	1990	-28 996	4.3
1963	-833	1.7	1977	-6 297	2.8	1991	-30 618	4.5
1964	-1 169	2.2	1978	-10 426	4.2	1992	-34 643	4.9
1965	-315	0.5	1979	-12 617	4.5	1993	-41 021	5.6
1966	-303	0.5	1980	-11 501	3.6	1994	-42 012	5.4
1967	-187	0.3	1981	-13 522	3.8	1995	-37 462	4.6
1968	-711	0.9	1982	-14 872	3.9	1996	-28 617	3.4
1969	-400	0.5	1983	-27 816	6.8	1997	-8 897	1.0
1970	332	0.4	1984	-32 399	7.2	1998	3 478	0.4
1971	-780	0.8	1985	-38 324	7.9	1999	2 884	0.3
1972	-1 542	1.4	1986	-34 404	6.7	2000	12 298	1.2
1973	-1 675	1.3	1987	-30 733	5.5	2001	17 148	1.7
						2002	8 907	0.8

Source: *Public Accounts of Canada*

(1) A minus (-) sign indicates a deficit. (2) GDP (Gross Domestic Product) represents the value (in current dollars at market prices) of all goods and services produced in Canada.

Per Capita Accumulated Federal Debt[1]

	(millions of dollars)		(dollars)	
	Net Debt	Interest on Debt	Net Debt Per Capita	Interest Per Capita
1940	3 271	139	288	12
1945	11 298	409	936	34
1950	11 645	440	849	32
1955	11 263	478	718	30
1960	12 089	736	677	41
1965	15 504	1 012	789	52
1970	16 943	1 676	796	79
1975	19 276	3 164	849	139
1980	72 159	8 494	2 853	353
1985	199 092	22 445	7 911	892
1986	233 496	25 441	9 210	1 003
1987	264 101	26 658	10 306	1 040
1988	292 184	29 028	11 276	1 120
1989	320 918	33 183	12 240	1 266
1990	357 811	38 820	13 484	1 472
1991	388 429	42 537	14 424	1 590
1992	423 072	41 020	15 469	1 499
1993	466 198	38 825	16 301	1 356
1994	508 210	37 982	17 381	1 299
1995	545 672	42 046	18 435	1 420
1996	574 289	46 905	19 908	1 626
1997	583 186	44 973	19 247	1 484
1998	579 708	40 931	19 166	1 353
1999	576 824	41 394	18 918	1 358
2000	564 526	41 647	18 358	1 354
2001	547 378	42 094	18 242	1 403
2002	583 432	37 735	18 492	1 196

Source: *Public Accounts of Canada*

(1) As of Mar. 31, on a public accounts basis.

FOREIGN TRADE

Canadian Imports – Top 50 Trading Partners

(millions of dollars)

Country	1990	%	2001	%	2002	%
TOTAL (ALL COUNTRIES)[1]	$136 245	100	343 075	100	348 653	100
United States	87 875	53.83	218 295	63.63	218 272	52.6
Japan.	9 525	6.99	14 635	4.27	15 412	4.42
China.	1 394	1.02	12 721	3.71	15 982	4.58
Mexico.	1 748	1.28	12 117	3.53	12 720	3.65
United Kingdom	4 898	3.59	11 714	3.41	9 728	2.79
Germany	3 835	2.81	7 970	2.32	8 293	2.39
France (incl. Monaco Fr. Antilles)	2 448	1.79	5 508	1.61	5 841	1.68
Korea South.	2 254	1.65	4 603	1.34	4 860	1.39
Taiwan (Taipei)	2 108	1.55	4 412	1.29	4 240	1.22
Italy (includes Vatican City State)	1 954	1.43	4 025	1.17	4 437	1.27
Norway	1 683	1.24	3 504	1.02	3 933	1.13
Malaysia	380	0.28	1 896	0.55	2 019	0.58
Sweden	893	0.65	1 707	0.50	1 859	0.53
Thailand.	406	0.30	1 691	0.49	1 777	0.51
Australia	764	0.56	1 623	0.47	1 721	0.49
Brazil	798	0.59	1 530	0.45	1 906	0.55
Ireland	257	0.19	1 440	0.42	1 736	0.50
Switzerland	646	0.47	1 406	0.41	1 516	0.43
Netherlands	719	0.53	1 388	0.40	1 464	0.42
Venezuela	577	0.42	1 353	0.39	1 231	0.35
Hong Kong	1 057	0.78	1 228	0.36	996	0.29
India	226	0.17	1 154	0.37	1 326	0.38
Algeria.	62	0.05	1 145	0.33	1 723	0.49
Singapore	551	0.40	1 137	0.33	988	0.28
Belgium	539	0.40	1 012	0.29	1 389	0.40
Philippines.	202	0.15	981	0.29	1 112	0.32
Indonesia (includes East Timor)	202	0.15	961	0.28	963	0.28
Spain	496	0.36	883	0.26	1 025	0.29
Iraq	112	0.08	874	0.25	1 089	0.31
Austria	406	0.30	872	0.25	1 007	0.29
Saudi Arabia	708	0.52	800	0.23	748	0.21
Denmark	248	0.18	764	0.22	1 024	0.29
Finland.	360	0.26	687	0.20	716	0.21
Chile	180	0.13	640	0.19	668	0.19
Israel	124	0.09	622	0.18	630	0.18
New Zealand	213	0.17	523	0.15	555	0.16
South Africa.	141	0.10	450	0.13	489	0.14
Colombia	132	0.10	415	0.12	392	0.11
Cuba	130	0.10	361	0.11	325	0.09
Russia	—	—	360	0.11	380	0.11
Argentina.	139	0.10	349	0.10	322	0.09
Jamaica.	157	0.16	324	0.09	270	0.08
Turkey	84	0.06	315	0.09	400	0.11
Poland.	78	0.06	295	0.09	312	0.09
Pakistan.	95	0.07	275	0.08	289	0.08
Portugal.	171	0.13	270	0.08	250	0.08
Peru.	128	0.94	251	0.07	293	0.08
Vietnam	15	0.01	237	0.07	284	0.08
Nigeria.	597	0.44	212	0.06	203	0.06
Guyana	24	0.02	209	0.06	225	0.06

Source: *Statistics Canada*   (1) 225 trading partners.

Canadian Exports – Top 50 Trading Partners

(millions of dollars)

(millions of dollars)	1990	%	2001	%	2002	%
TOTAL (ALL COUNTRIES)[1]	148 979	100	403 971	100	396 317	100
United States (U.S.).	111 556	74.88	351 751	87.07	345 427	87.16
Japan.	8 230	5.52	8 330	2.06	8 344	2.11
United Kingdom (U.K.)	3 541	2.38	5 057	1.25	4 430	1.12
China.	1 706	1.15	4 238	1.05	4 126	1.04
Germany	2 323	1.56	2 927	0.72	2 954	0.75
Mexico.	88 302	59.27	2 754	0.68	2 419	0.61
France (incl. Monaco French Antilles).	1 304	0.88	2 167	0.54	2 001	0.50
Korea South	1 554	1.04	2 013	0.50	1 998	0.50
Belgium.	1 249	0.84	1 922	0.48	1 907	0.48
Netherlands.	1 649	1.11	1 556	0.39	1 767	0.45
Italy (includes Vatican City State)	1 188	0.80	1 629	0.40	1 486	0.37
Hong Kong	685	0.46	1 241	0.31	1 206	0.30
Australia	902	0.61	1 077	0.27	1 169	0.29
Taiwan (Taipei)	798	0.54	1 014	0.25	1 119	0.28
Spain.	387	0.26	873	0.22	948	0.24
Norway	555	0.37	983	0.24	928	0.23
Brazil.	502	0.34	957	0.24	766	0.19
India	321	0.22	675	0.17	674	0.17
Singapore	406	0.27	395	0.10	576	0.15
Venezuela	287	0.19	834	0.21	545	0.14
Thailand.	505	0.34	442	0.11	530	0.13
Switzerland	1 054	0.71	338	0.08	518	0.13
Indonesia (includes East Timor)	312	0.21	466	0.12	492	0.12
Malaysia	256	0.17	344	0.09	491	0.12
Algeria.	294	0.20	297	0.07	442	0.11
Denmark	138	0.09	574	0.14	402	0.10
Israel.	145	0.10	351	0.09	388	0.10
Ireland.	139	0.09	321	0.08	363	0.09
Saudi Arabia	278	0.19	339	0.08	356	0.09
Colombia.	213	0.14	365	0.09	343	0.09
Philippines.	206	0.14	347	0.09	309	0.08
Sweden	327	0.22	310	0.08	286	0.07
Chile	200	0.13	369	0.09	282	0.07
Finland.	146	0.10	262	0.06	277	0.07
Cuba	176	0.12	394	0.10	276	0.07
United Arab Emirates.	30	0.02	208	0.05	272	0.07
Turkey	160	0.11	172	0.04	268	0.07
South Africa.	180	0.12	186	0.05	254	0.06
Austria.	158	0.11	304	0.08	243	0.06
Russia	—	—	290	0.07	239	0.06
New Zealand	158	0.11	216	0.05	211	0.05
Egypt.	76	0.05	221	0.05	184	0.05
Morocco	235	0.16	243	0.06	177	0.04
Peru.	58	0.04	189	0.05	169	0.04
Iran	360	0.24	496	0.12	167	0.04
Jamaica.	110	0.07	132	0.03	167	0.04
Trinidad and Tobago	63	0.04	187	0.05	146	0.04
Greece.	97	0.07	256	0.06	145	0.04
Portugal.	180	0.12	104	0.03	144	0.04
Tunisia.	53	0.04	62	0.02	137	0.03

Source: *Statistics Canada*

(1) 225 trading partners.

Canada's Top 50 Trading Partners by Balance of Trade

(millions of dollars)

Country	1990	%	2001	%	2002	%
TOTAL (ALL COUNTRIES)[1]	$136 245	100	343 075	100	348 653	100
United States	87 875	64.5	218 295	63.63	218 272	62.6
Japan.	9 525	6.99	14 635	4.27	15 412	4.42
China.	1 394	1.02	12 721	3.71	15 982	4.58
Mexico.	1 748	1.28	12 117	3.53	12 720	3.65
United Kingdom	4 898	3.59	11 714	3.41	9 728	2.79
Germany	3 835	2.81	7 970	2.32	8 293	2.38
France (incl. Monaco Fr. Antilles)	2 448	1.80	5 508	1.61	5 841	1.68
Korea South	2 254	1.65	4 603	1.34	4 860	1.39
Taiwan (Taipei)	2 108	1.55	4 412	1.29	4 240	1.22
Italy (includes Vatican City State)	1 954	1.43	4 025	1.17	4 437	1.27
Norway.	1 683	1.24	3 504	1.02	3 933	1.13
Malaysia	380	0.28	1 896	0.55	2 019	0.58
Sweden	893	0.66	1 707	0.50	1 859	0.53
Thailand.	406	0.30	1 691	0.49	1 777	0.51
Australia	764	0.56	1 623	0.47	1 721	0.49
Brazil	798	0.59	1 530	0.45	1 906	0.55
Ireland.	257	0.19	1 440	0.42	1 736	0.50
Switzerland	646	0.47	1 406	0.41	1 516	0.43
Netherlands	719	0.53	1 388	0.40	1 464	0.42
Venezuela	577	0.42	1 353	0.39	1 231	0.35
Hong Kong	1 057	0.78	1 228	0.36	996	0.29
India	226	0.17	1 154	0.34	1 326	0.38
Algeria.	62	0.05	1 145	0.33	1 723	0.49
Singapore	551	0.40	1 137	0.33	988	0.28
Belgium.	539	0.40	1 012	0.29	1 389	0.40
Philippines.	202	0.15	981	0.29	1 112	0.32
Indonesia (includes East Timor)	202	0.15	961	0.28	963	0.28
Spain.	496	0.36	883	0.26	1 025	0.29
Iraq	112	0.08	874	0.25	1 089	0.31
Austria.	406	0.30	872	0.25	1 007	0.29
Saudi Arabia	708	0.52	800	0.23	748	0.21
Denmark	248	0.18	764	0.22	1 024	0.29
Finland.	360	0.26	687	0.20	716	0.21
Chile	180	0.13	640	0.19	668	0.19
Israel	124	0.09	622	0.18	630	0.18
New Zealand	213	0.16	523	0.15	555	0.16
South Africa.	141	0.10	450	0.13	489	0.14
Colombia.	132	0.10	415	0.12	392	0.11
Cuba	130	0.10	361	0.11	325	0.09
Russia	—	—	360	0.10	380	0.11
Argentina.	139	0.10	349	0.10	322	0.09
Jamaica.	157	0.12	324	0.09	270	0.08
Turkey	84	0.06	315	0.09	400	0.11
Poland.	78	0.06	295	0.09	312	0.09
Pakistan.	95	0.07	275	0.08	289	0.08
Portugal.	171	0.13	270	0.08	250	0.07
Peru	128	0.09	251	0.07	293	0.08
Vietnam	15	0.01	237	0.07	284	0.08
Nigeria.	597	0.44	212	0.06	203	0.06
Guyana	24	0.02	209	0.06	225	0.06

Source: *Statistics Canada*   (1) 225 trading partners: total represents the sum of trade surpluses and trade deficits.

Trade Missions

Canada's small population means a small market for Canadian businesses. To create new jobs, these businesses must sell their goods and services elsewhere. According to the Department of Foreign Affairs and International Trade (DFAIT), exports accounted for more than 43 percent of all Canadian goods and services sold in 2002, and one in every three jobs in Canada was tied to exports. DFAIT estimates that every $1 billion in exports creates or supports 11,000 jobs in Canada.

As the tables on pages 215 and 216 show, Canada's biggest customer is the United States. The US is easily accessible, and it's compatible culturally and technologically too. But other foreign markets exist; e.g., in the Pacific Rim countries. DFAIT helps Canadian small or medium-sized firms export their products to these markets through high-profile Team Canada trade missions and regular trade missions.

Team Canada missions are led by the prime minister and include the federal minister for international trade, provincial premiers and territorial leaders. The missions often include academics and cultural ambassadors too. Business leaders—who must register beforehand and then be invited to participate—benefit through their association with high-profile Canadian figures in the destination countries.

Before a mission, DFAIT identifies the business sectors of greatest interest to the host countries. During a mission to Moscow in 2002, for example, officials focused on education, communications, metals, minerals, oil, gas, construction, agriculture and agri-food. In Munich in 2002, DFAIT added

media, film and technology transfer to the mix but dropped oil, gas, metals and minerals. DFAIT works with foreign officials to create the understanding necessary for business development. The results include joint ventures and the creation of facilities in destination countries.

In recent years, Team Canada has also promoted exporters from distinct Canadian regions. Team Canada Atlantic aids businesses based in the four Atlantic provinces, and Team Canada West aids firms in Western Canada. Junior Team Canada sends university students abroad to work in their areas of interest with business mentors.

Team Canada alone has helped more than 2,800 Canadian business representatives and organizations gain access to senior government and private-sector leaders in international markets. It's estimated that the new business generated is worth $30.6 billion.

Other trade missions, led by the federal minister of international trade, focus on specific market sectors abroad. Delegates meet with potential clients and gain knowledge of how to do business in target countries. (See "Canadian Trade Missions" below.)

A publicly held company, the Canadian Commercial Corporation, also aids Canadian exporters and foreign buyers in Canada. Established in 1946, the corporation supplies pre-contract, contract advisory and post-contract services for a fee. The organization provides a government-backed guarantee of performance for Canadian exporters. Visit http://www.ccc.ca for more information.

Team Canada Missions

Year	Destinations	Year	Destinations
1994	China	2001	USA (Atlanta)[1]
1996	India, Indonesia, Malaysia, Pakistan	2001	USA (Dallas, Los Angeles)[2]
1997	Korea, Philippines, Thailand	2001	China
1998	Argentina, Brazil, Chile, Mexico	2002	Germany, Russia
1999	Japan	2002	USA (New York)[1]
2000	USA (New England)[1]	2003	USA (Washington, DC)[1]

Regional missions: (1) Team Canada Atlantic; (2) Team Canada West

Canadian Trade Missions

Year	Destinations	Year	Destinations
1995	Argentina, Brazil, Chile	2000	Russia
1998	Italy	2000	Czech Republic, Hungary, Slovakia, Slovenia
1999	Poland, Ukraine		
1999	Israel, Palestine, Saudi Arabia, United Arab Emirates	2000	Algeria, Morocco, Portugal, Spain
1999	USA (California)	2002	India
1999	Ireland	2002	Mexico
2000	Australia	2002	Nigeria, Senegal, South Africa

Source: *Department of Foreign Affairs and International Trade, www.tcm-mec.gc.ca*

Foreign Investment in Canada

(millions of dollars)

	Total	United States	United Kingdom	Other EU[1]	Japan	Other OECD[2]	All Other
1930	2 427	1 993	392	–	–	–	42
1935	2 284	1 870	373	–	–	–	41
1940	2 477	2 064	362	–	–	–	51
1945	2 831	2 422	348	–	–	–	61
1950	4 098	3 549	468	–	–	–	81
1955	8 010	6 778	905	–	–	–	327
1960	13 583	11 210	1 550	553	–	–	270
1965	17 864	14 408	2 107	968	10	240	131
1970	27 374	22 054	2 641	1 617	103	580	379
1975	38 728	30 506	3 830	2 520	257	987	628
1980	64 708	50 368	5 773	5 168	605	1 524	1 270
1985	90 358	67 874	8 643	6 774	2 250	2 562	2 255
1990	130 932	84 089	17 185	14 339	5 222	5 871	4 227
1991	135 234	86 396	16 224	14 908	5 596	6 803	5 308
1992	137 918	88 161	16 799	15 056	5 962	6 913	5 027
1993	141 493	90 600	15 872	15 732	6 249	7 312	5 727
1994	154 594	102 629	14 693	16 824	6 587	7 989	5 873
1995	168 167	112 948	14 097	21 778	6 987	5 827	6 529
1996	182 126	121 943	14 292	24 406	7 873	6 748	6 865
1997	194 277	128 978	15 748	25 508	7 990	8 860	7 193
1998	219 389	146 893	17 042	31 126	8 393	8 958	6 978
1999	252 563	176 045	15 279	36 341	8 270	10 115	6 514
2000	307 591	191 870	23 184	63 240	8 126	13 050	8 121
2001	333 635	214 227	25 204	65 954	7 909	10 799	9 543
2002[3]	349 388	224 330	26 273	67 700	8 600	10 833	11 652

Source: © *Statistics Canada*

(1) Other European Union countries (EU) include Belgium, Denmark, Germany, France, Greece, Ireland, Italy, Luxembourg, Netherlands, Portugal, Spain; from January 1995, Austria, Finland and Sweden. (2) Other OECD countries include Australia, Iceland, New Zealand, Norway, Switzerland and Turkey; from July 1994, Mexico; from December 1995, Czech Republic; from May 1996, Hungary; from November 1996, Poland; and up to December 1994, Austria, Finland and Sweden. (3) Preliminary data.

Foreign Investment by Industry

(millions of dollars)

	Total	Wood & Paper	Energy & Metallic Minerals	Machinery & Transportation Equipment	Finance & Insurance	Services & Retailing	Other Industries
1991	135 234	7 902	31 706	18 212	25 939	10 363	41 112
1992	137 918	8 895	30 062	18 496	26 873	10 807	42 785
1993	141 493	9 109	30 846	20 641	26 685	11 010	43 203
1994	154 594	9 598	29 959	24 638	28 119	14 417	47 864
1995	168 167	10 010	29 061	25 305	29 086	16 885	57 820
1996	182 126	10 206	31 799	25 366	33 506	18 852	62 399
1997	194 277	12 595	33 923	28 043	35 781	19 460	64 476
1998	219 389	13 487	38 651	30 029	40 787	21 642	74 793
1999	252 563	15 345	42 884	30 563	52 755	23 462	87 555
2000	307 591	16 488	54 353	43 785	52 803	25 269	114 893
2001	333 635	14 750	70 324	45 674	66 174	26 692	110 020
2002[1]	349 388	14 773	79 659	49 109	67 182	29 117	109 549

Source: © *Statistics Canada* (1) Preliminary data.

Canadian Investment Abroad

(millions of dollars)

	Total	United States	United Kingdom	Other EU[1]	Japan	Other OECD[2]	All Other
1920	212	132	1	—	1	—	78
1925	246	144	1	—	1	—	100
1930	443	260	14	—	1	—	168
1935	485	266	46	—	—	—	173
1940	681	412	58	—	1	—	210
1945	720	455	54	—	2	—	209
1950	1 043	814	73	—	—	—	156
1955	1 835	1 362	145	—	6	—	322
1960	2 600	1 716	277	46	15	—	546
1965	3 655	2 178	510	125	28	44	769
1970	6 520	3 518	636	304	48	142	1 871
1975	11 091	5 975	1 105	633	74	699	2 605
1980	28 413	17 849	3 080	1 377	109	1 370	4 628
1985	60 292	41 851	4 865	2 868	276	2 293	8 139
1990	98 402	60 049	13 527	7 098	917	3 996	12 815
1991	109 068	63 379	15 262	8 505	2 182	3 548	16 192
1992	111 691	64 502	12 271	9 071	2 521	3 957	19 370
1993	122 427	67 677	12 907	11 478	2 845	4 355	23 165
1994	146 315	77 987	15 038	15 620	3 485	6 635	27 551
1995	161 237	84 562	16 412	18 106	2 739	7 166	32 251
1996	181 238	93 939	17 825	19 192	2 676	8 392	39 215
1997	218 607	110 707	22 722	22 416	2 985	9 284	50 493
1998	262 909	133 267	24 956	29 149	3 268	11 579	60 691
1999	290 730	151 775	25 686	28 384	3 853	12 381	68 651
2000	353 150	177 839	35 164	39 162	5 664	17 407	77 914
2001	389 660	188 791	39 742	41 607	7 033	25 904	86 582
2002[3]	431 819	201 792	45 241	546 123	9 203	33 815	87 156

Source: © *Statistics Canada*
(1) Other European Union countries (EU) include Belgium, Denmark, Germany, France, Greece, Ireland, Italy, Luxembourg, Netherlands, Portugal, Spain; from January 1995, Austria, Finland and Sweden. (2) Other OECD countries include Australia, Iceland, New Zealand, Norway, Switzerland and Turkey; from July 1994, Mexico; from December 1995, Czech Republic; from May 1996, Hungary; from November 1996, Poland; and up to December 1994, Austria, Finland and Sweden. (3) Preliminary data.

Canadian Investment Abroad by Industry

(millions of dollars)

	Total	Wood & Paper	Energy & Metallic Minerals	Machinery & Transportation Equipment	Finance & Insurance	Services & Retailing	Other Industries
1991	109 068	3 473	22 051	2 794	32 443	10 043	38 264
1992	111 691	3 576	24 198	3 188	32 140	10 263	38 326
1993	122 427	3 727	27 008	4 030	37 353	10 423	39 887
1994	146 315	4 358	32 189	4 681	44 725	12 066	48 297
1995	161 237	5 340	37 219	5 207	48 932	17 892	46 646
1996	181 238	4 710	44 703	5 867	58 098	19 724	48 138
1997	218 607	6 154	53 079	7 715	73 714	21 760	56 184
1998	262 909	7 053	58 700	11 752	85 562	31 643	68 199
1999	290 730	7 636	60 444	10 036	104 111	30 130	78 373
2000	353 150	7 321	67 747	20 949	118 891	45 839	92 404
2001	389 660	8 794	74 506	25 696	146 509	53 350	80 806
2002[1]	431 819	9 606	82 207	27 205	178 320	53 877	80 604

Source: © *Statistics Canada*   (1) Preliminary data.

BUSINESS

Agriculture in Canada

(millions of dollars)[1]

	1960	1970	1980	1990	2000	2001	2002[2]
Barley	69.4	144.7	553.6	545.2	582.5	711.1	547.5
Canola	14.8	96.7	673.6	789.6	1 560.0	1 718.6	1 624.3
Cattle	469.7	858.9	3 221.4	3 627.1	6 023.5	6 973.2	6 843.8
Corn	10.1	49.4	467.5	521.5	677.4	587.9	812.5
Dairy products	486.5	678.9	2 015.5	3 154.8	513.1	4 142.2	4 135.6
Eggs	137.8	172.8	407.0	482.3	482.4	563.5	584.1
Fruits	52.1	91.8	137.3	348.1	547.7	516.3	517.1
Ginseng	n.a.	n.a.	n.a.	30.5	52.2	69.7	54.2
Hogs	266.8	484.5	1 404.2	2 021.2	3 386.6	3 846.0	3 315.1
Honey	n.a.	n.a.	44.8	45.0	69.5	70.5	82.3
Lentils	n.a	n.a	n.a	n.a	241.9	189.7	133.8
Maple products	9.5	8.1	34.1	70.8	181.0	141.1	162.3
Nurseries	n.a.	n.a.	276.2	913.6	1 615.5	1 714.7	1 795.2
Oats	23.9	20.9	53.5	81.0	195.9	300.3	293.4
Potatoes	67.4	90.1	211.9	399.0	679.9	719.6	952
Poultry	135.5	262.7	670.2	1 201.6	1 625.1	1 769.8	1 708.6
Sheep	0.4	0.3	2.9	2.3	4.0	5.2	3.5
Soybeans	10.0	23.7	183.3	256.6	678.2	508.9	564.3
Sugar Beets	12.8	15.1	73.5	42.9	32.9	19.3	20.1
Tobacco	96.4	154.8	212.5	281.1	362.1	266.8	273.6
Vegetables	68.1	125.1	360.1	706.5	1 249.0	1 347.9	1 431.0
Wheat	442.7	570.1	2 774.5	2 351.5	3 061.9	3 465.4	3 223.8

Source: © Statistics Canada   (1) Not adjusted for inflation. (2) Preliminary statistics.

Canadian Agriculture by Province, 2002

(millions of dollars)

	N&L	PEI	NS	NB	Que	Ont	Man	Sask	Alta	BC
Barley	—	6.8	0.7	3.5	28.9	11.3	878	255.2	147.8	5.3
Canola	—	—	—	—	2.8	12.8	465.2	687.8	443.9	11.8
Cattle	1.5	25.8	27.9	29	231.1	1 071.1	485.5	883.4	3 850.1	238.6
Corn	—	—	3	—	323.8	450.7	34.5	—	0.5	—
Dairy products .	28	53.3	93.4	74.5	1 510.4	1 357.3	164	119.2	366.8	368.6
Eggs	11.1	3.5	23.4	14.5	102.8	223.2	64.9	23.2	42.4	75.2
Ginseng	—	—	—	—	—	32.4	—	—	—	21.8
Hogs	1.1	27.6	29.9	27.7	938.1	820.8	687.3	223.2	521.6	37.8
Honey	—	0.2	1	0.5	5.1	9.5	15.5	20.4	22.8	7.3
Lentils	—	—	—	—	—	—	0.5	132	1.3	—
Maple products .	—	—	1.1	5.8	144.5	10.8	—	—	—	—
Nurseries	10.4	2.3	36.4	52.6	189.4	900	38.9	26.7	125.3	43.5
Potatoes	1.4	194.2	10.6	125.9	123.8	101.9	135.5	47.9	146.8	63.9
Poultry	x	x	57	42.5	460.5	588.4	78.2	55.8	143.9	257.7
Soybeans	—	1.5	—	—	91.4	460.2	11.1	—	—	—
Sugar beets . . .	—	—	—	—	—	—	—	—	20.1	—
Tobacco	—	—	—	—	17.8	255.8	—	—	—	—
Vegetables	3	11.7	21.2	7.8	290.5	739.6	29.7	2.5	59.7	265.2
Wheat	—	3.5	2.6	1.4	17.5	209.8	598.6	959.3	636.3	13.5

Source: © Statistics Canada   (x) Confidential.

Mining in Canada

(millions of dollars)

	1960	1970	1980	1990	2000	2001	2002[2]
Total Value[1]	2 492.5	5 722.1	31 875.0	40 778.4	83 846.9	82967.8	76951.1
METALS							
Cadmium	3.3	15.3	7.6	11.6	.5	0.7	0.8
Cobalt	6.7	10.2	134.7	49.6	100.4	80.9	49
Copper	264.8	779.2	1 859.6	2 428.9	1 684.1	1 535.1	1 418.9
Gold	157.2	88.1	1 165.4	2 407.6	2 053.8	2 135.2	2 292.4
Iron Ore	175.1	588.6	1 700.9	1 258.8	1 424.5	1 188.9	1 391.7
Lead	43.9	123.1	273.7	279.3	96.6	109.4	70.7
Nickel	295.6	830.2	1 497.4	2 027.9	2 323.8	177.3	1 883.3
Platinum metals	28.9	43.6	159.1	189.4	478.5	651.9	449.5
Silver	30.2	81.9	828.8	249.7	279.0	277.9	314.5
Uranium	269.9	n.a.	702.0	887.9	473.2	605.4	608.4
Zinc	108.6	398.9	858.2	2 272.6	1 567.3	1 425.9	1 089.9
NON-METALS							
Asbestos	121.4	208.1	618.5	272.1	141.7	118.7	98
Diamonds					624.4	717.8	801.5
Gypsum	9.5	14.2	39.5	80.1	105.7	95.9	112.7
Potash	178.7	108.7	1 020.7	964.9	1 644.2	1 617.4	1 597.8
Salt	19.4	36.1	122.8	240.9	351.4	426.1	412.1
Sulphur (elemental)	4.3	28.4	444.1	368.9	92.4	1.3	0.6
STRUCTURAL MATERIALS							
Cement	93.3	155.7	581.4	991.4	1 258.7	1 348.3	1 387.5
Sand and gravel	111.2	133.6	508.4	817.3	971.2	1 062.2	1 047.4
Stone	60.6	87.9	341.2	663.4	881.3	957	971.8

Source: © *Statistics Canada*

(1) Total includes metals, non-metals, structural materials and fuels that are not shown. (2) Preliminary figures.

Mining by Province, 2002

(millions of dollars)

	N&L	PEI	NS	NB	Que	Ont	Man	Sask	Alta	BC	YT	NWT	NVT
METALS:													
Copper	—	—	—	22.1	213.2	466.6	92.8	24.8	—	599.3	—	—	—
Gold	22.9	—	—	3.8	505.7	1180.6	83.6	22.7	0.6	336.5	31.3	52.4	52.3
Iron Ore	895.5	—	—	—	...	—	—	—	—	—	—	—	—
Lead	—	—	—	52.3	—	—	—	—	—	1.6	—	—	16.8
Nickel	—	—	—	—	245.8	1239.8	397.6	—	—	—	—	—	—
Zinc	—	—	—	313.7	287.9	123.1	109	6.3	—	54.8	—	—	195.1
NON-METALS:													
Asbestos	—	—	—	—	98								
STRUCTURAL MATERIALS:													
Cement	—	—	...	—	293.5	552.4	—	—	...	247.6	—	—	—
Sand & Gravel	9.5	0.8	16	9.6	76.4	438.2	33.3	45.7	235.5	175.9	3.6	2.9	—
Stone	35.8	—	55.6	19.1	256.5	514.8	18.6	—	4.4	60.2	—	6.9	—

Source: © *Statistics Canada*

(...) Sample too small.

Manufacturing in Canada

(millions of dollars)

	2000		2001		
	Manufacturing shipments	Manufacturing value added	Manufacturing shipments	Manufacturing value added	% Change of Goods Shipped 2000–01
All industries	562 249.0	225 872.6	544 032.3	211 701.2	-3.2
Food manufacturing	57 294.2	18 590.1	61 480.3	19 827.8	7.3
Beverage and tobacco product . . .	11 611.4	7 234.7	11 684.9	7 256.4	0.6
Textile mills	4 199.3	1 745.2	4 083.4	1 828.7	-2.8
Textile product mills	2 775.4	1 247.3	2 665.8	1 304.5	-4.0
Clothing manufacturing	7 943.6	4 372.5	7 857.2	4 219.6	-1.1
Leather and allied product	957.7	465.1	982.7	444.2	2.6
Wood product manufacturing	31 658.3	12 422.5	30 124.5	11 761.4	-4.8
Paper manufacturing	38 275.9	18 241.3	35 923.2	16 017.3	-6.1
Printing and related support activities	11 113.1	6 226.7	11 679.1	6 662.6	5.1
Petroleum and coal products	33 918.0	3 678.2	33 954.1	4 919.1	0.1
Chemical manufacturing	37 147.9	15 194.0	38 619.4	14 924.8	4.0
Plastics and rubber products	22 060.4	10 449.7	22 716.9	10 741.8	3.0
Non-metallic mineral product	10 060.7	5 546.6	10 522.5	5 683.0	4.6
Primary metal manufacturing	36 236.0	14 435.0	34 153.9	12 251.8	-5.7
Fabricated metal product	29 570.8	15 166.5	30 111.9	14 969.7	1.8
Machinery manufacturing	26 304.9	13 879.2	26 495.1	13 796.6	0.7
Computer and electronic product .	37 459.7	15 523.0	27 152.9	7 971.6	-27.5
Electrical equipment appliance and component	11 607.1	5 214.6	11 707.0	4 943.7	0.9
Transportation equipment	132 785.4	46 140.9	122 195.8	41 634.4	-8.0
Furniture and related product	12 621.6	6 464.1	13 117.5	6 804.9	3.9
Miscellaneous manufacturing	6 647.5	3 635.2	6 804.1	3 737.3	2.4

Operating Profits by Major Industry

(millions of dollars)

Year	Primary (including oil and gas)	Utilities	Manufact- uring	Construction	Transpor- tation	Trade	Finance, Insurance & Real Estate
1990	5 033	1 686	15 702	19 678	1 282	11 527	31 328
1995	5 539	2 051	39 193	2 894	4 259	7 429	38 437
1999	6 550	2 528	46 185	3 598	5 061	15 959	62 665
2000	23 844	2 234	5 379	3 406	4 790	16 481	76 779
2001	21 536	2 946	34 058	2 275	2 643	15 058	53 812
2002	15 591	3 167	38 468	2 674	5 334	18 895	38 005

Year	Managerial & Related	Professional & Related	Information & Recreation	Accommodation & Food	Health & Social	Educational	Other Services
1990	22 107	675	4 604	126	705	86	526
1995	11 026	1 382	4 804	-88	742	-149	466
1999	14 975	1 168	6 496	1 840	1 486	108	1 057
2000	16 745	1 052	7 947	1 504	1 716	-9	1 111
2001 . . . . :	17 496	1 624	6 541	1 596	1 796	-133	642
2002	17 713	2 640	8 046	2 050	2 091	-97	943

Source: © *Statistics Canada*

Value of Manufacturing[1] by Province, 2002

(millions of dollars)

	Newfound- land and Labrador	Prince Edward Island	Nova Scotia	New Brunswick	Quebec	Ontario
All Industries	2 446.6	1 234.7	8 375.0	12 093.0	131 783.5	285 396.2
Food manufacturing	1 032.9	859.6	1 952.8	1 914.5	14 228.5	24 343.9
Beverage and tobacco product	118.3	x	x	207.2	3 728.6	5 282.4
Textile mills.	x	x	x	x	2 538.7	1 165.2
Textile product mills . . . . ,	3	2.8	x	x	1 071.9	1 201.2
Clothing manufacturing	x	x	x	x	4 745.5	1 953.5
Leather and allied product . . .	x	x	x	0.9	528.6	312.2
Wood product manufacturing	103.2	43.5	527.6	1 399.4	8 032.2	5 664.0
Paper manufacturing	x	x	1 040.5	2 191.7	11 993.3	11 115.0
Printing & related support activities	x	8.9	x	x	3 173.2	5 932.7
Petroleum and coal products	x	x	x	x	6 672.7	11 281.4
Chemical manufacturing	x	61.4	x	x	8 231.3	19 475.0
Plastics and rubber products	22.1	x	x	x	5 383.8	13 529.8
Non-metallic mineral product	x	x	x	x	2 346.1	5 169.7
Primary metal manufacturing	x	x	2.3	x	13 702.7	15 772.5
Fabricated metal product	61.9	22.5	x	x	6 440.8	17 460.0
Machinery manufacturing	35.1	19.3	150.7	155.3	5 180.1	14738.1
Computer and electronic product	x	x	x	x	8 626.3	13194.7
Electrical equipment, appliance and component manufacturing	7.6	x	x	x	3 077.3	6 983.9
Transportation equipment manufacturing	167.9	123.3	750.3	53.0	16 236.3	100 675.4
Furniture and related product	x	x	x	x	3 787.1	6 927.6
Miscellaneous manufacturing	x	5	x	x	2 058.4	3 218.2

	Manitoba	Saskat- chewan	Alberta	British Columbia	Yukon	Northwest Territories	Nunavut
All Industries.	11 311.7	7 434.6	45 565.0	38 332.1	16.5	39.0	4.3
Food manufacturing. . . .	2 434.7	1 782.0	8 423.4	4 508.1	—	—	—
Beverage and tobacco product	211.9	73.8	872.6	992.5	—	—	—
Textile mills	x	x	x	x	—	—	—
Textile product mills . . .	x	x	x	x	—	—	—
Clothing manufacturing .	406.4	28.3	135.7	x	—	—	—
Leather and allied product	x	3.5	x	9.1	—	—	—
Wood product manufacturing	—	623.0	314.9	2 599.9	10 816.9	—	—
Paper manufacturing . . .	549.1	493.3	1 715.3	6 264.1	—	—	—
Printing & related support activities	547.2	132.5	813.4	908.5	—	—	—
Petroleum and coal products	27.4	x	7 479.8	x	—	—	—
Chemical manufacturing	635.5	741.6	8 242.5	1 000.6	—	—	—
Plastics and rubber products	471.4	104.9	934.2	1 057.1	—	—	—
Non-metallic mineral product	153.7	92.5	1 258.7	1 058.9	—	—	—
Primary metal manufacturing	—	x	x	1 225.8	1 591.6	—	—
Fabricated metal product	515.3	396.7	2 938.9	1 702.6	—	—	—
Machinery manufacturing	—	797.9	621.8	3 257.7	1 539.1	—	—
Computer and electronic product	x	x	3 172.5	1 448.6	—	—	—
Electrical equipment, appliance and component manufacturing	—	229.9	384.8	288.4	x	—	—
Transportation equipment	1 661.3	256.2	703.2	1 568.8	—	—	—
Furniture and related product	498.9	54.9	979.7	671.5	—	—	—
Miscellaneous manufacturing	—	200.6	50.6	395.3	590.6	—	—

Source: *Statistics Canada*

(x) Data suppressed to protect confidentiality.

Retail Merchandising in Canada

(millions of dollars)[1]

	1997	1998	1999	2000	2001	2002	2003
Total retail, all stores	**59 459.2**	**61 668.7**	**65 194.9**	**69 258.3**	**72 282.5**	**76 644.6**	**75454.4**
Supermarkets and grocery stores	12 913.8	13 336.6	13 625.1	14 148.0	14 714.6	15 512.4	15 925.6
All other food stores	1 073.5	1 079.6	1 097.2	1 124.6	1 198.3	1 194.5	1 184.2
Drugs and patent medicine stores	3 074.4	3 236.0	3 333.7	3 374.7	3 604.0	3 883.8	3 872.8
Shoe stores	412.4	426.0	428.6	442.4	443.0	454.4	412.9
Men's clothing stores	392.4	395.4	384.0	382.8	355.3	340.8	284.2
Women's clothing stores	1 083.8	1 101.4	1 126.2	1 156.8	1 193.5	1 192.8	1 068.4
Other clothing stores	1 457.6	1 564.8	1 666.7	1 837.4	1 975.2	2 050.5	1 807.5
Household furniture and appliance stores . . .	2 326.4	2 526.8	2 770.5	3 069.0	3 313.6	3 665.5	3 350.8
Other household furnishings stores	575.0	607.2	643.0	720.6	777.6	901.6	862.3
Motor and recreational vehicle dealers	15 692.0	16 114.5	17 344.1	18 276.0	19 154.4	20 646.4	21 166.8
Gasoline service stations	4 232.0	4 046.7	4 500.1	5 590.9	5 603.7	5 812.3	6 091.4
Automotive parts, accessories and services . .	3 407.0	3 584.0	3 734.6	3 895.9	4 122.8	4 380.4	4 417.6
General merchandise stores	6 545.7	6 989.0	7 497.4	7 824.3	8 073.5	8 458.6	7 608
Department stores, excluding concessions . . .	3 837.4	4 050.9	4 288.2	4 373.2	4 685.0	4 956.1	4 328.1
Other general merchandise stores	2 708.4	2 938.0	3 209.2	3 451.1	3 388.5	3 502.4	3 280
Other semi-durable goods stores	2 046.9	2 054.4	2 123.2	2 180.2	2 238.1	2 362.6	2 125.2
Other durable goods stores	1 502.1	1 687.6	1 765.0	1 865.0	1 923.6	2 018.5	1 789.2
Other retail stores, not elsewhere classified . . .	2 724.2	2 918.8	3 155.3	3 369.5	3 591.4	3 769.5	3 487.6
Liquor, wine and beer stores	1 587.5	1 681.2	1 816.4	1 914.8	2 052.2	2 193.7	1 980.6
Other retail stores, not elsewhere classified, excluding liquor, wine and beer stores	1 136.7	1 237.6	1 338.8	1 454.7	1 539.2	1575.8	1 507

Source: © *Statistics Canada*   (1) Retail sales estimates exclude the Goods and Services Tax (GST).

Retail Merchandising by Province, 2002

(millions of dollars)

	N&L	PEI	NS	NB	Que.	Ont.	Man.	Sask.	Alta	BC	Terr.
Total retail, all stores . .	**1272.0**	**331.1**	**2293.1**	**1829.2**	**17477.6**	**28815.4**	**2662.2**	**2253.2**	**9364.2**	**10068.2**	**278.6**
Supermarkets & grocery .	311.6	90.2	587.2	449.8	3732.8	4899.4	604.6	536.9	1959.0	2285.1	55.9
Drugs & patent medicine . .	72.7	21.1	153.4	106.2	764.0	1603.6	98.5	103.7	398.7	551.7	x
Shoes	2.8	x	5.7	5.0	148.7	177.7	12.2	6.8	37.9	56.3	x
Men's clothing	3.0	x	4.4	6.9	69.6	158.5	11.0	7.1	42.5	35.9	x
Women's clothing	16.6	x	31.0	23.2	315.2	476.1	31.0	29.0	119.8	144.8	1.2
Other clothing	16.8	7.6	45.3	37.0	478.1	833.3	53.8	46.6	247.9	280.2	x
Household furn.& appliances	30.2	11.1	74.6	61.8	993.8	1327.3	108.6	77.5	478.0	494.8	7.7
Other household furnishings	3.4	3.9	16.3	16.5	142.2	413.7	21.1	20.6	127.6	134.7	1.6
Motor & recreational vehicles	355.0	62.9	533.8	474.4	4886.1	7857.4	782.8	610.1	2557.6	2473.0	x
Gasoline service stations .	115.0	35.8	207.2	170.1	1316.0	2057.8	228.7	190.0	723.1	752.6	x
Automotive parts, accessories & services . . .	63.1	20.4	110.4	111.1	1029.8	1679.8	133.7	135.6	566.5	512.1	x
General merchandise	183.0	30.9	252.1	192.5	1694.7	3312.2	331.4	292.0	1023.2	1067.6	78.9
Other semi-durable goods .	25.4	15.0	67.3	53.0	448.0	1073.3	63.8	50.7	250.6	307.6	7.8
Other durable goods	16.7	5.0	52.5	32.0	441.2	819.6	56.4	50.5	229.7	309.3	5.5
Other retail, not classified . .	43.8	14.1	124.7	74.7	622.9	1658.1	101.9	78.6	535.5	498.9	16.4

Source: © *Statistics Canada*

Internet Web Site Presence and Purchasing

	% of Enterprises with a Web site		% of Enterprises using the Internet to make purchases		
	2001	2002	2000	2001	2002
All private sector	**28.6**	**31.5**	**18.2**	**22.4**	**31.7**
Forestry, logging and support activities	15.3	9.4	4.5	11.0	20.1
Mining and oil and gas extraction	39.2	35.5	20.4	14.5	26.4
Utilities	45.1	47.4	25.5	31.5	41.6
Construction	24.3	22.9	n.a.	16.7	26.8
Manufacturing	45.9	54.7	21.3	29.1	40.5
Wholesale trade	37.6	40.7	22.9	26.4	36.3
Retail trade	26.7	30.7	13.5	16.9	29.1
Transportation and warehousing	11.1	15.8	15.0	11.6	19.2
Information and cultural industries	65.1	67.5	52.0	51.8	59.9
Finance and insurance	47.8	43.2	20.2	24.9	36.6
Real estate and rental and leasing	22.3	25.0	8.8	13.4	19.8
Professional, scientific and technical services	31.9	33.4	35.8	42.1	50.6
Management of companies and enterprises	13.8	23.2	8.5	8.4	21.1
Administration and support, etc.	39.7	35.1	22.5	30.9	28.5
Educational services (private sector)	61.7	74.4	41.0	39.3	46.1
Health care and social assistance (private sector)	18.6	18.2	14.4	20.0	29.5
Arts, entertainment and recreation	45.8	51.0	15.9	23.2	35.6
Accommodation and food services	20.1	21.7	10.1	9.4	18.2
Other services (except public administration)	24.5	30.4	10.5	14.8	23.4

Source: © *Statistics Canada*   (n.a.) Not available.

Internet Sales

	% of Enterprises that use the Internet to make sales		Internet sales 2001		
	2001	2002	as % of Total Revenue	% to Consumers	% outside Canada
All private sector	**6.7**	**7.5**	**0.6**	**27.4**	**21.9**
Forestry, logging and support activities	4.3	5.0	—	—	—
Mining and oil and gas extraction	0.2	3.2	—	n.a.	28.1
Utilities	1.0	1.6	—	—	—
Construction	0.7	4.1	—	—	—
Manufacturing	11.7	12.1	0.3	4.7	25.8
Wholesale trade	12.9	12.6	1.1	6.1	8.7
Retail trade	10.8	11.4	0.5	84.6	56.5
Transportation and warehousing	2.2	3.6	2.4	1.8	n.a.
Information and cultural industries	20.1	18.8	1.2	57.8	44.8
Finance and insurance	9.6	8.0	0.4	66.9	3.7
Real estate and rental and leasing	7.3	4.1	0.2	82.9	14.5
Professional, scientific and technical services	5.8	7.8	1.4	11.5	29.2
Management of companies and enterprises	4.8	5.9	0.6	1.2	12.4
Administration and support, etc.	10.7	11.0	1.0	39.9	41.8
Educational services (private sector)	14.0	21.3	1.5	27.0	31.1
Health care and social assistance (private sector)	0.6	1.4	n.a.	n.a.	n.a.
Arts, entertainment and recreation	10.0	14.1	1.2	97.2	27.8
Accommodation and food services	3.7	4.4	0.4	81.8	13.0
Other services (except public administration)	3.6	4.4	0.4	64.4	7.9

Source: © *Statistics Canada*   (n.a.) Not available.

Establishments by Industry and Number of Employees, 2002

	Total	# of Employees not reported	Total reporting staff	1–4
Total	2 204 782	1 157 641	1 047 141	600 303
GOODS PRODUCING				
Agriculture, Forestry, Fishing and Hunting ...	196 036	134 655	61 381	47 320
Mining and Oil and Gas Extraction..........	15 348	7 234	8 114	4 791
Utilities	1 916	731	1 185	517
Construction	245 625	135 667	109 958	69 950
Manufacturing...........................	104 669	40 269	64 400	27 516
SERVICES				
Wholesale Trade	122 202	55 960	66 242	32 496
Retail Trade..............................	218 462	86 403	132 059	59 277
Transportation and Warehousing	105 577	59 507	46 070	31 368
Information and Cultural Industries........	29 862	15 941	13 921	7 115
Finance and Insurance....................	104 709	69 710	34 999	17 857
Real Estate and Rental and Leasing........	161 478	121 644	39 834	25 648
Professional, Scientific and Technical Services.	287 029	173 361	113 668	79 740
Management of Companies and Enterprises ..	74 311	56 832	17 479	10 106
Administrative and Support, Waste .... Management and Remediation Services	100 711	53 761	46 950	27 696
Educational Services	19 668	8 283	11 385	6 021
Health Care and Social Assistance..........	92 591	11 228	81 363	46 309
Arts, Entertainment and Recreation.........	40 036	22 038	17 998	9 934
Accommodation and Food Services	111 657	36 567	75 090	28 094
Other Services (except Public Administration)	165 108	67 795	97 313	66 139
Public Administration	7 787	55	7 732	2 409

	Number of Employees						
	5–9	10–19	20–49	50–99	100–199	200–499	500 +
Total	179 441	123 068	88 129	31 857	14 742	6 842	2 759
GOODS PRODUCING							
Agriculture, Forestry, Fishing and Hunting.	7 183	3 937	2 106	571	194	63	7
Mining and Oil and Gas Extraction.......	1 031	873	713	344	187	124	51
Utilities.................................	205	144	135	68	39	43	34
Construction	17 586	11 083	7 630	2 443	902	305	59
Manufacturing........................	9 767	8 552	8 789	4 743	2 966	1 610	457
SERVICES							
Wholesale Trade	12 575	9 874	7 546	2 392	985	313	61
Retail Trade..........................	32 079	21 366	12 117	4 259	2 063	785	113
Transportation and Warehousing........	5 637	3 976	2 893	1 211	541	313	131
Information and Cultural Industries......	2 136	1 716	1 698	661	331	187	77
Finance and Insurance.................	5 680	4 610	4 824	1 094	529	248	157
Real Estate and Rental and Leasing......	6 033	3 950	2 748	976	333	112	34
Professional, Scientific and Technical Services	14 934	9 317	6 294	2 070	845	362	106
Management of Companies and Enterprises	2 672	1 921	1 638	718	309	67	48
Administrative and Support, Waste ..... Management and Remediation Services	7 818	5 057	3 853	1 369	682	354	121
Educational Services	1 762	1 265	1 043	392	251	216	435
Health Care and Social Assistance......	16 040	9 425	5 165	1 978	1 246	802	398
Arts, Entertainment and Recreation......	3 169	2 183	1 672	597	266	134	43
Accommodation and Food Services......	14 771	14 159	12 024	4 379	1 267	328	68
Other Services (except Public Administration)	16 742	8 649	4 195	1 016	400	135	37
Public Administration	1 621	1 011	1 046	576	406	341	322

Source: © *Statistics Canada*

LABOUR

Provincial Employment by Industry

1992

	N&L	PEI	NS	NB	Que	Ont	Man	Sask	Alta	BC
Total, all industries	242.4	65.3	426.6	341.5	3 483.4	5541.5	553.2	487.2	1 417.1	1 804.1
Goods-producing sector	62.5	21.3	104.9	89.8	938.1	1508.3	139.6	153.8	395.1	425.5
Agriculture.	2.2	5.7	9.5	7.3	69.6	117.7	41.6	83.8	99.6	36.8
Forestry, fishing, mining, oil and gas	17.2	4.1	20.3	14.2	50.9	56.2	8.5	14.5	80.7	57.8
Utilities	3.4	0.2	3.5	5.8	34.0	66.4	5.3	4.2	14.7	11.8
Construction	18.5	5.3	26.9	23.5	188.5	329.6	28.8	24.5	99.6	134.5
Manufacturing	21.3	5.9	44.7	39.1	595.1	938.4	55.3	26.7	100.4	184.7
Services-producing sector	167.8	43.0	308.4	241.6	2409.0	3 856.2	399.2	323.7	991.9	1341.0
Trade.	40.0	8.8	72.8	57.6	552.2	824.6	85.8	72.8	217.4	288.6
Wholesale trade	6.0	1.3	11.5	9.7	114.4	167.0	16.2	15.2	44.0	64.3
Retail trade	34.0	7.5	61.3	47.9	437.8	657.6	69.6	57.5	173.4	224.4
Transportation and warehousing . .	10.6	3.0	21.0	17.0	154.8	230.7	32.6	20.9	64.2	107.4
Finance, insurance, real estate & leasing	7.9	2.3	23.0	14.4	196.2	383.9	30.7	24.4	79.2	114.3
Finance and insurance	5.6	1.4	15.4	10.4	147.4	256.4	21.1	16.9	52.2	67.9
Real estate and leasing	2.3	0.9	7.7	4.0	48.8	127.6	9.6	7.5	26.9	46.4
Professional, scientific & technical services	5.8	1.4	12.9	8.7	132.4	284.8	17.3	11.8	66.4	92.0
Management of companies and										
administrative & other support services	4.8	1.2	10.1	8.1	78.7	167.6	12.4	9.5	40.6	47.9
Educational services	19.0	4.0	30.8	22.8	220.8	359.5	37.7	32.6	92.4	110.5
Health care and social assistance .	26.7	6.3	46.6	37.7	355.1	501.9	63.4	52.6	125.4	168.3
Information, culture and recreation	6.4	2.3	14.2	11.5	118.8	219.1	19.1	16.4	55.2	71.7
Accommodation and food services	13.3	4.8	22.7	20.8	204.4	316.8	36.9	28.7	92.3	147.6
Other services	12.5	3.3	20.9	17.0	162.9	237.1	26.5	22.9	68.5	89.7
Public administration	20.8	5.8	33.5	25.9	232.6	330.1	36.8	31.1	90.2	103.2
Unclassified industries	12.1	1.0	13.2	10.1	136.3	177.0	14.4	9.7	30.1	37.5

2002

	N&L	PEI	NS	NB	Que	Ont	Man	Sask	Alta	BC
Total, all industries	**257.4**	**76.3**	**474.2**	**385.7**	**3 929.9**	**6 531.5**	**598.0**	**511.1**	**1 767.6**	**2 157.8**
Goods-producing sector	62.2	21.7	108.3	94.0	1 029.2	1 733.3	146	132.4	483.4	439.3
Agriculture.	1.9	4.8	7.8	6.3	67.9	81.4	32.6	51.8	62.8	33.6
Forestry, fishing, mining, oil and gas	18.0	3.6	16.8	14.2	49.0	36.8	7.2	16.9	98.5	46.6
Utilities	2.9	0.4	3.0	4.6	30.3	52.5	6.3	4.2	17.7	12.8
Construction	15.7	5.5	30.1	24.2	179.5	380.9	27.7	28.5	150.5	134.1
Manufacturing	23.7	7.4	50.6	44.7	702.6	1 181.7	72.2	31.0	154.0	212.2
Services-producing sector	185.2	53.9	356.2	283.6	2 784.8	4 643.7	444.2	370.2	1265.5	1653.6
Trade.	42.6	10.3	80.6	56.8	627.6	968.9	91.1	81.2	264.1	334.6
Wholesale trade	6.5	1.3	13.8	11.1	135.5	235.4	19.0	18.6	62.4	76.3
Retail trade	36.1	9.0	66.8	45.7	492.1	733.4	72.1	62.6	201.6	258.3
Transportation and warehousing . .	12.1	2.8	21.5	21.5	158.1	296.9	35.9	25.9	102.2	116.7
Finance, insurance, real estate & leasing	8.2	2.2	22.1	15.1	197.5	408.2	29.0	28.1	86.2	122.7
Finance and insurance	5.4	1.6	15.5	10.8	149.4	309.1	21.9	21.4	54.8	79.6
Real estate and leasing	2.9	0.7	6.6	4.3	48.1	99.1	7.1	6.7	31.4	43.1
Professional, scientific & technical services	8.7	3.0	20.0	15.1	225.4	456.2	24.3	18.3	126.5	143.6
Management of companies and										
administrative & other support services	10.3	2.8	24.2	22.9	133.7	280.6	20.1	12.6	62.8	81.7
Educational services	19.3	5.0	34.9	23.0	246.0	393.1	42.7	37.8	107.5	144.4
Health care and social assistance .	31.7	7.9	52.9	43.8	413.4	573.9	75.1	58.8	161.6	223.6
Information, culture and recreation	8.0	3.3	19.3	14.2	174.1	311.7	25.6	19.8	72.8	112.6
Accommodation and food services	14.4	6.2	34.1	29.1	224.3	392.2	38.5	35.6	127.9	184.0
Other services	12.2	3.5	22.2	19.6	170.7	264.4	27.0	24.2	85.2	102.5
Public administration	17.5	6.7	24.4	22.5	214.0	297.7	34.8	28.0	68.7	87.3
Unclassified industries	10.0	0.8	9.7	8.2	115.9	154.5	7.8	8.5	18.7	64.9

Source: © *Statistics Canada*

Labour Force by Province, 2002

(thousands)

	Population 15 Years and Over	Labour Force[1]	Participation Rate[2]	Employed	Employment Rate (%)	Un- employed	Unemploy- ment Rate (%)
Canada	**25087.4**	**16925.3**	**67.5**	**15649.7**	**62.4**	**1275.6**	**7.5**
Newfoundland and Labrador	439.1	262.1	59.7	213.5	48.6	48.6	18.5
Prince Edward Island . . .	112.5	76.2	67.7	67.9	60.4	8.3	10.9
Nova Scotia.	757.7	476.9	62.9	432.3	57.1	44.6	9.4
New Brunswick	608.5	390.2	64.1	350.0	57.5	40.2	10.3
Quebec	6055.1	3991.7	65.9	3654.1	60.3	337.6	8.5
Ontario	9703.7	6633.1	68.4	6166.0	63.5	467.1	7.0
Manitoba	865.0	601.5	69.5	572.1	66.1	29.3	4.9
Saskatchewan	757.6	520.9	68.8	491.7	64.9	29.2	5.6
Alberta.	2445.1	1795.8	73.4	1707.5	69.8	88.4	4.9
British Columbia	3343.1	2176.9	65.1	1994.6	59.7	182.3	8.4

Source: © *Statistics Canada*

(1) The labour force consists of employed workers, and those who are unemployed but actively seeking work. (2) Participation rate is the percent of the population segment in the labour force.

Labour Force by Age, 2002

(thousands)

	Population	Labour Force[1]	Participation Rate[2]	Employed	Employment Rate (%)	Un- employed	Unemploy- ment Rate (%)
Men							
15 years and over	12 260.5	8989.8	73.3	8262	67.4	727.8	8.1
15-19 years	1048.7	568.5	54.2	453.4	43.2	115.1	20.2
20-24 years	1060.3	859.7	81.1	755.8	71.3	103.9	12.1
25-29 years	1052.8	957.1	90.9	870.1	82.6	87.0	9.1
30-34 years	1113.6	1037.2	93.1	959.5	86.2	77.7	7.5
35-39 years	1239.7	1150.3	92.8	1069.1	86.2	81.1	7.1
40-44 years	1362.9	1264.1	92.8	1188.3	87.2	75.8	6.0
45-49 years	1204.3	1099.7	91.3	1033.7	85.8	66.0	6.0
50-54 years	1055.8	925.8	87.7	871.9	82.6	53.9	5.8
55-59 years	851.8	629.2	73.9	588.1	69.0	41.1	6.5
60-64 years	643.3	327.5	50.9	306.3	47.6	21.2	6.5
65 years and over	1627.3	170.8	10.5	165.8	10.2	5.0	2.9
65-69 years	531.4	99.0	18.6	94.8	17.8	4.2	4.2
70 years and over	1095.8	71.8	6.6	71.0	6.5	—	—
Women							
15 years and over	12 684.6	7699.6	60.7	7149.8	56.4	549.8	7.1
15-19 years	997.3	545.1	54.7	461.5	46.3	83.6	15.3
20-24 years	1025.5	767.9	74.9	696.3	67.9	71.6	9.3
25-29 years	1036.1	835.3	80.6	777.9	75.1	57.5	6.9
30-34 years	1105.0	884.1	80.0	825.4	74.7	58.7	6.6
35-39 years	1233.0	1004.9	81.5	935.8	75.9	69.1	6.9
40-44 years	1365.4	1124.6	82.4	1052.7	77.1	71.8	6.4
45-49 years	1211.0	983.3	81.2	930.2	76.8	53.1	5.4
50-54 years	1073.4	798.9	74.4	756.6	70.5	42.4	5.3
55-59 years	873.3	473.1	54.2	444.7	50.9	28.4	6.0
60-64 years	674.7	205.0	30.4	194.1	28.8	11.0	5.4
65 years and over	2089.9	77.4	3.7	74.6	3.6	2.8	3.6
65-69 years	577.9	49.9	8.6	47.8	8.3	2.1	4.2
70 years and over	1512	27.5	1.8	26.8	1.8	—	—

Source: © *Statistics Canada*

(1) The labour force consists of employed workers, and those who are unemployed but actively seeking work. (2) Participation rate is the percent of the population segment that is in the labour force.

Average Weekly Earnings

All employees (including overtime) (dollars)

	1998	1999	2000	2001	2002
Average weekly earnings	**632.85**	**640.51**	**655.58**	**667.40**	**681.09**
Goods-producing industries	798.25	806.52	824.06	832.35	849.74
Forestry, logging and support	766.33	773.42	810.15	830.84	849.77
Mining and oil and gas extraction	1094.54	1101.04	1137.37	1153.12	1167.98
Utilities	1007.87	1018.23	1029.28	1038.83	1058.31
Construction	781.44	782.63	808.06	800.80	804.22
Manufacturing	770.92	782.43	796.89	808.10	830.14
Service-producing industries	583.19	590.22	603.93	617.70	630.88
Trade	525.01	531.18	536.87	543.47	545.39
Wholesale trade	759.05	758.60	762.84	774.87	778.70
Retail trade	416.97	423.00	425.62	431.06	434.46
Transportation and warehousing	704.87	715.98	725.10	741.65	764.40
Information and cultural industries	757.82	763.14	774.84	800.38	819.32
Finance and insurance	820.45	824.82	845.54	852.32	852.78
Real estate and rental and leasing	567.57	577.63	590.93	611.35	609.79
Professional, scientific & technical services	808.96	828.23	866.81	885.14	900.02
Management of companies & enterprises	860.89	855.85	829.82	839.66	846.25
Educational services	669.11	664.74	673.88	694.30	725.27
Health care and social assistance	543.45	544.78	562.39	581.36	605.12
Arts, entertainment and recreation	383.45	397.25	409.85	428.51	435.18
Other services (except public administration)	482.79	491.47	502.92	521.44	530.11
Public administration	734.05	761.05	781.15	791.95	833.52

Source: © *Statistics Canada*

Labour Income

(millions of dollars)

	1998	1999	2000	2001	2002
Labour income	**475 335**	**502 726**	**545 116**	**569 920**	**597 316**
Wages and salaries	419 190	445 384	483 861	504 765	528 907
All goods-producing industries	*119 934*	*126 108*	*136 602*	*141 407*	*147 532*
Agriculture, forestry, fishing and hunting	6 378	6 748	7 027	7 226	7 000
Mining and oil and gas extraction	9 101	8 531	10 023	11 433	11 775
Manufacturing	73 656	78 020	83 760	84 262	87 458
Construction	24 524	26 435	29 114	31 409	33 990
Utilities	6 276	6 374	6 678	7 076	7 308
All service-producing industries	*299 256*	*319 275*	*347 259*	*363 359*	*381 376*
Trade	58 751	61 475	65 658	69 171	72 174
Transportation and storage	23 538	24 823	26 066	26 526	27 428
Information and cultural industries	13 139	14 770	16 245	17 455	18 107
Finance, real estate and company management	38 910	41 103	46 993	49 128	50 913
Professional and personal services industries	67 649	74 209	81 310	86 057	90 791
Educational services	33 721	35 099	36 409	37 535	39 652
Health care and social assistance	33 649	35 958	38 969	41 569	44 722
Federal government public administration	13 258	14 750	17 875	17 362	18 456
Military	3 159	3 383	3 508	3 833	3 995
Federal public administration excluding military	10 099	11 367	14 368	13 530	14 461
Provincial and territorial public administration	8 641	9 018	9 433	9 938	10 216
Local public administration	8 000	8 069	8 302	8 617	8 917
Supplementary labour income	56 144	57 343	61 254	65 155	684 080

Source: © *Statistics Canada*

Employment in Manufacturing

(thousands)

	Labour Force	Employment	Full-time Employment[1]	Part-time Employment[2]	Unemployed	Unemployment Rate (%)
1988	2 246.3	2 104.3	2 025.2	79.1	142.0	6.3
1989	2 272.6	2 129.7	2 044.4	85.3	142.9	6.3
1990	2 227.7	2 052.5	1 978.2	74.4	175.2	7.9
1991	2 101.7	1 891.8	1 814.9	76.9	209.9	10.0
1992	2 011.6	1 821.5	1 740.5	81.0	190.2	9.5
1993	1 957.3	1 786.4	1 707.6	78.8	170.9	8.7
1994	1 962.6	1 820.3	1 741.9	78.4	142.3	7.3
1995	2 037.1	1 905.5	1 821.8	83.7	131.6	6.5
1996	2 079.7	1 931.1	1 842.5	88.6	148.5	7.1
1997	2 143.6	2 022.4	1 937.9	84.5	121.2	5.7
1998	2 248.0	2 113.8	2 028.7	85.0	134.2	6.0
1999	2 344.8	2 217.4	2 135.3	82.1	127.4	5.4
2000	2 392.8	2 280.2	2 202.1	78.1	112.6	4.7
2001	2 422.5	2 274.5	2 190.4	84.1	148.0	6.1
2002	2 480.0	2 326.2	2 244.2	82.0	153.8	6.2

Source: © *Statistics Canada*

(1) Full-time employment consists of persons who usually work 30 hours or more per week at their main or only job.
(2) Part-time employment consists of persons who usually work less than 30 hours per week at their main or only job.

Employment in Manufacturing by Sector

	Number of Manufacturing Establishments		Number of Production and Related Workers	
	1999	2000	1999	2000
Manufacturing	29 822	53 399	1 480 597	1 612 051
Food manufacturing	3 467	5 533	167 818	194 769
Beverage and tobacco product manufacturing	227	495	15 857	16 280
Textile mills	374	642	21 779	21 997
Textile product mills	422	936	14 856	16 999
Clothing manufacturing	1 342	2 874	70 744	121 070
Leather and allied product manufacturing	176	366	9 040	9 533
Wood product manufacturing	2 144	3 751	109 428	118 848
Paper manufacturing	663	872	82 254	79 146
Printing and related support activities	2 623	4 748	59 849	63 372
Petroleum and coal products manufacturing	204	220	6 691	7 124
Chemical manufacturing	1 274	2 061	55 052	52 267
Plastics and rubber products manufacturing	1 436	2 421	96 126	100 675
Non-metallic mineral product manufacturing	1 354	2 108	36 462	39 501
Primary metal manufacturing	478	643	75 594	75 515
Fabricated metal product manufacturing	4 283	7 807	140 548	152 198
Machinery manufacturing	2 653	4 972	105 705	111 762
Computer and electronic product manufacturing	956	2 049	63 812	66 004
Electrical equipment, appliance and component manufacturing	605	1 086	39 509	42 110
Transportation equipment manufacturing	1 332	2 223	195 255	190 801
Furniture and related product manufacturing	1 748	3 383	72 957	84 197
Miscellaneous manufacturing	2 061	4 209	41 261	47 883

Source: © *Statistics Canada*

Labour and Employment in Retail

(thousands)

	Labour Force		Employed		Full-time		Part-time		Unemployed		Unemployment Rate (%)	
	Men	Women	Men	Women	Men	Women	Men	Women	Men	Women	Men	Women
1988	832.6	900.7	783.2	841.5	626.9	485.8	156.3	355.7	49.4	59.2	5.9	6.6
1989	841.3	897.1	793.7	837.3	632.4	496.3	161.3	341.1	47.6	59.8	5.7	6.7
1990	843.2	922.5	790.6	858.4	627.8	501.3	162.8	357.1	52.6	64.1	6.2	6.9
1991	842.2	941.2	775.2	867.1	604.9	500.3	170.3	366.8	66.9	74.1	7.9	7.9
1992	855.2	915.8	787.8	844.6	614.0	492.9	173.8	351.7	67.5	71.2	7.9	7.8
1993	847.2	913.0	778.8	845.0	604.1	480.5	174.6	364.5	68.4	68.0	8.1	7.4
1994	847.8	923.5	786.1	863.8	606.5	494.7	179.6	369.0	61.7	59.7	7.3	6.5
1995	848.8	926.7	793.6	869.6	627.0	501.5	166.6	368.1	55.2	57.2	6.5	6.2
1996	851.6	919.1	795.0	866.3	623.8	488.5	171.3	377.8	56.6	52.8	6.6	5.7
1997	849.2	924.5	801.8	871.5	633.8	494.2	168.0	377.3	47.4	53.0	5.6	5.7
1998	836.9	953.0	794.1	901.3	622.2	523.6	172.0	377.7	42.7	51.6	5.1	5.4
1999	843.7	955.0	800.6	911.6	617.0	519.4	183.5	392.2	43.1	43.5	5.1	4.6
2000	854.8	999.3	816.1	953.8	631.9	566.5	184.2	387.3	38.7	45.5	4.5	4.6
2001	883.0	1033.3	841.5	988.0	645.8	580.1	195.7	407.8	41.6	45.3	4.7	4.4
2002	913.5	1064.2	865.2	1011.1	662.6	583.5	202.5	427.7	48.3	53.1	5.3	5.0

Source: © *Statistics Canada*

Retail Employment by Sector

	Total Number of Employees		Employees Paid by the Hour	
	2001	**2002**	**2001**	**2002**
Retail trade	148 8 916	1 550 141	1 054 276	1 091 068
Motor vehicle and parts dealers	154 467	162 230	67 111	71 425
Furniture stores	35 005	36 159	n.a.	n.a.
Home furnishings stores	22 172	23 957	n.a.	n.a.
Building material and supplies dealers	60 637	66 544	n.a.	n.a.
Lawn and garden equipment and supplies stores	9 635	10 109	n.a.	n.a.
Food and beverage stores	383 209	398 636	308 776	320 615
Health and personal care stores	120 166	124 646	n.a.	n.a.
Gasoline stations ...., ...	81 129	86 017	63 077	66 642
Clothing and clothing accessories stores	176 119	179 249	n.a.	n.a.
Sporting goods, hobby, book and music stores	72 427	75 073	51 409	53 382
Book, periodical and music stores	20 845	21 476	n.a.	n.a.
General merchandise stores	202 637	206 694	n.a.	n.a.
Miscellaneous store retailers....................	76 309	82 847	n.a.	n.a.
Electronic shopping and mail-order houses	9 776	10 424	6 351	6 738
Vending machine operators	6 315	6 062	4 051	3 929
Direct selling establishments	23 666	23 531	12 723	12 862
Information and cultural industries	342 757	347 780	131 827	130 138
Finance and insurance	555 641	568 837	115 723	116 387
Real estate and rental and leasing	215 859	227 985	95 848	101 432
Professional, scientific and technical services......	639 322	655 627	176 589	170 474
Management of companies and enterprises	83 802	89 191	n.a.	n.a.

Source: © *Statistics Canada*   (n.a.) Not available.

PERSONAL FINANCE

What's a Dollar Worth?[1]

This table shows how many current (2003) dollars it would take to equal the purchasing power of a single dollar in earlier years. For example, if you spent $30 a week on groceries in 1985 and want to know what that would be by today's standards, multiply $30 times the relative value of a 1985 dollar ($1.63) and you have your answer: $48.90. The relative value of a dollar for the years listed was calculated according to changes in the cost of living in Canada as measured by the Consumer Price Index (CPI).

Year	CPI	2003 Relative Value	Year	CPI	2003 Relative Value	Year	CPI	2003 Relative Value	Year	CPI	2003 Relative Value
1920	13.5	9.04	1962	18.9	6.46	1976	37.1	3.29	1990	93.1	1.31
1925	10.9	11.20	1963	19.2	6.36	1977	40.0	3.05	1991	98.9	1.23
1930	10.9	11.20	1964	19.6	6.23	1978	43.6	2.80	1992	100.0	1.22
1935	8.7	14.03	1965	20.0	6.11	1979	47.6	2.57	1993	101.6	1.20
1940	9.5	12.85	1966	20.8	5.87	1980	52.1	2.34	1994	101.6	1.20
1945	10.9	11.20	1967	21.5	5.68	1981	58.9	2.07	1995	104.4	1.17
1950	14.9	8.19	1968	22.4	5.45	1982	65.3	1.87	1996	105.9	1.15
1955	16.8	7.27	1969	23.4	5.22	1983	69.2	1.76	1997	107.7	1.13
1956	17.1	7.14	1970	24.2	5.05	1984	72.1	1.69	1998	108.8	1.12
1957	17.6	6.94	1971	24.9	4.90	1985	75.0	1.63	1999	110.5	1.10
1958	18.0	6.78	1972	26.1	4.68	1986	77.8	1.57	2000	113.7	1.07
1959	18.3	6.67	1973	28.1	4.35	1987	81.5	1.50	2001	117.5	1.04
1960	18.5	6.60	1974	31.1	3.93	1988	84.7	1.44	2002	119.0	1.03
1961	18.7	6.53	1975	34.5	3.54	1989	89.2	1.37	2003	122.1	1.00

Source: © *Statistics Canada*   (1) Based on Consumer Price Index as of June 2003. The current base period is 1992 = 100.

Personal Income and Savings

	Total Personal Income ($millions)	Annual Change in Personal Income (%)	Total Personal Disposable Income ($millions)	Total Personal Saving ($millions)	Personal Saving Rate (%)
1965	41 904	9.9	37 490	2 683	7.2
1970	67 932	8.4	56 042	4 284	7.6
1975	137 240	16.2	112 984	15 778	14.0
1980	248 761	13.9	206 266	32 065	15.5
1985	397 858	8.3	322 989	50 886	15.8
1986	425 757	7.0	340 403	45 761	13.4
1987	457 702	7.5	362 185	43 073	11.9
1988	502 542	9.8	395 217	48 691	12.3
1989	546 324	8.7	432 772	56 281	13.0
1990	586 566	7.4	457 400	59 286	13.0
1991	605 322	3.2	472 509	62 670	13.3
1992	620 653	2.5	483 370	62 879	13.0
1993	633 059	2.0	494 944	58 674	11.9
1994	646 348	2.1	501 678	47 427	9.5
1995	672 111	4.0	519 588	47 859	9.2
1996	687 203	2.2	527 783	37 041	7.0
1997	715 495	4.1	546 166	26 607	4.9
1998	748 321	4.6	568 766	27 610	4.9
1999	783 596	4.7	596 657	24 498	4.1
2000	838 880	7.1	637 673	30 422	4.8
2001	872 657	4.0	665 924	30 441	4.6
2002	903 278	3.5	698 479	29 278	4.2
2003	924 836	2.4	714 898	16 788	2.4

Source: © *Statistics Canada*

Sources of Income by Family Type, 2001

(%)

Canadian taxfilers report income from a number of sources during any given tax year. The table below shows the percentage of taxfilers reporting a specific type of income, broken down by family type.

	Total Family Types	Husband-Wife Families	Lone-Parent Families	Non-Family Persons
Total families.	13 324 980	7 187 680	1 406 400	4 730 900
% REPORTING:				
Employment income.	75	86	79	59
Wages/salaries/commissions.	72	82	76	55
Self-employment	16	23	9	8
Farm+fish self-employment	3	4	1	1
Other self-employment.	14	20	8	7
Investment	44	52	27	37
Government transfers.	82	80	96	81
Employment Insurance.	15	20	16	8
OAS/Net federal supp.	22	18	12	31
CPP/QPP	27	24	18	34
Canada Child Tax Benefit	25	33	64	n.a.
GST/HST credit.	55	41	82	69
Workers compensation	5	7	4	3
Social assistance	10	6	27	13
Provincial tax credits/Family benefits	46	37	74	53
Private pensions.	18	19	8	20
RRSP income.	3	3	1	3
Other income	27	33	26	18

Source: © *Statistics Canada*

Employment Income of Families with Children, 2001

	Total Families	Number of Children			
		0	**1**	**2**	**3+**
Total Couple Families	7 187 680	3 190 830	1 586 300	1 637 590	772 970
Median Employment Income of Husband in Single-Earner Family.	$29 700	$18 000	$33 600	$42 000	$37 600
Median Employment Income of Wife in Single-Earner Family.	$16 600	$15 200	$18 200	$20 000	$15 500
Median Employment Income of Couple in Dual-Earner Family	$64 200	$60 300	$63 800	$68 800	$64 000
Average Contribution of Wife in Dual-Earner Family	$27 500	$28 400	$27 400	$27 800	$24 900
LONE-PARENT FAMILIES					
Total Families with Employment Income	945 140	n.a	529 120	300 500	115 520
Median Employment Income of Parent.	$21 700	n.a	$22 400	$22 400	$16 800

Source: © *Statistics Canada*

Average Assets and Debts Held by Family Units, by Province, 1999

	Canada		Newfoundland & Labrador		Prince Edward Island	
Number of family units	12 215 629		198 630		54 205	
	% of Families[1]	$ Average	% of Families[1]	$ Average	% of Families[1]	$ Average
ASSETS	100.0	237 163	100.0	114 687	100.0	194 919
Financial assets	93.0	74 774	80.8	37 801	92.0	54 450
Within registered plans	61.0	56 442	42.0	34 112	52.2	60 380
RRSPs & LIRAs[2]	54.9	51 189	39.1	32 658	45.4	57 255
Other registered plans[3].	14.7	42 967	x	x	x	x
Outside registered plans.	90.0	39 047	79.5	20 424	88.5	21 016
Deposits in fin inst	87.9	14 970	78.1	7 657	84.6	8 060
Mutual & investmt funds. . . .	30.0	53 928	19.4	15 407	30.4	28 732
Other financial assets[4]	8.9	64 948	x	x	x	x
Non-financial assets	100.0	138 593	100.0	77 755	100.0	102 550
Principal residence.	60.4	149 661	73.2	66 440	67.2	92 108
Other real estate.	16.5	116 999	17.0	42 225	x	x
Vehicles	77.2	13 329	77.1	10 616	84.0	11 913
Other non-financial assets[5] .	100.0	18 689	100.0	13 767	100.0	19 184
Equity in business.	18.7	155 610	x	x	x	x
DEBTS	68.0	55 155	75.3	29 332	74.5	31 853
Mortgages.	35.1	82 844	25.1	46 332	31.8	49 491
Principal residence.	32.7	76 116	24.2	42 237	30.5	47 139
Other real estate.	4.7	88 550	x	x	x	x
Line of credit.	15.9	13 542	x	x	x	x
Cr card & installmt debt[6]. . . .	38.5	3 033	52.6	2 614	48.2	2 628
Student loans	11.8	10 361	19.8	15 831	x	x
Vehicle loans.	21.2	11 226	31.7	10 130	28.0	9 253
Other debt.	16.3	9 301	19.4	8 562	32.1	5 950
NET WORTH[7]	99.9	199 789	100.0	92 612	100.0	171 189

	Nova Scotia		New Brunswick		Quebec	
Number of family units	376 191		300 177		3 115 360	
	% of Families[1]	$ Average	% of Families[1]	$ Average	% of Families[1]	$ Average
ASSETS.	100.0	154 005	100.0	182 705	100.0	149 587
Financial assets	86.4	55 194	92.9	58 226	86.4	42 063
Within registered plans	54.0	43 020	57.2	49 632	48.0	41 585
RRSPs & LIRAs[2]	49.2	38 335	50.9	44 856	43.8	38 378
Other registered plans[3].	13.6	32 174	12.1	45 716	11.9	26 146
Outside registered plans. . . .	81.3	30 045	90.5	28 423	83.7	19 595
Deposits in fin inst	78.1	10 598	89.4	11 491	81.2	10 670
Mutual & investmt funds. . . .	30.4	31 983	21.8	49 374	23.3	27 992
Other financial assets[4]	9.9	65 025	6.3	74 464	x	x
Non-financial assets	100.0	94 340	100.0	101 815	100.0	91 874
Principal residence.	64.4	87 382	55.4	109 481	70.2	78 715
Other real estate.	19.4	50 615	16.8	101 942	19.7	52 090
Vehicles	76.9	12 122	72.8	11 740	82.2	12 779
Other non-financial assets[5] .	100.0	18 928	100.0	15 522	100.0	15 871
Equity in business.	14.1	84 989	14.4	186 422	x	x
DEBTS.	74.5	34 523	65.1	42 297	72.8	30 796
Mortgages.	32.4	51 732	32.6	65 594	33.1	40 762
Principal residence.	30.3	49 829	29.9	55 532	31.6	38 376
Other real estate.	x	x	5.2	93 151	x	x
Line of credit.	17.4	10 559	15.8	7 082	12.0	9 759
Cr card & installmt debt[6]. . . .	45.6	2 626	33.8	2 081	49.0	2 373
Student loans	13.7	11 178	11.9	7 971	18.3	10 137
Vehicle loans.	29.4	10 601	21.1	9 696	32.2	10 533
Other debt.	18.3	6 816	15.4	8 496	15.2	9 041
NET WORTH[7]	99.8	128 502	100.0	155 261	100.0	127 155 ▶

	Ontario		Manitoba		Saskatchewan	
Number of family units	4 480 409		446 152		401 649	
	% of Families[1]	$ Average	% of Families[1]	$ Average	% of Families[1]	$ Average
ASSETS	100.0	264 348	100.0	190 268	100.0	224 291
Financial assets	94.6	87 690	92.2	70 312	94.5	72 337
Within registered plans	64.9	62 377	62.9	52 422	63.3	51 155
RRSPs & LIRAs[2]	58.5	55 119	55.3	47 802	56.2	47 644
Other registered plans[3]	17.0	48 485	17.1	38 271	16.8	33 345
Outside registered plans	91.3	46 451	87.7	36 342	91.2	39 416
Deposits in fin inst	89.6	17 893	84.1	16 227	88.6	19 311
Mutual & investmt funds	34.0	65 386	33.4	43 895	34.2	41 637
Other financial assets[4]	8.3	50 412	9.8	36 364	16.4	28 118
Non-financial assets	100.0	160 277	100.0	96 467	100.0	104 626
Principal residence	60.5	181 395	64.1	91 348	69.1	82 091
Other real estate	16.3	128 634	17.7	57 351	18.0	90 831
Vehicles	76.7	13 062	78.8	13 079	84.3	15 595
Other non-financial assets[5]	100.0	19 513	100.0	17 504	100.0	18 337
Equity in business	19.6	108 038	17.3	167 572	28.9	177 529
DEBTS	68.0	63 579	62.9	37 604	66.2	38 418
Mortgages	36.3	94 406	33.0	51 196	30.6	48 616
Principal residence	34.1	88 689	31.2	49 201	29.2	45 424
Other real estate	4.5	88 417	x	x	x	x
Line of credit	16.1	16 978	12.4	8 556	16.2	11 090
Cr card & installmt debt[6]	39.9	3 373	33.5	3 069	38.6	2 690
Student loans	12.2	11 680	x	x	11.4	11 309
Vehicle loans	19.4	11 529	21.5	11 201	26.9	12 839
Other debt	13.9	9 078	18.3	8 447	19.7	15 068
NET WORTH[7]	99.9	221 233	100.0	166 628	100.0	198 911

	Alberta		British Columbia	
Number of family units	1 157 207		1 685 649	
	% of Families[1]	$ Average	% of Families[1]	$ Average
ASSETS	100.0	278 016	100.0	302 934
Financial assets	93.2	79 624	92.8	82 775
Within registered plans	63.4	55 611	61.0	60 882
RRSPs & LIRAs[2]	58.7	53 703	54.7	56 644
Other registered plans[3]	14.2	26 533	14.1	43 822
Outside registered plans	89.4	43 553	90.4	43 882
Deposits in financial institutions	86.1	15 771	87.5	14 231
Mutual funds & investment funds stocks & bonds (saving & other)	33.2	42 022	33.3	53 280
Other financial assets[4]	12.9	88 595	11.2	84 493
Non-financial assets	100.0	146 583	100.0	189 208
Principal residence	66.4	135 917	57.7	225 202
Other real estate	16.2	126 108	14.3	183 179
Vehicles	84.3	15 870	78.6	15 087
Other non-financial assets[5]	100.0	22 513	100.0	21 140
Equity in business	25.1	228 367	20.9	176 758
DEBTS	71.9	58 441	69.1	74 860
Mortgages	41.0	78 108	36.4	115 849
Principal residence	38.1	72 687	33.4	107 152
Other real estate	5.7	76 536	5.8	108 932
Line of credit	17.2	14 543	16.4	18 547
Credit card & installment debt[6]	39.7	3 379	38.3	3 814
Student loans	11.0	9 242	9.7	10 433
Vehicle loans	23.1	13 032	18.2	12 278
Other debt	18.1	11 688	20.3	9 034
NET WORTH[7]	99.9	236 198	99.9	251 517

Source: © *Statistics Canada*

x Data unavailable, not applicable or confidential.

(1) Family units: economic families (a group of two or more persons who live in the same dwelling & are related to each other by blood marriage common law or adoption) & unattached individuals (a person living either alone or with others to whom he or she is unrelated). (2) Registered Retirement Savings Plans (RRSPs) & Locked-in Retirement Accounts (LIRAs). (3) Plans other than RRSPs or LIRAs e.g. Registered Retirement Income Funds (RRIFs) Deferred Profit Sharing Plans (DPSPs) & Registered Education Savings Plans (RESPs). (4) Includes treasury bills mortgage-backed securities money held in trust annuities money owed to the respondent & other miscellaneous financial assets including shares of privately held companies not held within registered plans. (5) The value of the contents of the respondent's principal residence valuables & collectibles copyrights & patents etc. (6) Includes major credit cards & retail store cards gasoline station cards etc. Installment debt is the total amount owing on deferred payment or installment plans where the purchased item is to be paid for over a period of time. (7) Net worth = assets less debts.

Net Worth and Median Income by Family Type, 1998

	% of Family Units	% Economic Families	% Unattached Individuals	Median Net Worth	Median After-tax 1998 Income
All family units.................	100			**$81 000**	**$33 400**
Economic families of two or more...	68	100		$119 300	$43 000
Elderly families		14		$202 000	$32 000
Non-elderly families		86		$105 500	$48 400
Couples only		22		$125 800	$44 800
Couples with children under 18...		38		$100 500	$48 400
Lone-parent families		7		$14 600	$21 800
Other non-elderly families.......		18		$151 000	$52 300
Unattached individuals	32		100	$21 700	$16 700
Elderly men..................			7	$111 100	$17 700
Elderly women.................			20	$76 600	$15 300
Non-elderly men			42	$11 200	$19 800
Non-elderly women............			32	$12 000	$15 600

Source: © Statistics Canada

Distribution of Net Worth, 1998

For the 1998 tax year, the median net worth of the close to 12.2 million family units in Canada was around $81,000. However, when family units were ranked from highest net worth to lowest, the median net worth of the top 10 percent (or top decile) was nearly $703,500, while the median net worth of the lowest decile was $-2,100. Further analysis showed that the wealthiest 10 percent of family units held 53 percent of all personal wealth. (By comparison, in the US, the top 10 percent of family units and unattached individuals held approximately two-thirds of total net worth.)

Family units ranked by net worth in deciles (units of 10%)	% of Total Net Worth	Median Net Worth
All family units......................................	100	**$81 000**
Highest 10%..	53	$703 500
Ninth 10%..	17	$338 100
Eighth 10%...	11	$220 800
Seventh 10%..	8	$152 600
Sixth 10%..	5	$101 500
Fifth 10%..	3	$64 700
Fourth 10%...	2	$35 500
Third 10%..	1	$14 300
Second 10%..	...	$3 100
Lowest 10%...	...	$-2 100

Source: © Statistics Canada

Median Net Worth of Families by Income, 1998

After-tax Income in 1998	% of Family Units	Median Net Worth
All family units............................	100	**$81 000**
Less than $10 000	8	$1 700
$10 000 - $19 000	18	$14 600
$20 000 - $29 000	18	$52 000
$30 000 - $39 000	16	$82 800
$40 000 - $49 000	12	$109 200
$50 000 - $74 999	18	$153 500
$75 000 or more.........................	10	$314 200

Source: © Statistics Canada

Median Net Worth by Province, 1998

"Median" refers to the point in a data grouping at which half of those in the group fall below the median number and half are above it—the middle value or mid-point in the series. "Net worth" includes financial assets such as investments, non-financial assets such as property, and equity in businesses.

	% of Total Family Units	% Owning Principal Residence	% with After-tax Family Income under $20 000	Median Net Worth
All provinces.	100	60	26	**$81 000**
Newfoundland and Labrador.	2	73	31	$53 000
Prince Edward Island	...	67	30	$76 100
Nova Scotia.	3	64	32	$68 100
New Brunswick.	2	70	31	$65 400
Quebec	26	55	31	$61 300
Ontario	37	60	21	$101 400
Manitoba.	4	64	28	$79 300
Saskatchewan	3	69	30	$97 300
Alberta	9	66	24	$95 400
British Columbia	14	58	28	$94 800

Source: © *Statistics Canada*

Median Net Worth by Education, 1998

Highest Level of Education of Major Income Earner for Family	% of Family Units	Median Net Worth
Less than high school	27	$62 500
Graduated high school	23	$67 700
Non-university certificate	28	$78 700
University certificate:		
Bachelor's degree	15	$117 500
Master's or certificate above Bachelor's	5	$181 500
Doctorate.	1	$237 000
Degree in law, medicine, dentistry, veterinary medicine or optometry	1	$323 000

Source: © *Statistics Canada*

Median Net Worth by Occupation, 1998

Occupation of Major Income Earner for Family	% of Family Units	Median Net Worth	Median after-tax 1998 Income
All family units		**$81 000**	**$33 400**
Management	8	$192 800	$56 100
Primary industry	2	$155 000	$35 800
Social science, education, government and religion . .	5	$112 200	$49 600
Health	4	$111 600	$46 000
Natural and applied sciences.	6	$90 500	$47 500
Trades, transportation and equipment operators	12	$79 000	$41 800
Business, finance and administration	10	$77 900	$39 700
No occupation.	32	$76 500	$20 700
Processing, manufacturing and utilities	6	$66 900	$41 700
Art, culture, recreation and sport	2	$65 000	$35 400
Sales and service	13	$40 000	$28 400

Source: © *Statistics Canada*

Canadian Income Tax

Income tax was introduced in 1917 as a temporary measure to finance Canada's participation in World War I. The law introducing the tax (the Income War Tax Act) was shorter and much simpler than our current legislation. It imposed tax at graduated rates, ranging from 4 percent on the first $1,500 to 25 percent for income over $100,000.

This "temporary" tax was not repealed when the war ended. But on Jan. 1, 1949, the federal government removed "war" from the title and gave the statute the name it has today—the Income Tax Act. This act has been amended many times—most notably in 1972 when a major overhaul of the tax system broadened the tax base and introduced a tax on capital gains. This is still the basis of our federal income tax laws today.

In 1988, all personal exemptions and many deductions were changed to non-refundable tax credits. Unlike deductions, which reduce taxable income, credits are used to reduce the amount of tax payable. The term "non-refundable" refers to the fact that, although you can use these credits to reduce or eliminate your federal tax payable, any unused portion is not refundable to you. In some cases, however, you may be able to transfer the unused portion of the credits to someone else.

Because the credits are calculated by multiplying eligible amounts by 15 percent—the same as the lowest personal tax rate—the change makes no difference to those whose income falls within the lowest tax bracket. But it increases taxes for most of those with higher incomes.

Source: *Revenue Canada*

For the 2003 income tax year, the federal income tax rates for the individual are: 16 percent on income up to $32,182; $5,149 plus 22 percent on the next $32,182 up to $64,367; $12,230 plus 26 percent on the next $40,319 up to $104,647; and $22,703 plus 29 percent on income in excess of $104,648. There is a maximum total tax for the first three brackets, but no maximum tax for the over $104,648 bracket.

Provincial Income Tax

In previous years, all provinces and territories except Quebec computed income tax as a percentage of basic federal tax ("tax-on-tax" system). In 2000, five provinces switched to the "tax-on-income" system, with the other provinces and three territories following suit for the 2001 tax year. All jurisdictions, except for Quebec, continue to use the federal definition of taxable income. However, under a tax-on-income system, provinces set their own rates, brackets and credits.

Filing Tax Returns

Though corporations must file tax returns each year, individuals need only file if they owe taxes or if they are eligible to claim tax credits such as the Child Tax Credit, or the Goods and Services Tax Credit. Persons owing money must file a return by April 30 of the year following the taxation year. Failure to do so makes the taxpayer liable to a late-filing penalty of 5 percent of unpaid tax plus an additional penalty of 1 percent per month on the amount outstanding, to a maximum of 12 months, plus interest on amounts owing.

Federal Income Tax Rates on Individual Income, 2003

The federal components of personal income tax rates apply to all taxpayers.

Federal Tax Brackets, Marginal Rates and Minimum Amounts of Tax

Basic Federal Tax Brackets	Other than Quebec		Quebec	
	Marginal Rate	Minimum Federal Tax Payable	Marginal Rate[2]	Minimum Federal Tax Payable
$0 to $32 182	16%	$0[1]	13.36%	$0[1]
$32 183 to $64 367	22%	$5 149	18.37%	$4 300
$64 368 to $104 647	26%	$12 230	21.71%	$10 212
over $104 648	29%	$22 703	24.22%	$18 957

Source: © *"Tax Facts and Figures," PricewaterhouseCoopers*

(1) The basic personal credit eliminates federal tax for taxable income below $7,756. (2) Marginal rates for the federal component of personal tax are adjusted by a factor of 83.5 percent in Quebec: 13.36 percent = 16 percent x 83.5 percent; 18.37 = 22 percent x 83.5 percent; 21.71 percent = 26 percent x 83.5 percent; 24.215 percent = 83.5 percent x 29 percent. The federal surtax is not affected. The 83.5 percent factor is what remains after the 16.5 percent abatement.

Individual Provincial Income Tax Rates, 2003

For 2003, all provinces and territories compute income tax as "tax-on-income" systems. All jurisdictions, except for Quebec, continued to use the federal definition of taxable income. However, under a tax-on-income system, provinces set their own rates, brackets and credits.

Five provinces have surtaxes, calculated as a percentage of provincial tax. Manitoba and Saskatchewan eliminated their flat taxes in 2002, while several provinces have eliminated their surtaxes.

	Basic Tax Credit Amount	Basic Brackets					Provincial Surtax[1] On Provincial Tax Above:	Reduction for Low Incomes
Nfld & Lab.	$7 410	$0 to $29 589	$29 590 to $59 179	over $59 180			$7 032	No
Rates		10.57%	16.16%	18.02%			9% of tax	
PEI	$7 412	$0 to $30 753	$30 754 to $61 508	over $61 509			$5 200	Yes
Rates		9.8%	13.8%	16.7%			10% of tax	
N. Scotia	$7 231	$0 to $29 589	$29 590 to $59 179	over $59 180			$10 000	Yes
Rates		9.77%	14.95%	16.67%			10% of tax	
N. Brunswick	$7 756	$0 to $32 182	$32 183 to $64 368	$64 369 to $104 647	Over $104 648		n.a.	Yes
Rates		9.68%	14.82%	16.52%	17.84%			
Quebec[2]	$6 150	$0 to $27 094	$27 095 to $54 194	Over $54 195			n.a.	Yes
Rates		16%	20%	24%				
Ontario	$7 817	$0 to $32 434	$32 435 to $64 871	Over $64 872			$3 747 20% of tax $4 727 36% of tax	Yes
Rates		6.05%	9.15%	11.16%				
Manitoba	$7 634	$0 to $30 543	$30 544 to $64 999	Over $65 000			n.a.	Yes
Rates		10.9%	15.4%	17.4%				
Sask.	$8 000	$0 to $34 999	$35 000 to $99 999	over $100 000			n.a.	Yes
Rates		11%	13%	15%				
Alberta	$13 529	on taxable income					n.a.	Yes
Rates		10%						
B.C.	$8 307	$0 to $31 652	$31 653 to $63 307	$63 08 to $72 684	$72 685 to $88 259	Over $88 260	n.a.	No
Rates		6.05%	9.15%	11.7%	13.7%	14.7%		
Yukon	$7 634	$0 to $32 182	$32 183 to $64 367	$64 368 to $104 647	Over $104 648		$6 000	No
Rates		7.04%	9.68%	11.44%	12.76%		5% of tax	
Northwest Territories	$11 050	$0 to $32 182	$32 183 to $64 367	$64 368 to $104 647	Over $104 648		n.a.	No
Rates		7.2%	9.9%	11.7%	13.05%			
Nunavut	$10 160	$0 to $32 182	$32 183 to $64 367	$64 368 to $104 647	Over $104 648		n.a.	
Rates		4%	7%	9%	11.5%			
Non-residents	$7 756	$0 to $32 182	$32 183 to $64 367	$64 368 to $104 647	Over $104 648		n.a.	No
Rates		7.68%	10.56%	12.48%	13.92%			

Source: © "Tax Facts and Figures," PricewaterhouseCoopers   (n.a.) Not applicable.

(1) Surtax rates are the percentage of provincial tax above the basic provincial tax thresholds.
(2) Quebec's basic amount is $8,440 under the simplified tax system.

Personal Tax Credits, 2003

(dollars)

	Federal Amount[13]	Federal Credit[14]	Quebec Credit[15]
Basic	7 756	1 241	1 230
Spouse/Equivalent to Spouse[1]	6 586	1 054	1 230
Age 65[2]	3 787	606	440[16]
Disability[3]	6 279	1 005	440
Infirm dependant[4]	3 663	586	1 230
Care giver[5]			600
Dependant[6]			
— 1st	—	—	542
— Children (Additional)	—	—	500
Single parent	—	—	271
Living alone	—	—	219[16]
Pension income[7]	1 000	160	200[16]
CPP/QPP[8]	1 802	288	360
Employment Insurance (EI)	819	131	164
Education (per month)[9]			
— Full-time	400	64	344
— Part-time	120	19	344
CREDITS AS PERCENTAGE OF ACTUAL PAYMENT			
Dividends[10]	—[13]	13.33%[14]	10.83%
Charitable donations[11]			
First $200	—[13]	16%[14]	20%
Over $2000	—[13]	29%[14]	24%
Tuition[12]	—[13]	16%[14]	20%

Source: © *"Tax Facts and Figures," PricewaterhouseCoopers*
(1) The spousal and equivalent credits are reduced when the income of the spouse or qualifying dependent exceeds $659. Any net income of the spouse reduces the Quebec spouse credit. (2) The age credit is reduced if income exceeds $27,095. (3) Basic credit for individuals with severe and prolonged impairment. The under 18 supplement is reduced if childcare and attendant care expenses claimed for child exceed $2,145. (4) Reduced if dependent's income exceeds $5,115. Any income reduces the Quebec infirm dependant credit. (5) For providers of in-home care for an adult relative (reduced if relative's income exceeds $12,312). The caregiver credit for Quebec is refundable. (6) Quebec's childcare credit is refundable and depends on net family income, and ranges from 26% to 75% of the expense. To qualify for the additional credit for children, children must be full-time students or under 19 years of age at the end of the year. (7) Maximum pension credit is $160. (8) For employees, the maximum credit is $405, self-employed persons deduct half of CPP/QPP premiums paid for their own coverage and claim a credit for half of these premiums. (9) The education credit is $64/month for full-time students, $19/month for part-time students. Quebec's maximum education credit is $344 per term (maximum two terms per year) for a supporting Quebec parent, which is not transferable. (10) Credits for taxable Canadian dividends apply to the grossed-up amount (125 percent) of dividends. (11) Eligible donations are limited to 75% of net income. (12) Tuition credit is available only if at least $100 in fees is paid to an institution. (13) Provinces use their own amounts to determine credits. (14) Maximum dollar value of credits that are based on prescribed amounts. Provinces have their own maximum dollar value of credits. (15) Under Quebec's simplified tax regime, some credits shown are not available and are replaced by a $2,820 lump-sum amount. (16) The total of Quebec's age, pension and living alone credits is reduced if net family income exceeds $27,095.

Individual Tax Tables, 2002

This table shows the combined federal and provincial (or territorial) income taxes, including surtaxes and flat taxes, payable on the assumption that only the basic personal tax credit is available, and that all income is either interest or ordinary income (such as salary).

Amount of combined federal and provincial/territorial income tax

Taxable Income	$20 000	$30 000	$40 000	$50 000	$60 000	$70 000	$80 000	$90 000	$100 000
Newfoundland & Labr.	3 309	5 989	9 705	13 521	17 374	21 804	26 368	30 932	35 496
Prince Edward Island	3 212	5 792	9 241	12 821	16 514	20 768	25 205	29 642	34 079
Nova Scotia	3 176	5 824	9 419	13 114	16 823	20 956	25 231	29 664	34 098
New Brunswick	3 176	5 744	9 239	12 921	16 603	20 664	24 916	29 168	33 420
Quebec[1]	3 640	6 708	10 461	14 298	18 399	22 858	27 429	32 000	36 571
Ontario	2 724	4 929	7 884	10 999	14 185	18 052	22 393	26 734	31 075
Manitoba	3 301	6 016	9 631	13 371	17 111	21 217	25 557	29 897	34 237
Saskatchewan	3 329	6 054	9 478	13 003	-16 528	20 544	24 694	28 844	32 994
Alberta	2 548	5 245	8 344	11 544	14 744	18 210	21 810	25 410	29 010
British Columbia	2 694	4 899	7 879	10 994	14 109	17 687	21 628	25 630	29 700
Yukon	2 849	5 153	8 176	11 344	14 512	18 063	21 840	25 641	29 443
Northwest Territories	2 746	5 066	8 110	11 300	14 490	18 066	21 836	25 606	29 376
Nunavut	2 379	4 379	7 127	10 027	12 927	16 225	19 725	23 225	26 725

Source: © *"Tax Facts and Figures," PricewaterhouseCoopers* (1) In some situations, the calculation of taxable income for federal and Quebec purposes may be different, and the amounts shown may require adjustments.

INVESTMENT

Investment: A Glossary of Terms

Annual report: A report issued by a company to its shareholders at the end of the fiscal year. It contains a report on company operations and formal financial statements.

Bankers' acceptance: A commercial draft backed by the guarantee of a bank. The bankers' acceptance promises repayment on a certain date, usually not more than 90 days ahead, and bears a rate of return competitive with other chartered bank securities.

Bear market: A market in which prices are falling.

Bid and ask: The bid price is the highest price anyone is willing to pay to buy a stock; the ask is the lowest price anyone will accept to sell a stock. Together, the bid and ask prices are a quote.

Blue chip stocks: Stocks with good investment qualities, usually common shares of well-established companies with good earnings records and long-time dividend payments.

Board lot: A unit of trading. Board lots on the Toronto Stock Exchange are: under 10 cents each—1000 shares; between 10 cents and 99 cents each—500 shares; at and above $1 each—100 shares.

Bond: A written promise or IOU by the issuer to repay a fixed amount of borrowed money on a specified date, and to pay a set annual rate of interest in the meantime, generally at semi-annual intervals. Bonds are usually considered a safe investment because the borrower (whether a company or the government) must make interest payments before its money is spent on anything else.

Bull market: A market in which prices are rising.

Call: An option to buy a fixed amount of a certain stock at a specified price within a specified time.

Canada Savings Bonds: These are issued each fall, and are popular with small investors because they come in denominations starting at $100. They are not traded. They have a term of several years and a minimum guaranteed rate of interest. However, the government sets an effective rate during the issuing period each year, and adjusts it when necessary to conform with interest rate trends. Interest can be awarded yearly or compounded, depending upon the type of bond.

Capital gain or loss: Profit or loss resulting from the sale of an asset, such as a security. The gain or loss is the difference between the buying and selling price of the security with commissions figured in.

Commercial paper: Short-term negotiable securities issued by corporations that call for the payment of a specific amount of money at a given time.

Common shares: Securities issued by the company that represent part-ownership in the company. Common shares sometimes carry a voting privilege and entitle the holder to a share in the company's profits, usually issued in the form of dividends.

Convertible bond: A corporate bond (see below) that may be converted into a stated number of shares of the corporation's common stock. Its price tends to fluctuate with the price of the stock, as well as with changes in interest rates.

Corporate bonds: Evidence of debt by a corporation. The bond bears interest much like a government bond, and matures at a certain date in the future. Considered safer than the common or preferred stock of the same company.

Day order: An order to buy or sell a security valid only for the day the order is given.

Dividend: A portion of a company's profit paid to the common and preferred shareholders. The amount is decided upon by the company's board of directors, and may be paid in cash or stock.

Equities: Common and preferred stocks that represent a share in the ownership of a company.

Ex-dividend: Without dividend. The buyer of shares quoted ex-dividend is not entitled to receive an already declared dividend. When shares are un-dividend, the purchaser will receive the declared dividend.

Floor trader: A brokerage-firm employee who works on the stock exchange trading floor, and is responsible for executing buy and sell orders on behalf of the firm and its clients.

Futures: Contracts to buy or sell specific quantities of a commodity or financial instrument with delivery delayed until some agreed-upon time in the future.

Government of Canada bonds: These bear a fixed rate of interest and a maturation date in the future, and are traded on the market, with the price rising and falling in response to interest rate trends. ▶

▶ Long-term government bonds are considered a safe investment. Provinces and municipalities may also issue long-term bonds.

Index: Statistical measure of the state of the stock market or economy, based on the performance of stocks or other components. Examples are the TSE 300 Composite Index and the Toronto 35 Index.

Limit order: An order to buy or sell securities in which the client has specified the price. The order can be executed only at the specified price or a better one.

Liquidity: The measure of how quickly an investor can turn securities into cash. A security is liquid if it can be bought and sold quickly with small price changes between transactions.

Long: A term signifying ownership of securities. "I am long 100 XYZ" means that the speaker owns 100 shares of XYZ.

Margin: The amount paid by clients when they use credit to buy a security, the balance being loaned by their brokers.

Market order: An order to buy a security immediately at the best possible price.

Money market: Part of the capital market established for short-term borrowing and lending of funds. Money market dealers conduct business over the telephone, and trade securities such as short-term (three years and less) government bonds, government treasury bills and commercial paper.

Mutual fund: A portfolio, or selection, of professionally bought and managed stocks in which the investor pools money with thousands of others. A share price is based on net asset value, or the value of all the investments owned by the fund, less any debt, divided by the total number of shares. The major advantage is less risk—an investment is spread out over many stocks, and if one or two do badly, the remainder may shield the investor from the losses. Bond funds are mutual funds that deal in the bond market exclusively. Money market mutual funds concentrate on debt instruments sold on the money market. Equity mutual funds place their investments in the common shares of companies.

Odd lot: A number of shares less than a board lot.

Open order: An order to buy or sell a security at a specified price, valid until executed or cancelled.

Over-the-counter: The over-the-counter (OTC) or unlisted market is the market maintained by securities dealers for issues not listed on a stock exchange.

Penny stock: Low-priced, often speculative issues selling at less than $1 a share.

Preferred shares: Shares that carry dividends at fixed rates that must be paid before any dividends are paid to common shareholders.

Price/earnings ratio: A common stock's current market price divided by the company's annual per share earnings.

Prospectus: A legal document describing securities being offered for sale to the public. It must be prepared in accordance with provincial securities commission regulations.

Put: An option to sell a fixed amount of a certain stock at a specified price within a specified time.

Registered representative: A salesperson or broker employed by an investment firm. Salespersons must be registered with the provincial securities commission.

Right: A temporary privilege granted to existing common shareholders to purchase additional shares directly from the company at a stated price.

Settlement date: The date on which a securities buyer must pay for a purchase or a seller must deliver the securities sold. In general, settlement must be made on or before the third business day following the transaction date.

Short sale: The sale of shares that the seller does not own. The seller is speculating that the stock price will fall, in the hope of later purchasing the same number of securities at a lower price, thereby making a profit. Sellers must advise their brokers when they are selling short.

Stock yield: The percentage of the dividend paid in relation to the price of the stock. For example, a stock selling at $40 a share with an annual dividend of $2 a share yields 5 percent.

Transfer agent: A trust company appointed by a company to keep a record of the names, addresses and numbers of shares held by its shareholders. Transfer agents are often responsible for distributing dividend cheques.

Underwriting: The purchase for resale of a new issue of securities by an investment dealer or group of dealers.

Warrant: A certificate giving the holder the right to purchase securities at a stipulated price within a specified period of time. They are often detachable and may be traded separately.

Canadian Investors by Province, 2001

	% of Taxfilers with Investment Income	Average Age of Investor	Median Total Income of Investor	Median Investment Income	% Investment Income from Dividends
Canada	13	54	$37,700	$1,000	56
Newfoundland and Labrador	7	51	36,300	400	59
Prince Edward Island	12	53	32,100	600	58
Nova Scotia	12	55	35,300	800	68
New Brunswick	10	54	34,300	600	65
Quebec	13	52	36,300	800	60
Ontario	14	54	40,000	1,000	51
Manitoba	13	55	33,000	800	49
Saskatchewan	13	55	32,000	1,000	50
Alberta	15	52	39,900	1,100	63
British Columbia	14	55	36,100	1,400	55
Yukon	12	50	47,100	600	73
Northwest Territories	7	45	66,400	500	68
Nunavut	4	45	77,100	600	73

Source: © *Statistics Canada*

Canadian Investors by Age, 2001

	% Canadians with Investment Income					
	0-24	25-34	35-44	45-54	55-64	Over 65
Canada	4	8	18	24	20	26
Newfoundland and Labrador . .	3	7	21	32	21	16
Prince Edward Island	4	6	19	26	20	24
Nova Scotia	3	6	17	25	21	27
New Brunswick	3	6	17	27	21	26
Quebec	4	9	21	25	20	22
Ontario	4	8	17	23	19	29
Manitoba	4	7	16	24	20	29
Saskatchewan	4	6	17	24	19	30
Alberta	4	8	20	26	19	23
British Columbia	4	7	15	24	21	30
Yukon	3	8	22	34	20	13
Northwest Territories	4	12	30	35	14	5
Nunavut	4	17	23	38	15	4

Source: © *Statistics Canada*

Canadian Investors by Gender, 2001

	Taxfilers with Investment Income		Median Investment Income		
	% Male	% Female	Total	Male	Female
Canada	52	48	$1000	$800	$1100
Newfoundland and Labrador .	58	42	400	300	400
Prince Edward Island	55	45	600	500	600
Nova Scotia	53	47	800	700	900
New Brunswick	55	45	600	500	700
Quebec	55	45	800	800	800
Ontario	49	51	1000	800	1200
Manitoba	51	49	800	700	1000
Saskatchewan	54	46	1000	900	1100
Alberta	54	46	1100	1000	1100
British Columbia	49	51	1400	1200	1700
Yukon	51	49	600	700	500
Northwest Territories	57	43	500	500	400
Nunavut	61	39	600	600	600

Source: © *Statistics Canada*

Housing Affordability Table

The table below shows how expensive a home an individual or family could likely afford, using various income levels and mortgage interest rates—assuming a down-payment of 25 percent of the purchase price. As income rises, housing becomes more affordable, but it becomes less affordable as interest rates increase.

For example, most couples with a combined annual income of $60,000 would qualify for a mortgage on a home costing $192,170 at an 8 percent interest rate—provided they had a down-payment of $38,094 (25 percent of the purchase price). But at a 10 percent interest rate, the same couple earning the same income could only afford a $163,967 home.

The table assumes that mortgage payments, property taxes, heating costs and 50 percent of condominium fees should not exceed 32 percent of gross income (net income if self-employed). Most lending institutions use this percentage when calculating how large a mortgage you can afford. For this table, we have established annual costs of $2,400 for taxes and $2,400 for taxes and $2,400 for heating. Most lenders will also require that your total debt service ratio (mortgage payments, property taxes, heating cost, 50 percent of condo fees and any other liabilities such as car loans or other debts) does not exceed 40 percent of gross income.

Mortgage Interest Rate (%)[1]	Annual Income							
	$30 000	**$40 000**	**$50 000**	**$60 000**	**$70 000**	**$80 000**	**$90 000**	**$100 000**
4.00	25 348	109 838	194 332	278 823	363 314	439 357	506 951	574 546
4.25	24 707	107 062	189 420	271 776	354 132	428 252	494 138	560 024
4.50	24 090	104 391	184 693	264 993	345 294	417 564	481 806	546 048
4.75	23 497	101 818	180 142	258 464	336 785	407 275	469 934	532 593
5.00	22 925	99 341	175 760	252 176	328 592	397 367	458 501	519 636
5.25	22 374	96 955	171 538	246 119	320 700	387 823	447 489	507 155
5.50	21 844	94 658	167 471	240 283	313 095	378 627	436 878	495 129
5.75	21 333	92 440	163 550	234 658	305 766	369 764	426 652	483 539
6.00	20 840	90 334	159 771	229 236	298 701	361 220	416 793	472 386
6.25	20 364	88 244	156 127	224 007	291 887	352 980	407 285	461 591
6.50	19 906	86 257	152 611	218 863	185 315	345 032	398 115	451 197
6.75	19 463	84 340	149 219	214 096	278 973	337 363	389 265	441 169
7.00	19 036	82 490	145 946	209 399	272 853	329 962	380 726	431 490
7.25	18 624	80 704	142 785	204 865	256 945	322 817	372 482	422 147
7.50	18 226	78 979	139 733	200 486	261 239	315 917	364 520	413 124
7.75	17 842	77 313	136 785	196 257	255 728	309 252	356 830	404 408
8.00	17 470	75 703	133 937	192 170	250 403	302 813	349 400	395 987
8.25	17 111	74 147	131 184	188 220	245 256	296 589	342 219	387 848
8.50	16 764	72 643	128 523	184 402	240 281	290 572	335 276	379 981
8.75	16 428	71 188	125 950	180 170	235 470	284 754	328 583	372 372
9.00	16 103	69 781	123 461	177 138	230 816	279 127	322 070	365 013
9.25	15 789	68 420	121 052	173 683	226 314	273 682	315 787	357 893
9.50	15 485	67 103	118 722	170 339	221 958	268 413	309 707	351 002
9.75	15 191	65 827	116 465	167 102	217 738	263 312	303 822	344 332
10.00	14 906	64 593	114 281	163 967	213 654	258 372	296 122	337 873
10.25	14 630	63 397	112 165	160 932	209 698	253 588	292 602	331 616
10.50	14 363	62 238	110 115	157 990	205 865	248 953	287 254	325 555
10.75	14 104	61 115	108 128	155 139	202 151	244 462	282 072	319 682
11.00	13 852	60 027	106 202	152 376	198 550	240 108	277 048	313 988
11.25	13 609	58 971	104 335	149 697	195 060	235 886	272 177	308 468
11.50	13 373	57 948	102 524	147 099	191 674	231 792	267 453	303 114
11.75	13 144	56 955	100 767	144 579	188 390	227 820	262 870	297 920
12.00	12 921	55 991	99 063	142 133	185 203	223 966	258 423	292 880
12.25	12 705	55 058	97 408	139 759	182 110	220 225	254 107	287 988
12.50	14 496	54 148	95 802	137 454	179 196	216 594	249 917	283 239
12.75	12 292	53 267	94 242	135 216	176 190	213 067	245 847	278 627
13.00	12 095	52 410	92 727	133 042	173 358	209 642	241 895	274 148

Source: *The Royal Bank of Canada*

(1) Compounded semi-annually. Mortgage payments based on a 25-year amortization.

The Effect of Interest Rate Changes on Mortgage Payments

The table below shows the monthly mortgage payment (principal and interest) for each $1,000 of mortgage debt. To calculate your payment at a given interest rate, choose the corresponding amount in the amortization column you select and multiply the amount by the number of thousands of dollars of debt. For example, if you want to know the cost per month to carry an $85,000 mortgage amortized over 25 years at 7.00 percent, multiply 7 by 85 and the result, $595, is your monthly payment. If the same mortgage was coming up for renewal at 8.00 percent, the new payment amount would be $648.66 (7.63 x 85) or $53.56 more each month.

Monthly Payments for Each $1 000 of Mortgage

Interest Rate (%)	Amortization Period							
	1 Year	2 Years	3 Years	5 Years	10 Years	15 Years	20 Years	25 Years
4.00	$85.13	$43.41	$29.51	$18.40	$10.11	$7.38	$6.04	$5.26
4.25	85.25	43.52	29.62	18.51	10.23	7.50	6.17	5.40
4.50	85.36	43.63	29.73	18.62	10.34	7.63	6.30	5.53
4.75	85.47	43.74	29.84	18.74	10.46	7.75	6.44	5.67
5.00	85.58	43.85	29.95	18.85	10.58	7.88	6.57	5.82
5.25	85.70	43.96	30.06	18.96	10.70	8.01	6.71	5.95
5.50	85.81	44.07	30.17	19.07	10.82	8.14	6.84	6.10
5.75	85.92	44.18	30.28	19.19	10.94	8.27	6.98	6.25
6.00	86.03	44.29	30.39	19.30	11.07	8.40	7.12	6.40
6.25	86.14	44.40	30.50	19.41	11.19	8.53	7.26	6.55
6.50	86.26	44.51	30.61	19.53	11.31	8.66	7.41	6.70
6.75	86.37	44.62	30.72	19.64	11.43	8.80	7.55	6.85
7.00	86.48	44.73	30.83	19.75	11.56	8.93	7.69	7.00
7.25	86.59	44.84	30.94	19.87	11.68	9.07	7.84	7.16
7.50	86.70	44.95	31.05	19.98	11.81	9.21	7.99	7.32
7.75	86.82	45.06	31.16	20.10	11.94	9.34	8.13	7.47
8.00	86.93	45.17	31.28	20.21	12.06	9.48	8.28	7.63
8.25	87.04	45.28	31.39	20.33	12.19	9.62	8.43	7.79
8.50	87.15	45.39	31.50	20.45	12.32	9.76	8.59	7.95
8.75	87.26	45.50	31.61	20.56	12.45	9.90	8.74	8.12
9.00	87.38	45.61	31.72	20.68	12.58	10.05	8.89	8.28
9.25	87.49	45.72	31.84	20.80	12.71	10.19	9.05	8.44
9.50	87.60	45.83	31.95	20.91	12.84	10.33	9.20	8.61
9.75	87.71	45.94	32.06	21.03	12.97	10.48	9.36	8.78
10.00	87.82	46.05	32.17	21.15	13.10	10.62	9.52	8.94
10.25	87.93	46.16	32.28	21.27	13.24	10.77	9.68	9.11
10.50	88.04	46.27	32.40	21.38	13.37	10.92	9.83	9.28
10.75	88.16	46.38	32.51	21.50	13.50	11.06	10.00	9.45
11.00	88.27	46.49	32.62	21.62	13.64	11.21	10.16	9.63
11.25	88.38	46.61	32.74	21.74	13.77	11.36	10.32	9.80
11.50	88.49	46.72	32.85	21.86	13.91	11.51	10.48	9.97
11.75	88.60	46.83	32.96	21.98	14.04	11.66	10.65	10.14
12.00	88.71	46.94	33.08	22.10	14.18	11.82	10.81	10.32
12.25	88.82	47.05	33.19	22.22	14.32	11.97	10.98	10.49
12.50	88.94	47.16	33.30	22.34	14.46	12.12	11.14	10.67
12.75	89.05	47.27	33.42	22.46	14.59	12.28	11.31	10.85
13.00	89.18	47.38	33.53	22.58	14.73	12.43	11.48	11.02

Source: *The Royal Bank of Canada*

Average Resale Value of Canadian Homes[1]

In 2002 and 2003, the average resale value of Canadian homes continued to climb. The rate of housing sales remained strong across the country, despite an overall downward trend from the peak of January 2001. Particularly in the larger urban centres, a shortage of listings, combined with continued low interest levels, has been pushing prices up. Between March 2002 and March 2003, the national residential average price rose 8.6 percent to $201,662, setting a new record and breaking past the $200,000 level for the first time in history.

	1990	1995	2000	2001	2002	2003
Canada	139 922	150 321	164 091	171 897	184 855	208 525
Calgary	128 484	132 114	176 305	182 090	197 431	212 342
Edmonton	101 040	110 329	124 203	133 441	150 807	167 846
Halifax-Dartmouth	97 238	103 011	128 003	134 106	147 918	158 634
Montreal	111 956	109 929	125 333	128 851	144 280	173 813
Ottawa	141 562	143 127	159 623	175 972	203 283	225 381
Regina	71 054	76 629	94 518	96 943	98 512	99 318
Saint John	78 041	83 498	93 697	97 348	106 274	106 674
St. John's	88 939	89 655	100 763	105 237	113 860	124 468
Toronto[2]	254 890	203 028	243 249	251 508	282 765	297 175
Greater Vancouver	226 385	307 747	295 978	285 910	308 592	345 175
Victoria	160 743	210 669	251 398[3]	259 138[3]	287 279	337 638

Source: *The Canadian Real Estate Association; Victoria Real Estate Board*   (n.a.) Not available.
(1) Average price of all homes sold on the Multiple Listing Service in constant dollars.
(2) Includes Mississauga, Brampton, Durham, Orangeville and York Region figures.
(3) Figures from Victoria Real Estate Board; based on single family homes.

Mortgage Rates by Year[1]

	One-Year	Three-Year	Five-Year		One-Year	Three-Year	Five-Year
1980	13.98	n.a.	14.52	**1991**	10.08	10.90	11.13
1981	1812	18.33	18.38	**1992**	7.87	8.95	9.51
1982	16.85	17.83	18.04	**1993**	6.91	8.10	8.78
1983	10.98	12.52	13.23	**1994**	7.83	8.99	9.53
1984	12.00	13.21	13.58	**1995**	8.38	8.82	9.16
1985	10.31	11.54	12.12	**1996**	6.19	7.37	7.93
1986	10.15	10.88	11.21	**1997**	5.54	n.a.	7.07
1987	9.85	10.69	11.17	**1998**	6.50	n.a.	6.93
1988	10.83	11.42	11.65	**1999**	6.80	n.a.	7.56
1989	12.85	12.15	12.06	**2000**	7.85	n.a.	8.35
1990	13.40	13.38	13.35	**2001**	6.14	n.a.	7.40
				2002	4.70	6.28	7.01

Source: © *Bank of Canada, CMHC, Statistics Canada.*   (n.a.) Not available.
(1) Average typical mortgage rates.

GLOBAL INFORMATION

GLOBAL SUPERLATIVES

Size of the earth's surface		510 000 000 sq. km
Largest continent	Asia	44 485 900 sq. km
Smallest continent	Australia	7 682 300 sq. km
Largest ocean	Pacific	166 241 000 sq. km
Smallest ocean	Arctic	9 485 000 sq. km
Deepest point of any ocean	Marianas Trench, Pacific Ocean	11 022 m
Largest sea	South China Sea	2 974 600 sq. km
Largest lake	Caspian Sea, Russian Fed., Kazakhstan, Turkmenistan, Iran, Azerbaijan	371 000 sq. km
Deepest lake	Lake Baykal, Russia	1 620 m
Largest freshwater lake	Lake Superior, North America	82 100 sq. km
Highest major lake	Lake Titicaca, Bolivia-Peru, South America	3 809 m
Lowest major lake	Caspian Sea, Russian Fed., Kazakhstan, Turkmenistan, Iran, Azerbaijan	-28 m
Largest island	Greenland, Denmark	2 175 600 sq. km
Longest reef	Great Barrier Reef, Australia-Papua New Guinea	2 027 km
Longest river	Nile, Africa	6 670 km
Largest nation	Russia	17 075 272 sq. km
Smallest nation	Vatican City	.44 sq. km
Most populous nation	People's Republic of China (July 2003 est.)	pop. 1 286 975 468
Oldest city	Damascus, Syria	continuously inhabited since c. 2500 B.C.
Highest point	Mount Everest, Nepal-Tibet	8 846 m
Lowest point	Dead Sea, Israel-Jordan	-400 m
Highest city	Cerro de Pasco, Peru	4 259 m
Coldest city	Norilsk, Russia	average temp. -10.9°C
Hottest city	Djibouti, Djibouti	average temp. 30°C
Coldest place	Plateau Station, Antarctica	-56.7°C
Hottest place	Dalol, Danakil Depression, Ethiopia	35°C avg.
Coldest recorded temperature	Vostok, Antarctica (Australian territory), July 21, 1983	-89.2°C
Hottest recorded temperature (shade)	Al-Aziziyah, Libya, Sept. 13, 1922	58°C
Wettest spot	Mount Waialeale, Kauai, Hawaii	avg. ann. rainfall of 16 800 mm
Driest spot	Atacama Desert, Chile	avg. ann. precipitation barely measurable
Greatest snowfall in 24 hrs	Silver Lake, Colorado, U.S., Apr. 14–15, 1921	193 cm
Greatest rainfall in 24 hrs	Cilaos, Reunion Island, Indian Ocean, Mar. 15–16, 1952	1 870 mm
Largest desert	Sahara, Africa	9 million sq. km
Largest waterfall (by volume)	Khone, Kampuchea-Laos	11 610 cu. m/sec.
Tallest waterfall	Angel Falls, Venezuela	807 m
Largest gorge	Grand Canyon, Colorado River, Arizona	349 km long; 6–20 km wide; 1.6 km deep
Deepest gorge	Colca River Canyon, Peru	3 223 m
Oldest tree	a bristlecone pine, Wheeler's Peak, Nevada	approx. age of 5 100 yrs.
Greatest tides	Bay of Fundy, Nova Scotia	14.5 m
Most devastating volcanic eruption	Tambora, Sumbawa, Indonesia, Apr. 5–7, 1815	92 000 deaths
Longest bridge	Confederation, linking New Brunswick and Prince Edward Island	12.9 km
	(main span 11 km); bridge between the tip of Florida and Key West is also 11 km	
Largest man-made lake	Owen Falls, Uganda	2 700 000 cu. m
Tallest building	Sears Tower, Chicago, Illinois	110 storeys, 443 m

GEOGRAPHY

The Continents

Continent	Total Area (sq. km)	% of Earth's Land	Population	% of World Total
Asia	44 485 900	30.0	3 292 337 000	62.4
Africa	30 269 680	20.4	702 013 000	13.2
North and Central America	24 235 280	16.3	441 826 000	8.4
South America	17 820 770	12.0	309 634 000	5.9
Antarctica	13 209 000	8.9	uninhabited	
Europe	10 530 750	7.1	504 925 000	9.6
Oceania	7 830 682	5.3	27 752 000	.5

Source: *National Geographic Atlas of the World (1990), FAO Production Yearbook (1993)*

Highest and Lowest Points on Each Continent

Continent	Highest Point	(metres)	Lowest Point	(metres)
Asia	Everest	8 848	Dead Sea	-400
South America	Aconcagua	6 960	Valdés Peninsula	-40
North America	McKinley (Denali)	6 194	Death Valley	-86
Africa	Kilimanjaro	5 895	Lake Assal	-156
Europe	El'brus	5 642	Caspian Sea	-28
Antarctica	Vinson Massif	4 897	—	-2 538
Australia	Kosciusko	2 228	Lake Eyre	-16

Source: *National Geographic Atlas of the World (1990)*

World's Highest Cities

City	Altitude[1]	City	Altitude[1]
Cerro de Pasco, Peru	4 259 m	Quito, Ecuador	2 811 m
Shigatse, Tibet	3 800 m	Sucre, Bolivia	2 790 m
La Paz, Bolivia	3 636 m	Potosi, Bolivia	2 790 m
Lhasa, Tibet	3 606 m	Toluca de Lerdo, Mexico	2 680 m
Cuaco, Peru	3 400 m	Addis Ababa, Ethiopia	2 450 m

Source: *Global Atlas, Gage Educational Publishing Co., South American Handbook*
(1) Estimates vary, depending on source.

Oceans' Area and Depth

Ocean	Area (sq. km)	% of Earth's Water Area	Deepest Point	Depth (metres)
Pacific	166 241 000	46.0	Mariana Trench	10 924
Atlantic	86 557 000	23.9	Puerto Rico Trench	8 605
Indian	73 427 000	20.3	Java Trench	7 258
Arctic	9 485 000	2.6	Eurasia Basin	5 122

Source: *National Geographic Atlas of the World (1990)*

Major Seas of the World

Sea	Area (sq. km)	Average Depth (metres)	Sea	Area (sq. km)	Average Depth (metres)
South China	2 974 600	1 464	Sea of Japan	1 012 900	1 667
Caribbean	2 515 900	2 575	Hudson Bay	730 100	93
Mediterranean	2 510 000	1 501	East China	664 600	189
Bering	2 261 100	1 491	Andaman	564 900	1 118
Gulf of Mexico	1 507 600	1 615	Black	507 900	1 191
Sea of Okhotsk	1 392 100	973	Red	453 000	538

Source: *National Geographic Atlas of the World (1990)*

Largest Lakes of the World

Lake	Location	Area (sq. km)
Caspian (Sea)	Iran/Caspian Sea, Russian Fed., Kazakhstan, Turkmenistan, Iran, Azerbaijan	378 400
Superior	Canada/U.S.	82 260
Aral (Sea)	Kazakhstan-Uzbekistan	64 100
Victoria	Kenya/Tanzania/Uganda	62 940
Huron	Canada/U.S.	59 580
Michigan	U.S.	58 020
20 Tanganyika	Burundi/Tanzania/Zaire/Zambia	32 000
Baykal	Russia	31 500
Great Bear	**NWT, Canada**	**31 150**
Great Slave	**NWT, Canada**	**28 570**

Source: *World Facts and Figures, 1989; Victor Showers; John Wiley & Sons, Inc.*

Major Islands of the World

Island	Area (sq. km)	Island	Area (sq. km)
Greenland (Denmark)	2 175 600	Sumatra (Indonesia)	427 300
New Guinea (independent)	792 500	Honshu (Japan)	227 400
Borneo (Indonesia)	725 500	Great Britain (independent)	218 100
Madagascar (independent)	587 000	**Victoria (Canada)**	**217 300**
Baffin (Canada)	**507 500**	**Ellesmere (Canada)**	**196 200**

Source: *National Geographic Atlas of the World (1990)*

Highest Waterfalls in the World

Fall/Country	Height[1] (m)	Fall/Country	Height[1] (m)
Angel, Venezuela	807	Pilao, Brazil	524
Monge, Norway	774	Montoya, Venezuela	505
Itatinga, Brazil	628	Ribbon, United States	491
Ormeli, Norway	563	Great, Guyana	488
Tusse, Norway	533	Vestre Mardals, Norway	468

Source: *World Facts and Figures, 1989; Victor Showers; John Wiley & Sons Inc.*

(1) Height of the greatest individual leap.

Highest Mountains by Continent

Peak	Mountain Range or System	Location	Elevation[1] ft	m	First Ascent
■ Africa					
Kibo	n.a.	Tanganyika, Tanzania	19 340	5 890	1889
Mawensi	n.a.	Tanganyika, Tanzania	17 100	5 210	1912
Batian	n.a.	Kenya	17 050	5 200	1899
Nelion	n.a.	Kenya	17 020	5 190	1929
Margherita	Ruwenzori	Uganda/D. Rep. of Congo	16 760	5 110	1906
Alexandra	Ruwenzori	Uganda/D. Rep. of Congo	16 700	5 090	1906
Albert	Ruwenzori	Dem. Rep. of Congo	16 690	5 090	1932
Savoia	Ruwenzori	Uganda	16 330	4 980	1906
Elena	Ruwenzori	Uganda	16 300	4 970	1906
Elizabeth	Ruwenzori	Uganda	16 170	4 930	1953
■ Antarctica					
—	Sentinel	Antarctica	16 860	5140	1966
Tyree	Sentinel	Antarctica	16 290	4970	1967
Shinn	Sentinel	Antarctica	15 750	4800	1966
Gardner	Sentinel	Antarctica	15 370	4690	1966
Epperly	Sentinel	Antarctica	15 100	4600	n.a.
Kirkpatrick	Queen Alexandra	Antarctica	14 850	4530	n.a.
Elizabeth	Queen Alexandra	Antarctica	14 700	4480	n.a.
Markham	Queen Elizabeth	Antarctica	14 290	4360	n.a.
Bell	Queen Alexandra	Antarctica	14 120	4300	n.a.
Mackellar	Queen Alexandra	Antarctica	14 100	4300	n.a.
■ Asia					
Everest (alt Qomolangma, Chumulangma)	Nepal Himalaya	China/Nepal	29 030	8 850	1953
K2 (alt Chogori, Dapsang, Godwin Austen)	Karakoram	Pakistan-held Kashmir	28 250	8 610	1954
Kangchenjunga (alt Kanchenjunga): highest peak	Nepal Himalaya	India/Nepal	28 170	8 590	1955
Lhotse (alt E1, Luozi, Lotzu)	Nepal Himalaya	China/Nepal	27 890	8 500	1956
Kangchenjunga: S peak	Nepal Himalaya	India/Nepal	27 800	8 470	n.a.
Makalu I	Nepal Himalaya	China/Nepal	27 790	8 470	1955
Kangchenjunga: W peak	Nepal Himalaya	India/Nepal	27 620	8 420	1973
Lhotse Shar (alt Lhotse: E peak)	Nepal Himalaya	China/Nepal	27 500	8 380	1970
Dhaulagiri I (alt Daulagiri I)	Nepal Himalaya	Nepal	26 810	8 170	1960
Cho Oyu (alt Zhuoaoyu, Choaoyu): highest peak	Nepal Himalaya	China/Nepal	26 750	8 150	1954
■ Europe					
Elbrus (for Elborus): W peak	Caucasus (off Kavkaz)	Russia	18 480	5630	1874
Elbrus: E peak	Caucasus	Russia	18 360	5 590	1829
Shkhara: E peak	Caucasus	Georgia/Russia	17 060	5 200	1888
Dykh(-Tau): W peak	Caucasus	Russia	17 050	5 200	1888
Dykh(-Tau): E peak	Caucasus	Russia	16 900	5 150	1938
Koshtan(-Tau)	Caucasus	Russia	16 880	5 140	1888
Shkhara: W peak	Caucasus	Georgia/Russia	16 880	5 140	n.a.
Pushkina	Caucasus	Russia	16 730	5 100	1938
Dzhangi(-Tau): NW peak	Caucasus	Georgia	16 570	5 050	1903
Kazbek: E peak	Caucasus	Georgia	16 560	5 050	1868 ▶

▶ ■ **North America**

McKinley: S peak	Alaska	Alaska, U.S.	20 320	6 190	1913
Logan: central peak	Saint Elias	Yukon, Canada	19 520	5 959	1925
Logan: W peak	Saint Elias	Yukon, Canada	19 470	5 930	1925
McKinley: N peak	Alaska	Alaska, U.S.	19 470	5 930	1910
Logan: E peak	Saint Elias	Yukon, Canada	19 420	5 920	1957
Citlaltepetl (alt Orizaba)	Neovolcanica	Puebla-Veracruz, Mexico	18 410	5 610	1848
Logan: N peak	Saint Elias	Yukon, Canada	18 270	5 570	1959
Saint Elias	Saint Elias	Canada/U.S.	18 010	5 490	1897
Popocatepetl	Neovolcanica	Puebla, Mexico	17 930	5 460	1520
Foraker	Alaska	Alaska, U.S.	17 400	5 300	1934

■ **Oceania**

Jaya (for Carstensz, Djaja, Sukarno)	Sudirman (for Nassau)	Irian Jaya, Indonesia	16 500	5 030	1936
Daam	Jayawijaya (for Djajawidjaja, Orange)	Irian Jaya, Indonesia	16 150	4 920	n.a.
Pilimsit (for Idenburg)	Sudirman	Irian Jaya, Indonesia	15 750	4 800	1962
Trikora (for Wilhelmina)	Jayawijaya	Irian Jaya, Indonesia	15 580	4 750	1913
Mandala (for Juliana)	Jayawijaya	Irian Jaya, Indonesia	15 420	4 700	1959
Wilhelm	Bismarck	Papua New Guinea	15 400	4 690	n.a.
Wisnumurti (for Jan Pieterszoon Coen)	Jayawijaya	Irian Jaya, Indonesia	15 080	4 590	n.a.
Yamin (for Prins Hendrik)	Jayawijaya	Irian Jaya, Indonesia	14 860	4 530	n.a.
Kubor	Kubor	Papua New Guinea	14 300	4 360	n.a.
Herbert	Bismarck	Papua New Guinea	14 000	4 270	n.a.

■ **South America**

Aconcagua	Andes	Mendoza, Argentina	22 840	6 960	1897
Ojos del Salado: SE peak	Andes	Argentina/Chile	22 560	6 870	1937
Bonete	Andes	La Rioja, Argentina	22 550	6 870	1913
Pissis	Andes	Catamarca, La Rioja, Argentina	22 240	6 780	1937
Huascaran: S peak	Blanca (Andes)	Peru	22 210	6 770	1932
Mercedario	Andes	San Juan, Argentina	22 210	6 770	1934
Llullaillaco	Andes	Argentina/Chile	22 100[1]	6 730	bef 1550
Libertador (for Cachi: N peak)	Andes	Salta, Argentina	22 050	6 720	1950
Ojos del Salado: NW peak	Andes	Argentina/Chile	22 050	6 720	1937
Tupungato	Andes	Argentina/Chile	21 900	6 670	1897

Source: *World Facts and Figures, 1989; Victor Showers; John Wiley & Sons, Inc.*

(1) Rounded figures except from some Canadian peaks from Energy, Mines and Resources Canada. n.a. not available or not applicable.

Longest Rivers in the World

River	Outflow and Location	mi.	km
Nile-Kagera-Ruvuvu-Luvironza	Mediterranean Sea, Egypt	4 140	6 670
Amazon-Ucayali-Tambo-Ene-Apurimac	Atlantic Ocean, Amapa-Para, Brazil	4 080	6 570
Yangtze	East China Sea, Jiangsu, China	3 720	5 980
Mississippi-Missouri-Jefferson-Beaverhead-Red	Gulf of Mexico, Louisiana, U.S. Rock	3 710	5 970
Yenisey-Angara-Selenga-Ider	Yenisey Gulf of Kara Sea, Russia	3 650	5 870
Amur-Argun-Kerulen	Tatar Strait, Russia	3 590	5 780
Ob-Irtysh	Gulf of Ob of Kara Sea, Russia	3 360	5 410
Plata-Parana-Grande	Atlantic Ocean, Argentina-Uruguay	3 030	4 880
Huang	Gulf of Chihli of Yellow Sea, Shandong, China	3 010	4 840
Congo-Lualaba	Atlantic Ocean, Angola-Dem. Rep. of Congo	2 880	4 630

Source: *World Facts and Figures, 1989; Victor Showers; John Wiley & Sons, Inc.*

POPULATION

Global Population Trends

The Population Division of the United Nations carries out documentation and analytical work that is used by the UN General Assembly and the UN's Economic and Social Council, as well as by various conferences and member states. The information on population trends and other analysis that goes with the data gathering assists in the development of policy related to both population and social development at the national and international levels. The information below reflects projected population trends, based on population data as of July 1, 2002.

For more information about the United Nations Population Division, visit www.un.org/esa/population

Population Projections by Region

(000s)

Year	Africa	Asia	Europe	Latin America and the Caribbean[1]	Northern America[2]	Oceania[3]
2005	887 964	3 917 508	724 722	558 281	332 156	32 998
2010	984 225	4 148 948	719 714	594 436	348 139	34 821
2015	1 084 540	4 370 522	713 402	628 260	363 953	36 569
2020	1 187 584	4 570 131	705 410	659 248	379 589	38 275
2025	1 292 085	4 742 232	696 036	686 857	394 312	39 933
2030	1 398 004	4 886 647	685 440	711 058	407 532	41 468
2035	1 504 179	5 006 700	673 638	731 591	419 273	42 803
2040	1 608 329	5 103 021	660 645	747 953	429 706	43 938
2045	1 708 407	5 175 311	646 630	759 955	439 163	44 929

Source: *United Nations Population Division, World Populations Prospects Population Database*
(1) Includes South and Central America (2) Includes Bermuda, Canada, Greenland, Saint-Pierre-et-Miquelon, United States of America (3) Includes Australia, Melanesia, Micronesia, New Zealand, Polynesia

Projected Population Density by Region

(per square km)

Year	Africa	Asia	Europe	Latin America and the Caribbean	Northern America	Oceania
2005	29	123	32	27	15	4
2010	32	131	31	29	16	4
2015	36	138	31	31	17	4
2020	39	144	31	32	18	4
2025	43	149	30	33	18	5
2030	46	154	30	35	19	5
2035	50	158	29	36	19	5
2040	53	161	29	36	20	5
2045	56	163	28	37	20	5

Source: *United Nations Population Division, World Populations Prospects Population Database*

Projected Population Growth Rates by Region

(%)

Period	Africa	Asia	Europe	Latin America and the Caribbean	Northern America	Oceania
2005–2010	2.06	1.15	-0.14	1.26	0.94	1.08
2010–2015	1.94	1.04	-0.18	1.11	0.89	0.98
2015–2020	1.82	0.89	-0.23	0.96	0.84	0.91
2020–2025	1.69	0.74	-0.27	0.82	0.76	0.85
2025–2030	1.58	0.6	-0.31	0.69	0.66	0.76
2030–2035	1.46	0.49	-0.35	0.57	0.57	0.63
2035–2040	1.34	0.38	-0.39	0.44	0.49	0.52
2040–2045	1.21	0.28	-0.43	0.32	0.44	0.45
2045–2050	1.08	0.18	-0.46	0.2	0.4	0.39
2035–2040	1.55	0.51	-0.51	0.58	0.50	0.63
2040–2045	1.42	0.41	-0.55	0.49	0.46	0.55
2045–2050	1.26	0.32	-0.59	0.40	0.45	0.52

Source: *United Nations Population Division, World Populations Prospects Population Database*

Projected Net Migration Rate by Region

(per 1,000)

The net migration rate represents the number of immigrants minus the number of emigrants over the period shown, divided by the person-years lived by the population of the receiving country over that period.

Year	Africa	Asia	Europe	Latin America and the Caribbean	Northern America	Oceania
2005–2010	-0.2	-0.3	0.8	-1.0	3.9	2.5
2010–2015	-0.2	-0.3	0.8	-0.9	3.6	2.3
2015–2020	-0.2	-0.3	0.8	-0.8	3.4	2.0
2020–2025	-0.2	-0.3	0.8	-0.7	3.3	1.9
2025–2030	-0.2	-0.3	0.8	-0.7	3.2	1.9
2030–2035	-0.1	-0.2	0.8	-0.7	3.1	1.8
2035–2040	-0.1	-0.2	0.9	-0.6	3.0	1.8
2040–2045	-0.1	-0.2	0.9	-0.6	2.9	1.8
2045–2050	-0.1	-0.2	0.9	-0.6	2.9	1.7

Source: *United Nations Population Division, World Populations Prospects Population Database*

Median Age

The median age is the age at which there are as many persons with ages above the median as there are with ages below the median. In 2000, the median age in Canada was 36.9.

Year	Africa	Asia	Europe	Latin America and the Caribbean	Northern America	Oceania
2005	18.8	27.4	39.3	25.7	36.2	31.8
2010	19.3	28.6	40.8	27.4	36.7	32.8
2015	19.9	29.9	42.2	29.0	37.1	33.7
2020	20.6	31.4	43.6	30.7	37.6	34.7
2025	21.5	32.9	44.8	32.3	38.2	35.6
2030	22.5	34.3	46.1	34.0	38.8	36.7
2035	23.7	35.5	47.2	35.5	39.4	37.7
2040	24.8	36.7	47.9	37.1	39.7	38.6
2045	26.1	37.7	48.0	38.5	39.9	39.3
2050	27.5	38.7	47.7	39.8	40.2	39.9

Source: *United Nations Population Division, World Populations Prospects Population Database*

Sex Ratio

(number of males per 100 females)

Year	Africa	Asia	Europe	Latin America and the Caribbean	Northern America	Oceania
2005	99.2	104.0	93.1	97.8	96.8	100.7
2010	99.6	103.7	93.1	97.6	96.9	100.5
2015	100.1	103.3	93.1	97.4	97.0	100.4
2020	100.5	102.8	93.2	97.1	96.9	100.1
2025	100.8	102.2	93.2	96.9	96.8	99.9
2030	101.1	101.7	93.2	96.6	96.6	99.6
2035	101.3	101.2	93.2	96.3	96.5	99.4
2040	101.4	100.7	93.3	96.1	96.4	99.1
2045	101.5	100.2	93.4	95.8	96.5	99.0
2050	101.5	99.9	93.6	95.6	96.8	99.0

Source: *United Nations Population Division, World Populations Prospects Population Database*

Global Urbanization

% Urban Population, by Region

The continuing shift of Canada's population from rural to urban centres, as shown in the 2001 census data (see chapter entitled "The People"), is not happening in isolation—the urban dwelling trend is visible around the world. In March 2002, the United Nations Population Division (Department of Economic and Social Affairs) released population growth estimates based on 2001 population statistics that emphasized the growing trend.

The report, entitled *World Urbanization Prospects: The 2001 Revision*, suggested that by 2007, half of the world's population would live in urban areas. In 2000, 2.9 billion—47% of global population—lived in urban centres, compared to just 30% in 1950. By 2030, the proportion is expected to rise to 60%.

Year	Africa	Asia	Europe	Latin America and the Caribbean	Northern America	Oceania
2005	40.0	40.2	74.2	77.4	78.5	75.1
2010	42.7	43.0	75.1	79.0	79.8	75.7
2015	45.3	45.9	76.3	80.5	81.1	76.1
2020	47.9	48.7	77.6	81.8	82.3	76.4
2025	50.4	51.4	79.1	83.0	83.5	76.8
2030	52.9	54.1	80.5	84.0	84.5	77.3

Source: *United Nations Population Division, World Populations Prospects Population Database*

Cities with 10 Million Inhabitants or More

In 1950, just one city—New York—had a population of over 10 million (12.3 million). By 1975, five cities claimed the honour: Tokyo (19.8); New York (15.9); Shanghai (11.4); Mexico City (10.7); and Sao Paulo (10.3). By 2001, there were 17 such cities and by 2015 the UN projects that 21 cities (or "urban agglomerates") will have more than 10 million inhabitants. In fact, by 2015, Tokyo, Dhaka, Mumbai, Sao Paulo, Delhi and Mexico City are all expected to have more than 20 million residents each.

2001 City	Population (millions)	2015 City	Population (millions)
1. Tokyo	26.5	1. Tokyo	27.2
2. Sao Paulo	18.3	2. Dhaka	22.8
3. Mexico City	18.3	3. Mumbai	22.6
4. New York	16.8	4. Sao Paulo	21.2
5. Mumbai	16.5	5. Delhi	20.9
6. Los Angeles	13.3	6. Mexico City	20.4
7. Calcutta	13.3	7. New York	17.9
8. Dhaka	13.2	8. Jakarta	17.3
9. Delhi	13.0	9. Calcutta	16.7
10. Shanghai	12.8	10. Karachi	16.2
11. Buenos Aires	12.1	11. Lagos	16.0
12. Jakarta	11.4	12. Los Angeles	14.5
13. Osaka	11.0	13. Shanghai	13.6
14. Beijing	10.8	14. Buenos Aires	13.2
15. Rio de Janeiro	10.8	15. Metro Manila	12.6
16. Karachi	10.4	16. Beijing	11.7
17. Metro Manila	10.1	17. Rio de Janeiro	11.5
		18. Cairo	11.5
		19. Istanbul	11.4
		20. Osaka	11.0
		21. Tianjin	10.3

Source: *United Nations Population Division, World Urbanization Prospects: The 2001 Revision*

United Nations

The first United Nations declaration was signed by 22 Allied governments on January 1, 1942, and was an alliance against Germany, Italy and Japan. This anti-Axis coalition was converted into an international body in 1945 when 51 nations signed a United Nations Charter to form an organization that would "save succeeding generations from the scourge of war." The Charter was drawn up at the Conference on International Organization held in San Francisco from April 25 to June 26, 1945, and took effect October 24, 1945. UN membership has since grown to 191.

The UN has six parts, with the General Assembly—the central organ—acting as the main deliberative body. General Assembly meetings have been held at UN Headquarters in New York since 1946. The International Court of Justice in The Hague, Netherlands, is the only major UN organ not based in New York. Specialized agencies are located throughout the world.

Mail requests for information to the Public Inquiries Unit, Dept. of Public Information, Room GA-053, United Nations, New York, NY 10017. Visit the UN Web site at www.un.org or send e-mail to inquiries@un.org. Write also to the United Nations Association in Canada, 900–130 Slater St., Ottawa, ON, K1P 6E2 or send e-mail to info@unac.org.

■ Structure of the United Nations

General Assembly The General Assembly is the UN's forum for discussing issues, reviewing UN activities and setting the agenda for initiatives. All member states are represented, and each is entitled to one vote. Resolutions require a majority vote before adoption. A president, 21 vice-presidents and six committee chairs head the Assembly, which sits from mid-September to mid-December or as required for the rest of the year. The six committees study (a) disarmament and international security issues; (b) economics and finance issues; (c) social, humanitarian and cultural issues; (d) special political and decolonization issues; (e) UN administration and budgets; and (f) legal matters. The committees report to a plenary session of the Assembly.

The General Assembly sets UN policies, admits new members on recommendation of the Security Council, approves the budget and receives reports from all other UN bodies.

Security Council The Security Council has the power to act for the maintenance of peace and security. It can enforce military action or economic sanctions, and it can send peacekeeping units (the Blue Berets) to troubled areas. The Security Council may also try to negotiate a cease fire in the case of conflicts.

The Council has 15 members, five permanent and 10 elected by the General Assembly for two-year terms. Decisions require nine affirmative votes, but all permanent members have the right to veto. The permanent members are: China, France, the United Kingdom, the United States and the Russian Federation. Canada served its sixth term as a non-permanent member of the Council (from Jan. 1, 1999, to Dec. 31, 2000). The Security Council is permanently in session and representatives are on call 24 hours a day.

Economic and Social Council The Economic and Social Council co-ordinates the economic and social work of the UN and its related agencies. The Council's 54 members hold two month-long sessions each year: one in New York, the other in Geneva. Each member is elected by the General Assembly for a three-year term.

Trusteeship Council The council, created to oversee the independence of trust territories, is now in abeyance.

International Court of Justice (World Court) The Security Council elects 15 judges to the Court for nine-year terms. No two members may be from the same nation. The Court, located in The Hague, only sits in judgment on disputes between states. Both member and non-member states may submit grievances (border disputes, resource access, breach of treaty, etc.).

Countries can opt out of any proceeding, unless required to participate by treaty provisions. But after agreeing to become a party in a case, a nation must comply with the Court's decision, enforced by the Security Council.

Secretariat The Secretariat administers the programs and policies laid out by other UN bodies. The Secretary General is the Chief Administrative Officer of the Secretariat, which administers the work of the UN as directed by the General Assembly, Security Council and other organs.

Glossary of United Nations Acronyms

FAO: Food and Agriculture Organization

IAEA: International Atomic Energy Agency

IBRD: International Bank for Reconstruction and Development

ICAO: International Civil Aviation Organization

IDA: International Development Association

IFAD: International Fund for Agricultural Development

IFC: International Finance Corporation

ILO: International Labour Organization

IMF: International Monetary Fund

INSTRAW: International Research and Training Institute for the Advancement of Women

ITU: International Telecommunications Union

MINUCI: United Nations Mission in Côte d'Ivoire

MINUGUA: United Nations Mission for the Verification of Human Rights in Guatemala

MINURSO: United Nations Mission for the Referendum in Western Sahara

MONUC: United Nations Mission in the Democratic Republic of the Congo

UNAMA: United Nations Assistance Mission in Afghanistan

UNAMSIL: United Nations Mission in Sierra Leone

UNCTAD: United Nations Conference on Trade and Development

UNDOF: United Nations Disengagement Observer Force

UNDP: United Nations Development Programme

UNEP: United Nations Environment Programme

UNESCO: United Nations Educational, Scientific and Cultural Organization

UNFICYP: United Nations Peacekeeping Force in Cyprus

UNFPA: United Nations Population Fund

UN-Habitat: United Nations Human Settlements Programme

UNHCR: Office of the United Nations High Commissioner for Refugees

UNICEF: United Nations Children's Fund

UNIDO: United Nations Industrial Development Organization

UNIFIL: United Nations Interim Force in Lebanon

UNIKOM: United Nations Iraq-Kuwait Observation Mission (mission suspended in 2003)

UNITAR: United Nations Institute for Training and Research

UNMA: United Nations Mission in Angola

UNMEE: United Nations Mission in Ethiopia and Eritrea

UNMIK: United Nations Interim Administration Mission in Kosovo

UNMISET: United Nations Mission of Support in East Timor

UNMOGIP: United Nations Military Observer Group in India and Pakistan

UNOCHA: United Nations Office for the Coordination of Humanitarian Affairs

UNOMIG: United Nations Mission of Observers in Georgia

UNRWA: United Nations Relief and Works Agency for Palestine Refugees in the Near East

UNTSO: United Nations Truce Supervision Organization

UNU: United Nations University

UNV: United Nations Volunteers

UPU: Universal Postal Union

WFP: World Food Programme

WHO: World Health Organization

WIPO: World Intellectual Property Organization

WMO: World Meteorological Organization

WTO: World Trade Organization (formerly General Agreement on Tariffs and Trade)

■ Functional Commissions

Commission for Social Development

Commission of Sustainable Development

Commission on Human Rights

Commission on Narcotic Drugs

Commission on the Status of Women

Population Commission

Statistical Commission

■ Regional Commissions

ECA: Economic Commission for Africa

ECE: Economic Commission for Europe

ECLAC: Economic Commission for Latin America and the Caribbean

ESCAP: Economic and Social Commission for Asia and the Pacific

ESCWA: Economic and Social Commission for Western Asia

The United Nations System

Trusteeship Council

Security Council
- MINUCI
- MINURSO
- MONUC
- UNAMA
- UNAMSIL
- UNDOF
- UNFICYP
- UNIFIL
- UNIKOM
- UNMA
- UNMEE
- UNMIK
- UNMISET
- UNMOGIP
- UNOMIG
- UNTSO
- Military Staff Committee
- Standing Committees
- Ad Hoc Committees

Main Committees
Standing Committees
Other Ad Hoc/ Subsidiary Organs

International Court of Justice

General Assembly

Secretariat
- IAEA

MINUGUA
UNRWA

Economic and Social Council
- INSTRAW
- UN-HABITAT
- UNCTAD
- UNDP
- UNEP
- UNFPA
- UNHCR
- UNICEF
- UNITAR
- UNU
- UNV
- WFP
- Regional Commissions
- Functional Commissions
- Other Committees

- FAO
- ICAO
- IFAD
- ILO
- IMF
- IMO
- ITU
- UNESCO
- UNIDO
- UPU
- WHO
- WIPO
- WMO
- World Bank
  - IDA
  - IBRD
  - IFC
- WTO

○ Principal organs of the United Nations

● United Nations programs and organs

○ Specialized agencies and other autonomous organizations within the system

United Nations Association in Canada – August 2003

N.B. The International Criminal Court came into effect on July 1, 2002, but it is independent and not shown on this chart.

Roster of the United Nations

(as of October 2003)

The 191 members of the United Nations, with the years in which they became members.

Member	Year	Member	Year	Member	Year
Afghanistan	1946	Ethiopia	1945	Micronesia	1991
Albania	1955	Fiji	1970	Moldova	1992
Algeria	1962	Finland	1955	Monaco	1993
Andorra	1993	France	1945	Mongolia	1961
Angola	1976	Gabon	1960	Morocco	1956
Antigua and Barbuda	1981	Gambia	1965	Mozambique	1975
Argentina	1945	Georgia	1992	Myanmar (formerly Burma)	1948
Armenia	1992	Germany	1973	Namibia	1990
Australia	1945	Ghana	1957	Nauru	1999
Austria	1955	Greece	1945	Nepal	1955
Azerbaijan	1992	Grenada	1974	Netherlands	1945
Bahamas	1973	Guatemala	1945	New Zealand	1945
Bahrain	1971	Guinea	1958	Nicaragua	1945
Bangladesh	1974	Guinea-Bissau	1974	Niger	1960
Barbados	1966	Guyana	1966	Nigeria	1960
Belarus	1945	Haiti	1945	Norway	1945
Belgium	1945	Honduras	1945	Oman	1971
Belize	1981	Hungary	1955	Pakistan	1947
Benin	1960	Iceland	1946	Palau	1995
Bhutan	1971	India	1945	Panama	1945
Bolivia	1945	Indonesia	1950	Papua New Guinea	1975
Bosnia and Herzegovina	1992	Iran	1945	Paraguay	1945
Botswana	1966	Iraq	1945	Peru	1945
Brazil	1945	Ireland	1955	Philippines	1945
Brunei Darussalam	1984	Israel	1949	Poland	1945
Bulgaria	1955	Italy	1955	Portugal	1955
Burkina Faso	1960	Jamaica	1962	Qatar	1971
Burundi	1962	Japan	1956	Romania	1955
Cambodia	1955	Jordan	1955	Russian Federation	1945
Cameroon	1960	Kazakhstan	1992	Rwanda	1962
Canada	1945	Kenya	1963	Saint Kitts and Nevis	1983
Cape Verde	1975	Kiribati	1999	Saint Lucia	1979
Central African Republic	1960	Korea, North	1991	Saint Vincent and the	
Chad	1960	Korea, South	1991	Grenadines	1980
Chile	1945	Kuwait	1963	Samoa	1976
China	1945	Kyrgyzstan	1992	San Marino	1992
Colombia	1945	Laos	1955	São Tomé and Príncipe	1975
Comoros	1975	Latvia	1991	Saudi Arabia	1945
Congo	1960	Lebanon	1945	Senegal	1960
Costa Rica	1945	Lesotho	1966	Seychelles	1976
Côte d'Ivoire	1960	Liberia	1945	Sierra Leone	1961
Croatia	1992	Libya	1955	Singapore	1965
Cuba	1945	Liechtenstein	1990	Slovak Republic	1993
Cyprus	1960	Lithuania	1991	Slovenia	1992
Czech Republic	1993	Luxembourg	1945	Solomon Islands	1978
Democratic Republic of the		Macedonia, Former Yugoslav		Somalia	1960
Congo (formerly Zaire)	1960	Republic of	1993	South Africa	1945
Denmark	1945	Madagascar	1960	Spain	1955
Djibouti	1977	Malawi	1964	Sri Lanka	1955
Dominica	1978	Malaysia	1957	Sudan	1956
Dominican Republic	1945	Maldives	1965	Suriname	1975
Ecuador	1945	Mali	1960	Swaziland	1968
Egypt	1945	Malta	1964	Sweden	1946
El Salvador	1945	Marshall Islands	1991	Switzerland	2002
Equatorial Guinea	1968	Mauritania	1961	Syria	1945
Eritrea	1993	Mauritius	1968	Tajikistan	1992
Estonia	1991	Mexico	1945	Tanzania	1961

Member	Year	Member	Year	Member	Year
Thailand	1946	Tuvalu	2000	Vanuatu	1981
Timor-Leste	2002	Uganda	1962	Vietnam	1977
Togo	1960	Ukraine	1945	Venezuela	1945
Tonga	1999	United Arab Emirates	1971	Yemen	1947
Trinidad and Tobago	1962	United Kingdom	1945	Yugoslavia, Federal Republic of	
Tunisia	1956	United States of America	1945	(Serbia and Montenegro)	1945
Turkey	1945	Uruguay	1945	Zambia	1964
Turkmenistan	1992	Uzbekistan	1992	Zimbabwe	1980

Source: *United Nations Association www.un.org*

United Nations Secretaries-General

The Secretary-General, heading the Secretariat, is responsible for the UN's administration and for alerting the Security Council to any threats to international peace and security, and acts as spokesperson for the UN. The Secretary-General is elected by the General Assembly on the recommendation of the Security Council and cannot be from one of the five permanent members of the Security Council.

Secretary, Nation	Date Installed	Secretary, Nation	Date Installed
Trygve Lie, Norway	Feb. 1946	Javier Pérez de Cuéllar, Peru	Dec. 1981
Dag Hammarskjöld, Sweden	Apr. 1953	Boutros Boutros-Ghali, Egypt	Jan. 1992
U Thant, Burma	Nov. 1961	Kofi Annan, Ghana	Jan. 1997
Kurt Waldheim, Austria	Dec. 1971		(to Dec. 31, 2006)

Source: *United Nations Association*

Canadian Ambassadors to the United Nations

Ambassador	Date Appointed	Ambassador	Date Appointed
Andrew McNaughton	Jan. 1948	Saul Forbes Rae	June 1972
John Holmes	Jan. 1950	William Barton	May 1976
Gerald Riddell	June 1950	Michel Dupuy	Mar. 1980
David Johnson	Oct. 1951	Gérard Pelletier	Aug. 1981
Robert MacKay	June 1955	Stephen H. Lewis	Oct. 1984
Charles Ritchie	Nov. 1957	Yves Fortier	July 1988
Paul Tremblay	May 1962	Louise Fréchette	Jan. 1992
George Ignatieff	Mar. 1966	Robert K. Fowler	Jan. 1995
Yvon Beaulne	Jan. 196	Paul Heinbecker	June 2000

Source: *Dept. of Foreign Affairs*

Canada's Man on the International Criminal Court

*I*n 2003, a Canadian became the first president of the International Criminal Court (ICC). On March 11, Philippe Kirsch was inaugurated as one of the court's 18 judges in The Hague in the Netherlands. On the same day, Kirsch was unanimously elected president by his fellow judges.

Kirsch, a career diplomat and lawyer, has worked for the creation of a permanent international criminal court for years. In 1998, he chaired the main negotiating committee at the Rome Diplomatic Conference that adopted the court's founding statute. In subsequent years, he chaired the commission that drafted the court's rules of procedure and evidence.

The ICC was established to prosecute persons responsible for genocide, crimes against humanity and war crimes. The court has the conditional authority to act when national judicial systems fail to investigate or prosecute these offences. The court's jurisdiction is limited to crimes committed after July 1, 2002.

Kirsch will serve as a judge on the ICC for six years and as president for three years. For more information, visit www.icc.gc.ca

FOCUS ON...

The World Health Organization

The World Health Organization (WHO) is a specialized agency of the United Nations. The WHO declares in its constitution that every person has a right to good health and seeks to achieve the best possible health for all people in the world. The organization was established on April 7, 1948; its headquarters is in Geneva, Switzerland.

The WHO works with 192 governments to prevent and control the spread of disease. The agency promotes better sanitation and quarantine standards, cleaner water, proper food supply and nutrition, and better maternal and child care. The WHO sponsors medical research, encourages the investigation of new diseases, promotes immunization, and delivers medicine and medical equipment to needy countries. The agency can send teams to a site within 24 hours to control epidemics.

The WHO also promotes co-operation among non-governmental scientific and health organizations. These include UN agencies, bilateral agencies and "collaborating centres." The latter are national institutions (e.g., medical departments, research labs or training schools) that support the WHO's mandate and programs. Some publish medical information or devise new technologies; others provide advice on scientific, technical or policy issues.

The supreme decision-making body in the WHO is the World Health Assembly (WHA). This assembly consists of representatives from the WHO's 192 member states. The WHA decides major policy questions and approves the WHO's program and budget for the next two years. The assembly elects an executive board and appoints a director general. The WHA meets annually in Geneva in May.

The executive board consists of 32 health professionals who hold office for three-year terms. The board advises the WHA and implements the WHA's decisions. In January, the board prepares the agenda, reports and resolutions for the assembly's consideration in May. Another board meeting occurs in May after the assembly meets.

The WHO includes a secretariat of 3,500 health professionals and staff. These people work in Geneva, in the WHO's six regional offices and elsewhere. A director general leads the secretariat for five years. The director general is nominated by the executive board and approved by the assembly in May. The current director general is Dr. Lee Jong-wook of South Korea; he took office on July 21, 2003.

On May 19–28, 2003, the 56th session of the WHA occurred in Geneva. More than 2,000 people attended, including many ministers of health. The participants focused on the fight against tobacco use and a deadly new disease called severe acute respiratory syndrome (SARS).

On May 21, after four years of international negotiations, the WHA unanimously adopted the Framework Convention on Tobacco Control. This agreement—the world's first public health treaty—aims to protect people from the harmful effects of tobacco. The convention seeks to restrict tobacco advertising, increase tobacco taxes and eliminate the illegal cigarette trade. At least 40 governments must ratify the treaty before it enters into force, and ratification is expected to take one year.

The assembly also passed two resolutions about SARS. One declared that SARS was "the first severe infectious disease to emerge in the 21st century" and earmarked US$100 million in public and private funds to fight SARS. The other resolution confirmed the WHO's authority to verify outbreaks of disease by checking all official and unofficial sources and called for changes to international health law by 2005 to authorize the WHO to help control disease through on-site investigations.

The WHO will also continue its campaign against the epidemic of human immunodeficiency virus (HIV) and acquired immune deficiency syndrome (AIDS). The agency plans to reach its "three-by-five target" by providing anti-retroviral medicines to 3 million people in developing countries by the end of 2005.

WHO Regional Office Locations (Regions)

Brazzaville, Congo (Africa)
Cairo, Egypt (Eastern Mediterranean)
Copenhagen, Denmark (Europe)
Manila, Philippines (Western Pacific)
New Delhi, India (Southeast Asia)
Washington, DC, USA (The Americas)

Source: *World Health Organization www.who.int*

Asia-Pacific Economic Co-operation (APEC)

APEC is an association of 21 Pacific Rim countries seeking greater prosperity through freer trade. APEC's members include large, industrialized nations such as the United States and small, developing nations such as Papua New Guinea. The total population of APEC countries is 2.5 billion. In 2000, 47 percent of global trade moved through APEC countries; the combined gross domestic product of APEC's members was almost US$18 trillion.

APEC was established in 1989 at a conference of trade and foreign ministers in Canberra, Australia. The 12 founding countries (including Canada) agreed to meet annually in different member countries for informal ministerial talks. They also agreed to hold alternate ministerial meetings in APEC countries belonging to the Association of Southeast Asian Nations (ASEAN).

Subsequent meetings of trade and foreign ministers in the early 1990s produced several key decisions. In 1991, for example, APEC's members committed themselves to free enterprise and "open regionalism." In the same year, APEC admitted three Chinese states— China, Taiwan and Hong Kong—as members. In 1992, APEC decided to create a permanent Secretariat in Singapore and a central fund to cover its administration.

In 1993, APEC's international profile rose when, after a ministerial meeting in Seattle, all the political leaders of APEC countries met for a separate meeting on nearby Blake Island. They released an Economic Vision Statement that recognized the interdependence of all Pacific Rim economies. In subsequent years, APEC's political leaders have met for separate talks after each annual meeting of trade and foreign ministers.

In 1994, APEC's political leaders released the Bogor Declaration of Common Resolve in Indonesia. The statement pledged APEC's industrialized members to achieve total free trade and investment by 2010 and APEC's developing members to achieve the same goal by 2020. In 1998, during a serious financial crisis in Asia, APEC welcomed its three latest members: Russia, Vietnam and Peru.

APEC operates by consensus. Each year, a different country chairs and hosts the annual meetings of trade and foreign ministers and of political leaders. In 2003, Thailand is chairing and hosting these meetings; in 2004, Chile will assume these responsibilities.

At the annual ministerial meeting, APEC sets tasks for its three committees, one subcommittee, 11 working groups and other forums. The Committee on Trade and Investment pursues the liberalization of international trade; the Economic Committee analyzes economic trends; the Budget and Management Committee evaluates APEC's administration; and the ECOTECH Sub-committee assists senior officials in promoting economic and technical co-operation.

APEC's working groups—most of which were established in 1990 and 1991—focus on specific issues: small and medium-sized enterprises; energy; fisheries; human resources development; industrial science and technology; marine resource conservation; tourism; telecommunications and information; trade promotion; transportation; and agricultural technical co-operation. Other forums study issues such as the role of women in APEC and sustainable economic development.

Two other institutions provide advice. APEC's Secretariat provides research and technical support to APEC's member economies and committees. The Secretariat also promotes APEC to the world. The APEC Business Advisory Council (ABAC), which was created in Japan in 1995 and consists of business executives drawn from APEC countries, advises on the execution of APEC's plans.

Member Economies (date of membership)

Australia (1989)	Papua New Guinea
Brunei Darussalam	(1993)
(1989)	Peru (1998)
Canada (1989)	Philippines (1989)
Chile (1994)	Russia (1998)
China (1991)	Singapore (1989)
Hong Kong (1991)	South Korea (1989)
Indonesia (1989)	Taiwan (1991)
Japan (1989)	Thailand (1989)
Malaysia (1989)	United States (1989)
Mexico (1993)	Vietnam (1998)
New Zealand (1989)	

For more information about APEC, visit the official Web sites at www.apecsec.org.sg and http://dfait-maeci.gc.ca/canada-apec/

The European Union (EU)

The European Union (EU) represents a unique relationship among democratic nations, with the aim of constructing a united Europe. The EU is more than an international organization but not a full-blown federation. It is the world's largest trading entity, accounting for well over 20 percent of world trade. Its population totals about 379 million people.

The European Union originated as the European Coal and Steel Community (ECSC). Formed in 1951 by France, West Germany, Italy, the Netherlands, Belgium and Luxembourg, it became operational in 1952.

The success of the ECSC spurred the Six to apply the same approach to the entire economy. In 1957, the same six countries formed the European Economic Community (EEC), creating a common market for all sectors of the economy. The EEC committed the Six to dismantle trade barriers and to allow the free movement of goods, services, capital and people. At the same time, the Six formed the European Atomic Energy Community (Euratom) to further the use of nuclear energy for peaceful purposes.

In 1967, the institutions of the ECSC, Euratom and the EEC were merged. In 1973, Denmark, Ireland and the United Kingdom became members, as did Greece in 1981, Spain and Portugal in 1986 and Austria, Finland and Sweden in 1995. Ten more countries are expected to join on May 1, 2004, following the successful conclusion in 2002 of accession negotiations with Cyprus, the Czech Republic, Estonia, Hungary, Latvia, Lithuania, Malta, Poland, the Slovak Republic and Slovenia. They will create an EU of 25. Negotiations also continue with Romania and Bulgaria, and Turkey has been recognized as a candidate. The basic principle of the accession negotiations is that all applicants must accept existing EU law.

From its inception, the EU has been dedicated to ensuring economic and social progress and strengthening the unity of the economies of its member states. To help promote their harmonious development the EC uses the European Regional Development Fund, the European Social Fund, the European Agricultural Guidance and Guarantee Fund and the Cohesion Fund.

Part of the Single European Act, which came into force in 1987, was the Europe 1992 project. This aimed at completing the common market and creating a single internal market by dismantling the remaining physical, technical and fiscal barriers among the member states.

The Maastricht Treaty on European Union, signed in 1992, came into effect in November 1993. This treaty created a European Union of three pillars. The first pillar is the European Community with its joint supranational institutions. The two new pillars are intergovernmental co-operation in foreign and security policy and in justice and home affairs.

The Maastricht Treaty committed the member states to create an economic and monetary union, including the establishment of a European Central Bank in Frankfurt. In January 1999, the EURO was introduced as the new single European currency. In January 2002, EURO coins and banknotes began circulating in 12 member states, replacing their national currencies. The treaty also committed the Fifteen to political union, by developing a common foreign and security policy.

The treaty gave the regions a part to play in the Community by setting up a Committee of the Regions. It also introduced the principle of "subsidiarity," by which the EU deals only with matters it is better equipped to deal with than the member states.

In 1997, the Fifteen agreed to revise the Maastricht Treaty by drawing up a new treaty. Coming into force in May 1999, the Treaty of Amsterdam contained four major objectives. They were to
• ensure citizens' rights;
• ensure the free movement of citizens;
• strengthen the union's foreign policy; and
• make the union's decision-making process more effective.

The treaty also introduced the new position of high representative for the common foreign and security policy.

In Nice in 2000, the Fifteen concluded the Intergovernmental Conference on institutional reform by agreeing on the draft of a new treaty. The Treaty of Nice came into force in February 2003. It amended the Treaty on European Union and the treaties establishing the European Communities, and it included a Protocol on Enlargement of the EU to prepare the EU for the accession of more countries. The treaty allowed further qualified-majority voting for decisions that previously required unanimity. It also changed, from 2005, the weighting of votes in the council and reallocated the number of seats among the member states in the European Parliament.

In 2001, the European Council convened a Convention on the Future of Europe to prepare for the Intergovernmental Conference a draft treaty establishing a constitution for Europe. The conference began in October 2003.

■ INSTITUTIONS OF THE EU

The European Union creates its own laws and policies through the following institutions:

The European Commission proposes legislation, implements policy and enforces the treaties. It has investigative powers and can take legal action. It also represents the EU in trade negotiations. The Commission is headed by 20 commissioners: France, Germany, Italy, Spain and the UK each appoint two commissioners while the other member states appoint one commissioner each. The commissioners are appointed for five years.

The European Parliament is directly elected by the citizens of the union. Its members debate issues and question the commission and council. On a wide range of issues it shares legislative decision-making power equally with the council of the EU. It can dismiss the commission and has final approval over the EU budget. Elections take place every five years. Presently and until 2004, the number of MPs from each country are: Germany 99; UK 87; France 87; Italy 87; Spain 64; Netherlands 31; Belgium 25; Portugal 25; Greece 25; Sweden 22; Austria 21; Denmark 16; Finland 16; Ireland 15; and Luxembourg 6. MPs sit according to political affiliation and not nationality.

The Council of the European Union is composed of ministers from each of the member countries. The council acts on commission proposals and is, with the European Parliament, the EU's legislative decision-making body. Participation changes according to the agenda. Agricultural ministers, for instance, decide on agricultural matters and economic and finance ministers on economic and monetary matters. Ministers represent and defend the interests of their countries while seeking agreements that promote the union's goals. The presidency of the council rotates among the member states every six months. The Single European Act and subsequent treaties have gradually extended majority voting in the council in areas that previously required unanimity.

The European Council consists of the heads of state or government of the EU member states and the commission president. The group meets at least twice a year to define major internal and foreign policy orientations. The European Council does not legislate, but its written conclusions provide guidance.

The Court of Justice is the EU's supreme court. It interprets EU law and its rulings are binding—including on member states. The court has one judge from each member state, assisted by advocates-general. Both groups are appointed for six years by mutual consent of the member states.

The Court of Auditors audits the accounts of the EU and EU bodies.

The Committee of the Regions and the **Economic and Social Committee** must be consulted by the commission and the council on policies and proposals for legislation.

The European Central Bank governs monetary policy.

Members of the European Union

(as of October 2003)

Member	Year Joined	Member	Year Joined
Austria	1995	Italy	1952
Belgium	1952	Luxembourg	1952
Denmark	1973	Netherlands	1952
Finland	1995	Portugal	1986
France	1952	Spain	1986
Germany	1952	Sweden	1995
Greece	1981	United Kingdom	1973
Ireland	1973		

Source: *Commission of the European Communities*
For Internet information, visit: europa.eu.int and www.delcan.cec.eu.int

North Atlantic Treaty Organisation (NATO)

The North Atlantic Treaty Organisation (NATO) is a political and military alliance, created in Washington on April 4, 1949, when 12 states in Europe and North America signed the North Atlantic Treaty. NATO defends the peace and freedom of its members through collective security without sacrificing members' sovereignty. Headquarters is in Brussels, Belgium.

NATO was created to defend Western and Southern Europe from the threat of invasion by the Soviet Union following World War II. Western leaders began negotiating in 1948, after a Soviet attempt to deny Western access to West Berlin.

Today 19 countries belong, including the original 12: Belgium, Canada, Denmark, France, Iceland, Italy, Luxembourg, the Netherlands, Norway, Portugal, the United Kingdom and the United States, plus Greece and Turkey (1952), Germany (joined as West Germany, 1955) and Spain (1982). On March 12, 1999, NATO admitted its newest members—former members of the Soviet-led Warsaw Pact—Hungary, Poland and the Czech Republic.

The highest authority within NATO is the North Atlantic Council (NAC). It consists of permanent representatives, who act as ambassadors for their respective countries, and is directed by a secretary general. Meetings are weekly; the NAC also convenes less frequent meetings of foreign or defence ministers or heads of state. Discussions cover political, economic, military and scientific issues. The NAC reaches decisions only after all member states have been consulted. It cannot impose decisions on any of its members, although members can block the wishes of others by withholding consent.

The NAC can create subordinate committees and planning groups. The most important are the Defence Planning Committee and the Nuclear Planning Group. The Defence Planning Committee, which consists of permanent representatives and defence ministers, deals with collective defence planning. The Nuclear Planning Group, which consists of defence ministers, deals with nuclear weapons issues. Both are chaired by the NAC's secretary general. This post is currently held by Lord George Robertson, who took office on October 14, 1999, and who had previously served as the UK's Secretary of State for Defence.

At the Rome Summit in 1991, NATO outlined a new strategy for Europe after the collapse of the Soviet Union: co-operation with the ex-Warsaw Pact states, reduced dependence on nuclear weapons, reductions in the size and readiness of military forces, improvements in military flexibility, greater use of multinational military units and a new focus on peacekeeping.

Also concurrent with the disintegration of the Soviet Union, NATO created a number of mechanisms for consultation and co-operation with former Warsaw Pact states, including the North Atlantic Cooperation Council (NACC) (1991), the Partnership for Peace program (1994) and the Euro-Atlantic Partnership Council (1997). In 1997, NATO and Russia signed the NATO–Russia Founding Act, which obliged the signatories to co-operate as equal partners. In 2002, NATO and Russia strengthened their partnership by creating the NATO–Russia Council. The goal of these organizations was peaceful progress toward a new security environment in Europe.

In 1995, NATO first sent land troops outside NATO territory when 60,000 personnel went into Bosnia and Herzegovina under United Nations' authority to enforce the Dayton Peace Accord, negotiated to end armed conflict in the former Yugoslavia. NATO forces and troops from 19 non-NATO countries, including Russia, worked together during the mission, first as part of the Implementation Force (IFOR) and then as the Stabilisation Force (SFOR).

On March 23, 1999, the NAC authorized air strikes by NATO forces against targets in the Federal Republic of Yugoslavia in an effort to end that country's campaign against ethnic Albanians in Kosovo. The air strike campaign continued until June 10 when the withdrawal of Yugoslav forces from the Kosovo region began. As of June 12, 1999, NATO forces joined a UN-mandated peacekeeping force (Kosovo Force or KFOR), to enforce the withdrawal agreement.

On September 12, 2001, less than 24 hours after terrorist attacks on the United States, NATO declared that the attacks were against all 19 NATO countries and began to aid the United States in its campaign against terrorism. Today, NATO countries support US-led military operations against terrorists in Afghanistan and provide most of the troops in the UN-mandated International Security Assistance Force (ISAF) in Kabul to stabilize Afghanistan.

For more information about NATO, visit the Website at www.nato.int

The World Trade Organization (WTO)

The World Trade Organization presides over the rules of international trade for more than 140 countries. The organization seeks to make international trade predictable, open and smooth. The WTO also provides a forum for trade talks, promotes freer trade and resolves trade disputes. The organization's binding rules, which are called the WTO Agreements, are negotiated and signed by the WTO's member governments.

The WTO appeared on January 1, 1995, after trade representatives from 125 countries negotiated for eight years (1986–94) to reform the rules of international trade. The talks, which were known as the "Uruguay Round," aimed at overhauling the older General Agreement on Tariffs and Trade (GATT) and concluded with the signing of a 22,000-page agreement in Marrakesh, Morocco, on April 5, 1994.

The WTO's creation marked the biggest reform of international trade since the establishment of the GATT in 1948. The WTO took over the administration of the amended GATT, which covered trade in goods alone, and got the authority to preside over newer agreements covering trade in services and intellectual property (e.g., designs and inventions) as well. The reformed trading system also attracted more prospective member governments.

The GATT, however, remains at the centre of the WTO Agreements. Since 1995, the WTO has incorporated the GATT's basic principles—which are reflected in rules barring discrimination among trading partners and favouring lower tariffs—in the more recent General Agreement on Trade in Services (GATS) and the Agreement on Trade-Related Aspects of Intellectual Property Rights (TRIPS).

The WTO has 146 members. The majority are sovereign countries, but a few are customs territories that have control over their trade policies. (An example is the Separate Customs Territory of Taiwan, Penghu, Kinmen and Matsu.) The membership also includes most of the world's industrial powers—such as Canada, which signed the GATT in 1948—although more than three-quarters of the WTO's members are "developing" or "least developed" countries.

Thirty "observer governments" are negotiating to join the WTO. They must begin talks to join the WTO within five years of acquiring observer status. Current observers include significant states such as Russia and Saudi Arabia. The Vatican is also an observer, although it is exempt from the need to begin negotiations for membership within five years.

■ The Structure of the WTO

The WTO's highest executive authority is the Ministerial Conference. It consists of government ministers from all WTO members and meets at least once every two years. The Ministerial Conference rules on matters under the WTO Agreements. The most recent Ministerial Conference met in Cancun, Mexico, in 2003.

In between Ministerial Conferences, the General Council directs the WTO's daily business. The General Council consists of all WTO members, acts on behalf of the Ministerial Conference and reports to the Ministerial Conference. The General Council also convenes as the Trade Policy Review Body (to examine members' trade policies) and as the Dispute Settlement Body (to resolve conflicts between members and uphold the WTO Agreements).

Three more councils, each responsible for different areas of trade, report to the General Council: the Council for Trade in Goods, the Council for Trade in Services and the Council for Trade-Related Aspects of Intellectual Property. These councils also consist of all WTO members and have numerous subsidiary committees as well.

The WTO's Secretariat is located in Geneva, Switzerland. The Secretariat's roles include organizing the Ministerial Conference, providing technical help to the WTO's councils and committees, analyzing trends in world trade and providing information to the public. The Secretariat's director-general is Dr. Supachai Panitchpakdi of Thailand; he assumed his post on September 1, 2002, for a term of three years.

WTO Ministerial Conferences (date of occurrence)

Singapore (Dec. 9–13, 1996)

Geneva, Switzerland (May 18 and 20, 1998)

Seattle, USA (Nov. 30–Dec. 3,1999)

Doha, Qatar (Nov. 9–14, 2001)

Cancun, Mexico (Sept. 10–14, 2003)

Source: *World Trade Organization, www.wto.org*

Other International Organizations in the News

African Union
(formerly the Organization of African Unity)
African Union Headquarters
PO Box 3243
Roosevelt St (Old Airport Area)
W21K19
Addis Ababa, Ethiopia
Established: July 9, 2002, in Durban, Republic of South Africa
Aim: to promote solidarity, defend territorial integrity and accelerate socio-economic integration in Africa
Members: 53 governments including Western Sahara, a territory occupied by Morocco
Website: www.africa-union.org

Amnesty International
International Secretariat
1 Easton St
London WC1X 0DW
United Kingdom
Established: July 1961 in London, England
Aim: to prevent and end grave abuses to human rights worldwide
Members: more than 1.5 million members, supporters and subscribers in over 150 countries
Website: www.amnesty.org

Arctic Council
Arctic Council Secretariat
Ministry for Foreign Affairs of Iceland
Raudararstigur 25
IS-150 Reykjavik, Iceland
Established: Sept. 19, 1995, in Ottawa, Canada
Aim: to promote sustainable development and environmental protection throughout the circumpolar region
Members: (8) Canada, Denmark (including Greenland and the Faroe Islands), Finland, Iceland, Norway, Russia, Sweden and the USA; plus six international aboriginal organizations with permanent participant status
Website: www.arctic-council.org

Association of Southeast Asian Nations
ASEAN Secretariat
70A, Jalan Sisingamangaraja
Jakarta 12110, Indonesia
Established: Aug. 8, 1967, in Bangkok, Thailand
Aim: to encourage regional economic, social and cultural co-operation among member states
Members: (10) Brunei Darussalam, Cambodia, Indonesia, Laos, Malaysia, Myanmar, the Philippines, Singapore, Thailand and Vietnam
Website: www.aseansec.org

Christian Democrat International
CDI Headquarters
67 rue D'Arlon
B-1040 Brussels, Belgium
Established: Nov. 21, 1961
Aim: to promote co-operation among Christian democrat and people's parties worldwide; to protect human rights, families, the poor and nature within free-market societies
Members: 79 member parties worldwide; plus 14 observer parties
Website: www.idc-cdi.org

The Commonwealth
Commonwealth Secretariat
Marlborough House, Pall Mall
London SW1Y 5HX
United Kingdom
Established: Dec. 11, 1931, in London, England
Aim: to promote democracy and co-operation among former member countries of the British Empire
Members: 54 countries including Canada
Website: www.the commonwealth.org

Group of Eight (G8)
Established: November 1975 in Rambouillet, France
Aim: to manage macroeconomic issues, international trade, relations with developing countries, energy and regional security
Members: (8) Canada, France, Germany, Italy, Japan, Russia, the UK and the USA; plus the European Union
Website (unofficial): www.G8.utoronto.ca

International Civil Aviation Organization
ICAO, External Relations and Public Information Office
999 University St.
Montreal, PQ H3C 5H7
Established: Dec. 7, 1944, in Chicago, USA (a UN agency)
Aim: to promote international co-operation in civil aviation
Members: 188 countries including Canada
Website: www.icao.int

International Criminal Court
Maanweg, 174
2516 AB The Hague
The Netherlands
Founding Treaty Signed: July 17, 1998, in Rome, Italy
Aim: to prosecute persons resonsible for war crimes, crimes against humanity and genocide
Members: 91 countries including Canada
Website: www.icc.int

International Criminal Police Organization (Interpol)
General Secretariat
200, quai Charles de Gaulle
69006 Lyon, France
Established: Sept. 3–7, 1923, in Vienna, Austria, as the International Criminal Police Commission
Aim: to promote co-operation among national police forces in fighting international crime

Members: 181 countries including Canada
Website: www.interpol.int

International Federation of Journalists
IFJ Headquarters
IPC-Residence Palace, Bloc C
Rue de la Loi 155
B-1040 Brussels, Belgium
Established: 1926
Aim: to promote international action to defend press freedom and social justice through strong, free and independent trade unions of journalists
Members: 153 unions (including three Canadian unions) worldwide
Website: www.ifj.org

International Federation of Red Cross and Red Crescent Societies (formerly Red Cross)
IFRC Secretariat
PO Box 372
CH-1211 Geneva 19, Switzerland
Established: 1919 in Paris, France
Aim: to promote humanitarianism, prepare for disaster relief, provide relief after disasters and promote health in communities
Members: 178 national societies worldwide including Canada; plus nine observer "societies in formation"
Website: www.ifrc.org

International Labour Organization
International Labour Office
4, route des Morillons
CH-1211 Geneva 22, Switzerland
Established: April 1919 in Paris, France (now a UN agency)
Aim: to promote social justice and internationally recognized human and labour rights
Members: 175 countries including Canada
Website: www.ilo.org

International Monetary Fund
700 19th St NW
Washington, DC
20431 USA
Founding Conference: July 22, 1944, in Bretton Woods, USA (a UN agency)
Aim: to promote international monetary cooperation, exchange stability and orderly exchange arrangements; to foster economic growth and high levels of employment; and to provide temporary financial help to countries to ease balance of payments adjustment
Members: 184 countries including Canada
Website: www.imf.org

International Olympic Committee
Chateau de Vidy, CP 356
1007 Lausanne, Switzerland
Established: June 23, 1894, in France
Aim: to promote Olympic ideals and administer the Olympic games: 2004 Summer Olympics in Athens, Greece; 2006 Winter Olympics in Turin, Italy

Members: 199 National Olympic Committees worldwide including Canada
Website: www.olympic.org

International Organization for Standardization
ISO Central Secretariat
1, rue de Varembé, CP 56
CH-1211 Geneva 20, Switzerland
Established: Feb. 23, 1947, in Geneva, Switzerland
Aim: to promote the development of international standards to aid the international exchange of goods and services
Members: 96 (national) member bodies including Canada; 36 (national) correspondent member bodies
Website: www.iso.ch

Inter-Parliamentary Union
IPU Information Officer
5, chemin du Pommier, CP 330
CH-1218 Le Grand Saconnex
Geneva, Switzerland
Established: June 30, 1889, in Paris, France
Aim: to promote dialogue and co-operation among parliamentarians worldwide
Members: 145 national parliaments including Canada's; plus five associate international parliaments
Website: www.ipu.org

League of Arab States
(also known as the Arab League)
Midan Attahir, Tahir Square
PO Box 11642, Cairo, Egypt
Established: Mar. 22, 1945, in Cairo, Egypt
Aim: to promote economic, social, political and military co-operation among member states
Members: (22) Algeria, Bahrain, Comoros, Djibouti, Egypt, Iraq, Jordan, Kuwait, Lebanon, Libya, Mauritania, Morocco, Oman, Palestine, Qatar, Saudi Arabia, Somalia, Sudan, Syria, Tunisia, United Arab Emirates, Yemen
Website: www.leagueofarabstates.org

Liberal International
1 Whitehall Place
London SW1A 2HD
United Kingdom
Established: April, 1947 in Oxford, England
Aim: to strengthen ties among liberal political parties and governments worldwide
Members: 56 full member parties including Canada's; plus 25 observer parties; plus eight co-operating organizations
Website: www.liberal-international.org

Organisation Internationale de la Francophonie
Cabinet du Secrétaire général
28, rue de Bourgogne
75007 Paris, France
Founding Conference: Dec. 2–4, 1998, in Bucharest, Romania
Aim: to promote peace, democracy and French culture throughout the French-speaking world
Members: 51 governments including Canada,

New Brunswick, Quebec and French-speaking Belgium; plus five observer states
Website: www.francophonie.org

Organization for Economic Co-operation and Development
2, rue André Pascal
F-75775 Paris Cedex 16, France
Founding Conference: Dec. 14, 1960, in Paris, France; succeeded the Organisation for European Economic Co-operation (OEEC)
Aim: supports democracy and the market economy; researches economic and social issues to influence government policy throughout the industrialized world
Members: 30 countries including Canada
Website: www.oecd.org

Organization of American States
OAS Headquarters
17th St and Constitution Ave NW
Washington, DC
20006 USA
Established: Apr. 30, 1948, in Bogotá, Colombia
Aim: to strengthen democracy, advance human rights, promote peace and security, expand trade and reduce poverty, narcotics and corruption
Members: 35 states including Canada; plus 56 observer governments including the European Union and the Holy See. Cuba, although a member of the OAS, has been barred from participating by a resolution passed in 1962.
Website: www.oas.org

Organization of the Petroleum Exporting Countries
OPEC Secretariat
Obere Donaustrasse 93
A-1020 Vienna, Austria
Established: Sept. 10–14, 1960, in Baghdad, Iraq
Aim: to co-ordinate and stabilize oil and gas policies to benefit member states
Members: (11) Algeria, Indonesia, Iran, Iraq, Kuwait, Libya, Nigeria, Qatar, Saudi Arabia, United Arab Emirates and Venezuela
Website: www.opec.org

Organization of the Islamic Conference
OIC General Secretariat
(Temporary Headquarters)
VIP Centre, Madinah Rd
Jeddah, Saudi Arabia
Established: Sept. 25, 1969, in Rabat, Morocco
Aim: to strengthen Islamic solidarity and co-operation among member states; to protect the dignity, independence and national rights of Muslims
Members: 57 member states; plus three observer states
Website: www.oic-oci.org

Non-Aligned Movement
The NAM has no permanent headquarters or secretariat
Established: Sept. 1–6, 1961, in Belgrade, Yugoslavia
Aim: to promote Third World perspectives on colonialism, disarmament, minority rights, apartheid and poverty
Members: 116 national governments including Yugoslavia, which has been suspended; 17 observer national governments; seven observer organizations
Website: www.nam.gov.za

Socialist International
Maritime House
Old Town, Clapham
London SW4 0JW
United Kingdom
Established (in its present form): June 30–July 3, 1951, in Frankfurt, West Germany
Aim: to strengthen ties among social democratic, socialist and labour parties worldwide
Members: 89 full member parties including Canada's NDP; plus 25 consultative parties; plus 15 observer parties; plus other organizations
Website: www.socialistinternational.org

World Council of Churches
WCC Ecumenical Centre
PO Box 2100
1211 Geneva 2, Switzerland
Established: Aug. 23, 1948, in Amsterdam, The Netherlands
Aim: to promote the visible unity of Christianity
Members: 341 Christian churches in 120 countries
Website: www.wcc-coe.org

World Economic Forum
Media Inquiries e-mail:
public.affairs@weforum.org
Non-media Inquiries e-mail:
contact@weforum.org
Established: January 1971 in Davos, Switzerland
Aim: to provide collaborative opportunities for world leaders to address global issues and to promote entrepreneurship in the global public interest
Members: primarily drawn from the world's 1,000 leading global companies
Website: www.weforum.org

WWF International
(formerly the World Wildlife Fund)
WWF Secretariat
Avenue du Mont-Blanc
CH-1196, Gland, Switzerland
Established: Sept. 11, 1961, in Switzerland
Aim: to stop the degradation of the planet's natural environment and to help humans live in harmony with nature
Members: 1,600 members who pay an annual membership fee; plus 4.5 million supporters
Website: www.panda.org

■ Ancient History 5000 BC to AD 476

5000–3501 BC: The earliest known cities are in Mesopotamia—in southwest Asia between the Tigris and Euphrates Rivers—a plain rendered fertile by canals; the Egyptian calendar is regulated by the sun and moon; Sumerian writing exists, in southern Mesopotamia on clay tablets, consisting of 2,000 pictograph signs; the Neolithic period in western Europe is characterized by polished stone weapons and tools and agriculturally-based settlements; Cretan ships appear in the Mediterranean Sea; copper alloys are used, and there is smelting of gold and silver in Sumer and Egypt; harps and flutes are played in Egypt; painted pottery appears along the Mediterranean; coloured ceramic ware from Russia reaches China.

3500–2001: The Middle Eastern Bronze Age begins (c. 3500 BC); the height of Sumerian civilization (in the region of the Euphrates River valley) is noted for having a numerical system, irrigated agriculture, poetry, potters' wheels, linen, wheeled vehicles, wedge-shaped (cuneiform) script, barley, bread, beer, use of metal coins as legal tender, oil-burning lamps, brick temples and medicine; the dynasty of Pharoahs as god-kings in Egypt begins (2200–525 BC); the Great Sphinx of Gizeh is built; wrestling is the first highly developed sport; glass beads are worn in Egypt; the bow and arrow is first used in warfare; the Yao dynasty is the first recorded in China (2500–2300); the Indus civilization begins in India; the earliest Egyptian mummies are made; equinoxes and solstices are calculated in China; the first library is in Egypt.

2000–1501: The Egyptian height of power and achievement (18th dynasty) features an irrigation system, contraceptives, bathrooms with a water supply, an alphabet of 24 signs, and the oldest form of a novel (*Story of Sinuhe*); the Persian empire begins (1750–1550); the first legal system and laws of a kingdom are set up by Hammurabi, king of Babylonia; the first of seven periods of Chinese literature begins; Stonehenge is built; Abraham, the patriarch of the Jewish religion, lives (c. 1800); Babylonia uses geometry as the basis for astronomical measurements, and describes the signs of the Zodiac; religious dances are performed in Crete.

1500–1001: The Israelites, led by Moses, leave bondage in Egypt (eventually settling in Canaan in 1250), and receive the Ten Commandments and the world's first monotheistic belief at Mt Sinai; the decline of Egyptian power begins (1200–1090); Troy is destroyed during the Trojan War (1193–83) over Helen of Sparta (Greek legend); the Iron Age begins in the Mediterranean area (1000); obelisk structures are used as sundials in Egypt; the first Chinese dictionary is written; silk fabrics appear in China; leprosy spreads in India and Egypt; Phoenicia is the dominant trading power in the Mediterranean; the Mexican Sun Pyramid is built in Teotihuacan.

1000–901: Asiatic and Greek civilizations are linked by Phoenician trading; David is the king of the united kingdom of Judah and Israel (1000–960) with Jerusalem as its capital; David is succeeded by his son Solomon who presides over the height of Israel's ancient civilization (960–25); classical paganism reigns in Greece; pantheistic belief reigns in India (teaching reincarnation and the caste system); the Chou dynasty's rational philosophy reigns in China; Pinto Indians build huts in southwest North America; brush and ink painting appears in China; gold vessels and jewellery are made in northern Europe; the Hebrew alphabet and literature are developed; the Germanic peoples begin to migrate en masse.

900–601: Carthage is founded as a trading centre (813); *Iliad* and *Odyssey* are written and credited to the poet Homer (c. 800); according to legend, Rome is founded by the twins Romulus and Remus (753); the first recorded Olympic Games are held in Greece (776), and every four years thereafter during ancient times; the earliest record of music is a hymn on a Sumerian tablet; arts and crafts flourish in Asia Minor and Greece; a canal between the Nile River and the Red Sea is started under Pharoah Nechos; Etruscan art forms emerge in Tuscany; the Assyrians destroy Babylon and divert the Euphrates River to cover the site of the city; the Babylonians and their allies later destroy the Assyrian empire, which is then divided among the conquerors; the Acropolis, a fortified hill and religious centre, is built in Athens; limestone and marble are used in the construction of Greek temples; flutes and lyres accompany song; Greek choral and lyric poetry use strophe and antistrophe; Zoroaster, a religious teacher and prophet of ancient Persia, lives (c. 628–c. 551).

600–451: The Mayan civilization flourishes in Mexico; Nebuchadnezzer builds what may be the terraced Hanging Gardens of Babylon (600); Babylonian troops destroy the Jewish Temple at Jerusalem and take many Jews as slaves; Jews write the early books of the Bible during the Babylonian Captivity; Siddhartha Gautama, who becomes Buddha, the "enlightened" Indian philosopher and religious teacher, is born (563): at age 29 he renounces world luxuries and searches for enlightenment, which he attains at age 35 while meditating under a pipal tree at Bodh Gaya, and he teaches monks to continue his work; Confucius, the Chinese philosopher and teacher, is born (551); his moral and religious system governs China and is contained in the sayings of *Analects*; Cyrus II the Great of Persia conquers Babylon and surrounding areas and transforms Persia into a vast empire (c. 540): he frees the Jews from Babylon (536) and aids their return to Israel; Darius I divides the Persian empire into 20 provinces and introduces reforms including a common currency, regular taxes and a standing army; Solon's laws are adopted in Athens; Milo of Crotona, a legendary athlete, is crowned six times at the Olympic Games (536); Chinese feudal structure begins to weaken during Chou dynasty (c. 500–451); Greek cities are freed from Persian domination when the Greeks in Cyprus win the Persian Wars (490–49); the marble temple of Apollo is built at Delphi (478); the statue of Zeus, the centrepiece of the temple of Olympia, is built (460); Aeschylus writes *Prometheus Bound* (460); the *Fables of Aesop* is written by a former Phrygian slave.

450–301: The Greek Periclean Age unfolds with the philosophers Socrates and (his pupil) Plato, the dramatists Sophocles and Euripides and historians Thucydides and Herodotus; the beginning of the Indian empire is centred at Magadha (the "cradle of Buddhism"); the Torah becomes the moral code of the Jewish people; Celtic settlements begin in the British Isles; the Spartans use chemicals in warfare (charcoal, sulphur and pitch); the Parthenon, the masterpiece of Greek architecture, is built (447–32); the population of Greece reaches two million citizens and one million slaves; indigenous Indian civilization ends in Mexico; the Peloponnesian Wars between Athens and

Sparta (431–04) end when the Spartan navy destroys the Athenian navy at Aegospotami: this leads to the decline of Athens as a great power; the first horoscopes are developed in Mesopotamia (c. 410); Socrates is put to death for state offences (399); Brennus leads the Gauls from northern Italy to sack Rome (390); Rome is rebuilt (387) and city walls are built around it (377); Plato, a Greek philosopher, founds the most influential school in the world, the Academy (c. 387); the use of catapults as weapons of war begins; Aristotle, the Greek philosopher, is born (384); Alexander the Great, son of Philip II of Macedon, is born (356); Shung-tse founds Chinese monist philosophy (the doctrine that the universe can be explained by one principle) (350); Corinth becomes a trading centre (338); Philip II is assassinated (336); Alexander succeeds his father and conquers Persia, Jerusalem and Tyre, extending his empire to the Indus River in India where his generals force him to turn back; Alexander dies in Babylon (323) and his empire is divided among his generals who fight civil wars for a time (beginning in 321); the Hellenistic period of Greek arts begins (330–20) and the leading Greek schools of thought are: Stoics, Epicureans and Cynics; Euclid writes *Elements*, a standard work on geometry (323); Alexandria is the centre of Greek learning.

300–151: The Mexican sun temple Atetello is built at Teotihuacan (300); accurate star maps are compiled by Chinese astronomers (c. 300); full equality between patricians and plebeians is mandated in Rome (287); Archimedes, the Greek mathematician, is born (287); the practical end of the history of Babylon coincides with Babylonian re-establishment in the new city of Seleucia (275); Manetho, the high priest of Egypt, writes a history of Egypt in Greek (275); the Colossus at Rhodes is completed (275); the Lighthouse of Pharos is completed at Alexandria (275); the First Punic War between the Carthaginians and the Romans (264–41) arises out of a dispute involving the Sicilian cities of Messana and Syracuse: the Romans win naval battles at Mylae (260) and Cape Ecnomus (256) but lose in Africa (255); a Roman victory of the Aegadian Isles (241) brings a peace treaty that gives Sicily to Rome, but Rome reneges on the treaty and invades Sardinia and Corsica; the leap year is introduced into the Egyptian calendar (239); the Greeks and Romans play ball games, roll dice and play board games; the death of Sun-tsi marks the end of Chinese classical philosophy; the Great Wall of China (2,400 km long) is built to keep out invaders (215); the Second Punic War (218–01) opens when Hannibal and the Carthaginians conquer the Spanish city Saguntum, a Roman ally, and Rome declares war: Hannibal successfully invades Italy from the north (217) and makes an alliance with Philip V of Macedon (216), but is later defeated by the Romans at Zama (202) in Africa; Carthage surrenders its war fleet to Rome as well as its Spanish province; the Second Macedonian War (200–197) ends with the Romans under Flamius defeating Philip V of Macedon; the use of gears leads to the invention of the ox-driven water wheel for irrigation (200); an inscription is engraved on the Rosetta Stone (c. 200); Antiochus IV of Syria persecutes the Jews in Israel and desecrates their Temple of Jerusalem (168); the Jews revolt under Judas Maccabeus and repel the Syrians, then rededicate (Chanukah) the Temple (165); the inventor of trigonometry, Hipparchus of Nicaea, is born (160).

150–1 BC: During the Third Punic War (149–46) the Romans destroy Corinth and massacre the inhabitants of Carthage (due to alleged breach of treaty); the Roman Empire now consists of seven provinces; the Venus of Milo is sculpted (140); Cicero, the greatest Roman orator, is born (106); the first Chinese ships reach the east coast of India (100); the greatest of Roman poets, Virgil, is born (70): he pens the epic *Aeneid*; Horace, the lyric poet, is born (65); Julius Caesar, Roman military commander, organizes the First Triumvirate (60) with Pompey, commander-in-chief of the army, and Marcus Crassus; Caesar conquers the northern Gauls (55) and the Britons; Caesar and Pompey battle for control of Rome after Caesar crosses the Rubicon River and provokes a civil war; Caesar emerges victorious (48); the Julian calendar and leap year are adopted in Rome (46); Cleopatra, the last queen of Egypt, orders the death of Pompey; Caesar, now the dictator of Rome, is murdered by a group headed by Brutus and Cassius Longinus (44); Mark Antony, Octavian and Lepidus form the Second Triumvirate and defeat Brutus and Cassius at Phillipi (42); Mark Antony returns to Egypt (38) where he and Cleopatra commit suicide after being defeated by Octavian at Actium (31); Octavian, retitled Augustus, is a virtual emperor of Rome (30–AD 14); Herod the Great is appointed king

of Judea by the Romans (c. 40); the probable date of the birth of Jesus, the Jewish son of Mary, in Bethlehem (AD 4).

AD 1–150: Jesus, who is revered as the Son of God by his followers, the Christians, preaches for three years in Galilee (c. 30); in the third year of his preaching, Jesus is crucified in Jerusalem by Roman authorities at the request of local political and religious leaders; Caligula becomes emperor of Rome (37) and is known for his ruthlessness and insanity: he is assassinated by the Praetorian Guard (42) and is succeeded by Claudius I, who consolidates and reinvigorates the empire despite a paralysis (dies in 54); the apostle Paul sets out on his missionary travels (45) and spreads Christianity; Nero, emperor of Rome, is the first to persecute the Christians, for allegedly burning half of Rome (64); the Gospels according to Matthew, Mark and John are written; Jews revolt against Rome and the Romans destroy the second Temple at Jerusalem and enslave many inhabitants (70); 1,000 Jewish Zealots hold off the 15,000-member Roman legion for three years on the mountaintop fortress of Masada, and the Zealots commit suicide to escape capture (73); under Emperor Trajan, the Roman Empire reaches its greatest geographical extent when he conquers Dacia and much of Parthia (98–116); paper is made by the Chinese, though not for writing (by 100); Hadrian's Wall is built as the northern boundary and defence line of the Roman Empire (122–26); the medical authority to the 16th century, Greek physician and writer Galen (c. 130–200), demonstrates that arteries carry blood (not air) and establishes the importance of the spinal cord by correlating earlier medical knowledge with his discoveries based on experiments and animal dissection; the earliest known Sanskrit inscriptions are made in India (150).

151–300: Ptolemy, a Greco-Egyptian thinker, compiles *Almagest*, the 13-volume work on ancient astronomy (earth-centred universe), mathematics, geography and science, which is influential to the 16th century; the oldest known Maya monuments are built (c. 164); the period of Neo-Platonism, the last of the Greek philosophies, begins (c. 200); silkworms are exported from Korea to China and then to Japan (c. 200); citizenship is granted to every freeborn subject in the Roman Empire (212); Afghanistan is invaded by the Huns (200); the Goths invade Asia Minor and the Balkan

Peninsula (220); the end of the Han dynasty in China is followed by four centuries of division (220); the southern part of India breaks into several kingdoms; Rome celebrates its 1,000th anniversary (248); persecution of Christians increases and martyrs are revered as saints (c. 250); the first book of algebra is written by Diophantus of Alexandria (c. 250); the Goths attack the Black Sea area (257) as well as Athens, Sparta and Corinth (268); Pappus of Alexandria documents use of cogwheel, lever, pulley, screw and wedge (c. 285); Rome is partitioned into a western and an eastern empire; five distinct German dukedoms emerge (Saxons, Franks, Alemanni, Thuringians and Goths) (c. 300).

301–400: Constantine the Great reunites the western and eastern Roman Empires and becomes sole emperor (310–37); Constantine establishes toleration of Christianity with the Edict of Milan (313); the seat of the Roman Empire is moved to Constantinople (c. 331); the Basilican Church of St Peter is erected (330); Emperor Constantine is baptized on his deathbed (337) and is succeeded by his three sons, who again split Rome into two empires; the Huns invade Europe (360) and Russia (376); books begin to replace scrolls (360); Lo-Tsun, a Chinese monk, founds the Caves of the Thousand Buddhas in Kansu (360); Theodosius the Great becomes the last emperor of a united Roman Empire (392); Alaric, king of the Visigoths, invades Greece (396) and plunders Athens and the Balkans (398); the first definite records of Japanese history appear (400), although legend claims Japan was founded in 660 BC.

401–76: The Visigoths invade Italy (401); Alaric sacks Rome (410); Roman legions withdraw from Britain to defend Italy from the Visigoths (410); barbarians settle in Roman provinces (425); Attila becomes ruler of the Huns (433); St Augustine, Christian theologian, writes *The City of God* (411); alchemy begins with the search for the Philosopher's Stone and the Elixir of Life as chief objects; pre-Inca culture develops in Peru; Venice is founded by refugees from Attila's Huns (452); the Vandals sack Rome (455) and destroy the Roman fleet at Cartegena (460); the Huns leave Europe (470); the Mayan civilization flourishes in southern Mexico (c. 470); the first Shinto religious shrines are built in Japan (478): they deal primarily with nature and ancestor worship; the German barbarian

Odoacer takes Ravenna and deposes Emperor Romulus Augustulus, thereby ending the Western Roman Empire (476); Aryabhata, Hindu astronomer and mathematician, studies powers and roots of numbers (b. 476).

■ Middle or Dark Ages: 477–1450

477–529: Chi dynasty in southern China (479–502); Clovis, leader of the Franks (since 481), converts to Christianity (496); the first schism between the Western and Eastern Churches occurs when Pope Felix III excommunicates Patriarch Acacius of Constantinople (484–519); Armenian Church separates from Byzantium and Rome (491); the Moshica culture of the Chimic Indians flowers in Peru with agriculture, pottery and textiles; the Vatican Palace in Rome is first planned (500); Tamo carries tea from India to China (c. 500); Clovis kills Alaric II and annexes the Visigoth kingdom of Toulouse (507), and Clovis's realm is divided among his four sons upon his death (511); Emperor Wu-Ti converts to Buddhism and encourages the new religion in central China (517); Justinian I becomes the Byzantine Emperor (527): he is known for heavy taxes, public works and codifying Roman law; the Saxon kingdoms of Essex and Middlesex appear; Chosroes I is king of Persia (531–79) and encourages culture and art.

530–99: Arthur, the semi-legendary king of the Britons, is first mentioned at the Battle of Mt Badon (c. 540); the earliest Chinese roll paintings appear in Tun-huang (landscapes); war breaks out between Persia and the Byzantine Empire (539–62); St Gildas writes the first important source of early British history, *De excido et conquestu Brittaniae* (542); disastrous earthquakes occur around the world (543); the plague of Constantinople, imported by rats from Egypt and Syria, spreads throughout Europe and reaches Britain (547); the Golden Era of Byzantine art begins (550); Poles settle in western Galicia, Ukrainians in eastern Galicia (550); chess begins in India (c. 550); Buddhism is introduced into Japan by Emperor Shotoko Taishi (c.552–621), and the first Buddhist monastery in Japan is founded (587); Japanese prehistory ends and the Asuka period begins; Justinian sends missionaries to China and Ceylon to smuggle out silkworms and the European silk industry becomes a Byzantine state monopoly (553); Mohammed, the founder of Islam, is born (570); war is renewed between Persia and the Byzantine Empire (572–91), and again when Chosroes II ascends the throne of Persia (590–628); the plague ends after killing half the population of Europe (542–94); first verified account of decimal number system in India (595); probably the first English school is established at Canterbury (598); the authoritative Talmud Babli, a compilation of Jewish Oral Law with rabbinical interpretations, is compiled (c. 6th century).

600–749: Books printed in China (600); Czechs and Slovaks take up land in Bohemia and Moravia, Yugoslavs in Serbia (c. 600); smallpox spreads from India, via China and Asia Minor, to southern Europe; the oldest surviving wooden building in the world, the Horyuji temple and hospital, is completed in Japan (607); Mohammed experiences a religious vision on Mt Hira (610); "burning water" (petroleum) is used in Japan (615); orchestras are formed in China (619); porcelain is produced in China (620); the Hegira is named after Mohammed's flight from hostile Mecca to Yathrib (later renamed Medina), and is year one in the Muslim calendar (622); an encyclopedia of arts and sciences is written by Isidore of Seville (622); Shaka Trinity, the famous altarpiece of the Kondo in Japan, is built by Tori (623); Mohammed begins to dictate the Koran (the sacred book of Islam) in Arabic (625); the Byzantines decisively defeat the Persians at Nineveh (627); Mohammed captures Mecca and writes letters to world leaders explaining the Muslim faith (628); cotton is introduced in Arab countries (630); Buddhism becomes the state religion in Tibet (632); Medina is the seat of the first caliph (religious and political leader of Muslims) who is Abu Bekr, Mohammed's father-in-law; the Arabs attack Persia (633); Damascus is the new capital of the caliphs (635–70); Jerusalem is conquered by the Arabs (637); the book-copying industry of the west is destroyed by the Arabs and the Alexandrian school ceases to be the centre of Western culture (641); the Arabs under Omar destroy the Persian Empire: the caliphs rule the area (until 1258), and Islam replaces the religion of Zoroaster; the Eastern Roman Empire is weakened by the Arab conquest of Egypt, Mesopotamia and Syria (642); the Dome of the Rock, a Muslim mosque, is begun in Jerusalem (643); the Muslim fleet destroys the Byzantine fleet at Lycia (655); Croats and Serbs settle in Bosnia (650); Chinese artists invent lamp-black ink and

wood block printing (c. 650); Caliphs organize first news service (650); Japanese Buddhism and Shintoism are reconciled by the Korean-born priest Gyogi (c. 668–749); the Byzantines use "Greek Fire," a missile weapon of sulphur, rock, salt, resin and petroleum, against the Arabs at the siege of Constantinople (671–78); glass windows appear in English churches (674); the first Arab coinage is introduced (695); the Arabs destroy Carthage (697); Greek, instead of Latin, becomes the official language of the Eastern Roman Empire (700); the Arabs conquer Algiers (700) and virtually eliminate Christianity in northern Africa; mass migration of European peoples is followed by their subjection at the hands of property owners; China's population grows rapidly (700) and the first large urban developments appear there; the Great Mosque of Damascus is built (705); Buddhist monasteries in Japan become centres of civilization (710); the first written history of Japan, *Kojiki*, is compiled (712); the Lombard kingdom in northern Italy reaches its height (c. 600–c. 799); the Muslim empire now extends from the Pyrenees to China, with Damascus as its capital (715); the earliest Islamic paintings appear (715); Caliph Omar II grants tax exemption to all Muslim believers (717); the Chinese capital Ch'ang-an is the largest city in the world and Constantinople is the second largest (725); Casa Grande, a North American Indian fort and large irrigation works, is built in Arizona (725); Charles Martel (mayor of the Frankish court) wins victory over the Arabs in the battle of Tours and halts their westward advance (732); first printed newspaper published in Beijing (748).

750–849: Pueblos are built in southwest North America (750–900); Spain, under Arab influence, excels in mathematics, optics and chemistry (c. 750); Kiev, Russia, becomes known as a trading centre (750); the Turkish Empire is founded by a Tartar tribe in Armenia (760); Charlemagne becomes ruler of the Franks after the death of his father (Pepin the Short, son of Charles Martel) (768) and brother Carloman (771); Arabic learning flourishes under Harun-al-Rashid (790), peaks during reign of Caliph Mamun (813–33); the Byzantine Empress Irene overthrows her son Constantine (797), an act heralded by the Greek Church; Charlemagne is crowned Holy Roman Emperor (Western Empire) at Rome (800); the earliest records of Persian poetry and literature appear (800); the Vikings dominate Ireland

(802); Arabic numerals are created under Indian influence (814); the Arabs conquer Crete, proceed as far as the Greek isles (826) and begin their conquest of Italy and Sardinia (827); Prince Mimir founds the Great Moravian Empire (830) from a confederation of Slavs in Bohemia, Moravia, Slovakia, Hungary and Transylvania; the Treaty of Verdun divides the Frankish Empire into France, Germany and Italy (843); paper currency in China creates inflation and state bankruptcy (845); Abu Tamman writes _Hamasa_, a collection of Arabian legends, proverbs and heroic stories (845); the Arabs sack Rome (846), damage the Vatican and destroy the Venetian fleet.

850–99: Salerno University is founded (850); the discovery of coffee is credited to Arabia (850); Jews settling in Germany develop the Yiddish language (c. 850); the first important Japanese painter, Kudara Kuwanari, dies (853); Norse pirates enter the Mediterranean and sack the coast up to Asia Minor (859); Iceland is discovered by the Northmen (861); Russian Northmen sack parts of France (861) and attack Constantinople (865); Basil I, the Byzantine Emperor, compiles the Basilican code (reforming finance and law and restoring the prestige of the military), and begins the Macedonian dynasty (867); Alfred the Great, king of England, recaptures London from the Danes (878); Emperor Charles III becomes king of France and once more unites the empire of Charlemagne (884), he is deposed (887) and there is a final separation of Germany and France; England's King Alfred establishes a regular militia and navy, extends the power of the king's courts and institutes fairs and markets (890).

900–99: The Vikings discover Greenland (900); the Mayans relinquish their settlements in the lowlands of Mexico and emigrate to the Yucatan peninsula (900); England is divided into shires with county courts in order to safeguard the civil rights of the inhabitants (900); the Arabian tales _A Thousand and One Nights_ is begun (900); castles become the seats of the European nobility (900); Cordoba, Spain, is the seat of Arab learning, science, commerce and industry (930); Yenching becomes new capital city of China, later known as Beijing (938); revolts against imperial rule in Japan set off a period of civil war (939–1185); the Arab empire creates advanced postal and news services (942); the earliest record of the existence of a London bridge (963); a Chinese encyclo-

pedia of 1,000 volumes is begun (978–84); the rule of nobles in Rome ends (980); Venice and Genoa carry on a flourishing trade between Asia and Western Europe (983); systematic musical notation develops (990); canonization of Christian saints begins.

1000–99: The heroic poem _Beowulf_ is written in Old English by an unknown author (1000); Leif Ericsson, son of Eric the Red, sails to North America (1000); the Chinese invent gunpowder (1000); Mayan culture on the Yucatan peninsula achieves its zenith (1000); Sridhara, Indian mathematician, describes the importance of zero (1000); the Holy Sepulchre in Jerusalem is sacked by Muslims (1009); Danes under Canute control England (1016); Canute conquers Norway (1028); Jaroslav the Wise, Prince of Kiev (1020–54), codifies Russian law and builds cities, schools and churches; Byzantine power begins to decline (1025); Canute dies (1035) and his kingdom of England, Norway and Denmark is divided among his three sons; after murdering Duncan of Scotland, Macbeth becomes king (1040) and is later murdered by Malcolm (1057); time values are given to musical notes (1050); the separation of the Roman and Eastern Churches becomes permanent (1054); Westminster Abbey is consecrated (1065); William of Normandy is crowned William the Conqueror, of England (1066); the comet, later known as Halley's comet, appears (1066); She-tsung, Emperor of China, nationalizes agricultural production and distribution (1068); Constantine the African brings Greek medicine to the Western world (1071); the original Tower of London is built (1078); the Domesday Book, a survey of assessment for tax purposes, is compiled (1086); the start of the First Crusade (1096) is proclaimed by Pope Urban II to recapture the Holy Land from the Turks; Crusaders take Jerusalem (1099).

1100–99: Middle English supersedes Old English (1100); Islamic science begins to decline; secular music first appears; Robert of Normandy is appeased after invading England in the Treaty of Alton (1101); colonization of eastern Germany begins (1105); the earliest record of a miracle play is from Dunstable, England (1110): based on Scriptures and the lives of saints, they are widely performed until the 16th century; Bologna University founded (1119); the earliest account of a mariner's compass is by Alexander Neckham (1125); the

Second Crusade begins (1146) and fails one year later; Paris University is founded (1150); Bologna Medical School is founded (1150); the first recorded fire and plague insurance is in Iceland (1151); the Japanese clans Taira and Minamoto fight each other (1156); Eric of Sweden conquers Finland (1157); Thomas à Becket is elected Archbishop of Canterbury (1162) in an effort to curb church power, but he later quarrels with King Henry II over growing royal power; Becket is murdered by Norman knights (1170) and buried at Canterbury; jails are ordered erected in all English counties and boroughs (1166); Oxford University is founded (1167); rules for the canonization of saints are established by Pope Alexander III (1170); first authenticated influenza epidemics occur (1173); the Campanile ("Leaning Tower") of Pisa is built (1174); Walter Map organizes the Arthurian legends in their present form (1176); all Jews are banished from France (1182); the Third Crusade (1189–93) fails to recapture Jerusalem from the Muslims; Moses Maimonides, Jewish philosopher, introduces Aristotle to modern western philosophy when he attempts to reconcile Aristotle's theories with those of Jewish philosophy in *Guide to the Perplexed* (1190), and he is also credited with organizing all Jewish law for the layman as well as religious educators.

1200–49: Cambridge University founded (1200); Islam takes root in India; the Fourth Crusade begins with crusaders from Venice fighting Constantinople and establishing a Latin Kingdom of Jerusalem (1204); St Francis of Assisi issues the first rules of his brotherhood of educators and missionaries, the Franciscans (1209); in the Children's Crusade (1212), thousands of children from Europe leave for the Holy Land, but most are either sold as slaves or die of hunger or disease; Genghis Khan becomes chief prince of the Mongols (1206) and conquers most of the Chinese empire of north China (1213–15) as well as Turkistan, Afghanistan and Transoxania (1218–24), and he raids Persia and Eastern Europe; Genghis Khan's empire is divided among his descendants upon his death (1227); the Council of St Albans is the precursor to the British Parliament (1213); King John puts his seal on England's Magna Carta at Runnymede under compulsion by the barons (1215): it defines the limitations of royal power and sets out basic civil rights; the Fifth Crusade fails in Egypt (1217–21); the oldest national flag in the

world, Danneborg, is adopted by Denmark (1218); the form of the sonnet develops in Italian poetry (1221); St Thomas Aquinas (1225–74) theorizes philosophical proofs for the existence of God and reconciles Greek ideas with Christian theology; the Sixth Crusade is led by Emperor Frederick II (1228); crusaders bring back leprosy to Europe (1230), and they secure a temporary truce with the Muslims; three later crusades against Muslims in the 13th century fail; coal is mined for the first time in Newcastle, England (1233); the Inquisition begins as the pope makes Dominicans responsible for putting an end to heresy (1233); Alexander Nevski made Grand Duke of Novgorod (1236).

1250–99: Kublai Khan becomes governor of China (1251) and ruler of the Mongol peoples (1259–94); he fails to conquer Japan (1274), southeast Asia and Indonesia, but he defeats the Sung dynasty of China (1279); instruments of torture are first used in the Inquisition (1252); the Sorbonne is founded by Robert de Sorbon as the Paris School of Theology (1254); the House of Commons is established in England (1258); Mongols control Baghdad, end caliphate (1258); Roger Bacon writes *"De computo naturali"* (1264); the glass mirror is invented (1278); Marco Polo, the Venetian explorer, journeys to China (1271–95) and is in the diplomatic service of Kublai Khan (1275–92); Florence, Italy, is the leading European city in commerce and finance (c. 1282); the Teutonic Order, a German military and religious order, conquers Prussia (1283) after killing the native "heathens" and replacing them with Germans; spectacles (eyeglasses) are invented (1290); the crusades end and the Knights of St John of Jerusalem settle in Cyprus (1291).

1300–99: Trade fairs at Bruges, Antwerp, Lyons and Geneva (c. 1300); Edward I of England standardizes the yard and the acre (1305); Dante composes his *Divina Commedia* (1307–21); mechanical clocks are driven by weights in Europe; Salic Law, excluding women from succession to the throne, is adopted in France (1317); No plays originate in Japan (1325); the Aztecs establish Mexico City (1327); the sawmill is invented (1328); weaving at York first documented (1331); the Hundred Years War between France and England begins (1337) as a dispute over lands held by the English crown in France: it later becomes a dispute over the French crown itself; the first scientific weather forecasts are attempted by William Merlee of Oxford (1337); the Black Death (bubonic plague) devastates Europe, killing about 75 million people, more than one-third of the population (1347–51); Boccaccio writes *Decameron* (1348–53), which is intended to be a diversion from the horrors of the plague; Timur the Lame (Tamerlaine) begins his conquest of Asia (1363); the Aztecs of Mexico build their capital, Tenochtitlan (1364); the Mongol Yüan dynasty in China is overthrown by the national Ming dynasty (1368–1644); the building of the Bastille begins in Paris (1369); "Robin Hood," the legendary hero who robbed the rich to help the poor, appears in English ballads and literature; The Great Schism in the Catholic Church begins (1378–1417) when, after the death of Pope Gregory XI, two popes are elected, one each at Rome and Avignon; Venice wins its Hundred Years War against Genoa (1256–1381); Briton John Wyclif calls for the reform of church practices (1379); he is condemned as a heretic (1380, 1382) and inspires the first English translation of the Latin Bible, the Wyclif Bible; Chaucer writes *The Canterbury Tales*; the rival southern and northern courts of Japan's divided imperial family reunite after 50 years of strife; Denmark, Sweden and Norway unite under Queen Margaret of Denmark (1397) in the Union of Kalmar.

1400–39: Russia's greatest icon painter, Andrei Rublex, creates *Trinity* (1411); England and France sign a perpetual peace treaty upon the marriage of Henry V and Catherine of Valois (1420); Joan of Arc and her French followers defeat the British at Orleans (1429) and march triumphantly to Paris: she is then taken prisoner by the Burgundians (1430) and condemned and executed (1431) in a political inquisition and trial; complete suits of metal armor plate replace chain mail in Europe (1430); China shuts out the western world and bans voyages there (1433) because Confucian doctrine sees little merit in trade; the Portuguese find the way around Cape Bojador (on the west coast of Africa) under Henry the Navigator (1434); the Greek (Eastern or Byzantine) Church unites with the Roman church (1439) in order to save itself from the Turkish threat; Montezuma becomes ruler of the Aztecs in Mexico (1440) and begins to conquer surrounding tribes.

■ Renaissance: 1440–1650

1440–69: The rise of the Italian city-states heralds the Renaissance (1440–50), and the richest families (such as the Medici) vie with each other as patrons of art and learning (mainly in Florence); the first oil painter, Jan van Eyck, dies in Flanders (1441); France defeats England at Castillion, ending the Hundred Years War (1453), and the English give up everything except Calais, thus ending English rule in France; Zimbabwe, the great African kingdom, declines after 200 years of expansion (1450) because of food shortages; Constantinople, the old capital of the Byzantine empire, falls to the Ottomans (1453); a treaty unites rival Italian city-states (1454), requiring them to protect each other from outside aggression; Ming porcelain pottery appears in Europe (1460); the Bible is printed mechanically with metal typefaces and oil-based ink by Johann Gutenberg (1455); the Wars of the Roses begin in England (1455) as a struggle for the throne between the houses of York and Lancaster, and end (1485) when Henry VII of the house of Lancaster prevails over Richard III; Plato's writings are translated into Latin at the Platonic Academy in Florence (1469).

1470–99: Music sheets, maps and posters are mechanically printed (1470s); Vlad the Impaler dies in Transylvania (1477) and the mass murderer becomes the source for Dracula legends; Peruvian-centred Inca rule expands to include the entire Andean region (3,200 sq. km) under Pachacuti, and his son Topa Inca (1470), and it is characterized by terracing, irrigation, pantheistic religion with human sacrifice, advanced metalwork, tapestry making and construction; the Spanish Catholic Inquisition begins (1478); King Ferdinand V of Aragón and Queen Isabella I of Castile unite their crowns in Spain to ward off Alfonso V of Portugal (1479); Ivan the Great declares Russian independence (1480) from the Mongols when he refuses to continue paying them tribute; the first European manual of navigation and nautical almanac is prepared in Portugal by mathematical experts (1484) who calculate the latitude of the sun, based on the work of the Jewish astronomer Abraham Zacuto; the spread of witchcraft and heresy in Germany is attacked by Pope Innocent VIII (1484) and he authorizes Dominican inquisitors to torture and burn witches; the publication of an encyclopedia of witchcraft, *Malleus Maleficarum* (1486), adds to witch hunt hysteria; the Genoese seaman Christopher Columbus secures the sponsorship of Queen Isabella of Spain (1486) for his expedition to discover a western route to Asia (he sets sail with his three ships: Santa María, Pinta and Niña in 1492); the Aztecs of Mexico inaugurate the Great Temple of Tenochtitlan (1487) when they ritually sacrifice the hearts of 20,000 people; the Portuguese explorer Bartholomew Dias rounds the Cape of Good Hope off South Africa (1488); Leonardo da Vinci is in his prime in Italy (1488) as an artist, scientist, inventor and philosopher, with inventions centuries ahead of their time (e.g., he conceives of flying machines and an apparatus to enable humans to breathe under water); the Great Wall of China is rebuilt by Ming emperors as a defence against attacks by northern Barbarians (1488); the first terrestrial globe is made by Martin Behaim, a German (1492); Jews are ordered by Spain's Catholic rulers to choose between expulsion or forced conversion (1492), and the rulers change the options to conversion or death (1498); Spain conquers Granada (1492), the last Muslim kingdom in Spain; Spain and Portugal sign a treaty dividing lands discovered in the new world, but Spain benefits the most from the treaty (1494); French armies in Italy bring a virus later identified as syphilis to Naples and the epidemic spreads through Europe (1495); Columbus brings tobacco back from the new world (1496); the Chinese invent a toothbrush (1498); Vasco da Gama discovers a sea route around the Cape of Good Hope to India via the Indian Ocean (1498); the Italian navigator Amerigo Vespucci explores the northeast coast of South America (1499) and reports cannibals (1502); Portugal's Pedro Cabral discovers the east coast of Brazil and observes natives using stone to cut wood (1499).

1500–25: The discovery of plays and poems by Hroswitha of Gandersheim, a 10th-century Saxon, makes her the first European playwright since the Classical Age (1500); King Ferdinand of Spain sanctions a system of levying tribute payments from Indians in the new world and using Indians as forced labour (1501); Shi'ism becomes the state religion in Persia (1502) and Sunni Muslim dissenters are executed there; a hand-held timepiece, made possible by the invention of the coiled mainspring, is constructed by German locksmith Peter Henlein (1502); *David*, a 13-foot statue,

is completed by Michelangelo Buonarrotti (1504) in Florence, Italy; Leonardo da Vinci paints the *Mona Lisa* (1505); Venice dominates Mediterranean trade (c. 1507); a map calls the new world "America" after Amerigo Vespucci (1507) and shows it as a distinct continent; the first great German artist, Albrecht Dürer (painter/engraver), creates his *Adam and Eve* oil painting (1507); Michelangelo paints the ceiling of the Sistine Chapel (1508–12); Sebastian Cabot sails around Cuba, proving it is an island (1508) and later reaches Hudson Bay in search of a northwest passage; the first African slaves are brought to the Americas (Cuba) (1510); Erasmus, the Dutch humanist, writes the satirical *In Praise of Folly* (1511); Juan Ponce de Léon claims Florida for Spain (1513) while searching for the Fountain of Youth; Niccolo Machiavelli writes *The Prince* (1513) which discusses the uses and abuses of power; Vasco Núñez de Balboa discovers the "South Sea," or Pacific Ocean, for Spain (1513); Spain orders new world natives to convert to Christianity under threat of enslavement or death (1514); Henry VIII of England puts forth measures to protect peasants from enclosure—the dividing and closing off of common land (1515); Sir Thomas More writes *Utopia,* which depicts an ideal state (1516); Martin Luther, a German Augustinian monk, writes his *95 Theses*, attacking the Catholic Church's sale of indulgences granting the forgiveness of sins (1517) and nails it to the door of the Wittenberg church; English sailors complain to King Henry VIII about the growing number of French cod fishermen in Newfoundland (1517); the rule of Suleiman I the Magnificent sees the Ottoman Turks reach the zenith of their empire with the conquest of Egypt, Syria and Hungary (1520); Ferdinand Magellan begins a three-year voyage to circumnavigate the globe (1519); Hernando Cortes lands at Vera Cruz, Mexico, where Montezuma II and the Aztecs surrender (1519); chocolate is introduced to Europe from Mexico (1520); Nicholas Copernicus publishes his "Commentariolus" stating his theory that the earth revolves around the sun (1521); Martin Luther translates the Bible into German (1522).

1526–49: Lutheran German troops sack and burn Rome (1527); Hippocrates' ancient idea of the four humours governing bodily health is first disputed (1528); Henry VIII separates from the Church of Rome and becomes head of the English Church (1534) after he is refused an annulment of his first marriage; the Jesuit order of missionaries is founded by Ignatius Loyola (1534); Jacques Cartier searches for riches in North America along the St Lawrence River (1535); John Calvin, the French leader of the Protestant Reformation in Geneva, theorizes the concepts of predestination and God's omniscience (1536); the first mechanical artificial limbs appear for crippled war veterans (1539); the founder of the Sikh religion, Guru Nanak, dies in India (1539); Henry VIII becomes King of Ireland and Head of the Irish Church (1541); John Knox leads the Calvinist Reformation in Scotland (1541); oil is discovered in North America by the Spaniards (1543); Portuguese traders are the first to sell guns to Japan (1543); Nostradamus, the French astrologer, begins making predictions (1547); Ivan IV (the Terrible) is crowned the first czar of Russia (1547): he calls the first national assembly (1549).

1550–99: Jesuit missionaries protect natives in the new world from slavery (1551); Ivan the Terrible defeats the Mongols (1552), and conquers as far as the Caspian Sea (1556); Lady Jane Grey is executed for treason in England by Queen Mary Tudor (1554), who becomes known as "Bloody Mary" after persecuting Protestants (1555); Mary restores papal authority in England and Wales (1554); Charles V relinquishes the Holy Roman Empire and Spain to his brother and son, and goes to a monastery (1556); an influenza epidemic hits Europe (1557); Elizabeth I becomes Queen of England (1558) and rejects papal power in England (1559); the Huguenot (Calvinist French Protestant) conspiracy occurs at Amboise: liberty of worship is promised in France (1560); the Edict of Orleans suspends persecution of Huguenots (1561); the Peace of Amboise ends the first War of Religion in France and the Huguenots are granted limited toleration (1563); Andreas Vesalius, the Flemish founder of modern anatomy, dies (1564); Nobunaga deposes the Japanese shogunate and centralizes the government (1567); the Iroquois Confederacy of five North American nations (Mohawk, Oneida, Onondaga, Cayuga, Seneca) is founded (c. 1570); Huguenots are massacred on St Bartholomew's Day in Paris (1572); the Dutch War of Independence begins (1572); the Union of Utrecht is the foundation of the Dutch Republic (1579); William of Orange accepts the sovereignty of northern Netherlands and is

assassinated (1584); the first English colony in Newfoundland is founded (1582); Elizabeth of England orders Mary Queen of Scots beheaded for treason (1587); Christopher Marlowe completes *Dr. Faustus* (1588); the first Spanish Armada leaves for England and is defeated by the English under Charles Howard (1588); Sir Francis Drake, with 18,000 men, fails to take Lisbon for England (1589); William Shakespeare completes the play *Romeo and Juliet* (1594); the Second Spanish Armada leaves for England but is scattered by storms (1597); an English Act of Parliament calls for convicted criminals to serve their terms in the colonies (1597).

1600–49: France boasts the largest population in central Europe, with 16 million persons (1600); William Shakespeare completes *Hamlet* (1600); Dutch opticians invent the telescope (1600); the first modern public company is founded, the Dutch East India Company (1602); Guy Fawkes is arrested and accused of trying to blow up the House of Lords during James I's state opening of Parliament (The Gunpowder Plot, 1605); Fawkes is sentenced to death (1606); the first English settlement on the American mainland is founded at Jamestown, Virginia (1607); Shakespeare writes his *Sonnets* (1609); the first cheques appear in Netherlands as "cash letters" (1608); the *King James Bible* is published (1611); Peter Paul Rubens paints *Descent from the Cross* (1611); the North American Indian princess Pocahantas marries English colonist John Rolfe (1614); Galileo Galilei, Italian astronomer, faces the Inquisition for the first time for renouncing the Ptolemaic system of the earth-centred universe and embracing the Copernican sun-centred system (1615); the Thirty Years War begins in Prague as Protestants rebel against Catholic oppression (1618); slavery in North America begins when the first Africans are brought to Virginia (1619) and the triangular slave trade starts (British goods are sent to west Africa and are traded for slaves, who are traded for agricultural staples in the new world, which are sent back to Britain); pilgrims arriving on the *Mayflower* found Plymouth Colony, Massachusetts (1620); patent law is created in England to protect inventors (1623); construction begins on the Taj Mahal mausoleum in Agra, North India (1628); Charles I dissolves the English Parliament for 11 years (1629); Cardinal Richelieu, chief minister of Louis

XIII of France, rules France (1630–42); Galileo is forced by the Inquisition to cease promulgating the theories of Copernicus (1633); Japan forbids foreign books, Christianity and any European contacts (1637); René Descartes, called the father of modern philosophy, writes *Discourse on Method* (1637); the Ming dynasty in China ends and the Manchu dynasty takes power (1644–1912); Charles I of England, after a long struggle for power with Parliament (English Civil War 1642–48), is beheaded by Oliver Cromwell for treason (1649).

1650–99: Bishop James Ussher dates the creation of the world at October 23, 4004 BC (1650); the wholesale massacre of North American Indians by European settlers begins (1650); Thomas Hobbes writes *Leviathan*, a defence of absolute monarchy in England (1651); Oliver Cromwell becomes Lord Protector in England, dissolves Parliament, divides England into 11 districts, prohibits Anglican services (1653) and readmits Jews to England after 365 years (1655); Blaise Pascal (French) develops the basic laws of probability (1654); the Portuguese drive the Dutch out of Brazil (1654); the first London opera house opens (1656); Dutch peasants (Boers) first settle in South Africa (1660); the Royal Society is founded in London to promote scientific discussion among great thinkers (1660); the earliest condemnation of industrial pollution, *The Inconvenience of the Air and Smoke of London Dissipated*, is written by John Evelyn (1661); Louis XIV (the Sun King) begins to build the palace at Versailles (1662); Jean Baptiste Colbert forms the North American colony of New France with Quebec as its capital (1663); the British annex New Netherlands from the Dutch and rename the main city New York (1664); Isaac Newton begins to experiment with gravity and develops calculus (1664–66); the cell is named and described by Briton Robert Hooke (1665); the French army uses the first hand grenades (1667); Portugal gains independence from Spain through the Treaty of Lisbon (1668); micro-organisms are discovered by Anton van Leeuwenhoek (Dutch, 1669) who later observes bacteria (1683) for the first time; the Hudson's Bay Company is incorporated by a British royal charter to trade in the region of North America defined by those rivers which drain into Hudson Bay (1670); Dutch philosopher Baruch Spinoza writes *Ethics* (1675); the poems of Bashu (a pseudonym) popularize Japanese haiku poetry (1675); the *Declaration of the People of Virginia* by Nathaniel Bacon lends support to rebellion against authorities in the colonies (1676); Roman Catholics are excluded from both houses of Parliament in England (1678); the Habeas Corpus Amendment Act in England protects citizens from unjust imprisonment (1679); the French colonial empire of North America, reaching from Quebec to the mouth of the Mississippi River, is organized (1680); the large dodo bird with small, flightless wings becomes extinct (1680); Sir Isaac Newton writes *Principles of Natural Philosophy* (1687), which discusses universal gravitation; the Glorious Revolution establishes the constitutional monarchy in England (1688–89) and William of Orange III and Mary II ascend the throne; Peter the Great becomes czar of Russia (1689); John Locke writes *Essay Concerning Human Understanding* and *Two Treatises on Civil Government* (1690).

1700–49: The War of the Spanish Succession to the childless Charles II, Hapsburg king of Spain, is fought (1701–14) between the French Bourbons and Austrian Hapsburgs; rebellion occurs in Astrakhan against Czar Peter's westernization of Russia (1705); England and Scotland form Great Britain (1707); the Peace of Utrecht is signed between Spain and England: Spain cedes Gibraltar and Minorca to England (1713) and Philip of France retains the Spanish crown; D.G. Fahrenheit constructs a mercury thermometer with a temperature scale (1714); George F. Handel writes *Water Music* for King George I (1717); Daniel Defoe writes *The Life and Strange Surprising Adventures of Robinson Crusoe* (1719); the German composer and virtuoso organist J.S. Bach composes *The Brandenburg Concertos* (1721); Johnathan Swift writes *Gulliver's Travels* (1726); Benjamin Franklin, American statesman, scientist, printer and writer, writes *Poor Richard's Almanack* (1732); John Kay patents the fly shuttle loom, which revolutionizes weaving (1733); Alexander Pope, poet and English verse satirist, writes *Essay on Man* (1733); the modern classification system of plants and animals is introduced by Carolus Linnaeus (Swedish, 1735); Alaska is discovered by Victor Behring (1740); Frederick the Great introduces freedom of the press and freedom of worship in Prussia (1740); sign language for the deaf is created by Rodriguez Pereire (1749).

■ Industrial Revolution: 1750–1850

1750–99: Benjamin Franklin experimented with static electricity and invented the lightning conductor (1752); in the Seven Years War (1756–63) Britain declares war on France and, in the North American colonies, the French drive the British from the Great Lakes area (1756); the French lose Quebec to the British (1759) during the battle on the Plains of Abraham; Voltaire writes the philosophical novel *Candide* (1759); Catherine II (the Great) becomes czarina of Russia (1762); Swiss-French philosopher Jean Jacques Rousseau writes *Social Contract* (1762) which discusses his theory of "natural man"; the Peace of Paris (1763) ends the war between England and France and gives Canada to England; eight-year-old Mozart writes his first symphony (1764); the spinning jenny, which spins up to 120 threads at once, is invented by Briton James Hargreaves (1764); the British Parliament passes the Stamp Act for taxing American colonies: Virginia and New York challenge the right of Britain to taxation without representation (1766); the Mason-Dixon Line is drawn by English surveyors between Pennsylvania and Maryland (1767) and is later the boundary between "slave" and "free" states; Daniel Rutherford and Joseph Priestley independently discover nitrogen (1772); the Bolshoi Ballet is founded in Russia (1773); during the Boston Tea Party American colonists protesting British taxes dress as Indians and dump the cargo of three tea ships in the Boston, Mass., harbour (1773); James Watt, Scottish inventor, perfects the steam engine (1775); the American Revolution begins (1775); the Second Continental Congress assembles at Philadelphia and appoints George Washington commander-in-chief of the American forces; the Americans proclaim the *Declaration of Independence* (July 4, 1776); Edward Gibbon writes *Decline and Fall of the Roman Empire* (1776); Adam Smith completes *Wealth of Nations* (1776); after the American victory in the Saratoga Campaign (1777) France enters into an alliance with the Americans (1778); Washington's army suffers at Valley Forge (1778); Hawaii is discovered by James Cook (1778); Franz Mesmer practices mesmerism (hypnotism) (1778); Spain joins the American War of Independence against Britain (1779); the Dutch support the American side (1780); Sir William Herschel discovers Uranus (1781); British

General Cornwallis surrenders to the Americans (Oct. 1781) at the end of the Yorktown Campaign, and the Treaty of Paris recognizes American independence (1783); John Wesley writes the *Deed of Declaration*, the charter of Wesleyan Methodism (1784); the British colony of Australia is founded (1788); the French Revolution begins (1789); a Paris mob opposing the monarchy storms the Bastille jail; French royalists begin to emigrate; the French revolutionaries proclaim the Decrees of August 4 and the *Declaration of the Rights of Man and of the Citizen;* the government limits the monarchy's power, abolishes the French feudal system, extends religious tolerance to Jews and Protestants and reorganizes the Catholic Church; A.L. Lavoisier completes the *Table of Thirty-One Chemical Elements* (1790); the Constitutional Act divides Britain's Canadian colony into Upper Canada (English-speaking) and Lower Canada (French-speaking) (1791); Thomas Paine writes *The Rights of Man* in defence of the French Revolution (1791); the French King Louis XVI and Queen Marie Antoinette are beheaded for treason (Jan. 1793); the Reign of Terror (guillotine executions of prisoners) under the Jacobin government ends with the execution of Maximilien Robespierre; Robert Burns' *Auld Lang Syne* is published (1794); Edward Jenner discovers a smallpox vaccine (1796).

1800–09: Ottawa is founded (1800); Eli Whitney makes muskets with interchangeable parts (1800); the Library of Congress is established in Washington, D.C., by Thomas Jefferson (1800); the first battery is produced from zinc and copper plates by Alessandro Volto (1800); William Herschel discovers the existence of infrared solar rays (1800); the first submarine *Nautilus* is made by American civil engineer Robert Fulton (1801); the atomic theory of chemistry is put forth by John Dalton (1802); the U.S. buys land from France in the Louisiana Purchase (1803); Henry Shrapnel invents the shell used in warfare (1803); Napoleon crowns himself emperor of the French empire (1804) and king of Italy (1805); modern Egypt is established when Mehemet Ali becomes Pasha (1805); morphine is isolated by F.W.A. Satürner (1805); Napoleon wins his greatest victory, at Austerlitz, over the Austrians and Russians allied against him (1805); the American frigate *Chesapeake* is stopped and boarded by British naval officers looking for deserters, almost causing a war

(1807); Ludwig van Beethoven, the great German composer who brought together Classical and Romantic styles, performs his *Fifth Symphony* (written for Napoleon) and *Sixth Symphony* (1808); the first part of J.W. von Goethe's *Faust* is published (1808); Washington Irving writes *Rip van Winkle* (1809).

1810–19: Simón Bolívar becomes a leading figure in South American politics (1810) and liberates Greater Colombia (Panama, Venezuela, Ecuador and Colombia) (1819) and Peru (1824) from Spanish rule; a machine for spinning flax is invented by Philippe Girard (1812); German folklorist Jakob Grimm completes *Grimm's Fairy Tales* (1812–15); Napoleon Bonaparte's first military setback is in the Peninsular War (1808–14), and he later retreats from an unsuccessful invasion of Russia; the War of 1812 (1812–14) between Britain and the United States is foreshadowed by the battle at Tippecanoe (1811); Jane Austen writes *Pride and Prejudice* (1813), depicting English country life and mores; Austria, Russia and Prussia form an alliance against Napoleon and defeat him at Leipzig (1813) and recapture Paris (1814); Napoleon abdicates and is exiled to Elba Island; the War of 1812 continues in North America as the British capture Washington, DC (1814), but the Americans win battles at Fort McHenry, Thames (killing Tecumseh, an Indian ally of the British) and at Plattsburgh (1814); the British initiate peace in the Treaty of Ghent (1814) but this news travels too slowly to stop the Battle of New Orleans (1815), won by the Americans; Napoleon escapes from exile and returns to march on Paris; he is defeated at Waterloo (1815), abdicates again and is banished to St Helena Island; the German Confederation, dominated by Austria and Prussia, is created to replace the Holy Roman Empire (1815); Argentina declares its independence from Spain (1816); the classical economist David Ricardo (British) writes *The Principles of Political Economy and Taxation* (1817), discussing the determination of wage and value; Georg Hegel writes his all-embracing *Encyclopedia of the Philosophical Sciences* (1817); Mary Shelley writes *Frankenstein* (1818); Lord Byron begins *Don Juan* (1818–23); Chile proclaims its independence from Spain (1818); electromagnetism is discovered by Danish physicist Hans C. Oersted (1819); Greater Colombia (including Panama, Venezuela, Ecuador and Colombia) declares independence from Spain (1819).

1820–29: Andre Ampere (French) writes *Laws of Electrodynamic Action* (1820); Liberia is founded by the Washington Colonization Society, for the repatriation of black slaves (1820); Sir Walter Scott writes *Ivanhoe* (1820); John Keats writes *Ode to a Nightingale* (1820); an electric recording device for sound reproduction is invented by Sir Charles Wheatstone (1821); Peru and Guatemala declare their independence from Spain (1821); the Reign of Terror begins between the Greeks and the Turks (1821); Franz Liszt, the Hungarian pianist who revolutionizes Romantic music and invents the symphonic poem, makes his debut at age 11 in Vienna (1822); Brazil declares itself independent from Portugal (1822); the Monroe Doctrine closes the American continent to colonial settlement by European powers (1823); Spanish are defeated and Paris independence recognized (1824); Simón Bolívar creates his namesake, Bolivia (1825); the first steam-powered railroads carrying freight and passengers, operated by the Stockton and Darlington Railway, run in England (1825); the Erie Canal opens, linking the Hudson River and the Great Lakes (1825); the first major American author, James Fenimore Cooper, writes *The Last of the Mohicans* (1826); Felix Mendelssohn composes the Overture to *A Midsummer Night's Dream* (1826); the great cholera epidemic begins in India (1826) and spreads from Russia into Central Europe; J.J. Audubon writes *Birds of North America* (1827); Noah Webster writes the *American Dictionary of the English Language* (1828); Uruguay declares independence from Brazil (1828); the Peace of Adrianople ends the Russo-Turkish war and Turkey acknowledges the independence of Greece (1829); Frederic Chopin, the Polish pianist, debuts in Vienna (1829); Venezuela withdraws from Greater Colombia and becomes independent (1829).

1830–39: Charles Lyell of Scotland divides the geological system into three groups: Eocene, Miocene and Pliocene (1830); Ecuador declares independence (1830); mass demonstrations in Swiss cities lead to liberal reforms (1831); Charles Darwin sails on the HMS *Beagle* as a naturalist, surveying South America, New Zealand and Australia (1831–36); the leading antislavery leader in the United States, W.L. Garrison, begins publishing *The Liberator* in Boston (1831); the wealthy middle classes emerging from the Industrial Revolution are enfranchised in Britain, doubling the number of voters (1832); the New England antislavery society is founded in Boston (1832); slavery is abolished in the British Empire (1833); the Spanish Inquisition, begun during the 13th century, is finally abolished (1834); France's leading writer, Victor Hugo, writes *The Hunchback of Notre Dame* (1834); the Poor Law Amendment Act decrees that no able-bodied person (displaced by the Industrial Revolution) in Great Britain shall receive assistance unless he or she enters a workhouse (1834); Hans Christian Andersen writes his first stories for children (1835); the American writer Ralph Waldo Emerson writes *Nature* (1836); the People's Charter initiates Britain's first national working-class movement, calling for universal suffrage for men and voting by ballot (1836); the Dutch (Afrikaner) farmers begin "The Great Trek" of emigration across the Orange and Vaal rivers, South Africa (1836); the first botanical textbook, *The Elements of Botany*, is written by American Asa Gray (1836); Victoria becomes Queen of Great Britain (1837); citizens stage unsuccessful rebellions in Lower and Upper Canada (1837); Louis Braille invents his reading system for the blind (1837); Charles Dickens's *Oliver Twist*, a critique of British industrial society, is a bestseller (1838); the first bicycle is invented by a Scot, Kirkpatrick Macmillan (1839); the cell-growth theory is put forth by Theodor Schwann (1839); ozone is discovered by Christian Schönbein, a German-Swiss chemist (1839); American Charles Goodyear develops the process of vulcanization, making the commercial use of rubber possible (1839); a photograph produced on a silver-coated copperplate treated with iodine vapor, the daguerreotype, is invented by Louis Daguerre and Nicephore Niepce (French) (1839); the First Opium War between Britain and China begins (1839).

1840–49: New Zealand becomes a British colony (1840); philosopher Thomas Carlyle writes *On Heroes, Hero-Worship and the Heroic in History* in support of strong government (1841); the father of the guided tour, Thomas Cook (British), arranges his first trip (1841); showman P.T. Barnum gains fame after opening his American museum of "freak" exhibitions (1841); the Webster-Ashburton Treaty between Britain and the US settles

American border disputes with Canada (1842); the Treaty of Nanking ends the Opium War between Britain and China and confirms the cession of Hong Kong to Great Britain (1842); riots and strikes erupt in northern England's industrial areas (1842); Richard Wagner (German) finishes the opera *The Flying Dutchman* (1843); the amount of work required to produce a unit of heat, the joule, is determined by English physicist James P. Joule (1843); American social reformer Dorothea Dix reports on the shocking conditions in prisons and asylums, influencing the establishment of state hospitals for the insane in Europe and North America (1843); Samuel Morse's telegraph is used for the first time between Baltimore and Washington (1844); US troops are victorious over the Mexicans at Palo Alto (1846), Congress formally declares war, US forces take Santa Fe and annex New Mexico; the Smithsonian Institution, a research and educational centre, is founded in Washington, DC (1846); ether is first used as an anaesthetic by dentist W.T. Morton (1846); sisters Charlotte and Emily Brontë publish *Jane Eyre* and *Wuthering Heights* respectively (1847); US forces capture Mexico City (1847) and the Treaty of Guadalupe Hidalgo ends the Mexican–US war (1848), the US acquires Texas and much of the surrounding territory in return for $15 million; gold discoveries in California lead to the first gold rush (1848); a revolt in Paris causes Louis Philippe to abdicate (1848); a revolution in Vienna brings Metternich's resignation (1848); revolutions in Venice, Berlin, Milan, Rome and Parma (1848); the first Public Health Act is introduced in Britain (1848); the first women's rights convention, organized by Elizabeth Stanton and Lucretia Mott, is held in Seneca Falls, New York (1848); the *Communist Manifesto* is issued by Germans Karl Marx and Friedrich Engels (1848), championing the working class and establishing socialist theory.

1850–59: Harriet Beecher Stowe writes her antislavery novel *Uncle Tom's Cabin* (1852); the Transvaal is granted self-government (1852); the Crimean War (1853–56) begins when Russia occupies Moldavia and Walachia and Turkey declares war, the Russians destroy the Turkish fleet off Sinope, and England, France and Sardinia join Turkey's fight; after a long siege the Russian base Sebastopol falls to the allied forces (1855), and after the allied victory at Balaklava, Russia recognizes the integrity of Turkey (1856); English nurse Florence Nightingale founds modern nursing while tending soldiers during the Crimean War (1853–56); the first hypodermic syringe is used by Alexander Wood (1853); Samuel Colt revolutionizes the manufacture of small arms (1853); Commander Matthew Perry negotiates the first American–Japanese treaty, permitting US ships to use two Japanese ports (1854); the Elgin Reciprocity Treaty between Great Britain and the US implements free trade between Canada and the US (1854); steel making becomes inexpensive when Henry Bessemer introduces a converter into his process for making steel (1855); pure cocaine is extracted from coca leaves (1856); Gustave Flaubert, the French master of realistic novels, writes *Madame Bovary* (1856); Louis Pasteur discovers that fermentation is caused by microorganisms (1857), and later invents pasteurization and discovers a vaccine for rabies; the first Neanderthal skeleton is found in a cave in Neander Valley (near Düsseldorf, Germany); the Indian Mutiny against British rule (1857) causes the British siege and capture of Delhi; the British Royal Navy destroys the Chinese fleet, and Britain and France take Canton (1857); Giuseppe Garibaldi forms the Italian National Association for the unification of Italy (1857); the Treaty of Tientsin ends the Anglo–Chinese war (1858); Charles Darwin writes *On the Origin of Species by Natural Selection*, explaining his theory of evolution (1859); the German National Association is formed to unite Germany under Prussia (1859); John Stuart Mill (British) writes his essay *On Liberty* (1859).

■ Modern Era

1860–64: Garibaldi and his redshirts sail from Genoa to take Palermo and Naples; Victor Emmanuel II (king of Sardinia) invades the Papal States and defeats the Papal troops, Garibaldi proclaims Emmanuel II king of Italy (1860); Anglo–French troops defeat the Chinese at Pa-li-Chau (1860) and sign the Treaty of Peking; the first Food and Drugs Act is enacted in Britain (1860); Lenoir constructs the first internal-combustion engine (1860); a primitive form of typewriter is created by American Christopher L. Sholes (1860); hundreds of thousands of Irish and British citizens flee their homelands following the potato famine (by 1860); Russian troops fire at anti-Russian demonstrators in Poland during the Warsaw Massacre (1861); the first machine-chilled cold storage unit is built by T.S. Mort (1861); Krupp begins arms production in Essen, Germany (1861); the Archaeopteryx, the skeleton linking reptiles and birds, is discovered at Solnhofen, Germany (1861); the American Civil War (1861–65) begins after Abraham Lincoln, who views slavery as evil, is elected president; South Carolina secedes in protest, followed by 10 other southern states, to form the Confederacy fighting for states' rights and opposing the abolition of slavery; Lincoln issues the Emancipation Proclamation (1862) calling for the freeing of black slaves in Confederate territory; the Red Cross voluntary relief organization is proposed by Jean Henri Dunant, a Swiss humanist (1862); the first form of a machine gun is invented by the American Richard Gatling (1862); Otto von Bismarck becomes the prime minister of Prussia (1862) and begins his system of alliances and alignments that result in German pre-eminence in Europe; Victor Hugo writes *Les Miserables* (1862); Leo Tolstoy writes *War and Peace* (1864); the Geneva Convention establishes the neutrality of battlefield medical facilities (1864); liberalism, socialism and rationalism are condemned in *Syllabus Errorum*, issued by Pope Pius IX (1864); Cheyenne and Arapahoe Indians are massacred at Sand Creek, Colorado (1864); the First International Workingmen's Association is founded by Karl Marx in London and New York (1864); Confederate forces surrender finally at Appomattox, Virginia (1865), marking the end of the war and victory for the Union; slavery in the US is abolished by the Thirteenth Amendment; US Pres. Lincoln is assassinated by the actor John Wilkes Booth (1865).

1865–69: Lewis Carroll (British) writes *Alice's Adventures in Wonderland* (1865); Joseph Lister initiates antiseptic surgery by using carbolic acid on a compound wound (1865); line geometry is invented by German mathematician Julius Plücker (1865); Gregor Mendel, an Austrian monk, describes his Law of Heredity (1865); Bismarck, the Prussian foreign minister, provokes the brief Austro-Prussian War by invading the duchies of Schleswig-Holstein and overrunning the German states allied with Austria; after seven weeks a peace settlement gives Schleswig-Holstein, Hanover, Hesse, Nasau and Frankfurt to Prussia and excludes

Austria from influence in German affairs (1866); *Crime and Punishment* by Fyodor Dostoevsky is published (1866); Alfred Nobel invents dynamite (1866); Johann Strauss popularizes the Viennese waltz with Blue Danube (1866); the underwater torpedo is invented by Robert Whitehead, an English engineer (1866); the fundamental law of biogenetics, *General Morphology,* is published by Ernst Haeckel (1866); Claude Monet, a French founder of Impressionism, paints *Camille* (1866); Russia sells Alaska to the US for $7.2 million (1867); Karl Marx writes *Das Kapital*, volume I (1867); the British North America Act establishes the Dominion of Canada and John A. Macdonald becomes prime minister (1867); Louisa May Alcott describes Victorian American life in *Little Women* (1868); a skeleton of Cro Magnon man from the Upper Paleolithic age (the first Homo sapiens in Europe, successor to the Neanderthal man) is found in France by Louis Lartet (1868); the first regular Trades Union Congress is held at Manchester, England (1868); Dmitri Mendeleyev formulates his periodic law for the classification of the elements (1869); John Stuart Mill writes *On the Subjection of Women* (1869); the major early treatise on eugenics, *Hereditary Genius*, is published by Francis Galton (1869); J.W. Hyatt invents celluloid (plastic) (1869); the First Nihilist Congress is held at Basel, Switzerland (1869); the strategically important Suez Canal opens (1869); the doctrine of papal infallibility is established by Pope Pius IX during Vatican Council I (1869–79).

1870–79: US industrialist John D. Rockefeller founds the Standard Oil Company (1870); T.H. Huxley, English biologist and educator, writes the *Theory of Biogenesis* (1870); the Franco-Prussian War begins (1870) and France under Napoleon III capitulates; William I, king of Prussia, is proclaimed the German Emperor at Versailles, and in the Peace of Frankfurt France cedes Alsace-Lorraine to Germany (1871); the Italian Law of Guarantees allows the Pope possession of the Vatican (1871); labour unions become legal in Britain (1871); Charles Darwin writes *The Descent of Man* (1871); the Great Fire ravages Chicago (1871); explorer Sir Henry M. Stanley is sent to find David Livingstone in Africa (1871); the first modern luxury liner, SS *Oceanic*, is launched (1871); Civil War in Spain ends with the Carlists' defeat (1872); the Three Emperors

League is established in Berlin as an alliance between Germany, Russia and Austria–Hungary (1872); colour photographs are first developed (1873); James C. Maxwell writes *Electricity and Magnetism* (1873); Willhelm Wundt, known for the experimental method, writes *Physiological Psychology* (1873); under the direction of Benjamin Disraeli as prime minister, Britain expands its imperial power by annexing the Fiji islands (1874); Johannes Brahms composes the *Hungarian Dances* (1874); Johann Strauss II performs the operetta *Die Fledermaus* in Vienna (1874); Bosnia and Herzegovina rebel against Turkish rule (1875): Turkish sultan promises reforms (1875); Mary Baker Eddy writes *Science and Health* (1875) and she founds the Christian Science movement (1879); Georges Bizet performs *Carmen* in Paris (1875); British Queen Victoria is crowned empress of India (1876); Britain annexes the Transvaal (1877); US General George Custer is killed along with his cavalry by Cheyenne Indians in the Battle of Little Bighorn (1876); Alexander Graham Bell constructs a telephone (1876); first national lawn tennis championship played at Wimbledon (1877); German historian Heinrich Treitschke begins a racial anti-Semite movement (1878); Gilbert and Sullivan write *HMS Pinafore* (1878); British troops are massacred by Zulus in Isand-hlwana, Africa (1879); the British occupy the Khyber Pass near Afghanistan and are massacred in Kabul (1879); Norwegian Henrik Ibsen completes the play *A Doll's House* (1879); Chile invades Bolivia and its ally Peru after Bolivia cancels a Chilean company's contract to exploit Bolivia's nitrate deposits (1879).

1880–84: Auguste Rodin sculpts *The Thinker* (1880); France annexes Tahiti (1880); Transvaal declares its independence from Britain and the Boers establish a republic after a brief war with Britain (1880–81); the first practical electrical lights are independently made by Thomas Edison and J.W. Swan (1880); the malaria parasite is discovered by Charles Laveran (1880); the first large steel furnace is developed by American steel baron Andrew Carnegie (1880); the Vatican opens its archives to scholars (1881); the first Japanese political parties are founded (1881); violent government-condoned attacks (pogroms) are carried out against Russian Jews (1881–1917) causing large-scale Jewish emigration to North America; the Federation of Organized Trades and Labor Unions of the US and Canada is formed (1881); Germany, Austria and Italy form an alliance (1882); the three-mile limit for territorial waters is agreed upon at the Hague Convention (1882); Peter I. Tchaikovsky composes the *1812 Overture* (1882); psycho-analysis begins when Joseph Breuer (Austrian) uses hypnosis to treat hysteria (1882); Thomas Edison designs the first hydroelectric plant in Wisconsin (1882); the Orient Express train between Paris and Istanbul makes its first run (1883); *On the Size of Atoms* is published by British scientist William Thomson, later Lord Kelvin (1883); peace is restored between Peru and Chile (1883); Friedrich Nietzsche (German philosopher) begins *Thus Spake Zarathustra* (1884–91); gold is discovered in the Transvaal (1884) and this leads to the rise of Johannesburg; a truce is signed between Bolivia and Chile, with Bolivia forced to cede its only coastal territory to Chile (1884); the *Oxford English Dictionary* begins publication (1884–1928); the Berlin Conference of 14 nations on African affairs is held (1884).

1885–89: Karl Benz builds the single-cylinder engine for motor cars (1885); the individuality of fingerprints is proved by Sir Francis Galton (1885); the first Indian National Congress meets (1886); the Statue of Liberty is presented to the US by France (1886); steam is first used to sterilize surgical instruments by Ernst von Bergmann (1886); Irish politician Charles Parnell, the Fenians, and British Prime Min. William Gladstone try unsuccessfully to pass the first Irish Home Rule Bill to give Ireland control over domestic affairs (1886); Sir Arthur Conan Doyle writes the first Sherlock Holmes story, *A Study in Scarlet* (1887); William II (the Kaiser) becomes emperor of Germany (1888); Vincent Van Gogh paints the series of sunflowers (1888) and later, *Starry Night*; the electric motor is first constructed by Nikola A. Tesla and manufactured by George Westing-house (1888); radio waves are discovered to be of the same family as light waves by the inde-pendently working Heinrich Hertz and Oliver Lodge (1888); Kodak box camera produced by George Eastman (1888); "Jack the Ripper" murders six women in London (1888); Alexander G. Eiffel designs the Eiffel Tower for the Paris World Exhibition (1889).

1890–94: The first Japanese general election is held (1890); German Chancellor Bismarck dis-missed by Emperor William II (1890); the first moving picture shows appear in New York (1890); Oscar Wilde writes *The Picture of Dorian Gray* (1890); antitoxins are discovered by Emil von Behring (1890); the first entirely steel-framed building is erected in Chicago (1890); the Triple Alliance between Austria, Germany and Italy is renewed for 12 years (1891); Briton Thomas Hardy writes *Tess of the d'Urbervilles* (1891); Henri Toulouse-Lautrec produces his first music hall posters (1891); *Experiments in Aero-dynamics* is pub-lished by Samuel P. Langley (1891); the All-Deutschland Verband (Pan-Germany League) is founded (1891); Russia experiences wide-spread famine (1891); an earthquake in Japan kills ten thousand people (1891); the Java Man (*Pithecanthropus homo erectus*) is discovered by Dutch anthropologist Eugène Dubois, in Java (1891); Paul Gauguin (French) paints *By the Sea* in Tahiti (1892); Rudolph Diesel (German) patents his internal-combustion engine (1892); Tchaikovsky performs his *The Nutcracker* ballet score in St Petersburg (1892); Karl Benz constructs his four-wheel car (1893); Jewish French army captain Alfred Dreyfus is arrested under controversy and con-victed of spying for Germany (1894); Rudyard Kipling writes *The Jungle Book* (1894); after Japan sends troops to Seoul, Korea, Japan declares war on China and defeats the Chinese at Port Arthur (1894); Emil Berliner develops a horizontal gramophone disc, replacing the record cylinder for sound reproduction (1894).

1895–99: The Chinese–Japanese war ends with Japan victorious: Formosa and Port Arthur are first ceded to Japan and later returned to China for payment (1895); H.G. Wells writes *The Time Machine* (1895); William B. Yeats writes *Poems* (1895); X-rays are discovered by William Röntgen (1895); Marchese Marconi invents radio telegraphy (1895); the principle of rocket reaction propulsion is developed by Konstantin Isiolkovski (1895); the first modern Olympics is held in Athens, Greece (1896); Anton Chekhov (Russian) writes *The Sea Gull* (1896); five annual Nobel prizes are estab-lished by Alfred Nobel for persons who have contributed the most in the fields of physics, physiology and medicine, chemistry, literature and peace (1896); Wilfrid Laurier becomes the first French Canadian prime minister of Canada (1896–1911); the Klondike gold rush in Bonanza Creek, Canada, begins (1896); Edmond Rostand writes *Cyrano de Bergerac* (1897); Queen Victoria celebrates her Diamond Jubilee (1897); French writer Emile

Zola writes an open letter, *J'accuse*, condemning the Dreyfus espionage trial and he is imprisoned (1898), Col. Henry admits forging documents in the case (1898), and Captain Dreyfus is pardoned after a retrial (1899)—the case polarizes French politics for a decade; the US declares war on Spain over Cuba and destroys the Spanish fleet at Manila (1898); Spain cedes Cuba, Puerto Rico, Guam and the Philippines to the US for $20 million at the Treaty of Paris; Chinese Boxers, an anti-western organization, is formed (1898); the Boer War begins as the South African Republic (Transvaal) and the Orange Free State unite against the British (1898); Marie and Pierre Curie discover radium and polonium (1898); German Count Ferdinand von Zeppelin builds his airship (1898); photographs using artificial light are first taken (1898); Marchese Marconi invents the radio (1899).

1900: The Boer War continues and Canadian troops set sail for South Africa to fight for England in their first foreign war; Boxer rebellion against western influence, supported by the Dowager Empress Tzu-hsi, continues in China against Christian missionaries and foreigners; Sigmund Freud, the founder of psychoanalysis (Austrian), completes *The Interpretation of Dreams*; Wilhelm Wundt writes *Comparative Psychology*; Shintoism is reinstated in Japan to counter Buddhist influence; Commonwealth of Australia is created; Max Planck formulates the quantum theory; human speech is first transmitted via radio waves by the Canadian-born scientist R.A. Fessenden; Holland's senate creates an international arbitration court at The Hague; millions are reported starving in India; botanist Hugo de Vries rediscovers Gregor Mendel's laws of heredity after 30 years; 10,000 Ashanti natives attack a British force of 400 at Cape Coast, Ghana, and are defeated.

1901: Queen Victoria dies and is succeeded by her son Edward VII; the Dutch Boers begin organized guerrilla warfare against the British; the Cuba Convention makes Cuba a US protectorate; US Pres. William McKinley is assassinated and is succeeded by Theodore Roosevelt; a treaty is signed to build the Panama Canal under US supervision; the hormone adrenaline is first isolated; Walter Nernst postulates the "third law of thermodynamics"; John Pierpont Morgan organizes the US Steel Corp., the first billion-dollar corporation; the Peace of Peking ends the Boxer uprising and China is forced to pay an indemnity of $333 million to the Allies to amend commercial treaties in favour of foreign nationals and to allow foreign troops to be posted in Peking; French physicist Henri Becquerel determines that atoms have internal structure; there are racial riots in New Orleans when American black leader Booker T. Washington is invited to the White House; the Trans-Siberian railroad reaches Port Arthur on the east coast of Russia; oil drilling begins in Persia (Iran).

1902: An Anglo–Japanese treaty recognizes the independence of China and Korea; the Treaty of Vereeniging ends the Boer War and the Orange Free State becomes a British colony; the Triple Alliance between Germany, Austria and Italy is renewed for another six years; the US acquires perpetual control over the Panama Canal; the Colonial Conference meets in London; the Committee of Imperial Defence meets in London for the first time; Jean Sibelius, Finnish composer and conductor, completes *Symphony No. 2*; Egypt's Aswan Dam is opened.

1903: The "Entente Cordiale" between England and France is established to counter German imperialism; the Russian Social Democratic Party splits into Mensheviks (led by Plechanoff) and Bolsheviks (led by Vladimir Lenin and Leon Trotsky); *The Conduction of Electricity through Gases* is published by Joseph John Thomson; George Bernard Shaw (British) writes *Man and Superman*; Orville and Wilbur Wright successfully fly a powered airplane near Kitty Hawk, North Carolina; the electrocardiograph, which records heart action, is invented by William Einthoven; Emmeline Pankhurst (British) founds the National Women's Social and Political Union and campaigns for women's right to vote; Albert I, Prince of Monaco, founds the International Peace Institute; Henry Ford founds the Ford Motor Company.

1904: The Russo–Japanese War breaks out over Korea and Manchuria; the Japanese besiege Port Arthur and occupy Seoul; the Russian fleet is partially destroyed off Port Arthur; the Russians are defeated at Mukden and Toushima straits; Max Weber writes *The Protestant Ethic and the Birth of Capitalism*; the first performance of Giacomo Puccini's opera *Madama Butterfly* takes place in Milan; the first radio transmission of music is at Graz, Austria; the general theory of radioactivity is postulated by Ernest Rutherford and Frederick Soddy; W.C. Gorgas eradicates yellow fever in the Panama Canal Zone; silicones are discovered by F.S. Kipping.

1905: Albert Einstein publishes four papers detailing his special theory of relativity, the relationship between mass and energy, the Brownian theory of motion and another formulating the photon theory of light; the Russian city of Port Arthur surrenders to the Japanese; in Russia troops fire at peaceful protest marchers heading for the czar's Winter Palace in St Petersburg, and the event becomes known as "Bloody Sunday"; William II of Germany and Nicholas II of Russia sign the Treaty of Bjorko for mutual help in Europe; the Treaty of Portsmouth ends the Russo–Japanese War; a general strike in Russia in response to Bloody Sunday includes a sailors' mutiny on the battleship *Potemkin* and the creation of the first workers' soviet in St Petersburg; Czar Nicholas establishes a constitutional government (the Imperial Duma); the Norwegian Parliament decides to separate from Sweden; the Anglo–Japanese alliance is renewed for 10 years; the Sinn Fein nationalist party is formed in Ireland; George Santayana writes his philosophical work *The Life of Reason*.

1906: Reform laws are proposed in Russia and the Imperial Duma is dissolved by the czar to end the radical change; the All India Muslim League is founded by Aga Khan; the term "allergy" is introduced by Clemens von Pirquet; the position of the magnetic North Pole is determined by Norwegian explorer Roald Amundsen; night-shift work for women is forbidden in many countries; the San Francisco earthquake kills 700 people and causes $400 million in property loss; Transvaal and Orange River colonies are granted self-government.

1907: The second Russian Duma meets in March; its radical proposals lead to its dissolution five months later; the US prohibits Japanese immigration; Lenin leaves Russia and founds the newspaper *The Proletarian*; Grigori Rasputin, a Russian mystic, gains influence with the royal family when he treats the hemophiliac son of Nicholas II; New Zealand becomes a dominion within the British Empire; Baden-Powell forms the Boy Scout movement; Korea becomes a Japanese protectorate; Russian artist Marc Chagall paints *Peasant Women*; Gustav Mahler (Austrian)

composes *Symphony No. 8*; Ivan Pavlov (Russian) studies conditioned reflexes in dogs; the SS *Lusitania* beats the SS *Mauritania* in a race from Ireland to New York.

1908: Austria occupies Bosnia and Herzegovina; Bulgaria declares independence from Turkey; Isadora Duncan emerges as a popular modern dancer; the Zeppelin airship crashes near Echterdingen; General Motors Corporation is formed in the US; Henry Ford designs the inexpensive, standardized Model T automobile while pioneering assembly line techniques for autos; an earthquake in Sicily and Calabria kills 150,000; American Gertrude Stein writes *Three Lives*; French writer Anatole France completes the political satire *Penguin Island*; Canadian Lucy Maud Montgomery writes *Anne of Green Gables*.

1909: Turkey and Serbia acknowledge Austrian control of Bosnia and Herzegovina; sultan of Turkey is deposed and replaced by his brother; Ezra Pound writes *Exultations*; the first newsreels appear and director D.W. Griffith features Canadian-born Mary Pickford, who becomes the first film star; Sergei Diaghilev presents his *Ballets Russes*, revolutionizing dance, in Paris; Blériot flies from Calais to Dover in 37 minutes, and Farman makes the first 100-mile flight; W.E.B. Du Bois cofounds the National Negro Committee which becomes the National Association for the Advancement of Colored People in 1910; Girl Guides organized in Britain; Thomas Hunt Morgan begins research in genetics; US explorer Robert E. Peary reaches the North Pole.

1910: The Union of South Africa becomes a dominion within the British Empire with Louis Botha as premier; China abolishes slavery; Japan takes over Korea; Montenegro becomes an independent kingdom; Portugal becomes a republic after a revolution ends the monarchy; Albania rebels against Turkish rule; Roger Fry arranges the Post-Impressionist Exhibition in London with works by Cezanne, van Gogh and Matisse; Igor Stravinsky performs his ballet score *The Firebird* in Paris; the South American tango is the dance craze in Europe and North America; the first deep-sea research expedition is undertaken by Murray and Hjort; the five-day work week is instituted in the US, making the "week-end" possible.

1911: US–Japanese and Anglo–Japanese commercial treaties are signed; Diaz surrenders power in Mexico but revolutions continue; the Kaiser's Hamburg speech promises Germany's "Place in the Sun"; war erupts between Turkey and Italy and aircraft are first used for offensive measures; a revolution in Central China is followed by the fall of the Manchu dynasty (in power since 1644) and the proclamation of a Chinese Republic; Sun Yat-sen is elected president and he appoints Chiang Kai-shek as his military adviser; Russian premier, Peter Stolypin, is assassinated; Roald Amundsen reaches the South Pole; Marie Curie is the first person to win a second Nobel Prize, in chemistry; Rutherford formulates his theory of atomic structure.

1912: British dock workers, coal miners and transport workers strike; the German–Austro–Italian alliance is renewed again; Lenin becomes editor of *Pravda*; Sun Yat-sen founds Kuomintang (Chinese National Party); Montenegro declares war against Turkey and Bulgaria, Greece and Serbia mobilize; Carl Jung writes *The Theory of Psychoanalysis*; the term "vitamin" is coined by Polish chemist Kasimir Funk; Stefansson and Anderson explore Arctic Canada; Wilson's cloud chamber (particle detector) photographs lead to the detection of protons and electrons; the Royal Flying Corps (later RAF) is established in Britain; SS *Titanic* sinks on its first voyage after colliding with an iceberg: 1,513 people drown.

1913: The London Peace Treaty ending the First Balkan War is signed and Turkey loses all possessions in Europe except E. Thrace; the Second Balkan War breaks out as Bulgaria attacks Serbia and Greece; Russia declares war on Bulgaria, Bulgaria and Turkey settle a peace treaty and Turkey regains Thrace, Serbia invades Albania; Greece and Turkey make peace; police crack down on suffragist demonstrations led by Emmeline Pankhurst in London; Maxim Gorki, the father of Soviet literature, writes *My Childhood*; Charlie Chaplin first stars in movies; Niels Bohr formulates his theory of atomic structure; Albert Schweitzer, medical missionary, opens his famous hospital in Lambaréné, French Congo.

1914: Archduke Francis Ferdinand, heir to the Austrian throne, is assassinated in Sarajevo (capital of the Austro–Hungarian province of Bosnia) by a Serbian nationalist (June 28); Austria–Hungary challenges Serbia and declares war (July 28); Russia and France sup-

port Serbia and mobilize troops; Austria's ally Germany declares war on Russia and France in response; the members of the Triple Entente (Britain, France, Russia) declare war on Turkey after Turks attack Russia; Germany, Austria–Hungary and the Ottoman Empire (Turkey) form alliance of Central Powers, they are opposed by UK, members of British Empire, France, Russia, Belgium, Japan and Serbia (Allied Powers); Germany invades Belgium, attacks France, and establishes the Eastern Front against the Russians at Tannenberg and the Masurian Lakes; on the Western Front the Germans are held in check after battles at Marne River, France (Sept. 6); the First Battle of Ypres, Belgium, is waged to prevent the Germans from cutting British supply lines to France; Austria–Hungary fails in three attacks on Serbia and, after the Russians capture the province of Galicia, retreats to its own territory; by November 14, 1914, there is a deadlock along the Western Front (stretching 720 km across Belgium and northeast France to the Swiss border) that remains throughout the war; Irish writer James Joyce writes *Dubliners*; John B. Watson writes *Behavior: an Introduction to Comparative Psychology*; the first successful heart surgery is performed on a dog by Dr. Alexis Carrel; the Panama Canal opens; millions of immigrants leave southern and eastern Europe between 1905 and 1914.

1915: The Allied Gallipoli Campaign to neutralize Turkey fails and Australian and New Zealand troops suffer heavy losses; the first German submarine (U-boat) attack is at Le Havre; the German blockade of England begins; at the Second Battle of Ypres, Canadian forces hold off the German advance while under heavy fire and attacks from chlorine gas and newly introduced flame throwers; Italy joins the Allied Powers, declares war on Austria–Hungary (May 23) and an Italian Front soon opens; a German submarine sinks the *Lusitania* (May 7); the first Zeppelin air attack takes place on London; Ottoman-controlled Mesopotamia (now Iraq) surrenders to Britain; Italians fight Austria–Hungary in continuous battles at Isonzo (1915–17); Germans invade Warsaw and Brest-Litovsk; Allied troops land at Salonika; the first fighter airplane is constructed by Hugo Junkers; Henry Ford develops a farm tractor; the dysentery bacillus is isolated by British chemist James Kendall; the first book advocating birth control, by American Margaret Sanger, is published, and the author is sent to jail.

1916: Germany stages a Zeppelin raid on Paris and declares war on Portugal; Portugal and Rumania later join the Allied Powers; in the Middle East, T.E. Lawrence leads an Arab revolt against Turkey; heavy casualties occur at Verdun (Feb. 21); British and German fleets clash at the Battle of Jutland (May 31–June 1); the 1st Newfoundland Regiment is annihilated along with 624,000 Allied troops during the offensive at the Somme (launched July 1); HMS *Hampshire* is sunk; Italy declares war on Germany; the Germans first use gas masks and steel helmets; peace notes are exchanged between Germany and the Allies; Lloyd George becomes British prime minister; blood for transfusion is first refrigerated; the theory of shell shock is put forth by F.W. Mott; an underwater ultrasonic source for submarine detection is built by Paul Langevin; Britain initiates daylight-saving time; US purchases the Virgin Islands for $25 million.

1917: The United States enters the war on the Allied side (Apr. 6); Germans withdraw on the Western Front; the Russian Black Sea fleet mutinies at Sebastopol; there is revolution in Russia in February and the czar abdicates (Mar. 16); Kerensky becomes Russian premier and continues the war effort; Canadian forces seize Vimy Ridge in northern France; Germany stages air attacks on England; Greece joins the Allies (July); China declares war on Germany and Austria; the British-led offensive at the Third Battle of Ypres (Passchendaele) fails (July 31); the Italian army is defeated at Caporetto by Austria–Hungary; Kerensky's government is overthrown in Petrograd in October and Lenin is appointed chief commissar, Trotsky becomes commissar for foreign affairs and Russia seeks peace with Germany; the first tank battle is at Cambrai; starvation sweeps Germany; Finland declares independence from Russia; the Allies execute dancer Mata Hari as a spy; Lord Arthur Balfour, the British Foreign Secretary, issues the Balfour Declaration stating British support for a Jewish national homeland in Palestine; women are arrested for suffrage activities in the US.

1918: Russia, the Ukraine and the Central Powers conclude the Treaties of Brest-Litovsk: the first one establishes the independence of the Ukraine, the second strips Russia of its Baltic and Polish possessions; Turks surrender to British at Jerusalem; US Pres. Wilson puts forth Fourteen Points for world peace (including a proposal for a League of Nations); Rumania signs a peace treaty with the Central Powers; Germany launches three final offensives on the Western Front (Mar. 21); Germans bomb Paris; the Second Battle of the Marne (July 15–Aug. 6) is won by the Allies; the Allies win victories on all fronts in the fall; the Japanese push into Siberia; Germany and Austria agree to retreat to their own territory before an armistice is signed; the Hungarian premier is assassinated; the Turkish and Austro-Hungarian empires and Bulgaria surrender to the Allies (Nov. 3); the German fleet mutinies at Kiel and the emperor flees; an armistice between the Allies and Germany is signed (Nov. 11); Germany agrees to the provisions of the Treaty of Versailles after the Allies threaten to invade; Emperor Charles of Austria loses the throne; the map of Europe is reshaped: Austria becomes a republic and the Serbo-Croatian-Slovene Kingdom of Yugoslavia is proclaimed, Poland and Czechoslovakia are created; Iceland becomes an independent state; the Russian Revolution continues as Bolshevik workers take over government buildings, the Winter Palace and later Moscow and other cities; civil war between the Bolshevik (Red) and anti-Bolshevik (White) continues (until 1920); British, French and American troops intervene against the Reds; the British government abandons Home Rule for Ireland; former czar Nicholas II, and family are executed by Russian revolutionaries; Hsu-Shih-Chang becomes president of the Chinese Republic; women over 30 get the vote in Britain; controversy rages over the psychology of Freud and Jung; the true dimensions of the Milky Way are discovered by Harlow Shapley, an American astronomer.

1919: US Pres. Woodrow Wilson heads the first League of Nations meeting in Paris; the Peace Conference opens at Versailles; Benito Mussolini founds the Fasci del Combattimento in Italy; socialist governments are founded in Austria and Budapest, Hungary; the Treaty of Versailles is signed with Germany; the final treaty exacts heavy financial penalties on Germany, restricts the German army and navy, blames Germany for provoking the war and establishes the League of Nations; US refusal to ratify the treaty excludes it from League membership; the Allied peace treaty with Austria is signed at St Germain; the Treaty of Neuilly with Bulgaria is signed; the International Labor Congress in Washington endorses the eight-hour workday; the Red (Soviet) forces win successive battles in the Russian civil war; Soviets attack Finland; the first nonstop flight across the Atlantic is made from Newfoundland to Ireland by J.W. Alcock and A. Whitten Brown; Lady Astor is elected to Britain's Parliament, becoming the first female MP.

1920: The League of Nations is founded in Paris and establishes headquarters in Geneva; Russian civil war ends with Soviet victory; Great Britain gains control of Palestine from the Turks; The Hague becomes the International Court of Justice; the Little Entente between Czechoslovakia, Yugoslavia and Rumania is formed; the Treaty of Trianon is signed with Hungary; the Treaty of Sevres is signed with the Ottoman Empire; the 19th Amendment gives American women the vote; 200,000 Chinese die in an earthquake in Kansu province; the world population is 1.8 billion; Britain establishes separate parliaments for Northern and Southern Ireland; Adolph Hitler founds the Nazi party in Munich, Germany, and announces his 25-point program, blaming Germany's war defeat on Jews and Communists; Mohandas (Mahatma) Gandhi becomes India's leader in its struggle for independence from Britain; Prohibition goes into effect in the US, banning the sale and consumption of alcoholic beverages; a worldwide influenza epidemic, which began in 1918, leaves 22 million dead.

1921: The first Indian Parliament meets; German reparations payments totalling $33.3 million are fixed by the Allies at a Paris conference; Hitler's storm troopers (SA) begin to terrorize ideological opponents; Mackenzie King is elected prime minister of Canada; British Broadcasting Company is founded (changed to the British Broadcasting Corporation in 1927); the Spanish prime minister and Japanese premier are assassinated; founder of Portuguese republic is murdered; ex-emperor Charles stages two failed coup attempts to regain Hungarian throne; Britain and Ireland sign a peace treaty; German mark falls and rapid inflation plagues the economy; coal is successfully hydrogenated into oil by Friedrich Bergius; the tuberculosis vaccine (B-C-G) is developed by Albert Calmette and Camille Guerin; the chromosome theory of

heredity is put forth by American biologist Thomas Morgan; Albert Einstein wins Nobel Prize for Physics; Ku Klux Klan members terrorize blacks and black sympathizers in the southern US; one of the founders of modern aeronautics, Hermann J. Oberth, writes *The Rocket into Interplanetary Space*.

1922: Gandhi is sentenced to six years' imprisonment for civil disobedience; German reconstruction minister Walter Rathenau is assassinated by German nationalists; the Arab Congress at Nablus rejects the British control of Palestine; Austria denounces "Anschluss" (union with Germany); Mussolini stages the March on Rome and forms a Fascist government; Irish Free State is proclaimed; the tomb of Tutankhamen is discovered by Lord Carnarvaron and Howard Carter; a self-winding wristwatch is invented by John Harwood (patented in 1924); a stock market "boom" begins in the US; Soviet states form the USSR; insulin, prepared by Canadian physicians Frederick Banting, Charles Best and John Macleod, is first given to diabetic patients.

1923: An earthquake kills 120,000 people in Tokyo and Yokohama; Adolph Hitler tries (and fails) to overthrow the German government ("Beer Hall Putsch"); Greek army overthrows monarch; Jewish philosopher Martin Buber writes the theological *I and Thou*; the theory of acids and bases is postulated by J.N. Brönsted; Lee de Forest demonstrates the process for motion pictures with sound; the first commercial airline, Aeroflot, is founded in the USSR.

1924: Ramsay MacDonald forms the first Labour government in Britain; Adolph Hitler writes *Mein Kampf* during an eight-month jail term; R.C. Andrews discovers skulls and skeletons of Mesozoic dinosaurs in the Gobi desert; Winston Churchill, having switched from the Liberals to the Conservatives, is named Chancellor of the Exchequer in Britain; in Russia, Lenin dies and Stalin, Zinoviev and Kamenev ally against Trotsky; the "Zinoviev letter," purported to be calling for a communist revolution in Britain, is published by the British Foreign Office; Greece becomes a republic; elections are held in Italy and Mussolini wins support of 65 percent of the electorate; leader of Italian socialists is murdered; Albanian Republic is founded; Sigmund Freud begins *Collected Writings*

(12 vols. 1924–39); Gandhi fasts for 21 days, protesting feuding between Hindus and Muslims in India; British astronomer Arthur Eddington discovers that the luminosity of a star is approximately related to its mass; insecticides are used for the first time; a patent application for iconoscope (television) is filed by Russian-American inventor V.K. Zworkin; Danish polar explorer Knud Rasmussen completes the longest dog-sled journey ever made across the North American Arctic; British Imperial Airways begins commercial air flights.

1925: Locarno Conference creates a series of treaties between Germany, France, Belgium, Poland, UK, Italy and Czechoslovakia that set up a demilitarized zone in the Rhineland and confirmed borders between Belgium, France and Germany; Mrs Nellie Tayloe Ross of Wyoming becomes the first woman governor in the US; the United Church of Canada is founded; recognizable human features are transmitted by television by Scottish inventor John Logie Baird; Walter P. Chrysler founds the Chrysler Corporation; the (Franz) Fischer and (Hans) Tropsch synthesis leads to the industrial development of synthetic oil; Heisenberg, Bohr and Jordan develop quantum mechanics for atoms; the presence of cosmic rays in the upper atmosphere is discovered by US physicist Robert Andrews Millikan; the "flapper" era takes hold; an international convention condemns the illegal narcotics trade.

1926: Fascist youth organizations appear: "Balilla" in Italy and "Hitlerjugend" in Germany; Josef Pilsudski successfully stages a coup d'état in Poland and begins a military dictatorship; commerce in Britain is stopped by a general strike; Trotsky is expelled from Moscow; Hirohito succeeds his father Taisho as emperor of Japan; Robert H. Goddard fires the first liquid fuel rocket; vitamin B is isolated by B. Jansen and W. Donath; Kodak produces the first 16-mm movie film; British Imperial Chemical Industries (ICI) begins operations; H.L. Mencken writes *Notes on Democracy*; Turkish reforms include the abolition of polygamy, modernization of female attire and adoption of Latin alphabet (1926–28).

1927: The Allied military control of Germany ends; an economic conference in Geneva is attended by 52 nations; the economic system in Germany collapses ("Black Friday"); Trotsky

expelled from the Communist Party in the USSR; Nazis on trial in Austria for political murder are acquitted and socialists riot in Venice to protest; the first film with sound, a "talkie," *The Jazz Singer*, stars Al Jolson; Lev Theremin invents the earliest electronic musical instrument; Charles Lindbergh flies the monoplane *Spirit of St Louis* in the first solo transatlantic flight, nonstop from New York to Paris in 33.5 hours; Canadian forests are the first sprayed with insecticides by airplanes; the first vehicular tunnel, the Holland Tunnel, links New York and New Jersey.

1928: The Supreme Court of Canada rules that women may not hold public office because they are not "persons" as defined by the British North America Act, but the British Privy Council overturns the decision in a landmark Commonwealth case in 1929; the Kellogg-Briand Pact outlawing war is signed by 65 states; Josef Stalin emerges as leader of Soviet Union; the first economic five-year plan begins in the USSR; Chiang Kai-shek is elected president of China; overproduction of coffee leads to the collapse of Brazil's economy; penicillin is discovered by Alexander Fleming (Scottish); American anthropologist Margaret Mead writes *Coming of Age in Samoa;* the first colour motion pictures are exhibited by George Eastman in Rochester, New York; J.L. Baird presents colour television; Mickey Mouse makes his Disney debut.

1929: The US Stock Exchange collapses on October 28, Black Friday; the Great Depression, a world economic crisis, begins and is primarily caused by easy credit and stock market over-speculation, overproduction of goods and tariff and war-debt policies; six Chicago-area gangsters are machine-gunned to death in the St Valentine's Day Massacre; a dictatorship is established in Serbo-Croat-Slovene kingdom by the monarch and the country's name is changed to Yugoslavia; Trotsky is exiled from USSR; talks on Indian sovereignty begin between Indian leaders and the Viceroy; the Lateran Treaty establishes the independence of Vatican City; precise timekeeping is made possible with the quartz-crystal clocks by W.A. Morrison; the airship *Graf Zeppelin* flies around the world in 21 days.

1930: Austria and Italy sign a treaty of friendship; Britain, the US, Japan, France and Italy sign a treaty on naval disarmament; right-wing coalition comes to power in Germany,

Nazis later capture 107 more seats in an election; right-wing government is formed in Poland; Catholic-Fascist units are established in Austria; revolution in Argentina brings new military dictatorship to power; the planet Pluto is discovered by C.W. Tombaugh at Lowell Observatory; a yellow fever vaccine is developed by South African microbiologist Max Theiler; photoflash bulb is introduced; the word "technocracy," meaning the domination of technology, comes into use.

1931: A financial crisis in central Europe is caused by the collapse of Austria's Credit-Anstalt; all German banks close following the bankruptcy of the German Danatbank; Britain abandons the gold standard; Fascist party is formed in Britain; the Statute of Westminster establishes the British Commonwealth of Nations as a free association of autonomous nations sharing a common allegiance to the British crown, and declares that British Parliament can no longer legislate for any member states unless requested to do so; US Pres. Hoover proposes a one-year moratorium for reparations and war debts; the first trans-African railroad line is completed, Benguella-Katanga; the northern face of the Matterhorn is climbed for the first time by Franz and Toni Schmid.

1932: The Indian National Congress, a nationalist party dedicated to home rule, is declared illegal and its leader, Mahatma Gandhi, is arrested; the US criticizes Japanese aggression in Manchuria; the Nazis sweep the German Reichstag (Parliament) elections while WWI hero Hindenburg wins the presidential election; Hitler refuses Hindenburg's offer to become vice chancellor, and the Austrian-born Hitler receives German citizenship; Franklin D. Roosevelt wins the US presidential election and proposes domestic reform programs to provide recovery and relief from the Great Depression ("New Deal"); the USSR suffers famine; Zuider Zee, a huge dam and drainage project in Holland, is completed; Amelia Earheart is the first woman to fly solo across the Atlantic; Japan conquers world markets by undercutting prices; about 30 million people are unemployed worldwide; the neutron is discovered by James Chadwick; vitamin D is discovered.

1933: Reichstag building is burned in Berlin and Hitler uses the event to justify banning opposition parties and labour unions; Hitler is appointed German chancellor and granted dictatorial powers with the Enabling Law; Nazi Hermann Goering is named Prussian prime minister; Parliamentary government is suspended in Austria; starvation spreads in USSR; Paul Joseph Goebbels is named Hitler's minister of propaganda; Japan withdraws from the League of Nations; the first concentration camps are built by the Nazis in Germany to hold Jews and ideological opponents; books by non-Nazi and Jewish authors are burned in Germany; Germans begin to boycott and restrict Jewish services; an anti-Nazi treatise, *Judaism-Christendom-Germanism*, is published by Cardinal von Faulhaber in Munich; Assyrian Christians are massacred in Iraq; US goes off the gold standard and tries to stimulate its economy by creating the Tennessee Valley Authority to construct dams and generate electricity.

1934: A revolution in Austria overturns the Social Democrats and Austrian chancellor is assassinated by the Nazis; a general strike takes place in France; the USSR is admitted to the League of Nations; Winston Churchill warns the British Parliament of the German air menace; Hitler oversees purge of his associates and many are executed; a national vote grants him the title Führer (leader); Stalin's purge of the Soviet Communist party begins and he reportedly oversees the murder of millions of people; German scientist Albert Einstein is persecuted by the Nazis for being Jewish and he flees, settling in the US; Japan renounces the Washington treaties of 1922 and 1930; Mao Tse-tung, leader of the Chinese Communists, heads the Long March.

1935: Nazis repudiate the Treaty of Versailles and reintroduce compulsory military service; the autonomous territory of Saarland votes for reunion with Germany; an Anglo–German Naval Agreement is concluded; Nazis implement the Nuremberg Laws against Jews, stripping them of civic rights and forbidding intermarriage with non-Jews; Mussolini invades Ethiopia, and the League of Nations retaliates by imposing sanctions; the Chaco War, a bitter conflict between Paraguay and Bolivia begun in 1932 and fought over oil-rich but otherwise barren territory, ends after 100,000 lives were lost and both sides were exhausted (treaty not concluded until 1938); radar equipment to detect aircraft is built by Robert Watson Watt; oil pipelines between Iraq, Haifa and Tripoli open; Persia changes its name to Iran.

1936: King George V of England dies and is succeeded by Edward VIII; German troops occupy the Rhineland and Hitler wins the German elections with 99 percent of the vote; Italy, Austria and Hungary sign the Rome Pact; Britain, France and the US sign the London Naval Convention; an Austro-German convention acknowledges Austrian independence; the Spanish Civil War begins and Francisco Franco is appointed chief of state by the Nationalist insurgents against the government's Loyalist republicans; Franco begins the siege of Madrid, rebels take Malaga and destroy Guernica and Gijon and Franco begins a naval blockade (1937); Heinrich Himmler is appointed head of the Gestapo, responsible for Nazi concentration camps (1936–45); King Edward VIII abdicates in order to marry American divorcee Wallis Simpson; Mussolini and Hitler proclaim the Rome-Berlin Axis; the Anti-Comintern Pact is signed by Germany and Japan; Chiang Kai-shek declares war on Japan; Dr Alexis Carrel develops an artificial heart; the airship *Hindenburg* burns at Lakehurst, New Jersey, after a transatlantic flight; black American athlete Jesse Owens upsets the Nazis when he wins four gold medals at the Olympic Games in Berlin.

1937: Poland refuses to return Danzig to Germany; the first worldwide radio broadcast is heard when George VI is crowned King of Great Britain; Roosevelt signs a US Neutrality Act, intended to keep the US out of a possible European war; Trotsky, exiled from Russia in 1929, is forced to leave Norway and settles in Mexico; aggressive Japanese war policy begins when Prince Konoye is named the Japanese premier, and the Japanese seize major Chinese cities (Beijing, Tianjin, Shanghai, Nanjing and Hangzhou), forcing Chiang Kai-shek and the Communists, under Mao Tse-tung and Chou En-lai, to unite; the Chinese government makes Chungking its capital; the Royal Commission on Palestine recommends the establishment of Arab and Jewish states; Stalin initiates a purge of Soviet generals and show trials of political leaders; Britain signs naval agreements with Germany and the USSR; Germany guarantees Belgian sovereignty; Italy joins the Anti-Comintern Pact and withdraws from the League of Nations; Japanese planes sink US gunboat in Chinese waters; Amelia Earheart disappears during a Pacific flight.

1938: Germany annexes Austria, "Anschluss" (Mar.); France calls up reservists; Great Britain, France and Italy agree to let Germany absorb the Sudetenland, Czechoslovakia, in a policy of appeasement (Munich Pact, Sept.) and Germany promises to cease its aggressive expansion; British foreign minister Anthony Eden resigns in protest against the appeasement policy and Winston Churchill also voices opposition; Franco begins an offensive against the Spanish Loyalists in Catalonia; anti-Jewish legislation is enacted in Italy; Kristallnacht, or "Night of Broken Glass," is a large-scale pogrom by the Nazis against German Jews; the US and Germany recall their respective ambassadors; Japan withdraws from the League of Nations and sets up a puppet Chinese government in Nanking; Howard Hughes flies around the world in less than four days.

1939: US Pres. Roosevelt demands assurances from Hitler and Mussolini that they have no plans to attack other states; Germany breaks the Munich Pact and occupies Bohemia and Moravia; Slovakia is placed under "protection"; Italy invades Albania; Germany renounces the nonaggression pact with Poland and naval agreement with England, and concludes a 10-year alliance with Italy and a nonaggression pact with the USSR, secretly dividing Poland; Germany stages a surprise (blitzkrieg) invasion of Poland, and annexes Danzig (Sept. 1); Britain and France declare war on Germany (Sept. 3); the Allied powers are Britain and France and the Axis powers are led by Germany; Canada declares war (Sept. 10); US Pres. Roosevelt announces US neutrality; Soviets invade Poland from the east (Sept. 17); Germans overrun western Poland and reach Brest-Litovsk and Warsaw; France masses troops along the Maginot Line on the eastern frontier of France and Germany sends troops to its parallel Siegfried Line; the British Expeditionary Force is sent to France; the USSR invades Finland and is expelled from the League of Nations; Japan occupies Hainan and blockades the British at Tientsin; the US renounces the Japanese trade agreement of 1911; the Spanish Civil War ends with Franco's Nationalists (supported by Hitler and Mussolini) victorious over the Loyalists (supported by the USSR); Spain joins the Anti-Comintern Pact and leaves the League of Nations; England and Poland sign a treaty of mutual assistance; women and children are first evacuated from London; the first helicopter is built by Russian-American Igor Sikorsky; the US economy booms from arms sales to Europe.

1940: Food rationing begins in Britain; Finland surrenders (Mar.) and signs a peace treaty with the USSR; Germany invades Norway and Denmark (Apr. 9); Winston Churchill becomes British prime minister (May 10); Norway falls (June); Germany invades Belgium, Luxembourg and the Netherlands (May 10); Holland and Belgium surrender to Germany and 340,000 Allied forces are trapped in Belgium, but most are evacuated from Dunkirk, a French seaport on the English channel (May 29 to June 3); Italy declares war on France and Britain; Germans attack France from the north and enter Paris (June 14); France concludes an armistice with Germany; southern France remains unoccupied until 1942 and is ruled by the Vichy government; USSR seizes Estonia, Latvia and Lithuania (summer); the Royal Navy sinks the French fleet in Oran; the Royal Air Force begins night bombing of Germany; the Battle of Britain in August is the first battle fought completely in the air; Hitler begins bombing England (all-night blitzes) throughout fall and winter; Japan, Germany and Italy sign a military and economic pact; US destroyers are sold to Britain; Germany intensifies U-boat warfare; Italian forces attempt to take Egypt and Libya in order to cut off British access to Middle East oil and the Suez Canal; the British Eighth Army opens an offensive in North Africa and defeats the Italian forces; Trotsky is murdered in Mexico; Batista becomes president of Cuba; wall paintings dating to about 20,000 BC are discovered in France, the Lascaux caves; a giant cyclotron is built at the University of California for producing mesotrons from atomic nuclei.

1941: The British invade Ethiopia and defeat the Italians (by May); Germany opens a counter-offensive in North Africa to aid Italy; German General Rommel regains Libya and Egypt; Germans launch an airborne invasion against Crete, thereby securing an important base in the Mediterranean (by the end of May); England sinks the German battleship *Bismarck* in an effort to protect vital US shipments to Great Britain; Allies develop radar and sonar to track U-boats; German air raids over London continue; US freezes German and Italian assets in that country; Germans invade Russia (Operation Barbarossa, June 22); Churchill and Roosevelt sign the Atlantic charter (Aug. 14); German troops surround Leningrad and Moscow (Nov.), but an early, harsh winter stalls the German advance; Marshal Timoshenko launches the Russian counter-offensive; the US ambassador to Japan warns Pres. Roosevelt of possible Japanese attack; Japanese bomb Pearl Harbor (Dec. 7) and the US and Britain declare war on Japan (Dec. 8); China declares war on the Axis (Dec. 9); Japan invades the Philippines; Germany and Italy declare war on the US; the US declares war on Germany and Italy; British Hong Kong surrenders to the Japanese; Henry Moore draws refugees in London air raid shelters while an official war artist; Dmitri Shostakovich writes *Symphony No. 7* during the German siege of Leningrad; German dramatist Bertolt Brecht writes *Mother Courage and Her Children* while in exile from the Nazis.

1942: Hitler's Final Solution, the systematic murder of Jews in the Nazi gas chambers (Holocaust) is in full force at death camps such as Auschwitz and Dachau; the 26 Allied nations agree not to make separate treaties with the Axis powers; Rommel breaks through British lines and reaches El Alamein (320 km from the Suez Canal); Montgomery (British Eighth Army) scores the first decisive defeat of Rommel at El Alamein; Germans reach Stalingrad, Russia; 400,000 American troops land in French North Africa; Rommel, in full retreat, loses Tobruk and Benghazi; Japan invades Burma, the Dutch East Indies, and captures Singapore; the British bomb Cologne and Lübeck; the US and Canada intern residents of Japanese heritage in camps; many American and Philippine prisoners die in the Japanese-forced Bataan Death March; Americans bomb Tokyo; Americans begin successful island-hopping strategy against Japan and win the battles of the Coral Sea and Midway; French navy loses in Toulon; British and Indian troops advance in Burma; Fermi achieves the first controlled nuclear chain reaction when he splits the atom; the Manhattan Project of intensive US atomic research begins; the first electronic brain or automatic computer is developed in the US; a recorder using plastic magnetic recording tape is invented by German engineers; Gandhi demands independence from Britain and is arrested.

1943: German troops surrender at Stalingrad (Feb. 2) and begin to withdraw from the Caucasus; Churchill and Roosevelt meet in Casablanca; the Japanese are driven from Guadalcanal by US troops; the British Eighth Army reaches Tripoli; Axis powers surrender in North Africa (Tunisia, May 13); Russians destroy the German army southwest of Stalingrad; Russians recapture Rostov and Kharkov; the Royal Air Force raids Berlin; US planes sink the 22-ship Japanese convoy in the Battle of the Bismarck Sea; British and US armies in Africa link up and Rommel retreats; an armed Jewish uprising begins in the overcrowded Warsaw ghetto, but it is crushed by German troops (1943–44) who massacre Jewish inhabitants; the RAF bombs Ruhr dams; US forces land in New Guinea; US recaptures Aleutians; Allies land in Sicily (July 10); Churchill, Roosevelt and Mackenzie King meet in Quebec; US troops bomb Ploesti oil fields in Rumania and enter Messina; Allies land in Salerno Bay and invade Italy, which surrenders unconditionally (Sept. 8); Russians take Kiev; Chinese Gen. and Mme Chiang Kai-shek meet with Roosevelt and Churchill in Cairo and pledge to liberate Korea after Japan is defeated; Churchill, Stalin and Roosevelt hold the Teheran Conference; Allied round-the-clock bombing of Germany begins; the first fully electronic computer is used by the British government to crack German military codes; penicillin is used to treat chronic diseases; Bengal is swept by famine; rationing of selected foods begins in the US; major US cities are troubled by race riots.

1944: Germany continues air raids on London; Russian offensives continue in the Ukraine and Crimea; Allies bomb Berlin; Monte Cassino and Rome are liberated by the Allies June 4; D-day landings in Normandy (France, June 6): over 700 ships and 4,000 landing craft are involved and Canadian troops lead the trek from the Normandy beaches; Germans drop first flying bomb (V-1) on London; southern Japan is bombed by the US; US troops take Saipan; Russians capture 100,000 Germans at Minsk; German officers unsuccessfully attempt to assassinate Hitler; Russians reach Brest-Litovsk; Americans capture Guam from the Japanese; the British Eighth Army takes Florence; creation of a United Nations is discussed at the Dunbarton Oaks conference in Washington; Charles De Gaulle leads the Free French into Paris (Aug. 25); Allies liberate Belgium; the first V-2 rockets land in Britain; Churchill and Roosevelt meet in Quebec; Americans cross the German frontier near Trier; British airborne forces land at Eindhoven and Arnheim but have to withdraw; US troops land in the Philippines; Russians and Yugoslavs enter Belgrade; Russian Army

occupies Hungary; Japanese suffer heavy losses in Battle of Leyte Gulf; Battle of the Bulge (Ardennes Forest) results in Allied victory; France regains Lorraine; Rommel commits suicide; Vietnam, under Ho Chi Minh, declares independence from France; American playwright Tennessee Williams completes *The Glass Menagerie*; quinine is synthesized; Richard Strauss completes the opera *Die Liebe der Danae* in Austria but its performance is cancelled when the Nazis shut down the theatres; French playwright Jean-Paul Sartre writes the existentialist work *Being and Nothingness*.

1945: Britain begins major offensive in Burma; Russians take Warsaw, Krakow and reach Oder River; Churchill, Roosevelt and Stalin meet at the Yalta Conference; Americans enter Manila; Russians take Budapest; British troops reach the Rhine; US air raids on Tokyo, Cologne and Danzig; Okinawa is captured; the British Second Army crosses the Rhine; the last German V-2 rocket falls on Britain; Franklin D. Roosevelt dies and is succeeded by Harry S. Truman; Russians reach Berlin; Bologna is captured; US and Soviet troops meet at Torgau and both liberate Nazi death camps, finding gas chambers and crematoriums; anti-Axis coalition agrees to set up new international body to replace ineffective League of Nations; new United Nations charter drawn up at conference in San Francisco (Apr.–June); Bremen, Genoa, Verona and Venice are captured by the Allies; the Allies cross the Elbe; Mussolini is killed by Italian partisans; Hitler commits suicide (Apr. 30); the German army on the Italian front surrenders; Berlin surrenders to the Russians (May 2) and Germany capitulates to the Allies (May 7); V-E Day (Victory in Europe) ends the war in Europe (May 8); Germany is divided into four zones by the Allies and the three-power occupation of Berlin begins; Churchill, Truman and Stalin meet at Potsdam; Clement Attlee replaces Churchill as prime minister of Great Britain in a Labour landslide; the first atomic bomb is detonated near Alamogordo, New Mexico, after being developed by J. Robert Oppenheimer, Enrico Fermi and others (July 16); the Soviet Union declares war on Japan and occupied Manchuria; the US drops atomic bombs on Hiroshima (Aug. 6) and Nagasaki (Aug. 9); Japan surrenders and World War II ends; war dead are estimated at 35 million plus victims of Nazi concentration camps; the

Nuremberg trials of Nazi war criminals begin; the League of Nations holds its final meeting in Geneva and turns over its assets to the UN (Oct.); Charles De Gaulle is elected president of the French provisional government; Marshall Tito is chief of state of the newly created Federal People's Republic of Yugoslavia; Nationalists and Communists resume civil war in north China; the Arab League is founded to oppose the creation of a Jewish state; Shintoism is abolished in Japan; vitamin A is synthesized; black markets for food, clothing and cigarettes develop in Europe; the UN World Bank (International Bank for Reconstruction and Development) is founded with authorized share capital of $27 billion.

1946: Albania, Bulgaria, Hungary and Transjordan become sovereign states; the UN General Assembly holds its first session in London (Jan. 7), electing Trygve Lie of Norway as its first secretary-general, and its permanent headquarters is made in New York; Juan Perón is elected president of Argentina; a Peace Conference of 21 nations is held in Paris; 12 leading Nazis are sentenced to death following the Nuremberg trials and others get life imprisonment; power in Japan is transferred from the emperor to an elected assembly; the UN Atomic Energy Commission is formed to monitor member nations; after a referendum in Italy, the king abdicates, Italy becomes a republic and de Gasperi becomes head of state; xerography (photocopying) is invented by Chester Carlson; Dr Benjamin Spock writes *Baby and Child Care*, the "baby boom" reference book.

1947: British coal industry is nationalized; *The Diary of Anne Frank* is published by Anne's father, the only member of the German-Jewish Frank family to survive the Holocaust; Burma proclaims its independence; Paris Peace treaties signed; the Dead Sea Scrolls, dating from about 22 BC to AD 100, are discovered in Wadi Qumran, Palestine; American Chuck Yeager flies the first airplane at supersonic speeds; the transistor is invented by Bell Telephone Laboratory scientists; the UN divides Palestine, which is under British mandate, into a Jewish and an Arab state (Nov.) and the British withdraw six months later; India gains independence from Great Britain and is partitioned into India and East and West Pakistan.

1948: Mahatma Gandhi is assassinated by a Hindu opposing his tolerance of Muslims; a Communist coup d'état takes place in Czechoslovakia (Feb. 25); the Marshall Plan providing $17 billion in aid for Europe is passed by the US Congress; Winston Churchill chairs the Hague Congress for European unity; the Jewish state of Israel is proclaimed with Chaim Weizmann as president and David Ben-Gurion as premier (May 14); neighbouring Arab states declare war (1948–49) on Israel but by the end of the conflict Israel succeeds in increasing its territory; the Berlin airlift by the west begins after the USSR imposes a land and water blockade (1948–Sept. 1949); bread rationing ends in Britain; the World Council of Churches is organized in Amsterdam; American biologist Alfred C. Kinsey writes *Sexual Behavior in the Human Male*; the first World Health Assembly meets in Geneva; the first port radar system is installed in Liverpool, England.

1949: Tianjin, China, falls to the Communists, Chiang Kai-shek resigns as president of China, and removes his Nationalist forces to Formosa; the Communist People's Republic is proclaimed under Mao Tse-tung, with Chou En-lai as premier; the North Atlantic Treaty establishing a defence alliance (NATO) is signed by all parties (Belgium, Canada, Denmark, France, Iceland, Italy, Luxembourg, the Netherlands, Norway, Portugal, UK and US) in Washington; the Berlin blockade by the Soviet Union is lifted; the German Federal Republic (West Germany) comes into being with Bonn as its capital and Konrad Adenauer as chancellor; republic of Eire is proclaimed with its capital in Dublin; Transjordan is renamed the Hashemite Kingdom of Jordan; the state of Vietnam, under Ho Chi Minh, is established at Saigon; civil war looms in Korea; the apartheid program of official racial discrimination is established in South Africa; the Democratic Republic is established in East Germany with Pieck as president; India becomes a federal republic with Pandit Nehru as prime minister; Indonesia gains sovereignty from Holland; the USSR tests its first atomic bomb; the US launches a guided missile to a height of 400 km, the highest altitude yet; George Orwell publishes *Nineteen Eighty-Four*.

1950: Communist China and Russia sign a treaty of friendship and mutual assistance, Britain also recognizes Communist China; 18

protesters are killed in anti-apartheid riots in South Africa; Vietnam, Laos and Cambodia gain independence from France; North Korea invades South Korea, capturing Seoul and forcing Pres. Syngman Rhee to flee; US Atomic Energy Commission begins work on hydrogen bomb; UN forces under Gen. Douglas MacArthur land in South Korea and push north of the 38th parallel, prompting Communist China to enter the war; US recognizes Vietnam, sends military supplies and instructors and signs pact for military assistance with Vietnam, Laos, Cambodia and France.

1951: North Korean forces reach the 38th parallel and capture Seoul; attempts to negotiate peace fail; Gen. MacArthur is replaced as commander in Korea for threatening massive retaliation against China; Winston Churchill forms the government in Britain; Remington Rand produces UNIVAC, the first large-scale, general-purpose computer; electricity is produced from atomic energy in the US; heart-lung machine devised by J. Andre-Thomas; penicillin and streptomycin available in US.

1952: Dwight D. Eisenhower is elected US president; Britain produces an atomic bomb; Elizabeth II becomes Queen of England; Egypt rocked by anti-British riots: premier resigns and the army seizes power; Mau-maus rebel in Kenya and government declares a state of emergency; first hydrogen bomb at Eniwetok Atoll in the Pacific; British Overseas Airways introduces the world's first jet passenger service from London to Rome; the first pocket-sized transistor radio is marketed by Sony in Japan.

1953: An armistice ending the Korean War is signed at Panmunjom; Soviet leader Joseph Stalin dies and is replaced by Malenkov; Sweden's Dag Hammarskjöld is elected UN secretary-general; the Soviet Union explodes a hydrogen bomb; Yugoslavia proclaims a new constitution and Marshall Tito becomes president; Egyptian generals establish a dictatorship and proclaim a republic; rebels from Vietnam attack Laos; Fidel Castro begins a campaign to overthrow Cuban dictator Fulgencio Batista; Ethel and Julius Rosenberg are executed after being convicted of passing American atomic secrets to the Soviet Union; Edmund Hillary and Tenzing Norgay become the first to scale Mt Everest; the first successful open heart surgery is performed in the US; researchers associate lung cancer with cigarette smoking.

1954: Vietnamese Communists defeat the French at Dien Bien Phu; racial segregation in public schools is banned by the US Supreme Court; Gammal Abdel Nasser becomes leader in Egypt; the US Senate censures Sen. Joseph McCarthy for launching a Communist witch-hunt; Canada and the US plan a joint radar defence system in the north (Distant Early Warning, DEW Line); the US *Nautilus* becomes the first nuclear-powered submarine; Dr Jonas Salk begins inoculating children against polio; the oral contraceptive pill is introduced in the US; the first successful kidney transplant is performed in the US; Roger Bannister becomes the first to run a mile in less than four minutes.

1955: Churchill resigns in Britain and is succeeded by Anthony Eden; Bulganin succeeds Malenkov as Soviet premier; eight east-European Communist bloc countries adopt the Warsaw Pact mutual defence treaty; West Germany joins NATO; border clashes between Israel and Jordan increase; Juan Perón is ousted by a military coup in Argentina; the first optical fibres are produced in Britain.

1956: Nasser elected Egyptian president; Egypt seizes control of the Suez Canal; Israeli troops invade Egypt and push towards the canal; British and French forces invade Egypt; a United Nations force arrives in Egypt, prompting a cease-fire; UN truce proposals for dispute between Jordan and Israel accepted; Soviet Communist leader Nikita Khrushchev denounces Joseph Stalin's "cult of personality"; Soviet tanks and troops crush an anti-Communist rebellion in Hungary; Sudan becomes a democratic republic; Pakistan becomes an Islamic republic; Martin Luther King, Jr, leads the campaign against racial segregation in the US South; transatlantic telephone service begins; the first computer programming language (FORTRAN) is developed in the US.

1957: Israeli troops withdraw from Egypt and the Gaza Strip comes under UN jurisdiction; UN reopens the Suez Canal; the space race begins as the USSR launches the first earth-orbiting satellite *Sputnik 1*; Belgium, France, Italy, Luxembourg, the Netherlands and West Germany sign the Rome Treaty to extend the common market established for the steel industry to all sectors of the economy; Pres. Eisenhower warns that the US will oppose Communist takeovers in the Middle East;

Harold Macmillan leads the new Conservative government in Britain; John Diefenbaker becomes Canada's prime minister.

1958: Nikita Khrushchev becomes Soviet premier; Charles De Gaulle is elected president of France; Pope Pius XII dies and is succeeded by John XXIII; the first US space satellite, *Explorer I*, is launched; scientists in the USSR send two dogs into space and return them safely; Egypt and Syria form the United Arab Republic; Iraq's King Faisal is assassinated in a military coup; Alaska becomes the 49th US state.

1959: Fidel Castro overthrows Fulgencio Batista and establishes a Communist government in Cuba, expropriating sugar mills owned by the US; Soviet Prem. Khrushchev visits the US; American Vice-Pres. Richard Nixon visits the Soviet Union and has the "kitchen debate" with Khrushchev; the USSR sends a space probe to the moon and photographs its hidden side; the St Lawrence Seaway opens; the first commercial photocopier is introduced; the Dalai Lama flees Tibet; Hawaii becomes the 50th state of the US.

1960: An American U-2 spy plane is shot down over the USSR, prompting Soviet Prem. Nikita Khrushchev to cancel a Soviet-American summit meeting; 50 South African black protesters are massacred at Sharpeville; the Congo (Zaïre) gains independence from Belgium, sparking political instability and UN intervention; Cyprus becomes independent and Archbishop Makarios wins the first presidential election; Israeli agents capture former Gestapo chief Adolf Eichmann in Argentina and smuggle him to Israel for trial; Germany bans neo-Nazi political groups; John F. Kennedy is elected US president; the first weather and communications satellites are launched in the US; the first heart pacemaker is developed.

1961: Soviet Major Yuri Gagarin becomes the first man in space; US breaks off diplomatic ties with Cuba; the US-backed Bay of Pigs invasion by Cuban exiles fails to topple Cuba's Fidel Castro; astronaut Alan Shepard becomes the first American in space with a suborbital flight; East Germany builds the Berlin Wall to stop its citizens from moving to the West; Kuwait becomes independent from Britain, which sends troops to counter Iraqi annexation threats; UN Sec.-Gen. Dag Hammarskjöld dies in a plane crash over Northern Rhodesia; UK applies for membership in the Common

Market; the silicon chip is patented by Texas Instruments in the US.

1962: Fearing nuclear war, many North Americans build fallout shelters; John Glenn becomes the first American to orbit the earth; US establishes a military council in South Vietnam; the discovery of Soviet missile bases in Cuba leads to a US naval blockade; the Cuban Missile Crisis ends when Soviet leader Khrushchev agrees to dismantle the bases; UN troops quell rebellion in the Congo's Katanga province; Algeria, Uganda and Jamaica gain independence; the UN votes in favour of economic sanctions against South Africa; Pope John XXIII opens the Second Vatican Council which will modernize the Catholic church; the TV satellite *Telstar* is launched in the US.

1963: US Pres. John Kennedy is assassinated in Dallas and Lyndon Johnson succeeds him; the US, Soviet Union and Britain ban nuclear tests in the atmosphere; South Vietnamese leader Ngo Dinh Diem is assassinated following a military coup; US sends financial aid to South Vietnam; Zanzibar and Kenya gain independence; Dr. Martin Luther King leads the March on Washington seeking equality for US blacks; the "hot line" emergency communications link is established between the White House and the Kremlin; UK application to Common Market rejected after French opposition; British government rocked by the Profumo affair and the scandal forces the resignation of a senior minister; Pope John XXIII dies and is succeeded by Paul VI; archaeologists find the remains of a thousand-year-old Viking settlement in Newfoundland; the first liver and lung transplants are performed; Valentina Tereshkova becomes the first female astronaut.

1964: Harold Wilson becomes prime minister in Britain; Communist China announces it has developed an atomic bomb; the US escalates its military involvement in Vietnam following a reported North Vietnamese attack on US destroyers in the Gulf of Tonkin; the Palestine Liberation Organization (PLO) is formed; Zambia, Malta and Malawi become independent; the sultan of Zanzibar is banished and the country is declared a republic; Zanzibar unites with Tanganyika to form Tanzania; Northern Rhodesia declares independence and adopts the name Zambia; Leonid Brezhnev and Alexei Kosygin become Soviet leaders after Khrushchev is deposed; the first word processor is developed by IBM; the Beatles appear on the Ed Sullivan Show as "Beatlemania" sweeps North America.

1965: Ferdinand Marcos is elected president of the Philippines; Gambia and Rhodesia declare independence from Britain; Rhodesia's declaration is met by an oil embargo; a massive power failure blacks out most of the northeast US and eastern Canada; Pope Paul VI reaffirms the Catholic Church's opposition to birth control; a Soviet cosmonaut is the first to leave a spacecraft and "float" in space; two US Gemini capsules rendezvous in space.

1966: China's Red Guards demonstrate against western influences as Mao launches the Cultural Revolution; Indira Gandhi becomes India's prime minister; floods destroy art treasures in Florence, Italy; De Gaulle asks that NATO forces leave France; South African Pres. Hendrik Verwoerd is stabbed to death during a Parliamentary session; Lesotho and Guyana become independent; civilian protests against the Vietnam War escalate in the US; government in Ghana overthrown by military coup; an artificial heart is successfully implanted for the first time by Dr Michael De Bakey in Houston; the Soviet Union lands an unmanned spacecraft on the moon.

1967: Israel defeats Egypt, Syria and Jordan in the Six Day War and occupies the Sinai Peninsula, Golan Heights, Gaza Strip and the east bank of the Suez Canal; Expo 67 world fair opens in Montreal; a Soviet cosmonaut becomes the first reported casualty of the space race; US manned space flights are suspended after astronauts Grissom, White and Chaffee die in Apollo capsule fire; race riots erupt in US cities during the "long hot summer"; Canada celebrates its centennial; Dr Christiaan Barnard of South Africa performs the world's first successful human heart transplant: the patient survives for 18 days.

1968: The US intelligence ship *Pueblo* is captured by North Korea; US civil rights leader Martin Luther King, Jr, is assassinated in Memphis; presidential candidate Robert Kennedy is assassinated in Los Angeles; Soviet troops crush liberal reform in Czechoslovakia; a treaty limiting military use of outer space is signed by 62 nations; university student protest movement spreads worldwide; Richard Nixon is elected US president; Pierre Trudeau becomes prime minister in Canada; peace talks between the US and North Vietnam

begin in Paris; British colony of Mauritius becomes independent; Pope Paul VI issues an encyclical banning artificial birth control; three US astronauts circle the moon and return to Earth; *Surveyor 7*, uncrewed, lands on moon.

1969: US astronaut Neil Armstrong becomes the first man to walk on the moon as *Apollo 11* lands on the lunar surface; Yasser Arafat becomes PLO chairman; North Vietnamese leader Ho Chi Minh dies at age 79; the International Red Cross estimates that 1.5 million Biafrans have died, mostly by starvation, in the civil war with Nigeria; the US begins withdrawal of troops from Vietnam; Golda Meir becomes Israeli prime minister; the Concorde supersonic airliner makes its first flight; *Mariner* space probes transmit pictures of Mars back to earth.

1970: An earthquake kills about 30,000 people in Peru; US National Guardsmen kill four Kent State University students during antiwar protests at the campus and two students are killed at Jackson State following similar demonstrations; the first complete synthesis of a gene is announced by University of Wisconsin scientists; Arab commandos hijack three jets bound for New York from Europe; the civil wars in Nigeria end when Biafra capitulates to the federal government; the Front de Libération du Québec (FLQ) kidnaps British trade commissioner James Cross, and kidnaps and murders Quebec Cabinet minister Pierre Laporte; the Canadian federal government responds to this "October Crisis" by invoking the War Measures Act, temporarily suspending civil liberties in Canada; Israel and United Arab Republic declare a 99-day truce in latest conflict; Gambia becomes a republic; a cyclone and tidal wave hit the offshore islands in the Ganges Delta of East Pakistan, leaving at least 168,000 people dead and about 1 million homeless.

1971: US planes bomb Cambodia, attacking Vietcong supply routes; fighting in Indochina spreads to Laos and Cambodia; the US conducts large-scale bombing raids against North Vietnam; mainland China is admitted to the United Nations; women are granted the right to vote in Switzerland; violence in Northern Ireland escalates after Britain introduces policies of internment without trial; India fights with the Bengali rebels against Pakistan; the US and USSR sign a treaty banning nuclear weapons on the ocean floor; Algeria seizes majority control of all French oil and gas interests within its borders but promises restitution; Idi Amin takes control over Uganda; Mao Tse-tung's heir-apparent, Lin Piao, dies in a mysterious air crash; the USSR soft-lands a space capsule on Mars; a Los Angeles earthquake kills 60 people and causes $1 billion in damage; the hormone that controls human growth is synthesized by Dr Choh Hao Li at the University of California.

1972: The world's largest diamond (969.8 carats) is unearthed in Sierra Leone; US Pres. Richard Nixon meets Mao Tse-tung in China; Britain imposes direct rule on Northern Ireland and 467 people are killed in violence between Catholics and Protestants; Ceylon becomes a republic and changes its name to Sri Lanka; Philippine Pres. Ferdinand Marcos assumes near-dictatorial powers; a Soviet spacecraft soft-lands on Venus; more than 70 nations sign a treaty prohibiting the stockpiling of biological weapons; the US conducts its heaviest B-52 bombing raids of the war against North Vietnam but continues to withdraw troops, despite lack of progress at Paris peace talks; Arab terrorists massacre 11 Israeli Olympic athletes in a stand-off with West German police at the summer Olympic games in Munich; Richard Leakey and Glynn Isaac discover a 2.5-million-year-old human skull in northern Kenya; a US federal grand jury indicts seven persons, including two former White House aids, on charges of conspiracy to break into the Democratic national headquarters (in the Watergate building) in Washington, DC; Richard Nixon is re-elected as US president.

1973: A cease-fire agreement, intended to end the Vietnam war, is signed in Paris; fighting in the Middle East between Israeli and Arab forces (Yom Kippur War) is resolved by a shaky cease-fire; Arab oil-producing states cut petroleum exports to the US, western Europe and Japan because of their support of Israel; the US Senate begins televised hearings on the Watergate scandal and it is revealed that Pres. Nixon had secretly taped all conversations in his White House office; US vice-president resigns in an unrelated scandal; US combat involvement in Indochina officially ends as American planes halt their bombing of Cambodia; Typhoon Nora leaves 800,000 Filipinos homeless on the island of Luzon; Great Britain, Ireland and Denmark formally join the Common Market; the Bahamas are

granted independence from Britain after three centuries of colonial rule; Chilean Marxist Pres. Salvador Allende is overthrown by a CIA-backed military junta which claims Allende commits suicide; Shah of Iran nationalizes foreign-owned oil companies.

1974: Oil-producing nations boost their prices and worldwide inflation accelerates as economic growth slows to near zero in most industrialized nations; the government of China launches a new "Cultural Revolution" program aimed at condemning both the Chinese philosopher Confucius and former Defence Minister Lin Piao; West German Chancellor Willy Brandt resigns after a scandal involving an East German spy; the Tower of London and the British Houses of Parliament are bombed by the Irish Republican Army; Soviet Nobel Prize-winning author Aleksandr Solzhenitsyn is stripped of his citizenship and exiled; Portuguese dictatorship ended by military coup and democratic reforms are initiated; rebels supported by Greece overthrow government in Cyprus: Turkish forces invade and take over much of the island; India explodes a nuclear device; Syria and Israel agree to the boundaries of a demilitarized zone in the Golan Heights and they begin troop withdrawals from the region; US Pres. Richard Nixon resigns to avoid impeachment by Congress for his cover-up of the Watergate scandal; Gerald Ford is sworn in to replace Nixon; the US and Soviet Union reach a tentative agreement to limit the numbers of strategic offensive nuclear weapons and delivery vehicles; severe drought threatens millions in Africa; scientists warn of the effects of chloroflourocarbons (CFCs) on the ozone layer.

1975: Portugal's new constitution grants most power to the military; Angola, Cape Verde, Sâo Tomé and Principe and Mozambique gain independence from Portugal; Turkish Cypriots declare the establishment of a separate state in the northern half of the island; US evacuates as North Vietnam seizes Saigon; Egypt reopens the Suez Canal, which had been closed since the 1967 Arab–Israeli war; a UN Security Council resolution calling for the imposition of an arms embargo against South Africa is vetoed by the US, Great Britain and France; Generalissimo Franco, Spain's chief of state, dies and is replaced by King Juan Carlos I; Peru's president is ousted in a military coup and replaced by a general; a democratic republic is proclaimed in Laos; Papua New Guinea and Surinam become independent; civil war breaks out in Beirut between Christians and Muslims; rebels in Eritrea provoke battles with Ethiopian government.

1976: Chinese Prem. Chou En-lai and Communist Chinese leader Mao Tse-tung die within months of each other; riots against apartheid take place in the all-black township of Soweto outside of Johannesburg and spread to Cape Town in black townships and white areas; first reports surface that Libyan leader Col. Moammar Qaddafi is financing, training and arming a widespread terrorist network; the Parti Québécois wins power in Quebec's provincial election, raising the possibility of Quebec's secession from Canada; worldwide earthquakes kill an estimated 780,000 people; the Gang of Four (Mao Tse-tung's widow and three others) unsuccessfully attempt a coup in China; Venezuela nationalizes petroleum industry; president of Argentina overthrown by military junta; Spanish Sahara released from Spain's jurisdiction and divided between Morocco and Mauritania; North and South Vietnam reunited under Communist government; a military coup in Thailand topples the government; 9,000 refugees flee Angolan civil war.

1977: Cambodian refugees report economic and social disaster following the Communists' capture of Phnom Penh; Egypt severs diplomatic relations with Syria, Iraq, Libya, Algeria and South Yemen for attempting to disrupt its peace overtures to Israel; over 570 die in the world's worst aviation disaster when two Boeing 747s collide on the runway on the Canary Island of Tenerife; black South African leader Steven Biko dies in jail; French territories of Afars and Issa unite to form independent Republic of Djibouti; government of Pakistan is overthrown and martial law is imposed; Leonid Brezhnev becomes USSR president and Communist Party chief; Somalia-backed Eritrean guerrillas are stopped by Ethiopian army; Thailand government seized by military junta; Rhodesia's white government announces it will begin negotiations with black majority; cyclone in India leaves 20,000 dead and 2 million homeless; US unmanned spacecrafts *Voyager I* and *II* begin journeys to explore the outer solar system; the neutron bomb, which causes great loss of life but little property damage, is developed in the US.

1978: A Soviet-supported military junta takes power in Afghanistan and Soviet troops occupy the country; Lebanon is torn by Christian and Muslim militia activity as well as Palestinian guerrilla activity, and Arab League intervenes to restore peace; Israeli forces withdraw; Syria declares a unilateral cease-fire in and around Beirut, Lebanon; Egyptian Pres. Anwar Sadat and Israeli Prem. Menachem Begin sign peace accords, mediated by US Pres. Jimmy Carter; Shah Mohammed Riza Pahlevi of Iran imposes martial law to suppress antigovernment demonstrations; leftist Sandinista guerrillas attempt to overthrow the government of Nicaraguan Pres. Anastasio Somoza; US establishes full diplomatic relations with Communist China; the first peaceful transfer of power takes place in Dominican Republic; Zaïre invaded by secessionist rebels: defence aid comes from other African nations, and France and Belgium after the massacre of Europeans; military junta seizes power in Honduras; army seizes government power in Bolivia; former Italian Prem. Aldo Moro is kidnapped and murdered by the Red Brigades, a revolutionary terrorist group; John Paul II (Karol Wojtyla) of Poland becomes the first non-Italian Pope in four centuries; the first "test-tube baby" (human baby conceived outside the womb) is born in England.

1979: Armed Islamic revolutionary followers of Ayatollah Khomeini overthrow the government of Iran and the Shah flees; students demanding the Shah's return to stand trial seize hostages at US embassy; a malfunction in the cooling system of a nuclear reactor at Three Mile Island in Pennsylvania, US, closes down the reactor and radiation escapes into the air; Conservative Margaret Thatcher becomes Britain's first female prime minister; a black government is formally installed in Rhodesia and its name is changed to Zimbabwe; China and the US establish formal commercial relations for the first time since 1949; Vietnamese army invades Cambodia and installs new government; St Lucia, St Vincent and the Grenadines become independent; coup in Grenada replaces government leader; president of Uganda, Idi Amin, overthrown; Egypt is expelled from Arab League after signing Camp David peace treaty; first elections for European Parliament held; the US–USSR SALT (Strategic Arms Limitation Treaty) Agreement is signed in Vienna; Iran nationalizes remaining privately owned industries without compensation; sharp oil price increases contribute to high inflation worldwide; South Korean Pres. Park Chung Hee and his chief body guard are assassinated by a government official; emperor of Central African Empire overthrown; president of El Salvador is ousted by military coup.

1980: Soviet dissident Andrei Sakharov, a Nobel Prize-winning physicist, is arrested in Moscow; human interferon, a promising natural disease-fighting substance, is made by gene splicing; Mt St Helens erupts in Washington, in a blast that sends debris 20 km up into the atmosphere and is heard over 300 km away; in a political comeback, Indira Gandhi wins a landslide victory in India's parliamentary elections; Soviet war in Afghanistan escalates as the US imposes an embargo on the sale of grain and high technology to the Soviet Union in response to the continued occupation of Afghanistan, and 50 nations boycott the Moscow Olympics in protest; Roman Catholic Archbishop Oscar Arnulfo Romero, an El Salvadoran reformer, is assassinated while saying Mass; some 10,800 Cubans seek asylum in Peru's Cuban embassy and more than 125,000 Cubans escape by boat to the US; Liberian Pres. William Tolbert, Jr, is killed in a coup; military coup in Turkey unseats government; Zimbabwe gains independence from Britain; 350 Bengalis are massacred by native tribal people in India; black guerrillas successfully bomb two South African petroleum plants and a refinery; mass labour strikes in Poland force the government to allow independent trade unions, including Solidarity, led by Lech Walesa; 20 terrorist bomb attacks take place in France; the Iran–Iraq war begins when Iraqi fighter-bombers attack Iranian airfields and lay siege to its southwestern cities; 3,000 are killed in earthquakes centred in southern Italy; 20,000 die in two strong earthquakes in Algeria; *Voyager I* sends back the first pictures of Saturn; wreck of the *Titanic* found in North Atlantic.

1981: Aquired Immune Deficiency Syndrome (AIDS) is first recognized, in the US; in El Salvador, heavy fighting occurs between the government and leftist insurgents; the world's first reusable spacecraft, the Space Shuttle *Columbia*, is sent into space; clashes between Syrian troops and Christian militiamen in Lebanon are followed by Israeli bombing in support of Christian forces; artificial bone and skin are developed in the US; Pope John Paul II is shot and seriously wounded outside the Vatican by a Turkish terrorist; Israel is condemned worldwide after Israeli warplanes destroy an Iraqi atomic reactor near Baghdad; Irish prisoners in Belfast stage hunger strikes to force the British government to grant political prisoner status to Irish nationalist inmates, and some die; South African troops invade Angola in pursuit of guerrillas; Belize, formerly British Honduras, becomes independent from Britain; Pres. Anwar el-Sadat of Egypt is assassinated by Muslim extremists during a military parade; Israel formally annexes the Golan Heights; a five-day war between Ecuador and Peru erupts over a border dispute; Greece joins the European Community; Italian government rocked by revelation that nearly 1,000 key government, army and business leaders support a secret outlawed Masonic lodge; president of Bangladesh assassinated; Iranian president, prime minister and 29 others killed in bomb attack; 5,000 die when Indonesian ferry sinks in Java Sea; martial law is instituted in Poland in the face of continued labour unrest; the personal computer is introduced by IBM in the US.

1982: Argentina moves to reclaim Malvinas (the Falkland Islands) from UK by invading the territory; Britain defeats Argentina in the subsequent war; Canada gains the power to amend its own constitution from Britain; Israel withdraws from the Sinai and turns it over to Egypt, fulfilling their 1979 peace treaty; Israel invades Lebanon and the PLO leadership leaves Lebanon under UN protection; Lebanese Christian militiamen massacre Palestinians in refugee camps and Israel is accused of indirectly aiding the attack; Iran invades Iraq, but Iraq claims to have killed 27,000 Iranians in 18 days of battle; a series of IRA bombs explode in London, killing nine and wounding 51; western nations debate a proposed Soviet oil pipeline to western Europe; Lech Walesa, former leader of Solidarity, the outlawed Polish labour union, is freed after 11 months of imprisonment; military coups in Bangladesh and Guatemala force changes in government; Soviet leader Leonid Brezhnev dies and Yuri Andropov succeeds him; in Cambodia, support for Khmer Rouge grows as coalition against Vietnamese-backed government joined by Prince Sihanouk; up to 1,200 Afghan civilians and Soviet soldiers die in a tunnel explosion caused by the collision of two trucks; the first permanent artificial heart is transplanted into Dr Barney B. Clark, 61, in Utah; Mexican volcano, El Chichón, erupts, blasting debris into the stratosphere.

1983: Klaus Barbie, former chief of the German Gestapo in Lyons, France, during WW II, is deported to France from Bolivia to face charges of crimes against humanity; Soviet citizens and diplomats accused of espionage are expelled from France, Spain, the US and Britain; the US government is accused of having illegally aided Nicaraguan rebels; anti-government protests increase in Chile, governed by Gen. Pinochet; Ethiopia appeals for aid to 4 million victims of drought and famine; Sri Lankan Sinhalese and Tamil forces clash, killing hundreds and destroying the homes of thousands of others; 1,200 die in an earthquake in Turkey; martial law is formally lifted in Poland; the Organization of Petroleum Exporting Countries (OPEC) agrees to cut crude oil prices for the first time in its 23-year history; all 269 people aboard are killed when the Soviet Union shoots down a South Korean airliner, claiming that the plane had been on a spying mission and strayed into Soviet airspace; Benigno Aquino, opponent of Philippine Pres. Marcos, returns to Manila and is assassinated; 241 US Marines and sailors and 40 French paratroopers, members of a multinational peacekeeping force in Lebanon, are killed by suicide terrorists; the US and France support Chad's government against Libyan-supported guerrillas; Israeli withdrawal from Lebanon is followed by full-scale fighting between Lebanese ethnic and religious groups; US-led forces invade the small island of Grenada; US Cruise missiles in Europe are deployed in Britain despite Soviet and civilian opposition; white South Africans approve a new constitution granting limited political participation for persons of mixed race and Asians, but not for blacks, in a new tricameral legislature; Yasser Arafat and PLO guerrillas are evacuated from Lebanon to Tunis, under UN sponsorship; riots in Assam, India claim 5,000 lives and 300,000 refugees flee; the compact disc is introduced; after an 11-year journey, the *Pioneer 10* spacecraft leaves the solar system.

1984: Cholesterol is linked to heart disease following a 10-year study by US researchers; the Apple Macintosh with mouse enters the personal computer market; Konstantin Cher-

nenko becomes Soviet leader following the death of Yuri Andropov; US astronauts fly free of the space shuttle *Challenger*, the first humans to do so without a tether; US and UN forces are withdrawn from Lebanon; French and American researchers, working separately, report that they have identified viruses which appear to be the cause of AIDS; Saudi, Greek and Swiss tankers are attacked by both Iran and Iraq in the Persian Gulf and Saudi Arabia shoots down two Iranian jets; hundreds die during a battle for the Golden Temple in Amritsar between Sikh militants and police in India; Indian Prime Min. Indira Gandhi is slain by two of her Sikh bodyguards in New Delhi and widespread violence follows; Daniel Ortega, Sandinista leader, wins in Nicaraguan elections; the international community sends aid to starving Ethiopians; in a secret operation, Israel airlifts 25,000 Ethiopian Jews (Falashas) out of the Sudan; Britain and China finalize an agreement on Hong Kong's future, guaranteeing its capitalist system for 50 years after it is turned over to China in 1997; a Union Carbide chemical plant leak kills 2,500 in Bhopal, India; the European Space Agency launches the largest telecommunications satellite in the world.

1985: South African police kill 18 blacks commemorating the Sharpville massacre in 1960, 19 more are killed while participating in a funeral procession and later the government declares a state of emergency; Daniel Ortega becomes president of Nicaragua; US president urges military aid to Nicaraguan opposition forces but only humanitarian aid is approved; Mikhail Gorbachev succeeds Konstantin Chernenko as Soviet leader and he opens disarmament talks with the US; Iraq turns back an Iranian offensive, allegedly killing 30,000 to 50,000 Iranians; Shiite Muslim hijackers release hostages after 17 days of captivity in Beirut, having demanded the release of hundreds of Shiites detained by Israeli forces; Argentine president imposes drastic economic measures to cut 1,010 percent inflation rate; top French officials are linked to the bombing of a ship owned by Greenpeace; two leading Soviet KGB officials defect to Britain and the US, where both name Soviet spies in the two countries; a cyclone and tidal waves hit Bangladesh, killing 10,000; a Mexican earthquake kills more than 7,000 and causes widespread destruction, leaving thousands homeless; border dispute between Mali and

Burkina Faso leads to war but is eventually referred to International Court of Justice; Nicaragua suspends civil rights; four Palestinians seize the Italian cruise ship *Achille Lauro* off the coast of Egypt, murdering a wheelchair-bound American; Reagan and Gorbachev meet at the first superpower summit in six years; 95 Colombians die when 60 rebels seize the Palace of Justice in Bogotá and take more than 300 persons hostage; 60 die when Arab gunmen hijack an Egyptian jetliner, in an act allegedly backed by Libya's leader Col. Moammar Qaddafi; a Colombian volcanic eruption kills 20,000 people; Guatemala elects its first civilian president following three decades of military rule; Uruguay's military government replaced by civilian government; Sudanese and Ugandan presidents ousted by military coups; terrorists kill 20 people at two airports (in Rome and Vienna), both at the ticket counters of El Al, Israel's national airline; Live Aid rock concert in London, UK and Philadelphia, US raises over $60 million for African famine relief.

1986: Portugal and Spain join the European Community; Jean-Claude Duvalier, Haiti's "president for life," flees to France in the face of nationwide protest; Portugal elects its first civilian president in 60 years; Gorbachev calls for "radical reform" of Soviet economy and reshapes the leadership of the Communist party; Philippine Pres. Ferdinand Marcos flees to the US after allegations of electoral fraud; his opponent, Corazon Aquino, succeeds Marcos as president; Swedish Prime Min. Olof Palme is assassinated; former UN secretary general Kurt Waldheim is elected president of Austria; US planes bomb Libya citing retaliatory measures after missile attacks; radiation is spread following the meltdown of the Chernobyl nuclear power plant in the USSR; South African forces attack alleged African National Congress (ANC) bases in neighbouring Botswana, Zambia and Zimbabwe; the *New York Times* first links Panama's General Manuel Noriega with drug and arms trafficking; US president acknowledges a secret and illegal arms deal with Iran: the "Iran-Contra Affair" involving the US sale of arms in exchange for hostages is first reported in a Lebanese newspaper; the US space shuttle *Challenger* explodes one minute after liftoff and all seven crew members die instantly; *Voyager II* spacecraft passes Uranus.

1987: Soviet leader Mikhail Gorbachev begins a campaign for openness (glasnost) and reconstruction (perestroika); Tamil separatists kill hundreds of Sri Lankans, mostly Sinhalese, and clash with government forces; German pilot Mathias Rust, 19, embarrasses Soviets when he lands his single-engine Cessna in Red Square, Moscow; Moscow's Communist Party chief, Boris Yeltsin, is dismissed after criticizing Soviet leader Gorbachev; South Africa withdraws its troops from Angola; an Iraqi warplane's missile kills 37 US sailors in the Persian Gulf, and the US escorts Kuwaiti oil tankers despite danger posed by the Iran–Iraq war; 402 Iranian pilgrims to Mecca die in battles with Saudi police; 24 nations sign a treaty to protect the ozone layer; Portugal and China agree that the Portuguese colony of Macao will be returned to China in 1999; stock market prices plunge worldwide; the Palestinian intifada (uprising) begins against Israeli authorities in the Gaza Strip and West Bank, and thousands of protesters are imprisoned; Syrian troops enter Beirut in an attempt to bring a cease-fire; Lebanese prime minister dies in a bomb attack; a military coup ousts coalition government in Chad; 2,000 die in the Philippines when a ferry sinks.

1988: Nicaraguan contras and the Sandinista government reach a cease-fire agreement; the US and Soviet Union sign a treaty on intermediate-range nuclear forces (INF); Soviet troops begin to pull out of Afghanistan after a nine-year occupation; nationalist groups in Soviet-controlled Azerbaijan and Armenia clash; Colombian drug cartels defy government attempts to bring them to justice, and fight among themselves; a US navy warship accidentally shoots down a commercial Iranian airliner over the Persian Gulf, killing all 290 persons aboard; the Soviet Communist Party backs Gorbachev's plan for perestroika; Canadian and US governments ratify a free trade agreement, to take effect January 1, 1989; Iran and Iraq agree on a cease-fire to end their eight-year war; Iraq uses poison gas on its Kurdish minority and razes Kurdish villages; Libya and Chad formally end their war; Thailand and Laos do battle in a brief border dispute; Ethiopia and Somalia end 11 years of disputes over borders with a peace treaty; Solidarity supporters stage widespread strikes in Poland; Vietnamese troops leave Kampuchea; a military coup in Burma causes a change in leadership; Yugoslavia's inflation rate tops 250 percent, ethnic Albanians in Kosovo province demand freedom from Serbian rule; Benazir Bhutto, daughter of a former Pakistani president, becomes prime minister of Pakistan; 270 people die when a bomb blows up a Pan Am jetliner over Lockerbie, Scotland; 25,000 Armenians die during an earthquake.

1989: Iran's Ayatollah Khomeini calls for the execution of UK author Salman Rushdie for blaspheming the prophet Mohammed; the Soviet Union holds historic multicandidate parliamentary elections and Boris Yeltsin emerges as Russian leader; Japanese Prime Min. Noboru Takeshita is toppled by financial scandal, Emperor Hirohito dies and is succeeded by his son; Chinese students lead more than one million in demonstrations for democratic reforms, but spreading unrest is checked by a government crackdown in Tiananmen Square that is suspected to have killed thousands; Hungary opens its border with Austria and moves toward political and economic reform; anti-Communist forces continue to battle the government in Afghanistan; fighting between Christians and Muslims in Beirut intensifies; 90 people die in ethnic violence in Soviet Uzbekistan; Poles participate in their first open election in 40 years and Solidarity wins a solid victory; the three Baltic states (Estonia, Latvia and Lithuania) protest Soviet domination; a Colombian presidential candidate is slain, prompting a renewed crackdown on illegal drug traffickers; thousands of East Germans flee to West Germany and the East German government proposes political reforms; Vietnamese forces withdraw from Cambodia; East German communist leader Erich Honecker is removed from power, and is later charged with corruption; thousands demonstrate in Czechoslovakia and force the communist government to resign, Vaclav Havel is elected president; the spaceship *Atlantis* is launched on a journey to Jupiter; East Germany opens the Berlin Wall after 28 years and lifts visa and emigration restrictions; Panama's Gen. Manuel Noriega annuls presidential elections after an opposition party victory, the US invades Panama and Noriega goes into hiding; Romanian Pres. Nicolae Ceausescu is overthrown and executed with his wife for genocide, abuse of power and theft; 80 nations sign an agreement to limit production of chlorofluorocarbons (CFCs) to

protect the ozone layer; Paraguay's president is toppled by a military coup; the Exxon *Valdez* runs aground in Alaska and spills thousands of litres of oil; *Voyager II* spacecraft reaches Neptune.

1990: Panama's Manuel Noriega surrenders to US authorities; violence erupts in Soviet Azerbaijan as Azerbaijanis attack Armenians; Bulgaria and Yugoslavia switch to multiparty systems; Violeta Chamorro defeats Sandinista leader Daniel Ortega to become the Nicaraguan president; South African government lifts restrictions on opposition organizations and declares amnesty for political prisoners, black leader Nelson Mandela is freed after 27 years in prison; the US, France, Great Britain and the Soviet Union reach agreement on a reunited Germany; Lithuania proclaims its sovereignty and Soviet troops move in; Namibia gains independence from South Africa; newly released Soviet documents prove Soviet secret police killed 15,000 Polish military officers in the Katyn forest massacre of 1940; the $1.5-billion Hubble Space Telescope is sent into space, but flawed light-gathering mirrors distort transmissions; Iran's worst earthquake kills 40,000; more than 1,400 Muslim pilgrims to Mecca suffocate in a stampede in an overcrowded tunnel; Ukraine declares its sovereignty within the Soviet Union; the two Germanys reunite, merging their economic, legal and political systems; Czechoslovakia and Romania hold their first free elections in the postwar era (Aug. 2); Iraq invades Kuwait over disagreements regarding oil production levels and appears ready to invade Saudi Arabia; the UN passes sweeping trade and financial sanctions against Iraq, and aid and troops pour into Saudi Arabia; civil war in black South African townships kills hundreds; the first human gene therapy for disease is done by blood transfusion; South Africa bans racial discrimination in public places; following a political challenge from within her own party, British Prime Min. Margaret Thatcher resigns and is succeeded by John Major; Mozambique adopts a constitution allowing for a multiparty democracy; civil war in Chad ends with overthrow of president; a military coup in Bangladesh unseats the president; Soviet Pres. Mikhail Gorbachev proposes Union Treaty to restructure Soviet Union; Helmut Kohl elected chancellor of Unified Germany; Lech Walesa elected president of

Poland; African National Congress (ANC) holds first conference in South Africa in 31 years; Rev. Jean-Bertrand Aristide elected president of Haiti; Edward Shevardnadze resigns as Soviet foreign minister; Slovenia and Croatia initiate secession from Yugoslavian republic.

1991: Iraq ignores January 15 deadline for withdrawal from Kuwait and Allied forces (including the US, Canada, Britain, France, Italy, Japan, Pakistan and members of the Arab League) launch a six-week air attack; Soviets suppress independence movements in Baltic republics; US and Italy begin rescue of foreigners trapped in Somalian civil war; limited integration of schools begins in South Africa and sweeping reforms of apartheid law are proposed; Allies launch ground assault on Iraqi forces and informal cease-fire follows; 1,200 killed in an earthquake in Pakistan and Afghanistan; Lithuanians vote to secede from Soviet Union; Estonia and Latvia vote for independence from the Soviet Union; violent protests held in Belgrade to topple Yugoslavian government; Kuwaiti government forced to resign in wake of failure to establish postwar order; UN cease-fire formally ends Gulf War (Apr.) and Kurds flee from Iraq; Soviet republic of Georgia votes for independence; cease-fire declared in Angola's 16-year civil war; Rajiv Gandhi assassinated during Indian national election campaign; Boris Yeltsin elected president of Russia; Mt Pinatubo volcano erupts in Philippines; Population Registration Act repealed in South Africa; fighting between Yugoslav military and Slovenian nationalists escalates; Soviet hard-liners attempt a coup against Mikhail Gorbachev: its failure results in the dissolution of the Communist Party; rebels oust Haitian Pres. Jean-Bertrand Aristide; Serbia and Croatia reach political settlement but civil war continues; peace accord signed in El Salvador, paving the way to end of 11-year civil war; failed coup in Soviet Union speeds disintegration of the country as Lithuania, Estonia and Latvia act to enforce their independence; civil war in Croatia escalates; warring factions in Cambodia sign peace accord; talks on new constitution begin in South Africa; rebels fighting in Somalia claim to have taken over Mogadishu and deposed the president; Gorbachev resigns as USSR formally dissolves and Commonwealth of Independent States (CIS) created; fighting

escalates in Somalia; Slovenia and Croatia recognized as independent states by Germany; Islamic Salvation Front leads in Algerian elections; by year-end, cholera epidemic has killed 3,500 in Latin America and 12,500 in Africa.

1992: A Jan. military coup in Algeria gives power to a committee which cancels elections in progress; in June the Algerian president is assassinated and the defence minister assumes power. Brazil is the site of the Earth Summit, which sees 100 world leaders and 30,000 participants gather in Rio de Janeiro to discuss worldwide environmental protection; the country is rocked by political unrest in Aug., which ends the presidency of President Fernando Collor de Mello over an influence-peddling and bribery scandal. The European Community's Maastricht Treaty is first rejected by Denmark (June), then ratified by Irish (June) and French (Sept.) voters, and the Italian senate (Sept.). Czechoslovakia's president, Vaclav Havel, resigns on July 20 and the Parliament of Slovakia declares its sovereignty. An earthquake on Oct. 12 leaves 300 dead and thousands injured in Egypt. The Uruguay Round of the GATT (General Agreement on Tariffs and Trade) negotiations remains stalled over the issue of farm subsidies. Germany is plagued by riots and fire-bombings staged by right-wing extremists attacking foreign-born workers and refugees. Israel's national election results in a victory for the Labour Party and its leader, Yitzhak Rabin; in Aug., Rabin begins to hint that compromise in the area of peace and territorial disputes might be possible. Italy continues an anti-Mafia crackdown despite the assassination of two prominent judges and a police investigator. A ruptured petrol pipeline in Mexico's working-class district of Guadalajara is blamed for an explosion that kills 200 and injures nearly 1,500 in Apr. Peru's president, Alberto Fujimori, suspends sections of the country's constitution in Apr. and seizes power, citing a need to root out corruption and combat the combined forces of the Shining Path guerrillas and various drug barons. Russia's first experiments with free markets trigger soaring inflation and shortages. Civil war in Somalia brings 4.5 million of its people to the brink of starvation; by Aug. the UN brings in forces to ensure that food is distributed to the hungry, but is unable to restore order. The government in South

Africa continues to work towards a power-sharing agreement with the black majority after receiving nearly 70 percent support in a Mar. whites-only referendum; in Sept. troops from the Ciskei homeland open fire on ANC supporters massed at the border and talks on democratic reform are again delayed. Citizens in Thailand take to the streets in demonstrations that eventually force constitutional reforms and democratic elections. In the United Kingdom, the scandals of the royal family threaten the credibility of the monarchy; uncertainty over the fate of the Maastricht Treaty and pressure on UK currency force a withdrawal from the European Monetary System in Sept. and a devaluation of the UK pound. In the United States, riots in Los Angeles in late Apr./early May leave 42 dead. The US state of Florida is devastated by Hurricane Andrew (Aug.) which does an estimated $15-billion damage. On Oct. 12, the *Pioneer* spacecraft plunges into the scorching atmosphere surrounding the planet Venus and ends a 14-year space mission. In Nov., the Democrats, under Bill Clinton and Al Gore, are elected to a four-year term. Yugoslavia continues to disintegrate: the UN Security Council deploys peacekeepers in Jan.; Croatia and Slovenia are given diplomatic recognition by the European Community as well as 20 other countries (including Canada). By Feb., Serbia and Montenegro reach agreement on a common state retaining the Yugoslav flag, anthem and joint parliament; in Mar., citizens of the republic of Bosnia-Herzegovina vote for independence; however, ethnic fighting over Bosnian territory escalates throughout the year amid charges of ethnic cleansing and atrocities, and a series of cease-fires that rarely hold for more than a few days. On Sept. 22, Yugoslavia (Serbia and Montenegro) is expelled from the UN General Assembly.

1993: Both sides in the Bosnia-Herzegovina conflict reject peace plans to settle the conflict. In Burundi an abortive Oct. coup leaves the president and six ministers dead before the army decides to back the existing government and order is restored. Despite opposition and active interference by the Khmer Rouge, 90 percent of registered voters cast their ballots in Cambodia's national election in May. One of the longest civil wars in Africa ends when the separation of Eritrea from Ethiopia is approved in a referendum. After seven years of negotiation, the latest version of the GATT agreement is approved by 117 countries in late Dec. German military forces take part in missions outside Germany's borders for the first time since WWII; the German parliament bows to right-wing pressures and places limits on its liberal immigration laws. Neither the OAS nor the UN is able to restore Haiti's deposed president Jean-Bertrand Aristide to power despite intense negotiations and increased blockades. On Sept. 13, PLO leader Yasser Arafat and Israeli Prime Min. Yitzak Rabin meet in Washington to sign a peace agreement secretly negotiated in Norway; the agreement grants Palestinian autonomy over certain lands and recognizes Israel's right to exist. The results of the June election in Nigeria are nullified by the long-time dictator, despite protests which include a three-day general strike. A battle for power in the Russian parliament sees Pres. Boris Yeltsin strip Vice-Pres. Rutskoi of his powers and dissolve parliament to call Dec. elections; parliamentarians respond by barricading themselves in the building which is then surrounded by government troops. The seige is lifted when the insurgents surrender on Oct. 4; a new parliament is elected in Dec. and a new constitution is approved. Slovakia and the Czech Republic declare independence on Jan. 1. British Prime Min. John Major and his Irish counterpart announce a tentative peace plan for Northern Ireland that would allow the people to decide their own fate. US troops in Somalia hand the mission to re-establish order over to a UN force made up of personnel from 20 countries and announce they will pull out at the end of Mar. 1994. In Sept. an agreement is reached in South Africa that paves the way for a multiparty transitional council that includes blacks; in Oct. the United Nations lifts economic sanctions; in Nov. a new constitution is approved and national all-race elections are scheduled: white rule ends officially in Dec. In the United States, a stand-off outside the compound of a religious group in Waco, Texas, ends in tragedy when authorities storm the area and the buildings erupt in flames (Apr.). A rainy summer leads to record-breaking floods in nine states along the Mississippi River and in Oct. brush fires devastate six counties in California; in Nov. Pres. Clinton secures approval for NAFTA in the House of Representatives.

1994: Islamic fundamentalists in Algeria continue their fight to oust the government, targetting foreigners, journalists and intellectuals. In Feb. a Bosnian Serb mortar attack on a Sarajevo marketplace kills 66, injures 200 and prompts NATO to threaten punitive bombing if Serb guns are not pulled back from the city; in Aug. the Bosnian Serb rejection of a peace plan moves the government of Serbia to sever relations; in Dec. Bosnian Serbs kidnap UN peacekeepers and use them as human shields to halt NATO airstrikes. In Brazil, radical steps are taken to curb inflation; the currency (cruzeiro) is scrapped and replaced by the *real*, and severe budget cuts are instituted. Increasing numbers of Cuban citizens flee the country in the face of the effects of the trade embargo. A car ferry enroute from Estonia to Finland sinks, killing over 900 passengers and crew. Throughout the year German officials seize illegal shipments of plutonium apparently smuggled out of the former Soviet Union. A US-led force lands in Haiti on Sept. 19, and president-in-exile Jean-Bertrand Aristide returns to Haiti in Oct. In Jan. a heavily armed Jewish settler enters a mosque in Hebron on the West Bank and opens fire on Muslim worshippers; 40 Palestinians die and more than 250 are wounded in the riots that follow; throughout the year Islamic fundamentalists use suicide bombing in an effort to derail the peace talks. In May, Yasser Arafat and Israeli Prime Min. Rabin sign the peace accord that inaugurates Palestinian self-rule on the Gaza Strip and in Jericho; the PLO begins to create a government structure for the areas; in July, Jordan and Israel sign an agreement to normalize relations. Japan suffers a year of political uncertainty as a series of prime ministers fail to maintain a coalition government. A string of comet fragments known as Shoemaker-Levy 9 collide with Jupiter between July 16 and 22, causing massive explosions in the planet's atmosphere. The government of North Korea reluctantly agrees to allow nuclear inspectors to visit the majority of their nuclear sites. Ruler Kim Il Sung dies as negotiations end; his son and successor Kim Jong Il appears to have a tenuous grip on power. A New Year's day rebellion in Mexico sets the stage for a turbulent year—Zapatista rebels in the southern state of Chiapas demand land reforms; in Mar. Luis Colosio, the leading candidate in the national election, is gunned down at an outdoor rally; in Dec., the peso loses 40 percent of its value over eight days and trade allies move to prop up the economy. Workers try to bring down the military government in Nigeria by staging a general strike that drags on for six weeks. In Northern Ireland, the political wing of the IRA announces a "complete cessation of military operations" in Sept., paving the way for peace talks. In Oct., economic reforms lead to a steep plunge in the value of the ruble and widespread protests over unemployment; a leaky pipeline spills a massive quantity of oil onto the fragile permafrost and into surrounding rivers; in Dec., 40,000 Russian troops invade Chechnya to end the region's drive for independence. Plagued by racially motivated skirmishes at the beginning of the year, Rwanda dissolves into an ethnic blood bath after the death of the president in a plane crash; tens of thousands of Rwandans, mostly Tutsi, die at the hands of rival Hutus in a killing spree that lasts for months; Tutsi-led forces eventually regain control of the country and thousands more flee to refugee camps in neighbouring countries to escape feared reprisals. In Somalia, factional fighting reignites as both the US and the UN withdraw the forces policing the area. In Apr., all-race elections are held for the first time in South Africa, and Nelson Mandela is elected president; South Africa is given full membership to the UN in June. In the US, California is rocked by an earthquake in Jan.; in Feb., Aldrich Ames, a mid-level officer in the CIA, is exposed as a spy operating for Moscow since the mid-1980s. By June, the US dollar is in a record-breaking dive.

1995: The Algerian civil war continues, with Muslim extremists stepping up attacks on foreigners, collaborators, journalists, women who adopted modern ways of life, and the families of government officials. In the Atlantic region, a harsh hurricane season brings death and destruction to the Caribbean in the latter part of the year. In the Bosnian war, the blockade of Sarajevo continues for much of the year as truces fail to hold. In May NATO launches two days of airstrikes to break the impasse and Bosnian Serbs seize nearly 400 UN peacekeepers; the hostages are freed throughout May and June. In July Bosnian Serbs overrun the UN safe areas of Srebrenica and Zepa and clear the territory of Muslims. NATO resumes airstrikes in response to the shelling of a marketplace in Sarajevo. The bombing missions continue in Sept. to force the Bosnian Serbs to withdraw from positions around Sarajevo; a cease-fire is inaugurated in Oct. In Nov., negotiators for all sides in the Bosnian conflict meet at the Wright-Patterson Air Force Base outside Dayton, Ohio, for three weeks to hammer out a peace plan. By Dec. US and British military personnel are arriving in Bosnia to implement the agreement. Burmese officials free political dissident Aung San Suu Kyi from house arrest in July. In Burundi, murders by members of rival factions raise fears of Rwandan-style massacres; thousands of Rwandan refugees flee to Tanzania to escape the violence. The UN's Fourth World Conference on Women is held in China in Sept. In Croatia, Pres. Tudjman allows the UN peacekeeping mandate to lapse; in Aug. Croatian troops regain the territory in Krajina that had been lost to Croatian Serbs in 1991. France conducts three nuclear tests around the Muroroa Atoll in the South Pacific during the year, despite international protests and local demonstrations. Haitians vote on Dec. 17 in the first election since exiled Pres. Jean-Bertrand Aristide was returned to power. In Ireland, a bitter campaign over lifting the ban on divorce ends in narrow approval for liberalizing the laws (Nov.). Israel and the Palestinians struggle with the peace process throughout the year, postponing deadlines as suicide bomb attacks in Israel threaten to derail the process altogether. In Oct. Israeli forces begin to withdraw from parts of the West Bank in accordance with an agreement on Palestinian self rule. On Nov. 4, a 25-year-old militant Jewish law student shoots and kills Israeli Prime Min. Yitzak Rabin. On Jan. 17, the port of Kobe in Japan is struck by an earthquake measuring 7.2 on the Richter scale; 5,000 residents are killed, 25,000 are injured and 300,000 are left homeless. Also in Japan, a nerve-gas attack during rush hour in a Tokyo subway leaves 10 dead and 5,500 injured; two more incidents occur in Apr. in Yokohama; police trace the attacks to a religious cult known as Aum Shinrikyo and arrest its leader, Shoko Asahara. The Galileo space probe arrives at Jupiter in Dec. after a 3.7-billion km trip that took six years. Mexico grapples with a financial crisis that sees the peso fall to record lows; the US engineers a financial bail-out conditional upon austerity measures and the reform of the country's electoral process; loan repayments begin in Oct., ahead of schedule. In Nov. the military government in Nigeria condemns environmentalist and activist Ken Saro-Wiwa and eight others to death; the sentence is carried out on Nov. 10. Peru and Ecuador fight a month-long border war in the early part of the year. In Poland, long-time president Lech Walesa is defeated by a former Communist who promises to continue western-style reforms in Nov. Throughout the year Russia is unable to subdue guerrillas in the breakaway republic of Chechnya; bombing raids on the capital of Grozny reduce the city to rubble. A 7.5 (Richter scale) earthquake strikes Sakhalin Island in Russia's far east in May, killing nearly 2,000. UN forces pull out of Somalia after a two-year attempt to restore order amid drought, starvation and clan warfare. Sri Lanka's civil war with Tamil rebels continues as the Tamils refuse to consider peace proposals. In Singapore, at the 232-year-old Barings Bank, a rogue trader's speculation on the currency market costs the bank more than $1 billion; Barings collapses. In the US, on the anniversary of the FBI attack on the Branch Davidians in Waco, Texas, a bomb explodes outside a government building in Oklahoma City. One hundred and sixty-eight are killed and over 400 injured; police arrest Timothy McVeigh, a Gulf War veteran linked to American militia groups. On Oct. 16, Nation of Islam minister Louis Farrakhan rallies nearly a million black men in Washington.

1996: The Algerian civil war continues throughout the year. In Bosnia, prisoners are exchanged, residents are evacuated and Sarajevo is handed over to the Muslim-Croat federation. Bosnian Serb leader Radovan Karadzic withdraws from public life in July. In Sept. elections are held for the Serb Republic and the Muslim-Croat Federation. Bulgaria's currency collapses in May; hyperinflation paralyzes the economy. Rwandan refugees are forcibly repatriated in mid-July; days later the Tutsi-dominated army seizes power in a coup. Borders close as Rwanda's neighbours proclaim sanctions. On Aug. 3, top generals of the Khmer Rouge open amnesty negotiations with the Cambodian government to end decades of bloodshed. Hurricane Bertha hits the Caribbean islands and eastern US in July. In May, unrest in Tibet increases as Chinese authorities forbid demonstrations supporting the Dalai Lama. On July 29, the Chinese test an underground nuclear device and then declare a moratorium on testing. On Feb. 24, Cuban fighter planes shoot down two civilian US aircraft for violating Cuban air space. An Arab summit in Cairo in June calls for Israeli withdrawal from Palestinian territory, including Arab Jerusalem. France's former Pres. Francois Mitterand dies Jan. 8. France conducts a nuclear test on Jan. 27; on Jan. 29, Pres. Chirac announces a permanent end to nuclear tests and cancels the last two. Yasser Arafat is sworn in as president of the Palestinian Council's executive in Feb.; on Apr. 24 the PLO revokes the charter clauses that call for the destruction of Israel and the waging of war against the Jewish state. In Israel, a May election produces victory for Benjamin Netanyahu and the Likud party. In Sept., an archaeological tunnel bordering on Islam's third-holiest site, the Al Aqsa Mosque, is opened, touching off a wave of violent protest. The Bank of Tokyo and Mitsubishi Bank merge on Apr. 1 to create the world's largest bank. In South Korea, two former presidents are convicted of accepting bribes during their tenures. In Sept., a North Korean submarine runs aground in South Korea; most crew members die on South Korean soil. On Apr. 6, the Liberian capital of Monrovia is torn by factional fighting; UN troops take control of Monrovia on Apr. 21. In Nov., Pakistan's president dismisses Prime Min. Benazir Bhutto's government and calls for elections in the wake of corruption allegations. In Peru, Tupac Amaru guerrillas take diplomats hostage for several months. In June, Russian Pres. Yeltsin narrowly wins elections, and a run-off election in July confirms the victory. In Rwanda, clashes between Hutu and Tutsi soldiers occur in Jan.; by Nov. thousands of displaced Hutus (many of whom had been away since 1994) return home from Zaire. Serbian Pres. Milosevic orders the results of local elections annulled in Nov. when opposition parties win; outraged citizens protest well into 1997. On Mar. 29, leaders of Sierra Leone's military government transfer power to a democratically elected government. South Africa's main political parties agree on a new constitution on May 8; on May 9, F.W. de Klerk takes his National Party out of the government coalition. In Spain, Basque separatists detonate four bombs during July,

killing at least 35 and prompting demonstrations against the ETA. In the UK, the IRA ends a 17-month cease-fire in Feb. with three bombings; attacks continue through June. On Mar. 13, a gunman kills 16 kindergarten children and their teacher in Dunblane, Scotland, before killing himself. A "mad-cow disease" scare prompts the banning of British beef by the EC and the eventual destruction of thousands of cattle and embryos to contain the problem. Northern Ireland's July marching season sees renewed violence. On Apr. 3, an arrest is made in the 17-year-old Unabomber case. The Summer Olympics open in Atlanta on July 19. US Pres. Clinton is re-elected in Nov.

1997: In Afghanistan's civil war, the Taliban takes control of Kabul and other key cities; by year-end they impose strict Islamic rule in many areas. In Algeria, over 2,000 are killed in nearly 50 massacres as suspected Islamic terrorists continue their war against the government; a June election gives the military-backed regime a majority. The worst flooding of the century hits Central Europe in July, leaving hundreds dead as dams break and power fails. In Bulgaria, antigovernment strikes and political paralysis lead to economic collapse. In Cambodia, in July, Second Prime Min. Hun Sen seizes control of Phnom Penh. Chinese premier Deng Xiaoping dies on Feb. 19. In Nov., Egyptian terrorists kill 68 people in Luxor. On July 1, the British colony of Hong Kong returns to China, ending a 99-year lease agreement. In late Oct., Hong Kong's stock market drops over 10 percent in four days; global markets follow suit. Indonesia's slash-and-burn farming techniques and a delayed rainy season cover much of the country with smoke and threaten the health of more than 20 million people. Iraqi leader Saddam Hussein confronts the US in Nov. by barring American members of a UN weapons-inspection team; Allied mobilization prompts Hussein to allow the inspectors to continue their duties. In Japan, Yamichi Securities, one of the largest brokerages in the country, shuts down on Nov. 24 amid the collapse of stock prices and a payoff scandal; the closure leaves US$24 billion in debts. In Dec., representatives from 150 nations meet in Japan to devise controls on greenhouse gases to slow ozone damage and global warming. Liberia's former rebel Charles Taylor, a key figure in the country's seven-year civil war, wins 75 percent of the presidential vote and a legislative majority in the country's general election on July 24. In Pakistan, the Muslim League defeats former Prime Min. Bhutto's party in national elections on Feb. 3. In Russia, Pres. Boris Yeltsin is hospitalized on Jan. 8 with double pneumonia; the Duma begins discussing Yeltsin's impeachment. On Apr. 14, the World Bank agrees to loan US$6 billion over two years if Russia's economic reforms continue. Serbian protesters continue to demand that the results of the Nov. election be respected; by Feb., parliament recognizes the election results and allows the victors to take office. In Sierra Leone, in June, the third military coup in six years ends the fledgling civilian government. In Thailand, an economic crisis in Mar. forces the government to halt trading in all bank and financial stocks. The crisis continues as the government props up the baht, and Asian neighbours offer loans to help maintain foreign currency reserves. The Philippines, Malaysia and Indonesia devalue their currency, and the IMF offers aid throughout the region in exchange for economic reforms. The Turkish army wipes out Kurdish camps in Northern Iraq. In Scotland, embryologist Ian Wilmut and four colleagues at Roslin Institute near Edinburgh reveal that they had cloned a sheep. In Nevada, British pilot Andy Green breaks the sound barrier on Oct. 13 by driving a jet-propelled automobile at 1,229.775 kph. In the UK, Tony Blair and the Labour Party end 18 years of Conservative rule on May 1 in general elections. Historic peace talks in Northern Ireland begin on Oct. 7 as all parties, including Sinn Fein, try to end violence. British Prime Min. Tony Blair and Sinn Fein leader Gerry Adams meet at Downing Street on Dec. 11 to discuss Northern Ireland's peace—the first such meeting since the 1920s. Viewers around the world watch pictures sent back from Mars by the *Pathfinder* mission in July. On Oct. 6, the space shuttle *Atlantis* docks with the *Mir* space station. On Mars, *Pathfinder* falls silent. On Oct. 15, the space probe *Cassini* is launched for Saturn. In Zaire, Pres. Mobutu Sese Seko flees from an advancing rebel army on May 16; rebel troops subsequently enter Kinshasa, Laurent Kabila takes power, and the country is renamed Democratic Republic of the Congo.

1998: An earthquake in Afghanistan destroys 15,000 homes and kills about 5,000 people (Feb.). In Algeria, terrorist violence surges across the country before Ramadan. In Bangladesh, a 22-year-old war in the southeast ends when tribal fighters surrender their weapons and gain some autonomy for their Buddhist culture (Feb.); in July, monsoons strand 8 million people near the Bangladeshi capital. In Cambodia, Pol Pot, the Khmer Rouge leader responsible for the deaths of two million Cambodians in the 1970s, dies (Apr. 15). In Santiago, Chile, leaders from 34 American countries meet to talk about creating the Free Trade Area of the Americas (Apr. 19); Cuba is excluded. China orders the slaughter of over one million poultry in Hong Kong to end the threat of chicken flu; an earthquake measuring 6.2 on the Richter scale kills 50 and leaves 540,000 homeless in Hebei (Jan.); in Aug., China suffers its worst flood season in 50 years: 3,600 people killed and over 1.4 million people displaced. In Cuba, Pope John Paul II visits Catholics and Fidel Castro (Jan. 21–25). Ethiopia and Eritrea fight a border war (June). Eleven EU governments launch "The New European Way," a manifesto for a socialist Europe (Nov. 22). German Pres. Helmut Kohl, one of Europe's longest-serving leaders, is defeated at the polls by Social Democrat Gerhard Schroeder (Sept. 27). Hurricane Georges hits Haiti, the Dominican Republic and nearby islands, killing over 200 people and leaving hundreds of thousands homeless (Sept.); the following month, Hurricane Mitch devastates Central America over six days, killing more than 10,000 people and leaving 2 million homeless. India and Pakistan exchange artillery fire along the Kashmiri border (May); India explodes three nuclear devices in underground tests on May 11 and two more on May 13; Pakistan announces five successful underground nuclear tests (May 28). Massive flooding in northern and eastern India strands some 1.5 million (Aug. 27). In Indonesia, Pres. Suharto's troops fire on student demonstrators (May 12); a few hundred students occupy the parliament while thousands more gather outside (May 18); Suharto resigns (May 21); the military peacefully clears the parliament of 2,000 student demonstrators (May 22). In Iran, Pres. Khatami calls on the US to resume formal relations with his country for the first time since 1979 (Jan. 7). The Iraqi national assembly votes to suspend co-operation with UN weapons inspectors to protest more than eight years of economic sanctions (Aug. 15); the US and UK carry out air strikes against Iraq to "degrade" Pres. Saddam Hussein's military forces; the attacks, prompted by Iraq's refusal to co-operate with UN weapons inspectors, lack the UN Security Council's support (Dec. 16–20). Former Italian prime minister Silvio Berlusconi is sentenced for bribing tax inspectors (July). In Kenya, a car bomb explodes outside the US embassy; 263 people are killed and over 4,500 are injured; in Tanzania, a second car bomb explodes outside the US embassy, killing 10 and injuring 70 (Aug. 7); the US military fires missiles into the camp of Islamic terrorist Osama bin Laden in retaliation (Aug. 20). In Nigeria, following the death on June 8 of dictator Gen. Sani Abacha, Gen. Abubakar releases hundreds of prisoners and abolishes three discredited electoral bodies (July). In Russia, Pres. Yeltsin fires Prime Min. Viktor Chernomyrdin and his entire Cabinet; Yeltsin then appoints Sergei Kiriyenko as acting prime minister (Mar. 23); amidst economic woes, the IMF and other foreign lenders offer Russia a US$22.6-billion rescue package (July 13). The remains of Czar Nicholas and his family are interred in St. Petersburg (July 17). Pres. Yeltsin fires the entire Cabinet and reappoints Viktor Chernomyrdin as acting prime minister; the Duma refuses to confirm the appointment (Aug. 23); Yeltsin agrees to abandon some powers to get the confirmation (Aug. 29); Yeltsin and the Duma compromise with the confirmation of Yevgeni Primakov as prime minister (Sept.). South African Pres. Mandela receives the report of the Truth and Reconciliation Commission on crimes committed during apartheid (Oct. 29); Pres. Mandela also rules out a general amnesty for crimes committed during apartheid but repeats that amnesties are possible for those who apply for them (Dec. 6). In Sri Lanka, suicide bombers using boats packed with explosives ram a naval convoy transporting troops to Jaffna; two vessels sink and at least 40 soldiers die (Mar.). UN officials say 2.4 million Sudanese face starvation because of a two-year drought and a 15-year civil war (July). After 22 months of talks, the governments of the United Kingdom and Ireland and the warring factions in Ulster agree to permit a refer-

endum on the future of Northern Ireland and the creation of a self-governing Northern Ireland assembly (Apr. 10); while the IRA initially observes the cease-fire, dissident IRA groups cause violence; Sinn Fein votes to support the Easter peace agreement and allows its members to sit in Northern Ireland's new assembly (May 10); by month's end, most Irish (north and south) support the Easter pact; David Trimble, leader of the Ulster Unionist Party, is selected first minister of Northern Ireland's new assembly (July); an IRA splinter group detonates a car bomb in Omagh, killing 29 and injuring over 220 (Aug. 15); John Hume and David Trimble win the 1998 Nobel Peace Prize for their efforts in Northern Ireland (Oct. 16); British authorities arrest Chile's former dictator Augusto Pinochet in London (Oct. 16). The last US shuttle to Russia's *Mir* is launched to aid the aging space station (Jan. 22); US Pres. Clinton gives a deposition in the Paula Jones sexual harassment case (Jan. 17) and denies having sex with White House intern Monica Lewinsky (Jan. 26). US tobacco executives admit that smoking endangers health and agree to a US$368.5-billion settlement in exchange for immunity from further lawsuits (Jan. 29). Two boys, aged 11 and 13, gun down four classmates and a teacher in Jonesboro, Ark. (Mar. 24). The drug company Pfizer releases Viagra. In Florida, more than 120,000 people are evacuated from the paths of wildfires (July). The Dow Jones nosedives in late July—by Aug. 7 it has lost 10 percent of its value—and stock markets around the world follow suit. Monica Lewinsky testifies in Aug. before a grand jury that she had sex with Pres. Clinton between Nov. 1995 and May 1997; Pres. Clinton admits his affair with Lewinsky; the admission prompts calls for his impeachment because he had lied to the public (Sept. 11); Special Prosecutor Kenneth Starr delivers his report on the Lewinsky affair to the US Congress; his report is immediately posted on the Internet; the US House of Representatives asks its judiciary committee to begin an impeachment inquiry against Pres. Clinton for his role in the Lewinsky affair (Oct. 8). Pres. Clinton begins talks with Israeli Prime Min. Netanyahu and Palestinian leader Yasser Arafat in Wye, Md.; the talks break a 19-month impasse in Israeli–Palestinian relations over control of the West Bank (Oct. 15). The

US agrees to send US$600 million in food and food credits to Russia after a poor Russian harvest, and the EU agrees to send another US$500 million in food aid (Nov. 6). US Sen. John Glenn, 77, the oldest person to enter space, and the crew of the US space shuttle *Discovery*, return to earth after nine days in orbit (Nov. 7). Pres. Clinton agrees to pay US$850,000 to Paula Jones to settle her sexual harassment suit (Nov. 13); Kenneth Starr appears before the house judiciary committee to present his case against Pres. Clinton in the Lewinsky affair (Nov. 19); the US House of Representatives approves two articles of impeachment against Pres. Clinton (Dec. 18). In the Balkans, fighting erupts again in Kosovo between ethnic Albanians and Serbian police (Mar. 24) after a 10-day police action against the Kosovar Liberation Front causes about 100 civilian deaths. In May, the conflict spills into the Albanian republic. NATO warplanes fly over Kosovo to end Serbia's four-month battle with insurgents which has left about 300 dead and created 65,000 refugees (June). In Kosovo, 110 people are killed as Kosovar separatists try to enter the territory from Albania and fight the Yugoslavian army (July); fighting subsides in early Aug.; Yugoslavia's Pres. Milosevic and the West negotiate Yugoslavia's troop withdrawal from Kosovo (Oct.); the first unarmed international peacekeepers arrive in Kosovo under the command of the Organization for Security and Co-operation in Europe (Nov. 6).

1999: In Australia, Queensland suffers its worst floods in a century (Feb.). In Bangladesh, floods displace almost one million people (July). In China, more than 70,000 Hong Kong residents mark the 1989 massacre in Beijing's Tiananmen Square (June 4); the flooding of the Yangtze River and its tributaries displaces 1.84 million people (July); Chinese police arrest about 30,000 members of Falun Gong in 30 cities (July 21). In Colombia, FARC guerrillas attack 15 towns; about 200 people die in the fighting (July 8–12); 1.5 million unionized workers strike for two days to protest government austerity measures (Aug. 31–Sept. 1). In the Congo, following the collapse of a cease-fire signed by six African states, the rebel Congolese Rally for Democracy launches a new offensive and drives tens of thousands of refugees into Tanzania (July).

East Timorese vote overwhelmingly for independence from Indonesia after enduring 25 years of state violence (Aug. 30); pro-Jakarta militias step up attacks on East Timorese civilians; by mid-Sept., the Indonesian army withdraws at least 3,500 soldiers from East Timor while 8,000 UN troops under Australian command prepare to arrive and protect the tiny nation. The European Union launches the euro, the new single currency, in 11 countries (Jan. 1); the 20-member European Commission resigns en masse after an independent committee set up by the European Parliament finds the commission guilty of fraud, nepotism and mismanagement (Mar. 16); European Union leaders wrap up a successful summit in Finland, endowing the EU with new military powers and preparing for a peaceful eastward expansion (Dec. 11). In Germany, Berlin replaces Bonn as the capital (Aug. 9). On May 26, for the first time since 1971, Indian fighter jets attack Islamic guerrillas in Jammu and Kashmir; three Indian aircraft are shot down by Pakistan during border fighting (May 27–28); a supercyclone strikes the Bay of Bengal, killing 10,000 and leaving 15 million people homeless (Oct. 29). Indonesian officials confirm the victory of the Indonesian Democratic Party in the June 7 elections—the first held in 44 years (July 15). Iranian Pres. Mohammad Khatami becomes the first Iranian leader to visit the West since 1979 during a visit to Italy (Mar. 9–11). In Mar., US and UK aircraft hammer Iraqi air defences while patrolling "no-fly zones" over Iraq; Anglo-American air strikes continue throughout 1999. In Israel, 200,000 ultra-Orthodox Jews pray near the Supreme Court in Jerusalem to protest the court's alleged religious persecution of them (Feb. 14). In southern Mexico, rains cause flooding and mud slides that kill 450 and leave 315,000 homeless (Oct.). NATO admits three former Warsaw Pact states as members: Poland, Hungary and the Czech Republic (Mar. 12). North Korean officials say thousands of their people have died from famine since 1995 (May 8); US Sec. of State Madeleine Albright announces food aid for North Korea (May 17); North and South Korean navies battle in the Yellow Sea (June 15). In Pakistan, former prime minister Benazir Bhutto is convicted in absentia of corruption and sentenced to five years in prison (Apr. 15); Gen. Pervez Musharraf seizes power in a bloodless coup (Oct. 12). Panama takes control of the Panama Canal from the US (Dec. 31). Pope John Paul II speaks to 700,000 people near Gdansk, Poland (June 5). Portugal returns Macau to China, ending 442 years of colonial rule (Dec.). In Russia, Pres. Yeltsin dismisses the government of Prime Min. Primakov; Sergei Stepashin becomes prime minister (May 12); Russian troops attack Islamic rebels in Dagestan (Aug. 8); Pres. Yeltsin dismisses Prime Min. Stepashin's Cabinet and appoints Vladimir Putin as prime minister (Aug. 9); bombings in Moscow and other Russian cities kill more than 200 people; authorities blame Islamic rebels from Dagestan (Sept.); the Russian military gives the residents of Grozny, Chechnya, until Dec. 11 to evacuate the city; Russian troops assault and capture Grozny the next day; Pres. Yeltsin announces that he is stepping down and handing presidential powers to Prime Min. Vladimir Putin (Dec. 31). Sierra Leone's government agrees to share power with the rebel Revolutionary United Front, ending an eight-year civil war (July 7). South Africa's ANC wins landslide victories in national elections (June 2); Pres. Thabo Mbeki is sworn into office (June 16). In Sri Lanka, Pres. Kumaratunga is injured in one of two bomb blasts that kill at least 18 people and injure 150 others at election rallies (Dec. 18). In Switzerland, the International Olympic Committee, facing allegations of corruption in its selection of host cities, suspends six of its members (Jan. 23–24); in late Jan., four more IOC members resign. Turkish authorities capture Abdullah Ocalan, leader of the Kurdistan Workers' Party, in Kenya; Ocalan's return to Turkey sparks Kurdish protests around the world (Feb. 15); a Turkish court sentences Ocalan to death for leading the Kurdish rebellion (June 29). An earthquake shakes Izmit, Turkey: at least 12,000 people die, 30,000 people are injured and 200,000 are left homeless (Aug. 17). George Robertson, the UK's secretary of state for defence, says the British army has destroyed its stock of two million land mines (Feb. 22); British Prime Min. Tony Blair and Irish Prime Min. Bertie Ahern publish the Hillsborough Declaration, aimed at disarming Irish terrorists and bringing Sinn Fein into a power-sharing executive (Apr. 1); the UK's Prince Edward and Sophie Rhys-Jones wed at Windsor (June 19); more than 10,000 Catholics and Protestants unite in Omagh, Northern Ireland, to mark the anniversary of Ulster's worst IRA bombing (Aug. 15); later, peace talks produce an agreement that allows for a government of Sinn Fein and Ulster Unionists, despite the IRA's refusal to decommission its arsenal (Nov.); Protestant and Catholic adversaries join forces to form the Ulster Assembly (Nov. 29). An American rocket carrying the *Polar Lander* spacecraft takes off for Mars (Jan. 3); US Pres. Clinton delivers his sixth State of the Union Address, concentrating on social security, education and health care (Jan. 19); the US Senate acquits Pres. Clinton of perjury and obstruction charges stemming from the Paula Jones case and the Lewinsky scandal (Feb. 12); Pres. Clinton becomes the first sitting US president to be found in contempt of court when a judge declares that Clinton lied in his 1998 deposition in the Paula Jones case (Apr. 12); US astronomers announce the first discovery of a solar system outside our own orbiting the star Upsilon Andromeda (Apr. 15); two student gunmen attack a high school in Littleton, Colo., killing 13 people before killing themselves (Apr. 20); the space shuttle *Discovery*, carrying Canadian Julie Payette, returns to earth after a 10-day mission (June 6); Texas Gov. George W. Bush Jr declares his bid for the Republican presidential nomination (June 12); US Vice Pres. Al Gore declares his second bid for the Democratic presidential nomination (June 16); Hurricane Floyd batters the US east coast, forcing 3 million people to flee and killing at least six (Sept. 15–17); a US federal judge rules that Microsoft Corp. is a monopoly, declaring that actions by Bill Gates' software empire to protect its dominance hurt consumers (Nov. 5); the space shuttle *Discovery* returns from a 10-day mission with US Sen. John Glenn (Nov. 7); "anti-globalization" activists disrupt a World Trade Organization meeting in Seattle, Wash.; thousands of protesters face riot police armed with pepper spray and armoured cars (Nov. 30). The *Polar Lander* crashes on Mars (Dec. 3); NASA cannot establish contact. In Venezuela, flooding and mud slides create a crisis on Dec. 15 when 30,000 people are killed, 35,000 homes are destroyed and 400,000 people are left homeless. Under threats of NATO air strikes, Yugoslavian Serbs and Albanian Kosovars meet in Paris, France, for unsuccessful talks aimed at ending the fighting in Kosovo (Feb. 6–23); after the talks, NATO launches air strikes against Yugoslavia to force Pres. Milosevic to compromise over Kosovo (Mar. 24); Serbian forces in Kosovo step up "ethnic cleansing" of Albanian Kosovars, creating tens of thousands of refugees; Russian Pres. Yeltsin condemns NATO air strikes against Yugoslavia (Mar. 30); throughout May, NATO air forces hit targets in Serbia and Montenegro; on May 7, NATO mistakenly bombs the Chinese embassy in Belgrade, prompting anti-NATO protests in China; Yugoslavian Pres. Milosevic accepts NATO's peace terms (June 3); NATO's bombing campaign over Yugoslavia stops (June 10); NATO K-FOR and Russian troops enter Kosovo as peacekeepers (June 11–13); by June 20, Yugoslavia's troops in Kosovo are gone; in Belgrade, almost 150,000 demonstrators peacefully demand the resignation of Pres. Milosevic (Aug. 19).

2000: In Algeria, a six-month amnesty ends; the government claims that 6,000 Islamic guerrillas have surrendered and vows to fight the estimated 1,500 at large (Jan.). In Cambodia, the worst flooding in 70 years displaces 3.4 million people (Nov.). In Chile, former dictator Gen. Augusto Pinochet is arrested in Santiago for kidnapping and murder (Dec. 8). Colombia's National Liberation Army kidnaps 55 people (Sept. 17); three hostages die and the rest are not freed until Nov. The Dutch parliament votes by a margin of three to one to give same-sex couples the right to marry, adopt children and divorce (Sept. 12); Dutch parliamentarians follow up by voting to allow euthanasia and physician-assisted suicide in special cases (Nov. 28). Thousands of protesters storm Ecuador's national palace after a rebellion, led by Indians and backed by the military, forces the unpopular president to flee (Jan. 21). A drought in Ethiopia leaves more than eight million people short of food and seeking international aid (Apr.); Ethiopia announces the end of a two-year war with Eritrea (June); however, Eritreans vow to fight on until all disputed territory is returned to them; in Addis Ababa, the remains of Emperor Haile Selassie are laid to rest 25 years after his death (Nov. 5). In France, over 90 attacks occur on Jewish targets; authorities blame French-Arabs inspired by the Palestinian intifada (Oct.). Ariel Sharon's

visit to the Temple Mount in Sept. fuels continuing Israeli–Palestinian violence in Oct.; Israeli Prime Min. Ehud Barak announces his resignation (Dec. 10). In Japan, 16,000 people are evacuated from villages on Hokkaido as Mt Usu sends ash and rocks into the air and mud slides down its slopes (Apr.); over 13,000 Japanese suffer from food poisoning caused by contaminated milk products (July). In Korea, 100 families reunite in Seoul and Pyongyang 50 years after the nation's division into two antagonistic states (Aug.). South Lebanon descends into chaos after units of an Israeli-allied militia abandon their positions and Shiite Muslim guerrillas reclaim villages held by Israel for two decades (May 22). In Malaysia, the show trial of former deputy prime minister Anwar Ibrahim ends in a conviction on sodomy charges and a nine-year sentence (Aug.). In Mexico, Vicente Fox is elected president, ending 71 years of rule by the Institutional Revolutionary Party (July 2). In the Philippines, the House of Representatives impeaches Pres. Joseph Estrada for corruption, bribery and betrayal of public trust (Nov. 13). In Russia, acting Pres. Vladimir Putin announces that troops have captured the last rebel stronghold in Grozny (Feb. 6); Putin is elected president (Mar. 26); the lower house of the Russian parliament ratifies the START II Treaty between the US and Russia (Apr.): the agreement, approved by the US in 1996, calls for reducing the number of nuclear warheads on ballistic missiles to 3,500 each by 2007. The Russian nuclear submarine *Kursk* sinks to the floor of the Barents Sea with 118 sailors on board, after an explosion blows a hole through its starboard side (Aug. 14). The Serbian presidential election is marred by corruption and ballot irregularities, but Vojislav Kostunica clearly defeats Pres. Slobodan Milosevic (Sept. 24); Milosevic's refusal to leave office prompts the opposition to block roads, strike, burn parliament buildings and seize the government TV station; on Oct. 6, Milosevic concedes defeat. After almost a decade of chaos, more than 2,000 Somali clan leaders and citizens meet in Djibouti to form a central Somali government (Aug. 13). In Spain, one million people gather in Madrid to protest a car-bomb attack blamed on Basque terrorists (Jan. 22). In Uganda, more than 900 members of a religious cult are found dead (Mar.). On Dec. 15, Ukrainian engineers shut down the last nuclear reactor in Chernobyl, site of the world's worst nuclear accident in 1986. The UK resumes direct control over Northern Ireland when it becomes clear on Feb. 11 that the IRA will not meet conditions set for the Feb. 12 decommissioning of weapons; in May, the IRA agrees to international monitoring of arms dumps as a way around the impasse over weapons decommissioning. The UK incorporates the European Convention on Human Rights, establishing specific rights to privacy, family life, free expression and fair trials in its judicial system (Oct.). Eva Morris, the world's oldest woman, dies at age 114 (Nov. 2). In the US, Smith & Wesson agrees to install locks on its firearms to make them more childproof in exchange for the dropping of government lawsuits seeking damages for gun violence (Mar. 17). Technology stocks on the New York stock market suffer record drops in value: the NASDAQ index records a fall from US$6.71 trillion on Mar. 10 to US$5.61 trillion on Apr. 4. Celera Genomics says it has decoded all of the DNA pieces that make up the genetic pattern of a single human being (Apr. 6). Elian Gonzalez returns to Cuba from the US with his father (June 28), seven months after the boy's rescue at sea near Florida. The US and Vietnamese governments agree to lower trade barriers and increase US investment in Vietnam (July). The US House of Representatives votes to end restrictions on travel and limits on the sale of food and medicine to Cuba (July). In New York, Chase Manhattan Corp. reaches a deal to buy J.P. Morgan & Co. for about US$36 billion (Sept. 13); federal prosecutors conclude that insufficient evidence exists to charge Pres. Clinton or Hillary Clinton with fraud in the Whitewater affair (Sept. 20); the statement ends a six-year investigation into the Clintons' real estate transactions before they entered the White House; the US presidential election ends in stalemate (Nov. 7); Republican George W. Bush Jr is certified the winner on Nov. 26, but a ballot recount in Florida and legal challenges to Bush's victory continue into Dec. Pope John Paul II asks for God's forgiveness for the sins of Roman Catholics through the ages, including wrongs inflicted on Jews, women and minorities (Mar. 12); a terrorist's bomb explodes on the USS *Cole* in the harbour at Aden, Yemen, killing 17 and injuring 38 US sailors (Oct. 12). In Zimbabwe, Pres. Robert Mugabe

backs landless blacks as they take over commercial farms; the government passes a law allowing the government to confiscate white-owned farms (Apr. 6); Zimbabwe's highest court orders the government to remove squatters from about 1,000 mostly white-owned farms (Apr. 13), but police refuse to enforce the order; on Aug. 1, Zimbabwe's government confirms plans to confiscate more than half of all white-owned farmland and redistribute it to 500,000 poor black families.

2001: In Afghanistan, Taliban forces destroy art—including two huge fifth-century Buddhas carved into a mountainside in Bamiyan—because, government spokesmen say, art tempts Muslims to worship images, which is forbidden (Mar. 10); the Taliban order all non-Muslims to wear yellow cloth to identify themselves to officials (May); after the attacks on the US by terrorists on Sept. 11, tensions with the US increase; thousands of Afghans flee to Pakistan to avoid the coming war (Sept.); Arab TV station al-Jazeera broadcasts a videotape of al-Qaeda leader Osama bin Laden commending the Sept. 11 attacks (Oct. 7); on Oct. 7, the military phase of the US-led "war on terrorism" begins as US and UK air forces bomb military sites and suspected al-Qaeda camps in Afghanistan; Taliban forces flee Kabul (Nov.); al-Qaeda leader Mohammed Atef dies in a US raid (Nov. 13); US ground forces move in (Nov. 25); at a UN-led conference in Germany, Hamid Karzai emerges as head of an Afghan interim government (Dec. 5); the Taliban surrender Kandahar (Dec. 7). In Algeria, a student's death in police custody touches off two months of rioting (Apr. 18); at least 700 people die and hundreds more disappear after three days of rain, flooding and mud slides; Algiers is hardest hit (Nov. 10). Argentine Pres. Fernando de la Rua resigns (Dec. 20) amid demonstrations over the collapsing economy and austerity measures; Interim Pres. Adolpho Rodriguez Saa threatens the biggest government default in history (Dec. 23); Rodriguez, facing angry demonstrators, declares his resignation (Dec. 31). In Bosnia and Herzegovina, the government decides to co-operate with the International Criminal Tribunal for the Former Yugoslavia (Oct. 2); Radovan Karadzic and Ratko Mladic face arrest. In Brazil, over 20,000 prisoners stage co-ordinated riots, which kill 16 people, in prisons in Sao Paulo state (Feb. 18). Three explosions rock the Petrobras rig—the world's biggest offshore oil platform—killing 10 workers (Mar. 16), but over 160 people are saved before the rig sinks north of Rio de Janeiro (Mar. 20). In Chile, a court rules that Gen. Augusto Pinochet cannot be tried on human rights charges because of the former dictator's deteriorating mental health (July). China successfully launches its second unmanned spacecraft (Jan.). In Beijing, five Falun Gong supporters set themselves on fire in Tiananmen Square; one woman dies (Jan. 23). A US spy plane is forced to land in China after colliding with a Chinese fighter plane (Apr. 1); the Chinese pilot is killed when his plane crashes; the US crew is held for 11 days until the Chinese accept a US apology; 14 imprisoned members of the Falun Gong sect commit suicide in a labour camp (July). Chinese celebrate in Tiananmen Square when they learn that Beijing will host the 2008 Summer Olympic Games (July 13). In Colombia, two Liberal politicians are assassinated in Oct. amid revolutionary violence. In the Congo, Pres. Laurent Kabila dies after his bodyguard shoots him in Kinshasa (Jan. 17); Kabila's son, Joseph, becomes president. In Cuba, 750,000 are evacuated from homes when Hurricane Michelle hits the coast (Nov. 4); on Nov. 21, the government agrees to buy food from US companies to replace damaged crops, marking the first commercial export of food from the US to Cuba since 1959. In Ecuador, an oil tanker runs aground near the Galapagos Islands and threatens wildlife with a 1,200-sq. km oil slick. In El Salvador, an earthquake kills nearly 700 people, destroys 91,000 homes and causes US$1.5 billion in damage (Jan. 13); a second, more destructive, quake on Feb. 16 kills at least 280 people, injures more than 2,400 and leaves another 123,000 homeless. EU officials announce a moratorium on cod fishing in 20 percent of the North Sea to save dwindling cod stocks (Jan.). On the southern coast of France, a ship carrying about 1,500 people—mainly Kurds seeking asylum and work—runs aground (Feb. 23). In France, the first case of foot-and-mouth disease in livestock is confirmed (Mar. 12); new cases are also reported in Argentina, Saudi Arabia and the UAE; a surgical team in New York successfully performs a gallbladder operation on a patient in Strasbourg, France, by sending high-speed signals to robots (Sept. 7). In Germany, former chancellor Helmut Kohl agrees to pay a fine to settle a criminal investigation over illegal campaign contributions (Feb.). Flooding along Europe's Tizla River kills seven and forces the evacuation of 30,000 people in Hungary, Romania and Ukraine (Mar.). In India, an earthquake hits Gujarat, killing 15,000, injuring 60,000 and leaving 600,000 homeless (Jan. 26). Terrorist bombings occur in Oct. and Dec.; Indian and Pakistani troops exchange fire over Kashmir (Dec. 28). In Indonesia, over 7,000 Madurese immigrants flee Borneo for Java after Dayak tribesmen kill 469 of them during a week of violence (Feb. 24); 350 asylum seekers headed for Australia drown when their boat sinks near Java; fishermen rescue 44 survivors, who return to Indonesia (Oct. 20). Iraq and Egypt sign a free trade agreement (Jan.); US and UK jets bomb nearly 20 radar sites near Baghdad (Feb. 16). In Israel, Ariel Sharon defeats Ehud Barak in a prime ministerial election (Feb. 6). A Palestinian suicide bomber in Tel Aviv detonates a belt of explosives in a crowd, killing 18 and injuring 115 Israelis (June 1); the act brings the death toll from violence since Sept. 2000 to over 520 people. An Israeli military helicopter destroys the office of Palestinian Pres. Yasser Arafat (July); continuing violence prompts Israel to send tanks into the West Bank territory to engage Palestinian fighters (Aug. 14). On Oct. 2, US Pres. Bush expresses support for a Palestinian state so long as Israel's right to exist is respected; UK Prime Min. Tony Blair and Israeli Foreign Min. Shimon Peres follow suit (Oct.). Israeli forces kill Hamas leader Mahmoud Abu Hanoud (Nov. 23); Palestinian suicide bombers kill at least 25 people (Dec. 1–2); Israelis attack targets in the West Bank and Gaza Strip; Palestinian Pres. Yasser Arafat demands an end to attacks on Israelis (Dec. 16). In Italy, one demonstrator dies during a riot at the G8 summit meeting in Genoa (July 20). Ministers of 180 countries agree on the final details of the Kyoto Protocol, which commits signatories to reduce greenhouse gas emissions (Nov. 11). In Macedonia, Albanian rebels, fighting for independence in Kosovo, advance within mortar distance of the capital's airport as NATO and the country's government try to arrange a cease-fire and disarm the rebels (June); the Macedonian government announces a cease-fire with Albanian rebels in July, but a NATO-inspired peace deal sparks riots as forces attempt to move 300 Albanian fighters north (July); rival political leaders sign a peace accord aimed at ending six months of conflict and allowing NATO to disarm Albanian rebels (Aug.); the leader of Macedonia's Albanian rebels declares on Sept. 27 that his group has disbanded; NATO promises to provide security in Macedonia. Nepalese Crown Prince Dipendra kills his parents and nine other family members before turning the gun on himself (June 1). In the Netherlands, a Scottish court sitting in Camp Zeist convicts a Libyan agent of murder and sentences him to life in prison for the 1998 bombing of Pan Am Flight 103 over Lockerbie, Scotland, which killed 270 passengers; a second man is acquitted (Jan. 30). Norway resumes the export of whale products and angers conservationists opposed to commercial whaling (Jan. 22). Pakistan's military ruler, Gen. Pervez Musharraf, dismisses the president and takes the post himself (June 20); Musharraf dismisses hard-liners from senior military posts to distance Pakistan from Islamic militants and Taliban supporters (Oct. 7); gunmen kill about 15 people in a church in Bahawalpur (Oct. 28). An airplane flying to Portugal runs out of fuel in mid-flight but glides for 180 km and lands safely, without power, in the Azores (Aug. 24). Russia's space station *Mir* burns up in the earth's atmosphere over the South Pacific (Mar. 23). In Russian Yakutia, flooding displaces 42,000 people and causes $6 billion in damage along the Lena River; (May); Russia legalizes the sale of urban land for the first time since 1917 (Oct. 26). In Rwanda, four people get prison terms of 12 to 20 years for their roles in the 1994 Hutu extermination of Tutsis (June). In Saudi Arabia, 35 Muslim pilgrims are acci-dentally trampled to death outside Mecca (Mar. 5); in Medina, Saudi commandos storm a Russian airliner hijacked by Chechen rebels, freeing more than 100 passengers and crew (Mar. 16). In Durban, South Africa, a UN conference on racism sees controversy over a resolution equating Zionism and anti-Arab racism (Sept.). In Sri Lanka, a govern-ment ship sinks two boats belonging to Tamil rebels, killing 25 (Oct. 5); LTTE-owned boats sink a government oil tanker, killing 11 (Oct. 29). In Ukraine, a stray missile hits a Russian airliner over the Black Sea, killing all 78 on board (Oct. 4). British researchers say that the middle of the ice sheet in West Antarctica thinned by 10 m between 1992 and 1999 and fear that ice melting at a similar rate on Pine Island Glacier will raise ocean levels and threaten coastal cities around the world (Feb.). In the UK, an outbreak of foot-and-mouth disease first spotted in a slaughterhouse in Essex on Feb. 19 leads to the destruction of thousands of cattle and sheep. The worst riots in Belfast in three years injure 39 police (June 21); Belfast rioters injure 110 police officers after the Orange Order parades past a Catholic neigh-bourhood (July 13); 120 police officers in northern England are injured by mobs of white and South Asian youths armed with bats, rocks and firebombs (July 22); Protestant demonstrators scream and throw stones as Catholic girls walk to school in their Belfast neighbourhood (Sept.); Sinn Fein leader Gerry Adams and Martin McGuinness call on the IRA to disarm (Oct. 22); the IRA complies the next day. In the US, George W. Bush Jr is sworn in as 43rd president (Jan. 20); nine people die when the USS *Greeneville*, a nuclear submarine, surfaces underneath a Japanese fishing boat near Hawaii (Feb. 9); a California court rules that Napster, the Internet service used to swap music, must stop helping its users with illegal exchanges of copyrighted material (Feb.); Pres. Bush drops plans to support legislation that requires power plants to reduce carbon dioxide emissions, the chief greenhouse gas implicated in global warming (Mar.); a US court finds Ahmed Ressam, an Algerian, guilty of nine criminal offences— including conspiracy to commit terrorist acts by importing explosives into the US from Canada to disrupt millennium celebrations (Apr. 6). Two days of rioting and looting rock Cincinnati following the Apr. 7 killing of an unarmed black man by police—the fifth such killing by city police in seven months; protests subside on Apr. 11. California millionaire Dennis Tito, the world's first space tourist, spends six days at international space station *Alpha* (Apr. 28). Convicted Oklahoma City bomber Timothy McVeigh is executed (June 11). Microsoft wins a key legal battle when a US court overturns an order to break up the company. The US National Academy of Sciences releases a report confirming that global warming is a serious problem (June). Doctors in Kentucky implant the first self-contained artificial heart in a human, 59-year-old Robert Tools (July 2). Pres. Bush approves federal funding for limited medical research on stem cells extracted from human embryos (Aug.). On Sept. 11, the US suffers the worst terrorist attack in its history, with total casualties over 3,000; two US passenger airplanes hijacked by Islamic terrorists fly into both towers of New York's World Trade Center, exploding on impact and collapsing both towers; a third US passenger airplane hijacked by Islamic terrorists crashes into the Pentagon in Washington, DC; a fourth hijacked plane crashes into a field outside Shanksville, Pa.; after the attacks, the US administration builds a global alliance to combat terrorism; suspects are detained in Canada, the UK, Germany and other countries to find supporters of the suicide pilots; the US and its allies focus attention on the Taliban in Afghanistan and their "guest" Osama bin Laden, a Saudi terrorist; many countries mourn for the victims (Sept. 14); the US stock market falls, losing a trillion dollars in value; hundreds of thousands of airline and travel workers are laid off as people forsake air travel; news agencies and government offices receive mail containing deadly anthrax; four US citizens die (Oct.). Four men get life sentences in prison (Oct. 18) for the 1998 bombings of US embassies in Tanzania and Kenya. Energy giant Enron Corp. files for bankruptcy protection (Dec. 2). In Yugoslavia, commandos storm the retreat of ex-president Milosevic and arrest him for corruption after a two-day stand-off (Apr 1); Milosevic is extradited to The Hague (June 28) to stand before the war crimes tribunal on charges of crimes against humanity for the deaths of Albanian Kosovars in 1999. In Zimbabwe, the supreme court, recently stacked with Pres. Robert Mugabe's appointees, overturns rulings that declare the government's racially based program of land redistribution unconstitutional (Oct. 2).

2002: In Afghanistan, the US ground troops attack Taliban and al-Qaeda holdouts in Operation Anaconda (Mar. 1); Afghanistan's interim government reopens schools and girls attend for the first time since 1996 (Mar. 23); earthquakes kill as many as 1,800 people and leave 100,000 homeless (Mar. 25); King Mohammed Zahir Shah returns on Apr. 18 after living in Italy since 1973; Canadian soldiers launch Operation Torii (May 4). In Angola, UNITA founder and leader Jonas Savimbi dies in battle (Feb. 22). In Antarctica, scientists report on Mar. 19 that the Larsen B Shelf, a mass of ice 3,250 sq. km wide and

200 metres thick, has fallen into the ocean and broken apart in just a few months; scientists say that the rate of warming in the region is greater than elsewhere on earth. In Argentina, newly elected Pres. Eduardo Duhalde defaults on the nation's debt (Jan. 3); US Pres. Bush says that IMF and other financial help will continue as long as the government continues market reforms (Jan. 11); Argentina's supreme court rules that banking restrictions imposed in Dec. are unconstitutional (Feb. 1); the government declares Feb. 4–5 bank holidays to forestall a new run on the banks but rioting continues; banks close throughout Apr. 19–29 to control outflows of money after the lifting of banking restrictions. Bahrain becomes a constitutional monarchy (Feb. 14). The value of Brazil's currency enters a freefall after US Treasury Sec. Paul O'Neill criticizes financial aid to Latin America (July 28); Brazil's government announces the creation of Tumucumaque National Park, the world's largest rain forest reserve, in the northern Amazon (Aug. 23). The UN reports that at least 15 political killings occurred in Cambodia before elections on Feb 3. Political violence plagues Colombia: on Feb. 20, after the kidnapping of a senator, Pres. Andres Pastrana ends talks with FARC rebels and orders the military seizure of the FARC enclave, a demilitarized zone created in 1998; the bodies of a senator and two companions are discovered near Bogotá (Mar. 2); Catholic Archbishop Isaias Duarte is murdered in Cali (Mar. 16); the FARC kidnaps 12 legislators in a regional assembly (Apr. 11); presidential candidate Alvaro Uribe escapes a bomb blast that kills three and injures 15 (Apr. 14); 117 people die when the FARC mortars a church in Bojaya in the worst massacre of civilians in Colombia's 38-year civil war (May 2); FARC bombs kill 20 people at Pres. Uribe's inauguration (Aug. 6); at the UN, Pres. Uribe asks for help in his war against the rebel armies and the drug trade that finances them (Sept. 14). In Côte d'Ivoire, a military revolt provokes heavy fighting in three cities (Sept. 19); French and US soldiers subsequently evacuate foreigners trapped in the country. In the Democratic Republic of the Congo, Mt Nyiragogo erupts on Jan. 17, causing 500,000 people to flee their homes; on Sept. 6, DRC Pres. Joseph Kabila and Ugandan Pres. Yoweri Musevine sign a peace agreement to end a four-year war that has embroiled six African states. In Egypt, a military court sentences 51 Islamists to

prison for plotting to overthrow the government and assassinate Pres. Mubarak (Sept. 9). The euro, the single currency adopted by 12 members of the European Union, becomes legal tender (Jan. 1). In Europe, heavy rains cause rivers to flood cities in Austria, the Czech Republic, Germany, Hungary and Slovakia (mid-Aug.). In Greece, police arrest seven members of the terrorist organization called November 17, including leader Alexandros Giotopoulos (July 18). In Gujarat, India, sectarian violence kills hundreds of Hindus and Muslims in Feb. and Mar.; in May, violence breaks out in Kashmir; in Sept., before a state election in Kashmir, a government minister is assassinated and more than 600 people die; India blames the violence on Islamic militants based in Pakistan. In northwestern Iran, hundreds are killed and injured during an earthquake (June 22). In Iraq, Pres. Saddam Hussein warns that US attempts to change his regime will meet fierce resistance (Aug. 8); terrorist Abu Nidal is found dead, apparently of suicide, in his home in Baghdad (Aug. 20); Iraq agrees to allow UN weapons inspections, prompting dissension in the UN Security Council (Sept. 16); US jets bomb the civilian airport in Basra for the second time (Sept. 29); the chief UN weapons inspector and Iraqi officials begin talks in Vienna aimed at reopening UN weapons inspections in Iraq (Sept. 30). Violence plagues Israel and the Palestinian Territories: after a Palestinian suicide bomber attacks Jerusalem, Israel attacks Gaza City and destroys Palestinian Pres. Yasser Arafat's headquarters (Mar. 10); Israel raids a refugee camp in the Gaza Strip (Mar. 11); Israel occupies Ramallah (Mar. 12); the UN Security Council adopts a resolution supporting the creation of a Palestinian state (the US vetoed previous attempts) on Mar. 12; Israel attacks Pres. Arafat's Ramallah compound (Mar. 29); Israel occupies Palestinian towns in the West Bank (Apr. and June); a clash occurs at the Jenin refugee camp (Apr.); Palestinians and Israelis end a month-long stand-off at Bethlehem's Church of the Nativity (May 6); Israeli forces destroy Pres. Arafat's compound in Ramallah (June 6); Israel begins construction of a 115-km barrier to cordon off the West Bank; deadly Palestinian attacks continue (June–July); US Pres. Bush declares that a Palestinian state will be achieved if people abandon terrorism and if Pres. Arafat steps down (June 24); Israeli forces kill Hamas founder and military commander, Salah Shehada, along with 14 others in Gaza City (July 23); Israeli forces kill Nasir Jarrar, a Hamas military leader, in the West Bank (Aug. 14). In Italy, Interior Min. Claudio Scajola proclaims a state of emergency on Mar. 21 because of a sudden increase in illegal immigrants landing on the coast. Dozens of sailors are killed or injured in a naval battle between North and South Korea over a disputed sea boundary (June 30); both states blame each other for starting their biggest naval clash in three years; the two Koreas agree to clear land mines in the demilitarized zone (Sept. 14). In Myanmar, pro-democracy leader Aung San Suu Kyi is unconditionally freed (May 6); she had been under house arrest since Sept. 2000 and under heavy restrictions since 1989. In Nepal, battles between government soldiers and Maoist rebels leave more than 140 dead in Feb. In the Netherlands, Prime Min. Wim Kok and his government resign on Apr. 16 after the Netherlands Institute for War Documentation says that Dutch peacekeeping troops shared the blame for allowing the massacre of more than 8,000 Muslim males in Srebrenica, Bosnia, in 1995; on May 6, electoral candidate Pim Fortuyn is shot in the first political assassination in Dutch history. In Nigeria, the first execution under Islamic Sharia law—practised in northern states since Jan. 2000—is carried out (Jan. 3); explosions in a Lagos army barracks kill more than 600 people (Jan. 27); thousands flee and at least 100 people die in ethnic riots in Lagos (Jan. 4–6). In Pakistan, Pres. Pervez Musharraf emphasizes his commitment to ending terrorism and appeals for an end to extremism; police raid schools and mosques, arresting more than 300 Muslim extremists (Jan. 12); US journalist Daniel Pearl is confirmed dead (Feb. 21) when Pakistani officials receive a videotape of his murder; a grenade attack on a church in Islamabad kills a US diplomat and others (Mar. 17); al-Qanoon ("the Law") explodes a car bomb outside the US consulate in Karachi, killing 13 people (June 14); gunmen attack a Christian school and a church (Aug.). In the Philippines, US troops join government forces to fight Abu-Sayyaf, Islamic militants believed to be linked to al-Qaeda (Jan. 16). In Russia, TV-6, the last large independent TV station, is taken off the air (Jan. 21); a bomb explodes in Kaspiisk, a Caspian port city, during the Victory Day parade, killing at least 41 people (May 9); officials blame Chechen rebels for the attack; in Moscow,

Russian and US leaders sign the Strategic Offensive Reductions Treaty (SORT) on May 24, making official their Nov. 2001 pledge to reduce nuclear arsenals; Russia remains unreconciled to US plans for a missile defence program; during a Russia–EU summit in Moscow, the EU formally recognizes Russia as a market economy (May 30); Russian officials confirm that the *Kursk* sank after a faulty torpedo on board exploded (June 19); the Duma passes a bill allowing the sale of farmland (June 26); flash floods on the Black Sea coast kill at least 59 people (Aug. 10); fighting between Russian and Chechen forces continues in Chechnya. The leaders of Serbia, Montenegro and the Federal Republic of Yugoslavia agree to maintain a joint state named Serbia and Montenegro (Mar. 14). In Sierra Leone, Pres. Ahmed Tejan Kabbah leads a ceremony to mark the end of the 10-year-old civil war (Jan. 18); UN-sponsored elections occur in Sierra Leone and 17,000 peacekeepers observe them (May 14). In South Africa, Pres. Joseph Kabila of the Democratic Republic of the Congo and Rwandan Pres. Paul Kagame sign a peace agreement on July 30 to end a four-year war that killed about 2.5 million people. In Sri Lanka, the government and separatist Tamil Tigers sign an indefinite cease-fire agreement (Feb. 22); during peace talks in Sept., the Tamil Tigers drop their demand for an independent state. In the United Kingdom, cattle herds are declared free of foot-and-mouth disease on Jan. 14 after the destruction of more than four million sheep and cattle in two years; Colm Murphy is convicted for his role in the IRA bombing in Omagh, which killed 29 people in 1998 (Jan. 25); in Belfast, Protestant gunmen fire on Catholic homes (Apr.); 400 rioting youths throw homemade bombs at police (Apr. 3); police blame the Ulster Defence Association for orchestrating the riot; the IRA hands over another instalment of weapons to disarmament officials (Apr. 8); the IRA apologizes for the deaths of hundreds of non-combatants over 30 years in Northern Ireland (July 16). The Rome Statute of the International Criminal Court—the first permanent war crimes court—enters into force (July 1); the UN Security Council grants temporary immunity from the ICC to Americans serving with UN peacekeeping troops (July 12). The US begins moving captured Afghans to a naval base at Guantanamo Bay in Cuba; US officials refuse to guarantee that these "illegal combatants"

will be treated according to the Geneva Convention (Jan. 10); in his State of the Union address, Pres. Bush identifies Iran, Iraq and North Korea as an "axis of evil" of terrorist states (Jan. 12); Pres. Bush unveils the "Green Skies" plan—the US government alternative to the Kyoto agreement—to cut greenhouse gas emissions and pollution from power plants (Feb. 14); Vice-Pres. Dick Cheney begins a tour of Arab countries to win support for US plans to depose Iraqi Pres. Saddam Hussein (Mar. 12); the US rejects the International Criminal Court treaty (May 6); authorities reveal that a plot to set off a radioactive "dirty" bomb in the US has been thwarted (June 10); the US formally withdraws from the Antiballistic Missile Treaty (June 13); a Houston court finds accounting firm Arthur Andersen guilty of obstructing justice by shredding documents about the Enron financial scandal (June 15); WorldCom, the country's second-largest long-distance telecommunications company, announces on June 25 that it has overstated its cash flow by US$3.8 billion since the start of 2001; world markets enter a steep dive and WorldCom files for bankruptcy protection in July. Pres. Bush says the US will use "all the tools at [its] disposal" to remove Saddam Hussein under the policy of "regime change" (July 8); Pres. Bush signs a corporate responsibility law to reform business practices and restore investor confidence (July 30); Pres. Bush declares that the US will act unilaterally to remove Pres. Saddam Hussein if the UN cannot arrange unconditional weapons inspections in Iraq (Sept. 12). Pope John Paul II condemns child sexual abuse by priests, describing it as "grievously evil" (Mar. 22). In Zimbabwe, the government passes the Public Order and Security Bill, restricting freedom of expression, and the General Laws Amendment Bill, restricting foreign election monitors (Jan. 10); the government passes the Access to Information Bill, restricting the presence of foreign media (Jan. 31); EU officials impose sanctions on Pres. Robert Mugabe and his associates, including an arms embargo, a travel ban, a freezing of funds and the withdrawal of development aid (Feb. 18); Pres. Mugabe claims re-election in an election fraught with irregularities (Mar. 14); the Commonwealth suspends Zimbabwe's membership for one year (Mar. 19); police arrest dozens of white farmers who refuse to give up their land (Aug.). (See also "News Events" on pages 817–44.)

NATIONS OF THE WORLD

THE STATISTICS SHOWN ARE INTENDED TO PRESENT an informative and comparative picture of the various nations of the world and their dependent territories. All data, including the geographic, population and government data, are taken from the latest available sources. The economic and finance/trade data indicate the size of the national economies and the amount of economic activity in the respective countries; the population, health and education data, and communications and transportation data give some evidence of the quality of life and the state of the infrastructure in each nation.

All dollar amounts are in US dollars. International dollar price weights have been used instead of an official currency exchange rate in an attempt to make more equitable comparisons.

The "Total Fertility Rate" figure represents the number of children born per woman, and indicates the potential for population growth. A high total fertility rate will have an impact on a nation's workforce—women's participation may be limited; it may also have an impact on the amount of education available and the level of education achieved in the general population.

The information contained in this section reflects data available up to and including October 1, 2003. Sources used for information include:

CIA World Fact Book 2002 • *"Compendium of Statistics: Illiteracy" (UNESCO)* • *"Facts on File"* • *Demographic Yearbook (UN)* • *Encyclopedia Britannica* • *Direction of Trade Statistics (International Monetary Fund)* • *Foreign Affairs Canada* • *Government Finance Statistics Monthly (International Monetary Fund)* • *"Human Development Report" (UN Development Programme)* • *International Financial Statistics Yearbook (International Monetary Fund)* • *International Financial Statistics (monthly IMF update)* • *"Keesing's Record of World Events"* • *Monthly Bulletin of Statistics (UN Statistical Division)* • *"Population and Vital Statistics Report" (UN Dept. of International Economic and Social Affairs)* • *Statesman's Yearbook (Macmillan)* • *UNESCO Statistical Yearbook* • *World Bank Atlas (World Bank)* • *World Book Encyclopedia* • *World Culture Report (UNESCO)* • *World Debt Tables* • *"World Development Report" (World Bank)* • *"World Motor Vehicle Data" (Motor Vehicle Manufacturers Assoc. of the US Inc.)* • *"World Population" (UNESCO)* • *"World Population Data Sheet" (Population Reference Bureau Inc.)* • *World Resources (World Resources Institute)* • *World Statistics Pocketbook* • *"World Tables" (Johns Hopkins UP)* • *Worldwide Government Directory with International Organizations (Belmont Publications)* • *Year Book of Labour Statistics (International Labour Office, Geneva).*

Afghanistan

Long-Form Name: Islamic State of Afghanistan; **Capital:** Kabul

■ GEOGRAPHY

Area: 647,500 sq. km
Coastline: none: landlocked
Climate: arid to semi-arid; cold winters and hot summers, considerable snowfall
Environment: damaging earthquakes occur in Hindu Kush mountains; poor soil, flooding, desertification, overgrazing, deforestation (largely due to logging for building materials and fuel), pollution, soil degradation. Drought and land mines remaining from the war make it impossible in many areas to grow even the most essential food supplies

Terrain: mostly rugged mountains; plains in north and southwest
Land Use: 12% arable land; no permanent crops; 46% meadows and pastures; 3% forest and woodland; 39% other; includes about 24,000 sq. km of irrigated farmland
Location: SW Asia (Middle East)

■ PEOPLE

Population: 27,755,775 (July 2002 est.)
Nationality: Afghan
Age Structure: 0–14 yrs: 42.0%; 15–64: 55.2%; 65+: 2.8% (2002 est.)
Population Growth Rate: 3.43% (2002 est.)
Net Migration: 10.7 migrants/1,000 population (2002 est.)

Ethnic Groups: 38% Pathan, 25% Tajik, 6% Uzbek, 19% Hazara; minor ethnic groups include Charar Aimaks, Turkoman, Baloch and others
Languages: 35% Pushtu (official), 50% Afghan Persian (Dari), 11% Turkic languages (primarily Uzbek and Turmen), 4% thirty minor languages (primarily Balochi and Pahai); much bilingualism
Religions: Islam (84% Sunni Muslim, 15% Shi'a Muslim), 1% other
Birth Rate: 41.03/1,000 population (2002 est.)
Death Rate: 17.43/1,000 population (2002 est.)
Infant Mortality: 144.76 deaths/1,000 live births (2002 est.)
Life Expectancy at Birth: 47.32 years male, 45.85 years female (2002 est.)
Total Fertility Rate: 5.72 children born/woman (2002 est.)
Literacy: 31.5% (1999 est.)

■ **GOVERNMENT**

Leader(s): Pres. Hamid Karzai
Government Type: transitional
Administrative Divisions: 30 provinces (velayat, sing. & pl.)
Nationhood: Aug. 19, 1919 (from UK)
National Holiday: Victory of the Muslim Nation, Apr. 28; Remembrance Day for Martyrs and Disabled, May 4; Independence Day, August 19

■ **ECONOMY**

Overview: a poor country, largely dependent on farming (wheat) and livestock (sheep and goats); the economy is adversely affected by political and military disruptions; much of the population continues to suffer from insufficient food, clothing, housing and medical care; inflation remains a serious problem; government efforts to encourage foreign investment have failed
GDP: US$21 billion, per capita US$800; real growth rate n.a. (2000 est.)
Inflation: n.a.
Industries: accounts for 20% of GDP; small-scale production of textiles, soap, furniture, shoes, fertilizer and cement; handwoven carpets; natural gas, oil, coal, copper
Labour Force: 11.4 million (2001); 80% agriculture and animal husbandry, 10% industry, 10% services and other
Unemployment: n.a.
Agriculture: largely subsistence farming and nomadic animal husbandry; cash products—opium poppies, wheat, fruit, nuts, karakul pelts, wool, mutton, barley, corn; production is limited due to the shortage of modern machinery, high-grade seed and fertilizer. Accounts for 60% of GDP.

Natural Resources: natural gas, crude oil, copper, coal, salt, talc, barites, sulphur, lead, zinc, iron ore, slate, precious and semi-precious stones, especially lapis lazuli, amethysts, rubies

■ **FINANCE/TRADE**

Currency: afghani (Af) = 100 puls
International Reserves Excluding Gold: n.a.
Gold Reserves: n.a.
Budget: n.a.
Defence Expenditures: n.a.
Education Expenditures: n.a.
External Debt: n.a.
Exports: US$30 million (2000); commodities: natural gas 55%, fruit and nuts 24%, handwoven carpets, wool, cotton, hides, gemstones; partners: Pakistan, Germany, India, Belgium, Russia, United Arab Emirates
Imports: US$273 million (2000); commodities: capital goods, food and petroleum products, most consumer goods; partners: Pakistan, Kenya, Japan, India, South Korea, Turkmenistan

■ **COMMUNICATIONS**

Daily Newspapers: 5/1,000 inhabitants (2000)
Televisions: 14/1,000 inhabitants (2001)
Radios: 114/1,000 inhabitants (2001)
Telephones: 1 line/1,000 inhabitants (2001)

■ **TRANSPORTATION**

Motor Vehicles: 67,000; 35,000 passenger cars
Roads: 21,000 km; 2,793 km paved
Railway: 9.6 km from Kushka (Turkmenistan) to Towraghondi, and 15.0 km from Termez (Uzbekistan) to Kheyrabad
Air Traffic: 150,000 passengers carried (2001)
Airports: 46; 10 have paved runways (2002)

Canadian Embassy: c/o Canadian High Commission, Diplomatic Sector G-5, Islamabad; mailing address: GPO Box 1042, Islamabad, Pakistan. Tel: (011-92-51) 227-91. Fax: (011-92-51) 227-91-88. e-mail: isbad@dfait-maeci.gc.ca
Embassy in Canada: Embassy of Afghanistan, 246 Queen St., Suite 400, Ottawa, K1P 4E3 Tel: (613) 563-4223. Fax: (613) 563-4962 e-mail: afghanembott@hotmail.com

Albania

Long-Form Name: Republic of Albania
Capital: Tirana

■ **GEOGRAPHY**

Area: 28,748 sq. km
Coastline: 362 km

Climate: mild temperate; cool, cloudy, wet winters; hot, clear, dry summers; interior is cooler and wetter, with severe winters

Environment: subject to destructive earthquakes; soil erosion; water pollution; tsunami occur along southwestern coast; deforestation and water pollution are still current issues

Terrain: mostly mountains and hills; small plains along coast

Land Use: 21% arable land; 3% permanent crops; 15% meadows and pastures; 38% forest and woodland, including 30% scrub forest; 21% other; includes 3,400 sq. km irrigated

Location: SE Europe, bordering on Adriatic Sea

■ PEOPLE

Population: 3,544,841 (July 2002 est.)
Nationality: Albanian
Age Structure: 0–14 yrs: 28.8%; 15–64: 64.0%; 65+: 7.2% (2002 est.)
Population Growth Rate: 1.06% (2002 est.)
Net Migration: -1.46 migrants/1,000 population (2002 est.)
Ethnic Groups: 95% Albanian, 3% Greek, 2% others (Vlachs, Gypsies, Serbs and Bulgarians)
Languages: Albanian (Tosk is official dialect, also Gheg dialect), Greek
Religions: 70% Muslim, 20% Albanian Orthodox, 10% Roman Catholic
Birth Rate: 18.59/1,000 population (2002 est.)
Death Rate: 6.49/1,000 population (2002 est.)
Infant Mortality: 38.64 deaths/1,000 live births (2002 est.)
Life Expectancy at Birth: 69.27 years male, 75.14 years female (2002 est.)
Total Fertility Rate: 2.27 children born/woman (2002 est.)
Literacy: 84.7% (2000)

■ GOVERNMENT

Leader(s): Pres. Alfred Moisiu, Prime Min. Fatos Nano
Government Type: in transition to democracy
Administrative Divisions: 36 districts (rrethe, sing. —rreth) and 1 municipality (bashki)
Nationhood: Nov. 28, 1912 (from Ottoman Empire); People's Socialist Republic of Albania declared Jan. 11, 1946
National Holiday: Independence Day, Nov. 28

■ ECONOMY

Overview: the poorest country in Europe, it is a Stalinist-type economy (central planning and state ownership of the means of production); though largely self-sufficient in food until 1990, the recent break-up of co-operative farms and the general economic decline has forced Albania to rely increasingly on foreign aid; the government has taken strong measures to restore public order and to revive economic activity and trade

GDP: US$14 billion, per capita US$4,500; real growth rate 5.0% (2002 est.)
Inflation: 3.1% (2001)
Industries: accounts for 27% of GDP (2002); food processing, textiles and clothing, lumber, oil, cement, chemicals, basic metals, hydro-electricity; most industries produce at only fraction of past levels
Labour Force: 1.6 million (2001); 50% agriculture, 50% industry and services
Unemployment: officially 18% (2001), but likely to be as high as 25%
Agriculture: accounts for 49% of GDP (2002); arable land per capita among lowest in Europe; one-half of workforce engaged in farming; produces wide range of temperate-zone crops and livestock; claims self-sufficiency in grain output; 80% of all arable land is now in private ownership. Products include wheat, corn, potatoes, fruits, meat, dairy products.
Natural Resources: crude oil, natural gas, coal, chromium, copper, timber, nickel, petroleum

■ FINANCE/TRADE

Currency: lek (L) = 100 quintars
International Reserves Excluding Gold: US$403 million (Nov. 2002)
Gold Reserves: 0.111 million fine troy ounces (Dec. 2002)
Budget: revenues US$697 million; expenditures US$1.5 billion, including capital expenditures of US$368 million. (2002 est.)
Defence Expenditures: 3.7% of central government expenditures (2001)
Education Expenditures: 1.94% of central government expenditures (1998)
External Debt: US$1.094 billion (2001)
Exports: US$312 million (2002 est.); commodities: textiles, footwear, asphalt, bitumen, petroleum products, metals and metallic ores, electricity, oil, vegetables, fruit, tobacco; partners: Italy, Yugoslavia, Germany, Greece
Imports: US$1.431 billion (2002 est.); commodities: machinery, machine tools, iron and steel products, foodstuffs, textiles, chemicals, pharmaceuticals; partners: Italy, Greece, Turkey, Germany, Bulgaria

■ COMMUNICATIONS

Daily Newspapers: 35/1,000 inhabitants (2000)
Televisions: 123/1,000 inhabitants (2001)
Radios: 260/1,000 inhabitants (2001)
Telephones: 50 lines/1000 persons (2001)

■ TRANSPORTATION

Motor Vehicles: 154,000; 91,400 passenger cars (2000)
Roads: 18,000 km; 5,400 km paved
Railway: 447 km
Air Traffic: 146,000 passengers carried (2001)
Airports: 11; 3 have paved runways (2002)

Canadian Embassy: The Office of the Canadian Embassy, Rruga Brigada VIII, Pallat 2, Apt. 1, Tirana, Albania, Postal Address: P.O. Box 47, Tirana, Albania. Tel: (011-355-42) 57275. Fax: (011-355-42) 57273. e-mail: trana@dfait-maeci.gc.ca
Embassy in Canada: Embassy of the Republic of Albania, 130 Albert St, Ste 302, Ottawa ON K1P 5G4. Tel: (613) 236-4114. Fax: (613) 236-0804. e-mail: embassyrepublicofalbania@on.aivn.com

Algeria

Long-Form Name: Democratic and Popular Republic of Algeria
Capital: Algiers

■ GEOGRAPHY

Area: 2,381,740 sq. km
Coastline: 998 km
Climate: arid to semi-arid; mild, wet winters with hot, dry summers along coast; drier with cold winters and hot summers on high plateau; sirocco is a hot, dust/sand-laden wind especially common in summer
Environment: mountainous areas subject to severe earthquakes; desertification; industrial and domestic pollution and soil erosion contribute to environmental problems
Terrain: mostly high plateau and desert; some mountains; narrow, discontinuous coastal plain
Land Use: 3% arable land; 0% permanent crops; 13% meadows and pastures; 2% forest and woodland; 82% other; cattle, sheep and goat grazing on grassland and shrub regions; includes 5,600 sq. km irrigated
Location: N Africa, bordering on Mediterranean Sea

■ PEOPLE

Population: 32,277,942 (July 2002 est.)
Nationality: Algerian
Age Structure: 0–14 yrs: 33.5%; 15–64: 62.4%; 65+: 4.1% (2002 est.)
Population Growth Rate: 1.68% (2002 est.)
Net Migration: -0.42 migrants/1,000 population (2002 est.)
Ethnic Groups: 99% Arab-Berber, less than 1% European

Languages: Arabic (official), French, Berber dialects
Religions: 99% Sunni Muslim (state religion); 1% Christian and Jewish
Birth Rate: 22.34/1,000 population (2002 est.)
Death Rate: 5.15/1,000 population (2002 est.)
Infant Mortality: 39.15 deaths/1,000 live births (2002 est.)
Life Expectancy at Birth: 68.87 years male, 71.67 years female (2002 est.)
Total Fertility Rate: 2.63 children born/woman (2002 est.)
Literacy: 66.7% (2000)

■ GOVERNMENT

Leader(s): Pres. Abdelaziz Bouteflika, Prime Min. Ali Benflis
Government Type: republic
Administrative Divisions: 48 provinces (wilayas, sing. —wilaya)
Nationhood: July 5, 1962 (from France)
National Holiday: Anniversary of the Revolution, Nov. 1

■ ECONOMY

Overview: the economy is largely based on the exploitation of oil and natural gas products; dropping oil and gas prices have contributed to Algeria's most serious social and economic crisis since independence; recently, reforms have been implemented to combat social and economic problems
GDP: US$177 billion, per capita US$5,600; real growth rate 3.8% (2001 est.)
Inflation: 2% (2000 est)
Industries: petroleum, light industries, natural gas, mining, electrical, petrochemical, food processing. Accounts for 33% of GDP
Labour Force: 10.6 million (2001); 11% industry, 25% agriculture, 29% government, 15% construction and public works, 20% other
Unemployment: n.a.
Agriculture: accounts for 17% of GDP and employs 25% of labour force; products include wheat, barley, grapes, oats, olives, fruit, livestock; must import more than one-third of its food
Natural Resources: crude oil, natural gas, iron ore, phosphates, uranium, lead, zinc

■ FINANCE/TRADE

Currency: dinar (DA) = 100 centimes
International Reserves Excluding Gold: US$23.238 billion (Dec. 2002)
Gold Reserves: 5.583 million fine troy ounces (Dec. 2002)

Budget: revenues US$20.3 billion; expenditures US$18.8 billion, including capital expenditures US$5.8 billion (2001 est.)
Defence Expenditures: 12.0% of central government expenditure (2001)
Education Expenditures: 24.38% of central government expenditure (1999)
External Debt: US$22.503 billion (2001)
Exports: US$17.175 billion (2000); commodities: petroleum and natural gas 97%; partners: Italy, France, US, Spain, Brazil
Imports: US$10.459 billion (2000); commodities: capital goods, consumer goods, food and beverages; partners: France, Italy, Germany, US, Spain

■ COMMUNICATIONS

Daily Newspapers: 27/1,000 inhabitants (2000)
Televisions: 114/1,000 inhabitants (2001)
Radios: 244/1,000 inhabitants (2001)
Telephones: 61 lines/1,000 inhabitants (2001)

■ TRANSPORTATION

Motor Vehicles: 930,000; 500,000 passenger cars
Roads: 104,000 km; 71,656 km paved
Railway: 4,820 km
Air Traffic: 3,240,000 passengers carried (2001)
Airports: 136; 54 have paved runways (2002)

Canadian Embassy: The Canadian Embassy, 18 Mustapha Khalef St, Ben Aknoun, Algiers, Algeria; mailing address: P.O. Box 48, Alger-Gare, 16035 Alger, Algeria. Tel: (011-213-21) 914951. Fax: (011-213-21) 914973. e-mail: alger@dfait-maeci.gc.ca
Embassy in Canada: Embassy of the People's Democratic Republic of Algeria, 500 Wilbrod St. Ottawa, ON, K1N 6N2 Tel: (613) 789-8505 Fax: (613) 789-1406 e-mail: consalg@qc.aira.com

American Samoa

Long-Form Name: Territory of American Samoa
Capital: Pago Pago (on Tutuila Island)

■ GEOGRAPHY

Area: 199 sq. km
Climate: tropical maritime, plentiful rainfall, temperatures consistent throughout the year
Land Use: 5% arable land, 10% permanent crops; 0% meadows and pastures; 70% forest and woodland, 15% other; n.a. km irrigated
Location: S Pacific Ocean, E of Australia and New Zealand

■ PEOPLE

Population: 68,688 (July 2002 est.)

Nationality: American Samoan; nationals of the United States
Ethnic Groups: Samoan (Polynesian) 89%, Caucasian 2%, Tongan 4%, other 5%
Languages: Samoan (a Polynesian dialect), English

■ GOVERNMENT

Colony/Territory of: Dependent Territory of the United States
Leader(s): Pres. George W. Bush Jr.; Gov. Togiola Tulafono
Government Type: US dependency with democratically elected governor: unorganized unincorporated territory
National Holiday: Territorial Flag Day, Apr. 17

■ ECONOMY

Overview: agriculture: taro, bread-fruit, yams, bananas, coconuts; livestock includes pigs, goats, poultry; industries: fish (tuna) canning; economic activity is closely tied to US; tourism is slowly developing

■ FINANCE/TRADE

Currency: American dollar (US$) = 100 cents

Canadian Embassy: c/o The Canadian Embassy, 501 Pennsylvania Ave. NW, Washington DC. 20001 USATel: (202) 682-1740 Fax: (202) 682-7726 e-mail: wshdc@dfait-maeci.gc.ca
Representative to Canada: c/o Embassy of the United States of America, 490 Sussex Dr, Ottawa ON K1N 1G8. Tel: (613) 238-5335. Fax: (613) 688-3097. Email inquiries are not accepted

Andorra

Long-Form Name: Principality of Andorra
Capital: Andorra-la-Vella

■ GEOGRAPHY

Area: 468 sq. km
Coastline: none: landlocked
Climate: temperate; snowy, cold winters and warm, dry summers
Environment: deforestation, overgrazing, soil erosion; avalanches are a natural hazard
Terrain: rugged mountains separated by narrow valleys
Land Use: 4% arable land; 0% permanent crops; 45% meadows and pastures; 35% forest and woodland; 16% other; n.a. km irrigated
Location: SW Europe

■ PEOPLE

Population: 68,403 (July 2002 est.)
Nationality: Andorran
Age Structure: 0–14 yrs: 15.2%; 15–64: 71.9%; 65+: 12.9% (2002 est.)
Population Growth Rate: 1.11% (2002 est.)
Net Migration: 6.74 migrants/1,000 population (2002 est.)
Ethnic Groups: Catalan stock; 43% Spanish, 33% Andorran, 11% Portuguese, 7% French, 6% other
Languages: Catalan (official); many also speak some French and Spanish
Religions: predominantly Roman Catholic
Birth Rate: 9.97/1,000 population (2002 est.)
Death Rate: 5.57/1,000 population (2002 est.)
Infant Mortality: 4.07 deaths/1,000 live births (2002 est.)
Life Expectancy at Birth: 80.58 years male, 86.58 years female (2002 est.)
Total Fertility Rate: 1.26 children born/woman (2002 est.)
Literacy: approaching 100%

■ GOVERNMENT

Leader(s): Co-Heads of State: Jacques Chirac (France) and Joan Enric Vives Sicilia (Spain), Prem. Marc Forné Molné
Government Type: parliamentary democracy; retains as its heads of state a co-principality of president of France and Spanish bishop of Seo de Urgel, who are represented locally by officials called veguers
Administrative Divisions: 7 parishes (parroquies, sing.—parroquia)
Nationhood: 1278 (from France and Spain)
National Holiday: Mare de Deu de Meritxell, Sept. 8

■ ECONOMY

Overview: tourism is the backbone of the economy, due to its duty-free status and year-round resorts; most food is imported due to a scarcity of arable land
GDP: US$1.3 billion, per capita US$19,000; real growth rate 3.8% (2000 est.)
Inflation: n.a.
Industries: tourism (particularly skiing), sheep, timber, tobacco, banking
Labour Force: exact figures n.a.; 1% agriculture, 21% industry, 78% services
Unemployment: 0%
Agriculture: sheep raising, small quantities of tobacco, rye, wheat, barley, buckwheat, maize, oats and some vegetables, especially potatoes
Natural Resources: hydroelectricity, mineral water, timber, iron ore, lead

■ FINANCE/TRADE

Currency: French Franc = 100 centimes, Spanish peseta (F Ptas) = 100 centimos, Euro (€).
International Reserves Excluding Gold: n.a.
Gold Reserves: n.a.
Budget: n.a.
Defence Expenditures: defence is the responsibility of Spain and France
Education Expenditures: n.a.
External Debt: n.a.
Exports: exact figures unavailable; commodities: electricity, tobacco products, furniture; partners: France, Spain
Imports: exact figures unavailable; commodities: consumer goods, food; partners: France, Spain, US

■ COMMUNICATIONS

Daily Newspapers: 3 in total
Televisions: n.a.
Radios: n.a.
Telephones: 447 lines/1,000 inhabitants (1999)

■ TRANSPORTATION

Motor Vehicles: 36,000; 35,500 passenger cars
Roads: 269 km; 198 km paved
Railway: none
Air Traffic: n.a.
Airports: none

Canadian Embassy: The Canadian Embassy to Andorra, c/o The Canadian Embassy, Calle Nunez de Balboa, 35, Madrid, 28001, Spain; postal address: Apartado 587, 28080, Madrid, Spain. Tel: (011-34) 91-423-3252. Fax: (011-34) 91-423-3251. e-mail: mdrid@dfait-maeci.gc.ca
Embassy in Canada: c/o Embassy of the Principality of Andorra, 2 United Nations Plaza, 25th Fl, New York NY 10017, USA. Tel: (212) 750-8064. Fax: (212) 750-6630. e-mail: n.a.

Angola

Long-Form Name: Republic of Angola
Capital: Luanda

■ GEOGRAPHY

Area: 1,246,700 sq. km
Coastline: 1,600 km
Climate: semi-arid in south and along coast to Luanda; north has cool, dry season (May to October) and hot, rainy season (Nov. to Apr.)
Environment: locally heavy rainfall causes periodic flooding on plateau; desertification, especially on coastal plain, soil erosion and water pollution; deforestation

Terrain: narrow coastal plain rises abruptly to vast interior plain
Land Use: 2% arable land; 0% permanent crops; 23% meadows and pastures; 43% forest and woodland; 32% other; includes 750 sq. km irrigated
Location: SW Africa

■ PEOPLE

Population: 10,593,171 (July 2002 est.)
Nationality: Angolan
Age Structure: 0–14 yrs: 43.3%; 15–64: 53.9%; 65+: 2.8% (2002 est.)
Population Growth Rate: 2.18% (2002 est.)
Net Migration: 0 migrants/1,000 population (2002 est.)
Ethnic Groups: 37% Ovimbundu, 25% Kimbundu, 13% Bakongo, 2% Mestiço, 1% European, 22% other
Languages: Portuguese (official); Bantu dialects spoken include Ovimbundu, Kimbundu, Bakongo and Chokwe
Religions: 38% Roman Catholic, 15% Protestant, 47% Animist (indigenous beliefs)
Birth Rate: 46.18/1,000 population (2002 est.)
Death Rate: 24.35/1,000 population (2002 est.)
Infant Mortality: 191.66 deaths/1,000 live births (2002 est.)
Life Expectancy at Birth: 37.62 years male, 40.18 years female (2002 est.)
Total Fertility Rate: 6.43 children born/woman (2002 est.)
Literacy: 42% (1999 est.)

■ GOVERNMENT

Leader(s): Pres. José Eduardo dos Santos; Prime Min. Fernando da Piedade Dias dos Santos
Government Type: transitional government, nominally a democracy with strong presidential system
Administrative Divisions: 18 provinces (provincias, sing. —provincia)
Nationhood: Nov. 11, 1975 (from Portugal)
National Holiday: Independence Day, Nov. 11

■ ECONOMY

Overview: subsistence agriculture is the main livelihood of the population, but oil production is the most lucrative activity; recent internal war has weakened the economy, and food must be imported
GDP: US$13.3 billion, per capita US$1,330; real growth rate 5.4% (2001 est.)
Inflation: 152.6% (2001)
Industries: accounts for 70% of GDP (2000); petroleum, mining (phosphate rock, uranium, gold, iron ore, bauxite, feldspar, diamonds), fish

processing, brewing, tobacco, sugar, textiles, cement, food processing, building construction
Labour Force: 6.2 million (2001); 85% agriculture, 15% industry and services
Unemployment: extensive unemployment and underemployment affects more than half the population (2000 est.)
Agriculture: accounts for 6% of GDP (2000); cash crops—coffee, sisal, corn, cotton, sugar, manioc, tobacco; food crops—cassava, corn, vegetables, plantains, bananas and other local foodstuffs, fish
Natural Resources: petroleum, diamonds, iron ore, phosphates, copper, feldspar, gold, bauxite, uranium

■ FINANCE/TRADE

Currency: new kwanza (Kz) = 100 lwei
International Reserves Excluding Gold: US$376 million (Dec. 2002)
Gold Reserves: n.a.
Budget: n.a.
Defence Expenditures: 41.1% of total government expenditure (1999)
Education Expenditures: n.a.
External Debt: US$9.600 billion (2001)
Exports: US$4.940 billion (2000); commodities: oil, coffee, diamonds, sisal, fish and fish products, timber, cotton; partners: US, China, South Korea, countries of the European Union
Imports: US$1.550 billion (2000); commodities: machinery and electrical equipment, food, vehicles and spare parts, textiles and clothing, medicines, substantial military deliveries; partners: EU, Brazil, South Korea, South Africa

■ COMMUNICATIONS

Daily Newspapers: 11/1,000 inhabitants (2000)
Televisions: 19/1,000 inhabitants (2001)
Radios: 74/1,000 inhabitants (2001)
Telephones: 6 lines/1,000 inhabitants (2001)

■ TRANSPORTATION

Motor Vehicles: 225,000; 200,000 passenger cars
Roads: 76,626 km; 19,156 km paved
Railway: 2,771 km (2000)
Air Traffic: 193,000 passengers carried (2001)
Airports: 244; 32 have paved runways (2002)

Canadian Embassy: Consulate of Canada, Rua Rei Katyavala 113, Luanda, Angola; mailing address C.P. 3360, Luanda, Angola. Tel: (011-244-2) 448-371. Fax: (011-244-2) 44-94-94. e-mail: consul.can@angonet.org
Embassy in Canada: Embassy of the Republic of Angola, 189 Laurier Ave. E., Ottawa, ON

K1N 6P1. Tel: (613) 234-1152. Fax: (613) 234-1179. e-mail: info@embangola-can.org

Anguilla

Long-Form Name: Anguilla
Capital: The Valley

■ GEOGRAPHY

Area: 91 sq. km
Climate: dry and sunny, tropical with moderating northeast trade winds
Land Use: mostly rock, with sparse scrub, few trees, some commercial salt ponds; low rainfall limits agricultural potential
Location: West Indies, E of Puerto Rico

■ PEOPLE

Population: 12,446 (July 2002 est.)
Nationality: Anguillan
Ethnic Groups: of English ancestry, black/mixed-black African
Languages: English (official)

■ GOVERNMENT

Colony/Territory of: Dependent Territory of the United Kingdom
Leader(s): Head of State: Queen Elizabeth II, Gov. Peter Johnstone
Government Type: dependent overseas territory of the U.K.
National Holiday: Anguilla Day, May 30

■ ECONOMY

Overview: agriculture: pigeon peas, corn, sweet potatoes; fishing; livestock includes sheep, goats, cattle, poultry; main trading partner: U.K.; there are few natural resources and the economy depends heavily on tourism

■ FINANCE/TRADE

Currency: Eastern Caribbean dollar (EU$) = 100 cents

Canadian Embassy: c/o The Canadian High Commission, Macdonald House 1, Grosvenor Square, London W1K 4AB, England, UK. Tel: (011-44-20) 7258-6600. Fax: (011-44-20) 7258-6333. e-mail: ldn@dfait-maeci.gc.ca
Representative to Canada: c/o British High Commission, 80 Elgin St, Ottawa ON K1P 5K7. Tel: (613) 237-1530. Fax: (613) 237-7980. Email should be sent using the appropriate form at the British High Commission's Website at http://www.britain-in-canada.org

Antigua and Barbuda

Long-Form Name: Antigua and Barbuda
Capital: Saint John's (on Antigua)

■ GEOGRAPHY

Area: 442 sq. km; includes Redonda (1.3 sq. km)
Coastline: 153 km
Climate: tropical marine; little seasonal temperature variation
Environment: subject to hurricanes and tropical storms (July to Oct.); insufficient freshwater resources are decreased further by clear-cutting of trees, which promotes rain run-off; occasional long periods of drought; deeply indented coastline provides many natural harbours
Terrain: mostly low-lying limestone and coral islands with some higher volcanic areas
Land Use: 18% arable land; 0% permanent crops; 9% meadows and pastures; 11% forest and woodland; 62% other; n.a. km irrigated
Location: Caribbean islands, SE of Puerto Rico

■ PEOPLE

Population: 67,448 (July 2002 est.)
Nationality: Antiguan, Barbudan
Age Structure: 0–14 yrs: 28.0%; 15–64: 67.3%; 65+: 4.7% (2002 est.)
Population Growth Rate: 0.69% (2002 est.)
Net Migration: -6.23 migrants/1,000 population (2002 est.)
Ethnic Groups: almost entirely of black African origin; some of British, Portuguese, Lebanese and Syrian origin
Languages: English (official), local dialects
Religions: Anglican (predominant), other Protestant sects, some Roman Catholic
Birth Rate: 18.84/1,000 population (2002 est.)
Death Rate: 5.75/1,000 population (2002 est.)
Infant Mortality: 21.61 deaths/1,000 live births (2002 est.)
Life Expectancy at Birth: 68.72 years male, 73.45 years female (2002 est.)
Total Fertility Rate: 2.29 children born/woman (2002 est.)
Literacy: 96%

■ GOVERNMENT

Leader(s): Head of State: Queen Elizabeth II, Gov. Gen. James B. Carlisle, Prime Min. Lester Bird
Government Type: constitutional parliamentary democracy
Administrative Divisions: 6 parishes, 2 dependencies
Nationhood: Nov. 1, 1981 (from UK)
National Holiday: Independence Day, Nov. 1

■ ECONOMY

Overview: Tourism is the backbone of this service-oriented economy, therefore economic downturns, particularly in the US, can have adverse effects. A labour shortage is plaguing some sectors of the economy; agriculture is a minor but growing sector of the economy
GDP: US$674 million, per capita US$10,000; real growth rate 3.5% (2000 est.)
Inflation: 1.6% (1999 est.)
Industries: accounts for 19% of GDP; tourism, construction, light manufacturing (clothing, alcohol, household appliances)
Labour Force: 30,000; 82% commerce and services, 11% agriculture, 7% industry
Unemployment: 7% (1999 est.)
Agriculture: accounts for 4% of GDP; expanding output of cotton, fruit, vegetables and livestock; other crops—bananas, coconuts, sugar cane, cucumbers, mangoes; not self-sufficient in food
Natural Resources: negligible; pleasant climate and beautiful beaches foster tourism

■ FINANCE/TRADE

Currency: East Caribbean dollar ($EU) = 100 cents
International Reserves Excluding Gold: US$78 million (Oct. 2002)
Gold Reserves: n.a.
Budget: revenues US$123.7 million; expenditures US$145.9 million, including capital expenditures US$ n.a. (2000 est.)
Defence Expenditures: n.a.
Education Expenditures: n.a.
External Debt: n.a.
Exports: US$39 million (2000); commodities: petroleum products 48%, manufactures 23%, food and live animals 4%, machinery and transport equipment 17%; partners: Trinidad and Tobago, Barbados, US
Imports: US$410 million (2000); commodities: food and live animals, machinery and transport equipment, manufactures, chemicals, oil; partners: US, UK, OECS, Canada

■ COMMUNICATIONS

Daily Newspapers: 1 in total
Televisions: n.a.
Radios: n.a.
Telephones: 489 lines/1,000 inhabitants (1999)

■ TRANSPORTATION

Motor Vehicles: 14,800; 13,400 passenger cars
Roads: 1,165 km; 384 km paved (1999 est.)
Railway: 77 km
Air Traffic: 1,440,000 passengers carried (1999 est.)

Airports: 3; 2 have paved runways (2001 est.)

Canadian Embassy: c/o The Canadian High Commission, Bishop's Court Hill, Bridgetown, Barbados; mailing address: P.O. Box 404, Bridgetown, Barbados. Tel: 1-246-429-3550. Fax: 1-246-429-3780. e-mail: bdgtn@dfait-maeci.gc.ca
Embassy in Canada: c/o High Commission for the countries of the Organization of Eastern Caribbean States, 130 Albert St, Ste 700, Ottawa ON K1P 5G4. Tel: (613) 236-8952. Fax: (613) 236-3042. e-mail: echcc@travel-net.com

Argentina

Long-Form Name: Argentine Republic
Capital: Buenos Aires

■ GEOGRAPHY

Area: 2,766,890 sq. km
Coastline: 4,989 km
Climate: mostly temperate; arid in southeast; subantarctic in southwest
Environment: Tucamán and Mendoza areas in Andes subject to earthquakes; pamperos are violent windstorms that can strike the Pampas and northeast; irrigated soil degradation; desertification; air and water pollution in Buenos Aires; erosion is a current problem
Terrain: rich plains of the Pampas in northern half, flat to rolling plateau of Patagonia in south, rugged Andes along western border
Land Use: 9% arable land; 1% permanent crops; 52% meadows and pastures; 19% forest and woodland; 19% other; includes 15,610 sq. km irrigated
Location: SE South America

■ PEOPLE

Population: 37,812,817 (July 2002 est.)
Nationality: Argentine or Argentinian
Age Structure: 0–14 yrs: 26.3%; 15–64: 63.2%; 65+: 10.5% (2002 est.)
Population Growth Rate: 1.13% (2002 est.)
Net Migration: 0.63 migrants/1,000 population (2002 est.)
Ethnic Groups: 97% white (mostly Spanish and Italian), 3% mestizo, Indian, or other non-white groups
Languages: Spanish (official), English, Italian, German, French
Religions: 90% nominally Roman Catholic (less than 20% practising), 2% Protestant, 2% Jewish, 6% other
Birth Rate: 18.23/1,000 population (2002 est.)
Death Rate: 7.57/1,000 population (2002 est.)

Infant Mortality: 17.20 deaths/1,000 live births (2002 est.)
Life Expectancy at Birth: 72.1 years male, 79.03 years female (2002 est.)
Total Fertility Rate: 2.41 children born/woman (2002 est.)
Literacy: 96.8% (2000)

■ GOVERNMENT

Leader(s): Pres. Nestor Kirchner; V. Pres. Daniel Scioli
Government Type: republic
Administrative Divisions: 23 provinces (provincias, sing. — provincia) and 1 federal district (distrito federal)
Nationhood: July 9, 1816 (from Spain)
National Holiday: Revolution Day, May 25

■ ECONOMY

Overview: though the country possesses abundant natural resources and a diversified industrial base, burgeoning debt is weakening the economy; high unemployment rates have been a persistent problem, largely because of rigid labour laws
GDP: US$391 billion, per capita US$10,200; real growth rate -14.7% (2002 est.)
Inflation: -1.1% (2001)
Industries: accounts for 28% of GDP (2000); food processing (especially meat packing), motor vehicles, consumer durables, textiles, chemicals and petrochemicals, printing, metallurgy, steel
Labour Force: 15.4 million (2001); 13% agriculture, 34% industry, 53% services
Unemployment: 12.8% (2001)
Agriculture: accounts for 5% of GNP (including fishing) (2000); produces abundant food for both domestic consumption and exports; among world's top five exporters of grain and beef; principal crops—wheat, corn, sorghum, soybeans, sugar beets, peanuts, grapes, tea, lemons, tobacco
Natural Resources: fertile plains of the Pampas, lead, zinc, tin, copper, iron ore, manganese, crude oil, uranium

■ FINANCE/TRADE

Currency: nuevo peso argentino = 100 centavos
International Reserves Excluding Gold: US$10.489 billion (Dec. 2002)
Gold Reserves: 0.009 million fine troy ounces (Dec. 2002)
Budget: revenues US$44 billion; expenditures US$48 billion, including capital expenditures of US$ n.a. (2000 est.)

Defence Expenditures: 8.1% of total government expenditure (2001)
Education Expenditures: 6.28% of total government expenditure (2000)
External Debt: US$136.709 billion (2001)
Exports: US$25.329 billion (2002 est); commodities: meat, cereal grains, corn, oilseed, hides, wool; partners: US , Chile, Spain, Brazil
Imports: US$8.700 billion (2002 est.); commodities: machinery and equipment, metals, chemicals, motor vehicles, plastics, agricultural products; partners: US, Brazil, Germany, China

■ COMMUNICATIONS

Daily Newspapers: 37/1,000 inhabitants (2000)
Televisions: 326/1,000 inhabitants (2001)
Radios: 681/1,000 inhabitants (2001)
Telephones: 224 lines/1,000 inhabitants (2001)

■ TRANSPORTATION

Motor Vehicles: 6,770,000; 5,234,000 passenger cars (2000)
Roads: 215,434 km; 63,553 km paved
Railway: 33,744 km
Air Traffic: 5,739,000 passengers carried (2001)
Airports: 1,369; 145 have paved runways (2002)

Canadian Embassy: The Canadian Embassy, 2828 Tagle, 1425 Buenos Aires; mailing address: Casilla de Correo 1598 C1000WAP, Buenos Aires, Argentina. Tel: (011-54-11) 4808-1000. Fax: (011-54-11) 4808-1111. e-mail: bairs@dfait-maeci.gc.ca
Embassy in Canada: Embassy of the Argentine Republic, Royal Bank Centre, 90 Sparks St, Ste 910, Ottawa ON K1P 5B4. Tel: (613) 236-2351. Fax: (613) 235-2659. e-mail: n.a.

Armenia

Long-Form Name: Republic of Armenia
Capital: Yerevan

■ GEOGRAPHY

Area: 29,800 sq. km
Coastline: none: landlocked
Climate: severe winters; hot summers; dry year-round
Environment: prone to earthquakes; little land suitable for cultivation; air and water pollution; deforestation and drought; soil pollution is a current problem
Terrain: rugged highlands; 70% is mountains; little forest land; fast-flowing rivers; Aras River Valley has good soil
Land Use: 17% arable; 3% permanent crops; 24% meadows and pasture, 15% forests and

woodland, 41% other; includes 2,870 sq. km irrigated; most farmland lies in the Aras Valley; animal herding predominant in the highlands
Location: SW Asia

■ PEOPLE

Population: 3,330,099 (July 2002 est.)
Nationality: Armenian
Age Structure: 0–14 yrs: 22.2%; 15–64: 67.7%; 65+: 10.1% (2002 est.)
Population Growth Rate: -0.15% (2002 est.)
Net Migration: -3.51 migrants/1,000 population (2002 est.)
Ethnic Groups: 93% Armenians, 2% Russians, 3% Azerbaijanis, 2% other, predominantly Kurds
Languages: Armenian (official), Azerbaijan, Russian
Religions: predominantly Armenian Orthodox
Birth Rate: 12.00/1,000 population (2002 est.)
Death Rate: 9.94/1,000 population (2002 est.)
Infant Mortality: 41.07 deaths/1,000 live births (2002 est.)
Life Expectancy at Birth: 62.27 years male, 71.12 years female (2002 est.)
Total Fertility Rate: 1.53 children born/woman (2002 est.)
Literacy: 98.4% (2000)

■ GOVERNMENT

Leader(s): Pres. Robert Kocharian, Prime Min. Andranik Markaryan
Government Type: republic
Administrative Divisions: 10 provinces (marzer, sing. —marz) and 1 city (k'aghak'ner, sing. —k'aghak')
Nationhood: Sept. 21, 1991 (from Soviet Union)
National Holiday: Independence Day, Sept. 21

■ ECONOMY

Overview: predominantly manufacturing and agriculture; much of Armenia's population remains heavily dependent on remittances from relatives abroad
GDP: US$11.2 billion, per capita US$3,350; real growth rate 9.6% (2001 est.)
Inflation: 2.9% (2001)
Industries: accounts for 32% of GDP; electrical equipment and machinery, chemicals, machine tools, vehicles, textiles
Labour Force: 1.9 million (2001); 42% industry, 44% agriculture and forestry, 14% services
Unemployment: 9.3% (2001)
Agriculture: accounts for approximately 29% of GDP; fruit, grapes, vegetables, tobacco, grains, beetroot, potatoes, geranium oil, cattle and sheep herding

Natural Resources: marble, precious metals, iron, tufa, small deposits of gold, copper, molybdenum, zinc, alumina

■ FINANCE/TRADE

Currency: dram = 100 luma
International Reserves Excluding Gold: US$425 million (Dec. 2002)
Gold Reserves: 0.045 million fine troy ounces (Dec. 2002)
Budget: revenues US$358 million; expenditures US$458 million, including capital expenditures of US$ n.a (2001 est.)
Defence Expenditures: 20.2% of total government expenditure (1999)
Education Expenditures: n.a.
External Debt: US$1.001 billion (2001)
Exports: US$473 million (2002); commodities include cotton, diamonds, brandy, copper ore, fruit, olives, pomegranates, machine tools, instruments, shoes. Partners: Belgium, Iran, Russia, US.
Imports: US$899 million (2002 est.); commodities include machinery, energy, consumer goods, diamonds. Partners: Russia, US, Belgium, Iran

■ COMMUNICATIONS

Daily Newspapers: 5/1,000 inhabitants (2000)
Televisions: 230/1,000 inhabitants (2001)
Radios: 225/1,000 inhabitants (2001)
Telephones: 140 lines/1,000 persons (2001)

■ TRANSPORTATION

Motor Vehicles: n.a.
Roads: 11,300 km; 10,500 km paved
Railway: 825 km (does not include industrial lines)
Air Traffic: 369,000 passengers carried (2001)
Airports: 12; 5 have paved runways (2002)

Canadian Embassy: The Consulate of Canada, #21, 25 Demirjian St, Yerevan, Armenia. Tel: (011-3749) 401-238. Fax: (011-3741) 56-79-03; mailing address: c/o Starokonyushenny Per 23, Moscow 121002, Russian Federation. e-mail: aemin@freenet.am
Embassy in Canada: Embassy of the Republic of Armenia, 7 Delaware Ave, Ottawa ON K2P 0Z2. Tel: (613) 234-3710. Fax: (613) 234-3444. e-mail: erac@ican.net

Aruba

Long-Form Name: Aruba
Capital: Oranjestad

■ GEOGRAPHY

Area: 193 sq. km
Climate: tropical marine; little seasonal temperature variation
Land Use: 7% arable land; 0% permanent crops; 0% meadows and pastures; 0% forest and woodland; 93% other; 0.01 sq. km irrigated
Location: Caribbean island, off N coast of South America

■ PEOPLE

Population: 70,441 (July 2002 est.)
Nationality: Aruban
Ethnic Groups: 80% mixed European/Caribbean Indian
Languages: Dutch (official), Papiamento (a Spanish, Portuguese, Dutch, English dialect), English (widely spoken), Spanish

■ GOVERNMENT

Colony/Territory of: Dependent Territory of the Netherlands
Leader(s): Head of State: Queen Beatrix (Netherlands), Gov. Gen. Olindo Koolman, Prime Min. Nelson Oduber
Government Type: part of the Dutch realm; parliamentary democracy; autonomy in internal affairs obtained in 1986. Dutch government retains responsibility for defense and foreign affairs.
National Holiday: Flag Day, Mar. 18

■ ECONOMY

Overview: Tourism is the mainstay; banking and oil refinery are also important

■ FINANCE/TRADE

Currency: Aruban florin (Af) or guilder = 100 cents

Canadian Embassy: c/o The Canadian Embassy, Sophialaan 7, 2514JP, The Hague, Netherlands. Tel.: (011-31-70) 311-1600. Fax: (011-31-70) 311-1620. e-mail: hague@dfait-maeci.gc.ca
Representative to Canada: c/o Embassy of the Kingdom of the Netherlands, 350 Albert St, Ste 2020, Ottawa ON K1R 1A4. Tel: (613) 237-5030. Fax: (613) 237-6471. e-mail: nlgovott@netcom.ca

Australia

Long-Form Name: Commonwealth of Australia
Capital: Canberra

■ GEOGRAPHY

Area: 7,686,850 sq. km; includes Macquarie Island

Coastline: 25,760 km
Climate: generally arid to semi-arid; temperate in south and east; tropical in north
Environment: subject to severe droughts and floods; cyclones along coast; limited fresh water availability; soil degradation; regular, tropical, invigorating, sea breeze known as "the Doctor" occurs along west coast in summer; desertification. Shipping activities and tourism are threatening the Great Barrier Reef
Terrain: mostly low plateau with deserts; fertile plain in southeast
Land Use: 6% arable land; negligible permanent crops; 54% meadows and pastures; 19% forest and woodland; 21% other; includes 24,000 sq. km irrigated
Location: continent of the eastern hemisphere, SE of Asia and S. of the equator; divides Indian and Pacific Oceans

■ PEOPLE

Population: 19,546,792 (July 2002 est.)
Nationality: Australian
Age Structure: 0–14 yrs: 20.4%; 15–64: 67.0%; 65+: 12.6% (2002 est.)
Population Growth Rate: 0.96% (2002 est.)
Net Migration: 4.12 migrants/1,000 population (2002 est.)
Ethnic Groups: 92% Caucasian, 7% Asian, 1% Aboriginal and other
Languages: English, native languages
Religions: 26.1% Anglican, 26% Roman Catholic, 24.3% other Christian; most of the rest do not profess a religion
Birth Rate: 12.71/1,000 population (2002 est.)
Death Rate: 7.25/1,000 population (2002 est.)
Infant Mortality: 4.90 deaths/1,000 live births (2002 est.)
Life Expectancy at Birth: 77.15 years male, 83.0 years female (2002 est.)
Total Fertility Rate: 1.77 children born/woman (2002 est.)
Literacy: approaching 100% (2000)

■ GOVERNMENT

Leader(s): Head of State: Queen Elizabeth II, Gov. Gen. Michael Jeffrey, Prime Min. John Howard
Government Type: federal parliamentary state
Administrative Divisions: 6 states, 2 territories; dependent areas includes Ashmore and Cartier Islands (uninhabited), Australian Antarctic Territory (uninhabited except for scientific staff), Cocos (Keeling) Islands, Coral Sea Islands Territory (uninhabited), Christmas Island, Heard and McDonald Islands (uninhabited), Norfolk Island

Nationhood: Jan. 1, 1901 (federation of UK colonies)
National Holiday: Australia Day, Jan. 26

■ ECONOMY

Overview: successful Western-style capitalist economy and a major exporter of natural resources and agricultural products; is looking to increase exports of manufactured goods
GDP: US$582 billion, per capita US$27,000; real growth rate 3.6% (2002 est.)
Inflation: 4.4% (2001)
Industries: accounts for 25% of GDP (2001); mining, industrial and transportation equipment, food processing, chemicals, steel, motor vehicles
Labour Force: 9.9 million (2001); 73% services, 22% industry, 5% agriculture
Unemployment: 6.5% (Jan. 2003)
Agriculture: accounts for 3% of GDP and 30% of export revenues; world's largest exporter of beef and wool, second largest for mutton, and among top wheat exporters; major crops—wheat, barley, sugar cane, fruit; livestock—cattle, sheep, poultry
Natural Resources: bauxite, coal, iron ore, copper, tin, silver, uranium, nickel, tungsten, mineral sands, lead, zinc, diamonds, natural gas, crude oil

■ FINANCE/TRADE

Currency: dollar ($A) = 100 cents
International Reserves Excluding Gold: US$20.689 billion (Dec. 2002)
Gold Reserves: 2.563 million fine troy ounces (Dec. 2002)
Budget: revenues US$86.8 billion; expenditures US$84.1 billion, including capital expenditures US$ n.a. (FY2000/01 est.)
Defence Expenditures: 7.5% of central government expenditure (2001)
Education Expenditures: 7.6% of government expenditure (1999)
External Debt: US$220.6 billion (2000)
Exports: US$63.783 billion (2002 est.); commodities: wheat, barley, beef, lamb, dairy products, wool, gold, coal, iron ore; partners: developing countries, Japan, US, New Zealand, S Korea, Singapore, countries of the European Union
Imports: US$70.033 billion (2002 est.); commodities: manufactured raw materials, capital equipment, consumer goods; partners: developing countries, EU, US, Japan

■ COMMUNICATIONS

Daily Newspapers: 293/1,000 inhabitants (2000)
Televisions: 731/1,000 inhabitants (2001)

Radios: 1,999/1,000 inhabitants (2001)
Telephones: 519 lines/1,000 inhabitants (2001)

■ TRANSPORTATION

Motor Vehicles: 10,900,000; 9,000,000 passenger cars
Roads: 913,000 km; 353,331 km paved
Railway: 33,819 km
Air Traffic: 33,477,000 passengers carried (2001)
Airports: 421; 294 have paved runways (2002)

Canadian Embassy: The Canadian High Commission, Commonwealth Ave, Canberra A.C.T. 2600, Australia. Tel: (011-61-2) 6270-4000. Fax: (011-61-2) 6273-3285. e-mail: cnbra@dfait-maeci.gc.ca
Embassy in Canada: Australian High Commission, 50 O'Connor St, Ste 710, Ottawa ON K1P 6L2. Tel: (613) 236-0841. Fax: (613) 236-4376. e-mail: n.a.

Austria

Long-Form Name: Republic of Austria
Capital: Vienna

■ GEOGRAPHY

Area: 83,858 sq. km
Coastline: none: landlocked
Climate: temperate; continental, cloudy; cold winter with frequent rain in lowlands and snow in mountains; cool summers with occasional showers
Environment: because of steep slopes, poor soils and cold temperatures, population is concentrated on eastern lowlands; air and soil pollution is due to emissions by coal, and oil-fired power stations and industrial plants
Terrain: mostly mountains with Alps in west and south; flat, with gentle slopes along eastern and northern margins
Land Use: 17% arable land; 1% permanent crops; 23% meadows and pastures; 39% forest and woodland; 20% other; includes 457 sq. km irrigated
Location: C Europe

■ PEOPLE

Population: 8,169,929 (July 2002 est.)
Nationality: Austrian
Age Structure: 0–14 yrs: 16.4%; 15–64: 68.2%; 65+: 15.4% (2002 est.)
Population Growth Rate: 0.23% (2002 est.)
Net Migration: 2.45 migrants/1,000 population (2002 est.)
Ethnic Groups: 98% German, 2% Croatian, Slovene and others

Languages: German (official); Slovene, Hungarian, and a Croatian dialect also spoken
Religions: 85% Roman Catholic, 6% Protestant, 9% other
Birth Rate: 9.58/1,000 population (2002 est.)
Death Rate: 9.73/1,000 population (2002 est.)
Infant Mortality: 4.39 deaths/1,000 live births (2002 est.)
Life Expectancy at Birth: 74.85 years male, 81.31 years female (2002 est.)
Total Fertility Rate: 1.4 children born/woman (2002 est.)
Literacy: approaching 100% (2000)

■ GOVERNMENT

Leader(s): Chanc. Wolfgang Schuessel, Pres. Thomas Klestil
Government Type: federal republic
Administrative Divisions: 9 states (bundeslaender, sing. — bundesland)
Nationhood: Nov. 12, 1918 (from Austro-Hungarian Empire)
National Holiday: National Day, Oct. 26

■ ECONOMY

Overview: prosperous, Western capitalist economy, as well as substantial welfare benefits and extensive nationalized industry; unemployment is a continuing problem
GDP: US$226 billion, per capita US$27,700; real growth rate 0.6% (2002 est.)
Inflation: 2.7% (2001)
Industries: accounts for 33% of GDP (2002); foods, iron and steel, machines, textiles, chemicals, electrical, paper and pulp, tourism, mining
Labour Force: 3.8 million (2001); 67% services, 29% industry and crafts, 3% agriculture and forestry; an estimated 200,000 Austrians are employed in other European countries; foreign labourers in Austria number 177,840, about 6% of labour force
Unemployment: 6.9% (Jan. 2003)
Agriculture: accounts for 2% of GDP (including forestry) (2002); principal crops and animals— grains, fruit, potatoes, sugar beets, sawn wood, cattle, pigs, poultry; 80–90% self-sufficient in food
Natural Resources: iron ore, crude oil, timber, magnesite, lead, coal, lignite, copper, hydro-electricity

■ FINANCE/TRADE

Currency: schilling (S) = 100 groschen; Euro (€); on January 1, 2002 the Euro became the sole currency for everyday transactions.
International Reserves Excluding Gold: US$9.684 billion (Dec. 2002)

Gold Reserves: 11.172 million fine troy ounces (Jan. 2002)
Budget: revenues US$53 billion; expenditures US$54 billion, capital expenditures US$ n.a. (2001 est.)
Defence Expenditures: 2.0% of total government expenditure (2001)
Education Expenditures: n.a.
External Debt: US$16 billion (1999)
Exports: US$70.245 billion (2002 est.); commodities: machinery and equipment, iron and steel, lumber, textiles, paper products, chemicals; partners: countries of the European Union, Switzerland, US, Hungary
Imports: US$69.847 billion (2002 est.); commodities: petroleum, foodstuffs, machinery and equipment, vehicles, chemicals, textiles and clothing, pharmaceuticals; partners: Germany, Italy, France, Switzerland, US, Hungary

■ COMMUNICATIONS

Daily Newspapers: 296/1,000 inhabitants (2000)
Televisions: 542/1,000 inhabitants (2001)
Radios: 753/1,000 inhabitants (2001)
Telephones: 468 lines/1,000 inhabitants (2001)

■ TRANSPORTATION

Motor Vehicles: 4,400,000; 4,030,000 passenger cars (2000)
Roads: 133,361 km, all paved
Railway: 6,095.2 km (2001)
Air Traffic: 6,514,000 passengers carried (2001)
Airports: 55; 24 have paved runways (2002)

Canadian Embassy: The Canadian Embassy, Laurenzerberg 2 A-1010 Vienna, Austria. Tel: (011-43-1) 531-38-3000. Fax: (011-43-1) 531-38-3321. e-mail: vienn@dfait-maeci.gc.ca
Embassy in Canada: Embassy of the Republic of Austria, 445 Wilbrod St, Ottawa ON K1N 6M7. Tel: (613) 789-1444. Fax: (613) 789-3431. e-mail: embassy@austro.org

Azerbaijan

Long-Form Name: Azerbaijani Republic
Capital: Baku (or Baki)

■ GEOGRAPHY

Area: 86,600 sq. km
Coastline: none; landlocked. Inland coastline (Caspian Sea) approximately 800 km
Climate: Alpine to subtropical; dry, semi-arid steppe subject to drought
Environment: severe air and water pollution render Aspheron Peninsula, including Baku and

Sumgait, the "most ecologically devastated area in the world," according to local scientists
Terrain: fertile central lowlands; large flat Kura-Aras Lowland; Caucasus Mountains in north; western uplands
Land Use: 18% arable; 5% permanent crops; 11% forests and woodland, 25% meadows and pastures; 41% other (includes 14,550 sq. km irrigated); grazing land in the Caucasus Mountains; farming in lowlands
Location: SW Asia, bordering on Caspian Sea

■ PEOPLE

Population: 7,798,497 (July 2002 est.)
Nationality: Azerbaijani
Age Structure: 0–14 yrs: 28.3%; 15–64: 64.3%; 65+: 7.4% (2002 est.)
Population Growth Rate: 0.32% (2001 est.)
Net Migration: -5.41migrants/1,000 population (2002 est.)
Ethnic Groups: 90% Azerbaijani, 2.5% Russians, 2% Armenians, 3.2% Daghestanis, 2.3% other
Languages: Azerbaijani (official), Armenian, Russian, 6% other
Religions: Muslim 93.4%, Russian Orthodox 2.3%, Armenian Orthodox 2.3%, other 1.8%
Birth Rate: 18.84/1,000 population (2002 est.)
Death Rate: 9.61/1,000 population (2002 est.)
Infant Mortality: 82.74 deaths/1,000 live births (2002 est.)
Life Expectancy at Birth: 58.80 years male, 67.53 years female (2002 est.)
Total Fertility Rate: 2.29 children born/woman (2002 est.)
Literacy: 97% (1999)

■ GOVERNMENT

Leader(s): Pres. Heydar Aliyev, Prime Min. Ilham Aliyev
Government Type: republic
Administrative Divisions: 59 (rayonlar, sing. — rayon), 11 cities (saharlar, sing. — sahar), 1 autonomous republic (muxtar respublika, rayons)
Nationhood: Aug. 30, 1991 (from Soviet Union)
National Holiday: Independence Day (Founding of the Democratic Republic of Azerbaijan), May 28

■ ECONOMY

Overview: cotton and refining industries are most prominent; Azerbaijan is least industrially developed of the Transcaucasian States
GDP: US$27 billion, per capita US$3,300; real growth rate 6.1% (2002 est.)
Inflation: 1.5% (2001)

Industries: accounts for 33% of GDP (2001); oil extraction and refining, steel, cement, textiles, chemicals, petrochemicals
Labour Force: 3.7 million (2001); 41% agriculture and forestry, 7% industry, 53% services
Unemployment: 1.2% (2001)
Agriculture: accounts for 20% of GDP; cotton, grain, rice, grapes, tea, citrus fruit, vegetables, sheep and horse breeding, pigs and goats
Natural Resources: oil reserves, minerals, iron, aluminum

■ FINANCE/TRADE

Currency: manat = 100 gopik
International Reserves Excluding Gold: US$722 million (Dec. 2002)
Gold Reserves: none (Dec. 2001)
Budget: Revenues US$786 million, expenditures US$807 million, including capital expenditures of US $n.a. (2001)
Defence Expenditures: 10.2% of central government expenditure (2001)
Education Expenditures: 3.2 % of central government expenditure (2000 est.)
External Debt: US$1.219 billion (2001)
Exports: US$879 million (2000); oil and gas and related equipment, textiles, cotton. Partners: Italy, Turkey, Russia, Georgia, Israel
Imports: US$788 million (2000); machinery and parts, foodstuffs, textiles, consumer durables. Partners: US, Russia, Turkey, Kazakhstan, Germany

■ COMMUNICATIONS

Daily Newspapers: 27/1,000 inhabitants (2000)
Televisions: 321/1,000 inhabitants (2001)
Radios: 27/1,000 inhabitants (2001)
Telephones: 111 lines/1,000 persons (2001)

■ TRANSPORTATION

Motor Vehicles: 381,000; 295,000 passenger cars (2000)
Roads: 36,700 km; 31,800 km hard-surfaced
Railway: 2,125 km (does not include industrial lines)
Air Traffic: 544,000 passengers carried (2001)
Airports: 52; 9 have paved runways (2002)

Canadian Embassy: c/o The Canadian Embassy, Nenehatun Caddesi No. 75, Gaziosmanpasa 06700, Ankara, Turkey. Tel: (011-90-312) 459-9200. Fax: (011-90-312) 459-9361. e-mail: ankra@dfait-maeci.gc.ca
Embassy in Canada: c/o Embassy of the Republic of Azerbaijan, 2741, 34th St. NW, Washington DC 20008, USA. Tel: (202) 337-3500. Fax: (202) 337-5911. e-mail: azerbaijan@tidalwave.net

Bahamas

Long-Form Name: Commonwealth of The Bahamas
Capital: Nassau

■ GEOGRAPHY

Area: 13,940 sq. km
Coastline: 3,542 km
Climate: tropical marine; moderated by warm waters of Gulf Stream
Environment: subject to hurricanes and other tropical storms that cause extensive flood and wind damage; coral reef decay is a current issue
Terrain: long, flat coral islands with some low, rounded hills
Land Use: 1% arable land; 0% permanent crops; 0% meadows and pastures; 32% forest and woodland; 67% other; n.a. km irrigated
Location: Caribbean islands, E of Florida

■ PEOPLE

Population: 300,529 (July 2002 est.)
Nationality: Bahamian
Age Structure: 0–14 yrs: 29.0%; 15–64: 64.7%; 65+: 6.3% (2002 est.)
Population Growth Rate: 0.86% (2002 est.)
Net Migration: -2.63 migrants/1,000 population (2002 est.)
Ethnic Groups: 85% black, 12% white, 3% Asian and Hispanic
Languages: English; some Creole among Haitian immigrants
Religions: 32% Baptist, 20% Anglican, 19% Roman Catholic, smaller groups of other Protestants, Greek Orthodox and Jews
Birth Rate: 18.69/1,000 population (2002 est.)
Death Rate: 7.49/1,000 population (2002 est.)
Infant Mortality: 17.08 deaths/1,000 live births (2002 est.)
Life Expectancy at Birth: 66.32 years male, 73.49 years female (2002 est.)
Total Fertility Rate: 2.28 children born/woman (2002 est.)
Literacy: 95.4% (2000)

■ GOVERNMENT

Leader(s): Head of State: Queen Elizabeth II/Gov. Gen. Ivy Dumont. Prime Min. Perry Christie
Government Type: constitutional parliamentary democracy
Administrative Divisions: 21 districts
Nationhood: July 10, 1973 (from UK)
National Holiday: Independence Day, July 10

■ ECONOMY

Overview: tourism and offshore banking are features of this stable, middle-income developing nation
GDP: US$5 billion, per capita US$16,800; real growth rate 3.5% (2001 est.)
Inflation: 2.0% (2001)
Industries: accounts for 7% of GDP; banking, tourism, cement, oil refining and transshipment, salt production, rum, aragonite, pharmaceuticals, spiral welded steel pipe
Labour Force: approx. 156,000; 40% hotels and restaurants, 50% other services, 5% industry, 5% agriculture
Unemployment: n.a.
Agriculture: accounts for 3% of GDP; dominated by small-scale producers; principal products—citrus fruit, vegetables, poultry; large net importer of food
Natural Resources: salt, aragonite, timber

■ FINANCE/TRADE

Currency: Bahamian dollar ($B) = 100 cents
International Reserves Excluding Gold: US$381 million (Dec. 2002)
Gold Reserves: none (Jan. 2002)
Budget: revenues US$918.5 million; expenditures US$956.5 million, including capital expenditures US$106.7 million (FY1999/2000)
Defence Expenditures: 2.91% of central government expenditure (2001)
Education Expenditures: 19.8% of central government expenditure (2000)
External Debt: US$385.8 million (2000 est.)
Exports: US$572 million (2002 est.); commodities: pharmaceuticals, cement, rum, crawfish; partners: US, UK, France, Germany
Imports: US$1.564 billion (2002 est.); commodities: foodstuffs, manufactured goods, mineral fuels; partners: US, South Korea, Italy, Japan

■ COMMUNICATIONS

Daily Newspapers: 3 in total
Televisions: n.a.
Radios: n.a.
Telephones: 369 lines/1,000 inhabitants (1999)

■ TRANSPORTATION

Motor Vehicles: 59,000; 47,000 passenger cars
Roads: 2,693 km; 1,546 km paved
Railway: none
Air Traffic: 810,000 passengers carried (1999)
Airports: 67; 30 have paved runways (2002)

Canadian Embassy: Consulate of Canada, Shirley Street Plaza, Nassau; mailing address: Consulate of Canada, P.O. Box SS-6371, Nassau, Bahamas. Tel: (1-242) 393-2123. Fax: (1-242) 393-1305. e-mail: cdncon@bahamas.net.bs

Embassy in Canada: High Commission for the Commonwealth of the Bahamas, 50 O'Connor St, Ste 1313, Ottawa ON K1P 6L2. Tel: (613) 232-1724. Fax: (613) 232-0097. e-mail: ottawa-mission@bahighco.com

Bahrain

Long-Form Name: State of Bahrain
Capital: Manama

■ GEOGRAPHY

Area: 620 sq. km
Coastline: 161 km
Climate: arid; mild, pleasant winters; very hot, humid summers
Environment: there are no natural fresh water resources; ground water and sea water are the sole sources for all water needs; dust storms; desertification; drought; coastal degradation resulting from oil industry
Terrain: mostly low desert plain rising gently to low central escarpment
Land Use: 1% arable land; 1% permanent crops; 6% meadows and pastures; 0% forest and woodland; 92% other; includes 50 sq. km irrigated
Location: Persian Gulf, E of Saudi Arabia

■ PEOPLE

Population: 656,397 (July 2002 est.)
Nationality: Bahraini
Age Structure: 0–14 yrs: 29.2%; 15–64: 67.7%; 65+: 3.1% (2002 est.)
Population Growth Rate: 1.67% (2002 est.)
Net Migration: 1.09 migrants/1,000 population (2002 est.)
Ethnic Groups: 63% Bahraini, 19% Asian, 10% other Arab, 8% Iranian
Languages: Arabic (official); English also widely spoken; Farsi, Urdu
Religions: Muslim (70% Shi'a, 30% Sunni)
Birth Rate: 19.53/1,000 population (2002 est.)
Death Rate: 3.95/1,000 population (2002 est.)
Infant Mortality: 19.18 deaths/1,000 live births (2002 est.)
Life Expectancy at Birth: 71.05 years male, 75.96 years female (2002 est.)
Total Fertility Rate: 2.75 children born/woman (2002 est.)
Literacy: 87.6% (2000)

■ GOVERNMENT

Leader(s): King Hamad bin Isa al-Khalifa
Prime Min. Khalifa bin Salman Al Khalifa

Government Type: constitutional hereditary monarchy
Administrative Divisions: 12 municipalities (manatiq, sing. —mintaqah)
Nationhood: Aug. 15, 1971 (from UK)
National Holiday: National Day, Dec. 16

■ ECONOMY

Overview: petroleum production and processing are the backbone of the economy and any change in the world oil market affects the economy
GDP: US$8.4 billion, per capita US$13,000; real growth rate 4.0% (2001 est.)
Inflation: -0.7% (2000)
Industries: accounts for 35% of GDP (2001); petroleum processing and refining, aluminum smelting, offshore banking, ship repairing
Labour Force: exact figures n.a.; 42% of labour force is Bahraini; 79% industry, commerce and services, 20% government, 1% agriculture
Unemployment: n.a.
Agriculture: including fishing, accounts for 1% of GDP (2001); not self-sufficient in food production; heavily subsidized sector produces fruit, vegetables, poultry, dairy products, shrimp and fish
Natural Resources: oil, associated and non-associated natural gas, fish

■ FINANCE/TRADE

Currency: Bahraini dinar (BD) = 1,000 fils
International Reserves Excluding Gold: US$1.726 billion (Dec. 2002)
Gold Reserves: 0.15 million fine troy ounces (Dec. 2002)
Budget: revenues US$1.8 billion; expenditures US$2.2 billion, capital expenditures US$700 million (2002 est.)
Defence Expenditures: 15.23% of total government expenditures (2001)
Education Expenditures: 12.84% of central government expenditure (2000)
External Debt: US$2.7 billion (2000)
Exports: US$4.849 billion (2002 est.); commodities: petroleum 80%, aluminum 7%, other 13%; partners: US, Japan, Saudi Arabia, India, South Korea
Imports: US$4.467 billion (2002 est.); commodities: non-oil 59%, crude oil 41%; partners: UK, Saudi Arabia, US, France, Japan

■ COMMUNICATIONS

Daily Newspapers: 4 in total
Televisions: n.a.
Radios: n.a.
Telephones: 249 lines/1,000 inhabitants (1999)

■ TRANSPORTATION

Motor Vehicles: 178,000; 143,000 passenger cars
Roads: 3,164 km; 2,433 km paved
Railway: none
Air Traffic: 1,340,000 passengers carried (1999 est.)
Airports: 4; 3 have paved runways (2002)

Canadian Embassy: The Canadian Embassy to Bahrain, c/o The Canadian Embassy, P.O. Box 94321, Riyadh 11693, Saudi Arabia. Tel: (011-966-1) 488-2288. Fax: (011-966-1) 488-1997. e-mail: ryadh@dfait-maeci.gc.ca
Embassy in Canada: c/o The Embassy of the State of Bahrain, 3502 International Dr NW, Washington DC 20008, USA. Tel: (202) 312-0741. Fax: (202) 362-2192. e-mail: n.a.

Bangladesh

Long-Form Name: People's Republic of Bangladesh
Capital: Dhaka

■ GEOGRAPHY

Area: 144,000 sq. km
Coastline: 580 km
Climate: tropical; cool, dry winter (Oct. to Mar.); hot, humid summer (Mar. to June)
Environment: vulnerable to droughts; much of country routinely flooded during summer monsoon season (June to Oct.); overpopulation; deforestation; cyclones
Terrain: mostly flat alluvial plain; hilly in southeast
Land Use: 73% arable land; 2% permanent crops; 5% meadows and pastures; 15% forest and woodland; 5% other; includes 38,440 sq. km irrigated
Location: S Asia, bordering on Bay of Bengal

■ PEOPLE

Population: 133,376,684 (July 2002 est.)
Nationality: Bangladeshi
Age Structure: 0–14 yrs: 33.8%; 15–64: 62.8%; 65+: 3.4% (2002 est.)
Population Growth Rate: 1.59% (2002 est.)
Net Migration: -0.75 migrants/1,000 population (2002 est.)
Ethnic Groups: 98% Bengali, 250,000 Biharis, less than 1 million tribals
Languages: Bangla (official), English widely used, 5% tribal dialects
Religions: 83% Muslim, 16% Hindu, less than 1% Buddhist, Christian and other
Birth Rate: 25.12/1,000 population (2002 est.)
Death Rate: 8.47/1,000 population (2002 est.)

Infant Mortality: 68.05 deaths/1,000 live births (2002 est.)
Life Expectancy at Birth: 61.08 years male, 60.74 years female (2002 est.)
Total Fertility Rate: 2.72 children born/woman (2002 est.)
Literacy: 41.3% (2000)

■ GOVERNMENT

Leader(s): Pres. Iajuddin Ahmed, Prime Min. Khaleda Zia
Government Type: parliamentary democracy
Administrative Divisions: 5 divisions
Nationhood: Dec. 16, 1971 (from Pakistan; Bangladesh formerly known as East Pakistan)
National Holiday: Independence Day, Mar. 26 (date of independence from West Pakistan); Victory Day, Dec. 16 (commemorates the official creation of the state of Bangladesh.

■ ECONOMY

Overview: one of the poorest nations in the world; the economy is based on a small number of agricultural exports, which are vulnerable to natural disasters; few natural resources; frequent cyclones and floods, a rapidly growing labour force that cannot be absorbed by agriculture, a low level of industrialization, government interference with the economy, failure to exploit energy reserves, and inadequate power supplies all contribute to stifling economic growth
GDP: US$203 billion, per capita US$1,570; real growth rate 5.3% (2000 est.)
Inflation: 1.4% (2001)
Industries: accounts for 18% of GDP (2000), jute manufacturing, food processing, cotton textiles, petroleum, urea fertilizer
Labour Force: 70.8 million (2001); 63% agriculture, 26% services, 11% industry; extensive export of labour to Saudi Arabia, United Arab Emirates, Oman and Kuwait
Unemployment: n.a.
Agriculture: accounts for about 30% of GDP (2000), 65% of employment and 20% of exports; imports 10% of foodgrain requirements; world's largest exporter of jute; commercial products—jute, rice, wheat, tea, sugar cane, potatoes, tobacco, spices, beef, milk, poultry
Natural Resources: natural gas, arable land, timber

■ FINANCE/TRADE

Currency: taka (Tk) = 100 poisha
International Reserves Excluding Gold: US$1.683 billion (Dec. 2002)
Gold Reserves: 0.112 million fine troy ounces (Dec. 2002)

Budget: revenues US$4.9 billion; expenditures US$6.8 billion, including capital expenditures of US$ n.a. (FY1999/2000 est.)
Defence Expenditures: 11.2% of central government expenditure (2001)
Education Expenditures: n.a.
External Debt: US$15.215 billion (2001)
Exports: US$4.826 billion (2001); commodities: jute, tea, garments, leather, shrimp, manufacturing; partners: US, Germany, UK, France, Netherlands, Italy 4%
Imports: US$8.349 billion (2001); commodities: food, petroleum and other energy, non-food consumer goods, semi-processed goods and capital equipment; partners: India, EU, Japan, Singapore, China

■ COMMUNICATIONS

Daily Newspapers: 53/1,000 inhabitants (2000)
Televisions: 17/1,000 inhabitants (2001)
Radios: 49/1,000 inhabitants (2001)
Telephones: 4 lines/1,000 inhabitants (2001)

■ TRANSPORTATION

Motor Vehicles: 225,000; 152,000 passenger cars
Roads: 201,182 km; 19,112 km paved
Railway: 2,745 km
Air Traffic: 1,450,000 passengers carried (2001)
Airports: 18; 15 have paved runways (2002)

Canadian Embassy: The Canadian High Commission, House CWN 16/A, Rd. 48, Gulshan; mailing address: G.P.O. Box 569, Dhaka, Bangladesh. Tel: (011-880-2) 988-7091. Fax: (011-880-2) 882-30-43. e-mail: dhaka-da@dfait-maeci.gc.ca
Embassy in Canada: High Commission for the People's Republic of Bangladesh, 275 Bank St, Ste 302, Ottawa ON K2P 2L6. Tel: (613) 236-0138. Fax: (613) 567-3213. e-mail: bang@bellnet.ca

Barbados

Long-Form Name: Barbados
Capital: Bridgetown

■ GEOGRAPHY

Area: 430 sq. km
Coastline: 97 km
Climate: tropical; rainy season (June to Oct.)
Environment: subject to hurricanes, especially June to Oct.; water pollution and soil erosion; landslides
Terrain: relatively flat; rises gently to a central highland region
Land Use: 37% arable land; 0% permanent crops; 5% meadows and pastures; 12% forest and woodland; 46% other; includes 10 sq. km irrigated
Location: Caribbean islands, N of Venezuela

■ PEOPLE

Population: 276,607 (July 2002 est.)
Nationality: Barbadian, or Bajan (colloquial)
Age Structure: 0–14 yrs: 21.4%; 15–64: 69.8%; 65+: 8.8% (2002 est.)
Population Growth Rate: 0.46% (2002 est.)
Net Migration: -0.31 migrants/1,000 population (2002 est.)
Ethnic Groups: 80% African, 16% mixed, 4% European
Languages: English
Religions: 67% Protestant, 9% Methodist, 4% Roman Catholic, 9% other, including Moravian
Birth Rate: 13.32/1,000 population (2002 est.)
Death Rate: 8.38/1,000 population (2002 est.)
Infant Mortality: 11.71 deaths/1,000 live births (2002 est.)
Life Expectancy at Birth: 70.90 years male, 76.12 years female (2002 est.)
Total Fertility Rate: 1.64 children born/woman (2002 est.)
Literacy: 97% (1999)

■ GOVERNMENT

Leader(s): Head of State: Queen Elizabeth II, Gov. Gen. Sir Clifford Husbands. Prime Min. Owen Seymour Arthur
Government Type: parliamentary democracy
Administrative Divisions: 11 parishes
Nationhood: Nov. 30, 1966 (from UK)
National Holiday: Independence Day, Nov. 30

■ ECONOMY

Overview: has one of the highest standards of living of islands in the region; the tourist industry and traditional sugar cane cultivation are main parts of the economy; manufacturing and tourism have become increasingly important in recent years
GDP: US$4.0 billion, per capita US$14,500; real growth rate -2.0% (2001 est.)
Inflation: 2.6% (2001)
Industries: accounts for 16% of GDP; tourism, sugar, light manufacturing, component assembly for export
Labour Force: exact figures n.a.; 75% community, social and business services, 15% industry, 10% agriculture
Unemployment: 10% (Nov. 2001)
Agriculture: accounts for 6% of GDP; major cash crop is sugar cane; other crops—vegetables and cotton; not self-sufficient in food
Natural Resources: crude oil, fishing, natural gas

■ FINANCE/TRADE

Currency: Barbadian dollar ($BDS) = 100 cents
International Reserves Excluding Gold: US$651 million (Dec. 2002)
Gold Reserves: none (Jan. 2002)
Budget: revenues US$847 million; expenditures US$886 million, including capital expenditures of US$ n.a. (2000 est.)
Defence Expenditures: n.a.
Education Expenditures: n.a.
External Debt: US$701 million (2001)
Exports: US$206 million (2002); commodities: sugar and molasses, electrical components, clothing, rum, machinery and transport equipment; partners: Caribbean community, US, UK
Imports: US$1.039 billion (2002); commodities: foodstuffs, consumer durables, raw materials, crude oil; partners: US, CARICOM, Japan, UK, Canada

■ COMMUNICATIONS

Daily Newspapers: 2 in total
Televisions: n.a.
Radios: n.a.
Telephones: 427 lines/1,000 inhabitants (1999)

■ TRANSPORTATION

Motor Vehicles: 48,500; 45,000 passenger cars
Roads: 1,600 km; 1,682 km paved
Railway: none
Air Traffic: n.a.
Airports: 1, with a paved runway (2002)

Canadian Embassy: c/o The Canadian High Commission, Bishop's Court Hill, Bridgetown, Barbados; mailing address: P.O. Box 404, Bridgetown, Barbados. Tel: 1-246-429-3550. Fax: 1-246-429-3780. e-mail: bdgtn@dfait-maeci.gc.ca
Embassy in Canada: High Commission for Barbados, 130 Albert St, Ste 1204, Ottawa ON K1P 5G4. Tel: (613) 236-9517. Fax: (613) 230-4362. e-mail: ottawa@foreign.gov.bb

---

Belarus

Long-Form Name: Republic of Belarus
Capital: Minsk

■ GEOGRAPHY

Area: 207,600 sq. km
Coastline: none; landlocked
Climate: mild and moist, transitional between continental and maritime
Environment: southern region is badly contaminated with nuclear fallout from 1986 Chernobyl reactor accident; pesticide use results in extensive soil pollution
Terrain: land of forests, lakes, rivers, and marshes; soil poor, sandy, marshy
Land Use: 29% arable; 1% permanent crops and forest, 34% forests and woodland, 15% meadows and pastures; 21% other; includes 1,150 sq. km irrigated
Location: W Asia, bordering on Poland

■ PEOPLE

Population: 10,335,382 (July 2002 est.)
Nationality: Belarusian
Age Structure: 0–14 yrs: 17.3%; 15–64: 68.6%; 65+: 14.1% (2002 est.)
Population Growth Rate: -0.14% (2002 est.)
Net Migration: 2.78 migrants/1,000 population (2002 est.)
Ethnic Groups: 77.9% Byelorussian, 13.2% Russian, 4.1% Polish, 2.9% Ukrainian, 1.9% other
Languages: Byelorussian, Russian
Religions: predominantly Roman Catholic and Eastern Orthodox
Birth Rate: 9.86/1,000 population (2002 est.)
Death Rate: 13.99/1,000 population (2002 est.)
Infant Mortality: 14.12 deaths/1,000 live births (2002 est.)
Life Expectancy at Birth: 62.30 years male, 74.56 years female (2002 est.)
Total Fertility Rate: 1.31 children born/woman (2002 est.)
Literacy: 99.6% (2000)

■ GOVERNMENT

Leader(s): Pres. Aleksandr Lukashenko, Acting Prime Min. Sergei Sidorsky
Government Type: republic
Administrative Divisions: 6 regions (voblastsi, sing. — voblasts), 1 municipality (harady, sing. — horad)
Nationhood: Aug. 25, 1991 (from former Soviet Union)
National Holiday: Independence Day, July 3

■ ECONOMY

Overview: strong emphasis on mining and agriculture, with growing manufacturing (heavy machinery, chemicals, fertilizer) and services sector; Belarus is an important transport link for the former Soviet states
GDP: US$84.8 billion, per capita US$8,200; real growth rate 4.1% (2001 est.)
Inflation: 61.1% (2001)
Industries: accounts for 42% of GDP (2000); machinery, tools, refineries, fertilizer pro-

duction; about 50% of labour force is employed in industry

Labour Force: 5.3 million (2000); 27.4% manufacturing, 22.4% community, social and business services, 21.9% agriculture

Unemployment: 2%, but large numbers of underemployed (2001)

Agriculture: accounts for 13% of GDP (2000); potatoes, flax, rye, oats, barley, wheat, cattle breeding, milk, vegetables, pigs, potatoes, peat, forest resources

Natural Resources: oil and natural gas, potassium, forest land, peat deposits

■ FINANCE/TRADE

Currency: Belarusian ruble

International Reserves Excluding Gold: US$362 million (Nov. 2002)

Gold Reserves: n.a.

Budget: n.a.

Defence Expenditures: 4.5% of total government expenditures (2001)

Education Expenditures: 3.87% of total government expenditures (2000)

External Debt: US$869 million (2001)

Exports: US$7.836 billion (2002 est.); agricultural and transport machinery, chemicals, metals, textiles; partners: Russia, Ukraine, Poland, Germany

Imports: US$8.403 billion (2002 est.); commodities: fuels, raw materials, textiles, sugar; partners: Russia, Germany, Poland

■ COMMUNICATIONS

Daily Newspapers: 152/1,000 inhabitants (2000)

Televisions: 342/1,000 inhabitants (2001)

Radios: 199/1,000 inhabitants (2001)

Telephones: 279 lines/1,000 inhabitants (2001)

■ TRANSPORTATION

Motor Vehicles: 1,400,000; 1,350,000 passenger cars (2000)

Roads: 98,200 km; 66,100 km hard-surfaced

Railway: 5,563 km (does not include industrial lines) (2000)

Air Traffic: 222,000 passengers carried (2001)

Airports: 136; 33 have paved runways (2002)

Canadian Embassy: The Canadian Embassy to Belarus, c/o The Canadian Embassy, ul. Jana Matejki 1/5, 00-481 Warsaw, Poland. Tel: (011-48-22) 584-3100. Fax: (011-48-22) 584-3190 e-mail: wsaw@dfait-maeci.gc.ca

Embassy in Canada: Embassy of the Republic of Belarus, 130 Albert St, Ste 600, Ottawa ON K1P 5G4. Tel: (613) 233-9994. Fax: (613) 233-8500. e-mail: belamb@igs.net

Belgium

Long-Form Name: Kingdom of Belgium

Capital: Brussels

■ GEOGRAPHY

Area: 30,510 sq. km

Coastline: 66 km

Climate: temperate; mild winters, cool summers; rainy, humid, cloudy

Environment: air and water pollution; acid rain

Terrain: flat coastal plains in northwest central rolling hills, rugged mountains of Ardennes Forest in southeast

Land Use: 24% arable land; 1% permanent crops; 20% meadows and pastures; 21% forest and woodland; 34% other; includes 40 sq. km irrigated

Location: NW Europe, bordering on North Sea

■ PEOPLE

Population: 10,274,595 (July 2002 est.)

Nationality: Belgian

Age Structure: 0–14 yrs: 17.3%; 15–64: 65.6%; 65+: 17.1% (2002 est.)

Population Growth Rate: 0.15% (2002 est.)

Net Migration: 0.97 migrants/1,000 population (2002 est.)

Ethnic Groups: 58% Flemish, 31% Walloon, 11% mixed or other

Languages: Dutch or Flemish spoken in north (Flanders), French in south (Wallonia), both languages official; small English-speaking minority in east, German 1%

Religions: 75% Roman Catholic, remainder Protestant or other

Birth Rate: 10.58/1,000 population (2002 est.)

Death Rate: 10.08/1,000 population (2002 est.)

Infant Mortality: 4.64 deaths/1,000 live births (2002 est.)

Life Expectancy at Birth: 74.80 years male, 81.62 years female (2002 est.)

Total Fertility Rate: 1.61 children born/woman (2002 est.)

Literacy: approaching 100% (2000)

■ GOVERNMENT

Leader(s): Head of State: King Albert II. Prime Min. Guy Verhofstadt

Government Type: federal parliamentary democracy under a constitutional monarch

Administrative Divisions: 10 provinces and 1 region

Nationhood: Oct. 4, 1830 (from the Netherlands)

National Holiday: Independence Day, July 21

■ ECONOMY

Overview: a small, private enterprise-based economy possessing few natural resources, it is therefore highly vulnerable to the state of world markets; burgeoning public debt offsets economic growth
GDP: US$297.6 billion, per capita US$29,000; real growth rate 0.6% (2002 est.)
Inflation: 2.5% (2001)
Industries: accounts for 24% of GDP (2001); engineering and metal products, processed food and beverages, chemicals, basic metals, textiles, glass, petroleum, coal
Labour Force: 4.3 million (2001); 73% community, social and business services, 25% industry, 2% agriculture
Unemployment: 11.7% (Dec. 2002)
Agriculture: accounts for 1% of GDP (2001); emphasis on livestock production—beef, veal, pork, milk; major crops are sugar beets, fresh vegetables, fruit, grain and tobacco; net importer of farm products
Natural Resources: coal, natural gas

■ FINANCE/TRADE

Currency: Belgian franc (BF) = 100 centimes; Euro (€); on January 1, 2002 the Euro became the sole currency for everyday transactions.
International Reserves Excluding Gold: US$11.855 billion (Dec. 2002)
Gold Reserves: 8.294 million fine troy ounces (Dec. 2002)
Budget: revenues US$113.4 billion, expenditures US$106 billion, including capital expenditures of US$7.17 billion (2000)
Defence Expenditures: 3.2% of central government expenditure (2001)
Education Expenditures: n.a.
External Debt: US$28.3 billion (1999 est.)
Exports: US$208.763 billion (2002 est.) Belgium-Luxembourg Economic Union; commodities: iron and steel, transportation equipment, tractors, diamonds, petroleum products; partners: European Community, US
Imports: US$190.145 billion (2002 est.) Belgium-Luxembourg Economic Union; commodities: fuels, grains, chemicals, foodstuffs; partners: Netherlands, Germany, France, UK, US

■ COMMUNICATIONS

Daily Newspapers: 160/1,000 inhabitants (2000)
Televisions: 543/1,000 inhabitants (2001)
Radios: 793/1,000 inhabitants (2001)
Telephones: 498 lines/1,000 inhabitants (2001)

■ TRANSPORTATION

Motor Vehicles: 5,100,000; 4,600,000 passenger cars (2000 est.)
Roads: 145,774 km, 116,182 km paved
Railway: 3,422 km
Air Traffic: 8,489,000 passengers carried (2001)
Airports: 42; 25 have paved runways (2002)

Canadian Embassy: The Canadian Embassy, 2, Avenue de Tervuren, 1040 Brussels, Belgium. Tel: (011-32-2) 741-0611. Fax: (011-32-2) 741-0643. e-mail: bru@dfait-maeci.gc.ca
Embassy in Canada: Embassy of the Kingdom of Belgium, 80 Elgin St, 4th Fl, Ottawa ON K1P 1B7. Tel: (613) 236-7267. Fax: (613) 236-7882. e-mail: ambabel.ottawa@diplobel.org

Belize

Long-Form Name: Belize
Capital: Belmopan

■ GEOGRAPHY

Area: 22,960 sq. km
Coastline: 386 km
Climate: tropical; very hot and humid; rainy season (May to Feb.)
Environment: frequent devastating hurricanes (Sept. to Dec.) and coastal flooding, especially in south; deforestation; industrial and agricultural water pollution
Terrain: flat, swampy coastal plain; low mountains in south
Land Use: 10% arable land; 1% permanent crops; 2% meadows and pastures; 84% forest and woodland; 3% other; includes 30 sq. km irrigated
Location: Central (Latin) America, just S of Mexico bordering on Caribbean Sea

■ PEOPLE

Population: 262,999 (July 2002 est.)
Nationality: Belizean
Age Structure: 0–14 yrs: 41.6%; 15–64: 54.9%; 65+: 3.5% (2002 est.)
Population Growth Rate: 2.65% (2002 est.)
Net Migration: 0 migrants/1,000 population (2002 est.)
Ethnic Groups: 31% Creole, 44.1% Mestizo, 9.2% Maya, 6.2% Garifuna, 9.5% other
Languages: English (official), Spanish, Maya, Garifuna (Carib)
Religions: 62% Roman Catholic, 30% Protestant sects, 2% none, 6% other
Birth Rate: 31.08/1,000 population (2002 est.)
Death Rate: 4.60/1,000 population (2002 est.)
Infant Mortality: 24.31 deaths/1,000 live births (2002 est.)

Life Expectancy at Birth: 69.17 years male, 73.87 years female (2002 est.)
Total Fertility Rate: 3.96 children born/woman (2002 est.)
Literacy: 93.2% (2000)

■ GOVERNMENT

Leader(s): Head of State: Queen Elizabeth II, Gov. Gen. Colville Young. Prime Min. Said Musa
Government Type: parliamentary democracy
Administrative Divisions: 6 districts
Nationhood: Sept. 21, 1981 (from UK; Belize formerly known as British Honduras)
National Holiday: Independence Day, Sept. 21

■ ECONOMY

Overview: economy primarily based on agriculture and merchandising; sugar is the main crop; tourism and construction are becoming increasingly important
GDP: US$830 million, per capita US$3,250; real growth rate 3.0% (2001 est.)
Inflation: 1.2% (2001)
Industries: accounts for 24% of GDP (2001); sugar refining, clothing, timber and forest products, furniture, rum, soap, beverages, cigarettes, tourism, garment production, citrus concentrates
Labour Force: 71,000; 27% agriculture, 55% services, 18% industry
Unemployment: 12.8% (1999 est.)
Agriculture: accounts for 18% of GDP (including fish and forestry) and 75% of export earnings (2001); commercial crops include sugar cane, bananas, coca, citrus fruit; expanding output of lumber and cultured shrimp; net importer of basic foods
Natural Resources: arable land potential, timber, fish, hydroelectric power

■ FINANCE/TRADE

Currency: Belizean dollar ($BZ) = 100 cents
International Reserves Excluding Gold: US$115 million (Dec. 2002)
Gold Reserves: n.a.
Budget: revenues US$186 million; expenditures US$253 million, including capital expenditures of US$ n.a. (2000 est.)
Defence Expenditures: n.a.
Education Expenditures: n.a.
External Debt: US$708 million (2001)
Exports: US$178 million (2002 est.); commodities: sugar, clothing, seafood, molasses, bananas, citrus, wood and wood products; partners: EU, US, UK, CARICOM, Canada
Imports: US$510 million (2002 est.); commodities: machinery and transportation

equipment, food, beverages, tobacco, manufactured goods, fuels, chemicals, pharmaceuticals; partners: US, Mexico, Central America, UK

■ COMMUNICATIONS

Daily Newspapers: none
Televisions: n.a.
Radios: n.a.
Telephones: 156 lines/1,000 inhabitants (1999)

■ TRANSPORTATION

Motor Vehicles: 5,600; 2,400 passenger cars
Roads: 2,880 km; 490 km paved
Railway: none
Air Traffic: n.a.
Airports: 44; 4 have paved runways (2002)

Canadian Embassy: Consulate of Canada, 80 Princess Margaret Drive, Belize City, Belize. Mailing address: P.O. Box 610, Belize City, Belize. Tel: (011-501) 2-31-060. Fax: (011-501) 2-30060. e-mail: cdcon.bze@btl.net
Embassy in Canada: c/o High Commission for Belize, 2535 Massachusetts Ave NW, Washington DC 20008, USA. Tel: (202) 332-9636. Fax: (202) 332-6888. e-mail: belize@oas.org

---

Benin

Long-Form Name: Republic of Benin
Capital: Porto Novo (official); Cotonou (de facto)

■ GEOGRAPHY

Area: 112,620 sq. km
Coastline: 121 km
Climate: tropical; hot, humid in south; semi-arid in north
Environment: hot, dry, dusty harmattan wind may affect north in winter; deforestation; desertification; recent droughts have severely affected marginal agriculture in north; insufficient safe drinking water
Terrain: mostly flat to undulating plain; some hills and low mountains
Land Use: 13% arable land; 4% permanent crops; 4% meadows and pastures; 31% forest and woodland; 48% other; includes 120 sq. km irrigated
Location: WC Africa, bordering on South Atlantic Ocean

■ PEOPLE

Population: 6,787,625 (July 2002 est.)
Nationality: Beninese (sing. & pl.)
Age Structure: 0–14 yrs: 47.2%; 15–64: 50.5%; 65+:2.3% (2002 est.)

Population Growth Rate: 2.91% (2002 est.)
Net Migration: 0 migrants/1,000 population (2002 est.)
Ethnic Groups: 99% African (42 ethnic groups, most important being Fon, Adja, Yoruba, Bariba); 5,500 Europeans
Languages: French (official); also Fon, Yoruba, Fulami, Bariba
Religions: majority Animist, 15% Islam, 15% Christian
Birth Rate: 43.66/1,000 population (2002 est.)
Death Rate: 14.52/1,000 population (2002 est.)
Infant Mortality: 88.52 deaths/1,000 live births (2002 est.)
Life Expectancy at Birth: 48.81 years male, 50.61 years female (2002 est.)
Total Fertility Rate: 6.14 children born/woman (2002 est.)
Literacy: 39% (1999)

■ GOVERNMENT

Leader(s): Pres. Mathieu Kerekou
Government Type: republic under multiparty democratic rule
Administrative Divisions: 6 provinces
Nationhood: Aug. 1, 1960 (from France; Benin formerly known as Dahomey)
National Holiday: National Day, Aug. 1

■ ECONOMY

Overview: one of the least developed countries in the world; limited natural resources and an underdeveloped infrastructure characterize the economy; agricultural products are a major export
GDP: US$6.8 billion, per capita US$1,040; real growth rate 5.4% (2001 est.)
Inflation: 4.0% (2001)
Industries: accounts for 14% of GDP; palm oil and palm kernel oil processing, textiles, beverages, petroleum, cigarettes, construction materials, foodstuffs
Labour Force: 2.9 million (2001); 70.2% agriculture, 23.1% services, 6.6% industry
Unemployment: n.a.
Agriculture: accounts for 36% of GDP (2001); small farms produce 90% of agricultural output; production is dominated by food crops—corn, sorghum, cassava, yams, beans and rice; cash crops include cotton, palm oil and peanuts; poultry and livestock output has not kept up with consumption
Natural Resources: small offshore oil deposits, limestone, marble, timber

■ FINANCE/TRADE

Currency: Communauté financière africaine franc (CFAF) = 100 centimes
International Reserves Excluding Gold: US$582 million (Oct. 2002)
Gold Reserves: 0.011 million fine troy ounces (Jun. 2000)
Budget: revenues US$377.4 million; expenditures US$561.8 million, including capital expenditures of US$ n.a. (2001)
Defence Expenditures: 8.3% of central government expenditure (1999)
Education Expenditures: n.a
External Debt: US$1.665 billion (2001)
Exports: US$216 million (2002 est.); commodities: cotton, crude oil, cocoa, palm products; partners: Brazil, France, Indonesia, Thailand, Morocco, Portugal, Côte d'Ivoire
Imports: US$504 million (2002 est.); commodities: foodstuffs, tobacco, petroleum products, capital goods; partners: France, US, China, Côte d'Ivoire, Netherlands, Japan

■ COMMUNICATIONS

Daily Newspapers: 5/1,000 inhabitants (2000)
Televisions: 44/1,000 inhabitants (2001)
Radios: 441/1,000 inhabitants (2001)
Telephones: 9 lines/1,000 inhabitants (2001)

■ TRANSPORTATION

Motor Vehicles: 56,000; 36,400 passenger cars (1997 est.)
Roads: 6,787 km; 1,357 km paved
Railway: 578 km (2000)
Air Traffic: 46,000 passengers carried (2001)
Airports: 5; 1 has a paved runway (2002)

Canadian Embassy: The Canadian Embassy, Immeuble Trade Centre, 6th and 7th Floors, 23 Avenue Nogues, Le Plateau, Abidjan, 01 Côte d'Ivoire. Mailing address: c/o The Canadian Embassy, P.O. Box 4104, Abidjan 01, Côte d'Ivoire. Tel: (011-225) 20-21-30-07-00. Fax: (011-225) 20-30-07-20. e-mail: abdjn@dfait-maeci.gc.ca
Embassy in Canada: Embassy of the Republic of Benin, 58 Glebe Ave, Ottawa ON K1S 2C3. Tel: (613) 233-4429. Fax: (613) 233-8952. e-mail: ambaben2@on.aira.com

Bermuda

Long-Form Name: Commonwealth of Bermuda
Capital: Hamilton

■ GEOGRAPHY

Area: 58.8 sq. km

Climate: subtropical; mild, humid; gales, strong winds common in winter
Land Use: 6% arable land; 0% permanent crops; 0% meadows and pastures; 0% forest and woodland; 94% other; includes n.a. sq. km irrigated
Location: North Atlantic Ocean, E of United States

■ PEOPLE

Population: 64,482 (July 2003 est.)
Nationality: Bermudian
Age structure: 0–14 years: 19.2%;15–64 years: 69.3%; 65 years and over: 11.5% (2003 est.)
Population Growth Rate: 0.72% (2003 est.)
Net Migration: 2.56 migrant(s)/1,000 population (2003 est.)
Ethnic Groups: 58% black, 36% white, 6% other
Languages: English (official), Portuguese
Religions: 39% non-Anglican Protestant, 27% Anglican, 15% Roman Catholic, 19% other
Birth Rate: 12.13 births/1,000 population (2003 est.)
Death Rate: 7.46 deaths/1,000 population (2003 est.)
Infant Mortality: 9.05 deaths/1,000 live births
Life Expectancy at Birth: 75.38 years male, 79.49 years female (2003 est.)
Total Fertility Rate: 98% (1970 est.)

■ GOVERNMENT

Colony/Territory of: Dependent Territory of the United Kingdom
Leader(s): Head of State: Queen Elizabeth II, Gov. Thorold Masefield. Prem. Jennifer Smith
Government Type: dependent territory of the UK, with internal self-government
National Holiday: Bermuda Day, May 24

■ ECONOMY

Overview: a successful tourist industry accounts for its high per capita income; the industrial sector is small, and agriculture is limited by the lack of suitable land; 80% of food must be imported

■ FINANCE/TRADE

Currency: Bermudian dollar ($Ber) = 100 cents

Canadian Embassy: The Canadian Commission to Bermuda, c/o The Canadian Consulate General, 1251 Avenue of the Americas, New York NY, 10020-1175, USA. Tel: (212) 596-1628. Fax: (212) 596-1790. e-mail: cngny@dfait-maeci.gc.ca
Representative to Canada: c/o British High Commission, 80 Elgin St, Ottawa ON K1P 5K7. Tel: (613) 237-1530. Fax: (613) 237-7980.

Email should be sent using the appropriate form at the British High Commission's Website at http://www.britain-in-canada.org

Bhutan

Long-Form Name: Kingdom of Bhutan
Capital: Thimphu

■ GEOGRAPHY

Area: 47,000 sq. km
Coastline: none: landlocked
Climate: varies; tropical in southern plains; cool winters and hot summers in central valleys; severe winters and cool summers in Himalayas
Environment: violent storms coming from the Himalayas were the source of the country's name, which means Land of the Thunder Dragon; soil erosion and limited access to water are ongoing problems
Terrain: mostly mountainous with some fertile valleys and savanna
Land Use: 2% arable land; negligible permanent crops; 6% meadows and pastures; 66% forest and woodland; 26% other; includes 400 sq. km irrigated
Location: S Asia

■ PEOPLE

Population: 2,094,176 (July 2002 est.)
Nationality: Bhutanese (sing. & pl.)
Age Structure: 0–14 yrs: 39.8%; 15–64: 56.2%; 65+: 4.0% (2002 est.)
Population Growth Rate: 2.15% (2002 est.)
Net Migration: 0 migrants/1,000 population (2002 est.)
Ethnic Groups: 50% Bhote, 35% ethnic Nepalese, 15% indigenous or migrant tribes
Languages: Bhotes speak various Tibetan dialects—the most widely spoken dialect is Dzongkha (official); Nepalese speak various Nepalese dialects
Religions: 75% Mahayana Buddhism (state religion), Hinduism (25%, mainly ethnic Nepalese)
Birth Rate: 35.26/1,000 population (2002 est.)
Death Rate: 13.74/1,000 population (2002 est.)
Infant Mortality: 106.79 deaths/1,000 live births (2002 est.)
Life Expectancy at Birth: 53.53 years male, 52.83 years female (2002 est.)
Total Fertility Rate: 5.0 children born/woman (2002 est.)
Literacy: 42.0% (1999 est.)

■ GOVERNMENT

Leader(s): King Jigme Singye Wangchuk, Prime Min. Kinzang Dorji
Government Type: monarchy; special treaty relationship with India
Administrative Divisions: 18 districts (dzongkhag, sing. & pl.)
Nationhood: Aug. 8, 1949 (from India)
National Holiday: National Day, Dec. 17

■ ECONOMY

Overview: agriculture and forestry are the bedrock of the economy; it is poorly developed due to omnipresent rugged topography
GDP: US$2.5 billion, per capita US$1,200; real growth rate 6.0% (2001 est.)
Inflation: 3.9% (2001)
Industries: accounts for 20% of GDP (2001 est.); cement, chemical products, mining, distilling, food processing, handicrafts, wood products, calcium carbide. Industries are small and technologically underdeveloped
Labour Force: exact figures not available; there is a massive lack of skilled labour. 93% of the population is employed in agriculture, 5% in service, 2% in industry and commerce.
Unemployment: n.a.
Agriculture: accounts for 45% of GDP (2001), provides a living for 90% of the population; based on subsistence farming and animal husbandry; self-sufficient in food except for foodgrains; other production—rice, corn, root crops, citrus fruit, dairy and eggs
Natural Resources: timber, hydroelectricity, gypsum, calcium carbide, tourism potential

■ FINANCE/TRADE

Currency: ngultrum (Nu) = 100 chetrum; Indian currency is also legal tender
International Reserves Excluding Gold: US$275 million (Sept. 2002)
Gold Reserves: n.a.
Budget: exact figures n.a.; the government of India finances almost 60% of Bhutan's expenditures
Defence Expenditures: negligible
Education Expenditures: 15.14% of central government expenditure (2001)
External Debt: US$265 million (2001)
Exports: US$116 million (1999); commodities: cardamom, gypsum, timber, handicrafts, cement, fruit, electricity, precious stones, spices; partners: India, Bangladesh
Imports: US$182 million (1999); commodities: fuel and lubricants, grain, machinery and parts, vehicles, fabrics, rice; partners: India, Japan, UK, Germany, US

■ COMMUNICATIONS

Daily Newspapers: none
Televisions: n.a.
Radios: n.a.
Telephones: 18 lines/1,000 inhabitants (1999)

■ TRANSPORTATION

Motor Vehicles: n.a.
Roads: 3,285 km; 1,994 km surfaced
Railway: none
Air Traffic: 42,000 passengers carried (1999 est.)
Airports: 2; 1 has paved runway (2002)

Canadian Embassy: The Canadian High Commission, 7/8 Shantipath, Chanakyapuri, New Delhi 110021; mailing address: P.O. Box 5207, Chanakyapur, New Delhi, India. Tel: (011-91-11) 687-6500. Fax: (011-91-11) 687-6579. e-mail: delhi@dfait-maeci.gc.ca
Embassy in Canada: Consular Representation of Bhutan, 255 Consumers Road, Ste 401, Toronto ON M2J 5B6. Tel: (416) 498-3150. Fax: (416) 498-7296. e-mail: ecsondra@web.ca

Bolivia

Long-Form Name: Republic of Bolivia
Capital: La Paz (seat of government); Sucre (legal capital and seat of judiciary)

■ GEOGRAPHY

Area: 1,098,580 sq. km
Coastline: none: landlocked
Climate: varies with altitude; humid and tropical to cold and semi-arid
Environment: cold, thin air of high plateau is obstacle to efficient fuel combustion; over-grazing, soil erosion, desertification; defor-estation, pollution of drinking water
Terrain: Andes Mountains, high plateau, hills, lowland plains in Amazon basin
Land Use: 2% arable land; negligible permanent crops; 24% meadows and pastures; 53% forest and woodland; 21% other; includes 1,280 sq. km irrigated
Location: C South America

■ PEOPLE

Population: 8,445,134 (July 2002 est.)
Nationality: Bolivian
Age Structure: 0–14 yrs: 37.8%; 15–64: 57.7%; 65+: 4.5 (2001 est.)
Population Growth Rate: 1.69% (2002 est.)
Net Migration: -1.42 migrants/1,000 population (2002 est.)
Ethnic Groups: 30% Quechua, 25% Aymara, 30% mixed,15% European

Languages: Spanish, Quechua and Aymara (all official)
Religions: 95% Roman Catholic; 5% Protestant, especially Methodist
Birth Rate: 26.41/1,000 population (2002 est.)
Death Rate: 8.05/1,000 population (2002 est.)
Infant Mortality: 57.52 deaths/1,000 live births (2002 est.)
Life Expectancy at Birth: 61.86 years male, 67.10 years female (2002 est.)
Total Fertility Rate: 3.37 children born/woman (2002 est.)
Literacy: 85.5% (2000)

■ GOVERNMENT

Leader(s): Pres. Gonzalo Sanchez de Lozada Bustamante, V. Pres. Carlos Diego Mesa Gisbert
Government Type: republic
Administrative Divisions: 9 departments (departmentos, sing. —departmento)
Nationhood: Aug. 6, 1825 (from Spain)
National Holiday: Independence Day, Aug. 6

■ ECONOMY

Overview: a poor economy vulnerable to price fluctuations for its small number of exports; market-oriented economic reforms and tighter fiscal discipline are leading to generally improving economic conditions
GDP: US$21.4 billion, per capita US$2,600; real growth rate 0% (2001 est.)
Inflation: 1.6% (2001)
Industries: accounts for 31% of GDP (2000); mining, smelting, petroleum, food and beverage, tobacco, handicrafts, clothing; illicit drug industry reportedly produces the largest revenues
Labour Force: 3.5 million (2001); 29.1% trade and tourism, 26.2% community, social and business services, 19.4% manufacturing
Unemployment: n.a.
Agriculture: accounts for about 14% of GDP (including forestry and fisheries) (2000); principal commodities—soybeans, coffee, coca, cotton, corn, sugar cane, rice, potatoes, timber; self-sufficient in food
Natural Resources: tin, natural gas, crude oil, zinc, tungsten, antimony, silver, iron ore, lead, gold, timber, hydroelectric power

■ FINANCE/TRADE

Currency: Boliviano ($b) = 100 centavos
International Reserves Excluding Gold: US$580 million (Dec. 2002)
Gold Reserves: 0.911 million fine troy ounces (Dec. 2002)

Budget: revenues US$4 billion; expenditures US$4 billion, including capital expenditures of US$ n.a. (2002 est.)
Defence Expenditures: 6.1% of total government expenditure (2001)
Education Expenditures: 19.84% of government expenditure (2000)
External Debt: US$4.682 billion (2001)
Exports: US$1.724 billion (2001); commodities: metals 45%, natural gas 32%, coffee, soybeans, sugar, cotton, gold, timber; partners: US, Peru, Colombia, UK, Brazil
Imports: US$1.724 billion (2001); commodities: food, petroleum, consumer goods, capital goods; partners: US, Brazil, Argentina, Chile, Peru

■ COMMUNICATIONS

Daily Newspapers: 55/1,000 inhabitants (2000)
Televisions: 121/1,000 inhabitants (2001)
Radios: 676/1,000 inhabitants (2001)
Telephones: 62 lines/1,000 inhabitants (2001)

■ TRANSPORTATION

Motor Vehicles: 433,000; 200,000 passenger cars
Roads: 49,400 km; 2,500 km paved
Railway: 3,691 km
Air Traffic: 1,560,000 passengers carried (2001)
Airports: 1,109 airfields; 12 have paved runways (2002)

Canadian Embassy: The Consulate of Canada Calle Victor Sanjinez No. 2678 Edificio Barcelona, 2nd Floor, Plaza Espana, Sopacachi, La Paz; mailing address: Casilla Postal 13032, La Paz, Bolivia. Tel: (011-591-2) 241-5021. Fax: (011-591-2) 241-4453. e-mail: lapaz@dfait-maeci.gc.ca
Embassy in Canada: Embassy of the Republic of Bolivia, 130 Albert St, Ste 416, Ottawa ON K1P 5G4. Tel: (613) 236-5730. Fax: (613) 236-8237. e-mail: info@boliviaemb.ca

Bosnia and Herzegovina

Long-Form Name: Republic of Bosnia and Herzegovina
Capital: Sarajevo

■ GEOGRAPHY

Area: 51,129 sq. km
Coastline: 20 km
Climate: hot summers and cold winters; regions with high elevation have short, cool summers and long, severe winters; mild, rainy winters along the coast

Environment: air pollution; scarce water; waste disposal sites limited; subject to frequent destructive earthquakes
Terrain: mountains and valleys
Land Use: 14% arable; 5% permanent crops; 20% meadows and pastures; 39% forests; 22% other; includes 20 sq. km irrigated
Location: SE Europe

■ PEOPLE

Population: 3,964,388 (July 2002 est.)
Nationality: Bosnian, Herzegovinian
Age Structure: 0–14 yrs: 19.8%; 15–64: 70.6%; 65+: 9.6% (2002 est.)
Population Growth Rate: 0.76% (2002 est.)
Net Migration: 2.97 migrants/1,000 population (2002 est.)
Ethnic Groups: 31% Serb, Bosniak 44%, Croat 17%, Yugoslav 5.5%, other 2.5%; Note: Bosniak has replaced Muslim as an ethnic term, partly to avoid confusion with the religious term Muslim, an adherent of Islam.
Languages: Croatian, Serbian, Bosnian
Religions: 40% Muslim, 31% Orthodox, 15% Catholic, 4% Protestant, 10% other
Birth Rate: 12.76/1,000 population (2002 est.)
Death Rate: 8.10/1,000 population (2002 est.)
Infant Mortality: 23.53 deaths/1,000 live births (2002 est.)
Life Expectancy at Birth: 69.30 years male, 74.93 years female (2002 est.)
Total Fertility Rate: 1.71 children born/woman (2002 est.)
Literacy: n.a.

■ GOVERNMENT

Leader(s): Presidential Chairman Dragan Covic. Note: the central government. is headed by a tripartite presidency with one representative of each of the three major ethnic constituencies
Government Type: emerging federal democratic republic
Administrative Divisions: 2 first-order administrative divisions
Nationhood: Mar. 1, 1992 (from Yugoslavia)
National Holiday: Bilt National Day, Nov. 25

■ ECONOMY

Overview: though farms are almost entirely privately owned, they are small and inefficient, and food must be imported; inter-ethnic warfare has caused sharp decreases in industrial output and soaring unemployment
GDP: US$7 billion, per capita US$1,800; real growth rate 6.0% (2001 est.)
Inflation: 8% (2000 est.)

Industries: accounts for 28% of GDP; steel production, mining (esp. coal, iron ore, lead, zinc), manufacturing (esp. vehicle assembly, textiles, tobacco products, wood furniture), oil refining
Labour Force: 1.9 million (2000); 2% agriculture, 45% industry and mining
Unemployment: 35-40% (1999 est.)
Agriculture: accounts for 16% of GDP; regularly produces less than half the region's food needs; foothills of northern Bosnia support orchards, vineyards, livestock and some wheat and corn; long winters and heavy precipitation reduce agricultural output in mountains; farms are generally not very productive
Natural Resources: coal, iron, bauxite, manganese, timber, copper, lead, zinc, chromium, hydroelectric power

■ FINANCE/TRADE

Currency: convertible marka = 100 convertible pfenniga
International Reserves Excluding Gold: n.a.
Gold Reserves: n.a.
Budget: expenditures US$1.6 billion; revenues and capital expenditures n.a. (2000 est.)
Defence Expenditures: 24.3% of central government expenditure (1999)
Education Expenditures: n.a.
External Debt: US$2.226 billion (2001)
Exports: $1.082 billion (2001); partners include; Croatia, Switzerland, Italy, Germany
Imports: $3.217 billion (2001); commodities; foodstuffs, machinery and transport equipment, textiles, petroleum products. partners include: Croatia, Slovenia, Germany, Italy

■ COMMUNICATIONS

Daily Newspapers: 152/1,000 inhabitants (2000)
Televisions: 111/1,000 inhabitants (2001)
Radios: 243/1,000 inhabitants (2001)
Telephones: 111 lines/1,000 inhabitants (2001)

■ TRANSPORTATION

Motor Vehicles: n.a.
Roads: 21,846 km; 14,020 km paved
Railway: 1,021 km (2000)
Air Traffic: 65,000 passengers carried (2001)
Airports: 27; 8 have paved runways (2002)

Canadian Embassy: The Canadian Embassy, 4 Grbavicka, 71000 Sarajevo, Bosnia and Herzegovina. Tel: (011-387-33) 222-033. Fax: (011-387-33) 222-038. e-mail: sjevo@dfait-maeci.gc.ca
Embassy in Canada: Embassy of Bosnia and Herzogovina, 130 Albert St., Ste 805, Ottawa

ON K1P 5G4. Tel: (613) 236-0028. Fax: (613) 236-1139. e-mail: n.a.

Botswana

Long-Form Name: Republic of Botswana
Capital: Gaborone

■ GEOGRAPHY

Area: 600,370 sq. km
Coastline: none: landlocked
Climate: subtropical to semi-arid; warm winters and hot summers
Environment: overgrazing; desertification; limited resources of fresh water, periodic droughts, sand and dust storms
Terrain: predominantly flat to gently rolling tableland; Kalahari Desert in southwest
Land Use: 1% arable land; 0% permanent crops; 46% meadows and pastures; 47% forest and woodland; 6% other; includes 10 sq. km irrigated
Location: S Africa

■ PEOPLE

Population: 1,591,232 (July 2002 est.)
Nationality: Motswana (sing.), Batswana (pl.)
Age Structure: 0–14 yrs: 40.0%; 15–64: 55.8%; 65+: 4.2% (2002 est.)
Population Growth Rate: 0.18% (2002 est.)
Net Migration: 0 migrants/1,000 population (2002 est.)
Ethnic Groups: 95% Batswana; about 4% Kalanga, Basarwa and Kgalagadi; about 1% white
Languages: English (official), Setswana
Religions: 50% indigenous beliefs, 50% Christian
Birth Rate: 28.04/1,000 population (2002 est.)
Death Rate: 26.26/1,000 population (2002 est.)
Infant Mortality: 64.72 deaths/1,000 live births (2002 est.)
Life Expectancy at Birth: 35.15 years male, 35.43 years female (2002 est.)
Total Fertility Rate: 3.60 children born/woman (2002 est.)
Literacy: 77.2% (2000)

■ GOVERNMENT

Leader(s): Pres. Festus Gontebanye Mogae; V. Pres. Seretse Ian Khama
Government Type: parliamentary republic
Administrative Divisions: 10 districts and 4 town councils
Nationhood: Sept. 30, 1966 (from UK; Botswana formerly known as Bechuanaland)
National Holiday: Independence Day, Sept. 30

■ ECONOMY

Overview: economy based on mining (diamonds) and traditionally, cattle raising and crops; exhibits high unemployment
GDP: US$12.4 billion, per capita US$7,800; real growth rate 4.7% (2001 est.)
Inflation: 6.6% (2001)
Industries: accounts for 44% of GDP (2000); livestock processing; mining of diamonds, copper, nickel, coal, salt, soda ash, potash; tourism
Labour Force: 800,000 (2001); 36.6% community, social and business services; 18% trade and tourism, 11.2% manufacturing; 19,000 are employed in various mines in South Africa
Unemployment: 40% (2000 est.)
Agriculture: plagued by erratic rainfall and poor soil; accounts for only 4% of GDP; subsistence farming predominates; cattle raising supports 50% of the population; must import large share of food needs. Products include sorghum, millet, corn, peanuts, beans, livestock.
Natural Resources: diamonds, copper, nickel, salt, soda ash, potash, coal, iron ore, silver, natural gas

■ FINANCE/TRADE

Currency: pula (P) = 100 thebe
International Reserves Excluding Gold: US$5.521 billion (Dec. 2002)
Gold Reserves: n.a.
Budget: revenues US$2.3 billion; expenditures US$2.4 billion, including capital expenditures of US$ n.a. (FY2001/02)
Defence Expenditures: 9.8% of central government expenditure (1999)
Education Expenditures: n.a.
External Debt: US$370 million (2001)
Exports: US$2.480 billion (2001); commodities: diamonds 72%, copper and nickel 5%, meat 4%, cattle, animal products; partners: Switzerland, US, UK, other European Community-associated members of Southern African Customs Union
Imports: US$1.816 billion (2001); commodities: foodstuffs, vehicles, textiles, petroleum products; partners: Southern African Customs Union, EFTA, Zimbabwe

■ COMMUNICATIONS

Daily Newspapers: 27/1,000 inhabitants (2000)
Televisions: 30/1,000 inhabitants (2001)
Radios: 150/1,000 inhabitants (2001)
Telephones: 91 lines/1,000 inhabitants (2001)

■ TRANSPORTATION

Motor Vehicles: 111,000; 48,000 passenger cars (2000 est.)

Roads: 10,217 km; 5,620 km paved
Railway: 888 km
Air Traffic: 168,000 passengers carried (2001)
Airports: 92; 10 have paved runways (2002)

Canadian Embassy: The Consulate of Canada, Vision Hire Building, Plot 182, Queen's Road, Gaborone, Botswana; mailing address: P.O. Box 882, Gaborone, Botswana. Tel: (011-267) 39-44-11. Fax: (011-267) 39-44-11. e-mail: canada. consul@info.bw
Embassy in Canada: c/o High Commission for the Republic of Botswana, 1531-1533 New Hampshire Ave. NW, Washington DC 20036, USA. Tel: (202) 244-4990. Fax: (202) 244-4164. e-mail: n.a.

Brazil

Long-Form Name: Federative Republic of Brazil
Capital: Brasilia

■ GEOGRAPHY

Area: 8,511,965 sq. km; includes Arquipélago de Fernando de Noronha, Atol das Rocas, Ilha da Trindade, Ilhas Martin Vaz and Penedos de São Pedro e São Paulo
Coastline: 7,491 km
Climate: mostly tropical, but temperate in south
Environment: recurrent droughts in northeast; floods and frost in south; deforestation in Amazon basin; air and water pollution in Rio de Janeiro and São Paulo and several other large cities
Terrain: mostly flat to rolling lowlands in north; some plains, hills, mountains and narrow coastal belt
Land Use: 5% arable land; 1% permanent crops; 22% meadows and pastures; 58% forest and woodland; 14% other; includes 26,560 sq. km irrigated
Location: E South America

■ PEOPLE

Population: 176,029,560 (July 2002 est.)
Nationality: Brazilian
Age Structure: 0–14 yrs: 28.0%; 15–64: 66.4%; 65+: 5.6% (2002 est.)
Population Growth Rate: 0.87% (2002 est.)
Net Migration: -0.03 migrants/1,000 population (2002 est.)
Ethnic Groups: Portuguese, Italian, German, Japanese, black, Amerindian; 55% white, 38% mixed, 6% black, 1% other
Languages: Portuguese (official), Spanish, English, French
Religions: 70% Roman Catholic (nominal)

Birth Rate: 18.08/1,000 population (2002 est.)
Death Rate: 9.32/1,000 population (2002 est.)
Infant Mortality: 35.87 deaths/1,000 live births (2002 est.)
Life Expectancy at Birth: 59.40 years male, 67.91 years female (2002 est.)
Total Fertility Rate: 2.05 children born/woman (2002 est.)
Literacy: 85.2% (2000)

■ GOVERNMENT

Leader(s): Pres. Luiz Inacio Lula da Silva, V. Pres. Jose Alencar
Government Type: federative republic
Administrative Divisions: 26 states (estados, sing. — estado) and 1 federal district (distrito federal)
Nationhood: Sept. 7, 1822 (from Portugal)
National Holiday: Independence Day, Sept. 7

■ ECONOMY

Overview: inflation has dropped sharply and sweeping reforms have boosted the economy, but the domestic debt remains burdensome. Brazil's natural resources remain a major, long-term economic strength
GDP: US$1.34 trillion, per capita US$7,400; real growth rate 1.9% (2001 est.)
Inflation: 6.9% (2001)
Industries: accounts for 32% of GDP (2000); textiles and other consumer goods, shoes, chemicals, cement, lumber, iron ore, steel, motor vehicles and auto parts, metalworking, capital goods, tin
Labour Force: 80.7 million (2001); 53% community, social and business services, 23% agriculture, 24% industry
Unemployment: 9.6% (2001)
Agriculture: accounts for 9% of GDP (2000); world's largest producer and exporter of coffee and orange juice concentrate and second-largest exporter of soybeans; self-sufficient in food, except for wheat. Products also include rice, corn, cocoa
Natural Resources: iron ore, manganese, bauxite, nickel, uranium, phosphates, tin, hydro-electricity, gold, platinum, crude oil, timber

■ FINANCE/TRADE

Currency: real (CR$) = 100 centavos
International Reserves Excluding Gold: US$37.684 billion (Dec. 2002)
Gold Reserves: 0.442 million fine troy ounces (Dec. 2002)
Budget: revenues US$100.6 billion; expenditures US$91.6 billion, including capital expenditures of US$ n.a. (2000)

Defence Expenditures: 5.2% of total government expenditure (2001)
Education Expenditures: 6.14% of central government expenditure (1998)
External Debt: US$226.362 billion (2001)
Exports: US$58.024 billion (2002 est.); commodities: coffee, soybeans, footwear, metallurgical products, foodstuffs, iron ore, automobiles and parts; partners: US, Argentina, Germany, Japan, Italy, Netherlands
Imports: US$47.547 billion (2002 est.); commodities: crude oil, capital goods, chemical products, foodstuffs, coal; partners: US, Argentina, Germany, Japan, Italy

■ COMMUNICATIONS

Daily Newspapers: 43/1,000 inhabitants (2000)
Televisions: 349/1,000 inhabitants (2001)
Radios: 433/1,000 inhabitants (2001)
Telephones: 218 lines/1,000 inhabitants (2001)

■ TRANSPORTATION

Motor Vehicles: 16,700,000; 13,100,000 passenger cars
Roads: 1.98 million km; 184,140 km paved
Railway: 30,539 km (1999)
Air Traffic: 34,286,000 passengers carried (2001)
Airports: 3,365 airfields; 665 have paved runways (2002)

Canadian Embassy: Avenida das Nacoes, Quadra 803, Lote 16, Brasilia DF, 70410-900; mailing address: Caixa Postal 341, 70359-900 Brasilia DF, Brazil. Tel: (011-55-61) 424-5400. Fax: (011-55-61) 424-5490. e-mail: brsla@dfait-maeci.gc.ca
Embassy in Canada: Embassy of the Federative Republic of Brazil, 450 Wilbrod St, Ottawa ON K1N 6M8. Tel: (613) 237-1090. Fax: (613) 237-6144. e-mail: mailbox@brasembottawa.org

---

British Indian Ocean Territory

Long-Form Name: British Indian Ocean Territory
Capital: None; Victoria (Seychelles) is administrative headquarters

■ GEOGRAPHY

Area: 60 sq. km
Climate: tropical maritime, hot and humid, moderated by trade winds
Land Use: no arable land; 0% permanent crops; meadows or pastures; 100% other
Location: Indian Ocean, the Chagos Archipelago island group E of Madagascar, S of India

■ PEOPLE

Population: no indigenous inhabitants; US and UK military personnel
Nationality: n.a.
Ethnic Groups: n.a. — no indigenous population
Languages: n.a. — no indigenous population

■ GOVERNMENT

Colony/Territory of: Dependent Territory of the United Kingdom
Leader(s): Head of State: Queen Elizabeth II, Commissioner to the BIOT: Alan Huckle, Admin: Charles Hamilton
Government Type: dependent overseas territory of Great Britain
National Holiday: n.a.

■ ECONOMY

Overview: fishing, coconuts, guano fertilizer; all economic activity takes place on the largest island, Diego Garcia, where joint US–UK defence facilities are located; there are no industrial or agricultural activities on the islands

■ FINANCE/TRADE

Currency: pound sterling (£ or £ stg)

Canadian Embassy: c/o of the Canadian High Commission, Macdonald House, 1 Grosvenor Square, London W1K 4AB, England, UK. Tel: (011-44-20) 7258-6600. Fax: (011-44-20) 7258-6333. e-mail: ldn@dfait-maeci.gc.ca
Representative to Canada: c/o British High Commission, 80 Elgin St, Ottawa ON K1P 5K7. Tel: (613) 237-1530. Fax: (613) 237-7980. Email should be sent using the appropriate form at the British High Commission's Website at http://www.britain-in-canada.org

---

British Virgin Islands

Long-Form Name: British Virgin Islands
Capital: Road Town

■ GEOGRAPHY

Area: 150 sq. km; includes the island of Anegada
Climate: subtropical and humid; moderated by trade winds; hurricanes, and tropical storms occur from July to Oct.
Land Use: 20% arable; 7% permanent crops; 33% permanent pastures; 7% forests; 33% other
Location: Caribbean islands, E of Puerto Rico

■ PEOPLE

Population: 21,272 (July 2002 est.)
Nationality: British Virgin Islander

Ethnic Groups: 90% black, 10% white, Asian, and other
Languages: English (official)

■ GOVERNMENT

Colony/Territory of: Dependent territory of the UK
Leader(s): Head of State: Queen Elizabeth II, Gov. Thomas T. Macan, Chief Min. Orlando Smith
Government Type: overseas territory of Great Britain
National Holiday: Territory Day, July 1

■ ECONOMY

Overview: one of the most prosperous economies in the Caribbean; highly dependent on tourism

■ FINANCE/TRADE

Currency: US dollar ($) = 100 cents

Canadian Embassy: c/o The Canadian High Commission, Macdonald House, 1 Grosvenor Square, London, W1K 4AB, England, UK. Tel: (011-44-20) 7258-6600. Fax: (011-44-20) 7258-6333. e-mail: ldn@dfait-maeci.gc.ca
Representative to Canada: c/o British High Commission, 80 Elgin St, Ottawa ON K1P 5K7. Tel: (613) 237-1530. Fax: (613) 237-7980. Email should be sent using the appropriate form at the British High Commission's Website at http://www.britain-in-canada.org

Brunei Darussalam

Long-Form Name: Negara Brunei Darussalam
Capital: Bandar Seri Begawan

■ GEOGRAPHY

Area: 5,770 sq. km
Coastline: 161 km
Climate: tropical; hot, humid, rainy
Environment: typhoons, earthquakes and severe floods occasionally occur
Terrain: flat coastal plain rises to mountainous east; hilly lowland in west
Land Use: 1% arable land; 1% permanent crops; 1% meadows and pastures; 85% forest and woodland; 12% other; includes 10 sq. km irrigated
Location: Indonesia (island of Borneo), bordering on South China Sea and Malaysia

■ PEOPLE

Population: 350,898 (July 2002 est.)
Nationality: Bruneian
Age Structure: 0–14 yrs: 30.2%; 15–64: 67.0%; 65+: 2.8% (2002 est.)

Population Growth Rate: 2.06% (2002 est.)
Net Migration: 3.91 migrants/1,000 population (2002 est.)
Ethnic Groups: 62% Malay, 15% Chinese, 6% indigenous, 17% other
Languages: Malay (official), English and Chinese
Religions: Islam (official, mainly Sunni Muslims); majority of Chinese are Buddhist, Confucian or Taoist
Birth Rate: 20.06/1,000 population (2002 est.)
Death Rate: 3.38/1,000 population (2002 est.)
Infant Mortality: 13.91 deaths/1,000 live births (2002 est.)
Life Expectancy at Birth: 71.68 years male, 76.56 years female (2002 est.)
Total Fertility Rate: 2.40 children born/woman (2002 est.)
Literacy: 91.5% (2000)

■ GOVERNMENT

Leader(s): Sultan, Prime Min. and Min. of Defence Sir Hassanal Bolkiah
Government Type: constitutional sultanate
Administrative Divisions: 4 districts (daerah-daerah, sing. —daerah)
Nationhood: Jan. 1, 1984 (from UK)
National Holiday: National Day, Feb. 23

■ ECONOMY

Overview: economy is based on crude oil and natural gas exports and the per capita GDP is one of the highest for underdeveloped nations; almost totally supported by exports of crude oil and natural gas
GDP: US$6.2 billion, per capita US$18,000; real growth rate 3.0% (2001 est.)
Inflation: 1% (1999 est.)
Industries: accounts for 45% of GDP (2001 est.); petroleum, liquefied natural gas, construction
Labour Force: approx. 150,000; 42% production of oil, natural gas and construction; 48% government, 10% agriculture, forestry and fishing
Unemployment: n.a.
Agriculture: accounts for 5% of GDP; imports about 80% of its food needs; principal crops and livestock include rice, cassava, bananas, buffalo and pigs
Natural Resources: crude oil, natural gas, timber

■ FINANCE/TRADE

Currency: Bruneian dollar ($B) = 100 cents
International Reserves Excluding Gold: n.a.
Gold Reserves: n.a.
Budget: n.a.
Defence Expenditures: n.a.
Education Expenditures: n.a.

External Debt: none
Exports: exact figures n.a.; commodities: crude oil, liquefied natural gas, petroleum products; partners: Japan, US, South Korea, Thailand
Imports: exact figures n.a.; commodities: machinery and transport equipment, manufactured goods, food, beverages, tobacco, consumer goods; partners: Singapore, UK, Malaysia, US

■ COMMUNICATIONS

Daily Newspapers: 1 in total
Televisions: n.a.
Radios: n.a.
Telephones: 246 lines/1,000 inhabitants (1999)

■ TRANSPORTATION

Motor Vehicles: 166,000; 148,000 passenger cars
Roads: 1,712 km; 1,284 km paved
Railway: 13 km private line
Air Traffic: 1,001,000 passengers carried (1999 est.)
Airports: 2; 1 has paved runway (2001 est.)

Canadian Embassy: The High Commission of Canada, 5th Floor, Jalan McArthur Bldg., Bandar Seri Begawan; mailing address: P.O. Box 2808, Bandar Seri, Begawan B58675, Brunei Darussalam. Tel: (011-673-2) 22-00-43. Fax (011-673-2) 22-00-40. e-mail: bsbgn@dfait-maeci.gc.ca
Embassy in Canada: High Commission for Brunei, 395 Laurier Ave E, Ottawa ON K1N 6R4. Tel: (613) 234-5656. Fax: (613) 234-4397. e-mail: bhco@bellnet.ca

Bulgaria

Long-Form Name: Republic of Bulgaria
Capital: Sofia

■ GEOGRAPHY

Area: 110,910 sq. km
Coastline: 354 km
Climate: temperate; cold, damp winters; hot, dry summers
Environment: subject to earthquakes, landslides, deforestation, air and water pollution
Terrain: mostly mountains with lowlands in north and south
Land Use: 43% arable land; 2% permanent crops; 14% meadows and pastures; 38% forest and woodland; 3% other; includes 8,000 sq. km irrigated
Location: SE Europe, bordering on Black Sea

■ PEOPLE

Population: 7,621,337 (July 2002 est.)
Nationality: Bulgarian
Age Structure: 0–14 yrs: 14.6%; 15–64: 68.5%; 65+: 16.9% (2002 est.)
Population Growth Rate: -1.11% (2002 est.)
Net Migration: -4.74 migrants/1,000 population (2002 est.)
Ethnic Groups: 83% Bulgarian, 8.5% Turk, 2.6% Gypsy, 2.5% Macedonian, 3.4% Armenian, Russian, Tatar and other
Languages: Bulgarian (official), Turkish; secondary languages closely correspond to ethnic breakdown
Religions: 85% Bulgarian Orthodox, 13% Muslim (practised by Turkish and Pomak minorities), 0.8% Jewish, 0.7% Roman Catholic, 0.5% Protestant, Gregorian-Armenian and other
Birth Rate: 8.05/1,000 population (2002 est.)
Death Rate: 14.42/1,000 population (2002 est.)
Infant Mortality: 14.18 deaths/1,000 live births (2002 est.)
Life Expectancy at Birth: 67.98 years male, 75.22 years female (2002 est.)
Total Fertility Rate: 1.13 children born/woman (2002 est.)
Literacy: 98.4% (2000)

■ GOVERNMENT

Leader(s): Pres. Georgi Purvanov, Prime Min. Simeon Saxe-Coburg Gotha
Government Type: parliamentary democracy
Administrative Divisions: 28 provinces (oblasti, sing. —oblast)
Nationhood: March 3, 1878 (from Ottoman Empire)
National Holiday: Liberation Day, Mar. 3

■ ECONOMY

Overview: heavily in debt with low growth, the economy is also hindered by antiquated industrial plants; continues to adjust to a market economy; the government's structural reform program includes privatization and, where appropriate, liquidation of state-owned enterprises; agricultural policies have been liberalized
GDP: US$50.6 billion, per capita US$6,600; real growth rate 3.4% (2002 est.)
Inflation: 7.4% (2001)
Industries: accounts for 29% of GDP (2001); food processing, machine building and metal working, electronics, chemicals
Labour Force: 4.1 million (2001); 31% industry, 26% agriculture, 43% community, social and business services
Unemployment: 14.1% (2001)
Agriculture: accounts for 14% of GNP (2001); climate and soil conditions support livestock

raising and the growing of various grain crops, oilseeds, vegetables, fruit and tobacco; more than one-third of the arable land devoted to grain; world's fourth largest tobacco exporter; surplus food producer
Natural Resources: bauxite, copper, lead, zinc, coal, timber, arable land

■ FINANCE/TRADE

Currency: lev (pl. leva) (Lv) = 100 stotinki
International Reserves Excluding Gold: US$4.407 billion (Dec. 2002)
Gold Reserves: 1.282 million fine troy ounces (Dec. 2002)
Budget: revenues US$5.57 billion; expenditures US$5.68 billion, capital expenditures US$ n.a. (2001 est.)
Defence Expenditures: 7.9% of total government expenditure (2001)
Education Expenditures: 4.34% of central government expenditure (2000)
External Debt: US$9.615 billion (2001)
Exports: US$5.428 billion (2002 est.); commodities: machinery and equipment 60.5%, agricultural products 14.7%, manufactured consumer goods 10.6%, fuels, minerals, raw materials and metals 8.5%, other 5.7%; partners: Italy, Turkey, Germany, Greece, Serbia and Montenegro
Imports: US$7.292 billion (2002 est.); commodities: fuels, minerals, raw materials 45.2%, machinery and equipment 39.8%, manufactured consumer goods 4.6%, agricultural products 3.8%, other 6.6%; partners: Russia, Germany, Italy, France

■ COMMUNICATIONS

Daily Newspapers: 116/1,000 inhabitants (2000)
Televisions: 453/1,000 inhabitants (2001)
Radios: 543/1,000 inhabitants (2001)
Telephones: 359 lines/1,000 inhabitants (2001)

■ TRANSPORTATION

Motor Vehicles: 2,050,000; 1,800,000 passenger cars (2000 est.)
Roads: 37,288 km; 33,786 km paved
Railway: 4,294 km
Air Traffic: 234,000 passengers carried (2001)
Airports: 215; 128 have paved runways (2002)

Canadian Embassy: c/o The Canadian Embassy, 36 Nicolae Iorga, 71118 Bucharest, Romania; Postal Address: The Canadian Embassy, P.O. Box 117, Post Office No. 22, Bucharest, Romania. Tel (011-40-21) 307-5000. Fax (011-40-21) 307-5010. e-mail: bucst@dfait-maeci.gc.ca

Embassy in Canada: Embassy of the Republic of Bulgaria, 325 Stewart St, Ottawa ON K1N 6K5. Tel: (613) 789-3215. Fax: (613) 789-3524. e-mail: mailmn@storm.ca

Burma

see Myanmar

Burkina Faso

Long-Form Name: Burkina Faso
Capital: Ouagadougou

■ GEOGRAPHY

Area: 274,200 sq. km
Coastline: none: landlocked
Climate: tropical; warm, dry winters; hot, wet summers
Environment: recent droughts and desertification severely affecting marginal agricultural activities, population distribution, economy; overgrazing;
Terrain: mostly flat to dissected, undulating plains; hills in west and southeast
Land Use: 13% arable land; 0% permanent crops; 22% meadows and pastures; 50% forest and woodland; 15% other; includes 200 sq. km irrigated
Location: WC Africa

■ PEOPLE

Population: 12,603,185 (July 2002 est.)
Nationality: Burkinabe (sing. & pl.)
Age Structure: 0–14 yrs: 47.3%; 15–64: 49.8%; 65+: 2.9% (2002 est.)
Population Growth Rate: 2.64% (2002 est.)
Net Migration: -0.84 migrants/1,000 population (2002 est.)
Ethnic Groups: more than 50 tribes; principal tribe is Mossi (over 40% of pop.); other important groups are Gurunsi, Senufo, Lobi, Bobo, Mande and Fulani
Languages: French (official); tribal languages belong to Sudanic family, spoken by 90% of population
Religions: 40% indigenous beliefs, about 50% Muslim, 10% Christian (mainly Roman Catholic)
Birth Rate: 44.34/1,000 population (2002 est.)
Death Rate: 17.07/1,000 population (2002 est.)
Infant Mortality: 105.30 deaths/1,000 live births (2002 est.)
Life Expectancy at Birth: 45.45 years male, 46.78 years female (2002 est.)
Total Fertility Rate: 6.26 children born/woman (2002 est.)
Literacy: 23.0% (1999)

■ GOVERNMENT

Leader(s): Head of State: Capt. Blaise Compaoré, Prime Min. Paramango Ernest Yonli
Government Type: parliamentary democracy
Administrative Divisions: 45 provinces
Nationhood: Aug. 5, 1960 (from France; Burkina Faso formerly known as Upper Volta)
National Holiday: Republic Day — December 11

■ ECONOMY

Overview: a poor economy with high population density and few natural resources, it relies heavily on subsistence agriculture; economic development is hindered by a poor communications network; agriculture provides approximately one-third of national income
GDP: US$12.8 billion, per capita US$1,040; real growth rate 4.7% (2001 est.)
Inflation: 4.9% (2001)
Industries: accounts for 28% of GDP (2000); agricultural processing plants; brewery, cement and brick plants; soap, cigarettes, textiles, gold mining and extraction; a few other small consumer goods enterprises
Labour Force: 5.7 million (2001); 90% agriculture, 4.3% industry, 5% services; 20% of male labour force migrates annually to neighbouring countries for seasonal employment
Unemployment: n.a.
Agriculture: accounts for 31% of GDP (2000); cash crops—peanuts, shea nuts, sesame, cotton; food crops—sorghum, millet, corn, rice; livestock; not self-sufficient in foodgrains
Natural Resources: manganese, limestone, marble; small deposits of gold, antimony, copper, nickel, bauxite, lead, phosphates, zinc, silver

■ FINANCE/TRADE

Currency: Communauté financière africaine franc (CFAF) = 100 centimes
International Reserves Excluding Gold: US$234 million (Oct. 2002)
Gold Reserves: 0.011 million fine troy ounces (Aug. 2000)
Budget: revenues US$316 million; expenditures US$ n.a., including capital expenditures of US$ n.a. (2001)
Defence Expenditures: 5.9% of central government expenditure (1999)
Education Expenditures: n.a.
External Debt: US$1.490 billion (2001)
Exports: US$174 million (2002); commodities: oilseeds, cotton, live animals, gold; partners: Italy, France, Venezuela, Benelux

Imports: US$514 million (2002); commodities: grain, dairy products, petroleum, machinery; partners: Côte d'Ivoire, Venezuela, France

■ COMMUNICATIONS

Daily Newspapers: 1/1,000 inhabitants (2000)
Televisions: 103/1,000 inhabitants (2001)
Radios: 433/1,000 inhabitants (2001)
Telephones: 5 lines/1,000 inhabitants (2001)

■ TRANSPORTATION

Motor Vehicles: 55,000; 35,600 passenger cars
Roads: 12,506 km; 2,001 km paved
Railway: 622 km
Air Traffic: 100,000 passengers carried (2001)
Airports: 33; 2 have paved runways (2002)

Canadian Embassy: The Canadian Embassy, rue Agostino Neto, Ouagadougou; mailing address: Office of the Canadian Embassy, P.O. Box 548, Ouagadougou 01, Province du Kadiogo, Burkina Faso. Tel: (011-226) 31-18-95. Fax (011-226) 31-19-00. e-mail: ouaga@dfait-maeci.gc.ca
Embassy in Canada: Embassy of Burkina Faso, 48 Range Rd, Ottawa ON K1N 8J4. Tel: (613) 238-4796. Fax: (613) 238-3812. e-mail: burkina.faso@sympatico.ca

Burundi

Long-Form Name: Republic of Burundi
Capital: Bujumbura

■ GEOGRAPHY

Area: 27,830 sq. km
Coastline: none: landlocked
Climate: temperate; warm; occasional frost in uplands
Environment: soil exhaustion; soil erosion; deforestation; flooding and landslides are natural hazards
Terrain: mostly rolling to hilly highland; some plains
Land Use: 44% arable land; 9% permanent crops; 36% meadows and pastures; 3% forest and woodland; 8% other; includes 740 sq. km irrigated
Location: EC Africa

■ PEOPLE

Population: 6,373,002 (July 2002 est.)
Nationality: Burundian
Age Structure: 0–14 yrs: 46.5%; 15–64: 50.7%; 65+: 2.8% (2002 est.)
Population Growth Rate: 2.36% (2002 est.)

Net Migration: 0 migrants/ 1,000 population (2002 est.)
Ethnic Groups: Africans: 85% Hutu (Bantu), 14% Tutsi (Hamitic), 1% Twa (Pygmy); non-Africans: 3,000 Europeans, 2,000 South Asians
Languages: Kirundi and French (official); Swahili used commercially
Religions: about 67% Christian (62% Roman Catholic, 5% Protestant), 32% indigenous beliefs, 1% Muslim
Birth Rate: 39.87/1,000 population (2002 est.)
Death Rate: 16.30/1,000 population (2002 est.)
Infant Mortality: 69.97 deaths/1,000 live births (2002 est.)
Life Expectancy at Birth: 45.08 years male, 46.83 years female (2002 est.)
Total Fertility Rate: 6.07 children born/woman (2002 est.)
Literacy: 46.9% (1999)

■ GOVERNMENT

Leader(s): Pres. Domitien Ndayizeye; V. Pres. Alphonse Kadege
Government Type: republic
Administrative Divisions: 16 provinces
Nationhood: July 1, 1962 (from UN trusteeship under Belgian administration)
National Holiday: Independence Day, July 1

■ ECONOMY

Overview: economy is heavily dependent on the coffee crop and therefore vulnerable to market conditions; there are only a few basic industries; massive ethnic-based violence has also interfered with economic activity
GDP: US$3.7 billion, per capita US$600; real growth rate 1.4% (2001 est.)
Inflation: 9.2% (2001)
Industries: accounts for 18% of GDP (2001 est.); light consumer goods such as blankets, shoes, soap; assembly of imports; public works construction; food processing
Labour Force: 3.8 million (2001); 39.6% community, social and business services, 14.8% manufacturing
Unemployment: n.a.
Agriculture: accounts for 50% of GDP (2001 est.); 90% of population dependent on subsistence farming; marginally self-sufficient in food production; cash crops—coffee, cotton, tea; food crops—corn, sorghum, sweet potatoes, bananas, manioc; livestock—meat, milk, hides and skins
Natural Resources: nickel, uranium, rare earth oxide, peat, cobalt, copper, platinum (not yet exploited), vanadium, hydroelectric power

■ FINANCE/TRADE

Currency: Burundi franc (FBu) = 100 centimes
International Reserves Excluding Gold: US$59 million (Dec. 2002)
Gold Reserves: 0.001 million fine troy ounces (Dec. 2002)
Budget: revenues US$125 million, expenditures US$176 million, including capital expenditures of US$ n.a. (2000 est.)
Defence Expenditures: 27.1% of central government expenditure (2001)
Education Expenditures: 15.20% of central government expenditure (1999)
External Debt: US$1.065 billion (2001)
Exports: US$32 million (2002); commodities: coffee 88%, tea, sugar, cotton, hides and skins; partners: US, India, China, Japan, Singapore
Imports: US$134 million (2002); commodities: capital goods 31%, petroleum products 15%, foodstuffs, consumer goods; partners: EU, Tanzania, Zambia, India, China

■ COMMUNICATIONS

Daily Newspapers: 2/1,000 inhabitants (2000)
Televisions: 30/1,000 inhabitants (2001)
Radios: 220/1,000 inhabitants (2001)
Telephones: 3 lines/1,000 inhabitants (2001)

■ TRANSPORTATION

Motor Vehicles: 20,000; 8,200 passenger cars
Roads: 14,480 km; 1,028 km paved
Railway: none
Air Traffic: 12,000 passengers carried (2000)
Airports: 7; 1 has paved runways (2002)

Canadian Embassy: The Canadian High Commission, Comcraft House, 6th Floor, Haile Selassie Ave, Nairobi. Mailing address: c/o The Canadian High Commission, P.O. Box 30481, Nairobi, Kenya. Tel: (011-254-2) 21-48-04. Fax: (011-254-2) 22-69-87. e-mail: nrobi@dfait-maeci.gc.ca
Embassy in Canada: Embassy of the Republic of Burundi, 325 Dalhousie St., Suite 815, Ottawa ON K1N 7G2. Tel (613) 789-0414. Fax (613) 789-9537. e-mail: ambabucanada@infonet.ca

Cambodia

Long-Form Name: Kingdom of Cambodia
Capital: Phnom Penh

■ GEOGRAPHY

Area: 181,040 sq. km
Coastline: 443 km

Climate: tropical; rainy, monsoon season (May to Oct.); dry season (Dec. to Mar.); little seasonal temperature variation
Environment: a land of paddies and forests dominated by Mekong River and Tonle Sap; deforestation, monsoons; logging and strip mining are resulting in environmental degradation
Terrain: mostly low, flat plains; mountains in southwest and north
Land Use: 13% arable land; 0% permanent crops; 11% meadows and pastures; 66% forest and woodland; 10% other; includes 2,700 sq. km irrigated
Location: SE Asia, bordering on the Gulf of Siam

■ PEOPLE

Population: 12,775,324 (July 2002 est.)
Nationality: Cambodian
Age Structure: 0–14 yrs: 40.7%; 15–64: 55.8%; 65+: 3.5% (2002 est.)
Population Growth Rate: 2.24% (2002 est.)
Net Migration: 0 migrants/1,000 population (2002 est.)
Ethnic Groups: 90% Khmer (Cambodian), 5% Vietnamese, 1% Chinese, 4% other minorities
Languages: Khmer (official), French
Religions: 95% Theravada Buddhism, 5% Christianity
Birth Rate: 32.93/1,000 population (2002 est.)
Death Rate: 10.51/1,000 population (2002 est.)
Infant Mortality: 64.00 deaths/1,000 live births (2002 est.)
Life Expectancy at Birth: 54.81 years male, 59.50 years female (2002 est.)
Total Fertility Rate: 4.66 children born/woman (2002 est.)
Literacy: 67.8% (2000)

■ GOVERNMENT

Leader(s): King Norodom Sihanouk, Prime Min. Hun Sen
Government Type: liberal democracy under constitutional monarchy
Administrative Divisions: 20 provinces (khett, sing. & pl.) and 4 municipalities (krong, sing. & pl.)
Nationhood: Nov. 9, 1953 (from France)
National Holiday: Independence Day, Nov. 9

■ ECONOMY

Overview: a desperately poor country; the economy has suffered badly due to internal war; the country has not been able to feed its people; economy remains essentially rural, with 90% of the population dependent mainly on subsistence agriculture

GDP: US$18.7 billion, per capita US$1,500; real growth rate 5.3% (2001 est.)
Inflation: -0.6% (2001)
Industries: accounts for 15% of GDP (2000); rice milling, fishing, wood and wood products, rubber, cement, gem mining
Labour Force: 6.5 million (2001); 80% agriculture, 5% industry, 15% services
Unemployment: 2.8% (1999 est.)
Agriculture: accounts for 50% of GDP (2000), mainly subsistence farming except for rubber plantations; main crops—rice, rubber, corn; food shortages—rice, meat, vegetables, dairy products, sugar, flour
Natural Resources: timber, gemstones, some iron ore, manganese, phosphates, hydroelectricity potential

■ FINANCE/TRADE

Currency: new riel (KR) = 100 sen
International Reserves Excluding Gold: US$777 million (Dec. 2002)
Gold Reserves: n.a.
Budget: revenues US$363 million, expenditures US$532 million, including capital expenditures of US$225 (2000 est.)
Defence Expenditures: 26.0% of central government expenditure (1999)
Education Expenditures: n.a.
External Debt: US$2.704 billion total (2001)
Exports: US$1.296 billion (2001); commodities: timber, garments, rubber, rice, fish; partners: Singapore, US, Vietnam, Germany, UK
Imports: US$1.456 billion (2001); commodities: cigarettes, gold, construction materials, petroleum products, machinery, motor vehicles; partners: Singapore, Vietnam, Hong Kong, China, Thailand

■ COMMUNICATIONS

Daily Newspapers: 2/1,000 inhabitants (2000)
Televisions: 8/1,000 inhabitants (2001)
Radios: 119/1,000 inhabitants (2001)
Telephones: 2 lines/1,000 inhabitants (2001)

■ TRANSPORTATION

Motor Vehicles: 75,000; 62,000 passenger cars (2000)
Roads: 35,769 km, but some roads are in serious disrepair; 4,165 km paved
Railway: 603 km, much inoperational since 1973
Air Traffic: n.a.
Airports: 20; 5 have paved runways (2002)

Canadian Embassy: The Canadian Embassy, Villa 9, RV Senei Vinnavaut Oum, Chaktamouk, Daun Penh District, Phnom Penh. Tel: (011-

855-23) 213-470. Fax: (011-855-23) 211-389. e-mail: pnmpn@dfait-maeci.gc.ca
Embassy in Canada: c/o Embassy of the Kingdom of Cambodia, 866 UN Plaza, Ste. 420, New York, NY 10017, USA. Tel (212) 223-0676. Fax (212) 223-0425. e-mail: cambodia@un.int

Cameroon

Long-Form Name: Republic of Cameroon
Capital: Yaoundé

■ GEOGRAPHY

Area: 475,440 sq. km
Coastline: 402 km
Climate: varies with terrain from tropical along coast to semi-arid and hot in north
Environment: recent volcanic activity with release of poisonous gases; deforestation; overgrazing; desertification; diseases transmitted through the water supply are common
Terrain: coastal plain in southwest, dissected plateau in centre, mountains in west, plains in north
Land Use: 13% arable land; 2% permanent crops; 4% meadows and pastures; 78% forest and woodland; 3% other; includes 330 sq. km irrigated
Location: WC Africa, bordering on South Atlantic Ocean

■ PEOPLE

Population: 16,184,748 (July 2002 est.)
Nationality: Cameroonian
Age Structure: 0–14 yrs: 42.1%; 15–64: 54.5%; 65+: 3.4% (2002 est.)
Population Growth Rate: 2.36% (2002 est.)
Net Migration: 0 migrants/1,000 population (2001 est.)
Ethnic Groups: over 200 tribes of widely differing background; 31% Cameroon Highlanders, 19% Equatorial Bantu, 11% Kirdi, 10% Fulani, 8% Northwestern Bantu, 7% Eastern Nigritic, 13% other African, less than 1% non-African
Languages: English and French (official), 24 major African language groups, including Fang, Bamileke, Duala
Religions: 51% indigenous beliefs, 33% Christian, 16% Muslim
Birth Rate: 35.66/1,000 population (2002 est.)
Death Rate: 12.08/1,000 population (2002 est.)
Infant Mortality: 68.79 deaths/1,000 live births (2002 est.)
Life Expectancy at Birth: 53.51 years male, 55.23 years female (2002 est.)

Total Fertility Rate: 4.72 children born/woman (2002 est.)
Literacy: 75.8% (2000)

■ GOVERNMENT

Leader(s): Pres. Paul Biya, Prime Min. Peter Mafany Musonge
Government Type: unitary republic; multiparty presidential regime
Administrative Divisions: 10 provinces
Nationhood: Jan. 1, 1960 (from UN trusteeship under French administration; Cameroon formerly known as French Cameroon)
National Holiday: Republic Day, May 20

■ ECONOMY

Overview: an offshore oil industry has boosted the economy but the government is now emphasizing diversification, particularly in agriculture
GDP: US$26.4 billion, per capita US$1,700; real growth rate 4.9% (2001 est.)
Inflation: 4.5% (2001)
Industries: accounts for 20% of GDP (2000); crude oil products, small aluminum plant, food processing, light consumer goods industries, textiles, sawmills
Labour Force: 6.2 million (2001); 70% agriculture, 13% industry, 17% services
Unemployment: 30% (1998 est.)
Agriculture: the agriculture and forestry sectors provide employment for the majority of the population, contributing 44% to GNP (2000) and providing a high degree of self-sufficiency in staple foods
Natural Resources: crude oil, bauxite, iron ore, timber, hydroelectricity potential

■ FINANCE/TRADE

Currency: Communauté financière africaine franc (CFAF) = 100 centimes
International Reserves Excluding Gold: US$601 million (Nov. 2002)
Gold Reserves: 0.03 million fine troy ounces (Dec. 2002)
Budget: revenues US$2.2 billion; expenditures US$2.1 billion, including capital expenditures of US$ n.a. (FY2000/01 est.)
Defence Expenditures: 10.4% of total government expenditure (2001)
Education Expenditures: 12.00% of central government expenditure (1999)
External Debt: US$8.338 billion (2001)
Exports: US$1.489 billion (2000); commodities: petroleum products 56%, coffee, cocoa, cotton, aluminum, timber, manufacturing; partners: Italy, France, Netherlands

Imports: US$1.361 million (2000); commodities: machines and electrical equipment, transport equipment, chemical products, consumer goods; partners: France, Japan, US, Germany

■ COMMUNICATIONS

Daily Newspapers: 7/1,000 inhabitants (2000)
Televisions: 34/1,000 inhabitants (2001)
Radios: 163/1,000 inhabitants (2001)
Telephones: 7 lines/1,000 inhabitants (2001)

■ TRANSPORTATION

Motor Vehicles: 153,000; 92,000 passenger cars
Roads: 34,300 km; 4,288 km paved
Railway: 1,008 km
Air Traffic: 247,000 passengers carried (2001)
Airports: 49; 11 have paved runways (2002)

Canadian Embassy: The Canadian High Commission, Immeuble Stamiatades, Place de l'Hotel de Ville, Yaoundé, Cameroon; mailing address: P.O. Box 572, Yaounde, Cameroon. Tel: (011-237) 23-23-11. Fax: (011-237) 22-10-90. e-mail: yunde@dfait-maeci.gc.ca
Embassy in Canada: High Commission for the Republic of Cameroon, 170 Clemow Ave, Ottawa ON K1S 2B4. Tel: (613) 236-1522. Fax: (613) 236-3385. e-mail: cameroon@comnet.ca

Canada

Long-Form Name: Canada
Capital: Ottawa

■ GEOGRAPHY

Area: 9,976,140 sq. km
Coastline: 202,080 km
Climate: varies from temperate in south to subarctic and arctic in north
Environment: 80% of population concentrated within 160 km of US border; permafrost in north a serious obstacle to development; acid rain and ocean-water pollution resulting from industrial and agricultural activities are an increasing problem
Terrain: mostly plains with mountains in west and lowlands in southeast
Land Use: 5% arable land; negligible permanent crops; 3% meadows and pastures; 54% forest and woodland; 38% other; includes 7,200 sq. km irrigated
Location: N North America, bordering on North Atlantic Ocean, Arctic Ocean, North Pacific Ocean and United States

■ PEOPLE

Population: 32,207,113 (July 2003 est.)

Nationality: Canadian
Age Structure: 0–14 yrs: 18.5%; 15–64: 68.6%; 65+: 12.9% (2003 est.)
Population Growth Rate: 0.94% (2003 est.)
Net Migration: 6.07 migrants/1,000 population (2002 est.)
Ethnic Groups: 28% British, 23% French, 15% other European, 2% Amerindian, 6% Arab, 26% mixed background
Languages: English and French (both official)
Religions: 45% Roman Catholic, 12% United Church, 8% Anglican, 35% other
Birth Rate: 10.99/1,000 population (2003 est.)
Death Rate: 7.61/1,000 population (2003 est.)
Infant Mortality: 4.88 deaths/1,000 live births (2003 est.)
Life Expectancy at Birth: 76.44 years male, 83.38 years female (2003 est.)
Total Fertility Rate: 1.61 children born/woman (2003 est.)
Literacy: approaching 100% (2000)

■ GOVERNMENT

Leader(s): Head of State: Queen Elizabeth II, Gov. Gen. Adrienne Clarkson, Prime Min. Jean Chrétien
Government Type: confederation with parliamentary democracy
Administrative Divisions: 10 provinces, 3 territories
Nationhood: July 1, 1867 (from UK)
National Holiday: Canada Day, July 1

■ ECONOMY

Overview: abundant natural resources, skilled labour force, and high-tech industrialization characterize a market-oriented economy; Canada can anticipate solid economic prospects in the future
GDP: US$923 billion, per capita US$29,400; real growth rate 3.4% (2002 est.)
Inflation: 2.6% (2002 est.)
Industries: accounts for 27% of GDP (2001); processed and unprocessed minerals, food products, wood and paper products, transportation equipment, chemicals, fish products, petroleum, natural gas
Labour Force: 16.4 million (2001); 74% services, 15% manufacturing, 5% construction, 3% agriculture, 3% other
Unemployment: 8.0% (Feb. 2003)
Agriculture: accounts for 2% of GDP (2001); one of the world's major producers and exporters of grain (wheat and barley); key source of US agricultural imports; large forest resources cover 35% of total land area. Products also include

fruits, vegetables, tobacco, fish and dairy products

Natural Resources: nickel, zinc, copper, gold, lead, molybdenum, potash, silver, fish, timber, wildlife, coal, crude oil, natural gas

■ FINANCE/TRADE

Currency: dollar ($ or $Can) = 100 cents

International Reserves Excluding Gold: US$36.984 billion (Dec. 2002)

Gold Reserves: 0.599 million fine troy ounces (Dec. 2002)

Budget: revenues US$178.6 billion; expenditures US$161.4 billion, capital expenditures US$ n.a. (FY2000/01)

Defence Expenditures: 6.2% of central government expenditure (2001)

Education Expenditures: 2.29% of central government expenditure (2000)

External Debt: US $1.9 billion (2000)

Exports: US$250.191 billion (2002); commodities: newsprint, wood pulp, timber, grain, crude petroleum, natural gas, electricity, ferrous and non-ferrous ores, motor vehicles; partners: US, Japan, UK, Germany, other European Community

Imports: US$219.912 billion (2002 est.); commodities: processed foods, beverages, crude petroleum, chemicals, industrial machinery, motor vehicles, durable consumer goods, electronic computers; partners: US, Japan, UK, countries of the European Community

■ COMMUNICATIONS

Daily Newspapers: 159/1,000 inhabitants (2000)
Televisions: 700/1,000 inhabitants (2001)
Radios: 1,047/1,000 inhabitants (2001)
Telephones: 676 lines/1,000 inhabitants (2001)

■ TRANSPORTATION

Motor Vehicles: 18,400,000; 14,500,000 passenger cars (2000)

Roads: 901,902 km; 318,371 km paved

Railway: 36,114 km operational

Air Traffic: 24,204,000 passengers carried (2001)

Airports: 1,389; 507 have paved runways (2002)

Canadian Embassy: n.a.
Embassy in Canada: n.a.

Cape Verde

Long-Form Name: Republic of Cape Verde
Capital: Praia

■ GEOGRAPHY

Area: 4,033 sq. km
Coastline: 965 km

Climate: temperate; warm, dry, very erratic summer precipitation

Environment: subject to prolonged droughts; harmattan wind can obscure visibility; volcanically and seismically active; deforestation; desertification; overgrazing and overfishing

Terrain: steep, rugged, rocky, volcanic

Land Use: 11% arable land; negligible permanent crops; 6% meadows and pastures; negligible forest and woodland; 83% other; includes 30 sq. km irrigated

Location: Atlantic Ocean W of Africa

■ PEOPLE

Population: 408,760 (July 2002 est.)

Nationality: Cape Verdean

Age Structure: 0–14 yrs: 41.9%; 15–64: 51.5%; 65+: 6.6% (2002 est.)

Population Growth Rate: 0.85% (2002 est.)

Net Migration: -12.26 migrants/1,000 population (2002 est.)

Ethnic Groups: approx. 71% Creole (mulatto), 28% African, 1% European

Languages: Portuguese and Crioulo, a blend of Portuguese and West African tongues

Religions: Roman Catholicism fused with indigenous beliefs

Birth Rate: 27.81/1,000 population (2002 est.)

Death Rate: 7.01/1,000 population (2002 est.)

Infant Mortality: 51.86 deaths/1,000 live births (2002 est.)

Life Expectancy at Birth: 66.23 years male, 72.91 years female (2002 est.)

Total Fertility Rate: 3.91 children born/woman (2002 est.)

Literacy: 73.8% (2000)

■ GOVERNMENT

Leader(s): Pres. Pedro Pires, Prime Min. Jose Maria Pereira Neves

Government Type: republic

Administrative Divisions: 14 districts (concelhos, sing. —concelho)

Nationhood: July 5, 1975 (from Portugal)

National Holiday: Independence Day, July 5

■ ECONOMY

Overview: a service-oriented economy, which suffers from a poor natural resource base, a high birth rate and a long-term drought

GDP: US$600 million, per capita US$1,500; real growth rate 3.0% (2001 est.)

Inflation: 3.7% (2001)

Industries: accounts for 17% of GDP (2001), fish processing, salt mining, clothing factories, ship repair, construction materials, food and beverage production

Labour Force: n.a.; 52% agriculture (mostly subsistence), 25% services, 23% industry
Unemployment: 24% (1999 est.)
Agriculture: accounts for 11% of GDP (2001); largely subsistence farming; bananas are the only export crop; growth potential limited by poor soils and limited rainfall. Approximately 90% of food needs must be imported
Natural Resources: salt, basalt rock, pozzolana, limestone, kaolin, fish

■ FINANCE/TRADE

Currency: Cape Verdean escudo (C.V. Esc.) = 100 centavos
International Reserves Excluding Gold: US$77 million (Dec. 2002)
Gold Reserves: n.a.
Budget: revenues US$112 million; expenditures US$198 million, capital expenditures US$ n.a. (2000)
Defence Expenditures: n.a.
Education Expenditures: n.a.
External Debt: US$360 million (2001)
Exports: US$10 million (2001); commodities: fuel, shoes, garments, fish, bananas, salt; partners: Portugal, UK, Germany, Guinea-Bissau
Imports: US$248 million (2001); commodities: petroleum, foodstuffs, consumer goods, industrial products; partners: Portugal, Germany, France, UK

■ COMMUNICATIONS

Daily Newspapers: none
Televisions: n.a.
Radios: n.a.
Telephones: 112 lines/1,000 inhabitants (1999)

■ TRANSPORTATION

Motor Vehicles: 18,000; 11,000 passenger cars
Roads: 1,100 km; 858 km paved
Railway: none
Air Traffic: 273,000 passengers carried (1999 est.)
Airports: 9 (6 operational); 8 have paved runways (2002)

Canadian Embassy: c/o The Canadian Embassy, P.O. Box 3373, Dakar, Senegal. Tel: (011-221) 823-92-90. Fax: (011-221) 823-87-49. e-mail: dakar@dfait-maeci.gc.ca
Embassy in Canada: c/o Embassy of the Republic of Cape Verde, 3415 Massachusetts Ave NW, Washington DC 20007, USA. Tel: (202) 965-6820. Fax: (202) 965-1207. e-mail: n.a.

Cayman Islands

Long-Form Name: Cayman Islands
Capital: George Town (on Grand Cayman Island)

■ GEOGRAPHY

Area: 259 sq. km (three islands: Grand Cayman, Little Cayman, Cayman Brac)
Climate: tropical maritime; warm, rainy summers (May to Oct.); cool season: Nov. to March, hurricane-prone July to Nov.
Land Use: 0% arable; 0% permanent crops; 8% meadows and pastures; 23% forest and woodland; 69% other
Location: Caribbean Sea, S of Cuba

■ PEOPLE

Population: 36,273 (July 2002 est.)
Nationality: Caymanian
Ethnic Groups: 40% mixed, 20% white, 20% black, 20% expatriates of various ethnic groups, various Hispanic strains, descendants of European settlers
Languages: English (official)

■ GOVERNMENT

Colony/Territory of: Overseas territory of the United Kingdom
Leader(s): Head of State: Queen Elizabeth II, Gov. Bruce H. Dinwiddy
Government Type: British crown colony
National Holiday: Constitution Day (first Monday in July)

■ ECONOMY

Overview: chiefly tourism (75% of GDP and 75% of export earnings) and financial services; main export turtle products; imports: foodstuffs (about 90% of food and consumer goods must be imported), manufactured items, textiles, building materials, cars, petroleum products

■ FINANCE/TRADE

Currency: Caymanian dollar (CI$) = 100 cents

Canadian Embassy: c/o The Canadian High Commission, Macdonald House, 1 Grosvenor Square, London W1K 4AB, England, UK. Tel: (011-44-20) 7258-6600. Fax: (011-44-20) 7258-6333. e-mail: ldn@dfait-maeci.gc.ca
Representative to Canada: British High Commission, 80 Elgin St, Ottawa ON K1P 5K7. Tel: (613) 237-1530. Fax: (613) 237-7980. Email should be sent using the appropriate form at the British High Commission's Website at http://www.britain-in-canada.org

Central African Republic

Long-Form Name: Central African Republic
Capital: Bangui

■ GEOGRAPHY

Area: 622,984 sq. km
Coastline: none: landlocked
Climate: tropical; hot, dry winters; mild to hot, wet summers
Environment: hot, dry, dusty harmattan winds affect northern areas; poaching has diminished reputation as one of last great wildlife refuges; desertification and flooding; tap water is not safe to drink
Terrain: vast, flat to rolling, monotonous plateau; scattered hills in northeast and southwest
Land Use: 3% arable land; negligible permanent crops; 5% meadows and pastures; 75% forest and woodland; 17% other
Location: C Africa

■ PEOPLE

Population: 3,642,739 (July 2002 est.)
Nationality: Central African
Age Structure: 0–14 yrs: 43.0%; 15–64: 53.2%; 65+: 3.8% (2002 est.)
Population Growth Rate: 1.80% (2002 est.)
Net Migration: 0 migrants/1,000 population (2002 est.)
Ethnic Groups: about 80 ethnic groups, the majority of which have related ethnic and linguistic characteristics; 34% Baya, 27% Banda, 10% Sara, 21% Mandjia, 4% Mboum, 4% m'Baka; 6,500 Europeans, of whom 3,600 are French
Languages: French (official); Sangho (lingua franca and national language); Arabic, Hunsa, Swahili
Religions: 25% indigenous beliefs, 25% Protestant, 25% Roman Catholic, 15% Muslim, 10% other; animistic beliefs and practices strongly influence the Christian majority
Birth Rate: 36.60/1,000 population (2002 est.)
Death Rate: 18.62/1,000 population (2002 est.)
Infant Mortality: 103.81 deaths/1,000 live births (2002 est.)
Life Expectancy at Birth: 42.08 years male, 45.13 years female (2002 est.)
Total Fertility Rate: 4.77 children born/woman (2002 est.)
Literacy: 45.4% (1999)

■ GOVERNMENT

Leader(s): Pres. Francois Bozize, Prime Min. Abel Goumba

Government Type: republic
Administrative Divisions: 14 prefectures, 2 economic prefectures, 1 capital commune
Nationhood: Aug. 13, 1960 (from France; formerly known as Central African Empire)
National Holiday: Republic Day (proclamation of the republic), Dec. 1

■ ECONOMY

Overview: subsistence agriculture and forestry are the backbone of the economy. It suffers from a poor transportation infrastructure and a weak human resource base; diamond industry accounts for 54% of export earnings
GDP: US$4.6 billion, per capita US$1,300; real growth rate 1.8% (2001 est.)
Inflation: 3.0% (2000)
Industries: accounts for 20% of GDP (2001 est.); sawmills, breweries, diamond mining, textiles, footwear, assembly of bicycles and motorcycles
Labour Force: 1.8 million (2001); 32.6% construction industries, 30.5% manufacturing, 17.6% agriculture
Unemployment: n.a.
Agriculture: accounts for 55% of GDP (2001 est.); self-sufficient in food production except for grain; commercial crops—cotton, coffee, tobacco, timber; food crops—manioc, yams, millet, corn, bananas
Natural Resources: diamonds, uranium, timber, gold, oil, hydroelectric potential

■ FINANCE/TRADE

Currency: Communauté financière africaine franc (CFAF) = 100 centimes
International Reserves Excluding Gold: US$119 million (Nov. 2002)
Gold Reserves: 0.011 million fine troy ounces (Dec. 2002)
Budget: n.a.
Defence Expenditures: 15.4% of central government expenditure (1999)
Education Expenditures: n.a.
External Debt: US$822 million (2001)
Exports: US$143 million (2001); commodities: diamonds, cotton, coffee, timber, tobacco; partners: France, Benelux, Italy, Côte d'Ivoire, Spain, China
Imports: US$107 million (2001); commodities: food, textiles, petroleum products, machinery, electrical equipment, motor vehicles, chemicals, pharmaceuticals, consumer goods, industrial products; partners: France, Germany, Japan, Cameroon, Benelux, Côte d'Ivoire

■ COMMUNICATIONS

Daily Newspapers: 2/1,000 inhabitants (2000)
Televisions: 6/1,000 inhabitants (2000)

Radios: 80/1,000 inhabitants (2001)
Telephones: 2 lines/1,000 inhabitants (2001)

■ TRANSPORTATION

Motor Vehicles: 20,000; 11,000 passenger cars
Roads: 23,810 km; 429 km paved (2000)
Railway: none
Air Traffic: 46,000 passengers carried (2001)
Airports: 51; 3 have paved runways (2002)

Canadian Embassy: The Canadian High Commission, Immeuble Stamiatades, Place de l'Hotel de Ville, Yaoundé, Cameroon; mailing address: P.O. Box 572, Yaounde, Cameroon. Tel: (011-237) 22-32-311. Fax: (011-237) 22-21-090. e-mail: yunde@dfait-maeci.gc.ca
Embassy in Canada: c/o Embassy of the Central African Republic, 1618-22nd St NW, Washington DC 20008, USA. Tel: (202) 483-7800. Fax: (202) 332-9893. e-mail: n.a.

Chad

Long-Form Name: Republic of Chad
Capital: N'Djamena

■ GEOGRAPHY

Area: 1,284,000 sq. km
Coastline: none: landlocked
Climate: tropical in south, desert in north
Environment: hot, dry, dusty harmattan winds occur in north; drought and desertification adversely affecting south; subject to plagues of locusts; unsafe water supply
Terrain: broad, arid plains in centre, desert in north, mountains in northwest, lowlands in south
Land Use: 3% arable land; negligible permanent crops; 36% meadows and pastures; 26% forest and woodland; 35% others, includes 200 sq. km irrigated
Location: NC Africa

■ PEOPLE

Population: 8,997,237 (July 2002 est.)
Nationality: Chadian
Age Structure: 0–14 yrs: 47.8%; 15–64: 49.4%; 65+: 2.8% (2002 est.)
Population Growth Rate: 3.27% (2002 est.)
Net Migration: 0 migrants/1,000 population (2002 est.)
Ethnic Groups: some 200 distinct ethnic groups, most of whom are Muslims in the north and centre, and non-Muslims in the south; some 150,000 non-indigenous, of whom 1,000 are French

Languages: French and Arabic (official); Sara and Sango in south; more than 100 different languages and dialects are spoken
Religions: 50% Muslim, 25% Christian, 25% animism
Birth Rate: 47.74/1,000 population (2002 est.)
Death Rate: 15.06/1,000 population (2002 est.)
Infant Mortality: 93.46 deaths/1,000 live births (2002 est.)
Life Expectancy at Birth: 49.22 years male, 53.40 years female (2002 est.)
Total Fertility Rate: 6.50 children born/woman (2002 est.)
Literacy: 41% (1999)

■ GOVERNMENT

Leader(s): Pres. Lt.-Gen. Idriss Deby, Prime Min. Moussa Faki Mahamat
Government Type: republic
Administrative Divisions: 14 prefectures
Nationhood: Aug. 11, 1960 (from France)
National Holiday: Independence Day, Aug. 11

■ ECONOMY

Overview: one of the world's most under-developed countries; civil war, drought and food shortages have adversely affected the economy, which is based on subsistence farming and fishing
GDP: US$8.9 billion, per capita US$1,030; real growth rate 8.0% (2001 est.)
Inflation: 12.4% (2001)
Industries: accounts for 13% of GDP (2001 est.), cotton textile mills, slaughterhouses, soap, cigarettes, brewery, natron (sodium carbonate), construction materials
Labour Force: 3.8 million (2001); more than 80% of the labour force is engaged in agriculture.
Unemployment: n.a.
Agriculture: accounts for 38% of GDP (2001 est.); largely subsistence farming, herding, fishing; cotton most important cash crop; food crops include sorghum, millet, peanuts, rice, potatoes, manioc; livestock—cattle, sheep, goats, camels; self-sufficient in food in years of adequate rainfall
Natural Resources: small quantities of crude oil (unexploited but exploration beginning), uranium, natron, kaolin, fish (Lake Chad)

■ FINANCE/TRADE

Currency: Communauté financière africaine franc (CFAF) = 100 centimes
International Reserves Excluding Gold: US$194 million (Nov. 2002)
Gold Reserves: 0.011 million fine troy ounces (Dec. 2002)

Budget: n.a.
Defence Expenditures: 12.7% of central government expenditure (1999)
Education Expenditures: n.a.
External Debt: US$1.104 billion (2001)
Exports: US$166 million (2001); commodities: cotton 43%, cattle 35%, textiles 5%, fish; partners: Costa Rica, Nigeria, Portugal, Germany, Thailand, France
Imports: US$621 million (2001); commodities: machinery and transportation equipment 39%, industrial goods 20%, petroleum products 13%, foodstuffs 9%; partners: France, Cameroon, Nigeria, India

■ COMMUNICATIONS

Daily Newspapers: less than 1/1,000 inhabitants (2000)
Televisions: 1/1,000 inhabitants (2001)
Radios: 236/1,000 inhabitants (2001)
Telephones: 1 line/1,000 inhabitants (2001)

■ TRANSPORTATION

Motor Vehicles: 24,600; 10,000 passenger cars
Roads: 33,400 km; 450 km paved
Railway: none
Air Traffic: 46,000 passengers carried (2001)
Airports: 49; 7 have paved runways (2002)

Canadian Embassy: The Canadian High Commission, Immeuble Stamiatades, Place de l'Hotel de Ville, Yaoundé, Cameroon; mailing address: P.O. Box 572, Yaounde, Cameroon. Tel: (011-237) 22-32-311. Fax: (011-237) 22-21-090. e-mail: yunde@dfait-maeci.gc.ca
Embassy in Canada: c/o Embassy of the Republic of Chad, 2002 R St NW, Washington DC 20009, USA. Tel: (202) 462-4009. Fax: (202) 265-1937. e-mail: info@chadembassy.org

Channel Islands

Long-Form Name: Channel Islands; Guernsey: Bailiwick of Guernsey; Jersey: Bailiwick of Jersey
Capital: St. Helier (Jersey), St. Peter Port (Guernsey)

■ GEOGRAPHY

Area: Jersey: 116 sq. km; Guernsey: 194 sq. km
Climate: temperate, with mild winters and cool summers
Land Use: Jersey: 66% arable; remainder n.a.; Guernsey: n.a.
Location: English Channel, off the coast of France

■ PEOPLE

Population: Jersey: 89,775; Guernsey: 64,587 (July 2002 est.)
Nationality: Channel Islander
Ethnic Groups: English, French
Languages: English (official), French (official only on Jersey), Norman-French dialect

■ GOVERNMENT

Colony/Territory of: Dependent Territory of the United Kingdom
Leader(s): Head of State: Queen Elizabeth II; Jersey: Lt. Gov. A. J. C. Woodrow, Guernsey: Lt. Gov. and Commander-in-Chief Sir John Foley
Government Type: largely self-governing British Crown dependency
National Holiday: Liberation Day, May 9

■ ECONOMY

Overview: Jersey: economy is based chiefly on financial services, agriculture and tourism, vegetable and flower exports, Jersey cattle; Guernsey: tourism, financial services, Guernsey cattle, and tomato and flower exports make up backbone of the economy

■ FINANCE/TRADE

Currency: Jersey pound, Guernsey pound, both = 100 pence; both are at par with the British £

Canadian Embassy: c/o The Canadian High Commission, Macdonald House, 1 Grosvenor Square, London W1K 4AB, England, UK. Tel: (011-44-20) 7258-6600. Fax: (011-44-20) 7258-6333. e-mail: ldn@dfait-maeci.gc.ca
Representative to Canada: c/o British High Commission, 80 Elgin St, Ottawa ON K1P 5K7. Tel: (613) 237-1530. Fax: (613) 237-7980. Email should be sent using the appropriate form at the British High Commission's Website at http://www.britain-in-canada.org

Chile

Long-Form Name: Republic of Chile
Capital: Santiago

■ GEOGRAPHY

Area: 756,950 sq. km
Coastline: 6,435 km
Climate: temperate; desert in north; cool and damp in south
Environment: subject to severe earthquakes, active volcanism, tsunami; Atacama Desert one of world's driest regions; desertification; deforestation; air and water pollution

Terrain: low coastal mountains; fertile central valley; rugged Andes in east
Land Use: 5% arable land; negligible permanent crops; 18% meadows and pastures; 22% forest and woodland; 55% other; includes 18,000 sq. km irrigated
Location: SW South America

■ PEOPLE

Population: 5,498,930 (July 2002 est.)
Nationality: Chilean
Age Structure: 0–14 yrs: 26.9%; 15–64: 65.6%; 65+: 7.5% (2002 est.)
Population Growth Rate: 1.09% (2002 est.)
Net Migration: 0 migrants/1,000 population (2002 est.)
Ethnic Groups: 95% European and European-Amerindian, 3% Amerindian, 2% other
Languages: Spanish
Religions: 89% Roman Catholic, 11% Protestant and small Jewish population
Birth Rate: 16.46/1,000 population (2002 est.)
Death Rate: 5.59/1,000 population (2002 est.)
Infant Mortality: 9.12 deaths/1,000 live births (2002 est.)
Life Expectancy at Birth: 72.83 years male, 79.62 years female (2002 est.)
Total Fertility Rate: 2.13 children born/woman (2002 est.)
Literacy: 95.8% (2000)

■ GOVERNMENT

Leader(s): Pres. Ricardo Lagos
Government Type: republic
Administrative Divisions: 13 regions (regiones, sing. —region)
Nationhood: Sept. 18, 1810 (from Spain)
National Holiday: Independence Day, Sept. 18

■ ECONOMY

Overview: economy remains largely dependent on a few sectors, particularly copper mining (copper is the single largest export product), fishing and forestry
GDP: US$153 billion, per capita US$10,000; real growth rate 3.1% (2001 est.)
Inflation: 3.6% (2001)
Industries: accounts for 38% of GDP (2000); copper (Chile is the world's largest producer and exporter of copper), other minerals, foodstuffs, fish processing, iron and steel, wood and wood products, transport equipment, textiles, cement
Labour Force: 6.3 million (2001); 59% services, 27% industry, 14% agriculture
Unemployment: 7.8% (Nov. 2002)

Agriculture: accounts for about 8% of GDP (including fishing and forestry) (2000); major exporter of fruit, fish and timber products; major crops—wheat, corn, grapes, beans, sugar beets, potatoes, fruit; beef, poultry, fish; net agricultural importer
Natural Resources: copper, timber, iron ore, nitrates, precious metals, molybdenum

■ FINANCE/TRADE

Currency: peso ($CH) = 100 centavos
International Reserves Excluding Gold: US$15.341 billion (Dec. 2002)
Gold Reserves: 0.008 million fine troy ounces (Dec. 2002)
Budget: revenues US$16 billion; expenditures US$17 billion, including capital expenditures US$ n.a. (2000 est.)
Defence Expenditures: 12.4% of total government expenditure (2001)
Education Expenditures: 17.81% of central government expenditure (2000)
External Debt: US$38.360 billion (2001)
Exports: US$18.303 billion (2002 est.); commodities: copper 48%, industrial products 33%, molybdenum, iron ore, wood pulp, fishmeal, fruit; partners: US, Japan, UK, Brazil, China
Imports: US$17.237 billion (2002 est.); commodities: petroleum, wheat, capital goods, spare parts, raw materials; partners: US, Argentina, Brazil, China, Japan

■ COMMUNICATIONS

Daily Newspapers: 98/1,000 inhabitants (2000)
Televisions: 286/1,000 inhabitants (2001)
Radios: 759/1,000 inhabitants (2001)
Telephones: 233 lines/1,000 inhabitants (2001)

■ TRANSPORTATION

Motor Vehicles: 2,070,000; 1,300,000 passenger cars (2000 est.)
Roads: 79,800 km; 11,012 km paved
Railway: 6,701 km (2000)
Air Traffic: 5,301,000 passengers carried (2001)
Airports: 363; 71 have paved runways (2002)

Canadian Embassy: The Canadian Embassy, Edificio World Trade Centre, 12th Fl., Nueva Tajamar 481, Santiago, Chile; mailing address: Casilla 139-10, Santiago, Chile. Tel: (011-56-2) 362-9660. Fax: (011-56-2) 362-9663. e-mail: stago@dfait-maeci.gc.ca
Embassy in Canada: Embassy of the Republic of Chile, 50 O'Connor St, Ste 1413, Ottawa ON K1P 6L2. Tel: (613) 235-9940. Fax: (613) 235-1176. e-mail: echileca@chile.ca

China

Long-Form Name: People's Republic of China
Capital: Beijing

■ GEOGRAPHY

Area: 9,596,960 sq. km
Coastline: 14,500 km
Climate: extremely diverse; tropical in south to subarctic in north
Environment: frequent typhoons (about five times per year along southern and eastern coasts), damaging floods, tsunamis, earthquakes; deforestation; soil erosion; industrial pollution; water and air pollution; desertification; lack of safe drinking water
Terrain: mostly mountains, high plateaus, deserts in west; plains, deltas and hills in east
Land Use: 10% arable land; negligible permanent crops; 43% meadows and pastures; 14% forest and woodland; 33% other; includes 525,800 sq. km irrigated
Location: SE Asia, bordering on South China Sea, Yellow Sea

■ PEOPLE

Population: 1,284,303,705 (July 2002 est.)
Age Structure: 0–14 yrs: 24.3%; 15–64: 68.4%; 65+: 7.3% (2002 est.)
Population Growth Rate: 0.87% (2002 est.)
Net Migration: -0.38 migrants/1,000 population (2002 est.)
Ethnic Groups: 91.9% Han Chinese; 8.1% Zhuang, Uigur, Hui, Yi, Tibetan, Miao, Manchu, Mongol, Buyi, Korean and other nationalities
Languages: Standard Chinese (Putonghua) or Mandarin (based on the Beijing dialect), Yue (Cantonese), Wu (Shanghainese), Minbei (Fuzhou), Minnan. The Tibetans, Uigurs, Mongols and others have their own languages
Religions: officially atheist, but traditionally pragmatic and eclectic; Confucianism, Taoism and Buddhism; approx. 2–3% Muslim, 1% Christian
Birth Rate: 15.85/1,000 population (2002 est.)
Death Rate: 6.77/1,000 population (2002 est.)
Infant Mortality: 27.25 deaths/1,000 live births (2002 est.)
Life Expectancy at Birth: 70.02 years male, 73.86 years female (2002 est.)
Total Fertility Rate: 1.82 children born/woman (2002 est.)
Literacy: 84.1% (2000)

■ GOVERNMENT

Leader(s): Pres. Hu Jintao, Prem. Wen Jiabao
Government Type: Communist Party-led state
Administrative Divisions: 23 provinces (sheng, sing. & pl.), 5 autonomous regions (zizhigu, sing. & pl.), 4 government-controlled municipalities (shi, sing. & pl.)
Nationhood: People's Republic established Oct. 1, 1949
National Holiday: National Day, Oct. 1 (Founding of the People's Republic of China

■ ECONOMY

Overview: the Soviet-style, centrally planned economy has been recently altered to include increased local authority, which has led to greater production; population control is vital, but has been weakened by popular resistance and loss of authority by rural cadres. Decentralization of the economic system is slowly progressing
GDP: US$6 trillion, per capita US$4,600; real growth rate 8.0% (2002 est.)
Inflation: 0.3% (2001)
Industries: accounts for 49% of GDP (2001 est.); iron, steel, coal, machine building, armaments, textiles, petroleum, chemical fertilizer, cement, consumer durables, food processing
Labour Force: 763.2 million (2001); 50% agriculture, 23% industry, 27% services
Unemployment: 3.1% (2001)
Agriculture: accounts for 18% of GDP (2001 est.); among the world's largest producers of rice, potatoes, sorghum, peanuts, tea, millet, barley and pork; commercial crops include cotton, other fibres and oilseeds; produces variety of livestock products; self-sufficient in food
Natural Resources: coal, iron ore, crude oil, mercury, tin, tungsten, antimony, manganese, molybdenum, vanadium, magnetite, aluminum, lead, zinc, uranium, world's greatest hydroelectricity potential

■ FINANCE/TRADE

Currency: yuan (¥), pl. yen; = 10 jiao
International Reserves Excluding Gold: US$269.869 billion (Oct. 2002)
Gold Reserves: 16.100 million fine troy ounces (Oct. 2002)
Budget: revenues US$161.8 billion; expenditures US$191.8 billion, capital expenditures US$ n.a. (2000)
Defence Expenditures: 19.2% of total government expenditure (2001)
Education Expenditures: 1.69% of central government expenditure (1999)
External Debt: US$170.110 billion (2001)
Exports: US$310.104 billion (2002 est.); commodities: machinery and equipment, manufactured goods, agricultural products, oilseeds,

grain (rice and corn), oil, minerals; partners: US, Hong Kong, Japan, South Korea, Germany, Netherlands, UK
Imports: US$283.512 billion (2002 est.); commodities: grain (mostly wheat), chemical fertilizer, steel, industrial raw materials, machinery, equipment; partners: Japan, Taiwan, US, South Korea, Germany, Hong Kong, Russia, Malaysia

■ COMMUNICATIONS

Daily Newspapers: 39 in total
Televisions: 312/1,000 inhabitants (2001)
Radios: 339/1,000 inhabitants (2001)
Telephones: 1137 lines/1,000 inhabitants (2001)

■ TRANSPORTATION

Motor Vehicles: 11,450,000; 4,700,000 passenger cars
Roads: 1,400,000 km; 271,300 km paved
Railway: 67,524 km
Air Traffic: 72,661,000 passengers carried (2001)
Airports: 489; 324 have paved runways (2002)

Canadian Embassy: The Canadian Embassy, 19 Dong Zhi Men Wai St, Chao Yang District, Beijing 100600, People's Republic of China. Tel: (011-86-10) 6532-3536. Fax (011-86-10) 6532-4311. e-mail: bejing@dfait-maeci.gc.ca
Embassy in Canada: Embassy of the People's Republic of China, 515 St. Patrick St, Ottawa ON K1N 5H3. Tel: (613) 789-3434. Fax: (613) 789-1911. e-mail: n.a.

Christmas Island

Long-Form Name: Territory of Christmas Island
Capital: The Settlement

■ GEOGRAPHY

Area: 135 sq. km (land area); includes one of the largest coral islands in the Pacific
Climate: tropical, with little seasonal variation; heat and humidity moderated by trade winds
Land Use: dry sandy soil does not permit much cultivation
Location: SE Asia, between Australia and Indonesia

■ PEOPLE

Population: 474 (July 2002 est.)
Nationality: Christmas Islander
Ethnic Groups: 61% Chinese, 25% Malay, 11% European, 3% other. There is no indigenous population
Languages: English, Chinese, Oriental and European-speaking minorities

■ GOVERNMENT

Colony/Territory of: Dependent Territory of Australia
Leader(s): Head of State: Queen Elizabeth II, Administrator Bill Taylor appointed by Australian Commonwealth government.
Government Type: dependency of Australia
National Holiday: n.a.

■ ECONOMY

Overview: extraction and export of rock phosphate dust was the only significant economic activity until 1987, when the mine was closed; it was reopened in 1990

■ FINANCE/TRADE

Currency: Australian dollar = 100 cents

Canadian Embassy: c/o The Canadian High Commission, Commonwealth Ave, Canberra A.C.T. 2600, Australia. Tel: (011-61-2) 6270-4000. Fax: (011-61-2) 6273-3285. e-mail: cnbra@dfait-maeci.gc.ca
Representative to Canada: c/o Australian High Commission, 50 O'Connor St, Ste 710, Ottawa ON K1P 6L2. Tel: (613) 236-0841. Fax: (613) 236-4376. e-mail: n.a.

Cocos (Keeling) Islands

Long-Form Name: Territory of Cocos (Keeling) Islands
Capital: West Island

■ GEOGRAPHY

Area: 14 sq. km
Climate: tropical maritime modified by southeast trade wind for 9 months of the year; moderate rainfall
Land Use: primarily subsistence agriculture
Location: Indian Ocean, SW of Sumatra

■ PEOPLE

Population: 632 (July 2002 est.)
Nationality: Cocos Islander
Ethnic Groups: West Island: Europeans; Home Island: Cocos Malays
Languages: English, Malay

■ GOVERNMENT

Colony/Territory of: Dependent Territory of Australia
Leader(s): Head of State: Queen Elizabeth II, Administrator Bill Taylor (appointed by Gov. Gen. of Australia)
Government Type: territory of Australia; dependency placed under Australian govern-

ment. authority by Cocos (Keeling) Islands Act of 1955
National Holiday: n.a.

■ ECONOMY

Overview: little industrial activity; agriculture limited to copra and coconut cultivation

■ FINANCE/TRADE

Currency: Australian dollar = 100 cents

Canadian Embassy: c/o The Canadian High Commission, Commonwealth Ave, Canberra A.C.T. 2600, Australia. Tel: (011-61-2) 6270-4000. Fax: (011-61-2) 6273-3285. e-mail: cnbra@dfait-maeci.gc.ca
Representative to Canada: c/o Australian High Commission, 50 O'Connor St, Ste 710, Ottawa ON K1P 6L2. Tel: (613) 236-0841. Fax: (613) 236-4376. e-mail: n.a.

Colombia

Long-Form Name: Republic of Colombia
Capital: Bogotá

■ GEOGRAPHY

Area: 1,138,910 sq. km; includes Isla de Malpelo, Roncador Cay, Serrana Bank, and Serranilla Bank
Coastline: 3,208 km
Climate: tropical along coast and eastern plains; cooler in highlands
Environment: highlands subject to volcanic eruptions; deforestation; soil damage from overuse of pesticides; periodic droughts; air pollution
Terrain: mixture of flat coastal lowlands, plains in east, central highlands, some high mountains (Andes)
Land Use: 4% arable land; 1% permanent crops; 39% meadows and pastures; 48% forest and woodland; 8% other; includes 8,500 sq. km irrigated
Location: NW South America, bordering on Caribbean Sea, Pacific Ocean

■ PEOPLE

Population: 41,008,227 (July 2002 est.)
Nationality: Colombian
Age Structure: 0–14 yrs: 31.6%; 15–64: 63.6%; 65+: 4.8% (2002 est.)
Population Growth Rate: 1.60% (2002 est.)
Net Migration: -0.32 migrants/1,000 population (2002 est.)

Ethnic Groups: 58% mestizo, 20% white, 14% mulatto, 4% black, 3% mixed black-Amerindian, 1% Amerindian
Languages: Spanish
Religions: 95% Roman Catholic
Birth Rate: 21.99/1,000 population (2002 est.)
Death Rate: 5.66/1,000 population (2002 est.)
Infant Mortality: 23.21 deaths/1,000 live births (2002 est.)
Life Expectancy at Birth: 67.0 years male, 74.83 years female (2002 est.)
Total Fertility Rate: 2.64 children born/woman (2002 est.)
Literacy: 91.7% (2000)

■ GOVERNMENT

Leader(s): Pres. Alvaro Uribe Velez; V. Pres. Francisco Santos
Government Type: republic; executive branch dominates government structure
Administrative Divisions: 32 departments (departmentos, sing. —departmento), 1 capital district (distrito capital)
Nationhood: July 20, 1810 (from Spain)
National Holiday: Independence Day, July 20

■ ECONOMY

Overview: traditionally coffee has been the main export, though other industries such as oil and coal are developing; drug-related violence is an increasing threat to economic growth
GDP: US$255 billion, per capita US$6,300; real growth rate 1.5% (2001 est.)
Inflation: 8.7% (2001)
Industries: accounts for 26% of GDP (2001 est.); textiles, food processing, oil, clothing and footwear, beverages, chemicals, metal products, cement; mining—gold, coal, emeralds, iron, nickel, silver, salt
Labour Force: 18.9 million (2001); 46% community, social and business services, 24% industry, 30% agriculture
Unemployment: 20.5% (2001)
Agriculture: accounts for 19% of GDP (2001 est.); crops make up two-thirds and livestock one-third of agricultural output; climate and soils permit a wide variety of crops, such as coffee, bananas, rice, tobacco, corn, sugar cane, cocoa beans, oilseeds, vegetables; forest products and shrimp farming are increasing in importance
Natural Resources: crude oil, natural gas, coal, iron ore, nickel, gold, copper, emeralds

■ FINANCE/TRADE

Currency: peso ($Col) = 100 centavos
International Reserves Excluding Gold: US$10.732 billion (Dec. 2002)

Gold Reserves: 0.327 million fine troy ounces (Dec. 2002)

Budget: revenues US$24 billion; expenditures US$25.6 billion, including capital expenditures US$ n.a. (2001 est.)

Defence Expenditures: 18.8% of total government expenditure (2001)

Education Expenditures: 20.29% of central government expenditure (1999)

External Debt: US$36.699 billion (2001)

Exports: US$11.955 billion (2002 est.); commodities: coffee 30%, petroleum 24%, coal, bananas, fresh-cut flowers; partners: US, European Community, Andean Community of Nations

Imports: US$12.488 billion (2002 est.); commodities: industrial equipment, transportation equipment, foodstuffs, chemicals, paper products; partners: US, European Community, Andean Community of Nations, Japan

COMMUNICATIONS

Daily Newspapers: 46/1,000 inhabitants (2000)
Televisions: 286/1,000 inhabitants (2001)
Radios: 549/1,000 inhabitants (2001)
Telephones: 171 lines/1,000 inhabitants (2001)

TRANSPORTATION

Motor Vehicles: 2,060,000; 1,700,000 passenger cars (2000)
Roads: 110,000 km; 26,000 km paved
Railway: 3,304 km
Air Traffic: 9,566,000 passengers carried (2001)
Airports: 1,066; 96 have paved runways (2002)

Canadian Embassy: The Canadian Embassy, Carrera 7, No. 115-33, Piso 14, Bogotá, Colombia; mailing address: Apartado Aereo 110067, Bogotá 2, Colombia. Tel: (011-57-1) 657-9800. Fax (011-57-1) 657-9912. e-mail: bgota@dfait-maeci.gc.ca

Embassy in Canada: Embassy of the Republic of Colombia, 360 Albert St, Ste 1002, Ottawa ON K1R 7X7. Tel: (613) 230-3760. Fax: (613) 230-4416. e-mail: n.a.

Comoros

Long-Form Name: Union of the Comoros
Capital: Moroni

GEOGRAPHY

Area: 2,170 sq. km
Coastline: 340 km
Climate: tropical marine; rainy season (Nov. to May)

Environment: soil degradation and erosion, resulting from crop cultivation on slopes without proper terracing; deforestation; cyclones possible during rainy season

Terrain: volcanic islands, interiors vary from steep mountains to low hills

Land Use: 35% arable; 10% permanent crops; 7% meadows; 18% forest; 30% other

Location: E of Africa, Indian Ocean/ Mozambique Channel

PEOPLE

Population: 614,382 (July 2002 est.)
Nationality: Comoran
Age Structure: 0–14 yrs: 42.9%; 15–64: 54.2%; 65+: 2.9% (2002 est.)
Population Growth Rate: 2.99% (2002 est.)
Net Migration: 0 migrants/1,000 population (2002 est.)
Ethnic Groups: Antalote, Cafre, Makoa, Oimatsaha, Sakalava
Languages: French and Arabic (both official), Shaafi Islam (a Swahili dialect), Malagasy; majority speaks Comoran
Religions: 86% Sunni Muslim, 14% Roman Catholic
Birth Rate: 39.01/1,000 population (2002 est.)
Death Rate: 9.10/1,000 population (2002 est.)
Infant Mortality: 81.79 deaths/1,000 live births (2002 est.)
Life Expectancy at Birth: 58.56 years male, 63.09 years female (2002 est.)
Total Fertility Rate: 5.26 children born/woman (2002 est.)
Literacy: 55.9% (2000)

GOVERNMENT

Leader(s): Pres. of the Union Col. Assoumani Azali
Government Type: republic
Administrative Divisions: 3 islands and 4 municipalities
Nationhood: July 6, 1975 (from France)
National Holiday: Independence Day, July 6

ECONOMY

Overview: agriculture is the main sector of the economy, though it does not feed citizens adequately; lack of natural resources makes Comoros one of the world's poorest countries
GDP: US$424 million, per capita US$710; real growth rate 1.0% (2001 est.)
Inflation: 3.5% (1999)
Industries: accounts for 4% of GDP (2001 est.); perfume distillation, textiles, furniture, jewellery, soft drinks, construction materials

Labour Force: approx. 150,000; 80% agriculture, 6% industry, 14% services
Unemployment: 20% (1996 est.)
Agriculture: accounts for 40% of GDP (2001 est.); most of population works in subsistence agriculture and fishing; plantations produce cash crops for export—vanilla, cloves, perfume essences and copra; principal food crops—coconuts, bananas, cassava; large net food importer
Natural Resources: negligible

■ FINANCE/TRADE

Currency: Comoran franc (CFAF) = 100 centimes
International Reserves Excluding Gold: US$72 million (Nov. 2002)
Gold Reserves: 0.001 million fine troy ounces (June 1998)
Budget: revenues US$27.6 million; expenditures US$ n.a., including capital expenditures US$ n.a. (2001 est.)
Defence Expenditures: n.a.
Education Expenditures: n.a.
External Debt: US$246 million (2001)
Exports: US$20 million (2000); commodities: vanilla, cloves, perfume oil, copra; partners: France, US, Singapore, Germany
Imports: US$114 million (2000); commodities: rice and other foodstuffs, cement, petroleum products, consumer goods, paper products, fuels, electricity; partners: France, South Africa, Kenya, Pakistan

■ COMMUNICATIONS

Daily Newspapers: none
Televisions: n.a.
Radios: n.a.
Telephones: 10 lines/1,000 inhabitants (1999)

■ TRANSPORTATION

Motor Vehicles: n.a.
Roads: 880 km; 673 km paved
Railway: none
Air Traffic: 31,000 passengers carried (1999 est.)
Airports: 4; all have paved runways (2002)

Canadian Embassy: Canadian Embassy to the Comoros, c/o The Canadian High Commission, P.O. Box 1022, Dar-es-Salaam, Tanzania. Tel: (011-255-22) 211-2831. Fax: (011-255-22) 211-6897. e-mail: dslam@dfait-maeci.gc.ca
Embassy in Canada: Embassy of the Comoros, c/o Permanent Mission of the Comoros to the UN, 420 East 50th Street, New York, NY 10022, USA. Tel: (212) 972-8010. Fax: (212) 983-4712. e-mail: comun@undp.org

Congo

Long-Form Name: Republic of the Congo
Capital: Brazzaville

■ GEOGRAPHY

Area: 342,000 sq. km
Coastline: 169 km
Climate: tropical; rainy season (Mar. to June); dry season (June to Oct.); constant high temperatures and humidity; particularly enervating climate astride the equator
Environment: Deforestation; air and water pollution; unsafe water supply; about 70% of the population lives in Brazzaville, Pointe Noire or along the railroad between them
Terrain: coastal plain, southern basin, central plateau, northern basin
Land Use: 0% arable land; negligible permanent crops; 29% meadows; 62% forest; 9% other; includes 10 sq km irrigated
Location: WC Africa, bordering on South Atlantic Ocean

■ PEOPLE

Population: 2,958,448 (July 2002 est.)
Nationality: Congolese (sing. & pl.)
Age Structure: 0–14 yrs: 38.4%; 15–64: 58%; 65+: 3.6% (2003 est.)
Population Growth Rate: 1.53% (2003 est.)
Net Migration: 0 migrants/1,000 population (2002 est.)
Ethnic Groups: about 15 ethnic groups divided into some 75 tribes, almost all Bantu; most important ethnic groups are Kongo (48%) in south, Sangha (20%) and M'Bochi (12%) in the north, Teke (17%) in the centre; about 8,500 Europeans, mostly French
Languages: French (official); many African languages with Lingala and Kikongo most widely used
Religions: 50% Christian, 48% animist, 2% Muslim
Birth Rate: 29.46/1,000 population (2003 est.)
Death Rate: 14.2/1,000 population (2003 est.)
Infant Mortality: 94.34 deaths/1,000 live births (2003 est.)
Life Expectancy at Birth: 49.04 years male, 51.02 years female (2003 est.)
Total Fertility Rate: 3.65 children born/woman (2003 est.)
Literacy: 83.8% (2003 est.)

■ GOVERNMENT

Leader(s): Pres. Denis Sassou-Nguesso
Government Type: republic
Administrative Divisions: 9 regions, 1 commune

Nationhood: Aug. 15, 1960 (from France)
National Holiday: Congolese National Day, (Independence Day), Aug. 15

■ ECONOMY

Overview: oil revenues are responsible for one of the highest growth rates in Africa, though the country faces increasing foreign debt and is vulnerable to the oil market. Recent efforts at economic reform are beginning to show results
GDP: US$2.5 billion, per capita US$900; real growth rate 4.2% (2001 est.)
Inflation: 0.1% (2001)
Industries: accounts for 48% of GDP (2001 est.); petroleum, lumbering, cement, sawmills, brewery, sugar mills, palm oil, soap, cigarettes
Labour Force: 1.3 million (2001); 62.4% agriculture, 25.6% services, 11.9% industry
Unemployment: n.a.
Agriculture: accounts for 10% of GDP (including fishing and forestry); cassava accounts for 90% of food output; other crops—rice, corn, peanuts, vegetables; cash crops include coffee and cocoa; forest products important export earner; imports over 90% of food needs
Natural Resources: petroleum, timber, potash, lead, zinc, uranium, copper, phosphate, natural gas, hydroelectric potential

■ FINANCE/TRADE

Currency: Communauté financière africaine franc (CFAF) = 100 centimes
International Reserves Excluding Gold: US$41 million (Nov. 2002)
Gold Reserves: 0.011 million fine troy ounces (June 1998)
Budget: n.a.
Defence Expenditures: 8.4% of total government expenditure (1999)
Education Expenditures: n.a.
External Debt: US$4.496 billion (2001)
Exports: US$1.511 billion (2000); commodities: crude petroleum 50%, lumber, plywood, coffee, cocoa, sugar, diamonds; partners: US, South Korea, China, Germany
Imports: US$796 billion (2000); commodities: foodstuffs, consumer goods, intermediate manufactures, construction materials, capital equipment; partners: France, US, Italy, Belgium

■ COMMUNICATIONS

Daily Newspapers: 8/1,000 inhabitants (2000)
Televisions: 13/1,000 inhabitants (2000)
Radios: 123/1,000 inhabitants (2001)
Telephones: 7 lines/1,000 inhabitants (2001)

■ TRANSPORTATION

Motor Vehicles: 47,000; 30,000 passenger cars

Roads: 12,800 km; 1,242 km paved
Railway: 894 km (2000)
Air Traffic: 95,000 passengers carried (2001)
Airports: 33; 4 have paved runways (2002)

Canadian Embassy: The Canadian Embassy to the Republic of the Congo, P.O. Box 4037, Libreville, Gabon. Tel: (011-241) 73-73-54. Fax: (011-241) 73-73-88. e-mail: lbrve@dfait-maeci.gc.ca
Embassy in Canada: c/o Embassy of the Republic of the Congo, 4891 Colorado Ave NW, Washington DC 20011, USA. Tel: (202) 726-5500. Fax: (202) 726-1860. e-mail: n.a.

Congo (Democratic Republic)

Long-Form Name: Democratic Republic of the Congo (formerly known as Belgian Congo and also Zaire)
Capital: Kinshasa

■ GEOGRAPHY

Area: 2,345,410 sq. km
Coastline: 37 km
Climate: tropical; hot and humid in equatorial river basin; cooler and drier in southern highlands; cooler and wetter in eastern highlands
Environment: dense tropical rainforest in central river basin and eastern highlands; periodic droughts in south; water pollution, deforestation; poaching negatively affects wildlife populations
Terrain: vast central basin is a low-lying plateau; mountains in east
Land Use: 3% arable; negligible permanent crops; 7% meadows; 77% forest; 13% other; includes 110 sq. km irrigated
Location: C Africa, just barely bordering on South Atlantic Ocean

■ PEOPLE

Population: 55,225,478 (July 2002 est.)
Nationality: Congolese (sing. & pl.)
Age Structure: 0–14 yrs: 48.2%; 15–64: 49.3%; 65+: 2.5% (2002 est.)
Population Growth Rate: 2.79% (2002 est.)
Net Migration: -2.75 migrants/1,000 population (2002 est.)
Ethnic Groups: over 200 African ethnic groups, the majority are Bantu; four largest tribes—Mongo, Luba, Kongo (all Bantu) and the Mangbetu-Azande (Hamitic)—make up 45% of the population
Languages: French (official), Lingala, Swahili, Kinggwana, Kikongo, Tshiluba

Religions: 50% Roman Catholic, 20% Protestant, 10% Kimbanguist, 10% Muslim, 10% other syncretic sects and traditional beliefs
Birth Rate: 45.55/1,000 population (2002 est.)
Death Rate: 14.93/1,000 population (2002 est.)
Infant Mortality: 98.05 deaths/1,000 live births (2002 est.)
Life Expectancy at Birth: 44.27 years male, 51.24 years female (2002 est.)
Total Fertility Rate: 6.77 children born/woman (2002 est.)
Literacy: 60.3% (1999)

■ GOVERNMENT

Leader(s): Pres. Joseph Kabila
Government Type: dictatorship; ostensibly undergoing a transition to representative government
Administrative Divisions: 10 provinces and 1 city
Nationhood: June 30, 1960 (from Belgium)
National Holiday: Independence Day, June 30

■ ECONOMY

Overview: despite its vast potential wealth, the Democratic Republic of the Congo continues to suffer from a decline in the national economy; tight fiscal policies have curbed inflation and currency depreciation; a barter economy flourishes in all but the largest cities
GDP: US$32 billion, per capita US$590; real growth rate -4.0% (2001 est.)
Inflation: 540% (2000 est.)
Industries: accounts for 58% of GDP; mining, mineral processing, consumer products (including textiles, footwear and cigarettes), processed foods and beverages, cement, diamonds
Labour Force: 21.6 million (2001); 65% agriculture, 16% industry, 19% services
Unemployment: n.a.
Agriculture: accounts for 54% of GDP; cash crops: coffee, sugar, palm oil, rubber, quinine; food crops: cassava, bananas, root crops, corn, rice, peanuts, cocoa
Natural Resources: cobalt, copper, cadmium, crude oil, industrial and gem diamonds, gold, silver, zinc, manganese, tin, germanium, uranium, radium, bauxite, iron ore, coal, hydroelectric potential

■ FINANCE/TRADE

Currency: Congolese franc
International Reserves Excluding Gold: n.a.
Gold Reserves: n.a.
Budget: n.a.
Defence Expenditures: n.a.
Education Expenditures: n.a.
External Debt: US$11.392 billion (2001)

Exports: US$495 million (2000); commodities: copper 37%, coffee 24%, diamonds 12%, cobalt, crude oil; partners: US, Benelux, South Africa, Finland, Italy
Imports: US$396 million (2000); commodities: consumer goods, foodstuffs, mining and other machinery, transport equipment, fuels; partners: South Africa, Benelux, Nigeria, Kenya, China

■ COMMUNICATIONS

Daily Newspapers: 3/1,000 inhabitants (2000)
Televisions: 2/1,000 inhabitants (2000)
Radios: 386/1,000 inhabitants (2001)
Telephones: less than 1 line/1,000 inhabitants (2001)

■ TRANSPORTATION

Motor Vehicles: 530,000; 330,000 passenger cars
Roads: 157,000 km; n.a. km paved
Railway: 5,138 km (2000)
Air Traffic: n.a.
Airports: 232; 24 have paved runways (2002)

Canadian Embassy: The Canadian Embassy to the Democratic Republic of Congo, 17 avenue Pumbu, Commune de Gombe, Democratic Republic of Congo; mailing address: P.O. Box 8431, Kinshasa 1, Democratic Republic of Congo. Tel: (011-243) 884-1277. Fax: (011-243) 884-1277. e-mail: knsha@dfait-maeci.gc.ca
Embassy in Canada: Embassy of the Democratic Republic of Congo, 18 Range Rd, Ottawa ON K1N 8J3. Tel: (613) 230-6391. Fax: (613) 230-1945. e-mail: n.a.

Cook Islands

Long-Form Name: Cook Islands
Capital: Avarua (on Rarotonga Island)

■ GEOGRAPHY

Area: 240 sq. km
Climate: mild year-round, moderated by trade winds
Land Use: 9% arable; 13% permanent crops; negligible meadows and pastures; negligible forest and woodland; 78% other
Location: S Pacific Ocean, NE of New Zealand

■ PEOPLE

Population: 20,811 (July 2002 est.)
Nationality: Cook Islander
Ethnic Groups: Polynesian 81.3%, Polynesian-European mixture 7.7%, Polynesian-other mixture 7.7%, European 2.4%, other 0.9%
Languages: English (official), Cook Islands Maori

■ GOVERNMENT

Colony/Territory of: Self-governing territory in free association with New Zealand
Leader(s): Head of State: Queen Elizabeth II, Prime Min. Robert Woonton
Government Type: self-governing territory in free association with New Zealand; Cook Island is fully responsible for internal affairs; New Zealand retains responsibility for external affairs, in consultation with the Cook Islands
National Holiday: Constitution Day, first Monday in August

■ ECONOMY

Overview: agriculture provides the backbone of the economy: copra, fruits, tomatoes; livestock: pigs, goats; fishing; manufacturing is limited

■ FINANCE/TRADE

Currency: New Zealand dollar (NZ$) = 100 cents

Canadian Embassy: c/o The Canadian High Commission, 3rd Fl, 61 Molesworth St, Thorndon, Wellington, New Zealand; postal address: c/o Box 12-049, Thorndon, Wellington, New Zealand. Tel: (011-64-4) 473-9577. Fax: (011-64-4)471-2082. e-mail: wlgtn@dfait-maeci.gc.ca
Representative to Canada: c/o New Zealand High Commission, Clarica Centre, 99 Bank St, Ste 727, Ottawa ON K1P 6G3. Tel: (613) 238-5991. Fax: (613) 238-5707. e-mail: nzhcott@istar.ca

Costa Rica

Long-Form Name: Republic of Costa Rica
Capital: San José

■ GEOGRAPHY

Area: 51,100 sq. km; includes Isla del Coco
Coastline: 1,290 km
Climate: tropical; dry season (Dec. to Apr.); rainy season (May to Nov.)
Environment: subject to occasional earthquakes, hurricanes along Atlantic coast; frequent flooding of lowlands at onset of rainy season; active volcanoes; deforestation; soil erosion
Terrain: coastal plains separated by rugged mountains
Land Use: 6% arable; 5% permanent crops; 46% meadows; 31% forest; 12% other; includes 1,260 sq. km irrigated
Location: Central (Latin) America, bordering on Caribbean Sea, Pacific Ocean

■ PEOPLE

Population: 3,834,934 (July 2002 est.)
Nationality: Costa Rican
Age Structure: 0–14 yrs: 30.8%; 15–64: 63.9%; 65+: 5.3% (2002 est.)
Population Growth Rate: 1.61% (2002 est.)
Net Migration: 0.52 migrants/1,000 population (2002 est.)
Ethnic Groups: 94% white (including mestizo), 3% black, 1% Indian, 1% Chinese, 1% other
Languages: Spanish (official), English is spoken around Puerto Limon
Religions: 95% Roman Catholic
Birth Rate: 19.83/1,000 population (2002 est.)
Death Rate: 4.31/1,000 population (2002 est.)
Infant Mortality: 10.87 deaths/1,000 live births (2002 est.)
Life Expectancy at Birth: 73.68 years male, 78.89 years female (2002 est.)
Total Fertility Rate: 2.42 children born/woman (2002 est.)
Literacy: 95.6% (2000)

■ GOVERNMENT

Leader(s): Pres. Abel Pacheco
Government Type: democratic republic
Administrative Divisions: 7 provinces (provincias, sing. —provincia)
Nationhood: Sept. 15, 1821 (from Spain)
National Holiday: Independence Day, Sept. 15

■ ECONOMY

Overview: inflation and external debt are high, many people are underemployed; coffee and banana crops are vital
GDP: US$31.9 billion, per capita US$8,500; real growth rate 0.3% (2001 est.)
Inflation: 11.2% (2001)
Industries: accounts for 37% of GDP (2000); food processing, textiles and clothing, plastics products, construction materials, fertilizer, tourism
Labour Force: 1.6 million (2001); 58% community, social and business services, 20% agriculture, 22% industry
Unemployment: 6.1% (2001), but there is much underemployment
Agriculture: accounts for 11% of GDP (2000) and 70% of exports; cash commodities—coffee, pineapples, beef, bananas, sugar; normally self-sufficient in food except for grain; depletion of forest resources resulting in lower timber output
Natural Resources: hydroelectricity potential

■ FINANCE/TRADE

Currency: colón (pl. colones) (C/) = 100 centimes
International Reserves Excluding Gold: US$1.497 billion (Dec. 2002)
Gold Reserves: 0.002 million fine troy ounces (Dec. 2002)
Budget: revenues US$1.95 billion, expenditures US$2.4 billion, including capital expenditures of US$ n.a. (2000 est.)
Defence Expenditures: 2.0% of central government expenditure (1999)
Education Expenditures: 20.60% of central government expenditure (2000)
External Debt: US$4.586 billion (2001)
Exports: US$5.259 billion (2002); commodities: coffee, bananas, textiles, sugar, electronics, medical equipment; partners: US, EU, Central America, Puerto Rico, Mexico
Imports: US$7.175 billion (2002); commodities: petroleum, machinery, consumer durables, chemicals, fertilizer, foodstuffs; partners: US, EU, Mexico, Venezuela, Central America

■ COMMUNICATIONS

Daily Newspapers: 91/1,000 inhabitants (2000)
Televisions: 231/1,000 inhabitants (2001)
Radios: 816/1,000 inhabitants (2001)
Telephones: 230 lines/1,000 inhabitants (2001)

■ TRANSPORTATION

Motor Vehicles: 500,000; 300,000 passenger cars (2000)
Roads: 37,273 km; 7,827 km paved
Railway: 950 km
Air Traffic: 752,000 passengers carried (2001)
Airports: 152; 30 have paved runways (2002)

Canadian Embassy: The Canadian Embassy, Oficentro Ejecutivo La Sabana-detrás de la Contraloría, Sabana Sur, San José; mailing address: Canadian Embassy, P.O. Box 351-1007, Centro Colon, San José, Costa Rica. Tel: (011-506) 296-4149. Fax: (011-506) 296-4270. e-mail: sjcra@dfait-maeci.gc.ca
Embassy in Canada: Embassy of the Republic of Costa Rica, 325 Dalhousie St., Suite 407, Ottawa ON K1N 7G2. Tel: (613) 562-2855. Fax: (613) 562-2582. e-mail: n.a.

Côte d'Ivoire (Ivory Coast)

Long-Form Name: Republic of Côte d'Ivoire
Capital: Yamoussoukro; Abidjan remains the administrative centre.

■ GEOGRAPHY

Area: 322,460 sq. km
Coastline: 515 km
Climate: tropical along coast, semi-arid in far north; three seasons: warm and dry (Nov. to Mar.), hot and dry (Mar. to May), hot and wet (June to Oct.)
Environment: coast has heavy surf and no natural harbours; severe deforestation; water pollution; heavy flooding is possible during rainy season
Terrain: mostly flat to undulating plains; mountains in northwest
Land Use: 8% arable; 4% permanent crops; 41% permanent pastures; 22% forest; 25% other; includes 730 sq. km irrigated
Location: WC Africa, bordering on South Atlantic Ocean

■ PEOPLE

Population: 16,804,784 (July 2002 est.)
Nationality: Ivorian
Age Structure: 0–14 yrs: 46.0%; 15–64: 51.8%; 65+: 2.2% (2002 est.)
Population Growth Rate: 2.45% (2002 est.)
Net Migration: 1.22 migrants/1,000 population (2002 est.)
Ethnic Groups: over 60 ethnic groups; most important are the Baoule 23%, Bete 18%, Senoufou 15%, Malinke 11% and Agni; about 2 million foreign Africans mostly Burkinabe; about 130,000 to 330,000 non-Africans (30,000 French and 100,000–300,000 Lebanese)
Languages: French (official), 60 native dialects, of which Dioula is the most widely spoken
Religions: 28% indigenous, 60% Muslim, 12% Christian
Birth Rate: 39.99/1,000 population (2002 est.)
Death Rate: 16.74/1,000 population (2002 est.)
Infant Mortality: 92.23 deaths/1,000 live births (2002 est.)
Life Expectancy at Birth: 43.45 years male, 46.03 years female (2002 est.)
Total Fertility Rate: 5.61 children born/woman (2002 est.)
Literacy: 45.7% (1999)

■ GOVERNMENT

Leader(s): Pres. Laurent Gbagbo, Prime Min. Seydou Diarra
Government Type: republic; multiparty presidential regime
Administrative Divisions: 58 departments (departements, sing. —departement)
Nationhood: Aug. 7, 1960 (from France)
National Holiday: Independence Day, Aug. 7

■ ECONOMY

Overview: despite attempts to diversify, the economy is largely dependent on agriculture and related industries; highly sensitive to fluctuations in world prices for coffee and cocoa and to weather conditions

GDP: US$25.5 billion, per capita US$1,550; real growth rate -1.0% (2001)

Inflation: 4.3% (2001)

Industries: accounts for 29% of GDP (2000); foodstuffs, wood processing, oil refinery, automobile assembly, textiles, fertilizer, beverages

Labour Force: 6.6 million (2001); 45.4% community, social and business services, 15.6% industry, 13.8% agriculture

Unemployment: n.a.

Agriculture: contributes 28% to GDP and 80% to exports (2000); cash crops include coffee, cocoa beans, rice, timber, bananas, palm kernels, rubber; food crops; not self-sufficient in bread grain and dairy products

Natural Resources: crude oil, diamonds, manganese, iron ore, cobalt, bauxite, copper

■ FINANCE/TRADE

Currency: Communauté financière africaine franc (CFAF) = 100 centimes

International Reserves Excluding Gold: US$1.342 billion (Dec. 2002)

Gold Reserves: 0.045 million fine troy ounces (Jun. 2000)

Budget: revenues US$1.72 billion; expenditures US$2.4 billion, including capital expenditures of US$420 million (2001 est.)

Defence Expenditures: 3.7% of central government expenditure (2001)

Education Expenditures: n.a.

External Debt: US$11.582 billion (2001)

Exports: US$3.659 million (2001) commodities: cocoa 33%, coffee 20%, tropical woods 11%, cotton, bananas, pineapples, palm oil, petroleum; partners: France, Germany, Netherlands, US, Italy

Imports: US$2.548 million (2001) commodities: manufactured goods and semi-finished products 50%, consumer goods 40%, raw materials and fuels 10%; partners: France, Nigeria, China, Italy, Germany

■ COMMUNICATIONS

Daily Newspapers: 16/1,000 inhabitants (2000)
Televisions: 60/1,000 inhabitants (2001)
Radios: 183/1,000 inhabitants (2001)
Telephones: 18 lines/1,000 inhabitants (2001)

■ TRANSPORTATION

Motor Vehicles: 255,000; 160,000 passenger cars
Roads: 50,400 km; 4,889 km paved
Railway: 660 km
Air Traffic: 46,000 passengers carried (2001)
Airports: 36; 7 have paved runways (2002)

Canadian Embassy: The Canadian Embassy, Immeuble Trade-Center, 23 rue Nogues, Le Plateau, Abidjan; mailing address: BP 4104, Abidjan 01, Côte d'Ivoire. Tel: (011-225) 20-30-07-00. Fax: (011-225) 20-30-07-20. e-mail: abdjn@dfait-maeci.gc.ca

Embassy in Canada: Embassy of the Republic of Côte d'Ivoire, 9 Marlborough Ave, Ottawa ON K1N 8E6. Tel: (613) 236-9919. Fax: (613) 563-8287. e-mail: embaci@ican.net

Croatia

Long-Form Name: Republic of Croatia
Capital: Zagreb

■ GEOGRAPHY

Area: 56,542 sq. km

Coastline: 5,835 km

Climate: hot summers and cold winters; along coast, mild winters and dry summers

Environment: air pollution (including acid rain), damaged forests, coastal pollution; subject to frequent and destructive earthquakes

Terrain: flat plains along Hungarian border, low mountains and highlands along Adriatic coast, coastline and islands

Land Use: 21% arable; 2% permanent crops; 20% meadows and pastures; 38% forest and woodland, 19% other; includes 30 sq. km irrigated

Location: S Europe, bordering on Adriatic Sea

■ PEOPLE

Population: 4,390,751 (July 2002 est.)

Nationality: Croat

Age Structure: 0–14 yrs: 18.3%; 15–64: 66.3%; 65+: 15.4% (2002 est.)

Population Growth Rate: 1.12% (2002 est.)

Net Migration: 9.72 migrants/1,000 population (2002 est.)

Ethnic Groups: 78.1% Croat, 12.2% Serb, 0.9% Muslim, 0.5% Hungarian, 0.5% Slovenian, 0.4% Czech, 0.3% Albanian, 0.3% Montenegrin, 0.2% Roma, 6.6% other

Languages: Croatian 96%, other 4% (including Italian, Hungarian, Czech, Slovak and German)

Religions: 76.5% Catholic, 11.1% Orthodox, 1.2% Slavic Muslim, 0.4% Protestant, 10.8% others and unknown

Birth Rate: 12.80/1,000 population (2002 est.)
Death Rate: 11.31/1,000 population (2002 est.)
Infant Mortality: 7.06 deaths/1,000 live births (2002 est.)
Life Expectancy at Birth: 70.52 years male, 77.96 years female (2002 est.)
Total Fertility Rate: 1.93 children born/woman (2002 est.)
Literacy: 98.3% (2000)

■ GOVERNMENT

Leader(s): Pres. Stjepan Mesic, Prime Min. Ivica Racan
Government Type: parliamentary democracy
Administrative Divisions: 20 counties (zvpanije, sing. —zvpanija), 1 city
Nationhood: June 25, 1991, secession from federal Yugoslavia
National Holiday: Statehood Day, May 30

■ ECONOMY

Overview: tourism, manufacturing including chemicals, food products, petroleum, ships and textiles; war and internal strife have severely disrupted economy
GDP: US$38.9 billion, per capita US$8,800; real growth rate 3.0% (2002 est.)
Inflation: 4.8% (2001)
Industries: accounts for 33% of GDP (2002 est.); mining, fertilizers, plastics, chemicals, fabricated metal, pig iron and rolled steel products, paper, wood products, shipbuilding, food processing, beverages, sugar, cotton fabrics, machinery
Labour Force: 2.1 million (2001); 33.6% industry, 22.7% community, social and business services, 15.8% trade and tourism
Unemployment: 20.6% (2001)
Agriculture: accounts for 9% of GDP (2002 est.); Croatia normally produces a food surplus, but much land has been put out of production by fighting; products include wheat, maize, sugar, beets, olives, potatoes, plums, fish, livestock, esp. cattle, sheep, pigs, poultry, cereal grains, citrus fruit, vegetables
Natural Resources: oil, salt, coal, bauxite, brown coal and lignite, iron ore, china clay, silver, hydroelectric power, calcium, natural asphalt

■ FINANCE/TRADE

Currency: Croatian kuna = 100 lipas
International Reserves Excluding Gold: US$5.885 billion (Dec. 2002)
Gold Reserves: none (Dec. 2002)
Budget: revenues US$8.6 billion, expenditures US$9 billion, including capital expenditures of US$ n.a. (2001 est.)

Defence Expenditures: 5.9% of total government expenditure (2001)
Education Expenditures: 7.33% of central government expenditure (2001)
External Debt: US$10.742 billion (2001)
Exports: US$4.496 billion (2002 est.); machinery and transportation equipment, fuels, chemicals, textiles, and other manufactured goods; partners: Italy, Germany, Bosnia and Herzegovina, Slovenia, Austria, France
Imports: US$9.544 billion (2002 est.); machinery and transportation equipment, chemicals, raw materials. Partners: Germany, Italy, Russia, Slovenia, Austria, France

■ COMMUNICATIONS

Daily Newspapers: 114/1,000 inhabitants (2000)
Televisions: 293/1,000 inhabitants (2001)
Radios: 340/1,000 inhabitants (2001)
Telephones: 365 lines/1,000 inhabitants (2001)

■ TRANSPORTATION

Motor Vehicles: n.a.
Roads: 28,009 km; 23,695 km paved
Railway: 2,726 km
Air Traffic: 1,064,000 passengers carried (2001)
Airports: 67; 22 have paved runways (2002)

Canadian Embassy: The Canadian Embassy, Prilaz Gjure Dezelica #4, 10000 Zagreb. Tel: (011-385-1) 488-1200. Fax: (011-385-1) 488-1230. e-mail: zagrb@dfait-maeci.gc.ca
Embassy in Canada: Embassy of the Republic of Croatia, 229 Chapel St., Ottawa ON K1N 7Y6. Tel: (613) 562-7820. Fax: (613) 562-7821. e-mail: embcrott@sprint.ca

Cuba

Long-Form Name: Republic of Cuba
Capital: Havana

■ GEOGRAPHY

Area: 110,860 sq. km
Coastline: 3,735 km
Climate: tropical; moderated by trade winds; dry season (Nov. to Apr.); rainy season (May to Oct.)
Environment: averages one hurricane every two years; water pollution and deforestation
Terrain: mostly flat to rolling plains with rugged hills and mountains in the southeast
Land Use: 24% arable; 7% permanent crops; 27% pasture; 24% forest; 18% other; including 870 sq. km irrigated
Location: West Indies, bordering on Caribbean Sea, Atlantic Ocean

■ PEOPLE

Population: 11,224,321 (July 2002 est.)
Nationality: Cuban
Age Structure: 0–14 yrs: 20.6%; 15–64: 69.3%; 65+: 10.1% (2002 est.)
Population Growth Rate: 0.35% (2002 est.)
Net Migration: -1.21 migrants/1,000 population (2002 est.)
Ethnic Groups: 51% mulatto, 37% white, 11% black, 1% Chinese
Languages: Spanish
Religions: Christianity (majority Roman Catholic)
Birth Rate: 12.08/1,000 population (2002 est.)
Death Rate: 7.35/1,000 population (2002 est.)
Infant Mortality: 7.27 deaths/1,000 live births (2002 est.)
Life Expectancy at Birth: 74.20 years male, 79.15 years female (2002 est.)
Total Fertility Rate: 1.60 children born/woman (2002 est.)
Literacy: 96.7% (2000)

■ GOVERNMENT

Leader(s): Pres. of the Council of State: Fidel Castro Ruz
Government Type: communist state
Administrative Divisions: 14 provinces (provincias, sing. —provincia) and 1 special municipality (municipio especial)
Nationhood: May 20, 1902 (from Spain Dec. 10, 1898; administered by the US from 1898 to 1902)
National Holiday: Independence Day, Dec. 10

■ ECONOMY

Overview: state plays the primary role in the economy and controls practically all foreign trade; recent government reforms aim at alleviating serious shortages of food, consumer goods and services; tourism plays a key role in foreign currency earnings
GDP: US$25.9 billion, per capita US$2,300; real growth rate 0% (2002 est.)
Inflation: 0.3% (1999 est.)
Industries: accounts for 35% of GDP; sugar milling, petroleum refining, food and tobacco processing, textiles, chemicals, paper and wood products, metals (particularly nickel), cement, fertilizers, consumer goods, agricultural machinery
Labour Force: 5.6 million (2001); 51% services, 25% industry, 24% agriculture
Unemployment: 5.5% (2000 est.)
Agriculture: accounts for 8% of GDP (including fishing and forestry); key commercial crops—sugar cane, tobacco and citrus fruit; other products—coffee, rice, potatoes, meat, beans; world's largest sugar exporter; not self-sufficient in food
Natural Resources: cobalt, nickel, iron ore, copper, manganese, salt, timber, silica, petroleum

■ FINANCE/TRADE

Currency: peso ($) = 100 centavos
International Reserves Excluding Gold: n.a.
Gold Reserves: n.a.
Budget: revenues US$13.5 billion, expenditures US$14.3 billion, includes capital expenditures of US$ n.a. (2000 est.)
Defence Expenditures: n.a.
Education Expenditures: n.a.
External Debt: US$11.1 billion; another $15–20 billion is owed to Russia (2000).
Exports: US$2.420 billion (2000); commodities: sugar, nickel, shellfish, citrus, tobacco, coffee; partners: Netherlands, Russia, Canada, Spain, China
Imports: US$4.210 billion (2000); commodities: capital goods, industrial raw materials, machinery and transport equipment, food, petroleum; partners: Spain, France, Canada, China, Italy

■ COMMUNICATIONS

Daily Newspapers: 118/1,000 inhabitants (2000)
Televisions: 251/1,000 inhabitants (2001)
Radios: 185/1,000 inhabitants (2001)
Telephones: 51 lines/1,000 inhabitants (2001)

■ TRANSPORTATION

Motor Vehicles: 360,000; 175,000 passenger cars (2000)
Roads: 60,858 km; 29,820 km paved
Railway: 4,807 km
Air Traffic: 882,000 passengers carried (2001)
Airports: 172; 78 have paved runways (2002)

Canadian Embassy: The Canadian Embassy, Calle 30, No. 518 Esquina 7a, Avenida Miramar, Havana, Cuba. Tel: (011-53-7) 204-25-16. Fax: (011-53-7) 204-97-72. e-mail: havan@dfait-maeci.gc.ca
Embassy in Canada: Embassy of the Republic of Cuba, 388 Main St, Ottawa ON K1S 1E3. Tel: (613) 563-0141. Fax: (613) 563-0068. e-mail: cuba@iosphere.net

Cyprus

Long-Form Name: Republic of Cyprus
Capital: Nicosia

■ GEOGRAPHY

Area: 9,250 sq. km
Coastline: 648 km
Climate: temperate, Mediterranean with hot, dry summers and cool, wet winters
Environment: moderate earthquake activity; water resource problems (no natural reservoir catchments, seasonal disparity in rainfall and most potable resources concentrated in the Turkish-Cypriot area)
Terrain: central plain with mountains to north and south, plain along south coast
Land Use: 12% arable; 5% permanent crops; negligible permanent pastures; 13% forest; 70% other; including 400 sq. km irrigated
Location: Middle East, in the Mediterranean Sea

■ PEOPLE

Population: 767,314 (July 2002 est.)
Nationality: Cypriot
Age Structure: 0–14 yrs: 22.4%; 15–64: 66.6%; 65+: 11.0% (2002 est.)
Population Growth Rate: 0.57% (2002 est.)
Net Migration: 0.43 migrants/1,000 population (2002 est.)
Ethnic Groups: 78% Greek; 18% Turkish; 4% other
Languages: 80% Greek, Turkish, English
Religions: 78% Greek Orthodox; 18% Muslim; 4% Maronite, Armenian, Apostolic and other
Birth Rate: 12.91/1,000 population (2002 est.)
Death Rate: 7.63/1,000 population (2002 est.)
Infant Mortality: 7.71 deaths/1,000 live births (2002 est.)
Life Expectancy at Birth: 74.77 years male, 79.50 years female (2002 est.)
Total Fertility Rate: 1.90 children born/woman (2002 est.)
Literacy: 97.1% (2000)

■ GOVERNMENT

Leader(s): Pres. Tassos Papadopoulos
Government Type: republic; Greek Cypriots control the only internationally recognized government, however the country is divided by a UN-patrolled buffer zone. The northern portion of the island (approx. 40%) is a Turkish-Cypriot administered area. (In 1983 this area was declared the Turkish Republic of Northern Cyprus, but Turkey is the only nation to recognize this jurisdiction)
Administrative Divisions: 6 districts
Nationhood: Aug. 16, 1960 (from UK)

National Holiday: Independence Day, Oct. 1 (Nov. 15 is celebrated as Independence Day in the Turkish area)

■ ECONOMY

Overview: remains heavily dependent on agriculture and government service, which together employ about 50% of the workforce
GDP: Greek Cypriot area: revenues US$9.1 billion, per capita US$15,000; real growth rate 2.6%; Turkish Cypriot area: revenues US$1.1 billion, per capita US$7,000; real growth rate 0.8% (2001 est.)
Inflation: 2.0% (2001)
Industries: accounts for 20–21% of GDP; mining (iron pyrites, gypsum, asbestos); manufactured products—beverages, footwear, clothing and cement—are principally for local consumption, tourism
Labour Force: 377,300 (2000); Greek Cypriot area: 73% services, 22% industry, 5% agriculture; Turkish Cypriot area: 56% services, 23% industry, 21% agriculture
Unemployment: n.a.
Agriculture: accounts for 5–8% of GDP; major crops—potatoes, vegetables, barley, grapes, olives and citrus fruit; vegetables and fruit provide 25% of export revenues
Natural Resources: copper, pyrites, asbestos, gypsum, timber, salt, marble, clay earth pigment

■ FINANCE/TRADE

Currency: Cypriot pound (£ or £C) = 100 cents and Turkish lira (TL) = 100 kurus
International Reserves Excluding Gold: US$3.022 billion (Dec. 2002)
Gold Reserves: 0.465 million fine troy ounces (Dec. 2002)
Budget: Greek area: revenues US$2.4 billion; expenditures US$3.7 billion, including capital expenditures of US$539 million; Turkish area: revenues US$300 million; expenditures US$500 million, including capital expenditures of US$60 million (2001 est.)
Defence Expenditures: n.a.
Education Expenditures: n.a.
External Debt: n.a.
Exports: US$855 million (2002 est.); commodities: citrus, potatoes, grapes, wine, cement, clothing and shoes; partners: EU, Russia, Syria, Lebanon, Turkey, UK
Imports: US$3.959 billion (2002 est.); commodities: consumer goods 23%, petroleum and lubricants 12%, food and feed grains, machinery; partners: EU, US

■ COMMUNICATIONS

Daily Newspapers: 9 in total
Televisions: n.a.
Radios: n.a.
Telephones: 545 lines/1,000 inhabitants (1999)

■ TRANSPORTATION

Motor Vehicles: 340,000; 230,000 passenger cars
Roads: 13,013 km; 7,619 km paved
Railway: none
Air Traffic: 1,460,000 passengers carried (1999 est.)
Airports: 15; 13 have paved runways (2002)

Canadian Embassy: Consulate of Canada, P.O. Box 22125, 1095, Nicosia 1517. Mailing address: Consulate of Canada, P.O. Box 22125, 1095, Nicosia 1517, Cyprus. Tel. (011-357-2) 775-508, Fax. (011-357-2) 779-905. e-mail: n.a.
Embassy in Canada: c/o Embassy of the Republic of Cyprus, 2211 R St NW, Washington DC 20008, USA. Tel: (202) 462-5772. Fax: (202) 483-6710. e-mail: n.a.

Czech Republic

Long-Form Name: Czech Republic
Capital: Prague

■ GEOGRAPHY

Area: 78,866 sq. km
Coastline: none: landlocked
Climate: temperate; cool summers; cold, cloudy, humid winters
Environment: air and water pollution and acid rain, which also damages the forests; recently there has been severe flooding
Terrain: Bohemia in the west consists of rolling plains, hills and plateaus surrounded by low mountains; Moravia in east consists of very hilly country
Land Use: 41% arable; 2% permanent crops; 11% permanent pastures; 34% forests and woodland; 12% other; includes 240 sq. km irrigated
Location: C Europe

■ PEOPLE

Population: 10,256,760 (July 2002 est.)
Nationality: Czech
Age Structure: 0–14 yrs: 15.7%; 15–64: 70.3%; 65+: 14.0% (2002 est.)
Population Growth Rate: -0.07% (2002 est.)
Net Migration: 0.96 migrants/1,000 population (2002 est.)

Ethnic Groups: 81.2% Czech, 3.1% Slovak, 0.2% Hungarian, 0.5% German, 0.6% Polish, 13.2% Moravian, 0.4% Silesian, 0.3% Gypsy, 0.5% other
Languages: Czech and Slovak
Religions: 39.8% atheist, 39.2% Roman Catholic, 4.6% Protestant, 3% Orthodox, 13.4% other
Birth Rate: 9.08/1,000 population (2002 est.)
Death Rate: 10.76/1,000 population (2002 est.)
Infant Mortality: 5.46 deaths/1,000 live births (2002 est.)
Life Expectancy at Birth: 71.46 years male, 78.65 years female (2002 est.)
Total Fertility Rate: 1.18 children born/woman (2002 est.)
Literacy: approaching 100% (2000)

■ GOVERNMENT

Leader(s): Pres. Vaclav Klaus, Prem. Vladimir Spidla
Government Type: parliamentary democracy
Administrative Divisions: 13 regions (Kraje, sing. —Kraj), 1 capital city
Nationhood: Jan. 1, 1993 (from Czechoslovakia)
National Holiday: National Liberation Day, May 8; Founding of the Republic, Oct. 28

■ ECONOMY

Overview: economy is beginning the transition from a command to a market economy; economic growth is less important at this point than economic restructuring
GDP: US$155.9 billion, per capita US$15,300; real growth rate 2.6% (2002 est.)
Inflation: 4.7% (2001)
Industries: accounts for 41% of GDP (2001); fuels, ferrous metallurgy, machinery and equipment, coal, motor vehicles, glass, armaments
Labour Force: 5.7 million (2001); 35% industry, 5% agriculture, 60% services
Unemployment: 8.6% (May 2002)
Agriculture: accounts for 4% of GDP (2001); largely self-sufficient in food production; diversified crop and livestock production, including grains, sugar beets, potatoes, hops, fruit, hogs, cattle and poultry
Natural Resources: hard and soft coal, kaolin, clay, graphite

■ FINANCE/TRADE

Currency: koruna (pl. koruny) (Kcs) = 100 haleru
International Reserves Excluding Gold: US$23.556 billion (Dec. 2002)
Gold Reserves: 0.442 million fine troy ounces (Dec. 2002)

Budget: revenues US$16.7 billion; expenditures US$18 billion, including capital expenditures US$ n.a. (2001 est.)

Defence Expenditures: 5.4% of total government expenditure (2001)

Education Expenditures: 9.38% of central government expenditure (2000)

External Debt: US$21.691 billion (2001)

Exports: US$30.682 billion (2002); commodities: machinery and equipment 58.5%, industrial consumer goods 15.2%, fuels, chemicals, minerals and metals 10.6%, agricultural and forestry products 6.1%, other products 15.2%; partners: former USSR countries, Germany, Slovakia, UK, Austria, Poland

Imports: US$40.821 billion (2002); commodities: machinery and equipment 41.6%, fuels, minerals, metals 32.2%, agricultural and forestry products 11.5%, industrial consumer goods 6.7%, other products 8%; partners: Germany, Slovakia, Russia, Italy, Austria

■ **COMMUNICATIONS**

Daily Newspapers: 254/1,000 inhabitants (2000)
Televisions: 534/1,000 inhabitants (2001)
Radios: 803/1,000 inhabitants (2001)
Telephones: 375 lines/1,000 inhabitants (2001)

■ **TRANSPORTATION**

Motor Vehicles: 3,700,000; 3,400,000 passenger cars (2000)
Roads: 55,432 km; all paved (2000)
Railway: 9,444 km (2000)
Air Traffic: 2,560,000 passengers carried (2001)
Airports: 121; 44 have paved runways (2002)

Canadian Embassy: The Canadian Embassy, Mickiewiczova 6, 16000 Prague 6, Czech Republic. Tel: (011-420-2) 7210-1800. Fax: (011-420-2) 7210-1890. e-mail: prgue@dfait-maeci.gc.ca

Embassy in Canada: Embassy of the Czech Republic, 251 Cooper St. Ottawa ON, K2P 0G2. Tel: (613) 562-3875. Fax: (613) 562-3878. e-mail: ottawa@embassy.mzv.cz

---

Denmark

Long-Form Name: Kingdom of Denmark
Capital: Copenhagen

■ **GEOGRAPHY**

Area: 43,094 sq. km; includes the island of Bornholm in the Baltic Sea and the rest of metropolitan Denmark, but excludes the Faroe Islands and Greenland

Coastline: 7,314 km (includes fjords)
Climate: temperate; humid and overcast; mild, windy winters and cool summers
Environment: air and water pollution; pollution of drinking water
Terrain: low and flat to gently rolling plains
Land Use: 60% arable land; negligible permanent crops; 5% meadows; 10% forest; 25% other; includes 4,760 sq. km irrigated
Location: N Europe, bordering on North Sea, Baltic Sea

■ **PEOPLE**

Population: 5,368,854 (July 2002 est.)
Nationality: Dane
Age Structure: 0–14 yrs: 18.7%; 15–64: 66.4%; 65+: 14.9% (2002 est.)
Population Growth Rate: 0.29% (2002 est.)
Net Migration: 2.01 migrants/1,000 population (2002 est.)
Ethnic Groups: Scandinavian, Inuit, Faroese, German
Languages: Danish, Faroese, Greenlandic (an Inuit dialect); small German-speaking minority
Religions: 91% Evangelical Lutheran, 2% other Protestant and Roman Catholic, 7% other
Birth Rate: 11.74/1,000 population (2002 est.)
Death Rate: 10.81/1,000 population (2002 est.)
Infant Mortality: 4.97 deaths/1,000 live births (2002 est.)
Life Expectancy at Birth: 74.30 years male, 79.67 years female (2002 est.)
Total Fertility Rate: 1.73 children born/woman (2002 est.)
Literacy: approaching 100% (2000)

■ **GOVERNMENT**

Leader(s): Head of State: Queen Margrethe II, Prime Min. Anders Fogh Rasmussen
Government Type: constitutional monarchy
Administrative Divisions: 14 counties (amter, sing. —amt) and 2 kommunes; dependent areas includes Faroe Islands, Greenland (see Greenland entry for details)
Nationhood: became a constitutional monarchy in 1849
National Holiday: none designated. Constitution Day, June 5, is generally viewed as the National Day.

■ **ECONOMY**

Overview: advanced agriculture and industry; extensive government welfare measures; highly dependent on foreign trade
GDP: US$155.5 billion, per capita US$29,000; real growth rate 1.8% (2002 est.)

Inflation: 2.4% (2001)
Industries: accounts for 26% of GDP (2002 est.); food processing, machinery and equipment, textiles and clothing, chemical products, electronics, construction, furniture and other wood products
Labour Force: 22.9 million (2001); 79% community, social and business services, 17% industry, 4% agriculture
Unemployment: 4.9% (Dec. 2002)
Agriculture: accounts for 3% of GNP (2002 est.) and employs 5.6% of labour force (includes fishing); farm products account for nearly 15% of export revenues; principal products—meat, dairy, grain, potatoes, rape, sugar beets, fish; self-sufficient in food production
Natural Resources: crude oil, natural gas, fish, salt, limestone, sand and gravel

■ FINANCE/TRADE

Currency: krone (pl. kroner) (DKr) = 100 oere
International Reserves Excluding Gold: US$26.986 billion (Dec. 2002)
Gold Reserves: 2.140 million fine troy ounces (Dec. 2002)
Budget: revenues US$52.9 billion; expenditures US$51.3 billion, including capital expenditures US$500 million (2001 est.)
Defence Expenditures: 4.3% of total government expenditure (2001)
Education Expenditures: 12.69% of central government expenditure (2000)
External Debt: US$21.7 billion (2000)
Exports: US$53.437 billion (2002 est.); commodities: meat and meat products, dairy products, transport equipment, fish, chemicals, furniture, industrial machinery; partners: EU, US, Norway
Imports: US$46.177 billion (2002 est.); commodities: petroleum, machinery and equipment, chemicals, grain and foodstuffs, textiles, paper; partners: US, Germany, Netherlands, Sweden, UK, France, Italy

■ COMMUNICATIONS

Daily Newspapers: 283/1,000 inhabitants (2000)
Televisions: 857/1,000 inhabitants (2001)
Radios: 1,400/1,000 inhabitants (2001)
Telephones: 719 lines/1,000 inhabitants (2001)

■ TRANSPORTATION

Motor Vehicles: 2,200,000; 1,900,000 passenger cars (2000)
Roads: 71,437 km; all paved
Railway: 2,859 km operational
Air Traffic: 6,382,000 passengers carried (2001)

Airports: 116; 28 have paved runways (2002)

Canadian Embassy: The Canadian Embassy, Kr. Bernikowsgade 1, 1105 Copenhagen K, Denmark. Tel: (011-45) 33-48-32-00. Fax: (011-45) 33-48-32-20. e-mail: copen@dfait-maeci.gc.ca
Embassy in Canada: Embassy of the Kingdom of Denmark, 47 Clarence St, Ste 450, Ottawa ON K1N 9K1. Tel: (613) 562-1811. Fax: (613) 562-1812. e-mail: danemb@cyberus.ca

Djibouti

Long-Form Name: Republic of Djibouti
Capital: Djibouti

■ GEOGRAPHY

Area: 22,000 sq. km
Coastline: 314 km
Climate: desert; torrid, dry
Environment: vast wasteland; desertification; droughts and earthquakes; occasional cyclones; inadequate safe drinking water
Terrain: coastal plain and plateau separated by central mountains
Land Use: 0% arable; 0% permanent crops; 9% permanent pastures; negligible forest; 91% other; includes 10 sq. km irrigated
Location: E Africa, bordering on Gulf of Aden

■ PEOPLE

Population: 472,810 (July 2002 est.)
Nationality: Djiboutian
Age Structure: 0–14 yrs: 42.6%; 15–64: 54.5%; 65+: 2.9% (2002 est.)
Population Growth Rate: 2.59% (2002 est.)
Net Migration: 0 migrants/1,000 population (2002 est.)
Ethnic Groups: 60% Somali (Issa), 35% Afar, 5% French, Arab, Ethiopian and Italian
Languages: French and Arabic (both official); Somali and Afar widely used
Religions: 94% Muslim, 6% Christian
Birth Rate: 40.33/1,000 population (2002 est.)
Death Rate: 14.43/1,000 population (2002 est.)
Infant Mortality: 99.70 deaths/1,000 live births (2002 est.)
Life Expectancy at Birth: 49.73 years male, 53.52 years female (2002 est.)
Total Fertility Rate: 5.64 children born/woman (2002 est.)
Literacy: 64.6% (2000)

■ GOVERNMENT

Leader(s): Pres. Ismail Omar Guelleh, Prime Min. Mohamed Dileita
Government Type: republic
Administrative Divisions: 5 districts (cercles, sing. —cercle)
Nationhood: June 27, 1977 (from France; formerly known as French Territory of the Afars and Issao)
National Holiday: Independence Day, June 27

■ ECONOMY

Overview: based on service activities related to country's strategic location and status as a free trade zone; Djibouti is heavily dependent on foreign aid
GDP: US$586 million, per capita US$1,400; real growth rate 0% (2001 est.)
Inflation: 2.0% (2000 est.)
Industries: accounts for 10% of GDP (2001 est.); limited to a few small-scale enterprises, such as dairy products and mineral-water bottling
Labour Force: approx. 282,000; 75% agriculture, 11% industry, 14% services
Unemployment: 50% (2000 est.)
Agriculture: accounts for only 3% of GDP (2001 est.); scanty rainfall limits crop production to mostly fruit and vegetables; half of population pastoral nomads herding goats, sheep and camels; imports bulk of food needs
Natural Resources: geothermal areas

■ FINANCE/TRADE

Currency: Djiboutian franc (DF) = 100 centimes
International Reserves Excluding Gold: US$72 million (Nov. 2002)
Gold Reserves: n.a.
Budget: revenues US$133 million; expenditures US$187 million, including capital expenditures of US$ n.a. (1999 est.)
Defence Expenditures: n.a.
Education Expenditures: n.a.
External Debt: US$262 million (2001)
Exports: US$19 million (2000); commodities: hides and skins, coffee (in transit); partners: Somalia, Yemen, Ethiopia
Imports: US$271 million (2000); commodities: foods, beverages, transport equipment, chemicals, petroleum products; partners: France, Ethiopia, Italy, Saudi Arabia, UK

■ COMMUNICATIONS

Daily Newspapers: none
Televisions: n.a.
Radios: n.a.

Telephones: 14 lines/1,000 inhabitants (1999)

■ TRANSPORTATION

Motor Vehicles: 16,500; 13,500 passenger cars
Roads: 2,890 km; 364 km paved
Railway: 100 km
Air Traffic: n.a.
Airports: 12; 2 have paved runways (2002)

Canadian Embassy: The Canadian Embassy to Djibouti, c/o The Canadian Embassy, P.O. Box 1130, Addis Ababa, Ethiopia. Tel: (011-251-1) 71-30-22. Fax: (011-251-1) 71-30-33. e-mail: addis@dfait-maeci.gc.ca
Embassy in Canada: c/o Embassy of the Republic of Djibouti, 1156 15th St. NW, Ste 515, Washington DC 20005, USA. Tel: (202) 331-0270. Fax: (202) 331-0302. e-mail: n.a.

Dominica

Long-Form Name: Commonwealth of Dominica
Capital: Roseau

■ GEOGRAPHY

Area: 754 sq. km
Coastline: 148 km
Climate: tropical; moderated by northeast trade winds; heavy rainfall
Environment: flash floods a constant hazard; occasional hurricanes
Terrain: rugged mountains of volcanic origin
Land Use: 9% arable; 13% permanent crops; 3% meadows; 67% forest and woodland; 8% other; includes n.a. sq. km irrigated
Location: Caribbean islands, northern end of the Windward Islands

■ PEOPLE

Population: 70,158 (July 2002 est.)
Nationality: Dominican
Age Structure: 0–14 yrs: 28.3%; 15–64: 63.8%; 65+: 7.9% (2002 est.)
Population Growth Rate: -0.81% (2002 est.)
Net Migration: -18.26 migrants/1,000 population (2002 est.)
Ethnic Groups: mostly black; some Carib Indians
Languages: English (official); French patois widely spoken
Religions: 77% Roman Catholic; 15% Protestant, 2% none, 1% unknown, 5% other
Birth Rate: 17.30/1,000 population (2002 est.)
Death Rate: 7.11/1,000 population (2002 est.)
Infant Mortality: 15.94 deaths/1,000 live births (2002 est.)

Life Expectancy at Birth: 70.98 years male, 76.88 years female (2002 est.)
Total Fertility Rate: 2.01 children born/woman (2002 est.)
Literacy: 94%

■ GOVERNMENT

Leader(s): Pres. Vernon Shaw, Prime Min. Pierre Charles
Government Type: parliamentary democracy
Administrative Divisions: 10 parishes
Nationhood: Nov. 3, 1978 (from UK)
National Holiday: Independence Day, Nov. 3

■ ECONOMY

Overview: dependent on agriculture and vulnerable to climatic conditions; tourist potential (undeveloped)
GDP: US$262 million, per capita US$3,700; real growth rate -3.2% (2001 est.)
Inflation: 0.8% (2000)
Industries: agricultural processing, tourism, soap and other coconut-based products, cigars, pumice mining, cement blocks, shoes. Industries account for 23% of GDP (2001 est.)
Labour Force: approx. 25,000; agriculture 40%, industry and commerce 32%, services 28%
Unemployment: 20% (1999 est.)
Agriculture: accounts for 18% of GDP (2001 est.); principal crops—bananas, citrus fruit, mangoes, coconuts, root crops; bananas provide the bulk of export earnings; forestry and fisheries potential not exploited
Natural Resources: timber, hydroelectric power, arable land

■ FINANCE/TRADE

Currency: East Caribbean dollar ($EC) = 100 cents
International Reserves Excluding Gold: US$43 million (Oct. 2002)
Gold Reserves: n.a.
Budget: n.a.
Defence Expenditures: n.a.
Education Expenditures: n.a.
External Debt: US$206 million (2001)
Exports: US$48 million (2002 est.); commodities: bananas, coconuts, grapefruit, oranges, soap, galvanized sheets; partners: CARICOM countries, UK, US
Imports: US$115 million (2002 est.); commodities: food, oils and fats, chemicals, fuels and lubricants, manufactured goods, machinery and equipment; partners: US, CARICOM, UK, Netherlands, Canada

■ COMMUNICATIONS

Daily Newspapers: none
Televisions: n.a.
Radios: n.a.
Telephones: 279 lines/1,000 inhabitants (1999)

■ TRANSPORTATION

Motor Vehicles: 5,700; 2,800 passenger cars
Roads: 780 km; 390 km paved
Railway: none
Air Traffic: n.a.
Airports: 2; both have paved runways (2002)

Canadian Embassy: c/o The Canadian High Commission, Bishop's Court Hill, St. Michael, Barbados; mailing address: P.O. Box 404, Bridgetown, Barbados. Tel: (246) 429-3550. Fax: (246) 429-3780. e-mail: bdgtn@dfait-maeci.gc.ca
Embassy in Canada: c/o High Commission for the Countries of the Organization of Eastern Caribbean States, 130 Albert St, Ste 700, Ottawa ON K1P 5G4. Tel: (613) 236-8952. Fax: (613) 236-3042. e-mail: echcc@travel-net.com

Dominican Republic

Long-Form Name: Dominican Republic
Capital: Santo Domingo

■ GEOGRAPHY

Area: 48,730 sq. km
Coastline: 1,288 km
Climate: tropical maritime; little seasonal temperature variation
Environment: subject to occasional hurricanes (July to Oct.); deforestation; erosion and water shortage
Terrain: rugged highlands and mountains interspersed with fertile valleys
Land Use: 21% arable; 9% permanent crops; 43% meadows; 12% forest; 15% other; includes 2,590 sq. km irrigated
Location: West Indies, bordering on Haiti, Caribbean Sea, Atlantic Ocean

■ PEOPLE

Population: 8,721,594 (July 2002 est.)
Nationality: Dominican
Age Structure: 0–14 yrs: 33.7%; 15–64: 61.3%; 65+: 5.0% (2002 est.)
Population Growth Rate: 1.61% (2002 est.)
Net Migration: -3.59 migrants/1,000 population (2002 est.)

Ethnic Groups: 73% mixed, 16% white, 11% black
Languages: Spanish
Religions: 95% Roman Catholic
Birth Rate: 24.40/1,000 population (2002 est.)
Death Rate: 4.68/1,000 population (2002 est.)
Infant Mortality: 33.41 deaths/1,000 live births (2002 est.)
Life Expectancy at Birth: 71.57 years male, 75.91 years female (2002 est.)
Total Fertility Rate: 2.94 children born/woman (2002 est.)
Literacy: 83.6% (2000)

■ GOVERNMENT

Leader(s): Pres. Rafael Hipolito Mejia Dominguez, V. Pres. Milagros Ortiz Bosch
Government Type: representative democracy
Administrative Divisions: 29 provinces (provincias, sing. —provincia) and 1 district (distrito)
Nationhood: Feb. 27, 1844 (from Haiti)
National Holiday: Independence Day, Feb. 27

■ ECONOMY

Overview: agriculture is the backbone of the economy (sugar cane); tourism and a free trade zone help; hurricane damage has adversely affected agriculture and infrastructure; the government is attempting to increase electric generating capacity, but there have been numerous delays
GDP: US$50 billion, per capita US$5,800; real growth rate 1.5% (2001 est.)
Inflation: 8.9% (2001)
Industries: accounts for 34% of GDP (2000); tourism, sugar processing, nickel and gold mining, textiles, cement, tobacco
Labour Force: 3.8 million (2001); 17% agriculture, 59% services and government, 24% industry
Unemployment: 13.8% (2001)
Agriculture: accounts for 11% of GDP (2000) and employs almost half of labour force; sugar cane most important commercial crop, followed by coffee, cotton and cocoa; food crops include rice, beans, potatoes, corn; animal output; not self-sufficient in food
Natural Resources: nickel, bauxite, gold, silver

■ FINANCE/TRADE

Currency: Dominican peso ($RD) = 100 centavos
International Reserves Excluding Gold: US$553 million (Dec. 2002)
Gold Reserves: 0.018 million fine troy ounces (Dec. 2002)

Budget: revenues US$2.9 billion; expenditures US$3.2 billion, including capital expenditures of US$1.1 billion (2001 est.)
Defence Expenditures: 5.57% of total government expenditure (2000)
Education Expenditures: 16.37% of central government expenditure (1999)
External Debt: US$5.093 billion (2001)
Exports: US$868 million (2002 est.); commodities: sugar, coffee, cocoa, tobacco, gold, nickel; partners: US, Netherlands, Canada, France
Imports: US$5.989 billion (2002 est.); commodities: foodstuffs, petroleum, cotton and fabrics, chemicals and pharmaceuticals; partners: US, Mexico, Japan, Venezuela

■ COMMUNICATIONS

Daily Newspapers: 27/1,000 inhabitants (2000)
Televisions: 97/1,000 inhabitants (2000)
Radios: 181/1,000 inhabitants (2001)
Telephones: 110 lines/1,000 inhabitants (2001)

■ TRANSPORTATION

Motor Vehicles: 209,000; 114,200 passenger cars
Roads: 12,600 km; 6,224 km paved
Railway: 757 km
Air Traffic: 11,000 passengers carried (2000)
Airports: 29; 13 have paved runways (2002)

Canadian Embassy: The Canadian Embassy, Capitan Eugenio de Marchena, No. 39, La Esperilla, Santo Domingo; mailing address: Apartado 2054, Santo Domingo 1, Dominican Republic. Tel: (809) 685-1136. Fax: (809) 682-2691. e-mail: sdmgo@dfait-maeci.gc.ca
Embassy in Canada: Embassy of the Dominican Republic, 130 Albert St., Suite 418, Ottawa ON, K1P 5G4. Tel: (613) 569-9893. Fax: (613) 569-8673. e-mail: n.a.

East Timor

Long-Form Name: Democratic Republic of Timor-Leste
Capital: Dili

■ GEOGRAPHY

Area: 14,609 sq. km
Coastline: 706 km
Climate: tropical with little seasonal temperature variation and high annual rainfall.
Environment: lack of safe drinking water; water is mainly underground and often far from villages

Terrain: extremely mountainous, volcanic island, much of it covered in forest; flat and arable in the south

Land Use: n.a.; 1,065 sq. km irrigated

Location: eastern half of the island of Timor, which lies between Indonesia and Australia at the eastern end of Malay Archipelago.

■ PEOPLE

Population: 952,618 (July 2002 est.)

Nationality: East Timorese

Age Structure: 0–14 yrs: 49%; 15–64 yrs: 49%; 65 yrs +: 2%; (2001)

Population Growth Rate: 7.26% (2002 est.)

Net Migration: 51.07 migrants/1,000 population (2002 est.)

Ethnic Groups: Malay and Papuan, including 33% Tetum, 12% Mambai, 8% Kemak, 10% Makasai, 8% Galoli and 8% Tokodede

Languages: 9 Austronesian language groups: Tetum (spoken by about 60% of the population), Mambai, Tokodede, Kemak, Galoli, Idate, Waima'a, Naueti and 3 Papuan langauge groups (Bunak, Makasae, Fatuluku). Under Indonesian rule the official language was Bahasa. Some Timorese still speak Portuguese

Religions: Roman Catholic 91.4%; Other (Muslim, Protestant, Hindu, Buddhist)

Birth Rate: 28.07/1,000 population (2002 est.)

Death Rate: 6.52/1,000 population (2002 est.)

Infant Mortality: 51.99 deaths/1,000 live births (2002 est.)

Life Expectancy at Birth: 62.64 years male; 67.17 years female (2002 est.)

Total Fertility Rate: 3.88 children born/woman (2002 est.)

Literacy: 48% (2001 est.)

■ GOVERNMENT

Leader(s): Pres. Jose Alexandre ("Xanana") Gusmao, Prime Min. Mari Bin Amude Alkatiri

Government Type: republic

Administrative Divisions: 13 districts

Nationhood: May 20, 2002 is the official date of international recognition of East Timor's independence from Indonesia

National Holiday: Independence Day, August 30; National Day, November 28

■ ECONOMY

Overview: fierce fighting in struggle for independence has damaged or destroyed most of East Timor's infrastructure; East Timor hopes to revive its economy by export profits from its high-quality, organically grown coffee crop

GDP: US$145 million, per capita US$500; real growth rate 18.0% (2001 est.)

Inflation: 3.0% (2001), down from 76.7% in 1999

Industries: oil and natural gas, and the processing of agricultural products including coffee, fish, spices, coconuts and cacao. Industrial production accounts for 17% of DGP (2001)

Labour Force: 230,400 (2001 est.)

Unemployment: 6% (2001 est.)

Agriculture: cornerstone of East Timorese economy. It employs over 80% of the population and is the major source of foreign exchange revenue. While paddy and rain-fed rice is the leading cash crop, other principal crops include food crops 51%, plantations 25.8%, livestock 20.5%, forestry 1% and fisheries 1%. High-quality arabica coffee is also being produced. Agricultural production accounts for 25% of GDP (2001)

Natural Resources: extremely rich in oil, natural gas and manganese

■ FINANCE/TRADE

Currency: US dollar (US$) = 100 cents

International Reserves Excluding Gold: n.a.

Gold Reserves: n.a.

Budget: $584.1 million (proposed for 2000–2001)

Defence Expenditures: n.a.

Education Expenditures: n.a.

External Debt: n.a.

Exports: US$4 million (2001); commodities: coffee, copra, palm oil, rice, wax and hides; partners: Australia, Portugal

Imports: US$237 million (2001); partners: Australia, Portugal

■ COMMUNICATIONS

Daily Newspapers: n.a.

Televisions: n.a.

Radios: n.a.

Telephones: n.a.

■ TRANSPORTATION

Motor Vehicles: n.a.

Roads: 3,800 km; 428 km paved
Railway: n.a.
Air Traffic: n.a.
Airports: 8; 3 have paved runways (2002)

Canadian Embassy: n.a.
Embassy in Canada: n.a.

Ecuador

Long-Form Name: Republic of Ecuador
Capital: Quito

■ GEOGRAPHY

Area: 283,560 sq. km
Coastline: 2,237 km
Climate: tropical along coast becoming cooler inland
Environment: subject to frequent earthquakes, landslides, volcanic activity; deforestation; desertification; soil erosion; periodic droughts
Terrain: coastal plain, inter-Andean central highlands and flat to rolling eastern jungle
Land Use: 6% arable; 5% permanent crops; 18% meadows; 56% forest; 15% other; includes 8,650 sq. km irrigated
Location: NW South America, bordering on Pacific Ocean

■ PEOPLE

Population: 13,447,494 (July 2002 est.)
Nationality: Ecuadorian
Age Structure: 0–14 yrs: 35.4%; 15–64: 60.2%; 65+: 4.4% (2002 est.)
Population Growth Rate: 1.96% (2002 est.)
Net Migration: -0.53 migrants/1,000 population (2002 est.)
Ethnic Groups: 65% mestizo (mixed Indian and Spanish), 25% Indian, 7% Spanish, 3% black
Languages: Spanish (official), Indian languages, especially Quechua
Religions: 95% Roman Catholic
Birth Rate: 25.47/1,000 population (2002 est.)
Death Rate: 5.36/1,000 population (2002 est.)
Infant Mortality: 33.02 deaths/1,000 live births (2002 est.)
Life Expectancy at Birth: 68.79 years male, 74.57 years female (2002 est.)
Total Fertility Rate: 3.05 children born/woman (2002 est.)
Literacy: 91.6% (2000)

■ GOVERNMENT

Leader(s): Pres. Lucio Gutierrez Borbua, V. Pres. Alfredo Palacio

Government Type: republic
Administrative Divisions: 22 provinces (provincias, sing. —provincia)
Nationhood: May 24, 1822 (from Spain; Battle of Pichincha)
National Holiday: Independence Day, Aug. 10

■ ECONOMY

Overview: vulnerable to international oil prices; the banana crop, second in importance only to oil, has been hurt by EU import quotas and banana blight; strict austerity program has resulted in economic stabilization
GDP: US$39.6 billion, per capita US$3,000; real growth rate 4.3% (2001 est.)
Inflation: 37.7% (2001)
Industries: accounts for 25% of GDP (2000); food processing, textiles, metal works, paper products, chemicals, fishing, timber, petroleum
Labour Force: 5.1 million (2001); 30% agriculture, 45% services, 25% industry
Unemployment: 11.5% (2001)
Agriculture: accounts for 11% of GDP (2000) and 35% of labour force (including fishing and forestry); leading producer and exporter of bananas and balsawood; crop and livestock sector; coffee, cocoa, rice, potatoes, net importer of foodgrain, dairy products and sugar
Natural Resources: petroleum, fish, timber, hydroelectric power

■ FINANCE/TRADE

Currency: US dollar ($) = 100 cents
International Reserves Excluding Gold: US$715 million (Dec. 2002)
Gold Reserves: 0.845 million fine troy ounces (Dec. 2002)
Budget: revenues US$5.6 billion; expenditures US$5.6 billion, including capital expenditures of US$ n.a. (2001 est.)
Defence Expenditures: 16.2% of central government expenditure (1999)
Education Expenditures: n.a.
External Debt: US$13.910 billion (2001)
Exports: US$4.945 billion (2002 est.); commodities: petroleum 47%, coffee, bananas, cocoa products, shrimp, fish products; partners: US, Chile, Peru, Colombia, Italy
Imports: US$6.460 billion (2002 est.); commodities: transport equipment, vehicles, machinery, chemicals, petroleum; partners: US, Colombia, Japan, Venezuela, Brazil

■ COMMUNICATIONS

Daily Newspapers: 96/1,000 inhabitants (2000)
Televisions: 225/1,000 inhabitants (2001)

Radios: 413/1,000 inhabitants (2001)
Telephones: 104 lines/1,000 inhabitants (2001)

■ TRANSPORTATION

Motor Vehicles: 610,000; 540,000 passenger cars (2000 est.)
Roads: 43,197 km; 8,165 km paved (1999)
Railway: 965 km
Air Traffic: 1,251,000 passengers carried (2001)
Airports: 205; 61 have paved runways (2002)

Canadian Embassy: The Canadian Embassy, Avenida 6 de Diciembre, 2816 y Paul Rivet, Edificio Josueth Gonzalez, 4th Fl., Quito, Ecuador; mailing address: P.O. Box 17-11-6512, Quito, Ecuador. Tel: (011-593-2) 2564-795. Fax: (011-593-2) 2503-108. e-mail: quito@dfait-maeci.gc.ca
Embassy in Canada: Embassy of the Republic of Ecuador, 50 O'Connor St, Ste 316, Ottawa ON K1P 6L2. Tel: (613) 563-8206. Fax: (613) 235-5776. e-mail: mecuacan@sprint.ca

Egypt

Long-Form Name: Arab Republic of Egypt
Capital: Cairo

■ GEOGRAPHY

Area: 1,001,450 sq. km
Coastline: 2,450 km
Climate: desert; hot, dry summers with moderate winters
Environment: Nile is only perennial water source; increasing soil salinization below Aswan High Dam; hot, driving windstorm called khamsin occurs in spring; water pollution; desertification; urbanization and erosion are decreasing the arable land available
Terrain: vast desert plateau interrupted by Nile valley and delta
Land Use: 2% arable; 0% permanent crops; 0% meadows; negligible forest; 98% other; includes 33,000 sq. km irrigated
Location: NE Africa, bordering on Mediterranean Sea, Red Sea

■ PEOPLE

Population: 70,712,345 (July 2002 est.)
Nationality: Egyptian
Age Structure: 0–14 yrs: 34.0%; 15–64: 61.2%; 65+: 3.9% (2002 est.)
Population Growth Rate: 1.66% (2002 est.)
Net Migration: -0.24 migrants/1,000 population (2002 est.)
Ethnic Groups: 99% Eastern Hamitic stock; 1% Greek, Italian, Syro-Lebanese, Armenian

Languages: Arabic (official); English and French
Religions: 94% Muslim (mostly Sunni), 6% Coptic Christian and other
Birth Rate: 24.41/1,000 population (2002 est.)
Death Rate: 7.58/1,000 population (2002 est.)
Infant Mortality: 58.60 deaths/1,000 live births (2002 est.)
Life Expectancy at Birth: 61.96 years male, 66.24 years female (2002 est.)
Total Fertility Rate: 2.99 children born/woman (2002 est.)
Literacy: 55.3% (2000)

■ GOVERNMENT

Leader(s): Pres. Mohammed Hosni Mubarak, Prime Min. Atef Mohamed Ebeid
Government Type: republic
Administrative Divisions: 26 governorates (muhafazat, sing. —muhafazah)
Nationhood: Feb. 28, 1922 (from UK; formerly known as United Arab Republic)
National Holiday: Anniversary of the Revolution, July 23

■ ECONOMY

Overview: urban population growth puts pressure on the agricultural sector; having difficulty with its debt servicing; vulnerable to oil prices; unemployment has become a growing problem
GDP: US$258 billion, per capita US$3,700; real growth rate 2.5% (2001 est.)
Inflation: 2.3% (2001)
Industries: accounts for 30% of GDP (2001), textiles, food processing, tourism, chemicals, petroleum, construction, cement, metals
Labour Force: 25.2 million (2001); 29% agriculture, 49% community, social and business services, 22% industry
Unemployment: 8.2% (2001)
Agriculture: accounts for 14% of GDP (2001), employs more than one-third of labour force; dependent on irrigation water from the Nile; world's fifth largest cotton exporter; other crops include rice, corn, wheat, beans, fruit, vegetables; livestock production; not self-sufficient in food
Natural Resources: crude oil, natural gas, iron ore, phosphates, manganese, limestone, gypsum, talc, asbestos, lead, zinc

■ FINANCE/TRADE

Currency: Egyptian pound (LE) = 100 piasters
International Reserves Excluding Gold: US$13.242 billion (Dec. 2002)
Gold Reserves: 2.432 million fine troy ounces (Dec. 2002)
Budget: revenues US$21.5 billion; expenditures US$26.2 billion, including capital expenditures of US$5.9 billion (2001)

Defence Expenditures: 10.2% of central government expenditure (2001)
Education Expenditures: n.a.
External Debt: US$29.234 billion (2001)
Exports: US$4.852 billion (2002 est.); commodities: raw cotton, crude and refined petroleum, cotton yarn, textiles; partners: US, EU, Middle East, Asian countries
Imports: US$12.120 billion (2002 est.); commodities: foods, machinery and equipment, fertilizers, wood products, durable consumer goods, capital goods; partners: Germany, Italy, France, US, Asian countries, Middle East

■ COMMUNICATIONS

Daily Newspapers: 31/1,000 inhabitants (2000)
Televisions: 217/1,000 inhabitants (2001)
Radios: 339/1,000 inhabitants (2001)
Telephones: 104 lines/1,000 inhabitants (2001)

■ TRANSPORTATION

Motor Vehicles: 1,711,000; 1,300,000 passenger cars
Roads: 64,000 km; 49,984 km paved
Railway: 4,955 km (2000)
Air Traffic: 4,389,000 passengers carried (2001)
Airports: 92; 71 have paved runways (2002)

Canadian Embassy: The Canadian Embassy, #26 Kamel El Shenawy St., Garden City, Cairo, Egypt; mailing address: P.O. Box 1667, Cairo, Egypt. Tel: (011-20-2) 794-3110. Fax: (011-20-2) 796-3548. e-mail: cairo@dfait-maeci.gc.ca
Embassy in Canada: Embassy of the Arab Republic of Egypt, 454 Laurier Ave E, Ottawa ON K1N 6R3. Tel: (613) 234-4931. Fax: (613) 234-4398. e-mail: egyptemb@sympatico.ca

---

El Salvador

Long-Form Name: Republic of El Salvador
Capital: San Salvador

■ GEOGRAPHY

Area: 21,040 sq. km
Coastline: 307 km
Climate: tropical; rainy season (May to Oct.), dry season (Nov. to Apr.)
Environment: the Land of Volcanoes; subject to frequent and sometimes very destructive earthquakes; deforestation; soil erosion and pollution; water pollution
Terrain: mostly mountains with narrow coastal belt and central plateau
Land Use: 27% arable; 8% permanent crops; 29% meadows; 5% forest; 31% other; includes 360 sq. km irrigated

Location: Central (Latin) America, bordering on Pacific Ocean

■ PEOPLE

Population: 6,353,681 (July 2002 est.)
Nationality: Salvadoran
Age Structure: 0–14 yrs: 37.4%; 15–64: 57.5%; 65+: 5.1% (2002 est.)
Population Growth Rate: 1.83% (2002 est.)
Net Migration: -3.88 migrants/1,000 population (2002 est.)
Ethnic Groups: 90% mestizo, 1% Amerindian, 9% white
Languages: Spanish, Nahua spoken among some Indians
Religions: approx. 75% Roman Catholic, with activity by Protestant groups throughout the country
Birth Rate: 28.30/1,000 population (2002 est.)
Death Rate: 6.10/1,000 population (2002 est.)
Infant Mortality: 27.58 deaths/1,000 live births (2002 est.)
Life Expectancy at Birth: 66.72 years male, 74.11 years female (2002 est.)
Total Fertility Rate: 3.29 children born/woman (2002 est.)
Literacy: 78.7% (2000)

■ GOVERNMENT

Leader(s): Pres. Francisco Flores Perez, V. Pres. Carlos Quintanilla
Government Type: republic
Administrative Divisions: 14 departments (departmentos, sing. —departmento)
Nationhood: Sept. 15, 1821 (from Spain)
National Holiday: Independence Day; Sept. 15

■ ECONOMY

Overview: in recent years inflation has fallen to unprecedented levels and exports have grown considerably; even so, sizeable fiscal deficits persist; the trade deficit has been offset by remittances from the many Salvadorans living abroad
GDP: US$28.4 billion, per capita US$4,600; real growth rate 1.4% (2001 est.)
Inflation: 3.8% (2001)
Industries: accounts for 30% of GDP (2000); food processing, textiles, non-metallic products, tobacco, beverages, clothing, petroleum products, cement
Labour Force: 2.8 million (2001); 30% agriculture, 55% community, social and business services, 15% industry
Unemployment: 7.3% (2001)
Agriculture: accounts for 10% of GDP (2000) and 40% of labour force (including fishing and forestry); coffee most important commercial

crop; other products—sugar cane, corn, rice, beans, oilseeds, beef, dairy products, shrimp; not self-sufficient in food
Natural Resources: hydroelectricity and geothermal power, crude oil

■ FINANCE/TRADE

Currency: colón (pl. colones) (C/) = 100 centavos; also US dollar ($) =100 cents
International Reserves Excluding Gold: US$1.623 billion (Dec. 2002)
Gold Reserves: 0.469 million fine troy ounces (Dec. 2002)
Budget: revenues US$2.1 billion, expenditures US$2.5 billion, including capital expenditures of US$ n.a. (2001 est.)
Defence Expenditures: 31.2% of total government expenditure (2001)
Education Expenditures: 24.23% of central government expenditure (2000)
External Debt: US$4.683 billion (2001)
Exports: US$1.234 billion (2002); commodities: coffee 60%, sugar, cotton, shrimp, electricity; partners: US, Guatemala, Honduras, EU
Imports: US$3.908 billion (2002); commodities: petroleum products, electricity, consumer goods, foodstuffs, machinery, construction materials, fertilizer; partners: US, Guatemala, EU, Mexico

■ COMMUNICATIONS

Daily Newspapers: 28/1,000 inhabitants (2000)
Televisions: 201/1,000 inhabitants (2001)
Radios: 478/1,000 inhabitants (2001)
Telephones: 93 lines/1,000 inhabitants (2001)

■ TRANSPORTATION

Motor Vehicles: 380,000; 180,000 passenger cars (2000)
Roads: 10,029 km; 1,986 km paved
Railway: 562 km
Air Traffic: 2,192,000 passengers carried (2001)
Airports: 83; 4 have paved runways (2002)

Canadian Embassy: Office of the Canadian Embassy, Centro Financiero Gigante, Alameda Roosevelt y 63 Avenida Sur, Torre A, Lobby 2, Colonia Escalon, San Salvador, El Salvador. Tel: (011-503) 279-4655. Fax: (011-503) 279-0765. e-mail: ssal@dfait-maeci.gc.ca
Embassy in Canada: Embassy of the Republic of El Salvador, 209 Kent St, Ottawa ON K2P 1Z8. Tel: (613) 238-2939. Fax: (613) 238-6940. e-mail: embajada@elsalvador.ca.org

Equatorial Guinea

Long-Form Name: Republic of Equatorial Guinea
Capital: Malabo

■ GEOGRAPHY

Area: 28,051 sq. km
Coastline: 296 km
Climate: tropical; always hot, humid
Environment: subject to violent windstorms; desertification; unsafe drinking water
Terrain: coastal plains rise to interior hills; islands are volcanic
Land Use: 5% arable; 4% permanent crops; 4% meadows; 46% forest; 41% other; includes n.a. sq. km irrigated
Location: WC Africa, bordering on South Atlantic Ocean

■ PEOPLE

Population: 498,144 (July 2002 est.)
Nationality: Equatorial Guinean or Equato-guinean
Age Structure: 0–14 yrs: 42.4%; 15–64: 53.8%; 65+: 3.8% (2002 est.)
Population Growth Rate: 2.45% (2002 est.)
Net Migration: 0 migrants/1,000 population (2001 est.)
Ethnic Groups: indigenous population of Bioko, primarily Bubi, some Fernandinos; Rio Muni, primarily Fang; less than 1,000 Europeans, mostly Spanish
Languages: Spanish (official), pidgin English, Fang, Bubi, Ndowe, Bujeba, Anobones and Corisqueño
Religions: natives all nominally Christian and predominantly Roman Catholic; some pagan practices retained (5%)
Birth Rate: 37.33/1,000 population (2002 est.)
Death Rate: 12.83/1,000 population (2002 est.)
Infant Mortality: 90.96 deaths/1,000 live births (2002 est.)
Life Expectancy at Birth: 52.26 years male, 56.50 years female (2002 est.)
Total Fertility Rate: 4.81 children born/woman (2002 est.)
Literacy: 83.2% (2000)

■ GOVERNMENT

Leader(s): Pres. Teodoro Obiang Nguema Mbasogo, Prime Min. Candido Muatetema Rivas
Government Type: republic
Administrative Divisions: 7 provinces (provincias, sing. —provincia)

Nationhood: Oct. 12, 1968 (from Spain; formerly Spanish Guinea)
National Holiday: Independence Day, Oct. 12

■ ECONOMY

Overview: the economy is recovering from destruction by a past regime; subsistence agriculture, forestry and fishing predominate; little industry; many undeveloped natural resources, but increased exploitation of recently discovered natural gas resources is boosting the economy
GDP: US$1.04 billion, per capita US$2,100; real growth rate 6.0% (2001 est.)
Inflation: 6% (1999 est.)
Industries: accounts for 60% of GDP; petroleum, fishing, sawmilling
Labour Force: n.a.; 66% agriculture, 23% services, 11% industry
Unemployment: n.a.
Agriculture: accounts for 20% of GDP; cash crops—timber and coffee from Rio Muni, cocoa from Bioko; food crops—rice, yams, cassava, bananas, tobacco, oil, palm nuts, manioc, livestock, timber production
Natural Resources: timber, crude oil, small unexploited deposits of gold, manganese, uranium

■ FINANCE/TRADE

Currency: Communauté financière africaine franc (CFAF) = 100 centimes
International Reserves Excluding Gold: US$80 million (Nov. 2002)
Gold Reserves: n.a.
Budget: revenues US$200 million; expenditures US$158 million, capital expenditures US$ n.a. (2001 est.)
Defence Expenditures: 0.6% of GDP (1998)
Education Expenditures: n.a.
External Debt: US$239 million (2001)
Exports: US$396 million (2000); commodities: petroleum, coffee, timber, cocoa beans; partners: China, Japan, US, South Korea
Imports: US$30 million (2000); commodities: petroleum, food, beverages, clothing, machinery; partners: US, France, Spain, Italy

■ COMMUNICATIONS

Daily Newspapers: 1 in total
Televisions: n.a.
Radios: n.a.
Telephones: 13 lines/1,000 persons (1999)

■ TRANSPORTATION

Motor Vehicles: 10,500; 6,500 passenger cars
Roads: 2,880 km, none paved
Railway: none
Air Traffic: 24,000 passengers carried (1999 est.)
Airports: 3; 2 have paved runways (2002)

Canadian Embassy: The Canadian Embassy to Equatorial Guinea, c/o P.O. Box 4037, Libreville, Gabon. Tel: (011-241) 73-73-54. Fax (011-241) 73-73-88. e-mail: lbrve@dfait-maeci.gc.ca
Embassy in Canada: c/o Embassy of Equatorial Guinea, 2020 16th St, NW, Washington DC 20009, USA. Tel: (202) 518-5700. Fax: (202) 518-5252. e-mail: n.a.

Eritrea

Long-Form Name: State of Eritrea
Capital: Asmara (formerly Asmera)

■ GEOGRAPHY

Area: 121,320 sq. km
Coastline: 1,151 km mainland coast; 2,234 km including island coastlines
Climate: hot, dry desert along Red Sea coast, cooler and wetter in central highlands, semi-arid in west
Environment: frequent droughts, famine, deforestation, soil erosion, overgrazing
Terrain: highlands descending to coastal desert in east, hilly in northwest, flat to rolling plains in southwest
Land Use: 12% arable; 1% permanent crops; 49% meadows and pastures; 6% forests and woodland, 32% other; includes 220 sq. km irrigated
Location: E Africa

■ PEOPLE

Population: 4,465,651 (July 2002 est.)
Nationality: Eritrean
Age Structure: 0–14 yrs: 42.9%; 15–64: 53.9%; 65+: 3.2% (2002 est.)
Population Growth Rate: 3.80% (2002 est.)
Net Migration: 7.61 migrants/1,000 population (2002 est.)
Ethnic Groups: 50% ethnic Tigrinya, 40% Tigre and Kunama, 4% Afar, 3% Saho (Red Sea coast-dwellers), 3% other
Languages: Afar, Amharic, Tigre and Kunama, Cushitic dialects, Tigrinya, Nora Bana, Arabic
Religions: Muslim, Coptic Christian, Roman Catholic, Protestant
Birth Rate: 42.25/1,000 population (2002 est.)
Death Rate: 11.82/1,000 population (2002 est.)

Infant Mortality: 73.62 deaths/1,000 live births (2002 est.)
Life Expectancy at Birth: 54.09 years male, 59.13 years female (2002 est.)
Total Fertility Rate: 5.80 children born/woman (2002 est.)
Literacy: 52.78% (1999)

■ GOVERNMENT

Leader(s): Pres. Isaias Afworki
Government Type: transitional govt.
Administrative Divisions: 8 provinces (awraja)
Nationhood: May 24, 1993 (from Ethiopia)
National Holiday: National Day (independence from Ethiopia), May 24

■ ECONOMY

Overview: with independence from Ethiopia, Eritrea faces the bitter economic problems of a small and desperately poor nation; subsistence farming will continue to be the people's economic mainstay; production is augmented by remittances from abroad, and there are long-term prospects for revenue from offshore oil development, offshore fishing, and tourism; Ethiopia is largely dependent on Eritrean ports for foreign trade
GDP: US$3.2 billion, per capita US$740; real growth rate 7.0% (2001 est.)
Inflation: 14% (2000 est.)
Industries: accounts for 29% of GDP (2001 est.); food processing, beverages, textiles, clothing manufacture
Labour Force: 2.1 million (2001); 80% agriculture, 20% industry and commerce
Unemployment: n.a.
Agriculture: accounts for 17% of GDP (2001 est.); livestock, fish, vegetables, sorghum, lentils, vegetables, corn, cotton, coffee and tobacco
Natural Resources: gold, potash, copper, zinc, salt, fish

■ FINANCE/TRADE

Currency: nafka = 100 cents
International Reserves Excluding Gold: n.a.
Gold Reserves: n.a.
Budget: revenues US$206.4 million; expenditures US$615.7 million, capital expenditures US$ n.a. (2000 est.)
Defence Expenditures: 51.1% of GDP (1999)
Education Expenditures: 1.9% of GNP (1999 est.)
External Debt: US$410 million (2001)
Exports: US$17 million (1999); commodities: livestock, sorghum, textiles, food, small manufactures; partners: Ethiopia, Sudan, Japan, UAE, Italy

Imports: US$329 million (1999); commodities: processed goods, machinery, petroleum products; partners: Italy, United Arab Emirates, Germany, UK, Korea

■ COMMUNICATIONS

Daily Newspapers: none
Televisions: 39/1,000 inhabitants (2001)
Radios: 464/1,000 inhabitants (2001)
Telephones: 8 lines/1,000 inhabitants (2001)

■ TRANSPORTATION

Motor Vehicles: n.a.
Roads: 3,850 km, 810 km paved (2000)
Railway: 317 km; not operational
Air Traffic: n.a.
Airports: 21; 2 have paved runways (2002)

Canadian Embassy: The Canadian Embassy to Eritrea, c/o P.O. Box 1130, Addis Ababa, Ethiopia. Tel: (011-251-1) 71-30-22. Fax: (011-251-1) 71-30-33. e-mail: addis@dfait-maeci.gc.ca
Embassy in Canada: Embassy of the State of Eritrea, 75 Albert St., Suite 610, Ottawa, ON K1P 5E7. Tel: (613) 234-3989. Fax: (613) 234-6213. e-mail: n.a.

Estonia

Long-Form Name: Republic of Estonia
Capital: Tallinn

■ GEOGRAPHY

Area: 45,226 sq. km
Coastline: 3,794 km
Climate: wet, moderate winter; long windy autumn; warm sunny summer; late and short spring
Environment: severe air pollution, soil and ground water contamination (chemicals and petroleum products), radioactive waste; frequent spring floods are a natural hazard
Terrain: marshy lowlands, sloping coastal plain; islands account for 10% of the region
Land Use: 25% arable; negligible permanent crops; 11% meadows and pastures; 44% forest and woodland; 20% other; includes 40 sq. km irrigated
Location: NE Europe, bordering on Baltic Sea

■ PEOPLE

Population: 1,415,681 (July 2002 est.)
Nationality: Estonian
Age Structure: 0–14 yrs: 17.08%; 15–64: 68.14%; 65+: 14.78% (2001 est.)
Population Growth Rate: -0.52% (2002 est.)

Net Migration: -0.73 migrants/1,000 population (2002 est.)
Ethnic Groups: 65.1% Estonian, 28.1% Russian, 2.5% Ukrainian, 1.5% Byelorussian, 1% Finn, 1.8% other
Languages: Estonian (official), Russian, Latvian, Lithuanian, English and German also spoken
Religions: Lutheran, Orthodox Christian
Birth Rate: 8.96/1,000 population (2002 est.)
Death Rate: 13.44/1,000 population (2002 est.)
Infant Mortality: 12.32 deaths/1,000 live births (2002 est.)
Life Expectancy at Birth: 64.03 years male, 76.31 years female (2002 est.)
Total Fertility Rate: 1.24 children born/woman (2002 est.)
Literacy: approaching 100% (2000)

■ **GOVERNMENT**

Leader(s): Pres. Arnold Ruutel, Prime Min. Juhan Parts
Government Type: parliamentary democracy
Administrative Divisions: 15 counties (maakonnad, sing. —maakond)
Nationhood: Sept. 6, 1991 (from Soviet Union)
National Holiday: Independence Day, Feb. 24 (1918 from Soviet Russia); Sept. 6 (1991, from the Soviet Union)

■ **ECONOMY**

Overview: market reforms and stabilizing measures are rapidly transforming the economy; living standards and incomes are rising, but so are unemployment and inflation
GDP: US$15.2 billion, per capita US$10,900; real growth rate 4.4% (2002 est.)
Inflation: 5.7% (2001)
Industries: accounts for 29% of GDP (2001); electronics, electrical engineering, textiles, clothing, footwear, shipbuilding
Labour Force: 800,000 (2001); 20% industry, 69% community, social and business services, 11% agriculture
Unemployment: 11.3% (Nov. 2002); large numbers of underemployed
Agriculture: contributes 6% to GDP (2001), and employs 11% of labour force; dairy products, pork, poultry, eggs, fruit, vegetables; net exports of meat, fish, dairy products, potatoes
Natural Resources: fish, shale, phosphorites, amber, limestone, peat, dolomite, arable land

■ **FINANCE/TRADE**

Currency: kroon (pl. kroons) = 100 sents
International Reserves Excluding Gold: US$1.000 billion (Dec. 2002)

Gold Reserves: 0.008 million fine troy ounces (Dec. 2002)
Budget: revenues US$1.89 billion; expenditures US$1.89 billion, capital expenditures US$ n.a. (2002 est.)
Defence Expenditures: 5.6% of government expenditure (2001)
Education Expenditures: 10.24% of central government expenditure (2000)
External Debt: US$2.852 billion (2001)
Exports: US$3.439 billion (2002); dairy products, fish, furniture, electrical power, meat; partners: Latvia, Finland, Sweden, Germany, UK
Imports: US$4.811 billion (2002); machinery 45%, oil 13%, chemicals 12%, foodstuffs, textiles; partners: Finland, Russia, Sweden, Germany, Japan

■ **COMMUNICATIONS**

Daily Newspapers: 176/1,000 inhabitants (2000)
Televisions: 629/1,000 inhabitants (2001)
Radios: 1,136/1,000 inhabitants (2001)
Telephones: 352 lines/1,000 inhabitants (2001)

■ **TRANSPORTATION**

Motor Vehicles: 560,000; 470,000 passenger cars (2000)
Roads: 30,300 km; 29,200 km hard-surfaced
Railway: 968 km
Air Traffic: 278,000 passengers carried (2001)
Airports: 32; 8 have paved runways (2002)

Canadian Embassy: Office of the Canadian Embassy, Toom Kooli 13, 2nd Fl, 10130 Tallinn, Estonia. Tel: (011-372) 627-3311. Fax: (011-372) 627-3312. e-mail: tallinn@canada.ee
Embassy in Canada: c/o Embassy of the Republic of Estonia, 260 Dalhousie St, Ste 210, Ottawa ON K1N 7E4. Tel: (613) 789-4222. Fax: (613) 789-9555. e-mail: estoniaembassy@rogers.com

Ethiopia

Long-Form Name: Federal Democratic Republic of Ethiopia
Capital: Addis Ababa

■ **GEOGRAPHY**

Area: 1,127,127 sq. km
Coastline: none; landlocked
Climate: tropical with wide topographic-induced variation; prone to extended droughts
Environment: geologically active Great Rift Valley susceptible to earthquakes, volcanic eruptions; deforestation; overgrazing; soil

erosion; desertification; frequent droughts; famine

Terrain: high plateau with central mountain range divided by Great Rift Valley

Land Use: 12% arable; 1% permanent crops; 40% meadows; 25% forest; 22% other; includes 1,900 sq. km irrigated

Location: E Africa, between Somalia and Sudan

■ PEOPLE

Population: 67,673,031 (July 2002 est.)

Nationality: Ethiopian

Age Structure: 0–14 yrs: 47.2%; 15–64: 50.0%; 65+: 2.8% (2002 est.)

Population Growth Rate: 2.64% (2002 est.)

Net Migration: 0.11 migrants/1,000 population (2002 est.)

Ethnic Groups: 40% Oromo, 32% Amhara and Tigrean, 9% Sidamo, 6% Shankella, 6% Somali, 4% Afar, 2% Gurage, 1% other

Languages: Amharic (official), Tigrinya, Orominga, Guaraginga, Somali, Arabic, English (major foreign language taught in schools)

Religions: 45–50% Muslim, 35–40% Ethiopian Orthodox, 12% animist, 5% other

Birth Rate: 44.31/1,000 population (2002 est.)

Death Rate: 18.04/1,000 population (2002 est.)

Infant Mortality: 98.63 deaths/1,000 live births (2002 est.)

Life Expectancy at Birth: 43.36 years male, 45.09 years female (2002 est.)

Total Fertility Rate: 6.94 children born/woman (2002 est.)

Literacy: 37.4% (1999)

■ GOVERNMENT

Leader(s): Pres. Girma Woldegiorgis, Prem. Meles Zenawi

Government Type: federal republic

Administrative Divisions: 9 states and 2 self-governing administrations

Nationhood: oldest (at least 2,000 years) independent country in Africa and one of the oldest in the world

National Holiday: National Day, May 28

■ ECONOMY

Overview: remains one of the poorest and least developed countries in the world; its economy is based on agriculture and suffers from recent periods of drought, poor cultivation practices and the deterioration of internal security conditions

GDP: US$46 billion, per capita US$700; real growth rate 7.3% (2001 est.)

Inflation: -11.2% (2001)

Industries: accounts for 11% of GDP (2000), cement, textiles, food processing, beverages, chemicals, metals processing, oil refinery

Labour Force: 28.3 million (2001); 80% agriculture, 12% services, 8% industry

Unemployment: n.a.

Agriculture: accounts for 52% of GDP (2000) even though frequent droughts, poor cultivation practices and state economic policies keep farm output low; famines not uncommon; estimated 50% of agricultural production at subsistence level. Products include cereals, coffee, oilseed

Natural Resources: small reserves of gold, platinum, copper, potash, natural gas

■ FINANCE/TRADE

Currency: birr (Br) = 100 cents

International Reserves Excluding Gold: US$747 million (Nov. 2002)

Gold Reserves: 0.246 million fine troy ounces (Nov. 2002)

Budget: revenues US$1.8 billion; expenditures US$1.9 billion, capital expenditures US$600 million (2002 est.)

Defence Expenditures: 43.0% of central government expenditure (2001)

Education Expenditures: n.a.

External Debt: US$5.697 billion (2001)

Exports: US$508 million (2000); commodities: coffee 60%, gold, oilseed, hides; partners: Germany, Djibouti, Japan, Saudi Arabia

Imports: US$1.366 billion (2000); commodities: food, fuels, machinery and motor vehicles, capital goods; partners: Italy, US, Saudi Arabia, Russia

■ COMMUNICATIONS

Daily Newspapers: less than 1/1,000 inhabitants (2000)

Televisions: 6/1,000 inhabitants (2001)

Radios: 189/1,000 inhabitants (2001)

Telephones: 4 lines/1,000 inhabitants (2001)

■ TRANSPORTATION

Motor Vehicles: 69,000; 46,400 passenger cars

Roads: 24,145 km; 3,290 km paved

Railway: 681 km

Air Traffic: 1,028,000 passengers carried (2001)

Airports: 86; 14 have paved runways (2002)

Canadian Embassy: The Canadian Embassy, Old Airport Area, Higher 23, Kebele 12, House Number 122, Addis Ababa; mailing address: P.O. Box 1130, Addis Ababa, Ethiopia. Tel: (011-251-1) 71-30-22. Fax: (011-251-1) 71-30-33. e-mail: addis@dfait-maeci.gc.ca

Embassy in Canada: Embassy of the Federal Democratic Republic of Ethiopia, 151 Slater St,

Ste 210, Ottawa ON K1P 5H3. Tel: (613) 235-6637. Fax: (613) 235-4638. e-mail: infoethi @magi.com

Falkland Islands

Long-Form Name: Colony of the Falkland Islands
Capital: Stanley (on East Falkland)

■ GEOGRAPHY

Area: numerous islands covering 12,173 sq. km
Climate: damp, cool, temperate; strong winds, esp. in spring; occasional snow all year
Land Use: 99% pastureland
Location: S South America, in the South Atlantic Ocean

■ PEOPLE

Population: 2,967 (July 2002 est.)
Nationality: Falkland Islander
Ethnic Groups: almost 100% British descent
Languages: English

■ GOVERNMENT

Colony/Territory of: Dependent Territory of the United Kingdom
Leader(s): Head of State: Queen Elizabeth II, Gov. Howard J.S. Pearce
Government Type: overseas territory of the UK, although in 1990 Argentina declared the Falklands and other British-held South Atlantic Islands part of new Argentine province Tierra del Fuego
National Holiday: Liberation Day, June 14

■ ECONOMY

Overview: heavily agricultural, esp. sheep farming, with wool main product; fishing: illex squid; exports tend to outweigh imports in value; chief trading partner: United Kingdom

■ FINANCE/TRADE

Currency: Falkland Islands pound (FKP) = 100 pence, at parity with the British pound sterling

Canadian Embassy: c/o The Canadian High Commission, Macdonald House, 1 Grosvenor Square, London W1K 4AB, England, UK. Tel: (011-44-20) 7258-6600. Fax: (011-44-20) 7445-3302. e-mail: ldn@dfait-maeci.gc.ca
Representative to Canada: c/o British High Commission, 80 Elgin St, Ottawa ON K1P 5K7l. Tel: (613) 237-1530. Fax: (613) 237-7980. Email should be sent using the appropriate form at the British High Commission's Website at http://www.britain-in-canada.org

Faroe Islands

Long-Form Name: Faroe Islands
Capital: Tórshavn (island of Stremoy)

■ GEOGRAPHY

Area: 1,399 sq. km (total of 18 islands and some reefs)
Climate: cold and windy; mild winters, cool summers; foggy
Land Use: 6% arable; 94% other
Location: Norwegian Sea (N Atlantic Ocean), N of Scotland

■ PEOPLE

Population: 46,011 (July 2002 est.)
Nationality: Faroese (sing. & pl.)
Ethnic Groups: Scandinavian
Languages: Faroese (derived from Old Norse), Danish

■ GOVERNMENT

Colony/Territory of: Dependent Territory of Denmark
Leader(s): Queen Margrethe II of Denmark, High Comm. Birgit Kleis, Prime Min. Anfinn Kallsberg
Government Type: dependency with some degree of self-rule
National Holiday: Olaifest, July 29

■ ECONOMY

Overview: fishing main industry, now in decline, which poses great danger to the economy; steep coastline and treacherous currents make trading by sea difficult; exports: fish and fish products; partners: Denmark, Norway, Sweden, Germany, United States

■ FINANCE/TRADE

Currency: Danish krone (kr) = 100 oere

Canadian Embassy: c/o The Canadian Embassy, Kr. Bernikowsgade 1, 1105 Copenhagen K, Denmark. Tel: (011-45) 33-48-32-00. Fax: (011-45) 33-48-32-20. e-mail: copen@dfait-maeci.gc.ca
Representative to Canada: c/o Embassy of the Kingdom of Denmark, 47 Clarence St, Ste 450, Ottawa ON K1N 9K1. Tel: (613) 562-1811. Fax: (613) 562-1812. e-mail: danemb@cyberus.ca

Fiji

Long-Form Name: Republic of the Fiji Islands
Capital: Suva

■ GEOGRAPHY

Area: 18,270 sq. km; includes 332 islands of which approx. 110 are inhabited
Coastline: 1,129 km
Climate: tropical marine; only slight seasonal temperature variation
Environment: subject to hurricanes from Nov. to Jan.; deforestation and soil erosion
Terrain: mostly mountains of volcanic origin
Land Use: 10% arable; 4% permanent crops; 10% meadows; 65% forest; 11% other; includes 30 sq. km irrigated
Location: Pacific Ocean, N of New Zealand

■ PEOPLE

Population: 856,346 (July 2002 est.)
Nationality: Fijian
Age Structure: 0–14 yrs: 32.5%; 15–64: 63.8%; 65+: 3.7% (2002 est.)
Population Growth Rate: 1.41% (2002 est.)
Net Migration: -3.35 migrants/1,000 population (2002 est.)
Ethnic Groups: 44% Indian, 51% Fijian, 5% European, other Pacific Islanders, overseas Chinese and others
Languages: English (official); Fijian; Hindi
Religions: Christianity 52%, Hinduism 38%, Muslim 8%, other 2%
Birth Rate: 23.20/1,000 population (2002 est.)
Death Rate: 5.72/1,000 population (2002 est.)
Infant Mortality: 13.72 deaths/1,000 live births (2002 est.)
Life Expectancy at Birth: 66.13 years male, 71.11 years female (2002 est.)
Total Fertility Rate: 2.83 children born/woman (2002 est.)
Literacy: 92.9% (2000)

■ GOVERNMENT

Leader(s): Pres. Ratu Josefa Iloilo, Prime Min. Laisenia Qarase
Government Type: republic. The government was destabilized by a coup and hostage taking that began May 19, 2000; it ended with the release of final hostages of deposed elected government on July 13, 2000. A new president was elected by the Great Council of Chiefs on July 13
Administrative Divisions: 4 divisions and 1 dependency
Nationhood: Oct. 10, 1970 (from UK)
National Holiday: Independence Day, second Monday in October

■ ECONOMY

Overview: the economy, based on agriculture, has recovered from military coups, droughts and a drop in tourism; sugar exports are a major source of income
GDP: US$4.4 billion, per capita US$5,200; real growth rate -8% (2001 est.)
Inflation: 4.3% (2001)
Industries: accounts for 25% of GDP (2000); sugar, copra, tourism, gold, silver, fishing, clothing, lumber, small cottage industries
Labour Force: approx. 235,000; 70% of the population is engaged in agriculture and subsistence farming
Unemployment: n.a.
Agriculture: accounts for 17% of GDP (2000); principal cash crop is sugar cane; coconuts, cassava, rice, sweet potatoes and bananas; small livestock sector includes cattle, pigs, horses and goats; annual fish catch is significant
Natural Resources: timber, fish, gold, copper, offshore oil potential

■ FINANCE/TRADE

Currency: Fijian dollar ($F) = 100 cents
International Reserves Excluding Gold: US$359 million (Dec. 2002)
Gold Reserves: 0.001 million fine troy ounces (Dec. 2002)
Budget: revenues US$427 million; expenditures US$531.4 million, including capital expenditures US$ n.a. (2000 est.)
Defence Expenditures: n.a.
Education Expenditures: n.a.
External Debt: US$188 million (2001)
Exports: US$537 million (2001); commodities: sugar 49%, garments, gold, copra, processed fish, lumber; partners: Australia, US, UK, Japan, other Pacific island countries, New Zealand
Imports: US$793 million (2001); commodities: food 15%, petroleum products, machinery, consumer goods; partners: New Zealand, Australia, Singapore, Japan, Hong Kong, US, Taiwan

■ COMMUNICATIONS

Daily Newspapers: 1 in total
Televisions: n.a.
Radios: n.a.
Telephones: 101 lines/1,000 inhabitants (1999)

■ TRANSPORTATION

Motor Vehicles: 59,000; 30,000 passenger cars
Roads: 3,440 km; 1,692 km paved
Railway: 597 km

Air Traffic: 590,000 passengers carried (1999 est.)
Airports: 27; 3 have paved runways (2002)

Canadian Embassy: The Canadian Embassy to Fiji, c/o The Canadian High Commission, P.O. Box 12-049, Thorndon, Wellington, New Zealand. Tel: (011-679) 721-936. Fax: (011-679) 750-666. e-mail: wlgtn@dfait-maeci.gc.ca
Embassy in Canada: c/o Embassy of the Republic of Fiji, 630 Third Ave, 7th Fl, New York NY 10017, USA. Tel: (212) 687-4130. Fax: (212) 687-3963. e-mail: n.a.

Finland

Long-Form Name: Republic of Finland
Capital: Helsinki

■ GEOGRAPHY

Area: 337,030 sq. km
Coastline: 1,126 km excluding islands and coastal indentations
Climate: cold temperate; potentially subarctic, but comparatively mild because of moderating influence of the North Atlantic Current, Baltic Sea and more than 60,000 lakes
Environment: permanently wet ground covers approx. 30% of land; air and water pollution
Terrain: mostly low, flat to rolling plains interspersed with lakes and low hills
Land Use: 8% arable; 0% permanent crops; 0% meadows; 76% forest; 16% other; includes 640 sq. km irrigated
Location: N Europe, bordering on Baltic Sea

■ PEOPLE

Population: 5,183,545 (July 2002 est.)
Nationality: Finn
Age Structure: 0–14 yrs: 17.9%; 15–64: 66.9%; 65+: 15.2% (2002 est.)
Population Growth Rate: 0.14% (2002 est.)
Net Migration: 0.62 migrants/1,000 population (2002 est.)
Ethnic Groups: 93% Finn, 6% Swede, 0.11% Lapp, 0.12% Gypsy, 0.02% Tatar
Languages: 93.5% Finnish, 6.3% Swedish (both official); small Lapp- and Russian-speaking minorities; business language is English
Religions: 89% Evangelical Lutheran, 9% atheist, 1% Eastern Orthodox, 1% other
Birth Rate: 10.60/1,000 population (2002 est.)
Death Rate: 9.78/1,000 population (2002 est.)
Infant Mortality: 3.76 deaths/1,000 live births (2002 est.)
Life Expectancy at Birth: 74.10 years male, 81.52 years female (2002 est.)

Total Fertility Rate: 1.70 children born/woman (2002 est.)
Literacy: approaching 100% (2000)

■ GOVERNMENT

Leader(s): Pres. Tarja Halonen, Prime Min. Matti Taneli Vanhanen
Government Type: republic
Administrative Divisions: 6 provinces (laanit, sing. -laani)
Nationhood: Dec. 6, 1917 (from Soviet Union)
National Holiday: Independence Day, Dec. 6

■ ECONOMY

Overview: the manufacturing sector and trade are vital to this highly industrialized, largely free market economy; because of the climate, agricultural development is limited to maintaining self-sufficiency in basic products. Unemployment is a continuing problem.
GDP: US$136.2 billion, per capita US$26,200; real growth rate 1.1% (2002 est.)
Inflation: 2.6% (2001)
Industries: accounts for 34% of GDP (2002 est.); metal manufacturing and shipbuilding, forestry and wood processing (pulp, paper), copper refining, foodstuffs, textiles, clothing
Labour Force: 2.6 million (2001); 32% community, social and business services, 22% industry, 14% commerce, 32% other
Unemployment: 9.5% (Jan. 2003)
Agriculture: accounts for 4% of GDP (2002 est.) (including forestry); livestock production, especially dairy cattle, predominates; forestry is an important export earner; main crops—cereals, sugar beets, potatoes; 85% self-sufficient, but short of food and fodder grains
Natural Resources: timber, copper, zinc, iron ore, silver

■ FINANCE/TRADE

Currency: markkaa, or Finmark = 100 pennia; Euro (€); on January 1, 2002 the Euro became the sole currency for everyday transactions.
International Reserves Excluding Gold: US$9.285 billion (Dec. 2002)
Gold Reserves: 1.577 million fine troy ounces (Dec. 2002)
Budget: revenues US$36.1 billion; expenditures US$31 billion, including capital expenditures of US$ n.a. (2000 est.)
Defence Expenditures: 4.4% of central government expenditure (2001)
Education Expenditures: n.a.
External Debt: n.a.
Exports: US$42.385 billion (2002 est.); commodities: timber, paper and pulp, ships,

machinery, clothing and footwear; partners: Germany, US, UK, Sweden, Russia, France
Imports: US$32.395 billion (2002 est.); commodities: foodstuffs, petroleum and petroleum products, chemicals, transport equipment, iron and steel, machinery, textile yarn and fabrics, fodder grains; partners: Germany, Sweden, Russia, US, UK, France

■ COMMUNICATIONS

Daily Newspapers: 445/1,000 inhabitants (2000)
Televisions: 678/1,000 inhabitants (2001)
Radios: 1,624/1,000 inhabitants (2001)
Telephones: 548 lines/1,000 inhabitants (2001)

■ TRANSPORTATION

Motor Vehicles: 2,400,000; 2,100,000 passenger cars (2000 est.)
Roads: 77,831 km; 49,789 km paved
Railway: 5,865 km
Air Traffic: 6,698,000 passengers carried (2001)
Airports: 160; 74 have paved runways (2002)

Canadian Embassy: The Canadian Embassy, Pohjois Esplanadi 25B, 00100 Helsinki; mailing address: Box 779, 00101 Helsinki, Finland. Tel: (011-358-9) 22-85-30. Fax (011-358-9) 60-10-60. e-mail: hsnki@dfait-maeci.gc.ca
Embassy in Canada: Embassy of Finland, 55 Metcalfe St, Ste 850, Ottawa ON K1P 6L5. Tel: (613) 236-2389. Fax: (613) 238-1474. e-mail: finembott@synapse.net

France

Long-Form Name: French Republic
Capital: Paris

■ GEOGRAPHY

Area: 547,030 sq. km; includes Corsica and the rest of metropolitan France, but excludes the overseas administrative divisions
Coastline: 3,427 km (includes Corsica, 644 km)
Climate: generally cool winters and mild summers, but mild winters and hot summers along the Mediterranean
Environment: most of large urban areas and industrial centres in Rhône, Garonne, Seine or Loire River basins; occasional warm, tropical winds known as mistrals are in central south; air and water pollution; acid rain
Terrain: mostly flat plains or gently rolling hills in north and west; remainder is mountainous, especially Pyrenees in south and Alps in east
Land Use: 33% arable; 2% permanent crops; 20% meadows; 27% forest; 18% other; includes 20,000 sq. km irrigated

Location: W Europe, bordering on Atlantic Ocean, Mediterranean Sea

■ PEOPLE

Population: 59,765,983 (July 2002 est.)
Nationality: Frenchman, Frenchwoman
Age Structure: 0–14 yrs: 18.5%; 15–64: 65.2%; 65+: 16.3% (2002 est.)
Population Growth Rate: 0.35% (2002 est.)
Net Migration: 0.64 migrants/1,000 population (2002 est.)
Ethnic Groups: Celtic and Latin with Teutonic, Slavic, North African, Indochinese and Basque minorities
Languages: French (100% of population); rapidly declining regional dialects (Provençal, Breton, Alsatian, Corsican, Catalan, Basque, Flemish)
Religions: 90% Roman Catholic, 2% Protestant, 1% Jewish, 1% Muslim (North African workers), 6% unaffiliated
Birth Rate: 11.94/1,000 population (2002 est.)
Death Rate: 9.04/1,000 population (2002 est.)
Infant Mortality: 4.41 deaths/1,000 live births (2002 est.)
Life Expectancy at Birth: 75.17 years male, 83.14 years female (2002 est.)
Total Fertility Rate: 1.74 children born/woman (2002 est.)
Literacy: approaching 100% (2000)

■ GOVERNMENT

Leader(s): Pres. Jacques Chirac, Prime Min. Jean-Pierre Raffarin
Government Type: republic
Administrative Divisions: 22 regions; dependent areas includes Bassas da India, Clipperton Island, Europa Island, Glorioso Islands, Juan de Nova Island, Tromelin Island, French Polynesia, Guadeloupe, Guiana (French Guiana), Martinique, Mayotte, New Caledonia, Réunion, St. Pierre and Miquelon, Southern and Antarctic Territories, Wallis and Futuna Islands
Nationhood: unified by Clovis in 486, First Republic proclaimed in 1792
National Holiday: Taking of the Bastille, July 14

■ ECONOMY

Overview: one of the world's most developed economies; largely self-sufficient in agricultural products; the leading agricultural producer in Western Europe; highly diversified industrial sector; economic integration into the European Community has unknown consequences; unemployment is rising rapidly
GDP: US$1.54 trillion, per capita US$25,700 real growth rate 1.1% (2002 est.)

Inflation: 1.6% (2001)
Industries: accounts for 26% of GDP (2002 est.); steel, machinery, chemicals, automobiles, metallurgy, aircraft, electronics, mining, textiles, food processing, tourism
Labour Force: 26.8 million (2001); 71% community, social and business services, 25% industry, 4% agriculture
Unemployment: 10.0% (2001)
Agriculture: accounts for 3% of GNP (2002 est.) (including fishing and forestry); one of the world's top five wheat producers; self-sufficient for most temperate-zone foods; shortages include fats and oils and tropical produce, but overall net exporter of farm products
Natural Resources: coal, iron ore, bauxite, fish, timber, zinc, potash

■ FINANCE/TRADE

Currency: franc (F or FF) = 100 centimes; Euro (€); on January 1, 2002, the Euro became the sole currency for everyday transactions
International Reserves Excluding Gold: US$28.365 billion (Dec. 2002)
Gold Reserves: 97.247 million fine troy ounces (Dec. 2002)
Budget: revenues US$210 billion; expenditures US$240 billion, including capital expenditures of US$ n.a. (2000 est.)
Defence Expenditures: 6.4% of central government expenditure (2001)
Education Expenditures: n.a.
External Debt: n.a.
Exports: US$299.675 billion (2002 est.); commodities: machinery and transportation equipment, chemicals, foodstuffs, agricultural products, iron and steel products, textiles and clothing; partners: Germany, UK, Spain, Italy, US
Imports: US$297.703 billion (2002 est.); commodities: crude oil, machinery and equipment, agricultural products, chemicals, iron and steel products; partners: Germany, Benelux, Italy, UK, US

■ COMMUNICATIONS

Daily Newspapers: 201/1,000 inhabitants (2000)
Televisions: 632/1,000 inhabitants (2001)
Radios: 950/1,000 inhabitants (2001)
Telephones: 573/1,000 inhabitants (2001)

■ TRANSPORTATION

Motor Vehicles: 33,600,000; 28,000,000 passenger cars (2000)
Roads: 892,900 km; all paved
Railway: 31,939 km

Air Traffic: 50,817,000 passengers carried (2001)
Airports: 477; 273 have paved runways (2002)

Canadian Embassy: The Canadian Embassy, 35-37 avenue Montaigne, 75008, Paris, France. Tel: (011-33-1) 44-43-29-00. Fax: (011-33-1) 44-43-29-99. e-mail: paris@dfait-maeci.gc.ca
Embassy in Canada: Embassy of France, 42 Sussex Dr, Ottawa ON K1M 2C9. Tel: (613) 789-1795. Fax: (613) 562-3735. e-mail: politique@ambafrance-ca.org

French Guiana

Long-Form Name: Department of Guiana
Capital: Cayenne

■ GEOGRAPHY

Area: 91,000 sq. km
Coastline: 378 km
Climate: tropical, warm and humid, little seasonal temperature variation
Terrain: low-lying coastal plains rising to hills and small mountains
Land Use: 90% forest and woodland; interior is uncultivated wilderness, with mineral and forest resources that have not been tapped; 10% of land is under cultivation; 20 sq. km are irrigated
Location: N South America, bordering on Atlantic Ocean

■ PEOPLE

Population: 186,917 (July 2003 est.)
Nationality: French Guianese
Ethnic Groups: 66% black or mulatto, 12% Caucasian, 12% East Indian, Chinese, Amerindian, 10% other
Languages: French (official), Creole patois

■ GOVERNMENT

Colony/Territory of: Overseas Department of France
Leader(s): Head of State: Pres. Jacques Chirac (France); Prefect Ange Mancini, Pres. of General Council Joseph Ho-Ten-Yu
Government Type: overseas department of France
National Holiday: Taking of the Bastille, July 14

■ ECONOMY

Overview: economy is closely tied to that of France through subsidies and imports; agriculture: rice, manioc, sugar cane, livestock; forestry, fisheries, food processing industry; chief trading partners: France, EU countries,

Japan, US; unemployment is particularly serious among younger workers

■ FINANCE/TRADE

Currency: French franc = 100 centimes, Euro (€)

Canadian Embassy: c/o The Canadian Embassy, 35-57 avenue Montaigne, Paris 75008, France. Tel: (011-33-1) 44-43-29-00. Fax: (011-3-1) 44-43-29-99. e-mail: paris@dfait-maeci.gc.ca
Representative to Canada: c/o Embassy of France, 42 Sussex Dr, Ottawa ON K1M 2C9. Tel: (613) 789-1795. Fax: (613) 562-3735. e-mail: politique@ambafrance-ca.org

French Polynesia

Long-Form Name: Territory of French Polynesia
Capital: Papeete (Windward Islands)

■ GEOGRAPHY

Area: 4,167 sq. km, consisting of five island archipelagoes scattered widely over Eastern Pacific; uninhabited Clipperton Territory is a dependency of French Polynesia but does not form part of the territory
Climate: warm and humid; tropical but moderate
Environment:
Land Use: 1% arable; 6% permanent crops; 5% meadows and pastures; 31% forest and woodland, 57% other
Location: south Pacific Ocean, NE of New Zealand

■ PEOPLE

Population: 257,847 (July 2002 est.)
Nationality: French Polynesian
Ethnic Groups: 78% Polynesian, 12% Chinese, 6% local French, 4% metropolitan French
Languages: French and Tahitian (both official)

■ GOVERNMENT

Colony/Territory of: Overseas Territory of France
Leader(s): Pres. Jacques Chirac (France), represented by High Commissioner to French Polynesia Michel Mathieu
Government Type: French overseas territory
National Holiday: Taking of the Bastille, July 14

■ ECONOMY

Overview: agriculture: copra, tropical fruits grown for local consumption; tourism accounts for approximately 20% of GDP and is primary source of revenue; trading partners: France, UK, US

■ FINANCE/TRADE

Currency: CFP franc = 100 centimes

Canadian Embassy: c/o The Canadian Embassy, 35-37 avenue Montaigne, Paris 75008, France. Tel: (011-33-1) 44-43-29-00. Fax: (011-33-1) 44-43-29-99. e-mail: paris@dfait-maeci.gc.ca
Representative to Canada: c/o Embassy of France, 42 Sussex Dr, Ottawa ON K1M 2C9. Tel: (613) 789-1795. Fax: (613) 562-3735. e-mail: politique@ambafrance-ca.org

Gabon

Long-Form Name: Gabonese Republic
Capital: Libreville

■ GEOGRAPHY

Area: 267,667 sq. km
Coastline: 885 km
Climate: tropical; always hot, humid
Environment: deforestation and poaching
Terrain: narrow coastal plain; hilly interior; savanna in east and south
Land Use: 1% arable; 1% permanent crops; 18% meadows; 77% forest; 3% other; includes 150 sq. km irrigated
Location: WC Africa, bordering on South Atlantic Ocean

■ PEOPLE

Population: 1,233,353 (July 2002 est.)
Nationality: Gabonese (sing. & pl.)
Age Structure: 0–14 yrs: 33.3%; 15–64: 60.6%; 65+: 6.1% (2002 est.)
Population Growth Rate: 0.97% (2002 est.)
Net Migration: 0 migrants/1,000 population (2002 est.)
Ethnic Groups: about 40 Bantu tribes, including four major tribal groupings (Fang, Eshira, Bapounou, Bateke); approx. 154,000 other Africans and Europeans, including 6,000 French and 11,000 persons of mixed background
Languages: French (official), Fang, Myene, Bateke, Bapounou/Eschira, Bandjabi
Religions: 55–75% Roman Catholic, 1% Muslim, remainder animist
Birth Rate: 27.24/1,000 population (2002 est.)
Death Rate: 17.59/1,000 population (2002 est.)
Infant Mortality: 93.50 deaths/1,000 live births (2002 est.)
Life Expectancy at Birth: 48.01 years male, 50.25 years female (2002 est.)
Total Fertility Rate: 3.65 children born/woman (2002 est.)
Literacy: 63.0% (1999)

■ GOVERNMENT

Leader(s): Pres. El Hadj Omar Bongo, Prem. Jean-François Ntoutoume-Emane
Government Type: republic; multiparty presidential regime
Administrative Divisions: 9 provinces
Nationhood: Aug. 17, 1960 (from France)
National Holiday: Founding of the Gabonese Democratic Party, March 12

■ ECONOMY

Overview: economy is dependent on oil, which has contributed to an increase in per capita income; agricultural and industrial sectors are relatively underdeveloped
GDP: US$6.7 billion, per capita US$5,500; real growth rate 2.5% (2001 est.)
Inflation: 0.5% (2000)
Industries: accounts for 60% of GDP; sawmills, cement, petroleum, food and beverages; mining of increasing importance (especially manganese and uranium)
Labour Force: 600,000 (2001); 60% agriculture, 15% industry, 25% services
Unemployment: n.a.
Agriculture: accounts for 10% of GDP (including fishing and forestry); cash crops—cocoa, coffee, palm oil; livestock not developed; importer of food; okoume (a tropical softwood) is the most important timber product; rubber; fish
Natural Resources: crude oil, manganese, uranium, gold, timber, iron ore

■ FINANCE/TRADE

Currency: Communauté financière africaine franc (CFAF) = 100 centimes
International Reserves Excluding Gold: US$109 million (Nov. 2002)
Gold Reserves: 0.013 million fine troy ounces (Dec. 2002)
Budget: revenues US$1.8 billion; expenditures US$1.8 billion, capital expenditures US$310 million (2002 est.)
Defence Expenditures: 7.3% of central government expenditure (1999)
Education Expenditures: n.a.
External Debt: US$3.409 billion (2001)
Exports: US$2.643 billion (2000); commodities: crude oil 70%, manganese 11%, wood 12%, uranium 6%; partners: France, US, China, Netherlands Antilles
Imports: US$973 million (2000); commodities: foodstuffs, chemical products, petroleum products, construction materials, manufacturers, machinery; partners: France, US, Belgium, Côte d'Ivoire

■ COMMUNICATIONS

Daily Newspapers: 30/1,000 inhabitants (2000)
Televisions: 326/1,000 inhabitants (2001)
Radios: 501/1,000 inhabitants (2001)
Telephones: 30 lines/1,000 inhabitants (2001)

■ TRANSPORTATION

Motor Vehicles: 39,500; 23,800 passenger cars
Roads: 8,454 km; 838 km paved
Railway: 649 km
Air Traffic: 374,000 passengers carried (2001)
Airports: 59; 10 have paved runways (2002)

Canadian Embassy: The Canadian Embassy, P.O. Box 4037 Libreville, Gabon. Tel: (011-241) 73-73-54. Fax: (011-241) 73-73-88. e-mail: lbrve@dfait-maeci.gc.ca
Embassy in Canada: Embassy of the Gabonese Republic, 4 Range Rd, Ottawa ON K1N 8J5. Tel: (613) 232-5301. Fax: (613) 232-6916. e-mail: ambgabon@sprint.ca

Gambia

Long-Form Name: Republic of the Gambia
Capital: Banjul

■ GEOGRAPHY

Area: 11,300 sq. km
Coastline: 80 km
Climate: tropical; hot, rainy season (June to Nov.); cooler, dry season (Nov. to May)
Environment: deforestation and desertification; diseases spread through the water supply are common
Terrain: flood plain of the Gambia River flanked by some low hills
Land Use: 18% arable; 0% permanent crops; 9% meadows; 28% forest; 45% other; includes 20 sq. km irrigated
Location: W Africa, bordering on Atlantic Ocean

■ PEOPLE

Population: 1,455,842 (July 2002 est.)
Nationality: Gambian
Age Structure: 0–14 yrs: 45.1%; 15–64: 52.3%; 65+: 2.6% (2002 est.)
Population Growth Rate: 3.09% (2002 est.)
Net Migration: 2.23 migrants/1,000 population (2002 est.)
Ethnic Groups: 99% African (42% Mandinka, 18% Fula, 16% Wolof, 10% Jola, 9% Serahuli, 4% other); 1% non-Gambian

Languages: English (official); Mandinka, Wolof, Fula, other indigenous vernaculars
Religions: 90% Muslim, 9% Christian, 1% indigenous beliefs
Birth Rate: 41.25/1,000 population (2002 est.)
Death Rate: 12.63/1,000 population (2002 est.)
Infant Mortality: 76.39 deaths/1,000 live births (2002 est.)
Life Expectancy at Birth: 52.02 years male, 56.01 years female (2002 est.)
Total Fertility Rate: 5.61 children born/woman (2002 est.)
Literacy: 35.7% (1999)

■ GOVERNMENT

Leader(s): Head of State Yahya Jammeh, V. Pres. Isatou Njie-Saidy
Government Type: republic
Administrative Divisions: 5 divisions and 1 city (Banjul)
Nationhood: Feb. 18, 1965 (from UK)
National Holiday: Independence Day, Feb. 18

■ ECONOMY

Overview: a poor country, lacking in natural resources and possessing a limited agricultural base of peanut products; the recent rebound in tourism has helped the economy
GDP: US$2.5 billion, per capita US$1,770; real growth rate 5.7% (2001 est.)
Inflation: 0.8% (2000)
Industries: accounts for 12% of GDP; peanut processing, tourism, beverages, agricultural machinery assembly, woodworking, metal-working, clothing
Labour Force: 700,000 (2001); 75% agriculture, 19% industry, commerce and services, 6% government
Unemployment: 13.8% (2001)
Agriculture: accounts for 21% of GDP; imports one-third of food requirements; major export crop is peanuts; also millet, sorghum, rice, corn; forestry and fishing resources not fully exploited
Natural Resources: fish

■ FINANCE/TRADE

Currency: dalasi (D) = 100 butut
International Reserves Excluding Gold: US$96 million (May 2002)
Gold Reserves: n.a.
Budget: revenues US$90.5 million; expenditures US$80.9 million, including capital expenditures US$4.1 million (2001 est.)
Defence Expenditures: 5.4% of central government expenditure (1999)
Education Expenditures: n.a.

External Debt: US$489 million (2001)
Exports: US$9 million (2000); commodities: peanuts and peanut products, fish, cotton lint, palm kernels; partners: Benelux, Japan, UK, Brazil
Imports: US$210 million (2000); commodities: foodstuffs, manufacturers, raw materials, fuel, machinery and transport equipment; partners: China, UK, Netherlands, France, Brazil

■ COMMUNICATIONS

Daily Newspapers: 2/1,000 inhabitants (2000)
Televisions: 3/1,000 inhabitants (2001)
Radios: 396/1,000 inhabitants (2001)
Telephones: 26 lines/1,000 inhabitants (2001)

■ TRANSPORTATION

Motor Vehicles: 9,000; 8,000 passenger cars
Roads: 2,700 km; 956 km paved
Railway: none
Air Traffic: n.a.
Airports: 1, with paved runway (2002)

Canadian Embassy: The Canadian High Commission to the Gambia, c/o The Canadian Embassy, P.O. Box 3373, Dakar, Senegal. Tel: (011-221) 823-92-90. Fax: (011-221) 823-87-49. e-mail: dakar@dfait-maeci.gc.ca
Embassy in Canada: c/o High Commission for the Republic of the Gambia, 1155 15th St NW, Ste 1000, Washington DC 20005-2 USA. Tel: (202) 785-1399. Fax: (202) 785-1430. e-mail: n.a.

Gaza Strip

Long-Form Name: none
Capital: none

■ GEOGRAPHY

Area: 360 sq. km
Climate: temperate, mild winters, dry and warm to hot summers
Land Use: 24% arable; 39% permanent crops; 0% permanent pastures; 11% forests and woodland; 26% other; includes 120 sq. km irrigated
Location: Middle East, bordering on Mediterranean Sea, Egypt and Israel.

■ PEOPLE

Population: 1,225,911, plus more than 5,000 Israeli settlers (July 2002 est.)
Nationality: n.a.
Ethnic Groups: Palestinian Arab and other 99.4%, Jewish 0.6%

Languages: Arabic, Hebrew (spoken by Israeli settlers and many Palestinians), English (widely understood)

■ GOVERNMENT

Colony/Territory of: claimed and occupied by Israel

Leader(s): local Palestinian authority is headed by Yasser Arafat, subject to Israeli authority

Government Type: Palestinian Legislative Council (Jan. 1996) has limited powers under interim self-governing agreements with Israel. Originally designated as a five-year interim arrangement in 1993, permanent status still under negotiation

National Holiday: n.a.

■ ECONOMY

Overview: economic conditions in the Gaza Strip, under the responsibility of the Palestinian Authority since the Cairo Agreement of May 1994, have deteriorated since the early 1990s; the most serious negative social effect has been the emergence of chronic unemployment, which has risen to over 20%

■ FINANCE/TRADE

Currency: 1 new Israeli shekel = 100 new agorot

Canadian Embassy: n.a.
Representative to Canada: n.a.

Georgia

Long-Form Name: Republic of Georgia
Capital: T'bilisi

■ GEOGRAPHY

Area: 69,700 sq. km
Coastline: 310 km
Climate: Alpine to subtropical with warm, humid coastlands
Environment: soil, air and water pollution from toxic chemicals
Terrain: largely mountainous in north and south; lowlands open to Black Sea in west; Kura River Basin in east; good soils in river valley, flood plains and lowlands
Land Use: 34% forests and woodlands; 9% arable; 4% permanent crops; 25% meadows and pastures; 28% other; includes 4,700 sq. km irrigated
Location: SW Asia, bordering on Black Sea

■ PEOPLE

Population: 4,960,951 (July 2002 est.)
Nationality: Georgian

Age Structure: 0–14 yrs: 19.0%; 15–64: 68.2%; 65+: 12.8% (2002 est.)
Population Growth Rate: -0.55% (2002 est.)
Net Migration: -2.39 migrants/1,000 population (2002 est.)
Ethnic Groups: 70.1% Georgian, 8.1% Armenian, 6.3% Russian, 5.7% Azerbaijani, 3% Ossetian, 1.9% Greek, 1.8% Abkhazian, 1% Ukrainian, 2.1% other
Languages: Armenian 7%, Azeri 6%, Georgian 71% (official), Russian 9%, other 7%
Religions: Christian Orthodox 75%, Muslim 11%, Armenian Apostolic 8%, unknown 6%
Birth Rate: 11.48/1,000 population (2002 est.)
Death Rate: 14.61/1,000 population (2002 est.)
Infant Mortality: 51.81 deaths/1,000 live births (2002 est.)
Life Expectancy at Birth: 61.19 years male, 68.32 years female (2002 est.)
Total Fertility Rate: 1.48 children born/woman (2002 est.)
Literacy: approaching 100% (2000)

■ GOVERNMENT

Leader(s): Pres. Eduard A. Shevardnadze
Government Type: republic
Administrative Divisions: 53 rayons (raionebi, sing. —raioni), 9 cities (k'alak'ebi, sing. — k'alak'i) and 2 autonomous regions (avtomnoy respubliki, sing. —avtom respublika)
Nationhood: April 9, 1991 (from Soviet Union)
National Holiday: Independence Day, May 26

■ ECONOMY

Overview: Steel processing and light industry predominate; agriculture hindered by extensive wooded areas; international transportation services through key ports are Georgia's main hope for the future
GDP: US$15 billion, per capita US$3,100; real growth rate 4.0% (2002 est.)
Inflation: 4.6% (2001)
Industries: accounts for 25% of GDP (2002 est.); coal and non-ferrous metals refining, machinery and instruments, electrical engineering, chemical production, food processing, cloth, hosiery, shoes, vehicles, mining, esp. manganese, coal, baryta
Labour Force: 2.5 million (2000); 20% industry and construction, 40% agriculture and forestry, 40% services
Unemployment: 13.8% (2000 est.)
Agriculture: accounts for 20% of GDP (2002 est.); grapes, tobacco, bay leaves, tea, citrus fruit, sugar, vegetables, grains, tobacco, tung, silk, orchard fruit, potatoes, livestock

Natural Resources: manganese deposits; sulphur and other medicinal springs, forest resources, hydro power, coal and oil

■ FINANCE/TRADE

Currency: lari (GEL) = 100 tetri
International Reserves Excluding Gold: n.a.
Gold Reserves: none (Jan. 2002)
Budget: revenues US$499 million; expenditures US$554 million, including capital expenditures of US$ n.a. (2001 est.)
Defence Expenditures: 4.42% of total government expenditure (2002)
Education Expenditures: 3.65% of central government expenditure (2000)
External Debt: US$1.714 billion (2001)
Exports: US$176 million (2000); grain, fruit, vegetables, tea, electric mine cars, seamless pipes; partners: Russia, Turkey, Azerbaijan, US, Germany
Imports: US$961 million (2000); fuel, food-stuffs, machinery, equipment; partners: Russia, Turkey, Azerbaijan, Germany, US

■ COMMUNICATIONS

Daily Newspapers: 5/1,000 inhabitants (2000)
Televisions: 474/1,000 inhabitants (2001)
Radios: 556/1,000 inhabitants (2001)
Telephones: 159 lines/1,000 inhabitants (2001)

■ TRANSPORTATION

Motor Vehicles: 314,000; 244,000 passenger cars (2000)
Roads: 33,900 km; 29,500 km hard-surfaced
Railway: 1,583 km
Air Traffic: 111,000 passengers carried (2001)
Airports: 31; 16 have paved runways (2002)

Canadian Embassy: The Canadian Embassy to Georgia, c/o The Canadian Embassy, Nenehatun Caddesi No. 75, Gaziosmanpasa 06700, Ankara, Turkey. Tel: (011-90-312) 459-9200. Fax: (011-90-312) 459-9362. e-mail: ankra@dfait-maeci.gc.ca
Embassy in Canada: c/o Embassy of the Republic of Georgia, 1615 New Hampshire Ave. NW, Suite 300, Washington DC 20009, USA. Tel: (202) 387-2390. Fax: (202) 393-4537. e-mail: n.a.

Germany

Long-Form Name: Federal Republic of Germany
Capital: Berlin

■ GEOGRAPHY

Area: 357,021 sq. km
Coastline: 2,389 km

Climate: temperate; cool, wet summers; cool to cold, cloudy winters with frequent rain and snow; occasional warm, tropical föhn wind; high relative humidity
Environment: air and water pollution; significant deforestation in mountain regions due to environmental pollution
Terrain: flat plains; lowlands in north; central uplands; Bavarian Alps in southwest
Land Use: 33% arable land; 1% permanent crops; 15% meadows and pastures; 31% forest and woodland; 20% other; includes 4,850 sq. km irrigated
Location: NC Europe, bordering on North Sea, Baltic Sea

■ PEOPLE

Population: 83,251,851 (July 2002 est.)
Nationality: German
Age Structure: 0–14 yrs: 15.4%; 15–64: 67.6%; 65+: 17.0% (2002 est.)
Population Growth Rate: 0.26% (2002 est.)
Net Migration: 3.99 migrants/1,000 population (2002 est.
Ethnic Groups: German 91.5%, Turkish 2.4%, Italian 0.7%, Greek 0.4%. Polish 0.4%, other 4.6%
Languages: German (official)
Religions: 45% Protestant, 37% Roman Catholic, 18% unaffiliated
Birth Rate: 8.99/1,000 population (2002 est.)
Death Rate: 10.36/1,000 population (2002 est.)
Infant Mortality: 4.65 deaths/1,000 live births (2002 est.)
Life Expectancy at Birth: 74.64 years male, 81.09 years female (2002 est.)
Total Fertility Rate: 1.39 children born/woman (2002 est.)
Literacy: approaching 100% (2000)

■ GOVERNMENT

Leader(s): Chanc. Gerhard Schroeder, Pres. Johannes Rau
Government Type: federal republic
Administrative Divisions: 16 states (Laender, sing. —Land)
Nationhood: January 18, 1871 (unification of German Empire); West Germany and East Germany were unified on Oct. 3, 1990
National Holiday: German Unity Day, Oct. 3

■ ECONOMY

Overview: possesses the world's third most technologically powerful economy, after the US and Japan, but its capitalistic economy has begun to struggle under the burden of generous social benefits; unemployment is a long-term,

not just cyclical, problem; the integration and upgrading of the Eastern German economy remains a costly long-term problem
GDP: US$2.184 trillion, per capita US$26,600; real growth rate 0.4% (2002 est.)
Inflation: 2.5% (2001)
Industries: accounts for 31% of GDP (2002 est.); iron, steel, coal, chemicals, vehicles, ships, machinery, food and beverages, electronics, brown coal, shipbuilding, textiles, petroleum refining
Labour Force: 41 million (2001); 33% industry, 64% community, social and business services, 3% agriculture
Unemployment: 10.5% (Sept. 2002)
Agriculture: agriculture, including fishing and forestry, accounts for about 1% of GDP (2000); diversified crop and livestock farming, including wheat, potatoes, barley, sugar beets, fruit, cabbages, livestock products; net importer of food
Natural Resources: iron ore, coal, potash, natural gas, copper, salt, nickel, timber

■ FINANCE/TRADE

Currency: Deutsche Mark (DM) = 100 Pfennige; Euro (€); on January 1, 2002, the Euro became the sole currency for everyday transactions
International Reserves Excluding Gold: US$51.170 billion (Dec. 2002)
Gold Reserves: 110.786 million fine troy ounces (Dec. 2002)
Budget: revenues US$802 billion; expenditures US$825 billion, including capital expenditures US$ n.a. (2001 est.)
Defence Expenditures: 4.7% of central government expenditure (2001)
Education Expenditures: n.a.
External Debt: n.a.
Exports: US$612.908 billion (2002); manufactured goods 88%, agricultural products 5%, raw materials 2.3%, other 4.7%; partners: France, US, UK, Netherlands, Austria, Belgium, Spain, Switzerland
Imports: US$493.753 billion (2002); manufactured goods 74%, agricultural products 10%, fuels 6.4%, raw materials 6%, other 3.6%; partners: France, Netherlands, US, UK, Italy, Belgium, Japan, Austria

■ COMMUNICATIONS

Daily Newspapers: 305/1,000 inhabitants (2000)
Televisions: 586/1,000 inhabitants (2001)
Radios: 570/1,000 inhabitants (2001)
Telephones: 634 lines/1,000 inhabitants (2001)

■ TRANSPORTATION

Motor Vehicles: 47,000,000; 42,200,000 passenger cars (2000)
Roads: 656,140 km; 650,891 km paved
Railway: 44,000 km (2000)
Air Traffic: 57,334,000 passengers carried (2001)
Airports: 625; 328 have paved runways (2002)

Canadian Embassy: The Canadian Embassy, Friedrichstrasse 95, 10117, Berlin, Germany. Tel: (011-49-30) 20-312-0. Fax: (011-49-30) 20-312-590. e-mail: brlin@dfait-maeci.gc.ca
Embassy in Canada: Embassy of the Federal Republic of Germany, 1 Waverley St, Ottawa ON K2P 0T8. Tel: (613) 232-1101. Fax: (613) 594-9330. e-mail: GermanEmbassyOttawa@ on.aibn.com

Ghana

Long-Form Name: Republic of Ghana
Capital: Accra

■ GEOGRAPHY

Area: 238,540 sq. km
Coastline: 539 km
Climate: tropical; warm and comparatively dry along southeast coast; hot and humid in southwest; hot and dry in north
Environment: recent drought in north severely affecting marginal agricultural activities; deforestation; overgrazing; soil erosion; dry, northeasterly harmattan wind (Jan. to Mar.); water pollution and insufficient safe drinking water
Terrain: mostly low plains with dissected plateau in south-central area
Land Use: 12% arable; 7% permanent crops; 22% meadows; 35% forest; 24% other; includes 110 sq. km irrigated
Location: WC Africa, bordering on South Atlantic Ocean

■ PEOPLE

Population: 20,244,154 (July 2002 est.)
Nationality: Ghanaian
Age Structure: 0–14 yrs: 40.4%; 15–64: 56.1%; 65+: 3.5% (2002 est.)
Population Growth Rate: 1.70% (2002 est.)
Net Migration: -0.74 migrants/1,000 population (2002 est.)
Ethnic Groups: 99.8% black African (major tribes—44% Akan, 16% Moshi-Dagomba, 13% Ewe, 8% Ga, 18.8% other), 0.2% European and other
Languages: English (official); African languages include Akan, Moshi-Dagomba, Ewe and Ga

Religions: 38% indigenous beliefs, 30% Muslim, 24% Christian, 8% other
Birth Rate: 28.08/1,000 population (2002 est.)
Death Rate: 10.31/1,000 population (2002 est.)
Infant Mortality: 55.64 deaths/1,000 live births (2002 est.)
Life Expectancy at Birth: 55.66 years male, 58.51years female (2002 est.)
Total Fertility Rate: 3.69 children born/woman (2002 est.)
Literacy: 71.5% (2000)

■ GOVERNMENT

Leader(s): Pres. John Agyekum Kufuor, V. Pres. Aliu Mahama
Government Type: constitutional democracy
Administrative Divisions: 10 regions
Nationhood: Mar. 6, 1957 (from UK, formerly known as Gold Coast)
National Holiday: Independence Day, Mar. 6

■ ECONOMY

Overview: heavily dependent on cocoa, gold and timber exports; international assistance boosts this economy, which depends on good harvests; population growth is a burden
GDP: US$39.4 billion, per capita US$1,980; real growth rate 3.0% (2001 est.)
Inflation: 32.9% (2001)
Industries: accounts for 25% of GDP (2000); mining, lumbering, light manufacturing, fishing, aluminum, food processing
Labour Force: 9.4 million (2001); 60% agriculture, 15% industry, 25% services
Unemployment: n.a.
Agriculture: accounts for 36% of GDP (2000); major cash crop is cocoa; other crops: rice, coffee, cassava, peanuts, corn, bananas, timber; normally self-sufficient in food
Natural Resources: gold, timber, industrial diamonds, bauxite, manganese, fish, rubber

■ FINANCE/TRADE

Currency: cedi (C/) = 100 pesewas
International Reserves Excluding Gold: US$485 million (Oct. 2002)
Gold Reserves: 0.281 million fine troy ounces (Oct. 2002)
Budget: revenues US$1.603 billion; expenditures US$1.975 billion, capital expenditures US$ n.a. (2001 est.)
Defence Expenditures: 3.1% of central government expenditure (1999)
Education Expenditures: n.a.
External Debt: US$6.759 billion (2001)
Exports: US$1.413 billion (2000); commodities: cocoa 60%, timber, gold, tuna, bauxite, and aluminum; partners: Togo, UK, Italy, Netherlands, Germany, US, France
Imports: US$2.973 billion (2001); commodities: petroleum 16%, consumer goods, foods, intermediate goods, capital equipment; partners: US, UK, Nigeria, Germany, Italy, Spain

■ COMMUNICATIONS

Daily Newspapers: 14/1,000 inhabitants (2000)
Televisions: 118/1,000 inhabitants (2001)
Radios: 710/1,000 inhabitants (2001)
Telephones: 12 lines/1,000 inhabitants (2001)

■ TRANSPORTATION

Motor Vehicles: 135,000; 90,000 passenger cars
Roads: 38,940 km; 9,346 km hard-surfaced
Railway: 953 km
Air Traffic: 301,000 passengers carried (2001)
Airports: 12; 7 have paved runways (2002)

Canadian Embassy: Canadian High Commission, 42 Independence Ave, Accra, Ghana; P.O. Box 1639, Accra, Ghana. Tel: (011-233-21) 22-85-55. Fax: (011-233-21) 77-37-92. e-mail: accra@ dfait-maeci.gc.ca
Embassy in Canada: High Commission for the Republic of Ghana, 1 Clemow Ave, Ottawa ON K1S 2A9. Tel: (613) 236-0871. Fax: (613) 236-0874. e-mail: n.a.

Gibraltar

Long-Form Name: Gibraltar
Capital: Gibraltar

■ GEOGRAPHY

Area: 6.5 sq. km
Climate: warm, temperate, low precipitation, mild winters, warm summers
Land Use: almost 100% bare limestone (Rock of Gibraltar) and/or built up; no farmland
Location: Iberian Peninsula of S Spain, bordering on Mediterranean Sea

■ PEOPLE

Population: 27,714 (July 2002 est.)
Nationality: Gibraltarian
Ethnic Groups: Portuguese, Maltese, Spanish, Italian, English
Languages: English (used in schools and for official purposes), Spanish, Italian, Portuguese, Russian

■ GOVERNMENT

Colony/Territory of: Dependent Territory of United Kingdom

Leader(s): Head of State: Queen Elizabeth II, Gov. David Durie, Chief Min. Peter Caruana
Government Type: dependent overseas territory of the UK
National Holiday: Commonwealth Day (second Monday in March), National Day, Sept. 10

■ ECONOMY

Overview: tourism most important; industries: construction materials, beverage bottling; re-exports: tobacco, petroleum, wine; exports of local products negligible; must import all food; more than 70% of the economy is in the public sector

■ FINANCE/TRADE

Currency: Gibraltar pound = 100 pence

Canadian Embassy: c/o The Canadian High Commission, Macdonald House, 1 Grosvenor Square, London W1K 4AB, England, UK. Tel: (011-44-20) 7258-6600. Fax: (011-44-20) 7258-6333. e-mail: ldn@dfait-maeci.gc.ca
Representative to Canada: c/o British High Commission, 80 Elgin St, Ottawa ON K1P 5K7. Tel: (613) 237-1530. Fax: (613) 237-7980. Email should be sent using the appropriate form at the British High Commission's Website at http://www.britain-in-canada.org

Greece

Long-Form Name: Hellenic Republic
Capital: Athens

■ GEOGRAPHY

Area: 131,940 sq. km
Coastline: 13,676 km
Climate: temperate; mild, wet winter; hot, dry summer
Environment: subject to severe earthquakes; air pollution; archipelago of 2,000 islands; water pollution
Terrain: mostly mountainous with ranges extending into sea as peninsulas or chains of islands
Land Use: 19% arable; 8% permanent crops; 41% meadows; 20% forest; 12% other; includes 14,220 sq. km irrigated
Location: S Europe, bordering on Adriatic Sea

■ PEOPLE

Population: 10,645,343 (July 2002 est.)
Nationality: Greek
Age Structure: 0–14 yrs: 14.8%; 15–64: 67.1%; 65+: 18.1% (2002 est.)
Population Growth Rate: 0.20% (2002 est.)

Net Migration: 1.96 migrants/1,000 population (2002 est.)
Ethnic Groups: 98% Greek, 2% others
Languages: Greek (official); English, German and French widely understood
Religions: 98% Greek Orthodox, 1.3% Muslim, 0.7% other
Birth Rate: 9.82/1,000 population (2002 est.)
Death Rate: 9.79/1,000 population (2002 est.)
Infant Mortality: 6.25 deaths/1,000 live births (2002 est.)
Life Expectancy at Birth: 76.17 years male, 81.48 years female (2002 est.)
Total Fertility Rate: 1.34 children born/woman (2002 est.)
Literacy: 97.2% (2000)

■ GOVERNMENT

Leader(s): Pres. Konstandinos "Kostis" Stefano-poulos, Prime Min. Konstandinos Simitis
Government Type: presidential parliamentary government
Administrative Divisions: 51 prefectures (nomoi, sing. —omós) and 1 autonomous region
Nationhood: 1829 (from the Ottoman Empire)
National Holiday: Independence Day (proclamation of the war of independence), Mar. 25

■ ECONOMY

Overview: a large commodity trade deficit is offset by the successful tourism industry; economy is characterized by low GDP growth and high national debt
GDP: US$201.1 billion, per capita US$19,000; real growth rate 3.5% (2002 est.)
Inflation: 3.4% (2001)
Industries: accounts for 20% of GDP (2000); food and tobacco processing, textiles, chemicals, metal products, tourism, mining, petroleum
Labour Force: 4.6 million (2001); 20% agriculture, 59% community, social and business services, 21% industry
Unemployment: 10.8% (2001)
Agriculture: accounts for 7% of GDP (2000) (including fishing and forestry); self-sufficient in food; principal products—wheat, corn, barley, sugar beets, olives, tomatoes, wine, tobacco, potatoes, beef, mutton, pork, dairy products
Natural Resources: bauxite, lignite, magnesite, crude oil, marble, hydro power

■ FINANCE/TRADE

Currency: drachma (Dr) = 100 lepta; Euro (€); on January 1, 2002 the Euro became the sole currency for everyday transactions.
International Reserves Excluding Gold: US$8.083 billion (Dec. 2002)

Gold Reserves: 3.935 million fine troy ounces (Dec. 2002)

Budget: revenues US$37 billion; expenditures US$45 billion, capital expenditures US$ n.a. (1998 est.)

Defence Expenditures: 15.6% of central government expenditure (2001)

Education Expenditures: n.a.

External Debt: US$57 billion (2000 est.)

Exports: US$9.483 billion (2001); commodities: manufactured goods, food and live animals, fuels and lubricants, raw materials; partners: Germany, Italy, UK, US

Imports: US$29.928 billion (2001); commodities: machinery and transport equipment, light manufactures, fuels and lubricants, foodstuffs, chemicals; partners: Italy, Germany, France, Netherlands

■ COMMUNICATIONS

Daily Newspapers: 23/1,000 inhabitants (2000)
Televisions: 519/1,000 inhabitants (2001)
Radios: 478/1,000 inhabitants (2001)
Telephones: 529 lines/1,000 inhabitants (2001)

■ TRANSPORTATION

Motor Vehicles: 3,700,000; 2,700,000 passenger cars (2000)
Roads: 117,000 km; 107,406 km paved
Railway: 2,571 km (2000)
Air Traffic: 7,303,000 passengers carried (2001)
Airports: 79; 66 have paved runways (2002)

Canadian Embassy: The Canadian Embassy, 4 Ioannou Gennadiou St, Athens 115 21, Greece. Tel: (011-30-10) 727-3400. Fax: (011-30-10) 727-3460. e-mail: athns@dfait-maeci.gc.ca
Embassy in Canada: Embassy of the Hellenic Republic, 80 MacLaren St, Ottawa ON K2P 0K6. Tel: (613) 238-6271. Fax: (613) 238-5676. e-mail: greekembott@travel-net.com

Greenland

Long-Form Name: Grønland
Capital: Nuuk (Godthab)

■ GEOGRAPHY

Area: 2,175,600 sq. km
Climate: arctic to subarctic; cool summers, cold winters
Land Use: 1% meadow and pastures; negligible forest and woodland; 99% bare rock, snow and ice

Location: N North America, bordering on Atlantic Ocean, Greenland Sea, Arctic Ocean, Baffin Bay

■ PEOPLE

Population: 56,376 (July 2002 est.)
Nationality: Greenlander
Ethnic Groups: 87% Greenlander (Inuit and Greenland-born Caucasians), 13% Danish and others
Languages: Inuit dialects, Danish

■ GOVERNMENT

Colony/Territory of: Dependent Territory of Denmark
Leader(s): Queen Margrethe II of Denmark, represented by High Comm. Peter Lauritzen, Prem. Hans Enoksen
Government Type: part of the Danish realm; self-governing overseas administrative division
National Holiday: June 21 (longest day of the year)

■ ECONOMY

Overview: dependent on annual subsidy from the Danish government; unemployment is on the increase; fishing is the most important industry; mineral resource exploitation is limited to lead and zinc

■ FINANCE/TRADE

Currency: Danish krone (DKr) = 100 oere

Canadian Embassy: c/o The Canadian Embassy, Kr. Bernikowsgade 1, 1105 Copenhagen K, Denmark. Tel: (011-45) 33-48-32-00. Fax: (011-45) 33-48-32-20. e-mail: copen@dfait-maeci.gc.ca
Representative to Canada: c/o Royal Danish Embassy, 47 Clarence St Ste 450, Ottawa ON K1N 9K1. Tel: (613) 562-1811. Fax: (613) 562-1812. e-mail: danemb@cyberus.ca

Grenada

Long-Form Name: Grenada
Capital: Saint George's

■ GEOGRAPHY

Area: 340 sq. km
Coastline: 121 km
Climate: tropical; tempered by northeast trade winds
Environment: lies on edge of hurricane belt; hurricane season lasts from June to Nov.
Terrain: volcanic in origin with central mountains

Land Use: 15% arable; 18% permanent crops; 3% meadows; 9% forest; 55% other
Location: Caribbean islands, just north of Venezuela

■ PEOPLE

Population: 89,211 (July 2002 est.)
Nationality: Grenadian
Age Structure: 0–14 yrs: 35.9%; 15–64: 60.3%; 65+: 3.8% (2002 est.)
Population Growth Rate: 0.02% (2002 est.)
Net Migration: -15.21 migrants/1,000 population (2002 est.)
Ethnic Groups: 82% black, some East Indians, Europeans, a few Arawak
Languages: English (official); some French patois
Religions: largely Roman Catholic; Anglican; other Protestant sects
Birth Rate: 23.05/1,000 population (2002 est.)
Death Rate: 7.63/1,000 population (2002 est.)
Infant Mortality: 14.63 deaths/1,000 live births (2002 est.)
Life Expectancy at Birth: 62.74 years male, 66.31 years female (2002 est.)
Total Fertility Rate: 2.50 children born/woman (2002 est.)
Literacy: 96%

■ GOVERNMENT

Leader(s): Head of State: Queen Elizabeth II, Gov. Gen. Daniel Williams, Prime Min. Keith Mitchell
Government Type: constitutional democracy
Administrative Divisions: 6 parishes and 1 dependency
Nationhood: Feb. 7, 1974 (from UK)
National Holiday: Independence Day, Feb. 7

■ ECONOMY

Overview: economy is based on agriculture (spices, tropical plants) and tourism; unemployment is high
GDP: US$424 million, per capita US$4,750; real growth rate 6.5% (2001 est.)
Inflation: 2.5% (2000 est.)
Industries: accounts for 24% of GDP (2000); food and beverage, textiles, light assembly operations, tourism, construction
Labour Force: approx. 45,000; services 62%, agriculture 24%, construction 8%, manufacturing 5%, other 1%
Unemployment: n.a.
Agriculture: accounts for 8% of GDP (2000), 80% of exports and employs 24% of the labour force; bananas, cocoa, nutmeg and mace are major crops; citrus, root crops, avocados; small-scale farms predominate
Natural Resources: timber, tropical fruit, deep-water harbours

■ FINANCE/TRADE

Currency: East Caribbean dollar ($EC) = 100 cents
International Reserves Excluding Gold: US$76 million (Oct. 2002)
Gold Reserves: n.a.
Budget: n.a.
Defence Expenditures: n.a.
Education Expenditures: n.a.
External Debt: US$215 million (2001)
Exports: US$23 million (2000); commodities: nutmeg 35%, cocoa beans 15%, bananas 13%, mace 7%, textiles; partners: CARICOM countries, UK, US, Netherlands
Imports: US$175 million (2000); commodities: machinery 24%, food 22%, manufactured goods 19%, petroleum 8%; partners: US, CARICOM, UK, Japan

■ COMMUNICATIONS

Daily Newspapers: n.a.
Televisions: n.a.
Radios: n.a.
Telephones: 315 lines/1,000 inhabitants (1999)

■ TRANSPORTATION

Motor Vehicles: n.a.
Roads: 1,040 km; 638 km paved
Railway: none
Air Traffic: n.a.
Airports: 3; all have paved runways (2002)

Canadian Embassy: The Canadian High Commission to Grenada, c/o The Canadian High Commission, Bishop's Court Hill, Bridge-town, Barbados; mailing address: P.O. Box 404, Bridgetown, Barbados. Tel: 1-246-429-3550. Fax: 1-246-429-3780. e-mail: bdgtn@dfait-maeci.gc.ca
Embassy in Canada: c/o High Commission for the Countries of the Organization of Eastern Caribbean States, 130 Albert St, Ste 700, Ottawa ON K1P 5G4. Tel: (613) 236-8952. Fax: (613) 236-3042. e-mail: echcc@travel-net.com

Guadeloupe

Long-Form Name: Department of Guadeloupe
Capital: Basse-Terre (seat of government); each of the 7 inhabited islands has its own chief town

■ GEOGRAPHY

Area: 1,780 sq. km (2 main islands, 5 small islands, one small island group called Iles des Saintes)
Climate: subtropical tempered by trade winds; hot and humid May–Dec., cool and dry Dec.–April
Land Use: 14% arable; 4% permanent crops; 14% meadows and pastures; 39% forest and woodland, 29% other; includes 20 sq. km irrigated
Location: Caribbean, halfway along the Lesser Antilles arch between Puerto Rico and S America

■ PEOPLE

Population: 435,739 (July 2002 est.)
Nationality: Guadeloupian
Ethnic Groups: 90% black or mulatto, 5% white, less than 5% East Indian, Lebanese, Chinese
Languages: French, Creole dialect

■ GOVERNMENT

Colony/Territory of: Overseas Department of France
Leader(s): Head of State: Pres. Jacques Chirac (France), Prefect Dominique Vian, Pres. of the General Council Jacques Gillot
Government Type: overseas department of France
National Holiday: Taking of the Bastille, July 14

■ ECONOMY

Overview: economy depends on agriculture, tourism, light industry and services; unemployment is especially high among youth; agriculture: includes bananas, sugar cane, rum, flowers, livestock; vegetables and tobacco grown for local consumption; forestry, fisheries, tourism, food processing; partners: France, Martinique

■ FINANCE/TRADE

Currency: French franc = 100 centimes; Euro as of March 1, 2002

Canadian Embassy: c/o The Canadian Embassy, 35-37 avenue Montaigne, Paris, 75008, France. Tel: (011-331) 44-43-29-00. Fax: (011-331) 44-43-29-99. e-mail: paris@dfait-maeci.gc.ca
Representative to Canada: c/o Embassy of France, 42 Sussex Dr, Ottawa ON K1M 2C9. Tel: (613) 789-1795. Fax: (613) 562-3735. e-mail: politique@ambafrance-ca.org

Guam

Long-Form Name: Territory of Guam

Capital: Hagatna (Agana)

■ GEOGRAPHY

Area: 549 sq. km
Climate: tropical maritime, with little seasonal variation, but typhoon-prone and suffers from earthquakes; wet all year
Land Use: 11% arable; 11% permanent crops; 15% meadows and pastures; 18% forest and woodland, 45% other; interior is mountainous and volcanic hills dominate the south, but many forests in northern Guam have been cleared for farming and the construction of airfields; coconut trees grow throughout the island
Location: N Pacific Ocean, E of the Philippines

■ PEOPLE

Population: 160,796 (July 2002 est.)
Nationality: Guamanian
Ethnic Groups: 47% Chamorro, 25% Filipino, 10% Caucasian, 18% Chinese, Japanese, Korean and other
Languages: English (official), Chamorro, Japanese

■ GOVERNMENT

Colony/Territory of: Unincorporated Outlying Territory of the United States
Leader(s): Head of State: Pres. George W. Bush, Jr. (US), Gov. Felix P. P. Camacho
Government Type: unincorporated outlying territory of the US; executive powers of the legislature similar to those of an American state legislature
National Holiday: Guam Discovery Day (first Monday in March); also Liberation Day, July 21

■ ECONOMY

Overview: economy depends mainly on US military spending and on tourism; agriculture: corn, coconuts, sweet potatoes, cucumbers, watermelons, beans, livestock, esp. cattle and pigs, fruit, vegetables, fish; industry: textile manufacture, cement, petroleum, printing, plastics, ship repair; tourism of growing importance

■ FINANCE/TRADE

Currency: American dollar = 100 cents

Canadian Embassy: c/o The Canadian Embassy, 501 Pennsylvania Avenue NW, Washington DC 20001, USA. Tel: (202) 682-1740. Fax: (202) 682-7726. e-mail: wshdc@dfait-maeci.gc.ca
Representative to Canada: c/o Embassy of the United States of America, 490 Sussex Drive, Ottawa ON, K1N 1G8. Tel: (613) 238-5335.

Fax: (613) 688-3097. Email inquiries are not accepted

Guatemala

Long-Form Name: Republic of Guatemala
Capital: Guatemala

■ GEOGRAPHY

Area: 108,890 sq. km
Coastline: 400 km
Climate: tropical; hot, humid in lowlands; cooler in highlands
Environment: numerous volcanoes in mountains, with frequent violent earthquakes; Caribbean coast subject to hurricanes and other tropical storms; deforestation; soil erosion; water pollution
Terrain: mostly mountainous with narrow coastal plains and rolling limestone plateau (Petén)
Land Use: 12% arable; 5% permanent crops; 24% permanent pastures; 54% forest; 5% other; includes 1,250 sq. km irrigated
Location: northernmost Central (Latin) America, bordering on Caribbean Sea, Pacific Ocean

■ PEOPLE

Population: 13,314,079 (July 2002 est.)
Nationality: Guatemalan
Age Structure: 0–14 yrs: 41.8%; 15–64: 54.5%; 65+: 3.7% (2002 est.)
Population Growth Rate: 2.57% (2002 est.)
Net Migration: -1.79 migrants/1,000 population (2002 est.)
Ethnic Groups: 56% Ladino (mestizo-mixed Indian and European ancestry), 44% Indian
Languages: 60% Spanish, but 40% of the population speaks an Indian language as a primary tongue (23 Indian dialects, including Quiche, Cakchiquel, Kekchi)
Religions: predominantly Roman Catholic; also Protestant, traditional Mayan
Birth Rate: 34.17/1,000 population (2002 est.)
Death Rate: 6.67/1,000 population (2002 est.)
Infant Mortality: 44.55 deaths/1,000 live births (2002 est.)
Life Expectancy at Birth: 66.14 years male, 69.66 years female (2002 est.)
Total Fertility Rate: 4.51 children born/woman (2002 est.)
Literacy: 68.6% (2000)

■ GOVERNMENT

Leader(s): Pres. Alfonso Portillo Cabrera, V. Pres. Juan Francisco Reyes Lopez

Government Type: constitutional democratic republic
Administrative Divisions: 22 departments (departamento, pl. departamentos)
Nationhood: Sept. 15, 1821 (from Spain)
National Holiday: Independence Day, Sept. 15

■ ECONOMY

Overview: the inflation rate has dropped significantly as a result of government economic reforms, but political uncertainty casts a shadow over the agriculturally based economy
GDP: US$48.3 billion, per capita US$3,700; real growth rate 2.3% (2001 est.)
Inflation: 7.6% (2001)
Industries: accounts for 20% of GDP (2000); sugar, textiles and clothing, furniture, chemicals, petroleum, metals, rubber, tourism
Labour Force: 4.4 million (2001); 35% community, social and business services, 50% agriculture, 15% industry
Unemployment: 7.5% (1999 est.)
Agriculture: accounts for 23% of GDP (2000) and employs 60% of the labour force; principal crops—sugar cane, corn, bananas, coffee, beans, cardamom; livestock—cattle, sheep, pigs, chickens; food importer
Natural Resources: crude oil, nickel, rare woods, fish, chicle, hydro power

■ FINANCE/TRADE

Currency: quetzal (pl. quetzales) (Q) = 100 centavos, also US ($) = 100 cents
International Reserves Excluding Gold: US$2.299 billion (Dec. 2002)
Gold Reserves: 0.216 million fine troy ounces (Dec. 2002)
Budget: revenue US$2.2 billion, expenditures US$1.8 billion, including capital expenditures of US$ n.a. (2001 est.)
Defence Expenditures: 5.0% of central government expenditure (1999)
Education Expenditures: n.a.
External Debt: US$4.526 billion (2001)
Exports: US$2.244 billion (2002 est.); commodities: coffee 38%, bananas 7%, sugar 7%, cardamom 4%; partners: US, El Salvador, Costa Rica, Nicaragua, Germany
Imports: US$6.011 billion (2002 est.); commodities: fuel and petroleum products, machinery, grain, fertilizers, motor vehicles; partners: US, Mexico, South Korea, El Salvador, Venezuela

■ COMMUNICATIONS

Daily Newspapers: 33/1,000 inhabitants (2000)

Televisions: 61/1,000 inhabitants (2001)
Radios: 79/1,000 inhabitants (2001)
Telephones: 65 lines/1,000 inhabitants (2001)

■ TRANSPORTATION

Motor Vehicles: 199,000; 102,000 passenger cars
Roads: 13,856 km; 4,370 km paved
Railway: 884 km (2000)
Air Traffic: 506,000 passengers carried (2000)
Airports: 475; 11 have paved runways (2002)

Canadian Embassy: The Canadian Embassy, 13 Calle 8-44, Zone 10, Guatemala City; mailing address: P.O. Box 400, Guatemala City, Guatemala, C.A. Tel: (011-502) 333-61-02. Fax: (011-502) 333-61-61. e-mail: gtmla@dfait-maeci.gc.ca
Embassy in Canada: Embassy of the Republic of Guatemala, 130 Albert St, Ste 1010, Ottawa ON K1P 5G4. Tel: (613) 233-7237. Fax: (613) 233-0135. e-mail: embassy1@embguate-canada.com

Guinea

Long-Form Name: Republic of Guinea
Capital: Conakry

■ GEOGRAPHY

Area: 245,857 sq. km
Coastline: 320 km
Climate: generally hot and humid; monsoonal-type rainy season (June to Nov.) with south-westerly winds; dry season (Dec. to May) with northeasterly harmattan winds
Environment: hot, dry, dusty harmattan haze may reduce visibility during dry season; deforestation; insufficient safe drinking water
Terrain: generally flat coastal plain, hilly to mountainous interior
Land Use: 2% arable; negligible permanent crops; 22% permanent pastures; 59% forest; 17% other; includes 950 sq. km irrigated
Location: W Africa, bordering on Atlantic Ocean

■ PEOPLE

Population: 7,775,065 (July 2002 est.)
Nationality: Guinean
Age Structure: 0–14 yrs: 42.8%; 15–64: 54.5%; 65+: 2.7% (2002 est.)
Population Growth Rate: 2.23% (2002 est.)
Net Migration: 0 migrants/1,000 population (2002 est.)
Ethnic Groups: 40% Peuhl, 30% Malinke, 20% Sousou, 10% smaller tribes
Languages: French (official); each tribe has its own language; 8 official languages are taught in schools, including Fulani, Malinke, Soussou

Religions: 85% Muslim, 7% indigenous beliefs, 8% Christian
Birth Rate: 39.49/1,000 population (2002 est.)
Death Rate: 17.24/1,000 population (2002 est.)
Infant Mortality: 127.08 deaths/1,000 live births (2002 est.)
Life Expectancy at Birth: 43.81 years male, 48.82 years female (2002 est.)
Total Fertility Rate: 5.32 children born/woman (2002 est.)
Literacy: 35.0% (1999)

■ GOVERNMENT

Leader(s): Pres. Gen. Lansana Conté, Premier Lamine Sidime
Government Type: republic
Administrative Divisions: 33 prefectures and 1 special zone (zone speciale)
Nationhood: Oct. 2, 1958 (from France; formerly known as French Guinea)
National Holiday: Anniversary of the Second Republic, Apr. 3. Independence Day, Oct. 2

■ ECONOMY

Overview: although possessing numerous natural resources and potential for agricultural development, it is one of the poorest countries in the world; mining accounts for the bulk of Guinea's exports, and apart from the bauxite industry, foreign investment remains low
GDP: US$15 billion, per capita US$1,970; real growth rate 3.3% (2001 est.)
Inflation: 6% (2000 est.)
Industries: accounts for 38% of GDP (2000); bauxite mining, alumina, diamond mining, light manufacturing and agricultural processing industries
Labour Force: 3.6 million (2001); 80% agriculture, 20% industry and services
Unemployment: n.a.
Agriculture: accounts for 24% of GDP (2000) and employs 80% of the workforce (including fishing and forestry); mostly subsistence farming; principal products—rice, coffee, pineapples, palm kernels, cassava, sweet potatoes, timber; livestock—cattle, sheep and goats
Natural Resources: bauxite, iron ore, diamonds, gold, uranium, hydroelectricity, fish

■ FINANCE/TRADE

Currency: Guinean franc = 100 centimes
International Reserves Excluding Gold: US$194 million (June 2002)
Gold Reserves: n.a.
Budget: revenues US$ n.a., expenditures US$417.7 million, including capital expenditures US$ n.a. (2000 est.)

Defence Expenditures: 8.5% of central government expenditure (2001)
Education Expenditures: n.a.
External Debt: US$3.254 billion (2001)
Exports: exact figures n.a.; commodities: alumina, bauxite, gold, diamonds, coffee, pineapples, bananas, palm kernels; partners: Belgium, US, Ireland, Russia
Imports: exact figures n.a.; commodities: petroleum products, metals, machinery, transport equipment, foodstuffs, textiles and grain; partners: US, France, Belgium, Côte d'Ivoire

■ COMMUNICATIONS

Daily Newspapers: none
Televisions: 44/1,000 inhabitants (2001)
Radios: 52/1,000 inhabitants (2001)
Telephones: 3 lines/1,000 inhabitants (2001)

■ TRANSPORTATION

Motor Vehicles: 33,000; 13,700 passenger cars
Roads: 30,500 km; 5,033 km paved
Railway: 1,086 km
Air Traffic: 61,000 passengers carried (2000)
Airports: 15; 5 have paved runways (2002)

Canadian Embassy: The Canadian Embassy, P.O. Box 99, Conakry, Guinea. Tel: (011-224) 46-23-95. Fax: (011-224) 46-42-35. e-mail: cnaky@dfait-maeci.gc.ca
Embassy in Canada: Embassy of the Republic of Guinea, 483 Wilbrod St, Ottawa ON K1N 6N1. Tel: (613) 789-8444. Fax: (613) 789-7560. e-mail: ambaguineaott@sympatico.ca

Guinea-Bissau

Long-Form Name: Republic of Guinea-Bissau
Capital: Bissau

■ GEOGRAPHY

Area: 36,120 sq. km
Coastline: 350 km
Climate: tropical; generally hot and humid; monsoon-type rainy season (June to Nov.) with southwesterly winds; dry season (Dec. to May) with northeasterly harmattan winds
Environment: hot, dry, dusty harmattan haze may reduce visibility during dry season; deforestation, soil erosion
Terrain: mostly low coastal plain rising to savanna in east
Land Use: 11% arable; 1% permanent crops; 38% meadows; 38% forest; 12% other; includes 170 sq. km irrigated
Location: W Africa, bordering on Atlantic Ocean

■ PEOPLE

Population: 1,345,479 (July 2002 est.)
Nationality: Guinean
Age Structure: 0–14 yrs: 41.9%; 15–64: 55.2%; 65+: 2.9% (2002 est.)
Population Growth Rate: 2.23% (2002 est.)
Net Migration: -1.62 migrants/1,000 population (2002 est.)
Ethnic Groups: approx. 99% African (including 30% Balanta, 20% Fula, 14% Manjaca, 13% Mandinga, 7% Papel); less than 1% European and mulatto
Languages: Portuguese (official); Crioulo (a Portuguese-based Creole), Balante and numerous African languages
Religions: 65% indigenous beliefs, 30% Muslim, 5% Christian
Birth Rate: 38.95/1,000 population (2002 est.)
Death Rate: 15.05/1,000 population (2002 est.)
Infant Mortality: 108.54 deaths/1,000 live births (2002 est.)
Life Expectancy at Birth: 47.47 years male, 52.20 years female (2002 est.)
Total Fertility Rate: 5.13 children born/woman (2002 est.)
Literacy: 37.7% (1999)

■ GOVERNMENT

Leader(s): Pres. Kumba Yala, Prime Min. Mario Pires
Government Type: republic
Administrative Divisions: 9 regions (regiões, singular–região)
Nationhood: Sept. 10, 1974 (from Portugal; formerly known as Portuguese Guinea)
National Holiday: Independence Day, Sept. 24

■ ECONOMY

Overview: this poor country is focusing on agricultural development; exploitation of mineral deposits is hampered by a weak infrastructure and high costs. The heavy foreign debt is a burden
GDP: US$1.2 billion, per capita US$900; real growth rate 7.2% (2001 est.)
Inflation: 3.3% (2001)
Industries: accounts for 15% of GDP; agricultural processing, beer, soft drinks
Labour Force: 600,000 (2001); 82% agriculture, 18% other
Unemployment: n.a.
Agriculture: accounts for 54% of GDP; nearly 100% of exports and 80% of employment; rice is the staple; not self-sufficient in food; fishing and forestry not fully exploited; crops include corn, beans, cassava, cashew nuts, peanuts, palm kernels, cotton, timber and fish

Natural Resources: unexploited deposits of petroleum, bauxite, phosphates; fish, timber

■ FINANCE/TRADE

Currency: Communauté financière africaine (CFAF) franc = 100 centimes
International Reserves Excluding Gold: US$97 million (Oct. 2002)
Gold Reserves: none (Dec. 2002)
Budget: n.a.
Defence Expenditures: 6.1% of central government expenditure (1999)
Education Expenditures: n.a.
External Debt: US$668 million (2001)
Exports: US$62 million (2001); commodities: cashews, fish, peanuts, palm kernels; partners: India, Italy, South Korea, Belgium
Imports: US$86 million (2001); commodities: capital equipment, consumer goods, semi-processed goods, foods, petroleum; partners: Portugal, Senegal, Thailand, China

■ COMMUNICATIONS

Daily Newspapers: 5/1,000 inhabitants (2000)
Televisions: 36/1,000 inhabitants (2001)
Radios: 204/1,000 inhabitants (2001)
Telephones: 10 lines/1,000 inhabitants (2001)

■ TRANSPORTATION

Motor Vehicles: 6,900; 4,000 passenger cars
Roads: 4,400 km; 453 km paved
Railway: none
Air Traffic: 20,000 passengers carried (2000)
Airports: 28; 3 have paved runways (2002)

Canadian Embassy: The Canadian Embassy to Guinea-Bissau, c/o The Canadian Embassy, P.O. Box 3373, Dakar, Senegal. Tel: (011-221) 823-92-90. Fax: (011-221) 823-87-49. e-mail: dakar@dfait-maeci.gc.ca
Embassy in Canada: c/o Embassy of the Republic of Guinea-Bissau, 15929 Yukon Lane (Rockville, Maryland), Washington DC 20855, USA. Tel: (301) 947-3958. Fax: (301) 947-3958. e-mail: n.a.

Guyana

Long-Form Name: Co-operative Republic of Guyana
Capital: Georgetown

■ GEOGRAPHY

Area: 214,970 sq. km
Coastline: 459 km

Climate: tropical; hot, humid, moderated by northeast trade winds; two rainy seasons (May to mid-Aug., mid-Nov. to mid-Jan.)
Environment: flash floods a constant threat during rainy seasons; water pollution; deforestation
Terrain: mostly rolling highlands; low coastal plain; savanna in south
Land Use: 2% arable; negligible permanent crops; 6% meadows; 84% forest; 8% other; includes 1,500 sq. km irrigated
Location: N South America, bordering on Atlantic Ocean

■ PEOPLE

Population: 698,209 (July 2002 est.)
Nationality: Guyanese
Age Structure: 0–14 yrs: 27.6%; 15–64: 67.4%; 65+: 5.0% (2002 est.)
Population Growth Rate: 0.23% (2002 est.)
Net Migration: -6.28 migrants/1,000 population (2002 est.)
Ethnic Groups: 51% East Indian, 44% black and mixed, 4% Amerindian, 1% European and Chinese
Languages: English, Hindi, Urdu, Amerindian dialects
Religions: 60% Christian, 30% Hindu, 9% Muslim, 1% other
Birth Rate: 17.89/1,000 population (2002 est.)
Death Rate: 9.33/1,000 population (2002 est.)
Infant Mortality: 38.37 deaths/1,000 live births (2002 est.)
Life Expectancy at Birth: 59.96 years male, 65.34 years female (2002 est.)
Total Fertility Rate: 2.09 children born/woman (2002 est.)
Literacy: 98.5% (2000)

■ GOVERNMENT

Leader(s): Pres. Bharrat Jagdeo, Prime Min. Samuel Hinds
Government Type: republic
Administrative Divisions: 10 regions
Nationhood: May 26, 1966 (from UK; formerly known as British Guyana)
National Holiday: Republic Day, Feb. 23

■ ECONOMY

Overview: one of the world's poorest countries, with a per capita income less than one-fifth the South American average; electricity has been in short supply and constitutes a major barrier to production
GDP: US$2.5 billion, per capita US$3,600; real growth rate 2.8% (2000)
Inflation: 2.6% (2001)

Industries: accounts for 32% of GDP (2000); bauxite mining, sugar, rice milling, timber, fishing (shrimp), textiles, gold mining
Labour Force: exact figures n.a.; 26% industry, 27% agriculture, 47% services
Unemployment: n.a.
Agriculture: most important sector, accounting for 36% of GDP (2000); sugar and rice are main crops; livestock include beef, pork, poultry; not self-sufficient in food; development potential exists for fishing and forestry, wheat, vegetable oils
Natural Resources: bauxite, gold, diamonds, hardwood timber, shrimp, fish

■ **FINANCE/TRADE**

Currency: Guyanese dollar ($G) = 100 cents
International Reserves Excluding Gold: US$284 million (Dec. 2002)
Gold Reserves: n.a.
Budget: revenues US$227 million; expenditures US$235.2 million, including capital expenditures of US$93.4 million (2000)
Defence Expenditures: n.a.
Education Expenditures: n.a.
External Debt: US$1.406 billion (2001)
Exports: US$473 million (2002 est.); commodities: bauxite, sugar, rice, shrimp, gold, molasses, timber, rum; partners: Canada, US, UK, Netherlands Antilles
Imports: US$552 million (2002 est.); commodities: manufactures, machinery, food, petroleum; partners: US, Trinidad and Tobago, Netherlands Antilles, UK

■ **COMMUNICATIONS**

Daily Newspapers: 2 in total
Televisions: n.a.
Radios: n.a.
Telephones: 75 lines/1,000 inhabitants (1999)

■ **TRANSPORTATION**

Motor Vehicles: 33,000; 24,000 passenger cars
Roads: 7,970 km; 590 km paved
Railway: 187 km; no public railroads
Air Traffic: 145,000 passengers carried (1999 est.)
Airports: 51; 8 have paved runways (2002)

Canadian Embassy: Canadian High Commission, High and Young Streets, Georgetown; mailing address: P.O. Box 10880, Georgetown, Guyana. Tel: (011-592) 227-2081. Fax: (011-592) 225-8380. e-mail: grgtn@dfait-maeci.gc.ca
Embassy in Canada: High Commission for the Co-operative Republic of Guyana, Burnside Bldg, 151 Slater St, Ste 309, Ottawa ON K1P 5H3. Tel: (613) 235-7249. Fax: (613) 235-1447. e-mail: n.a.

Haiti

Long-Form Name: Republic of Haiti
Capital: Port-au-Prince

■ **GEOGRAPHY**

Area: 27,750 sq. km
Coastline: 1,771 km
Climate: tropical; semi-arid where mountains in east cut off trade winds
Environment: lies in the middle of the hurricane belt and subject to severe storms from June to Oct.; occasional flooding and earthquakes; deforestation; soil erosion, insufficient safe drinking water
Terrain: mostly rough and mountainous
Land Use: 20% arable; 13% permanent crops; 18% meadows; 5% forest; 44% other; includes 750 sq. km irrigated
Location: West Indies, bordering on Caribbean Sea, Atlantic Ocean

■ **PEOPLE**

Population: 7,063,722 (July 2002 est.)
Nationality: Haitian
Age Structure: 0–14 yrs: 39.5%; 15–64: 56.3%; 65+: 4.2% (2002 est.)
Population Growth Rate: 1.42% (2002 est.)
Net Migration: -2.31 migrants/1,000 population (2002 est.)
Ethnic Groups: 95% black, 5% mulatto and European
Languages: French (official) spoken by only 10% of population; all speak Creole
Religions: 80% Roman Catholic (of which an overwhelming majority also practice Voodoo), 16% Protestant, 4% other
Birth Rate: 31.42/1,000 population (2002 est.)
Death Rate: 14.88/1,000 population (2002 est.)
Infant Mortality: 93.35 deaths/1,000 live births (2002 est.)
Life Expectancy at Birth: 47.88 years male, 51.29 years female (2002 est.)
Total Fertility Rate: 4.30 children born/woman (2002 est.)
Literacy: 49.8% (2000)

■ **GOVERNMENT**

Leader(s): Pres. Jean-Bertrand Aristide, Prem. Yvon Neptune
Government Type: elected government
Administrative Divisions: 9 départements (départements, sing. —département)
Nationhood: Jan. 1, 1804 (from France)

National Holiday: Independence Day, Jan. 1

■ ECONOMY

Overview: about 75% of the population live in absolute poverty, and do not have access to safe drinking water, medical care or sufficient food; agriculture based on small-scale subsistence farming; trade sanctions have further damaged the economy

GDP: US$12 billion, per capita US$1,700; real growth rate -1.2% (2001 est.)

Inflation: 14.2% (2001)

Industries: accounts for 20% of GDP (2001 est.); sugar refining, textiles, flour milling, cement manufacturing, bauxite mining, tourism, light assembly industries based on imported parts

Labour Force: 3.6 million (2001); 66% agriculture, 25% services, 9% industry

Unemployment: 70%; widespread underemployment (1999)

Agriculture: accounts for 30% of GDP (2001 est.) and employs 70% of workforce; mostly small-size subsistence farms; commercial crops include coffee, mangoes, and sugar cane; staple crops include rice, corn, sorghum and mangoes

Natural Resources: bauxite, copper, gold, calcium carbonate

■ FINANCE/TRADE

Currency: gourde (G) = 100 centimes

International Reserves Excluding Gold: US$100 million (Aug. 2002)

Gold Reserves: 0.001 million fine troy ounces (Dec. 2002)

Budget: revenues US$273 million; expenditures US$361 million, including capital expenditures US$ n.a. (FY2000/01 est.).

Defence Expenditures: n.a.

Education Expenditures: n.a.

External Debt: US$1.250 billion (2001)

Exports: US$277 million (2002 est.); commodities: light manufactures 65%, coffee 17%, other agriculture 8%, other products 10%; partners: US, EU

Imports: US$1.103 billion (2002 est.); commodities: machines and manufactures 36%, food and beverages 21%, petroleum products 11%, fats and oils 12%, chemicals 12%; partners: US, EU, Dominican Republic

■ COMMUNICATIONS

Daily Newspapers: 3/1,000 inhabitants (2000)

Televisions: 6/1,000 inhabitants (2001)

Radios: 18/1,000 inhabitants (2001)

Telephones: 10 lines/1,000 inhabitants (2001)

■ TRANSPORTATION

Motor Vehicles: 53,000; 32,000 passenger cars

Roads: 4,160 km; 1,011 km paved

Railway: 40 km (2001)

Air Traffic: n.a.

Airports: 12; 2 have paved runways (2002)

Canadian Embassy: The Canadian Embassy, Édifice Banque de Nova Scotia, route de Delmas, Port-au-Prince, Haiti; mailing address: C.P. 826, Port-au-Prince, Haiti. Tel: (011-509) 298-3050. Fax: (011-509) 298-3801. e-mail: prnce@dfait-maeci.gc.ca

Embassy in Canada: Embassy of the Republic of Haiti, 130 Albert St, Ste 1409, Ottawa ON K1P 5G4. Tel: (613) 238-1628. Fax (613) 238-2986. e-mail: bohio@sympatico.ca

Honduras

Long-Form Name: Republic of Honduras

Capital: Tegucigalpa

■ GEOGRAPHY

Area: 112,090 sq. km

Coastline: 820 km

Climate: subtropical in lowlands, temperate in mountains

Environment: subject to frequent, but generally mild, earthquakes; damaging hurricanes along Caribbean coast; deforestation; soil erosion; mining pollution of freshwater resources

Terrain: mostly mountainous in interior, narrow coastal plains

Land Use: 15% arable; 3% permanent crops; 14% permanent pastures; 54% forest and woodlands; 14% other; includes 760 sq. km irrigated

Location: Central (Latin) America, bordering on Caribbean Sea, Pacific Ocean

■ PEOPLE

Population: 6,560,608 (July 2002 est.)

Nationality: Honduran

Age Structure: 0–14 yrs: 41.8%; 15–64: 54.6%; 65+: 3.6% (2002 est.)

Population Growth Rate: 2.34% (2002 est.)

Net Migration: -2.07 migrants/1,000 population (2002 est.)

Ethnic Groups: 90% mestizo (mixed Indian and European), 7% Indian, 2% black, 1% white

Languages: Spanish, Indian dialects

Religions: about 97% Roman Catholic; small Protestant minority

Birth Rate: 31.21/1,000 population (2002 est.)

Death Rate: 5.74/1,000 population (2002 est.)
Infant Mortality: 30.48 deaths/1,000 live births (2002 est.)
Life Expectancy at Birth: 67.11 years male, 70.51 years female (2002 est.)
Total Fertility Rate: 4.03 children born/woman (2002 est.)
Literacy: 74.6% (2000)

■ GOVERNMENT

Leader(s): Pres. Ricardo Maduro
Government Type: democratic constitutional republic
Administrative Divisions: 18 departments (departamentos, sing. —departamento, plus 1 probable central district)
Nationhood: Sept. 15, 1821 (from Spain)
National Holiday: Independence Day, Sept. 15

■ ECONOMY

Overview: one of the poorest countries in the western hemisphere, with a high population growth rate, a high unemployment rate, a lack of basic services and an export sector vulnerable to world prices (coffee, bananas)
GDP: US$17 billion, per capita US$2,600; real growth rate 2.1% (2001 est.)
Inflation: 9.7% (2001)
Industries: accounts for 32% of GDP (2000); agricultural processing (sugar and coffee), textiles, clothing, wood products
Labour Force: 2.5 million (2001); 34% agriculture, 45% community, social and business services, 21% industry
Unemployment: 3.7% (2001)
Agriculture: accounts for 18% of GDP (2000), over 60% of the labour force and 20% of exports; main products include bananas, coffee, timber, beef, citrus fruit, shrimp; importer of wheat
Natural Resources: timber, gold, silver, copper, lead, zinc, iron ore, antimony, coal, fish

■ FINANCE/TRADE

Currency: lempira (L) = 100 centavos
International Reserves Excluding Gold: US$1.524 billion (Dec. 2002)
Gold Reserves: 0.021 million fine troy ounces (Dec. 2002)
Budget: revenues US$607 million; expenditures US$411.9 billion, including capital expenditures of US$106 million (1999 est.)
Defence Expenditures: 2.6% of central government expenditure (1999)
Education Expenditures: n.a.
External Debt: US$5.051 billion (2001)

Exports: US$1.287 billion (2002 est.); commodities: bananas, coffee, shrimp, lobster, minerals, lumber; partners: US, El Salvador, Germany, Belgium, Guatemala
Imports: US$2.863 billion (2002 est.); commodities: machinery and transport equipment, chemical products, manufactured goods, fuel and oil, foodstuffs; partners: US, Guatemala, El Salvador, Mexico, Japan

■ COMMUNICATIONS

Daily Newspapers: 55/1,000 inhabitants (2000)
Televisions: 96/1,000 inhabitants (2001)
Radios: 413/1,000 inhabitants (2001)
Telephones: 47 lines/1,000 inhabitants (2001)

■ TRANSPORTATION

Motor Vehicles: 400,000; 330,000 passenger cars (2000)
Roads: 15,400 km; 3,126 km paved
Railway: 595 km (2000)
Air Traffic: 545,000 passengers carried (1999 est.)
Airports: 117; 12 have paved runways (2002)

Canadian Embassy: The Office of the Canadian Embassy, Centro Financiero BANEXPO, 3rd Floor, Bulevar San Juan Bosco, Colonia Payaqui, Tegucigalpa, Honduras, Postal Address: The Office of the Canadian Embassy, P.O. Box 3552, Tegucigalpa, Honduras. Tel: (011 504) 232-4551. Fax: (011 504) 239-7767. e-mail: tglpa@dfait-maeci.gc.ca
Embassy in Canada: Embassy of the Republic of Honduras, 151 Slater St, Ste 805, Ottawa ON K1P 5H3. Tel: (613) 233-8900. Fax: (613) 232-0193. e-mail: scastell@magma.ca

Hong Kong

Long-Form Name: Hong Kong Special Administrative Region
Capital: none

■ GEOGRAPHY

Area: 1,092 sq. km
Climate: tropical monsoon; cool and humid in winter, hot and rainy from spring through summer, warm and sunny in fall
Land Use: 6% arable land; 1% permanent crops; 1% meadows; 20% forest; 72% other; includes 20 sq. km irrigated
Location: SE Asia, bordering on South China Sea

■ PEOPLE

Population: 7,303,334 (July 2002 est.)
Nationality: Chinese
Ethnic Groups: 95% Chinese, 5% other
Languages: Chinese (Cantonese), English

■ GOVERNMENT

Colony/Territory of: Special Administrative Region (SAR) of the People's Republic of China
Leader(s): Pres. Hu Jintao (China); Chief Exec. Tung Chee-hwa
Government Type: reverted to China July 1, 1997
National Holiday: National Day, Oct. 1; July 1 is celebrated as Hong Kong Special Administrative Region Establishment Day

■ ECONOMY

Overview: manufacturing and services (finance, business and professional) are the basis of the economy; natural resources are limited and food and raw materials must be imported

■ FINANCE/TRADE

Currency: Hong Kong dollar (HK$) = 100 cents

Canadian Embassy: c/o The Canadian Embassy, 19 Dong Zhi Men Wai, Chao Yang District 100600, Beijing, PDR China. Tel: (011-86-10) 6532-3536. Fax: (011-86-10) 6532-4311. e-mail: bejing@dfait-maeci.gc.ca
Representative to Canada: c/o Embassy of the People's Republic of China, 515 St. Patrick St, Ottawa ON K1N 5H3. Tel: (613) 789-3434. Fax: (613) 789-1911. e-mail: n.a.

Hungary

Long-Form Name: Republic of Hungary
Capital: Budapest

■ GEOGRAPHY

Area: 93,030 sq. km
Coastline: none: landlocked
Climate: temperate; cold, cloudy, humid winter; warm summer
Environment: levees are common along many streams, but flooding occurs almost every year; pollution of air, soil and underground water resources
Terrain: mostly flat to rolling plains
Land Use: 51% arable; 3.6% permanent crops; 12.4% permanent pastures; 19% forest; 14% other; includes 2,100 sq. km irrigated
Location: C Europe

■ PEOPLE

Population: 10,075,034 (July 2002 est.)
Nationality: Hungarian
Age Structure: 0–14 yrs: 16.4%; 15–64: 68.8%; 65+: 14.8% (2002 est.)
Population Growth Rate: -0.30% (2002 est.)
Net Migration: 0.76 migrants/1,000 population (2002 est.)
Ethnic Groups: 89.9% Hungarian, 4% Gypsy, 2% Serb, 2.6% German, 0.8% Slovak, 0.7% Romanian
Languages: Hungarian (Magyar, official), 1.8% other
Religions: 67.5% Roman Catholic, 20% Calvinist, 5% Lutheran, 7.5% atheist and other
Birth Rate: 9.34/1,000 population (2002 est.)
Death Rate: 13.09/1,000 population (2002 est.)
Infant Mortality: 8.77 deaths/1,000 live births (2002 est.)
Life Expectancy at Birth: 67.55 years male, 76.55 years female (2002 est.)
Total Fertility Rate: 1.25 children born/woman (2002 est.)
Literacy: 99.3% (2000)

■ GOVERNMENT

Leader(s): Pres. Ferenc Madl, Prime Min. Peter Medgyessy
Government Type: parliamentary democracy
Administrative Divisions: 19 counties (megyek, sing. —megye), 20 urban counties and 1 capital city (fovaros)
Nationhood: 1001 (unification by King Stephen I)
National Holiday: St. Stephen's Day, Aug. 20 (National Day)

■ ECONOMY

Overview: consolidated its stabilization program and undergone enough restructuring to become an established market economy; it appears to have entered a period of sustainable growth, gradually falling inflation, and stable external balances; the government's main economic priorities are to complete structural reforms, particularly in pension, taxation, and health-care reforms
GDP: US$134.7 billion, per capita US$13,300; real growth rate 3.2% (2002 est.)
Inflation: 9.1% (2001)
Industries: accounts for 34% of GDP (2000); mining, metallurgy, engineering industries, processed foods, textiles, chemicals (especially pharmaceuticals)
Labour Force: 4.9 million (2001); 27% industry, 65% community, social and business services, 8% agriculture
Unemployment: 6.5% (2001)

Agriculture: accounts for 4% of GDP (2000) (including forestry) and 16% of employment; highly diversified crop-livestock farming; main crops—wheat, corn, sunflowers, potatoes, sugar beets; livestock—hogs, cattle, poultry and dairy products; self-sufficient in food
Natural Resources: bauxite, coal, natural gas, fertile soils, arable land

■ FINANCE/TRADE

Currency: forint (Ft) = 100 filler
International Reserves Excluding Gold: US$10.349 billion (Dec. 2002)
Gold Reserves: 0.101 million fine troy ounces (Dec. 2002)
Budget: revenues US$13 billion; expenditures US$14.4 billion, including capital expenditures of US$ n.a. (2000 est.)
Defence Expenditures: 4.3% of central government expenditure (2001)
Education Expenditures: 6.28% of total government expenditure (2000)
External Debt: US$30.289 billion (2001)
Exports: US$33.256 billion (2002 est.); commodities: capital goods 36%, foods 24%, consumer goods 18%, fuels and minerals 11%, other 11%; partners: Germany, Austria, Italy, US
Imports: US$35.909 billion (2002 est.); commodities: machinery and transport 28%, fuels 20%, chemical products 14%, manufactured consumer goods 16%, agriculture 6%, other 16%; partners: former USSR countries 43%, Germany, Italy, Austria, Russia

■ COMMUNICATIONS

Daily Newspapers: 456/1,000 inhabitants (2000)
Televisions: 445/1,000 inhabitants (2001)
Radios: 690/1,000 inhabitants (2001)
Telephones: 374 lines/1,000 inhabitants (2001)

■ TRANSPORTATION

Motor Vehicles: 2,750,000; 2,400,000 passenger cars (2000)
Roads: 188,203 km; 81,680 km paved
Railway: 7,869 km
Air Traffic: 2,075,000 passengers carried (2001)
Airports: 43; 16 have paved runways (2002)

Canadian Embassy: The Canadian Embassy, Zugligeti vt. 51-53, 1121 Budapest, Hungary. Tel.: (011-36-1) 392-3360. Fax: (011-36-1) 392-3390. e-mail: bpest@dfait-maeci.gc.ca
Embassy in Canada: Embassy of the Republic of Hungary, 299 Waverley St, Ottawa ON K2P 0V9. Tel: (613) 230-2717. Fax: (613) 230-7560. e-mail: sysadmin@huembott.org

Iceland

Long-Form Name: Republic of Iceland
Capital: Reykjavik

■ GEOGRAPHY

Area: 103,000 sq. km
Coastline: 4,988 km
Climate: temperate; moderated by North Atlantic Current; mild, windy winters; damp, cool summers
Environment: subject to earthquakes and volcanic activity; water pollution
Terrain: mostly plateau interspersed with mountain peaks, ice fields; coast deeply indented by bays and fjords
Land Use: 0% arable; 0% permanent crops; 23% meadows; 1% forest; 76% other
Location: NW Europe, island in Norwegian Sea, Atlantic Ocean

■ PEOPLE

Population: 279,384 (July 2002 est.)
Nationality: Icelander
Age Structure: 0–14 yrs: 23.0%; 15–64: 65.1%; 65+: 11.9% (2002 est.)
Population Growth Rate: 0.52% (2002 est.)
Net Migration: -2.27 migrants/1,000 population (2002 est.)
Ethnic Groups: homogeneous mixture of descendants of Norwegians and Celts
Languages: Icelandic
Religions: Christianity (predominantly Protestant)
Birth Rate: 14.37/1,000 population (2002 est.)
Death Rate: 6.93/1,000 population (2002 est.)
Infant Mortality: 3.53 deaths/1,000 live births (2002 est.)
Life Expectancy at Birth: 77.42 years male, 82.07 years female (2002 est.)
Total Fertility Rate: 1.99 children born/woman (2002 est.)
Literacy: approaching 100% (2000)

■ GOVERNMENT

Leader(s): Pres. Olafur Ragnar Grimsson, Prime Min. David Oddsson
Government Type: constitutional republic
Administrative Divisions: 23 counties (syslar, sing. —sysla) and 14 independent towns (kaupstadhir, sing. —kaupstadhur)
Nationhood: June 17, 1944 (from Denmark)
National Holiday: Anniversary of the Establishment of the Republic, June 17

■ ECONOMY

Overview: basically capitalistic, but it has an extensive welfare system, low unemployment,

and an unusually even distribution of income; depends heavily on the fishing industry and is vulnerable to changing world fish prices
GDP: US$7.7 billion, per capita US$27,100; real growth rate -0.7% (2002 est.)
Inflation: 6.4% (2001)
Industries: accounts for 21% of GDP (2001 est.); fish processing, aluminum smelting, ferro-silicon production, hydroelectricity
Labour Force: 159,000 (2000); 55% commerce, finance and services, 13% other manufacturing, 5.1% agriculture, 12% fish processing, 15% other
Unemployment: 3.0% (Nov. 2002)
Agriculture: accounts for about 15% of GDP (includes fishing) (2001 est.); fishing is the most important economic activity, contributing nearly 75% to export earnings; principal crops include potatoes and turnips; livestock—cattle, sheep; self-sufficient in crops
Natural Resources: fish, hydroelectric and geothermal power, diatomite

■ FINANCE/TRADE

Currency: króna (pl. krónur) (ISK) = 100 aurar
International Reserves Excluding Gold: US$440 million (Dec. 2002)
Gold Reserves: 0.063 million fine troy ounces (Dec. 2002)
Budget: revenues US$3.5 billion; expenditures US$3.3 billion, including capital expenditures of US$467 million (1999)
Defence Expenditures: none
Education Expenditures: n.a.
External Debt: US$2.6 billion (1999)
Exports: US$2.213 billion (2002 est.); commodities: fish and fish products, animal products, aluminum, diatomite; partners: UK, Germany, Netherlands, US, Portugal, Spain, Norway
Imports: US$2.245 billion (2002 est.); commodities: machinery and transportation equipment, petroleum, foodstuffs, textiles; partners: Germany, US, Denmark, Norway, UK, Netherlands

■ COMMUNICATIONS

Daily Newspapers: 5 in total
Televisions: n.a.
Radios: n.a.
Telephones: 677 lines/1,000 inhabitants (1999)

■ TRANSPORTATION

Motor Vehicles: 144,000; 125,300 passenger cars
Roads: 12,691 km; 3,262 km paved
Railway: none
Air Traffic: 1,530,000 passengers carried (1999 est.)

Airports: 86; 13 have paved runways (2002)

Canadian Embassy: The Consulate General of Canada, Tungata 14, 101 Reykjavik, Iceland, Postal Address: The Consulate General of Canada, P.O. Box 1510, 121 Reykjavik, Iceland. Tel: (011 354) 575-6500. Fax: (011-354) 575-6501. e-mail: n.a.
Embassy in Canada: Embassy of the Republic of Iceland, 360 Albert St, 7th Fl Ste 710, Ottawa ON K1R 7X7. Tel: (613) 482-1944. Fax: (613) 482-1945. e-mail: n.a.

India

Long-Form Name: Republic of India
Capital: New Delhi

■ GEOGRAPHY

Area: 3,287,590 sq. km
Coastline: 7,000 km
Climate: varies from tropical monsoon in south to temperate in north
Environment: deforestation; soil erosion; overgrazing; air and water pollution; desertification; droughts, flash floods, severe thunderstorms common; earthquakes are a hazard
Terrain: upland plain (Deccan Plateau) in south, flat to rolling plain along the Ganges, deserts in west, Himalayas in north
Land Use: 56% arable; 1% permanent crops; 4% meadows; 23% forest; 16% other; includes 590,000 sq. km irrigated
Location: S Asia, bordering on Arabian Sea, Indian Ocean, Bay of Bengal

■ PEOPLE

Population: 1,045,845,226 (July 2002 est.)
Nationality: Indian
Age Structure: 0–14 yrs: 32.7%; 15–64: 62.6%; 65+: 4.7% (2002 est.)
Population Growth Rate: 1.51% (2002 est.)
Net Migration: -0.07 migrants/1,000 population (2002 est.)
Ethnic Groups: 72% Indo-Aryan, 25% Dravidian, 3% Mongoloid and other
Languages: Hindi (official, spoken by 30%); English; 19 regional languages, including Bengali, Tlegu, Marathi, Tamil, Urdu, Gujarati, Malayalam, Kannada, Oriya, Punjabi, Assamese, Kashmiri, Sindhi and Sanskrit; 24 languages spoken by a million or more persons each; numerous other languages
Religions: 80% Hindu, 14% Muslim, 2.4% Christian, 2% Sikh, 0.7% Buddhist, 0.5% Jains, 0.4% other
Birth Rate: 23.79/1,000 population (2002 est.)

Death Rate: 8.62/1,000 population (2002 est.)
Infant Mortality: 61.47 deaths/1,000 live births (2002 est.)
Life Expectancy at Birth: 62.55 years male, 63.93 years female (2002 est.)
Total Fertility Rate: 2.98 children born/woman (2002 est.)
Literacy: 57.2% (2000)

■ GOVERNMENT

Leader(s): Pres. A.P.J. Abdul Kalam, Prime Min. Atal Bihari Vajpayee
Government Type: federal republic
Administrative Divisions: 28 states and 7 union territories
Nationhood: Aug. 15, 1947 (from UK)
National Holiday: Anniversary of the Proclamation of the Republic, Jan. 26

■ ECONOMY

Overview: a mixture of traditional village farming and handicrafts, modern agriculture, old and new branches of industry and a multitude of support services; millions still live in poverty, hoping to benefit from modern farming techniques
GDP: US$2.66 trillion, per capita US$2,540; real growth rate 4.3% (2002 est.)
Inflation: 3.7% (2001)
Industries: accounts for 25% of GDP (2002 est.), textiles, food processing, steel, machinery, transportation equipment, cement, jute manufactures, mining, petroleum, power, chemicals, pharmaceuticals, electronics
Labour Force: 460.5 million (2001); 60% agriculture, 17% industry, 23% services
Unemployment: n.a.
Agriculture: accounts for 25% of GDP (2002 est.) and employs two-thirds of labour force; self-sufficient in foodgrains; main crops—rice, wheat, oilseeds, cotton, jute, tea, sugar cane, potatoes; livestock—cattle, buffalo, sheep, goats and poultry; in top 10 of fishing nations
Natural Resources: coal, iron ore, manganese, mica, bauxite, titanium ore, chromite, petroleum, natural gas, diamonds, crude oil, limestone

■ FINANCE/TRADE

Currency: rupee (Rs) = 100 paise
International Reserves Excluding Gold: US$67.666 billion (Dec. 2002)
Gold Reserves: 11.502 million fine troy ounces (Dec. 2002)
Budget: revenues US$48.3 billion; expenditures US$78.2 billion, including capital expenditures of US$13.5 billion (FY2001/02 est.)

Defence Expenditures: 14.0% of central government expenditure (2001)
Education Expenditures: 2.63% of central government expenditure (2000)
External Debt: US$97.320 billion (2001)
Exports: US$48.048 billion (2002 est.); commodities: tea, coffee, iron ore, fish products, manufactures; partners: US, UK, Germany, Japan, Benelux
Imports: US$54.268 billion (2002 est.); commodities: petroleum, edible oils, textiles, clothing, capital goods; partners: UK, US, Belgium, Japan, Germany

■ COMMUNICATIONS

Daily Newspapers: 60/1,000 inhabitants (2000)
Televisions: 83/1,000 inhabitants (2001)
Radios: 120/1,000 inhabitants (2001)
Telephones: 38 lines/1,000 inhabitants (2001)

■ TRANSPORTATION

Motor Vehicles: 8,200,000; 5,150,000 passenger cars (2000)
Roads: 3,319,644 km; 1,517,077 km hard-surfaced
Railway: 63,693 km (2001
Air Traffic: 17,272,000 passengers carried (2001)
Airports: 335; 232 have paved runways (2002)

Canadian Embassy: The Canadian High Commission, 7/8 Shantipath, Chanakyapuri, New Delhi 110021; mailing address: The Canadian High Commission, P.O. Box 5207, Chanakyapuri, New Delhi 110021, India. Tel: (011-91-11) 687-6500. Fax: (011-91-11) 687-6579. e-mail: delhi@dfait-maeci.gc.ca
Embassy in Canada: High Commission for the Republic of India, 10 Springfield Rd, Ottawa ON K1M 1C9. Tel: (613) 744-3751. Fax: (613) 744-0913. e-mail: hicomind@sprint.ca

Indonesia

Long-Form Name: Republic of Indonesia
Capital: Jakarta

■ GEOGRAPHY

Area: 1,919,440 sq. km (13,677 islands)
Coastline: 54,716 km
Climate: tropical; hot, humid; more moderate in highlands
Environment: archipelago of more than 13,500 islands (6,000 inhabited); occasional floods, severe droughts and tsunamis; deforestation; environmental pollution
Terrain: mostly coastal lowlands; larger islands have interior mountains

Land Use: 10% arable; 7% permanent crops; 7% meadows; 62% forest; 14% other; includes 48,150 sq. km irrigated
Location: SE Asia, bordering on Indian Ocean

■ PEOPLE

Population: 231,328,092 (July 2002 est.)
Nationality: Indonesian
Age Structure: 0–14 yrs: 30.26%; 15–64: 65.11%; 65+: 4.63% (2001 est.)
Population Growth Rate: 1.54% (2002 est.)
Net Migration: -0.21 migrants/1,000 population (2002 est.)
Ethnic Groups: majority of Malay stock comprising 45% Javanese, 14% Sundanese, 7.5% Madurese, 7.5% coastal Malays, 26% other
Languages: Bahasa Indonesia (modified form of Malay; official); English and Dutch leading foreign languages; 25 local dialects, the most widely spoken of which is Javanese
Religions: 87% Muslim, 6% Protestant, 3% Roman Catholic, 2% Hindu, 1% Buddhist, 1% other
Birth Rate: 21.87/1,000 population (2002 est.)
Death Rate: 6.28/1,000 population (2002 est.)
Infant Mortality: 39.40 deaths/1,000 live births (2002 est.)
Life Expectancy at Birth: 66.24 years male, 71.13 years female (2002 est.)
Total Fertility Rate: 2.54 children born/woman (2002 est.)
Literacy: 86.9% (2000)

■ GOVERNMENT

Leader(s): Pres. Sukarnoputri Megawati, V. Pres. Hamzah Haz
Government Type: republic
Administrative Divisions: 27 provinces (propinsi-propinsi, sing. —propinsi), 2 special regions (daerah-daerah istimewa, sing. —daerah istimewa) and 1 special capital city district (daerah khusus ibukota)
Nationhood: Aug. 17, 1945 (Indonesia became legally independent from the Netherlands on Dec. 27, 1949; formerly known as Netherlands or Dutch East Indies)
National Holiday: Independence Day, Aug. 17

■ ECONOMY

Overview: a mixed economy with many socialist institutions and central planning but with a recent emphasis on deregulation and private enterprise; hampered by large population growth; possesses abundant natural wealth

GDP: US$687 billion, per capita US$3,000; real growth rate 3.3% (2001 est.)
Inflation: 11.5% (2001)
Industries: accounts for 41% of GDP (2001 est.); petroleum, textiles, mining, cement, chemical fertilizer production, timber, food, rubber
Labour Force: 102.0 million (2001); 45% agriculture, 16% industry, 39% services
Unemployment: 6.1%; 50% underemployment (2001 est.)
Agriculture: accounts for 17% of GDP (2001 est.); subsistence food production; small-holder and plantation production for export; rice, cassava, peanuts, rubber, cocoa, coffee, copra, other tropical products; poultry, beef, pork, eggs; the staple crop is rice; once the world's largest rice importer, Indonesia is now nearly self-sufficient
Natural Resources: crude oil, tin, natural gas, nickel, timber, bauxite, copper, fertile soils, coal, gold, silver

■ FINANCE/TRADE

Currency: rupiah (Rp) = 100 sen
International Reserves Excluding Gold: US$30.501 billion (Dec. 2002)
Gold Reserves: 3.101 million fine troy ounces (Dec. 2002)
Budget: revenues US$26 billion; expenditures US$30 billion, including capital expenditures of US$ n.a. (2000 est.)
Defence Expenditures: 4.6% of central government expenditure (2001)
Education Expenditures: 6.66% of central gov't expenditure (1999)
External Debt: US$135.704 billion (2001)
Exports: US$52.115 billion (2001); commodities: petroleum and liquefied natural gas 40%, timber 15%, textiles 7%, rubber 5%, coffee 3%; partners: Japan, US, Singapore, South Korea, China, Malaysia
Imports: US$31.010 billion (2001); commodities: machinery 39%, chemical products 19%, manufactured goods 16%; partners: Japan, Singapore, US, South Korea, China, Australia

■ COMMUNICATIONS

Daily Newspapers: 23/1,000 inhabitants (2000)
Televisions: 153/1,000 inhabitants (2001)
Radios: 159/1,000 inhabitants (2001)
Telephones: 35 lines/1,000 inhabitants (2001)

■ TRANSPORTATION

Motor Vehicles: 5,700,000; 3,200,000 passenger cars (2000)
Roads: 342,700 km; 158,670 km paved

Railway: 6,458 km (2001)
Air Traffic: 10,049,000 passengers carried (2001)
Airports: 490; 153 have paved runways (2002)

Canadian Embassy: The Canadian Embassy, Jalan Jendral Sudirman, Jakarta 12920; mailing address: P.O. Box 8324/JKS.MP, Jakarta 12083, Indonesia. Tel: (011-62-21) 2550-7800. Fax: (011-62-21) 2550-7811. e-mail: jkrta@dfait-maeci.gc.ca
Embassy in Canada: Embassy of the Republic of Indonesia, 55 Parkdale Ave, Ottawa ON K1Y 1E5. Tel: (613) 724-1100. Fax: (613) 724-1105. e-mail: info@prica.org

Iran

Long-Form Name: Islamic Republic of Iran
Capital: Tehran

■ GEOGRAPHY

Area: 1,648,000 sq. km
Coastline: 2,440 km
Climate: mostly arid or semi-arid, subtropical along Caspian coast
Environment: deforestation; overgrazing; desertification; air and water pollution; periodic droughts and floods
Terrain: rugged mountainous rim; high, central basin with deserts, mountains; small, discontinuous plains along both coasts
Land Use: 10% arable; 1% permanent crops; 27% meadows; 7% forest; 55% other; includes 75,620 sq. km irrigated
Location: SW Asia (Middle East), bordering on Persian Gulf

■ PEOPLE

Population: 66,622,704 (July 2002 est.)
Nationality: Iranian
Age Structure: 0–14 yrs: 31.6%; 15–64: 63.7%; 65+: 4.7% (2002 est.)
Population Growth Rate: 0.77% (2002 est.)
Net Migration: -4.46 migrants/1,000 population (2002 est.)
Ethnic Groups: 51% Persian, 24% Azerbaijani, 7% Kurd, 8% Gilaki and Mazandarani, 2% Lur, 2% Baloch, 3% Arab, 2% Turkmen, 1% other
Languages: Farsi (Persian) (official) 58%, Turkic and Turkic dialects 26%, Kurdish 9%, Luri 2%, Balochi 1%, Turkish 1%, Arabic 1%, 2% other
Religions: 99% Muslim (89% Shia, 10% Sunni); Christianity, Judaism, Zoroastrianism 1%
Birth Rate: 17.54/1,000 population (2002 est.)
Death Rate: 5.39/1,000 population (2002 est.)

Infant Mortality: 28.07 deaths/1,000 live births (2002 est.)
Life Expectancy at Birth: 68.87 years male, 71.69 years female (2002 est.)
Total Fertility Rate: 2.01 children born/woman (2002 est.)
Literacy: 76.3% (2000)

■ GOVERNMENT

Leader(s): Pres. Mohammed Khatami, Supreme Religious Leader Ayatollah Mohammed Ali Hoseini Khamenei
Government Type: theocratic republic
Administrative Divisions: 28 provinces (ostanha, sing. —ostan)
Nationhood: Apr. 1, 1979, Islamic Republic of Iran proclaimed
National Holiday: Islamic Republic Day, Apr. 1

■ ECONOMY

Overview: economy is a mixture of central planning, state ownership of oil and other large enterprises, village agriculture, and small-scale private trading and service ventures; soaring external debt and high unemployment impede progress towards recovery from the economic devastation of the war with Iraq
GDP: US$456 billion, per capita US$7,000; real growth rate 5.0% (2002 est.)
Inflation: 11.3% (2001)
Industries: accounts for 26% of GDP (2002 est.); petroleum, petrochemicals, textiles, cement and other building materials, food processing (particularly sugar refining and vegetable oil production), metal fabricating (steel and copper)
Labour Force: 20.4 million (2001); 30% agriculture, 25% industry, 45% services
Unemployment: 14% (2000 est.)
Agriculture: accounts for 19% of GDP (2002 est.); principal products—rice, other grains, sugar beets, fruits, nuts, cotton, wheat, dairy products, wool, caviar; not self-sufficient in food
Natural Resources: petroleum, natural gas, coal, chromium, copper, iron ore, lead, manganese, zinc, sulphur

■ FINANCE/TRADE

Currency: 10 rials (RIs) = 1 toman
International Reserves Excluding Gold: n.a.
Gold Reserves: n.a.
Budget: revenues US$24 billion; expenditures US$22 billion, including capital expenditures of US$ n.a. (2001 est.)
Defence Expenditures: 17.2% of central government expenditure (2001)

Education Expenditures: 18.60% of central government expenditure (2000)
External Debt: US$7.483 billion (2001)
Exports: US$24.444 billion (2002 est.); commodities: petroleum 90%, carpets, fruit, nuts, hides; partners: Japan, Italy, UAE, France, China
Imports: US$22.091 billion (2002 est.); commodities: machinery, military supplies, metal works, foodstuffs, pharmaceuticals, technical services, refined oil products; partners: Germany, Italy, China, Japan, UAE

■ COMMUNICATIONS

Daily Newspapers: 28/1,000 inhabitants (2000)
Televisions: 163/1,000 inhabitants (2001)
Radios: 281/1,000 inhabitants (2001)
Telephones: 169 lines/1,000 inhabitants (2001)

■ TRANSPORTATION

Motor Vehicles: 2,239,000; 1,630,000 passenger cars
Roads: 140,200 km; 49,440 km paved
Railway: 6,130 km
Air Traffic: 9,318,000 passengers carried (2001)
Airports: 322 airfields; 122 have paved runways (2002)

Canadian Embassy: The Canadian Embassy to the Islamic Republic of Iran, 57 Shahid Javad-e-Sarafraz, Ostad-Motahari Ave, 15868 Tehran; mailing address: P.O. Box 11365-4647, Tehran, Iran. Tel: (011-98-21) 873-2623. Fax: (011-98-21) 873-3202. e-mail: teran@dfait-maeci.gc.ca
Embassy in Canada: Embassy of the Islamic Republic of Iran, 245 Metcalfe St, Ottawa ON K2P 2K2. Tel: (613) 235-5105. Fax: (613) 238-0379. e-mail: n.a.

Iraq

Long-Form Name: Republic of Iraq
Capital: Baghdad

■ GEOGRAPHY

Area: 437,072 sq. km
Coastline: 58 km
Climate: desert; mild to cool winters with dry, hot, cloudless summers; northern mountainous regions experience cold winters with occasionally heavy snows
Environment: development of Tigris-Euphrates river systems contingent upon agreements with upstream riparians (Syria and Turkey); air and water pollution; soil degradation (salinization) and erosion; desertification

Terrain: mostly broad plains; reedy marshes in southeast; mountains along borders with Iran and Turkey
Land Use: 12% arable; 0% permanent crops; 9% meadows; 0% forest; 79% other; includes 35,250 sq. km irrigated
Location: SW Asia (Middle East), bordering on Persian Gulf

■ PEOPLE

Population: 24,001,816 (July 2002 est.)
Nationality: Iraqi
Age Structure: 0–14 yrs: 41.1%; 15–64: 55.9%; 65+: 3.0% (2002 est.)
Population Growth Rate: 2.82% (2002 est.)
Net Migration: 0 migrants/1,000 population (2002 est.)
Ethnic Groups: 75–80% Arab, 15–20% Kurdish, 5% Turkoman and other
Languages: Arabic (official), Kurdish (official in Kurdish region), Assyrian, Armenian
Religions: 97% Muslim (60–65% Shi'a, 32–37% Sunni), 3% Christian or other
Birth Rate: 34.20/1,000 population (2002 est.)
Death Rate: 6.02/1,000 population (2002 est.)
Infant Mortality: 57.61 deaths/1,000 live births (2002 est.)
Life Expectancy at Birth: 66.31 years male, 68.50 years female (2002 est.)
Total Fertility Rate: 4.63 children born/woman (2002 est.)
Literacy: 58%

■ GOVERNMENT

Leader(s): US Chief Admin. (Interim): L. Paul Bremer III
Government Type: republic (in transition following April 2003 defeat of Saddam Hussein regime by US-led coalition)
Administrative Divisions: 18 provinces (muhafazat, sing. —muhafazah)
Nationhood: Oct. 3, 1932 (from League of Nations mandate under British administration)
National Holiday: Anniversary of the Revolution, July 17

■ ECONOMY

Overview: Iraq's economy is dominated by the oil sector, which has traditionally provided about 95% of foreign exchange earnings. Political instability (the eight-year war with Iran during the 1990s; the invasion of Kuwait and the hostilities and sanctions that followed) has been at the root of Iraq's substantial debt-load. The drop in GDP in 2001–02 was largely the result of the global economic slowdown and lower oil prices. Most recently, the military victory of the US-led coalition in March/April 2003 resulted in the shutdown of much of the country's central economic administrative structure.

GDP: US$58 billion, per capita US$2,400; real growth rate -3% (2002 est.)

Inflation: 70% (2002 est.)

Industries: accounts for 13% of GDP; petroleum, chemicals, textiles, construction materials, food processing

Labour Force: 6.5 million (2002)

Unemployment: n.a.

Agriculture: principal products: wheat, barley, rice, vegetables, dates, other fruit, cotton, wool; livestock: cattle, sheep; not self-sufficient in food output

Natural Resources: petroleum, natural gas, phosphates, sulphur

■ FINANCE/TRADE

Currency: dinar = 1,000 fils

International Reserves Excluding Gold: n.a.

Gold Reserves: n.a.

Budget: n.a.

Defence Expenditures: n.a.

Education Expenditures: n.a.

External Debt: US$120 billion (2002 est.)

Exports: US$13 billion (2002); commodities: crude oil and refined products, machinery, chemicals, dates; partners: US, Italy, France, Netherlands

Imports: US$7.8 billion (2002); commodities: manufactures, medicines, food; partners: France, Australia, Italy, Germany

■ COMMUNICATIONS

Daily Newspapers: 19/1,000 inhabitants (2000)

Televisions: 83/1,000 inhabitants (2001)

Radios: 222/1,000 inhabitants (2001)

Telephones: 29 lines/1,000 inhabitants (2001)

■ TRANSPORTATION

Motor Vehicles: 1,040,000; 672,000 passenger cars

Roads: 45,550 km; 38,400 km paved

Railway: 1,963 km (2003)

Air Traffic: n.a.

Airports: 150; 77 have paved runways (2002)

Canadian Embassy: The Canadian Embassy to Iraq, c/o The Canadian Embassy, P.O. Box 815403, Amman, Jordan, 11180. Tel: (011-962-6) 566-61-24. Fax: (011-962-6) 568-92-27. e-mail: amman@dfait-maeci.gc.ca

Embassy in Canada: Embassy of the Republic of Iraq, 215 McLeod St, Ottawa ON K2P 0Z8. Tel: (613) 236-9177. Fax: (613) 567-1101. e-mail: n.a.

Ireland

Long-Form Name: Ireland

Capital: Dublin

■ GEOGRAPHY

Area: 70,280 sq. km

Coastline: 1,448 km

Climate: temperate maritime; modified by North Atlantic Current; mild winters, cool summers; consistently humid; overcast about half the time

Environment: deforestation and water pollution, especially of lakes, from agricultural runoff

Terrain: mostly level to rolling interior plains surrounded by rugged hills and low mountains; sea cliffs on west coast

Land Use: 13% arable; negligible permanent crops; 68% meadows; 5% forest; 14% other; includes n.a. sq. km irrigated

Location: NW Europe, (British Isles), bordering on Atlantic Ocean and Irish Sea

■ PEOPLE

Population: 3,883,159 (July 2002 est.)

Nationality: Irish

Age Structure: 0–14 yrs: 21.3%; 15–64: 67.3%; 65+: 11.4% (2002 est.)

Population Growth Rate: 1.07% (2002 est.)

Net Migration: 4.12 migrants/1,000 population (2002 est.)

Ethnic Groups: Celtic, with English minority

Languages: Irish (official first language, but use is limited) and English; English is the language generally used, with Gaelic spoken in a few areas, mostly along the western seaboard

Religions: 93% Roman Catholic, 3% Anglican, 1% atheist, 3% other

Birth Rate: 14.62/1,000 population (2002 est.)

Death Rate: 8.01/1,000 population (2002 est.)

Infant Mortality: 5.43 deaths/1,000 live births (2002 est.)

Life Expectancy at Birth: 74.41 years male, 80.12 years female (2002 est.)

Total Fertility Rate: 1.90 children born/woman (2002 est.)

Literacy: approaching 100% (2000)

■ GOVERNMENT

Leader(s): Pres. Mary McAleese, Prime Min. Bertie Ahern

Government Type: republic

Administrative Divisions: 26 counties

Nationhood: Dec. 6, 1921 (from UK)

National Holiday: St. Patrick's Day, Mar. 17

■ ECONOMY

Overview: a small, open economy that is trade dependent; unemployment is high but inflation has been considerably lowered and the deficit burden relieved

GDP: US$111.3 billion, per capita US$28,500; real growth rate 3.9% (2002 est.)

Inflation: 4.9% (2001)

Industries: account for 36% of GDP (2001), 80% of exports and employs almost 30% of the workforce; food products, brewing, textiles, clothing, chemicals, pharmaceuticals, machinery, transportation equipment, glass and crystal

Labour Force: 1.6 million (2001); 64% community, social and business services, 28% industry, 8% agriculture

Unemployment: 4.7% (2001)

Agriculture: accounts for 4% of GDP (2001) and 8% of the labour force; principal crops include turnips, barley, potatoes, sugar, beets, wheat; livestock—meat and dairy products; 85% self-sufficient in food; food shortages include bread grain, fruits, vegetables

Natural Resources: zinc, lead, natural gas, barite, copper, gypsum, limestone, dolomite, peat, silver

■ FINANCE/TRADE

Currency: Irish pound (£ or £Ir) = 100 pence; Euro (€); on January 1, 2002 the Euro became the sole currency for everyday transactions.

International Reserves Excluding Gold: US$5.414 billion (Dec. 2002)

Gold Reserves: 0.176 million fine troy ounces (Dec. 2002)

Budget: revenues US$34 billion; expenditures US$27 billion, including capital expenditures of US$ n.a. (2001)

Defence Expenditures: 2.8% of central government expenditure (2001)

Education Expenditures: n.a.

External Debt: US$11 billion (1998)

Exports: US$87.536 billion (2002 est.); commodities: live animals, animal products, chemicals, data processing equipment, industrial machinery; partners: European Community, US

Imports: US$51.596 billion (2002 est.); commodities: food, animal feed, chemicals, petroleum and petroleum products, machinery, textiles, clothing; partners: UK, Germany, France, Netherlands, US, Japan

■ COMMUNICATIONS

Daily Newspapers: 150/1,000 inhabitants (2000)

Televisions: 399/1,000 inhabitants (2001)

Radios: 695/1,000 inhabitants (2001)

Telephones: 485 lines/1,000 inhabitants (2001)

■ TRANSPORTATION

Motor Vehicles: 1,320,000; 1,100,000 passenger cars

Roads: 92,500 km; 87,042 km paved

Railway: 3,314 km (2001)

Air Traffic: 16,374,000 passengers carried (2001)

Airports: 41; 16 have paved runways (2002)

Canadian Embassy: The Canadian Embassy, 65 St Stephen's Green, Dublin 2, Ireland. Tel: (011-353-1) 417-4100. Fax: (011-353-1) 417-4101. e-mail: dubln@dfait-maeci.gc.ca

Embassy in Canada: Embassy of Ireland, 130 Albert St, Ste 1105, Ottawa ON K1P 5G4. Tel: (613) 233-6281. Fax: (613) 233-5835. e-mail: emb.ireland@sympatico.ca

Isle of Man

Long-Form Name: Isle of Man

Capital: Douglas

■ GEOGRAPHY

Area: 572 sq. km

Climate: temperate maritime, cool summers and mild winters, humid, overcast about half the time

Land Use: 9% arable; 0% permanent crops; 46% permanent pastures; 6% forests and woodland; 39% other;

Location: Irish Sea, between Great Britain and Northern Ireland

■ PEOPLE

Population: 73,873 (July 2002 est.)

Nationality: Manxman, Manxwoman

Ethnic Groups: Manx (Norse-Celtic descent), Briton

Languages: English, Manx, Gaelic

■ GOVERNMENT

Colony/Territory of: Dependency of United Kingdom

Leader(s): Head of State: Queen Elizabeth II, Lt.-Gov. Ian David Macfadyen, Chief Min. Richard Corkill

Government Type: parliamentary democracy

National Holiday: Tynwald Day, July 5

■ ECONOMY

Overview: offshore banking, manufacturing, and tourism are key sectors of the economy; the government's policy of offering incentives to high-technology companies and financial institutions to locate on the island has paid off in expanding employment opportunities in high-income industries

■ FINANCE/TRADE

Currency: Manx pound = 100 pence; on a par with British pound sterling

Canadian Embassy: c/o The Canadian High Commission, Macdonald House, 1 Grosvenor Square, London W1K 4AB, England, UK. Tel: (011-44-20) 7258-6600. Fax: (011-44-20) 7258-6333. e-mail: Ldn@dfait-maeci.gc.ca
Representative to Canada: c/o British High Commission, 80 Elgin St, Ottawa ON K1P 5K7. Tel: (613) 237-1530. Fax: (613) 237-7980. Email should be sent using the appropriate form at the British High Commission's Website at http://www.britain-in-canada.org

Israel

Long-Form Name: State of Israel
Capital: Jerusalem

■ GEOGRAPHY

Area: 20,770 sq. km
Coastline: 273 km
Climate: temperate; hot and dry in desert areas
Environment: sandstorms may occur during spring and summer; limited arable land and natural water resources pose serious constraints; deforestation
Terrain: Negev Desert in the south; low coastal plain; central mountains; Jordan Rift Valley
Land Use: 17% arable; 4% permanent crops; 7% permanent pastures; 6% forest; 66% other; includes 1,990 sq. km irrigated
Location: SW Asia (Middle East), bordering on Mediterranean Sea

■ PEOPLE

Population: 6,029,529; includes about 187,000 Israeli settlers in the West Bank, about 20,000 in the Israeli-occupied Golan Heights, more than 5,000 in the Gaza Strip, and fewer than 177,000 in East Jerusalem (July 2002 est.)
Nationality: Israeli
Age Structure: 0–14 yrs: 27.1%; 15–64: 63.0%; 65+: 9.9% (2002 est.)
Population Growth Rate: 1.48% (2002 est.)
Net Migration: 2.11 migrants/1,000 population (2002 est.)
Ethnic Groups: 80.1% Jewish, 19.9% non-Jewish (mostly Arab)

Languages: Hebrew (official); Arabic used officially for Arab minority; European languages (mostly English)
Religions: 82% Judaism, 14% Islam (mostly Sunni Muslim), 2% Christian and Druze, 2% other
Birth Rate: 18.91/1,000 population (2002 est.)
Death Rate: 6.21/1,000 population (2002 est.)
Infant Mortality: 7.55 deaths/1,000 live births (2002 est.)
Life Expectancy at Birth: 76.82 years male, 81.01 years female (2002 est.)
Total Fertility Rate: 2.54 children born/woman (2002 est.)
Literacy: 94.6% (2000)

■ GOVERNMENT

Leader(s): Prime Min. Ariel Sharon, Pres. Moshe Katzav
Government Type: parliamentary democracy
Administrative Divisions: 6 districts (mehozot, sing. —mehoz)
Nationhood: May 14, 1948 (from League of Nations mandate under British administration)
National Holiday: Independence Day, May 14; the Jewish calendar is lunar and the holiday may occur in Apr. or May

■ ECONOMY

Overview: a market economy with government participation; despite limited natural resources, this country has strong agriculture and industry sectors; transfer payments and foreign loans offset the deficit; the Palestinian uprising and Russian immigration stifle growth; high Jewish immigration from the former Soviet states has created massive housing problems
GDP: US$122 billion, per capita US$19,000; real growth rate -1.1% (2002 est.)
Inflation: 1.1% (2001)
Industries: accounts for 37% of GDP (2001 est.); food processing, diamond cutting and polishing, textiles, clothing, chemicals, metal products, military equipment, transport equipment, electrical equipment, miscellaneous machinery, potash mining, high-technology electronics, tourism
Labour Force: 2.8 million (2001); 77% services, 20% industry, 3% agriculture
Unemployment: 11.2% (Aug. 2002)
Agriculture: accounts for 3% of GDP (2001 est.); largely self-sufficient in food production, except for bread grains; principal products—citrus and other fruit, vegetables, cotton; livestock products—beef, dairy and poultry

Natural Resources: copper, phosphates, bromide, potash, clay, sand, sulphur, asphalt, manganese, small amounts of natural gas and crude oil

■ FINANCE/TRADE

Currency: new Israeli shekel (NIS) = 100 new agorot
International Reserves Excluding Gold: US$24.076 billion (Dec. 2002)
Gold Reserves: none (Dec. 2002)
Budget: revenues US$40 billion; expenditures US$42.4 billion, capital expenditures US$ n.a. (2000 est.)
Defence Expenditures: 16.6% of central government expenditure (2001)
Education Expenditures: 13.54% of central government expenditure (2000)
External Debt: US$38 billion (2000 est.)
Exports: US$29.468 billion (2002); commodities: polished diamonds, citrus and other fruit, textiles and clothing, processed foods, fertilizer and chemical products, military hardware, electronics; partners: US, Benelux, Hong Kong, Germany, UK, Japan
Imports: US$32.424 billion (2002 est.); commodities: military equipment, rough diamonds, oil, chemicals, machinery, iron and steel, cereals, textiles, vehicles, ships, aircraft; partners: US, Benelux, Germany, UK, Switzerland, Italy

■ COMMUNICATIONS

Daily Newspapers: 290/1,000 inhabitants (2000)
Televisions: 335/1,000 inhabitants (2001)
Radios: 526/1,000 inhabitants (2001)
Telephones: 476 lines/1,000 inhabitants (2001)

■ TRANSPORTATION

Motor Vehicles: 1,600,000; 1,300,000 passenger cars (2000)
Roads: 15,965 km, all paved
Railway: 647 km
Air Traffic: 3,990,000 passengers carried (2001)
Airports: 54; 28 have paved runways (2002)

Canadian Embassy: The Canadian Embassy, 3 Nirim St., 4th Fl, Tel Aviv, 67060; mailing address: P.O. Box 9442, Tel Aviv, Israel. Tel: (011-972-3) 636-3300. Fax: (011-972-3) 636-3380. e-mail: taviv@dfait-maeci.gc.ca
Embassy in Canada: Embassy of Israel, 50 O'Connor St, Ste 1005, Ottawa ON K1P 6L2. Tel: (613) 567-6450. Fax: (613) 237-8865. e-mail: ottawa@israel.org

Italy

Long-Form Name: Italian Republic
Capital: Rome

■ GEOGRAPHY

Area: 301,230 sq. km; includes Sardinia and Sicily
Coastline: 7,600 km
Climate: predominantly Mediterranean; Alpine in far north; hot, dry in south
Environment: regional risks include landslides, mudflows, snowslides, earthquakes, volcanic eruptions, flooding; land sinkage in Venice; serious air and water pollution
Terrain: mostly rugged and mountainous; some plains, coastal lowlands
Land Use: 31% arable; 10% permanent crops; 15% meadows; 23% forest; 21% other; includes 26,980sq. km irrigated
Location: S Europe, bordering on Adriatic Sea, Mediterranean Sea

■ PEOPLE

Population: 57,715,625 (July 2002 est.)
Nationality: Italian
Age Structure: 0–14 yrs: 14.1%; 15–64: 67.3%; 65+: 18.6% (2002 est.)
Population Growth Rate: 0.05% (2002 est.)
Net Migration: 1.73 migrants/1,000 population (2002 est.)
Ethnic Groups: primarily Italian but population includes small clusters of German-, French- and Slovene-Italians in the north and Albanian-Italians in the south; Sicilians; Sardinians
Languages: Italian; parts of Trentino-Alto Adige region are predominantly German-speaking; significant French-speaking minority in Valle d'Aosta region; Slovene-speaking minority in the Trieste-Gorizia area
Religions: almost 100% nominally Roman Catholic
Birth Rate: 8.93/1,000 population (2002 est.)
Death Rate: 10.13/1,000 population (2002 est.)
Infant Mortality: 5.76 deaths/1,000 live births (2002 est.)
Life Expectancy at Birth: 76.08 years male, 82.63 years female (2002 est.)
Total Fertility Rate: 1.19 children born/woman (2002 est.)
Literacy: 98.4% (2000)

■ GOVERNMENT

Leader(s): Pres. Carlo Azeglio Ciampi, Prime Min. Silvio Berlusconi
Government Type: republic

Administrative Divisions: 20 regions (regioni, sing. —regione)
Nationhood: Mar. 17, 1861, Kingdom of Italy proclaimed
National Holiday: Anniversary of the Republic, June 2

ECONOMY

Overview: country is divided into a developed industrial north and an undeveloped agricultural south; an inadequate communications system, high pollution and economic integration into the European Union pose continuing challenges
GDP: US$1.438 trillion, per capita US$25,000; real growth rate 0.4% (2002 est.)
Inflation: 2.8% (2001)
Industries: accounts for 30% of GDP (2001 est.); machinery and transportation equipment, iron and steel, chemicals, food processing, textiles, motor vehicles
Labour Force: 25.8 million (2001); 32% industry, 5% agriculture, 63% community, social and business services
Unemployment: 10.8% (2001)
Agriculture: accounts for 2% of GDP (2001 est.) and 10% of the workforce; self-sufficient in foods other than meat and dairy products; principal crops—fruit, vegetables, grapes, potatoes, sugar beets, soybeans, grain, olives
Natural Resources: mercury, potash, marble, sulphur, dwindling natural gas and crude oil reserves, fish, coal

FINANCE/TRADE

Currency: lira (Lit) = 100 centesimi; Euro (€); on January 1, 2002 the Euro became the sole currency for everyday transactions.
International Reserves Excluding Gold: US$28.603 billion (Dec. 2002)
Gold Reserves: 78.829 million fine troy ounces (Dec. 2002)
Budget: revenues US$504 billion; expenditures US$517 billion, including capital expenditures US$ n.a. (2001 est.)
Defence Expenditures: 4.8% of central government expenditure (2001)
Education Expenditures: n.a.
External Debt: n.a.
Exports: US$241.639 billion (2002 est.); commodities: textiles, wearing apparel, metals, transportation equipment, chemicals; partners: EU, US
Imports: US$233.289 billion (2002 est.); commodities: petroleum, industrial machinery, chemicals, metals, foods, agricultural products; partners: Germany, France, Netherlands, UK, US

COMMUNICATIONS

Daily Newspapers: 104/1,000 inhabitants (2000)
Televisions: 494/1,000 inhabitants (2001)
Radios: 878/1,000 inhabitants (2001)
Telephones: 471 lines/1,000 inhabitants (2001)

TRANSPORTATION

Motor Vehicles: 34,000,000; 31,100,000 passenger cars (2000)
Roads: 668,669 km; all paved
Railway: 19,786 km
Air Traffic: 31,031,000 passengers carried (2001)
Airports: 135; 96 have paved runways (2002)

Canadian Embassy: The Canadian Embassy, Via G.B. de Rossi 27, 00161 Rome, Italy. Tel: (011-39-06) 445981. Fax: (011-39-06) 445 98750. e-mail: rome@dfait-maeci.gc.ca
Embassy in Canada: Embassy of the Italian Republic, 275 Slater St, 21st Fl, Ottawa ON K1P 5H9. Tel: (613) 232-2401. Fax: (613) 233-1484. e-mail: ambital@italyincanada.org

Jamaica

Long-Form Name: Jamaica
Capital: Kingston

GEOGRAPHY

Area: 10,990 sq. km
Coastline: 1,022 km
Climate: tropical; hot, humid; temperate interior
Environment: subject to hurricanes (especially July to Nov.); deforestation; water pollution
Terrain: mostly mountainous with narrow, discontinuous coastal plain
Land Use: 14% arable; 6% permanent crops; 24% meadows; 17% forest; 39% other; includes 250 sq. km irrigated
Location: West Indies, island in Caribbean Sea, just south of Cuba

PEOPLE

Population: 2,680,029 (July 2002 est.)
Nationality: Jamaican
Age Structure: 0–14 yrs: 29.1%; 15–64: 64.1%; 65+: 6.8% (2002 est.)
Population Growth Rate: 0.56% (2002 est.)
Net Migration: -6.65 migrants/1,000 population (2002 est.)
Ethnic Groups: 90.9% African, 7.3% mixed, 1.3% East Indian and Afro-East Indian, 0.2%

white, 0.2% Chinese and Afro-Chinese, 0.1% other
Languages: English (official), Creole
Religions: 60% Protestant, 5% Roman Catholic, 35% other
Birth Rate: 17.74/1,000 population (2002 est.)
Death Rate: 5.45/1,000 population (2002 est.)
Infant Mortality: 13.71 deaths/1,000 live births (2002 est.)
Life Expectancy at Birth: 73.65 years male, 77.73 years female (2002 est.)
Total Fertility Rate: 2.05 children born/woman (2002 est.)
Literacy: 86.9% (2000)

■ GOVERNMENT

Leader(s): Head of State: Queen Elizabeth II, Gov. Gen. Howard Cooke
Government Type: parliamentary democracy
Administrative Divisions: 14 parishes
Nationhood: Aug. 6, 1962 (from UK)
National Holiday: Independence Day, first Monday in Aug.

■ ECONOMY

Overview: key sectors in this island economy are bauxite and tourism; continued tight fiscal policies have helped slow inflation and stabilize the exchange rate, but have resulted in the slowdown of economic growth
GDP: US$9.8 billion, per capita US$3,700; real growth rate 1.1% (2001 est.)
Inflation: 7.0% (2001)
Industries: accounts for 28% of GDP (2000); tourism, bauxite mining, textiles, food processing, light manufactures
Labour Force: 1.4 million (2001); 21% agriculture, 60% community, social and business services, 19% industry
Unemployment: 15.7% (2001)
Agriculture: accounts for about 7% of GDP (2000), 22% of workforce and 17% of exports; principal crops—sugar cane, bananas, coffee, citrus, potatoes and vegetables; not self-sufficient in grain, meat and dairy products
Natural Resources: bauxite, gypsum, limestone

■ FINANCE/TRADE

Currency: Jamaican dollar ($J) = 100 cents
International Reserves Excluding Gold: US$1.646 billion (Dec. 2002)
Gold Reserves: n.a.
Budget: revenues US$2.23 billion; expenditures US$2.56 billion, including capital expenditures of US$232.5 million (1999–2000 est.)
Defence Expenditures: 1.63% of central government expenditure (2001)

Education Expenditures: 14.27% of central government expenditure (2000)
External Debt: US$4.956 billion (2001)
Exports: US$1.126 billion (2002 est.); commodities: bauxite, alumina, sugar, bananas; partners: US, EU, UK, Canada
Imports: US$3.296 billion (2002 est.); commodities: petroleum, machinery, food, consumer goods, construction goods; partners: US, CARICOM countries, Latin America, EU

■ COMMUNICATIONS

Daily Newspapers: 62/1,000 inhabitants (2000)
Televisions: 194/1,000 inhabitants (2001)
Radios: 796/1,000 inhabitants (2001)
Telephones: 197 lines/1,000 inhabitants (2001)

■ TRANSPORTATION

Motor Vehicles: 58,900; 43,500 passenger cars
Roads: 19,000 km; 13,433 km paved
Railway: 272 km
Air Traffic: 1,946,000 passengers carried (2001)
Airports: 35; 11 have paved runways (2002)

Canadian Embassy: The Canadian High Commission, 3 West Kings House Road, Kingston 10, Jamaica; mailing address: The Canadian High Commission, P.O. Box 1500, Kingston 10, Jamaica. Tel: (876) 926-1500. Fax: (876) 511-3494. e-mail: kngtn@dfait-maeci.gc.ca
Embassy in Canada: Jamaican High Commission, 275 Slater St, Ste 800, Ottawa ON K1P 5H9. Tel: (613) 233-9311. Fax: (613) 233-0611. e-mail: jhcott@comnet.ca

Japan

Long-Form Name: Japan
Capital: Tokyo

■ GEOGRAPHY

Area: 377,835 sq. km; includes Bonin Islands (Ogasawara-gunto), Daito-shoto, Minamijima, Okinotori-shima, Ryukyu Islands (Nansei-shoto) and Volcano Islands (Kazan-retto)
Coastline: 29,751 km
Climate: varies from tropical in south to cool temperate in north
Environment: many dormant and some active volcanoes; about 1,500 seismic occurrences (mostly tremors) every year; subject to tsunamis; acid rain caused by industrial emissions
Terrain: mostly rugged and mountainous
Land Use: 11% arable; 1% permanent crops; 2% permanent pastures; 67% forest and woodland; 19% other; includes 27,820 sq. km irrigated

Location: E Asia, bordering on Sea of Japan, North Pacific Ocean

■ PEOPLE

Population: 126,974,628 (July 2002 est.)
Nationality: Japanese
Age Structure: 0–14 yrs: 14.5%; 15–64: 67.5%; 65+: 18.0% (2002 est.)
Population Growth Rate: 0.15% (2002 est.)
Net Migration: 0 migrants/1,000 population (2002 est.)
Ethnic Groups: 99.4% Japanese, 0.6% other (mostly Korean)
Languages: Japanese
Religions: most Japanese observe both Shinto and Buddhist rites; about 16% belong to other faiths, including 0.8% Christian
Birth Rate: 10.03/1,000 population (2002 est.)
Death Rate: 8.53/1,000 population (2002 est.)
Infant Mortality: 3.84 deaths/1,000 live births (2002 est.)
Life Expectancy at Birth: 77.73 years male, 84.25 years female (2002 est.)
Total Fertility Rate: 1.42 children born/woman (2002 est.)
Literacy: approaching 100% (2000)

■ GOVERNMENT

Leader(s): Emperor Tsegu no Miya Akihito, Prime Min. Junichiro Koizumi
Government Type: constitutional monarchy with a parliamentary government
Administrative Divisions: 47 prefectures
Nationhood: 660 BC, traditional founding by Emperor Jimmu; May 3, 1947 constitutional monarchy established
National Holiday: Birthday of the Emperor, Dec. 23

■ ECONOMY

Overview: impressive economic growth and status as the second largest industrial economy in the world is due to government-industry co-operation and a strong work ethic; known for high-tech industry; the crowding of habitable land and the ageing population are two major long-term problems
GDP: US$3.55 trillion, per capita US$28,000; real growth rate -0.3% (2002 est.)
Inflation: -0.7% (2001)
Industries: accounts for 31% of GDP (2001 est.), metallurgy, engineering, electrical and electronics, textiles, chemicals, automobiles, fishing
Labour Force: 68.2 million (2001); 70% community, social and business services, 25% industry; 5% agriculture
Unemployment: 5% (Dec. 2002)

Agriculture: accounts for 1% of GDP (2001 est.); highly subsidized and protected sector, with crop yields among highest in the world; main crops—rice, sugar beets, vegetables, fruit; animal products include fish, pork, poultry, dairy and eggs; about 50% self-sufficient in food
Natural Resources: negligible mineral resources, fish

■ FINANCE/TRADE

Currency: yen (pl. yen) (¥)
International Reserves Excluding Gold: US$461.186 billion (Dec. 2002)
Gold Reserves: 24.602 million fine troy ounces (Dec. 2002)
Budget: revenues US$441 billion; expenditures US$718 billion, including capital expenditures of US$84 billion (2001–2002 est.)
Defence Expenditures: 3.69% of central government expenditure (2001)
Education Expenditures: n.a.
External Debt: n.a.
Exports: US$406.195 billion (2002 est.); commodities: manufactures 97% (including machinery 38%, motor vehicles 17%, consumer electronics 10%); partners: US, China, South Korea, Taiwan, Hong Kong
Imports: US$327.271 billion (2002 est.); commodities: manufactures 42%, fossil fuels 30%, foodstuffs 15%, non-fuel raw materials 13%; partners: US, China, South Korea, Taiwan, Indonesia

■ COMMUNICATIONS

Daily Newspapers: 578/1,000 inhabitants (2000)
Televisions: 731/1,000 inhabitants (2001)
Radios: 956/1,000 inhabitants (2001)
Telephones: 597 lines/1,000 inhabitants (2001)

■ TRANSPORTATION

Motor Vehicles: 71,000,000; 50,000,000 passenger cars (2000)
Roads: 1,152,207 km; 863,003 km paved
Railway: 23,654 km (2000)
Air Traffic: 107,870,000 passengers carried (2001)
Airports: 173; 141 have paved runways (2002)

Canadian Embassy: The Canadian Embassy, 3-38 Akasaka 7-chome, Minato-ku, Tokyo 107-8503, Japan. Tel: (011-81-3) 5412-6200. Fax: (011-81-3) 5412-6303. e-mail: tokyo@dfait-maeci.gc.ca
Embassy in Canada: Embassy of Japan, 255 Sussex Dr, Ottawa ON K1N 9E6. Tel: (613) 241-8541. Fax: (613) 241-2232. e-mail: n.a.

Jordan

Long-Form Name: Hashemite Kingdom of Jordan
Capital: Amman

■ GEOGRAPHY

Area: 92,300 sq. km
Coastline: 26 km
Climate: mostly arid desert; rainy season in west (Nov. to Apr.)
Environment: lack of natural water resources; deforestation; overgrazing; soil erosion; desertification
Terrain: mostly desert plateau in east, highland area in west; Great Rift Valley separates East and West Banks of the Jordan River
Land Use: 4% arable land; 1% permanent crops; 9% permanent pastures; 1% forest; 85% other; includes 750 sq. km irrigated
Location: SW Asia (Middle East), on Arabian Peninsula

■ PEOPLE

Population: 5,307,470 (July 2002 est.)
Nationality: Jordanian
Age Structure: 0–14 yrs: 36.6%; 15–64: 60.0%; 65+: 3.4% (2002 est.)
Population Growth Rate: 3.0% (2001 est.)
Net Migration: 6.97 migrants/1,000 population (2002 est.)
Ethnic Groups: 98% Arab, 1% Circassian, 1% Armenian
Languages: Arabic (official); English widely understood among upper and middle classes
Religions: Islam (92% Sunni Muslim, Shia minority), 8% Christianity
Birth Rate: 24.58/1,000 population (2002 est.)
Death Rate: 2.62/1,000 population (2002 est.)
Infant Mortality: 19.61 deaths/1,000 live births (2002 est.)
Life Expectancy at Birth: 75.26 years male, 80.30 years female (2002 est.)
Total Fertility Rate: 3.15 children born/woman (2002 est.)
Literacy: 89.7% (2000)

■ GOVERNMENT

Leader(s): King Abdullah II, Prem. Ali Abu al-Ragheb
Government Type: constitutional monarchy
Administrative Divisions: 12 governorates (muhafazat, sing. —muhafazah)
Nationhood: May 25, 1946 (from League of Nations mandate under British administration; formerly known as Trans-Jordan)

National Holiday: Independence Day, May 25

■ ECONOMY

Overview: imports are outweighing exports and foreign aid makes up the difference; droughts are a potential threat; debt, poverty and unemployment remain problems; economic recovery is unlikely without substantial foreign aid, debt relief and economic reform
GDP: US$22.8 billion, per capita US$4,300; real growth rate 3.5% (2002 est.)
Inflation: 1.8% (2001)
Industries: accounts for 26% of GDP (2001 est.); phosphate mining, petroleum refining, cement, potash, light manufacturing
Labour Force: 1.5 million (2001); 83% services, 13% industry, 5% agriculture
Unemployment: 13.2% (2001)
Agriculture: accounts for 4% of GDP (2001 est.); principal products are wheat, barley, citrus fruit, tomatoes, melons, olives; livestock—sheep, goats, poultry; large net importer of food
Natural Resources: phosphates, potash, shale oil

■ FINANCE/TRADE

Currency: Jordanian dinar (JD) = 1,000 fils
International Reserves Excluding Gold: US$3.976 billion (Dec. 2002)
Gold Reserves: 0.410 million fine troy ounces (Dec. 2002)
Budget: revenues US$2.9 billion; expenditures US$3.1 billion, including capital expenditures of US$ n.a. (2001 est.)
Defence Expenditures: 26.5% of central government expenditure (2000)
Education Expenditures: 15.93% of central government expenditure (2001)
External Debt: US$7.480 billion (2001)
Exports: US$2.588 billion (2002 est.); commodities: fruit and vegetables, phosphates, fertilizers; partners: India, US, Saudi Arabia, Israel
Imports: US$4.534 billion (2002 est.); commodities: crude oil, textiles, capital goods, motor vehicles, foodstuffs; partners: Germany, US, Italy, France

■ COMMUNICATIONS

Daily Newspapers: 75/1,000 inhabitants (2000)
Televisions: 111/1,000 inhabitants (2001)
Radios: 372/1,000 inhabitants (2001)
Telephones: 127 lines/1,000 inhabitants (2001)

■ TRANSPORTATION

Motor Vehicles: 265,000; 175,000 passenger cars
Roads: 8,000 km, all paved (2000 est.)

Railway: 677 km (2001)
Air Traffic: 1,178,000 passengers carried (2001)
Airports: 18; 15 have paved runways (2002)

Canadian Embassy: The Canadian Embassy, Pearl of Shmeisani Bldg, Shmeisani, Amman, Jordan; mailing address: P.O. Box 815403, Amman, Jordan 11180. Tel: (011-962-6) 566-61-24. Fax: (011-962-6) 568-92-27. e-mail: amman@dfait-maeci.gc.ca
Embassy in Canada: Embassy of the Hashemite Kingdom of Jordan, 100 Bronson Ave, Ste 701, Ottawa ON K1R 6G8. Tel: (613) 238-8090. Fax: (613) 232-3341. e-mail: n.a.

Kazakhstan

Long-Form Name: Republic of Kazakhstan
Capital: Astana; in December 1998 the government was moved from Almaty to Astana

■ GEOGRAPHY

Area: 2,717,300 sq. km
Coastline: none; landlocked; Kazakhstan borders the Aral Sea (1,070 km) and the Caspian Sea (1,894 km)
Climate: dry desert climate; arid and semi-arid; hot summers and cold winters
Environment: drought and desertification; lack of fresh water; drying up of Aral Sea is causing increased concentrations of chemical pesticides and natural salts; industrial pollution, including radioactive or toxic chemical sites
Terrain: desert and steppe; plains in western Siberia to oasis and desert in Central Asia
Land Use: 12% arable; 11% permanent crops; 57% meadows and pastures; 4% forests; 16% other; includes 23,320 sq. km irrigated
Location: C Asia, bordering on Caspian Sea

■ PEOPLE

Population: 16,741,519 (July 2002 est.)
Nationality: Kazakhstani
Age Structure: 0–14 yrs: 26.0%; 15–64: 66.5%; 65+: 7.5% (2002 est.)
Population Growth Rate: 0.10% (2002 est.)
Net Migration: -6.16 migrants/1,000 population (2002 est.)
Ethnic Groups: 46% Kazakh, 34.7% Russian, 4.9% Ukrainian, 3.1% German, 2.3% Uzbek, 1.9% Tatar, 7.1% other
Languages: Kazakh (official, spoken by over 40% of population), Russian (official, spoken by two-thirds of population), German, Ukrainian

Religions: primarily Sunni Muslim (47%) and Eastern Orthodox (44%), Protestant (2%), other 7%
Birth Rate: 17.83/1,000 population (2002 est.)
Death Rate: 10.69/1,000 population (2002 est.)
Infant Mortality: 58.95 deaths/1,000 live births (2002 est.)
Life Expectancy at Birth: 57.02 years male, 69.01 years female (2002 est.)
Total Fertility Rate: 2.12 children born/woman (2002 est.)
Literacy: 99% (1999)

■ GOVERNMENT

Leader(s): Pres. Nursultan A. Nazarbayev, Prime Min. Daniyal Akhmetov
Government Type: republic
Administrative Divisions: 14 oblasts (oblystar, sing. —oblysy) and 3 cities (gala, sing. —galasy)
Nationhood: Dec. 16, 1991 (from Soviet Union)
National Holiday: Day of the Republic, Oct. 25

■ ECONOMY

Overview: predominantly mining and manufacturing; agriculture possible only with irrigation; serious pollution problems, lack of modern technology and little experience in foreign markets hamper economic progress
GDP: US$98.1 billion, per capita US$5,900; real growth rate 12.2% (2001 est.)
Inflation: 8.4% (2001)
Industries: accounts for 30% of GDP (2000); coal refining, oil and natural gas extraction, mining, agricultural machinery, electric motors, construction materials
Labour Force: 7.3 million (2001) 50% community, social and business services, 20% agriculture, 30% industry
Unemployment: 13.7%; large numbers of underemployed (2001)
Agriculture: accounts for 9% of GDP (2000), and employs one-fifth of labour force; wheat, cotton, rice, vineyard and orchard crops, sheep, cattle
Natural Resources: fish, oil, natural gas, zinc, coal, lead, iron ore, rare metals, tungsten, copper, zinc, manganese, bauxite, gold

■ FINANCE/TRADE

Currency: tenge = 100 tiyn
International Reserves Excluding Gold: US$2.551 billion (Dec. 2002)
Gold Reserves: 1.708 million fine troy ounces (Dec. 2002)

Budget: revenues US$4.2 billion; expenditures US$5.1 billion, including capital expenditures of US$ n.a. (2001 est.)
Defence Expenditures: 6.8% of central government expenditure (2001)
Education Expenditures: 3.64% of central government expenditure (2000)
External Debt: US$14.372 billion (2001)
Exports: US$9.092 billion (2002 est.): fuels, karakul fleece, wool, industrial products; partners: Russia, China, Germany
Imports: US$6.399 billion (2002 est.): fuel, industrial products; partners: Russia, Germany, US

■ COMMUNICATIONS

Daily Newspapers: 3 in total
Televisions: 241/1,000 inhabitants (2001)
Radios: 411/1,000 inhabitants (2001)
Telephones: 113 lines/1,000 inhabitants (2001)

■ TRANSPORTATION

Motor Vehicles: 1,440,000; 1,100,000 passenger cars (2000)
Roads: 189,000 km; 108,100 km hard-surfaced
Railway: 13,601 km
Air Traffic: 501,000 passengers carried (2001)
Airports: 449 airfields; 28 have paved runways (2002)

Canadian Embassy: The Canadian Embassy, 34 Karasai Batir St, Almaty 480100, Kazakhstan. Tel: (011-7-3272) 50-11-51. Fax: (011-7-3272) 582-493. e-mail: almat@dfait-maeci.gc.ca
Embassy in Canada: c/o The Embassy of the Republic of Kazhakstan, 1401 16th Street NW, Washington, DC 20036, USA. Tel: (202) 232-5488. Fax: (202) 232-5845. e-mail: kazak@intr.net

Kenya

Long-Form Name: Republic of Kenya
Capital: Nairobi

■ GEOGRAPHY

Area: 582,650 sq. km
Coastline: 536 km
Climate: varies from tropical along coast to arid in interior
Environment: unique physiography supports abundant and varied wildlife of scientific and economic value, but poaching is a continuing problem; deforestation; soil erosion; desertification; glaciers on Mt Kenya; deteriorating water quality
Terrain: low plains rise to central highlands bisected by Great Rift Valley; fertile plateau in west

Land Use: 7% arable; 1% permanent crops; 37% permanent pastures; 30% forest; 25% other; includes 670 sq. km irrigated
Location: E Africa, bordering on Indian Ocean

■ PEOPLE

Population: 31,138,735 (July 2002 est.)
Nationality: Kenyan
Age Structure: 0–14 yrs: 41.1%; 15–64: 56.1%; 65+: 2.8% (2002 est.)
Population Growth Rate: 1.15% (2002 est.)
Net Migration: -1.48 migrants/1,000 population (2002 est.)
Ethnic Groups: 22% Kikuyu, 14% Luhya, 13% Luo, 12% Kalenjin, 11% Kamba, 6% Kisii, 6% Meru, 1% Asian, European and Arab, 15% other
Languages: English and Swahili (official); Kikuyu and Luo are widely spoken; numerous indigenous languages
Religions: 28% Roman Catholic, 26% indigenous beliefs, 38% Protestant, 8% other
Birth Rate: 27.61/1,000 population (2002 est.)
Death Rate: 14.68/1,000 population (2002 est.)
Infant Mortality: 67.24 deaths/1,000 live births (2002 est.)
Life Expectancy at Birth: 46.20 years male, 47.85 years female (2002 est.)
Total Fertility Rate: 3.34 children born/woman (2002 est.)
Literacy: 82.4% (2000)

■ GOVERNMENT

Leader(s): Pres. Mwai Kibaki, V. Pres. Wamalwa Kijana
Government Type: republic
Administrative Divisions: 7 provinces and 1 area
Nationhood: Dec. 12, 1963 (from UK; formerly known as British East Africa)
National Holiday: Independence Day, Dec. 12

■ ECONOMY

Overview: a large annual population growth, a deteriorating infrastructure and a shortage of arable land threaten economic growth; vulnerable to weather conditions
GDP: US$31 billion, per capita US$1,000; real growth rate 1.0% (2001 est.)
Inflation: 0.8% (2001)
Industries: accounts for 16% of GDP (2000); small-scale consumer goods (plastic, furniture, batteries, textiles, soap, cigarettes, flour), agricultural processing, oil refining, cement, tourism
Labour Force: 15.9 million (2001); 75–80% of the population is engaged in agriculture
Unemployment: 50% in urban areas (1998 est.)

Agriculture: accounts for 23% of GDP (2000) and 65% of exports; cash crops include coffee, tea, sisal, pineapple; food products—corn, wheat, sugar cane, fruit, vegetables, dairy products, poultry, eggs; food output not sufficient for existing population

Natural Resources: gold, limestone, diatomite, salt barytes, magnesite, feldspar, sapphires, fluorspar, garnets, wildlife, hydro power

■ FINANCE/TRADE

Currency: Kenyan shilling (KSh) = 100 cents
International Reserves Excluding Gold: US$1.068 billion (Dec. 2002)
Gold Reserves: 0.001 million fine troy ounces (Dec. 2002)
Budget: revenues US$2.91 billion; expenditures US$2.97 billion, including capital expenditures of US$ n.a. (2000 est.)
Defence Expenditures: 5.8% of central government expenditure (2001)
Education Expenditures: 25.64% of central government expenditure (1998)
External Debt: US$5.833 billion (2001)
Exports: US$2.084 billion (2002 est.); commodities: coffee 20%, tea 18%, manufactures 15%, petroleum products 10%; partners: US, Tanzania, Uganda, Germany
Imports: US$3.556 billion (2002 est.); commodities: machinery and transportation equipment 36%, raw materials 33%, fuels and lubricants 20%, food and consumer goods 11%; partners: UK, UAE, Japan, India

■ COMMUNICATIONS

Daily Newspapers: 10/1,000 inhabitants (2000)
Televisions: 26/1,000 inhabitants (2001)
Radios: 221/1,000 inhabitants (2001)
Telephones: 10 lines/1,000 inhabitants (2001)

■ TRANSPORTATION

Motor Vehicles: 364,900; 271,000 passenger cars
Roads: 63,300 km; 8,940 km paved
Railway: 2,778 km
Air Traffic: 1,418,000 passengers carried (2001)
Airports: 231; 19 have paved runways (2002)

Canadian Embassy: The Canadian High Commission, Comcraft House, Hailé Sélassie Ave, Nairobi; mailing address: The Canadian High Commission, P.O. Box 30481, Nairobi, Kenya. Tel: (011-254-2) 21-48-04. Fax: (011-254-2) 22-69-87. e-mail: nrobi@dfait-maeci.gc.ca
Embassy in Canada: High Commission for the Republic of Kenya, 415 Laurier Ave E, Ottawa ON K1N 6R4. Tel: (613) 563-1773. Fax: (613) 233-6599. e-mail: kenrep@on.aibn.com

Kiribati

Long-Form Name: Republic of Kiribati
Capital: Tarawa

■ GEOGRAPHY

Area: 717 sq. km
Coastline: 1,143 km
Climate: tropical; marine, hot and humid, moderated by trade winds
Environment: typhoons can occur anytime, but usually Nov. to Mar.
Terrain: mostly low-lying coral atolls surrounded by extensive reefs
Land Use: negligible arable; 51% permanent crops; 0% meadows; 3% forest; 46% other; includes n.a. sq. km irrigated
Location: SW Pacific Ocean, NE of Australia

■ PEOPLE

Population: 96,335 (July 2002 est.); only 20 of Kiribati's 33 islands are inhabited
Nationality: I-Kiribati (sing. & pl.)
Age Structure: 0–14 yrs: 40.2%; 15–64: 56.6%; 65+: 3.2% (2002 est.)
Population Growth Rate: 2.28% (2002 est.)
Net Migration: 0 migrants/1,000 population (2002 est.)
Ethnic Groups: Micronesian
Languages: English (official), Gilbertese
Religions: 52.6% Roman Catholic, 40.9% Protestant (Congregational), some Seventh-Day Adventist and Baha'i
Birth Rate: 31.58/1,000 population (2002 est.)
Death Rate: 8.76/1,000 population (2002 est.)
Infant Mortality: 52.63 deaths/1,000 live births (2002 est.)
Life Expectancy at Birth: 57.61 years male, 63.62 years female (2002 est.)
Total Fertility Rate: 4.32 children born/woman (2002 est.)
Literacy: 90.6%

■ GOVERNMENT

Leader(s): Pres. Atone Tong, V. Pres. Teima Onorio
Government Type: republic
Administrative Divisions: 3 units
Nationhood: July 12, 1979 (from UK; formerly known as Gilbert Islands)
National Holiday: Independence Day, July 12

■ ECONOMY

Overview: economy has fluctuated widely in recent years and copra production and a good fish catch have provided a boost; at present there is a moderate but steady growth trend

GDP: US$79 million, per capita US$840; real growth rate 1.5% (2001 est.). Kiribati's revenues are supplemented by a nearly equal amount from external sources
Inflation: 2% (1999 est.)
Industries: accounts for 7% of GDP; fishing, handicrafts
Labour Force: n.a.
Unemployment: n.a., but massive underemployment
Agriculture: accounts for 30% of GDP (including fishing); copra and fish contribute 65% to exports; subsistence farming predominates; food crops—taro, breadfruit, sweet potatoes, vegetables, fish; not self-sufficient in food
Natural Resources: tuna fishing

■ **FINANCE/TRADE**

Currency: Australian dollar ($A) = 100 cents
International Reserves Excluding Gold: n.a.
Gold Reserves: n.a.
Budget: revenues US$28.4 million; expenditures US$37.2 million, capital expenditures US$ n.a. (2000 est.)
Defence Expenditures: n.a.
Education Expenditures: n.a.
External Debt: US$10 million (1999 est.)
Exports: US$6 million (2000); commodities: fish 55%, copra 42%; partners: Japan, Bangladesh, US, Australia, Brazil, Poland
Imports: US$29 million (2000); commodities: foodstuffs, fuel, transportation equipment; partners: Australia, Japan, Fiji, Poland, US

■ **COMMUNICATIONS**

Daily Newspapers: none
Televisions: n.a.
Radios: n.a.
Telephones: 43 lines/1,000 inhabitants (1999)

■ **TRANSPORTATION**

Motor Vehicles: n.a.
Roads: 670 km; n.a. km paved
Railway: none
Air Traffic: 32,000 passengers carried (1999 est.)
Airports: 21; 4 have paved runways (2002)

Canadian Embassy: The Canadian High Commission to Kiribati, c/o The Canadian High Commission, P.O. Box 12-049, Thorndon, Wellington, New Zealand. Tel: (011-64-4) 473-9577. Fax: (011-64-4) 471-2082. e-mail: wlgtn@dfait-maeci.gc.ca
Embassy in Canada: c/o New Zealand High Commission, Clarica Centre, 99 Bank St, Ste 727, Ottawa, ON K1P 6G3. Tel: (613) 238-5991. Fax: (613) 238-5707. e-mail: nzhcott@istar.ca

Korea (North)

Long-Form Name: Democratic People's Republic of Korea
Capital: P'yongyang

■ **GEOGRAPHY**

Area: 120,540 sq. km
Coastline: 2,495 km
Climate: temperate with rainfall concentrated in summer
Environment: isolated mountainous interior, nearly inaccessible and sparsely populated; late-spring droughts often followed by severe flooding
Terrain: mostly hills and mountains separated by deep, narrow valleys; coastal plains wide in west, discontinuous in east
Land Use: 14% arable; 2% permanent crops; negligible meadows; 61% forest; 23% other; includes 14,600 sq. km irrigated
Location: E Asia, bordering on Yellow Sea, Sea of Japan

■ **PEOPLE**

Population: 22,224,195 (July 2002 est.)
Nationality: Korean
Age Structure: 0–14 yrs: 25.4%; 15–64: 67.4%; 65+: 7.2% (2002 est.)
Population Growth Rate: 1.10% (2002 est.)
Net Migration: 0 migrants/1,000 population (2002 est.)
Ethnic Groups: Korean (racially homogeneous)
Languages: Korean
Religions: Buddhism and Confucianism; Taoism, Shamanism, Chonodogyu; autonomous religious activities are now almost nonexistent; government-sponsored religious groups exist to provide an illusion of religious freedom
Birth Rate: 17.95/1,000 population (2002 est.)
Death Rate: 6.96/1,000 population (2002 est.)
Infant Mortality: 22.80 deaths/1,000 live births (2002 est.)
Life Expectancy at Birth: 68.31 years male, 74.44 years female (2002 est.)
Total Fertility Rate: 2.22 children born/woman (2002 est.)
Literacy: 99%

■ **GOVERNMENT**

Leader(s): Chairman National Defense Commission Kim Jong-I, Chairman of Supreme People's Assembly Kim Yong-nam
Government Type: authoritarian socialist state; one-person dictatorship
Administrative Divisions: 9 provinces (do, sing. & pl.) and 3 special cities (si, sing. & pl.)

Nationhood: Sept. 9, 1948
National Holiday: Independence Day (DPRK Foundation Day), Sept. 9

■ ECONOMY

Overview: a command economy that is almost completely socialized, with state-owned industry and collectivization of agriculture; state control over economic affairs is unusually tight even for a socialist country
GDP: US$22.0 billion, per capita US$1,000; real growth rate 1.0% (2002 est.)
Inflation: n.a.
Industries: accounts for 32% of GDP (2000); machine building, military products, electric power, chemicals, mining, metallurgy, textiles, food processing
Labour Force: 11.7 million (2001); 36% agricultural, 64% services and industry
Unemployment: n.a.
Agriculture: accounts for about 30% of GNP (2000) and 36% of workforce; principal crops—rice, corn, potatoes, soybeans, pulses; fish; livestock and livestock products—cattle, hogs, pork, eggs; not self-sufficient in grain
Natural Resources: coal, lead, tungsten, zinc, graphite, magnesite, iron ore, copper, gold, pyrites, salt, fluorspar, hydroelectricity

■ FINANCE/TRADE

Currency: North Korean won (Wn) = 100 chon
International Reserves Excluding Gold: n.a.
Gold Reserves: n.a.
Budget: n.a.
Defence Expenditures: n.a.
Education Expenditures: n.a.
External Debt: n.a.
Exports: exact figures n.a.; commodities: minerals, metallurgical products, agricultural products, manufactures; partners: former USSR countries, China, Japan, South Korea
Imports: exact figures n.a.; commodities: petroleum, machinery and equipment, coking coal, grain; partners: China, South Korea, Japan

■ COMMUNICATIONS

Daily Newspapers: 208/1,000 inhabitants (2000)
Televisions: 59/1,000 inhabitants (2001)
Radios: 154/1,000 inhabitants (2001)
Telephones: 22 lines/1,000 inhabitants (2001)

■ TRANSPORTATION

Motor Vehicles: n.a.
Roads: 31,200 km; 1,997 km paved
Railway: 5,000 km
Air Traffic: 79,000 passengers carried (2001)
Airports: 87; 39 have paved runways (2002)

Canadian Embassy: The Canadian Embassy to the Democratic People's Republic of Korea, c/o The Canadian Embassy, 19 Dong Zhi Men Wai St., Chao Yang District, Beijing 100600, People's Republic of China. Tel: (011-86-10) 6532-3536. Fax: (011-86-10) 6532-4311. e-mail: bejing@dfait-maeci.gc.ca
Embassy in Canada: c/o Permanent Mission of the Democratic People's Republic of Korea to the United Nations, 820 Second Ave., 13th Floor, New York 10017, USA. Tel: (212) 972-3105. Fax: (212) 972-3154. e-mail: n.a.

Korea (South)

Long-Form Name: Republic of Korea
Capital: Seoul

■ GEOGRAPHY

Area: 98,480 sq. km
Coastline: 2,413 km
Climate: temperate, with rainfall heavier in summer than winter
Environment: occasional typhoons bring high winds and floods; earthquakes in southwest; air and water pollution in large cities
Terrain: mostly hilly and mountainous; wide coastal plains in west and south
Land Use: 19% arable; 2% permanent crops; 1% meadows; 65% forest; 13% other; includes 11,590 sq. km irrigated
Location: E Asia, bordering on Yellow Sea, Sea of Japan

■ PEOPLE

Population: 48,324,000 (July 2002 est.)
Nationality: Korean
Age Structure: 0–14 yrs: 21.4%; 15–64: 71.0%; 65+: 7.6% (2002 est.)
Population Growth Rate: 0.85% (2002 est.)
Net Migration: 0 migrants/1,000 population (2002 est.)
Ethnic Groups: homogeneous; small Chinese minority (about 20,000)
Languages: Korean; English widely taught in high school
Religions: 48.6% Christianity, 47.4% Buddhism, 3% Confucianism, 1% other
Birth Rate: 14.55/1,000 population (2002 est.)
Death Rate: 6.02/1,000 population (2002 est.)
Infant Mortality: 7.58 deaths/1,000 live births (2002 est.)
Life Expectancy at Birth: 71.20 years male, 78.95 years female (2002 est.)
Total Fertility Rate: 1.72 children born/woman (2002 est.)
Literacy: 97.8% (2000)

■ GOVERNMENT

Leader(s): Pres. No Mu-hyon, Prime Min. Ko Kon
Government Type: republic
Administrative Divisions: 9 provinces (do, sing. & pl.) and 7 special cities (gwangyoksi, sing. & pl.)
Nationhood: Aug. 15, 1948
National Holiday: Independence Day, Aug. 15

■ ECONOMY

Overview: dynamic growth is attributed to the planned development of an export-oriented economy in a strongly entrepreneurial society; labour unrest has hurt its record of non-inflationary growth; economic growth has recovered in recent years
GDP: US$931 billion, per capita US$19,400; real growth rate 5.8% (2002 est.)
Inflation: 4.3% (2001)
Industries: accounts for 42% of GDP (2002 est.); textiles, clothing, footwear, food processing, chemicals, steel, electronics, automobile production, shipbuilding
Labour Force: 24.3 million (2001); 69% services, 22% industry, 10% agriculture
Unemployment: 3.5% (Jan. 2003)
Agriculture: accounts for 4% of GDP (2002 est.) and 21% of workforce (including fishing and forestry); main crops—rice, root crops, barley, vegetables, fruit; livestock and livestock products—cattle, hogs, chickens, milk, eggs; self-sufficient in food, except for wheat; fish catch is seventh largest in the world
Natural Resources: coal, tungsten, graphite, molybdenum, lead, hydroelectricity

■ FINANCE/TRADE

Currency: South Korean won (W) = 100 chun
International Reserves Excluding Gold: US$121.345 billion (Dec. 2002)
Gold Reserves: 0.444 million fine troy ounces (Dec. 2002)
Budget: revenues US$118.1 billion; expenditures US$95.7 billion, including capital expenditures of US$22.6 billion (2000)
Defence Expenditures: 16.6% of central government expenditure (2001)
Education Expenditures: n.a.
External Debt: US$134.417 billion (2000)
Exports: US$162.822 billion (2002); commodities: textiles, clothing, electronic and electrical equipment, footwear, machinery, steel, automobiles, ships, fish; partners: US, China, Japan, Hong Kong, Taiwan
Imports: US$141.098 billion (2002); commodities: machinery, electronics and electronic equip-

ment, oil, steel, transport equipment, textiles, organic chemicals, grains; partners: Japan, US, China, Saudi Arabia, Australia

■ COMMUNICATIONS

Daily Newspapers: 393/1,000 inhabitants (2000)
Televisions: 363/1,000 inhabitants (2001)
Radios: 1,034/1,000 inhabitants (2001)
Telephones: 486/1,000 inhabitants (2001)

■ TRANSPORTATION

Motor Vehicles: 11,400,000; 8,000,000 passenger cars (2000)
Roads: 87,534 km; 65,388 km paved (1999)
Railway: 3,124 km
Air Traffic: 32,638,000 passengers carried (2001)
Airports: 102; 69 have paved runways (2002)

Canadian Embassy: The Canadian Embassy, Fl. 10 & 11, Kolon Building, 45 Mugyo-Dong, Jung-Ku, Seoul 100-170, Korea; mailing address; P.O. Box 6299, Seoul 100-662 Korea. Tel: (011-82-2) 3455-6000. Fax: (011-82-2) 755-0686. e-mail: seoul@dfait-maeci.gc.ca
Embassy in Canada: Embassy of the Republic of Korea, 150 Boteler St, Ottawa ON K1N 5A6. Tel: (613) 244-5010. Fax: (613) 244-5043. e-mail: cultural@emb-korea.ottawa.on.ca

Kuwait

Long-Form Name: State of Kuwait
Capital: Kuwait

■ GEOGRAPHY

Area: 17,820 sq. km
Coastline: 499 km
Climate: dry desert; intensely hot summers; short, cool winters
Environment: large and sophisticated desalination plants are required for adequate drinking water supply; air and water pollution; desertification
Terrain: flat to slightly undulating desert plain
Land Use: negligible arable; 0% permanent crops; 8% meadows; negligible forest; 92% other; includes 60 sq. km irrigated
Location: SW Asia (Middle East), on Arabian Peninsula, bordering on Persian Gulf

■ PEOPLE

Population: 2,111,561; includes 1,159,913 non-nationals (July 2002 est.)
Nationality: Kuwaiti
Age Structure: 0–14 yrs: 28.3%; 15–64: 69.2%; 65+: 2.5% (2002 est.)
Population Growth Rate: 3.33% (2002 est.)

Net Migration: 13.88 migrants/1,000 population (2002 est.)
Ethnic Groups: 45% Kuwaiti, 35% other Arab, 9% South Asian, 4% Iranian, 7% other
Languages: Arabic (official); Kurdish, Farsi, English (commercial) widely spoken
Religions: 85% Muslim (30% Shi'a, 45% Sunni, 10% other), 15% Christian, Hindu, Parsi and other
Birth Rate: 21.84/1,000 population (2002 est.)
Death Rate: 2.46/1,000 population (2002 est.)
Infant Mortality: 10.87 deaths/1,000 live births (2002 est.)
Life Expectancy at Birth: 75.56 years male, 77.39 years female (2002 est.)
Total Fertility Rate: 3.14 children born/woman (2002 est.)
Literacy: 82.0% (2000)

■ GOVERNMENT

Leader(s): Prime Min. Sabah al-Ahmad al-Jabir al-Sabah, Emir Shaikh Jabir al-Ahmad al-Jabir al-Sabah
Government Type: nominal constitutional monarchy
Administrative Divisions: 5 governorates (muhafazat, sing. -muhafazah)
Nationhood: June 19, 1961 (from UK)
National Holiday: National Day, Feb. 25

■ ECONOMY

Overview: a small and relatively open economy with crude oil reserves of about 10% of world reserves; lacks water and has practically no arable land, thus preventing development of agriculture; with the exception of fish, it depends almost wholly on food imports
GDP: US$30.9 billion, per capita US$15,100; real growth rate 4.0% (2001 est.)
Inflation: 1.7% (2001)
Industries: petroleum (accounts for 60% of GDP and 90% of export revenues), petrochemicals, desalination, food processing, salt, construction
Labour Force: 800,000 (2001); 45% services, 20% construction, 12% trade, 9% manufacturing, 3% finance and real estate, 2% agriculture, 2% power and water, 1% mining and quarrying
Unemployment: n.a.
Agriculture: virtually none; dependent on imports for food; about 75% of potable water (adversely affected by the Gulf War) must be distilled or imported
Natural Resources: petroleum, fish, shrimp, natural gas

■ FINANCE/TRADE

Currency: dinar (KD) = 1,000 fils
International Reserves Excluding Gold: US$9.208 billion (Dec. 2002)
Gold Reserves: 2.539 million fine troy ounces (Dec. 2002)
Budget: revenues US$11.5 billion; expenditures US$17.2 billion, including capital expenditures US$ n.a. (FY2001/02)
Defence Expenditures: 18.8% of central government expenditure (2001)
Education Expenditures: 13.91% of central government expenditure (1999)
External Debt: US$6.9 billion (2000 est.)
Exports: US$16.203 billion (2001); commodities: oil 90%; fertilizers; partners: Japan, US, South Korea, Singapore, Netherlands, Pakistan, Indonesia, UK
Imports: US$7.869 billion (2001); commodities: food, construction material, vehicles and parts, clothing; partners: Japan, US, Germany, UK, France, Australia, Netherlands

■ COMMUNICATIONS

Daily Newspapers: 374/1,000 inhabitants (2000)
Televisions: 482/1,000 inhabitants (2001)
Radios: 624/1,000 inhabitants (2001)
Telephones: 240 lines/1,000 inhabitants (2001)

■ TRANSPORTATION

Motor Vehicles: 693,000; 538,000 passenger cars
Roads: 4,450 km; 3,590 km paved
Railway: none
Air Traffic: 2,085,000 passengers carried (2001)
Airports: 7; 3 have paved runways (2002)

Canadian Embassy: The Canadian Embassy, Villa 24, Area 4, 24 Mutawakel St, Da Aiyah, Kuwait; mailing address: P.O. Box 25281, 13113, Safat, Kuwait City, Kuwait. Tel: (011-965) 256-3025. Fax: (011-965) 256-0173. e-mail: kwait@dfait-maeci.gc.ca
Embassy in Canada: Embassy of the State of Kuwait, 80 Elgin St, Ottawa, ON K1P 1C6. Tel: (613) 780-9999. Fax: (613) 780-9905. e-mail: info@embassyofkuwait.com

Kyrgyzstan

Long-Form Name: Kyrgyz Republic
Capital: Bishkek

■ GEOGRAPHY

Area: 198,500 sq. km
Coastline: none: landlocked

Climate: dry continental to polar in high Tien Shan; subtropical in south; glacial Alpine; moderate in valley regions

Environment: frequent severe earthquakes; water pollution and water-borne diseases are widespread

Terrain: mountainous; 75% of land covered by snow and glaciers; peaks of Tien Shan rise to 7,000 meters, and associated valleys and basins encompass the entire nation

Land Use: land is cultivated mainly in valleys; 7% arable; negligible permanent crops; 44% meadows and pastures; 4% forest and woodland; 45% other; includes 10,740 sq. km irrigated

Location: C Asia, bordering on China

■ PEOPLE

Population: 4,822,166 (July 2002 est.)

Nationality: Kyrgyzstani

Age Structure: 0–14 yrs: 34.4%; 15–64: 59.4%; 65+: 6.2% (2002 est.)

Population Growth Rate: 1.45% (2002 est.)

Net Migration: -2.51 migrants/1,000 population (2002 est.)

Ethnic Groups: 52.4% Kirghiz, 18% Russian, 12.9% Uzbeks, 2.5% Ukrainian, 2.4% German, 1.6% Tatars, 10.2% other

Languages: Kirghiz and Russian (both official) and Dungan

Religions: 75% Muslim, 20% Eastern Orthodox, 5% other

Birth Rate: 26.11/1,000 population (2002 est.)

Death Rate: 9.10/1,000 population (2002 est.)

Infant Mortality: 75.92 deaths/1,000 live births (2002 est.)

Life Expectancy at Birth: 59.35 years male, 67.98 years female (2002 est.)

Total Fertility Rate: 3.16 children born/woman (2002 est.)

Literacy: approaching 100% (2000)

■ GOVERNMENT

Leader(s): Pres. Askar Akayev, Prime Min. Nikolai Tanayev

Government Type: republic

Administrative Divisions: 7 provinces (oblastar, pl., sing. —oblasty) and 1 city

Nationhood: August 31, 1991 (from Soviet Union)

National Holiday: National Day, Dec. 2; also Independence Day, Aug. 31

■ ECONOMY

Overview: a small, poor, mountainous country with a predominantly agricultural economy; has been one of the most progressive countries of the former Soviet Union in carrying out market reforms; foreign assistance played a substantial role in the country's recent economic turnaround

GDP: US$13.5 billion, per capita US$2,800; real growth rate 5% (2001 est.)

Inflation: 6.9% (2001)

Industries: accounts for 27% of GDP (2000); small machinery, cement, shoes, furniture and appliances, electronics, electrical engineering, silk making, rare earth metals

Labour Force: 2.2 million (2001); 55% agriculture and forestry, 15% industry and construction, 30% other services

Unemployment: n.a.

Agriculture: accounts for 38% of GDP (2000); irrigation required; wheat, barley, beets, cotton, fruit, vegetables, potatoes, cotton, grain, tobacco, livestock: sheep, goats, cattle

Natural Resources: mercury, antimony, zinc, tungsten deposits, coal, natural gas, oil, nepheline, bismuth, mercury, lead, zinc

■ FINANCE/TRADE

Currency: Kyrgyzstani som = 100 tyiyn

International Reserves Excluding Gold: US$289 million (Dec. 2002)

Gold Reserves: 0.083 million fine troy ounces (Dec. 2002)

Budget: revenues US$207.4 million, expenditures US$238.7 million, including capital expenditures of US$ n.a. (1999 est.)

Defence Expenditures: 10.0% of central government expenditure (2001)

Education Expenditures: 19.5% of central government expenditure (2000)

External Debt: US$1.717 billion (2001)

Exports: US$480 million (2001); agricultural products, antimony, silk, carpets, non-ferrous metals, electrical equipment, cotton, wool, meat, tobacco, gold, mercury, hydro power, machinery, consumer goods; partners: Germany, Russia, Kazakhstan, Uzbekistan, China

Imports: US$472 million (2001); grain, lumber, industrial products, metals, fuel, machinery, consumer goods; partners: Russia, Kazakhstan, Uzbekistan, US, Turkey

■ COMMUNICATIONS

Daily Newspapers: 27/1,000 inhabitants (2000)

Televisions: 49/1,000 inhabitants (2001)

Radios: 110/1,000 inhabitants (2001)

Telephones: 78 lines/1,000 inhabitants (2001)

■ TRANSPORTATION

Motor Vehicles: 185,000; 180,000 passenger cars (2000)

Roads: 30,300 km; 22,600 km paved or graveled

Railway: 370 km, plus industrial lines
Air Traffic: 192,000 passengers carried (2001)
Airports: 50; 4 have paved runways (2002)

Canadian Embassy: c/o The Canadian Embassy, 34 Karasai Batir St, Almaty 480100, Kazakhstan. Tel: (011-7-3272) 50-11-51. Fax: (011-7-3272) 582-493. e-mail: almat@dfait-maeci.gc.ca
Embassy in Canada: c/o Embassy of the Kyrgyz Republic, 1732 Wisconsin Ave NW, Washington DC 20007, USA. Tel: (202) 338-5141. Fax: (202) 338-5139. e-mail: n.a.

Laos

Long-Form Name: Lao People's Democratic Republic
Capital: Vientiane

■ GEOGRAPHY

Area: 236,800 sq. km
Coastline: none: landlocked
Climate: tropical monsoon; rainy season (May to Nov.); dry season (Dec. to Apr.)
Environment: deforestation; soil erosion; subject to floods; limited safe drinking water
Terrain: mostly rugged mountains; some plains and plateaus
Land Use: 3% arable land; negligible permanent crops; 3% meadows; 54% forest; 40% other; includes between 750 and 1,640 sq. km irrigated
Location: SE Asia

■ PEOPLE

Population: 5,777,180 (July 2002 est.)
Nationality: Laotian or Lao
Age Structure: 0–14 yrs: 42.5%; 15–64: 54.2%; 65+: 3.3% (2002 est.)
Population Growth Rate: 2.47% (2002 est.)
Net Migration: 0 migrants/1,000 population (2002 est.)
Ethnic Groups: mostly Laotian; Vietnamese, Kha, Thai, Meo, Hmong, Yao, Chinese, European, Indian and Pakistani minorities
Languages: Lao (official), French, English, tribal languages
Religions: 60% Buddhist, 40% animist and other
Birth Rate: 37.39/1,000 population (2002 est.)
Death Rate: 12.71/1,000 population (2002 est.)
Infant Mortality: 90.98 deaths/1,000 live births (2002 est.)
Life Expectancy at Birth: 51.95 years male, 55.87 years female (2002 est.)
Total Fertility Rate: 5.03 children born/woman (2002 est.)
Literacy: 48.7% (2000)

■ GOVERNMENT

Leader(s): Pres. Khamtai Siphandon, Prime Min. Boungnang Volachit
Government Type: communist state
Administrative Divisions: 16 provinces (khoueng, sing. & pl.) and 1 municipality (kampheng nakhon, sing. & pl.) and 1 special zone (khetphiset, sing. & pl.)
Nationhood: July 19, 1949 (from France)
National Holiday: National Day (proclamation of the Lao People's Democratic Republic), Dec. 2

■ ECONOMY

Overview: one of the world's poorest nations, landlocked with a primitive infrastructure; while traditionally a communist centrally planned economy with government ownership and control of productive enterprises, the government is now decentralizing control and encouraging some private enterprise; heavily dependent on foreign aid
GDP: US$9.2 billion, per capita US$1,630; real growth rate 5.0% (2001 est.)
Inflation: 7.8% (2001)
Industries: accounts for 22% of GDP (2000); tin mining, timber, electric power, agricultural processing
Labour Force: 2.6 million (2001); 80% agriculture, 5% industry, 15% services
Unemployment: n.a.
Agriculture: accounts for 53% of GDP (2000) and employs most of the labour force; subsistence farming predominates; normally self-sufficient; principal crops—rice (80% of cultivated land), potatoes, vegetables, coffee, tea, sugar cane, cotton
Natural Resources: timber, hydroelectricity, gypsum, tin, gold, gemstones

■ FINANCE/TRADE

Currency: new kip (NK) = 100 at
International Reserves Excluding Gold: US$192 million (Nov. 2002)
Gold Reserves: 0.072 million fine troy ounces (Dec. 2002)
Budget: n.a.
Defence Expenditures: 11.1% of central government expenditure (1999)
Education Expenditures: n.a.
External Debt: US$2.495 billion (2001)
Exports: US$298 million (2002); wood products, electricity, tin, consumer goods; partners: Thailand, Germany, France, UK, Belgium
Imports: US$431 million (2002); machinery and equipment, fuel, vehicles; partners: Thailand, Japan, China, Singapore, Hong Kong

■ COMMUNICATIONS

Daily Newspapers: 4/1,000 inhabitants (2000)
Televisions: 52/1,000 inhabitants (2001)
Radios: 148/1,000 inhabitants (2001)
Telephones: 10 lines/1,000 inhabitants (2001)

■ TRANSPORTATION

Motor Vehicles: 21,000; 10,000 passenger cars
Roads: 14,000 km; 3,360 km paved
Railway: none
Air Traffic: 211,000 passengers carried (2001)
Airports: 51; 9 have paved runways (2002)

Canadian Embassy: The Canadian Embassy to Laos, c/o P.O. Box 2090, Bangkok 10501 Thailand. Tel: (011-66-2) 636-0540. Fax: (011-66-2) 636-0565. e-mail: bngkk@dfait-maeci.gc.ca
Embassy in Canada: c/o Embassy of the Lao People's Democratic Republic, 2222 S St NW, Washington DC 20001, USA. Tel: (202) 332-6416. Fax: (202) 332-4923. e-mail: n.a.

Latvia

Long-Form Name: Republic of Latvia
Capital: Riga

■ GEOGRAPHY

Area: 64,589 sq. km
Coastline: 531 km
Climate: maritime, wet, moderate winters
Environment: air and water pollution, soil and groundwater contaminated with chemicals and petroleum products at military bases
Terrain: hilly, forested land with many lakes and shallow valleys
Land Use: 27% arable; negligible permanent crops; 13% meadows and pastures; 46% forest; 14% other; includes 200 sq. km irrigated
Location: NE Europe, bordering on Baltic Sea

■ PEOPLE

Population: 2,366,515 (July 2002 est.)
Nationality: Latvian
Age Structure: 0–14 yrs: 15.8%; 15–64: 68.6%; 65+: 15.6% (2002 est.)
Population Growth Rate: -0.77% (2002 est.)
Net Migration: -1.23 migrants/1,000 population (2002 est.)
Ethnic Groups: 56.5% Latvian, 30.4% Russian, 4.3% Belorussian, 2.8% Ukrainian, 2.6% Polish, 3.4% other
Languages: Lettish (official), Lithuanian, Russian, some others
Religions: Lutheran, Catholic, Russian Orthodox
Birth Rate: 8.27/1,000 population (2002 est.)
Death Rate: 14.74/1,000 population (2002 est.)

Infant Mortality: 14.96 deaths/1,000 live births (2002 est.)
Life Expectancy at Birth: 63.13 years male, 75.17 years female (2002 est.)
Total Fertility Rate: 1.18 children born/woman (2002 est.)
Literacy: 99.8% (2000)

■ GOVERNMENT

Leader(s): Pres. Vaira Vike-Freiberga, Prime Min. Einars Repse
Government Type: parliamentary democracy
Administrative Divisions: 26 counties (sing. — rajons) and 7 municipalities
Nationhood: Aug. 21, 1991 (from Soviet Union)
National Holiday: Independence Day, Nov. 18

■ ECONOMY

Overview: lacks natural resources, aside from its arable land and small forests; its most valuable economic asset is its workforce, which is better educated and disciplined than in most of the former Soviet republics; rapidly moving towards a dynamic market economy,
GDP: US$20 billion, per capita US$8,300; real growth rate 4.5% (2002 est.)
Inflation: 2.5% (2001)
Industries: accounts for 26% of GDP (2001) and 31% of labour force; manufacturing of railroad cars, paper, woollen goods, electronics and engineering, food processing
Labour Force: 1.3 million (2001); 25% industry, 15% forestry and agriculture, 60% services
Unemployment: 7.9% (June 2002)
Agriculture: accounts for 5% of GDP (2001), employs 9% of labour force and has become largely privatized; poor soil hinders agriculture products including grain, beets, potatoes, cattle and dairy farming, poultry, eggs, fishing
Natural Resources: forests, peat deposits, amber, dolomite, hydroelectric power, arable land

■ FINANCE/TRADE

Currency: lat = 100 santims
International Reserves Excluding Gold: US$1.241 billion (Dec. 2002)
Gold Reserves: 0.249 milllion fine troy ounces (Dec. 2002)
Budget: revenues US$2.4 billion, expenditures US$2.6 billion, including capital expenditures of US$ n.a. (2002 est.)
Defence Expenditures: 3.9% of central government expenditure (2001)
Education Expenditures: 5.62% of central government expenditure (2000)
External Debt: US$5.710 billion (2001)

Exports: US$2.223 billion (2002); vehicles, household appliances, electric power, textiles; partners: Germany, UK, Sweden, Lithuania, Russia

Imports: US$3.831 billion (2002): fuels, cars, chemicals and metal products; partners: Russia, Germany, Lithuania, Finland, Sweden

■ COMMUNICATIONS

Daily Newspapers: 135/1,000 inhabitants (2000)
Televisions: 840/1,000 inhabitants (2001)
Radios: 700/1,000 inhabitants (2001)
Telephones: 308 lines/1,000 inhabitants (2001)

■ TRANSPORTATION

Motor Vehicles: 620,000; 520,000 passenger cars (2000)
Roads: 59,178 km; 22,843 km paved
Railway: 2,412 km (2001)
Air Traffic: 305,000 passengers carried (2001)
Airports: 25; 13 have paved runways (2002)

Canadian Embassy: The Canadian Embassy, Doma Laukums 4, 4th Fl, Riga LV-1977, Latvia. Tel. (011-371) 783-0141. Fax: (011-371) 783-1040. e-mail: riga@dfait-maeci.gc.ca
Embassy in Canada: Embassy of the Republic of Latvia, 280 Albert St Ste 300, Ottawa, ON, K1P 5G8. Tel: (613) 238-6014. Fax: (613) 238-7044. e-mail: embassy.canada@mfa.gov.lv

Lebanon

Long-Form Name: Lebanese Republic
Capital: Beirut

■ GEOGRAPHY

Area: 10,400 sq. km
Coastline: 225 km
Climate: Mediterranean; mild to cool, wet winters with hot, dry summers; heavy snowfall in winter in Lebanon Mountains
Environment: deforestation; soil erosion; air and water pollution; desertification
Terrain: narrow coastal plain; al Biqa' separates Lebanon and Anti-Lebanon Mountains; rugged terrain historically helped isolate, protect and develop numerous factional groups based on religion, clan and ethnicity
Land Use: 18% arable; 9% permanent crops; 1% meadow; 8% forest; 64% other; includes 1,200 sq. km irrigated
Location: SW Asia (Middle East), bordering on Mediterranean Sea

■ PEOPLE

Population: 3,627,774 (July 2001 est.)
Nationality: Lebanese (sing. & pl.)

Age Structure: 0–14 yrs: 27.3%; 15–64: 65.9%; 65+: 6.8% (2002 est.)
Population Growth Rate: 1.36% (2002 est.)
Net Migration: 0 migrants/1,000 population (2002 est.)
Ethnic Groups: 95% Arab, 4% Armenian, 1% other
Languages: Arabic and French (both official); Armenian, English, Kurdish
Religions: Muslim 70% (Sunni, Shia and Druse), Christian 30% (mainly Maronite; also, Armenian, Greek and Syrian sects and Protestants)
Birth Rate: 19.96/1,000 population (2002 est.)
Death Rate: 6.35/1,000 population (2002 est.)
Infant Mortality: 27.39 deaths/1,000 live births (2002 est.)
Life Expectancy at Birth: 69.38 years male, 74.32 years female (2002 est.)
Total Fertility Rate: 2.02 children born/woman (2002 est.)
Literacy: 86.0% (2000)

■ GOVERNMENT

Leader(s): Pres. Emile Jamil Lahud, Prime Min. Rafiq Hariri
Government Type: republic
Administrative Divisions: 5 governorates (muhafazat, sing. —muhafazah)
Nationhood: Nov. 22, 1943 (from League of Nations mandate under French administration)
National Holiday: Independence Day, Nov. 22

■ ECONOMY

Overview: Factional infighting has led to deterioration of the infrastructure and disrupted normal economic activity in what used to be the centre for Middle Eastern banking; high unemployment; growing shortages; international aid is vital
GDP: US$18.8 billion, per capita US$5,200; real growth rate 1.0% (2001 est.)
Inflation: 0% (2000 est.)
Industries: accounts for 21% of GDP (2000); banking, food processing, textiles, cement, oil refining, chemicals, jewellery, some metal fabricating
Labour Force: 1.6 million (2001); 27.4% industry, 58.4% services, 14.3% agriculture
Unemployment: n.a.
Agriculture: accounts for about 12% of GDP (2000); principal products—citrus fruit, grapes, tomatoes, apples, vegetables, potatoes, olives, tobacco, hemp (hashish), sheep and goats; not self-sufficient in grain
Natural Resources: limestone, iron ore, salt; water-surplus state in a water-deficit region

■ FINANCE/TRADE

Currency: Lebanese pound (£L) = 100 piasters
International Reserves Excluding Gold: US$7.244 billion (Dec. 2002)
Gold Reserves: 9.222 million fine troy ounces (Dec. 2002)
Budget: revenues US$4.6 billion; expenditures US$8.9 billion, including capital expenditures of US$ n.a. (2001 est.)
Defence Expenditures: 14% of central government expenditure (2001)
Education Expenditures: 7.23% of central government expenditure (1999)
External Debt: US$12.450 billion (2001)
Exports: US$717 million (2000); commodities: agricultural products, chemicals, tobacco, textiles, metals and jewellery; partners: 21% Saudi Arabia, UAE, Switzerland, US, France, Iraq, Jordan, Kuwait, Syria
Imports: US$6.253 billion (2000); commodities: consumer goods, machinery and transport equipment, metals, petroleum products; partners: Italy, France, Germany, US, Switzerland, Japan, China, Syria, UK

■ COMMUNICATIONS

Daily Newspapers: 107/1,000 inhabitants (2000)
Televisions: 336/1,000 inhabitants (2001)
Radios: 182/1,000 inhabitants (2001)
Telephones: 195 lines/1,000 inhabitants (2001)

■ TRANSPORTATION

Motor Vehicles: 1,200,000; 1,135,000 passenger cars (2000)
Roads: 7,300 km; 6,200 km paved
Railway: 399 km; railroad system in disrepair, considered inoperable
Air Traffic: 816,000 passengers carried (2001)
Airports: 8; 5 have paved runways (2002)

Canadian Embassy: The Canadian Embassy, 43 Jal-el-Dib Highway, 1st floor, Jal-ed-Dib, Lebanon; mailing address: P.O. Box 60163, Jal-el-Dib, Beirut, Lebanon. Tel: (011-961-4) 713-900. Fax: (011-961-4) 710-595. e-mail: berut@dfait-maeci.gc.ca
Embassy in Canada: Embassy of the Lebanese Republic, 640 Lyon St, Ottawa ON K1S 3Z5. Tel: (613) 236-5825. Fax: (613) 232-1609. e-mail: info@lebanonembassy.ca

---

Lesotho

Long-Form Name: Kingdom of Lesotho
Capital: Maseru

■ GEOGRAPHY

Area: 30,355 sq. km
Coastline: none: landlocked
Climate: temperate; cool to cold, dry winters; hot, wet summers
Environment: population pressure forcing settlement in marginal agricultural areas results in overgrazing, severe soil erosion, soil exhaustion; desertification
Terrain: mostly highland with some plateaus, hills and mountains
Land Use: 11% arable; 0% permanent crops; 66% meadows; 0% forest; 23% other; includes 10 sq. km irrigated
Location: S Africa

■ PEOPLE

Population: 2,207,954 (July 2002 est.)
Nationality: Mosotho (sing.), Basotho (pl.)
Age Structure: 0–14 yrs: 39.0%; 15–64: 56.3%; 65+: 4.7% (2002 est.)
Population Growth Rate: 1.33% (2002 est.)
Net Migration: -0.63 migrants/1,000 population (2002 est.)
Ethnic Groups: 99.7% Sotho; 0.3% Europeans, Asians and other
Languages: Sesotho (southern Sotho) and English (official); also Zulu and Xhosa
Religions: 80% Christian, indigenous beliefs
Birth Rate: 30.72/1,000 population (2002 est.)
Death Rate: 16.81/1,000 population (2002 est.)
Infant Mortality: 82.57 deaths/1,000 live births (2002 est.)
Life Expectancy at Birth: 46.30 years male, 47.80 years female (2002 est.)
Total Fertility Rate: 4.01 children born/woman (2002 est.)
Literacy: 83.4% (2000)

■ GOVERNMENT

Leader(s): King Letsie III, Prime Min. Bethuel Pakalitha Mosisili
Government Type: parliamentary constitutional monarchy
Administrative Divisions: 10 districts
Nationhood: Oct. 4, 1966 (from UK: formerly known as Basutoland)
National Holiday: Independence Day, Oct. 4

■ ECONOMY

Overview: the economy is hampered by the geography of the country (small, landlocked and mountainous) and the lack of natural resources other than water; subsistence farming is the main occupation; labourers in South Africa make remittances; industry is growing in importance

GDP: US$5.3 billion, per capita US$2,450; real growth rate 2.6% (2001 est.)
Inflation: -9.6% (2001)
Industries: accounts for 38% of GDP (2001); light manufacturing, milling, canning, leather, jute production, textiles, clothing, light engineering, food, beverages, handicrafts, tourism
Labour Force: 900,000 (2001); 86% agriculture
Unemployment: 45% (2000 est.)
Agriculture: accounts for 18% of GDP (2001); very primitive, mostly subsistence farming and livestock; principal crops are corn, wheat, pulses, sorghum and barley
Natural Resources: some diamonds and other minerals, water, agricultural and grazing land

■ FINANCE/TRADE

Currency: loti, maloti (pl.) = 100 lisente; also the South African rand
International Reserves Excluding Gold: US$411 million (Nov. 2002)
Gold Reserves: n.a.
Budget: revenues US$76 million, expenditures US$80 million, including capital expenditures of $US n.a. (FY1999/2000 est.)
Defence Expenditures: 6.4% of central government expenditure (2001)
Education Expenditures: n.a.
External Debt: US$593 million (2001)
Exports: US$280 million (2001); commodities: wool, mohair, wheat, cattle, peas, beans, corn, hides, skins, baskets; partners: South African Customs Union, North American countries
Imports: US$682 million (2001); commodities: corn, building materials, clothing, vehicles, machinery, medicines, petroleum, oil and lubricants; partners: South African Customs Union, Asian countries

■ COMMUNICATIONS

Daily Newspapers: 8/1,000 inhabitants (2000)
Televisions: 16/1,000 inhabitants (2001)
Radios: 53/1,000 inhabitants (2001)
Telephones: 10 lines/1,000 inhabitants (2001)

■ TRANSPORTATION

Motor Vehicles: n.a.
Roads: 4,955 km; 887 km paved
Railway: 2.6 km, owned, operated by and included in the statistics for South Africa
Air Traffic: n.a.
Airports: 28; 4 have paved runways (2002)

Canadian Embassy: The Canadian High Commission to Lesotho, 1103 Arcadia St., Hatfield, Pretoria 0028. Mailing address: c/o Canadian Embassy, Private Bag X13, Hatfield 0028, Pretoria, South Africa. Tel: (011-27-12) 422-3000. Fax: (011-27-12) 422-3052. e-mail: pret@dfait-maeci.gc.ca
Embassy in Canada: c/o High Commission for the Kingdom of Lesotho, 2511 Massachusetts Ave NW, Washington DC 20008, USA. Tel: (202) 797-5533. Fax: (202) 234-6815. e-mail: n.a.

Liberia

Long-Form Name: Republic of Liberia
Capital: Monrovia

■ GEOGRAPHY

Area: 111,370 sq. km
Coastline: 579 km
Climate: tropical; hot, humid; dry winters with hot days and cool to cold nights; wet, cloudy summers with frequent heavy showers
Environment: West Africa's largest tropical rainforest, subject to deforestation; soil erosion is increasingly a problem; river pollution
Terrain: mostly flat to rolling coastal plains rising to rolling plateau and low mountains in northeast
Land Use: 1% arable; 3% permanent crops; 59% permanent pastures; 18% forest; 19% other; includes 30 sq. km irrigated
Location: W Africa, bordering on South Atlantic Ocean

■ PEOPLE

Population: 3,288,198 (July 2002 est.)
Nationality: Liberian
Age Structure: 0–14 yrs: 43.3%; 15–64: 53.2%; 65+: 3.5% (2002 est.)
Population Growth Rate: 1.91% (2002 est.)
Net Migration: -10.80 migrants/1,000 population (2002 est.)
Ethnic Groups: 95% indigenous African tribes, including Kpelle, Bassa, Gio, Kru, Grego, Mano, Krahn, Gola, Gbandi, Lom, Kissi, Vai and Bella; 2.5% descendants of repatriated slaves known as Americo-Liberians, and 2.5% Congo People (descendants of immigrants from the Caribbean who had been slaves)
Languages: English (official); 20 local languages of the Niger-Congo language group; English used by approx. 20%
Religions: 70% traditional, 20% Muslim, 10% Christian
Birth Rate: 45.95/1,000 population (2002 est.)
Death Rate: 16.05/1,000 population (2002 est.)
Infant Mortality: 130.21 deaths/1,000 live births (2002 est.)

Life Expectancy at Birth: 50.33 years male, 53.33 years female (2002 est.)
Total Fertility Rate: 6.29 children born/woman (2002 est.)
Literacy: 48.4%

■ GOVERNMENT

Leader(s): Pres. Moses Zeh Blah
Government Type: republic
Administrative Divisions: 13 counties
Nationhood: July 26, 1847
National Holiday: Independence Day, July 26

■ ECONOMY

Overview: civil war since 1990 has destroyed much of Liberia's economy, especially the infrastructure in and around Monrovia; many businesspeople have fled the country, taking capital and expertise with them; the government must encourage foreign investment to restore the infrastructure and to raise incomes
GDP: US$3.6 billion, per capita US$1,100; real growth rate 5.0% (2001 est.)
Inflation: 5% (2000 est.)
Industries: accounts for 10% of GDP; rubber processing, food processing, construction materials, furniture, palm oil processing, mining (iron ore, diamonds)
Labour Force: 1.3 million (2001); 70% agriculture, 22% services, 8% industry
Unemployment: 70%
Agriculture: including fishing and forestry, accounts for 60% of GDP (2001 est.); principal products—rubber, timber, coffee, cocoa, rice, cassava, palm oil, sugar cane, bananas, sheep and goats; not self-sufficient in food, imports 25% of rice consumption
Natural Resources: iron ore, timber, diamonds, gold, hydro power

■ FINANCE/TRADE

Currency: Liberian dollar ($L) = 100 cents
International Reserves Excluding Gold: none (Aug. 2002)
Gold Reserves: n.a.
Budget: revenues US$85.4 million; expenditures US$90.5 million, capital expenditures US$ n.a. (2000 est.)
Defence Expenditures: 8.3% of central government expenditure (1999)
Education Expenditures: n.a.
External Debt: US$1.987 billion (2001)
Exports: US$1.328 billion (2000); commodities: diamonds, iron ore, rubber, timber, coffee, cocoa; partners: Belgium, Germany, Italy, US

Imports: US$1.036 billion (2000); commodities: mineral fuels, chemicals, machinery, foodstuffs; partners: France, South Korea, Japan, Singapore

■ COMMUNICATIONS

Daily Newspapers: 12/1,000 inhabitants (2000)
Televisions: 25/1,000 inhabitants (2001)
Radios: 274/1,000 inhabitants (2001)
Telephones: 2 lines/1,000 inhabitants (2001)

■ TRANSPORTATION

Motor Vehicles: 28,700; 17,800 passenger cars
Roads: 10,600 km; 657 km paved
Railway: 490 km
Air Traffic: n.a.
Airports: 47; 2 have paved runways (2002)

Canadian Embassy: The Canadian Embassy, Immeuble Trade-Center, 23 rue Nogues, Le Plateau, Abidjan; mailing address: BP 4104, Abidjan 01, Côte d'Ivoire. Tel: (011-225) 20-30-07-00. Fax: (011-225) 20-30-07-20. e-mail: abdjn@dfait-maeci.gc.ca
Embassy in Canada: c/o Consulate of Liberia, 1441 Ontario St., Burlington, ON, L7S 1G5. Tel: (905) 333-4000. Fax: (905)632-4000. e-mail: n.a.

Libya

Long-Form Name: Socialist People's Libyan Arab Jamahiriya
Capital: Tripoli

■ GEOGRAPHY

Area: 1,759,540 sq. km
Coastline: 1,770 km
Climate: Mediterranean along coast; dry, extreme desert interior
Environment: hot, dry, dust-laden ghibli (a southern wind lasting one to four days in spring and fall); desertification; dust storms; sparse natural surface-water resources
Terrain: mostly barren, flat to undulating plains, plateaus, depressions
Land Use: 1% arable; 0% permanent crops; 8% meadows; 0% forest; 91% other; includes 4,700 sq. km irrigated
Location: N Africa, bordering on Mediterranean Sea

■ PEOPLE

Population: 5,368,585; includes 662,669 non-nationals (July 2002 est.)
Nationality: Libyan

Age Structure: 0–14 yrs: 35.0%; 15–64: 61.0%; 65+: 4.0% (2002 est.)
Population Growth Rate: 2.41% (2002 est.)
Net Migration: 0 migrants/1,000 population (2002 est.)
Ethnic Groups: 97% Berber and Arab; some Greeks, Maltese, Italians, Egyptians, Pakistanis, Turks, Indians and Tunisians
Languages: Arabic (official); Italian and English widely understood in major cities, Berber
Religions: 97% Sunni Muslim, 3% Christian and other
Birth Rate: 27.59/1,000 population (2002 est.)
Death Rate: 3.50/1,000 population (2002 est.)
Infant Mortality: 27.90 deaths/1,000 live births (2002 est.)
Life Expectancy at Birth: 73.71 years male, 78.11 years female (2002 est.)
Total Fertility Rate: 3.57 children born/woman (2002 est.)
Literacy: 80% (2000)

■ GOVERNMENT

Leader(s): Leader Col. Mu'ammar Abu Minyar al-Qadhafi, Sec. Gen. of People's Congress Muhammad al-Zanati
Government Type: Jamahiriya (a state of the masses); in theory, governed by the populace through local councils; in fact, a military dictatorship
Administrative Divisions: 25 municipalities (baladiyat, sing. —baladiyah)
Nationhood: Dec. 24, 1951 (from Italy)
National Holiday: Revolution Day, Sept. 1

■ ECONOMY

Overview: a socialist-oriented economy that depends largely on revenues from the oil sector; cutbacks on imports due to declining oil revenues have led to shortages of foodstuffs and basic goods; must import 75% of its food needs, as poor soil and climate limit agricultural production
GDP: US$40 billion, per capita US$7,600; real growth rate 3.0% (2001 est.)
Inflation: 18.5% (2000 est.)
Industries: accounts for 47% of GDP; petroleum, food processing, textiles, handicrafts, cement
Labour Force: 1.6 million (2001); 29% industry, 54% services, 17% agriculture
Unemployment: 30% (2000 est.)
Agriculture: accounts for 7% of GDP; cash crops—wheat, barley, olives, dates, citrus fruit, peanuts, soybeans; 75% of food is imported
Natural Resources: crude oil, natural gas, gypsum

■ FINANCE/TRADE

Currency: Libyan dinar (LD) = 1,000 dirhams
International Reserves Excluding Gold: US$14.769 billion (Dec. 2002)
Gold Reserves: n.a.
Budget: revenues US$9.3 billion; expenditures US$9.2 billion, including capital expenditures of US$ n.a. (2001 est.)
Defence Expenditures: 3.9% of GDP (2000)
Education Expenditures: n.a.
External Debt: US$4.1 billion (2000 est.)
Exports: US$9.021 billion (2001); commodities: petroleum, peanuts, hides; partners: Italy, Germany, Spain, Turkey, France, Tunisia
Imports: US$4.449 billion (2001); commodities: machinery, transport equipment, food, manufactured goods; partners: Italy, Germany, UK, Tunisia, France, South Korea.

■ COMMUNICATIONS

Daily Newspapers: 15/1,000 inhabitants (2000)
Televisions: 137/1,000 inhabitants (2001)
Radios: 273/1,000 inhabitants (2001)
Telephones: 109 lines/1,000 inhabitants (2001)

■ TRANSPORTATION

Motor Vehicles: 904,000; 592,000 passenger cars
Roads: 83,200 km; 47,590 km paved
Railway: none
Air Traffic: 583,000 passengers carried (2001)
Airports: 136; 58 have paved runways (2002)

Canadian Embassy: The Canadian Embassy, Al-Fateh Tower, 7th Fl, P.O. Box 93392, Al-Fateh Tower Post Office, Tripoli, Libya. Tel: (011-218-21) 335-1633. Fax: (011-218-21) 335-1630. e-mail: trpli@dfait-maeci.gc.ca
Embassy in Canada: Embassy of the Socialist People's Libyan Arab Jamahiriya, 81 Metcalfe St Ste 1000, Ottawa ON K1P 6K7. Tel: (613) 230-0919. Fax: (613) 230-0683. e-mail: n.a.

Liechtenstein

Long-Form Name: Principality of Liechtenstein
Capital: Vaduz

■ GEOGRAPHY

Area: 160 sq. km
Coastline: none: landlocked
Climate: continental; cold, cloudy winters with frequent snow or rain; cool to moderately warm, cloudy, humid summers
Environment: variety of microclimatic variations based on elevation

Terrain: mostly mountainous (Alps) with Rhine Valley in western third.

Land Use: 24% arable; 0% permanent crops; 16% meadows; 35% forest; 25% other; includes n.a. sq. km irrigated

Location: C Europe, bordering on Switzerland and Austria

■ PEOPLE

Population: 32,842 (July 2002 est.)

Nationality: Liechtensteiner

Age Structure: 0–14 yrs: 18.3%; 15–64: 70.5%; 65+: 11.2% (2002 est.)

Population Growth Rate: 0.94% (2002 est.)

Net Migration: 4.93 migrants/1,000 population (2002 est.)

Ethnic Groups: 87.5% Alemannic, 12.5% Italian, Turkish and other

Languages: German (official), also Alemannic dialect

Religions: 87.3% Roman Catholic, 8.3% Protestant, 2.8% other; 1.6% unknown

Birth Rate: 11.24/1,000 population (2002 est.)

Death Rate: 6.76/1,000 population (2002 est.)

Infant Mortality: 4.92 deaths/1,000 live births (2002 est.)

Life Expectancy at Birth: 75.47 years male, 82.74 years female (2002 est.)

Total Fertility Rate: 1.5 children born/woman (2002 est.)

Literacy: approaching 100%

■ GOVERNMENT

Leader(s): Head of State: Prince Hans Adam II von und zu Liechtenstein, Prime Min. Otmar Hasler

Government Type: hereditary constitutional monarchy

Administrative Divisions: 11 communes (gemeinden, sing. —gemeinde)

Nationhood: Jan. 23, 1719, Imperial Principality of Liechtenstein established

National Holiday: Assumption Day, Aug. 15

■ ECONOMY

Overview: a prosperous economy based mainly on small-scale light industry and some farming; economy closely tied to that of Switzerland in a customs union; known for low business taxes and easy incorporation rules

GDP: n.a.

Inflation: n.a.

Industries: electronics, metal manufacturing, textiles, ceramics, pharmaceuticals, food products, precision instruments, tourism

Labour Force: approx. 23,500, of which 13,847 are foreigners; 48% industry, trade and building, 51% services, 1% agriculture, fishing, forestry and horticulture

Unemployment: 1.8% (Feb. 1999)

Agriculture: livestock, vegetables, corn, barley, wheat, potatoes, grapes

Natural Resources: hydroelectric potential, arable land

■ FINANCE/TRADE

Currency: Swiss franc, franken, or franco (SwF) = 100 centimes, rappen, or centesimi

International Reserves Excluding Gold: n.a.

Gold Reserves: n.a.

Budget: n.a.

Defence Expenditures: defence is the responsibility of Switzerland

Education Expenditures: n.a.

External Debt: none

Exports: exact figures not available; small speciality machinery, dental products, stamps, hardware, pottery; partners: EU, US, Switzerland

Imports: exact figures not available; commodities: machinery, metal goods, textiles, foodstuffs, motor vehicles; partners: EU countries, Switzerland

■ COMMUNICATIONS

Daily Newspapers: 2 in total

Televisions: n.a.

Radios: n.a.

Telephones: 609 lines/1,000 inhabitants (1999)

■ TRANSPORTATION

Motor Vehicles: n.a.

Roads: 250 km; all paved

Railway: 18.5 km, owned, operated and included in statistics for Austria

Air Traffic: n.a.

Airports: none

Canadian Embassy: The Canadian Embassy, Kirchenfeldstrasse 88, Bern, 3005, Switzerland. Mailing address: The Canadian Embassy to Liechtenstein, c/o the Canadian Embassy, P.O. Box 3000, Berne 6, Switzerland. Tel: (011-41-31) 357-32-00. Fax: (011-41-31) 357-32-10. e-mail: bern@dfait-maeci.gc.ca

Embassy in Canada: Embassy of Liechtenstein, c/o Embassy of Switzerland, 5 Marlborough Ave, Ottawa ON K1N 8E6. Tel: (613) 235-1837. Fax: (613) 563-1394. e-mail: vertretung@ott.rep.admin.ch

Lithuania

Long-Form Name: Republic of Lithuania
Capital: Vilnius

■ GEOGRAPHY

Area: 65,200 sq. km
Coastline: 99 km
Climate: transitional, between maritime and continental; mild, with moderate precipitation
Environment: risk of accidents from the two Chernobyl-type reactors; at military bases, contamination of soil and groundwater with chemicals and petroleum products
Terrain: undulating glacial terrain; rivers, lakes and swamps predominate
Land Use: 39% arable; 9% permanent crops; 6% permanent pastures; 31% forest; 15% other; includes 90 sq. km irrigated
Location: NE Europe, bordering on Baltic Sea

■ PEOPLE

Population: 3,601,138 (July 2002 est.)
Nationality: Lithuanian
Age Structure: 0–14 yrs: 18.2%; 15–64: 68.0%; 65+: 13.8% (2002 est.)
Population Growth Rate: -0.25% (2002 est.)
Net Migration: 0.15 migrants/1,000 population (2002 est.)
Ethnic Groups: 80.6% Lithuanian, 8.7% Russian, 7% Polish, 1.6% Byelorussian, 2.1% other
Languages: Lithuanian (official), Russian, Polish
Religions: predominantly Protestant, Roman Catholic, Russian Orthodox
Birth Rate: 10.22/1,000 population (2002 est.)
Death Rate: 12.87/1,000 population (2002 est.)
Infant Mortality: 14.34 deaths/1,000 live births (2002 est.)
Life Expectancy at Birth: 63.54 years male, 75.60 years female (2002 est.)
Total Fertility Rate: 1.40 children born/woman (2002 est.)
Literacy: 99.6% (2000)

■ GOVERNMENT

Leader(s): Pres. Rolandas Paksas, Prime Min. Algirdas Mikolas Brazauskas
Government Type: parliamentary democracy
Administrative Divisions: 10 counties (apskritys, sing. —apskritis)
Nationhood: Sept. 6, 1991 (from Soviet Union)
National Holiday: Independence Day, Feb. 16

■ ECONOMY

Overview: arable land and strategic location are Lithuania's only important natural resources; Lithuania remains highly dependent on Russia for energy, raw materials, grains and markets for its products
GDP: US$29.2 billion, per capita US$8,400; real growth rate 4.5% (2002 est.)
Inflation: 1.2% (2001)
Industries: accounts for 31% of GDP (2001 est.) and employs 42% of labour force; heavy engineering, shipbuilding, production of building materials, nuclear and electric power production; electric motors, television sets, appliances, refining, fertilizer
Labour Force: 1.8 million (2001); 30% industry, 50% community, social and business services, 20% agriculture
Unemployment: 10.9% (Dec. 2002)
Agriculture: accounts for 8% of GDP (2001 est.) and employs approximately 18% of labour force; beef and dairy cattle and related products, pigs, poultry, grains, flax, potatoes and other vegetables, eggs, fish, dairy products; net exporter of meat, milk, eggs and fish
Natural Resources: amber, peat

■ FINANCE/TRADE

Currency: litas (pl. litai) = 100 centas
International Reserves Excluding Gold: US$2.356 billion (Dec. 2002)
Gold Reserves: 0.186 million fine troy ounces (Dec. 2002)
Budget: revenues US$1.59 billion; expenditures US$1.77 billion, capital expenditures US$ n.a. (2001 est.)
Defence Expenditures: 6.8% of central government expenditure (2001)
Education Expenditures: 5.82% of central government expenditure (2000)
External Debt: US$5.248 billion (2001)
Exports: US$5.299 billion (2002); 18% electronics, 5% petroleum products, 10% food, 6% chemicals; partners: UK, Latvia, Germany, Russia, Poland
Imports: US$7.245 billion (2002); 24% oil, 14% machinery, 8% chemicals, grain, textiles and clothing; partners: Russia, Germany, Poland, Italy, France

■ COMMUNICATIONS

Daily Newspapers: 29/1,000 inhabitants (2000)
Televisions: 422/1,000 inhabitants (2001)
Radios: 524/1,000 inhabitants (2001)
Telephones: 313 lines/1,000 inhabitants (2001)

■ TRANSPORTATION

Motor Vehicles: 1,160,000; 1,000,000 passenger cars (2000)

Roads: 44,000 km; 35,500 km paved (2000)
Railway: 1,998 km
Air Traffic: 304,000 passengers carried (2001)
Airports: 72; 9 have paved runways (2002)

Canadian Embassy: Office of the Canadian Embassy, Gedimino pr. 64, 2001 Vilnius, Lithuania. Tel: (011-370) 249-7865. Fax: (011-370) 249-6884. e-mail: vilnius@canada.lt
Embassy in Canada: Embassy of the Republic of Lithuania, 130 Albert St, Ste 204, Ottawa, ON K1P 5G4. Tel: (613) 567-5458. Fax: (613) 567-5315. e-mail: litemb@storm.ca

Luxembourg

Long-Form Name: Grand Duchy of Luxembourg
Capital: Luxembourg

■ GEOGRAPHY

Area: 2,586 sq. km
Coastline: none: landlocked
Climate: modified continental with mild winters, cool summers
Environment: deforestation; air and water pollution in urban areas
Terrain: mostly gently rolling uplands with broad, shallow valleys; uplands to slightly mountainous in the north; steep slope down to Moselle floodplain in the southeast
Land Use: 24% arable; 1% permanent crops; 20% meadows; 21% forest; 34% other; including 40 sq. km irrigated shared with Belgium
Location: NC Europe, bordering on Belgium, France and Germany

■ PEOPLE

Population: 448,569 (July 2002 est.)
Nationality: Luxembourger
Age Structure: 0–14 yrs: 18.9%; 15–64: 67.0%; 65+: 14.1% (2002 est.)
Population Growth Rate: 1.25% (2002 est.)
Net Migration: 9.26 migrants/1,000 population (2002 est.)
Ethnic Groups: Celtic base, with French and German blend; also guest and worker residents
Languages: Luxembourgisch (official), German (written language of commerce and press), French (administrative), English
Religions: 97% Roman Catholic, 3% Protestant and Jewish
Birth Rate: 12.06/1,000 population (2002 est.)
Death Rate: 8.83/1,000 population (2002 est.)
Infant Mortality: 4.71 deaths/1,000 live births (2002 est.)

Life Expectancy at Birth: 74.20 years male, 80.97 years female (2002 est.)
Total Fertility Rate: 1.70 children born/woman (2002 est.)
Literacy: approaching 100% (2000)

■ GOVERNMENT

Leader(s): Head of State: Henri, Grand Duke of Luxembourg, Prime Min. Jean-Claude Juncker
Government Type: constitutional monarchy
Administrative Divisions: 3 districts
Nationhood: 1839 (Grand Duchy)
National Holiday: National Day (public celebration of the Grand Duke's birthday), June 23

■ ECONOMY

Overview: a stable economy featuring moderate growth, low inflation and negligible unemployment; is in an economic union with Belgium for trade and most financial matters, and is also closely connected economically with the Netherlands; financial sector is strong; industrial sector is becoming increasingly diversified
GDP: US$20 billion, per capita US$44,000; real growth rate 2.3% (2002 est.)
Inflation: 2.7% (2001)
Industries: accounts for 30% of GDP; banking, iron and steel, food processing, chemicals, metal products, engineering, tires, glass, aluminum
Labour Force: 248,000 (2000); 90% community, social and business services, 8% industries, 2% agriculture
Unemployment: 3.4% (Dec. 2002)
Agriculture: accounts for only 1% of GDP (including forestry); principal products—barley, oats, potatoes, wheat, fruits, wine grapes; cattle-raising widespread
Natural Resources: iron ore (no longer exploited), arable land

■ FINANCE/TRADE

Currency: Luxembourg franc (LuxF) = 100 centimes; Euro (€); on January 1, 2002 the Euro became the sole currency for everyday transactions.
International Reserves Excluding Gold: US$152 million (Dec. 2002)
Gold Reserves: 0.076 million fine troy ounces (Dec. 2002)
Budget: revenues US$5.5 billion; expenditures US$5.5 billion, including capital expenditures US$760 million (2002 est.)
Defence Expenditures: n.a.
Education Expenditures: n.a
External Debt: n.a.
Exports: US$6.304 billion (2002 est.); commodities: finished steel products, chemicals,

rubber products, glass, aluminum, other industrial products; partners: Germany, France, Belgium, US
Imports: US$11.109 billion (2002 est.); commodities: minerals, metals, foodstuffs, quality consumer goods; partners: Germany, Belgium, France, US

■ COMMUNICATIONS

Daily Newspapers: 5 in total
Televisions: n.a.
Radios: n.a.
Telephones: 724 lines/1,000 inhabitants (1999)

■ TRANSPORTATION

Motor Vehicles: 251,000; 233,000 passenger cars
Roads: 5,166 km; all paved (1999)
Railway: 274 km (2001)
Air Traffic: 640,000 passengers carried (1999 est.)
Airports: 2; 1 has paved runways (2002)

Canadian Embassy: The Canadian Embassy to Luxembourg, c/o 2, Avenue de Tervuren, 1040 Brussels, Belgium. Tel: (011-32-2) 741-0611. Fax: (011-32-2) 741-0643. e-mail: bru@dfait-maeci.gc.ca
Embassy in Canada: c/o Embassy of the Grand Duchy of Luxembourg, 2200 Massachusetts Ave NW, Washington DC 20008, USA. Tel: (202) 265-4171. Fax: (202) 328-8270. e-mail: info@luxembourg-usa.org

Macau

Long-Form Name: Macau Special Administrative Region
Capital: none

■ GEOGRAPHY

Area: 21 sq. km (a peninsula and three small islands)
Climate: subtropical maritime; marine with cool winters, warm summers
Land Use: 98% built-up; almost no agricultural lands or fresh water resources
Location: SE coast of China, bordering on South China Sea

■ PEOPLE

Population: 461,833 (July 2002 est.)
Nationality: Chinese
Ethnic Groups: Chinese 95%, Portuguese 3%, other 2%
Languages: Portuguese (official), Cantonese, English widely spoken

■ GOVERNMENT

Colony/Territory of: Special Administrative Region of China
Leader(s): Pres. Hu Jintao (China), Chief Exec. Edmund Ho Hau-wah
Government Type: reverted to China Dec. 20, 1999
National Holiday: National Day, Oct. 1; Dec. 20 is celebrated as Macau Special Administrative Region Establishment Day

■ ECONOMY

Overview: gambling and tourism; industry confined to textiles, fireworks, toy-making, plastics; imports almost all energy, food and water from China

■ FINANCE/TRADE

Currency: pataca (pl. patacas) = 100 avos

Canadian Embassy: n.a.
Representative to Canada: none

Macedonia

Long-Form Name: The Former Yugoslav Republic of Macedonia
Capital: Skopje

■ GEOGRAPHY

Area: 25,333 sq. km
Coastline: none: landlocked
Climate: hot, dry summers and autumns; winters relatively cold with heavy snowfall
Environment: high earthquake hazard; air pollution from metallurgical plants
Terrain: mountainous, with deep valleys and basins; three large lakes
Land Use: 24% arable land; 2% permanent crops; 25% permanent pastures; 39% forests; 10% other; includes 550 sq. km irrigated
Location: SE Europe

■ PEOPLE

Population: 2,054,800 (July 2002 est.)
Nationality: Macedonian
Age Structure: 0–14 yrs: 22.4%; 15–64: 67.2%; 65+: 10.4% (2002 est.)
Population Growth Rate: 0.41% (2002 est.)
Net Migration: -1.49 migrants/1,000 population (2002 est.)
Ethnic Groups: 66.6% Macedonian, 22.7% Albanian, 4% Turkish, 2.1% Serb, 2.2% Gypsies, 2.4% other
Languages: 70% Macedonian, 21% Albanian, 3% Turkish, 3% Serbo-Croatian, 3% other

Religions: 67% Eastern Orthodox, 30% Muslim, 3% other
Birth Rate: 13.35/1,000 population (2002 est.)
Death Rate: 7.74/1,000 population (2002 est.)
Infant Mortality: 12.54 deaths/1,000 live births (2002 est.)
Life Expectancy at Birth: 72.01 years male, 76.68 years female (2002 est.)
Total Fertility Rate: 1.77 children born/woman (2002 est.)
Literacy: 94% (1999)

■ GOVERNMENT

Leader(s): Pres. Boris Trajkovski, Prem. Branko Crvenkovski
Government Type: parliamentary democracy
Administrative Divisions: 123 municpalities (opstini, sing. —opstina)
Nationhood: Sept. 17, 1991 (from Yugoslavia)
National Holiday: Independence Day, Sept. 8; Uprising Day, Aug. 2

■ ECONOMY

Overview: although it is the poorest of the six republics of the dissolved Yugoslav federation, Macedonia can meet its basic food requirements; new economic ties are necessary, however, to keep living standards from falling to a bare subsistence level; all oil, gas, modern machinery and parts must be imported; continued political upheaval prevents return to settled economic conditions; an important supplement to GDP is the remittances from thousands of Macedonians working in Germany and other West European countries; continued recovery depends on Macedonia's ability to attract investment, to redevelop trade ties with Greece and Serbia and Montenegro, and to maintain its commitment to economic liberalization
GDP: US$10 billion, per capita US$5,000; real growth rate 3.8% (2002 est.)
Inflation: 11.0% (2000)
Industries: accounts for 31% of GDP (2001 est.); level of technology is generally low; basic liquid fuels, coal, metallic chromium, lead, zinc; Macedonia is one of the seven legal cultivators of the opium poppy for the world pharmaceutical industry
Labour Force: 1 million (2001); 35.2% industry, 20.2% community, social and business services, 11.6% trade and tourism
Unemployment: 34.5% (2001)
Agriculture: highly labour-intensive; accounts for 11% of GDP (2001 est.). Rice, tobacco, corn, sesame, citrus, millet and wheat are the chief crops; livestock production includes beef, pork and poultry
Natural Resources: chromium, lead, zinc, manganese, tungsten, nickel, iron ore, asbestos, timber

■ FINANCE/TRADE

Currency: denar = 100 deni
International Reserves Excluding Gold: US$721 million (Dec. 2002)
Gold Reserves: 0.918 million fine troy ounces (Dec. 2002)
Budget: revenues US$850 million; expenditures US$950 million, capital expenditures US$ n.a. (2001 est.)
Defence Expenditures: 2.17% of GDP (2000–2001)
Education Expenditures: n.a.
External Debt: US$1.423 billion (2001)
Exports: US$1.083 billion (2002 est.); manufactured goods, machinery and transportation equipment, raw materials, food and livestock, tobacco and beverages, chemicals; partners: Serbia and Montenegro, Germany, Greece, Italy, US
Imports: US$1.840 billion (2002 est.); fuel and lubricants, machinery and transport equipment, food and livestock, chemicals, raw materials, manufactures; partners: Germany, Greece, Serbia and Montenegro, Russia, Slovenia

■ COMMUNICATIONS

Daily Newspapers: 21/1,000 inhabitants (2000)
Televisions: 282/1,000 inhabitants (2001)
Radios: 205/1,000 inhabitants (2001)
Telephones: 263 lines/1,000 inhabitants (2001)

■ TRANSPORTATION

Motor Vehicles: n.a.
Roads: 8,684 km; 5,540 km paved
Railway: 699 km (2001)
Air Traffic: 316,000 passengers carried (2001)
Airports: 17; 10 have paved runways (2002)

Canadian Embassy: Office of the Canadian Embassy, 44 Mitropolit Teodosij Gologanov, 1000 Skopje, Former Yugoslav Republic of Macedonia, Tel: (011-389-2) 125-228. Fax: (011-389-2) 122-681. e-mail: skpje@dfait-maeci.gc.ca
Embassy in Canada: Embassy of the Former Yugoslav Republic of Macedonia, 130 Albert St Ste 1006, Ottawa, ON, K1P 5G4. Tel: (613) 234-3882. Fax: (613) 233-1852. e-mail: emb.macedonia.ottawa@sympatico.ca

Madagascar

Long-Form Name: Republic of Madagascar
Capital: Antananarivo

■ GEOGRAPHY

Area: 587,040 sq. km
Coastline: 4,828 km
Climate: tropical along coast, temperate inland, arid in south
Environment: subject to periodic cyclones; deforestation; overgrazing; soil erosion; desertification; water pollution
Terrain: narrow coastal plain; high plateau and mountains in centre
Land Use: 4% arable; 1% permanent crops; 41% permanent pastures; 40% forest; 14% other; includes 10,900 sq. km irrigated
Location: island in the Indian Ocean, E of Africa

■ PEOPLE

Population: 16,473,477 (July 2002 est.)
Nationality: Malagasy
Age Structure: 0–14 yrs: 45.0%; 15–64: 51.8%; 65+: 3.2% (2002 est.)
Population Growth Rate: 3.03% (2002 est.)
Net Migration: 0 migrants/1,000 population (2002 est.)
Ethnic Groups: basic split between highlanders of predominantly Malayo-Indonesian origin (Merina and Betsileo) and coastal tribes, collectively termed the Côtiers, with mixed African, Malayo-Indonesian and Arab ancestry (Betsimisaraka, Tsimihety, Antaiska, Sakalava)
Languages: French and Malagasy (both official)
Religions: 52% indigenous beliefs; approx. 41% Christian, 7% Muslim
Birth Rate: 42.41/1,000 population (2002 est.)
Death Rate: 12.15/1,000 population (2002 est.)
Infant Mortality: 81.90 deaths/1,000 live births (2002 est.)
Life Expectancy at Birth: 53.45 years male, 58.11 years female (2002 est.)
Total Fertility Rate: 5.77 children born/woman (2002 est.)
Literacy: 66.5% (2000)

■ GOVERNMENT

Leader(s): Pres. Marc Ravalomanana, Prime Min. Jacques Sylla
Government Type: republic
Administrative Divisions: 6 provinces (faritany)
Nationhood: June 26, 1960 (from France; formerly known as Malagasy Republic)
National Holiday: Independence Day, June 26

■ ECONOMY

Overview: a poor country, hampered by high population growth and a GDP growth rate that is not keeping pace; agriculture is the basis of the economy; industrial development is hurt by government policies restricting imports of equipment and spare parts
GDP: US$14 billion, per capita US$870; real growth rate 5.0% (2001 est.)
Inflation: 6.9% (2001)
Industries: accounts for 14% of GDP (2000); agricultural processing (meat canneries, soap factories, breweries, tanneries, sugar refining), light consumer goods industries (textiles, glassware), cement, automobile assembly plant, paper, petroleum
Labour Force: 7.6 million (2001); 59.2% community, social and business services, 26.7% agriculture
Unemployment: n.a.
Agriculture: accounts for 30% of GDP (2000); cash crops—coffee, vanilla, sugar cane, cloves, cocoa; food crops—rice, cassava, beans, bananas, peanuts; almost self-sufficient in rice
Natural Resources: graphite, chromite, coal, bauxite, salt, quartz, tar sands, semi-precious stones, mica, fish

■ FINANCE/TRADE

Currency: Malagasy franc (FMG) = 100 centimes
International Reserves Excluding Gold: US$373 million (Nov. 2002)
Gold Reserves: n.a.
Budget: n.a.
Defence Expenditures: 7.1% of central government expenditure (2001)
Education Expenditures: n.a.
External Debt: US$4.701 billion (2000)
Exports: US$238 million (2000); commodities: coffee 45%, vanilla 15%, cloves 11%, shellfish, sugar, petroleum products; partners: France, Japan, Italy, Germany, US, UK
Imports: US$501 million (2000); commodities: intermediate manufactures 30%, capital goods 28%, petroleum 15%, consumer goods 14%, food 13%; partners: France, Hong Kong, China, Singapore, Japan

■ COMMUNICATIONS

Daily Newspapers: 5/1,000 inhabitants (2000)
Televisions: 24/1,000 inhabitants (2001)
Radios: 216/1,000 inhabitants (2001)
Telephones: 4 lines/1,000 inhabitants (2001)

■ TRANSPORTATION

Motor Vehicles: 74,700; 58,900 passenger cars

Roads: 49,837 km; 5,781 km paved
Railway: 893 km (2001)
Air Traffic: 624,000 passengers carried (2001)
Airports: 130; 29 have paved runways (2002)

Canadian Embassy: The Canadian Embassy to Madagascar, P.O. Box 1022, Dar-es-Salaam, Tanzania. Tel: (011-255-22) 211-2831. Fax: (011-255-22) 211-6897. e-mail: dslam@dfait-aeci.gc.ca
Embassy in Canada: Embassy of the Republic of Madagascar, 649 Blair Rd, Ottawa, ON KIJ 7M4. Tel: (613) 744-7995. Fax: (613) 744-2530. e-mail: ambamadott@on.aibn.com

Malawi

Long-Form Name: Republic of Malawi
Capital: Lilongwe

■ GEOGRAPHY

Area: 118,480 sq. km
Coastline: none: landlocked
Climate: tropical; rainy season (Nov. to May); dry season (May to Nov.)
Environment: deforestation; water pollution; soil degradation
Terrain: narrow elongated plateau with rolling plains, rounded hills, some mountains
Land Use: 34% arable; 0% permanent crops; 20% meadows; 39% forest; 7% other; includes 280 sq. km irrigated
Location: SE Africa

■ PEOPLE

Population: 10,701,824 (July 2002 est.)
Nationality: Malawian
Age Structure: 0–14 yrs: 44.0%; 15–64: 53.2%; 65+: 2.8% (2002 est.)
Population Growth Rate: 1.39% (2002 est.)
Net Migration: 0 migrants/1,000 population (2002 est.)
Ethnic Groups: Chewa, Nyanja, Tumbuko, Yao, Lomwe, Sena, Tonga, Ngoni, Ngonde, Asian, European
Languages: English and Chichewa (both official); other languages important regionally
Religions: 55% Protestant, 20% Roman Catholic, 25% Muslim, traditional indigenous beliefs
Birth Rate: 37.13/1,000 population (2002 est.)
Death Rate: 23.20/1,000 population (2002 est.)
Infant Mortality: 119.96 deaths/1,000 live births (2002 est.)
Life Expectancy at Birth: 36.05 years male, 37.15 years female (2002 est.)

Total Fertility Rate: 5.04 children born/woman (2002 est.)
Literacy: 59.2% (1999)

■ GOVERNMENT

Leader(s): Pres. Bakili Muluzi, Vice Pres. Justin Malewezi
Government Type: multiparty democracy
Administrative Divisions: 24 districts
Nationhood: July 6, 1964 (from UK; formerly known as Nyasaland)
National Holiday: Independence Day, July 6; Republic Day, July 6

■ ECONOMY

Overview: one of the world's least developed countries; the economy is predominantly agricultural, with about 90% of the population living in rural areas; economy depends heavily on foreign aid
GDP: US$7 billion, per capita US$660; real growth rate 1.7% (2001 est.)
Inflation: 29.5% (2000)
Industries: accounts for 19% of GDP (2000); agricultural processing (tea, tobacco, sugar), sawmilling, cement, consumer goods
Labour Force: 5.1 million (2001); 86% agriculture, 14% industry and services
Unemployment: n.a.
Agriculture: accounts for 40% of GDP (2000); crops: tobacco, sugar cane, cotton, tea, corn, potatoes, cassava; subsistence crops: cattle and goats
Natural Resources: limestone; unexploited deposits of uranium, coal and bauxite

■ FINANCE/TRADE

Currency: kwacha (K) = 100 tambala
International Reserves Excluding Gold: US$165 million (Dec. 2002)
Gold Reserves: 0.010 million fine troy ounces (Dec. 2002)
Budget: revenues US$490 million, expenditures US$523 million, including capital expenditures of US$ n.a. (FY1999/2000 est.)
Defence Expenditures: 2.2% of central government expenditure (1999)
Education Expenditures: n.a.
External Debt: US$2.602 billion (2001)
Exports: US$415 million (2002 est.); commodities: tobacco, tea, sugar, coffee, peanuts; partners: US, UK, South Africa, Germany, Japan, Netherlands
Imports: US$599 million (2002 est.); commodities: food, petroleum, semi-manufactures, consumer goods, transportation equipment;

partners: South Africa, Japan, US, UK, Zimbabwe, Germany, Zambia

■ COMMUNICATIONS

Daily Newspapers: 3/1,000 inhabitants (2000)
Televisions: 4/1,000 inhabitants (2001)
Radios: 499/1,000 inhabitants (2001)
Telephones: 5 lines/1,000 inhabitants (2001)

■ TRANSPORTATION

Motor Vehicles: 54,300; 25,400 passenger cars
Roads: 28,400 km; 5,254 km paved
Railway: 797 km (2001)
Air Traffic: 113,000 passengers carried (2001)
Airports: 44; 6 have paved runways (2002)

Canadian Embassy: The Canadian High Commission to Malawi, c/o The Canadian High Commission, 5199 United Nations Ave, Lusaka; mailing address: P.O. Box 31313 Lusaka, Zambia. Tel: (011-260-1) 25-08-33. Fax: (011-260-1) 25-41-76. e-mail: lsaka@dfait-maeci.gc.ca
Embassy in Canada: High Commission for the Republic of Malawi, 7 Clemow Ave, Ottawa ON K1S 2A9. Tel: (613) 236-8931. Fax: (613) 236-1054. e-mail: malawi.highcommission@sympatico.ca

Malaysia

Long-Form Name: Malaysia
Capital: Kuala Lumpur

■ GEOGRAPHY

Area: 329,750 sq. km; includes Sabah and Sarawak
Coastline: 4,675 km total (2,068 km Peninsular Malaysia, 2,607 km East Malaysia)
Climate: tropical; annual southwest (Apr. to Oct.) and northeast (Oct. to Feb.) monsoons
Environment: subject to flooding; air and water pollution; deforestation
Terrain: coastal plains rising to hills and mountains
Land Use: 3% arable; 12% permanent crops; negligible meadows; 68% forest; 17% other; includes 3,650 sq. km irrigated
Location: SE Asia, bordering on South China Sea

■ PEOPLE

Population: 22,622,365 (July 2002 est.)
Nationality: Malaysian
Age Structure: 0–14 yrs: 34.1%; 15–64: 61.6%; 65+: 4.3% (2002 est.)

Population Growth Rate: 1.91% (2002 est.)
Net Migration: 0 migrants/1,000 population (2002 est.)
Ethnic Groups: 58% Malay and other indigenous, 26% Chinese, 7% Indian, 9% other
Languages: Peninsular Malaysia: Malay (official), English, Chinese dialects, Tamil; State of Sabah: English, Malay, numerous tribal dialects; Chinese State of Sarawak: English, Malay, Mandarin, numerous tribal languages
Religions: Peninsular Malaysia: Muslim (Malays), Buddhist (Chinese), Hindu (Indians); State of Sabah: 38% Muslim, 17% Christian, 45% other; Chinese State of Sarawak: 35% tribal religions, 24% Buddhist and Confucianist, 20% Muslim, 16% Christian, 5% other
Birth Rate: 24.22/1,000 population (2002 est.)
Death Rate: 5.16/1,000 population (2002 est.)
Infant Mortality: 19.66 deaths/1,000 live births (2002 est.)
Life Expectancy at Birth: 68.75 years male, 74.12 years female (2002 est.)
Total Fertility Rate: 3.18 children born/woman (2002 est.)
Literacy: 87.5% (2000)

■ GOVERNMENT

Leader(s): Paramount Ruler: Tuanka Syed Sirajuddin ibni Almarhum Tuanka Syed Putra Jamalullail, Prime Min. Mahathir bin Mohamad
Government Type: constitutional monarchy nominally headed by the paramount ruler (king) and a bicameral parliament
Administrative Divisions: 13 states (negeri-negeri, sing. —negeri) and 2 federal territories (wilaya-wilaya persekutuan, sing. —wilayah persekutuan)
Nationhood: Aug. 31, 1957 (from UK)
National Holiday: Independence/Malaysia Day, Aug. 31

■ ECONOMY

Overview: vulnerable to recession or a fall in world commodity prices because of its high export dependence; the world's largest producer of semiconductor devices; the majority of the rural population subsists at the poverty level but recent increases in economic output have improved living standards and real income; foreign investment has increased significantly in recent years
GDP: US$200 billion, per capita US$9,000; real growth rate 0.3% (2001 est.)
Inflation: 1.4% (2001)
Industries: accounts for 40% of GDP (2001); rubber and oil palm processing and manu-

facturing, light manufacturing industries, electronics, tin mining and smelting, logging and processing timber, petroleum production, agriculture processing

Labour Force: 10.0 million (2001); 16% agriculture, 27% industry, 10% services, trade and tourism 28%, other 19%

Unemployment: 3.0% (2001)

Agriculture: accounts for 12% of GDP (2001); Peninsular Malaysia—natural rubber, palm oil, cocoa, rice; Sabah—mainly subsistence; main crops—rubber, timber, coconut, rice; Sarawak—main crops—rubber, timber, pepper; there is a deficit of rice in all areas

Natural Resources: tin, crude oil, timber, copper, iron ore, natural gas, bauxite

■ FINANCE/TRADE

Currency: ringgit ($M) = 100 sen

International Reserves Excluding Gold: US$34.222 billion (Dec. 2002)

Gold Reserves: 1.170 million fine troy ounces (Dec. 2002)

Budget: revenues US$20.3 billion; expenditures US$27.2 billion, including capital expenditures of US$9.4 billion (2001 est.)

Defence Expenditures: 10.6% of central government expenditure (2001)

Education Expenditures: n.a.

External Debt: US$43.351 billion (2001)

Exports: US$92.240 billion (2002 est.); commodities: natural rubber, palm oil, tin, timber, petroleum, electronics, light manufactures; partners: US, Singapore, Japan, Hong, Kong, Netherlands, China, Thailand

Imports: US$79.589 billion (2002 est.); commodities: food, crude oil, consumer goods, intermediate goods, capital equipment, chemicals; partners: Japan, US, Singapore, Taiwan, China, Germany, Thailand

■ COMMUNICATIONS

Daily Newspapers: 158/1,000 inhabitants (2000)

Televisions: 201/1,000 inhabitants (2001)

Radios: 420/1,000 inhabitants (2001)

Telephones: 196 lines/1,000 inhabitants (2001)

■ TRANSPORTATION

Motor Vehicles: 4,400,000; 3,700,000 passenger cars (2000)

Roads: 64,672 km; 48,707 km paved

Railway: Peninsular Malaysia: 1,672 km; Sabah: 134 km; Sarawak: none (2001)

Air Traffic: 16,311,000 passengers carried (2001)

Airports: 116; 35 have paved runways (2002)

Canadian Embassy: The Canadian High Commission, Menara Tan + Tan, 17th floor, 207 Jalan Tun Razak, 50400 Kuala Lumpur, Malaysia; mailing address: P.O. Box 10990, 50732 Kuala Lumpur, Malaysia. Tel: (011-60-3) 2718-3333. Fax: (011-60-3) 2718-3399. e-mail: klmpr@dfait-maeci.gc.ca

Embassy in Canada: High Commission for Malaysia, 60 Boteler St, Ottawa ON K1N 8Y7. Tel: (613) 241-5182. Fax: (613) 241-5214. e-mail: mwottawa@istar.ca

Maldives

Long-Form Name: Republic of Maldives

Capital: Malé

■ GEOGRAPHY

Area: 300 sq. km; 1,190 coral islands grouped in 26 atolls

Coastline: 644 km

Climate: tropical; hot, humid; dry, northeast monsoon (Nov. to Mar.); rainy, southwest monsoon (June to Aug.)

Environment: future rise in ocean level could obliterate large parts of the country; freshwater supplies are limited

Terrain: flat with elevations of only 2.5 metres

Land Use: 10% arable; 0% permanent crops; 3% meadows; 3% forest; 84% other; includes n.a. sq. km irrigated

Location: islands in the Indian Ocean, S of India

■ PEOPLE

Population: 320,165 (July 2002 est.)

Nationality: Maldivian

Age Structure: 0–14 yrs: 45.3%; 15–64: 51.7%; 65+: 3% (2002 est.)

Population Growth Rate: 2.95% (2002 est.)

Net Migration: 0 migrants/1,000 population (2002 est.)

Ethnic Groups: mixtures of Sinhalese, Dravidian, Arab and African

Languages: Dhivehi (Maldivian dialect of Sinhara; script derived from Arabic); English spoken by most government officials

Religions: Sunni Muslim

Birth Rate: 37.41/1,000 population (2002 est.)

Death Rate: 7.86/1,000 population (2002 est.)

Infant Mortality: 61.93 deaths/1,000 live births (2002 est.)

Life Expectancy at Birth: 61.72 years male, 64.20 years female (2002 est.)

Total Fertility Rate: 5.38 children born/woman (2002 est.)

Literacy: 96.7% (2000)

■ GOVERNMENT

Leader(s): Pres. Maumoun Abdul Gayoom
Government Type: republic
Administrative Divisions: 19 atolls (atolhu, sing. & pl.) and 1 other first-order administrative division
Nationhood: July 26, 1965 (from UK)
National Holiday: Independence Day, July 26

■ ECONOMY

Overview: Based on fishing, tourism and shipping; fishing is the largest industry; tourism has become one of the largest and most important sources of revenue
GDP: US$1.2 billion, per capita US$3,870; real growth rate 7% (2001 est.)
Inflation: 0.6% (2001)
Industries: accounts for 18% of GDP (2000); fishing and fish processing, tourism, shipping, boat building, some coconut processing, garments, woven mats, coir (rope), handicrafts
Labour Force: approx. 70,000; 22% agriculture, 18% industry, 60% services
Unemployment: negligible
Agriculture: accounts for almost 20% of GDP (including fishing); fishing more important than farming; limited production of coconuts, corn, sweet potatoes; most staple foods must be imported
Natural Resources: fish

■ FINANCE/TRADE

Currency: rufiyaa (Rf) = 100 laari
International Reserves Excluding Gold: US$133 million (Dec. 2002)
Gold Reserves: 0.002 million fine troy ounces (Dec. 2002)
Budget: revenues US$166 million, expenditures US$192 million, including capital expenditures US$80 million (1999 est.)
Defence Expenditures: 11.46% of central government expenditure (2001)
Education Expenditures: 17.79% of central government expenditure (2000)
External Debt: US$235 million (2001)
Exports: US$87 million (2002 est.); commodities: fish 57%, clothing 39%; partners: Japan, UK, Sri Lanka, US.
Imports: US$369 million (2002 est.); commodities: intermediate and capital goods 47%, consumer goods 42%, petroleum products 11%; partners: Singapore, India, Sri Lanka, Japan, Canada

■ COMMUNICATIONS

Daily Newspapers: 2 in total
Televisions: n.a.
Radios: n.a.
Telephones: 80 lines/1,000 inhabitants (1999)

■ TRANSPORTATION

Motor Vehicles: n.a.
Roads: Malé has 9.6 km of coral highways within the city
Railway: none
Air Traffic: 215,000 passengers carried (1999 est.)
Airports: 5; 2 have paved runways (2002)

Canadian Embassy: The Canadian High Commission to Maldives, c/o The Canadian High Commission, P.O. Box 1006, Colombo 7, Sri Lanka. Tel: (011-94-75) 69-58-41. Fax: (011-94-1) 35-38-29. e-mail: clmbo@dfait-maeci.gc.ca
Embassy in Canada: Embassy of the Maldives, c/o High Commission for the Democratic Socialist Republic of Sri Lanka, 333 Laurier Ave W, Ste 1204, Ottawa ON K1P 1C1. Tel: (613) 233-8449. Fax: (613) 238-8448. e-mail: lankacom@magi.com

Mali

Long-Form Name: Republic of Mali
Capital: Bamako

■ GEOGRAPHY

Area: 1,240,000 sq. km
Coastline: none: landlocked
Climate: subtropical to arid; hot and dry Feb. to June; rainy, humid and mild June to Nov.; cool and dry Nov. to Feb.
Environment: hot, dust-laden harmattan haze common during dry seasons; soil erosion; desertification; deforestation
Terrain: mostly flat to rolling northern plains covered by sand; savanna in south, rugged hills in northeast
Land Use: 2% arable; 0% permanent crops; 25% meadows; 6% forest; 67% other; includes 1,380 sq. km irrigated
Location: NW Africa

■ PEOPLE

Population: 11,340,480 (July 2002 est.)
Nationality: Malian
Age Structure: 0–14 yrs: 47.2%; 15–64: 49.8%; 65+: 3.0% (2002 est.)

Population Growth Rate: 2.97% (2002 est.)
Net Migration: -0.35 migrants/1,000 population (2002 est.)
Ethnic Groups: 50% Mande (Bambara, Malinke, Sarakole), 17% Peul, 12% Voltaic, 6% Songhai, 10% Tuareg and Moor, 5% other
Languages: French (official); Bambara spoken by about 80% of the population; numerous African languages
Religions: 90% Muslim, 9% indigenous beliefs, 1% Christian
Birth Rate: 48.37/1,000 population (2002 est.)
Death Rate: 18.32/1,000 population (2002 est.)
Infant Mortality: 119.63 deaths/1,000 live births (2002 est.)
Life Expectancy at Birth: 46.18 years male, 48.64 years female (2002 est.)
Total Fertility Rate: 6.73 children born/woman (2002 est.)
Literacy: 39.8% (1999)

■ GOVERNMENT

Leader(s): Pres. Amadou Toumani Toure, Prime Min. Ahmed Mohamed Ag Hamani
Government Type: republic
Administrative Divisions: 8 regions
Nationhood: Sept. 22, 1960 (from France; formerly French Sudan)
National Holiday: Anniversary of the Proclamation of the Republic, Sept. 22

■ ECONOMY

Overview: among the poorest countries in the world, with 65% of its land area desert or semi-desert; economic activity is largely confined to the area irrigated by the Niger; industrial activity is concentrated on processing farm commodities
GDP: US$9.2 billion, per capita US$840; real growth rate -1.2% (2001 est.)
Inflation: 5.2% (2001)
Industries: accounts for 17% of GDP (2001 est.); small local consumer goods and processing, construction, phosphate, gold, fishing
Labour Force: 5.4 million (2001); 80% agriculture and fishing
Unemployment: n.a.
Agriculture: accounts for 45% of GDP (2001 est.); most production based on small subsistence farms; cotton and livestock products account for over 70% of exports; other crops—millet, rice, corn, vegetables, peanuts; livestock—cattle, sheep and goats
Natural Resources: gold, phosphates, kaolin, salt, limestone, uranium, bauxite, iron ore, manganese, tin and copper deposits are known but not exploited

■ FINANCE/TRADE

Currency: Communauté financière africaine franc (CFAF) = 100 centimes
International Reserves Excluding Gold: US$513 million (Oct. 2002)
Gold Reserves: 0.19 million fine troy ounces (Aug. 2000)
Budget: revenues US$764 million; expenditures US$828 million, capital expenditures US$ n.a. (2002 est.)
Defence Expenditures: 8.7% of central government expenditure (1999)
Education Expenditures: n.a.
External Debt: US$2.890 billion (2001)
Exports: US$739 million (2001); commodities: livestock, peanuts, dried fish, cotton, skins; partners: Brazil, South Korea, Italy, Canada
Imports: US$656 million (2001); commodities: textiles, vehicles, petroleum products, machinery, sugar, cereals; partners: Côte d'Ivoire, France, Senegal, Germany, Benelux

■ COMMUNICATIONS

Daily Newspapers: 1/1,000 inhabitants (2000)
Televisions: 17/1,000 inhabitants (2001)
Radios: 180/1,000 inhabitants (2001)
Telephones: 4 lines/1,000 inhabitants (2001)

■ TRANSPORTATION

Motor Vehicles: 41,800; 24,700 passenger cars
Roads: 15,100 km; 1,827 km paved
Railway: 729 km (2001)
Air Traffic: 46,000 passengers carried (2001)
Airports: 27; 7 have paved runways (2002)

Canadian Embassy: The Canadian Embassy, P.O. Box 198, Bamako, Mali. Tel: (011-223) 21-22-36. Fax: (011-223) 21-22-36. e-mail: bmako@dfait-maeci.gc.ca
Embassy in Canada: Embassy of the Republic of Mali, 50 Goulburn Ave, Ottawa ON K1N 8C8. Tel: (613) 232-1501. Fax: (613) 232-7429. e-mail: n.a.

Malta

Long-Form Name: Republic of Malta
Capital: Valletta

■ GEOGRAPHY

Area: 316 sq. km
Coastline: 196.8 km

Climate: Mediterranean with mild, rainy winters and hot, dry summers

Environment: numerous bays provide good harbours; fresh water very scarce, increasing reliance on desalination

Terrain: mostly low, rocky, flat to dissected plains; many coastal cliffs

Land Use: 32% arable; 3% permanent crops; 0% meadows; 4% forest; 61% other; includes 20 sq. km irrigated

Location: Mediterranean Sea, S of Sicily

■ PEOPLE

Population: 397,499 (July 2002 est.)

Nationality: Maltese (sing. & pl.)

Age Structure: 0–14 yrs: 19.7%; 15–64: 67.5%; 65+: 12.8% (2002 est.)

Population Growth Rate: 0.73% (2002 est.)

Net Migration: 2.36 migrants/1,000 population (2002 est.)

Ethnic Groups: mixture of Arab, Sicilian, Norman, Spanish, Italian, English

Languages: Maltese and English (both official), Italian widely spoken

Religions: 98% Roman Catholic

Birth Rate: 12.76/1,000 population (2002 est.)

Death Rate: 7.77/1,000 population (2002 est.)

Infant Mortality: 5.72 deaths/1,000 live births (2002 est.)

Life Expectancy at Birth: 75.78 years male, 80.96 years female (2002 est.)

Total Fertility Rate: 1.91 children born/woman (2002 est.)

Literacy: 92.0% (2000)

■ GOVERNMENT

Leader(s): Pres. Guido De Marco, Prime Min. Eddie Fenech Adami

Government Type: republic

Administrative Divisions: none

Nationhood: Sept. 21, 1964 (from UK)

National Holiday: Independence Day, Sept. 21

■ ECONOMY

Overview: manufacturing and tourism are important; economy is dependent on foreign trade and services (food, water and energy); Malta produces only 20% of its food needs, has a limited supply of fresh water and lacks domestic energy sources

GDP: US$7 billion, per capita US$17,000; real growth rate 2.2% (2002 est.)

Inflation: 2.9% (2001)

Industries: accounts for 26% of GDP; tourism, ship repair, clothing, construction, food manufacturing, textiles, footwear, beverages, tobacco

Labour Force: approx. 146,000; 24% industry, 71% services, 5% agriculture

Unemployment: 4.5% (Sept. 2000)

Agriculture: accounts for 3% of GDP; 20% self-sufficient overall; main products—potatoes, cauliflower, grapes, wheat, barley, tomatoes, citrus, cut flowers, green peppers, hogs, poultry, eggs; adequate supplies of vegetables, milk, pork products; seasonal or periodic shortages

Natural Resources: limestone, salt

■ FINANCE/TRADE

Currency: Maltese lira (LM) = 100 cents

International Reserves Excluding Gold: US$2.118 million (Nov. 2002)

Gold Reserves: 0.004 million fine troy ounces (Nov. 2002)

Budget: revenues US$1.5 billion; expenditures US$1.6 billion, including capital expenditures of US$ n.a. (2000)

Defence Expenditures: n.a.

Education Expenditures: n.a.

External Debt: US$1.531 billion (2001)

Exports: US$2.044 billion (2002 est.); commodities: clothing, textiles, footwear, ships; partners: US, Germany, France, UK, Italy

Imports: US$2.743 billion (2002 est.); commodities: food, beverages, tobacco, petroleum, non-food raw materials; partners: Italy, France, US, UK, Germany

■ COMMUNICATIONS

Daily Newspapers: 2 in total

Televisions: n.a.

Radios: n.a.

Telephones: 512 lines/1,000 inhabitants (1999)

■ TRANSPORTATION

Motor Vehicles: 141,200; 122,100 passenger cars

Roads: 1,742 km; 1,677 km paved

Railway: none

Air Traffic: 1,200,000 passengers carried (1999 est.)

Airports: 1, with a paved runway (2002)

Canadian Embassy: The Canadian High Commission to Malta, c/o The Canadian Embassy, Via G.B. de Rossi 27, 00161 Rome, Italy. Tel: (011-39-06) 445981. Fax: (011-39-06) 445 98750. e-mail: rome@dfait-maeci.gc.ca

Embassy in Canada: c/o High Commission for Malta, 2017 Connecticut Ave NW, Washington DC 20008, USA. Tel: (202) 462-3611. Fax: (202) 387-5470. e-mail: n.a.

Marshall Islands

Long-Form Name: Republic of the Marshall Islands
Capital: Majuro

■ GEOGRAPHY

Area: 181.3 sq. km; 2 island chains of 30 atolls and 1,152 islands
Coastline: 370.4 km
Climate: islands border typhoon belt; wet season, May to Nov.; hot and humid
Environment: occasional typhoons; insufficient fresh water
Terrain: low coral limestone and sand islands
Land Use: 0% arable; 60% permanent crops; 0% meadows or forests; 40% other; includes no irrigated land
Location: Oceania, in North Pacific Ocean, SW of Hawaii

■ PEOPLE

Population: 73,630 (July 2002 est.)
Nationality: Marshallese (sing. & pl.)
Age Structure: 0–14 yrs: 49.1%; 15–64: 48.9%; 65+: 2.0% (2002 est.)
Population Growth Rate: 3.89% (2002 est.)
Net Migration: 0 migrants/1,000 population (2002 est.)
Ethnic Groups: Micronesian
Languages: English (official), two major Marshallese dialects, Japanese
Religions: Christian (predominantly Protestant)
Birth Rate: 44.98/1,000 population (2002 est.)
Death Rate: 6.07/1,000 population (2002 est.)
Infant Mortality: 38.68 deaths/1,000 live births (2002 est.)
Life Expectancy at Birth: 64.35 years male, 68.09 years female (2002 est.)
Total Fertility Rate: 6.49 children born/woman (2002 est.)
Literacy: 93%

■ GOVERNMENT

Leader(s): Pres. Kessai Note
Government Type: constitutional government in free association with the US
Administrative Divisions: 33 municipalities
Nationhood: Oct. 21, 1986 (from US-administered UN trusteeship)
National Holiday: Constitution Day, May 1

■ ECONOMY

Overview: agriculture and tourism are the backbone of the economy; industry is on a small scale, limited to handicrafts, copra and fish processing; imports far exceed exports; foreign aid is vital
GDP: US$115 million, per capita US$1,600; real growth rate 1.0% (2001 est.)
Inflation: n.a.
Industries: accounts for 16% of GDP (2000); copra, fish, tourism, crafts; offshore banking is in its infancy
Labour Force: n.a.; 21% agriculture, 21% industry, 58% services
Unemployment: n.a.
Agriculture: accounts for 14% of GDP (2000); coconuts, taro, cacao, breadfruit, fruits, poultry, tomatoes, melons, cattle, pigs
Natural Resources: phosphate, marine products, minerals

■ FINANCE/TRADE

Currency: US$ = 100 cents
International Reserves Excluding Gold: n.a.
Gold Reserves: n.a.
Budget: n.a.
Defence Expenditures: defence is the responsibility of the US
Education Expenditures: n.a.
External Debt: n.a.
Exports: exact figures n.a.; fish, coconut oil, trochus shells; partners: US, Japan, Australia
Imports: exact figures n.a.; foodstuffs, machinery, equipment, fuels, beverages, tobacco; partners: US, Japan, Australia, New Zealand, Singapore, Fiji, China, Philippines

■ COMMUNICATIONS

Daily Newspapers: n.a.
Televisions: n.a.
Radios: n.a.
Telephones: 62 lines/ 1,000 inhabitants (1999)

■ TRANSPORTATION

Motor Vehicles: n.a.
Roads: paved roads on major islands only
Railway: none
Air Traffic: 35,000 passengers carried (1999 est.)
Airports: 17; 4 have paved runways (2002)

Canadian Embassy: The Canadian Embassy to the Marshall Islands, c/o The Canadian High Commission, Commonwealth Ave., Canberra A.C.T., Australia. Tel: (011-61-2) 6270-4000. Fax: (011-61-2) 6273-3285. e-mail: cnbra@dfait-maeci.gc.ca
Embassy in Canada: c/o Embassy of the Republic of the Marshall Islands, 2433 Massachusetts Ave NW, Washington DC 20008, USA. Tel: (202) 234-5414. Fax: (202) 232-3236. e-mail: n.a.

Martinique

Long-Form Name: Department of Martinique
Capital: Fort-de-France

■ GEOGRAPHY

Area: 1,100 sq. km
Climate: tropical, moderated by trade winds; rainy season (June to Oct.)
Land Use: 8% arable; 8% permanent crops; 17% permanent pastures; 44% forest; 23% other; includes 30 sq. km irrigated
Location: Caribbean Islands, halfway along the Lesser Antilles arch between Puerto Rico and Venezuela

■ PEOPLE

Population: 422,277 (July 2002 est.)
Nationality: Martiniquais
Ethnic Groups: 90% black, remainder a mix of black African and Latin ancestry, Caucasian 5%
Languages: French (official), majority speak Creole

■ GOVERNMENT

Colony/Territory of: Overseas Department of France
Leader(s): Pres. Jacques Chirac (France), Prefect Michel Cadot
Government Type: overseas department of France
National Holiday: Taking of the Bastille, National Day, July 14

■ ECONOMY

Overview: most of the meat, vegetable and grain requirements must be imported; industry: food processing, oil refining, chemical engineering; agriculture: pineapples, tobacco, cotton, bananas, sugar, rum, livestock; forest products; fishing; chief trading partners: France, UK, Guadeloupe

■ FINANCE/TRADE

Currency: French franc (F) = 100 centimes, Euro (€)

Canadian Embassy: c/o The Canadian Embassy 35-37 avenue Montaigne, 75008 Paris, France. Tel: (011-33-1) 44-43-29-00. Fax: (011-33-1) 44-43-29-99. e-mail: paris@dfait-maeci.gc.ca
Representative to Canada: c/o Embassy of France, 42 Sussex Dr, Ottawa ON K1M 2C9. Tel: (613) 789-1795. Fax: (613) 562-3735. e-mail: politique@ambafrance-ca.org

Mauritania

Long-Form Name: Islamic Republic of Mauritania
Capital: Nouakchott

■ GEOGRAPHY

Area: 1,030,700 sq. km
Coastline: 754 km
Climate: desert; constantly hot, dry, dusty
Environment: hot, dry, dust/sand-laden sirocco wind blows primarily in Mar. and Apr.; desertification; only perennial river is the Senegal; overgrazing and insufficient fresh water
Terrain: mostly barren, flat plains of the Sahara; some central hills
Land Use: 0% arable; 0% permanent crops; 38% meadows; 4% forest; 58% other; includes 490 sq. km irrigated
Location: NW Africa, bordering on Atlantic Ocean

■ PEOPLE

Population: 2,828,858 (July 2002 est.)
Nationality: Mauritanian
Age Structure: 0–14 yrs: 46.1%; 15–64: 51.7%; 65+: 2.2% (2002 est.)
Population Growth Rate: 2.92% (2002 est.)
Net Migration: 0 migrants/1,000 population (2002 est.)
Ethnic Groups: 30% Maur, 40% mixed Maur-black, 30% black
Languages: Hasaniya Arabic and Wolof (both official), Pular, Soninke
Religions: nearly 100% Muslim
Birth Rate: 42.54/1,000 population (2002 est.)
Death Rate: 13.34/1,000 population (2002 est.)
Infant Mortality: 75.25 deaths/1,000 live births (2002 est.)
Life Expectancy at Birth: 49.42 years male, 53.71 years female (2002 est.)
Total Fertility Rate: 6.15 children born/woman (2002 est.)
Literacy: 41.6% (1999)

■ GOVERNMENT

Leader(s): Pres. Maaouya Ould Sid Ahmed Taya, Prime Min. Sghair Ould Mbareck
Government Type: republic
Administrative Divisions: 12 regions and 1 capital district
Nationhood: Nov. 28, 1960 (from France)
National Holiday: Independence Day, Nov. 28

■ ECONOMY

Overview: most of the population is engaged in agricultural and livestock production; sub-

stantial iron ores; threatened by foreign overexploitation of fishing areas; in recent years, droughts, conflicts with Senegal, rising energy costs and economic mismanagement have resulted in a substantial build-up of foreign debt
GDP: US$5 billion, per capita US$1,800; real growth rate 4.0% (2001 est.)
Inflation: 4.7% (2001)
Industries: accounts for 29% of GDP (2001 est.); fishing, fish processing, mining of iron ore and gypsum
Labour Force: 1.3 million (2001); 50% agriculture, 40% services, 10% industry
Unemployment: n.a.
Agriculture: accounts for 25% of GDP (including fishing) (2001 est.); largely subsistence farming, nomadic cattle and sheep herding except in Senegal river valley; crops—dates, millet, sorghum, root crops, rice, corn; fish products number-one export; large food deficit in years of drought
Natural Resources: iron ore, gypsum, fish, copper, phosphate

■ **FINANCE/TRADE**

Currency: ouguiya (UM) = 5 Khoums
International Reserves Excluding Gold: US$281 million (Apr. 2001)
Gold Reserves: 0.012 million fine troy ounces (Apr. 2001)
Budget: n.a.
Defence Expenditures: 18.9% of central government expenditure (1999)
Education Expenditures: n.a.
External Debt: US$2.164 billion (2001)
Exports: US$592 million (2000); commodities: iron ore, processed fish, small amounts of gum arabic and gypsum, unrecorded but numerically significant cattle exports to Senegal; partners: France, Japan, Italy, Spain
Imports: US$294 million (2000); commodities: foodstuffs, consumer goods, petroleum products, capital goods; partners: France, US, Spain, Algeria, Germany, Benelux, Senegal

■ **COMMUNICATIONS**

Daily Newspapers: less than 1/1,000 inhabitants (2000)
Televisions: 96/1,000 inhabitants (2000)
Radios: 149/1,000 inhabitants (2001)
Telephones: 7 lines/1,000 inhabitants (2001)

■ **TRANSPORTATION**

Motor Vehicles: 27,000; 17,800 passenger cars
Roads: 7,660 km; 866 km paved

Railway: 704 km (2001)
Air Traffic: 156,000 passengers carried (2001)
Airports: 26; 10 have paved runways (2002)

Canadian Embassy: The Canadian Embassy to Mauritania, c/o The Canadian Embassy, P.O. Box 3373, Dakar, Senegal. Tel: (011-221) 823-9290. Fax: (011-221) 823-8749. e-mail: dakar@dfait-maeci.gc.ca
Embassy in Canada: Embassy of the Islamic Republic of Mauritania, 121 Sherwood Dr, Ottawa ON K1V 3V1. Tel: (613) 237-3283. Fax: (613) 237-3287. e-mail: info@mauritania-canada.ca

Mauritius

Long-Form Name: Republic of Mauritius
Capital: Port Louis

■ **GEOGRAPHY**

Area: 1,860 sq. km; includes Agalega Islands, Cargados Carajos Shoals (St. Brandon) and Rodriques
Coastline: 177 km
Climate: tropical modified by southeast trade winds; warm, dry winter (May to Nov.); hot, wet, humid summer (Nov. to May)
Environment: subject to cyclones (Nov. to Apr.); almost completely surrounded by reefs; water pollution is a growing problem
Terrain: small coastal plain rising to discontinuous mountains encircling central plateau
Land Use: 49% arable; 3% permanent crops; 3% meadows; 22% forest; 23% other; includes 200 sq. km irrigated
Location: Indian Ocean, E of Africa (E of Madagascar)

■ **PEOPLE**

Population: 1,200,206 (July 2002 est.)
Nationality: Mauritian
Age Structure: 0–14 yrs: 25.4%; 15–64: 68.3%; 65+: 6.3% (2002 est.)
Population Growth Rate: 0.86% (2002 est.)
Net Migration: -0.92 migrants/1,000 population (2002 est.)
Ethnic Groups: 68% Indo-Mauritian, 27% Creole, 3% Sino-Mauritian, 2% Franco-Mauritian
Languages: English (official), Creole, French, Hindi, Urdu, Hakka, Bojpoori
Religions: 52% Hindu, 28% Christian (mostly Roman Catholic with a few Anglicans), 17% Muslim, 3% other
Birth Rate: 16.34/1,000 population (2002 est.)
Death Rate: 6.81/1,000 population (2002 est.)

Infant Mortality: 16.65 deaths/1,000 live births (2002 est.)
Life Expectancy at Birth: 67.54 years male, 75.58 years female (2002 est.)
Total Fertility Rate: 2.00 children born/woman (2002 est.)
Literacy: 84.5% (2000)

■ GOVERNMENT

Leader(s): Pres. Carl Auguste Offmann, Prime Min. Anerood Jugnauth
Government Type: parliamentary democracy
Administrative Divisions: 9 administrative districts and 3 dependencies
Nationhood: Mar. 12, 1968 (from UK)
National Holiday: Independence Day, Mar. 12

■ ECONOMY

Overview: based on sugar, manufacturing (textiles) and tourism; industrialization programs stress increasing exports
GDP: US$12.9 billion, per capita US$10,800; real growth rate 5.2% (2001 est.)
Inflation: 5.4% (2001)
Industries: accounts for 33% of GDP; food processing (largely sugar milling), textiles, wearing apparel, chemical and chemical products, metal products, transport equipment, non-electrical machinery, tourism
Labour Force: 500,000 (2001); 14% agriculture, 36% industry, 24% community, social and business services, 26% other
Unemployment: 6.4% (1999 est.)
Agriculture: accounts for 6% of GDP; about 90% of cultivated land in sugar cane (which accounts for 40% of export earnings); other products—tea, corn, potatoes, bananas, pulses, cattle, goats, fish; net food importer, especially rice and fish
Natural Resources: arable land, fish

■ FINANCE/TRADE

Currency: rupee (Mau Rs) = 100 cents
International Reserves Excluding Gold: US$1.227 billion (Dec. 2002)
Gold Reserves: 0.062 million fine troy ounces (Dec. 2002)
Budget: revenues US$1.1 billion, expenditures US$1.2 billion, including capital expenditures US$ n.a. (1999 est.)
Defence Expenditures: 0.8% of total government expenditure (2001)
Education Expenditures: 16.15% of central government expenditure (2000)
External Debt: US$1.724 billion (2001)

Exports: US$1.765 billion (2002 est.); commodities: textiles 44%, sugar 40%, light manufactures 10%; partners: UK, France, US, South Africa, Germany, Italy
Imports: US$2.055 billion (2002 est.); commodities: manufactured goods 50%, capital equipment 17%, foodstuffs 13%, petroleum products 8%, chemicals 7%; partners: South Africa, France, India, Hong Kong, UK

■ COMMUNICATIONS

Daily Newspapers: 119/1,000 inhabitants (2000)
Televisions: 301/1,000 inhabitants (2001)
Radios: 379/1,000 inhabitants (2001)
Telephones: 257 lines/1,000 inhabitants (2001)

■ TRANSPORTATION

Motor Vehicles: 116,000; 87,000 passenger cars (2000)
Roads: 1,860 km; 1,786 km paved
Railway: none
Air Traffic: 997,000 passengers carried (2001)
Airports: 5; 2 have paved runways (2002)

Canadian Embassy: The Canadian High Commission to Mauritius, c/o 1103 Arcadia St., Hatfield, Pretoria 0028. Mailing address: c/o Canadian Embassy, Private Bag X13, Hatfield 0028, Pretoria, South Africa. Tel: (011-27-12) 422-3000. Fax: (011-27-12) 422-3052. e-mail: pret@dfait-maeci.gc.ca
Embassy in Canada: c/o Embassy of Mauritius, 4301 Connecticut Avenue NW, Ste 441, Washington DC 20008, USA. Tel: (202) 244-1491. Fax: (202) 966-0983. e-mail: mauritius.embassy@prodigy.net

Mayotte

Long-Form Name: Territorial Collectivity of Mayotte
Capital: Mamoutzou

■ GEOGRAPHY

Area: 374 sq. km
Climate: tropical maritime; hot, humid rainy season during northeastern monsoon (Nov. to May), dry season is cooler (May to Nov.)
Land Use: 20,000 acres under agricultural cultivation
Location: Mozambique Channel, off E coast of Africa

■ PEOPLE

Population: 170,879 (July 2002 est.)
Nationality: Mahorais (sing. & pl.)

Ethnic Groups: Antalote, Cafre, Makoa, Oimatsaha, Sakalava
Languages: French (official), Mahorian (a Swahili dialect)

■ GOVERNMENT

Colony/Territory of: Territorial Collectivity of France
Leader(s): Pres. Jacques Chirac (France), Prefect Jean-Jacques Brot
Government Type: French territorial collectivity
National Holiday: Taking of the Bastille, July 14

■ ECONOMY

Overview: industry: lobster, shrimp; agriculture: pineapples, bananas, mangoes, breadfruit, cassava, ylang-ylang, vanilla, coffee, spices; must import a large portion of its food requirements, mainly from France; chief trading partners: France, UK, South Africa, Bahrain, Thailand, Réunion

■ FINANCE/TRADE

Currency: French franc (F) = 100 centimes; also Euro as of March 1, 2002

Canadian Embassy: c/o The Canadian Embassy, 35-37 avenue Montaigne, 75008 Paris, France. Tel: (011-33-1) 44-43-29-00. Fax: (011-33-1) 44-43-29-99. e-mail: paris@dfait-maeci.gc.ca
Representative to Canada: c/o Embassy of France, 42 Sussex Dr., Ottawa ON K1M 2C9. Tel: (613) 789-1795. Fax: (613)562-3735. e-mail: politique@ambafrance-ca.org

---

Mexico

Long-Form Name: United Mexican States
Capital: Mexico City

■ GEOGRAPHY

Area: 1,972,550 sq. km
Coastline: 9,330 km
Climate: varies from tropical to desert
Environment: subject to tsunamis along the Pacific coast and destructive earthquakes in the centre and south; natural water resources scarce and polluted; deforestation; erosion widespread; desertification; serious air pollution
Terrain: high, rugged mountains, low coastal plains, high plateaus and desert
Land Use: 12% arable; 1% permanent crops; 39% meadows; 26% forest; 22% other; includes 65,000 sq. km irrigated
Location: Central (Latin) America, bordering on United States, Gulf of Mexico, Pacific Ocean

■ PEOPLE

Population: 103,400,165 (July 2002 est.)
Nationality: Mexican
Age Structure: 0–14 yrs: 32.8%; 15–64: 62.7%; 65+: 4.5% (2002 est.)
Population Growth Rate: 1.47% (2002 est.)
Net Migration: -2.71 migrants/1,000 population (2002 est.)
Ethnic Groups: 60% mestizo (Indian-Spanish), 30% Amerindian or predominantly Amerindian, 9% white or predominantly white, 1% other
Languages: Spanish, also indigenous (Mayan) languages
Religions: 89% Roman Catholic, 6% Protestant, 5% other
Birth Rate: 22.36/1,000 population (2002 est.)
Death Rate: 4.99/1,000 population (2002 est.)
Infant Mortality: 24.52 deaths/1,000 live births (2002 est.)
Life Expectancy at Birth: 68.99 years male, 75.21 years female (2002 est.)
Total Fertility Rate: 2.57 children born/woman (2002 est.)
Literacy: 91.4% (2000)

■ GOVERNMENT

Leader(s): Pres. Vicente Fox Quesada
Government Type: federal republic operating under a centralized government
Administrative Divisions: 31 states (estados, sing. —estado) and 1 federal district (distrito federal)
Nationhood: Sept. 16, 1810 (from Spain)
National Holiday: Independence Day, Sept. 16

■ ECONOMY

Overview: outlook remains positive, but this country still needs to overcome many structural problems as it strives to modernize its economy and raise living standards; income distribution is very unequal, with the top 20% of income earners accounting for 55% of income; trade with the US and Canada has nearly doubled since NAFTA was implemented in 1994
GDP: US$920 billion, per capita US$9,000; real growth rate -0.3% (2001 est.)
Inflation: 6.4% (2001)
Industries: accounts for 26% of GDP (2001 est.); food and beverages, tobacco, chemicals, iron and steel, petroleum, mining, textiles, clothing, transportation equipment, tourism
Labour Force: 41.3 million (2001); 56% services, 20% agriculture, 24% industry
Unemployment: 2.0% (2001); plus considerable underemployment
Agriculture: accounts for 5% of GDP (2001 est.) and 20% of labour force; large number of small farms at subsistence level; major food crops—

corn, wheat, rice, beans, soybeans; cash crops—cotton, coffee, fruit, tomatoes, beef, poultry, dairy products
Natural Resources: crude oil, silver, copper, gold, lead, zinc, natural gas, timber

■ FINANCE/TRADE

Currency: peso ($Mex) = 100 centavos
International Reserves Excluding Gold: US$50.594 billion (Dec. 2002)
Gold Reserves: 0.225 million fine troy ounces (Dec. 2002)
Budget: revenues US$136 billion; expenditures US$140 billion, capital expenditures US$ n.a. (2001 est.)
Defence Expenditures: 3.2% of central government expenditure (2001)
Education Expenditures: 25.54% of central government expenditure (1999)
External Debt: US$158.290 billion (2001)
Exports: US$159.287 billion (2002 est.); commodities: crude oil, oil products, silver, fruits, vegetables, coffee, shrimp, engines, cotton; partners: US, Canada, Germany, Spain, Netherlands Antilles, Japan, UK, Venezuela
Imports: US$165.367 billion (2002 est.); commodities: grain, metal manufactures, agricultural machinery, electrical equipment, motor vehicle and aircraft parts; partners: US, Japan, Germany, Canada, China, South Korea, Taiwan, Italy, Brazil

■ COMMUNICATIONS

Daily Newspapers: 94/1,000 inhabitants (2000)
Televisions: 283/1,000 inhabitants (2001)
Radios: 330/1,000 inhabitants (2001)
Telephones: 137 lines/1,000 inhabitants (2001)

■ TRANSPORTATION

Motor Vehicles: 15,400,000; 10,400,000 passenger cars (2000 est.)
Roads: 323,977 km; 96,221 km paved
Railway: 18,000 km
Air Traffic: 20,043,000 passengers carried (2001)
Airports: 1,852; 231 have paved runways (2002)

Canadian Embassy: The Canadian Embassy, Calle Schiller no. 529, Rincon del Bosque, Colonia Polanco, 11580 Mexico; mailing address: Apartado Postal 105-05, 11580 Mexico, Mexico. Tel: (011-52-5) 724-7900. Fax: (011-52-5) 724-7980. e-mail: mxico@dfait-maeci.gc.ca
Embassy in Canada: Embassy of the United Mexican States, 45 O'Connor St, Ste 1500, Ottawa ON K1P 1A4. Tel: (613) 233-8988. Fax: (613) 235-9123. e-mail: info@embamexcan.com

Micronesia

Long-Form Name: Federated States of Micronesia
Capital: Palikir

■ GEOGRAPHY

Area: 702 sq. km.; 4 major island groups totalling 607 islands
Coastline: 6,112 km
Climate: tropical; heavy rainfall all year long, particularly in the eastern islands
Environment: occasional severe typhoons mostly from June to Dec.
Terrain: varies from high, mountainous islands to low coral atolls; volcanic outcroppings
Land Use: n.a.
Location: Oceania, in the N Pacific Ocean, NE of Australia

■ PEOPLE

Population: 135,869 (July 2002 est.)
Nationality: Micronesian
Age Structure: n.a.
Population Growth Rate: 3.28% (2000 est.)
Net Migration: 11.65 migrants/1,000 population (2000 est.)
Ethnic Groups: 9 Micronesian and Polynesian groups
Languages: English (official and common), local languages including Pohnpeian, Yapese, Trukese and Kosrean
Religions: Roman Catholic 50%, Protestant 47%, other or none 3%
Birth Rate: 27.09/1,000 population (2000 est.)
Death Rate: 5.95/1,000 population (2000 est.)
Infant Mortality: 33.48 deaths/1,000 live births (2000 est.)
Life Expectancy at Birth: 66.67 years male, 70.62 years female (2000 est.)
Total Fertility Rate: 3.83 children born/woman (2000 est.)
Literacy: 89%

■ GOVERNMENT

Leader(s): Pres. Joseph J. "Joe" Urusemal, V. Pres. Redley Killion
Government Type: constitutional government in free association with the United States
Administrative Divisions: 4 states
Nationhood: Nov. 3, 1986 (from US-administered UN Trusteeship)
National Holiday: Proclamation of the Federated States of Micronesia, May 10

■ ECONOMY

Overview: mostly subsistence farming and fishing; few economically viable mineral

deposits; region's remote location and lack of adequate facilities hinders development of tourism potential; considerably dependent on financial assistance from the US
GDP: US$269 million, per capita US$2,000; real growth rate 2.0% (2001 est.)
Inflation: 2.6% (1999 est.)
Industries: accounts for 4% of GDP; fish processing, crafts, tourism, construction
Labour Force: n.a.; two-thirds are government employees
Unemployment: 16% (1999 est.)
Agriculture: accounts for 50% of GDP (2000); pepper, tropical fruits and vegetables, coconuts, sweet potatoes, pigs, chickens
Natural Resources: forests, marine products, deep-sea minerals

■ FINANCE/TRADE

Currency: US dollar ($) = 100 cents
International Reserves Excluding Gold: US$116 million (Nov. 2002)
Gold Reserves: n.a.
Budget: n.a.
Defence Expenditures: n.a.
Education Expenditures: n.a.
External Debt: n.a.
Exports: exact figures not available; commodities: fish, garments, bananas, pepper; partners: Japan, US, Guam
Imports: exact figures not available; commodities: food, manufactures, machinery and equipment, beverages; partners: US, Japan, Australia

■ COMMUNICATIONS

Daily Newspapers: n.a.
Televisions: n.a.
Radios: n.a.
Telephones: 80 lines/1,000 inhabitants (1999)

■ TRANSPORTATION

Motor Vehicles: n.a.
Roads: 240 km; 42 km paved
Railway: none
Air Traffic: n.a.
Airports: 7; 6 have paved runways (2002)

Canadian Embassy: Canadian Embassy to the Federated States of Micronesia, c/o The Canadian High Commission, Commonwealth Avenue, Canberra ACT 2600, Australia, Tel: (011 61 2) 6270-4000. Fax: (011 61 2) 6273-3285. e-mail: cnbra@dfait-maeci.gc.ca
Embassy in Canada: c/o The Embassy of the Republic of the Philippines, 130 Albert St Ste 606, Ottawa, ON K1P 5G4. Tel: (613) 233-

1121. Fax: (613) 233-4165. e-mail: ottawape@istar.ca

Moldova

Long-Form Name: Republic of Moldova
Capital: Chisinau

■ GEOGRAPHY

Area: 33,843 sq. km
Coastline: none: landlocked
Climate: mild sunny winters; warm rainy summers; long dry autumns
Environment: heavy use of agricultural chemicals, including banned pesticides such as DDT, has contaminated groundwater and soil; erosion severe due to poor farming methods
Terrain: hilly plains in north; southern steppe
Land Use: 53% arable; 14% permanent crops; 13% permanent pastures; 13% forest; 7% other; includes 3,070 sq. km irrigated
Location: E Europe, bordering on Ukraine and Romania

■ PEOPLE

Population: 4,434,547 (July 2002 est.)
Nationality: Moldovan
Age Structure: 0–14 yrs: 21.7%; 15–64: 68.2%; 65+: 10.1% (2002 est.)
Population Growth Rate: 0.09% (2002 est.)
Net Migration: -0.28 migrants/1,000 population (2002 est.)
Ethnic Groups: 64.5% Moldavian, 13.8% Ukrainian, 13% Russian, 3.5% Gagauz, 1.5% Jews, 3.7% other
Languages: Moldavan (official), Russian, Ukrainian, Gagauz (a Turkish dialect)
Religions: 98.5% Eastern Orthodox, 1.5% Jewish, minority Baptists (note that almost all churchgoers are ethnic Moldovan; the Slavic population are not churchgoers)
Birth Rate: 13.82/1,000 population (2002 est.)
Death Rate: 12.64/1,000 population (2002 est.)
Infant Mortality: 42.16 deaths/1,000 live births (2002 est.)
Life Expectancy at Birth: 60.39 years male, 69.31 years female (2002 est.)
Total Fertility Rate: 1.71 children born/woman (2002 est.)
Literacy: 98.9% (2000)

■ GOVERNMENT

Leader(s): Pres. Vladimir Voronin, Prime Min. Vasile Tarlev
Government Type: republic

Administrative Divisions: 10 juletule (sing. juletul), 1 autonomous territorial unit and 1 municipality
Nationhood: Aug. 27, 1991 (from Soviet Union)
National Holiday: Independence Day, Aug. 27

■ ECONOMY

Overview: predominantly agricultural, with important manufacturing sector; Moldova has a climate favourable to agriculture, and this is where the bulk of economic development has taken place
GDP: US$11 billion, per capita US$3,000; real growth rate 4.0% (2000)
Inflation: 9.8% (2001)
Industries: accounts for 23% of GDP (2000); machinery and appliances, hosiery, refined sugar, vegetable oil, canned food, shoes, textiles
Labour Force: 2.2 million (2001); 40% agriculture, 46% other; 14% industry
Unemployment: 11.1%; also large numbers of underemployed (2001)
Agriculture: accounts for 28% of GDP (2000); grapes and other fruits, vegetables, sugar, wheat and cereal grains, tobacco, oil, essential oil crops, beets, wine; beef, milk.
Natural Resources: lignite, phosphorites, gypsum, arable land

■ FINANCE/TRADE

Currency: leu (pl. lei)
International Reserves Excluding Gold: US$269 million (Dec. 2002)
Gold Reserves: n.a.
Budget: revenues US$536 million; expenditures US$594 million, including capital expenditures of US$ n.a. (1998 est.)
Defence Expenditures: 1.8% of central government expenditures (2001)
Education Expenditures: 3.98% of central government expenditure (2000)
External Debt: US$1.214 billion (2001)
Exports: US$449 million (2000); wine, grapes, other agricultural products, machinery, pumps; partners: Russia, Ukraine, Italy, Germany, Romania
Imports: US$617 million (2000); fuels, metals and metal products, consumer products, foodstuffs; partners: Russia, Romania, Ukraine, Germany, Italy

■ COMMUNICATIONS

Daily Newspapers: 13/1,000 inhabitants (2000)
Televisions: 296/1,000 inhabitants (2001)
Radios: 758/1,000 inhabitants (2001)
Telephones: 154 lines/1,000 inhabitants (2001)

■ TRANSPORTATION

Motor Vehicles: 310,000; 240,000 passenger cars (2000)
Roads: 20,000 km; 13,900 km hard-surfaced
Railway: 1,328 km, which does not include industrial lines
Air Traffic: 120,000 passengers carried (2001)
Airports: 30; 7 have paved runways (2002)

Canadian Embassy: The Canadian Embassy to Moldova, 36 Nicolae Iorga St., 71118 Bucharest, Romania. Mailing address: c/o The Canadian Embassy, P.O. Box 117, Post Office No. 22, 71118 Bucharest, Romania. Tel: (011-40-21) 307-5000. Fax: (011-40-21) 307-5010. e-mail: bucst@dfait-maeci.gc.ca
Embassy in Canada: Embassy of the Republic of Moldova, 2101 S. St NW, Washington DC 20008, USA. Tel: (202) 667-1130. Fax: (202) 667-1204. e-mail: ciobanu@dgsys.com

Monaco

Long-Form Name: Principality of Monaco
Capital: Monaco

■ GEOGRAPHY

Area: 1.95 sq. km
Coastline: 4.1 km
Climate: Mediterranean with mild, wet winters and hot, dry summers
Environment: almost entirely urban
Terrain: hilly, rugged, rocky
Land Use: almost 100% urban
Location: W Europe, bordering on France and Mediterranean Sea

■ PEOPLE

Population: 31,987 (July 2002 est.)
Nationality: Monegasque or Monacan
Age Structure: 0–14 yrs: 15.5%; 15–64: 62.1%; 65+: 22.4% (2002 est.)
Population Growth Rate: 0.45% (2002 est.)
Net Migration: 7.82 migrants/1,000 population (2002 est.)
Ethnic Groups: 47% French, 16% Monegasque, 16% Italian, 21% other
Languages: French (official), English, Italian, Monegasque
Religions: 95% Roman Catholic
Birth Rate: 9.60/1,000 population (2002 est.)
Death Rate: 12.91/1,000 population (2002 est.)
Infant Mortality: 5.73 deaths/1,000 live births (2002 est.)
Life Expectancy at Birth: 75.21 years male, 83.25 years female (2002 est.)

Total Fertility Rate: 1.76 children born/woman (2002 est.)
Literacy: 99%

■ GOVERNMENT

Leader(s): Prince Rainier III, Min. of State Patrick Leclercq
Government Type: constitutional monarchy
Administrative Divisions: 4 districts (quartiers, sing. —quartier)
Nationhood: 1419, rule by the House of Grimaldi
National Holiday: National Day, Nov. 19

■ ECONOMY

Overview: a popular resort, attracting tourists to its casinos and pleasant climate; no income tax and low business taxes make it a tax haven; no data is published on the economy
GDP: n.a.
Inflation: n.a.
Industries: pharmaceuticals, food processing, precision instruments, glassmaking, printing, tourism
Labour Force: n.a.
Unemployment: n.a.
Agriculture: none
Natural Resources: none

■ FINANCE/TRADE

Currency: French franc (F) = 100 centimes; also Euro as of March 1, 2002
International Reserves Excluding Gold: n.a.
Gold Reserves: n.a.
Budget: n.a.
Defence Expenditures: defence is the responsibility of France
Education Expenditures: n.a.
External Debt: n.a.
Exports: n.a.; full customs integration with France, which collects and rebates Monegasque trade duties
Imports: n.a.; full customs integration with France, which collects and rebates Monegasque trade duties

■ COMMUNICATIONS

Daily Newspapers: 1 in total
Televisions: n.a.
Radios: n.a.
Telephones: n.a.

■ TRANSPORTATION

Motor Vehicles: 21,000; 17,000 passenger cars
Roads: 50 km paved city streets only (2001)
Railway: 1.7 km
Air Traffic: 48,000 passengers carried (1999 est.)

Airports: Monaco is linked to the airport in Nice, France, by helicopter service

Canadian Embassy: The Canadian Consulate General, c/o The Canadian Embassy, 35 av Montaigne, 75008 Paris, France. Tel: (011-33-1) 44-43-22-51. Fax: (011-33-1) 44-43-29-99. e-mail: paris@dfait-maeci.gc.ca
Embassy in Canada: Consulate of Monaco, 20 Queen St. W., Suite 3300, Toronto, ON, M5H 3R3. Tel: (416) 971-4848, Fax: (416) 971-4849. e-mail: blette@lette.com

Mongolia

Long-Form Name: Mongolia
Capital: Ulan Bator, or Ulaanbaatar

■ GEOGRAPHY

Area: 1,565,000 sq. km
Coastline: none: landlocked
Climate: desert; continental (large daily and seasonal temperature ranges)
Environment: harsh and rugged; water resources are severely limited; deforestation is a problem; spring dust storms are a natural hazard
Terrain: vast semi-desert and desert plains; mountains in west and southwest; Gobi Desert in southeast
Land Use: 5.7% arable; 0% permanent crops; 81% meadows; 11.4% forest; 1.9% other; includes 840 sq. km irrigated
Location: EC Asia, bordering China and Russia

■ PEOPLE

Population: 2,694,432 (July 2002 est.)
Nationality: Mongolian
Age Structure: 0–14 yrs: 32.0%; 15–64: 64.1%; 65+: 3.9% (2002 est.)
Population Growth Rate: 1.48% (2002 est.)
Net Migration: 0 migrants/1,000 population (2002 est.)
Ethnic Groups: 90% Mongol, 4% Kazakh, 2% Chinese, 2% Russian, 2% other
Languages: Kazakh and Khalkha Mongol is spoken by over 90% of population; minor languages include Turkic, Russian, Chinese and English
Religions: no state religion; predominantly Buddhist Lamaism and Shamanism, Islam 4%
Birth Rate: 21.80/1,000 population (2002 est.)
Death Rate: 7.01/1,000 population (2002 est.)
Infant Mortality: 51.97 deaths/1,000 live births (2002 est.)
Life Expectancy at Birth: 62.47 years male, 66.87 years female (2002 est.)

Total Fertility Rate: 2.37 children born/woman (2002 est.)
Literacy: 98.9% (2000)

■ GOVERNMENT

Leader(s): Pres. Natsagiin Bagabandi, Prime Min. Nambaryn Enkhbayar
Government Type: republic
Administrative Divisions: 18 provinces (aymguud, sing. —aymag) and 3 municipalities (hotuud, sing. —hot)
Nationhood: July 11, 1921 (from China; formerly known as Outer Mongolia)
National Holiday: Independence/Revolution Day, July 11

■ ECONOMY

Overview: severe climate, widely dispersed population and largely unproductive land have hindered economic development; one-quarter of the population lives below the poverty line; economy is traditionally based on agriculture and the breeding of livestock (has highest number of livestock per person in the world); recently extensive mineral resources have been developed
GDP: US$4.7 billion, per capita US$1,770; average real growth rate 2.4% (2001 est.)
Inflation: 7.6% (1999)
Industries: accounts for 30% of GDP (2000); processing of animal products, building materials, food and beverage, mining (particularly coal), copper
Labour Force: 1.2 million (2001); primarily engaged in herding and agriculture
Unemployment: 5.7% (2001)
Agriculture: accounts for 32% of GDP (2000) and 90% of exports, and provides livelihood for about 50% of the population; livestock raising predominates (sheep, goats, cattle, camels, horses); crops—wheat, barley, potatoes, forage
Natural Resources: oil, coal, copper, molybdenum, tungsten, phosphates, tin, nickel, zinc, wolfram, fluorspar, gold

■ FINANCE/TRADE

Currency: tughrik (Tug) = 100 mongos
International Reserves Excluding Gold: US$350 million (Dec. 2002)
Gold Reserves: 0.142 million fine troy ounces (Dec. 2002)
Budget: revenues US$262 million, expenditures of US$328 million, including capital expenditures of US$ n.a. (2000 est.)
Defence Expenditures: 7.5% of central government expenditure (2001)

Education Expenditures: 8.68% of central government expenditure (2000)
External Debt: US$885 million (2001)
Exports: US$435 million (2000); commodities: livestock, animal products, wool, hides, cashmere, copper, fluorspar, non-ferrous metals, minerals; partners: China, US, Russia, Japan
Imports: US$455 million (2000); commodities: machinery and equipment, fuels, food products, industrial consumer goods, chemicals, building materials, sugar, tea; partners: Russia, China, Japan, South Korea, US

■ COMMUNICATIONS

Daily Newspapers: 30/1,000 inhabitants (2000)
Televisions: 72/1,000 inhabitants (2001)
Radios: 50/1,000 inhabitants (2001)
Telephones: 52 lines/1,000 inhabitants (2001)

■ TRANSPORTATION

Motor Vehicles: 80,000; 45,000 passenger cars (2000)
Roads: 49,250 km; 1,674 km paved (2000)
Railway: 1,815 km
Air Traffic: 255,000 passengers carried (2001)
Airports: 34; 8 have paved runways (2002)

Canadian Embassy: The Canadian Embassy to Mongolia, c/o The Canadian Embassy, 19 Dong Zhi Men Wai St, Chao Yang District, Beijing 100600, China. Tel: (011-86-10) 6532-3536. Fax: (011-86-10) 6532-4311. e-mail: bejing@dfait-maeci.gc.ca
Embassy in Canada: Embassy of Mongolia, 151 Slater St. Suite 503, Ottawa, ON, K1P 5H3. Tel: (613)569-3830 Fax: (613)569-3916. e-mail: mail@mongolembassy.org

---

Montserrat

Long-Form Name: Montserrat
Capital: Plymouth (abandoned in 1997 due to volcanic activity); interim government buildings are located in Brades

■ GEOGRAPHY

Area: 100 sq. km
Climate: tropical, no well-defined rainy season; June to Nov. hottest; prone to hurricanes
Land Use: 20% arable; 0% permanent crops; 10% meadows and pastures; 40% forests; 30% other; includes n.a. sq. km irrigated
Location: Caribbean island, SE of Puerto Rico

■ PEOPLE

Population: 8,437 (July 2002 est.)
Nationality: Montserratian

Ethnic Groups: descendants of British, French, Irish settlers; also black
Languages: English (official)

■ GOVERNMENT

Colony/Territory of: Crown Colony of the United Kingdom
Leader(s): Head of State: Queen Elizabeth II, Gov. Anthony J. Longrigg, Chief Min. John Osborne
Government Type: dependent territory of the UK
National Holiday: Celebration of the Birthday of the Queen, second Saturday in June

■ ECONOMY

Overview: manufacturing accounts for 85% of exports: leather goods, cotton clothing, electronics, plastic bags, herbal teas, ornamental plants, tropical fruit; the economy is heavily dependent on imports, making it vulnerable to fluctuations in world prices; ongoing major volcanic activity is hindering economic activity

■ FINANCE/TRADE

Currency: Eastern Caribbean dollar = 100 cents

Canadian Embassy: c/o Macdonald House, 1 Grosvenor Square, London WIK 4AB, England, UK. Tel: (011-44-20) 7258-6600. Fax: (011-44-20) 7258-6333. e-mail: ldn@dfait-maeci.gc.ca
Representative to Canada: c/o High Commission for the Countries of the Organization of Eastern Caribbean States, 130 Albert St, Ste 700, Ottawa ON K1P 5G4. Tel: (613) 236-8952. Fax: (613) 236-3042. e-mail: echcc@travel-net.com

Morocco

Long-Form Name: Kingdom of Morocco
Capital: Rabat

■ GEOGRAPHY

Area: 446,550 sq. km
Coastline: 1,835 km
Climate: Mediterranean, becoming more extreme in the interior
Environment: northern mountains geologically unstable and subject to earthquakes; desertification; unsafe water supply; land degradation
Terrain: mostly mountains with rich coastal plains
Land Use: 21% arable; 1% permanent crops; 47% permanent pastures; 20% forest; 11% other; includes 12,910 sq. km irrigated
Location: NW Africa, bordering on Atlantic Ocean

■ PEOPLE

Population: 31,167,783 (July 2002 est.)
Nationality: Moroccan
Age Structure: 0–14 yrs: 33.8%; 15–64: 61.5%; 65+: 4.7% (2002 est.)
Population Growth Rate: 1.68% (2002 est.)
Net Migration: -1.09 migrants/1,000 population (2002 est.)
Ethnic Groups: 99.1% Arab-Berber, 0.7% non-Morrocan, 0.2% Jewish
Languages: Arabic (official); several Berber dialects; French is language of business, government, diplomacy and post-primary education
Religions: 98.7% Sunni Muslim, 1.1% Christian, 0.2% Jewish
Birth Rate: 23.69/1,000 population (2002 est.)
Death Rate: 5.86/1,000 population (2002 est.)
Infant Mortality: 46.49 deaths/1,000 live births (2002 est.)
Life Expectancy at Birth: 67.49 years male, 72.08 years female (2002 est.)
Total Fertility Rate: 2.97 children born/woman (2002 est.)
Literacy: 48.9% (2000)

■ GOVERNMENT

Leader(s): King Sidi Mohammed VI, Prime Min. Driss Jettou
Government Type: constitutional monarchy
Administrative Divisions: 37 provinces and 2 municipalities (wilayas)
Nationhood: Mar. 2, 1956 (from France)
National Holiday: Throne Day or Sete de Throne, July 30 (anniversary of King Mohammed VI's accession to the throne)

■ ECONOMY

Overview: faces the problems typical of developing countries: restraining government spending, reducing constraints on private activity and foreign trade, and keeping inflation manageable
GDP: US$112 billion, per capita US$3,700; real growth rate 5.0% (2001 est.)
Inflation: 0.6% (2001)
Industries: accounts for 33% of GDP (2000), phosphate rock mining and processing, food processing, leather goods, textiles, construction, tourism
Labour Force: 11.8 million (2001); 50% agriculture, 35% services, 15% industry
Unemployment: 22.0% (2001)
Agriculture: accounts for 15% of GDP (2000); 50% of employment and 30% of export value; not self-sufficient in food; cereal farming and

livestock raising predominate; barley, wheat, citrus fruit, wine, vegetables, olives
Natural Resources: phosphates, iron ore, manganese, lead, zinc, fish, salt

■ FINANCE/TRADE

Currency: dirham (DH) = 100 centimes
International Reserves Excluding Gold: US$10.133 billion (Dec. 2002)
Gold Reserves: 0.708 million fine troy ounces (Dec. 2002)
Budget: revenues US$13.8 billion; expenditures of US$14.6 billion, including capital expenditures of US$2.1 billion (2001)
Defence Expenditures: 12.4% of central government expenditure (2001)
Education Expenditures: 17.78% of central government expenditure (1999)
External Debt: US$16.962 billion (2001)
Exports: US$7.647 billion (2002 est.); commodities: food and beverages 30%, semiprocessed goods 23%, consumer goods 21%, phosphates 17%; partners: France, Spain, UK, Italy, Germany, India, US
Imports: US$11.163 billion (2002 est.); commodities: capital goods 24%, semi-processed goods 22%, raw materials 16%, fuel and lubricants 16%, food and beverages 13%, consumer goods 10%; partners: France, Spain, Germany, Italy, UK, US

■ COMMUNICATIONS

Daily Newspapers: 28/1,000 inhabitants (2000)
Televisions: 159/1,000 inhabitants (2001)
Radios: 243/1,000 inhabitants (2001)
Telephones: 41 lines/1,000 inhabitants (2001)

■ TRANSPORTATION

Motor Vehicles: 1,600,000; 1,250,000 passenger cars (2000)
Roads: 57,847 km; 30,254 km paved
Railway: 1,907 km
Air Traffic: 3,681,000 passengers carried (2001)
Airports: 67; 26 have paved runways (2002)

Canadian Embassy: The Canadian Embassy, 13 bis, rue Jaafar As-Sadik; Rabat-Agdal; mailing address: CP 709, Rabat-Agdal, Morocco. Tel: (011-212-37) 68-74-00. Fax: (011-212-37) 68-74-30. e-mail: rabat@dfait-maeci.gc.ca.
Embassy in Canada: Embassy of the Kingdom of Morocco, 38 Range Rd, Ottawa ON K1N 8J4. Tel: (613) 236-7391. Fax: (613) 236-6164. e-mail: sifamaot@videotron.net

Mozambique

Long-Form Name: Republic of Mozambique
Capital: Maputo

■ GEOGRAPHY

Area: 801,590 sq. km
Coastline: 2,470 km
Climate: tropical to subtropical
Environment: severe drought and floods occur in south; desertification; water pollution; danger of cyclones
Terrain: mostly coastal lowlands, uplands in centre, high plateaus in northwest, mountains in west
Land Use: 4% arable; negligible permanent crops; 56% meadows; 18% forest; 22% other; includes 1,070 sq. km irrigated
Location: SE Africa, bordering on Mozambique Channel

■ PEOPLE

Population: 19,607,519 (July 2002 est.)
Nationality: Mozambican
Age Structure: 0–14 yrs: 42.5%; 15–64: 54.7%; 65+: 2.8% (2002 est.)
Population Growth Rate: 1.13% (2002 est.)
Net Migration: 0 migrants/1,000 population (2002 est.)
Ethnic Groups: 99.66% indigenous tribal groups; about 0.06% Europeans, 0.2% Euro-Africans, 0.08% Indians
Languages: Portuguese (official); English; many indigenous dialects
Religions: 50% indigenous beliefs, 30% Christian, 20% Muslim
Birth Rate: 36.41/1,000 population (2002 est.)
Death Rate: 25.13/1,000 population (2002 est.)
Infant Mortality: 138.55 deaths/1,000 live births (2002 est.)
Life Expectancy at Birth: 36.25 years male, 34.65 years female (2002 est.)
Total Fertility Rate: 4.71 children born/woman (2002 est.)
Literacy: 43.2% (1999)

■ GOVERNMENT

Leader(s): Pres. Joaquím Alberto Chissano, Prime Min. Pascoal Manuel Mocumbi
Government Type: republic
Administrative Divisions: 10 provinces (provincias, sing. —provincia)
Nationhood: June 25, 1975 (from Portugal)
National Holiday: Independence Day, June 25

■ ECONOMY

Overview: internal disorder, lack of government administrative control and a growing foreign

debt have contributed to the country's failure to exploit the economic potential of its agricultural, hydro power and transportation resources; depends on much foreign aid; industry operates at only 20–40% of capacity
GDP: US$17.5 billion; per capita US$900; real growth rate 9.2% (2001 est.)
Inflation: 11.4% (2000 est.)
Industries: accounts for 25% of GDP (2000); food, beverages, chemicals (fertilizer, soap, paints), petroleum products, textiles, non-metallic mineral products (cement, glass, asbestos), tobacco
Labour Force: 9.4 million (2001); 81% agriculture, 6% industry, 13% services
Unemployment: n.a.
Agriculture: accounts for 33% of GDP (2000), over 90% of labour force and about 90% of exports; cash crops—cotton, cashew nuts, sugar cane, tea, shrimp; other crops—cassava, corn, rice, tropical fruit; beef, poultry, not self-sufficient in food
Natural Resources: coal, titanium, natural gas, hydro power

■ FINANCE/TRADE

Currency: metical (pl. meticais) (Mt) = 100 centavos
International Reserves Excluding Gold: US$755 million (Nov. 2002)
Gold Reserves: n.a.
Budget: revenues US$393.1 million; expenditures US$1.025 billion, including capital expenditures US$479.4 million (2001 est.)
Defence Expenditures: 9.1% of central government expenditure (1999)
Education Expenditures: n.a.
External Debt: US$4.466 billion (2001)
Exports: US$190 million (2000); commodities: shrimp 48%, cashews 21%, sugar 10%, copra 3%, citrus 3%, cotton, electricity; partners: South Africa, Zimbabwe, Spain, Portugal
Imports: US$939 million (2000); commodities: food, clothing, farm equipment, petroleum, chemicals, metals; partners: South Africa, Portugal, US, Australia

■ COMMUNICATIONS

Daily Newspapers: 2/1,000 inhabitants (2000)
Televisions: 5/1,000 inhabitants (2001)
Radios: 44/1,000 inhabitants (2001)
Telephones: 4 lines/1,000 inhabitants (2001)

■ TRANSPORTATION

Motor Vehicles: 88,800; 67,600 passenger cars
Roads: 30,400 km; 5,685 km paved
Railway: 3,131 km (2001)
Air Traffic: 264,000 passengers carried (2001)
Airports: 166; 22 have paved runways (2002)

Canadian Embassy: The Canadian Embassy, avenida Julius Nyerere, No. 1128, Maputo; mailing address: P.O. Box 1578, Maputo, Mozambique. Tel: (011-258-1) 492-623. Fax: (011-258-1) 492-667. e-mail: canembas@ ecanada.uem.mz
Embassy in Canada: c/o High Commission for the Republic of Mozambique, 1990 M St NW, Ste 570, Washington DC 20036, USA. Tel: (202) 293-7146. Fax: (202) 835-0245. e-mail: n.a.

Myanmar

Long-Form Name: Union of Myanmar (formerly Burma)
Capital: Rangoon (Yangon)

■ GEOGRAPHY

Area: 678,500 sq. km
Coastline: 1,930 km
Climate: tropical monsoon; cloudy, rainy, hot, humid summers (southwest monsoon, June to Sept.); less cloudy, scant rainfall, mild temperatures, lower humidity during winter (northeast monsoon, Dec. to Apr.)
Environment: subject to destructive earthquakes and cyclones; flooding and landslides common during rainy season (June to Sept.); deforestation
Terrain: central lowlands ringed by steep, rugged highlands
Land Use: 15% arable land; 1% permanent crops; 1% meadows and pastures; 49% forest and woodland; 34% other; includes 15,920 sq. km irrigated
Location: SE Asia, bordering on Bay of Bengal

■ PEOPLE

Population: 42,238,224 (July 2002 est.)
Nationality: Burmese
Age Structure: 0–14 yrs: 28.6%; 15–64: 66.6%; 65+: 4.8% (2002 est.)
Population Growth Rate: 0.56% (2002 est.)
Net Migration: -1.83 migrants/1,000 population (2002 est.)
Ethnic Groups: 68% Burmese, 9% Shan, 7% Karen, 4% Rakhine, 3% Chinese, 2% Mon, 2% Indian, 5% other
Languages: Myanmar (Burmese); minority ethnic groups have their own languages
Religions: 89% Buddhist, 11% animist beliefs, Muslim, Christian or other
Birth Rate: 19.65/1,000 population (2002 est.)
Death Rate: 12.25/1,000 population (2002 est.)
Infant Mortality: 72.11 deaths/1,000 live births (2002 est.)
Life Expectancy at Birth: 53.85 years male, 57.07 years female (2002 est.)
Total Fertility Rate: 2.23 children born/woman (2002 est.)

Literacy: 84.7% (2000)

■ GOVERNMENT

Leader(s): Chairman and Prime Min. General Than Shwe
Government Type: military regime
Administrative Divisions: 7 divisions (yin-mya, sing. —yin), 7 states (pyine-mya, sing. —pyine)
Nationhood: Jan. 4, 1948 (from UK)
National Holiday: Independence Day, Jan. 4

■ ECONOMY

Overview: dependent on agriculture and vulnerable to world market conditions (especially for rice); has been unable to achieve much improvement in export earnings due to falling prices for many of its export commodities
GDP: US$63 billion, per capita US$1,500; real growth rate 2.3% (2001 est.)
Inflation: 21.1% (2001)
Industries: accounts for 9% of GDP (2000); agricultural processing; textiles and footwear; wood and wood products; petroleum refining; mining of copper, tin, tungsten, iron; construction materials; pharmaceuticals; fertilizer
Labour Force: 25.8 million (2001); 65% agriculture, 25% services, 10% industry
Unemployment: n.a.
Agriculture: accounts for 60% of GDP (2000); self-sufficient in food; principal crops: rice, corn, oilseed, sugar cane, pulses; world's largest stand of hardwood trees; rice and teak account for 55% of exports; world's largest producer of opium poppies
Natural Resources: crude oil, timber, tin, antimony, zinc, copper, tungsten, lead, coal, some marble, limestone, precious stones, natural gas

■ FINANCE/TRADE

Currency: kyat (K) = 100 pyas
International Reserves Excluding Gold: US$450 million (Sept. 2002)
Gold Reserves: 0.231 million fine troy ounces (Sept. 2002)
Budget: n.a.
Defence Expenditures: 26.6% of central government expenditure (2001)
Education Expenditures: 7.90% of central government expenditure (1999)
External Debt: US$5.670 billion (2001)
Exports: US$2.870 billion (2002 est.); commodities: teak, rice, oilseed, metals, rubber, gems; partners: US, India, China, Japan, Singapore
Imports: US$2.006 billion (2002 est.); commodities: machinery, transport equipment, chemicals, food products; partners: China, Singapore, South Korea, Japan, Taiwan

■ COMMUNICATIONS

Daily Newspapers: 9/1,000 inhabitants (2000)
Televisions: 8/1,000 inhabitants (2001)
Radios: 65/1,000 inhabitants (2001)
Telephones: 6 lines/1,000 inhabitants 2001)

■ TRANSPORTATION

Motor Vehicles: 69,000; 35,000 passenger cars
Roads: 28,200 km; 3,440 km paved
Railway: 3,991 km
Air Traffic: 398,000 passengers carried (2001)
Airports: 80; 8 have paved runways (2002)

Canadian Embassy: The Canadian Embassy to Myanmar, c/o The Canadian Embassy, 990 Rama IV, Abdulrahim Place, 15th Fl, Bangrak, Bangkok 10500, Thailand; mailing address: P.O. Box 2090, Bangkok 10501, Thailand. Tel: (011-66-2) 636-0540. Fax: (011-66-2) 636-0566. e-mail: bngkk@dfait-maeci.gc.ca
Embassy in Canada: c/o Embassy of the Union of Myanmar, 85 Range Rd, Ste 902/903, Ottawa ON K1N 8J6. Tel: (613) 232-6434. Fax: (613) 232-6435. e-mail: meott@magma.ca

Namibia

Long-Form Name: Republic of Namibia
Capital: Windhoek

■ GEOGRAPHY

Area: 825,418 sq. km
Coastline: 1,572 km
Climate: desert; hot, dry; rainfall sparse and erratic
Environment: inhospitable with very limited natural water resources; drought and desertification
Terrain: mostly high plateau; Namib Desert along coast; Kalahari Desert in east
Land Use: 1% arable; 0% permanent crops; 46% permanent pastures; 22% forest; 31% other; includes 70 sq. km irrigated
Location: SW Africa, bordering on South Atlantic Ocean

■ PEOPLE

Population: 1,820,916 (July 2002 est.)
Nationality: Namibian
Age Structure: 0–14 yrs: 42.6%; 15–64: 53.7%; 65+: 3.7% (2002 est.)
Population Growth Rate: 1.19% (2002 est.)
Net Migration: 0 migrants/1,000 population (2002 est.)
Ethnic Groups: 87.5% black, 6% white, 6.5% mixed; about 50% of the population belong to the Ovambo tribe and 9% to the Kavangos tribe

Languages: white population: 60% Afrikaans, 33% German, 7% English (all official); several indigenous languages
Religions: 90% Christian, 10% traditional religions
Birth Rate: 34.17/1,000 population (2002 est.)
Death Rate: 22.28/1,000 population (2002 est.)
Infant Mortality: 72.43 deaths/1,000 live births (2002 est.)
Life Expectancy at Birth: 40.81 years male, 37.07 years female (2002 est.)
Total Fertility Rate: 4.77 children born/woman (2002 est.)
Literacy: 82.0% (2000)

■ GOVERNMENT

Leader(s): Pres. Sam Nujoma, Prime Min. Theo-Ben Gurirab
Government Type: republic
Administrative Divisions: 13 regions
Nationhood: Mar. 21, 1990 (from South Africa)
National Holiday: Independence Day, Mar. 21

■ ECONOMY

Overview: very dependent on the mining industry to extract and process minerals for export; world's fifth largest producer of uranium; rich diamond deposits; more than 50% of the population depends on subsistence agriculture
GDP: US$8.1 billion, per capita US$4,500; real growth rate 4.0% (2001 est.)
Inflation: 9.5% (2001)
Industries: meat packing, fish processing, dairy products; mining accounts for 28% of GDP (2000)(copper, lead, zinc, diamonds, uranium)
Labour Force: 700,000 (2001); 47% agriculture, 20% industry, 33% services
Unemployment: n.a.
Agriculture: accounts for 11% of GDP (2000)(including fishing); mostly subsistence farming; livestock raising major source of cash income; crops: millet, sorghum, peanuts; large unfulfilled fish catch potential; needs to import food
Natural Resources: diamonds, copper, uranium, gold, lead, tin, zinc, salt, vanadium, natural gas, fish, hydroelectric potential; suspected deposits of coal and iron ore

■ FINANCE/TRADE

Currency: Namibian dollar = 100 cents, also the South African Rand
International Reserves Excluding Gold: US$323 million (Dec. 2002)
Gold Reserves: none (Jan. 2002)
Budget: n.a.
Defence Expenditures: 9.1% of central government expenditure (2001)
Education Expenditures: n.a.

External Debt: US$217 million (2000 est.)
Exports: US$1.244 billion (1999); commodities: diamonds, uranium, zinc, copper, meat, processed fish, karakul skins; partners: South Africa, UK, Spain, Japan
Imports: US$1.50 billion (1999 est.); commodities: foodstuffs, manufactured consumer goods, machinery and equipment, chemicals; partners: South Africa, Germany, US

■ COMMUNICATIONS

Daily Newspapers: 19/1,000 inhabitants (2000)
Televisions: 38/1,000 inhabitants (2001)
Radios: 141/1,000 inhabitants (2001)
Telephones: 66 lines/1,000 inhabitants (2001)

■ TRANSPORTATION

Motor Vehicles: 129,000; 62,500 passenger cars
Roads: 64,800 km; 5,378 km paved
Railway: 2,382 km
Air Traffic: 212,000 passengers carried (2001)
Airports: 137; 21 have paved runways (2002)

Canadian Embassy: The Canadian High Commission to Namibia, c/o The Canadian High Commission, 1103 Arcadia St, Hatfield 0028, Pretoria; mailing address: Private Bag X13, Hatfield 0028, Pretoria, South Africa. Tel.: (011-27-12) 422-3000. Fax: (011-27-12) 422-3052. e-mail: pret@dfait-maeci.gc.ca
Embassy in Canada: High Commission for the Republic of Namibia, 1605 New Hampshire Ave NW, Washington DC 20009, USA. Tel: (202) 986-0540. Fax: (202) 986-0443. e-mail: n.a.

Nauru

Long-Form Name: Republic of Nauru
Capital: no capital city as such; government offices in Yaren

■ GEOGRAPHY

Area: 21 sq. km
Coastline: 30 km
Climate: tropical; monsoonal; rainy season (Nov. to Feb.)
Environment: only 53 km south of equator; periodic droughts; water supply limited and unreliable
Terrain: sandy beach rises to fertile ring around raised coral reefs with phosphate plateau in centre
Land Use: 0% arable; 0% permanent crops; 0% meadows; 0% forest; 100% other
Location: island in the Pacific Ocean, NE of Australia

■ PEOPLE

Population: 12,329 (July 2002 est.)
Nationality: Nauruan

Age Structure: 0–14 yrs: 39.6%; 15–64: 58.7%; 65+: 1.7% (2002 est.)
Population Growth Rate: 1.96% (2002 est.)
Net Migration: 0 migrants/1,000 population (2002 est.)
Ethnic Groups: 58% Nauruan, 26% other Pacific Islander, 8% Chinese, 8% European
Languages: Nauruan, a distinct Pacific Island language (official); English widely understood, spoken and used for most government and commercial purposes
Religions: Christian (two-thirds Nauruan Protestant, one-third Roman Catholic)
Birth Rate: 26.60/1,000 population (2002 est.)
Death Rate: 7.06/1,000 population (2002 est.)
Infant Mortality: 10.52 deaths/1,000 live births (2002 est.)
Life Expectancy at Birth: 58.05 years male, 65.26 years female (2002 est.)
Total Fertility Rate: 3.50 children born/woman (2002 est.)
Literacy: n.a.

■ GOVERNMENT

Leader(s): Pres. Rene Harris
Government Type: republic
Administrative Divisions: 14 districts
Nationhood: Jan. 31, 1968 (from UN trusteeship under Australia, New Zealand and UK; formerly known as Pleasant Island)
National Holiday: Independence Day, Jan. 31

■ ECONOMY

Overview: most resources are imported; has one of the highest per capita incomes in the Third World; the rehabilitation of mined land and the replacement of income from phosphates are serious long-term considerations
GDP: US$60 million; per capita US$5,000; real growth rate n.a. (2001 est.)
Inflation: n.a.
Industries: phosphate mining, financial services, coconuts
Labour Force: n.a.
Unemployment: 0%
Agriculture: coconuts; other agricultural activities are negligible; almost completely dependent on imports for food and water
Natural Resources: phosphates

■ FINANCE/TRADE

Currency: Australian dollar ($A) = 100 cents
International Reserves Excluding Gold: n.a.
Gold Reserves: n.a.
Budget: n.a.
Defence Expenditures: no formal defence structure
Education Expenditures: n.a.
External Debt: n.a.

Exports: n.a.; commodities: phosphates; partners: Australia, New Zealand, South Korea, US
Imports: n.a.; commodities: food, fuel, manufacturers, building materials, machinery; partners: Australia, US, UK, Indonesia, India

■ COMMUNICATIONS

Daily Newspapers: none
Televisions: n.a.
Radios: n.a.
Telephones: n.a.

■ TRANSPORTATION

Motor Vehicles: n.a.
Roads: 30 km; 24 km paved
Railway: 5 km
Air Traffic: 155,000 passengers carried (1999 est.)
Airports: 1, with a paved runway (2002)

Canadian Embassy: c/o The Canadian High Commission, Commonwealth Ave, Canberra A.C.T. 2600, Australia. Tel: (011-61-2) 6270-4000. Fax: (011-61-2) 6273-3285. e-mail: cnbra@dfait-maeci.gc.ca
Embassy in Canada: c/o Australian High Commission, 50 O'Connor St, Ste 710, Ottawa ON K1P 6L2. Tel: (613) 236-0841. Fax: (613) 236-4376. e-mail: n.a.

Nepal

Long-Form Name: Kingdom of Nepal
Capital: Kathmandu

■ GEOGRAPHY

Area: 140,800 sq. km
Coastline: none: landlocked
Climate: varies from cool summers and severe winters in north to subtropical summers and mild winters in south
Environment: contains eight of the world's 10 highest peaks; flooding, drought, landslides; deforestation; soil erosion; water pollution
Terrain: flat river plain of the Ganges in south, central hilly region, rugged Himalayas in north
Land Use: 17% arable; negligible permanent crops; 15% meadows; 42% forest; 26% other; includes 11,350 sq. km irrigated
Location: SC Asia, bordering on India and Tibet

■ PEOPLE

Population: 25,873,917 (July 2002 est.)
Nationality: Nepalese
Age Structure: 0–14 yrs: 40.0%; 15–64: 56.4%; 65+: 3.6% (2002 est.)
Population Growth Rate: 2.29% (2002 est.)
Net Migration: 0 migrants/1,000 population (2002 est.)
Ethnic Groups: Newars, Indians, Tibetans, Gurungs, Magars, Tamangs, Bhotias, Rais,

Limbus, Sherpas, as well as many smaller groups

Languages: Nepali (official); 20 languages divided into numerous dialects

Religions: 90% Hindu, 5% Buddhist, 3% Muslim, 2% other; only official Hindu state in the world, although no sharp distinction between many Hindu and Buddhist groups; small groups of Muslims and Christians

Birth Rate: 32.49/1,000 population (2002 est.)

Death Rate: 10.03/1,000 population (2002 est.)

Infant Mortality: 72.36 deaths/1,000 live births (2002 est.)

Life Expectancy at Birth: 59.01 years male, 58.20 years female (2002 est.)

Total Fertility Rate: 4.48 children born/woman (2002 est.)

Literacy: 41.8% (2000)

■ GOVERNMENT

Leader(s): King Gyanendra Bir Bikram Shah Dev, Prime Min. Surya Bahadur Thapa

Government Type: parliamentary democracy

Administrative Divisions: 14 zones (anchal, sing. & pl.)

Nationhood: 1768, unified by Prithvi Narayan Shah

National Holiday: Birthday of His Majesty the King, July 7

■ ECONOMY

Overview: one of the poorest and most underdeveloped countries in the world; agriculture provides the backbone of the economy, employing more than 80% of the population; there have been attempts to expand into other economic sectors

GDP: US$35.6 billion, per capita US$1,400; real growth rate 2.6% (2001 est.)

Inflation: 2.8% (2001)

Industries: accounts for 22% of GDP; small rice, jute, sugar and oilseed mills, cigarettes, textiles, cement, brick; tourism, carpet production

Labour Force: 11.0 million (2001); 81% agriculture, 16% services, 3% industry

Unemployment: 1.1% (2001)

Agriculture: accounts for 41% of GDP and 80% of workforce; farm products—rice, corn, wheat, sugar cane, root crops, milk, buffalo meat; not self-sufficient in food, particularly in drought years

Natural Resources: quartz, water, timber, hydroelectric potential, scenic beauty; small deposits of lignite, copper, cobalt, iron ore

■ FINANCE/TRADE

Currency: rupee (NRs) = 100 paisa

International Reserves Excluding Gold: US$1.018 billion (Dec. 2002)

Gold Reserves: 0.153 million fine troy ounces (Dec. 2002)

Budget: revenues US$665 million; expenditures US$1.1 billion, capital expenditures US$ n.a. (FY1999/2000 est.)

Defence Expenditures: 6.5% of central government expenditure (2001)

Education Expenditures: 15.24% of central government expenditure (2001)

External Debt: US$2.700 billion (2001)

Exports: US$738 million (2001); commodities: clothing, carpets, leather goods, grain; partners: India, US, Germany

Imports: US$1.474 billion (2001); commodities: petroleum products 20%, fertilizer 11%, machinery and equipment 10%; partners: India, Singapore, China, Hong Kong

■ COMMUNICATIONS

Daily Newspapers: 12/1,000 inhabitants (2000)

Televisions: 8/1,000 inhabitants (2001)

Radios: 39/1,000 inhabitants (2001)

Telephones: 13 lines/1,000 inhabitants (2001)

■ TRANSPORTATION

Motor Vehicles: n.a.

Roads: 13,223 km; 4,073 km paved

Railway: 59 km

Air Traffic: 641,000 passengers carried (2001)

Airports: 45; 9 have paved runways (2002)

Canadian Embassy: The Canadian Embassy to Nepal, c/o The Canadian Cooperation Office, Lazimpat, Kathmandu, Nepal; mailing address: P.O. Box 4574, Kathmandu, Nepal. Tel: (011-9771) 415-193. Fax: (011-9771) 410-422. e-mail: cco@cco.org.np

Embassy in Canada: Embassy of the Kingdom of Nepal, 2131 Leroy Place NW, Washington DC 20008, USA. Tel: (202) 667-4550. Fax: (202) 667-5534. e-mail: nepali@erols.com

Netherlands

Long-Form Name: Kingdom of the Netherlands

Capital: Amsterdam; seat of government: The Hague

■ GEOGRAPHY

Area: 41,526 sq. km

Coastline: 451 km

Climate: temperate; marine; cool summers and mild winters

Environment: nearly half of the land area is below sea level and protected from the North Sea by dikes; water and air pollution

Terrain: mostly coastal lowland and reclaimed land (polders); some hills in southeast

Land Use: 25% arable; 3% permanent crops; 25% permanent pastures; 8% forest; 39% other; includes 5,650 sq. km irrigated
Location: NW Europe, bordering on North Sea

■ PEOPLE

Population: 16,067,754 (July 2002 est.)
Nationality: Dutchman, Dutchwoman
Age Structure: 0–14 yrs: 18.3%; 15–64: 67.9%; 65+: 13.8% (2002 est.)
Population Growth Rate: 0.53% (2002 est.)
Net Migration: 2.35 migrants/1,000 population (2002 est.)
Ethnic Groups: 91% Dutch, 9% Moroccans, Turks and others
Languages: Dutch, Frisian
Religions: 62% Christianity, of which 34% is Roman Catholic and 25% is Protestant; most of the rest do not profess a religion
Birth Rate: 11.58/1,000 population (2002 est.)
Death Rate: 8.67/1,000 population (2002 est.)
Infant Mortality: 4.31 deaths/1,000 live births (2002 est.)
Life Expectancy at Birth: 75.70 years male, 81.59 years female (2002 est.)
Total Fertility Rate: 1.65 children born/woman (2002 est.)
Literacy: approaching 100% (2000)

■ GOVERNMENT

Leader(s): Head of State: Queen Beatrix, Prem. Jan Peter Balkenende
Government Type: constitutional monarchy
Administrative Divisions: 12 provinces (provincien, sing. provincie); dependent areas: Aruba, Netherlands Antilles
Nationhood: 1579 (from Spain)
National Holiday: Queen's Day, Apr. 30

■ ECONOMY

Overview: a highly developed and affluent economy based on private enterprise; numerous government-backed welfare programs; trade and financial sectors are the strongest part of the economy
GDP: US$434 billion, per capita US$26,900; real growth rate 0.3% (2002 est.)
Inflation: 4.5% (2001)
Industries: contributes 26% to the GDP (2001 est.); agro-industries, metal and engineering products, electrical machinery and equipment, chemicals, petroleum, fishing, construction, micro-electronics
Labour Force: 7.4 million (2001); 73% community, social and business services, 23% industry, 4% agriculture
Unemployment: 2.7% (Dec. 2002)
Agriculture: accounts for 3% of GDP (2001 est.) and 4% of labour force; animal production

predominates; crops—grains, potatoes, sugar beets, fruits, vegetables; shortages of grain, fats and oils
Natural Resources: natural gas, crude oil, fertile soil

■ FINANCE/TRADE

Currency: guilder, gulden or florin (f.) = 100 cents; Euro (€); on January 1, 2002 the Euro became the sole currency for everyday transactions.
International Reserves Excluding Gold: US$9.563 billion (Dec. 2002)
Gold Reserves: 27.382 million fine troy ounces (Dec. 2002)
Budget: revenues US$134 billion; expenditures US$134 billion, including capital expenditures of US$ n.a. (2001 est.)
Defence Expenditures: 4.0% of central government expenditures (2001)
Education Expenditures: n.a.
External Debt: none
Exports: US$215.388 billion (2002 est.); commodities; agricultural products, processed foods and tobacco, natural gas, chemicals, metal products, textiles, clothing; partners: EU (Germany, Benelux, UK, France, Italy)
Imports: US$187.033 billion (2002 est.); commodities: raw materials and semi-finished products, consumer goods, transportation equipment, crude oil, food products; partners: Germany, Benelux, UK, France, US

■ COMMUNICATIONS

Daily Newspapers: 306/1,000 inhabitants (2000)
Televisions: 553/1,000 inhabitants (2001)
Radios: 980/1,000 inhabitants (2001)
Telephones: 621 lines/1,000 inhabitants (2001)

■ TRANSPORTATION

Motor Vehicles: 6,800,000; 6,100,000 passenger cars (2000)
Roads: 116,500 km; 104,850 km paved
Railway: 2,808 km
Air Traffic: 20,474,000 passengers carried (2001)
Airports: 28; 21 have paved runways (2002)

Canadian Embassy: The Canadian Embassy, Sophialaan 7, 2514JP, The Hague, Netherlands. Tel: (011-31-70) 311-1600. Fax: (011-31-70) 311-1620. e-mail: hague@dfait-maeci.gc.ca
Embassy in Canada: Embassy of the Kingdom of the Netherlands, 350 Albert St, Ste 2020, Ottawa ON K1R 1A4. Tel: (613) 237-5030. Fax: (613) 237-6471. e-mail: nlgovott@netcom.ca

Netherlands Antilles

Long-Form Name: Netherlands Antilles

Capital: Willemstad

■ GEOGRAPHY

Area: 960 sq. km, 2 island groups
Climate: tropical maritime, moderated by northeasterly trade winds, short rainy season
Land Use: islands mostly too rocky for agriculture; only 10% is arable land; 0% permanent crops; 0% meadows and pastures; 0% forest, 90% other; includes n.a. sq. km irrigated
Location: West Indies, just north of Venezuela

■ PEOPLE

Population: 214,258 (July 2002 est.)
Nationality: Netherlands Antillean, or Dutch Antillean
Ethnic Groups: mixed African 85%, Carib Indian, European, Latin, Oriental
Languages: Dutch (official), Papiamento (derived from Dutch, Spanish, Portuguese), English

■ GOVERNMENT

Colony/Territory of: Dependent Territory of the Netherlands
Leader(s): Chief of State: Queen Beatrix, Gov. Frits Goedgedrag, Prime Min. Etienne Ys
Government Type: dependency with internal self-government; the Dutch government retains responsibility for defense and foreign affairs.
National Holiday: Queen's Day, Apr. 30

■ ECONOMY

Overview: unlike many Latin American countries, the Netherlands Antilles has avoided crushing external debt; Curaçao has one of the largest ship-repair dry docks in the western hemisphere; almost all consumer goods must be imported; chief trading partner: UK

■ FINANCE/TRADE

Currency: Netherlands Antilles guilder, gulden or florin = 100 cents; also the Euro

Canadian Embassy: c/o The Canadian Embassy, 7, 2514JP The Hague, Netherlands. Tel: (011-31-70) 311-1600. Fax: (011-31-70) 311-1620. e-mail: hague@dfait-maeci.gc.ca
Representative to Canada: c/o Embassy of the Kingdom of the Netherlands, 350 Albert St, Ste 2020, Ottawa ON K1R 1A4. Tel: (613) 237-5030. Fax: (613) 237-6471. e-mail: nlgovott@netcom.ca

New Caledonia

Long-Form Name: Territory of New Caledonia and Dependencies
Capital: Nouméa

■ GEOGRAPHY

Area: 19,060 sq. km (a peninsula and three small islands)
Climate: humid, subtropical maritime, modified by southeast trade winds
Land Use: 0% arable; 0% permanent crops; 12% meadow and pasture, 39% forest and woodland, 49% other; includes 160 sq. km irrigated
Location: SW Pacific Ocean (Melanesia), E of Australia

■ PEOPLE

Population: 207,858 (July 2002 est.)
Nationality: New Caledonian
Ethnic Groups: 42.5% Melanesian, 37.1% European, 8.4% Wallisian, 3.8% Polynesian, 3.6% Indonesian, 1.6% Vietnamese, 3% other
Languages: French (official), 28 Melanesian and Polynesian languages

■ GOVERNMENT

Colony/Territory of: Overseas Territory of France
Leader(s): Pres. Jacques Chirac (France), High Comm. Daniel Constantin
Government Type: overseas territory of France since 1956
National Holiday: Taking of the Bastille, July 14

■ ECONOMY

Overview: only a negligible portion of the land is arable; and most food must be imported; the backbone of the economy is nickel export

■ FINANCE/TRADE

Currency: CFP franc = 100 centimes

Canadian Embassy: c/o The Canadian Embassy, 35-37 avenue Montaigne 75008 Paris, France. Tel: (011-33-1) 44-43-29-00. Fax: (011-33-1) 44-43-29-99. e-mail: paris@dfait-maeci.gc.ca
Representative to Canada: c/o Embassy of France, 42 Sussex Dr, Ottawa ON K1M 2C9. Tel: (613) 789-1795. Fax: (613) 562-3735. e-mail: politique@ambafrance-ca.org

New Zealand

Long-Form Name: New Zealand
Capital: Wellington

■ GEOGRAPHY

Area: 268,680 sq. km
Coastline: 15,134 km
Climate: temperate with sharp regional contrasts
Environment: earthquakes are common though usually not severe; deforestation and soil degradation are increasing; occasional volcanic activity
Terrain: predominantly mountainous with some large coastal plains

Land Use: 9% arable; 5% permanent crops; 50% meadows and pastures; 28% forest and woodland; 8% other; includes 2,850 sq. km irrigated
Location: SE of Australia, bordering on Tasman Sea, Pacific Ocean

■ PEOPLE

Population: 3,908,037 (July 2002 est.)
Nationality: New Zealander
Age Structure: 0–14 yrs: 22.2%; 15–64: 66.3%; 65+: 11.5% (2002 est.)
Population Growth Rate: 1.12% (2002 est.)
Net Migration: 4.48 migrants/1,000 population (2002 est.)
Ethnic Groups: 79.1% European, 9.7% Maori, 3.8% Pacific Islander, 7.4% other
Languages: English (official), Maori
Religions: 75% Christian, 18% unspecified, 7% Hindu, Confucian, other
Birth Rate: 14.23/1,000 population (2002 est.)
Death Rate: 7.55/1,000 population (2002 est.)
Infant Mortality: 6.18 deaths/1,000 live births (2002 est.)
Life Expectancy at Birth: 75.17 years male, 81.27 years female (2002 est.)
Total Fertility Rate: 1.80 children born/woman (2002 est.)
Literacy: approaching 100% (2000)

■ GOVERNMENT

Leader(s): Head of State: Queen Elizabeth II, Gov. Gen. Silvia Cartwright, Prime Min. Helen Clark
Government Type: parliamentary democracy
Administrative Divisions: 93 counties, 9 districts, 3 town districts; dependent areas includes the Cook Islands, the Kermadec Islands, Niue, the Ross Dependency (uninhabited except for scientific personnel), Tokelau
Nationhood: Sept. 26, 1907 (from UK)
National Holiday: Waitangi Day, Feb. 6

■ ECONOMY

Overview: government has been reorienting from an agrarian to an open, free-market economy that can compete in the global community; inflation and unemployment have been reduced
GDP: US$75.4 billion, per capita US$19,500; real growth rate 3.1% (2001 est.)
Inflation: 2.6% (2001)
Industries: accounts for 23% of GDP; food processing, wool production, wood and paper products, textiles, machinery, transportation equipment, banking and insurance, tourism, mining
Labour Force: 1.9 million (2000); 6.5% community, social and business services, 25% industry, 10% agriculture
Unemployment: 5.3% (Aug. 2002)

Agriculture: accounts for 8% of GDP and 10% of workforce; livestock predominates: wool, meat, dairy products; crops: wheat, barley, potatoes, pulses, fruit and vegetables; fish; surplus producer of farm products
Natural Resources: natural gas, iron ore, sand, coal, timber, hydroelectricity, gold, limestone

■ FINANCE/TRADE

Currency: New Zealand dollar (NZ$) = 100 cents
International Reserves Excluding Gold: US$3.739 billion (Dec. 2002)
Gold Reserves: none (Jan. 2002)
Budget: revenues US$16.7 billion; expenditures US$16.6 billion, including capital expenditures US$ n.a. (FY2000/01)
Defence Expenditures: 4.0% of central government expenditure (2001)
Education Expenditures: 16.29% of central government expenditure (2000)
External Debt: US$30.8 billion (2000 est.)
Exports: US$14.364 billion (2002 est.); commodities: wool, lamb, mutton, beef, fruit, fish, cheese, manufactures, chemicals, forestry products; partners: Japan, Australia, US, UK, South Korea, China
Imports: US$15.078 billion (2002); commodities: petroleum, consumer goods, motor vehicles, industrial equipment; partners: Australia, US, Japan, UK, China, Germany

■ COMMUNICATIONS

Daily Newspapers: 362/1,000 inhabitants (2000)
Televisions: 557/1,000 inhabitants (2001)
Radios: 997/1,000 inhabitants (2001)
Telephones: 477 lines/1,000 inhabitants (2001)

■ TRANSPORTATION

Motor Vehicles: 2,100,000; 1,900,000 passenger cars (2000)
Roads: 92,200 km; 53,568 km paved
Railway: 3,908 km (2001)
Air Traffic: 11,095,000 passengers carried (2001)
Airports: 106; 46 have paved runways (2002)

Canadian Embassy: The Canadian High Commission, 61 Molesworth St, 3rd Floor, Thorndon, Wellington; mailing address: P.O. Box 12049, Thorndon, Wellington, New Zealand. Tel: (011-64-4) 473-9577. Fax: (011-64-4) 471-2082. e-mail: wlgtn@dfait-maeci.gc.ca
Embassy in Canada: c/o New Zealand High Commission, Clarica Centre, 99 Bank St, Ste 727, Ottawa ON K1P 6G3. Tel: (613) 238-5991. Fax: (613) 238-5707. e-mail: nzhcott@istar.ca

Nicaragua

Long-Form Name: Republic of Nicaragua

Capital: Managua

■ GEOGRAPHY

Area: 129,494 sq. km
Coastline: 910 km
Climate: tropical in lowlands, cooler in highlands
Environment: subject to destructive earthquakes, volcanoes, landslides and occasional severe hurricanes; deforestation; soil erosion; water pollution
Terrain: extensive Atlantic coastal plains rising to central interior mountains; narrow Pacific coastal plain interrupted by volcanoes
Land Use: 9% arable; 1% permanent crops; 46% meadows; 27% forest; 17% other; includes 880 sq. km irrigated
Location: Central (Latin) America, bordering on Caribbean Sea, Pacific Ocean

■ PEOPLE

Population: 5,023,818 (July 2002 est.)
Nationality: Nicaraguan
Age Structure: 0–14 yrs: 38.3%; 15–64: 58.7%; 65+: 3.0% (2002 est.)
Population Growth Rate: 2.09% (2002 est.)
Net Migration: -1.30 migrants/1,000 population (2002 est.)
Ethnic Groups: 69% mestizo, 17% white, 9% black, 5% Indian
Languages: Spanish (official); English- and Indian-speaking minorities on Atlantic coast
Religions: 95% Roman Catholic, 5% Protestant
Birth Rate: 26.98/1,000 population (2002 est.)
Death Rate: 4.76/1,000 population (2002 est.)
Infant Mortality: 32.52 deaths/1,000 live births (2002 est.)
Life Expectancy at Birth: 67.39 years male, 71.44 years female (2002 est.)
Total Fertility Rate: 3.09 children born/woman (2002 est.)
Literacy: 66.5% (2000)

■ GOVERNMENT

Leader(s): Pres. Enrique Bolanos, V. Pres. Jose Rizo
Government Type: republic
Administrative Divisions: 15 departments (departamentos, sing. —departamento) and 2 autonomous regions (regiones autonomistas, sing. —region autonomista)
Nationhood: Sept. 15, 1821 (from Spain)
National Holiday: Independence Day, Sept. 15

■ ECONOMY

Overview: based on the export of coffee and cotton; government control is extensive, including the financial system, wholesale purchasing, production, sales, foreign trade and distribution of goods; many shortages; high inflation

GDP: US$12.3 billion, per capita US$2,500; real growth rate 2.5% (2001 est.)
Inflation: 11.00% (2000 est.)
Industries: accounts for 23% of GDP (2000); food processing, chemicals, metal products, textiles, clothing, petroleum refining and distribution, beverages, footwear
Labour Force: 2.1 million (2001); 43% services, 42% agriculture, 15% industry
Unemployment: 13.3%; underemployment approximately 36% (2001 est.)
Agriculture: accounts for 33% of GDP (2000); cash crops—coffee, bananas, sugar cane, cotton, tobacco; food crops—rice, corn, cassava, citrus fruit, beans; variety of animal products—beef, veal, pork, poultry, dairy; war has lowered self-sufficiency in food
Natural Resources: gold, silver, copper, tungsten, lead, zinc, timber, fish

■ FINANCE/TRADE

Currency: gold córdoba ($C) = 100 centavos
International Reserves Excluding Gold: US$448 million (Dec. 2002)
Gold Reserves: n.a.
Budget: revenues US$726 million; expenditures US$908 million, including capital expenditures US$ n.a. (2000 est.)
Defence Expenditures: 3.1% of central government expenditure (2001)
Education Expenditures: na
External Debt: US$6.391 billion (2001)
Exports: US$607 million (2001); commodities: coffee, cotton, sugar, bananas, seafood, meat, chemicals; partners: US, Germany, Canada, Costa Rica, Honduras
Imports: US$1.776 billion (2001); commodities: petroleum, food, chemicals, machinery, clothing; partners: US, Costa Rica, Venezuela, Guatemala, Mexico

■ COMMUNICATIONS

Daily Newspapers: 30/1,000 inhabitants (2000)
Televisions: 69/1,000 inhabitants (2001)
Radios: 270/1,000 inhabitants (2001)
Telephones: 31 lines/1,000 inhabitants (2001)

■ TRANSPORTATION

Motor Vehicles: 148,000; 73,000 passenger cars
Roads: 16,382 km; 1,818 km paved
Railway: 6 km (2001)
Air Traffic: 61,000 passengers carried (2001)
Airports: 182; 11 have paved runways (2002)

Canadian Embassy: The Office of the Canadian Embassy, Costado Oriental de la Casa Nazareth, Una Quadra Arriba, Calle Noval, Managua. Mailing address: The Office of the Canadian Embassy, Apartado Postal 25, Managua, Nicaragua. Tel: (011-505) 268-0433. Fax: (011-

505) 268-0437. e-mail: mngua@dfait-maeci.gc.ca

Embassy in Canada: c/o Embassy of the Republic of Nicaragua, 1627 New Hampshire Ave NW, Washington DC 20009, USA. Tel: (202) 939-6570. Fax: (202) 939-6545. e-mail: n.a.

Niger

Long-Form Name: Republic of Niger
Capital: Niamey

■ GEOGRAPHY

Area: 1,267,000 sq. km
Coastline: none: landlocked
Climate: mostly hot, dry, dusty; tropical in extreme south
Environment: recurrent drought and desertification severely affecting marginal agricultural activities; overgrazing; soil erosion
Terrain: desert and sand dunes; hills in north
Land Use: 3% arable land; 0% permanent crops; 7% meadows; 2% forest; 88% other; includes 660 sq. km irrigated
Location: WC Africa

■ PEOPLE

Population: 10,639,744 (July 2002 est.)
Nationality: Nigerien
Age Structure: 0–14 yrs: 47.9%; 15–64: 49.8%; 65+: 2.3% (2002 est.)
Population Growth Rate: 2.70% (2002 est.)
Net Migration: -0.71 migrants/1,000 population (2002 est.)
Ethnic Groups: 56% Hausa; 22% Djerma; 8.5% Fula; 8% Tuareg; 4.3% Beri Beri (Kanouri); 1.2% Arab, Toubou and Gourmantche; about 1,200 French expatriates
Languages: French (official); Hausa (50%), Djerma, also Tuareg, Fulani
Religions: 80% Muslim, remainder indigenous beliefs and Christians
Birth Rate: 49.95/1,000 population (2002 est.)
Death Rate: 22.25/1,000 population (2002 est.)
Infant Mortality: 122.23 deaths/1,000 live births (2002 est.)
Life Expectancy at Birth: 42.04 years male, 41.77 years female (2002 est.)
Total Fertility Rate: 7.00 children born/woman (2002 est.)
Literacy: 15.3% (1999)

■ GOVERNMENT

Leader(s): Pres. Mamadou Tandja, Prime Min. Hama Amadou
Government Type: republic
Administrative Divisions: 7 departments (departements, sing. —departement); 1 capital district (capitale district)
Nationhood: Aug. 3, 1960 (from France)

National Holiday: Republic Day, Dec. 18

■ ECONOMY

Overview: about 90% of the population is engaged in livestock rearing and farming; depends heavily on exploitation of uranium deposits, thus vulnerable to demand for uranium; increasing external debt is a problem; GDP growth cannot keep pace with the rapid population growth
GDP: US$8.4 billion, per capita US$820; real growth rate 3.1% (2001 est.)
Inflation: 4.0% (2001)
Industries: accounts for 17% of GDP (2000); cement, brick, rice mills, small cotton gins, textiles, chemicals, oilseed presses, slaughterhouses and a few other small light industries; uranium production began in 1971
Labour Force: 5.3 million (2001); 90% agriculture, 6% industry, 4% government
Unemployment: n.a.
Agriculture: accounts for 41% of GDP (2000) and 90% of labour force; cash crops—cowpeas, cotton, peanuts; food crops—millet, sorghum, cassava, rice; livestock—cattle, sheep, goats, camels, poultry; self-sufficient in food except in drought years
Natural Resources: uranium, coal, iron ore, tin, phosphates, gold, petroleum

■ FINANCE/TRADE

Currency: Communauté financière africaine franc (CFAF) = 100 centimes
International Reserves Excluding Gold: US$140 million (Oct. 2002)
Gold Reserves: 0.011 million fine troy ounces (Aug. 2000)
Budget: revenues US$320 million; expenditures US$320 million, including capital expenditures of US$178 million (2002 est.)
Defence Expenditures: 6.4% of central government expenditure (1999)
Education Expenditures: n.a.
External Debt: US$1.555 billion (2001)
Exports: US$270 million (2001); commodities: uranium 76%, livestock, cowpeas, onions, hides, skins; partners: France, Nigeria, Spain, US
Imports: US$320 million (2001); commodities: petroleum products, primary materials, machinery, vehicles and parts, electronic equipment, pharmaceuticals, chemical products, cereals, foodstuffs; partners: France, Côte d'Ivoire, Nigeria, US

■ COMMUNICATIONS

Daily Newspapers: less than 1/1,000 inhabitants (2000)
Televisions: 37/1,000 inhabitants (2001)
Radios: 121/1,000 inhabitants (2001)

Telephones: 2 lines/1,000 inhabitants (2001)

■ TRANSPORTATION

Motor Vehicles: 51,600; 37,500 passenger cars
Roads: 10,100 km; 798 km paved
Railway: none
Air Traffic: 46,000 passengers carried (2001)
Airports: 26; 9 have paved runways (2002)

Canadian Embassy: Office of the Canadian Embassy, Boulevard Mali Béro, Niamey, Niger; mailing address: Box 362, Niamey, Niger. Tel: (011-227) 75-36-86. Fax: (011-227) 75-31-07. e-mail: niamy@dfait-maeci.gc.ca
Embassy in Canada: Embassy of the Republic of Niger, 38 Blackburn Ave, Ottawa ON K1N 8A3. Tel: (613) 232-4291. Fax: (613) 230-9808. e-mail: n.a.

Nigeria

Long-Form Name: Federal Republic of Nigeria
Capital: Abuja

■ GEOGRAPHY

Area: 923,768 sq. km
Coastline: 853 km
Climate: varies; equatorial in south, tropical in centre, arid in north
Environment: recent droughts in north severely affecting marginal agricultural activities; desertification; soil degradation, rapid deforestation
Terrain: southern lowlands merge into central hills and plateaus; mountains in southeast, plains in north
Land Use: 33% arable; 3% permanent crops; 44% permanent pastures; 12% forest; 8% other; includes 2,330 sq. km irrigated
Location: WC Africa, bordering on South Atlantic Ocean

■ PEOPLE

Population: 129,934,911 (July 2002 est.)
Nationality: Nigerian
Age Structure: 0–14 yrs: 43.6%; 15–64: 53.6%; 65+: 2.8% (2002 est.)
Population Growth Rate: 2.54% (2002 est.)
Net Migration: 0.27 migrants/1,000 population (2002 est.)
Ethnic Groups: more than 250 tribal groups; Hausa and Fulani of the north, Yoruba of the southwest and Ibos of the southeast make up 65% of the population; about 27,000 non-Africans
Languages: English (official); Hausa, Yoruba, Ibo, Fulani and several other languages also widely used

Religions: 50% Muslim, 40% Christian, 10% indigenous beliefs
Birth Rate: 39.22/1,000 population (2002 est.)
Death Rate: 14.10/1,000 population (2002 est.)
Infant Mortality: 72.49 deaths/1,000 live births (2002 est.)
Life Expectancy at Birth: 50.58 years male, 50.60 years female (2002 est.)
Total Fertility Rate: 5.49 children born/woman (2002 est.)
Literacy: 63.9% (2000)

■ GOVERNMENT

Leader(s): Pres. Olusegun Obasanjo, V. Pres. Atiku Abubakar
Government Type: republic in transition from military to civilian rule.
Administrative Divisions: 36 states and 1 territory
Nationhood: Oct. 1, 1960 (from UK)
National Holiday: Independence Day, Oct. 1

■ ECONOMY

Overview: dependent on oil and vulnerable to oil prices; agricultural production cannot keep pace with rapid population growth and Nigeria, once a large exporter of food, must now import foodstuffs; high inflationary pressures are a concern; government efforts to reduce Nigeria's dependence on oil exports and to sustain non-inflationary economic growth have been hampered by inadequate new investment and endemic corruption
GDP: US$105.9 billion, per capita US$840; real growth rate 3.5% (2001 est.)
Inflation: 16.5% (2001)
Industries: accounts for 33% of GDP (2000); crude oil, natural gas, coal, tin, columbite; palm oil, peanut, cotton, rubber, petroleum, wood, hides and skins; textiles, cement, building materials, food products, footwear, chemicals, printing, ceramics, steel
Labour Force: 51.6 million (2001); 70% agriculture, 20% services, 10% industry
Unemployment: n.a.
Agriculture: accounts for 39% of GDP (2000) and half of labour force; inefficient small-scale farming dominates; once a large net exporter of food and now an importer; cash crops—cocoa, peanuts, palm oil, rubber; food crops—corn, rice, sorghum, millet, cassava, yams, fishing and forestry, livestock
Natural Resources: crude oil, tin, columbite, iron ore, coal, limestone, lead, zinc, natural gas

■ FINANCE/TRADE

Currency: naira (N) = 100 kobo
International Reserves Excluding Gold: US$9.227 billion (May 2002)

Gold Reserves: 0.687 million fine troy ounces (Sept. 2002)
Budget: revenues US$3.4 billion; expenditures US$3.6 billion, including capital expenditures of US$ n.a. (2000 est.)
Defence Expenditures: 8.1% of central government expenditure (1999)
Education Expenditures: n.a.
External Debt: US$31.119 billion (2001)
Exports: US$15.107 billion (2002); commodities: oil 95%, cocoa, palm kernels, rubber; partners: US, Spain, India, France, Brazil
Imports: US$7.547 billion (2002); commodities: consumer goods, capital equipment, chemicals, raw materials; partners: UK, US, France, Germany, China

■ COMMUNICATIONS

Daily Newspapers: 24/1,000 inhabitants (2000)
Televisions: 68/1,000 inhabitants (2001)
Radios: 200/1,000 inhabitants (2001)
Telephones: 5 lines/1,000 inhabitants (2001)

■ TRANSPORTATION

Motor Vehicles: 970,000; 590,200 passenger cars
Roads: 193,200 km; 59,892 km paved, but much of the road system is barely usable.
Railway: 3,557 km
Air Traffic: 529,000 passengers carried (2001)
Airports: 70; 36 have paved runways (2002)

Canadian Embassy: The Canadian High Commission, 3A Bobo St, Maitama, Abuja FCT, Nigeria. Tel: (011-234-9) 413-9910. Fax: (011-234-9) 413-9911. e-mail: abuja@dfait-maeci.gc.ca
Embassy in Canada: High Commission for the Federal Republic of Nigeria, 295 Metcalfe St, Ottawa, ON K2P 1R9. Tel: (613) 236-0522. Fax: (613) 236-0529. e-mail: hc@nigeriahigh commottawa.com

Niue

Long-Form Name: Niue
Capital: Alofi

■ GEOGRAPHY

Area: 260 sq. km, world's largest uplifted coral island
Climate: tropical maritime, modified by southeasterly trade winds
Land Use: 19% arable; 8% permanent crops; 4% meadows and pastures; 19% forest, 50% other; includes n.a. sq. km irrigated
Location: Pacific Ocean, NE of New Zealand

■ PEOPLE

Population: 2,134 (July 2002 est.)
Nationality: Niuean
Ethnic Groups: Polynesian
Languages: English, Polynesian closely related to Tongan and Samoan

■ GOVERNMENT

Colony/Territory of: Self-governing territory in free association with New Zealand
Leader(s): Head of State: Queen Elizabeth II, NZ High Comm. Sandra Lee-Vercoe, Prem. Young Vivian
Government Type: self-governing parliamentary democracy in free association with New Zealand
National Holiday: Waitangi Day, Feb. 6

■ ECONOMY

Overview: heavily dependent on aid from New Zealand; government expenditures regularly exceed revenues; agriculture includes coconuts, honey, limes, root crops, livestock; chief trading partner: New Zealand

■ FINANCE/TRADE

Currency: New Zealand dollar = 100 cents

Canadian Embassy: c/o The Canadian High Commission, 3rd Fl, 61 Molesworth St, Thorndon, Wellington, New Zealand; Mailing address: c/o P.O. Box 12-049, Thorndon, Wellington, New Zealand. Tel: (011-64-4) 473-9577. Fax: (011-64-4) 471-2082. e-mail: wlgtn@dfait-maeci.gc.ca
Representative to Canada: c/o New Zealand High Commission, Clarica Centre, 99 Bank St, Ste 727, Ottawa ON K1P 6G3. Tel: (613) 238-5991. Fax: (613) 238-5707. e-mail: nzhcott@istar.ca

Norfolk Island

Long-Form Name: Territory of Norfolk Island
Capital: Kingston (administrative centre), Burnt Pine (commercial centre)

■ GEOGRAPHY

Area: 34.6 sq. km
Climate: subtropical, mild, little seasonal variation
Land Use: 0% arable; 0% permanent crops; 25% meadows and pastures; 0% forests; 75% other; includes no irrigated land
Location: S Pacific Ocean, E of Australia

■ PEOPLE

Population: 1,866 (July 2002 est.)
Nationality: Norfolk Islander

Ethnic Groups: majority descendants of Polynesians and British (the latter crew members of the British naval ship *Bounty*)
Languages: English (official), Norfolk (a mixture of 18th-century English and ancient Tahitian)

■ GOVERNMENT

Colony/Territory of: Dependent Territory of Australia
Leader(s): Queen Elizabeth II, represented by Admin. Anthony J. Messner; Min. for Regional Services Wilson Tuckey
Government Type: a largely self-governing dependency, territory of Australia
National Holiday: Pitcairners' Arrival Day Anniversary, June 8

■ ECONOMY

Overview: tourism is backbone of economy; revenues from tourism have helped the agricultural sector become self-sufficient in beef, poultry and eggs; export of indigenous fruit and vegetables

■ FINANCE/TRADE

Currency: Australian dollar = 100 cents

Canadian Embassy: c/o The Canadian High Commission, Commonwealth Ave, Canberra, A.C.T. 2600, Australia. Tel: (011-61-2) 6270-4000. Fax: (011-61-2) 6273-3285. e-mail: cnbra@dfait-maeci.gc.ca
Representative to Canada: c/o Australian High Commission, 50 O'Connor St, Ste 710, Ottawa ON K1P 6L2. Tel: (613) 236-0841. Fax: (613) 236-4376. e-mail: n.a.

Northern Marianas

Long-Form Name: The Commonwealth of the Northern Mariana Islands
Capital: Saipan

■ GEOGRAPHY

Area: 477 sq. km (combined land area of 14 islands)
Coastline: 1,482 km
Climate: tropical maritime, moderated by northeasterly trade winds; little seasonal temperature variation
Terrain: southern islands are limestone with level terraces and fringing coral reefs; northern islands are volcanic
Land Use: 21% arable on Saipan Island; volcanic islands too mountainous for cultivation; chief agricultural use is grazing; 19% meadows and pastures; no irrigated land
Location: Pacific Ocean, E of the Philippines

■ PEOPLE

Population: 77,311 (July 2002 est.)
Nationality: no descriptive term; American citizenship
Ethnic Groups: Chamorro, Carolinians and other Micronesians, Caucasian, Japanese, Chinese, Korean
Languages: English (official), Chamorro, Carolinian, Japanese; 86% of the population speaks a language other than English at home

■ GOVERNMENT

Colony/Territory of: Commonwealth in political union with the United States
Leader(s): Head of State: Pres. George W. Bush Jr. (US), Gov. Juan N. Babauta
Government Type: commonwealth in political union with the US; self-governing with locally elected governing body
National Holiday: Commonwealth Day, Jan. 8

■ ECONOMY

Overview: economy benefits from US financial assistance, but the rate of funding has declined as local revenues have increased; tourism is growing in importance and now employs approximately 50% of the workforce; agriculture: cattle, coconuts, breadfruit, vegetables

■ FINANCE/TRADE

Currency: American dollar = 100 cents

Canadian Embassy: c/o The Canadian Embassy, 501 Pennsylvania Ave. NW, Washington DC 20001, USA. Tel: (202) 682-1740. Fax: (202) 456-7726. e-mail: wshdc-outpack@dfait-maeci.gc.ca
Representative to Canada: c/o Embassy of the United States of America, 490 Sussex Dr., Ottawa, ON, K1N 1G8. Tel: (613) 238-5335. Fax: (613) 688-3097. Email inquiries are not accepted

Norway

Long-Form Name: Kingdom of Norway
Capital: Oslo

■ GEOGRAPHY

Area: 324,220 sq. km
Coastline: 21,925 km (3,491 km mainland; 2,413 km large islands; 16,093 km long fjords; numerous small islands and minor indentations); one of the longest and most rugged coastlines in the world
Climate: temperate along coast, modified by North Atlantic Current; colder interior; rainy year-round on west coast

Environment: air and water pollution; acid rain damages forests and adversely affects lakes and threatens fish stocks

Terrain: glaciated; mostly high plateaus and rugged mountains broken by fertile valleys; small, scattered plains; coastline deeply indented by fjords; arctic tundra in north

Land Use: 3% arable; 0% permanent crops; negligible meadows; 27% forest; 70% other; includes 1,270 sq. km irrigated

Location: N Europe, bordering on Norwegian Sea, North Sea

■ PEOPLE

Population: 4,525,116 (July 2002 est.)

Nationality: Norwegian

Age Structure: 0–14 yrs: 20.0%; 15–64: 65.0%; 65+: 15.0% (2002 est.)

Population Growth Rate: 0.47% (2002 est.)

Net Migration: 2.10 migrants/1,000 population (2002 est.)

Ethnic Groups: Germanic (Nordic, Alpine, Baltic) and racial-cultural minority of 20,000 Lapps

Languages: Norwegian (official); small Lapp- and Finnish-speaking minorities

Religions: Lutheran (88%, state church), other Protestant and Roman Catholic 4%, none 3.2%, other 4.8%

Birth Rate: 12.39/1,000 population (2002 est.)

Death Rate: 9.78/1,000 population (2002 est.)

Infant Mortality: 3.90 deaths/1,000 live births (2002 est.)

Life Expectancy at Birth: 76.01 years male, 82.07 years female (2002 est.)

Total Fertility Rate: 1.80 children born/woman (2002 est.)

Literacy: approaching 100% (2000)

■ GOVERNMENT

Leader(s): King Harald V, Prime Min. Kjell Magne Bondevik

Government Type: constitutional monarchy

Administrative Divisions: 19 provinces (fylker, sing. —fylke); dependent areas include Bouvet Island (uninhabited), Jan Mayen (uninhabited), Peter I Island (uninhabited), Queen Maud Land (uninhabited), Svalbard

Nationhood: Oct. 26, 1905 (from Sweden)

National Holiday: Constitution Day, May 17

■ ECONOMY

Overview: a small country with high dependence on international trade; a prosperous capitalist nation that has extensive welfare measures; concerns are the ageing population, increased economic integration with Europe and the balance between private and public influence in economic decisions

GDP: US$143 billion, per capita US$31,800; real growth rate 1.6% (2002 est.)

Inflation: 3.0% (2001)

Industries: accounts for 31% of GDP (2000); petroleum and gas, food processing, shipbuilding, pulp and paper products, metal, chemicals, timber, mining, textiles, fishing

Labour Force: 2.3 million (2001); 74% community, social and business services, 22% industry, 4% agriculture, forestry and fishing

Unemployment: 3.4% (Dec. 2002)

Agriculture: accounts for 2% of GDP (2000); among world's top 10 fishing nations; livestock output exceeds value of crops; over half of food needs imported. Domestic products include barley, other grains, potatoes, beef, milk and fish.

Natural Resources: rich in natural resources: crude oil, copper, natural gas, pyrites, nickel, iron ore, zinc, lead, fish, timber, hydro power

■ FINANCE/TRADE

Currency: krone (pl. kroner) (NKr) = 100 oere

International Reserves Excluding Gold: US$20.682 billion (Dec. 2002)

Gold Reserves: 1.184 million fine troy ounces (Dec. 2002)

Budget: revenues US$71.7 billion, expenditures US$57.6 billion, including capital expenditures US$ n.a. (2000)

Defence Expenditures: 5.9% of central government expenditure (2001)

Education Expenditures: n.a.

External Debt: none

Exports: US$54.996 billion (2002 est.); commodities: petroleum and petroleum products 25%, natural gas 11%, fish 7%, aluminum 6%, ships 3.5%, pulp and paper; partners: UK, France, Germany, Netherlands, Sweden, US

Imports: US$29.700 billion (2002 est.); commodities: machinery, fuels and lubricants, transportation equipment, chemicals, foodstuffs, clothing, ships; partners: Sweden, Germany, UK, Denmark, France, US

■ COMMUNICATIONS

Daily Newspapers: 569/1,000 inhabitants (2000)

Televisions: 883/1,000 inhabitants (2001)

Radios: 3,324/1,000 inhabitants (2001)

Telephones: 720 lines/1,000 inhabitants (2001)

■ TRANSPORTATION

Motor Vehicles: 2,300,000; 1,800,000 passenger cars (2000)

Roads: 91,180 km; 67,838 km paved

Railway: 4,006 km

Air Traffic: 14,559,000 passengers carried (2001)

Airports: 102; 66 have paved runways (2002)

Canadian Embassy: The Canadian Embassy, Wergelandsveien #7, 0244 Oslo, Norway. Tel: (011-47) 22-99-53-00. Fax: (011-47) 22-99-53-01. e-mail: oslo@dfait-maeci.gc.ca

Embassy in Canada: Embassy of the Kingdom of Norway, Royal Bank Centre, 90 Sparks St, Ste 532, Ottawa ON K1P 5B4. Tel: (613) 238-6571. Fax: (613) 238-2765. e-mail: emb.ottawa@mfa.no

Oman

Long-Form Name: Sultanate of Oman
Capital: Masqat or Muscat

■ GEOGRAPHY

Area: 212,460 sq. km
Coastline: 2,092 km
Climate: dry desert; hot, humid along coast; hot, dry interior; strong southwest summer monsoon (May to Sept.) in far south
Environment: summer winds often raise large sandstorms and dust storms in interior; sparse natural freshwater resources are threatened by increasing soil salinity
Terrain: vast central desert plain, rugged mountains in north and south
Land Use: 0% arable; negligible permanent crops; 5% meadows; 0% forest; 95% other; includes 620 sq. km irrigated
Location: SW Asia (Middle East), bordering on Arabian Sea

■ PEOPLE

Population: 2,713,462; includes 527,078 non-nationals (July 2002 est.)
Nationality: Omani
Age Structure: 0–14 yrs: 41.9%; 15–64: 55.7%; 65+: 2.4% (2002 est.)
Population Growth Rate: 3.41% (2002 est.)
Net Migration: 0.35 migrants/1,000 population (2002 est.)
Ethnic Groups: almost entirely Arab, with small Balochi, Zanzibari, Pakistani and Indian groups
Languages: Arabic (official); English, Balochi, Urdu, Indian dialects
Religions: 75% Ibadhi Muslim; remainder Sunni Muslim, Shi'a Muslim, Hindu minority
Birth Rate: 37.76/1,000 population (2002 est.)
Death Rate: 4.03/1,000 population (2002 est.)
Infant Mortality: 21.77 deaths/1,000 live births (2002 est.)
Life Expectancy at Birth: 70.15 years male, 74.57 years female (2002 est.)
Total Fertility Rate: 5.99 children born/woman (2002 est.)
Literacy: 71.7 (2000)

■ GOVERNMENT

Leader(s): Sultan and Prime Min. Qaboos Bin Sa'id
Government Type: absolute monarchy; independent, with residual UK influence
Administrative Divisions: 6 regions (mintaqat, sing. —mintaqah) and 2 governorates (muhafazat, sing. —muhafazah)
Nationhood: 1650; expulsion of the Portuguese
National Holiday: National Day (Birthday of Sultan Qaboos), Nov. 18

■ ECONOMY

Overview: depends on the success of its oil industry, which has 15 years' supply at the current rate of extraction; subsistence agriculture is the major employment, and the general populace relies on imported food
GDP: US$21.5 billion, per capita US$8,200; real growth rate 7.4% (2001 est.)
Inflation: -1.1% (2001)
Industries: accounts for 40% of GDP; crude oil production and refining, natural gas production, construction, cement, copper
Labour Force: 700,000 (2001); 50% agriculture, 21.8% industry, 28.6% services; 58% of labour force are non-Omani
Unemployment: n.a.
Agriculture: accounts for 3% of GDP and 50% of labour force (including fishing); less than 2% of land cultivated; largely subsistence farming (dates, limes, bananas, alfalfa, vegetables, camels, cattle); not self-sufficient in food
Natural Resources: crude oil, copper, asbestos, some marble, limestone, chromium, gypsum, natural gas

■ FINANCE/TRADE

Currency: Omani rial (RO) = 1,000 baiza
International Reserves Excluding Gold: US$3.173 billion (Dec. 2002)
Gold Reserves: 0.001 million fine troy ounces (Dec. 2002)
Budget: revenues US$9.2 billion; expenditures US$6.9 billion, including capital expenditures of US$ n.a. (2000 est.)
Defence Expenditures: 40.70% of central government expenditure (2001)
Education Expenditures: 15.17% of central government expenditure (2000)
External Debt: US$6.025 billion (2001)
Exports: US$7.750 billion (2000); commodities: petroleum, re-exports, processed copper, dates, nuts, fish; partners: Japan, South Korea, Thailand, China, United Arab Emirates, US
Imports: US$5.798 billion (2001); commodities: machinery, transportation equipment, manufactured goods, food, livestock, lubricants;

partners: Japan, United Arab Emirates, UK, Germany, US, Italy.

■ COMMUNICATIONS

Daily Newspapers: 29/1,000 inhabitants (2000)
Televisions: 563/1,000 inhabitants (2001)
Radios: 621/1,000 inhabitants (2001)
Telephones: 90 lines/1,000 inhabitants (2001)

■ TRANSPORTATION

Motor Vehicles: 300,000; 209,000 passenger cars
Roads: 32,800 km; 9,840 km paved
Railway: none
Air Traffic: 1,980,000 passengers carried (2001)
Airports: 143; 6 have paved runways (2002)

Canadian Embassy: The Canadian Embassy to Oman, c/o The Canadian Embassy, P.O. Box 94321, Riyadh 11693, Saudi Arabia. Tel: (011-966-1) 488-2288. Fax: (011-966-1) 488-1997. e-mail: ryadh@dfait-maeci.gc.ca
Embassy in Canada: c/o Embassy of the Sultanate of Oman, 2535 Belmont Rd. NW, Washington DC 20008, USA. Tel: (202) 387-1980. Fax: (202) 745-4933. e-mail: n.a.

Pakistan

Long-Form Name: Islamic Republic of Pakistan
Capital: Islamabad

■ GEOGRAPHY

Area: 803,940 sq. km
Coastline: 1,046 km along Gulf of Oman and Arabian Sea
Climate: mostly hot, dry desert; temperate in northwest; arctic in north
Environment: frequent earthquakes, occasionally severe especially in north and west; flooding along the Indus after heavy rains (July and Aug.); deforestation; soil erosion; desertification; water pollution from raw sewage
Terrain: flat Indus plain in east; mountains in north and northwest; Balochistan plateau in west
Land Use: 27% arable; 1% permanent crops; 6% meadows; 5% forest; 61% other; includes 180,000 sq. km irrigated
Location: SW Asia (Middle East), bordering on Arabian Sea

■ PEOPLE

Population: 147,663,429 (July 2002 est.)
Nationality: Pakistani
Age Structure: 0–14 yrs: 39.9%; 15–64: 56.0%; 65+: 4.1% (2002 est.)
Population Growth Rate: 2.06% (2002 est.)
Net Migration: -0.79 migrants/1,000 population (2002 est.)

Ethnic Groups: Punjabi, Sindhi, Pashtun (Pathan), Baloch, Muhajir (immigrants from India and their descendants)
Languages: Urdu (official), Punjab (spoken by majority), Sindhi, Pushto, English
Religions: 97% Muslim (77% Sunni, 20% Shi'a), 3% Christian, Hindu and other
Birth Rate: 30.40/1,000 population (2002 est.)
Death Rate: 9.02/1,000 population (2002 est.)
Infant Mortality: 78.52 deaths/1,000 live births (2002 est.)
Life Expectancy at Birth: 60.96 years male, 62.73 years female (2002 est.)
Total Fertility Rate: 4.25 children born/woman (2002 est.)
Literacy: 43.2% (2000)

■ GOVERNMENT

Leader(s): Pres. Pervez Musharraf
Government Type: federal republic
Administrative Divisions: 4 provinces, 1 territory and 1 capital territory
Nationhood: Aug. 14, 1947 (from UK; formerly West Pakistan)
National Holiday: Republic Day (proclamation of the republic), Mar. 23

■ ECONOMY

Overview: long-standing economic weaknesses such as indebtedness, a small tax base, large population and dependence on cotton exports hamper the economy
GDP: US$299 billion, per capita US$2,100; real growth rate 3.3% (2001 est.)
Inflation: 3.1% (2001)
Industries: accounts for 24% of GDP (2001 est.); textiles, food processing, beverages, petroleum products, construction materials, clothing, paper products, international finance, shrimp
Labour Force: 51.73.5 million (2001); 44% agriculture, 17% industry, 39% community, social and business services
Unemployment: 5.9% (2001)
Agriculture: 26% of GDP (2000), over 50% of labour force; world's largest continuous irrigation system; cotton, wheat, rice, sugar cane, fruits, vegetables, livestock (milk, beef, mutton, eggs); self-sufficient in foodgrain
Natural Resources: land, extensive natural gas reserves, limited crude oil, poor quality coal, iron ore, copper, salt, limestone

■ FINANCE/TRADE

Currency: Pakistani rupee (PRs) = 100 paisa
International Reserves Excluding Gold: US$8.078 billion (Dec. 2002)
Gold Reserves: 2.093 million fine troy ounces (Dec. 2002)

Budget: revenues US$8.9 billion; expenditures US$11.6 billion, including capital expenditures US$ n.a. (FY2000/01 est.)
Defence Expenditures: 23.0% of central government expenditure (2001)
Education Expenditures: 0.97% of central government expenditure (2001)
External Debt: US$32.020 billion (2001)
Exports: US$9.724 billion (2002 est.); commodities: rice, cotton, textiles, clothing; partners: US, UK, UAE, Hong Kong, Germany
Imports: US$10.964 billion (2002 est.); commodities: petroleum, petroleum products, machinery, transportation, equipment, vegetable oils, animal fats, chemicals; partners: Kuwait, UAE, Saudi Arabia, US, Japan

■ COMMUNICATIONS

Daily Newspapers: 40/1,000 inhabitants (2000)
Televisions: 148/1,000 inhabitants (2001)
Radios: 105/1,000 inhabitants (2001)
Telephones: 23 lines/1.000 inhabitants (2001)

■ TRANSPORTATION

Motor Vehicles: 1,200,000; 723,000 passenger cars (2000)
Roads: 247,811 km; 141,252 km paved
Railway: 8,163 km
Air Traffic: 4,871,000 passengers carried (2001)
Airports: 120; 87 have paved runways (2002)

Canadian Embassy: The Canadian High Commission, Diplomatic Enclave, Sector G-5, Islamabad; mailing address: The Canadian High Commission, G.P.O. Box 1042, Islamabad, Pakistan. Tel: (011-92-51) 227-91-00. Fax: (011-92-51) 227-91-88. e-mail: isbad@dfait-maeci.gc.ca
Embassy in Canada: High Commission for the Islamic Republic of Pakistan, Burnside Bldg, 151 Slater St, Ste 608, Ottawa ON K1P 5H3. Tel: (613) 238-7881. Fax: (613) 238-7296. e-mail: parepottawa@sprint.ca

Palau

Long-Form Name: Republic of Palau
Capital: Koror (on Koror Island); a new capital is being built 20 km northeast

■ GEOGRAPHY

Area: 458 sq. km (26 islands and 300+ islets)
Coastline: 1,519 km
Climate: tropical, warm year-round; wet season, May to Dec.; dry season, Jan. to April; typhoon-prone with violent winds and heavy rain, esp. in July

Environment: inadequate facilities for waste management; typhoons
Terrain: about 200 islands; topography varies from high and mountainous to low coral reef islands; northern islands of volcanic origin, fertile and extensively cultivated; southern islands too rugged for habitation
Land Use: n.a.
Location: W Pacific Ocean (Micronesia), E of the Philippines

■ PEOPLE

Population: 19,409 (July 2002 est.)
Nationality: Palauan
Age Structure: 0–14 yrs: 26.8%; 15–64: 68.6%; 65+: 4.6% (2002 est.)
Population Growth Rate: 1.61% (2002 est.)
Net Migration: 3.86 migrants/1,000 population (2002 est.)
Ethnic Groups: Polynesian, Malayan, Melanesian, mixtures
Languages: English (official in all states), Sonsorolese, Angaur, Japanese, Tobi, Palauan
Religions: Christian, Modekngei, a religion indigenous to Palau
Birth Rate: 19.32/1,000 population (2002 est.)
Death Rate: 7.11/1,000 population (2002 est.)
Infant Mortality: 16.21 deaths/1,000 live births (2002 est.)
Life Expectancy at Birth: 65.07 years male, 72.50 years female (2002 est.)
Total Fertility Rate: 2.47 children born/woman (2002 est.)
Literacy: 92%

■ GOVERNMENT

Leader(s): Pres. Tommy Remengesau, V. Pres. Sandra Pierantozzi
Government Type: constitutional government in free association with the US
Administrative Divisions: 18 states
Nationhood: Oct. 1, 1994 (from US-administered UN trusteeship)
National Holiday: Constitution Day, July 9

■ ECONOMY

Overview: subsistence agriculture and fishing; some tourism; government is main employer; phosphate deposits on northern islands; largely dependent on imports from the US
GDP: US$174 million, per capita US$9,000; real growth rate 1.0% (2001 est.)
Inflation: n.a.
Industries: some fishing and agriculture, tourism, crafts, garment making
Labour Force: exact figures n.a.; 20% agriculture
Unemployment: 2.3% (2000 est.)

Panama 489

Agriculture: subsistence-level cultivation of coconuts, copra, yams, cassava
Natural Resources: marine resources, minerals (especially gold), forests

■ FINANCE/TRADE

Currency: American dollar (US$) = 100 cents
International Reserves Excluding Gold: n.a.
Gold Reserves: n.a.
Budget: revenues US$57.7 million; expenditures US$80.8 million, including capital expenditures of US$17.1 million (1999 est.)
Defence Expenditures: defence is the responsibility of the US
Education Expenditures: n.a.
External Debt: none (2000)
Exports: US$11 million (1999); fish, copra, handicrafts; partners: US, Japan, Singapore
Imports: US$123 million (2000); machinery, equipment, fuels; partners: US

■ COMMUNICATIONS

Daily Newspapers: n.a.
Televisions: n.a.
Radios: n.a.
Telephones: n.a.

■ TRANSPORTATION

Motor Vehicles: n.a.
Roads: 61 km; 36 km paved
Railway: none
Air Traffic: n.a.
Airports: 3; 1 has a paved runway (2002)

Canadian Embassy: c/o The Canadian Embassy, 501 Pennsylvania Ave NW, Washington DC 20001, USA. Tel: (202) 682-1740. Fax: (202) 456-7726. e-mail: washdc-outpack@dfait-maeci.gc.ca
Embassy in Canada: c/o Embassy of the United States of America, 490 Sussex Drive, Ottawa, ON, K1N 1G8, Tel: (613) 238-5335. Fax: (613) 688-3097. Email inquiries are not accepted

---

Panama

Long-Form Name: Republic of Panama
Capital: Panama

■ GEOGRAPHY

Area: 78,200 sq. km
Coastline: 2,490 km
Climate: tropical; hot, humid, cloudy; prolonged rainy season (May to Jan.), short dry season (Jan. to May)
Environment: dense tropical forest in east and northwest is threatened by deforestation; water pollution and soil degradation

Terrain: interior mostly steep, rugged mountains and dissected, upland plains; coastal areas largely plains and rolling hills
Land Use: 7% arable; 2% permanent crops; 20% meadows; 44% forest; 27% other; includes 320 sq. km irrigated
Location: Central (Latin) America, bordering on S America, Caribbean Sea, Pacific Ocean

■ PEOPLE

Population: 2,882,329 (July 2002 est.)
Nationality: Panamanian
Age Structure: 0–14 yrs: 29.6%; 15–64: 64.3%; 65+: 6.1% (2002 est.)
Population Growth Rate: 1.26% (2002 est.)
Net Migration: -1.04 migrants/1,000 population (2002 est.)
Ethnic Groups: 70% mestizo (mixed Indian and European ancestry), 14% West Indian, 10% white, 6% Indian
Languages: Spanish (official), 14% English; many Panamanians are bilingual
Religions: 85% Roman Catholic, 15% Protestant
Birth Rate: 18.60/1,000 population (2002 est.)
Death Rate: 4.96/1,000 population (2002 est.)
Infant Mortality: 19.57 deaths/1,000 live births (2002 est.)
Life Expectancy at Birth: 73.14 years male, 78.74 years female (2002 est.)
Total Fertility Rate: 2.22 children born/woman (2002 est.)
Literacy: 91.9% (2000)

■ GOVERNMENT

Leader(s): Pres. Mireya Elisa Moscoso de Gruber, First V. Pres. Arturo Ulises Vallarino
Government Type: constitutional republic
Administrative Divisions: 9 provinces (provincias, sing. provincia) and 1 territory (comarca)
Nationhood: Nov. 3, 1903 (from Colombia; became independent from Spain Nov. 28, 1821)
National Holiday: Independence Day, Nov. 3

■ ECONOMY

Overview: political instability, lack of credit and the erosion of business confidence have drastically hurt the economy resulting in a recent overall economic slump; exports are stagnant; unemployment and economic reform are two of the greatest challenges the government must face
GDP: US$16.9 billion, per capita US$5,900; real growth rate 1.4% (2001 est.)
Inflation: 0.3% (2001)
Industries: accounts for 17% of GDP (2000); manufacturing and construction activities, petroleum refining, brewing, cement and other construction materials, sugar mills

Labour Force: 1.2 million (2001); 61% community, social and business services; 21% agriculture, 18% industry
Unemployment: 13.3% (2001)
Agriculture: accounts for 7% of GDP (2000) and almost one-third of labour force; bananas, rice, corn, coffee, sugar cane, livestock, fishing, importer of foodgrain, vegetables, milk products
Natural Resources: copper, mahogany forests, shrimp, hydroelectric potential

■ FINANCE/TRADE

Currency: balboa (B) = 100 centesimos, also the US dollar ($) = 100 cents.
International Reserves Excluding Gold: US$1.183 million (Dec. 2002)
Gold Reserves: n.a.
Budget: revenues US$2.8 billion; expenditures US$2.9 billion, including capital expenditures of US$471 million (2000 est.)
Defence Expenditures: 4.2% of central government expenditure (2001)
Education Expenditures: 16.98% of central government expenditure (1999)
External Debt: US$8.245 billion (2001)
Exports: US$911 million (2002); commodities: bananas 40%, shrimp 27%, coffee 4%, sugar, petroleum products; partners: US, Sweden, Benelux, Costa Rica
Imports: US$2.964 billion (2001); commodities: foodstuffs 16%, capital goods 9%, crude oil 16%, consumer goods, chemicals; partners: US, Ecuador, Venezuela, Japan

■ COMMUNICATIONS

Daily Newspapers: 62/1,000 inhabitants (2000)
Televisions: 194/1,000 inhabitants (2001)
Radios: 300/1,000 inhabitants (2001)
Telephones: 148 lines/1,000 inhabitants (2001)

■ TRANSPORTATION

Motor Vehicles: 320,000; 230,000 passenger cars (2000)
Roads: 11,592 km; 4,079 km paved (2000)
Railway: 335 km
Air Traffic: 1,115,000 passengers carried (2001)
Airports: 107; 41 have paved runways (2002)

Canadian Embassy: The Canadian Embassy, World Trade Center, 1st Floor, Calle 53 Este Marbella y Calle 5 B Sur, Urbanización Marbella, Panama City, Panama; Postal Address: The Canadian Embassy, Apartado Postal 0832-2446, Estafeta World Trade Center, Panama City, Panama. Tel: (011-507) 264-9731. Fax: (011-507) 263-8083. e-mail: panam@dfait-maeci.gc.ca
Embassy in Canada: Embassy of the Republic of Panama, 130 Albert St, Ste 300, Ottawa ON

K1P 5G4. Tel: (613) 236-7177. Fax: (613) 236-5775. e-mail: pancanem@travel-net.com

Papua New Guinea

Long-Form Name: Independent State of Papua New Guinea
Capital: Port Moresby

■ GEOGRAPHY

Area: 462,840 sq. km
Coastline: 5,152 km
Climate: tropical; northwest monsoon (Dec. to Mar.), southeast monsoon (May to Oct.); slight seasonal temperature variation
Environment: one of the world's largest swamps along southwest coast; some active volcanoes; frequent earthquakes and mudslides; pollution and deforestation
Terrain: mostly mountains with coastal lowlands and rolling foothills
Land Use: 0.1% arable; 1% permanent crops; negligible meadows; 92.9% forest; 6% other; includes n.a. sq. km irrigated
Location: Pacific Ocean, Coral Sea N of Australia

■ PEOPLE

Population: 5,172,033 (July 2002 est.)
Nationality: Papua New Guinean
Age Structure: 0–14 yrs: 38.6%; 15–64: 57.7%; 65+: 3.7% (2002 est.)
Population Growth Rate: 2.39% (2002 est.)
Net Migration: 0 migrants/1,000 population (2002 est.)
Ethnic Groups: predominantly Melanesian and Papuan; some Negrito, Micronesian and Polynesian
Languages: pidgin, English, Motu (all official); also 715 local languages
Religions: 22% Roman Catholic, 16% Lutheran, 8% Presbyterian/Methodist/London Missionary Society, 5% Anglican, 4% Evangelical Alliance, 1% Seventh-Day Adventists, 10% other Protestant sects, 34% indigenous beliefs
Birth Rate: 31.61/1,000 population (2002 est.)
Death Rate: 7.75/1,000 population (2002 est.)
Infant Mortality: 56.53 deaths/1,000 live births (2002 est.)
Life Expectancy at Birth: 61.73 years male, 66.03 years female (2002 est.)
Total Fertility Rate: 4.21 children born/woman (2002 est.)
Literacy: 63.9% (2000)

■ GOVERNMENT

Leader(s): Head of State: Queen Elizabeth II, Gov. Gen. Silas Atopare, Prime Min. Michael Somare
Government Type: parliamentary democracy

Administrative Divisions: 20 provinces
Nationhood: Sept. 16, 1975 (from UN trusteeship under Australian administration)
National Holiday: Independence Day, Sept. 16

■ ECONOMY

Overview: country has abundant natural resources but exploitation has been hampered by the rugged terrain and the high cost of developing an infrastructure; subsistence agriculture is the livelihood for 85% of the population; mining accounts for about 60% of export earnings
GDP: US$12.2 billion, per capita US$2,400; real growth rate -2.5% (2001 est.)
Inflation: 9.3% (2001)
Industries: accounts for 44% of GDP (2000); copra crushing, palm oil processing, plywood processing, wood chip production, gold, silver, copper, construction, tourism
Labour Force: 2.6 million (2001); 85% agriculture, 10% industry, 5% other
Unemployment: n.a.
Agriculture: accounts for 26% of GDP (2000); fertile soils and favourable climate permit cultivating a wide variety of crops; cash crops: coffee, cocoa, coconuts, palm kernels; other products: tea, rubber, sweet potatoes, fruit, vegetables, poultry, pork; net importer of food for urban centres
Natural Resources: gold, copper, silver, natural gas, timber, oil potential, fisheries

■ FINANCE/TRADE

Currency: kina (K) = 100 toea
International Reserves Excluding Gold: US$330 million (Dec. 2002)
Gold Reserves: 0.063 million fine troy ounces (Dec. 2002)
Budget: revenues US$894 million; expenditures US$1.1 billion, including capital expenditures of US$344 million (2000 est.)
Defence Expenditures: 3.3% of central government expenditures (2001)
Education Expenditures: 22.06% of central government expenditure (1999)
External Debt: US$2.521 billion (2001)
Exports: US$1.805 billion (2001); commodities: gold, copper ore, coffee, copra, palm oil, timber, lobster; partners: Germany, Japan, Australia, China, South Korea, UK, Philippines, US
Imports: US$1.072 billion (2001); commodities: machinery and transport equipment, fuels, food, chemicals, consumer goods; partners: Australia, Singapore, Japan, New Zealand, Indonesia, Malaysia, US

■ COMMUNICATIONS

Daily Newspapers: 14/1,000 inhabitants (2000)
Televisions: 19/1,000 inhabitants (2001)

Radios: 86/1,000 inhabitants (2001)
Telephones: 12 lines/1,000 inhabitants (2001)

■ TRANSPORTATION

Motor Vehicles: 99,300; 21,600 passenger cars
Roads: 19,600 km; 686 km paved
Railway: none
Air Traffic: 1,188,000 passengers carried (2001)
Airports: 490; 21 have paved runways (2002)

Canadian Embassy: The Canadian High Commission to Papua New Guinea, c/o The Canadian High Commission, Commonwealth Ave, Canberra A.C.T. 2600, Australia. Tel: (011-61-2) 6270-4000. Fax: (011-61-2) 6273-3285. e-mail: cnbra@dfait-maeci.gc.ca
Embassy in Canada: c/o High Commission for Papua New Guinea, 1779 Massachusetts Ave NW, Ste 805, Washington DC 20036, USA. Tel: (202) 745-3680. Fax: (202) 745-3679. e-mail: n.a.

Paraguay

Long-Form Name: Republic of Paraguay
Capital: Asunción

■ GEOGRAPHY

Area: 406,750 sq. km
Coastline: none: landlocked
Climate: subtropical; varies from temperate in east to semi-arid in far west
Environment: local flooding in southeast (early Sept. to June); poorly drained plains may become boggy (early Oct. to June); deforestation and water pollution are increasing
Terrain: grassy plains and wooded hills east of Río Paraguay; Gran Chaco region west of Río Paraguay mostly low, marshy plain near the river and dry forest and thorny scrub elsewhere
Land Use: 6% arable; 0% permanent crops; 55% permanent pastures; 32% forest; 7% other; includes 670 sq. km irrigated
Location: C South America

■ PEOPLE

Population: 5,884,491 (July 2002 est.)
Nationality: Paraguayan
Age Structure: 0–14 yrs: 38.7%; 15–64: 56.6%; 65+: 4.7% (2002 est.)
Population Growth Rate: 2.57% (2002 est.)
Net Migration: -0.09 migrants/1,000 population (2002 est.)
Ethnic Groups: 95% mestizo (Spanish and Indian), 5% white and Indian
Languages: Spanish (official), Guarani
Religions: 90% Roman Catholic; 10% Mennonite and other Protestant denominations
Birth Rate: 30.50/1,000 population (2002 est.)
Death Rate: 4.69/1,000 population (2002 est.)

Infant Mortality: 28.75 deaths/1,000 live births (2002 est.)
Life Expectancy at Birth: 71.67 years male, 76.77 years female (2002 est.)
Total Fertility Rate: 4.07 children born/woman (2002 est.)
Literacy: 93.3% (2000)

■ GOVERNMENT

Leader(s): Pres. Nicanor Duarte Frutos, V. Pres. Luis Castiglioni
Government Type: constitutional republic
Administrative Divisions: 17 departments (departamentos, sing. —departamento) and 1 capital city
Nationhood: May 14, 1811 (from Spain)
National Holiday: Independence Days, May 14–15

■ ECONOMY

Overview: in the absence of significant mineral or petroleum resources, the economy is based on agriculture; has a large hydroelectric power potential; is vulnerable to climatic conditions and international commodity prices for agricultural exports; non-traditional exports are growing rapidly
GDP: US$26.2 billion, per capita US$4,600; real growth rate 0% (2001 est.)
Inflation: 7.3% (2001)
Industries: accounts for 26% of GDP (2000); meat packing, oilseed crushing, milling, brewing, textiles, other light consumer goods, cement, construction
Labour Force: 2.1 million (2001); 45% agriculture
Unemployment: 16% (2000 est.)
Agriculture: accounts for 29% GDP (2000) and 45% of labour force; cash crops: cotton, sugar cane; other crops: corn, wheat, tobacco, soybeans, cassava, fruit and vegetables; animal products: beef, pork, eggs, milk; surplus producer of timber; self-sufficient in most foods
Natural Resources: iron ore, manganese, limestone, hydro power, timber

■ FINANCE/TRADE

Currency: guaraní (pl. guaraníes) (G/) = 100 centimos
International Reserves Excluding Gold: US$629 million (Dec. 2002)
Gold Reserves: 0.035 million fine troy ounces (Dec. 2002)
Budget: revenues US$1.3 billion, expenditures US$2 billion, including capital expenditures of US$700 million (1999 est.)
Defence Expenditures: 5.0% of central government expenditure (2001)
Education Expenditures: n.a.

External Debt: US$2.817 billion (2001)
Exports: US$1.237 billion (2000); commodities: cotton, soybeans, timber, vegetable oils, coffee, tung oil, meat products, electricity; partners: Brazil, Uruguay, Argentina
Imports: US$3.697 billion (2000); commodities: capital goods 35%, consumer goods 20%, fuels and lubricants 19%, raw materials 16%, foodstuffs, beverages and tobacco 10%; partners: Argentina, Brazil, Uruguay

■ COMMUNICATIONS

Daily Newspapers: 43/1,000 inhabitants (2000)
Televisions: 218/1,000 inhabitants (2001)
Radios: 182/1,000 inhabitants (2001)
Telephones: 51 lines/1,000 inhabitants (2001)

■ TRANSPORTATION

Motor Vehicles: 121,000; 71,000 passenger cars
Roads: 25,901 km; 3,067 km paved (2001)
Railway: 971 km
Air Traffic: 281,000 passengers carried (2001)
Airports: 899; 11 have paved runways (2002)

Canadian Embassy: The Canadian Embassy to Paraguay, The Canadian Embassy, 2828 Tagle, 1425 Buenos Aires; mailing address: Casilla de Correo 1598 C1000WAP, Buenos Aires, Argentina. Tel: (011-54-11) 4808-1000. Fax: (011-54-11) 4808-1111. e-mail: bairs@dfait-maeci.gc.ca
Embassy in Canada: Embassy of the Republic of Paraguay, 151 Slater St, Ste 501, Ottawa, ON K1P 5H3. Tel: (613) 567-1283. Fax: (613) 567-1679. e-mail: embapar@magmacom.com

Peru

Long-Form Name: Republic of Peru
Capital: Lima

■ GEOGRAPHY

Area: 1,285,220 sq. km
Coastline: 2,414 km
Climate: varies from tropical in east to dry desert in west
Environment: subject to earthquakes, tsunamis, landslides, mild volcanic activity; deforestation; overgrazing; soil erosion; desertification; air pollution in Lima; shares control of Lago Titicaca, world's highest navigable lake, with Bolivia
Terrain: western coastal plain (costa), high and rugged Andes in centre (sierra), eastern lowland jungle of Amazon Basin (selva)
Land Use: 3% arable: negligible permanent crops; 21% meadows; 66% forest; 10% other; includes 11,950 sq. km irrigated

Location: W South America, bordering on Pacific Ocean

■ PEOPLE

Population: 27,949,639 (July 2002 est.)
Nationality: Peruvian
Age Structure: 0–14 yrs: 34.0%; 15–64: 61.1%; 65+: 4.9% (2002 est.)
Population Growth Rate: 1.66% (2002 est.)
Net Migration: -1.05 migrants/1,000 population (2002 est.)
Ethnic Groups: 45% Indian; 37% mestizo (mixed Indian and European ancestry); 15% white; 3% black, Japanese, Chinese and other
Languages: Spanish and Quechua (official), Aymara
Religions: predominantly Roman Catholic
Birth Rate: 23.36/1,000 population (2002 est.)
Death Rate: 5.74/1,000 population (2002 est.)
Infant Mortality: 38.18 deaths/1,000 live births (2002 est.)
Life Expectancy at Birth: 68.18 years male, 73.12 years female (2002 est.)
Total Fertility Rate: 2.89 children born/woman (2002 est.)
Literacy: 89.9% (2000)

■ GOVERNMENT

Leader(s): Pres. Alejandro Toledo, Prime Min. Beatriz Merino
Government Type: constitutional republic
Administrative Divisions: 24 departments (departamentos, sing. —departamento) and 1 constitutional province (provincia constitucional)
Nationhood: July 28, 1821 (from Spain)
National Holiday: Independence Day, July 28

■ ECONOMY

Overview: revival of growth in GDP continues to be restricted by the large amount of public and private resources being devoted to strengthening internal security; deficit spending and poor relations with international lenders are problems; labour unrest has cut production; food shortages; world's largest producer of coca (for cocaine)
GDP: US$132 billion, per capita US$4,800; real growth rate -0.3% (2001 est.)
Inflation: 2.0% (2001)
Industries: accounts for 35% of GDP (2001 est.), mining of metals, petroleum, fishing, textiles, clothing, food processing, cement, auto assembly, steel, shipbuilding, metal fabrication
Labour Force: 10.1 million (2001); 34.1% trade and tourism, 28.6% community, social and business services, 6% finance
Unemployment: 8.0%, plus extensive underemployment (2001)

Agriculture: accounts for 10% of GDP (2001 est.) and 35% of labour force; commercial crops: coffee, cotton, sugar cane; other crops: rice, wheat, potatoes, plantains, coca; animal products: poultry, meats, dairy, wool; not self-sufficient in grain or vegetable oil; fish catch of 6.9 million metric tons
Natural Resources: copper, silver, gold, petroleum, timber, fish, iron ore, coal, phosphate, potash

■ FINANCE/TRADE

Currency: nuevo sol (pl. soles) (S/.) = 100 centimos
International Reserves Excluding Gold: US$9.339 billion (Dec. 2002)
Gold Reserves: 1.115 million fine troy ounces (Dec. 2002)
Budget: revenues US$10.4 billion, expenditures US$10.4 billion, including capital expenditures of US$ n.a. (2002 est.)
Defence Expenditures: 9.2% of central government expenditure (2001)
Education Expenditures: n.a.
External Debt: US$27.512 billion (2001)
Exports: US$6.592 billion (2001 est.); commodities: fishmeal, cotton, sugar, coffee, copper, iron ore, refined silver, lead, zinc, crude petroleum and by-products; partners: US, UK, Switzerland, China, Japan, Chile, Brazil
Imports: US$8.797 billion (2000); commodities: foodstuffs, machinery, transport equipment, iron and steel semi-manufactures, chemicals, pharmaceuticals; partners: US, Chile, Spain, Venezuela, Colombia, Brazil, Japan

■ COMMUNICATIONS

Daily Newspapers: 74 in total
Televisions: 148/1,000 inhabitants (2001)
Radios: 269/1,000 inhabitants (2001)
Telephones: 78 lines/1,000 inhabitants (2001)

■ TRANSPORTATION

Motor Vehicles: 1,000,000; 740,000 passenger cars (2000)
Roads: 72,900 km; 8,700 km paved
Railway: 2,102 km
Air Traffic: 1,605,000 passengers carried (2001)
Airports: 239; 49 have paved runways (2002)

Canadian Embassy: The Canadian Embassy, Calle Libertad 130, Miraflores, Lima 18, Peru; mailing address: Casilla 18-1126, Correo Miraflores, Lima, Peru. Tel: (011-51-1) 444-4015. Fax: (011-51-1) 242-4050. e-mail: lima@dfait-maeci.gc.ca
Embassy in Canada: Embassy of the Republic of Peru, 130 Albert St, Ste 1901, Ottawa ON K1P

5G4. Tel: (613) 238-1777. Fax: (613) 232-3062.
e-mail: embperuca@bellnet.ca

Philippines

Long-Form Name: Republic of the Philippines
Capital: Manila

■ GEOGRAPHY

Area: 300,000 sq. km
Coastline: 36,289 km
Climate: tropical marine; northeast monsoon
(Nov. to Apr.); southwest monsoon (May to
Oct.)
Environment: astride typhoon belt, usually
affected by 15 and struck by five to six cyclonic
storms per year; subject to landslides, active
volcanoes, destructive earthquakes, tsunami;
deforestation; soil erosion; water pollution
Terrain: mostly mountains with narrow to
extensive coastal lowlands
Land Use: 19% arable; 12% permanent crops;
4% meadows; 46% forest; 19% other; includes
15,500 sq. km irrigated
Location: SE of China, bordering on South
China Sea, Pacific Ocean

■ PEOPLE

Population: 84,525,639 (July 2002 est.)
Nationality: Filipino
Age Structure: 0–14 yrs: 36.6%; 15–64: 59.7%;
65+: 3.7% (2002 est.)
Population Growth Rate: 1.99% (2002 est.)
Net Migration: -1.00 migrants/1,000 population
(2002 est.)
Ethnic Groups: 91.5% Christian Malay, 4%
Muslim Malay, 1.5% Chinese, 3% other
Languages: Pilipino (native national language
based on Tagalog) and English (both official);
Spanish also spoken, also 76 indigenous
languages including Cebuano, Tagalog, Iloco,
Ifugao
Religions: 83% Roman Catholic, 9% Protestant,
5% Muslim, 3% Buddhist and other
Birth Rate: 26.88/1,000 population (2002 est.)
Death Rate: 5.95/1,000 population (2002 est.)
Infant Mortality: 27.87 deaths/1,000 live births
(2002 est.)
Life Expectancy at Birth: 65.26 years male, 71.12
years female (2002 est.)
Total Fertility Rate: 3.35 children born/woman
(2002 est.)
Literacy: 95.3% (2000)

■ GOVERNMENT

Leader(s): Pres. Gloria Macapagal-Arroyo, V.
Pres. Teofisto Guingona
Government Type: republic
Administrative Divisions: 14 regions, divided into
73 provinces and 61 chartered cities

Nationhood: July 4, 1946 (from US)
National Holiday: Independence Day (from
Spain), June 12

■ ECONOMY

Overview: drought and power supply problems
have hampered production; world's largest
exporter of coconuts and coconut products
GDP: US$335 billion, per capita US$4,000; real
growth rate 2.8% (2001 est.)
Inflation: 6.1% (2001)
Industries: accounts for 30% of GDP (2000);
textiles, pharmaceuticals, chemicals, wood
products, food processing, electronics assembly,
petroleum refining, fishing
Labour Force: 33.3 million (2001); 40% agriculture, 18% services, 18% manufacturing
Unemployment: 10.1% (2001)
Agriculture: accounts for 17% of GDP (2000)
and 45% of labour force; major crops: rice,
coconuts, corn, sugar cane, bananas, pineapples,
mangoes; animal products: pork, eggs, beef; net
exporter of farm products: fish catch of 2
million metric tons annually
Natural Resources: timber, crude oil, nickel,
cobalt, silver, gold, salt, copper

■ FINANCE/TRADE

Currency: peso (P) = 100 centavos
International Reserves Excluding Gold: US$13.136
billion (Dec. 2002)
Gold Reserves: 8.729 million fine troy ounces
(Dec. 2002)
Budget: revenues US$10.9 billion; expenditures
US$13.8 billion, including capital expenditures
US$ n.a. (2001 est.)
Defence Expenditures: 5.1% of central
government expenditure (2001)
Education Expenditures: 18.72% of central
government expenditure (2000)
External Debt: US$52.356 billion (2001)
Exports: US$34.700 billion (2002 est.);
commodities: electrical equipment 19%, textiles
16%, minerals and ores 11%, farm products
10%, coconut 10%, chemicals 5%, fish 5%,
forest products 4%; partners: US, Japan,
Netherlands, Singapore, Taiwan, Hong Kong
Imports: US$35.183 billion (2002 est.); com-
modities: raw materials 53%, capital goods
17%, petroleum products 17%; partners: Japan,
US, EU, South Korea, Singapore, Taiwan

■ COMMUNICATIONS

Daily Newspapers: 82/1,000 inhabitants (2000)
Televisions: 173/1,000 inhabitants (2001)
Radios: 161/1,000 inhabitants (2001)
Telephones: 42 lines/1,000 inhabitants (2001)

■ TRANSPORTATION

Motor Vehicles: 2,600,000; 828,000 passenger cars (2000)
Roads: 199,950 km; 39,590 km paved
Railway: 897 km
Air Traffic: 5,652,000 passengers carried (2001)
Airports: 275; 82 have paved runways (2002)

Canadian Embassy: The Canadian Embassy, 9th and 11th Fl, Allied Bank Centre, 6754 Ayala Ave, Makati, Manila, Philippines; mailing address: P.O. Box 2168, Makati CPO 1261, Manila, Philippines. Tel: (011-63-2) 867-0001. Fax: (011-63-2) 810-4299. e-mail: manil@dfait-maeci.gc.ca
Embassy in Canada: Embassy of the Republic of the Philippines, 130 Albert St, Ste 606, Ottawa ON K1P 5G4. Tel: (613) 233-1121. Fax: (613) 233-4165. e-mail: ottawape@istar.ca

---

Pitcairn Islands

Long-Form Name: Pitcairn, Henderson, Ducie and Oeno Islands
Capital: Adamstown

■ GEOGRAPHY

Area: 47 sq. km (Pitcairn and 3 small uninhabited islands)
Climate: tropical, hot, humid, modified by southeasterly trade winds; rainy season from Nov. to March
Land Use: rugged but fertile interior
Location: S Pacific Ocean, E of French Polynesia

■ PEOPLE

Population: 47 (July 2002 est.)
Nationality: Pitcairn Islander
Ethnic Groups: descendants of Polynesians and British (the latter crew members of the British naval ship *Bounty*)
Languages: English (official), Tahitian-English dialect

■ GOVERNMENT

Colony/Territory of: Dependent Territory of the United Kingdom
Leader(s): Queen Elizabeth II (UK), High Comm. to New Zealand Richard Fell
Government Type: dependency of the UK
National Holiday: Celebration of the birthday of the Queen, second Saturday in June

■ ECONOMY

Overview: inhabitants subsist on fishing and farming; fertile soil of the valleys produces wide variety of fruit and vegetables; bartering is an important part of the economy; imports: fuel oil, machinery, building materials; no exports other than small tourist trade with passing ships

■ FINANCE/TRADE

Currency: New Zealand dollar = 100 cents

Canadian Embassy: c/o The Canadian High Commission, Macdonald House, 1 Grosvenor Square, London, W1K 4AB. Tel: (011-44-20) 7258-6600. Fax: (011-44-20) 7258-6333. e-mail: ldn@dfait-maeci.gc.ca
Representative to Canada: c/o British High Commission, 80 Elgin St, Ottawa ON K1P 5K7. Tel: (613) 237-1530. Fax: (613) 237-7980. Email should be sent using the appropriate form at the British High Commission's Website at http://www.britain-in-canada.org

---

Poland

Long-Form Name: Republic of Poland
Capital: Warsaw

■ GEOGRAPHY

Area: 312,683 sq. km
Coastline: 491 km along Baltic Sea
Climate: temperate with cold, cloudy, moderately severe winters with frequent precipitation; mild summers with frequent showers and thundershowers
Environment: plain crossed by a few meandering streams; severe air and water pollution in south; flat terrain; lack of natural barriers; recently there has been severe flooding
Terrain: mostly flat plain, mountains along southern border
Land Use: 47% arable; 1% permanent crops; 13% meadows; 29% forest; 10% other; includes 1,000 sq. km irrigated
Location: NE Europe, bordering on Baltic Sea

■ PEOPLE

Population: 38,625,478 (July 2002 est.)
Nationality: Polish, Pole
Age Structure: 0–14 yrs: 17.9%; 15–64: 69.5%; 65+: 12.6% (2002 est.)
Population Growth Rate: -0.02% (2002 est.)
Net Migration: -0.49 migrants/1,000 population (2002 est.)
Ethnic Groups: 97.6% Polish, 1.3% German, 0.6% Ukrainian, 0.5% Byelorussian
Languages: Polish
Religions: 95% Roman Catholic (about 75% practising), 5% Russian Orthodox, Protestant and other
Birth Rate: 10.29/1,000 population (2002 est.)
Death Rate: 9.97/1,000 population (2002 est.)
Infant Mortality: 9.17 deaths/1,000 live births (2002 est.)

Life Expectancy at Birth: 69.52 years male, 78.05 years female (2002 est.)
Total Fertility Rate: 1.37 children born/woman (2002 est.)
Literacy: 99.7% (2000)

■ GOVERNMENT

Leader(s): Pres. Aleksander Kwasniewski, Prem. Leszek Miller
Government Type: republic
Administrative Divisions: 16 provinces (wojewodztwa, sing. —wojewodztwo)
Nationhood: Nov. 11, 1918, independent republic proclaimed
National Holiday: Constitution Day, May 3; Independence Day, Nov. 11

■ ECONOMY

Overview: continues to make good progress in the difficult transition to a free-market economy; in contrast to the vibrant expansion of private non-farm activity, the large agricultural component remains handicapped by structural problems, surplus labour, inefficient small farms, and lack of investment
GDP: US$368.1 billion, per capita US$9,500; real growth rate 1.2% (2002 est.)
Inflation: 5.5% (2001)
Industries: accounts for 32% of GDP (2000), machine building, iron and steel, extractive industries, chemicals, shipbuilding, food processing, glass, beverages, textiles
Labour Force: 19.9 million (2001); 28% agriculture, 22.1% industry, 50% community, social and business services
Unemployment: 18.7% (Jan. 2003)
Agriculture: accounts for 3% GDP (2000) and 27% of labour force; 75% of output from private farms, 25% from state farms; low productivity; leading European producer of rye, rapeseed and potatoes; wide variety of other crops and livestock; major exporter of pork products
Natural Resources: coal, sulphur, copper, natural gas, silver, lead, salt

■ FINANCE/TRADE

Currency: zloty (pl. zlotych) (Zl) = 100 groszy
International Reserves Excluding Gold: US$28.450 billion (Nov. 2002)
Gold Reserves: 3.309 million fine troy ounces (Nov. 2002)
Budget: revenues US$49.6 billion; expenditures US$52.3 billion, including capital expenditures US$ n.a. (1999)
Defence Expenditures: 5.3% of central government expenditure (2001)
Education Expenditures: 4.71% of total government expenditure (2000)
External Debt: US$62.393 billion (2001)

Exports: US$39.157 billion (2002 est.); commodities: machinery and equipment 63%, fuels, minerals and metals 14%, manufactured consumer goods 14%, agricultural and forestry products 5%; partners: Germany, Italy, France, UK
Imports: US$52.841 billion (2002 est.); commodities: machinery and equipment 36%, fuels, minerals and metals 35%, manufactured consumer goods 9%, agricultural and forestry products 12%; partners: Germany, Russia, Italy, France

■ COMMUNICATIONS

Daily Newspapers: 102/1,000 inhabitants (2000)
Televisions: 401/1,000 inhabitants (2001)
Radios: 523/1,000 inhabitants (2001)
Telephones: 295 lines/1,000 inhabitants (2001)

■ TRANSPORTATION

Motor Vehicles: 11,000,000; 9,200,000 passenger cars (2000)
Roads: 381,046 km; 249,966 km paved
Railway: 23,420 km
Air Traffic: 2,670,000 passengers carried (2001)
Airports: 122; 83 have paved runways (2002)

Canadian Embassy: The Canadian Embassy, ul. Jana Matejki 1/5, 00-481, Warsaw, Poland. Tel: (011-48-22) 584-3100. Fax: (011-48-22) 584-3190. e-mail: wsaw@dfait-maeci.gc.ca
Embassy in Canada: Embassy of the Republic of Poland, 443 Daly Ave, Ottawa ON K1N 6H3. Tel: (613) 789-0468. Fax: (613) 789-1218. e-mail: n.a.

Portugal

Long-Form Name: Portuguese Republic
Capital: Lisbon

■ GEOGRAPHY

Area: 92,391 sq. km; includes Azores and Madeira Islands
Coastline: 1,793 km
Climate: maritime temperature; cool and rainy in north, warmer and drier in south
Environment: air pollution and soil degradation are accelerating; coastal water pollution; Azores subject to severe earthquakes
Terrain: mountainous north, rolling plains in south
Land Use: 26% arable; 9% permanent crops; 9% meadows; 36% forest; 20% other; includes 6,320 sq. km irrigated
Location: SW Europe, bordering on North Atlantic Ocean

■ PEOPLE

Population: 10,084,245 (July 2002 est.)
Nationality: Portuguese

Age Structure: 0–14 yrs: 16.9%; 15–64: 67.3%; 65+: 15.8% (2002 est.)
Population Growth Rate: 0.18% (2002 est.)
Net Migration: 0.50 migrants/1,000 population (2002 est.)
Ethnic Groups: homogeneous Mediterranean stock in mainland, Azores and Madeira Islands; citizens of black African descent who immigrated to mainland during decolonization number less than 100,000
Languages: Portuguese (official), English, French
Religions: 97% Roman Catholic, 1% Protestant, 2% other
Birth Rate: 11.50/1,000 population (2002 est.)
Death Rate: 10.21/1,000 population (2002 est.)
Infant Mortality: 5.84 deaths/1,000 live births (2002 est.)
Life Expectancy at Birth: 72.65 years male, 79.87 years female (2002 est.)
Total Fertility Rate: 1.48 children born/woman (2002 est.)
Literacy: 92.2% (2000)

■ GOVERNMENT

Leader(s): Pres. Jorge Sampaio, Prem. José Manuel Durao Barroso
Government Type: parliamentary democracy
Administrative Divisions: 18 districts (distritos, sing. —distrito) and 2 autonomous regions (regioes autonomas, sing. —regiao autonoma)
Nationhood: 1143; independent republic proclaimed Oct. 5, 1910
National Holiday: Day of Portugal, June 10

■ ECONOMY

Overview: the economy has grown recently due to strong domestic consumption and investment spending; government is promoting privatization measures; the global slowdown and tight financial policies to combat inflation have caused economic growth to slow
GDP: US$182 billion, per capita US$18,000; real growth rate 0.8% (2001 est.)
Inflation: 4.4% (2001)
Industries: accounts for 29% of GDP (2001); textiles and footwear; wood pulp, paper and cork; metalworking; oil refining; chemicals; fish canning; wine; tourism
Labour Force: 5.1 million (2001); 60% community, social and business services, 30% industry, 10% agriculture
Unemployment: 4.1% (Oct. 2001)
Agriculture: accounts for 4% of GDP (2001) and 20% of labour force; small inefficient farms; imports more than half of food needs; major crops: grain, potatoes, olives, grapes; livestock sector: sheep, cattle, goats, poultry, meat, dairy products

Natural Resources: fish, forests (cork), tungsten, iron ore, uranium ore, marble

■ FINANCE/TRADE

Currency: escudo (Esc) = 100 centavos; Euro (€); on January 1, 2002 the Euro became the sole currency for everyday transactions.
International Reserves Excluding Gold: US$11.179 billion (Dec. 2002)
Gold Reserves: 19.028 million fine troy ounces (Dec. 2002)
Budget: revenues US$45 billion, expenditures US$48 billion, including capital expenditures of US$ n.a. (2001 est.)
Defence Expenditures: 5.4% of central government expenditures (2001)
Education Expenditures: n.a.
External Debt: n.a.
Exports: US$23.901 billion (2001); commodities: cotton textiles, cork and cork products, canned fish, wine, timber and timber products, resin, machinery, appliances; partners: EU, US
Imports: US$37.902 billion (2001); commodities: petroleum, cotton, foodgrains, industrial machinery, iron and steel, chemicals; partners: Spain, Germany, France, Italy, UK, US, Japan

■ COMMUNICATIONS

Daily Newspapers: 32/1,000 inhabitants (2000)
Televisions: 415/1,000 inhabitants (2001)
Radios: 304/1,000 inhabitants (2001)
Telephones: 427 lines/1,000 inhabitants (2001)

■ TRANSPORTATION

Motor Vehicles: 3,500,000; 3,100,000 passenger cars (2000)
Roads: 68,732 km; 59,110 km surfaced (1999)
Railway: 2,850 km
Air Traffic: 6,651,000 passengers carried (2001)
Airports: 67; 40 have paved runways (2002)

Canadian Embassy: The Canadian Embassy, Avenida da Liberdade, 196-200, 3rd Floor, 1269-121 Lisbon, Portugal. Tel: (011-351) 21-316-46-00. Fax: (011-351) 21-316-46-91. e-mail: lsbon@dfait-maeci.gc.ca
Embassy in Canada: Embassy of Portugal, 645 Island Park Dr, Ottawa ON K1Y 0B8. Tel: (613) 729-0883. Fax: (613) 729-4236. e-mail: embportugal@embportugal-ottawa.org

Puerto Rico

Long-Form Name: Commonwealth of Puerto Rico
Capital: San Juan

■ GEOGRAPHY

Area: 9,104 sq. km
Climate: tropical marine, mild, little seasonal temperature variation
Land Use: 4% arable; 5% permanent crops; 26% permanent pastures; 16% forest; 49% other; includes 400 sq. km irrigated
Location: West Indies, bordering on Caribbean Sea, Atlantic Ocean

■ PEOPLE

Population: 3,957,988 (July 2002 est.)
Nationality: Puerto Rican (US citizens)
Ethnic Groups: almost entirely Hispanic
Languages: Spanish (official); English is widely understood

■ GOVERNMENT

Colony/Territory of: Commonwealth associated with the US
Leader(s): Pres. George W. Bush Jr., Gov. Sila Maria Calderon
Government Type: Commonwealth associated with the US
National Holiday: US Independence Day, July 4

■ ECONOMY

Overview: economy (one of the most dynamic in the Caribbean region) has benefited from heavy US investment; new industries include pharmaceuticals and electronics; tourism is important; sugar production has lost out to dairy production and other livestock products as the main facet of the agricultural sector

■ FINANCE/TRADE

Currency: American dollar ($US) = 100 cents

Canadian Embassy: c/o The Canadian Embassy, 501 Pennsylvania Ave NW, Washington DC 20001, USA. Tel: (202) 682-1740. Fax: (202) 456-7726. e-mail: wshdc@dfait-maeci.gc.ca
Representative to Canada: c/o Embassy of the United States of America, 490 Sussex Drive, Ottawa, ON, K1N 1G8. Tel: (613) 238-5335. Fax: (613) 688-3097. Email inquiries are not accepted

Qatar

Long-Form Name: State of Qatar
Capital: Doha

■ GEOGRAPHY

Area: 11,437 sq. km
Coastline: 563 km
Climate: desert; hot, dry; humid and sultry in summer
Environment: haze, dust storms, sandstorms common; limited freshwater resources mean increasing dependence on large-scale desalination facilities
Terrain: mostly flat and barren desert covered with loose sand and gravel
Land Use: 1% arable; 0% permanent crops; 5% meadows; 0% forest; 94% other; includes 130 sq. km irrigated
Location: SW Asia (Middle East, Arabian Peninsula), bordering on Persian Gulf

■ PEOPLE

Population: 793,341 (July 2002 est.)
Nationality: Qatari
Age Structure: 0–14 yrs: 25.2%; 15–64: 72.1%; 65+: 2.7% (2002 est.)
Population Growth Rate: 3.02% (2002 est.)
Net Migration: 18.75 migrants/1,000 population (2002 est.)
Ethnic Groups: 40% Arab, 18% Pakistani, 18% Indian, 10% Iranian, 14% other
Languages: Arabic (official); English is commonly used as second language
Religions: Islam (native Qataris—less than one-third of the population—principally adhere to orthodox Wahhabi sect of Sunni Muslims)
Birth Rate: 15.78/1,000 population (2002 est.)
Death Rate: 4.34/1,000 population (2002 est.)
Infant Mortality: 20.73 deaths/1,000 live births (2002 est.)
Life Expectancy at Birth: 70.40 years male, 75.48 years female (2002 est.)
Total Fertility Rate: 3.10 children born/woman (2002 est.)
Literacy: 81.2% (2000)

■ GOVERNMENT

Leader(s): Amir Shaykh Hamad bin Khalifa Al Thani, Prime Min. Shaykh Abdallah bin Khalifa Al Thani
Government Type: traditional monarchy
Administrative Divisions: 9 municipalities (baladiyah, sing. —baladiyah)
Nationhood: Sept. 3, 1971 (from UK)
National Holiday: Independence Day, Sept. 3

■ ECONOMY

Overview: has one of the highest per capita GDPs in the world, due to oil revenues; reserves should not be completely depleted for about 20 years; production and export of natural gas is becoming increasingly important; oil has given Qatar a per capita GDP comparable to the leading West European industrial countries
GDP: US$16.3 billion, per capita US$21,200; real growth rate 5.6% (2001 est.)
Inflation: -1.0% (2000)
Industries: accounts for 49% of GDP; crude oil production and refining, fertilizers, petrochemicals, steel, cement

Labour Force: n.a.; 3% agriculture, 28% industry, 69% services; 83% of labour force in private sector is non-Qatari
Unemployment: n.a.
Agriculture: farming and grazing on small scale, less than 1% of GDP; commercial fishing increasing in importance; most food imported. Domestic products include fruits, vegetables, poultry, dairy products.
Natural Resources: crude oil, natural gas, fish

■ FINANCE/TRADE

Currency: Qatari riyal (QR) = 100 dirhams
International Reserves Excluding Gold: US$1.503 billion (Nov. 2002)
Gold Reserves: 0.019 million fine troy ounces (Nov. 2002)
Budget: revenues US$5 billion; expenditures US$4.8 billion, including capital expenditures of US$900 million (FY2001/02 est.)
Defence Expenditures: 8.1% of GDP (1999–2000)
Education Expenditures: n.a.
External Debt: US$13.1 billion (2000 est.)
Exports: US$4.125 billion (2000); commodities: petroleum products 90%, steel, fertilizers; partners: Japan, Singapore, South Korea, US, UAE
Imports: US$3.575 billion (2000); commodities: foodstuffs, beverages, animal and vegetable oils, chemicals, machinery and equipment; partners: UK, Japan, Germany, US, Italy

■ COMMUNICATIONS

Daily Newspapers: 5 in total
Televisions: n.a.
Radios: n.a.
Telephones: 263 lines/1,000 inhabitants (1999)

■ TRANSPORTATION

Motor Vehicles: 184,000; 97,000 passenger cars
Roads: 1,230 km; 1,107 km paved
Railway: none
Air Traffic: 1,300,000 passengers carried (1999 est.)
Airports: 4; 2 have paved runways (2002)

Canadian Embassy: The Canadian Embassy to Qatar, c/o The Canadian Embassy, Villa 24, Area 4, Plot 121, 24 Al-Mutawakel St, Da Aiyah, Kuwait City, Kuwait; mailing address: P.O. Box 25281, 13113, Safat, Kuwait City, Kuwait. Tel: (011-965) 256-3025. Fax: (011-965) 256-0173. e-mail: kwait@dfait-maeci.gc.ca
Embassy in Canada: Embassy of the State of Qatar, c/o Permanent Mission of the State of Qatar to the United Nations, 809 UN Plaza, First Ave 4th Fl, New York NY 10017, USA. Tel: (212) 486-9335. Fax: (212) 758-4952. e-mail: n.a.

Réunion

Long-Form Name: Department of Réunion
Capital: Saint-Denis

■ GEOGRAPHY

Area: 2,512 sq. km; uninhabited islands of Juan de Nova, Europa, Bassas da India, Iles Glorieuses, Tromelin administered by Réunion but do not form part of the territory; Mauritius and the Seychelles claim Tromelin, Madagascar claims all 5 islands
Climate: tropical, but more moderate at higher elevations; May to Nov.: cool and dry; Nov. to April: hot and rainy
Land Use: volcanic island; some cultivation of indigenous plants and cash crops such as corn; 17% arable; 2% permanent crops; 5% meadows and pastures; 35% forest, 41% other; includes 120 sq. km irrigated
Location: Indian Ocean, E of Africa (E of Madagascar)

■ PEOPLE

Population: 743,981 (July 2002 est.)
Nationality: Réunionese
Ethnic Groups: French Creoles, African, Malagasy, Pakistani, Indian and Chinese minorities
Languages: French (official), Creole vernacular

■ GOVERNMENT

Colony/Territory of: Overseas Department of France
Leader(s): Pres. Jacques Chirac (France), Prefect Gonthier Friederici
Government Type: overseas department of France
National Holiday: Taking of the Bastille, July 14

■ ECONOMY

Overview: agriculture-based economy, of which sugar cane is the backbone; government is promoting the development of the tourist industry; socio-economic tensions between classes with widely disparate living standards; economy heavily depends on financial assistance from France

■ FINANCE/TRADE

Currency: French franc = 100 centimes

Canadian Embassy: c/o The Canadian Embassy, 35-37 avenue Montaigne, 75008, Paris, France. Tel: (011-33-1) 44-43-29-00. Fax: (011-33-1) 44043-29-99. e-mail: paris@dfait-maeci.gc.ca
Representative to Canada: c/o Embassy of France, 42 Sussex Dr, Ottawa ON K1M 2C9. Tel: (613) 789-1795. Fax: (613) 562-3735. e-mail: politique@ambafrance-ca.org

Romania

Long-Form Name: Romania
Capital: Bucharest

■ GEOGRAPHY

Area: 237,500 sq. km
Coastline: 225 km
Climate: temperate; cold, cloudy winters with frequent snow and fog; sunny summers with frequent showers and thunderstorms
Environment: frequent earthquakes most severe in south and southwest; geologic structure and climate promote landslides; water pollution; air pollution in south; soil degradation
Terrain: central Transylvanian Basin is separated from the plain of Moldavia on the east by the Carpathian Mountains and separated from the Walachian Plain on the south by the Transylvanian Alps
Land Use: 41% arable; 3% permanent crops; 21% meadows; 29% forest; 6% other; includes 28,800 sq. km irrigated
Location: SE Europe, bordering on Black Sea

■ PEOPLE

Population: 22,317,730 (July 2002 est.)
Nationality: Romanian
Age Structure: 0–14 yrs: 17.4%; 15–64: 68.8%; 65+: 13.8% (2002 est.)
Population Growth Rate: -0.21% (2002 est.)
Net Migration: -0.6 migrants/1,000 population (2002 est.)
Ethnic Groups: 89.5% Romanian; 7.1% Hungarian; 0.5% German; 2.9% Ukrainian, Serb, Croat, Russian, Turk and Gypsy
Languages: Romanian (official), Hungarian, German; French and English also spoken
Religions: 70% Romanian Orthodox; 6% Roman Catholic; 24% Calvinist, Lutheran, Jewish, Baptist, unaffiliated
Birth Rate: 10.81/1,000 population (2002 est.)
Death Rate: 12.27/1,000 population (2002 est.)
Infant Mortality: 18.88 deaths/1,000 live births (2002 est.)
Life Expectancy at Birth: 66.62 years male, 74.39 years female (2002 est.)
Total Fertility Rate: 1.35 children born/woman (2002 est.)
Literacy: 98.1% (2000)

■ GOVERNMENT

Leader(s): Pres. Ion Iliescu, Prime Min. Adrian Nastase
Government Type: republic
Administrative Divisions: 40 counties (judete, sing. —judet) and 1 municipality (municipiu)
Nationhood: 1881 (from Turkey); republic proclaimed Dec. 30, 1947

National Holiday: National Day/Unification Day, Dec. 1

■ ECONOMY

Overview: industry suffers from an ageing capital plant and shortages of energy; agriculture sector has suffered from drought and mismanagement; private enterprise is increasing in importance; growing budget deficit, inflation, unemployment and a deteriorating infrastructure hamper economic progress
GDP: US$152.7 billion, per capita US$6,800; real growth rate 4.8% (2001 est.)
Inflation: 34.5% (2001)
Industries: accounts for 30% of GDP (2000); mining, timber, construction materials, metallurgy, chemicals, machine building, food processing, petroleum
Labour Force: 10.8 million (2001); 25% industry, 40% agriculture, 35% community, social and business services
Unemployment: 8.1% (Dec. 2002)
Agriculture: accounts for 15% of GDP (2000) and 28% of labour force; major wheat and corn producer, sugar beets, sunflower seeds, grapes, potatoes, milk, eggs, meat
Natural Resources: crude oil (reserves being exhausted), timber, natural gas, coal, iron ore, salt, arable land, hydro power

■ FINANCE/TRADE

Currency: leu (pl. lei) = 100 bani
International Reserves Excluding Gold: US$7.211 billion (Dec. 2002)
Gold Reserves: 3.386 million fine troy ounces (Dec. 2002)
Budget: revenues US$11.2 billion; expenditures US$12.7 billion, including capital expenditures of US$ n.a. (1999 est.)
Defence Expenditures: 8.1% of central government expenditure (2001)
Education Expenditures: 9.83% of total government expenditure (1999)
External Debt: US$11.653 billion (2001)
Exports: US$13.870 billion (2002); commodities: machinery and equipment 34.7%, fuels, minerals and metals 24.7%, manufactured consumer goods 16.9%, agricultural materials and forestry products 11.9%, other 11.6%; partners: Italy, Germany, France, Turkey, US
Imports: US$18.847 billion (2002); commodities: fuels, minerals and metals 51%, machinery and equipment 26.7%, agricultural and forestry products 11%, manufactured consumer goods 4.2%; partners: Italy, Germany, France, Russia

■ COMMUNICATIONS

Daily Newspapers: 300/1,000 inhabitants (2000)
Televisions: 379/1,000 inhabitants (2001)

Radios: 358/1,000 inhabitants (2001)
Telephones: 184 lines/1,000 inhabitants (2001)

■ TRANSPORTATION

Motor Vehicles: 3,400,000; 3,000,000 passenger cars (2000)
Roads: 153,359 km; 103,671 km paved
Railway: 11,385 km
Air Traffic: 1,135,000 passengers carried (2001)
Airports: 61; 25 have paved runways (2002)

Canadian Embassy: The Canadian Embassy, 36, Nicolae Iorga, 71118 Bucharest, Romania; Postal Address: P.O. Box 117, Post Office No. 22, Bucharest, Romania. Tel: (011-40-1) 307-5000. Fax: (011-40-1) 307-5010. e-mail: bucst@dfait-maeci.gc.ca
Embassy in Canada: Embassy of Romania, 655 Rideau St, Ottawa ON K1N 6A3. Tel: (613) 789-3709. Fax: (613) 789-4365. e-mail: romania@cyberus.ca

Russia

Long-Form Name: Russian Federation
Capital: Moscow

■ GEOGRAPHY

Area: 17,075,200 sq. km
Coastline: 37,653 km
Climate: ranges from steppes in south through humid continental, subarctic in Siberia to tundra in polar north; winters vary—cool along Black Sea, frigid in Siberia; summers—warm in the steppes to cool along Arctic coast
Environment: cold desert in north; volcanic activity; only small percentage of land is arable—much is too far north; permafrost over much of Siberia; severe land, air and water pollution; deforestation and soil erosion
Terrain: rolling western plains, north-south ridge of Ural Mountains, central plateau, rugged eastern uplands
Land Use: 8% arable; 46% forests and woodland; 4% meadows and pastures; 42% steppe and cold desert; includes 46,630 sq. km irrigated
Location: E Europe and N Asia, bordering on Barents Sea, Baltic Sea, Black Sea, Caspian Sea

■ PEOPLE

Population: 144,978,573 (July 2002 est.)
Nationality: Russian
Age Structure: 0–14 yrs: 16.7%; 15–64: 70.2%; 65+: 13.1% (2002 est.)
Population Growth Rate: -0.33% (2002 est.)
Net Migration: 0.94 migrants/1,000 population (2002 est.)
Ethnic Groups: 81.5% Russians; 3.8% Tatars, 1.2% Chuvash, 0.9% Bashkir, 0.8% Belorussian, 3% Ukrainian, remainder includes Chechens, Germans, Udmurts, Mari, Kazakhs, Avars, Jews, Moldavians and Armenians
Languages: Russian (official), Tartar, Ukrainian
Religions: Christianity (Russian Orthodox) with substantial Muslim populations and other religious minorities
Birth Rate: 9.71/1,000 population (2002 est.)
Death Rate: 13.91/1,000 population (2002 est.)
Infant Mortality: 19.78 deaths/1,000 live births (2002 est.)
Life Expectancy at Birth: 62.29 years male, 72.97 years female (2002 est.)
Total Fertility Rate: 1.30 children born/woman (2002 est.)
Literacy: 99.6% (2000)

■ GOVERNMENT

Leader(s): Pres. Vladimir V. Putin, Prem. Mikhail Kasyanov
Government Type: federation
Administrative Divisions: 49 oblasts (oblastey, sing. —oblast), 21 autonomous republics (avtonomnyk respublik, sing. —avtonomnaya respublika), 10 autonomous okrugs (avtonomnykh okrugov, sing. —avtonomnyy okrug), 6 krays (krayer, sing. — kray), 2 federal cities (gorod) and 1 autonomous oblast (avtonomnaya oblast)
Nationhood: Aug. 24, 1991 (from Soviet Union)
National Holiday: Independence Day, June 12

■ ECONOMY

Overview: a vast country with a great many natural resources, a well-educated population, and a diverse but declining industrial base; 25% of the population live below the poverty line and the country continues to experience formidable difficulties in moving from its old centrally planned economy to a modern market economy; the severity of Russia's economic problems is dramatized by the large annual decline in population, caused by environmental hazards, poor health care, and other factors
GDP: US$1.27 trillion, per capita US$8,800; real growth rate 4.0% (2002 est.)
Inflation: 21.5% (2001)
Industries: accounts for 39% of GDP (2001); natural gas refining, steel and coal production and processing, all forms of machine building, shipbuilding, transportation equipment, consumer durables, communications and agricultural equipment, medical and scientific instruments
Labour Force: 77.6 million (2001); 28% industry, 61% community, social and business services, 11% agriculture
Unemployment: 11.4% (2001)
Agriculture: accounts for 7% of GDP (2001); grain, sugar beets, sunflower seeds, meat, milk, vegetables, fruit

Natural Resources: iron ore, coal, oil, gold, platinum, copper, zinc, lead, tin, rare metals; climate, terrain and distance hinder exploitation

■ FINANCE/TRADE

Currency: ruble (rbl.) = 100 kopeks
International Reserves Excluding Gold: US$44.054 billion (Dec. 2002)
Gold Reserves: 12.464 million fine troy ounces (Dec. 2002)
Budget: revenues US$45 billion; expenditures US$43 billion, including capital expenditures US$ n.a. (2001 est.)
Defence Expenditures: 15.4% of central government expenditure (2001)
Education Expenditures: 2.26% of total government expenditure (2000)
External Debt: US$152.649 billion (2001)
Exports: US$100.877 billion (2002 est.); commodities: fuels, wood products, metals, chemicals, wide range of manufactured products; partners: Germany, US, Italy, China, Belarus, Ukraine
Imports: US$43.721 billion (2002 est.); commodities: machinery, medicine, foodstuffs, consumer products; partners: Germany, Belarus, Ukraine, US, Kazakhstan, Italy

■ COMMUNICATIONS

Daily Newspapers: 105/1,000 inhabitants (2000)
Televisions: 538/1,000 inhabitants (2001)
Radios: 418/1,000 inhabitants (2001)
Telephones: 243 lines/1,000 inhabitants (2001)

■ TRANSPORTATION

Motor Vehicles: 22,250,000; 17,500,000 passenger cars (2000 est.)
Roads: 952,000 km; 752,000 km hard-surfaced
Railway: 87,157 km
Air Traffic: 20,235,000 passengers carried (2001)
Airports: 2,743; 471 have paved runways (2002)

Canadian Embassy: The Canadian Embassy, Starokonyushenny Per 23, Moscow 119002, Russia. Tel: (011-7-095) 105-6000. Fax: (011-7-095) 105-6025. e-mail: mosco@dfait-maeci.gc.ca
Embassy in Canada: Embassy of the Russian Federation, 285 Charlotte St, Ottawa ON K1N 8L5. Tel: (613) 235-4341. Fax: (613) 236-6342. e-mail: rusemb@intranet.ca

Rwanda

Long-Form Name: Rwandese Republic
Capital: Kigali

■ GEOGRAPHY

Area: 26,338 sq. km
Coastline: none: landlocked
Climate: temperate; two rainy seasons (Feb. to Apr., Nov. to Jan.); mild in mountains with frost and snow possible
Environment: deforestation; overgrazing; soil exhaustion; soil erosion; periodic droughts
Terrain: mostly grassy uplands and hills; mountains in west
Land Use: 35% arable; 13% permanent crops; 18% meadows; 22% forest; 12% other; includes 40 sq. km irrigated
Location: EC Africa

■ PEOPLE

Population: 7,398,074 (July 2002 est.)
Nationality: Rwandan
Age Structure: 0–14 yrs: 41.7%; 15–64: 55.4%; 65+: 2.9% (2002 est.)
Population Growth Rate: 1.16% (2002 est.)
Net Migration: -1.32 migrants/1,000 population (2002 est.)
Ethnic Groups: 84% Hutu, 15% Tutsi, 1% Twa (Pygmoid)
Languages: Kinyarwanda, French, English (all official); Kiswahili used in commercial centres
Religions: 65% Christian (mostly Roman Catholic), 9% Protestant, 1% Muslim, 25% indigenous beliefs and other
Birth Rate: 33.28/1,000 population (2002 est.)
Death Rate: 21.39/1,000 population (2002 est.)
Infant Mortality: 117.79 deaths/1,000 live births (2002 est.)
Life Expectancy at Birth: 38.14 years male, 39.20 years female (2002 est.)
Total Fertility Rate: 4.72 children born/woman (2002 est.)
Literacy: 65.8% (1999)

■ GOVERNMENT

Leader(s): Pres. Paul Kagame, Prime Min. Bernard Makuza
Government Type: republic; presidential system in which military leaders hold key offices
Administrative Divisions: 12 prefectures
Nationhood: July 1, 1962 (from UN trusteeship under Belgian administration)
National Holiday: Independence Day, July 1

■ ECONOMY

Overview: a poor nation whose economy is severely hampered by civil war, which has damaged infrastructure and economic prospects; agricultural sector dominates, with coffee and tea making up 80–90% of total exports; manufacturing is largely restricted to the processing of agricultural products

GDP: US$7.2 billion, per capita US$1,000; real growth rate 5.0% (2001 est.)
Inflation: 3.3% (2001)
Industries: accounts for 20% of GDP (2000); mining of cassiterite (tin ore) and wolframite (tungsten ore), tin, cement, agricultural processing, small-scale beverage production, soap, furniture, shoes, plastic goods, textiles, cigarettes
Labour Force: 4.7 million (2001); 90% agriulture
Unemployment: n.a.
Agriculture: accounts for 46% of GDP (2000) and about 90% of labour force; cash crops: coffee, tea, pyrethrum (insecticide made from chrysanthemums); main food crops: bananas, beans, sorghum, potatoes; stock raising; self-sufficiency declining; country imports food-stuffs as farm production fails to keep up with population growth; coffee and tea constitute 80–90% of total exports
Natural Resources: gold, cassiterite (tin ore), wolframite (tungsten ore), natural gas, hydro power

■ FINANCE/TRADE

Currency: Rwandan franc (RF) = 100 centimes
International Reserves Excluding Gold: US$244 million (Dec. 2002)
Gold Reserves: none (Dec. 2002)
Budget: revenues US$199.3 million; expenditures US$443 million, including capital expenditures of US$ n.a. (2001 est.)
Defence Expenditures: 22.7% of central government expenditure (1999)
Education Expenditures: n.a.
External Debt: US$1.283 billion (2001)
Exports: US$64 million (2002 est.); commodities: coffee 85%, tea, tin, cassiterite, wolframite, pyrethrum; partners: EU, Pakistan, US, China, Malaysia
Imports: US$204 million (2002); commodities: textiles, foodstuffs, machines and equipment, capital goods, steel, petroleum products, cement and construction material; partners: Kenya, EU, US, India, Tanzania

■ COMMUNICATIONS

Daily Newspapers: less than 1/1,000 inhabitants (2000)
Televisions: 0/1,000 inhabitants (2000)
Radios: 76/1,000 inhabitants (2001)
Telephones: 3 lines/1,000 inhabitants (2001)

■ TRANSPORTATION

Motor Vehicles: 27,800; 11,900 passenger cars
Roads: 12,000 km; 1,000 km paved
Railway: none
Air Traffic: n.a.

Airports: 8; 4 have paved runways (2002)

Canadian Embassy: Office of the Canadian Embassy, rue Akagera, P.O. Box 1177, Kigali, Rwanda. Tel: (011-250) 573210. Fax: (011-250) 572719. e-mail: kgali@dfait-maeci.gc.ca
Embassy in Canada: c/o Embassy of the Republic of Rwanda, 1714 New Hampshire NW, Washington DC 20009, USA. Tel: (202) 232-2882. Fax: (202) 232-4544. e-mail: n.a.

Saint Helena

Long-Form Name: Saint Helena
Capital: Jamestown

■ GEOGRAPHY

Area: 410 sq. km
Climate: tropical marine; little seasonal variation
Land Use: 6% arable; 0% permanent crops; 6% meadows and pastures; 6% forests; 82% other; includes n.a. sq. km irrigated
Location: S Atlantic Ocean, SW of Africa

■ PEOPLE

Population: 7,317 (July 2002 est.)
Nationality: Saint Helenian
Ethnic Groups: Europeans, East Indians, Africans
Languages: English (official)

■ GOVERNMENT

Colony/Territory of: Dependent Territory of the United Kingdom
Leader(s): Head of State: Queen Elizabeth II, Gov. and Commander-in-Chief David James Hollamby
Government Type: dependent territory of the UK
National Holiday: Celebration of the Birthday of the Queen, second Saturday in June

■ ECONOMY

Overview: depends primarily on financial assistance from UK; fishing, livestock raising and sale of handicrafts provide income for local population; due to the lack of jobs, many inhabitants have emigrated

■ FINANCE/TRADE

Currency: Saint Helenian pound = 100 pence (at par with British pound)

Canadian Embassy: c/o The Canadian High Commission, Macdonald House, 1 Grosvenor Square, London W1K 4AB, England, UK. Tel: (011-44-20) 7258-6600. Fax: (011-44-20) 7258-6333. e-mail: ldn@dfait-maeci.gc.ca
Representative to Canada: c/o British High Commission, 80 Elgin St, Ottawa ON K1P 5K7. Tel: (613) 237-1530. Fax: (613) 237-7980.

Email should be sent using the appropriate form at the British High Commission's Website at http://www.britain-in-canada.org

Saint Kitts and Nevis

Long-Form Name: Federation of Saint Kitts and Nevis
Capital: Basseterre

■ GEOGRAPHY

Area: 261 sq. km
Coastline: 135 km
Climate: subtropical tempered by constant sea breezes; little seasonal temperature variation; rainy season (May to Nov.)
Environment: subject to hurricanes (July to Oct.)
Terrain: volcanic with mountainous interiors
Land Use: 22% arable; 17% permanent crops; 3% meadows; 17% forest; 41% other; includes n.a. sq. km irrigated
Location: Caribbean islands E of Puerto Rico

■ PEOPLE

Population: 38,736 (July 2002 est.)
Nationality: Kittsian or Kittitian, Nevisian
Age Structure: 0–14 yrs: 29.4%; 15–64: 61.9%; 65+: 8.7% (2002 est.)
Population Growth Rate: 0.01% (2002 est.)
Net Migration: -9.5 migrants/1,000 population (2002 est.)
Ethnic Groups: mainly of black African descent
Languages: English
Religions: Anglican, other Protestant sects, Roman Catholic
Birth Rate: 18.61/1,000 population (2002 est.)
Death Rate: 9.04/1,000 population (2002 est.)
Infant Mortality: 15.83 deaths/1,000 live births (2002 est.)
Life Expectancy at Birth: 68.49 years male, 74.26 years female (2002 est.)
Total Fertility Rate: 2.39 children born/woman (2002 est.)
Literacy: 90.0%

■ GOVERNMENT

Leader(s): Head of State: Queen Elizabeth II, Gov. Gen. Cuthbert Montraville Sebastian, Prime Min. Denzil Douglas
Government Type: constitutional monarchy
Administrative Divisions: 14 parishes
Nationhood: Sept. 19, 1983 (from UK)
National Holiday: Independence Day, Sept. 19

■ ECONOMY

Overview: traditionally dependent on the growing and processing of sugar cane and on remittances from overseas workers; tourism and export-oriented manufacturing are increasing

GDP: US$339 million, per capita US$8,700; real growth rate 1.0% (2001 est.)
Inflation: 2.5% (2000 est.)
Industries: accounts for 26% of GDP (2001); sugar processing, tourism, cotton, salt, copra, clothing, footwear, beverages
Labour Force: approx. 20,000 (1999)
Unemployment: n.a.
Agriculture: accounts for 4% of GDP (2001); cash crop: sugar cane; subsistence crops: rice, yams, vegetables, bananas; fishing potential but not fully exploited; most food imported
Natural Resources: negligible

■ FINANCE/TRADE

Currency: East Caribbean dollar ($EC) = 100 cents
International Reserves Excluding Gold: US$56 million (Oct. 2002)
Gold Reserves: n.a.
Budget: revenues US$85.7 million, expenditures US$95.6 million, including capital expenditures of US$ n.a. (2001 est.)
Defence Expenditures: n.a.
Education Expenditures: n.a.
External Debt: US$189 million (2001)
Exports: US$39 million (2000); commodities: sugar, manufactures, electronics, tobacco, postage stamps; partners: US, UK, CARICOM countries
Imports: US$151 million (2000); commodities: foodstuffs, intermediate manufactures, machinery, fuels; partners: US, CARICOM countries, UK

■ COMMUNICATIONS

Daily Newspapers: none
Televisions: n.a.
Radios: n.a.
Telephones: 518 lines/1,000 inhabitants (1999)

■ TRANSPORTATION

Motor Vehicles: n.a.
Roads: 320 km; 136 km paved
Railway: 58 km
Air Traffic: n.a.
Airports: 2, both with paved runways (2002)

Canadian Embassy: The Canadian High Commission to Saint Kitts and Nevis, c/o The Canadian High Commission, Bishop's Court Hill, St. Michael, Barbados; mailing address: P.O. Box 404, Bridgetown, Barbados. Tel: (246) 429-3550. Fax: (246) 429-3780. e-mail: bdgtn@dfait-maeci.gc.ca

Embassy in Canada: c/o High Commission for the Countries of the Organization of Eastern Caribbean States, 130 Albert St Ste 700, Ottawa ON K1P 5G4. Tel: (613) 236-8952. Fax: (613) 236-3042. e-mail: echcc@travel-net.com

Saint Lucia

Long-Form Name: Saint Lucia
Capital: Castries

■ GEOGRAPHY

Area: 620 sq. km
Coastline: 158 km
Climate: tropical, moderated by northeast trade winds; dry season from Jan. to Apr., rainy season from May to Aug.
Environment: subject to hurricanes and volcanic activity; deforestation; soil erosion
Terrain: volcanic and mountainous with some broad, fertile valleys
Land Use: 8% arable; 21% permanent crops; 5% meadow; 13% forest; 53% other; includes 30 sq. km irrigated
Location: Caribbean islands, N of Venezuela

■ PEOPLE

Population: 158,178 (July 2000 est.)
Nationality: Saint Lucian
Age Structure: 0–14 yrs: 31.6%; 15–64: 63.1%; 65+: 5.3% (2002 est.)
Population Growth Rate: 1.23% (2001 est.)
Net Migration: -3.64 migrants/1,000 population (2002 est.)
Ethnic Groups: 90% African descent, 6% mixed, 3% East Indian, 1% Caucasian.
Languages: English (official), French patois
Religions: 90% Roman Catholic, 7% Protestant, 3% Anglican
Birth Rate: 21.37/1,000 population (2002 est.)
Death Rate: 5.30/1,000 population (2002 est.)
Infant Mortality: 14.80 deaths/1,000 live births (2002 est.)
Life Expectancy at Birth: 69.26 years male, 76.64 years female (2002 est.)
Total Fertility Rate: 2.34 children born/woman (2002 est.)
Literacy: 82.0%

■ GOVERNMENT

Leader(s): Head of State: Queen Elizabeth II, Gov. Gen. Calliopa Pearlette Louisy, Prime Min. Kenny Anthony
Government Type: parliamentary democracy
Administrative Divisions: 11 quarters
Nationhood: Feb. 22, 1979 (from UK)
National Holiday: Independence Day, Feb. 22

■ ECONOMY

Overview: depends on strong agricultural (bananas) and tourist industry sectors; expanding industrial base supported by foreign investment in manufacturing and activities such as data processing; vulnerable to droughts and tropical storms
GDP: US$700 million, per capita US$4,400; real growth rate -2.5% (2000 est.)
Inflation: 2.5% (2000 est.)
Industries: accounts for 20% of GDP (2000); clothing, electronic component assembly, beverages, tourism, lime and coconut processing
Labour Force: 43,800; 43% agriculture, 39% services, 18% industry and commerce
Unemployment: n.a.
Agriculture: accounts for 8% GDP (2000) and 43% of labour force; crops: bananas, coconuts, vegetables, citrus fruit, root crops, cocoa; imports food for the tourist industry
Natural Resources: forests, sandy beaches, minerals (pumice), mineral springs, geothermal potential

■ FINANCE/TRADE

Currency: East Caribbean dollar (EC$) = 100 cents
International Reserves Excluding Gold: US$107 million (Oct. 2002)
Gold Reserves: n.a.
Budget: n.a.
Defence Expenditures: n.a.
Education Expenditures: n.a.
External Debt: US$238 million (2001)
Exports: US$38 million (2002 est.); commodities: bananas 67%, cocoa, vegetables, fruit, coconut oil, clothing; partners: UK, US, CARICOM countries
Imports: US$254 million (2002 est.); commodities: manufactured goods 22%, machinery and transportation equipment 21%, food and live animals 20%, mineral fuels, foodstuffs, machinery and equipment, fertilizers, petroleum products; partners: US, CARICOM countries, Japan, Canada

■ COMMUNICATIONS

Daily Newspapers: none
Televisions: n.a.
Radios: n.a.
Telephones: 266 lines/1,000 inhabitants (1999)

■ TRANSPORTATION

Motor Vehicles: 12,300; 11,400 passenger cars
Roads: 1,210 km; 63 km paved
Railway: none
Air Traffic: n.a.
Airports: 2, both with paved runways (2002)

Canadian Embassy: The Canadian High Commission to Saint Lucia, c/o The Canadian High Commission, Bishop's Court Hill, St. Michael, Barbados; mailing address: P.O. Box 404, Bridgetown, Barbados. Tel: (246) 429-3550. Fax: (246) 429-3780. e-mail: bdgtn@dfait-maeci.gc.ca

Embassy in Canada: c/o High Commission for the Countries of the Organization of Eastern Caribbean States, 130 Albert St Ste 700, Ottawa ON K1P 5G4. Tel: (613) 236-8952. Fax: (613) 236-3042. e-mail: echcc@travel-net.com

Saint Pierre and Miquelon

Long-Form Name: Territorial Collectivity of Saint Pierre and Miquelon
Capital: Saint-Pierre

■ GEOGRAPHY

Area: 242 sq. km, 8 small islands
Climate: cold and wet, misty and foggy, windy spring and autumn, moist, temperate summers, cold and snowy winters
Land Use: 13% arable; 0% permanent crops; 0% meadows and pastures; 4% forest, 83% other; includes n.a. km irrigated
Location: N Atlantic Ocean, S of Newfoundland

■ PEOPLE

Population: 6,954 (July 2002 est.)
Nationality: Frenchman, Frenchwoman
Ethnic Groups: descendants of French settlers, Basques and Bretons (French fishermen)
Languages: French, English

■ GOVERNMENT

Colony/Territory of: Territorial Collectivity of France
Leader(s): Pres. Jacques Chirac (France), Prefect Claude Valleix
Government Type: territorial collectivity with internal self-government
National Holiday: Taking of the Bastille, July 14

■ ECONOMY

Overview: fishing, and the servicing of fishing fleets operating off the coast of Newfoundland, have long been an important part of the economy; agriculture: some vegetables and livestock for local consumption; partners: UK, Canada, EU

■ FINANCE/TRADE

Currency: French franc = 100 centimes; also the Euro

Canadian Embassy: c/o The Canadian Embassy, 35-37 avenue Montaigne, 75008 Paris, France.
Tel: (011-33-1) 44-43-29-00. Fax: (011-33-1) 44-43-29-99. e-mail: paris@dfait-maeci.gc.ca
Representative to Canada: c/o Embassy of France, 42 Sussex Dr, Ottawa ON K1M 2C9. Tel: (613) 789-1795. Fax: (613) 562-3735. e-mail: politique@ambafrance-ca.org

Saint Vincent and the Grenadines

Long-Form Name: Saint Vincent and the Grenadines
Capital: Kingstown

■ GEOGRAPHY

Area: 389 sq. km
Coastline: 84 km
Climate: tropical; little seasonal temperature variation; rainy season (May to Nov.)
Environment: subject to hurricanes; Soufrière volcano is a constant threat; water pollution along coasts
Terrain: volcanic, mountainous; Soufrière volcano on the island of Saint Vincent
Land Use: 10% arable; 18% permanent crops; 5% meadows; 36% forest; 31% other; includes 10 sq. km irrigated
Location: Caribbean islands, N of Venezuela

■ PEOPLE

Population: 116,394 (July 2002 est.)
Nationality: Saint Vincentian or Vincentian
Age Structure: 0–14 yrs: 28.9%; 15–64: 64.8%; 65+: 6.3% (2002 est.)
Population Growth Rate: 0.37% (2002 est.)
Net Migration: -7.69 migrants/1,000 population (2002 est.)
Ethnic Groups: 66% black African descent; remainder mixed, with some white, East Indian, Carib Indian
Languages: English (official), some French patois
Religions: Anglican, Methodist, Roman Catholic, Seventh-Day Adventist
Birth Rate: 17.54/1,000 population (2002 est.)
Death Rate: 6.12/1,000 population (2002 est.)
Infant Mortality: 16.15 deaths/1,000 live births (2002 est.)
Life Expectancy at Birth: 71.07 years male, 74.63 years female (2002 est.)
Total Fertility Rate: 2.01 children born/woman (2002 est.)
Literacy: 82.0%

■ GOVERNMENT

Leader(s): Head of State: Queen Elizabeth II, Gov. Gen. Frederick Nathaniel Ballantyne, Prime Min. Ralph Gonsalves
Government Type: parliamentary democracy
Administrative Divisions: 6 parishes
Nationhood: Oct. 27, 1979 (from UK)
National Holiday: Independence Day, Oct. 27

■ ECONOMY

Overview: overdependence on the weather-plagued banana crop as a major export earner has caused high unemployment; has been unsuccessful in diversifying into new industries
GDP: US$339 million, per capita US$2,900; real growth rate -0.8% (2001 est.)
Inflation: 0.8% (2001)
Industries: accounts for 26% of GDP (2001 est.); food processing (sugar, flour), cement, furniture, rum, starch, sheet metal, beverage
Labour Force: n.a.
Unemployment: n.a.
Agriculture: accounts for 10% of GDP (2001 est.) and 60% of labour force; provides bulk of exports; products: bananas, arrowroot (world's largest producer), coconuts, sweet potatoes, spices; small numbers of cattle, sheep, hogs, goats; small fish catch used locally
Natural Resources: negligible

■ FINANCE/TRADE

Currency: East Caribbean dollar ($EC) = 100 cents
International Reserves Excluding Gold: US$56 million (Oct. 2002)
Gold Reserves: n.a.
Budget: n.a.
Defence Expenditures: negligible
Education Expenditures: 16.45% of total government expenditure (2000)
External Debt: US$194 million (2001)
Exports: US$38 million (2002 est.); commodities: bananas, eddoes and dasheen (taro), arrowroot starch, copra; partners: CARICOM, UK, US
Imports: US$159 million (2002 est.); commodities: foodstuffs, machinery and equipment, chemicals and fertilizers, minerals and fuels; partners: US, CARICOM countries, UK

■ COMMUNICATIONS

Daily Newspapers: none
Televisions: n.a.
Radios: n.a.
Telephones: 209 lines/1,000 inhabitants (1999)

■ TRANSPORTATION

Motor Vehicles: 8,200; 5,000 passenger cars
Roads: 1,040 km; 320 km paved
Railway: none
Air Traffic: n.a.
Airports: 6, 5 with paved runways (2002)

Canadian Embassy: The Canadian High Commission to Saint Vincent and the Grenadines, c/o The Canadian High Commission, Bishop's Court Hill, St. Michael, Barbados; mailing address: P.O. Box 404, Bridgetown, Barbados. Tel: (246) 429-3550. Fax: (246) 429-3780. e-mail: bdgtn@dfait-maeci.gc.ca
Embassy in Canada: c/o High Commission for the Countries of the Organization of Eastern Caribbean States, 130 Albert St Ste 700, Ottawa ON K1P 5G4. Tel: (613) 236-8952. Fax: (613) 236-3042. e-mail: echcc@travel-net.com

Samoa

Long-Form Name: Independent State of Samoa
Capital: Apia

■ GEOGRAPHY

Area: 2,860 sq. km
Coastline: 403 km
Climate: tropical; rainy season lasts from Oct. to March, dry season from May to Oct.
Environment: volcanism and typhoons are natural hazards; soil erosion
Terrain: interior is rocky, with volcanic mountains; narrow coastal plain
Land Use: 19% arable; 24% permanent crops; 0% meadows and pastures; 47% forest and woodland, 10% other; includes n.a. sq. km irrigated
Location: South Pacific Ocean, E of Australia and NE of New Zealand

■ PEOPLE

Population: 178,631 (July 2002 est.)
Nationality: Samoan
Age Structure: 0–14 yrs: 30.6%; 15–64: 63.5%; 65+: 5.9% (2002 est.)
Population Growth Rate: -0.25% (2002 est.)
Net Migration: -11.64 migrants/1,000 population (2002 est.)
Ethnic Groups: 92.6% Samoan, 7% European-Polynesian; 0.4% Europeans
Languages: Samoan (Polynesian), also English
Religions: almost 100% Christianity
Birth Rate: 15.53/1,000 population (2002 est.)
Death Rate: 6.35/1,000 population (2002 est.)
Infant Mortality: 30.74 deaths/1,000 live births (2002 est.)
Life Expectancy at Birth: 67.06 years male, 72.69 years female (2002 est.)
Total Fertility Rate: 3.30 children born/women (2002 est.)
Literacy: 80.2% (2000)

■ GOVERNMENT

Leader(s): Head of State Tanumafili II Malietoa, Prime Min. Sailele Malielegaoi Tuialepa
Government Type: constitutional monarchy under a native chief
Administrative Divisions: 11 districts
Nationhood: Jan. 1, 1962
National Holiday: Independence Day, June 1

■ ECONOMY

Overview: Recent economic growth has been impressive, but overall the ecenomy remains heavily agriculture-oriented, and disease and pests have done much damage in recent years; tourism has become the most important growth industry; the flexibility of the labour market is a basic strength for future economic gains

GDP: US$618 million; per capita US$3,500, real growth rate 6.0% (2001 est.)

Inflation: 4.0% (2001)

Industries: accounts for 18% of GDP (2000); fishing, timber, food processing, tourism

Labour Force: 90,000 (2000 est.); 65% agriculture, 30% services, 5% industry

Unemployment: n.a.

Agriculture: makes up 16% of GDP (2000); mostly coconuts and fruit

Natural Resources: fish, forest resources, hydroelectric potential

■ FINANCE/TRADE

Currency: tala ($WS) = 100 sene

International Reserves Excluding Gold: US$63 million (Dec. 2002)

Gold Reserves: n.a.

Budget: revenues US$105 million; expenditures US$119 million, including capital expenditures US$ n.a. (FY2001/02)

Defence Expenditures: n.a.

Education Expenditures: n.a.

External Debt: US$204 million (2001)

Exports: US$16 million (2002 est.); commodities: coconut oil and cream, copra, fish, beer; partners: New Zealand, American Samoa, Australia, Indonesia, US

Imports: US$140 million (2002 est.); commodities: intermediate goods, food, capital goods; partners: New Zealand, Australia, Fiji, US, Japan

■ COMMUNICATIONS

Daily Newspapers: none

Televisions: n.a.

Radios: n.a.

Telephones: 49 lines/1,000 inhabitants (1999)

■ TRANSPORTATION

Motor Vehicles: 2,600; 1,200 passenger cars

Roads: 835 km; 267 km paved

Railway: none

Air Traffic: 85,000 passengers carried (1999 est.)

Airports: 3, all with paved runways (2002)

Canadian Embassy: The Canadian High Commission to Western Samoa, c/o The Canadian High Commission, P.O. Box 12049, Thorndon, Wellington, New Zealand. Tel: (011-64-4) 473-9577. Fax: (011-64-4) 471-2082. e-mail: wlgtn@dfait-maeci.gc.ca

Embassy in Canada: c/o Samoa High Commission, 800 Second Ave, Ste 400J, New York NY 10017, USA. Tel: (212) 599-6196. Fax: (212) 599-0797. e-mail: samoa@un.int

San Marino

Long-Form Name: Republic of San Marino

Capital: San Marino

■ GEOGRAPHY

Area: 60.5 sq. km

Coastline: none: landlocked

Climate: Mediterranean; mild to cool winters; warm, sunny summers

Environment: dominated by the Apennines

Terrain: rugged mountains

Land Use: 17% arable; 0% permanent crops; 0% meadows; 0% forest; 83% other; includes n.a. sq. km irrigated

Location: S Europe (E Italy)

■ PEOPLE

Population: 27,730 (July 2002 est.)

Nationality: Sammarinese

Age Structure: 0–14 yrs: 16.1%; 15–64: 67.5%; 65+: 16.4% (2002 est.)

Population Growth Rate: 1.41% (2002 est.)

Net Migration: 11.29 migrants/1,000 population (2002 est.)

Ethnic Groups: Sammarinese, Italian

Languages: Italian

Religions: Roman Catholic

Birth Rate: 10.64/1,000 population (2002 est.)

Death Rate: 7.79/1,000 population (2002 est.)

Infant Mortality: 6.09 deaths/1,000 live births (2002 est.)

Life Expectancy at Birth: 77.79 years male, 85.18 years female (2002 est.)

Total Fertility Rate: 1.30 children born/woman (2002 est.)

Literacy: 96%

■ GOVERNMENT

Leader(s): Captains-Regent: Piermarino Menicucci and Giovanni Giannoni

Government Type: republic

Administrative Divisions: 9 municipalities (castelli, sing. —castello)

Nationhood: 301 (by tradition)

National Holiday: Anniversary of the Foundation of the Republic, Sept. 3

■ ECONOMY

Overview: tourism and the sale of postage stamps are vital to the economy; tourism itself contributes more than 50% to the GDP; key industries are clothing, electronics, ceramics, agricultural products, wine and cheese
GDP: US$940 million, per capita $34,600; real growth rate 7.5% (2001 est.)
Inflation: 2.2% (2000)
Industries: wine, olive oil, cement, leather, textiles, tourism
Labour Force: 18,500 (1999); 57% services, 42% industry, 1% agriculture
Unemployment: 2.8% (Dec. 2000)
Agriculture: employs 2% of labour force; products: wheat, grapes, corn, olives, meat, cheese, hides; small numbers of cattle, pigs, horses; depends on Italy for food imports
Natural Resources: building stone

■ FINANCE/TRADE

Currency: Italian lire (Lit) = 100 centesimi; also the Euro. San Marino also mints its own coins
International Reserves Excluding Gold: n.a.
Gold Reserves: n.a.
Budget: revenues US$400 million, expenditures US$400 million, including capital expenditures of US$ n.a. (2000 est.)
Defence Expenditures: n.a.
Education Expenditures: n.a.
External Debt: n.a.
Exports: n.a.; trade data are included in the statistics for Italy. Products include building stone, lime, wood, chestnuts, wheat, wine, baked goods, hides, ceramics
Imports: n.a.; trade data are included in the statistics for Italy. Products include a wide variety of consumer manufactures and food-stuffs

■ COMMUNICATIONS

Daily Newspapers: 3 in total
Televisions: n.a.
Radios: n.a.
Telephones: 689 lines/1,000 inhabitants (1999)

■ TRANSPORTATION

Motor Vehicles: 30,000; 25,000 passenger cars
Roads: 220 km; all km paved
Railway: none
Air Traffic: n.a.
Airports: none

Canadian Embassy: The Canadian Consulate to San Marino, c/o The Canadian Embassy, Via G.B. de Rossi, 27, 00161 Rome, Italy. Tel: (011-39-06) 445981. Fax: (011-39-06) 445 98750. e-mail: rome@dfait-maeci.gc.ca

Embassy in Canada: c/o Consulate of San Marino, 20 Queen St W Ste 3300, P.O. Box 33, Toronto ON M5H 3R3. Tel: (416) 971-4848. Fax: (416) 971-4849. e-mail: n.a.

São Tomé and Príncipe

Long-Form Name: Democratic Republic of São Tomé and Príncipe
Capital: São Tomé

■ GEOGRAPHY

Area: 1,001 sq. km
Coastline: 209 km
Climate: tropical; hot, humid; one rainy season (Oct. to May)
Environment: deforestation; soil degradation
Terrain: volcanic, mountainous
Land Use: 2% arable; 36% permanent crops; 1% meadows; 0% forest; 61% other; includes 100 sq. km irrigated
Location: S Atlantic Ocean, off W African Coast

■ PEOPLE

Population: 170,730 (July 2002 est.)
Nationality: São Toméan
Age Structure: 0–14 yrs: 47.7%; 15–64: 48.3%; 65+: 4.0% (2002 est.)
Population Growth Rate: 3.18% (2002 est.)
Net Migration: -3.15 migrants/1,000 population (2002 est.)
Ethnic Groups: mestiço, angolares (descendants of Angolan slaves), forros (descendants of freed slaves), servicais (contract labourers from Angola, Mozambique and Cape Verde), tongas (children of servicais born on the islands) and European (primarily Portuguese)
Languages: Portuguese (official), Crioulo
Religions: Roman Catholic, Evangelical Protestant, Seventh-Day Adventist
Birth Rate: 42.30/1,000 population (2002 est.)
Death Rate: 7.32/1,000 population (2002 est.)
Infant Mortality: 47.50 deaths/1,000 live births (2002 est.)
Life Expectancy at Birth: 64.47 years male, 67.45 years female (2002 est.)
Total Fertility Rate: 5.95 children born/woman (2002 est.)
Literacy: 75%

■ GOVERNMENT

Leader(s): Pres. Fradique de Menezes, Prime Min. Maria das Neves
Government Type: republic
Administrative Divisions: 2 provinces
Nationhood: July 12, 1975 (from Portugal)
National Holiday: Independence Day, July 12

■ ECONOMY

Overview: the economy is hampered by over-dependence on cocoa production, which has substantially declined in recent years because of drought and mismanagement; imports 90% of food needs as well as all fuels and most manu-factured goods; government is attempting to restructure economy and reduce debt burden

GDP: US$189 million, per capita US$1,200; real growth rate 4.0% (2001 est.)

Inflation: 5% (2000 est.)

Industries: accounts for 19% of GDP; light construction, shirts, soap, beer, fisheries, shrimp processing

Labour Force: n.a.; most of population engaged in subsistence agriculture and fishing. There are shortages of skilled workers

Unemployment: 50% (1998 est.)

Agriculture: 23% of GDP; primary source of exports; cash crops: cocoa (85%), coconuts, palm kernels, coffee, copra, cinnamon, pepper; food products: bananas, papayas, beans, poultry, fish; not self-sufficient in foodgrain and meat

Natural Resources: fish, hydro power

■ FINANCE/TRADE

Currency: dobra (Db) = 100 centimos

International Reserves Excluding Gold: n.a.

Gold Reserves: n.a.

Budget: n.a.

Defence Expenditures: n.a.

Education Expenditures: n.a.

External Debt: US$313 million (2001)

Exports: US$4.90 million (1999 est.); com-modities: cocoa 85%, copra, coffee, palm oil; partners: Spain, Netherlands, Portugal

Imports: US$19.50 million (1999 est.); com-modities: machinery and electrical equipment 54%, food products 23%, other 23%; partners: Portugal, France, UK

■ COMMUNICATIONS

Daily Newspapers: none

Televisions: n.a.

Radios: n.a.

Telephones: 31 lines/1,000 inhabitants (1999)

■ TRANSPORTATION

Motor Vehicles: n.a.

Roads: 320 km; 218 km paved

Railway: none

Air Traffic: 27,000 passengers carried (1999 est.)

Airports: 2, both with paved runways (2002)

Canadian Embassy: The Canadian Embassy to São Tomé and Príncipe, c/o The Canadian Embassy, P.O. Box 4037 Libreville, Gabon. Tel: (011-241) 73-73-54. Fax: (011-241) 73-73-88. e-mail: lbrve@dfait-maeci.gc.ca

Embassy in Canada: c/o Embassy of São Tomé and Príncipe, 400 Park Ave, 7th Fl, New York, NY 10022. Tel: (212) 317-0533. Fax: (212) 317-0580. e-mail: n.a.

Saudi Arabia

Long-Form Name: Kingdom of Saudi Arabia

Capital: Riyadh (royal); Jeddah (administrative)

■ GEOGRAPHY

Area: 1,960,582 sq. km

Coastline: 2,640 km

Climate: harsh, dry desert with great extremes of temperature

Environment: no perennial rivers or permanent water-bodies; developing extensive coastal seawater desalination facilities; desertification; coastal pollution; frequent dust and sandstorms

Terrain: mostly uninhabited, sandy desert

Land Use: 2% arable; 0% permanent crops; 56% permanent pastures; 1% forest; 41% other; includes 16,200 sq. km irrigated

Location: SW Asia (Middle East), bordering on Persian Gulf, Arabian Sea, Red Sea

■ PEOPLE

Population: 23,513,330; includes 5,360,526 non-nationals (July 2002 est.)

Nationality: Saudi

Age Structure: 0–14 yrs: 42.4%; 15–64: 54.8%; 65+: 2.8% (2002 est.)

Population Growth Rate: 3.27% (2002 est.)

Net Migration: 1.28 migrants/1,000 population (2002 est.)

Ethnic Groups: 90% Arab, 10% Afro-Asian

Languages: Arabic (official); English (business language)

Religions: Muslim (85% Sunni, 15% Shia)

Birth Rate: 37.25/1,000 population (2002 est.)

Death Rate: 5.85/1,000 population (2002 est.)

Infant Mortality: 49.59 deaths/1,000 live births (2002 est.)

Life Expectancy at Birth: 66.70 years male, 70.20 years female (2002 est.)

Total Fertility Rate: 6.21 children born/woman (2002 est.)

Literacy: 76.3% (2000)

■ GOVERNMENT

Leader(s): King and Prime Min. Fahd bin Abdul Aziz al Saud

Government Type: monarchy

Administrative Divisions: 13 provinces (mintaqat, sing. —mintaqah)

Nationhood: Sept. 23, 1932 (unification)

National Holiday: Unification of the Kingdom, Sept. 23

■ ECONOMY

Overview: has the largest reserves of petroleum in the world and is the largest exporter of petroleum; the government is working toward the privatization of the economy

GDP: US$241 billion, per capita US$10,600; real growth rate 1.6% (2001 est.)

Inflation: -0.5% (2001)

Industries: accounts for 48% of GDP (2000); crude oil production, petroleum refining, basic petrochemicals, cement, small steel-rolling mill, construction, fertilizer, plastic

Labour Force: 7.1 million (4 million foreign workers) (2001); 25% industry, 63% services, 12% agriculture

Unemployment: n.a.

Agriculture: accounts for 7% of GDP (2000); fastest growing economic sector; subsidized by government; products: wheat, barley, tomatoes, melons, dates, citrus fruit, mutton, chickens, eggs, milk; approaching self-sufficiency in food

Natural Resources: crude oil, natural gas, iron ore, gold, copper

■ FINANCE/TRADE

Currency: riyal (SR) = 100 halalah

International Reserves Excluding Gold: US$20.610 billion (Dec. 2002)

Gold Reserves: 4.596 million fine troy ounces (Dec. 2002)

Budget: revenues US$42 billion; expenditures US$54 billion, including capital expenditures US$ n.a. (2002 est.)

Defence Expenditures: 43.2% of central government expenditure (1999)

Education Expenditures: n.a.

External Debt: US$26.3 billion (2000 est.)

Exports: US$68.064 billion (2001); commodities: petroleum and petroleum products 89%; partners: Japan, US, South Korea, Singapore, India

Imports: US$31.223 billion (2001); commodities: manufactured goods, transportation equipment, construction materials, processed food products; partners: US, Japan, Germany, UK

■ COMMUNICATIONS

Daily Newspapers: 326/1,000 inhabitants (2000)
Televisions: 264/1,000 inhabitants (2001)
Radios: 326/1,000 inhabitants (2001)
Telephones: 145 lines/1,000 inhabitants (2001)

■ TRANSPORTATION

Motor Vehicles: 3,000,000; 1,710,000 passenger cars
Roads: 146,524 km; 44,104 km paved
Railway: 1,392 km
Air Traffic: 12,836,000 passengers carried (2001)
Airports: 209; 70 have paved runways (2002)

Canadian Embassy: The Canadian Embassy, Diplomatic Quarter, Riyadh; mailing address: P.O. Box 94321, Riyadh 11693, Saudi Arabia. Tel: (011-966-1) 488-2288. Fax: (011-966-1) 488-1997. e-mail: ryadh@dfait-maeci.gc.ca

Embassy in Canada: Royal Embassy of Saudi Arabia, 99 Bank St, Ste 901, Ottawa ON K1P 6B9. Tel: (613) 237-4100. Fax: (613) 237-0567. e-mail: n.a.

Senegal

Long-Form Name: Republic of Senegal
Capital: Dakar

■ GEOGRAPHY

Area: 196,190 sq. km
Coastline: 531 km
Climate: tropical; hot, humid; rainy season (Dec. to Apr.) has strong southeast winds; dry season (May to Nov.) dominated by hot, dry harmattan wind
Environment: lowlands seasonally flooded; deforestation; overgrazing; soil degradation; wildlife populations are endangered by poaching
Terrain: generally low, rolling, plains rising to foothills in southeast
Land Use: 12% arable; 0% permanent crops; 16% permanent pastures; 54% forest; 18% other; includes 710 sq. km irrigated
Location: W Africa, bordering on Atlantic Ocean

■ PEOPLE

Population: 10,589,571 (July 2002 est.)
Nationality: Senegalese (sing. & pl.)
Age Structure: 0–14 yrs: 43.5%; 15–64: 53.4%; 65+: 3.1% (2002 est.)
Population Growth Rate: 2.91% (2002 est.)
Net Migration: 0.21 migrants/1,000 population (2002 est.)
Ethnic Groups: 43.3% Wolof, 23.8% Fulani, 14.7% Serer, 3.7% Diola, 3% Mandingo, 1% European and Lebanese, 10.5% other
Languages: French (official); Wolof, Pulaar, Diola, Mandingo
Religions: 92% Muslim, 6% indigenous beliefs, 2% Christian (mostly Roman Catholic)
Birth Rate: 36.99/1,000 population (2002 est.)
Death Rate: 8.14/1,000 population (2002 est.)
Infant Mortality: 55.41 deaths/1,000 live births (2002 est.)
Life Expectancy at Birth: 61.29 years male, 64.61 years female (2002 est.)
Total Fertility Rate: 5.03 children born/woman (2002 est.)
Literacy: 36.4% (1999)

■ GOVERNMENT

Leader(s): Pres. Abdoulaye Wade, Prime Min. Idrissa Seck
Government Type: republic under multiparty democratic rule
Administrative Divisions: 10 regions
Nationhood: April 4, 1960 (from France)
National Holiday: Independence Day, Apr. 4

■ ECONOMY

Overview: tourism has emerged as a great boon to the economy; fishing is the main economic resource; mining (phosphate) has been hurt by reduced worldwide demand for fertilizers in recent years; limited resource base, environmental degradation and very high population growth continue to delay improvements
GDP: US$16.2 billion, per capita US$1,580; real growth rate 5.7% (2001 est.)
Inflation: 3.1% (2001)
Industries: accounts for 26% of GDP (2000); fishing, agricultural processing, phosphate mining, petroleum refining, building materials
Labour Force: 4.4 million (2001); 70% agriculture
Unemployment: n.a.; urban youth 40%
Agriculture: including fishing, accounts for 18% of GDP (2000); major products: peanuts (cash crop), millet, corn, sorghum, rice, cotton, tomatoes, green vegetables; estimated two-thirds self-sufficient in food, cattle, poultry, pigs; fish catch of 354,000 metric tons
Natural Resources: fish, phosphates, iron ore

■ FINANCE/TRADE

Currency: Communauté financière africaine franc (CFAF) = 100 centimes
International Reserves Excluding Gold: US$620 million (Oct. 2002)
Gold Reserves: none (Dec. 2002)
Budget: revenues US$1.373 billion, expenditures US$1.373 billion, including capital expenditures of US$357 million (2002 est.)
Defence Expenditures: 6.8% of central government expenditure (2001)
Education Expenditures: n.a.
External Debt: US$3.461 billion (2001)
Exports: US$1.000 billion (2002); commodities: manufactures 30%, fish products 27%, peanuts 11%, petroleum products 11%, phosphates 10%; partners: France, Italy, Spain, Côte d'Ivoire
Imports: US$1.544 billion (2001); commodities: semi-manufactures 30%, food 27%, durable consumer goods 17%, petroleum 12%, capital goods 14%; partners: France, Nigeria, Germany, US, Italy

■ COMMUNICATIONS

Daily Newspapers: 5/1,000 inhabitants (2000)

Televisions: 79/1,000 inhabitants (2001)
Radios: 126/1,000 inhabitants (2001)
Telephones: 25 lines/1,000 inhabitants (2001)

■ TRANSPORTATION

Motor Vehicles: 160,000; 110,000 passenger cars
Roads: 14,576 km; 4,271 km paved
Railway: 906 km
Air Traffic: 6,000 passengers carried (2001)
Airports: 20; 9 have paved runways (2002)

Canadian Embassy: The Canadian Embassy, 45 av. de la République, P.O. Box 3373, Dakar, Senegal. Tel: (011-221) 823-92-90. Fax: (011-221) 823-87-49. e-mail: dakar@dfait-maeci.gc.ca
Embassy in Canada: Embassy of the Republic of Senegal, 57 Marlborough Ave, Ottawa ON K1N 8E8. Tel: (613) 238-6392. Fax: (613) 238-2695. e-mail: ambassn@sympatico.ca

Serbia and Montenegro

Long-Form Name: Serbia and Montenegro
Capital: Belgrade (Serbia), Podgorica (Montenegro)

■ GEOGRAPHY

Area: 102,350 sq. km (Serbia 88,412 sq. km, Montenegro 13,938 sq. km)
Coastline: 199 km (Montenegro 199 km, Serbia 0 km)
Climate: continental in north; continental and Mediterranean in central region; south—Adriatic climate along coast, hot and dry summers, relatively cold winters, with heavy snowfall inland
Environment: coastal water pollution from sewage outlets, esp. in tourist-related areas; air and water pollution; subject to earthquakes
Terrain: varied: rich fertile plain in north, limestone ranges and basins in east, mountains and hills in southeast, high shoreline with no islands in southwest
Land Use: 40% arable; 0% permanent crops; 20.7% meadows and pastures; 17.3% forests, 22% other; includes 570 sq. km irrigated
Location: S Europe, bordering Adriatic Sea

■ PEOPLE

Population: 10,656,929 (July 2002 est.)
Nationality: Serb, Montenegrin
Age Structure: 0–14 yrs: 19.6%; 15–64: 65.3%; 65+: 15.1% (2002 est.)
Population Growth Rate: -0.12% (2002 est.)
Net Migration: -3.38 migrants/1000 population (2002 est.)
Ethnic Groups: 62.6% Serb, 16.5% Albanian, 5% Montenegrin, 3.4% Yugoslav, 3.3% Hungarian, 9.2% other

Languages: 95% Serbian, 5% Albanian
Religions: 65% Orthodox, 19% Muslim, 4% Roman Catholic, 1% Protestant, 11% other
Birth Rate: 12.80/1000 population (2002 est.)
Death Rate: 10.59/1,000 population (2002 est.)
Infant Mortality: 17.36 deaths/1,000 live births (2002 est.)
Life Expectancy at Birth: 70.78 years male, 76.89 years female (2002 est.)
Total Fertility Rate: 1.78 children born/woman (2002 est.)
Literacy: n.a.

■ GOVERNMENT

Leader(s): Pres. and Chair. of the Council of Ministers: Svetozar Marovic
Government Type: republic
Administrative Divisions: 2 republics (republike, sing. —republika) and 2 nominally autonomous provinces (autonomna pokrajine, sing. — autonomna pokrajina)
Nationhood: April 11, 1992 (from Yugoslavia)
National Holiday: St. Vitus Day, June 28

■ ECONOMY

Overview: ethnic warfare has caused destabilization of republic boundaries and the break-up of important inter-republic trade connections; the economic boom anticipated by the government after the suspension of UN sanctions has failed to take place, largely due to government mismanagement of the economy. International sanctions have now been lifted, and Serbia and Montenegro is in the initial stages of economic reform
GDP: US$25.3 billion, per capita US$2,370; real growth rate 3.5% (2002 est.)
Inflation: n.a.
Industries: accounts for 36% of GDP (2001 est.); machine building, metallurgy, mining, consumer goods, electronics, petroleum products, chemicals, pharmaceuticals
Labour Force: 5.1 million (2001); 41% industry, 35% services, 12% trade and tourism, 7% transportation and communication, 5% agriculture
Unemployment: 30% (2000 est.)
Agriculture: accounts for 26% of GDP (2001 est.); cereals, cotton, oilseed plants, chicory, fodder crops, fruit, vegetables, tobacco, olives, citrus, rice, livestock (sheep, goats)
Natural Resources: oil, gas, coal, antimony, copper, lead, gold, chrome, pyrite, hydro power

■ FINANCE/TRADE

Currency: Yugoslav New Dinar (YD) = 100 paras. Also the Euro: in Montenegro the Euro is legal tender, in Kosovo both the Euro and the Dinar are legal tender.
International Reserves Excluding Gold: n.a.

Gold Reserves: n.a.
Budget: revenues US$3.9 billion, expenditures US$4.3 billion, including capital expenditures of US$ n.a. (2001 est.)
Defence Expenditures: 6.5% of GDP (1999)
Education Expenditures: n.a.
External Debt: US$11.740 billion (2001)
Exports: US$2.004 billion (2002 est.); manufactured goods, food, live animals, raw materials; partners: Italy, Bosnia and Herzegovina, Macedonia, Germany
Imports: US$5.624 billion (2002 est.); machinery, transport equipment, fuels and lubricants, manufactured goods, chemicals, food, live animals, raw materials; partners: Germany, Italy, Russia, Greece

■ COMMUNICATIONS

Daily Newspapers: 107/1,000 inhabitants (2000)
Televisions: 282/1,000 inhabitants (2001)
Radios: 297/1,000 inhabitants (2001)
Telephones: 229 lines/1,000 inhabitants (2001)

■ TRANSPORTATION

Motor Vehicles: 2,000,000; 1,800,000 passenger cars (2000)
Roads: 48,603 km; 28,822 km paved
Railway: 4,095 km (2000)
Air Traffic: 1,117,000 passengers carried (2001)
Airports: 46; 19 have paved runways (2002)

Canadian Embassy: The Canadian Embassy, 75 Kneza Milosa, 11000 Belgrade, Yugoslavia. Tel: (011-381-11) 306-3000. Fax: (011-381-11) 306-3042. e-mail: bgrad@dfait-maeci.gc.ca
Embassy in Canada: c/o Embassy of Serbia and Montenegro, 17 Blackburn Ave, Ottawa ON K1N 8A2. Tel: (613) 233-6289. Fax: (613) 233-7850. e-mail: diplomat@yuemb.ca

Seychelles

Long-Form Name: Republic of Seychelles
Capital: Victoria

■ GEOGRAPHY

Area: 455 sq. km
Coastline: 491 km
Climate: tropical marine; humid; cooler season during southeast monsoon (late May to Sept.); warmer season during northwest monsoon (Mar. to May)
Environment: lies outside the cyclone belt, so severe storms are rare; short droughts possible; no fresh water, catchments collect rain
Terrain: 40 granitic and about 50 coralline islands; Mahé Group is granitic, narrow coastal strip, rocky, hilly; others are coral, flat, elevated reefs

Land Use: 2% arable; 13% permanent crops; 0% meadows; 11% forest; 74% other; includes n.a. sq. km irrigated
Location: Indian Ocean, NE of Madagascar

■ PEOPLE

Population: 80,098 (July 2002 est.)
Nationality: Seychellois (sing. & pl.)
Age Structure: 0–14 yrs: 27.8%; 15–64: 66.0%; 65+: 6.2% (2002 est.)
Population Growth Rate: 0.47% (2002 est.)
Net Migration: -5.99 migrants/1,000 population (2002 est.)
Ethnic Groups: Seychellois (mixture of Asians, Africans, Europeans)
Languages: English, French (both official), Creole
Religions: 90% Roman Catholic, 8% Anglican, 2% other
Birth Rate: 17.27/1,000 population (2002 est.)
Death Rate: 6.57/1,000 population (2002 est.)
Infant Mortality: 16.86 deaths/1,000 live births (2002 est.)
Life Expectancy at Birth: 65.48 years male, 76.63 years female (2002 est.)
Total Fertility Rate: 1.81 children born/woman (2002 est.)
Literacy: 58%

■ GOVERNMENT

Leader(s): Pres. France Albert René, V. Pres. James Michel
Government Type: republic
Administrative Divisions: 23 administrative districts
Nationhood: June 29, 1976 (from UK)
National Holiday: Constitution Day, June 18 (1993 adoption of a new constitution)

■ ECONOMY

Overview: the government is moving to reduce the high dependence on tourism by promoting the development of farming, fishing and small-scale manufacturing, yet it is also encouraging foreign investment in order to upgrade hotels and other services
GDP: US$605 million, per capita US$7,600; real growth rate 1.5% (2001 est.)
Inflation: 6.0% (2001)
Industries: accounts for 26.3% of GDP; tourism employs 30% of labour force; mostly subsistence farming; cash crops: coconuts, cinnamon, vanilla; other products: sweet potatoes, cassava, bananas; broiler chickens; large share of food needs imported; expansion of tuna fishing under way
Labour Force: n.a.; 19% industry, 71% services, 10% agriculture
Unemployment: n.a.

Agriculture: accounts for 4% of GDP, mostly subsistence farming; cash crops: coconuts, cinnamon, vanilla, yams, bananas; large share of food needs to be imported; tuna fishing is increasing in importance
Natural Resources: fish, copra, cinnamon trees

■ FINANCE/TRADE

Currency: Seychelles rupee (SRe) = 100 cents
International Reserves Excluding Gold: US$85 million (Nov. 2002)
Gold Reserves: n.a.
Budget: n.a.
Defence Expenditures: 3.17% of total government expenditure (2000)
Education Expenditures: 7.10% of government expenditure (2000)
External Debt: US$215 million (2001)
Exports: US$216 million (2001); commodities: fish, copra, cinnamon bark, petroleum products (re-exports); partners: France, Italy, UK, Netherlands
Imports: US$523 million (2001); commodities: manufactured goods, food, tobacco, beverages, machinery and transportation equipment, petroleum products; partners: Italy, South Africa, France, UK, Singapore

■ COMMUNICATIONS

Daily Newspapers: 1 in total
Televisions: n.a.
Radios: n.a.
Telephones: 248 lines/1,000 inhabitants (1999)

■ TRANSPORTATION

Motor Vehicles: 8,500; 6,800 passenger cars
Roads: 280 km; 176 km paved
Railway: none
Air Traffic: 430,000 passengers carried (1999 est.)
Airports: 14; 7 have paved runways (2002)

Canadian Embassy: The Canadian High Commission to Seychelles, c/o The Canadian High Commission, 38 Mirambo St, Dar-es-Salaam; mailing address: P.O. Box 1022, Dar-es-Salaam, Tanzania. Tel: (011-255-22) 211-2831. Fax: (011-255-22) 211-6897. e-mail: dslam@dfait-maeci.gc.ca
Embassy in Canada: c/o High Commission for the Republic of Seychelles, 800 Second Ave, Ste 400C, New York NY 10017, USA. Tel: (212) 972-1785. Fax: (212) 972-1786. e-mail: seychelles@un.int

Sierra Leone

Long-Form Name: Republic of Sierra Leone
Capital: Freetown

■ GEOGRAPHY

Area: 71,740 sq. km
Coastline: 402 km
Climate: tropical; hot, humid; summer rainy season (May to Dec.); winter dry season (Dec. to Apr.)
Environment: extensive mangrove swamps hinder access to sea; sand and dust storms; deforestation; soil degradation; population pressure negatively affects land
Terrain: coastal belt of mangrove swamps, wooded hill country, upland plateau, mountains in east
Land Use: 7% arable; 1% permanent crops; 31% meadows; 28% forest; 33% other; includes 290 sq. km irrigated
Location: W Africa, bordering on North Atlantic Ocean

■ PEOPLE

Population: 5,614,743 (July 2002 est.)
Nationality: Sierra Leonean
Age Structure: 0–14 yrs: 44.7%; 15–64: 52.1%; 65+: 3.2% (2002 est.)
Population Growth Rate: 3.21% (2002 est.)
Net Migration: 6.32 migrants/1,000 population (2002 est.)
Ethnic Groups: 90% native African (30% Temne, 39% Mende, 30% other); 10% Creole, European, Lebanese and Asian
Languages: English (official); regular use limited to literate minority; principal vernaculars are Mende in south and Temne in north; Krio is the language of the resettled ex-slave population of the Freetown area and is lingua franca
Religions: 60% Muslim, 10% Christian, 30% traditional beliefs
Birth Rate: 44.58/1,000 population (2002 est.)
Death Rate: 18.83/1,000 population (2002 est.)
Infant Mortality: 144.38 deaths/1,000 live births (2002 est.)
Life Expectancy at Birth: 43.01 years male, 49.01 years female (2002 est.)
Total Fertility Rate: 5.94 children born/woman (2002 est.)
Literacy: 32.0% (1999)

■ GOVERNMENT

Leader(s): Pres. Ahmad Tejan Kabbah, V. Pres. Solomon Berewa
Government Type: constitutional democracy
Administrative Divisions: 3 provinces and 1 area
Nationhood: Apr. 27, 1961 (from UK)
National Holiday: Independence Day, Apr. 27

■ ECONOMY

Overview: the economic and social infrastructure is underdeveloped; subsistence agriculture is the backbone of the economy; problems include unemployment, large trade deficits; diamond mining is an important source of national income
GDP: US$2.7 billion, per capita US$500; real growth rate 3.0% (2001 est.)
Inflation: 2.1% (2001)
Industries: accounts for 27% of GDP (2000); mining (diamonds, bauxite, rutile), small-scale manufacturing (beverages, textiles, cigarettes, footwear), petroleum refinery
Labour Force: 1.9 million (2001); 69.6% agriculture, 14.1% industry, 16.4% services
Unemployment: n.a.
Agriculture: accounts for 43% of GDP (2000) and two-thirds of the labour force, largely subsistence farming; cash crops: coffee, cocoa, palm kernels; harvest of food staple rice meets 80% of domestic needs; annual fish catch averages 53,000 metric tons
Natural Resources: diamonds, titanium ore, bauxite, iron ore, gold, chromite

■ FINANCE/TRADE

Currency: leone (Le) = 100 cents
International Reserves Excluding Gold: US$84 million (Dec. 2002)
Gold Reserves: n.a.
Budget: revenues US$96 million, expenditures US$351 million, including capital expenditures of US$ n.a. (2000 est.)
Defence Expenditures: 6.5% of central government expenditure (2001)
Education Expenditures: n.a.
External Debt: US$1.188 billion (2001)
Exports: US$29 million (2001); commodities: rutile 50%, bauxite 17%, cocoa 11%, diamonds 3%, coffee 3%; partners: New Zealand, US, Belgium, France
Imports: US$182 million (2001); commodities: capital goods 40%, food 32%, petroleum 12%, consumer goods 7%, light industrial goods; partners: Czech Republic, US, UK, Netherlands

■ COMMUNICATIONS

Daily Newspapers: 4/1,000 inhabitants (2000)
Televisions: 13/1,000 inhabitants (2001)
Radios: 259/1,000 inhabitants (2001)
Telephones: 5 lines/1,000 inhabitants (2001)

■ TRANSPORTATION

Motor Vehicles: 42,500; 21,000 passenger cars
Roads: 11,700 km; 936 km paved
Railway: 84 km
Air Traffic: 14,000 passengers carried (2001)
Airports: 10; 1 has paved runway (2002)

Canadian Embassy: The Canadian High Commission to Sierra Leone, c/o The Canadian

Embassy, PO Box 99, Conakry, Guinea. Tel: (011-224) 46-23-95. Fax: (011-224) 46-42-35. e-mail: cnaky@dfait-maeci.gc.ca

Embassy in Canada: c/o High Commission for the Republic of Sierra Leone, 1701-19th St NW, Washington DC 20009, USA. Tel: (202) 939-9261. Fax: (202) 483-1793. e-mail: slehoc@starpower.net

Singapore

Long-Form Name: Republic of Singapore
Capital: Singapore

■ GEOGRAPHY

Area: 647.5 sq. km
Coastline: 193 km
Climate: tropical; hot, humid, rainy; no pronounced rainy or dry seasons; thunderstorms occur on 40% of all days (67% of days in Apr.)
Environment: mostly urban and industrialized; water supply is limited
Terrain: lowland; gently undulating central plateau contains water catchment area and nature preserve
Land Use: 2% arable; 6% permanent crops; 0% meadows; 5% forest; 87% other; includes n.a. sq. km irrigated
Location: SE Asia (southern tip of Malaysia), bordering on South China Sea

■ PEOPLE

Population: 4,452,732 (July 2002 est.)
Nationality: Singaporean
Age Structure: 0–14 yrs: 17.6%; 15–64: 75.3%; 65+: 7.1% (2002 est.)
Population Growth Rate: 3.46% (2002 est.)
Net Migration: 26.11 migrants/1,000 population (2002 est.)
Ethnic Groups: 77% Chinese, 14% Malay, 7.6% Indian, 1.4% other
Languages: Chinese (Mandarin), Malay, Tamil and English (all official); Malay (national)
Religions: majority of Chinese are Buddhists or atheists; Malays nearly all Muslim (minorities are Christians, Hindus, Sikhs, Taoists, Confucianists)
Birth Rate: 12.78/1,000 population (2002 est.)
Death Rate: 4.28/1,000 population (2002 est.)
Infant Mortality: 3.60 deaths/1,000 live births (2002 est.)
Life Expectancy at Birth: 77.34 years male, 83.47 years female (2002 est.)
Total Fertility Rate: 1.23 children born/woman (2002 est.)
Literacy: 92.3% (2000)

■ GOVERNMENT

Leader(s): Pres. Sellapan Rama Nathan, Prime Min. Goh Chok Tong

Government Type: parliamentary republic within Commonwealth
Administrative Divisions: none
Nationhood: Aug. 9, 1965 (from Malaysia)
National Holiday: Independence Day, Aug. 9

■ ECONOMY

Overview: has an open entrepreneurial economy with strong service and manufacturing sectors and good international trading links; growth has traditionally run at high rates; per capita GDP is among the highest in Asia; rising labour costs continue to adversely affect Singapore's competitiveness
GDP: US$106.3 billion, per capita US$24,700; real growth rate -2.2% (2001 est.)
Inflation: 1.0% (2001)
Industries: accounts for 33% of GDP (2001 est.); petroleum refining, electronics, oil drilling equipment, rubber processing and rubber products, processed food and beverages, ship repair, entrepôt trade, financial services, biotechnology
Labour Force: 2 million (2001); 27% industry, 22.8% trade and tourism, 21.6% community, social and business services
Unemployment: 9.3% (Dec. 2001)
Agriculture: minor importance in the economy; self-sufficient in poultry and eggs; must import most other food; major crops: rubber, copra, fruit, vegetables, fish
Natural Resources: fish, deepwater ports

■ FINANCE/TRADE

Currency: Singapore dollar ($S) = 100 cents
International Reserves Excluding Gold: US$82.021 billion (Dec. 2002)
Gold Reserves: n.a.
Budget: revenues US$18.1 billion; expenditures US$17.1 billion, including capital expenditures US$9.5 billion (1999–2000 est.)
Defence Expenditures: 22.8% of central government expenditure (2001)
Education Expenditures: 21.03% of central government expenditure (2000)
External Debt: US$9.7 billion (2000)
Exports: US$122.483 billion (2002 est.); commodities (includes transshipments to Malaysia): petroleum products, rubber electronics, manufactured goods; partners: US, Malaysia, Hong Kong, Japan, Taiwan, Thailand, China, South Korea
Imports: US$115.047 billion (2002 est.); commodities (includes transshipments from Malaysia): capital equipment, petroleum, chemicals, manufactured goods, foodstuffs; partners: Japan, Malaysia, US, China, Taiwan, Thailand, South Korea, Saudi Arabia

■ COMMUNICATIONS

Daily Newspapers: 298/1,000 inhabitants (2000)
Televisions: 300/1,000 inhabitants (2001)
Radios: 672/1,000 inhabitants (2001)
Telephones: 471 lines/1,000 inhabitants (2001)

■ TRANSPORTATION

Motor Vehicles: 570,000; 420,000 passenger cars (2000)
Roads: 3,150 km; 3,066 km paved (2000)
Railway: 38.6 km
Air Traffic: 16,704,000 passengers carried (2000)
Airports: 9; all have paved runways (2002)

Canadian Embassy: Canadian High Commission, IBM Towers, 14th & 15th Fls, 80 Anson Rd, Singapore 079907; mailing address: Robinson Rd, P.O. Box 845, Singapore 901645. Tel: (011-65) 6325-3200. Fax: (011-65) 6325-3297. e-mail: spore@dfait-maeci.gc.ca
Embassy in Canada: c/o High Commission for the Republic of Singapore, 231 East 51st St, New York NY 10022, USA. Tel: (212) 826-0840. Fax: (212) 826-2964. e-mail: n.a.

Slovakia

Long-Form Name: Slovak Republic
Capital: Bratislava

■ GEOGRAPHY

Area: 48,845 sq. km
Coastline: none: landlocked
Climate: temperate: cool summers, cold, cloudy, humid winters
Environment: severe damage to forests from acid rain; industrial air pollution from metallurgical plants poses risks to human health
Terrain: rugged mountains in central region and north, lowlands in south
Land Use: 31% arable; 3% permanent crops; 17% permanent pastures; 41% forests; 8% other; includes 1,740 sq. km irrigated
Location: C Europe

■ PEOPLE

Population: 5,422,366 (July 2002 est.)
Nationality: Slovak
Age Structure: 0–14 yrs: 18.3%; 15–64: 70.1%; 65+: 11.6% (2002 est.)
Population Growth Rate: 0.14% (2002 est.)
Net Migration: 0.53 migrants/1,000 population (2002 est.)
Ethnic Groups: 85.7% Slovak, 10.6% Hungarian, 1.6% Gypsy, 1.0% Czech, 0.3% Ruthenian, 0.3% Ukrainian, 0.1% German, 0.1% Polish, 0.3% other
Languages: Slovak (official), Hungarian

Religions: 60.3% Roman Catholic, 9.7% atheist, 8.4% Protestant, 4.1% Orthodox, 17.5% other
Birth Rate: 10.09/1,000 population (2002 est.)
Death Rate: 9.22/1,000 population (2002 est.)
Infant Mortality: 8.76 deaths/1,000 live births (2002 est.)
Life Expectancy at Birth: 70.19 years male, 78.41 years female (2002 est.)
Total Fertility Rate: 1.25 children born/woman (2002 est.)
Literacy: approaching 100% (2000)

■ GOVERNMENT

Leader(s): Pres. Rudolf Schuster, Prime Min. Mikulas Dzurinda
Government Type: parliamentary democracy
Administrative Divisions: 8 regions (kraje, sing. —kraj)
Nationhood: Jan. 1, 1993 (from Czechoslovakia)
National Holiday: Slovak Constitution Day, Sept. 1; Anniversary of Slovak National Uprising, Aug. 29

■ ECONOMY

Overview: continues the difficult transition from a centrally controlled economy to a modern market-oriented economy; private activity now makes up more than two-thirds of GDP. Slovakia continues to experience difficulty in attracting foreign investment
GDP: US$66 billion, per capita US$12,200; real growth rate 4.0% (2002 est.)
Inflation: 7.3% (2001)
Industries: accounts for 32% of GDP (2000); mining, chemicals, metalworking, consumer appliances, plastics, armaments
Labour Force: 3.0 million (2001); 29.3% industry, 26.4% community, social and business services, 12.4% agriculture
Unemployment: 18.9% (2001)
Agriculture: accounts for 4% of GDP (2000); very diversified crop and livestock production including grains, livestock, poultry; mostly self-sufficient in food
Natural Resources: brown coal and lignite, iron ore, copper, manganese, salt, gas

■ FINANCE/TRADE

Currency: koruna (pl. koruny) (Kc) = 100 halierov
International Reserves Excluding Gold: US$8.809 billion (Dec. 2002)
Gold Reserves: 1.129 million fine troy ounces (Dec. 2002)
Budget: revenues US$5.2 billion; expenditures US$5.6 billion, including capital expenditures US$ n.a. (1999)
Defence Expenditures: 4.9% of central government expenditure (2001)

Education Expenditures: 9.84% of central government expenditure (2000)
External Debt: US$11.121 billion (2001)
Exports: US$13.729 billion (2002); machinery and transport equipment, chemicals, fuels, minerals, agricultural products; partners: Germany, Italy, Austria, Czech Republic
Imports: US$16.248 billion (2002); machinery and transport equipment, fuels, lubricants, manufactured goods, chemicals, agricultural products; partners: Germany, Italy, Czech Republic, Russia

■ COMMUNICATIONS

Daily Newspapers: 131/1,000 inhabitants (2000)
Televisions: 407/1,000 inhabitants (2001)
Radios: 695/1,000 inhabitants (2001)
Telephones: 288 lines/1,000 inhabitants (2001)

■ TRANSPORTATION

Motor Vehicles: 1,400,000; 1,200,000 passenger cars (2000)
Roads: 17,710 km; 17,533 km paved
Railway: 3,660 km
Air Traffic: 43,000 passengers carried (2001)
Airports: 34; 17 have paved runways (2002)

Canadian Embassy: The Canadian Embassy to Slovakia, Misikova 28D, 81100 Bratislava, Slovak Republic. Tel: (011-421-2) 5244-2175. Fax: (011-421-2) 5249-9995. e-mail: masson yensen@canemb.sk
Embassy in Canada: Embassy of the Slovak Republic, 50 Rideau Terrace, Ottawa ON K1M 2A1. Tel: (613) 749-4442. Fax: (613) 749-4989. e-mail: slovakemb@sprint.ca

---

Slovenia

Long-Form Name: Republic of Slovenia
Capital: Ljubljana

■ GEOGRAPHY

Area: 20,253 sq. km
Coastline: 46.6 km
Climate: Mediterranean climate on the coast, continental climate with mild to hot summers and cold winters in the plateaus and eastern valleys
Environment: pollution of Sava River; heavy metals and toxic chemicals along coast; forest damage from air pollution; subject to flooding and earthquakes
Terrain: short coastal strip, alpine mountain region; mixed mountains and valleys and numerous rivers in east
Land Use: 12% arable; 3% permanent crops; 24% meadows and pastures; 54% forests and woodland; 7% other; includes 20 sq. km irrigated

Location: southern Europe, bordering on Adriatic Sea

■ PEOPLE

Population: 1,932,917 (July 2002 est.)
Nationality: Slovene
Age Structure: 0–14 yrs: 15.7%; 15–64: 69.8%; 65+: 14.5% (2002 est.)
Population Growth Rate: 0.14% (2002 est.)
Net Migration: 2.24 migrants/1,000 population (2002 est.)
Ethnic Groups: 88% Slovene, 3% Croat, 2% Serb, 1% Bosniak, 0.6% Yugoslav, 0.4% Hungarian, 5% other
Languages: 91% Slovenian, 6% Serbo-Croatian, 3% other
Religions: 71% Roman Catholic, 1% Lutheran, 1% Muslim, 4.3% athiest, 23% other
Birth Rate: 9.27/1,000 population (2002 est.)
Death Rate: 10.07/1,000 population (2002 est.)
Infant Mortality: 4.47 deaths/1,000 live births (2002 est.)
Life Expectancy at Birth: 71.42 years male, 79.37 years female (2002 est.)
Total Fertility Rate: 1.28 children born/woman (2002 est.)
Literacy: 99.6% (2000)

■ GOVERNMENT

Leader(s): Pres. Janez Drnovsek, Prime Min. Anton Rop
Government Type: parliamentary democratic republic
Administrative Divisions: 136 municipalities (obcine, sing. —obcina) and 11 urban municipalities (obcine mestne, sing. —obcina mestna)
Nationhood: June 25, 1991 (from Yugoslavia)
National Holiday: National Statehood Day, June 25

■ ECONOMY

Overview: tourism has suffered due to internal strife; destruction of trade channels and the influx of tens of thousands of refugees have interfered with economic recovery after secession from Yugoslavia; there are efforts toward the privatization of major industrial firms; inflation and unemployment rates are gradually beginning to drop
GDP: US$36 billion, per capita US$18,000; real growth rate 3% (2002 est.)
Inflation: 9.4% (2001)
Industries: accounts for 36% of GDP (2001 est.); metallurgy, furniture, sports equipment, steel, cars, sugar, cement, textiles, machine tools
Labour Force: 1.0 million (2001); 39.3% industry, 23.1% community, social and business services, 11.1% trade and tourism
Unemployment: 7.5% (2001)

Agriculture: accounts for 3% of GDP (2001 est.); products include wheat, maize, grapes, sugar beets, potatoes, cabbages, livestock (esp. cattle, sheep, pigs, poultry); fishing, forestry; many other agricultural products must be imported
Natural Resources: brown coal and lignite deposits, lead, zinc, mercury, uranium, silver, hydro power

■ FINANCE/TRADE

Currency: Slovenian tolar = 100 stotins (at parity with Yugoslav dinar)
International Reserves Excluding Gold: US$6.980 billion (Dec. 2002)
Gold Reserves: 0.243 million fine troy ounces (Dec. 2002)
Budget: n.a.
Defence Expenditures: 3.5% of central government expenditure (2001)
Education Expenditures: n.a.
External Debt: US$6.2 billion (2000)
Exports: US$8.913 billion (2002 est.); machinery, semi-finished goods, raw materials, electric motors, transportation equipment, clothing, foodstuffs; partners: Germany, Italy, Croatia, Austria, France
Imports: US$10.531 billion (2002 est.); raw materials, semi-finished goods, machinery, foodstuffs; partners: Germany, Italy, France, Austria, Croatia

■ COMMUNICATIONS

Daily Newspapers: 169/1,000 inhabitants (2000)
Televisions: 367/1,000 inhabitants (2001)
Radios: 405/1,000 inhabitants (2001)
Telephones: 401 lines/1,000 inhabitants (2001)

■ TRANSPORTATION

Motor Vehicles: 900,000; 800,000 passenger cars (2000)
Roads: 19,586 km; 17,745 km paved
Railway: 1,201 km
Air Traffic: 690,000 passengers carried (2001)
Airports: 14; 6 have paved runways (2002)

Canadian Embassy: The Canadian Embassy to Slovenia, c/o The Canadian Embassy Zugligeti ut. 51-53, 1121 Budapest, Hungary. Tel.: (011-36-1) 392-3360. Fax: (011-36-1) 392-3390. e-mail: bpest@dfait-maeci.gc.ca
Embassy in Canada: Embassy of the Republic of Slovenia, 150 Metcalfe St, Ste 2101, Ottawa, ON K2P 1P1. Tel: (613) 565-5781. Fax: (613) 565-5783. e-mail: vot@mzz-dkp.sigov.si

Solomon Islands

Long-Form Name: Solomon Islands
Capital: Honiara (on island of Guadalcanal)

■ GEOGRAPHY

Area: 28,450 sq km
Coastline: 5,313 km
Climate: tropical monsoon; few extremes of temperature and weather
Environment: subject to typhoons, which are rarely destructive; geologically active region with frequent earth tremors; soil degradation and deforestation; deterioration of coral reefs
Terrain: mostly rugged mountains with some low coral atolls
Land Use: 1% arable; 1% permanent crops; 1% meadows; 88% pastures; 9% other; includes n.a. sq. km irrigated
Location: Melanesia, Pacific Ocean, E of New Guinea

■ PEOPLE

Population: 494,786 (July 2002 est.)
Nationality: Solomon Islander
Age Structure: 0–14 yrs: 43.4%; 15–64: 53.5%; 65+: 3.1% (2002 est.)
Population Growth Rate: 2.91% (2002 est.)
Net Migration: 0 migrants/1,000 population (2002 est.)
Ethnic Groups: 93% Melanesian, 4% Polynesian, 1.5% Micronesian, 0.8% European, 0.3% Chinese, 0.4% other
Languages: English (official), Pidgin, 120 local languages
Religions: 34% Anglican, 19% Roman Catholic, 17% South Seas Evangelical, 25% other Protestant, 5% other
Birth Rate: 33.26/1,000 population (2002 est.)
Death Rate: 4.19/1,000 population (2002 est.)
Infant Mortality: 23.68 deaths/1,000 live births (2002 est.)
Life Expectancy at Birth: 69.38 years male, 74.39 years female (2002 est.)
Total Fertility Rate: 4.50 children born/woman (2002 est.)
Literacy: 62%

■ GOVERNMENT

Leader(s): Head of State: Queen Elizabeth II, Gov. Gen. John Lapli, Prime Min. Sir Allan Kemakeza
Government Type: parliamentary democracy
Administrative Divisions: 7 provinces and 1 town
Nationhood: July 7, 1978 (from UK; formerly known as British Solomon Islands)
National Holiday: Independence Day, July 7

■ ECONOMY

Overview: about 90% of the population depend on subsistence agriculture, fishing and forestry for at least part of their livelihood; possesses an abundance of undeveloped mineral resources; little manufacturing activity—most manufactured

goods must be imported; uncontrolled government spending is leading to national financial ruin despite a rich natural resource base
GDP: US$800 million, per capita US$1,700; real growth rate -10.0% (2001 est.)
Inflation: 10% (1999)
Industries: account for 11% of GDP; copra, fish (tuna)
Labour Force: approx. 27,000; 20% community, social and business services, 75% agriculture, 5% industry
Unemployment: n.a.
Agriculture: including fishing and forestry, accounts for approx. 42% of GDP; mostly subsistence farming; cash crops: cocoa, beans, coconuts, palm kernels, timber; other products: rice, potatoes, vegetables, fruit, cattle, pigs; not self-sufficient in foodgrains; 90% of fish catch is exported
Natural Resources: fish, forests, gold, bauxite, phosphates, lead, zinc, nickel

■ FINANCE/TRADE

Currency: Solomon Islands dollar ($SI) = 100 cents
International Reserves Excluding Gold: US$30 million (Oct. 2001)
Gold Reserves: n.a.
Budget: revenues US$38 million, expenditures US$ n.a., including capital expenditures of US$ n.a. (2001)
Defence Expenditures: negligible
Education Expenditures: n.a.
External Debt: US$163 million (2001)
Exports: US$130 million (2000); commodities: fish 46%, timber 31%, copra 5%, palm oil 5%; partners: Japan, China, Philippines, South Korea, UK, Thailand
Imports: US$145 million (2000); commodities: equipment and machinery 30%, fuel 19%, food 16%; partners: Australia, Singapore, New Zealand, Japan, US

■ COMMUNICATIONS

Daily Newspapers: none
Televisions: n.a.
Radios: n.a.
Telephones: 19 lines/1,000 inhabitants (1999)

■ TRANSPORTATION

Motor Vehicles: n.a.
Roads: 1,360 km; 34 km paved
Railway: none
Air Traffic: 100,000 passengers carried (1999 est.)
Airports: 31; 2 have paved runways (2002)

Canadian Embassy: The Canadian High Commission to Solomon Islands, c/o The Canadian High Commission, Commonwealth Ave, Canberra A.C.T. 2600, Australia. Tel: (011-61-2) 6270-4000. Fax: (011-61-2) 6273-3285. e-mail: cnbra@dfait-maeci.gc.ca
Embassy in Canada: c/o High Commission for the Solomon Islands, 800-2nd Ave, Ste 400L, New York NY 10017, USA. Tel: (212) 599-6192. Fax: (212) 661-8925. e-mail: simny@solomons.com

Somalia

Long-Form Name: Somalia
Capital: Mogadishu

■ GEOGRAPHY

Area: 637,657 sq. km
Coastline: 3,025 km
Climate: desert; northeast monsoon (Dec. to Feb.), cooler southwest monsoon (May to Oct.); irregular rainfall; hot, humid periods (tangambili) between monsoons
Environment: recurring droughts; frequent dust storms over eastern plains in summer; deforestation; overgrazing; soil erosion; desertification
Terrain: mostly flat to undulating plateau rising to hills in north
Land Use: 2% arable; negligible permanent crops; 69% permanent pastures; 26% forest; 3% other; includes 1,800 sq. km irrigated
Location: E Africa, bordering on Gulf of Aden, Indian Ocean

■ PEOPLE

Population: 7,753,310 (July 2002 est.)
Nationality: Somali
Age Structure: 0–14 yrs: 44.7%; 15–64: 52.6%; 65+: 2.7% (2002 est.)
Population Growth Rate: 3.46% (2002 est.)
Net Migration: 5.75 migrants/1,000 population (2002 est.)
Ethnic Groups: 85% Somali, rest mainly Bantu; 30,000 Arabs, 3,000 Europeans, 800 Asians
Languages: Somali (official); Arabic, Italian, English
Religions: almost entirely Sunni Muslim, small Christian community
Birth Rate: 46.83/1,000 population (2002 est.)
Death Rate: 17.99/1,000 population (2002 est.)
Infant Mortality: 122.15 deaths/1,000 live births (2002 est.)
Life Expectancy at Birth: 44.33 years male, 48.65 years female (2002 est.)
Total Fertility Rate: 7.05 children born/woman (2002 est.)
Literacy: 24%

■ GOVERNMENT

Leader(s): Pres. Abdikassim Salad Hassan, Prime Min. Hassan Abshir Farah
Government Type: parliamentary
Administrative Divisions: 18 regions (plural n.a., sing. —gobolka)
Nationhood: July 1, 1960 (from a merger of British Somaliland, which became independent from the UK on June 26, 1960, and Italian Somaliland, which became independent from the Italian-administered UN trusteeship on July 1, 1960, to form the Somali Republic)
National Holiday: Anniversary of the Revolution, Oct. 21, Foundation of the Somali Republic, July 1

■ ECONOMY

Overview: nomads or semi-nomads who are dependent upon livestock for their livelihoods make up about 50% of the population; one of the world's least developed countries, possessing few resources; problems include high external debt, triple-digit inflation and bitter civil war, which has devastated much of the economy
GDP: US$4.1 billion, per capita US$550; real growth rate 3.0% (2001 est.)
Inflation: over 100%; businesses print their own money (2000)
Industries: accounts for 10% of GDP (2000); based on processing of agricultural products; sugar refining, textiles, petroleum refining
Labour Force: 3.9 million (2001); 71% agriculture, 29% industry and services
Unemployment: n.a.
Agriculture: livestock accounts for 65% of GDP (2000) and 65% of export revenue: cattle, sheep, goats; fishing potential largely unexploited; crops: bananas, sorghum, corn, mangoes, sugar cane, beans, fish; not self-sufficient in food
Natural Resources: uranium and largely unexploited reserves of iron ore, tin, gypsum, bauxite, copper, salt

■ FINANCE/TRADE

Currency: Somali shilling (So.Sh.) = 100 cents
International Reserves Excluding Gold: n.a.
Gold Reserves: n.a.
Budget: n.a.
Defence Expenditures: n.a.
Education Expenditures: n.a.
External Debt: US$2.531 billion (2001)
Exports: US$41 million (2000); commodities: livestock, hides, skins, bananas, fish; partners: Saudi Arabia, UAE, Yemen
Imports: US$45 million (2000); commodities: textiles, petroleum products, foodstuffs, construction materials; partners: Djibouti, Kenya, India

■ COMMUNICATIONS

Daily Newspapers: 1/1,000 inhabitants (2000)

Televisions: 14/1,000 inhabitants (2001)
Radios: 60/1,000 inhabitants (2001)
Telephones: 4 lines/1,000 inhabitants (2001)

■ TRANSPORTATION

Motor Vehicles: 20,000; 10,000 passenger cars
Roads: 22,100 km; 2,608 km paved
Railway: none
Air Traffic: n.a.
Airports: 54; 6 have paved runways (2002)

Canadian Embassy: The Canadian Embassy to Somalia, c/o The Canadian High Commission, Comcraft House, 6th Fl, Hailé Sélassie Ave, Nairobi, Kenya; mailing address: The Canadian High Commission, P.O. Box 30481, Nairobi, Kenya. Tel: (011-254-2) 21-48-04. Fax: (011-254-2) 22-69-87. e-mail: nrobi@dfait-maeci.gc.ca
Embassy in Canada: c/o The High Commission for the Republic of Kenya, 415 Laurier Ave E, Ottawa ON K1N 6R4. Tel: (613) 563-1773. Fax: (613) 233-6599. e-mail: kenrep@on.aibn.com

South Africa

Long-Form Name: Republic of South Africa
Capital: Pretoria (administrative), Cape Town (legislative), Bloemfontein (judicial)

■ GEOGRAPHY

Area: 1,219,912 sq. km; includes Walvis Bay, Marion Island and Prince Edward Island
Coastline: 2,798 km
Climate: mostly semi-arid; subtropical along coast; sunny days, cool nights
Environment: lack of important arterial rivers or lakes requires extensive water conservation and control measures; prolonged droughts and increasing water pollution exacerbate the problem
Terrain: vast interior plateau rimmed by rugged hills and narrow coastal plain
Land Use: 10% arable; 1% permanent crops; 67% meadows; 7% forest; 15% other; includes 13,500 sq. km irrigated
Location: S Africa, bordering on Indian Ocean, South Atlantic Ocean

■ PEOPLE

Population: 43,647,658 (July 2002 est.)
Nationality: South African
Age Structure: 0–14 yrs: 31.6%; 15–64: 63.4%; 65+: 5.0% (2002 est.)
Population Growth Rate: 0.02% (2002 est.)
Net Migration: -1.56 migrants/1,000 population (2002 est.)
Ethnic Groups: 75.2% black, 13.6% white, 8.6% coloured, 2.6% Indian

Languages: 11 official languages: Afrikaans, English, Ndebele, Pedi, Sotho, Swazi, Tsonga, Tswana, Venda, Xhosa, Zulu
Religions: most of whites, coloureds and approx. 60% of blacks are Christian; approx. 60% of Indians are Hindu, 20% Muslim
Birth Rate: 20.63/1,000 population (2002 est.)
Death Rate: 18.86/1,000 population (2002 est.)
Infant Mortality: 61.76 deaths/1,000 live births (2002 est.)
Life Expectancy at Birth: 45.19 years male, 45.68 years female (2002 est.)
Total Fertility Rate: 2.38 children born/woman (2002 est.)
Literacy: 85.3% (2000)

■ GOVERNMENT

Leader(s): Pres. Thabo Mvuyelwa Mbeki
Government Type: republic
Administrative Divisions: 9 provinces; after the election bringing Mandela to power, all 10 black homelands and 4 provinces existing earlier were dissolved
Nationhood: May 31, 1910 (from UK)
National Holiday: Freedom Day, April 27

■ ECONOMY

Overview: there is great disparity in living standards between the white minority (favoured) and the black majority; international embargoes against the country (because of its policy of apartheid) hurt the economy; other problems include crime, corruption and HIV/AIDS; burgeoning unemployment; has rich mineral resources (diamonds)
GDP: US$412 billion, per capita US$9,400; real growth rate 2.6% (2001 est.)
Inflation: 5.7% (2001)
Industries: accounts for 31% of GDP (2000); mining (world's largest producer of platinum, gold, chrome), automobile assembly, metal-working, machinery, textile, iron and steel, chemical, fertilizer, foodstuffs
Labour Force: 17.2 million (2001); 25% industry, 45% community, social and business services, 30% agriculture
Unemployment: 23.3% (2001)
Agriculture: accounts for 3% of GDP (2000) and 30% of labour force; diversified agriculture, with emphasis on livestock; products: cattle, poultry, sheep, wool, milk, beef, corn, wheat, sugar cane, fruit, vegetables; self-sufficient in food
Natural Resources: gold, chromium, antimony, coal, iron ore, manganese, nickel, phosphates, tin, uranium, gem diamonds, platinum, copper, vanadium, salt, natural gas

■ FINANCE/TRADE

Currency: rand (R) = 100 cents

International Reserves Excluding Gold: US$5.904 billion (Dec. 2002)
Gold Reserves: 5.580 million fine troy ounces (Dec. 2002)
Budget: revenues US$22.6 billion, expenditures US$24.7 billion, including capital expenditures of US$ n.a. (FY2002/03)
Defence Expenditures: 5.4% of central government expenditure (2001)
Education Expenditures: n.a.
External Debt: US$24.050 billion (2001)
Exports: US$26.042 billion (2000); commodities: gold 40%, minerals and metals 23%, food 6%, chemicals 3%; partners: EU, US, Japan, Mozambique
Imports: US$26.811 billion (2000); commodities: machinery 27%, chemicals 11%, vehicles and aircraft 11%, textiles, scientific instruments, base metals; partners: EU, US, Saudi Arabia, Japan

■ COMMUNICATIONS

Daily Newspapers: 32/1,000 inhabitants (2000)
Televisions: 152/1,000 inhabitants (2001)
Radios: 338/1,000 inhabitants (2001)
Telephones: 112 lines/1,000 inhabitants (2001)

■ TRANSPORTATION

Motor Vehicles: 6,230,000; 4,100,000 passenger cars (2000)
Roads: 534,131 km; 63,027 km paved
Railway: 20,384 km (2001)
Air Traffic: 7,948,000 passengers carried (2001)
Airports: 740; 143 have paved runways (2002)

Canadian Embassy: The Canadian High Commission, 1103 Arcadia, Hatfield 0028, Pretoria; mailing address: Private Bag X13, Hatfield 0028, South Africa. Tel: (011-27-12) 422-3000. Fax: (011-27-12) 422-3052. e-mail: pret@dfait-maeci.gc.ca
Embassy in Canada: Embassy of the Republic of South Africa, 15 Sussex Dr, Ottawa ON K1M 1M8. Tel: (613) 744-0330. Fax: (613) 741-1639. e-mail: rsafrica@sympatico.ca

Spain

Long-Form Name: Kingdom of Spain
Capital: Madrid

■ GEOGRAPHY

Area: 504,782 sq. km; includes Balaeric Islands, Canary Islands, Ceuta, Melilla, Islas Chafarinas, Peñón de Vélez de la Gomera
Coastline: 4,964 km
Climate: temperate; clear, hot summers in interior, more moderate and cloudy along coast; cloudy, cold winters in interior, partly cloudy and cool along coast

Environment: deforestation; air and water pollution; soil degradation; desertification; periodic droughts

Terrain: large, flat to dissected, rugged hills; Pyrenees in north

Land Use: 30% arable; 9% permanent crops; 21% meadows; 32% forest; 8% other; includes 36,400 sq. km irrigated

Location: SW Europe, bordering on Mediterranean Sea and N Atlantic Ocean

■ PEOPLE

Population: 40,077,100 (July 2002 est.)

Nationality: Spanish or Spaniard

Age Structure: 0–14 yrs: 14.5%; 15–64: 68.1%; 65+: 17.4% (2002 est.)

Population Growth Rate: 0.09% (2002 est.)

Net Migration: 0.87 migrants/1,000 population (2002 est.)

Ethnic Groups: composite of Mediterranean and Nordic types

Languages: Castilian Spanish; second languages include 17% Catalan (northeast), 7% Galician (northwest), 2% Basque (north)

Religions: 99% Roman Catholic, 1% other sects

Birth Rate: 9.29/1,000 population (2002 est.)

Death Rate: 9.22/1,000 population (2002 est.)

Infant Mortality: 4.85 deaths/1,000 live births (2002 est.)

Life Expectancy at Birth: 75.63 years male, 82.76 years female (2002 est.)

Total Fertility Rate: 1.16 children born/woman (2002 est.)

Literacy: 97.6% (2000)

■ GOVERNMENT

Leader(s): King Juan Carlos I, Pres. Jose Maria Aznar

Government Type: parliamentary monarchy

Administrative Divisions: 17 autonomous communities (comunidades autonomas, sing. — comunidad autonoma)

Nationhood: 1492 (expulsion of the Moors and unification)

National Holiday: National Day, Oct. 12

■ ECONOMY

Overview: advocates liberalization, privatization, and deregulation of the economy, and has introduced some tax reforms to that end; adjustment to the monetary and other economic policies of an integrated Europe will pose difficult challenges in the next few years

GDP: US$828 billion, per capita US$20,700; real growth rate 2.0% (2002 est.)

Inflation: 3.6% (2001)

Industries: accounts for 28% of GDP (2000); textiles and apparel (including footwear), food and beverages, metals and metal manufacturing, chemicals, shipbuilding, automobiles, machine tools

Labour Force: 18.2 million (2001); 64% services, 29% manufacturing and mining, 7% agriculture

Unemployment: 14.1% (2001)

Agriculture: accounts for 4% of GDP (2000) and 14% of labour force; major products: grain, vegetables, olives, wine grapes, sugar beets, citrus fruit, beef, pork, poultry, dairy; largely self-sufficient in food; fish catch of 1.4 million metric tons

Natural Resources: coal, lignite, iron ore, uranium, mercury, pyrites, fluorspar, gypsum, zinc, lead, tungsten, copper, kaolin, potash, hydro power

■ FINANCE/TRADE

Currency: peseta (Pta) = 100 centimos; Euro (€) on January 1, 2002 the Euro became the sole currency for everyday transactions

International Reserves Excluding Gold: US$34.535 billion (Dec. 2002)

Gold Reserves: 16.828 million fine troy ounces (Dec. 2002)

Budget: revenues US$105 billion, expenditures US$109 billion, including capital expenditures US$12.8 billion (2000 est.)

Defence Expenditures: 4.2% of central government expenditure (2001)

Education Expenditures: n.a.

External Debt: n.a.

Exports: US$118.153 billion (2002 est.); commodities: foodstuffs, live animals, wood, footwear, machinery, chemicals; partners: EU, Latin America, US

Imports: US$153.728 billion (2002 est.); commodities: petroleum, footwear, machinery, chemicals, grain, soybeans, coffee, tobacco, iron and steel, timber, cotton, transport equipment; partners: France, Germany, Italy, Benelux, UK, OPEC countries, US, Japan, Latin America

■ COMMUNICATIONS

Daily Newspapers: 100/1,000 inhabitants (2000)

Televisions: 598/1,000 inhabitants (2001)

Radios: 330/1,000 inhabitants (2001)

Telephones: 431 lines/1,000 inhabitants (2001)

■ TRANSPORTATION

Motor Vehicles: 18,900,000; 15,600,000 passenger cars (2000 est.)

Roads: 346,858 km; 343,389 km paved

Railway: 15,171 km

Air Traffic: 41,470,000 passengers carried (2001)

Airports: 133; 93 have paved runways (2002)

Canadian Embassy: The Canadian Embassy, Calle Nunez de Balboa, 35, 28001 Madrid; mailing address: Apartado 587, 28080 Madrid,

Spain. Tel: (011-34) 91-423-3252. Fax: (011-34) 91-423-3251. e-mail: mdrid@dfait-maeci.gc.ca

Embassy in Canada: Embassy of the Kingdom of Spain, 74 Stanley Ave, Ottawa ON, K1M IP4. Tel: (613) 747-2252. Fax: (613) 744-1224. e-mail: embespca@mail.mae.es

Sri Lanka

Long-Form Name: Democratic Socialist Republic of Sri Lanka
Capital: Colombo (administrative); Sri Jayewardenepura Kotte (legislative)

■ GEOGRAPHY

Area: 65,610 sq. km
Coastline: 1,340 km
Climate: tropical; monsoonal; northeast monsoon (Dec. to Mar.); southwest monsoon (June to Oct.)
Environment: occasional cyclones, tornadoes; deforestation; soil erosion; pollution of fresh water resources
Terrain: mostly low, flat to rolling plain; mountains in south-central interior
Land Use: 14% arable; 15% permanent crops; 7% meadows; 32% forest; 32% other; includes 6,510 sq. km irrigated
Location: Indian Ocean, S of India

■ PEOPLE

Population: 19,576,783 (July 2002 est.)
Nationality: Sri Lankan
Age Structure: 0–14 yrs: 25.6%; 15–64: 67.7%; 65+: 6.7% (2002 est.)
Population Growth Rate: 0.85% (2002 est.)
Net Migration: -1.39 migrants/1,000 population (2002 est.)
Ethnic Groups: 74% Sinhalese; 18% Tamil; 7% Moor; 1% Burgher, Malay and Veddha
Languages: Sinhala (official); Sinhala and Tamil are the national languages; Sinhala spoken by about 74% of population, Tamil spoken by about 18%; English commonly used in government and spoken by about 10% of the population
Religions: 69% Buddhist, 15% Hindu (Tamil speakers), 8% Christian, 8% Muslim
Birth Rate: 16.36/1,000 population (2002 est.)
Death Rate: 6.45/1,000 population (2002 est.)
Infant Mortality: 15.65 deaths/1,000 live births (2002 est.)
Life Expectancy at Birth: 69.83 years male, 75.00 years female (2002 est.)
Total Fertility Rate: 1.93 children born/woman (2002 est.)
Literacy: 91.6% (2000)

■ GOVERNMENT

Leader(s): Pres. Chandrika Bandaranaike Kumaratunga, Prime Min. Ranil Wickremesinghe
Government Type: republic
Administrative Divisions: 8 provinces
Nationhood: Feb. 4, 1948 (from UK; formerly known as Ceylon)
National Holiday: Independence and National Day, Feb. 4

■ ECONOMY

Overview: sustained economic growth, coupled with low population growth, has pushed Sri Lanka from the ranks of the poorest countries, however civil war between Sinhalese and Tamils continues to disrupt economic progress
GDP: US$62.7 billion, per capita US$3,250; real growth rate -1.0% (2001 est.)
Inflation: 14.2% (2001)
Industries: accounts for 27% of GDP (2000); processing of rubber, tea, coconuts and other agricultural commodities; cement, petroleum refining, textiles, tobacco. The apparel industry has surpassed all other kinds of manufacturing
Labour Force: 8.3 million (2001); 38% agriculture, 45% community, social and business services, 17% industry
Unemployment: 10.6% (2001)
Agriculture: accounts for 21% of GDP (2000) and almost 45% of labour force; most important staple crop is paddy rice; other field crops: sugar cane, grains, pulses, oilseeds, roots; spices; cash crops: tea, rubber, coconuts; animal products: milk, eggs, hides, meat; not self-sufficient in rice production
Natural Resources: limestone, graphite, mineral sands, gems, phosphates, clay, hydro power

■ FINANCE/TRADE

Currency: rupee (SL Re) = 100 cents
International Reserves Excluding Gold: US$1.455 billion (Nov. 2002)
Gold Reserves: 0.663 million fine troy ounces (Nov. 2002)
Budget: revenues US$2.8 billion; expenditures US$4.1 billion, including capital expenditures of US$ n.a. (2001 est.)
Defence Expenditures: 14.7% of central government expenditure (2001)
Education Expenditures: 9.60% of government expenditure (2000)
External Debt: US$8.529 billion (2001)
Exports: US$4.552 billion (2002 est.); commodities: tea, textiles and garments, petroleum products, coconut, rubber, agricultural products, gems and jewellery, marine products; partners: US, UK, Middle East, Germany, Japan

Imports: US$5.820 billion (2002 est.); commodities: petroleum, machinery and equipment, textiles and textile materials, wheat, transportation equipment, electrical machinery, sugar, rice; partners: Japan, India, Hong Kong, Singapore, South Korea

■ COMMUNICATIONS

Daily Newspapers: 29/1,000 inhabitants (2000)
Televisions: 117/1,000 inhabitants (2001)
Radios: 215/1,000 inhabitants (2001)
Telephones: 44 lines/1,000 inhabitants (2001)

■ TRANSPORTATION

Motor Vehicles: 660,000; 290,000 passenger cars (2000)
Roads: 11,285 km; 10,721 km paved
Railway: 1,463 km
Air Traffic: 1,719,000 passengers carried (2001)
Airports: 15, 14 have paved runways (2002)

Canadian Embassy: The Canadian High Commission, 6 Gregory's Rd, Cinnamon Gardens, Colombo 7, Sri Lanka; mailing address: P.O. Box 1006, Colombo 7, Sri Lanka. Tel: (011-94-1) 69-58-41. Fax: (011-94-75) 35-38-29. e-mail: clmbo@dfait-maeci.gc.ca
Embassy in Canada: High Commission for the Democratic Socialist Republic of Sri Lanka, 333 Laurier Ave W, Ste 1204, Ottawa ON K1P 1C1. Tel: (613) 233-8449. Fax: (613) 238-8448. e-mail: lankacom@magi.com

---

Sudan

Long-Form Name: Republic of the Sudan
Capital: Khartoum

■ GEOGRAPHY

Area: 2,505,810 sq. km
Coastline: 853 km
Climate: tropical in south; arid desert in north; rainy season (Apr. to Oct.)
Environment: dominated by the Nile and its tributaries; dust storms; desertification; unsafe drinking water resources; overhunting threatens wildlife population
Terrain: generally flat, featureless plain; mountains in east and west
Land Use: 5% arable; negligible permanent crops; 46% permanent pastures; 19% forest; 30% other; includes 19,500 sq. km irrigated
Location: NE Africa, bordering on Red Sea

■ PEOPLE

Population: 37,090,298 (July 2002 est.)
Nationality: Sudanese

Age Structure: 0–14 yrs: 44.2%; 15–64: 53.6%; 65+: 2.2% (2002 est.)
Population Growth Rate: 2.73% (2002 est.)
Net Migration: -0.07 migrants/1,000 population (2002 est.)
Ethnic Groups: 52% black, 39% Arab, 6% Beja, 2% foreigners, 1% other
Languages: Arabic (official), Nubian, Ta Bedawie, diverse dialects of Nilotic, Nilo-Hamatic and Sudanic languages, English; program of Arabization in process
Religions: 70% Sunni Muslim (in north), 25% indigenous beliefs, 5% Christian (mostly in south and Khartoum)
Birth Rate: 37.21/1,000 population (2002 est.)
Death Rate: 9.81/1,000 population (2002 est.)
Infant Mortality: 67.14 deaths/1,000 live births (2002 est.)
Life Expectancy at Birth: 56.22 years male, 58.50 years female (2002 est.)
Total Fertility Rate: 5.22 children born/woman (2002 est.)
Literacy: 57.8% (2000)

■ GOVERNMENT

Leader(s): Pres. Omar Hassan Ahmed al-Bashir
Government Type: authoritarian regime
Administrative Divisions: 26 states (wilayat, sing. —wilayah)
Nationhood: Jan. 1, 1956 (from Egypt and UK; formerly known as Anglo-Egyptian Sudan)
National Holiday: Independence Day, Jan. 1

■ ECONOMY

Overview: a very poor country, hurt by civil war, chronic political instability, adverse weather and counterproductive governmental economic policies; agriculture is the economic base. It employs 80% of the labour force and focuses chiefly on processing agricultural produce; international aid is helping the country manage a high foreign debt, but creditors want economic reform
GDP: US$49.3 billion, per capita US$1,360; real growth rate 5.5% (2001 est.)
Inflation: 6.4% (2001)
Industries: accounts for 17% of GDP; cotton ginning, textiles, cement, edible oils, sugar, soap distilling, shoes, petroleum refining
Labour Force: 12.7 million (2001); 80% agriculture, 10% industry, 6% services, 4% other
Unemployment: n.a.
Agriculture: accounts for 39% of GDP and 80% of labour force; untapped potential for higher farm production; water shortages; two-thirds of land area suitable for crops and livestock; major products: cotton, oilseeds, sorghum, millet,

wheat, gum arabic, papaya, bananas, sheep; marginally self-sufficient in most foods
Natural Resources: modest reserves of crude oil, iron ore, copper, chromium ore, zinc, tungsten, mica, silver

■ FINANCE/TRADE

Currency: Sudanese dinar (LSd) = 100 piastres; Sudanese pound was discontinued in July 1999
International Reserves Excluding Gold: US$478 million (Dec. 2002)
Gold Reserves: n.a.
Budget: revenues US$1.6 billion; expenditures US$1.9 billion, including capital expenditures of US$ n.a. (2001 est.)
Defence Expenditures: 27.4% of central government expenditure (2001)
Education Expenditures: 7.64% of central government expenditure (1999)
External Debt: US$15.348 billion (2001)
Exports: US$1.756 billion (2002 est.); commodities: cotton 43%, sesame, gum arabic, peanuts, livestock, sugar; partners: Japan, China, Saudi Arabia, Germany
Imports: US$1.816 billion (2002 est.); commodities: petroleum products, manufactured goods, machinery and equipment, medicines and chemicals; partners: China, Saudi Arabia, UK, Germany

■ COMMUNICATIONS

Daily Newspapers: 26/1,000 inhabitants (2000)
Televisions: 386/1,000 inhabitants (2001)
Radios: 466/1,000 inhabitants (2001)
Telephones: 14 lines/1,000 inhabitants (2001)

■ TRANSPORTATION

Motor Vehicles: 75,000; 35,000 passenger cars (1996)
Roads: 11,900 km; 4,320 km paved
Railway: 5,995 km
Air Traffic: 415,000 passengers carried (2001)
Airports: 65; 12 have paved runways (2002)

Canadian Embassy: The Canadian Embassy to the Sudan, 10th St, Off Sharia al Baladia, Khartoum East, Sudan. Tel: (011-249-11) 79-03-20. Fax: (011-249-11) 79-03-21. e-mail: nicholas.coghlan@dfait-maeci.gc.ca
Embassy in Canada: Embassy of the Republic of the Sudan, 354 Stewart St, Ottawa ON K1N 6K8. Tel: (613) 235-4000. Fax: (613) 235-6880. e-mail: sudanembassy-canada@home.com

Suriname

Long-Form Name: Republic of Suriname

Capital: Paramaribo

■ GEOGRAPHY

Area: 163,270 sq. km
Coastline: 386 km
Climate: tropical; moderated by trade winds
Environment: mostly tropical rainforest; deforestation resulting from logging for export; mining causes pollution of inland waterways
Terrain: mostly rolling hills; narrow coastal plain with swamps
Land Use: 0.37% arable; 0% permanent crops; 0% meadows; 96% forest; 4% other; includes 490 sq. km irrigated
Location: N South America, bordering on Atlantic Ocean

■ PEOPLE

Population: 436,494 (July 2002 est.)
Nationality: Surinamer
Age Structure: 0–14 yrs: 31.1%; 15–64: 63.1%; 65+: 5.8% (2002 est.)
Population Growth Rate: 0.55% (2002 est.)
Net Migration: -8.82 migrants/1,000 population (2002 est.)
Ethnic Groups: 37% Hindustani (East Indian), 31% Creole (black and mixed), 15% Javanese, 10% Maroons, 2% Amerindian, 2% Chinese, 1% European, 2% other
Languages: Dutch (official), Hindustani 32%, Javanese 15%; the majority can speak the native language Sranang Tongo (Taki-Taki); English is also widely spoken
Religions: 27.4% Hindu, 19.6% Muslim, 22.8% Roman Catholic, 25.2% Protestant (predominantly Moravian), about 5% indigenous beliefs
Birth Rate: 19.97/1,000 population (2002 est.)
Death Rate: 5.67/1,000 population (2002 est.)
Infant Mortality: 23.48 deaths/1,000 live births (2002 est.)
Life Expectancy at Birth: 69.23 years male, 74.70 years female (2002 est.)
Total Fertility Rate: 2.44 children born/woman (2002 est.)
Literacy: 93.0% (1999)

■ GOVERNMENT

Leader(s): Pres. Ronald Venetiaan, V. Pres and Prime Min. Jules R. Ajodhia
Government Type: constitutional democracy
Administrative Divisions: 10 districts (distrikten, sing. distrikt)
Nationhood: Nov. 25, 1975 (from Netherlands; formerly known as Netherlands Guiana or Dutch Guiana)
National Holiday: Independence Day, Nov. 25

■ ECONOMY

Overview: the economy is vulnerable to world prices for its bauxite, which provides more than 15% of the GDP and 65+% of export earnings. Guerrilla activity has targeted the economic infrastructure; high inflation, high unemployment, widespread black-market activity and hard currency shortfalls continue to characterize the economy
GDP: US$1.5 billion, per capita US$3,500; real growth rate -5.5% (2000 est.)
Inflation: 64.3% (2000)
Industries: accounts for 22% of GDP; bauxite mining, alumina and aluminum production, lumbering, food processing, fishing
Labour Force: approx. 100,000; 20% agriculture, 8.9% industry, 49.4% services, 15.2% trade and tourism
Unemployment: n.a.
Agriculture: accounts for 13% of GDP and 25% of export earnings; paddy rice planted on 85% of arable land and represents 60% of total farm output; other products: bananas, palm kernels, coconuts, plantains, peanuts, beef, chicken; shrimp and forestry products of increasing importance
Natural Resources: timber, hydro power potential, fish, shrimp, bauxite, iron ore and modest amounts of nickel, copper, platinum, gold

■ FINANCE/TRADE

Currency: Surinamese guilder, gulden or florin (Sf) = 100 cents
International Reserves Excluding Gold: US$106 million (Dec. 2002)
Gold Reserves: 0.021 million fine troy ounces (Dec. 2002)
Budget: n.a.
Defence Expenditures: n.a.
Education Expenditures: n.a.
External Debt: US$512 million (2002 est.)
Exports: US$414 million (2000); commodities: alumina, bauxite, aluminum, rice, wood and wood products, shrimp and fish, bananas; partners: Netherlands, US, Norway, France, Japan, UK
Imports: US$439 million (2000); commodities: capital equipment, petroleum, foodstuffs, cotton, consumer goods; partners: US, Netherlands, Trinidad and Tobago, Brazil, UK, Japan

■ COMMUNICATIONS

Daily Newspapers: 2 in total
Televisions: n.a.
Radios: n.a.
Telephones: 171 lines/1,000 inhabitants (1999)

■ TRANSPORTATION

Motor Vehicles: 66,000; 46,900 passenger cars
Roads: 4,530 km; 1,178 km paved
Railway: 166 km
Air Traffic: 315,000 passengers carried (1999 est.)
Airports: 46; 5 have paved runways (2002)

Canadian Embassy: The Canadian Embassy to Suriname, c/o Canadian High Commission, High and Young Streets, Georgetown; mailing address: P.O. Box 10880, Georgetown, Guyana. Tel. (011-592) 227-2081. Fax: (011-592) 225-8380. e-mail: grgtn@dfait-maeci.gc.ca
Embassy in Canada: c/o Embassy of the Republic of Suriname, Van Ness Center, 4301 Connecticut Ave NW, Ste 460, Washington DC 20008, USA. Tel: (202) 244-7488. Fax: (202) 244-5878. e-mail: embsur@erols.com

Svalbard

Long-Form Name: Svalbard
Capital: Longyearbyen

■ GEOGRAPHY

Area: 62,049 sq. km, 5 large islands, many smaller ones
Climate: arctic, tempered by mild Atlantic winds, cool summers, cold winters
Land Use: undeveloped except for mining establishments; no trees—the only bushes are crowberry and cloudberry
Location: Arctic Ocean, midway between Norway and the North Pole

■ PEOPLE

Population: 2,868 (July 2002 est.)
Nationality: Norwegian
Ethnic Groups: 62% Russian and Ukrainian; 38% Norwegian
Languages: Norwegian, Russian

■ GOVERNMENT

Colony/Territory of: Dependent Territory of Norway
Leader(s): Head of State: King Harald V (Norway), District Gov. Odd Olsen Ingerø
Government Type: Territory of Norway
National Holiday: n.a.

■ ECONOMY

Overview: tourism most important; coal mining only industry (the Norwegian state-owned company employs almost 60% of the population); some trapping of seal, polar bear, fox and walrus

■ FINANCE/TRADE

Currency: Norwegian krone = 100 oere

Canadian Embassy: c/o The Canadian Embassy, Wergelandsveien 7, 0244 Oslo, Norway. Tel: (011-47) 22-99-53-00. Fax: (011-47) 22-99-53-01. e-mail: oslo@dfait-maeci.gc.ca

Representative to Canada: c/o Embassy of the Kingdom of Norway, Royal Bank Centre, 90 Sparks St, Ste 532, Ottawa ON K1P 5B4. Tel: (613) 238-6571. Fax: (613) 238-2765. e-mail: emb.ottawa@mfa.no

Swaziland

Long-Form Name: Kingdom of Swaziland
Capital: Mbabane (administrative); Lobamba (legislative)

■ GEOGRAPHY

Area: 17,363 sq. km
Coastline: none: landlocked
Climate: varies from tropical to near temperate
Environment: overhunting and overgrazing; soil degradation; soil erosion; limited safe drinking water
Terrain: mostly mountains and hills; some moderately sloping plains
Land Use: 11% arable; 0% permanent crops; 62% meadows; 7% forest; 20% other; includes 690 sq. km irrigated
Location: S Africa

■ PEOPLE

Population: 1,123,605 (July 2002 est.)
Nationality: Swazi
Age Structure: 0–14 yrs: 45.5%; 15–64: 51.9%; 65+: 2.6% (2002 est.)
Population Growth Rate: 1.63% (2002 est.)
Net Migration: 0 migrants/1,000 population (2002 est.)
Ethnic Groups: 97% African, 3% European
Languages: English and siSwati (official); government business conducted in English
Religions: 60% Christian, 40% indigenous beliefs
Birth Rate: 39.59/1,000 population (2002 est.)
Death Rate: 23.26/1,000 population (2002 est.)
Infant Mortality: 109.43 deaths/1,000 live births (2002 est.)
Life Expectancy at Birth: 36.35 years male, 37.66 years female (2002 est.)
Total Fertility Rate: 5.77 children born/woman (2002 est.)
Literacy: 79.6% (2000)

■ GOVERNMENT

Leader(s): King Mswati III, Premier Barnabas Sibusiso Dlamini

Government Type: monarchy; independent member of Commonwealth
Administrative Divisions: 4 districts
Nationhood: Sept. 6, 1968 (from UK)
National Holiday: Somhlolo (Independence) Day, Sept. 6

■ ECONOMY

Overview: is based on subsistence agriculture and is closely tied to that of its neighbour, South Africa, from which it receives 90% of its imports and to which it sends about half of its exports; manufacturing focuses on the processing of agricultural products; mining is becoming less important; overgrazing, soil deterioration and recurrent droughts are persistent problems
GDP: US$4.6 billion, per capita US$4,200; real growth rate 2.5% (2001 est.)
Inflation: 5.9% (2001)
Industries: accounts for 46% of GDP; mining (coal and asbestos), wood pulp, sugar; asbestos is declining in importance
Labour Force: 400,000 (2000); 74% agriculture, 17% services, 9% industry; 24,000–29,000 employed in South Africa
Unemployment: n.a.
Agriculture: accounts for 10% of GDP and over two-thirds of labour force; mostly subsistence agriculture; cash crops: sugar cane, citrus fruit, cotton, tobacco, pineapple; other crops and livestock: corn, sorghum, peanuts, cattle, goats, sheep; not self-sufficient in grain
Natural Resources: asbestos, coal, clay, tin, hydroelectric power, quarry stone, talc, forests and small gold and diamond deposits

■ FINANCE/TRADE

Currency: lilangeni (pl. emalangeni) (E) = 100 cents
International Reserves Excluding Gold: US$276 million (Dec. 2002)
Gold Reserves: n.a.
Budget: revenues US$448 million, expenditures US$506.9 million, including capital expenditures of US$147 million (FY2001/02)
Defence Expenditures: 5.2% of central government expenditure (2001)
Education Expenditures: 19.84% of central government expenditure (2000)
External Debt: US$308 million (2001)
Exports: US$825 million (1999); commodities: sugar, asbestos, wood pulp, citrus, canned fruit, soft drink concentrates; partners: South Africa, US, Mozambique, EU, UK
Imports: US$1.05 billion (1999); commodities: motor vehicles, machinery, transport equipment, chemicals, petroleum products, foodstuffs; partners: South Africa, EU, Japan, Singapore

■ COMMUNICATIONS

Daily Newspapers: 26/1,000 inhabitants (2000)
Televisions: 128/1,000 inhabitants (2001)
Radios: 162/1,000 inhabitants (2001)
Telephones: 31 lines/1,000 inhabitants (2001)

■ TRANSPORTATION

Motor Vehicles: 77,000; 37,000 passenger cars (2000)
Roads: 3,000 km; 1,064 km paved
Railway: 297 km
Air Traffic: 90,000 passengers carried (2001)
Airports: 18; 1 has a paved runway (2002)

Canadian Embassy: The Canadian High Commission to Swaziland, c/o The Canadian Embassy, 1103 Arcadia St, Hatfield 0028, Pretoria; mailing address: Private Bag X13, Hatfield 0028, Pretoria, South Africa. Tel: (011-27-12) 422-3000. Fax (011-27-12) 422-3052. e-mail: pret@dfait-maeci.gc.ca
Embassy in Canada: c/o High Commission for the Kingdom of Swaziland, 3400 International Dr NW, Ste 3M, Washington DC, 20008, Tel: (202) 234-5002, Fax: (202) 234-8254. e-mail: swaziland@compuserve.com

Sweden

Long-Form Name: Kingdom of Sweden
Capital: Stockholm

■ GEOGRAPHY

Area: 449,964 sq. km
Coastline: 3,218 km
Climate: temperate in south with cold, cloudy winters and cool, partly cloudy summers, subarctic in north
Environment: water pollution; acid rain; ice floes in coastal waters hinder navigation
Terrain: mostly flat or gently rolling lowlands; mountains in west
Land Use: 7% arable; 0% permanent crops; 1% meadows; 68% forest; 24% other; includes 1,150 sq. km irrigated
Location: N Europe, bordering on Baltic Sea

■ PEOPLE

Population: 8,875,053 (July 2001 est.)
Nationality: Swedish, Swede
Age Structure: 0–14 yrs: 18.0%; 15–64: 64.7%; 65+: 17.3% (2002 est.)
Population Growth Rate: 0.02% (2002 est.)
Net Migration: 0.95 migrants/1,000 population (2002 est.)
Ethnic Groups: homogeneous white population; small Lappish minority; about 12% foreign born or first-generation immigrants (Finns, Yugoslavs, Danes, Norwegians, Greeks, Turks)

Languages: Swedish (official), small Lapp- and Finnish-speaking minorities; immigrants speak native languages
Religions: 94% Evangelical Lutheran, 1.5% Roman Catholic, 4.5% other
Birth Rate: 9.81/1,000 population (2002 est.)
Death Rate: 10.60/1,000 population (2002 est.)
Infant Mortality: 3.44 deaths/1,000 live births (2002 est.)
Life Expectancy at Birth: 77.19 years male, 82.64 years female (2002 est.)
Total Fertility Rate: 1.54 children born/woman (2002 est.)
Literacy: approaching 100% (2000)

■ GOVERNMENT

Leader(s): King Carl XVI Gustaf, Prime Min. Goran Persson
Government Type: constitutional monarchy
Administrative Divisions: 21 counties (lan, sing. & pl.)
Nationhood: June 6, 1523, constitutional monarchy established
National Holiday: Day of the Swedish Flag, June 6

■ ECONOMY

Overview: a mixed system of high-tech capitalism and extensive welfare benefits; has benefited from neutrality in world wars; economy is heavily oriented toward foreign trade; has excellent communications systems
GDP: US$227.4 billion, per capita US$25,400; real growth rate 1.8% (2002 est.)
Inflation: 2.4% (2001)
Industries: accounts for 28% of GDP (2001); iron and steel, precision equipment (bearings, radio and telephone parts, armaments), wood pulp and paper products, processed foods, motor vehicles
Labour Force: 4.8 million (2000); 74% community, social and business services, 24% industry, 2% agriculture
Unemployment: 5.1% (Jan. 2003)
Agriculture: accounts for 2% of GDP (2001); animal husbandry predominates, with milk and dairy products accounting for 37% of farm income; main crops: grains, sugar beets, potatoes; 100% self-sufficient in grains and potatoes, 85% self-sufficient in sugar beets
Natural Resources: zinc, iron ore, lead, copper, silver, timber, uranium, hydro power potential

■ FINANCE/TRADE

Currency: krona (pl. kronor) (Skr) = 100 oere
International Reserves Excluding Gold: US$17.127 billion (Dec. 2002)
Gold Reserves: 5.961 million fine troy ounces (Dec. 2002)

Budget: revenues US$119 billion, expenditures US$110 billion, including capital expenditures of US$ n.a. (2001 est.)
Defence Expenditures: 5.4% of government expenditure (2001)
Education Expenditures: 6.58% of total government expenditure (1999)
External Debt: n.a.
Exports: US$78.196 billion (2002 est.); commodities: machinery, motor vehicles, paper products, pulp and wood, iron and steel products, chemicals, petroleum and petroleum products; partners: Germany, UK, Denmark, Finland, US, Norway
Imports: US$63.332 billion (2002 est.); commodities: machinery, petroleum and petroleum products, chemicals, motor vehicles, foodstuffs, iron and steel, clothing; partners: Germany, UK, Denmark, Netherlands, US, France, Norway

■ COMMUNICATIONS

Daily Newspapers: 410/1,000 inhabitants (2000)
Televisions: 965/1,000 inhabitants (2001)
Radios: 2,811/1,000 inhabitants (2001)
Telephones: 739 lines/1,000 inhabitants (2001)

■ TRANSPORTATION

Motor Vehicles: 4,200,000; 3,900,000 passenger cars (2000)
Roads: 210,907 km; 163,453 km paved
Railway: 12,821 km
Air Traffic: 13,123,000 passengers carried (2001)
Airports: 255; 145 have paved runways (2002)

Canadian Embassy: The Canadian Embassy, Tegelbacken 4 (Flr 7), Stockholm, Sweden; mailing address: P.O. Box 16129; S-10323 Stockholm, Sweden. Tel: (011-46-8) 453-3000. Fax: (011-46-8) 453-3016. e-mail: stkhm@dfait-maeci.gc.ca
Embassy in Canada: Embassy of Sweden, Mercury Court, 377 Dalhousie St, Ottawa ON K1N 9N8. Tel: (613) 241-8553. Fax: (613) 241-2277. e-mail: sweden@cyberus.ca

---

Switzerland

Long-Form Name: Swiss Confederation
Capital: Bern

■ GEOGRAPHY

Area: 41,290 sq. km
Coastline: none: landlocked
Climate: temperate, but varies with altitude; cold, cloudy, rainy/snowy winters; cool to warm, cloudy, humid summers with occasional showers

Environment: dominated by Alps; air and water pollution; avalanches, flash floods and landslides are natural hazards
Terrain: mostly mountains (Alps in south, Jura in northwest) with a central plateau of rolling hills, plains and large lakes
Land Use: 10% arable; 2% permanent crops; 28% permanent pastures; 32% forest; 28% other; includes 250 sq. km irrigated
Location: C Europe

■ PEOPLE

Population: 7,301,994 (July 2002 est.)
Nationality: Swiss (sing. & pl.)
Age Structure: 0–14 yrs: 16.8%; 15–64: 67.7%; 65+: 15.5% (2002 est.)
Population Growth Rate: 0.24% (2002 est.)
Net Migration: 1.37 migrants/1,000 population (2002 est.)
Ethnic Groups: total population: 65% German, 18% French, 10% Italian, 1% Romansch, 6% other
Languages: 65% German, 18% French, 12% Italian, 1% Raeto-Romansch (all official), 4% other
Religions: 47.6% Roman Catholic, 44.3% Protestant, 8.1% other
Birth Rate: 9.84/1,000 population (2002 est.)
Death Rate: 8.79/1,000 population (2002 est.)
Infant Mortality: 4.42 deaths/1,000 live births (2002 est.)
Life Expectancy at Birth: 76.98 years male, 82.89 years female (2002 est.)
Total Fertility Rate: 1.47 children born/woman (2002 est.)
Literacy: approaching 100% (2000)

■ GOVERNMENT

Leader(s): Pres. Pascal Couchepin, V. Pres. Ruth Metzler-Arnold
Government Type: federal republic
Administrative Divisions: 26 cantons
Nationhood: Aug. 1, 1291
National Holiday: Anniversary of the Founding of the Swiss Confederation, Aug. 1

■ ECONOMY

Overview: country has the highest per capita output, general living standards, education and science, health-care and diet standards in Europe; important banking and tourist sectors; low inflation and negligible unemployment are due partly to government policies; has rejected membership in the European Economic Community
GDP: US$231 billion, per capita US$31,700; real growth rate 2.0% (2002 est.)
Inflation: 1.0% (2001)

Industries: accounts for 34% of GDP (2002 est.); machinery, chemicals, watches, textiles, precision instruments
Labour Force: 3.9 million (2001); 26% industry, 69% community, social and business services, 5% agriculture
Unemployment: 3.8% (Jan. 2003)
Agriculture: accounts for 2% of GDP (2002 est.); dairy farming predominates; less than 50% self-sufficient; food shortages: fish, refined sugar, fats and oils (other than butter), grains, eggs, fruit, vegetables, meat
Natural Resources: hydro power potential, timber, salt; scenic beauty

■ **FINANCE/TRADE**

Currency: Swiss franc, franken, or franco (SwF) = 100 centimes, rappen, or centesimi
International Reserves Excluding Gold: US$40.155 billion (Dec. 2002)
Gold Reserves: 61.623 million fine troy ounces (Dec. 2002)
Budget: revenues US$30 billion; expenditures US$30 billion, including capital expenditures of US$ n.a. (2001 est.)
Defence Expenditures: 4.2% of central government expenditure (2001)
Education Expenditures: 2.44% of total government expenditure (1999)
External Debt: n.a.
Exports: US$83.922 billion (2002); commodities: machinery and equipment, precision instruments, metal products, foodstuffs, textiles and clothing; partners: Germany, France, Italy, UK, US, Japan
Imports: US$79.130 billion (2002); commodities: agricultural products, machinery and transportation equipment, chemicals, textiles, construction materials; partners: Germany, France, Italy, Netherlands, UK, US

■ **COMMUNICATIONS**

Daily Newspapers: 373/1,000 inhabitants (2000)
Televisions: 554/1,000 inhabitants (2001)
Radios: 1,002/1,000 inhabitants (2001)
Telephones: 746 lines/1,000 inhabitants (2001)

■ **TRANSPORTATION**

Motor Vehicles: 3,800,000; 3,500,000 passenger cars (2000)
Roads: 71,059 km; all paved
Railway: 4,406 km
Air Traffic: 16,915,000 passengers carried (2001)
Airports: 66; 41 have paved runways (2002)

Canadian Embassy: The Canadian Embassy, Kirchenfeldstrasse 88, Bern, 3005, Switzerland. Mailing address: P.O. Box 3000, Berne 6, Switzerland. Tel: (011-41-31) 357-32-00. Fax: (011-41-31) 357-32-10. e-mail: bern@dfait-maeci.gc.ca
Embassy in Canada: Embassy of Switzerland, 5 Marlborough Ave, Ottawa ON K1N 8E6. Tel: (613) 235-1837. Fax: (613) 563-1394. e-mail: vertretung@ott.rep.admin.ch

Syria

Long-Form Name: Syrian Arab Republic
Capital: Damascus

■ **GEOGRAPHY**

Area: 185,180 sq. km; including 1,295 sq. km of Israeli-occupied territory
Coastline: 193 km
Climate: mostly desert; hot, dry, sunny summers (June to Aug.) and mild, rainy winters (Dec. to Feb.) along coast
Environment: deforestation; overgrazing; soil erosion; desertification; unsafe drinking water
Terrain: primarily semi-arid and desert plateau; narrow coastal plain; mountains in west
Land Use: 28% arable; 4% permanent crops; 43% meadows; 3% forest; 22% other; includes 12,130 sq. km irrigated
Location: SW Asia (Middle East), bordering on Mediterranean Sea

■ **PEOPLE**

Population: 17,155,814 (July 2002 est.)
Nationality: Syrian
Age Structure: 0–14 yrs: 39.3%; 15–64: 57.5%; 65+: 3.2% (2002 est.)
Population Growth Rate: 2.50% (2002 est.)
Net Migration: 0 migrants/1,000 population (2002 est.)
Ethnic Groups: 90.3% Arab; 9.7% Kurds, Armenians and other
Languages: Arabic (official), Kurdish, Armenian, Aramaic, Circassian; English and French widely understood
Religions: 74% Sunni, 16% Alawite, Druze and other Muslim sects, 10% Christian
Birth Rate: 30.11/1,000 population (2002 est.)
Death Rate: 5.12/1,000 population (2002 est.)
Infant Mortality: 32.73 deaths/1,000 live births (2002 est.)
Life Expectancy at Birth: 67.90 years male, 70.32 years female (2002 est.)
Total Fertility Rate: 3.84 children born/woman (2002 est.)
Literacy: 74.4% (2000)

■ **GOVERNMENT**

Leader(s): Pres. Bashar al-Asad, V. Pres. Abd al-Halim ibn Said Khaddam and Mohammad

Zuheir Masharka, Prime Min. Muhammad Mustafa Miru
Government Type: republic under left-wing military regime
Administrative Divisions: 14 provinces (muhafazat, sing. —muhafazah)
Nationhood: Apr. 17, 1946 (from League of Nations mandate under French administration; formerly known as United Arab Republic)
National Holiday: Independence Day, Apr. 17

■ ECONOMY

Overview: economic difficulties are due, in part, to severe drought in several recent years, costly but unsuccessful attempts to match Israel's military strength, a fall-off in Arab aid and insufficient foreign exchange earnings to buy needed imports; agricultural output is poor; a major long-term concern is the additional drain of upstream Euphrates water by Turkey once its vast dam and irrigation projects are completed
GDP: US$54.2 billion; per capita US$3,200; real growth rate 2.0% (2001 est.)
Inflation: -0.4% (2000)
Industries: accounts for 23% of GDP (2000), textiles, food processing, beverages, tobacco, phosphate rock mining, petroleum
Labour Force: 5.4 million (2001); 40% services, 40% agriculture, 20% industry
Unemployment: 20% (2000 est.)
Agriculture: accounts for 27% of GDP (2000); all major crops (wheat, barley, cotton, lentils, chickpeas) grown on rain-fed land causing wide swings in yields; animal products: beef, lamb, eggs, poultry, milk; not self-sufficient in grain or livestock products
Natural Resources: crude oil, phosphates, chrome and manganese ores, asphalt, iron ore, rock salt, marble, gypsum

■ FINANCE/TRADE

Currency: Syrian pound (£S) = 100 piastres
International Reserves Excluding Gold: n.a.
Gold Reserves: 0.833 million fine troy ounces (Dec. 2002)
Budget: revenues US$5 billion; expenditures US$7 billion, including capital expenditures of US$ n.a. (2001 est.)
Defence Expenditures: 24.2% of central government expenditure (2001)
Education Expenditures: n.a.
External Debt: US$21.305 billion (2001)
Exports: US$5.254 billion (2001); commodities: petroleum, textiles, fruit and vegetables, phosphates; partners: Italy, Germany, France, Turkey, Saudi Arabia
Imports: US$4.757 billion (2001); commodities: petroleum, machinery, base metals, foodstuffs and beverages, textiles and chemicals; partners:

France, Italy, Lebanon, China, Germany, South Korea, Turkey, US

■ COMMUNICATIONS

Daily Newspapers: 20/1,000 inhabitants (2000)
Televisions: 67/1,000 inhabitants (2001)
Radios: 276/1,000 inhabitants (2001)
Telephones: 103 lines/1,000 inhabitants (2001)

■ TRANSPORTATION

Motor Vehicles: 500,000; 151,000 passenger cars (2000)
Roads: 41,451 km; 9,575 km hard-surfaced
Railway: 2,750 km
Air Traffic: 761,000 passengers carried (2001)
Airports: 99; 24 have paved runways (2002)

Canadian Embassy: The Canadian Embassy, Lot 12, Mezzeh Autostrade, Damascus, Syria; mailing address: P.O. Box 3394, Damascus, Syria. Tel: (011-963-11) 611-6692. Fax: (011-963-11) 611-4000. e-mail: dmcus@dfait-maeci.gc.ca
Embassy in Canada: Embassy of the Syrian Arab Republic, 151 Slater St., Suite 1000, Ottawa, ON, K1P 5H3, Tel: (613) 569-5556, Fax: (613) 569-3800. e-mail: syrianembassy@on.aibn.com

Taiwan

Long-Form Name: Taiwan
Capital: Taipei

■ GEOGRAPHY

Area: 35,980 sq. km; includes the Pescadores, Matsu and Quemoy
Coastline: 1,566.3 km
Climate: tropical; marine; rainy season during southwest monsoon (June to Aug.)
Environment: subject to earthquakes and typhoons; water and air pollution
Terrain: eastern two-thirds mostly rugged mountains; flat to gently rolling plains in west
Land Use: 24% arable; 1% permanent crops; 5% meadows; 55% forest; 15% other; includes n.a. sq. km irrigated
Location: island, SE of China, bordering on South and East China Seas, Pacific Ocean

■ PEOPLE

Population: 22,548,009 (July 2002 est.)
Nationality: Taiwanese
Age Structure: 0–14 yrs: 21%; 15–64: 70%; 65+: 9% (2002 est.)
Population Growth Rate: 0.78% (2002 est.)
Net Migration: -0.30 migrants/1,000 population (2002 est.)
Ethnic Groups: 84% Taiwanese, 14% mainland Chinese, 2% aborigine

Languages: Mandarin Chinese (official); Taiwanese and Hakka dialects also used
Religions: 93% mixture of Buddhist, Islam, Confucian and Taoist, 5% Christian, 2% other
Birth Rate: 14.21/1,000 population (2002 est.)
Death Rate: 6.08/1,000 population (2002 est.)
Infant Mortality: 6.80 deaths/1,000 live births (2002 est.)
Life Expectancy at Birth: 73.99 years male, 79.71 years female (2002 est.)
Total Fertility Rate: 1.76 children born/woman (2002 est.)
Literacy: 94%

■ GOVERNMENT

Leader(s): Pres. Chen Shui-bian, V. Pres. Annette Lu, Prem. Yu Shyi-Kun
Government Type: multiparty democratic regime
Administrative Divisions: 16 counties (hsien, sing. & pl.), 5 municipalities (shih, sing. & pl.), 2 special municipalities (chuan-shih, sing. & pl.)
Nationhood: Taiwanese
National Holiday: National Day (Anniversary of the Revolution), Oct. 10

■ ECONOMY

Overview: dynamic capitalist economy with gradually decreasing guidance of investment and foreign trade by government authorities and partial government ownership of some large banks and industrial firms
GDP: US$386 billion, per capita US$17,200; real growth rate -2.2% (2001 est.)
Inflation: 1.3% (2000 est.)
Industries: accounts for 32% of GDP (2000), textiles, clothing, chemicals, electronics, food processing, plywood, sugar milling, cement, shipbuilding, petroleum
Labour Force: 9.8 million (2000 est.); 56% services, 36% industry, 8% agriculture
Unemployment: 3% (2000 est.)
Agriculture: accounts for 2% of GDP (2000); heavily subsidized sector; major crops: rice, sugar cane, sweet potatoes, fruit, vegetables, tea; livestock: hogs, poultry, beef, milk, cattle; not self-sufficient in wheat, soybeans, corn; fish catch expanding, 1.4 million metric tons
Natural Resources: small deposits of coal, natural gas, limestone, marble and asbestos

■ FINANCE/TRADE

Currency: New Taiwan dollar (NT$) = 100 cents
International Reserves Excluding Gold: n.a.
Gold Reserves: n.a.
Budget: revenues US$36 billion; expenditures US$36.1 billion, including capital expenditures of US$ n.a. (2002 est.)
Defence Expenditures: n.a.
Education Expenditures: n.a.

External Debt: US$40 billion (2000)
Exports: US$121.528 billion (1999); commodities: textiles 16%, electrical machinery 19%, general machinery and equipment 14%, telecommunications equipment 9%, basic metals and metal products 5%, foodstuffs 0.9%, plywood and wood products 1.3%; partners: US Hong Kong, Europe, Japan
Imports: US$110.961 billion (1999); commodities: machinery and equipment 15.9%, crude oil 5%, chemical and chemical products 11.1%, basic metals 7.4%, foodstuffs 2%, minerals, precision equipment; partners: Japan, US, European countries, South Korea

■ COMMUNICATIONS

Daily Newspapers: n.a.
Televisions: n.a.
Radios: n.a.
Telephones: n.a.

■ TRANSPORTATION

Motor Vehicles: 5,225,000; 4,300,000 passenger cars
Roads: 34,901 km; 31,271 km paved
Railway: 1,108 km
Air Traffic: n.a.
Airports: 39; 37 have paved runways (2002)

Canadian Embassy: none
Embassy in Canada: none

Tajikistan

Long-Form Name: Republic of Tajikistan
Capital: Dushanbe

■ GEOGRAPHY

Area: 143,100 sq. km
Coastline: none; landlocked
Climate: continental; severe winters in east; extremely hot summers; wet spring; semi-arid to polar in Pamir mountains
Environment: lack of fresh water; little land suitable for cultivation; industrial pollution
Terrain: mountains and glaciers constitute 93% of land area, predominantly herding and non-agricultural
Land Use: 6% arable; negligible permanent crops; 25% meadows and pastures; 4% forest and woodland, 65% other; includes 7,200 sq. km irrigated
Location: C Asia, bordering on China and Afghanistan

■ PEOPLE

Population: 6,719,567 (July 2002 est.)
Nationality: Tajik, Tajikistani

Age Structure: 0–14 yrs: 40.4%; 15–64: 54.9%; 65+: 4.7% (2002 est.)
Population Growth Rate: 2.12% (2002 est.)
Net Migration: -3.27 migrants/1,000 population (2002 est.)
Ethnic Groups: 64.9% Tajik, 25% Uzbek, 3.5% Russian (declining due to emigration), 6.6% other
Languages: Tajik (official), Uzbek, Russian
Religions: 80% Sunni Muslim, 5% Shia Muslim, 15% other
Birth Rate: 32.99/1,000 population (2002 est.)
Death Rate: 8.51/1,000 population (2002 est.)
Infant Mortality: 114.77 deaths/1,000 live births (2002 est.)
Life Expectancy at Birth: 61.24 years male, 67.46 years female (2002 est.)
Total Fertility Rate: 4.23 children born/woman (2002 est.)
Literacy: 99.2% (2000)

■ **GOVERNMENT**

Leader(s): Pres. Emomali Rahmonov, Prime Min. Oqil Oqilov
Government Type: republic
Administrative Divisions: 2 oblasts (viloyatho, sing. —viloyat) and 1 autonomous oblast (viloyati mukhtori)
Nationhood: Sept. 9, 1991 (from Soviet Union)
National Holiday: Independence Day, Sept. 9

■ **ECONOMY**

Overview: mostly mining and manufacturing with strong agricultural sector; industry and agriculture have been producing at reduced capacity due to civil unrest; currency incompatibility with neighbouring countries is straining trade relations; depends on aid from Russia and Uzbekistan and on international aid for much of its basic subsistence needs
GDP: US$7.5 billion, per capita US$1,140; real growth rate 8.3% (2001 est.)
Inflation: 33% (2000 est.)
Industries: accounts for 25% of GDP (2000); aluminum and electrochemical plants, textile machinery, silk and carpet mills; zinc, lead, chemicals and fertilizers, cement, vegetable oil, refrigerators and freezers
Labour Force: 2.5 million (2001); 67% agriculture and forestry, 8% industry, 25% services
Unemployment: n.a.
Agriculture: accounts for 19% of GDP (2000); cotton, grapes, fruit, grains, silkworm farming, cattle breeding, sheep, goats, pigs
Natural Resources: coal, oil, rare metals, rock crystal, mica, gold, hydro power potential, uranium, mercury, zinc, lead

■ **FINANCE/TRADE**

Currency: Tajik somoni
International Reserves Excluding Gold: n.a.
Gold Reserves: 0.009 million fine troy ounces (May 2002)
Budget: revenues US$146 million, expenditures US$196 million, including capital expenditures of US$ n.a. (2000 est.)
Defence Expenditures: 10.1% of central government expenditure (2001)
Education Expenditures: 3.15% of total government expenditure (2000)
External Debt: US$1.086 billion (2001)
Exports: US$727 million (2000); commodities: fruit, plant products, aluminum, electricity; partners: European countries, Uzbekistan, Russia
Imports: US$696 million (2000); commodities: fuel, machinery, foodstuffs; partners: European nations, Uzbekistan, Russia

■ **COMMUNICATIONS**

Daily Newspapers: 20/1,000 inhabitants (2000)
Televisions: 326/1,000 inhabitants (2001)
Radios: 141/1,000 inhabitants (2001)
Telephones: 36 lines/1,000 inhabitants (2001)

■ **TRANSPORTATION**

Motor Vehicles: n.a.
Roads: 29,900 km; 21,400 km hard-surfaced
Railway: 482 km, not including industrial lines
Air Traffic: 274,000 passengers carried (2001)
Airports: 53; 2 have paved runways (2002)

Canadian Embassy: The Canadian Embassy to Tajikistan, c/o The Canadian Embassy, 34 Kasarai Batir St, Almaty 480100, Kazakhstan. Tel: (011-7-3272) 50-11-51. Fax: (011-7-3272) 582-493. e-mail: almat@dfait-maeci.gc.ca
Embassy in Canada: n.a.

Tanzania

Long-Form Name: United Republic of Tanzania
Capital: Dar es Salaam

■ **GEOGRAPHY**

Area: 945,087 sq. km (includes the islands of Mafia, Pemba and Zanzibar)
Coastline: 1,424 km
Climate: varies from tropical along coast to temperate in highlands
Environment: deforestation; lack of water limits agriculture; recent droughts affected marginal agriculture
Terrain: plains along coast; central plateau; highlands in north, south; Kilimanjaro is highest point in Africa

Land Use: 3% arable; 1% permanent crops; 40% meadows; 38% forest; 18% other; includes 1,550 sq. km irrigated
Location: E Africa, bordering on Indian Ocean

■ PEOPLE

Population: 37,187,939 (July 2002 est.)
Nationality: Tanzanian
Age Structure: 0–14 yrs: 44.6%; 15–64: 52.5%; 65+: 2.9% (2002 est.)
Population Growth Rate: 2.60% (2002 est.)
Net Migration: -0.08 migrants/1,000 population (2002 est.)
Ethnic Groups: 99% native African consisting of well over 100 tribes; 1% Asian, European and Arab
Languages: Swahili and English (official); English primarily language of commerce, administration and higher education; Swahili widely understood and generally used for communication between ethnic groups
Religions: mainland: 30% Christian, 35% Muslim, 35% indigenous beliefs; Zanzibar: almost all Muslim
Birth Rate: 39.12/1,000 population (2002 est.)
Death Rate: 13.02/1,000 population (2002 est.)
Infant Mortality: 77.85 deaths/1,000 live births (2002 est.)
Life Expectancy at Birth: 50.76 years male, 52.67 years female (2002 est.)
Total Fertility Rate: 5.33 children born/woman (2002 est.)
Literacy: 74.7% (1999)

■ GOVERNMENT

Leader(s): Pres. Benjamin William Mkapa, Prem. Frederick Sumaye
Government Type: republic
Administrative Divisions: 25 regions
Nationhood: April 26, 1964; Tanganyika became independent on Dec. 9, 1961 (from UN trusteeship under British administration); Zanzibar became independent Dec. 19, 1963 (from UK); Tanganyika united with Zanzibar Apr. 26, 1964 to form the political unit that was renamed Tanzania on Oct. 29, 1964
National Holiday: Union Day, Apr. 26

■ ECONOMY

Overview: world aid is increasing the availability of imports and providing funds to rehabilitate this country's deteriorated economic infrastructure; this poor economy is heavily dependent on agriculture; industry is largely confined to processing agricultural products; mining is increasing in importance; recent banking reforms have helped increase private sector growth and investment
GDP: US$22.1 billion; per capita US$610; real growth rate 5.0% (2001 est.)

Inflation: 5.1% (2001)
Industries: accounts for 15% of GDP (2000); primarily agricultural processing (sugar, beer, cigarettes, sisal twine), diamond mines, oil refineries, shoes, cement, textiles, wood products, fertilizer
Labour Force: 17.7 million (2001); 80% agriculture, 20% industry and commerce
Unemployment: n.a.
Agriculture: accounts for 45% of GDP (2000), 85% of exports and employs 90% of workforce; topography and climatic conditions limit cultivated crops to only 5% of land area; cash crops: coffee, sisal, tea, cotton, pyrethrum (insecticide made from chrysanthemums), cashews, tobacco, cloves (Zanzibar); corn, wheat, beans, fruit and vegetables grown for local consumption
Natural Resources: hydro power potential, tin, phosphates, iron ore, coal, diamonds, gemstones, gold, natural gas, nickel

■ FINANCE/TRADE

Currency: Tanzania shilling (TSh) = 100 cents
International Reserves Excluding Gold: US$1.451 billion (Nov. 2002)
Gold Reserves: n.a.
Budget: revenues US$1.01 billion; expenditures US$1.38 billion, including capital expenditures of US$ n.a. (FY2000/01 est.)
Defence Expenditures: 10.1% of central government expenditure (1999)
Education Expenditures: n.a.
External Debt: US$6.676 billion (2001)
Exports: US$749 million (2002 est.); commodities: gold, coffee, cashew nuts, manufactures, cotton; partners: Germany, Japan, India, Belgium
Imports: US$1.691 billion (2002 est.); commodities: manufactured goods, machinery and transportation equipment, cotton piece goods, crude oil, foodstuffs; partners: Australia, Japan, UK, South Africa

■ COMMUNICATIONS

Daily Newspapers: 4/1,000 inhabitants (2000)
Televisions: 42/1,000 inhabitants (2001)
Radios: 406/1,000 inhabitants (2001)
Telephones: 4 lines/1,000 inhabitants (2001)

■ TRANSPORTATION

Motor Vehicles: 133,800; 55,000 passenger cars
Roads: 85,000 km; 4,250 paved
Railway: 3,569 km
Air Traffic: 171,000 passengers carried (2001)
Airports: 125; 11 have paved runways (2002)

Canadian Embassy: The Canadian High Commission, 38 Mirambo St, Dar-es-Salaam; mailing address: P.O. Box 1022, Dar-es-Salaam,

Tanzania. Tel: (011-255-22) 211-2831. Fax: (011-255-22) 211-6897. e-mail: dslam@dfait-maeci.gc.ca

Embassy in Canada: High Commission for the United Republic of Tanzania, 50 Range Rd, Ottawa ON, K1N 8J4. Tel: (613) 232-1500. Fax: (613) 232-5184. e-mail: tzottawa@synapse.net

Thailand

Long-Form Name: Kingdom of Thailand
Capital: Bangkok

■ GEOGRAPHY

Area: 514,000 sq. km
Coastline: 3,219 km
Climate: tropical; rainy, warm, cloudy southwest monsoon (mid-May to Sept.); dry, cool, north-east monsoon (Nov. to mid-Mar.); southern isthmus always hot and humid
Environment: air and water pollution; land subsidence in Bangkok area; deforestation; soil erosion; illegal hunting threatens wildlife populations
Terrain: central plain; eastern plateau (Khorat); mountains elsewhere
Land Use: 34% arable; 6% permanent crops; 2% permanent pastures; 26% forest; 32% other; includes 47,490 sq. km irrigated
Location: SE Asia, bordering on Gulf of Siam and Andaman Sea

■ PEOPLE

Population: 62,354,402 (July 2002 est.)
Nationality: Thai (sing. & pl.)
Age Structure: 0–14 yrs: 23.3%; 15–64: 69.9%; 65+: 6.8% (2002 est.)
Population Growth Rate: 0.88% (2002 est.)
Net Migration: 0 migrants/1,000 population (2002 est.)
Ethnic Groups: 75% Thai, 14% Chinese, 11% other
Languages: Thai; English is the secondary language of the elite; small minorities speak Chinese, Malay, indigenous languages
Religions: 95% Buddhist (Theravada), 3.8% Muslim, 0.5% Christianity, 0.1% Hinduism, 0.6% other
Birth Rate: 16.39/1,000 population (2002 est.)
Death Rate: 7.55/1,000 population (2002 est.)
Infant Mortality: 29.50 deaths/1,000 live births (2002 est.)
Life Expectancy at Birth: 66.00 years male, 72.51 years female (2002 est.)
Total Fertility Rate: 1.86 children born/woman (2002 est.)
Literacy: 95.5% (2000)

■ GOVERNMENT

Leader(s): King Phumiphon Adunyadet (Rama IX), Prem. Thaksin Chinnawat
Government Type: constitutional monarchy
Administrative Divisions: 76 provinces (changwat, sing. & pl.)
Nationhood: 1238 (traditional founding date); never colonized
National Holiday: Birthday of His Majesty the King, Dec. 5

■ ECONOMY

Overview: with the currency depreciation and the collapse of domestic demands, imports have fallen by more than a third recently; foreign investment for new projects, the long-time catalyst of Thailand's economic growth, has also slowed
GDP: US$410 billion, per capita US$6,600; real growth rate 1.4% (2001 est.)
Inflation: 1.7% (2001)
Industries: accounts for 40% of GDP (2000), tourism is the largest source of foreign exchange; textiles and garments, agricultural processing, beverages, tobacco, cement, other light manufacturing, such as jewellery; electric appliances and components, integrated circuits, furniture, plastics
Labour Force: 37.2 million (2001); 54% agriculture, 31% services, 15% industry
Unemployment: 2.4% (2001)
Agriculture: accounts for 11% of GDP (2001) and 57% of labour force; leading producer and exporter of rice and cassava; other crops: rubber, corn, sugar cane, coconuts, soybeans; self-sufficient in food except for wheat
Natural Resources: tin, rubber, natural gas, tungsten, tantalum, timber, lead, fish, gypsum, lignite, fluorite

■ FINANCE/TRADE

Currency: baht (pl. baht) (B) = 100 satang
International Reserves Excluding Gold: US$38.046 billion (Dec. 2002)
Gold Reserves: 2.503 million fine troy ounces (Dec. 2002)
Budget: revenues US$19 billion; expenditures US$21 billion, including capital expenditures of US$ n.a. (2000 est.)
Defence Expenditures: 7.1% of central government expenditure (2001)
Education Expenditures: 22.45% of government expenditure (2000)
External Debt: US$67.384 billion (2001)
Exports: US$68.852 billion (2002); commodities: textiles 12%, fishery products 12%, rice 8%, tapioca 8%, jewellery 6%, manufactured gas, corn, tin; partners: US, Japan, Singapore, Malaysia, Hong Kong, China

Imports: US$64.721 billion (2002); commodities: machinery and parts 23%, petroleum products 13%, chemicals 11%, iron and steel, electrical appliances; partners: Japan, US, Singapore, Malaysia, China, Taiwan

■ COMMUNICATIONS

Daily Newspapers: 64/1,000 inhabitants (2000)
Televisions: 300/1,000 inhabitants (2001)
Radios: 235/1,000 inhabitants (2001)
Telephones: 99 lines/1,000 inhabitants (2001)

■ TRANSPORTATION

Motor Vehicles: 5,700,000; 1,550,000 passenger cars
Roads: 64,600 km; 62,985 km paved
Railway: 4,071 km
Air Traffic: 17,662,000 passengers carried (2001)
Airports: 110; 62 have paved runways (2002)

Canadian Embassy: The Canadian Embassy, 990 Rama IV, Abdulrahim Place, 15th Fl, Bangkok 10500, Thailand; mailing address: P.O. Box 2090, Bangkok 10501, Thailand. Tel: (011-66-2) 636-0540. Fax: (011-66-2) 636-0566. e-mail: bngkk@dfait-maeci.gc.ca
Embassy in Canada: The Royal Thai Embassy, 180 Island Park Dr, Ottawa ON K1Y 0A2. Tel: (613) 722-4444. Fax: (613) 722-6624. e-mail: thaicommott@sympatico.ca

Togo

Long-Form Name: Togolese Republic
Capital: Lomé

■ GEOGRAPHY

Area: 56,785 sq. km
Coastline: 56 km
Climate: tropical; hot, humid in south; semi-arid in north
Environment: hot, dry harmattan wind; recent droughts affecting agriculture; deforestation
Terrain: gently rolling savanna in north; low coastal plain with extensive lagoons and marshes
Land Use: 38% arable; 7% permanent crops; 4% meadows; 17% forest; 34% other; includes 70 sq. km irrigated
Location: WC Africa, bordering on South Atlantic Ocean

■ PEOPLE

Population: 5,285,501 (July 2002 est.)
Nationality: Togolese (sing. & pl.)
Age Structure: 0–14 yrs: 45.1%; 15–64: 52.4%; 65+: 2.5% (2002 est.)
Population Growth Rate: 2.48% (2002 est.)
Net Migration: 0 migrants/1,000 population (2002 est.)

Ethnic Groups: 37 tribes; largest and most important are Ewe, Mina and Kabyè; under 1% European and Syrian-Lebanese
Languages: French, both official and language of commerce; major African languages are Ewe and Mina in the south and Dagomba and Kabyè in the north
Religions: about 70% indigenous beliefs, 20% Christian, 10% Muslim
Birth Rate: 36.11/1,000 population (2002 est.)
Death Rate: 11.30/1,000 population (2002 est.)
Infant Mortality: 69.32 deaths/1,000 live births (2002 est.)
Life Expectancy at Birth: 52.03 years male, 56.07 years female (2002 est.)
Total Fertility Rate: 5.14 children born/woman (2002 est.)
Literacy: 57.1% (2000)

■ GOVERNMENT

Leader(s): Pres. Gen. Gnassingbé Eyadéma, Prime Min. Koffi Sama
Government Type: republic; one-party presidential regime under transition to multiparty democratic rule
Administrative Divisions: 5 regions
Nationhood: Apr. 27, 1960 (from UN trusteeship under French administration; formerly known as French Togo)
National Holiday: Independence Day, Apr. 27

■ ECONOMY

Overview: an underdeveloped country that is heavily dependent on subsistence agriculture and phosphate mining; self-sufficient in basic foodstuffs when harvests are normal; political unrest and widespread strikes have interfered with economic activity
GDP: US$7.6 billion, per capita US$1,500; real growth rate 2.2% (2001 est.)
Inflation: 5.4% (2001)
Industries: accounts for 21% of GDP (2001 est.); phosphate mining, agricultural processing, cement, handicrafts, textiles, beverages
Labour Force: 1.9 million (2001); 65% agriculture, 5% industry, 30% services
Unemployment: n.a.
Agriculture: accounts for 42% of GDP (2001 est.) and 64% of labour force; cash crops: coffee, cocoa, cotton; food crops: yams, cassava, corn, beans, rice, millet, sorghum, fish, livestock
Natural Resources: phosphates, limestone, marble, arable land

■ FINANCE/TRADE

Currency: Communauté financière africaine franc (CFAF) = 100 centimes
International Reserves Excluding Gold: US$199 million (Oct. 2002)

Gold Reserves: none (Dec. 2002)
Budget: n.a.
Defence Expenditures: 9.4% of central government expenditure (1999)
Education Expenditures: n.a.
External Debt: US$1.406 billion (2001)
Exports: US$251 million (2002); commodities: phosphates, cocoa, coffee, cotton, manufactures, palm kernels; partners: Benin, Nigeria, Belgium, Ghana
Imports: US$590 million (2001); commodities: food, fuels, durable consumer goods, other intermediate goods, capital goods; partners: Ghana, China, France, Côte d'Ivoire

■ COMMUNICATIONS

Daily Newspapers: 2/1,000 inhabitants (2000)
Televisions: 37/1,000 inhabitants (2001)
Radios: 265/1,000 inhabitants (2001)
Telephones: 10 lines/1,000 inhabitants (2001)

■ TRANSPORTATION

Motor Vehicles: 110,000; 75,000 passenger cars
Roads: 7,520 km; 2,376 km paved
Railway: 525 km
Air Traffic: 46,000 passengers carried (2001)
Airports: 9; 2 have paved runways (2002)

Canadian Embassy: The Canadian Embassy to Togo, c/o Canadian High Commission, 42 Independence Ave, Accra, Ghana; P.O. Box 1639, Accra, Ghana. Tel: (011-233-21) 22-85-55. Fax: (011-233-21) 77-37-92. e-mail: accra@dfait-maeci.gc.ca
Embassy in Canada: Embassy of the Republic of Togo, 12 Range Rd, Ottawa ON K1N 8J3. Tel: (613) 238-5916. Fax: (613) 235-6425. e-mail: n.a.

Tokelau

Long-Form Name: Tokelau
Capital: none; each atoll has its own administrative centre

■ GEOGRAPHY

Area: 10 sq. km, 3 atolls
Climate: tropical maritime, moderated by trade winds (April–Nov.)
Land Use: 0% arable; permanent crops; meadows/pastures or forests; 100% other; includes no irrigated land
Location: S Pacific Ocean, NE of Australia

■ PEOPLE

Population: 1,431 (July 2002 est.)
Nationality: Tokelauan
Ethnic Groups: Polynesian
Languages: Tokelauan, English

■ GOVERNMENT

Colony/Territory of: Overseas Territory of New Zealand
Leader(s): Head of State: Queen Elizabeth II, Administrator Lindsay Watt
Government Type: territory of New Zealand
National Holiday: Waitangi Day, Feb. 6

■ ECONOMY

Overview: Tokelau's small size, great distance from markets and lack of resources greatly hinder economic development; copra is only agricultural product of significance; the people rely on aid from New Zealand, supplemented by revenue from postage stamps, souvenir coins, and handicrafts

■ FINANCE/TRADE

Currency: New Zealand dollar = 100 cents

Canadian Embassy: c/o The Canadian High Commission, 3rd Fl, 61 Molesworth St. Thorndon, Wellington, New Zealand; mailing address: P.O. Box 12049, Thorndon, Wellington, New Zealand. Tel: (011-64-4) 6270-4000. Fax: (011-64-4) 471-2082. e-mail: wlgtn@dfait-maeci.gc.ca
Representative to Canada: c/o New Zealand High Commission, Clarica Centre, 99 Bank St, Ste 727, Ottawa ON K1P 6G3. Tel: (613) 238-5991. Fax: (613) 238-5707. e-mail: nzhcott@istar.ca

Tonga

Long-Form Name: Kingdom of Tonga
Capital: Nuku'alofa

■ GEOGRAPHY

Area: 748 sq. km; archipelago of 170 islands, of which 36 are inhabited
Coastline: 419 km
Climate: tropical; modified by trade winds; warm season (Dec. to May), cool season (May to Dec.)
Environment: subject to cyclones (Oct. to Apr.); deforestation and overhunting of native animals
Terrain: most islands have limestone base formed from uplifted coral formation; others have limestone overlying volcanic base
Land Use: 24% arable; 43% permanent crops; 6% meadows; 11% forest; 16% other; includes n.a. sq. km irrigated
Location: Pacific Ocean, NW of New Zealand

■ PEOPLE

Population: 106,137 (July 2002 est.)
Nationality: Tongan
Age Structure: 0–14 yrs: 39.5%; 15–64: 56.4%; 65+: 4.1% (2002 est.)
Population Growth Rate: 1.85% (2002 est.)

Net Migration: 0 migrants/1,000 population (2002 est.)
Ethnic Groups: Polynesian; about 300 Europeans
Languages: Tongan, English
Religions: Christian; Free Wesleyan Church claims over 30,000 adherents
Birth Rate: 24.08/1,000 population (2002 est.)
Death Rate: 5.63/1,000 population (2002 est.)
Infant Mortality: 13.72 deaths/1,000 live births (2002 est.)
Life Expectancy at Birth: 66.13 years male, 71.11 years female (2002 est.)
Total Fertility Rate: 3.0 children born/woman (2002 est.)
Literacy: n.a.

■ GOVERNMENT

Leader(s): King Taufa'ahau Tupou IV, Prime Min. Prince Lavaka ata Ulukalala
Government Type: hereditary constitutional monarchy
Administrative Divisions: three island groups
Nationhood: June 4, 1970 (from UK; formerly known as Friendly Islands)
National Holiday: Independence Day, June 4

■ ECONOMY

Overview: the economy's base is agriculture though the country must import a high proportion of its food, for the most part from New Zealand; tourism is the main source of hard currency; the country also remains dependent on sizeable external aid and remittances to offset its trade deficit
GDP: US$225 million, per capita US$2,200; real growth rate 5.3% (2000 est.)
Inflation: 8.3% (2001)
Industries: accounts for 10% of GDP (2001 est.); tourism, fishing
Labour Force: n.a.; 65% agriculture, 35% mining
Unemployment: n.a.
Agriculture: accounts for 30% of GDP and 70% of labour force; dominated by coconut, copra and banana production; squash, vanilla beans, cocoa, coffee, ginger, black pepper, fish
Natural Resources: fish, fertile soil

■ FINANCE/TRADE

Currency: pa'anga ($T) = 100 seniti
International Reserves Excluding Gold: US$28 million (Dec. 2002)
Gold Reserves: n.a.
Budget: revenues US$39.9 million, expenditures US$54.2 million, including capital expenditures of US$1.9 million (FY1999/2000 est.)
Defence Expenditures: n.a.
Education Expenditures: n.a.
External Debt: US$63 million (2001)
Exports: US$12 million (2000); commodities: coconut oil, desiccated coconut, copra, bananas, taro, vanilla beans, fruit, vegetables, fish; partners: New Zealand, Australia, US, Fiji, Japan
Imports: US$74 million (2000); commodities: food products, beverages, tobacco, fuels, machinery, transport equipment, chemicals, building materials; partners: New Zealand, Australia, Japan, US, Fiji

■ COMMUNICATIONS

Daily Newspapers: 1 in total
Televisions: n.a.
Radios: n.a.
Telephones: 93 lines/1,000 inhabitants (1999)

■ TRANSPORTATION

Motor Vehicles: n.a.
Roads: 680 km; 184 km paved
Railway: none
Air Traffic: 54,000 passengers carried (1999 est.)
Airports: 6; 1 has a paved runways (2002)

Canadian Embassy: The Canadian High Commission to Tonga, c/o The Canadian High Commission, 61 Molesworth St, 3rd Floor, Thorndon, Wellington; mailing address: P.O. Box 12-049, Thorndon, Wellington, New Zealand. Tel: (011-64-4) 473-9577. Fax: (011-64-4) 471-2082. e-mail: wlgtn@dfait-maeci.gc.ca
Embassy in Canada: c/o Embassy of the Kingdom of Tonga, 250 East 51st St, New York NY 10022, USA. Tel: (917) 369-1025. Fax: (917) 369-1024. e-mail: n.a.

Trinidad and Tobago

Long-Form Name: Republic of Trinidad and Tobago
Capital: Port of Spain

■ GEOGRAPHY

Area: 5,128 sq. km
Coastline: 362 km
Climate: tropical; rainy season (June to Dec.)
Environment: outside usual path of hurricanes and other tropical storms; water pollution and soil deterioration; oil pollution of beaches
Terrain: mostly plains with some hills and low mountains
Land Use: 15% arable; 9% permanent crops; 2% meadows; 46% forest; 28% other; includes 30 sq. km irrigated
Location: West Indies, off N coast of South America

■ PEOPLE

Population: 1,163,724 (July 2002 est.)
Nationality: Trinidadian, Tobagonian
Age Structure: 0–14 yrs: 23.0%; 15–64: 70.2%; 65+: 6.8% (2002 est.)

Population Growth Rate: -0.52% (2002 est.)
Net Migration: -10.02 migrants/1,000 population (2002 est.)
Ethnic Groups: 40% black, 40% East Indian, 14% mixed, 1% white, 1% Chinese, 4% other
Languages: English (official), Hindi, French, Spanish, Chinese
Religions: Christianity 61%, Hinduism 24%, Islam 6%, 9% other
Birth Rate: 13.66/1,000 population (2002 est.)
Death Rate: 8.81/1,000 population (2002 est.)
Infant Mortality: 24.20 deaths/1,000 live births (2002 est.)
Life Expectancy at Birth: 66.04 years male, 71.25 years female (2002 est.)
Total Fertility Rate: 1.80 children born/woman (2002 est.)
Literacy: 93.8% (2000)

■ GOVERNMENT

Leader(s): Pres. George Maxwell Richards, Prime Min. Patrick Manning
Government Type: parliamentary democracy
Administrative Divisions: 8 counties, 3 municipalities and 1 ward
Nationhood: Aug. 31, 1962 (from UK)
National Holiday: Independence Day, Aug. 31

■ ECONOMY

Overview: the economy has suffered in recent years because of the sharp decline in the price of oil; the unemployment rate has risen due to the government's austerity programs; the government is seeking to diversify the country's export base
GDP: US$10.6 billion, per capita US$9,000; real growth rate 4.0% (2001 est.)
Inflation: 3.6% (2000)
Industries: accounts for 43% of GDP (2000); petroleum, chemicals, tourism, food processing, cement, beverage, cotton textiles
Labour Force: 600,000 (2001); 64% community, social and business services, 10% agriculture, 12% construction
Unemployment: 13.1% (2001)
Agriculture: accounts for approx. 2% of GDP (2000); highly subsidized sector; major crops: cocoa and sugar cane; sugar cane acreage is being shifted into rice, citrus, coffee, vegetables; must import large share of food needs
Natural Resources: crude oil, natural gas, asphalt

■ FINANCE/TRADE

Currency: Trinidad and Tobago dollar ($TT) = 100 cents
International Reserves Excluding Gold: US$2.062 billion (Oct. 2002)
Gold Reserves: 0.061 million fine troy ounces (Oct. 2002)
Budget: n.a.

Defence Expenditures: 5.5% of central government expenditure (1999)
Education Expenditures: n.a.
External Debt: US$2.422 billion (2001)
Exports: US$3.928 billion (2002 est.); commodities (including re-exports): petroleum and petroleum products 70%, fertilizer, chemicals 15%, steel products, sugar, cocoa, coffee, citrus; partners: US, CARICOM countries, Latin America, EU
Imports: US$3.428 billion (2002 est.); commodities: raw materials 41%, capital goods 30%, consumer goods 29%; partners: US, Venezuela, EU, CARICOM countries

■ COMMUNICATIONS

Daily Newspapers: 123/1,000 inhabitants (2000)
Televisions: 340/1,000 inhabitants (2001)
Radios: 532/1,000 inhabitants (2001)
Telephones: 240 lines/1,000 inhabitants (2001)

■ TRANSPORTATION

Motor Vehicles: 155,000; 128,000 passenger cars
Roads: 8,320 km; 4,252 km paved
Railway: minimal agricultural railway system near San Fernando
Air Traffic: 1,124,000 passengers carried (2001)
Airports: 6; 3 have paved runways (2002)

Canadian Embassy: The Canadian High Commission, Maple House, 3-3A Sweet Briar Road, St. Clair, Port-of-Spain, Trinidad and Tobago; mailing address: P.O. Box 1246, Port-of-Spain, Trinidad and Tobago. Tel: (868) 622-6232. Fax: (868) 628-1830. e-mail: pspan-ag@dfait-maeci.gc.ca
Embassy in Canada: High Commission for the Republic of Trinidad and Tobago, 200 First Ave, 3rd Level, Ottawa ON K1S 2G6. Tel: (613) 232-2418. Fax: (613) 232-4349. e-mail: ottawa@ttmissions.com

Tunisia

Long-Form Name: Republic of Tunisia
Capital: Tunis

■ GEOGRAPHY

Area: 163,610 sq. km
Coastline: 1,148 km
Climate: temperate in north with mild, rainy winters and hot, dry summers; desert in south
Environment: deforestation; overgrazing; soil erosion; desertification; ineffective disposal of toxic and hazardous wastes
Terrain: mountains in north; hot, dry central plain; semi-arid south merges into the Sahara
Land Use: 19% arable; 13% permanent crops; 20% meadows; 4% forest; 44% other; includes 3,800 sq. km irrigated

Location: N Africa, bordering on Mediterranean Sea

■ PEOPLE

Population: 9,815,644 (July 2002 est.)
Nationality: Tunisian
Age Structure: 0–14 yrs: 27.8%; 15–64: 65.9%; 65+: 6.3% (2002 est.)
Population Growth Rate: 1.12% (2002 est.)
Net Migration: -0.63 migrants/1,000 population (2002 est.)
Ethnic Groups: 98% Arab-Berber, 1% European, less than 1% Jewish
Languages: Arabic (official); Arabic and French (commerce)
Religions: 98% Muslim, 1% Christian, less than 1% Jewish
Birth Rate: 16.83/1,000 population (2002 est.)
Death Rate: 5.00/1,000 population (2002 est.)
Infant Mortality: 27.97 deaths/1,000 live births (2002 est.)
Life Expectancy at Birth: 72.56 years male, 75.89 years female (2002 est.)
Total Fertility Rate: 1.94 children born/woman (2002 est.)
Literacy: 71.0% (2000)

■ GOVERNMENT

Leader(s): Pres. Gen. Zine El Abidine Ben Ali, Prime Min. Mohamed Ghannouchi
Government Type: republic
Administrative Divisions: 23 governorates
Nationhood: Mar. 20, 1956 (from France)
National Holiday: Independence Day, Mar. 20

■ ECONOMY

Overview: diverse economy, with important agriculture, mining, energy, tourism, and manufacturing sectors; governmental control of economic affairs has gradually lessened over the past decade with increasing privatization of trade and commerce, simplification of the tax structure, and a prudent approach to debt
GDP: US$64.5 billion, per capita US$6,600; real growth rate 4.8% (2001 est.)
Inflation: 1.9% (2001)
Industries: accounts for 28% of GDP (2000); petroleum, mining (particularly phosphate and iron ore), textiles, footwear, food, beverages, tourism
Labour Force: 3.9 million (2001); 22% agriculture, 23% industry, 55% services
Unemployment: 15.6% (2000 est.)
Agriculture: accounts for 12% of GDP (2000); output subject to severe fluctuations because of frequent droughts; export crops: olives, dates, oranges, almonds; other products: grain, sugar beets, wine grapes, poultry, beef, dairy; not self-sufficient in food

Natural Resources: crude oil, phosphates, iron ore, lead, zinc, salt, arable land

■ FINANCE/TRADE

Currency: Tunisian dinar (D) = 1,000 millimes
International Reserves Excluding Gold: US$2.211 billion (Oct. 2002)
Gold Reserves: 0.218 million fine troy ounces (Oct. 2002)
Budget: revenues US$5.7 billion; expenditures US$6.3 billion, including capital expenditures of US$1.5 billion (2001 est.)
Defence Expenditures: 5.2% of central government expenditure (2001)
Education Expenditures: 18.01% of total government expenditure (2000)
External Debt: US$10.884 billion (2001)
Exports: US$6.799 billion (2002); commodities: hydrocarbons, agricultural products, phosphates and chemicals; partners: France, Italy, Germany, Belgium, Libya
Imports: US$9.527 billion (2002); commodities: industrial goods and equipment 57%, hydrocarbons 13%, food 12%, consumer goods; partners: France, Germany, Italy, Spain, Belgium

■ COMMUNICATIONS

Daily Newspapers: 19/1,000 inhabitants (2000)
Televisions: 198/1,000 inhabitants (2001)
Radios: 158/1,000 inhabitants (2001)
Telephones: 109 lines/1,000 inhabitants (2001)

■ TRANSPORTATION

Motor Vehicles: 531,000; 248,000 passenger cars
Roads: 23,100 km; 18,226 km paved
Railway: 2,168 km (2001)
Air Traffic: 1,926,000 passengers carried (2001)
Airports: 30; 14 have paved runways (2002)

Canadian Embassy: Canadian Embassy, 3, rue du Sénégal, Place d'Afrique, 1002 Tunis-Belvedere, Tunisia; mailing address: CP 31, Le Belvédère, 1002, Tunis-Belvedere, Tunisia. Tel: (011-216-71) 104-000. Fax: (011-216-71) 104-191. e-mail: tunis@dfait-maeci.gc.ca
Embassy in Canada: Embassy of the Republic of Tunisia, 515 O'Connor St, Ottawa ON, K1S 3P8. Tel: (613) 237-0330. Fax: (613) 237-7939. e-mail: n.a.

Turkey

Long-Form Name: Republic of Turkey
Capital: Ankara

■ GEOGRAPHY

Area: 780,580 sq. km
Coastline: 7,200 km

Climate: temperate; hot, dry summers with mild, wet winters; harsher in interior
Environment: subject to severe earthquakes, especially along major river valleys in west; water and air pollution; desertification
Terrain: mostly mountains; narrow coastal plain; high central plateau (Anatolia)
Land Use: 32% arable; 4% permanent crops; 16% meadows; 26% forest; 22% other; includes 42,000 sq. km irrigated
Location: SW Asia (Near East), bordering on Mediterranean Sea, Black Sea, Aegean Sea

■ PEOPLE

Population: 67,308,928 (July 2002 est.)
Nationality: Turk
Age Structure: 0–14 yrs: 27.8%; 15–64: 65.9%; 65+: 6.3% (2002 est.)
Population Growth Rate: 1.20% (2002 est.)
Net Migration: 0 migrants/1,000 population (2002 est.)
Ethnic Groups: 80% Turkish, 20% Kurd
Languages: Turkish (official), Kurdish 7%, Arabic; English (business language)
Religions: 99.8% Muslim (mostly Sunni), 0.2% other (mostly Christian and Jewish)
Birth Rate: 17.95/1,000 population (2002 est.)
Death Rate: 5.95/1,000 population (2002 est.)
Infant Mortality: 45.77 deaths/1,000 live births (2002 est.)
Life Expectancy at Birth: 69.15 years male, 74.01 years female (2002 est.)
Total Fertility Rate: 2.07 children born/woman (2002 est.)
Literacy: 85.1% (2000)

■ GOVERNMENT

Leader(s): Pres. Ahmet Necdet Sezer, Prime Min. Recep Tayyip Erdogan
Government Type: republican parliamentary democracy
Administrative Divisions: 80 provinces (iller, sing. —il)
Nationhood: Oct. 29, 1923 (successor state to the Ottoman Empire)
National Holiday: Anniversary of the Declaration of the Republic, Oct. 29

■ ECONOMY

Overview: has a strong and rapidly growing private sector, yet the state still plays a major role in basic industry, banking, transport and communications; its most important industry and largest export is textiles and clothing, which are almost entirely in private hands. Note: Major economic disruption in August 1999 due to a massive earthquake
GDP: US$468 billion, per capita US$7,000; real growth rate 4.2% (2002 est.)
Inflation: 54.4% (2001)

Industries: accounts for 30% of GDP (2001); textiles, food processing, mining (coal, chromite, copper, boron minerals), steel, petroleum, construction, lumber, paper
Labour Force: 31.9 million (2001); 40% agriculture, 22% industry, 38% community, social and business services; about 1,000,000 Turks work abroad
Unemployment: 8.3% (2001).
Agriculture: accounts for 13% of GDP (2001) and 46% the labour force; products: tobacco, cotton, grain, olives, sugar beets, pulses, citrus fruit, variety of animal products; self-sufficient in food most years
Natural Resources: antimony, coal, chromium, mercury, copper, borate, sulphur, iron ore

■ FINANCE/TRADE

Currency: Turkish lira (TL) = 100 kurus
International Reserves Excluding Gold: US$27.069 billion (Dec. 2002)
Gold Reserves: 3.733 million fine troy ounces (Dec. 2002)
Budget: revenues US$42.4 billion; expenditures US$69.1 billion, including capital expenditures of US$ n.a. (2001)
Defence Expenditures: 10% of central government expenditure (2001)
Education Expenditures: 9.63% of total government expenditure (2000)
External Debt: US$115.118 billion (2001)
Exports: US$33.277 billion (2002 est.); commodities: industrial products 70%, crops and livestock products 25%; partners: Germany, US, Italy, UK, France, Russia
Imports: US$46.828 billion (2002 est.); commodities: crude oil, machinery, transport equipment, metals, pharmaceuticals, dyes, plastics, rubber, mineral fuels, fertilizers, chemicals; partners: Germany, Italy, Russia, US, France, UK

■ COMMUNICATIONS

Daily Newspapers: 511/1,000 inhabitants (2000)
Televisions: 319/1,000 inhabitants (2001)
Radios: 487/1,000 inhabitants (2001)
Telephones: 285 lines/1,000 inhabitants (2001)

■ TRANSPORTATION

Motor Vehicles: 5,600,000; 4,200,000 passenger cars (2000)
Roads: 382,059 km; 106,976 km paved (1999)
Railway: 8,607 km operational (2001)
Air Traffic: 9,905,000 passengers carried (2001)
Airports: 120; 86 have paved runways (2002)

Canadian Embassy: The Canadian Embassy, Nenehatun Caddesi 75, Gaziosmanpasa, 06700 Ankara, Turkey. Tel: (011-90-312) 459-9200.

Fax: (011-90-312) 459-9361. e-mail: ankra@
dfait-maeci.gc.ca
Embassy in Canada: Embassy of the Republic of
Turkey, 197 Wurtemburg St, Ottawa ON K1N
8L9. Tel: (613) 789-4044. Fax: (613) 789-3442.
e-mail: turkishottawa@mfa.gov.tr

Turkmenistan

Long-Form Name: Turkmenistan
Capital: Ashkhabad

■ GEOGRAPHY

Area: 488,100 sq. km
Coastline: landlocked; 1,768 km inland coastline
along Caspian Sea
Climate: subtropical desert; long, extremely hot
summers; short and cold winters; rainfall occurs
only in the mountains
Environment: soil and groundwater contaminated
with chemicals and pesticides; salinization and
waterlogging of soil due to poor irrigation
methods; desertification in some areas; prone to
earthquakes
Terrain: flat to rolling sandy desert; Caspian Sea
in west
Land Use: 3% arable; 0% permanent crops; 63%
pastures and meadows; 8% forests; 26% other;
includes 18,000 sq. km irrigated
Location: WC Asia, bordering on Caspian Sea

■ PEOPLE

Population: 4,688,963 (July 2002 est.)
Nationality: Turkmen
Age Structure: 0–14 yrs: 37.3%; 15–64: 58.6%;
65+: 4.1% (2002 est.)
Population Growth Rate: 1.84% (2002 est.)
Net Migration: -0.98 migrants/1,000 population
(2002 est.)
Ethnic Groups: 77% Turkmen, 6.7% Russian,
9.2% Uzbek, 2% Kazakh, 5.1% other
Languages: 72% Turkmen (official), 12%
Russian, 9% Uzbek, 7% other
Religions: 89% Muslim, 9% Eastern Orthodox,
2% unknown
Birth Rate: 28.27/1,000 population (2002 est.)
Death Rate: 8.92/1,000 population (2002 est.)
Infant Mortality: 73.21 deaths/1,000 live births
(2002 est.)
Life Expectancy at Birth: 57.57 years male, 64.80
years female (2002 est.)
Total Fertility Rate: 3.54 children born/woman
(2002 est.)
Literacy: 98% (1999)

■ GOVERNMENT

Leader(s): Pres. Saparmurad Niyazov
Government Type: republic
Administrative Divisions: 5 regions (welayatlar,
sing. —welayat)

Nationhood: Oct. 27, 1991 (from Soviet Union)
National Holiday: Independence Day, Oct. 27

■ ECONOMY

Overview: mining produces the greatest part of
Turkmenistan's economic production value, but
agriculture is the chief occupation; industry
leans heavily toward the energy sector (gas, oil),
but the lack of pipeline access to hard currency
markets limits expansion; efforts at gas and oil
export expansion will take many more years to
pay off. Privatization goals remain limited.
GDP: US$21.5 billion, per capita US$4,700; real
growth rate 10.0% (2001 est.)
Inflation: 14% (2000 est.)
Industries: accounts for 45% of GDP (2000); oil
production and refining, natural gas extraction,
chemicals, electrical engineering, fertilizer,
carpets, textiles and clothing, food processing
Labour Force: 2.4 million (2001); 48% agriculture and forestry, 15% industry and construction, 37% services
Unemployment: n.a.
Agriculture: accounts for 27% of GDP (2000);
irrigation is mandatory for agriculture; products
include cotton, grains, livestock, fish
Natural Resources: extensive mineral deposits,
including the world's largest sulfur deposits; oil,
natural gas, coal, potassium, salts, sulphur

■ FINANCE/TRADE

Currency: manat = 100 tenesi
International Reserves Excluding Gold: n.a.
Gold Reserves: n.a.
Budget: revenues US$588.6 million, expendi-
tures US$658.2 million, including capital
expenditures of US$ n.a. (1999 est.)
Defence Expenditures: 16.0% of central govern-
ment expenditure (1999)
Education Expenditures: n.a.
External Debt: US$2.5 billion (2000 est.)
Exports: US$2.333 billion (2000); oil, natural
gas, electric power, clothing and textiles,
petroleum products, carpets; partners: Turkey,
Ukraine, Iran, Italy, Switzerland
Imports: US$1.014 billion (2000); machinery,
foodstuffs, consumer products, plastics and
rubber, textiles; partners: Ukraine, Russia,
Turkey, UAE, France

■ COMMUNICATIONS

Daily Newspapers: 7/1,000 inhabitants (2000)
Televisions: 196/1,000 inhabitants (2001)
Radios: 256/1,000 inhabitants (2001)
Telephones: 80 lines/1,000 inhabitants (2001)

■ TRANSPORTATION

Motor Vehicles: n.a.
Roads: 24,000 km; 19,488 km paved
Railway: 2,440 km (2001)

Air Traffic: 1,407,000 passengers carried (2001)
Airports: 76; 13 have paved runways (2002)

Canadian Embassy: c/o The Canadian Embassy, Nenehatun Caddesi 75, Gaziosmanpasa 06700, Ankara, Turkey. Tel: (011-90-312) 459-9200. Fax: (011-90-312) 459-9361. e-mail: ankra@ dfait-maeci.gc.ca

Embassy in Canada: c/o Embassy of the Republic of Turkmenistan, 2207 Massachusetts Ave NW, Washington DC 20008, USA. Tel: (202) 588-1500. Fax: (202) 588-0697. e-mail: n.a.

Turks and Caicos

Long-Form Name: The Turks and Caicos Islands
Capital: Cockburn Town (on Grand Turk Island)

■ GEOGRAPHY

Area: 430 sq. km; 30+ small cays, of which only 8 are inhabited
Climate: sunny, relatively dry, equable climate with moderating winds; occasional hurricanes
Land Use: 2% arable; 0% permanent crops; meadows; forests; 98% other; includes n.a. sq. km irrigated
Location: West Indies (S Atlantic Ocean), N of Dominican Republic

■ PEOPLE

Population: 18,738 (July 2002 est.)
Nationality: none (British citizens)
Ethnic Groups: black majority
Languages: English (official)

■ GOVERNMENT

Colony/Territory of: Colony of the United Kingdom
Leader(s): Head of State: Queen Elizabeth II, Gov. Mervyn Jones, Head of government: Chief Min. Derek H. Taylor
Government Type: dependent territory of the United Kingdom
National Holiday: Constitution Day, Aug. 30

■ ECONOMY

Overview: fishing is the most important activity; exports include lobster, conch, other fish products; imports include food and drink, tobacco, maufactured goods; tourism; offshore banking; chief trading partner: US

■ FINANCE/TRADE

Currency: US dollar (US$) = 100 cents

Canadian Embassy: c/o The Canadian High Commission, Macdonald House, 1 Grosvenor Square, London W1K 4AB, England, UK. Tel: (011-44-20) 7258-6600. Fax: (011-44-20) 7258-6333. e-mail: ldn@dfait-maeci.gc.ca

Representative to Canada: c/o British High Commission, 80 Elgin St, Ottawa ON K1P 5K7. Tel: (613) 237-1530. Fax: (613) 237-7980. Email should be sent using the appropriate form at the British High Commission's Website at http://www.britain-in-canada.org

Tuvalu

Long-Form Name: Tuvalu
Capital: Funafuti

■ GEOGRAPHY

Area: 26 sq. km
Coastline: 24 km
Climate: tropical; moderated by easterly trade winds (Mar. to Nov.); westerly gales and heavy rain (Nov. to Mar.)
Environment: severe tropical storms are rare; no natural safe drinking water resources
Terrain: very low-lying and narrow coral atolls
Land Use: the 9 coral atolls have just enough soil to allow for subsistence agriculture; there are also coconut groves
Location: S Pacific Ocean, NE of Australia

■ PEOPLE

Population: 11,146 (July 2002 est.)
Nationality: Tuvaluan
Age Structure: 0–14 yrs: 32.6%; 15–64: 62.3%; 65+: 5.1% (2002 est.)
Population Growth Rate: 1.40% (2002 est.)
Net Migration: 0 migrants/1,000 population (2002 est.)
Ethnic Groups: 96% Polynesian
Languages: Tuvaluan, English
Religions: 97% Congregationalist (Church of Tuvalu), 1.4% Seventh Day Adventists, 1% Baha'i, 0.6% other
Birth Rate: 21.44/1,000 population (2002 est.)
Death Rate: 7.45/1,000 population (2002 est.)
Infant Mortality: 22.00 deaths/1,000 live births (2002 est.)
Life Expectancy at Birth: 64.83 years male, 69.23 years female (2002 est.)
Total Fertility Rate: 3.07 children born/woman (2002 est.)
Literacy: n.a.

■ GOVERNMENT

Leader(s): Head of State: Queen Elizabeth II, Gov. Gen. Sir Tomasi Puapua, Prime Min. Koloa Talake
Government Type: constitutional monarchy with a parliamentary democracy
Administrative Divisions: none
Nationhood: Oct. 1, 1978 from UK (formerly known as Ellice Islands)
National Holiday: Independence Day, Oct. 1

■ ECONOMY

Overview: scattered group of 9 coral atolls with poor soil; a small economy, no known mineral resources and few exports; receives money from the sale of stamps and coins and worker remittances as well as an international trust fund; subsistence farming and fishing are the primary economic activities
GDP: US$12.2 million; per capita US$1,100; real growth rate 3.0% (2000 est.)
Inflation: 7% (1999 est.)
Industries: fishing, tourism, copra, fish
Labour Force: n.a.
Unemployment: n.a.
Agriculture: coconuts, copra, fish
Natural Resources: fish

■ FINANCE/TRADE

Currency: Australian dollar ($A) or Tuvaluan dollar ($T) = 100 cents
International Reserves Excluding Gold: n.a.
Gold Reserves: n.a.
Budget: revenues US$22.5 million, expenditures US$11.2 million, including capital expenditures of US$4.2 million (2000 est.)
Defence Expenditures: n.a.
Education Expenditures: n.a.
External Debt: n.a.
Exports: n.a.; commodities: copra; partners: Fiji, Germany, Iceland, Sweden
Imports: n.a.; commodities: food, animals, fuels, machinery, manufactures; partners: Fiji, Australia, Portugal, New Zealand

■ COMMUNICATIONS

Daily Newspapers: none
Televisions: n.a.
Radios: n.a.
Telephones: n.a.

■ TRANSPORTATION

Motor Vehicles: n.a.
Roads: 8 km gravel roads
Railway: none
Air Traffic: n.a.
Airports: 1; no paved runway (2002)

Canadian Embassy: The Canadian High Commission to Tuvalu, c/o The Canadian High Commission, 61 Molesworth St, 3rd Fl, Thorndon, Wellington; mailing address: P.O. Box 12-049, Thorndon, Wellington, New Zealand. Tel: (011-64-4) 473-9577. Fax: (011-64-4) 471-2082. e-mail: wlgtn@dfait-maeci.gc.ca
Embassy in Canada: c/o New Zealand High Commission, Clarica Centre, 99 Bank St, Ste 727, Ottawa, ON K1P 6G3. Tel: (613) 238-5991. Fax: (613) 238-5707. e-mail: nzhcott@istar.ca

U.S. Virgin Islands

Long-Form Name: Virgin Islands of the United States
Capital: Charlotte Amalie

■ GEOGRAPHY

Area: 352 sq. km
Climate: subtropical, tempered by easterly trade winds, relatively low humidity, little seasonal temperature variation; rainy season May to Nov.
Land Use: 15% arable; 6% permanent crops; 26% meadows; 6% forest; 47% other; includes n.a. sq. km irrigated
Location: Caribbean islands, just E of Puerto Rico

■ PEOPLE

Population: 123,498 (July 2002 est.)
Nationality: Virgin Islander
Ethnic Groups: 74% West Indian (45% born in the Virgin Islands and 29% born elsewhere in the West Indies), 13% US mainland, 5% Puerto Rican, 8% other (80% black, 15% white, 5% other); 14% of Hispanic origin
Languages: English (official), but Spanish and Creole are widely spoken

■ GOVERNMENT

Colony/Territory of: Dependent Territory of the United States
Leader(s): Head of State: Pres. George W. Bush Jr., Gov. Charles Wesley Turnbull
Government Type: organized, unincorporated territory of the US
National Holiday: Transfer Day, Mar. 27 (1917, from Denmark to the US)

■ ECONOMY

Overview: tourism is the primary economic activity accounting for more than 70% of GDP and 70% of employment; some manufacturing; small agricultural sector (most food is imported); international business and financial services are a small but growing sector

■ FINANCE/TRADE

Currency: US dollar ($) = 100 cents

Canadian Embassy: c/o The Canadian Embassy, 501 Pennsylvania Ave NW, Washington DC 20001, USA. Tel: (202) 682-1740. Fax: (202) 456-7726. e-mail: wshdc@dfait-maeci.gc.ca
Representative to Canada: c/o Embassy of the United States of America, 490 Sussex Dr, Ottawa, ON, K1N 1G8. Tel: (613) 238-5335. Fax: (613) 688-3097. Email inquiries are not accepted

Uganda

Long-Form Name: Republic of Uganda
Capital: Kampala

■ GEOGRAPHY

Area: 236,040 sq. km
Coastline: none: landlocked
Climate: tropical; generally rainy with two dry seasons (Dec. to Feb., June to Aug.); semi-arid in northeast
Environment: straddles equator; deforestation; overgrazing; soil erosion; widespread poaching
Terrain: mostly plateau with rim of mountains
Land Use: 25% arable; 9% permanent crops; 9% permanent pastures; 28% forest; 29% other; includes 90 sq. km irrigated
Location: EC Africa

■ PEOPLE

Population: 24,699,073 (July 2002 est.)
Nationality: Ugandan
Age Structure: 0–14 yrs: 50.9%; 15–64: 47.0%; 65+: 2.1% (2002 est.)
Population Growth Rate: 2.94% (2002 est.)
Net Migration: -0.28 migrants/1,000 population (2002 est.)
Ethnic Groups: 17% Baganda, 12% Karamojong, 8% Basogo, 8% Iteso, 6% Langi, 6% Rwanda, 5% Bagisu, 4% Acholi, 4% Lugbara, 3% Bunyro, 27% other
Languages: English (official); Luganda and Swahili widely used; other Bantu and Nilotic languages
Religions: 33% Roman Catholic, 33% Protestant, 16% Muslim, rest indigenous beliefs
Birth Rate: 47.15/1,000 population (2002 est.)
Death Rate: 17.53/1,000 population (2002 est.)
Infant Mortality: 89.35 deaths/1,000 live births (2002 est.)
Life Expectancy at Birth: 42.97 years male, 44.67 years female (2002 est.)
Total Fertility Rate: 6.80 children born/woman (2002 est.)
Literacy: 67.1% (2000)

■ GOVERNMENT

Leader(s): Pres. Yoweri Kaguta Museveni, Prime Min. Apollo Nsibambi
Government Type: republic
Administrative Divisions: 45 districts
Nationhood: Oct. 9, 1962 (from UK)
National Holiday: Independence Day, Oct. 9

■ ECONOMY

Overview: despite substantial natural resources, the economy has been ruined by years of political instability, mismanagement and civil war; the government has started a reform program that is partly aimed at lowering high inflation and increasing export earnings; agriculture is the most important economic sector
GDP: US$29 billion, per capita US$1,200; real growth rate 5.1% (2001 est.)
Inflation: 0.1% (2002 est.)
Industries: accounts for 18% of GDP (2000); sugar, brewing, tobacco, cotton textiles, cement
Labour Force: 12 million (2001); 82% agriculture, 5% industry, 13% services
Unemployment: n.a.
Agriculture: accounts for 44% (2000) of GDP; coffee, tea and tobacco are the main export crops. Domestic products also include cotton, corn, millet and livestock
Natural Resources: copper, cobalt, limestone, salt, hydro power, arable land

■ FINANCE/TRADE

Currency: Ugandan shilling (USh) = 100 cents
International Reserves Excluding Gold: US$934 million (Dec. 2002)
Gold Reserves: n.a.
Budget: revenues US$959 million; expenditures US$1.04 billion, including capital expenditures of US$ n.a. (1999)
Defence Expenditures: 10.1% of central government expenditure (2001)
Education Expenditures: n.a.
External Debt: US$3.733 billion (2001)
Exports: US$413 million (2002 est.); commodities: coffee 97%, fish and fish products, cotton, tea; partners: Germany, Netherlands, US, Spain, Belgium
Imports: US$1.119 billion (2002 est.); commodities: petroleum products, machinery, cotton piece goods, metals, transportation equipment, food; partners: Kenya, US, India, South Africa, Japan

■ COMMUNICATIONS

Daily Newspapers: 2/1,000 inhabitants (2000)
Televisions: 27/1,000 inhabitants (2001)
Radios: 127/1,000 inhabitants (2001)
Telephones: 3 lines/1,000 inhabitants (2001)

■ TRANSPORTATION

Motor Vehicles: 120,000; 48,400 passenger cars (2000)
Roads: 27,000 km; 1,800 km paved
Railway: 1,241 km
Air Traffic: 41,000 passengers carried (2001)
Airports: 27; 4 have paved runways (2002)

Canadian Embassy: The Canadian High Commission to Uganda, c/o The Canadian High Commission, Comcraft House, Hailé Sélassie Ave, Nairobi, Kenya; mailing address: The Canadian High Commission, P.O. Box 30481, Nairobi, Kenya. Tel: (011-254-2) 21-48-04.

Fax: (011-254-2) 22-69-87. e-mail: nrobi@ dfait-maeci.gc.ca
Embassy in Canada: High Commission for the Republic of Uganda, 231 Cobourg St, Ottawa ON K1N 8J2. Tel: (613) 789-7797. Fax: (613) 789-8909. e-mail: ugacom@comnet.ca

Ukraine

Long-Form Name: Ukraine
Capital: Kiev

■ GEOGRAPHY

Area: 603,700 sq. km
Coastline: 2,782 km
Climate: temperate continental; subtropical on southern Crimean coast; moderate rainfall in north; drier in southern regions
Environment: air and water pollution, unsafe drinking water, deforestation, radiation contamination around Chernobyl nuclear power plant
Terrain: Carpathian mountains in west, marshy in north, remainder flat fertile plains (steppes) and plateaux
Land Use: 58% arable; 2% permanent crops; 13% meadows and pastures; 18% forest, 9% other; includes 24,540 sq. km irrigated
Location: E Europe, bordering on Black Sea

■ PEOPLE

Population: 48,396,470 (July 2002 est.)
Nationality: Ukrainian
Age Structure: 0–14 yrs: 16.8%; 15–64: 68.7%; 65+: 14.5% (2002 est.)
Population Growth Rate: -0.72% (2002 est.)
Net Migration: -0.42 migrants/1,000 population (2002 est.)
Ethnic Groups: 73% Ukrainian, 22% Russian, 1% Jewish, 4% other
Languages: Ukrainian, Russian, Romanian, Polish
Religions: predominantly Eastern Orthodox and Roman Catholic; Uniate Church re-legalized in 1991; also, Autocephalous Orthodox Church, Greek rite Catholic
Birth Rate: 9.59/1,000 population (2002 est.)
Death Rate: 16.40/1,000 population (2002 est.)
Infant Mortality: 21.14 deaths/1,000 live births (2002 est.)
Life Expectancy at Birth: 60.86 years male, 72.06 years female (2002 est.)
Total Fertility Rate: 1.32 children born/woman (2002 est.)
Literacy: 99.6% (2000)

■ GOVERNMENT

Leader(s): Pres. Leonid Kuchma, Prime Min. Viktor Yanukovych
Government Type: republic

Administrative Divisions: 24 oblasts (oblasti, sing. —oblast), 1 autonomous republic (avtomnaya respublika), 2 municipalities (mista, sing. —misto) with oblast status
Nationhood: Aug. 24, 1991 (from Soviet Union)
National Holiday: Independence Day, Aug. 24

■ ECONOMY

Overview: mining and heavy industry, with very strong agricultural sector; food surplus area of former USSR
GDP: US$205 billion, per capita US$4,200; real growth rate 9.0% (2001 est.)
Inflation: 25.8% (2000 est.)
Industries: accounts for 40% of GDP (2000) and 33% of labour force; industries include: mining, manufacturing of machinery, food processing, chemicals, electric and electronic equipment, coal, electric power, food processing (esp. sugar)
Labour Force: 25.0 million (2001); 32% industry and construction, 24% agriculture and forestry, 17% health and cultural services, 27% other
Unemployment: 11.9% (2001)
Agriculture: accounts for about 13% of GDP (2000); corn, wheat, sugar beets, sunflower seeds, barley, tobacco; livestock includes cattle, pigs, goats, sheep, vegetables, milk
Natural Resources: coal, manganese, oil, gypsum, iron, lead, zinc, titanium, natural gas, oil, salt, sulphur, graphite, mercury, timber, arable land

■ FINANCE/TRADE

Currency: hryvnia (pl. hryvni) = 100 kopiykas
International Reserves Excluding Gold: US$4.241 billion (Dec. 2002)
Gold Reserves: 0.504 million fine troy ounces (Dec. 2002)
Budget: revenues US$10.2 billion; expenditures US$11.1 billion, including capital expenditures US$ n.a. (2002 est.)
Defence Expenditures: 9.8% of central government expenditure (2001)
Education Expenditures: 5.72% of central government expenditure (2000)
External Debt: US$12.811 billion (2001)
Exports: US$14.767 billion (2000): minerals, agricultural products, heavy machinery, vehicles, airplanes; partners: Russia, Turkey, Italy, Germany
Imports: US$18.465 billion (2000): machinery and equipment, chemicals, textiles, energy; partners: Russia, Turkmenistan, Germany, US

■ COMMUNICATIONS

Daily Newspapers: 175/1,000 inhabitants (2000)
Televisions: 456/1,000 inhabitants (2001)
Radios: 889/1,000 inhabitants (2001)
Telephones: 212 lines/1,000 inhabitants (2001)

■ TRANSPORTATION

Motor Vehicles: 5,000,000 passenger cars (2000)
Roads: 273,700 km; n.a. km paved
Railway: 22,510 km
Air Traffic: 996,000 passengers carried (2001)
Airports: 718; 114 have paved runways (2002)

Canadian Embassy: The Canadian Embassy, 31 Yaroslaviv Val St, Kiev 01901, Ukraine. Tel: (011-380-44) 464-1144. Fax: (011-380-44) 464-0598. e-mail: kiev@dfait-maeci.gc.ca
Embassy in Canada: Embassy of Ukraine, 310 Somerset St W, Ottawa ON K2P 0J9. Tel: (613) 230-2961. Fax: (613) 230-2400. e-mail: ukrembassy@on.aibn.com

---

United Arab Emirates

Long-Form Name: United Arab Emirates
Capital: Abu Dhabi

■ GEOGRAPHY

Area: 82,880 sq. km
Coastline: 1,318 km
Climate: desert; cooler in eastern mountains
Environment: frequent dust- and sandstorms; lack of natural freshwater resources being overcome by desalination plants; desertification
Terrain: flat, barren coastal plain; desert wasteland; mountains in east
Land Use: 2% permanent pastures; 98% other; includes 720 sq. km irrigated
Location: SW Asia (Middle East), Arabian Peninsula bordering on Persian Gulf

■ PEOPLE

Population: 2,445,989 (July 2002 est.)
Nationality: Emirati
Age Structure: 0–14 yrs: 27.7%; 15–64: 69.7%; 65+: 2.6% (2002 est.)
Population Growth Rate: 1.58% (2002 est.)
Net Migration: 1.41 migrants/1,000 population (2002 est.)
Ethnic Groups: 19% Emiri, 23% other Arab, 50% South Asian (fluctuating); 8% other expatriates (includes Westerners and East Asians); less than 20% of the population are United Arab Emirates citizens
Languages: Arabic (official); Farsi and English widely spoken in major cities; Hindi, Urdu
Religions: 96% Muslim (16% Shi'a); 4% Christian, Hindu and other
Birth Rate: 18.30/1,000 population (2002 est.)
Death Rate: 3.90/1,000 population (2002 est.)
Infant Mortality: 16.12 deaths/1,000 live births (2002 est.)
Life Expectancy at Birth: 72.06 years male, 77.10 years female (2002 est.)

Total Fertility Rate: 3.16 children born/woman (2002 est.)
Literacy: 76.3% (2000)

■ GOVERNMENT

Leader(s): Pres. Zayid bin Sultan Al Nuhayyan, V. Pres. and Prime Min. Maktoum bin Rashid al-Maktoum
Government Type: federation with specified powers delegated to the United Arab Emirates central government and other powers reserved to member emirates
Administrative Divisions: 7 emirates (imarat, sing. -imarah)
Nationhood: Dec. 2, 1971 (from UK; formerly known as Trucial States)
National Holiday: Independence Day, Dec. 2

■ ECONOMY

Overview: an open economy tied to the world prices for oil and gas; currently has a high standard of living; crude oil reserves should last for over 100 years at present levels of production; the government is encouraging privatization measures
GDP: US$51 billion, per capita US$21,100; real growth rate 5.6% (2001 est.)
Inflation: 4.5% (2000 est.)
Industries: accounts for 46% of GDP (2000); petroleum, fishing, petrochemicals, construction materials, some boat building, handicrafts, pearling
Labour Force: 1.5 million (2001): 15% industry, 7% agriculture, 78% services
Unemployment: n.a.
Agriculture: accounts for 3% of GDP (2000) and 8% of labour force; cash crop: dates; food products: vegetables, watermelons, poultry, eggs, dairy, fish; only 25% self-sufficient in food
Natural Resources: crude oil and natural gas

■ FINANCE/TRADE

Currency: Emirian dirham (Dh) = 100 fils
International Reserves Excluding Gold: US$15.253 billion (Nov. 2002)
Gold Reserves: 0.397 million fine troy ounces (Nov. 2002)
Budget: revenues US$6.5 billion; expenditures US$7.3 billion, including capital expenditures US$ n.a. (2000 est.)
Defence Expenditures: 30.1% of central government expenditure (2001)
Education Expenditures: 17.33% of central government expenditure (1999)
External Debt: US$12.6 billion (2000 est.)
Exports: US$43.506 billion (2000); commodities: crude oil 75%, natural gas, re-exports, dried fish, dates; partners: US, European Community, Japan, Singapore, Korea, India, Oman, Iran

Imports: US$35.575 billion (2000); commodities: food, consumer and capital goods; partners: Japan, US, UK, Italy, Germany, South Korea

■ COMMUNICATIONS

Daily Newspapers: 156/1,000 inhabitants (2000)
Televisions: 252/1,000 inhabitants (2001)
Radios: 318/1,000 inhabitants (2001)
Telephones: 340 lines/1,000 inhabitants (2001)

■ TRANSPORTATION

Motor Vehicles: 400,000; 320,000 passenger cars
Roads: 4,835 km, all paved
Railway: none
Air Traffic: 7,676,000 passengers carried (2001)
Airports: 38; 19 have paved runways (2002)

Canadian Embassy: The Canadian Embassy, Villa No. 440, 26th St, Rowdah District, Abu Dhabi, UAE; mailing address: P.O. Box 6970, Abu Dhabi, UAE. Tel: (011-971-2) 407-1300. Fax: (011-971-2) 407-1399. e-mail: abdbi@dfait-maeci.gc.ca
Embassy in Canada: c/o Embassy of the United Arab Emirates, 45 O'Connor St, Ste 1800 World Exchange Plaza, Ottawa, ON, K1P 1A4, Tel: (613) 565-7272, Fax: (613) 565-8007. e-mail: safara@uae-embassy.com

United Kingdom

Long-Form Name: United Kingdom of Great Britain and Northern Ireland
Capital: London

■ GEOGRAPHY

Area: 244,820 sq. km
Coastline: 12,429 km
Climate: temperate; moderated by prevailing southwest winds over the North Atlantic Current; more than half of the days are overcast
Environment: pollution control measures improving air, water quality; because of heavily indented coastline, no location is more than 125 km from tidal waters
Terrain: mostly rugged hills and low mountains; level to rolling plains in east and southeast
Land Use: 25% arable; negligible permanent crops; 46% meadows; 10% forest; 19% other; includes 1,080 sq. km irrigated
Location: NW Europe, bordering on North Sea, Atlantic Ocean

■ PEOPLE

Population: 59,778,002 (July 2002 est.)
Nationality: British or Briton
Age Structure: 0–14 yrs: 18.7%; 15–64: 65.5%; 65+: 15.8% (2002 est.)
Population Growth Rate: 0.21% (2002 est.)

Net Migration: 1.06 migrants/1,000 population (2002 est.)
Ethnic Groups: 81.5% English, 9.6% Scottish, 2.4% Irish, 1.9% Welsh, 1.8% Ulster, 2.8% West Indian, Indian, Pakistani and other
Languages: English, Welsh (about 26% of population of Wales), Scottish form of Gaelic (about 60,000 in Scotland)
Religions: 73% Anglican, 23% Roman Catholic, 3% Muslim, 0.1% Sikh, 0.2% Presbyterian, 0.5% Methodist, 0.2% Jewish
Birth Rate: 11.34/1,000 population (2002 est.)
Death Rate: 10.30/1,000 population (2002 est.)
Infant Mortality: 5.45 deaths/1,000 live births (2002 est.)
Life Expectancy at Birth: 75.29 years male, 80.84 years female (2002 est.)
Total Fertility Rate: 1.73 children born/woman (2002 est.)
Literacy: approaching 100% (2000)

■ GOVERNMENT

Leader(s): Head of State: Queen Elizabeth II, Prime Min. Tony Blair
Government Type: constitutional monarchy
Administrative Divisions: England: 47 boroughs, 36 counties, 29 London boroughs, 12 cities and boroughs, 10 counties, 12 cities, 3 royal boroughs, Northern Ireland: 24 districts, 2 cities; Scotland: 32 council areas; Wales: 11 county boroughs, 9 counties, 2 cities and counties. Dependent areas include: Anguilla, Bermuda, British Antarctic Territory (uninhabited except for variable population of research stations — about 300 persons), British Indian Ocean Territory, British Virgin Islands, Cayman Islands, Channel Islands, Falkland Islands, Gibraltar, Guernsey, Isle of Man, Jersey, Montserrat, Pitcairn, Saint Helena, South Georgia (uninhabited except for scientific station and 500 persons in a whaling/sealing settlement), South Sandwich Islands (uninhabited), Turks and Caicos Islands
Nationhood: Jan. 1, 1801, United Kingdom established
National Holiday: Celebration of the Birthday of the Queen, second Saturday in June

■ ECONOMY

Overview: essentially capitalist economy; intensive agricultural practices produce 60% of domestic food needs with only 1% of the labour force; strong service sector; industry is declining in importance
GDP: US$1.52 trillion, per capita US$25,300; real growth rate 1.6% (2002 est.)
Inflation: 1.8% (2001)
Industries: accounts for 25% of GDP (2000) and 25% of labour force; machinery and transportation equipment, metals, food processing,

paper and paper products, textiles, chemicals, clothing, other consumer goods, motor vehicles, aircraft, shipbuilding, petroleum, coal

Labour Force: 29.4 million (2001); 74% services, 25% industry, 1% agriculture

Unemployment: 3.0% (Nov. 2002)

Agriculture: accounts for only 1% of GDP (2000); highly mechanized and efficient farms; wide variety of crops and livestock products produced; about 60% self-sufficient in food and feed needs

Natural Resources: coal, crude oil, natural gas, tin, limestone, iron ore, salt, clay, chalk, gypsum, lead, silica

■ FINANCE/TRADE

Currency: pound sterling (£ or £ stg) = 100 pence

International Reserves Excluding Gold: US$39.359 billion (Dec. 2002)

Gold Reserves: 10.091 million fine troy ounces (Dec. 2002)

Budget: revenues US$565 billion; expenditures US$540 billion, including capital expenditures US$ n.a. (2001)

Defence Expenditures: 7.0% of central government expenditure (2001)

Education Expenditures: 3.73% of total government expenditure (1999)

External Debt: n.a.

Exports: US$273.976 billion (2002 est.); commodities: manufactured goods, machinery, fuels, chemicals, semi-finished goods, transport equipment; partners: Germany, France, Netherlands, Ireland, US

Imports: US$330.064 billion (2002 est.); commodities: manufactured goods, machinery, semi-finished goods, foodstuffs, consumer goods; partners: Germany, France, Netherlands, Benelux, US

■ COMMUNICATIONS

Daily Newspapers: 329/1,000 inhabitants (2000)

Televisions: 950/1,000 inhabitants (2001)

Radios: 1,446/1,000 inhabitants (2001)

Telephones: 588 lines/1,000 inhabitants (2001)

■ TRANSPORTATION

Motor Vehicles: 25,000,000; 22,300,000 passenger cars (2000)

Roads: 371,603 km, all paved

Railway: 16,878 km

Air Traffic: 72,772,000 passengers carried (2001)

Airports: 470; 334 have paved runways (2002)

Canadian Embassy: The Canadian High Commission, Macdonald House, 1 Grosvenor Square, London W1K 4AB, England, UK. Tel: (011-44-20) 7258-6600. Fax: (011-44-20) 7258-6333. e-mail: ldn@dfait-maeci.gc.ca

Embassy in Canada: British High Commission, 80 Elgin St, Ottawa ON K1P 5K7. Tel: (613) 237-1530. Fax: (613) 237-7980. Email should be sent using the appropriate form at the British High Commission's Website at http://www.britain-in-canada.org

United States

Long-Form Name: United States of America
Capital: Washington, D.C.

■ GEOGRAPHY

Area: 9,629,091 sq. km; includes only the 50 states and District of Columbia

Coastline: 19,924 km

Climate: mostly temperate, but varies from tropical (Hawaii) to arctic (Alaska); arid to semi-arid in west with occasional warm, dry chinook wind

Environment: pollution control measures improving air and water quality; acid rain; agricultural fertilizer and pesticide pollution; management of sparse natural water resources in west; desertification; tsunamis, volcanoes and earthquake activity around Pacific; permafrost in Alaska

Terrain: vast central plain, mountains in west, hills and low mountains in east; rugged mountains and broad river valleys in Alaska; rugged, volcanic topography in Hawaii

Land Use: 19% arable; negligible permanent crops; 25% meadows; 30% forest; 26% other; includes 207,000 sq. km irrigated

Location: North America, bordering on Canada, Mexico, Pacific Ocean, Atlantic Ocean

■ PEOPLE

Population: 280,562,489 (July 2002 est.)

Nationality: American

Age Structure: 0–14 yrs: 21.0%; 15–64: 66.4%; 65+: 12.6% (2002 est.)

Population Growth Rate: 0.89% (2002 est.)

Net Migration: 3.5 migrants/1,000 population (2002 est.)

Ethnic Groups: 83.5% white, 12.4% black, 3.3% Asian, 0.8% other

Languages: predominantly English; sizable Spanish-speaking minority

Religions: 56% Protestant (including 21% Baptist, 12% Methodist, 8% Lutheran, 4% Presbyterian, 3% Episcopalian), 28% Roman Catholic, 2% Jewish, 4% other; 10% none

Birth Rate: 14.10/1,000 population (2002 est.)

Death Rate: 8.70/1,000 population (2002 est.)

Infant Mortality: 6.69 deaths/1,000 live births (2002 est.)

Life Expectancy at Birth: 74.50 years male, 80.20 years female (2002 est.)

Total Fertility Rate: 2.07 children born/woman (2002 est.)
Literacy: approaching 100% (2000)

■ GOVERNMENT

Leader(s): Pres. George W. Bush Jr., V. Pres. Richard B. Cheney
Government Type: federal republic
Administrative Divisions: 50 states and 1 district; dependent areas include: American Samoa, Baker Island, Federated States of Micronesia, Guam, Howland Island, Jarvis Island, Johnston Atoll, Kingman Reef, Marshall Islands, Midway Islands (inhabited by U.S. military personnel), Northern Marianas, Palau, Palymyra Atoll, Puerto Rico (for details see Puerto Rico entry), Virgin Islands (for details see Virgin Islands entry), Wake Island (military base), Navassa Island
Nationhood: July 4, 1776 (from England)
National Holiday: Independence Day, July 4

■ ECONOMY

Overview: market-oriented economy with a very large private sector; a powerful and diversified economy, with high per capita GNP; problems include the significant budget and trade deficits, large medical costs for the ageing population and inadequate investment in industry and infrastructure
GDP: US$10.082 trillion, per capita US$36,300; real growth rate 2.45% (2002 est.)
Inflation: 1.6% (2002)
Industries: accounts for 18% of GDP and 25.3% of labour force (2001 est.); highly diversified industry; petroleum, steel, motor vehicles, aerospace, telecommunications, chemicals, electronics, food processing, consumer goods, fishing, lumber, mining
Labour Force: 146.7 million (2001); 30.2% managerial and professional, 29.2% technical, sales and administrative support, 13.5% services, 24.6% manufacturing, mining, transportation and crafts, 2.5% farming, forestry and fishing.
Unemployment: 5.7% (Dec. 2002)
Agriculture: accounts for 2% of GDP and 2.5% of labour force; favourable climate and soils support a wide variety of crops and livestock production; world's second largest producer and top exporter of grain; surplus food producer; fish catch of 4.4 million metric tons
Natural Resources: coal, copper, lead, phosphates, uranium, bauxite, gold, iron, mercury, nickel, potash, silver, tungsten, zinc, crude oil, natural gas, timber

■ FINANCE/TRADE

Currency: $US = 100 cents
International Reserves Excluding Gold: US$67.962 billion (Dec. 2002)

Gold Reserves: 262.000 million fine troy ounces (Dec. 2002)
Budget: revenues US$1.828 trillion; expenditures US$1.703 trillion, including capital expenditures US$ n.a. (1999)
Defence Expenditures: 16.0% of central government expenditure (2001)
Education Expenditures: 1.78% of government expenditure (2000)
External Debt: n.a.
Exports: US$688.960 billion (2002 est.); commodities: capital goods, automobiles, industrial supplies and raw materials, consumer goods, agricultural products; partners: Canada, Mexico, Japan, UK, Germany, France, Netherlands
Imports: US$1.177 trillion (2002 est.); commodities: crude and partly refined petroleum, machinery, automobiles, consumer goods, industrial raw materials, food and beverages; partners: Japan, Canada, China, Mexico, Germany, UK, Taiwan

■ COMMUNICATIONS

Daily Newspapers: 213/1,000 inhabitants (2000)
Televisions: 835/1,000 inhabitants (2000)
Radios: 2,117/1,000 inhabitants (2001)
Telephones: 667 lines/1,000 inhabitants (2001)

■ TRANSPORTATION

Motor Vehicles: 211,000,000; 133,000,000 passenger cars (2000)
Roads: 6,370,031 km; 5,733,028 km paved
Railway: 212,433 km
Air Traffic: 619,262,000 passengers carried (2001)
Airports: 14,695; 5,132 have paved runways (2002)

Canadian Embassy: The Canadian Embassy, 501 Pennsylvania Ave, NW, Washington DC 20001, USA. Tel: (202) 682-1740. Fax: (202) 682-7726. e-mail: wshdc-outpack@dfait-maeci.gc.ca
Embassy in Canada: Embassy of the United States of America, 490 Sussex Dr, Ottawa, ON, K1N 1G8. Tel: (613) 238-5335. Fax: (613) 688-3097. Email inquiries are not accepted

Uruguay

Long-Form Name: Oriental Republic of Uruguay
Capital: Montevideo

■ GEOGRAPHY

Area: 176,220 sq. km
Coastline: 660 km
Climate: warm temperate; freezing temperatures almost unknown
Environment: subject to seasonally high winds, droughts, floods; industrial pollution from Brazil

Terrain: mostly rolling plains and low hills; fertile coastal lowland
Land Use: 7% arable; negligible permanent crops; 77% meadows; 6% forest; 10% other; includes 1,800 sq. km irrigated
Location: SE South America, bordering on Atlantic Ocean

■ PEOPLE

Population: 3,386,575 (July 2002 est.)
Nationality: Uruguayan
Age Structure: 0–14 yrs: 24.4%; 15–64: 62.6%; 65+: 13.0% (2002 est.)
Population Growth Rate: 0.79% (2002 est.)
Net Migration: -0.41 migrants/1,000 population (2002 est.)
Ethnic Groups: 88% white, 8% mestizo, 4% black
Languages: Spanish, Brazilero
Religions: 66% nominally Roman Catholic, 2% Protestant, 2% Jewish, 30% other
Birth Rate: 17.28/1,000 population (2002 est.)
Death Rate: 9.00/1,000 population (2002 est.)
Infant Mortality: 14.25 deaths/1,000 live births (2002 est.)
Life Expectancy at Birth: 72.32 years male, 79.17 years female (2002 est.)
Total Fertility Rate: 2.35 children born/woman (2002 est.)
Literacy: 97.7% (2000)

■ GOVERNMENT

Leader(s): Pres. Jorge Batlle Ibanez, V. Pres. Luis Hierro
Government Type: constitutional republic
Administrative Divisions: 19 departments (departamentos, sing. —departamento)
Nationhood: Aug. 25, 1828 (from Brazil)
National Holiday: Independence Day, Aug. 25

■ ECONOMY

Overview: a small economy with favourable climate, good soils and considerable hydro power potential; problems include high inflation rates, a large and growing domestic debt and frequent strikes; growth in the agriculture and fishing sectors has spurred recovery; unemployment is on the rise and hobbles economic progress
GDP: US$31 billion, per capita US$9,200; real growth rate -1.5% (2001 est.)
Inflation: 4.4% (2001)
Industries: accounts for 29% of GDP (2001) and 19% of labour force; meat packing, oil refining, manufacturing, foodstuffs, engineering, transport equipment, sugar, textiles, leather apparel, tires
Labour Force: 1.5 million (2001); 70% community, social and business services, 16% industry, 14% agriculture

Unemployment: 11.3% (2001)
Agriculture: accounts for 6% of GDP (2000) and 11% of labour force; meat processing, wool and hides, sugar, textiles, footwear, leather apparel, tires, cement, fishing, petroleum refining, wine, wheat, rice, corn, sorghum; livestock and fish; self-sufficient in most basic foods
Natural Resources: arable land, hydro power potential, minor minerals

■ FINANCE/TRADE

Currency: new peso (N$Ur) = 100 centesimos
International Reserves Excluding Gold: US$769 million (Dec. 2002)
Gold Reserves: 0.008 million fine troy ounces (Dec. 2002)
Budget: revenues US$3.7 billion; expenditures US$4.6 billion, including capital expenditures of US$500 million (2000)
Defence Expenditures: 4.2% of central government expenditure (2001)
Education Expenditures: 7.10% of total government expenditure (2000)
External Debt: US$9.706 billion (2001)
Exports: US$1.859 billion (2002 est.); commodities: hides and leather goods 17%, beef 10%, wool 9%, fish 7%, rice 4%; partners: EU, US
Imports: US$2.051 billion (2002 est.); commodities: fuels and lubricants 15%, metals, machinery, transportation equipment, industrial chemicals; partners: MERCOSUR partners, EU, US

■ COMMUNICATIONS

Daily Newspapers: 293/1,000 inhabitants (2000)
Televisions: 530/1,000 inhabitants (2001)
Radios: 603/1,000 inhabitants (2001)
Telephones: 283 lines/1,000 inhabitants (2001)

■ TRANSPORTATION

Motor Vehicles: 585,000; 530,000 passenger cars (2000)
Roads: 8,764 km; 7,800 km paved
Railway: 2,993 km
Air Traffic: 559,000 passengers carried (2001)
Airports: 64; 15 have paved runways (2002)

Canadian Embassy: The Canadian Embassy, Plaza Independencia 749, off. 102, 11100 Montevideo, Uruguay. Tel: (011-598-2) 902-20-30. Fax: (011-598-2) 902-20-29. e-mail: mvdeo@dfait-maeci.gc.ca
Embassy in Canada: Embassy of the Eastern Republic of Uruguay, 130 Albert St, Ste 1905, Ottawa ON K1P 5G4. Tel: (613) 234-2727. Fax: (613) 233-4670. e-mail: uruott@iosphere.net

Uzbekistan

Long-Form Name: Republic of Uzbekistan
Capital: Tashkent

■ GEOGRAPHY

Area: 447,400 sq. km
Coastline: landlocked; 420 km inland coastline along Aral Sea
Climate: dry continental; warm to hot summers; cool to cold winters; semi-arid grassland in east
Environment: drying up of the Aral Sea is resulting in increasing concentrations of chemical pesticides and natural salts; water and soil pollution
Terrain: flat to rolling deserts and semi-deserts, mountains, shrinking Aral Sea in west
Land Use: 9% arable; 1% permanent crops; 46% meadows and pastures; 3% forest, 41% other; includes 42,810 sq. km irrigated
Location: C Asia

■ PEOPLE

Population: 25,155,064 (July 2001 est.)
Nationality: Uzbekistani
Age Structure: 0–14 yrs: 35.5%; 15–64: 59.8%; 65+: 4.7% (2002 est.)
Population Growth Rate: 1.62% (2002 est.)
Net Migration: -1.94 migrants/1,000 population (2002 est.)
Ethnic Groups: 80% Uzbek, 5.5% Russian, 1.5% Tartars, 5% Tajiks, 3% Kazakhs, 2.5% Kara-Kalpaks, 2.5% other
Languages: 74.3% Uzbek (official), 14.2% Russian, 4.4% Tajik, 7.1% other
Religions: predominantly Sunni Muslim and Eastern Orthodox
Birth Rate: 26.09/1,000 population (2002 est.)
Death Rate: 7.98/1,000 population (2002 est.)
Infant Mortality: 71.72 deaths/1,000 live births (2002 est.)
Life Expectancy at Birth: 60.38 years male, 67.60 years female (2002 est.)
Total Fertility Rate: 3.03 children born/woman (2002 est.)
Literacy: 99.2% (2000)

■ GOVERNMENT

Leader(s): Pres. Islam À. Karimov, Prem. Otkir Sultonov
Government Type: republic
Administrative Divisions: 12 (wiloyatlar, sing. — wiloyat), 1 autonomous republic (respublikasi), 1 city (shahri)
Nationhood: Aug. 31, 1991 (from Soviet Union)
National Holiday: Independence Day, Sept. 1

■ ECONOMY

Overview: despite the need for irrigation, agriculture is the predominant economic sector; small industrial sector, mining; inflation is skyrocketing and economic problems are numerous; more than 60% of the population is living in overcrowded rural villages
GDP: US$62 billion, per capita US$2,500; real growth rate 3.0% (2001 est.)
Inflation: 40% (2000 est.)
Industries: accounts for 24% of GDP (2000); chemicals and gas, machine building, metal-making, textile manufacture, clothing, butter, preserves, vegetable oil, textiles
Labour Force: 10.7 million (2001); 44% agriculture and forestry, 20% industry and construction, 36% services
Unemployment: 10% (1999 est.); also large numbers of underemployed
Agriculture: accounts for 33% of GDP (2000), vegetables, cotton, grains, almonds, fruit, livestock; 97% of all crops are grown on irrigated land
Natural Resources: gold, non-ferrous metals, coal, natural gas, petroleum, uranium, silver, copper

■ FINANCE/TRADE

Currency: Uzbekistani sum
International Reserves Excluding Gold: n.a.
Gold Reserves: n.a.
Budget: revenues US$4 billion, expenditures US$4.1 billion, including capital expenditures of US$ n.a. (1999 est.)
Defence Expenditures: 5.3% of central government expenditure (1999)
Education Expenditures: n.a.
External Debt: US$4.627 billion (2001)
Exports: US$3.217 billion (2000): cotton, agricultural products, machinery, gold, natural gas; partners: Russia, Switzerland, UK, Ukraine, South Korea, Kazakhstan
Imports: US$3.247 billion (2000): foodstuffs, machinery, consumer products; partners: Russia, South Korea, Germany, US, Ukraine, Kazakhstan

■ COMMUNICATIONS

Daily Newspapers: 3/1,000 inhabitants (2000)
Televisions: 276/1,000 inhabitants (2001)
Radios: 456/1,000 inhabitants (2001)
Telephones: 66 lines/1,000 inhabitants (2001)

■ TRANSPORTATION

Motor Vehicles: n.a.
Roads: 81,600 km; 71,237 km hard-surfaced
Railway: 3,656 km, (2000)
Air Traffic: 2,256,000 passengers carried (2001)
Airports: 267 airfields; 10 have paved runways (2002)

Canadian Embassy: c/o The Canadian Embassy, 23 Starokonyushenny Perculok, Moscow 121002, Russia. Tel: (011-7-095) 105-6000.

Fax: (011-7-095) 105-6025. e-mail: mosco@
dfait-maeci.gc.ca
Embassy in Canada: c/o The Embassy of the
Republic of Uzbekistan, 1746 Massachusetts
Ave. NW, Washington, DC 20036. Tel: (202)
887-5300. Fax: (202) 293-6804. e-mail: n.a.

Vanuatu

Long-Form Name: Republic of Vanuatu
Capital: Port Vila

■ GEOGRAPHY

Area: 12,200 sq. km
Coastline: 2,528 km
Climate: tropical; moderated by southeast trade
winds
Environment: subject to tropical cyclones or
typhoons (Jan. to Apr.); volcanism causes minor
earthquakes; lack of safe drinking water
Terrain: mostly mountains of volcanic origin;
narrow coastal plains
Land Use: 2% arable; 10% permanent crops; 2%
meadows; 75% forests and woodlands; 11%
other; includes n.a. sq. km irrigated
Location: South Pacific Ocean, NE of Australia

■ PEOPLE

Population: 196,178 (July 2002 est.)
Nationality: Ni-Vanuatu (sing. & pl.)
Age Structure: 0–14 yrs: 36.6%; 15–64: 61.1%;
65+: 3.3% (2002 est.)
Population Growth Rate: 1.66% (2002 est.)
Net Migration: 0 migrants/1,000 population
(2002 est.)
Ethnic Groups: 94% indigenous Melanesian, 4%
French, remainder Vietnamese, Chinese and
various Pacific Islanders
Languages: English and French (both official);
pidgin (known as Bislama or Bichelama)
Religions: 36.7% Presbyterian, 15% Anglican,
15% Catholic, 7.6% indigenous beliefs, 6.2%
Seventh-Day Adventist, 3.8% Church of Christ,
15.7% other
Birth Rate: 24.83/1,000 population (2002 est.)
Death Rate: 8.25/1,000 population (2002 est.)
Infant Mortality: 59.58 deaths/1,000 live births
(2002 est.)
Life Expectancy at Birth: 59.93 years male, 62.80
years female (2002 est.)
Total Fertility Rate: 3.08 children born/woman
(2002 est.)
Literacy: 64.0%

■ GOVERNMENT

Leader(s): Pres. John Bani, Prime Min. Edward
Natapei
Government Type: republic
Administrative Divisions: 6 provinces

Nationhood: July 30, 1980 (from France and UK;
formerly known as New Hebrides)
National Holiday: Independence Day, July 30

■ ECONOMY

Overview: economy is based on subsistence
farming, fishing and tourism; few mineral
deposits; a small light industry sector sees to
local needs; tax revenues come largely from
import duties
GDP: US$257 million, per capita US$1,300; real
growth rate -2.7% (2000 est.)
Inflation: 3.7% (2001)
Industries: accounts for 12% of GDP (2000);
food and fish freezing, meat canning, wood
processing
Labour Force: n.a.; 65% agriculture, 30% services,
5% industry
Unemployment: n.a.
Agriculture: accounts for 26% of GDP (2000)
and 65% of labour force; export crops: cocoa,
coffee and fish; subsistence crops: copra, taro,
yams, coconuts, fruit and vegetables
Natural Resources: manganese, hardwood
forests, fish

■ FINANCE/TRADE

Currency: vatu (VT) = 100 centimes
International Reserves Excluding Gold: US$37
million (Dec. 2002)
Gold Reserves: n.a.
Budget: n.a.
Defence Expenditures: negligible
Education Expenditures: n.a.
External Debt: US$66 million (2001)
Exports: US$16 million (2001 est.); com-
modities: copra 37%, cocoa 11%, meat 9%, fish
8%, timber 4%; partners: Japan, Belgium, US,
Germany
Imports: US$74 million (2001 est.); com-
modities: machines and vehicles 25%, food and
beverages 23%, basic manufactures 18%, raw
materials and fuels 11%, chemicals 6%;
partners: Australia, Singapore, New Zealand,
Japan, US

■ COMMUNICATIONS

Daily Newspapers: none
Televisions: n.a.
Radios: n.a.
Telephones: 28 lines/1,000 inhabitants (1999)

■ TRANSPORTATION

Motor Vehicles: 6,300; 4,000 passenger cars
Roads: 1,070 km; 256 km paved
Railway: none
Air Traffic: 85,000 passengers carried (1999 est.)
Airports: 31; 2 have paved runways (2001 est.)

Canadian Embassy: The Canadian High Commission to Vanuatu, c/o The Canadian High Commission, Commonwealth Ave, Canberra A.C.T. 2600, Australia. Tel: (011-61-2) 6270-4000. Fax: (011-61-2) 6273-3285. e-mail: cnbra@dfait-maeci.gc.ca
Embassy in Canada: n.a.

Vatican City

Long-Form Name: State of the Vatican City, or the Holy See
Capital: Vatican City

■ GEOGRAPHY

Area: 0.44 sq. km
Coastline: none: landlocked
Climate: temperate; mild, rainy winters (Sept. to mid-May) with hot, dry summers (May to Sept.)
Environment: urban
Terrain: low hill
Land Use: 100% built-up
Location: S Europe (W Italy)

■ PEOPLE

Population: 900 (July 2002 est.)
Nationality: n.a.
Age Structure: n.a.
Population Growth Rate: 1.15% (2002 est.)
Net Migration: n.a.
Ethnic Groups: primarily Italians and Swiss but also many other nationalities
Languages: Italian, Latin and various other languages
Religions: Roman Catholic
Birth Rate: n.a.
Death Rate: n.a.
Infant Mortality: n.a.
Life Expectancy at Birth: n.a.
Total Fertility Rate: n.a.
Literacy: 100%

■ GOVERNMENT

Leader(s): Head, Roman Catholic Church, Pope John Paul II (Karol Wojtyla)
Government Type: monarchical-sacerdotal state
Administrative Divisions: none
Nationhood: Feb. 11, 1929 (from Italy)
National Holiday: Installation Day of the Pope (John Paul II), Oct. 22; also Christmas, Easter, Feast of Saints Peter and Paul (June 29), and other holy days of obligation

■ ECONOMY

Overview: economy is supported financially by contributions (known as Peter's Pence) from Roman Catholics throughout the world, the sale of postage stamps, tourist mementos, fees for admission to museums and the sale of publications

GDP: n.a.
Inflation: n.a.
Industries: printing and production of a small amount of mosaics and staff uniforms; worldwide banking and financial activities
Labour Force: approximately 1,500 Vatican City employees divided into three categories: executives, office workers, salaried employees
Unemployment: n.a.
Agriculture: none
Natural Resources: none

■ FINANCE/TRADE

Currency: Vatican Lira (Lit) = 100 centesimi (at par with Italian lira)
International Reserves Excluding Gold: n.a.
Gold Reserves: n.a.
Budget: n.a.
Defence Expenditures: defence is the responsibility of Italy
Education Expenditures: n.a.
External Debt: n.a.
Exports: n.a.
Imports: n.a.

■ COMMUNICATIONS

Daily Newspapers: 1 in total
Televisions: n.a.
Radios: n.a.
Telephones: n.a.

■ TRANSPORTATION

Motor Vehicles: n.a.
Roads: no highways, all city streets
Railway: 862 m
Air Traffic: none
Airports: none

Canadian Embassy: The Canadian Embassy, Via della Conciliazione 4/D, 00193 Rome, Italy. Tel. (011-39-06) 6830-7316. Fax: (011-39-06) 6880-6283. e-mail: vatcn@dfait-maeci.gc.ca
Embassy in Canada: Apostolic Nunciature, 724 Manor Ave, Rockcliffe Park, Ottawa ON K1M 0E3. Tel: (613) 746-4914. Fax: (613) 746-4786. e-mail: nuncioap@istar.ca

Venezuela

Long-Form Name: The Bolivarian Republic of Venezuela
Capital: Caracas

■ GEOGRAPHY

Area: 912,050 sq. km
Coastline: 2,800 km
Climate: tropical; hot, humid; more moderate in highlands

Environment: subject to floods, rockslides, mud slides; periodic droughts; increasing industrial pollution in Caracas and Maracaibo
Terrain: Andes Mountains and Maracaibo lowlands in northwest; central plains (llanos); Guyana highlands in southwest
Land Use: 4% arable; 1% permanent crops; 20% meadows; 34% forest; 41% other; includes 540 sq. km irrigated
Location: N South America, bordering on Caribbean Sea

■ PEOPLE

Population: 24,287,670 (July 2002 est.)
Nationality: Venezuelan
Age Structure: 0–14 yrs: 31.6%; 15–64: 63.6%; 65+: 4.8% (2002 est.)
Population Growth Rate: 1.52% (2002 est.)
Net Migration: -0.11 migrants/1,000 population (2002 est.)
Ethnic Groups: 67% mestizo, 21% white, 10% black, 2% Indian
Languages: Spanish (official); Indian dialects spoken by approximately 200,000 Amerindians in the remote interior
Religions: 96% nominally Roman Catholic, 2% Protestant, 2% other
Birth Rate: 20.22/1,000 population (2002 est.)
Death Rate: 4.91/1,000 population (2002 est.)
Infant Mortality: 24.58 deaths/1,000 live births (2002 est.)
Life Expectancy at Birth: 70.53 years male, 76.81 years female (2002 est.)
Total Fertility Rate: 2.41 children born/woman (2002 est.)
Literacy: 92.6% (2000)

■ GOVERNMENT

Leader(s): Pres. Hugo Chavez Frias, V. Pres. Jose Vicente Rangel
Government Type: republic
Administrative Divisions: 23 states (estados, sing. —estado), 1 federal district (distrito federal) and 1 federal dependency (dependencia federal)
Nationhood: July 5, 1811 (from Spain)
National Holiday: Independence Day, July 5

■ ECONOMY

Overview: petroleum is the backbone of the economy, accounting for 27% of GDP, 78% of total exports and more than half of government revenue; it is likely to become even more important as the state petroleum company plans to double its production over the next 10 years
GDP: US$146.2 billion, per capita US$6,100; real growth rate 2.7% (2001 est.)
Inflation: 12.5% (2001)
Industries: accounts for 40% of GDP (2001 est.); petroleum, iron-ore mining, construction

materials, food processing, textiles, steel, aluminum, motor vehicle assembly
Labour Force: 10.2 million (2001); 64% community, social and business services, 23% industry, 13% agriculture
Unemployment: 14.9% (2001)
Agriculture: accounts for 5% GDP (2001 est.); products: corn, sorghum, sugar cane, rice, bananas, vegetables, coffee, beef, pork, milk, eggs, fish; not self-sufficient in food other than meat
Natural Resources: crude oil, natural gas, iron ore, gold, bauxite, other minerals, hydro power, diamonds

■ FINANCE/TRADE

Currency: bolívar (Bs) = 100 centimos
International Reserves Excluding Gold: US$8.592 billion (Dec. 2002)
Gold Reserves: 10.560 million fine troy ounces (Dec. 2002)
Budget: revenues US$26.4 billion; expenditures US$27 billion, including capital expenditures of US$ n.a. (2000 est.)
Defence Expenditures: 6.1% of central government expenditure (2001)
Education Expenditures: 22.13% of central government expenditure (2000)
External Debt: US$34.660 billion (2001)
Exports: US$24.889 billion (2002 est.); commodities: petroleum 81%, bauxite and aluminum, iron ore, agricultural products, basic manufactures; partners: US, Brazil, Colombia, Italy, Spain
Imports: US$14.564 billion (2002 est.); commodities: foodstuffs, chemicals, manufactures, machinery and transport equipment; partners: US, Colombia, Brazil, Germany, Italy

■ COMMUNICATIONS

Daily Newspapers: 206/1,000 inhabitants (2000)
Televisions: 185/1,000 inhabitants (2001)
Radios: 294/1,000 inhabitants (2001)
Telephones: 109 lines/1,000 inhabitants (2001)

■ TRANSPORTATION

Motor Vehicles: 2,025,000; 1,500,000 passenger cars
Roads: 96,155 km; 32,308 km paved
Railway: 682 km
Air Traffic: 4,052,000 passengers carried (2001)
Airports: 372; 127 have paved runways (2002)

Canadian Embassy: The Canadian Embassy, Avenida Francisco de Miranda con Avenida Sur de Altamira, Altamira, Caracas, Venezuela. mailing address: Apartado 62302, Caracas 1060A, Venezuela. Tel: (011-58-212) 264-0833. Fax: (011-58-212) 261-8741. e-mail: crcas@ dfait-maeci.gc.ca

Embassy in Canada: Embassy of the Republic of Venezuela, 32 Range Rd, Ottawa ON K1N 8J4. Tel: (613) 235-5151. Fax: (613) 235-3205. e-mail: embavene@travel-net.com

Vietnam

Long-Form Name: Socialist Republic of Vietnam
Capital: Hanoi

■ GEOGRAPHY

Area: 329,560 sq. km
Coastline: 3,444 km (excluding islands)
Climate: tropical in south; monsoonal in north with hot, rainy season (mid-May to mid-Sept.) and warm, dry season (mid-Oct. to mid-Mar.)
Environment: occasional typhoons (May to Jan.) with extensive flooding; soil deterioration; inadequate supply of safe drinking water
Terrain: low, flat delta in south and north; central highlands; hilly, mountainous far north and northwest
Land Use: 17% arable; 4% permanent crops; 1% meadows; 30% forest; 48% other; includes 30,000 sq. km irrigated
Location: SE Asia, bordering on South China Sea

■ PEOPLE

Population: 81,098,416 (July 2002 est.)
Nationality: Vietnamese (sing. & pl.)
Age Structure: 0–14 yrs: 31.6%; 15–64: 62.9%; 65+: 5.5% (2002 est.)
Population Growth Rate: 1.43% (2002 est.)
Net Migration: -0.47 migrants/1,000 population (2002 est.)
Ethnic Groups: 85–90% predominantly Vietnamese; 3% Chinese; more than 60 ethnic minorities including Muong, Thai, Meo, Khmer, Man, Cham; other mountain tribes
Languages: Vietnamese (official), French, Chinese, English, Khmer, tribal languages (Mon-Khmer and Malayo-Polynesian)
Religions: Buddhist, Confucian, Taoist, Roman Catholic, indigenous beliefs, Islamic, Protestant
Birth Rate: 20.89/1,000 population (2002 est.)
Death Rate: 6.14/1,000 population (2002 est.)
Infant Mortality: 29.34 deaths/1,000 live births (2002 est.)
Life Expectancy at Birth: 67.40 years male, 72.50 years female (2002 est.)
Total Fertility Rate: 2.44 children born/woman (2002 est.)
Literacy: 93.4% (2000)

■ GOVERNMENT

Leader(s): Pres. Tran Duc Luong, Prime Min. Phan Van Khai
Government Type: communist state

Administrative Divisions: 58 provinces (tinh, sing. & pl.), 3 municipalities (thu do, sing. & pl.)
Nationhood: Sept. 2, 1945 (from France)
National Holiday: Independence Day, Sept. 2

■ ECONOMY

Overview: centrally planned, developing economy with extensive government ownership and control of production facilities; dependent on foreign aid; high rate of population growth and high unemployment combine to form the economy's most serious problem
GDP: US$168.1 billion, per capita US$2,100; real growth rate 4.7% (2001 est.)
Inflation: -0.4% (2001)
Industries: accounts for 34% of GDP (2000); food processing, textiles, machine building, mining, cement, chemical fertilizer, glass, tires, oil, fishing
Labour Force: 41.1 million (2001); 67% agriculture, 33% industry and services
Unemployment: n.a.
Agriculture: accounts for 25% of GDP (2000); rice, corn, potatoes make up 50% of farm output; commercial crops (rubber, soybeans, coffee, tea, bananas) and animal products other 50%; not self-sufficient in rice
Natural Resources: phosphates, coal, manganese, bauxite, chromate, offshore oil deposits, forests

■ FINANCE/TRADE

Currency: dong (pl. dong) (D) = 100 xu
International Reserves Excluding Gold: US$3.982 billion (Nov. 2002)
Gold Reserves: n.a.
Budget: revenues US$5.3 billion, expenditures US$5.6 billion, including capital expenditures of US$1.8 billion (1999 est.)
Defence Expenditures: 11.6% of central government expenditure (1999)
Education Expenditures: 13.93% of total government expenditure (2000)
External Debt: US$12.578 billion (2001)
Exports: US$15.876 billion (2002 est.); commodities: agricultural and handicraft products, coal, minerals, ores, coffee, rubber, tea; partners: Israel, Jordan, Gaza Strip
Imports: US$17.863 billion (2002 est.); commodities: petroleum, steel products, railroad equipment, chemicals, medicines, raw cotton, fertilizer, grain; partners: Japan, Singapore, South Korea, Taiwan, China, Thailand, Hong Kong

■ COMMUNICATIONS

Daily Newspapers: 4/1,000 inhabitants (2000)
Televisions: 186/1,000 inhabitants (2001)
Radios: 109/1,000 inhabitants (2001)
Telephones: 38 lines/1,000 inhabitants (2001)

■ TRANSPORTATION

Motor Vehicles: 178,000; 80,000 passenger cars
Roads: 93,300 km; 23,418 km paved
Railway: 3,142 km (2001)
Air Traffic: 3,410,000 passengers carried (2001)
Airports: 34; 17 have paved runways (2002)

Canadian Embassy: The Canadian Embassy, 31 Hung Vuong Street, Hanoi, Vietnam, Tel: (011 84 4) 823-5500, Fax: (011 84 4) 823-5333. e-mail: hanoi@dfait-maeci.gc.ca
Embassy in Canada: Embassy of the Socialist Republic of Vietnam, 470 Wilbrod St, Ottawa, ON KIN 6M8. Tel: (613) 236-0772. Fax: (613) 236-2704. e-mail: vietem@istar.ca

Wallis and Futuna

Long-Form Name: Territory of the Wallis and Futuna Islands
Capital: Mata-Utu

■ GEOGRAPHY

Area: 274 sq. km
Climate: tropical maritime, rainy season (Nov. to April); cool, dry season (May to Oct.)
Land Use: 5% arable; 20% permanent crops; 0% meadows and pasture; 0% forests; 75% other; includes n.a. sq. km irrigated
Location: SW Pacific Ocean, E of Australia

■ PEOPLE

Population: 15,585 (July 2002 est.)
Nationality: Wallisian, Futunan, or Wallis and Futuna Islanders
Ethnic Groups: Polynesians, and descendants of French settlers
Languages: Wallisian, Futunian (Polynesian languages), French

■ GOVERNMENT

Colony/Territory of: Overseas Territory of France
Leader(s): Head of State: Pres. Jacques Chirac (France), High Administrator: Christian Job
Government Type: overseas territory of France
National Holiday: Bastille Day, July 14

■ ECONOMY

Overview: agriculture includes copra, cassava, yams, taro roots, bananas; livestock includes pigs and goats; considerable imports, negligible exports

■ FINANCE/TRADE

Currency: CFP franc = 100 centimes

Canadian Embassy: c/o The Canadian Embassy, 35-37 avenue Montaigne, 75008, Paris, France. Tel: (011-33-1) 44-43-29-00. Fax: (011-33-1) 44-43-29-99. e-mail: paris@dfait-maeci.gc.ca

Representative to Canada: c/o Embassy of France, 42 Sussex Dr, Ottawa ON K1M 2C9. Tel: (613) 789-1795. Fax: (613) 562-3735. e-mail: politique@ambafrance-ca.org

West Bank

Long-Form Name: none
Capital: none

■ GEOGRAPHY

Area: 5,860 sq. km
Climate: temperate, temperature and precipitation vary with altitude, warm to hot summers, cool to mild winters
Land Use: 27% arable; 0% permanent crops; 32% permanent pastures; 1% forests and woodland; 40% other; includes n.a. sq. km irrigated
Location: Middle East, between Israel and Jordan

■ PEOPLE

Population: 2,163,667 (Feb. 2002 est.)
Nationality: n.a.
Ethnic Groups: Palestinian Arab and other 83%, Jewish 17%
Languages: Arabic, Hebrew (spoken by Israeli settlers and many Palestinians), English (widely understood)

■ GOVERNMENT

Colony/Territory of: claimed and occupied by Israel
Leader(s): local Palestinian authority is headed by Yasser Arafat, subject to Israeli authority
Government Type: Palestinian Legislative Council (Jan. 1996) has limited powers under interim self-governing agreements with Israel. Originally designated as a five-year interim arrangement in 1993, permanent status still under negotiation.
National Holiday: n.a.

■ ECONOMY

Overview: as for Gaza Strip

■ FINANCE/TRADE

Currency: 1 new Israeli shekel= 100 new agorot; 1 Jordanian dinar = 1,000 fils.

Canadian Embassy: n.a.
Representative to Canada: n.a.

Western Sahara

Long-Form Name: Western Sahara
Capital: none

■ GEOGRAPHY

Area: 266,000 sq. km

Coastline: 1,110 km
Climate: Mediterranean to arid; hot, dry desert; rain is rare; cold offshore air currents produce fog and heavy dew
Environment: desertification, sparse water and arable land; hot and dry and dust/sand-laden sirocco wind; harmattan haze
Terrain: mostly barren rocky desert; small mountains in south and northeast
Land Use: 0% arable; 0% permanent crops; 19% permanent pastures; 0% forests; 81% other; includes n.a. sq. km irrigated
Location: NW Africa, bordering on Atlantic Ocean

■ PEOPLE

Population: 256,177 (July 2002 est.)
Nationality: Sahrawi, Sahraoui
Age Structure: n.a.
Population Growth Rate: 2.29% (2000 est.)
Net Migration: -6.05 migrants/1,000 population (2000 est.)
Ethnic Groups: Arabs, Berbers
Languages: Hassaniya Arabic, Moroccan Arabic
Religions: Islam (almost 100% Sunni Muslim)
Birth Rate: 45.07/1,000 population (2000 est.)
Death Rate: 16.11/1,000 population (2000 est.)
Infant Mortality: 133.59 deaths/1,000 live births (2000 est.)
Life Expectancy at Birth: 48.65 years male, 51.33 years female (2000 est.)
Total Fertility Rate: 6.64 children born/woman (2000 est.)
Literacy: n.a.

■ GOVERNMENT

Leader(s): under de facto control of Morocco
Government Type: under Moroccan occupation; legal status and matters of sovereignty remain unresolved
Administrative Divisions: none (under de facto control of Morocco)
Nationhood: n.a.
National Holiday: n.a.

■ ECONOMY

Overview: economy severely disrupted by Moroccan occupation and ongoing guerrilla warfare; poor in natural resources and with inadequate rainfall, most food must be imported; all aspects of the economy are controlled by the Moroccan government
GDP: n.a.
Inflation: n.a.
Industries: phosphate mining, fishing, handicrafts
Labour Force: approx. 12,000; 50% of the people are engaged in subsistence farming and animal husbandry
Unemployment: n.a.
Agriculture: limited to subsistence agriculture; some grain production, livestock (esp. sheep,

goats, camels); cash economy exists largely for the garrison forces
Natural Resources: rich phosphate deposits, iron ore

■ FINANCE/TRADE

Currency: Moroccan dirham (DH) = 100 centimes
International Reserves Excluding Gold: n.a.
Gold Reserves: n.a.
Budget: n.a.
Defence Expenditures: n.a.
Education Expenditures: n.a.
External Debt: n.a.
Exports: exact figures n.a.; phosphates main export product; Morocco claims and administers Western Sahara, so trade partners are included in overall Moroccan accounts
Imports: exact figures n.a.; fuel for fishing fleet; most of the country's food supply must be imported; partners, see exports

■ COMMUNICATIONS

Daily Newspapers: n.a.
Televisions: n.a.
Radios: n.a.
Telephones: n.a.

■ TRANSPORTATION

Motor Vehicles: n.a.
Roads: 6,200 km; 1,350 km surfaced
Railway: none
Air Traffic: n.a.
Airports: 11; 3 have paved runways (2002)

Canadian Embassy: none
Embassy in Canada: none

Yemen

Long-Form Name: Republic of Yemen
Capital: Sana'a (political capital); Aden (commercial capital)

■ GEOGRAPHY

Area: 527,970 sq. km
Coastline: 1,906 km
Climate: hot, dry desert in the south to temperate in central region and north; harsh desert in the east
Environment: desertification, overgrazing, lack of natural fresh water, soil erosion, summer dust and sandstorms
Terrain: narrow coastal plain; western mountains, northern desert interior
Land Use: 3% arable land; 13% permanent crops; 33.5% meadows and pasture; 4% forest and woodland; 46.5% other; includes 5,674 sq. km irrigated
Location: SW Asia (Middle East), bordering on Red Sea

■ PEOPLE

Population: 18,701,257 (July 2002 est.)
Nationality: Yemeni
Age Structure: 0–14 yrs: 47.0%; 15–64: 50.1%; 65+: 2.9% (2002 est.)
Population Growth Rate: 3.40% (2002 est.)
Net Migration: 0 migrants/1,000 population (2002 est.)
Ethnic Groups: predominantly Arab; Afro-Arab, Indian, Somali and European minorities
Languages: Arabic
Religions: predominantly Muslim; Christian and Hindu minorities in the south
Birth Rate: 43.30/1,000 population (2002 est.)
Death Rate: 9.31/1,000 population (2002 est.)
Infant Mortality: 66.78 deaths/1,000 live births (2002 est.)
Life Expectancy at Birth: 58.81 years male, 62.46 years female (2002 est.)
Total Fertility Rate: 6.90 children born/woman (2002 est.)
Literacy: 46.3% (2000)

■ GOVERNMENT

Leader(s): Pres. Ali Abdallah Salih, Prime Min. Abd al-Qadir Ba Jamal
Government Type: republic
Administrative Divisions: 17 governorates (muhafazat, sing. —muhafazah)
Nationhood: May 22, 1990
National Holiday: Unification Day, May 22

■ ECONOMY

Overview: future economic level depends heavily on Western assistance; North: low level of domestic industry once self-sufficient in food but now dependent on imports; South: economic growth among the slowest of all Arab countries
GDP: US$14.8 billion, per capita US$820; real growth rate 4.0% (2001 est.)
Inflation: 10% (2000 est.)
Industries: accounts for 40% of GDP (2000); petroleum, cotton, textiles, leather goods, food processing, handicrafts, cement, small aluminum products factory
Labour Force: 5.7 million (2001); most people are employed in agriculture
Unemployment: n.a.
Agriculture: in the north, agriculture accounts for 20% GDP; main crops include fruit (grapes) and cotton; in the south, agriculture accounts for 17% GDP and 45% of the labour force; the main agricultural product is livestock (cattle, camels, sheep, goats, poultry)
Natural Resources: salt deposits, petroleum, fish, marble, coal, gold, lead, nickel, copper

■ FINANCE/TRADE

Currency: Yemeni rial (YR) = 100 fils
International Reserves Excluding Gold: US$4.148 billion (Oct. 2002)

Gold Reserves: 0.050 million fine troy ounces (Oct. 2002)
Budget: revenues US$3 billion; expenditures US$3.1 billion, including capital expenditures of US$ n.a. (2001 est.)
Defence Expenditures: 18.8% of central government expenditure (2001)
Education Expenditures: 21.81% of government expenditure (1999)
External Debt: US$4.954 billion (2001)
Exports: US$3.214 billion (2001); crude oil, cotton, coffee, vegetables, cotton, animal hides, fish; partners: Saudi Arabia, Japan, Singapore, Thailand, China, South Korea
Imports: US$2.309 billion (2001); textiles and other manufactured consumer goods, petroleum products, sugar, grain, flour, other foodstuffs, cement, consumer goods, crude oil, machinery, chemicals; partners: Saudi Arabia, UAE, US, France, Italy

■ COMMUNICATIONS

Daily Newspapers: 15/1,000 inhabitants (2000)
Televisions: 283/1,000 inhabitants (2001)
Radios: 65/1,000 inhabitants (2001)
Telephones: 22 lines/1,000 inhabitants (2001)

■ TRANSPORTATION

Motor Vehicles: 516,000; 230,000 passenger cars
Roads: 69,263 km; 9,963 km paved (1999)
Railway: none
Air Traffic: 841,000 passengers carried (2001)
Airports: 49; 16 have paved runways (2002)

Canadian Embassy: The Canadian Embassy to Yemen, c/o Canadian Embassy, Diplomatic Quarter, P.O. Box 94321, Riyadh 11693, Saudi Arabia. Tel: (011-966-1) 488-2288. Fax: (011-966-1) 488-1997. e-mail: ryadh@dfait-maeci.gc.ca
Embassy in Canada: Embassy of the Republic of Yemen, 788 Island Park Drive, Ottawa ON K1Y OC2. Tel: (613) 729-6627. Fax: (613) 729-8915. e-mail: info@yemenembassy.ca

Yugoslavia

see Serbia and Montenegro

Zambia

Long-Form Name: Republic of Zambia
Capital: Lusaka

■ GEOGRAPHY

Area: 752,614 sq. km
Coastline: none: landlocked
Climate: tropical; modified by altitude; rainy season (Oct. to Apr.)
Environment: deforestation; soil erosion; desertification; air pollution and resultant acid

rain; tropical storms are a natural hazard from Nov. to Apr.

Terrain: mostly high plateau with some hills and mountains

Land Use: 7% arable; 0% permanent crops; 40% meadows; 39% forest; 14% other; includes 460 sq. km irrigated

Location: SC Africa

■ PEOPLE

Population: 9,959,037 (July 2002 est.)

Nationality: Zambian

Age Structure: 0–14 yrs: 47.1%; 15–64: 50.4%; 65+: 2.5% (2002 est.)

Population Growth Rate: 1.90% (2002 est.)

Net Migration: -0.16 migrants/1,000 population (2002 est.)

Ethnic Groups: 98.7% African, 1.1% European, 0.2% other

Languages: English (official); about 70 indigenous languages

Religions: 50–75% Christian, 24–49% Muslim and Hindu, remainder indigenous beliefs

Birth Rate: 41.01/1,000 population (2002 est.)

Death Rate: 21.89/1,000 population (2002 est.)

Infant Mortality: 89.39 deaths/1,000 live births (2002 est.)

Life Expectancy at Birth: 37.05 years male, 37.66 years female (2002 est.)

Total Fertility Rate: 5.43 children born/woman (2002 est.)

Literacy: 77.2% (1999)

■ GOVERNMENT

Leader(s): Pres. Levy Mwanawasa, V. Pres. Nevers Mumba

Government Type: republic

Administrative Divisions: 9 provinces

Nationhood: Oct. 24, 1964 (from UK; formerly known as Northern Rhodesia)

National Holiday: Independence Day, Oct. 24

■ ECONOMY

Overview: economy continues to decline due to a sustained drop in copper production and ineffective economic policies; problems include a high inflation rate, high population growth and severe drought

GDP: US$8.5 billion, per capita US$870; real growth rate 3.9% (2001 est.)

Inflation: 27.3% (2000 est.)

Industries: accounts for 25% of GDP (2000); copper mining and processing, transport, construction, foodstuffs, beverages, chemicals, textiles and fertilizer

Labour Force: 4.4 million (2001); 85% agriculture, 6% industry, 9% services

Unemployment: 50% (2000 est.)

Agriculture: accounts for 24% of GDP (2000) and 85% of labour force; food production is insufficient for country's needs; crops: corn (food staple), sorghum, rice, peanuts, sunflower, tobacco, cotton, sugar cane, cassava; cattle, goats, beef, eggs produced; marginally self-sufficient in corn

Natural Resources: copper, cobalt, zinc, lead, coal, emeralds, gold, silver, uranium, hydro power potential

■ FINANCE/TRADE

Currency: kwacha (K) = 100 ngwee

International Reserves Excluding Gold: US$362 million (Oct. 2002)

Gold Reserves: n.a.

Budget: revenues US$1.2 billion; expenditures US$1.25 billion, including capital expenditures of US$ n.a. (2001 est.)

Defence Expenditures: 3.93% of government expenditure (1999)

Education Expenditures: 14.45% of government expenditure (1999)

External Debt: US$5.671 billion (2001)

Exports: US$698 million (2000); commodities: copper, zinc, cobalt, lead, tobacco, electricity; partners: UK, South Africa, Switzerland, Malawi

Imports: US$682 million (2000); commodities: machinery, transportation equipment, foodstuffs, fuels, manufactures; partners: South Africa, UK, Zimbabwe, US

■ COMMUNICATIONS

Daily Newspapers: 12/1,000 inhabitants (2000)

Televisions: 113/1,000 inhabitants (2001)

Radios: 169/1,000 inhabitants (2001)

Telephones: 8 lines/1,000 inhabitants (2001)

■ TRANSPORTATION

Motor Vehicles: 215,500; 142,000 passenger cars

Roads: 66,781 km; n.a. km paved

Railway: 2,157 km (2001)

Air Traffic: 49,000 passengers carried (2001)

Airports: 111; 11 have paved runways (2002)

Canadian Embassy: The Canadian High Commission, 5199 United Nations Ave, Lusaka; mailing address: P.O. Box 31313, 10101 Lusaka, Zambia. Tel: (011-260-1) 25-08-33. Fax: (011-260-1) 25-41-76. e-mail: lsaka@dfait-maeci.gc.ca

Embassy in Canada: c/o High Commision for the Republic of Zambia, Embassy of Zambia, 2419 Massachusetts Ave NW, Washington DC 20008, USA. Tel: (202) 265-9717. Fax: (202) 332-0826. e-mail: zambia@tmn.com

Zimbabwe

Long-Form Name: Republic of Zimbabwe

Capital: Harare

■ GEOGRAPHY

Area: 390,580 sq. km

Coastline: none: landlocked

Climate: tropical; moderated by altitude; rainy season (Nov. to Mar.)
Environment: recurring droughts; floods and severe storms are rare; deforestation; soil erosion; air and water pollution; desertification; poaching has significantly reduced the black rhinoceros population, which was once the largest concentration of the species anywhere in the world
Terrain: mostly high plateau with higher central plateau (high veld); mountains in east
Land Use: 7% arable; less than 1% permanent crops (coffee plantations); 13% meadows; 23% forest and woodland; 57% other; includes 1,930 sq. km irrigated
Location: S Africa

■ PEOPLE

Population: 11,376,676 (July 2002 est.)
Nationality: Zimbabwean
Age Structure: 0–14 yrs: 37.9%; 15–64: 58.4%; 65+: 3.7% (2002 est.)
Population Growth Rate: 0.05% (2002 est.)
Net Migration: 0 migrants/1,000 population (2002 est.)
Ethnic Groups: 98% African (71% Shona, 16% Ndebele, 11% other), 1% white, 1% mixed and Asian
Languages: English (official); Shona and Sindebele, numerous minor tribal dialects
Religions: 50% syncretic (part Christian, part indigenous beliefs), 25% Christian, 24% indigenous beliefs, a few Muslim
Birth Rate: 24.59/1,000 population (2002 est.)
Death Rate: 24.06/1,000 population (2002 est.)
Infant Mortality: 62.97 deaths/1,000 live births (2002 est.)
Life Expectancy at Birth: 37.87 years male, 35.10 years female (2002 est.)
Total Fertility Rate: 3.21 children born/woman (2002 est.)
Literacy: 88.7% (2000)

■ GOVERNMENT

Leader(s): Pres. Robert Mugabe
Government Type: parliamentary democracy
Administrative Divisions: 8 provinces and 2 cities with provincial status
Nationhood: Apr. 18, 1980 (from UK; formerly known as Southern Rhodesia)
National Holiday: Independence Day, Apr. 18

■ ECONOMY

Overview: severe droughts have adversely affected this agriculture-based economy in recent years; the government is working to consolidate earlier progress in developing a market-oriented economy
GDP: US$28 billion, per capita US$2,450; real growth rate -6.5% (2001 est.)
Inflation: 76.7% (2001)
Industries: accounts for 14% of GDP (2000); mining (minerals and metals account for 40% of exports), steel, clothing and footwear, chemicals, foodstuffs, fertilizer, beverages, transportation equipment, wood products
Labour Force: 5.9 million (2001); 24% community, social and business services, 66% agriculture, 10% industry
Unemployment: 6.0% (2001)
Agriculture: accounts for 11% of GDP (2000); 40% of land area divided into 4,500 large commercial farms and 42% in communal lands; crops: corn (food staple), cotton, tobacco, wheat, coffee, sugar cane, peanuts; livestock: cattle, sheep, goats, pigs; self-sufficient in food
Natural Resources: coal, chromium ore, asbestos, gold, nickel, copper, iron ore, vanadium, lithium, tin

■ FINANCE/TRADE

Currency: Zimbabwean dollar ($Z) = 100 cents
International Reserves Excluding Gold: US$82 million (Aug. 2002)
Gold Reserves: 0.139 million fine troy ounces (Aug. 2002)
Budget: revenues US$2.5 billion; expenditures US$2.6 billion, including capital expenditures US$ n.a. (2000 est.)
Defence Expenditures: 9.4% of central government expenditure (2001)
Education Expenditures: n.a.
External Debt: US$3.780 billion (2001)
Exports: US$1.927 billion (2000); commodities: agriculture 34% (tobacco 21%, other 13%), manufactures 19%, gold 11%, ferrochrome 11%, cotton 6%; partners: South Africa, UK, Japan, Germany, China
Imports: US$2.564 billion (2000); commodities: machinery and transportation equipment 37%, other manufactures 22%, chemicals 16%, fuels 15%; partners: South Africa, UK, Germany, US, Japan

■ COMMUNICATIONS

Daily Newspapers: 18/1,000 inhabitants (2000)
Televisions: 30/1,000 inhabitants (2000)
Radios: 362/1,000 inhabitants (2001)
Telephones: 19 lines/1,000 inhabitants (2001)

■ TRANSPORTATION

Motor Vehicles: 358,000; 250,000 passenger cars
Roads: 18,338 km; 8,692 km paved
Railway: 3,077 km (2001)
Air Traffic: 495,000 passengers carried (2001)
Airports: 454; 17 have paved runways (2002)

Canadian Embassy: The Canadian High Commission, 45 Baines Ave, Harare, Zimbabwe; mailing address: P.O. Box 1430, Harare, Zimbabwe. Tel: (011-263-4) 252-181. Fax: (011-263-4) 252-186. e-mail: hrare@dfait-maeci.gc.ca
Embassy in Canada: High Commission for the Republic of Zimbabwe, 332 Somerset St W, Ottawa ON K2P 0J9. Tel: (613) 237-4388. Fax: (613) 563-8269. e-mail: zim.highcomm@sympatico.ca

SCIENCE AND NATURE

Astronomy has taught us that the universe is more complex than the ancients thought. Though less dependent on the "patterns" in the sky, we continue the exploration. The skies act not simply as a guide, but also as a frontier to be explored.

Our Solar System

Our solar system consists of our sun, at least nine planets and smaller bodies such as asteroids, comets and moons. The dominant member of this family is the sun, our nearest star. The sun is an enormous ball of hot, glowing gas, mostly hydrogen and helium. Its powerful pull of gravity holds the planets, asteroids and comets in orbit around it.

The planets have been known since people first turned their gaze skyward. The ancient Greeks called them "wanderers" because they moved through the sky relative to the fixed stars. Five planets can be seen without a telescope: Mercury, Venus, Mars, Jupiter and Saturn. They are visible because they reflect the light of the sun.

In order of distance from the sun, the planets are Mercury, Venus, Earth, Mars, Jupiter, Saturn, Uranus, Neptune and Pluto.

All the planets revolve (orbit) around the sun in the same counter-clockwise direction. The closer to the sun, the greater their speed. Except for Pluto, all the orbits lie in nearly the same plane in space, like marbles rolling on a table top.

Our Place in the Universe Although the solar system seems enormous, it is quite small compared to the whole universe. Our sun is only one star among the hundreds of billions that make up our spiral-shaped galaxy, the **Milky Way**. It takes our sun, with planets in tow, about 250 million years to orbit around the Milky Way just once. All the stars that we see at night are in a small, nearby portion of our galaxy. There may be billions of galaxies in the universe, each containing billions of stars of its own.

The Birth of Our Solar System Approximately 4.6 billion years ago (billions of years after the galaxies were formed) astronomers believe that a vast cloud of gas and dust collapsed and formed a spinning disk. Gravitation compacted so much material in the centre that extremely high pressures and temperatures lit a nuclear fire—our sun began to shine. Meanwhile, any remaining lumps of hot solids and gases slowly collected to become the planets, moons, asteroids and comets.

Our Solar System The planets of the solar system can be divided into two groups. The inner planets, Mercury, Venus, Earth and Mars, are the **terrestrial**, or Earth-like, planets. These are small rocky worlds with metal cores and thin atmospheres, except for airless Mercury. Jupiter, Saturn, Uranus and Neptune make up the realm of the **gas giants**. These planets do not have a solid surface, but are made up of layers of gases and clouds, possibly with rocky cores the size of Earth. The gas giants are huge: a thousand Earths could easily fit inside Jupiter. Saturn's rings may be the most famous feature of the solar system but rings are also found around Jupiter, Uranus and Neptune.

Pluto is unique and does not fit into either of these two groups. It is a tiny world of rock and ice, smaller than the Earth's moon, and with an extremely thin atmosphere.

Separating the terrestrial planets from the gas giants is the **asteroid belt**, a region of space between Mars and Jupiter where as many as 50,000 rocky objects may orbit the sun. Asteroids, often called minor planets, range from gravel-size, or smaller, to the 1,000-km-wide Ceres. They may be the remains of a small, shattered planet.

More than 60 moons, or satellites, are found in the solar system. All the planets, except for Mercury and Venus, have at least one moon orbiting them. Some of these moons are fascinating worlds in their own right: **Phobos** and **Deimos**, the moons of Mars, may be captured asteroids; **Io**, one of Jupiter's moons, has many active volcanoes; **Europa**, another one of Jupiter's moons, may have a frozen ocean; **Titan**, a moon of Saturn, has an atmosphere thicker than Earth's. Jupiter with its 39 known moons, Saturn with its 30 and Uranus with its 20 are like miniature solar systems.

Exploring the Solar System Most of the planets have been visited by space probes from Earth: Mercury was visited in 1974 by *Mariner 10*, Soviet *Venera* spacecraft landed on Venus several times in the 1970s while *Viking 1* and *2* landed on Mars in 1976. The best spacecraft views of Jupiter and Saturn were obtained by *Voyager 1* and *2* in 1979 and 1980–81 respectively. *Voyager 2* went on to Uranus in 1986 and Neptune in August 1989. These spacecraft made discoveries not possible from the Earth: craters on Mercury, volcanoes and great valleys on Mars, Jupiter's ring and 10 new moons of Uranus were only a few.

Recent missions include the *Ulysses* mission, launched in 1990, which finished its second orbit of the sun in 1997–98. The spacecraft performed a south polar pass of the sun from September 2000 to January 2001. The combined NASA/ESA (European Space Agency) *Cassini* mission to Saturn was launched in October 1997. *Cassini* will enter orbit around Saturn in July 2004.

Mars has been the target of several missions, and the pace of exploration is increasing. In 1997, the *Pathfinder* mission to Mars made a successful landing, sending back data and pictures. In November 1996 the *Mars Global Surveyor* (MGS) was launched on a mapping and photography mission. Mapping began in March 1999 and pictures taken in June 2000 showed features resembling water erosion in over 200 places. In 2002, the *Mars Odyssey* spacecraft detected quantities of undergound ice. A 2003 European mission, the *Mars Express*, will use radar to continue the search for water. Two NASA missions in 2003 will land robotic explorers—dubbed *Spirit* and *Opportunity*—to send back detailed data about the surface. Visit http://mars.jpl.nasa.gov for details.

Our Solar System at a Glance

	Distance from Sun (million km)	Equatorial Diameter (km)	Gravity (Earth=1)	Mass (Earth=1)	Period of Orbit about the Sun	Period of Rotation on Axis (days)	Number of Known Moons
Sun	—	1 392 000	27.90	332 830	—	25.38	—
Mercury	57.9	4 878	0.38	0.06	88.0 days	58.60	0
Venus	108.2	12 104	0.91	0.8	224.7 days	243.00	0
Earth	149.6	12 756	1.00	1.0	365.3 days	0.99	1
Mars	227.9	6 787	0.38	0.1	1.88 years	1.02	2
Jupiter	778.4	142 800	2.54	317.8	11.86 years	0.41	52
Saturn	1 426.7	120 000	1.08	95.2	29.63 years	0.42	30
Uranus	2 868.7	51 200	0.91	14.5	83.97 years	0.71	21
Neptune	4 498.2	48 680	1.19	17.2	164.80 years	0.67	11
Pluto	5 906.3	2 390	0.06	0.002	248.63 years	6.38	1

Source: *NASA 2001; http://solarsystem.nasa.gov/features/planets/planetsfeat.html*

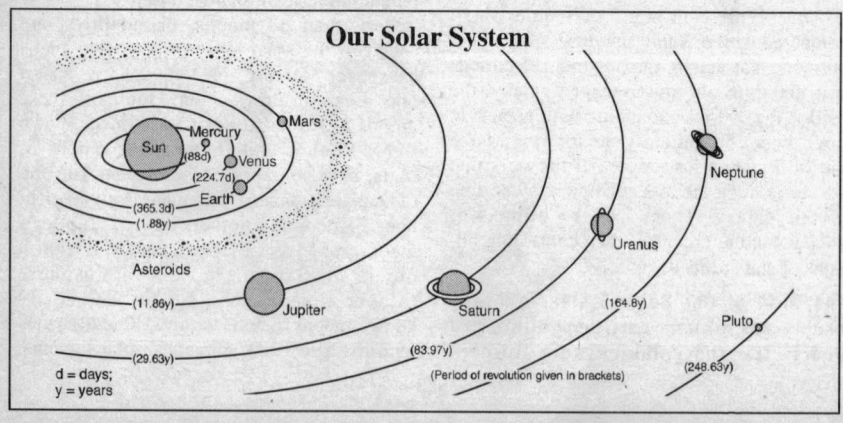

Our Solar System

Mercury (88d) — Venus (224.7d) — Earth (365.3d) (1.88y) — Mars — Asteroids — Jupiter (11.86y) — Saturn (29.63y) — Uranus (83.97y) — Neptune (164.8y) — Pluto (248.63y)

d = days; y = years

(Period of revolution given in brackets)

International Space Station (ISS)

Sixteen countries have been contributing to the International Space Station (ISS), a project that first got serious attention (and funding) in 1993. That project is now a reality that orbits 400 km above the Earth, at an inclination of 51.6° to the equator.

The assembly of the ISS began in 1998, when the first stage—the Functional Cargo Block—was launched from Kazakhstan. That first launch put the propulsion, command and control systems in place with the Zarya module. A six-man crew went up in December 1998 to do some assembly of the space station in orbit—they added the Unity module. In June 1999, tools and a crane were added to assist in construction. On May 19, 2000, a seven-member crew began to ready the space station for residents. On July 25, 2000, the third big component of the station, Zvezda, docked with the ISS. A NASA mission in mid-September took supplies up after a Russian supply ship with oxygen generators, toilet components and other gear had made Zvezda habitable. The September NASA mission installed equipment such as power and data cables as well as bringing supplies.

Canada's Marc Garneau visited the station as part of a mission (Nov. 30–Dec. 11, 2000) to install the station's first solar panels, which will generate 110 kilowatts of power. Col. Chris Hadfield became the first Canadian to walk in space (Apr. 19–May 1, 2001), when he installed CANADARM2.

Canada's contribution to the ISS is the Mobile Servicing System (MSS); the sophisticated CANADARM2 is part of this system, as is a robotic hand (known formally as a Special Purpose Dexterous Manipulator or SPDM). These pieces and the CANADARM2 will be used for assembly and maintenance tasks on the space station. The arm, together with the hand, can manipulate delicate objects; the CANADARM2 can work with large objects. The Canadian Space Agency is developing a Canadian Space Vision System to assist those using the equipment. Ground support for the devices will be at CSA headquarters in St. Hubert, Quebec.

The station is expected to be finished in 2006.

Other contributions to the project include a pressurized lab and logistics transport vehicles (European Space Agency); a lab with "attached exposed facility" and logistics transport vehicles (Japan); and research modules, a service module with its own life support and habitation system, a science power platform to supply electrical power, more logistics transport vehicles and a Soyuz spacecraft for emergency crew return and transfer (Russia).

The completed station would weigh almost 450 metric tons, were it on Earth. It will be 108 m by 88 m, with about the same volume as the fuselage of Boeing 747 or three ordinary houses. It will accommodate up to seven people at once. Its orbit was chosen because it can be reached by launch vehicles from each of the international partners; the orbit also allows observation of 85 percent of the globe and 95 percent of the world's population.

The ISS was originally planned to establish a permanent laboratory where gravity, temperature and air pressure could be manipulated to create conditions that would be impossible to achieve in Earth-bound labs. The participants in the ISS program are the United States; Canada; European Space Agency partners Belgium, Denmark, France, Germany, Italy, the Netherlands, Norway, Spain, Sweden, Switzerland, and the United Kingdom; plus Japan, Russia and Brazil. Each partner will contribute astronauts to crew the finished station, and have access to its labs for research and experiments.

For more news and information, visit spaceflight.nasa.gov/station or www.space.gc.ca

Some Astronomical Terms

Asteroid: Any of the thousands of small, rocky objects that orbit the Sun. Some pass closer to the Sun than Earth does and others have orbits that take them well beyond Jupiter. The largest asteroid is one called Ceres.

Big Bang: The primeval explosion that most astronomers think gave rise to the universe as we see it today, in which clusters of galaxies are moving apart from one another. Astronomers calculate the Big Bang happened about 15 to 20 billion years ago.

Black Hole: An object whose gravitational pull is so strong that—within a certain distance of it—nothing can escape, not even light. Black holes are thought to result from the collapse of certain very massive stars, but other kinds have been postulated as well: **mini black holes**, for example, which might have been formed in the turbulence shortly after the Big Bang. **Supermassive black holes**—with masses millions of times the Sun's—may exist in the cores of large galaxies.

Comet: A small chunk of ice, dust and rocky material (a few kilometres across) which, when it comes close enough to the Sun, can develop a tenuous "tail." The tail of a comet is made of gas and dust that have been driven off the comet's surface by the Sun's energy. The tail always points away from the Sun (no matter in what direction the comet is moving).

Eclipse: The blocking of all or part of the light from one object by another.

Galaxy: A large assemblage of stars (and sometimes interstellar gas and dust), typically containing millions to hundreds of billions of member stars. A galaxy is held together by the gravitational attraction of its member stars (and other material) to one another.

Light-Year: The distance light travels in one year in a vacuum. Since light travels at a speed of about 300,000 km per second, a light-year is roughly 9.5 trillion km long.

Magnitude: A way of expressing the brightness of astronomical objects, inherited from the Greeks. In the magnitude system, a lower number indicates a brighter object (for example, a 1st-magnitude star is brighter than a 3rd-magnitude star). Each step in magnitude corresponds to a brightness difference of about 2.5. Stars of the 6th magnitude are the faintest unaided human eye can see.

Meteor: A bit of solid debris from space, burning up in the Earth's atmosphere because of friction with the air. Before entering Earth's atmosphere, the body is called a meteoroid. If any of the object survives its fiery passage through the air, the parts that hit the ground are called **meteorites.**

Milky Way Galaxy: A spiral galaxy, with a disk approximately 100,000 light-years across, containing roughly 400 billion stars. Our Sun is in the disk about two-thirds of the way from the centre. It takes about 200 million years to orbit the centre of the Milky Way once.

Neutron Star: A crushed remnant left over when a very massive star explodes. Some neutron stars are known to spin very rapidly, at least at the beginning, and can be detected as **pulsars**: rapidly flashing sources of radio radiation or visible light. The pulses are produced by the spinning of a neutron star, much as a lighthouse beacon appears to flash off, on and off.

Nova: A star that abruptly and temporarily increases its brightness by a factor of hundreds of thousands.

Orbit: The path of one body around another (such as the Moon around the Earth) or around the centre of gravity of a number of objects (such as the Sun's 200-million-year path around the centre of our galaxy).

Planet: A major object that orbits around a star.

Quasar: One of a class of very distant (typically billions of light years away), extremely bright, and very small objects. Quasar means "quasi-star"—that is, something that looks like a star but can't actually be a star.

Red Giant: A very large, distended, and relatively cool star in the final stages of its life.

Solar System: The Sun and all things orbiting it, including the nine major planets, their satellites, and all the asteroids and comets.

Supernova: An explosion that marks the end of a very massive star's life. When it occurs, the star can outshine all the other stars in a galaxy in total for several days, and may leave behind a crushed core (perhaps a neutron star or a black hole).

White Dwarf: The collapsed remnant of a relatively low-mass star (roughly one and a half times the Sun's mass and less), which has exhausted the fuel for its nuclear reactions and shines only by radiating its stored-up heat.

Source: *The Astronomical Society of the Pacific, San Francisco, CA*

Phases of the Moon, 2004

(Eastern Standard Time)

New Moon	First Quarter	Full Moon	Last Quarter
		Jan 7 10:40 AM	Jan 14 11:46 PM
Jan 21 16:05 PM	Jan 29 1:03 AM	Feb 6 3:47 AM	Feb 13 8:39 AM
Feb 20 4:18 AM	Feb 27 10:24 PM	Mar 6 6:14 PM	Mar 13 4:01 PM
Mar 20 17:41 PM	Mar 28 18:48 PM	Apr 5 7:03 AM	Apr 11 11:46 PM
Apr 19 9:21 AM	Apr 27 1:32 PM	May 4 4:33 PM	May11 7:04 AM
May 19 12:52 AM	May 27 3:57 AM	June 3 12:20 AM	Jun 9 4:02 PM
Jun 17 4:27 PM	Jun 25 3:08 PM	Jul 2 7:09 AM	Jul 9 3:33 AM
Jul 17 7:24 AM	Jul 24 11:37 PM	Jul 31 2:05 PM	Aug 7 6:01 PM
Aug 15 9:24 PM	Aug 23 6:12 AM	Aug 29 10:22 PM	Sep 6 4:01 PM
Sep 14 10:29 AM	Sep 21 11:53 AM	Sep 28 9:09 AM	Oct 6 6:12 AM
Oct 13 10:48 PM	Oct 20 5:59 PM	Oct 27 11:07 PM	Nov 5 6:25 PM
Nov12 9:27 AM	Nov 19 12:50 AM	Nov 26 3:07 PM	Dec 4 7:53 PM
Dec 11 8:29 PM	Dec 18 11:39 AM	Dec 26 10:06 AM	

Daylight Saving Time (Summer Time) is kept in most places across Canada. It starts at 2 a.m. on the first Sunday in April, when clocks go forward one hour. Clocks return to Standard Time at 2 a.m. on the last Sunday in October, when clocks go back one hour. To get wristwatch time in the Eastern Time Zone during daylight saving *add* one hour to the times listed.

Across Canada, there are six Standard Time Zones. To adjust to wristwatch time in another time zone, add or subtract the following to the times listed in the table: Newfoundland (+1hr 30m), Atlantic (+1hr), Central (-1hr), Mountain (-2hr), Pacific (-3hr).

Organizations

Canadian Astronomical Society

An organization of professional astronomers. Contact: Hugh Couchman, CASCA Secretary Department of Physics & Astronomy, McMaster University, Hamilton, ON L8S 4M1
Business office: R. Hanes
Dept. of Physics, Queen's University, Kingston, ON K7L 3N6
Tel: (613) 533-6439; Fax: (613) 533-6463
Web site: www.casca.ca

Royal Astronomical Society of Canada (RASC)

The Society is an organization of amateur and professional astronomers that is open to anyone interested in astronomy. The Society publishes the annual *Observer's Handbook* as well as other publications. It has more than 4,500 members in 26 centres across Canada. National Headquarters: 136 Dupont Street, Toronto, ON M5R 1V2
Tel: (888) 924-RASC
Web site: www.rasc.ca

Look Out... It's a Starquake!

*S*tarquakes—the stellar equivalent of earthquakes—are helping scientists uncover clues about how distant stars are put together. Canadian astrophysicist Gilles Fontaine at the University of Montreal is a leading figure in this field. He and his team work very much like geophysicists who analyse seismic waves on Earth to establish a picture of the planet's deep structures. When there's a similar seismic disturbance in a distant star, the light from it develops oscillations—it "shakes." Using new numerical techniques to analyse those vibrations, Fontaine and his team were able to establish the mass, dimension, surface temperature, internal chemical composition, period of rotation and distance from our sun of a star called PG0014+067 that is so faint it's invisible to the naked eye. Detailed analysis of such stars—known as white dwarfs and sub dwarfs—is allowing astrophysicists to deduce new information about the characteristics of galaxies and even the age of the universe itself.

Source: *NSERC*

Events in the 2004 Sky

January

3–5   Quadrantids Meteor Shower. The near full moon will be a problem for the Quadrantids this year. Best viewing will be to the east after midnight.

March

4   Jupiter at Opposition. The giant planet will be at its closest approach to Earth. This is the best time to view and photograph Jupiter and its moons.

20   The vernal equinox occurs at 1:49 p.m. EST. There will be equal amounts of day and night. This is also the first day of spring.

April

21–23   Lyrid Meteor Shower. This should be a great year for the Lyrids. The thin crescent moon will set early in the evening leaving a dark sky for the show. Look for meteors radiating from the constellation of Lyra after midnight.

May

4   Total lunar eclipse. (See Eclipses, p. 571, for details.)

5–6   Eta Aquarids Meteor Shower. This will be a disappointing year for the Eta Aquarids. The nearly full moon will hide all but the brightest meteors. Best viewing will be to the east, well after midnight.

June

8   Transit of Venus across the sun. This extremely rare event will only be visible in Asia, Africa and Europe. The dark disk of the planet will be seen moving across the face of the Sun over a period of about six hours.

20   The summer solstice occurs at 8:57 p.m. EDT. The sun is at its highest point in the sky and it will be the longest day of the year. This is the first day of summer in the northern hemisphere.

July

28–29   Southern Delta Aquarids Meteor Shower. The near full moon will be a problem this year. The radiant point for this shower is in the constellation of Aquarius. The brightest meteors can be seen to the east after midnight.

August

11–13   Perseids Meteor Shower. The thin crescent moon should provide good viewing for the Perseids this year. Best viewing should be to the east after midnight. The shower will peak on August 12.

27   Uranus at Opposition. The giant blue planet will be at its closest approach to Earth. Those with good telescopes should be able to make out the planet's tiny blue disk.

September

22   The autumnal equinox begins at 12:30 p.m. EDT. There will be equal amounts of day and night. This is also the first day of autumn.

October

21–22   Orionids Meteor Shower. The near quarter moon may make early evening viewing difficult. The radiant point for this shower is in the constellation of Orion. The best time to see the Orionids this year will be after the moon sets, well after midnight. Look to the east.

28   Total solar eclipse. (See Eclipses, p. 571, for details.)

November

17–18   Leonid Meteor Shower. The near quarter moon will make viewing difficult in the early evening. Look for this shower radiating from the constellation Leo well after midnight, when the moon has set.

December

13–15   Geminids Meteor Shower. This will be a great year for the Geminids. The moon will be totally absent after sunset so even the faintest meteors can be seen. The radiant point for this shower will be in the constellation of Gemini. Look to the east after midnight.

21   The winter solstice occurs at 7:42 a.m. EST. The sun is at its lowest point in the sky and it will be the shortest day of the year. This is the first day of winter in the northern hemisphere.

Eclipses in 2004

The year 2004 features two partial eclipses of the sun and two total eclipses of the moon. Unfortunately for viewers in Canada, neither of the solar eclipses will be visible and only one of the lunar eclipses.

April 19

The first eclipse of the year will be a partial eclipse of the sun, visible in Antarctica, the southeast Atlantic Ocean, and the southern half of Africa and Madagascar.

May 4

The beginning of the first total eclipse of the moon will be visible in Asia, Europe, Africa, Indonesia, Australia, New Zealand, Antarctica, the eastern South Atlantic Ocean, the Indian Ocean, and the western Pacific Ocean; the end will be visible in Africa, Europe, western Asia, western Australia, Antarctica, South America, the eastern North Atlantic Ocean, the South Atlantic Ocean, the Indian Ocean, and the extreme southeastern South Pacific Ocean.

October 14

A partial eclipse of the sun will be visible in northeast Asia, Japan, the western Pacific Ocean, the Hawaiian Islands, and the western part of Alaska.

October 28

The beginning of the last eclipse of the year—a total eclipse of the moon – will be visible in Africa, Europe, Greenland, the Arctic, North America except the extreme northwest, Central America, South America, extreme western Asia, part of Queen Maud Land and Antarctica, the Atlantic Ocean, the eastern South Pacific Ocean, and the western Indian Ocean; the end will be visible in North America, the Arctic, Greenland, Central America, South America, Europe, western Africa, Antarctic peninsula, the eastern Pacific Ocean, and the Atlantic Ocean.

> **WARNING: SPECIAL PRECAUTIONS MUST BE TAKEN TO OBSERVE THE SUN AT ALL TIMES. AT NO TIME DURING A PARTIAL SOLAR ECLIPSE CAN THE SUN BE OBSERVED SAFELY WITH THE UNPROTECTED HUMAN EYE.**

Space Information on the World Wide Web

NASA Home Page: *www.nasa.gov*
NASA provides links to the massive amount of information the agency has placed on the Web, as well as links to other space-related sites in the United States and other countries.
Space Telescope Science Institute: *www.stsci.edu*
This is the site for the Hubble Telescope.

Cassini Mission to Saturn: *http://saturn.jpl.nasa.gov*
Images, mission status, student activities.

Getting down on Mars: *A one-stop shopping site for people interested in all aspects of the Red Planet is http://mars.jpl.nasa.gov/. Learn about the evidence for water, the search for traces of former life, and the spacecraft that are studying Mars' surface. If you dream of walking on the ochre dunes of Mars, try http://spaceflight.nasa.gov/mars/, where you'll learn about plans for human exploration of the solar system.*

Canadian Space Agency: *The agency has a home page dedicated to its activities in space. You'll find details of past work and plans for the future, as well as information about space science, a huge gallery of images of current and past Canadian astronauts, and details about all of the agency's programs. (See p. 570.)*
Visit www.space.gc.ca

The Canadian Space Agency (CSA)

With the launch of *Alouette I* on September 9, 1962, Canada became the third country—after the USSR and the U.S.—to have a satellite orbiting the Earth. *Alouette I* was the first satellite to return useful information; its goal was to study the ionosphere (the layer of the atmosphere that affects long-distance radio and television transmissions). The Canadian Space Agency, created by Parliament on December 14, 1990, carries on a long tradition of activity in space for Canadians—a tradition that continues to this day.

Alouette paved the way for further scientific satellites, and, in 1972, Canada broke new ground with the launch of *Anik A-1*, making us the first country to have a commercial communications satellite. It made nation-wide, real-time television possible, and—for the first time—brought reliable telephone service to the far North. A successor satellite, *Anik E-2*, still provides services to television networks and facilitates activities such as the transmission of newspaper copy to printing plants around the country. (A new satellite in the same tradition, *Anik F-2*, was slated to be launched late in 2003.)

Joint ventures with other countries are the norm for Canadian space activities; starting with *Alouette*, our satellites have been launched using boosters provided by other nations. In 1976, the U.S. and Canada launched Hermes, a joint venture communications satellite that became the prototype for direct broadcast satellites. And in 1981, the Canadian-designed and built Remote Manipulator System was installed on the U.S. space shuttle *Columbia*. The RMS—soon to be better known as the Canadarm—was operated by two hand controls from inside the *Columbia*'s cabin, allowing astronauts to take satellites from the cargo bay and place them in space. The Canadarm is also designed to snare satellites from orbit and put them in the cargo bay for repair or a return to Earth.

The Canadian Astronaut Program has been in operation since 1983. (See the next page for the role Canada's astronauts and science have played in building the International Space Station.)

But much of Canada's space activity was undertaken by different departments; the creation of the CSA was intended to co-ordinate Canada's space programs and manage our space-related activities. Its formal mission is to "promote the peaceful use and development of space for the social and economic benefit of Canadians."

Working with scientists and the private sector, the CSA has been involved in a series of important commercial and scientific satellites.

RadarSat, launched in 1995, is the country's first Earth Observation satellite. This remote sensing satellite is in a near-polar orbit 800 km above the Earth. *RadarSat* produces images of the Earth's surface using a microwave Synthetic Aperture Radar (SAR) system. (Similar devices use optical sensors; unlike them, *RadarSat* can function night or day, and through clouds, fog or smoke.)

Among projects for the future is the second *RadarSat*, intended to be launched in early 2004.

But one of the most exciting new projects is Canada's first space telescope, the Microvariability and Oscillations of STars or MOST. No bigger than a suitcase, and costing less than $10 million, MOST was launched the day before Canada Day, 2003, using a Russian Stiletto rocket, and was immediately seen to be working perfectly.

The 54-kilogram MOST's main job is to study nearby sunlike stars, but one of its first tasks will be to try to verify the existence of a planet orbiting the star 51 Pegasi A, which is 42 light-years away. Scientists are hoping MOST will provide clues to the origin of the planet—if it exists.

MOST will also be used to help determine the age of the universe by training its modest telescope on the same distant star for as long as seven weeks—something that previously would have needed a huge satellite to get the necessary accuracy.

But a Toronto space technology company, Dynacon Enterprises Ltd., came up with a tiny device to accurately control what's called the satellite's orientation, which determines where the telescope points.

Another small satellite, the 150-kilogram SCISAT-1, was launched in early August 2003. The $42-million spacecraft houses pioneering instruments to decipher chemical reactions in the atmosphere.

Depending on how much money is available, the CSA wants to launch either a microsat (like MOST, under 100 kilograms) or a smallsat (like SCISAT, under 500 kilograms) every year.

Also depending on money is Canada's participation in the biggest space mission of the decade: a science laboratory destined to land on Mars in 2009. NASA has invited the CSA to take part, but that may require Parliament to open its purse strings—something the agency is seeking.

Canada's Astronauts

The Canadian Astronaut Program began in 1983 when Canada was invited to send an astronaut on the U.S. space shuttle. A permanent corps of Canadian astronauts who could co-ordinate and conduct Canadian experiments in space was created as a result.

Dr. Marc Garneau was the first Canadian astronaut to fly in space. He conducted a set of experiments in space science, space technology, and life sciences during Mission 41-G, from October 5 to 13, 1984, aboard the space shuttle *Challenger*.

Dr. Steve MacLean flew aboard the shuttle *Columbia* from October 22 to November 1, 1992, and conducted a second set of these experiments.

Dr. Roberta Bondar flew aboard *Discovery* from January 22 to 30, 1992, as the prime Canadian Payload Specialist for the first International Microgravity Laboratory mission; she conducted more than 43 experiments on behalf of 13 countries.

Col. Chris Hadfield, in November 1995, was the first Canadian to serve as a full crew member and the first Canadian on board the Russian Space Station *Mir* when he flew aboard *Atlantis* from November 12 to 20, 1995.

Dr. Marc Garneau made his second space flight in May 1996, as a Mission Specialist aboard Space Shuttle *Endeavor*.

Dr. Robert Thirsk flew as a Payload Specialist on June 20, 1996, aboard *Columbia*.

Bjarni Tryggvason was Payload Specialist on August 7, 1997, for *Discovery*.

Dr. Dave Williams flew on board *Columbia* from April 17 to May 3, 1998.

Julie Payette flew aboard *Discovery* in August 1996, as part of a 10-day logistics and resupply mission to the International Space Station (ISS).

Dr. Marc Garneau flew his third space mission November 30, 2000, when he installed the first of four sets of solar panels on the ISS.

Col. Chris Hadfield became the first Canadian to walk in space in April 2001, when he installed and tested CANADARM2 (part of Canada's contribution to the multi-billion-dollar-project) on the ISS.

Dr. Steve MacLean was scheduled to fly on *Endeavor* in late May 2003, but all flights were grounded in the wake of the February 1, 2003, mishap that destroyed the shuttle *Columbia*.

Source: *Canadian Space Agency www.space.gc.ca*

Constellations

Astronomers have divided the sky into 88 well-defined areas called constellations. They are named after people, animals or objects. The pattern of bright stars in some constellations (such as Orion or Scorpius) resembles the person, animal, or object they are named after, but in most constellations it is difficult to see a pattern among the stars. The largest constellation is Hydrus, followed by Virgo and Ursa Major. The smallest is Crux.

Constellation	Meaning	Constellation	Meaning
Andromeda	Daughter of Cassiopeia	Lacerta	The Lizard
Antlia	The Air Pump	Leo	The Lion
Apus	Bird of Paradise	Leo Minor	The Little Lion
Aquarius	The Water-bearer	Lepus	The Hare
Aquila	The Eagle	Libra	The Balance
Ara	The Altar	Lupus	The Wolf
Aries	The Ram	Lynx	The Lynx
Auriga	The Charioteer	Lyra	The Lyre
Bootes	The Herdsman	Mensa	Table Mountain
Caelum	The Chisel	Microscopium	The Microscope
Camelopardalis	The Giraffe	Monoceros	The Unicorn
Cancer	The Crab	Musca	The Fly
Canes Venatici	The Hunting Dogs	Norma	The Square
Canis Major	The Big Dog	Octans	The Octant
Canis Minor	The Little Dog	Ophiuchus	The Serpent-bearer
Capricornus	The Horned Goat	Orion	The Hunter
Carina	The Keel	Pavo	The Peacock
Cassiopeia	The Queen	Pegasus	The Winged Horse
Centaurus	The Centaur	Perseus	Rescuer of Andromeda
Cepheus	The King	Phoenix	The Phoenix
Cetus	The Whale	Pictor	The Painter
Chamaeleon	The Chameleon	Pisces	The Fishes
Circinus	The Compasses	Piscis Austrinus	The Southern Fish
Columba	The Dove	Puppis	The Stern
Coma Berenices	Berenice's Hair	Pyxis	The Compass
Corona Australis	The Southern Crown	Reticulum	The Reticule
Corona Borealis	The Northern Crown	Sagitta	The Arrow
Corvus	The Crow	Sagittarius	The Archer
Crater	The Cup	Scorpius	The Scorpion
Crux	The Cross	Sculptor	The Sculptor
Cygnus	The Swan	Scutum	The Shield
Delphinus	The Dolphin	Serpens	The Serpent
Dorado	The Goldfish	Sextans	The Sextant
Draco	The Dragon	Taurus	The Bull
Equuleus	The Little Horse	Telescopium	The Telescope
Eridanus	A River	Triangulum	The Triangle
Fornax	The Furnace	Triangulum Australe	The Southern Triangle
Gemini	The Twins	Tucana	The Toucan
Grus	The Crane (bird)	Ursa Major	The Great Bear[1]
Hercules	The Son of Zeus	Ursa Minor	The Little Bear[2]
Horologium	The Clock	Vela	The Sails
Hydra	The Water Snake (f)	Virgo	The Maiden
Hydrus	The Water Snake (m)	Volans	The Flying Fish
Indus	The Indian	Vulpecula	The Fox

(1) Commonly known as the Big Dipper. (2) Commonly known as the Little Dipper.

Observatories in Canada

Maritime Region

☐ **Burke-Gaffney Observatory**
Department of Astronomy and Physics, Saint Mary's University, Halifax, NS B3H 3C3. From November to March, open at 7 pm; from April to June at 9 pm, every 1st and 3rd Saturday; from June to September, open every Saturday. Tel: (902) 496-8257.
Web site: http://apwww.stmarys.ca/bgo

Central Canada

☐ **David Dunlap Observatory**
Richmond Hill, Ont. Tours are held Saturday evenings from May to September, and Friday and Saturdays in July and August. Tickets are sold on a first-come, first-served basis. Tel: (905) 884-2112. Web site: http://ddo.astro.utoronto.ca/ddohome/index.html

☐ **Helen B. Hogg Observatory**
Canada Science and Technology Museum. 1867 St. Laurent Blvd, Ottawa, ON K1G 5A3. Tel: (613) 991-3044.

☐ **Hume Cronyn Memorial Observatory**
University of Western Ontario, London, ON N6A 3K7.
Open late October to early April by reservation, and
from June to August on Saturday evenings at 8:30 pm.
Tel: (519) 661-2111. Web site: phobos.astro.uwo.ca/
~dfgray/pub-nit.html

Western Canada

☐ **Climenhaga Observatory**
Dept. of Physics and Astronomy, University of Victoria,
PO Box 3055, Stn Csc, Victoria, BC V8W 3P6.
Tel: (250) 721-7700. Open daily. Web site:
http://astrowww.phys.uvic.ca/climenhaga/obs/telescope.html

☐ **Rothney Astrophysical Observatory**
Physics and Astronomy Dept., University of Calgary,
Calgary, AB T2N 1N4. Tel: (403) 220-5385. Web site:
http://phas.ucalgary.ca/rao/

☐ **Dominion Astrophysical Observatory**
Little Saanich Mountain, 5071 West Saanich Road,
Victoria, BC, Canada V9E 2E7. Open from 10:00 am to
6:00 pm daily, but closed Mondays from November 1st
to April. Some Saturday evenings are open for star
parties and other special events. Tel: (250) 363-8262.

☐ **Dominion Radio Astrophysical Observatory**
PO Box 248, Penticton, BC V2A 6K3. Guide available
on weekends, 10 am to 5 pm, at the visitors' centre.
The grounds and visitors' centre are open during normal
business hours during the week, but there are no guides
available. Tel: (250) 493-2277.

☐ **H.R. MacMillan Planetarium and Gordon
Southam Observatory** 1100 Chestnut St., Vancouver,
BC V6J 3J9. Tel: (604) 738-7827.

☐ **Devon Observatory** Dept. of Physics, University
of Alberta, Edmonton, AB T6G 2J1.

☐ **University of Saskatchewan Observatory**
Wiggins Avenue off College Drive, 116 Science Place,
Saskatoon, SK S7N 5E2. Open to the public every
Saturday evening. Tel: (306) 966-6429.

☐ **University of British Columbia Observatory**
2219 Main Mall, Vancouver, BC V6T 1W5. Free public
observing on clear Saturday evenings. Tel: (604) 224-6186.

Planetariums

Maritime Region

☐ **The Halifax Planetarium**
The education section of the Nova Scotia Museum of
Natural History is located in the Sir James Dunn Building
at Dalhousie University.1747 Summer St., Halifax, NS
B3H 3A6. Tel: (902) 424-7370 or (902) 424-7353.
Web site: Halifax.rasc.ca/hp/

Central Canada

☐ **Doran Planetarium**
Laurentian University, Ramsey Lake Rd, Sudbury, ON
P3E 2C6. Tel: (705) 675-1151, ext. 2227. Web site:
http://laurentian.ca/physics/PLANETARIUM/Planetarium.html/

☐ **Planetarium de Montréal** 1000 St. Jacques St.
W., Montreal, QC H3C 1G7. Tel: (514) 872-4530. Live
shows in French and English. Open daily. Web site:
www.planetarium.montreal.qc.ca/

☐ **Roberta Bondar Planetarium**
Seneca College, Newnham Campus, on Finch Ave. E.
between Highway 404 and Don Mills Road.
Tel: (416) 491-5050, ext. 2227. Closed during the
2003-04 academic year.

☐ **William J. McCallion Planetarium**
Department of Physics and Astronomy, McMaster
University, 1280 Main Street, Hamilton, ON L8S 4M1.
Tel: (905) 525-9140, ext. 27777.

Western Canada

☐ **Calgary Science Centre**
15 701–11 St. S.W., Calgary, AB Tel: (403) 268-8300
Web site: www.calgaryscience.ca

☐ **Edmonton Odyssium**
1121-142 St., Edmonton, AB T5M 4A1.
Tel: (780) 452-9100 or (780) 451-3344. Features
planetarium Star Theatre, IMAX film theatre, exhibit
galleries, telescope shop and bookstore. Open daily.
Web site: www.odyssium.com

☐ **H.R. MacMillan Planetarium**
1100 Chestnut St., Vancouver, BC V6J 3J9. Tel: (604)
738-7827. Web site: http://pacific-space-centre.bc.ca/

☐ **Manitoba Planetarium**
190 Rupert Ave., Winnipeg, MB R3B 0N2.
Tel: (204) 956-2830 (switchboard). Shows daily except
some Mondays. Museum gift shop has scientific books
and equipment. Web site: wwwmanitobamusem.ca

EARTH SCIENCES

The earth sciences include **geology** (the study of earth's origin and composition), **oceanography** (the study of ocean water, currents, life-forms and the ocean floor), **paleontology** (the study of fossils and ancient life-forms), and **meteorology** (the study of earth's atmosphere, including weather and climate).

The Geological Survey of Canada

The Geological Survey of Canada (GSC) is Canada's first scientific agency, and one of the first of its kind in the world. The agency was created to survey and map mineral deposits in Canada's nearly 1 million square kilometres of land and freshwater lakes, and more than 6 million square kilometres of coastal boundaries.

The Survey began life in Montreal in 1842. Under the first director, William Edmond Logan, a Canadian businessman turned geologist, its initial task was a search for coal, the main industrial fuel at the time. The search, throughout Upper and Lower Canada, was unsuccessful, but Logan did find mineable deposits of copper and other metallic minerals.

Soon Survey geologists were undertaking expeditions westward. In the 1880s another director, George Mercer Dawson, became a noted ethnologist in Western Canada, as well as a pioneer geologist. His reports included observations of the Haida people of British Columbia. During his expeditions he took many photographs of settlements and totem poles, capturing a glimpse of a vanishing landscape.

In 1992 the Geological Survey marked its 150th anniversary. While the task of mapping Canada's geology remains its central focus, the computerized Survey of the 1990s is very different from the one started by Sir William Logan. The Survey now undertakes an ever-expanding range of research—from exploring questions related to global change to those concerning natural hazards such as earthquakes, landslides, volcanoes, floods and ground instability.

For more information on the Geological Survey and its programs, contact: Communications Office, Geological Survey of Canada, 601 Booth Street, Ottawa, Ontario K1A OE8.

Sea-bottom Energy

*C*anada may have another energy resource, thanks to a discovery made by ocean researcher Ross Chapman at the University of Victoria. Off the coast of Vancouver Island, Chapman and colleagues found huge amounts of methane hydrates—a potential alternative energy source, since methane is a cheap and clean fuel. However, there is also an environmental concern: Methane is a greenhouse gas and is known to contribute to global warming. As long as the methane is locked up in hydrates at the bottom of the sea, it's safe, but extraction has the potential to let gas escape, increasing the pace of climate change. Methane hydrates are ice-like formations of methane molecules, which are individually surrounded by a cage of water molecules. The deposit Chapman found takes up three or four square kilometres of the sea floor, at depths around 850 metres below the ocean's surface.

Source: *NSERC*

Common Geological Terms

Continental shelf: Submerged edge of continent, extending to depths of less than 200 metres, and largely made up of sedimentary rock.

Earthquake: A sudden motion or trembling in the earth caused by the release of slowly accumulated strain along a fault line or through volcanic activity.

Echo Sounding: A determination of water depth by measuring the time required for a sonic or ultrasonic signal to travel to the bottom of a body of water and back to the ship emitting the signal.

Epicentre: Point on the earth's surface directly above the focus of an earthquake, usually the location of the most severe damage.

Erosion: Breakdown and wearing away of rocks on the earth's surface by the action of water, waves, glaciers, wind and underground water. ▶

▶ **Fault:** A fracture in the earth's crust along which there has been displacement of the rock on either side, relative to one another.

Geothermal Energy: Energy that can be extracted from the earth's internal heat, usually in the form of emissions of hot water, steam, and gas.

Glacier: A large ice mass formed on land by recrystallization of compacted snow.

Ice Field: An extensive area of interconnected glaciers. An ice field is known as pack ice when floating on the sea.

Igneous Rock: Rock formed when a mass of molten magma cools and solidifies on or below earth's surface. One of three main classes of rock.

Magma: Molten rocky material (mostly silica) beneath the earth's surface. Reaching the surface red hot through volcanic activity, it cools and becomes lava.

Metamorphic Rock: Rock formed when pre-existing rocks are altered by marked changes in temperature, pressure, or shearing stress. One of three major rock groups.

Sedimentary Rock: Rock formed from the accumulation of loose material deposited by water, wind and ice, and solidified by compaction.

Seismograph: A device that records the seismic vibrations of an earthquake. The wave disturbances caused by earthquakes have different speeds and require different lengths of time to reach the surface.

Tectonic Plates: Rigid outer layer of the earth's crust consists of about ten large plates, which "float" horizontally across the denser inner crust.The boundaries of these plates are zones of intense activity, and give rise to mountain building, volcanoes, changes in the ocean floor, and earthquakes.

Tsunami: Particular form of ocean wave produced by an earthquake in the ocean floor, noted for its destructive force.

Volcano: A vent in the earth's crust through which magma, rock fragments, dust, gases and ash are ejected from below earth's surface.

Composition of the Earth

Core: The earth's core lies about 2,900 km below the surface, and consists of two layers: a solid inner core and an outer liquid layer. The inner core is a solid mass, 3,200 km in diameter, probably composed of compressed iron with small amounts of other metals such as nickel. The outer core (the only liquid layer) is about 3,470 km in radius and gives rise to earth's magnetic fields.

Mantle: Accounting for about 82 percent of earth's volume, the mantle is denser than the crust, and probably increases in density close to the core. The mantle extends from the core to about 90 km below the higher mountains, and to about 5 km beneath parts of the ocean crust.

Crust: The outside crust of planet earth ranges in thickness from 5 to 50 km. The relatively light, granite-like rock forming the continents overlies a thinner magnesium-iron layer that makes up the ocean floor. The continental blocks "float" on the denser layer forming the ocean bed.

Hydrosphere: A layer of water covering over 70 percent of the earth's crust, including all water on or near the surface of the planet.

Atmosphere: The lightest part of earth is the atmosphere, a gaseous envelope surrounding the planet. The atmosphere consists of nitrogen, oxygen, water vapour and argon. Less than 0.1 percent is composed of other gases. Gases have weight, so the atmosphere is densest near earth's surface, and thins towards the vacuum of space.

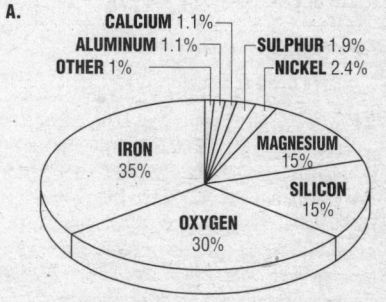

A.

CALCIUM 1.1%
ALUMINIUM 1.1%
OTHER 1%
SULPHUR 1.9%
NICKEL 2.4%
IRON 35%
MAGNESIUM 15%
SILICON 15%
OXYGEN 30%

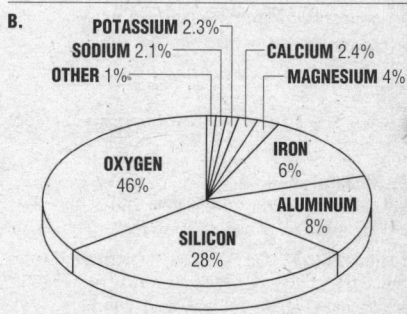

B.

POTASSIUM 2.3%
SODIUM 2.1%
OTHER 1%
CALCIUM 2.4%
MAGNESIUM 4%
OXYGEN 46%
IRON 6%
ALUMINUM 8%
SILICON 28%

▲

Relative abundance of elements by weight of elements in the whole earth (A) and in the earth's crust (B).

Earthquakes

Although the earth's surface seems completely stable, it is constantly moving and changing. Layers of rock in the earth's crust, called plates, push and pull each other until they bend or stretch.

Vibrations or "seismic waves" emanate from the source of the breakage out through the earth, causing the planet to quiver or ring like a tuning fork. The waves can be so minor that the quake will not be felt by humans, or so severe it will change the physical landscape of the area.

Earthquakes can happen all over the world, but they tend to recur along weaknesses in the crust, called faults. By studying the patterns of earthquakes, scientists determine the areas at greatest risk and compile the information in seismic zoning maps. In this way, building regulations can be applied to earthquake zones to minimize possible damage.

The most common method of measuring an earthquake's magnitude is the Richter Scale. It estimates the force from recordings of seismic waves taken by an instrument called a seismometer. The scale is logarithmic, so that each numeric reading is ten times greater in recorded amplitude.

The intensity of an earthquake can also be measured through the Modified Mercali Scale. In addition to mechanical recordings, it uses witness accounts to describe the effects of an earthquake.

Measuring Earthquakes

Richter		Modified Mercali	
2.5	Generally felt, but not recorded.	I	Not felt except by a very few.
		II	Felt only by a few persons at rest, especially on upper floors of buildings.
3.5	Felt by many people.	III	Felt noticeably indoors. Standing cars may rock slightly. Most people do not recognize.
		IV	During daytime felt by many indoors, outdoors by a few. Dishes, windows and doors disturbed; walls creak. At night, some awaken. Sensation like a heavy truck passing.
		V	Felt by nearly everyone; many awakened. Some dishes and windows broken; some objects over-turned. Trees, poles and other tall objects disturbed.
4.5	Some local damage may occur.	VI	Felt by all, many run outdoors. Heavy furniture moves; occasionally plaster falls and chimneys damaged. Overall damage slight.
		VII	Everyone runs outdoors. Well-built structures suffer negligible damage; slight to moderate damage in well-built homes; poorly constructed buildings suffer considerable damage. Noticed by people in moving cars.
6.0	A destructive earthquake	VIII	Damage slight in specially designed structures; considerable in ordinary substantial buildings, with partial collapse; great in poorly built structures. Chimneys fall. Heavy furniture overturned. Disturbs people driving cars. Sand and mud ejected in small amounts.
		IX	Damage to specially designed structures considerable. Buildings shifted off foundations. Conspicuous ground cracks. Underground pipes broken.

▶ Richter		Modified Mercali	
7.0	A major earthquake, about 10 occur each year	X	Some well-built wooden structures destroyed; most masonry and frame structures destroyed. Ground badly cracked. Rails bent. Landslides considerable.
8.0	Great earthquake, occurs once every five to 10 years	XI	Few masonry structures remain standing. Bridges destroyed. Broad fissures in ground. Underground pipelines out of service. Earth slumps, and land slips in soft ground.
		XII	Damage total. Waves seen on ground surface. Lines of sight and levels distorted. Objects thrown upward into air.

World's Major Earthquakes

Date	Location	Deaths	Magnitude
1902 Dec. 16	Turkestan	4 500	—
1905 Apr. 4	India, Kangra	19 000	8.6
1905 Sep. 8	Italy, Calabria	2 500	7.9
1906 Aug. 17	Chile, Santiago	20 000	8.6
1907 Oct. 21	Central Asia	12 000	8.1
1908 Dec. 28	Italy, Messina	83 000	7.5
1915 Jan. 13	Italy, Avezzano	29 980	7.5
1920 Dec. 16	China, Gansu	200 000	8.6
1923 Sep. 1	Japan, Kwanto-Tokyo-Yokohama	143 000	8.3
1925 Mar. 16	China, Yunnan	5 000	7.1
1927 Mar. 7	Japan, Tango	3 020	7.9
1927 May 22	China, near Xining	200 000	8.3
1929 May 1	Iran	3 300	7.4
1932 Dec. 25	China, Gansu	70 000	7.6
1933 Mar. 2	Japan, Sanriku	2 990	8.9
1934 Jan. 15	India, Behar-Nepal	*10 700	8.4
1935 Apr. 20	Formosa	3 280	7.1
1935 May 30	Pakistan, Quetta	30 000	7.6
1939 Jan. 25	Chile, Chillan	28 000	8.3
1939 Dec. 26	Turkey, Erzincan	30 000	7.6
1948 June 28	Japan, Fukui	5 390	7.3
1949 Aug. 5	Ecuador, Ambato	6 000	6.8
1960 Feb. 29	Morocco, Agadir	15 000	5.9
1960 May 22	Chile	5 000	7.3
1966 Aug. 19	Turkey, Varto	2 520	7.1
1968 Aug. 31	Iran	20 000	7.3
1970 May 31	Peru	66 000	7.8
1972 Apr. 10	Southern Iran	5 054	7.1
1972 Dec. 23	Nicaragua, Managua	5 000	6.2
1974 Dec. 28	Pakistan	5 300	6.2
1976 Feb. 4	Guatemala	23 000	7.5
1976 June 30	Indonesia, Westirian	5 000	7.1
1976 July 27	China, Tangshan	255 000	8.0
1976 Aug. 16	Philippines, Mindanao	8 000	7.9
1976 Nov. 24	Turkey	4 000	7.3
1978 Sep. 16	Iran	25 000	7.8
1980 Oct. 10	Algeria	4 500	7.7
1980 Nov. 23	Southern Italy	4 800	7.2
1981 June 11	Southern Iran	3 000	6.9
1985 Sep. 19	Mexico, Michoacan	15 000	8.1
1988 Dec. 7	USSR, Turkey	25 000	7.0
1990 June 20	Western Iran	50 000	7.7
1993 Sept. 30	India	9 500	6.4
1995 Jan. 17	Kobe, Japan	6 000	7.2
1998 Feb. 1	Afghanistan	5 000	6.9
1999 Aug. 17	Turkey	12 000	7.4
2001 Jan. 26	India, Gujarat	20 085	7.7
2003 May 21	Algeria	2 666	6.8

Source: *U.S. Geological Survey*

Earthquakes in Canada

Scientists estimate that more than 1,000 earthquakes are recorded in Canada each year. Most measure less than 3 on the Richter scale. The southwest corner of British Columbia is the most active earthquake region (more than 200 every year). Other active regions include coastal BC, the southern Yukon, the Mackenzie Valley in the Northwest Territories, the Arctic Islands, and parts of Ontario and Quebec (especially the Ottawa and St Lawrence valleys).

Date		Location	Magnitude
1918	Dec. 6	Vancouver Island	7.0
1925	Mar. 1	Charlevoix-Kamouraska region, Québec	6.7
1929	May 6	Off Queen Charlotte Islands	7.0
1929	Nov. 18	Atlantic Ocean, south of Newfoundland	7.2
1933	Nov. 20	Baffin Bay	7.3
1935	Nov. 1	Québec–Ontario border	6.2
1946	June 23	Vancouver Island	7.3
1949	Aug. 22	Off Queen Charlotte Islands	8.1
1958	July 10	Alaska–BC border	7.9
1970	June 24	South of Queen Charlotte Islands	7.4
1976	Dec. 20	West of Vancouver Island	6.8
1979	Feb. 28	Yukon–Alaska border	7.5
1980	Dec. 17	West of Vancouver Island	6.8
1985	Dec. 23	Mackenzie region, NWT	6.9
1988	Nov. 25	Saguenay region, Quebec	6.0
1989	Dec. 25	Northern Quebec	6.1
1992	Apr. 6	West of Vancouver Island	6.8
2001	Sept. 14	West of Vancouver Island	6.0

Source: *Geological Survey of Canada*

For more information, contact the National Earthquake Hazards Program of the Geological Survey of Canada (www.seismo.nrcan.gc.ca):

East
7 Observatory Cres.
Ottawa, ON
K1A 0Y3
(613) 995-5548

West
P.O. Box 6000
9860 West Saanich
Sidney, BC V8L 4B2
(604) 363-6500

Geological Time Periods

The story of planet earth is one of continuous change. Fossils, rock records and radioactive dating show three marked changes in the patterns of plant and animal life. These times of change in the most recent 570 million years of the earth's history are divided by geologists into three eras: Paleozoic (ancient life); Mesozoic (age of reptiles); and Cenozoic (age of mammals). The more than 4 billion years before the start of the Paleozoic era are referred to as Precambrian time. Each

geological unit is divided further: the eras into periods, the periods into epochs.

The names of the time periods are taken either from the geographic locality where the fossil information was best displayed or first studied, or from some characteristic of the geological formations. For example, the Jurassic period is named from the Jura Mountains of France and Switzerland, and the Carboniferous is named from the coal-bearing sedimentary rocks.

▶

Era	Period	Epoch	Years Ago	Changes and Characteristics
▶ **Precambrian Time**			4.5 bil.?	Cooling and melting of the earth's crust. Evidence of bacteria, the first known living things, about 3.5 billion years ago.
Paleozoic	Cambrian		575 mil.	Seas spread across North America. First fish appear. Greatest development of invertebrates.
	Ordovician		480 mil.	Floods sometimes cover two-thirds of North America. Jawless fish appear. Algae become plentiful.
	Silurian		435 mil.	Coral reefs are formed. First amphibians and forests of fernlike trees appear.
	Devonian		405 mil.	Gas and oil are formed. Many kinds of fish in seas and fresh water. First insects appear.
	Carboniferous —Mississippian		350 mil.	Warm, moist climate produces great forests that later become coal beds. Fish and amphibians plentiful.
	—Pennsylvanian		310 mil.	Appalachian Mountains are formed. Large amounts of coal are formed. First reptiles appear.
	Permian		270 mil.	Ural Mountains are formed. Glaciers in southern hemisphere melt. Gas, oil and salt are formed. Reptiles developing.
Mesozoic	Triassic		225 mil.	Reptiles dominate the earth. First mammals appear.
	Jurassic		180 mil.	Shallow seas invade continents. Dinosaurs reach their largest size. First birds appear.
	Cretaceous		130 mil.	Seas spread over the land. Flowering plants appear. Dinosaurs die out. Most chalk deposits are made.
Cenozoic	Tertiary	Paleocene	65 mil.	Mountains become higher. Climates less uniform. Mammals, flowering plants become common.
		Eocene	50 mil.	Climate mild. Seas flood shores of continents. Primitive apes, early horses and elephants appear.
		Oligocene	38 mil.	Climate mild. Alps and Himalayas begin to rise. Many volcanoes. Oil and natural gas are formed.
		Miocene	27 mil.	Climate mild. Rocky Mountains and Sierra Nevadas forming. Flowering plants and trees resemble modern kinds.
		Pliocene	10 mil.	Climate cooling. Mountains rising in western Canada. Many volcanoes. Birds and mammals spread around the world. Humans appear near end of epoch.
	Quaternary	Pleistocene	1.5 mil.	Great ice sheets cover northern hemisphere. Climate cool. Mountains continue to rise in North America. Early humans reach Europe and North America.
		Recent, or Holocene	10 000	Glaciers melt and Great Lakes are formed. Climate warm. Humans live in most parts of the earth, develop agriculture, use metals, domesticate animals.

Lithoprobe

(by Horst Heise, Communications Adviser)

Imagine the world's surface as a jigsaw puzzle—many small pieces fitted together. That's how geoscientists—those who study the Earth—now see the planet. But stretch your mind a bit further and imagine that the pieces change and move over time, so that the puzzle today is not like the puzzle of a few million years ago. This insight—that the continents and oceans are not firmly in place, but constantly move and jostle with each other—arose in the 1960s, and changed the way geoscientists think about geological processes. This notion of geological turmoil gave new insights into such things as volcanoes and earthquakes, how mountains arise, or where to expect certain minerals, such as ore deposits or diamonds. It was as revolutionary a view as Darwin's evolution or Einstein's relativity.

■ How Canada was built—over four billion years

Canada's Lithoprobe project is investigating the jigsaw puzzle of our continent to its deep roots and exploring its 4-billion-year past. In other words, Lithoprobe is studying the birth and evolution of Canada—not as a country, but as a collection of rocky structures. Lithoprobe—the title comes from the lithosphere, the name given to Earth's rocky crust and uppermost mantle—was conceived by a group of Canada's solid-earth scientists (geologists, geophysicists and geochemists) from universities and the Geological Survey of Canada (GSC) during a meeting in Toronto in 1981. When field investigations started in 1984, this now $100-million-plus fundamental research project became fully funded by the Natural Sciences and Engineering Research Council of Canada (NSERC), the GSC and other sources.

These Canadian scientists set out to answer some fundamental questions. Specifically, where did our continent come from, how was it built, what is its history, and how deep does it extend into the Earth? The Lithoprobe project was made possible in part because a study of the continent's growth could be conducted within Canada. As well,

Canada's development is so tied to our natural resources that our geoscientists themselves are one of the country's great resources. Earth-science teams, including more than 900 specialists (about 400 of them undergraduate, post-graduate and post-doctoral students) from various branches of the earth sciences have been tracing the growth (and partial destruction) of our continent since the project started in 1984.

■ World's first continental study

Now in its final stage, Lithoprobe has been the world's first national and multidisciplinary investigation of the origin and growth of a continent. You can find information, maps, illustrations, and a slide set for teachers at www.lithoprobe.ca, along with links to the participating earth-science groups at universities, the GSC, and provincial agencies. You can request hard copies either on the Web site, or by mail from the Lithoprobe Secretariat, EOS South, University of British Columbia, 6339 Stores Road, Vancouver, BC, V6T 1Z4.

Earth's outer, hard shell consists of an unsteady mosaic of large and small crustal plates, including the North American plate, which all move, driven by heat-convection flows in the planet's mantle. Earth's interior acts like a gigantic nuclear power plant, driven by the heat generated by atomic decay. Heat pushes hot mantle plumes—molten rock—upward from the interior of Earth, against the overlying crust; if the crust splits, for instance along the mid-oceanic ridges, the magma oozes through. This pushes the split plate portions in opposite directions. In the middle of the Atlantic Ocean, for example, there is a two-sided movement away from the so-called mid-Atlantic ridge, which is widening the distance between the coasts of Europe and Africa on one side, and the Americas on the other. Not that we need to worry about it: it's a slow process. The plates move at, maybe, the speed our fingernails grow, or 5 to 6 centimetres a year. That's 50 to 60 kilometres every million years or 5,000 to 6,000 km in

100 million years. If we wait long enough, then, even the mighty Pacific Ocean—more than 6,000 kilometres across—might one day disappear, squeezed out of existence by the opposing coasts.

■ Today is just a snapshot

Naturally, what's happening today is fascinating, but it is only a snapshot of a planet in motion. There have been many very different such pictures from the dynamic movements of the Earth's surface during the past 4 billion years. (Four billion, by the way, is a 4 with 9 zeroes after it; it's also abbreviated 4 Ga.) Not only do plates collide, pieces of crust are constantly being recycled, pushed deeper into the mantle as the plates slowly slam into each other. To trace the origins of today's puzzle pieces geoscientists use many clues. For instance, Earth's magnetic field aligns magnetic minerals as rocks solidify from either cooling magma or new sediments. If, later, tectonic plates bearing these rock formations twist and wander, their original magnetic position still can be read. Different minerals form at certain depths in the crust, depending on heat and pressure. Geologists can see where deeper, denser crust was pushed onto lighter crust. The age of very ancient rock formations can be read with astounding accuracy, another craft perfected only two decades ago. Rocks carry more such markers, including their gravity, density, and chemistry. Then there are such phenomena as Earth's interior heat flow, which can be measured, and which also determines how flexible or brittle a rock formation may be. Electric conductivity independently complements gravity, and so on.

■ An early start for our continent

Earth's geological history began with our planet's cooling 4.6 billion years ago, eventually leading to the formation of the planet's outer crust, part of the lithosphere, which also includes a portion of the upper mantle. Canada's oldest rock is more than 4 Ga old, and was found in the Slave (geological) province or "craton" in the Northwest Territories. This is one of six small micro-continents that later formed the core of the Canadian Shield, all older than 2.5 Ga (see accompanying map). They

include Slave, Rae, Hearne, Wyoming in the west, Superior in the centre and Nain in the northeast. Younger (but still very old) regions now lie between them, and also on their outsides.

These old cratons were much farther apart during the Archean than they are now, separated by oceanic crust and oceans, and subsequently brought together by the unceasing movements of crustal plates. When the plates are being moved and pushed by the convection flows they have to escape either on top of adjacent plates as accretions, or by sliding below another in a process called subduction, in which part of the subducted plate may attach to the underside of the invaded host plate, while most of it sinks back into the mantle to be melted and recycled.

In this manner, the old cratons eventually collided with each other during the Early Proterozoic (between 1.7 and 2 billion years ago). Islands in the oceans between them, and the ocean floor itself, were squeezed into a series of mountain belts (or "orogens") in the most widely spread round of continental collisions the world has ever seen. These ribbons in between the cratons welded together the core of the Canadian Shield, and clearly show up on our tectonic-domain map of Canada. Among the new mountain belts, the Trans-Hudson Orogen was the largest. It reaches from the Dakotas in the U.S. north through Saskatchewan, turns east to cross Hudson Bay, and shows up in various places east and north, notably in northwestern Labrador, to continue in Greenland and onward.

■ Building a supercontinent

The next really big, crustal-scale push came from the east and southeast (about 1 billion years ago) when the towering Middle Proterozoic Grenville Orogen was squeezed against and partly heaved onto the Canadian Shield by an aggressive continent (Gondwana), moving in from the east and southeast. This led to the formation of a supercontinent, which geoscientists call Rodinia, surrounded by oceans. This is how regions of what is now eastern and southern Ontario and adjacent parts of Quebec (plus much territory beyond, which later was again lost) made it on to the map of Canada. But this area then looked like the Himalayas and Tibetan Highlands—until the forces of erosion brought it down to its present level. The Grenville Orogen completed the tectonic frame of our Canadian Shield, part of Laurentia, as the then-North American continent is called.

At about the same time that the huge Grenville mountains were being shaped, a nearby part of Laurentia was almost split apart by what is called the Keweenawan Rift. This was caused by a rising mantle plume that almost tore our continent apart and, along the opening crack, poured out stupendous amounts of lavas. The 2,000-kilometre crack—now curved—is clearly visible in the Great Lakes region on the tectonic map. (It's the wiggly crescent marked as 1,100 million years old.)

Not much was quiet on the western side of Laurentia, either. During Middle and Late Proterozoic times and extending into the Early Paleozoic (half a billion to 1.85 billion years ago), rifting did turn into continent splitting when an unknown large block, perhaps now part of Australia, broke away. This left a wide continental shelf upon which sediments were deposited, which now cover most of Alberta and parts of Saskatchewan and Manitoba, and the western NWT, including portions of the pushed-up grandeur of the Rocky Mountains.

In the east, the massive supercontinent that had—by a billion years ago—resulted from the Grenville orogen, split roughly where the St. Lawrence River is today. This happened about 600 million years ago, and a wide sea, dubbed the Iapetus Ocean, developed. But it didn't take long, geologically speaking, for a reversal in direction. Iapetus was pushed out of existence in a series of tectonic squeezes that ended with the creation of the Appalachian Mountains (between about 275 and 475 million years ago). Today we can see the old Iapetus ocean floor trending up north-northeast through the middle of Newfoundland, with the island's eastern side having come from the old, separated continental block (Gondwana) and the west belonging to our own Laurentia.

■ Here comes the Atlantic

The Atlantic opened quite recently (about 160 million years ago), and still is widening today, but that opening occurred farther east this time, leaving the newly acquired Appalachians attached to Laurentia. And the Atlantic is now doing what the Iapetus had done before, pushing Europe and Africa (which then was part of Gondwana) eastward, and our own Laurentian plate westward.

While Canada's eastern coast is passive, and only its offshore continental shelves are growing as they receive the sediments from inland, our west coast is active, as our continent bulldozes onto the adjacent ocean floor, and the underlying ocean plate is subducting under Vancouver Island, causing the volcanoes and earthquakes on the west coast. Farther inland, the Rockies formed during the period 160–60 million years ago, following two major crustal-plate pushes, while plate movements bringing accretions have kept B.C. growing westward since Jurassic times (about 180 million years ago).

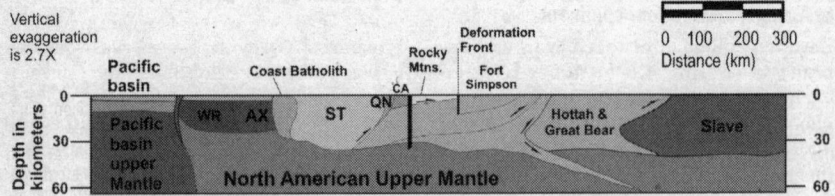

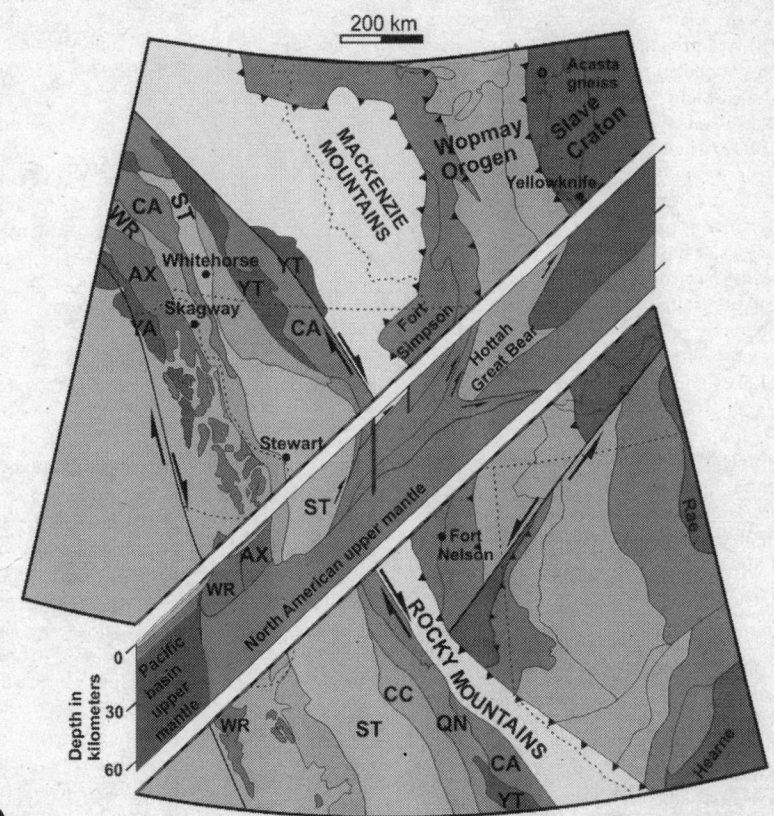

A simplified geological map of the tectonic elements of northwestern Canada, the study area for the SNORCLE transect (see the tectonic element map of Canada on the next page for location of SNORCLE). Along the location of the cross-section of the previous page, the map has been slit and the same cross-section inserted to give a sense of the three-dimensional extent of the tectonic elements. The oldest rocks on Earth, the Acasta gneiss, are located at the small open circle north of Yellowknife. The Hottah-Great Bear and Fort Simpson blocks form the Wopmay Orogen.

Note how the area west of the Rocky and Mackenzie mountains is made up of a collage of accreted terranes that represent the westward growth of North America since about 180 million years ago. Terrane abbreviations additional to those in the previous figure are: Cache Creek (CC); Yakutat (YA) and Yukon-Tanana (YT). The black lines with arrows in opposite directions show major strike-slip faults in the region; the arrows distinguish the sense of relative motion along the faults.

A simplified lithospheric cross-section across northwestern Canada one of the most recent results from the SNORCLE transect. On the right, the Slave block contains the world's oldest rocks and was fully established about 2.6 Ga. A younger block, the Hottah and Great Bear, collided with the Slave from the west about 1.92-1.88 Ga. Shortly after, another block, Fort Simpson, collided with the Hottah and Great Bear about 1.84-1.80 Ga. Part of this block was shoved over the Hottah and Great Bear, but part of it was forced deeper into the mantle. For more than a billion years, sediments accumulated on the then western

margin of North America; some pushing and stretching of these occurred. Much later, about 180-60 million years ago, some big pushes occurred as smaller blocks called accreted terranes collided with western North America forming the Rocky Mountains and adding westward growth to the continent. West of the Queen Charlotte Islands (represented by WR), a major strike-slip fault (just like the San Andreas fault in California) separates the Pacific basin lithosphere from that of North America. Terrane abbreviations (east to west) are: Cassiar (CA); Quesnellia (QN); Stikinia (ST); Alexander (AX); and Wrangellia (WR).

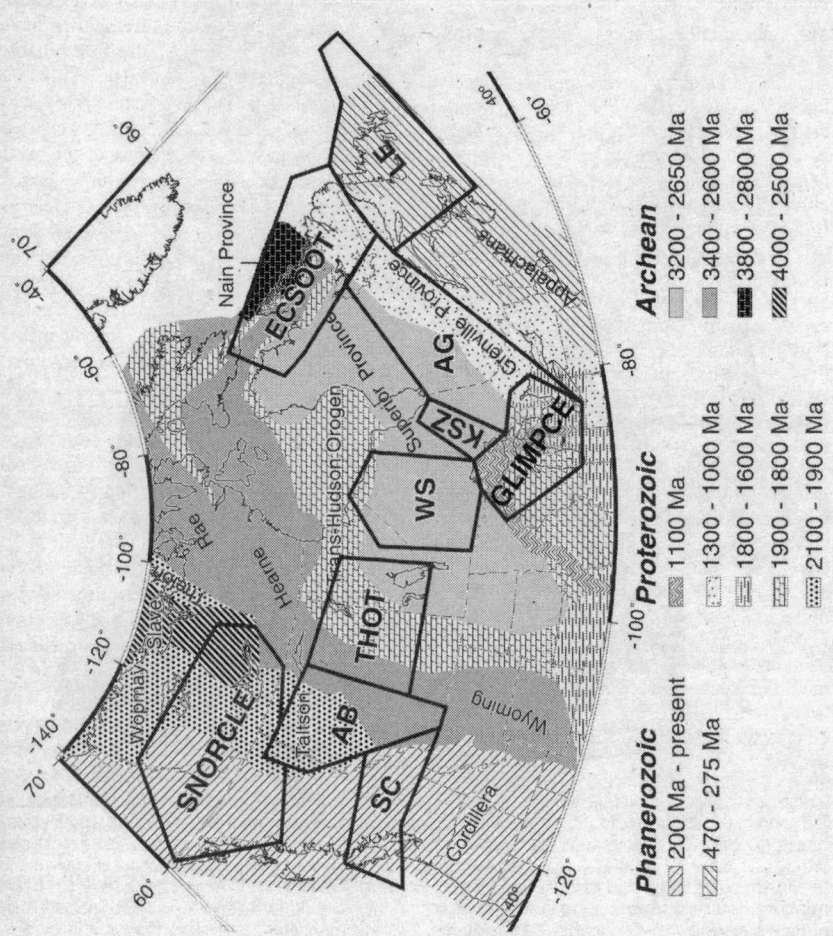

A geological map of Canada showing the tectonic elements described in our text. The legend gives the age of the regions or elements. The heavy-lined boxes outline the study areas with their acronyms. From west to east these are the: Slave Northern Cordillera Lithosphere Evolution (SNORCLE); Southern Cordillera (SC); Alberta Basement (AB); Trans-Hudson Orogen (THOT); Kapuskasing Structural Zone (KSZ); Great Lakes International Multidisciplinary Program on Crustal Evolution (GLIMPCE); Abitibi-Grenville (AG); Lithoprobe East (LE); and Eastern Canadian Shield Onshore-Offshore (ECSOOT) transects.

Minerals

Minerals are all around us—everything from ice on the sidewalk in winter to the salt you sprinkle on French fries. Each mineral species has a definite chemical composition and a crystal structure. Therefore, ice is mineral because it is solid, but water, is not because it is liquid. Sea shells are not minerals because, although they are solid, they are organic—formed by living creatures.

The physical properties of minerals—their form and hardness—are easy to recognize. Specimens may be composed of large showy crystals or millions of tiny crystals fused together. The external shape (or habit) is determined by the internal arrangement of atoms. The atoms are joined together in a framework to form minute building blocks. Called the crystal structure, the arrangement of atoms is unique for each mineral. The habit is also partly the result of the environment in which a mineral grows. If there is enough space during growth, the mineral develops smooth external crystals. However, conditions are seldom ideal and more often than not, minerals grow together as masses of fibres, grains, plates or spheres. The hardness of a mineral—its resistance to scratching—is measured by the Mohs scale.

The optical properties of minerals—lustre, colour and transparency—are easily observed by the unaided eye; other optical properties are determined with microscopes. Lustre is the quality of light reflected from the surface of a mineral. For instance, the highly reflective surfaces of pyrite produce the metallic lustre characteristics of most sulphide minerals. Many silicates, carbonates and other minerals have a softer, but still bright, glassy or vitreous lustre. Minerals with surfaces that reflect light more diffusely, such as serpentine asbestos or cyanotrichite, are said to have silky or earthly lustres. Lustre is a reliable means of distinguishing minerals.

Colour can also be very distinctive, but is not always reliable in identifying most minerals because even minerals of the same species can occur in many colours. Quartz, which is quite common, can be as clear as water or the deepest purple because of flaws in the mineral's crystal structure. Colour can also be affected by the presence of major elements in the mineral: copper in azurite produces an intense azure blue; arsenic makes realgar appear red; and curite is coloured orange by uranium. Colour can also be produced by physical structure. When light strikes very thin layers within the structure of labradorite, the mineral glows with iridescent colours, an effect much like that of sunlight striking a film of gasoline on a puddle, causing a rainbow of colour.

Determining the chemical composition and crystal structure of minerals requires laboratory techniques and tools such as the electron microbe, a reliable tool for analysing chemical composition. Crystal structure is determined using an X-ray diffractometer. Other mineral properties such as magnetism, fluorescence and radioactivity are more easily detected: magnetite and pyrrhotite are noticeably magnetic; some minerals, such as scheelite, fluoresce strongly in ultra-violet light; and all uranium and thorium-bearing minerals are radioactive. The radiation can easily be detected with a Geiger counter or scintillometer.

Mohs Scale of Hardness

Mohs scale indicates the relative hardness of minerals. Each mineral listed is hard enough to scratch a smooth surface of those below it. On this scale, a polymer-like polyethylene would have a hardness of about 1, a finger nail 2.5, a penny 5, window glass 5.5, and the blade of a pocket knife 6.5. Tool steel has a hardness of about 7, and easily cuts glass.

10	Diamond
9	Corundum
8	Topaz
7	Quartz
6	Orthoclase
5	Apatite
4	Fluorite
3	Calcite
2	Gypsum
1	Talc

Source: *Geological Survey of Canada*

Earth Sciences Museums

Maritime Region:

☐ **St. Lawrence Miner's Museum**
PO Box 128, St. Lawrence, NL A0E 2V0. Tel: (709) 873-2222. No charge. Open in summer.

☐ **Fundy Geological Museum**
TTwo Island Road, PO Box 640, Parrsboro, NS B0M 1S0. Tel: 902-254-3814. Open daily from 9:30 am to 5:30 pm, June 1 to October 15; open Tuesday to Saturday from 9 am to 5 pm, Sundays from 1 to 5 pm, from October 16 to May 31. Web site: http://museum.gov.ns.ca/fgm/

☐ **Inverness Miner's Museum**
Lower Railway St., Inverness NS B0E 1N0. Tel: (902) 258-2097. Donations. Open from June to September, 9 am to 5 pm weekdays, and noon to 5 pm on weekends.

☐ **Springhill Miner's Museum**
PO Box 610, Black River Road, Springhill, NS B0M 1X0. Tel: (902) 597-3449. Open spring, summer and fall.

Central Canada:

☐ **Canadian Museum of Nature,**
Viola Macmillan Mineral Gallery
240 McLeod St., Ottawa, ON K1P 6P4. Tel: (613) 566-4700. Open daily. Web site: www.nature.ca

☐ **Logan Hall**
Geological Survey of Canada, 601 Booth St., Ottawa, ON K1A 0E8. Tel: (613) 996-5763. Open 8 am to 4 pm weekdays, year-round.

☐ **Musée de Géologie**
Laval University, Pavillon Pouliot, 4th floor, Sainte Foy, QC G1K 7P4. Tel: (418) 656-2131. Open all year.

☐ **Musée mineralogique et minier de Thetford Mines** 711 Smith Blvd. S., Thetford Mines, QC G6G 5T3. Tel: (418) 335-2123. Open all year. Web site: www.mmmtm.qc.ca/

☐ **Musée régional mines de Malartic**
650 rue da la Paix, Malartic, QC J0Y 1Z0. Tel: (819) 757-4677. Open daily in summer; weekdays in winter. Web site: http://museemalartic.qc.ca/

☐ **Earth Sciences Museum**
University of Waterloo, Waterloo, ON N2L 3G1. Tel: (519) 888-4567, ext. 2469. Web site: www.science.uwaterloo.ca/earth/museum/museum.html

☐ **Miller Museum of Geology**
Queen's University, Miller Hall, Kingston, ON K7L 3N6. Tel: (613) 533-6767. Open all year.

☐ **Oil Museum of Canada**
2423 Kelly Road, Oil Springs, ON N0N 1P0. Tel: (519) 834-2840. Open in summer and fall; tours available.

☐ **The Petrolia Discovery Foundation**
4381 Discovery Line, Petrolia, ON N0N 1R0. Tel: (519) 882-0897. Open in summer and fall.

☐ **Royal Ontario Museum,**
INCO Gallery of Earth Sciences
1100 Queen's Park, Toronto, ON M5S 2C6. Tel: (416) 586-5549. Closed Christmas, New Year's Day.

☐ **Timmins Museum**
70 Legion Drive, South Porcupine, ON P4N 1B3. Tel: (705) 235-5066. Open all year.

Western Canada:

☐ **Stonewall Quarry Park**
200 North Main Street, Stonewall, MB R0C 2Z0. Tel: (204) 467-5354. Open in summer.

☐ **Royal Saskatchewan Museum**
2445 Albert Street, Regina, SK S4P 3V7. Tel: (306) 787-2815. Open all year. Web site: www.royalsaskmuseum.ca/

☐ **Frank Slide Interpretive Centre**
PO Box 959, Blairmore, AB T0K 0E0. Located 1 km north of Frank, Alta. Tel: (403) 562-7388. Open all year.

☐ **Royal Tyrrell Museum of Palaeontology**
Hwy. 838, Midland Provincial Park, Drumheller, AB T0J 0Y0. Tel: (403) 823-7707. Open all year. Web site: www.tyrrellmuseum.com

☐ **Dinosaur Provincial Park**
Patricia, AB T0J 2K0. Tel: (403) 378-4342. Open all year.

☐ **British Columbia Museum of Mining**
PO Box 188, Britannia Beach, BC V0N 1J0. Tel: 1-800-896-4044. Open in summer and fall; all year for groups.

☐ **Pacific Mineral Museum**
848 West Hastings St., Vancouver, BC V6C 1C8. Tel: (604) 689-8700. Entrance fee. Closed Mondays during the winter. Web site: www.pacificmineralmuseum.org

☐ **Princeton and District Museums**
167 Vermilion St., Princeton, BC V0X 1W0. Tel: (250) 295-7588. Open from June 30 to August 31.

☐ **Keno City Mining Museum**
Centre St., Keno City, YT Y0B 1M0. Tel: (867) 995-2792. Open in summer.

PHYSICAL SCIENCES

Physics and chemistry constitute the physical sciences. **Chemistry** concerns itself with the composition, properties and reactions of substances. Organic chemistry, one of the two main branches of chemistry, specializes in the composition, properties and reactions of hydrocarbon compounds. The other branch, inorganic chemistry, deals primarily with the elements and compounds that do not include hydrocarbons. **Physics** concerns itself with universal aspects of nature—forces, energy, structure of matter, and their interactions. Some of its particular fields are: plasma physics, optics and quantum optics, particle physics, geophysics, biophysics and acoustics. As basic sciences, physics and chemistry permeate all sciences and technologies.

Common Chemistry Terms

Acid: A substance that in liquid form will turn blue litmus paper red, react with alkalis (bases) to form salts, and dissolve metals to form salts.

Alkali: Any compound that has chemical qualities of a base, such as reacting with acid to form salts.

Atomic Weight (Mass): The relative mass of an atom, based on a scale in which a specific carbon atom is assigned a mass value of 12.

Base: An alkaline substance, either molecular or ionic in form, that will accept or receive a proton from another chemical unit.

Catalyst: A substance that accelerates a chemical reaction without becoming a part of the end product of the reaction.

Compound: A substance formed by the combination of two or more chemical elements that cannot be separated from the combination by physical means. The constituent atoms, however, can usually be separated by means of chemical reactions.

Electron: A negatively charged particle that moves in orbit about the nucleus of an atom.

Element: A substance composed of atoms with the same atomic number or the same number of protons in their nuclei.

Isotope: One of two or more atoms having the same atomic number, but a different mass number.

Mass Number: The atomic weight of an isotope, calculated from the number of protons and neutrons in the nucleus.

Matter: Anything that has weight or fills space, such as a solid, liquid or gas.

Polymer: A huge molecule composed of repeating units of the same molecule.

Valence: A number that represents the combining power of an element, ion or radical.

Common Physics Terms

Acceleration: The rate of change of velocity with respect to time.

Anode: The positive terminal of an electric current flow. In a vacuum tube, electrons flow from the cathode to the anode.

Cathode: The negative terminal of an electric current system. In vacuum tube, the filament serves as the source electrons.

Conduction: The transfer of heat by molecular motion from a source of high temperature to a region of lower temperature, tending towards a result of equalized temperatures.

Convection: The mechanical transfer of heated molecules of a gas or liquid from a source to another area, as when a room is warmed by the movement of air molecules heated by a radiator.

Electromotive Force: The force that causes the movement of electrons through an electrical circuit.

Energy: The ability to perform work. Energy may be changed from one form to another, as from heat to light, but normally it cannot be created or destroyed.

Force: The influence on a body that causes it to accelerate.

Heat: A form of energy that results from the disordered motion of molecules. As the motion becomes more rapid and disordered, the amount of heat is increased.

Mass: A measure of the amount of matter. Near the surface of the Earth, it is roughly equivalent to weight.

Momentum: The mathematical product of the mass of a moving object and its velocity.

Velocity: The speed with which an object travels over a specified distance during a measured amount of time.

Weight: The force on a body produced by the downward pull of gravity on it.

Basic Laws of Physics

■ Newton's Laws of Motion

Newton's laws apply to objects in a vacuum, and are difficult to observe in the "real" world where forces such as friction affect all objects.

First Law: Any object at rest tends to stay at rest, and a body in motion will continue that motion with a constant velocity unless acted upon by some external unbalanced force.

Second Law: The acceleration of an object is directly proportional to the force acting upon it, and is inversely proportional to the mass of the object.

Third Law: Every action generates an equal and opposite reaction.

■ Gravity

When an object is dropped near the surface of the Earth, it increases in speed as it falls. By rolling balls down inclined planes Galileo discovered that acceleration due to gravity is the same for all objects, independent of their weight (mass). For example, if you drop this book and a brick simultaneously, they will reach to floor at the same time. You can try the same experiment with a heavy book and a single sheet of paper. The paper is affected by the resistance of the air. Then crumple the paper, and try again.

Gravity is the force that tends to attract objects to the centre of a celestial body, such as the Earth, the moon or Mars. The weight of an object at the Earth's surface is mainly due to the force of gravity between the Earth and the object. The force exerted by the Earth varies with the object's distance from the centre of the Earth. Therefore the weight of an object is not the same at the Earth's surface as it is on the moon or in space.

■ Laws of Thermodynamics

Sadi Carnot (1796–1832) stated in his work *Reflections on the Motive Power of Fire* that mechanical energy could be produced by the simple transfer of heat.

First Law: In a closed system, energy appears to be conserved in all but nuclear reactions and other extreme conditions.

Second Law: In a closed system, heat never travels from a low to a higher temperature in a self sustaining process. In a closed system, entropy (disorder) always increases.

■ Two Basic Laws of Quantum Physics

Heisenberg's Uncertainty Principle: It is impossible to specify completely the position and momentum of a particle, such as an electron.

Pauli's Exclusion Principle: No two electrons of the same atom can have identical values for all four quantum numbers: at least one quantum number must be different.

Loudness of Sounds

Sound is measured in decibels. A decibel is a unit for measuring the relative intensity of a sound, equal to one-tenth of a bel. A bel indicates the amount of energy in the form of sound transmitted to one square centimetre of the ear. The bel was named after Alexander Graham Bell.

The decibel scale advances geometrically instead of arithmetically. Twenty decibels represents not twice as much noise as ten, but 10 times as much. The 80-decibel level of a pneumatic drill is 100 times as noisy as the 60-decibel level of a quiet motor.

Source: *Dictionary of Science, Barnhardt, American Heritage Series*

Intensity (decibels)	Loudness	Intensity (decibels)	Loudness
0	Threshold of hearing	70	Loud conversation
10 (1 bel)	Virtual silence	80	Door slamming
20	Quiet room	90	Busy typing room
30	Watch ticking at 1 m	100	Near loud motor horn
40	Quiet street	110	Pneumatic drill
50	Quiet conversation	120	Near airplane engine
60	Quiet motor at 1 m	130	Threshold of pain

The Elements

An element is a substance composed of atoms that are chemically alike—each atom has an identical number of protons in its nucleus. Furthermore, there is no known process to break these elements down into more fundamental substances.

Name	Symbol	Number	Name	Symbol	Number	Name	Symbol	Number
actinium	Ac	89	gold	Au	79	potassium	K	19
aluminum	Al	13	hafnium	Hf	72	praseodymium	Pr	59
americium	Am	95	hassium	Hs	108	promethium	Pm	61
antimony	Sb	51	helium	He	2	protactinium	Pa	91
argon	Ar	18	holmium	Ho	67	radium	Ra	88
arsenic	As	33	hydrogen	H	1	radon	Rn	86
astatine	At	85	indium	In	49	rhenium	Re	75
barium	Ba	56	iodine	I	53	rhodium	Rh	45
berkelium	Bk	97	iridium	Ir	77	rubidium	Rb	37
beryllium	Be	4	iron	Fe	26	ruthenium	Ru	44
bismuth	Bi	83	krypton	Kr	36	rutherfordium	Rf	104
bohrium	Bh	107	lanthanum	La	57	samarium	Sm	62
boron	B	5	lawrencium	Lr	103	scandium	Sc	21
bromine	Br	35	lead	Pb	82	seaborgium	Sg	106
cadmium	Cd	48	lithium	Li	3	selenium	Se	34
calcium	Ca	20	lutetium	Lu	71	silicon	Si	14
californium	Cf	98	magnesium	Mg	12	silver	Ag	47
carbon	C	6	manganese	Mn	25	sodium	Na	11
cerium	Ce	58	meitnerium	Mt	109	strontium	Sr	38
cesium	Cs	55	mendelevium	Md	101	sulfur	S	16
chlorine	Cl	17	mercury	Hg	80	tantalum	Ta	73
chromium	Cr	24	molybdenum	Mo	42	technetium	Tc	43
cobalt	Co	27	neodymium	Nd	60	tellurium	Te	52
copper	Cu	29	neon	Ne	10	terbium	Tb	65
curium	Cm	96	neptunium	Np	93	thallium	Tl	81
darnstadtium	Ds	110	nickel	Ni	28	thorium	Th	90
dubnium	Db	105	niobium	Nb	41	thulium	Tm	69
dysprosium	Dy	66	nitrogen	N	7	tin	Sn	50
einsteinium	Es	99	nobelium	No	102	titanium	Ti	22
erbium	Er	68	osmium	Os	76	tungsten	W	74
europium	Eu	63	oxygen	O	8	unununium*	Uuu	111
fermium	Fm	100	palladium	Pd	46	ununbium*	Uub	112
fluorine	F	9	phosphorus	P	15	ununquadium*	Uuq	114
francium	Fr	87	platinum	Pt	78	ununhexium*	Uuh	116
gadolinium	Gd	64	plutonium	Pu	94	ununoctium*	Uuo	118
gallium	Ga	31	polonium	Po	84	uranium	U	92
germanium	Ge	32				vanadium	V	23
						xenon	Xe	54
						ytterbium	Yb	70
						yttrium	Y	39
						zinc	Zn	30
						zirconium	Zr	40

*temporary name

What is the Periodic Table?

*T*he Periodic Table of Elements (shown on the next page) has its roots in the 19th century when chemists calculated how much one atom of an element weighed in comparison to another. The resulting weight was known as the atomic mass and measured in atomic mass units (amu). (An amu is a mass equal to $1/12$ of the mass of the most common form of carbon atom.) As the list of elements was compiled and ranked in order of mass, chemists noted that every seven or eight elements had similar properties.

By 1869 Dimitri Mendeleyev was confident enough to rearrange the list of elements to group those with similar properties and leave blanks for the missing ones. Mendeleyev only had 63 elements; the table now has 110 named elements (some artificially created) and at least five others have been found but not named.

Early in the 20th century, the table was further refined when atoms were found to be made up of protons and electrons. The number of protons and electrons is equal in one atom and this number was designated the element's atomic number. The table now shows the elements in order according to their atomic number and their atomic mass.

Periodic Table of Elements

1 H 1.00																	**2** He 4.00
3 Li 6.94	**4** Be 9.01											**5** B 10.81	**6** C 12.01	**7** N 14.01	**8** O 15.99	**9** F 18.99	**10** Ne 20.18
11 Na 22.98	**12** Mg 24.30											**13** Al 26.98	**14** Si 28.08	**15** P 30.97	**16** S 32.06	**17** Cl 35.45	**18** Ar 39.95
19 K 39.09	**20** Ca 40.08	**21** Sc 44.95	**22** Ti 47.88	**23** V 50.94	**24** Cr 51.99	**25** Mn 54.94	**26** Fe 55.84	**27** Co 58.93	**28** Ni 58.69	**29** Cu 63.54	**30** Zn 65.39	**31** Ga 69.72	**32** Ge 72.61	**33** As 74.92	**34** Se 78.96	**35** Br 79.90	**36** Kr 83.80
37 Rb 85.46	**38** Sr 87.62	**39** Y 88.90	**40** Zr 91.22	**41** Nb 92.91	**42** Mo 95.94	**43** Tc (98)	**44** Ru 101.07	**45** Rh 102.91	**46** Pd 106.42	**47** Ag 107.87	**48** Cd 112.41	**49** In 114.82	**50** Sn 118.71	**51** Sb 121.76	**52** Te 127.60	**53** I 126.90	**54** Xe 131.29
55 Cs 132.90	**56** Ba 137.33	**71** Lu 174.97	**72** Hf 178.49	**73** Ta 180.95	**74** W 183.84	**75** Re 186.21	**76** Os 190.2	**77** Ir 192.22	**78** Pt 195.08	**79** Au 196.97	**80** Hg 200.59	**81** Tl 204.38	**82** Pb 207.2	**83** Bi 208.98	**84** Po (209)	**85** At (210)	**86** Rn (222)
87 Fr (223)	**88** Ra 226.02	**103** Lr (262)	**104** Rf (263)	**105** Db (262)	**106** Sg (266)	**107** Bh (264)	**108** Hs (269)	**109** Mt (268)	**110** Ds (271)	**111** Uuu (272)	**112** Uub (277)		**114** Uuq (289)		**116** Uuh (289)		**118** Uuo (293)

transition metals — *non-metals* — *gases* — *other metals*

lanthanoids

57 La 138.91	**58** Ce 140.12	**59** Pr 140.91	**60** Nd 144.24	**61** Pm (145)	**62** Sm 150.36	**63** Eu 151.96	**64** Gd 157.25	**65** Tb 158.93	**66** Dy 162.50	**67** Ho 164.93	**68** Er 167.26	**69** Tm 168.93	**70** Yb 173.04

actinoids

89 Ac 227.03	**90** Th 232.04	**91** Pa 231.04	**92** U 238.03	**93** Np 237.05	**94** Pu (244)	**95** Am (243)	**96** Cm (247)	**97** Bk (247)	**98** Cf (251)	**99** Es (252)	**100** Fm (257)	**101** Md (258)	**102** No (259)

rare earth elements

This is a table which shows the properties of the elements, in the order of their atomic mass or number, and arranged in horizontal rows (periods) and vertical columns (groups) to illustrate the occurence of similarities in the structure of their atoms. When the elements are arranged in this order, their chemical and physical properties show repeatable trends. This pattern in properties occurs periodically; that is, the pattern is repeated in an orderly manner over time.

The order of the elements is that of their atomic numbers, the integers which are equal to the positive electrical charges of the atomic nuclei expressed in electronic units.

Elements that are listed with their atomic weights in brackets are radioactive and have variable weights. Since the various isotopes weigh differently at different times due to decay (that is, an isotope will be heavier at its creation than later on), the atomic mass of the most stable isotope is listed.

FOCUS ON...

Canadian Light Source

In one corner of the University of Saskatchewan's campus is Canada's biggest science project in decades—the Canadian Light Source (CLS). With a price-tag of $174 million, the CLS will give Canadian scientists a cutting-edge tool for research ranging from archaeology to zoology.

The CLS is a synchrotron—a device for creating intense beams of light that can be used to probe deep inside almost anything, showing details hidden to other methods of investigation. It has been described as a "Swiss army knife" for scientific research because of its enormous versatility.

Information obtained by scientists using the synchrotron can be employed to help design new drugs, examine the structure of surfaces in order to develop more effective motor oils, build more powerful computer chips, develop new materials for safer medical implants, and help with clean-up of mining wastes, to name just a few applications.

■ Research Tool

Indeed, Canadian scientists already use synchrotrons in other countries—even Brazil, Korea and Taiwan have their own—because they have become indispensable in many areas of research. For example:

- Mineralogist Jenne Percival of Natural Resources Canada wants to use the CLS to study how uranium binds to clay. This will have important implications for the way uranium mining is done.
- Biochemist Michele Loewen of the National Research Council is using off-shore synchrotrons to study the behaviour of proteins. She's looking forward to doing the work in Canada.
- Geochemist Alan Anderson of St. Francis Xavier University wants to use the CLS to study how ore deposits are formed by hot fluids, which may shed light on where to develop new mines.

The synchrotron is based on some fundamental facts of physics. First, a moving electron (or any subatomic particle) that is forced to change direction will lose energy. Second, that energy comes in packets called photons, the particles of light.

■ Brighter Than Sunlight

The CLS speeds billions of electrons up to nearly the speed of light, using microwave energy. Then the (now highly energetic) electrons are sent into a large ring, 171.5 metres in circumference, where they are propelled in a multi-sided near-circle by 24 guide magnets, as well as by 108 smaller focussing magnets. Every time the electrons pass one of the guide magnets, they change direction, forcing them to emit photons, in a beam millions of times as bright as sunlight.

A similar phenomenon happens every winter, when charged particles from the sun approach the earth in a straight line. But when they hit the earth's magnetic field, they are forced into a spiral motion and begin shedding the photons that we see as the northern lights.

The difference is that the CLS lets researchers capture, tune, and use different parts of the light spectrum, from infrared to x-rays, in what are called "beamlines." In principle, the CLS could have a beamline for every guide magnet and still more to use light created when the focussing magnets herd the electrons back into line.

Initially, however, only seven are being built, with more being added later as money is available and demand grows. The first seven are:

- High Resolution Far-Infrared Spectroscopy
- Mid-Infrared Microscopy
- Plane Grating Monochromator
- Spherical Grating Monochromator
- Soft X-ray Spectromicroscopy
- Macromolecular Protein Crystallography
- X-ray Absorption Spectroscopy with Microprobe Capabilities.

At least six of the beamlines are to be up and running when the CLS "takes first light" early in 2004. Because of the beamlines, publicity for the CLS often calls it "Canada's Field of Beams."

More than 2,000 academic and industrial researchers a year from across Canada and from other countries are expected to use the facility once the full complement of beamlines is developed.

■ Wide Range of Support

The University of Saskatchewan is the home of the CLS, but dozens of other Canadian universities are supporting it, as well as industrial partners, such as the pharmaceutical giant GlaxoSmithKline, and research organizations, such as the Canadian Institute for Health Research.

The CLS began as an idea floated by the Natural Sciences and Engineering Council, Canada's largest scientific granting council, in 1994. Two years later, an international committee recommended the bid put together by the University of Saskatchewan. And in 1999, the Canada Foundation for Innovation gave the green light, when it announced a $56.4-million contribution toward building costs.

That was slightly more than a third of the $141 million needed to construct the machine and the building to house it (an existing building and equipment accounted for the other $33 million of the $174 million price-tag).

So the CLS consortium had to raise the rest; it came from various sources, including $2.4 million from the city of Saskatoon, $500,000 for the drug company Boehringer Ingelheim, $25 million from the Saskatchewan government, and so on.

■ "Third-Generation" Synchrotron

The CLS is one of only 17 "third-generation" synchrotrons either in existence or planned. Third-generation synchrotrons have devices inserted to produce even more light from the electron stream. This makes it possible to do such things as medical imaging faster and cheaper and to "see" much smaller entities than has been possible before.

This first-in-Canada 2.9 GeV (giga-electron volt) synchrotron light source will be fully competitive with the best available internationally and is expected to attract industrial and academic researchers from coast to coast.

■ Reverse "Brain Drain"

Indeed, a reverse brain drain began happening even before the CLS was ready to start work. Physicist Dean Chapman of the Illinois Institute of Technology, world-renowned for his use of synchrotron light in medical and biological applications, agreed to relocate to Saskatoon. CLS Director Bill Tomlinson, with more than 25 years of experience in developing synchrotrons, came from the European Synchrotron Radiation Facility. All told, more than 25 researchers have moved to the University of Saskatchewan to take advantage of the CLS, and still others have taken up posts at nearby universities.

As well, an independent consulting firm estimated in 1996 that the CLS, once it's running, will attract $35 million a year to Canada in commercial research and development spending, add $12 million a year to Canada's gross domestic product and create 200 permanent jobs.

Building the CLS was an engineering challenge. Because it must be absolutely rock-steady, the main hall that houses the machine is anchored by 632 concrete piles driven between 10 and 20 metres into the Prairie soil. The main hall itself has an area of 6,806 square metres or about 1.7 acres—that's roughly the same size as four double tennis courts or 50 sheets of curling ice. But that's still only about half the area of the whole facility, including office space and other areas.

Building the structure took 7,000 cubic metres of concrete—enough for 160 new 1,200-square-foot homes. That's equivalent to 1,200 truckloads of concrete, weighing about 16,800 tonnes. Also needed was 1,300 tonnes of steel to frame the building and 5,280 square metres of wall sheathing.

The CLS Web site is at www.lightsource.ca

The International System of Units (SI)

The Systeme Internationale (SI) or metric system was developed in France in 1799. By 1880 many European countries and much of South America had adopted the system as a common language of measurements.

The pressures of global trade have persuaded many of the English-speaking countries to adopt a uniform international standard of measure. Canada adopted the metric system in 1970.

Name	Symbol	Quantity
■ SI Base Units		
metre	m	length
kilogram	kg	mass
second	s	time
ampere	A	electric current
kelvin	K	thermodynamic temperature
mole	mol	amount of substance
candela	cd	luminous intensity
■ SI Supplementary Units		
radian	rad	plane angle
steradian	sr	solid angle
■ Common SI Derived Units With Special Names		
hertz	Hz	frequency
pascal	Pa	pressure, stress
watt	W	power, radiant flux
volt	V	electric potential, electromotive force
newton	N	force
joule	J	energy, work
coulomb	C	electric charge
ohm	Ω	electric resistance
farad	F	electric capacitance
■ Common Units Used With the SI		
litre	L	volume or capacity (= 1 dm^3)
degree Celsius	°C	temperature (= 1 K; 0°C = 273.2 K)
hectare	ha	area (= 10 000 m^2)
tonne	t	mass (= 1000 kg)
electronvolt	eV	energy (= 0.160 aJ)
nautical mile	M	distance (navigation) (= 1852 m)
knot	kn	speed (navigation) (= 1 M/h)
standard atmosphere	atm	atmospheric pressure (= 101.3 kPa)

■ SI Prefixes

Name	Symbol	Multiplying Factor*
exa-	E	10^{18}
peta-	P	10^{15}
tera-	T	10^{12}
giga-	G	10^{9}
mega-	M	10^{6}
kilo-	k	10^{3}
hecto-	h	10^{2}
deca-	da	10
deci-	d	10^{-1}
centi-	c	10^{-2}
milli-	m	10^{-3}
micro-	μ	10^{-6}
nano-	n	10^{-9}
pico-	p	10^{-12}
femto-	f	10^{-15}
atto-	a	10^{-18}

*10^2 = 100; 10^3 = 1 000; 10^{-1} = 0.1; 10^{-2} = 0.01; Thus, 2 km = 2 x 1 000 = 2 000 m ; 3 cm = 3 x 0.01 = 0.03 m

Source: *Gage Canadian Dictionary*

Large Numbers

1 thousand	1 000
1 million	1 000 000 or 10^6
1 milliard: used in Europe, USSR, former French possessions	1 000 000 000 or 10^9
1 billion:	1 000 000 000 000 or 10^{12}
—Canada, the United States and France	1 000 000 000 or 10^9
1 trillion:	1 000 000 000 000 000 000 or 10^{18}
—Canada and the United States	1 000 000 000 000 or 10^{12}

Source: *World Weights and Measures*

Science Centres and Museums

Maritime Region:

☐ **Discovery Centre**
1593 Barrington St., Halifax, NS. Open daily.
Tel: (902) 492-4422.
Web site: www.discoverycentre.ns.ca

☐ **Nova Scotia Museum of Industry**
147 N. Foord St., Stellarton, NS B0K 1S0.
Open daily. Tel: (902) 755-5425.
Web site: www.museum.gov.ns.ca/moi

☐ **Nova Scotia Museum of Natural History**
1747 Summer St., Halifax, NS B3H 3A6
Tel: (902) 424-7353 Open daily.
Web site: www.museum.gov.ns.ca/mnh

Central Canada:

☐ **Museum of Visual Science and Optometry**
University of Waterloo, 200 University Ave. W.,
Waterloo, ON N2L 3G1. Open weekdays. Web site:
www.optometry.uwaterloo.ca/~museum

☐ **Hamilton Museum of Steam and Technology**
900 Woodward Ave., Hamilton, ON L8H 7N2.
Tel: (905) 546-4797. Open all year.

☐ **National Museum of Science and Technology**
1867 St. Laurent Blvd, Ottawa, ON K1G 5A3.
Tel: (613) 991-3044. Open all year.
Web site: www.science-tech.technomuses.ca

☐ **Ontario Science Centre**
7770 Don Mills Rd, Toronto, ON M3C 1T3.
Tel : (416) 696-1000. Open daily.
Web site: www.ontariosciencecentre.ca/

☐ **Science North**
100 Ramsay Lake Rd, Sudbury, ON P3E 5S9.
Tel: (705) 522-3700. Open all year.
Web site: www.sciencenorth.on.ca

Western Canada:

☐ **Calgary Science Centre**
701-11 Street S.W., Calgary, AB T2P 2M5.
Tel: (403) 221-3700. Open all year.
Web site: www.calgaryscience.ca

☐ **Odyssium**
11211-142 St., Edmonton, AB T5M 4A1.
Tel: (403) 452-9100. Open all year.
Web site: www.odyssium.com

☐ **Okanagan Science Centre**
2704 Highway 6, Vernon, BC V1T 5G5.
Tel : (250) 545-3644. Closed Sundays.
Web site: www.okscience.ca

☐ **Saskatchewan Science Centre**
2903 Powerhouse Dr., Regina, SK S4N 0A1.
Tel: 1-800-667-6300. Open all year.
Web site: www.sciencecentre.sk.ca

☐ **Science World**
1455 Quebec St., Vancouver, BC V6A 3Z7.
Tel: (604) 443-7440. Open daily, except Christmas
Day. Web site: www.scienceworld.bc.ca

Upping the Ante in Computer Games

*U*niversity of Alberta computer scientists are betting that it's only a matter of time before the world's best poker players are folding their cards in the face of a digital opponent. Jonathan Schaeffer, who heads up the University of Alberta's Games Research Group, says poker is an ideal way to test an artificial intelligence program designed to deal with incomplete information and uncertainty. And their latest program—dubbed PsOpti—is good enough that it gave one of the world's top players a hard time. "After 7,000 hands it was clear that the human was the better player, but it took him a long time to figure out how to win against the program," said Schaeffer, who already has one world man-machine games title under his belt—his Chinook program jumped to checkers world champion in 1994. PsOpti is designed as a defensive player. The program is based on a mathematical formula developed by game theory founder John Nash (the subject of the Academy Award-winning film A BEAUTIFUL MIND. This mathematical approach emphasizes the best strategy to ensure that you don't lose.

Source: *NSERC*

SCIENCE AT WORK

Individual Canadians have been awarded recognition in the ranks of the world's pre-eminent scientists and researchers, as our lists of Nobel Prize winners and the Canadian Engineering and Science Hall of Fame both show.

Canadian Nobel Laureates in Science and Medicine

1923	Drs. Banting, Macleod and Collip	Medicine and Physiology	For the discovery of insulin
1971	Dr. Gerhard Herzberg	Chemistry	For his contributions to the knowledge of electronic structure, particularly free radicals
1986	Dr. John Polanyi	Chemistry	For contributions concerning the dynamics of elementary chemical reactions
1993	Dr. Michael Smith	Chemistry	Co-winner for work on genetic codes
1994	Bertram Brockhouse	Physics	Co-winner for study on atoms

Canadian Science and Engineering Hall of Fame

The inductees into the Canadian Science and Engineering Hall of Fame are outstanding researchers, inventors and innovators who have won worldwide recognition for their accomplishments. The Hall of Fame web site can be accessed at www.nrc.ca

The Inductees

Maude Abbott (1869–1940) . . . . Pathologist and specialist in congenital heart disease
Sir Frederick Banting (1891–1941) . . . . Co-discoverer of insulin; Nobel laureate
Alexander Graham Bell (1847–1922) . . . . . Inventor of the telephone
J. Armand Bombardier (1907–1964) . . . . Inventor of the snowmobile
Bertram Brockhouse (1918–) . . . . Physicist who pioneered use of neutron scattering in study of atoms; Nobel laureate
Douglas Harold Copp (1915–1998) . . . . Discoverer of calcitonin, a hormone used in the treatment of osteoporosis
Pierre Dansereau (1911–) . . . . Pioneered a new approach to the study of ecology
Reginald Fessenden (1866–1932) . . . . Pioneer in the development of the radio
Sir Sanford Fleming (1827–1915) . . . . Architect of the transcontinental railway; inventor of time zones
Gerald Heffernan (1919–) . . . . Innovation in steel production, developer of the environment-friendly "mini-mill"
Gerhard Herzberg (1904–99) . . . . Astrophysicist; Nobel laureate
Harold Elford Johns (1915–1998) . . . . Developer of the cobalt-60 cancer therapy unit in 1951.
George J. Klein (1904–92) . . . . Design engineer, the most productive inventor in 20th century Canada
Hugh Le Caine (1914–77) . . . . Physicist; designed the first musical synthesizer
Sir William Logan (1798–1875) . . . . First director of the Geological Survey of Canada
Elizabeth "Elsie" MacGill (1905–80) . . . . . . Aeronautical engineer, oversaw WWII production of Hawker Hurricane fighter aircraft
Frances G. McGill (1877–1959) . . . . Pioneer in forensic pathology
Frère Marie-Victorin (1885–1944) . . . . Botanist, author and teacher
Andrew G.L. MacNaughton (1887–1966) . . . Inventor of cathode-ray detection finder and military leader
Margaret Newton (1887–1971) . . . . Plant pathologist who developed techniques to combat wheat rust
Joseph-Alphonse Ouimet (1908–88) . . . . Inventor, engineer and CBC president
Wilder Penfield (1891–1976) . . . . Neurosurgeon who developed surgical treatments for epilepsy
John Polanyi (1929–) . . . . Contributed to the development of laser chemistry; Nobel laureate
Charles E. Saunders (1867–1937) . . . . Developed fast-ripening Marquis wheat
Charles Scriver (1930–) . . . . Innovator in medical genetics
Michael Smith (1932–2000) . . . . Chemistry researcher, genetic codes and DNA; Nobel laureate
Edgar William Richard Steacie (1900–62) . . Researcher (free radical chemistry), educator
Wallace Turnbull (1870–1954) . . . . Inventor of the variable pitch propeller
John Tuzo Wilson (1908–1993) . . . . Contributed to development of plate tectonics

Source: *National Research Council*

The National Research Council

Canada's National Research Council was established in 1916, with the country at war and millions of men and women serving overseas. The NRC's goal was to develop Canadian science—a goal that is still its focus. Some highlights from the NRC's history:

1916–1927: Magnesite, a mineral used in the coating of high-temperature industrial furnaces, was imported for years because domestic ores weren't pure enough. NRC-financed researchers found a simple way of eliminating the impurities, so Canada could cut its dependence on imports.

1928–1932: From 1924 to 1938, Canadian medical researchers worked with the NRC to find a vaccine against tuberculosis. Their work helped make the BCG vaccine the main weapon against the disease.

George Klein (1904–1992), a Canadian inventor and a longtime NRC employee, produced an almost endless list of inventions: aircraft skis, an electric wheelchair for quadriplegics, a microsurgery staple gun and a retractable antenna that is still standard equipment on satellites

1933–1945: The NRC helped develop radar (for "radio distance and ranging") during World War II. Today, radar is essential to make travel safer by air, land and sea.

Before World War II began, the NRC enlisted **Sir Frederick Banting**, the discoverer of insulin, to lead research on combat-related medicine. Banting's team worked on wound infections, shock, penicillin, a typhus vaccine, blood substitutes and plastic surgery.

If you've ever played a **synthesizer**, you owe the experience to an NRC scientist. Hugh Le Caine invented the world's first in 1945.

1946–1952: Canola oil, which can sometimes take the place of butter on popcorn, is used to make margarine, cooking oils, lubricants and inks. In the 1940s, the NRC helped to develop a hybrid canola plant, and today canola is one of Canada's leading cash crops.

If you or someone you know wears a **pacemaker,** the technology that made it possible was developed by the NRC in the late 1940s by Jack Hopps.

1953–1963: The NRC's Harry Stevinson developed a reliable emergency locator beacon for downed aircraft. In 1957, the Crash Position Indicator was introduced for military use, and by 1960 was available for commercial aircraft.

In 1958, the NRC built one of the world's earliest cesium beam atomic clocks—accurate to a few millionths of a second per year. By the 1970s, NRC time was being used to set official time scales and clocks around the world.

1964–1971: In 1971, Dr. Gerhard Herzberg of the NRC won a Nobel Prize in chemistry for his work in identifying molecules in space.

1972–1980: In 1973, the NRC opened a centre to retrieve and analyse data from flight recorders (more commonly known as black boxes).

Also in 1973, the **Canada–France–Hawaii Telescope** opened, high on the frigid, barren top of the Hawaiian volcano Mauna Kea. It can produce images almost as sharp as those from the Hubble Space Telescope—and it's much easier to repair.

1981–1989: The NRC developed an optical security patch that changes colour in different lights. The patch is used on paper money and drivers' licences to prevent counterfeiting.

Saran Narang made a major medical breakthrough when he produced **synthetic insulin** for use by diabetics.

1990-2001: In May 1996, Canadian astronaut Marc Garneau retrieved a satellite in flight using the CANADARM—with the help of the Space Vision System, a technology developed by the NRC.

In the early 1990s, NRC experts introduced various fingerprint detection methods that are still used by the RCMP and other police forces.

Exhausting Research on Edmonton's Roads

A 1993 GM pickup truck cruising the streets and highways around Edmonton may play a key role in setting future emissions standards—it's the only vehicle on the road in Canada whose every emission is being constantly monitored by a web of sensors that record everything from engine speed to fuel flow and exhaust gas composition. Vehicle emission standards are now based on vehicles tested on a dynamometer—a sort of indoor treadmill for cars—rather than real-world conditions, says project leader David Checkel of the University of Alberta.

The research could help point the way to more efficient and less polluting engine systems.

Source: *NSERC*

2002 Nobel Prize Winners

Each October the Swedish academies for physics, chemistry and medicine announce the winners of the Nobel Prizes in science. The awards are named after Alfred Nobel, the Swedish-born chemist and businessman who invented dynamite and smokeless gunpowder. The science prizes, as well as a prize for literature and one for peace, are financed by an endowment from Nobel's estate. The prize for economics is financed by the Swedish national bank. The peace prize went to former U.S. President Jimmy Carter for working to find peaceful solutions to conflict and to promote human welfare. The Hungarian writer Imre Kertesz was awarded the literature prize. And the economics prize went to Daniel Kahneman of Princeton University and Vernon L. Smith of George Mason University for new approaches to economics.

In 2002, Raymond Davis Jr. of the University of Pennsylvania, and Masatoshi Koshiba of the University of Tokyo, shared half the **physics** prize for helping detect cosmic neutrinos; half went to Riccardo Giacconi of Associated Universities Inc., for work on cosmic X-ray sources.

Half the **chemistry** prize was shared by John Fenn of Virginia Commonwealth University and Koichi Tanaka of Shimadzu Corp. for studies of biological macromolecules; half went to Kurt Wuthrich of the Swiss Federal Institute of Technology for determining the structure of such macromolecules.

Sydney Brenner of the Molecular Sciences Institute, Robert Horvitz of the Massachusetts Institute of Technology, and John Sulston of the Sanger Institute shared the **medicine and physiology** prize for work on genetic regulation of organ development and programmed cell death.

The official Web site of the Nobel Foundation can be found at www.nobel.se

2002 Manning Award Winners

The Manning Awards recognize and encourage innovation in Canada by honouring individuals who have created and promoted a new concept, process or product that is beneficial to society. Administered by the Calgary-based Ernest C. Manning Foundation, the awards are presented annually. For the 2003 winners, visit www.manningawards.ca

PRINCIPAL AWARD: Mike Lazaridis and Gary Mousseau, of Waterloo, Ont., developed the architecture for the BlackBerry, the first handheld, totally integrated, wireless e-mail system. BlackBerry is the world's leading wireless enterprise solution for mobile professionals to stay continuously connected to their corporate e-mail, while meeting the security and manageability requirements of IT departments.

AWARD OF DISTINCTION: Dr. Harold Jennings, of Ottawa, Ont., spent nearly 25 years researching, developing and bringing to commercialization the world's first synthetic vaccine that protects infants against Group C meningitis—the most common form of the disease to strike youngsters.

INNOVATION AWARD: David Martin and Nancy Knowlton, of Calgary, Alta., through their company SMART Technologies, Inc., developed the first interactive whiteboard system to provide touch control of computer applications, annotation over top of standard Windows applications and the ability to save these notes.

Malcolm Jefferson, of Ottawa, Ont., invented the Centric-Safe Haven bicycle child carrier, which enhances safety and makes cycling a shared experience by placing the child securely in the carrier in front of the adult rider.

YOUNG CANADIAN INNOVATION AWARDS: Dan Carew and Adam Panter, of Fenelon Falls, Ont. (Moving Molecular Mountains); Jean-Philippe Demers, St. Athanase, Que. (Defective Cell Division); Russ Dickson, Niagara, Ont. (Simplification of Antibodies via Computer Program); Mahvish Jafri and Faizal Ismail, Toronto, Ont. (Boundary Layer Acceleration).

Source: *The Manning Awards*

Patents

If you have an idea for a new gizmo, what is required to have it patented? The Patent Office judges the idea based the following criteria:

1) the device must be the first of its kind in the world;
2) it must be useful, and most importantly, it must work;
3) it must be obviously ingenious to others familiar with the field.

A patent gives you the right to exclude others from making, using or selling an invention from the day the patent is granted until 20 years after filing. Patents also provide useful technical information to the public. Although individual inventors still apply for patents, the majority of applications now come from large corporations. Patents are granted by individual countries; so the protection of a Canadian patent extends throughout Canada alone. Patent rights in the United States or elsewhere must be applied for separately in the individual countries.

A Canadian patent application can be filed from any Canada Post outlet across the country. Detailed information on the application procedure for Patents, Trademarks, Copyrights and Industrial and Integrated Circuits Designs can be obtained from the Canadian Intellectual Property Office in Hull, Québec. (819) 997-1936.

There are now a number of Internet sites that are of interest to inventors. These include:

The Canadian Intellectual Property Office (CIPO)
http://cipo.gc.ca
CIPO's web site has information on Canadian Patents, Trademarks, Copyrights, Industrial Designs and Integrated Circuit Topographies. Trademarks can now be filed on line.

The Canadian Innovation Centre
www.innovationcentre.ca
The Canadian Innovation Centre is a not-for-profit corporation dedicated to helping Canadians commercialize their technological innovations. The Centre issues a publication, *Eureka!*, quarterly.

Canadian Technology Network
http://ctn-rct.nrc-cnrc.gc.ca/
Part of the National Reseearch Council site, CTN gives small and medium-sized technology businesses access to a cross-country network of expert advisers.

U.S. Patent and Trademark Office
www.uspto.gov/
General information about U.S. Patents and Trademarks is available, and the site has direct links to other national patent offices.

Canada Foundation for Innovation
www.innovation.ca/
The Canada Foundation for Innovation (CFI) is an independent corporation, established by the Government of Canada in 1997, to strengthen the capability of Canadian universities, colleges, research hospitals and other not-for-profit institutions to carry out world-class research and technology development.

When Practice Doesn't Make Perfect

Only one in 10,000 people has absolute or perfect pitch—they can identify or produce a specific musical note to order. When he's touring with the Rolling Stones, guitarist Keith Richards employs a man with perfect pitch whose sole job is to keep his guitars tuned. New York's renowned Juilliard School of Music has tried to train people in perfect pitch but has failed. But why is perfect pitch so rare? That's one of the questions puzzling McGill University psychology professor Daniel Levitin, who researches the mental processes involved in making and listening to music. In the long run, the research into auditory processing could enhance our understanding of how the brain works.

Source: *NSERC*

ATMOSPHERIC SCIENCE

A Glossary of Weather Terms

Air mass: An extensive body of air with a fairly uniform distribution of moisture and temperature throughout.

Alberta clipper: Named after the clipper sailing ships, which at one time were the fastest vessels on the seas. These storms zip along at 64 km/h, preceded by about 5 cm of light, powdery snow and followed by violent winds capable of reaching 100 km/h. This often results in severe blowing and drifting with blizzard conditions that can leave many roads impassable.

Atmosphere: The envelope of air surrounding the earth. Most weather events are confined to the lower 10 km of the atmosphere.

Atmospheric pressure: The force exerted on the earth by the weight of the atmosphere.

Blizzard: Severe winter weather condition characterized by low temperatures, strong winds above 40 km/h, and visibility of less than 1 km due to blowing snow; condition lasts three hours or more.

Blowing snow: Snow lifted from the earth's surface by the wind to a height of two metres or more. Blowing snow is higher than drifting snow.

Bright sunshine: Sunshine intense enough to burn a mark on recording paper mounted in the Campbell-Stokes sunshine recorder. The daily period of bright sunshine is less than that of visible sunshine because the sun's rays are not intense enough to burn the paper just after sunrise, near sunset and under cloudy conditions.

Chinook (also snow-eater): A dry, warm, strong wind that blows down the eastern slopes of the Rocky Mountains in North America. The warmth and dryness are due principally to heating by compression as the air descends the mountain slope.

Cold wave: An occurrence of dangerous cold conditions, when temperatures often dip below -18°C, that usually lasts longer than a few days.

Crepuscular rays: Clouds to excite any sky photographer, crepuscular rays are caused by streaks or beams of sunlight shining through openings in large cumulonimbus clouds on the horizon. The beams reach down and outward from behind the clouds. If they focus upward, toward a point in the sky opposite the sun, they are called anticrepuscular rays. Sometimes they are called sun beams crossing the sky or Jacob's ladder. Sailors refer to them as "the sun drawing water." The dark bands you see crossing the sky are the shadows from clouds.

Cyclone: A generic term that describes all classes of storms from local thunderstorms and tiny dust devils to monstrous hurricanes and typhoons. It comes from the Greek word *kyklon*, meaning cycle, circle or coil of a snake and refers to all circular wind systems.

Deep low: Used to describe the central barometric pressure of a low (usually when it is about 975 millibars [97.50 kPa or less]). Often has winds of gale to storm force around the low.

Developing low: A low in which the central pressure is decreasing with time. Winds normally increase as the low deepens.

Dew point temperature: The temperature at which air becomes saturated, allowing condensation of water vapour as frost, fog, dew, mist or precipitation.

Drizzle: Precipitation consisting of numerous minute water droplets which appear to float; the droplets are much smaller than in rain.

El Niño: Near the end of most years, the normally cold Peru Current that sweeps northward along the South American coast from southern Chile to the equator is replaced by a warm southward flowing coastal current. Centuries ago the local fishermen named this the "Christ child current," because it appeared around the Christmas season. Every few years it was unusually intense and over time the term El Niño became more closely associated with occasional intense warmings.

Filling low: A low in which the central pressure is increasing with time., i.e., the low is gradually weakening.

Flash floods: A very rapid rise of water with little or no advance warning, most often when an intense thunderstorm drops a huge rainfall on a fairly small area in a very short space of time.

Fog: A cloud based at the earth's surface consisting of tiny water droplets or, under very cold conditions, ice crystals or ice fog; generally found in calm or low wind conditions. Under foggy conditions, visibility is reduced to less than one kilometre.

▶

▶ **Frazil ice:** [French Canadian] During the freeze-up period ice forms on the river surface and ice crystals or frazil develop within the river, especially in open, turbulent water slightly below 0°C. Frazil ice is very common in rapids.

Freezing precipitation: Supercooled water drops of drizzle, or rain which freeze on impact to form a coating of ice upon the ground or any objects they strike.

Front: The boundary between two different air masses which have originated from widely separated regions. A cold front is the leading edge of an advancing cold air mass, while a warm front is the trailing edge of a retreating cold air mass.

Frost: The deposit of ice crystals that occurs when the air temperature is at or below the freezing point of water. The term frost is also used to describe the icy deposits of water vapor that may form on the ground or on other surfaces like car windshields, which are colder than the surrounding air and which have a temperature below freezing.

Gale: A strong wind. A gale warning is issued for expected winds of 65 to 100 km/h (34 to 47 knots).

Gust: A sudden, brief increase in wind speed, for generally less than 20 seconds.

Heat wave: A period with more than three consecutive days of maximum temperatures at or above 32°C.

High pressure: A term for an area of high (maximum) pressure with a closed, clockwise (in the Northern Hemisphere) circulation of air.

Humidex: A measure of what hot weather "feels like." Air of a given temperature and moisture content is equated in comfort to air with a higher temperature and that of negligible moisture content. At a humidex of 30°C some people begin to experience discomfort. (See chart on p. 603.)

Hurricanes: Tropical systems are classed into several categories depending on maximum strength, usually measured by maximum sustained wind speed. A *tropical disturbance* is simply a moving area of thunderstorms in the tropics that maintains its identity for 24 hours or more. A *tropical depression* is a cyclonic system originating over the tropics with a highest sustained wind speed of up to 61 km/h. A *tropical storm* has a highest sustained wind speed of between 62 and 117 km/h. A *hurricane* has wind speeds of 118 km/h or more.

Ice pellets: Precipitation consisting of fragments of ice, 5 mm or less in diameter, that bounce when hitting a hard surface, making a sound upon impact.

Inversion: The term refers to a temperature increase with height, where the usual pattern is a decrease in temperature within increasing height.

Isobar: A line on a weather map or chart connecting points of equal pressure. The large concentric lines on television or newspaper weather maps are isobars.

Killing frost: A frost severe enough to end the growing season, usually when the air temperature falls below −2°C.

Land breeze: A small-scale wind set off when the air temperature over water is warmer than that over adjacent land. The land breeze develops at night and blows from the land out to the sea or onto the lake. Its counterpart is the sea or lake breeze.

Low pressure: An area of low (minimum) atmospheric pressure that has a closed counter-clockwise circulation in the Northern Hemisphere.

Peak wind (gust): The highest instantaneous wind speed recorded for a specific time period.

Plough winds: These belong to a family of strong, straight-line downburst winds found in thunderstorms. These winds rush to the ground with great force, maybe 100 to 150 km/h and occasionally even higher. Damage usually covers an area less than 3 km across. Plough winds are capable of toppling trees, lifting roofs, and ripping apart houses and other structures.

Precipitation: Any and all forms of water, whether liquid or solid, that fall from the atmosphere and reach the earth's surface. A day with measurable precipitation is a day when the water equivalent of the precipitation is equal to or greater than 0.2 mm.

Probability of precipitation (POP): Subjective numerical estimates of your chances of encountering measurable precipitation at some time during the forecast period. For example, a 40% probability of rain means there are four chances in 10 of getting wet. They cannot be used to predict when, where or how much precipitation will occur.

Relative humidity: The ratio of water vapour in the air at a given temperature to the maximum which could exist at that temperature. It is usually expressed as a percentage.

Ridge: An elongated area of high pressure extending from the centre of a high pressure region; the opposite of a trough. ▶

▶ **Sea breeze:** A small-scale wind set off when the air temperature over land is greater than that over the adjacent sea. The sea breeze develops during the day and blows from the sea to the land. Its counterpart is the land breeze.

Sleet: This is not what you think. In the United States, sleet is frozen raindrops that bounce when they hit the surface. It is not as treacherous to drive on as is freezing rain. What Americans call sleet a Canadian would call ice pellets or frozen raindrops. They are spherical or irregular shapes with a diameter of 5 mm or less. Pellets do not stick to trees or wires. On the other hand, sleet to a British weather watcher is a mix of rain and partly melted snowflakes.

Small craft warning: Issued when winds over the coastal marine areas are expected to reach and maintain speeds of 20 to 33 knots.

Snow: Precipitation consisting of white or translucent ice crystals and often agglomerated into snowflakes. A day with measurable snow is a day when the total snowfall is at least 0.2 cm.

Squall: A strong, sudden wind which generally lasts a few minutes then quickly decreases in speed. Squalls are generally associated with severe thunderstorms.

Storm track: The path taken by a low-pressure centre.

Storm warning: The wind warning that is issued to mariners when winds are expected to be from 48 to 63 knots.

Thunderstorm: A local storm, usually produced by a cumulonimbus cloud, and always accompanied by thunder and lightning. A thunderstorm day is a day when thunder is heard or when lightning is seen (rain and snow need not have fallen).

Tornado (also twister): A violently rotating column of air that is usually visible as a funnel cloud hanging from dark thunderstorm clouds. It is one of the least extensive of all storms, but in violence, it is the most destructive.

Trough: An elongated area of low pressure extending from the centre of a low pressure region; the opposite of a ridge.

Tsunami: Also known (incorrectly) as a tidal wave. "Tsunami" is a Japanese word that means "harbour wave." It is a wave set in motion by an undersea movement such as an earthquake or a landslide. These waves can travel up to 1,000 km/h over long distances, hitting the shore with tremendous force.

Typhoon: A severe tropical cyclone in the Western Pacific Ocean, counterpart of the Atlantic hurricane.

Virga: Streaks of falling rain that evaporate before reaching the ground.

Watches and warnings: Environment Canada alerts Canadians to severe storms by issuing weather watches and warnings. Usually the first message is the severe thunderstorm watch. If a watch is issued in your area, maintain your routine, but keep an eye skyward for threatening weather, and listen to radio and television for further weather information. When severe local storms are building, or have actually been sighted or detected by radar, then warnings are issued and updated. These may be either severe thunderstorm warnings or tornado warnings. Warnings mean you should be on the alert.

Waterspout: A waterspout is not really a waterspout. Often called a tornado over water, the actual water spray involved does not extend from the surface to the cloud, but 3 to 10 metres above the water surface. Like the tornado, the waterspout is very brief. Sailors believed one way of breaking up a waterspout was to fire a cannon through it.

Weatheradio: This is the name of Environment Canada's weather information broadcast network. The network has transmitters in every region and listeners need a receiver, which can be purchased from electronic equipment dealers, to pick up the broadcasts. Weatheradio signals warnings of severe weather automatically to receivers equipped with special alarm devices for that purpose.

Westerlies (west-wind belt): The pronounced west-to-east motion of the atmosphere centred over middle latitudes from about 35° to 65° latitude.

Willy-willies: Refers to small, circular winds such as dust devils or whirlwinds in Australia, not very hazardous. Before 1950, willy-willies referred to much larger, more destructive typhoons or hurricanes.

Wind chill: A measure of the effect we feel when strong winds are combined with freezing temperatures. The index is in temperature-like units, explaining the way skin feels in a comparable temperature on a calm day, i.e., if it's −10°C and the wind chill is −20, it means your skin feels as cold as it would on a calm day at −20°C.

Wind direction: The direction from which the wind is blowing.

Humidex

RELATIVE HUMIDITY (%)

DRY BULB TEMP (°C)	100	95	90	85	80	75	70	65	60	55	50	45	40	35	30	25	20
43													56	54	51	49	47
42												56	54	52	50	48	46
41											56	54	52	50	48	46	44
40										57	54	52	51	49	47	44	43
39							57	56	56	54	53	51	49	47	45	43	41
38					58	57	55	53	54	52	51	49	47	46	43	42	40
37			58	57	56	54	53	51	51	50	49	47	45	43	42	40	
36		58	57	56	54	52	51	49	50	48	47	45	43	42	40	38	
35	58	57	55	53	52	51	49	48	48	47	45	43	42	41	38	37	
34	55	54	52	51	50	48	47	46	47	45	43	42	41	39	37	36	
33	52	51	50	49	47	46	45	43	44	43	42	40	38	37	36	34	
32	50	49	48	46	45	44	43	41	42	41	39	38	37	36	34	33	
31	48	47	46	44	43	42	41	40	40	39	38	38	35	34	33	31	
30	46	45	44	43	42	41	39	38	38	37	36	36	34	33	31	31	
29	43	42	41	41	39	38	37	36	37	36	34	35	32	31	30		
28	41	40	39	38	37	36	35	34	35	34	33	33	31	29	28		
27	39	38	37	36	35	34	33	32	34	32	31	32	29	28	28		
26	37	36	35	34	33	33	32	31	31	31	29	30	28	27			
25	35	34	33	33	32	31	30	29	30	29	28	28	27	26			
24	33	32	32	31	30	29	28	27	28	28	27	27	26	25			
23	33	29	29	28	28	27	26	27	27	26	25	26	23				
22		29	28	27	27	26	26	26	24	24	23	24					
21	29							24	24	23	23	23					

DRY BULB TEMPERATURE (DEGREES CELSIUS)

Humidex (°C)	Degree of Comfort
20–29	Comfortable
30–39	Varying degrees of discomfort
40–45	Almost everyone uncomfortable
46 and over	Many types of labour must be restricted

■ In hot weather, our bodies regulate core temperature by using our sweat glands to shed water. Sweating doesn't cool the body, but the evaporation of sweat on your skin removes heat because it takes energy (heat) to change the liquid on your skin to vapour in the air. However, when it's humid, the air itself is already full of moisture and it can't absorb the moisture we are trying to shed, making us sticky and uncomfortable.

Ultra-Violet Index

Ultra-violet radiation is short-wavelength radiation that is part of the spectrum, just beyond visible violet light. These waves can harm both plant and animal life—the shorter of the UV wavelengths, known as UV-B, can cause sunburn, skin cancer and cataracts in humans and animals, and can also reduce agricultural productivity.

These rays are usually blocked by the protective ozone layer in the stratosphere, found between 10 and 50 km above the earth. Ozone is a form of oxygen that has three atoms instead of two and is created when ordinary oxygen interacts with ultraviolet radiation from the sun. Ozone can be destroyed by chemicals released into the air—most notably by the breakdown of chlorofluorocarbons (CFCs). CFCs have been used in air-conditioning, refrigeration and in some plastics manufacturing and CFC molecules are stable enough to last 100 years in the atmosphere—long enough to drift into the stratosphere where UV-B rays can break them down to produce free chlorine atoms. It is the chlorine atoms that destroy ozone.

In the 1970s, scientists had a theory that the chemicals drifting in the atmosphere could destroy the ozone layer. In the winter of 1985 NASA discovered a hole in the ozone layer over Antarctica. In recent years the continuing depletion of the ozone layer has resulted in its general thinning, and in holes of varying sizes at the poles from time to time. Various attempts have been made to phase out the use of ozone-depleting chemicals all over the world, particularly at the Earth Summit in Rio de Janeiro in June 1992. While progress has been made, it is important to realize that more UV-B rays are getting through the atmosphere and there is a higher risk of UV-B generated health problems.

In May 1992, Canada's weather service launched a daily ultraviolet index as part of the forecast, the first country in the world to do so. The purpose of the index is to warn people about the dangers of over-exposure to the sun. Several other countries, including Australia, New Zealand, the Netherlands, Germany, Great Britain and the United States, have now started their own programs closely modelled on the Canadian UV index.

The amount of UV-B is measured on a scale of 0 to 10, with 10 being a typical amount you would receive on a summer day in the tropics. The higher the number, the faster you'll sunburn. (Sunburn times are for light, untanned skin; times would be somewhat longer for those with darker skin.)

UV Index	Category	Sunburn Time
over 9	extreme	less than 15 minutes
7–9	high	about 20 minutes
4–7	moderate	about 30 minutes
0–4	low	more than one hour

Source: *Environment Canada*

Sailing on the Solar Wind

*O*utside of science fiction, space travel has always meant large, noisy rockets, powered by burning enormous amounts of fuel. But the Planetary Society, based in Pasadena, Calif., wants to try something different—a spacecraft powered by sunlight. The photons of light emitted by the sun actually exert a measurable pressure—and that can be used to push a so-called solar sail. Late in 2002, the Society, in a joint project with the Russian Babakin Space Centre, near Moscow, planned to begin the first space tests of a solar sail placed in orbit by a Volna rocket. The spacecraft, dubbed Cosmos I, is a 90-centimetre metal pod, with eight 11-metre-long sail blades.

In orbit around Earth, constant tacking will be needed because the sun's light—like a constant wind—comes from one direction only. But longer journeys, especially outward bound, would be easier. The motto for the project comes from the words of scientist and visionary Carl Sagan: "We have lingered long enough on the shores of the cosmic ocean. We are ready at last to set sail for the stars."

Source: *The Planetary Society*

Weather Records

	Canada	United States	World
Highest maximum air temperature	45.0˚ Midale and Yellowgrass, Sask. July 5, 1937	56.7˚ Death Valley, CA July 10, 1913	58.0˚ Al'azizyah, Libya Sept. 13, 1922
Lowest minimum air temperature	-63.0˚ Snag, YT Feb. 3, 1947	-62.1˚ Prospect Creek Camp, AK Jan. 23, 1971	-89.6˚ Vostok, Antarctica July 21, 1983
Coldest month	-47.9˚ Eureka, NWT Feb. 1979		
Highest sea-level pressure	107.95 kPa Dawson, YT Feb. 2, 1989	107.86 kPa Northway, AK Jan. 31, 1989	108.38 kPa Agata, Siberia USSR Dec. 31, 1968
Lowest sea-level pressure	94.02 kPa St. Anthony, Nfld Jan. 20, 1977	89.23 kPa Matecumbe Key, FL Sept. 2, 1935	87 kPa in eye of Typhoon Tip (Pacific Ocean) Oct. 12, 1979
Greatest precipitation in 24 hrs	489.2 mm Ucluelet Brynnor Mines, BC Oct. 6, 1967	1 090 mm Alvin, TX	1 869.9 mm Cilaos, La Réunion Is. March 15, 1952
Greatest precipitation in one month	2 235.5 mm Swanson Bay, BC Nov. 1917	2 717.8 mm Kukui, HI March 1942	9 300 mm Cherrapunji, India July 1861
Greatest precipitation in one year	9 341.1 mm Henderson Lake, BC 1998	17 902.7 mm Kukui, HI 1982	26 461.2 mm Cherrapunji, India Aug. 1860-July 1861
Greatest average annual precipitation	6.65 m Henderson Lake, BC	11 684 mm Mt. Waialeaie, Kauai, HI	11 684 mm Mt. Waialeaie, Kauai, HI
Least annual precipitation	12.7 mm Arctic Bay, NWT 1949	0.0 Bagdad, CA Oct. 3, 1912 to Nov. 8, 1914	0.0 Arica, Chile—no rain for 14 years
Greatest average annual snowfall	1 433 cm Glacier Mt. Fidelity, BC	1 461 cm Rainer Paradise Ranger Station, WA	
Greatest snowfall in one season	2 446.9 cm Revelstoke/Mt. Copeland, BC 1971–72	2 850 cm Mt. Baker, WA 1998–99	
Greatest snowfall in one month	535.9 cm Haines Apps. No 2, BC Dec. 1959	990.6 cm Tamarack, CA Jan. 1911	
Greatest snowfall in one day	145 cm Tahtsa Lake West, BC Feb. 11, 1999	193 cm Silver Lake, CO April 14–15, 1921	
Highest average annual number of thunderstorm days	36 days London, Ont.	96 days Fort Meyers, FL	322 days Bogor, Indonesia
Heaviest hailstone	290 g Cedoux, Sask. Aug. 27, 1973	758 g Coffeyville, KS Sept. 3, 1970	15 000 g Guangdong province of China April 19, 1995
Highest average annual wind speed	36 km/h Cape Warwick, Resolution Island, NWT	56.3 km/h Mt. Washington, NH	
Highest wind speed for 1 hr	201.1 km/h Cape Hopes Advance (Quaqtaq), Que. Nov. 18, 1931	362.0 km/h Mt. Washington, NH April 12, 1934	
Highest average hours of fog	1 890 hrs Argentia, Nfld	2 552 hrs Cape Disappointment, WA	

Source: *Environment Canada*

Wind Chill Hazards

Check the wind chill before you go outdoors in the winter, and make sure you are well prepared for the weather. Even moderate wind chills can be dangerous if you are outside for long periods.

In parts of the country with a milder climate (Southern Ontario, Southern British Columbia and the Atlantic provinces except Labrador), a wind chill warning is issued at –35°C. Further north,

people have grown more accustomed to the cold, and have adapted to the more severe conditions. Because of this, Environment Canada issues warnings at progressively colder wind chill values as you move north. Most of Canada hears a warning at –45°C. The residents of the Arctic and Northern Manitoba, Northern Ontario and Northern Quebec are warned at –53°C, and –63°C in the high Arctic.

Wind Chill (°C)	Description	Health Concern	What to do
0 to –9	Low	• Slight increase in discomfort.	• Dress warmly, with the outside temperature in mind.
–9 to –24	Moderate	• Uncomfortable. • Exposed skin feels cold. • Risk of hypothermia if outside for long periods without adequate protection.	• Dress in layers of warm clothing, with an outer layer that is wind resistant • Wear a hat, mittens and scarf. • Keep active.
–25 to –44	Cold	• Risk of skin freezing (frostbite). Check extremities (fingers, toes, ears and face) for numbness or whiteness. Risk of hypothermia if outside for long periods without adequate protection.	• Dress in layers of warm clothing, with an outer layer that is wind resistant. • Cover all exposed skin, particularly your face and hands. Wear a hat, mittens and a scarf, neck tube or face mask. • Keep active.
–45 to –62 WARNING LEVEL	Very cold	• Exposed skin may freeze in minutes. Check extremities frequently for numbness or whiteness (frostbite). Serious risk of hypothermia if outside for long periods.	• Be careful. Dress very warmly in layers of clothing, with an outer layer that is wind resistant. Cover all exposed skin, particularly your face and hands. Wear a hat, mittens and a scarf, neck tube or face mask. Limit outdoor activities to short periods. Be ready to cut short or cancel outdoor activities. Keep active.
–63 and colder DANGER!	Extreme	• Outdoor conditions are hazardous. Exposed skin may freeze in seconds.	• Stay indoors.

Source: *Environment Canada*

Why Wind Chill Matters

On a calm winter day, our bodies insulate us from cold temperatures by warming a thin layer of air close to our skin (the boundary layer). When the wind blows, it takes away this protective layer, exposing our skin to cold, moving air. Our bodies expend more energy warming up a new layer, and if each one keeps getting blown away, our skin temperature will drop, and we will feel colder.

How much heat you keep or lose depends not just on the wind. Good-quality clothing with high insulating properties traps air, for a thicker boundary layer around the body to keep in the heat. Wet clothing or footwear loses this property; the water creates body-heat loss that nearly equals the condition of exposed skin.

Your body type also determines how quickly you lose or increase heat—people with a tall, slim build become cold much faster than those who are shorter and heavier. Physical activity (walking or skiing) increases metabolism and generates body heat; those with less muscle mass (children or the elderly) find it harder to get warm.

The Beaufort Wind Scale

Beaufort forces range from 0 in calm conditions, to 12 in a hurricane. Rear-Admiral Sir Francis Beaufort of the British Royal Navy devised the scale in 1805. It originally referred to the amount of sail a full-rigged ship could carry in specific wind conditions. In light air, just one sail would be taken in; in a moderate gale, seven would come down; and in a heavy storm the number would be eleven, therefore Beaufort force 11. The Beaufort scale has been modified and modernized several times. Basically, however, the idea is to estimate wind speed by watching the effects of wind on such things as flags, trees, smoke, water surface and even people. The scale is still widely used today.

Beaufort Wind Force	Wind Speed (km/h)	Wind Type	Descriptive Effects
0	0–1	calm	smoke rises vertically
1	2–5	light air	smoke drifts slowly
2	6–11	light breeze	leaves rustle; wind vanes move
3	12–19	gentle breeze	leaves and twigs in constant motion
4	20–29	moderate breeze	small branches move; raises dust and loose paper moves along
5	30–38	fresh breeze	small trees sway
6	39–50	strong breeze	large branches in continuous motion; telephone wires whistle
7	51–61	near gale	whole trees in motion; wind affects walking
8	62–74	gale	twigs and small branches break off trees
9	75–87	strong gale	branches break; shingles blow from roofs
10	88–101	storm	trees snap and uproot; some damage to buildings
11	102–117	violent storm	property damage widespread
12	118–	hurricane	severe and extensive damage

Source: *Environment Canada*

Tornado Intensity Scale

Tornadoes are classified by the destruction they leave behind. They are rated from F0 to F5, F standing for Fujita, one of the world's leading experts on tornadoes.

F-Scale	Winds (km/h)	Length (km)	Width	Damage
0 (very weak)	under 116	< 1.5	under 15m	Light damage; minor roof, tree, chimney, antenna and sign damage
1 (weak)	117–180	1.6–5	16–50m	Moderate damage; barns torn apart; mobile homes pushed off foundations; trees snapped; cars pushed off roads; sheet metal buildings destroyed
2 (strong)	181–252	5.1–15.9	51–160m	Considerable damage; roofs torn off schools, homes and businesses; debris from barns scattered; trailers disintegrated; large trees uprooted; concrete block buildings destroyed
3 (severe)	253–332	16–50	161–500m	Severe damage; roofs and walls of schools, homes and buildings blown away; large trees uprooted; weaker homes completely disappear
4 (devastating)	333–419	51–159	0.5–1.4km	Interior and exterior walls of all homes blown apart; cars thrown more than 300m in the air
5 (incredible)	420–512	160–507	1.5–16km	Strongly built homes completely blown away; bizarre phenomena such as straw driven through fence posts

Source: *Environment Canada*

The Saffir-Simpson Hurricane Intensity Scale

Category	Maximum Sustained Wind Speed (km/h)	Minimum Surface Pressure (kPa)	Storm Surge (m)	Remarks
1 (minimal)	119–153	>=98.0	1.0–1.7	Damage to trees and signs. Low-lying flooding. Small craft torn from mooring.
2 (moderate)	154–177	97.9–96.5	1.8–2.6	Trees blown down; damage to mobile homes and roofs. Marinas flooded; evacuation of shores.
3 (extensive)	178–209	96.4–94.5	2.7–3.8	Some structural damage to small buildings; serious coastal flooding; mobile homes destroyed.
4 (extreme)	210–249	94.4–92.0	3.9–5.6	Extensive damage: doors, roofs, windows; major damage to lower floors of buildings near shore. Major beach erosion. Massive evacuation from shore possible.
5 (catastrophic)	>250	<92.0	>5.6	Small buildings blown away; complete destruction of mobile homes; massive evacuation within 10 to 20 km of shore possible.

Source: *H.S. Saffir, P.E. and Dr. R. Simpson*

Hurricane Names in 2004

*T*he names chosen for tropical storms in the Atlantic Ocean, Gulf of Mexico and the Caribbean Sea for 2004 are: Alex, Bonnie, Charley, Danielle, Earl, Frances, Gaston, Hermine, Ivan, Jeanne, Karl, Lisa, Matthew, Nicole, Otto, Paula, Richard, Shary, Tomas, Virginie, and Walter. The names for eastern Pacific tropical storms (those west of 140°W) are: Agatha, Blas, Celia, Darby, Estelle, Frank, Georgette, Howard, Isis, Javier, Kay, Lester, Madeline, Newton, Orlene, Paine, Roslyn, Seymour, Tina, Virgil, Winifred, Xavier, Yolanda, and Zeke. Other regions of the world have their own naming systems: see www.nhc.noaa.gov/aboutnames.html*

Since 1953, Atlantic tropical storms have been named from lists originated by the National Hurricane Centre and now maintained and updated by an international committee of the World Meteorological Organization (WMO). The lists featured only women's names until 1979, when men's and women's names were alternated. Six lists are used in rotation. Thus, the 2004 list will be used again in 2010.

Hurricanes that have a severe impact on lives or the economy are remembered for generations, and some go into weather history. If a hurricane has had a major impact, any country affected by the storm can request that the name of the hurricane be "retired" by agreement of the WMO. Retiring a name actually means that it cannot be reused for at least 10 years, to facilitate historic references, legal actions, insurance claim activities, etc. and avoid public confusion with another storm of the same name. The WMO does more than name hurricanes. The organization sets international standards for monitoring weather and climate, and acts to foster the exchange of ideas and best practices. Visit www.wmo.ch

Air Quality

Poor quality air—or air pollution—affects the health of all of us, especially children, the elderly and people with lung conditions (bronchitis or asthma) or heart problems. Effects can range from irritation to eyes, nose and throat to decreased lung capacity, or an intensifying of the impact of existing respiratory diseases. Even healthy, active Canadians can feel the effects of pollution. They may notice they're breathing less efficiently when they are active during times of high pollution levels.

When we think of air pollution, we usually think of smog. Smog is composed mostly of ground-level ozone and fine particles.

Ozone (O_3), is a colourless, odourless gas. It's the result of a chain of chemical reactions between nitrogen oxides and volatile organic compounds warmed by sunlight. High levels typically occur from May to September, between noon and early evening, when the warm temperatures (over 25°C) accelerate the process. (Areas in Canada that have been experiencing warmer summers have also experienced an increase in air quality problems or smog alerts during the last few years for this reason.)

Nitrogen oxides are emitted by burning fossil fuels (coal and oil); volatile organic compounds are found in the unburned gasoline emitted in car exhaust; they are also emitted by solvents, oil-based paints or similar materials.

Exposure to high levels of O_3 results in chest tightness, coughing and wheezing. People with respiratory and heart problems are at a higher risk for these problems. Ozone also causes noticeable damage in many crops, garden plants and trees—reducing crop yields and stunting growth.

Fine suspended particles in the atmosphere consist of either solid particles or fine liquid droplets. They include aerosols, smoke, fumes, dust, fly ash (fine ash from the fuel burned in power stations or at brick works) and pollen.

Particles in the atmosphere have been characterized according to size, mainly because of the different health effects from particles of different diameters. Particles with diameters less than 100 microns (millionths of a metre) are classified as total suspended particles (TSP). Most particle emissions from human activity fall into the TSP size range. Particles less than 10 microns and 2.5 microns in diameter are defined as inhalable particles (PM_{10}) and respirable particles ($PM_{2.5}$), respectively. The smaller the particle, the further it will penetrate into the lungs—respirable particles penetrate the furthest and aggravate bronchitis, asthma and other respiratory diseases the most.

Levels of Inhalable Airborne Particles in Canadian Cities (PM_{10} and $PM_{2.5}$)

| Year | PM_{10} (mg/m3) | | $PM_{2.5}$ (mg/m3) | |
	mean	mean peak	mean	mean peak
1991	23.1	48.4	11.9	30.6
1992	27.5	67.6	13.9	30.9
1993	22.9	53.3	11.9	33.0
1994	21.2	53.9	11.1	28.3
1995	18.0	44.5	9.0	24.5
1996	17.0	36.1	8.6	19.9
1997	18.1	36.9	9.3	20.8
1998	20.7	49.2	10.1	26.7
1999	19.7	46.9	9.4	23.6
2000	18.0	39.2	8.9	22.3
2001	18.1	41.3	9.0	24.4
2002	18.1	48.6	10.2	27.4

Source: *Environmental Technology Centre, Environment Canada, Ottawa, Ontario*   Last update: 2003

▶ Particles come from both natural and man-made sources. Natural sources include wind-blown soil and mineral particles, volcanic ash, sea salt spray and biological materials such as pollen, spores, bacteria and smoke from forest fires. Man-made sources include wind-blown dust from agricultural soil, roads and construction sites and particles from combustion of fossil fuels.

Aside from smog, the air can also include the following:

Nitrogen dioxide (NO_2), a reddish-brown gas with a pungent and irritating odour, transforms in the air to make gaseous nitric acid and toxic organic nitrates. NO_2, of course, plays a major role in the production of ground-level ozone, and is also a precursor to nitrates, which contribute to increased respirable particle levels.

All combustion in air produces oxides of nitrogen, of which NO_2 is the major one. Much of it comes from the transportation sector—cars and trucks. Most of the remainder comes from power generation, metal production and incineration. There are also a few natural sources of NO_2.

NO_2 irritates the lungs and can lower resistance to respiratory infection. People with asthma and bronchitis are especially sensitive.

Sulphur dioxide (SO_2), a colourless gas, smells like burnt matches. It can be oxidized to sulphur trioxide, which in the presence of water is transformed to sulphuric acid mist or rain. SO_2 can be oxidized to form acid aerosols. It is also a precursor to sulphates, one of the main components of particles in the atmosphere that can penetrate deep into the lungs. SO_2 comes mainly from smelters and utilities, iron and steel mills, petroleum refineries and pulp and paper mills. Small sources include residential, commercial and industrial space heating.

Exposure to high levels of SO_2 can cause breathing problems, respiratory illness, a weakening of the lung's defences and a worsening of respiratory and cardiovascular disease. People with asthma or chronic lung or heart disease are the most sensitive to SO_2. It also damages trees and crops.

Carbon monoxide (CO), a colourless, odourless and tasteless but poisonous gas, is produced primarily by incomplete burning of fossil fuels. Most of it comes from cars and trucks, but a significant amount is produced by metal production.

CO enters the bloodstream and reduces oxygen delivery to the organs and tissues. People with heart disease are particularly sensitive. Exposure to high levels is linked to impairment of vision, work capacity, learning ability and performance of difficult tasks, as well as premature death.

Total reduced sulphur compounds (TRS) produce offensive odours similar to those of rotten eggs or cabbage. Industrial sources of TRS include the steel industry, pulp and paper mills, refineries and sewage treatment facilities. Natural sources include swamps, bogs and marshes.

TRS compounds are not normally considered a health hazard. They are, however, a primary cause of odours.

How Is Air Quality Measured?

The federal government, the provinces and many municipalities have created a measure known as an Air Quality Index (AQI). This uses real-time data from measuring stations to calculate the amount of the above common pollutants in the air. The list of measured pollutants varies from place to place, but Ontario's Air Quality Index serves as an example.

In Ontario, a network of 33 monitoring stations continuously measures the six common pollutants: ozone, suspended particles, nitrogen dioxide, sulphur dioxide, carbon monoxide and total reduced sulphur compounds. The quantity of each is measured on an appropriate scale and the AQI for a locality is based on whichever is highest on a particular day. (See Ontario's air quality Web site: www.airqualityontario.com)

If the AQI falls below 32, the air is considered good or very good. An AQI reading between 32 and 49 indicates moderate air quality, and an AQI reading from 50 to 99 indicates poor air quality. A reading over 100 indicates very poor air quality.

Sources: *Government of Ontario, Environment Canada*

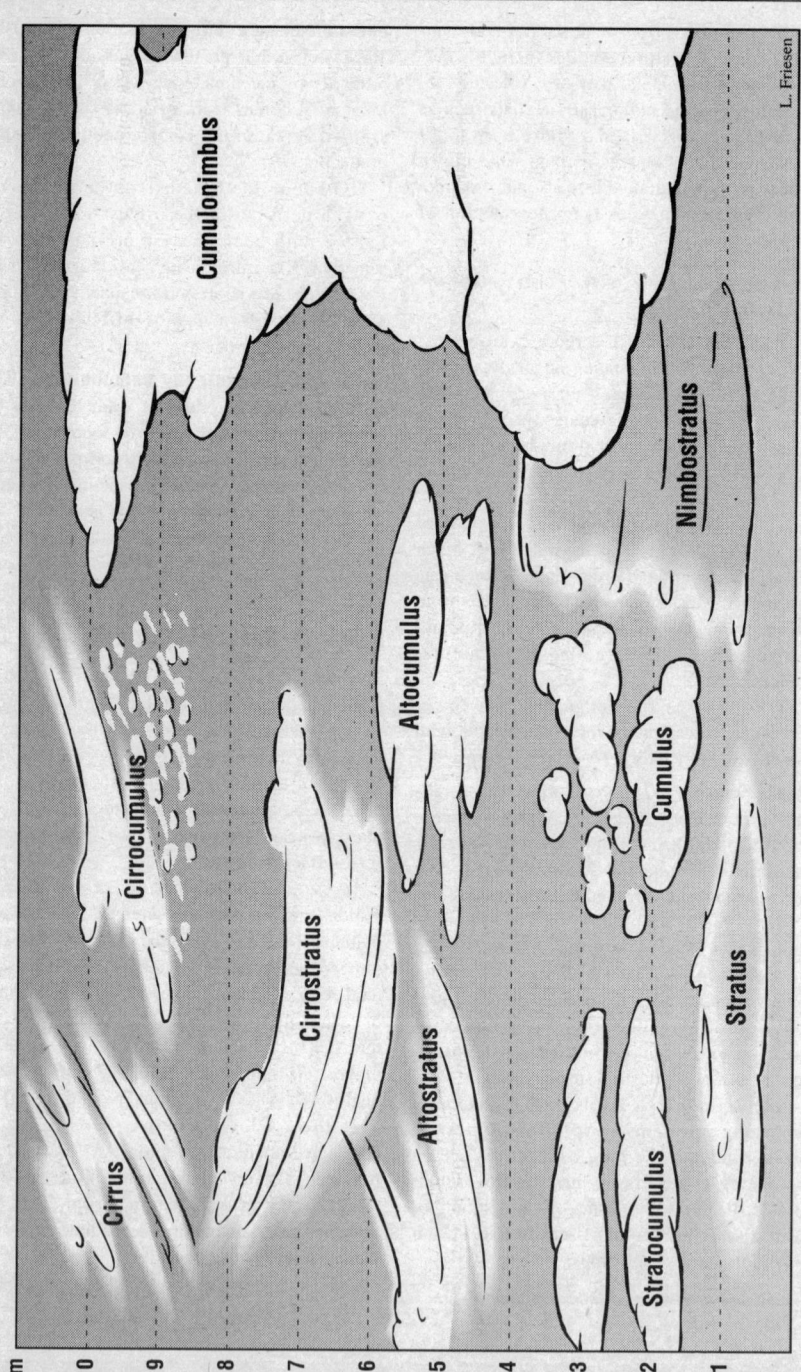

L. Friesen

Ten Basic Cloud Types

1. Cirrus
Thin wispy small white clouds that often occur as feathery filaments or long streamers stretching across the sky. Often their ends are swept by strong winds giving it the look of a mare's tail.

2. Cirrostratus
White uniform veil of thin transparent cloud. Sky still appears bright with a halo around the sun. Cloud sheets are small or extensive.

3. Cirrocumulus
Thin bands of either continuous or patchy small clouds, white or pale grey in colour. Cloud base occurs above 6,000 m.; ripple or rib pattern gives it a look of fish-scales, often referred to as a "mackerel sky."

4. Altocumulus
Either patchy or continuous middle cumulus cloud with a dappled or rippled appearance. Thicker and lower version of cirrocumulus that is associated with changeable weather and perhaps rain.

5. Altostratus
Grey pale uniform layer of cloud in which the sun may appear weakly. Too thick and low for halos to be seen; however, through the overcast, the sun can be seen weakly. A sign of precipitation within a few hours.

6. Stratocumulus
Low layers of grey or whitish clouds with occasional dark patches that have a well-defined rounded or undulating appearance. May have a few breaks, but usually total cloud cover extends for hundreds of kilometres.

7. Stratus
A grey uniform low blanket of cloud that may be continuous or patchy, often producing light drizzle. The base is between the surface and 300 m, often obscuring hill tops and tall buildings. Looks like high drifting fog or making for a dull, grey day.

8. Nimbostratus
A thick low-level (600 m) deck of cloud providing continuous rain or snow. Usually covers the entire sky and completely hides the sun.

9. Cumulus
White puffy clouds that often form by day and disappear by night. Well-defined base begins at 600 to 1,200 m; upper parts are cauliflower-like. Associated with fair weather, blue sky and no precipitation.

10. Cumulonimbus
Giant impressive cumulus clouds with dark base and a smooth anvil-shaped top. Called the kings of the sky, they are the biggest of all clouds, often towering in excess of 10 km. Often associated with severe thunderstorms and sometimes hail or tornadoes. In heavy rain, cumulonimbus clouds have a dark ominous base and a curtain of rain.

Source: *Environment Canada*

Weather Symbols

Meteorologists all around the world use a standard set of symbols in constructing detailed weather maps. Here are some samples of these universal weather symbols:

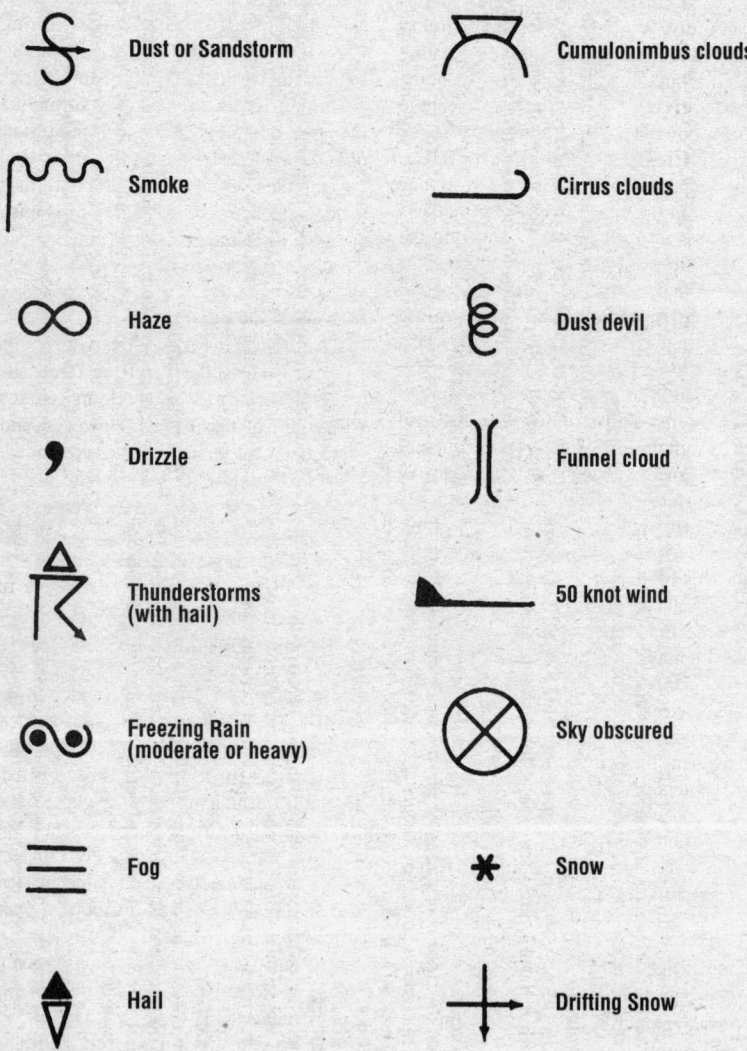

Dust or Sandstorm

Smoke

Haze

Drizzle

Thunderstorms (with hail)

Freezing Rain (moderate or heavy)

Fog

Hail

Cumulonimbus clouds

Cirrus clouds

Dust devil

Funnel cloud

50 knot wind

Sky obscured

Snow

Drifting Snow

Revisiting the Kyoto Protocol

■ Signing on to Kyoto

Climate change is a global problem that affects all countries; a central cause of climate change is greenhouse gases (GHGs), such as methane and carbon dioxide. Many GHGs form naturally, but without human activity, it's unlikely there would be a crisis. Heating and cooling buildings, using energy at home and work, driving vehicles to move people and goods, powering industrial processes—all these activities contribute extra GHGs. Greenhouse gases are so named because they form a layer in the upper atmosphere that acts like the glass in a greenhouse—trapping the warmth of the sun. This is a good thing for hothouse tomatoes, but a bad thing for the earth. Scientists believe that the warming trend they see is contributing to damage to the polar ice caps, causing sea levels to rise, increasing the number of extremely violent weather events and causing agricultural patterns to change. The Intergovernmental Panel on Climate Control (IPCC), set up by the World Meteorological Organization and United Nations Environment Program, estimates that world temperatures will rise on average by between 1.4 and 5.8 C degrees this century. In Canada, climate change will affect fishing, farming, forestry, lakes, rivers and coastal communities. To deal with the issue, more than 160 countries from around the world gathered in Kyoto, Japan, in December 1997, and agreed to reduce GHG emissions. The agreement that set out those targets, and the options available to countries to achieve them, became known as the Kyoto Protocol. Canada ratified the Protocol Dec. 17, 2002, after a fractious debate. Our target is to reduce GHG emissions to 6 percent below 1990 levels by the period between 2008 and 2012.

■ Implementing Kyoto

The Kyoto climate accord comes into effect when enough countries have agreed to it. But the actual number needed for international ratification reflects a compromise between environmentalism and economic development. There are two key numbers. The accord comes into effect when a minimum of 55 nations have ratified it—provided those 55 nations include enough developed nations to account for 55 percent of the world's 1990 carbon dioxide emissions. By June 2003, 110 countries had signed on, but there were not enough of the developed nations to bring the treaty into force. The Russian Federation was expected to ratify the agreement, which would put Kyoto over the top. Complicating the issue is the fact that the United States—one of the largest emitters of carbon dioxide—has pulled out of the negotiations, arguing that the science behind the accord is unsound and that implementing the agreement would harm the U.S. economy.

■ What Is the Cost?

Economists are divided on the costs of climate control. Clearly there will be losses in the traditional industries related to the production and export of fossil fuels. However, another view says that changing our economies and lifestyles to slow global climate change is likely to add jobs and growth—although not in the conventional energy sector. Alternative technologies such as solar and wind power, as well as the production of alternative fuels, would be the new growth areas. There is also, of course, a cost for doing nothing. One of the prime costs, according to the World Health Organization (WHO), is the impact on public health care. WHO estimates that the penalty for failing to reduce the levels of air pollution could be as high as 8 million additional premature deaths around the world between 2000 and 2020. Prime Minister Jean Chrétien has said Canada wants to meet most of its Kyoto obligations through "domestic action" and the government has produced a plan for climate change. Canada is already set to reduce emissions by 65 megatons—one third of the Kyoto target—and will be looking for ways to achieve the rest in the next few years. For various views on the issues surrounding the Kyoto Protocol, start with these Web sites: climatechange.gc.ca; www.davidsuzuki.org/; www3.gov.ab.ca/env/ or www.chamber.ca/newpages/policy.html

LIFE SCIENCES

The life sciences consist of diverse disciplines that share a knowledge base centred on the same fundamental question, "What is life?" Beginning with biology (the study of living organisms), the life sciences soon included: zoology (the study of animals), botany (the study of plants), and taxonomy (the study of the classification of living things).

Over the last century, an ever-increasing variety of subdisciplines and approaches to studying life have arisen: microbiology (the study of microorganisms), genetics (the study of heredity), biochemistry (the study of chemical compounds and reactions in living organisms), ecology (the study of the relationships between living things and their environment), and ethology (the study of animal behaviour). Most recently these disciplines have been joined by biotechnology (the study and use of organisms or their components for the manufacture or production of commercial substances, aided by techniques of genetic manipulation).

Common Life Sciences Terms

Aerobic: Life processes that depend on the presence of oxygen.

Algae: Simple rootless plants that grow in bodies of water in relative proportion to the amount of nutrients available.

Allergen: Any of various sorts of material that, as a result of coming into contact with appropriate tissues, induce a state of sensitivity and/or resistance to infection or toxic substances.

Anaerobic: Life processes that occur in the absence of oxygen.

Animal: A vertebrate (having a bony skeleton or one made of cartilage) or invertebrate (lacking a spine or skeleton) species including, but not limited to, humans and other mammals, birds, fish, and shellfish.

Bacteria: Single cell microorganisms that possess cell walls. Some cause disease and some are beneficial.

Baleen: Horny plates with fringed inner edges attached to the upper jaw of Mysticeti type whales, such as right and blue whales. The baleen are used to filter plankton and other food from water.

Biodiversity: The total diversity within an ecosystem, including genetic variation among species, diversity of life forms, and ecosystem diversity.

Biomass: The amount of living matter in a given unit of the environment.

Biosphere: The portion of earth (upwards at least to a height of 10,000 m and downward to the ocean floor and 100 km below the planet's surface) and the atmosphere surrounding it that supports life.

Bloom: A seasonal, dense growth of small marine plants, i.e., phytoplankton.

Coniferous: Refers to a softwood, cone-bearing tree.

Deciduous: Refers to a hardwood, leaf-dropping tree.

Effluent Waste: Material discharged into the environment, treated or untreated.

Flood Tide: Interim period of tide between low and high water; a rising tide.

Lagoon: Shallow pond where sunlight, bacterial action and oxygen work to purify waste water.

Marsh: Wet, soft, low-lying land that provides a natural habitat for many plants and animals.

Molt: The periodic casting off or shedding of the outer body covering (feathers, hair, skin or cuticle) by birds, mammals, arachnids and reptiles.

Nutrients: Elements or compounds essential to growth and development of living things: carbon, oxygen, nitrogen, potassium and phosphorus.

Osmosis: Tendency of a fluid to pass through a permeable membrane, such as the wall of a living cell, into a less concentrated solution, so as to equalize concentrations on both sides of the membrane.

Photosynthesis: A process of biochemical change in which plant cells, using light as an energy source, manufacture simple sugars from oxygen and carbon dioxide.

Regeneration (forests): The renewal of a forest by natural processes (self-sown seed or root suckers), as well as by sowing or planting new tree stock.

Synthesis: Production of a substance by the union of elements or simpler chemical compounds.

Tailings: Residue of raw materials or waste separated out during the processing of wood or minerals products.

Tidal Marsh: Low, flat marshlands crossed by interlaced channels and tidal sloughs, and subject to tidal inundation from the ocean, normally, the only vegetation present is salt-tolerant rushes and grasses.

Tide: Alternate rising and falling of water levels twice each lunar day, due to gravitational attraction of the moon and the sun in conjunction with the earth's rotational force.

Major Groups of Living Organisms

All life forms are classified in a hierarchical series of groups. Taxonomy, the science of such classification, was introduced by Swedish scientist Carolus Linneaus (1707–78).

The purpose of classification is to provide each plant or animal on the planet with a unique name by which it is known; to describe it so it may be recognized by anyone; and to place it within a system that shows its relationship to other plants and animals.

The system is flexible, allowing updating as more is learned about individual species and their history.

Naming
The scientific naming of species involves two Latin names. The first word in the species name denotes the Genus the species belongs to. For example, the first word in the scientific name of the Monarch butterfly is *Danaus*. The Monarch belongs to the Genus Danaus.

The second word in the scientific name is particular to a species and can be quite arbitrary. Sometimes species names refer to a person, a country, a particular feature of the animal or plant, or a food source. The second word in the scientific name for the Monarch is *plexippus*. Thus, the scientific name of the Monarch is *Danaus plexippus*.

A species usually also has a common or more familiar name. For example, people seldom refer to the Monarch butterfly as Danaus plexippus.

Species
The basic level in the system is species. The interpretation of differences and similarities between species is often subjective, so the number and name of a species may change. New species are still being found and identified.

Genus
Species with a number of common features are grouped together in Genera. The number of different species in a genus can vary from one to several hundred. Again identification is subjective and the number of genera is not fixed.

Family
Genera are further grouped into Families. Butterfly genera are broadly divided into four major families: 1) Papilionidae (swallowtails); 2) Pierodae (whites and sulphurs); 3) Nymphalidae (brush-footed); and 4) Lycaenidae (hairstreaks, coppers and blues).

Order
Families that share major characteristics are grouped into Orders. For example, butterflies, along with moths, belong to the Order Lepidoptera or insects with scales. The word comes from the Greek words *lepis* (scale) and *pteron* (wing). Classification at this level can be a very complex structure of orders, sub-orders, and sub-sub-orders.

Class
Further up the hierarchy, all Orders belong to a Class. Members of each class show characteristics indicating a common evolutionary descent.

Phylum
At the next level, butterflies, for example, are members of the Phylum Arthropoda, along with millipedes, spiders, and crustaceans, among others. The word Phylum comes from the Greek *phulon* or race.

Kingdom
At the highest level of the hierarchy, butterflies, along with other living creatures, including humans, are members of the Animal Kingdom.

Extinct and Endangered Species in Canada, 2003

The following list has been prepared by the Committee on the Status of Endangered Wildlife in Canada.

The "Extinct" category refers to any species that was indigenous to Canada that no longer exists anywhere in the world. The "Extirpated" category refers to any species that no longer exists in the wild but does occur elsewhere. The "Endangered" category refers to any species threatened with imminent extinction or extirpation throughout all or most of its Canadian range.

For more information, visit the web site www.speciesatrisk.gc.ca.

Species	Habitat	Year Documented
EXTINCT CATEGORY		
Mammals		
Caribou, Woodland	(Queen Charlotte Islands population) BC	1920s, 1984
Mink, Sea	Atlantic coastal waters	1894
Birds		
Auk, Great	QC, NB, NS, NF	1844
Duck, Labrador	QC, NB, NS, NF	1875
Pigeon, Passenger	SK, MB, ON, QC, NB, NS, PE	1914
Fish		
Cisco, Deepwater	ON	1952
Dace, Banff Longnose	AB	1986
Stickleback, Benthic (Hadley Lake)	BC	1999
Stickleback, Limnetic (Hadley Lake)	BC	1999
Walleye, Blue	ON	1965
Molluscs		
Limpet, Eelgrass	QC, NS, NF	1929
Mosses		
Moss, Macoun's Shining	ON	not observed since 1864
EXTIRPATED CATEGORY		
Mammals		
Bear, Grizzly	(Prairie population) AB, SK, MB	1880s
Ferret, Black-footed	AB, SK, MB	1974
Walrus, Atlantic	Atlantic coastal waters	1850
Whale, Grey	Atlantic population	prior 1800
Birds		
Grouse, Sage	(British Columbia population) BC	not observed since 1960's
Prairie-Chicken, Greater	AB, SK, MB, ON	last reported 1987 (SK)
Reptiles		
Lizard, Pygmy Short-Horned	(British Columbia population) BC	last reported 1898, near Osoyoos, BC
Rattlesnake, Timber	ON	1941
Snake, Pacific Gopher	BC	Not seen since 1957
Turtle, Pacific Pond	BC	Not seen since 1959
Fish		
Chub, Gravel	ON	last reported 1958, Thames River drainage
Paddlefish	ON	1917
Amphibians		
Salamander, Tiger	ON	Not observed since 1915
Molluscs		
Wedgemussel, Dwarf	NB	1968
Snail, Puget Oregonian	BC	not observed since 1905
Lepidopterans[1]		
Blue, Karner	ON	1991
Elfin, Frosted	ON	1988
Marble, Island	BC	prior 1910
Plants		
Blue-eyed Mary	ON	not observed since 1954
Tick-trefoil, Illinois	ON	not observed since 1888
Mosses		
Moss, Incurved Grizzled	ON	2002

▶

ENDANGERED CATEGORY

Mammals

Badger, American	BC, ON	2000
Caribou, Peary	(Banks Island population) (High Arctic population) NT, NU	1991
Caribou, Woodland	(Atlantic - Gaspésie population) QC	2000
Fox, Swift	AB, SK	1998
Marmot, Vancouver Island	BC	1997
Marten, American	(Newfoundland population) NF	1996
Whale, Beluga	St. Lawrence River population	1997
	Ungava Bay population	1988
	Southeast Baffin Island–Cumberland Sound population	1990
Whale, Blue	Atlantic and Pacific populations	2002
Whale, Bowhead	Eastern Arctic population	1980
	Western Arctic population	1986
Whale, Killer	Northeast Pacific southern resident population	2001
Whale, Right	Atlantic and Pacific Oceans	1990
Wolverine	(Eastern population) QC, NF	1989

Birds

Bobwhite, Northern	ON	1994
Chat, Western Yellow-breasted	BC	2000
Crane, Whooping	NT, NU	1978
Curlew, Eskimo	All provinces and territories except BC	2000
Flycatcher, Acadian	ON	1994
Grouse, Sage	(Prairie population) AB, SK	1998
Owl, Barn	(Eastern population) ON, QC	1999
Owl, Burrowing	BC, AB, MB, SK	1995
Owl, Northern Spotted	BC	1999
Plover, Mountain	AB, SK	1987
Plover, Piping	AB, SK, MB, ON, QC, NB, NS, PE, NF	1985
Rail, King	ON	1994
Screech-owl, Western	BC	2002
Shrike, Loggerhead	(Eastern population) MB, ON, QC	1991
Sparrow, Henslow's	ON	1993
Tern, Roseate	QC, NB, NS	1999
Thrasher, Sage	BC, AB, SK	1992
Warbler, Kirtland's	ON	1999
Warbler, Prothonotary	ON	1996
Woodpecker, White-headed	BC	2000

Amphibians

Frog, Northern Cricket	ON	1990
Frog, Northern Leopard	(Southern Mountain population) BC	1998
Frog, Oregon Spotted	BC	1999
Frog, Rocky Mountain Tailed	BC	2000

Reptiles

Racer, Blue	ON	1991
Salamander, Tiger	BC	2001
Snake, Lake Erie Water	ON	1991
Snake, Night	BC	2001
Snake, Sharp-tailed	BC	1999
Turtle, Leatherback	Atlantic & Pacific Oceans	1981

Fish

Dace, Nooksack	BC	1996
Lamprey, Morrison Creek	BC	1999
Salmon, Atlantic	(Inner Bay of Fundy populations) NB, NS	2001
Stickleback, Benthic Paxton Lake (Texada Island)	BC	1999
Stickleback, Benthic Vananda Creek	BC	1999
Stickleback, Limnetic Paxton Lake (Texada Island)	BC	1999
Stickleback, Limnetic Vananda Creek	BC	1999
Sucker, Salish	BC	1986
Trout, Aurora	ON	2000
Whitefish, Atlantic (Acadian)	NS	1984

Molluscs

Bean, Rayed	ON	1999
Lampmussel, Wavy-rayed	ON	1999

▶

▶ Mussel, Mudpuppy . . . . ON 2001
Physa, Hotwater . . . . BC 1998
Riffleshell, Northern . . . . ON 1999
Snail, Banff Springs . . . . ~. . . AB 1997
Snuffbox . . . . ON 2001

Lepidopterans[1]
Blue, Island . . . . BC 2000
Checkerspot, Taylor's . . . . BC 2000
Moth, Yucca . . . . AB 2002
Ringlet, Maritime . . . . QC, NB 1997

Plants
Agalinis, Gattinger's . . . . ON 1999
Agalinis, Skinner's . . . . ON 1999
Ammannia, Scarlet . . . . BC, ON 1999
Avens, Eastern Mountain . . . . NS 1999
Balsamroot, Deltoid . . . . BC 1996
Bluehearts . . . . ON 1998
Braya, Long's . . . . NF 1997
Bugbane, Tall . . . . BC 2001
Bulrush, Bashful (Few-flowered Club-rush) . . . . . ON 2000
Bush-clover, Slender . . . . ON 1999
Buttercup, Water-plantain . . . . BC 1996
Cactus, Eastern Prickly Pear . . . . ON 1998
Coreopsis, Pink . . . . NS 1999
Cryptanthe, Tiny . . . . AB, SK 1998
Fern, Southern Maidenhair . . . . BC 1998
Gentian, White Prairie . . . . ON 1991
Ginseng, American . . . . ON, QC 1999
Goat's-rue, Virginia . . . . ON 1996
Goldenrod, Showy . . . . ON 1999
Lady's-slipper, Small White . . . . MB, ON 1999
Lotus, Seaside Birds-foot . . . . BC 1996
Lousewort, Furbish's . . . . NB 1998
Lupine, Prairie . . . . BC 1996
Milkwort, Pink . . . . ON 1998
Mountain-mint, Hoary . . . . ON 1998
Mulberry, Red . . . . ON 1999
Orchid, Western Prairie Fringed . . . . MB 2000
Owl-clover, Bearded . . . . BC 1998
Paintbrush, Golden . . . . BC 1995
Plantain, Heart-leaved . . . . ON 1998
Pogonia, Large Whorled . . . . ON 1998
Pogonia, Nodding . . . . ON 1999
Pogonia, Small Whorled . . . . ON 1998
Quillwort, Engelmann's . . . . ON 1992
Sanicle, Bear's-foot . . . . BC 2001
Sedge, False Hop . . . . ON, QC 1997
Sedge, Juniper . . . . ON 1999
Sprike-rush, Horsetail . . . . ON 2000
Sundew, Thread-leaved . . . . NS 1991
Thistle, Pitcher's . . . . ON 1999
Toothcup . . . . BC, ON 1999
Tree, Cucumber . . . . ON 1999
Trillium, Drooping . . . . ON 1996
Twayblade, Purple . . . . ON 1999
Violet, Bird's-foot . . . . ON 2002
Willow, Barrens . . . . NF 2001
Wintergreen, Spotted . . . . YT, NT, BC, AB 2000
Wood-poppy . . . . ON 1993
Woodsia, Blunt-lobed . . . . ON, QC 1994
Woolly-heads, Tall . . . . (Pacific population) BC 2001

Lichens
Lichen, Boreal Felt . . . . NB, NS 2002
Seaside Centipede . . . . BC 1996

Mosses
Moss, Apple . . . . BC 1997
Moss, Poor Pocket . . . . BC 2001

Source: *Committee on Status of Endangered Wildlife in Canada*
(1) Lepidopteran: Order of insects with four wings covered by fine scales; butterflies and moths.

FOCUS ON...

Emerging Diseases

On July 5, 2003, the World Health Organization announced that the global outbreak of severe acute respiratory syndrome (SARS) had been "contained"—after more than 800 deaths around the world. The announcement came three days after Toronto—the hardest-hit place outside Asia—was removed from the UN agency's list of SARS hot spots.

But as the SARS crisis slowly ebbed, other emerging diseases—West Nile virus and monkeypox—claimed their share of public dismay. They follow in the wake of such headline-grabbers as Ebola, Legionnaires Disease and HIV/AIDS. Many of the new diseases have this in common: they are animal infections that make the jump to humans, in a process called zoonosis.

Carried by Birds

West Nile virus, for instance, is carried by birds and spread by mosquitoes. Until a few years ago, it was found only in Europe and Africa. Then—no one knows how—the virus made it to North America. Possibly an infected bird was blown across the Atlantic by a storm. Once here, mosquitoes picked up the virus and transmitted it, first to other birds, and then to mammals, including humans.

SARS is thought to have originated in a Chinese mammal, the civet cat. HIV, the human immuno-deficiency virus, probably jumped from chimpanzees or other primates.

But what's happening? After all, not long ago, top medical experts thought infectious disease was pretty much a dead issue. Vaccines had taken care of polio and smallpox. Malaria, once a scourge in the southern U.S., had been vanquished from that region. In 1967, then-U.S. surgeon-general William Stewart had the temerity to say that "the war on infectious diseases has been won."

Unfortunately, Stewart didn't reckon on economic and social changes that have meant a constant parade of new diseases—and the public disquiet that they bring. Those changes include increased travel, global trade, changes in land use, alterations in weather, climate or ecosystems, poverty, war, inequality and even such technological advances as antibiotics, whose inappropriate use can spawn drug-resistant germs.

Take monkeypox, for instance, which originated when African rats and mice, imported to the U.S. to be sold as exotic pets, infected pet Prairie dogs, who then made their owners sick. The monkeypox virus can be fatal in humans.

SARS became an international story when an infected doctor from China stayed in a Hong Kong hotel. He passed the flu-like disease to several others, including a woman who later flew home to Toronto, starting the Canadian outbreak. Others spread the disease to other countries, while China—where it originated—suffered more than 5,000 cases and 348 deaths. (Canada's toll was 377 probable or suspected cases and more than 40 deaths.)

It is likely, experts think, that we will see more emerging diseases. But at least in North America, officials are putting together early-warning systems to detect outbreaks. The Laboratory Response Network, for instance, links more than 120 labs in the U.S. and Canada; as soon as a new disease is suspected, the labs can begin trying to pinpoint the cause.

Swift Response Needed

Swift scientific response was important in the SARS outbreak; several tests for the virus that is linked to the disease were quickly developed, with varying levels of reliability. Canadian scientists at the University of British Columbia were the first to find the genetic sequence of the SARS virus, which may prove to be a key step in developing a vaccine.

And, in the long run, a vaccine may be what will be needed. Experts—including the World Health Organization—are warning that SARS, like other emerging diseases, is not likely to go away.

The greatest fear is that the next outbreak of SARS or something like it will not take place in North America, Europe, or even relatively developed regions like Hong Kong and China. Instead, experts fear the effects on places like Africa, where medical infrastructure is limited and where millions of people have weakened immune systems, owing to HIV.

For more information, try these Web sites: www.cdc.gov/ncidod/EID, www.fas.org/promed, and www.hcsc.gc.ca/hpb/lcdc/fedlab

Zoos and Aquariums*

Maritime Region:

☐ **Aquarium and Marine Centre**
100 Aquarium St., Shippigan, NB E0B 2P0.
Tel: (506) 336-3013. Open May to September.
Web site: www.gnb.ca/0181/index-e.asp

☐ **Cherry Brook Zoo**
901 Foster Thurston Dr., Saint John, NB E2K 5H9.
Tel: (506) 634-1440. Open all year.
Web site: www.cbzoo.com/

☐ **Magnetic Hill Zoo**
100 Worthington Ave., Moncton, NB E1C 9Z3.
Tel: (506) 384-0303. Open May to October, with
limited openings on winter weekends. Web site:
http://new-brunswick.net/new-brunswick/moncton/
zoo.html

Central Canada:

☐ **Aquarium du Québec**
1675, ave. des Hotels, Ste-Foy, QC G1W 4S3 Tel :
(418) 659-5264. Web site: www.spsnq.qc.ca/

☐ **The Biodome de Montréal**
4777, ave. Pierre-de Coubenin, Montréal, QC
H1V 1B3. Tel: (514) 868-3000. Open all year.
Web site: www.ville.montreal.qc.ca/biodome/ebdm.htm

☐ **Parc safari Africain**
850 Route 202, Hemmingford, QC J0L 1H0.
Tel: (514) 247-2727. Open mid-May to Labour Day.
Web site: www.parcsafari.com

☐ **Saint-Félicien Zoo**
2230 boul. du Jardin, Saint-Félicien, QC G8K 2P8.
Tel: 1-800-667-5687. Open mid-May to mid-October.
Web site: www.zoosauvage.qc.ca/indexfr.html

☐ **Zoo de Granby**
525, rue Saint-Hubert, Granby, QC J2G 5P3.
Tel: 1-877-472-6299. Open May to September.
Web site: www.zoogranby.qc.ca

☐ **African Lion Safari and Game Farm**
RR #1, Cambridge, ON N1R 5S2. Tel: (519) 623-2620.
Open summer. Web site: www.lionsafari.com/index2.asp

☐ **Bowmanville Zoo**
340 King St. E., Bowmanville, ON L1C 3K5.
Tel: (905) 623-5655. Open daily in summer.
Web site: www.bowmanvillezoo.com

☐ **Jungle Cat World**
3667 Concession 6, Orono, ON L0B 1M0.
Tel: (905) 983-5016. Open daily.
Web site: www.junglecatworld.com

☐ **Toronto Zoo**
361A Old Finch Ave., Scarborough, ON M1B 5K7.
Tel: (416) 392-5900. Open all year.
Web site: www.torontozoo.com

Western Canada:

☐ **Assiniboine Park Zoo**
2355 Corydon Ave., Winnipeg, MB R3P 0R5.
Tel: (204) 982-0660. Open all year.
Web site: www.zoosociety.com

☐ **Saskatoon Zoo**
1903 Forest Dr., Saskatoon, SK S7S 1G9.
Tel: (306) 975-3395. Open all year.

☐ **Alberta Birds of Prey**
PO Box 1150, Coaldale, AB T1M 1M9.
Tel: (403) 345-4262. Open daily in summer.
Web site: www.albertabirds.com

☐ **Calgary Zoo**
1300 Zoo Road N.E., Calgary, AB T2M 4R8.
Tel: (403) 232-9300. Open all year.
Web site: www.calgaryzoo.ab.ca

☐ **Dolphin Lagoon**
West Edmonton Mall, #2472, 8770-170 St.,
Edmonton, AB T5T 4M2. Tel: 1-800-661-8890.
Web site: www.westedmall.com/entertainment/
dolphin.shtml

☐ **Valley Zoo**
PO Box 2359, 13315 Buena Vista Rd, Edmonton, AB
T5J 2R7. Tel: (780) 496-8787. Open all year.
Web site: www.gov.edmonton.ab.ca/valleyzoo/

☐ **Crystal Garden**
613 Pandora Ave., Victoria, BC V8W 1N8.
Tel: (250) 953-8800. Open all year.
Web site: www.bcpcc.com/crystal

☐ **Greater Vancouver Zoological Centre**
5048-264 St., Aldergrove, BC V4W 1N7.
Tel: (604) 856-6825. Open daily.
Web site: www.greatervancouverzoo.com

☐ **Kamloops Wildlife Park**
PO Box 698, East Trans Canada Highway, Kamloops,
BC V2C 5L7. Tel: (250) 573-3242. Open all year.
Web site: www.kamloopswildlife.org

☐ **Mountain View Farms Breeding and
Conservation Centre** 8011-240th St., Langley, BC
V3A 4P9. Tel: (604) 882-9313.
Web site: www.mtnviewfarms.com

☐ **Vancouver Aquarium Marine Science Centre**
PO Box 3232, Stanley Park, Vancouver, BC
V6B 3X8. Tel: (604) 659-3474. Open all year.
Web site: www.vanaqua.org

*Accredited by the Canadian Association of Zoos and
Aquariums.

Canada may well have been one of the best kept secrets on the world's arts and entertainment scene, but the secret is getting harder and harder to keep as artists like Atom Egoyan, Alanis Morissette, Robert LePage, and Yann Martel make their mark. Historically, the small size and scattered nature of the Canadian market made dissemination of Canadian works of art and entertainment products difficult. But the years following World War II saw an explosion of activity in every sector, fuelled by public institutions such as the CBC, the Canada Council for the Arts, and the National Film Board and similar provincial and local agencies. Canadian content requirements for broadcasters and tax and investment measures favouring Canadian publishers have also helped foster successful, if fragile, publishing and recording industries. In 2001–2002 all levels of government devoted $6.1 billion to culture (this includes federal support for the CBC and provincial and local support for public libraries). Restraints on public spending over the past two decades have caused emphasis to be placed on private investment and on production for foreign markets. During the 1990s, film and TV production saw a 200 percent increase in foreign investment and a 33 percent increase in private sector Canadian investment. At the same time Canadian authors, agents and publishers found the sale of foreign rights to be a lucrative stream of revenue in a world hungry to read the work of writers such as Carol Shields, Michael Ondaatje, Anne Michaels and Ann-Marie MacDonald.

MAJOR ARTS COUNCILS

The Canada Council: 350 Albert St, Box 1047, Ottawa, ON K1P 5V8, tel: (613) 566-4414 (toll-free: 1-800-263-5588); fax: (613) 566-4390; e-mail: [employee name]@canadacouncil.ca (see personnel directory at Web site); Web site: www.canadacouncil.ca

Alberta Foundation for the Arts: Alberta Community Development, 901 Standard Life Centre, 10405 Jasper Ave, Edmonton, AB T5J 4R7; tel: (780) 427-9968; fax: (780) 422-9132; e-mail: afa@mcd.gov.ab.ca; Web site: www.affta.ab.ca

British Columbia Arts Council: Box 9819, Stn Prov. Govt, Victoria, BC V8W 9W3; tel: (250) 356-1718; fax: (250) 387-4099; e-mail: BCArtsCouncil @gems2.gov.bc.ca; Web site: www.bcartscouncil.ca

Manitoba Arts Council: 525-93 Lombard Ave, Winnipeg, MB R3B 3B1; tel: (204) 945-2237; fax: (204) 945-5925; e-mail: info@artscouncil.mb.ca; Web site: www.artscouncil.mb.ca

New Brunswick Arts Board: 634 Queen St, Ste 300, Fredericton, NB E3B 1C2; tel: 1-866-460-ARTS; e-mail: [employee name]@artsnb.ca (see personnel directory at Web site); Web site: www.artsnb.ca

Newfoundland and Labrador Arts Council: Box 98, St. John's, NF A1C 5H5; tel: 1-866-726-2212; fax: (709)726-0619; e-mail: nlacmail@nfld.net; web site: www.nlac.nf.ca

Northwest Territories Arts Council: Department of Education, Culture and Employment, Government of the Northwest Territories, Box 1320, Yellowknife, NT X1A 2L9; tel: (867) 920-3103; fax: (867) 873-0205

Nova Scotia Arts and Culture Partnership Council: World Trade and Convention Centre, 1800 Argyle St, Ste 402, PO Box 456, Halifax, NS B3J 2R5; tel: (902) 424-6471; fax (902) 424-0170; e-mail: turnerpm@gov.ns.ca

Ontario Arts Council: 151 Bloor St W, 5th floor Toronto, ON M5S 1T6; tel: (416) 961-1660 (toll-free in Ontario: 1-800-387-0058); fax: (416) 961-7796; e-mail: info@arts.on.ca; Web site: www.arts.on.ca

P.E.I. Council of the Arts: 115 Richmond St, Charlottetown, PE C1E 1H7; tel: (902) 368-6176; fax: (902) 368-4418; e-mail: peiarts@peiartscouncil.com; Web site: www.peiartscouncil.com

Consell des arts et des lettres du Quebec: Quebec bureau: 79, boul René-Lévesque Est, 3e étage, Quebec, QC G1R 5N5; tel: (418) 643-1707 (toll-free: 1-800-897-1707); fax: (418) 643-4558; Montreal bureau: 500, Place d'Armes, 15e étage, Montréal, QC H2Y 2W2; tel: (514) 864-3350 (toll-free1-800-608-3350); fax: (514) 864-4160; e-mail: affaires.publiques@calq.gouv.qc.ca; Web site: www.calq.gouv.qc.ca

Saskatchewan Arts Board: 2135 Broad St, Regina, SK S4P 3V7; tel: (306) 787-4056 (toll-free in Saskatchewan: 1-800-667-7526); fax: (306) 787-4199; e-mail: sab@artsboard.sk.ca; Web site: www.artsboard.sk.ca

Yukon Tourism, Arts Branch: PO Box 2703, Whitehorse, YT Y1A 2C6; tel: (867) 667-5386 (toll-free in Yukon: 1-800-661-0408); fax: (867) 667-8023; e-mail: arts@gov.yk.ca; Web site: www.btc.gov.yk.ca/cultural/MAJOR ARTS

TELEVISION

Television first reached Canada in the 1940s from border stations in the United States. The Canadian Broadcasting Corporation's TV services were launched in 1952. The launch in English Canada was less than auspicious; the first image to appear on the screen was the CBC logo presented upside down. The CBC recovered its poise and the network grew rapidly, opening stations across the country and broadcasting its programs on affiliated private stations.

CBC TV was joined by the private Canadian Television Network in 1961. The CanWest/Global system began in the 1970s and has become Canada's third major television network. Through the 1980s and 1990s the CRTC has licensed dozens of specialty cable services to ensure that Canadian services offer viewers a full range of choices.

While the most-watched television programs in Canada continue to be American dramas and situation comedies, Canadian broadcasters have scored considerable success with programs such as *Traders* and *DaVinci's Inquest*, *Street Legal*, and *Due South*. Canadian producers have been particularly successful with children's programs such as *Mr. Dressup* and with sketch comedy programs including *SCTV*, *Codco*, and *This Hour Has 22 Minutes*.

Today the television market accounts for 70 percent of the 14,000 film projects undertaken in Canada each year. Much of that production is destined for air in the United States and other countries as international coproduction becomes an increasingly popular way of funding television programs around the world.

Canada's Television Classification System

In the fall of 1997, a television classification system was formally launched on Canadian airwaves to help Canadians identify programming suitable to various age groups. There are seven classification levels. Although violence is the most important content consideration, each classification also includes information on coarse language, nudity and sex. The classifications are designed for use with V-chip technology which enables parents to block reception of undesirable programs. A Canadian V-chip system using the following classifications is expected to be operational in 2001.

 Children: Might contain occasional comedic, unrealistic depictions of violence. No offensive language. No sex or nudity.

 Children Over 8 Years: Might include mild physical violence, comedic violence, comic horror, special effects; fantasy, supernatural, or animated violence. No profanity. No sex or nudity.

 General: Violence is minimal and infrequent. Contains no frightening special effects not required by the storyline. May contain inoffensive slang. No profanity. No sex or nudity.

 Parental Guidance: Moderate violence which must be justified within the context of the storyline. Might contain mild profanity, suggestive language, some nudity.

 Over 14 Years: Might contain intense scenes of violence. Could include frequent profanity. Might include scenes of nudity and/or sexual activity.

 Adults: Depictions of violence are intended for adult viewing, and thus are not suitable for audiences under 18 years of age. Might contain graphic language and explicit portrayals of sex and/or nudity.

Exempt: News, sports, documentaries, and other information programming, talk shows, music videos, and variety programming.

Source: *Media Awareness Network, www.media-awareness.ca*

The CRTC: Canada's Communications Watchdog

The Canadian Radio-television and Telecommunications Commission (CRTC) regulates all aspects of the Canadian broadcasting system. It grants licences to radio and television broadcasters, enforces the conditions of those licences and reviews broadcaster performance at regularly scheduled hearings. Created under the Broadcasting Act of 1968, the Commission inherited a long tradition of government supervision of broadcasting in Canada. Radio broadcasting was regulated in its early days under the Radiotelegraph Act. In the 1930s responsibility for radio was shifted to the newly created Canadian Broadcasting Corporation. Private broadcasters were unhappy with a system that gave their public sector competitor the right to supervise their businesses and so an independent regulator, the Board of Broadcast Governors (BBG) was formed in 1958. The Broadcasting Act of 1968 replaced the BBG with the CRTC. The commission scored a success with the establishment of Canadian content regulations in 1971 for radio. Through the 1980s and 1990s it insisted on higher levels of quality Canadian programming from private television broadcasters and oversaw the introduction of dozens of new specialty services on cable and satellite television. While the CRTC also supervises telecommunications it announced in 1999 that it would not attempt to regulate the Internet.

Web site: www.crtc.gc.ca

The Gemini Awards, 2002

The Gemini Awards were established in 1986 to honor outstanding contributions to the Canadian television industry. Given out annually by the Academy of Canadian Cinema and Television, the Geminis grew out of the former ACTRA Awards, last presented in 1985. The 17th annual Geminis were held Nov. 2–4, 2002, in Toronto.

Dramatic series . . . . *DaVinci's Inquest*
Comedy series . . . . *An American In Canada*
TV movie . . . . *Torso*
Actor (dramatic series) . . . . Donnelly Rhodes, *DaVinci's Inquest*
Actor (dramatic program) . . . . Colm Feore, *Trudeau*
Supporting actor (dramatic program or mini-series) . . . . Sam Waterston, *The Matthew Shepard Story*
Supporting actor (dramatic series) . . . . Garry Chalk, *Cold Squad*
Actress (dramatic series . . . . Julie Stewart, *Cold Squad*
Actress (dramatic program) . . . . Aeofie McMahon, *Random Passage*
Supporting actress (dramatic program or mini-series)-Jackie Burroughs, *Armistead Maupin's Further Tales of the City*
Supporting actress (dramatic series) . . . . Dixie Seatle, *Paradise Falls*
Performance (performing arts program or series) . . . . Mirko Hector, Jason Shipley-Jones, Naomi Stikeman, Zofia Tujaka, *Montreal Dance*
Ensemble performance (comedy program or series) . . . . Rick Mercer, Jackie Torrens, Peter Keleghan, Dan Lett, Leah Pinsent, *Made In Canada*, "Everyone's a Critic"
Performance (variety program or series) . . . . Steven Page, Jim Creeggan, Kevin Hearn, Ed Robertson, Tyler Stewart, *2002 Juno Awards*
Animated program or series . . . . *Aagh! It's The Mr. Hell Show!*, p. Christopher Brough, J. Falconer
Children's or Youth program or series . . . . *he Famous Jett Jackson*, p. Shawn Levy, Bruce Kalish, Kevin May
Documentary series . . . . *Witness*, p. Marie Natanson, Hilary Armstrong, Charlotte Odele
Lifestyle/General Interest series . . . . *Opening Soon*, p. Tim O'Brian, Rachel Low
Best talk series . . . . *Health On The Line*, p. Indra Seja
Sports program . . . . *The Olympians*, p. Paul Harrington, Mike Brannagan, Peter Findlay
Newscast . . . . *The National*, p. Cynthia Kinch, Mark Harrison, Lynn Kelly, Fred Parker, Jonathan Whitten
News Anchor . . . . . . Peter Mansbridge, CBC News: *The National*, "Attack on the USA"/"Bethlehem Tour"/"Big Picture"
News information series . . . . *the fifth estate*, p. David Studer, Jim Williamson
Performing arts program . . . . *Dracula: Pages From A Virgin's Diary*, p. Vonnie Von Helmolt, Robert Sherrin
Science, technology, nature, environment or adventure documentary program . . . . *The Secret World of Gardens: Frogs*, p. Susan Fleming

Source: *Academy of Canadian Cinema and Television*

The Most-Watched Television Programs in Canada[1]

Top 10 Programs[2]

1. Academy Awards (CTV)
2. Grey Cup Game 2002 (CBC)
3. Golden Globe Awards (CTV)
4. Academy Awards Pre-show (CTV)
5. Juno Awards (CTV)
6. Emmy Awards (CTV)
7. Céline in Las Vegas (CBC)
8. Golden Globe Pre-show (CTV)
9. Toronto Rocks (CBC)
10. American Music Awards (CTV))

Top 10 Regularly Scheduled Programs[3]

1. *C.S.I.* (CTV)
2. *American Idol 2* Tuesday (CTV)
3. *American Idol 2* Wednesday (CTV)
4. *Canadian Idol* (CTV)
5. *C.S.I. Miami* (CTV)
6. *E.R.* (CTV)
7. NHL Playoffs Round 1 (CBC)
8. *Law and Order* (CTV)
9. *The Amazing Race 4* (CTV)
10. NHL Playoffs Round 2 (CBC)

Source: *Nielsen Media Research, 2003 Copyright Nielsen Media Research*
(1) Persons two years and older for the period Sept. 2, 2002–Aug. 31, 2003. (2) Specials, not including sports. (3) Five telecasts minimum.

The Prime-Time Emmy Awards, 2002–2003

The Emmy Awards are presented annually on behalf of the U.S. Academy of Television Arts and Sciences. The 55th annual Prime-Time Emmy Awards were presented September 21, 2003, at the Shrine auditorium in Los Angeles, California.

OUTSTANDING DRAMA SERIES . . . . *The West Wing*, NBC
Actor (drama series) . . . . James Gandolfini, *The Sopranos*, HBO
Actress (drama series) . . . . Edie Falco, *The Sopranos*, HBO
Supporting actor (drama series) . . . . Joe Pantoliano, *The Sopranos*, HBO
Supporting actress (drama series) . . . . Tyne Daly, *Judging Amy*, CBS
Directing (drama series) . . . . Christopher Misiano, *The West Wing*, "Twenty-Five," NBC
Writing (drama series) . . . . Robin Green, Mitchell Burgess, David Chase, *The Sopranos*, "White Caps," HBO

OUTSTANDING COMEDY SERIES . . . . *Everybody Loves Raymond*, CBS
Actor (comedy series) . . . . Tony Shalhoub, *Monk*, USA
Actress (comedy series) . . . . Debra Messing, *Will & Grace*, NBC
Supporting actor (comedy series) . . . . Brad Garrett, *Everybody Loves Raymond*, CBS
Supporting actress (comedy series) . . . . Doris Roberts, *Everybody Loves Raymond*, CBS
Directing (comedy series) . . . . Robert B. Weide, *Curb Your Enthusiasm*, "Krazee-Eyez Killa," HBO
Writing (comedy series) . . . . Tucker Cawley, *Everybody Loves Raymond*, "Baggage," CBS

OUTSTANDING MINISERIES . . . . *Steven Spielberg Presents Taken*, Sci Fi
Actor (miniseries or movie) . . . . William H. Macy, *Door to Door*, TNT
Actress (miniseries or movie) . . . . Maggie Smith, *My House in Umbria*, HBO
Supporting actor (miniseries or movie) . . . . Ben Gazzara, *Hysterical Blindness*, HBO
Supporting actress (miniseries or movie) . . . . Gena Rowlands, *Hysterical Blindness*, HBO
Directing (miniseries or movie) . . . . Steven Shachter, *Door to Door*, TNT
Writing (miniseries or movie) . . . . William H. Macy, Steven Shachter, *Door to Door*, TNT
OUTSTANDING VARIETY, MUSIC OR COMEDY SERIES . . . . *The Daily Show With Jon Stewart*, Comedy Central

OUTSTANDING VARIETY, MUSIC OR COMEDY SPECIAL . . . . *Cher—The Farewell Tour*, NBC
Directing (variety or music) . . . . Glen Weiss, *The 56th Annual Tony Awards*, CBC
Writing (variety or music) . . . . David Javerbaum *et. al.*, *The Daily Show With Jon Stewart*, Comedy Central
Performance (variety or music) . . . . Wayne Brady, *Whose Line Is It Anyway?*, ABC

OUTSTANDING TV MOVIE . . . . *Door to Door*, TNT

Television Networks and Cable Services

Arts & Entertainment Network (A&E):
235 E 45th St, New York, NY 10017
(212) 210-1400 www.aetv.com

Atlantic Television System & Atlantic Satellite Network: 2885 Robie St, Halifax, NS B3K 5Z4
(902) 453-4000 www.atv.ca

Bravo!: 299 Queen St W, Toronto, ON
M5V 2Z5 (416) 591-5757 www.bravo.ca

Canadian Broadcasting Corporation (CBC):
Box 500, Stn A, Toronto, ON M5W 1E6
(416) 205-3311 www.cbc.ca

Canal Famille: 2100 Sainte-Catherine ouest,
Bureau 800, Montreal, QC H3H 2T3
(514) 939-3150

CanWest/Global Communications Corp.:
201 Portage Ave, 31st Flr, TD Centre,
Winnipeg, MB R3B 3L7 (204) 956-2025

CTV Television Network Ltd: Box 9, Stn O,
9 Channel Nine Ct, Scarborough, ON M1S 4B5
(416) 332-5000 www.ctv.ca

Discovery Channel: 9 Channel Nine Ct,
Scarborough, ON M1S 4B5 (416) 332-5000
www.discovery.ca

The Family Channel Inc.: BCE Place,
181 Bay St, Box 787, Toronto, ON M5J 2T3
(416) 956-2030 www.family.ca

Global Television Network: 81 Barber Greene
Rd, Don Mills, ON M3C 2A2 (416) 446-5311
www.canada.com

Life Network: 121 Bloor St E, Ste 200, Toronto, ON
M4W 3M5 (416) 967-0022 www.lifenetwork.ca

The Movie Network/Viewers Choice: BCE Place,
181 Bay St, Box 787, Toronto, ON M5J 2T3

(416) 956-2010, www.themovienetwork.ca,
www.viewerschoice.ca

MuchMusic, MuchMoreMusic: 299 Queen St W,
Toronto, ON M5V 2Z5 (416) 591-5757
www.muchmusic.com, www.muchmore
music.com

MusiquePlus: 355 Sainte-Catherine est,
Montreal, QC H3B 1A5 (514) 284-7587
www.musiqueplus.com

Showcase Television Inc.: 121 Bloor St E,
#200, Toronto, ON M4W 1B9 (416) 967-3253
www.showcase.ca

Télé-Québec: 1000, rue Fullum, Montreal,
QC H2K 3L7 1-800-361-4301 www.telequebec.
qc.ca

The Sports Network (TSN): 9 Channel Nine Ct,
Scarborough, ON M1S 4B5 (416) 332-5000
www.tsn.ca

Telelatino Network Inc.: 5125 Steeles Ave W,
Weston, ON M9L 1R5 (416) 744-8200
www.tlntv.com

TVOntario (TVO): Box 200, Stn Q, Toronto, ON
M4T 2T1 (416) 484-2600 www.tvo.org

Vision TV: 80 Bond St, Toronto, ON M5B 1X2
(416) 368-3194 www.visiontv.ca

W Network: W Network, 64 Jefferson Ave,
Unit 18, Toronto, ON M6K 3H4 (416) 534-1191
ext. 5155 www.wnetwork.com

YTV Canada Inc.: 64 Jefferson Ave, Unit 18,
Toronto, ON M6K 3H4. (416) 534-1191
www.ytv.com

Al Jazeera: Changing the TV Landscape

*T*he events of September 11, 2001, brought the world's attention to a new presence in the
media landscape. With its broadcast of tapes of speeches and discussions with Al Quaeda
leader Osama bin Laden, Al Jazeera, the 24-hour Arabic satellite news channel based in Quatar,
showed the world that western media no longer had a monopoly on international coverage of
events in the Arab world. The service claims 40 million viewers world wide, including 150,000 in
the United States. As of spring 2002 it was not licensed for distribution in Canada. In stark
contrast to its stranglehold on coverage of the 1991 war in Iraq, CNN turned to Al Jazeera for
help in covering the war in Afghanistan, featuring interviews with the latter's correspondents in
Kandahar and New York. Al Jazeera drew accusations of anti-American bias from the US
government after it broadcast the bin Laden tapes, but the Committee to Protect Journalists said
that criticisms of the service in the Arab world for alleged pro-Israeli and pro-US bias suggest
the service is providing balanced coverage.

MUSIC

The watershed year in the Canadian music industry was 1971, when the federal government imposed Canadian content regulations on the country's radio stations. These regulations helped build a domestic recording industry that has produced several generations of world-class pop stars including Bryan Adams, Céline Dion, Sarah MacLachlan and Shania Twain.

Montreal, Toronto and Vancouver have consistently served as centres for the Canadian popular music industry. But other cities have served as hotbeds at various periods. Winnipeg in the 1960s was dubbed the Liverpool of Canada for a scene that launched the careers of Neil Young and The Guess Who. The Ottawa Valley has long been a place of musical ferment owing to the interaction of Irish, Scottish and French settlers. Bruce Cockburn and Alanis Morrissette are two of the National Capital Region's best-known alumni.

Nova Scotia and Newfoundland have historically been home to vibrant Celtic folk traditions and the 1990s saw the rise of Atlantic Canada as a major centre for music production in Canada. Those traditions have been parlayed into commercial success for artists such as Great Big Sea, The Rankins, singer Rita MacNeil, and folk/rock fiddlers Ashley MacIsaac and Natalie MacMaster.

Avril Lavigne: Canada's #1 Sk8er Girl

2003 *witnessed a tidal wave of recognition for a rebel tomboy from Napanee, Ontario, who in the previous year had turned the pop world upside down. Riding the overwhelming success of her debut CD,* **Let Go,** *Avril Lavigne set a whole new standard for chic among female rock stars, as she eschewed Spandex, thongs and belly tops for jeans, neck ties and a Napanee Home Hardware T-shirt.*

Let Go *netted Lavigne four Juno Awards at the annual awards ceremonies in Ottawa in early April. She won for Single of the Year ("Complicated"), Album and Pop Album of the Year, as well as Best New Solo Artist.*

Lavigne's success has extended world-wide, with accolades pouring in from Europe and the United States. **Let Go** *was ranked North America's top-selling debut CD in 2002 and it garnered Lavigne five nominations for the 2003 Grammy Awards. She was nominated for Best New Artist, Song of the Year and Best Female Pop Performance for "Complicated," Best Pop Vocal Album for* **Let Go,** *and Best Female Rock Vocal Performance for her second single "Sk8er Boi." The string of nominations tied her for the year's most nominated artist with Norah Jones, Bruce Springsteen, Nelly and Eminem. A strong favourite in all categories, Lavigne was shutout by Jones, whose softer, jazz-influenced style is in stark contrast to the Canadian's biting, punky sound.*

The middle child of a religious family, Lavigne broke out of Napanee (population 5,000) at age 16, heading for New York and almost immediately grabbing the attention of Arista Records. "I'm just coming out and I'm going to clearly be myself—I write what I feel, I never worry what others think," Avril avows. "I'm gonna dress what's me, I'm gonna act what's me and I'm gonna sing what's me."

In spite of Lavigne's rebellious image, many parents of teen and pre-teen girls are grateful to her for providing their daughters with a more independently minded and less body-centred role model than glamour divas such as Britney Spears, Christina Aguilera and Shakira, who had dominated the female pop world prior to her arrival.

That didn't stop Britain's **New Music Express** *from presenting Lavigne with the Carling Award for Most Sexy Woman, beating out Aguilera and Kylie Minogue.*

The Juno Awards, 1994–2003

The Juno Awards were established in 1975 to honour achievement in the Canadian recording industry. The name was chosen to honour Pierre Juneau, former head of the Canadian Radio-television and Telecommunications Commission (CRTC) which instituted "Canadian content" requirements in the nation's broadcast industry.

Nominations for most major Juno categories are determined by record sales, although the actual winners are selected by a vote of members of the Canadian Academy of Recording Arts & Sciences.

Nominees must be Canadian citizens or landed immigrants and must have resided in Canada during the year prior to their nomination. Eligible recordings don't require national distribution, but must be available for retail sale in Canada.

The latest awards were announced April 5–6, 2003. The awards ceremony was broadcast live from Ottawa.

Canadian Entertainer of the Year

1994	The Rankin Family
1995	The Tragically Hip
1996	Shania Twain

Juno Fan Choice Award

2003	Shania Twain

Best Selling Album (Foreign or Domestic)

2000	*Millennium*, Backstreet Boys
2001	*The Marshall Mathers LP*, Eminem
2002	*Hotshot*, Shaggy

International Album of the Year

2003	*The Eminem Show*, Eminem

Best Album

1994	*Harvest Moon*, Neil Young
1995	*Colour of My Love*, Céline Dion
1996	*Jagged Little Pill*, Alanis Morissette
1997	*Trouble at the Henhouse*, The Tragically Hip
1998	*Clumsy*, Our Lady Peace
1999	*Let's Talk About Love*, Céline Dion
2000	*Supposed Former Infatuation Junkie*, Alanis Morissette
2001	*Maroon*, The Barenaked Ladies
2002	*The Look of Love*, Diana Krall
2003	*Let Go*, Avril Lavigne

Best Single

1994	"Fare Thee Well Love," The Rankin Family
1995	"Could I Be Your Girl," Jann Arden
1996	"You Oughta Know," Alanis Morissette
1997	"Ironic," Alanis Morissette
1998	"Building a Mystery," Sarah McLachlan
1999	"One Week," The Barenaked Ladies
2000	"Bobcaygeon," The Tragically Hip
2001	"I'm Like A Bird," Nelly Furtado
2002	"How You Remind Me," Nickelback
2003	"Complicated," Avril Lavigne

Best Artist

2002	Diana Krall
2003	Shania Twain

Best Female Artist

1994	Céline Dion
1995	Jann Arden
1996	Alanis Morissette
1997	Céline Dion
1998	Sarah McLachlan
1999	Céline Dion
2000	Chantal Kreviazuk
2001	Jann Arden

Best Male Artist

1994	Roch Voisine
1995	Neil Young
1996	Colin James
1997	Bryan Adams
1998	Paul Brandt
1999	Jim Cuddy
2000	Bryan Adams
2001	Neil Young

Best Group

1994	The Rankin Family
1995	The Tragically Hip
1996	Blue Rodeo
1997	The Tragically Hip
1998	Our Lady Peace
1999	The Barenaked Ladies
2000	Matthew Good Band
2001	The Barenaked Ladies
2002	Nickelback
2003	Sum 41

Best Songwriter

1994	Leonard Cohen
1995	Jann Arden
1996	Alanis Morissette, Glen Ballard
1997	Alanis Morissette, Glen Ballard
1998	Sarah McLachlan, Pierre Marchand
1999	Bryan Adams, Phil Thornalley "On A Day Like Today"; Bryan Adams, Eliott Kennedy,"When You're Gone"
2000	Shania Twain, Robert John "Mutt" Lange, "Man! I Feel Like A Woman," "You've Got A Way," "That Don't Impress Me Much"
2001	Nelly Furtado, "Turn Off The Light," "I'm Like A Bird," "...on the radio (remember the days)"
2002	Jann Arden, Russell Brown, "Never Mind,"
2003	Chad Kroeger/Nickelback, "Hero"; Nickelback, "Too Bad," "How You Remind Me" ▶

Best New Solo Artist

1994	Jann Arden
1995	Susan Aglukark
1996	Ashley MacIsaac
1997	Terri Clark
1998	Holly McNarland
1999	Melanie Doane
2000	Tal Bachman
2001	Nelly Furtado
2002	Hawksley Workman
2003	Avril Lavigne

Best New Group

1994	The Waltons
1995	Moist
1996	The Philosopher Kings
1997	The Killjoys
1998	Leahy
1999	Johnny Favourite Swing Orchestra
2000	Sky
2001	Nickelback
2002	Default
2003	Theory of a Deadman

Best Francophone Album

1994	*Album de Peuple: Tome 2*
1995	*Coup de tête*
1996	*D'eux*
1997	*Live À Paris*
1998	*Marie Michèle Desrosiers Chante Les Classiques de Noël*
1999	*S'il Suffisait D'Aimer*, Céline Dion
2000	*En Catimini*, La Chicane
2001	*Un grand noël d'amour*, Ginette Reno
2002	*Les Vents ont changé*, Kevin Parent
2003	*Rêver Mieux*, Daniel Bélanger

Best Country Recording

2003	"I'm Gonna' Getcha' Good," Shania Twain

Best Country Artist

2002	Carolyn Dawn Johnson
2003	Shania Twain

Best Country Female Artist

1994	Cassandra Vasik
1995	Michelle Wright
1996	Shania Twain
1997	Shania Twain
1998	Shania Twain
1999	Shania Twain
2000	Shania Twain
2001	Terri Clark

Best Country Male Artist

1994	Charlie Major
1995	Charlie Major
1996	Charlie Major
1997	Paul Brandt
1998	Paul Brandt
1999	Paul Brandt
2000	Paul Brandt
2001	Paul Brandt

Best New Country Artist/Group

2002	Ennis Sisters

Best Country Group or Duo

1994	The Rankin Family
1995	Prairie Oyster
1996	Prairie Oyster
1997	The Rankin Family
1998	Farmer's Daughter
1999	Leahy
2000	The Rankins
2001	The Wilkinsons

Best Pop Album

2000	*Colour Moving And Still*, Chantal Kreviazuk
2001	*Maroon*, The Barenaked Ladies
2002	*Morning Orbit*, David Usher
2003	*Let Go*, Avril Lavigne

Best Rock Album

1994	*Dig*, I, Mother Earth
1995	*Suffersystem*, Monster Voodoo Machine
1996	*Jagged Little Pill*, Alanis Morissette
2000	*Beautiful Midnight*, Matthew Good Band
2001	*Music @ Work*, The Tragically Hip
2002	*Silver Side Up*, Nickelback
2003	*Gravity*, Our Lady Peace

Best Alternative Album

1998	*Glee*, Bran Van 3000
1999	*Rufus Wainwright*, Rufus Wainwright
2000	*Julie Doiron and the Wooden Stars*, Julie Doiron and the Wooden Stars
2001	*Mass Romantic*, The New Pornographers
2002	*Poses*, Rufus Wainwright
2003	*You Forgot It In People*, Broken Social Scenes

Best Rap Recording

1994	"*One Track Mind*," TBTBT
1995	"*Certified*," Ghetto Concept
1996	"*E-Z On Tha Motion*," Ghetto Concept
1997	"*What It Takes*," Choclair
1998	"*Cash Crop*," Rascalz
1999	"*Northern Touch*," Rascalz featuring Choclair, Kardinal Offishall, Thrust and Checkmate
2000	"*Ice Cold*," Choclair
2001	"*Balance*," Swollen Members
2002	"*Bad Dreams*," Swollen Members
2003	"Monsters in the Closet," Swollen Members

Best Dance Recording

1994	"Thankful (Raw Club Mix)," Red Light
1995	"Higher Love (Club Mix)," Capital Sound
1996	"A Deeper Shade of Love (Extended Mix)," Camille
1997	"Astroplane" (City of Love Mix)," BKS
1998	"Euphoria" (Rabbit in the Moon Mix)," Delerium
1999	"*Broken Bones*," Love Inc.
2000	"*Silence*," Delerium

2001 . . . . "*Into the Night*," Love Inc.
2002 . . . . "*Spaced Invaders*," Hatiras
2003 . . . . "The Sound Bluntz," Billie Jean

Best Contemporary Jazz Album

1994 . . . . *Don't Smoke in Bed*, Holly Cole Trio
1995 *The Merlin Factor*, Jim Hillman & The Merlin Factor
1996 . . . . *NOJO*, Neufeld-Occhipinti Jazz Orchestra
1997 . . . . *Africville Suite*, Joe Sealy
1998 . . . . *Metalwood*, Metalwood
1999 . . . . *Metalwood 2*, Metalwood
2000 . . . .*so far*, D.D Jackson
2001 . . . . *Compassion*, François Carrier Trio
2002 . . . . *Live*, François Bourassa Trio + André LeRoux
2003 . . . . .*tales from the blue lounge*, Richard Underhill

Best Vocal Jazz Album

2000 . . . . *When I Look In Your Eyes*, Diana Krall
2001 . . . . *Both Sides Now*, Joni Mitchell
2002 . . . . *The Look of Love*, Diana Krall
2003 . . . . *Live In Paris*, Diana Krall

Best Mainstream/Traditional Jazz Album

1994 . *Fables and Dreams*, Dave Young/Phil Dwyer Quartet
1995 . . . . *Free Trade*, Free Trade
1996 . . . . *Vernal Fields*, Ingrid Jensen
1997 . . . . *Ancestors*, Renee Rosnes
1998 . . . . . . *In the Mean Time*, The Hugh Fraser Quintet
1999 . . . . *The Atlantic Sessions*, Kirk MacDonald
2000 . . . . *Deep In A Dream*, Pat LaBarbera
2001 . . . . *Rob McConnell Tentet*, Rob McConnell Tentet
2002 . . . . *Murley, Bickert & Wallace: Live at the Senator*
2003 . . . . *Life On Earth*, Renee Rosnes Mike Murley

Best R&B/Soul Recording

1994 . . . . "The Time is Right," Rupert Gayle
1995 . . . . . "First Impressions for the Bottom Jigglers,"
                                                    Bass is Base
1996 . . . . "Deborah Cox," Deborah Cox
1997 . . . . "Feelin' Alright," Carlos Morgan
1998 . . . ."Things Just Ain't the Same," Deborah Cox
1999 . . . . "One Wish," Deborah Cox
2000 . . . . "Thinkin' About You," 2Rude
                                  featuring Latoya & Miranda
2001 . . . . "Sleepless," jacksoul
2002 . . . . "Don't You Forget It," Glenn Lewis
2003 . . . . "The Way I Feel," Remy Shand

Best Blues/Gospel Album

1994 . . . . *South at Eight/North at Nine*, Colin Linden
1995 . . . . *Joy to the World Jubilation V*,
                          Montreal Jubilation Gospel Choir
1996 . . . . *That River*, Jim Byrnes
1997 . . . . . . *Right To Sing The Blues*, Long John Baldry

Best Blues Album

1998 . . . . *National Steel*, Colin James
1999 . . . . *Blues Weather*, Fathead
2000 . . . . *Gust Of Wind*, Ray Bonneville
2001 . . . . *Love Comin' Down*, Sue Foley
2002 . . . . *Big Mouth*, Colin Linden

2003 . . . . *6-String Lover*, Jack de Keyzer

Best Gospel Album

1998 . . . . *Romantics and Mystics*, Steve Bell
1999 . . . . *Life Is*, Sharon Riley & Faith Chorale
2000 . . . . *Legacy Of Hope*, Deborah Klassen
2001 . . . . *Simple Songs*, Steve Bell
2002 . . . . *Downhere*, Downhere
2003 . . . . *Instrument of Praise*, Toronto Mass Choir

Best Reggae/Calypso Recording

1994 . . . . *Informer*, Snow
1995 . . . . *Class and Credential*, Carla Marshall
1996 . . . . *Now and Forever*, Sattalites
1997 . . . . *Nana Maclean*, Nana Maclean
1998 . . . . *Catch de Vibe*, Messenjah
1999 . . . . *Vision*, Frankie Wilmot
2000 . . . . *Heart & Soul*, Lazo
2001 . . . . *Lenn Hammond*, Lenn Hammond
2002 . . . . *Love (African Woman)*, Blessed
2003 . . . . *You Won't See Me Any More*, Sonia Collymore

Best Global/ World Music Album

1994 . . . . *El Camino Real*, Ancient Cultures
1995 . . . . *Africa+*, Eval Manigat
1996 . . . . *Music From Africa*, Takadja
1997 . . . . *Africa Do Brasil*, Paulo Ramos Group
1998 . . . . *La Llorona*, Lhasa
1999 . . . . *La Llorona*, Lhasa
2000 . . . . *Omnisource*, Madagascar Slim
2001 . *Ritmo + Soul*, Jane Bunnett and the Spirits of Havana
2002 . . . . *The Journey*, Alpha Yaya Diallo
2003 . . . . *Balagane*, Jeszcze Raz

Best Roots and Traditional Album

1994 . . . . *My Skies*, James Keelaghan
1995 . . . . *The Mask and Mirror*, Loreena McKennitt
1996 . *Hi: How Are You Today?*, Ashley MacIsaac (solo);
     Gypsies & Lovers, The Irish Descendants (group)
1997 . . . . *drive-in movie*, Fred Eaglesmith (solo);
     Matapedia, Kate & Anna McGarrigle (group)
1998 . . . . *Other Songs*, Ron Sexsmith (solo)
     Molinos, The Paperboys (group)
1999 . . . .*Heartstrings*, Willie P Bennett (solo)
     The McGarrigle Hour, Kate & Anna McGarrigle (group)
2000 . . . *Breakfast In New Orleans, Dinner In Timbuktu*,
                                  Bruce Cockburn (solo)
     Kings Of Love, Blackie & The Rodeo Kings (group)
2001 . . . . *Jenny Whiteley*, Jenny Whiteley (solo)
     Tri-Continental, Tri-Continental, Bill Bourne,
     Lester Quitzau, Madagascar Slim (group)
2002 . . . . *Cordial*, La Bottine Souriante
2003 . . . .*Unravel*, Lynn Miles (solo),
     Chicken Scratch, Zubot & Dawson (group)

Instrumental Artist(s) of the Year

1994 . . . . Ofra Harnoy
1995 . . . . André Gagnon
1996 . . . . Liona Boyd
1997 . . . . Ashley MacIsaac
1998 . . . . Leahy ▶

Best Instrumental Album

1999	*My Roots Are Showing*, Natalie MacMaster
2000	*In My Hands*, Natalie MacMaster
2001	*Free Fall*, Jesse Cook
2002	*Armando's Fire*, Oscar Lopez

Best Classical Album (solo or chamber ensemble)

1994	*Beethoven: Piano Sonatas, Op 10, No. 1-3*, Louis Lortie
1995	*Erica Goodman Plays Canadian Harp Music*, Erica Goodman
1996	*Aikan: Grande Sonate/Sonatine*, Marc-André Hamelin
1997	*Scriabin: The Complete Piano Sonatas*, Marc-André Hamelin
1998	*Marc-André Hamelin plays Franz Liszt*, Marc-André Hamelin
1999	*Bach: Well-Tempered Clavier – Book 1*, Angela Hewitt
2000	*Schumann: String Quartets*, St. Lawrence String Quartet
2001	*Bach: The Six Sonatas & Partitas For Solo Violin*, James Ehnes
2002	*Bach Arrangements*, Angela Hewitt
2003	*Allegro*, Robert Michaels

Best Classical Album (large ensemble)

1994	*Handel: Concerti Grossi, Op. 3, No 1-6*, Tafelmusik
1995	*Bach: Brandenburg Concertos Nos 1-6*, Tafelmusik
1996	*Shostakovich: Symphonies 5 & 9*, Orchestra Symphonique de Montréal
1997	*Ginastera/Villa-Lobos/Evangelista*, I Musici de Montreal
1998	*Mozart Horn Concertos*, James Sommerville, CBC Vancouver Orchestra, Mario Bernardi
1999	*Handel: Music For The Royal Fireworks*, Tafelmusik, Jeanne Lamon (Musical Director)
2000	*Respighi: La Boutique Fantasque*, Orchestra Symphonique de Montréal
2001	*Sibelius: Lemminkäinen Suite — Night Ride And Sunrise*, Toronto Symphony Orchestra
2002	*Max Bruch, Concertos 1 & 3*, James Ehnes, violin—Orchestra Symphonique de Montréal
2003	*Bruch Concertos: Vol II*, James Ehnes/Mario Bernardi/Orchestre symphonique de Montréal

Best Classical Album (vocal or choral performance)

1995	*Berlioz: Les Troyens*, Vocal Soloists, Choeur et Orchestre symphonique de Montréal
1995	*Ben Heppner Sings Richard Strauss*, Ben Heppner, Toronto Symphony Orchestra, Andrew Davis, conductor
1997	*Berlioz: La Damnation de Faust*, Choeur et Orchestre symphonique de Montreal, Charles Dutoit, Conductor
1998	*Soirée Francaise*, Michel Schade, Russel Braun, Canadian Opera Company Orchestra, Richard Bradshaw
1999	*Songs Of Travel*, Gerald Finley (baritone), Stephen Ralls (piano)
2000	*German Romantic Opera*, Ben Heppner
2001	*G.F Handel: Apollo e Dafne Silete Venti*, Karina Gauvin; Russell Braun; Les violons du Roy
2002	*Air Français*, Ben Heppner
2003	*Mozart Requiem*, Les Violons du roi

Best Classical Composition

1994	"*Among Friends*" Chan Ka Nin
1995	"*Sketches From Natal*," Malcolm Forsyth
1996	"Concerto For Violin and Orchestra," Andrew P MacDonald
1997	"*Picasso Suite*," Harry Somers
1998	"*Electra Rising*," Malcolm Forsyth
1999	"*Concerto for Wind Orchestra*," Colin McPhee
2000	"*Shattered Night, Shivering Stars*, "Alexina Louie
2001	" *From The Diary of Anne Frank*," Oskar Morawetz
2002	"*Par-çi, par la*," Chan Ka Nin
2003	"Requiem for a Charred Skull," Bramwell Tovey

Best Children's Album

1994	*Tchaikovsky Discovers America*, Susan Hammond/Classical Kids
1995	*Bananaphone*, Raffi
1996	*Celery Stalks at Midnight*, Al Simmons
1997	*Songs From the Treehouse*, Martha Johnson
1998	*Livin' in a Shoe*, Judy & David
1999	*Mozart's Magnificent Voyage*, Susan Hammond's Classical Kids
2000	*Skinnamarink TV*, Sharon, Lois and Bram
2001	*Sing & Dance*, Jack Grunsky
2002	*A Classical Kids Christmas*, Susan Hammond
2003	*Sing with Fred*, Fred Penner

Producer of the Year

1994	Steve MacKinnon/Marc Jordan (Greg Penny, co-producer)
1995	Robbie Robertson
1996	Michael-Phillip Wojewoda
1997	Garth Richardson
1998	Pierre Marchand
1999	Colin James (co-producer, Joe Hardy)
2000	Tal Bachman and Bob Rock
2001	Gerald Eaton, Brian West and Nelly Furtado
2002	Daniel Lanois (co-producer Brian Eno), "Beautiful Day," "Elevation," U2
2003	Alannis Morrissette, "Hands Clean," "So Unsexy"

Best Video

1994	"*I Would Die For You*" (Jann Arden), Jeth Weinrich
1995	"*Tunnel of Trees*" (Gogh Van Go), Lyne Charlebois
1996	"*Good Mother*" (Jann Arden), Jeth Weinrich
1997	"*Burned Out Car*" (Junkhouse), Jeth Weinrich
1998	"*Gasoline*" (Moist), Javier Aguilera
1999	"*Forestfire*" (David Usher), Javier Aguilera
2000	"*So Pure,*" Alanis Morrissette
2001	"Alive" (Edwin), Rob Heydon
2002	"Jealous of Your Cigarette" (Hawksley Workman), Sean Michael Turrell
2003	Weapon, Ante Kovac, Matthew Good

Best Music of Aboriginal Canada Recording

1995	Susan Aglukark
1996	Jerry Alfred & The Medicine Beat
1997	Buffy Ste. Marie
2000	*Falling Down*, Chester Knight & The Wind
2001	*Nipaiamianan*, Florent Vollant
2002	*On and On*, Eagle & Hawk
2003	*Lovesick Blues*, Derek Miller

Source: *Canadian Academy of Recording Arts & Sciences*

The East Coast Music Awards, 2003

The East Coast Music Awards were established in 1989 to honor outstanding contributions to the Canadian music industry by artists performing, recording, or rooted in Atlantic Canada, and to celebrate that region's distinct musical heritage in English and in French. The 14th annual ECMAs were presented February 20, 2003, in Halifax, NS.

Male Artist of the Year . . . . Lennie Gallant
Female Artist of the Year . . . . Natalie MacMaster
Group of the Year . . . . Great Big Sea
Bluegrass Artist/Group of the Year . . . . Ray Legere
Songwriter of the Year . . . . Jimmy Rankin,
"Midnight Angel"
Single of the Year . . . . "Here," Crush
Video of the Year . . . . "Sea of No Cares," Great Big Sea
Album of the Year . . . . . *Sea of No Cares*, Great Big Sea
New Artist of the Year. . . . . The Cottars
Entertainer of the Year . . . . Great Big Sea
Country Artist/Group of the Year . . . . Julian Austin
Pop Artist/Group of the Year . . . . Great Big Sea
Rock Artist/Group of the Year . . . . Human
Instrumental Artist/Group of the Year . . . . . J.P. Cormier
Alternative Artist/Group of the Year . . . . . Nathan Wiley

Jazz Artist/Group of the Year . . . . Harvey Millar
Blues Artist/Group of the Year . . . . Charlie A'Court
Gospel Artist/Group of the Year . . . . The LaPointes
Urban Recording of the Year . . . . *Square*, Buck 65
Classical Recording of the Year . . . . *Denise Djokic*,
Denise Djokic
Roots/Traditional Solo Artist of the Year. . . . Terry Kelly
Roots/Traditional Group of the Year . . . . Barachois
Francophone Recording of the Year . . . *Levent bohème*,
Lennie Gallant
African-Canadian Recording of the Year. . *Nice to Wear*
Scott Parsons
Aboriginal Recording of the Year . . . . . *Way Back Then*,
The Flummies
Video of the Year . . . . "Sea of No Cares," Great Big Sea

The Grammy Awards, 1998–2002

Grammy winners are selected annually by the 6,000 voting members of The Recording Academy, based on artistic and/or technical excellence.

The titles for song of the year are followed by the names of the songwriters. The 2002 Grammy winners were announced Feb. 23, 2003.

Best Record

1998 . . . . "My Heart Will Go On," Céline Dion
1999 . . . . . . "Smooth," Santana featuring Rob Thomas
2000 . . . . "Beautiful Day," U2
2001 . . . . "Walk On," U2
2002 . . . . "Don't Know Why," Norah Jones

Best Album

1998 . . . . . *The Miseducation of Lauryn Hill*, Lauryn Hill
1999 . . . . *Supernatural*, Santana
2000 . . . . *Two Against Nature*, Steely Dan
2001 . . . . *O Brother, Where Art Thou?* (soundtrack),
Various Artists
2002 . . . . *Come Away With Me*, Norah Jones

Best Song

1998 "My Heart Will Go On," James Harper, Will Jennings
1999 . "Smooth," Itaal Shur & Rob Thomas, songwriters
2000 . . . . "Beautiful Day," U2
2001 . . . . "Fallin,'" Alicia Keys
2002 . . . . "Don't Know Why," Jesse Harris

Best Male Pop Vocal

1998 . . . . "My Father's Eyes," Eric Clapton
1999 . . . . "Brand New Day," Sting
2000 . . . . "Again," Lenny Kravitz
2001 . . "Don't Let Me Be Lonely Tonight," James Taylor
2002 . . . . "Your Body Is a Wonderland," John Mayer

Best Female Pop Vocal

1998 . . . . "My Heart Will Go On," Céline Dion

1999 . . . . . "I Will Remember You," Sarah McLachlan
2000 . . . . "There Goes the Neighborhood," Sheryl Crow
2001 . . . . "I'm Like a Bird," Nelly Furtado
2002 . . . . "Don't Know Why," Norah Jones

Best Rap Album

1998 . . . . *Vol.2 Hard Knock Life*, Jay-Z
1999 . . . . *The Slim Shady LP*, Eminem
2000 . . . . *The Marshall Mathers LP*, Eminem
2001 . . . . *Stankonia*, Outkast
2002 . . . . *The Eminem Show*, Eminem

Best Male Country Vocal Performance

1998 . . . . "If You Ever Had Forever In Mind," Vince Gill
1999 . . . . "Choice," George Jones
2000 . . . . "Solitary Man," Johnny Cash
2001 . . . . "O Death," Ralph Stanley
2002 . . . . "Give My Love to Rose," Johnny Cash

Best Female Country Vocal Performance

1998 . . . . "You're Still The One," Shania Twain
1999 . . . . "Man! I Feel Like A Woman!" Shania Twain
2000 . . . . "Breathe," Faith Hill
2001 . . . . "Shine," Dolly Parton
2002 . . . . "Cry," Faith Hill

Best Jazz Vocal Performance

1998 . . . . "I Remember Miles," Shirley Horn
1999 . . . . "When I Look In Your Eyes," Diana Krall
2000 "In the Moment—Live in Concert," Dianne Reeves
2001 . . . . *The Calling*, Dianne Reeves ▶

▶ **Best Instrumental Soloist(s) Performance**
(with Orchestra)

1998 . "Penderecki: Violin Con. No. 2 Metamorphosen,"
Anne-Sophie Mutter & Krzysztof Penderecki
1999 "Prokofiev: Piano Concertos. Nos. 1 & 3; Bartók:
Piano Con. No. 3," Martha Argerich & the Montreal
Symphony Orchestra
2000 . . . . "Maw: Violin Concerto,"
Joshua Bell & the London Philharmonic Orchestra
2001 . . "Strauss Wind Concertos (Horn Concerto; Obo
Concerto, Etc.)," Daniel Barenboim
2002. "Brahms/Stravinsky Violin Concertos," Hilary Hahn

Best New Artist

1998 . . . . Lauryn Hill
1999 . . . . Christina Aguilera
2000 . . . . Shelby Lynne
2001 . . . . Alicia Keys
2002 . . . . Norah Jones

Source: *National Academy of Recording Arts & Sciences*

The ADISQ ("Félix") Awards, 2002

The Felix Awards have been presented annually since 1978 by ADISQ, the umbrella group representing the Québec music, video, and performance industry, to acknowledge achievement in Canada's French language music and performance scene. The 24th awards were held at ADISQ's annual gala, October 26, 2002.

Popular Song of the Year . . . ."*Je n'ai que mon âme,*"
Natasha St.-Pier
Group of the Year . . . . .Les Respectables
Best Female Vocalist . . . . .Isabelle Boulay
Best Male Vocalist . . . . .Garou
Album of the Year (pop-rock) . . . .*Rêver Mieux,*
Daniel Bélanger
Album of the Year (popular) . . . .*Rendez-vous,*
Sylvain Cossette
Album of the Year (rock) . . . .*Adrénaline,* Eric Lapointe
Album of the Year (contemporary folk) .*Doux sauvage,*
Robert Charlebois
Album of the Year (hip-hop) . . .*Influences,* Dubmatique
Album of the Year (jazz) *Versant Jazz-Live au Lion d'Or,*
Sylvain Lelièvre
Bestselling Album . . . . .*Rêver Mieux,* Daniel Bélanger
Album of the Year (electronic/techno) *Jérôme Minière,*
Jérôme·Minière présente Herri Kopter
Best Quebec Artist In a Language Other Than French .
Céline Dion, *Productions Feeling*
Best Artist from "la francophonie" . .Charles Aznavour

Album of the Year (traditional) . . . .*Cordial,*
La Bottine Souriante
Best World Music Artist (Québecois) . . . .*Beat*
Writer/Composer of the Year . . . . .Pierre Flynn
Album of the Year (country) . . . .
Chansons du patrimoine-Volume 1, Georges Hamel
Album of the Year (classical, large ensemble) *Concert*
français, James Ehnes et l'Orchestre
symphonique de Québec
Album of the Year (classical, soloist/small ensemble),
Rachmaninov & Moussorgsky—Moments musicaux—
Les tableaux d'une exposition, Alain Lefèvre
Video of the Year . . . .*Le poète des temps gris,*
Daniel Boucher
Album of the Year (children's) . . . .*Ma p'tite pouponne,*
Shilvi
Album of the Year (instrumental) . . . .*Histoires rêvées,*
André Gagnon
Album of the Year (humour) . . . .*Grandes Gueules*
Le Disque, Grandes Gueules, Réal Béland
Album of the Year (original soundtrack) . .*Les Boys III*
Various Artists

www.musiccentre.ca: The Canadian Music Centre On-line

*W**ith offices in Toronto, Montreal, Vancouver, Calgary and Sackville, the Canadian Music Centre promotes the works of its Associate Composers, and encourages the performance and appreciation of Canadian music, making it available to the public through its sales operations and through lending libraries at each of its locations. These services have now been enhanced by on-line services available on the CMC web site. An on-line catalogue search gives visitors access to the centre's database of nearly 600 composers' works, including score samples and audio clips. Scores may be borrowed free of charge. A selection of published and unpublished music is available for purchase. The site's "Buy a Recording" area offers access to the most complete commercial CD catalogue in the world of recorded music by Canadian composers, listing over 700 independent titles available for purchase. A directory of the centre's Associate Composers offers biographical information and a list of their works available at the CMC. The CMC site also includes an interactive introduction to the compositional trends of the 20th century of Canadian composers entitled Sound Progression.*

The Canadian Academy of Recording Arts and Sciences (CARAS)

This organization was originally created to administer and promote the Juno Awards. It has since expanded its mandate to link members of the Canadian music community and members of the public interested in the Canadian music and recording industry. The Junos themselves remain the centrepiece, to recognize (and reward) outstanding achievement in recorded music. The broadcast of the Junos brings singers, musicians, songwriters, producers and other creative talent together and to the attention of both a national audience and foreign markets.

Beginning with jazz and big band legends Oscar Peterson and Guy Lombardo in 1978, CARAS has inducted a figure from the Canadian music scene into the Canadian Music Hall of Fame each year. A database of these inductees is maintained on the Juno awards web site, www. juno-awards.ca. Just click the Juno History button on the Junos' home page. CARAS is in the process of expanding this database to provide complete biographical information on each inductee. The Junos' web site offers complete contact information on CARAS and information on the Junos nomination process.

Canadian Music Hall of Fame

The Canadian Academy of Recording Arts and Sciences instituted a Hall of Fame Award in 1978 to honour Canadians who have contributed to the greater international recognition of Canadian artists and music.

■ Winners

1978	Guy Lombardo	1986	Gordon Lightfoot			John Kay
	Oscar Peterson	1987	The Guess Who			Zal Yanovsky
1979	Hank Snow	1989	The Band	1997		Lenny Breau
1980	Paul Anka	1990	Maureen Forrester			Gil Evans
1981	Joni Mitchell	1991	Leonard Cohen			Maynard Ferguson
1982	Neil Young	1992	Ian & Sylvia			Moe Kauffman
1983	Glenn Gould	1993	Anne Murray			Rob McConnell
1984	The Crewcuts	1994	Rush	1998		David Foster
	The Diamonds	1995	Buffy Sainte-Marie	1999		Luc Plamondon
	The Four Lads	1996	David Clayton-Thomas	2000		Bruce Fairbairn
1985	Wilf Carter		Denny Doherty	2001		Bruce Cockburn
			Domenic Troiano	2002		Daniel Lanois

2002 INDUCTEE

■ Tom Cochrane

Tom Cochrane was born in Lynn Lake, Manitoba, the son of a bush pilot. At age 11, he got his first guitar and, by the early 1970s, he was performing folk-oriented material in coffeehouses in Yorkville. In 1973, a single on Daffodil Records, "You're Driving Me Crazy," marked his recording debut, followed by an album, *Hang On To Your Resistance*. Toronto band Red Rider took Cochrane on as lead singer/songwriter and, from 1980 to 1984, the band released four acclaimed studio albums that included the songs "Lunatic Fringe" and "White Hot." "Lunatic Fringe" went on to become one of the most played songs in history on American Rock radio. The group became Tom Cochrane & Red Rider in 1986. The album of that name produced major hits in "Boy Inside the Man" and "Untouchable One." It was followed by the hit albums "The Symphony Sessions" and 1988's *Victory Day*, an album that included one of Tom's signature songs the haunting Canadian tune "Big League." A Juno Award (one of many) as Songwriter of the Year in 1989 confirmed the respect Tom now enjoyed within the industry. Cochrane's 1991 solo album, *Mad Mad World*, became one of the highest-selling Canadian records of all time, scoring diamond status (for a million sales) here. Thanks to the smash hit single "Life Is A Highway," the album notched two million in international sales.

Source: *Canadian Academy of Recording Arts and Sciences* www.juno-awards.ca/caras/

Canadian Country Music Awards, 2003

Fans' Choice Award	Terri Clark
Female Artist of the Year	Shania Twain
Male Artist of the Year	Aaron Lines
Single of the Year	"I Just Wanna' Be Mad," Terri Clark
Album of the Year	*Up!*, Shania Twain
Duo or Group of the Year	Emerson Drive
Music Video of the Year	"I'm Gonna' Getcha' Good," Shania Twain
Song of the Year	"Rocket Girl," Jason McCoy, Denny Carr
Roots Artist or Group of the Year	Sean Hogan
Rising Star	Aaron Lines

Source: *Canadian Country Music Awards*

Top 50 Albums in Canada, 2002

Artist, Title

1) Shania Twain, *Up!*
2) Eminem, *The Eminem Show*
3) Céline Dion, *A New Day Has Come*
4) Avril Lavigne, *Let Go*
5) Elvis Presley, *Elvis: 30 Number 1 Hits*
6) Shakira, *Laundry Service*
7) Soundtrack, *8 Mile*
8) Nickelback, *Silver Side Up*
9) Nelly, *Nellyville*
10) Pink, *M!SSUNDAZTOOD*
11) Diana Krall, *The Look of Love*
12) Josh Groban, *Josh Groban*
13) Enrique Iglesias, *Escape*
14) Various Artists, *Big Shiny Tunes 7*
15) Rolling Stones, *Forty Licks*
16) Various Artists, *Now! 7*
17) Norah Jones, *Come Away With Me*
18) Various Artists, *MuchDance 2003/DansePlus*
19) Soundtrack, *O Brother, Where Art Thou?*
20) Dixie Chicks, *Home*
21) Various Artists, *Big Shiny Tunes 6*
22) Diana Krall, *Live in Paris*
23) Our Lady Peace, *Gravity*
24) Kylie Minogue, *Fever*
25) Creed, *Weathered*

Artist, Title

26) Ja Rule, *Pain Is Love*
27) Linkin Park, *Hybrid Theory*
28) Soundtrack, *Shrek*
29) U2, *Best of 1990-2000 & B-Sides*
30) Alan Jackson, *Drive*
31) Ashanti, *Ashanti*
32) Various Artists, *MuchDance 2002*
33) Red Hot Chili Peppers, *By The Way*
34) Soundtrack, *Spiderman*
35) Coldplay, *Rush of Blood to the Head*
36) Santana, *Shaman*
37) Faith Hill, *Cry*
38) Various Artists, *Mixmania*
39) Remy Shand, *The Way I Feel*
40) Sheryl Crow, *C'mon C'mon*
41) Alicia Keys, *Songs In a Minor*
42) Alanis Morissette, *Under Rug Swept*
43) No Doubt, *Rock Steady*
44) Various Artists, *Women & Songs 5*
45) Christina Aguilera, *Stripped*
46) Enya, *A Day Without Rain*
47) Britney Spears, *Britney*
48) Soundtrack, *I Am Sam*
49) Rod Stewart, *Great American Song Book*
50) Jennifer Lopez, *This Is Me ... Then*

Source: *Chart Information Supplied By Soundscan. Copyright (C) 2002 By Soundscan, Inc. All Rights Reserved.* Nielsen SoundScan
Note: Canadian artists set in bold type.

Top 50 Singles in Canada, 2002

Artist, Title	Artist, Title
1) Kelly Clarkson, *"Moment Like This/Before You"*	26) U2, *"Electrical Storm"* (DVD Single)
2) Madonna, *"Die Another Day"*	**27) Alanis Morrissette, "Hands Clean"**
3) U2, *"Electrical Storm" #1 & #2*	28) Radio Head, *"My Iron Lung"* (Import)
4) Elvis vs. JXL, *"A Little Less Conversation"*	**29) Pink, "Just Like a Pill"**
5) Nelly, *"Hot In Here"*	30) Nine Inch Nails, *"Closer"*
6) Shania Twain, "I'm Gonna' Getcha' Good"	31) Oasis, *"Stop Crying Your Heart Out"*
7) Las Ketchup, "Ketchup Song (Hey Hay)"	32) Red Hot Chili Peppers, *"By the Way"*
8) Chad Kroeger, featuring Josey S, *"Hero"*	**33) George Harrison, "My Sweet Lord"**
9) Jennifer Lopez, *"Jenny From The Block"*	34) Dixie Chicks, *"Landslide"*
10) Shaggy, *"Hey Sexy Lady"*	35) IIO, *"Rapture"*
11) Boomtang, "Movin' On"	36) Keith Urban, *"Somebody Like You"*
12) Nelly, *"Dilemma"*	**37) P Diddy, "I Need A Girl" I & II**
13) Faith Hill, *"Cry"*	38) U2, *"Stuck In A Moment"*
14) Paul Brandt, "Canadian Man"	39) Céline Dion, *"A New Day Has Come"*
15) Christina Aguilera, *"Dirrty"*	40) Tori Amos, *"Sort of Fairyville"*
16) Oasis, *"Hindu Times"*	41) Blink 182, *"I Won't Be Home For Christmas"*
17) Shawn Desman, *"Get Ready"*	**42) Tea Party, "Soul Breaking"**
18) N'SYNC, *"Girlfriend"*	43) Portishead, *"Glory Times"*
19) Coldplay, *"In My Place"*	**44) Snow, "Legal"**
20) Pearl Jam, *"I Am Mine"*	45) Sean Paul, *"Gimme' the Light"*
21) Enya, *"Only Time"*	46) Craig David, *"What's Your Flava"*
22) Mariah Carey, *"Through the Rain"*	47) Oasis, *"Little By Little"*
23) Dirty Vegas, *"Days Go By"*	48) Laura Pausini, *"Surrender"*
24) Bon Jovi, "Everyday"	**49) Matthew Good Band, "Raygun"**
25) Faith Hill, *"There You'll Be"*	**50) Hampton The Hampster, "Hampsterdance Song"**

Source: *Chart Information Supplied By Soundscan. Copyright (C) 2000 By Soundscan, Inc. All Rights Reserved.* Ｎ Nielsen SoundScan
Note: Canadian artists set in bold type.

MTV Video Music Awards, 2003

Best Video of the Year	"Work It," Missy "Misdemeanor" Elliott
Best Rock Video	"Somewhere I Belong," Linkin Park
Best R&B Vide	"Crazy In Love," Beyonce (f/Jay-Z)
Best Hip Hop Video	"Work It," Missy "Misdemeanor" Elliott
Best Rap Video	"In Da Club," 50 Cent
Best Direction	"The Scientist," Coldplay
Best Female Video	"Crazy In Love," Beyonce (f/Jay-Z)
Best Pop Video	"Cry Me A River," Justin Timberlake
Best Video from a Film	"Lose Yourself," Eminem
Best New Artist	"In Da Club," 50 Cent
Best Group Video	"The Scientist," Coldplay
Best Male Video	"Cry Me A River," Justin Timberlake
Best Dance Video	"Rock Your Body," Justin Timberlake
Best Breakthrough Video	"The Scientist," Coldplay
Best Art Direction	"There There," Radiohead
Special Effects	"Go With The Flow," Queens of the Stone Age
Best Editing	"Seven Nation Army," The White Stripes
Best Choreography	"Crazy In Love," Beyonce (f/Jay-Z)
Best Cinematography	"Hurt," Johnny Cash

Source: *MTV: Music Television*

MuchMusic Video Awards, 2003

Favourite International Group. . . . . Good Charlotte, "The Anthem"
Favourite International Artist . . . . Eminem, "Lose Yourself"
Favourite Canadian Group . . . . **Simple Plan, "I'd Do Anything"**
Favourite Canadian Artist . . . . **Avril Lavigne, "Sk8er Boi"**
Best International Video By A Canadian . . . . **Avril Lavigne, "Sk8er Boi"**
Best Video . . . . **Our Lady Peace, "Innocent"**
Best Pop Video. . . . . Shawn Desman, "Get Ready"
MuchLOUD Best Rock Video. . . . . Treble Charger, "Hundred Million"
Best French Video . . . . **Daniel Bélanger, "dans un spoutnik"**
MuchVIBE Best Rap Video . . . . **Swollen Members, Nelly Furtado, "Breathe"**
Best Director. . . . . Treble Charger, "Hundred Million"
Best Post-Production . . . . Danko Jones, "Lovercall"
Best Cinematography . . . . **Our Lady Peace, "Innocent"**
Best Independent Video . . . . **Not By Choice, "Now That You Are Leaving"**
MuchMoreMusic Award . . . . **Shania Twain, "Up!"**
Best International Video Artist . . . . Sean Paul, "Gimme the Light"
Best International Video Group. . . . . The White Stripes, "Seven Nation Army"
Source: *MuchMusic Network*

Recording Industry Sales, 2002–2003[1]

These two charts examine the amount—and dollar value—of music purchased in a variety of forms between June 30–May 31, for 2002 and 2003. Sales information is supplied by members of the Canadian Recording Industry Association. Units and dollar amounts are expressed in the thousands.

'000s Units Shipped	2003	2002	% change
VHS	240	409	−41%
DVDs	1076	527	104%
Total Music Video	*1316*	*936*	*41%*
Total Singles	*421*	*203*	*107%*
Cassette	138	367	−62%
CD	18 449	19 292	−4%
Total Albums	*18 587*	*19 659*	*−5%*
Grand Total	**20 324**	**20 798**	**−2%**

Net Value of Sales ($000s)	2003	2002	% change
VHS	1776	3563	−50%
DVD	18 183	9511	91%
Total Music Videos	*19 959*	*13 074*	*53%*
Total Singles	*1373*	*653*	*110%*
Cassette	403	1659	−76%
CD	211 927	223 954	−5%
Total Albums	*225*	*613*	*−6%*
Grand Total	**$233,662**	**$239 340**	**−2%**

Note: The categories of DCC/Mini Disc and Cassette Single have been eliminated from the report due to negligible sales.

Source: *Canadian Recording Industry Association*   (1) For the period ending June 30.

The Rock and Roll Hall of Fame

The Rock and Roll Hall of Fame was established in 1984. The Rock and Roll Hall of Fame and Museum opened in September 1995 in Cleveland, Ohio.

■ **ARTISTS (Year Elected)**

Aerosmith (2001)
The Allman Brothers Band (1995)
The Animals (1994)
LaVern Baker (1991)
Hank Ballard (1990)
The Band (1994)
The Beach Boys (1988)
The Beatles (1988)
The Bee Gees (1997)
Chuck Berry (1986)

Bobby "Blue" Bland (1992)
Booker T. & The MG's (1992)
David Bowie (1996)
James Brown (1986)
Ruth Brown (1993)
Buffalo Springfield (1997)
Solomon Burke (2001)
The Byrds (1991)
David Byrne (2002)
Johnny Cash (1992)
Ray Charles (1986)

Eric Clapton (2000)
The Clash (2003)
The Coasters (1987)
Eddie Cochran (1987)
Sam Cooke (1986)
Elvis Costello and the Attractions (2003)
Cream (1993)
Creedence Clearwater Revival (1993)
Crosby, Stills and Nash (1997)
Bobby Darin (1990)
Bo Diddley (1987)

▶

Dion (1989)
Fats Domino (1986)
The Doors (1993)
The Drifters (1988)
Bob Dylan (1988)
The Eagles (1998)
Earth, Wind and Fire (2000)
Duane Eddy (1994)
The Everly Brothers (1986)
The Flamingos (2001)
Fleetwood Mac (1998)
The Four Seasons (1990)
The Four Tops (1990)
Aretha Franklin (1987)
Marvin Gaye (1987)
The Grateful Dead (1994)
Al Green (1995)
Bill Haley (1987)
Isaac Hayes (2002)
Buddy Holly (1986)
The Jimi Hendrix Experience (1992)
John Lee Hooker (1991)
The Impressions (1991)
The Isley Brothers (1992)
Michael Jackson (2001)
Etta James (1993)
Jefferson Airplane (1996)
Billy Joel (1999)
Elton John (1994)
Janis Joplin (1995)
B.B. King (1987)
The Jackson Five (1997)
The Kinks (1990)
Gladys Knight and the Pips (1996)
Led Zeppelin (1995)
Lloyd Price (1998)
Brenda Lee (2002)
John Lennon (1994)
Jerry Lee Lewis (1986)
Little Richard (1986)
Little Willie John (1996)
The Lovin' Spoonful (2000)
Frankie Lyman and the Teenagers
  (1993)
The Mamas and the Papas (1998)
Bob Marley (1994)
Martha and the Vandellas (1995)
Curtis Mayfield (1999)
Paul McCartney (1999)
Joni Mitchell (1997)
Clyde McPhatter (1987)
The Moonglows (2000)
Van Morrison (1993)
Ricky Nelson (1987)

Roy Orbison (1987)
Parliament Funkadelic (1997)
Carl Perkins (1987)
Tom Petty (2002)
Wilson Pickett (1991)
Pink Floyd (1996)
Gene Pitney (2002)
The Platters (1990)
Elvis Presley (1986)
Queen (2001)
Bonnie Raitt (2000)
Dee Dee Ramone (2002)
Otis Redding (1989)
Jimmy Reed (1991)
The Righteous Brothers (2003)
Smokey Robinson (1987)
The Rolling Stones (1989)
Sam & Dave (1992)
Santana (1998)
Del Shannon (1999)
The Shirelles (1996)
Paul Simon (2001)
Simon and Garfunkel (1990)
Sly and the Family Stone (1993)
Dusty Springfield (1999)
Bruce Springsteen (1999)
Steely Dan (2001)
Rod Stewart (1994)
The Supremes (1988)
The Staple Singers (1999)
James Taylor (2000)
The Temptations (1989)
Ike and Tina Turner (1991)
Big Joe Turner (1987)
Ritchie Valens (2001)
Gene Vincent (1998)
The Velvet Underground (1996)
Muddy Waters (1987)
The Who (1990)
Jackie Wilson (1987)
Stevie Wonder (1989)
The Yardbirds (1992)
The Young Rascals (1997)
Neil Young (1995)
Frank Zappa (1995)

■ NON-PERFORMERS

Paul Ackerman (1995)
Dave Bartholomew (1991)
Ralph Bass (1991)
Chris Blackwell (2001)
Leonard Chess (1987)
Dick Clark (1993)
Clive Davis (2000)

Tom Donahue (1996)
Lamont Dozier, Brian Holland
  & Eddie Holland (1990)
Ahmet Ertegun (1987)
Leo Fender (1992)
Alan Freed (1986)
Milt Gabler (1993)
Gerry Goffin & Carole King (1990)
Berry Gordy, Jr. (1988)
Bill Graham (1992)
Jerry Leiber & Mike Stoller (1987)
George Martin (1999)
Syd Nathan (1997)
Johnny Otis (1994)
Sam Phillips (1986)
Doc Pomus (1992)
Phil Spector (1989)
Allen Toussaint (1998)
Jerry Wexler (1987)

■ LIFETIME ACHIEVEMENT AWARDS

Willie Dixon (1994)
Nesuhi Ertegun (1991)
John Hammond (1986)

■ EARLY INFLUENCES

Louis Armstrong (1990)
Charles Brown (1999)
Charlie Christian (1990)
Nat "King" Cole (2000)
Willie Dixon (1994)
Woody Guthrie (1988)
Billie Holiday (2000)
Howlin' Wolf (1991)
The Ink Spots (1989)
Mahalia Jackson (1997)
Elmore James (1992)
Robert Johnson (1986)
Louis Jordan (1987)
Lead Belly (1988)
Bill Monroe (1997)
Jelly Roll Morton (1998)
The Orioles (1995)
Les Paul (1988)
Professor Longhair (1992)
Ma Rainey (1990)
Jimmie Rodgers (1986)
Pete Seeger (1996)
Bessie Smith (1989)
The Soul Stirrers (1989)
T-Bone Walker (1987)
Dinah Washington (1993)
Hank Williams (1987)
Bob Wills & His Texas Playboys (1999)
Jimmy Yancey (1986)

FOCUS ON ...

SarsStock: An Emotional Rescue for Toronto

On July 23, 2003, Toronto played host to the largest ticketed, single-day event in rock music history. An estimated 490,000 people attended the Molson Canadian Rocks for Toronto concert. Headlined by "the world's greatest rock'n'roll band," The Rolling Stones, the concert was held at the city's Downsview Park, a former air force base which, the previous year, had been the setting for the Papal Mass on World Youth Day. The purpose of the event was to raise funds for those affected by outbreaks of Severe Acute Respiratory Syndrome in Toronto earlier in the year, and to send a signal to the world that Canada's largest city was fully recovered and open for business.

The 11-hour concert kicked off at 1:00 pm EST with a series of short sets from Montreal-born Sam Roberts, Ottawa's Kathleen Edwards, Quebec's La Chicane, Tea Party from Windsor, Ontario, Montreal's Sass Jordan (who appeared with Toronto guitarist Jeff Healey), and Toronto's Blue Rodeo. From the US came The Flaming Lips, r'n'b greats, The Isley Brothers and (incongruously to many in the crowd) former 'NSYNC star Justin Timberlake. Longer evening sets were provided by classic Canadian bands The Guess Who and Rush, followed by Australian heavy metal stars AC/DC and finally The Rolling Stones. The Stones played for an hour and forty minutes, performing songs including "Start Me Up," "Brown Sugar," "Sympathy for the Devil," and "You Can't Always Get What You Want."

Hosted by actors Dan Aykroyd and Jim Belushi, the concert was the brainchild of Toronto MP Dennis Mills and Senator Jerry Grafstein. It came together with help from local, provincial and federal governments, sponsorship from Molson's breweries and the assistance of Toronto concert promoter and Rolling Stones tour manager Michael Cohl.

The Rolling Stones played for a minimal fee and donated merchandising revenue from the concert to relief for the families of SARS victims and those who have suffered unemployment due to lost revenues in the city's hospitality industry.

"We've got to remember the ones who took the hit," said guitarist Keith Richards, rock's most famous Soul Survivor, of those who had fallen to SARS. "All you can do is say goodbye and give them a song."

Music Festivals in Canada

Classical music festivals and competitions across Canada have played an essential role in the development of the country's musical talent since the first local music festival was organized in Edmonton in 1908. By 1953, every province had at least one festival in operation. The Federation of Canadian Music Festivals was founded in 1949 to coordinate their activities and, in Canada's centennial year (1967), the first all-Canadian music competition was held in Saint John, N.B.

Today, the Federation reports a total of 230 festivals occurring in Canada each year. These festivals attract some 140,000 entries involving the participation of as many as half a million people. Attendance at local festivals averages 450,000, while provincial festivals average audiences of 6,000 people. The festivals are important to young musicians as much for the prestige they bestow on participants as for the prizes and scholarships offered to help with their studies. The Federation is made up of provincial associations that are responsible for supporting local festivals and organizing festivals to determine the provincial champions at various levels. These champions represent their home province at the National Music Festival. In 1973, the national competition was instituted on an annual basis. Since 1981, the national festival has been held in a different province each year.

Major Classical and New Music Festivals

In addition to the network of amateur music festivals sponsored by the Federation of Canadian Music Festivals, a number of other amateur music festivals and professional festivals take place across Canada each year.

The Banff International String Quartet Competition
Banff, Alberta, Aug. 31, 2003–Sept. 5, 2004. This triennial competition was created in 1983 to mark the 50th anniversary of the Banff Centre for the Arts. The Banff International String Quartet Competition (BISQC) has since become recognized as one of the world's leading international music competitions. (403) 762-6100

The Winnipeg Symphony Orchestra New Music Festival
Winnipeg, Manitoba, Jan. 24–30, 2004. First presented in January 1992, the Festival has drawn international participation, earned critical acclaim, and enjoyed a growing audience. It is now considered one of Canada's most important forums for new work. (204) 949-3999

The Ottawa International Chamber Music Festival
Ottawa, July–Aug. The Ottawa Chamber Music Society produces a two-week summer programme of chamber music featuring the highest calibre of local, national and international artists. Concerts take place in downtown Ottawa, mostly in churches. (613) 234-8008 www.chamberfest.com

Festival of the Sound
Parry Sound, Ont. July–Aug. Talks by renowned scholars, open Rehearsals, and concerts reflecting a wide variety of classical genres make this a noted Ontario festival on the shores of Georgian Bay. (705) 746-2410 www.festivalofthesound.on.ca

The Saskatoon Symphony Festival of New Music
Saskatoon, Saskatchewan, Apr. Events include small chamber groups, a jazz brunch, concerts by the Saskatchewan Chamber Orchestra, and an after-hours club. Also includes world premieres of new works such as *Batoche,* a chamber opera based on the life of Louis Riel, by composer Bill Pura. The Festival of New Music puts the Prairies on the cutting edge of creative music making. (306) 665-6414

Festival international de Lanaudière
Joliette, Qué., June–Aug. This six-week event is one of the largest and longest classical music festivals in Canada. Some 30 concerts are presented by as many as 1,300 musicians for up to 48,000 visitors. Most concerts for soloists and smaller ensembles are held in the many churches of the Joliette area. Larger groups such as the Montreal Symphony Orchestra perform at the Lanaudière Amphitheatre. The festival is renowned for its emphasis on new work and young artists. 1-800-245-7636 www.lanaudiere.org

MusicFest Canada
Montreal, Que., May 24–29. This six-day annual national event brings together more than 11,000 of Canada's finest young musicians who perform for recognition as the country's foremost musical ensembles. Participants range in age from 12 to 24 years and are drawn from the elementary, high school, college and university levels. (403) 717-1766 www.musicfest.ca

MOVIES

Canada has been a world leader in documentary filmmaking, producing renowned artists such as Donald Brittain and Harry Rasky primarily through the National Film Board of Canada. The film board has also helped bring Canada to prominence as a producer of animation, and short subjects. Canadians have made an enormous contribution to the Hollywood feature film industry, from film mogul Louis B. Mayer to acclaimed director Norman Jewison to stars including Mary Pickford, Dan Aykroyd, Michael J. Fox, John Candy and Keanu Reeves. The Department of Canadian Heritage estimates that 20 percent of those employed in the Hollywood film industry are Canadian and that about 60 percent of the software used in U.S. film productions was developed by Canadians. Made-in-Canada features by filmmakers such as Denys Arcand, David Cronenberg, Atom Egoyan and Patricia Rozema have enjoyed considerable critical and "art house" success around the world. In the 1990s, Canadian features twice won the Special Grand Jury Prize at the Cannes Film Festival. However, with US distribution houses controlling 85 percent of the theatrical market, only one in twenty features gaining commercial release in Canada is produced in Canada.

Toronto International Film Festival, 2003

The 28th annual festival was held September 4 to 13, 2003, showing 339 films from 55 countries. This is widely regarded as North America's major film festival.

People's Choice Award . . . . *Zatoichi*, Takeshi Kitano (Japan)

Discovery Award . . . . *Rhinoceros Eyes*, **Aaron Woodley** (USA)

Fipresci Award . . . . *November*, Achero Mañas (Spain)

Best Canadian First Feature . . . . **Love, Sex and Eating the Bones, Sudz Sutherland**

Best Canadian Feature Film . . . . **Les Invasions barbares, Denys Arcand**

Best Canadian Short Film . . . . **Aspiration, Constant Mentzas**

Source: *Toronto International Film Festival*

Montreal World Film Festival, 2003

The 27th annual Festival des Films du Monde was held from August 27 to Sept 7, 2003.

Grand Prix of the Americas . . . . *The Cordon*, Goran Markovic (Serbia and Montenegro)

Special Grand Prix of the Jury . . . . **Gaz Bar Blues, Louis Bélanger (Canada)**

Best Director . . . . Antonio Mercero, *4th Floor* (Spain)

Best Actress . . . . Marima Glazer, *The Little Polish* (Argentina/Spain)

Best Actor . . . . Silvio Orlando, *The Soul's Haven* (Italy)

Best Screenplay . . . . Dusan Kovacevic, *The Professional* (Serbia and Montenegro)

Best Short Film . . . . *Life and Death of a Boring Moment*, Patrick Bossard (France)

Jury Prize (Short Film) . . . . *In Bed With My Books*, Michael Bergman (USA)

People's Choice Award . . . . *4th Floor*, Antonio Mercero (Spain)

Source: *Montreal World Film Festival*

Genie Awards, 1992–2002

The Genie Awards have been presented since 1980 by the Academy of Canadian Cinema and Television to honor achievement in the Canadian film industry. Awards apply to films released in the previous year. Voting is conducted in a two-step process whereby the winners are chosen by all academy members from among the five nominees selected in each category by their respective craft branches. The 2002 awards were presented Feb. 13, 2003.

1992

Picture .... *Naked Lunch*
Actor .... Tony Nardi, *La Sarrasine*
Actress .... Janet Wright, *Bordertown Café*
Sup. Actor .... Michael Hogan, *Solitaire*
Sup. Actress .... Monique Mercure, *Naked Lunch*
Director .... David Cronenberg, *Naked Lunch*

1993

Picture .... *Thirty-Two Short Films about Glenn Gould*
Actor .... Tom McCamus, *I Love A Man in Uniform*
Actress .... Sheila McCarthy, *The Lotus Eaters*
Sup. Actor .... Kevin Tighe, *I Love A Man in Uniform*
Sup. Actress .... Nicola Cavendish, *The Grocer's Wife*
Director .... François Girard, *Thirty-Two Short Films about Glenn Gould*

1994

Picture .... *Exotica*
Actor .... Maury Chaykin, *Whale Music*
Actress .... Sandra Oh, *Double Happiness*
Sup. Actor .... Don McKellar, *Exotica*
Sup. Actress .... Martha Henry, *Mustard Bath*
Director .... Atom Egoyan, *Exotica*

1995

Picture .... *Le Confessionnal*
Actor .... David La Haye, *L'Enfant D'Eau*
Actress .... Helena Bonham Carter, *Margaret's Museum*
Sup. Actor .... Kenneth Welsh, *Margaret's Museum*
Sup. Actress .... Kate Nelligan, *Margaret's Museum*
Director .... Robert Lepage, *Le Confessionnal*

1996

Picture .... *Lilies*
Actor ...... William Hutt, *Long Day's Journey Into Night*
Actress ... Martha Henry, *Long Day's Journey Into Night*
Sup. Actor ... Peter Donaldson, *Long Day's Journey Into Night*
Sup. Actress .... Martha Burns, *Long Day's Journey Into Night*
Director .... David Cronenberg, *Crash*

1997

Picture .... *The Sweet Hereafter*
Actor .... Ian Holm, *The Sweet Hereafter*
Actress......................... Molly Parker, *Kissed*
Sup. Actor .... Peter MacNeill, *The Hanging Garden*
Sup. Actress..... Seana McKenna, *The Hanging Garden*
Director.......... Atom Egoyan, *The Sweet Hereafter*

1998

Picture................................ *The Red Violin*
Actor............. Roshan Seth, *Such a Long Journey*

Actress .... Sandra Oh, *Last Night*
Sup. Actor .... Callum Keith Rennie, *Last Night*
Sup. Actress .... Monique Mercure, *Conquest*
Director .... François Girard, *The Red Violin*

1999

Picture... *Sunshine*
Actor .... Bob Hoskins, *Felicia's Journey*
Actress .... Sylvie Moreau, *Post Mortem*
Sup. Actor................. Mark McKinney, *Dog Park*
Sup. Actress..... Catherine O'Hara, *The Life Before This*
Director .... Jeremy Podeswa, *The Five Senses*

2000

Picture .... *Maelström*
Actor................. Tony Nardi, *My Father's Angel*
Actress .... Marie-Josée Croze, *Maelström*
Sup. Actor........ Martin Cummins, *Love Come Down*
Sup. Actress .... Helen Shaver, *We All Fall Down*
Director.................. Denis Villeneuve, *Maelström*

2001

Picture .... *Atanarjuat (The Fast Runner)*
Actor .... Brendan Fletcher, *The Law of Enclosures*
Actress .... Élise Guilbault, *La femme qui boit (The Woman Who Drinks)*
Sup. Actor .... Vincent Gale, *Last Wedding*
Sup. Actress .... Molly Parker, *Last Wedding*
Director . Zacharias Kunuk, *Atanarjuat (The Fast Runner)*

2002

Picture .... *Ararat*
Actor...................... Luc Picard, *Savage Messiah*
Actress .... Arsinée Khanjian, *Ararat*
Sup. Actor........................ Elias Koteas, *Ararat*
Sup. Actress .... Pascale Montpetit, *Savage Messiah*
Directo .... David Cronenberg, *Spider*
Original Screenplay Deepa Mehta, *Bollywood/Hollywood*
Cinematography .... Paul Sarossy, *Perfect Pie*
Film Editing .... Lara Mazur, *Suddenly Naked*
Art Direction .... Francois Seguin, *Almost America*
Costume Design................ Beth Pasternak, *Ararat*
Overall Sound . Tom Hidderly, Todd Beckett, Keith Elliott, Mark Szivgovitz, *Between Strangers*
Sound Editing ...... Fred Brennan, Roderick Deogrades, Barry Gillmore, Goro Koyama, Andy Malcolm, David McCallum, Jane Tattersall, *Max*
Music Score .... Mychael Danna, *Ararat*
Best Feature Length Documentar .... *Gambling, Gods and LSD*
Best Animated Short .... *The Hungry Squid*
Best Live Action Short Drama .... *Shout Love*

Motion Picture Academy Awards (Oscars™), 1992–2002

1992

Picture . . . . *Unforgiven*, Clint Eastwood, producer
Actor . . . . Al Pacino, *Scent of A Woman*
Actress . . . . Emma Thompson, *Howards End*
Sup. Actor . . . . Gene Hackman, *Unforgiven*
Sup. Actress . . . . Marisa Tomei, *My Cousin Vinny*
Director . . . . Clint Eastwood, *Unforgiven*

1993

Picture . . . . *Schindler's List*, Steven Spielberg,
Gerald R. Molen, Branko Lustig, producers
Actor . . . . Tom Hanks, *Philadelphia*
Actress . . . . Holly Hunter, *The Piano*
Sup. Actor . . . . Tommy Lee Jones, *The Fugitive*
Sup. Actress . . . . Anna Paquin, *The Piano*
Director . . . . Steven Spielberg, *Schindler's List*

1994

Picture . . . . *Forrest Gump*, SteveTisch,
Wendy Finerman, Steve Sharkey, producers
Actor . . . . Tom Hanks, *Forrest Gump*
Actress . . . . Jessica Lange, *Blue Sky*
Sup. Actor . . . . Martin Landau, *Ed Wood*
Sup. Actress . . . . Dianne Wiest, *Bullets Over Broadway*
Director . . . . Robert Zemeckis, *Forrest Gump*

1995

Picture . . . . . . *Braveheart*, Mel Gibson, Alan Ladd, Jr., and
Bruce Davey, producers
Actor . . . . Nicolas Cage, *Leaving Las Vegas*
Actress . . . . Susan Sarandon, *Dead Man Walking*
Sup. Actor . . . . Kevin Spacey, *The Usual Suspects*
Sup. Actress . . . . Mira Sorvino, *Mighty Aphrodite*
Director . . . . Mel Gibson, *Braveheart*

1996

Picture . . . . . *The English Patient*, Saul Zaentz, producer
Actor . . . . Geoffrey Rush, *Shine*
Actress . . . . Frances McDormand, *Fargo*
Sup. Actor . . . . Cuba Gooding, Jr., *Jerry Maguire*
Sup. Actress . . . . . Juliette Binoche, *The English Patient*
Director . . . . Anthony Minghella, *The English Patient*

1997

Picture . . . . *Titanic*, James Cameron,
Jon Landau, producers
Actor . . . . Jack Nicholson, *As Good as It Gets*
Actress . . . . Helen Hunt, *As Good as It Gets*
Sup. Actor . . . . Robin Williams, *Good Will Hunting*
Sup. Actress . . . . Kim Basinger, *L.A. Confidential*
Director . . . . **James Cameron, *Titanic***

1998

Picture . . . . *Shakespeare in Love*, Donna Gigliotti,
Marc Norman, David Parfitt, Harvey Weinstein,
Edward Zwick, producers
Actor . . . . Roberto Benigni, *Life is Beautiful*
Actress . . . . Gwyneth Paltrow, *Shakespeare in Love*
Sup. Actor . . . . James Coburn, *Affliction*

Sup. Actress . . . . Judi Dench, *Shakespeare in Love*
Director . . . . Steven Spielberg, *Saving Private Ryan*

1999

Picture . . . . *American Beauty*, Bruce Cohen
and Dan Jinks, producers
Actor . . . . Kevin Spacey, *American Beauty*
Actress . . . . Hilary Swank, *Boys Don't Cry*
Sup. Actor . . . . . . Michael Caine, *The Cider House Rules*
Sup. Actress . . . . Angelina Jolie, *Girl Interrupted*
Director . . . . Sam Mendes, *American Beauty*

2000

Picture . . . . . . *Gladiator*, Douglas Wick, David Franzoni,
Branko Lustig, producers
Actor . . . . Russell Crowe, *Gladiator*
Actress . . . . Julia Roberts, *Erin Brockovich*
Sup. Actor . . . . Benicio Del Toro, *Traffic*
Sup. Actress . . . . Marcia Gay Harden, *Pollock*
Director . . . . Steven Soderbergh, *Traffic*

2001

Picture . . . *A Beautiful Mind*, Douglas Wick, Brian Grazer
and Ron Howard; producers
Actor . . . . Denzel Washington, *Training Day*
Actress . . . . Halle Berry, *Monster's Ball*
Sup. Actor . . . . Jim Broadbent, *Iris*
Sup. Actress . . . . . . Jennifer Connelly, *A Beautiful Mind*
Director . . . . Ron Howard, *A Beautiful Mind*

2002

Picture . . . . *Chicago*, Martin Richards, producer
Actor . . . . Adrien Brody, *The Pianist*
Actress . . . . Nicole Kidman, *The Hours*
Sup. Actor . . . . Chris Cooper, *Adaptation*
Sup. Actress . . . . Catherine Zeta-Jones, *Chicago*
Director . . . . Roman Polanski, *The Pianist*
Foreign-Language Film. . . . *Nowhere In Africa*, Germany
Original Screenplay . . . . . Pedro Almodovar, *Talk to Her*
Screenplay Adaptation . . . Ronald Harwood, *The Pianist*
Cinematography . . . . . Conrad L. Hall, *Road to Perdition*
Editing . . . . Martin Walsh, *Chicago*
Original Score . . . . **Eliot Goldenthal, *Frida***
Original Song. . . . . Eminem, Jeff Bass, Luis Resto,
"Lose Yourself" (*8 Mile*)
Art Direction . . . . . . John Myhre, Gordon Sim, *Chicago*
Costume Design . . . . Colleen Atwood, *Chicago*
Sound . . . . Mike Minkler, Dominick Travella,
David Lee, *Chicago*
Sound Editing. . . . Ethan Van der Ryn, Michael Hopkins,
The Lord of the Rings: The Two Towers
Makeup . . . . John Jackson, Beatrice de Alba, *Frida*
Visual Effects . . . . Jim Rygiel, Joe Letteri,
Randall William Cook, Alex Funke,
The Lord of the Rings: The Two Towers
Documentary Feature. . . . . Michael Moore,
Michael Donovan, *Bowling for Columbine*
Documentary Short Subject . . . . Bill Guttentag,
Robert David Port, *Twin Towers*

Source: © *Academy of Motion Picture Arts and Sciences* Oscars® for the 75th Annual Academy Awards were presented on March 22, 2003, by the Academy of Motion Picture Arts and Sciences.

2002 Oscar™ Nominations

Picture: *Chicago, Gangs of New York, The Hours, The Lord of the Rings: The Two Towers, The Pianist*

Actor: Adrien Brody, *The Pianist*; Nicolas Cage, *Adaptation*; Michael Caine, *The Quiet American*; Daniel Day-Lewis, *Gangs of New York*; Jack Nicholson, *About Schmidt*

Actress: Nicole Kidman, *The Hours*; Salma Hayek, *Frida*; Diane Lane, *Unfaithful*; Renée Zellweger, *Chicago*; Julianne Moore, *Far from Heaven*

Supporting Actor: Chris Cooper, *Adaptation*; Ed Harris, *The Hours*; Paul Newman, *Road to Perdition*; John C. Reilly, *Chicago*; Christopher Walken, *Catch Me If You Can*

Supporting Actress: Catherine Zeta-Jones, *Chicago*; Kathy Bates, *About Schmidt*; Julianne Moore, *The Hours*; Queen Latifah, *Chicago*; Meryl Streep, *Adaptation*

Director: Rob Marshall, *Chicago*; Martin Scorsese, *Gangs of New York*; Stephen Daldry, *The Hours*; Roman Polanski, *The Pianist*; Pedro Almodovar, *Talk to Her*

Foreign-Language Film: *Nowhere In Africa*, Germany; *El Crimen Del Padre Amaro*, Mexico; *Hero*, China; *The Man Without A Past*, Finland; *Zus & Zo*, Netherlands

Original Screenplay: Todd Haynes, *Far from Heaven*; Jay Cocks, Steve Zaillian, Kenneth Lonnergan, *Gangs of New York*; **Nia Vardalos, *My Big Fat Greek Wedding*;** Pedro Almodovar, *Talk to Her*; Carlos Cuarón, Alfonso Cuarón, *Y Tu Mamá También*

Screenplay Adaptation: Ronald Harwood, *The Pianist*; Peter Hedges, Chris Weitz, Paul Weitz, *About A Boy*; Charlie Kaufman, Donald Kaufman, *Adaptation*; Bill Condon, *Chicago*; David Hare, *The Hours*; Michael Horton, *The Lord of the Rings: The Two Towers*

Cinematography: Martin Walsh, *Chicago*; Edward Lachman, *Far from Heaven*; Michael Ballhaus, *Gangs of New York*; Pawel Edelman, *The Pianist*; Conrad L. Hall, *Road to Perdition*

Original Song: Eminem, Jeff Bass, Luis Resto, "Lose Yourself"; John Kander, Fred Ebb, "I Move On"; Elliot Goldenthal, Julie Taymor, "Burn It Blue"; Bono, The Edge, Adam Clayton, Larry Mullen, "The Hands That Built America"; Paul Simon, "Father and Daughter"

Source: © Academy of Motion Picture Arts and Sciences

The Sundance Film Festival Awards

The Sundance Film Festival was held January 16–26, 2003, in Park City, Utah.

Documentary Grand Jury Prize . . . . *Capturing the Friedmans*, dir. Andrew Jarecki

Dramatic Grand Jury Prize . . . . . . *American Splendour*, dir. Shari Springer Berman, Robert Pulcini

Documentary Audience Award . . . . *My Flesh and Blood*, dir. Jonathan Karsh

Dramatic Audience Award . . . . *The Station Agent*, dir. Tom McCarthy

World Cinema Audience Award . . . . *Whale Rider*, dir. Nick Caro

Documentary Directing Award . . . . Jonathan Karsh, *My Flesh and Blood*

Dramatic Directing Award . . . . . . Catherine Hardwicke, *Thirteen*

The Freedom of Expression Award . . . *What I Want My Words To Do To You*, dir. Judith Katz, Madeleine Gavin, Gary Sunshine

Waldo Salt Screenwriting Award . . . . . . Tom McCarthy, *The Station Agent*

Documentary Special Jury Prize . . . . . . (joint winners) *The Murder of Emmett Till*, dir. Stanley Wilson; *A Certain Kind of Death*, dir. Blue Hadaegh, Grover Babcock

Special Jury Prize for Outstanding Performance . . . . . (joint winners) Patricia Clarkson, *The Station Agent*, *All the Real Girls, Pieces of April*; Charles Busch, *Die Mommie Die*

Jury Prize in Short Filmmaking . . . . . . *Terminal Bar*, dir. Stefan Nadelman

Source: *Sundance Film Festival*

The Berlin Film Festival Awards

The awards of the 53rd annual Berlin Film Festival (also known as the "Berlinale") were announced February 16, 2003.

Golden Berlin Bear . . . . *In This World*, dir. Michael Winterbottom

Silver Berlin Bear . . . . *Adaptation*, dir. Spike Jonze

Best Actress . . . . (joint winners) Nicole Kidman, Meryl Streep, Juliannne Moore, *The Hours*

Best Actor . . . . Sam Rockwell, *Confessions of a Dangerous Mind*

Best Director . . . . Patrice Chéreau, *Son Frère*

Alfred Bauer Prize (for innovation) Ying Xiong, dir., *Hero*

Blue Angel Award (best European film) *Good-by Lenin*, dir. Wolfgang Becker

Source: *Berlin Film Festival*

The Cannes Film Festival Awards, 1997–2003

1997

Special Grand Jury Prize   *The Sweet Hereafter* (Canada)
Best Director .... Wong Kar-Wai, *Happy Together*
(Hong Kong)
Best Actor .... Sean Penn, *She's So Lovely* (USA)
Best Actress .... Kathy Burke, *Nilby Mouth* (UK)
Palme d'Or............. (tie) *Unagi* (The Eel) (Japan)
The Taste of Cherry (Iran)

1998

Grand Jury Prize .... *La Vita e Bella* (Italy)
Special Jury Prize .... *La Classe de Neige* (France);
Festen (Denmark)
Best Director ....John Boorman, *The General* (UK)
Best Actor........ Peter Mullan, *My Name Is Joe* (UK)
Best Actress...... Elodie Bouchez and Natacha Regnier,
La Vie Revee des Anges (France)
Palme d'Or........................ *Eternity and a Day*,
Theo Angelopoulos (Greece)

1999

Grand Jury Prize .... *L'humanité* (France)
Jury Prize .... *A Carta* (Portugal)
Best Director...................... Pedro Almodovar,
Todo Sobre Mi Madre (Spain)
Best Actor .... Emmanuel Schotté, *L'humanité* (France)
Best Actress (tie) Séverine Cancele, *L'humanité* (France)
and Emilie Dequenne, *Rosetta* (Belgium)
Palme d'Or......................... *Rosetta*, Luc and
Jean-Pierre Dardenne (Belgium)

2000

Grand Prize.......... *Guizi Lai Le*, Jiang Wen (China)
Jury Prize..... *Sånger Från Andra Våningen* (Sweden),
Takhté Siah (Iran)
Best Director............. Edward Yang, *Yi Yi* (Taiwan)
Best Actor .... Tony Leung Chiu-Wai,
In the Mood for Love (China)

Best Actress ..... Björk, *Dancer in the Dark* (Denmark)
Palme d'Or *Dancer in the Dark*,
Lars von Trier (Denmark)

2001

Grand Prize.................... *The Piano Teacher*,
Michael Haneke (Austria/France)
**Caméra d'Or .... *Atanarjuat (The Fast Runner)*,
Zacharias Kunuk (Canada)**
Best Director .... (tie) Joel Coen,
The Man Who Wasn't There (USA);
David Lynch, *Mulholland Drive* (USA)
Best Actor. Benoit Magimel, *The Piano Teacher* (France)
Best Actress .... Isabelle Huppert,
The Piano Teacher (France)
Palme d'Or ..... *The Son's Room*, Nanni Moretti (Italy)

2002

Grand Prize .... *The Man Without a Past*,
Aki Kaurismäki dir. (Iceland)
Caméra d'Or . *Bord de mer*, Julie Lopes-Curval (France)
Best Director .... (tie) Im Kwon-Taek,
Chihwaseon (South Korea);
Paul Thomas Anderson, *Punch-Drunk Love (USA)*
Best Actor .... Olivier Gourmet, *Les Fils*
Best Actress Kati Outinen, *The Man Without a Past* (Iceland)
Palme d'Or .. *The Pianist*, Roman Polanski dir. (France)

2003

Grand Prize...... *Uzak*, Nuri Bilge Cevlan, dir. (Turkey)
Caméra d'Or*Reconstruction*, Christopher Boe (Denmark)
Best Director ....Gus Van Sant, *Elephant* (USA)
Best Actor .... (tie) Muzaffer Ozdemir,
Mehmen Ermin Toprak, *Uzak*
**Best Actress .... Marie Josée Croze,
Barbarian Invasions (Canada)**
Palme d'Or........ *Elephant*, Gus Van Sant, dir. (USA)

Source: *The Cannes Film Festival*

Arcand Comes Close at Cannes

*W*hen Quebec film-maker Denys Arcand entered competition with his latest project at the 2003 Cannes Film Festival, it looked for a moment like it just might be Canada's year. Arcand's **Barbarian Invasions** drew such a warm response from its audience that the film became highly touted for the festival's prestigious Palme d' Or award. In the past, Canadian directors David Cronenberg (**Crash**), Atom Egoyan (**The Sweet Hereafter**), Zacharias Kunuk (**Atanarjuat: The Fast Runner***) and Arcand himself (for **Jesus of Montreal**) have returned from Cannes with major prizes. But no Canadian has yet claimed the Palme, the festival's top honour. When this year's jury (which included director Stephen Soderburgh and actress Meg Ryan) awarded the Palme d' Or to US director Gus Van Sant for **Elephant**, Arcand said he was not surprised. But his leading lady, Quebec actress Marie Josée Croze, did pick up the prize for best actress. **Barbarian Invasions** is the sequel to Arcand's much-loved 1986 hit **The Decline of the American Empire.**

CANADIAN ARTS AWARDS

Governor General's Performing Arts Awards

The Governor General's Performing Arts Awards were inaugurated in 1992 to pay tribute to the lifetime achievements of outstanding artists in a variety of creative fields. The motto of the awards, "The Arts Engage and Inspire Us," reflects the cultural contribution made by recipients chosen from theatre, dance, classical music/opera, popular music, film and broadcasting. The awards are presented annually in November by the Governor General and are administered by the Governor General's Performing Arts Awards Foundation.

■ Winners 1998–2002

1998
Paul Buissoneau
Bruce Cockburn
Rock Demers
The Royal Canadian Air Farce
Arnold Spohr
Jon Vickers
Joseph H. Shoctor
Denis Marleau

1999
Mario Bernardi
David Cronenberg
Denise Filiatrault
Mavor Moore

Louis Quilico
Ginette Reno
Sam Sniderman
Michel Tremblay

2000
Janette Bertrand
Walter Carsen
Tom C. ("Stompin' Tom") Connors
Fernand Nault
Christopher Newton
Teresa Stratas
Donald Sutherland

2001
Mario Bernardi
Diane Dufresne

Max Ferguson, O.C.
Evelyn Hart, C.C.
Christopher Plummer, C.C.
Anne-Claire Poirier
Thea Borlase
Édouard Lock

2002
André Brassard
Joy Coghill
The Guess Who
Karen Kain
Phil Nimmons
Jean-Pierre Perreault
Father Fernand Lindsay
Angela Hewitt

2003 Winners

■ Pierrette Alaire

Born in Montreal in 1921, Pierrette Alarie made her stage debut as an actress. Coming from a family of musicians, she began singing in 1940 while frequenting the studio of tenor Salvator Issaurel. In 1943 she continued her studies at the Curtis Institute of Philadelphia. Two years later, under the direction of celebrated conductor Bruno Walter, she made her debut at the Metropolitan Opera of New York in the role of Oscar in Verdi's *A Masked Ball*. In 1949, the Alarie Simoneau couple joined the Opéra Comique and the Opéra de Paris. Madame Alarie's career took a new turn, and during the next ten years she was a featured

performer at many leading European festivals. Her career in North America is equally impressive. In 1954, she became one of the pioneers of Radio Canada television through her contributions to the earliest televised classical concert programs.

■ Dave Broadfoot

Following his early careers in the Merchant Navy and the clothing business, Dave became involved with amateur theatre and soon quit his day job and headed for Toronto. Within weeks he was on TV, as a stand-up comedian in *The Big Revue,* which led to a 10-year association with the legendary satirical revue

Photo Credit: Michael Assaly

Spring Thaw. In 1973 Dave became one of the founders of The Royal Canadian Air Farce and for 15 years told the Canadian story through the iconic Canadian figures of Corporal Renfrew, Big Bobby Clobber and the Member for Kicking Horse Pass. His first solo television special in 1996, at the age of 70, was a tour-de-force and won one of the highest audience numbers of the season. Two more specials (with equally impressive numbers) have followed, and his autobiography, *Old Enough To Say What I Want,* was published in 2002—and re-published in 2003.

■ Douglas Campbell

Douglas Campbell arrived in Canada exactly 50 years ago to take a leading role in the inaugural season at Stratford. His career there has included more than 50 roles, among them the celebrated 1954 production of *Oedipus Rex* and his definitive performances of

Falstaff and Lear. Campbell created the Canadian Players, taking classical theatre to communities across the country, allowing

many who were to become great names in Canadian theatre to develop their craft and build careers here. In 1992, he began a long relationship with Vancouver's Bard on the Beach company, whose new studio theatre bears his name. He has directed for Bard on the Beach and at Stratford and served as artistic director of The Piggery summer theatre in North Hatley, Quebec. His television career has included the role of Inspector Alistair Cameron in CBC's successful series *The Great Detective* which aired from 1979 to 1982.

■ Marie Chouinard

The works of choreographer and performer Marie Chouinard reflect her view of dance as a sacred art, her respect for the body as a vehicle for that art, and a virtuoso approach

Photo Credit: Laurence Labat

to performance. In 1978, Chouinard presented her first creation, *Cristallisation*. This was followed by some 50 works in which she refined her interest in the mysteries of the human body. For the next 12 years she performed solo, as she travelled throughout the world and absorbed various cultures. In 1990 she founded the Compagnie Marie Chouinard, which permitted her to develop a repertoire for group dance. Her first ensemble piece, *Les Trous du ciel* (1991), was acclaimed in Canada, the United States, and Europe. *The Rite of Spring* followed in 1993, and from 1994 on would be performed with *L'Après-midi d'un faune* in a dual programme. In 1996, the Company created *L'Amande et le Diamant* in which Chouinard continued her research on the links between sound and movement. In 1999, she created *Des feux dans la nuit*, and *24 Preludes by Chopin*. In 2000, she created *Le Cri du monde*, a study of morphological division, and in 2001, *Étude nº 1*, a solo work for female dancer.

■ Norman Jewison

A respected force in the motion picture industry for more than four decades, Toronto-born Norman Jewison has been nominated for four Oscars, while his films have received 46 nominations and 12 Academy Awards. He received the Irving Thalberg Award in 1999 and the Ramon John Hnatyshyn Award in the inaugural year of the Governor General's Performing Arts Awards for his vision in establishing the Canadian Film Centre. In the 1950s in his native Toronto, Jewison found occasional work as an actor on stage and in radio which led to training with the BBC and several years at the CBC writing, directing and producing dramas, musicals and specials. In 1958 he joined CBS in the U.S. where he earned three Emmys for his music specials featuring all the leading stars of the time. In the early 1960s he began directing feature films. His 1966 hit, *The Russians are Coming! The Russians are Coming!*, established him as a star. Other hits include *In the Heat of the Night* (which won the best picture Oscar in 1967), *The Thomas Crown Affair*, *Fiddler on the Roof*, *Jesus Christ Superstar*, *Hurricane*, and the multiple Oscar-winner *Moonstruck*.

■ Micheline Lanctôt

Born in Montreal in 1947, actor/filmmaker Micheline Lanctôt began her career in film animation. While working at Potterton Productions, she met director Gilles Carle, who, in 1972, offered her a role in *La Vraie Nature de Bernadette*, for which she won a

Photo Credit: Paul-Émile Rioux

Photo Credit: Columbia Pictures Industries, Inc.

Genie award for best female performance. After that, Lanctôt's acting career took off with films including *Voyage en Grande Tartarie*, *The Apprenticeship of Duddy Kravitz*, *Mourir à tuetête* and *Blood & Guts*.

In 1979, she scripted her first full-length film, *L'Homme à tout faire*, which won the silver medal at the San Sebastian Festival in 1980 as well as eight nominations at the Canadian Film Awards. In 1984, her second feature, *Sonatine*, garnered numerous awards, including among others the Lion d'Argent at the Venice Film Festival. In 1992, she produced *Deux Actrices*, a film that received the grand prize at the 1994 Rendezvous du cinéma québécois. Her television acting credits include *Jamais deux sans toi*, *Bunker*, *Les Héritiers Duval*, *Scoop*, *Omerta*, and *Le Pollock*. Most recently, film audiences have seen her in the new Denys Arcand film, *Les Invasions barbares*.

■ Jim and Sandra Pitblado

Born and raised in Winnipeg, Jim and Sandra Pitblado have nurtured the growth of numerous institutions and artists. As chairman of the National Ballet from 1990 to 1997, Jim was an exemplary leader while the

Photo Credit: Cylla von Tiedemann

couple's contributions affected every aspect of the Ballet's operations. Sandra's commitment to the world of theatre has been no less impressive. She served as chair of Toronto's Tarragon Theatre for six years. During her tenure as chair of the Stratford Festival, the Endowment Foundation was organized, the Conservatory for Classical Theatre Training was established, the Avon Theatre was rebuilt and a new fourth stage established in part with a significant leading gift from the Pitblados. Sandra is currently a director of

the Stratford Festival Endowment Foundation, chair of the Canadian Arts Summit, a board member of the Creative Trust and is an honourary member of the Board at Tarragon. Jim remains chair of the National Ballet's Endowment Foundation and serves on the boards of the Ontario Arts Council Foundation, the Council for Business and the Arts, and Soulpepper Theatre Company.

■ Ian Tyson

Born in Victoria, Ian Tyson spent his early years in Alberta learning about ranching and music. While recuperating in a Calgary hospital from a rodeo accident, he learned the guitar and then hitchhiked to Toronto where

Photo Credit: Richard Siemens

he sang in coffee-houses, teaming up with Sylvia Fricker. As Ian and Sylvia, the couple created a folk music sensation. After more than a dozen albums and a musical migration into the country-rock sound of The Great Speckled Bird (which hosted its own television show), Ian and Sylvia went their separate ways in the mid-70s. Following his move back to Alberta, Ian experienced a musical renaissance inspired by his need to make a statement about "Western" culture as something distinct from mainstream North American culture, investing the cowboy story-song with a sound that is both deeply personal and very deeply felt.

The National Aboriginal Achievement Awards, 2003

The National Aboriginal Achievements Foundation established these awards in conjunction with the United Nations' International Decade of the World's Indigenous peoples. The awards recognize career achievements by Aboriginal professionals in diverse occupations. The foundation presents awards to outstanding First Nations citizens in the fields of arts and culture, medicine, business, law, heritage and sports, education, the environment, public service and community development. The 10th annual National Aboriginal Achievement Awards were held March 28, 2003, in Ottawa. The following biographies are of those who received awards in the arts.

■ Winners, Arts and Culture, 1997–2002[1]

1997	2000	2002
Kiawak Ashoona	Tsa-qwa-supp (Art	Ohito Ashoona
Gil Cardinal	Thompson)	Freda Diesing
Graham Greene	Leetia Ineak	Gail Guthrie Valaskakis
1998	**2001**	
Tantoo Cardinal	Tomson Highway	
Daphne Odjig	Zacharias Kunuk	
Buffy Sainte-Marie		

(1) In 1999, there were no recipients in the area of arts and culture.

2003 Winners

■ **John Arcand, musician:** John Arcand fiddles to a historic tune. The undisputed master of the Métis fiddle, his music is more than passionate. He "bleeds Métis music," a fan once enthused. Now 60, Arcand has written 250 original tunes that are played across North America and has seven original recordings under his belt. A ninth-generation Métis fiddler, he's ensured the Métis tunes of his grandfather and father remain a part of his people and still flourish today. Arcand is also thinking about the future—a Métis future where his people's culture remains vibrant and strong. He helped found and is an instructor at the Emma Lake Fiddle Camp, an intensive camp dedicated to teaching the art of fiddling. He also started the renowned John Arcand Fiddle Fest in 1998. Along the way, he worked at the Gabriel Dumont Institute of Native Studies and Applied Research in the area of fiddle music research and compilation. The end result? *Drops of Brandy*, a four-CD set that brought together the best Métis fiddlers in Canada. To see Arcand perform is to witness a man serious about his music and in harmony with all that is good. Arcand is happiest and most at home when a fiddle is in his hands. "I knew from childhood I would be a fiddler," he says. "I love the constant challenge because you cannot ever master the fiddle." John Arcand, however, has come close.

■ **Tom King, author:** The world owes Helen Hoy a big thank you. "I needed to impress her," famed novelist, scholar, screenwriter and literary giant Tom King said of his partner. "She loved good food and good writing. My cooking didn't impress her so I tried to impress her with my writing." It's a good thing King tried.

Years after he put down the frying pan and took up a pen, he is one of Canada's leading authors. Tom King has written four best-selling novels, numerous television scripts and award-winning works of short fiction and non-fiction featuring Aboriginal themes. "Native people in the contemporary world, it's a topic I could write about until the day I die," he says. Millions of Canadians know him as the creative force behind CBC Radio's *Dead Dog Café Comedy Hour*. With humour as his vehicle, King has brought First Nations issues to the forefront of Canadian society. He has cleverly used *Dead Dog Café* as a vehicle for mainstream Canada to learn about some serious issues affecting Aboriginal communities and a window into Aboriginal culture. By making Canadians laugh, King makes us all think about and face the country's Aboriginal reality. A Professor at the University of Guelph, King will be giving this year's Massey Lectures. In doing so, this Cherokee joins a select group that includes John Kenneth Galbraith, Martin Luther King and Noam Chomsky. A recent member of the jury selection panel for the esteemed Giller book prize, Tom King is much more than an artist, he is a Renaissance man. And a funny one at that. Just ask Helen.

■ **Lifetime Achievement Award: Robbie Robertson, musician:** A Mohawk from the Six Nations Reserve in Ontario, Robbie Robertson is one of the most influential musicians of our times. When folk legend Bob Dylan made the historic decision to synthesize folk and rock music, it was Robertson and The Band he turned to for backup. Robertson toured the world in 1965/66 with Dylan and recorded the legendary *Basement Tapes*. "I had no idea that we were entering not only another world but a music revolution. This was a time and a music that was going to change the course of music forever," he remembers today. Separately, Robertson's group The Band released *Music From Big Pink*, featuring hits such as "The Weight" and "Up On Cripple Creek" and were soon a force on their own. Later, Robertson was the driving force behind the Martin Scorsese-directed film *The Last Waltz*, the Band's 1976 farewell concert that was turned into one of the greatest rock movies of all time. As a solo artist, Robertson began to explore his Aboriginal roots as no other rock musician of his stature had yet done. At the 2002 Olympic Winter Games opening ceremonies in Salt Lake City, Robertson—along with Rita Coolidge, Sadie Buck and Jackie Bird—brought Aboriginal talent to the world by performing "The Stomp Dance (Unity Song)" for an audience of three billion people. "My education is my upbringing," he says of his Aboriginal roots. "But basically I'm still just that kid from Six Nations who had a lot of big dreams." And so much more.

Source: *The National Aboriginal Achievement Foundation*

THEATRE

Toronto is now considered the third-largest production centre of live theatre in the English-speaking world (following New York, and London, England). The English Canadian theatre scene has undergone exponential growth since the birth of the Stratford Shakespearean Festival at Stratford, Ont., in 1953. The alternative theatre movement that swept English Canada in the 1970s established producers of Canadian drama in every large centre. Diminishing government support in the 1980s and 1990s led to more emphasis on commercial Canadian productions of British, French and American "megamusicals" while development of new and experimental work has passed increasingly to independent artists often appearing at a cross-Canada network of "fringe" festivals.

Theatrical activity in French Canada burgeoned in the 1950s and 1960s as playwrights such as Marcel Dubé (*Un Simple Soldat*) and Gratien Gélinas (*'Tit Coq*) explored the social and moral issues confronting Québecers in their own dialect. This movement reached its apex in the work of Michel Tremblay in the early 1970s. More recently, Quebec theatre has also excelled in less verbal forms of theatre such as the spectacles produced by Cirque du Soleil, while the "total theatre" productions of Quebec City writer/performer/director Robert Lepage have garnered critical acclaim around the world.

Dora Mavor Moore Awards, 2003

The Doras, honouring excellence in Toronto theatrical productions, were first handed out in 1981. Named for Dora Mavor Moore, a teacher and director who helped establish professional theatre in Canada in the 1930s and 1940s, the awards are chosen annually from over 200 productions. The 2002 Dora Mavor Moore Awards, honouring the best of the Toronto community's performing arts, were held June 23, 2003 at the Princess of Wales Theatre.

General Theatre

Outstanding New Play . . . . *Girl In The Goldfish Bowl*, Morris Panych
Outstanding New Musical . . . . *Little Mercy's First Murder*, Morwyn Brebner, Jay Turvey and Paul Sportelli
Outstanding Production of a Play . . . . *Girl In The Goldfish Bowl*, Tarragon Theatre
Outstanding Production of a Musical . . . . *Little Mercy's First Murder*, Tarragon Theatre
Outstanding Direction of a Play . . . . *Girl In The Goldfish Bowl*, Morris Panych
Outstanding Direction of a Musical . . . . Eda Holmes, *Little Mercy's First Murder*
Outstanding Performance by a Male in a Principal Role (Play) . . . . Richard McMillan, *Through the Eyes*
Outstanding Performance by a Female in a Principal Role (Play) . . . . Kristina Nicoll, *Girl In The Goldfish Bowl*
Outstanding Performance by a Male in a Principal Role (Musical) . . . . Peter Millard, *Little Mercy's First Murder*
Outstanding Performance by a Female in a Principal Role (Musical) . . . . Melody Johnson, *Little Mercy's First Murder*
Outstanding Performance in a Featured Role (Play or Musical) . . . . Tanja Jacobs, *Girl In The Goldfish Bowl*
Outstanding Production for Young Audiences . . . . *Patty's Cake*, Carousel Productions
Outstanding Set Design . . . . Astrid Janson, *The Maids*
Outstanding Costume Design . . . . David Boechler, *Swollen Tongues*

Independent Theatre

Outstanding New Play or Musical . . . . *Poochwater*, Mike McPhaden
Outstanding Production . . . . *Mump & Smoot in "Flux"*, Mump & Smoot
Outstanding Direction . . . . Karen Hines, *Mump & Smoot in "Flux"*
Outstanding Performance by a Female . . . . Hazel Desbarats, *The Sea*
Outstanding Performance by a Male . . . . Nigel Shawn Williams, *Two Words for Snow*
Outstanding Set Design . . . . Teresa Przybylski, *Two Words for Snow*
Outstanding Costume Design . . . . Joanne Dente, *Grendelmaus*

Source: *Toronto Theatre Alliance*

Jessie Awards, 2003

Named for professional theatre pioneer Jessie Richardson, these awards honour excellence in and raise awareness of professional theatre in Vancouver. Winners of the 20th Jessies were announced June 16, 2003, in the Commodore Ballroom.

Small Theatre

Outstanding Original Play or Musical. . . . . . . Drew McCreadie, *The Cat Who Ate Her Husband, Ruby Slippers Theatre*
Outstanding Production . . . . *The Fall*, The Electric Company
Larry Lillo Award for Outstanding Direction . . . . Diane Brown, *The Cat Who Ate Her Husband, Ruby Slippers Theatre*
Outstanding Performance by an Actress in a Lead Role . . . . Lois Anderson, *Killjoy*, Solo Collective
Outstanding Performance by an Actor in a Lead Role . . . . Derek Metz, *Snowman, Section 8 Theatre*
Outstanding Performance by an Actress in a Supporting Role   Colleen Wheeler, *The Birth of Freedom*, The Virtual Stage
Outstanding Performance by an Actor in a Supporting Role . . . . Alex Ferguson, *The Cat Who Ate Her Husband, Ruby Slippers Theatre*
Outstanding Costume Design. . . . . Rebekka Sorenson, *The Cat Who Ate Her Husband, Ruby Slippers Theatre*
Outstanding Set Design . . . . *Catherine Mudryk, Mon Joyau*, Théâtre de la Seizième
Outstanding Lighting Design . . . . Adrian Muir, *The Fall*, The Electric Company
Outstanding Sound Design or Original Composition . . . . Patrick Pennefather, *The Fall*, The Electric Company

Large Theatre

Outstanding Production . . . . *Fiddler On The Roof*, Vancouver Playhouse
Larry Lillo Award for Outstanding Direction . . . . Dean Paul Gibson, *Twelfth Night,* Bard on the Beach
Outstanding Performance by an Actress in a Lead Role . . . . . Gabrielle Rose, *The Memory of Water*, Arts Club Theatre
Outstanding Performance by an Actor in a Lead Role . . . . . . Jay Brazeau, *Fiddler On The Roof*, Vancouver Playhouse
Outstanding Performance by an Actress in a Supporting Role . . Terra C. MacLeod, *West Side Story*, Arts Club Theatre
Outstanding Performance by an Actor in a Supporting Role . . . . Bob Frazer, *Zadie's Shoes*. Arts Club Theatre
Outstanding Set Design . . . . Brian Perchaluk, *Mary's Wedding*, Vancouver Playhouse
Outstanding Lighting Design . . . . Alan Brodie, *Mary's Wedding*, Vancouver Playhouse
Outstanding Sound Design or Original Composition . . . . Tobin Stokes, *Mary's Wedding*, Vancouver Playhouse
Outstanding Costume Design . . . . Mara Gottler, *Henry V*, Bard on the Beach

Source: *Jessie Richardson Society*

Theatre Highlights for 2004

Arts Club Theatre, Vancouver

A plump, bald film archivist and an impulsive failed actress meet at Mae West's tomb in Claudia Shear's *Dirty Blonde* (Jan. 30-Feb. 29). The legendary revue *Jacques Brel Is Alive and Well and Living In Paris,* by Eric Blau, Mort Shuman and Jacques Brel runs Feb.13-Mar. 13. A powerful portrait of the world and human emotions, *Jacques Brel Is Alive and Well...* is full of musical observations that reverberate with love, loss, poignancy and the changes that come with age. Noel Coward's *Private Lives* follows Mar. 12–Apr. 11. It's a comic account of what happens when Elyot and Amanda, a former husband and wife, find themselves in adjoining rooms at a seaside Normandy hotel while on honeymoon with their new spouses, Sibyl and Victor. Vancouver's own Morris Panych presents *7 Stories*, Apr. 16-May 15. In this absurdist comedy, a man contemplates suicide from the seventh-story ledge of an apartment building, while his neighbours pop in and out of his deliberations.

Vancouver Playhouse, Vancouver

Arms and the Man, Bernard Shaw's slyly farcical attack on the romantic notions of war, runs Jan. 17-Mar. 20. Shifting realities, black & white movies and the legendary golfer Ben Hogan help a family struggling to cope with their golden years in *One Last Kiss*, by Aaron Bushkowski (Feb. 21-Mar. 20). A shattering confrontation between passion and normalcy, *Equus* (Mar. 27-Apr. 24) examines the psychological shackles placed on all of us by a "civilized" society. In Peter Shaffer's groundbreaking drama, a child psychiatrist, haunted by doubts about his life and work, confronts his own demons when he treats a teenager who has brutally maimed six horses.

Theatre Calgary, Calgary

There's a Whole Lotta Shakin' Goin' On! in *Fire* (Feb. 3-22) by Paul Ledoux and David Young. Two Arkansas brothers follow in the father's footsteps, one by preaching the good word to his flock, the other by singin' and dancin' to the devil's beat of rock and roll. Modelled on the true story of Jimmy Swaggart and Jerry Lee Lewis. Beth Henley's Pulitzer Prize-winning comedy, *Crimes of the Heart*, runs Mar. 16-Apr. 4. A successful Manhattan lawyer struggles with a ghost from his past in *Counselor-At-Law* by Elmer Rice, Apr. 20-May 9.

Globe Theatre, Regina

The Globe's Sandbox series (Jan.15-18) showcases new works by Saskatchewan writers. It's two paws up for A.R. Gurney's *Sylvia* (Jan. 28-Feb. 14), a hilarious romp about a woman struggling with the ups and downs of pet ownership. Floyd Favel's new play, *The Sleeping Land* (Feb. 14-28), explores a mysterious explosion in Siberia in 1908. A shy countess and a musician facing a dwindling career are united when a cruel count plots to humiliate his wife in Mieko Ouchi's *The Red Priest* (Mar. 10-27). In *Lunch* (Mar. 23-28), Alberta's Old Trout Puppet Workshop "explores the outer edges of the puppet medium." Robert Bolt's classic, *A Man For All Seasons*, offers a glimpse into the tortured mind of Sir Thomas More, one of history's most tragic heroes (Apr. 21-May 8).

Manitoba Theatre Centre, Winnipeg

Lerner and Loewe's classic musical, *My Fair Lady*, based on Bernard Shaw's *Pygmalion*, runs Jan. 7-31. *Tuesdays With Morrie*, by Jeff Hatcher and Mitch Albom, chronicles the last class ever taught by professor Morrie Schwartz to his last pupil, Albom. Based on a true event, *The Winslow Boy* by Terrence Rattigan is a story about a father's two-year campaign to clear his son's name, and the price his family pays to "let right be done."

Mirvish Productions, Toronto

The Adventures of a Black Girl In Search of God runs to Mar. 21, Harbourfront Centre. This acclaimed masterpiece from Governor General's Award-winning playwright Djanet Sears is about a remarkable love, an incredible heist, an extraordinary funeral, and a burning search for answers to the profound mysteries of being alive. *Copenhagen* (Jan.-Feb., Winter Garden Theatre), tells the story of a war-time meeting between Werner Heisenberg and Niels Bohr, two nuclear scientists on opposite sides of WWII. The Royal Shakespeare Company brings to Toronto its famous production of John Barton's *The Hollow Crown* (Feb.-Mar., Princess of Wales Theatre), a history of the kings and queens of England—but nothing like any schoolbook history you've ever read. *Hairspray* (beginning May, Princess of Wales Theatre), Broadway's biggest musical comedy phenomenon, takes you back to 1962 as 16-year-old Tracy Turnblad sets out to dance her way onto TV's most popular show.

Tarragon Theatre, Toronto

One of Canada's pre-eminent playwrights, Judith Thompson, returns with *Capture Me* (Jan. 6-Feb. 8), the story of a funny, free-spirited kindergarten teacher and a mysterious refugee who find unexpected love. Kristen Thomson's Dora Award-winning *I, Claudia* (Dec. 30, 2003-Feb. 8) explores, with both hilarity and heartbreak, the anxieties of an "official pre-teen" facing her parents' separation and her father's impending re-marriage. *Rune Arledge* by Micheal Healey (Mar 2-Apr. 4) examines a family of women—the eldest incapable of keeping stories to herself, her two daughters on the verge of making life-altering decisions, a granddaughter wise beyond her years. *The Red Priest* runs Mar. 30-May 2 (see Globe Theatre). The Marx Brothers meet Bertolt Brecht in *Simpl* by Peter Froehlich (Apr. 27-May 30). It's a funny and at times disturbing play about German beer-hall comedians Karl Valentin and Liesl Karlstadt, whose genius for physical comedy and elegant verbal acrobatics made them hugely popular from early in the 20th century through the grim days of the Third Reich. Tarragon's Spring Arts Fair, a celebration of the performing arts and works-in-progress, runs May 29 & 30.

The National Arts Centre, Ottawa

The NAC presents Shakespeare's revenge tragedy, *Hamlet*, Jan. 8-24. *The Well Being* (Jan. 27-Feb. 7), by Andrew Buckland, Lionel Newton and Lara Foot-Newton, is a modern fable from South Africa that explores the relationship between man and his natural environment. The world English-language premiere of *Written On Water*, by Michel Marc Bouchard, runs Feb. 26-Mar. 13. When a flood destroys their town, a writing group decides whether or not to re-create the manuscripts containing their life stories. *Simpl* by Peter Froehlich runs Mar. 30-Apr. 10 (see Tarragon Theatre). Antonine

Maillet's celebrated Acadian novel, *Pélagie la Charette*, is the inspiration for *Pélagie* (May 13-29), a musical by Vincent de Tourdonnet and Allen Cole. NAC's family series includes Theatre Direct's *I Met a Bully on the Hill*, by Martha Brooks and Maureen Hunter (Feb. 14-15), and *Jack and the Three Giants*, by Andy Jones and Philip Dinn (May 15-16).

Centaur Theatre, Montreal
With a powerful tale of delusion, deception and misplaced romantic obsession, Michel Tremblay takes us back to the Plateau area of Montreal, circa 1930, in *Past Perfect*, a "prequel" to his hit play *Albertine In Five Times* (Jan. 27-Mar. 7). Centaur presents the play's English-language world premiere. Two reclusive farmers, boyhood friends and WWII veterans, share a mysterious secret in Michael Healey's *The Drawer Boy* (Mar. 2-28). U.S. playwright Neil Labute's *The Shape of Things* (Mar. 30-May 9), peels back the skin of two modern-day relationships in a power-packed evening of theatrical revelation. *Tiger's Heart* by Mark Lambert (May 4-30), tells the story of a young Englishwoman who, in the early 19th century, disguises herself as a man to study medicine.

Theatre New Brunswick, Fredericton
Set in 15th-century Italy, *Vinci* (Mar. 12-Apr. 3), by Maureen Hunter, is the story of a priest's struggle between what his friends want him to do, what his God tells him to do and what his heart knows he should do. Dealing with a town obsessed with the fate of Leonardo, a child born out of wedlock, the priest must choose "for the good of the child." TNB presents Dan Needles' *Wingfield On Ice* (Mar. 12-Apr. 3). As the first frosts come to Persephone Township, Walt and Maggie Wingfield are all set to welcome new life on the farm. She's expecting and he's nesting. But Walt is alarmed about the old feuds that divide the neighbours and disturb the tranquility of the community.

Neptune Theatre, Halifax
One of the most acclaimed plays of recent years, 2001 Pulitzer Prize-winner *Proof* (Jan. 27-Feb. 22), by David Auburn, explores the unknowability of love as much as it does the mysteries of mathematics. Neptune presents Arthur Miller's classic modern tragedy, *Death of a Salesman*, Mar. 2-28. Andrew Lloyd Webber's legendary musical *Cats*, based on *Old Possum's Book of Practical Cats* by T.S. Eliot, runs Apr. 13-May 30. In *Blue/Orange* (Feb. 23-Mar. 14), by Joe Penhall, an enigmatic patient in a London psychiatric hospital claims to be the son of an African dictator. In nine scenes that backpedal through time, playwright Harold Pinter chronicles the progress and regression of an illicit love affair in *Betrayal* (Mar. 23-Apr. 11).

Summer Theatre in Canada

Blyth Festival
PO Box 10, Blyth, ON
N0M 1H0

Charlottetown Festival
Confederation Centre of Arts
145 Richmond St
Charlottetown, PE, C1A 1J1

Huron Country Playhouse
RR #1, Grand Bend, ON
N0M 1T0

Kawartha Summer Theatre
PO Box 161, 2 Lindsay St S
Lindsay, ON K9V 4S1

Lighthouse Festival Theatre
PO Box 1208, Port Dover, ON
N0A 1N0

Nanaimo Festival
PO Box 626, Nanaimo, BC
V9R 5L9

Port Credit Summer Theatre
161 Lakeshore Road W
Mississauga, ON L5H 1G3

Red Barn Theatre
PO Box 291,
Jackson's Point, ON L0E 1L0

Shaw Festival Theatre
PO Box 774
Niagara-on-the-Lake
ON L0S 1J0

Stephenville Festival
149 Montana Dr
Stephenville, NF A2N 2T4

Stratford Shakespearean Festival
PO Box 520, Stratford, ON
N5A 6V2

Theatre Orangeville
Orangeville Opera House
87 Broadway,
Orangeville, ON
L9W 1K1

Thousand Islands Playhouse
PO Box 241
Gananoque, ON
K7G 2T8

Upper Canada Playhouse
PO Box 852
Morrisburg, ON
K0C 1X0

Major Theatre Companies in Canada

MARITIMES

Mermaid Theatre of Nova Scotia: PO Box 2697, Windsor, NS B0N 2T0

Mulgrave Road Co-op Theatre: PO Box 219, Guysborough, NS B0H 1N0

Neptune Theatre Foundation: #B24, 1903 Barrington St, Halifax, NS B3J 3L7

Ship's Company Theatre: PO Box 275, Parrsboro, NS B0M 1S0

Theatre New Brunswick: PO Box 566, Fredericton, NB E3B 5A6

CENTRAL CANADA

Buddies in Bad Times: 12 Alexander St, Toronto, ON M5R 1E8

Canadian Stage Company: 26 Berkeley St, Toronto, ON M5A 2W3

Centaur Theatre Company: 453, rue Saint-François-Xavier, Montreal, QC H2Y 2T1

La Compagnie Jean Duceppe: 1400 rue Saint-Urbain, Montreal, QC H2X 2M5

Company of Sirens: 736 Bathurst St, Toronto, ON M5S 2R4

Factory Theatre: 125 Bathurst St, Toronto, ON M5V 2R2

Grand Theatre Company (Theatre London): 471 Richmond St, London, ON N6A 3E4

Great Canadian Theatre Company: 910 Gladstone Ave, Ottawa, ON K1R 6Y4

Gryphon Theatre: PO Box 454, Barrie, ON L4M 4T7

Magnus Theatre Company: The Central School Bldg, 10 South Algoma St, Thunder Bay, ON P7B 3A7

National Arts Centre: PO Box 1534, Stn B, Ottawa, ON K1P 5W1

Native Earth Performing Arts: 503-720 Bathurst St, Toronto, ON M5S 2R4

Nightwood Theatre: 6000-317 Adelaide St W, Toronto, ON M5V 1T2

The Piggery: PO Box 390, North Hatley, QC J0B 2C0

Princess of Wales Theatre: 300 King St W, Toronto, ON M5V 1J2

Royal Alexandra Theatre: 260 King St W, Toronto, ON M5V 1H9

Saidye Bronfman Centre for the Arts: 5170 Chemin de la Côte, Ste-Catherine, Montreal, QC H3Y 1M7

Soulpepper Theatre Company: PO Box 199, 260 Adelaide St E, Toronto, ON M5A 1N1

Sudbury Theatre Centre: PO Box 641, Stn B, Sudbury, ON P3E 4P8

Tarragon Theatre: 30 Bridgman Ave, Toronto, ON M5R 1X3

Theatre Aquarius: 190 King William St, Hamilton, ON L8R 1A8

Théâtre de la Bordée: 1105, rue Saint-Jean, #201, Quebec, QC G1R 1S3

Théâtre du Nouveau Monde: 137, Saint-Ferdinand, #201, Montreal, QC H4C 2S7

Théâtre du Rideau Vert: 269 René Levésque G, Quebec, QC GIR 2B3

Le Théâtre du Trident: 580, ave Grande-Allée est, #20, Quebec, QC G1R 2K2

Theatre Passe Muraille: 16 Ryerson Ave, Toronto, ON M5T 2P3

Young People's Theatre: 165 Front St E, Toronto, ON M5A 3Z4

WESTERN CANADA

Alberta Theatre Projects: 220-9th Ave SE, Calgary, AB T2G 5C4

Arts Club Theatre: 1585 Johnson St, Vancouver, BC V6H 3R9

Belfry Theatre: 1291 Gladstone Ave, Victoria, BC V8T 1G5

Citadel Theatre: 9828-101A Ave, Edmonton, AB T5J 3C6

Globe Theatre: 1801 Scarth St, Regina, SK S4P 2G9

Manitoba Theatre Centre: 174 Market Ave, Winnipeg, MB R3B 0P8

Manitoba Theatre for Young People: 89 Princess St, Winnipeg, MB R3B 2X5

New Bastion Theatre Company: 625 Superior Ave, Victoria, BC V8V 1V1

Nightcap Productions: PO Box 1646, Saskatoon, SK S7K 3R8

Persephone Theatre: 2802 Rusholme Rd, Saskatoon, SK S7L 0H2

Popular Theatre Alliance of Manitoba: 2-413 Selkirk Ave, Winnipeg, MB R2W 2M4

Prairie Theatre Exchange: 389 Portage Ave, Portage Place, Unit Y300, Winnipeg, MB R3B 3H6

Tamahnous Theatre Workshop Society: 222-275 Woodland Dr, Vancouver, BC V5L 3S7

Theatre Calgary: 220-9th Ave SE, Calgary, AB T2G 5C4

Theatre Network Society: 10708-124th St, Edmonton, AB T5M 0H1

25th Street Theatre: 420 Duchess St, Saskatoon, SK S7K 0R1

Vancouver Playhouse: 160 West 1st Ave, Vancouver, BC V5Y 1A4

Western Canada Theatre Company: PO Box 329, Kamloops, BC V2C 5K9

Sources Include: *The Professional Association of Canadian Theatres*

DANCE

Canada is home to strong traditions in both classical and contemporary dance. Founded in 1938, The Royal Winnipeg Ballet is the second oldest company in North America and was the first in the Commonwealth to receive a Royal charter. Since 1951, the Toronto-based National Ballet of Canada has provided a home to major talents including prima ballerinas Karen Kain and Veronica Tennant. It has also been a favoured stopping place for international greats such as the late Rudolph Nureyev. The National Ballet was instrumental in facilitating the 1979 defection of Russia's Mikhail Baryshnikov in Toronto. Baryshnikov danced his first performances as a free man with the National Ballet, an event whose anniversary was marked in 1999 with the presentation of an honorary doctorate to Baryshnikov at the University of Toronto.

Major Ballet Companies

Alberta Ballet: 141-18th Avenue SW, Calgary, AB T2S 0B8

Ballet British Columbia: #102, 1101 West Broadway, Vancouver, BC V6H 1G2

Ballet Jorgen: 213B Glebeholme Blvd, Toronto, ON M4J 1S8

Ballet North: 12245-131 St, Edmonton, AB T5L 1M8

Les Grands Ballets Canadiens: 4816 rue Rivard, Montreal, QC H2J 2N6

Royal Winnipeg Ballet: 380 Graham Ave, Winnipeg, MB R3C 4K2

The National Ballet of Canada: The Walter Carson Centre, 470 Queen's Quay W, Toronto, ON M5V 3K4

Major Contemporary and Jazz Dance Companies

Les Ballets Jazz de Montréal: 3450 rue St-Urbain, Montreal, QC H2X 2N5

Contemporary Dancers Canada: 109 Pulford St, Winnipeg, MB R3L 1X8

Dancemakers: 927 Dupont St, Toronto, ON M6H 1Z1

Decidedly Jazz Danceworks: 1514-4th St SW, Calgary, AB T2R 0Y4

Desrosiers Dance Theatre: 103-219 Broadview Ave, Toronto, ON M4M 2G3

Fortier Danse Création: PO Box 605, Stn C, Montreal, QC H2L 4L5

Margie Gillis Dance Foundation: 502-3575 boul St Laurent, #502, Montreal, QC H2X 2T7

Danny Grossman Dance Company: 511 Bloor St W, Toronto, ON M5S 1Y4

LaLaLa Human Steps: #206, 5655 ave du Parc, Montreal, QC H2V 4H2

Le Groupe de la Place Royale: 2 Daly Ave, Ste 2, Ottawa, ON K1N 6E2

Karen Jamieson Dance Company: 221 E 16th Ave, Vancouver, BC V5T 2T5

Kompany!: #810, 10136-100th St, Edmonton, AB T5J 0P1

Mascall Dance: 1130 Jervis St, Vancouver, BC V6E 2C7

O Vertigo Danse: 4455 rue de Rouen, Montreal, QC H1V 1H1

La Fondation Jean-Pierre Perreault: 2022 rue Sherbrooke est, Montreal, QC H2K 1B9

Gina Lori Riley Dance Enterprises: 3277 Sandwich St, Windsor, ON N9C 1A9

Toronto Dance Theatre: 80 Winchester St, Toronto, ON M4X 1B2

Canadian Children's Dance Theatre: 509 Parliament St, Toronto, ON M4X 1P3

Compagnie Marie Chouinard: #615-3981 boul St-Laurent, Montreal, QC H2W 1Y5

Dance Arts Vancouver: #402-873 Beatty St, Vancouver, BC V6B 2M6

Source: *Dance Umbrella of Ontario*

BOOKS, MAGAZINES, NEWSPAPERS

According to the Association of Canadian Book Publishers, book publishing is a $1.7-billion enterprise in Canada. Eleven million English-speaking Canadians regularly read books, twice as many as in 1978, and Canadian-owned publishing firms publish over 80 percent of Canadian-authored titles. The association also reports that export of Canadian books has tripled since 1989. Canadian authors regularly win international acclaim and in recent years Canadians have won the Pulitzer Prize, the Booker Prize, and the Orange Prize for Fiction. In 2002, the Canadian publishing industry experienced a major crisis with the collapse of Stoddart Publishing. Most critical was the failure of Stoddart's distribution arm, which handled the books of several important small publishers.

Magazine publishing in Canada is an $866-million business in which domestic magazines take a 30 percent share of the market. The industry was dealt a serious blow in 2000 when the federal government was forced by the World Trade Organization to abandon tax measures aimed at protecting the advertising market from nominally Canadian "split run" editions of U.S. magazines. In 2001 the federal government responded with the creation of the $150,000,000 Canada Magazine Fund designed to offset revenue losses due to increased foreign competition.

Recent years have seen major shifts in newspaper ownership. Montreal-based Québecor Inc. took control of the Sun newspaper chain. Canada's oldest newspaper dynasty, that of the Thomson family, divested itself of most of its newspaper holdings, while in 2000 the newspaper empire of Conrad Black's Hollinger Inc. sold its interests in Southam Newspapers to Winnipeg television magnate Izzy Asper's Canwest/Global Corporation.

The Governor General's Literary Awards, 1993–2002

The Governor General's Literary Awards, Canada's foremost literary prizes, are presented annually to recognize and reward Canadian writers. The awards were initiated in 1937 by the Canadian Authors' Association with the agreement of Governor General Baron Tweedsmuir (novelist John Buchan), and were administered by the Association until 1958.

The Awards are now administered by the Canada Council, which appoints juries composed of literary specialists who select the best English- and French-language works in each of six categories: drama, fiction, poetry, non-fiction, and, beginning in 1987, children's literature (text and illustration) and translation. The juries review all books by Canadian authors, illustrators and translators published in Canada or abroad during the previous year (Oct. 1–Sept. 30). In the case of translation, the original work must also be a Canadian-authored title. Winners receive a medal from the Governor General, $10,000 and a specially bound copy of their award-winning book. The 2002 winners were announced November 12, 2002, in Ottawa.

English

—1993—

Fiction . . . . *The Stone Diaries*, Carol Shields
Non-fiction . . . . *Touch the Dragon*, Karen Connelly
Poetry . . . . *Forest of the Medieval World*, Don Coles
Drama . . . . *Fronteras Americanas*, Guillermo Verdecchia

—1994—

Fiction . . . . *A Discovery of Strangers*, Rudy Wiebe
Non-fiction . . . . . *Rogue Primate: An Exploration of Human Domestication*, John A. Livingston
Poetry . . . . *Cantos from a Small Room*, Robert Hilles
Drama . . . . *The Ends of the Earth*, Morris Panych

—1995—

Fiction	*The Roaring Girl*, Greg Hollingshead
Non-fiction	*Shadow Maker: The Life of Gwendolyn MacEwen*, Rosemary Sullivan
Poetry	*Voice*, Anne Szumigalski
Drama	*Three in the Back, Two in the Head*, Jason Sherman

—1996—

Fiction	*The Englishman's Boy*, Guy Vanderhaeghe
Non-fiction	*The Unconscious Civilization*, John Ralston Saul
Poetry	*Apostrophes: Woman at a Piano*, E.D. Blodgett
Drama	*The Monument*, Colleen Wagner

—1997—

Fiction	*The Underpainter*, Jane Urquhart
Non-fiction	*Drumblair—Memories of a Jamaican Childhood*, Rachel Manley
Poetry	*Land to Light On*, Dionne Brand
Drama	*fareWel*, Ian Ross

—1998—

Fiction	*Forms of Devotion*, Diane Schoemperlen
Non-fiction	*Lines on the Water—A Fisherman's Life on the Miramichi*, David Adams Richards
Poetry	*White Stone: The Alice Poems*, Stephanie Bolster
Drama	*Harlem Duet*, Djanet Sears

—1999—

Fiction	*Elizabeth and After*, Matt Cohen
Non-fiction	*Water*, Marq de Villiers
Poetry	*Songs for Relinquishing the Earth*, Jan Zwicky
Drama	*The Drawer Boy*, Michael Healey

—2000—

Fiction	*Anil's Ghost*, Michael Ondaatje
Non-fiction	*Notes from the Hyena's Belly*, Nega Mezlekia
Poetry	*Another Gravity*, Don McKay
Drama	*Elizabeth Rex*, Timothy Findley

—2001—

Fiction	*Clara Callan*, Richard B. Wright
Non-fiction	*The Ingenuity Gap*, Thomas Homer-Dixon
Poetry	*Execution Poems*, George Elliott Clarke
Drama	*The Harps of God*, Kent Stetson

—2002—

Fiction	*A Song for Nettie Johnson*, Gloria Sawai
Non-fiction	*Saboteurs: Wiebo Ludwig's War Against Big Oil*, Andrew Nikiforuk
Poetry	*Surrender*, Roy Miki
Drama	*Unity (1918)*, Kevin Kerr
Translation	*Thunder and Light*, Nigel Spencer
Children's Literature (Illustration)	*Alphabeasts*, Wallace Edwards
Children's Literature (Text)	*True Confessions of a Heartless Girl*, Martha Brooks

French

—1993—

Fiction	*Cartique des Plaines*, Nancy Huston
Non-fiction	*Le littérature de l'exiguité*, François Paré
Poetry	*Le Saut de L'ange*, Denise Desautels
Drama	*Celle-là*, Daniel Danis

—1994—

Fiction	*Le Petit Aigle à tête blanche*, Robert Lalonde
Non-fiction	*Du sida*, Chantal Saint-Jarre
Poetry	*Aknos*, Fulvio Caccia
Drama	*French Town*, Michel Ouellette

—1995—

Fiction	*Les Oiseaux de Saint-John Perse*, Nicole Houde
Non-fiction	*Louis-Antoine Dessaulles*, Yvan Lamonde
Poetry	*Pour orchestre et poète seul*, Émile Martel
Drama	*Les Quatre Morts de Marie*, Carole Fréchette

—1996—

Fiction	*Soifs*, Marie-Claire Blais
Non-fiction	*Le Naufrage de l'université*, Michel Freitag
Poetry	*Le Quatuor de l'errance*, Serge Patrice Thibodeau
Drama	*Le Passage de l'Indiana*, Normand Chaurette

—1997—

Fiction	*Cet imperceptible mouvement*, Aude
Non-fiction	*Enfants du néant et mangeurs d'âmes—Guerre, culture et société en Iroquoisie ancienne*, Roland Viau
Poetry	*Romans-fleuves*, Pierre Nepveu
Drama	*Dits et Inédits*, Yvan Bienvenue

—1998—

Fiction	*La Terre ferme*, Christiane Frenette
Non-fiction	*Intérieurs du Nouveau Monde*, Pierre Nepveu
Poetry	*Le Part de feu/Le Deuil de la rancune*, Suzanne Jacob
Drama	*15 secondes*, François Archambault

—1999—

Fiction	*La Danse juive*, Lise Tremblay
Non-fiction	*Le Mal du Nord*, Pierre Perrault
Poetry	*Conversations*, Herménégilde Chiasson
Drama	*Il n'y a que l'amour*, Jean Marc Dalpé

—2000—

Fiction	*Un vent se lève qui éparpille*, Jean Marc Dalpé
Non-fiction	*Genèse des nations et cultures du Nouveau Monde*, Gérard Bouchard
Poetry	*La Marche de l'aveugle sans son chien*, Normand de Bellefeuille
Drama	*Littoral*, Wajdi Mouawad

—2001—

Fiction	*Le ravissement*, Andrée A. Michaud
Non-fiction	*Quel Canada pour les Autochtones? La fin de l'exclusion*, Renée Dupuis
Poetry	*Des ombres portées*, Paul Chanel Malenfant
Drama	*Le Petit Köchel*, Normand Chaurette

—2002—

Fiction	*La Gloire de Cassiodore*, Monique LaRue
Non-fiction	*Mark Twain et la parole noire*, Judith Lavoie
Poetry	*Humains paysages en temps de paix relative*, Robert Dickson
Drama	*Le Langue-à-Langue des chiens de roche*, Daniel Danis
Translation	*Histoire universelle de la chasteté et du célibat*, Paule Pierce-Noyart
Children's Literature (Illustration)	*Le grand voyage de Monsieur*, Luc Melanson
Children's Literature (Text)	*L'oiseau de passage*, Hélène Vachon

Source: *The Canada Council*

The Giller Prize, 1994–2002

The Giller Prize awards $25,000 annually to the author of the best Canadian novel or short story collection published in English. The award was founded in 1994 by Toronto businessman Jack Rabinovitch in honour of his late wife, literary journalist Doris Giller.

The 2002 Giller Prize was presented November 5, 2002.

Year	Author	Title
1994	M.G. Vassanji	*The Book of Secrets*
1995	Rohinton Mistry	*A Fine Balance*
1996	Margaret Atwood	*Alias Grace*
1997	Mordecai Richler	*Barney's Version*
1998	Alice Munro	*The Love of a Good Woman*
1999	Bonnie Burnard	*A Good House*
2000 (joint winners)	Michael Ondaatje	*Anil's Ghost*
	David Adams Richards	*Mercy Among the Children*
2001	Richard B. Wright	*Clara Callan*
2002	Austin Clarke	*The Polished Hoe*

The Man-Booker Prize, 1994–2002

The Man-Booker Prize recognizes the best work of English fiction published in the Commonwealth, South Africa and Ireland. Since April 2002 it has been sponsored by Man Group plc, a global provider of alternative investment funds, and administered by the Booker Prize Book Foundation, a British educational charity. Since 1984, the value of the Booker Prize has been £15,000.

Year	Author	Title
1994	James Kelman	*How Late It Was, How Late*
1995	Pat Barker	*The Ghost Road*
1996	Graham Swift	*Last Orders*
1997	Arundhati Roy	*The God of Small Things*
1998	Ian McEwan	*Amsterdam*
1999	J.M. Coetzee	*Disgrace*
2000	**Margaret Atwood**	***The Blind Assassin***
2001	Peter Carey	*The True Story of the Kelly Gang*
2002	**Yann Martel**	***Life of Pi***

Pulitzer Prizes, 2002

The winners of these annual American literary awards were announced on April 7, 2003.

Fiction	Jeffrey Eugenides, *Middlesex*
Non-fiction	Samantha Power, *"A Problem From Hell": America and the Age of Genocide*
Poetry	Paul Muldoon, *Moy Sand and Gravel*
Drama	Nilo Cruz, *Anna in the Tropics*
Biography	Robert A. Caro, *Master of the Senate*
History	Rick Atkinson, *An Army at Dawn: The War in North Africa 1942–1943*
News Reporting	Staff, *The Eagle-Tribune*, Lawrence, Mass.
Investigative Reporting	Clifford J. Levy, *The New York Times*

The Griffin Poetry Prize, 2002–2003

Consisting of two $40,000 awards presented annually, the Griffin Poetry Prize is one of the world's largest awards for poets. The Griffin Trust for Excellence in Poetry gives one prize to a Canadian poet and one to an international poet. The competition is judged by a panel of Canadian and international literary figures. The 2003 Griffin Prize was announced June 12 in Toronto.

■ Canada

Year	Author	Title
2002	Christian Bök	*Eunoia*
2003	Margaret Avison	*Concrete and Wild Carrot*

■ International

Year	Author	Title
2002	Alice Notley (USA)	*Disobedience*
2003	Paul Muldoon (UK)	*Moy Sand and Gravel*

The Stephen Leacock Medal for Humour, 1999–2003

Stephen Butler Leacock was born in England in 1869. He was educated at Upper Canada College, University of Toronto (B.A.), and the University of Chicago (Ph.D.). He taught at UCC, and later lectured in political science at McGill. His literary output included works in history, economics and political science, although by far the most popular were his humour books. By the time of his death in 1944, he was the best-known humourist in the English-speaking world.

Canada's highest award for humour is given annually at a ceremony in Leacock's hometown of Orillia, Ontario.

Year	Author	Title
1999	Stuart McLean	*Home from the Vinyl Café*
2000	Arthur Black	*Black Tie and Tales*
2001	Stuart McLean	*Vinyl Café Unplugged*
2002	Will Ferguson	*Generica*
2003	Dan Needles	*With Axe and Flask—A History of Persephone Township from Pre-Cambrian Times to the Present*

Source: *The Leacock Home*

www.archives.ca: The National Archives On-line

*I*n May 2001, the National Archives of Canada launched its official web site designed as an introduction to its collections and services. Digitization of the archives' materials is ongoing, but for the moment the site gives visitors an opportunity to get a glimpse of the fascinating items in the archival vaults. The "Living Memory" segment of the site was inspired by the **Treasured Memories** exhibition held in 1999 to mark the archives' 125th anniversary. Among the documents and artefacts displayed are the Canadian Bill of Rights, illustrations from the Log book of the HMS Pegasus as it carried out the first visit by a member of the Royal family to Canada in 1820 and the Torah of the Shearith Israel Congregation of 18th-century Montreal. The database is searchable by Theme, Period and Media Type. It contains maps, documentary art, photographs and government records. A short description of each item is provided with selections from the item in question: for example, a page of former Governor General Georges Vanier's report on his 1945 visit to the recently liberated concentration camp at Buchenwald in his capacity as Canada's Ambassador to France.

The research section of the web site offers an introduction to Research Services at the National Archives. The ArchiviaNet on-line research and consultation tool gives access to information about items stored in the archives' general inventory.

Bestselling Books in Canada, 2002

Fiction

1. *Unless*, Carol Shields
2. *Family Matters*, Rohinton Mistry
3. *Questions*, Maeve Binchy
4. *Crow Lake*, Mary Lawson
5. *The Smelters of Stone*, Jean M. Auel
6. *The Navigator of New York*, Wayne Johnston
7. *The Lovely Bones*, Alice Sebold
8. *Clara Callan*, Richard B. Wright
9. *Atonement*, Ian McEwan
10. *The Last Crossing*, Guy Vanderhaeghe

Source: *The Globe and Mail*   Canadian books set in bold type.

Non-fiction

1. *Stupid White Men*, Michael Moore
2. *9-11*, Noam Chomsky
3. *How To Be A Canadian*, Will & Ian Ferguson
4. *Dropped Threads*, edited by Carol Shields and Marjorie Anderson
5. *Souvenir of Canada*, Douglas Coupland
6. *Lucky Man*, Michael J. Fox
7. *On Equilibrium*, John Ralston Saul
8. *Shakey: Neil Young's Biography*, Jimmy McDonough
9. *Jack: Straight from the Gut*, Jack Welch and Jack A. Byrne
10. *Negotiating with the Dead*, Margaret Atwood

National Magazine Awards, 2003

These annual awards were presented May 30, 2003, by the National Magazine Awards Foundation. In 2003 there were gold and silver awards in 33 categories, including writing, design, illustration, and photography and art direction. Gold award winners are listed below.

One-of-a-Kind Articles . . . . Andy Lamey, "My Life As A Pimp," *Toronto Life*
Humour . . . . Ken Hegan, "*I Can Do That*," *BC Business*
Business . . . . David Hayes, "Song Corpse," *Toronto Life*
Science & Technology . . . . David Lees, "Coral Champions," *Canadian Geographic*
Health and Medicine . . . . James Fitzgerald, "Sins of the Fathers," *Toronto Life*
Still-Life Photography . . . . Colin Faulkner, "Cherries Jubilation," *Food & Drink*
Fashion . . . . Denis Desro, Chris Nicolls, Isabelle Long, "Blow Out," *Elle Canada*
Politics . . . . John Lorinc, "Dirty Rotten Scandal," *Toronto Life*
Investigative Reporting . . . . Daniel Sanger, "The Many Lives and Singular Death of Danny Kane," *Saturday Night*
Fiction . . . . Anne Fleming, "Gay Dwarves of America," *The New Quarterly*
Arts and Entertainment . . . . Michael Posner, "Schtick Figure," *Toronto Life*
Sports and Recreation . . . . Charles Wilkins, "The Last Fish He Ever Caught," *Outdoor Canada*
Photojournalism . . . . Naomi Harris, "RawshiftFreedom," *Shift*
Personal journalism . . . . Daniel Wood, "Hammering Away At Eternity," *explore*
Portrait Photography . . . . K.C. Armstrong, "The Man Who Reads Faces," *Elm Street*
Columns . . . . Robert Fulford, "Man Bites Man, Personal Loyalty Mourning Show," *Toronto Life*
Service . . . . Jonathan Trudel, Véronique Robert, "Alerte à la santé des hommes," *L'actualité*
Travel . . . . J.B. MacKinnon, "Behind the Grass Curtain," *explore*
Spot Illustration . . . . Greg Mably, "Pills, Profits and ... Perils," *Maclean's*
How-To . . . . Kevin Callan, "Secrets of Algonquin," *explore*
Essays . . . . Mark Kingwell, "Meaning To Get To: Procrastination and the Art of Life," *Queen's Quarterly*
Profiles . . . . Geoff Powter, "The Happy Tormented Life of a Mountain Legend," *explore*
Poetry . . . . Alison Pick, "Question & Answer," *The New Quarterly*
Art Direction for a Single Article . . . . *Adbusters* Art Dept., "The Lilly Suicides," *Adbusters*
Editorial Package . . . . Staff, "Food Issue," *Canadian Geographic*
Words and Pictures . . . . . Nancy Clark, Ian O'Neill, Steve Manley, Mick Coulas, "Camp! Around the Clock," *Seasons*
Magazine Covers . . . . Marcello Biagioni, "Body Flop," *R.O.B. Magazine*
President's Medal . . . . *Outpost*
Alexander Ross Award for Best New Magazine Writer . . . . Jean-François Bégin
Foundation Award for Outstanding Achievement . . . . Sally Armstrong

Source: *National Magazine Awards Foundation*

Top Canadian Paid-Circulation Magazines, 2003

Magazine	Circulation[1]
Reader's Digest (Canadian English edition)	1 000 000
Chatelaine (English-language edition)	704 466
Canadian Living	543 825
TV Guide	429 003
Maclean's	445 022
Time (Canadian edition)	240 684
Sélection du Reader's Digest (Canadian French edition)	232 767
Canadian Geographic	227 799
Coupe de Pouce	217 068
Châtelaine (French language edition)	91 399
L'Actualité	187 700
TV Hebdo	166 873
Flare	57 025

Source: *CARD: Media Information Network* (1) Average total paid circulation for most recently reported 6-month period as of August 2003.

Canada's Newspapers On-Line

Southam Newspapers—www.canada.com: *Operated by CanWest Interactive, this site links to sites for Southam newspapers in major Canadian cities including* **The Vancouver Sun**, *the* **Vancouver Province**, *the* **Calgary Herald**, *the* **Edmonton Journal**, *the* **Ottawa Citizen** *and the* **Montreal Gazette**. *The sites each offer a home page containing the day's lead story plus "sections" such as a "front" section, news section, sports, entertainment, etc., each containing a selection of stories from that day's edition. The newspapers' archives can be accessed on a pay basis at www.infomart.ca.*

The Toronto Star—www.thestar.com: *The official site of Canada's largest circulation daily offers a selection of articles from sections including the Greater Toronto, Sports, Business and Entertainment sections of each day's edition, plus access to stories from weekly sections. A 14-day archive may be searched free of charge. Paid archive searches for articles dating as far back as January 1985 may be conducted for a nominal fee payable by credit card.*

The Globe and Mail—www.globeandmail.com: *"Canada's National Newspaper" includes a selection of approximately 10 stories per section of its daily print edition. Weekly features such as columns by the paper's 31 columnists are also available. A free seven-day archive search is offered plus a complete index of the print edition's headlines for the day.*

National Post—www.nationalpost.com: *As well as a selection of stories from each day's edition, the National Post site offers a 14-day searchable database of its stories. Weekly features such as Saturday Post, Post Movies and Driver's Edge are available, as are specials such as* **Inside Entertainment** *and* **National Post Business Magazine**.

The Winnipeg Free Press—www.winnipegfreepress.com: *The* **Free Press** *offers full on-line access only to subscribers of its print edition inside Manitoba. Readers outside Manitoba may subscribe to the paper on-line for a charge of $5.00 per month. Available free on the web site are auto listings, classifieds, obituaries, careers and special sections.*

The Chronicle Herald, Mail Star and **Sunday Herald,** Halifax—www.herald.ns.ca: *As well as selections from the day's news, the site gives access to weekly features such as Travel, Arts, Living, Science and Technology and to a seven-day archive of selections from the newspapers. Subscribers to the print edition can register for free access to the full edition on-line. On-line subscriptions to the papers are $13 per month.*

Top Canadian Daily Newspapers, 2003

Newspaper	Circulation[1]		
	Daily[2]	Saturday	Sunday
Toronto Star	463 215	673 988	430 520
Globe and Mail	318 009	402 216	
Journal de Montreal	268 527	326 085	270 006
National Post	251 803	288 192	
Toronto Sun	210 957	175 426	362 119
La Presse	185 609	268 236	194 012
Vancouver Sun	180 888 (M-Th.) 209 906 (F.)	238 848	
Vancouver Province	160 165	197 660	
Montreal Gazette	141 517	169 355	138 640
Ottawa Citizen	133 977	171 231	130 499
Edmonton Journal	127 507 (M-Th./Sat.); 148 639 (Fri.)	126 479	
Winnipeg Free Press	120 489	174 299	119 466
Calgary Herald	114 475 (M-Th.) 143 210 (Fri.)	127 338	114 020
Halifax Chronicle Herald	07 225	61 451	
Hamiltion Spectator	105 195	122 197	
Le Journal de Quebec	97 188	123 100	99 516
London Free Press	92 544	113 864	
Le Soleil	81 045	112 951	90 304
Windsor Star	75 114	85 447	
Edmonton Sun	72 830 (Mon.-Sat.)	101 668	
Victoria-Times Columnist	72 588 (Mon.-Th.)	77 537	75 898

Sources: *CARD: Media Information Network, Canadian Newspaper Association*
(1) Average total paid circulation for most recently reported 6-month period as of August 2003. Ranked by weekday circulation.
(2) Monday to Friday unless otherwise indicated.

National Newspaper Awards, 2003

These annual awards were announced in Calgary on May 2, 2003.

Editorial Writing . . . . Russell Wangersky, *St. John's Telegram*
News Photography . . . . Jim Young, *Reuters*
Feature Photography . . . . Dave Chan, *Globe and Mail*
Breaking News Reporting . . . . Lindsay Kines, Kim Bolan, *The Vancouver Sun*
International Reporting . . . . Stephen Thorne, *Canadian Press*
Sports Writing . . . . Gary Mason, *The Vancouver Sun*
Long Feature Writing . . . . Dan Gardner, *Ottawa Citizen*
Short Feature Writing . . . . Anthony Reinhart, *Kitchener-Waterloo Record*
Columns . . . . Josh Freed, *Montreal Gazette*
Sports Photography . . . . Peter Power, *TheToronto Star*
Local Reporting . . . . Chris Lambie, *Halifax Daily News*
Arts and Entertainment . . . . Alison Rose, *National Post*
Presentation . . . . Geneviève Dinel, *La Presse*
Editorial Cartooning . . . . Serge Chapleau, *La Presse*
Business Reporting . . . . Jacquie McNish, Brian Laghi, John Partridge Simon Tuck, *Globe and Mail*
Investigations . . . . Jim Rankin, Scott Simmie, John Duncanson, Michele Shephard, Jennifer Quinn, *Toronto Star*

Source: *Canadian Newspaper Association*

GALLERIES AND MUSEUMS

Canadian art is a time-honoured tradition with the oldest surviving work of prehistoric First Nations carving dating back to 5,000 B.C. European traditions were slow to take hold in the colonial regime. Bishop Laval established the country's first school of art near Quebec in 1675 and religious art dominated the Canadian scene until the 19th century when Paul Kane and Cornelius Krieghoff became the country's first genre painters, rendering scenes of native and settler life respectively. After the establishment of major art institutions such as the Royal Canadian Academy of Art (1880) and the Ontario College of Art (1875), landscape became the dominant form of Canadian painting, a trend that peaked with the formation of the Group of Seven in 1920 (see article below). Abstract art reached Canada in the 1940s and gained its first domestic expression in the work of Montreal's automatiste painters, lead by Jean Paul Riopelle and Paul-Émile Borduas, working under the influence of cubism and the French surrealists. Art in English Canada remained under the sway of the Group of Seven and that of British representational trends in portraiture and urban landscape until the formation in 1954 and subsequent international success of Painters Eleven in Toronto. This group, which featured Jack Bush, Kazuo

Nakamura, Jock MacDonald, William Ronald, and Harold Town, drew heavily on the abstract expressionist movement in the United States for inspiration and its members scored success in New York critical circles of the period. Leadership reverted to Montreal in the 1960s with the emergence of painters devoted to the op art school focussing on experiments in visual effects and surface dynamics. While hyper-realist painters such as Nova Scotia's Alex Colville, and Newfoundland's Christopher Pratt and Manitoba-born naïve painter William Kurelek kept representational painting popular through the 1970s, a new generation of artists such as Michael Snow, Greg Curnoe, General Idea, and Iain Baxter followed the international trend away from painting into conceptual art exploring new media such as film, photography, performance and installation art. The 1980s saw a rebirth in interest in representational painting with the emergence of neo-expressionist–influenced work from groups such as Vancouver's New Romantics and Toronto's ChromaZone Collective. Today the Canadian art scene features artists working in every conceivable medium and genre. Their work is shown in artist-run collectives, commercial galleries and larger public galleries in every major centre.

The Group of Seven

The Group of Seven held its first exhibition at the Art Gallery of Toronto in May 1920. The original members included J.E.H. MacDonald, Lawren Harris, A.Y. Jackson, Arthur Lismer, F.H. Varley, Frank Johnston and Franklin Carmichael.

In 1924, Johnston resigned from the Group and, in 1926, A.J. Casson was invited to join. In the later years of the Group, two new members, Edwin Holgate and Lionel Lemoine FitzGerald, were added. The Group held its final exhibition in Dec. 1931 and disbanded in 1932.

Tom Thomson, who drowned in 1917, was never a member of the Group of Seven, though his boldly coloured works depicting the rugged landscape of northern Ontario became associated with its style of painting.

By breaking with the traditional, European, painting style popular in Canada in the

1920s, the Group of Seven made a huge impact on Canadian art. Although originally reviled by critics, the Group had gained wide acceptance and popularity by the 1930s. Today, the Group's paintings are exhibited in every major gallery in Canada.

J.E.H. **MacDonald** (1873–1932)
Lawren **Harris** (1885–1970)
Alexander Young (A.Y.) **Jackson** (1882–1974)
Arthur **Lismer** (1885–1969)
Frederick Horsman (F.H.) **Varley** (1881–1969)
Frank Hans **Johnston** (1888–1949)
Frank **Carmichael** (1890–1945)
Alfred Joseph (A.J.) **Casson** (1898–1992)
Edwin **Holgate** (1892–1977)
Lionel Lemoine **FitzGerald** (1890–1956)
Tom **Thomson** (1877–1917)

Source: *Looking at Landscape*, Dwight Siegner, The McMichael Canadian Art Collection

Gallery and Museum Highlights, 2004

Vancouver Art Gallery

Chagall: Storyteller (Oct. 16, 2003–Feb. 8, 2004)—Marc Chagall occupies a unique place in 20th-century art. Born in Russia, he was part of the Jewish diaspora and spent most of his working life in France. Yet his art was deeply influenced by his childhood in Vitebsk, and many of his most famous works are based on memories of his homeland. Largely narrative, much of his printmaking illustrates texts such as Gogol's Dead Souls, the Bible and Longus' Daphnis and Chloe. This exhibition, the first important showing of Chagall's work in Vancouver, will examine his work as a printmaker and include a select number of gouaches and canvases.

From state-endorsed images to personal experiences, *Canvas of War:*

Painting the Canadian Experience, 1914–1945 (Feb.14–May 30) examines

Canada's role in war and conflict and its impact on civilians and the military. It features treasures from the collection of the Canadian War Museum in Ottawa.

Other exhibitions for 2004 include: *Baja to Vancouver: The West Coast and Contemporary Art* (June 5–Sept. 6), *Massive Change: The Future of Design Culture* (June 24–Sept. 26), *Arthur Erickson* (Oct. 21, 2004–Jan. 23, 2005).

Glenbow Museum, Calgary

The Mysterious Bog People: Exclusive International Tour Partner (Oct. 2003–Feb. 2004) is the first international touring exhibition to tell the story of life in Northern Europe from the Stone Age to the end of the 16th century. It reveals the importance of the discoveries in European bogs that shed light on the everyday lives, ideas and beliefs of ancient peoples.

Winnipeg Art Gallery

The Jerry Twomey Collection at the Winnipeg Art Gallery: Inuit Sculpture from the Canadian Arctic (through Mar. 7, 2004): Jerry Twomey was the first collector to research the individual artists who were creating sculpture in the 1950s and 1960s. He exhaustively classified and organized his collection by community and artist, identifying artists by family group. In order to determine the most talented

artists carving at that time, he bought widely from literally every dealer and wholesale agency in the country. He made several trips to Arctic communities, taking photographs of artists he met on his travels. His collection included carvings from every art-producing community at that time—30 in all. It is a definitive overview of Inuit carving activity across the Canadian Arctic in the first two decades that Inuit sculpture was marketed in Southern Canada.

Art Gallery of Ontario, Toronto

Present Tense: Maria Sheriff (Oct. 29, 2003–Jan. 11, 2004)—A new sculpture and video installation by Montreal artist Maria Sheriff poetically finds likeness and incongruity in substance and light. *Re-play: Stan Douglas* (Oct. 22, 2003–Jan. 11, 2004)—A landmark in video art, Vancouver artist Stan Douglas's "Hors-champs," shows a jazz quartet from two simultaneous points of view. Among the most celebrated works of contemporary Canadian art, "Hors-champs" has not been seen in Toronto in nearly ten years. *Woman as Goddess: Liberated Nudes by Robert Markle and Joyce Wieland* (Nov. 29, 2003–Feb. 29, 2004)—A provocative conversation about the nude, an icon of Western art that was radicalized by the 1960s counterculture. Approximately 100 works, dating from the late 1950s through the 1990s, epitomize both artists' distinct reinterpretations of the nude.

Royal Ontario Museum, Toronto

The next few years will be a time of renewal for the Royal Ontario Museum as Renaissance ROM, the major expansion and restoration project, adds new galleries and restores historic buildings. The Museum will remain open during the construction (May 2003–Dec. 2006), offering a series of touring exhibitions including *Eternal Egypt: Masterworks of Ancient Art from The British Museum* (Feb. 28–June 6, 2004), which illustrates the development and achievements of ancient Egyptian art over more than 3,000 years, from the pre-Dynastic to the Roman Periods (c. 3100 BC to 30 BC). The diverse works include mummy masks, coffins and other funerary items, sculpture and reliefs, papyri, ostraca (pottery shards used as writing surfaces), jewellery and cosmetic objects. Many of the 150 exceptional objects have never before left The British Museum or have not been exhibited for years. *Pearls: A Natural History* (Sept. 18, 2004–Jan. 9, 2005) traces both the natural and cultural history of pearls across the continents. It features more than 600 objects and nearly half a million pearls. Among the exhibition's highlights are exquisite ornaments worn by luminaries such as Queen Victoria, Marie Antoinette, Marilyn Monroe, Audrey Hepburn and Joan Crawford, as well as spectacular gems from renowned jewellers such as Cartier, Tiffany, and Harry Winston.

National Gallery of Canada, Ottawa

Lucius O'Brien: "Sunrise on the Saguenay," (through Feb. 8, 2004) highlights a landmark painting in the history of Canadian art, Lucius O'Brien's "Sunrise on the Saguenay." It has become a key image linked to the identity of Quebec City. *David Rabinowitch* (Feb.6–May 2, 2004) surveys the work of the Canadian sculptor who, since the 1960s, has developed a singular body of work that combines the apparently contrasting fields of gravity and perspective. This is one of the first large-scale Canadian presentations of work by Rabinowitch. It will highlight the cyclical development of his rigorous and concise sculptural and drawing techniques. *French Drawings from Canadian Collections* (May 21–Aug. 29, 2004) brings together over eighty French drawings done between the 16th and 19th centuries, selected to highlight some of the major stages in the development of art in France. Antoine Watteau, François Boucher, Jean-Honoré Fragonard, Jacques-Louis David, Anne-Louis Girodet, Eugène Delacroix and Théodore Géricault, Edgar Degas, Pierre Puvis de Chavannes and Odilon Redon are among the artists included. *The Great Parade: Portrait of the Artist as Clown* (June 26–Sept. 19) will examine the condition of the modern artist. From the mid-19th century to the beginning of 21st century, the circus became the locale for artists' imaginative expression, and the clown a metaphoric figure. Approximately 175 works by artists as varied as Daumier, Renoir, Seurat, Lautrec, Degas, Picasso, Rouault, Beckmann, Léger, Chagall, Calder and several contemporary artists will be installed in thematic groupings.

Canadian Museum of Civilization, Hull

Ancient Treasures and the Dead Sea Scrolls (Dec. 5, 2003–Apr. 12, 2004) presents over 100 ancient treasures from the Israel Museum and the Israel Antiquities Authority, dating from 3,200 to 1,300 years ago, many exhibited for the first time in North America. The artifacts include some of the 20th century's most remarkable discoveries, including three of the Dead Sea Scrolls, from among the first scrolls found in 1947. *The Rocket, Maurice Richard* (Apr. 8, 2004–Mar. 13, 2005) traces the story of hockey immortal Maurice "The Rocket" Richard, illustrated by treasures from his own memorabilia collection, plus fan scrapbooks, newspaper clippings, music, photographs, video and rare artifacts, all showing the special relationship of Number 9 to Quebec and Canada. With *Living in New France* (June 10, 2004–Mar. 28, 2005), the Canadian Museum of Civilization celebrates the 400th anniversary of French settlement in North America with a must-see exhibition on New France. Through rich artifacts from over 40 collections, the exhibition provides a look at life in New France in the 17th and 18th centuries.

Montreal Museum of Fine Art

Global Village: The 60s (Oct. 2, 2003–Jan. 18, 2004) will provide a sweeping overview of the forces of the imagination that were at work in this eventful decade, as manifested in art, design, photography, fashion and architecture. It will feature about 250 works, each an example of what was brand new in the 1960s. Featuring approximately 180 works of statuary, pottery and painting, *Tanagra: Myth and Archaelogy* (Feb. 5–May 9) will tell of the discovery of Boeotian tombs in central Greece in 1870 and examine the effect this had on European artistic and literary creation. From a reflection on the place and date of the original production of these famous terra-cotta figures known as "tanagras," the exhibition will study how this theme was taken up and developed in the other principal regions of the Hellenistic world. *Jean Cocteau: Universal Creator* (Apr. 15–Aug. 29) will reflect the abundance of Cocteau's *oeuvre*, in which disciplines and personalities cross-fertilized and influenced each other. The curatorial team has chosen a multi-disciplinary approach to the show, presenting recreated décors and stage sets alongside the paintings and drawings. The exhibition will also feature a festival of Cocteau's films. *Max Stern: Collector, Art Dealer and Patron* (Sept. 16–Dec. 12) includes works by Paul-Émile Borduas, Emily Carr, Jean-Philippe Dallaire, J.E.H. MacDonald, Arthur Lismer, James Wilson Morrice, Jean-Paul Riopelle, Goodridge Roberts and Jori Smith.

Beaverbrook Museum, Fredericton

Exhibitions at the Beaverbrook for 2004 include: *Alex Colville: Return Paintings, Drawings and Prints 1994–2002* (through Feb. 29); *Bruno Bobak: A Legacy in Art* (through Feb. 29); *Atlantic Canadian Artists: A Selection II* (through Feb. 29); *Portraits* (Feb. 7–Sept. 5); *Abstracts/Colourfield* (Feb. 9–May 31); *Marion McCain Atlantic Art Exhibition* (Mar.13–Apr. 25); *Sixteenth-Century Italian Drawings: The Century of Mannerism* (May 1–July 1); *Dalí 100th Birthday Celebration Exhibition* (May 9–Sept. 5); *Contemporary Acadian Art* (May 9–Sept. 5); *New Brunswick First Nations Art* (June–Aug.); *The Changing Land: Modern British Landscape Painting 1900–1950* (Sept. 11–Nov. 7); *Glenn Priestly: From Tabor Hill to Keswick Ridge* (Sept.–Dec.); *Dutch and Flemish Drawings from the National Gallery of Canada* (Nov. 21, 2004–Feb.20, 2005). Permanent exhibitions: *The Beaverbrook Art Gallery Collection of Cornelius Krieghoff*, "Santiago El Grande by Salvador Dalí."

Museums Online

*M*ost major museums have Web sites that offer the public access to their collections, research documents, and education resources and activities. Here's a description of what you'll find at sites for some major Canadian and international museums:

The British Museum, London, England (www.thebritishmuseum.ac.uk) *The "Compass" section of this site gives the visitor access to a database containing images and descriptions of 5,000 objects from the museum collections. Virtual tours are available on a variety of subjects. A "Children's Compass" is available for young visitors.*

The Canadian Museum of Civilization, Hull, Quebec (www.civilization.ca)

This site's "Collections Storage Space" offers images and descriptions of furnishings, tools, personal items and other artifacts in the fields of archaeology, ethnology, folk culture and history. A virtual tour of the museum's Canada Hall is available, as well as an extensive selection of articles and images concerning the collections and recent exhibitions.

The Kunsthistorisches Museum, Vienna, Austria (www.khm.at) *Visitors may survey collections from a dozen departments. Notable are collections of 15th- to 18th-century art and items from the treasuries of the Hapsburg-Lorraine household and the Holy Roman Empire.*

Musée du Louvre, Paris, France (www.louvre.fr) *The site offers a selection of works from each of nine departments. A virtual tour offers 70 images drawn from 50 rooms in the museum.*

The Royal British Columbia Museum, Victoria, B.C. (rbcm1.rbcm.gov.bc.ca)

This site reflects the RBCM's mandate to explore and preserve B.C.'s cultural and natural heritage. Its "Object Database" provides an opportunity to survey a collection rich in artifacts from Northwest First Nations peoples, as well as from pioneer and modern periods.

The Royal Ontario Museum, Toronto, Ont. (www.rom.on.ca) *An "Interactive" section offers quizzes, contests, electronic postcards from the collection, and activities such as how to make a dinosaur out of chicken bones.*

The Smithsonian Institution, Washington, D.C., U.S.A. (www.si.edu) *An extensive "Explore and Learn" online resource section includes floor-by-floor virtual tours, audio presentations by famous performing artists, "Closer Look" brochures on museum installations, photo exhibits, and games and activities for children.*

Major Public Art Galleries in Canada

Art Gallery of Greater Victoria: 1040 Moss St, Victoria, BC V8V 4P1 (604) 384-4101

Art Gallery of Nova Scotia: PO Box 2262, Halifax, NS B3J 3C8 (902) 424-7542

Art Gallery of Ontario: 317 Dundas St W, Toronto, ON M5T 1G4 (416) 979-6648

Art Gallery of Windsor: 3100 Howard Ave, Windsor, ON N8X 3Y8 (519) 258-7111

Beaverbrook Art Gallery: PO Box 605, Fredericton, NB E3B 5A6 (506) 458-8545

Confederation Centre Art Gallery and Museum: 145 Richmond St, Charlottetown, PE C1A 1J1 (902) 628-6111

Dunlop Art Gallery: PO Box 2311, Regina, SK S4P 3Z5 (306) 777-6040

Edmonton Art Gallery: 2 Sir Winston Churchill Sq, Edmonton, AB T5J 2C1 (403) 422-6223

McMichael Canadian Art Collection: 10365 Islington Ave, Kleinburg, ON L0J 1C0 (905) 893-1121

Montreal Museum of Fine Arts: 1379-1380 Sherbrooke St W, PO Box 3000, Stn H, Montreal, QC H3G 2T9 (514) 285-1600

Musee d'Art Contemporain de Montreal: 185, rue Ste Catherine ouest, Montreal, QC H2X 1Z8 (514) 847-6212

Musée du Québec: Parc des Champs de Bataille, 1, rue Wolfe/Montcalm, Quebec, QC G1R 5H3 (418) 643-2150

National Gallery of Canada: 380 Sussex Dr, Ottawa, ON K1N 9N4 (613) 990-1985

Thunder Bay Art Gallery: PO Box 1193, Stn F, Thunder Bay, ON P7C 4X9 (807) 577-6427

Vancouver Art Gallery: 750 Hornby St, Vancouver, BC V6Z 2H7 (604) 662-4700

Winnipeg Art Gallery: 300 Memorial Blvd, Winnipeg, MB R3C 1V1 (204) 786-6641

Major Public Museums in Canada

Canadian Centre for Architecture: 1920 rue Baile, Montreal, QC H3A 1E9 (514) 939-7000

Canadian Museum of Civilization: 100 Laurier St, Box 3100, Stn B, Hull, QC J8X 4H2 (819) 776-7000

Canadian Museum of Contemporary Photography: 1 Rideau Canal, PO Box 465, Stn A, Ottawa, ON K1N 9N6 (613) 990-8257

Canadian Museum of Nature: PO Box 3443, Stn D, Ottawa, ON K1P 6P4 (613) 566-4700

Canadian War Museum: 330 Sussex Dr, Ottawa, ON K1A 0M8 (613) 996-1420

Glenbow-Alberta Institute: 130-9th Ave. SE, Calgary, AB T2G 0P3 (403) 268-4100

Manitoba Museum of Man and Nature: 190 Rupert Ave, Winnipeg, MB R3B 0N2 (204) 956-2830

Maritime Museum of the Atlantic: 1675 Lower Water St, Halifax, NS B3J 1S3 (902) 429-7490

McCord Museum of Canadian History: 690, rue Sherbrooke ouest, Montreal, QC H3A 1E9 (514) 398-7100

Musée de la Civilisation: 85, rue Dalhousie, CP 155, Succursale B, Quebec, QC G1K 7A6 (418) 643-2158

New Brunswick Museum: 277 Douglas Ave, Saint John, NB E2K 1E5 (506) 643-2300

Newfoundland Museum: 285 Duckworth St, PO Box 8700, St. John's, NF A1B 4J6 (709) 729-2329

Nova Scotia Museum: 1747 Summer St, Halifax, NS B3H 3A6 (902) 424-6471

Prince of Wales Northern Heritage Centre: PO Box 1320, Yellowknife, NT X1A 2L9 (867) 873-7551

Provincial Museum of Alberta: 12845-102nd Ave, Edmonton, AB T5N 0M6 (403) 453-9100

Royal British Columbia Museum: PO Box 9815, Stn Prov. Govt, Victoria, BC V8W 9W2 (250) 387-3701

Royal Ontario Museum: 100 Queen's Park, Toronto, ON M5S 2C6 (416) 586-8000

Royal Saskatchewan Museum: Wascana Park, College and Albert, Regina, SK S4P 3V7 (306) 787-2815

Vancouver Museum: 1100 Chestnut St, Vancouver, BC V6J 3J9 (604) 736-4431

Prince Edward Island Museum and Heritage Foundation: 2 Kent St, Charlottetown, PE C1A 1M6 (902) 368-6600

Governor General's Awards in Visual and Media Arts

These annual awards, funded and administered by the Canada Council for the Arts, were created in June 1999. Six prizes are awarded for distinguished career achievement in the visual and media arts, and one prize for distinguished contributions to the visual and media arts through voluntarism, philanthropy, board governance or community outreach activities. The fourth annual Governor General's Awards were announced March 4, 2003.

2003 Winners

■ **Robert Archambeau:** Manitoba artist Robert Archambeau has been internationally recognized for excellence in wood-fired ceramics. Born and educated in Toledo, Ohio, he moved to Winnipeg in 1968 to become a professor in the School of Art at the University of Manitoba, where he taught for 23 years before retiring in 1991. As a senior artist and influential teacher, Archambeau has inspired students and remains an active figure in the provincial arts scene.

■ **Alex Colville:** Alex Colville is one of Canada's most celebrated artists, whose paintings and prints are in public and private collections across Canada and around the world. Born in Toronto, he received his Bachelor of Fine Arts degree at Mount Allison University in Sackville, New Brunswick. He was an official war artist during World War II, then became a professor of art at Mount Allison, retiring in 1963 to devote himself full-time to his art. In 1966, he represented Canada at the Venice Biennale, the world's oldest and most prestigious exhibition of visual art. Colville has lived and worked in Wolfville, Nova Scotia, for the past 30 years.

■ **Gathie Falk:** Gathie Falk is best known as a painter, sculptor and performance artist whose work reflects the objects and activities of everyday life. Born in Alexander, Manitoba, she moved to Vancouver as a teenager and received her formal education in art at the University of British Columbia. In the late 1960s, Falk switched from painting to ceramic sculpture and was introduced to performance art, creating and performing 15 works between 1968 and 1977. Her paintings and sculptures have been exhibited in numerous venues and are in many public collections.

■ **Betty Goodwin:** Montreal artist Betty Goodwin has been a dominant figure in Canadian art for the past 35 years. A creator whose art has delved into diverse fields of interest—printmaking, drawing, collage, photography, sculpture and installation—she continues to have an influence in Canada and abroad. In 1989, Goodwin represented Canada at the Sao Paulo International Biennial, and her work was included in the 1995 Venice Biennale. She has won the Prix Paul-Émile Borduas (1986) and the Gershon Iskowitz Prize (1995).

■ **Walter Harris:** Walter Harris is a hereditary Gitxsan chief whose totem poles and carved sculptures are well known across Canada and around the world. He has received dozens of commissions from government and the private sector and has created works for, among others, the Vancouver International Airport, Golden Gate Park in San Francisco, Victoria Island in Ottawa, the Westar Sawmill office in Japan, the Canadian Embassy in Paris and the House of Commons.

■ **Takao Tanabe:** Born in Prince Rupert, B.C., Takao Tanabe attended the Winnipeg School of Art, the Brooklyn Museum Art School and the Central School of Arts and Crafts in London. Tanabe was at the forefront of non-objective painting in the 1950s and was included in numerous international exhibitions as well as solo and group exhibitions in Canada. While head of the Art Department at the Banff School of Fine Arts between 1973 and 1980, he began to paint the landscapes for which he is best known.

■ **Suzanne Rivard Le Moyne:** Suzanne Rivard Le Moyne began her career as a painter, but is best known as an arts educator and the creator of the Canada Council Art Bank. Born in Quebec City, she obtained her diploma at Quebec's École des beaux-arts in 1950 then taught at l'École des beaux-arts de Montréal. She came to Ottawa in the 1960s, where she worked for the Arts and Culture Division of the Department of the Secretary of State and was head of visual arts for the Canada Council. Between 1974 and 1982, she headed the Department of Visual Arts and Theatre at the University of Ottawa.

FESTIVALS AND EVENTS, 2004

In addition to festivals in the various branches of the performing arts, communities across Canada celebrate local, national and international culture with a wide variety of events. Here is a sample of the fairs and festivals available to visitors across Canada. Note that dates are subject to change and interested visitors should contact the numbers given, or the tourist bureaus of the respective provinces and territories.

■ Newfoundland and Labrador

Gander's Annual Festival of Flight, Gander, Jul. 28-Aug. 2: Described as "Newfoundland's Biggest Kitchen Party," the festival includes live music, seafood, fireworks and demolition derbies. (709) 651-5927

Trinity-Conception Fall Fair, Harbour Grace, Sept. 23-29: The annual fair will include the Miss Newfoundland & Labrador Pageant, a talent search contest, farm days, arts & crafts contest, agricultural contests, amusement park, parade, and nightly entertainment. (709) 596-6201

Grand Falls-Windsor Red Maple Festival, Grand Falls-Windsor, Oct. 29-Nov. 5: This community fall festival features swimming, hockey, tournament, ball hockey tournament, teen dances, adult dances and community skating. It concludes with a huge bonfire and mini-fireworks at Centennial Field. (709) 489-0450

■ Prince Edward Island

Lucy Maud Montgomery Festival, Cavendish and Area, Aug. 13-5: Two days of wholesome family fun and an opportunity to learn more about Montgomery and her time. Experience old-fashioned community events and hear readings from Montgomery's work. Improve your writing skills at writers' workshops. Enjoy traditional and children's entertainment. (902) 963-7874

Festival of Lights, Charlottetown Waterfront, June 30-Aug. 3: The Festival of Lights has become the premier celebration of the Canada Day weekend in Atlantic Canada. Festivities include nightly concerts, international buskers, carnival midway and the July 1st fireworks over Charlottetown Harbour. Toll-free: 1-800-955-1864

Summerside Highland Gathering, College of Piping, Summerside, June 25-27: Competitions for pipe bands, solo pipers and drummers, Highland and step dancers, and heavy-weight athletes. Celtic entertainment with concerts, ceilidhs, fiddling, clans, and children's activities. Daily and weekend passes available. (902) 436-5377, toll-free: 1-877-BAGPIPE

Festival Rendez-vous Rustico, Rustico, July 30-Aug. 1: An Acadian festival of traditional music, dance, culture, food and games, featuring ECMA award winner Lenny Gallant. Horse and wagon rides, games, races, carnival blow-ups, face painting are among the family activities. (902) 963-3252

The Indian River Festival Midsummer Magic Weekend, Indian River, July 29-Aug. 1: Four nights of fabulous music performed by internationally acclaimed musicians, recorded for broadcast by CBC Radio. Music you can hear with your heart in an acoustic and architectural treasure. (902) 836-4933, toll-free: 1-800-565-3688

■ Nova Scotia

Yarmouth Seafest, Yarmouth, July 14-18: This community event celebrates Yarmouth's connection to a seafaring heritage. Key elements include a giant street parade, antique car show, bagpiper's walk and tea with the Mayor. It also features the largest fireworks display in Southwest Nova Scotia and the fabulous Fish Feast. (902) 742-5355

Festival Acadien de Clare, Clare, July 5-11: Canada's largest and oldest Acadian festival. Theatre, hikes, races, parades, a deep-sea fishing tournament and other competitions are all part of the event. (902) 769-3655

Nova Scotia International Tattoo, Halifax, June 29-July 7: The world's largest annual indoor show presents acts performed by over 2,000 military and civilian performers from Canada and around the world. The program offers a unique combination of music, dance, drama, gymnastics, comedy and military displays. (902) 420-1114

Antigonish Highland Games, Antigonish, July 11-13: A traditional Scottish Highland Games including clan gatherings, Scottish heritage workshops and concerts. Concentrated in the last three days are piping, dancing, drumming and heavy event competitions, along with one of Canada's finest outdoor tattoos and the "Concert Under the Stars." (902) 863-4275

Congrès mondial acadien, provincewide, July 31–Aug. 15: In 2004, the 3rd Congrès mondial acadien will celebrate a homecoming to the birthplace of L'Acadie. Over 250,000 participants will walk the land where their ancestors once lived. Music, song, dance, pageantry and joyful reunions will abound. (902) 424-7104

Celtic Colours, Cape Breton, Oct. 8-16: Voted one of the "Top 100 Events in North America" for 2003 by the American Bus Association. Autumn is the time when the sounds of fiddles, pipes and voices in song echo over the island with Celtic Colours International Festival. An event to remember with over 250 musicians, dancers, singers, and storytellers at venues across the Island with Celtic Colours International Festival. The festival's goal is to increase international awareness of Cape Breton's own world-class Celtic talent and to help preserve Cape Breton's "living" Celtic culture. (902) 539-8800

■ **New Brunswick**

Shediac Lobster Festival, Shediac, second week of July: The Shediac Lobster Festival is an annual event held in the first week of July. Visitors are invited to discover the region's lobster and Acadian culture. Parades, races, entertainment and fireworks are all part of the festivities. (506) 532-1122

New Brunswick Highland Games and Scottish Festival, Fredericton, late July: This event features pipeband competitions, individual piping and drumming competitions, highland dancing competitions, heavy events contests, clan heritage genealogy workshop, Celtic music, ceilidh and concerts under the stars. It also includes fiddling, whisky tasting, Celtic guitar and step dancing. (506) 452-9244, toll-free: 1-888-368-4444

La Foire Brayonne, Edmundston, August: Internationally renowned, this popular festival offers three main activities: concerts, cultural activities and sports events. It celebrates the heritage of local Francophones and it is one of the biggest Francophone festivals outside Québec. (506) 739-6608

■ **Quebec**

The Québec Winter Carnival, Quebec City, Feb.: This is a unique and exciting event that enlivens the world's snow capital. It draws nearly 1,000,000 visitors every year. For 17 consecutive days, the Carnival offers sporting, artistic, and cultural activities that provide grown-ups

and children alike an opportunity to rediscover the wonders of winter. The main Carnival attractions are located in the heart of Old Québec. These include dogsled races, canoe races, parades, ice fishing, flapjack breakfasts and toboggan runs. Toll-free: 1-877-BONJOUR

Journées de la culture, Abitibi-Témiscamingue, Bas-Saint-Laurent, Centre-du-Québec, Charlevoix, Chaudière-Appalaches, Duplessis, Gaspésie, Greater Québec City Area, Îles-de-la-Madeleine, Lanaudière, Laurentians, Laval, Manicouagan, Mauricie, Montérégie, Montréal, Northern Québec, Outaouais, Saguenay-Lac-Saint-Jean, Eastern Townships. Late Sept: Each year, artists, craftspeople and cultural workers hold their own original activities to reveal the secrets of their art or throw a spotlight on the hidden treasures of their community. With 2000 activities all over Québec, they extend a hand to the people not normally reached and open the art and culture for all. Toll-free: 1-877-BONJOUR

Quebec Summer Festival, Quebec City, July: This is the biggest French-language stage and street performance event in North America. Over 1,000 artists from up to 20 countries perform in as many as 500 shows. Toll-free: 1-877-BONJOUR

■ **Ontario**

The Toronto International Carnival, Toronto, Aug.: Formerly known as Caribana, this is the largest festival rooted in Caribbean culture in North America. The two-week festival attracts over a million participants annually. (416) 465-4884

Winterlude, Ottawa, weekends in Feb.: The world's largest skating rink (the Rideau Canal) is the centrepiece of this annual winter carnival. But the bed races, polar bear golf, buskers on ice, hot air balloon fiesta, ice sculptures and figure skating that contribute to the festivities take place throughout the National Capital Region. Toll-free: 1-800-363-4465

Great Rendezvous Festival, Thunder Bay, second week of July: This 10-day festival commemorates the historic arrival of the voyageur brigades and features rustic camps, authentic canoes, unique crafts, historic games, music and spirited fun. (807) 625-2149

■ **Manitoba**

Northern Manitoba Trapper's Festival, The Pas, Feb. 11-15: This winter festival, originating in 1916, celebrates the cultural heritage of the northern pioneer with skill displays and entertainments. Events include the World Championship Dog Race and King Trapper events, including canoe packing, trap setting, moose calling, bannock baking and more. An arts and crafts show, beard-growing contest and children's games are also part of the fun. (204) 623-2912

Festival du Voyageur, Winnipeg, Feb. 13-22: This is western Canada's largest winter festival: a celebration of Canada's fur-trading era combines the joie de vivre of the voyageurs with more than 400 music performances, magnificent snow sculptures, historical interpretation of early 19th-century life at Fort Gibraltar, live entertainment, traditional dishes, arets and crafts, the voyageur International Sled Dog Classic and governor's ball. (204) 237-7692; www.festivalvoyageur.mb.ca

Royal Manitoba Winter Fair, Keyston Centre, Brandon, Mar. 29-Apr. 3: A week of continuous excitement with world-class equestrian events, children's shows, agricultural shows and auctions. (204) 726-3590; www.brandon.com/provinciale

Red River Exhibition, Winnipeg, June 24-July 3: Family entertainment starts with a parade and continues with a giant midway, nightly entertainment and attractions, innovative displays and creative exhibits. (204) 888-6990; www.redriverex.com

Flin Flon Trout Festival, Flin Flon, June 28-July 1: Starting at sunrise at the beginning of June, the official cast opens the month-long catch-and-release lake trout fishing derby. The July 1st long weekend is a celebrated festival event with pancake breakfast, parade, ceremonies, Main Street extravaganzas, amusements, sporting events and a regional showcase. Take part in a day of canoeing in the Canadian Open Gold Rush Canoe Derby. (204) 687-3469

A Taste of Manitoba, Winnipeg, July: Twenty-eight of Manitoba's great restaurants dish out over 80 different menu items along with a main stage, children's entertainment, buskers and attractions. (204) 783-9955

Canada's National Ukrainian Festival, Dauphin, Aug. 1-3: Special celebration of Ukraine's independence is an opportunity to experience the flavour of the old traditions and culture through song, dance, costume and delectably satisfying Ukrainian cuisine. (204) 622-4600; www.cnuf.ca

Winnipeg International Children's Festival, Winnipeg, June 10-13: The Winnipeg International Children's Festival provides world-standard performing arts and participatory activities that are educational, entertaining and accessible to young people from all social, economic and ethnic backgrounds. Activities include Authors' Reading Tent, Circus and Magic Partnership Tent, hands-on activities, puppet-making and more. (204) 958-4730; www.kidsfest.ca

■ Saskatchewan

The Prince Albert Winter Festival, Prince Albert, Feb.: The 26th annual Prince Albert Winter Festival includes children's carnival, talent shows, arts & crafts, international food and entertainment, guest artists, sled dog races and snow sculptures. (306) 764-7595

Vesna Festival, Saskatoon, May: A celebration of Ukrainian culture including artisans, fine arts, cultural displays and, of course, lots of dancing. (306) 934-1803

Taste of Saskatchewan, Saskatoon, July: More than 24 Saskatoon restaurants serve three of their favourite house dishes in an outdoor setting in Friendship Park. Available for sampling are Chinese, Greek, Italian, Indian, Native and Cajun foods. Live entertainment includes some of Saskatchewan's finest performers. (306) 975-3175

■ Alberta

Stampede 2004, Calgary, July: The Calgary Stampede is Canada's premiere celebration of western heritage and culture and one of the top such events in all of North America. Organizers promise visitors more to see and do over 10 days than they will ever be able to manage—from midway rides to pancakes, horses to light shows, rodeos to stage shows, chuckwagons to displays of Alberta Agriculture and top name entertainers. Western duds are a must! General information: 1-800-661-1260; tickets: 1-800-661-1767; www.calgarystampede.com

Klondike Days, Edmonton, July 18-27: More than 750,000 fair visitors attend this exposition which starts with a colourful parade and continues with 10 days of midway rides and attractions, excellent live entertainment, chuckwagon racing, the Feature Country Showcase, great shopping and the mini-donuts that have become the fair's trademark. Each afternoon, there is live entertainment with bathtub racing and the Taste of Edmonton restaurant showcase downtown. Each night a show of fireworks completes the day's excitement. Toll-free: 1-888-800-7275; www.klondikedays.com

Cold Lake-Maple Flag Event, Cold Lake, mid-May to mid-June: Airforce flying demonstrations take place at the Cold Lake airbase for six weeks every summer. Fighter pilots are training for the Canadian Forces and Top Gun crews from all over the world. Toll-free: 1-800-840-6140; www.airforce.forces.ca/4wing/index_e.cfm

■ British Columbia

Kamloops Cowboy Festival, Kamloops, Mar.: The B.C. Cowboy Heritage Society presents this festival, which includes a western trade show, art, music and cowboy poetry. It supports the preservation of cowboy heritage in B.C. and institutions such as the B.C. Cowboy Hall of Fame, which holds its induction ceremony at the festival. Toll-free: 1-888-763-2224; www.bcchs.com/festival.htm

Victoria Harbour Festival, Victoria, May: This 10-day celebration bridges two holiday long weekends, Canada's Victoria Day and U.S. Memorial Day. Featured under the festival umbrella are events ranging from a literary festival to a rodeo, with many family-oriented entertainment, cultural and sporting events in between. The Victoria Day Parade and internationally renowned Swiftsure International Yacht Race are part of the festivities. Swiftsure: (250) 592-9098

Nanaimo Marine Festival, Nanaimo, fourth weekend of July: The main event of this four-day sea festival on Vancouver Island is a bathtub race featuring a variety of unusual home-made watercraft. (250) 753-7223; www.bathtub.island.net/

HSBC Power Smart Celebration of Light, Vancouver, July-Aug.: Three countries put on fabulous fireworks displays in this dazzling competition in the skies over Vancouver. The four-night competition attracts 1.2 million viewers, including residents from all over the lower mainland, tourists and cruise ship passengers. Jugglers, face painters, magicians and musicians entertain visitors on their way from parking lots to the fireworks festival viewing areas at English Bay, Kitsilano, Vanier Park, Jericho Beach and West Vancouver. (604) 641-1193; www.celebration-of-light.com

Okanagan Wine Festivals, Okanagan Valley, throughout the year: The Okanagan Ice Wine Festival in January incorporates winter recreation with wine education and cuisine. The Okanagan Spring Wine Festival in April and May focusses on the culinary arts and features a vine cycling event. The Okanagan Summer Wine Festival in August is a relaxing and tasty event. And the Okanagan Fall Wine Festival in October celebrates the harvest. (250) 861-6654; www.thewinefestivals.com

■ Yukon

Yukon Sourdough Rendezvous Festival, Whitehorse, Feb.: This winter festival has sports, arts, as well as traditional games. The entertainment ranges from dog races to cancan dancers, from snowshoe shufflers to the International Winter Air Show. (867) 667-2148

■ Northwest Territories

Caribou Carnival, Yellowknife, March: The Caribou Carnival is Yellowknifers' favourite spring event. The Queen and Princess contests are featured, as well as snowmobile races. Also included in the carnival is the NMI Mobility Canadian Championship Dog Derby. The biggest purse in the Northwest Territories is offered for this three-day, 240-km (142-mile) race on Great Slave Lake. The annual race will feature mushers from across North America and around the world. (867) 873-4262

■ Nunavut

Nunavut Day, throughout Nunavut, July 9: Residents of Nunavut celebrate both the coming of summer and the founding of Nunavut on this day. Events take place across the new territory. Among the activities in Baker Lake are foot and bicycle races, a tea-boiling contest and traditional Inuit games. Toll-free: 1-800-491-7910

CANADIAN HALL OF FAME

The following list is not meant to be exhaustive, but rather a general listing of prominent Canadians, and those whose reputation is inextricably linked to Canada.

A

ABBOTT, John Joseph Caldwell (Sir), politics. St Andrews, Lower Canada, 1821–93. Canada's third prime minister.

ABBOTT, Maude Elizabeth Seymour, medicine. St Andrews, Que., 1869–1940. Specialist in congenital heart disease. *History of Medicine in the Province of Quebec.*

ABBOTT, Roger, performing arts. Eng., 1946. Actor and co-producer of CBC's *Royal Canadian Air Farce*; noted for impersonation of Jean Chrétien.

ABEL, Sidney Gerald (Sid), sports. Melville, Sask., 1918–2000. Hockey player; 1949–52 considered best offensive unit when centred with Gordie Howe and Ted Lindsay (Detroit Red Wings); four-time all-star.

ABERDEEN, Ishbel Maria Marjoribanks Gordon (Lady), reformer. Eng., 1857–1939. Helped create National Council of Women, Victorian Order of Nurses.

ABERHART, William "Bible Bill," politics. Hibbard Twp, Ont., 1878–1943. Founded Social Credit party; Alberta premier 1935–43.

ACORN, Milton, literary arts. Charlottetown, PEI, 1923–86. Radical poet. "The Island Means Minago."

ADAIR, Jean, performing arts. Toronto, Ont., 1873–1953. Character actress best known in her role as Aunt Martha Brewster in the movie *Arsenic and Old Lace*. Also *Something in the Wind; Living in a Big Way.*

ADAMS, Bryan, performing arts. Kingston, Ont., 1959. Singer/songwriter; rock star. *Reckless.*

ADAMS, Ian, literary arts. Tanzania, 1937. Novelist, non-fiction writer. *S, Portrait of a Spy; The Trudeau Papers.*

ADAMS, Lawrence, performing arts. St. Boniface, Man., 1937–2003. Dancer with the National Ballet of Canada 1954–69; after his retirement he and his wife, Miriam Weinstein, created Dance Collection Danse, Canada's largest dance archive and publisher. *Encyclopedia of Theatre Dance in Canada.*

ADAMS, Thomas, city planner. Scot., 1871–1940. Father of the Canadian Planning Movement.

AFFLECK, Raymond Tait, visual arts. Penticton, BC, 1922–89. Architect; designed Place Ville Marie, Place Bonaventure.

AGAR, Carlyle Clare, exploration and discovery. Lion's Head, Ont., 1901–68. Revolutionized helicopter maneuvers for high-altitude landing and takeoff in inaccessible places; instrumental in building BC's Palisade Lake Dam.

AGLUKARK, Susan, performing arts. Arviat, NWT, 1966. Singer/songwriter; first Inuit recording artist. *Unsung Heroes; This Child.*

AIRD, John Black, politics. Toronto, Ont., 1923–95. Liberal senator; Ontario lieutenant-governor 1980–85.

AISLIN (b. Christopher Terry Mosher), visual arts. Ottawa, Ont., 1942. *Montreal Gazette* cartoonist; sports caricaturist.

AITKEN, William Maxwell (Lord Beaverbrook), literary arts. Maple, Ont., 1879–1964. Publisher; newspaper magnate; British Conservative cabinet minister.

AKEEAKTASHUK, visual arts. Hudson Bay, Ont., 1898–1954. Sculptor; first important Inuit carver.

ALBANI, Emma (b. Louise Cecile Emma Lajeunesse), performing arts. Chambly, Que., 1847–1930. Opera singer; grand diva excelled in Wagnerian opera, popular in Britain and US.

ALCOCK, John Alfred, science. Scot., 1938. Expert in laser and plasma physics; winner of Herzberg medal in 1975.

ALEXANDER, Lincoln MacCauley, politics. Toronto, Ont., 1922. First Black in Parliament; Ont. lieutenant-governor 1985–91.

ALLAN, Hugh (Sir), business. Scot., 1810–82. Railway promoter; suspected of electoral bribery for soliciting favours in Pacific Scandal (1873).

ALLAN, Ted (b. Allan Herman), performing arts. Montreal, Que., 1916–95. Author; screenwriter. *Lies My Father Told Me; Bethune: The Making of a Hero.*

ALLEMAGNE, John Cameron, literary arts. Toronto, Ont., 1951. Reporter, columnist, food writer. *The Importance of Lunch.*

ALLEN, Charlotte Vale, literary arts. Toronto, Ont., 1941. Writer, lecturer on child abuse. *Daddy's Girl.*

ALLEN, John F. (Jack), science. Winnipeg, Man., 1908. Co-discoverer of superfluidity in liquid helium.

ALLEN, Montagu (Sir), sports. Montreal, Que., 1860–1951. Financier and sportsman who donated Allen Cup in 1908 for senior amateur competition in Canada.

ALLEN, Ralph, literary arts. Winnipeg, Man., 1913–66. Influential *Maclean's* editor (1946–60).

ALMOND, Paul, performing arts. Montreal, Que., 1931. Film director. *Act of the Heart.*

ALTMAN, Sidney, science. Montreal, Que., 1939. Microbiologist; 1989 Nobel Prize in chemistry for role in research into chemical cell reactions.

AMIEL, Barbara, media. Eng., 1940s. Journalist; conservative political and social columnist.

AMOS, Beth (b. Bessie Rymer), performing arts. St Catharines, Ont., 1915–95. Actor. *Jake and the Kid; Miracle at Indian Creek; Canadian Bacon.*

ANDERSON, Doris Hilda, literary arts. Toronto, Ont., 1921. Writer; feminist; editor, *Chatelaine* 1958–77.

ANDERSON, Frank Ross, sports. Edmonton, Alta, 1938–1980. International chess master; won gold medals in Amsterdam (1954) and in Munich (1958).

ANDERSON, Pamela Denise, performing arts. Ladysmith, BC, 1967. Voluptuous actress who has starred in *Baywatch, Barb Wire.*

ANDERSON, Reid Bryce, performing arts. New Westminster, BC, 1949. Dancer; ballet director of National Ballet of British Columbia; later National Ballet of Canada.

ANDRÉ, Brother (b. Alfred Bissette), religion. St Gregoire d'Iberville, Lower Canada, 1845–1937. Mystic; built Montreal's St Joseph's Oratory.

ANGILIK, Paul Apak, performing arts. Hall Beach, NWT, 1954–98. Documentary filmmaker of Inuit life; adventurer; contributor to Inuit Broadcasting Corporation.

ANKA, Paul Albert, performing arts. Ottawa, Ont., 1941. Singer/songwriter; composed more than 400 songs. "My Way."

APPLEBAUM, Louis, performing arts. Toronto, Ont., 1918–2000. Composer; writer of opera, concerts, film scores.

APPLEYARD, Peter, performing arts. Eng., 1928. Jazz musician; vibraphonist; TV personality. "Swing Fever."

APPS, Charles Joseph Sylvanus (Syl), sports. Paris, Ont., 1915–98. Hockey player; Toronto Maple Leafs (1936–48); 3-time all-star; pole vault contender in 1936 Olympics; 1937 Canadian Athlete of the Year.

AQUIN, Hubert, literary arts. Montreal, Que., 1929–77. Novelist; modernist writer. *Neige Noire.*

ARBOUR, Louise, law. Montreal, Que., 1947. Judge of Supreme Court of Ontario; appointed to Supreme Court of Canada in 1999. From 1996–99 was chief prosecutor for UN's international war crimes tribunal.

ARCAND, Denys, performing arts. Deschambault, Que., 1941. Film director. *Decline of the American Empire.*

ARCHAMBAULT, Louis, visual arts. Montreal, Que., 1915–2003. Sculptor; his work is in many museum collections.

ARCHER, Violet, performing arts. Montreal, Que., 1913–2000. Internationally recognized classical music composer, inspired by Canadian folk music. *Prairie Profiles.*

ARCHIBALD, William Munroe, exploration and discovery. Truro, NS, 1876–1949. Nicknamed "Canada's Flying Businessman," Archibald was the first person to fly into the BC interior to locate mining opportunities in remote areas.

ARDEN, Elizabeth (b. Florence Nightingale Graham), business. Woodbridge, Ont., 1884–1966. Founder of the Elizabeth Arden cosmetics empire, Arden was a pioneer in mass advertising and built the business from a small shop in New York City in 1914 to a vast chain of spas and beauty salons.

ARDEN, Jann (b. Jann Arden Richards), performing arts. Calgary, Alta, 1962. Juno-award winning pop singer, songwriter. *Happy?; Time for Mercy.*

ARMSTRONG, Neil J., exploration and discovery. Alvinston, Ont., 1920–94. First helicopter pilot/geologist in North America; in the 1960s he was first to make contact with Inuit of the Barren Lands by flying into their territory. He pioneered the use of electromagnetic systems to detect mineral conductors in earth from a helicopter, and invented the hover sight, which is used universally as an inexpensive method of airborne surveying.

ARTHUR, Eric Ross, visual arts. New Zealand, 1898–1982. Architectural conservancy advocate; writer. *Toronto: No Mean City; The Barn: A Vanishing Landmark in North America.*

ASPER, Israel Harold, business. Minnedosa, Man., 1932. Financier; founder Global-TV; columnist; author.

ATHANS, George S. Jr., sports. Kelowna, BC, 1952. Three-time world water ski champion.

ATKIN, Harvey, performing arts. Toronto, Ont., 1942. Versatile character actor portrayed Desk Sergeant Ronald Coleman on the long-running TV program *Cagney & Lacey;* also in films including *Atlantic City* and *Meatballs.*

ATKINSON, Joseph, media. Newcastle, Ont., 1865–1948. Journalist; built *Toronto Star* into nation's largest newspaper.

ATWOOD, Margaret Eleanor, literary arts. Ottawa, Ont., 1939. Prolific and award-winning novelist with international following. *The Handmaid's Tale, Alias Grace, The Blind Assassin* (Booker Prize).

AUBERT de GASPE, Philippe-Ignace François, literary arts. Quebec City, Que., 1814–41. Novelist; wrote first French-Cdn novel. *L'influence d'un livre* (1837).

AUBERT, Rosemary, literary arts. USA. Novelist, poet, biographer who specializes in crime writing; winner of the 1995 Arthur Ellis Award for her short story "The Midnight Boat to Palermo"; also author of Ellis Portal mystery series: *Free Reign; Feast of Stephen.*

AUDETTE, Julien Joseph, science. Radville, Sask., 1914–86. First Canadian to break 300,000 ft (9144 m) in a sailplane, only Canadian to hold all eight competitive soaring awards. His "Audette Project" was a data-collection program that connected climatological information with nonpowered aviation.

AUF DER MAUR, Nick, journalism. Montreal, Que., 1942–98. Long-time columnist for *Montreal Gazette;* cowrote biography of Brian Mulroney: *The Boy from Baie Comeau.*

AUGUSTINE, Joseph M., exploration and discovery. Big Cove, Nfld, 1911. Native leader and historian who, in 1972, discovered the Augustine Mound, a trove of ancient artifacts dating back 2000 years, near the community of Red Bank on the Miramichi River.

AUGUSTYN, Frank Joseph, performing arts. Hamilton, Ont., 1953. Former principal dancer, National Ballet of Canada; director, Ottawa Ballet.

AUSTIN, John Alexander McDonald, business. Renfrew, Ont., 1912–84. Co-founder, with brother Charles, of Austin Airways; he pioneered air service to remote communities in the Hudson Bay and James Bay regions; working with the federal government, he also was instrumental in aerial surveying of the regions and in improving contact with remote communities. Former director of Air Industries and Transport Association.

AVERY, Oswald, science. Halifax, NS, 1877–1955. First person to show agent responsible for transferring genetic information was DNA, not a protein as previously thought.

AXELRAD, Arthur Aaron, medicine. Montreal, Que., 1923. Histologist; won international acclaim for his research into leukemia and hemapaiesis, specializing in blood cell differentiation. Head of University of Toronto's anatomy department 1966–85.

AXWORTHY, Norman Lloyd, politics. North Battleford, Sask., 1939. Liberal minister of external affairs; defense.

AYKROYD, Daniel Edward (Dan), performing arts. Ottawa, Ont., 1952. Actor/comedian. *Saturday Night Live, Ghostbusters.*

BACHLE, Leo, visual arts. Toronto, Ont., 1923–2003. In 1942 Bachle originated the Johnny Canuck comic books, "Canada's answer to Nazi oppression." After the war ended he became a stand-up comic under the name Les Barker, playing with such stars as Dean Martin, Jerry Lewis, Rich Little and Tiny Tim.

BACHMAN, Randy, performing arts. Winnipeg, Man., 1946. Rock musician; guitarist for Guess Who, Bachman-Turner Overdrive. Released a retrospective of Canadian guitarist Lenny Breau. *American Woman.*

BADAY, Lida, business. Hamilton, Ont., 1957. Fashion designer of women's clothing; began own label in 1987. Her clothing is sold across Canada and the US, distinctive for her stylish workmanship with wool jersey.

BAETZ, Reuben, politics. Chelsey, Ont., 1923–96. Executive director of Canadian Council on Social Development; proponent of national unemployment insurance program.

BAFFIN, William, exploration and discovery. Eng., 1584–1622. Made two Arctic voyages in search of the Northwest Passage; first to conclude Hudson Bay did not lead westward; explored Baffin Island.

BAGSHAW, Elizabeth Catherine, medicine. Victoria County, Ont., 1881–1982. Pioneering woman doctor who, from 1932–66, was medical director of Canada's first (illegal) birth control clinic in Hamilton, Ont., responding to women's financial needs during Depression years.

BAILEY, Brian, business. Galahad, Alta, 1958. Women's sportswear designer; launched label with own name in 1988; later under Iscariot Design; active fashion business promoter.

BAILEY, Donovan, sports. Jamaica, 1967. Track star who won 100 m race at world record time, 9.84, at 1996 Olympics in Atlanta.

BAIN, Conrad, performing arts. Lethbridge, Alta, 1923. Actor who appeared most famously as "Mr. Drummond" on *Different Strokes*, also on soaps *The Edge of Night* and *Search for Tomorrow*, and on film. *Postcards from the Edge; I Never Sang for My Father.*

BAIRD, Elizabeth Carol, literary arts. Stratford, Ont., 1939. Food writer with *Canadian Living Magazine* and the *Toronto Star*; author of several cookbooks. *Classic Canadian Cooking; Elizabeth Baird's Favourites.*

BAKER, Carroll, performing arts. Bridgewater, NS, 1949. Singer; country music star.

BAKER, Edmund Albert, education. Collins Bay, Ont., 1893–1968. Founder of the Canadian National Institute for the Blind in 1918; from 1920–62 he was the general secretary and managing director of the CNIB, and in 1951 he became the first president of the World Council for the Welfare of the Blind.

BALCHEN, Bernt, invention. Norway, 1899–1973. Pilot/engineer who piloted Raoul Amundsen's North Pole expedition; developer of world's northernmost airbase on west coast of Greenland; designed the first commercial air route between Scandinavia and Canada; mapped remote areas of Canada's north.

BALDWIN, Robert, politics. York, Ont., 1804–58. Proponent of responsible government; co-premier (with LaFontaine) of Upper Canada.

BALFOUR, St. Clair, business. Hamilton, Ont., 1910–2002. Grandson of Southam Press's founder, Balfour became president of Southam Press in 1961; chairman of Southam Inc. 1975–85. A noted philanthropist and fundraiser for the University of Toronto, he established the Southam Fellowships Program (later the Canadian Journalism Fellowships) in 1962.

BALLARD, Harold Edwin, sports. Toronto, Ont., 1903–90. Sports capitalist; irascible owner of Toronto Maple Leafs, Hamilton Tiger Cats.

BANKS, Thomas (Tommy), performing arts. Calgary, Alta, 1936. Internationally recognized jazz pianist and conductor who performs with trio members Bob Miller and Tom Doran; appointed to the Senate in 2000.

BANTING, Frederick Grant (Sir), medicine. Alliston, Ont., 1891–1941. Medical researcher; co-discoverer of insulin; Nobel Prize for medicine, 1923.

BARBEAU, Charles Marius, ethnologist. St-Marie-de-Beauce, Que., 1883–1969. Eminent folklorist.

BARFOOT, Joan Louise, literary arts. Owen Sound, Ont., 1947. Novelist. *Dancing in the Dark; Family News; Charlotte and Claudia Keeping in Touch.*

BARKER, William George (Billy), military. Dauphin, Man., 1894–1930. Fighter pilot awarded Victoria Cross for 60 solo combat missions against German aircraft during WWI.

BARLOW, Maude Victoria, politics. Toronto, Ont., 1947. Political/human rights activist, author. Chair, Council of Canadians.

BARR, Murray Llewellyn, medicine. Belmont, Ont., 1908–95. Anatomist; developed chromosome analysis to diagnose genetic disorders.

BARR, Robert, literary arts. Scot., 1850–1912. Early Canadian crime writer. *The Measure of the Rule; The Girl in the Case.*

BARRON, Colin Fraser, military. Scot., 1893–59. Victoria Cross recipient, WWI, Battle of Passchendaele, 1917. Corporal, 3rd Battalion.

BARRY, James (b. Miranda Stewart), medicine. Eng., 1795–1865. In 1857 appointed inspector general of military hospitals in Province of Canada; as a woman disguised as a man, was the first woman doctor to work in Canada.

BARTLEMAN, James Karl, politics. Orillia, Ont., 1939. In 2002 became Ontario's first aboriginal lieutenant governor; previously high commissioner in South Africa and Australia; foreign policy advisor to Prime Minister Jean Chrétien 1994–98.

BASINSKI, Zbigniew Stanislaw, science. Poland, 1928. Outstanding metal physics researcher.

BASSETT, John White Hughes, media. Ottawa, Ont., 1915–98. Media executive.

BASSETT-SEGUSO, Carling Kathrin, sports. Toronto, Ont., 1967. Top-ranked Canadian tennis player.

BATA, Sonja Ingrid, public service. Switzerland, 1926. Founder of the Bata Shoe Museum in Toronto; wife of shoe retailing entrepreneur Thomas Bata.

BATA, Thomas John, business. Czech., 1914. Industrialist; chairman, Bata Shoes; in over 70 countries.

BATEMAN, Robert McLellan, visual arts. Toronto, Ont., 1930. Painter; major international wildlife artist.

BATTLE, Helen Irene, science. London, Ont., 1903–94. World-renowned zoologist; one of the first zoologists to work in the laboratory, specializing in marine biology and using histology and physiology in her research.

BAUER, David William (Father), sports. Kitchener, Ont., 1925–88. Hockey coach; father of Cdn Olympic hockey.

BAUMANN, Alexander (Sasha), sports. Czech., 1964. Swimmer; gold medals in 200 m, 400 m individual medley, 1984 Olympics; 1984 top male athlete.

BEARDY, Quentin Pickering Jackson, visual arts. Island Lake, Man., 1944–84. Graphic stylist using Cree legends.

BEATTY, Henry Perrin, politics. Toronto, Ont., 1950. President of CBC, 1995–98; former PC cabinet minister.

BECK, Adam (Sir), business. Baden, Canada W, 1857–1925. Hydro commissioner; built Ontario Hydro.

BECKER, Abigail, military. Frontenac Cty, UC, 1831–1905. Heroine; saved men shipwrecked on Lake Erie.

BECKWITH, John, literary arts/performing arts. Victoria, BC, 1927. Composer; writer; critic. *The Shivaree.*

BEDARD, Myriam, sports. Loretteville, Que., 1969. Biathlete; two gold medals, biathlon, '94 Olympics.

BEDDOES, Dick, media. Daysland, Alta, 1926–91. Colourful sportswriter, broadcaster, hockey commentator with the Vancouver *Sun, Globe & Mail, Edmonton Bulletin;* broadcaster on CFRB radio in Toronto. *Pal Hal,* a profile of Harold Ballard.

BEECROFT, Norma Marian, performing arts. Oshawa, Ont., 1934. Composer; avant-garde musician. "From Dreams of Brass."

BEERS, William George, medicine/sports. Montreal, Que., 1843–1900. Popularized lacrosse; dean, Canada's first dental college.

BEGIN, Monique, politics. Italy, 1936. First Quebec woman in Commons; health minister.

BEIQUE, Pierre, performing arts. Pointe aux Trembles, Que., 1910–2003. In 1939 became managing director of the Société des Concertes symphoniques de Montréal, the forerunner of the Orchestre symphonique de Montréal; Béique transformed the orchestra into an international force.

BELANGER, Michel, business. Lévis, Que., 1929–97. President of Quebec's National Bank; 1991–92 was cochairman of Belanger-Campeau Commission which examined constitutional concerns in Quebec.

BELIVEAU, Jean Arthur, sports. Trois-Rivières, Que., 1931. Hockey player; stylish Montreal Canadiens centre, 1953–71; 507 goals.

BELL, Alexander Graham, invention. Scot., 1847–1922. Invented telephone; worked on iron lung, phonograph, seawater desalination.

BELL, George Maxwell (Max), business. Regina, Sask., 1912–72. Industrialist; principal, FP Publications, and sportsman.

BELL, Marilyn, sports. Toronto, Ont., 1937. First person to swim Lake Ontario (1954).

BELL, Robert Edward, science. Ladner, BC, 1918–92. Nuclear physicist; discovered proton radioactivity.

BELLEW, Edward Donald, military. India, 1882–1974. Victoria Cross recipient, WWI, Second Battle of Ypres, 1915. Lieutenant, British Columbia Regiment, 7th Canadian Infantry Battalion.

BELLOW, Saul, literary arts. Lachine, Que., 1915. Nobel Prize for Literature. *Herzog.*

BELZBERG, Samuel, business. Calgary, Alta, 1928. Financier; developed real estate financing in W Canada; founder, First City Trust.

BENMERGUI, Ralph, performing arts. Morocco, 1955. CBC radio and television personality; host of television programs *Friday Night!* ; CBC's *Midday;* frequent host for CBC Radio's *This Morning.*

BENNETT, Richard Bedford, first Viscount, politics. Hopewell Hill, NB, 1870–1947. Prime minister of Canada 1930–35.

BENNETT, William Andrew Cecil (W.A.C.), politics. Hastings, NB, 1900–79. Social Credit premier of BC, 1952–72.

BENNETT, William Richards, politics. Kelowna, BC, 1932. Social Credit premier of BC, 1975–86.

BENOIT, Jehane, media. Montreal, Que., 1904–87. Food expert; cookbook writer; featured on TV; authority on Cdn/Québécois cooking.

BENT, Philip Eric, military. Halifax, NS, 1891–1917. Victoria Cross recipient, WWI, Battle of Passchendaele, 1917. Lieutenant colonel, 9th Battalion, Leicestershire Regiment.

BENY, Roloff (b. Wilfred Roy), visual arts. Medicine Hat, Alta, 1924–84. Photographer; lavish travel books. *India.*

BERBICK, Trevor, sports. Jamaica, 1952. Boxer; Canadian heavyweight champion (1978–85); WBC world heavyweight champion (1986).

BERCZY, William (b. Johann Albrecht Ulrich Moll), visual arts. Germany, 1744–1813. Painter, architect; most famous for his portraits of the native leader Joseph Brant. Also designed church decorations for Christ Church Montreal, in 1903.

BERESFORD-HOWE, Constance Elizabeth, literary arts. Montreal, Que., 1922. Novelist. *Night Studies.*

BERGER, Thomas Rodney, politics. Victoria, BC, 1933. Jurist; proponent of aboriginal rights; commissioner, Mackenzie Valley Pipeline Inquiry.

BERLIN, Boris, performing arts. Russia, 1907–2001. Long associated with Toronto's Royal Conservatory of Music, taught many of Canada's leading pianists; author and coauthor of major pedagogical works. *Basics of Ear Training.*

BERNARDI, Mario, performing arts. Kirkland Lake, Ont., 1930. Conductor, Calgary Philharmonic.

BERNIER, Sylvie, sports. Quebec City, Que., 1964. Diver; gold medal, 3 m springboard, 1984 Olympics.

BERTON, Pierre, literary arts. Whitehorse, YT, 1920. Popular historian; author and media personality. *The Last Spike.*

BESRE, Jean, performing arts. Sherbrooke, Que., 1936–2001. Beloved Quebec television and stage actor; for many years starred in popular TV series *Jamais deux sans toi* and *La P'tite Semaine;* also performed in children's programs and wrote musical comedy *Madeleine de Verchères.*

BESSETTE, Gerard, literary arts. Ste-Anne-de-Sabrevois, Que., 1920. Novelist, poet, literary critic. *Mes romans et moi.*

BEST, Charles Herbert, medicine. USA, 1899–1978. Physiologist; co-discoverer of insulin.

BETHUNE, Henry Norman, medicine. Gravenhurst, Ont., 1890–1939. Surgeon; hero in China, where he died helping revolutionary army.

BEY, Salome, performing arts. USA, 1938?. Singer, songwriter, actress. Noted for jazz, blues, spirituals. Wrote and starred in *Indigo,* a history of blues. *Shimmytime.*

BIDDLE, Charles, performing arts. USA, 1926–2003. Jazz bassist who, after arriving in Montreal from the US in 1948, played the city's jazz clubs until he opened his own, Biddles, in the 1980s; instrumental in the organization of the Montreal Jazz Festival.

BIG BEAR, politics. Ft. Carlton, Sask., 1825–88. Cree leader; opposed treaties on grounds they would destroy Cree way of life.

BIGELOW, Dr. Wilfred Gordon, medicine. Brandon, Man., 1913. Surgeon; developed first cardiac pacemaker.

BILLES, Alfred Jackson, business. Toronto, Ont., 1902–95. Co-founder in 1922 of Canada-wide chain Canadian Tire Corporation.

BILLES, John William, business. Toronto, Ont., 1896–1956. Original founder of Canadian Tire chain of hardware stores.

BINNS, Patrick George, politics. Weyburn, Sask., 1948. PC premier of PEI, 1996.

BIRDSELL, Sandra, literary arts. Hamiota, Man., 1942. Novelist who weaves domestic and feminist themes into her work. *The Missing Child; The Chrome Suite.*

BIRKS, Henry, business. Montreal, Que., 1840–1928. Silversmith who founded national jewelry chain Henry Birks and Sons, opening his first store in 1879 in Montreal.

BIRNEY, Alfred Earle, literary arts. Calgary, Alta, 1904–1995. Narrative poet and professor. *David and Other Poems.*

BISHOP, William Avery (Billy), military. Owen Sound, Ont., 1894–1956. WWI flying ace; downed 72 enemy planes.

BISSELL, Keith, performing arts. Meaford, Ont., 1912–92. Composer of choral, vocal, organ, orchestral and chamber music; folksong arrangements for piano and voice; commissioned by Lois Marshall, Charles Peaker and others.

BISSOONDATH, Neil Devindra, literary arts. Trinidad, 1955. Novelist; short story writer. *A Casual Brutality.*

BITOV, John, business. Toronto, Ont., 1928. Founder of Bitove Corp., food service and hospitality company that has influenced Canadian food catering in hospitals, airlines and railway companies.

BJORSON, Rosella Marie, business. Lethbridge, Alta, 1947. First woman pilot in Canada to fly a commercial flight (Transair); first female flight officer in North America; in 1990 became first female flight captain in Canada (Canadian Airlines).

BLACK, Arthur, media. Toronto, Ont., 1943. Syndicated journalist and broadcaster; host of CBC Radio's *Basic Black,* a program incorporating humour, interviews and music. *Wit and Wisdom of Arthur Black.*

BLACK, Conrad Moffat, business. Montreal, Que., 1944. Press baron; owner of Hollinger Inc. newspaper empire.

BLACK, Davidson, medicine. Toronto, Ont., 1884–1934. China-based anatomist, scholar and anthropologist; identified Peking Man, an ancient human species of *Homo erectus.*

BLAIS, Marie-Claire, literary arts. Quebec City, Que., 1939. Influential novelist. *Une Saison dans la vie d'Emmanuel.*

BLAISE, Clark Lee, literary arts. USA, 1940. Writer; explorer of the displaced person. *Resident Alien.*

BLAKE, Hector "Toe," sports. Victoria Mines, Ont., 1912–95. Hockey player; coached Montreal Canadiens to eight Stanley Cups, 1955–68.

BLAKENEY, Allan Emrys, politics. Bridgewater, NS, 1925. NDP premier of Saskatchewan 1971–82.

BLISS, John William Michael, politics. Leamington, Ont., 1941. Author, history commentator. *Right Honorable Men: The Descent of Canadian Politics from Macdonald to Mulroney.*

BLOHM, Hans Ludwig, visual arts. Germany, 1927. Photographer; author of many photography books. *The Beauty of the Maritimes.*

BLONDIN-ANDREWS, Ethel, politics. Fort Norman, NWT, 1951. In 1988, first native woman elected to Parliament, for Western Arctic (Lib).

BLUMENFELD, Hans, city planner. Germany, 1892–1988. Urban planner; author. *The Modern Metropolis.*

BLYTHE, Dominic, performing arts. Eng., 1947. Actor with Stratford Festival, Ont.

BOBACK, Molly Lamb, visual arts. Vancouver, BC, 1922. As the only woman war artist assigned during World War II, she documented the Canadian Women's Corp; also a writer and broadcaster.

BOCHNER, Lloyd, performing arts. Toronto, Ont., 1924. Character actor who has appeared in IV series *Dynasty* and *Santa Barbara* and in movies. *Naked Gun 2 1/2.*

BODOGH, Marilyn, sports. Toronto, Ont., 1955. Curling. Two-time world champion (skip) in women's curling; member of Team Canada.

BOGGS, Jean Sutherland, visual arts. Peru, 1922. Art curator; National Gallery curator, 1966–76.

BOLDT, Arnie, sports. Osler, Sask., 1957. One-legged high jumper holds disabled world record (2.08 m).

BOLT, Carol, literary arts. Winnipeg, Man., 1941. Playwright; socially conscious writer. *One Night Stand.*

BOMBARDIER, Joseph Armand, invention. Valcourt, Que., 1908–64. Inventor; developer of snowmobiles.

BONDAR, Roberta Lynn, science. Sault Ste Marie, Ont., 1945. Astronaut; first Canadian woman in space.

BONISTEEL, Roy, media. Ameliasburg Ont., 1930. Host of CBC television's *Man Alive* series 1967–89; early career as a radio producer for church organizations. *In Search of Man Alive.*

BORDEN, Robert Laird (Sir), politics. Grand Pré, NS, 1854–1937. Canada's prime minister throughout WWI (1911–20).

BORDUAS, Paul-Emile, visual arts. St-Hilaire, Que., 1905–60. Painter; founded Automatistes. *L'etoile noire.*

BORSOS, Phillip, performing arts. Tasmania, 1954–95. Filmmaker. *The Grey Fox* (winner of Best Picture and Best Director, 1982 Genie Awards); *Bethune.*

BOSSY, Michael, sports. Montreal, Que., 1957. Hockey player; NY Islanders winger; nine 50-goal seasons.

BOTSFORD, Sara, performing arts. Dobie, Ont., 1952. Stage, film and TV actress. *Bay Boy; E.N.G.*

BOTTERELL, Edmund Henry, science. Vancouver, BC, 1906–97. Neurosurgeon who initiated program into spinal chord injury research; during WWII devoted to rehabilitation of veterans.

BOUCHARD, Lucien, politics. St-Coeur-de-Marie, Que., 1938. Founder and leader of Bloc Québécois; leader of Parti Québécois; premier of Quebec, 1996–2001.

BOUCHER, Gaetan, sports. Charlesbourg, Que., 1958. Speedskater; two gold medals (1000 m, 1500 m) and a bronze medal (500 m) 1984 Winter Olympics.

BOUEY, Gerald Keith, business. Axford, Sask., 1920. Banker; governor.

BOURASSA, Henri, politics. Montreal, Que., 1868–1952. Federalist; founded *Le Devoir* newspaper.

BOURASSA, Jocelyne, sports. Shawinigan-Sud, Que., 1947. Golf champion, winner of many awards, including La Canadienne 1973 LPGA event; Golf Personality of the Year, Golf Canada, 1972.

BOURASSA, Robert, politics. Montreal, Que., 1933–96. Quebec premier 1970–76, 1985–93.

BOURGAULT, Pierre, politics. East-Angus, Que., 1934–2003. Journalist, politician; president of Rassemblement pour l'indépendence nationale (RIN), which merged with PQ in 1968. Later advisor to Jacques Parizeau. Journalist with *Le Journal de Montréal* and contributor to national newspapers. *Moi, je m'en souviens.*

BOURGEOYS, Marguerite, religion. France, 1620–1700. Religious educator; canonized, 1982.

BOURGET, Ignace, religion. Lauzon, Que., 1799–1885. Catholic bishop of Montreal; avid ultra-Montanist opposed secular Quebec.

BOURNE, Shae-Lynn, sports. Chatham, Ont., 1976. Ice dancing; with Victor Kraatz won Canadian title, 1993–96; third in World Championships, 1996.

BOURQUE, James, politics. Wandering River, Alta, 1935–96. Aboriginal activist appointed to Privy Council, 1992. Co-director of policy for Royal Commission on Aboriginal Peoples, 1994.

BOURQUE, Raymond, sports. Montreal, Que., 1960. Hockey player; Boston Bruins defenceman; four-time Norris Trophy winner.

BOWELL, Mackenzie (Sir), politics. Eng., 1823–1917. Canada's fifth prime minister (1894–96).

BOWER, John William (Johnny), sports. Prince Albert, Sask., 1924. Hockey player. Long-time goalkeeper for New York Rangers, Toronto Maple Leafs; led Leafs to four Stanley Cup wins.

BOWERING, George Harry, literary arts. Penticton, BC, 1935. Prolific poet and prose writer: "Burning Water."

BOWMAN, Scotty, sports. Montreal, Que., 1933. Hockey coach; won nine Stanley Cups; five with Montreal.

BOYD, Liona, performing arts. Eng., 1950. Acclaimed classical guitarist. *The Guitar–Liona Boyd.*

BOYLE, Harry J., media. St. Augustine, Ont., 1915. Producer; media executive; novelist. Joined CBC in 1942, working as co-producer and in executive positions; in 1968 joined the Canadian Radio Television and Telecommunications Commission. Wrote *The Canadian Novel; The Luck of the Irish.*

BOYLE, Joseph Whiteside, exploration and discovery. Toronto, Ont., 1867–1923. Adventurer "Klondike Joe"; mining entrepreneur; national hero in Romania.

BOYLE, Willard S., invention. Amherst, NS, 1924. Physicist who co-invented the charge-coupled device for camcorders and telescopes.

BRACKEN, John, politics. Ellisville, Ont., 1883–1969. Cons. Manitoba premier 1922–42.

BRADFORD, Robert William, visual arts/business. Toronto, Ont., 1923. Aviation artist and historian; cofounder of National Aviation Museum in Ottawa, Ont.

BRAITHWAITE, Max, literary arts. Nokomis, Sask., 1911–95. Prairie novelist noted for autobiographical novel *Why Shoot the Teacher?*

BRAKHAGE, James Stanley (Stan), performing arts. USA, 1933–2003. Award-winning cinematographer whose avant-garde methods were expressed by his use of handheld cameras, rapid scene changes and physical alterations to the film itself. *Dog Star Man; Stan's Window.*

BRAND, Oscar, performing arts. Winnipeg, Man., 1920. Folksinger; recorded 80 albums; author folk song collections. *Squid Jiggin' Ground.*

BRANT, Joseph (b. Thayendanegea), politics/religion. USA, 1742–1807. Mohawk leader; British loyalist during American Revolution; translated Bible into Mohawk.

BRANT, Mary "Molly," politics. USA, c1736–96. Sister of Joseph Brant; influential leader of Six Nations women's federation, selected chiefs for Mohawk Confederacy; staunch Loyalist.

BRASSARD, Jean-Luc, sports. Valleyfield, Que., 1972. Skier; gold medal moguls 1994 Olympics.

BRASSEUR, Isabelle, sports. Kingsbury, Que., 1970. Skater; with Lloyd Eisler won 1993 pairs world title, two Olympic bronze medals (1992).

BRAULT, Jacques, literary arts. Montreal, Que., 1933. Poet; playwright; novelist. *Agonie.*

BRAUN, Eric, performing arts. Windsor, Ont., 1934–2001. Internationally renowned baritone opera singer; Braun's repertoire spanned classical and modern works, with a special emphasis on Schubert, Wagner and Schumann.

BREAU, Lenny, performing arts. USA, 1941–84. Guitarist, singer, composer of jazz, country, folk and pop; aired on CBC radio in 1940s and 1950s.

BRÉBEUF, Jean de, religion. France, 1593–1649. Jesuit martyr; missionary at Sainte Marie among the Hurons.

BRILL, Debbie, sports. Mission, BC, 1953. High jumper; originated "Brill bend" jumping style.

BRITTAIN, Donald, visual arts. Ottawa, Ont., 1928–89. Documentary filmmaker. *On Guard for Thee.*

BROADBENT, John Edward (Ed), politics. Oshawa, Ont., 1936. National leader, NDP 1975–89.

BROADFOOT, Dave, performing arts. Toronto, Ont., 1925. Comedian; Sergeant Renfrew character on *Royal Canadian Air Farce.*

BROCK, Isaac (Sir), military. Eng., 1769–1812. Soldier; War of 1812 hero; died at Queenston Heights.

BROCKHOUSE, Bertram Neville, science. Lethbridge, Alta, 1918. Pioneer of use of thermal neutrons to study aspects of behaviour of condensed matter systems at atomic level. Won 1994 Nobel Prize for physics.

BROCKINGTON, Leonard Walter, business. Wales, 1888–1966. First chairman of the CBC 1936–39; also expert labour arbitrator, representing clients including the US government, the Toronto Transit Commission and the Seafarers Union. Special assistant to Prime Minister Mackenzie King 1939–42.

BRONFMAN, Charles Rosner, business. Montreal, Que., 1931. Industrialist; chairman, Cemp Investments Ltd; former owner, Montreal Expos.

BRONFMAN, Edgar M., business. Montreal, Que., 1929. Industrialist; CEO, Seagram's Ltd; president, World Jewish Congress.

BRONFMAN, Samuel, business. Brandon, Man., 1891–1971. Capitalist; distiller (Seagram Co. Ltd) and philanthropist.

BROOKS, Marilyn, business. USA, 1932. Fashion designer launched innovative Unicorn boutique in Toronto, Ont., in 1963; founder of Marilyn Brooks boutique chain.

BROSSARD, Nicole, literary arts. Montreal, Que., 1943. Formalist poet and novelist. "Mecanique jongleuse suivi de masculin grammaticale."

BROWN, George, media/politics. Scot., 1818–80. Journalist; founded *Toronto Globe* (1844); as reformer, played major role in Confederation.

BROWN, Harry, military. Gananoque, Ont., 1898–1917. Victoria Cross recipient, WWI, Battle of Hill 70, 1917. Private, 10th Battalion.

BROWN, John George "Kootenai," exploration and discovery. Ire., 1839–1916. Adventurer; army official; prospector; whisky trader; established Waterton Lakes Natl Park.

BROWN, Rosemary, politics. Jamaica, 1930–2003. Activist; head, Ontario Human Rights Comm; former NDP leadership candidate.

BROWNING, Kurt, sports. Rocky Mountain House, Alta, 1966. World figure skating champion, 1989–91, 1993.

BRUHN, Erik Belton Evers, performing arts. Denmark, 1928–86. Dancer; choreographer; guiding figure for National Ballet.

BRULE, Etienne, exploration and discovery. France, 1592–1633. Explorer; first known European to reach Lake Superior.

BRZOZOWICZ, Czelaw Peter, engineering. Poland, 1911–97. Structural engineer consulted on Toronto's original subway line, Niagara Falls Skylon Tower and CN Tower in Toronto.

BUCHAN, John, first Baron Tweedsmuir, literary arts. Scot., 1875–1940. Thriller novelist, wrote *The Thirty-nine Steps*; governor general, 1935–40.

BUCHANAN, John MacLennan, politics. Sydney, NS, 1931. Conservative premier of NS, 1978–90.

BUCK, Tim, politics. Eng., 1891–1973. Radical politician; led Canadian Commmunist Party, 1929–61.

BUCKE, Richard Maurice, medicine. Eng., 1837–1902. Physician; writer; advocate for the mentally ill; spiritual writer. *Cosmic Consciousness*.

BUCZYNSKI, Walter, performing arts. Toronto, Ont., 1933. Pianist and composer of orchestral, chamber, vocal and piano music; soloist internationally in 1960s and 1970s. *Songs of War; Ressurrection II.*

BUJOLD, Geneviève, performing arts. Montreal, Que., 1942. Actress; international star. *Dead Ringers.*

BULL, Gerald Vincent, invention. North Bay, Ont., 1928–90. Inventor; weapons designer; murdered mysteriously.

BURKA, Petra, sports. Holland, 1946. Figure skater; women's world champion, 1965.

BURNARD, Bonnie, literary arts. Petrolia, Ont., 1945. Novelist; her *A Good House* won the 1999 Giller Prize. *Women of Influence*, short stories.

BURNS, Tommy (b. Noah Brusso), sports. Hanover, Ont., 1881–1955. Boxer; world heavyweight champion, 1906–08.

BURR, Raymond William Stacy, performing arts. New Westminster, BC, 1917–93. Actor; TV's Perry Mason, 1957–66, 1985–93.

BURROUGHS, Jackie, performing arts. Eng., 1942. Actress; versatile performer; Hetty in *Road to Avonlea.*

BUSH, John Hamilton (Jack), visual arts. Toronto, Ont., 1909–77. Abstract artist. "Bridge Passage."

BUSHNELL, Ernest Leslie, media. Lindsay, Ont., 1900–87. Started Canada's first radio advertising agency; VP of CBC 1945–58; founder of CJOH-TV in Ottawa, an affiliate of CTV.

BUTALA, Sharon Annette, literary arts. Nipawin, Sask., 1940. Novelist, short story writer, playwright. *Coming Attractions; The Fourth Archangel.*

BUTCHART, Robert Pim, business. Owen Sound, Ont., 1856–1943. In 1888 founded Owen Sound Portland Cement Co.; later turned quarries in Victoria, BC, into famed Butchart Gardens.

BY, John, military. Eng., 1779–1836. Engineer; built Rideau Canal, Quebec fortifications.

BYNG, Julian Hedworth George, first Viscount, military. Eng., 1862–1935. Soldier; governor general, 1921–26.

C

CABOT, John (b. Giovanni Caboto), exploration and discovery. Italy, c. 1450–99. First N American landing since the Vikings.

CABOT, Sebastian, performing arts. Eng., 1918–76. Portly, bearded character actor in film and television. *The Captain's Paradise; The Beachcombers; Family Affair.*

CAIN, Larry, sports. Toronto, Ont., 1963. Canoeist; gold (500 m) and silver (1000 m) medals, 1984 Olympics.

CALDER, Frank Arthur, politics. Nass Harbour, BC, 1915. Native politician; Nishga leader; BC MLA.

CALDWELL, Zoe, performing arts. Australia, 1933. Actor, director. *The Prime of Miss Jean Brodie.*

CALLAGHAN, Barry, literary arts. Toronto, Ont., 1937. Founder of *Exile: A Literary Quarterly*; novelist, journalist; son of Morley Callaghan.

CALLAGHAN, Morley Edward, literary arts. Toronto, Ont., 1903–90. Novelist; memoirist. *The Loved and the Lost.*

CALLBECK, Catherine, politics. Central Bedeque, PEI, 1939. First woman to be elected premier. Liberal premier of PEI 1993–96.

CALLWOOD, June, public service. Chatham, Ont., 1924. Journalist; civil libertarian, AIDS activist.

CALVERT, Lorne Albert, politics. Moose Jaw, Sask., 1952. NDP premier of Saskatchewan 2001–; formerly minister of social services.

CAMERON, Elspeth MacGregor, literary arts. Toronto, Ont., 1943. Biographer. *Robertson Davies: An Appreciation; Hugh MacLennan: A Writer's Life; Irving Layton: A Portrait.*

CAMERON, James, literary arts. Eng., 1910. Philosopher; essayist; poet. "Images of Authority."

CAMERON, James, performing arts. Kapuskasing, Ont., 1954. Hollywood-based director of action movies including *Terminator* series, *Aliens, True Lies, Titanic.*

CAMERON, Michelle, sports. Calgary, Alta, 1962. Gold medalist in sychronized swimming with Carolyn Waldo, 1988 Olympics.

CAMERON, Silver Donald, literary arts. Toronto, Ont., 1937. Novelist, critic, editor, playwright. *Dragon Lady; Wind, Whales and Whisky: A Cape Breton Voyage.*

CAMERON, Thomas Wright Moir, medicine. Scot., 1894–1947. Parasitologist; pioneered study of parasitic worms.

CAMP, Dalton Kingsley, politics. Woodstock, NB, 1920–2002. PC consultant; newspaper columnist.

CAMPBELL, Alexander (Sir), politics. Eng., 1822–92. Tory leader; Father of Confederation.

CAMPBELL, Avril Phaedra (Kim), politics. Port Alberni, BC, 1947. First woman prime minister of Canada, June 1993–December 1993.

CAMPBELL, Cassie, sports. Brampton, Ont., 1973. Captain of women's gold-medal winning hockey game in 2002 Salt Lake City Olympics; Campbell plays defense.

CAMPBELL, Clarence, sports. Fleming, Sask., 1905–84. Sports administrator; headed NHL, 1946–77.

CAMPBELL, Douglas, performing arts. Scot., 1922. Actor at Stratford Festival, Ont. Co-founder of Canadian Players.

CAMPBELL, Frederick William, military. Mount Forest, Ont., 1867–1915. Victoria Cross recipient, WWI, Battle of Givenchy, 1915. Lieutenant, 1st Battalion of the 1st Brigade.

CAMPBELL, Gordon, politics. Vancouver, BC, 1948. Liberal party premier of British Columbia 2001–; formerly mayor of Vancouver.

CAMPBELL, Neve, performing arts. Guelph, Ont., 1973. Actress/dancer noted for role in Canadian TV series *Catwalk;* appeared in the US TV series *Party of 5;* also films *The Craft;* and the cult hit *Scream.*

CAMPBELL, Nicholas, performing arts. Toronto, Ont., 1952. Versatile actor, screenwriter, director; star of CBC's *DaVinci's Inquest;* also film *The Omen;* and TV production of *Come Back Little Sheba.*

CAMPBELL, Norman Kenneth, performing arts. USA, 1924. Music producer; innovative developer of ballet and musicals.

CAMPEAU, Robert, business. Sudbury, Ont., 1923. Financier; exemplar of 1980s expansionist business mania; developer; retail store magnate.

CANDY, John Franklin, performing arts. Toronto, Ont., 1950–94. Actor; comedian; bearish *SCTV* regular (Johnny LaRue, William B.); film star. *Uncle Buck; Planes, Trains and Automobiles.*

CAPLAN, Elinor, politics. Toronto, Ont., 1944. Liberal MP; former chairman of management board, has held various portfolios in provincial government, including minister of citizenship and immigration.

CAPLAN, Gerald Lewis, politics. Toronto, Ont., 1938. National director of federal NDP in 1982, campaign director in 1984. Advisor to Stephen Lewis; co-chair of Task Force on Broadcasting Policy in 1985; Chairman of Ontario Royal Commission on Education in 1993.

CARDINAL, Douglas Joseph, visual arts. Red Deer, Alta, 1934. Métis architect; Canadian Museum of Civilization.

CARDINAL, Tantoo, performing arts. Fort McMurray, Alta, 1951. Native actress who has appeared in films, *Big Bear, Smoke Signals, Black Robe* and CBC's *North of 60.*

CARELESS, James Maurice Stockford, literary arts. Toronto, Ont., 1919. Historian; has written extensively on the effect of cities expanding into the hinterland. *Canada: A Story of Challenge; Brown of the Globe.*

CARIOU, Len, performing arts. St Boniface Man., 1939. Theatre director and actor; associated with Manitoba Theatre Centre; Stratford Festival, Ont.; and in England and US. Tony Award for Stephen Sondheim's *Sweeney Todd* in New York, 1979.

CARLE, Gilles, visual arts. Maniwaki, Que., 1929. Film director. *La Vrai Nature de Bernadette.*

CARLETON, Guy (Sir), first Baron Dorchester, politics. Ire., 1724–1808. Quebec governor, 1768–78, 1785–95; supporter of French traditions.

CARMAN, William Bliss, literary arts. Fredericton, NB, 1861–1929. Poet; journalist. "The Pipes of Pan."

CARMICHAEL, Franklin, visual arts. Orillia, Ont., 1890–1945. Group of Seven founding member.

CARNEGIE, Herb, sports. Toronto, Ont., 1919. Outstanding hockey player, winner of four MVP awards with Black Aces, a semipro team with Quebec Senior Hockey League, during the 1940s and '50s; Carnegie, whose parents were Jamaican, was barred from NHL because of his race.

CARNEY, Patricia, politics. China, 1935. PC minister of energy, mines and resources and international trade; entered Senate in 1990.

CARR, Emily, visual arts. Victoria, BC, 1871–1945. Painter of NW coastal Indians and nature.

CARR, Shirley, politics. Niagara Falls, Ont. First Woman to lead CUPE, Canada's largest union. President Emeritus, Canadian Labour Congress.

CARR, William Keir, military. Grand Bank, Nfld, 1923. Known as the "Father of the Canadian Air Force" for his work in consolidating military aviation after the unification of the armed forces.

CARREY, James (Jim), performing arts. Jackson's Point, Ont., 1962. Comedic actor. *Ace Ventura; The Mask; Batman Forever.*

CARRICK, William Henesey, performing arts. Toronto, Ont., 1920–2002. Wildlife filmmaker who worked extensively with the NFB and Ducks Unlimited. His discovery that wild geese would follow a light aircraft to learn forgotten migratory routes led to the film *Fly Away Home,* for which he acted as a consultant. *World in a Marsh.*

CARRIER, Roch, literary arts. Beauce, Que., 1937. Novelist; playwright. *La Guerre, Yes Sir!*

CARSON, John Elmer (Jack), performing arts. Carman, Man., 1910–63. Square-jawed film actor. *Mildred Pierce.*

CARTER, Emmett (Cardinal), religion. Montreal, Que., 1912–2003. As Toronto Cardinal, helped get full funding for Catholic schools.

CARTER, Wilf, performing arts. Port Hilford, NS, 1904–96. Singer; father of Canadian country music.

CARTIER, Georges-Etienne (Sir), politics. St Antoine, UC, 1814–73. Father of Confederation; joint premier of United Canada, 1857–62.

CARTIER, Jacques, exploration and discovery. France, 1491–1557. Credited with European discovery of Canada; first explorer of St. Lawrence River.

CARVER, Brent, performing arts. Cranbrook, BC, 1951. Actor at Ontario's Stratford Festival (*Hamlet; Pirates of Penzance*); television (CBC's *Street Legal*); in musical comedy (*Jacques Brel Is Alive and Well and Living in Paris*); and on film (*The Wars*).

CARVER, Humphrey Stephen Mumford, politics. Eng., 1902–95. Key figure in Central Mortgage and Housing Corporation 1950s–60s; formed Co-operative Commonwealth Federation, forerunner of NDP.

CASAVANT, Joseph, business. Saint-Hyacinthe, Que., 1807–74. Blacksmith who became Canada's first organ maker; he built 17 organs before his death. His sons took over the business, naming it Casavant Frères; the company's instruments continue to be internationally famous for their quality.

CASGRAIN, Thérèse, politics. Montreal, Que., 1896–1981. Won Quebec women the right to vote (1940) and hold provincial office; leader of Quebec's CCF party in 1951.

CASSON, Alfred Joseph (A.J.), visual arts. Toronto, Ont., 1898–1992. Member, Group of Seven. *Country Store.*

CATHERWOOD, Ethel, sports. Haldimand Cty, Ont., 1909–87. High jumper; gold in high jump, 1928 Olympics.

CAVOUKIAN, Artin and Lucie, visual arts. Egypt, Armenia, 1915–95, 1923–95. Clientele of photographer Artin with wife Lucie included world leaders.

CHALMERS, Floyd Sherman, public service. USA, 1898–1993. Instituted Floyd S. Chalmers Foundation funding for arts in Canada.

CHAMBERLAIN, Douglas Thomas, performing arts. Toronto, Ont., 1933. Character actor; roles in classics, comedy and light opera, associated with Ontario's Stratford Festival; *Spring Thaw* revue; also at Charlottetown Festival and Vancouver Playhouse Theatre.

CHAMPLAIN, Samuel de, exploration and discovery. France, 1567–1635. Explorer; important cartographer/geographer; "Father of New France."

CHANG, Simon, business. China, 1950. Fashion designer; also branched into fragrances, accessories, uniforms for restaurants and salon design.

CHANG, Thomas Ming Sui, medicine/science. China, 1933. Physiologist; expert on artificial cells and organs.

CHANT, Donald Alfred, science. Toronto, Ont., 1928. Pioneer in environmental movement in the 1960s, specializing in pesticides, pollution, wildlife preservation and ecosystems. In 1980 was chairman of Ontario Waste Management.

CHAPMAN, John Herbert, science. London, Ont., 1921–79. Physicist; lead role in Canada's satellite program.

CHAPUT-ROLLAND, Solange, media. Montreal, Que., 1919–2001. Writer; broadcaster; Québécoise federalist.

CHAREST, Jean J., politics. Sherbrooke, Que., 1958. Led PC party after '93 federal electoral debacle; elected PC premier of Quebec 2003.

CHARLEBOIS, Robert, performing arts. Montreal, Que., 1945. Singer/songwriter. "Solidaritude."

CHARLEVOIX, Pierre François Xavier de, literary arts. France, 1682–1761. Historian; first complete history of New France.

CHAYKIN, Maury, performing arts. USA, 1949. Prolific actor has appeared in *Jacob Two-Two Meets the Hooded Fang; Dances with Wolves.*

CHEE CHEE, Benjamin (b. Kenneth Thomas Benjamin), visual arts. Temagami, Ont., 1944–77. Ojibwa artist; block-stamped abstract and animal, bird images; noted for use of movement and humour.

CHERRY, Don, sports. Kingston, Ont., 1934. Hockey coach; commentator; feisty nationalist.

CHEVALIER, Leo, business. Montreal, Que., 1934–2000. Fashion designer of international lines.

CHING, Julia, academia. China, 1934–2001. Leading scholar in Chinese history and religion, specializing in neo-Confucian philosophy. *Probing China's Soul.*

CHIPMAN, Ward, law. St John, NB, 1787–1851. Jurist; chief justice of NB; noted abolitionist.

CHIRAEFF, Ludmilla, performing arts. Latvia, 1924. Choreographer; founder, Les Grands Ballets Canadiennes.

CHISHOLM, George Brock, medicine. Oakville, Ont., 1896–1971. Psychiatrist; early opponent of pollution, nuclear arms; first head of World Health Org.

CHONG, Rae Dawn, performing arts. Vancouver, BC, 1962. Film actress. *Quest for Fire.*

CHONG, Thomas (Tommy), performing arts. Edmonton, Alta, 1938. Actor; half of Cheech and Chong comedy team. *Cheech and Chong's Nice Dreams.*

CHOUART DES GROSEILLIERS, Medard, exploration and discovery. France, 1618–90. Explorer; fur trader; with Radisson opened western fur trade.

CHOUINARD, Josée, sports. Rosemont, Que., 1969. Three-time Canadian figure skating champion.

CHRÉTIEN, Joseph Jacques Jean, politics. Shawinigan, Que., 1934. Prime minister of Canada, Liberal party, 1993–2004.

CHRETIEN, Raymond, politics. Shawinigan, Que., 1942. Canadian ambassador to the United States, France.; nephew of Prime Minister Jean Chrétien.

CHRISTENSEN, Hayden, performing arts. Vancouver, BC, 1981. Actor; has gained new role in *Star Wars* series as the young Anakin Skywalker. *Higher Ground.*

CHRISTIE, Robert Wallace, performing arts. Toronto, Ont., 1920–96. Played at Ontario's Stratford Festival; Old Vic in London, England; famous for portrayal of John A. Macdonald.

CHRISTIE, William Mellis, business. Scot., 1829–1900. Biscuit manufacturer; Christie Biscuits founder.

CHUVALO, George, sports. Toronto, Ont., 1937. Boxer; fought three world champions; never knocked down. Antidrug crusader.

CLAIR, Frank, sports. USA, 1917. Football coach; 174 wins (Ottawa Rough Riders) tops CFL coaches. Also coached Toronto Argonauts to 1950, 1952 Grey Cups.

CLANCY, Francis Michael "King," sports. Ottawa, Ont., 1903–86. Hockey player; defenceman, Ottawa Senators; Toronto Maple Leafs; lively raconteur.

CLARK, Charles Joseph (Joe), politics. High River, Alta, 1939. Prime minister of Canada 1979–80. Leader of federal Progressive Conservative Party, 1998–2003.

CLARK, Greg, literary arts. Toronto, Ont., 1892–1977. Journalist and humorist, winner of Leacock Award for Humour.

CLARK, Karl Adolf, invention. Georgetown, Ont., 1888–1966. Discovered hot-water recovery process used in oil extraction from tar sands, crucial to growth of industry.

CLARK, Susan, performing arts. Sarnia, Ont., 1940. Actress who has appeared in Hollywood movies, television. *Murder by Decree; Coogan's Bluff; Webster.*

CLARK, Wayne, business. Drumheller, Alta, 1949. Canadian fashion designer noted for his dramatic evening wear and high-quality sportswear.

CLARKE, Austin Chesterfield, literary arts. Barbados, 1934. Novelist, short story writer. *The Origin of Waves; The Polished Hoe* won the 2002 Giller Prize, 2003 Commonwealth Writers Prize.

CLARKE, Larry Denman, business. Eng., 1925. Founder of SPAR Aerospace, an internationally recognized company for its major contribution to the development of the CANADARM, used for manoeuvring objects while in orbit.

CLARKE, Lionel Beaumaurice, military. Waterdown, Ont., 1892–1916. Victoria Cross recipient, WWI, the Somme, 1916. Corporal, 2nd Battalion.

CLARKSON, Adrienne Louise, media/politics. Hong Kong, 1939. Broadcaster; long-time CBC host. *Take Thirty.* Appointed governor-general of Canada, 1999.

CLAYTON-THOMAS, David, performing arts. Eng., 1941. Singer; member, Blood, Sweat and Tears. *Spinning Wheel.*

COCHRANE, Tom, performing arts. Lynn Lake, Man., 1953. Singer, songwriter, guitarist. Led Toronto-based quintet, Tom Cochrane and Red Rider, formed in 1976. *Breaking Curfew.* Went solo in 1991 with *Mad, Mad World.* "Life is a Highway."

COCKBURN, Bruce, performing arts. Ottawa, Ont., 1945. Singer/songwriter; politically conscious performer. *You've Never Seen Everything.*

COCKBURN, Hampden Zane Churchill, military. Toronto, Ont., 1867–1913. Victoria Cross recipient, Boer War, 1900. Lieutenant, Royal Canadian Dragoons.

COE-JONES, Dawn, sports. Lake Cowichan, BC, 1961. Golfer; leading pro; 1993 LPGA title.

COHEN, Leonard, literary arts/performing arts. Montreal, Que., 1934. Poet, lyricist, singer. *Flowers for Hitler, I'm Your Man.*

COHEN, Matt, literary arts. Kingston, Ont., 1942–2000. Short story writer, novelist, translator. *The Colour of War; Living on Water; Freud: The Paris Notebooks.*

COHEN, Morris (Moishe) Abraham "Two-Gun," military. Eng., 1889–1970. China hand; confidant of Sun Yat-sen; general in Chinese army.

COHEN, Samuel Nathan, literary arts. Sydney, NS, 1923–71. Critic; Canada's first serious drama critic.

COHON, George, business. USA, 1937. CEO, Cdn McDonald's restaurants; philanthropist.

COLDWELL, James William (Major), politics. Eng., 1888–1974. CCF founder; leader, 1942–60.

COLE, Holly, performing arts. Halifax, NS, 1963. Jazz/pop singer with distinctive contralto voice; founder of the Holly Cole Trio. *Don't Smoke in Bed; Christmas Blues; Dear Dark Heart.*

COLE, Jack, business. Toronto, Ont., 1920–97. With brother Carl started Coles chain of bookstores in Toronto, which later became national; created Coles Notes, study booklets for students, in 1947.

COLEMAN, Kathleen Blake (Kit), media. Toronto, Ont., 1864–1915. First woman war correspondent.

COLICOS, John, performing arts. Toronto, Ont., 1928–2000. Stage actor; Stratford Festival regular.

COLLENETTE, David M., politics. Eng., 1946. Liberal MP; has been minister of transportation, national defense and veteran affairs.

COLLIP, James Bertram, medicine. Belleville, Ont., 1892–1965. Biochemist; co-discoverer of insulin.

COLOMBO, John Robert, literary arts. Kitchener, Ont., 1936. Anthologist; prolific compiler of reference books. *Colombo's Canadian Quotations.*

COLVILLE, Alexander, visual arts. Toronto, Ont., 1920. Realistic painter; designed centennial coins.

COMBE, Robert Grierson, military. Scot., 1880–1917. Victoria Cross recipient, WWI, Acheville, France, 1917. Lieutenant, 27th Battalion.

COMFORT, Charles Fraser, visual arts. Scot., 1900–94. Artist, graphic designer, created murals for Toronto Stock Exchange; director of National Gallery of Canada 1960–65.

CONACHER, Lionel Pretoria, sports. Toronto, Ont., 1901–54. Canada's Athlete of the Half-Century (1900–1950).

CONIBEAR, Kenneth Wilfred, literary arts. Orrville, Ont., 1907–2002. Novelist, outdoorsman, lecturer; Conibear managed Grey Owl's lecture tour of the UK in 1937. His memoir: *Arctic Adventures with the Lady Greenbelly.*

CONNOR, Ralph (b. Charles William Gordon), literary arts. West Indian Lands, Glengarry County, Canada West 1860–1937. Popular novelist, preacher of "red-blooded" Christianity. *The Sky Pilot.*

CONNORS, Charles Thomas "Stompin' Tom," performing arts. Saint John, NB, 1936. Country singer; nationalist performer. *Across This Land with Stompin' Tom.*

COOK, George Ramsay, literary arts. Alameda, Sask., 1931. Prolific historian. *Canada: A Modern Study; The Maple Leaf Forever.*

COOK, James, exploration and discovery. Eng., 1728–79. Navigator; explored Newfoundland and Northwest coasts.

COOK, Myrtle, sports. Toronto, Ont., 1902–85. Member of the women's track and field team in the 1928 Amsterdam Olympics, setting world record in 100 m race during Olympic trials; sports journalist for the *Montreal Star,* active on Olympic committees throughout career.

COOKE, Jack Kent, business. Hamilton, Ont., 1912–97. Capitalist; flamboyant owner of newspapers, radio stations, sports teams (Washington Redskins; L.A. Lakers; L.A. Kings).

COOMBS, Ernest Arthur (Ernie), performing arts. USA, 1927–2001. Children's entertainer; CBC's *Mr. Dressup.*

COON COME, Matthew, politics. Mistassini, Que., 1956. Grand Chief of the Assembly of First Nations 2000–.

COOP, Jane Austin, performing arts. Saint John, NB, 1950. Classical pianist; has appeared with both national and international orchestras; Beethoven specialist.

COPP, Harold, science. Toronto, Ont., 1915–1998. Physiologist; discovered calcitonin, hormone that regulates calcium in blood.

COPPS, Sheila Maureen, politics. Hamilton, Ont., 1952. Appointed Liberal deputy prime minister 1993.

CORBEIL, Carole, literary arts. Montreal, Que., 1952–2000. Award-winning journalist and novelist wrote *Voice-Over,* which won City of Toronto Book Award in 1993, and *In the Wings.*

CORBETT, Edward Annand, education. Truro, NS, 1887–1964. Internationally recognized as a pioneer in adult education. From 1936–51 he was director of Canadian Association for Adult Education; organized the Banff School of Fine Arts and was first director 1933–36; worked with CBC to develop the Farm Radio Forum starting in 1942 to promote adult education over the airwaves.

CORBETT, Percy Ellwood, education. Tyne Valley, PEI, 1892–1983. Legal educator, activist against injustice; one of the world's leading experts on international law. *Law and Society in the Relations of States; The Growth of World Law.*

CORMIER, Ernest, visual arts. Montreal, Que., 1885–1980. Architect; designed University of Montreal.

CORNISH, Judith, business. Toronto, Ont., 1958. With partner Joyce Gunhouse designs Comrags fashion design label.

CORRIGAL, Jim, sports. Barrie, Ont., 1946. Football player. Lineman with Toronto Argonauts 1970–81; fourtime CFL all-star.

COSENTINO, Frank, sports. Hamilton, Ont., 1937. Football player; CFL quarterback, 1960–69; sports history writer; prof., physical education.

COSTAIN, Thomas Bertram, literary arts. Brantford, Ont., 1885–1965. Historical novelist. *High Towers.*

COUGHTRY, Graham, visual arts. St Lambert, Que., 1931–99. Abstract figurative painter; exhibited in New York's Guggenheim Museum, Museum of Modern Art, as well as across Canada.

COULTHARD, Jean, performing arts. Vancouver, BC, 1908–2000. Composer. "The Pines of Emily Carr."

COUPLAND, Douglas Campbell, literary arts. Germany, 1961. Novelist; humorist. *Generation X, Microserfs.*

COURNOYEA, Nellie J., politics. Aklavik, NWT, 1940. First woman aboriginal leader of Northwest Territories.

COWAN, Garry, sports. Kitchener, Ont., 1938. Golfer; twice US amateur champion (1966, 1971).

COXETER, Harold Scott Macdonald "H.S.M.," science. Eng., 1907–2003. Mathematician dubbed as the "world's greatest geometer," Coxeter specializes in dimensional analogy, a process of stretching geometric shapes into higher dimensions, a geometric concept known as "Coxeter groups."

CRANSTON, Toller, sports. Hamilton, Ont., 1949. Skater; brought innovation and artistry to men's figure skating.

CRAWLEY, Frank Radford "Budge," visual arts. Ottawa, Ont., 1911–87. Film producer. *The Rowdyman.*

CREIGHTON, Donald Grant, literary arts. Toronto, Ont., 1902–79. Historian; developed literary side of history.

CREIGHTON, Mary Helen, performing arts. Dartmouth, NS, 1899–1989. Folk music expert specializing in English, French, Gaelic, Mi'kmaq and Nova Scotian music; associated with National Museum of Canada.

CREMAZIE, Claude Joseph Olivier "Octave," literary arts. Quebec City, Que., 1827–79. Father of French Canadian poetry. "Le Drapeau de Carillon."

CREMO, Lee, performing arts. Cape Breton, NS, 1939–99. Six-time winner of Maritime Old-Time Fiddling Contest; mix of Irish, Scottish, Mi'kmaq Indian music; winner of Canadian title at Alberta Tar Sands Competition.

CREWSON, Wendy, performing arts. Hamilton, Ont., 1956. Actress in TV and film, starred in *At the End of the Day: The Sue Rodriguez Story*. Also, *I'll Never Get to Heaven; Getting Married in Buffalo Jump*.

CROLL, David Arnold, politics. Russia, 1900–91. Liberal MLA in 1934; first Jewish Cabinet minister (1955).

CROMBIE, David Edward, politics. Toronto, Ont., 1936. Civic reformer; Toronto mayor 1973–78.

CRONENBERG, David, visual arts. Toronto, Ont., 1943. Film director; inventive horror; science fiction filmmaker. *Videodrome, Crash*.

CRONYN, Hume (b. Hume Blake), performing arts. London, Ont., 1911–2003. Stage actor; film character player. *Cocoon*.

CROSBIE, John Carnell, politics. St John's, Nfld. 1931. PC minister of fisheries and oceans; international trade; justice.

CROTHERS, William, sports. Markham, Ont., 1940. Runner; silver medal (800 m), 1964 Olympics.

CROW, John William, business. Eng., 1937. Economist; governor of Bank of Canada, 1987–94.

CROWFOOT, military. Belly R, Alta, 1830–90. Blackfoot chief, diplomat.

CUDDY, James Gordon (Jim), performing arts. Toronto, Ont., 1955. Lead singer for rock group Blue Rodeo.

CUMMINGS, Burton, performing arts. Winnipeg, Man., 1947. Rock singer; lead singer, The Guess Who; later solo artist. *My Own Way to Rock*.

CUNARD, Samuel (Sir), business. Halifax, NS, 1787–1865. Shipowner; founded Cunard Line forerunner.

CURNOE, Gregory Richard, visual arts. London, Ont., 1936–92. Fine artist whose paintings often incorporated written words; also created collages, drawings, prints.

CURRIE, Arthur William (Sir), military. Strathroy, Ont., 1875–1933. Commander, Canadian corps, WWI.

CURRIE, Philip, science. Toronto, Ont., 1948. Curator of dinosaurs for Alberta's Royal Tyrrel Museum in Drumheller and world leader in paleontology; recently discovered a feathered dinosaur that proved birds were dinosaurs.

CURTOLA, Robert Allen (Bobby), performing arts. Thunder Bay, Ont., 1944. Singer; early teen idol. "Fortune Teller."

CYR, Louis, sports. Napierville, Que., 1863–1912. World's strongest man, 1880–1990.

D

DAFOE, Allan Roy, medicine. Madoc, Ont., 1883–1943. Small-town physician who delivered the Dionne quintuplets, May 28, 1934; later faced accusations of exploiting the sisters.

DAFOE, John Wesley, media. Combermere, Ont., 1866–1944. Journalist; influential editor, *Winnipeg Free Press*.

DAIGLE, Sylvie, sports. Sherbrooke, Que., 1962. Won gold in 1988 Calgary Olympics in short track speed skating, as well as silver and bronze medals; five-time world champion.

DAIR, Carl, visual arts. Welland, Ont., 1912–67. Internationally recognized designer, topographer; created Cartier, first modern Canadian typeface. *Design with Type*.

DALE, Cynthia, performing arts. Toronto, Ont., 1961. Actress known for roles in TV series *Street Legal; Taking the Falls*, and for numerous roles at Stratford Festival.

DANBY, Kenneth Edison (Ken), visual arts. Sault Ste Marie, Ont., 1940. Painter of realistic sports figures.

DANCE, Helen Oakley, performing arts. Toronto, Ont., 1913–2001. Record producer, jazz and blues historian and journalist, Dance was a contemporary of jazz greats such as Duke Ellington; also civil-rights supporter.

DANKO, Rick, performing arts. Simcoe, Ont., 1943–99. Founder and vocal/bass member of folk, blues, rock group The Band, subject of director Martin Scorcese's film *The Last Waltz*.

DAUDELIN, Charles, visual arts. Granby, Que., 1920–2001. Abstract artist, sculptor whose spiritually themed works are displayed in Canada and France. Designed awards for France-Canada and Jutra prizes.

DAUDELIN, Robert, performing arts. West Shefford, Que., 1939. Film administrator; writer; producer; director. Founder of movie critic magazine *Objectif*; International Film Festival in Montreal; director of Cinémathèque québécoise.

DAVEY, Keith, politics. Toronto, Ont., 1926. Long-time Liberal Party strategist.

DAVIES, Robertson William, literary arts. Thamesville, Ont., 1913–95. Novelist; playwright. *Fifth Business*.

DAVIS, Andrew, performing arts. Eng., 1944. Conductor of Toronto Symphony Orchestra 1975–88; participated in 1978 TSO visit to People's Republic of China.

DAVIS, Donald, performing arts. Newmarket, Ont., 1928–98. Distinguished Shakespearean actor, played Ontario's Stratford Festival; also appeared in TV roles: *Mission Impossible*. Co-founder of Toronto's Crest Theatre.

DAVIS, Fred, media. Toronto, Ont., 1921–96. Broadcaster and host of long-running CBC panel show *Front Page Challenge* (1957–95).

DAVIS, Victor, sports. Guelph, Ont., 1964–89. Swimmer; three medals 1984 Olympics; gold in 200 m breaststroke.

DAVIS, Warren, performing arts. Peterborough, Ont., 1926–95. CBC newsman. *The National; This Hour Has Seven Days*.

DAVIS, William Grenville, politics. Brampton, Ont., 1929. PC premier of Ontario, 1971–85.

DAWSON, George Mercer, science. Pictou, NS, 1849–1901. Geologist; surveyed much of northern and western Canada.

DAWSON, John William (Sir), science. Pictou, NS, 1820–99. Geologist; made McGill a leading university; founded Royal Society of Canada.

DAY, James, sports. Thornhill, Ont., 1946. Equestrian; team gold medal, 1968 Olympics.

DAY, Stockwell, politics. Barrie, Ont., 1950. Former provincial treasurer for Alberta; Canadian Reform Alliance Conservative Party leader, 2000–02.

DE CARLO, Yvonne (b. Peggy Yvonne Middleton), performing arts. Vancouver, BC, 1924. Actress; film/TV star. *The Munsters*.

DE LA ROCHE, Mazo (b. Maisie Roche), literary arts. Newmarket, Ont., 1879–1961. Prolific popular novelist. *Jalna*.

de VILLIERS, Priscilla, politics. S. Africa, 1942. Activist and founder of CAVEAT, Canadians Against Violence Everywhere Advocating Its Termination.

DEL GRANDE, Louis, performing arts. USA, 1942. Actor, producer, writer. Starred in CBC TV series *Seeing Things*.

DENNYS, Louise, literary arts. Egypt, 1948. Vicepresident and publisher at Knopf Canada.

DEPOE, Norman Reade, media. USA, 1917–80. CBC's Ottawa correspondent in the 1960s, Depoe was respected for his high standards in both national and international reporting during his career; also helped build CBC network in the 1950s.

DESCHENES, Jules, law. Montreal, Que., 1923–2000. Jurist; Que. chief justice; chairman, Inquiry of War Criminals in Canada.

DESJARDINS, Alphonse, business. Lévis, Que., 1854–1920. Banker; established first Caisse populaire (credit union) in 1900.

DESMARAIS, Paul, business. Sudbury, Ont., 1927. Industrialist; chairman of Power Corp., controlling trust, insurance and paper companies.

DESMOND, Trudy, performing arts. USA, 1946–99. Ballad and jazz singer, appeared in 1970 revue Spring Thaw. *My One and Only Love,* a tribute to Gershwin.

DEWAR, Marion, politics. Montreal, Que., 1928. Mayor, Ottawa, 1978–85; NDP MP.

DEWDNEY, Christopher, literary arts. London, Ont., 1951. Eclectic poet. *The Immaculate Perception: The Recent Artifacts from the Institute of Applied Fiction.*

DEWHURST, Colleen, performing arts. Montreal, Que., 1926–91. Actress who cultivated an earth-mother persona; noted for TV and film roles and performances in Albee and O'Neill plays. *Annie Hall; Murphy Brown.*

DE WIND, Edmund, military. Ire., 1883–1918. Victoria Cross recipient, WWI, Race Course Redoubt (Grougie, France), 1918. 2nd Lieutenant, 31st and 15th Battalions.

DeWOLF, Harry George, military. Bedford, NS, 1903–2000. Most decorated officer in Canadian Armed Forces; at helm of HMS *Haida* during Allied invasion of Normandy.

DHALIWAL, Herb, politics. India, 1952. Liberal MP, minister of fisheries and oceans.

DIAMOND, Abel Joseph (Jack), visual arts. South Africa, 1932. Leading architect; designed Toronto's central YMCA; York University (Toronto) Student Centre; Jerusalem City Hall; Burns Building, Calgary.

DIAMOND, Billy, politics/business. Waskaganish, Que., 1949. Cree chief who successfully negotiated for native rights during James Bay hydroelectric project in Quebec; founder of Cree-owned airline Air Creebec.

DICKENS, Francis Jeffrey, military. Eng., 1844–86. Policeman; novelist's son; inspector in NWMP.

DICKINS, Clennell Haggerston "Punch," exploration and discovery. Portage la Prairie, Man., 1899–1995. Adventurer. First to fly length of MacKenzie River and above Arctic Circle.

DICKINSON, Peter Allgood Rastall, visual arts. Eng., 1925–61. International style architect responsible for postwar development: Benvenuto Apartments, Prudential Building (Toronto); CIBC, Windsor Plaza (Montreal).

DICKSON, Robert George Brian, law. Yorkton, Sask., 1916–98. Chief justice of Canada, 1984–90.

DIEFENBAKER, John George, politics. Neustadt, Ont., 1895–1979. Prime minister of Canada 1957–63. (PC)

DION, Celine, performing arts. Montreal, Que., 1968. Popular Quebec chanteuse. "My Heart Will Go On."

DION, Stéphane, politics. Quebec City, Que., 1955. Political scientist; Liberal minister of intergovernmental affairs 1996–.

DIONNE, Marcel, sports. Drummondville, Que., 1951. Hockey player; centre; 731 goals, third all-time.

DIONNE sisters, medicine. Corbeil, Ont., 1934. Annette, Émilie (d. 1954), Yvonne (d. 2001), Cecile and Marie (d. 1970), identical quintuplets born to poor rural family, became tourist attraction through government exploitation.

DMYTRYK, Edward, visual arts. Grand Forks, BC, 1908–99. Film director; film noir specialist. One of Hollywood Ten during McCarthy era. *Detour.*

DOBBS, Kildare Robert Eric, literary arts. India, 1923. Short story writer, essayist. *Coastal Canada; Historic Canada.*

DOER, Gary, politics. Winnipeg, Man., 1948. NDP premier of Manitoba, elected in 1999.

DOHERTY, Denny, performing arts. Halifax, NS, 1941. Pop singer; founding member, The Mamas and the Papas.

DONKIN, Eric Albert, performing arts. Eng., 1930–98. Classical actor who played 26 seasons at Ontario's Stratford Festival.

DONOHUE, Jack, sports. USA, 1931–2003. Basketball coach who brought Canadian teams to the top six in the world during his 18-year career, including a gold medal win at the 1982 World University Games in Edmonton.

DOOHAN, James Montgomery, performing arts. Vancouver, BC, 1920. Actor; played Scotty (Lt. Commander Montgomery Scott) in *Star Trek* series.

DOSANJH, Ujjah, politics. India, 1947. NDP premier of BC 2000–01.

DOUGHTY, Arthur George (Sir), archivist. Eng., 1860–1936. Established Public Archives of Canada.

DOUGLAS, Campbell Mellis, military. Quebec City, LC, 1840–1909. Victoria Cross recipient, Andaman Islands Expedition, 1867. Assistant surgeon, 24th Regiment of Foot.

DOUGLAS, James (Sir), politics. British Guiana, 1803–77. Administrator; governor of BC, 1858–64.

DOUGLAS, Robert John Wilson, science. Southampton, Ont., 1920. Geologist; famous for geographical survey of structure of Rockies and foothills of southern Alberta.

DOUGLAS, Thomas Clement (Tommy), politics. Scot., 1904–86. Eloquent socialist; Sask. premier, 1944–61; NDP federal leader, 1961–71.

DOYLE, Richard (Dic) James, media. Toronto, Ont., 1923–2003. Editor of the *Globe and Mail* from 1963–83, Doyle transformed the paper from a PC party mouthpiece to a more independent voice; appointed to the Senate in 1985.

DRABINSKY, Garth Howard, performing arts. Toronto, Ont., 1948. Impresario; Cineplex founder, theatrical producer. *Show Boat.*

DRAPEAU, Jean, politics. Montreal, Que., 1916–99. Montreal mayor for 29 years; brought city Expo 67, 1976 Olympics, Montreal Expos.

DRESSLER, Marie (b. Leila von Koerber), performing arts. Cobourg, Ont., 1869–1934. Actress; oversize film star. *Min and Bill.*

DRYDEN, Kenneth Wayne, sports. Hamilton, Ont., 1947. Hockey goaltender; six-time all-star for Montreal; president and general manager of the Toronto Maple Leafs in 1997. Also lawyer and writer. *The Game.*

DUCKWORTH, Henry Edmison, science. Brandon, Man., 1915. With associates constructed highy accurate mass spectrometers for determination of atomic masses.

DUDEK, Louis, literary arts. Montreal, Que., 1918–2001. Poet, professor and literary critic, Dudek co-founded with Irving Layton and Raymond Souster Contact Press, which published major Canadian poets in the 1950s and '60s. *Surface of Time.*

DUGUID, Don, sports. Winnipeg, Man., 1935. Curler; Canadian and world champion, 1970, 1971.

DUMONT, Fernand, politics. Montmorency, Que., 1927–97. Quebec sovereigntist named deputy minister of cultural development for PQ in 1976; drafter of Bill 101, French Language Charter.

DUMONT, Gabriel, military. Red River, Sask., 1837–1906. Métis leader; guerrilla leader in NW Rebellion.

DUNBAR, Isobel Moira, science. Scot., 1918. Member of the Arctic section of the Defense Research Board; specialized in the study of sea ice and its relationship to climate. *Arctic Canada from the Air.*

DUNN, Alexander Roberts, military. York, Upper Canada, 1833–68. First Canadian-born soldier to receive the Victoria Cross, Charge of the Light Brigade, Crimean War, 1854. Lieutenant, 11th Hussars.

DUNNING, George, performing arts. Toronto, Ont., 1920. Animator and director; creator of Beatles *Yellow Submarine* film animation.

DUPLESSIS, Maurice Le Noblet, politics. Trois-Rivières, Que., 1890–1959. Powerful premier of Quebec, 1936–39, 1944–59.

DURBIN, Deanna (b. Edna Mae Durbin), performing arts. Winnipeg, Man., 1921. Actress; singer; teenage movie star. *3 Smart Girls.*

DURELLE, Yvon, sports. Baie Ste Anne, Que., 1929. Canadian middleweight boxing title 1953; light heavyweight 1953–54; British empire light heavyweight champion 1957.

DURHAM, John George Lambton, first Earl of, politics. Eng., 1792–1840. Statesman; "Radical Jack" urged union of English and French Canada.

DURNAN, William Arnold (Bill), sports. Toronto, Ont., 1915–72. Hockey goaltender; six-time Vezina Trophy winner for Montreal Canadiens.

DUTOIT, Charles Edouard, performing arts. Switz., 1936. Conductor of Montreal Symphony Orchestra.

DWAN, Allan, visual arts. Toronto, Ont., 1885–1981. Film director from silent era, made over 200 Hollywood films. *Sands of Iwo Jima.*

E

EATON, Cyrus Stephen, business. Pugwash, NS, 1883–1979. Financier; promoter of international peace.

EATON, Fredrik Stefan, business. Toronto, Ont., 1938. Retailer; former chairman, T. Eaton Co.

EATON, Timothy, business. Ire., 1834–1907. Retailer; innovative founder of T. Eaton Co. in 1867.

EDWARDS, Henrietta, public service. Montreal, Que., 1849–1931. In 1875 published first women's magazine in Canada, *Women's Work in Canada*; with Lady Aberdeen co-established the National Council of Women and the Victorian Order of Nurses.

EDWARDS, Robert Chambers (Bob), media. Scot., 1864–1922. Journalist; published satirical *Calgary Eye Opener.*

EGGLETON, Arthur C., politics. Toronto, Ont., 1943. Liberal MP; mayor of Toronto 1980–91 (Toronto's longest-serving mayor).

EGOYAN, Atom, visual arts. Egypt, 1960. Film director; guitarist; playwright. *The Sweet Hereafter.*

EISLER, Lloyd, sports. Seaforth, Ont., 1963. Figure skater; with Isabelle Brasseur won world pairs title, 1993; Olympic bronze medals.

ELDER, Jim, sports. Toronto, Ont., 1934. Equestrian; team gold medal, 1968 Olympics.

ELGAARD, Ray, sports. Edmonton, Alta, 1959. Football player; Sask. Roughriders star wide receiver.

ELGIN, James Bruce, eighth Earl of, politics. Eng., 1811–63. Governor general, 1847–54.

ELLIOTT, David James, performing arts. Milton, Ont., 1960. A member of the Young Company at Stratford Festival in Ontario; cast as Nick Del Gado in CBC drama *Street Legal;* has appeared on American TV programs. *The Untouchables.*

ELVIN-LEWIS, Memory, science. Vancouver, BC, 1933. Ethnobotanist who, with husband Walter Lewis, is a leading world expert on airborne and allergenic pollens, as well as the medicinal uses of tropical plants.

EMERY, Victor, sports. Montreal, Que., 1933. Bobsledder; piloted 1964 Olympic gold medal team.

EMSLIE, Robert Daniel, sports. Guelph, Ont., 1859–1943. Major league baseball pitcher; won 32 games for Baltimore Orioles in 1884; umpire in National League, strove to improve working conditions and umpires' image.

ENGEL, Howard, literary arts. Toronto, Ont., 1931. Mystery writer. *Murder Sees the Light.*

ENGEL, Marian, literary arts. Toronto, Ont., 1933–85. Novelist. *Bear.*

ERASMUS, Georges Henry, politics. Ft Rae, NWT, 1948. Dene leader; former head, Assembly of First Nations.

ERICKSON, Arthur Charles, visual arts. Vancouver, BC, 1924. Architect; Simon Fraser University (Burnaby, BC).

ESPOSITO, Phillip Anthony (Phil), sports. Sault Ste Marie, Ont., 1942. Hockey player; Boston, Chicago, New York Rangers centre; 717 goals, fourth all-time.

ESTEY, Willard Zebedee "Bud," law. Saskatoon, Sask., 1919–2002. Supreme Court justice, 1977–88; headed several royal commissions.

ETROG, Sorel, visual arts. Romania, 1933. Monumental sculptor; designer. "Ritual Head."

EVANGELISTA, Linda, media. St Catharines, Ont., 1965. International top model.

EVANS, Gil, performing arts. Toronto, Ont., 1912–88. Composer, arranger, pianist. Played free jazz, rock and funk. Gil Evans Orchestra.

EVANS, James, education. Eng., 1801–46. English Methodist missionary, invented Cree syllabic writing system. *Cree Syllabic Hymn Book.*

EVANSHEN, Terrance Anthony (Terry), sports. Montreal, Que., 1944. Football player; outstanding CFL receiver.

EVES, Ernie, politics. Windsor, Ont., 1946. Became PC premier of Ontario 2002, replacing Mike Harris; from 1995–2001, deputy premier and minister of finance.

EYTON, Trevor, business. Quebec City, Que., 1934. Executive; president, Brascan Ltd; many corporate boards.

F

FACKENHEIM, Emil Ludwig, literary arts. Germany, 1916. Philosopher; works on religion and the Holocaust. *Quest for Past and Future.*

FAIRCLOUGH, Ellen Louks, politics. Hamilton, Ont., 1905. First woman Cabinet minister (1957).

FAIRFIELD, Robert, visual arts. St Catharines, Ont., 1918–95. Designed Stratford Festival Theatre, Ont.; Ontario pavilion at Expo 67.

FAIRLEY, Barker, visual arts. Eng., 1887–1986. Critic; essential Goethe scholar; portrait painter.

FAITH, Percy, performing arts. Toronto, Ont., 1908–76. Bandleader; top music arranger. "Canadian Sunset."

FALK, Gathie, visual arts. Alexander, Man., 1928. Multimedia artist, specializes in performance art, watercolour, drawings. Work shown at National Gallery of Canada.

FALONEY, Bernie, sports. USA, 1932. Football player; long-time star QB for Edmonton, Hamilton.

FARQUHARSON, Ray, medicine. Claude, Ont., 1897–1965. Doctor who discovered Farquharson phenomenon, a hormone-related theory in secretion activity; his 1958 Farquharson Report led to the formation of the Medical Research Council in 1960.

FAVREAU, Marc, performing arts. Montreal, Que., 1929. Actor; author, noted for role as the hapless, naïve clown Sol, performed on TV and in theatre. *Sol et Gobelet.*

FEINBERG, Abraham (Rabbi) (b. Abraham Nisselevicz, aka Anthony Frome), politics. USA, 1899–1986. Peace activist; champion of radical causes.

FEORE, Colm, performing arts. USA, 1958. Actor; played Glenn Gould in *Thirty-two Short Films About Glenn Gould.* Roles at Stratford Festival, Ont.; also in film *The Red Violin.*

FERGUSON, Don, performing arts. Montreal, Que., 1946. Actor, writer, director of CHC documentaries; on team of CBC's *Royal Canadian Air Farce.* Impersonates Lucien Bouchard, Preston Manning.

FERGUSON, Ivan Graeme, invention. Toronto, Ont., 1929. Inventor; developed IMAX and OMNIMAX film systems.

FERGUSON, James Francis, performing arts. Ire., 1940–97. Founder, with George Millar, of the Irish Rovers, a singing group that popularized Irish pub music from the sixties on; appeared on CBC television.

FERGUSON, Max "Rawhide," media. Eng., 1924. Broadcaster; popular host of CBC Radio's *Rawhide.*

FERGUSON, Maynard, performing arts, Verdun, Que., 1928. Jazz trumpeter; versatile stylist made 50 albums.

FERRON, Jacques, literary arts/politics. Louiseville, Que., 1921–85. Playwright, *Contes du pays incertain;* Rhinoceros Party founder.

FESSENDEN, Reginald Aubrey, invention. Milton-Est, Canada E, 1866–1932. Inventor; transmitted world's first radio broadcast (1906).

FIELDING, Joy, literary arts. Toronto, Ont., 1945. Novelist, journalist, scriptwriter. *Tell Me No Stories.*

FILION, Herve, sports. Angers, Que., 1940. Harness driver; all-time leader in victories; 12,000+.

FILMON, Gary Albert, politics. Winnipeg, Man., 1942. PC Manitoba premier, 1988–1999.

FINDLEY, Timothy, literary arts. Toronto, Ont., 1930–2002. Novelist/playwright. *The Wars; The Piano Man's Daughter.*

FISHER, Ruby, sports. Eng., 1908–2001. Winner of the Canadian Open women's tennis doubles championship 1938 and 1948; gold medal in the 1985 World Masters Games.

FITZ-JONES, Philip Chester, science. Vancouver, BC, 1920. Researched structure and chemical nature of bacterial spores.

FITZGERALD, Lionel LeMoine, visual arts. Winnipeg, Man., 1890–1956. Impressionist turned to abstracts. "Doc Snider's House."

FLAVELLE, Joseph Wesley (Sir), business. Peterborough, Ont., 1858–1939. Financier; executive for Canada Packers, Bank of Commerce, National Trust.

FLEMING, Sandford (Sir), invention. Scot., 1827–1915. Engineer; developed standard time; designed Canada's first postage stamp; built railways.

FLOWERDEW, Gordon Muriel, military. Eng., 1885–1918. Victoria Cross recipient, WWI, Race Course Redoubt (Grougie, France), 1918. Lieutenant, Lord Strathcona's Horse.

FOLEY, Dave, performing arts. Toronto, Ont., 1963. Actor; role of Dave Nelson in TV series *News Radio;* member of comedy troupe Kids in the Hall.

FOLLOWS, Megan, performing arts. Toronto, Ont., 1969. Actor who portrayed Anne of Green Gables in CBC·TV series. *Silver Bullet.*

FONYO, Stephen Charles (Steve), sports. Montreal, Que., 1965. Handicapped runner; "Journey for Lives" raised funds for cancer research, 1985.

FORBES, Kenneth, visual arts. Toronto, Ont., 1892–1980. War artist, portrait painter (John Diefenbaker); works displayed in Canadian War Museum.

FORD, Glenn (b. Gwyllyn Samuel Newton Ford), performing arts. Quebec City, Que., 1916. Noted American actor of the 1940s and 1950s. *Gilda; Teahouse of the August Moon.*

FORRESTER, Helen, literary arts. Eng., 1919. Novelist. Wrote semiautobiographical Liverpool series: *Twopence to Cross the Mersey; Liverpool Miss; By the Waters of Liverpool; Lime Street at Two.*

FORRESTER, Maureen, performing arts. Monteal, Que., 1930. Operatic contralto; Canada's prima diva.

FORSEY, Eugene Alfred, politics. Grand Bank, Nfld, 1904–91. Intellectual; commentator on public affairs; social radical; strong federalist.

FORTIER, L. Yves, politics. Quebec City, Que., 1935. Former Canadian ambassador to the United Nations.

FOSTER, David Walter, performing arts. Victoria, BC, 1949. Musician; produced many major acts (Chicago, Barbra Streisand); 12 Grammy awards.

FOSTER, George Eulas (Sir), politics. Carleton, NB, 1847–1931. Statesman; central in Cdn political life; acting PM during Borden's illness (1920).

FOTHERINGHAM, Allan, media. Hearne, Sask., 1932. Journalist; popular political columnist.

FOULIS, Robert, invention. Scot., 1796–1866. Civil engineer, inventor, artist who invented the steam fog horn; developed New Brunswick's first iron foundry in Saint John.

FOWKE, Edith Margaret, literary arts. Lumsden, Sask., 1913–96. Music ethnologist, published traditional Canadian folksongs. *Penguin Book of Canadian Folksongs; Sally Go Round the Sun.*

FOX, Michael James (J.), performing arts. Edmonton, Alta, 1961. Actor; diminutive leading man. *Back to the Future.*

FOX, Terrance Stanley (Terry), sports. Winnipeg, Man., 1958–81. Began "Marathon of Hope" cross-Canada run to raise funds for cancer research; Lou Marsh Trophy as Canada's top athlete, 1980.

FRANCA, Celia (b. Celia Franks), performing arts. Eng., 1921. Choreographer; founder of National Ballet of Canada.

FRANCK, Albert Jacques, visual arts. Holland, 1899–1973. Painter especially noted for his depiction of old houses and back lanes in the old city of Toronto.

FRANCKS, Don Harvey, performing arts. Burnaby, BC, 1932. Veteran actor, jazz musician, appeared in revue Spring Thaw. Also TV and film roles. *The Man From U.N.C.L.E.; Finian's Rainbow.*

FRANKLIN, John (Sir), exploration and discovery. Eng., 1786–1847. Bold, doomed Arctic explorer.

FRANKLIN, Ursula Martius, science. Germany, 1921. Physicist and educator; specialist in field of archeometry, which relates materials analysis with archeology; advocate for Science for Peace.

FRANKS, Wilbur Rounding, invention. Weston, Ont., 1901–86. Inventor; devised pressure suit for airplane pilots.

FRAPPIER, Armand, science. Valleyfield, Que., 1904–91. Influential microbiologist.

FRASER, Anna, sports. Ottawa, Ont., 1963. Free-style skier; World Cup Aerial Champion (1986).

FRASER, Brendan, performing arts. USA, 1968. Comedic actor who has appeared in films *George of the Jungle*, *Airheads* and *Dudley Do-Right*.

FRASER, John Anderson, literary arts. Montreal, Que., 1944. Author; former editor of *Saturday Night* magazine; master of Massey College, Toronto. *The Chinese: A Portrait of a People.*

FRASER, Simon, exploration and discovery. USA, 1776–1862. First white man to explore Fraser River.

FRASER, Sylvia Lois, literary arts. Hamilton, Ont., 1935. Novelist. *Pandora; Berlin Solstice; My Father's House; The Emperor's Virgin.*

FRECHETTE, Sylvie, sports. Laval, Que., 1967. Received post-event gold medal in synchronized swimming, 1992 Olympics.

FREEDMAN, Harry, performing arts. Poland, 1922. Composer of chamber, symphonic, instrumental music; also wrote scores for stage and film (*The Pyx*). *Encounter.*

FRENCH, David, literary arts. Coley's Point, Nfld. 1939. Playwright. *Salt-Water Moon; Jitters; Leaving Home.*

FREUND, Kurt, medicine. Czech., 1914–96. Psychiatrist; noted researcher into human sexuality.

FROBISHER, Martin (Sir), exploration and discovery. Eng., 1539–94. Mariner; discovered Frobisher Bay.

FRONTENAC ET PALLUAU, (Louis de Buade) Comte de, politics. France, 1622–98. Gov. gen, New France, 1672–82, 1689–98.

FROST, Leslie Miscampbell, politics. Orillia, Ont., 1895–1973. PC premier of Ontario, 1949–61.

FRUM, Barbara Ruth, media. USA, 1937–92. Broadcaster; interviewer. *As It Happens; The Journal.*

FRUM, David, literary arts. Toronto, Ont., 1960. Journalist of "new right."

FRYE, Herman Northrop, literary arts. Sherbrooke, Que., 1912–91. Canada's most influential literary critic. *Anatomy of Criticism.*

FULFORD, Robert Marshall Blount, media. Ottawa, Ont., 1932. Journalist; former editor, *Saturday Night;* columnist.

FULTON, E. Davie, politics. Kamloops, BC, 1916–2000. Justice minister in John Diefenbaker's government, beginning 1957; became BC Supreme Court judge 1973–81.

FUNG, Donna Lori, sports. Vancouver, BC, 1963. Rhythmic gymnast; gold medal, 1984 Olympics.

FURST, Judith, performing arts. New Westminster, BC, 1943. Opera singer; internationally renowned diva.

FURTADO, Nelly, performing arts. Victoria, BC, 1978. Singer of popular music including folk, hip-hop, bossa nova and reggae, and a Grammy Award winner. *Whoa, Nelly!*

GABEREAU, Vicki Frances, media. Vancouver, BC, 1946. Broadcaster, author. Host of CBC Radio's *Gabereau,* 1988–97. Host of TV talk show on Baton Broadcasting.

GABRIEL, Tony, sports. Hamilton, Ont., 1948. Football player; CFL tight end; held record 138 straight games with receptions until 1995.

GAGNON, André, performing arts. Saint-Pacôme-de-Kamouraska, Que., 1942. Pianist; composer. "Le Saint-Laurent."

GAGNON, André Phillipe, performing arts. Loretteville, Que., 1961. Comedian, impressionist, noted for one-man shows.

GAGNON, Charles, visual arts. Montreal, Que., 1934–2003. An abstract painter, photographer, filmmaker and sculptor; his film *The Eighth Day* was created for the Christian Pavilion at Expo 67 in Montreal, a statement against the war in Vietnam.

GAGNON, Marc, sports. Chicoutimi, Que., 1975. Four-time gold medal winner in Salt Lake City 2002 Olympics for men's speed skating and men's relay team; overall, with a record-breaking total of five gold medals in three Olympic seasons. Also a four-time world champion short-track speed skater.

GALBRAITH, John Kenneth, business/literary arts. Iona Station, Ont., 1908. Economist; author; influential intellectual. *The Affluent Society.*

GALDIKAS, Biruté, science. Germany, 1946. Anthropologist; world's foremost expert on the physical anthropology of orangutans.

GALLANT, Mavis Leslie, literary arts. Montreal, Que., 1922. Author of more than 100 short stories. "A Fairly Good Time."

GALLEY, Harry A., invention. Montreal, Que., 1903–95. Inco employee; designer of first mass-produced stainless steel sink.

GALLIVAN, Danny, sports. Montreal, Que., 1917–93. Hockey announcer; voice of the Montreal Canadiens.

GALT, Alexander Tilloch, politics. Eng., 1817–93. Railway promoter; proposed union of all British colonies.

GARBER, Victor, performing arts. London, Ont., 1949. Character actor in Hollywood, formerly led folk band The Sugar Shoppe. Roles include Jesus in *Godspell;* also appeared in films *Titanic* and *First Wives Club.*

GARNEAU, François Xavier, literary arts. Quebec City, Que., 1809–66. Writer; early historian. *Histoire du Canada.*

GARNEAU, Hector de Saint Denys, literary arts. Montreal, Que., 1912–43. Poet. "Regards et jeux dans l'espace."

GARNEAU, Marc, science. Quebec City, Que., 1949. First Canadian astronaut (1984) to achieve liftoff.

GARNER, Hugh, literary arts. Eng., 1913–79. Working class novelist. *Cabbagetown.*

GASCON, Jean, performing arts. Montreal, Que., 1921–88. Actor; director; influential man of the theatre; headed Stratford Festival, Natl Arts Centre.

GAYFORD, Thomas Franklin, sports. Toronto, Ont., 1928. Equestrian; won gold medal Prix des Nations in 1968 Olympics.

GEDGE, Pauline, literary arts. New Zealand, 1945. Novelist. *Scroll of Saqqara; The Twelfth Transforming; The Covenant.*

GEHRY, Frank, visual arts. Toronto, Ont., 1929. Internationally recognized architect. Guggenheim Museum in Bilbao, Spain; Art and Teaching Museum, University of Minnesota.

GELBER, Arthur Ellis, public service. Toronto, Ont., 1915–98. Philanthropist who was prominent on arts boards, including National Arts Centre, National Ballet of Canada and the Ontario Arts Council.

GELINAS, Gratien, performing arts. St Tite, Que., 1909–99. Actor; director; playwright; crucial to modern Quebec theatre.

GEOFFRION, Joseph André Bernard "Boom Boom," sports. Montreal, Que., 1931. Hockey player; right-winger, Montreal Canadiens (1950–64), noted for strength and speed.

GEORGE, Dan (Teswahno), performing arts. Burrard Reserve, BC, 1899–1981. Actor; helped redefine image of Aboriginal peoples in media. *Little Big Man.*

GERUSSI, Bruno, performing arts. Medicine Hat, Alta, 1928–95. Actor; regular on *The Beachcombers.*

GESNER, Abraham, invention. Cornwallis, NS, 1797–1864. Inventor of kerosene oil.

GETTY, Donald Ross, politics/sports. Montreal, Que., 1933. Edmonton Eskimos quarterback; PC premier of Alberta; 1985–92.

GHERMEZIAN, Jacob, business. Azerbaijan, 1902–2000. Founder of Triple Five Corp., he built the West Edmonton Mall in Alberta, the world's largest mall; also developed the Mall of America in Bloomington, Minnesota.

GHIZ, Joseph Atallah, politics. Charlettetown, PEI, 1945–97. Liberal premier of PEI 1986–93. Avid supporter of Meech Lake Accord and Charlottetown Accord.

GIAUQUE, William Francis, science. Niagara Falls, Ont., 1895–1982. Chemist who won 1949 Nobel Prize in chemistry for studies of properties of substances at temperatures near absolute zero.

GIBSON, George "Mooney," sports. London, Ont., 1880–1967. Baseball player; pro catcher, 1905–18.

GIBSON, Graeme C., literary arts. London, Ont., 1934. Novelist. *Five Legs; Perpetual Motion.*

GILLIS, Margie, performing arts. Montreal, Que., 1953. Dancer, choreographer; depicts social and political themes; an internationally acclaimed soloist, she has toured with Les Grands Ballet Canadiens, and introduced modern dance to China after the revolution. *Mercy.*

GILMOUR, Clyde, media. Calgary, Alta, 1912–97. Journalist; arts radio broadcaster. *Gilmour's Albums.*

GIMBY, Bobbie (b. Robert Stead), performing arts. Cabri, Sask., 1918–98. Trumpeter, songwriter. Appeared in CBC radio series *The Happy Gang.* Composed "CA-NA-DA" in 1967 for centennial celebrations.

GISBORNE, Frederick Newton, invention. Eng., 1824–92. Inventor; developed undersea telegraph cable (1852).

GIVENS, Philip, politics. Toronto, Ont., 1922–95. Mayor of Toronto 1964–66; responsible for acquisition of Henry Moore's *The Archer* sculpture at Toronto's New City Hall.

GOLDSMITH, Robert, literary arts. St Andrews, NB, 1794–1861. First Canadian-born poet to write in English: *The Rising Village* described Acadian experience.

GOMEZ, Avelino, sports. Cuba, 1928–80. Jockey; over 4,000 career wins, including four Queen's Plates.

GOODERHAM, William, business. Eng., 1790–1881. With nephew James built Canada West's largest distillery, in 1859; Gooderham and Worts eventually had interests in distilleries, railways, transportation and retailing.

GOODIS, Jerry, business. Toronto, Ont., 1929–2002. A singer with the Canadian folk group the Travellers in the 1950s, Goodis wrote a Canadian version of "This Land Is Your Land," originally written by Woody Guthrie; he later co-founded one of Canada's top advertising firms, Goodis Goldberg Soren.

GOODMAN, Henry George, business. USA, 1907–97. Philanthropist, volunteer and lawyer who helped initiate and served as president of the Jewish Children's Aid Society in Toronto.

GOODYEAR, Scott, sports. Toronto, Ont., 1959. Indy car driver; winner of Canadian Racing Drivers Association Driver of the Year award; first Canadian to win oval race.

GORDON, Charles William, literary arts. Glengarry City, Canada W, 1860–1937. Presbyterian minister who wrote western-style novels, *The Sky Pilot, The Prospector,* as well as *Glengarry School Days.*

GORDON, Donald, business. Scot., 1901–69. Executive; controversial head of CNR, 1950–66.

GORDON, Walter Lockhart, politics. Toronto, Ont., 1906–87. Economic nationalist; inspired creation of Committee for an Independent Canada.

GORMAN, Charles, sports. Saint John, NB, 1897–1940. Speed skater; held seven world records.

GOTLIEB, Allan Ezra, politics. Winnipeg, Man., 1928. Career public servant; Canadian ambassador to US 1981–89.

GOTLIEB, Calvin Carl "King," education. Toronto, Ont., 1921. Pioneer in computer education, beginning at the University of Toronto in 1951; co-founder of the Computing and Data Processing Association of Canada. *Social Issues in Computing* (co-author); *Economics of Computers.*

GOTLIEB, Phyllis Fay, literary arts. Toronto, Ont., 1926. Poet, science fiction writer. *Heart of Red Iron; The Kingdom of the Cats.*

GOUGEON, Hélène Carroll, media. Ottawa, Ont., 1924–2000. Veteran journalist on radio, TV and in print; culinary expertise led to her *The Original Canadian Cookbook.* Also wrote for *Weekend, Toronto Star, Ottawa Journal.*

GOUIN, Jean-Lomer (Sir), politics. Canada E, 1861–1929. Liberal premier of Quebec, 1905–20.

GOULD, Glenn Herbert, performing arts. Toronto, Ont., 1932–82. Classical pianist; *Goldberg Variations* stand out in brilliant, eccentric career.

GOULET, Robert Gerard, performing arts. USA, 1933. Singer/actor, noted for romantic male leads. *South Pacific; Camelot.*

GOUZENKO, Igor Sergeievich, military. USSR, 1919–82. Spy; defector exposed Soviet espionage network.

GOVIER, Katherine Mary, literary arts. Edmonton, Alta, 1948. Novelist, short story writer. *Random Descent; Angel Walk.*

GOWAN, Elsie Park, literary arts. Scot., 1905–99. Internationally recognized playwright for radio and stage. *Beeches from Bond Street; The Building of Canada.*

GOWDY, Barbara, literary arts. Windsor, Ont., 1950. Novelist. *Mister Sandman; The White Bone; The Romantic.*

GOY, Luba, performing arts. Germany, 1946. Comedian on *Royal Canadian Air Farce;* impersonations include Sheila Copps, Pamela Wallin.

GRAHAM, William (Bill) Carvel, politics. Montreal, Que., 1939. Appointed minister of foreign affairs 2002 in Chrétien government.

GRANT, Charles, law. Toronto, Ont., 1902–80. Activist; fought anti-Semitism, racism, bigotry.

GRANT, George Parkin, literary arts. Toronto, Ont., 1918–88. Philosopher; influential pessimistic thinker and nationalist. *Lament for a Nation.*

GRAY, George H., sports. Canada W, 1865–1933. Shot putter; world record holder during 1880s.

GRAY, Herbert Eser, politics. Windsor, Ont., 1931. Liberal Party stalwart; has served as government leader; solicitor general; deputy prime minister for Jean Chrétien 1997–2000.

GRAY, James Henry, literary arts. Whitemouth, Man., 1906–98. Social historian whose works reflected Western Canadian society. *The Winter Years,* a story about the Depression; *The Boy From Winnipeg.*

GREEN, Tom, performing arts. Pembroke, Ont., 1971. Satirical "shock" comedian, stages outrageous publicity stunts. *The Tom Green Show.*

GREENAWAY, Keith Rogers, invention. Woodville, Ont., 1916. Co-inventor of the RCAF Twilight Computer, which is used worldwide for high-latitude navigation; also developed the Earth Convergency Grid, which used gyro-steering techniques.

GREENE, Graham, performing arts. Six Nations Reserve, Ont., 1952. Film/TV actor. *Dances with Wolves.*

GREENE, Lorne Hyman, performing arts. Ottawa, Ont., 1915–87. Actor; Ben Cartwright on TV's *Bonanza* for 14 years.

GREENE, Nancy Catherine, sports. Ottawa, Ont., 1943. Skier; World Cup winner, 1967, 1968; gold and silver slalom medals.

GREENOUGH, Gail, sports. Edmonton, Alta, 1960. Equestrian; 1986 world champion, individual show jumping.

GREENSPAN, Edward Leonard, law. Niagara Falls, Ont., 1944. Distinguished criminal lawyer.

GRENFELL, Wilfred Thomason (Sir), medicine. Eng., 1865–1940. Medical missionary; builder of hospitals in Nfld.

GRETZKY, Wayne, sports. Brantford, Ont., 1961. Hockey player; all-time leading NHL scorer (894 goals).

GREY, Deborah C., politics. Vancouver, BC, 1952. Canadian Alliance MP; deputy parliamentary leader; cofounder of Reform Party.

GREY OWL (b. Archibald Stansfield Belaney), literary arts. Eng., 1888–1938. Writer; conservationist who identified with Aboriginal peoples. *Pilgrims of the Wild.*

GRIERSON, John, visual arts. Scot., 1898–1972. Documentarist; creator of National Film Board.

GRIFFITH, Linda, performing arts. Toronto, Ont., 1953. Film, TV and stage actress. *Maggie and Pierre.*

GRIMES, Roger D., politics. Grand Falls, Nfld, 1950. Liberal premier of Nova Scotia 2001–; formerly minister of education.

GROSS, Paul, performing arts. Calgary, Alta, 1959. Actor, playwright; starred in TV series *Due South.*

GROSSMAN, Daniel Williams, performing arts. USA, 1942. Founder of the Danny Grossman Dance Co.; specializes in contemporary dance, set to jazz, rock music. *Higher; Nobody's Business.*

GROSSMAN, Lawrence S. (Larry), politics. Toronto, Ont., 1943–97. High-profile minister in Bill Davis's Ontario PC government, ran unsuccessfully as Tory leader against David Peterson in 1975.

GROULX, Lionel Adolphe, religion. Vaudreuil, Que., 1878–1967. Historian; Quebec religious nationalist.

GROVE, Frederick Philip, literary arts. Prussia, 1879–1948. Writer. *In Search of Myself.*

GUERIN, Gertrude Ettershank (Klaw Law We Leth), politics. Mission Reserve, N. Vancouver, BC. A Musqueam chief, considered to be the first native woman to hold such a high-ranking position.

GUILLET, James Edwin Dr., invention. Toronto, Ont., 1927. Inventor of biodegradable plastics.

GUNHOUSE, Joyce, business. Toronto, Ont., 1961. With partner Judith Cornish designs Comrags fashion design label.

GUSTAFSON, Ralph Barker, literary arts. Lime Ridge, Que., 1909–95. Founder of League of Canadian Poets. Governor General's Award, 1974. *Fire and Stone.*

GWYN, Richard, media. Eng., 1934. Long-time journalist with the *Toronto Star;* freelance journalist and political commentator. *The 49th Paradox: Canada in North America.*

GWYN, Sandra (Alexandra) Jean Fraser, literary arts. St John's, Nfld, 1935–2000. Governor General's Award, 1984. *The Private Capital; Tapestry of War.*

GWYNNE, Horace "Lefty," sports. Toronto, Ont., 1912–2001. Boxer; bantamweight gold medal, 1932 Olympics.

GZOWSKI, Casimir Stanislaus (Sir), exploration and discovery. Russia, 1813–98. Engineer; built roads, bridges and railroads.

GZOWSKI, Peter, media. Toronto, Ont., 1934–2002. Broadcaster; author; long-time CBC Radio host. *Morningside.*

HACKNER, Allan, sports. Nipigon, Ont., 1954. Curler; Canadian and world champion, 1982, 1985.

HADFIELD, Chris Austin, science. Sarnia, Ont., 1959. Astronaut, first Canadian mission specialist on space shuttle, 1996.

HAIG, Don, performing arts. Winnipeg, Man., 1933–2002. Co-founder of the Canadian Film Editors Guild and active in the CBC and National Film Board, Haig was instrumental in the development of the Canadian film industry.

HAILEY, Arthur, literary arts. Eng., 1920. Writer; produced string of best-sellers. *Airport.*

HAIM, Corey, performing arts. Toronto, Ont., 1972. Actor, producer. *Demolition High; Life 101.*

HALDER, Walter (Wally), sports. Toronto, Ont., 1925–94. Leading goal scorer on Canada's gold medallist team at 1948 Olympic Winter Games.

HALIBURTON, Thomas Chandler, literary arts. Windsor, NS, 1796–1865. Writer; social satirist. *The Clockmaker.*

HALL, Emmett Matthew, public service. Saint-Columban, Que., 1898–1995. Chief Justice of Saskatchewan; coauthor of Ontario's 1966 Hall-Dennis education report.

HALL, Frederick William, military. Ire., 1885–1915. Victoria Cross recipient, WWI, Second Battle of Ypres, 1915. Company sergeant-major, 8th Battalion.

HALL, Glenn Henry, sports. Humboldt, Sask., 1931. Hockey goaltender; 11-time all-star; record 502 consecutive games.

HALL, Monty, performing arts. Winnipeg, Man., 1925. Long-time TV host of *Let's Make a Deal* show.

HALL, William Edward, military. Horton Bluffs, NS, 1827–1904. First black soldier to receive the Victoria Cross, Indian Mutiny, 1857. Able seaman, Naval Brigade.

HALPERT, Herbert, literary arts. USA, 1911–2000. Newfoundland folklorist and academic; author of *Folktales of Newfoundland; Christmas Mumming in Newfoundland: Folklore and History.*

HAMEL, Theophile, visual arts. Ste-Foy, LC, 1817–70. Painted life-like official portraits.

HAMILTON, Barbara, performing arts. Toronto, Ont., 1926–96. Veteran screen and stage actor. *Anne of Green Gables; Crazy for You.*

HAMM, John F., politics. New Glasgow, NS, 1938. PC premier of Nova Scotia, 1999–.

HAMPSON, Sharon, performing arts. Toronto, Ont., 1943. Member of children's musical entertainment group Sharon, Lois and Bram; live and on TV. *The Elephant Show.*

HANLAN, Edward (Ned), sports. Toronto, Ont., 1855–1908. World champion oarsman, 1880–84.

HANNA, Robert Hill, military. Ire., 1887–1967. Victoria Cross recipient, WWI, Battle of Hill 70, 1917. Company sergeant-major, 29th Battalion.

HANSEN, Rick, sports. Port Alberni, BC, 1957. Wheelchair athlete; "Man in Motion" tour raised $20M for medical research.

HANSON, Melvin "Fritzie," sports. USA, 1912. Football player; led Winnipeg to first western Grey Cup (1935).

HARCOURT, Michael Franklin, politics. Edmonton, Alta, 1943. NDP Premier of BC 1991–96.

HARDY, Hagood, performing arts. USA, 1937–97. Pop/jazz pianist and composer; Juno award-winner. "The Homecoming"; scores for *Anne of Green Gables, Road to Avonlea.*

HARE, Frederick Kenneth, science. Eng., 1919–2002. Environmentalist; expert on climate change, greenhouse effect.

HARNOY, Ofra, performing arts. Israel, 1965. International virtuoso cellist.

HARPER, Elijah, politics. Red Sucker L, Man., 1949. MLA in Manitoba legislature who blocked passage of Meech Lake Accord.

HARPER, J. Russell, visual arts. Caledonia, Ont., 1914–83. Art historian; pioneered study of art history.

HARPER, Stephen, politics. Toronto, Ont., 1959. Elected leader of the Canadian Alliance party in 2002; former president of National Citizens Coalition.

HARRINGTON, Michael Francis, performing arts. St John's, Nfld, 1916–99. Supporter of an independent Newfoundland prior to 1949 confederation, Harrington hosted popular 1940s Newfoundland radio program *The Barrelman;* co-edited complete National Convention debates.

HARRINGTON, Rex Howard, performing arts. Peterborough, Ont., 1962. Internationally recognized ballet dancer; principal with National Ballet of Canada.

HARRINGTON, Richard, visual arts. Germany, 1911. Photographer whose stark portraits of a starving Inuit population in the late 1940s brought world attention to the grim situation caused partly by the disappearance of the caribou. *The Inuit: Life as It Was; Richard Harrington's Yukon.*

HARRIS, Christie, literary arts. USA, 1907–2002. Expert in West Coast Haida Indian culture, Harris interpreted Haida legends on radio, in classrooms and in literary works. *Raven's Cry; Once Upon a Totem.*

HARRIS, Lawren Stewart, visual arts. Brantford, Ont., 1885–1970. Founder of Group of Seven; noted for stark landscapes, *Above Lake Superior.*

HARRIS, Micheal Deane, politics. Toronto, Ont., 1945. PC premier of Ontario 1995–2002.

HARRIS, Mike, sports. Georgetown, Ont., 1967. Skip of the silver-medal-winning curling team during the 1998 winter Olympics in Nagano, Japan.

HARRIS, Wayne, sports. USA, 1938. Football player; outstanding Calgary Stampeders linebacker.

HARRON, Donald (Don), performing arts. Toronto, Ont., 1924. Actor; comedian; host of *Morningside* 1977–82; also noted for portraying Charlie Farquharson.

HART, Corey Mitchell, performing arts. Montreal, Que., 1962. Pop singer; teen heartthrob. *Boy in the Box.*

HART, Evelyn Anne, performing arts. Toronto, Ont., 1956. Prima ballerina, Royal Winnipeg Ballet.

HART, Julia, literary arts. Fredericton, NB, 1797–1867. Novelist whose *St. Ursula's Convent* written in 1824 was the first work of fiction by a Canadian-born writer to be published in Canada.

HARTMAN, Grace, business. Toronto, Ont., 1918–1993. Labour leader; first woman to head Canadian Union of Public Employees (1975–83).

HARVEY, Douglas N. (Doug), sports. Montreal, Que., 1924–90. Hockey player; Montreal Canadiens defenceman; won seven Norris Trophies.

HARVEY, Frederick Maurice Watson, military. Ire., 1888–1980. Victoria Cross recipient, WWI, Guyencourt, France, 1917. Lieutenant, Lord Strathcona's Horse.

HARVIE, Eric Lafferty, business/philanthropy. Orillia, Ont., 1892–1975. Founder of mining companies Western Leaseholds and Western Minerals; with wealth derived from oil discovery on properties he initiated the Glenbow Foundation and Heritage Park in Calgary; he was also a founding officer of the Canada Council.

HARWOOD, Vanessa Clare, performing arts. Eng., 1947. National Ballet soloist.

HATFIELD, Richard Bennett, politics. Woodstock, NB, 1931–91. PC premier of NB, 1970–87.

HAWKINS, Ronald "Rompin' Ronnie," performing arts. USA, 1935. Pop/country singer; pioneer of Canadian rock. "Mary Lou."

HAWLEY, Sanford Desmond (Sandy), sports. Oshawa, Ont., 1949. Jockey; winner of more than 6,000 races.

HAYDEN, Melissa (b. Mildred Herman), performing arts. Toronto, Ont., 1923. Virtuoso with New York City Ballet.

HEALEY, Jeff, performing arts. Toronto, Ont., 1966. Blind vocalist and guitarist, rock, blues music; Jeff Healey Trio. "Angel Eyes"; "See the Light."

HEARNE, Samuel, exploration and discovery. Eng., 1745–92. Explorer; *A Journey from Prince of Wales's Fort in Hudson's Bay to the Northern Ocean* is one of the great travel narratives.

HEATH, John Geoffrey (Jeff), sports. Ft William, Ont., 1915–75. Baseball player; hit .293 in 14-year career.

HEBB, Donald Olding, science. Chester, NS, 1904–85. Psychologist; developmental work showed importance of environmental stimulation.

HÉBERT, Anne, literary arts. Ste-Catherine-de-Fossambault, Que., 1916–2000. Novelist. *Kamouraska.*

HÉBERT, Louis-Philippe, visual arts. Megantic, Que., 1850–1917. Commemorative sculptor of many public monuments. *Queen Victoria.*

HEDDLE, Kathleen, sports. Vancouver, BC, 1965. With Marnie McBean won women's double sculls rowing medals: two golds in 1992 at Barcelona Olympics; one gold, one bronze in 1996 Olympics in Atlanta.

HEES, George Harris, politics. Toronto, Ont., 1910–96. PC Cabinet minister for John Diefenbaker and Brian Mulroney.

HEGGTVEIT, Anne, sports. Ottawa, Ont., 1939. Skier; Canada's first Olympic gold medal in skiing; women's slalom, 1960.

HELLSTROM, Sheila Anne (Brig-Gen.), military. Bridgewater, NS, 1935. Soldier; first Cdn woman general.

HELWIG, David Gordon, literary arts. Toronto, Ont., 1938. Poet; novelist. "Figures in a Landscape."

HEMSWORTH, Albert Wade, performing arts. Brantford, Ont., 1916–2002. Folksinger, banjo and guitar player; Hemsworth's songs were featured on NFB documentaries and sung by contemporary artists such as Kate and Anna McGarrigle. "Foolish You"; "The Blackfly Song."

HENLEY, Garney, sports. USA, 1935. Football player; Hamilton star CFL's most versatile player.

HENNING, Douglas, performing arts. Ft Garry, Man., 1947–2000. Magician; co-founder, Natural Law Party.

HENRY, Martha, performing arts. USA, 1938. TV/film actress; Stratford regular. *The Wars.*

HENSON, Josiah, politics. USA, 1789–1883. Black leader; escaped slave; model for *Uncle Tom's Cabin.*

HENSTRIDGE, Natasha, performing arts. Springdale, Nfld. 1974. Model turned actress; appeared in *Species* movie series; also films *Dog Park* and *The Whole Nine Yards.*

HEPBURN, Doug, sports. Vancouver, BC, 1926. Weight lifter; world heavyweight title, 1953.

HEPBURN, Mitchell Frederick, politics. St Thomas, Ont., 1896–1953. Liberal Ontario premier, 1934–42.

HEPPNER, Ben, performing arts. Murrayville, BC, 1956. Tenor opera singer, Metropolitan debut in 1991.

HERBERT, Paul, performing arts. Thetford Mines, Que., 1924. Actor; screenwriter; director.

HERIOT, George, visual arts. Scot., 1759–1839. Watercolourist. *Lake St Charles Near Quebec.*

HEROUX, Denis, visual arts. Montreal, Que., 1940. Film producer. *Atlantic City.*

HERZBERG, Gerhard, medicine. Germany, 1904–99. Physicist; molecular analyst; Nobel Prize, chemistry, 1971.

HEWITT, Angela Mary, performing arts. Ottawa, Ont., 1958. Internationally renowned classical pianist; Bach specialist. Winner of 1985 International Bach Competition in Toronto, Ont.

HEWITT, Foster William, sports. Toronto, Ont., 1903–85. Hockey announcer; voice of Toronto Maple Leafs.

HIBBERT, Curtis, sports. Mississauga, Ont., 1966. Gymnast; won five gold medals in 1990 Commonwealth Games.

HIGHWAY, Tomson, literary arts. Brovchet, Man., 1951. Playwright; novelist. *Dry Lips Oughta Move to Kapuskasing.*

HILL, Arthur, performing arts. Melfort, Sask., 1922. Stage and film performer. *The Ugly American.*

HILL, Dan Jr, performing arts. Toronto, Ont., 1954. Ballad singer and composer. "Sometimes When We Touch."

HILL, Daniel Grafton Sr, politics. USA, 1923–2003. Reformer; human rights; black history activist and writer.

HILL, James Jerome, business. Rockwood, Ont., 1838–1916. In 1890 consolidated vast railway holdings into the Great Northern Railway Co., also was integral in the building of the Canadian Pacific Railway.

HILLER, Arthur Garfin, visual arts. Edmonton, Alta, 1923. Filmmaker/director. *Love Story.*

HILLIARD, Anna Marion, medicine. Morrisburg, Ont., 1902–58. In 1947 helped develop the Pap test to detect cervical cancer; facilitated its initiation at Women's College Hospital in Toronto in 1948. Wrote *A Woman Doctor Looks at Love and Life.*

HILLIER, James, invention. Brantford, Ont., 1915. Inventor; pioneered electron microscopes.

HIRSCH, John Stephen, performing arts. Hungary, 1930–89. Stage director; founded Manitoba Theatre Centre; headed Stratford Festival, CBC TV drama.

HITSCHMANOVA, Lotta, politics. Czech., 1909–80. Activist; founding director, Unitarian Service Committee of Canada development agency.

HNATYSHYN, Ramon John, politics. Saskatoon, Sask., 1934–2002. Governor general of Canada 1990–95.

HOBSON, Frederick "Hobbie," military. Eng., 1875–1917. Victoria Cross recipient, WWI, Battle of Hill 70. Sergeant, 20th Battalion.

HODGINS, Jack Stanley, literary arts. Comox, BC, 1938. Novelist. *The Resurrection of Joseph Bourne.*

HODGSON, George Ritchie, sports. Montreal, Que., 1893–1983. Swimmer; first Canadian Olympic gold medals in swimming; 400 m, 1500 m freestyle in 1912.

HOFFMAN, Abigail (Abbie), sports. Toronto, Ont., 1947. Sports feminist; director of Sport Canada.

HOFFMEISTER, Bertram Meryl, military. Vancouver, BC, 1907–99. Canadian general in WWII, considered brilliant battle strategist, later chairman of lumber conglomerate MacMillan Bloedel.

HOGG-PRIESTLY, Helen Battles, science. USA, 1905–93. Astronomer; star clusters expert; asteroid named for her.

HOHL, Elmer, sports. Wellesley, Ont., 1919–87. Horseshoe pitcher; world champion, 1965–87.

HOLGATE, Edwin, visual arts. Allandale, Ont., 1892–1977. Group of Seven artist, noted for portraiture; member of Royal Canadian Academy of Arts.

HOLLAND, Edward James Gibson, military. Ottawa, Ont., 1878–1948. Victoria Cross recipient, Boer War, 1900. Sergeant, Royal Canadian Dragoons.

HOLLINGSHEAD, Gregory Albert Frank, literary arts. Toronto, Ont., 1947. Governor General's Award for fiction, 1995, *The Roaring Girl.*

HOLMAN, Derek, performing arts. Eng., 1931. Composer, organist, choir director; led the Canadian Children's Opera Chorus 1975–85; wrote theatrical and liturgical choral music. *Doctor Canon's Cure; The Invisible Reality.*

HOLMES, Thomas William, military. Montreal, Que., 1898–1950. Victoria Cross recipient, WWI, Battle of Passchendaele, 1917. Private, 4th Canadian Mounted Rifles.

HOMME, Robert, performing arts. USA, 1919–2000. Portrayed the Friendly Giant on long-running CBC children's program of same name.

HOOD, Hugh John Blagdon, literary arts. Toronto, Ont., 1928. Novelist; essayist. *The Swing in the Garden.*

HORTON, Miles Gilbert "Tim," sports. Cochrane, Ont., 1930–74. Toronto Maple Leaf hockey player, five Stanley Cup wins; founder of national doughnut chain.

HOSPITAL, Janette Turner, literary arts. Australia, 1942. Winner of the Seal First Novel Award, 1982, *The Ivory Swing. Isobars.*

HOUSSER, Yvonne McKague, visual arts. Toronto, Ont., 1898–1996. Group of Seven-influenced paintings: National Art Gallery; Art Gallery of Ontario; McMichael Gallery.

HOUSTON, Heather, sports. Thunder Bay, Ont., 1959. Curler; skip of 1989 world championship team; Canadian championships 1988, 1989.

HOUSTON, James Archibald, literary/visual arts. Toronto, Ont., 1921. In the 1950s became a major buyer and supporter of Inuit art. *White Dawn; Confessions of an Igloo Dweller.*

HOWARD, Russ, sports. Penetanguishene, Ont., 1955. Curler; Canadian and world champion, 1987, 1993.

HOWE, Clarence Decatur (C.D.), business/politics. USA, 1886–1960. Foremost grain elevator builder of his day, Howe was a Liberal minister of transport; helped create Trans-Canada Airlines, forerunner of Air Canada.

HOWE, Gordon (Gordie), sports. Floral, Sask., 1928. Hockey player; Detroit Red Wings great; 801 NHL goals.

HOWE, Joseph, politics. Halifax, NS, 1804–73. Led fight against Nova Scotia entry into Confederation; later joined cabinet.

HUBEL, David Hunter, science. Windsor, Ont., 1926. Winner of 1981 Nobel Prize in medicine and physiology for research in processing the visual system.

HUGGINS, Charles Brenton, science. Halifax, NS, 1901–97. Won Nobel Prize for medicine in 1966 for discoveries concerning hormonal treatment of prostate cancer.

HUGHES, Monica, literary arts. Eng., 1925–2003. A popular writer of children's fiction, Hughes was widely acclaimed for her science fiction themes in titles including *Hunter in the Dark, Blaine's Way* and *The Seven Magpies.*

HULL, Robert Marvin, sports. Pte Anne, Ont., 1939. Hockey player; "Golden Jet," left winger for Chicago and Winnipeg; 610 NHL goals.

HUMPHREY, Jack Weldon, visual arts. Saint John, NB, 1901–67. Internationally recognized painter; his watercolours of landscapes and people were inspired by cubist and expressionist influences.

HUMPHREY, John Peters, public service. Hampton, NB, 1905–95. Principal author of the Universal Declaration of Human Rights; founder of the Canadian Human Rights Foundation and Amnesty International (Can.).

HUNGERFORD, George William, sports. Vancouver, BC, 1944. Rower; gold medal, coxless pairs, 1964 Olympics.

HUNTER, Thomas James (Tommy), performing arts. London, Ont., 1937. Country singer; *Tommy Hunter Show* on CBC, 1965–92.

HUNTSMAN, Archibald Gowanlock, science. Tintern, Ont., 1883–1973. Biologist; pioneered fisheries science.

HUOT, Juliette, performing arts. Tétraultville, Que., 1912–2001. Quebec television, theatre and film actress, beloved for matriarchal roles. *Les Plouffes; Jamais deux sans toi.*

HURTIG, Melvyn (Mel), literary arts. Edmonton, Alta, 1932. Publisher; Canadian nationalist. *The Canadian Encyclopedia.*

HUSTON, Walter (b. Walter Houghston), performing arts. Toronto, Ont., 1884–1960. Actor. *Treasure of the Sierra Madre.*

HUTCHISON, William Bruce, literary arts. Prescott, Ont., 1901–92. Political historian; biogapher of W.L. Mackenzie King, *The Incredible Canadian.*

HUTT, William Ian deWitt, performing arts. Toronto, Ont., 1920. Stage actor; distinguished Stratford leading player.

HYLAND, Francis, performing arts. Regina, Sask., c. 1932. Actor with Stratford Festival, Ont.

IBERVILLE, Pierre Le Moyne, Sieur d', military. Montreal, Que., 1661–1706. Soldier; daring, often cruel, adventurer.

IDE, Thomas Ranald (Ran), media. Ottawa, Ont., 1919–96. Appointed in 1966 to set up TVOntario, an innovative education network.

IGALI, Baraladei Daniel, sports. Nigeria, 1974. Won gold medal in 2000 Sydney Olympics in freestyle wrestling.

IGNATIEFF, George, politics. Russia, 1913–89. Diplomat; expert in East-West relations; UN ambassador.

IGNATIEFF, Michael, literary arts/media. Toronto, Ont., 1947. Writer; broadcaster. *The Russian Album.*

IMLACH, George "Punch," sports. Toronto, Ont., 1918–87. Hockey coach and manager; during 11 seasons with Toronto Maple Leafs won four Stanley Cups.

INNIS, Harold Adams, politics. Otterville, Ont., 1894–1952. Political economist; communications theorist. *Empire and Communications.*

IRELAND, John, performing arts. Vancouver, BC, 1914–1992. Actor; often played a heavy. *Red River*

IRONSIDE, Michael, performing arts. Toronto, Ont., 1950. Character actor, specializes in thugs; has appeared in films *Top Gun; Highlander II.* Also on TV's *ER* series.

IRVIN, Dick Sr, sports. Limestone Ridge, Ont., 1892–1957. Hockey executive; innovative coach/mgr of Montreal Canadiens, Toronto Maple Leafs.

IRVING, Kenneth Colin (K.C.), business. Buctouche, NB, 1899–1992. Industrialist; founder of NB business empire, from oil to broadcasting.

IRWIN, Mary (b. May Campbell), performing arts. Whitby, Ont., 1862–1938. Broadway, vaudeville star; famous for first screen kiss in film *The Kiss,* in 1896. Sang "After the Ball."

ISELER, Elmer Walter, performing arts. Port Colbourne, Ont., 1927–98. Choral conductor who founded Festival Singers of Canada; from 1964 to 1997 conductor of the Toronto Mendelssohn Choir; also founded the Elmer Iseler Singers.

ISRAEL, Werner, science. Germany, 1931. Physicist; pioneered study of black holes, gravitation.

ISSAJENKO, Angella (Taylor), sports. Jamaica, 1958. Sprinter; many medals in 100 m races.

JACKS, Terry, performing arts. Winnipeg, Man., 1944. Singer; founding member, the Poppy Family.

JACKSON, Alexander Young (A.Y.), visual arts. Montreal, Que., 1882–1974. Painter; landscape artist; member, Group of Seven. *Barns.*

JACKSON, Donald, sports. Oshawa, Ont., 1940. Figure skater; men's world champion, 1962.

JACKSON, Roger, sports. Toronto, Ont., 1942. Rower; gold medal, coxless pairs, 1964 Olympics.

JACKSON, Russell Stanley (Russ), sports. Hamilton, Ont., 1936. Football player; Ottawa quarterback; 3-time Schenley Award winner as CFL top player.

JACKSON, Tom, performing arts. Winnipeg, Man. Native actor and singer, has appeared on CBC's *North of 60, Medicine River, The Diviners.*

JACOBI, Lou, performing arts. Toronto, Ont., 1913. Character actor; has appeared in Spring Thaw revue; on Broadway; and in film *(Irma la Douce).*

JACOBS, "Indian" Jack, sports. USA, 1920–74. Football player; fiery quarterback for Winnipeg Blue Bombers; helped popularize CFL.

JACOBS, Jane, literary arts. USA, 1916. Urban critic; major urban thinker. *Systems of Survival.*

JACQUES, Elliott, science. Toronto, Ont., 1917–2003. Psychologist and social scientist whose Jacques' Stratified Systems Theory studied employee patterns in the workplace; he also coined the term "midlife crisis."

JAMES, Colin, performing arts. Regina, Sask., 1964. Songwriter, guitarist; plays blues, pop, swing. *Hook, Line & Single; Colin James.*

JAMES, Gerry, sports. Regina, Sask., 1934. Football/hockey player; rare pro double; Winnipeg Blue Bombers, Toronto Maple Leafs.

JANES, Percy Maxwell, literary arts. St John's, Nfld, 1922–99. Newfoundland writer whose gritty works depicted the reality of life on the island. *House of Hate.*

JARVIS, Graham, performing arts. Toronto, Ont., 1930–2003. Character actor best known as Charlie Haggers in the 1970s sitcom *Mary Hartman, Mary Hartman,* Jarvis appeared widely on television and film. *M*A*S*H; 7th Heaven; The Drew Carey Show; Alice's Restaurant; Silkwood.*

JELINEK, Otto John, sports/politics. Czech., 1940. PC minister; with sister Maria won world pairs figure skating title (1972).

JENKINS, Ferguson Arthur, sports. Chatham, Ont., 1943. Baseball pitcher; only Canadian in Hall of Fame, 284 career wins.

JENNESS, Diamond, literary arts. New Zealand, 1886–1969. Anthropologist; author; expert on native Canadians. *The People of the Twilight.*

JENNINGS, Peter Charles, media. Toronto, Ont., 1938. Broadcaster; anchorman, *ABC Evening News.*

JEROME, Harry Winston, sports. Prince Albert, Sask., 1940–82. Sprinter; one-time world record holder in 100 m.

JEWISON, Norman Frederick, visual arts. Toronto, Ont., 1926. Film director; founded Canadian Film Centre in Toronto. *In the Heat of the Night.*

JOHANSSON, Herman Smith "Chief Jackrabbit," sports. Norway, 1875–1986. Skier; popularizer of cross-country skiing.

JOHNS, Harold Elford (Dr), medicine. China, 1915–1998. Physician; developed cobalt bomb for treating cancer.

JOHNSON, Ben, sports. Jamaica, 1961. Sprinter; stripped of 100 m world record time gold medal in 1988 Olympics for using banned drug.

JOHNSON, Daniel, politics. Montreal, Que., 1944. Liberal opposition leader in Quebec 1994–98.

JOHNSON, Edward, performing arts. Guelph, Ont., 1878–1959. Opera singer, performed at Metropolitan Opera in New York; later chairman of board of Royal Conservatory of Music in Toronto.

JOHNSON, Emily Pauline "Tekahionwake," literary arts. Six Nations Reserve, UC, 1861–1913. Her poetry celebrated Canada and her native heritage. "Flint and Feather."

JOHNSTON, Francis Hans (Franz), visual arts. Toronto, Ont., 1888–1949. Early Group of Seven member. *Batchawana Falls.*

JOHNSTON, Lynn, visual arts. Collingwood, Ont., 1947. Cartoonist; creator, "For Better or For Worse."

JOHNSTON, Rita Margaret, politics. Melville, Sask., 1935. First woman premier in Canada (BC) in 1991, succeeded Bill Vander Zalm.

JOLIAT, Aurèle, sports. Ottawa, Ont., 1908–86. Hockey player; left winger for Montreal Canadiens.

JOLLIET, Louis, exploration and discovery. Quebec City, Que., 1645–1700. Co-discoverer of the Mississippi R.

JONAS, George, literary arts. Hungary, 1935. Poet, writer, scriptwriter. Script for CBC's *The Scales of Justice; Vengeance; By Persons Unknown: The Strange Death of Christine Demeter.*

JONES KONIHOWSKI, Diane, sports. Vancouver, BC, 1951. Canadian pentathlon record holder.

JONES, Oliver Theophilus, performing arts. Montreal, Que., 1934. Internationally acclaimed jazz pianist famous for his lively keyboard style. *Just 88; From Lust to Lively.*

JONES, Richard, public service. USA, 1905–2001. Founder of the Canadian Council of Christians and Jews in 1948; initiator of national Brotherhood Week, in response to the horrors of the then recent Holocaust in Europe.

JORY, Victor, performing arts. Yukon, 1902–82. Actor; Hollywood villain. *Huckleberry Finn.*

JUCKES, Gordon, sports. Watrous, Sask., 1914–95. Hockey and Sports Hall of Fame member, established national team program.

JULIEN, Pauline, performing arts. Trois-Rivières, Que., 1928–98. Quebec singer, political activist, separatist and feminist, Julien embodied the spirit of Quebec through songs of her own composition as well as Kurt Weill, Bertolt Brecht and Gilles Vigneault.

JULIETTE (b. Juliette Augustina Sysak), performing arts. Winnipeg, Man., 1927. Singer; early TV star; own show, 1954–66.

JUNEAU, Pierre, business. Verdun, Que., 1922. Broadcast executive; headed CRTC, 1968–75.

JUTRA, Claude, visual arts. Montreal, Que., 1930–87. Film director. *Mon Oncle Antoine.*

K

KAIN, Karen, performing arts. Hamilton, Ont., 1951. Prima ballerina, National Ballet of Canada.

KALVAK, Helen, visual arts. Victoria I., NWT, 1901–84. Inuit artist; over 300 prints portray the life of the Copper Inuit, frequent spiritual themes. *Kidnapper.*

KANE, Lori, sports. Charlottetown, PEI, 1964. Golfer; member of Canadian Inernational Team 1989–92; member of Commonwealth Team in 1991; 1992 Canadian World Amateur Team; 1997, Canadian Athlete of the Year.

KANE, Paul, visual arts. Ire., 1810–71. Painter of the Canadian West and native peoples.

KAREDA, Urjo, performing arts. Estonia, 1944–2002. Mentor to many of Canada's top playwrights, Kareda was artistic director of Toronto's Tarragon Theatre for 20 years; past director of Stratford Festival in Ontario; and theatre and opera critic for the *Toronto Star* and the *Globe and Mail.*

KARPIS, Alvin (b. Albin Karpowicz). Montreal, Que., 1908–79. Barker Gang member; US Public Enemy No. 1.

KARSH, Malak, visual arts. Armenia, 1915–2001. Nature and landscape photographer famous for his image of a log jam on the Ottawa River that graced Canada's $1 bill prior to the introduction of the loonie; initiated Ottawa's annual Tulip Festival.

KARSH, Yousuf, visual arts. Armenia, 1908–2002. Photographer; portraitist of the famous, e.g., Churchill.

KAYFETZ, Benjamin Kershon, public service. Toronto, Ont., 1919–2002. Director of community relations for the Canadian Jewish Congress for nearly forty years; lobbyist for anti-discrimination legislation through Canada's human rights code.

KEDROVA, Lila Howard, performing arts. Russia, 1920–2000. Actress noted for role as Madame Hortense in film *Zorba the Greek,* also appeared in *High Wind in Jamaica.*

KEELER, Ruby (b. Ethel Keeler), performing arts. Halifax, NS, 1909–93. Actress; dancer. *42nd Street.*

KEITH, Vicki, sports. Winnipeg, Man., 1961. Swam all five Great Lakes in 1988.

KELESI, Helen Mersi, sports. Victoria, BC, 1969. Tennis player; Canadian women's championship 1987–90.

KELLY, Leonard "Red," sports. Simcoe, Ont., 1927. Hockey player; star defenceman with Detroit and Toronto; two-time Liberal MP.

KELLY, Milton Terrence (M.T.), literary arts. Toronto, Ont., 1947. Poet, playwright, novelist. *A Dream Like Mine.*

KELSO, John Joseph, politics. Ire., 1864–1935. Reformer; founded Toronto Humane Society, Children's Aid.

KENOJUAK Ashevak, visual arts. Baffin Island, NWT, 1927. Artist noted for bird graphics.

KEON, David Michael, sports. Noranda, Que., 1940. Hockey player with Toronto Maple Leafs 1960–75. Team Canada member 1977. Winner of Conn Smythe trophy, 1967.

KERR, John Chipman, military. Fox River, NS, 1887–1963. Victoria Cross recipient, WWI, the Somme, 1916. Private, 49th Canadian Infantry Battalion.

KERR, Robert Allan, performing arts. Calgary, Alta, 1918–2003. Host of CBC's national classical music program *Off the Record* 1960–96, Kerr had an encyclopedic knowledge, especially in the field of organ music.

KHANJIAN, Arsinée, performing arts. Lebanon, 1958. Film and theatre actress, wife of film director Atom Egoyan. *Next of Kin; Exotica.*

KHORANA, Har Gobind, science. India, 1922. Chemist; Nobel Prize in medicine (1968) for DNA research.

KIDD, Bruce, sports. Ottawa, Ont., 1943. Runner; many wins at various distances; outstanding athlete in Canada, 1961 and 1962.

KIDDER, Margot, performing arts. Yellowknife, NWT, 1948. Actress; Hollywood star. *Superman.*

KIERANS, Eric William, politics. Montreal, Que., 1914. Economist; outspoken nationalist.

KILBOURN, William, literary arts. Toronto, Ont., 1926–95. Writer; historian; biographer of C.D. Howe.

KILLAM, Isaac Walton, business. Yarmouth, NS, 1885–1955. Industrialist; built business empire; known for philanthropy.

KING, Allan Winton, visual arts. Vancouver, BC, 1930. Filmmaker; documentarist. *Warrendale.*

KING, Charmion, performing arts. Toronto, Ont., 1925. Film, radio, TV and stage actress who has appeared at Ontario's Stratford Festival. *Who Has Seen the Wind; Wind at My Back.*

KING, Thomas, literary arts. USA, 1943. Aboriginal writer, novelist. Creator of "Dead Dog Café" on CBC Radio programs *Morningside* and *This Morning. Medicine River; Green Grass, Running Water.*

KING, William Lyon Mackenzie, politics. Kitchener, Ont., 1874–1950. Lib. prime minister of Canada during WWII.

KINROSS, Cecil John, military. Eng., 1896–1957. Victoria Cross recipient, WWI, Battle of Passchendaele, 1917. Private, 49th Battalion.

KINSELLA, William Patrick (W.P.), literary arts. Edmonton, Alta, 1935. Writer; known for poetic baseball fiction. *Shoeless Joe.*

KIRCK, Harvey (b. Harvey Krick), media. New Liskeard, Ont., 1928–2002. Anchor and co-anchor with Lloyd Robertson, of CTV's national news desk; the gruff Kirck also appeared on *Canada A.M.* and *Inside Canada. Nobody Calls Me Mr. Kirck.*

KIRKE, David (Sir), exploration and discovery. France, 1597–1654. First governor of Nfld, 1637.

KLEIN, Abraham Moses (A.M.), literary arts. Ukraine, 1909–72. Poet of Jewish themes. "Portrait of the Poet as Landscape."

KLEIN, George John, invention. Hamilton, Ont., 1904–92. Productive inventor: wind tunnels, gearing systems, Canadarm gear design.

KLEIN, Ralph Philip, politics. Calgary, Alta, 1942. PC premier of Alberta, 1992–.

KNOTT, Elsie Marie, politics. Curve Lake, Ont., 1922–95. First native woman in Canada to be elected chief, at Ojibwa reserve near Peterborough, Ont.

KNOWLES, Stanley Howard, politics. USA, 1908–97. A founder of the New Democratic Party; represented Winnipeg North Centre riding 1942–81. Admired for his support of old-age pensions; president of Canadian Labour Congress 1958–62.

KNUDSON, George, sports. Winnipeg, Man., 1937–89. Golfer; Canada's top pro; 12 PGA tour victories.

KOFFLER, Murray Bernard, business. Toronto, Ont., 1924. Entrepreneur; made Shopper's Drug Mart Canada's largest pharmacy chain.

KOFFMAN, Morris (Moe), performing arts. Toronto, Ont., 1928–2001. Jazz flautist. "Swinging Shepherd Blues."

KOGAWA, Joy Nozomi, literary arts. Vancouver, BC, 1935. Writer. *Obasan; Itsuka.*

KONOWAL, Filip, military. Russia, 1887–1959. Victoria Cross recipient, WWI, Battle of Hill 70, 1917. Corporal, 47th Battalion.

KOTCHEFF, William Theodore (Ted), visual arts. Toronto, Ont., 1931. Film director. *The Apprenticeship of Duddy Kravitz.*

KRAATZ, Victor, sports. Germany, 1971. Ice dancing; with Shae-Lynn Bourne won Canadian title, 1993–96; third in World Championships, 1996.

KRALL, Diana, performing arts. Nanaimo, BC, 1964. Sultry jazz vocalist. *When I Look Into Your Eyes.*

KREBS, Charles J., science. USA, 1936. Zoologist specializing in animal ecology; his *The Experimental Analysis of Distribution and Abundance* is widely read by students of ecology. The Krebs Effect, or Fence Effect, explains the effect fencing has on animal populations.

KREINER, Kathy, sports. Timmins, Ont., 1957. Skier; gold medal, giant slalom, 1976 Olympics.

KREVER, Horace, law. Montreal, Que., 1929. Judge who led Royal Commission of Inquiry on the Blood System in Canada, 1993–97.

KRIEGHOFF, Cornelius David, visual arts. Holland, 1815–72. Known for paintings of Quebec life. *The Habitant Farm.*

KROL, Joseph "Joe King," sports. Hamilton, Ont., 1919. Football player; Toronto Argos star; top athlete, 1946.

KUDELKA, James, performing arts. Newmarket, Ont., 1955. Artistic director for the National Ballet of Canada; also choreographer, dancer. Critically acclaimed work with classical and modern influences. *Spring Awakening.*

KUERTI, Anton Emil, performing arts. Austria, 1938. Leading pianist; composer; Beethoven specialist.

KURELEK, William (Wasyl), visual arts. Whitfield, Alta, 1927–77. Symbolist religious painter.

KUWABARA, Bruce, visual arts. Hamilton, Ont., 1949. Partner with Toronto-based architecture firm Kuwabara Payne McKenna Blumberg; award-winning designer of Kitchener, Ont., City Hall; City Hall in Richmond, BC.

LA SALLE, Rene Robert Cavelier, Sieur de, exploration and discovery. France, 1643–87. Became commandant of Fort Frontenac in present-day Kingston, Ont., 1673.

LA VERENDRYE, Pierre Gaultier de Varennes, Sieur de, exploration and discovery. Trois-Rivières, Que., 1685–1749. Explorer of W Canada.

LABATT, John Kinder, business. Ire., 1803–66. In 1855 became owner of a small brewery in London, Ont., the origin of the giant brewery empire.

LAFLEUR, Guy Damien, sports. Thurso, Que., 1951. Hockey player; Canadiens star right winger; 560 goals. .

LAFONTAINE, Louis Hippolyte (Sir), politics. Boucherville, LC, 1807–64. In effect, Canada's first PM, 1848–51.

LALONDE, Donny, sports. Kitchener, Ont., 1960. Boxer; WBC light heavyweight champion (1987–88).

LALONDE, Edouard Charles, sports. Cornwall, Ont., 1887–1970. In 1950 named as one of Canada's outstanding lacrosse players of the half-century; played NHL Montreal Canadiens, scoring 124 goals in 98 games 1913–18.

LALONDE, Marc, politics. Île-Perrot, Que., 1929. Pierre Trudeau's principle secretary 1968–72; held various portfolios until retirement in 1984.

LAMBERT, Natalie, sports. Montreal, Que., 1963. Speed skater; short track title, 500 m, 1993.

LAMBERTS, Heath, performing arts. Toronto, Ont., 1941. Actor at Stratford Festival, Ont. *Glengarry Glen Ross; Cyrano de Bergerac.*

LAMER, Antonio, law. Montreal, Que., 1933. Chief justice of the Supreme Court 1990–99.

LAMPMAN, Archibald, literary arts. Morpeth, Canada W, 1861–99. Nature poet. "Lyrics of Earth."

LANCASTER, Ron, sports. USA, 1938. Football player; coach; quarterback set 30 CFL records.

LANCTOT, Françoise, performing arts. Montreal, Que., 1947. Actress, film director; winner of Etrog for *La vrai nature du Bernadette. The Apprenticeship of Duddy Kravitz.*

LANDRY, G. Yves, business. Thetford Mines, Que., 1938–98. Died while chairman, president and CEO of Chrysler Canada; co-chairman of Automotive Advisory Committee to the Minister of Industry Canada.

LANDRY, Jean-Bernard, politics. Saint-Jacques, Montcalm Co, Que., 1937. Parti Québécois premier of Quebec 2001–2003; former deputy premier and minister of finance.

LANG, Katherine Dawn (k.d.), performing arts. Consort, Alta, 1961. Country-torch singer; vegetarian activist. *Shadowlands.*

LANGFORD, Sam, sports. Weymouth Falls, NS, 1886–1956. Boxer; great fighter; denied title shot.

LANOIS, Daniel, performing arts. Hamilton, Ont., 1953. Singer; producer of Peter Gabriel's "Sledgehammer" and with Brian Eno U2's *Joshua Tree.*

LANTOS, Robert, visual arts. Hungary, 1949. Film producer; CEO, Alliance Communications. *Black Robe.*

LAPIERRE, Laurier L., media. Megantic, Que., 1929. TV personality, author; co-host, *This Hour Has Seven Days.*

LAPOINTE, Louise Marguerite Renaude, media. Disraeli, Que., 1912–2002. First French Canadian woman to be appointed Speaker of the Senate, 1974–79; journalist with Montreal's *La Presse.* Member of the Group of 78, which called upon Canada to aid the world's poor in 1982.

LASKIN, Bora, law. Ft William, Ont., 1912–84. Chief justice of Canada, 1973–84.

LASTMAN, Melvin Douglas (Mel), politics. Toronto, Ont., 1933. Mayor of the amalgamated City of Toronto 1997–2003; formerly long-time mayor of North York, a satellite "city" of the former Metropolitan Toronto.

LAU, Evelyn, literary arts. Vancouver, BC, 1971. Poet, novelist, short story writer, used own experiences to portray the lives of street kids. *Runaway: Diary of a Street Kid; You Are Not Who You Claim; Oedipal Dreams.*

LAUMANN, Silken, sports. Toronto, Ont., 1964. Rower; braved broken leg for bronze medal in 1992 Olympics; Athlete of the Year 1991, 1992.

LAURE, Carole (b. Carol Champagne), performing arts. Montreal, Que., 1949. Actress; screen star. *Maria Chapdelaine.*

LAURENCE, Jean Margaret, literary arts. Neepawa, Man., 1926–87. Writer; created fictional setting of Manawaka. *The Diviners; The Stone Angel.*

LAURENDEAU, Joseph-Edmond-André, politics. Montreal, Que., 1912–68. Co-chairman of Royal Commission on Bilingualism and Biculturalism 1963–68; editor of Montreal's *Le Devoir 1958–68.*

LAURIER, Wilfrid (Sir), politics. St-Lin, Canada E, 1841–1919. Canada's first French-speaking prime minister.

LAURIN, Camille, politics. Charlemagne, Que., 1922–99. Drafted Bill 101, Quebec's French Language Charter; joined Quebec National Assembly in 1970, member of Parti Québécois.

LAVAL, François de, religion. France, 1623–1708. First bishop of Quebec (1674–88).

LAVALLÉE, Calixa, performing arts. Verchères, Canada E, 1842–1891. Composer of "O Canada."

LAVIGNE, Avril, performing arts. Napanee, Ont., 1984. Outspoken skater/punk rock singer/songwriter; she reached instant fame with her videos *Sk8ter Boi* and *I'm With You,* and album *Let Go.*

LAW, Andrew Bonar, politics. Rexton, NB, 1858–1923. Prime Minister of Britain 1922–23; signed Treaty of Versailles on behalf of Great Britain in 1919.

LAWRENCE, Florence, performing arts. Hamilton, Ont., 1890–1938. Film and vaudeville actress; first to use publicity stunt to launch career. *Daniel Boone; Resurrection.*

LAYTON, Irving Peter, literary arts. Romania, 1912. Prolific, flamboyant poet. "A Red Carpet for the Sun."

LEARNMONTH, Okill Massey, military. Quebec City, Que., 1894–1917. Victoria Cross recipient, WWI, Battle of Hill 70, 1917. Major, 2nd Battalion.

LE CAINE, Hugh, performing arts/science. Port Arthur, Ont., 1914–77. Physicist; composer; designed the sackbut, the first musical synthesizer.

LEACOCK, Stephen Butler, literary arts. Eng., 1869–1944. Humorist. *Sunshine Sketches of a Little Town.*

LEBLANC, Romeo, politics. Memramcook, NB, 1927. Governor general of Canada 1994–99; former Liberal MP.

LEBLOND, Charles Philippe, science. France, 1910. Anatomist; pioneer in cell biology.

LECAVALIER, René, media. Montreal, Que., 1918. In 1952 called first televised hockey game on TV on Radio-Canada; remained as commentator for *La Soirée du hockey* till 1985.

LECLERC, Felix, performing arts. La Tuque, Que., 1914–88. Singer/songwriter; influential chansonnier and Quebec nationalist.

LEE, Dennis Beynon, literary arts. Toronto, Ont., 1939. Poet, children's writer. *Alligator Pie; Garbage Delight.*

LEE, Geddy, performing arts. Toronto, Ont., 1953. Singer/songwriter; lead singer for Rush. *Moving Pictures.*

LEE-GARTNER, Kerrin, sports. Trail, BC, 1966. Skier; gold medal, women's downhill, 1992 Olympics.

LEGER, Gabrielle Carmel, politics. Montreal, Que., 1916–98. Wife of the late governor general Jules Leger; acted for her husband when he suffered a stroke shortly after taking office.

LEGER, Jules, politics. St-Anicet, Que., 1913–80. Canada's governor general, 1974–79.

LEGER, Paul-Émile, religion. Valleyfield, Que., 1904–91. Cardinal; eloquent, compassionate religious leader; became missionary in Africa.

LEMELIN, Roger, literary arts. Quebec City, Que., 1919–92. Writer; creator of the popular Plouffe family.

LEMIEUX, Jean-Paul, visual arts. Quebec City, Que., 1904–90. Landscape painter. *Le Visiteur du Soir; Lazare.*

LEMIEUX, Mario, sports. Montreal, Que., 1965. Hockey player; Pittsburgh Penguins centre, one of two players to average two points per game.

LEMIEUX, Raymond Urgel, medicine. La Biche, Alta, 1920. Scientist with National Research Council, solved riddle of synthesis of sucrose; pioneer in blood-typing serum.

LENNOX, Edward James, visual arts. Toronto, Ont., 1854–1933. Architect of "Richardson Romanesque" style. Toronto's Old City Hall, Casa Loma; powerhouse at Niagara Falls, Ont.

LEONARD, Stanley, sports. Vancouver, BC, 1915. Golfer; won many Canadian titles; three US tour wins.

LEPAGE, Robert, performing arts. Quebec City, Que., 1957. Actor, screenwriter, director; former artistic director of Ottawa's National Arts Centre; Théatre francais. *Secret War Tour.*

LESAGE, Jean, politics. Montreal, Que., 1912–80. Liberal premier of Quebec, 1960–66.

LETHEREN, Carol Anne, sports. Toronto, Ont., 1942–2001. Chief executive of Canadian Olympic Association.

LEVESQUE, Georges-Henri, politics. Roberval, Que., 1902–2000. Dominican priest, founded Faculty of Social Sciences at Laval University; major figure in Quebec's Quiet Revolution.

LEVESQUE, Jean-Louis, business. Nouvelle, Que., 1911–1994. Financier; co-founder of Levesque Beaubien Inc., Quebec's largest brokerage house.

LEVESQUE, René, politics. New Carlisle, Que., 1922–87. Led Parti Québécois; Quebec premier 1976–85.

LEVY, Eugene, performing arts. Hamilton, Ont., 1946. Actor; comedian; *SCTV* regular (Earl Camembert, Bobby Bitman).

LEVY, Julia, science. Singapore, 1934. Microbiologist and immunologist who co-discovered photodynamic anti-cancer drugs and who developed Photofrin after taking over American Cyanide's Johnson & Johnson subsidiary, which produced it previously.

LEWIS, David, politics. Russia, 1909–81. Federal NDP leader, 1971–75; eloquent speaker.

LEWIS, Lennox, sports. Eng., 1965. Boxer; super heavyweight gold medal, 1988 Olympics.

LEWIS, Stephen Henry, politics. Ottawa, Ont., 1937. Ont. NDP leader; Cdn UN ambassador.

LEWIS, Walter, science. Ottawa, Ont., 1930. Ethnobotanist who, with wife, Memory Elvin-Lewis, is a leading world expert on airborne and allergenic pollens, as well as the medicinal uses of tropical plants.

LEWIS, Wilfrid Bennett, science. Eng., 1908–87. Physicist; prime role in developing CANDU reactor.

LEYRAC, Monique, performing arts. Montreal, Que., 1928. Actress; popular Quebec chanteuse.

LIGHTFOOT, Gordon Meredith, performing arts. Orillia, Ont., 1938. Singer/songwriter; popular vocalist with many hits. "Canadian Railroad Trilogy."

LILIENSTEIN, Lois, performing arts. USA, 1936. Member of children's musical entertainment group Sharon, Lois and Bram; live and on TV. *The Elephant Show.*

LILLIE, Beatrice Gladys, performing arts. Toronto, Ont., 1894–1989. Stage comedienne. *Auntie Mame.*

LINDER, Cec, performing arts. Poland, 1921–92. Television, stage and film character actor. *Goldfinger; A Touch of Class; The Edge of Night.*

LINDROS, Eric, sports. London, Ont., 1973. Hockey player; centre for Philadelphia Flyers; winner of Hart Trophy, 1995.

LINDSAY, Robert Blake Theodore (Ted), sports. Renfrew, Ont., 1925. Hockey player; left winger 17 seasons with Detroit and Chicago.

LINKLETTER, Art (b. Arthur Brown), performing arts. Moose Jaw, Sask., 1912. Radio/TV host. *People Are Funny.*

LISMER, Arthur, visual arts. Eng., 1885–1969. Painter; Group of Seven founding member. *September Gale.*

LITTLE, Jean, literary arts. Taiwan, 1932. Popular writer of children's literature, poetry; blends themes of alienation and troubled relationships. *From Anna; Mama's Going to Buy You a Mockingbird; His Banner Over Me.*

LITTLE, Richard Carruthers (Rich), performing arts. Ottawa, Ont., 1938. Impersonator; night club and television performer.

LIVESAY, Dorothy, literary arts. Winnipeg, Man., 1909–96. Poet; sensitive feminist writer. *Poems for People.*

LOATES, Glen Martin, visual arts. Toronto, Ont., 1945. Wildlife artist; painter and naturalist.

LOCKHART, Gene, performing arts. London, Ont., 1891–1957. Character actor appeared in *Miracle on 34th Street, Carousel,* and on Broadway. Father of actress June Lockhart.

LOGAN, William Edmond (Sir), science. Montreal, Que., 1798–1875. Geologist; first head of Geological Survey of Canada; first to map Laurentian Shield.

LOMBARDI, Johnny, business. Toronto, Ont., 1915–2002. Pioneer broadcaster whose CHIN Radio in Toronto, Ont., became first multicultural broadcasting voice in Ontario.

LOMBARDO, Gaetano Alberto "Guy," performing arts. London, Ont., 1902–77. Bandleader; his Royal Canadians most popular band in N America; 300 million records sold. Also won International World Cup in speed boating in 1946; US champion 1946–49; Canadian title in 1955, 1956.

LONGBOAT, Thomas Charles, sports. Brantford, Ont., 1887–1949. Runner; set record in 1907 Boston Marathon.

LONGDEN, John (Johnny), sports. Eng., 1910–2003. Jockey; first N American with 4,000 winners (career: 6,032).

LORD, Bernard, politics. Moncton, NB, 1965. PC premier of NB, elected in 1999.

LORTIE, Louis, performing arts. Montreal, Que., 1959. Pianist; five-time winner of Canadian Music Competition, 1968–72; 1990 Juno for Best Classical Album.

LOUGHEED, Edgar Peter, politics. Calgary, Alta, 1928. PC premier of Alberta, 1971–85; played strong role in federal politics.

LOVELL, Jocelyn, sports. Eng., 1950. Canada's leading cyclist 1970–83; winner of 1000 m silver medal in 1978 world championships; paralysed in training accident 1983.

LOWRY, (Clarence) Malcolm, literary arts. Eng., 1909–57. British novelist whose powerful novels reflected his turbulent life; lived in BC 1937–54. *Under the Volcano.*

LUBA (b. Luba Kowalchyk), performing arts. Montreal, Que., 1958. Pop singer-songwriter. "Between the Earth and Sky"; "All or Nothing."

LUCAS, Clarence, performing arts. Six Nations Reserve, Brantford, Ont., 1866–1947. Internationally recognized composer, conductor for voice, piano, chamber and orchestral music. Wrote score for D.W. Griffith's film *Intolerance;* cantata *The Birth of Christ;* and overtures for Shakespearean plays.

LUND, Alan, performing arts. Toronto, Ont., 1927–92. Dancer/choreographer. With wife Blanche Harris performed as an Astaire/Rogers-style dancing team; Stratford Festival, Charlottetown Festival.

LUNDSTROM, Linda, business. Red Lake, Ont., 1951. Founder of fashion business with boutiques across North America; her signature LaParka has long been her Canadian culture statement, as are her all-Canadian-made clothes.

M

MACDONALD, Donald Stovel, politics. Ottawa, Ont., 1932. In 1975 became finance minister for federal Liberals, introduced Wage and Price Controls; in 1982 became chairman of the Royal Commission on Economic Union and Development Prospects for Canada; high commissioner to UK 1988–91.

MacDONALD, Finlay, politics. Sydney, NS, 1923–2002. Nova Scotia PC senator and broadcasting executive (founding director of CTV); backroom politician for Robert Stanfield and prime ministers Joe Clark and Brian Mulroney.

MacDONALD, Flora Isabel, politics. Sydney, NS, 1926. First woman to hold senior Cabinet post; external affairs in Clark govt (1979).

MacDONALD, James Edward Hervey (J.E.H.), visual arts. Eng., 1874–1932. Landscape painter; Group of Seven founder. *Mist Fantasy.*

MacDONALD, James Williamson Galloway (Jock), visual arts. Scot., 1897–1960. Early abstract painter; member, Painters Eleven.

MACDONALD, John Alexander (Sir), politics. Scot., 1815–91. Canada's first official prime minister.

MacDONALD, Norm, performing arts. Quebec City, Que., 1963. Comedian and impersonator (Bob Dole, Burt Reynolds, David Letterman); starred in the TV program *The Norm Show* and appeared in the film *People Against Larry Flynt.*

MacDOUGALL, Fraser, media. Stratford, Ont., 1907–2000. Longtime journalism figure; Ottawa bureau chief for Canadian Press; active on Ontario Press Council; chairman of Michener journalism awards.

MacDOWELL, Thain Wendell, military. Lachute, Que., 1890–1960. Victoria Cross recipient, Vimy Ridge, 1917. Captain, 38th Battalion.

MacEACHEN, Allan Joseph, politics. Inverness, NS, 1921. Liberal MP, portfolios in finance, external affairs; deputy MP in Trudeau government.

MacEWEN, Gwendolyn, literary arts. Toronto, Ont., 1941–87. Poet. *The Shadow-Maker.*

MacGREGOR, Roy, literary arts. Whitney, Ont., 1948. Novelist, columnist. *Home Game: Hockey and Life in Canada; The Last Season.*

MacGUIGAN, Mark Rudolph, politics. Charlottetown, PEI, 1931–98. Liberal politician who served with Pierre Trudeau, ran unsuccessfully for leader in 1984, later appointed judge of the Federal Court of Appeal. Founding member of the Canadian Civil Liberties Association.

MacISAAC, Ashley, performing arts. Antigonish, NS, 1975. Eclectic musician who blends pop music with traditional Celtic sound. *How Are You Today?; Fine Thank You Very Much.*

MacKAY, James William (Jim), performing arts. Beaverton, Ont., 1916–2002. Pioneer film animator who began his career with the National Film Board in 1942, succeeding the legendary Norman McLaren as head of animation in 1945. With George Dunning founded Graphic Associates, producing some of Canada's first TV commercials. In the 1950s he founded Film Design Ltd., which produced work for *Sesame Street,* among others.

MacKAY, Peter, politics. New Glasgow, NS, 1966. Elected federal PC leader 2003, replacing former prime minister Joe Clark.

MACKENZIE, Alexander, politics. Scot., 1822–1892. Canada's second prime minister (Lib).

MacKENZIE, Alexander (Sir), exploration and discovery. Scot., 1764–1820. Charted MacKenzie R. (1789); crossed from L. Athabasca to Pacific Ocean (1793).

MacKENZIE, Maj.-Gen. Lewis W., military. Truro, NS, 1940. Soldier; led UN soldiers from 33 nations (incl. Canada) in opening Sarajevo airport for delivery of humanitarian aid during Bosnian civil war.

MacKENZIE, William Lyon, politics. Scot., 1795–1861. Led 1837 rebellion for reform in Upper Canada; Toronto's first mayor.

MacLEAN, John Angus, politics. Lewes, PEI, 1914–2000. Premier PEI 1979–81; instigator of equalization payments for troubled Atlantic fisheries.

MACLEAN, John Bayne, media. Crieff, Ont., 1862–1950. Founder of *Maclean's* magazine in 1905; also of *Financial Post, Chatelaine.*

MacLEAN, Steven Glenwood, science. Ottawa, Ont., 1954. Laser physicist who trained with NASA's astronaut program, specializes with NASA's robotics branch.

MacLENNAN, John Hugh, literary arts. Glace Bay, NS, 1907–90. Novelist. *The Watch That Ends the Night; Barometer Rising.*

MacLEOD, Alistair, literary arts. North Battleford, Sask., 1936. Short story writer, novelist; his Cape Breton saga, *No Great Mischief,* winner of Trillium Book Award. *Island: The Collected Stories.*

MacLEOD, John James Rickard, medicine. Scot., 1876–1935. Medical researcher, co-winner with Drs. Banting and Best of Nobel Prize in 1923 for discovery of insulin.

MacMILLAN, Ernest Campbell (Sir), performing arts. Mimico, Ont., 1893–1973. Renowned conductor, composer, arranger; championed Canadian works.

MacMILLAN, Harvey Reginald (H.R.), business. Newmarket, Ont., 1885–1976. Industrialist; established forerunner of logging giant MacMillan Bloedel.

MacMILLAN, Margaret Olwen, literary arts. Toronto, Ont., 1943. Historian; author of award-winning *Paris 1919: Six Months That Changed the World.* Also *Women of the Raj.*

MacNAUGHTON, Andrew George Latta, military. Moosomin, NWT, 1887–1966. Soldier; led Cdn army in WWII; endorsed Dieppe raid; diplomat; UN Atomic Energy Assn.

MacNEIL, Rita, performing arts. Big Pond, NS, 1944. Cape Breton country singer; star of CBC's *Rita MacNeil Show.*

MacNEIL, Robert Breckenridge Ware, media. Toronto, Ont., 1932. TV host, newscaster, reporter, co-hosted public television series in USA, *MacNeil-Lehrer Newshour.*

MacNUTT, Walter, performing arts. Charlottetown, PEI, 1910–96. Composer of orchestral, chamber, choral, vocal, and keyboard music; noted for compositions for Anglo-Catholic service.

MACPHAIL, Agnes Campbell, politics. Proton Twp, Ont., 1890–1954. Only woman MP in 1921 (first women's vote); founded Elizabeth Fry Society.

MacPHERSON, Cluny, invention. St John's, Nfld, 1879–1966. Invented the gas helmet.

MacPHERSON, Duncan, visual arts. Toronto, Ont., 1925–93. Long-time *Toronto Star* cartoonist.

MAGEE, Helen Gagan, journalism. Toronto, Ont., 1908–98. Author and food writer for the Toronto *Globe and Mail* and former *Telegram.*

MAGNUSSEN, Karen Diane, sports. North Vancouver, BC, 1952. Figure skater; world champion, 1973.

MAHOVLICH, Francis William, sports. Timmins, Ont., 1938. Toronto Maple Leaf hockey player, 1957–68; winner of Calder Trophy, 1958; in 1998 appointed to the Senate.

MAILLET, Antonine, literary arts. Buctouche, NB, 1929. Novelist of Acadian life. Winner of France's *La Prix Goncourt La Sagouine.*

MAISONNEUVE, Paul de Chomedey, Sieur de, politics. France, 1612–76. Founder of Montreal, 1642.

MAITLAND, (Herbert) Alan, performing arts. Lilburn, Ont., 1920–99. Long-running CBC radio host noted for his rich, resonant voice; appeared on *Maitland Manor, Read to Me* and most notably, *As It Happens,* with co-hosts Barbara Frum and Michael Enright, among others, from 1974–93.

MAK, Tak Wah, medicine. China, 1946. Research led him to discover the T-cell receptor, crucial to understanding the human immune system.

MANDEL, Howie, performing arts. Toronto, Ont., 1955. Manic comic and TV actor. *St Elsewhere.*

MANGUEL, Alberto Adrian, literary arts. Argentina, 1948. Critic, anthologist, novelist. *News from a Foreign Country; The Oxford Book of Canadian Ghost Stories.*

MANKIEWICZ, Francis, performing arts. China, 1944–93. Celebrated director noted for his powerful films *Les Bons débarras* and *Les Portes Tourantes.* Also directed many CBC dramas.

MANLEY, Elizabeth, sports. Belleville, Ont., 1965. Figure skater; silver medal, 1988 Olympics.

MANLEY, John, politics. Ottawa, Ont., 1950. Liberal MP; Cabinet portfolios have included foreign affairs, industry and finance.

MANNERS, David (b. Rauff de Ryther Duan Acklom), performing arts. Halifax, NS, 1900–98. Actor; novelist. Manners was a leading Hollywood actor of the 1930s, appearing in films such as *Journey's End; Dracula; The Mummy* and *Jalna.* Wrote novels: *Convenient Season; Under Running Laughter.*

MANNING, Ernest Charles, politics. Carnduff, Sask., 1908–96. Alberta's Social Credit premier 1943–68; father of Reform Party leader Preston Manning.

MANNING, Ernest Preston, politics. Edmonton, Alta, 1942. Led Reform Party to breakthrough in 1993 federal election; leader to 2000.

MANNING, Thomas Henry, exploration and discovery. Eng., 1911–98. Mapmaker who charted vast territories of the Arctic; also biologist and naturalist focusing on Arctic environment.

MANNIS, Harry, media. Toronto, Ont., 1920–2003. Veteran CBC announcer noted for his impeccable delivery; after many years as a radio announcer, notably on the Toronto news program *What's New?* He moved on to television, hosting *Themes and Variations* and *Anthology.*

MANSBRIDGE, Peter, media. Eng., 1948. Broadcaster; anchorman, CBC national news.

MANSOURI, Lotfallah (Lotfi), performing arts. Iran, 1929. Former general director of Canadian Opera Company; creator of "surtitles," English translations of opera house librettos screened above stage.

MARCHAND, Leonard Stephen, politics. Vernon, BC, 1933. Native politician; first native federal cabinet minister.

MARCHILDON, Philip Edward, sports. Penetanguishene, Ont., 1913. Began career with Philadelphia Athletics in 1940; won 68 major league games before retirement in 1950.

MARCUS, Rudolph A., science. Montreal, Que., 1923. Winner of 1992 Nobel Prize in chemistry for work on electron transfer reactions in chemical systems.

MARGISON, Richard, performing arts. Victoria, BC, 1953. Tenor opera singer whose repertoire includes Verdi, Puccini and Bizet; international reputation.

MARIE-VICTORIN, Frère, science. Kingsley Falls, Que., 1885–1944. Distinguished botanist, author of *Croquis laurentiens; Les filicinée de Québec.*

MARK, J. Carson, science. Lindsay, Ont., 1913–97. Head of theoretical division of Los Alamos Scientific Library, influence in creation of hydrogen bomb.

MARQUETTE, Jacques, exploration and discovery. France, 1637–75. Jesuit priest explored North America with Louis Jolliet; served at Sault Ste Marie, 1666.

MARSHALL, Donald, law. Sydney, NS, 1953. Acquitted of murder after serving 11 years in prison.

MARSHALL, Lois Catherine, performing arts. Toronto, Ont., 1924–97. Soprano, career began with Sir Ernest MacMillan's Bach's *St Matthew's Passion* with Mendelssohn Choir and Toronto Symphony; Toronto Arts Award for Music, 1989.

MARSHALL, Phyllis, performing arts. Barrie, Ont., 1921–96. Jazz singer; pioneer among black Canadian performers; performed with Cab Calloway, Percy Faith; 1949–52 on CBC Radio's *Blues for Friday.*

MARTIN, Andrea, performing arts. USA, 1947. Stage, television and film actor particularly well known for comic roles in *SCTV* series.

MARTIN, Clara Brett, law. Toronto, Ont., 1874–1923. First woman lawyer in British Empire.

MARTIN, Paul Edgar Philippe, politics. Windsor, Ont., 1938. Liberal minister of finance 1993–2002.

MARTIN, Paul Joseph James, politics. Ottawa, Ont., 1903–92. Long-time Liberal Cabinet minister.

MARTIN, Peter, literary arts. Ottawa, Ont., 1934–2003. Founder with his wife, Carol, of the Readers Club of Canada, publishing Canadian authors' books under the Peter Martin Associates imprint. His roster included Hugh Hood, Robert Fulford, John Robert Colombo and Marjorie Lamb.

MARTINI, Paul, sports. Weston, Ont., 1960. Figure skater; world pairs champion (with Barbara Underhill), 1984.

MASON, Roger Burford, literary arts. Eng., 1943–98. Editor and writer, short stories: *The Beaver Picture & Other Stories;* biography of John Evans, who devised a Cree alphabet (*Travels in the Shining Island*); and a biography of artist Franz Johnson.

MASSE, Marcel, politics. St-Jean-de-Matha, Que., 1936. Leader of Union Nationale 1966–70; later minister of communications; national defense in PC federal government.

MASSEY, Charles Vincent, politics. Toronto, Ont., 1887–1967. First Canadian-born governor general, 1952–59.

MASSEY, Hart Almerrin, business. Haldemand Twp, Ont., 1823–96. Capitalist; developed Massey-Ferguson Ltd.

MASSEY, Raymond Hart, performing arts. Toronto, Ont., 1896–1983. Craggy-faced actor often played Lincoln. *Dr. Kildare.*

MASSON, Henri Leopold, visual arts. Belgium, 1907–96. Paintings of city and landscapes in the 1940s; National Gallery.

MAXWELL, Lois (b. Lois Ruth Hooker), performing arts. Kitchener, Ont., 1927. Actress, columnist. Played character Moneypenny in James Bond movie series from 1963–83. Former columnist for Toronto *Sun.*

MAYER, Louis B. (Burt) (b. Eliezer Maéyer), performing arts. Russia, 1885–1957. Grew up in Saint John, NB; with Samuel Goldwyn formed MGM movie studio in 1924; cofounded the Academy of Motion Picture Arts and Sciences in 1927.

McBEAN, Marnie, sports. Toronto, Ont., 1968. With Kathleen Heddle won women's double sculls rowing medals: two gold in 1992 Barcelona Olympics; one gold, one bronze in 1996 Olympics in Atlanta.

McBRIDE, Robert Bruce (Bob), performing arts. Toronto, Ont., 1946–98. Juno–award-winning lead singer of the 1970s rock band Lighthouse.

McCAIN, H. Harrison, business. Florenceville, NB, 1927. Industrialist; turned potato-processing plant into international firm.

McCALLUM, John, politics. Montreal, Que., 1950. Appointed minister of defense in 2002 in Chrétien government.

McCARTHY, Doris, visual arts. Calgary, Alta, 1910. Artist, calligrapher, more than 90 solo exhibitions.

McCLELLAND, John Gordon (Jack), literary arts. Toronto, Ont., 1922. Publisher; his McClelland & Stewart nurtured Canadian writing; over 5,000 Canadian titles.

McCLUNG, Nellie Letitia, law. Chatsworth, Ont., 1873–1951. Reformer; fought for women's suffrage.

McCONNELL, Robert Murray Gordon, performing arts. London, Ont., 1935. Jazz musician; founded Boss Brass, major big band.

McCOY, Elijah, invention. Colchester, Ont., 1844–1892. Son of American slaves, McCoy invented a lubrication process for steam engines in 1872; the "real McCoy" refers to his oiling device for machinery. Also invented the ironing board and lawn sprinkler.

McCRAE, John, literary arts. Guelph, Ont., 1872–1918. Poet/physician who wrote "In Flanders Fields."

McCULLOCH, Bruce Ian, performing arts. Edmonton, Alta, 1961. Versatile comedic actor and founding member of Kids in the Hall comedy troupe; director; writer. *Dog Park; Stealing Harvard.*

McCURDY, Edward Potts, performing arts. USA, 1919–2000. Folk singer, played in Ontario's Mariposa Folk Festival; noted for his huge repertoire of folk music that reflected the cultural history of Canada, specializing in Maritimes music.

McCURDY, Howard Douglas, politics. London, Ont., 1932. Black activist; also biologist.

McCURDY, John Alexander Douglas, exploration and discovery. Baddeck, NS, 1886–1961. Pilot; first airplane flight in British Empire in Silver Dart (1909).

McDERMOTT, Dennis, business. Eng., 1922–2003. Labour leader; former president, Canadian Labour Congress.

McDONALD, Bruce, performing arts. Kingston, Ont., 1959. Film director. *Roadkill; Highway 61; Dance Me Outside.*

McDONALD, Kevin Hamilton, performing arts. Montreal, Que., 1961. Comedian who began his career with the comedy troupe Kids in the Hall with CBC. He has appeared widely on Canadian and US TV and film. *The Martin Short Show; Friends.*

McDONOUGH, Pat, business. Ire., 1935. Successful Canadian fashion designer; formerly designed costumes for Diana Rigg in British TV series *The Avengers* and for Princess Diana.

McDOUGALL, Barbara Jean, politics. Toronto, Ont., 1937. PC external affairs minister 1991–93; political commentator and journalist.

McFARLANE, Leslie (Franklin W. Dixon), literary arts. Ottawa, Ont., 1903–77. Author of *Hardy Boys* adventure series.

McFARLENE, Todd, literary arts. Calgary, Alta, 1961. Creator of cult comic book *Spawn;* the first issue in 1992 was best-selling independent comic at 1.7 million copies sold.

McGARRIGLE, Anna and Kate, performing arts. Montreal, Que., 1944, 1946. Songwriters/ singers. Unique duo sings folk, own compositions. "Love Over and Over."

McGEE, Thomas D'Arcy, politics. Ire., 1825–68. Eloquent proponent of Confederation; assassinated 1868.

McGIBBON, Pauline Emily, politics. Sarnia, Ont., 1910–2002. Cda's first woman lieutenant-governor (Ont., 1974).

McINTOSH, John, invention. USA, 1777–1845. Inventor; breeder of McIntosh apple.

McKELLAR, Don, performing arts. Toronto, Ont., 1963. Filmmaker, screenwriter, actor. *Thirty-Two Short Films About Glenn Gould; Last Night.*

McKENNA, Frank Joseph, politics. Apolaqui, NB, 1948. Liberal premier of NB 1987–97.

McKENNA, Patrick Ivan Peter, performing arts. Hamilton, Ont., 1960. Comic actor played Harold on *Red Green Show*. Also on drama series *Traders.*

McKENNITT, Loreena, performing arts. Morden, Man., 1957. Singer; harpist; Celtic music repertoire.

McKENZIE, Hugh, military. Eng., 1885–1917. Victoria Cross recipient, WWI, Battle of Passchendaele, 1917. Lieutenant, 7th Canadian Machine Gun Company.

McKENZIE, Robert Tait, visual arts. Almonte, Ont., 1867–1938. Sculptor, orthopedic surgeon; designer of war memorials, sculptures.

McKINNEY, Louise, politics. Frankville, Ont., 1868–1931. First woman in Commonwealth to serve as an MLA (Alberta, 1917), the first year women could vote and run for office.

McKINNEY, Mark, performing arts. Ottawa, Ont., 1959. Comedian who was a member of the Kids in the Hall comedy troupe; has appeared on *Saturday Night Live,* as well as films *Dog Park, The Ladies Man* and *Superstar.*

McKINNON, Catherine, performing arts. Saint John, NB, 1944. Singer, actress. Appeared in CBC's *Don Messer's Jubilee;* Spring Thaw revue; *The Catherine McKinnon Show; Charlottetown Festival.* Married to actor/humorist Don Harron.

McKOY, Mark, sports. Guyana, 1961. Hurdler; gold medal, 110 m hurdles, 1992 Olympics.

McLACHLAN, Beverly, public service. Pincher Creek, Alta, 1943. Former BC Chief Justice of Supreme Court; in January 2000 became Chief Justice of Supreme Court of Canada.

McLACHLAN, Sara, performing arts. Halifax, NS, 1968. Singer-songwriter of pop music. *Surfacing.*

McLAREN, Norman, visual arts. Scot., 1914–87. Filmmaker; innovative NFB animator. *Pas de deux.*

McLARNIN, Jimmy, sports. Ire., 1907. Boxer; world welterweight champion, 1933–35.

McLAUCHLAN, Murray Edward, performing arts. Scot., 1948. Country performer; *Swingin' on a Star,* CBC Radio (1990); seven-time Juno award winner.

McLAUGHLIN, Audrey, politics. Dutton, Ont., 1936. NDP national leader 1989–95. First woman to lead a national party.

McLAUGHLIN, Robert Samuel (Col.), business. Enniskillen, Ont., 1871–1972. Industrialist; founded firm that became General Motors of Canada.

McLEAN, Stuart, media. Montreal, Que., 1948. Broadcaster on CBC's *Morningside; Vinyl Café;* author of *Welcome Home: Travels in Small Town Canada.*

McLEAN, Grant, performing arts. Yorkton, Sask., 1921–2002. Director of production and acting commissioner at the National Film Board 1941–67, McLean was a pioneer of the cinema verité genre. His imaginative and sometimes controversial works included *Target Berlin, The People Between* and *Labyrinth,* which was created for Expo 67.

McLUHAN, Herbert Marshall, media. Edmonton, Alta, 1911–80. Media theorist; developed theory about "hot" and "cool" media. *The Gutenburg Galaxy.*

McMURTRY, Roland Roy, politics. Toronto, Ont., 1932. Chief Justice of Ontario Court of Justice.

McNAUGHTON, Andrew George Latta, military. Moosomin, NWT, 1887–1966. Army officer, scientist, as chief of general staff of Armed Forces 1929–35 began modernization of nonpermanent militia; 1935–39 president of National Research Council of Canada.

McNAUGHTON, Duncan Anderson, sports. Cornwall, Ont., 1910–1998. High jumper; 1932 Olympic high jump gold medal.

McNEIL, Bill, media. Glace Bay, NS, 1924–2003. Radio host with the CBC; he hosted *Assignments* and *Fresh Air,* and adapted his series of social history books for television: *Voice of the Pioneer.*

McPHERSON, Aimee Semple, religion. Ingersoll, Ont., 1890–1944. Controversial evangelist.

McPHERSON, Donald, sports. Windsor, Ont., 1945. World professional champion figure skater, 1965.

McTAGGART, David, environment. Vancouver, BC, 1932–2001. Co-founder of environmental protectionist organization Greenpeace International. McTaggart came to prominence when protesting French nuclear testing in 1972 in Polynesia; the French rammed his boat and testing was postponed.

MEAGHER, Blanche Margaret, public service. Halifax, NS, 1911–99. Canada's first woman ambassador beginning in 1942, Meagher was posted in various locations: Mexico, Israel, Sweden, Uganda and London.

MEHTA, Deepa, performing arts. India, 1950. Award-winning film director, producer and screenwriter. *Sam and Me; Camilla Fire.*

MEIGHEN, Arthur, politics. Anderson, Ont., 1874–1960. Succeeded Sir Robert Borden as prime minister of Canada.

MEIGS, Mary, visual/literary/performing arts. USA, 1917–2002. Painter, illustrator and writer who illustrated several of Marie-Claire Blais's novels; wrote novels including *Lily Broscoe, a Self-Portrait* and *The Medusa Head;* also *In the Company of Strangers,* based on her acting debut in the NFB film *The Company of Strangers.*

MEILLEUR, Marie Louise Febronie Chasse, Kamouraska, Que., 1880–1998. Recognized in 1997 as the world's oldest person, lived in rural Ontario for most of her life.

MERCER, Ruby, performing arts. USA, 1906–99. Former opera singer who debuted at New York's Metropolitan Opera in 1936, Mercer was instrumental in the development of Canadian opera; founder of *Opera Canada* magazine, Canadian Children's Opera Chorus and host of CBC radio's *Opera Time* and *Opera in Stereo.*

MERCREDI, Ovide William, politics. Grand Rapids, Man., 1946. National chief of the Assembly of First Nations, 1991–2000.

MERRIL, Judith, literary arts. USA, 1923–97. Science fiction writer, novelist, editor, short story writer, critic. *Survival Ship and Other Stories; Daughters of the Earth and Other Stories.*

MESSER, Donald Charles Frederick (Don), performing arts. Tweedside, NB, 1909–73. Bandleader; popular maker of traditional fiddle and dance music. *Don Messer's Jubilee.*

METCALF, John Wesley, literary arts. Eng., 1938. Essayist; short story writer. *Going Down Slow; Private Parts: A Memoir; Adult Entertainment.*

MICHAELS, Lorne (b. Lorne Lipowitz), media. Toronto, Ont., 1945. TV producer; founding producer, *Saturday Night Live.*

MICHENER, Daniel Roland, politics. Lacombe, Alta, 1900–91. Governor general of Canada, 1967–74.

MIKITA, Stan (b. Stanislaus Gvoth), sports. Czech., 1940. Hockey player; centre with Chicago Blackhawks (1959–80); first Czech to play in NHL.

MILLAR, Ian D., sports. Halifax, NS, 1947. Eight-time Canadian show-jumping champian; Cdn Athlete of the Year, 1987, 1989.

MILLAR, Margaret, literary arts. Kitchener, Ont., 1915. Thriller writer. *Beast in View.*

MILNE, David Brown, visual arts. Paisley, Ont., 1882–1953. Versatile painter. *Raspberry Jam.*

MILNE, William, military. Scot., 1892–1917. Victoria Cross recipient, WWI, Vimy Ridge, 1917. Private, 50th Battalion.

MILNER, Brenda, science. Eng., 1915. Neuropsychologist; ground-breaking brain researcher.

MINER, John Thomas (Jack), science. USA, 1865–1944. Conservationist; pioneered bird sanctuaries, migratory banding.

MIRVISH, Edwin (Ed) (b. Yehudi Mirvish), business. USA, 1914. Entrepreneur; retailer (Honest Ed's) and theatre owner in Toronto, Ont.

MISTRY, Rohinton, literary arts. India, 1952. Novelist, short story writer. *Such a Long Journey; A Fine Balance.*

MITCHELL, Joni (b. Roberta Joan Anderson), performing arts. Ft Macleod, Alta, 1943. Singer/songwriter; influential lyricist. *Court and Spark.*

MITCHELL, Ray, sports. Peace River, Alta, 1931. Bowler; winner of 1972 Canadian and world 10-pin championship.

MITCHELL, William Ormond (W.O.), literary arts. Weyburn, Sask., 1914–98. Prairie novelist. *Who Has Seen the Wind?*

MOCHRIE, Colin Andrew, performing arts. Scot., 1957. Popular comedian who has appeared on American improv show *Whose Line Is It, Anyway?* as well as CBC's *This Hour Has 22 Minutes,* and Global TV's *Blackfly.*

MOLSON, John, business. Eng., 1764–1836. Founded Molson brewery; built railroads.

MONK, Lorraine, visual arts. Montreal, Que. Head of the Still Photography division of the National Film Board for many years; first director of the Canadian Museum of Contemporary Photography in Ottawa. *A Year in the Land; The Female Eye.*

MONTCALM DE SAINT VERAN, Louis Joseph de Montcalm Grozon, military. France, 1712–59. Soldier; French commander in Seven Years War; died on Plains of Abraham.

MONTGOMERY, Lucy Maud, literary arts. Clifton, PEI, 1874–1942. Writer; creator of *Anne of Green Gables.*

MONTGOMERY, Robert Douglas, performing arts. Bradford, Ont., 1908–66. Movie actor, played Laurie in 1933 version of *Little Women* opposite Katharine Hepburn.

MOODIE, Susanna, literary arts. Eng., 1803–85. Writer; pioneer author of *Roughing It in the Bush.*

MOORE, Brian, literary arts. N Ire., 1921–99. Prolific novelist; winner of two Governor General's Awards. *The Luck of Ginger Coffey; Black Robe.*

MOORE, Dora Mavor, performing arts. Scot., 1888–1979. Actress appeared in Canada and US; founded Village Players in 1938 in Toronto, Ont.; toured schools. *Spring Thaw.*

MOORE, Gregory William, sports. Vancouver, BC, 1975–99. Four time winner of Championship Auto Racing Teams (CART) circuit; died in Marlboro 500 race in California.

MOORE, James Mavor, literary arts. Toronto, Ont., 1919. TV producer; librettist; columnist; critic.

MOORES, Frank Duff, politics. Carbonear, Nfld, 1933. PC premier of Newfoundland, 1972–79.

MORANIS, Rick, performing arts. Toronto, Ont., 1953. Comedian; actor; *SCTV* regular. *Ghostbusters.*

MORAWETZ, Oskar, performing arts. Czech., 1917. Composer. *From the Diary of Anne Frank.*

MORENZ, Howarth Williams (Howie), sports. Mitchell, Ont., 1902–37. Hockey player; centre; Canada's player of half century (CP), 1950; died of on-ice injuries.

MORGAN, Henry, business. Scot., 1819–93. In 1852 Morgan founded a dry goods store in Montreal, which by 1950 became the national chain Henry Morgan & Co.; merged with Hudson's Bay Company in 1960.

MORGAN, John, performing arts. Wales. Comedian who appeared on CBC's *Royal Canadian Air Farce,* roles include Jock McBile and Mike from Canmore.

MORGENTALER, Henry, medicine. Poland, 1923. Physician; challenge of abortion laws led to Supreme Court ruling them unconstitutional.

MORISSETTE, Alanis Nadine, performing arts. Ottawa, Ont., 1974. Singer-songwriter. Juno award winner 1996 for *Jagged Little Pill* (Best Album) and Female Vocalist of the Year; Grammy Award winner, 1996.

MORIYAMA, Raymond, visual arts. Vancouver, BC, 1929. Architect; Ontario Science Centre.

MORRICE, James Wilson (J.W.), visual arts. Montreal, Que., 1864–1924. Artist; early modernist. *The Ice Bridge.*

MORRIS, Alwyn, sports. Montreal, Que., 1957. With Hugh Fisher won gold medal in 1000 m and bronze in 500 m kayak doubles at 1984 Olympics.

MORRIS, Joseph (Joe), politics. Eng., 1913–96. Former president of Canadian Labour Congress; chairman of International Labour Organization.

MORRISON, Bram, performing arts. Toronto, Ont., 1940. Member of children's musical entertainment group Sharon, Lois and Bram; live and on TV. *The Elephant Show.*

MORRISSEAU, Norval, visual arts. Sand Point Reserve, Ont., 1932. Ojibwa artist originated pictographic style.

MORSE, Barry, performing arts. Eng., 1918. Stage/film/TV actor; regular on *The Fugitive.*

MORTON, William Lewis (W.L.), literary arts. Gladstone, Man., 1908–80. Historian. *Manitoba: A History.*

MOSS, Carrie-Anne, performing arts. Vancouver, BC, 1967. Model turned actress who has appeared in *Dark Justice* TV series, as well as *Matrix, Models Inc.,* and *F/X The Series.*

MOWAT, Claire Angel, literary arts. Toronto, Ont., 1933. Graphic artist, fiction writer, wife of writer Farley Mowat. *The Girl From Away; The Outport People; The French Isles.*

MOWAT, Farley McGill, literary arts. Belleville, Ont., 1921. Controversial, popular naturalist writer. *A Whale for the Killing.*

MOWAT, Oliver (Sir), politics. Kingston, UC, 1820–1903. Ontario premier, 1872–96; lieutenant governor, 1897–1903.

MUKHERJEE, Bharati, literary arts. India, 1940. Novelist. *The Middleman and Other Stories; Jasmine.*

MULLIN, George Harry, military. USA, 1892–1963. Victoria Cross recipient, WWI, Battle of Passchendaele, 1917. Sergeant, 7th Canadian Machine Gun Company.

MULRONEY, Brian Martin, politics. Baie Comeau, Que., 1939. PC prime minister of Canada 1984–93.

MUNDELL, Robert, business. Kingston, Ont., 1932. Winner of 1999 Nobel Prize for economics for 1960s study of exchange rates and their relationship to monetary policy.

MUNK, Peter, business. Hungary, 1927. Capitalist; CEO, American Barrick Resources gold mining company.

MUNRO, Alice, literary arts. Wingham, Ont., 1931. Short story writer. Winner of 1998 Giller prize. *Lives of Girls and Women.*

MUNSCH, Robert, literary arts. USA, 1945. Children's writer. *The Paper Bag Princess; Love You Forever.*

MURPHY, Emily Cowan, law. Cookstown, Ont., 1868–1933. Legal reformer; first woman magistrate in British Empire; fought for women's rights.

MURPHY, Rex, media. Carbonear, Nfld, 1947. CBC news journalist with acerbic style. *Cross Country Checkup.*

MURRAY, Anne, performing arts. Springhill, NS, 1945. Singer; Canada's most successful performer; many Junos and Grammys. "Snowbird."

MURRAY, George Henry, politics. Grand Narrows, NS, 1861–1929. Lib. premier of NS, 1896–1923.

MURRAY, John Wilson, law. Scot., 1840–1906. Detective; pioneered scientific crime detection.

MURRAY, Margaret Teresa "Ma," media. USA, 1888–1982. Journalist; pungent editorialist in own magazines.

MURRAY, Robert George Everitt, science. Eng., 1919. With Philip Fitz-Jones, researched structure and chemical nature of bacterial spores.

MUSGRAVE, Susan, literary arts. USA, 1951. Poet, novelist, children's writer. *The Embalmer's Art: Poems; The Charcoal Burners.*

MUSTARD, James Fraser, medicine. Toronto, Ont., 1927. Physician; medical humanitarian; found connection between aspirin and blood clotting.

MUSTARD, William, medicine. Clinton, Ont., 1914–87. Physician; beloved children's surgeon developed operations for blue babies, polio victims.

MYERS, Barton, visual arts. USA, 1934. Architect. Seagram Museum in Waterloo, Ont.; U of Toronto's Woodsworth College; UCLA Northwest Commons and Housing; Housing Union Building, U of Alta.

MYERS, Mike, performing arts. Toronto, Ont., 1963. Comic actor has appeared in movies *Austin Powers; It's a Dog's Life; Wayne's World* also appeared on *Saturday Night Live.*

MYLES, Alannah, performing arts. Toronto, Ont., 1958. Pop singer/composer of hard rock, ballads. "Lover of Mine"; *Black Velvet; Al-Lan-Nah.*

N

NAISMITH, James A., sports. Almonte, Ont., 1861–1939. Physician; invented basketball in 1891.

NAKAMURA, Kazuo, visual arts. Vancouver, BC, 1926–2002. Abstract artist, member of Painters Eleven with such luminaries as William Ronald and Harold Town, noted for his subdued style. *Reflections; Block Structure.*

NAMARO, James (Jimmy), performing arts. USA, 1913–98. A member of the CBC's *Happy Gang,* the longest-running program on the radio network; also led his own jazz band.

NANOGAK, Agnes, visual arts. Baillie I., NWT, 1925. Inuit artist whose prints depict Inuit myths and legends, operating out of Holman I. artist co-op. Illustrated *Tales from the Igloo.*

NASH, Cyril Knowlton, media. Toronto, Ont., 1927. Broadcaster; former anchorman, CBC national news.

NATTRASS, Susan Marie, sports. Medicine Hat, Alta, 1950. Shooter; six women's world trapshooting titles.

NAULT, Fernand (b. Fernand-Noel Boissonneault), performing arts. Montreal, Que., 1921. Dancer; choreographer, Les Grands Ballets Canadiens.

NELLIGAN, Émile, literary arts. Montreal, Que., 1879–1941. Romantic poet. "Romance du Vin."

NELLIGAN, Kate, performing arts. London, Ont., 1951. Actor; appears on both stage and film. *Eleni.*

NEMETZ, Nathaniel "Sonny," law. Winnipeg, Man., 1913–97. Chief Justice of British Columbia 1979–88, leading judicial administrator in BC.

NEVILLE, John, performing arts. Eng., 1925. Actor, director. Stratford Festival, Ont.; director of Stratford's The Young Company.

NEWMAN, Peter Charles, media. Austria, 1929. Journalist; popular historian. *The Canadian Establishment, Maclean's* editor, 1971–82.

NEWTON, Margaret, science. Montreal, Que., 1887–1971. Plant pathologist; first scientist to research rust in wheat.

NICHOL, Barrie Phillip (bp), literary arts. Vancouver, BC, 1944–88. Concrete and sound poet, novelist. *Journeying and Returns; Love: A Book of Remembrance.*

NICHOL, Dave, business. Chatham, Ont., 1940. Made Loblaws stores market leader with President's Choice label.

NICHOLAS, Cynthia (Cindy), sports. Toronto, Ont., 1957. Marathon swimmer; first woman to swim English Channel both ways.

NICKERSON, William Henry Snyder, military. Saint John, NB, 1875–1954. Victoria Cross recipient, Boer War, 1900. Lieutenant, Mounted Infantry.

NICOL, Eric, media. Kingston, Ont., 1919. Humour columnist. "Girdle Me a Globe."

NIELSEN, Erik Hersholt, politics. Regina, Sask., 1924. PC MP elected in Yukon 1957, served as deputy prime minister in Mulroney government.

NIELSEN, Leslie, performing arts. Regina, Sask., 1926. Deadpan film/TV comedian. *Naked Gun.*

NORQUAY, John, politics. St Andrews, Man., 1841–89. Manitoba premier of mixed European and native ancestry, 1878–87.

NORTHCOTT, Ronald Charles, sports. Innisfail, Alta, 1935. Curler; skipped three Brier and world champion rinks.

NOTMAN, William, visual arts. Scot., 1826–91. Innovative Montreal-based portrait photographer who sent his studio photographers across Canada and the US to record social landscape, recording the growth and character of the continent.

NOWLAN, Alden, literary arts. Windsor, NS, 1933–83. Poet. "Bread, Wine and Salt."

OAKS, Sir Harry, business. USA, 1874–1943. Oaks made his fortune through gold mine near Swastika, Ont., became North America's second largest gold mine; retired to the Bahamas; victim of unsolved murder.

O'BRIEN, Mary, public service. Scot., 1926–98. Midwife, philosopher; founding member of the Feminist Party of Canada, wrote *The Politics of Reproduction; Reproducing the World.*

ODJIG, Daphne, visual arts. Manitoulin Island, Ont., 1919. Blends western and native styles. *The Indian in Transition.*

OH, Sandra, performing arts. Nepean, Ont., 1971. Korean-Canadian actress appeared in TV version of *The Diary of Evelyn Lau;* also stage production of *Oleanna.*

O'HARA, Catherine, performing arts. Toronto, Ont., 1954. Actor; comedian; *SCTV* regular (Lola Heatherton).

OKALIK, Paul, politics. Pangnirtung, NWT, 1964. First premier of 19-member Legislative Assembly for Nunavit in the Eastern Arctic, created in 1999.

O'KELLY, Christopher Patrick, military. Winnipeg, Man., 1895–1923. Victoria Cross recipient, WWI, Battle of Passchendaele, 1917. Captain, 52nd Battalion.

OLCOTT, Sidney, performing arts. Toronto, Ont., 1873–1949. Director of Hollywood silent films, pioneered locations shots, westerns. *Ben Hur.*

O'LEARY, Michael John, military. Ire., 1889–1961. Victoria Cross recipient, WWI, Cuinchy, France, 1915. Lance-corporal, 1st Battalion of the Irish Guards.

OLIPHANT, Betty, performing arts. Eng., 1918. Founded National Ballet School.

OLSEN, Horace "Bud," politics. Iddesleigh, Alta, 1925–2002. Liberal Cabinet minister during Trudeau years; lieutenant governor of Alberta 1996–2000; noted parliamentarian.

ONDAATJE, Christopher, business/literary arts. Sri Lanka, 1933. Financier; author. *Leopard in the Afternoon.*

ONDAATJE, Michael, literary arts. Sri Lanka, 1943. Poet; editor; novelist. *The English Patient* (Booker Prize).

O'NEILL, James Edward "Tip," sports. Canada W, 1859–1918. Baseball player; batted .326 in 10-year career.

OONARK, Jessie, visual arts. Back River, NWT, 1906–85. Inuit artist who employed brilliant colours to depict both traditional images and Christian themes in her drawings and wall hangings.

ORBINSKI, James, medicine. Eng., 1960. President, International Council, for Doctors Without Borders; accepted 1999 Nobel Peace Prize on behalf of the international organization.

ORONHYATEKHA (Peter Martin), business. Six Nations Reserve, Ont., 1841–1907. First native Canadian to receive a degree from a Canadian university; founder of the Independent Order of Foresters, a fraternal life insurance organization.

O'ROURKE, Michael James, military. Ire., 1878–1957. Victoria Cross recipient, WWI, Battle of Hill 70, 1917. Private, 7th Battalion.

ORR, Robert Gordon (Bobby), sports. Parry Sound, Ont., 1948. Hockey player; spectacular offensive defenceman; won eight consecutive Norris trophies.

ORSER, Brian Ernest, sports. Belleville, Ont., 1961. Figure skater; 1987 world champion, twice Olympic silver medallist (1984, 1988).

ORTON, George W., sports. Strathroy, Ont., 1873–1958. Runner; Canada's first Olympic gold medallist, winning for USA in 1900 (2500 m steeplechase).

OSGOODE, William, law. Eng., 1754–1824. First chief justice of Upper Canada; played key role in development of Canadian legislation.

OSLER, William (Sir), medicine. Bond Head, UC, 1849–1919. Physician; renowned medical educator; author of authoritative textbooks.

OSTANEK, Walter, performing arts. Duparket, Que., 1935. "King of Polka"; popular piano accordionist with more than 60 polka recordings and multiple Grammy awards.

OTTENBRITE, Anne, sports. Whitby, Ont., 1966. Swimmer; gold medal, 200 m, 1984 Olympics.

OUIMET, Joseph Alphonse, media. Montreal, Que., 1908–88. TV executive; designed first Canadian TV receiver; CBC president, 1958–67.

PACE, Kate, sports. North Bay, Ont., 1969. Skier; World Cup downhill champion, 1993.

PACHTER, Charles, visual arts. Toronto, Ont., 1942. Painter famous for flag series; 1973 acrylic sketch titled *Queen on Moose.*

PAGE, Patricia Kathleen, (P.K.), literary arts. Eng., 1916. Poet; novelist; artist. "The Metal and the Flower."

PANNETON, Philippe (Ringuet), literary arts. Trois-Rivières, Que., 1895–1960. Man of letters; acclaimed Quebec writer. *Trente Arpents.*

PAPINEAU, Louis Joseph, politics. Montreal, Que., 1786–1871. Led political reform movement in Lower Canada.

PARENT, Etienne, politics. Beauport, Upper Canada, 1802–74. Editor of *La Gazette de Québec* and *Le Canadien;* early advocate for French-Canadian nationalism, later lectured at Institut Canadien to promote business and industry, education reform and political economy.

PARIS, Erna, literary arts. Toronto, Ont., 1938. Writer. *The Garden and the Gun; End of Days.*

PARIZEAU, Jacques, politics. Montreal, Que., 1930. Leader, Parti Québécois 1987–95.

PARKER, Cecilia, performing arts. Fort William, Ont., 1905–93. Famous for playing Andy Hardy's older sister in the *Andy Hardy* film series; also appeared in Hollywood westerns and action films of the 1930s.

PARKER, Jackie, sports. USA, 1932. Football player; coach; Edmonton Eskimos star quarterback; named CFL outstanding player three times.

PARKER, Jon Kimura, performing arts. Vancouver, BC, 1959. Concert pianist, performed for Queen, prime ministers, and at Carnegie Hall.

PARKIN, John Burnett, visual arts. Toronto, Ont., 1911–75. Partnered with John Cresswell Parkin (no relation) to build major public buildings, including hospitals, schools, airports. Largest firm in Canada in the 1950s and '60s. Union Station (Ottawa), IBM head office (Toronto).

PARROT, Jean-Claude, business. Montreal, Que., 1936. Labour leader; leader of militant postal union.

PARRY, Sir William Edward, exploration and discovery. Eng., 1790–1855. Parry's explorations into the Arctic led to the discovery of the North Pole and the charting of the Northwest Passage.

PARTRIDGE, Edward Alexander, business. Canada W, 1862–1931. Farm reformer; visionary in grain industry fought monopolies, started growers' cooperative.

PASSAGLIA, Lui, sports. Vancouver, BC, 1954. Football player; kicker with BC Lions; CFL's all-time scoring leader.

PATRICK, Lester, sports. Drummondville, Que., 1883–1960. Hockey executive; NHL builder.

PATTISON, James Allen, business. Saskatoon, Sask., 1928. Industrialist; developed car dealership into business empire; chairman, Expo 86.

PATTISON, John George, military. 1875–1917. Victoria Cross recipient, WWI, Vimy Ridge, 1917. Private, 50th Battalion.

PAUL, Robert, sports. Toronto, Ont., 1937. Figure skater; with Barbara Wagner, won four pairs titles, 1960 Olympic gold.

PAYETTE, Julie, science. Montreal, Que., 1963. Astronaut and mission specialist on crew of STS-96 Atlantis, a 10-day logistics and resupply mission that launched in May 1999.

PAYETTE, Lise, media/politics. Montreal, Que., 1931. Broadcaster, writer, politician; her radio show with Radio-Canada, *Place Aux Femmes,* aired in the 1960s; Parti Québécois MNA 1976–80.

PEAKER, Charles, performing arts. Eng., 1899–1978. Organist, choirmaster, writer. Foremost concert organist in Canada. Edited *Organ Music of Canada.*

PEARKES, George Randolph, military. Eng., 1888–1984. Victoria Cross recipient, WWI, Battle of Passchendaele, 1917. Major, 5th Canadian Mounted Rifles Battalion.

PEARSON, Lester Bowles, politics. Newtonbrook, Ont., 1897–1972. Lib. prime minister of Canada 1963–1968; awarded Nobel Peace Prize in 1957.

PECKFORD, Alfred Brian, politics. Whitbourne, Nfld, 1942. PC premier of Nfld, 1979–89.

PEEL, Paul, visual arts. London, Ont., 1860–92. Painter famous for *After the Bath,* which depicts two children warming themselves before a fireplace. *The Tired Model; Good News, Toronto.*

PELADEAU, Pierre, media. Outremont, Que., 1925–97. Publisher; head of newspaper giant Quebecor.

PELLAN, Alfred, visual arts. Quebec City, Que., 1906–88. Painter; cubist and surrealist artist.

PELLATT, Henry Mill (Sir), military. Kingston, Canada W, 1860–1939. Soldier; builder of eccentric Toronto mansion, Casa Loma.

PELLETIER, David, sports. Sayabec, Que., 1974. With Jamie Salé won gold medal in pairs figure skating at 2002 Salt Lake City Winter Olympics; the award was presented after controversy over prior judging that placed Russian team at top while Salé and Pelletier first winning silver.

PELLETIER, Gerard, politics. Victoriaville, Que., 1919–97. Chief editor for *La Presse* (1961–65); federal deputy minister for Montreal riding of Hochelaga 1965–75. Later ambassador for Canada in Paris and for United Nations.

PENFIELD, Wilder Groves Dr, medicine. USA, 1891–1976. Neurologist; writer; pioneered mapping of brain functions; founded Montreal Neurological Inst.

PENNELL, Nicholas, performing arts. Eng., 1938–95. Former actor at Stratford Festival; starred in British TV series *The Forsyte Saga.*

PENNER, Fredrick Ralph, performing arts. Winnipeg, Man., 1946. Popular children's entertainer; host of CBC TV's *Fred Penner's Place;* former national spokesperson for UNICEF. *Moonlight Express.*

PENTLAND, Barbara Lally, performing arts. Winnipeg, Man., 1912–2000. Celebrated avant-garde composer; noted for anti-tonal style. *Concerto for Piano and String Orchestra.*

PEPIN, Jean-Luc, politics. Drummondville, Que., 1924–95. Longtime Liberal cabinet minister; served on Anti-Inflation Board, co-chairman of 1977 unity task force.

PEPIN, Marcel, politics. Montreal, Que., 1926–2000. Became president of Confederation of National Trade unions in 1965; responsible for uniting public service unions in Quebec and instigator of illegal Common Front Strike of 1972; later head of World Confederation of Labour.

PERCIVAL, Lloyd, sports. Toronto, Ont., 1913–1974. Sports enthusiast; in 1941 founded CBC Radio Sports College; founder of Fitness Institute and coach to many successful athletes.

PERCY, Karen, sports. Edmonton, Alta, 1966. Skier; won two bronze medals, 1988 Olympics.

PERRAULT, Jean-Pierre, performing arts. Montreal, Que., 1947–2002. Montreal-based dancer and choreographer whose signature style—complex lighting and staging techniques dubbed Perraultesque—gained him worldwide notoriety. Founder of the dance company Fondation Jean-Pierre Perrault.

PERRAULT, Pierre, visual arts. Montreal, Que., 1927. Filmmaker; realist director. *L'Acadie, L'Acadie.*

PETERSON, Eric, performing arts. Indian Head, Sask., 1946. Actor. *Billy Bishop Goes to War;* CBC's *Street Legal* series.

PETERSON, Oscar Emmanuel, performing arts. Montreal, Que., 1925. Jazz pianist/composer. As leader of the Oscar Peterson Trio, he has recorded more than 100 albums. *Canadiana Suite; Night Train.*

PETRIE, Daniel, performing arts. Glace Bay, NS, 1920. Film director, won Genie award for *Bay Boy; A Raisin in the Sun.*

PETTIGREW, Pierre, politics. Quebec City, Que., 1951. Liberal MP; minister of international trade; strong federalist voice against Quebec separatism.

PEZER, Vera, sports. Melfort, Sask., 1939. Curler; Canadian women's champion, 1971–73.

PFLUG, Christiane, visual arts. Germany, 1936–72. Painter of melancholy landscapes and domestic scenes. *Cottingham School After the Rain; Kitchen Door with Esther.*

PHILLIPS, Robin, performing arts. Eng., 1942. Director, Stratford Festival, 1975–80, 1986–87.

PICKERSGILL, John Whitney, politics. Wyecombe, Ont., 1905–97. Public servant, politician and historian who advised 'prime ministers Mackenzie King and Louis St. Laurent on policy; became president of Canadian Transport Commission in 1967. Wrote *My Years With Louis St. Laurent.*

PICKFORD, Mary (b. Gladys Smith), performing arts. Toronto, Ont., 1893–1979. Actress; "America's Sweetheart" was early movie star. *Sparrows.*

PIDGEON, Walter, performing arts. E Saint John, NB, 1897–1984. Leading man. *Mrs. Miniver.*

PINSENT, Gordon Edward, performing arts. Grand Falls, Nfld, 1930. Versatile actor. *The Rowdyman; Due South.*

PINSENT, Leah, performing arts. Toronto, Ont., 1964. Actress, daughter of Gordon Pinsent. Has appeared on film (*The Bay Boy*) and TV (*More Tears; Made in Canada*).

PITSEOLAK Ashoona, visual arts. NWT, 1904–83. Artist of Inuit myth and legend.

PITSEOLAK, Peter, visual arts. NWT, 1902–73. Photographer; recorded passing of traditional Inuit life.

PLAMONDON, Antoine, visual arts. Lorette, Que., 1804–95. Portraitist and religious painter.

PLAMONDON, Luc, performing arts. St Raymond-de-Portneuf, Que., 1945. Lyricist; wrote rock opera *Starmania;* collaborated with Britain's Tim Rice; has written songs for Céline Dion.

PLANTE, Jacques, sports. Mt Carmel, Que., 1929–86. Hockey goaltender; seven-time Vezina winner; originated face mask.

PLAUNT, Alan Butterworth, media. Ottawa, Ont., 1904–41. With Graham Spry founded the Canadian Radio League in 1930, an association that promoted public broadcasting. The association was a precursor to the Canadian Broadcasting Corporation, and Plaunt sat on the first board of governors.

PLAUT, Gunther, religion. Germany, 1912. Rabbi (Toronto's Holy Blossom Temple); author; advocate of modern secular Judaism. Wrote *The Torah: A Modern Commentary; The Man Who Would Be Messiah,* a novel.

PLUMMER, Arthur Christopher Orme, performing arts. Toronto, Ont., 1929. Stage and film star. *The Sound of Music.*

POCKLINGTON, Peter H., business. Regina, Sask., 1941. Entrepreneur; owner of Edmonton Oilers.

POCOCK, Nancy Meek, philanthropy. USA, 1911–98. Quaker and pacifist, an antiwar and refugee advocate; won the Medal of Friendship from Socialist Republic of Vietnam.

PODBORSKI, Steve, sports. Toronto, Ont., 1957. Skier; world downhill champion, 1982.

POITRAS, Jean-Claude, business. Montreal, Que., 1949. Designer of couture-quality fashion under own label; founder of Fashion Société Design collections.

POLANYI, John Charles, science. Germany, 1929. Chemist; Nobel Prize (1986) for work on infrared chemiluminescence.

POLLEY, Sarah, performing arts. Toronto, Ont., 1979. Actress; *The Road to Avonlea; The Sweet Hereafter.*

POLLOCK, Sam, sports. Montreal, Que., 1925. Hockey executive; built Montreal Canadiens dynasty.

POLLOCK, Sharon, literary arts. Fredericton, NB, 1936. Playwright; writer of conscience. *Blood Relations.*

PONTIAC, military. USA, 1720?–69. Ottawa Indian chief who formed alliance with various Indian federations to attack English, including a fort at Point Pelee, Ont.; in 1765 key signer of peace treaties with the English.

PORTER, Anna Maria, literary arts. Hungary. Publisher, author. CEO and director of Key Porter Books; mystery writer. *The Bookfair Murders; Mortal Sins.*

POST, Sandra, sports. Oakville, Ont., 1943. Golfer; Canada's first woman touring professional.

POTTS, Jerry (b. Ky-yo-Kosi), military. USA, 1840–96. Native scout; Blackfoot became NWMP special constable.

POTVIN, Dennis, sports. Ottawa, Ont., 1953. Hockey player; as defenceman with New York Islanders (1973–88) all-time leader in goals and assists.

POWELL, Marion, medicine. Toronto, Ont., 1923–97. Former president of Planned Parenthood in Toronto; a pioneer in introducing birth control information in the 1960s.

POWLESS, Alex, sports. Six Nations Reserve, Ont., 1926–2003. Lacrosse champion whose team, the Peterborough Timbermen, won four Mann Cups; he also coached his son Gaylord Powless, a celebrated lacrosse player who died in 2001.

PRATLEY, Gerald Arthur, performing arts. Eng., 1923. Film critic; founder of Ontario Film Institute in 1968; CBC's first film critic 1948–75. *Pratley at the Movies.*

PRATT, Edwin James (E.J.), literary arts. Western Bay, Nfld, 1883–1964. Leading pre-WWII poet. "Newfoundland Verse."

PRATT, John Christopher, visual arts. St John's, Nfld, 1935. Artist; developed style of "conceptual realism."

PRATT, Mary, visual arts. Fredericton, NB, 1935. Artist; her paintings portray kitchen imagery and domestic themes. Illustrated Cynthia Wine's *Across the Table: An Indulgent Look at Food in Canada.*

PREVOST, André, performing arts. Hawkesbury, Ont., 1934–2001. Quebec-based composer whose humanistic works included *Terre des Hommes (Man and His World); Cantate pour cordes* and *Chorégraphie,* which was inspired by the 1972 assassination of Olympic athletes in Munich.

PRIESTLEY, Jason Bradford, performing arts. Vancouver, BC, 1969. Popular actor noted for his brooding looks. *Beverly Hills, 90210.*

PURDY, Alfred Wellington, literary arts. Wooler, Ont., 1918–2000. Working-class poet. "The Cariboo Horses."

Q

QUARRINGTON, Paul Lewis, literary arts. Toronto, Ont., 1953. Governor General's Award for Fiction, 1990. *Home Game; Whale Music.*

QUILICO, Louis, performing arts. Montreal, Que., 1925–2000. Operatic baritone; appeared with most major companies.

R

RADDAL, Thomas Head, literary arts. Eng., 1903–94. Governor General's Award-winning historical novelist. *The Pied Piper of Dipper Creek and Other Tales; His Majesty's Yankees.*

RADISSON, Pierre Esprit, exploration and discovery. France, 1636–1710. Explorer; fur trader; important in early history of Hudson's Bay Co as guide and advisor.

RAE, John, exploration and discovery. Orkney, 1813–1893. Explorer who found evidence of Sir John Franklin's fated expedition in the Canadian north; surveyor for the Hudson's Bay Company, charting northern regions and western Canada.

RAE, Robert Keith (Bob), politics. Ottawa, Ont., 1948. NDP premier of Ontario 1990–95.

RAFFI (b. Raffi Cavoukian), performing arts. Egypt, 1948. Singer. *Baby Beluga.*

RAIN, Douglas, performing arts. Winnipeg, Man., 1928. Actor; has played more than 30 seasons with Ontario's Stratford Festival; voice of Hal the Computer in the films *2001* and *2002.*

RANKIN, John Morris, performing arts. Mabou, NS, 1959–2000. Head of musical group The Rankin Family, later The Rankins, Cape Breton musicians instrumental in popular revival of East Coast Celtic tradition.

RASKY, Harry, performing arts. Toronto, Ont., 1928. Filmmaker; noted documentarist. *The Dispossessed: The War Against the Indians.*

RASMINSKY, Louis, business. Montreal, Que., 1908–98. Governor, Bank of Canada, 1961–72.

RAYNER, Gordon, visual arts. Toronto, Ont., 1935. Realist, abstract painter, landscapes and cityscapes; northern Ontario landscapes. *Magnetawan No. 2.*

READ, Ken, sports. USA, 1955. Skier; winner of five World Cup downhill victories (1975–80).

READE, Herbert Taylor, military. Perth, Upper Canada, 1828–97. Victoria Cross recipient, Indian Mutiny, 1857. Surgeon, 61st Gloucestershire Regiment of Foot.

REANEY, James Crerar, literary arts. Easthope, Ont., 1926. Playwright; poet; critic. "A Suit of Nettles."

REBICK, Judy, politics. USA, 1945. Former head, Natl Action Committee on Status of Women.

REED, George Robert, sports. USA, 1939. Football player; running back with Sask. Roughriders; 44 CFL records.

REEVES, Keanu, performing arts. Lebanon, 1965. Actor. *Bill and Ted's Excellent Adventure; My Own Private Idaho.*

REGAN, Gerald Augustine, politics. Windsor, NS, 1928. Liberal premier of NS, 1970–78.

REICHMANN, Paul, business. Austria, 1930. Developer; philanthropist; with brothers Albert and Ralph, built Olympia & York into world's largest real estate developers in 1980s.

REID, Daphne Kate, performing arts. Eng., 1930–93. Primarily stage actress; Stratford mainstay.

REID, Fiona, performing arts. Eng., 1951. Dramatic and comedic actor. CBC's *King of Kensington* series; Stratford Festival, Ont.

REID, William Ronald (Bill), visual arts. Victoria, BC, 1920–98. Noted artist who promoted Northwest Coast native carving; also a sculptor whose works appear in major galleries and buildings.

REITMAN, Ivan, visual arts. Czech., 1946. Film director; producer; went from exploitation movies to blockbusters. *Ghostbusters.*

RENNIE, Callum Keith, performing arts. Eng., 1960. Actor noted for role as Stanley Raymond Kowalski in CBC Mountie comedy/drama *Due South;* also appeared in movies *My Life as a Dog; Hard Core Logo*; and in TV series *The X-Files.*

RENO, Ginette, performing arts. Montreal, Que., 1946. Popular chanteuse of sentimental ballads. "Tu vivras toujours dans mon coeur"; "A ma manière."

RICCI, Nino Pio, literary arts. Leamington, Ont., 1959. Novelist, recipient of Governor General's Award for Fiction, 1990, for *Lives of the Saints.*

RICHARD, Joseph Henry Maurice "Rocket," sports. Montreal, Que., 1921–2000. Hockey player; legendary right winger; hockey's first 50-goal, 500-goal scorer.

RICHARDS, David Adams, literary arts. Newcastle, NB, 1950. Author of fiction, stage and screen plays, and poetry; co-winner of 2000 Giller Prize for *Mercy Among the Children.*

RICHARDSON, Arthur Herbert Lindsay, military. Eng., 1873–1923. Victoria Cross recipient, Boer War, 1900. Sergeant, Lord Strathcona's Horse.

RICHARDSON, Ernie, sports. Stoughton, Sask., 1931. Curler; skipped four Brier and world title rinks.

RICHARDSON, James Armstrong, business. Kingston, Ont., 1885–1939. Financier; founded family grain business and investment house.

RICHARDSON, James Cleland, military. Scot., 1895–1916. Victoria Cross recipient, WWI, the Somme, 1916. Piper, 16th Battalion.

RICHLER, Mordecai, literary arts. Montreal, Que., 1931–2001. Novelist; essayist; acerbic comic writer. *St Urbain's Horseman.*

RICKER, William Edwin, science. Waterdown, Ont., 1908–2001. Creator of the Ricker Curve, an internationally recognized formula for helping fishermen to increase their catch by calculating supply as affected by rate of fishing and spawning success.

RIDOUT, Godfrey, performing arts. Toronto, Ont., 1918–84. Composer of chamber, symphonic and religious choral works.

RIEL, Louis, politics. St Boniface, Man., 1844–85. Métis leader; led North West Rebellion, 1870 and 1885; hanged for treason; rehabilitated and recognized as a founder of Manitoba in 1992.

RIOPELLE, Jean-Paul, visual arts. Montreal, Que., 1923–2002. Acclaimed painter, sculptor. *Autrich.*

RITCHIE, Albert Edgar, politics. Andover, NB, 1916–2002. Ambassador to the US 1966–69, during the Johnson and Nixon administrations; key advisor to Prime Minister Pierre Trudeau during the October Crisis of 1970.

RITCHIE, Charles Stewart Almon, politics. Halifax, NS, 1906–95. Diplomat post–WWII; author of a number of books. *The Siren Years.*

RITTER, Erika, literary arts. Regina, Sask., 1948. Playwright, essayist, broadcaster. Her plays are a light-hearted look at serious women's issues. *The Visitor From Charleston; Automatic Pilot; Urban Scrawl.*

ROBARTS, John Parmenter, politics. Banff, Alta, 1917–82. PC premier of Ontario, 1961–71.

ROBERSTON, Jaime Robbie, performing arts. Toronto, Ont., 1944. Singer, songwriter, played with Ronnie Hawkins and the Band; wrote scores for films including *Raging Bull, King of Comedy.*

ROBERTS, Charles George Douglas (Sir), literary arts. Douglas, NB, 1860–1943. Poet; animal story writer. *Eyes of the Wilderness.*

ROBERTSON, Heather Margaret, literary arts. Winnipeg, Man., 1942. Novelist, critic. *More Than a Rose: Prime Ministers, Wives and Other Women.*

ROBERTSON, James Peter, military. Pictou, NS, 1883–1917. Victoria Cross recipient, WWI, Battle of Passchendaele, 1917. Private, 27th Battalion.

ROBERTSON, John Ross, business. Toronto, Ont., 1841–1918. Financier; publisher and philanthropist.

ROBERTSON, Lloyd, media. Stratford, Ont., 1934. Broadcaster; chief anchor, CTV news.

ROBICHAUD, Louis Joseph, politics. St-Antoine, NB, 1925. Liberal premier of NB, 1960–70.

ROBILLARD, Lucienne, politics. Montreal, Que., 1945. Liberal MP active in Quebec referendum debate; president of treasury board; formerly minister of citizenship and immigration.

ROBINETTE, John Josiah (J.J.), law. Toronto, Ont., 1906–96. Lawyer; prominent in criminal and constitutional law.

ROBINSON, Svend J., politics. USA, 1952. NDP MP, British Columbia; social activist, gay rights.

ROBLIN, Dufferin (Duff), politics. Winnipeg, Man., 1917. PC premier of Manitoba, 1958–67.

ROBLIN, Rodmond Palen (Sir), politics. Sophiasburg, Canada W, 1853–1937. PC premier of Manitoba, 1900–15.

ROCK, Allan Michael, politics. Ottawa, Ont., 1947. Liberal MP made minister of justice and attorney general in 1993, introduced major changes in Young Offender's Act and gun control legislation, minister of health in Chrétien government.

RODRIGUEZ, Sue, public service. Winnipeg, Man., 1959–94. Lou Gehrig's disease victim who championed right to die.

ROGERS, Edward S. (Ted), business. Toronto, Ont., 1933. Cable TV executive; runs Canada's largest cable system; 1994 take-over of Maclean Hunter.

ROGERS, Edward Samuel, invention. Toronto, Ont., 1900–39. Radio inventor; perfected alternating current radio tube, revolutionizing the industry.

ROGERS, Shelagh, media. Ottawa, Ont., 1956. CBC radio personality. Host of CBC's *This Morning; Take Five with Shelagh Rogers.*

ROGERS, Stan, performing arts. Hamilton, Ont., 1949–83. Folk singer/songwriter. "Between the Breaks."

ROHMER, Richard, literary arts. Hamilton, Ont., 1924. Writer. *Triad, Red Arctic, Death by Deficit.*

ROLPH, John, medicine. Eng., 1793–1870. Physician; ran medical school; constitutional reformer.

ROMAN, Stephen Boleslav, business. Slovakia, 1921–88. Industrialist; founded Denison Mines Ltd.

ROMANOW, Roy John, politics. Saskatoon, Sask., 1939. NDP premier of Sask 1991–2001.

RONALD, William (b. William Smith), visual arts. Stratford, Ont., 1926–98. Abstract artist; host, *As It Happens.*

ROOKE, Leon, literary arts. USA, 1934. Short story writer, novelist, playwright. *Krokodile; Shakespeare's Dog; How I Saved the Province; A Bit of White Cloth.*

ROSE, Fred (b. Fred Rosenburg), politics. Poland, 1907–83. Only Canadian Communist MP (1945); jailed as spy.

ROSENFELD, Fanny "Bobbie," sports. Russia, 1905–69. Track star; Canada's female athlete of half century.

ROSS, Anne Glass, medicine. Ukraine, 1911–98. Executive director of Winnipeg's Mount Carmel community health clinic, the first of its kind in Canada; birth control advocate. *Pregnant and Alone; Clinic with a Heart.*

ROSS, James Sinclair, literary arts. Shellbrook, Sask., 1908–96. Novelist. *As for Me and My House.*

ROSS, Sir James Clark, exploration and discovery. Eng., 1800–62. With Sir William Edward Parry searched for North Pole; discovered magnetic pole on Boothia Peninsula in 1831.

ROSS, Malcolm, literary arts. Fredericton, NB, 1911–2002. With Jack McClelland initiated the New Canadian Library paperback series under the McClelland & Stewart imprint, which enabled Canadians to have ready access to writers such as Frederick Philip Grove, Margaret Laurence and Morley Callaghan. Author of *Our Sense of Identity, the Arts in Canada; The Impossible Sum of Our Traditions.*

ROTHSTEIN, Aser, science. Vancouver, BC, 1918. Physiologist; introduced radioisotopes in biology.

ROULEAU, Joseph, performing arts. Matane, Que., 1929. Operatic bass; internationally famous singer.

ROUX, Jean-Louis, performing arts/politics. Montreal, Que., 1923. Actor, playwright with successful career was rejected as proposed lieutenant governor of Quebec in 1997 due to youthful support of Nazi regime during WWII; appointed head of Canada Council in 1998.

ROY, Gabrielle, literary arts. St Boniface, Man., 1909–83. Popular novelist. *The Tin Flute.*

ROY, Patrick, sports. Quebec City, Que., 1965. Hockey player with Montreal Canadiens, Colorado Avalanche; youngest ever to win Conn Smythe trophy; in 1989–92 considered to be one of best goalies in the world.

ROZEMA, Patricia, politics. Kingston, Ont., 1958. Filmmaker. *I've Heard the Mermaids Singing, White Room.*

RUBENSTEIN, Louis, sports. Montreal, Que., 1861–1931. Canadian figure skating champion 1883–89; in 1890 won unofficial world title in Russia; also cyclist, bowler.

RUBES, Jan, performing arts. Czech., 1920. Singer; actor; operatic bass; TV host; film actor.

RUBINEK, Saul, performing arts. Toronto, Ont., 1948. Versatile character player. *The Quarrel.*

RUBINSKY, Yuri, business. Lebanon, 1952–96. Founder of Banff Publishing Workshop; co-director of SoftQuad Inc.; software designer.

RULE, Jane Vance, literary arts. USA, 1931. Novelist, short story writer. *Desert of the Heart; After the Fire; Contract With the World.*

RUSSELL, Loris Shano, science. USA, 1904. Paleontologist; suggested dinosaurs might be warm-blooded.

RUTHERFORD, Ann, performing arts. Toronto, Ont., 1917. Actress who appeared as Andy Hardy's girlfriend, Polly Benedict, in 12 Hardy films. *Secret Life of Walter Mitty.*

RUTHERFORD, Ernest (Rutherford of Nelson), science. NZ, 1871–1937. Physicist; much of his seminal work done at McGill University.

RYAN, Claude, politics. Montreal, Que., 1925. Editor of *Le Devoir* 1965–78; supporter of Quiet Revolution in Quebec. In 1978 became leader of Quebec Liberal party, losing to René Lévesque in 1982.

RYAN, Pat, sports. Winnipeg, Man., 1955. Curler; skip of world championship team in 1989; Canadian championship 1988, 1989.

RYAN, Thomas F. (Tommy), business. Guelph, Ont., 1872–1961. Entrepreneur; invented five-pin bowling (1909).

RYBCZYNSKI, Witold, literary arts/visual arts. Scot., 1943. Architect; critic; writer. *Home; City Life; A Clearing in the Distance.*

RYERSON, Adolphus Egerton, politics. Norfolk County, UC, 1803–82. Leading figure in 19th century politics and education.

RYGA, George, literary arts. Deep Creek, Alta, 1932–87. Playwright, novelist. *Ecstasy of Rita Joe; Night Desk.*

S

SABIA, Laura Louise, public service. Pembroke, Ont., 1916–96. Headed Royal Commission on the Status of Women in 1960s; became president of National Action Committee on the Status of Women 1973.

SAFDIE, Moshe, visual arts. Israel, 1938. Architect; Habitat, National Gallery of Canada.

SAFER, Morley, media. Toronto, Ont., 1931. Broadcaster; co-host, *60 Minutes,* since 1971.

SAHL, Mort, performing arts. Montreal, Que., 1926. Comedian; delivered political satire in monologues.

SAINTE-MARIE, Buffy, performing arts. Craven, Sask., 1941. Native singer. "Soldier Blue."

SALABERRY, Charles Michel D'Irumberry de, military. Beauport, Que., 1778–1829. Soldier; repelled American force in Battle of Chateauguay (1813).

SALÉ, Jamie, sports. Calgary, Alta, 1977. With David Pelletier won gold medal in pairs figure skating at 2002 Salt Lake City Winter Olympics; the award was given after controversy over prior judging that placed Russian team at top with Salé and Pelletier first winning silver.

SALTZMAN, Harry, performing arts. Saint John, NB, 1915–94. Co-producer of James Bond films. *The Man With the Golden Gun; The Ipcress File.*

SALUTIN, Rick, literary arts. Toronto, Ont., 1942. Playwright, columnist; commentator. *Marginal Notes; Challenges to the Mainstream; Globe and Mail* columnist.

SARLOS, Andrew, business. Hungary, 1931–97. Financial trader with Toronto Stock Exchange. Realized $22-million profit from Hiram-Walker–Consumer's Gas merger.

SARRAZIN, Michael, performing arts. Quebec City, Que., 1940. Leading man. *They Shoot Horses, Don't They?.*

SAUL, John Ralston, literary arts. Ottawa, Ont., 1947. Novelist, essayist. *The Paradise Eater; Voltaire's Bastards: The Dictatorship of Reason in the West.*

SAUNDERS, Charles Edward (Sir), science. London, Ont., 1867–1937. Agriculturalist; introduced Marquis wheat to W Canada.

SAUVE, Jeanne Mathilde, politics. Prud'homme, Sask., 1922–93. Governor general, 1984–89.

SAVAGE, John, politics. Wales, 1932. Liberal premier of NS 1993–97; as a medical doctor he treated HIV patients in Africa, as well as running a free clinic for a disadvantaged community outside of Halifax.

SAWCHUK, Terrence Gordon, sports. Winnipeg, Man., 1929–70. Hockey goaltender; all-time shutouts leader (103).

SAWYER, Robert, literary arts. Ottawa, Ont., 1960. Science fiction writer, winner of US Nebula award, awards in Japan, France, Spain. *Flashforward; Factoring Humanity.*

SCHAEFER, Carl Fellman, visual arts. Hanover, Ont., 1903–95. Painter of rural Ontario landscapes, director of Ontario College of Art.

SCHAFER, Raymond Murray, performing arts. Sarnia, Ont., 1933. Composer of contemporary music, first recipient of Glenn Gould Award in 1987.

SCHALLY, Andrew Victor, science. Poland, 1926. Winner of 1977 Nobel Prize in medicine and physiology, for research into understanding peptide hormones in the brain.

SCHAWLOW, Arthur, science. USA, 1921–99. Canadian-educated scientist, winner of 1964 Nobel Prize with Charles Hand Townes, co-patented the laser.

SCHLESINGER, Joe, media. Austria, 1928. Journalist; long-time CBC foreign correspondent.

SCHMIRLER, Sandra Marie, sports. Biggar, Sask., 1963–2000. Skip of the gold-medal-winning curling team at the 1998 Winter Olympics in Nagano, Japan.

SCHNARRE, Monika, performing arts. Toronto, Ont., 1971. Won 1986 Face of the 1980s modeling award; acting career includes role on *The Bold and the Beautiful.*

SCHOLES, Myron, economics. Timmins, Ont., 1941. Stanford University-based co-winner (with Harvard academic Robert Merton) of Nobel Prize for economics, for developing a mathematical formula for estimating values in the worldwide market of derivatives, known as the Black-Scholes formula.

SCHREYER, Edward Richard, politics. Beausejour, Man., 1935. NDP premier of Man., 1969–77; governor general of Canada, 1979–84.

SCHULTZ, Albert, performing arts. Port Hope, Ont., 1963. Stage, film and TV actor, co-founder of Toronto's Soulpepper Theatre Co. Has performed at Ontario's Stratford Festival, Edmonton's Citadel Theatre, and appeared on CBC drama *Street Legal.*

SCHULTZ, Erik, performing arts. Hamilton, Ont., 1952–2002. An internationally renowned trumpeter, Schultz specialized in Baroque music and toured with organist Jan Overduin; with his father established the IBS label, which recorded music of new Canadian artists.

SCOTT, Barbara Ann, sports. Ottawa, Ont., 1928. Figure skater; women's world champion, 1947–48; Olympic gold medal, 1948.

SCOTT, Duncan Campbell, literary arts. Ottawa, Ont., 1862–1947. Poet. "New World Lyrics and Ballads."

SCOTT, Francis (Frank) Reginald, literary arts. Quebec City, Que., 1899–1985. Poet. *Collected Poems.*

SCOTT, Jack, performing arts. Windsor, Ont., 1936. Singer; 1950s rockabilly star. "My True Love."

SCRIMGER, Francis Alexander Caron, military. Montreal, Que., 1881–1937. Victoria Cross recipient, WWI, Second Battle of Ypres, 1915. Captain, 14th Battalion, Royal Montreal Regiment.

SCRIVEN, Joseph Medlicott, religion. Ire., 1919–86. Hymn writer; wrote "What a Friend We Have in Jesus."

SEAGRAM, Joseph Emm, business. Fishers Mills, Ont., 1841–1919. Founder of world's largest distillery for spirits and wine-making; active as race horse owner; PC MP in Waterloo, Ont.

SECORD, Laura, military. USA, 1775–1868. Heroine; warned British of American attack (1813).

SEGAL, Hugh, politics. Montreal, Que., 1950. Backroom PC advisor to Robert Stanfield, William Davis and Brian Mulroney.

SELKIRK, George, sports. Huntsville, Ont., 1899–1987. Baseball player; outfielder on several NY Yankee championship teams; replaced Babe Ruth in 1934.

SELKIRK, Thomas Douglas, fifth Earl of, exploration and discovery. Scot., 1771–1820. Colonizer; established Red River settlement in Manitoba.

SELYE, Hans, medicine. Austria, 1907–82. Endocrinologist; author; pioneer in stress research. *The Stress of Life.*

SENNETT, Mack (b. Mikail Sinnott), visual arts. Danville, Que., 1880–1960. Producer; silent comedy pioneer; Keystone Kops.

SERVICE, Robert William, literary arts. Eng., 1874–1958. Poet of the Yukon. "Songs of a Sourdough."

SETON, Ernest Thompson, literary arts. Eng., 1860–1946. Naturalist; writer. *Wild Animals I Have Known.*

SEYMOUR, Lynn (b. Lynn Springbett), performing arts. Wainwright, Alta, 1939. Celebrated ballet dancer who performed with Sadler's Wells and the Royal Ballet in London, Eng., and has appeared with the National Ballet of Canada.

SHADBOLT, John Leonard (Jack), visual arts. Eng., 1909–98. BC artist noted for nature and native Canadian influenced work.

SHANKLAND, Robert, military. Scot., 1887–1968. Victoria Cross recipient, WWI, Battle of Passchendaele, 1917. Lieutenant, 43rd Cameron Highlands Battalion.

SHANNON, Kathleen, performing arts. Vancouver, BC, 1935–98. Founder of National Film Board's Studio D in 1974, which provided female filmmakers an opportunity to create documentaries with a feminist perspective. *If You Love This Planet; Not a Love Story.*

SHARP, Mitchell, politics. Winnipeg, Man., 1911. From 1942 to 1978 Liberal Party luminary; personal adviser to Prime Minister Jean Chrétien.

SHARPE, Isadore Nathaniel, business. Toronto, Ont., 1931. Opened first Four Seasons Hotel in Toronto in 1961 on Jarvis Street, now a worldwide chain of luxury hotels.

SHATNER, William, performing arts. Montreal, Que., 1931. Actor; Capt. Kirk on TV/movies *Star Trek.*

SHATTO, Dick, sports. USA, 1936–2003. Star running back for the CFL, Shatto played with the Toronto Argonauts for 12 seasons; upon retirement he led the league with touchdowns, passes and offensive yardage; established 15 records during his career.

SHAVER, Helen, performing arts. St Thomas, Ont., 1951. Actress appeared in *The Amityville Horror; Bethune: the Making of a Hero.*

SHEARER, Douglas, performing arts. Westmount, Que., 1899–1971. Sound recording technician, 40 years with MGM; won 12 Academy Awards; brother of actress Norma Shearer. *The Great Caruso; The Big House.*

SHEARER, Norma, performing arts. Edmonton, Alta, 1900–83. Actress; Hollywood star. *Romeo and Juliet.*

SHEBIB, Donald, visual arts. Toronto, Ont., 1939. Acclaimed filmmaker: *Goin' Down the Road; Heartaches.*

SHIELDS, Carol, literary arts. USA, 1935–2003. Writer; won 1993 Booker and Pulitzer prizes for *The Stone Diaries.*

SHORE, Eddie, sports. Ft Qu'Appelle, Sask., 1902–85. Hockey player; Boston defenceman; four-time Hart Trophy winner.

SHORT, Martin, performing arts. Toronto, Ont., 1951. Comedian; TV/film star; *SCTV*'s Ed Grimley. *3 Amigos.*

SHULMAN, Morton (Dr), business/medicine. Toronto, Ont., 1925–2000. Investor; physician; author; stock promoter; introduced anti-Parkinson's disease drug into Canada.

SHUSTER, Frank, performing arts. Toronto, Ont., 1918–2002. Comedian; straighter half of Wayne & Shuster team.

SHUSTER, Joe, visual arts. Toronto, Ont., 1914–92. Cartoonist; co-creator of Superman.

SIBERRY, Jane, performing arts. Ottawa, Ont., 1955. Singer, songwriter, guitarist. Contemporary folk style. *Jane Siberry; No Borders Here.*

SIFTON, Clifford (Sir), politics. Arva, Canada W, 1861–1929. Promoted immigration to settle western Canada.

SIFTON, Ellis Welwood, military. Wallacetown, Ont., 1891–1917. Victoria Cross recipient, WWI, Vimy Ridge, 1917. Lance-sergeant, 18th Battalion.

SILVERHEELS, Harold Jay Smith, performing arts. Six Nations Reserve, Ont., 1919–80. Actor; played Tonto in *Lone Ranger.*

SIMARD, Réné, performing arts. Chicoutimi, Que., 1961. Quebec pop singer began as boy soprano turned international pop star. *The Réné Simard Show* on CBC.

SIMCOE, Elizabeth Posthuma, literary arts. Eng., 1766–1850. Wife of John Graves Simcoe, first governor of Upper Canada; her diary and watercolours of Upper Canada provide a unique picture of contemporary life in the colony.

SIMCOE, John Graves, politics. Eng., 1752–1806. Upper Canada's first lieutenant governor, 1792–96.

SIMPSON, Allan John, public service. Ottawa, Ont., 1939–98. Co-founder of Canadians with Disabilities and the Canadian Association of Independent Living Centres; created first Pan-Am Wheelchair Games and Canadian Wheelchair Sports Association. Lobbied to have disabled included in Charter of Rights and Freedoms.

SIMPSON, Sir George, business. Scot., 1787–1860. Financier; governor, Hudson's Bay Co., 1820–60.

SINCLAIR, Gordon Allan, media. Toronto, Ont., 1900–84. Journalist; feisty commentator; long-time *Front Page Challenge* panelist.

SITTLER, Darryl Glen, sports. St Jacob's, Ont., 1950. Hockey player; with Toronto Maple Leafs set NHL record 10 points in one game.

SKRESLET, Laurie Grant, exploration and discovery. Calgary, Alta, 1949. In 1982 became first Canadian to conquer Mount Everest with the Canadian Mount Everest Expedition.

SKVORECKY, Josef, literary arts. Czech., 1924. Writer; novelist; critic. *The Engineer of Human Souls.*

SLADE, Bernard (b. Bernard Slade Newbound), performing arts. St Catharines, Ont., 1930. Sitcom pilot writer for *The Flying Nun; The Partridge Family; Bridget Loves Bernie.* Wrote screenplay for *Same Time Next Year.*

SLOCUM, Joshua, literary arts. Wilmot Twp, NS, 1844–1909. Sailor; wrote classic *Sailing Alone Around the World.*

SMALLWOOD, Joseph Roberts (Joey), politics. Gambo, Nfld, 1900–92. Led Newfoundland into Confederation, 1949; premier 1949–72.

SMART, Elizabeth, literary arts. Ottawa, Ont., 1913–86. Novelist. *By Grand Central Station I Sat Down and Wept.*

SMELLIE, Elizabeth Lawrie, medicine. Port Arthur, Ont., 1884–1968. Nurse; builder, Victorian Order of Nurses.

SMITH, Alexis, performing arts. Penticton, BC, 1921–93. Film and television actress appeared in *Marcus Welby; Rhapsody in Blue; Of Human Bondage.*

SMITH, Byron, exploration and discovery. Winnipeg, Man., 1960. Leader of AGF Everest 2000 expedition; reached summit May 21, 2000, with team members Tim Rippel and Brad Wrobleski.

SMITH, Donald Graham, sports. Edmonton, Alta, 1958. Swimmer; six gold medals, 1978 Commonwealth Games.

SMITH, Ernest Alvia "Smokey," military. New Westminster, BC, 1914. First Canadian private to win the Victoria Cross; last living Canadian recipient, WWII, Italian front, 1944. Private, Seaforth Highlanders.

SMITH, Lois Irene, performing arts. Vancouver, BC, 1929. National Ballet's first prima ballerina.

SMITH, Michael, science. Eng., 1932–2000. Biochemist; 1993 Nobel Prize winner in chemistry.

SMITH, Michael, sports. Kenora, Ont., 1967. Decathlete; silver medal, 1991 world championships.

SMITH, Stephen Richard (Steve), performing arts. Toronto, Ont., 1945. Comedian who stars in *Red Green Show* also plays stand-up comedy.

SMITH, Wilfred Cantwell, literary arts. Toronto, Ont., 1916–2000. Founder of McGill University's Islamic Institute; co-founder of Harvard's Center for Study of World Religions. *Islam in Modern History.*

SMITS, Sonja, performing arts. Sudbury, Ont., 1958. Star of CBC series *Street Legal;* CBC's *The Diviners.* Appeared in stage production of *Nothing Sacred.*

SMYTHE, Constantine Falkland Cary (Conn), sports. Toronto, Ont., 1895–1980. Hockey executive; owner of Toronto Maple Leafs, 1930–61.

SNIDERMAN, Sam, business. Toronto, Ont., 1920. Retailer; established Sam the Record Man; 130 stores.

SNOW, Clarence Eugene "Hank," performing arts. Liverpool, NS, 1914–2000. Country music singer. "I'm Movin' On."

SNOW, Michael James Aleck, visual arts. Toronto, Ont., 1929. Painter; sculptor; filmmaker; photographer.

SOBEY, Frank, business. Lyons Brook, NS, 1902–85. Industrialist; turned family grocery business into a major industry.

SOMERS, Harry Stewart, performing arts. Toronto, Ont., 1925–99. Composer of opera, orchestral, vocal and ballet music, acclaimed for operas *Louis Riel* and *The Fool;* commissioned by Yehudi Menuhin to write *Music for Solo Violin.*

SOPINKA, John, law/sports. Broderick, Sask., 1933–97. Supreme Court justice; former CFL player.

SOUSTER, Raymond Holmes, literary arts. Toronto, Ont., 1921. Poet; editor. "The Colour of the Times."

SOUTHAM, William, media. Montreal, Que., 1843–1932. Publisher; founded Southam newspaper dynasty.

SPARLING, Gordon, performing arts. Toronto, Ont., 1900–94. Pioneer director, writer and producer of about 200 films; responsible for Canadian Cameo Series 1932–55, which brought Canada to international attention. Supervised newsreels during WW II, later worked with NFB.

SPICER, Keith, media. Toronto, Ont., 1934. Civil servant; chairman, Canadian Radio-Television and Telecommunications Commission.

SPOHR, Arnold, performing arts. Rhein, Sask., 1927. Ballet teacher; led Royal Winnipeg Ballet to world fame.

SPRY, Graham, media. St, Thomas, Ont., 1900–83. Journalist and political organizer who, with Alan Plaunt, co-founded the Canadian Radio League in 1930, which promoted public broadcasting. The organization was a precursor of the Canadian Broadcasting Corporation.

ST LAURENT, Louis Stephen, politics. Compton, Que., 1882–1973. Prime minister of Canada 1948–57; one of the architects of NATO.

STAEBLER, Edna, media. Kitchener, Ont., 1906. Journalist, cookbook writer, specializing in Mennonite cuisine. *Food That Really Schmecks; Whatever Happened to Maggie?*

STANFIELD, Robert Lorne, politics. Truro, NS, 1914. PC premier of NS, 1956–67; as federal PC leader, lost three elections to Trudeau.

STANLEY, George Frances Gillman, literary arts. Westmount, Que., 1907–2002. Historian; proposed basic design of Maple Leaf flag in 1965.

STAROWICZ, Marc, performing arts. Eng., 1946. Longtime CBC luminary; producer of radio and television documentaries and current affairs programming. *Witness; Life & Times; The Journal; As It Happens;* and *Canada: A People's History.*

STARYK, Steven, performing arts. Toronto, Ont., 1932. Violinist; virtuoso performer and teacher.

STEACIE, Edgar William Richard, science. Montreal, Que., 1900–62. Chemist; authority on free radical kinetics.

STEELE, Samuel Benfield (Sir), military. Purbrook, Canada W, 1849–1919. NWMP and WWI officer.

STEFANSSON, Vilhjalmur, exploration and discovery. Arnes, Man., 1879–1962. Controversial Arctic explorer. Wrote *My Life with the Eskimo; The Friendly Arctic.*

STEINBERG, David (b. Duddy Steinberg), performing arts. St Boniface, Man., 1942. Stand-up comic; talk show host.

STEINBERG, Samuel, business. Hungary, 1905–78. Retailer; turned family grocery into supermarket empire.

STEPHENSON, William Samuel (Sir), military. Winnipeg, Man., 1896–1989. Spy; "Intrepid," head of British counterespionage during WWII; invented wirephotos.

STERN, Bonnie Susan, business. Toronto, Ont., 1947. Food commentator and cookbook editor; founder of Bonnie Stern Cooking Schools; host of WTN TV show *Bonnie Stern Entertains.* Author of *Bonnie Stern Cooks; Simply Heart Smart Cooking.*

STEWART, Walter Douglas, literary arts. Toronto, Ont., 1931. Journalist, editor, social commentator; noted for acerbic wit. Author of *Shrug: Trudeau in Power; Towers of Gold, Feet of Clay;* and. *True Blue, a History of United Empire Loyalists.*

STOJKO, Elvis, sports. Newmarket, Ont., 1972. Figure skater; two-time Olympic silver medallist; three-time world champion.

STOWE, Emily Howard, medicine. Norwich, UC, 1831–1903. Physician; first Canadian woman to practice medicine; had to obtain degree in US.

STRACHAN, Gordon Muriel, military. Eng., 1885–1918. Victoria Cross recipient, WWI, Battle of Cambrai, 1917.

STRACHAN, John, religion. Scot., 1778–1867. Anglican bishop; strove to keep Upper Canada British.

STRATAS, Teresa (b. Anastasia Stratakis), performing arts. Toronto, Ont., 1938. Opera soprano; diva with strong stage presence.

STRATHCONA, Donald Alexander Smith (Sir), first Baron, politics. Scot., 1820–1914. Politician, businessman, diplomat; drove the Last Spike.

STRATTON, Dorothy (b. Dorothy Ruth Hoogstratten), performing arts. Vancouver, BC, 1960–80. Playboy model; murdered by estranged husband. Her story was told in film *Star 80,* starring Mariel Hemingway.

STREIT, Marlene Stewart, sports. Cereal, Alta, 1934. Golfer; won many international titles. Canadian Athlete of the Year, 1951, 1956.

STRONACH, Frank, business. Austria, 1954. Industrialist; chairman, Magna Intl; built machine company into global enterprise.

STRONG, Lori, sports. Toronto, Ont., 1972. Gymnast; winner of four gold medals at 1990 Commonwealth Games.

STRONG, Maurice Frederick, business. Oak Lake, Man., 1929. Headed Canadian International Development Agency; secretary-general of UN Conference in the Human Environment; head of Petro-Canada and Ontario Hydro; Canadian Ambassador to the UN.

SULLIVAN, Kevin Roderick, performing arts. Toronto, Ont., 1955. Producer; made *Anne of Green Gables;* launched popular *Road to Avonlea* TV series.

SUNG, Alfred (b. Sung Wang Moon), business. Toronto, Ont., 1948. Fashion designer; top designer of the 1980s.

SURIN, Bruny, sports. Haiti, 1967. Sprinter; world 100 m outdoor champion, 1993.

SUTHERLAND, Donald, performing arts. Saint John, NB, 1934. Versatile actor of Hollywood and Canadian films. *Murder by Decree; Don't Look Now.*

SUTHERLAND, Kiefer, performing arts. Eng., 1964. Actor. *Bay Boy; Flatliners; Stand By Me.*

SUZUKI, David Takayoshi, media/science. Vancouver, BC, 1936. Geneticist; promoter of environmental causes; columnist; host of CBC's *The Nature of Things.*

SWAN, Anna Haining, performing arts. Mill Brook, NS, 1846–88. Giantess, at 7 ft. 6 in., 352 lbs; was P.T. Barnum star.

SWAN, Susan, literary arts. Midland, Ont., 1945. Novelist. *Women of the World; The Last of the Golden Girls.*

SWINTON, George, performing arts. Austria, 1917–2002. Artist, art historian. Leading expert on Inuit art. *Sculpture of the Eskimo.*

SYDOR, Alison, sports. Vancouver, BC, 1966. Champion mountain biker; won 1996 Olympics silver award, threetime World MTB champion, 1994, 1995, 1996.

SZNAJDER, Andrew, sports. Toronto, Ont., 1968. Fourtime Canadian singles tennis champ.

TALBOT, Thomas, politics. Ire., 1771–1853. Personal secretary to Lieutenant Governor of Upper Canada John Graves Simcoe; fostered creation of Talbot Trail, the first transport artery to be built across southwestern Ontario.

TALON, Jean-Baptiste, politics. France, 1625–94. Governor; as intendant, sought to diversify economy of New France with minerals, timber, farming.

TANNER, Elaine, sports. Vancouver, BC, 1951. Canada's best woman swimmer by age 15; world records in individual medley and butterfly; won silver and bronze medals in 1968 Olympics.

TASCHEREAU, Louis-Alexandre, politics. Quebec City, Que., 1867–1952. Liberal premier of Quebec, 1920–36; anti-nationalist leader.

TAUBE, Henry, science. Neudorf, Sask., 1915. Nobel Prize winner in 1983 in chemistry for research into electron transfer reactions, especially in metal complexes.

TAYLOR, Edward Plunket (E.P.), business. Ottawa, Ont., 1901–89. Industrialist; founded Argus Corp; notable horseman.

TAYLOR, Fred "Cyclone," sports. Tara, Ont., 1883–1979. Hockey's first great star.

TAYLOR, Kenneth Douglas, politics. Calgary, Alta, 1934. Diplomat; engineering freedom for six US hostages in Iran made him an instant celebrity in 1980.

TAYLOR, Richard Edward, science. Medicine Hat, Alta, 1929. Physicist; nuclear accelerator pioneer; 1990 Nobel Prize in physics.

TAYLOR, Ronald, medicine/sports. Toronto, Ont., 1937. Major league relief pitcher (1962–72) and sports medicine pioneer.

TECUMSEH, military. USA, 1768–1813. Chief of Shawnee Indians, ally of Britain and Canada during the War of 1812.

TEMPLETON, Charles Bradley, media. Toronto, Ont., 1915–2001. Author, broadcaster, playwright, evangelist, journalist; wrote controversial *Act of God.*

TENNANT, Veronica, performing arts. Eng., 1947. Prima ballerina, National Ballet of Canada.

TEWKSBURY, Mark, sports. Calgary, Alta, 1968. Swimmer; gold medal, 100 m backstroke, 1992 Olympics.

THERIAULT, Yves, literary arts. Quebec City, Que., 1915–83. Novelist, dramatist. *Contes pour un homme seul; Agaguk.*

THICKE, Alan (b. Alan Jeffery), performing arts. Kirkland Lake, Ont., 1948. Actor and talk show host, host of TV game show *Pictionary,* formerly host of talk show *Thicke of the Night.*

THIRSK, Robert Brent (Bob), science. New Westminster, BC, 1953. In 1996 flew a 17-day journey on space shuttle Columbia, conducting experiments on space sickness and researching other areas.

THOM, Linda, sports. Hamilton, Ont., 1943. Shooter; gold medal, women's sports pistol, 1984 Olympics.

THOM, Ronald James, visual arts. Penticton, BC, 1923. Architect; Shaw Festival Theatre, Toronto Zoo.

THOMAS, Dave, performing arts. Toronto, Ont., 1953. Comedic actor noted for roles on *SCTV* portrayed with Rick Moranis; one of the McKenzie Brothers in *Strange Brew.*

THOMPSON, David, exploration and discovery. Eng., 1770–1857. Charted Columbia River.

THOMPSON, John Sparrow David (Sir), politics. Halifax, NS, 1845–94. Canada's fourth prime minister, 1892–94; largely responsible for establishment of the Criminal Code.

THOMPSON, Scott, performing arts. North Bay, Ont., 1959. Founding member of Kids in the Hall comedy troupe; has appeared in films *Millennium* and *Popcorn* and the TV series *The Larry Sanders Show.*

THOMSON, Andrew, science. Dobbington, Ont., 1893–1974. Co-founder of World Meteorological Organization; established weather-forecasting centres across Canada.

THOMSON, David Kenneth Roy, business. Toronto, Ont., 1923. Businessman; art collector; chairman, Thomson Newspapers Ltd.

THOMSON, Roy Herbert (R.H.), performing arts. Toronto, Ont., 1947. Stage and television actor. *Charlie Grant's War; Cry from the Heart; Ticket to Heaven.*

THOMSON, Roy (Lord Thomson of Fleet), media. Toronto, Ont., 1894–1976. Publisher; owned major newspapers in English-speaking world.

THOMSON, Thomas John (Tom), visual arts. Claremont, Ont., 1877–1917. Influential painter. *Autumn Foliage.*

THORBURN, Clifford Charles Devlin, sports. Victoria, BC, 1948. Snooker player; world champion, 1980.

TILLY, Jennifer, performing arts. USA, 1959. Actress, appeared in Woody Allen's *Bullets Over Broadway.*

TILLY, Margaret (Meg), performing arts. Texada Is., BC, 1960. Actress whose winsome face appeared in *The Body Snatchers; The Big Chill.*

TIMMINS, Noah Anthony, business. Mattawa, Ont., 1867–1936. Mining operator; developed N America's largest gold mine; town named for him.

TINTNER, Georg, performing arts. Vienna, 1917–99. Conductor of Nova Scotia Symphony Orchestra 1987–94; noted for recordings of Anton Bruckner.

TOBIN, Brian Vincent, politics. Stephenville, Nfld, 1954. Began "cod war" with Spain while serving as Liberal Minister of Fisheries and Oceans, 1995; premier of Nfld, 1996–2001.

TORGOV, Morley Edward, literary arts. Sault Ste Marie, Ont., 1927. Story writer. *The Abramsky Variations; The Outside Chance of Maximilian Glick.*

TORY, Henry Marshall, educator. Pt Shoreham, NS, 1864–1947. University founder: UBC, Carleton.

TOTH, Jerry (Jaroslav), performing arts. Windsor, Ont., 1929–99. Saxophonist, clarinetist, arranger, conductor and producer. Toth was responsible for the *Hockey Night in Canada* theme on CBC, as well as many other network productions: *Wayne and Shuster; Parade.* Member of Boss Brass ensemble for 20 years.

TOWN, Harold Barling, visual arts. Toronto, Ont., 1924–90. Influential painter, sculptor, writer.

TOWNSEND, Eleanor, performing arts. Goderich, Ont., 1944–98. Fiddling champion who was first woman to win North American Fiddle Championship at Shelburne, Ont.; member of both Canada's and US Fiddling Halls of Fame.

TRACY, Paul, sports. Scarborough, Ont., 1968. Auto racer; winner of three Indy titles in 1993.

TRAILL, Catharine Parr, literary arts. Eng., 1802–99. Writer. *The Backwoods of Canada.*

TRAVERS, Mary (La Bolduc), performing arts. Newport, Que., 1894–1941. Singer, songwriter, fiddler whose songs in colloquial French about common people's concerns were widely recorded and hugely popular.

TREBEK, Alex, performing arts. Sudbury, Ont., 1940. TV host of *Jeopardy* quiz show.

TREMBLAY, Gilles, performing arts. Arvida, Que., 1932. Composer of soundtrack for Quebec pavilion for Expo 67 (*Sonorisation du Pavillon du Québec*); composer for major Canadian orchestras. *Kékoba; Les Vépres de la Vierge.*

TREMBLAY, Jean-Claude, sports. Bagotville, Ont., 1939–94. Star defenceman for Montreal Canadiens in 1960s.

TREMBLAY, Michel, literary arts. Montreal, Que., 1942. Playwright; novelist. *Le Vrai Monde.*

TROIANO, Dominic, performing arts. Italy, 1946. Rock guitarist collaborated with the Mandalas, The Guess Who; wrote for CBC TV. *Night Heat; Diamonds.*

TROUT, Jennie Kidd, medicine. Scot., 1841–1921. First woman in Canada licensed to practice medicine; established Ontario Medical College for Women in Kingston, Ont.

TRUDEAU, Pierre Elliott, politics. Montreal, Que., 1919–2000. Prime minister of Canada 1968–79, 1980–84.

TRYGGVASON, Bjarni V., science. Iceland, 1945. Astronaut who flew aboard the *Discovery* in 1997 for 11 days to test Canadian-made equipment at zero gravity.

TSUI, Lap-Chee, medicine. China, 1950. Molecular geneticist who, in 1989, found gene that causes cystic fibrosis and developed the Cystic Fibrosis Transmembrane Regulator principle.

TUBMAN, Harriet Ross (b. Araminta Ross), public service. USA, 1820–1913. Former slave who was instrumental in freeing slaves via the Underground Railroad; escaped persecution in St. Catharines, Ont.

TULK, Robert Raymond, literary arts. Deer Lake, Nfld, 1938–2001. Author of humorous *Newfie Jokes* series; its eight editions were published between 1969 and 1991. Although some found the title derogatory, he was praised for their comedic insights into both island and mainlander foibles.

TULVING, Endel, medicine. Estonia, 1927. Cognitive psychologist who is world authority on human memory function.

TUPPER, Charles (Sir), politics. Amherst, NS, 1821–1915. Appointed as Canada's sixth prime minister, 1896.

TURCOTTE, Ron, sports. Drummond, NB, 1941. Jockey; long-time leading jockey rode Secretariat to Triple Crown (1973).

TURNBULL, Wallace, invention. Saint John, NB, 1870–1954. Inventor of variable pitch propeller in 1927, contributed to improved flying safety.

TURNER, John Napier, politics. Eng., 1929. Prime minister of Canada June 1984–July 1984.

TURNER, Richard Ernest William, military. Quebec City, Que., 1871–1961. Victoria Cross recipient, Boer War, 1900. Lieutenant, Royal Canadian Dragoons.

TUROFSKY, Riki, performing arts. Toronto, Ont., 1944. Debuted in 1972 at New York City Opera in *Carmen;* host of CBC's *Summer Festival* in 1978; *Festival Today* in 1984.

TWAIN, Shania (b. Eileen Regina Edwards), performing arts. Windsor, Ont., 1965. Winner of Country Music of the Year Award (US) 1995. *The Woman in Me.*

TYRRELL, Joseph Burr, science. Weston, Canada W, 1858–1957. Geologist; discovered S Alberta dinosaur beds.

TYSON, Ian Dawson, performing arts. Victoria, BC, 1933. Singer/songwriter; half of Ian and Sylvia. "Four Strong Winds."

TYSON, Sylvia Fricker, performing arts. Chatham, Ont., 1940. Singer; half of Ian and Sylvia. "You Were on My Mind."

UCHIDA, Irene Ayako, medicine. Vancouver, BC, 1917. Cytogeneticist who is world expert on Down Syndrome and other diseases caused by chromosomal abnormalities.

UNDERHILL, Barbara Ann, sports. Pembroke, Ont., 1963. Figure skater; world pairs champion (with Paul Martini), 1984.

UNDERHILL, Frank Hawkins, literary arts. Stouffville, Ont., 1889–1971. Historian and political critic who contributed often to the *Canadian Forum,* he was first president of the League for Social Reconstruction, and predicted Canada would weaken its ties to Britain while strengthening those with the USA.

UNGER, James, visual arts. Eng., 1937. Cartoonist; creator of popular "Herman" cartoon strip.

URQUHART, Jane, literary arts. Little Long Lac, Que., 1949. Novelist; short story writer. *Away; The Underpainter; The Whirlpool.*

UTECK, Lawrence (Larry), sports. Thornhill, Ont., 1952–2002. Star CFL defensive back who played with BC, Toronto, Ottawa and Montreal teams; later successfully coached St. Mary's Huskies in Halifax; served as deputy mayor of Halifax. Died of Lou Gehrig's disease.

VAILLANCOURT, Armand J.R., visual arts. Black L., Que., 1932. Sculpts in aid of social activism.

VALDY, (b. Vladimir Horsdal), performing arts. Ottawa, Ont., 1946. Country-folk singer-songwriter, guitarist. "Rock and Roll Song"; *Valdy; Notes from Places.*

VALLIERES, Pierre, politics. Montreal, Que., 1938–98. Journalist and former leader of Front de Libération de Québec (FLQ); author of *White Niggers of America,* which compared Québécois with American Blacks; fell out with FLQ after murder of labour minister Pierre Laporte.

VAN, Billy (b. Billy Van Evera), performing arts. Toronto, Ont., 1934–2003. Veteran comic actor, appeared on CBC television shows *Nightcap* and *The Hilarious House of Frightenstein;* TVO's *Bits and Bytes;* as well as American series *The Sonny & Cher Comedy Hour* and *The Bobby Vinton Show.*

VAN HERK, Aritha, literary arts. Wetaskiwin, Alta, 1954. Novelist. *Judith; No Fixed Address; Places Far from Ellesmere.*

VAN HORNE, William Cornelius (Sir), business. USA, 1843–1915. Driving force behind Canadian Pacific Railroad.

VAN VOGT, Alfred Elton (A.E.), literary arts. Winnipeg, Man., 1912. Writer; science fiction standout. *Slan.*

VANCOUVER, George, exploration and discovery. Eng., 1757–98. Navigator; surveyor of BC coastline.

VANDER ZALM, William Nick, politics. Holland, 1934. Social Credit premier of BC 1986–91, proponent of free trade.

VANDERBURG, Helen, sports. Calgary, Alta, 1959. Synchronized swimmer; dominated sport in 1979.

VANDERHAEGHE, Guy Clarence, literary arts. Esterhazy, Sask., 1951. Novelist, won 1982 Governor General's Award for *Man Descending. My Present Age; Homesick; The Englishman's Boy* (Governor General's Award).

VANIER, Georges Phileas, politics. Montreal, Que., 1888–1967. Governor general, 1959–67.

VANIER, Jean, public service. Switz., 1928. Spiritual leader; man of great moral conviction established homes for handicapped around the world.

VANNELLI, Gino, performing arts. Montreal, Que., 1954. Pop singer. *Brother to Brother; Nightwalker.*

VARLEY, Frederick Horsman (F.H.), visual arts. Eng., 1881–1969. Member, Group of Seven. *Vera.*

VEREGIN, Peter Vasilevich, religion. Russia, 1859–1924. Charismatic Doukhobor leader.

VERNON, John, performing arts. Montreal, Que., 1931. TV and film actor. *Wojeck.*

VEZINA, Georges, sports. Chicoutimi, Que., 1887–1926. Hockey goalie; NHL trophy named for him.

VICKERS, Jonathan Stewart (Jon), performing arts. Prince Albert, Sask., 1926. Tenor; operatic star; Wagner specialist.

VICKREY, William, economics. Victoria, BC, 1914–96. Winner of Nobel Prize in economics in 1996. Worked with United Nations on tax issues in African countries.

VIGNEAULT, Gilles, performing arts. Natashquan, Que., 1928. Beloved poet and cultural icon of Québécois. "Mon Pays."

VILLENEUVE, Gilles, sports. St-Jean, Que., 1950–82. Auto racer; won six Grand Prix titles.

VILLENEUVE, Jacques, sports. St-Jean, Que., 1971. Winner of Indianapolis 500 in 1995; Lou Marsh trophy for Canadian Athlete of the Year, 1995.

VINCENT, Anthony Gustave, public service. Eng., 1939. Canadian ambassador to Peru when, in December 1996, Tupac Amaru guerrillas stormed Japanese ambassador's residence in Lima, taking 575 hostages. Vincent attempted negotiations with leader Nestor Cerpa; the remaining hostages were freed when troops stormed residence in April 1997.

VOYER, Bernard, sports. Rimouski, Que., 1953. Mountain climber who has reached the tallest summit on every continent on earth, including Antarctica's Mount Vinson, Mount Everest and Mount Kilimanjaro.

WAGNER, Barbara Aileen, sports. Toronto, Ont., 1938. Figure skater; with Robert Paul, won four pairs titles and 1960 Olympic gold.

WALDO, Carolyn, sports. Montreal, Que., 1964. Synchronized swimmer; two gold medals, 1988 Olympics.

WALKER, Larry, sports. Maple Ridge, BC, 1966. Baseball player; star outfielder for Montreal Expos, Colorado Rockies. NL MVP, 1997. NL batting champion, 1998.

WALLIN, Pamela, media. Wadena, Sask., 1953. Longtime CBC journalist and independent news magazine host. In 2002 appointed Canadian consul general for New York City.

WALLS, Earl, sports. Puce, Ont., 1928–96. Canadian heavyweight boxing champion, 1952.

WALSH, Richard "Hock," Toronto, Ont., 1948–2000. performing arts. Co-founder in 1969 with brother Donnie of Downchild Blues Band; inspiration for Dan Aykroyd and John Belushi in movie *The Blues Brothers.*

WALTERS, Angus, exploration and discovery. Lunenburg, NS, 1882–1968. *Bluenose* captain; skipper of celebrated schooner.

WALTERS, Eric, literary arts. Toronto, Ont., 1957. Popular writer of young people's adventure books. *Tiger by the Tail; Trapped in Ice.*

WARD, Maxwell William, business. Edmonton, Alta, 1921. Capitalist; charter flights pioneer; founded Wardair.

WARNER, Jack L., performing arts. London, Ont., 1892–1978. Head of production at Warner Brothers in 1927; launched talkies with *The Jazz Singer,* starring Al Jolson.

WARREN, Earl (b. Earl Warren Segal), media. Regina, Sask., 1933–2002. Popular host of Toronto's CFRB radio program *House of Warren* from 1996–83, after a radio career in several Canadian cities. Also hosted *The Earl Warren Show.*

WASHINGTON, Jackie, performing arts. Hamilton, Ont., 1919. Jazz/blues musician and actor who originally sang with the Four Washington Brothers and has retained a thriving career with hit albums. *Midnight Choo Choo; Where Old Friends Meet.*

WATKINS, Melville Henry, business. Toronto, Ont., 1932. Economist; founded left-wing Waffle Movement.

WATSON, Harold Percival "Whipper," sports. Saskatoon, Sask., 1923–2002. Left winger hockey player who won four Stanley Cups with the Toronto Maple Leafs between 1947 and 1951 and with the Detroit Red Wings in 1943.

WATSON, Hilda Pauline, politics. Kuest, Sask., 1922–96. Leader of the Yukon Territorial Progressive Conservatives, 1978. First woman to lead a political party in Canada.

WATSON, Homer Ransford, visual arts. Doon, Canada W, 1855–1936. Landscape painter. *The Pioneer Mill.*

WATSON, John, literary arts. Scot., 1847–1939. Philosopher; metaphysician. "Kant and His English Critics."

WATSON, Ken, sports. Minnedosa, Man., 1904–86. Curler; three-time Brier winner; curling teacher.

WATSON, Patrick, media. Toronto, Ont., 1929. TV host; actor; writer; producer.

WATSON, Sheila Doherty, literary arts. New Westminster, BC, 1909–98. Author of *Double Hook,* considered to be the first modern Canadian novel; also *Deep Hollow Creek.* Described experiences as schoolteacher in central BC in the 1930s.

WATSON, William "Whipper Billy," sports. Toronto, Ont., 1917–1990. Wrestler; twice world pro champion.

WAXMAN, Albert Samuel (Al), performing arts. Toronto, Ont., 1935–2001. Movie and TV performer. *King of Kensington.*

WAYNE, John Louis (Johnny), performing arts. Toronto, Ont., 1918–90. Comedian; wilder half of Wayne and Shuster comedy team.

WEBSTER, Donald Colin "Ben," invention. Montreal, Que., 1928–97. Founder of high-tech Helix Investments (Canada), credited with introduction of the fastening material Velcro.

WEBSTER, John Edgar (Jack), media. Scot., 1918–99. Broadcaster; journalist on *Vancouver Sun.* Noted for outspoken opinions.

WEINZWEIG, John Jacob, performing arts. Toronto, Ont., 1913. Influential composer using 12-tone technique. "Red Ear of Corn."

WEIR, Michael Richard, sports. Sarnia, Ont., 1970. Winner of 2000 World Golf Championship and American Express Championship; 1999 PGA Air Canada Championship.

WEIR, Robert Stanley, literary arts. Hamilton, Ont., 1856–1926. Jurist; author; wrote English lyrics of national anthem, "O Canada."

WELLS, Clyde Kirby, politics. Buchans Junction, Nfld, 1937. Newfoundland premier 1989–96.

WELSH, Kenneth, politics. Edmonton, Alta, 1942. Versatile actor noted for roles in *Empire Inc.; And Then You Die; The Tar Sands.*

WESTON, Hilary M., politics. Ire., 1942. Appointed lieutenant governor of Ontario in 1997, wife of grocery magnate Galen Weston.

WESTON, W. Galen Gordon, business. Eng., 1940. Industrialist; Canadian head for George Weston Ltd.

WESTON, Willard Garfield, business. Toronto, Ont., 1893–1978. Industrialist; pioneer in food retailing.

WHEELER, Anne, visual arts. Edmonton, Alta, 1946. Filmmaker. *A Change of Heart; Bye Bye Blues.*

WHEELER, Lucille, sports. Montreal, Que., 1935. Skier; first N American to win world title, downhill and slalom (1958).

WHITE, Bob, business. Ire., 1935. Labour leader; first head of Canadian Auto Workers' Union.

WHITFIELD, Simon, sports. Victoria, BC, 1975. Gold medallist for triathlon in 2000 Sydney Olympics; 1998, 1999 Canadian champion.

WHITTON, Charlotte Elizabeth, politics. Renfrew, Ont., 1896–1975. Reformer; outspoken Ottawa mayor.

WIEBE, Rudy Henry, literary arts. Speedwell, Sask., 1934. Mennonite novelist. *Temptations of Big Bear.*

WILLAN, James Healey, performing arts. Eng., 1880–1968. Classical composer and musician. "O Lord, Our Governour" sung at Queen Elizabeth II's coronation in Westminster Abbey.

WILLIAMS, Daffyd (Dave) Rhys, science. Saskatoon, Sask., 1954. Astronaut, flew on 16-day Spacelab flight aboard Space Shuttle Columbia in 1998; coordinator of Canadian Astronaut Program Space Unit Life Simulation (CAPSULS) project.

WILLIAMS, Percy Alfred, sports. Vancouver, BC, 1908–82. Sprinter; Olympic gold in 100 m and 200 m, 1928.

WILSON, Bertha, law. Scot., 1923. First woman named to Supreme Court of Canada (1982).

WILSON, Cairine Reay, politics. Montreal, Que., 1885–1962. Canada's first woman senator, 1930 (Lib.).

WILSON, Daniel (Sir), educator. Scot., 1816–92. Darwinian opposed idea of natural selection; energetic administrator, author, scholar.

WILSON, Ethel Davis, literary arts. S Africa, 1888–1980. BC novelist. *Swamp Angel.*

WILSON, John Tuzo, science. Ottawa, Ont., 1908–93. Geophysicist; pioneered plate tectonics theory.

WILSON, Lois Miriam, religion. Winnipeg, Man., 1927. First woman president of Canadian Council of Churches, in 1976; first woman Moderator of United Church of Canada in 1980. Peace advocate and active in antipoverty initiatives.

WILSON, Michael Holcombe, politics. Toronto, Ont., 1937. PC minister of industry, science and technology; international trade; finance minister (1984–91).

WISEMAN, Adele, literary arts. Winnipeg, Man., 1928–92. Novelist, poet. *The Sacrifice; Crackpot.*

WISEMAN, Joseph, performing arts. Montreal, Que., 1918. Actor; title role in James Bond movie, *Dr. No.*

WOLFE, James, military. Eng., 1727–59. Soldier; took Quebec for British; died on Plains of Abraham.

WONG, Celia Jan, media. Montreal, Que., 1952. *Globe and Mail* correspondent in China, 1988–94. *Red China Blues.*

WOOD, Elizabeth Wyn, visual arts. Orillia, Ont., 1903–66. Sculptor; fountains and panels for Rainbow Bridge Gardens, monument to King George VI, Niagara Falls.

WOOD, Sharon Adele, exploration and discovery. Halifax, NS, 1957. First woman from the Western Hemisphere to successfully climb Mount Everest as a member of the Canadian Everest Light Expedition, in 1986.

WOODCOCK, George, literary arts. Winnipeg, Man., 1912–95. Historian; journalist; activist. *Anarchism.*

WOODSWORTH, James Shaver, politics. Etobicoke, Ont., 1874–1942. Founder Cooperative Commonwealth Federation (later NDP).

WRAY, Fay, performing arts. Medicine Hat, Alta, 1910. Famous as screaming heroine in *King Kong.*

WRIGHT, Eric Stanley, literary arts. Eng., 1929. Mystery writer. *A Senstive Case; Final Cut.*

WRIGHT, Michelle, performing arts. Merlin, Ont., 1960. Sultry country songstress. "Now and Then."

WRIGHT, Richard B., literary arts. Midland, Ont., 1937. Award-winning novelist whose works reflect the personal identity crises of dwellers in urban settings. *The Age of Longing; Clara Callan* (winner of the Giller Prize and Governor General's Award).

YANOFSKY, Abe (b. Daniel Abraham), sports. Poland, 1925–2000. First chess grandmaster in Commonwealth; child prodigy in 1939 Chess Olympics in Buenos Aires; active in Winnipeg city council.

YANOVSKY, Zal, performing arts. Toronto, Ont., 1944–2002. Singer; member of folk-rock group The Lovin' Spoonful.

YOST, Elwy, performing arts. Toronto, Ont., 1925. Affable and knowledgeable host of TVOntario's popular *Saturday Night at the Movies.*

YOUNG, Neil Percival, performing arts. Toronto, Ont., 1945. Singer/songwriter; seminal rocker. *After the Gold Rush.*

YOUNG, Scott Alexander, literary arts. Glenboro, Man., 1918. Novelist, short story writer, children's writer, biographer. *The Boys of Saturday Night; Power Play.*

YOUVILLE, Marie Marguerite d', religion. Varennes, Que., 1701–71. First Canadian to be beatified by Pope; founded Grey Nuns.

ZEIDLER, Eberhard Heinrich, visual arts. Germany, 1936. Award-winning architect of Toronto Eaton Centre, Toronto's Queen's Quay Terminal, Ontario Place.

ZERAFA, Boris, visual arts. Egypt, 1933–2002. Architect who designed both Canadian and global landmarks, including Toronto's Lothian Mews, Royal Bank Plaza and Hazelton Lanes; Montreal's Bank of Paris; Calgary's Bow Valley Square; and King Abdul Aziz University in Saudi Arabia.

ZNAIMER, Moses, business. Toronto, Ont., 1942. TV executive; founder of CITY-TV, Much Music.

ZOLF, Larry, media. Winnipeg, Man., 1934. Broadcaster; journalist; writer. CBC's *Fifth Estate.*

ZUCKERMAN, Mortimer, business. Montreal, Que., 1937. Financier; developer, magazine publisher.

BASEBALL

American League Final Standings, 2003

Eastern Division

TEAM	W	L	PCT	GB
Y-New York	101	61	.623	-
X-Boston	95	67	.586	6.0
Toronto	**86**	**76**	**.531**	**15.0**
Baltimore	71	91	.438	30.0
Tampa Bay	63	99	.389	38.0

Central Division

TEAM	W	L	PCT	GB
Y-Minnesota	90	72	.556	-
Chicago	86	76	.531	4.0
Kansas City	83	79	.512	7.0
Cleveland	68	94	.420	22.0
Detroit	43	119	.265	47.0

Western Division

TEAM	W	L	PCT	GB
Y-Oakland	96	66	.593	-
Seattle	93	69	.574	3.0
Anaheim	77	85	.475	19.0
Texas	71	91	.438	25.0

Source: *Major League Baseball*

X — Wild Card   Y — Division Title.

American League Leaders, 2003

Batting

Batting Average

B. Mueller, Bos	.326
M. Ramirez, Bos	.325
D. Jeter, NY	.324
M. Ordonez, CWS	.317
V. Wells, Tor	**.317**
G. Anderson, Ana	.315
A. Pierzynski, Min	.312
I. Suzuki, Sea	.312
A. Huff, TB	.311
C. Beltran, KC	.307
S. Stewart, Min	.307

On-Base Percentage

M. Ramirez, Bos	.427
C. Delgado, Tor	**.426**
J. Giambi, NYY	.412
E. Martinez, Sea	.406
J. Posada, NYY	.405
B. Mueller, Bos	.398
T. Nixon, Bos	.396
A. Rodriguez, Tex	.396
D. Jeter, NY	.393
C. Koskie, Min.	**.393**
D. Mientkiewicz, Min	.393

Runs

A. Rodriguez, Tex	124
N. Garciaparra, Bos	120
V. Wells, Tor	**118**
C. Delgado, Tor	**117**
M. Ramirez, Bos	117
A. Soriano, NYY	114
B. Boone, Sea	111
I. Suzuki, Sea	111
M. Young, Tex	106
J. Damon, Bos	103
R. Winn, Sea	103

Hits

V. Wells, Tor	**215**
I. Suzuki, Sea	212
M. Young, Tex	204
G. Anderson, Ana	201
N. Garciaparra, Bos	198
A. Huff, TB	198
A. Soriano, NYY	198
M. Ordonez, CWS	192
M. Ramirez, Bos	185
R. Baldelli, TB	184

Runs Batted In

C. Delgado, Tor	**145**
A. Rodriguez, Tex	118
B. Boone, Sea	117
V. Wells, Tor	**117**
G. Anderson, Ana	116
C. Lee, CWS	113
R. Palmeiro, Tex	112
J. Giambi, NYY	107
A. Huff, TB	107
H. Matsui, NYY	106
M. Tejada, Oak	106

Doubles

G. Anderson, Ana	49
V. Wells, Tor	**47**
A. Huff, TB	47
M. Ordonez, CWS	46
E. Hinske, Tor	**45**
B. Mueller, Bos	45
S. Stewart, Min	44
H. Matsui, NYY	42
M. Tejada, Oak	42
3 players tied with	39

Triples

C. Guzman, Min	14
N. Garciaparra, Bos	13
C. Beltran, KC	10
E. Byrnes, Oak	9
C. Crawford, TB	9
L. Rivas, Min	9
M. Young, Tex	9
R. Baldelli, TB	8
I. Suzuki, Sea	8
3 players tied with	7

Home Runs

A. Rodriguez, Tex	47
C. Delgado, Tor	**42**
F. Thomas, CWS	42
J. Giambi, NYY	41
R. Palmeiro, Tex	38
A. Soriano, NYY	38
M. Ramirez, Bos	37
B. Boone, Sea	35
A. Huff, TB	34
V. Wells, Tor	**33**

Slugging Percentage

A. Rodriguez, Tex	.600
C. Delgado, Tor	**.593**
D. Ortiz, Bos	.592
M. Ramirez, Bos	.587
T. Nixon, Bos	.578
F. Thomas, CWS	.562
A. Huff, TB	.555
V. Wells, Tor	**.550**
M. Ordonez, CWS	.546
G. Anderson, Ana	.541

Stolen Bases

C. Crawford, TB	55
A. Sanchez, Det	44
C. Beltran, KC	41
A. Soriano, NYY	35
I. Suzuki, Sea	34
J. Damon, Bos	30
R. Baldelli, TB	27
B. Roberts, Bal	23
R. Winn, Sea	23
A. Kennedy, Ana	22

Walks

J. Giambi, NYY	129
C. Delgado, Tor	**109**
E. Durazo, Oak	100
F. Thomas, CWS	100
M. Ramirez, Bos	97
J. Posada, NYY	93
E. Martinez, Sea	92
A. Rodriguez, Tex	87
J. Olerud, Sea	84
R. Palmeiro, Tex	84

Total Bases

V. Wells, Tor	**373**
A. Rodriguez, Tex	364
A. Soriano, NYY	358
A. Huff, TB	353
G. Anderson, Ana	345
N. Garciaparra, Bos	345
C. Delgado, Tor	**338**
M. Ramirez, Bos	334
B. Boone, Sea	333
M. Ordonez, CWS	331

Pitching

Wins – Losses		Winning Percentage		Earned Run Average	
R. Halladay, Tor	22-7	J. Santana, Min	.800	P. Martinez, Bos	2.22
J. Moyer, Sea	21-7	P. Martinez, Bos	.778	T. Hudson, Oak	2.70
A. Pettitte, NYY	21-8	R. Halladay, Tor	.759	E. Loaiza, CWS	2.90
E. Loaiza, CWS	21-9	J. Moyer, Sea	.750	M. Mulder, Oak	3.13
D. Lowe, Bos	17-7	A. Pettitte, NYY	.724	R. Halladay, Tor	3.25
M. Mussina, NYY	17-8	D. Lowe, Bos	.708	J. Moyer, Sea	3.27
R. Clemens, NYY	17-9	E. Loaiza, CWS	.700	B. Zito, Oak	3.30
T. Hudson, Oak	16-7	S. Ponson, Bal	.700	M. Mussina, NYY	3.40
J. Pineiro, Sea	16-11	T. Hudson, Oak	.696	R. Franklin, Sea	3.57
R. Ortiz, Ana	16-13	D. Wells, NYY	.682	C. Sabathia, Cle	3.60

Strikeouts		Saves		Shutouts	
E. Loaiza, CWS	207	K. Foulke, Oak	43	R. Halladay, Tor	2
P. Martinez, Bos	206	E. Guardado, Min	41	T. Hudson, Oak	2
R. Halladay, Tor	204	M. Rivera, NYY	40	J. Lackey, Ana	2
M. Mussina, NYY	195	J. Julio, Bal	36	M. Mulder, Oak	2
R. Clemens, NYY	190	T. Percival, Ana	33	J. Pineiro, Sea	2
A. Pettitte, NYY	180	M. MacDougal, KC	27	20 players tied with	1
B. Colon, CWS	173	L. Carter, TB	26		
J. Santana, Min	169	U. Urbina, Tex	26		
T. Wakefield, Bos	169	D. Baez, Cle	25		
T. Hudson, Oak	162	S. Hasegawa, Sea	16		
		B. Kim, Bos	16		

Innings Pitched		Pitched Games		Complete Games	
R. Halladay, Tor	266.0	T. Miller, Tor	79	B. Colon, CWS	9
B. Colon, CWS	242.0	J. Walker, Det	78	R. Halladay, Tor	9
T. Hudson, Oak	241.0	J. Grimsley, KC	76	M. Mulder, Oak	9
B. Zito, Oak	231.2	B. Ryan, Bal	76	S. Ponson, Bal	4
M. Buehrle, CWS	230.1	L. Hawkins, Min	74	D. Wells, NYY	4
E. Loaiza, CWS	226.1	D. Baez, Cle	73	B. Zito, Oak	4
J. Thomson, Tex	217.0	F. Cordero, Tex	73	6 players tied with	3
J. Moyer, Sea	215.0	J. Romero, Min	73		
M. Mussina, NYY	214.2	4 players tied with	72		
D. Wells, NYY	213.0				

Source: *Major League Baseball*

National League Final Standings, 2003

Eastern Division	W	L	PCT	GB
Y-Atlanta	101	61	.623	-
X-Florida	91	71	.562	10.0
Philadelphia	86	76	.531	15.0
Montreal	**83**	**79**	**.512**	**18.0**
New York	66	95	.410	34.5

Central Division	W	L	PCT	GB
Y-Chicago	88	74	.543	-
Houston	87	75	.537	1.0
St. Louis	85	77	.525	3.0
Pittsburgh	75	87	.463	13.0
Cincinnati	69	93	.426	19.0
Milwaukee	68	94	.420	20.0

Western Division	W	L	PCT	GB
Y-San Francisco	100	61	.621	-
Los Angeles	85	77	.525	15.5
Arizona	84	78	.519	16.5
Colorado	74	88	.457	26.5
San Diego	64	98	.395	36.5

Source: *Major League Baseball*   X — Wild Card Y — Division Title.

National League Leaders, 2003

Batting

Batting Average		On-Base Percentage		Runs	
A. Pujols, StL	.359	B. Bonds, SF	.529	A. Pujols, StL	137
T. Helton, Col	.358	T. Helton, Col	.458	T. Helton, Col	135
B. Bonds, SF	.341	A. Pujols, StL	.439	R. Furcal, Atl	130
E. Renteria, StL	.330	B. Giles, Pit	.427	G. Sheffield, Atl	126
G. Sheffield, Atl	.330	L. Walker, Col	.422	B. Bonds, SF	111
J. Kendall, Pit	.325	G. Sheffield, Atl	.419	J. Thome, Phi	111
M. Giles, Atl	.316	L. Berkman, Hou	.412	L. Berkman, Hou	110
L. Castillo, Fla	.314	B. Abreu, Phi	.409	J. Bagwell, Hou	109
M. Grudzielanek, CHC	.314	L. Gonzalez, Ari	.402	C. Jones, Atl	103
M. Loretta, SD	.314	C. Jones, Atl	.402	C. Biggio, Hou	102
S. Podsednik, Mil	.314				

Hits

A. Pujols, StL	212
T. Helton, Col	209
J. Pierre, Fla	204
R. Furcal, Atl	194
E. Renteria, StL	194
J. Kendall, Pit	191
G. Sheffield, Atl	190
L. Castillo, Fla	187
O. Cabrera, Mon	**186**
M. Loretta, SD	185

Runs Batted In

P. Wilson, Col	141
G. Sheffield, Atl	132
J. Thome, Phi	131
A. Pujols, StL	124
R. Sexson, Mil	124
T. Helton, Col	117
A. Jones, Atl	116
J. Lopez, Atl	109
C. Jones, Atl	106
A. Ramirez, CHC	106

Doubles

A. Pujols, StL	51
M. Giles, Atl	49
S. Green, LA	49
T. Helton, Col	49
S. Rolen, StL	49
O. Cabrera, Mon	**47**
E. Renteria, StL	47
L. Gonzalez, Ari	46
C. Biggio, Hou	44
R. Hidalgo, Hou	43
P. Wilson, Col	43

Triples

S. Finley, Ari	10
R. Furcal, Atl	10
K. Lofton, CHC	8
S. Podsednik, Mil	8
A. Nunez, Pit	7
C. Patterson, CHC	7
J. Pierre, Fla	7
L. Walker, Col	**7**
10 players tied with	6

Home Runs

J. Thome, Phi	47
B. Bonds, SF	45
R. Sexson, Mil	45
J. Lopez, Atl	43
A. Pujols, StL	43
S. Sosa, CHC	40
J. Bagwell, Hou	39
J. Edmonds, StL	39
G. Sheffield, Atl	39
A. Jones, Atl	36
P. Wilson, Col	36

Slugging Percentage

B. Bonds, SF	.749
A. Pujols, StL	.667
T. Helton, Col	.630
J. Edmonds, StL	.617
G. Sheffield, Atl	.604
J. Thome, Phi	.573
R. Hidalgo, Hou	.572
S. Sosa, CHC	.553
R. Sexson, Mil	.548
G. Jenkins, Mil	.538

Stolen Bases

J. Pierre, Fla	65
S. Podsednik, Mil	43
D. Roberts, LA	40
E. Renteria, StL	34
K. Lofton, CHC	30
E. Young, SF	28
R. Furcal, Atl	25
O. Cabrera, Mon	**24**
B. Abreu, Phi	22
L. Castillo, Fla	21
D. Lee, Fla	21

Walks

B. Bonds, SF	148
T. Helton, Col	111
J. Thome, Phi	111
B. Abreu, Phi	109
L. Berkman, Hou	107
B. Giles, Pit	105
J. Cruz, SF	102
R. Sexson, Mil	98
L. Walker, Col	**98**
L. Gonzalez, Ari	94
C. Jones, Atl	94

Total Bases

A. Pujols, StL	394
T. Helton, Col	367
G. Sheffield, Atl	348
R. Sexson, Mil	332
J. Thome, Phi	331
P. Wilson, Col	322
J. Bagwell, Hou	317
J. Lopez, Atl	314
L. Gonzalez, Ari	308
J. Payton, Col	307

Pitching

Wins – Losses

R. Ortiz, Atl	21-7
M. Prior, CHC	18-6
W. Williams, StL	18-9
J. Schmidt, SF	17-5
S. Trachsel, NYM	16-10
R. Wolf, Phi	16-10
G. Maddux, Atl	16-11
H. Nomo, LA	16-13
A. Leiter, NYM	15-9
J. Robertson, Hou	15-9
L. Hernandez, Mon	**15-10**

Winning Percentage

J. Schmidt, SF	.773
J. Nathan, SF	.750
R. Ortiz, Atl	.750
M. Prior, CHC	.750
H. Ramirez, Atl	.750
D. Willis, Fla	.700
R. Oswalt, Hou	.667
K. Rueter, SF	.667
W. Williams, StL	.667
M. Hampton, Atl	.636

Earned Run Average

J. Schmidt, SF	2.34
K. Brown, LA	2.39
M. Prior, CHC	2.43
B. Webb, Ari	2.84
C. Schilling, Ari	2.95
H. Nomo, LA	3.09
C. Zambrano, CHC	3.11
L. Hernandez, Mon	**3.20**
K. Wood, CHC	3.20
J. Vazquez, Mon	**3.24**

Strikeouts

K. Wood, CHC	266
M. Prior, CHC	245
J. Vazquez, Mon	**241**
J. Schmidt, SF	208
C. Schilling, Ari	194
K. Brown, LA	185
L. Hernandez, Mon	**178**
H. Nomo, LA	177
R. Wolf, Phi	177
B. Webb, Ari	172

Saves

E. Gagne, LA	**55**
J. Smoltz, Atl	45
B. Wagner, Hou	44
T. Worrell, SF	38
R. Biddle, Mon	**34**
J. Borowski, CHC	33
M. Mantei, Ari	29
B. Looper, Fla	28
M. Williams, Phi	28
J. Mesa, Phi	24

Shutouts

K. Millwood, Phi	3
M. Morris, StL	3
J. Schmidt, SF	3
H. Nomo, LA	2
C. Schilling, Ari	2
J. Suppan, Pit	2
S. Trachsel, NYM	2
D. Willis, Fla	2
R. Wolf, Phi	2
K. Wood, CHC	2

Innings Pitched

L. Hernandez, Mon	**233.1**
J. Vazquez, Mon	**230.2**
K. Millwood, Phi	222.0
B. Sheets, Mil	220.2
W. Williams, StL	220.2
G. Maddux, Atl	218.1
H. Nomo, LA	218.1
C. Zambrano, CHC	214.0
R. Ortiz, Atl	212.1
M. Prior, CHC	211.1

Pitched Games

P. Quantrill, LA	89
O. Villarreal, Ari	86
R. King, Atl	80
T. Martin, LA	80
S. Kline, StL	78
B. Lidge, Hou	78
J. Nathan, SF	78
B. Wagner, Hou	78
4 players tied with	77

Complete Games

L. Hernandez, Mon	**8**
K. Millwood, Phi	5
M. Morris, StL	5
J. Schmidt, SF	5
J. Vazquez, Mon	**4**
K. Wood, CHC	4
M. Prior, CHC	3
M. Redman, Fla	3
C. Schilling, Ari	3
J. Suppan, Pit	3
C. Zambrano, CHC	3

Source: *Major League Baseball*

Major League Pennant Winners, 1961–2003

	National League					American League			
	Winner	**Won**	**Lost**	**%**		**Winner**	**Won**	**Lost**	**%**
1961	Cincinnati	93	61	.604	**1961**	New York	109	53	.673
1962	San Francisco	103	62	.624	**1962**	New York	96	66	.593
1963	Los Angeles	99	63	.611	**1963**	New York	104	57	.646
1964	St. Louis	93	69	.574	**1964**	New York	99	63	.611
1965	Los Angeles	97	65	.599	**1965**	Minnesota	102	60	.630
1966	Los Angeles	95	67	.586	**1966**	Baltimore	97	63	.606
1967	St. Louis	101	60	.627	**1967**	Boston	92	70	.568
1968	St. Louis	97	65	.599	**1968**	Detroit	103	59	.636
1969	New York	100	62	.617	**1969**	Baltimore	109	53	.673
1970	Cincinnati	102	60	.630	**1970**	Baltimore	108	54	.667
1971	Pittsburgh	97	65	.599	**1971**	Baltimore	101	57	.639
1972	Cincinnati	95	59	.617	**1972**	Oakland	93	62	.600
1973	New York	82	79	.509	**1973**	Oakland	94	68	.580
1974	Los Angeles	102	60	.630	**1974**	Oakland	90	72	.556
1975	Cincinnati	108	54	.667	**1975**	Boston	95	65	.594
1976	Cincinnati	102	60	.630	**1976**	New York	97	62	.610
1977	Los Angeles	98	64	.605	**1977**	New York	100	62	.617
1978	Los Angeles	95	67	.586	**1978**	New York	100	63	.613
1979	Pittsburgh	98	64	.605	**1979**	Baltimore	102	57	.642
1980	Philadelphia	91	71	.562	**1980**	Kansas City	97	65	.599
1981	Los Angeles	63	47	.573	**1981**	New York	59	48	.551
1982	St. Louis	92	70	.568	**1982**	Milwaukee	95	67	.586
1983	Philadelphia	90	72	.556	**1983**	Baltimore	98	64	.605
1984	San Diego	92	70	.568	**1984**	Detroit	104	58	.642
1985	St. Louis	101	61	.623	**1985**	Kansas City	91	71	.562
1986	New York	108	54	.667	**1986**	Boston	95	66	.590
1987	St. Louis	95	67	.586	**1987**	Minnesota	85	77	.525
1988	Los Angeles	94	67	.584	**1988**	Oakland	104	58	.642
1989	San Francisco	92	70	.568	**1989**	Oakland	99	63	.611
1990	Cincinnati	91	71	.562	**1990**	Oakland	103	59	.636
1991	Atlanta	94	68	.580	**1991**	Minnesota	95	67	.586
1992	Atlanta	98	64	.605	**1992**	**Toronto**	**96**	**66**	**.593**
1993	Philadelphia	97	65	.599	**1993**	**Toronto**	**95**	**67**	**.586**
1994[1]	no winner				**1994**[1]	no winner			
1995	Atlanta	90	54	.625	**1995**	Cleveland	100	44	.694
1996	Atlanta	96	66	.593	**1996**	New York	92	70	.569
1997	Florida	92	70	.568	**1997**	Cleveland	86	75	.534
1998	San Diego	98	64	.605	**1998**	New York	114	48	.704
1999	Atlanta	103	59	.639	**1999**	New York	98	64	.605
2000	New York	94	68	.580	**2000**	New York	87	74	.540
2001	Arizona	92	70	.568	**2001**	New York	95	65	.594
2002	San Francisco	95	66	.590	**2002**	Anaheim	99	63	.611
2003	Florida	91	71	.562	**2003**	New York	101	61	.623

Source: *Canadian Press*   (1) Players strike Aug. 12, 1994; owners suspended season, Sept. 14, 1994.

World Series Results, 1963–2003

	Champion	Final Opponent	Series Result
1963	Los Angeles Dodgers, NL	New York Yankees, AL	4–0
1964	St. Louis Cardinals, NL	New York Yankees, AL	4–3
1965	Los Angeles Dodgers, NL	Minnesota Twins, AL	4–3
1966	Baltimore Orioles, AL	Los Angeles Dodgers, NL	4–0
1967	St. Louis Cardinals, NL	Boston Red Sox, AL	4–3
1968	Detroit Tigers, AL	St. Louis Cardinals, NL	4–3
1969	New York Mets, NL	Baltimore Orioles, AL	4–1
1970	Baltimore Orioles, AL	Cincinnati Reds, NL	4–1
1971	Pittsburgh Pirates, NL	Baltimore Orioles, AL	4–3
1972	Oakland Athletics, AL	Cincinnati Reds, NL	4–3
1973	Oakland Athletics, AL	New York Mets, NL	4–3
1974	Oakland Athletics, AL	Los Angeles Dodgers, NL	4–1
1975	Cincinnati Reds, NL	Boston Red Sox, AL	4–3
1976	Cincinnati Reds, NL	New York Yankees, AL	4–0
1977	New York Yankees, AL	Los Angeles Dodgers, NL	4–2
1978	New York Yankees, AL	Los Angeles Dodgers, NL	4–2
1979	Pittsburgh Pirates, NL	Baltimore Orioles, AL	4–3
1980	Philadelphia Phillies, NL	Kansas City Royals, AL	4–2
1981	Los Angeles Dodgers, NL	New York Yankees, AL	4–2
1982	St. Louis Cardinals, NL	Milwaukee Brewers, AL	4–3
1983	Baltimore Orioles, AL	Philadelphia Phillies, NL	4–1
1984	Detroit Tigers, AL	San Diego Padres, NL	4–1
1985	Kansas City Royals, AL	St. Louis Cardinals, NL	4–3
1986	New York Mets, NL	Boston Red Sox, AL	4–3
1987	Minnesota Twins, AL	St. Louis Cardinals, NL	4–3
1988	Los Angeles Dodgers, NL	Oakland Athletics, AL	4–1
1989	Oakland Athletics, AL	San Francisco Giants, NL	4–0
1990	Cincinnati Reds, NL	Oakland Athletics, AL	4–0
1991	Minnesota Twins, AL	Atlanta Braves, NL	4–3
1992	**Toronto Blue Jays, AL**	Atlanta Braves, NL	4–2
1993	**Toronto Blue Jays, AL**	Philadelphia Phillies, NL	4–2
1994	No World Series: season suspended Sept. 15, 1994		
1995	Atlanta Braves, NL	Cleveland Indians, AL	4–2
1996	New York Yankees, AL	Atlanta Braves, NL	4–2
1997	Florida Marlins, NL	Cleveland Indians, AL	4–3
1998	New York Yankees, AL	San Diego Padres, NL	4–0
1999	New York Yankees, AL	Atlanta Braves, NL	4–0
2000	New York Yankees, AL	New York Mets, NL	4–1
2001	Arizona Diamondbacks, NL	New York Yankees, AL	4–3
2002	Anaheim Angels, AL	San Francisco Giants, NL	4–3
2003	Florida Marlins, NL	New York Yankees, AL	4–2

Source: *Canadian Press*

World Series MVPs, 1973–2003

1973	Reggie Jackson, Oak	1982	Darrell Porter, StL	1993	**Paul Molitor, Tor**
1974	Rollie Fingers, Oak	1983	Rick Dempsey, Bal	1994	No award
1975	Pete Rose, Cin	1984	Alan Trammell, Det	1995	Tom Glavine, Atl
1976	Johnny Bench, Cin	1985	Bret Saberhagen, KC	1996	John Wetteland, NY
1977	Reggie Jackson, NY (AL)	1986	Ray Knight, NY (NL)	1997	Livan Hernandez, Fla
1978	Bucky Dent, NY (AL)	1987	Frank Viola, Min	1998	Scott Brosius, NY
1979	Willie Stargell, Pgh	1988	Orel Hershiser, LA	1999	Mariano Rivera, NY
1980	Mike Schmidt, Pha	1989	Dave Stewart, Oak	2000	Mariano Rivera, NY
1981	Ron Cey, LA[1]	1990	Jose Rijo, Cin	2001	Curt Schilling/Randy Johnson, AR[1]
1981	Pedro Guerrero, LA[1]	1991	Jack Morris, Min	2002	Troy Glaus, Ana
1981	Steve Yeager, LA[1]	1992	**Pat Borders, Tor**	2003	Josh Beckett, Fla

Source: *Canadian Press*

(1) Joint winners.

Cy Young Award Winners, 1964–2003

	Player, Club		Player, Club
1964[1]	Dean Chance, California Angels	1985 (NL)	Dwight Gooden, New York Mets
1965[1]	Sandy Koufax, Los Angeles Dodgers	(AL)	Bret Saberhagen, Kansas City Royals
1966[1]	Sandy Koufax, Los Angeles Dodgers	1986 (NL)	Mike Scott, Houston Astros
1967 (NL)	Mike McCormick, San Francisco Giants	(AL)	Roger Clemens, Boston Red Sox
(AL)	Jim Lonborg, Boston Red Sox	1987 (NL)	Steve Bedrosian, Philadelphia Phillies
1968 (NL)	Bob Gibson, St. Louis Cardinals	(AL)	Roger Clemens, Boston Red Sox
(AL)	Dennis McLain, Detroit Tigers	1988 (NL)	Orel Hershiser, Los Angeles Dodgers
1969 (NL)	Tom Seaver, New York Mets	(AL)	Frank Viola, Minnesota Twins
(AL)	Dennis McLain, Detroit Tigers	1989 (NL)	Mark Davis, San Diego Padres
(AL)	Mike Cuellar, Baltimore Orioles	(AL)	Bret Saberhagen, Kansas City Royals
1970 (NL)	Bob Gibson, St. Louis Cardinals	1990 (NL)	Doug Drabek, Pittsburgh Pirates
(AL)	Jim Perry, Minnesota Twins	(AL)	Bob Welch, Oakland A's
1971 (NL)	Ferguson Jenkins, Chicago Cubs	1991 (NL)	Tom Glavine, Atlanta Braves
(AL)	Vida Blue, Oakland A's	(AL)	Roger Clemens, Boston Red Sox
1972 (NL)	Steve Carlton, Philadelphia Phillies	1992 (NL)	Greg Maddux, Chicago Cubs
(AL)	Gaylord Perry, Cleveland Indians	(AL)	Dennis Eckersley, Oakland A's
1973 (NL)	Tom Seaver, New York Mets	1993 (NL)	Greg Maddux, Atlanta Braves
(AL)	Jim Palmer, Baltimore Orioles	(AL)	Jack McDowell, Chicago White Sox
1974 (NL)	Mike Marshall, Los Angeles Dodgers	1994 (NL)	Greg Maddux, Atlanta Braves
(AL)	Jim (Catfish) Hunter, Oakland A's	(AL)	David Cone, Kansas City Royals
1975 (NL)	Tom Seaver, New York Mets	1995 (NL)	Greg Maddux, Atlanta Braves
(AL)	Jim Palmer, Baltimore Orioles	(AL)	Randy Johnson, Seattle Mariner
1976 (NL)	Randy Jones, San Diego Padres	1996 (NL)	John Smoltz, Atlanta Braves
(AL)	Jim Palmer, Baltimore Orioles	**(AL)**	**Pat Hentgen, Toronto Blue Jays**
1977 (NL)	Steve Carlton, Philadelphia Phillies	**1997 (NL)**	**Pedro Martinez, Montreal Expos**
(AL)	Sparky Lyle, New York Yankees	**(AL)**	**Roger Clemens, Toronto Blue Jays**
1978 (NL)	Gaylord Perry, San Diego Padres	1998 (NL)	Tom Glavine, Atlanta Braves
(AL)	Ron Guidry, New York Yankees	**(AL)**	**Roger Clemens, Toronto Blue Jays**
1979 (NL)	Bruce Sutter, Chicago Cubs	1999 (NL)	Randy Johnson, Arizona Diamondbacks
(AL)	Mike Flanagan, Baltimore Orioles	(AL)	Pedro Martinez, Boston Red Sox
1980 (NL)	Steve Carlton, Philadelphia Phillies	2000 (NL)	Randy Johnson, Arizona Diamondbacks
(AL)	Steve Stone, Baltimore Orioles	(AL)	Pedro Martinez, Boston Red Sox
1981 (NL)	Fernando Valenzuela, Los Angeles Dodgers	2001 (NL)	Randy Johnson, Arizona Diamondbacks
(AL)	Rollie Fingers, Milwaukee Brewers	(AL)	Roger Clemens, New York Yankees
1982 (NL)	Steve Carlton, Philadelphia Phillies	2002 (NL)	Randy Johnson, Arizona Diamondbacks
(AL)	Pete Vuckovich, Milwaukee Brewers	(AL)	Barry Zito, Oakland A's
1983 (NL)	John Denny, Philadelphia Phillies	2003 (NL)	Eric Gagne, Los Angeles Dodgers
(AL)	LaMarr Hoyt, Chicago White Sox	(AL)	Roy Halladay, Toronto Blue Jays
1984 (NL)	Rick Sutcliffe, Chicago Cubs		
(AL)	Willie Hernandez, Detroit Tigers		

Source: *Canadian Press*   (1) One award, 1962–66.

Most Valuable Player, 1962–2002

	National League	American League
1962	Maury Wills, Los Angeles Dodgers	Mickey Mantle, New York Yankees
1963	Sandy Koufax, Los Angeles Dodgers	Elston Howard, New York Yankees
1964	Ken Boyer, St. Louis Cardinals	Brooks Robinson, Baltimore Orioles
1965	Willie Mays, San Francisco Giants	Zoilo Versalles, Minnesota Twins
1966	Roberto Clemente, Pittsburgh Pirates	Frank Robinson, Baltimore Orioles
1967	Orlando Cepeda, St. Louis Cardinals	Carl Yastrzemski, Boston Red Sox
1968	Bob Gibson, St. Louis Cardinals	Denny McLain, Detroit Tigers
1969	Willie McCovey, San Francisco Giants	Harmon Killebrew, Minnesota Twins
1971	Joe Torre, St. Louis Cardinals	Vida Blue, Oakland Athletics
1972	Johnny Bench, Cincinnati Reds	Dick Allen, Chicago White Sox
1975	Joe Morgan, Cincinnati Reds	Fred Lynn, Boston Red Sox
1976	Joe Morgan, Cincinnati Reds	Thurman Munson, New York Yankees
1979	Keith Hernandez, St. Louis Cardinals; Willie Stargell, Pittsburgh Pirates	Don Baylor, California Angels
1980	Mike Schmidt, Philadelphia Phillies	George Brett, Kansas City Royals
1981	Mike Schmidt, Philadelphia Phillies	Rollie Fingers, Milwaukee Brewers
1982	Dale Murphy, Atlanta Braves	Robin Yount, Milwaukee Brewers
1983	Dale Murphy, Atlanta Braves	Cal Ripken, Jr., Baltimore Orioles
1984	Ryne Sandberg, Chicago Cubs	Willie Hernandez, Detroit Tigers
1985	Willie McGee, St. Louis Cardinals	Don Mattingly, New York Yankees
1986	Mike Schmidt, Philadelphia Phillies	Roger Clemens, Boston Red Sox
1987	André Dawson, Chicago Cubs	**George Bell, Toronto Blue Jays**
1988	Kirk Gibson, Los Angeles Dodgers	Jose Canseco, Oakland Athletics
1989	Kevin Mitchell, San Francisco Giants	Robin Yount, Milwaukee Brewers
1990	Barry Bonds, Pittsburgh Pirates	Rickey Henderson, Oakland Athletics
1991	Terry Pendleton, Atlanta Braves	Cal Ripken, Jr., Baltimore Orioles
1992	Barry Bonds, Pittsburgh Pirates	Dennis Eckersley, Oakland A's
1993	Barry Bonds, San Francisco Giants	Frank Thomas, Chicago White Sox
1994	Jeff Bagwell, Houston Astros	Frank Thomas, Chicago White Sox
1995	Barry Larkin, Cincinnati Reds	Mo Vaughn, Boston Red Sox
1996	Ken Caminiti, San Diego Padres	Juan Gonzalez, Texas Rangers
1997	Larry Walker, Colorado Rockies	Ken Griffey Jr., Seattle Mariners
1998	Sammy Sosa, Chicago Cubs	Juan Gonzalez, Texas Rangers
1999	Chipper Jones, Atlanta Braves	Ivan Rodriguez, Texas Rangers
2000	Jeff Kent, San Francisco Giants	Jason Giambi, Oakland A's
2001	Barry Bonds, San Francisco Giants	Ichiro Suzuki, Seattle Mariners
2002	Barry Bonds, San Francisco Giants	Miguel Tejada, Oakland A's

Source: *Baseball Almanac*

Who was Cy Young?

*T*he Cy Young award is given to the most outstanding pitcher in each league. Although Cy Young pitched in the late 1800s and early 1900s, he is as well known today as any pitcher in history. Dent Young, who was raised on a farm in eastern Ohio, was pretty green when he came to the big leagues but before long he was nicknamed "Cy," as in Cyclone, because of his blinding fastball. Over a 22-year career he was the winning pitcher of record 511 times, 95 ahead of second-place Walter Johnson. The fact that he averaged over 23 wins a season is amazing enough, but that he did it over 22 years is truly astounding. Young was inducted into baseball's Hall of Fame in 1937.

Batting Champions, 1963–2003

National League

	Player, Club	%
1963	Tommy Davis, Los Angeles	.326
1964	Roberto Clemente, Pittsburgh	.339
1965	Roberto Clemente, Pittsburgh	.329
1966	Matty Alou, Pittsburgh	.342
1967	Roberto Clemente, Pittsburgh	.357
1968	Pete Rose, Cincinnati	.335
1969	Pete Rose, Cincinnati	.348
1970	Rico Carty, Atlanta	.366
1971	Joe Torre, St. Louis	.363
1972	Billy Williams, Chicago	.333
1973	Pete Rose, Cincinnati	.338
1974	Ralph Garr, Atlanta	.353
1975	Bill Madlock, Chicago	.354
1976	Bill Madlock, Chicago	.339
1977	Dave Parker, Pittsburgh	.338
1978	Dave Parker, Pittsburgh	.334
1979	Keith Hernandez, St. Louis	.344
1980	Bill Buckner, Chicago	.324
1981	Bill Madlock, Pittsburgh[1]	.341
1982	**Al Oliver, Montreal**	**.331**
1983	Bill Madlock, Pittsburgh	.323
1984	Tony Gwynn, San Diego	.351
1985	Willie McGee, St. Louis	.353
1986	**Tim Raines, Montreal**	**.334**
1987	Tony Gwynn, San Diego	.370
1988	Tony Gwynn, San Diego	.313
1989	Tony Gwynn, San Diego	.336
1990	Willie McGee, St. Louis	.335
1991	Terry Pendleton, Atlanta	.319
1992	Gary Sheffield, San Diego	.330
1993	Andres Galarraga, Colorado	.370
1994	Tony Gwynn, San Diego[1]	.394
1995	Tony Gwynn, San Diego	.368
1996	Tony Gwynn, San Diego	.353
1997	Tony Gwynn, San Diego	.372
1998	Larry Walker, Colorado	.363
1999	Larry Walker, Colorado	.379
2000	Todd Helton, Colorado	.372
2001	Larry Walker, Colorado	.350
2002	Barry Bonds, San Francisco	.370
2003	Albert Pujols, St. Louis	.359

American League

	Player, Club	%
1963	Carl Yastrzemski, Boston	.321
1964	Tony Oliva, Minnesota	.323
1965	Tony Oliva, Minnesota	.321
1966	Frank Robinson, Baltimore	.316
1967	Carl Yastrzemski, Boston	.326
1968	Carl Yastrzemski, Boston	.301
1969	Rod Carew, Minnesota	.332
1970	Alex Johnson, California	.329
1971	Tony Oliva, Minnesota	.337
1972	Rod Carew, Minnesota	.318
1973	Rod Carew, Minnesota	.350
1974	Rod Carew, Minnesota	.364
1975	Rod Carew, Minnesota	.359
1976	George Brett, Kansas City	.333
1977	Rod Carew, Minnesota	.388
1978	Rod Carew, Minnesota	.333
1979	Fred Lynn, Boston	.333
1980	George Brett, Kansas City	.390
1981	Carney Lansford, Boston	.336
1982	Willie Wilson, Kansas City	.332
1983	Wade Boggs, Boston	.361
1984	Don Mattingly, New York	.343
1985	Wade Boggs, Boston	.368
1986	Wade Boggs, Boston	.357
1987	Wade Boggs, Boston	.363
1988	Wade Boggs, Boston	.366
1989	Kirby Puckett, Minnesota	.339
1990	George Brett, Kansas City	.329
1991	Julio Franco, Texas	.341
1992	Edgar Martinez, Seattle	.343
1993	**John Olerud, Toronto**	**.363**
1994	Paul O'Neill, New York[1]	.359
1995	Edgar Martinez, Seattle	.356
1996	Alex Rodriguez, Seattle	.358
1997	Frank Thomas, Chicago	.347
1998	Bernie Williams, New York	.339
1999	Nomar Garciaparra, Boston	**.357**
2000	Nomar Garciaparra, Boston	.372
2001	Ichiro Suzuki, Seattle	.350
2002	Manny Ramirez, Boston	.349
2003	Bill Mueller, Boston	.326

Source: *Canadian Press*   (1) Strike abbreviated season.

Home Run Seasons

HR	Player, Team	Year	HR	Player, Team	Year	HR	Player, Team	Year
73	Barry Bonds, SF	2001	57	Alex Rodriguez,	2002	52	Mark McGwire, Oak	1996
70	Mark McGwire, StL	1998	57	Luis Gonzalez, Ari	2001	52	Alex Rodriguez,Tex	2001
66	Sammy Sosa, Chi Cubs	1998	56	Hack Wilson, Chi Cubs	1930	51	Ralph Kiner, Pit	1947
65	Mark McGwire, StL	1999	56	Ken Griffey Jr., Sea	1998	51	Johnny Mize,	
64	Sammy Sosa, Chi Cubs	2001	56	Ken Griffey Jr., Sea	1997		NY Giants	1947
63	Sammy Sosa, Chi Cubs	1999	54	Babe Ruth, NYY	1920	51	Willie Mays, NY Giants	1955
61	Roger Maris, NYY	1961	54	Babe Ruth, NYY	1928	51	Cecil Fielder, Det	1990
60	Babe Ruth, NYY	1927	54	Ralph Kiner, Pit	1949	50	Jimmie Foxx, Bos	1938
59	Babe Ruth, NYY	1921	54	Mickey Mantle, NYY	1961	50	Albert Belle, Cle	1995
58	Jimmie Foxx, Phi Athletics	1932	52	Mickey Mantle, NYY	1956	50	Brady Anderson, Bal	1996
58	Hank Greenberg, Det	1938	52	Willie Mays, SF	1965	50	Greg Vaughn, SD	1998
58	Mark McGwire, Oak/ StL	1997	52	George Foster, Cin	1977			

Source: *Canadian Press*

Individual Earned Run Average Leaders, 1962–2003

National League

Player, Team	ERA
1962 . . . . Sandy Koufax, LA	2.54
1963 . . . . Sandy Koufax, LA	1.88
1964 . . . . Sandy Koufax, LA	1.74
1965 . . . . Sandy Koufax, LA	2.04
1966 . . . . Sandy Koufax, LA	1.73
1967 . . . . Phil Niekro, Atl	1.87
1968 . . . . Bob Gibson, StL	1.12
1969 . . . . Juan Marichal, SF	2.10
1970 . . . . Tom Seaver, NY	2.81
1971 . . . . Tom Seaver, NY	1.76
1972 . . . . Steve Carlton, Pha	1.97
1973 . . . . Tom Seaver, NY	2.08
1974 . . . . Buzz Capra, Atl	2.28
1975 . . . . Randy Jones, SD	2.24
1976 . . . . John Denny, StL	2.52
1977 . . . . John Candelaria, Pgh	2.34
1978 . . . . Craig Swan, NY	2.43
1979 . . . . J.R. Richard, Hou	2.71
1980 . . . . Don Sutton, LA	2.21
1981 . . . . Nolan Ryan, Hou	1.69[1]
1982 . . . . Steve Rogers, Mtl	2.40
1983 . . . . Atlee Hammaker, SF	2.25
1984 . . . . Alejandro Pena, LA	2.48
1985 . . . . Dwight Gooden, NY	1.53
1986 . . . . Mike Scott, Hou	2.22
1987 . . . . Nolan Ryan, Hou	2.76
1988 . . . . Joe Magrane, StL	2.18
1989 . . . . Scott Garrelts, SF	2.28
1990 . . . . Danny Darwin, Hou	2.21
1991 . . . . Dennis Martinez, Mtl	2.39
1992 . . . . Bill Swift, SF	2.08
1993 . . . . Greg Maddux, Atl.	2.36
1994 . . . . Greg Maddux, Atl	1.56[1]
1995 . . . . Greg Maddux, Atl	1.63
1996 . . . . Kevin Brown, Fla.	1.89
1997 . . . . Pedro Martinez, Mtl	1.90
1998 . . . . Greg Maddux, Atl.	2.22
1999 . . . . Randy Johnson, Ari	2.48
2000 . . . . Kevin Brown, LA.	2.58
2001 . . . . Randy Johnson, Ari	2.49
2002 . . . . Randy Johnson, Ari	2.32
2003 . . . . Jason Schmidt, SF	2.34

American League

Player, Team	ERA
1962 . . . . Hank Aguirre, Det	2.21
1963 . . . . Gary Peters, Chi	2.33
1964 . . . . Dean Chance, LA	1.65
1965 . . . . Sam McDowell, Cle	2.18
1966 . . . . Gary Peters, Chi	1.98
1967 . . . . Joel Horlen, Chi	2.06
1968 . . . . Luis Tiant, Cle	1.60
1969 . . . . Dick Bosman, Wash	2.19
1970 . . . . Diego Segui, Oak	2.56
1971 . . . . Vida Blue, Oak	1.82
1972 . . . . Luis Tiant, Bos	1.91
1973 . . . . Jim Palmer, Bal	2.40
1974 . . . . Catfish Hunter, Oak	2.49
1975 . . . . Jim Palmer, Bal	2.09
1976 . . . . Mark Fidrych, Det	2.34
1977 . . . . Frank Tanana, Cal	2.54
1978 . . . . Ron Guidry, NY	1.74
1979 . . . . Ron Guidry, NY	2.78
1980 . . . . Rudy May, NY	2.47
1981 . . . . Steve McCatty, Oak	2.32[1]
1982 . . . . Rick Sutcliffe, Cle	2.96
1983 . . . . Rick Honeycutt, Tex	2.42
1984 . . . . Mike Boddicker, Bal	2.79
1985 . . . . Dave Stieb, Tor	2.48
1986 . . . . Roger Clemens, Bos	2.48
1987 . . . . Jimmy Key, Tor	2.76
1988 . . . . Allan Anderson, Min	2.45
1989 . . . . Bret Saberhagen, KC	2.16
1990 . . . . Roger Clemens, Bos	1.93
1991 . . . . Roger Clemens, Bos	2.62
1992 . . . . Roger Clemens, Bos	2.41
1993 . . . . Kevin Appier, KC	2.56
1994 . . . . Steve Ontiveras, Oak	2.65[1]
1995 . . . . Randy Johnson, Sea	2.48
1996 . . . . Juan Guzman, Tor	2.93
1997 . . . . Roger Clemens, Tor	2.05
1998 . . . . Roger Clemens, Tor	2.65
1999 . . . . Pedro Martinez, Bos	2.07
2000 . . . . Pedro Martinez, Bos	1.74
2001 . . . . Freddy Garcia, Sea	3.05
2002 . . . . Pedro Martinez, Bos	2.26
2003 . . . . Pedro Martinez, Bos	2.22

(1) Strike abbreviated season.

Directory of Selected Baseball Organizations in Canada

Canadian Federation of Amateur Baseball
2212 Gladwin Crescent,
Suite A7
Ottawa, ON K1B 5N1
Tel: (613) 748-5606
Fax: (613) 748-5767
www.baseball.ca

Major League Baseball
350 Park Ave.
New York, NY 10022
Tel: (212) 339-7800
www.mlb.com

Montreal Expos Baseball Club
P.O. Box 500, Station M
Montreal, Que
H1V 3P2
Tel: (514) 253-3434
Fax: (514) 253-8282
www.montrealexpos.com

Toronto Blue Jays
The Skydome
300 The Esplanade West,
Suite 3200
Toronto, Ont.
M5V 3B3
Tel: (416) 341-1000
www.bluejays.ca

Canadian Players in Major League Baseball, 2003

Player	TEAM	POS	G	AB	R	H	2B	3B	HR	RBI	TB	BB	SO	SB	CS	OBP	SLG	AVG
Matt Stairs	PIT	OF	121	305	49	89	20	1	20	57	171	45	64	0	1	.389	.561	.292
Corey Koskie	MIN	3B	131	469	76	137	29	2	14	69	212	77	113	11	5	.393	.452	.292
Jason Bay	PIT/SD	OF	30	87	15	25	7	1	4	14	46	19	29	3	1	.421	.529	.287
Larry Walker	COL	OF	143	454	86	129	25	7	16	79	216	98	87	7	4	.422	.476	.284
Aaron Guiel	KC	OF	99	354	63	98	30	0	15	52	173	27	63	3	5	.346	.489	.277
Danny Klassen	DET	3B	22	73	9	18	3	1	1	7	26	4	26	0	1	.286	.356	.247
Justin Morneau	MIN	1B	40	106	14	24	4	0	4	16	40	9	30	0	0	.287	.377	.226
Pete Laforest	TB	C	19	48	0	8	2	0	0	6	10	1	14	0	0	.196	.208	.167

POS = position; G = games played; AB = at bats; R = runs; H = hits; 2B = doubles; 3B = triples; HR = home runs; RBI = runs batted in; TB = total bases; BB = walks; SO = strikeouts; SB = stolen bases; CS = caught stealing; OBP = on-base percentage; SLG = slugging percentage; AVG = batting average

Pitcher	TEAM	W	L	ERA	G	GS	CG	SHO	SV	SVO	IP	H	R	ER	HR	HBP	BB	SO
Eric Gagne	LA	2	3	1.20	77	0	0	0	55	55	82.1	37	12	11	2	3	20	137
Rheal Cormier	PHI	8	0	1.70	65	0	0	0	1	4	84.2	54	18	16	4	1	25	67
Paul Quantrill	LA	2	5	1.75	89	0	0	0	1	5	77.1	61	18	15	2	3	15	44
Chris Reitsma	CIN	9	5	4.29	57	3	0	0	12	18	84.0	92	41	40	14	0	19	53
Rich Harden	OAK	5	4	4.46	15	13	0	0	0	0	74.2	72	38	37	5	1	40	67
Chris Mears	DET	1	3	5.44	29	3	0	0	5	5	41.1	50	28	25	5	3	11	21
Ryan Dempster	CIN	3	7	6.54	22	20	0	0	0	0	115.2	134	89	84	14	5	70	84
Aaron Myette	CLE	0	0	23.62	2	0	0	0	0	0	2.2	7	7	7	1	1	2	1

W = wins; L = losses; ERA = earned run average; G = games played; GS = games started; CG = complete games; SHO = shutouts; SV = saves; SVO = save opportunities; IP = innings pitched; H = hits; R = runs; ER = earned runs; HR = home runs allowed; HBP = hit by pitch; BB = walks; SO = strikeouts

Source: *Major League Baseball; SLAM! Sports*

Career Records of Some Canadian Major League Players of the Past

Player	Years	G	AB	R	H	HR	RBI	AVG	OBP	SLG	BB	SO	SB	CS
Tip O'Neill	1922-23	1054	4255	880	1386	52	757	.326	.392	.458	421	146	161	—
Pop Smith	1880-91	1110	4230	642	939	24	358	.300	.287	.313	325	345	169	—
Doc Mille	1910-14	557	1717	184	507	12	235	.295	.343	.390	121	149	64	—
Jeff Heath	1936-49	1383	4937	777	1447	194	887	.293	.370	.509	593	670	56	47
Goody Rosen .	1937-46	551	1916	310	557	22	197	.291	.364	.398	218	166	12	—
George Selkirk	1934-42	846	2790	503	810	108	576	.290	.400	.483	486	319	49	32
Terry Puhl	1977-91	1531	4855	676	1361	62	435	.280	.349	.388	505	507	217	99
Bill Phillips . . .	1879-88	1038	4255	562	1130	17	534	.266	.299	.374	178	215	39	—

Pitcher	Years	W	L	IP	ERA	G	GS	CG	SV	H	ER	BB	K
Fergie Jenkins	1965-83	284	226	4500.2	3.34	664	594	267	7	4142	1669	997	3192
Kirk McCaskill	1985-96	106	108	1729.0	4.12	380	242	30	7	1748	791	665	1003
Reggie Cleveland . .	1969-81	105	106	1809.0	4.02	428	203	57	25	1843	807	543	930
John Hiller	1965-80	87	76	1242.0	2.83	545	43	13	125	1040	391	535	1036
Phil Marchildon . . .	1940-50	68	75	1214.1	3.93	185	162	82	2	1084	530	684	481
Dick Fowler	1941-52	66	79	1303.0	4.11	221	170	75	4	1367	595	578	382
Claude Raymond . .	1959-71	46	53	721.0	3.66	449	7	2	83	711	293	225	497
Ron Taylor	1962-72	45	43	800.0	3.93	491	17	3	72	794	349	209	464

G = Games played. AB = At bats. R = Runs. H = Hits. 2B = Doubles. 3B = Triples. HR = Home runs. RBI = Runs batted in. BA = Batting average. OBA = On-base percentage. SA = Slugging average.
W = Wins. L = Losses. % = Percentage. G = Games pitched. SHO = Shutouts. SV = Saves. IP = Innings pitched. H = Hits allowed. BB = Walks. SO = Strikeouts. ERA = Earned run average.
(1) Marchildon was in the Canadian Armed Forces in 1943–44.

Source: *Sportspic.com*

Montreal Expos Year-By-Year Record, 1969–2003

	Won	Lost	%	Pos.	Home Attendance	Manager		Won	Lost	%	Pos.	Home Attendance	Manager
1969...	52	110	.321	6th	1 212 608	Gene Mauch	**1986**...	78	83	.484	4th	1 128 981	Buck Rodgers
1970...	73	89	.451	6th	1 424 683	Gene Mauch	**1987**...	91	71	.562	3rd	1 850 324	Buck Rodgers
1971...	71	90	.441	5th	1 290 963	Gene Mauch	**1988**...	81	81	.500	3rd	1 478 659	Buck Rodgers
1972...	70	86	.449	5th	1 142 145	Gene Mauch	**1989**...	81	81	.500	4th	1 783 533	Buck Rodgers
1973...	79	83	.488	4th	1 246 863	Gene Mauch	**1990**...	85	77	.525	3rd	1 421 388	Buck Rodgers
1974...	79	82	.491	4th	1 019 134	Gene Mauch	**1991**...	70	91	.441	6th	978 045	B. Rodgers/
1975...	75	87	.463	5th	908 292	Gene Mauch							T. Runnells
1976...	55	107	.340	6th	646 704	K. Kuehl/C. Fox	**1992**...	87	75	.537	2nd	1 731 566	T. Runnells/
1977...	75	87	.463	5th	1 433 757	Dick Williams							F. Alou
1978...	76	86	.469	4th	1 427 007	Dick Williams	**1993**...	94	68	.580	2nd	1 641 437	Felipe Alou
1979...	95	65	.594	2nd	2 102 173	Dick Williams	**1994**...	74	40	.649	1st(a)	1 276 250	Felipe Alou
1980...	90	72	.556	2nd	2 208 175	Dick Williams	**1995**...	66	78	.458	5th	1 309 618	Felipe Alou
1981...	60	48	.556	—	1 534 564	D. Williams/	**1996**...	88	74	.543	2nd	1 618 573	Felipe Alou
						J.Fanning	**1997**...	78	84	.481	4th	1 175 000	Felipe Alou
1982...	86	76	.531	3rd	2 318 292	Jim Fanning	**1998**...	65	97	.401	4th	914 909	Felipe Alou
1983...	82	80	.506	3rd	2 320 651	Bill Virdon	**1999**...	68	94	.420	4th	773 277	Felipe Alou
1984...	78	83	.484	5th	1 606 531	B. Virdon/	**2000**...	67	95	.414	4th	926 427	Felipe Alou
						J. Fanning	**2001**...	68	94	.420	5th	642 745	F. Alou/J. Torborg
1985...	84	77	.522	3rd	1 502 494	Buck Rodgers	**2002**...	83	79	.512	2nd	749 104	Frank Robinson
							2003...	83	79	.512	4th	1 025 640	Frank Robinson

Source: *Canadian Press*

(a) Eastern Division: first year with three divisions.

Montreal Expos Individual Statistics, 2003

Batting

Player	POS	G	AB	R	H	2B	3B	HR	RBI	TB	BB	SO	SB	CS	OBP	SLG	AVG
J Vitiello	OF	38	76	12	26	6	0	3	13	41	7	14	0	0	.407	.539	.342
V Guerrero	OF	112	394	71	130	20	3	25	79	231	63	53	9	5	.426	.586	.330
J Vidro	2B	144	509	77	158	36	0	15	65	239	69	50	3	2	.397	.470	.310
O Cabrera	SS	162	626	95	186	47	2	17	80	288	52	64	24	2	.347	.460	.297
W Cordero	1B	130	436	57	121	27	0	16	71	196	49	90	1	1	.354	.450	.278
B Wilkerson	OF	146	504	78	135	34	4	19	77	234	89	155	13	10	.380	.464	.268
T Tucker	P	44	19	1	5	1	0	0	0	6	0	6	0	0	.263	.316	.263
J Carroll	3B	105	227	31	59	10	1	1	10	74	19	39	5	2	.323	.326	.260
T Zeile	3B	34	113	11	29	2	2	5	19	50	10	18	1	0	.331	.442	.257
E Chavez	OF	141	483	66	121	25	5	5	47	171	31	59	18	7	.294	.354	.251
M Cepicky	OF	5	8	0	2	1	0	0	0	3	0	2	0	0	.250	.375	.250
J Eischen	P	67	4	1	1	0	0	0	0	1	0	2	0	0	.250	.250	.250
E Guzman	3B	52	146	15	35	5	0	1	14	43	5	17	0	0	.263	.295	.240
H Mateo	2B	100	154	29	37	3	1	0	7	42	11	38	11	1	.304	.273	.240
J Macias	OF	111	272	31	65	15	2	4	22	96	11	45	4	3	.273	.353	.239
R Calloway	OF	126	340	36	81	17	1	9	52	127	20	80	9	2	.282	.374	.238
B Schneider	C	108	335	34	77	26	1	9	46	132	37	75	0	2	.309	.394	.230
M Barrett	C	70	226	33	47	9	2	10	30	90	21	37	0	0	.280	.398	.208
T Armas	P	5	10	0	2	0	0	0	0	2	0	2	0	0	.200	.200	.200
F Tatis	3B	53	175	15	34	6	0	2	15	46	18	40	2	1	.281	.263	.194
J Liefer	1B	35	88	6	17	3	0	3	18	29	3	26	0	1	.217	.330	.193
L Hernandez	P	31	74	2	14	1	0	0	6	15	1	14	0	0	.211	.203	.189
T Ohka	P	33	55	2	10	0	0	0	3	10	2	10	0	0	.211	.182	.182
J Vazquez	P	32	65	5	10	0	1	0	6	12	2	8	0	0	.179	.185	.154
Z Day	P	23	47	2	2	0	0	0	2	2	1	22	0	0	.063	.043	.043

POS = position; G = games played; AB = at bats; R = runs; H = hits; 2B = doubles; 3B = triples; HR = home runs; RBI = runs batted in; TB = total bases; BB = walks; SO = strikeouts; SB = stolen bases; CS = caught stealing; OBP = on-base percentage; SLG = slugging percentage; AVG = batting average

Source: *Major League Baseball*

Pitching

Player	W	L	ERA	G	GS	CG	SHO	SV	SVO	IP	H	R	ER	HR	HBP	BB	SO
J Mercedes	0	0	0.00	5	0	0	0	0	0	7.1	6	3	0	0	0	5	3
R Corcoran	0	0	1.23	5	0	0	0	0	0	7.1	7	2	1	0	0	3	2
C Cordero	1	0	1.64	12	0	0	0	1	1	11.0	4	2	2	1	0	3	12
T Armas	2	1	2.61	5	5	0	0	0	0	31.0	25	9	9	4	1	8	23
L Ayala	10	3	2.92	65	0	0	0	5	8	71.0	65	27	23	8	5	13	46
J Eischen	2	2	3.06	70	0	0	0	1	4	53.0	57	27	18	7	3	13	40
L Hernandez	15	10	3.20	33	33	8	0	0	0	233.1	225	92	83	27	10	57	178
J Vazquez	13	12	3.24	34	34	4	1	0	0	230.2	198	93	83	28	4	57	241
S Stewart	3	1	3.98	51	0	0	0	0	1	43.0	52	22	19	5	1	13	29
J Manon	1	2	4.13	23	0	0	0	1	1	28.1	26	13	13	3	1	17	15
T Ohka	10	12	4.16	34	34	2	0	0	0	199.0	233	106	92	24	9	45	118
Z Day	9	8	4.18	23	23	1	1	0	0	131.1	132	64	61	8	10	59	61
C Vargas	6	8	4.34	23	20	0	0	0	0	114.0	111	59	55	16	7	41	62
R Biddle	5	8	4.65	73	0	0	0	34	41	71.2	71	43	37	10	6	40	54
T Tucker	2	3	4.73	45	7	0	0	0	2	80.0	90	49	42	8	4	20	47
E Knott	1	2	5.12	13	1	0	0	0	0	19.1	23	12	11	2	0	6	17
D Smith	2	2	5.26	32	0	0	0	0	1	37.2	42	23	22	11	2	18	35
A Ferrari	0	0	6.75	4	0	0	0	0	0	4.0	4	3	3	1	1	5	1
H Almonte	1	1	6.83	28	0	0	0	0	0	29.0	34	22	22	4	2	17	26
V Darensbourg	0	0	8.00	9	0	0	0	0	0	9.0	17	9	8	2	0	1	4
S Kim	0	1	8.36	4	3	0	0	0	0	14.0	24	13	13	6	4	8	5
T Drew	0	2	12.46	6	1	0	0	0	0	8.2	12	12	12	3	0	8	3
B Hebson	0	0	13.50	2	0	0	0	0	0	2.0	4	3	3	1	1	1	1
B Reames	0	0	27.00	2	0	0	0	0	0	1.1	4	4	4	0	0	2	1

W = wins; L = losses; ERA = earned run average; G = games played; GS = games started; CG = complete games; SHO = shutouts; SV = saves; SVO = save opportunities; IP = innings pitched; H = hits; R = runs; ER = earned runs; HR = home runs allowed; HBP = hit by pitch; BB = walks; SO = strikeouts

Source: *Major League Baseball*

Montreal Expos Team Records, through 2003 Season

Batting

Single Season

Batting Average: Vladimir Guerrero, 2000, .345
At Bats: Warren Cromartie, 1979, 659
Games: Rusty Staub, 1971, 162; Ken Singleton, 1973, 162; Warren Cromartie, 1980, 162; Orlando Cabrera, 2001, 2003, 162
Hits: Vladimir Guerrero, 2002, 206
Runs: Tim Raines, 1983, 133
Singles: Tim Raines, 1986, 140
Doubles: Mark Grudzielanek, 1997, 54
Triples: Rodney Scott, 1980, 13; Tim Raines, 1985, 13; Mitch Webster, 1986, 13
Home Runs: Vladimir Guerrero, 2000, 44
Runs Batted In: Vladimir Guerrero, 1999, 131
Total Bases: Vladimir Guerrero, 2000, 379
Slugging Percentage: Vladimir Guerrero, 2000, .664
On-Base Percentage: Tim Raines, 1987, .431
Stolen Bases: Ron LeFlore, 1980, 97
Strikeouts: Andres Galarraga, 1990, 169
Walks: Ken Singleton, 1973, 123

Career Leaders

Batting average: .323, Vladimir Guerrero
At Bats: Tim Wallach, 6 529
Games: Tim Wallach, 1 767
Hits: Tim Wallach, 1 694
Runs: Tim Raines, 947
Singles: Tim Raines, 1,148
Doubles: Tim Wallach, 360
Triples: Tim Raines, 82
Home Runs: Vladimir Guerrero, 234
Runs Batted In: Tim Wallach, 905
Total Bases: Tim Wallach, 2,728
Slugging Percentage: V. Guerrero, .588
On-Base Percentage: Rusty Staub, .402
Stolen Bases: Tim Raines, 635
Strikeouts: Tim Wallach, 1,009
Walks: Tim Raines, 793

Pitching

Single Season

Games: Mike Marshall, 1973, 92
Games Started: Steve Rogers, 1977, 40
Complete Games: Bill Stoneman, 1971, 20
Innings Pitched: Steve Rogers, 1977, 302
Wins: Ross Grimsley, 1978, 20
Losses: Steve Rogers, 1974, 22
Saves: John Wetteland, 1993, 43
Earned Run Average: Ugueth Urbina, 1998, 1.30
Strikeouts: Pedro Martinez, 1997, 305

Career Leaders

Games: Tim Burke, 425
Games Started: Steve Rogers, 393
Complete Games: Steve Rogers, 129
Innings Pitched: Steve Rogers, 2 838
Wins: Steve Rogers, 158
Losses: Steve Rogers, 152
Saves: Jeff Reardon, 152
Earned Run Average: Tim Burke, 2.61
Strikeouts: Steve Rogers, 1,621

Source: *Major League Baseball*

Montreal Expos Player of the Year, 1969–2002

1969	Rusty Staub	1978	Ross Grimsley	1986	Tim Raines	1995	David Segui
1970	Carl Morton	1979	Larry Parrish	1987	Tim Wallach	1996	Hank Rodriguez
1971	Ron Hunt	1980	Gary Carter	1988	Andres Galarraga	1997	Pedro Martinez
1972	Mike Marshall	1981	Andre Dawson	1989	Tim Wallach	1998	Vladimir Guerrero
1973	Mike Marshall	1982	Al Oliver	1990	Tim Wallach	1999	Vladimir Guerrero
1974	Willie Davis	1983	Andre Dawson; Tim Raines (tie)	1991	Dennis Martinez	2000	Vladimir Guerrero
1975	Gary Carter			1992	Larry Walker	2001	Orlando Cabrera
1976	Woodie Fryman	1984	Gary Carter	1993	Marquis Grissom	2002	Vladimir Guerrero
1977	Gary Carter	1985	Tim Raines	1994	Moises Alou		

Gary Carter first Expo in Baseball Hall of Fame

Catcher Gary Carter, who spent 12 years with the Montreal Expos organization, was inducted to the National Baseball Museum and Hall of Fame in Cooperstown, New York, in 2003. Carter is the first Montreal player to be inducted into the prestigious Hall of Fame who played more games with Montreal than with any other team; Carter's player bust, therefore, is topped with a Montreal Expos cap. Carter's major league career spanned 19 years; he also played with the New York Mets, the San Francisco Giants, and the Los Angeles Dodgers. Carter hit 324 home runs during his career, was an 11-time All-Star (and twice an All Star Game MVP), and holds the all-time catching record with 12,988 chances. Carter's only World Series ring came with the 1986 New York Mets.

Source: *Canadian Press*

Want to Surf for Sports Info?

Basketball
Basketball Canada
www.basketball.ca/
Official site of Canadian basketball, providing information on national teams and all national basketball associations.

FIBA (Federation Internationale Basketall Association)
www.fiba.com/
Official site of the international governing body of basketball, featuring tournament information, press releases and rules.

Cycling
Canadian Cycling Association
www.canadian-cycling.com/
Governing body of cycling in Canada with information on national teams, championships, coaching and rules.

Lacrosse
National Lacrosse League
www.nationallacrosse.com/
Official site of the National Lacrosse league with schedules, team rosters, standings and statistics.

Football
Canadian Football League
www.cfl.ca
All you need to know about the CFL

National Football League
www.nfl.com
All the information you want on the NFL

Canadian Junior Football League
www.cjfl.ca
Scores, standings and stats

Rugby
Rugby Canada
www.rugbycanada.ca/
Official site of Canadian rugby with information on Canadian national teams, super league, national championships, refereeing and coaching.

Soccer
Canadian Soccer Association
www.canadasoccer.com/
Governing body for both men's and women's soccer in Canada with constantly upadated information on competitions, national teams and players.

Toronto Blue Jays Year-By-Year Record, 1977–2003

	Won	Lost	%	Pos.	Home Attendance	Manager		Won	Lost	%	Pos.	Home Attendance	Manager
1977	54	107	.335	7th	1 701 052	Roy Hartsfield	**1989**	89	73	.549	1st	3 375 573	Williams/Gaston
1978	59	102	.366	7th	1 562 585	Roy Hartsfield	**1990**	86	76	.531	2nd	3 885 284	Cito Gaston
1979	53	109	.327	7th	1 431 651	Roy Hartsfield	**1991**	91	71	.562	1st	4 001 526	Cito Gaston
1980	67	95	.414	7th	1 400 327	Bob Mattick	**1992**	96	66	.593	1st	4 028 318	Cito Gaston
1981	37	69	.349	—	755 083	Bob Mattick	**1993**	95	67	.586	1st	4 057 947	Cito Gaston
1st half ..	16	42	.276	7th	—		**1994** ..	55	60	.476	3rd[2]	2 907 933	Cito Gaston
2nd half	21	27	.438	7th	—		**1995**	56	88	.389	5th	2 826 483	Cito Gaston
1982	78	84	.481	6th[1]	1 275 978	Bobby Cox	**1996**	74	88	.457	4th	2 559 563	Cito Gaston
1983	89	73	.549	4th	1 930 415	Bobby Cox	**1997**	76	86	.469	5th	2 589 297	Cito Gaston[3]
1984	89	73	.549	2nd	2 110 009	Bobby Cox	**1998**	88	74	.543	3rd	2 454 303	Tim Johnson
1985	99	62	.615	1st	2 468 925	Bobby Cox	**1999**	84	78	.518	3rd	2 163 473	Jim Fregosi
1986	86	76	.531	4th	2 455 477	Jimy Williams	**2000**	83	78	.516	3rd	1 819 886	Jim Fregosi
1987	96	66	.593	2nd	2 778 459	Jimy Williams	**2001**	80	82	.494	3rd	1 915 438	Buck Martinez
1988	87	75	.537	3rd	2 595 175	Jimy Williams	**2002**	78	84	.481	3rd	1 637 900	Martinez/Tosca
							2003	86	76	.531	3rd	1 799 458	Carlos Tosca

(1) Tied. (2) Eastern Division: first year with three divisions (3) Gaston was fired with five games remaining in the 1997 season.

Source: *Canadian Press*

Toronto Blue Jays Individual Statistics, 2003

Batting

Player	POS	G	AB	R	H	2B	3B	HR	RBI	TB	BB	SO	SB	CS	OBP	SLG	AVG
J Tam	P	5	1	0	1	1	0	0	1	2	0	0	0	0	1.000	2.000	1.000
H Clark	3B	38	70	9	25	3	1	0	7	30	3	6	0	1	.400	.429	.357
C Lidle.........	P	2	6	1	2	0	0	0	0	2	0	0	0	0	.333	.333	.333
V Wells	OF	161	678	118	215	49	5	33	117	373	42	80	4	1	.359	.550	.317
G Myers	C	121	329	51	101	19	0	15	52	165	37	57	0	3	.374	.502	.307
C Delgado	1B	161	570	117	172	38	1	42	145	338	109	137	0	0	.426	.593	.302
F Catalanotto..	OF	133	489	83	146	34	6	13	59	231	35	62	2	2	.351	.472	.299
R Johnson	OF	114	412	79	121	21	2	10	52	176	20	67	5	3	.353	.427	.294
M Bordick.....	SS	102	343	39	94	18	2	5	54	131	33	60	3	1	.340	.382	.274
O Hudson	2B	142	474	54	127	21	6	9	57	187	39	87	5	4	.328	.395	.268
J Phelps......	DH	119	396	57	106	18	1	20	66	186	39	115	1	2	.358	.470	.268
C Woodward...	SS	104	349	49	91	22	2	7	45	138	28	72	1	2	.316	.395	.261
T Wilson	C	96	256	37	66	19	0	5	35	100	28	80	0	0	.331	.391	.258
D Berg........	2B	61	161	26	41	6	1	4	18	61	11	34	0	1	.301	.379	.255
M Hendrickson ..	P	2	4	1	1	0	0	1	1	4	0	1	0	0	.250	1.000	.250
B Kielty	OF	137	427	71	104	26	1	13	57	171	71	92	8	3	.358	.400	.244
E Hinske	3B	124	449	74	109	45	3	12	63	196	59	104	12	2	.329	.437	.243
J Werth........	OF	26	48	7	10	4	0	2	10	20	3	22	1	0	.255	.417	.208
K Huckaby......	C	5	11	1	2	1	0	0	2	3	0	4	0	0	.182	.273	.182
K Escobar	P	2	6	1	1	0	0	0	1	1	0	3	0	0	.167	.167	.167
K Cash	C	34	106	10	15	3	0	1	8	21	4	22	0	0	.179	.198	.142
R Halladay......	P	2	9	2	1	0	0	0	0	1	0	3	0	0	.111	.111	.111

POS = position; G = games played; AB = at bats; R = runs; H = hits; 2B = doubles; 3B = triples; HR = home runs; RBI = runs batted in; TB = total bases; BB = walks; SO = strikeouts; SB = stolen bases; CS = caught stealing; OBP = on-base percentage; SLG = slugging percentage; AVG = batting average

Source: *Major League Baseball*

Pitchers

Player	W	L	ERA	G	GS	CG	SHO	SV	SVO	IP	H	R	ER	HR	HBP	BB	SO
▶ B Bowles	0	0	2.57	5	0	0	0	0	0	7.0	8	4	2	1	2	2	2
D Linton	0	0	3.00	7	0	0	0	0	0	9.0	7	3	3	2	0	4	7
J Kershner	3	3	3.17	40	0	0	0	0	1	54.0	43	21	19	5	2	15	32
R Halladay	22	7	3.25	36	36	9	2	0	0	266.0	253	111	96	26	9	32	204
D Creek	0	0	3.29	21	0	0	0	0	1	13.2	14	6	5	2	2	12	11
A Lopez	1	3	3.42	72	0	0	0	14	16	73.2	58	31	28	5	5	34	64
K Escobar	13	9	4.29	41	26	1	1	4	5	180.1	189	94	86	15	9	78	159
J Towers	8	1	4.48	14	8	1	0	1	1	64.1	67	34	32	15	4	7	42
S Service	0	0	4.50	15	0	0	0	0	0	16.0	17	8	8	3	0	6	17
T Miller	2	2	4.61	79	0	0	0	4	5	52.2	46	30	27	7	5	28	44
P Walker	2	2	4.88	23	7	0	0	0	0	55.1	59	31	30	11	2	24	29
V Chulk	0	0	5.06	3	0	0	0	0	1	5.1	6	3	3	0	0	3	2
D Davis	4	6	5.37	13	12	0	0	0	0	57.0	74	37	34	8	1	30	27
M Hendrickson . .	9	9	5.51	30	30	1	1	0	0	158.1	207	111	97	24	0	40	76
J Tam	0	4	5.64	44	0	0	0	1	2	44.2	58	30	28	5	1	25	26
C Politte	1	5	5.66	54	0	0	0	12	18	49.1	52	32	31	11	1	17	40
C Lidle	12	15	5.75	31	31	2	0	0	0	192.2	216	133	123	24	5	60	112
T Sturtze	7	6	5.94	40	8	0	0	0	0	89.1	107	67	59	14	7	43	54
D Reichert	0	0	6.06	15	0	0	0	0	1	16.1	28	12	11	2	2	8	13
C Thurman	1	1	6.46	6	3	0	0	0	0	15.1	21	11	11	3	0	9	11
J Acevedo	1	5	6.57	39	0	0	0	6	8	38.1	52	32	28	6	2	18	28
J Wasdin	0	1	23.40	3	2	0	0	0	0	5.0	16	13	13	2	0	4	5

W = wins; L = losses; ERA = earned run average; G = games played; GS = games started; CG = complete games; SHO = shutouts; SV = saves; SVO = save opportunities; IP = innings pitched; H = hits; R = runs; ER = earned runs; HR = home runs allowed; HBP = hit by pitch; BB = walks; SO = strikeouts

Source: *Major League Baseball*

Toronto Blue Jays Team Records, through 2003 Season

Batting

Single Season

Batting Average: John Olerud, 1993, .363

At Bats: Tony Fernandez, 1986, 687

Games: Tony Fernandez, 1986, 163

Hits: Vernon Wells, 2003, 215

Runs: Shawn Green, 1999, 134

Singles: Tony Fernandez, 1986, 161

Doubles: Carlos Delgado, 2000, 57

Triples: Tony Fernandez, 1990, 17

Home Runs: George Bell, 1987, 47

Runs Batted In: Carlos Delgado, 2003, 145

Total Bases: Carlos Delgado, 2000, 378

Slugging Percentage: Carlos Delgado, 2000, .664

On-Base Percentage: John Olerud, 1993, .473

Stolen Bases: Dave Collins, 1984, 60

Strikeouts: José Canseco, 1998, 159

Walks: Carlos Delgado, 2000, 123

Career Leaders

Batting Average: Roberto Alomar, .307

At Bats: Tony Fernandez, 5,335

Games: Tony Fernandez, 1,450

Hits: Tony Fernandez, 1,583

Runs: Carlos Delgado, 815

Singles: Tony Fernandez, 1,035

Doubles: Carlos Delgado, 317

Triples: Tony Fernandez, 72

Home Runs: Carlos Delgado, 304

Runs Batted In: George Bell, 959

Total Bases: Carlos Delgado, 2,541

Slugging Percentage: Carlos Delgado, .558

On-Base Percentage: Carlos Delgado, .395

Stolen Bases: Lloyd Moseby, 255

Strikeouts: Carlos Delgado, 1,127

Walks: Carlos Delgado, 758

▶

Pitching

Single Season	Career Leaders
Games: Mark Eichhorn, 1987, 89	**Games:** Duane Ward, 452
Games Started: Jim Clancy, 1982, 40	**Games Started:** Dave Stieb, 408
Complete Games: Dave Stieb, 1982, 19	**Complete Games:** Dave Stieb, 103
Innings Pitched: Dave Stieb, 1982, 288	**Innings Pitched:** Dave Stieb, 2,873
Wins: Roy Halladay, 2003, 22	**Wins:** Dave Stieb, 175
Losses: Jerry Garvin, 1977, 18; Phil Huffman, 1979, 18	**Losses:** Jim Clancy, 140
Saves: Duane Ward, 1993, 45	**Saves:** Tom Henke, 217
Earned Run Average: Mark Eichhorn, 1986, 1.72	**Earned Run Average:** Tom Henke, 2.48
Strikeouts: Roger Clemens, 1997, 292	**Strikeouts:** Dave Stieb, 1 658

Source: *Major League Baseball*

Toronto Blue Jays Player of the Year, 1977–2002

1977	Bob Bailor	1986	Jesse Barfield	1995	Roberto Alomar
1978	Bob Bailor	1987	George Bell	1996	Ed Sprague
1979	Alfredo Griffin	1988	Fred McGriff	1997	Carlos Delgado
1980	John Mayberry	1989	George Bell	1998	Carlos Delgado
1981	Dave Stieb	1990	Kelly Gruber	1999	Shawn Green
1982	Damaso Garcia	1991	Roberto Alomar	2000	Carlos Delgado
1983	Lloyd Moseby	1992	Roberto Alomar	2001	Jose Cruz Jr.
1984	Dave Collins	1993	Paul Molitor	2002	Vernon Wells
1985	Jesse Barfield	1994	Joe Carter		

Blue Jays' Hinske named 2002 AL rookie of the year

*T*oronto Blue Jays' third baseman Eric Hinske was voted the American League's rookie of the year for the 2002 season. Hinske earned 19 of 28 first-place votes and 9 second-place votes to claim the prize over second-place votegetter Rodrigo Lopez of the Baltimore Orioles. Hinske is the second Blue Jay to be named rookie of the year; in 1979, Alfredo Griffin was the co-winner with John Castino of the Minnesota Twins. Hinske earned the award after a 2002 campaign in which he batted .279, hit 24 home runs, and drove in 84 runs. Hinske's home run and RBI totals, along with his 38 doubles, 99 runs, and 77 walks, are all Blue Jays' rookie records.

Source: *Canadian Press*

National Basketball Association, 2002–03

Final Regular Season Standings

Eastern Conference

■ Atlantic Division

	W	L	PCT	GB
New Jersey (2)[a]	49	33	.598	—
Philadelphia (4)	48	34	.585	1
Boston (6)	44	38	.537	5
Orlando (8)	42	40	.512	7
Washington	37	45	.451	12
New York	37	45	.451	12
Miami	25	57	.305	24

■ Central Division

	W	L	PCT	GB
Detroit (1)[b]	50	32	.610	—
Indiana (3)	48	34	.585	2
New Orleans[c] (5)	47	35	.573	3
Milwaukee (7)	42	40	.512	8
Atlanta	35	47	.427	15
Chicago	30	52	.366	20
Toronto	24	58	.293	26
Cleveland	17	65	.207	33

Western Conference

■ Midwest Division

	W	L	PCT	GB
San Antonio (1)[d]	60	22	.732	—
Dallas (3)	60	22	.732	—
Minnesota (4)	51	31	.622	9
Utah (7)	47	35	.573	13
Houston	43	39	.524	17
Memphis	28	54	.341	32
Denver	17	65	.207	43

■ Pacific Division

	W	L	PCT	GB
Sacramento (2)	59	23	.720	—
L.A. Lakers (5)	50	32	.610	9
Portland (6)	50	32	.610	9
Phoenix (8)	44	38	.537	15
Seattle	40	42	.488	19
Golden State	38	44	.463	21
L.A. Clippers	27	55	.329	32

a Number in brackets indicates seeding in conference playoffs b Top seed in Eastern Conference playoffs c Played 2001–02 season in Charlotte d Top seed in Western Conference playoffs

Source: *NBA*

NBA Playoff Results, 2002–03

Eastern Conference

First Round (best-of-7 series)
Detroit defeated Orlando, 4–3
New Jersey defeated Milwaukee, 4–2
Boston defeated Indiana 4–2
Philadelphia defeated New Orleans 4–2

Semifinals (best-of-7 series)
Detroit defeated Philadelphia 4–2
New Jersey defeated Boston 4–0

Finals (best-of-7 series)
New Jersey defeated Detroit 4–0

Source: *NBA*

Western Conference

First Round (best-of-7 series)
San Antonio defeated Phoenix 4–2
Sacramento defeated Utah 4–1
Dallas defeated Portland 4–3
L.A. Lakers defeated Minnesota 4–2

Semifinals (best-of-7 series)
San Antonio defeated L.A. Lakers 4–2
Dallas defeated Sacramento 4–3

Finals (best-of-7 series)
San Antonio defeated Dallas 4–2

NBA FINALS

San Antonio Spurs defeated New Jersey Nets 4–2

Game 1:
San Antonio 101 – New Jersey 89
Game 2:
San Antonio 85 – **New Jersey 87**
Game 3:
San Antonio 84 – New Jersey 79
Game 4:
San Antonio 76 – **New Jersey 77**
Game 5:
San Antonio 93 – New Jersey 83
Game 6:
San Antonio 88 – New Jersey 77

Former ABA Teams Square Off for NBA Championship

For the first time, two teams from the old American Basketball Association (ABA) played for the NBA championship. The San Antonio Spurs and the New Jersey Nets were two of the four teams to join the NBA when the two leagues merged before the 1976–77 NBA season. Former ABA teams had contended for the NBA championship in three of the previous four years, with San Antonio becoming the first to win, in 1999, an NBA championship, but never before had two former ABA teams faced each other in the NBA Finals. San Antonio defeated New Jersey, four games to two, to capture its second NBA championship.

Source: *NBA*

Individual Statistical Leaders, Regular Season, 2002–03

Points Per Game

■ Points Per Game

Player	G	FG	FT	P	PG
1. Tracy McGrady (Orlando Magic)	75	829	576	2,407	32.1
2. Kobe Bryant (Los Angeles Lakers)	82	868	601	2,461	30.0
3. Allen Iverson (Philadelphia 76ers)	82	804	570	2,262	27.6
4. Shaquille O'Neal (Los Angeles Lakers)	67	695	451	1,841	27.5
5. Paul Pierce (Boston Celtics)	79	663	604	2,048	25.9
6. Dirk Nowitzki (Dallas Mavericks)	80	690	483	2,011	25.1
7. Tim Duncan (San Antonio Spurs)	81	714	450	1,884	23.3
8. Chris Webber (Sacramento Kings)	67	661	215	1,542	23.0
8. Kevin Garnett (Minnesota Timberwolves)	82	743	377	1,883	23.0
10. Ray Allen (Seattle SuperSonics)	76	598	316	1,713	22.5

■ Rebounds Per Game

Player	G	OFF	DEF	REB	RPG
1. Ben Wallace (Detroit Pistons)	73	4.0	11.4	1,126	15.4
2. Kevin Garnett (Minnesota Timberwolves)	82	3.0	10.5	1,102	13.4
3. Tim Duncan (San Antonio Spurs)	81	3.2	9.7	1,043	12.9
4. Jermaine O'Neal (Indiana Pacers)	77	2.6	7.7	796	10.3
5. Brian Grant (Miami Heat)	82	2.9	7.3	837	10.2
5. Troy Murphy (Golden State Warriors)	79	2.9	7.3	806	10.2
7. Dirk Nowitzki (Dallas Mavericks)	80	1.0	8.9	791	9.9
8. Shawn Marion (Phoenix Suns)	81	2.5	7.1	773	9.5
9. **Jerome Williams (Toronto Raptors)**	71	3.3	5.9	650	9.2
10. P.J. Brown (New Orleans Hornets)	78	3.1	5.9	701	9.0
10. Donyell Marshall (Chicago Bulls)	78	3.0	6.0	699	9.0

■ Field Goal Percentage

Player	FGM	FGA	%
1. Eddy Curry (Chicago Bulls)	335	573	.585
2. Shaquille O'Neal (Los Angeles Lakers)	695	1,211	.574
3. Carlos Boozer (Cleveland Cavaliers)	331	618	.536
4. P.J. Brown (New Orleans Hornets)	319	601	.531
5. Radoslav Nesterovic (Minnesota Timberwolves)	400	762	.525
6. Nene Hilario (Denver Nuggets)	321	619	.519
7. Tim Duncan (San Antonio Spurs)	714	1,392	.513
8. Matt Harpring (Utah Jazz)	521	1,020	.511
9. Pau Gasol (Memphis Grizzlies)	569	1,116	.510
10. Brian Grant (Miami Heat)	344	676	.509

■ Free Throw Percentage

Player	FTM	FTA	%
1. Allan Houston (New York Knicks)	363	395	.919
2. Ray Allen (Seattle SuperSonics)	316	345	.916
3. **Steve Nash (Dallas Mavericks)**	308	339	.909
4. Troy Hudson (Min. Timberwolves)	208	231	.900
4. Reggie Miller (Indiana Pacers)	207	230	.900
6. Jason Terry (Atlanta Hawks)	259	292	.887
7. Dirk Nowitzki (Dallas Mavericks)	483	548	.881
8. Chauncey Billups (Detroit Pistons)	318	362	.878
8. Jerry Stackhouse (Wash. Wizards)	455	518	.878
8. Darrell Armstrong (Orlando Magic)	165	188	.878

■ Assists Per Game

Player	GP	AST	AVG
1. Jason Kidd (New Jersey Nets)	80	711	8.9
2. Jason Williams (Memphis Grizzlies)	76	631	8.3
2. Gary Payton (Milwaukee Bucks)	80	663	8.3
4. Stephon Marbury (Phoenix Suns)	81	654	8.1
5. John Stockton (Utah Jazz)	82	629	7.7
6. Jamaal Tinsley (Indiana Pacers)	73	548	7.5
7. Jason Terry (Atlanta Hawks)	81	600	7.4
8. **Steve Nash (Dallas Mavericks)**	82	598	7.3
9. Andre Miller (Los Angeles Clippers)	80	537	6.7
10. Eric Snow (Philadelphia 76ers)	82	544	6.6

■ Three-Point Field Goals Percentage

Player	3FG	3FGA	%
1. Bruce Bowen (San Antonio Spurs)	101	229	.441
2. Michael Redd (Milwaukee Bucks)	182	416	.438
3. Wesley Person (Memphis Grizzlies)	100	231	.433
4. David Wesley (New Orleans Hornets)	134	316	.424
5. Wally Szczerbiak (Min. Timberwolves)	61	145	.421
6. **Steve Nash (Dallas Mavericks)**	111	269	.413
6. Matt Harpring (Utah Jazz)	66	160	.413
8. Anthony Peeler (Min. Timberwolves)	87	212	.410
9. Mike Bibby (Sacramento Kings)	56	137	.409
10. Eddie Jones (Miami Heat)	98	241	.407
10. Jon Barry (Detroit Pistons)	87	214	.407

■ **Steals Per Game**

Player	GP	STL	SPG
1. Allen Iverson (Philadelphia 76ers)	82	225	2.74
2. Ron Artest (Indiana Pacers)	69	159	2.30
3. Shawn Marion (Phoenix Suns)	81	185	2.28
4. Doug Christie (Sacramento Kings)	80	180	2.25
5. Jason Kidd (New Jersey Nets)	80	179	2.24
6. Kobe Bryant (Los Angeles Lakers)	82	181	2.21
7. Paul Pierce (Boston Celtics)	79	139	1.76
8. Caron Butler (Miami Heat)	78	137	1.76
9. Steve Francis (Houston Rockets)	81	141	1.74
10. Jamaal Tinsley (Indiana Pacers)	73	125	1.71

Source: *NBA*

■ **Blocked Shots Per Game**

Player	GP	BLK	AVG
1. Theo Ratliff (Atlanta Hawks)	81	262	3.23
2. Ben Wallace (Detroit Pistons)	73	230	3.15
3. Tim Duncan (San Antonio Spurs)	81	237	2.93
4. Elton Brand (Los Angeles Clippers)	62	158	2.55
5. Adonal Foyle (Golden State Warriors)	82	205	2.50
6. Shaquille O'Neal (Los Angeles Lakers)	67	159	2.37
7. Jermaine O'Neal (Indiana Pacers)	77	178	2.31
8. Andrei Kirilenko (Utah Jazz)	80	175	2.19
9. Shawn Bradley (Dallas Mavericks)	81	170	2.10
10. Erick Dampier (Golden State Warriors)	82	154	1.88
10. Zydrunas Ilgauskas (Clev. Cavaliers)	81	152	1.88
10. Keon Clark (Sacramento Kings)	80	150	1.88

All-Time NBA Statistical Leaders

(as of the end of the 2002–03 season)

■ **Total points, career**

Player	GP	FG	FT	PPG	PTS
1. Kareem Abdul-Jabbar	1,560	15,837	6,712	24.6	38,387
2. Karl Malone*	1,434	13,335	9,619	25.4	36,374
3. Michael Jordan*	1,072	12,192	7,327	30.1	32,292
4. Wilt Chamberlain	1,045	12,681	6,057	30.1	31,419
5. Moses Malone	1,329	9,435	8,531	20.6	27,409
6. Elvin Hayes	1,303	10,976	5,356	21.0	27,313
7. Hakeem Olajuwon	1,238	10,749	5,423	21.8	26,946
8. Oscar Robertson	1,040	9,508	7,694	25.7	26,710
9. Dominique Wilkins	1,074	9,963	6,031	24.8	26,668
10. John Havlicek	1,270	10,513	5,369	20.8	26,395

■ **Total rebounds, career**

Player	GP	OFF	DEF	RPG	REB
1. Wilt Chamberlain	1,045	0[a]	0	22.9	23,924
2. Bill Russell	963	0	0	22.5	21,620
3. Kareem Abdul-Jabbar	1,560	2,975	9,394	11.2	17,440
4. Elvin Hayes	1,303	2,778	6,973	12.5	16,279
5. Moses Malone	1,329	6,731	9,481	12.2	16,212
6. Robert Parish	1,611	4,598	10,117	9.1	14,715
7. Karl Malone*	1,434	3,501	11,100	10.2	14,601
8. Nate Thurmond	964	744	1,827	15.0	14,464
9. Walt Bellamy	1,043	264	481	13.7	14,241
10. Wes Unseld	984	2,085	4,974	14.0	13,769

[a] Offensive and defensive rebounds were not recorded prior to 1973–74 season.

■ **Total assists, career**

Player	GP	APG	AST
1. John Stockton*	1,504	10.5	15,806
2. Mark Jackson*	1,254	8.1	10,215
3. Magic Johnson	906	11.2	10,141
4. Oscar Robertson	1,040	9.5	9,887
5. Isiah Thomas	979	9.3	9,061
6. Rod Strickland*	1,017	7.6	7,704
7. Gary Payton*	1,027	7.4	7,590
8. Maurice Cheeks	1,101	6.7	7,392
9. Lenny Wilkens	1,077	6.7	7,211
10. Terry Porter	1,274	5.6	7,160

■ **Total blocked shots, career**

Player	GP	AVG	BLK
1. Hakeem Olajuwon	1,238	3.09	3,830
2. Kareem Abdul-Jabbar	1,560	2.57	3,189
3. Mark Eaton	875	3.50	3,064
4. David Robinson*	987	2.99	2,954
5. Patrick Ewing	1,183	2.45	2,894
6. Dikembe Mutombo*	864	3.33	2,873
7. Tree Rollins	1,156	2.20	2,542
8. Robert Parish	1,611	1.47	2,361
9. Manute Bol	624	3.34	2,086
10. George T. Johnson	904	2.46	2,082

Source: *NBA*   * Active player during 2002–03 season

[a] Blocked shots were not recorded prior to the 1973–74 season.

Toronto Raptors Individual Statistics, 2002–03

Player	G	MIN	FGM-A	FG%	3PM-A	3P%	FTM-A	FT%	PTS	PPG
Vince Carter	43	1,471	355-760	.467	45-131	.344	129-160	.806	884	20.6
Voshon Lenard	63	1,929	325-809	.402	92-252	.365	156-194	.804	898	14.3
Morris Peterson	82	2,949	421-1,073	.392	116-344	.337	195-247	.789	1,153	14.1
Antonio Davis	53	1,894	261-641	.407	0-0	.000	216-280	.771	738	13.9
Alvin Williams	78	2,638	396-905	.438	48-146	.329	187-239	.782	1,027	13.2
Jerome Williams	71	2,346	267-535	.499	1-6	.167	156-281	.555	691	9.7
Lindsey Hunter	29	673	106-302	.351	34-107	.318	34-47	.723	280	9.7
Rafer Alston	47	980	139-335	.415	51-130	.392	37-54	.685	366	7.8
Jelani McCoy	67	1,367	194-395	.491	0-0	.000	69-126	.548	457	6.8
Damone Brown	5	115	11-35	.314	0-2	.000	6-8	.750	28	5.6
Mamadou N'diaye	22	364	43-96	.448	0-0	.000	34-47	.723	120	5.5
Michael Bradley	67	1,314	151-314	.481	1-6	.167	35-67	.522	338	5.0
Greg Foster	29	539	47-122	.385	1-4	.250	26-32	.813	121	4.2
Chris Jefferies	51	666	75-194	.387	18-54	.333	29-43	.674	197	3.9
Nate Huffman	7	76	9-25	.360	0-0	.000	5-8	.625	23	3.3
Art Long	7	80	9-25	.360	1-2	.500	1-5	.200	20	2.9
Maceo Baston	16	106	15-25	.600	0-0	.000	10-12	.833	40	2.5
Zendon Hamilton	3	12	2-5	.400	0-0	.000	2-2	1.000	6	2.0

Player	REB	OFF	DEF	RPG	AST	APG	STL	BLK	TO	PF
Vince Carter	188	59	129	4.40	143	3.3	48	41	74	121
Voshon Lenard	212	48	164	3.40	144	2.3	59	21	103	156
Morris Peterson	363	97	266	4.40	188	2.3	88	32	128	232
Antonio Davis	437	130	307	8.20	131	2.5	23	62	118	150
Alvin Williams	245	55	190	3.10	416	5.3	111	21	128	170
Jerome Williams	650	231	419	9.20	95	1.3	116	26	98	197
Lindsey Hunter	59	15	44	2.00	71	2.4	35	5	57	50
Rafer Alston	107	21	86	2.30	192	4.1	38	15	86	120
Jelani McCoy	355	95	260	5.30	43	.6	28	60	96	162
Damone Brown	15	3	12	3.00	3	.6	1	0	6	14
Mamadou N'diaye	82	29	53	3.70	7	.3	8	32	21	58
Michael Bradley	409	162	247	6.10	67	1.0	16	32	76	125
Greg Foster	102	30	72	3.50	13	.4	1	9	30	82
Chris Jefferies	59	16	43	1.20	22	.4	19	16	45	56
Nate Huffman	23	9	14	3.30	5	.7	1	3	3	13
Art Long	20	8	12	2.90	4	.6	3	1	11	13
Maceo Baston	23	4	19	1.40	0	.0	4	11	6	16
Zendon Hamilton	4	1	3	1.30	0	.0	1	0	1	2

Source: *NBA*

G= games played; MIN = total minutes (season); FGM-A = field goals made-attempts; FG% = field goal percentage; 3PM-A = three-point field goals made-attempts; 3P% = three-point field goal percentage; FTM-A = free throws made-attempts; FT% = free throw percentage; PTS = total points (season); PPG = points per game; REB = total rebounds (season); OFF = total offensive rebounds (season); DEF = total defensive rebounds (season); RPG = rebounds per game; AST = total assists (season); APG = assists per game; STL = total steals (season); BLK = total blocked shots (season); TO = total turnovers (season); PF = total personal fouls (season)

Shanghai Sensation Yao Ming Attracts New Fan Base to NBA

*W*hen the Houston Rockets used the first overall pick in the 2002 NBA Draft on centre Yao Ming of China, pundits wondered whether the team had made a worthy basketball pick; no one questioned the impact that the 7'5" Yao would have in attracting fans. Arenas around the league sold out weeks in advance when the Rockets came to town, led by legions of fans of Chinese descent. In Toronto, Chinese Canadians came out in force—including a block of 2,000 tickets purchased by the Canadian Chinese Youth Athletic Association—for the single game in March 2003 that the Rockets played at the Air Canada Centre against the Raptors. As it turns out, Yao also has game—he finished second in the voting for Rookie of the Year, behind Amare Stoudemire of the Phoenix Suns.

Source: *NBA; Canadian Press*

Men's Olympic Games Qualifying Tournament, 2003

Pan-American Olympic Qualifying Tournament for Men 2003
San Juan, Puerto Rico—August 20–31, 2003

Preliminary Round Standings

■ Group A				■ Group B		
Team	W	L		Team	W	L
Argentina	3	1		Brazil	3	1
Canada	**3**	**1**		Dominican Republic	2	2
Mexico	2	2		USA	4	0
Puerto Rico	2	2		Venezuela	1	3
Uruguay	0	4		Virgin Islands	0	4

Note: Top four teams in each group qualify for second round.

Preliminary Round Scores

Wednesday, August 20	Thursday, August 21	Friday, August 22	Saturday, August 23	Sunday, August 24
Mexico 91, Argentina 89	Argentina 91, Uruguay 60	Mexico 80, Uruguay 68	**Canada 90**, Uruguay 84	**Canada 108**, Mexico 72
Dominican Republic 78, Venezuela 76	Brazil 100, Virgin Islands 74	Argentina 94, **Canada 90**	U.S. 113, Virgin Islands 55	Venezuela 87, Virgin Islands 84
Puerto Rico 91, Uruguay 78	**Canada 89**, Puerto Rico 79	Dominican Republic 69, Virgin Islands 65	Puerto Rico 92, Mexico 70	Argentina 85, Puerto Rico 80
U.S. 110, Brazil, 76	U.S. 111, Dominican Republic 73	U.S. 98, Venezuela 69	Brazil 96, Venezuela 89	Brazil 104, Dominican Republic 72

Second Round Standings

Team	W	L		Team	W	L
USA	7	0		Venezuela	3	4
Argentina	4	3		Mexico	3	4
Canada	**4**	**3**		Brazil	2	5
Puerto Rico	4	3		Dominican Republic	1	6

Note: Top four teams qualify for final round.

Second Round Scores

Monday, August 25	Tuesday, August 26	Wednesday, August 27	Thursday, August 28
Mexico 100, Dominican Republic 91	Venezuela 98, Mexico 95	**Canada 78**, Dominican Republic 75	Venezuela 93, **Canada 86** (OT)
Argentina 76, Brazil 74	U.S. 94, Argentina 86	Venezuela 97, Argentina 92	Mexico 102, Brazil 92
Puerto Rico 84, Venezuela 59	Puerto Rico 94, Dominican Republic 61	Puerto Rico 72, Brazil 70	Argentina 102, Dominican Republic 72
U.S. 111, **Canada 71**	**Canada 101**, Brazil 97	U.S. 96, Mexico 69	U.S. 91, Puerto Rico 65

Final Round Standings

Team	W	L		Team	W	L
USA	10	0		Puerto Rico	6	4
Argentina	6	4		**Canada**	**5**	**5**

Note: Top three teams qualify for 2004 Olympic Games in Athens.

Final Round Scores

Saturday, August 30	Sunday, August 31
	Bronze Medal game, Puerto Rico 79, **Canada 66** (Puerto Rico qualifies for 2004 Olympics)
Medal Semifinals — Argentina 88, **Canada 72**	
Medal Semifinals — U.S. 87, Puerto Rico 71	Gold Medal game, U.S. 106, Argentina 73 (U.S and Argentina qualify for 2004 Olympics)

Source: *FIBA*

Canadian Men's National Team

Name	Hometown	Name	Hometown
Rowan Barrett (G)	Mississauga, ON	Andrew Kwiatkowski (F)	Cambridge, ON
Denham Brown (G)	Toronto, ON	Steve Nash (G)	Victoria, BC
Greg Francis (G)	Toronto, ON	Greg Newton (C)	Niagara Falls, ON
Peter Guarasci (C)	Niagara Falls, ON	Shawn Swords (G)	Sudbury, ON
Prosper Karangwa (G)	Montreal, QC	Novell Thomas (G)	Richmond, BC
Mike King (F)	Guelph, ON	Jesse Young (F)	Peterborough, ON

Coach Jay Triano

Source: *Basketball Canada*

Women's Olympic Games Qualifying Tournament, 2003

Pan-American Olympic Qualifying Tournament for Women 2003
Culiacan, Mexico—September 17–21, 2003

Preliminary Round Standings

■ Group A						■ Group B					
Team	W	L	PF	PA	PTS	Team	W	L	PF	PA	PTS
Brazil	2	0	216	98	4	Cuba	3	0	258	171	6
Mexico	1	1	107	167	3	Canada	2	1	212	168	5
Chile	0	2	98	156	2	Argentina	1	2	218	209	4
						Dominican Rep.	0	3	158	298	3

Note: Top two teams in each group qualify for semi-final round.

Preliminary Round Scores

Wednesday, September 17

Brazil 102, Chile 45

Cuba 102, Dominican Republic 50

Canada 57, Argentina 56

Thursday, September 18

Argentina 104, Dominican Republic 73

Brazil 114, Mexico 53

Cuba 77, **Canada** 63

Friday, September 19

Mexico 54, Chile 53

Cuba 79, Argentina 58

Canada 92, Dominican Republic 35

Semi-final Round

Saturday, September 20

Brazil 71, **Canada 65**

Cuba 76, Mexico 49

Bronze Medal Game

Sunday, September 21

Gold Medal Game

Sunday, September 21

Brazil 90, Cuba 81

Source: *FIBA*   Note: Only gold medal winner advances to 2004 Summer Olympic Games in Athens, Greece.

Canadian Women's National Team

Name	Hometown	Name	Hometown
Cal Bouchard (G)	Aurora, ON	Nikki Johnson (G/F)	Niagara Falls, ON
Claudia Brassard (F)	Quebec City, QC	Teresa Kleindienst (G)	Abbotsford, BC
Leighann Doan (G)	Halkirk, AB	Susan Murray (C)	Mississauga, ON
Carolyn Ganes (C)	Saskatoon, SK	Dianne Norman (F)	Fredericton, NB
Isabelle Grenier (G)	Sainte-Foy, QC	Kim Smith (F)	Mission, BC
Michelle Hendry (F)	Kamloops, BC	Shona Thorburn (G)	Hamilton, ON

Coach   Allison McNeill

Source: *Basketball Canada*

Canadian Football League

(2002 Regular Season Standings)

Team	GP	W	L	T	OTL	F	A	PTS
East Division								
Montreal	18	13	5	0	1	587	407	27
Toronto	18	8	10	0	0	344	482	16
Hamilton	18	7	11	0	1	427	524	15
Ottawa	18	4	14	0	2	356	550	10

Note: Teams losing in overtime are awarded one point.

Team	GP	W	L	T	OTL	F	A	PTS
West Division								
Edmonton	18	13	5	0	0	516	450	26
Winnipeg	18	12	6	0	0	566	421	24
B. Columbia . .	18	10	8	0	0	480	399	20
Saskatchewan .	18	8	10	0	2	435	393	18
Calgary	18	6	12	0	2	438	509	14

Playoffs

Sunday, November 10, 2002
Eastern Division Semi-Final —
Saskatchewan 14 at Toronto 24
Attendance: 23,124
Western Division Semi-Final —
British Columbia 3 at Winnipeg 30
Attendance: 22,508

Sunday, November 17, 2002
Eastern Division Final —
Toronto 18 at Montreal 35
Attendance: 57,125
Western Division Final —
Winnipeg 30 at Edmonton 33
Attendance: 34,322

Sunday, November 24, 2002—Montreal **25** vs Edmonton **16**
Grey Cup Championship at Olympic Stadium, Montreal—Attendance: 62,531

Source: *Canadian Football League*

CFL All-Stars, 2002

(voted by Football Reporters of Canada)

Offence

Quarterback: Anthony Calvillo, Montreal
Running Back: John Avery, Edmonton
Running Back: Charles Roberts, Winnipeg
Slotback: Milt Stegall*, Winnipeg
Slotback: Terry Vaughn, Edmonton
Wide Receiver: Derick Armstrong, Saskatchewan
Wide Receiver: Jason Tucker, Edmonton
Centre: Bryan Chiu, Montreal
Tackle: Uzooma Okeke, Montreal
Tackle: Dave Mudge, Winnipeg
Guard: Scott Flory, Montreal
Guard: Jay McNeil, Calgary

Defence

Defensive Tackle: Denny Fortney, Winnipeg
Defensive Tackle: Doug Brown, Winnipeg
Defensive End: Elfrid Payton, Edmonton
Defensive End: Joe Montford, Toronto
Linebacker: Barrin Simpson, British Columbia
Linebacker: John Grace, Ottawa
Linebacker: Brendon Ayanbadejo, British Columbia
Cornerback: Eric Carter, British Columbia
Cornerback: Omar Morgan, Saskatchewan
Defensive Back: Barron Miles, Montreal
Defensive Back: Clifford Ivory, Toronto
Safety: Rob Hitchcock, Hamilton

Special Teams

Punter:
Noel Prefontaine, Toronto

Placekicker:
Sean Fleming, Edmonton

Special Team:
Corey Holmes, Saskatchewan

Source: *Canadian Football League*   * - Unanimous selection

Troubled CFL Franchises

The summer of 2003 was a taxing time for the CFL's two southern Ontario franchises. The league announced that it was taking control of the management of the Toronto Argonauts and the Hamilton Tiger-Cats franchises until new ownership stepped forward for each franchise. Money problems were the crowning blows that led to the league's action — Toronto's management stopped paying its bills; Hamilton's leadership failed to meet its players' payroll. The league promises to find the right ownership groups that will revitalize both of these storied franchises.

The Grey Cup, 1909–2002

The Grey Cup was donated in 1909 by Governor General Earl Grey for the "Rugby Football Championship of Canada." Since 1954, only teams in the Canadian Football League have challenged for the trophy, with the winners of the East and West divisions meeting in the championship game.

1909	U. of Toronto 26, Parkdale 6	**1957**	Hamilton 32, Winnipeg 7
1910	U. of Toronto 16, Ham. Tigers 7	**1958**	Winnipeg 35, Hamilton 28
1911	U. of Toronto 14, Toronto 7	**1959**	Winnipeg 21, Hamilton 7
1912	Ham. Alerts 11, Toronto 4	**1960**	Ottawa 16, Edmonton 6
1913	Ham. Tigers 44, Parkdale 2	**1961**	Winnipeg 21, Hamilton 14
1914	Toronto 14, U. of Toronto 2	**1962**	Winnipeg 28, Hamilton 27
1915	Ham. Tigers 13, Tor. R.A.A. 7	**1963**	Hamilton 21, BC 10
1916–19	No games held.	**1964**	BC 34, Hamilton 24
1920	U. of Toronto 16, Toronto 3	**1965**	Hamilton 22, Winnipeg 16
1921	Toronto 23, Edmonton 0	**1966**	Saskatchewan 29, Ottawa 14
1922	Queen's U. 13, Edmonton 1	**1967**	Hamilton 24, Saskatchewan 1
1923	Queen's U. 54, Regina 0	**1968**	Ottawa 24, Calgary 21
1924	Queen's U. 11, Balmy Beach 3	**1969**	Ottawa 29, Saskatchewan 11
1925	Ott. Senators 24, Winnipeg 1	**1970**	Montreal 23, Calgary 10
1926	Ott. Senators 10, U. of Toronto 7	**1971**	Calgary 14, Toronto 11
1927	Balmy Beach 9, Ham. Tigers 6	**1972**	Hamilton 13, Saskatchewan 10
1928	Ham. Tigers 30, Regina 0	**1973**	Ottawa 22, Edmonton 18
1929	Ham. Tigers 14, Regina 3	**1974**	Montreal 20, Edmonton 7
1930	Balmy Beach 11, Regina 6	**1975**	Edmonton 9, Montreal 8
1931	Mtl. A.A.A. 22, Regina 0	**1976**	Ottawa 23, Saskatchewan 20
1932	Ham. Tigers 25, Regina 6	**1977**	Montreal 41, Edmonton 6
1933	Toronto 4, Sarnia 3	**1978**	Edmonton 20, Montreal 13
1934	Sarnia 20, Regina 12	**1979**	Edmonton 17, Montreal 9
1935	Winnipeg 18, Ham. Tigers 12	**1980**	Edmonton 48, Hamilton 10
1936	Sarnia 26, Ott. R.R. 20	**1981**	Edmonton 26, Ottawa 23
1937	Toronto 4, Winnipeg 3	**1982**	Edmonton 32, Toronto 16
1938	Toronto 30, Winnipeg 7	**1983**	Toronto 18, BC 17
1939	Winnipeg 8, Ottawa 7	**1984**	Winnipeg 47, Hamilton 17
1940[1]	Ottawa 12, Balmy Beach 5	**1985**	BC 37, Hamilton 24
	Ottawa 8, Balmy Beach 2	**1986**	Hamilton 39, Edmonton 15
1941	Winnipeg 18, Ottawa 16	**1987**	Edmonton 38, Toronto 36
1942	Tor. R.C.A.F. 8, Win. R.C.A.F. 5	**1988**	Winnipeg 22, BC 21
1943	Ham. F. Wild 23, Win. R.C.A.F. 14	**1989**	Saskatchewan 43, Hamilton 40
1944	Mtl. St. H.D. Navy 7, Ham. F. Wild 6	**1990**	Winnipeg 50, Edmonton 11
1945	Toronto 35, Winnipeg 0	**1991**	Toronto 36, Calgary 21
1946	Toronto 28, Winnipeg 6	**1992**	Calgary 24, Winnipeg 10
1947	Toronto 10, Winnipeg 9	**1993**	Edmonton 33, Winnipeg 23
1948	Calgary 12, Ottawa 7	**1994**	BC 26, Baltimore 23
1949	Mtl. Als. 28, Calgary 15	**1995**	Baltimore 37, Calgary 20
1950	Toronto 13, Winnipeg 0	**1996**	Toronto 43, Edmonton 37
1951	Ottawa 21, Saskatchewan 14	**1997**	Toronto 47, Saskatchewan 23
1952	Toronto 21, Edmonton 11	**1998**	Calgary 26, Hamilton 24
1953	Hamilton 12, Winnipeg 6	**1999**	Hamilton 32, Calgary 21
1954	Edmonton 26, Montreal 25	**2000**	BC 28, Montreal 26
1955	Edmonton 34, Montreal 19	**2001**	Calgary 27, Winnipeg 19
1956	Edmonton 50, Montreal 27	**2002**	Montreal 25, Edmonton 16

Source: *Canadian Press*

(1) A 2-game total point series.

All-Time Leading CFL Players

(up to the end of the 2002 season)

Playing Records

Games Played, Career

408 . . . . . Lui Passaglia (B.C.) 1976–2000
394 . . . . . Bob Cameron (Winnipeg) 1980–2002
321 . . . . . Miles Gorrell (five teams) 1978–1996
299 . . . . . Damon Allen (five teams) 1985–2002
290 . . . . . Paul Osbaldiston (three teams) 1986–2002

Consecutive Games Played

353 . . . . . Bob Cameron (Winnipeg) 1980–2000
268 . . . . . Paul Osbaldiston (three teams) 1988–2002
262 . . . . . Mark McLoughlin (Calgary) 1988–2002
253 . . . . . Dave Cutler (Edmonton) 1969–1984
252 . . . . . Leo Groenewegen (three teams) 1987–2000

Seasons Played, Career

25 . . . . . . Lui Passaglia (B.C.) 1976–2000
23 . . . . . . Bob Cameron (Winnipeg) 1980–2002
22 . . . . . . Eddie Emerson (Ottawa) 1911–1937
20 . . . . . . Hank Ilesic (three teams) 1977–1993, 1995, 1998, 2001
19 . . . . . . Ron Lancaster (two teams) 1960–1978
19 . . . . . . Miles Gorrell (five teams) 1978–1996

Consecutive Seasons Played

25 . . . . . . Lui Passaglia (B.C.) 1976–2000
21 . . . . . . Bob Cameron (Winnipeg) 1980–2002
19 . . . . . . Miles Gorrell (Five teams) 1978–1997
19 . . . . . . Ron Lancaster (Two Teams) 1960–1978
18 . . . . . . Damon Allen (five teams) 1985–2002

Scoring Records

Points, Career

3991 . . . . . Lui Passaglia (B.C.) 1976–2000
2852 . . . . . Paul Osbaldiston (three teams) 1986–2002
2848 . . . . . Mark McLoughlin (Calgary) 1988–2002
2374 . . . . . Dave Ridgway (Saskatchewan) 1982–1994
2237 . . . . . Dave Cutler (Edmonton) 1969–1984

Most Points, One Season

236 . . . . . Lance Chomyc (Toronto) 1991
235 . . . . . Roman Anderson (San Antonio) 1995
233 . . . . . Paul Osbaldiston (Hamilton) 1989
233 . . . . . Dave Ridgway (Saskatchewan) 1990
228 . . . . . Carlos Huerta (Baltimore) 1995

Most Points, One Game

36 . . . . . . Bob McNamara (Winnipeg) Oct 13, 1956
30 . . . . . . Ernie Pitts (Winnipeg) Aug 29, 1959
30 . . . . . . Fred Burket (Saskatchewan) Oct 26, 1959
30 . . . . . . Earl Lunsford (Calgary) Sept 2, 1962
30 . . . . . . Martin Patton (Shreveport) Aug 5, 1995
30 . . . . . . Eric Blount (Edmonton) Sept 15, 1995

Most Touchdowns, One Season

23 . . . . . . Milt Stegall (Winnipeg) 2002
22 . . . . . . Cory Philpot (B.C.) 1995
21 . . . . . . Allen Pitts (Calgary) 1994
20 . . . . . . Pat Abbruzzi (Montreal) 1956
20 . . . . . . Darrell K. Smith (Toronto) 1990
20 . . . . . . Blake Marshall (Edmonton) 1991
20 . . . . . . Jon Volpe (B.C.) 1991

Touchdowns, Career

137 . . . . . George Reed (Saskatchewan) 1963–1975
117 . . . . . Allen Pitts (Calgary) 1990–2000
113 . . . . . Mike Pringle (four teams) 1992–2001
97 . . . . . . Brian Kelly (Edmonton) 1979–1987
91 . . . . . . Dick Shatto (Toronto) 1954–1965
91 . . . . . . Tom Scott (three teams) 1974–1984

Most Touchdowns, One Game

6 . . . . Eddie James (Winnipeg) Sept 28, 1932
6 . . . . Bob McNamara (Winnipeg) Oct 13, 1956
5 . . . . Ernie Pitts (Winnipeg) Aug 29, 1959
5 . . . . Fred Burket (Saskatchewan) Oct 26, 1959
5 . . . . Earl Lunsford (Calgary) Sept 2, 1962
5 . . . . Martin Patton (Shreveport) Aug 5, 1995
5 . . . . Eric Blount (Edmonton) Sept 15, 1995

Source: *Canadian Football League*

CFL Outstanding Player Awards (1982–2002)[1]

Outstanding Player

1982	Condredge Holloway, Tor	1989	Tracy Ham, Edm	1996	Doug Flutie, Tor
1983	Warren Moon, Edm	1990	Mike Clemons, Tor	1997	Doug Flutie, Tor
1984	Willard Reaves, Wpg	1991	Doug Flutie, BC	1998	Mike Pringle, Mtl
1985	Mervyn Fernandez, BC	1992	Doug Flutie, Cal	1999	Danny McManus, Ham
1986	James Murphy, Wpg	1993	Doug Flutie, Cal	2000	Dave Dickenson, Cal
1987	Tom Clements, Wpg	1994	Doug Flutie, Cal	2001	Khari Jones, Wpg
1988	David Williams, BC	1995	Mike Pringle, Bal	2002	Milt Stegall, Wpg

Outstanding Canadian

1982	Rocky DiPietro, Ham	1989	Rocky DiPietro, Ham	1996	Leroy Blugh, Edm
1983	Paul Bennett, Wpg	1990	Ray Elgaard, Sask	1997	Sean Millington, BC
1984	Nick Arakgi, Mtl	1991	Blake Marshall, Edm	1998	Mike Morreale, Ham
1985	Paul Bennett, Ham	1992	Ray Elgaard, Sask	1999	Mike O'Shea, Tor
1986	Joe Poplawski, Wpg	1993	Dave Sapunjis, Cal	2000	Sean Millington, BC
1987	Scott Flagel, Wpg	1994	Gerald Wilcox, Wpg	2001	Doug Brown, Wpg
1988	Ray Elgaard, Sask	1995	Dave Sapunjis, Cal	2002	Ben Cahoon, Mtl

Outstanding Defensive Player

1982	James Parker, Edm	1989	Danny Bass, Edm	1996	Willie Pless, Edm
1983	Greg Marshall, Ott	1990	Greg Battle, Wpg	1997	Willie Pless, Edm
1984	James Parker, BC	1991	Greg Battle, Wpg	1998	Joe Montford, Ham
1985	Tyrone Jones, Wpg	1992	Willie Pless, Edm	1999	Calvin Tiggle, Ham
1986	James Parker, BC	1993	Jearld Baylis, Sask	2000	Joe Montford, Ham
1987	Gregg Stumon, BC	1994	Willie Pless, Edm	2001	Joe Montford, Ham
1988	Grover Covington, Ham	1995	Willie Pless, Edm	2002	Elfrid Payton, Edm

Outstanding Offensive Lineman

1982	Rudy Phillips, Ott	1989	Rod Connop, Edm	1996	Mike Kiselak, Tor
1983	Rudy Phillips, Ott	1990	Jim Mills, BC	1997	Mike Kiselak, Tor
1984	John Bonk, Wpg	1991	Jim Mills, BC	1998	Fred Childress, Cal
1985	Nick Bastaja, Wpg	1992	Rob Smith, Ott	1999	Uzooma Okeke, Mtl
1986	Roger Aldag, Sask	1993	Chris Walby, Wpg	2000	Pierre Vercheval, Mtl
1987	Chris Walby, Wpg	1994	Shar Pourdanesh, Bal	2001	Dave Mudge, Wpg
1988	Roger Aldag, Sask	1995	Mike Withycombe, Bal	2002	Brian Chiu, Mtl

Outstanding Rookie

1982	Chris Isaac, Ott	1989	Stephen Jordan, Ham	1996	Kelvin Anderson, Cal
1983	Johnny Shepherd, Ham	1990	Reggie Barnes, Ott	1997	Derrell Mitchell, Tor
1984	Dwaine Wilson, Mtl	1991	Jon Volpe, BC	1998	Steve Muhammad, BC
1985	Michael Gray, BC	1992	Mike Richardson, Wpg	1999	Pat LaCoste, BC
1986	Harold Hallman, Cal	1993	Michael O'Shea, Ham	2000	Albert Johnson III, Wpg
1987	Gill Fenerty, Tor	1994	Matt Goodwin, Bal	2001	Barrin Simpson, BC
1988	Orville Lee, Ott	1995	Shalon Baker, Edm	2002	Jason Clermont, BC

Source: *Canadian Football League*

(1) Winners are chosen by a vote of the Football Reporters of Canada; prior to 1989 they were known as the Schenley Awards.

Canadian Football Hall of Fame

(players only)

Player, Year Elected, Team(s)

Ah You, Junior (1997) Mtl
Aldag, Roger, (2002) Sask
Atchison, Ron, (1978) Sask
Bailey, Byron (1975) BC
Baker, Bitt (1994) Sask/BC
Barrow, John (1976) Ham
Bass, Danny (2000) Tor/Cgy/Edm
Batstone, Harry (1963) Tor/Queen's
Beach, Ormond (1963) Sarnia
Benecick, Al (1996) Sask
Bennett, Paul (2002) Tor/Wpg/Ham
Box, Ab (1965) Balmy Beach/Tor
Breen, Joseph (1963) U of Toronto/Tor
Bright, Johnny (1970) Edm/Cal
Brock, Ralph Dieter (1995) Wpg/Ham
Brown, Tom (1984) BC
Browne, Less (2002) Ham/Wpg/Ott/BC
Burden, Willie (2001) Cal
Campbell, Jerry "Soupy" (1996) Cal/Ott
Casey, Tom (1964) Wpg
Charlton, Ken (1992) Ott/Sask
Clements, Tom (1994) Ott/Sask/Ham/Wpg
Clark, Bill (1996) Sask
Coffey, Tommy Joe (1977) Edm/Cal
Conacher, Lionel (1963) Tor
Copeland, Royal (1988) Tor
Corrigal, Jim (1990) Tor
Covington, Grover (2000) Ham
Cox, Ernest (1963) Ham
Craig, Ross (1964) Ham
Cronin, Carl (1967) Wpg
Cutler, Dave (1998) Edm
Cutler, Wes (1968) Tor
Dalla Riva, Peter (1993) Mtl
Dipietro, Rocky (1997) Ham
Dixon, George (1974) Mtl
Elgaard, Ray (2002) Sask
Eliowitz, Abe (1969) Ott/Mtl
Emerson, Eddie (1963) Ott
Estay, Ron (2003) BC/Edm
Etcheverry, Sam (1969) Mtl
Evanshen, Terry (1984) Mtl/Cal/Ham/Tor
Faloney, Bernie (1974) Edm/Ham
Fear, Cap (1967) Tor/Mtl/Ham
Fennell, Dave (1990) Edm
Ferraro, John (1966) Ham/Mtl
Fieldgate, Norm (1979) BC
Fleming, Willie (1982) BC
Frank, Bill (2001) BC/Tor/Wpg

Player, Year Elected, Team(s)

Gabriel, Tony (1984) Ham/Ott
Gaines, Geve (1994) Mtl/Ott
Gall, Hugh (1963) U of Toronto
Golab, Tony (1964) Ott
Grant, Tom (1995) Ham/Wpg
Gray, Herb (1983) Wpg
Griffing, Dean (1965) Sask/Cal
Hanson, Fritz (1963) Wpg
Harris, Dickie (1998) Mtl
Harris, Wayne (1976) Cal
Harrison, Herman (1993) Cal
Helton, John (1985) Cal/Wpg
Henley, Garney (1979) Ham
Hinton, Tom (1991) BC
Holloway, Condredge (1998) O/Tor/BC
Huffman, Dick (1987) Wpg/Cal
Isbister, Bob (1965) Ham
Jackson, Russ (1973) Ott
Jacobs, Jack (1963) Wpg
James, Eddie (1963) Wpg/Reg
James, Gerry (1981) Wpg
Kabat, Greg (1966) Wpg
Kapp, Joe (1984) Cal/BC
Keeling, Jerry (1989) Cal/Ott/Ham
Kelly, Brian (1991) Edm
Kelly, Ellison (1992) Edm/Ham
Kepley, Dan (1996) Edm
Krol, Joe (1963) Tor/Ham
Kwong, Normie (1969) Cal/Edm
Lawson, Smirle (1963) U. of Toronto
Leadlay, Frank (1963) Queen's/Ham
Lear, Les (1974) Wpg/Cal
Lewis, Leo (1973) Wpg
Lunsford, Earl (1983) Cal
Luster, Marv (1990) Mtl/Tor
Luzzi, Don (1985) Cal
McCance, Chester (1976) Wpg/Mtl
McGill, Frank (1965) Mtl
McGowan, George (2003) Edm
McQuarters, Ed (1988) Sask
Miles, Rollie (1980) Edm
Moon, Warren (2001) Edm
Morris, Frank (1983) Tor/Edm
Morris, Ted (1964) Tor
Mosca, Angelo (1987) Ham
Murphy, James (2000) Wpg
Nelson, Roger (1985) Edm
Neumann, Peter (1979) Ham
O'Quinn, Red (1981) Mtl

Player, Year Elected, Team(s)

Pajaczkowski, Tony (1988) Cal/Mtl
Parker, Jackie (1971) Edm/Tor/BC
Parker, James (2001) Edm/BC/Tor
Patterson, Hal (1971) Mtl/Ham
Perry, Gordon (1970) Mtl
Perry, Norman (1963) Sarnia
Ploen, Ken (1975) Wpg
Poplawski, Joe (1998) Wpg
Quilty, Silver (1966) U. of Ottawa
Raimy, Dave (2000) Wpg/Tor
Rebholz, Russ (1963) Wpg
Reed, George (1979) Sask
Reeve, Ted (1963) Tor
Ridgway, Dave (2003) Sask
Rigney, Frank (1984) Wpg
Robinson, Larry (1998) Cal
Rodden, Michael (1964) Queen's/Tor
Rowe, Paul (1964) Cal
Ruby, Martin (1974) Sask
Russel, Jeff (1963) Ott
Scott, Tom (1998) Wpg/Edm
Scott, Vince (1982) Ham
Shatto, Dick (1975) Tor
Simpson, Benjamin (1963) Ham
Simpson, Bob (1976) Ott
Sprague, David (1963) Ham/Ott
Stevenson, Art (1969) Wpg
Stewart, Ron (1977) Ott
Stirling, Bummer (1966) Sarnia
Sutherin, Don (1992) Ham/Ott
Symons, Bill (1997) BC/Tor
Thelen, Dave (1989) Ott/Tor
Timmis, Brian (1963) Ham/Ott
Tinsley, Buddy (1982) Wpg
Tommy, Andrew (1989) Ott/Tor
Trawick, Herb (1975) Mtl
Tubman, Joe (1968) Ott
Tucker, Whit (1993) Ott
Urness, Ted (1989) Sask
Vaughn, Kaye (1978) Ott
Wagner, Virgil (1980) Mtl
Walby, Chris (2003) Mtl/Wpg
Welch, Huck (1964) Ham/Mtl
Wilkinson, Tom (1987) Edm
Wilson, Al (1997) BC
Wylie, Harvey (1980) Cal
Young, Jim (1991) BC
Zock, William (1984) Tor/Edm

Source: *Canadian Football League*

2003 CFL Hall of Fame Inductees

These five individuals were formally inducted into the Canadian Football Hall of Fame during the Induction Week festivities in Calgary, Alberta, September 11–14, 2003.

■ Ron Estay (Player):

Defensive end Ron Estay began his CFL career as a B.C. Lion in 1972. He was traded to the Edmonton Eskimos in 1973 and the team's defensive captain for four seasons. Estay was a two-time CFL All-Star (1977 and 1980) and four-time Western All-Star (1973, 1977, 1978, and 1980). He played in nine Grey Cup championships and was on the winning end six times. Estay retired in 1982 after nine years in the CFL. He has since been recognized for his contributions to football through his induction into the Louisiana State University Hall of Fame and the Alberta Sports Hall of Fame. For the past three years, Estay has been the defensive line coach for the Saskatchewan Roughriders.

■ Ed Henick (Builder):

A true, devoted football supporter, Ed Henick began his involvement in football while in high school in Saskatoon. Henick joined the Saskatoon Hilltops in 1947 as a player for two seasons. He quickly moved into coaching and administration and became president of the Hilltops in 1963 and 1964. Henick helped form the Saskatoon Minor Flag Football League, was commissioner of the Kinsmen Tackle Football League, president of Football Saskatchewan, president of the Prairie Junior Football Conference, among many more awards and honours. Henick passed away on November 24, 2000, shortly after handing out plaques at the Hilltops year-end banquet.

■ George McGowan (Player):

Wide receiver George McGowan played eight years with the Edmonton Eskimos, beginning in 1971. He led the CFL in pas receptions in 1973 and 1975, with 81 and 98 receptions, respectively. McGowan was a CFL All-Star three times and a Western All-Star three times. He received the Schenley Most Outstanding Player Award in 1973 and was named the Jeff Nicklin Award Winner as well in 1973. McGowan played in five Grey Cup games in eight years and was on the winning end two times.

■ Dave Ridgway (Player):

Kicker Dave Ridgway played his entire fourteen-year CFL career with the Saskatchewan Roughriders, beginning in 1982. Ridgway holds the CFL league record for most field goals in a regular season (59 field goals in 1990), most field goals in a regular season game (8 field goals), and most consecutive field goals during the regular season (28). He was a CFL All-Star six times and a Western All-Star seven times. Dave Ridgway was a three-time Dave Dryburgh Memorial Trophy Winner. He played in the 1989 Grey Cup game, kicking the winning field goal in the final seconds of the game. Ridgway retired from the Roughriders in 1996 and has since become a member of the Saskatchewan Plaza of Honour and had his jersey #36 retired by the team.

■ Chris Walby (Player):

Chris Walby began his CFL career with the Montreal Alouettes in 1981. After playing five games with the team, he finished off the season with the Winnipeg Blue Bombers. This towering offensive tackle played sixteen years in the CFL and was known for making players feel part of the group. Walby won CFL All-Star honours nine times, was a Western All-Star four times, and an Eastern All-Star seven times. He won the Schenley Most Outstanding Offensive Lineman Award in 1987 and the CFL Most Outstanding Offensive Lineman Award in 1993. Chris Walby played in five Grey Cup games, winning three. He retired from CFL action in 1996 and continues his involvement as a colour commentator for CBC during the CFL season.

Source: *Canadian Football League*

Canadian Football Hall of Fame

*I*nterested in Canadian Football? Visit the Canadian Football Hall of Fame. In the Hands-On zone you can kick a virtual field goal and view videos showing production of football equipment and in the Heritage zone you can view photos of Gridiron Greats. The Hall also offers student education programs that help kids build language skills as they discover the star players and explore exhibits. The CFL Hall of Fame itself is located at 58 Jackson Street West, Hamilton, Ontario and is open year round Tuesday to Saturday, 9:30 a.m. till 4:30 p.m. It's closed Statutory holidays and long weekends. For information call (905) 528-7566 or click on www.footballhof.com.

NFL Final Standings, 2002–03

American Football Conference

■ AFC East	W	L	T	PCT	PF	PA
NY Jets (Y)	9	7	0	.562	359	336
New England	9	7	0	.562	381	346
Miami	9	7	0	.562	378	301
Buffalo	8	8	0	.500	379	397

■ AFC North	W	L	T	PCT	PF	PA
Pittsburgh (Y)	10	5	1	.656	390	345
Cleveland (X)	9	7	0	.562	344	320
Baltimore	7	9	0	.438	316	354
Cincinnati	2	14	0	.125	279	456

■ AFC South	W	L	T	PCT	PF	PA
Tennessee (YZ)	11	5	0	.688	367	324
Indianapolis	10	6	0	.625	349	313
Jacksonville	6	10	0	.375	328	315
Houston	4	12	0	.250	213	356

■ AFC West	W	L	T	PCT	PF	PA
Oakland (*YZ)	11	5	0	.688	450	304
Denver	9	7	0	.562	392	344
San Diego	8	8	0	.500	333	367
Kansas City	8	8	0	.500	467	399

Source: *National Football League*

National Football Conference

■ NFC East	W	L	T	PCT	PF	PA
Philadelphia (*YZ)	12	4	0	.750	415	241
NY Giants (X)	10	6	0	.625	320	279
Washington	7	9	0	.438	307	365
Dallas	5	11	0	.312	217	329

■ NFC North	W	L	T	PCT	PF	PA
Green Bay (Y)	12	4	0	.750	398	328
Minnesota	6	10	0	.375	390	442
Chicago	4	12	0	.250	281	379
Detroit	3	13	0	.188	306	451

■ NFC South	W	L	T	PCT	PF	PA
Tampa Bay (YZ)	12	4	0	.750	346	196
Atlanta (X)	9	6	1	.594	402	314
New Orleans	9	7	0	.562	432	388
Carolina	7	9	0	.438	258	302

■ NFC West	W	L	T	PCT	PF	PA
San Francisco (Y)	10	6	0	.625	367	351
St Louis	7	9	0	.438	316	369
Seattle	7	9	0	.438	355	369
Arizona	5	11	0	.312	262	417

(X) Clinched Playoff Berth (Y) Clinched Division Title (Z) Clinched First Round Bye (*) Clinched Home Field Advantage in Playoffs

Playoffs

■ Wild Cards

Saturday, Jan. 4, 2003
At New York Jets 41
Indianapolis Colts 0

Saturday, Jan. 4, 2003
Atlanta Falcons 27
At Green Bay Packers 7

Sunday, Jan. 5, 2003
At Pittsburgh Steelers 36
Cleveland Browns 33

Sunday, Jan. 5, 2003
At San Francisco 49ers 39
New York Giants 38

■ Divisional Playoffs

Saturday, Jan. 11, 2003
At Tennessee Titans 34
Pittsburgh Steelers 31

Saturday, Jan. 11, 2003
At Philadelphia Eagles 20
Atlanta Falcons 6

Sunday, Jan. 12, 2003
At Tampa Bay Buccaneers 31
San Francisco 49ers 6

Sunday, Jan. 12, 2003
At Oakland Raiders 30
New York Jets 10

■ Conference Championship

Sunday, Jan. 19, 2003
Tampa Bay Buccaneers 27
Philadelphia Eagles 10

Sunday, Jan. 19, 2003
At Oakland Raiders 41
Tennessee Titans 24

■ Super Bowl XXXVII at Qualcomm Stadium San Diego, California

Sunday, Jan. 26, 2003
Tampa Bay Buccaneers 48
Oakland Raiders 21

Source: *National Football League*

Super Bowl Results, 1992–2003

Date	Results	MVP
Jan. 26, 1992	Washington 37, Buffalo 24	Mark Rypien, Washington
Jan. 31, 1993	Dallas 52, Buffalo 17	Troy Aikman, Dallas
Jan. 30, 1994	Dallas 30, Buffalo 13	Emmitt Smith, Dallas
Jan. 29, 1995	San Francisco 49, San Diego 26	Steve Young, San Francisco
Jan. 28, 1996	Dallas 27, Pittsburgh 17	Larry Brown, Dallas
Jan. 26, 1997	Green Bay 35, New England 21	Desmond Howard, Green Bay
Jan. 25, 1998	Denver 31, Green Bay 24	Terrell Davis, Denver
Jan. 31, 1999	Denver 34, Atlanta 19	John Elway, Denver
Jan. 30, 2000	St. Louis 23, Tennessee 16	Kurt Warren, St. Louis
Jan. 28, 2001	Baltimore 34, New York Giants 7	Ray Lewis, Baltimore
Feb. 3, 2002	New England 20, St. Louis 17	Tom Brady, New England
Jan. 26, 2003	Tampa Bay 48, Oakland 21	Dexter Jackson, Tampa Bay

National Football League Individual Leaders, 2002

■ PASSING

PLAYER	TEAM	YDS	ATT	CMP	TDS	INTS	LONG	RATING
Rich Gannon	OAK	4689	618	418	26	10	75	97.3
Drew Bledsoe	BUF	4359	610	375	24	15	73	86.0
Peyton Manning	IND	4200	591	392	27	19	69	88.8
Kerry Collins	NYG	4073	545	335	19	14	82	85.4
Daunte Culpepper	MIN	3853	549	333	18	23	61	75.3
Tom Brady	NE	3764	601	373	28	14	49	85.7
Trent Green	KC	3690	470	287	26	13	99	92.6
Brett Favre	GB	3658	551	341	27	16	85	85.6
Aaron Brooks	NO	3572	528	283	27	15	64	80.1
Steve McNair	TEN	3387	492	301	22	15	55	84.0

■ RECEIVING

PLAYER	TEAM	REC	YDS	AVG	TDS	LONG
Marvin Harrison	IND	143	1722	12.0	11	69
Hines Ward	PIT	112	1329	11.9	12	72
Randy Moss	MIN	106	1347	12.7	7	60
Eric Moulds	BUF	100	1292	12.9	10	70
Terrell Owens	SF	100	1300	13.0	13	76
Troy Brown	NE	97	890	9.2	3	38
Marty Booker	CHI	97	1189	12.3	6	54
Peerless Price	BUF	94	1252	13.3	9	73
Jerry Rice	OAK	92	1211	13.2	7	75
Charlie Garner	OAK	91	941	10.3	4	69
Torry Holt	STL	91	1302	14.3	4	58

■ RUSHING

PLAYER	TEAM	YDS	ATT	AVG	TDS	LONG
Ricky Williams	MIA	1853	383	4.8	16	63
LaDainian Tomlinson	SD	1683	372	4.5	14	76
Priest Holmes	KC	1615	313	5.2	21	56
Clinton Portis	DEN	1508	273	5.5	15	59
Travis Henry	BUF	1438	325	4.4	13	34
Deuce McAllister	NO	1388	325	4.3	13	62
Tiki Barber	NYG	1387	304	4.6	11	70
Jamal Lewis	BAL	1327	308	4.3	6	75
Fred Taylor	JAC	1314	287	4.6	8	63
Corey Dillon	CIN	1311	314	4.2	7	67

■ SACKS

PLAYER	TEAM	SACKS	TAC
Jason Taylor	MIA	18.5	45.0
Simeon Rice	TB	15.5	41.0
Dwight Freeney	IND	13	40.0
Hugh Douglas	PHI	12.5	44.0
Andre Carter	SF	12.5	45.0
Kabeer Gbaja-Biamila	GB	12	35.0
Julius Peppers	CAR	12	28.0
Leonard Little	STL	12	37.0
Roderick Coleman	OAK	11	32.0
Michael Strahan	NYG	11	55.0
LaVar Arrington	WAS	11	67.0

■ SCORING

PLAYER	TEAM	POINTS	TDS	XPT	FG
Priest Holmes	KC	144	24	0	0
Jay Feely	ATL	138	0	42	32
David Akers	PHI	133	0	43	30
John Carney	NO	130	0	37	31
Sebastian Janikowski	OAK	128	0	50	26
Ryan Longwell	GB	128	0	44	28
Martin Gramatica	TB	128	0	32	32
Jason Elam	DEN	120	0	42	26
Adam Vinatieri	NE	117	0	36	27
Morten Andersen	KC	117	0	51	22

Source: *NFL*

2003 PGA Scoring Leaders

(as of October 5, 2003)

Rank	Player (Country)	Average Strokes per Round
1	Tiger Woods (USA)	68.13
2	Vijay Singh (Fiji)	68.68
3	Ernie Els (South Africa)	68.76
4	**Mike Weir (Canada)**	**68.82**
5	Jim Furyk (USA)	68.86
6	Retief Goosen (South Africa)	69.18
7	Davis Love III (USA)	69.34
8	Kenny Perry (USA)	69.39
9	Darren Clarke (N. Ireland)	69.59
10	Nick Price (Zimbabwe)	69.69
10	David Toms (USA)	69.69
12	Chad Campbell (USA)	69.70
13	Robert Allenby (Australia)	69.73
14	Jay Haas (USA)	69.76
15	Fred Couples (USA)	69.79
16	Niclas Fasth (Sweden)	69.88
17	Loren Roberts (USA)	69.89
18	Tim Herron (USA)	69.93
19	Scott Verplank (USA)	69.95
20	Fred Funk (USA)	69.96
21	Bob Estes (USA)	69.99
22	Dicky Pride (USA)	70.02
23	Stewart Cink (USA)	70.05
24	Dennis Paulson (USA)	70.10
25	Phil Mickelson (USA)	70.11
150	**Ian Leggatt (Canada)**	**71.48**
156	**Glen Hnatiuk (Canada)**	**71.54**

Source: *Professional Golf Association*

2003 PGA Tour Money Leaders

(as of October 5, 2003 — in US dollars)

Rank	Player (Country)	Events	Earnings
1	Tiger Woods (USA)	16	$6 278 746
2	Vijay Singh (Fiji)	24	$6 107 507
3	Davis Love III (USA)	19	$5 541 096
4	Jim Furyk (USA)	23	$4 815 355
5	**Mike Weir (Canada)**	**19**	**$4 716 410**
6	Kenny Perry (USA)	23	$4 164 976
7	David Toms (USA)	24	$3 589 255
8	Ernie Els (South Africa)	15	$3 226 997
9	Chad Campbell (USA)	24	$2 612 464
10	Bob Tway (USA)	23	$2 361 750
11	Jay Haas (USA)	23	$2 328 752
12	Jonathan Kaye (USA)	25	$2 270 837
13	Justin Leonard (USA)	21	$2 257 325
14	Chris DiMarco (USA)	24	$2 228 030
15	Nick Price (Zimbabwe)	15	$2 171 591
16	Tim Herron (USA)	26	$2 077 390
17	Fred Funk (USA)	30	$1 971 508
18	Brad Faxon (USA)	23	$1 957 445
19	Steve Flesch (USA)	29	$1 947 532
20	J.L. Lewis (USA)	28	$1 945 659
21	Jerry Kelly (USA)	26	$1 876 149
22	Chris Riley (USA)	26	$1 851 533
23	Kirk Triplett (USA)	22	$1 835 361
24	Retief Goosen (S. Africa)	15	$1 819 523
25	Shaun Micheel (USA)	26	$1 817 492
123	**Glen Hnatiuk (Canada)**	**26**	**$ 468 083**
159	**Ian Leggatt (Canada)**	**23**	**$ 271 014**

Source: *Professional Golf Association*

Canadian PGA Tour Tournament Champions

Al Balding	1955 Mayfair Open		1967 New Orleans Open
	1957 Miami Beach Open		1968 Phoenix Open
	1957 West Palm Beach Open		1968 Tucson Open
	1957 Havana Invitational		1972 Robinson Open
Dave Barr	1981 Quad Cities Open	Ian Leggatt	2002 Tucson Open
	1987 Georgia-Pacific Atlanta Golf Classic	Stan Leonard	1957 Greater Greensboro Open
			1958 Tournament of Champions
	2003 Royal Caribbean Golf Classic (Champions Tour)		1960 Western Open
		Mike Weir	1999 Air Canada Championship
Kenneth Black (amateur)	1936 Vancouver Golden Jubilee		2000 WGC-American Express Championship
Dan Halldorson	1980 Pensacola Open		
	1986 Deposit Guaranty Golf Classic		2001 The Tour Championship
			2003 Bob Hope Chrysler Classic
George Knudson	1961 Coral Gables Open		2003 Nissan Open
	1963 Portland Open		2003 Masters
	1964 Fresno Open	Richard Zokol	1992 Greater Milwaukee Open

Official World Golf Ranking

(as of October 5, 2003)

Rank	Player (Country)	Pts. Avg.	Rank	Player (Country)	Pts. Avg.	Rank	Player (Country)	Pts. Avg.
1	Tiger Woods (USA)	17.07	35	Chad Campbell (USA)	2.99	69	Rory Sabbatini (South Africa)	2.06
2	Ernie Els (South Africa)	9.89	36	Alex Cejka (Germany)	2.95	70	J L Lewis (USA)	2.03
3	Vijay Singh (Fiji)	9.27	37	Ben Curtis (USA)	2.92	71	Craig Parry (Australia)	2.00
4	Davis Love-III (USA)	8.24	38	Fredrik Jacobson (Sweden)	2.88	72	Bernhard Langer (Germany)	1.96
5	Jim Furyk (USA)	7.77	39	Stephen Leaney (Australia)	2.85	73	Brian Davis (England)	1.95
6	**Mike Weir (Canada)**	**7.61**	40	Colin Montgomerie (Scotland)	2.80	74	Mathias Gronberg (Sweden)	1.93
7	David Toms (USA)	6.01	41	Justin Rose (England)	2.78	75	Bradley Dredge (Wales)	1.91
8	Kenny Perry (USA)	5.76	42	Eduardo Romero (Argentina)	2.70	76	Todd Hamilton (USA)	1.90
9	Retief Goosen (South Africa)	5.45	43	Tim Herron (USA)	2.66	77	Robert Gamez (USA)	1.90
10	Padraig Harrington (Ireland)	5.41	44	Scott Verplank (USA)	2.65	78	Tom Lehman (USA)	1.88
11	Phil Mickelson (USA)	5.10	45	Ian Poulter (England)	2.65	79	Scott McCarron (USA)	1.88
12	Nick Price (Zimbabwe)	5.06	46	Michael Campbell (New Zealand)	2.65	80	Mark Calcavecchia (USA)	1.87
13	Darren Clarke (N. Ireland)	4.87	47	Peter Lonard (Australia)	2.65	81	Dan Forsman (USA)	1.85
14	Justin Leonard (USA)	3.88	48	Shaun Micheel (USA)	2.64	82	Ignacio Garrido (Spain)	1.81
15	K.J. Choi (Korea)	3.83	49	Loren Roberts (USA)	2.61	83	Shingo Katayama (Japan)	1.81
16	Chris DiMarco (USA)	3.79	50	Scott Hoch (USA)	2.59	84	Geoff Ogilvy (Australia)	1.78
17	Robert Allenby (Australia)	3.51	51	Trevor Immelman (S. Africa)	2.53	85	Lee Janzen (USA)	1.77
18	Adam Scott (Australia)	3.40	52	Len Mattiace (USA)	2.53	86	Duffy Waldorf (USA)	1.77
19	Jay Haas (USA)	3.36	53	Niclas Fasth (Sweden)	2.52	87	Kevin Sutherland (USA)	1.77
20	Stuart Appleby (Australia)	3.30	54	Phillip Price (Wales)	2.47	88	Phil Tataurangi (New Zealand)	1.72
21	Rocco Mediate (USA)	3.30	55	John Huston (USA)	2.44	89	Ben Crane (USA)	1.71
22	Sergio Garcia (Spain)	3.24	56	Kirk Triplett (USA)	2.36	90	Steve Lowery (USA)	1.71
23	Paul Casey (England)	3.21	57	Jeff Sluman (USA)	2.35	91	Andre Stolz (Australia)	1.71
24	Thomas Björn (Denmark)	3.21	58	Angel Cabrera (Argentina)	2.35	92	Briny Baird (USA)	1.68
25	Charles Howell III (USA)	3.17	59	Tim Clark (South Africa)	2.33	93	Gary Evans (England)	1.65
26	Fred Funk (USA)	3.14	60	Steve Flesch (USA)	2.32	94	Jose M Olazabal (Spain)	1.62
27	Jonathan Kaye (USA)	3.14	61	John Rollins (USA)	2.29	95	Tim Petrovic (USA)	1.59
28	Jerry Kelly (USA)	3.14	62	Toshimitsu Izawa (Japan)	2.28	96	Aaron Baddeley (Australia)	1.56
29	Brad Faxon (USA)	3.13	63	Lee Westwood (England)	2.22	97	Toru Taniguchi (Japan)	1.55
30	Chris Riley (USA)	3.06	64	Nick Faldo (England)	2.13	98	Peter Jacobsen (USA)	1.55
31	Fred Couples (USA)	3.04	65	Jonathan Byrd (USA)	2.12	99	David Smail (New Zealand)	1.55
32	Rich Beem (USA)	3.03	66	Paul Lawrie (Scotland)	2.11	100	Robert Karlsson (Sweden)	1.50
33	Bob Tway (USA)	3.00	67	Stewart Cink (USA)	2.09	207	**Ian Leggatt (Canada)**	**0.75**
34	Bob Estes (USA)	3.00	68	Shigeki Maruyama (Japan)	2.06	224	**Glen Hnatiuk (Canada)**	**0.70**

Source: *The Official World Golf Ranking*

Weir wins Masters to become first Canadian to win a golf major championship

*M*ike Weir, a native of Bright's Grove, Ontario, became the first Canadian to win one of the men's professional golf tour's four major championships when he won the Masters Tournament in a sudden-death playoff against Len Mattiace of the United States. Weir also is the second left-handed golfer to win a major; Bob Charles of New Zealand won the British Open in 1963. The Masters victory was just one of many highlights of a stellar 2003 that kept Weir in contention for the PGA Tour's prestigious Player of the Year honour. The Masters was Weir's third win of the year, following victories at the Bob Hope Chrysler Classic and the Nissan Open. He also played well in the three other major championships, finishing tied for 3rd at the U.S. Open, tied for 7th at the PGA Championship, and tied for 28th at the British Open. And after finishing the 2002 campaign as the 46th-ranked golfer in the world, Weir climbed as high as the 3rd position in the Official World Golf Rankings. Weir's success simply added to the pressure to become the first Canadian in 49 years to capture Canada's national championship, the Bell Canadian Open, at Hamilton (Ontario) Golf Club in September, but his 3-under par score of 277 was only enough for a 10th-place finish.

Source: *PGA Tour*

2002–03 PGA Tour Tournament Champions

(October 6, 2002–October 5, 2003)

Date	Tournament	Location	Champion
Oct. 3–6, 2002	Michelob Championship at Kingsmill	Williamsburg, VA	Charles Howell III
Oct. 10–13, 2002	Invensys Classic at Las Vegas	Las Vegas, NV	Phil Tataurangi
Oct. 17–20, 2002	The Disney Golf Classic	Lake Buena Vista, FL	Bob Burns
Oct. 24–27, 2002	Buick Challenge	Pine Mountain, GA	Jonathan Byrd
Oct. 31–Nov. 3, 2002	THE TOUR Championship presented by Coca-Cola	Atlanta, GA	Vijay Singh
Oct. 31–Nov. 3, 2002	Southern Farm Bureau Classic	Madison, MS	Luke Donald
Jan. 9–12, 2003	Mercedes Championships	Kapalua, HI	Ernie Els
Jan. 16–19, 2003	Sony Open in Hawaii	Honolulu, HI	Ernie Els
Jan. 23–26, 2003	Phoenix Open	Scottsdale, AZ	Vijay Singh
Jan. 29–Feb. 2, 2003	Bob Hope Chrysler Classic	La Quinta, CA	**Mike Weir**
Feb. 6–9, 2003	AT&T Pebble Beach National Pro-Am	Pebble Beach, CA	Davis Love III
Feb. 13–16, 2003	Buick Invitational	San Diego, CA	Tiger Woods
Feb. 20–23, 2003	Nissan Open	Pacific Palisades, CA	**Mike Weir**
Feb. 27–March 2, 2003	WGC-Accenture Match Play Championship	Carlsbad, CA	Tiger Woods
Feb. 27–March 2, 2003	Chrysler Classic of Tucson	Tucson, AZ	Frank Lickliter II
March 6–9, 2003	Ford Championship at Doral	Miami, FL	Scott Hoch
March 13–16, 2003	The Honda Classic	Palm Beach Gardens, FL	Justin Leonard
March 20–23, 2003	Bay Hill Invitational Presented by Cooper Tires	Orlando, FL	Tiger Woods
March 27–30, 2003	THE PLAYERS Championship	Ponte Vedra Beach, FL	Davis Love III
April 3–6, 2003	BellSouth Classic	Duluth, GA	Ben Crane
April 10–13, 2003	The Masters #	Augusta, GA	**Mike Weir**
April 17–20, 2003	The MCI Heritage	Hilton Head Island, SC	Davis Love III
April 24–27, 2003	Shell Houston Open	Houston, TX	Fred Couples
May 1–4, 2003	HP Classic of New Orleans	New Orleans, LA	Steve Flesch
May 8–11, 2003	Wachovia Championship	Charlotte, NC	David Toms
May 15–18, 2003	EDS Byron Nelson Championship	Irving, TX	Vijay Singh
May 22–25, 2003	Bank of America Colonial	Fort Worth, TX	Kenny Perry
May 29–June 1, 2003	Memorial Tournament	Dublin, OH	Kenny Perry
June 5–8, 2003	Booz Allen Open	Potomac, MD	Rory Sabbatini
June 12–15, 2003	U.S. Open #	Olympia Fields, IL	Jim Furyk
June 19–22, 2003	Buick Classic	Harrison, NY	Jonathan Kaye
June 26–29, 2003	FedEx St. Jude Classic	Memphis, TN	David Toms
July 3–6, 2003	100th Western Open	Lemont, IL	Tiger Woods
July 10–13, 2003	Greater Milwaukee Open	Milwaukee	Kenny Perry
July 17–20, 2003	British Open #	Sandwich, England	Ben Curtis
July 17–20, 2003	B.C. Open	Endicott, NY	Craig Stadler
July 24–27, 2003	Greater Hartford Open	Cromwell, CT	Peter Jacobsen
July 31–Aug. 3, 2003	Buick Open	Grand Blanc, MI	Jim Furyk
Aug. 7–10, 2003	The INTERNATIONAL	Castle Rock, CO	Davis Love III
Aug. 14–17, 2003	PGA Championship #	Rochester, NY	Shaun Micheel
Aug. 21–24, 2003	WGC-NEC Invitational	Akron, OH	Darren Clarke
Aug. 21–24, 2003	Reno-Tahoe Open	Reno, NV	Kirk Triplett
Aug. 29–Sept. 1, 2003	Deutsche Bank Championship	Norton, MA	Adam Scott
Sept. 4–7, 2003	**Bell Canadian Open**	**Ancaster, Ontario, Canada**	**Bob Tway**
Sept. 11–14, 2003	John Deere Classic	Silvis, IL	Vijay Singh
Sept. 18–21, 2003	84 Lumber Classic of Pennsylvania	Farmington, PA	J.L. Lewis
Sept. 25–28, 2003	Valero Texas Open	San Antonio, TX	Tommy Armour III
Oct. 2–5, 2003	WGC-American Express Championship	Woodstock, GA	Tiger Woods
Oct. 2–5, 2003	Southern Farm Bureau Classic	Madison, MS	John Huston

Source: *Professional Golf Association*   # Major Championships

2003 LPGA Scoring Leaders

(as of October 5, 2003)

Rank	Player (Country)	Average Strokes per Round	Rank	Player (Country)	Average Strokes per Round
1	Annika Sorenstam (Sweden)	69.18	15	Meg Mallon (USA)	70.97
2	Rosie Jones (USA)	69.96	16	Mi-Hyun Kim (Korea)	71.02
3	Se Ri Pak (Korea)	70.01	17	Rachel Teske (Australia)	71.04
4	Grace Park (Korea)	70.14	18	Michele Redman (USA)	71.12
5	Karrie Webb (Australia)	70.19	19	Becky Morgan (Wales)	71.16
6	Juli Inkster (USA)	70.28	20	Suzann Pettersen (Norway)	71.19
7	Patricia Meunier-Lebouc (France)	70.40	21	Soo-Yun Kang (Korea)	71.22
8	Hee-Won Han (Korea)	70.57	22	Laura Davies (England)	71.28
9	Cristie Kerr (USA)	70.68	T23	Sophie Gustafson (Sweden)	71.35
10	Lorena Ochoa (Mexico)	70.76	T23	Pat Hurst (USA)	71.35
11	Beth Daniel (USA)	70.82	25	Jennifer Rosales (Philippines)	71.42
12	Catriona Matthew (Scotland)	70.86	**55**	**A.J. Eathorne (Canada)**	**72.37**
T13	**Lorie Kane (Canada)**	**70.93**	**61**	**Dawn Coe-Jones (Canada)**	**72.61**
T13	Candie Kung (Taiwan)	70.93			

Source: *Ladies Professional Golf Association*

2003 LPGA Tour Money Leaders

(as of October 5, 2003 — in US dollars)

Rank	Player (Country)	Earnings	Rank	Player (Country)	Earnings
1	Annika Sorenstam (Sweden)	$1 695 006.00	15	**Lorie Kane (Canada)**	**$ 587 593.00**
2	Se Ri Pak (Korea)	$1 346 248.00	16	Cristie Kerr (USA)	$ 586 097.00
3	Grace Park (Korea)	$1 157 572.00	17	Meg Mallon (USA)	$ 523 070.00
4	Hee-Won Han (Korea)	$ 993 575.00	18	Catriona Matthew (Scotland)	$ 457 613.00
5	Juli Inkster (USA)	$ 967 145.00	19	Becky Morgan (Wales)	$ 441 100.00
6	Candie Kung (Taiwan)	$ 874 108.00	20	Michele Redman (USA)	$ 435 918.00
7	Lorena Ochoa (Mexico)	$ 756 174.00	21	Mi-Hyun Kim (Korea)	$ 432 259.00
8	Rosie Jones (USA)	$ 737 255.00	22	Wendy Ward (USA)	$ 421 234.00
9	Beth Daniel (USA)	$ 736 349.00	23	Jeong Jang (Korea)	$ 416 223.00
10	Karrie Webb (Australia)	$ 703 766.00	24	Pat Hurst (USA)	$ 405 625.00
11	Rachel Teske (Australia)	$ 700 664.00	25	Kelly Robbins (USA)	$ 399 245.00
12	Patricia Meunier-Lebouc (France)	$ 654 572.00	**83**	**Dawn Coe-Jones (Canada)**	**$ 82 100.00**
13	Angela Stanford (USA)	$ 608 637.00	**99**	**A.J. Eathorne (Canada)**	**$ 64 745.00**
14	Hilary Lunke (USA)	$ 606 274.00			

Bell Canadian Open Champions

The Bell Canadian Open is the world's third oldest national open championship, behind the Open Championship in Great Britain and the United States Open Championship. Seven Canadians have won the national championship, but none since Pat Fletcher of Saskatoon did so in 1954. The following list of past championship winners includes the winning scores (in parentheses) and host courses.

1980 Bob Gilder (274) Royal Montreal	1989 Steve Jones (271) Glen Abbey	1998 Billy Andrade (275) Glen Abbey
1981 Peter Oosterhuis (280) Glen Abbey	1990 Wayne Levi (278) Glen Abbey	1999 Hal Sutton (275) Glen Abbey
1982 Bruce Lietzke (277) Glen Abbey	1991 Nick Price (273) Glen Abbey	2000 Tiger Woods (266) Glen Abbey
1983 John Cook (277) Glen Abbey	1992 Greg Norman (280) Glen Abbey	2001 Scott Verplank (266) Royal Montreal
1984 Greg Norman (278) Glen Abbey	1993 David Frost (279) Glen Abbey	
1985 Curtis Strange (279) Glen Abbey	1994 Nick Price (275) Glen Abbey	2002 John Rollins (272) Angus Glen
1986 Bob Murphy (280) Glen Abbey	1995 Mark O'Meara (274) Glen Abbey	2003 Bob Tway (272) Hamilton Golf
1987 Curtis Strange (276) Glen Abbey	1996 Dudley Hart (202) Glen Abbey	Club
1988 Ken Green (275) Glen Abbey	1997 Steve Jones (275) Royal Montreal	

NATIONAL HOCKEY LEAGUE, 2002–03

Conference Standings

Conference standings reflect the order in which teams qualify for the playoffs. Teams with the best record in the conference (marked with a *z*) and division leaders (marked with a *y*) are automatically seeded first through third. Other playoff participants are marked with an *x*.

Eastern Conference

Rank	Team	GP	W	L	T	OTL	GF	GA	PTS
1	z-**Ottawa**	82	52	21	8	1	263	182	113
2	y-New Jersey	82	46	20	10	6	216	166	108
3	y-Tampa Bay	82	36	25	16	5	219	210	93
4	x-Philadelphia	82	45	20	13	4	211	166	107
5	x-**Toronto**	82	44	28	7	3	236	208	98
6	x-Washington	82	39	29	8	6	224	220	92
7	x-Boston	82	36	31	11	4	245	237	87
8	x-NY Islanders	82	35	34	11	2	224	231	83
9	NY Rangers	82	32	36	10	4	210	231	78
10	**Montreal**	82	30	35	8	9	206	234	77
11	Atlanta	82	31	39	7	5	226	284	74
12	Buffalo	82	27	37	10	8	190	219	72
13	Florida	82	24	36	13	9	176	237	70
14	Pittsburgh	82	27	44	6	5	189	255	65
15	Carolina	82	22	43	11	6	171	240	61

Western Conference

Rank	Team	GP	W	L	T	OTL	GF	GA	PTS
1	z-Dallas	82	46	17	15	4	245	169	111
2	y-Detroit	82	48	20	10	4	269	203	110
3	y-Colorado	82	42	19	13	8	251	194	105
4	x-**Vancouver**	82	45	23	13	1	264	208	104
5	x-St Louis	82	41	24	11	6	253	222	99
6	x-Minnesota	82	42	29	10	1	198	178	95
7	x-Anaheim	82	40	27	9	6	203	193	95
8	x-**Edmonton**	82	36	26	11	9	231	230	92
9	Chicago	82	30	33	13	6	207	226	79
10	Los Angeles	82	33	37	6	6	203	221	78
11	Phoenix	82	31	35	11	5	204	230	78
12	**Calgary**	82	29	36	13	4	186	228	75
13	Nashville	82	27	35	13	7	183	206	74
14	San Jose	82	28	37	9	8	214	239	73
15	Columbus	82	29	42	8	3	213	263	69

Source: *National Hockey League*

GP - Games Played; **W** – Wins; **L** – Losses; **T** – Ties; **GF** – Goals; **GA** - Goals Against; **OTL** - Overtime Losses (worth one point); **PTS** - Points

Division Standings

Eastern Conference

■ ATLANTIC	GP	W	L	T	OTL	PTS	GF	GA	HOME	AWAY
y-New Jersey	82	46	20	10	6	108	216	166	25-11-3-2	21-9-7-4
x-Philadelphia . . .	82	45	20	13	4	107	211	166	21-10-8-2	24-10-5-2
x-NY Islanders . . .	82	35	34	11	2	83	224	231	18-18-5-0	17-16-6-2
NY Rangers	82	32	36	10	4	78	210	231	17-18-4-2	15-18-6-2
Pittsburgh	82	27	44	6	5	65	189	255	15-22-2-2	12-22-4-3

■ NORTHEAST	GP	W	L	T	OTL	PTS	GF	GA	HOME	AWAY
*-Ottawa	82	52	21	8	1	113	263	182	28-9-3-1	24-12-5-0
x-Toronto	82	44	28	7	3	98	236	208	24-13-4-0	20-15-3-3
x-Boston	82	36	31	11	4	87	245	237	23-11-5-2	13-20-6-2
Montreal	82	30	35	8	9	77	206	234	16-16-5-4	14-19-3-5
Buffalo	82	27	37	10	8	72	190	219	18-16-5-2	9-21-5-6

■ SOUTHEAST	GP	W	L	T	OTL	PTS	GF	GA	HOME	AWAY
y-Tampa Bay	82	36	25	16	5	93	219	210	22-9-7-3	14-16-9-2
x-Washington. . . .	82	39	29	8	6	92	224	220	24-13-2-2	15-16-6-4
Atlanta	82	31	39	7	5	74	226	284	15-19-4-3	16-20-3-2
Florida	82	24	36	13	9	70	176	237	8-21-7-5	16-15-6-4
Carolina	82	22	43	11	6	61	171	240	12-17-9-3	10-26-2-3

Western Conference

■ CENTRAL	GP	W	L	T	OTL	PTS	GF	GA	HOME	AWAY
y-Detroit.	82	48	20	10	4	110	269	203	28-6-5-2	20-14-5-2
x-St. Louis	82	41	24	11	6	99	253	222	23-11-4-3	18-13-7-3
Chicago	82	30	33	13	6	79	207	226	17-15-7-2	13-18-6-4
Nashville	82	27	35	13	7	74	183	206	18-17-5-1	9-18-8-6
Columbus	82	29	42	8	3	69	213	263	20-14-5-2	9-28-3-1

■ NORTHWEST	GP	W	L	T	OTL	PTS	GF	GA	HOME	AWAY
y-Colorado	82	42	19	13	8	105	251	194	21-9-8-3	21-10-5-5
x-Vancouver.	82	45	23	13	1	104	264	208	22-13-6-0	23-10-7-1
x-Minnesota	82	42	29	10	1	95	198	178	25-13-3-0	17-16-7-1
x-Edmonton	82	36	26	11	9	92	231	230	20-12-5-4	16-14-6-5
Calgary.	82	29	36	13	4	75	186	228	14-16-10-1	15-20-3-3

■ PACIFIC	GP	W	L	T	OTL	PTS	GF	GA	HOME	AWAY
z-Dallas	82	46	17	15	4	111	245	169	28-5-6-2	18-12-9-2
x-Anaheim	82	40	27	9	6	95	203	193	22-10-7-2	18-17-2-4
Los Angeles	82	33	37	6	6	78	203	221	19-19-2-1	14-18-4-5
Phoenix	82	31	35	11	5	78	204	230	17-16-6-2	14-19-5-3
San Jose	82	28	37	9	8	73	214	239	17-16-5-3	11-21-4-5

Source: *ESPN.com*

x- clinched playoff spot

y- clinched division title

z- clinched best record in conference

*- clinched President's Trophy (best regular-season record)

NHL Playoff Results 2002–2003

■ **CONFERENCE QUARTER-FINALS**

Eastern Conference – 1

Matchup	Result
Ottawa vs. NY Islanders	
Game 1:	NY Islanders 3, at Ottawa 0
Game 2:	At Ottawa 3, NY Islanders 0
Game 3:	Ottawa 3, at NY Islanders 2 (2OT)
Game 4:	Ottawa 3, at NY Islanders 1
Game 5:	At Ottawa 4, NY Islanders 1

Ottawa wins series 4-1

Eastern Conference – 2

Matchup	Result
New Jersey vs. Boston	
Game 1:	At New Jersey 2, Boston 1
Game 2:	At New Jersey 4, Boston 2
Game 3:	New Jersey 3, at Boston 0
Game 4:	At Boston 5, New Jersey 1
Game 5:	At New Jersey 3, Boston 0

New Jersey wins series 4-1

Eastern Conference – 3

Matchup	Result
Tampa Bay vs. Washington	
Game 1:	Washington 3, at Tampa Bay 0
Game 2:	Washington 6, at Tampa Bay 3
Game 3:	Tampa Bay 4, at Washington 3 (OT)
Game 4:	Tampa Bay 3, at Washington 1
Game 5:	At Tampa Bay 2, Washington 1
Game 6:	Tampa Bay 2, at Washington 1 (3OT)

Tampa Bay wins series 4-2

Eastern Conference – 4

Matchup	Result
Toronto vs. N.Y. Islanders	
Philadelphia vs. Toronto	
Game 1:	Toronto 5, at Philadelphia 3
Game 2:	At Philadelphia 4, Toronto 1
Game 3:	At Toronto 4, Philadelphia 3 (2OT)
Game 4:	Philadelphia 3, at Toronto 2 (3OT)
Game 5:	At Philadelphia 4, Toronto 1
Game 6:	At Toronto 2, Philadelphia 1 (2OT)
Game 7:	At Philadelphia 6, Toronto 1

Philadelphia wins series 4-3

Western Conference – 1

Matchup	Result
Dallas vs. Edmonton	
Game 1:	Edmonton 2, at Dallas 1
Game 2:	At Dallas 6, Edmonton 1
Game 3:	At Edmonton 3, Dallas 2
Game 4:	Dallas 3, at Edmonton 1
Game 5:	At Dallas 5, Edmonton 2
Game 6:	Dallas 3, at Edmonton 2

Dallas wins series 4-2

Western Conference – 2

Matchup	Result
Detroit vs. Anaheim	
Game 1:	Anaheim 2, at Detroit 1 (3OT)
Game 2:	Anaheim 3, at Detroit 2
Game 3:	At Anaheim 2, Detroit 1
Game 4:	At Anaheim 3, Detroit 2 (OT)

Anaheim wins series 4-0

Western Conference – 3

Matchup	Result
Colorado vs. Minnesota	
Game 1:	Minnesota 4, at Colorado 2
Game 2:	At Colorado 3, Minnesota 2
Game 3:	Colorado 3, at Minnesota 0
Game 4:	Colorado 3, at Minnesota 1
Game 5:	Minnesota 3, at Colorado 2
Game 6:	At Minnesota 3, Colorado 2 (OT)
Game 7:	Minnesota 3, at Colorado 2 (OT)

Minnesota wins series 4-3

Western Conference – 4

Matchup	Result
Vancouver vs. St. Louis	
Game 1:	St. Louis 6, at Vancouver 0
Game 2:	At Vancouver 2, St. Louis 1
Game 3:	At St. Louis 3, Vancouver 1
Game 4:	At St. Louis 4, Vancouver 1
Game 5:	At Vancouver 5, St. Louis 3
Game 6:	Vancouver 4, at St. Louis 3
Game 7:	At Vancouver 4, St. Louis 1

Vancouver wins series 4-3

▶ ■ CONFERENCE SEMI-FINALS

Eastern Conference – 1
Matchup	Result
Ottawa vs. Philadelphia	
Game 1:	At Ottawa 4, Philadelphia 2
Game 2:	Philadelphia 2, at Ottawa 0
Game 3:	Ottawa 3, at Philadelphia 2 (OT)
Game 4:	At Philadelphia 1, Ottawa 0
Game 5:	At Ottawa 5, Philadelphia 2
Game 6:	Ottawa 5, at Philadelphia 1
Ottawa wins series 4-2	

Western Conference – 1
Matchup	Result
Dallas vs. Anaheim	
Game 1:	Anaheim 4, at Dallas 3 (5OT)
Game 2:	Anaheim 3, at Dallas 2 (OT)
Game 3:	Dallas 3, at Anaheim 2
Game 4:	At Anaheim 1, Dallas 0
Game 5:	At Dallas 4, Anaheim 1
Game 6:	At Anaheim 4, Dallas 3
Anaheim wins series 4-2	

Eastern Conference – 2
Matchup	Result
New Jersey vs. Tampa Bay	
Game 1:	At New Jersey 3, Tampa Bay 0
Game 2:	At New Jersey 3, Tampa Bay 2 (OT)
Game 3:	At Tampa Bay 4, New Jersey 3
Game 4:	New Jersey 3, at Tampa Bay 1
Game 5:	At New Jersey 2, Tampa Bay 1 (3OT)
New Jersey wins series 4-1	

Western Conference – 2
Matchup	Result
Vancouver vs. Minnesota	
Game 1:	At Vancouver 4, Minnesota 3 (OT)
Game 2:	Minnesota 3, at Vancouver 2
Game 3:	Vancouver 3, at Minnesota 2
Game 4:	Vancouver 3, at Minnesota 2 (OT)
Game 5:	Minnesota 7, at Vancouver 2
Game 6:	At Minnesota 5, Vancouver 1
Game 7:	Minnesota 4, at Vancouver 2
Minnesota wins series 4-3	

■ CONFERENCE FINALS

EASTERN CONFERENCE FINAL
Matchup	Result
Ottawa vs. New Jersey	
Game 1:	At Ottawa 3, New Jersey 2 (OT)
Game 2:	New Jersey 4, at Ottawa 1
Game 3:	At New Jersey 1, Ottawa 0
Game 4:	At New Jersey 5, Ottawa 2
Game 5:	At Ottawa 3, New Jersey 1
Game 6:	Ottawa 2, at New Jersey 1 (OT)
Game 7:	New Jersey 3, at Ottawa 2
New Jersey wins series 4-3	

WESTERN CONFERENCE FINAL
Matchup	Result
Minnesota vs. Anaheim	
Game 1:	Anaheim 1, at Minnesota 0 (2OT)
Game 2:	Anaheim 2, at Minnesota 0
Game 3:	At Anaheim 4, Minnesota 0
Game 4:	At Anaheim 2, Minnesota 1
Anaheim wins series 4-0	

STANLEY CUP FINALS
New Jersey vs. Anaheim
Game 1: At New Jersey 3, Anaheim 0
Game 2: At New Jersey 3, Anaheim 0
Game 3: At Anaheim 3, New Jersey 2 (OT)
Game 4: At Anaheim 1, New Jersey 0 (OT)
Game 5: At New Jersey 6, Anaheim 3
Game 6: At Anaheim 5, New Jersey 2
Game 7: At New Jersey 3, Anaheim 0
New Jersey wins Stanley Cup 4-3

Source: *The Hockey Nut*

Stanley Cup Champions, 1926–2003

The Stanley Cup, the oldest trophy competed for by professional athletes in North America, was donated by Frederick Arthur, Lord Stanley of Preston, in 1893. Originally presented to the amateur hockey champions of Canada, it has been awarded to the top professional team since 1910 and, since 1926, has been competed for only by NHL teams.

Year	Champion	Final Opponent	Series Result	Winning Coach	Winning Manager
1926	Montreal Maroons	Victoria	3-1	Eddie Gerard	Eddie Gerard
1927	Ottawa Senators	Boston	2-0	Dave Gill	Dave Gill
1928	New York Rangers	Montreal	3-2	Lester Patrick	Lester Patrick
1929	Boston Bruins	New York	2-0	Cy Denneny	Art Ross
1930	Montreal Canadiens	Boston	2-0	Cecil Hart	Cecil Hart
1931	Montreal Canadiens	Chicago	3-2	Cecil Hart	Cecil Hart
1932	Toronto Maple Leafs	New York	3-0	Dick Irvin	Conn Smythe
1933	New York Rangers	Toronto	3-1	Lester Patrick	Lester Patrick
1934	Chicago Black Hawks	Detroit	3-1	Tommy Gorman	Tommy Gorman
1935	Montreal Maroons	Toronto	3-0	Tommy Gorman	Tommy Gorman
1936	Detroit Red Wings	Toronto	4-0	Jack Adams	Jack Adams
1937	Detroit Red Wings	New York	3-2	Jack Adams	Jack Adams
1938	Chicago Black Hawks	Toronto	4-1	Bill Stewart	Bill Stewart
1939	Boston Bruins	Toronto	4-1	Art Ross	Art Ross
1940	New York Rangers	Toronto	4-2	Frank Boucher	Lester Patrick
1941	Boston Bruins	Detroit	4-0	Cooney Weiland	Art Ross
1942	Toronto Maple Leafs	Detroit	4-3	Hap Day	Conn Smythe
1943	Detroit Red Wings	Boston	4-0	Jack Adams	Jack Adams
1944	Montreal Canadiens	Chicago	4-0	Dick Irvin	Tommy Gorman
1945	Toronto Maple Leafs	Detroit	4-3	Hap Day	Conn Smythe
1946	Montreal Canadiens	Boston	4-1	Dick Irvin	Tommy Gorman
1947	Toronto Maple Leafs	Montreal	4-2	Hap Day	Conn Smythe
1948	Toronto Maple Leafs	Detroit	4-0	Hap Day	Conn Smythe
1949	Toronto Maple Leafs	Detroit	4-0	Hap Day	Conn Smythe
1950	Detroit Red Wings	New York	4-3	Tommy Ivan	Jack Adams
1951	Toronto Maple Leafs	Montreal	4-1	Joe Primeau	Conn Smythe
1952	Detroit Red Wings	Montreal	4-0	Tommy Ivan	Jack Adams
1953	Montreal Canadiens	Boston	4-1	Dick Irvin	Frank Selke
1954	Detroit Red Wings	Montreal	4-3	Tommy Ivan	Jack Adams
1955	Detroit Red Wings	Montreal	4-3	Jimmy Skinner	Jack Adams
1956	Montreal Canadiens	Detroit	4-1	Toe Blake	Frank Selke
1957	Montreal Canadiens	Boston	4-1	Toe Blake	Frank Selke
1958	Montreal Canadiens	Boston	4-2	Toe Blake	Frank Selke
1959	Montreal Canadiens	Toronto	4-1	Toe Blake	Frank Selke
1960	Montreal Canadiens	Toronto	4-0	Toe Blake	Frank Selke
1961	Chicago Black Hawks	Detroit	4-2	Rudy Pilous	Tommy Ivan
1962	Toronto Maple Leafs	Chicago	4-2	Punch Imlach	Punch Imlach
1963	Toronto Maple Leafs	Detroit	4-1	Punch Imlach	Punch Imlach
1964	Toronto Maple Leafs	Detroit	4-3	Punch Imlach	Punch Imlach
1965	Montreal Canadiens	Chicago	4-3	Toe Blake	Sam Pollock
1966	Montreal Canadiens	Detroit	4-2	Toe Blake	Sam Pollock
1967	Toronto Maple Leafs	Montreal	4-2	Punch Imlach	Punch Imlach
1968	Montreal Canadiens	St. Louis	4-0	Toe Blake	Sam Pollock
1969	Montreal Canadiens	St. Louis	4-0	Claude Ruel	Sam Pollock
1970	Boston Bruins	St. Louis	4-0	Harry Sinden	Milt Schmidt
1971	Montreal Canadiens	Chicago	4-3	Al MacNeil	Sam Pollock
1972	Boston Bruins	New York	4-2	Tom Johnson	Milt Schmidt
1973	Montreal Canadiens	Chicago	4-2	Scotty Bowman	Sam Pollock
1974	Philadelphia Flyers	Boston	4-2	Fred Shero	Keith Allen
1975	Philadelphia Flyers	Buffalo	4-2	Fred Shero	Keith Allen
1976	Montreal Canadiens	Philadelphia	4-0	Scotty Bowman	Sam Pollock
1977	Montreal Canadiens	Boston	4-0	Scotty Bowman	Sam Pollock
1978	Montreal Canadiens	Boston	4-2	Scotty Bowman	Sam Pollock

▶

Year	Champion	Final Opponent	Series Result	Winning Coach	Winning Manager
1979	Montreal Canadiens	New York	4-1	Scotty Bowman	Irving Grundman
1980	N.Y. Islanders	Philadelphia	4-2	Al Arbour	Bill Torrey
1981	N.Y. Islanders	Minnesota	4-1	Al Arbour	Bill Torrey
1982	N.Y. Islanders	Vancouver	4-0	Al Arbour	Bill Torrey
1983	N.Y. Islanders	Edmonton	4-0	Al Arbour	Bill Torrey
1984	Edmonton Oilers	New York	4-1	Glen Sather	Glen Sather
1985	Edmonton Oilers	Philadelphia	4-1	Glen Sather	Glen Sather
1986	Montreal Canadiens	Calgary	4-1	Jean Perron	Serge Savard
1987	Edmonton Oilers	Philadelphia	4-3	Glen Sather	Glen Sather
1988	Edmonton Oilers	Boston	4-0	Glen Sather	Glen Sather
1989	Calgary Flames	Montreal	4-2	Terry Crisp	Cliff Fletcher
1990	Edmonton Oilers	Boston	4-1	John Muckler	Glen Sather
1991	Pittsburgh Penguins	Minnesota	4-2	Bob Johnson	Craig Patrick
1992	Pittsburgh Penguins	Chicago	4-0	Scotty Bowman	Craig Patrick
1993	Montreal Canadiens	Los Angeles	4-1	Jacques Demers	Serge Savard
1994	New York Rangers	Vancouver	4-3	Mike Keenan	Neil Smith
1995	New Jersey Devils	Detroit	4-0	Jacques Lemaire	Lou Lamoriello
1996	Colorado Avalanche	Florida	4-0	Marc Crawford	Pierre Lacroix
1997	Detroit Red Wings	Philadelphia	4-0	Scotty Bowman	Scotty Bowman
1998	Detroit Red Wings	Washington	4-0	Scotty Bowman	Ken Holland
1999	Dallas Stars	Buffalo	4-2	Ken Hitchcock	Bob Gainey
2000	New Jersey Devils	Dallas	4-2	Larry Robinson	Lou Lamoriello
2001	Colorado Avalanche	New Jersey	4-3	Bob Harley	Pierre Lacroix
2002	Detroit Red Wings	Carolina	4-1	Scotty Bowman	Ken Holland
2003	New Jersey Devils	Anaheim	4-3	Pat Burns	Lou Lamoriello

Source: *National Hockey League*

Selected Hockey Organizations

Hockey Hall of Fame
BCE Place
30 Yonge St.
Toronto, Ont.
M5E 1X8
Tel: (416) 360-7735
Fax: (416) 360-1501
http://www.hhof.com

National Hockey League
1251 Avenue of the Americas
New York, NY
10020
Tel: (212) 789-2000
http://www.nhl.com

National Hockey League Players' Association
777 Bay St., Suite 2400
Toronto, Ont.
M5G 2C8
Tel: (416) 313-2300
Fax: (416) 313-2301
http://www.nhlpa.com

Hockey Information web sites

Canadian Hockey League
www.chl.ca
Info on Canadian junior
hockey with links to various
leagues

The Hockey News
www.thn.com
News and stats

Ontario Hockey League
www.ontariohockeyleague.com
Scores, standings, game
recaps and news

Hockey Future: The Hockey Propects Resource
www.hockeysfuture.com
Learn about the stars of
tomorrow today

American Hockey League
www.theahl.com
Stats, rosters and team info

The Hockey Nut
www.hockeynut.com/
An ice hockey webzine with
up-to-date news, scores and
statistics.

Source: *The Hockey Nut*

NHL Scoring Leaders, 2002–2003

Regular Season

Player	Team	GP	G	A	Pts	+/-	PIM
Peter Forsberg	COL	75	29	77	106	52	70
Markus Naslund	VAN	82	48	56	104	6	52
Joe Thornton	BOS	77	36	65	101	12	109
Milan Hejduk	COL	82	50	48	98	52	32
Todd Bertuzzi	VAN	82	46	51	97	2	144
Pavol Demitra	STL	78	36	57	93	0	32
Glen Murray	BOS	82	44	48	92	9	64
Mario Lemieux	PIT	67	28	63	91	-25	43
Dany Heatley	ATL	77	41	48	89	-8	58
Zigmund Palffy	LOS	76	37	48	85	22	47
Mike Modano	DAL	79	28	57	85	34	30
Sergei Fedorov	DET	80	36	47	83	15	52
Marian Hossa	OTT	80	45	35	80	8	34
Paul Kariya	ANA	82	25	55	80	-3	48
Alexander Mogilny	TOR	73	33	46	79	4	12
Daniel Alfredsson	OTT	78	27	52	79	15	42
Vaclav Prospal	TAM	80	22	57	79	9	53
Vincent Lecavalier	TAM	80	34	44	78	0	39
Alexei Kovalev	NYR	78	37	40	77	-9	70
Jaromir Jagr	WAS	75	36	41	77	5	38
Brett Hull	DET	82	37	39	76	11	22
Miroslav Satan	BUF	79	26	50	76	-3	20
Ray Whitney	CLB	81	24	52	76	-26	22
Brad Richards	TAM	80	17	57	74	3	24
Mats Sundin	TOR	75	37	35	72	1	58

Playoffs

Player	Team	GP	G	A	Pts	+/-	PIM
Jamie Langenbrunner	NJD	24	11	7	18	11	16
Scott Niedermayer	NJD	24	2	16	18	11	16
Marian Gaborik	MIN	18	9	8	17	2	6
John Madden	NJD	24	6	10	16	10	2
Marian Hossa	OTT	18	5	11	16	-1	6
Mike Modano	DAL	12	5	10	15	2	4
Jeff Friesen	NJD	24	10	4	14	10	6
Markus Naslund	VAN	14	5	9	14	-6	18
Sergei Zubov	DAL	12	4	10	14	2	4
Andrew Brunette	MIN	18	7	6	13	-3	4
Wes Walz	MIN	18	7	6	13	5	14
Doug Weight	STL	7	5	8	13	0	2
Patrik Elias	NJD	24	5	8	13	5	26
Adam Oates	ANA	21	4	9	13	2	6
Petr Sykora	ANA	21	4	9	13	3	12
Sergei Zholtok	MIN	18	2	11	13	-7	0
Martin St. Louis	TAM	11	7	5	12	5	0
Paul Kariya	ANA	21	6	6	12	0	6
Jay Pandolfo	NJD	24	6	6	12	9	2
Scott Gomez	NJD	24	3	9	12	3	2
Radek Bonk	OTT	18	6	5	11	2	10
Martin Havlat	OTT	18	5	6	11	4	14
Brendan Morrison	VAN	14	4	7	11	-4	18
Mike Leclerc	ANA	21	2	9	11	3	12
Brian Rafalski	NJD	23	2	9	11	7	8

Source: *The Hockey Nut*

GP – games played; G – goals; A – assists; Pts – total points; +/- – plus/minus (the number of goals scored against the number of goals scored against per 60 minutes of play; PIM – penalty minutes

NHL Goalie Statistics, 2002–03 Season

Regular Season

■ WINS

Goaltender	Team	GPI	W	L	T
Martin Brodeur........	NJD	73	41	23	9
Patrick Lalime	OTT	67	39	20	7
Ed Belfour	TOR	62	37	20	5
Patrick Roy	COL	63	35	15	13
Curtis Joseph........	DET	61	34	19	6
Jean-Sebastien Giguere .	ANA	65	34	22	6
Roman Cechmanek	PHI	58	33	15	10
Dan Cloutier..........	VAN	57	33	16	7
Olaf Kolzig	WAS	66	33	25	6
Marty Turco	DAL	55	31	10	10
Nikolai Khabibulin	TAM	65	30	22	11

■ SHUTOUTS

Goaltender	Team	GPI	SO
Martin Brodeur........	NJD	73	9
Jocelyn Thibault.......	CHI	62	8
Jean-Sebastien Giguere .	ANA	65	8
Patrick Lalime	OTT	67	8
Marty Turco	DAL	55	7
Ed Belfour	TOR	62	7
Roman Cechmanek	PHI	58	6
Roberto Luongo.......	FLA	65	6
Kevin Weekes.........	CAR	51	5
Mike Dunham.........	NYR	58	5
Curtis Joseph.........	DET	61	5
Patrick Roy	COL	63	5
Marc Denis...........	CLB	77	5

■ GOALS-AGAINST AVERAGE (minimum 27 games)

Goaltender	Team	GPI	GA	AVG
Marty Turco	DAL	55	92	1.72
Roman Cechmanek	PHI	58	102	1.83
Dwayne Roloson ..	MIN	50	98	2.00
Martin Brodeur ...	NJD	73	147	2.02
Patrick Lalime	OTT	67	142	2.16
Patrick Roy	COL	63	137	2.18
Robert Esche	PHI	30	60	2.20
Tomas Vokoun....	NAS	69	146	2.20
Manny Fernandez..	MIN	35	74	2.24
Ed Belfour	TOR	62	141	2.26
Jean-Sebastien Giguere	ANA	65	145	2.30
Garth Snow	NYI	43	92	2.31
Jocelyn Thibault...	CHI	62	144	2.37
Olaf Kolzig	WAS	66	156	2.40
Dan Cloutier......	VAN	57	136	2.42

■ SAVE PERCENTAGE (minimum 27 GPI)

Goaltender	Team	GPI	GA	SA	SPCT
Marty Turco	DAL	55	92	1359	.932
Dwayne Roloson .	MIN	50	98	1334	.927
Roman Cechmanek	PHI	58	102	1368	.925
Manny Fernandez.	MIN	35	74	972	.924
Ed Belfour	TOR	62	141	1816	.922
Jean-Sebastien Giguere	ANA	65	145	1820	.920
Patrick Roy	COL	63	137	1723	.920
Olaf Kolzig	WAS	66	156	1925	.919
Garth Snow	NYI	43	92	1120	.918
Tomas Vokoun ...	NAS	69	146	1771	.918
Roberto Luongo .	FLA	65	164	2011	.918

Playoffs

■ WINS

Goaltender	Team	GPI	W	L
Martin Brodeur...	NJD	24	16	8
Jean-Sebastien Giguere	ANA	21	15	6
Patrick Lalime ...	OTT	18	11	7
Dan Cloutier.....	VAN	14	7	7
Marty Turco	DAL	12	6	6
Roman Cechmanek	PHI	13	6	7
Nikolai Khabibulin	TAM	10	5	5
Dwayne Roloson .	MIN	11	5	6

■ GOALS-AGAINST AVERAGE

Goaltender	Team	GPI	GA	AVG
Jean-Sebastien Giguere	ANA	21	38	1.62
Martin Brodeur...	NJD	24	41	1.65
Jeff Hackett	BOS	3	5	1.68
Patrick Lalime ...	OTT	18	34	1.82
Marty Turco	DAL	12	25	1.88
Manny Fernandez.	MIN	9	18	1.96
Curtis Joseph....	DET	4	10	2.08
Olaf Kolzig	WAS	6	14	2.08
Roman Cechmanek	PHI	13	31	2.15
Patrick Roy......	COL	7	16	2.27
Garth Snow	NYI	5	12	2.36

■ SHUTOUTS

Goaltender	Team	GPI	SO
Martin Brodeur........	NJD	24	7
Jean-Sebastien Giguere .	ANA	21	5
Roman Cechmanek	PHI	13	2
Patrick Lalime	OTT	18	1
Garth Snow	NYI	5	1
Olaf Kolzig	WAS	6	1
Chris Osgood.........	STL	7	1
Patrick Roy	COL	7	1

■ SAVE PERCENTAGE

Goaltender	Team	GPI	GA	SA	SPCT
Jean-Sebastien Giguere	ANA	21	38	659	.945
Martin Brodeur....	NJD	24	41	581	.934
Jeff Hackett	BOS	3	5	71	.934
Manny Fernandez.	MIN	9	18	235	.929
Olaf Kolzig	WAS	6	14	178	.927
Patrick Lalime ...	OTT	18	34	415	.924
Marty Turco	DAL	12	25	285	.919
Curtis Joseph	DET	4	10	110	.917
Ed Belfour	TOR	7	24	258	.915
Nikolai Khabibulin	TAM	10	26	273	.913

Source: *The Hockey Nut*

AVG = Average; GPI = Games Played; GA = Goals Against; L = Losses; SA = Saves; SO = Shut outs; SPCT = Save percentage; T = Ties; W = Wins.

Regular Season NHL Scoring Champions, 1960–2003

Season	Player, Team	GP	G	A	PTS	Season	Player, Team	GP	G	A	PTS
1959–60	Bobby Hull, Chi	70	39	42	81	1981–82	Wayne Gretzky, Edm	80	92	120	212
1960–61	Bernie Geoffrion, Mtl	64	50	45	95	1982–83	Wayne Gretzky, Edm	80	71	125	196
1961–62	Bobby Hull, Chi	70	50	34	84	1983–84	Wayne Gretzky, Edm	74	87	118	205
1962–63	Gordie Howe, Det	70	38	48	86	1984–85	Wayne Gretzky, Edm	80	73	135	208
1963–64	Stan Mikita, Chi	70	39	50	89	1985–86	Wayne Gretzky, Edm	80	52	163	215
1964–65	Stan Mikita, Chi	70	28	59	87	1986–87	Wayne Gretzky, Edm	79	62	121	183
1965–66	Bobby Hull, Chi	65	54	43	97	1987–88	Mario Lemieux, Pitt	77	70	98	168
1966–67	Stan Mikita, Chi	70	35	62	97	1988–89	Mario Lemieux, Pitt	76	85	114	199
1967–68	Stan Mikita, Chi	72	40	47	87	1989–90	Wayne Gretzky, L.A.	73	40	102	142
1968–69	Phil Esposito, Bos	74	49	77	126	1990–91	Wayne Gretzky, L.A.	78	41	122	163
1969–70	Bobby Orr, Bos	76	33	87	120	1991–92	Mario Lemieux, Pitt	64	44	87	131
1970–71	Phil Esposito, Bos	78	76	76	152	1992–93	Mario Lemieux, Pitt	60	69	91	160
1971–72	Phil Esposito, Bos	76	66	67	133	1993–94	Wayne Gretzky, L.A.	81	38	92	130
1972–73	Phil Esposito, Bos	78	55	75	130	1994–95	Jaromir Jagr[1], Pitt	48[2]	32	38	70
1973–74	Phil Esposito, Bos	78	68	77	145	1995–96	Mario Lemieux, Pitt	70	69	92	161
1974–75	Bobby Orr, Bos	80	46	89	135	1996–97	Mario Lemieux, Pitt	76	50	72	122
1975–76	Guy Lafleur, Mtl	80	56	69	125	1997–98	Jaromir Jagr, Pitt	77	35	67	102
1976–77	Guy Lafleur, Mtl	80	56	80	136	1998–99	Jaromir Jagr, Pitt	81	44	83	127
1977–78	Guy Lafleur, Mtl	78	60	72	132	1999–00	Jaromir Jagr, Pitt	63	42	54	96
1978–79	Bryan Trottier, NYI	76	47	87	134	2000–01	Jaromir Jagr, Pitt	81	52	69	121
1979–80	Marcel Dionne, L.A.	80	53	84	137	2001–02	Jarome Iginla, Cal.	82	52	44	96
1980–81	Wayne Gretzky, Edm	80	55	109	164	2002–03	Peter Forsberg, Col.	75	29	77	106

Source: *StatsHockey.com*

(1) Jagr tied with Lindros (Phi); awarded title based on most goals scored. (2) Season shortened to 48 games due to owner/player dispute.

Hockey Hall of Fame

*I*nterested in learning about ice hockey? Visit the Hockey Hall of Fame inside Toronto's BCE Place. Tours last about three hours and educational programs exist for junior, intermediate and senior students. Outreach programs such as Shut Out, Shutdown, and the Legends of Hockey Mobile Exhibit are also available.

In 2002, the Hockey Hall of Fame unveiled a special display honouring the Salt Lake Olympics and Canada's gold-medal-winning men's and women's hockey teams. The new display, which is part of the Royal Canadian Mint World of Hockey Zone, recounts the Salt Lake City Olympic hockey tournaments and honours its champions.

The Olympic tribute display tells the story of the Salt Lake Loonie. The Salt Lake Loonie was buried surreptitiously at centre ice before the 2002 Olympic Ice Hockey tournaments. The Canadian in charge of monitoring ice conditions in Salt Lake City felt the Loonie would not only make a perfect centre-ice dot in the E-Centre Arena, but would also bring luck to his hockey-playing countrymen and women. After Team Canada's second hockey gold-medal victory, the Loonie was dug up and presented to Team Canada General Manager Wayne Gretzky. (From March 8 until Labour Day (September 2, 2002) hockey enthusiasts had the opportunity to touch the Salt Lake Loonie in hope of picking up some of its good luck.)

The Hockey Hall of Fame is in BCE Place at 30 Yonge Street, Toronto. It's open every day except Christmas, New Year's Day and Induction Day. See their web site at http://www.hhof.com or call (416) 360-7735 for more information.

2003 NHL Draft — First Round Selections

PICK, TEAM, PLAYER, POSITION, PREVIOUS TEAM, PREVIOUS LEAGUE

1 Pittsburgh (from Florida), Marc-Andre Fleury, G, Cape Breton, QMJHL
2 Carolina, Eric Staal, C, Peterborough, OHL
3 Florida (from Pittsburgh), Nathan Horton, C, Oshawa, OHL
4 Columbus, Nikolai Zherdev, F/W, HC CSKA, RUS
5 Buffalo, Thomas Vanek, LW, U. of Minnesota, WCHA
6 San Jose, Milan Michalek, RW, Budejovice, CZE
7 Nashville, Ryan Suter, D, US Nat'l U-18, USA
8 Atlanta, Braydon Coburn, D, Portland, WHL
9 Calgary, Dion Phaneuf, D, Red Deer, WHL
10 Montreal, Andrei Kastsitsyn, F, HC CSKA, RUS
11 Philadelphia (from Phoenix), Jeff Carter, C, Sault-Ste-Marie, OHL
12 NY Rangers, Hugh Jessiman, RW, Dartmouth Coll., ECAC
13 Los Angeles, Dustin Brown, RW, Guelph, OHL
14 Chicago, Brent Seabrook, D, Lethbridge, WHL
15 NY Islanders, Robert Nilsson, C F W, Leksand, SWE
16 San Jose (from Boston), Steve Bernier, RW, Moncton, QMJHL

17 New Jersey (from Edmonton), Zach Parise, C, U. of North Dakota, WCHA
18 Washington, Eric Fehr, RW, Brandon, WHL
19 Anaheim, Ryan Getzlaf, C, Calgary, WHL
20 Minnesota, Brent Burns, RW, Brampton, OHL
21 Boston (from Toronto), Mark Stuart, D, Colorado College, WCHA
22 Edmonton (from St. Louis), Marc-Antoine Pouliot, C, Rimouski, QMJHL
23 Vancouver, Ryan Kesler, C, Ohio State, CCHA
24 Philadelphia, Mike Richards, C, Kitchener, OHL
25 Florida (from Tampa Bay), Anthony Stewart, C/RW, Kingston, OHL
26 Los Angeles (from Colorado), Brian Boyle, C, St. Sebastian's, USHSE
27 Los Angeles (from Detroit), Jeff Tambellini, LW, U. of Michigan, CCHA
28 Anaheim (from Dallas), Corey Perry, RW, London, OHL
29 Ottawa, Patrick Eaves, RW, Boston College, H-EAST
30 St. Louis (from New Jersey), Shawn Belle, D, Tri-City, WHL

Source: *National Hockey League*

NHL All-Stars, 1998–2003

First Team	Second Team	First Team	Second Team
1998		**2001**	
Dominik Hasek, Buf, G	Martin Brodeur, NJ, G	Dominik Hasek, Det, G	Roman Cechmanek, Phil, G
Rob Blake, LA, D	Raymond Bourque, Bos, D	Ray Bourque, Col, D	Rob Blake, Col, D
Nicklas Lidstrom, Det, D	Chris Pronger, StL, D	Nicklas Lidstrom, Det, D	Scott Stevens, NJD, D
Peter Forsberg, Col, C	Wayne Gretzky, NYR, C	Joe Sakic, Col, C	Mario Lemieux, Pitt. C
Jaromir Jagr, Pitt, RW	Teemu Selanne, Ana, RW	Jaromir Jagr, Wash, RW	Pavel Bure, Fla, RW
John LeClair, Phi, LW	Keith Tkachuk, Pho, LW	Patrik Elias, NJD, LW	Luc Robitaille, Det, LW
1999		**2002**	
Dominik Hasek, Buf, G	Bryon Dafoe, Bos, G	Patrick Roy, Col, G	Jose Theodore, Mtl, G
Al MacInnis, StL, D	Raymond Bourque, Bos, D	Nicklas Lidstrom, Det, D	Rob Blake, Col, D
Nicklas Lidstrom, Det, D	Eric Desjardins, Pha, D	Chris Chelios, Det, D	Sergei Gonchar, Was, D
Peter Forsberg, Col, C	Alexei Yashin, Ott, C	Markus Naslund, Van, LW	Brendan Shanahan, Det, LW
Jaromir Jagr, Pitt, RW	Teemu Selanne, Ana, RW	Joe Sakic, Col, C	Mats Sundin, Tor, C
Paul Kariya, Ana, LW	John LeClair, Phil, LW	Jarome Iginla, Cal, RW	Bill Guerin, Bos, RW
2000		**2003**	
Olaf Kolzig, Was, G	Roman Turek, StL, G	Martin Brodeur, NJ, G	Marty Turco, Dal, G
Chris Pronger, StL, D	Rob Blake, LA, D	Marcus Naslund, Van, LW	Paul Kariya, Ana, LW
Nicklas Lidstrom, Det, D	Eric Desjardins, Phil, D	Todd Bertuzzi, Van, RW	Milan Hejduk, Col, RW
Steve Yzerman, Det, C	Mike Modano, Dal, C	Peter Forsberg, Col, C	Joe Thornton, Bos, C
Jaromir Jagr, Pitt, RW	Pavel Bure, Fla, RW	Al MacInnis, StL, D	Sergei Gonchar, Was, D
Brendan Shanahan, Det, LW	Paul Kariya, Ana, LW	Nicklas Lidstrom, Det, D	Derian Hatcher, Dal, D

Source: *National Hockey League*   As selected by members of the Professional Hockey Writers' Association.

NHL Individual Award Winners, 1983–2003

Hart Trophy (Most Valuable Player)[1]

1983 Wayne Gretzky, Edm	**1990** Mark Messier, Edm	**1997** Dominik Hasek, Buf
1984 Wayne Gretzky, Edm	**1991** Brett Hull, StL	**1998** Dominik Hasek, Buf
1985 Wayne Gretzky, Edm	**1992** Mark Messier, NYR	**1999** Jaromir Jagr, Pitt
1986 Wayne Gretzky, Edm	**1993** Mario Lemieux, Pitt	**2000** Chris Pranger, StL
1987 Wayne Gretzky, Edm	**1994** Sergei Fedorov, Det	**2001** Joe Sakic, Col
1988 Mario Lemieux, Pitt	**1995** Eric Lindros, Phil	**2002** Jose Theodore, Mtl
1989 Wayne Gretzky, LA	**1996** Mario Lemieux, Pitt	**2003** Peter Forsberg, Col

Calder Trophy (Best Rookie)[1]

1983 Steve Larmer, Chi	**1990** Sergei Makarov, Cal	**1997** Bryan Berard, NYI
1984 Tom Barrasso, Buf	**1991** Ed Belfour, Chi	**1998** Sergei Samsonov, Bos
1985 Mario Lemieux, Pitt	**1992** Pavel Bure, Vcr	**1999** Chris Drury, Col
1986 Gary Suter, Cal	**1993** Teemu Selanne, Wpg	**2000** Scott Gomez, NJ
1987 Luc Robitaille, LA	**1994** Martin Brodeur, NJ	**2001** Evgeni Nabokov, SJ
1988 Joe Nieuwendyk, Cal	**1995** Peter Forsberg, Que	**2002** Dany Heatley, Atl
1989 Brian Leetch, NYR	**1996** Daniel Alfredsson, Ott	**2003** Barret Jackman, StL

James Norris Trophy (Best Defenceman)[1]

1983 Rod Langway, Wash	**1990** Raymond Bourque, Bos	**1997** Brian Leetch, NYR
1984 Rod Langway, Wash	**1991** Raymond Bourque, Bos	**1998** Rob Blake, LA
1985 Paul Coffey, Edm	**1992** Brian Leetch, NYR	**1999** Al MacInnis, StL
1986 Paul Coffey, Edm	**1993** Chris Chelios, Chi	**2000** Chris Pranger, StL
1987 Raymond Bourque, Bos	**1994** Raymond Bourque, Bos	**2001** Nicklas Lidstrom, Det
1988 Raymond Bourque, Bos	**1995** Paul Coffey, Det	**2002** Nicklas Lidstrom, Det
1989 Chris Chelios, Mtl	**1996** Chris Chelios, Chi	**2003** Nicklas Lidstrom, Det

Veniza Trophy (Best Goalkeeper)[2]

1983 Pete Peeters, Bos	**1990** Patrick Roy, Mtl	**1997** Dominik Hasek, Buf
1984 Tom Barrasso, Buf	**1991** Ed Belfour, Chi	**1998** Dominik Hasek, Buf
1985 Pelle Lindbergh, Phil	**1992** Patrick Roy, Mtl	**1999** Dominik Hasek, Buf
1986 John Vanbiesbrouck, NYR	**1993** Ed Belfour, Chi	**2000** Olaf Kolzig, Wash
1987 Ron Hextall, Phil	**1994** Dominik Hasek, Buf	**2001** Dominik Hasek, Buf
1988 Grant Fuhr, Edm	**1995** Dominik Hasek, Buf	**2002** Jose Theodore, Mtl
1989 Patrick Roy, Mtl	**1996** Jim Carey, Wash	**2003** Martin Brodeur, NJ

Lady Byng Trophy (Most Sportsmanlike)[1]

1983 Mike Bossy, NYI	**1990** Brett Hull, StL	**1997** Paul Kariya, Ana
1984 Mike Bossy, NYI	**1991** Wayne Gretzky, LA	**1998** Ron Francis, Pitt
1985 Jari Kurri, Edm	**1992** Wayne Gretzky, LA	**1999** Wayne Gretzky, NYR
1986 Mike Bossy, NYI	**1993** Pierre Turgeon, NYI	**2000** Pavol Demitra, StL
1987 Joe Mullen, Cal	**1994** Wayne Gretzky, LA	**2001** Joe Sakic, Col
1988 Mats Naslund, Mtl	**1995** Ron Francis, Pitt	**2002** Ron Francis, Car
1989 Joe Mullen, Cal	**1996** Paul Kariya, Ana	**2003** Alexander Mogilny, Tor

▶

(1) As selected at the end of the regular season by members of the Professional Hockey Writers' Association in the NHL cities. (2) Since the 1981–82 season, Vezina Trophy winners have been selected by general managers of the NHL clubs. In earlier seasons the trophy was awarded to the goalkeeper(s) of the team allowing the fewest goals during the regular season.

▶

Conn Smythe Trophy (Most Valuable in Playoffs)[3]

1983 Bill Smith, NYI	**1990** Bill Ranford, Edm	**1997** Mike Vernon, Det
1984 Mark Messier, Edm	**1991** Mario Lemieux, Pitt	**1998** Steve Yzerman, Det
1985 Wayne Gretzky, Edm	**1992** Mario Lemieux, Pitt	**1999** Joe Nieuwendyk, Dal
1986 Patrick Roy, Mtl	**1993** Patrick Roy, Mtl	**2000** Scott Stevens, NJ
1987 Ron Hextall, Phil	**1994** Brian Leetch, NYR	**2001** Patrick Roy, Col
1988 Wayne Gretzky, Edm	**1995** Claude Lemieux, NJ	**2002** Nicklas Lidstrom, Det
1989 Al MacInnis, Cal	**1996** Joe Sakic, Col	**2003** Jean-Sebastien Giguere, Ana

Frank J. Selke Trophy (Best Defensive Forward)[1]

1983 Bobby Clarke, Phil	**1990** Rick Meagher, StL	**1997** Mike Peca, Buf
1984 Doug Jarvis, Wash	**1991** Dirk Graham, Chi	**1998** Jere Lehtinen, Dal
1985 Craig Ramsay, Buf	**1992** Guy Carbonneau, Mtl	**1999** Jere Lehtinen, Dal
1986 Troy Murray, Chi	**1993** Doug Gilmour, Tor	**2000** Steve Yzerman, Det
1987 Dave Poulin, Phil	**1994** Sergei Fedorov, Det	**2001** John Madden, NJ
1988 Guy Carbonneau, Mtl	**1995** Ron Francis, Det	**2002** Mike Peca, NYI
1989 Guy Carbonneau, Mtl	**1996** Sergei Fedorov, Det	**2003** Jere Lehtinen, Dal

Jack Adams Trophy (Coach of the Year)

1983 Orval Tessier, Chi	**1990** Bob Murdoch, Wpg	**1997** Ted Nolan, Buf
1984 Bryan Murray, Wash	**1991** Brian Sutter, StL	**1998** Pat Burns, Bos
1985 Mike Keenan, Phil	**1992** Pat Quinn, Van	**1999** Jacques Martin, Ott
1986 Glen Sather, Edm	**1993** Pat Burns, Tor	**2000** Joel Quenneville, StL
1987 Jacques Demers, Det	**1994** Jacques Lemaire, NJ	**2001** Bill Barber, Phil
1988 Jacques Demers, Det	**1995** Marc Crawford, Que	**2002** Bob Francis, Phnx
1989 Pat Burns, Det	**1996** Scotty Bowman, Det	**2003** Jacques Lemaire, Min

Source: *HickokSports.com*

(3) As selected by members of the Professional Hockey Writers' Association at the end of the last game of the Stanley Cup finals.

Top NHL Draft Picks Since 1980

Player, Team Selected by, Position, Junior Team	**Player, Team Selected by, Position, Junior Team**
1980 Doug Wickenheiser, Montreal, C, Regina (WHL)	**1993** Alexandre Daigle, Ottawa, C, Victoriaville (QMJHL)
1981 Dale Hawerchuk, Winnipeg, C, Cornwall (QMJHL)	**1994** Ed Jovanovski, Florida, D, Windsor (OHL)
1982 Gord Kluzak, Boston, D, Billings (WHL)	**1995** Bryan Berard, Ottawa, D, Detroit (OHL)
1983 Brian Lawton, Minnesota, C, Mount St. Charles HS	**1996** Chris Phillips, Ottawa, D, Prince Albert (WHL)
1984 Mario Lemieux, Pittsburgh, C, Laval (QMJHL)	**1997** Joe Thornton, Boston, C, Sault Ste. Marie (OHL)
1985 Wendel Clark, Toronto, LW-D, Saskatoon (WHL)	**1998** Vincent Lecavalier, Tampa Bay, C, Rimouski
1986 Joe Murphy, Detroit, C, Michigan State	(QMJHL)
1987 Pierre Turgeon, Buffalo, C, Granby (QMJHL)	**1999** Patrik Stefan, Atlanta, C, Long Beach (IHL)
1988 Mike Modano, Minnesota, C, Prince Albert (WHL)	**2000** Rick DiPietro, N.Y. Islanders, G, Boston University
1989 Mats Sundin, Quebec, RW, Nacka (Sweden)	**2001** Ilya Kovalchuk, Atlanta, C, Spartak (Russia, Div. 1)
1990 Owen Nolan, Quebec, RW, Cornwall (OHL)	**2002** Rick Nash, Columbus, LW, London (OHL)
1991 Eric Lindros, Quebec, C, Oshawa (OHL)	**2003** Marc-Andre Fleury, Pittsburgh, G, Cape Breton
1992 Roman Hamrlik, Tampa Bay, D, ZPS Zin (Czech)	(QMJHL)

Source: *The Sports Network Inc.*

Men's World Hockey Championships, 2003

Held in Finland, April 26–May 11

Canada Wins World Championship

Team Canada breezed through the 2003 International Ice Hockey Federation Men's World Hockey Championship undefeated to claim its 18th gold medal in World Championship play. Anson Carter from Toronto (who plays for the NHL's New York Rangers) scored the winning goal in overtime to lift Canada to a 3–2 victory over Sweden. Slovakia, the 2002 gold medal winner, took the bronze medal with a 4–2 victory over the Czech Republic.

PRELIMINARY ROUND STANDINGS: (Top three in each group advance to qualification round)

■ **Group A**

Team	W	L	T	GF	GA	PTS
Slovakia	3	0	0	22	5	6
Germany	2	1	0	9	8	4
Ukraine	1	2	0	9	13	2
Japan	0	3	0	6	20	0

■ **Group C**

Team	W	L	T	GF	GA	PTS
Canada	3	0	0	12	2	6
Sweden	2	1	0	6	5	4
Latvia	1	2	0	6	9	2
Belarus	0	3	0	1	9	0

■ **Group B**

Team	W	L	T	GF	GA	PTS
Russia	3	0	0	14	5	6
Switzerland	2	1	0	9	7	4
Denmark	1	2	0	8	14	2
USA	0	3	0	4	9	0

■ **Group D**

Team	W	L	T	GF	GA	PTS
Czech Republic	3	0	0	15	4	6
Finland	2	1	0	18	3	4
Austria	1	2	0	8	15	2
Slovenia	0	3	0	4	23	0

QUALIFICATION ROUND STANDINGS: (Top four in each group advance to quarterfinals)

■ **Group E**

Team	W	L	T	GF	GA	PTS
Slovakia	4	0	1	27	9	9
Czech Republic	4	0	1	22	7	9
Finland	2	2	1	18	10	5
Germany	2	2	1	11	11	5
Austria	1	4	0	9	27	2
Ukraine	0	5	0	8	31	0

■ **Group F**

Team	W	L	T	GF	GA	PTS
Canada	4	0	1	18	6	9
Sweden	4	1	0	20	9	8
Russia	2	3	0	16	14	4
Switzerland	2	3	0	14	16	4
Latvia	2	3	0	10	16	4
Denmark	0	4	1	8	25	1

Quarterfinal

Canada 3, Germany 2 (1-0, 1-0, 0-2, 1-0)

Slovakia 3, Switzerland 1 (0-1, 2-0, 1-0)

Czech Republic 3, Russia 0 (1-0, 2-0, 0-0)

Sweden 6, Finland 5 (1-3, 3-2, 2-0)

Semifinal

Canada 8, Czech Republic 4 (1-0, 2-2, 5-2)

Sweden 4, Slovakia 1 (1-0, 1-1, 2-0)

Bronze Medal Game

Slovakia 4, Czech Republic 2 (2-1, 1-1, 1-0)

Gold Medal Game

Canada 3, Sweden 2 (1-2, 0-0, 1-0, 1-0)

Source: *International Ice Hockey Federation*

2003 World Championship Scoring Leaders

Scoring leaders

Player	Team	GP	G	A	P	Pim	+/-
Zigmund Palffy	SVK	9	7	8	15	18	9
Jozef Stumpel	SVK	9	4	11	15	0	7
Lubomir Visnovsky	SVK	9	4	8	12	2	11
Teemu Selanne	FIN	7	8	3	11	2	3
Saku Koivu	FIN	7	1	10	11	4	3
Dany Heatley	**CAN**	**9**	**7**	**3**	**10**	**10**	**9**
Mats Sundin	SWE	7	6	4	10	10	8
Miroslav Satan	SVK	9	6	4	10	2	2
Martin Straka	CZE	9	6	4	10	4	5
Kimmo Rintanen	FIN	7	5	4	9	0	3
Peter Forsberg	SWE	8	4	5	9	6	5
Daniel Brière	**CAN**	**9**	**4**	**5**	**9**	**6**	**8**
Richard Zednik	SVK	9	5	3	8	6	9
Robert Reichel	CZE	8	4	4	8	2	4
Ladislav Nagy	SVK	9	4	4	8	10	5
Peter Nordstrom	SWE	9	2	6	8	4	7
Per-Johan Axelsson	SWE	9	4	3	7	16	7
John Pohl	USA	6	3	4	7	0	1
Ville Peltonen	FIN	7	3	4	7	2	2
Shawn Horcoff	**CAN**	**9**	**3**	**4**	**7**	**0**	**4**
Henrik Zetterberg	SWE	9	3	4	7	2	4
Jay Bouwmeester	**CAN**	**9**	**3**	**4**	**7**	**4**	**3**
Kimmo Timonen	FIN	7	2	5	7	2	1
Petr Kadlec	CZE	9	1	6	7	12	-3
Tomas Kaberle	CZE	7	0	7	7	2	-1

Source: *International Ice Hockey Federation*
GP – games played; G – goals; A – assists; Pts – total points; +/- – plus/minus (the number of goals scored against per 60 minutes of play; PIM – penalty minutes

2003 World Championship Team Canada Statistics

Player	Birthplace	Position	GP	G	A	Pts	PIM	+/-
Dany Heatley	Freiburg, Germany	F	9	7	3	10	10	9
Daniel Brière	Gatineau, QC	F	9	4	5	9	6	8
Shawn Horcoff	Trail, BC	F	9	3	4	7	0	4
Jay Bouwmeester	Edmonton, AB	D	9	3	4	7	4	3
Shane Doan	Halkirk, AB	F	9	4	2	6	12	1
Steven Reinprecht	Edmonton, AB	F	8	0	6	6	2	1
Mike Comrie	Edmonton, AB	F	9	3	2	5	6	1
Mathieu Dandenault	Sherbrooke, QC	D	9	2	3	5	12	9
Ryan Smyth	Banff, AB	F	9	2	2	4	2	1
Kirk Maltby	Guelph, ON	F	9	2	2	4	8	1
Patrick Marleau	Aneroid, SK	F	9	0	4	4	4	11
Anson Carter	Toronto, ON	F	9	2	1	3	8	1
Cory Cross	Lloydminster, AB	D	8	1	2	3	4	6
Eric Brewer	Vernon, BC	D	9	1	2	3	8	5
Steve Staios	Hamilton, ON	D	9	0	3	3	4	4
Kris Draper	Toronto, ON	F	9	0	3	3	10	1
Kyle Calder	Mannville, AB	F	9	1	1	2	0	3
Craig Rivet	North Bay, ON	D	9	0	1	1	6	3
Krys Kolanos	Calgary, AB	F	9	0	1	1	6	1
James Heward	Regina, SK	D	9	0	0	0	2	-1

Player	Birthplace	Position	GPI	GA	GAA	SA	SPCT	SO
Martin Biron	Lac St-Charles, QC	GK	0	0	0.00	0	.000	0
Sean Burke	Windsor ON	GK	6	7	1.28	149	.955	1
Roberto Luongo	Montreal, QC	GK	4	7	1.98	93	.930	1

Head coach: Andy Murray, Souris, MB (Los Angeles Kings, NHL)

Source: *International Ice Hockey Federation; Hockey Canada*
GP – games played; G – goals; A – assists; Pts – total points; +/- – plus/minus (the number of goals scored against the number of goals scored against per 60 minutes of play; PIM – penalty minutes; GPI – games played; GAA – average goals against per game; SO – shutouts; SA – saves; GA – goals against; SPCT – percentage of saves made on attempted shots

World Hockey Championships, 1981–2003
Team Canada's Leading Scorers

		GP	G	A	PTS			GP	G	A	PTS
1981	Dennis Maruk	8	5	3	8	1993	Eric Lindros	8	11	6	17
1982	Wayne Gretzky	10	6	8	14	1994	Paul Kariya	8	5	7	12
1983	Michel Goulet	10	1	8	9	1995	Andrew McKim	8	6	7	13
1984	Marcel Dionne	10	6	3	9	1996	Yanic Perrault	8	6	3	9
1985	Mario Lemieux	9	4	6	10	1997	Travis Green	11	3	5	8
1986	Brent Sutter	8	4	7	11	1998	Ray Whitney	6	4	2	6
1987	Tony Tanti	10	6	2	8	1999	Corey Stillman	10	4	4	8
1989[1]	Brian Bellows	10	8	7	15	2000	Todd Bertuzzi	9	5	4	9
1990	Steve Yzerman	10	9	10	19	2001	Brad Richards	7	3	3	6
1991	Joe Sakic	10	6	5	11	2002	Andy McDonald	7	4	1	5
1992	Steve Thomas	6	2	2	4	2003	Dan Heatley	9	7	3	10

Source: *International Ice Hockey Federation* (1) No championship held in 1988.

World Junior Hockey Medal Winners, 1981–2003

1981 . . . . Sweden, Finland, Soviet Union	1993 . . . . **Canada**, Sweden, Czech-Slovak
1982 . . . . **Canada**, Czechoslovakia, Finland	1994 . . . . **Canada**, Sweden, Russia
1983 . . . . Soviet Union, Czechoslovakia, **Canada**	1995 . . . . **Canada**, Russia, Sweden
1984 . . . . Soviet Union, Finland, Czechoslovakia	1996 . . . . **Canada**, Sweden, Russia
1985 . . . . **Canada,** Czechoslovakia, Soviet Union	1997 . . . . **Canada**, United States, Russia
1986 . . . . Soviet Union, **Canada**, United States	1998 . . . . Finland, Russia, Switzerland
1987 . . . . Finland, Czechoslovakia, Sweden	1999 . . . . Russia, **Canada**, Slovakia
1988 . . . . **Canada**, Soviet Union, Finland	2000 . . . . Czech Republic, Russia, **Canada**
1989 . . . . Soviet Union, Sweden, Czechoslovakia	2001 . . . . Czech Republic, Finland, **Canada**
1990 . . . . **Canada**, Soviet Union, Czechoslovakia	2002 . . . . Russia, **Canada**, Finland
1991 . . . . **Canada**, Soviet Union, Czechoslovakia	2003 . . . . Russia, **Canada**, Finland
1992 . . . . C.I.S., Sweden, United States	

Source: *The Sports Network Inc.*

Nunavut History at World Junior Hockey Championships

eam Canada's 2003 World Junior Hockey Championship roster included a first: the first player from the territory of Nunavut to be selected to the national junior team. Jordin Tootoo comes from Rankin Inlet, a village of just over 2,000 residents on Hudson Bay just north of Manitoba. Starting in minor hockey in his home territory before playing on teams in Alberta and Manitoba, Tootoo has played for four years with the WHL's Brandon Wheat Kings. Tootoo became the first player from Nunavut to be selected in the NHL draft when he was selected by the Nashville Predators in the fourth round of the 2001 draft. Tootoo played in his first regular season NHL game on October 9, 2003, becoming the first Inuit to play in the league.

Source: *Hockey Canada*

2003 World Junior Hockey Championship

(Halifax/Sydney, Nova Scotia, December 26, 2002 to January 5, 2003)

■ **Preliminary Round Standings**

Group A	W	L	T	GF	GA	Pts	Group B	W	L	T	GF	GA	Pts
Russia	4	0	0	21	7	8	Canada	4	0	0	21	6	8
USA	3	1	0	15	9	6	Finland	2	1	1	12	9	5
Slovakia	2	2	0	15	8	4	Czech Republic	2	1	1	8	7	5
Switzerland	1	3	0	10	15	2	Sweden	1	3	0	12	16	2
Belarus	0	4	0	6	28	0	Germany	0	4	0	3	18	0

■ **Quarterfinal**

Russia advances with a bye

Canada advances with a bye

USA 4, Czech Republic 3 (2-0, 2-2, 0-1)

Finland 6, Slovakia 0 (3-0, 3-0, 0-0)

■ **Semifinal**

Russia 4, Finland 1 (1-1, 0-0, 3-0)

Canada 3, USA 2 (1-1, 1-0, 1-1)

■ **Bronze Medal Game**

Finland 3, USA 2 (2-0, 1-0, 0-2)

■ **Gold Medal Game**

Russia 3, **Canada** 2 (1-1, 0-1, 2-0)

Source: *International Ice Hockey Federation*

■ **Canada Captures Second Consecutive Silver Medal**

Team Canada earned the silver medal in the 2003 International Ice Hockey Federation World Junior Hockey Championship, losing to Russia in the gold medal game for the second consecutive year. Finland defeated the United States to capture the bronze medal.

2003 World Junior Hockey Championship Team Canada Statistics

Player	Hometown	Position	GP	G	A	Pts	PIM	+/-
Carlo Colaiacovo	Ottawa, ON	D	6	1	9	10	2	-1
Pierre-Alexandre Parenteau	Hull, QC	F	6	4	3	7	2	2
Ian White	Steinbach, MB	D	6	2	4	6	0	1
Brooks Laich	Wawota, SK	F	6	2	4	6	0	0
Scottie Upshall	Ft. McMurray, AB	F	6	4	1	5	18	0
Pierre-Marc Bouchard	Boucherville, QC	F	6	2	3	5	2	-2
Kyle Wellwood	Oldcastle, ON	F	6	1	4	5	0	0
Joffrey Lupul	Edmonton, AB	F	6	2	1	3	27	-1
Derek Roy	Rockland, ON	F	6	1	2	3	4	2
Jay McClement	Kingston, ON	F	6	1	2	3	4	1
Jeff Woywitka	Vermilion, AB	D	6	1	1	2	0	2
Matthew Stajan	Mississauga, ON	D	6	1	1	2	0	1
Gregory Campbell	Tillsonburg, ON	F	6	1	1	2	4	3
Jordin Tootoo	Rankin Inlet, NV	F	6	1	1	2	4	-2
Brendan Bell	Ottawa, ON	D	6	1	1	2	6	-3
Steve Eminger	Woodbridge, ON	D	6	0	2	2	16	-1
Nathan Paetsch	Leroy, SK	D	6	1	0	1	4	4
Alexandre Rouleau	Mont-Laurier, QC	D	6	0	1	1	0	2
Boyd Gordon	Unity, SK	F	6	0	0	0	0	0
Daniel Paillé	Welland, ON	F	6	0	0	0	2	0

Player	Hometown	Position	GPI	GA	GAA	SA	SPCT	SO
Marc-Andre Fleury	Sorel, QC	GK	5	7	1.57	90	.928	1
David Le Neveu	Fernie, BC	GK	2	4	2.63	21	.840	0

Head coach: Marc Habscheid, Kelowna (WHL)

Source: *International Ice Hockey Federation; Hockey Canada*

GP – games played; G – goals; A – assists; Pts – total points; +/- – plus/minus (the number of goals scored against the number of goals scored against per 60 minutes of play; PIM – penalty minutes; GPI – games played; GAA – average goals against per game; SO – shutouts; SA – saves; GA – goals against; SPCT – percentage of saves made on attempted shots

International Hockey Competitions

■ WORLD CHAMPIONSHIP

	GOLD	SILVER	BRONZE
1920...	Canada	United States..	Czechoslovakia
1924...	Canada	United States..	Britain
1928...	Canada	Sweden	Switzerland
1930...	Canada	Germany	Switzerland
1931...	Canada	United States..	Austria
1932...	Canada	United States..	Germany
1933...	United States..	Canada	Czechoslovakia
1934...	Canada	United States..	Germany
1935...	Canada	Switzerland...	Britain
1936...	Britain	Canada	United States
1937...	Canada	Britain	Switzerland
1938...	Canada	Britain	Czechoslovakia
1939...	Canada	United States..	Switzerland
1940-46 WORLD WAR II — NO EVENT HELD			
1947...	Czechoslovakia	Sweden	Austria
1948...	Canada	Czechoslovakia	Switzerland
1949...	Czechoslovakia	Canada	United States
1950...	Canada	United States..	Switzerland
1951...	Canada	Sweden	Switzerland
1952...	Canada	United States..	Sweden
1953...	Sweden	Germany	Switzerland
1954...	Soviet Union..	Canada	Sweden
1955...	Canada	Soviet Union..	Czechoslovakia
1956...	Soviet Union..	United States..	Canada
1957...	Sweden	Soviet Union..	Czechoslovakia
1958...	Canada	Soviet Union..	Sweden
1959...	Canada	Soviet Union..	Czechoslovakia
1960...	United States..	Canada	Soviet Union
1961...	Canada	Czechoslovakia	Soviet Union
1962...	Sweden	Canada	United States
1963...	Soviet Union..	Sweden	Czechoslovakia
1964...	Soviet Union..	Sweden	Czechoslovakia
1965...	Soviet Union..	Czechoslovakia	Sweden
1966...	Soviet Union..	Czechoslovakia	Canada
1967...	Soviet Union..	Sweden	Canada
1968...	Soviet Union..	Czechoslovakia	Canada
1969...	Soviet Union..	Sweden	Czechoslovakia
1970...	Soviet Union..	Sweden	Czechoslovakia
1971...	Soviet Union..	Czechoslovakia	Sweden
1972...	Czechoslovakia	Soviet Union..	Sweden
1973...	Soviet Union..	Sweden	Czechoslovakia
1974...	Soviet Union..	Czechoslovakia	Sweden
1975...	Soviet Union..	Czechoslovakia	Sweden
1976...	Czechoslovakia	Soviet Union..	Sweden
1977...	Czechoslovakia	Sweden	Soviet Union
1978...	Soviet Union..	Czechoslovakia	Canada
1979...	Soviet Union..	Czechoslovakia	Sweden
1981...	Soviet Union..	Sweden	Czechoslovakia
1982...	Soviet Union..	Czechoslovakia	Canada
1983...	Soviet Union..	Czechoslovakia	Canada
1985...	Czechoslovakia	Canada	Soviet Union
1986...	Soviet Union..	Sweden	Canada
1987...	Sweden	Soviet Union..	Czechoslovakia
1989...	Soviet Union..	Canada	Czechoslovakia
1990...	Soviet Union..	Sweden	Czechoslovakia
1991...	Sweden	Canada	Soviet Union
1992...	Sweden	Finland	Czechoslovakia
1993...	Russia	Sweden	Czechoslovakia
1994...	Canada	Finland	Sweden
1995...	Finland	Sweden	Canada
1996...	Czech Republic	Canada	United States
1997...	Canada	Sweden	Czech Republic
1998...	Sweden	Finland	Czech Republic
1999...	Czech Republic	Finland	Sweden
2000...	Czech Republic	Slovakia	Finland
2001...	Czech Republic	Finland	Sweden
2002...	Slovakia	Russia	Sweden
2003...	Canada	Sweden	Slovakia

■ OLYMPIC GAMES

	GOLD	SILVER	BRONZE
1924...	Canada	United States..	Britain
1928...	Canada	Sweden	Switzerland
1932...	Canada	United States..	Germany
1936...	Britain	Canada	United States
1948...	Canada	Czechoslovakia	Switzerland
1952...	Canada	United States..	Sweden
1956...	Soviet Union..	United States..	Canada
1960...	United States..	Canada	Soviet Union
1964...	Soviet Union..	Sweden	Czechoslovakia
1968...	Soviet Union..	Czechoslovakia	Canada
1972...	Soviet Union..	United States..	Czechoslovakia
1976...	Soviet Union..	Czechoslovakia	Germany
1980...	United States..	Soviet Union..	Sweden
1984...	Soviet Union..	Czechoslovakia	Sweden
1988...	Soviet Union..	Finland	Sweden
1992...	Unified Team..	Canada	Czechoslovakia
1994...	Sweden	Canada	Finland
1998...	Czech Republic	Russia	Finland
2002...	Canada	United States..	Russia

■ WORLD CUP OF HOCKEY

	WINNER	RUNNER-UP
1996...	United States..	Canada

■ CANADA CUP

	WINNER	RUNNER-UP
1976...	Canada	Czechoslovakia
1981...	Soviet Union..	Canada
1984...	Canada	Sweden
1987...	Canada	Soviet Union
1991...	Canada	United States

Memorial Cup Winners, 1962–2003

(Canadian Junior Hockey Champions)

1962	Hamilton Red Wings	1983	Portland Winter Hawks
1963	Edmonton Oil Kings	1984	Ottawa 67's
1964	Toronto Marlboros	1985	Prince Albert Raiders
1965	Niagara Falls Flyers	1986	Guelph Platers
1966	Edmonton Oil Kings	1987	Medicine Hat Tigers
1967	Toronto Marlboros	1988	Medicine Hat Tigers
1968	Niagara Falls Flyers	1989	Swift Current Broncos
1969	Montreal Jr. Canadiens	1990	Oshawa Generals
1970	Montreal Jr. Canadiens	1991	Spokane Chiefs
1971	Quebec Ramparts	1992	Kamloops Blazers
1972	Cornwall Royals	1993	Sault Ste. Marie Greyhounds
1973	Toronto Marlboros	1994	Kamloops Blazers
1974	Regina Pats	1995	Kamloops Blazers
1975	Toronto Marlboros	1996	Granby Predateurs
1976	Hamilton Fincups	1997	Hull Olympiques
1977	New Westminster Bruins	1998	Portland Winter Hawks
1978	New Westminster Bruins	1999	Ottawa 67s
1979	Peterborough Petes	2000	Rimouski Oceanic
1980	Cornwall Royals	2001	Red Deer Rebels
1981	Cornwall Royals	2002	Kooteny Ice
1982	Kitchener Rangers	2003	Kitchener Rangers

Source: *Canoe Limited Partnership*

World Women's Hockey Championship Medal Winners, 1990–2001

Year	Gold	Silver	Bronze	Host City
1990	Canada	United States	Finland	Ottawa, ON, Canada
1992	Canada	United States	Finland	Tampere, Finland
1994	Canada	United States	Finland	Lake Placid, NY, USA
1997	Canada	United States	Finland	Kitchener, ON, Canada
1999	Canada	United States	Finland	Espoo, Finland
2000	Canada	United States	Finland	Mississauga, ON, Canada
2001	Canada	United States	Russia	Minneapolis, MN, USA
2003*	—	—	—	Beijing, China

*-Cancelled due to SARS outbreak.

Wickenheiser Breaks Through "Ice Ceiling"

Hayley Wickenheiser, a standout leader on the Canadian Women's National Team since 1994, became the first woman to score a point in a professional men's hockey game. Her assist to teammate Matti Tevanen in January 2003 was the first of her 11 points in 23 games for the Kirkkonummi Salamat, a second-division team in the Finnish League. Wickenheiser follows Maren Valenti as the only two women to play on a professional men's hockey team; Valenti played 24 games for a German second-division team in the late 1990s but did not score a point. Wickenheiser has signed on for a second season with Kirkkonummi, which has been elevated to the Finnish League's first division for the 2003–04 season.

Source: *Canadian Press*

Summer Olympics

Location	Date of Competition	Competitors Men	Women	Nations Represented	Unofficial Winners
1896 Athens, Greece	Apr. 6–15	311	0	13	United States
1900 Paris, France	May 20–Oct. 28	1 319	11	22	United States
1904 St. Louis, United States	July 1–Nov. 23	681	6	12	United States
1906[1] Athens, Greece	Apr. 22–May 2	877	7	20	United States
1908 London, England	Apr. 27–Oct. 31	1 999	36	23	United States
1912 Stockholm, Sweden	May 5–July 22	2 490	57	28	United States
1916 Cancelled because of World War I					
1920 Antwerp, Belgium	Apr. 20–Sept. 12	2 543	64	29	United States
1924 Paris, France	May 4–July 27	2 956	136	44	United States
1928 Amsterdam, Netherlands	May 17–Aug. 12	2 724	290	46	United States
1932 Los Angeles, United States	July 30–Aug. 14	1 281	127	37	United States
1936 Berlin, Germany	Aug. 1–16	3 738	328	49	Germany
1940 Cancelled because of World War II					
1944 Cancelled because of World War II					
1948 London, England	July 29–Aug. 14	3 714	385	59	United States
1952 Helsinki, Finland	July 19–Aug. 3	4 407	518	69	United States
1956 Melbourne, Australia[2]	Nov. 22–Dec. 8	2 958	384	67	USSR
1960 Rome, Italy	Aug. 25–Sept. 11	4 738	610	83	USSR
1964 Tokyo, Japan	Oct. 10–24	4 457	683	93	United States
1968 Mexico City, Mexico	Oct. 12–27	4 750	781	112	United States
1972 Munich, West Germany	Aug. 26–Sept. 10	5 848	1 299	122	USSR
1976 Montreal, Canada	July 17–Aug. 1	4 834	1 251	92[3]	USSR
1980 Moscow, USSR	July 19–Aug. 3	4 265	1 088	81	USSR
1984 Los Angeles, United States	July 28–Aug. 12	5 458	1 620	141	United States
1988 Seoul, South Korea	Sept. 17–Oct. 2	7 105	2 476	160	USSR
1992 Barcelona, Spain	July 25–Aug. 9	7 555	3 008	172	Unified Team
1996 Atlanta, United States	July 19–Aug. 4	7 000	3 800	197	United States
2000 Sydney, Australia	Sept. 16–Oct. 1	6 582	4 069	199	United States
2004 Athens, Greece	Aug. 13–29				
2008 Beijing, China	Aug. 8–24				

Source: *Canadian Olympic Association, International Olympic Committee*
(1) 1906 Games were not recognized by the International Olympic Committee.
(2) The equestrian events were held in Stockholm, Sweden, June 10–17, 1956.
(3) Most sources list this figure as 88. Cameroon, Egypt, Morocco and Tunisia all boycotted the 1976 Olympics; however, their athletes had already competed before the boycott was officially announced.

Winter Olympics

Year	Location	Date of Competition	Competitors Men	Women	Nations Represented	Unofficial Winners
1924	Chamonix, France	Jan. 25–Feb. 4	281	13	16	Norway
1928	St. Moritz, Switzerland	Feb. 11–19	468	27	25	Norway
1932	Lake Placid, United States	Feb. 4–15	274	32	17	United States
1936	Garmisch-Partenkirchen, Germany	Feb. 6–16	675	80	28	Norway
1940	Cancelled because of World War II					
1944	Cancelled because of World War II					
1948	St. Moritz, Switzerland	Jan. 30–Feb. 8	636	77	28	Sweden
1952	Oslo, Norway	Feb. 14–25	623	109	30	Norway
1956	Cortina d'Ampezzo, Italy	Jan. 26–Feb. 5	686	132	32	U.S.S.R.
1960	Squaw Valley, United States	Feb. 18–28	521	144	30	U.S.S.R.
1964	Innsbruck, Austria	Jan. 29–Feb. 9	986	200	36	U.S.S.R.
1968	Grenoble, France	Feb. 6–18	1 081	212	37	Norway
1972	Sapporo, Japan	Feb. 3–13	1 015	217	35	U.S.S.R.
1976	Innsbruck, Austria	Feb. 4–15	900	228	37	U.S.S.R.
1980	Lake Placid, United States	Feb. 14–23	833	234	37	East Germany
1984	Sarajevo, Yugoslavia	Feb. 7–19	1 180	409	49	U.S.S.R.
1988	Calgary, Canada	Feb. 13–28	1 128	317	57	U.S.S.R.
1992	Albertville, France	Feb. 8–23	1 545	602	64	Germany
1994	Lillehammer, Norway	Feb. 12–27	1 216	521	67	Norway
1998	Nagano, Japan	Feb. 7–22	1 488	814	72	Germany
2002	Salt Lake City, United States	Feb. 8–24	1 513	886	77	Germany
2006	Turin, Italy	Feb. 10–26				
2010	Vancouver/Whistler, Canada	Feb. 12–26				

Source: *International Olympic Committee, Canadian Olympic Association*

Vancouver to Host 2010 Winter Olympics

By a slim three-vote margin, Vancouver won the right to host the 2010 Winter Olympic Games. On the second ballot of the International Olympic Committee's vote to award the 2010 Games, Vancouver/Whistler was selected over Pyeongchang, South Korea (Salzburg, Austria's bid was eliminated in the first ballot), to become the third Canadian city to host an Olympic Games and the second to host the Winter Games. The Games will take place over a 17-day period in February 2010 at a variety of existing and yet-to-be-constructed facilities in Vancouver and Whistler.

Source: *Canadian Press*

Canada's Olympic Medalists, 1900–2002

Summer Olympic Games

1900

Bronze: Men's athletics, 400m hurdles George Orton (Although a Canadian citizen, he represented the University of Pennsylvania; Canada did not officially appear at the Olympics until 1904.)

1904

Gold: Men's athletics, 56lb weight throw Étienne Desmarteau
Gold: Men's golf George Lyon
Gold: Men's team football (soccer)
Gold: Men's team lacrosse
Silver: Men's rowing, eight with coxswain

1908

Gold: Men's athletics, 200m Robert Kerr
Gold: Men's team lacrosse
Gold: Men's trapshooting Walter Ewing
Silver: Men's team shooting, clay pigeons
Silver: Men's trapshooting George Beattie
Silver: Men's athletics, triple jump J. Garfield MacDonald
Bronze: Men's athletics, 100m Robert Kerr
Bronze: Men's freestyle wrestling, bantamweight Aubert Cote
Bronze: Men's athletics, hammer throw Cornelius Walsh
Bronze: Men's athletics, long jump Calvin Bricker
Bronze: Men's athletics, pole vault Edward Archibald
Bronze: Men's rowing, coxless pair Norman Jackes Fred Toms
Bronze: Men's rowing, eight with coxswain
Bronze: Men's team cycling (1 980-yard pursuit) William Anderson Walter Andrews Frederick McCarthy William Morton
Bronze: Men's team shooting (rifle)

1912

Gold: Men's athletics, 10 000m walk George Goulding
Gold: Men's swimming, 1 500m freestyle George Hodgson
Gold: Men's swimming, 400m freestyle George Hodgson
Silver: Men's athletics, hammer throw Duncan Gillis
Silver: Men's athletics, long jump Calvin Bricker
Bronze: Men's athletics, pentathlon Frank Lukeman
Bronze: Men's athletics, pole vault William Happenny
Bronze: Men's rowing, single sculls Everard Butler

1920

Gold: Men's athletics, 110m hurdles Earl Thomson
Gold: Men's boxing, welterweight Julius Schneider
Silver: Men's boxing, bantamweight Clifford Graham
Silver: Men's boxing, middleweight George Prud'homme
Silver: Men's swimming, 1 500m freestyle George Vernot
Bronze: Men's boxing, lightweight Clarence Newton
Bronze: Men's boxing, middleweight Montgomery Herscovitch
Bronze: Men's swimming, 400m freestyle George Vernot

1924

Silver: Men's rowing, eight with coxswain
Silver: Men's rowing, four without coxswain Archibald Black, George MacKay, A. Mariacher, William Wood
Silver: Men's team shooting, clay pigeons
Bronze: Men's boxing, welterweight Douglas Lewis

1928

Gold: Men's athletics, 100m Percy Williams
Gold: Men's athletics, 200m Percy Williams
Gold: Women's athletics, 4x100m relay Myrtle Cook, Fanny Rosenfeld, Ethel Smith, Jean Thompson
Gold: Women's athletics, high jump Ethel Catherwood
Silver: Men's athletics, 400m James Ball
Silver: Men's freestyle wrestling, middleweight Donald Stockton
Silver: Men's rowing, double sculls John Guest, Joseph Wright Jr.
Silver: Women's athletics, 100m Fanny Rosenfeld
Bronze: Men's athletics, 4x400m relay James Ball, Philip Edwards, Stanley Glover, Alexander Wilson
Bronze: Men's boxing, welterweight Raymond Smillie
Bronze: Men's freestyle wrestling, bantamweight James Trifunov
Bronze: Men's freestyle wrestling, welterweight Maurice Letchford
Bronze: Men's rowing, eight with coxswain
Bronze: Men's swimming, 4x200m freestyle relay Garnet Ault, Frederick Bourne, Walter Spence, James Thompson
Bronze: Women's athletics, 100m Ethel Smith

1932

Gold: Men's athletics, high jump Duncan McNaughton
Gold: Men's boxing, bantamweight Horace Gwynne

▶

▶ Silver: **Men's athletics, 800m** Alexander Wilson
Silver: **Men's freestyle wrestling, welterweight** Daniel
　　MacDonald
Silver: **Sailing, 8m mixed**
Silver: **Women's athletics, 100m** Hilda Strike-Sisson
Silver: **Women's athletics, 4x100m relay** Mary Frizzell,
　　Mildred Frizzell, Lillian Palmer-Alderson, Hilda
　　Strike-Sisson
Bronze: **Men's athletics, 1 500m** Philip Edwards
Bronze: **Men's athletics, 400m** Alexander Wilson
Bronze: **Men's athletics, 4x400m relay** James Ball,
　　Philip Edwards, Raymond Lewis, Alexander
　　Wilson
Bronze: **Men's athletics, 800m** Philip Edwards
Bronze: **Men's rowing, double sculls** Noel De Mille,
　　Charles Pratt
Bronze: **Men's rowing, eight with coxswain**
Bronze: **Sailing, 6m mixed** Gardner Boultbee, Kenneth
　　Glass, Philip Rogers, Gerald Wilson
Bronze: **Women's athletics, high jump** Eva Dawes-
　　Spinks

1936

Gold: **Men's 1 000m canoe single** Frank Amyot
Silver: **Men's 10 000m canoe double** Harvey Charters,
　　Frank Saker
Silver: **Men's athletics, 400m hurdles** John Loaring
Silver: **Men's team basketball**
Bronze: **Men's 1 000m canoe double** Harvey Charters,
　　Frank Saker
Bronze: **Men's athletics, 800m** Philip Edwards
Bronze: **Men's freestyle wrestling, welterweight**
　　Joseph Schleimer
Bronze: **Women's athletics, 4x100m relay** Dorothy
　　Brookshaw, Hilda Cameron, Mildred Dolson-
　　Cavill, Aileen Meagher
Bronze: **Women's athletics, 80m hurdles** Elizabeth
　　Taylor-Campbell

1948

Silver: **Men's 1 000m canoe single** Douglas Bennett
Bronze: **Men's 10 000m canoe single** Norman Lane
Bronze: **Women's athletics, 4x100m relay** Dianne
　　Foster, Patricia Jones, Nancy MacKay-Murrall,
　　Violet Meyers

1952

Gold: **Men's trapshooting** George Genereux
Silver: **Men's 10 000m canoe double** Donald Hawgood,
　　Kenneth Lane
Silver: **Men's weightlifting, middleweight** Gerald Gratton

1956

Gold: **Men's shooting, 50m rifle prone** Gerald Ouellette
Gold: **Men's rowing, four without coxswain** Donald
　　Arnold, Ignace D'Hondt, Lorne Loomer, Archibald
　　MacKinnon
Silver: **Men's rowing, eight with coxswain**
Bronze: **Men's shooting, 50m rifle prone** Gilmore Boa
Bronze: **Mixed team equestrian**
Bronze: **Women's diving, 3m springboard** Irene
　　MacDonald

1960

Silver: **Men's rowing, eight with coxswain**

1964

Gold: **Men's rowing, coxless pair** George Hungerford,
　　Roger Jackson
Silver: **Men's athletics, 800m** William Crothers
Silver: **Men's judo, heavyweight** Alfred Rogers
Bronze: **Men's athletics, 100m** Harry Jerome

1968

Gold: **Mixed team equestrian**
Silver: **Men's swimming, 400m freestyle** Ralph Hutton
Silver: **Women's swimming, 100m backstroke** Elaine
　　Tanner
Silver: **Women's swimming, 200m backstroke** Elaine
　　Tanner
Bronze: **Women's swimming, 4x100m freestyle relay**
　　Marilyn Corson-Whitney, Angela Coughlaw,
　　Marion Lay, Elaine Tanner

1972

Silver: **Men's swimming, 100m butterfly** Bruce
　　Robertson
Silver: **Women's swimming, 400m individual medley**
　　Leslie Cliff
Bronze: **Mixed sailing, fleet/match race keelboat open**
　　Paul Cote, John Ekels, David Miller
Bronze: **Men's swimming, 4x100m medley relay** Erik
　　Fish, Robert Kasting, William Mahony, Bruce
　　Robertson

1976

Silver: **Men's 1 500m canoe single** John Wood
Silver: **Men's athletics, high jump** Gregory Joy
Silver: **Men's swimming, 4x100 medley relay** Clayton
　　Evans, Gary MacDonald, Stephen Pickell, Graham
　　Smith
Silver: **Mixed individual equestrian** Michel Vaillancourt ▶

Silver: Women's swimming, 400m individual medley Cheryl Gibson

Bronze: Women's swimming, 100m backstroke Nancy Garapick

Bronze: Women's swimming, 200m backstroke Nancy Garapick

Bronze: Women's swimming, 400m freestyle Shannon Smith

Bronze: Women's swimming, 400m individual medley Rebecca Smith

Bronze: Women's swimming, 4x100 medley relay Wendy Cook-Hogg, Robin Corsiglia, Anne Jardin, Susan Smith-Sloan

Bronze: Women's swimming, 4x100m freestyle relay Gail Amundrud, Barbara Clark, Anne Jardin, Rebecca Smith

1984

Gold: Men's 1 000m kayak double Lawrence Cain, Hugh Fisher

Gold: Men's 1 000m kayak double Hugh Fisher, Alwyn Morris

Gold: Men's rowing, eight with coxswain

Gold: Men's swimming, 200m breaststroke Victor Davis

Gold: Men's swimming, 200m individual medley Alexander Baumann

Gold: Men's swimming, 400m individual medley Alexander Baumann

Gold: Women's diving, 3m springboard Sylvie Bernier

Gold: Women's shooting, 25m pistol Linda Thom

Gold: Women's swimming, 200m breaststroke Anne Ottenbrite

Silver: Men's 1 000m canoe single Lawrence Cain

Silver: Men's boxing, heavyweight Willie Dewit

Silver: Men's boxing, light-middleweight Shawn O'Sullivan

Silver: Men's cycling, 1km time trial Curtis Harnett

Silver: Men's cycling, individual road race Stephen Bauer

Silver: Men's freestyle wrestling, super heavyweight Robert Molle

Silver: Men's swimming, 100m breaststroke Victor Davis

Silver: Men's swimming, 4x100m medley relay Victor Davis, Donald Goss, Thomas Ponting, Michael West

Silver: Men's weightlifting, middleweight Jacques Demers

Silver: Mixed sailing, flying Dutchman Terence McLaughlin, Evert Bastet

Silver: Women's 500m kayak double Alexandra Barre, Susan Holloway

Silver: Women's athletics, 4x100m relay Angela Bailey, France Gareau, Marita Payne-Wiggins, Angella Taylor-Issajenko

Silver: Women's athletics, 4x400m relay Charmaine Crooks, Molly Killingbeck, Marita Payne-Wiggins, Jillian Richardson-Briscoe

Silver: Women's rowing, four-oared shell with coxswain Barbara Armbrust, Marilyn Brain, Angela Schneider, Lesley Thompson, Jane Tregunno

Silver: Women's rowing, pair without coxswain Elizabeth Craig, Patricia Smith

Silver: Women's swimming, 100m breaststroke Anne Ottenbrite

Silver: Women's synchronized swimming, duet Sharon Hambrook, Kelly Kryczka

Silver: Women's synchronized swimming, solo Carolyn Waldo

Bronze: Men's 500m kayak double Hugh Fisher, Alwyn Morris

Bronze: Men's athletics, 100m Ben Johnson

Bronze: Men's athletics, 4x100m relay Sterling Hinds, Ben Johnson, Anthony Sharpe, Desai Williams

Bronze: Men's boxing, bantamweight Dale Walters

Bronze: Men's freestyle wrestling, middleweight Christopher Rinke

Bronze: Men's judo, heavyweight Marc Berger

Bronze: Men's rowing, quadruple sculls without coxswain Bruce Ford, Douglas Hamilton, Michael Hughes, Philip Monckton

Bronze: Men's rowing, single sculls Robert Mills

Bronze: Men's sailing, single-handed dinghy Terence Neilson

Bronze: Men's swimming, 100m backstroke Michael West

Bronze: Men's swimming, 200m backstroke Cameron Henning

Bronze: Mixed sailing, fleet/match race keelboat open Stephen Calder, Hans Fogh, John Kerr

Bronze: Women's 500m kayak four Alexandra Barre, Lucie Guay, Susan Holloway, Barbara Olmstead

Bronze: Women's athletics, 3 000m Lynn Williams

Bronze: Women's rowing, double sculls Daniele Laumann, Silken Laumann

Bronze: Women's swimming, 4x100m medley relay Reema Abdo, Michelle MacPherson, Anne Ottenbrite, Pamela Rai

1988

Gold: Men's boxing, super heavyweight Lennox Lewis

Gold: Women's synchronized swimming, duet Michelle Cameron, Carolyn Waldo

▶ Gold: **Women's synchronized swimming, solo** Carolyn Waldo

Silver: **Men's boxing, middleweight** Egerton Marcus

Silver: **Men's swimming, 4x100m medley relay** Victor Davis, Donald Goss, Thomas Ponting, Mark Tewksbury

Bronze: **Men's athletics, decathlon** David Steen

Bronze: **Men's boxing, light-middleweight** Raymond Downey

Bronze: **Mixed sailing, flying Dutchman** Frank McLaughlin, John Millen

Bronze: **Mixed team equestrian**

Bronze: **Women's swimming, 4x100m medley relay** Allison Higson, Jane Kerr, Lori Melien, Andrea Nugent

1992

Gold: **Men's athletics, 110m hurdles** Mark McKoy

Gold: **Men's rowing, eight with coxswain**

Gold: **Men's swimming, 100m backstroke** Mark Tewksbury

Gold: **Women's rowing, coxless four** Jennifer Barnes, Jessica Monroe, Brenda Taylor, Kay Worthington

Gold: **Women's rowing, eight with coxswain**

Gold: **Women's rowing, pair without coxswain** Kathleen Heddle, Marnie McBean

Gold: **Women's synchronized swimming, solo** Sylvie Frechette

Silver: **Men's athletics, 20km race walk** Guillaume Leblanc

Silver: **Men's boxing, light-welterweight** Mark Leduc

Silver: **Men's freestyle wrestling, super heavyweight** Jeffrey Thue

Silver: **Women's synchronized swimming, duet** Penny Vilagos, Vicky Vilagos

Bronze: **Men's boxing, middleweight** Christopher Johnson

Bronze: **Men's cycling, sprint** Curtis Harnett

Bronze: **Men's judo, middleweight** Nicolas Gill

Bronze: **Men's swimming, 4x100m medley relay** Stephen Clarke, Jonathan Cleveland, Marcel Gery, Mark Tewksbury

Bronze: **Mixed sailing, two-person keelboat open** Eric Jespersen, Ross MacDonald

Bronze: **Women's athletics, 3 000m** Angela Chalmers

Bronze: **Women's rowing, single sculls** Silken Laumann

1996

Gold: **Men's athletics, 100m** Donovan Bailey

Gold: **Men's athletics, 4x100m relay** Donovan Bailey, Robert Esmie, Glenroy Gilbert, Bruny Surin

Gold: **Women's rowing, double sculls** Kathleen Heddle, Marnie McBean

Silver: **Men's boxing, heavyweight** David Defiagbon

Silver: **Men's cycling, points race** Brian Walton

Silver: **Men's freestyle wrestling, bantamweight** Giuvi Sissaouri

Silver: **Men's rowing, lightweight coxless four** Dave Boyes, Gavin Hassett, Jeffrey Lay, Brian Peaker

Silver: **Men's rowing, single sculls** Derek Porter

Silver: **Women's 500m kayak single** Caroline Brunet

Silver: **Women's mountain bike, cross-country** Alison Sydor

Silver: **Women's rowing, eight with coxswain**

Silver: **Women's rowing, single sculls** Silken Laumann

Silver: **Women's swimming, 200m individual medley** Marianne Limpert

Silver: **Women's team synchronized swimming**

Bronze: **Men's beach volleyball** John Child, Mark Heese

Bronze: **Men's cycling, sprint** Curtis Harnett

Bronze: **Men's swimming, 200m individual medley** Curtis Myden

Bronze: **Men's swimming, 400m individual medley** Curtis Myden

Bronze: **Women's cycling, individual road race** Clara Hughes

Bronze: **Women's cycling, individual time trial** Clara Hughes

Bronze: **Women's diving, 3m springboard** Annie Pelletier

Bronze: **Women's rowing, quadruple sculls without coxswain** Laryssa Biesenthal, Kathleen Heddle, Marnie McBean, Diane O'Grady

2000

Gold: **Men's freestyle wrestling, 63–69kg** Daniel Igali

Gold: **Men's tennis, doubles** Sebastien Lareau, Daniel Nestor

Gold: **Men's triathlon, individual** Simon Whitfield

Silver: **Men's judo, half-heavyweight** Nicolas Gill

Silver: **Women's 500m kayak single** Caroline Brunet

Silver: **Women's synchronized diving, 10m platform** Emilie Heymans, Anne Montminy

Bronze: **Men's 1 000m canoe single** Stephen Giles

Bronze: **Men's swimming, 400m individual medley** Curtis Myden

Bronze: **Men's trampoline, individual** Mathieu Turgeon

Bronze: **Women's diving, 10m platform** Anne Montminy

Bronze: **Women's rowing, eight with coxswain**

Bronze: **Women's team synchronized swimming**

Bronze: **Women's trampoline, individual** Karen Cockburn

Source: *International Olympic Committee*

Winter Olympic Games

1920

Gold: Men's ice hockey (Although the Winter Games did not begin until 1924, ice hockey was an official event at the 1920 Summer Games.)

1924

Gold: Men's ice hockey

1928

Gold: Men's ice hockey

1932

Gold: Men's ice hockey
Silver: Men's speed skating, 1 500m Alexander Hurd
Bronze: Men's figure skating Montgomery Wilson
Bronze: Men's speed skating, 1 500m William Logan
Bronze: Men's speed skating, 10 000m Frank Stack
Bronze: Men's speed skating, 5 000m William Logan
Bronze: Men's speed skating, 500m Alexander Hurd

1936

Silver: Men's ice hockey

1948

Gold: Men's ice hockey
Gold: Women's figure skating Barbara Ann Scott
Bronze: Pairs figure skating Wallace Diestelmeyer, Suzanne Morrow

1952

Gold: Men's ice hockey
Bronze: Men's speed skating, 500m Gordon Audley

1956

Silver: Pairs figure skating Norris Bowden, Frances Dafoe
Bronze: Men's ice hockey
Bronze: Women's alpine skiing, downhill Lucile Wheeler

1960

Gold: Pairs figure skating Robert Paul, Barbara Wagner
Gold: Women's alpine skiing, slalom Anne Heggtveit
Silver: Men's ice hockey
Bronze: Men's figure skating Donald Jackson

1964

Gold: Men's bobsleigh, four-man Douglas Anakin, John Emery, Victor Emery, Peter Kirby
Bronze: Pairs figure skating Debbi Wilkes, Guy Revell
Bronze: Women's figure skating Petra Burka

1968

Gold: Women's alpine skiing, giant slalom Nancy Greene
Bronze: Men's ice hockey
Bronze: Women's alpine skiing, slalom Nancy Greene

1972

Silver: Women's figure skating Karen Magnussen

1976

Gold: Women's alpine skiing, giant slalom Kathy Kreiner
Silver: Women's speed skating, 500m Cathy Priestner
Bronze: Men's figure skating Toller Cranston

1980

Silver: Men's speed skating, 1 000m Gaetan Boucher
Bronze: Men's alpine skiing, downhill Steve Podborski

1984

Gold: Men's speed skating, 1 000m Gaetan Boucher
Gold: Men's speed skating, 1 500m Gaetan Boucher
Silver: Men's figure skating Brian Orser
Bronze: Men's speed skating, 500m Gaetan Boucher

1988

Silver: Men's figure skating Brian Orser
Silver: Women's figure skating Elizabeth Manley
Bronze: Pairs ice dancing Robert McCall, Tracy Wilson
Bronze: Women's alpine skiing, downhill Karen Percy
Bronze: Women's alpine skiing, super-G Karen Percy

1992

Gold: Women's alpine skiing, downhill Kerrin Lee-Gartner
Gold: Women's short track speed skating, 3 000m relay Angela Cutrone, Sylvie Daigle, Nathalie Lambert, Annie Perreault

▶ **Silver: Men's ice hockey**
Silver: Men's short track speed skating, 1 000m Frédéric Blackburn
Silver: Men's short track speed skating, 5 000m relay Frédéric Blackburn, Laurent Daignault, Michel Daignault, Sylvain Gagnon, Mark Lackie
Bronze: Pairs figure skating Isabelle Brasseur, Lloyd Eisler
Bronze: Women's biathlon, 15km Myriam Bedard

1994

Gold: Men's freestyle skiing, moguls Jean-Luc Brassard
Gold: Women's biathlon, 15km Myriam Bedard
Gold: Women's biathlon, 7.5km Myriam Bedard
Silver: Men's figure skating Elvis Stojko
Silver: Men's freestyle skiing, aerials Philippe Laroche
Silver: Men's ice hockey
Silver: Women's short track speed skating, 1 000m Nathalie Lambert
Silver: Women's short track speed skating, 3 000m relay Christine Boudrias, Isabelle Charest, Angela Cutrone, Sylvie Daigle, Nathalie Lambert
Silver: Women's speed skating, 500m Susan Auch
Bronze: Men's alpine skiing, downhill Ed Podivinsky
Bronze: Men's freestyle skiing, aerials Lloyd Langlois
Bronze: Men's short track speed skating, 1 000m Marc Gagnon
Bronze: Pairs figure skating Isabelle Brasseur, Lloyd Eisler

1998

Gold: Men's bobsleigh, two-man Pierre Lueders, David MacEachern
Gold: Men's short track speed skating, 5 000m relay Eric Bedard, Derrick Campbell, François Drolet, Marc Gagnon
Gold: Men's snowboard, giant-slalom Ross Rebagliati
Gold: Women's curling Jan Betker, Atina Ford, Marcia Gudereit, Joan McCusker, Sandra Schmirler
Gold: Women's short track speed skating, 500m Annie Perreault
Gold: Women's speed skating, 500m Catriona LeMay Doan
Silver: Men's curling Mike Harris, Richard Hart, George Karrys, Collin Mitchell, Paul Savage
Silver: Men's figure skating Elvis Stojko
Silver: Men's speed skating, 500m Jeremy Wotherspoon

Silver: Women's ice hockey
Silver: Women's speed skating, 500m Susan Auch
Bronze: Men's short track speed skating, 1 000m Eric Bedard
Bronze: Men's speed skating, 500m Kevin Overland
Bronze: Women's short track speed skating, 3 000m relay Christine Boudrias, Isabelle Charest, Annie Perreault, Tania Vicent
Bronze: Women's speed skating, 1 000m Catriona LeMay Doan

2002

Gold: Men's ice hockey
Gold: Men's short track speed skating, 5 000m relay Eric Bedard, Marc Gagnon, Jonathan Guilmette, François-Louis Tremblay, Mathieu Turcotte
Gold: Men's short track speed skating, 500m Marc Gagnon
Gold: Pairs figure skating David Pelletier, Jamie Sale
Gold: Women's ice hockey
Gold: Women's speed skating, 500m Catriona LeMay Doan
Silver: Men's curling Don Bartlett, Kevin Martin, Carter Rycroft, Ken Tralnberg, Don Walchuk
Silver: Men's short track speed skating, 500m Jonathan Guilmette
Silver: Women's cross-country skiing, 5km pursuit Beckie Scott
Silver: Women's freestyle skiing, aerials Veronica Brenner
Bronze: Men's short track speed skating, 1 000m Mathieu Turcotte
Bronze: Men's short track speed skating, 1 500m Marc Gagnon
Bronze: Women's curling Kelley Law, Diane Nelson, Cheryl Noble, Julie Skinner, Georgina Wheatcroft
Bronze: Women's freestyle skiing, aerials Deidra Dionne
Bronze: Women's short track speed skating, 3 000m relay Isabelle Charest, Marie-Eve Drolet, Amelie Goulet-Nadon, Alanna Kraus, Tania Vicent
Bronze: Women's speed skating, 3 000m Cindy Klassen
Bronze: Women's speed skating, 5 000m Clara Hughes

Source: *International Olympic Committee*

The XIVth Pan American Games

Santo Domingo, Dominican Republic
August 2–17, 2003

■ Final Medal Standings

Country	Gold	Silver	Bronze	Total
USA	115	81	75	271
Cuba	72	41	38	151
Canada	**29**	**56**	**42**	**127**
Brazil	28	39	53	120
Mexico	20	28	32	80
Venezuela	16	20	28	64
Argentina	16	18	26	60
Colombia	10	8	23	41
Dominican Republic	10	12	19	41
Chile	2	10	10	22
Puerto Rico	3	4	8	15
Jamaica	5	2	7	14
Guatemala	0	3	8	11
Peru	1	1	8	10
Ecuador	3	1	5	9
Uruguay	2	1	5	8
Trinidad & Tobago	2	4	1	7
El Salvador	0	2	2	4
Barbados	2	0	1	3
Haiti	0	1	2	3
Bahamas	0	2	0	2
Bolivia	0	0	2	2
Grenada	0	1	1	2
Guyana	0	0	2	2
Panama	0	0	2	2
Cayman Islands	0	1	0	1
Bermuda	0	1	0	1
Costa Rica	0	0	1	1
Honduras	0	0	1	1
Netherlands Antilles	0	0	1	1
St. Lucia	0	0	1	1

Canadian Medal Winners

■ GOLD

Artistic Gymnastics
Floor — Brandon O'Neill
Athletics
Discus — Jason Tunks
800m — Achraf Tadili
Long Jump — Alice Falaiye
Badminton
Singles — Mike Beres
Mixed Doubles — Denyse Julien, Philippe Bourret
Doubles — Charmaine Reid, Helen Nichol
Canoe-Kayak
K-4 500m — Jen Adamson, Jill D'Alessio, Émelie Fournel, Victoria Tuttle
C-1 1000m — Tom Hall
Cycling
Points Race — Clara Hughes
Diving
3m Synchronized — Blythe Hartley, Émilie Heymans
10m Synchronized — Alexandre Despatie, Philippe Comtois
3m Springboard — Blythe Hartley
10m Synchronized — Émilie Heymans, Marie-Ève Marleau
3m Springboard — Alexandre Despatie
3m Synchronized — Alexandre Despatie, Phillipe Comtois
10m Platform — Émilie Heymans
Equestrian
Individual Dressage — Leslie Reid
Rowing
Lightweight Double Sculls — Gen Meredith, Fiona Milne
Double Sculls — Stacey Norwood, Marilyn Taylor
Softball
Team — Men's Team
Squash
Team — Viktor Berg, Shahier Razik, Graham Ryding
Singles — Shahier Razik
Swimming
200m Butterfly — Audrey Lacroix
200m Individual Medley — Joanne Malar-Morreale
Triathlon
Individual — Jill Savege
Water Ski
Tricks — Jaret Llewellyn
Slalom — Drew Ross
Jump — Karissa Wedd

■ SILVER

Artistic Gymnastics
Team — Mélanie Banville, Heather Purnell, Lydia Williams, Richelle Aiko-Simpson, Gael Mackie, Kylie Stone
Athletics
Pole vault — Stephanie McCann
100m hurdles — Perdita Felicien
Marathon — Bruce Deacon
Heptathlon — Nicole Haynes
3,000m Steeple-chase — Joël Bourgeois
Badminton
Doubles — Mike Beres, Kyle Hunter
Singles — Andrew Dabeka
Singles — Anna Rice
Mixed Double — Mike Beres, Jody Patrick
Doubles — Denyse Julien, Anna Rice
Bowling
Doubles — Danyck Brière, George Lambert
Canoe-Kayak
K-2 500m — Émelie Fournel, Victoria Tuttle
C-1 500m — Scott Dickey
Cycling
Individual Road Time Trial — Clara Hughes
Diving
3m Springboard — Émilie Heymens
Equestrian Dressage
Team Dressage — Evi Strasser, Leslie Reid, Jacquelyn Brooks, Ashley Holzer

▶ **Fencing**

Ind. Épée	Sherraine Mackay

Field Hockey

Team	Men's Team

Football

Team	Women's Team

Judo

Heavyweight 100kg	Nicolas Gill
Middleweight 90kg	Keith Morgan
Extra lightweight 48 kg	Carolyne Lepage

Karate

Kumite Individual 68kg	Saeed Baghbani
Kumite Individual 58kg	Btissama Essadiqi

Racquetball

Mens Single	Mike Green

Rhythmic Gymnastics

Clubs	Alexandra Orlando
Ribbon	Alexandra Orlando
Group All-around	Roxana Cervantes, Irina Funtikova, Pam Jewell, Emilie Livingston, Sarah Stock
Hoops	Alexandra Orlando

Roller Sports – Hockey

Inline Hockey	Inline Hockey Team

Rowing

Eight with Cox	Neil Armour, Iain Brambell, Kevin Burt, Chris Davidson, Geoff Hodgson, David Kay, Mike Lewis, Michael Simonson, Dallas Smith-cox
Lightweight Coxless Fours	Iain Brambell, Chris Davidson, Mike Lewis, Michael Simonson
Single Sculls	Fiona Milne
Lightweight Single Sculls	Gen Meredith

Sailing

Laser	Bernard Luttmer
Laser Radial	Keamia Rasa
Sailboard	Dominique Vallée

Shooting

Double Trap	Cynthia Meyer
Trap	Cynthia Meyer

Softball

Team	Women's Softball Team

Squash

Team	Marnie Baizley, Melanie Jans, Carolyn Russell
Singles	Graham Ryding
Singles	Melanie Jans

Swimming

4x100m medley relay	Elizabeth Collins, Audrey Lacroix, Joanne Malar-Morreale, Kathleen Stoody
100m Butterfly	Audrey Lacroix
4x100m Relay	Audrey Lacroix, Elizabeth Collins, Joanne Malar-Morreale, Kelly Doody

Synchronized Swimming

Team	Synchronized Swim Team
Duet	Fanny Letourneau, Courtney Stewart

Water Ski

Jump	Jaret Llewellyn

Water-polo

Team	Women's Water-polo

Wrestling

84kg	Carl Rainville
60kg	Gia Sissaouri
Freestyle 48kg	Lyndsay Belisle
Freestyle 55kg	Tonya Verbeek
Freestyle 63kg	Viola Yanik
Freestyle 72kg	Ohenewa Akuffo

■ **BRONZE**

Athletics

Pole Vault	Stephanie McCann
Shot Put	Brad Snyder

Badminton

Doubles	Michael Beres, Kyle Hunter
Singles	Kyle Hunter

Boxing

Heavyweight 91kg	Jason Douglas
Middleweight 75kg	Jean Pascal

Canoe-Kayak

K-1 500m	Jill D'Allessio
C-2 500m	Thomas Hall, Ian Mortimer
K-1 500m	Mark de Jonge

Cycling

Individual Pursuit	Clara Hughes

Diving

10m Platform	Alexandre Despatie
10m Platform	Blythe Hartley

Fencing

Team Épée	Catherine Dunnette, Sherraine MacKay, Marie-Ève Pelletier
Ind. Sabre	Michel Boulos

Judo

Heavyweight +78kg	Olia Berger
Half-Heavyweight	Amy Cotton
63kg	Isabelle Pearson
73kg	Jean-François Marceau

Karate

Kumite Individual +58kg	Nassim Varasteteh

Racquetball

Doubles	Josée Grand'Maître, Julie Neubauer

Rhythmic Gymnastics

Ball	Alexandra Orlando
Group - 3 Hoops & 2 Balls	Roxana Cervantes, Irina Funtikova, Pam Jewell, Emilie Livingston, Sarah Stock
Balls	Alexandra Orlando

Sailing

Sailboard	Kevin Stittle

Shooting

Skeet	Linda Conley
Double Trap	Susan Nattrass
Air Pistol	Lynda Hare

Squash

Singles	Marnie Baizley
Singles	Marnie Baizley

Swimming

4x100m Medley Relay	Sean Sepulis, Scott Dickens, Chad Murray, Matt Ross
100m Breaststroke	Kathleen Stoody
4x100m Freestyle Relay	Brian Edey, Matt Rose, Colin Russell, Chad Murray
4x200m Freestyle Relay	Maya Beaudry, Elizabeth Collins, Audrey Lacroix, Joanne Malar-Morreale

Water Ski

Jump	Ryan Dodd

Water-polo

Team	Men's Water-polo

Wrestling

74kg	Zoltan Hunyady
55kg	Mischa Japaridze

Source: *Canadian Olympic Committee*

Canadian Curling Champions

Men

Skip, Province	Skip, Province	Skip, Province
1928 Gordon Hudson, Man.	1956 Billy Walsh, Man.	1981 Kerry Burtnyk, Man.
1929 Gordon Hudson, Man.	1957 Matt Baldwin, Alta	1982 Al Hackner, N. Ont.
1930 Howard Wood, Man.	1958 Matt Baldwin, Alta	1983 Ed Werenich, Ont.
1931 Bob Gourley, Man.	1959 Ernie Richardson, Sask.	1984 Mike Riley, Man.
1932 Jim Congalton, Man.	1960 Ernie Richardson, Sask.	1985 Al Hackner, N. Ont.
1933 Cliff Manahan, Alta	1961 Hec Gervais, Alta	1986 Ed Lukowich, Alta
1934 Leo Johnson, Man.	1962 Ernie Richardson, Sask.	1987 Russ Howard, Ont.
1935 Gordon Campbell, Ont.	1963 Ernie Richardson, Sask.	1988 Pat Ryan, Alta
1936 Ken Watson, Man.	1964 Lyall Dagg, BC	1989 Pat Ryan, Alta
1937 Cliff Manahan, Alta	1965 Terry Braunstein, Man.	1990 Ed Werenich, Ont.
1938 Ab Gowanlock, Man.	1966 Ron Northcott, Alta	1991 Kevin Martin, Alta
1939 Bert Hall, Ont.	1967 Alf Phillips, Jr., Ont.	1992 Vic Peters, Man.
1940 Howard Wood, Man.	1968 Ron Northcott, Alta	1993 Russ Howard, Ont.
1941 Howard Palmer, Alta	1969 Ron Northcott, Alta	1994 Rick Folk, BC
1942 Ken Watson, Man.	1970 Don Duguid, Man.	1995 Kerry Burtnyk, Man
1946 Billy Rose, Alta	1971 Don Duguid, Man.	1996 Jeff Stoughton, Man
1947 Jimmy Welsh, Man.	1972 Orest Meleschuk, Man.	1997 Kevin Martin, Alta
1948 Frenchy D'Amour, BC	1973 Harvey Mazinke, Sask.	1998 Wayne Middaugh, Ont.
1949 Ken Watson, Man.	1974 Hector Gervais, Alta	1999 Jeff Stoughton, Man.
1950 Tom Ramsay, N. Ont.	1975 Bill Tetley, N. Ont.	2000 Greg McAuley, BC
1951 Don Oyler, NS	1976 Jack MacDuff, Nfld.	2001 Randy Ferbey, Alta
1952 Billy Walsh, Man.	1977 Jim Ursel, Que.	2002 Randy Ferbey, Alta
1953 Ab Gowanlock, Man.	1978 Ed Lukowich, Alta	2003 Randy Ferbey, Alta
1954 Matt Baldwin, Alta	1979 Barry Fry, Man.	
1955 Garnet Campbell, Sask.	1980 Rick Folk, Sask.	

Women

Skip, Province	Skip, Province	Skip, Province
1961 Joyce McKee, Sask.	1976 Lindsay Davie, BC	1991 Julie Sutton, BC
1962 Ina Hansen, BC	1977 Myrna McQuarrie, Alta.	1992 Connie Laliberte, Man.
1963 Mabel DeWare, NB	1978 Cathy Pidzarko, Man.	1993 Sandra Peterson, Sask.
1964 Ina Hansen, BC	1979 Lindsay Sparkes, BC	1994 Sandra Peterson, Sask
1965 Peggy Casselman, Man.	1980 Marj Mitchell, Sask.	1995 Connie Laliberte, Man.
1966 Gail Lee, Alta.	1981 Susan Seitz, Alta.	1996 Marilyn Bodogh, Ont.
1967 Betty Duguid, Man.	1982 Colleen Jones, NS	1997 Sandra Schmirler, Sask.
1968 Hazel Jamieson, Alta.	1983 Penny LaRocque, NS	1998 Cathy Borst, Alta.
1969 Joyce McKee, Sask.	1984 Connie Laliberte, Man.	1999 Colleen Jones, NS
1970 Dorenda Schoenhais, Sask.	1985 Linda Moore, BC	2000 Kelly Law, BC
1971 Vera Pezer, Sask.	1986 Marilyn Darte, Ont.	2001 Colleen Jones, NS
1972 Vera Pezer, Sask.	1987 Pat Sanders, BC	2002 Colleen Jones, NS
1973 Vera Pezer, Sask.	1988 Heather Houston, Ont.	2003 Colleen Jones, NS
1974 Emily Farnham, Sask.	1989 Heather Houston, Ont.	
1975 Lee Tobin, Que.	1990 Alison Goring, Ont.	

Source: *Canadian Press*

Association of Tennis Professionals' Ranking

(as of September 30, 2003)

The top ranking in men's tennis will be determined following the season-ending Tennis Masters Cup, to be held Nov. 8–16, 2003, in Houston, Texas.

Rank	Player (Country)	Rank	Player (Country)
1	Andy Roddick (USA)	11	Mark Philippoussis (Australia)
2	Juan Carlos Ferrero (Spain)	12	Sebastien Grosjean (France)
3	Roger Federer (Switzerland)	12	Paradorn Srichaphan (Thailand)
4	Andre Agassi (USA)	14	Younes El Aynaoui (Morocco)
5	Guillermo Coria (Argentina)	14	Martin Verkerk (Netherlands)
6	Rainer Schuettler (Germany)	16	Gustavo Kuerten (Brazil)
7	Carlos Moya (Spain)	16	Tommy Robredo (Spain)
8	David Nalbandian (Argentina)	18	Felix Mantilla (Spain)
9	Lleyton Hewitt (Australia)	19	Agustin Calleri (Argentina)
10	Sjeng Schalken (Netherlands)	20	Jiri Novak (Czech Republic)

Source: *Association of Tennis Professionals*

Association of Tennis Professionals' Top Money Earners

(as of September 30, 2003)

Ranking	Player (Country)	Earnings (in US$)	Ranking	Player (Country)	Earnings (in US$)
1	Andy Roddick (USA)	$2 705 662	6	Rainer Schuettler (Germany)	$1 167 002
2	Juan Carlos Ferrero (Spain)	$2 413 330	7	Carlos Moya (Spain)	$999 705
3	Roger Federer (Switzerland)	$2 147 580	8	David Nalbandian (Argentina)	$986 783
4	Andre Agassi (USA)	$1 830 929	9	Lleyton Hewitt (Australia)	$873 598
5	Guillermo Coria (Argentina)	$1 588 982	10	Martin Verkerk (Netherlands)	$798 261

Source: *Association of Tennis Professionals*

Women's Tennis Association Rankings

(as of October 13, 2003)

Rank	Player (Country)	Rank	Player (Country)
1	Kim Clijsters (Belgium)	11	Ai Sugiyama (Japan)
2	Justine Henin-Hardenne (Belgium)	12	Vera Zvonareva (Russia)
3	Serena Williams (USA)	13	Conchita Martinez (Spain)
4	Lindsay Davenport (USA)	14	Nadia Petrova (Russia)
5	Jennifer Capriati (USA)	15	Daniela Hantuchova (Slovakia)
6	Venus Williams (USA)	16	Anna Pistolesi (Israel)
7	Amelie Mauresmo (France)	17	Paola Suarez (Argentina)
8	Elena Dementieva (Russia)	18	Patty Schnyder (Switzerland)
9	Anastasia Myskina (Russia)	19	Magdalena Maleeva (Bulgaria)
10	Chanda Rubin (USA)	20	Meghann Shaughnessy (USA)

Source: *Women's Tennis Association*

Women's Tennis Association Top Money Earners

(as of October 13, 2003)

Ranking	Player (Country)	Earnings (in US$)	Ranking	Player (Country)	Earnings (in US$)
1	Justine Henin-Hardenne (Belgium)	$3 088 264	6	Venus Williams (USA)	$998 222
2	Kim Clijsters (Belgium)	$2 910 264	7	Ai Sugiyama (Japan)	$901 074
3	Serena Williams (USA)	$2 249 038	8	Paola Suarez (Argentina)	$879 966
4	Lindsay Davenport (USA)	$1 293 743	9	Amelie Mauresmo (France)	$780 906
5	Jennifer Capriati (USA)	$1 011 181	10	Anastasia Myskina (Russia)	$730 006

Source: *Women's Tennis Association*

Davis Cup 2004

The Davis Cup international tennis competition began in 1900, and with 142 nations competing for a spot in the World Group, it is the largest annual international team competition in world sport. Only 16 countries each year can qualify for a spot in the World Group first playoff round to compete for the Davis Cup. During each round, nations face off in five-match—or *rubber*—competitions—called *ties*—over a three-day period. In each tie, the first day features two singles matches, followed the doubles match on day two, with two final singles matches to wrap up the tie on day three. In the Davis Cup's 103-year history, the United States and Australia have dominated the competition, winning 32 and 28 Davis Cups, respectively. Canada advanced to the 2004 World Group with a 3-2 win over Brazil at a tie in Calgary in September 2003. This win gets Canada back in the World Group for the first time since 1992.

World Group, Playoff Ties 2003

(winner advances to 2004 World Group)

Austria 3, Belgium 2
Canada 3, Brazil 2
R1: Flavio Saretta (Brazil) def.
    Frederic Niemeyer (Canada)
    6-4, 7-6(5), 6-7(4), 6-4
R2: **Daniel Nestor (Canada)** def.
    Gustavo Kuerten (Brazil)
    6-7(7), 7-6(0), 6-3, 6-7(7), 7-5

R3: **Daniel Nestor / Frederic
    Niemeyer (Canada)** def. Gustavo
    Kuerten / Andre Sa (Brazil)
    6-3, 6-2, 1-6, 6-2
R4: Gustavo Kuerten (Brazil) def.
    Simon Larose (Canada)
    7-6(4), 7-6(4), 3-6, 7-6(10)
R5: **Frank Dancevic (Canada)** def.

Flavio Saretta (Brazil)
    6-3, 7-5, 3-6, 7-6(7)
Czech Republic 4, Thailand 1
Belarus 3, Germany 2
Morocco 3, Great Britain 2
Netherlands 5, India 0
Romania 3, Ecuador 2
USA 3, Slovak Republic 2

Draw for World Group 2004

Dates:

First Round: February 6–8, 2004
Quarterfinals: April 9–11, 2004

Semifinals: September 24–26, 2004
Final: December 3–5, 2004

■ **First Round Ties**

Australia vs. Sweden
United States vs. Austria
Russia vs. *Belarus*
Argentina vs. *Morocco*

Romania vs. Switzerland
Croatia vs. *France*
Canada vs. *Netherlands*
Czech Republic vs. Spain
(host nation in italics)

Team Canada Davis Cup History

First year played: 1913
Years played: 76
Ties played (W-L): 122 (49–73)
Years in World Group (1981 onwards): 3 (0–2)
Best performance: World Group finalist, 1913

Most total wins: Daniel Nestor (29–17)
Most singles wins: Sebastien Lareau (17–16)
Most double wins: Grant Connell (15–6)
Best doubles team: Sebastien Lareau & Grant Connell (6–0)
Most ties played: Daniel Nestor (24)
Most years played: Glenn Michibata (11), Daniel Nestor (11), Jack Wright (11)

LACROSSE

National Lacrosse League (NLL), 2003

■ 2002–03 FINAL STANDINGS

Eastern Division	GP	W	L	PCT	GB	FOR	AG
Colorado Mammoth[1]	16	9	7	.562	—	226	223
Philadelphia Wings	16	8	8	.500	1	203	209
New Jersey Storm	16	3	13	.188	6	187	220
New York Saints	16	3	13	.188	6	198	239

Central Division	GP	W	L	PCT	GB	FOR	AG
Rochester Knighthawks[1]	16	12	4	.750	—	214	173
Buffalo Bandits[2]	16	12	4	.750	—	231	188
Columbus Landsharks	16	8	8	.500	4	184	203
Albany Attack	16	8	8	.500	4	198	191

Northern Division	GP	W	L	PCT	GB	FOR	AG
Toronto Rock[1]	16	11	5	.687	—	195	164
Vancouver Ravens[2]	16	9	7	.562	2	208	196
Calgary Roughnecks[2]	16	9	7	.562	2	209	207
Ottawa Rebel	16	4	12	.250	7	174	214

(1) clinched division title
(2) clinched playoff berth

■ PLAYOFFS

Wild Card Round
Sat. April 19
Buffalo Bandits 16 **Calgary Roughnecks 9**
Colorado Mammoth 15 **Vancouver Ravens 12**

Semi-Finals
Sat. April 26
Toronto Rock 15 Colorado Mammoth 11
Rochester Knighthawks 16 Buffalo Bandits 13

Championship Game
Sat. May 3
Toronto Rock 8 Rochester Knighthawks 6
Game MVP: Bob Watson (Toronto)

Source: *National Lacrosse League*

NLL Scoring Leaders, 2003

Player, Team	GP	G	A	PTS	AVG/G
John Tavares, Buf	16	49	58	107	6.69
John Grant, Roc	16	46	53	99	6.19
Gary Gait, Col	16	61	35	96	6.00
Colin Doyle, Tor	16	**39**	**55**	**94**	**5.88**
Tom Marechek, Phi	15	42	45	87	5.80
Blaine Manning, Tor	16	**40**	**38**	**78**	**4.88**
Chris Driscoll, NYK	12	30	46	76	6.33
Josh Sanderson, Alb	15	25	51	76	5.07
Gary Rosyski, Alb	16	36	38	74	4.62
Derek Malawsky, Roc	16	27	47	74	4.62

Source: *National Lacrosse League*

Lacrosse—The Mann Cup, 1910–2003

The Mann Cup was presented by the late Sir Donald Mann, builder of the Canadian Northern Railway, for the Senior Amateur Championship of Canada and was originally a challenge cup.

1910	Young Torontos, Toronto, Ont.	1960	Sailors, Port Credit, Ont.
1911	Vancouver Athletic Club, Vancouver, BC	1961	Burrards, Vancouver, BC
1912	Vancouver Athletic Club, Vancouver, BC	1962	O'Keefes, New Westminster, BC
1913	Vancouver Athletic Club, Vancouver, BC	1963	Carlings, Vancouver, BC
1914	Vancouver Athletic Club, Vancouver, BC	1964	Carlings, Vancouver, BC
1915	Salmonbellies, New Westminster, BC	1965	Salmonbellies, New Westminster, BC
1916	Salmonbellies, New Westminster, BC	1966	Lakers, Peterborough, Ont.
1917	Salmonbellies, New Westminster, BC	1967	Carlings, Vancouver, BC
1918	Coughlans, Vancouver, BC	1968	Redmen, Brooklin, Ont.
1919	Foundation Club, Vancouver, BC	1969	Redmen, Brooklin, Ont.
1920–1925	Salmonbellies, New Westminster, BC	1970	Salmonbellies, New Westminster, BC
1926	Westonmen, Weston, Ont.	1971	Warriors, Brantford, Ont.
1927	Salmonbellies, New Westminster, BC	1972	Salmonbellies, New Westminster, BC
1928	Emmets, Ottawa, Ont.	1973	Lakers, Peterborough, Ont.
1929	Generals, Oshawa, Ont.	1974	Salmonbellies, New Westminster, BC
1930	Excelsiors, Brampton, Ont.	1975	Burrards, Vancouver, BC
1931	Excelsiors, Brampton, Ont.	1976	Salmonbellies, New Westminster, BC
1932	Mountaineers, Mimico, Ont.	1977	Burrards, Vancouver, BC
1933	Tigers, Hamilton, Ont.	1978	Red Oaks, Peterborough, Ont.
1934	Terriers, Orillia, Ont.	1979	Shamrocks, Victoria, BC
1935	Terriers, Orillia, Ont.	1980	Excelsiors, Brampton, Ont.
1936	Terriers, Orillia, Ont.	1981	Salmonbellies, New Westminster, BC
1937	Salmonbellies, New Westminster, BC	1982	Lakers, Peterborough, Ont.
1938	Athletics, St. Catharines, Ont.	1983	Payless, Victoria, BC
1939	Adanacs, New Westminster, BC	1984	Lakers, Peterborough, Ont.
1940	Athletics, St. Catharines, Ont.	1985	Redmen, Brooklin, Ont.
1941	Athletics, St. Catharines, Ont.	1986	Salmonbellies, New Westminster, BC
1942	Combines, Mimico/Brampton, Ont.	1987	Redmen, Brooklin, Ont.
1943	Salmonbellies, New Westminster, BC	1988	Redmen, Brooklin, Ont.
1944	Athletics, St. Catharines, Ont.	1989	Salmonbellies, New Westminster, BC
1945	Burrards, Vancouver, BC	1990	Redmen, Brooklin, Ont.
1946	Athletics, St. Catharines, Ont.	1991	Salmonbellies, New Westminster, BC
1947	Adanacs, New Westminster, BC	1992	Excelsiors, Brampton, Ont.
1948	Tigers, Hamilton, Ont.	1993	Excelsiors, Brampton, Ont.
1949	Burrards, Vancouver, BC	1994	Chiefs, Six Nations, Ont.
1950	Crescents, Owen Sound, Ont.	1995	Chiefs, Six Nations, Ont.
1951	Timbermen, Peterborough, Ont.	1996	Chiefs, Six Nations, Ont.
1952	Timbermen, Peterborough, Ont.	1997	Shamrocks, Victoria, BC
1953	Timbermen, Peterborough, Ont.	1998	Excelsiors, Brampton, Ont.
1954	Timbermen, Peterborough, Ont.	1999	Shamrocks, Victoria, BC
1955	Shamrocks, Victoria, BC	2000	Redmen, Brooklin, Ont.
1956	Timbermen, Nanaimo, BC	2001	Adanacs, Coquitlam, BC
1957	Shamrocks, Victoria, BC	2002	Excelsiors, Brampton, Ont.
1958	Salmonberries, New Westminster, BC	2003	Shamrocks, Victoria, BC
1959	O'Keefes, New Westminster, BC		

Source: *Canadian Lacrosse Association*

Figure Skating Champions, 1957–2003

	Canadian Champions		World Champions	
	Men	**Women**	**Men**	**Women**
1957	Charles Snelling	Carole Jane Pachl	Dave Jenkins, US	Carol Heiss, US
1958	Charles Snelling	Margaret Crosland	Dave Jenkins, US	Carol Heiss, US
1959	Donald Jackson	Margaret Crosland	Dave Jenkins, US	Carol Heiss, US
1960	Donald Jackson	Wendy Griner	Alain Giletti, France	Carol Heiss, US
1961	Donald Jackson	Wendy Griner	—[1]	—[1]
1962	Donald Jackson	Wendy Griner	Don Jackson, Canada	Sjoukje Dijkstra, Neth.
1963	Donald McPherson	Wendy Griner	Don McPherson, Canada	Sjoukje Dijkstra, Neth.
1964	Charles Snelling	Petra Burka	Manfred Schnelldorfer, W. Germany	Sjoukje Dijkstra, Neth.
1965	Donald Knight	Petra Burka	Alain Calmat, France	Petra Burka, Canada
1966	Donald Knight	Petra Burka	Emmerich Danzer, Austria	Peggy Fleming, US
1967	Donald Knight	Valerie Jones	Emmerich Danzer, Austria	Peggy Fleming, US
1968	Jay Humphry	Karen Magnussen	Emmerich Danzer, Austria	Peggy Fleming, US
1969	Jay Humphry	Linda Carbonetto	Tim Wood, US	Gabriele Seyfert, E. Germany
1970	David McGillivray	Karen Magnussen	Tim Wood, US	Gabriele Seyfert, E. Germany
1971	Toller Cranston	Karen Magnussen	Ondrej Nepela, Czech.	Beatrix Schuba, Austria
1972	Toller Cranston	Karen Magnussen	Ondrej Nepela, Czech.	Beatrix Schuba, Austria
1973	Toller Cranston	Karen Magnussen	Ondrej Nepela, Czech.	Karen Magnussen, Canada
1974	Toller Cránston	Lynn Nightingale	Jan Hoffman, E. Germany	Christine Errath, E. Germany
1975	Toller Cranston	Lynn Nightingale	Sergei Volkov, USSR	Dianne de Leeuw, Neth.-US
1976	Toller Cranston	Lynn Nightingale	John Curry, Gr. Brit.	Dorothy Hamill, US
1977	Ron Shaver	Lynn Nightingale	Vladimir Kovalev, USSR	Linda Fratianne, US
1978	Brian Pockar	Heather Kemkaran	Charles Tickner, US	Anett Poetzsch, E. Germany
1979	Brian Pockar	Janet Morrisey	Vladimir Kovalev, USSR	Linda Fratianne, US
1980	Brian Pockar	Heather Kemkaran	Jan Hoffmann, E. Germany	Anett Poetzsch, E. Germany
1981	Brian Orser	Tracey Wainman	Scott Hamilton, US	Denise Biellmann, Switzerland
1982	Brian Orser	Kay Thomson	Scott Hamilton, US	Elaine Zayak, US
1983	Brian Orser	Kay Thomson	Scott Hamilton, US	Rosalyn Sumners, US
1984	Brian Orser	Kay Thomson	Scott Hamilton, US	Katarina Witt, E. Germany
1985	Brian Orser	Elizabeth Manley	Alexandre Fadeev, USSR	Katarina Witt, E. Germany
1986	Brian Orser	Tracey Wainman	Brian Boitano, US	Debi Thomas, US
1987	Brian Orser	Elizabeth Manley	Brian Orser, Canada	Katarina Witt, E. Germany
1988	Brian Orser	Elizabeth Manley	Brian Boitano, US	Katarina Witt, E. Germany
1989	Kurt Browning	Karen Preston	Kurt Browning, Canada	Midori Ito, Japan
1990	Kurt Browning	Lisa Sargeant	Kurt Browning, Canada	Jill Trenary, US
1991	Kurt Browning	Josée Chouinard	Kurt Browning, Canada	Kristi Yamaguchi, US
1992	Michael Slipchuk	Karen Preston	Victor Petrenko, Russia	Kristi Yameguchi, US
1993	Kurt Browning	Josée Chouinard	Kurt Browning, Canada	Oksana Baiul, Ukraine
1994	Elvis Stojko	Josée Chouinard	Elvis Stojko, Canada	Yuka Sato, Japan
1995	Sebastien Britten	Netty Kim	Elvis Stojko, Canada	Lu Chen, China
1996	Elvis Stojko	Jennifer Robinson	Todd Eldredge, US	Michelle Kwan, US
1997	Elvis Stojko	Susan Humphreys	Elvis Stojko, Canada	Tara Lapinski, US
1998	Elvis Stojko	Angela Derochie	Alexei Yagudin, Russia	Michelle Kwan, US
1999	Elvis Stojko	Jennifer Robinson	Alexei Yagudin, Russia	Maria Butyrskaya, Russia
2000	Elvis Stojko	Jennifer Robinson	Alexei Yagudin, Russia	Michelle Kwan, US
2001	Emmanuel Sandhu	Jennifer Robinson	Evgeny Plushenko, Russia	Michelle Kwan, US
2002	Elvis Stojko	Jennifer Robinson	Alexei Yagudin, Russia	Irina Slutskaya, Russia
2003	Emmanuel Sandhu	Jennifer Robinson	Evgeny Plushenko, Russia	Michelle Kwan, US

Source: *Canadian Figure Skating Association*

(1) The 1961 world championships were cancelled after an air crash killed the entire US team travelling to the competition.

The Queen's Plate, 1970–2003

The Queen's Plate, first run in 1860, is North America's oldest annual sports event. The race for 3-year-olds foaled in Canada is run at Toronto's Woodbine Race Track in late June or July.

	Winner	Jockey	Time		Winner	Jockey	Time
1970	Almoner	Sandy Hawley	2:04.4	1987	Market Control	Ken Skinner	2:03.2
1971	Kennedy Road	Sandy Hawley	2:03	1988	Regal Intention	Jack Lauzon	2:06.1
1972	Victoria Song	Robin Platts	2:03.1	1989	With Approval	Don Seymour	2:03
1973	Royal Chocolate	Ted Colangelo	2:08	1990	Izvestia	Don Seymour	2:01.4
1974	Amber Herod	Robin Platts	2:09.1	1991	Dance Smartly	Pal Day	2:03.2
1975	L'Enjoleur	Sandy Hawley	2:02.3	1992	Alydeed	Craig Perret	2:04.6
1976	Norcliffe	Jeffrey Fell	2:05	1993	Peteski	Craig Perret	2:04.2
1977	Sound Reason	Robin Platts	2:06.3	1994	Basqueian	Jack Laron	2:03.4
1978	Regal Embrace	Sandy Hawley	2:02	1995	Regal Discovery	Todd Kabel	2:03.4
1979	Steady Growth	Brian Swatuk	2:06.3	1996	Victor Cooley	Emke Ramsammy	2:03.8
1980	Driving Home	Bill Parsons	2:04.1	1997	Awesome Again	A.E. Smith	2:04
1981	Fiddle Dancer Boy	David Clark	2:04.4	1998	Archer's Bay	Kent Desormeaux	2:02.1
1982	Son of Briartic	John-Paul Souter	2:04.3	1999	Woodcarver	Mickey Walls	2:03
1983	Bompago	Larry Attard	2:04.1	2000	Scatter the Gold	Todd Kabel	1:56.0
1984	Key to the Moon	Robin Platts	2:03.4	2001	Dancethruthedawn	Gary Boulanger	2:03.8
1985	La Lorgnette	David Clark	2:04.3	2002	TJ's Lucky Moon	Steven Bahen	2:06.8
1986	Golden Choice	Vince Bracciale	2:07.1	2003	Wando	Patrick Husbands	2:02.4

Source: *Woodbine Entertainment Group*

Thoroughbred Racing

Thoroughbred racing's coveted Triple Crown has only been won 11 times: Sir Barton (1919); Gallant Fax (1930); Omaha (1935); War Admiral (1937); Whirlaway (1941); Count Fleet (1943); Assault (1946); Citation (1948); Secretariat (1973); Seattle Slew (1977) and Affirmed (1978). The challenge will be taken up anew in 2004: The Kentucky Derby will be held at Churchill Downs on May 1, 2004; The Preakness Stakes will be held at Pimlico on May 15, 2004; and The Belmont Stakes will be held at Belmont Park on June 5, 2004.

Triple Crown	Date	Winner
Kentucky Derby	May 3, 2003	Funny Cide
Preakness Stakes	May 17, 2003	Funny Cide
Belmont Stakes	June 7, 2003	Empire Maker

Source: *ESPN Network*

Harness Racing

	Date	Winner	Driver	Time
North American Cup	June 21, 2003	Yankee Cruiser	Dean Magee	1:49.3
The Canadian Pacing Derby	August 16, 2003	Art Major	John Campbell	1:49.1
The Metro Pace	August 30, 2003	Camelot Hall	George Brennan	1:51.4
Maple Leaf Trot	September 13, 2003	Rotation	Trevor Ritchie	1:53.2
Canadian Trotting Classic	September 20, 2003	Mr. Muscleman	Ron Pierce	1:54:3

Source: *Woodbine Entertainment Group*

Prince of Wales Stakes, 1962–2003

	Winner	Jockey	Time[1]		Winner	Jockey	Time[1]
1962	King Gorm	Hugo Dittfach	2:21.1	1983	Archdeacon	Vince Bracciale	2:32.0
1963	Canebora	Hugo Dittfach	2:30.3	1984	Val Dansant	John LeBlanc	2:48.3
1964	Canadillis	Avelino Gomez	2:35.0	1985	Imperial Choice	Irwin Driedger	2:34.3
1965	Good Old Mort	S. McComb	2:22.4	1986	Golden Choice	Vince Bracciale	2:44.2
1966	He's A Smoothie	Hugo Dittfach	2:19.0	1987	Coryphee	Brian Swatuk	2:39.3
1967	Battling	Hugo Dittfach	2:21.0	1988	Regal Classic	Sandy Hawley	2:00.1
1968	Rouletabille	Richard Grubb	2:18.3	1989	With Approval	Don Seymour	1:56.4
1969	Sharp-Eyed Quillo	H. Gustines	2:16.3	1990	Izvestia	Don Seymour	1:56.2
1970	Almoner	Sandy Hawley	2:19.4	1991	Dance Smartly	Pal Day	1:56.3
1971	New Pro	Jim Kelly	2:15.1	1992	Benburb	Larry Attard	1:57.2
1972	Presidial	John LeBlanc	2:16.3	1993	Peteski	Dave Penna	1:34.4
1973	Tara Road	Sandy Hawley	2:16.4	1994	Bruce's Mill	Craig Perret	1:53.4
1974	Rushton's Corsair	Jim Kelly	2:23.2	1995	Kiridashi	Larry Attard	1:55.0
1975	L'Enjoleur	Sandy Hawley	2:32.2	1996	Stephanotis	Mickey Walls	1:55.2
1976	Norcliffe	Jeff Fell	2:30.1	1997	Cryptocloser	W. Martinez	1:56
1977	Dance in Time	Gary Stahlbaum	2:31.4	1998[2]	Archer's Bay	Robert Landry	1:55.1
1978	Overskate	Robin Platts	2:34.2	1999	Gandria	Constant Montpellier	1:56.4
1979	Mass Rally	George Ho Sang	2:33.2	2000	Scatter the Gold	Todd Kabel	1:56.0
1980	Allan Blue	Joe Belowus	2:34.4	2001	Fantastic Light	Frankie Dettori	2:04.4
1981	Cadet Corps	Robin Platts	2:34.4	2002	Le Cinquieme Essai	Brian Bochinski	1:56.5
1982	Runaway Groom	Robin Platts	2:38.2	2003	Wando	Patrick Husbands	1:55.8

Source: *Ontario Jockey Club*   (1) Fractions of a second are in fifths. (2) Held July 25, 1999.

Breeders Stakes, 1962–2003

	Winner	Jockey	Time[1]		Winner	Jockey	Time[1]
1962	Crafty Lace	Ron Turcotte	2:52	1983	Kingsbridge	Robin Platts	2:32.2
1963	Canebora	Manuel Ycaza	2:32.1	1984	Bounding Away	David Clark	2:32.3
1964	Artic Hills	R. Armstrong	2:33.3	1985	Crowning Honors	Brian Swatuk	2:50
1965	Good Old Mort	P. Kallai	2:43	1986	Carotene	Richard Dos Ramos	2:32.3
1966	Titled Hero	Avelino Gomez	2:31.2	1987	Hangin On a Star	Dave Penna	2:30
1967	Pine Point	Avelino Gomez	2:32.1	1988	King's Deputy	Sandy Hawley	2:30.3
1968	No Parando	John LeBlanc	2:30	1989	With Approval	Don Seymour	2:29
1969	Grey Whiz	John LeBlanc	2:29	1990	Izvestia	Don Seymour	2:33.2
1970	Mary of Scotland	Richard Grubb	2:38.2	1991	Dance Smartly	Pal Day	2:31.2
1971	Belle Geste	Noel Turcotte	2:28	1992	Blitzer	Don Seymour	2:35.3
1972	Nice Dancer	Sandy Hawley	2:35.4	1993	Peteski	Craig Perret	2:30.4
1973	Come In Dad	Wayne Green	2:33.3	1994	Basqueian	Jack Lauzon	2:47.4
1974	Haymaker's Jig	Robin Platts	2:30.4	1995	Charlie's Dewan	Craig Perret	2:26.4
1975	Momigi	Gary Melanson	2:38.1	1996	Chief Bearheart	Mickey Walls	2:28.3
1976	Tiny Tinker	Sandy Hawley	2:31.1	1997	John The Magician	Steven Bahen	2:35
1977	Dance in Time	Gary Stahlbaum	3:01.3	1998[2]	Pinafore Park	Robert Landry	2:30.1
1978	Overskate	Robin Platts	2:29.2	1999	Free Vacation	Laurie Gulas	2:28.4
1979	Bridle Path	Sandy Hawley	2:29.3	2000	Lodge Hill	Todd Pletcher	2:28
1980	Ben Fab	Gary Stahlbaum	2:31.3	2001	Sweetest Thing	James McAleney	2:29.9
1981	Social Wizard	George Ho Sang	2:48.4	2002	Portcullis	Slade Callaghan	2:29.8
1982	Runaway Groom	Robin Platts	2:32.1	2003	Wando	Patrick Husbands	2:28.7

Source: *Ontario Jockey Club*   (1) Fractions of a second are in fifths. (2) August 15, 1999.

Championship Auto Racing Teams (CART), 2003

(as of September 30, 2003)

Race	Date	Winner
Grand Prix of St. Petersburg	February 23	Paul Tracy
Tecate Telmex Monterrey Grand Prix	March 23	Paul Tracy
Toyota Grand Prix of Long Beach	April 13	Paul Tracy
London Champ Car Trophy	May 5	Sebastien Bourdais
German 500	May 11	Sebastien Bourdais
Milwaukee Mile Centennial 500	May 31	Michel Jourdain Jr.
Grand Prix of Monterey	June 15	Patrick Carpentier
G.I. Joe's 200 (Portland)	June 22	Adrian Fernandez
The Cleveland Grand Prix	July 5	Sebastien Bourdais
Molson Indy Toronto	July 13	Paul Tracy
Molson Indy Vancouver	July 27	Paul Tracy
Mario Andretti Grand Prix (Elkhart Lake)	August 3	Bruno Junqueira
Champ Car Grand Prix of Mid-Ohio	August 10	Paul Tracy
Molson Indy Montreal	August 24	Michel Jourdain Jr.
Centrix Financial Grand Prix of Denver	August 31	Bruno Junqueira
Grand Prix Americas (Miami)	September 26	Mario Dominguez
Gran Premio Telmex (Mexico City)	October 12, 2003	Paul Tracy

CART races for the balance of the 2003 season:

Lexmark Indy 300 (Queensland, Australia)	October 26, 2003
Champ Car 500 (Fontana, CA)	November 2, 2003

Source: *CART Inc.*

CART Champions

Year	Winner	Team	Points
1979	Rick Mears	Penske Racing	4 060
1980	Johnny Rutherford	Chaparral Racing	4 723
1981	Rick Mears	Penske Racing	304
1982	Rick Mears	Penske Racing	294
1983	Al Unser	Penske Racing	151
1984	Mario Andretti	Newman/Haas Racing	176
1985	Al Unser	Penske Racing	151
1986	Bobby Rahal	Truesports	179
1987	Bobby Rahal	Truesports	188
1988	Danny Sullivan	Penske Racing	182
1989	Emerson Fittipaldi	Patrick Racing	196
1990	Al Unser, Jr	Galles-Kraco Racing	210
1991	Michael Andretti	Newman/Haas Racing	234
1992	Babby Rahal	Rahal-Hogan Racing	196
1993	Nigel Mansell	Newman/Haas	191
1994	Al Unser, Jr	Malboro Team Penske	225
1995	Jacques Villeneuve	Team Green	172
1996	Jimmy Vasser	Target Chip Ganassi	154
1997	Alex Zanardi	Targe Chip Ganassi	195
1998	Alex Zanardi	Target Chip Ganassi	285
1999	Juan Montoya	Target Chip Ganassi	212
2000	Gil de Ferran	Marlboro Team Penske	168
2001	Gil de Ferran	Marlboro Team Penske	199
2002	Cristiano da Matta	Newman/Haas Racing	237

Source: *CART Inc.*

Tour de France: Winners, 1983–2003

1983	Laurent Fignon, France	1994	Miguel Indurain, Spain
1984	Laurent Fignon, France	1995	Miguel Indurain, Spain
1985	Bernard Hinault, France	1996	Bjarne Riis, Denmark
1986	Greg LeMond, United States	1997	Jan Ullrich, Germany
1987	Stephen Roche, Ireland	1998	Marco Pantani, Italy
1988	Pedro Delgado, Spain	1999	Lance Armstrong, United States
1989	Greg LeMond, United States	2000	Lance Armstrong, United States
1990	Greg LeMond, United States	2001	Lance Armstrong, United States
1991	Miguel Indurain, Spain	2002	Lance Armstrong, United States
1992	Miguel Indurain, Spain	2003	Lance Armstrong, United States
1993	Miguel Indurain, Spain		

Source: *sports.excite.com*

Mountain Bike World Championships

■ Cross Country Elite Men

Place	Name	UCI Points
1.	Meirhaeghe, Filip (Bel)	2:25:02
2.	Hesjedal, Ryder (Can)	2:25:48
3.	Paulissen, Roel (Bel)	2:26:54
4.	Naef, Ralph (Sui)	2:27:43
5.	Peters, Bas (Ned)	2:27:53
16.	Sheppard, Chris (Can)	2:33:43
19.	Green, Roland (Can)	2:35:03
28.	Kabush, Geoff (Can)	2:38:12
31.	Wedge, Peter (Can)	2:39:00
57.	Hestler, Andreas (Can)	-2 laps
68.	Toulouse, Mathieu (Can)	-3 laps

■ Cross Country Elite Women

Place	Name	UCI Points
1.	Spitz, Sabine (Ger)	2:07:59
2.	Sydor, Alison (Can)	2:08:15
3.	Kalentieva, Irina (Rus)	2:09:58
4.	Kraft, Ivonne (Ger)	2:10:57
5.	Premont, Marie-Helene (Can)	2:12:14
19.	Bisaro, Kiara (Can)	2:20:48
33.	De Wolfe, Karen (Can)	2:26:05
38.	Sinclair, Trish (Can)	2:27:53
45.	Redden, Chrissy (Can)	-2 laps
63.	Walter, Sandra (Can)	-2 laps

■ The Espoir

Place	Name	UCI Points
1.	Weber, Balz (Sui)	2:09:45
2.	Fumic, Manuel (Ger)	2:10:22
3.	Alvarez, Ivan (Esp)	2:10:57
4.	Killeen, Liam (GBr)	2:11:19
5.	Filippi, Nicolas (Fra)	2:14:43
12.	Federau, Ricky (Can)	2:17:48
27.	Sneddon, Kris (Can)	2:25:02
30.	Watson, Andrew (Can)	2:26:47
38.	Van Toever, James (Can)	-1 lap
43.	Garrigan, Mike (Can)	-1 lap
47.	Routley, Will (Can)	-2 laps
56.	Hadley, Matthew (Can)	-2 laps

The CONCACAF Gold Cup 2003

Held in the United States and Mexico
July 12–27, 2003

Mexico won its fourth CONCACAF Gold Cup, sailing through the 2003 tournament undefeated.

2003 COMPETITION

■ Group A

Team	MP	W	D	L	F	A	Pts
Mexico	2	1	1	0	1	0	4
Brazil	2	1	0	1	2	2	3
Honduras	2	0	1	1	1	2	1

■ Group A Scores

Mexico 1, Brazil 0
Brazil 2, Honduras 1
Mexico 0, Honduras 0

■ Group B

Team	MP	W	D	L	F	A	Pts
Colombia	2	1	1	0	2	1	4
Jamaica	2	1	0	1	2	1	3
Guatemala	2	0	1	1	1	3	1

■ Group B Scores

Colombia 1, Jamaica 0
Jamaica 2, Guatemala 0
Colombia 1, Guatemala 1

■ Group C

Team	MP	W	D	L	F	A	Pts
USA	2	2	0	0	4	0	6
El Salvador	2	1	0	1	1	2	3
Martinique	2	0	0	2	0	3	0

■ Group C Scores

USA 2, El Salvador 0
USA 2, Martinique 0
El Salvador 1, Martinique 0

■ Group D

Team	MP	W	D	L	F	A	Pts
Costa Rica	2	1	0	1	3	1	3
Cuba	2	1	0	1	2	3	3
Canada	2	1	0	1	1	2	3

■ Group D Scores

Canada 1, Costa Rica 0
Cuba 2, **Canada 0**
Costa Rica 3, Cuba 0

■ Quarter Finals

USA 5, Cuba 0
Costa Rica 5, El Salvador 2
Brazil 2, Colombia 0
Mexico 5, Jamaica 0

■ Semi Finals

Brazil 2, USA 1
Mexico 2, Costa Rica 0

■ Championship Final

Mexico 1, Brazil 0

Source: *Canadian Soccer Association*   (1) advancing teams decided by drawing

■ History

USA and Mexico have dominated the tournament as the two strongest teams of the region and entered the 2000 tournament as favourites. The previous results in the final are:

YEAR	WINNER	LOSER	SCORE
1991	USA	Honduras	0-0, 4-3 on penalties
1993	Mexico	USA	4-0
1996	Mexico	Brazil	2-0
1998	Mexico	USA	1-0
2000	Canada	Columbia	2-0
2002	USA	Costa Rica	2-0

Rugby World Cup, 2003

Australia, Oct. 10–Nov. 22, 2003

Canada's national rugby team qualified for the 2003 Rugby World Cup by winning the Americas Rugby World Cup qualifying group in August 2002. Team Canada begins play on Sunday, October 12, in Melbourne, Australia, against Wales, the first of four matches in its preliminary round pool.

Pool A	Pool B	Pool C	Pool D
Australia	France	South Africa	New Zealand
Argentina	Scotland	England	Wales
Ireland	Fiji	Samoa	Italy
Namibia	Japan	Georgia	**Canada**
Romania	USA	Uruguay	Tonga

■ Canada's Team Schedule for Rugby World Cup

October 12	**Canada** vs. Wales	November 8–9	Quarterfinal matches
October 17	**Canada** vs. New Zealand	November 15–16	Semifinal matches
October 21	**Canada** vs. Italy	November 22	Final
October 29	**Canada** vs. Tonga		

■ Canada's Team Roster for Rugby World Cup

Name	Hometown	Position
Ryan Banks	Burnaby, BC	Number 8
Jared Barker	Victoria, BC	Flyhalf
John Cannon	Abbotsford, BC	Centre
Leif Carlson	Vancouver, BC	Lock/Back row
Al Charron (c)	Ottawa, ON	Flanker
Garth Cooke	Merritt, BC	Prop
Jamie Cudmore	Squamish, BC	Lock
Marco Di Girolamo	Maple, ON	Scrumhalf
Jim Douglas	Kelowna, BC	Flanker
Pat Dunkley	Victoria, BC	Hooker
Ed Fairhurst	Victoria, BC	Scrumhalf
Sean Fauth	Calgary, AB	Wing
Quentin Fyffe	Calgary, AB	Fullback
Josh Jackson	Lantzville, BC	Lock
Mike James	Burnaby, BC	Lock
Matt King	Toronto, ON	Centre/Wing
Ed Knaggs	Cole Harbour, NS	Lock
Mark Lawson	Vancouver, BC	Hooker
David Lougheed	Calgary, AB	Wing
James Pritchard	Regina, SK	Fullback/Wing
Jeff Reid	Sydney, Australia	Lock/Flanker
Bob Ross	Victoria, BC	Fullback
Ryan Smith	Caledon, ON	Flyhalf
Rod Snow	St. John's, NL	Prop
Winston Stanley	Victoria, BC	Wing
Jon Thiel	White Rock, BC	Prop
Kevin Tkachuck	Regina, SK	Prop
Adam van Staveren	Pickering, ON	Flanker
Morgan Williams	Cole Harbour, NS	Scrumhalf
Nik Witkowski	Montreal, QC	Centre
Colin Yukes	Edmonton, AB	Lock/Back row

Canada's Sports Hall of Fame

(living members as of October 1, 2003)[1]

Anakin, Douglas, bobsled
Arnold, Don, rowing
Athans, George, Jr., water skiing
Aubut, Marcel, hockey builder
Balding, Al, golf
Baldwin, Matt, curling
Bassett-Seguso, Carling, tennis
Baumann, Alex, swimming
Bédard, Myriam, biathlon
Bedard, Robert, tennis
Béliveau, Jean, hockey
Bell, Marilyn, marathon swimming
Bernier, Sylvie, diving
Betger, Jan, curling
Boldt, Arnie, field high jump
Boucher, Gaetan, speed skating
Bower, Johnny, hockey
Box, Ab, football
Boys, Bev, diving
Brasseur, Isabelle, figure skating
Brooks, Lela, speed skating
Brouillard, Lou, boxing
Browning, Kurt, figure skating
Burka, Ellen, figure skating builder
Burka, Petra, figure skating
Burka, Sylvia, speed skating
Cain, Larry, canoeing
Cameron, Michelle, synchro swimming
Carnegie, Herb, hockey
Chuvalo, George, boxing
Cliff, Leslie, swimming
Clifford, Betsy, skiing
Cowan, Gary, golf
Cranston, Toller, figure skating
Crothers, Bill, track mid-distance
D'hondt, Walter, rowing
Dafoe, Frances, figure skating
Day, James, equestrian
Dexter, Glen, yachting
Dionne, Marcel, hockey
Dojack, Paul, football builder
Drake, Clare, hockey builder
Drayton, Jerome, marathon running
Dryden, Ken, hockey
Duguid, Don, curling
Dunnell, Milt, sports broadcaster
Durrelle, Yvon, boxing

Eisler, Lloyd, figure skating
Elder, James, equestrian
Emery, Dr. John, bobsled
Emery, Victor, bobsled
Esaw, Johnny, all-around builder
Esposito, Phil, hockey
Filion, Hervé, harness racing
Fisher, Hugh, canoeing
Fogh, Hans, yachting
Fortier, Sylvie, synchro swimming
Frechette, Sylvie, synchro swimming
Gabriel, Tony, football
Gainey, Bob, hockey
Galbraith, Sheldon, figure skating builder
Gate, George, swimming builder
Gaudaur, Jake, Jr., football builder
Gayford, Tom, equestrian
Geoffrion, Bernard "Boom Boom," hockey
Golab, Tony, football
Gowan, Geoff, builder
Graham, Laurie, skiing
Greene, Nancy, skiing
Grenier, Jean, speed skating builder
Gretzky, Wayne, hockey
Gudereit, Marcia, curling
Hall, Glenn, hockey
Hartman, Barney, skeet shooting
Hawley, Sandy, horse racing
Heddle, Kathleen, rowing
Heggtveit, Anne, skiing
Henderson, Paul, hockey
Hepburn, Doug, weightlifting
Hildebrand, Ike, lacrosse
Hiller, John, baseball
Howe, Gordie, hockey
Hull, Bobby, hockey
Hungerford, George W., rowing
Hunter, Bill, builder
Huot, Jules, golf
Hutton, Ralph, swimming
Jackson, Donald, figure skating
Jackson, Dr. Roger, rowing
Jackson, Russ, football
Jelinek, Maria, figure skating
Jelinek, Otto, figure skating
Jenkins, Ferguson, baseball
Josenhans, Andreas, yachting

▶ **Kelly,** Leonard (Red), hockey
Kidd, Bruce, track mid-distance
Kirby, Peter, bobsled
Kreiner, Kathy, skiing
Krol, Joe, football
Kwong, Norm, football
Lafleur, Guy, hockey
Lambert, Nathalie, speed skating
Lancaster, Ron, football
Laumann, Silken, rowing
Lee-Gartner, Kerrin, skiing
Lemieux, Mario, hockey
Leonard, Stan, golf
Lessard, Lucille, archery
Lidstone, Dorothy, archery
Lindsay, Robert B.T. (Ted), hockey
Loney, Don, football builder
Longden, Johnny, horse racing
Loomer, Lorne, rowing
Lovell, Jocelyn, cycling
Luftspring, Sammy, boxing
MacDonald, Irene, diving
MacDonald, Noel, basketball
MacMillan, Sandy, yachting
Magnussen, Karen, figure skating
Mahovlich, Frank, hockey
Mara, George, multi-sport builder
Martini, Paul, figure skating
McBean, Marnie, rowing
McCusker, Joan, curling
McLarnin, Jimmy, boxing
McPherson, Donald, figure skating
Miles, John C., marathon swimming
Millar, Ian, equestrian
Mitchell, Ray, bowling
Morris, Alwyn, canoeing
Muir, Debbie, synchro swim builder
Nattrass, Susan, trap shooting
Nicholas, Cindy, marathon swimming
Northcott, Ron, curling
O'Donnell, Bill, harness racing
Orr, Robert (Bobby), hockey
Orser, Brian, figure skating
Ottenbrite, Anne, swimming
Parker, Jackie, football
Pashby, Dr. Tom, multi-sport builder
Paul, Robert, figure skating
Peden, Doug, multi-sport
Percy, Karen, skiing

Perry, Gordon, football
Podborski, Steve, skiing
Pollock, Sam, hockey builder
Post, Sandra, golf
Potvin, Denis, hockey
Presley, Gerald, bobsled
Primrose, John, trap shooting
Ramage, Pat, skiing builder
Read, Ken, skiing
Reed, George, football
Richard, Henri, hockey
Richardson, Arnold, curling
Richardson, Ernie, curling
Richardson, Garnet, curling
Richardson, Wes, curling
Robertson, Bruce, swimming
Rogers, Doug, judo
Saunders, Claude, rowing builder
Schmidt, Milt, hockey
Scott, Barbara Ann, figure skating
Shedd, Marjory, badminton
Smith, Graham, swimming
Sorensen, Gerry, skiing
Steen, Dave, decathlon
Stewart, Marlene, golf
Stewart, Ron, football
Storey, R.A. (Red), all-around
Stukus, Annis, football builder
Tanner, Elaine, swimming
Taylor, Ron, baseball
Tewksbury, Mark, swimming
Thom, Linda, pistol shooting
Thompson, James, speedboating builder
Thorburn, Cliff, snooker
Townsend, Cathy, bowling
Turcotte, Ron, horse racing
Underhill, Barbara, figure skating
Van Vliet, Maury, builder
Vanderburg, Helen, synchro swimming
Wagner, Barbara, figure skating
Waldo, Carolyn, synchro swimming
Waples, Keith, harness racing
Weslock, Nick, golf
Wheeler, Lucille, skiing
Whitaker, Brig. Gen. Denis, equestrian builder
Wilson, Bruce, soccer
Worrall, Jim, builder
Young, Jim, football
Young, Michael, bobsled

Source: *Canada's Sports Hall of Fame*
(1) No new members were inducted in 2003.

Temperature Equivalents

(Celsius and Fahrenheit)

°C	°F	°C	°F	°C	°F	°C	°F	°C	°F
-50	-58	-30	-22	-10	14	10	50	30	86
-49	-56.2	-29	-20.2	-9	15.8	11	51.8	31	87.8
-48	-54.4	-28	-18.4	-8	17.6	12	53.6	32	89.6
-47	-52.6	-27	-16.6	-7	19.4	13	55.4	33	91.4
-46	-50.8	-26	-14.8	-6	21.2	14	57.2	34	93.2
-45	-49	-25	-13	-5	23	15	59	35	95
-44	-47.2	-24	-11.2	-4	24.8	16	60.8	36	96.8
-43	-45.4	-23	-9.4	-3	26.6	17	62.6	37	98.6
-42	-43.6	-22	-7.6	-2	28.4	18	64.4	38	100.4
-41	-41.8	-21	-5.8	-1	30.2	19	66.2	39	102.2
-40	-40	-20	-4	0	32	20	68	40	104
-39	-38.2	-19	-2.2	1	33.8	21	69.8	41	105.8
-38	-36.4	-18	-0.4	2	35.6	22	71.6	42	107.6
-37	-34.6	-17	1.4	3	37.4	23	73.4	43	109.4
-36	-32.8	-16	3.2	4	39.2	24	75.2	44	111.2
-35	-31	-15	5	5	41	25	77	45	113
-34	-29.2	-14	6.8	6	42.8	26	78.8	50	122
-33	-27.4	-13	8.6	7	44.6	27	80.6	100	212
-32	-25.6	-12	10.4	8	46.4	28	82.4	150	302
-31	-23.8	-11	12.2	9	48.2	29	84.2	200	392

Household Measures, Metric Equivalents

Volume

Imperial	Metric	Imperial	Metric	Imperial	Metric
1/4 tsp	1 mL	1/4 cup	50 mL	4 cups	1 L
1/2 tsp	2 mL	1/3 cup	75 mL	5 cups	1.25 L
3/4 tsp	4 mL	1/2 cup	125 mL	6 cups	1.5 L
1 tsp	5 mL	2/3 cup	150 mL	7 cups	1.75 L
2 tsp	10 mL	3/4 cup	175 mL	8 cups	2 L
1 tbsp (3 tsp)	15 mL	1 cup	250 mL		

Weight

Imperial	Metric	Imperial	Metric	Imperial	Metric
1 oz	25 g	1/2 lb	250 g	1 3/4 lb	875 g
2 oz	50 g	2/3 lb	350 g	2.2 lb	1 kg
3 oz	75 g	3/4 lb	375 g	3 lb	1.5 kg
1/4 lb	125 g	1 lb	500 g	5 lb	2.2 kg
1/3 lb	175 g	1 1/2 lb	750 g	10 lb	4.5 kg

Oven Temperatures

Imperial (°F)	Metric (°C)	Imperial (°F)	Metric (°C)	Imperial (°F)	Metric (°C)
250	120	350	180	450	230
275	135	375	190	475	245
300	150	400	200	500	260
325	160	425	220		

Canadian Imperial and Metric Measures

Name	Abbrev.	Equivalent in Related Units	Metric Equivalent
■ Length			
inch	in.	—	2.54 cm
foot	ft.	12 in.	30.48 cm
yard	yd.	3 ft.; 36 in.	0.91 m
mile	mi.	1 760 yd.; 5 280 ft.	1.609 km
■ Mass (Weight)			
grain	gr.	—	0.06 g
dram	dr.	27.343 gr.	1.77 g
ounce	oz.	16 dr.	28.35 g
pound	lb.	16 oz.	0.453 kg
hundredweight			
(short)	cwt.	100 lb.	45.36 kg
(long)	cwt.	112 lb.	50.80 kg
ton (short)	—	2 000 lb.	0.907 t
ton (long)	—	2 240 lb.	1.016 t
■ Volume and Capacity			
fluid dram	fl. dr.	0.22 cu. in.	3.55 cm^3
fluid ounce	fl. oz.	8 fl. dr.; 1.7 cu. in.	28.41 cm^3
pint	pt.	20 fl. oz.; 34.7 cu. in.	568.3 cm^3
quart	qt.	2 pt.; 69.4 cu. in.	1.14 dm^3
gallon	gal.	4 qt.; 277 cu. in.	4.55 dm^3
peck	pk.	2 gal.; 555 cu. in.	9.09 dm^3
bushel	bu.	4 pk.; 2 219 cu. in.	36.37 dm^3
barrel (oil)	bbl	35 gal.	0.159 m^3
cubic foot	ft.^{3}	1 728 in.^{3}	0.028 m^3
cubic yard	yd.^{3}	27 ft.^{3}	0.765 m^3
■ Area			
square foot	ft.^{2}	144 sq. in.	0.09 m^2
square yard	yd.^{2}	9 sq. ft.	0.836 m^2
acre	—	4 840 sq. yd.	4 047 m^2
square mile	sq. mi.	640 acres	2.590 km^2

Source: *Gage Canadian Dictionary*

Roman Numerals

I	1	VII	7	XX	20	C	100	$\overline{V}$	5 000
II	2	VIII	8	XXX	30	CC	200	$\overline{X}$	10 000
III	3	IX	9	XL	40	CD	400	$\overline{L}$	50 000
IV	4	X	10	L	50	D	500	$\overline{C}$	100 000
V	5	XI	11	LX	60	CM	900	$\overline{D}$	500 000
VI	6	XIX	19	XC	90	M	1 000	$\overline{M}$	1 000 000

Canada's Food Guide To Healthy Eating[1]

Canada's Food Guide, revised in November of 1992, recognizes that the amount of food each Canadian needs every day from the four food groups and other foods depends on age, body size, activity level, whether the individual is male or female, and if the individual is pregnant or breast-feeding. That's why the Food Guide gives a range of possible servings for each food group—young children can choose the lower number of recommended servings from a particular group, while male teenagers can go to the higher number. Most other people can choose servings somewhere in between.

Canada's Food Guide recommends, every day:

■ 5 to 12 servings from the grain products group. An example of one serving would be one slice of bread; 30 g of cold cereal or 175 mL of hot cereal. Two servings would be a bagel, pita or bun; or 250 mL of rice or pasta.

■ 5 to 10 servings of vegetables and fruit.

One serving would be one medium size vegetable or fruit; 125 mL of fresh, frozen or canned vegetables or fruit; 250 mL of salad; or 125 mL of juice.

■ 2 to 3 servings of meat or alternatives. One serving would be 50-100 g of meat, poultry or fish; 1-2 eggs; 125-250 mL of beans; 100 g of tofu; or 30 mL of peanut butter.

■ Recommended servings of milk products vary according to age: 2-3 servings for children aged 4-9; 3-4 servings for young people aged 10-16; 2-4 servings for adults; and 3-4 servings for pregnant or breast-feeding women. Examples of one serving would be 250 mL of milk, 50 g of cheese or 175 g of yogurt.

Taste and enjoyment can also come from other foods and beverages that are not part of the four food groups. Some of these foods are higher in fat or calories, so it is recommended that these foods be used in moderation. The important things to remember are: enjoy a variety of foods from each group every day and choose lower-fat foods more often.

Source: *Health and Welfare Canada*   (1) For people four years and over.

Functions of Nutrients

Calcium aids in the formation and maintenance of strong bones and teeth; promotes healthy nerve function and normal blood clotting.

Carbohydrate supplies energy; assists in the utilization of fats.

Fat supplies energy; aids in the absorption of fat-soluble vitamins.

Fibre provides undigestible bulk, which encourages the normal elimination of body wastes.

Folacin (folic acid) aids red blood cell formation.

Iodine aids in function of the thyroid gland.

Iron combines with protein to form hemoglobin, the red blood cell constituent that transports oxygen and carbon dioxide.

Magnesium aids in formation and maintenance of strong bones and teeth; aids in energy metabolism and tissue formation.

Phosphorus aids in formation and maintenance of strong bones and teeth.

Protein builds and repairs body tissues; builds antibodies, the blood components that fight infection.

Riboflavin (vitamin B_2) maintains healthy skin and eyes; maintains a normal nervous system; releases energy to body cells during metabolism.

Thiamin (vitamin B_1) releases energy from carbohydrate; aids normal growth and appetite.

Vitamin A aids normal bone and tooth development; promotes good night vision; maintains the health of skin and membranes.

Vitamin B_{12} (cobalamin) aids in red blood cell formation; maintains healthy nerve and gastrointestinal tissues.

Vitamin C (ascorbic acid) maintains healthy teeth and gums; maintains strong vessel walls.

Vitamin E (tocopherol) protects the fat in body tissues from oxidation.

Zinc aids in energy and metabolism and tissue formation.

Source: *Canada's Food Guide Handbook*

Health Canada   Santé Canada

CANADA'S
Food Guide
TO HEALTHY EATING
FOR PEOPLE FOUR YEARS
AND OVER

Enjoy a variety
of foods from each
group every day.

Choose lower-
fat foods
more often.

Grain Products
Choose whole grain
and enriched
products more often.

Vegetables and Fruit
Choose dark green and
orange vegetables and
orange fruit more often.

Milk Products
Choose lower-fat milk
products more often.

Meat and Alternatives
Choose leaner meats,
poultry and fish, as well
as dried peas, beans
and lentils more often.

Canada

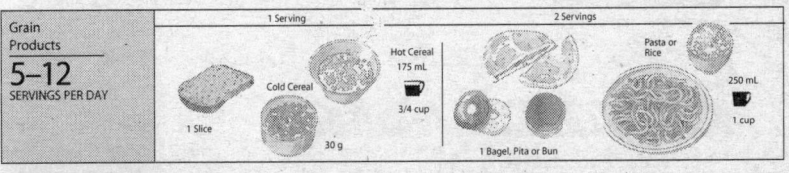

Grain Products **5–12** SERVINGS PER DAY	1 Serving	2 Servings

1 Slice · Cold Cereal 30 g · Hot Cereal 175 mL 3/4 cup · 1 Bagel, Pita or Bun · Pasta or Rice 250 mL 1 cup

Vegetables and Fruit **5–10** SERVINGS PER DAY	1 Serving

1 Medium Size Vegetable or Fruit · Fresh, Frozen or Canned Vegetables or Fruit 125 mL 1/2 cup · Salad 250 mL 1 cup · Juice 125 mL 1/2 cup

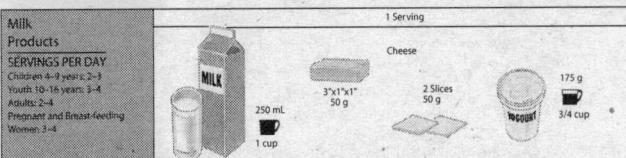

Milk Products SERVINGS PER DAY Children 4–9 years: 2–3 Youth 10–16 years: 3–4 Adults: 2–4 Pregnant and Breast-feeding Women: 3–4	1 Serving

MILK 250 mL 1 cup · Cheese 3"x1"x1" 50 g · 2 Slices 50 g · 175 g 3/4 cup

Other Foods

Taste and enjoyment can also come from other foods and beverages that are not part of the 4 food groups. Some of these foods are higher in fat or calories, so use these foods in moderation.

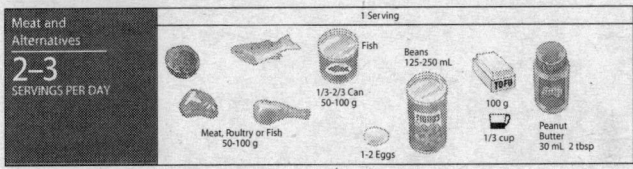

Meat and Alternatives **2–3** SERVINGS PER DAY	1 Serving

Meat, Poultry or Fish 50-100 g · Fish 1/3-2/3 Can 50-100 g · 1-2 Eggs · Beans 125-250 mL · 100 g · Peanut Butter 30 mL 2 tbsp 1/3 cup

Different People Need Different Amounts of Food

The amount of food you need every day from the 4 food groups and other foods depends on your age, body size, activity level, whether you are male or female and if you are pregnant or breast-feeding. That is why the Food Guide gives a lower and higher number of servings for each food group. For example, young children can choose the lower number of servings, while male teenagers can go to the higher number. Most other people can choose servings somewhere in between.

Consult Canada's Physical Activity Guide to Healthy Active Living to help you build physical activity into your daily life.

Enjoy eating well, being active and feeling good about yourself. That's **VITALIT**

© Minister of Public Works and Government Services Canada, 1997
Cat. No. H39-252/1992E ISBN 0-662-19648-1
No changes permitted. Reprint permission not required.

In 1997, Federal, Provincial and Territorial Ministers responsible for fitness, active living, recreation and sport recognized physical inactivity as a serious health issue and set a target to reduce inactivity by 10 percent by 2003. In response, Health Canada and partners launched "Canada's Physical Activity Guide to Healthy Active Living" in 1998, our first-ever set of national guidelines designed to help Canadians improve their health through regular physical activity. In 1999, "Canada's Physical Activity Guide for Older Adults" was launched. To order free copies of both Guides, call toll free 1-888-334-9769, or visit the Guide's Web site (http://www.paguide.com).

Choose a variety of activities from these three groups:

Endurance

4-7 days a week
Continuous activities for your heart, lungs and circulatory system.

Flexibility

4-7 days a week
Gentle reaching, bending and stretching activities to keep your muscles relaxed and joints mobile.

Strength

2-4 days a week
Activities against resistance to strengthen muscles and bones and improve posture.

Starting slowly is very safe for most people. Not sure? Consult your health professional.

For a copy of the *Guide Handbook* and more information: **1-888-334-9769**, or **www.paguide.com**

Eating well is also important. Follow *Canada's Food Guide to Healthy Eating* to make wise food choices.

Get Active Your Way, Every Day–For Life!

Scientists say accumulate 60 minutes of physical activity every day to stay healthy or improve your health. As you progress to moderate activities you can cut down to 30 minutes, 4 days a week. Add-up your activities in periods of at least 10 minutes each. Start slowly... and build up.

Time needed depends on effort

Very Light Effort	Light Effort 60 minutes	Moderate Effort 30-60 minutes	Vigorous Effort 20-30 minutes	Maximum Effort
• Strolling • Dusting	• Light walking • Volleyball • Easy gardening • Stretching	• Brisk walking • Biking • Raking leaves • Swimming • Dancing • Water aerobics	• Aerobics • Jogging • Hockey • Basketball • Fast swimming • Fast dancing	• Sprinting • Racing

Range needed to stay healthy

You Can Do It – Getting started is easier than you think

Physical activity doesn't have to be very hard. Build physical activities into your daily routine.

- Walk whenever you can get off the bus early, use the stairs instead of the elevator.
- Reduce inactivity for long periods, like watching TV.
- Get up from the couch and stretch and bend for a few minutes every hour.
- Play actively with your kids.
- Choose to walk, wheel or cycle for short trips.

- Start with a 10 minute walk – gradually increase the time.
- Find out about walking and cycling paths nearby and use them.
- Observe a physical activity class to see if you want to try it.
- Try one class to start – you don't have to make a long-term commitment.
- Do the activities you are doing now, more often.

Benefits of regular activity:

- better health
- improved fitness
- better posture and balance
- better self-esteem
- weight control
- stronger muscles and bones
- feeling more energetic
- relaxation and reduced stress
- continued independent living in later life

Health risks of inactivity:

- premature death
- heart disease
- obesity
- high blood pressure
- adult-onset diabetes
- osteoporosis
- stroke
- depression
- colon cancer

Be changes permitted. Permission to photocopy
This document is strictly not required.
Cat. No. H39-429/1998 1E   ISBN 0-662-8602-7

Laundry Care Symbols

The Canadian Care Labelling Program is a voluntary one that provides consumer information on the care of textiles, usually clothing. It uses five basic symbols, illustrated in the conventional "traffic light" colours. The program takes into consideration the fabric's colourfastness (i.e. whether the dye will bleed into the water and other clothing); whether it will shrink or stretch; how bleach will affect the garment; and how it may be ironed safely.

This labelling program does not apply to upholstered furniture, mattresses, carpets, leather, fur or yarn.

The basic symbols represent washing, bleaching, drying, ironing and dry cleaning, and the colours represent stop/do not (red), be careful (yellow) and go ahead (green). The red/crossed out symbol is only used when the procedure would damage the article.

Symbol	Red	Yellow	Green
	Stop	**Be careful**	**Go ahead**
Washing	Do not wash	Hand wash in cool water; 30°C Machine wash in cool water at a gentle setting—reduced agitation; 40°C Machine wash in lukewarm water at a gentle setting—reduced agitation; 50°C Machine wash in warm water at a gentle setting—reduced agitation	50°C Machine wash in warm water at a normal setting; 70°C Machine wash in hot water at a normal setting
Bleaching	Do not use chlorine bleach	Use chlorine bleach with care	
Drying		Dry flat; Tumble dry at low temperature	Tumble dry at medium to high temperature; Hang to dry; Drip dry
Ironing	Do not iron	110°C or Iron at low setting; 150°C or Iron at medium setting	200°C or Iron at high setting
Dry Cleaning	Do not dry clean	Dry clean—with caution	Dry clean

Source: *Industry Canada*

Product Safety Symbols

Health Canada has devised a set of safety symbols for containers of household chemicals and other materials. These symbols indicate possible hazards associated with various products such as cleaning liquids and powders, paint thinners, drain cleaners, windshield washer fluids and polishes, as well as some glues and treatments for household surfaces such as brick and metal, and garden chemicals.

The symbols indicate the type of danger and are contained in a frame that indicates the degree of danger—the more sides the frame has, the more dangerous the product is. In addition to the symbols, the labels on most of these containers include a safety warning. Learn the symbols opposite and handle the materials with care, especially if children live in the home or visit often.

Follow these steps to Safety:

- Teach children that the symbols mean Danger! Do Not Touch!
- Chemical product containers, even if sealed or empty, are not toys. Never let children play with them.
- If there is anything in the label instructions that you don't understand, ask for help. Make sure the symbols and labels on containers are not removed or covered up.
- Keep household chemicals in their original containers. Never mix them together. Some mixtures can produce harmful gases.
- Close the cap on the container tightly, even if you set it down for just a moment. Make sure that child-resistant containers are working.
- Keep all chemical products out of sight and out of reach of children.

Corrosive: the product can burn skin or eyes, and if swallowed, will damage the throat and stomach.

Explosive: the container can explode if heated or punctured. Flying pieces of metal or plastic from the container can cause serious injury, especially to the eyes.

Flammable: the product or its vapours will catch fire easily if it is near heat, flames or sparks

Poison: if the product is swallowed, licked or even, in some cases inhaled, it can cause sickness or death

If someone is injured:

- Call your doctor or the Poison Control Centre immediately.
- Give the information from the label to the person answering.
- Take the container with you when you go for help.

CANADIAN IDENTITY

Basic Canadian identification includes birth certificates and driver's licences, plus passports or permanent resident cards for use outside Canada's borders. These documents are necessary to prove identity (including citizenship) or establish eligibility for social benefits.

■ Birth certificate

A birth certificate is the document that establishes legal identity. Individuals should be registered at birth; the Canadian certificate that is issued is necessary to obtain health cards, Social Insurance Numbers and passports. Foreign birth certificates are also a starting point for establishing identity or eligibility in Canada.

If you need to register a birth or replace a lost Canadian birth certificate, contact the Vital Statistics department of your provincial government.

■ Canadian Passports

The best of proof of citizenship when you are travelling outside Canada is a valid passport. It is the only proof that is accepted in all countries. While passports are not required for entry into the U.S., many Canadians have been stopped for failure to have photo identification and proof of citizenship. In the aftermath of September 11, 2001, valid and trusted identification has become even more important. Passports can also be useful when cashing travellers' cheques or completing legal transactions in the U.S., and a passport is essential if the U.S. is only one stop in a multi-destination tour.

Any Canadian citizen may obtain a passport. It is valid for five years; it cannot be renewed or extended. Make sure that you will be home before the expiry date. (Some countries will not allow entry unless the passport is valid long after you plan to return home.) Many countries require a visa in addition to a passport. Always check with your travel agent, the Department of Foreign Affairs or that country's representative in Canada (listed in "Nations of the World") before you leave home, to ensure you have all of the required documentation.

How do you get a passport? Application forms are available at post offices and passport offices (there are 28 of them across the country). The form requires information about birth, citizenship, marital status and residence, in addition to two copies of a photo, which must conform to requirements relating to size and type of shot.

(Passport photos can be obtained at many photo supply stores as well as other outlets. They can be in black and white or colour. Family snapshots are not suitable.)

The completed form must be witnessed by a "guarantor": someone who has known you for at least two years and can attest to the truth of the information submitted. A guarantor must come from a recognized profession such as engineering, medicine or clergy or be in a senior administrative position in an academic or financial institution.

A passport is a valuable document. To ensure your passport is safe, consider locking it up when away from home—many hotels offer safe places for valuables. If you carry your passport with you, check for it and other valuables at least once a day. You have a better chance of retracing your steps to find a misplaced passport (or reporting a stolen credit card before too much damage is done) if it has been missing for less than 24 hours.

While it is your responsibility to protect your passport and other valuables during your trip, the nearest Canadian diplomatic or consular mission can help **if your passport is lost or stolen.** The loss must also be reported to the local police. (The same applies if your passport is lost or stolen at home. The police must be notified as well as the nearest passport office.)

Canada's Department of Foreign Affairs and International Trade (DFAIT) maintains a network of 250 offices, embassies, high commissions, consulates, honorary consuls and development offices in over 180 countries. (Australian diplomatic officers provide services where Canada does not have a presence.) For a list of Canadian representation abroad, consult the country-by-country listings in "Nations of the World." The offices are also listed in a government booklet entitled *Bon Voyage, But....*

Should you become ill, incapacitated or a victim of crime (or arrested), local consular staff can provide assistance. In addition, **emergency consular services** can be obtained by calling (613) 996-8885 at any time. (Collect calls will be accepted.)

■ The Permanent Resident Card

Also known as the Maple Leaf Card or the PR card, this is a new, wallet-sized plastic card for people who have completed the immigration process and have Permanent Resident status, but are not Canadian citizens. It replaces the IMM 1000 as the document to be presented by permanent residents who are re-entering Canada on a commercial carrier (plane, boat, train or bus) as of December 31, 2003.

As of June 28, 2002, new permanent residents began receiving the card. As of October 15, 2002, current permanent residents may apply for one. For more information about this new piece of identification, visit www.cic.gc.ca or contact your local Citizenship and Immigration office.

■ Pre-trip Planning

Make sure that you have proper identification before you leave, plus any required visas. Take out-of-country medical insurance and enough medication or other medical appliances you may require. It may be difficult to obtain them elsewhere—"common" items can be hard to find in some places. In addition, DFAIT suggests that detailed travel plan information should be left with family or friends in Canada.

Check to see if DFAIT has issued any Travel Advisories. Call 1 800 575 2500 or visit the government's web site at http://www.voyage.gc.ca/destinations/menu_e.htm. Travel advisories can cover anything from the local political situation to an outbreak of Yellow Fever.

If you are travelling by air or crossing into the U.S., give yourself extra time to clear security checks. Ensure that you can answer detailed questions about your belongings and provide quick access to everything. There will be random, thorough checks. No sharp objects of any kind will be allowed in aircraft cabins, and casual joking about threats will be taken seriously.

Social Insurance Number (SIN)

Social Insurance Numbers are issued by Human Resources Development Canada (HRDC). The nine-digit number is a file number that identifies you for taxation, premiums (and payments) for pensions and employment insurance. Your SIN will be requested once you've been hired for a job—your employer will use it to report earnings to the government.

How do you get a SIN? Apply for one at a Human Resources Centre (check the blue pages in your telephone book for the closest office) or by mail. You can obtain the form by downloading it from HRDC's web site (http://www.hrdc-drhc.gc.ca).

You must complete the application with your name, date of birth, place of birth and your mother's and father's birth names. You must also provide the original (or a certified copy) of the document(s) that prove your identity and your status in Canada. If you are a Canadian citizen born in Canada, a birth certificate or passport is acceptable; in Quebec and Newfoundland, a baptismal certificate is also acceptable. If you are a Canadian citizen born outside the country, a Certificate of Canadian Citizenship or a valid passport is required. A Permanent Resident can use the new Permanent Resident card (see above).

If the name you now use is different from the one on original documents, you must also supply evidence that your name was legally changed.

If the card is lost or stolen, notify the local HRDC office. The staff will advise you of the steps needed to protect yourself from SIN fraud. (This usually takes the form of someone else applying for government benefits under your name. SIN fraud includes: knowingly applying for more than one SIN; using someone else's number to obtain financial benefits or establish an identity; loaning or selling a SIN or card to another party; or manufacturing a card.)

Your SIN is not intended to be a piece of identification and there is no need to supply the number for purposes other than employment or financial transactions such as investments. Store the card in a secure place rather than carrying it with you.

Canadian Postal Rates

(as of January 14, 2002)

		Within Canada	To the USA (airmail)	International
Lettermail and postcards (letter size max. 245 mm x 150 mm x 5 mm)	0-29 g	$0.48[1]	$0.65	$1.25
	30-50 g	$0.77[1]	$0.90	$1.75
Non-standard and oversize items (max. 380 mm x 270 mm x 20 mm)	0-100 g	$0.96	$1.40	$3.00
	101-200 g	$1.60	$2.60	$5.20
	201-500 g	$2.10	$4.60	$10.00
Registered mail		$4.00 plus applicable postage	$4.00 plus applicable postage	$4.00 plus applicable postage

Note: GST is applicable to all postal charges. Other services for parcels, bulk mailings or expedited delivery are also available. (1) Surcharges apply if mail is not coded. Postal rates for uncoded letter 0–29g: $0.62; 30–50g: $0.96. (2) Postages varies by size and weight of mail item.

■ What's the best way to address an envelope?

A wide variety of packages and styles of address make it through Canada Post's system, however there are ways to ensure that your mail is handled most efficiently. While the computerized systems can read a range of addresses—including handwriting—the system's preferred style is as follows:

Line 1: name of the recipient
Line 2: title, floor number, attention line
Line 3: If business, company name
Line 4: unit number (if applicable):
street number and name
If post office box, information should appear above municipality name
Line 5: municipality, province   postal code

While the system can read upper and lower case, upper case is preferred, with an aligned left margin. Address lines should be less than 40 characters long. The first three elements of the postal code should be separated from the final three by a space, never a hyphen.

The return address should be formatted the same way, in the upper left corner (or on the back at the top). If on the front, it should be clearly separated from the destination address and preferably be smaller than the destination address.

Characters should be larger than 2 mm and smaller than 5 mm (10 to 12 point).

When addressing mail to the United States, the U.S. Postal Service prefers the use of the two-character state symbol rather than having the name of the state spelled out. The ZIP code should come two spaces after the state code and appear on the same line. The final line should be USA. When addressing international mail, the name of the country should be spelled out in full (GREAT BRITAIN) and should appear on the last line of the address, below any other municipality, city name or code information.

■ Province and Territory Symbols

The two-character symbols have been designated by Canada Post in order to make mailing more efficient. The codes for Canada's ten provinces and three territories are:

Newfoundland & Labrador (changed from NF as of Oct. 21, 2002)	NL
Prince Edward Island	PE
Nova Scotia	NS
New Brunswick	NB
Quebec	QC
Ontario	ON
Manitoba	MB
Saskatchewan	SK
Alberta	AB
British Columbia	BC
Yukon Territory	YT
Northwest Territories	NT
Nunavut	NU

Source: *Canada Post*

October 1, 2002–September 30, 2003

ADAMS, Lawrence, 66. A dancer with the National Ballet of Canada 1954–69; subsequently, with his wife, dancer Miriam Weinstein, co-founded Dance Collection Danse, Canada's largest dance archive and dance publisher. February 26, 2003.

ALLEN, Edward George (Eddie), 95. Youthful-looking member of the CBC radio comedy troupe, The Happy Gang, which ran from 1937–59; Allen was the lead singer and sometimes emcee. July 5, 2003.

AMIES, Sir Hardy, 93. From 1955–90 Amies was Queen Elizabeth II's couturier, following the Queen's request in 1951 that he design her wardrobe for a royal visit to Canada. March 5, 2003.

AMIN, Idi (b. Idi Amin Dada Oumee), 77. Military dictator of Uganda 1971–79, Amin was held responsible for the deaths of 300,000 Ugandans during his bloody rule; after his deposition by Tanzanian troops, he lived in exile in Saudi Arabia. August 16, 2003.

ARCHAMBAULT, Louis, 87. An internationally recognized Quebec-based sculptor, Archambault represented Canada in the Expo 67 sculpture pavilion, at the Milan Triennale in 1954 and the Venice Biennale in 1956. *Un Grand Couple; Mystical Symbols.* January 27, 2003.

ASPER, Israel Harold (Izzy), 71. Media tycoon who founded CanWest Global Communications Corp., a multinational newspaper and television station empire. CanWest was considerably strengthened when Asper bought Southam newspapers from Conrad Black in 2000. He was noted for his staunch support of Israel, his penchant for lawsuits and his generous philanthropic works. October 7, 2003.

BACHLE, Leo, 79. In 1942, as a teenager, Bachle approached Bell Comics in Toronto with his Johnny Canuck comic book series, inspired by a cousin who was a WWII fighter pilot; "Canada's answer to Nazi oppression"

became immensely popular. After the war Bachle became a stand-up comic under the name Les Barker. May 2003.

BALLARD, Hank (b. John H. Kendricks), 67 or 76. Wrote the hit song "The Twist," which launched a 1960s dance craze and was later recorded by pop singer Chubby Checker. As lead singer of the Midnighters beginning in the 1950s, he was a prolific songwriter. "Let's Go, Let's Go, Let's Go." March 2, 2003.

BEIQUE, Pierre, 92. In 1939 became managing director of the Société des Concerts symphoniques de Montréal, later known as the Orchestre Symphonique de Montréal. Béique was credited with transforming the minor orchestra into a magnet for international conductors and performers. February 27, 2003.

BELL, George Derek Fleetman, 66. A harpist with the Irish Celtic band the Chieftains, Bell was a classical musician and composer who appeared with symphony orchestras in his native Belfast as well as internationally. He also wrote three piano sonatas and two symphonies. *Three Images of Ireland in Druid Times.* October 17, 2002.

BERRIGAN, Philip, 79. Former Roman Catholic priest who was a pioneer in the civil rights and anti-war movements in the US, leading to multiple arrests. With his brother Daniel, he led the Catonsville Nine, a group that stole draft documents from a draft board office in Catonsville, Maryland, in 1968, and burned them in protest. December 6, 2002.

BIDDLE, Charles, 76. US-born Biddle, a jazz bassist, spent many years playing his brand of melodic swing tunes at clubs in Montreal until he opened his own club, Biddles, in the early 1980s. Co-organizer of the first Montreal Jazz Festival. February 4, 2003.

BLUMES, Mark, 59. In 1977 Blumes founded the Mark's Work Wearhouse clothing store chain in Calgary; primarily aimed to supply durable clothing for oil rig workers, the store's inventory became more fashion-conscious. November 16, 2002.

BOURGAULT, Pierre, 69. A fine orator, Bourgault, a left-wing Quebec separatist and journalist, co-founded, in the 1960s, the Rassemblent pour l'indépendance nationale, which in 1968 evolved into the Parti Québécois led by René Lévesque. As a journalist he wrote for *La Presse, The Gazette* and *Journal de Montréal.* Bourgault was an adviser to premier Jacques Parizeau. *Moi, je m'en souviens.* June 16, 2003.

BOYD, Eva Narcissus "Little Eva," 57. American pop singer who came to prominence with her 1962 hit, "Loco-Motion," which she performed with her distinctive dance of the same name. Also recorded "Little Eva by the Loco-Motions" and "Dance to the Loco-Motion." April 10, 2003.

BRAKHAGE, James Stanley (Stan), 70. Award-winning cinematographer whose avant-garde methods broke new ground, beginning in the 1950s, through the use of hand-held cameras, rapid scene changes and physical alterations to the film itself. *Dog Star Man; Stan's Window.* March 9, 2003.

BRINKLEY, David, 82. Blunt, no-nonsense co-anchor with Chet Huntley on NBC's *Huntley-Brinkley Report* from 1956–80; after Huntley retired, Brinkley went on to host *This Week With David Brinkley* until 1996; he ranked in popularity with CBS's Walter Cronkite. June 11, 2003.

BRONSON, Charles (b. Charles Buchinsky), 81. Rugged American actor well known for his *Death Wish* series of vigilante movies; also appeared in films including *The Great Escape, The Magnificent Seven, The Valachi Papers* and *The Sandpiper.* August 30, 2003.

BROWN, Dorris "Dee" Alexander, 94. American writer from the South whose book *Bury My Heart at Wounded Knee: An Indian History of the American West* challenged the conventional Eurocentric view of white settlement in the West between 1860 and 1890. Also wrote *The Gentle Tamers: Women of*

the Old Wild West and *Hear That Lonesome Whistle Blow.* December 12, 2002.

BROWN, Rosemary, 72. The first black woman elected to a Canadian legislature, in BC, the Jamaica-born Brown, an NDP member, served on the Canadian Security Intelligence Review Committee, was a chief commissioner of the Ontario Human Rights Commission and was a founding member of the Vancouver Status of Women committee. April 26, 2003.

CALVERT, Phyllis, 87. British actress noted for her gracious persona and dry wit, Calvert appeared in films written by Terence Rattigan, J.M. Barrie, Graham Greene and Noel Coward. Among her films were *Peter Pan, The Complaisant Lover, Blithe Spirit* and *Punch Without Judy.* October 8, 2002.

CARRICK, William Henesey, 81. Wildlife filmmaker whose discovery that geese would follow a light aircraft to relearn forgotten migratory patterns led to the creation of the film *Fly Away Home.* Among his films were *World in a Marsh* and *Audubon Wildlife,* an IMAX production. October 7, 2002.

CARTER, Bennett Lester "Benny," 95. Jazz composer, arranger and bandleader, Carter, who played saxophone, trumpet and clarinet, was a pioneer of the big band swing era in the 1930s and '40s; he also arranged music for major jazz stars including Ella Fitzgerald, Billie Holiday and Louis Armstrong. July 12, 2003.

CARTER, Cardinal Gerald Emmett, 91. Although a conservative Roman Catholic leader, Cardinal Carter promoted a variety of social justice issues. His initiatives led to the controversial full financing of Catholic schools in Ontario; he was also head of the International Committee for English in Liturgy, which oversaw the translation of Latin religious texts. April 6, 2003.

CASH, Johnny, 71. Veteran country-western singer/songwriter dubbed the Man in Black, Cash sang melancholy, gritty songs of the darker aspects of life such as failed romance and the despair of the ordinary workingman. "A Boy Named Sue"; "The Ballad of Ira Hayes." September 12, 2003.

CASWELL, Moira Lenore, 66. Well-respected Ontario Supreme Court judge whose cases included sprinter Ben Johnson's failed appeal to be released from the sporting ban that arose from his use of banned drugs in 1993, following the loss of his gold medal in the 1988 Olympics. Died in a freak skiing accident in Collingwood, Ontario. March 2, 2003.

CHADWICK, Lynn, 88. An English sculptor regarded as Henry Moore's successor, Chadwick was a master metalwork craftsman whose bold sculptures evocative of the greatness of humankind are on display in 22 countries. *Standing Figure IV; Three Elektras.* April 25, 2003.

CHRÉTIEN, Maurice, 91. Eldest brother and mentor to Prime Minister Jean Chrétien and father of Raymond Chrétien, ambassador to France and former US ambassador, the elder Chrétien was a prominent gynecologist in Montreal. November 29, 2002.

COBURN, James, 74. Veteran American actor whose crusty persona and rugged good looks lent to his distinctive screen presence. His credits include lead roles in *Our Man Flint, The Great Escape* and *The Magnificent Seven.* He also appeared on stage, and, in the 1950s, on the TV shows *Studio One* and *General Electric Theater.* November 18, 2002.

CONIBEAR, Kenneth Wilfred, 95. A hunter, trapper, university lecturer and writer, Conibear managed the Indian impersonator Grey Owl's lecture tour of England in 1937; he published three novels between 1936 and 1940, then resumed writing in 1995 with his book *The Nothing Man* and his autobiography, *Arctic Adventures with the Lady Greenbelly.* October 4, 2002.

COXETER, Harold Scott MacDonald, 96. One of the world's top geometers, Coxeter specialized in dimensional analogy, a process of stretching geometric shapes into higher dimensions, a geometric concept known as the "Coxeter group." Wrote *Introduction to Geometry* in 1961, which is still a standard text today. March 31, 2003.

CRENNA, Richard, 75. American actor whose prolific career began in the late 1930s, on the radio programs *Burns and Allen* and *Our Miss Brooks.* He had a lead role in the 1950s series *The Real McCoys* and later appeared in films such as *Wait Until Dark, The Sand Pebbles* and *The Flamingo Kid.* He was taping a new series, *Judging Amy,* at the time of his death. January 17, 2003.

CRONYN, Hume, 91. Veteran film and stage actor whose long career led him to co-star with his late wife, Jessica Tandy, in plays including *The Gin Game, Fourposter* and *The Petition.* Born in London, Ont., and related to the Labatt family, Cronyn appeared in early films such as *The Ziegfeld Follies* and enjoyed later success in the comedy *Cocoon* and its sequel. June 15, 2003.

De MELLO, Sergio Vieira, 55. Head of the UN's Iraqi operations and a probable successor to the UN's Secretary-General Kofi Annan, de Mello was killed in a truck-bomb attack at the Canal Hotel, the headquarters for the UN in Iraq. August 19, 2003.

DOBBS, Glenn "The Dobber," 82. American-born football star who was instrumental in the Saskatchewan Roughriders' Grey Cup win in 1951. After coaching the team for a short time he spent four years in the All-American Football Conference, a rival to the NFL. November 12, 2002.

DONEGAN, Anthony James "Lonnie," 71. Britain's first pop music superstar and inspiration for the Beatles, Donegan became famous with his skiffle-style music. He peaked in the 1950s with hits such as "Does Your Chewing Gum Lose Its Flavour on the Bedpost Overnight" and "My Old Man's a Dustman." November 3, 2002.

DONOHUE, Jack, 71. Basketball coach who has been credited with taking Canadian teams to top world competitions; for 18 years under his tutelage, Canadian teams were among the top six in the world, including a gold medal win at the 1983 World University Games in Edmonton. April 16, 2003.

DOWNING, Robert, 67. Sculptor, painter, photographer and digital artist, Downing employed geometric shapes into his prolific works; though he struggled financially throughout his life, his work is exhibited worldwide, and in Canadian locations including the Art Gallery of Ontario and Ottawa's National Gallery. July 22, 2003.

DOYLE, Richard "Dic" James, 80. Editor of the *Globe and Mail* newspaper 1963–83, Doyle was credited with turning the paper from a Progressive Conservative party mouthpiece to an independent voice. In 1985 Brian Mulroney appointed him to the Senate. March 20, 2003.

EBSEN, Christian Rudolph "Buddy," 95. Tall, gangly American character actor most remembered for his lead role as Jed Clampett in the long-running TV series *The Beverly Hillbillies,* Ebsen began his career in MGM musicals and on Broadway; he later starred in the TV series *Barnaby Jones* and appeared in films including *Breakfast at Tiffany's*. July 6, 2003.

FACKENHEIM, Emil, 87. Born in Germany, Fackenheim, a world-renowned rabbi and philosopher, wrote extensively on the concept of reconciling one's belief in God in the face of the Holocaust; he taught at the University of Toronto for 36 years. *God's Presence in History.* September 26, 2003.

FERGUSON, Ronald, 71. Father of Sarah Ferguson, the Duchess of York, and former polo coach for Prince Charles, Ferguson led a stormy life, which he documented in his tell-all memoir, *The Galloping Major.* March 16, 2003.

GAGNON, Charles Fernand, 68. Painter of bold abstract works, as well as a photographer, filmmaker and sculptor, Gagnon reached fame in the 1970s and '80s, showing his work across Canada; his film *The Eighth Day,* created for the Christian Pavilion at Expo 67, demonstrated his anti Vietnam war sentiments. April 16, 2003.

GETTY, Sir John Paul Jr., 70. American-born oil tycoon and philanthropist who took residence in Britain in the early 1970s, Getty was son of the founder of Standard Oil. April 17, 2003.

GIBB, Maurice, 53. A member of the hugely successful pop group the Bee Gees, with twin brother, Robin, and older brother, Barry. Gibb and his fellow musicians had six consecutive number-one hits in the US, including "Stayin' Alive" in 1977, composed for the disco movie *Saturday Night Fever.* He died following intestinal surgery. "New York Mining Disaster." January 12, 2003.

GOODIS, Jerry, 73. A former singer with the Canadian folk group the Travellers, in the 1950s, and co-author of the Canadian version of "This Land Is Your Land," originally written by Woody Guthrie, Goodis was a luminary in Canada's advertising business; his client list included Pierre Trudeau, who hired Goodis to advise on his election campaigns. November 8, 2002.

GREEN, Cecil Howard, 102. Co-founder of Texas Instruments; when he became president in 1950, the company cashed in on the new electronics industry. Green donated huge amounts to hospitals and educational institutions. Born in England, he spent most of his childhood in Vancouver, BC. April 11, 2003.

HACKETT, Leonard "Buddy," 78. American comedian who started his career in the 1950s TV shows of Jack Paar and Arthur Godfrey; popular on the comedy circuit, he also appeared on stage (*Viva Madison Avenue; I Had a Ball*) and in movies (*The Music Man; The Love Bug*). Television appearances included *Sabrina the Teenage Witch* and *The Late Late Show with Craig Kilborn.* June 30, 2003.

HARRIS, Richard, 72. Rakish Irish-born actor who appeared in countless British and Hollywood films, including *Camelot, The Sporting Life, The Field* and, latterly, two Harry Potter movies. October 25, 2002.

HAWTHORNE, George Vickers, 93. Hawthorne served as deputy minister in the federal government while Allan MacEachen was minister of labour; in this capacity he was instrumental in the setting of Canada's first minimum wage program, as well as setting minimum hours of labour and providing vacation pay to workers. November 22, 2002.

HAY, Henry (Harry), 90. A pioneering American gay activist, Hay wrote *The Call*, a groundbreaking manifesto in support of gay rights. He later founded the Mattechine Society, which supported gay rights, but from which Hay was eventually ousted due to his Communist leanings during the McCarthy era. October 24, 2002.

HELMS, Richard McGarrah, 89. Director of the CIA 1966–73, when he was fired by Richard Nixon for refusing to block the FBI investigation into the 1972 Watergate scandal; he was subsequently named ambassador to Iran. Frequently called back to Washington to testify about the CIA's assassination attempts of world leaders such as Fidel Castro, he was eventually fined for his lack of cooperation. October 22, 2002.

HEPBURN, Katharine, 96. Unsurpassed winner of four Academy Awards, Hepburn epitomized the upper-class East Coast society woman in many of her acting roles throughout her film career, which ran from 1932 to 1994. Among her most memorable roles were with her real-life partner, Spencer Tracy, in *Woman of the Year, Keeper of the Flame* and *Guess Who's Coming to Dinner*. She starred as Jo March in *Little Women*, with Cary Grant in *Bringing Up Baby*, and with Humphrey Bogart in *The African Queen*. June 29, 2003.

HILL, Daniel Grafton, 79. In 1962 the American-born Hill was appointed director of the Ontario Human Rights Commission, and was chairman 1971–73; also appointed Ontario ombudsman in 1984. Author of *Negroes in Toronto* and *The Freedom Seekers: Blacks in Early Canada*. Hill was father to singer/songwriter Dan Hill and writer Lawrence Hill. June 26, 2003.

HILL, George Roy, 81. Award-winning director of movies including *The Sting, Butch Cassidy and the Sundance Kid*, both starring Robert Redford and Paul Newman, and *The World According to Garp*. Hill also directed the TV rendition of the *Titanic* story, *A Night to Remember*, as well as Broadway hits including *Look Homeward, Angel* and *Period of Adjustment*. December 27, 2002.

HILL, (John Edward) Christopher, 91. British Marxist historian whose writings on seventeenth-century British politics remain essential reading for history students. His theory that the English Revolution was not an aberration in peaceful British history but a sign of class struggle has been long debated by scholars. *The English Revolution 1640*. February 24, 2003.

HILLER, Wendy (Dame), 90. Veteran British actress whose Manchester accent endeared her to audiences. She had a huge stage repertoire: Shakespeare, Ibsen, O'Neill, Wilde, among others. Film roles included *Pygmalian, Separate Tables* and *A Man for All Seasons*. May 14, 2003.

HINES, Gregory, 57. American tap dancer/choreographer who also acted on Broadway, in films and on TV; he appeared in the movies *The Cotton Club* and *White Nights*, as well as his own sitcom, *The Gregory Hines Show*, and recently on *The West Wing*. August 9, 2003.

HNATYSHYN, Ramon John, 68. Canada's twenty-fourth governor general 1990–95, Hnatyshyn first served as a PC MP from Saskatoon; he was credited with opening up the gardens of Rideau Hall in Ottawa to the public and for his common touch to a job that had been previously served in a much more formal manner. December 18, 2002.

HOPE, Bob (b. Leslie Townes Hope), 100. British-born iconic American comic actor whose morale-boosting appearances on American military bases during wars, starting with WWII in 1941 to Desert Storm in 1991, became legendary. His best-known films were the "Road" movies made with Bing Crosby; he also appeared in NBC TV specials throughout his lengthy career. "Thanks for the Memory." July 27, 2003.

HUGHES, Monica, 77. A popular writer of children's fiction, Hughes was widely acclaimed for her science fiction themes in titles including *Hunter in the Dark, The Keeper of the Isis Light* (the first of a trilogy), *Blaine's Way* and *The Seven Magpies*. She was a recipient of a Canada Council Children's Literature Prize and the Phoenix Award. March 7, 2003.

JACK, Donald, 78. Three-time winner of the Leacock Award for his three volumes of *The Bandy Papers*, which were lighthearted chronicles with characterizations drawn from inhabitants of the Ottawa Valley; also a scriptwriter and author of nonfiction. Wrote a radio history titled *Sinc, Betty and the Morning Man*. June 2, 2003.

JACQUES, Elliott, 86. Psychologist and social scientist whose Jacques' Stratified Systems Theory demonstrated how workers, from low level to upper management, work on various time frames for completion of tasks; he coined the term "midlife crisis" in 1965 while studying the career turns many artists experience around the age of 35. March 8, 2003.

JARVIS, Graham Powely, 72. Character actor best known as Charlie Haggers in the 1970s sitcom *Mary Hartman, Mary Hartman*, Jarvis was a familiar face in movies, television and theatre, appearing in such productions as *M*A*S*H, 7th Heaven, The Drew Carey Show, Alice's Restaurant* and *Silkwood*, as well as theatre productions *Much Ado About Nothing* and *The Rocky Picture Horror Show*. April 16, 2003.

JENKINS, Roy, 82. British MP first elected to the Labour Party in 1948; in 1981 founded the Social Democratic Party. Served as the chancellor of the exchequer as well as president of the European Commission. January 5, 2003.

JUMP, Gordon, 71. American comic actor best known for his role as Arthur Carlson, the radio station general manager in the CBS sitcom *WKRP in Cincinnati*, which aired 1978–82; for the past 14 years he portrayed the lonely Maytag repairman, retiring in July 2003. September 22, 2003.

KAY, Dorothy "Dottie" Blanche, 80. The Manitoba-born Kay led her All-American Girls Baseball League team, the Rockford Peaches, to win four championships between 1945 and 1954. Her character was played by Madonna in the film *A League of Their Own*. May 8, 2003.

KAZAN, Eli, 94. Pulitzer Prize and Oscar-winning American director whose films and plays enjoyed huge success. He directed Broadway plays including *Death of a Salesman* and *A Streetcar Named Desire*, and major films: *On the Waterfront; Splendor in the Grass; The Last Tycoon; A Face in the Crowd*. September 28, 2003.

KELLY, Craig, 36. A four-time world champion snowboarder, Kelly pioneered the sport and promoted it worldwide. Born in Illinois, Kelly was latterly based in Nelson, BC; he died in an avalanche with six other snowboarders near Revelstoke, BC. January 20, 2003.

KELLY, David, 59. British microbiologist whose expertise on Iraq's weaponry capabilities was crucial when he appeared as a witness in the House of Commons in 2003 to comment on a BBC report that the government had misled the populace by depending on misleading reports regarding Saddam Hussein's alleged build-up of nuclear weapons. He subsequently committed suicide. July 17, 2003.

KERR, Robert Allan, 84. Host of CBC Radio's national classical music program *Off the Record* 1960–96, at which time he semi-retired with a monthly program and weekly spots on the CBC's *In Performance*. April 8, 2003.

LAVIGNE, Conrad, 86. Founder of CFCL, Canada's first French language station, in 1951, based in Timmins, Ont. In 1956 he brought northern Ontario French-speakers CFCL-TV, appearing each week on *The President's Corner*. The station, which later became Mid-Canada Television, was the largest privately owned network in the world at the time. April 16, 2003.

LECKY, John MacMillan Stirling, 62. In 1988 Lecky founded the airline that became Canada 3000, which was the country's second-largest airline next to Air Canada. Following the Sept. 11, 2001, terrorist attacks, the airline experienced huge financial losses and became bankrupt later that year. Lecky was also an avid rugby player, and won the silver medal for rowing at the 1960 Olympics in Rome. February 25, 2003.

LEE, Arthur, 86. A businessman and generous philanthropist, Lee, through his Montreal company, Wing's Noodles, offered the world's first kosher French-English fortune cookies. Avidly patriotic, he donated an elaborate pagoda to Montreal's Chinatown in celebration of Expo 67. November 10, 2002.

LONGDEN, John (Johnny) Eric, 96. A legendary jockey who was born in England, raised in Canada, then became a US citizen, Longden had 6032 wins; he was the world's leading jockey in 1938, '47 and '48, and won the Triple Crown in 1943. February 14, 2003.

MacKAY, James William, 86. Pioneer film animator whose career began with the National Film Board in 1942. He succeeded the legendary Norman McLaren as head of the animation department in 1945, and in 1952 joined George Dunning to form Graphic Associates, producing some of Canada's first TV commercials. In the 1950s his Film Design Ltd. produced animation for clients including *Sesame Street* and TVOntario's *Join In.* October 26, 2002.

MANNIS, Harry, 82. A veteran CBC Radio and television announcer, Mannis was noted for his impeccable delivery. He joined the network in the late 1940s, eventually anchoring the Toronto metro news desk and hosting *Themes and Variations* and *Anthology.* He appeared on CBC TV into the 1980s. January 2, 2003.

MARTIN, Peter, 68. Martin founded, with his first wife, Carol, the Readers' Club of Canada and, shortly after, in 1965, Peter Martin Associates, publishing Canadian authors including Hugh Hood, Robert Fulford and John Robert Colombo under the Peter Martin Associates imprint. March 15, 2003.

McDERMOTT, Dennis, 81. President of the Canadian Labour Congress 1978–86 and director of the Canadian branch of the United Auto Workers, McDermott was a leading labour activist in the 1970s and '80s. In 1981 he organized a huge rally on Parliament Hill to protest high interest rates. Between 1986

and 1989 he served as Canadian ambassador to Ireland. February 13, 2003.

McLEAN, Grant, 81. McLean was with the National Film Board, 1941–67; he was director of production for 10 years, acting commissioner for 15. A pioneer of the cinema verité genre, McLean filmed groundbreaking subjects that included Inuit society, the Chinese civil war of the 1940s, and racial prejudice. *Target Berlin; The People Between; Labyrinth* (created especially for Expo 67 in Montreal). December 19, 2002.

McNEIL, Bill, 78. A radio host whose career began with the CBC in his native Cape Breton, McNeil moved to CBC Toronto in 1953, hosting national broadcasts *Assignments* and *Fresh Air.* His series *Voice of the Pioneer* led him to write a series of social history books. January 29, 2003.

McQUEEN, Glenn John, 41. A Toronto-born computer animator who worked with Pixar Animation Studios in California, following his association with Pacific Data Images; McQueen was instrumental in the creation of characters in films including *Toy Story, It's a Bug's Life* and *Monsters, Inc.* October 29, 2002.

MEIGS, Mary, 85. US-born painter, illustrator and writer who illustrated several of the books of France-based Canadian writer Marie-Claire Blais. Among her novels were *Lily Broscoe* and *The Medusa Head;* her *In the Company of Strangers* was a memoir of her participation in the NFB's *The Company of Strangers.* November 15, 2002.

MILES, Johnny, 97. Cape Bretoner who won record-breaking races in the Boston Marathon in 1926 and 1929, and became an Olympian contender in the 1928 and 1932 games. The Johnny Miles Race Event is held annually in New Glasgow, NS. June 15, 2003.

MILNE, Amy-Rae, 20. At the age of 7 in 1970, as part of her school's Earth Day project, Milne began a Saskatoon business to charge homeowners to pick up their recycling materials and deliver them to a recycling depot; as a result she spoke at the UN's Earth Day celebrations in New York and was appointed the youth ambassador for UN publications. September 11, 2002.

MODI, Vinod Jayantilal, 73. Born in India, Modi was an award-winning science professor at the University of British Columbia and inventor who refused to patent his discoveries, preferring to sustain public access to his inventions, which were in the fields of aerodynamics, biomechanics and oceanic engineering. He also worked with the Canadian Space Agency's program on the ionosphere, the Oedipus Project. February 12, 2003.

MOSLEY, Diana, 93. One of the notorious Mitford sisters, a family of eccentric British aristocrats, Mosley was a supporter of Hitler, whom she befriended through her marriage to Sir Oswald Mosley, leader of the British Union of Fascists during WWII. August 11, 2003.

MUNROE, John, 72. Liberal Cabinet minister during the Trudeau years, representing the Hamilton-East riding in Ontario 1962–84; among his portfolios: health and welfare, labour and Indian affairs. August 19, 2003.

NEILSON, Roger Paul, 69. Hockey coach who earned the nickname Captain Video for his innovative use of video as a training aid for hockey players. Throughout his 50-year career he coached teams in Toronto, Buffalo, Vancouver, New York and LA, among others. June 21, 2003.

O'CONNOR, Donald David Dixon Ronald, 78. An American actor and dancer, O'Connor is best known for his acrobatic footwork during the "Make 'Em Laugh" number in the film *Singin' in the Rain.* He also appeared in the *Francis* (the talking mule) series of movies. *Anything Goes; Call Me Madam.* September 27, 2003.

OBNEY, Nicholas, 84. Prominent herniologist who, from 1965 to 1988, was chief surgeon of the world-renowned Shouldice Hospital, founded by the late Dr. E. Earle Shouldice. Dr. Obney was credited with performing 32,000 hernia operations; his revolutionary techniques allowed patients to walk about just hours after surgery. February 15, 2003.

OLLIVIER, Emile, 62. A Haitian-born novelist and essayist, Ollivier was forced into exile by the Duvalier regime and arrived in Montreal in 1967, where he became active in Quebec literary circles as well as the Haitian community. *La Discourse aux Cent Voix; Les Urnes Scelles.* November 10, 2002.

PALMER, Robert, 54. British rock singer/songwriter who blended rock, soul, blues and reggae music; his career began in the 1970s, but recently he achieved increased notoriety and success. "Addicted to Love"; "Simply Irresistible." September 26, 2003.

PARKER, Suzy (b. Cecilia Ann Renée Parker), 69. A top model of the 1950s, the red-haired Parker was the first in her profession to earn more than $100 an hour. Said to be the inspiration behind the Audrey Hepburn character in *Funny Face,* in which Parker played a cameo role, she became an actress and also a professional photographer after studying with Henri Cartier-Bresson. April 3, 2003.

PAYCHECK, Johnny (b. Donald Eugene Lytle), 64. Country singer whose career took off in the 1960s and resulted in his biggest hit, "Take This Job and Shove It," in 1977. Despite his prolific career, Paycheck ran afoul with the law for many years, and only later settled down to a quiet life. "Don't Take Her, She's All I Got." February 15, 2003.

PECK, Eldred Gregory, 87. A giant of the Hollywood film industry, Peck had a long and versatile career, in dramatic roles in *To Kill a Mockingbird, Cape Fear, Spellbound* and *Moby Dick,* as well as comedic ones in *Roman Holiday* with Audrey Hepburn and in *Arabesque* with Sophia Loren. His characters revealed a moral rectitude and gravity that Peck exemplified in his personal life. June 12, 2003.

PERREAULT, Jean-Pierre, 55. Montreal-based choreographer and dancer whose complex signature style was dubbed Perreaultesque. He started his career with Le Groupe de la Place Royale and later founded his own company, Fondation Jean-Pierre Perrault. December 4, 2002.

PLIMPTON, George, 78. Noted American editor and journalist who founded the prestigious *Paris Review* in 1953. Dubbed the "participatory journalist," Plimpton was famous for his attempts at activities including boxing, circus acrobatics, baseball and football to research his writings. September 25, 2003.

POWLESS, Alex Ross, 76. An inductee to the Ontario and Canadian Lacrosse halls of fame, Powless won four Mann Cups while playing with the Peterborough Timbermen 1951–54; he also coached six of his sons, including the late Gaylord Powless, on the First Nations Team. May 26, 2003.

PRATT, John Robert, 96. An engineer, architect, politician and actor, Pratt appeared in Canada and the UK in the wartime revue *Meet the Army,* for which he wrote and sang "You'll Get Used to It." Elected mayor of Dorval, Que., in 1955, and as a PC MP from 1957 to 1962. April 6, 2003.

RAWLS, John Bordley, 82. American political theorist noted for his innovative books on justice and liberalism, especially his *A Theory of Justice,* which stressed the rights of minorities, including those of women as they became more active in academic circles. November 24, 2002.

REGAN, Donald, 84. Treasury secretary and White House chief of staff for president Ronald Reagan 1981–87, when he was forced to resign due to the Iran–Contra affair. His tell-all memoir was titled *For the Record: From Wall Street to Washington.* June 10, 2003.

RITTER, John, 54. American comic actor best known for his starring role in the 1970s sitcom *Three's Company,* with co-stars Suzanne Somers and Joyce DeWitt; Ritter also appeared in movies including *Sling Blade* and *Tadpole* and frequently on television, most recently the sitcom *8 Simple Rules... for Dating My Teenage Daughter.* September 11, 2003.

RITTS, Herb, 50. American celebrity photographer who created almost iconoclastic portraits, especially during the 1980s and '90s. Among his subjects: Elizabeth Taylor, the Dalai Lama, Cindy Crawford and Madonna. December 26, 2002.

ROGERS, Fred McFeely, 74. The kindly, soft-spoken host of the long-running (1963–2001) *Mr. Rogers' Neighborhood,* the popular children's series in which the cardigan-clad Mr. Rogers addressed his young audience with gentleness and respect. In 1962 Rogers hosted the CBC television show *Misterogers,* accompanied by the late Ernie Coombs (the CBC's Mr. Dressup). Shortly after, Rogers returned to the US to host his more well-known show, based in Pittsburgh, for the PBS network. February 27, 2003.

ROSS, Ian, 44. World-renowned wildlife biologist whose specialty was studying the habits of cougars in the Albertan foothills; Ross was killed in a light-plane crash in Kenya, where he was involved in a project designed to help the local population live in harmony with big cats. June 29, 2003.

ROSS, Malcolm, 91. Credited as the patriarch of Canadian literature, Ross, with Jack McClelland, initiated in the early 1950s the New Canadian Library paperback series, which, published by McClelland & Stewart, was developed when Ross was dismayed that Canadian literature was barely taught or read in Canada. Ross's career began with the NFB during World War II; he later taught English at the University of Manitoba, with Margaret Laurence and Adele Wiseman among his students, and subsequently at Queen's University, the University of Toronto and Dalhousie University. *Our Sense of Identity; The Arts in Canada; The Impossible Sum of Our Traditions.* November 4, 2002.

RUGHEIMER, Gunnar, 79. The first head of CBC TV news programming, the Swedish-born Rugheimer inaugurated in 1946 CBC's *Newsmagazine*, which replaced the familiar newsreel footage that preceded movies. The program lasted until 1986, when it was replaced by *The Journal.* Among Rugheimer's innovative ideas was to bring footage of Queen Elizabeth's coronation to Canada just hours after the event, in 1953. February 21, 2003.

RUSSELL, John Robert, 13th Duke of Bedford, 85. Although estranged from his family and his ancestral home, Woburn

Abbey, in Bedfordshire, England, Russell took over the stately home upon his father's death in 1955 and opened it to the public, complete with children's zoo, a playground and a tearoom, turning the costly estate into a profitable business and much sought-after tourist destination. October 25, 2002.

SAID, Edward, 67. An American English and comparative literature professor at New York's Columbia University, Said championed the Palestinian quest for justice in Israel. Despite his stance, he criticized Yasser Arafat for what he perceived as his weak role in the 1993 Oslo peace accord. In his book *Orientalism*, Said explored the West's perception of modern Islam. *The Question of Palestine*. September 24, 2003.

SAVAGE, John, 70. NS Liberal premier, 1993–97. Savage was also a medical doctor, treating HIV patients in Africa and in Nova Scotia, as well as running a free clinic in North Preston, a disadvantaged community outside of Halifax. May 13, 2003.

SCHESLINGER, John, 77. British-born Hollywood director whose hard-hitting, dramatic films included *Midnight Cowboy, Sunday Bloody Sunday, The Day of the Locust* and *Marathon Man*. July 25, 2003.

SCHULTZ, Erik, 50. An internationally renowned trumpeter, Schultz specialized in Baroque music; his recordings and tours with organist Jan Overduin were well received in Canada and abroad. In 1993 he and his father created the IBS label, which recorded the music of beginning Canadian artists. December 1, 2002.

SEGUNDO, Compay, 95. Cuban guitarist and singer whose Buena Vista Social Club band brought Cuban music to world attention with its blend of African and Spanish sounds. July 13, 2003.

SHATTO, Dick, 69. One of the finest running backs for the CFL, US-born Shatto played 12 seasons with the Toronto Argonauts. At the time of his retirement he led the league with touchdowns, passes and offensive yardage. February 4, 2003.

SHAUGHNESSY, Lord (b. William Graham Shaughnessy), 81. Grandson of Baron Shaughnessy, former president of the Canadian Pacific Railway, Lord Shaughnessy was the only Canadian in Britain's House of Lords to speak in favour of Canada's repatriation of the Constitution in 1982. A successful businessman in Canada, he also appeared in the House of Lords until 1999, when its legislative powers were cancelled. May 22, 2003.

SHAWCROSS, Lord Hartley William, 101. A British Liberal MP, Shawcross was the chief prosecutor at the Nuremberg Nazi war crimes tribunal, following the end of WWII, as well as acting on other high-profile cases. July 10, 2003.

SHIELDS, Carol, 68. Novelist, author, playwright, poet and academic, the US-born Shields was best known for her award-winning novels, many of which portrayed the sometimes ordinary but absolutely extraordinary lives of women as they pursued their domestic routines. *Swann; The Stone Diaries; Larry's Party; Unless*. July 16, 2003.

SIMMONS, Richard (Dick), 89. American actor best remembered in his role as Sergeant Frank Preston of the Northwest Mounted Police in the 1950s television series *Sergeant Preston of the Yukon;* Simmons also appeared in films such as *The Three Musketeers* and *Lady in the Lake*. January 11, 2003.

SIMONE, Nina (b. Kathleen Waymon), 70. American-born jazz and blues singer who resided in France, Simone was noted not only for her rich vocal talent, but for her fight against racism in the US. Inspired by the murder of four black children in the 1963 bombing of a church in Birmingham, Ala., she wrote "Mississippi Goddam" as well as other civil-rights–themed songs. "Little Girl Blue." April 21, 2003.

SISULU, Walter, 90. With Nelson Mandela joined the African National Congress to fight apartheid in South Africa in the early 1940s. After serving a life imprisonment sentence from 1964 to 1989, he became the party's deputy president until 1994 when he retired. May 5, 2003.

SOLOMON, Starr, 64. Prominent in the Ottawa social scene for many years, Solomon worked variously for the *Ottawa Citizen,* the CBC in Toronto as a writer and producer, and in public relations. Among her passions was a campaign to save the CNR's cabooses, and the furthering of women's rights through the Legal Education and Action Fund (LEAF), which she co-founded. January 3, 2003.

STACK, Robert, 84. Ruggedly handsome American actor best remembered for his role as Eliot Ness in the 1959–63 TV series *The Untouchables.* Also narrated the *Unsolved Mysteries* series that debuted in 1988. Among his more than 40 films: *The High and the Mighty; Sayonara; Good Morning Miss Dove.* May 14, 2003.

STRUMMER, Joe (b. John Graham Mellor), 50. A member, with Paul Simonon and Mick Jones, of the British punk rock group the Clash, whose hard-hitting music helped launch the punk genre of the late 1970s. Strummer, a vocalist, guitarist and songwriter, wrote music with a sharp political edge; he also appeared in the films *King of Comedy* and *Rude Boy.* "London Calling." December 22, 2002.

STUEMER, Diane, 43. Writer, journalist and advertising executive, Stuemer, after being diagnosed with cancer, sailed around the world on a four-year journey starting in 1997 with her husband and their four children, chronicling their adventures for the *Ottawa Citizen* and later in her book *The Voyage of the Northern Magic.* March 15, 2003.

THATCHER, Sir Denis, 88. A successful businessman in his own right, Thatcher was the husband of former British Conservative prime minister Margaret Thatcher, who held office 1979–90; Thatcher managed to remain supportive of his wife while keeping a low profile in the highly charged atmosphere of British politics. June 25, 2003.

THESIGER, Sir Wilfred, 93. Intrepid British explorer who immersed himself in the cultures of the countries he mapped, photographed and wrote about, particularly Arabia's Empty Quarter and the home of the Shiite Marsh Arabs. He held great disdain

for the modern comforts that his younger contemporaries employed during their travels. *Arabian Sands; The Marsh Arabs.* August 24, 2003.

THOMPSON, Arthur Ivan, 54. Artist from the Nuu-chah-nulth band of Vancouver Island whose skill in blending traditional native art with modern graphic art techniques led to his designing the logo for the Commonwealth Games held in Victoria in 1994. His bold, dramatic works have been shown worldwide. Also an advocate for victims of sexual abuse in residential schools. March 30, 2003.

THURMOND, James Strom, 100. The longest-running senator (for South Carolina) in US history, Thurmond served from 1928 to 2003; his extreme right-wing views led him to support segregation and denounce communism and the civil rights movement. June 26, 2003.

URBANI, Dr. Carlo, 46. Italian specialist in communicable diseases, Urbani was the first doctor who identified Severe Acute Respiratory Syndrome (SARS), the flu-like virus that originated in China in 2003 and quickly spread throughout the world. Dr. Urbani died of the disease after contracting it from an American businessman he was treating in Hanoi. March 29, 2003.

URIS, Leon, 78. American best-selling novelist whose massive tomes often chronicled major historical events. *Exodus* told the history of European Jews in the twentieth century; *Trinity* followed the tribulations of the Irish; *Topaz* was a spy story set in France. His *O'Hara's Choice* will be published posthumously. June 21, 2003.

UTECK, Lawrence (Larry), 50. Star CFL defensive back who played with the BC, Toronto, Ottawa and Montreal teams, Uteck later led a successful coaching career with the St. Mary's Huskies in Halifax, as well as serving as deputy mayor of Halifax. He died from complications of Lou Gehrig's disease. December 25, 2002.

VAN, Billy (b. Billy Van Evera), 68. Veteran comic actor who appeared on Canadian television shows including the CBC's 1960s satirical series, *Nightcap,* and *The Hilarious House of Frightenstein;* TVOntario's *Bits and Bytes;* as well as American series such as *The Sonny & Cher Comedy Hour* and *The Bobby Vinton Show.* January 8, 2003.

WARREN, Earl Warren, 69. Popular host of Toronto's CFRB radio program *House of Warren,* 1961–83. His folksy, down-home commentary on everyday events contributed to his popularity, but after the radio network's switch to a younger audience demographic, Warren went on to start his own travel agency and to host *The Earl Warren Show.* October 19, 2002.

WATSON, Harold Percival "Whipper," 79. Leftwinger hockey player who won four Stanley Cups with the Toronto Maple Leafs 1947–51 and one with the Detroit Red Wings in 1943. At six-two he was one of the biggest players in the NHL; he eschewed the recent trend toward on-rink fighting. November 21, 2002.

WELLSTONE, Paul, 58. Popular Minnesota Democrat senator died with his wife, daughter and three aides in the crash of his campaign aircraft near Eveleth, Minn., only 11 days before the midterm Congressional elections in which he was running for a third six-year term. Wellstone, a vocal opponent of the impending war on Iraq, was replaced by former vice president Walter Mondale, who lost the election to Republican Norm Coleman. October 25, 2002.

WESLEY, Mary, 90. British novelist whose literary career took off when she was 70. Her dramatic, sexually explicit novels mirrored the dark side of upper-class English society; many were developed into films. *The Camomile Lawn; Harnessing Peacocks; Part of the Furniture.* December 30, 2002.

WHITE, Barry, 58. American rhythm and blues singer/songwriter whose rich, seductive baritone and suggestive lyrics brought him fame. "Can't Get Enough of Your Love, Baby"; Love Serenade." July 4, 2003.

WILLIAMS, Sir Bernard, 73. British professor whose writings on moral philosophy, focussing on personal identity and the self, were highly regarded in the academic community. *Morality: An Introduction to Ethics; Problems of the Self; Ethics and the Limits of Philosophy.* June 10, 2003.

WILSON, Kemmons, 90. In 1951 Wilson founded the Holiday Inn hotel chain in Memphis, Tenn., inspired by the need for affordable family-style lodgings. The chain, named after the film of the same name starring Bing Crosby, now holds properties across North America as well as globally. January 12, 2003.

YANOVSKY, Zalman (Zal), 57. Founding member along with John Sebastian of the pop group the Lovin' Spoonful, whose folk-blues-rock style shot them to fame with singles including "Do You Believe in Magic?" "Summer in the City" and "Daydream." After the group broke up, Yanovsky opened Chez Piggy, a popular restaurant in Kingston, Ont. December 13, 2002.

ZERAFA, Boris, 69. Egyptian-born architect who designed both Canadian and global architectural landmarks. Among his most famous buildings: Toronto's innovative Lothian Mews, a shop-filled courtyard that has since been demolished, the Royal Bank Plaza and the Hazelton Lanes shopping/condo complex; Montreal's Bank of Paris; Calgary's Bow Valley Square; and King Abdul Aziz University in Saudi Arabia. November 2, 2002.

ZEVON, Warren, 56. Singer/songwriter whose often bizarre themes reflected the dark side of ordinary life as well as the humorous aspects. He wrote the theme song "He Quit Me" for the movie *Midnight Cowboy* in the 1960s, and went on to a successful career writing music for television and recording several albums in the past decades. *Excitable Boy; Mr. Bad Example.* September 7, 2003.

NOTE: Names in boldface indicate Canadian-born.

October 1, 2002, to September 30, 2003

(See also Obituaries pages 805–816.)

October 2002

INTERNATIONAL

Brazil: On October 27, Luiz Inacio Lula da Silva, leader of the left-wing Worker's Party and a former factory worker known for his anti-capitalist rhetoric, won Brazil's presidential election after a run-off ballot. **Columbia:** On October 19, the government's war against the Revolutionary Armed Forces of Columbia (FARC) spilled into Medellin, its second-largest city, as President Alvaro Uribe ordered a surprise offensive to eject the leftist rebels from a slum district. **Côte d'Ivoire:** Following a failed coup attempt on September 19 and after 30 days of turmoil nearing civil war, the government and rebels reached a cease-fire agreement on October 17, under the supervision of the Economic Community of West African States (ECOWAS). **Democratic Republic of the Congo:** As part of the Pretoria peace agreement, foreign troops finally began pulling out of the Democratic Republic of the Congo in early October. In what is considered Africa's "first world war," rebel fighting in the DRC drew in troops from neighbouring countries Rwanda, Uganda, Burundi (supporting the rebels), Zimbabwe, Angola, Namibia and Chad (supporting the government). **European Union:** On October 9, the European Commission formally recommended that up to ten countries could join the EU in 2004. It offered no date, however, for when accession negotiations might even begin with Turkey, Bulgaria or Romania. **Guinea:** A discovery of mass graves on October 22 suggested that the late dictator and liberation hero, Sekou Toure, killed more people than previously thought. **Indonesia:** On October 12, a car bomb destroyed the heart of the nightclub district on the island of Bali, killing 202 people and injuring more than 300. Many of the victims were Australian tourists. Ali Imron, the suspect in the bombing, said the attacks were targeted at Americans. Imron's organization has been linked to al-Qaeda. **Iraq:** On October 12, Iraq sent a letter to UN weapons inspection chiefs saying that it would let UN weapons inspectors return under rules set out by the Security Council in 1998. On October 16, Saddam Hussein won 100 percent of the votes, with 100 percent turnout in a referendum on whether he should rule for another seven years. The result topped even the last vote, held in 1995, when Saddam received a 99.96 percent "yes" vote. **Israel and the Palestinian Territories:** Israel said its troops were searching for Hamas militants. The Israeli army resumed positions outside Yasser Arafat's largely destroyed Ramallah compound on October 1, after pulling out under American pressure in September. Fourteen Palestinians were killed in an Israeli army raid on an alleged Hamas stronghold in southern Gaza on October 7. **Jamaica:** Sitting Prime Minister P.J. Patterson, leader of the People's National Party, won a fourth consecutive term, but with a reduced majority. About 60 people were killed during the run-up to the election. **Kuwait:** In an apparent terrorist incident, an American marine was shot dead and another injured by two Kuwaiti gunmen during a military exercise in Kuwait. **The Netherlands:** The three-month-old coalition government collapsed on October 16, over "unacceptable" conflicts within the three-party coalition. A new election was set for January 2003. **North Korea:** The government disclosed to U.S. envoy James Kelly that it had defied a 1994 agreement with the United States and has a secret and active nuclear weapons program. **Pakistan:** In Pakistan's first general election since a military coup in 1999 and its first ever parliamentary elections, General Pervez Musharaff stayed on as president. A civilian prime minister was also elected, Mir Zafarullah Khan Jamali. Jamali promised to continue Musharaff's antiterrorism policy. **Philippines:** Bomb blasts in Zamboanga City on October 2 and 16 killed four and seven people, respectively. Philippine authorities blamed the Abu Sayyaf terrorist group for the attacks. **Russia:** On October 23, about 50 Chechen terrorists took 700 people hostage in a Moscow theatre. When the terrorists threatened to begin killing hostages if the Russian government did not meet their demands to end the war in Chechyna, Russian special forces troops pumped an unidentified gas through the air conditioning system and subsequently stormed the theatre on the morning of October 26. Most of the Chechens, but also nearly 120 hostages, were killed in the siege. **United Kingdom:** The peace process in Northern Ireland faced a crisis after an October 4 police raid found that an official of Sinn Fein had secretly photocopied documents holding details of potential terrorist targets and of communications between British and Irish ministers, including British Prime Minister Tony Blair. **United Nations:** Chief Weapons Inspector Hans Blix recommended to the Security Council on October 4 that inspections for weapons of mass destruction in Iraq should not begin until Iraq releases a full inventory of its weapons. **United States:** On October 2, Andrew Fastow, former chief financial officer of Enron, was charged with fraud, money laundering and conspiracy in connection with an accounting scandal that hid millions in debt at the bankrupt energy-trading company. On October 7, President George Bush laid out his case for war against Saddam Hussein on television, calling for urgent measures for disarming Iraq. Twenty-eight west coast ports reopened on October 8 after a 10-day man-

agement lockout caused by a dispute with the dockers' union. President George Bush invoked the Taft-Hartley Act for the first time since 1978, imposing an 80-day cooling-off period. On October 11, former U.S. President Jimmy Carter won the Nobel Peace Prize for "decades of untiring effort to find peaceful solutions to international conflicts, to advance democracy and human rights, and to promote economic and social development." Sam Waksal, former chief executive at ImClone, pleaded guilty to six charges in an insider-trading case on October 15. Prosecutors were also probing whether Martha Stewart, America's queen of home style, sold around $230,000 worth of ImClone shares based on inside information from Waksal. On October 24, federal police arrested two men, John Allen Muhammed, 41, and John Lee Malvo, 17, in connection with sniper shootings in the Washington, D.C., area that left 10 dead and three wounded, and sparked one of the largest manhunts in the region's history. Police were unclear as to the motive. **Yemen:** On October 6, a French oil tanker was crippled by an explosion off the south-east coast of Yemen. The tanker crew claimed the ship, which was carrying nearly 400,000 barrels of crude oil, was rammed by a small craft packed with explosives. One member of the crew remained unaccounted for.

CANADA

Tensions escalated between Canadian and American diplomats over the October 2 deportation of Canadian citizen Maher Arar, a 32-year-old engineer from Ottawa. Arar was arrested for alleged terrorist ties at New York's JFK airport during a trip back to Canada from Tunisia and was deported to Syria. U.S. officials claimed the arrest was justified, but Foreign Affairs Minister Bill Graham filed an official protest with Washington, demanding to know why Arar was arrested. As Britain's Queen Elizabeth began a 12-day tour of Canada on October 4, Deputy Prime Minister John Manley said it is unnecessary for Canada to continue under the monarchical system, causing a furor among Canadian monarchists. On October 9, 45 charges were laid against members of a criminal organization involved in smuggling illegal migrants from South Asia into Canada for $40,000 per person. In her 2002 status report on October 9, Auditor General Sheila Fraser said that almost all the provinces contravened the Canada Health Act, but that Ottawa doesn't have the manpower or the will to crack down. On October 16, Peter Ritchie, the lawyer representing accused serial killer Robert Pickton, quit the case over a funding dispute with the B.C. government, possibly delaying the trial for months. Pickton is charged with the first-degree murder of 15 women from Vancouver's Downtown Eastside area. New Brunswick Premier Bernard Lord announced on October 22 that he would not run for the federal Conservative leadership, ending months of speculation. A Senate committee called for a $5-billion-per-year infusion of new money into the health-care system, to be raised by an increase in the GST or through insurance premiums. The committee also recommended the appointment of an independent health-care commissioner and expanding Medicare to cover "catastrophic" drug costs (October 25). In the wake of a *Toronto Star* exposé alleging that members of Toronto's 7,200-strong police force treat blacks far more harshly than whites, Chief Julian Fantino announced an inquiry into the police department's race relations (October 25). Foreign Minister Bill Graham confirmed on October 31 that U.S. officials transferred Canadian Omar Khadr from Afghanistan to Guantanamo Bay, where 600 suspected al-Qaeda combatants are being held.

NOVEMBER 2002

INTERNATIONAL

Austria: Wolfgang Schüessel was re-elected as chancellor on November 24. Schüessel's center-right People's Party won 42 percent of the vote. **China:** On November 8, the Chinese Communist Party convened its 16th Congress to name a replacement for outgoing president, party chief and military leader, Jiang Zemin. On November 14, Zemin officially retired and Hu Jintao was named as his successor. Zemin, however, maintained his chairmanship of the Central Military Commission, effectively the head of the armed forces. **Czech Republic:** At a meeting in Prague on November 21, NATO governments formally invited Bulgaria, Estonia, Latvia, Lithuania, Romania and Slovenia to join the military alliance. **Ethiopia:** On November 11, Prime Minister Meles Zenawi warned that if food aid was not increased, Ethiopia faced a famine worse than that of 1984, which killed one million people. Zenawi predicted that the number facing starvation could rise to 15 million. **Indonesia:** On November 21, Indonesian police arrested Imam Samudra, the suspected mastermind behind the terrorist bombings in Bali in October 2002. He confessed to his involvement in the attacks. **Iran:** On November 8, a university professor was sentenced to death for saying that Muslims should not "blindly" follow religious leaders. The ruling sparked a wave of student protests across the country. **Iraq:** UN arms inspectors, led by Chief Weapons Inspector Hans Blix and Chief of the International Atomic Energy Agency Mohamed El-Baradei, arrived in Iraq on November 18 to begin their search for weapons of mass destruction. **Israel and the Palestinian Territories:** Prime Minister Ariel Sharon's 20-month national unity government collapsed on November 3 when the Labour Party walked out, led by the defence and foreign ministers. Former Israeli Prime Minister Benjamin Netanyahu agreed to serve as foreign minister on the condition that Sharon call for new elections, which he did on November 5. A Palestinian gunman killed five people, including two children, in a November 10 attack on a kibbutz in Israel.

The Al-Aksa Martyrs Brigade, the militant arm of Yasser Arafat's Fatah movement, claimed responsibility. In response, the Israeli army reoccupied Nablus and raided Gaza. **Kenya:** In attacks on Israeli targets in Kenya on November 28, missiles narrowly missed an Israeli charter plane taking off from Mombasa airport, and a car bomb destroyed an Israeli-owned seaside hotel, killing at least 12 people. Al-Qaeda was believed to be involved. **North Korea:** In response to North Korea's October 2002 acknowledgement that it had been secretly working to develop nuclear weapons, on November 13 the United States threatened to cut fuel shipments to that country. South Korean warships fired warning shots at a North Korean patrol boat that crossed a disputed maritime border on November 20. **Qatar:** On November 12, a tape claiming to feature the voice of Osama bin Laden was broadcast by Qatar's al-Jazeera television network. The man on the audiotape praised the recent terrorist attacks in Indonesia and Russia, and threatened future attacks. **Spain:** An oil tanker broke in half 130 miles off the northwest coast of Spain on November 19. The Greek-owned vessel, the *Prestige*, was carrying more than 19.6 million gallons of oil. **Switzerland:** On November 5 in Interlaken, 40 countries endorsed the Kimberly Process, which guarantees that only diamonds mined legally in Africa could be traded on the international market. The intent of the pact is to deny the rebel armies who mine "conflict" diamonds the cash to buy weapons. **Turkey:** Voters gave the Justice and Development Party, led by Recep Erdogan, a solid victory with 34.1 percent of the vote on November 3. A former Islamicist, he promised to push ahead Turkey's application for EU membership. **United Nations:** The Security Council unanimously passed a resolution on November 8 calling on Iraq to disarm or else face "serious consequences." Five days later, Iraq accepted the resolution without conditions, but denied that it had any weapons

of mass destruction. A UN report released on November 26 revealed that 42 million people are infected with HIV worldwide. The cumulative death toll of deaths and infections exceeds the number killed during the Second World War. **United States:** On November 1, the US Justice Department reached a settlement with Microsoft in the three-year-old anti-trust case against the software giant. The agreement fell far short of the original government aim of breaking up the company and most of the stiff penalties sought were rejected. Microsoft was, however, forced to stop all retaliatory actions against competing companies and to deal with licensing partners on uniform terms. The Republicans celebrated a victory in America's mid-term elections on November 5, retaking the Senate and increasing their majority in the House of Representatives. President Bush became the first president to make mid-term gains in both houses in nearly 70 years. Attorney-General John Ashcroft stated on November 7 that the Washington snipers would be tried in Virginia instead of Maryland: Virginia is thought more likely to impose the death penalty if the suspects are convicted. At least 36 people were killed by a series of unusually severe tornadoes in Tennessee, Alabama, Ohio, Pennsylvania and Mississippi on November 11. On November 14, Democrat Nancy Pelosi became the first woman to be elected as House minority leader, and the first women to lead a party in Congress. On November 19, the U.S. Senate voted 90-9 to create the Cabinet-level Department of Homeland Security. The new department will have a budget of $37 billion, and combine 22 security agencies and 170,000 workers. Six days later, President Bush nominated Tom Ridge as secretary of the department. On November 26, President Bush signed a terrorism insurance bill into law. The new legislation requires the federal government to pay 90 percent of the cost of attack on losses of more than $10 billion, making the government the insurer of last resort in the event of another large attack. **Venezuela:** On November 17, President Hugo Chavez sent troops into Caracas to wrest control of the capital's police force from the mayor, his staunch opponent. The move sparked widespread demonstrations and clashes with police. **Yemen:** On November 4, a missile fired from an unmanned CIA Predator aircraft killed Qaed Salim Sinan al-Harethi, a senior al-Qaeda leader, and his five companions travelling in his car in remote northwestern Yemen.

CANADA

In a 5 to 4 ruling on November 1, the Supreme Court of Canada gave federal penitentiary inmates the right to vote in federal elections. The court said that denying inmates the right to vote does more to undermine their respect for democracy than enhance it. In an embarrassing defeat in the House of Commons, on November 6 Prime Minister Chrétien lost the ability to single-handedly appoint the chairs of parliamentary committees. Upset about Chrétien's decision to stay in power for another 18 months, and looking to minimize the Prime Minister's power, a number of Liberal MPs sided with the Canadian Alliance on the vote. Lucille Poulin, 78, a former Catholic nun, was sentenced to eight months in jail on November 8 for assaulting children in the religious commune she presided over on Prince Edward Island. Amid rising consumer anger over high electricity bills, the Ontario government said it would bring in measures to take the sting out of deregulation. The program is expected to include rebates, initially averaging $45 per household (November 11). In a symbolic move, Quebec Premier Bernard Landry skipped official Remembrance Day ceremonies on November 11 to attend an event held by the nationalist Société St-Jean Baptiste instead. At the event, Landry linked the struggle of Quebec separatists to that of the soldiers in both World Wars, saying, "Quebec is a nation, and very

democratically and peacefully is searching for full liberty." Larry Campbell, a former Mountie and coroner who inspired a CBC Television series, won a landslide election on November 18 to become the mayor of Vancouver. Representing the left-wing Coalition of Progressive Electors, Campbell ended a 16-year conservative hold on the mayoralty. On November 21, the RCMP laid 33 charges against four individuals, the Armour Pharmaceutical Co., and the Canadian Red Cross Society in connection with the tainted-blood scandal in the 1980s. Thousands of people were infected with HIV and Hepatitis C through tainted blood and tainted blood products. On November 25, health experts announced that the source of the encephalitis that killed Joyce Kimmel of Kitchener, Ontario, was probably West Nile virus, contracted through one of her numerous blood transfusions. Up to 80 percent of those who contract West Nile virus experience no symptoms and could unwittingly give blood. The Romanow report on Canada's health-care system was released on November 28, calling for a $15-billion infusion in federal funding by 2006, along with extensive modernization and streamlining. The report also stated that increasing private provisions was unnecessary.

DECEMBER 2002

INTERNATIONAL

Australia: Prime Minister John Howard stated on December 2 that he was prepared to launch pre-emptive action against terrorists in neighbouring Asian countries if they threatened Australia. The comments drew the ire of several Asian states. **Burundi:** The government and the main rebel group agreed to a cease-fire on December 3, ending a war that had left more than 300,000 dead. A day later, another rebel group rejected the deal. A week later, fresh fighting erupted. **Chile:** After 11 years of talks, the United States and Chile concluded a bilateral free-trade deal on December 11.

The pact abolishes tariffs on 85 percent of consumer and industrial goods. **Democratic Republic of the Congo:** On December 17, President Joseph Kabila signed a peace deal with the country's two main rebel groups, ending four years of civil war. Both groups were given a share of Cabinet posts, and elections are to be held in two years. **East Timor:** In the capital of Dili, five people were reported dead after police fired on a crowd protesting against the arrest of a student on December 5. The prime minister's house was burned down. **European Union:** On December 13 at the Copenhagen Summit, 10 countries were formally invited to join the European Union. Expansion, set for May 2004, will increase membership to 25 countries and 450 million people. The new members, mostly former Communist countries, are: Poland, Czech Republic, Hungary, Slovakia, Lithuania, Latvia, Estonia, Slovenia, Cyprus and Malta. **Indonesia:** The government and separatist rebels in Aceh signed a peace deal on December 9 that would end 26 years of fighting. The deal granted autonomy and free elections to Aceh in exchange for the rebels' disarming. **Israel and the Palestinian Territories:** On December 4, Prime Minister Ariel Sharon accepted U.S. President George Bush's plan for a Palestinian state in parts of the West Bank and Gaza Strip, so long as Yasser Arafat is removed from power. Leaders of the Palestinian Authority postponed presidential elections on December 22, saying they cannot be held while movement in the West Bank is restricted by Israeli troops. **Kenya:** On December 28, Kenya's opposition won a presidential and parliamentary election for the first time since independence in 1963. The new president, Mwai Kibaki, garnered 63 percent of the vote. **North Korea:** The government threatened to end an eight-year freeze on its plutonium-producing reactors on December 12, in response to the suspension of oil supplies to the country. On December 22, North Korea removed the seals protecting its stockpile of plutonium. Five days later, officials expelled UN inspectors monitoring a nuclear reactor at Yongbyon. U.S. officials said that North Korea was capable of producing about five nuclear weapons within six months. **Russia:** Rebel Chechen suicide bombers blew up the headquarters of the pro-Russian government in Grozny on December 27. At least 46 people died in the blasts. **South Korea:** The acquittal in a military court of two American soldiers charged with the negligent homicide of two South Korean teenagers crushed by an armoured vehicle sparked massive anti-American protests across South Korea on December 15. The protests marked another sign of deteriorating American-South Korean relations. On December 19, South Korea elected No Mu-hyon as its new president in a tight race. No, the candidate of the ruling party, favours a policy of engagement with North Korea. **United Nations:** Iraq delivered a 12,000-page weapons report to the United Nations on December 7. The report said that Iraq neither possesses weapons of mass destruction nor has programs for creating them. Disagreement arose in the Security Council as to how the report would be reviewed; the U.S. took charge of the report, distributing full copies to the other four permanent members, but edited copies to the non-permanent members, for fear of disclosing nuclear "recipes." On December 19, U.S. Secretary of State Colin Powell stated that after a review of the Iraqi weapons declaration, Iraq was in "material breach" of November's Security Council resolution because of omissions and inconsistencies. **United States:** The Bush administration published a new strategy document on December 10, hinting that it might use nuclear weapons if its troops or allies were attacked with non-conventional weapons. On December 13, Cardinal Bernard Law resigned as archbishop of Boston before the Pope. His resignation followed the public release of clergy personnel records that revealed additional cases of sexual abuse by priests and further cover-up by church leadership. Former Vice-President Al Gore announced on December 16 that he would not make a bid for the Presidency in 2004, leaving the race for the Democratic candidacy wide open. On December 17, President Bush ordered the production of a limited missile defence shield within two years, including the upgrading of early-warning radar stations in Britain and Greenland. A spokeswoman for the Raëlians, a sect that believes space travellers created humans by cloning, said on December 26 that the group had created the first human clone, a 7-pound baby girl. Many in the international community, including President George Bush, condemned the unsubstantiated claim. Already a millionaire, Andrew J. Whittaker claimed a record $314.9-million jackpot in a U.S. lottery on December 26. Opting for the lump-sum payment, Whittaker cleared about $133.4 million after taxes. On December 30, the budget director for the Bush administration revised the estimated cost of a war in Iraq, to between $50 and $60 billion from earlier estimates of $200 billion. **Venezuela:** On December 2, opponents of President Hugo Chávez called a general, nationwide strike against the government in an effort to force the president to call a referendum on his rule. **Yemen:** A North Korean ship stopped and searched by Spanish warships on December 9 was found to be carrying 15 Scud missiles, warheads and chemicals. The ship was later released when the missiles were revealed to be legal purchases by the government of Yemen. On December 30, three American missionaries were killed at a Baptist missionary hospital in Jibla by an Islamic militant. **Yugoslavia:** For the second time in three months, less than 50 percent of voters participated in the Yugoslavian presidential election, invalidating incumbent President Vojislav Kostunica's victory.

CANADA

Police arrested 14 members of Montreal's so-called West End Gang on December 5 on a multitude of drug charges, including the importation of $2.1 billion worth of cocaine and hashish since 1999. In two federal by-elections on December 9, the Bloc Québécois squeezed out narrow victories over the Liberals, winning 50.1 percent of the vote in Berthier-Montcalm and 48.1 percent in Lac-Saint-Jean-Saguenay. On December 10, the House of Commons voted to support ratification of the Kyoto Protocol by a vote of 195 to 77. Canadian Alliance leader Stephen Harper slammed the government for pushing ahead without full details on how the protocol's targets would be met. Statistics Canada announced on December 10 that between 1996 and 2001 the number of people in Canada whose mother tongue was neither English nor French grew by 12.5 percent. After French and English, Chinese was the third most common mother tongue. Six hundred members of the Innu band of Davis Inlet in northern Labrador, one of Canada's most troubled native communities, began the move to nearby Natuashish as part of a $152-million relocation project (December 12). After intense pressure from Jewish organizations and others for not banning Hezbollah outright, the federal government indicated on December 13 that it would change its policy on the Lebanese guerrilla group and ban its political arm. Ottawa had banned only Hezbollah's military arm in late 2001. Following the largest investigation in the city's history, Quebec City police announced on December 18 that they had dismantled a juvenile prostitution ring involving at least 17 girls between the ages of 14 and 17 who had been forced into the trade. In all, 33 men, many of them prominent local businessmen, were charged. On December 20, the Supreme Court ruled that, unlike married couples, people in common-law relationships do not have an automatic right to a 50-50 division of assets in the event of a breakup.

JANUARY 2003

INTERNATIONAL

Afghanistan: On January 28, in the heaviest fighting in months, American and Afghan-government forces exchanged fire with about 80 fighters believed to be loyal to the Taliban. No American or government casualties were reported. **Australia:** Bushfires circled the capital of Canberra on January 19, eventually destroying more than 450 homes and killing four people. **Burundi:** Up to 60,000 civilians fled Burundi amid fighting between the army and ethnic Hutu rebels. Each side was trying to capture as much territory as possible ahead of scheduled peace talks (January 22). **China:** Officials announced on January 2 that China plans to put an astronaut in space during 2003. **Côte d'Ivoire:** On January 25, the government of Cote d'Ivoire agreed in Paris that it would share power with rebel groups. Within hours of the deal being signed, however, tens of thousands of government supporters took to the streets to protest the deal, sparking a week of violence and renewed fighting between rebels and the government. **Cyprus:** In long-awaited talks, Rauf Denktash and Glafcos Clerides, leaders of the rival Cypriot communities, met on January 20 to discuss a UN plan to reunify the island. No agreement was reached, but talks did not break down either. **European Union:** Europeans Jacques Chirac and Gerhard Schroeder met on January 22 and agreed on a joint proposal to the convention drawing up a draft constitution for the EU. The proposal included a stronger president for the European Commission and a longer-term one for the European Council. **Iraq:** Secretary of Defense Donald Rumsfeld ordered about 62,000 troops to the Persian Gulf on January 10, bringing the total deployment in the region to nearly 80,000. On January 16, UN weapons inspectors discovered 11 empty chemical warheads in southern Iraq. Iraq claimed they were listed in their weapons declaration. **Israel and the Palestinian Territories:** In coordinated attacks, two suicide bombers struck a crowded downtown Tel Aviv market on January 5, killing 23 people and injuring more than 100 others. The Al-Aksa Martyrs Brigade claimed responsibility for the attacks. On January 29, Prime Minister Ariel Sharon and his Likud Party soundly beat the Labour Party, almost doubling its seats in the Knesset. **Japan:** On January 14, Prime Minister Junichiro Koizumi angered neighbouring countries by visiting for the third year in a row the controversial Yasukuni shrine, dedicated to the memory of Japan's 2.5 million war dead, including some war criminals. **Mexico:** Foreign Minister Jorge Castañeda resigned on January 10 over frustration at being unable to reach an accord on migration with the United States. After an earthquake on January 22 killed nearly 30 people and injured about 300 others in Colima, President Vicente Fox declared a state of emergency. **Nepal:** After nearly seven years of fighting and more than 7,000 dead, the government of Nepal and Maoist rebels agreed on January 29 to a cease-fire designed to lead to peace talks. **The Netherlands:** In their second general election in nine months, Dutch voters gave the Christian Democrats a narrow victory over the Labour Party on January 23. The anti-immigration party of Pim Fortuyn, who was murdered in 2002, was badly beaten. **North Korea:** The North Korean government announced on January 9 that it was withdrawing from the Treaty on the Nonproliferation of Nuclear Weapons. In a Cabinet-level meeting with South Korea on January 22, North Korean officials announced that it had "no intention of producing nuclear weapons at this stage." After snubbing a South Korean envoy on January 29, President Kim Jong Il called for a promise by America not to attack North Korea. The next day, Kim called U.S. President Bush's State of the Union address a "declaration of aggression." **Sri Lanka:** On January 6 the government and rebel Tamil Tigers began a fourth round of talks aimed at bringing an end to 19 years of civil war and providing the island's minority Tamils with a homeland. **United Kingdom:** Six terror suspects were arrested on January 5 when police found traces of the toxic agent ricin in a London apartment. Authorities believed that the suspects were planning to poison the food supply of British troops. **United Nations:** Minister of Foreign Affairs Dominique de Villepin announced on January 20 that France may use its veto in the Security Council to thwart the U.S. push for a resolution justifying early action against Iraq. German chancellor Gerhard Schroeder also signaled his country's reluctance. Both argued for giving weapons inspections more time. Despite its record on human rights, Libya was chosen to chair the UN Human Rights Commission for 2003 on January 20. Just three members voted against Libya: the United States, Canada and Guatemala. Chief weapons inspector Hans Blix reported to the UN Security Council on January 27 that Iraq was not fully cooperating with inspectors, and had failed to prove it has destroyed its banned weapons. Mohammed El-Baradei, chief of the International Atomic Energy Agency, reported that his team did not turn up any evidence that Iraq had revived its nuclear weapons program. **United States:** On January 3, Democratic North Carolina senator John Edwards announced that he will run for President in 2004. A commuter plane crashed into a building seconds after takeoff on January 8 in North Carolina. All 21 aboard died. In an unprecedented move, on January 11 outgoing Illinois governor George Ryan commuted the death sentences of 156 inmates on death row. The decision was made because of doubts about the Illinois justice system, which he called "arbitrary and capricious." On January 13, Connecticut senator and former vice-presidential candidate Joseph Lieberman announced that he would run for President in 2004. President Bush announced on January 14 that if North Korea agreed not

to continue developing nuclear weapons, he would consider starting a "bold initiative" of food aid. North Korea rejected the advance, insisting on a non-aggression pact. In his January 28 State of the Union address, President Bush presented his case for war with Iraq. Bush also presented plans for a $674-billion tax cut package to help boost the economy, and $400 billion over ten years to modernize Medicare. A January 29 explosion at a Kingston, North Carolina, medical supplies plant killed four people and wounded 36. Richard Reid, accused of attempting to blow up a plane with explosives in his shoes in December 2001, was sentenced to life in prison on January 30. **Yemen:** An overloaded boat carrying Somalis to Yemen caught fire and capsized in the Gulf of Aden on January 15. At least 80 people died.

CANADA

Justice Minister Martin Cauchon stated on January 8 that Ottawa would not back away from its controversial firearms registry, despite a projected $1-billion cost over-run and the renewed opposition of eight provincial governments. Despite being first in division standings, the National Hockey League's Ottawa Senators were granted bankruptcy protection on January 9. The hearing for two U.S. Air Force pilots facing potential court-martial for dropping a 500-pound bomb on a Canadian squad in Afghanistan in April 2002 began on January 14. Four Canadian soldiers died and eight were wounded in the incident. Nova Scotia MP Peter MacKay and Calgary lawyer Jim Prentice were the first two candidates to announce for the federal Progressive Conservative leadership race (January 16). Both candidates emphasized the need to "unite the right" as part of efforts to reconstruct a national alternative to the Liberal Party. On January 20, an Ontario Superior Court judge ordered a new trial for Nicholas Ribic, an Edmonton man who joined the Serbian army and was accused of kidnapping two UN observers in 1995—including

Canadian Captain Patrick Rechner—and using them as human shields in an attempt to stop UN bombing of Serbian positions. In advance of federal-provincial talks on health care, federal Health Minister Anne McLellan stated that Ottawa wants universal home care, a better drug plan and improved efficiencies before it invests billions of dollars of new money. The provinces responded by arguing that they know best how to spend health dollars (January 22). On January 22, the federal government announced that it will invest $172.5 million over five years to upgrade security at Canada's major seaports. Ports will become more like air terminals, with restricted access areas and better scanning capabilities. On January 29, a British Columbia judge threw out the portion of the Elections Act that prohibits publishing how Atlantic Canada voted before western polls close. Elections Canada appealed the decision. Officials revealed on January 29 that Prime Minister Chrétien's campaign finance bill will cost taxpayers $40 million in an election year and $23 million between elections. The proposed law is intended to change the notion that money buys influence by capping donations.

FEBRUARY 2003

INTERNATIONAL

Bolivia: Rioting in the capital of La Paz on February 12 and 13 caused 27 deaths and forced the government to abandon plans to raise taxes in order to secure new loans from the International Monetary Fund. Most of the dead were police shot by soldiers. **Bosnia & Herzegovina:** Former Bosnian President Biljana Plavsic was sentenced to 11 years in prison on February 27 for the persecution of thousands of Muslims and Croats in Bosnia between 1992 and 1995. Plavsic is the only woman to be indicted for war crimes in the former Yugoslavia. **Germany:** In a Hamburg courtroom on February 19, Mounir El-Motassadeq was found guilty of 3,066 counts of being an accessory to murder, attempted murder, and of belonging to a terrorist organization. El-Motassadeq is the first September 11 suspect to be convicted. **Iran:** An Iranian military transport plane carrying 302 members of the elite Republican Guard crashed in southeast Iran on February 20, killing everyone on board. **Iraq:** A UN-appointed panel of arms experts concluded on February 12 that Iraq's al-Samoud 2 ballistic missiles violate the 90-mile range limit imposed on the country. **Israel and the Palestinian Territories:** The Knesset approved the newly established Israeli government on February 28. Prime Minister Ariel Sharon will preside over the hawkish four-party coalition. **NATO:** A rift was exposed in the North Atlantic Alliance on February 10 as France, Germany and Belgium vetoed the U.S. request for NATO to begin sending military hardware to Turkey as a defence for that country in case of war with Iraq. Six days later, a compromise was reached that excluded France from the planning process. **North Korea:** In the latest exchange of words with the United States, North Korea threatened to pull out of the armistice agreement that ended the Korean War in 1953 (February 18). The U.S. announced on February 26 that North Korea has reactivated its nuclear plant at Yongbyon, which allowed the country to convert nuclear waste into weapons-grade plutonium. **Philippines:** U.S. marines and special operations forces were dispatched to the Philippines on February 20 to help the Filipino military root out and destroy the Muslim extremist group Abu Sayyaf. **Qatar:** On February 11, Qatar's al-Jazeera television network released a recording believed to be of Osama bin Laden, warning of future attacks against the U.S. and encouraging Iraq to defend against a possible U.S.-led attack. The Bush administration cited the recording as further evidence of Iraqi connections with al-Qaeda. **Serbia & Montenegro:** On February 4, the Yugoslavian parliament voted to rename the country Serbia and

Montenegro. The change reflects Montenegro's desire for independence. The NATO-led peacekeeping force in the autonomous province of Kosovo arrested three ethnic-Albanian former guerillas wanted by the UN war crimes tribunal (February 17). **South Korea:** On February 18, two subway cars were engulfed in flames when a suicidal man ignited a bottle filled with paint thinner; 133 passengers died, but the suspect, Kim Dae Han, survived. **Turkey:** Following a February 21 offer of $15 billion in economic and military aid in exchange for allowing the U.S. to launch an offensive against Iraq from their territory, Turkey signaled its willingness to host U.S. troops. **United Kingdom:** Some 2,300 soldiers and police, complete with armoured vehicles, were deployed to London's Heathrow airport on February 12 in response to a possible terrorist missile attack. Dolly, the sheep famous for being the first mammal to be cloned from an adult cell, was put down on February 14 after she was found to be suffering from a progressive lung disease. It was unclear whether her early death was in any way connected to the fact that she was a clone. **United Nations:** U.S. Secretary of State Colin Powell pressed the U.S. case for war against Iraq, telling the Security Council on February 5 that Saddam Hussein was an imminent threat to world security, had continually deceived UN weapons inspectors, had links to al-Qaeda, and possessed mobile biological weapons factories. A second report by chief weapons inspectors Hans Blix and Mohamed El-Baradei to the Security Council on February 14 concluded that Iraq is becoming more cooperative and forthcoming about its weapons programs. The U.S. and U.K. claimed this was a delay tactic; France and Germany used the findings to intensify their opposition to military action against Iraq. On February 22, Chief Weapons Inspector Hans Blix told Iraq to dismantle its al-Samoud 2 missiles. Five days later, Iraqi leader Saddam Hussein agreed "in principle" to begin dismantling the missiles. In a draft resolution submitted to the Security Council on February 22, the U.S., U.K. and Spain stated that "Iraq has failed to take the final opportunity" to disarm, and that it was time to authorize the use of military force against the country. On February 24, France, Germany and Russia submitted a counter-resolution seeking intensified and extended inspections. **United States:** Space shuttle *Columbia* broke up on February 1 as it re-entered Earth's atmosphere on its way to the Kennedy Space Center. All seven crew were killed. On February 13, a panel commissioned to investigate the accident announced that their preliminary conclusion into the accident was that a hole in the left wing allowed superheated gas into the shuttle. President Bush submitted his fiscal year 2004 budget to Congress on February 3. The budget totaled $2.23 trillion and predicted record deficits in coming years. Included in the budget: $380 billion for defense, a 4.2 percent increase over 2003. Not included: funding for the war in Iraq. The attorneys-general of Connecticut, Massachusetts, Maine, New Jersey, Rhode Island, Washington and New York sued the Environmental Protection Agency on February 19 for not regulating carbon dioxide emissions under the Clean Air Act. On February 21, a pyrotechnics display set off during a concert by the rock band Great White ignited an inferno that engulfed a small nightclub in West Warwick, Rhode Island. The fire killed 97 people. Signaling a policy shift, the White House announced that Iraq must disarm and that Saddam Hussein must go into exile if Iraq is to avoid war. **Venezuela:** A crippling nation-wide strike ended on February 2, although oil-industry workers remained behind the picket lines. **Worldwide:** On February 15, millions of protesters gathered in New York, London, Melbourne, Paris, Seoul, Toronto and other cities around the globe to rally against military action in Iraq.

CANADA

A February 2 ice storm hit south-central New Brunswick. Officials said the storm was worse than the 1998 ice storm that crippled parts of Quebec and eastern Ontario. Days later, a second ice storm hit the region, leaving about 60,000 homes and businesses without power. On February 4, Regina, Saskatchewan, police recovered a missing computer hard drive with personal and financial information on approximately one million Canadians. Federal and provincial health care officials emerged from talks on February 5 with a deal that would see billions more dollars going to health care over the next three years. The federal government will give $13.5 billion in new money, including $9.5 billion for programs resulting from the Roy Romanow report. In the wake of a $428-million loss for 2002, Air Canada warned on February 6 that it may undertake large-scale layoffs, wage cuts, and the sale of its newly launched Jazz regional airline. On February 13, Alberta's privacy commissioner rejected the province's decision to put photos, health and personal information on the Internet about potential adoptees under provincial care as "insensitive and badly thought out." One girl in foster care discovered she was up for adoption when told by a classmate. The race for the leadership of the Liberal Party formally began on February 13, as Heritage Minister Sheila Copps announced her candidacy to replace Prime Minister Chrétien. The family of Private Richard Green, one of four Canadians killed on a training mission in Afghanistan last year, filed a wrongful death claim against the U.S. government on February 13. On February 17, forty Edmontonians whose families were touched by cancer skated their way into the *Guinness Book of World Records* by playing the world's longest outdoor hockey game. After 80 hours of play, they raised more than $83,000 for cancer research. On February 20, twelve years after 17-year-old Neil Stonechild was found dead in a frozen field outside Saskatoon, Saskatchewan Justice Minister Eric Cline announced a judicial inquiry to provide "a public airing" into police actions involving the Cree teen on the day he died. Brian Doyle, a St. John's, Newfoundland, man who killed his friend's mother and stayed silent while another man went to prison, pleaded guilty to the 1991 murder on February 20. He will spend at least the next 18 years behind bars.

MARCH 2003

INTERNATIONAL

Afghanistan: In their largest operation in more than a year, about 1,000 U.S. soldiers raided Kandahar on March 20 to root out al-Qaeda members. **Cyprus:** Talks to reunify Greek and Turkish Cypriots fell apart after Turkish Cypriot leader Rauf Denktash rejected a UN-sponsored agreement on March 11. **Germany:** In an effort to revive Germany's flagging economy, Chancellor Gerhard Schroeder unveiled a package of reforms aimed at cutting unemployment benefits, easing stifling labour laws, and helping small business. While trade unions widely disagreed with the plans, many on the right thought it too timid (March 14). **Greece:** The trial of 19 people accused of belonging to the leftist November 17 terrorist group opened on March 2. Officials say the organization has murdered 23 people since 1973. **European Union:** For the first time, a military force under the aegis of the EU undertook a peacekeeping role. The 300-plus troops, under the overall command of a German admiral, replaced a NATO-led force monitoring peace in Macedonia (March 31). **Iraq:** On March 19, the U.S. officially launched Operation Iraqi Freedom, with a "decapitation attack" targeting Saddam Hussein and other leaders in Baghdad. The U.S. launched a second round of air strikes against critical targets in Baghdad and ground troops entered the country for the first time on March 20. The major phase of the war began on March 21 with heavy aerial attacks on Baghdad and other cities. The campaign, dubbed "shock and awe," was intended to promptly overwhelm Iraqi forces. Coalition forces encountered fierce resistance near the southern city of Nasiriya on March 23. Iraqi troops captured 12 members of the 50th Ordnance Maintenance Company on March 23; al-Jazeera subsequently broadcast images of the captives, some of them apparently dead with gunshot wounds to the forehead. On March 24, coalition troops reached within 50 miles of Baghdad. Significance resistance was met from Iraqi soldiers and paramilitary fighters in Nasiriya and Basra. On March 25, the U.S. military was forced to adjust its ground strategy in the face of increasing attacks from Iraq militias (called fedayeen). The northern front of the Iraq war opened on March 26 as about 1,000 coalition paratroopers landed in Kurdish-controlled northern Iraq. U.S. forces intensified their bombardment of Baghdad on March 27, targeting government buildings. An Iraqi suicide bomber killed four U.S. soldiers from the Third Infantry Division near Najaf. Iraqi officials praised the attacks and promised more of its kind. On March 30, U.S. marines and army troops launched the first attack on Iraq's Republican Guard forces, about 65 miles outside Baghdad. **Israel and the Palestinian Territories:** A suicide bomber struck a bus on March 5 in Haifa, killing 15 people. Hamas claimed responsibility for the attack. Israel retaliated by seizing territory in Gaza. On March 10, the Palestinian parliament approved the establishment of the post of prime minister; Yasser Arafat nominated Mahmoud Abbas, second-in-command of the Palestine Liberation Organization, to fill it. The prime minister will be responsible for domestic matters, while Arafat will continue to handle foreign relations. **Kashmir:** On March 23, 24 Hindu Brahmins were executed in an attack at Nandimarg. India blamed the attack on Pakistani militants. **The Netherlands:** The Hague-based International Criminal Court

officially opened on March 11. The court will prosecute human rights abuses. The U.S. did not sign the treaty that created the court. **North Korea:** Four North Korean fighter jets came within 50 feet of an unarmed U.S. Air Force spy plane over the Sea of Japan on March 3. The U.S. said the plane was on a reconnaissance mission to track the launching of ballistic missiles. **Philippines:** A bomb attack at an airport in Davao killed 21 people on March 4. Officials suspected the Muslim separatist group Moro Islamic Liberation Front to be behind the attack. **Serbia & Montenegro:** Prime Minister Zoran Djindjic, a Serb, was gunned down outside his Belgrade office on March 12. Six days later, the Serbian parliament elected pro-Western reformer Zoran Zivkovic to replace Djindjic. **Turkey:** On March 1, the Turkish parliament rejected the U.S. plan to base 62,000 troops in Turkey in support of an offensive against Iraq. In a special vote on March 9, Recep Tayyip Erdogan of the Justice and Development Party won a seat in parliament and became prime minister. He had been barred from becoming prime minister following his party's dominance of the November 2002 election because of a 1998 conviction for "inciting religious hatred." A constitutional amendment allowed him to run again and assume the post. **United Nations:** On March 5, France and Russia threatened to veto the resolution introduced by the U.S., U.K. and Spain calling for the use of force to disarm Iraq. Chief weapons inspectors Hans Blix and Mohammed El-Baradei told the Security Council on March 7 that pressure on Iraq had been effective in getting the country to disarm. El-Baradei stated that documents showing that Iraq tried to buy uranium from Niger were forged, and that the Bush administration had used the evidence to justify a pre-emptive strike against Iraq. In debate following the weapons inspection report on March 7, U.K. foreign minister Jack Straw proposed a compromise that would give Iraq until March 17 to completely disarm. France, Russia and Germany said they would not vote for the resolution. When it became clear that France would veto a joint UN resolution that authorized the use of force against Iraq, the U.S., U.K. and Spain withdrew their proposed resolution. **United States:** In a nationally televised press conference on March 6, President Bush told his country that Saddam Hussein is a direct threat to the U.S. and that the U.S. will attack Iraq unilaterally if necessary. On March 13, the Senate voted 64 to 33 to outlaw partial-birth abortions, a procedure used to end pregnancies in their second and third trimesters. Abortion-rights advocates promised to challenge the constitutionality of the law if signed by President Bush. On March 17, President Bush told his country that war with Iraq would be avoided only if Saddam Hussein stepped down within 48 hours. After a bitter fight, the Senate voted 52 to 48 on March 19 against drilling for oil in the Arctic National Wildlife Refuge. **Worldwide:** The World Health Organization reported on March 15 that a mystery illness with origins in Asia is a virus called Severe Acute Respiratory Syndrome (SARS), and is a "worldwide health threat." On March 25, the U.S.-based Center for Disease Control said that a "previously unrecognized virus from the coronavirus family" was the root of the illness.

CANADA

On March 5, the Canadian Forces destroyer HMCS *Iroquois* set sail again for the Persian Gulf to be the flagship of an international naval group, but without a helicopter. The government was criticized for not being able to find a spare helicopter to outfit the ship. The United States imposed a 3.94 percent tariff on Canadian wheat, angering Canadian farmers who claimed the U.S. has among the world's most heavily subsidized farm economies. U.S. farmers were seeking a tariff in the 14-25 percent range (March 5). On March 11, Edmonton passed a bylaw that would allow police to ticket schoolyard bullies who repeatedly push, shove and name-call

their peers. It is the first of its kind in Canada. An overnight blaze on March 13 destroyed much of Edmonton's Old Strathcona area, a historic district that was once the staging ground for the Yukon gold rush. Two former Saskatoon police officers were convicted on March 13 of abandoning an aboriginal man on the outskirts of town three years ago on a cold January night. The pair were sent to jail for eight months. A sudden turnaround in the Quebec public opinion polls provoked Premier Bernard Landry into calling an April election (March 15). Landry also unveiled the Parti Québécois platform for the election. The plan included a promise to draw up a blueprint for sovereignty, as well as a four-day workweek, improved health services and better schools. Ottawa pledged a further $250 million in aid to war-torn Afghanistan on March 17. The commitment doubled the amount given to Afghanistan since 1990, and is the largest Canadian aid commitment ever made to a single country. On March 20, the military hearing on the "friendly fire" deaths of four Canadian soldiers in Afghanistan last year recommended against court-martial and criminal charges, opting instead for administrative punishment. Families of the slain soldiers were upset by the decision and its timing: the day after the U.S. invasion of Iraq. On March 25, Ottawa pledged to establish 10 new national parks and protected marine areas over the next five years, at a cost of $220 million. In an effort to revitalize an industry hit hard by the softwood lumber dispute with the United States, British Columbia said it would relax its timber-cutting rules (March 26).

APRIL 2003

INTERNATIONAL

China: In a dramatic about-face, the Chinese government admitted on April 20 that it had under-reported the number of SARS victims in the country. Officials also cancelled the week-long May Day celebrations and fired the health minister. **Cuba:** On April 1, hijackers commandeered a plane bound for Havana and demanded that it land in Key West, Florida. On April 2, armed men hijacked a government-run ferry; they surrendered to Cuban authorities on April 4. A week later, Cuba executed the three men who hijacked the ferry and gave life sentences to four others. In a further crackdown on dissident activity, Cuban courts handed stiff sentences to advocates of democratic reform on April 7. Nearly 80 people, including journalists and librarians, face terms of up to 27 years in prison. **European Union:** Hungary voted overwhelmingly in favour of joining the EU on April 12, though voter turnout was low. In the largest expansion in the European Union's history, leaders of the 10 acceding nations met at the Acropolis in Athens, Greece, and signed accession treaties (April 16). They will formally join the other 15 members in May 2004. **Iran:** On April 28, the Bush administration confirmed that it had reached a cease-fire agreement with the People's Mujahedeen, a terrorist organization that was active in Iran and Iraq. **Iraq:** U.S. troops seized Saddam International Airport outside Baghdad on April 4. In a symbolic gesture, it was renamed Baghdad International Airport. On April 5, U.S. forces rolled into the capital city of Baghdad in tanks and other vehicles and engaged in firefights with Iraqi troops. Iraqi casualties were heavy, though resistance was much weaker than anticipated. Allies bombed the Basra home of Iraqi General Ali Hassan al-Majid, known as "Chemical Ali" for launching chemical attacks on the Kurds in the late 1980s. The general was believed to have died in the attacks. British forces took control of Basra, Iraq's second-largest city, on April 7. Reportedly countering sniper fire, U.S. tanks fired on the Palestine Hotel (April 8), a building where many foreign journalists were based and which served as the Iraq bureau for the al-Jazeera network. Three journalists were killed. On April 9,

Baghdad fell as U.S. forces took control of the city. On April 10, a major statue of Saddam Hussein was symbolically toppled. The oil-rich northern city of Kirkuk fell to Kurd fighters on April 11. The U.S. assumed control of the city as part of efforts to allay Turkish fears about a Kurdish independence movement spreading to within its borders. The Pentagon officially declared the end of Saddam Hussein's regime after Tikrit— Saddam's hometown—fell to U.S. forces on April 14. On April 15, U.S. forces captured Abu Abbas, a leader of the Palestine Liberation Front, the group that seized the Italian cruise ship *Achille Lauro* in 1985 and killed an American passenger. Retired Lieutenant-General Jay Garner arrived in Baghdad on April 21 to assume the post of civil administrator. Garner, charged with reconstruction and humanitarian aid in post-Saddam Iraq, promised to restore services and establish an interim government as soon as possible. Tariq Aziz, deputy prime minister of the Saddam regime, turned himself in to U.S. troops in Baghdad on April 24. On April 28, U.S. administrators and about 300 Iraqi leaders agreed to hold a national conference to elect a transitional government. **Israel and the Palestinian Territories:** Yasser Arafat endorsed a Cabinet in a last-minute compromise with Prime Minister Mahmoud Abbas on April 23, paving the way for the U.S. to introduce a new peace plan. On April 30, U.S. officials presented Israeli Prime Minister Ariel Sharon and Palestinian Prime Minister Mahmoud Abbas a "road map" for peace in the Middle East. The plan calls on both sides to make concessions and end violence, and envisions the creation of a Palestinian state by 2005. **New Zealand:** In Antarctic waters off the New Zealand coast, fishermen caught a young female colossal squid on April 4, weighing 330 pounds and measuring 16 feet. It was only the second such squid ever caught. **Nigeria:** On April 22, an election commission declared incumbent president Olusegun Obasanjo victorious over opposition leader Muhammadu Buhari, by a margin of 60 percent to 20 percent. Accusing Obasanjo's party of election fraud, Buhari rejected the count. **North Korea:** In a move that ended months of impasse, North Korean officials agreed to direct, one-on-one talks with Washington. In a first, China would also be invited to the meetings (April 16). During talks with American and Chinese officials on April 24, North Korean officials admitted that the country actually possessed a nuclear bomb, and threatened to "test, export or use" the weapon. In a reversal of Clinton-era policies towards North Korea, on April 29 the U.S. rejected the idea of making economic concessions to North Korea in exchange for a commitment to abandon its nuclear program. **Philippines:** In the second such attack in a month, a bomb was detonated near a ferry terminal in Davao on April 2, killing 16 people. Officials blamed the Muslim separatist group the Moro Islamic Liberation Front. **Saudi Arabia:** The U.S. government announced on April 29 that it plans to withdraw its combat troops from Saudi Arabia by the summer. Defense Secretary Donald Rumsfeld cited the fall of Saddam Hussein as the reason for the decision. **Sierra Leone:** The first public hearings of the Truth and Reconciliation Commission took place on April 14. The commission will take testimony from some 700 victims and participants in Sierra Leone's decade-long civil war, which ended in 2001. **South Korea:** Stating his interest in maintaining close ties with the United States, President No Mu-hyon agreed to send about 700 medical and other non-combat personnel to support coalition forces in Iraq. **South Africa:** In a landmark decision on April 15, the South African government agreed to pay reparations of $85 million to the families of more than 19,000 apartheid victims. **United Kingdom:** On April 27, Gerry Adams, president of Sinn Fein, announced that the Irish Republican Army would disarm and ban paramilitary activity as long as other groups meet their commit-

ments to the Good Friday Peace Accord. **United Nations:** On April 16, U.S. President Bush urged the UN to lift sanctions on Iraq now that Saddam Hussein was out of power. Lifting the sanctions was seen as a way to enable Iraqi oil money to help pay for the reconstruction of the battered country. **United States:** President Bush appointed Alan Greenspan, chairman of the Federal Reserve Board, to a fifth term on April 22. Greenspan's current term expires in June 2004.

CANADA

On April 1, Newfoundland and Labrador became the first province to ban the use of hand-held cellphones while driving, replicating measures taken in 30 countries around the world. Following 10 years of negotiations, the federal government granted Yukon Territory full control over its natural resources on April 1. The move is one of the final steps on the road to becoming a province. Massive downpours and sudden snowmelt flooded homes and destroyed roads and bridges in Nova Scotia, New Brunswick and parts of Newfoundland. Two people died when their car was swept from the road near Bridgewater, N.S., and into the LeHave River (April 3). Robert Ghiz, the 29-year-old son of the late Prince Edward Island premier Joe Ghiz, followed in his father's footsteps to win the leadership of P.E.I.'s Liberal Party on April 5. On April 9, Alberta announced its 10th straight budgetary surplus ($1.1 billion) alongside a spending increase of nearly five percent. Finance Minister John Manley finally tossed his hat into the Liberal leadership race on April 10, joining Heritage Minister Sheila Copps and former Finance Minister Paul Martin. A new Liberal leader will be chosen in November 2003. The Quebec Liberal Party knocked the sovereigntist Parti Québécois out of power after nine years in office after elections on April 14. Jean Charest's Liberals won 76 of 125 seats in the snap election, called by Premier Bernard Landry in March. Stan and Frank Koebel, the brothers at the centre of the tainted water scandal in Walkerton, Ontario, in 2000, were charged with 12 offences, including breach of trust and public endangerment. Seven people died when deadly E. coli bacteria contaminated the town's water supply, which the Koebel brothers were responsible for (April 23). Eleven years after its initial moratorium, the federal government closed what remained of the Atlantic cod fishery, ending a centuries-old industry. Despite increasingly stringent conservation attempts, cod stocks showed no signs of recovery. About 1,000 commercial fishermen were offered $44 million in compensation (April 24). Two Sikhs, Ripudaman Singh Malik, 56, a wealthy Vancouver businessman, and Ajaib Singh Bagri, 53, a Kamloops, B.C., mill worker, pleaded not guilty to the murder of 329 people as the long-awaited trial into the 1985 Air India bombing began in Vancouver on April 28.

MAY 2003

INTERNATIONAL

Algeria: A 6.7 magnitude earthquake struck near the capital Algiers, killing more than 2,200 people and injuring roughly 7,000 (May 21). **Argentina:** Former president Carlos Menem withdrew from the presidential runoff on May 14, handing the presidency to Néstor Kirchner. **Australia:** Governor-General Peter Hollingworth resigned on May 11 after controversy about his conduct. Hollingworth was alleged to have protected pedophiles in the church while he was the Anglican archbishop of Brisbane, and to have raped a woman in the mid-1960s. **Belgium:** The Flemish Liberals, led by incumbent Prime Minister Guy Verhofstadt, won the May 18 general election. While the Green Party was wiped out in the election, the far-right Vlaams Blok, which wants Flemish independence, gained ground. **France:** On May 13, more than 850,000 public workers participated in a one-day strike to protest against the proposed pension reform plan. **India:** In a move to curb hostilities with Pakistan, Prime Minister Atal Bihari Vajpayee resumed dialogue with Pakistan and announced the restoration of civilian air travel between the two countries (May 2). A month-long heatwave in southern India, with temperatures as high as 50 degrees Celsius, killed over 1,300 people. **Indonesia:** On May 18, President Megawati Sukarnoputri declared martial law in Aceh in an attempt to crack down on the separatist Free Aceh Movement after continued violence ended a cease-fire. A day later, more than 1,000 Indonesian troops begin offensive operations in Aceh. **Iraq:** On May 16, U.S. and British diplomats postponed self-rule in Iraq, by deciding against allowing Iraqi opposition groups to form an interim government. Instead, Iraqi exiles and opposition leaders were to have a consultative role. **Israel and the Palestinian Territories:** In the highest level talks between Israelis and Palestinians in two years, Palestinian Prime Minister Mahmoud Abbas and Israeli Prime Minister Ariel Sharon met on May 17 to discuss the U.S.-proposed "road map" for peace in the Middle East. The pair failed to make any progress. A Palestinian suicide bomber killed two settlers in Hebron hours before the meeting. Prime Minister Sharon convinced the Israeli Cabinet to accept the "road map" on May 25. While this was the first time an Israeli government had formally endorsed the creation of a Palestinian state, the acceptance came with a long list of conditions. **Morocco:** On May 17, twelve suicide bombers launched coordinated attacks in Casablanca, killing more than 40 people. A Moroccan terrorist cell was suspected to be behind the attacks. **Myanmar:** The ruling military regime announced on May 30 that it had put Aung San Suu Kyi and other members of the National League for Democracy in "protective custody." **Peru:** On May 29, a student was killed and more than 70 people were injured as troops clashed with protestors across Peru after President Alejandro Toledo, faced with strikes by teachers and health workers, declared a 30-day state of emergency. **Russia:** More than 40 people died when a truck carrying explosives blew up near a government complex in Znamenskoye, Chechnya, on May 12. **Saudi Arabia:** Thirty-four people died in three separate but coordinated terrorist attacks inside residential compounds in Saudi Arabia on May 12. Al-Qaeda is suspected to be behind the attack, which the U.S. government had previously warned Saudi Arabia about. **Switzerland:** Members of the World Health Organization adopted the Framework Convention on Tobacco Control on May 21. If sufficiently ratified by member nations, the anti-smoking treaty will ban tobacco advertising and force warning labels to occupy 30 percent of tobacco products. **Turkey:** A 6.4 magnitude earthquake in southeastern Turkey on May 1 destroyed a bridge and dozens of buildings, killing more than 100 people. **United Kingdom:** On May 1, Prime Minister Tony Blair postponed a Northern Ireland vote for power-sharing until the fall because, he said, the Irish Republican Army had failed to commit to end violence. **United Nations:** On May 9, the U.S., Britain and Spain submitted a proposal to the UN Security Council to give the United States and Britain authority over Iraq's government and finances. The proposal also calls on the UN to lift sanctions against Iraq. The Security Council voted unanimously on May 22 to end 13 years of economic sanctions against Iraq. The decision also gave the U.S. and Britain broad power to run Iraq's government and economy until an Iraqi government was in place. On May 23, UN Secretary-General Kofi Annan appointed Sérgio Vieira de Mello of Portugal as his Special Representative to Iraq. De Mello will coordinate aid from the UN and non-governmental organizations, oversee the return of refugees, and ensure that human rights are upheld. **United States:** In a nationally televised speech from the aircraft carrier *Abraham Lincoln* on May 1, President Bush declared U.S. victory in the war in Iraq and combat operations over. Bush also declared an end to combat operations in Afghanistan, marking the formal transition from military operations to rebuilding. On May 1, the House of Representatives voted 375 to 41 in favour of a $15-billion program to fight HIV/AIDS around the world. The decision included a provision that one-third of the money was to be used to encourage abstinence. President Bush announced on May 6 that L. Paul Bremer, a former diplomat and former chief of counterterrorism, would replace Jay Garner as top civilian administrator in Iraq. On May 9, the House of Representatives voted 222 to 203 in favour of a 10-year, $550-billion tax cut proposed by President Bush. The plan provides the greatest relief to wealthier Americans, by reducing taxes on dividends and capital gains. The U.S. government ordered the expulsion of 14 Cuban diplomats on May 13, citing "inappropriate and unacceptable activities," a euphemism for spying. On May 27, Secretary of Defense Donald Rumsfeld acknowledged that Saddam Hussein may have ordered the destruction of all his biological and chemical weapons before the U.S.-led invasion began. Scientists announced on May 29 the creation of a cloned mule, named Idaho Gem, from a cell from a mule fetus and a horse egg. This was the first cloning of a member of the horse family. Secretary of State Colin Powell denied on May 30 that intelligence about Iraq's biological and chemical weapons was distorted or exaggerated to justify an attack on Iraq. British Prime Minister Tony Blair also denied such accusations in a similar speech that day. **Zimbabwe:** In a meeting in Harare on May 5, the presidents of South Africa, Nigeria and Malawi failed to resolve the growing turmoil between Zimbabwe's President Robert Mugabe and opposition head Morgan Tsvangirai.

CANADA

In a landmark ruling on May 1, the British Columbia Court of Appeal gave Ottawa and the provinces until July 2004 to change existing marriage laws to allow for gay wedlock. This was the most senior Canadian court to endorse same-sex marriage. Ottawa declared infamous Holocaust denier Ernst Zundel a national security risk on May 2, a designation that should hasten his deportation to Germany where he faces charges of incitement of hatred. The federal government announced on May 5 that Canada would take over international command of the peacekeeping mission in Kabul, Afghanistan. Nearly 1,800 troops will deploy with the force, beginning in August 2003. On May 14, the World Health Organization removed Toronto from its list of SARS-affected areas. Only twelve days later, however, Toronto was placed back on the list after the city informed the WHO of eight new probable and 26 suspected cases, its first new cases in a month. A cow in Alberta was diagnosed with Mad Cow disease on May 20. The news immediately prompted the U.S., Australia, South Korea and Japan to ban imports of Canadian beef, cattle and animal feed. A group of 25 peacekeepers announced on May 27 that it was suing the Canadian Forces for $60 million because of psychological stress suffered while on duty. The lawsuit alleged that Ottawa did not offer enough counseling for depression and trauma. In a preliminary ruling on May 27, the World Trade Organization said Canada's softwood lumber royalties are not an unfair subsidy, as U.S. lumber interests have claimed. On May 28, the Ontario government announced that it would spend $720 million on assisting health-care workers and facilities involved in the SARS fight. Despite having only one confirmed case of Mad Cow disease, food inspectors singled out nearly 1,000 cattle for slaughter and quarantined 17 farms in Alberta, British Columbia and Saskatchewan on May 28. With the approval of

Vancouver-area Bishop Michael Ingham, an Anglican priest blessed a same-sex union using a special rite. The head of the Anglican Church, the Archbishop of Canterbury, said he was "saddened" by the event (May 29).

JUNE 2003

INTERNATIONAL

Afghanistan: A suicide bomber struck a military bus on June 7, killing four German peacekeepers and wounding 30 others. Al-Qaeda was suspected to be behind the attack. **Democratic Republic of the Congo:** On June 6, a French-led peacekeeping force began arriving in Bunia to bolster UN efforts to stem the brutal inter-tribal violence between the Lendus and Hema ethnic groups. **European Union:** The Convention on the Future of Europe ended on June 12 with a draft EU constitution that included more than 400 articles. The constitution calls for the establishment of two permanent presidents, a parliament and a foreign minister. If approved, the constitution will give EU laws precedence over those of the individual nations. Voters in Poland and the Czech Republic overwhelmingly approved entry to the EU in referendums on June 9 and 14, respectively. **Finland:** Finland's first female prime minister, Anneli Jaatteenmaki, resigned on June 18 after only two months in office. She was accused of failing to tell the truth about documents with which she embarrassed her main opponent during the April elections. **France:** At a meeting of the Group of Eight leading industrial countries in Evian, leaders discussed the nuclear weapons programs of North Korea and Iran (June 1). The next day, summit leaders urged the two countries to dismantle their programs. Large strikes and demonstrations were held across France on June 10, in a continuation of strike activity against proposals for pension reform. **Iran:** Both the U.S. and EU announced on June 19 that they would not tolerate an Iranian nuclear bomb and intimated that force could be used, as a last resort, to stop countries from obtaining them. Also that day, the International Atomic Energy Agency accused Iran of concealing some of its nuclear activities. **Iraq:** On June 16, U.S. forces apprehended Abed Hamid Mahmud al-Tikrit, Saddam Hussein's presidential secretary and fourth on the most-wanted list in Iraq. In an attempt to end a series of deadly attacks on U.S. and British troops, American troops carried out about 20 raids in the Tigris River valley on June 29. **Israel and the Palestinian Territories:** On June 6, the militant Islamic group Hamas withdrew from cease-fire negotiations with Prime Minister Mahmoud Abbas, claiming he yielded too much at his summit with Israeli Prime Minister Ariel Sharon. The "road map" peace process faced its first major obstacles after a series of suicide attacks and counterattacks. On June 9, three militant Islamic groups collaborated in an attack on Israeli soldiers in Hebron, killing four. On June 10, Israel attempted to assassinate Hamas leader Dr. Abdel Aziz Rantisi. On June 11, a Palestinian suicide bomber blew himself up on a bus in Jerusalem, killing 16 and wounding more than 100. On June 27, Israeli troops began leaving parts of the Gaza Strip as part of a pullout agreement. Palestinians were to assume a security role there and work to intercept attacks by Islamic militants. The pullout and assumption of security duties were the first coordinated steps in the "road map" peace process. Palestinian militant groups Hamas and Islamic Jihad announced a cease-fire on June 29, vowing to end attacks on Israeli targets for three months. The group al-Fatah announced a six-month truce. **Italy:** On June 18, the Italian government passed legislation protecting five senior politicians, including Prime Minister Silvio Berlusconi, from prosecution while in office. Berlusconi, who would assume

the presidency of the European Union only two weeks later, was on trial for charges of corruption. The trial was suspended. **Jordan:** At a June 4 summit meeting with Israeli, Palestinian and Jordanian leaders, U.S. President Bush discussed his "road map" for Middle Eastern peace. On June 17, in its first election since King Abdullah dissolved parliament two years ago, independents loyal to the king won most of the 110 seats in the expanded legislature. **Libya:** On June 14, leader Moammar Qaddafi fired his prime minister and called for the radical reform or abolition of the country's public sector, signaling that Libya may open up to foreign companies. **Mauritania:** An attempted rebel coup against President Maaouya Ould Sid Ahmed Taya was suppressed after heavy fighting in the capital Nouakchott on June 8. The uprising was the most serious challenge so far to the rule of President Taya, who had recently cracked down on suspected Islamists. **Myanmar:** On June 16, members of the Association of Southeast Asian Nations condemned the Myanmar government for its crackdown on opposition leader Aung San Suu Kyi and her supporters. **North Korea:** On June 9, North Korea continued its nuclear diplomacy, by saying it needed nuclear weapons to counter America's "hostile policy" towards it, but also for cutting its armed forces and putting more cash into the economy. **Pakistan:** At a June 24 meeting at Camp David, U.S. President George Bush offered Pakstani president Pervez Musharraf a $3-billion package in military aid, but not the F-16 fighters that Musharraf specifically wanted. **South Korea:** On June 5, the U.S. and South Korean governments agreed that 14,000 soldiers would be gradually withdrawn from the border with North Korea. **United Kingdom:** Gordon Brown, chancellor of the Exchequer, announced on June 9 that Britain would not adopt the euro, saying that England had not met certain economic conditions required before changing its currency. **United States:** On June 3, government officials indicated that former CIA analysts were being employed to review top-secret National Intelligence estimates to determine if the intelligence community exaggerated Iraq's biological and chemical weapons capabilities. The Senate and the House of Representatives also indicated that they plan to request a similar review. Homemaking diva Martha Stewart was indicted on June 4 on charges of conspiracy, obstruction of justice and securities fraud, stemming from her December 2001 sale of shares in ImClone Systems. The House of Representatives voted 282 to 139 to ban late-term "partial-birth" abortions on June 4. Amid concern about the growing number of U.S. combat deaths in Iraq, President Bush said on June 21 that Hussein loyalists were trying to "kill and intimidate" Americans. In a bipartisan vote, Congress approved the largest-ever expansion of Medicare. The drug plan will cost about $400 billion over 10 years. **Worldwide:** The widely anticipated fifth instalment of the Harry Potter series, *Harry Potter and the Order of the Phoenix,* enjoyed record sales upon its release on June 21.

CANADA

McGill University nutritionists announced on June 4 that they had developed a healthier cooking oil. The blend of plant sterols and olive, flaxseed, coconut and tropical oils was said to increase the body's metabolism rather than being stored as fat. Former Native leader David Ahenakew, who provoked a national furor when he called Jews "a disease," was charged with promoting hate on June 11. Prime Minister Chrétien's reform of election financing was pushed through Parliament on June 11. Corporate donations were cut back but taxpayers will be required to pay $1.75 per vote per party, based on the previous election. In its first budget since taking power in April, the new Liberal government in Quebec slashed business subsidies by nearly $800 million,

cut government expenditures, and increased health and education funding (June 12). Though defeated in recent elections, Bernard Landry won the right to remain the leader of the Parti Québécois until spring 2005 (June 14). On June 17, Ottawa introduced legislation to make same-sex marriages legal, while at the same time permitting churches and religious groups to "sanctify marriages as they see it." The decision follows rulings in favour of same-sex marriages by courts in British Columbia, Quebec and Ontario. The federal government promised $190 million in compensation for farmers affected by the Mad Cow crisis, and up to $300 million if the provinces also contributed to the plan (June 19). Montreal-based photojournalist Zahra Kazemi, a dual citizen of Iran and Canada, was arrested in Iran on June 23 while taking pictures of protestors. She died of a fractured skull while in custody, though Iranian officials said she had suffered a stroke. After diplomatic pressure, Vice-President Mohammad Ali Abtahi admitted that Kazemi had been beaten while being questioned by the security force loyal to the hard-line clerics. Privacy Commissioner George Radwanski resigned on June 24 amid investigations by the Auditor General and a parliamentary committee into his lavish food and travel spending. Radwanski and a female assistant expensed $500,000 over two years for travel and meals, much of it enjoyed together.

JULY 2003

INTERNATIONAL

Burundi: A nascent cease-fire broke down on July 21 as rebels shelled the capital Bujumbura and fought with the army in the streets. At least 170 were killed and thousands had fled their homes. **China:** On July 1, about 500,000 people in Hong Kong protested against the establishment of proposed anti-subversion laws that would impose lengthy jail terms for sedition, secession or treason. A powerful explosion at a fireworks factory in northern China on July 29 left 29 dead and more than 100 injured. **European Union:** On July 27, France and Germany, whose economies have struggled in recent years, called for a more flexible interpretation of the stability and growth pact rules, which require countries using the euro to keep their public deficits to less than 3 percent of GDP. Most of the EU's smaller governments disagreed with the proposal. **Iraq:** With allied troops under continued attacks by Baath Party loyalists, U.S. officials announced on July 3 a bounty of $25 million for the capture of Saddam Hussein or evidence confirming his death. A governing council of 25 diverse Iraqi leaders (including two women) was established on July 13 as the interim government in Iraq. Among the group's first decisions was to abolish six holidays celebrated under the Hussein regime and to create a committee to set up a criminal court for trying top officials in Hussein's government for war crimes. Saddam Hussein's sons Uday and Qusay were killed in a firefight in a Mosul palace on July 22. American troops stormed the residence after receiving a tip from an Iraqi citizen. As the hunt for Saddam Hussein intensified, on July 29, U.S. troops raided dozens of sites in Hussein's hometown of Tikrit, capturing about 175 people believed to be Hussein loyalists. **Israel and the Palestinian Territories:** Israeli soldiers continued their withdrawal from parts of Bethlehem and the West Bank on July 2. As planned, Palestinian forces assumed a security role. The Israeli Cabinet agreed to release Palestinian prisoners, and began by freeing about 300 on July 6. Palestinians wanted many more to be released (up to 5,500) for the cease-fire to hold. On July 7, Prime Minister Mahmoud Abbas threatened to resign in the face of rising criticism about his handling of peace negotiations with Israel. A week later, Abbas and Arafat agreed to a power-sharing deal

that requires Abbas to consider negotiating guidelines created by the Palestine Liberation Organization when dealing with Israel. During a July 29 meeting with President Bush at the White House, Israeli Prime Minister Ariel Sharon refused to dismantle a security fence cutting through the West Bank. **Liberia:** On July 3, President Bush announced that he was considering U.S. intervention in Liberia. Bush said that Liberian president Charles Taylor must step down before the U.S. sends any peacekeeping forces to oversee a fragile cease-fire between rebels and government. Taylor, indicted for war crimes, later stated that he would resign after international peacekeepers arrived and accepted an offer of safe haven in Nigeria. On July 19, the opposition Liberians United for Reconciliation and Democracy laid siege to the capital Monrovia. Six days later, U.S. President Bush deployed 2,300 marines to the Liberian coast. **North Korea:** The U.S. government reported on July 14 that North Korea informed them of plans to use weapons-grade plutonium from spent fuel rods to build six nuclear weapons. The CIA could not confirm the claim. **Pakistan:** A suicide bomber attacked a Shiite mosque in Quetta on July 4, killing 48 Muslims. **Peru:** Five policemen and two civilians were killed in a July 11 clash with the left-wing Shining Path guerrilla organization, raising fears that the Maoist terrorist group was resurging. On July 31, Peru formally asked Japan to extradite former Peruvian president Alberto Fujimori to face charges for murder and kidnapping. **Philippines:** In an attempted coup on July 27, about 50 junior officers of the Philippine military called for the resignation of President Gloria Macapagal Arroyo and the defense secretary. The mutiny ended peacefully. **São Tomé and Príncipe:** In a July 16 military coup, Maj Fernando Pereira toppled the government and took over the capital, São Tomé. **Solomon Islands:** The vanguard elements of an Australian-led peacekeeping force of 2,200 arrived on July 24 to restore order and disarm ethnic gangs. The government asked for foreign assistance after years of ongoing violence threatened to descend into full-scale anarchy. **United Kingdom:** On July 7, a foreign affairs parliamentary committee reported that Prime Minister Tony Blair did not tamper with evidence to justify a war in Iraq. The committee did say, however, that Blair unwittingly misled Parliament when he presented it with a dossier in February that included unverified information about Iraq's weapons capabilities. **United States:** The Pope appointed Sean P. O'Malley as leader of the beleaguered Boston archdiocese on July 1. O'Malley replaced Cardinal Bernard Law, who resigned in December amid a sexual abuse controversy. Government officials announced on July 1 that the U.S. would withhold military aid to 35 countries that did not give American exemption to prosecution by the International Criminal Court. President Bush admitted on July 7 that evidence regarding an alleged Iraqi purchase of uranium from Africa, cited in his January State of the Union address, was unsubstantiated and should not have been included in his speech. Secretary of Defense Donald Rumsfeld told the Senate Armed Services Committee on July 9 that the price of the war in Iraq had nearly doubled the April estimate, to about $3.9 billion per month. General Tommy Franks also reported that the troop strength in Iraq, about 145,000, was not likely to be reduced in the near future. The White House reported on July 15 that the 2003 budget deficit would reach $455 billion, the largest in U.S. history. An 87-year-old man crashed his car through an outdoor market in Santa Monica, California, on July 16, killing 10 and injuring dozens of others. The incident stirred debate about age limits for senior drivers. Visiting British Prime Minister Tony Blair told a joint session of Congress on July 17 that the war in Iraq was justified, even if no biological, chemical or nuclear weapons are ever found. **Worldwide:** On July 5, the World Health Organization declared that the SARS virus had been contained, with no new cases reported since June 15. Officials warned, however, that the lack of cases could be seasonally related.

CANADA

As the July 1 deadline to register guns with the federal firearms registry passed, six provinces—Alberta, Manitoba, Saskatchewan, Newfoundland and Labrador, Nova Scotia and Ontario—had considered refusing or decided to refuse to prosecute gun owners who failed or declined to register their firearms with the newly created registry. On July 9, Canada became the first country to distribute marijuana to individuals with a medical right to use it. The measure was introduced in response to a court order that required Ottawa to create a new policy. The eight-team Canadian Baseball League announced on July 18 that it would shut down halfway through its first season, following the July 23 all-star game in Calgary. On July 22, Liberal leadership contender John Manley quit the leadership race, saying that to continue would be "irresponsible" in the face of insufficient party support. On July 25, Canada recalled Philip MacKinnon, its ambassador to Iran, and will consider trade or travel sanctions against the theocratic regime after it ignored diplomatic requests to return the body of Montreal photojournalist Zahra Kazemi. Statistics Canada reported on July 25 that the national crime rate for 2002 represented a drop of 27 percent since 1992. Armed robberies declined by an even larger 62 percent over the decade. At a World Trade Organization meeting in Montreal from July 27 to 29, thousands of demonstrators protesting against globalization clashed with riot police. Hundreds were arrested. Responding to increasingly vocal public concern over high automobile insurance rates, on July 29 the New Brunswick legislature passed a law forcing a 20 percent reduction in auto premiums, retroactive to July 1. On July 29, a British Columbia provincial court judge threw out a controversial federal program that allowed three native bands along the lower Fraser River to fish commercially for salmon when others could not, saying that the program discriminated on the basis of race. Ottawa subsequently halted the 11-year-old pilot project, angering native leaders. Close to 450,000 people filled Downsview Airport in Toronto for a SARS benefit concert on July 30. Headlined by the Rolling Stones, it was Canada's largest-ever rock concert.

AUGUST 2003

INTERNATIONAL

Afghanistan: In its first mission outside Europe, the North Atlantic Treaty Organization assumed formal command of the peacekeeping forces in Afghanistan on August 11. In the most deadly 24-hour period over the last year, terrorist attacks, counter-terrorist operations and political violence on August 13 claimed the lives of more than 60 people in Khost, Uruzgan, Helmand, Kabul and Ghazni provinces. **France:** As many as 11,435 people, most of them elderly, died in France during Europe's worst heat wave of recent memory. Slow reaction to the crisis by authorities prompted the resignation of France's director of public health on August 18. **India:** More than 50 people were killed and over 150 injured when two bombs exploded in Mumbai's (formerly Bombay) financial centre on August 25. Authorities blamed the attack on a Pakistan-based terrorist organization. **Indonesia:** A car bomb demolished part of an American-run hotel in Jakarta, killing 10 and injuring about 150 on August 5. Indonesian police said the explosives and methods used in the attack resembled those of the October 2002 bombing of a Bali nightclub. **Iran:** Amid growing concern about Iran's nuclear ambitions, a leaked

International Atomic Energy Agency report stated that inspectors found traces of highly enriched uranium in samples taken from the Natanz nuclear facility. Iran claimed that the samples were contaminated by imported equipment (August 26). **Iraq:** A car bomb exploded outside the Jordanian embassy on August 7, killing 11 and wounding about 70 others. On August 19, a suicide bomber drove a truck into the UN's headquarters in Iraq, killing 23 people and injuring 100 others. The attack, the deadliest against the UN in history, also claimed the life of Sérgio Vieira de Mello, a Brazilian diplomat who was the Secretary-General's special representative in Iraq. On August 21, U.S. officials announced that they had captured and detained Ali Hassan al-Majid, also known as "Chemical Ali," for his attack on Iraqi Kurds with poison gas in 1988. **Israel and the Palestinian Territories:** Israel announced on August 15 that it would cede control of Jericho and Qalqilya to Palestinian authorities, and allow Palestinian chairman Yasser Arafat to travel outside his Ramallah compound. The decision was contingent on Palestinians ending violence and the disarmament of Palestinian militants. A devastating suicide bombing on a crowded bus in Jerusalem killed 20 and wounded more than 100 on August 19. After Israeli retaliation two days later, Hamas and Islamic Jihad formally withdrew from the cease-fire. **Liberia:** Nigerian peacekeepers landed at Monrovia airport on August 4 in an effort to control vicious fighting between the government and rebel factions. The Nigerians represented the vanguard of an anticipated 3,000-plus strong West African peacekeeping force. After weeks of promising to step down, President Charles Taylor resigned on August 11 and left for Nigeria. Vice-President Moses Blah took over the presidency. On August 21, Liberia's rival political parties selected businessman Charles Gyude as chairman of the interim government until October 2005, when elections are scheduled to take place. **Libya:** In a landmark move, the government of Libya accepted the blame for the 1988 bombing of Pan Am Flight 103 that killed 270 people over Lockerbie, Scotland. The agreement, which includes payments totaling $2.7 billion to the families of the victims, paved the way for the UN to lift sanctions against the country (August 15). **Morocco:** Four men were sentenced to death on August 19 for their part in the suicide bombings that killed 45 people in Casablanca in May. Eighty-three others went to prison, many for life. **Nepal:** After a deadlock in peace talks, Nepal's Maoist rebels declared on August 27 that the country's seven-month-old cease-fire was over. **North America:** In the continent's largest-ever power blackout, 50 million people across eight U.S. states as well as Ontario and Quebec lost electricity for up to 48 hours on August 14. The exact cause was unknown, but officials blamed the region's aging electricity grid. **Pakistan:** On August 5, former Prime Minister Benazir Bhutto and her husband were found guilty by a Swiss court of money laundering and given suspended sentences of six months in jail. Bhutto, who currently lives in exile in London, said she would appeal the ruling. **Portugal:** A forest fire that began in early August ravaged 531,000 acres of woodland before finally being extinguished on 18 August. The fires claimed at least 18 lives, with damage estimated at over $1 billion. **Russia:** An August 1 truck bomb explosion at a military hospital in Mozdok killed 35 and injured dozens of others. The Russian government blamed the attacks on Chechen separatists. On August 30, the Russian Defence Ministry reported the loss of a nuclear-powered submarine with 10 crew in the Barents Sea. The submarine was being towed to a scrapyard, but the conning-tower hatch was left open. **Rwanda:** In an election that was orderly but possibly tainted by intimidation, President Paul Kagame, a Tutsi, won 95 percent of the vote in a presidential

election on August 25. **Uganda:** Idi Amin, the former Ugandan president notorious for committing numerous atrocities, died in exile in Saudi Arabia on August 16. **United Kingdom:** On August 11, Lord Hutton opened an inquiry into scientist David Kelly's death. Kelly was a scientist with the Ministry of Defence who committed suicide in July, after reportedly telling a BBC journalist that the government had "sexed up" intelligence about Iraq's alleged weapons of mass destruction to help justify the war in Iraq. On August 28, Prime Minister Tony Blair gave evidence to the inquiry; he stated that if the allegations against the government had in fact been true, he would have had to resign. **United States:** In a move that threatened to split the Episcopalian Church, diocesan bishops voted to confirm V. Gene Robinson as the church's first openly gay bishop on August 5. Pledging "no retreat" in Iraq, on August 27 President Bush claimed that U.S. forces were making good progress in restoring order to the country. The State Department, however, signaled that, for the first time, they might consider a multinational force under the UN, provided an American led it. The Department of Justice reported on August 25 that 23 million serious crimes were committed in America in 2002, the lowest level in 30 years. In an election on whether to recall California Governor Gray Davis, 135 candidates were officially accepted on to the ballot on August 10. Leading contenders to replace the incumbent Democratic governor included the Republican front-runner, actor Arnold Schwarzenegger, and the Democratic lieutenant-governor, Cruz Bustamante. **Venezuela:** Tens of thousands of people marched into the capital, Caracas, in support of a referendum to force president Hugo Chàvez out of office. Earlier in the day, opposition groups delivered a petition signed by 2.5 million people demanding a recall referendum (August 20).

CANADA

A state of emergency was declared in British Columbia on August 2 and extended throughout the month and into September, in response to massive forest fires that ravaged the Okanagan and Kamloops regions. At its peak, over 2,200 Canadian Forces troops joined firefighters and a fleet of 27 aircraft and 115 helicopters battling the fires. On August 5, Nova Scotians gave Tory Premier John Hamm another mandate, albeit as leader of a minority government. Hamm's party emerged from the election holding 25 seats of the 52-seat legislature, compared to 15 for the NDP and 12 for the Liberals. After several storms dropped over 150 millimetres of rain over Quebec, devastating floods tore through the province on August 6, crashing through homes and uprooting trees. A blast in a grain elevator in Halifax on August 7 forced up to 400 people from their homes. Combustible grain dust was considered to be the most likely cause of the explosion. No one was injured. On August 12, Ottawa unveiled a $1.3-billion plan to cut greenhouse gas emissions in line with the Kyoto Protocol. The new measures include a $100-million subsidy for ethanol fuel and a $1,000 inducement to homeowners to make houses more energy efficient. On August 13, Dr Nestor Yanga became the 44th person to die of SARS in the Toronto area. On August 21, Saskatchewan and the city of North Battleford reached a $3.2-million settlement with 700 residents who became violently ill after the city's water supply was infected by a parasite in 2001. No one died in the incident, but court documents showed North Battleford failed to test its water properly and had built the treatment plant two kilometres downstream of its sewage plant. RCMP and Ontario police arrested 19 Muslim men, most from Pakistan, on suspicion of terrorism. One of the men was enrolled in a flight school and was making training flights over the Pickering nuclear power plant outside Toronto (August 22). In an August 25 deal with Ottawa, Dogrib natives in the Northwest Territories assumed ownership of approximately 39,000 square kilometres of territory just north of Great Slave Lake. The band will also have a say over resource development and royalties in the area, which includes Canada's two largest diamond mines.

SEPTEMBER 2003

INTERNATIONAL

China: Ceding to months of public pressure, Hong Kong's chief executive, Tung Chee-hwa, withdrew his government's controversial internal-security, anti-subversion bill on September 5. The bill would have made it easier for the government to stifle opposition. **Democratic Republic of the Congo:** French troops in Bunia formally handed over their duties to UN forces on September 1, ending their three-month deployment to protect civilians from ethnic bloodshed. The UN force in the Bunia region, which will total 5,000, is largely made up of Uruguayan and Bangladeshi soldiers. **Israel and the Palestinian Territories:** In response to Israel's September 6 attempt to kill Hamas founder and spiritual leader Sheikh Yassin, Hamas suicide bombers killed 15 Israelis in Jerusalem and Tel Aviv. Palestinian Prime Minister Mahmoud Abbas resigned on September 6 after losing his party's confidence. He was replaced by Ahmed Qurei, the speaker of parliament. On September 11, the Israeli Cabinet decided "in principle" to expel Yasser Arafat from the area. The decision was met with widespread international condemnation. **Iraq:** The Arab League recognized the American-appointed Governing Council on September 9, allowing it to take up the seat left vacant by the fall of Saddam Hussein's regime. On September 12, American soldiers killed eight Iraqi policemen in a gun battle in Falluja, the heart of Iraqi resistance to the occupation. Following a September 24 bomb attack against UN workers, the second such incident in a month, UN Secretary-General Kofi Annan ordered most remaining staff to leave Iraq. Responding to demands from France and others for a rapid timetable for self-rule, U.S. Secretary of State Colin Powell gave the Governing Council six months to write a new constitution (September 25). **Iran:** On September 15, the International Atomic Energy Agency announced that it would give Iran until the end of October to disprove suspicions that it is not secretly building a nuclear bomb. **Italy:** A massive blackout, similar to the grid failure that hit North America in August, left most of the country without power on September 28. Authorities blamed malfunctioning supply lines from France. **Japan:** On September 20, Prime Minister Junichiro Koizumi was comfortably re-elected as leader of the governing Liberal Democratic Party. Despite facing internal criticism for his reform agenda and the slow pace of economic recovery, he was widely supported because of his public popularity—vital to his party winning the next general election. An earthquake with a magnitude of 8.0 shook northern Japan on September 26, causing power failures and setting fires. At least 164 people were injured; no deaths were reported. **Liberia:** As their numbers grew, the Nigerian-led peacekeeping force in Liberia, known as ECOMIL, began deploying outside the capital Monrovia on September 9. By September 14, the force had reached Liberia's second-largest city, Buchanan. **Mexico:** On September 15, the World Trade Organization's talks in Cancun broke down over a proposal to maintain the level of agricultural subsidies in the developed world. Poorer countries were hoping to significantly reduce the $300 billion in agricultural subsidies paid every year to farmers in the world's rich nations.

NATO: Dutch Foreign Minister Jaap de Hoop Scheffer was named as the next Secretary-General of the military alliance on September 22. **Singapore:** In the first new case of the disease in five months, a new case of SARS was reported in Singapore on September 9. The World Health Organization, however, said that the case was unlikely to herald another mass outbreak. **South Korea:** The strongest typhoon to hit the country in over 100 years devastated portions of the southeastern coast, killing 87 people and causing billions of dollars in damage. **Sudan:** On September 25, the government agreed to withdraw most of its troops from the rebel-held south of the country and concluded a security pact. The accord with the Sudan People's Liberation Army was seen as a significant step towards ending one of Africa's longest-running and deadliest civil wars. **Sweden:** Shocked Swedes went into mourning when their popular foreign minister, Anna Lindh, died after an assailant stabbed her in the chest, arms and stomach in a Stockholm department store on September 10. **Syria:** President Bashar al-Asad appointed a new, reformist prime minister on September 10, the first sign of major change since he took over after his father's death in 2000. **Taiwan:** Up to 150,000 Taiwanese demonstrated in Taipei's streets to demand a formal change of the island's name from the Republic of China to Taiwan. **United Kingdom:** A parliamentary committee concluded on September 11 that Geoff Hoon, Britain's Minister of Defence, was "unhelpful and potentially misleading" in failing to reveal concerns within his ministry about the dossier on Iraq's weapons of mass destruction. **United Nations:** In Geneva on September 13 with the four other permanent members of the Security Council, U.S. Secretary of State Colin Powell continued his push to approve a resolution calling for the creation of a multinational force in Iraq. No agreement was reached. The French continued to signal great reluctance to endorse any resolution that appears to give retroactive blessing to the war. Opening the 58th General Assembly on September 23, Secretary-General Kofi Annan said the organization had come to a "fork in the road" and argued that fundamental weaknesses had to be addressed if it was to remain relevant. **United States:** Calling Iraq the "central front" in the war on terror in a September 7 address, President George Bush asked Congress for $87 billion for further military and reconstruction costs. On September 10, Boston's Catholic church agreed to pay $85 million to 552 people who say their priests sexually abused them. On the eve of the women's World Cup of soccer, the Women's United Soccer Association announced that it was suspending operations after three seasons (September 16). Retired General Wesley Clark, former supreme allied commander of NATO and leader of the Kosovo air campaign, announced his entrance into the presidential race as a Democratic candidate on September 16. Clark had been highly critical of the Bush administration and the war in Iraq. Hurricane Isabel lashed a huge swath of the Eastern seaboard on September 18, leaving nearly two dozen dead, flooded cities and two million without power from North Carolina to New Jersey. On September 29, allegations surfaced that the White House illegally disclosed the identity of a CIA operative as revenge for her husband's criticism of the war against Iraq. The following day, prominent Democrats called for an independent inquiry into the allegations. **Zimbabwe:** The country's only independent newspaper, the Daily News, was shut down by the government on September 12. The government said it was operating illegally, but the incident was widely seen as another attack on press freedoms by the Mugabe regime.

CANADA

On September 5, a North American Free Trade panel ruled that the U.S. had not proven that Canadian softwood exports threatened to harm U.S. lumber firms. The ruling could eventually force the U.S. to drop its 27.2 percent duty on Canadian softwood lumber. Overturning a lower court decision, on September 13 the New Brunswick Court of Appeal ruled that Mi'kmaq logger Joshua Bernard has the right to harvest and sell trees from Crown lands that were historically occupied by first nations people. The decision has significant implications for New Brunswick's $4-billion-a-year forestry industry. On September 16, the House of Commons narrowly rejected a Canadian Alliance Party motion to reaffirm that marriage is, by definition, a union between a man and a woman. The 137 to 132 vote was key to efforts to extend marriage rights to same-sex couples. A parliamentary committee launched a probe into Governor-General Adrienne Clarkson's budget and spending habits on September 22, amid rising controversy over a $1-million trip to Russia, Finland and Iceland. The Ward Hunt ice shelf on Ellesmere Island, which had jutted into the Arctic Ocean for more than 3,000 years, broke up on September 21, providing fresh evidence that the region is warming. Health officials in Saskatchewan confirmed the death of three people from West Nile virus on September 23, bringing the provincial total to six. Saskatchewan had more than 400 confirmed and probable cases of the virus this year, making it the province with the highest reported number of cases in the country. About 6,000 day-care workers in Quebec held walkouts on September 26, affecting more than 300 day-care centres throughout the province. The child-care workers claimed the contract they signed with the former Parti Québécois government in March was not being respected by the new Liberal government. On September 29, Hurricane Juan–the strongest in decades–touched down in Nova Scotia, killing two and causing extensive flooding and damage in Halifax. Pat Binns and his Progressive Conservative Party won their third consecutive majority government in Prince Edward Island elections on September 29.

Index

H

CALENDARS AND HOLIDAYS

2004

JANUARY
S	M	T	W	T	F	S
				1	2	3
4	5	6	7	8	9	10
11	12	13	14	15	16	17
18	19	20	21	22	23	24
25	26	27	28	29	30	31

FEBRUARY
S	M	T	W	T	F	S
1	2	3	4	5	6	7
8	9	10	11	12	13	14
15	16	17	18	19	20	21
22	23	24	25	26	27	28
29						

MARCH
S	M	T	W	T	F	S
	1	2	3	4	5	6
7	8	9	10	11	12	13
14	15	16	17	18	19	20
21	22	23	24	25	26	27
28	29	30	31			

APRIL
S	M	T	W	T	F	S
				1	2	3
4	5	6	7	8	9	10
11	12	13	14	15	16	17
18	19	20	21	22	23	24
25	26	27	28	29	30	

MAY
S	M	T	W	T	F	S
						1
2	3	4	5	6	7	8
9	10	11	12	13	14	15
16	17	18	19	20	21	22
23	24	25	26	27	28	29
30	31					

JUNE
S	M	T	W	T	F	S
		1	2	3	4	5
6	7	8	9	10	11	12
13	14	15	16	17	18	19
20	21	22	23	24	25	26
27	28	29	30			

JULY
S	M	T	W	T	F	S
				1	2	3
4	5	6	7	8	9	10
11	12	13	14	15	16	17
18	19	20	21	22	23	24
25	26	27	28	29	30	31

AUGUST
S	M	T	W	T	F	S
1	2	3	4	5	6	7
8	9	10	11	12	13	14
15	16	17	18	19	20	21
22	23	24	25	26	27	28
29	30	31				

SEPTEMBER
S	M	T	W	T	F	S
			1	2	3	4
5	6	7	8	9	10	11
12	13	14	15	16	17	18
19	20	21	22	23	24	25
26	27	28	29	30		

OCTOBER
S	M	T	W	T	F	S
					1	2
3	4	5	6	7	8	9
10	11	12	13	14	15	16
17	18	19	20	21	22	23
24	25	26	27	28	29	30
31						

NOVEMBER
S	M	T	W	T	F	S
	1	2	3	4	5	6
7	8	9	10	11	12	13
14	15	16	17	18	19	20
21	22	23	24	25	26	27
28	29	30				

DECEMBER
S	M	T	W	T	F	S
			1	2	3	4
5	6	7	8	9	10	11
12	13	14	15	16	17	18
19	20	21	22	23	24	25
26	27	28	29	30	31	

New Year's Day (January 1), Good Friday (April 9), Easter Sunday (April 11), Victoria Day (May 24), Canada Day (July 1), Labour Day (September 6), Thanksgiving (October 11), Christmas Day and Boxing Day (December 25 and 26).

Other Holidays and Holy Days, 2004

Government and bank holidays: April 12 (Easter Monday), November 11 (Remembrance Day).
Islamic Holy Days: These are subject to the sighting of the moon. The key days are: Nuzulul Qur'an; Eidul Fitri; Eidul Adha; Islamic New Year; Ashoora; Maulid Nabi; Isra'and Miraj; First Day of Ramadhan.

Jewish Holy Days: Purim—March 17; Passover—April 6–12; Shavuot—May 26–27; Rosh Hashanah—September 16; Yom Kippur—September 25; Sukkot—September 30–October 7; Simchat Torah—October 7–8; Hanukkah—December 9–15.
Chinese New Year—January 22, 2004.

2003

JANUARY
S	M	T	W	T	F	S
			1	2	3	4
5	6	7	8	9	10	11
12	13	14	15	16	17	18
19	20	21	22	23	24	25
26	27	28	29	30	31	

FEBRUARY
S	M	T	W	T	F	S
						1
2	3	4	5	6	7	8
9	10	11	12	13	14	15
16	17	18	19	20	21	22
23	24	25	26	27	28	29

MARCH
S	M	T	W	T	F	S
						1
2	3	4	5	6	7	8
9	10	11	12	13	14	15
16	17	18	19	20	21	22
23	24	25	26	27	28	29
30	31					

APRIL
S	M	T	W	T	F	S
		1	2	3	4	5
6	7	8	9	10	11	12
13	14	15	16	17	18	19
20	21	22	23	24	25	26
27	28	29	30			

MAY
S	M	T	W	T	F	S
				1	2	3
4	5	6	7	8	9	10
11	12	13	14	15	16	17
18	19	20	21	22	23	24
25	26	27	28	29	30	31

JUNE
S	M	T	W	T	F	S
1	2	3	4	5	6	7
8	9	10	11	12	13	14
15	16	17	18	19	20	21
22	23	24	25	26	27	28
29	30					

JULY
S	M	T	W	T	F	S
		1	2	3	4	5
6	7	8	9	10	11	12
13	14	15	16	17	18	19
20	21	22	23	24	25	26
27	28	29	30	31		

AUGUST
S	M	T	W	T	F	S
					1	2
3	4	5	6	7	8	9
10	11	12	13	14	15	16
17	18	19	20	21	22	23
24	25	26	27	28	29	30
31						

SEPTEMBER
S	M	T	W	T	F	S
	1	2	3	4	5	6
7	8	9	10	11	12	13
14	15	16	17	18	19	20
21	22	23	24	25	26	27
28	29	30				

OCTOBER
S	M	T	W	T	F	S
			1	2	3	4
5	6	7	8	9	10	11
12	13	14	15	16	17	18
19	20	21	22	23	24	25
26	27	28	29	30	31	

NOVEMBER
S	M	T	W	T	F	S
						1
2	3	4	5	6	7	8
9	10	11	12	13	14	15
16	17	18	19	20	21	22
23	24	25	26	27	28	29
30						

DECEMBER
S	M	T	W	T	F	S
	1	2	3	4	5	6
7	8	9	10	11	12	13
14	15	16	17	18	19	20
21	22	23	24	25	26	27
28	29	30	31			

2005

JANUARY
S	M	T	W	T	F	S
						1
2	3	4	5	6	7	8
9	10	11	12	13	14	15
16	17	18	19	20	21	22
23	24	25	26	27	28	29
30	31					

FEBRUARY
S	M	T	W	T	F	S
		1	2	3	4	5
6	7	8	9	10	11	12
13	14	15	16	17	18	19
20	21	22	23	24	25	26
27	28					

MARCH
S	M	T	W	T	F	S
		1	2	3	4	5
6	7	8	9	10	11	12
13	14	15	16	17	18	19
20	21	22	23	24	25	26
27	28	29	30	31		

APRIL
S	M	T	W	T	F	S
					1	2
3	4	5	6	7	8	9
10	11	12	13	14	15	16
17	18	19	20	21	22	23
24	25	26	27	28	29	30

MAY
S	M	T	W	T	F	S
1	2	3	4	5	6	7
8	9	10	11	12	13	14
15	16	17	18	19	20	21
22	23	24	25	26	27	28
29	30	31				

JUNE
S	M	T	W	T	F	S
			1	2	3	4
5	6	7	8	9	10	11
12	13	14	15	16	17	18
19	20	21	22	23	24	25
26	27	28	29	30		

JULY
S	M	T	W	T	F	S
					1	2
3	4	5	6	7	8	9
10	11	12	13	14	15	16
17	18	19	20	21	22	23
24	25	26	27	28	29	30
31						

AUGUST
S	M	T	W	T	F	S
	1	2	3	4	5	6
7	8	9	10	11	12	13
14	15	16	17	18	19	20
21	22	23	24	25	26	27
28	29	30	31			

SEPTEMBER
S	M	T	W	T	F	S
				1	2	3
4	5	6	7	8	9	10
11	12	13	14	15	16	17
18	19	20	21	22	23	24
25	26	27	28	29	30	

OCTOBER
S	M	T	W	T	F	S
						1
2	3	4	5	6	7	8
9	10	11	12	13	14	15
16	17	18	19	20	21	22
23	24	25	26	27	28	29
30	31					

NOVEMBER
S	M	T	W	T	F	S
		1	2	3	4	5
6	7	8	9	10	11	12
13	14	15	16	17	18	19
20	21	22	23	24	25	26
27	28	29	30			

DECEMBER
S	M	T	W	T	F	S
				1	2	3
4	5	6	7	8	9	10
11	12	13	14	15	16	17
18	19	20	21	22	23	24
25	26	27	28	29	30	31